17TH EDITION **2020**

BECKETT

THE #1 AUTHORITY ON COLLECTIBLES

GRADED
CARD PRICE GUIDE

THE HOBBY'S MOST RELIABLE AND RELIED UPON SOURCE ™

Founder: Dr. James Beckett III
Edited by the Price Guide Staff of BECKETT MEDIA

BECKETT is a registered trademark of BECKETT MEDIA LLC, DALLAS, TEXAS
Manufactured in the United States of America | Published by Beckett Media LLC

Beckett Media LLC
4635 McEwen Dr.
Dallas, TX 75244
(972)991-6657
beckett.com

First Printing ISBN: 978-1-936681-32-7

TABLE OF
CONTENTS

STAFF

EDITORIAL

MIKE PAYNE
Editorial Director

RYAN CRACKNELL
Hobby Editor

ERIC KNAGG
Graphic Design

COLLECTIBLES DATA PUBLISHING

BRIAN FLEISCHER
Manager | Sr. Market Analyst

PRICE GUIDE STAFF
Lloyd Almonguera, Ryan Altubar, Matt Bible, Jeff Camay, Steve Dalton, Justin Grunert, Junel Magale, Eric Norton, Kristian Redulla, Arsenio Tan, Sam Zimmer

ADVERTISING

TED BARKER
Senior Sales Executive
tbarker@beckett.com
972.448.9147

ALEX SORIANO
Advertising Sales Executive
alex@beckett.com
619.392.5299

BECKETT GRADING SERVICES

JEROMY MURRAY
VP, Grading & Authentication
4635 McEwen Road,
Dallas, TX 75244
jmurray@beckett.com

GRADING SALES/ SHOW STAFF

DEREK FICKEN
Midwest/Southeast
Regional Sales Manager
dficken@beckett.com
Office: 972.448.9144

NEW YORK OFFICE
484 White Plains Rd, 2nd Floor,
Eastchester, N.Y. 10709

CHARLES STABILE
Northeast Regional
Sales Manager
cstabile@beckett.com
Office: 914.268.0533

CALIFORNIA OFFICE
17900 Sky Park Circle, Suite
200, Irvine, CA 92614

MICHAEL GARDNER
Western Regional
Sales Manager
mgardner@beckett.com
Office: 714.200.1934
Fax: 714.388.3741

DONGWOON LEE
Asia/Pacific Sales Manager
dongwoonl@beckett.com
Cell +82.10.6826.6868

Grading Customer Service:
972.448.9188 or
grading@beckett.com

BECKETT DIGITAL STUDIO
DANIEL MOSCOSO

OPERATIONS
ALBERTO CHAVEZ
Sr. Logistics & Facilities
Manager

EDITORIAL, PRODUCTION & SALES OFFICE
4635 McEwen Road,
Dallas TX 75244

972.991.6657
beckett.com

BECKETT MEDIA, LLC
SANDEEP DUA - President
KEVIN ISAACSON - Vice President

COVER IMAGE BY GETTY IMAGES

How to Use

What's listed?

Beckett Graded Card Price Guide features a multi-sport format comprised of baseball, basketball, football, golf, hockey and Magic the Gathering. Our goal is to include all significant professionally graded cards from 1887-present.

What's not listed?

Unlike the raw card price guides featured within our magazine titles, Beckett Graded Card Price Guide focuses solely on material that is most frequently submitted to the top professional grading companies.

How do I find what I'm looking for?

The Price Guide is structured alphabetically by sport (baseball first, followed by basketball then football, etc.) and chronologically within each sport.

Why aren't prices listed for every condition?

After analyzing market conditions, it was determined that eight columns for vintage and four columns for modern era material best captured the range of graded cards trading hands in collectible condition. There's little need to list values for graded NM or ExMt modern era cards because material in less than NmMt condition is rarely submitted for grading. Conversely, Mint and Gem Mint graded cards are so rare in many vintage sets that providing accurate values is nearly impossible.

Why are some fields blank within the pricing grids?

Because the Price Guide is based on real-world transactions, we've deliberately left fields blank where populations are too low to derive consistent valuations. Rather than list highly dubious values for "low population" cards, we've chosen to augment the pricing grids for each set by reporting historical sales on significant rarities at the end of each set listing.

Additionally, prices are not listed for some low-end cards valued under $4 (about half the cost to grade a card). If you see a blank field for a low-end condition, you can assume the card is worth less than five dollars in that grade.

Why are vintage common cards individually listed but not modern era singles in the pricing grids?

We've gone to great lengths to extensively research market conditions for commons and minor stars. In vintage releases with a healthy community of set builders, the impact of Population Reports can be significant on the values of scarce commons and minor stars in high grade so we've included prices for every card. Frankly, it's pretty easy to figure out how much a 1957 Topps Mickey Mantle is worth in NM or NmMt since there are plenty of copies in circulation. But the task is tougher when determining the value for the Max Surkont card in similar condition - there are only a handful of high-end copies available and they sell at a premium.

There are relatively few graded card set builders for modern era releases thus the truncated listings.

How do I differentiate values between the various grading companies?

The market for professionally graded sports cards is today predominantly comprised of three companies BGS/BVG, PSA and SGC. Rather than try to break down listings for every card in every condition by every company (a bewildering option on the printed page and a virtual impossibility given the inherent inconsistencies in trading volume), we've chosen to simplify matters by providing the value that the card is most commonly traded for in that grade.

The catch is that not all company's cards always trade for equal value (in equal grade) from the various eras. We approached this dilemma by looking at market share as the primary arbiter of value. For example, the majority of 1950s graded baseball cards circulating within the secondary market are encapsulated by PSA, thus the values we list for these cards largely reflect PSA trading levels. Conversely, SGC has a significant presence and status in tobacco-era material, thus the values we list for this material is demonstrably based upon SGC transactions. In the modern era material, BGS is a market leader and the listed values are thus noticeably based on transactions of BGS cards.

None of this, however, clarifies values for the consumer dealing in vintage Beckett graded cards or modern-era SGC material. To that effect, we've added some specific sales listings to the beginning of the pricing grid for each applicable set. It's here that you'll find specific information for companies with lower trading volume in that era for some key cards, illuminating potential differences in the sales levels listed in the pricing grid.

How do I reference PSA cards with qualifiers?

In general, PSA cards with qualifiers sell for about two levels lower than the grade on the label for post-WWII material (i.e. a PSA 7 OC will sell for about the same as a standard PSA 5) and one level below the grade on the label for pre-WWII material. We don't list specific values for these cards due to low trading volume on the secondary market. Significant PSA cards with qualifiers will, however, be referenced within our sales notes at the end of each set listing.

Where do you get your sales information from?

Every card sale from every major auction house over the past few years (Goodwin, Heritage, Lelands, Legendary, Memory Lane, Mile High, Robert Edward, etc.) has been gathered and analyzed. The unending stream of sales from eBay and other online community-based auctions also have been reviewed. Dealers at the leading shows across America have and will continue to be interviewed by our staff of analysts throughout the year.

Furthermore, a community message board on beckett.com devoted specifically to pricing is available to all. If you've got some feedback, wish to voice your opinion or simply want to provide some sales data, you'll have a venue to do so on your own time in your own home ... and our analysts will be reading (and responding when appropriate) alongside fellow collectors and dealers.

BASEBALL

1887 - 1980

1887 Allen and Ginter N28

		PrFr 1	GD 2	VG 3	VgEx 4	EX 5	ExMt 6	NM 7	NmMt 8
1	Cap Anson#{Baseball	900	1,200	1,800	2,500	3,000	4,000	8,800	12,000
2	Charles Bennett#{Baseball	150	225	275	350	800			
3	Robert L. Caruthers#{Baseball	150	200	250	300	500	600	1,000	3,200
4	John Clarkson#{Baseball	300	400	500	800	1,000	1,500	2,500	9,500
5	Charles Comiskey#{Baseball	350	450	600	800	1,200	2,000	3,000	
6	Captain Jack Glasscock#{Baseball	150	250	300	400	600	900	1,200	2,000
7	Timothy Keefe#{Baseball	325	400	550	750	1,000	1,500	2,500	9,500
8	Mike Kelly#{Baseball	350	600	750	1,000	1,200	1,800	3,000	10,500
9	Joseph Mulvey#{Baseball	125	175	250	300	400	700	1,000	2,800
10	John M. Ward#{Baseball	350	450	600	750	1,200	1,800	2,500	6,000

—Cap Anson SGC 88 (NmMt) sold for $26,450 (Hunt; 11/06)
—Charles Bennett PSA 7 (NM) sold for $2,492 (eBay; 5/06)
—John Clarkson GAI 8.5 (NmMt) sold for $2,585 (Memory Lane; 12/07)
—John Clarkson GAI 8 (NmMt) sold for $3,435 (Mile High; 8/07)
—Charles Comiskey GAI 8 (NmMt) sold for $2,806 (Mastro; 12/06)
—Tim Keefe GAI 8 (NmMt) sold for $2,827 (SCP; 7/08)
—Mike Kelly GAI 8.5 (NmMt+) sold for $7,967 (Mile High; 11/05)

1887-90 Old Judge N172

		PrFr 1	GD 2	VG 3	VgEx 4	EX 5	ExMt 6	NM 7	NmMt 8
1	Gus Albert	120	150	200	300	350	500		
3	Alexander	100	120	150	250	350	500		
4	Myron Allen	100	120	150	250	350	500		
5	Bob Allen	100	120	150	400	500	600		
6	Uncle Bill Alvord	100	120	150	250	350	500		
7	Varney Anderson	1,200	1,500	2,000	2,500	3,000	4,000		
8	Ed Andrews	100	120	150	250	350	500		
9	Ed Andrews w/B.Hoover	100	120	150	250	350	500		
10	Wally Andrews	100	120	150	250	350	500		
11	Bill Annis	100	120	150	250	350	500		
12B	Cap Anson Street Clothes	2,500	3,000	4,000	5,000	6,000	8,000		
13	Old Hoss Ardner	100	120	150	250	350	500		
14	Tug Arundel	100	120	150	250	350	500		
15	Jersey Bakley	100	120	150	250	350	500		
16	Clarence Baldwin	100	120	150	250	350	500		
17	Mark (Fido) Baldwin	150	120	250	300	500	700		
18	Lady Baldwin	100	120	150	250	350	500		
19	James Banning	100	120	150	250	350	500		
20	Samuel Barkley	100	200	250	300	500	700		
21	Bald Billy Barnie MG	100	120	150	250	350	500		
22	Charles Bassett	100	120	150	250	350	500		
23	Charles Bastian	100	120	300	350	400	500		
24	Charles Bastian w/P.Schriver	100	120	150	250	350	500		
25	Ebenezer Beatin	100	120	150	250	350	500		
26	Jake Beckley	1,000	1,200	1,500	200	2,500	4,000		
28	Charles Bennett	100	120	150	250	350	500		
29	Louis Bierbauer	100	120	150	500	600	800		
30	Louis Bierbauer w/R.Gamble	100	120	150	250	350	500		
31	Bill Bishop	100	120	200	250	350	500		
32	William Blair	100	200	250	300	350	500		
33	Ned Bligh	120	150	200	250	350	500		
34	Bogart	100	120	150	250	350	500		
35	Boyce	100	120	300	350	400	500		
36	Jake Boyd	100	120	150	250	350	500		
37	Honest John Boyle	100	120	150	250	350	500		
38	Handsome Henry Boyle	100	120	300	400	500	600		
39	Nick Bradley	100	120	150	250	350	500		
40	George (Grin) Bradley	400	600	800	1,000	1,200	2,500		
43	Timothy Brosnan Minn	100	120	150	250	400	1,500		
44	Timothy Brosnan Sioux	100	120	200	300	350	500		
45	Cal Broughton	100	120	150	250	350	500		
46	Dan Brouthers	400	1,200	1,300	1,400	1,500	4,000		
47	Thomas Brown	100	120	250	300				
48	California Brown	100	200	250	300				
50	Charles Brynan	100	120	150	250	350	500		
51	Al Buckenberger MG	100	120	150	250	350	500		
52	Dick Buckley	100	200	250	300	350	500		
53	Charles Buffington	100	120	150	300	400	500		
54	Ernest Burch	100	120	150	300	350	500		
55	Bill Burdick	100	120	150	250	350	500		
56	Black Jack Burdock	100	120	300	350	400	500		
57	Robert Burks	100	120	150	250	350	500		
59	James Burns Omaha	100	120	150	250	400	800		
60	Jimmy Burns KC	100	120	150	250	350	500		
61	Tommy (Oyster) Burns	150	200	350	400	500	800		
62	Thomas E. Burns	100	120	150	300	350	500		
63	Doc Bushong Brooklyn	100	120	150	250	350	500		
64	Doc Bushong Browns Champs	150	200	400	500	800	1,200		
65	Patsy Cahill	100	120	150	900	1,000	1,200		
66	Count Campau	100	120	150	250	350	500		
67	Jimmy Canavan	100	120	150	250	350	500		
68	Bart Cantz	120	150	200	600	800	1,200		
69	Handsome Jack Carney	100	120	150	250	350	500		
70	Hick Carpenter	150	200	250	400	500	800		
71	Cliff Carroll	200	400	600	1,000	1,200	1,500		
72	Scrappy Carroll	100	120	150	250	350	500		
73	Frederick Carroll	100	250	300	400	500	600		
74	Jumbo Cartwright	150	200	250	400				
75	Bob Caruthers Brooklyn	200	250	350	1,800	2,000	2,500		
76	Bob Caruthers Browns Champs	200	300	350	400	500	800		
77	Daniel Casey	100	120	150	250	350	500		
78	Icebox Chamberlain	100	120	150	250	400	500		
79	Cupid Childs	100	120	150	250	350	500		
80	Bob Clark	150	200	300	400	500	800		
81	Owen (Spider) Clark	150	200	250	400	500	800		
83	William (Dad) Clarke	100	120	150	250	500	800		
84	Pete Connell	100	120	150	250	350	500		
85	John Clarkson	500	600	800	1,000	1,200			
86	Jack Clements	100	120	300	400	500	600		
87	Elmer Cleveland	120	150	350	400	450	500		
88	Monk Cline	100	150	200	250	350	500		
89	Mike Cody	100	120	250	300	350	500		
90	John Coleman	100	120	200	250	400	1,000		
91	Bill Collins	120	150	350	600	800	1,200		
92	Hub Collins	100	120	150	250	350	500		
93	Charles Comiskey	500	1,000	1,200	3,000	6,000	8,000		
94	Commy Comiskey Brown's	500	600	800	2,000	2,500	4,000		
95	Roger Connor Script	1,200	1,500	2,000	3,000	4,000	4,000		
96	Roger Connor New York	1,000	1,200	1,500	2,000	2,500	4,000		
97	Richard Conway	100	120	200	250	350	500		
98	Peter Conway	100	120	150	250	350	500		
99	James Conway	100	120	150	250	350	500		
100	Paul Cook	100	120	150	250	350	500		
101	Jimmy Cooney	120	150	200	250	350	500		
102	Larry Corcoran	150	200	250	2,500				
103	Pop Corkhill	100	120	150	250	350	500		
104	Cannon Ball Crane	120	300	350	400	450	500		
105	Samuel Crane	150	200	250	300	400	600		
106	Jack Crogan	100	450	550	650	800	1,000		
107	John Crooks	100	200	250	300	350	500		
108	Lave Cross	100	120	150	250	350	500		
109	Bill Crossley	100	120	150	250	350	500		
111	Joe Crotty	120	150	200	250	350	500		
112	Billy Crowell	100	120	150	250	350	500		
113	Jim Cudworth	100	120	150	250	350	500		
114	Bert Cunningham	100	120	150	250	350	500		
115	Tacks Curtis	100	120	150	250	350	500		

#	Name	PrFr 1	GD 2	VG 3	VgEx 4	EX 5	ExMt 6	NM 7	NmMt 8
117	Ed Cushman	1,200	1,500	2,400	3,000	3,600	5,000		
118	Tony Cusick	1,200	1,500	2,000	2,500	3,000	4,000		
120	Edward Dailey Phi-Wash	100	150	200	250	350	500		
121	Edward Dailey Columbus	150	200	250	400	500	800		
122	Bill Daley	100	120	150	250	350	500		
123	Con Daley	100	200	250	300	350	500		
124	Abner Dalrymple	100	120	150	350	400	500		
125	Tom Daly	120	200	250	300	350	500		
126	James Daly	100	120	150	250	350	500		
127	Law Daniels	120	150	200	300	400	600		
128	Dell Darling	100	200	250	300	350	500		
129	William Darnbrough	100	120	150	250	350	500		
130	D.J. Davin	400	500	600	1,000	1,200	1,500		
131	Jumbo Davis	100	120	150	300	350	500		
132	Pat Dealey	100	120	300	400	500	600		
133	Thomas Deasley Throwing	100	120	150	250	400	500		
134	Thomas Deasley Fielding	120	150	200	400	500	600		
135	Edward Decker	100	120	200	250	350	500		
136	Ed Delahanty	3,000	7,500	9,000					
137	Jeremiah Denny	100	120	300	350	400	500		
138	James Devlin	100	120	200	250	350	500		
139	Thomas Dolan	100	120	150	250	350	500		
142	James Donahue	120	150	200	250	350	500		
143	James Donnelly	150	200	250	400	500	800		
146	Mike Dorgan	150	200	300	400	500	600		
148	Home Run Duffe	150	200	250	300	350	500		
149	Hugh Duffy	400	700	1,000	1,500	2,000	3,000		
150	Dan Dugdale	100	120	150	250	350	500		
151	Duck Duke	100	120	150	250	350	500		
152	Sure Shot Dunlap	150	200	250	300	350	500		
153	J. Dunn	150	200	250	400	500	800		
154	Jesse (Cyclone) Duryea	100	120	200	800	1,000	1,200		
155	John Dwyer	100	120	200	800	1,000	1,200		
156	Billy Earle	100	120	150	250	400	1,000		
157	Buck Ebright	100	120	150	250	350	500		
158	Red Ehret	100	120	150	250	350	500		
159	R. Emmerke	120	150	200	250	350	500		
160	Dude Esterbrook	100	120	150	1,500	2,000	2,800		
161	Henry Esterday	100	120	150	250	350	500		
162	Long John Ewing	100	120	150	250	350	500		
163	Buck Ewing	800	1,000	1,600	2,000	3,000	4,000		
164	Buck Ewing w/Mascot	800	1,000	2,000	4,000	6,000	8,000		
165	Jay Faatz	100	120	250	300	350	500		
166	Clinkgers Fagan	100	200	250	300	350	500		
167	William Farmer	100	150	200	250	350	500		
168	Sidney Farrar	120	150	200	250	300	500		
169	Jack (Moose) Farrell	150	150	200	300	400	600		
170	Charles(Duke) Farrell	100	120	150	250	350	500		
171	Frank Fennelly	100	150	200	250	350	500		
172	Charlie Ferguson	100	120	200	250	350	600		
173	Colonel Ferson	100	120	150	250	350	500		
175	Jocko Fields	120	250	300	400	500	600		
176	Fischer - Maroons	100	120	150	250	350	500		
177	Thomas Flanigan	100	120	150	250	350	500		
178	Silver Flint	120	200	250	300	400	1,000		
179	Thomas Flood	100	120	150	250	350	500		
180	Jocko Flynn Omaha	400	500	800	1,000	1,200	1,500		
181	James Fogarty	150	200	250	300	400	1,500		
182	Frank (Monkey) Foreman	100	120	150	250	350	500		
183	Thomas Forster	100	120	150	250	350	500		
185	Elmer Foster NY-Chi	100	120	150	400	600	800		
187	Scissors Foutz Brown's	120	300	400	500	600	800		
188	Scissors Foutz Brooklyn	100	120	150	250	350	600		
189	Julie Freeman	100	120	250	300	350	500		
190	Will Fry	100	120	150	250	350	500		
192	William Fuller	100	300	350	400	450	500		
193	Shorty Fuller	100	200	300	400	500	600		
194	Christopher Fullmer	100	120	150	300	400	500		
195	Christopher Fullmer w/T.Tucker	100	120	150	250	350	500		
196	Honest John Gaffney MG	120	150	200	300	400	600		
197	Pud Galvin	1,000	1,800	5,700	6,200				
198	Robert Gamble	100	250	300	400	500	600		
199	Charles Ganzel	120	150	200	250	350	500		
200	Gid Gardner	100	120	150	250	350	600		
201	Gid Gardner w/M.Murray	100	120	150	250	350	500		
202	Hank Gastreich	100	120	150	400	500	600		
203	Emil Geiss	100	120	150	250	350	500		
204	Frenchy Genins	100	120	300	400	500	600		
205	William George	100	150	200	250	350	500		
206	Joe Gerhardt	100	120	150	250	350	500		
207	Pretzels Getzein	100	150	200	250	350	500		
208	Lee Gibson	100	120	150	250	350	500		
209	Robert Gilks	100	150	200	400	500	600		
210	Pete Gillespie	100	250	300	350	400	800		
211	Barney Gilligan	100	120	150	250	350	500		
212	Frank Gilmore	100	120	150	250	350	500		
213	Pebbly Jack Glasscock	350	400	450	550	800	1,000		
214	Kid Gleason	120	150	200	500	600	1,500		
215	Brother Bill Gleason	200	250	300	500	800	1,000		
216	William Bill Gleason	120	200	300	400	500	600		
217	Mouse Glenn	100	150	200	250	350	500		
218	Michael Goodfellow	100	120	150	250	350	500		
219	George (Piano Legs) Gore	150	250	300	350	400	500		
220	Frank Graves	100	120	150	250	350	500		
221	William Greenwood	100	120	150	250	350	500		
222	Michael Greer	100	120	150	250	350	500		
223	Mike Griffin	250	300	400					
224	Clark Griffith	600	800	1,000	1,200	2,500	3,000		
225	Henry Gruber	100	120	200	250	350	500		
226	Addison Gumbert	100	120	150	250	350	500		
227	Thomas Gunning	100	120	150	250	350	500		
228	Joseph Gunson	100	120	150	250	350	500		
229	George Haddock	100	120	300	350	400	500		
230	William Hafner	100	120	150	250	350	600		
231	Willie Hahm Mascot	100	120	150	250	350	500		
232	William Hallman	100	120	200	250	350	500		
233	Billy Hamilton	600	800	1,000	1,200	2,000	1,000		
234	Willie Hamm w/N.Williamson	120	150	200	300	400	600		
237	Ned Hanlon	400	500	1,000	1,200	2,000	3,000		
238	William Hanrahan	100	120	150	250	350	500		
240	Pa Harkins	100	150	200	1,200	1,500	2,000		
241	William Hart	100	120	150	250	350	500		
242	William (Bill) Hasamdear	100	120	150	250	350	500		
243	Colonel Hatfield	120	150	200	250	350	675		
244	Egyptian Healey Wash-Ind	100	150	200	250	400	500		
245	Egyptian Healey Washington	100	120	150	250	350	500		
246	J.C. Healy	100	120	150	250	400	1,000		
247	Guy Hecker	100	120	150	250	350	500		
248	Tony Hellman	100	120	150	250	350	500		
249	Hardie Henderson	100	120	150	250	350	500		
250	Hardie Henderson w/M.Greer	100	120	150	250	350	500		
251	Moxie Hengle	100	120	150	250	350	500		
252	John Henry	100	120	150	250	350	500		
253	Edward Herr	150	200	250	300	350	500		
254	Hunkey Hines	100	120	150	250	350	500		
255	Paul Hines	100	120	150	250	350	500		
256	Texas Wonder Hoffman	100	120	150	250	350	500		
257	Eddie Hogan	100	120	150	250	350	500		
259	William Holbert	100	120	800	1,000	1,200	1,500		
260	James (Bugs) Holliday	100	120	200	250	400	500		
261	Charles Hoover	100	120	150	250	350	500		
262	Buster Hoover	100	120	150	250	350	500		
263	Jack Horner	300	500	700	900	1,200	5,000		
264	Jack Horner w/E.Warner	100	120	150	250	350	500		
265	Michael Hornung	100	120	300	400	500	800		
266	Pete Hotaling	100	120	150	250	350	500		
267	William Howes	100	120	200	250	350	500		
268	Dummy Hoy	1,200	1,500	2,000	2,500	3,000	4,000	6,000	
269	Nat Hudson Brown's	120	150	300	400	600	800		
270	Nat Hudson St. Louis	100	120	150	250	350	500		
271	Mickey Hughes	100	120	150	250	350	500		
272	Hungler	100	120	200	250	350	500		
273	Wild Bill Hutchinson	100	120	150	250	350	500		
274	John Irwin	100	120	150	250	350	500		
275	Arthur (Cut Rate) Irwin	100	120	150	250	350	600		
276	A.C. Jantzen	100	120	300	350	400	500		
277	Frederick Jevne	100	120	600	800	1,000	1,200		
278	John Johnson	120	150	200	250	350	500		
279	Richard Johnston	100	120	250	300	400	500		
280	Jordan	800	1,000	2,000					
281	Heinie Kappell	100	120	250	300	350	500		
282	Timothy Keefe	600	800	1,000	1,200	1,500	2,500		
283	Tim Keefe w/D.Richardson	500	600	800	1,000	2,300	2,500		
284	George Keefe	100	120	150	250	350	500		

#	Player	PrFr 1	GD 2	VG 3	VgEx 4	EX 5	ExMt 6	NM 7	NmMt 8
285	James Keenan	100	120	150	250	350	500		
286	Mike (King) Kelly	1,500	2,400	3,000	3,500	4,000	5,000		
287	Honest John Kelly MGR	350	400	450	550	800	1,000		
288	Kelly UMP	100	120	150	250	350	500		
289	Charles Kelly	200	250	1,000	1,100	1,200	1,500		
290	Kelly and Powell UMP-MGR	100	120	150	250	350	500		
291	Rudolph Kemmler Brown's	120	150	400	800	1,000	1,200		
292	Rudolph Kemmler St. Paul	100	120	150	250	350	500		
293	Theodore Kennedy	100	120	150	250	400	500		
294	J.J. Kenyon	100	120	150	250	350	500		
295	John Kerins	100	250	300	400	500	600		
296	Matthew Kilroy	100	120	150	250	350	500		
298	August Kloff	200	400	1,000	1,200	1,500	2,000		
299	William Klusman	100	120	150	250	350	500		
300	Phillip Knell	100	120	150	250	350	500		
301	Fred Knouf	100	150	200	300	350	500		
303	William Krieg	100	200	250	300	350	500		
304	William Krieg w/A.Kloff	100	120	150	250	350	500		
305	Gus Krock	120	200	350	400	450	600		
306	Willie Kuehne	100	120	150	250	350	500		
307	Frederick Lange	100	120	150	250	350	500		
308	Ted Larkin	100	120	150	250	350	500		
309	Arlie Latham Brown's	200	300	350	500	600	1,000		
310	Arlie Latham Stl-Chi	120	150	200	300	400	600		
311	John Lauer	100	120	150	250	350	500		
312	John Leighton	200	250	300	350	450	600		
314	Tom Loftus MGR	100	400	450	500	550	650		
315	Herman (Germany) Long	120	150	200	300	400	600		
317	Tom Lovett	100	120	150	250	350	500		
318	Bobby (Link) Lowe	120	150	200	300	400	600		
321	Dennis Lyons	100	120	150	250	350	500		
322	Harry Lyons	120	150	200	250	350	500		
323	Connie Mack	2,000	2,500	3,000	4,000	5,000	6,000		
324	Joe (Reddie) Mack	100	120	150	250	350	500		
325	James (Little Mack) Macullar	100	120	150	250	350	500		
326	Kid Madden	100	120	400	600	800	1,200		
327	Daniel Mahoney	100	120	150	250	350	500		
328	Willard (Grasshopper) Maines	100	120	150	250	350	500		
329	Fred Mann	100	120	150	400	500	700		
330	Jimmy Manning	100	120	150	250	350	500		
331	Charles (Lefty) Marr	100	120	150	250	350	500		
332	Mascot (Willie) Breslin	100	120	150	250	350	500		
333	Samuel Maskery	100	120	150	250	350	500		
335	Michael Mattimore	200	250	300	350	600	800		
336	Albert Maul	100	120	150	250	350	500		
338	Albert Mays	100	120	150	300	350	500		
339	James McAleer	100	120	150	250	350	500		
340	Tommy McCarthy	300	600	800	1,500	2,000	2,500		
341	John McCarthy	100	120	150	250	350	700		
342	James McCauley	100	120	150	250	350	500		
343	William McClellan	100	120	150	250	400	1,000		
344	John McCormack	150	200	250	350	450	600		
345	Big Jim McCormick	100	120	150	300	1,000	1,200		
346	McCreachery MGR	300	400	500	800	1,000	1,200		
347	James (Chippy) McGarr	100	120	150	250	350	500		
348	Jack McGeachy	100	150	200	350	450	600		
349	John McGlone	100	120	150	250	350	500		
350	James (Deacon) McGuire	200	250	300	400	500	600		
351	Bill McGunnigle MGR	120	200	250	300	400	500		
352	Ed McKean	100	120	150	250	350	500		
353	Alex McKinnon	100	250	300	350	400	500		
355	Bid McPhee	3,000	6,000	7,000	8,000	10,000	10,000		
356	James McQuaid	100	120	150	250	350	500		
357	John McQuaid UMP	100	120	150	250	350	500		
358	Jame McTamany	175	200	250	400	500	800		
359	George McVey	100	120	150	250	350	500		
362	George (Doggie) Miller	100	120	250	300	350	500		
363	Joseph Miller	100	120	150	250	350	500		
364	Jocko Milligan	100	120	200	250	350	500		
365	E.L. Mills	100	120	150	250	350	600		
366	Daniel Minnehan	100	120	150	250	-350	500		
367	Samuel Moffet	100	120	150	250	350	500		
368	Honest Morrell	150	200	250	400	500	800		
369	Ed Morris	120	150	200	250	350	500		
370	Morrisey	100	120	150	250	350	500		
371	Tony (Count) Mullane	120	150	200	500	600	800		
372	Joseph Mulvey	100	120	300	400	500	700		
373	P.L. Murphy	100	120	150	250	350	500		
374	Pat J. Murphy	100	120	150	250	350	500		
375	Miah Murray	100	120	150	250	350	500		
376	Truthful Mutrie MGR	350	400	450	500	800	1,000		
377	George Myers	100	200	250	300	350	500		
378	Al (Cod) Myers	120	200	250	300	400	800		
379	Thomas Nagle	100	120	150	250	350	500		
380	Billy Nash	200	250	300	400	500	800		
382	Kid Nichols	1,500	2,000	2,500	3,000	6,000	8,000		
383	Samuel Nichols	100	120	150	250	350	500		
384	J.W. Nicholson	100	120	150	250	350	500		
385	Tom Nicholson (Parson)	150	200	250	300	350	500		
386	Nick Nicholl Brown's	120	250	350	450	600	800		
387	Hugh Nicol	100	120	150	250	350	500		
388	Hugh Nicol w/J.Reilly	100	120	150	250	350	500		
389	Frederick Nyce	100	120	150	250	350	500		
390	Doc Oberlander	120	150	200	300	400	600		
391	Jack O'Brien	150	200	250					
392	Billy O'Brien	100	120	150	250	350	500		
393	Billy O'Brien w/J.Irwin	100	120	150	250	350	500		
394	Darby O'Brien	100	200	250	350	450	600		
395	John O'Brien	120	150	200	250	400	500		
396	P.J. O'Connell	100	120	150	250	400	500		
398	Hank O'Day	300	800	1,000	1,100	1,200	1,500		
399	O'Day	100	120	150	250	400	500		
400	James O'Neil Stl-Chi	120	150	200	250	500	800		
401	James O'Neil Brown's	120	150	200	400	500	600		
403	Jim O'Rourke	600	1,200	1,500	2,000	2,500	3,000		
404	Thomas O'Rourke	100	120	200	250	350	500		
406	David Orr	100	120	250	300	400	500		
407	Parsons	100	120	150	250	400	800		
408	Owen Patton	100	120	150	300	400	500		
409	James Peeples	100	120	150	250	400	500		
410	James Peeples w/H.Henderson	100	120	150	250	350	500		
412	Patrick Pettee	100	500	600	700	800	1,000		
413	Patrick Pettee w/B.Lowe	100	120	150	250	350	500		
414	Dandelion Pfeffer	150	200	250	500	600	800		
415	Dick Phelan	100	120	250	500	800	1,000		
416	William Phillips	100	120	200	250	350	500		
418	George Pinkney	100	120	250	300	350	500		
419	Thomas Poorman	100	200	250	300	350	500		
420	Henry Porter	250	300	400	450	600	800		
421	James Powell	100	150	200	300	400	500		
423	Bill (Blondie) Purcell	100	120	300	350	400	500		
424	Thomas Quinn	100	150	200	250	350	500		
425	Joseph Quinn	100	150	200	350	400	500		
426	Old Hoss Radbourne Portrait	1,200	2,000	2,200	2,500	4,000	5,000		
427	Old Hoss Radbourne In Action	1,200	2,000	2,200	2,500	3,000	4,000		
428	Shorty Radford	100	120	150	300	350	500		
429	Tom Ramsey	100	120	150	250	350	500		
430	Rehse	100	120	150	250	350	500		
431	Long John Reilly	100	120	150	250	600	800		
432	Charles (Princeton) Reilly	100	120	150	250	350	500		
433	Charles Reynolds	100	120	150	250	350	500		
434	Hardie Richardson	100	120	150	250	350	500		
435	Danny Richardson	100	200	250	350	450	600		
437	John Roach	100	200	250	400	500	600		
438	Wilbert Robinson	1,000	1,200	1,500	2,000	2,500	3,000		
439	M.C. Robinson	100	120	150	300	350	500		
440	Yank Robinson Stl	100	120	150	250	350	500		
441	Yank Robinson Brown's	200	250	300	500	600	800		
442	George Rooks	100	120	150	250	350	500		
445	Jack Rowe	100	120	150	250	350	500		
446	Amos Rusie	1,500	2,000	2,500	3,000				
447	Amos Rusie New York	1,500	2,000	3,000	4,000				
448	James Ryan	120	150	250	300	400	600		
449	Henry Sage	100	120	150	250	350	500		
450	Henry Sage w/W.Van Dyke	100	120	150	250	350	500		
451	Sanders	100	120	150	250	350	500		
452	Al (Ben) Sanders	100	120	200	250	350	500		
453	Frank Scheibeck	100	120	150	250	350	500		
454	Albert Schellhase	100	120	150	250	350	500		
455	William Schenkle	100	120	150	250	400	500		
456	Bill Schildknecht	100	120	150	250	350	500		
457	Gus Schmelz MG	100	120	150	250	350	500		
458	Lewis (Jumbo) Schoeneck	100	120	150	350	450	600		
459	Pop Schriver	100	150	200	250	350	600		

#	Name	PrFr 1	GD 2	VG 3	VgEx 4	EX 5	ExMt 6	NM 7	NmMt 8
460	John Seery	100	120	200	250	350	500		
461	William Serad	100	120	150	250	350	500		
462	Edward Seward	120	150	200	250	350	500		
463	George (Orator) Shafer	100	120	150	250	350	500		
464	Frank Shafer	100	120	150	250	350	500		
465	Daniel Shannon	100	120	150	250	350	500		
466	William Sharsig	100	120	150	250	350	500		
467	Samuel Shaw	100	120	150	250	350	500		
468	John Shaw	100	120	150	250	600	800		
469	William Shindle	100	120	150	250	350	500		
470	George Shoch	175	250	350	450	550	800		
471	Otto Shomberg	100	120	150	250	500	600		
472	Lev Shrev	100	250	350	450	550	700		
473	Ed (Baldy) Silch	100	150	200	250	350	500		
474	Michael Slattery	100	120	250	300	350	500		
475	Sam (Sky Rocket) Smith	100	120	150	800	1,000	1,200		
476	John Smith Portrait	400	500	600	1,500	2,000	2,500		
477	John Smith Non-Portrait	120	150	200	300	400	600		
478	Elmer Smith	100	120	150	250	350	500		
479	Fred (Sam) Smith	100	120	150	250	350	500		
480	George (Germany) Smith	100	120	150	250	350	500		
481	Pop Smith	100	120	150	250	800	1,000		
482	Nick Smith	100	120	200	250	350	500		
483	P.T. Somers	100	120	150	250	350	500		
484	Joe Sommer	100	120	150	300	350	500		
485	Pete Sommers	100	120	200	250	350	500		
486	William Sowders	120	150	200	250	350	500		
487	John Sowders	100	120	150	600	800	1,000		
488	Charles Sprague	100	120	150	250	350	500		
489	Edward Sproat	100	150	200	250	350	500		
490	Harry Staley	150	200	250	300	400	500		
491	Daniel Stearns	120	150	200	250	400	600		
492	Billy (Cannonball) Stemmyer	100	200	300	400	500	700		
493	B.F. Stephens	100	120	150	250	350	500		
494	John C. Sterling	100	120	150	250	350	500		
496	Harry Stovey	200	300	900	1,000	1,200	1,500		
497	C. Scott Stratton	100	120	500	600	800	1,200		
498	Joseph Straus	100	120	150	250	350	500		
499	John (Cub) Stricker	100	120	150	250	350	500		
500	Marty Sullivan	100	120	300	400	500	700		
501	Michael Sullivan	100	200	250	350	450	600		
502	Billy Sunday	500	800	1,000	2,000	2,500	6,000		
503	Sy Sutcliffe	100	120	150	250	350	500		
504	Ezra Sutton	100	400	450	500	600	800		
505	Ed Cyrus Swartwood	150	200	250	400	500	800		
506	Parke Swartzel	100	120	150	250	350	500		
507	Peter Sweeney	100	120	150	250	350	500		
509	Ed (Dimples) Tate	100	200	250	300	350	500		
510	Patsy Tebeau	120	150	200	300	400	600		
511	John Tener	100	120	150	425	550	800		
512	Bill (Adonis) Terry	100	120	150	250	350	500		
513	Sam Thompson	1,200	1,400	1,800	2,000	5,000	5,000		
514	Silent Mike Tiernan	120	200	250	300	400	600		
515	Ledell Titcomb	100	250	300	400	500	700		
516	Phillip Tomney	100	120	150	250	350	500		
517	Stephen Toole	150	200	250	400	500	600		
518	George Townsend	100	250	350	450	550	700		
519	William Traffley	100	120	150	250	500	1,000		
520	George Treadway	100	200	250	300	350	500		
521	Samuel Trott	100	120	150	250	800	1,000		
522	Samuel Trott w/T.Burns	100	120	150	250	800	1,000		
523	Tom (Foghorn) Tucker	100	120	150	250	350	500		
524	William Tuckerman	150	200	250	300	400	500		
525	George Turner	100	120	150	250	350	500		
526	Lawrence Twitchell	300	350	400	450	500	600		
527	James Tyng	100	120	150	250	350	500		
529	George (Rip) Van Haltren	150	200	250	400	500	800		
530	Farmer Harry Vaughn	100	120	150	250	350	500		
531	Peek-a-Boo Veach St. Paul	150	200	250	400	500	800		
533	Leon Viau	100	120	200	250	350	600		
534	William Vinton	100	120	150	250	350	500		
535	Joseph Visner	100	120	150	250	350	500		
537	Joseph Walsh	100	120	150	250	350	500		
538	John M. Ward	1,000	1,200	1,500	2,000	2,500	4,000		
539	E.H. Warner	150	200	250	400	500	800		
540	William Watkins MGR	100	300	400	500	600	800		
541	Farmer Bill Weaver	100	250	300	400	500	650		

#	Name	PrFr 1	GD 2	VG 3	VgEx 4	EX 5	ExMt 6	NM 7	NmMt 8
542	Charles Weber	150	200	250	300	400	500		
543	George (Stump) Weidman	150	200	250	350	450	800		
544	William Widner	100	120	150	250	350	500		
545	Curtis Welch Brown's	120	250	350	450	600	800		
546	Curtis Welch A's	100	120	150	400	500	600		
547	Curtis Welch w/B.Gleason	120	150	200	300	400	600		
548	Smilin Mickey Welch	1,000	1,500	1,800	2,000	4,000	5,000		
549	Jake Wells	100	120	150	250	350	500		
550	Frank Wells	100	120	150	250	350	500		
551	Joseph Werrick	100	120	150	250	350	500		
552	Milton (Buck) West	100	120	150	250	350	500		
553	Gus (Cannonball) Weyhing	100	120	150	250	350	500		
554	John Weyhing	100	120	150	300	400	500		
555	Bobby Wheelock	100	200	250	300	350	500		
556	Whitacre	100	120	150	250	400	500		
557	Pat Whitaker	100	120	150	250	350	500		
558	Deacon White	1,000	2,000	3,000	5,000	6,000	8,000		
559	William White	100	120	150	250	350	500		
560	Jim (Grasshopper) Whitney	120	150	200	300	400	600		
561	Arthur Whitney	120	150	500	600	800	1,000		
562	G. Whitney	100	120	150	250	350	500		
563	James Williams MG	100	120	150	2,500	3,000	5,000		
564	Ned Williamson	120	200	300	400	500	700		
565	Williamson and Mascot	100	120	150	250	350	500		
566	C.H. Willis	100	120	400	500	600	700		
567	Walt Wilmot	100	120	150	500	800	1,000		
568	George Winkleman Hartford	250	300	400	600	5,000	7,000		
569	Samuel Wise	100	300	400	500	600	800		
570	William (Chicken) Wolf	100	120	150	250	350	500		
571	George (Dandy) Wood	120	200	300	400	600	800		
572	Peter Wood	200	250	300	400	500	650		
573	Harry Wright	2,500	3,000	4,000	5,000	6,000	10,000		
574	Charles (Chief) Zimmer	100	120	150	250	350	500		
575	Frank Zinn	100	150	200	250	350	500		

—Many subjects within the N172 Old Judge set appear in multiple poses and/or text variations. Listed prices refer to all variations unless noted.

—High grade Commons and Minor Stars generally trade as follows: NM - $600-$1,000, NmMt - $1,200-$2,000 and Mint - $2,500-$4,000 per.

—Cap Anson Street Clothes PSA 8 (NmMt) sold for $31,900 (REA; 4/06)

—Jake Beckley SGC 88 (NmMt) sold for $15,829 (Goodwin; 5/14)

—Stephen Behel Dotted Tie SGC 40 (VG) sold for $5,948 (Mastro; 8/07)

—John Clarkson Boston PSA 7 (NM) sold for $4,915 (Mastro; 8/07)

—John Clarkson Boston PSA 7 (NM) sold for $3,480 (REA 5/05)

—John Clarkson Chicago GAI 7 (NM) sold for $2,520 (Mastro; 4/07)

—John Clarkson Chicago GAI 7 (NM) sold for $2,430 (Sloate; 1/08)

—Charles Comiskey Brown's Champs SGC 84 (NM) sold for $7,919 (Mastro; 4/07)

—Charles Comiskey Brown's Champs SGC 84 (NM) sold for $6,926 (Sloate; 1/08)

—Ed Delahanty Hands at Waist SGC 88 (NmMt) sold for $31,598 (Goodwin; 7/10)

—Ed Delahanty Hands at Waist PSA 8 (NmMt) sold for $19,720 (REA; 4/06)

—Ed Delahanty Hands at Waist SGC 84 (NM) sold for $16,450 (REA; 5/10)

—Ed Delahanty Hands at Waist SGC 84 (NM) sold for $16,440 (Goodwin; 7/13)

—Ed Delahanty Hands at Waist SGC 84 (NM) sold for $13,916 (Sloate; 1/08)

—Ed Delahanty Hands at Waist SGC 84 (NM) sold for $10,780 (Mastro; 4/07)

—John Doran SGC 30 (Good) sold for $50,000 (Legendary; 11/12)

—Clark Griffith Ball in Hands SGC 84 (NM) sold for $5,415 (Memory Lane; 11/05)

—Clark Griffith Right Hand at Head SGC 84 (NM) sold for $4,468 (Mastro; 4/07)

—Billy Hamilton w/Bat PSA 8 (NmMt) sold for $6,691 (Mastro; 4/07)

—Billy Hamilton w/Bat PSA 8 (NmMt) sold for $5,418 (Sloate; 1/08)

—Frank Hankinson Dotted Tie SGC 60 (EX) sold for $5,531 (Goodwin; 11/05)

—Dummy Hoy Right Arm Over Head SGC 84 (NM) sold for $4,640 (REA; 4/06)

—$10,000 Kelly Portrait w/Cap Chicago SGC 84 (NM) sold for $5,800 (REA 4/06)

—Tommy McCarthy St. Louis Fielding PSA 8 (NmMt) sold for $6,555 (Sloate; 3/07)

—Bid McPhee Catching Ball SGC 84 (NM) sold for $9,595 (Mastro; 8/06)

—Bid McPhee Catching Ball SGC 84 (NM) sold for $7,361 (Mastro; 4/07)

—John McQuaid UMP PSA 3.5 (VG+) sold for $16,035 (Goodwin; 7/13)

—John McQuaid UMP PSA 3.5 (VG+) sold for $8,030 (Goodwin; 6/12)

—Jim O'Rourke Bat in Hand SGC 88 (NmMt) sold for $7,049 (Mastro; 8/06)

—Jim O'Rourke Throwing PSA 9 (MT) sold for $11,611 (Mastro; 8/06)

—Jim O'Rourke #403 SGC 88 (NmMt) sold for $6,032 (Goodwin; 6/12)

—Amos Rusie SGC 60 (EX) sold for $6,500 (REA; 05/12)

—David Orr Dotted Tie SGC 60 (EX) sold for $2,963 (Mastro; 8/07)

—David Orr Dotted Tie SGC 60 (EX) sold for $2,644 (REA; 4/07)

—Old Hoss Radbourne Hands on Hips SGC 84 (NM) sold for $7,199 (Mastro; 4/07)

—Old Hoss Radbourne Hands on Hips SGC 84 (NM) sold for $6,773 (Sloate; 1/08)

—Captain John Ward PSA 9 (MT) sold for $29,375 (REA; 5/08)

—Captain John Ward Sliding PSA 8 (NmMt) sold for $7,361 (Mastro; 12/06)
—John Ward Portrait PSA 7 (NM) sold for $8,878 (SCP; 7/08)
—Arthur Whitney #561 SGC 70 (EX+) sold for $5,729 (Goodwin; 8/12)
—Harry Wright Portrait PSA 8 (NmMt) sold for $19,720 (REA; 4/06)
—Harry Wright Portrait PSA 7 (NM) sold for $10,755 (Heritage; 5/07)

1888 Allen and Ginter N29

		PrFr 1	GD 2	VG 3	VgEx 4	EX 5	ExMt 6	NM 7	NmMt 8
1	Buck Ewing#(Baseball	600	800	1,000	1,200	1,500	2,500	3,000	6,000

—Buck Ewing PSA 9 (MT) sold for $15,080 (REA; 4/06)
—James Ryan PSA 9 (MT) sold for $3,355 (Mastro; 12/06)

1888 Goodwin Champions N162

		PrFr 1	GD 2	VG 3	VgEx 4	EX 5	ExMt 6	NM 7	NmMt 8
1	Ed Andrews (Baseball)	400	600	800	1,000	1,200	2,500		
2	Cap Anson (Baseball)	2,000	2,500	3,000	4,000	6,000	12,000		
3	Dan Brouthers (Baseball)	800	1,000	1,200	1,500	2,500	4,000		
4	Bob Caruthers (Baseball)	400	600	800	1,000	1,500	2,500	3,000	
5	Fred Dunlap (Baseball)	400	600	800	1,000	1,500	2,500		
6	Jack Glasscock (Baseball)	400	600	800	1,000	1,500	3,000		
7	Tim Keefe (Baseball)	600	800	1,000	1,800	2,500			
8	King Kelly (Baseball)	1,000	1,500	2,000	3,000	5,000	8,000		

—Ed Andrews PSA 7 (NM) sold for $6,600 (Mastro; 5/08)
—Ed Andrews PSA 7 (NM) sold for $3,884 (Heritage; 10/07)
—Cap Anson PSA 7 (NM) sold for $25,831 (Memory Lane; 5/08)
—Cap Anson PSA 7 (NM) sold for $23,184 (Goodwin; 3/09)
—Cap Anson PSA 7 (NM) sold for $10,443 (Mastro; 12/05)
—Cap Anson SGC 80 (ExMt) sold for $13,698 (Mastro; 4/07)
—Dan Brouthers PSA 7 (NM) sold for $11,596 (Mastro; 4/07)
—Dan Brouthers PSA 7 (NM) sold for $6,600 (Mastro; 5/08)
—Fred Dunlap PSA 7.5 (NM+) sold for $9,000 (mastro; 5/08)
—Tim Keefe PSA 8 (NmMt) sold for $18,448 (Goodwin; 11/07)
—Tim Keefe PSA 7 (NM) sold for $13,394 (Mastro; 4/07)
—Tim Keefe SGC 80 (ExMt) sold for $7,050 (REA; 5/08)
—Tim Keefe PSA 6 (ExMt) sold for $3,680 (Superior; 3/05)
—King Kelly PSA 8 (NmMt) sold for $66,337 (SCP; 7/08)
—King Kelly PSA 8 (NmMt) sold for $18,975 (SCP Sotheby's 8/03)
—King Kelly PSA 7 (NM) sold for $12,000 (Mastro; 5/08)

1895 Mayo's Cut Plug N300

		PrFr 1	GD 2	VG 3	VgEx 4	EX 5	ExMt 6	NM 7	NmMt 8
1	Charlie Abbey	350	500	650	700	1,000			
2	Cap Anson	2,000	2,500	4,000	6,000	8,000			
3	Jimmy Bannon	200	300	400	500	800			
4A	Dan Brouthers Baltimore	1,200	2,000	2,500	3,000	4,000			
4B	Dan Brouthers Louisville	1,200	2,000	2,500	3,000	4,000			
5	Ed Cartwright	200	300	450	500	800			
6	John Clarkson	500	800	1,200	1,500	2,500	4,000		
7	Tommy Corcoran	200	300	400	500				
8	Lave Cross	200	300	400	500	800			
9	William Dahlen	300	400	1,000	1,200				
10	Tom Daly	200	300	400	500	800			
11	Ed Delehanty UER	1,500	2,800	3,000	4,000	6,000			
12	Hugh Duffy	500	800	1,500	2,500				
13A	Buck Ewing Cincinnati	1,200	2,000	2,500	3,000	5,000			
13B	Buck Ewing Cleveland	1,200	2,200	2,500	3,000	5,000			
14	Dave Foutz	200	300	400	500	800			
15	Bill Joyce	200	250	400	600	800			
16	Charlie Ganzel	200	300	400	500	800			
17A	Jack Glasscock Louisville	200	300	400	500	800			
17B	Jack Glasscock Pittsburgh	300	500	800	1,000				
18	Mike Griffin	200	300	400	500	800			
19A	George Haddock No Team	400	700	1,200					
19B	George Haddock Philadelphia	200	300	400	500	800			
20	Bill Hallman	200	300	500	500	1,000			
21	Billy Hamilton	600	1,000	1,600	2,000	3,300			
22	Brickyard Kennedy	250	400	500	700	1,000			
23A	Tom Kinslow No Team	400	600	1,000					
23B	Tom Kinslow Pittsburgh	300	500	800	1,000	1,200			
24	Arlie Latham	200	350	400	500	800			
25	Herman Long	200	300	400	500	800			
26	Tom Lovett	200	300	400	500	800			
27	Link Lowe	200	300	400	500	800			
28	Tommy McCarthy	500	800	1,200	1,500	2,000			
29	Yale Murphy	250	400	500	700	1,000			

		PrFr 1	GD 2	VG 3	VgEx 4	EX 5	ExMt 6	NM 7	NmMt 8
30	Billy Nash	200	350	400	500	800			
31	Kid Nichols	1,500	2,500	3,000	4,000	7,500			
32A	Fred Pfeffer 2nd Base	250	400	500	700	1,000			
32B	Fred Pfeffer Retired	250	400	500	700	1,000			
33	Wilbert Robinson	1,000	1,500	2,000	2,500	4,000			
34A	Amos Rusie COR	800	2,000	2,500	3,000	5,000			
34B	Amos Russie ERR	1,000	1,500	2,000	2,500	4,000			
35	Jimmy Ryan	200	300	400	500	800			
36	Bill Shindle	200	300	400	500	800			
37	Germany Smith	200	300	400	500	800			
38	Otis Stockdale UER	200	300	400	500	800			
39	Tommy Tucker	200	300	400	500	800			
40A	John Ward 2nd Base	1,000	1,500	2,500	3,000	4,000			
40B	John Ward Retired	1,000	1,500	2,000	2,500	4,000			

—Cap Anson PSA 7 (NM) sold for $18,832 (SCP; 7/08)
—Cap Anson SGC 80 (ExMt) sold for $14,100 (REA; 5/08)
—Tommy Corcoran SGC 60 (EX) sold for $4,406 (REA; 5/08)
—Buck Ewing Cincinnati PSA 6 (ExMt) sold for $9,860 (REA; 5/05)
—Buck Ewing Cleveland #13B SGC 84 (NrMt) sold for $9,960 (Greg Bussineau; 7/12)
—Buck Ewing Cleveland SGC 84 (NM) sold for $13,853 (eBay; 4/07)
—Buck Ewing Cleveland SGC 7 (Nm) sold for $9,400 (REA; 05/11)
—Jack Glasscock Pittsburgh SGC 60 (EX) sold for $3,231 (REA; 5/08)
—Tommy McCarthy SGC 80 (ExMt) sold for $4,113 (REA; 5/08)
—Kid Nichols PSA 8 (NmMt) sold for $16,450 (REA; 05/11)
—Kid Nichols PSA 8 (NmMt) sold for $15,600 (SCP Sotheby's; 12/05)
—Amos Rusie COR SGC 80 (ExMt) sold for $7,050 (REA; 5/08)
—John Ward Retired SGC 80 (ExMt) sold for $8,120 (REA; 5/05)
—John Ward Retired SGC 80 (ExMt) sold for $5,581 (REA; 5/08)

1903-04 Breisch-Williams E107

	PrFr 1	GD 2	VG 3	VgEx 4	EX 5	ExMt 6	NM 7	NmMt 8

—Jake Beckley SGC 30 (Good) sold for $7,845 (Mastro; 4/06)
—Jack Chesbro SGC 40 (VG) sold for $15,103 (Mastro; 8/07)
—Jack Chesbro SGC 30 (Good) sold for $15,600 (eBay; 12/05)
—Jack Chesbro SGC 10 (Poor) sold for $4,468 (Mastro; 4/07)
—Fred Clarke SGC 10 (Poor) sold for $8,676 (eBay; 12/06)
—Fred Clarke SGC 10 (Poor) sold for $2,092 (Brockelman and Luckey; 6/08)
—Jimmy Collins SGC 40 (VG) sold for $11,732 (Mastro; 8/07)
—Tommy Corcoran SGC 10 (Poor) sold for $11,000 (Legendary; 8/13)
—Ed Delahanty SGC 10 (Poor) sold for $74,750 (Huggins and Scott; 10/07)
—Ed Delahanty SGC 10 (Poor) sold for $23,700 (REA; 5/13)
—Ed Delahanty SGC 10 (Poor) sold for $17,000 (Legendary; 8/13)
—Ed Delahanty SGC Authentic sold for $15,600 (eBay; 12/05)
—Elmer Flick SGC 30 (Good) sold for $5,205 (Memory Lane; 5/08)
—Addie Joss SGC 45 (VG+) sold for $14,220 (REA; 5/13)
—Addie Joss SGC 40 (VG) sold for $13,200 (Mastro; 5/08)
—Addie Joss PSA 1 (Poor) sold for $5,368 (eBay; 12/06)
—Addie Joss SGC 10 (Poor) sold for $3,355 (Mastro; 4/07)
—Willie Keeler SGC 30 (Good) sold for $15,600 (eBay; 12/05)
—Willie Keeler SGC 30 (Good) sold for $14,383 (Mastro; 8/07)
—Willie Keeler SGC 20 (Fair) sold for $10,665 (REA; 5/13)
—Christy Mathewson SGC 30 (Good) sold for $119,500 (Heritage; 8/10)
—Christy Mathewson SGC 20 (Fair) sold for $120,000 (Mastro; 12/08)
—Christy Mathewson SGC 20 (Fair) sold for $67,500 (Legendary; 11/13)
—Joe McGinnity SGC 10 (Poor) sold for $5,288 (REA; 5/08)
—Joe McGinnity SGC 10 (Poor) sold for $4,046 (Mastro; 4/07)
—Eddie Plank SGC 30 (Good) sold for $16,816 (Mastro; 4/07)
—Eddie Plank SGC 10 (Poor) sold for $7,800 (Mastro; 5/08)
—Eddie Plank #120 SGC 10 (Poor) sold for $6,115 (Goodwin; 7/12)
—Rube Waddell #148 SGC 20 (Fair) sold for $5,558 (Goodwin; 7/12)
—Honus Wagner SGC 40 (VG) sold for $133,933 (Mastro; 4/07)
—Vic Willis SGC 20 (Fair) sold for $5,118 (Mastro; 6/07)
—Cy Young SGC 60 (EX) sold for $79,068 (Mile High; 03/09)
—Cy Young PSA 5 (EX) sold for $68,150 (Memory Lane; 12/07)
—Cy Young SGC 40 (VG) sold for $72,000 (Mastro; 8/07)
—Cy Young SGC 10 (Poor) sold for $15,859 (Mastro; 4/07)

1906 Fan Craze AL WG2

		GD 2	VG 3	VgEx 4	EX 5	ExMt 6	NM 7	NmMt 8	MT 9
1	Nick Altrock	30	40	50	60	80	120	200	400
2	Jim Barrett	25	30	40	50	60	80	120	400
3	Harry Bay	25	30	40	50	60	80	120	300
4	Chief Bender	100	120	150	200	250	400	600	1,200
5	Bill Bernhardt	25	30	40	50	60	80	120	300
6	Bill Bradley	25	30	40	50	60	80	120	300

#		GD 2	VG 3	VgEx 4	EX 5	ExMt 6	NM 7	NmMt 8	MT 9
7	Jack Chesbro	100	120	150	200	400	600	800	1,200
8	Jimmy Collins	80	100	120	150	200	300	500	1,000
9	Sam Crawford	120	150	200	250	300	500	800	1,500
10	Lou Criger	25	30	40	50	60	80	120	300
11	Lave Cross	25	30	40	50	60	80	120	300
12	Monty Cross	25	30	40	50	60	80	120	300
13	Harry Davis	25	30	40	50	60	80	120	300
14	Bill Dineen	25	30	40	50	60	80	120	300
15	Pat Donovan	25	30	40	50	60	80	120	300
16	Pat Dougherty	25	30	40	50	60	80	120	300
17	Norman Elberfeld	25	30	40	50	60	80	120	300
18	Hobe Ferris	25	30	40	50	60	80	120	300
19	Elmer Flick	80	100	120	150	200	300	500	1,000
20	Buck Freeman	25	30	40	50	60	80	120	300
21	Fred Glade	25	30	40	50	60	80	120	300
22	Clark Griffith	80	100	120	150	200	300	500	1,000
23	Charles Hickman	25	30	40	50	60	80	120	300
24	William Holmes	25	30	40	50	60	80	120	300
25	Harry Howell	25	30	40	50	60	80	120	300
26	Frank Isbell	25	30	40	50	60	80	120	300
27	Albert Jacobson	25	30	40	50	60	80	120	300
28	Ban Johnson PRES	120	150	200	250	300	500	800	1,500
29	Fielder Jones	25	30	40	50	60	80	120	300
30	Adrian Joss	120	150	200	250	300	500	800	1,500
31	Willie Keeler	100	120	150	200	250	400	600	1,200
32	Nap Lajoie	120	150	200	250	300	500	800	1,500
33	Connie Mack MG	150	200	200	250	300	500	800	2,000
34	Jimmy McAleer	25	30	40	50	60	80	120	300
35	Jim McGuire	25	30	40	50	60	100	120	300
36	Earl Moore	25	30	40	50	60	80	120	300
37	George Mullen	40	50	60	80	100	120	200	500
38	Billy Owen	25	30	40	50	60	80	120	300
39	Fred Parent	25	30	40	50	60	80	120	300
40	Case Patten	25	30	40	50	80	100	120	300
41	Eddie Plank	150	200	250	300	400	500	800	1,500
42	Ossie Schreckengost	25	30	40	50	80	100	120	300
43	Jake Stahl	30	40	50	60	80	120	200	400
44	Fred Stone	25	40	50	60	80	100	120	300
45	William Sudhoff	25	30	40	50	60	80	120	300
46	Roy Turner	25	30	40	80	100	120	120	300
47	Rube Waddell	80	100	120	150	200	300	500	1,000
48	Bob Wallace	60	80	100	120	150	250	400	800
49	G. Harris White	25	30	40	50	60	80	120	300
50	George Winter	25	30	40	50	60	80	120	300
51	Cy Young	250	300	600	700	800	1,500	2,000	

—A handful of PSA 10 (Gem) Commons & Minor Stars have sold on eBay in recent times between $400-$800 per.
—Jimmy Collins PSA 10 (Gem) sold for $3,000 (eBay; 12/06)
—Eddie Plank PSA 10 (Gem) sold for $4,446 (SCP; 3/09)
—Eddie Plank PSA 10 (Gem) sold for $3,000 (eBay; 11/06)

1906 Fan Craze NL WG3

#		GD 2	VG 3	VgEx 4	EX 5	ExMt 6	NM 7	NmMt 8	MT 9
1	Red Ames	25	30	40	50	60	80	120	300
2	Ginger Beaumont	25	30	40	50	60	80	120	300
3	Jake Beckley	100	120	150	200	250	400	600	1,200
4	Billy Bergen	25	30	40	50	60	80	120	300
5	Roger Bresnahan	100	120	150	200	250	400	600	1,200
6	George Brown	25	30	40	60	80	100	120	300
7	Mordacai Brown (Mordecai)	100	120	150	200	250	400	600	1,200
8	Doc Casey	25	30	40	50	60	80	120	300
9	Frank Chance	80	100	120	150	200	300	500	1,000
10	Fred Clarke	80	100	120	150	200	300	500	1,000
11	Tommy Corcoran	25	30	40	50	60	80	200	300
12	Bill Dahlen	30	60	80	100	120	150	200	400
13	Mike Donlin	25	30	40	50	60	80	120	300
14	Charley Dooin	25	30	40	50	60	80	120	300
15	Mickey Doolin (Doolan)	25	30	40	50	60	80	120	300
16	Hugh Duffy	80	100	120	150	200	300	500	1,000
17	John E. Dunleavy	25	30	40	50	60	80	120	300
18	Bob Ewing	25	30	40	50	60	80	120	350
19	Chick Fraser	25	30	40	50	60	80	120	300
20	Ned Hanlon MG	80	100	120	150	300	400	500	1,000
21	Del Howard	25	30	40	50	60	80	120	300
22	Miller Huggins	80	100	120	150	200	300	500	1,000
23	Joe Kelley	80	100	120	150	200	300	500	1,300
24	John Kling	25	30	40	50	60	80	150	300
25	Tommy Leach	25	30	40	50	60	80	120	300
26	Harry Lumley	25	30	40	50	60	80	120	300
27	Carl Lundgren	25	30	40	50	60	80	120	300
28	Bill Maloney	25	30	40	50	60	80	120	800
29	Dan McGann	25	30	40	50	60	80	120	300
30	Joe McGinnity	80	100	120	150	200	300	500	1,000
31	John McGraw MG	80	100	120	150	200	300	500	1,000
32	Harry McIntire	25	30	40	50	60	80	120	300
33	Kid Nichols	50	60	80	300	400	500	700	1,200
34	Mike O'Neil	25	30	40	50	60	80	120	350
35	Orval Overall	25	30	40	50	80	100	120	300
36	Frank Pfeffer	25	30	40	50	60	80	120	300
37	Deacon Philippe	25	30	40	50	60	80	120	300
38	Charley Pittinger	25	30	40	50	60	80	120	350
39	Harry C. Pulliam PRES	25	30	40	50	60	80	120	300
40	Ed Reulbach	25	30	40	50	60	80	120	350
41	Claude Ritchey	25	30	40	60	80	100	120	350
42	Cy Seymour	25	30	40	50	60	80	120	800
43	Jim Sheckard	25	30	40	50	60	80	120	300
44	Jack Taylor	25	30	40	60	80	100	120	300
45	Dummy Taylor	25	30	40	100	120	150	200	1,000
46	Fred Tenny (Tenney)	25	30	40	50	60	80	120	300
47	Harry Theilman	25	30	40	50	60	80	100	300
48	Roy Thomas	25	30	40	50	60	80	120	300
49	Honus Wagner	800	1,500	1,800	2,000	2,500	3,000	4,000	
50	Jake Weimer	25	30	40	50	60	80	120	350
51	Bob Wicker	25	30	40	50	60	80	120	300
52	Vic Willis	80	100	120	150	200	300	500	1,000
53	Lew Wiltsie	25	30	40	50	60	80	400	600
54	Irving Young	25	30	40	60	80	100	120	300

1909 E92-1 Dockman and Sons

#		PrFr 1	GD 2	VG 3	VgEx 4	EX 5	ExMt 6	NM 7	NmMt 8
1	Harry Bemis	30	60	100	200	350	500		
2	Chief Bender	80	200	250	400				
3	Bill Bergen	30	120	150	200	350	500		
4	Bob Bescher	30	120	150	200	350	500		
5	Al Bridwell	30	60	150	200	350	600		
6	Joe Casey	30	60	100	200	350	500		
7	Frank Chance	100	250	350	600	800			
8	Hal Chase	60	120	200	300	500	800		
9	Sam Crawford	150	200	350	600	1,000			
10	Harry Davis	30	100	120	200	350	500		
11	Art Devlin	30	60	150	200	350	500		
12	Bill Donovan	30	60	100	200	350	500		
13	Mickey Doolan	30	60	100	200	350	500		
14	Patsy Dougherty	30	60	100	200	350	500		
15	Larry Doyle Batting	30	60	120	200	350	500		
16	Larry Doyle Throwing	30	60	150	200	350	500		
17	George Gibson	30	60	150	200	500	800		
18	Topsy Hartsel	30	60	100	200	350	500		
19	Hugh Jennings	100	250	350	600	1,000	1,200		
20	Red Kleinow	30	120	150	200	350	1,000		
21	Nap Lajoie	200	300	500	800	1,200			
22	Hans Lobert	30	60	100	200	350	500		
23	Sherry Magee	30	60	100	200	350	500		
24	Christy Matthewson	400	800	1,200	2,000	3,000	5,000		
25	John McGraw	100	250	350	600	1,000			
26	Larry McLean	30	120	150	200	350	500		
27	Dots Miller Batting	30	60	100	200	350	500		
28	Danny Murphy	30	60	100	120	350	500		
29	Bill O'Hara	30	80	100	200	350	500		
30	Germany Schaefer	30	80	100	200	550	600		
31	Admiral Schlei	30	150	200	250	350	500		
32	Boss Schmidt	30	80	100	200	350	600		
33	John Siegle	60	100	150	250	350	1,500		
34	Dave Shean	30	60	150	200	350	500		
35	Frank Smith	30	60	100	200	350	500		
36	Joe Tinker	100	250	350	600	1,000			
37	Honus Wagner Batting	1,000	1,500	2,800	4,000				
38	Honus Wagner Throwing	1,000	2,000	2,800	3,500	5,000			
39	Cy Young Cleveland	400	800	1,100	1,500	2,500			
40	Heinie Zimmerman	35	60	100	200	350	500		

—Hughie Jennings PSA 8 (NmMt) sold for $4,6692 (Goodwin; 11/07)
—Christy Mathewson PSA 7 (NM) sold for $6,289 (eBay; 8/06)

—Christy Matthewson SGC 86 (NrMt+) sold for $14,034 (Goodwin; 10/12)
—Christy Matthewson SGC 86 (NrMt+) sold for $11,212 (Goodwin; 5/14)
—John McGraw PSA 7 (NM) sold for $4,201 (Goodwin; 6/06)
—Honus Wagner Batting PSA 5 (EX) sold for $7,307 (Goodwin; 11/07)
—Honus Wagner Throwing PSA 6 (ExMt) sold for $9,950 (eBay; 2/07)
—Honus Wagner Throwing #38 PSA 6 (ExMt) sold for $6,462 (Huggins and Scott; 8/12)

1909 E92-2 Croft's Candy

		PrFr 1	GD 2	VG 3	VgEx 4	EX 5	ExMt 6	NM 7	NmMt 8
1	Jack Barry	50	100	150	200	350	500		
2	Harry Bemis	50	100	120	300	350	500		
3	Chief Bender Striped Cap	100	250	350	600	1,000			
4	Chief Bender White Cap	100	250	350	600	1,000			
5	Bill Bergen	50	100	120	200	350	500		
6	Bob Bescher	50	100	120	200	350	500		
7	Al Bridwell	50	100	120	200	350	500		
8	Doc Casey	50	100	120	200	350	500		
9	Frank Chance	100	300	350	600	1,000			
10	Hal Chase	80	150	200	300	500	800		
11	Ty Cobb	2,000	3,000	4,000	14,000				
12	Eddie Collins	100	250	350	725	1,000			
13	Sam Crawford	100	250	350	600	1,000			
14	Harry Davis	50	100	120	200	350	500		
15	Art Devlin	50	100	120	200	350	500		
16	Bill Donovan	50	100	120	200	350	500		
17	Red Dooin	50	100	120	200	350	500		
18	Mickey Doolan	50	100	120	200	350	500		
19	Patsy Dougherty	50	100	120	200	350	500		
20	Larry Doyle Batting	50	300	400	500	600	800		
21	Larry Doyle Throwing	50	100	120	200	350	500		
22	Johnny Evers	100	250	350	600	1,000			
23	George Gibson	50	100	120	200	350	500		
24	Topsy Hartsel	50	100	120	200	350	500		
25	Fred Jacklitsch	50	100	120	200	350	500		
26	Hugh Jennings	50	100	120	200	350	950		
27	Red Kleinow	50	100	120	200	350	500		
28	Otto Knabe	50	100	120	200	350	500		
29	John Knight	50	100	120	200	350	500		
30	Nap Lajoie	120	300	500	800	1,200			
31	Hans Lobert	50	100	120	200	350	500		
32	Sherry Magee	50	100	120	200	350	500		
33	Christy Matthewson	600	1,000	1,200	3,000				
34	John McGraw	100	250	350	600	1,000			
35	Larry McLean	50	100	120	200	350	500		
36	Dots Miller Batting	50	100	120	200	350	500		
37	Dots Miller Fielding	50	100	120	200	350	500		
38	Danny Murphy	50	100	120	200	350	500		
39	Bill O'Hara	50	100	120	200	350	500		
40	Germany Schaefer	50	100	120	200	350	500		
41	Admiral Schlei	50	100	120	200	350	500		
42	Boss Schmidt	50	100	120	200	350	500		
43	Dave Shean	50	150	200	250	350	500		
44	John Siegle	50	100	120	200	350	500		
45	Frank Smith	50	100	120	200	350	500		
46	Joe Tinker	100	250	350	600	1,000			
47	Honus Wagner Batting	1,000	1,500	2,500	4,000				
48	Honus Wagner Throwing	1,400	1,800	2,000	3,000				
49	Cy Young	500	800	1,000	1,500	2,500			
50	Heinie Zimmerman	50	100	120	200	350	500		

—Cy Young PSA 7 (NM) sold for $13,045 (Mastro; 8/07)

1909 E92-3 Croft's Cocoa

		PrFr 1	GD 2	VG 3	VgEx 4	EX 5	ExMt 6	NM 7	NmMt 8
1	Jack Barry	50	150	200	250	350	500		
2	Harry Bemis	50	100	120	200	350	500		
3	Chief Bender Striped Cap	100	250	350	600	1,000			
4	Chief Bender White Cap	100	250	350	600	1,000			
5	Bill Bergen	50	100	120	200	350	500		
6	Bob Bescher	50	100	120	200	350	500		
7	Al Bridwell	50	150	200	250	400	500		
8	Doc Casey	50	100	120	200	350	500		
9	Frank Chance	100	500	600	700	1,000			
10	Hal Chase	80	150	200	500	600	800		
11	Ty Cobb	2,000	3,000	4,000	6,000	10,000			
12	Eddie Collins	100	250	350	600	1,000			

		PrFr 1	GD 2	VG 3	VgEx 4	EX 5	ExMt 6	NM 7	NmMt #
13	Sam Crawford	100	250	350	600	1,000			
14	Harry Davis	50	100	120	200	350	500		
15	Art Devlin	50	100	120	200	350	500		
16	Bill Donovan	50	200	250	350	450	600		
17	Red Dooin	50	100	150	200	350	500		
18	Mickey Doolan	50	100	200	300	400	550		
19	Patsy Dougherty	50	100	120	200	350	500		
20	Larry Doyle Batting	50	100	120	200	350	500		
21	Larry Doyle Throwing	50	100	120	200	350	500		
22	Johnny Evers	100	250	350	600	1,000			
23	George Gibson	50	100	120	200	350	500		
24	Topsy Hartsel	50	100	120	200	350	500		
25	Fred Jacklitsch	50	100	120	200	350	500		
26	Hugh Jennings	100	250	400	600	1,000	1,200		
27	Red Kleinow	50	100	120	200	350	500		
28	Otto Knabe	50	100	120	200	350	500		
29	Jack Knight	50	100	120	200	350	500		
30	Nap Lajoie	120	300	600	800	1,200			
31	Hans Lobert	50	100	120	200	350	500		
32	Sherry Magee	50	100	120	200	350	500		
33	Christy Matthewson	600	1,000	2,000	3,000	3,500	5,000		
34	John McGraw	100	250	350	600	1,000			
35	Larry McLean	50	100	250	350	450	600		
36	Dots Miller Batting	50	100	120	200	350	500		
37	Dots Miller Fielding	50	150	200	250	350	500		
38	Danny Murphy	50	100	120	200	350	500		
39	Bill O'Hara	50	100	120	200	350	500		
40	Germany Schaefer	50	100	120	200	350	500		
41	Admiral Schlei	50	100	120	200	350	500		
42	Boss Schmidt	50	200	250	350	450	600		
43	Dave Shean	50	100	120	200	350	500		
44	John Siegle	50	100	120	200	350	500		
45	Frank Smith	50	100	120	200	350	500		
46	Joe Tinker	100	250	350	600	1,500			
47	Honus Wagner Batting	1,000	1,500	2,500	4,000				
48	Honus Wagner Throwing	1,000	1,500	3,300	4,300				
49	Cy Young Cleveland	500	800	1,200	1,700	2,800			
50	Heinie Zimmerman	50	100	120	200	350	500		

—Ty Cobb PSA 6 (ExMt) sold for $15,100 (eBay; 12/05)
—Cy Young PSA 7 (NM) sold for $5,510 (REA; 5/05)

1909 E92-4 Nadja Caramel

		PrFr 1	GD 2	VG 3	VgEx 4	EX 5	ExMt 6	NM 7	NmMt 8
1	Bill Bailey	50	100	150	200	350	500		
2	Jack Barry	50	100	120	200	350	500		
3	Harry Bemis	50	100	120	200	350	500		
4	Chief Bender Striped Cap	100	800	1,000	1,200	1,500			
5	Chief Bender White Cap	100	250	400	600	1,000			
6	Bill Bergen	50	100	120	200	350	500		
7	Bob Bescher	50	100	120	200	350	500		
8	Roger Bresnahan	100	200	250	300	500			
9	Al Bridwell	50	100	120	200	350	500		
10	Doc Casey	50	100	120	200	350	500		
11	Frank Chance	100	250	350	600	1,000			
12	Hal Chase	80	150	200	300	500	800		
13	Ty Cobb	2,000	3,000	4,000	6,000				
14	Eddie Collins	100	250	350	600	1,000			
15	Sam Crawford	100	250	350	600	1,000			
16	Harry Davis	50	100	120	200	350	500		
17	Art Devlin	50	100	120	200	350	500		
18	Bill Donovan	50	100	120	200	350	500		
19	Red Dooin	50	100	120	200	350	500		
20	Mickey Doolan	50	100	120	200	350	500		
21	Patsy Dougherty	50	100	120	200	350	500		
22	Larry Doyle Batting	50	100	120	200	350	500		
23	Larry Doyle Throwing	50	100	120	200	350	500		
24	Rube Ellis	50	100	120	200	350	500		
25	Johnny Evers	100	250	350	600	1,000			
26	George Gibson	50	100	120	200	350	500		
27	Topsy Hartsel	50	100	120	200	350	500		
28	Roy Hartzell Batting	50	100	120	200	300	500		
29	Roy Hartzell Fielding	50	80	100	120	250	500		
30	Harry Howell Follow Through	50	100	120	200	300	500		
31	Harry Howell Ready to Pitch	50	120	150	200	250	500		
32	Fred Jacklitsch	50	100	120	200	350	500		
33	Hugh Jennings	100	250	350	600	1,000	500		

	PrFr 1	GD 2	VG 3	VgEx 4	EX 5	ExMt 6	NM 7	NmMt 8
Red Kleinow	50	100	120	200	350	500		
Otto Knabe	50	100	120	200	350	500		
Jack Knight	50	100	120	200	350	500		
Nap Lajoie	120	300	500	800	1,200			
Hans Lobert	50	100	120	200	350	500		
Sherry Magee	60	100	120	200	350	500		
Christy Matthewson	600	1,000	1,200	2,000	3,000	5,000		
John McGraw	100	250	350	600	1,000	1,200		
Larry McLean	50	100	120	200	350	500		
Dots Miller Batting	60	100	120	300	400	500		
Dots Miller Fielding	50	100	120	200	350	500		
Danny Murphy	50	100	120	200	350	500		
Rebel Oakes	120	150	200	250	300	500		
Bill O'Hara	50	100	120	200	350	500		
Ed Phelps	50	100	120	200	350	500		
Germany Schaefer	50	100	120	200	350	500		
Admiral Schlei	50	100	120	200	350	500		
Boss Schmidt	50	100	120	200	350	500		
Dave Shean	50	100	120	200	350	500		
Johnny Seigle (Siegle)	50	100	120	200	350	500		
Frank Smith	50	100	120	200	350	500		
George Stone Blue Back	50	100	120	200	250	500		
George Stone Green Back	50	100	120	200	300	500		
Joe Tinker	100	250	350	600	1,000			
Honus Wagner Batting	1,000	1,500	6,000	8,000				
Honus Wagner Throwing	1,000	1,500	2,000	3,000				
Bobby Wallace	80	150	250	400	600	1,000		
Cy Young	500	800	1,000	1,500	2,500			
Heinie Zimmerman	50	100	120	200	350	500		

—Roger Bresnahan SGC 84 (NM) sold for $2,569 (Mastro; 6/06)
—Johnny Evers PSA 4 (VgEx) sold for $3,055 (Goodwin; 11/07)
—Honus Wagner Throwing PSA 5 (EX) sold for $12,948 (Goodwin; 11/07)
—Cy Young PSA 4 (VgEx) sold for $5,034 (Goodwin; 11/07)

1909 Philadelphia Caramel E95

		PrFr 1	GD 2	VG 3	VgEx 4	EX 5	ExMt 6	NM 7	NmMt 8
1	Chief Bender	150	200	400	600	1,000			
2	Bill Carrigan	40	80	100	200	300	600		
3	Frank Chance	150	200	300	500	800			
4	Ed Cicotte	150	300	550	850	1,400			
5	Ty Cobb	1,000	1,500	2,500	4,000	6,000	10,000		
6	Eddie Collins	120	200	300	500	800			
7	Sam Crawford	120	200	300	500	800			
8	Art Devlin	40	60	100	200	300	600		
9	Larry Doyle	40	60	100	200	300	600		
10	Johnny Evers	120	300	400	550	800			
11	Solly Hoffman	40	60	100	200	300	600		
12	Harry Krause	40	60	100	200	300	600		
13	Tommy Leach	40	80	120	350	450	1,000		
14	Harry Lord	40	60	100	200	300	600		
15	Nick Maddox	40	80	100	120	575	1,100		
16	Christy Mathewson	400	500	1,000	1,500	3,000	5,000		
17	Matty McIntyre	40	60	100	300	400	600		
18	Fred Merkle	60	100	150	250	400	800		
19	Cy Morgan	40	80	120	200	300	600		
20	Eddie Plank	800	1,000	1,200	2,000				
21	Ed Reulbach	40	120	150	200	300	600		
22	Honus Wagner	1,200	2,000	2,500	3,500	5,500	9,000		
23	Ed Willetts (Willett)	60	80	100	200	300	900		
24	Vic Willis	120	200	250	300	800	2,000		
25	Hooks Wiltse	50	60	100	200	300	600		

—Chief Bender PSA 7 (NM) sold for $7,500 (eBay; 12/06)
—Chief Bender PSA 6 (ExMt) sold for $4,827 (eBay; 11/06)
—Frank Chance PSA 7 (NM) sold for $9,382 (Mastro; 4/06)
—Ed Cicotte PSA 7 (NM) sold for $8,070 (SCP; 7/08)
—Ed Cicotte PSA 7 (NM) sold for $4,201 (Goodwin; 11/05)
—Ty Cobb SGC 60 (EX) sold for $9,582 (Mastro; 4/07)
—Ty Cobb GAI 5.5 (EX+) sold for $4,652 (Mastro; 6/07)
—Eddie Collins PSA 6 (ExMt) sold for $3,586 (Mastro; 8/07)
—Eddie Collins SGC 80 (ExMt) sold for $3,586 (Mastro; 4/07)
—Sam Crawford SGC 70 (EX+) sold for $1,913 (Goodwin; 2/06)
—Johnny Evers PSA 6 (ExMt) sold for $3,826 (Mile High; 8/07)
—Johnny Evers SGC 80 (ExMt) sold for $3,598 (Mastro; 12/06)

—Eddie Plank SGC 70 (EX+) sold for $4,305 (eBay; 8/07)
—Eddie Plank SGC 70 (EX+) sold for $3,957 (Memory Lane; 5/08)
—Eddie Plank SGC 70 (EX+) sold for $3,355 (Mastro; 12/07)
—Eddie Plank PSA 5 (EX) sold for $8,711 (Mastro; 8/07)
—Honus Wagner SGC 84 (NM) sold for $12,490 (Mastro; 12/05)

1909 Ramly T204

		PrFr 1	GD 2	VG 3	VgEx 4	EX 5	ExMt 6	NM 7	NmMt 8
1	Whitey Alperman	120	200	250	300	500			
2	John J. Anderson	80	120	200	250	500			
3	Jimmy Archer	80	120	150	250	500			
4	Frank Arrelanes (Arellanes)	120	200	250	400	800			
5	Jim Ball	80	150	200	250	500			
6	Neal Ball	80	150	200	250	500			
7	Frank Bancroft	100	150	275	350	600			
8	Johnny Bates	120	150	200	250	500			
9	Fred Beebe	80	150	200	250	500			
10	George Bell	80	120	150	250	500			
11	Chief Bender	400	500	600	1,000	3,600			
12	Walter Blair	80	120	150	250	500			
13	Cliff Blankenship	80	120	150	250	500			
14	Frank Bowerman	80	120	150	250	500			
15	Kitty Bransfield	120	200	250	400	800			
16	Roger Bresnahan	250	400	800	1,500	2,000			
17	Al Bridwell	80	120	150	250	500			
18	Mordecai Brown	300	500	800	1,200	2,900			
19	Fred Burchell	80	120	200	850	1,600			
20	Jesse Burkett	1,600	2,500	4,300	5,000	7,000			
21	Bobby Byrnes (Byrne)	80	120	150	250	500			
22	Bill Carrigan	80	120	150	250	750			
23	Frank Chance	250	400	700	900	1,500			
24	Charles Chech	100	150	250	350	600			
25	Eddie Cicotte	250	400	500	800	1,500			
26	Otis Clymer	80	120	150	250	500			
27	Andrew Coakley	80	120	150	250	500			
28	Eddie Collins	300	500	800	1,200	2,000			
29	Jimmy Collins	250	400	600	1,000	1,500			
30	Wid Conroy	80	120	150	250	500			
31	Jack Coombs	120	200	250	400	800			
32	Doc Crandall	80	120	250	350	500			
33	Lou Criger	80	120	150	250	500			
34	Harry Davis	80	120	150	250	1,000			
35	Art Devlin	80	120	150	250	500			
36	Bill Dineen (Dineen)	80	120	150	275	500			
37	Pat Donahue	80	120	200	250	500			
38	Mike Donlin	80	120	150	250	500			
39	Bill Donovan	100	150	250	300	600			
40	Gus Dorner	80	120	200	250	500			
41	Joe Dunn	80	120	150	250	500			
42	Kid Elberfield	80	120	150	1,000	1,500			
43	Johnny Evers	300	600	1,000	2,000				
44	Bob Ewing	80	120	150	250	500			
45	George Ferguson	80	120	150	250	500			
46	Hobe Ferris	80	120	150	250	500			
47	Jerry Freeman	80	120	150	250	500			
48	Art Fromme	100	120	200	250	500			
49	Bob Ganley	80	120	150	250	500			
50	Doc Gessler	80	120	150	250	500			
51	Peaches Graham	80	120	150	250	500			
52	Clark Griffith	250	400	600	1,000	2,000			
53	Roy Hartzell (Topsy Hartsel Pictured)	80	120	150	250		500		
54	Charlie Hemphill	80	120	150	300	500			
55	Dick Hoblitzel (Hoblitzell)	80	120	150	250	500			
56	George Howard	80	120	325	425	600			
57	Harry Howell	80	120	150	250	500			
58	Miller Huggins	250	400	500	800	2,000			
59	John Hummel	80	120	150	250	500			
60	Walter Johnson	3,500	6,000	10,000	18,000	25,000			
61	Tom Jones	80	150	200	250	500			
62	Mike Kahoe	80	150	200	250	500			
63	Ed Kargar (Karger)	100	150	300	400	600			
64	Willie Keeler	400	600	1,200	1,500	2,200			
65	Red Kleinon (Kleinow)	80	120	150	300	500			
66	John Knight	80	120	250	300	500			
67	Ed Konetchey (Konetchy)	80	120	150	250	500			
68	Vive Lindaman	80	120	200	250	500			

#	Player	PrFr 1	GD 2	VG 3	VgEx 4	EX 5	ExMt 6	NM 7	NmMt 8
69	Hans Loebert (Lobert)	80	120	250	350	500			
70	Harry Lord	80	150	200	250	500			
71	Harry Lumley	80	120	150	250	500			
72	Ernie Lush	80	120	150	250	500			
73	Rube Manning	80	120	150	300	500			
74	Jimmy McAleer	80	120	150	250	500			
75	Amby McConnell	80	120	150	250	500			
76	Moose McCormick	80	120	150	250	500			
77	Matty McIntyre	80	120	250	300	500			
78	Larry McLean	80	120	150	250	500			
79	Fred Merkle	120	200	250	400	800			
80	Clyde Milan	80	120	150	250	500			
81	Mike Mitchell	80	120	150	250	500			
82	Pat Moran	200	250	300	350	500			
83	Cy Morgan	120	150	200	300	500			
84	Tim Murname (Murnane)	100	150	200	300	500			
85	Danny Murphy	80	120	150	275	500			
86	Red Murray	80	120	150	250	500			
87	Doc Newton	80	120	150	250	600			
88	Simon Nichols (Nicholls)	80	120	150	600	700			
89	Harry Niles	80	120	150	250	500			
90	Bill O'Hare (O'Hara)	80	120	150	250	500			
91	Charley O'Leary	80	120	150	400	600			
92	Dode Paskert	80	120	150	250	500			
93	Barney Pelty	120	300	350	500	800			
94	Jack Pfeister (Pfiester)	80	120	150	250	500			
95	Eddie Plank	1,000	1,800	2,800	3,200	10,000			
96	Jack Powell	80	120	150	250	500			
97	Bugs Raymond	80	120	150	250	500			
98	Tom Reilly	80	120	150	250	500			
99	Claude Ritchey	80	120	150	250	500			
100	Nap Rucker	80	150	200	300	500			
101	Ed Ruelbach (Reulbach)	80	120	150	275	500			
102	Slim Sallee	80	120	150	250	500			
103	Germany Schaefer	80	120	150	250	500			
104	Jimmy Schekard (Sheckard)	80	120	150	250	500			
105	Admiral Schlei	80	120	150	250	500			
106	Wildfire Schulte	80	120	150	250	500			
107	Jimmy Sebring	80	120	150	250	500			
108	Bill Shipke	80	120	150	250	500			
109	Charlie Smith	80	120	250	350	500			
110	Tubby Spencer	80	120	150	250	500			
111	Jake Stahl	120	200	250	400	800			
112	Jim Stephens	80	120	200	250	500			
113	Harry Stienfeldt (Steinfeldt)	120	200	250	400	800			
114	Gabby Street	80	120	150	250	500			
115	Bill Sweeney	80	120	200	250	500			
116	Fred Tenney	80	120	400	600	800			
117	Ira Thomas	80	120	150	250	500			
118	Joe Tinker	400	600	800	2,400	2,500			
119	Bob Unglane (Unglaub)	80	120	150	250	500			
120	Heinie Wagner	80	120	250	500	700			
121	Bobby Wallace	250	400	500	800	1,500			

—Neal Ball PSA 8 (NmMt) sold for $5,513 (SCP; 7/08)
—Chief Bender SGC 84 (NM) sold for $6,544 (Mastro; 4/07)
—Kitty Bransfield PSA 8 (NmMt) sold for $21,047 (Mastro; 4/06)
—Mordecai Brown PSA 6 (ExMt) sold for $2,448 (Mastro; 4/07)
—Jesse Burkett SGC 80 (ExMt) sold for $9,696 (Mastro; 8/07)
—Jesse Burkett (TTT Back) SGC 80 (ExMt) sold for $10,541 (Mastro; 4/07)
—Jesse Burkett (TTT Back) SGC 20 (Fair) sold for $3,205 (Sloate; 5/08)
—Eddie Collins #28 PSA 8 (NmMt) sold for $16,286 (Mile High; 1/13)
—Eddie Collins #28 PSA 8 (NmMt) sold for $13,080 (Goodwin; 8/12)
—Miller Huggins PSA 7 (NM) sold for $7,621 (Memory Lane; 12/07)
—Walter Johnson SGC 9 (Mint) sold for $59,250 (REA; Spring '14)
—Walter Johnson SGC 7 (NM) sold for $42,000 (REA; Spring '15)
—Walter Johnson SGC 6 (ExMt) sold for $29,718 (Mile High; 10/13)
—Walter Johnson SGC 80 (ExMt) sold for $21,330 (REA; Spring '14)
—Willie Keeler PSA 6 (ExMt) sold for $5,220 (REA; 4/06)
—Eddie Plank PSA 7 (NrMt) sold for $10,0000 (Legendary; 8/10)
—Eddie Plank PSA 6 (ExMt) sold for $8,693 (Memory Lane; 12/07)
—Eddie Plank #95 PSA 8 (NmMt) sold for $40,825 (Mile High; 1/12)
—Eddie Plank SGC 70 (EX+) sold for $5,295 (Mastro; 12/05)
—Bobby Wallace PSA 7 (NM) sold for $7,672 (Goodwin; 3/08)
—Bobby Wallace SGC 80 (ExMt) sold for $3,944 (Mastro; 4/07)

1909-11 Colgan's Chips E254

#	Player	PrFr 1	GD 2	VG 3	VgEx 4	EX 5	ExMt 6	NM 7	NmMt 8
1	Ed Abbaticchio	8	10	15	20	25	30		
2	Fred Abbott	8	10	15	20	25	30		
3A	Bill Abstein Pittsburg	8	10	15	20	25	30		
3B	Bill Abstein Jersey City	8	10	15	20	25	30		
4	Babe Adams	8	10	15	20	25	30		
5	Merle (Doc) Adkins	8	10	15	20	25	30		
6	Joe Agler	8	10	15	20	25	30		
7	Alperman	8	10	15	20	25	30		
8A	Dave Altizer Cincinnati	8	10	15	20	25	30		
8B	Dave Altizer Minneapolis	8	10	15	20	25	30		
9	Nick Altrock	8	10	15	20	25	30		
10A	Red Ames Cincinnati	8	10	15	20	25	30		
10B	Red Ames New York	8	10	15	20	25	30		
11	Jimmy Archer	8	10	15	20	25	30		
12A	Atkins Atlanta	8	10	15	20	25	30		
12B	Atkins Fort Wayne	8	10	15	20	25	30		
13	Jake Atz	8	10	15	20	25	30		
14A	Jimmy Austin New York	8	10	15	20	25	30		
14B	Jimmy Austin St. Louis	8	10	15	20	25	30		
15A	Charlie Babb Memphis	8	10	15	20	25	30		
15B	Charlie Babb Norfolk	8	10	15	20	25	30		
16	Rudolph Baerwald	8	10	15	20	25	30		
17	Bill Bailey	8	10	15	20	25	30		
18	Frank Baker	30	40	60	80	150	200		
19	Jack Barry	8	10	15	20	25	30		
20	Bill Bartley	8	10	15	20	25	30		
21A	Johnny Bates Cincinnati	8	10	15	20	25	30		
21B	Johnny Bates Philadelphia	8	10	15	20	25	30		
22	Dick Bayless	8	10	15	20	25	30		
23A	Ginger Beaumont Boston	8	10	15	20	25	30		
23B	Ginger Beaumont Chicago	8	10	15	20	25	30		
23C	Ginger Beaumont St. Paul	8	10	15	20	25	30		
24	Beals Becker	8	10	15	20	25	40		
25	Fred Beebe	8	10	15	20	25	30		
26	George Bell	8	10	15	20	25	30		
27A	Harry Bemis Cleveland	8	10	15	20	25	30		
27B	Harry Bemis Columbus	8	10	15	20	25	30		
28A	Heinie Berger Cleveland	8	10	15	20	25	30		
28B	Heinie Berger Columbus	8	10	15	20	25	30		
29	Bob Bescher	8	10	15	20	25	30		
30	Beumiller	8	10	15	20	25	30		
31	Joe Birmingham	8	10	15	20	25	30		
32	Kitty Bransfield	8	10	15	20	25	30		
33A	Roger Bresnahan St. Louis	30	40	60	80	100	120		
33B	Roger Bresnahan Chicago	30	40	60	80	100	120		
34	Al Bridwell	8	10	15	20	25	30		
35	Lew Brockett	8	10	15	20	25	30		
36	Brown	8	10	15	20	25	30		
37A	Al Burch Brooklyn	8	10	15	20	25	30		
37B	Burch Louisville	8	10	15	20	25	30		
38A	William Burke Ft. Wayne	8	10	15	20	25	30		
38B	William Burke Indianapolis	8	10	15	20	25	30		
39	Burns	8	10	15	20	25	30		
40	Donie Bush	8	10	15	20	25	30		
41	Bill Byers	8	10	15	20	25	30		
42	Bobby Byrne	8	10	15	20	25	30		
43	Callahan	8	10	15	20	25	30		
44	Howie Camnitz	8	10	15	20	25	30		
45	Campbell	8	10	15	20	25	30		
46A	Charlie Carr Indianapolis	8	10	15	20	25	30		
46B	Charlie Carr Utica	8	10	15	20	25	30		
46C	Charlie Carr Kansas City	8	10	15	20	25	30		
47	Cashion Washington	8	10	15	20	25	30		
48A	Frank Chance	30	40	60	80	100	120		
48B	Frank Chance New York	8	10	15	20	25	30		
49	Hal Chase	20	50	80	100	150	200		
50	Eddie Cicotte	8	10	15	20	25	30		
51	Clancy	8	10	15	20	25	30		
52	Nig Clarke	12	15	25	30	40	50		
53	Fred Clarke	25	30	50	60	80	100		
54	Clarke	8	10	15	20	25	30		
55	Clemons	8	10	15	20	25	30		
56	Otis Clymer	8	10	15	20	25	30		

	PrFr 1	GD 2	VG 3	VgEx 4	EX 5	ExMt 6	NM 7	NmMt 8
A Ty Cobb w/Name	200	300	400	900	1,200	1,600		
B Ty Cobb w/o Name	200	250	500	600	800	1,000		
Eddie Collins	30	40	60	80	100	120		
A Buck Congalton Columbus	8	10	15	20	25	30		
B Buck Congalton Omaha	8	10	15	20	25	30		
C Buck Congalton Toledo	8	10	15	20	25	30		
Wid Conroy	8	10	15	20	50	60		
Cook	8	10	15	20	25	30		
Coombs	8	10	15	20	25	30		
Corcoran	8	10	15	20	25	30		
Courtney	8	10	15	20	25	30		
A Harry Coveleski	8	10	15	20	25	30		
B Stan Coveleski	12	15	25	30	40	50		
Doc Crandall	8	10	15	20	25	30		
Gavvy Cravath	8	10	15	20	25	30		
Sam Crawford	8	10	15	20	25	30		
Dode Criss	8	10	15	20	25	30		
Bill Dahlen	8	10	15	20	25	30		
Bernard Daniels	8	10	15	20	25	30		
A Jake Daubert Memphis	8	10	15	20	25	30		
B Jake Daubert Brooklyn	8	10	15	20	25	30		
Harry Davis	8	10	15	20	25	30		
George Davis	12	15	25	30	40	50		
Jim Delahanty	8	10	15	20	25	30		
A Ray Demmett New York	8	10	15	20	25	30		
B Ray Demmett Montreal	8	10	15	20	25	30		
C Ray Demmett St. Louis	8	10	15	20	25	30		
Art Devlin	8	10	15	20	25	30		
A Joshua Devore Cincinnati	8	10	15	20	25	30		
B Joshua Devore New York	8	10	15	20	25	30		
Turkey Mike Donlin	8	10	15	20	25	30		
Bill Donovan	8	10	15	20	25	30		
Charles Dooin	8	10	15	20	25	30		
Mickey Doolan	8	10	15	20	25	30		
Patsy Dougherty	8	10	15	20	25	30		
Tom Downey	8	10	15	20	25	30		
Larry Doyle	8	10	15	20	25	30		
Drake	8	10	15	20	25	30		
Jack Dunn	8	10	15	20	25	30		
Charles Eagan	8	10	15	20	25	30		
A Kid Elberfield Washington	8	10	15	20	25	30		
B Kid Elberfield Chattanooga	8	10	15	20	25	30		
C Kid Elberfield New York	8	10	15	20	25	30		
Roy Ellam	8	10	15	20	25	30		
Elliott	8	10	15	20	25	30		
Rube Ellis	8	10	15	20	25	30		
Elwert	8	10	15	20	25	30		
94A Clyde Engle New York	8	10	15	20	25	30		
94B Clyde Engle Boston	8	10	15	20	25	30		
95 James Esmond	8	10	15	20	25	30		
96 Steve Evans	8	10	15	20	25	30		
97 Johnny Evers	30	40	60	80	100	120		
98 George Ferguson	8	10	15	20	25	30		
99 Hobe Ferris	8	10	15	20	25	30		
100 James Field	8	10	15	20	25	30		
101 Fisher	8	10	15	20	25	30		
102 Matthew Fitzgerald	8	10	15	20	25	30		
103A Patrick Flaherty Kansas City	8	10	15	20	25	30		
103B Patrick Flaherty Atlanta	8	10	15	20	25	30		
104 John Flater	8	10	15	20	25	30		
105A Elmer Flick Cleveland	25	30	50	60	80	100		
105B Elmer Flick Toledo	25	30	50	60	80	100		
106 Russ Ford	8	10	15	20	25	30		
107 George Foster	8	10	15	20	25	30		
108A Freck Balt	8	10	15	20	25	30		
108B Freck Tor	8	10	15	20	25	30		
109 Freeman	8	10	15	20	25	30		
110 Bill Friel	8	10	15	20	25	30		
111 John Frill	8	10	15	20	25	30		
112 Art Fromme	8	10	15	20	25	30		
113A Larry Gardner Boston	8	10	15	20	25	30		
113B Larry Gardner New York	8	10	15	20	25	30		
114 Gus Gaspar	8	10	15	20	25	30		
115A Gus Getz Boston	8	10	15	20	25	30		
115B Gus Getz Pittsburgh	8	10	15	20	25	30		
116 George Gibson	8	10	15	20	25	30		
117 Graham	8	10	15	20	25	30		
118A Ed Grant Cincinnati	8	10	15	20	25	30		
118B Ed Grant New York	8	10	15	20	25	30		
119 Grief	8	10	15	20	25	30		
120A Moose Grimshaw Toronto	8	10	15	20	25	30		
120B Moose Grimshaw Louisville	8	10	15	20	25	30		
121 Bob Groom	8	10	15	20	25	30		
122 Noodles Hahn	8	10	15	20	25	30		
123 John Halla	8	10	15	20	25	30		
124 Hally	8	10	15	20	25	30		
125 Charles Hanford	8	10	15	20	25	30		
126A Topsy Hartsel Philadelphia	8	10	15	20	25	30		
126B Topsy Hartsel Toledo	8	10	15	20	25	30		
127A Roy Hartzel St. Louis	8	10	15	20	25	30		
127B Roy Hartzell New York	8	10	15	20	25	30		
128 Weldon Henley	8	10	15	20	25	30		
129 Harry Hinchman	8	10	15	20	25	30		
130 Richard Hoblitzell	8	10	15	20	25	30		
131 Solly Hofman	8	10	15	20	25	30		
132 William Hogan	8	10	15	20	25	30		
133A Harry Hooper Boston AL	25	30	150	200	250	300		
133B Harry Hooper Boston NL	25	30	80	100	120	150		
134 Del Howard	8	10	15	20	25	30		
135 Miller Huggins	8	10	15	20	25	30		
136A Thomas Hughes Milwaukee	8	10	15	20	25	30		
136B Thomas Hughes Louisville	8	10	15	20	25	30		
136C Thomas Hughes Louisville C	8	10	15	20	25	30		
137 Thomas Hughes Rochester	8	10	15	20	25	30		
138A Rudy Hulswitt St. Louis	8	10	15	20	25	30		
138B Rudy Hulswitt Chattanooga	8	10	15	20	25	30		
138C Rudy Hulswitt Louisville	8	10	15	20	25	30		
139 John Hummel	8	10	15	20	25	30		
140 George Hunter	8	10	15	20	25	30		
142 Hugh Jennings	25	50	60	80	100	120		
143 Johns	8	10	15	20	25	30		
144 Davy Jones	8	10	15	40	50	60		
145 Tom Jones	8	10	15	20	25	30		
146A Jordon Toronto	8	10	15	20	25	30		
146B Jordon Atlanta	8	10	15	20	25	30		
146C Jordon Atlanta	8	10	15	20	25	30		
146D Jordon Louisville	8	10	15	20	25	30		
147 Addie Joss	25	30	50	60	250	300		
148 Kaiser Louisville	8	10	15	20	25	30		
149 Keefe Rochester	8	10	15	20	25	30		
150 Willie Keeler	25	30	50	60	80	100		
151A Kelly Jersey City	8	10	15	20	25	30		
151B Kelly Toronto	8	10	15	20	25	30		
152A William Killefer St. Louis	8	10	15	20	25	30		
152B William Killefer Philadelphia	8	10	15	20	25	30		
153A Ed Killian Detroit	8	10	15	20	25	30		
153B Ed Killian Toronto	8	10	15	20	25	30		
154 Johnny Kling	8	10	15	20	25	30		
155 Klipfer	8	10	15	20	25	30		
156 Otto Knabe	8	10	15	20	25	30		
157A John Knight New York	8	10	15	20	25	30		
157B John Knight Jersey City	8	10	15	20	25	30		
158 Ed Konetchy	8	10	15	20	25	30		
159 Paul Krichell St. Louis	8	10	15	20	25	30		
160 Rube Kroh	8	10	15	20	25	30		
161A Doc Lafitte Rochester	8	10	15	20	25	30		
161B Doc Lafitte Providence	8	10	15	20	25	30		
162 Nap Lajoie	40	50	80	100	120	150		
163 Lakoff	8	10	15	20	25	30		
164 Frank Lange	8	10	15	20	25	30		
165A Frank LaPorte St. Louis	8	10	15	20	25	30		
165B Frank LaPorte New York	8	10	15	20	25	30		
166 Tommy Leach	8	10	15	20	25	30		
167 Lee	8	10	15	20	25	30		
168 William Lelivelt	8	10	15	20	25	30		
169A Lewis Milwaukee	8	10	15	20	25	30		
169B Lewis Indianapolis	8	10	15	20	25	30		
170A Vivian Lindaman Boston	8	10	15	20	25	30		
170B Vivian Lindaman Louisville	8	10	15	20	25	30		
170C Vivian Lindaman Indianapolis	8	10	15	20	25	30		
171 Bris Lord	8	10	15	20	25	30		
172A Harry Lord Boston	8	10	15	20	25	30		
172B Harry Lord Chicago	8	10	15	20	25	30		
173A William Ludwig Milwaukee	8	10	15	20	25	80		

#	Player	PrFr 1	GD 2	VG 3	VgEx 4	EX 5	ExMt 6	NM 7	NmMt 8
173B	William Ludwig St. Louis	8	10	15	20	25	30		
174	Lush Toronto	8	10	15	20	25	30		
175	Thomas Madden	8	10	15	20	25	30		
176A	Nick Maddox Pittsburg	8	10	15	20	25	30		
176B	Nick Maddox Louisville	8	10	15	20	25	30		
177A	Manser Jersey City	8	10	15	20	25	30		
177B	Manser Rochester	8	10	15	20	25	30		
178	Rube Marquard	25	30	50	60	80	100		
179	Al Mattern	8	10	15	20	25	30		
180	Matthews Atlanta	8	10	15	20	25	30		
181	McAllister Atlanta	8	10	15	20	25	30		
182	George McBride	8	10	15	20	25	30		
183	Alex McCarthy	8	10	15	20	25	30		
184	Ambrose McConnell Rochester	8	10	15	20	25	30		
185	Ambrose McConnell Toronto	8	10	15	20	25	30		
186	Moose McCormick	8	10	15	20	25	30		
187	Dennis McGann	8	10	15	20	25	30		
188	James McGinley	8	10	15	20	25	30		
189	Joe McGinnity	25	30	50	60	80	100		
190A	Matty McIntyre Detroit	8	10	15	20	25	30		
190B	Matty McIntyre Chicago	8	10	15	20	25	30		
191A	Larry McLean Cincinnati	8	10	15	20	25	30		
191B	Larry McLean St. Louis	8	10	15	20	25	30		
192	Fred Merkle	8	10	15	20	25	30		
193A	George Merritt Buffalo	8	10	15	20	25	30		
193B	George Merritt Jersey City	8	10	15	20	25	30		
194	Lee Meyer	8	10	15	20	25	30		
195	Chief Meyers	8	10	15	20	25	30		
196	Clyde Milan	8	10	15	20	25	30		
197	Dots Miller	8	10	15	20	25	30		
198	Miller Columbus	8	10	15	20	25	30		
199A	Mike Mitchell Cincinnati	8	10	15	20	25	30		
199B	Mike Mitchell Chicago	8	10	15	20	25	30		
200	Mitchell Providence	8	10	15	20	25	30		
201	Albert Mitchell	8	10	15	20	25	30		
202	Carlton Molesworth	8	10	15	20	25	30		
203	Joseph H. Moran	8	10	15	20	80	100		
204	Pat Moran	8	10	15	20	25	30		
205	George Moriarty Detroit	8	10	15	20	25	30		
206A	George Moriarty Louisville	8	10	15	20	25	30		
206B	George Moriarty Omaha	8	10	15	20	25	30		
207	George Mullin	8	10	15	20	25	30		
208A	Simmy Murch Chattanooga	8	10	15	20	25	30		
208B	Simmy Murch Indianapolis	8	10	15	20	25	30		
209	Danny Murphy	8	10	15	20	25	30		
210A	Red Murray	8	10	15	20	25	30		
210B	Red Murray	8	10	15	20	25	30		
211	Murray Buffalo	8	10	15	20	25	30		
212	Bill Nattress	8	10	15	20	25	30		
213A	Red Nelson St. Louis	8	10	15	20	25	30		
213B	Red Nelson Toledo	8	10	15	20	25	30		
214	George Northrop	8	10	15	20	25	30		
215	Rebel Oakes	8	10	15	20	25	30		
216	Frederick Odwell	8	10	15	20	25	30		
217	Rube Oldring	8	10	15	20	25	30		
218	Steve O'Neill	8	10	15	20	25	30		
219A	O'Rourke St. Paul	8	10	15	20	25	30		
219B	O'Rourke Columbus	8	10	15	20	25	30		
220A	Al Orth New York	8	10	15	20	25	30		
220B	Al Orth Indianapolis	8	10	15	20	25	30		
221	Wilfred Osborn	8	10	15	20	25	30		
222	Orvie Overall	8	10	15	20	25	30		
223	Frank Owens	8	10	15	20	25	30		
224	Lawrence Pape	8	10	15	20	25	30		
225A	Freddie Parent	8	10	15	20	25	30		
225B	Freddy Parent	8	10	15	20	25	30		
226A	Dode Paskert Cincinnati	8	10	15	20	25	30		
226B	Dode Paskert Philadelphia	8	10	15	20	25	30		
227	Heinie Peitz	8	10	15	20	25	30		
228	Perry Providence	8	10	15	20	25	30		
229	Robert A. Peterson	8	10	15	20	25	60		
230	John Pfeister	8	10	15	20	25	30		
231	Deacon Phillipe	8	10	15	20	25	30		
232A	Oliver Pickering Louisville	8	10	15	20	25	30		
232B	Oliver Pickering Minneapolis	8	10	15	20	25	30		
232C	Oliver Pickering Omaha	8	10	15	20	25	30		
233A	Billy Purtell Chicago	8	10	15	20	25	30		

#	Player	PrFr 1	GD 2	VG 3	VgEx 4	EX 5	ExMt 6	NM 7	NmMt #
233B	Billy Purtell Boston	8	10	15	20	25	30		
233C	Billy Purtell Jersey City	8	10	15	20	25	30		
234	Bill Rariden	8	10	15	20	25	30		
235	Morrie Rath	8	10	15	20	25	30		
236	Bugs Raymond	8	10	15	20	25	30		
237	Michael Regan	8	10	15	20	25	30		
238	Thomas Reilly Chicago	8	10	15	20	25	30		
239	Thomas Reilly Louisville	8	10	15	20	25	30		
240	Ed Reulbach	8	10	15	20	25	30		
241	Claude Ritchey	8	10	15	20	25	30		
242	Lou Ritter	8	10	15	20	25	30		
243	Clyde Robinson	8	10	15	20	25	30		
244	Royal Rock	8	10	15	20	25	30		
245A	Jack Rowan Cin	8	10	15	20	25	30		
245B	Jack Rowan Phil	8	10	15	20	25	30		
246	Nap Rucker	8	10	15	20	25	30		
247A	Dick Rudolph New York	8	10	15	20	25	30		
247B	Dick Rudolph Toronto	8	10	15	20	25	30		
248	Buddy Ryan St. Paul	8	10	15	20	25	30		
249	Buddy Ryan Cleveland	8	10	15	20	25	30		
250	Slim Sallee	8	10	15	20	25	30		
251	Ray Schalk	8	10	15	20	25	30		
252A	Bill Schardt Birmingham	8	10	15	20	25	30		
252B	Bill Schardt Milwaukee	8	10	15	20	25	30		
253	Jimmy Sheckard (Scheckard)	8	10	15	20	25	30		
254A	George Schirm Birmingham	8	10	15	20	25	30		
254B	George Schirm Buffalo	8	10	15	20	25	30		
255	Larry Schlafly	8	10	15	20	25	30		
256	Frank Schulte	8	10	15	20	25	30		
257A	James Seabaugh Nashville	8	10	15	20	25	30		
258	Selby Louisville	8	10	15	20	25	30		
259A	Cy Seymour New York	8	10	15	20	25	30		
259B	Cy Seymour Baltimore	8	10	15	20	25	30		
260	Bob Shawkey	8	10	15	20	25	30		
261	Shelton Columbus	8	10	15	20	25	30		
262	Hosea Siner	8	10	15	20	25	30		
263A	Smith Atlanta	8	10	15	20	25	30		
263B	Smith Buffalo	8	10	15	20	25	30		
264	Smith Newark	8	10	15	20	25	30		
265	George Henry Smith	8	10	15	20	25	30		
266	Fred Snodgrass	8	10	15	20	25	30		
267A	Robert Spade Cincinnati	8	10	15	20	25	30		
267B	Robert Spade Newark	8	10	15	20	25	30		
268A	Tully Sparks Philadelphia	8	10	15	20	25	30		
268B	Tully Sparks Richmond	8	10	15	20	25	30		
269A	Tris Speaker Boston AL	40	50	80	100	120	150		
269B	Tris Speaker Boston NL	40	50	80	100	120	150		
270	Tubby Spencer	8	10	15	20	25	30		
271	Jake Stahl	8	10	15	20	25	30		
272	Stansberry Louisville	8	10	15	20	25	30		
273	Harry Steinfeldt	8	10	15	20	25	30		
274	George Stone	8	10	15	20	25	30		
275	George Stovall	8	10	15	20	25	30		
276	Gabby Street	8	10	15	20	25	30		
277	Amos Strunk	8	10	15	20	25	30		
278A	Billy Sullivan Louisville	8	10	15	20	25	30		
278B	Billy Sullivan Omaha	8	10	15	20	25	30		
279	Billy Sullivan Indianapolis	8	10	15	20	25	30		
280	J. Sullivan Louisville	8	10	15	20	25	30		
281	Ed Summers	8	10	15	20	25	30		
282	Swacina Newark	8	10	15	20	25	30		
283	Jeff Sweeney	8	10	15	20	25	30		
284	Bill Sweeney	8	10	15	20	25	30		
285	Lee Tannehill	8	10	15	20	25	30		
286	John Taylor Kansas City	8	10	15	20	25	30		
287	John Taylor Montreal	8	10	15	20	25	30		
288	Jim Thorpe	8	10	15	20	25	30		
289A	Joe Tinker	30	40	80	100	120	150		
289B	Joe Tinker Cincinnati	8	10	15	20	25	30		
290A	John Titus Philadelphia	8	10	15	20	25	30		
290B	John Titus Boston	8	10	15	20	25	30		
291	Terry Turner	8	10	15	20	25	30		
292A	Bob Unglaub Washington	8	10	15	20	25	30		
292B	Bob Unglaub Lincoln	8	10	15	20	25	30		
292C	Bob Unglaub Minneapolis	8	10	15	20	25	30		
293	Viebahn Jersey City	8	10	15	20	25	30		
294A	Rube Waddell St. Louis	25	30	50	100	120	150		

	PrFr 1	GD 2	VG 3	VgEx 4	EX 5	ExMt 6	NM 7	NmMt 8
4B Rube Waddell Minneapolis	25	30	50	60	80	100		
4C Rube Waddell Newark	25	30	50	60	80	100		
5 Honus Wagner	200	250	600	700	1,200	1,500		
6 Walker Atlanta	8	10	15	20	25	30		
7 Bobby Wallace	8	10	15	20	25	30		
8 Waller Jersey City	8	10	15	20	25	30		
9 Ed Walsh	8	10	15	20	25	30		
0 Jack Warhop	8	10	15	20	25	30		
1 Wauner Memphis	8	10	15	20	25	30		
2 Wiesman Nashville	8	10	15	20	25	30		
3 Zach Wheat	8	10	15	20	25	30		
4 White Buffalo	8	10	15	20	25	30		
5 Kirby White	8	10	15	20	25	30		
6 Kaiser Wilhelm	8	10	15	20	25	30		
7 Ed Willett	8	10	15	20	25	30		
8A Williams Indianapolis	8	10	15	20	25	30		
8B Williams Minneapolis	8	10	15	20	25	30		
9 Owen Wilson	8	10	15	20	25	30		
0 Hooks Wiltse	8	10	15	20	25	30		
1 Joe Wood Boston	8	10	15	20	25	30		
2A Orville Woodruff Indianapolis	8	10	15	20	25	30		
2B Orville Woodruff Louisville	8	10	15	20	25	30		
3 Walter Woods Buffalo	8	10	15	20	25	30		
4 Joseph Yeager	8	10	15	20	25	30		
5 Cy Young	100	120	200	250	300	400		
6 Heinie Zimmerman Chicago	12	15	25	30	40	50		
7A Heinie Zimmerman Newark	12	15	25	30	40	50		
7B Zimmerman Newark	8	10	15	20	25	30		

—Ty Cobb SGC 88 (NmMt) sold for $1,998 (REA; 5/08)
—Ty Cobb PSA 8 (NmMt) sold for $1,852 (Memory Lane; 8/06)
—Addie Joss PSA 8 (NmMt) sold for $1,470 (Memory Lane; 12/07)
—Honus Wagner Curved Letters PSA 8 (NmMt) sold for $2,443 (Goodwin; 11/07)
—Honus Wagner GAI 8 (NmMt) sold for $899 (eBay; 5/07)
—Honus Wagner SGC 80 (ExMt) sold for $1,410 (REA; 4/07)
—Cy Young PSA 7 (NM) sold for $983 (Memory Lane; 8/06)

1909-11 American Caramel E90-1

	PrFr 1	GD 2	VG 3	VgEx 4	EX 5	ExMt 6	NM 7	NmMt 8
Bill Bailey	25	50	80	120	200	400		
Home Run Baker	80	150	400	500	800	1,800		
Jack Barry	25	50	120	150	200	400		
George Bell	25	50	100	150	200	400		
Harry Bemis	150	200	250	300	400			
Chief Bender	80	150	250	300	800	1,800		
Bob Bescher	50	100	150	250	400			
Cliff Blankenship	25	50	80	150	200	400		
John Bliss	25	50	80	120	200	400		
0 Bill Bradley	25	100	120	150	300	500		
1 Kitty Bransfield P on Shirt	25	50	80	150	250	400		
2 Kitty Bransfield No P on Shirt	30	100	150	250	400	600		
3 Roger Bresnahan	70	135	250	400	1,200			
4 Al Bridwell	25	50	80	120	200	400		
5 Buster Brown Horizontal	50	120	200	250	400	800		
6 Mordecai Brown	150	250	400	800				
7 Donie Bush	25	50	80	120	250	400		
8 John Butler	25	50	80	150	200	400		
9 Howie Camnitz	25	50	80	200	250	400		
20 Frank Chance	80	150	250	400	600	1,500		
21 Hal Chase	50	200	250	350	500	1,200		
22 Fred Clarke Philadelphia	80	150	250	400	800			
23 Fred Clarke Pittsburgh	300	400	600	1,000				
24 Wally Clement	30	60	100	150	400	1,200		
25 Ty Cobb	800	1,200	2,000	3,000	6,000			
26 Eddie Collins	80	150	300	400	800			
27 Frank Corridon	25	50	80	120	200	400		
28 Sam Crawford	80	150	250	500	600	1,500		
29 Lou Criger	25	50	80	120	200	600		
30 George Davis	100	200	300	500	800			
31 Jasper Davis	25	50	80	120	200	400		
32 Ray Demmitt	50	100	150	250	400			
33 Mike Donlin	40	80	120	200	300	600		
34 Wild Bill Donovan	30	60	100	200	250	500		
35 Red Dooin	25	50	100	120	200	400		
36 Patsy Dougherty	150	250	350	500	600	800		
37 Hugh Duffy	300	600	1,200	2,000				
38 Jimmy Dygert	25	80	100	120	200	400		
39 Rube Ellis	25	80	100	150	250	400		
40 Clyde Engle	25	50	80	150	300	500		
41 Art Fromme	50	100	150	250	400			
42 George Gibson Back View	50	100	350	450	700			
43 George Gibson Front View	25	100	120	200	250	400		
44 George Graham	250	400	800	2,000				
45 Eddie Grant	30	60	100	150	250	500		
46 Dolly Gray	30	60	100	150	250	500		
47 Bob Groom	25	80	100	120	200	400		
48 Charles Hall Horizontal	30	60	100	150	250	500		
49 Roy Hartzell Fielding	25	50	80	150	200	400		
50 Roy Hartzell Batting	40	80	120	200	300	600		
51 William Heitmuller	25	80	100	120	200			
52 Harry Howell Follow Through	25	50	80	120	200	400		
53 Harry Howell Wind Up	30	60	100	150	250	600		
54 Tex Irwin (Erwin)	25	50	80	150	250	400		
55 Frank Isbell	25	50	80	150	200	400		
56 Joe Jackson	12,000	20,000	25,000	30,000				
57 Hughie Jennings	80	120	200	250	300			
58 Tim Jordan	25	50	80	150	200	400		
59 Addie Joss Pitching	100	400	600	1,000				
60 Addie Joss Portrait	150	250	600	800	1,200	3,000		
61 Ed Karger	150	400	500	800				
62 Willie Keeler Portrait Pink	100	200	400	700	1,200	2,000		
63 Willie Keeler Portrait Red	300	600	1,000	1,500				
64 Willie Keeler Throwing	250	600	1,000	1,500	2,500			
65 John Knight	25	50	150	250	400	800		
66 Harry Krause	25	50	80	150	250			
67 Nap Lajoie	200	350	500	800	1,500	2,500		
68 Tommy Leach Batting	30	60	120	150	300	500		
69 Tommy Leach Throwing	30	60	100	150	250	500		
70 Sam Leever	25	50	100	120	200	400		
71 Hans Lobert	50	300	400	500	600			
72 Harry Lumley	25	50	120	150	200	400		
73 Rube Marquard	80	200	250	400	800			
74 Christy Mathewson	375	500	800	1,500	3,000	5,000		
75 Stuffy McInnes (McInnis)	40	80	100	150	250	500		
76 Harry McIntyre	25	50	80	120	200	400		
77 Larry McLean	175	250	350	450	600			
78 George McQuillan	25	50	80	120	350	500		
79 Dots Miller#(w/o sunset in background)	25	50	100	120	200		400	
81 Mike Mitchell	2,000	3,000	4,000	5,000				
82 Fred Mitchell	25	50	80	200	400	600		
83 George Mullin	30	60	100	150	250	500		
84 Rebel Oakes	80	150	300	400	500	600		
85 Patrick O'Connor	30	60	100	150	250			
86 Charley O'Leary	25	50	80	120	200	400		
87 Orval Overall	60	120	250	300	600			
88 Jim Pastorius	25	80	150	200	300	400		
89 Ed Phelps	25	50	80	120	200	400		
90 Eddie Plank	250	500	600	1,000	1,500	4,000		
91 Lew Richie	25	50	80	120	200	400		
92 Germany Schaefer	30	60	120	150	250			
93 Victor Schlitzer	30	120	250	300	400	600		
94 Johnny Siegle	50	100	150	250	400			
95 Dave Shean	50	100	250	350	500			
96 Jimmy Sheckard	30	60	100	150	250	500		
97 Tris Speaker	1,400	1,600	3,000					
98 Jake Stahl	250	500	800	1,200				
99 Oscar Stanage	25	60	80	150	200	400		
100 George Stone Left Hand	25	250	400	600	1,000	2,000		
101 George Stone No Hands	25	60	80	150	200	400		
102 George Stovall	25	50	150	200	250	400		
103 Ed Summers	25	50	80	120	200	1,500		
104 Bill Sweeney	300	600	1,000	1,500				
105 Jeff Sweeney	25	50	80	120	200	400		
106 Jesse Tannehill	25	50	80	120	200	400		
107 Lee Tannehill	25	50	120	150	200	400		
108 Fred Tenney	40	80	120	200	300	600		
109 Ira Thomas	30	60	100	150	250	500		
110 Roy Thomas	25	50	80	120	200	400		
111 Joe Tinker	100	150	300	400	500			
112 Bob Unglaub	30	50	80	120	300	800		
113 Jerry Upp	120	250	400	600	1,000			
114 Honus Wagner Batting	800	1,500	2,000					
115 Honus Wagner Throwing	800	1,200	2,000					
116 Bobby Wallace	50	100	150	300	500			

		PrFr 1	GD 2	VG 3	VgEx 4	EX 5	ExMt 6	NM 7	NmMt 8
117	Ed Walsh	500	800	1,500					
118	Vic Willis	100	200	300	500	1,000			
119	Hooks Wiltse	40	80	120	200	300	600		
120	Cy Young Boston	400	800	1,600	2,000	3,500	6,000		
121	Cy Young Cleveland	400	800	1,200	2,000				

—A near-complete set (119 of 120 cards minus Joe Jackson) sold for $149,112 (Mile High; 01/07)
—A near-complete set (119 of 120 cards minus Joe Jackson) sold for $87,000 (REA; 4/06)
—Mordecai Brown PSA 5 (EX) sold for $2,806 (eBay; 5/06)
—Frank Chance PSA 7 (NM) sold for $3,258 (eBay; 5/08)
—George Davis PSA 6 (ExMt) sold for $2,070 (eBay; 6/06)
—George Graham SGC 60 (EX) sold for $2,514 (Old Judge; 11/07)
—Joe Jackson PSA 8 (NmMt) sold for $667,189 (SCP; 8/16)
—Joe Jackson SGC 70 (EX+) sold for $86,976 (Goodwin; 9/08)
—Joe Jackson SGC 70 (EX+) sold for $77,021 (Leland's; 12/06)
—Joe Jackson PSA 5 (Ex) sold for $44,063 (REA; 5/10)
—Joe Jackson GAI 3.5 (VG+) sold for $17,986 (Goodwin; 3/09)
—Joe Jackson PSA 2.5 (G/VG) sold for $23,448 (Goodwin; 12/11)
—Joe Jackson PSA 2.5 (G/VG) sold for $18,800 (eBay; 1/13)
—Joe Jackson SGC 20 (Fair) sold for $10,280 (Goodwin; 2/14)
—Addie Joss Pitching PSA 7 (NM) sold for $4,629 (Mile High; 1/07)
—Addie Joss Pitching SGC 60 (EX) sold for $2,693 (Mastro; 12/06)
—Mike Mitchell SGC 60 (EX) sold for $13,797 (Old Judge; 11/07)
—Mike Mitchell PSA 5 (EX) sold for $11,155 (Mile High; 1/07)
—Honus Wagner Batting PSA 6 (ExMt) sold for $5,541 (Mile High 1/07)
—Honus Wagner Throwing PSA 6 (ExMt) sold for $7,186 (Mile High 1/07)
—Bobby Wallace PSA 7 (NM) sold for $1,339 (Mile High; 1/07)

1909-11 T206

		PrFr 1	GD 2	VG 3	VgEx 4	EX 5	ExMt 6	NM 7	NmMt 8
1	Ed Abbaticchio Blue Sleeves	25	30	100	120	350	450		
2	Ed Abbaticchio Brown Sleeves	25	30	50	100	200	300	800	
3	Fred Abbott ML	40	50	80	120	200	500	600	
4	Bill Abstein	20	50	80	120	200	300	500	
5	Doc Adkins ML	40	50	100	200	400	500		
6	Whitey Alperman	30	50	60	120	200	300	600	
7	Red Ames Hands at Chest	30	40	80	120	400	600		
8	Red Ames Hands over Head	20	25	60	100	250	300		
9	Red Ames Portrait	20	30	50	100	200	400	500	
10	John Anderson ML	25	60	80	100	200	250	800	
11	Frank Arellanes	20	25	80	100	150	200	500	
12	Herman Armbruster ML	20	40	60	120	150	350		
13	Harry Arndt ML	20	50	60	120	200	300	1,000	
14	Jake Atz	20	25	40	100	200	300	400	
15	Home Run Baker	80	150	400	500	800	1,400	2,500	
16	Neal Ball Cleveland	20	25	40	80	120	200	500	
17	Neal Ball New York	30	40	60	100	200	250	400	
18	Jap Barbeau	25	50	60	100	200	300	500	
19	Cy Barger ML	30	50	80	120	250	300		
20	Jack Barry	25	30	60	100	200	250	500	
21	Shad Barry ML	40	50	60	100	150	250	800	
22	Jack Bastian SL	40	80	150	300	500	600		
23	Emil Batch ML	25	40	60	100	200	400		
24	Johnny Bates	30	50	60	100	250	300	500	
25	Harry Bay SL	50	60	150	300	600	800		
26	Ginger Beaumont	30	60	80	150	200	400	800	
27	Fred Beck	30	40	80	100	250	300	500	
28	Beals Becker	20	25	60	100	200	300	400	
29	Jake Beckley ML	80	120	200	300	600	800	2,000	
30	George Bell Follow Through	20	25	60	120	150	300		
31	George Bell Hands above Head	20	25	40	50	150	250		
32	Chief Bender Pitching No Trees	60	100	200	250	600	1,000	2,700	
33	Chief Bender Pitching Trees	100	120	150	250	350	800	1,900	
34	Chief Bender Portrait	120	150	200	300	600	1,200	2,000	
35	Bill Bergen Batting	20	30	40	60	100	250	500	
36	Bill Bergen Catching	20	25	60	120	150	200	500	
37	Heinie Berger	20	25	60	80	250	300	500	
38	Bill Bernhard SL	50	80	300	400	500	600		
39	Bob Bescher Hands in Air	20	25	50	100	150	300	400	
40	Bob Bescher Portrait	20	25	120	150	200	250	400	
41	Joe Birmingham Horizontal	30	80	120	150	250	300		
42	Lena Blackburne ML	20	50	60	100	200	400	500	
43	Jack Bliss	20	25	50	120	150	400	500	
44	Frank Bowerman	40	60	80	120	150	300	500	
45	Bill Bradley with Bat	25	30	60	100	200	250	600	
46	Bill Bradley Portrait	30	80	100	120	150	300	500	
47	Dave Brain ML	20	60	80	100	200	400	600	

		PrFr 1	GD 2	VG 3	VgEx 4	EX 5	ExMt 6	NM 7	NmMt 8
48	Kitty Bransfield	20	50	80	100	120	400	1,000	
49	Roy Brashear ML	40	50	60	120	200	250	500	
50	Ted Breitenstein SL	80	120	250	400	500	600	1,200	
51	Roger Bresnahan Portrait	80	120	150	250	350	1,000	1,800	
52	Roger Bresnahan with Bat	60	100	150	250	400	600	1,500	
53	Al Bridwell No Cap	20	25	50	100	120	200	500	
54	Al Bridwell with Cap	20	25	60	100	150	250	400	
55	George Brown Chicago	30	40	80	120	200	500		
56	George Brown Washington	80	120	200	500	600	1,200	3,600	
57	Mordecai Brown Chicago Shirt	120	150	200	400	500	800	2,500	
58	Mordecai Brown Cubs Shirt	100	150	250	400	500	1,500	2,500	
59	Mordecai Brown Portrait	120	150	250	400	600	1,400	2,000	
60	Al Burch Batting	40	50	80	120	350	500		
61	Al Burch Fielding	20	25	40	100	150	200	400	
62	Fred Burchell ML	20	50	60	120	200	300	500	
63	Jimmy Burke ML	20	25	40	50	120	200	400	
64	Bill Burns	20	60	100	120	250	400		
65	Donie Bush	20	25	50	100	150	250		
66	John Butler ML	20	25	40	120	200	250	500	
67	Bobby Byrne	20	25	50	150	200	300	400	
68	Howie Camnitz Arm at Side	60	80	100	125	200	350	600	
69	Howie Camnitz Arms Folded	20	30	60	100	150	200	600	
70	Howie Camnitz Hands above Head	25	30	40	150	200	400	600	
71	Billy Campbell	20	25	40	100	150	250	500	
72	Scoops Carey SL	40	50	100	300	500	800	2,400	
73	Charley Carr ML	20	25	40	80	200	250	500	
74	Bill Carrigan	30	40	60	120	150	250		
75	Doc Casey ML	20	25	50	100	120	250	400	
76	Peter Cassidy ML	30	50	60	100	150	300	750	
77	Frank Chance Batting	60	100	300	400	500	100	2,000	
78	Frank Chance Portrait Red	100	200	300	400	1,000	1,200	2,500	
79	Frank Chance Portrait Yellow	80	120	200	350	600	1,500	2,000	
80	Bill Chappelle ML	20	30	60	80	120	200	425	
81	Chappie Charles	25	30	50	80	150	200	400	
82	Hal Chase Throwing Dark Cap	25	30	100	150	250	450	1,000	
83	Hal Chase Holding Trophy	30	80	120	300	400	800		
84	Hal Chase Portrait Blue	30	50	120	200	300	400	800	
85	Hal Chase Portrait Pink	50	80	100	300	400	1,100		
86	Hal Chase Throwing White Cap	30	40	100	150	300	400	1,200	
87	Jack Chesbro	120	200	400	500	800	1,200	2,500	
88	Ed Cicotte	60	150	200	300	400	700		
89	Bill Clancy (Clancey) ML	20	25	50	60	300	400	600	
90	Fred Clarke Holding Bat	50	100	150	300	400	600	1,500	
91	Fred Clarke Portrait	60	100	150	250	400	600	2,000	
92	Josh Clark (Clarke) ML	20	25	60	80	150	200	575	
93	J.J. (Nig) Clarke	20	25	40	150	200	250	400	
94	Bill Clymer ML	20	40	80	100	150	200	600	
95	Ty Cobb Bat off Shoulder	1,000	1,500	2,000	4,000	6,000	8,000	15,000	
96	Ty Cobb Bat on Shoulder	1,000	2,000	2,500	4,000	6,000	8,000	15,000	
97	Ty Cobb Portrait Green	1,500	4,000	5,000	8,000	10,000	25,000		
98	Ty Cobb Portrait Red	1,200	2,000	3,000	5,000	6,000	10,000	15,000	
99	Cad Coles SL	20	25	120	200	300	600	3,000	
100	Eddie Collins Philadelphia	120	250	300	500	800	1,000	2,500	
101	Jimmy Collins Minneapolis ML	120	150	300	400	500	600	1,200	
102	Bunk Congalton ML	20	25	40	100	200	250	1,200	
103	Wid Conroy Fielding	20	25	40	100	150	250	800	
104	Wid Conroy with Bat	20	25	40	60	100	250	500	
105	Harry Covaleski	40	50	120	150	200	300	800	
106	Doc Crandall No Cap	20	25	60	80	200	250	400	
107	Doc Crandall with Cap	20	25	40	120	150	200	500	
108	Bill Cranston SL	50	60	100	150	500	600		
109	Gavvy Cravath ML	20	25	100	120	150	300	700	
110	Sam Crawford Throwing	60	100	200	300	600	1,200	1,500	
111	Sam Crawford with Bat	60	120	200	250	600	600	20,000	
112	Birdie Cree	25	30	50	150	200	250		
113	Lou Criger	20	40	60	80	250	300		
114	Dode Criss UER	20	25	60	100	150	250	500	
115	Monte Cross ML	20	25	40	60	100	200	400	
116	Bill Dahlen Boston	20	50	80	150	200	250	800	
117	Bill Dahlen Brooklyn	100	120	400	800	2,000	4,500	5,000	
118	Paul Davidson ML	20	50	60	80	20	350	500	
119	George Davis	80	200	250	300	500	800	2,000	
120	Harry Davis (Davis on Front)	20	25	40	120	150	200	500	
121	Harry Davis (H.Davis on Front)	20	25	40	50	150	200	500	
122	Frank Delehanty (Delahanty) ML	20	40	60	120	200	250	500	
123	Jim Delehanty	20	25	80	120	200	800		
124	Ray Demmitt New York	25	30	50	100	150	300	600	

	PrFr 1	GD 2	VG 3	VgEx 4	EX 5	ExMt 6	NM 7	NmMt 8
Ray Demmitt St. Louis	1,500	2,000	2,500	8,000				
Rube Dessau ML	20	30	40	60	175	300	600	
Art Devlin	20	25	40	60	150	250	400	
Josh Devore	20	50	60	120	150	200	600	
Bill Dineen	25	30	40	60	150	200	800	
Mike Donlin Fielding	40	50	80	120	200	400		
Mike Donlin Seated	20	25	40	60	120	350	500	
Mike Donlin with Bat	20	25	60	120	300	350	400	
Jiggs Donahue (Donohue)	20	25	40	50	100	200	1,000	
Wild Bill Donovan Portrait	30	40	60	100	150	250	1,000	
Wild Bill Donovan Throwing	20	25	80	100	200	275	600	
Red Dooin	20	25	40	80	150	200	500	
Mickey Doolan Batting	30	40	60	120	150	250	500	
Mickey Doolan Fielding	20	25	100	120	150	200	400	
Mickey Doolin Portrait	20	25	40	50	200	300	400	
Gus Dorner ML	20	25	60	80	120	300	400	
Patsy Dougherty Portrait	20	25	40	200	250	300	400	
Tom Downey Batting	30	40	60	80	150	250		
Tom Downey Fielding	20	30	40	80	120	200	400	
Jerry Downs ML	30	40	60	100	120	400	600	
Joe Doyle Hands Above Head	150	200	250	500	800			
Larry Doyle Portrait	20	25	40	60	300	350		
Larry Doyle Throwing	20	25	60	100	200	300		
Larry Doyle with Bat	30	40	50	80	250	300	400	
Jean Dubuc	50	60	80	120	250	200	500	
Hugh Duffy	120	200	250	400	600	800	2,000	
Jack Dunn Baltimore ML	20	25	60	120	300	400	500	
Joe Dunn Brooklyn	20	25	120	150	200	250	700	
Bull Durham	25	30	50	200	400	600		
Jimmy Dygert	20	25	40	50	120	250	400	
Ted Easterly	20	30	40	100	150	200	600	
Dick Egan	20	30	40	100	120	250	800	
Kid Elberfeld Fielding	50	60	100	120	200	300		
Kid Elberfeld Portrait New York	25	30	50	150	300	400		
Kid Elberfeld Portrait Wash	300	400	600	1,000	2,500			
Roy Ellam SL	60	100	120	500	600	800		
Clyde Engle	20	25	40	80	150	250	500	
Steve Evans	30	40	60	100	120	300	500	
Johnny Evers Portrait	120	200	300	400	800	1,500	2,500	
Johnny Evers w/Bat Chi Shirt	80	120	150	400	500	1,500	2,000	
Johnny Evers w/Bat Cubs Shirt	150	200	300	500	1,000	2,000		
Bob Ewing	20	25	60	120	150	250	800	
Cecil Ferguson	20	25	40	100	120	250	500	
Hobe Ferris	20	25	120	150	200	250	500	
Lou Fiene Portrait	30	40	60	120	300	500	600	
Lou Fiene Throwing	20	25	50	80	150	250	400	
Steamer Flanagan ML	20	25	60	80	200	300	500	
Art Fletcher	20	25	40	80	120	200	400	
Elmer Flick	60	120	200	300	400	800	2,000	
Russ Ford	20	50	80	120	250	300	500	
Ed Foster SL	50	60	250	500	600			
Jerry Freeman ML	20	25	80	120	250	400	600	
John Frill	20	60	100	120	150	200	500	
Charlie Fritz SL	40	80	100	200	400	1,200		
Art Fromme	40	50	60	120	200	400	600	
Chick Gandil	60	120	200	400	1,000	1,500		
Bob Ganley	25	30	100	120	200	400		
John Ganzel ML	30	50	60	100	200	300	500	
Harry Gasper (Gaspar)	20	30	60	200	250	300	400	
Rube Geyer	20	40	60	80	120	300	500	
George Gibson	25	60	80	120	150	250	500	
Billy Gilbert	20	40	50	100	120	200	500	
Wilbur Goode	30	40	80	120	200	400	500	
Bill Graham St. Louis	20	25	40	80	150	300	400	
Peaches Graham Boston	30	50	80	100	120	300	600	
Dolly Gray	20	25	40	60	200	250	500	
Ed Greminger SL	50	60	100	300	400	800	1,500	
Clark Griffith Batting	50	60	100	250	350	500	2,000	
Clark Griffith Portrait	50	100	120	200	400	800	2,000	
Moose Grimshaw ML	20	25	60	80	150	200	400	
Bob Groom	20	50	60	80	200	250	400	
Tom Guiheen SL	60	100	200	300	500	600	3,000	
Ed Hahn	20	50	80	100	250	300	400	
Bob Hall ML	20	25	40	80	120	400		
Bill Hallman ML	25	30	40	60	150	250		
Jack Hannifan (Hannifin) ML	20	25	50	80	100	200	400	
Bill Hart Little Rock SL	40	50	120	200	300	850	1,200	

	PrFr 1	GD 2	VG 3	VgEx 4	EX 5	ExMt 6	NM 7	NmMt 8
205 Jimmy Hart Montgomery SL	50	60	100	200	400	700		
206 Topsy Hartsel	30	40	60	80	150	200		
207 Jack Hayden ML	20	25	40	120	150	200	500	
208 J.Ross Helm SL	40	50	120	250	400	800	1,500	
209 Charlie Hemphill	20	25	40	100	150	250	500	
210 Buck Herzog Boston	20	25	60	120	250	350	700	
211 Buck Herzog New York	20	25	50	100	150	250		
212 Gordon Hickman SL	60	100	150	300	500	600	3,000	
213 Bill Hinchman Cleveland	20	25	40	50	150	200	500	
214 Harry Hinchman Toledo ML	50	60	80	100	150	250	400	
215 Dick Hoblitzell	20	25	50	100	150	200	400	
216 Danny Hoffman St. Louis	30	40	60	120	150	250	600	
217 Izzy Hoffman Providence ML	20	30	50	100	150	250		
218 Solly Hofman	20	25	40	60	250	300	400	
219 Bock Hooker SL	100	150	200	250	400	650		
220 Del Howard Chicago	20	25	50	100	200	500		
221 Ernie Howard Savannah SL	50	80	120	200	400	800		
222 Harry Howell Hand at Waist	20	25	40	120	200	250	500	
223 Harry Howell Portrait	30	40	120	150	200	250	400	
224 Miller Huggins Hands at Mouth	100	120	150	200	500	600	1,500	
225 Miller Huggins Portrait	50	60	200	250	400	600	1,500	
226 Rudy Hulswitt	30	60	80	120	200	300	400	
227 John Hummel	20	25	100	120	200	400	800	
228 George Hunter	25	30	80	100	200	300	400	
229 Frank Isbell	40	50	60	120	150	400		
230 Fred Jacklitsch	40	50	80	100	150	250	500	
231 Jimmy Jackson ML	20	30	60	100	150	300	500	
232 Hughie Jennings Both Hands	60	120	200	250	500	600	1,500	
233 Hughie Jennings One Hand	80	100	120	200	600	800	2,000	
234 Hughie Jennings Portrait	80	150	200	250	500	600	2,000	
235 Walter Johnson Hands at Chest	200	500	800	1,200	2,500	4,000	10,000	
236 Walter Johnson Portrait	500	600	1,200	2,000	3,000	5,000	20,000	
237 Davy Jones Detroit	25	30	40	100	120	250	800	
238 Fielder Jones Hands at Hips	20	25	40	100	150	250		
239 Fielder Jones Portrait	20	25	40	80	120	500	800	
240 Tom Jones St. Louis	20	25	40	80	100			
241 Dutch Jordan Atlanta SL	40	50	100	300	500	600		
242 Tim Jordan Brooklyn Batting	20	25	40	80	250	350	500	
243 Tim Jordan Brooklyn Portrait	20	25	40	50	150	200	400	
244 Addie Joss Pitching	60	100	200	300	500	700	2,000	
245 Addie Joss Portrait	80	200	250	300	500	1,200	4,000	
246 Ed Karger	20	25	50	80	100	300	500	
247 Willie Keeler Portrait	100	200	250	500	600	1,000	3,500	
248 Willie Keeler with Bat	100	150	200	400	600	1,800	2,000	
249 Joe Kelley ML	100	120	200	300	400	600		
250 J.F. Kiernan SL	80	100	150	400	500			
251 Ed Killian Pitching	20	25	40	60	150	200	400	
252 Ed Killian Portrait	20	25	40	120	200	250	400	
253 Frank King SL	60	80	150	400	500	600		
254 Rube Kisinger (Kissinger) ML	25	30	40	60	150	400		
255 Red Kleinow Boston	80	100	200	300	500	800	2,500	
256 Red Kleinow New York Catching	25	30	120	150	250	500	600	
257 Red Kleinow New York with Bat	30	40	60	80	150	300	400	
258 Johnny Kling	20	25	60	80	200	500		
259 Otto Knabe	20	25	40	60	120	300	400	
260 Jack Knight Portrait	20	25	50	100	150	250		
261 Jack Knight with Bat	20	25	40	100	250	300	500	
262 Ed Konetchy Glove Near Ground	30	40	100	120	200	300	600	
263 Ed Konetchy Glove Above Head	20	25	40	120	150	250	500	
264 Harry Krause Pitching	20	25	50	120	150	200	400	
265 Harry Krause Portrait	30	40	80	120	150	250	400	
266 Rube Kroh	20	25	40	50	100	200	500	
267 Otto Kruger (Krueger) ML	20	25	40	60	250	350	800	
268 James LaFitte SL	40	120	200	400	500	800		
269 Nap Lajoie Portrait	120	300	400	600	1,000	2,000	6,000	
270 Nap Lajoie Throwing	120	200	300	400	600	1,000	2,000	
271 Nap Lajoie with Bat	120	250	400	600	800	1,200	3,000	
272 Joe Lake New York	30	40	80	100	150	250		
273 Joe Lake St. Louis No Ball	20	25	40	80	120	200	400	
274 Joe Lake St. Louis with Ball	20	25	40	80	150	500		
275 Frank LaPorte	30	40	60	100	200	400	800	
276 Arlie Latham	20	25	50	100	200	300	800	
277 Bill Lattimore ML	20	30	40	60	100	200	400	
278 Jimmy Lavender ML	20	25	60	150	200	250	500	
279 Tommy Leach Bending Over	20	25	60	80	150	300	500	
280 Tommy Leach Portrait	20	25	60	100	150	250		
281 Lefty Leifield Batting	30	40	50	100	200	300	400	

#		PrFr 1	GD 2	VG 3	VgEx 4	EX 5	ExMt 6	NM 7	NmMt 8
282	Lefty Leifield Pitching	20	30	60	80	200	300		
283	Ed Lennox	20	25	40	80	120	200	400	
284	Harry Lentz (Sentz) SL	60	80	150	250	500	1,500		
285	Glenn Liebhardt	30	40	80	100	200	250	400	
286	Vive Lindaman	20	25	40	50	150	300		
287	Perry Lipe SL	40	80	150	400	500	800		
288	Paddy Livingstone	40	50	60	100	150	300	400	
289	Hans Lobert	20	25	100	150	200	500		
290	Harry Lord	25	50	80	120	250	300	400	
291	Harry Lumley	20	50	80	100	150	400	600	
292	Carl Lundgren Chicago	120	200	300	500	800	2,500		
293	Carl Lundgren Kansas City ML	25	30	100	200	250	800		
294	Nick Maddox	20	25	40	50	100	200	400	
294	Sherry Magie Portrait (Magee)	8,000	10,000	15,000	25,000				
295	Sherry Magee with Bat	20	25	60	120	250	450	500	
296	Sherry Magee Portrait	40	60	200	300	400	500		
298	Bill Malarkey ML	20	25	40	80	100	250	800	
299	Billy Maloney ML	20	30	40	80	120	400	600	
300	George Manion SL	50	60	150	250	500	600		
301	Rube Manning Batting	20	25	50	80	120	200	400	
302	Rube Manning Pitching	20	25	50	80	120	200		
303	Rube Marquard Follow Through	50	80	120	250	600	800	1,700	
304	Rube Marquard Hands at Thighs	80	100	200	250	400	500	1,700	
305	Rube Marquard Portrait	80	100	150	250	500	1,200	2,000	
306	Doc Marshall	20	25	40	80	120	200	400	
307	Christy Mathewson Dark Cap	300	400	500	1,000	2,000	3,000	6,000	
308	Christy Mathewson Portrait	250	400	800	1,500	2,000	4,000	8,000	
309	Christy Mathewson White Cap	300	400	600	1,000	2,000	2,500	5,000	
310	Al Mattern	40	50	60	100	150	250	400	
311	John McAleese	30	50	60	80	100	200	500	
312	George McBride	40	50	60	120	250	300	400	
313	Pat McCauley SL	40	50	150	300	400	800	4,000	
314	Moose McCormick	25	30	60	80	150	200	400	
315	Pryor McElveen	30	40	60	100	120	250	400	
316	Dan McGann ML	20	25	40	60	120	200	400	
317	Jim McGinley ML	20	25	40	60	100	250	400	
318	Iron Man McGinnity ML	60	80	120	200	450	600	2,000	
319	Stoney McGlynn ML	30	40	60	80	150	200	500	
320	John McGraw Finger in Air	60	100	150	250	500	800	2,000	
321	John McGraw Glove at Hip	100	120	200	300	500	800	2,000	
322	John McGraw Portrait No Cap	60	100	200	300	500	800	1,500	
323	John McGraw Portrait with Cap	60	80	200	300	400	600	1,500	
324	Harry McIntyre Brooklyn	20	25	40	80	150	200	400	
325	Harry McIntyre Brooklyn-Chicago	20	25	40	60	100	200	400	
326	Matty McIntyre Detroit	20	25	40	80	150	350		
327	Larry McLean	20	25	40	60	150	200	400	
328	George McQuillan Ball in Hand	20	25	50	80	150	300	500	
329	George McQuillan with Bat	30	40	60	120	250	300	800	
330	Fred Merkle Portrait	25	100	120	150	250	300	800	
331	Fred Merkle Throwing	25	30	60	150	250	500		
332	George Merritt ML	20	60	80	100	150	250	800	
333	Chief Meyers	20	25	40	80	200	400	600	
334	Chief Myers Batting (Meyers)	20	25	40	80	120	250		
335	Chief Myers Fielding (Meyers)	20	25	40	120	300	400	800	
336	Clyde Milan	25	50	60	80	200	400	500	
337	Molly Miller Dallas SL	40	50	200	300	400	600		
338	Dots Miller Pittsburgh	30	40	60	100	150	250	500	
339	Bill Milligan ML	20	25	40	100	150	250		
340	Fred Mitchell Toronto ML	20	50	80	100	120	250		
341	Mike Mitchell Cincinnati	20	25	40	80	150	250	600	
342	Dan Moeller ML	20	25	50	80	100	200	600	
343	Carleton Molesworth SL	40	100	150	300	400	600		
344	Herbie Moran Providence ML	20	25	40	60	120	200	500	
345	Pat Moran Chicago	30	50	60	100	200	250		
346	George Moriarty	20	25	60	100	150	200	500	
347	Mike Mowrey	20	25	40	60	120	200	400	
348	Dom Mullaney SL	40	80	150	300	500	700	1,200	
349	George Mullen (Mullin)	30	40	80	100	150	250	500	
350	George Mullin with Bat	20	25	40	80	100	250		
351	George Mullin Throwing	25	30	100	150	200	300		
352	Danny Murphy Batting	20	25	40	100	200	250		
353	Danny Murphy Throwing	25	30	60	100	150	250	800	
354	Red Murray Batting	20	25	40	80	150	200	400	
355	Red Murray Portrait	20	25	40	80	150	200	400	
356	Billy Nattress ML	20	25	40	60	200	250	500	
357	Tom Needham	30	40	60	100	200	300		
358	Simon Nicholls Hands on Knees	20	25	40	120	200	250	800	

#		PrFr 1	GD 2	VG 3	VgEx 4	EX 5	ExMt 6	NM 7	NmMt
359	Simon Nichols Batting (Nicholls)	20	25	60	80	350	500		
360	Harry Niles	20	50	60	100	250	300	400	
361	Rebel Oakes	20	25	60	80	120	250		
362	Frank Oberlin ML	40	50	60	100	200	400	500	
363	Peter O'Brien ML	40	50	60	120	150	250		
364	Bill O'Hara New York	20	25	40	120	150	300		
365	Bill O'Hara St. Louis	1,500	2,000	4,000	8,000				
366	Rube Oldring Batting	20	25	60	80	120	300	400	
367	Rube Oldring Fielding	20	25	40	80	120	200	500	
368	Charley O'Leary Hands on Knees	20	25	40	60	120	200	400	
369	Charley O'Leary Portrait	30	40	60	100	150	200	600	
370	William O'Neil ML	25	40	100	120	200	500		
371	Al Orth SL	40	50	100	300	350	600	1,200	
372	William Otey SL	50	100	200	400	500	1,000		
373	Orval Overall Hand at Face	20	30	50	100	150	200	400	
374	Orval Overall Hands at Waist	20	25	60	100	200	250		
375	Orval Overall Portrait	20	25	50	80	150	200	500	
376	Frank Owen (Owens)	20	40	60	80	150	300	400	
377	George Paige SL	50	60	150	400	500	800	2,500	
378	Fred Parent	20	25	50	80	150	200	600	
379	Dode Paskert	20	25	40	100	120	200	700	
380	Jim Pastorius	20	25	40	100	120	250		
381	Harry Pattee	80	100	150	200	400	500	2,000	
382	Fred Payne	20	25	50	80	300	400	600	
383	Barney Pelty Horizontal	30	80	200	250	300	500	1,200	
384	Barney Pelty Vertical	20	25	50	120	250	800	1,000	
385	Hub Perdue SL	40	50	150	250	600	800	1,500	
386	George Perring	40	50	60	120	150	300	500	
387	Arch Persons SL	40	50	150	200	450	600		
388	Francis Pfeffer	30	40	60	100	200	250	600	
389	Jeff Pfeffer ERR#{Chicago								
390	Jake Pfeister Seated (Pfiester)	30	40	60	120	150	200	400	
391	Jake Pfeister Throwing (Pfiester)	20	25	50	100	200	300		
392	Jimmy Phelan ML	20	25	40	80	150	250		
393	Eddie Phelps	20	25	40	80	150	200	400	
394	Deacon Phillippe	20	25	40	100	150	200	450	
395	Ollie Pickering ML	20	25	50	80	100	250		
396	Eddie Plank	50,000	60,000						
397	Phil Poland ML	20	25	40	120	150	200		
398	Jack Powell	25	30	100	120	200	250	1,000	
399	Mike Powers	25	60	80	200	250	500		
400	Billy Purtell	20	30	40	50	200	300	500	
401	Ambrose Puttman (Puttmann) ML	40	80	100	120	250	400		
402	Lee Quillen (Quillin) ML	20	25	40	100	150	250	400	
403	Jack Quinn	30	40	50	60	200	300	400	
404	Newt Randall ML	20	25	50	60	120	200	1,000	
405	Bugs Raymond	20	25	40	80	200	250	500	
406	Ed Reagan SL	40	50	100	250	400	800		
407	Ed Reulbach Glove Showing	30	60	80	150	300	400		
408	Ed Reulbach No Glove	25	30	60	100	250	350	500	
409	Dutch Revelle SL	40	50	80	150	400	1,000	1,200	
410	Bob Rhoades Hands at Chest	20	25	40	60	100	300	500	
411	Bob Rhoades Right Arm Out	30	40	60	100	150	200	500	
412	Charlie Rhodes	20	25	150	200	250	300	400	
413	Claude Ritchey	30	40	50	150	200	400		
414	Lou Ritter ML	20	25	40	60	120	300		
415	Ike Rockenfeld SL	40	60	100	200	500	600		
416	Claude Rossman	30	50	80	120	300	400	500	
417	Nap Rucker Portrait	25	30	40	120	150	200	600	
418	Nap Rucker Throwing	30	40	50	100	250	500	700	
419	Dick Rudolph ML	20	30	80	150	300	400	500	
420	Ray Ryan SL	60	100	250	300	500	1,000		
421	Germany Schaefer Detroit	20	50	60	150	300	400	500	
422	Germany Schaefer Washington	30	40	60	80	150	200	500	
423	George Schirm ML	20	50	60	80	150	400		
424	Larry Schlafly ML	20	25	40	100	120	250	400	
425	Admiral Schlei Batting	20	25	60	80	150	200	500	
426	Admiral Schlei Catching	20	40	60	80	200	300	500	
427	Admiral Schlei Portrait	40	50	60	120	200	350	1,200	
428	Boss Schmidt Portrait	20	25	40	60	150	200	400	
429	Boss Schmidt Throwing	20	25	40	80	150	250	400	
430	Ossee Schreck (Schreckengost) ML	20	25	40	80	200	250	850	
431	Wildfire Schulte Back View	20	30	40	120	150	350	500	
432	Wildfire Schulte Front View	30	50	80	150	600			
433	Jim Scott	20	30	60	80	150	250	600	
434	Charles Seitz SL	80	100	150	200	500	600		
435	Cy Seymour Batting	20	25	40	60	120	200	400	

	PrFr 1	GD 2	VG 3	VgEx 4	EX 5	ExMt 6	NM 7	NmMt 8
Cy Seymour Portrait	20	25	40	80	150	200	500	
Cy Seymour Throwing	20	25	40	120	200	400	500	
Spike Shannon ML	20	25	40	60	150	200	1,000	
Bud Sharpe ML	20	25	40	50	150	250	400	
Bud Shappe (Sharpe) ML	300	500	800					
Shag Shaughnessy SL	100	150	400	450	1,000	1,200		
Al Shaw St. Louis	20	50	60	120	150	250		
Hunky Shaw Providence ML	20	25	40	50	200	250		
Jimmy Sheckard Glove Showing	20	25	40	80	150	300	600	
Jimmy Sheckard No Glove	30	40	80	100	120	200	500	
Bill Shipke	20	25	40	60	200	300	500	
Jimmy Slagle ML	25	30	40	60	150	200		
Carlos Smith Shreveport SL	50	80	150	250	600	1,000		
Frank Smith Chicago-Boston	100	120	150	250	600			
Frank Smith Chicago F.Smith	40	50	60	80	150	250	500	
Frank Smith Chicago White Cap	25	30	40	80	150	250	400	
Heinie Smith Buffalo ML	25	30	60	150	200	200	500	
Happy Smith Brooklyn	20	25	40	100	150	200	800	
Sid Smith Atlanta SL	40	60	120	250	500	1,500		
Fred Snodgrass Batting	30	40	60	100	200	600		
Fred nodgrass (Snodgrass) Batting	400	600	1,000					
Fred Snodgrass Catching	20	25	50	120	200	250	500	
Bob Spade	20	25	40	80	120	300	500	
Tris Speaker	400	500	800	1,500	2,500	3,000	4,000	
Tubby Spencer	20	25	60	80	150	350		
Jake Stahl Glove Shows	20	40	60	80	150	300		
Jake Stahl No Glove Shows	20	25	60	120	150	200	400	
Oscar Stanage	25	50	80	120	200	300	400	
Dolly Stark SL	60	80	150	200	300	600		
Charlie Starr	20	25	40	120	200	300	600	
Harry Steinfeldt with Bat	20	25	50	80	150	200	600	
Harry Steinfeldt Portrait	30	40	60	100	150	250	600	
Jim Stephens	20	25	40	80	120	200	500	
George Stone	30	60	80	200	400	500	800	
George Stovall Batting	20	25	40	80	150	400	800	
George Stovall Portrait	20	25	40	80	150	200	500	
Sam Strang ML	20	25	40	80	150	250	400	
Gabby Street Catching	20	25	60	100	200	250	400	
Gabby Street Portrait	30	40	60	100	200	250	500	
Billy Sullivan	20	25	50	80	150	250	800	
Ed Summers	20	40	50	80	120	250	600	
Bill Sweeney Boston	20	25	50	80	120	300	600	
Jeff Sweeney New York	40	50	80	150	300	400	600	
Jesse Tannehill Washington	30	60	80	120	200	300	500	
Lee Tannehill Chicago L.Tannehill	20	25	40	80	120	250	600	
Lee Tannehill Chicago Tannehill	20	25	40	80	120	250	1,000	
Dummy Taylor ML	25	50	80	100	300	400	1,000	
Fred Tenney	25	50	100	150	400	500	600	
Tony Thebo SL	60	80	120	250	400	1,200		
Jake Thielman ML	20	25	40	80	200	250	600	
Ira Thomas	20	50	60	100	250	300	400	
Woodie Thornton SL	50	120	150	250	500	800	1,200	
Joe Tinker Bat off Shoulder	80	100	250	300	800	1,200	3,000	
Joe Tinker Bat on Shoulder	100	120	200	300	500	1,000	2,000	
Joe Tinker Hands on Knees	80	120	200	400	700	1,200	6,000	
Joe Tinker Portrait	100	200	300	500	3,000	4,000		
John Titus	100	200	250	400	600			
Terry Turner	20	50	60	120	200	300	800	
Bob Unglaub	20	25	40	80	150	400	600	
Juan Violat (Viola) SL	50	60	200	250	400	1,000		
Rube Waddell Portrait	80	120	250	400	500	800	2,000	
Rube Waddell Throwing	50	120	200	500	600	1,000	2,500	
Heinie Wagner Bat on Left	25	30	50	120	150	250	600	
Heinie Wagner Bat on Right	25	30	60	200	250	300		
Honus Wagner	▲800,000	▲1500,000						
Bobby Wallace	50	120	150	250	400	600	2,000	
Ed Walsh	150	200	250	▲500	800	1,500	2,000	
Jack Warhop	20	25	50	80	150	200	600	
Jake Weimer	20	25	40	80	150	250	400	
James Westlake SL	50	100	200	300	400	600		
Zack Wheat	80	150	200	600	800	1,000	2,000	
Doc White Chicago Pitching	20	25	50	80	120	300	800	
Doc White Chicago Portrait	40	50	80	100	120	400		
Foley White Houston SL	80	120	150	300	400	600		
Jack White Buffalo ML	20	25	40	60	120	200	400	
Kaiser Wilhelm Hands at Chest	25	30	40	120	200	300	500	
Kaiser Wilhelm with Bat	25	30	40	120	200	250	500	

	PrFr 1	GD 2	VG 3	VgEx 4	EX 5	ExMt 6	NM 7	NmMt 8
513 Ed Willett with Bat	20	25	60	100	200	250	500	
514 Ed Willetts Throwing	20	25	40	50	200	300	500	
515 Jimmy Williams	20	25	60	80	150	200	400	
516 Vic Willis Pittsburgh Portrait	50	80	150	250	450	1,200	1,500	
517 Vic Willis St. Louis Throwing	50	80	120	200	500	800	1,500	
518 Vic Willis St. Louis with Bat	50	80	150	200	400	600	2,000	
519 Owen Wilson	25	30	80	120	150	250	400	
520 Hooks Wiltse Pitching	25	30	40	120	150	250	400	
521 Hooks Wiltse Portrait No Cap	40	50	60	100	150	300		
522 Hooks Wiltse Portrait with Cap	20	25	40	150	200	400	2,000	
523 Lucky Wright ML	20	25	40	80	150	250	400	
524 Cy Young Bare Hand Shows	250	600	800	1,500	2,000	2,500	6,000	
525 Cy Young Glove Shows	500	600	800	1,500	2,000	2,500	4,000	
526 Cy Young Portrait	400	800	1,500	2,500	5,000	6,000	8,000	
527 Irv Young Minneapolis ML	50	60	80	120	200	400		
528 Heinie Zimmerman	50	60	80	120	200	300		

—Prices listed above pertain to Piedmont and Sweet Caporal backs. The scarcer backs command premium values.

—ML and SL notations signify Minor Leaguers and Southern Leaguers.

—A near-complete set (520 of 524 excluding Doyle Nat'l, Magie, Plank and Wagner) rated #3 on PSA Set Registry sold for $255,200 (REA; 4/06).

—Listed pricing for Commons & Minor Stars in NmMt, Mint and Gem is unavailable due to scarcity. In general, NmMt cards sell for $1,250-$2,500 and Mint 9's sell for $7,000-$10,000 per.

—Doc Adkins PSA 8 (NmMt) sold for $5,802 (eBay; 6/06)

—Home Run Baker PSA 8 (NmMt) sold for $21,510 (Heritage; 8/10)

—Home Run Baker (Red Hindu) PSA 5 (EX) sold for $4,025 (eBay; 5/08)

—Jake Beckley ML PSA 8 (NmMt) sold for $33,958 (Goodwin; 10/12)

—Chief Bender Pitching No Trees PSA 8 (NmMt) sold for $14,103 (Goodwin; 4/11)

—Chief Bender Pitching No Trees SGC 88 (NmMt) sold for $6,407 (Mastro; 12/05)

—Chief Bender Portrait PSA 9 (Mint) sold for $30,090 (Goodwin; 6/12)

—Chief Bender Portrait PSA 9 (MT) sold for $16,261 (Mastro; 4/07)

—Chief Bender Portrait PSA 8 (NmMt) sold for $7,200 (Mastro; 5/08)

—Chief Bender Portrait PSA 8 (NmMt) sold for $7,162 (SCP Sotheby's; 11/06)

—Chief Bender Portrait PSA 8 (NmMt) sold for $6,341 (Mile High; 2/08)

—Chief Bender Portrait PSA 8 (NmMt) sold for $4,915 (Mastro; 12/06)

—Chief Bender Portrait PSA 8 (NmMt) sold for $4,780 (Heritage; 10/06)

—Jake Beckley PSA 8 (NmMt) sold for $33,958 (Goodwin; 9/12)

—Roger Bresnahan Portrait SGC 96 (MT) sold for $8,908 (Mastro; 12/07)

—Roger Bresnahan Portrait PSA 8 (NmMt) sold for $4,891 (SCP Sotheby's; 11/06)

—George Brown Chicago PSA 8 (NmMt) sold for $4,252 (eBay; 2/06)

—Mordecai Brown Cubs Shirt PSA 8 (NmMt) sold for $4,554 (SCP Sotheby's; 11/06)

—Mordecai Brown Chicago Shirt (Red Hindu) SGC 4 (VG/Ex) sold for $13,252 (Goodwin; 09/11)

—Mordecai Brown Cubs Shirt PSA 2 (Good) (Black Lennox) sold for $7,770 (Goodwin; 6/12)

—Mordecai Brown Portrait PSA 8 (NmMt) sold for $10,434 (Goodwin; 6/06)

—Mordecai Brown Portrait PSA 8 (NmMt) sold for $3,376 (eBay; 2/08)

—Mordecai Brown Portrait PSA 8 (NmMt) sold for $3,049 (Mastro; 8/07)

—Al Burch Fielding (Brown Lenox) PSA 4 (VG/Ex) sold for $12,334 (Goodwin; 09/11)

—Howie Camnitz Arm at Side PSA 8 (NmMt) sold for $11,054 (Memory Lane 8/06)

—Hal Chase Portrait Pink PSA 7 (NM) sold for $5,117 (Goodwin; 03/12)

—Frank Chance Batting SGC 96 (Mint) sold for $10,809 (Goodwin; 10/12)

—Frank Chance Batting PSA 8 (NmMt) sold for $6,083 (Mastro; 4/07)

—Frank Chance Portrait Red PSA 8 (NmMt) sold for $7,750 (eBay; 2/06)

—Frank Chance Portrait Yellow PSA 7 (NM) sold for $5,207 (Mile High; 05/11)

—Frank Chance Portrait Yellow (Lenox Back) PSA 4 (VgEx) sold for $7,500 (REA; 05/12)

—Frank Chance Portrait Yellow (Red Hindu Back) PSA 3 (VG) sold for $16,980 (SCP; 12/12)

—Jack Chesbro PSA 9 (MT) sold for $15,859 (Mastro; 4/07)

—Jack Chesbro PSA 8 (NmMt) sold for $7,477 (Goodwin; 8/12)

—Eddie Cicotte PSA 8 (NmMt) sold for $2,500 (eBay; 6/07)

—Fred Clarke Holding Bat PSA 8 (NmMt) sold for $6,668 (eBay; 7/08)

—Fred Clarke Holding Bat PSA 8 (NmMt) sold for $6,177 (Goodwin; 8/12)

—Fred Clarke Holding Bat PSA 8 (NmMt) sold for $5,463 (eBay; 11/06)

—Fred Clarke Portrait PSA 8 (NmMt) sold for $8,908 (SCP; 5/12)

—Fred Clarke Portrait PSA 8 (NmMt) sold for $5,381 (SCP Sotheby's; 11/06)

—Ty Cobb Bat off Shoulder PSA 9 (Mint) sold for $488,425 (SCP; 8/16)

—Ty Cobb Bat off Shoulder PSA 8 (NmMt) sold for $29,625 (REA; 5/13)

—Ty Cobb Bat on Shoulder PSA 8 (NmMt) sold for $24,619 (Goodwin; 4/11)

—Ty Cobb Bat on Shoulder PSA 8 (NmMt) sold for $23,645 (Mastro; 12/06)

—Ty Cobb Bat off Shoulder PSA 8 (NmMt) sold for $17,986 (Mastro; 12/05)

—Ty Cobb Bat off Shoulder (Uzit) PSA 2 (Good) sold for $17,775 (REA; 5/13)

—Ty Cobb Bat off Shoulder (Uzit) SGC 1.5 (Fair) sold for $14,403 (Mile High; 10/11)

—Ty Cobb Portrait Green PSA 8 (NmMt) sold for $64,506 (Goodwin; 2/11)

—Ty Cobb Portrait Green SGC 86 (NM+) sold for $14,394 (Goodwin; 7/10)

—Ty Cobb Portrait Green PSA 7 (NM) sold for $34,073 (SCP Sotheby's; 9/07)

—Ty Cobb Portrait Green PSA 7 (NM) sold for $32,588 (REA; 5/13)

—Ty Cobb Portrait Green PSA 7 (NM) sold for $18,705 (Mastro; 4/06)

—Ty Cobb Portrait Green PSA 7 (NM) sold for $17,625 (REA; 4/07)

—Ty Cobb Portrait Red PSA 8 (NmMt) sold for $27,584 (SCP; 12/14)

—Ty Cobb Portrait Red PSA 8 (NmMt) sold for $26,663 (REA; 5/13)
—Ty Cobb Portrait Red PSA 8 (NmMt) sold for $24,930 (Memory Lane; 5/08)
—Ty Cobb Portrait Red PSA 8 (NmMt) sold for $18,832 (SCP; 7/08)
—Ty Cobb Portrait Red PSA 8 (NmMt) sold for $18,800 (REA; 05/11)
—Ty Cobb Portrait Red PSA 8 (NmMt) sold for $17,834 (Mile High; 2/08)
—Ty Cobb Portrait Red PSA 8 (NmMt) sold for $13,397 (Goodwin; 2/07)
—Ty Cobb Portrait Red SGC 86 (NM+) sold for $6,573 (Heritage; 10/07)
—Ty Cobb Portrait Red (Uzit) PSA 6 (ExMt) sold for $29,375 (REA; 4/07)
—Ty Cobb Portrait Red (Hindu Red) PSA 3 (VG) sold for $45,510 (SCP; 12/12)
—Ty Cobb Portrait Red (Lennox) PSA 3 (VG) sold for $27,000 (REA; Spring '15)
—Ty Cobb Portrait Red (Cobb Back) SGC 30 (Good) sold for $132,000 (REA; Spring '15)
—Ty Cobb Portrait Red (Cobb Back) SGC 30 (Good) sold for $66,000 (Mastro; 8/08)
—Ty Cobb Portrait Red (Cobb Back) SGC 30 (Good) sold for $60,000 (Mastro; 8/07)
—Ty Cobb Portrait Red (Cobb Back) SGC 30 (Good) sold for $29,000 (REA; 5/05)
—Ty Cobb Portrait Red (Cobb Back) SGC 20 (Fair) sold for $64,625 (REA; 5/08)
—Ty Cobb Portrait Red (Cobb Back) SGC 20 (Fair) sold for $28,970 (Mastro; 12/05)
—Ty Cobb Portrait Red (Blank Back) SGC A (Authentic) sold for $15,654 (Goodwin; 09/11)
—Ty Cobb Portrait Red (Hindu Red) PSA 1 (Poor) sold for $29,336 (SCP; 4/13)
—Eddie Collins PSA 9 (Mint) sold for $26,335 (Goodwin; 12/10)
—Eddie Collins PSA 8 (NmMt) sold for $18,705 (Goodwin; 11/07)
—Eddie Collins Philadelphia PSA 8 (NmMt) sold for $7,500 (REA; 05/12)
—Sam Crawford with Bat (Uzit) PSA 8 (NmMt) sold for $57,159 (Goodwin; 12/11)
—Sam Crawford with Bat PSA 8 (NmMt) sold for $3,950 (eBay; 3/07)
—Ray Demmitt St. Louis PSA 5 (Ex) sold for $12,925 (REA; 5/08)
—Ray Demmitt St. Louis SGC 60 (Ex) sold for $9,718 (Goodwin; 04/12)
—Ray Demmitt St. Louis SGC 60 (EX) sold for $5,000 (REA; 05/12)
—Gus Dorner Dopner PSA 2 (Good) sold for $5,500 (REA; 05/12)
—Joe Doyle Hands Above Head PSA 7 (NM) sold for $1,248 (eBay; 3/07)
—Joe Doyle Hands Above Head PSA 6 (ExMt) sold for $3,961 (eBay; 8/06)
—Joe Doyle Hands Above Head PSA 6 (ExMt) sold for $2,301 (eBay; 6/08)
—Joe Doyle Hands Above Head Nat'l PSA 3 (Vg) sold for $350,000 (REA; 05/12)
—Larry Doyle with Bat PSA 2 (Good) (Drum) sold for $5,362 (Goodwin; 6/12)
—Hugh Duffy PSA 8 (NmMt) sold for $6,797 (Goodwin; 6/12)
—Kid Elberfeld Fielding (Broad Leaf 460) PSA 6 (ExMt) sold for $7,638 (REA; 5/08)
—Kid Elberfeld Wash. Portrait PSA 7 (NM) sold for $4,278 (eBay; 10/07)
—Kid Elberfeld Wash. Portrait PSA 6 (ExMt) sold for $3,130 (eBay; 11/07)
—Kid Elberfeld Wash. Portrait GAI 5 (EX) sold for $1,432 (Old Judge; 11/05)
—Kid Elberfeld Wash. Portrait GAI 5 (EX) sold for $1,324 (eBay; 1/06)
—Johnny Evers Portrait PSA 8 (NmMt) sold for $12,440 (Goodwin; 8/12)
—Johnny Evers Portrait PSA 8 (NmMt) sold for $10,690 (Goodwin; 7/14)
—Johnny Evers Portrait PSA 8 (NmMt) sold for $8,878 (SCP Sotheby's 11/30/06)
—Johnny Evers w/Bat Chicago Shirt PSA 8 (NmMt) sold for $4,183 (Heritage; 10/06)
—Johnny Evers w/Bat Chicago Shirt SGC 88 (NmMt) sold for $4,067 (Goodwin; 3/08)
—Johnny Evers w/Bat Chicago Shirt SGC 88 (NmMt) sold for $3,716 (eBay; 3/07)
—Johnny Evers w/Bat Cubs Shirt PSA 8 (NmMmt) sold for $13,145 (Heritage; 10/06)
—Johnny Evers w/Bat Cubs Shirt PSA 7 (NM) sold for $5,378 (Heritage; 10/06)
—Johnny Evers w/Bat Cubs Shirt PSA 7 (NM) sold for $4,674 (Goodwin; 3/08)
—Johnny Evers w/Bat Cubs Shirt PSA 4.5 (Vg/Ex+) (Hindu) sold for $9,306 (SCP; 5/12)
—Hobe Ferris PSA 8 (NmMt) sold for $12,936 (Goodwin; 2/11)
—Lou Fiene Throwing SGC 40 (VG) (Drum) sold for $5,484 (Goodwin; 10/12)
—Elmer Flick PSA 8 (NmMt) sold for $7,477 (Goodwin; 8/12)
—Clark Griffith Batting (Drum) PSA 7 (NM) sold for $10,541 (Mastro; 4/07)
—Clark Griffith Batting PSA 4 (Vg/Ex) (Drum) sold for $8,755 (Goodwin; 10/12)
—Clark Griffith Batting (Red Hindu) PSA 2 (Good) sold for $2,949 (Sloate; 5/08)
—Clark Griffith Portrait PSA 9 (MT) sold for $12,773 (Mastro; 4/06)
—Clark Griffith Portrait PSA 8 (NmMt) sold for $2,629 (Heritage; 10/06)
—Miller Huggins Hands at Mouth PSA 9 (MT) sold for $10,555 (Mastro; 4/06)
—Miller Huggins Hands at Mouth PSA 8 (NmMt) sold for $4,922 (Goodwin; 2/07)
—Miller Huggins Hands at Mouth PSA 8 (NmMt) sold for $3,976 (Mastro; 4/06)
—Miller Huggins Hands at Mouth PSA 8 (NmMt) sold for $2,986 (Mastro; 12/05)
—Miller Huggins Hands at Mouth (Drum) SGC 40 (VG) sold for $14,578 (Goodwin; 6/13)
—Miller Huggins Portrait PSA 8 (NmMt) sold for $6,177 (Goodwin; 8/12)
—Miller Huggins Portrait PSA 8 (NmMt) sold for $3,614 (Mastro; 12/05)
—Hughie Jennings Both Hands PSA 8 (NmMt) sold for $8,225 (Goodwin; 8/12)
—Hughie Jennings One Hand PSA 8 (NmMt) sold for $4,780 (Heritage; 10/06)
—Hughie Jennings One Hand PSA 8 (NmMt) sold for $3,285 (Mastro; 12/05)
—Hughie Jennings One Hand PSA 8 (NmMt) sold for $3,231 (REA; 5/08)
—Hughie Jennings Portrait SGC 92 (NmMt+) sold for $3,355 (Mastro; 12/07)
—Hughie Jennings Portrait PSA 8 (NmMt) sold for $5,672 (Goodwin; 10/06)
—Hughie Jennings Portrait PSA 8 (NmMt) sold for $4,042 (SCP Sotheby's; 11/06)
—Hughie Jennings Portrait PSA 8 (NmMt) sold for $3,938 (Memory Lane; 3/06)
—Walter Johnson Hands at Chest PSA 9 (Mint) sold for $47,853 (Goodwin; 11/08)
—Walter Johnson Hands at Chest PSA 8 (NmMt) sold for $10,780 (Mastro; 12/06)
—Walter Johnson Hands at Chest PSA 8 (NmMt) sold for $10,280 (Goodwin; 7/13)
—Walter Johnson Hands at Chest PSA 8 (NmMt) sold for $9,664 (SCP; 7/08)
—Walter Johnson Hands at Chest PSA 8 (NmMt) sold for $8,856 (eBay; 11/07)
—Walter Johnson Hands at Chest (Hindu Red) SGC 55 (VgEx+) sold for $10,073 (REA; 5/13)

—Walter Johnson Hands at Chest (Hindu Red) SGC 4 (VgEx) sold for $11,000 (REA; 05/12)
—Walter Johnson Hands at Chest (Hindu Red) PSA 4 (VgEx) sold for $10,780 (SCP; 4/13)
—Walter Johnson Hands at Chest (Hindu Red) PSA 4 (VgEx) sold for $9,799 (SCP; 12/12)
—Walter Johnson Portrait PSA 9 (MT) sold for $44,428 (Mastro; 12/06)
—Walter Johnson Portrait PSA 9 (MT) sold for $37,700 (REA; 5/05)
—Walter Johnson Portrait PSA 8 (NmMt) sold for $28,090 (SCP; 7/08)
—Walter Johnson Portrait PSA 8 (NmMt) sold for $23,971 (Goodwin; 3/15)
—Walter Johnson Portrait PSA 8 (NmMt) sold for $22,440 (Bussineau; 7/13)
—Walter Johnson Portrait PSA 8 (NmMt) sold for $20,191 (SCP Sotheby's; 11/06)
—Walter Johnson Portrait PSA 8 (NmMt) sold for $18,827 (Mastro; 8/07)
—Walter Johnson Portrait PSA 8 (NmMt) sold for $16,000 (eBay; 10/08)
—Walter Johnson Portrait PSA 8 (NmMt) sold for $15,811 (Mastro; 12/05)
—Walter Johnson Portrait PSA 8 (NmMt) sold for $14,600 (eBay; 6/08)
—Walter Johnson Portrait (Brown Hindu) PSA 3 (VG) sold for $3,525 (REA; 5/08)
—Addie Joss Pitching PSA 9 (MT) sold for $18,705 (Goodwin; 10/06)
—Addie Joss Pitching PSA 8 (NmMt) sold for $3,355 (Mastro; 8/07)
—Addie Joss Pitching PSA 8 (NmMt) sold for $2,510 (SCP Sotheby's; 1/08)
—Addie Joss Portrait PSA 9 (MT) sold for $35,202 (Goodwin; 2/11)
—Addie Joss Portrait PSA 8 (NmMt) sold for $7,272 (Mile High; 12/05)
—Addie Joss Portrait PSA 8 (NmMt) sold for $5,801 (Goodwin; 8/12)
—Addie Joss Portrait PSA 8 (NmMt) sold for $5,533 (Memory Lane; 9/07)
—Addie Joss Portrait PSA 8 (NmMt) sold for $5,273 (Goodwin; 10/12)
—Addie Joss Portrait PSA 8 (NmMt) sold for $4,780 (Heritage; 10/06)
—Addie Joss Portrait PSA 8 (NmMt) sold for $4,041 (SCP Sotheby's 9/07)
—Addie Joss Portrait PSA 8 (NmMt) sold for $3,614 (Mastro; 12/05)
—Addie Joss Portrait GAI 8 (NmMt) sold for $2,300 (eBay; 2/06)
—Willie Keeler Portrait PSA 8 (NmMt) sold for $30,792 (SCP Sotheby's; 11/06)
—Willie Keeler Portrait PSA 8 (NmMt) sold for $19,404 (Goodwin; 6/12)
—Willie Keeler with Bat PSA 9 (MT) sold for $12,536 (SCP Sotheby's; 11/06)
—Willie Keeler with Bat PSA 9 (MT) sold for $8,908 (Mastro; 12/07)
—Willie Keeler with Bat PSA 8 (NmMt) sold for $5,801 (Goodwin; 8/12)
—Willie Keeler with Bat PSA 8 (NmMt) sold for $3,285 (Mastro; 12/05)
—Joe Kelley PSA 7 (NM) sold for $7,109 (Mile High; 6/15/06)
—Rube Kisinger ML PSA 8 (NmMt) sold for $8,550 (Goodwin; 10/12)
—Red Kleinow Boston SGC 30 (Good) (Broad Leaf 460) sold for $5,425 (Memory Lane; 8/12)
—Ed Konetchy Glove Near Ground (Drum) PSA 1 (Poor) sold for $10,347 (Goodwin; 3/13)
—Otto Krueger PSA 8 (NmMt) sold for $5,512 (SCP Sotheby's; 11/06)
—Nap Lajoie Portrait PSA 8 (NmMt) sold for $11,814 (SCP Sotheby's; 11/06)
—Nap Lajoie Portrait PSA 8 (NmMt) sold for $8,495 (Goodwin; 6/12)
—Nap Lajoie Throwing PSA 8 (NmMt) sold for $6,032 (Mile High; 5/12)
—Nap Lajoie Throwing PSA 8 (NmMt) sold for $5,616 (Goodwin; 11/12)
—Nap Lajoie Throwing PSA 8 (NmMt) sold for $5,381 (SCP Sotheby; 11/06)
—Nap Lajoie Throwing PSA 8 (NmMt) sold for $5,105 (Goodwin; 10/12)
—Nap Lajoie Throwing PSA 8 (NmMt) sold for $5,034 (Goodwin; 2/07)
—Nap Lajoie Throwing PSA 8 (NmMt) sold for $4,438 (Mastro; 12/06)
—Nap Lajoie Throwing PSA 8 (NmMt) sold for $4,183 (eBay; 3/06)
—Nap Lajoie Throwing PSA 8 (NmMt) sold for $4,061 (Mastro; 8/07)
—Nap Lajoie Throwing PSA 8 (NmMt) sold for $3,999 (eBay; 7/07)
—Nap Lajoie Throwing PSA 8 (NmMt) sold for $3,614 (Mastro; 12/05)
—Nap Lajoie with Bat PSA 8 (NmMt) sold for $8,495 (Goodwin; 6/12)
—Nap Lajoie with Bat PSA 8 (NmMt) sold for $5,956 (eBay; 6/07)
—Carl Lundgren Chicago PSA 7 (NM) MK sold for $16,459 (SCP Sotheby's; 11/06)
—Sherry Magie Portrait (Magee) PSA 8 (NmMt) sold for $27,660 (Greg Bussineau; 12/15)
—Sherry Magie Portrait (Magee) SGC 80 (ExMt) sold for $80,077 (Goodwin; 04/12)
—Sherry Magie Portrait (Magee) SGC 60 (EX) sold for $30,600 (Greg Bussineau; 12/12)
—Sherry Magie Portrait (Magee) PSA 2.5 (G+) sold for $15,036 (SCP; 3/09)
—Sherry Magie Portrait (Magee) PSA 2.5 (G+) sold for $15,000 (REA; 05/12)
—Sherry Magie Portrait (Magee) SGC 20 (Fair) sold for $8,215 (Goodwin; 8/12)
—Sherry Magee Portrait PSA 2.5 (G+) sold for $7,848 (Memory Lane; 8/12)
—Rube Marquard Hands Thighs PSA 9 (MT) sold for $10,977 (Goodwin; 11/07)
—Rube Marquard Hands Thighs PSA 8 (NmMt) sold for $3,674 (SCP Sotheby's; 11/06)
—Rube Marquard Hands Thighs PSA 8 (NmMt) sold for $3,037 (SCP Sotheby's; 1/08)
—Rube Marquard Portrait PSA 8 (NmMt) sold for $3,976 (Mastro; 12/05)
—Christy Mathewson Dark Cap PSA 8.5 (NmMt+) sold for $34,693 (Mile High; 10/13)
—Christy Mathewson Portrait PSA 8 (NmMt) sold for $32,588 (REA; 5/13)
—Christy Mathewson Portrait PSA 8 (NmMt) sold for $29,339 (Goodwin; 6/12)
—Christy Mathewson Portrait PSA 8 (NmMt) sold for $25,468 (Mastro; 12/05)
—Christy Mathewson Dark Cap PSA 8 (NmMt) sold for $35,502 (Goodwin; 8/12)
—Christy Mathewson White Cap PSA 8 (NmMt) sold for $11,611 (Mastro; 4/06)
—Christy Mathewson White Cap PSA 8 (NmMt) sold for $10,025 (Mastro; 12/06)
—Christy Mathewson White Cap PSA 8 (NmMt) sold for $9,929 (Sloate; 11/06)
—Iron Man McGinnity PSA 9 (MT) sold for $20,336 (Mastro; 8/06)
—Iron Man McGinnity SGC 96 (MT) sold for $11,239 (Goodwin; 9/08)
—John McGraw Finger in Air PSA 9 (MT) sold for $6,995 (eBay; 1/06)
—John McGraw Finger in Air PSA 9 (MT) sold for $4,024 (Mastro; 12/05)
—John McGraw Finger in Air PSA 8 (NmMt) sold for $6,670 (SCP; 7/08)
—John McGraw Finger in Air PSA 8 (NmMt) sold for $4,328 (Goodwin; 10/06)

John McGraw Finger in Air PSA 8 (NmMt) sold for $3,938 (Memory Lane; 3/06)
John McGraw Finger in Air PSA 8 (NmMt) sold for $2,988 (Heritage; 10/07)
John McGraw Glove at Hip PSA 8 (NmMt) sold for $5,801 (Goodwin; 10/12)
John McGraw Glove at Hip PSA 8 (NmMt) sold for $3,884 (Heritage; 5/07)
John McGraw Portrait No Cap PSA 8 (NmMt) sold for $6,611 (Mile High; 12/05)
John McGraw Portrait with Cap PSA 8 (NmMt) sold for $4,375 (Mastro; 4/06)
George McQuillan with Bat PSA 1 (Poor) (Brown Lennox) sold for $5,484 (Goodwin; 8/12)
Carleton Molesworth PSA 8 (NmMt) sold for $11,878 (Goodwin; 7/10)
Danny Murphy Batting PSA 2 (Red Hindu Back) (Good) sold for $31,328 (SCP; 12/12)
Bill O'Hara St. Louis PSA 7 (NM) sold for $44,325 (Mile High; 10/11)
Bill O'Hara St. Louis PSA 5 (EX) sold for $22,325 (REA; 5/10)
Bill O'Hara St. Louis PSA 5 (EX) sold for $11,500 (Superior; 8/05)
Jim Pastorius PSA 10 (Gem) sold for $23,311 (Goodwin; 5/07)
Deacon Phillipe PSA 9 (MT) sold for $11,020 (REA; 4/06)
Eddie Plank PSA 6 (ExMt) sold for $239,000 (Heritage; 7/16)
Eddie Plank PSA 6 (ExMt) sold for $193,767 (Goodwin; 4/11)
Eddie Plank PSA 6 (ExMt) sold for $188,000 (REA; 5/09)
Eddie Plank PSA 6 MC (ExMt, Miscut) sold for $102,000 (SCP Sotheby's; 6/07)
Eddie Plank SGC 70 (Ex+) (Piedmont 150 Back) sold for $330,826 (Goodwin; 04/12)
Eddie Plank SGC 60 (EX) sold for $106,650 (REA; 5/13)
Eddie Plank PSA 5 (EX) sold for $85,237 (Lelands; 12/12)
Eddie Plank PSA 5 (EX) sold for $78,959 (Mile High; 10/13)
Eddie Plank PSA 5 (EX) sold for $75,600 (Bussineau; 7/13)
Eddie Plank PSA 5 (EX) sold for $52,200 (REA; 5/05)
Eddie Plank PSA 4.5 (VgEx+) sold for $66,000 (REA; Spring '15)
Eddie Plank SGC 50 (VgEx) sold for $43,500 (REA; 4/06)
Eddie Plank PSA 4 (VgEx) sold for $94,000 (REA; 05/11)
Eddie Plank PSA 4 (VgEx) sold for $88,875 (REA; 5/13)
Eddie Plank PSA 4 (VgEx) sold for $83,300 (Memory Lane; 5/12)
Eddie Plank PSA 4 (VgEx) sold for $80,000 (REA; 05/12)
Eddie Plank PSA 4 (VgEx) sold for $42,000 (eBay; 3/06)
Eddie Plank SGC 40 (VG) sold for $77,675 (Heritage; 5/08)
Eddie Plank PSA 3 (VG) sold for $65,725 (Heritage; 4/10)
Eddie Plank SGC 40 (VG) sold for $58,750 (REA; 5/10)
Eddie Plank GAI 3 (VG) sold for $40,828 (SCP; 7/08)
Eddie Plank PSA 3 (VG) sold for $40,388 (Mastro; 12/06)
Eddie Plank SGC 40 (VG) sold for $39,704 (Sloate; 11/06)
Eddie Plank GAI 3 (VG) sold for $17,250 (SCP; 12/04)
Eddie Plank SGC 2.5 (G/VG) sold for $42,000 (REA; Spring '15)
Eddie Plank SGC 20 (F) sold for $29,375 (REA; 5/09)
Eddie Plank PSA Authentic (Missing Color) sold for $92,762 (Goodwin; 1/13)
Ike Rockenfeld PSA 7 (NM) sold for $6,914 (SCP; 7/08)
George Schirm PSA 7 (NM) sold for $8,100 (eBay; 6/06)
Ossie Schreck PSA 9 (MT) sold for $12,760 (REA; 4/06)
Germany Schaefer Detroit PSA 9 (Mint) sold for $5,558 (Memory Lane; 8/12)
Charles Seitz PSA 8 (NmMt) sold for $11,759 (Goodwin; 2/11)
Cy Seymour Throwing (Drum) PSA 1 (Poor) sold for $24,406 (Goodwin; 3/13)
Frank Smith Chicago-Boston PSA 7 (NM) sold for $8,700 (REA; 4/06)
Frank Smith Chicago-Boston PSA 6 (ExMt) sold for $2,994 (eBay; 2/06)
Frank Smith Chicago-Boston PSA 6 (ExMt) sold for $1,622 (Memory Lane; 12/07)
Sid Smith Atlanta SL SGC A (Authentic) (Old Mill Brown) sold for $24,000 (REA; Fall '14)
Tris Speaker PSA 8 (NmMt) sold for $22,041 (Goodwin; 4/11)
Tris Speaker PSA 8 (NmMt) sold for $13,920 (REA; 4/06)
Tris Speaker PSA 8 (NmMt) sold for $12,720 (Greg Bussineau; 12/12)
Tris Speaker GAI 7.5 (NM+) sold for $2,395 (eBay; 1/06)
Tris Speaker (Drum) PSA 4 (VgEx) sold for $7,534 (SCP; 7/08)
Jake Stahl Glove Shows PSA 8 (NmMt) sold for $4,150 (eBay; 9/06)
Gabby Street Catching SGC 40 (Vg) (Broadleaf 460) sold for $15,307 (Goodwin; 01/12)
Cy Seymour Throwing (Red Hindu Back) PSA 3 (VG) sold for $12,173 (SCP; 12/12)
Joe Tinker Bat off Shoulder PSA 8 (NmMt) (EPDG) sold for $15,054 (Goodwin; 8/12)
Joe Tinker Bat off Shoulder PSA 8 (NmMt) sold for $7,365 (Memory Lane; 9/07)
Joe Tinker Hands on Knees PSA 8 (NmMt) sold for $8,923 (Goodwin; 11/07)
Rube Waddell Portrait PSA 9 (MT) sold for $28,969 (Goodwin 2/10)
Rube Waddell Portrait PSA 8 (NmMt) sold for $13,252 (Goodwin; 8/12)
Rube Waddell Portrait PSA 8 (NmMt) sold for $5,512 (SCP Sotheby's; 11/06)
Rube Waddell Throwing PSA 9 (MT) sold for $27,096 (Mastro; 8/06)
Rube Waddell Throwing PSA 9 (Mint) sold for $23,520 (Greg Bussineau; 4/12)
Rube Waddell Throwing PSA 8 (NmMt) sold for $7,049 (Mastro; 12/05)
Rube Waddell Throwing PSA 8 (NmMt) sold for $4,540 (eBay; 3/07)
Honus Wagner PSA 8 (NmMt) sold privately by SCP for $2.8M in September, 2007
Honus Wagner PSA 8 (NmMt) purchased for $2.35M in March, 2007 by SCP
Honus Wagner PSA 8 (NmMt) purchased for $1.265M on eBay in 2000 by B.Seigel
Honus Wagner PSA 8 (NmMt) purchased for $640K at Christy's, 1996 by M.Gidwitz
Honus Wagner PSA 8 (NmMt) sold by Gretzky for $500,000 to Treat Ent. in 1995
Honus Wagner PSA 8 (NmMt) purchased for $451,000 in 1991 by Gretzky & McNall
Honus Wagner PSA 5 MC (EX, Miscut) sold for $2.10M (Goldin; 4/13)
Honus Wagner PSA 5 MC (EX, Miscut) sold for $1.62M (Mastro; 8/08)

—Honus Wagner GAI 3.5 (VG+) sold for $456,057 (Mastro; 12/05)
—Honus Wagner PSA 3 (Vg) sold for $1,320,000 (REA; Spring '15)
—Honus Wagner SGC 40 (Vg) sold for $1,232,466 (Goodwin; 04/12)
—Honus Wagner SGC 40 (Vg) sold for $925,000 (Memory Lane Private Sale; 7/09)
—Honus Wagner SGC 40 (Vg) sold for $791,000 (Phillip Weiss; 11/08)
—Honus Wagner PSA 2 (Good) sold for $654,500 (Memory Lane; 5/12)
—Honus Wagner PSA 2 (Good) sold for $651,150 (REA; 5/12)
—Honus Wagner PSA 2 (Good) sold for $294,337 (Memory Lane; 12/06)
—Honus Wagner PSA 1 (Poor) sold for $402,900 (REA; 5/13)
—Honus Wagner PSA 1 (Poor) sold for $399,500 (REA; 5/09)
—Honus Wagner BVG 1 (Poor) sold for $317,250 (REA; 5/08)
—Honus Wagner PSA 1 (Poor) sold for $282,000 (REA; 5/10)
—Honus Wagner SGC 10 (Poor) sold for $227,050 (Heritage; 5/08)
—Honus Wagner SGC 10 (Poor) sold for $192,000 (Mastro; 8/07)
—Honus Wagner PSA 1 (Poor) sold for $132,000 (SCP/Sotheby's; 6/05)
—Honus Wagner SGC Authentic sold for $262,000 (Heritage; 11/10)
—Honus Wagner PSA Authentic sold for $222,000 (Legendary; 7/09)
—Honus Wagner PSA Authentic sold for $219,225 (Legendary; 3/10)
—Honus Wagner SGC Authentic sold for $198,850 (Goodwin; 8/12)
—Honus Wagner PSA Authentic sold for $188,000 (REA; 5/11)
—Bobby Wallace PSA 9 (Mint) sold for $48,523 (Goodwin; 3/09)
—Ed Walsh PSA 8 (NmMt) sold for $8,529 (Mastro; 12/05)
—Ed Walsh PSA 8 (NmMt) sold for $5,676 (Heritage; 10/06)
—Ed Walsh PSA 8 (NmMt) sold for $5,144 (SCP; 7/08)
—Zack Wheat (Red Hindu) SGC 30 (Good) sold for $2,307 (Sloate; 5/08)
—Vic Willis St. Louis with Bat PSA 8 (NmMt) sold for $7,477 (Goodwin; 8/12)
—Vic Willis Throwing PSA 8 (NmMt) sold for $5,975 (Heritage; 10/06)
—Cy Young Bare Hand Shows PSA 9 (MT) sold for $61,885 (Goodwin; 4/11)
—Cy Young Bare Hand Shows PSA 9 (MT) sold for $26,482 (SCP Sotheby's; 5/04)
—Cy Young Bare Hand Shows PSA 8 (NmMt) sold for $13,901 (Memory Lane; 4/05)
—Cy Young Bare Hand Shows PSA 8 (NmMt) sold for $10,798 (Goodwin; 7/10)
—Cy Young Bare Hand Shows SGC 8 (NmMt) sold for $5,000 (Mastro; 12/08)
—Cy Young Bare Hand Shows GAI 8 (NmMt) sold for $4,554 (eBay; 7/06)
—Cy Young Glove Shows PSA 8 (NmMt) sold for $37,230 (Mastro; 12/06)
—Cy Young Glove Shows PSA 8 (NmMt) sold for $28,373 (Goodwin; 4/11)
—Cy Young Portrait PSA 8 (NmMt) sold for $35,225 (Goodwin; 3/15)
—Cy Young Portrait PSA 8 (NmMt) sold for $33,900 (Mastro; 12/05)
—Cy Young Portrait PSA 8 (NmMt) sold for $27,240 (Bussineau; 7/13)

1910 American Caramel Pirates E90-2

		PrFr 1	GD 2	VG 3	VgEx 4	EX 5	ExMt 6	NM 7	NmMt 8
1	Babe Adams	120	200	250	800				
2	Fred Clarke	120	250	400	800				
3	George Gibson	120	200	400	500				
4	Ham Hyatt	120	200	400	800				
5	Tommy Leach	120	200	300	800				
6	Sam Leever	120	200	400	800				
7	Nick Maddox	120	200	400	800				
8	Dots Miller	120	200	400	800				
9	Deacon Phillippe	120	200	300	800				
10	Honus Wagner	2,500	4,000	6,000	9,000	10,000			
11	Chief Wilson	120	200	400	800				

—Ham Hyatt PSA 6 (ExMt) sold for $4,565 (eBay; 5/08)
—Deacon Phillipe PSA 6 (ExMt) sold for $3,021 (eBay; 5/08)
—Honus Wagner PSA 3.5 (VG+) sold for $6,420 (Goodwin; 12/11)

1910 E98 Set of 30

		PrFr 1	GD 2	VG 3	VgEx 4	EX 5	ExMt 6	NM 7	NmMt 8
1	Chief Bender	120	250	400	800	1,500			
2	Roger Bresnahan	150	300	400	800	1,500			
3	Al Bridwell	150	200	250	500	1,000			
4	Miner Brown	150	500	600	1,000	1,500			
5	Frank Chance	120	400	500	800	1,500			
6	Hal Chase	150	400	500	1,000				
7	Fred Clarke	120	400	500	800	1,500			
8	Ty Cobb	1,500	2,000	3,000	6,000				
9	Eddie Collins	120	300	400	800	3,000			
10	Jack Coombs	100	150	250	500	1,000			
11	Bill Dahlen	100	150	250	500	1,000			
12	Harry Davis	100	150	250	500	1,000			
13	Red Dooin	100	150	400	500	1,000			
14	Johnny Evers	150	300	400	800	1,500			
15	Russ Ford	80	200	250	500	1,000			
16	Hughey Jennings	150	300	400	800	1,500			
17	Johnny Kling	80	150	250	600	1,000			

#		PrFr 1	GD 2	VG 3	VgEx 4	EX 5	ExMt 6	NM 7	NmMt 8
18	Nap Lajoie	200	400	600	1,200	2,500			
19	Connie Mack	150	600	1,000	1,500	3,000			
20	Christy Mathewson	800	2,500	3,000					
21	John McGraw	150	250	400	800	1,500			
22	Larry McLean	80	150	250	500	1,000			
23	Chief Meyers	100	150	300	500	1,000			
24	George Mullin	80	200	250	500	1,000			
25	Fred Tenney	80	150	250	500	1,000			
26	Joe Tinker	120	250	400					
27	Hippo Vaughn	120	250	500					
28	Hans Wagner	1,000	1,600	2,500	6,500				
29	Ed Walsh	250	300	600	800	1,500			
30	Cy Young	600	1,200	2,000	3,000				

—Chief Bender PSA 6 (ExMt) sold for $5,391 (Mile High; 8/07)
—Chief Bender PSA 6 (ExMt) sold for $3,523 (Mastro; 12/06)
—Roger Bresnahan PSA 7 (NM) sold for $8,284 (Mastro; 8/06)
—Roger Bresnahan PSA 6 (ExMt) sold for $7,050 (REA; 5/08)
—Miner Brown PSA 7 (NM) sold for $7,783 (Mile High; 1/07)
—Ty Cobb PSA 7 (NM) sold for $31,827 (Mile High; 1/07)
—Ty Cobb PSA 5 (Ex) sold for $8,812 (REA; 5/09)
—Johnny Evers PSA 6 (ExMt) sold for $7,264 (Mile High; 1/07)
—Joe Tinker PSA 6 (ExMt) sold for $7,442 (Mile High; 8/07)
—Joe Tinker PSA 6 (ExMt) sold for $6,603 (Mile High; 1/07)
—Joe Tinker PSA 4 (VgEx) sold for $3,301 (Mile High; 1/07)
—Hans Wagner SGC 5.5 (Ex+) sold for $5,435 (Goodwin; 09/11)
—Honus Wagner PSA 5 (EX) sold for $16,944 (Mile High; 1/07)
—Cy Young #30 PSA 8 (NmMt) sold for $5,273 (Mile High; 1/13)
—Cy Young SGC 60 (EX) sold for $4,702 (Mile High; 3/09)

1910 Old Mill T210

—Joe Jackson PSA 5 ST (EX w/stain) sold for $112,022 (Mastro; 4/06)
—Joe Jackson SGC 40 (VG) sold for $168,000 (REA; Spring '15)
—Joe Jackson SGC 40 (VG) sold for $116,000 (REA; 4/06)
—Joe Jackson PSA 2 (Good) sold for $165,486 (SCP; 7/08)
—Joe Jackson SGC 30 (Good) sold for $118,500 (REA; 5/13)
—Joe Jackson PSA 2 (Good) sold for $96,631 (SCP; 12/12)
—Joe Jackson SGC 30 (Good) sold for $80,000 (Legendary; 11/13)
—Joe Jackson PSA 1.5 (Fair) sold for $77,820 (SCP; 4/13)
—Joe Jackson PSA Authentic sold for $102,000 (Mastro; 12/08)
—Joe Jackson PSA Authentic sold for $92,800 (REA; 5/05)
—Joe Jackson SGC Authentic sold for $57,500 (Lgendary; 5/14)
—Joe Jackson PSA Authentic sold for $56,028 (Goodwin; 11/15)
—Casey Stengel PSA 6 (ExMt) sold for $41,903 (SCP; 7/08)
—Casey Stengel PSA 6 (ExMt) sold for $23,500 (REA; 9/10)
—Casey Stengel SGC 5 (Ex) sold for $27,000 (REA; Sping '15)
—Casey Stengel PSA 4 (VgEx) sold for $41,125 (REA; 5/08)
—Casey Stengel PSA 3 (VG) sold for $20,880 (REA; 4/06)
—Casey Stengel PSA 3 (VG) sold for $18,360 (Mastro; 4/07)
—Casey Stengel PSA 3 (VG) sold for $17,075 (eBay; 1/07)

1910 Philadelphia Caramel E96

#		PrFr 1	GD 2	VG 3	VgEx 4	EX 5	ExMt 6	NM 7	NmMt 8
1	Babe Adams	60	120	200	300				
2	Red Ames	60	120	200	300				
3	Frank Arellanes	60	120	200	300	1,500			
4	Home Run Baker	200	300	400	800				
5	Mordecai Brown	100	200	600	800				
6	Fred Clark (Clarke)	100	200	300	500				
7	Harry Davis	60	120	200	300	600			
8	Jim Delehanty	60	120	200	300				
9	Bill Donovan	60	150	200	300				
10	Red Dooin	60	120	200	300				
11	George Gibson	60	120	200	500				
12	Buck Herzog	60	120	200	300				
13	Hugh Jennings MG	80	150	250	400				
14	Ed Karger	60	120	200	300	600			
15	Johnny Kling	60	120	200	300				
16	Ed Konetchy	60	120	200	300				
17	Napoleon Lajoie	325	400	800	1,000				
18	Connie Mack MG	300	800	1,000	1,200				
19	Rube Marquard	100	250	400	400				
20	George McQuillan	60	150	200	300				
21	Chief Meyers	60	120	200	300	600			
22	Mike Mowrey	60	120	200	300	600			

#		PrFr 1	GD 2	VG 3	VgEx 4	EX 5	ExMt 6	NM 7	NmM
23	George Mullin	60	120	200	300				
24	Red Murray	60	120	200	300	600			
25	Jack Pfeister (Pfiester)	60	120	200	300				
26	Claude Rossman	60	120	150	300				
27	Nap Rucker	60	120	250	300				
28	Tubby Spencer	60	120	200	300				
29	Ira Thomas	60	120	300	350				
30	Joe Tinker	100	200	300	800				

—Frank Baker SGC 70 (EX+) sold for $2,826 (Mastro; 6/06)
—Home Run Baker PSA 6.5 (ExMt+) sold for $5,307 (Mile High; 05/11)
—Mordecai Brown PSA 5 (EX) sold for $1,725 (eBay; 11/06)
—Fred Clarke SGC 70 (EX+) sold for $1,746 (Memory Lane; 8/06)
—Bill Donovan PSA 6 (ExMt) sold for $9,068 (Goodwin; 09/11)
—Hugh Jennings PSA 6 (ExMt) sold for $6,573 (Heritage; 5/08)
—Hugh Jennings SGC 80 (ExMt) sold for $2,693 (Mastro; 4/07)
—Connie Mack PSA 6 (ExMt) sold for $4,730 (eBay; 6/08)
—Claude Rossman PSA 6 (ExMt) sold for $9,068 (Goodwin; 09/11)
—Tubby Spencer PSA 6 (ExMt) sold for $4,930 (eBay; 6/08)

1910 Standard Caramel E93

#		PrFr 1	GD 2	VG 3	VgEx 4	EX 5	ExMt 6	NM 7	NmM
1	Red Ames	60	80	100	120	650	1,200		
2	Chief Bender	120	200	350	400	600	800		
3	Mordecai Brown	200	300	500	800	1,500	2,500		
4	Frank Chance	175	250	350	600	1,200	2,000		
5	Hal Chase	100	150	200	250	600	1,500		
6	Ty Cobb	800	1,500	2,500	4,000	6,000	8,000		
7	Eddie Collins	100	150	300	500	800	1,000		
8	Harry Coveleskie (Coveleski)	50	80	150	400	800	1,500		
9	Fred Clarke	100	150	250	500	800	1,500		
10	Jim Delehanty	50	80	200	250	350	400		
11	Bill Donovan	50	80	150	400	800			
12	Red Dooin	50	80	150	250	350	1,200		
13	Johnny Evers	150	250	400	600	1,500	2,500		
14	George Gibson	50	80	150	300	500	800		
15	Clark Griffith	100	150	250	500	600	1,500		
16	Hugh Jennings	100	150	250	500	1,000	1,500		
17	Davy Jones	50	80	150	325	500	1,200		
18	Addie Joss	150	250	400	600	1,000	2,500		
19	Napoleon Lajoie	200	300	500	800	2,000	3,000		
20	Tommy Leach	50	80	150	300	500	3,600		
21	Christy Mathewson	600	1,000	1,500	2,500	4,000	6,000		
22	John McGraw	100	150	200	300	1,000	1,500		
23	Jim Pastorius	50	80	150	300	500	1,300		
24	Deacon Phillippe	50	80	200	300	500	800		
25	Eddie Plank	250	500	550	600	1,000	3,000		
26	Joe Tinker	100	150	300	500	1,000	1,500		
27	Rube Waddell	120	200	400	600	1,200			
28	Honus Wagner	1,200	2,000	2,500	3,500	6,000	8,000		
29	Hooks Wiltse	50	80	150	250	300	1,500		
30	Cy Young	500	800	1,200	2,000	3,500	6,000		

—Chief Bender PSA 7 (NM) sold for $7,144 (Goodwin; 5/08)
—Chief Bender PSA 7 (NM) sold for $6,404 (eBay; 2/08)
—Frank Chance PSA 7 (NM) sold for $15,898 (Memory Lane; 3/06)
—Ty Cobb SGC 80 (ExMt) sold for $27,600 (Hunt; 11/06)
—Ty Cobb PSA 7 (NM) sold for $11,894 (Goodwin; 7/10)
—Wild Bill Donovan SGC 84 (NM) sold for $10,058 (Mastro; 12/06)
—Clark Griffith PSA 7 (NM) sold for $5,650 (eBay; 8/06)
—Hugh Jennings SGC 82 (NmMt+) sold for $10,157 (Heritage; 11/10)
—Hugh Jennings PSA 7 (NM) sold for $10,158 (Heritage; 10/07)
—Hugh Jennings PSA 7 (NM) sold for $9,562 (Memory Lane; 12/06)
—Napoleon Lajoie PSA 8 (NmMt) sold for $11,352 (Heritage; 11/10)
—Christy Mathewson PSA 8 (NM) sold for $24,000 (REA; Fall '14)
—Christy Mathewson SGC 84 (NM) sold for $13,045 (Mastro; 12/06)
—Eddie Plank PSA 7 (NM) sold for $11,316 (Memory Lane; 3/06)
—Eddie Plank PSA 7 (NM) sold for $8,962 (Memory Lane; 12/06)
—Eddie Plank PSA 7 (NM) sold for $8,386 (Memory Lane; 12/07)
—Honus Wagner SGC 88 (NmMt) sold for $19,120 (Heritage; 11/10)
—Honus Wagner SGC 88 (NmMt) sold for $17,101 (Mile High; 1/12)
—Honus Wagner SGC 88 (NmMt) sold for $16,440 (Goodwin; 6/12)
—Honus Wagner PSA 7 (NM) sold for $20,315 (Heritage; 5/08)
—Honus Wagner PSA 7 (NM) sold for $13,342 (Memory Lane; 12/06)
—Honus Wagner SGC 7 (NM) sold for $7,050 (REA; 05/11)
—Rube Waddell PSA 7 (NM) sold for $4,994 (REA; 4/07)

310-11 Sporting Life M116

	PrFr 1	GD 2	VG 3	VgEx 4	EX 5	ExMt 6	NM 7	NmMt 8
Ed Abbaticchio	25	30	40	50	80	120	150	400
Babe Adams Black Back	25	30	40	50	80	120	200	400
Babe Adams Blue Back	25	30	40	50	80	120	200	400
Red Ames	25	30	40	60	80	120	200	400
Jimmy Archer	25	30	40	50	80	120	200	400
Frank Arellanes	25	30	40	50	80	120	200	400
Tommy Atkins	25	30	40	50	80	120	200	400
Jimmy Austin	25	30	40	50	80	120	200	400
Les Bachman	25	30	40	50	80	120	200	400
Bill Bailey	25	30	40	50	80	120	200	400
Frank Baker Black Back	120	150	200	250	300	400	600	1,200
Frank Baker Blue Back	100	120	150	350	450	600	800	1,000
Cy Barger	25	30	40	50	80	120	200	400
Jack Barry	25	30	40	50	80	120	200	400
Johnny Bates Philadelphia	25	30	40	50	80	120	200	400
Ginger Beaumont	25	30	40	50	80	120	200	400
Fred Beck	25	30	40	50	80	120	200	400
Heine Beckendorf	25	30	40	50	80	120	200	400
Fred Beebe	25	30	40	50	80	120	200	400
George Bell	25	30	40	50	80	120	200	400
Harry Bemis	25	30	40	50	80	120	200	400
Chief Bender Blue	120	150	200	250	300	500	900	1,500
Chief Bender Pastel	100	120	150	200	250	400	600	1,000
Bill Bergen	25	30	40	50	80	120	200	400
Charles Berger	25	30	40	50	80	120	200	400
Bob Bescher	25	30	40	50	80	120	200	400
Joseph Birmingham	25	30	40	50	80	120	200	400
Lena Blackburn	25	30	40	50	80	120	200	400
Jack Bliss	25	30	40	50	80	120	200	400
James J. Block	25	30	40	50	80	120	200	400
Hugh Bradley	25	30	40	50	80	120	200	400
Kitty Bransfield	25	30	40	50	100	120	200	400
Roger Bresnahan Blue	120	150	200	250	300	500	800	1,500
Roger Bresnahan Pastel	100	120	150	200	400	500	700	1,000
Al Bridwell	25	30	40	50	80	120	200	400
Buster Brown	25	30	40	50	80	120	200	400
Mordecai Brown Blue	120	150	200	350	400	600	800	1,500
Mordecai Brown Pastel	120	150	200	350	400	600	850	1,000
Al Burch	25	30	40	50	80	120	200	400
Donie Bush	25	30	40	50	80	120	200	400
Bobby Byrne	25	30	40	50	80	120	200	400
Howie Camnitz	25	30	40	50	80	120	200	400
Vin Campbell	25	30	40	50	80	120	200	400
Bill Carrigan	25	30	40	50	100	120	200	400
Frank Chance Blue	120	150	200	250	300	500	900	1,500
Frank Chance Pastel	100	120	200	250	300	400	600	1,000
Chappy Charles	25	30	40	50	80	120	200	400
Hal Chase Blue	80	100	120	150	200	300	600	1,200
Hal Chase Pastel	80	100	120	150	200	300	600	1,000
Ed Cicotte	100	120	150	200	300	400	800	1,200
Fred Clarke Black Back	100	120	150	200	250	400	600	1,000
Fred Clarke Blue Back	100	120	150	200	250	400	600	1,000
Nig Clarke	25	30	40	50	80	120	200	400
Tommy Clarke	25	30	40	50	80	120	200	400
Ty Cobb Blue	1,000	1,500	2,500	3,500	4,000	5,000	6,000	
Ty Cobb Pastel	800	1,000	1,500	2,000	2,500	3,000	5,000	
Eddie Collins Blue	150	200	250	300	500	600	1,000	2,500
Eddie Collins Pastel	120	150	200	250	300	500	800	1,200
Ray Collins	25	30	40	50	80	120	200	400
Wid Conroy	25	30	40	50	80	120	200	400
Jack Coombs	25	30	40	50	80	120	200	400
Frank Corridon	25	30	40	50	80	120	200	400
Harry Coveleski ML	30	40	50	60	100	150	250	500
Doc Crandall	25	30	40	50	80	120	200	400
Sam Crawford Blue	120	150	200	250	400	500	800	1,500
Sam Crawford Pastel	100	120	150	200	300	400	600	1,000
Birdie Cree	25	30	40	50	80	120	200	625
Lou Criger	25	30	40	50	80	120	200	400
Dode Criss	25	30	40	50	80	120	200	400
Cliff Curtis	25	30	40	50	80	120	200	400
Bill Dahlen MG	25	30	40	50	80	120	200	400
William Davidson	25	30	40	50	80	120	200	400
Harry Davis Blue	30	40	50	60	150	200	250	500

		PrFr 1	GD 2	VG 3	VgEx 4	EX 5	ExMt 6	NM 7	NmMt 8
62B	Harry Davis Pastel	25	30	40	50	80	120	200	400
63	Jim Delehanty	25	30	40	50	80	120	200	400
64	Ray Demmitt	25	30	40	50	80	120	200	400
65	Frank Dessau	25	30	40	50	80	120	200	400
66A	Art Devlin Black Back	25	30	40	50	80	120	200	400
66B	Art Devlin Blue Back	25	30	40	50	80	120	200	400
67	Josh Devore	25	30	40	50	80	120	200	400
68	Pat Donahue	25	30	40	50	80	120	200	400
69	Patsy Donovan MG	25	30	40	50	80	120	200	400
70A	Bill Donovan Blue	25	30	40	50	100	120	200	400
70B	Bill Donovan Pastel	25	30	40	50	100	120	200	400
71A	Red Dooin Blue	30	40	50	100	150	200	250	500
71B	Red Dooin Pastel	25	30	40	50	80	120	200	400
72	Mickey Doolan	25	30	40	50	80	120	200	400
73	Patsy Dougherty	25	30	40	50	80	120	200	400
74	Tom Downey	25	30	40	50	80	120	200	400
75	Jim Doyle	25	30	40	50	80	120	200	400
76A	Larry Doyle Blue	30	40	50	60	100	150	250	500
76B	Larry Doyle Pastel	25	30	40	50	80	120	200	400
77	Hugh Duffy MG	100	120	250	300	350	400	600	1,000
78	Jimmy Dygert	25	30	40	50	80	120	150	400
79	Dick Eagan	25	30	40	50	80	120	200	400
80	Kid Elberfeld	25	30	40	50	80	120	200	400
81	Rube Ellis	25	30	40	50	80	120	200	400
82	Clyde Engle	25	30	40	50	80	120	200	400
83	Tex Erwin	25	30	40	50	80	120	300	400
84	Steve Evans	25	30	40	50	80	120	200	400
85A	Johnny Evers Black Back	120	150	200	250	300	500	800	1,500
85B	Johnny Evers Blue Back	120	150	200	250	300	500	800	1,200
86	Bob Ewing	25	30	40	50	80	120	200	400
87	Cy Falkenberg	25	30	40	80	100	200	150	400
88	George Ferguson	25	30	40	50	80	120	200	400
89	Art Fletcher	25	30	40	50	80	120	200	400
90	Elmer Flick	100	120	150	200	250	400	600	1,000
91	John Flynn	25	30	40	50	80	120	200	400
92	Russ Ford	25	30	40	50	80	120	200	400
93	Ed Foster ML	25	30	40	50	120	200	300	400
94	Bill Foxen	25	30	40	50	80	120	200	400
95	John Frill ML	25	30	40	50	80	120	200	400
96	Samuel Frock	25	30	40	50	80	120	200	400
97	Art Fromme	25	30	40	50	80	120	200	400
98	Earle Gardner New York	25	30	40	50	80	120	200	400
99	Larry Gardner Boston	25	30	40	80	120	200	300	400
100	Harry Gaspar	25	30	40	50	80	120	200	400
101	Doc Gessler	25	30	40	50	80	120	150	400
102A	George Gibson Blue	30	40	50	60	150	250		
102B	George Gibson Pastel	25	30	40	60	150	250		
103	Bert Graham	25	30	40	50	80	120	200	400
104	Peaches Graham	25	30	40	50	80	120	200	400
105	Eddie Grant	25	30	40	50	80	120	200	400
106	Clark Griffith MG	100	120	150	200	300	400	600	1,000
107	Ed Hahn	25	30	40	50	80	150	250	
108	Charles Hall	25	30	40	50	80	120	200	400
109	Bob Harmon	25	30	40	50	80	120	200	400
110	Topsy Hartsel	25	30	40	50	80	120	200	400
111	Roy Hartzell	25	30	40	50	80	120	200	400
112	Heinie Heitmuller	25	30	40	50	80	120	200	400
113	Buck Herzog	25	30	40	50	80	120	200	400
114	Doc Hoblitzel	25	30	40	50	80	120	200	400
115	Danny Hoffman	25	30	40	50	80	120	200	400
116	Solly Hofman	25	30	40	50	80	120	200	400
117	Harry Hooper	100	120	150	200	250	400	600	1,500
118	Harry Howell	25	30	40	50	80	120	200	400
119	Miller Huggins	100	120	150	200	250	400	600	1,200
120	Tom Hughes ML	25	30	40	50	80	120	200	400
121	Rudy Hulswitt	25	30	40	50	80	120	200	400
122	John Hummel	25	30	40	50	80	120	200	400
123	George Hunter	25	30	40	50	80	120	200	400
124	Ham Hyatt	25	30	40	50	80	120	200	400
125	Fred Jacklitsch	25	30	50	60	80	120	200	400
126A	Hugh Jennings MG Blue	120	150	200	250	400	500	800	1,500
126B	Hugh Jennings MG Pastel	100	120	150	200	250	400	600	1,000
127	Walter Johnson	500	600	800	1,000	1,800	2,000	4,000	5,000
128A	Davy Jones Blue	30	40	50	60	100	150	250	1,500
128B	Davy Jones Pastel	25	30	40	50	80	120	200	400
129	Tom Jones	25	30	40	50	80	120	200	400
130A	Tim Jordan Blue	30	40	50	60	100	150	250	500

#	Player	PrFr 1	GD 2	VG 3	VgEx 4	EX 5	ExMt 6	NM 7	NmMt 8
130B	Tim Jordan Pastel	25	30	40	50	80	120	200	400
131	Addie Joss	100	120	200	250	300	1,100	1,800	
132	John Kane	25	30	40	50	80	120	200	400
133	Edwin Karge	25	30	40	50	80	120	200	400
134	Red Killifer	25	30	40	50	120	120	200	625
135	Johnny Kling	25	30	40	50	80	120	200	400
136	Otto Knabe	25	30	40	50	80	120	200	400
137	John Knight	25	30	40	50	80	120	200	400
138	Ed Konetchy	25	30	40	50	80	120	200	400
139	Harry Krause	25	30	40	50	80	120	200	400
140	Rube Kroh	25	30	40	50	80	120	200	400
141	Otto Krueger ML	25	30	40	50	80	120	200	400
142A	Nap Lajoie Blue	300	400	500	600	800	1,000	1,500	
142B	Nap Lajoie Pastel	200	300	400	500	600	800	1,200	
143	Joe Lake	25	30	40	50	80	120	200	400
144	Fred Lake MG	25	30	40	50	80	120	200	400
145	Frank LaPorte	25	30	40	50	80	120	200	400
146	Jack Lapp	25	30	40	80	120	200	300	400
147	Chick Lathers	25	30	40	60	80	120	200	400
148A	Tommy Leach Blue	30	40	50	120	150	200	300	500
148B	Tommy Leach Pastel	25	30	40	50	80	120	200	400
149	Sam Leever	25	30	40	50	80	120	200	400
150	Lefty Leifield	25	30	40	50	80	120	200	400
151	Ed Lennox	25	30	40	50	80	120	200	400
152	Frederick Link	25	30	40	50	80	120	200	400
153	Paddy Livingstone	25	30	40	50	80	120	200	400
154	Hans Lobert	25	30	40	50	80	120	200	400
155	Bris Lord	25	30	40	50	80	120	200	400
156A	Harry Lord Blue	30	40	50	60	100	150	250	500
156B	Harry Lord Pastel	25	30	40	50	80	120	200	400
157	Johnny Lush	25	30	40	50	80	100	120	400
158	Connie Mack MG	150	200	250	300	400	700		
159	Thomas Madden	25	30	40	50	80	120	200	400
160	Nick Maddox	25	30	40	50	80	120	200	400
161	Sherry Magee	25	30	40	50	80	120	200	400
162A	Christy Mathewson Blue	500	600	800	1,000	1,200	1,500	2,500	
162B	Christy Mathewson Pastel	500	600	800	1,000	1,200	1,500	2,500	5,000
163	Al Mattern	25	30	40	60	80	120	200	400
164	Jimmy McAleer MG	25	30	40	50	80	120	200	400
165	George McBride	25	30	40	50	80	120	200	400
166A	Amby McConnell Boston	25	30	40	50	80	120	200	400
167	Pryor McElveen	25	30	40	50	80	120	200	400
168	John McGraw MG	80	100	200	250	300	500	800	1,200
169	Deacon McGuire MG	25	30	40	50	80	120	200	400
170	Stuffy McInnis	25	30	40	50	80	120	200	400
171	Harry McIntire	25	30	40	50	80	120	200	400
172	Matty McIntyre	25	30	40	50	80	120	250	
173	Larry McLean	25	30	40	50	80	120	200	400
174	Tommy McMillan	25	30	40	50	80	120	200	400
175B	George McQuillan Phil Blue	30	40	50	80	100	150	250	500
175C	George McQuillan Phil Pastel	25	30	40	50	80	120	200	400
176	Paul Meloan	25	30	40	80	120	200	300	400
177	Fred Merkle	25	30	40	50	80	120	200	400
178	Chief Meyers	25	30	40	50	120	150	200	400
179	Clyde Milan	25	30	40	50	80	120	200	400
180	Dots Miller	25	30	40	50	80	120	200	400
181	Warren Miller	25	30	40	50	80	120	200	750
182	Fred Mitchell ML	25	30	40	50	80	120	200	400
183	Mike Mitchell	25	30	40	50	80	120	200	400
184	Earl Moore	25	30	40	50	80	120	200	400
185	Pat Moran	25	30	40	50	80	120	200	400
186A	Lew Moren Black Back	25	30	40	50	80	120	200	400
186B	Lew Moren Blue Back	30	40	50	60	100	150	250	500
187	Cy Morgan	25	30	40	50	80	120	200	400
188	George Moriarty	25	30	40	50	80	120	200	400
189	Mike Mowery	25	30	40	50	80	120	200	400
190A	George Mullin Black Back	25	30	40	50	80	120	200	400
190B	George Mullin Blue Back	30	40	50	60	100	150	250	500
191	Danny Murphy	25	30	40	50	80	120	200	400
192	Red Murray	25	30	40	50	80	175	200	400
193	Tom Needham	25	30	40	50	80	120	200	400
194	Harry Niles	25	30	40	50	80	120	200	400
195	Rebel Oakes	25	30	40	80	100	120	300	400
196	Jack O'Connor	25	30	40	50	80	120	200	400
197	Paddy O'Connor	25	30	40	50	80	120	150	400
198	Bill O'Hara ML	25	30	40	50	80	120	200	400
199	Rube Oldring	25	30	40	50	80	120	200	400

#	Player	PrFr 1	GD 2	VG 3	VgEx 4	EX 5	ExMt 6	NM 7	NmMt 8
200	Charley O'Leary	25	30	40	50	80	150	200	4
201	Orval Overall	25	30	40	50	80	120	200	4
202	Fred Parent	25	30	40	60	80	120	200	4
203	Dode Paskert	25	30	40	50	80	120	200	4
204	Frederick Payne	25	30	40	50	80	120	200	4
205	Barney Pelty	25	30	40	50	80	120	200	4
206	Hub Pernoll	25	30	40	80	120	200	300	
207	George Perring ML	25	30	40	50	80	300	400	
208	Big Jeff Pfeffer	25	30	40	50	80	120	200	4
209	Jack Pfiester	25	30	40	50	80	120	200	4
210	Art Phelan	25	30	40	50	120	200	300	4
211	Ed Phelps	25	30	40	50	80	120	200	4
212	Deacon Phillipe	25	30	40	50	80	120	200	4
213	Eddie Plank	400	500	600	800	1,000	1,200	2,000	
214	Jack Powell	25	30	40	50	80	120	200	4
215	Billy (William) Purtell	25	30	40	50	80	120	200	4
216	Farmer Ray ML	25	30	40	50	80	120	200	5
217	Bugs Raymond	25	30	40	50	450	500	600	4
218	Doc Reisling	25	30	40	50	80	120	200	4
219	Ed Reulbach	25	30	40	50	80	120	200	4
220	Lew Richie	25	30	40	50	80	120	200	4
221	Jack Rowan	25	30	40	50	80	120	200	4
222A	Nap Rucker Black Back	25	30	40	50	80	120	200	4
222B	Nap Rucker Blue Back	25	30	60	80	100	120	200	4
223	Slim Sallee	25	30	40	50	80	120	200	4
224	Doc Scanlon	25	30	40	60	80	120	200	4
225	Germany Schaefer	25	30	40	50	80	120	200	4
226	Lou Schettler	25	30	40	50	80	150	200	4
227	Admiral Schlei	25	30	40	50	80	120	200	4
228	Boss Schmidt	25	30	40	50	80	120	200	4
229	Wildfire Schulte	25	30	40	50	80	120	200	4
230	Al Schweitzer	25	30	40	50	80	120	200	4
231	James Scott	25	30	40	50	80	120	200	4
232	James Seymour	25	30	40	50	80	120	200	4
233	Tillie Shafer	25	30	40	50	80	120	200	4
234	David Shean	25	30	40	50	80	120	200	4
235	Bayard Sharpe	25	30	40	50	80	120	200	4
236	Jimmy Sheckard	25	30	40	50	80	120	200	4
237	Mike Simon	25	30	40	50	80	120	200	4
238	Charlie Smith	25	30	40	50	80	120	200	4
239	Frank Smith	25	30	40	50	80	120	200	6
240	Harry Smith	25	30	40	50	80	120	200	4
241	Fred Snodgrass	25	30	40	50	80	120	200	4
242	Bob Spade UER	25	30	40	50	80	120	200	4
243	Tully Sparks	25	30	40	50	80	120	200	4
244	Tris Speaker	500	600	800	1,000	1,200	2,000	3,000	5,0
245	Jake Stahl	25	30	40	50	120	200	200	4
246	George Stallings MG	25	30	40	50	80	120	200	4
247	Oscar Stanage	25	30	40	50	80	120	200	4
248	Harry Steinfeldt	25	30	40	50	80	120	200	4
249	Jim Stephens	25	30	40	50	80	120	200	4
250	George Stone	25	30	40	50	80	120	200	4
251	George Stovall	25	30	40	80	100	120	200	4
252	Gabby Street	25	30	40	50	80	120	150	4
253	Sailor Stroud	25	30	40	50	80	120	200	4
254	Amos Strunk	25	30	40	50	80	120	200	4
255	George Suggs	25	30	40	50	80	120	200	52
256	Billy Sullivan	25	30	40	50	80	120	150	4
257A	Ed Summers Black Back	25	30	40	50	80	120	200	4
257B	Ed Summers Blue Back	25	30	40	50	80	120	200	4
258	Bill Sweeney	25	30	40	50	80	120	200	4
259	Jeff Sweeney	25	30	40	50	80	120	200	4
260	Lee Tannehill	25	30	40	50	80	120	200	40
261A	Fred Tenney Blue	30	40	50	60	250	300	400	6
262B	Fred Tenney Pastel	25	30	40	50	100	120	200	4
262A	Ira Thomas Blue	30	40	50	80	100	250	400	6
262B	Ira Thomas Pastel	25	30	40	50	80	120	200	4
263	John Thoney	25	30	40	50	80	120	200	4
264A	Joe Tinker Black Back	120	150	200	250	300	500	800	1,5
264B	Joe Tinker Blue Back	100	120	150	200	250	400	1,400	2,2
265	John Titus	25	30	40	50	80	120	200	4
266	Terry Turner	25	30	40	50	80	120	200	40
267	Bob Unglaub	25	30	40	50	80	120	200	4
268A	Rube Waddell Black Back	120	200	250	300	300	500	800	1,5
268B	Rube Waddell Blue Back	100	120	150	300	350	400	600	1,0
269A	Hans Wagner Blue	2,000	3,000	4,000	5,000	6,000	8,000		
269B	Hans Wagner Pastel	1,200	1,500	3,000	4,000	5,000	6,000	12,000	

	PrFr 1	GD 2	VG 3	VgEx 4	EX 5	ExMt 6	NM 7	NmMt 8
0 Heinie Wagner	25	30	40	50	80	120	200	400
4 Bobby Wallace	80	100	120	150	200	300	500	1,000
2 Ed Walsh	100	120	150	250	300	400	900	1,500
3 Jimmy Walsh Gray	60	80	100	120	150	250	500	800
4 Jimmy Walsh White	80	100	120	150	250	300	600	1,000
5 Doc White	25	30	40	50	80	120	200	400
6 Kaiser Wilhelm	25	30	40	50	80	120	200	400
7 Ed Willett	25	30	40	50	80	120	200	400
8 Vic Willis	100	120	150	200	250	400	600	1,500
9 Art Wilson	25	30	40	50	80	200	200	400
0 Chief Wilson	25	30	40	50	80	120	200	400
1 Hooks Wiltse	25	30	40	50	80	120	200	400
2 Harry Wolter	25	30	40	50	80	120	200	400
Joe Wood	300	400	500	800	1,200	2,800		
4 Ralph Works	25	30	40	50	80	120	200	400
5A Cy Young Black Back	500	600	800	1,000	1,200	1,500	2,500	4,000
5B Cy Young Blue Back	500	600	800	1,000	1,200	1,500	2,500	
6 Irv Young	25	30	40	50	80	120	200	400
7 Heinie Zimmerman	25	30	40	50	80	120	200	400
8 Dutch Zwilling	25	30	40	50	80	200	250	400

Frank Baker Blue PSA 9 (MT) sold for $4,249 (Mastro; 4/06)
Ty Cobb Pastel PSA 8 (NmMt) sold for $12,592 (Memory Lane; 9/07)
Ty Cobb Pastel PSA 8 (NmMt) sold for $12,134 (SCP Sotheby's; 9/07)
Ty Cobb Pastel PSA 8 (NmMt) sold for $8,400 (Mastro; 5/08)
Walter Johnson PSA 9 (MT) sold for $12,925 (REA; 4/07)
Addie Joss PSA 8 (NmMt) sold for $1,790 (eBay; 6/08)
Nap Lajoie Blue PSA 9 (MT) sold for $8,924 (Mile High; 1/07)
Nap Lajoie Blue PSA 8 (NmMt) sold for $6,531 (Memory Lane; 9/07)
Christy Mathewson Pastel PSA 9 (MT) sold for $18,727 (Memory Lane; 8/05)
Christy Mathewson Pastel PSA 9 (MT) sold for $16,955 (Goodwin; 6/06)
Amby McConnell Chicago SGC 60 (EX) sold for $31,024 (Old Judge; 11/07)
George McQuillan Cincinnati SGC 70 (EX+) sold for $3,819 (REA; 4/07)
George McQuillan Cincinnati PSA 3 (VG) sold for $3,455 (Old Judge; 11/07)
Hans Wagner Pastel PSA 8 (NmMt) sold for $14,664 (SCP Sotheby's; 9/07)
Hans Wagner Pastel PSA 8 (NmMt) sold for $12,469 (Memory Lane 4/07)

910-12 Sweet Caporal Pins P2

	PrFr 1	GD 2	VG 3	VgEx 4	EX 5	ExMt 6	NM 7	NmMt 8
Ed Abbaticchio	6	8	10	12	20	25	40	60
Red Ames	6	8	10	12	20	25	40	60
Jimmy Archer Small Letters	6	8	10	12	20	25	40	60
Jimmy Archer Large Letters	8	10	12	15	20	30	50	80
Jimmy Austin Small Letters	6	8	10	12	20	25	40	80
Jimmy Austin Large Letters	8	10	12	15	20	30	50	80
Home Run Baker	12	15	20	25	30	80	100	200
Neal Ball	6	8	10	12	20	25	40	60
Cy Barger	6	8	10	12	20	25	40	60
Jack Barry	6	8	10	12	20	25	40	60
Johnny Bates	6	8	10	12	20	25	40	60
Beals Becker	6	8	10	12	20	25	40	60
Fred Beebe	6	8	10	12	20	25	40	60
A George Bell Small Letters	6	8	10	12	20	25	40	60
B George Bell Large Letters	8	10	12	15	20	30	50	80
A Chief Bender Small Letters	12	15	20	25	30	50	80	150
B Chief Bender Large Letters	20	25	30	40	50	80	120	300
Bill Bergen	6	8	10	12	20	25	40	60
Bob Bescher	6	8	10	12	20	25	40	60
Joe Birmingham	6	8	10	12	20	25	40	60
Kitty Bransfield	6	8	10	12	15	50	60	80
A R.Bresnahan Mouth Closed Sm Ltr	12	15	20	25	30	50	80	200
B R.Bresnahan Mouth Closed Lg Ltr	20	25	30	40	60	80	120	400
Al Bridwell	6	8	10	12	20	25	40	60
A Mordecai Brown Small Letters	12	15	20	25	30	50	80	120
B Mordecai Brown Large Letters	20	25	30	40	80	100	175	250
Bobby Byrne	6	8	10	12	20	25	40	60
Nixey Callahan	6	8	10	12	20	25	40	
A Howie Camnitz Small Letters	6	8	10	12	20	25	40	60
B Howie Camnitz Large Letters	8	10	12	15	20	30	50	80
A Bill Carrigan Small Letters	6	8	10	12	20	25	40	60
B Bill Carrigan Large Letters	8	10	12	15	20	30	50	80
A Frank Chance Small Letters	20	25	30	40	80	250	300	500
B Frank Chance Large Letters	12	15	20	25	60	250	300	500
A Hal Chase Small Letters	12	15	20	25	30	80	100	120
B Hal Chase Large Letters	12	15	20	25	30	50	80	120
Ed Cicotte	12	15	20	25	80	100	120	200
A Fred Clarke Small Letters	12	15	20	25	30	50	80	120

	PrFr 1	GD 2	VG 3	VgEx 4	EX 5	ExMt 6	NM 7	NmMt 8
28B Fred Clarke Large Letters	20	25	30	40	50	100	120	200
29A Ty Cobb Small Letters	150	200	250	300	400	600	800	1,200
29B Ty Cobb Large Letters	200	250	300	400	500	700	1,000	
30A Eddie Collins Small Letters	12	15	20	25	80	120	150	
30B Eddie Collins Large Letters	20	25	30	40	50	80	120	200
31 Doc Crandall	6	8	10	12	20	25	40	60
32A Birdie Cree	6	8	10	12	20	25	40	60
32B Bill Dahlen Large Letters	6	8	10	12	20	25	40	60
33 Jim Delahanty	6	8	10	12	20	25	40	60
34 Art Devlin	6	8	10	12	20	25	40	60
35 Josh Devore	6	8	10	12	20	25	40	60
36 Bill Donovan	6	8	10	12	20	25	40	60
37A Red Dooin Small Letters	6	8	10	12	20	25	40	60
37B Red Dooin Large Letters	8	10	12	15	20	30	50	80
38A Mickey Doolan Small Letters	6	8	10	12	20	25	40	60
38B Mickey Doolan Large Letters	8	10	12	15	20	30	50	80
39 Patsy Dougherty	6	8	10	12	20	25	40	60
40A Tom Downey Small Letters	6	8	10	12	20	25	40	80
40B Tom Downey Large Letters	8	10	12	15	20	30	50	80
41A Larry Doyle Small Letters	6	8	10	12	20	25	40	60
41B Larry Doyle Large Letters	8	10	12	15	20	30	50	80
42 Louis Drucke	6	8	10	12	20	25	40	60
43A Hugh Duffy Small Letters	12	15	20	25	30	50	80	200
43B Hugh Duffy Large Letters	20	25	30	40	50	80	120	200
44 Jimmy Dygert	6	8	10	12	20	25	80	120
45A Kid Elberfeld Small Letters	6	8	10	12	20	25	40	60
45B Kid Elberfeld Large Letters	8	10	12	15	20	30	50	80
46A Clyde Engle Small Letters	6	8	10	12	20	25	40	60
46B Clyde Engle Large Letters	8	10	12	15	20	30	50	80
47 Tex Erwin	6	8	10	12	20	25	40	60
48 Steve Evans	6	8	10	12	20	25	40	60
49 Johnny Evers	12	15	20	25	100	120	150	250
50 Cecil Ferguson	6	8	10	12	20	25	40	60
51 John Flynn	6	8	10	12	20	25	40	60
52A Russ Ford Small Letters	6	8	10	12	20	25	40	60
52B Russ Ford Large Letters	8	10	12	15	20	30	50	80
53 Art Fromme	6	8	10	12	20	25	40	60
54 Harry Gaspar	6	8	10	12	20	25	40	60
55 George Gibson	6	8	10	12	20	25	60	80
56 Eddie Grant	6	8	10	12	20	25	40	60
57 Dolly Gray	6	8	10	12	20	25	40	60
58A Clark Griffith Small Letters	12	15	20	25	30	50	80	120
58B Clark Griffith Large Letters	20	25	30	40	50	80	120	200
59 Bob Groom	6	8	10	12	20	25	40	60
60 Bob Harmon	6	8	10	12	20	25	40	60
61 Topsy Hartsel	6	8	10	12	20	25	40	60
62 Arnold Hauser	6	8	10	12	15	80	100	60
63 Ira Hemphill	6	8	10	12	20	25	40	60
64 Buck Herzog Large Letters	6	8	10	12	20	25	40	60
65 Buck Herzog Large Letters	6	8	10	12	20	25	40	60
66 Dick Hoblitzell	6	8	10	12	20	25	60	80
67 Danny Hoffman	6	8	10	12	20	25	40	60
68 Harry Hooper	12	15	20	25	30	80	100	120
69A Miller Huggins Small Letters	12	15	20	25	30	50	150	200
69B Miller Huggins Large Letters	20	25	30	40	60	100	120	200
70 John Hummel	6	8	10	12	20	25	40	80
71A Hugh Jennings Small Letters	12	15	20	25	30	50	200	250
71B Hugh Jennings Large Letters	20	25	30	40	50	120	150	200
72A Walter Johnson Small Letters	50	60	80	150	200	250	400	500
72B Walter Johnson Large Letters	100	120	150	200	250	300	400	600
73 Tom Jones	6	8	10	12	20	25	40	60
74 Ed Karger	6	8	10	12	20	25	40	60
75 Ed Killian	6	8	10	12	20	25	50	60
76A Jack Knight Small Letters	6	8	10	12	20	25	40	80
76B Jack Knight Large Letters	8	10	12	15	20	30	50	80
77 Ed Konetchy	6	8	10	12	20	25	40	60
78 Harry Krause	6	8	10	12	20	25	40	60
79 Rube Kroh	6	8	10	12	20	25	40	60
80 Nap Lajoie	30	40	50	60	120	150	250	300
81A Frank LaPorte Small Letters	6	8	10	12	20	25	40	60
81B Frank LaPorte Large Letters	8	10	12	15	20	30	50	80
82 Arlie Latham	6	8	10	12	20	25	40	60
83A Tommy Leach Small Letters	6	8	10	12	20	25	40	60
83B Tommy Leach Large Letters	8	10	12	15	20	30	40	80
84 Sam Leever	6	8	10	12	20	25	40	60
85 Lefty Leifield	6	8	10	12	20	25	40	60
86 Paddy Livingston	6	8	10	12	20	25	40	60

		PrFr 1	GD 2	VG 3	VgEx 4	EX 5	ExMt 6	NM 7	NmMt 8
87	Hans Lobert	6	8	10	12	20	25	40	60
88A	Harry Lord Small Letters	6	8	10	12	20	25	40	60
88B	Harry Lord Large Letters	8	10	12	15	20	30	50	120
89	Nick Maddox	6	8	10	12	20	25	40	60
90	Sherry Magee	6	8	10	12	15	30	40	80
91	Rube Marquard	25	30	40	50	60	100	150	
92A	Christy Mathewson Small Ltr	50	60	80	120	150	300	350	500
92B	Christy Mathewson Large Ltr	60	80	100	120	200	250	400	600
93A	Al Mattern Small Letters	6	8	10	12	20	25	40	60
93B	Al Mattern Large Letters	8	10	12	15	20	30	50	80
94	George McBride	6	8	10	12	20	25	40	60
95A	John McGraw Small Letters	12	15	20	25	30	50	80	300
95B	John McGraw Large Letters	20	25	30	40	50	150	200	400
96	Harry McIntire	6	8	10	12	20	25	40	60
97A	Matty McIntyre Small Letters	6	8	10	12	20	25	120	200
97B	Matty McIntyre Large Letters	8	10	12	15	20	30	50	80
98A	Larry McLean Small Letters	6	8	10	12	20	25	40	60
98B	Larry McLean Large Letters	8	10	12	15	20	30	50	175
99	Fred Merkle	6	8	10	12	20	25	60	80
100	Chief Meyers	6	8	10	12	15	60	80	100
101	Clyde Milan	6	8	10	12	20	25	40	60
102	Dots Miller	6	8	10	12	20	25	40	60
103	Mike Mitchell	6	8	10	12	20	25	40	60
104	Pat Moran	6	8	10	12	20	25	40	60
105A	George Mullen (Mullin) Small Ltr	6	8	10	12	20	25	40	60
105B	George Mullen (Mullin) Large Ltr	8	10	12	15	20	30	60	80
106	Danny Murphy	6	8	10	12	20	25	40	60
107	Red Murray	6	8	10	12	20	25	40	60
108	Tom Needham	6	8	10	12	15	60	80	100
109A	Rebel Oakes Small Letters	6	8	10	12	20	25	40	300
109B	Rebel Oakes Large Letters	8	10	12	15	20	30	50	350
110	Rube Oldring	6	8	10	12	20	25	40	60
111	Charley O'Leary	6	8	10	12	20	25	40	60
112	Orval Overall	6	8	10	12	20	25	40	60
113	Fred Parent	6	8	10	12	20	25	40	80
114A	Dode Paskert Small Letters	6	8	10	12	20	25	40	60
114B	Dode Paskert Large Letters	8	10	12	15	20	30	50	80
115	Barney Pelty	6	8	10	60	80	100	120	150
116	Jake Pfiester	6	8	10	12	20	25	40	60
117	Eddie Phelps	6	8	10	12	15	25	40	60
118	Deacon Phillippe	6	8	10	12	20	25	40	60
119	Jack Quinn	6	8	10	12	20	25	40	60
120	Ed Reulbach	6	8	10	12	20	25	40	60
121	Lew Richie	6	8	10	12	20	25	40	60
122	Jack Rowan	6	8	10	12	20	25	40	60
123A	Nap Rucker Small Letters	6	8	10	12	20	25	40	60
123B	Nap Rucker Large Letters	8	10	12	15	20	30	50	80
124	Doc Scanlon	6	8	10	12	20	25	40	60
125	Herman Schaefer	6	8	10	12	20	25	40	80
126A	Boss Schmidt Small Letters	6	8	10	12	20	25	40	60
126B	Boss Schmidt Large Letters	12	15	20	25	30	60	80	120
127	Wildfire Schulte	6	8	10	12	20	25	40	60
128	Jimmy Sheckard	6	8	10	12	20	25	40	60
129	Hap Smith	6	8	10	12	20	25	40	60
130A	Tris Speaker Small Letters	30	40	50	60	100	120	200	300
130B	Tris Speaker Large Letters	40	50	60	80	120	150	250	400
131	Oscar Stanage	6	8	10	12	20	25	40	
132	Harry Steinfeldt	6	8	10	12	20	25	40	60
133	George Stone	6	8	10	12	15	60	80	100
134A	George Stovall Small Letters	6	8	10	12	20	25	40	60
134B	George Stovall Large Letters	8	10	12	15	20	30	50	80
135A	Gabby Street Small Letters	6	8	10	12	20	25	40	60
135B	Gabby Street Large Letters	8	10	12	15	20	30	50	80
136	George Suggs	6	8	10	12	20	25	40	
137A	Ira Thomas Small Letters	6	8	10	12	20	25	40	80
137B	Ira Thomas Large Letters	8	10	12	15	20	30	50	80
138A	Joe Tinker Small Letters	12	15	20	25	30	80	100	120
138B	Joe Tinker Large Letters	20	25	30	40	50	80	120	200
139A	John Titus Small Letters	6	8	10	12	20	25	40	60
139B	John Titus Large Letters	8	10	12	15	20	30	50	80
140	Terry Turner	6	8	10	12	20	25	80	100
141	Heinie Wagner	6	8	10	12	20	25	40	60
142A	Bobby Wallace w/Cap Small Ltr	8	10	12	15	20	30	50	80
142B	Bobby Wallace w/Cap Large Ltr	12	15	20	25	30	50	80	120
143	Bobby Wallace without Cap	12	15	20	25	30	40	50	80
144	Ed Walsh	12	15	20	25	30	50	100	120
145	Jack Warhop	6	8	10	12	20	25	60	80

		PrFr 1	GD 2	VG 3	VgEx 4	EX 5	ExMt 6	NM 7	NmMt
146B	Zach Wheat Large Letters	20	25	30	40	50	100	120	20
146A	Zach Wheat Small Letters	20	25	30	40	50	100	120	30
147	Doc White	6	8	10	12	20	25	40	6
148A	Art Wilson Small Letters	6	8	10	12	20	25	40	6
148B	Art Wilson Large Letters	8	10	12	15	20	30	50	8
149	Owen Wilson	6	8	10	12	20	25	40	6
150	Hooks Wiltse	6	8	10	12	20	25	40	6
151	Harry Wolter	6	8	10	12	20	25	40	6
152A	Cy Young C on Cap	50	60	100	120	150	300	400	60
152B	Old Cy Young Plain Cap	50	60	100	120	150	300	400	60

—Ty Cobb Small Letters PSA 9 (MT) sold for $2,326 (eBay; 5/07)
—Ty Cobb Small Letters PSA 9 (MT) sold for $1,527 (eBay; 10/07)
—Ty Cobb Large Letters PSA 8 (NmMt) sold for $2,750 (eBay; 4/07)
—Walter Johnson Small Letters PSA 9 (MT) sold for $1,416 (eBay; 8/08)
—Walter Johnson Small Letters PSA 9 (MT) sold for $1,220 (eBay; 5/08)
—Cy Young C on Cap Small Letters PSA 9 (MT) sold for $729 (eBay; 4/08)

1911 Close Candy E94

		PrFr 1	GD 2	VG 3	VgEx 4	EX 5	ExMt 6	NM 7	NmMt
1	Jimmy Austin	100	250	500	700				
2	Johnny Bates	100	350	500	1,200	1,800			
3	Bob Bescher	120	250	350	400				
4	Bobby Byrne	100	250	500	1,100				
5	Frank Chance	250	600	900					
6	Eddie Cicotte	250	500	1,200	1,300	2,000			
7	Ty Cobb	300	3,500	8,200	8,500	12,000			
8	Sam Crawford	250	550	925	1,200				
9	Harry Davis	100	250	350					
10	Art Devlin	100	250	400	700				
11	Josh Devore	120	250	350					
12	Mickey Doolan	120	250	350	500				
13	Patsy Dougherty	100	250	700					
14	Johnny Evers	250	500	800					
15	Eddie Grant	100	250	500					
16	Hugh Jennings	200	450	600					
17	Red Kleinow	100	250	500					
18	Napoleon Lajoie	250	500	800	1,500				
19	Joe Lake	100	250	450	600				
20	Tommy Leach	100	250	350	600	1,000			
21	Hans Lobert	100	250	350					
22	Harry Lord	100	250	800					
23	Sherry Magee	100	300	500	700	1,500			
24	John McGraw	250	500	1,000	1,200				
25	Earl Moore	120	400	500	600				
26	Red Murray	100	250	350	850				
27	Tris Speaker	700	1,000	1,800	2,000				
28	Terry Turner	100	250	500	1,400				
29	Honus Wagner	2,000	2,500	4,800	6,000	10,400			
30	Cy Young	1,000	2,500	3,800					

—Frank Chance #5 PSA 8 (NmMt) sold for $11,212 (Goodwin; 6/12)
—Ty Cobb SGC 86 (NM+) sold for $21,047 (Mastro; 12/05)
—Sam Crawford PSA 8 (NmMt) sold for $9,582 (Mastro; 4/07)
—Sam Crawford PSA 8 (NmMt) sold for $7,170 (Heritage; 10/07)
—Hugh Jennings PSA 6 (ExMt) sold for $4,593 (Mastro; 8/06)
—John McGraw SGC 70 (EX+) sold for $3,795 (Mastro; 12/05)
—John McGraw PSA 5 (EX) sold for $1,995 (Madec; 11/07)
—Tris Speaker SGC 80 (ExMt) sold for $8,120 (REA; 4/06)
—Tris Speaker PSA 6 (ExMt) sold for $4,275 (eBay; 5/06)
—Cy Young SGC 50 (VgEx) sold for $4,674 (Mastro; 12/05)

1911 Mecca Double Folders T201

		PrFr 1	GD 2	VG 3	VgEx 4	EX 5	ExMt 6	NM 7	NmMt
1	Abstein/Butler	25	40	100	150	250	300	400	1,00
2	Baker/Downie	25	30	50	100	120	150	400	8
3	Barrett/McGlyn	25	30	40	60	120	200	300	8
4	Bender/Oldring	50	60	120	150	175	250	400	1,50
5	Brown/Hofman	60	80	100	150	200	250	400	1,20
6	Chase/Sweeney	30	40	60	80	120	200	500	8
7	Cicotte/Thoney	30	60	80	100	120	250	500	1,20
8	Clarke/Byrne	30	40	60	80	150	250	400	8
9	Collins/Baker	50	80	100	120	250	300	800	1,5
10	Crawford/Cobb	250	400	500	700	1,200	2,000	2,500	8,00
11	Donovan/Stroud	25	30	40	60	100	150	350	8
12	Downs/Odell	25	30	50	60	100	150	300	8
13	Doyle/Meyers	25	30	40	60	100	150	250	8

	PrFr 1	GD 2	VG 3	VgEx 4	EX 5	ExMt 6	NM 7	NmMt 8
Evers/Chance	60	80	120	200	250	400	700	2,000
Ford/Johnson	25	30	40	60	100	150	300	800
Foster/Ward	25	30	40	60	100	150	300	800
Gaspar/Clarke	25	30	40	60	100	150	300	800
Grant/McLean	25	30	60	80	100	150	300	800
Hartzell/Blair	25	30	40	60	100	150	300	800
Hickman/Hinchman	25	30	40	60	100	200	300	1,000
Huggins/Bresnahan	50	60	100	120	200	300	600	1,500
Johnson/Street	120	150	200	300	500	700	1,500	4,000
Killian/Fitzpatrick	25	30	40	60	100	250	350	800
Kling/Cole	25	30	60	80	100	150	300	800
Lajoie/Falkenberg	120	150	200	250	600	700	800	2,000
Lake/Wallace	30	60	80	100	150	200	400	1,300
LaPorte/Stephens	25	30	40	60	100	150	250	800
Lapp/Barry	25	30	40	60	100	200	300	800
Leach/Gibson	25	30	40	60	100	150	300	800
Leifield/Simon	25	30	40	60	100	150	300	800
Lobert/Moore	25	30	50	60	100	150	300	800
Lord/Dougherty	40	50	60	100	200	400	500	1,500
Lush/Hauser	25	30	40	60	100	150	300	800
Mattern/Graham	25	30	40	60	100	150	300	800
Mathewson/Bridwell UER	120	150	300	350	600	800	1,800	4,000
McBride/Elberfeld	25	40	50	60	100	150	300	800
McCabe/Starr	25	30	40	60	100	150	300	800
McGinnity/McCarty	30	60	80	100	200	300	500	1,200
Miller/Herzog	25	30	40	60	100	150	300	800
Rucker/Daubert	25	30	40	60	100	150	300	800
Seymour/Dygert	25	30	40	60	100	150	300	800
Speaker/Gardner	60	80	150	200	400	450	800	2,000
Summers/Jennings	30	40	50	80	150	200	400	1,200
Thomas/Coombs	25	30	40	60	100	150	300	800
Titus/Dooin	25	30	40	60	100	150		
Turner/Stovall	25	30	40	60	120	150	300	800
Walsh/Payne	40	50	60	100	150	200	400	1,200
Wheat/Bergen	30	80	100	150	200	250	400	1,200
Wiltse/Merkle	25	30	40	80	100	150	300	800
Woodruff/Williams	25	30	40	80	100	150	150	800

Crawford/Cobb SGC 86 (NM+) sold for $4,061 (Mastro; 8/07)
Mathewson/Bridwell SGC 92 (NmMt+) sold for $4,945 (Superior; 12/05)
McBride/Elberfeld PSA 9 (MT) sold for $5,011 (Mastro; 10/06)

911 T205 Gold Border

	PrFr 1	GD 2	VG 3	VgEx 4	EX 5	ExMt 6	NM 7	NmMt 8
Ed Abbaticchio	15	25	30	50	120	250		
Doc Adkins	30	50	80	200	250	500		
Leon K. Ames	15	25	30	60	175	300		
Jas. P. Archer	15	25	60	80	120	300		
Jimmy Austin	15	25	40	80	120	300		
Bill Bailey	15	25	30	▲80	100	250		
Home Run Baker	100	150	200	250	500	800		
Neal Ball	15	25	30	50	100	250		
E.B. Barger Full B on Cap	15	25	30	80	120	350		
E.B. Barger Partial B on Cap	60	100	120	250	450	800		
Jack Barry	15	25	30	50	120	250		
Emil Batch	25	40	80	120	250			
John W. Bates	30	50	60	▲100	120	250		
Fred Beck	15	▲30	▲40	50	120	250		
Beals Becker	15	25	30	50	150	300		
George Bell	15	25	30	60	100	300		
Chas. Bender	60	100	150	200	400	800		
William Bergen	15	25	50	60	120	250		
Bob Bescher	15	25	50	▲100	200	250		
Joe Birmingham	15	25	30	80	100	300		
Lena Blackburne	15	25	40	60	120	250		
William Bransfield	25	40	50	80	150	300		
Roger Bresnahan Mouth Closed	60	100	200	250	300	600		
Roger Bresnahan Mouth Open	80	120	300	350	600	1,000		
A.H. Bridwell	15	25	30	80	120	200		
Mordecai Brown	60	120	150	250	400	1,000		
Robt. Byrne	15	25	30	50	120	250		
Hick Cady	30	50	60	120	300	600		
Howie Camnitz	15	25	40	60	150	200		
Bill Carrigan	15	25	40	60	120	200		
Frank Chance	60	80	100	200	350	600		
A Hal Chase Both Border Ends	30	50	80	120	300	600		
B Hal Chase Both Border Extends	30	50	60	200	350	600		

	PrFr 1	GD 2	VG 3	VgEx 4	EX 5	ExMt 6	NM 7	NmMt 8
33 Hal Chase Left Ear	60	120	200	300	400	1,000		
34 Ed Cicotte	40	80	150	200	400	900		
35 Fred Clarke	40	100	120	200	300	800		
36 Ty Cobb	600	1,200	1,500	2,000	4,000	10,000		
37 Eddie Collins Mouth Closed	50	100	150	300	400	1,000		
38 Eddie Collins Mouth Open	120	200	300	500	600	1,800		
39 Jimmy Collins	60	120	225	350	500	800		
40 Frank Corridon	15	25	50	120	150	200		
41A Otis Crandall T Crossed	20	30	40	80	250			
41B Otis Crandall T Not Crossed	20	30	40	60	200			
42 Lou Criger	15	25	40	60	120	250		
43 W.F. Dahlen	60	100	120	300	400			
44 Jake Daubert	15	25	30	50	100	250		
45 Jim Delahanty	15	25	30	60	120	250		
46 Art Devlin	30	50	60	100	150	400		
47 Josh Devore	15	25	30	80	120	200		
48 W.R. Dickson	15	25	30	50	200	800		
49 Jiggs Donohue (Donahue)	60	100	150	250	400	800		
50 Chas. S. Dooin	25	40	50	80	120	200		
51 Michael J. Doolan	15	25	30	50	100	250		
52A Patsy Dougherty Red Sock	30	50	100	150	350			
52B Patsy Dougherty White Sock	30	50	80	100	300	700		
53 Thomas Downey	15	25	30	50	100	250		
54 Larry Doyle	15	25	40	80	150	250		
55 Hugh Duffy	50	80	120	175	300	600		
56 Jack Dunn	50	80	100	150	400	500		
57 Jimmy Dygert	15	40	50	60	120	250		
58 R. Egan	15	25	30	60	175	300		
59 Kid Elberfeld	15	25	40	60	100	250		
60 Clyde Engle	15	25	30	50	150	250		
61 Louis Evans	15	25	60	80	100	200		
62 John J. Evers	80	120	150	350	500	1,000		
63 Bob Ewing	25	40	50	80	120	300		
64 G.C. Ferguson	15	25	50	60	100	200		
65 Ray Fisher	40	100	120	150	300	900		
66 Arthur Fletcher	15	25	30	50	200	300		
67 John Flynn	20	25	30	50	100	250		
68 Russ Ford Black Cap	15	25	60	80	120	250		
69 Russ Ford White Cap	60	80	120	150	400			
70 Wm. A. Foxen	15	25	50	80	120	250		
71 Jimmy Frick	30	50	50	150				
72 Arthur Fromme	15	25	▲40	50	100	250		
73 Earl Gardner	15	25	30	60	100	200		
74 H.L. Gaspar	15	25	40	60	100	250		
75 George Gibson	15	25	40	80	150	250		
76 William Goode (Good)	15	50	60	80	150	250		
77 George Graham Cubs	60	100	150	250	500	1,000		
78 George Graham Rustlers	15	25	40	50	120	350		
79 Edward L. Grant	50	150	350	450	800	1,200		
80A Dolly Gray No Stats on Back	40	60	100	120	250	500		
80B Dolly Gray Stats on Back	200	300	400	800	1,000	3,500		
81 Clark Griffith	50	80	120	150	300	800		
82 Bob Groom	15	25	30	50	100	250		
83 Charlie Hanford	30	50	60	100	250			
84 Bob Harmon Both Ears	15	25	30	60	120	200		
85 Bob Harmon Left Ear	50	80	120	200	475	800		
86 Topsy Hartsel	15	25	30	50	100	250		
87 Arnold J. Hauser	15	25	30	80	120	250		
88 Charlie Hemphill	30	50	60	80	125	200		
89 C.L. Herzog	15	25	30	50	100	200		
90A R.Hoblitzell No Stats on Back	6,000	8,000	10,000	12,000				
90B R.Hoblitzell Cin. after 1908	25	40	60	120	450	600		
90C R.Hoblitzel Name Incorrect	100	150	200	300	600	1,200		
90D R.Hoblitzell No Cin. after 1908	100	150	200	800				
91 Danny Hoffman	15	40	50	80	120	600		
92 Miller J. Huggins	40	60	120	200	350	700		
93 John Hummell	15	25	30	60	100	250		
94 Fred Jacklitsch	15	25	30	50	120	250		
95 Hughie Jennings	80	100	120	150	300	1,000		
96 Walter Johnson	250	400	700	1,000	1,500	5,500		
97 David Jones	15	25	50	80	150	250		
98 Tom Jones	15	25	40	50	120	300		
99 Addie Joss	400	500	▲1,200	▲1,500	2,000			
100 Ed Karger	50	80	150	200	400	1,000		
101 Ed Killian	15	25	30	50	150			
102 Red Kleinow	60	100	120	200	400	800		
103 John G. Kling	15	25	30	50	100	300		

#	Name	PrFr 1	GD 2	VG 3	VgEx 4	EX 5	ExMt 6	NM 7	NmMt 8
104	Jack Knight	15	30	40	80	120	200		
105	Ed Konetchy	15	25	50	60	120	250		
106	Harry Krause	15	25	30	60	120	200		
107	Floyd M. Kroh	15	25	50	60	100	200		
108	Frank Lang	15	25	30	50	100	200		
109	Frank LaPorte	15	25	40	60	120			
110A	Arlie Latham A.Latham	25	40	50	80	300	400		
110B	Arlie Latham W.A. Latham	60	120	150	400	500			
111	Thomas W. Leach	15	25	50	80	120	225		
112	Wyatt Lee	25	40	60	120	175	400		
113	Sam Leever	20	25	30	60	120	200		
114A	A. Leifield A. on Front	40	60	80	120	400	800		
114B	A.P. Leifield A.P. on Front	40	60	80	135	400			
115	Edgar Lennox	15	25	50	80	120	550		
116	Paddy Livingston	15	25	30	50	150	200		
117	John B. Lobert	15	25	40	80	120	250		
118	Briscoe Lord	15	25	40	60	175	250		
119	Harry Lord	15	25	30	50	100	200		
120	John Lush	15	25	30	60	150	250		
121	Nick Maddox	15	25	30	50	120	300		
122	Sherwood R. Magee	15	25	30	50	100	350		
123	R.W. Marquard	50	100	120	150	300	1,000		
124	Christy Mathewson	250	400	▲800	▲1,500	2,500	3,000		
125	A.A. Mattern	15	25	30	60	120			
126	Lewis McAllister	25	40	80	100	200			
127	George McBride	15	25	40	60	120	250		
128	Amby McConnell	15	25	50	80	120			
129	Pryor McElveen	15	25	30	50	200	250		
130	J.J. McGraw	50	80	150	250	300	600		
131	Harry McIntire	15	25	30	80	100	200		
132	Matty McIntyre	15	25	30	50	100	225		
133	M.A. McLean	15	25	30	60	150	300		
134	Fred Merkle	15	25	30	80	120	500		
135	George Merritt	30	50	60	100	250	500		
136	J.T. Meyers	15	25	30	50	120	200		
137	Clyde Milan	15	25	40	50	120	250		
138	J.D. Miller	15	25	40	80	100	250		
139	M.F. Mitchell	15	25	30	50	150	200		
140A	Pat Moran Stray Line	400	600	1,200	1,500	4,000			
140B	Pat Moran No Stray Line	15	25	30	60	120	300		
141	George Moriarty	15	25	30	60	150	300		
142	George Mullin	15	25	50	80	150	250		
143	Danny Murphy	15	25	30	50	100	250		
144	Jack Murray	15	25	30	50	200	350		
145	John Nee	30	50	100	150	400			
146	Thos. J. Needham	15	25	50	60	100	600		
147	Rebel Oakes	15	50	60	100	150	250		
148	Rube Oldring	15	25	40	50	150	250		
149	Charley O'Leary	15	25	30	60	120	200		
150	Fred Olmstead	15	25	40	60	120	200		
151	Orval Overall	15	30	60	80	120	600		
152	Freddy Parent	15	30	40	50	100	200		
153	George Paskert	15	25	30	50	100	300		
154	Fred Payne	15	25	30	60	120	200		
155	Barney Pelty	15	25	40	60	120	200		
156	John Pfiester	15	25	30	50	120	250		
157	Jimmy Phelan	30	50	60	100	250	800		
158	E.J. Phelps	15	25	50	80	100	250		
159	Charles Phillippe	15	25	30	50	100	200		
160	Jack Quinn	30	60	80	100	200	400		
161	Bugs Raymond	60	100	120	200	400	800		
162	E.M. Reulbach	15	25	40	60	120	225		
163	Lewis Richie	15	25	30	50	100	200		
164	John A. Rowan	40	60	100	120	250	600		
165	Geo N. Rucker	15	25	30	50	100	250		
166	W.D. Scanlan	50	80	100	200	400	900		
167	Germany Schaefer	15	25	30	50	100	200		
168	Admiral Schlei	15	40	50	60	120	200		
169	Boss Schmidt	15	25	30	50	225	350		
170	F.M. Schulte	15	25	40	60	150	300		
171	Jim Scott	15	25	30	60	120	250		
172	B.H. Sharpe	15	25	30	60	120	200		
173	David Shean Cubs	40	60	80	150	400	800		
174	David Shean Rustlers	15	25	40	100	150	250		
175	Jas. T. Sheckard	15	25	30	80	120	350		
176	Hack Simmons	15	25	30	80	120	400		
177	Tony Smith	15	30	40	50	100	300		

#	Name	PrFr 1	GD 2	VG 3	VgEx 4	EX 5	ExMt 6	NM 7	NmMt 8
178	Fred Snodgrass	15	25	40	60	100	250		
179	Tris Speaker	120	250	350	500	1,000	1,400		
180	Jake Stahl	15	25	30	50	120	350		
181	Oscar Stanage	15	25	50	80	150	300		
182	Harry Steinfeldt	15	40	50	60	150	200		
183	George Stone	25	40	50	80	150	250		
184	George Stovall	15	25	40	60	250	400		
185	Gabby Street	15	25	30	50	100	300		
186	George Suggs	60	100	120	200	500	800		
187	Ed Summers	15	25	30	60	200	300		
188	Jeff Sweeney	50	80	100	200	450			
189	Lee Tannehill	15	25	30	50	100	200		
190	Ira Thomas	15	25	30	60	120	250		
191	Joe Tinker	60	80	120	200	400	850		
192	John Titus	15	25	30	50	200	250		
193	Terry Turner	50	80	100	120	200	400		
194	James Vaughn	60	100	120	200	500			
195	Heinie Wagner	50	100	120	200	300	800		
196	Bobby Wallace with Cap	40	80	100	250	400	600		
197A	Bobby Wallace No Cap 1 Line	500	800	1,000	1,500	2,400			
197B	Bobby Wallace No Cap 2 Lines	150	300	400	750	1,200			
198	Ed Walsh	100	150	200	350	800	1,500		
199	Z.D. Wheat	60	100	200	250	300	1,200		
200	Doc White	15	25	30	50	120	800		
201	Kirb White	50	80	100	200	400			
202A	Irvin K. Wilhelm	100	150	200	300	600	1,200		
202B	Irvin K. Wilhelm Suffe ed in Bio	150	200	350	800				
203	Ed Willett	15	25	30	50	120	300		
204	J. Owen Wilson	15	25	40	50	120	300		
205	George R. Wiltse Both Ears	15	25	40	80	120	250		
206	George R. Wiltse Right Ear	40	60	80	150	400	800		
207	Harry Wolter	15	25	30	80	150	250		
208	Cy Young	300	500	1,000	1,200	1,800	4,000		

—Frank Baker PSA 7 (NM) sold for $2,610 (REA; 5/05)
—Chas. Bender PSA 8 (NmMt) sold for $15,103 (Mastro; 8/07)
—Chas. Bender PSA 7 (NM) sold for $2,610 (REA; 4/06)
—Roger Bresnahan Mouth Closed PSA 8 (NmMt) sold for $8,908 (Mastro; 8/07)
—Roger Bresnahan Mouth Closed PSA 7 (NM) sold for $1,528 (REA; 5/08)
—Roger Bresnahan Mouth Open PSA 8 (NmMt) sold for $6,691 (Mastro; 12/07)
—Roger Bresnahan Mouth Open PSA 7 (NM) sold for $2,550 (eBay; 1/07)
—Roger Bresnahan Mouth Open PSA 7 (NM) sold for $2,115 (REA; 5/08)
—Mordecai Brown PSA 8 (NmMt) sold for $8,098 (Mastro; 8/07)
—Mordecai Brown PSA 7 (NM) sold for $2,390 (Heritage; 10/06)
—Hick Cady PSA 8 (NmMt) sold for $5,777 (Mastro; 8/07)
—Frank Chance PSA 9 (MT) sold for $19,785 (Mastro; 12/05)
—Frank Chance PSA 8 (NmMt) sold for $6,702 (Goodwin; 11/07)
—Frank Chance PSA 7 (NM) sold for $2,458 (Mastro; 8/07)
—Frank Chance PSA 7 (NM) sold for $1,793 (Heritage; 10/07)
—Frank Chance PSA 7 (NM) sold for $1,793 (Heritage; 5/07)
—Frank Chance #31 PSA 8 (NmMt) sold for $6,000 (Greg Bussineau; 7/12)
—Hal Chase Both Ears Frame Below Shoulders sold for $5,251 (Mastro; 8/07)
—Eddie Cicotte PSA 7 (NM) sold for $3,259 (Mastro; 8/07)
—Eddie Cicotte PSA 7 (NM) sold for $2,643 (eBay; 1/08)
—Fred Clarke SGC 84 (NM) sold for $1,680 (Mastro; 5/08)
—Ty Cobb PSA 8 (NmMt) sold for $84,000 (Mastro; 8/07)
—Ty Cobb SGC 84 (NM) sold for $28,800 (Mastro; 5/08)
—Ty Cobb SGC 84 (NM) sold for $22,634 (Mastro; 8/06)
—Ty Cobb SGC 84 (NM) sold for $18,000 (Legendary; 3/10)
—Ty Cobb PSA 7 (NM) sold for $15,288 (Sloate; 11/06)
—Ty Cobb SGC 84 (NM) sold for $15,000 (Mastro; 12/08)
—Ty Cobb PSA 7 (NM) sold for $14,220 (REA; Fall '13)
—Ty Cobb SGC 84 (NM) sold for $10,665 (REA; Spring '14)
—Eddie Collins Mouth Closed PSA 8 (NmMt) sold for $6,691 (Mastro; 12/07)
—Eddie Collins Mouth Closed PSA 7 (NM) sold for $3,525 (REA; 4/07)
—Eddie Collins Mouth Open PSA 8 (NmMt) sold for $15,1030 (Mastro; 8/07)
—Eddie Collins Mouth Open PSA 8 (NmMt) sold for $10,665 (REA; Fall '13)
—Eddie Collins Mouth Open PSA 7 (NM) sold for $7,000 (eBay; 6/06)
—Jimmy Collins PSA 7 (NM) sold for $4,061 (Mastro; 8/07)
—Jimmy Collins PSA 7 (NM) sold for $3,046 (Memory Lane; 5/08)
—Otis Crandall T Not Crossed PSA 8 (NmMt) sold for $5,407 (Mastro; 8/07)
—John Evers PSA 7 (NM) sold for $5,407 (Mastro; 8/07)
—John Evers PSA 7 (NM) sold for $2,151 (Heritage; 5/07)
—George Graham Cubs PSA 7 (NM) sold for $4,915 (Mastro; 8/07)
—George Graham Cubs PSA 7 (NM) sold for $3,862 (Goodwin; 2/07)
—Dolly Gray No Stats on Back PSA 7 (NM) sold for $4,050 (eBay; 10/06)
—Dolly Gray No Stats on Back PSA 7 (NM) sold for $3,523 (Mastro; 8/07)
—Dolly Gray Stats on Back PSA 7 (NM) sold for $4,800 (Mastro; 5/08)

Clark Griffith #81 PSA 8 (NmMt) sold for $9,049 (Goodwin; 8/12)

Richard Hoblitzell No Stats PSA 6 (ExMt) sold for $33,000 (SCP Sotheby's; 12/05)

Richard Hoblitzell No Stats PSA 6 (ExMt) sold for $32,209 (Mastro; 8/07)

Richard Hoblitzell No Stats PSA 6 (ExMt) sold for $26,438 (REA; 5/10)

Richard Hoblitzell No Stats PSA 6 (ExMt) sold for $24,000 (Mastro; 8/08)

Richard Hoblitzell No Stats PSA 6 (ExMt) sold for $19,876 (Mile High; 11/10)

Richard Hoblitzell No Stats PSA 6 (ExMt) sold for $18,000 (Legendary; 11/10)

Richard Hoblitzell No Stats SGC 60 (EX) sold for $14,351 (Mastro; 12/06)

Richard Hoblitzell No Stats PSA 5 (EX) sold for $11,309 (Mile High; 1/13)

Richard Hoblitzell No Stats SGC 60 (EX) sold for $10,280 (Mile High; 12/13)

Miller J. Huggins PSA 8 (NmMt) sold for $7,800 (Mastro; 5/08)

Hughie Jennings PSA 7 (NM) sold for $1,800 (Mastro; 5/08)

Walter Johnson SGC 92 (NmMt+) sold for $28,063 (Goodwin; 9/13)

Walter Johnson GAI 8.5 (NmMt+) sold for $16,197 (Mile High; 1/07)

Walter Johnson GAI 8.5 (NmMt+) sold for $13,145 (Heritage; 4/10)

Walter Johnson PSA 8 (NmMt) sold for $48,000 (Mastro; 5/08)

Walter Johnson PSA 8 (NmMt) sold for $26,335 (Mastro; 8/06)

Walter Johnson GAI 7.5 (NM+) sold for $6,019 (Mastro; 12/06)

Walter Johnson PSA 7 (NM) sold for $7,768 (Heritage; 10/07)

Davey Jones PSA 7 (NM) sold for $1,598 (eBay; 2/08)

Addie Joss PSA 6 (ExMt) sold for $6,420 (Mile High; 1/13)

Addie Joss PSA 6 (ExMt) sold for $5,040 (Greg Bussineau; 7/12)

Addie Joss PSA 6 (ExMt) sold for $4,774 (Mastro; 8/07)

A.P. Leifield A.P. on Front PSA 6 (ExMt) sold for $1,327 (eBay; 4/08)

A.P. Leifield A.P. on Front PSA 6 (ExMt) sold for $781 (eBay; 2/08)

Briscoe Lord (Drum Back) SGC 70 (EX+) sold for $13,661 (Mastro; 4/07)

Rube Marquard SGC 88 (NmMt) sold for $12,490 (Mastro; 4/06)

Rube Marquard PSA 7 (NM) sold for $1,912 (Heritage; 5/07)

Christy Mathewson PSA 8 (NmMt) sold for $24,720 (Greg Bussineau; 4/15)

Christy Mathewson PSA 8 (NmMt) sold for $23,700 (REA; Fall '13)

Christy Mathewson PSA 8 (NmMt) sold for $17,657 (Mastro; 12/07)

Christy Mathewson SGC 86 (NM+) sold for $12,500 (eBay; 10/06)

Christy Mathewson SGC 86 (NM+) sold for $10,575 (REA; 4/06)

Christy Mathewson PSA 7 (NM) sold for $10,665 (Memory Lane; 5/08)

Christy Mathewson PSA 7 (NM) sold for $8,700 (REA; 4/06)

Christy Mathewson PSA 7 (NM) sold for $8,205 (Memory Lane; 3/06)

Christy Mathewson SGC 84 (NM) sold for $8,134 (Memory Lane; 8/06)

Christy Mathewson PSA 7 (NM) sold for $8,098 (Mastro; 8/07)

Christy Mathewson PSA 7 (NM) sold for $7,676 (eBay; 11/05)

Christy Mathewson PSA 7 (NM) sold for $7,619 (Goodwin; 2/06)

Christy Mathewson SGC 84 (NM) sold for $7,284 (Mastro; 4/07)

Christy Mathewson PSA 7 (NM) sold for $6,600 (Mastro; 5/08)

Christy Mathewson SGC 84 (NM) sold for $6,400 (eBay; 1/06)

Lewis McAllister SGC 84 (NM) sold for $3,523 (Mastro; 4/07)

Lewis McAllister SGC 84 (NM) sold for $2,400 (Mastro; 5/08)

J.J. McGraw PSA 8 (NmMt) sold for $8,098 (Mastro; 8/07)

J.J. McGraw PSA 7 (NM) sold for $1,612 (Sloate; 5/08)

J.J. McGraw PSA 7 (NM) sold for $1,434 (Heritage; 10/07)

Pat Moran Stray Line Under Stats PSA 7 (NM) sold for $9,600 (Mastro; 5/08)

Tris Speaker PSA 8 (NmMt) sold for $14,045 (Mastro; 8/07)

Tris Speaker PSA 8 (NmMt) sold for $11,878 (Goodwin; 6/06)

Tris Speaker PSA 8 (NmMt) sold for $10,280 (Mile High; 6/13)

Tris Speaker PSA 7 (NM) sold for $2,520 (Mastro; 4/07)

Tris Speaker #179 PSA 8 (NmMt) sold for $10,440 (Greg Bussineau; 7/12)

Heinie Wagner PSA 7 (NM) sold for $3,554 (eBay; 4/06)

Bobby Wallace No Cap 1 Line 1910 PSA 6 (ExMt) sold for $18,289 (Mastro; 12/05)

Bobby Wallace No Cap 1 Line 1910 PSA 6 (ExMt) sold for $4,500 (Mastro; 5/08)

Irvin K. Wilhelm Missing Letter PSA 6 (ExMt) sold for $2,880 (Mastro; 5/08)

Irvin K. Wilhelm #202B PSA 5 (EX) sold for $5,094 (Memory Lane; 5/12)

Cy Young PSA 8 (NmMt) sold for $23,666 (Mastro; 4/07)

Cy Young PSA 8 (NmMt) sold for $18,827 (Mastro; 12/07)

Cy Young PSA 8 (NmMt) sold for $17,775 (REA; Fall '13)

Cy Young PSA 7 (NM) sold for $12,773 (Mastro; 4/06)

Cy Young PSA 7 (NM) sold for $11,611 (Goodwin; 10/06)

1910-11 Turkey Red T3

	PrFr 1	GD 2	VG 3	VgEx 4	EX 5	ExMt 6
Mordecai Brown	400	600	1,000	1,500	2,500	
Roger Bresnahan	200	300	500	1,000	1,750	
Sam Crawford	300	500	800	1,200	2,000	
Hal Chase	200	300	500	800	1,500	
Fred Clarke	300	400	600	1,000	2,000	
Ty Cobb	2,500	4,000	5,000	8,000	20,000	30,000
Johnny Evers	300	500	800	1,200	2,300	
Clark Griffith	250	400	600	1,000	1,750	
Hughie Jennings	300	500	800	1,200	2,000	

		PrFr 1	GD 2	VG 3	VgEx 4	EX 5	ExMt 6
19	Addie Joss	400	600	1,000	1,500	2,500	
23	Napoleon Lajoie	500	800	1,200	2,000	3,000	
26	John McGraw	300	400	600	1,200	2,000	
27	Christy Mathewson	1,000	2,000	3,000	6,000	12,000	18,000
35	Joe Tinker	300	400	600	1,200	2,500	
36	Tris Speaker	500	800	1,500	2,500	4,000	6,000
39	Rube Waddell	200	400	600	1,000	2,000	
40	Vic Willis	200	300	500	800	1,500	3,500
42	Cy Young	1,000	1,500	2,700	4,000	6,000	
47	Frank Chance At Bat	400	600	1,000	1,500	3,000	
48	Jack Murray At Bat	150	200	500	800	2,000	
49	Close Play At Second	150	200	500	800		
50	Chief Myers At Bat UER	150	200	675	800		
78	Frank Baker	120	300	500	800	2,000	
80	Chief Bender	300	500	800	1,200	2,500	
87	Eddie Collins	300	400	600	1,000	2,500	
99	Walter Johnson	1,000	1,500	2,500	4,000	10,600	
101	Willie Keeler	300	500	800	1,200	2,500	
114	Bob Rhoads	600	800	1,000	1,500	2,500	
122	Fred Tenney	500	800	1,200	2,000	3,000	
124	Bobby Wallace	250	300	500	800	1,500	3,000
125	Ed Walsh	250	400	600	1,000	2,000	
126	Chief Wilson	200	300	500	1,000		

—Close Play at Second #49 PSA 5 (EX) sold for $6,159 (Memory Lane; 12/07)

—Ty Cobb #9 PSA 8 (NmMt) sold for $92,160 (Mastro; 12/05)

—Ty Cobb #9 SGC 60 (EX) sold for $27,400 (Mastro; 4/07)

—Ty Cobb #9 SGC 60 (EX) sold for $17,709 (Goodwin; 2/07)

—Ty Cobb #9 GAI 5 (EX) sold for $10,978 (Mastro Classic; 2/07)

—Harry Coveleski #88 PSA 6 (ExMt) sold for $3,586 (Mastro; 12/06)

—Harry Coveleski #88 PSA 5 (EX) sold for $4,207 (Memory Lane; 12/07)

—Lou Criger #89 PSA 5 (EX) sold for $3,477 (Memory Lane; 12/07)

—Bill Dahlen PSA 6 (ExMt) sold for $11,136 (SCP Sotheby's; 9/07)

—Clark Griffith #17 SGC 84 (NM) sold for $8,843 (Goodwin; 2/07)

—Clark Griffith #17 PSA 7 (NM) sold for $7,500 (eBay; 1/06)

—Hughie Jennings #18 SGC 80 (ExMt) sold for $5,533 (Memory Lane; 5/08)

—Walter Johnson #99 PSA 6 (ExMt) sold for $17,817 (Mile High; 1/07)

—Walter Johnson #99 PSA 6 (ExMt) sold for $12,925 (REA; 4/07)

—Jordan/Herzog PSA 5 (EX) sold for $4,207 (Memory Lane; 12/07)

—Red Kleinow #21 PSA 5 (EX) sold for $5,269 (Memory Lane; 5/08)

—Harry Krause #22 PSA 5 (EX) sold for $3,825 (Memory Lane; 12/07)

—Christy Mathewson #27 SGC 80 (ExMt) sold for $19,769 (Mastro; 4/07)

—George McBride #110 PSA 6 (ExMt) sold for $18,802 (Memory Lane; 5/08)

—Harry McIntire #28 PSA 6 (ExMt) sold for $19,977 (Memory Lane; 5/08)

—Harry McIntire #28 PSA 5 (EX) sold for $3,477 (Memory Lane; 12/07)

—Chief Myers at Bat #50 PSA 5 (EX) sold for $5,584 (Memory Lane; 9/07)

—Bob Rhoads #114 PSA 6 (ExMt) sold for $10,024 (Mastro; 8/06)

—Bob Rhoads #114 PSA 5 (EX) sold for $4,761 (Goodwin; 11/07)

—Bob Rhoads #114 PSA 5 (EX) sold for $2,650 (eBay; 11/07)

—Fred Tenney #122 PSA 6 (ExMt) sold for $8,176 (Memory Lane; 4/07)

—Fred Tenney #122 PSA 6 (ExMt) sold for $6,846 (Mastro; 8/06)

—Fred Tenney #122 PSA 6 (ExMt) sold for $4,339 (Mastro; 5/08)

—Vic Willis #40 PSA 7 (NM) sold for $7,754 (Mastro; 4/06)

—Chief Wilson #126 PSA 6 (ExMt) sold for $5,142 (Mastro; 8/06)

—Chief Wilson #126 PSA 5 (ExMt) sold for $4,627 (Memory Lane; 12/07)

—Cy Young #42 SGC 80 (ExMt) sold for $18,827 (Mastro; 4/07)

—Cy Young #42 GAI 6 (ExMt) sold for $5,530 (Mastro; 12/06)

1912 Hassan Triple Folders T202

		PrFr 1	GD 2	VG 3	VgEx 4	EX 5	ExMt 6	NM 7	NmMt 8
1	A Close Play (Wallace, LaPorte)	60	80	100	150	250	400	1,000	
2	A Close Play (Wallace, Pelty)	60	80	100	150	250	400	800	
3	A Desperate (O'Leary, Cobb)	300	450	600	1,000	1,750	3,500		
4	A Great Batsman (Barger. Bergen)	30	40	60	100	150	300	800	
5	A Great Batsman (Rucker, Bergen)	30	50	60	100	150	250	600	
6	A Wide Throw (Mullin, Stanage)	30	40	60	120	150	250	600	
7	Ambrose McCon (Blair, Quinn)	30	40	60	100	150	250	800	
8	Baker Gets His (Collins, Baker)	100	120	150	250	400	800	1,500	
9	Birmingham Gets (Johnson, Street)	150	200	300	400	700	900		1,200
10	Birmingham's HR (Birm, Turner)	60	80	100	150	250	400	1,000	
11	Bush Just (Moran, Magee)	30	40	60	100	150	300	600	
12	Carrigan (Gaspar, McLean)	30	40	60	100	200	250	600	
13	Carrigan (Wagner, Carrigan)	30	50	60	100	200	250	600	
14	Catching (Oakes, Bresnahan)	60	80	100	150	250	500	1,000	
15	Caught (Bresnahan, Harmon)	60	80	100	150	250	400	1,000	
16	Chance Beats (Chance, Foxen)	60	80	100	150	250	400	1,000	
17	Chance Beats (McIntire, Archer)	30	40	60	120	200	250	800	

#	Card	PrFr 1	GD 2	VG 3	VgEx 4	EX 5	ExMt 6	NM 7	NmMt 8
18	Chance Beats (Overall, Archer)	30	40	60	100	200	250	800	
19	Chance Beats (Rowan, Archer)	30	40	60	100	200	250	600	
20	Chance Beats (Shean, Chance)	60	80	100	150	250	400	1,000	
21	Chase Dives (Chase, Wolter)	30	40	60	100	200	250	600	
22	Chase Dives (Gibson, Clarke)	60	80	100	150	250	400	1,000	
23	Chase Dives (Phillippe, Gibson)	30	40	60	100	150	250	600	
24	Chase Gets (Egan, Mitchell)	30	40	60	100	200	250	600	
25	Chase Gets (Wolter, Chase)	30	40	60	200	250	300	600	
26	Chase Guard (Chase, Wolter)	30	40	80	100	200	400	900	
27	Chase Guard (Gibson, Clarke)	30	40	60	120	200	250	1,200	
28	Chase Guard (Leifield, Gibson)	30	40	60	100	200	250	600	
29	Chase Ready (Paskert, Magee)	30	40	60	100	150	450	600	
30	Chase Safe (Barry, Baker)	80	100	120	200	500			
31	Chief Bender (Bender, Thomas)	60	100	120	200	250	400	1,000	
32	Clarke Hikes (Bridwell, Kling)	30	40	80	100	150	400	1,800	
33	Close at First (Ball, Stovall)	30	40	60	100	150	250	600	
34	Close at the Plate (Payne, White)	30	40	80	120	150	400	800	
35	Close at the Plate (Walsh, Payne)	60	80	120	200	250	450	800	
36	Close at Third (Carrigan, Wagner)	30	40	60	100	200	250	600	
37	Close at Third (Wood, Speaker)	200	250	300	350	500	1,200		
38	Collins Easily (Byrne, Clarke)	60	80	100	150	250	450	1,000	
39	Collins Easily (Collins, Baker)	100	120	200	250	400	700	1,800	
40	Collins Easily (Collins, Murphy)	60	80	100	150	300	400	1,000	
41	Crawford (Stanage, Summers)	30	40	60	100	150	250	600	
42	Cree Rolls (Daubert, Hummel)	30	40	60	100	150	250	600	
43	Davy Jones (Delahanty, Jones)	30	40	60	120	150	250	800	
44	Devlin (Devlin G, Mathewson)	150	300	800	1,000	1,200			
45	Devlin (Devlin R, Mathewson)	120	150	250	350	700	1,400	2,500	
46	Devlin (Fletcher, Mathewson)	120	150	250	350	500	1,500		
47	Devlin (Meyers, Mathewson)	150	200	250	350	500	1,000	2,000	
48	Donlin Out (Camnitz, Gibson)	30	40	60	100	150	300	600	
49	Donlin Out (Dooin, Magee)	30	40	60	100	150	250	600	
50	Donlin Out (Doyle, Merkle)	30	40	60	100	150	250	900	
51	Donlin Out (Gibson, Phillippe)	30	40	60	100	150	250	600	
52	Donlin Out (Leach, Wilson)	30	40	60	100	150	400	600	
53	Dooin Gets (Dooin, Doolan)	30	40	80	100	200	250	600	
54	Dooin Gets (Dooin, Lobert)	30	40	60	100	150	300	1,200	
55	Dooin Gets (Dooin, Titus)	30	40	60	100	200	250	800	
56	Easy for Larry (Doyle, Merkle)	30	40	60	100	200	300	1,000	
57	Elberfeld Beats (Elberfeld, Milan)	30	40	60	100	150	300	600	
58	Elberfeld Gets (Elberfeld, Milan)	30	40	60	100	150	300	600	
59	Engle in a (Speaker, Engle)	80	100	200	250	350	500	1,200	
60	Evers Makes (Archer, Evers)	60	80	100	150	250	450	1,000	
61	Evers Makes (Archer, Overall)	30	40	100	120	150	250	1,000	
62	Evers Makes (Archer, Ruelbach)	30	40	60	100	200	400	600	
63	Evers Makes (Chance, Evers)	100	120	150	400	500	800		
64	Evers Makes (Tinker, Chance)	200	300	300	500	700	1,200	3,000	
65	Fast Work (O'Leary, Cobb)	400	450	600	1,000	1,700	2,500	4,000	
66	Ford Putting (Ford, Sweeney)	30	40	60	150	200	250	800	
67	Ford Putting (Ford, Vaughn)	30	40	60	120	200	250	800	
68	Good Play (Moriarty, Cobb)	300	500	600	800	1,800	3,000		
69	Grant Gets (Grant, Hoblitzell)	40	80	100	120	150	300	600	
70	Hal Chase (McConnell, McIntyre)	30	40	60	100	200	400	700	
71	Hal Chase (McLean, Suggs)	30	40	60	100	150	300	600	
72	Harry Lord at (Lennox, Tinker)	60	80	120	150	275	400	1,000	
73	Hartsel Strikes (Gray, Groom)	30	40	60	100	200	400	1,200	
74	Hartzell (Dahlen, Scanlan)	30	40	60	100	150	300	600	
75	Held at Third (Lord, Tannehill)	30	40	60	100	200	250	600	
76	Jake Stahl (Cicotte, Stahl)	30	40	80	120	200	250	600	
77	Jim Delahanty (Delahanty, Jones)	30	40	80	100	200	350	1,000	
78	Just Before (Ames, Meyers)	30	40	60	150	200	400	600	
79	Just Before (Becker, Devore)	30	40	60	120	200	250	600	
80	Just Before (Bresnahan, McGraw)	100	120	150	250	400	600	1,500	
81	Just Before (Crandall, Meyers)	30	40	80	100	150	250	600	
82	Just Before (Fletcher, Mathewson)	150	200	250	400	600	1,500		
83	Just Before (Marquard, Meyers)	60	80	100	250	300	600		
84	Just Before (McGraw, Jennings)	80	100	120	200	400	600	1,500	
85	Just Before (Meyers, Mathewson)	120	150	200	500	700	800	1,800	
86	Just Before (Meyers, Wiltse)	30	40	80	150	250	300	600	
87	Just Before (Murray, Snodgrass)	30	40	60	200	250	300	600	
88	Knight Catches (Knight, Johnson)	150	200	250	400	600	1,000	1,500	
89	Lobert Almost (Bridwell, Kling)	30	40	60	100	200	250	600	
90	Lobert Almost (Kling, Steinfeldt)	30	40	60	100	150	250	600	
91	Lobert Almost (Kling, Young)	150	300	350	450	600	1,000		
92	Lobert Gets (Kling, Mattern)	30	40	60	100	150	250	600	
93	Lobert Gets (Dooin, Lobert)	30	40	60	100	150	250	600	
94	Lobert Catches (Lord, Tannehill)	30	40	60	100	150	500		
95	McConnell (Needham, Richie)	30	40	60	100	150	250	600	
96	McIntyre (McConnell, McIntyre)	30	40	60	100	150	250	900	
97	Moriarty Spiked (Stanage, Willett)	30	40	60	100	200	250	600	
98	Nearly Caught (Bates, Bescher)	30	40	60	100	150	250	800	
99	Oldring Almost (Lord, Oldring)	30	40	60	120	150	300	900	
100	Schaefer On (McBride, Milan)	30	40	60	100	150	250	600	
101	Schaefer Steals (McBride, Griffith)	30	40	60	100	200	250	800	
102	Scoring From (Lord, Oldring)	30	40	60	100	150	250	650	
103	Scrambling (Barger, Bergen)	30	40	60	100	250	350	600	
104	Scrambling (Chase, Wolter)	30	40	80	100	150	400	600	
105	Speaker Almost (Miller, Clarke)	60	80	120	150	300	400	1,000	
106	Speaker Round (Wood, Speaker)	200	250	300	500	600	1,200		
107	Speaker Scores (Speaker, Engle)	120	200	250	300	500	1,000		
108	Stahl Safe (Austin, Stovall)	30	40	60	100	150	250	600	
109	Stone About (Schulte, Sheckard)	30	40	60	100	150	250	600	
110	Sullivan Puts (Evans, Huggins)	60	80	100	150	250	400		
111	Sullivan Puts (Gray, Groom)	30	40	60	120	150	250	800	
112	Sweeney Gets (Ford, Sweeney)	30	40	60	100	200	250	600	
113	Sweeney Gets (Ford, Vaughn)	30	40	60	100	150	400	1,200	
114	Tenney Lands (Latham, Raymond)	30	40	60	300	400	500	600	
115	The Athletic (Barry, Baker)	80	100	150	200	300	500		
116	The Athletic (Brown, Graham)	30	40	60	100	150	300	800	
117	The Athletic (Hauser, Konetchy)	30	40	60	100	150	250	600	
118	The Athletic (Krause, Thomas)	30	40	60	100	150	250	600	
119	The Pinch Hitter (Egan, Hoblitzell)	30	40	60	100	200	250	600	
120	The Scissors (Birmingham, Turner)	30	40	80	100	200		250	6
121	Tom Jones (Fromme, McLean)	30	40	60	150	200	250	600	
122	Tom Jones (Gaspar, McLean)	30	40	60	100	150	250	600	
123	Too Late (Ames, Meyers)	30	40	60	100	150	250	1,200	
124	Too Late (Crandall, Meyers)	30	50	60	100	250	300	600	
125	Too Late (Devlin G, Mathewson)	250	300	400	825	1,200			
126	Too Late (Devlin R, Mathewson)	300	400	500	800	1,500			
127	Too Late (Marquard, Meyers)	60	80	100	200	400			
128	Too Late (Meyers, Wiltse)	30	40	60	100	150	300	600	
129	Ty Cobb Steals (Jennings, Cobb)	400	600	800	1,400	2,000	3,200	6,400	
130	Ty Cobb Steals (Moriarty, Cobb)	350	450	750	1,000	1,750	3,000		
131	Ty Cobb Steals (Stovall, Austin)	200	250	400	600	1,000	1,500	3,000	
132	Wheat Strikes (Dahlen, Wheat)	60	80	100	200	300	400	1,000	

—A Desperate (O'Leary, Cobb) #3 PSA 7 (NrMt) sold for $7,800 (Greg Bussineau; 4/12)
—Ty Cobb Steals (Moriarty/Cobb) PSA 8.5 (NmMt+) sold for $35,592 (Goodwin; 9/08)
—Ty Cobb Steals (Jennings/Cobb) PSA 8 (NmMt) sold for $10,192 (Goodwin; 9/14)
—Collins Easily Safe (Collins/Baker) PSA 8 (NmMt) sold for $5,728 (Goodwin; 2/07)
—Devlin Gets (Devlin R, Matty) PSA 8 (NmMt) sold for $11,071 (Goodwin; 2/07)
—Devlin Gets (Devlin R, Matty) PSA 8 (NmMt) sold for $5,398 (Memory Lane; 12/07)
—Devlin (Fletcher, Mathewson) PSA 8 (NmMt) sold for $12,521 (Goodwin; 12/11)
—Fast Work (O'Leary/Cobb) PSA 8 (NmMt) sold for $13,767 (Memory Lane; 12/07)
—Fast Work (O'Leary/Cobb) PSA 8 (NmMt) sold for $10,267 (Goodwin; 8/07)
—Good Play (Moriarty/Cobb) PSA 8 (NmMt) sold for $,920 (Bussineau; 7/14)
—Good Play (Moriarty/Cobb) PSA 8 (NmMt) sold for $11,086 (Mile High; 2/08)
—Good Play (Moriarty/Cobb) PSA 7 (NM) sold for $5,676 (Memory Lane; 3/08)
—Just Before (Meyers, Mathewson) PSA 8 (NmMt) sold for $5,999 (Mastro; 8/06)
—Lobert Almost Caught (Kling/Young) PSA 7 (NM) sold for $1,936 (eBay; 2/08)
—Lobert Catches his Man (Lord, Tannehill) PSA 7 (NM) sold for $3,363 (eBay; 6/06)
—The Athletic Infield (Baker, Barry) PSA 8 (NmMt) sold for $10,058 (Mastro; 4/07)
—Too Late for Devlin (Devlin R, Mathewson) PSA 6 (ExMt) sold for $5,100 (eBay; 4/07)

1912 T207 Brown Background

#	Card	PrFr 1	GD 2	VG 3	VgEx 4	EX 5	ExMt 6	NM 7	NmM
2	Eddie Ainsmith	25	40	50	60	100			
4	Jimmy Austin Insignia	25	40	50	60	100			
5	Jimmy Austin No Insignia	40	60	80	100	150			
6	Neal Ball	40	60	80	100	150			
7	Eros Barger	25	40	50	80	100	200		
8	Jack Barry	40	60	80					
10	Beals Becker	25	40	50	80	100	200		
11	Chief Bender	60	80	120	200	350	500		
13	Robert Bescher	25	40	50	60	120	200		
15	Lena Blackburne	80	120	150	250				
18	Ping Bodie	25	40	50	80	100			
19	Hugh Bradley	25	40	150	200	250	300		
20	Roger Bresnahan	50	80	120	200	325	500		
23	Robert M. Byrne	25	40	50	80	120			
24	Nixey Callahan	25	40	50	60	100			
25	Howie Camnitz	25	40	100	120	200	250		
26	Max Carey	100	150	200	400	500	750		
28	Bill Carrigan Wagner Back	40	60	80	100	150			

	PrFr 1	GD 2	VG 3	VgEx 4	EX 5	ExMt 6	NM 7	NmMt 8
George Chalmers	25	40	50	60	100	200		
Frank Chance	50	80	120	200	350	500		
Eddie Cicotte	150	250	300	500	1,000			
Tommy Clarke	25	40	50	120	150			
King Cole	25	40	50	60	100	200		
John Collins	40	60	80					
Robert Coulson	25	40	50	60	100	200		
Tex Covington	25	40	50	60	100	200		
Otis Crandall	25	40	50	60	150	200		
Dave Danforth	25	80	100	120	150			
Bert Daniels	25	40	50	60	100	200		
Jake Daubert	40	60	80	100	150			
Harry Davis	25	40	50	100	200			
Jim Delahanty	25	40	50	60	100	200		
Claud Derrick	25	40	50	60	120	200		
Art Devlin	25	40	50	60	120	200		
Joshua Devore	25	40	50	60	100	250		
Red Dooin	25	40	50	60	100	200		
Lawrence Doyle	25	40	50	60	120	200		
Dellos Drake	25	40	50	120	150			
Tex Erwin	25	40	50	150	200	250		
Steve Evans	25	40	50	60	120			
John Ferry	25	40	50	60	100	200		
Ray Fisher Blue Cap	25	40	200	200	250	300		
Ray Fisher White Cap	40	60	80	250	300			
Art Fletcher	25	40	50	60	120	200		
Art Fromme	25	40	50	60	100			
Del Gainor	25	40	50	60	100			
Larry Gardner	25	40	50	60	150	250		
Roy Golden	25	40	50	80	100	200		
Hank Gowdy	25	60	80	150				
Peaches Graham	40	60	80	100	150			
Jack Graney	25	40	50	150	200	250		
Vean Gregg	80	150	400	450	500			
Sea Lion Hall	25	40	50	60	250			
Ed Hallinan	40	60	80	100	200			
Earl Hamilton	25	40	50	60	100			
Robert Harmon	25	40	50	120	150	200		
Olaf Henriksen	25	40	50	60	100	250		
John Henry	40	60	80	100	250			
Buck Herzog	60	100	120	150	250			
Willie Hogan	25	40	60	100				
Harry Hooper	150	250	300	500				
Walter Johnson	200	350	500	600	1,000	2,500		
George Kaler (Kahler)	25	40	50	60	100			
Billy Kelly	40	80	100	120	150			
Jay Kirke	60	100	150					
Otto Knabe	25	40	50	60	100	200		
Ed Konetchy	25	40	50	60	100	250		
Harry Krause	25	40	50	60	120			
Jack Lapp	25	40	50	60	100			
Arlie Latham	25	40	50	60	100	200		
Tommy Leach	25	40	50	350	400			
Lefty Leifield	25	40	50	60				
Ed Lennox	25	40	50	60	120			
Duffy Lewis Boston	80	120	250	300				
105A Irving Lewis Emblem	1,500	2,500	4,000	6,000				
105B Irving Lewis No Emblem	1,500	2,500	14,000	16,000				
Jack Lively	25	40	50	60	250	300		
Paddy Livingston A on Shirt	40	60	100	200				
Paddy Livingston Small C	40	60	100					
Bris Lord Philadelphia	25	40	50	60	100			
Harry Lord Chicago	25	40	50	60	100			
Louis Lowdermilk	1,000	1,500	2,800	3,500				
Richard Marquard	50	80	100	200	300	500		
Armando Marsans	40	60	150	200	250			
George McBride	25	40	50	60	100	200		
Ed McDonald	25	40	120	150	200			
John McGraw	50	100	120	150	200			
Harry McIntire	25	40	50	60	100	200		
Matty McIntyre	25	40	50	60	150			
Bill McKechnie	150	250	300	600				
Larry McLean	25	40	60	80	100			
Clyde Milan	25	40	50	60	100	250		
Doc Miller Boston	80	120	300	400				

	PrFr 1	GD 2	VG 3	VgEx 4	EX 5	ExMt 6	NM 7	NmMt 8
125 Dots Miller Pittsburgh	25	40	50	60	100	200		
127 Ward Miller Chicago	800	1,400	1,500	2,000				
128 Mike Mitchell Cincinnati	25	40	50	60	100			
129 Willie Mitchell Cleveland	25	40	50	60	100			
132 Pat Moran	25	40	50	60	100	200		
133 Cy Morgan Philadelphia	30	50	60	80	120			
134 Ray Morgan Washington	40	60	80					
135 George Moriarty	60	100	300					
136 George Mullin D Cap	40	60	80	100	150			
137 George Mullin No D on Cap	40	60	80	100	250	350		
138 Tom Needham	25	40	50	60	150			
140 Hub Northen	25	40	50					
141 Les Nunamaker	25	40	50	150	250			
142 Rebel Oakes	25	40	50	60	100	200		
143 Buck O'Brien	25	40	100	120	200	300		
144 Rube Oldring	25	40	50	60	100	200		
145 Ivy Olson	25	40	150	200	250	300		
146 Martin J. O'Toole	25	40	50	60	100	200		
147 George Paskart (Paskert)	25	40	50	80	100	200		
149 Hub Perdue	25	40	80					
152 Jack Quinn	25	40	50	200	250	300		
153 Pat Ragan	100	150	200	300				
154 Arthur Rasmussen	100	250	300	350				
156 Ed Reulbach	25	40	50	80				
157 Nap Rucker	40	100	200					
159 Vic Saier	400	500	1,200					
160 Doc Scanlon (Scanlan)	25	40	50	60	120	200		
161 Germany Schaefer	25	40	50	60	100	200		
162 Bill Schardt	30	50	60	80	120			
163 Frank Schulte	30	50	60	80	120			
164 Jim Scott	30	50						
165 Hank Severeid	25	40	50	60	100	200		
166 Mike Simon	25	40	50	60	100	200		
167 Frank Smith Cincinnati	30	50	120					
168 Wallace Smith St. Louis	30	50	60					
169 Fred Snodgrass	25	40	50	60	100			
170 Tris Speaker	250	400	700	1,200	1,800	2,200		
171 Harry Spratt	25	40	50	80	100			
172 Eddie Stack	25	40	50	100	120	200		
173 Oscar Stanage	25	40	50	80	150			
174 Bill Steele	60	100	150					
175 Harry Steinfeldt	25	40	100	120	150	250		
176 George Stovall	30	50	120					
177 Gabby Street	25	40	50	60	100			
178 Amos Strunk	25	40	50	60	100	200		
179 Billy Sullivan	25	40	50					
181 Lee Tannehill	25	40	50	60	100			
183 Joe Tinker	60	100	200	250	350	500		
184 Bert Tooley	25	40	50	60	100			
185 Terry Turner	25	40	50	60	150	200		
186 Lefty Tyler	250	400	500	600				
187 Hippo Vaughn	40	60	80	100	200			
188 Heine Wagner	40	200	250	300	400			
189 Dixie Walker	25	40	50	60	150	200		
190 Bobby Wallace	80	120	150					
191 Jack Warhop	25	40	50	250	400			
192 Buck Weaver	500	800	1,000	2,000	3,000			
193 Zack Wheat	80	120	150	250	400			
195 Dewey Wilie	25	40	50	60	120	200		
196 Bob Williams	30	50	60	80	120			
197 Art Wilson New York	25	40	50	60	100	200		
198 Chief Wilson Pittsburgh	25	40	50	60	100			
199 George Wiltse	25	40	50	80	100	200		
201 Harry Wolverton	25	40	50	60	120	200		
202 Joe Wood	300	600	800	1,000				
204 Ralph Works	200	300	400	500				
205 Steve Yerkes	40	60	80					

—Roger Bresnahan PSA 8 (NmMt) sold for $3,306 (eBay; 10/06)
—Roger Bresnahan PSA 7 (NM) sold for $1,388 (Memory Lane; 5/08)
—Roger Bresnahan PSA 7 (NM) sold for $832 (eBay; 10/07)
—Max Carey PSA 7 (NM) sold for $2,214 (Sloate; 6/07)
—Mike Donlin SGC 40 (VG) sold for $1,137 (eBay; 2/07)
—Mike Donlin (Broad Leaf) SGC 30 (Good) sold for $3,851 (Sloate; 5/08)
—Irving Lewis (No Emblem) PSA 6 (ExMt) sold for $17,625 (REA; 5/10)
—Irving Lewis (No Emblem) PSA 2.5 (GVg) sold for $12,936 (Goodwin; 2/14)

—Irving Lewis (Emblem) SGC 60 (EX) sold for $9,345 (Goodwin; 12/12)
—Louis Lowdermilk PSA 7 (NM) sold for $15,405 (REA; 5/13)
—Louis Lowdermilk PSA 7 (NM) sold for $13,513 (Mastro; 8/06)
—Louis Lowdermilk PSA 7 (NM) sold for $11,163 (REA; 5/10)
—Louis Lowdermilk Red Cross SGC 40 (VG) sold for $16,590 (REA; 5/13)
—John McGraw PSA 6 (ExMt) sold for $1,215 (Memory Lane; 12/07)
—Ward Miller Chicago PSA 8 (NmMt) sold for $13,035 (REA; Spring '14)
—Ward Miller Chicago PSA 6 (ExMt) sold for $2,271 (Heritage; 10/07)
—Zack Wheat PSA 6 (ExMt) sold for $1,334 (Memory Lane; 12/07)

1913 Tom Barker Game WG6

		PrFr 1	GD 2	VG 3	VgEx 4	EX 5	ExMt 6	NM 7	NmMt 8
1	Grover Alexander	120	150	200	250	300	400	500	600
3	Chief Bender	15	20	25	30	40	60	80	100
4	Bob Bescher	8	10	12	15	20	25	30	50
5	Joe Birmingham	8	10	12	15	20	25	30	50
6	Roger Bresnahan	20	25	30	40	50	60	80	120
7	Nixey Callahan	8	10	12	15	20	25	30	50
8	Bill Carrigan	8	10	12	15	20	25	30	50
9	Frank Chance	20	25	30	40	50	60	80	120
10	Hal Chase	10	12	15	20	25	30	40	60
11	Fred Clarke	15	20	25	30	40	50	60	100
12	Ty Cobb	120	250	300	350	400	425	600	1,000
13	Sam Crawford	20	25	30	40	50	60	80	120
14	Jake Daubert	8	10	12	15	20	25	30	50
15	Red Dooin	8	10	12	15	20	25	30	50
16	Johnny Evers	20	25	30	40	50	60	100	150
17	Vean Gregg	8	10	12	15	20	25	30	50
18	Clark Griffith	15	20	25	30	40	50	60	100
19	Dick Hoblitzel	8	10	12	15	20	25	30	50
20	Miller Huggins	15	20	25	30	40	50	60	100
21	Joe Jackson	500	600	750	1,000	1,200	1,500	2,000	2,500
22	Hugh Jennings	15	20	25	30	40	50	60	100
23	Walter Johnson	50	60	80	100	120	150	200	350
24	Ed Konetchy	8	10	12	15	20	25	30	50
25	Nap Lajoie	25	30	40	50	60	80	100	150
26	Connie Mack	20	25	30	40	50	60	100	200
27	Rube Marquard	15	20	25	30	60	80	100	100
28	Christy Mathewson	50	60	80	100	120	250	400	500
29	John McGraw	20	25	30	40	50	60	80	120
30	Chief Meyers	8	10	12	15	20	25	30	50
31	Clyde Milan	8	10	12	15	20	25	30	50
32	Marty O'Toole	8	10	12	15	20	25	30	50
33	Nap Rucker	8	10	12	15	20	25	30	50
34	Tris Speaker	25	30	40	50	80	150	200	250
35	George Stallings	8	10	12	15	20	25	30	50
36	Bill Sweeney	8	10	12	15	20	25	30	50
37	Joe Tinker	20	25	30	40	50	60	80	120
38	Honus Wagner	120	150	200	250	300	400	500	800
40	Zack Wheat	15	20	30	40	50	60	80	120
42	Joe Wood	15	20	25	30	100	120	150	200
43	Cy Young	50	60	80	100	120	150	200	350

—A complete 52-card set plus original box with 30 PSA 9's, including Cobb and Jackson, sold for $15,080 (REA; 4/06)
—Ty Cobb PSA 9 (MT) sold for $1,554 (Heritage; 5/08)
—Christy Mathewson PSA 10 (Gem) sold for $2,077 (eBay; 8/07)
—Tris Speaker PSA 10 (Gem) sold for $1,252 (eBay; 8/07)
—Tris Speaker PSA 9 (MT) sold for $416 (Goodwin; 3/08)

1913 National Game WG5

		PrFr 1	GD 2	VG 3	VgEx 4	EX 5	ExMt 6	NM 7	NmMt 8
1	Grover Alexander	100	120	150	200	250	300	400	500
2	Frank Baker	20	25	30	40	50	60	80	200
3	Chief Bender	15	20	25	30	40	50	60	150
4	Bob Bescher	8	10	12	15	20	25	30	50
5	Joe Birmingham	8	10	12	15	20	25	30	120
6	Roger Bresnahan	20	25	30	40	50	60	80	150
7	Nixey Callahan	8	10	12	15	20	25	30	60
8	Frank Chance	20	25	30	40	50	60	80	120
9	Hal Chase	10	12	15	20	25	30	40	60
10	Fred Clarke	15	20	25	30	40	50	60	100
11	Ty Cobb	120	150	200	250	400	700	800	1,000
12	Sam Crawford	20	25	30	40	50	60	100	120
13	Bill Dahlen	8	10	12	15	20	25	30	150
14	Jake Daubert	8	10	12	15	20	25	30	80

		PrFr 1	GD 2	VG 3	VgEx 4	EX 5	ExMt 6	NM 7	NmMt
15	Red Dooin	8	10	12	15	20	25	30	12
16	Johnny Evers	20	25	30	120	150	200	250	20
17	Vean Gregg	8	10	12	15	20	25	30	12
18	Clark Griffith MG	15	20	25	30	40	50	60	15
19	Dick Hoblitzel	8	10	12	15	20	25	30	12
20	Miller Huggins	15	20	25	30	40	50	60	10
21	Joe Jackson	500	600	700	800	1,000	1,200	1,500	2,50
22	Hugh Jennings MG	15	20	25	30	40	50	60	10
23	Walter Johnson	40	50	150	200	250	300	400	50
24	Ed Konetchy	8	10	12	15	20	25	30	5
25	Nap Lajoie	25	30	40	50	120	150	200	20
26	Connie Mack MG	20	25	30	40	50	80	120	20
27	Rube Marquard	15	20	25	30	40	50	80	10
28	Christy Mathewson	40	50	60	120	150	200	250	30
29	John McGraw MG	20	25	30	40	50	60	80	12
30	Larry McLean	8	10	12	15	20	25	30	5
31	Clyde.Milan	8	10	12	15	20	25	30	12
32	Marty O'Toole	8	10	12	15	20	25	30	12
33	Nap Rucker	8	10	12	15	20	25	30	10
34	Tris Speaker	25	30	40	50	60	80	120	15
35	Jake Stahl	8	10	12	15	20	25	30	5
36	George Stallings MG	8	10	12	15	20	25	30	5
37	George Stovall	8	10	12	15	20	25	30	5
39	Joe Tinker	20	25	50	60	80	100	120	15
40	Honus Wagner	120	150	250	300	350	500	600	80
42	Joe Wood	15	20	25	30	40	50	100	15
43	Cy Young	50	60	80	100	200	250	300	40

—Grover Alexander PSA 9 (MT) sold for $1,047 (eBay; 7/07)
—Frank Baker PSA 9 (MT) sold for $665 (eBay; 2/08)
—Ty Cobb PSA 10 (Gem) sold for $3,876 (Mastro; 4/07)
—Joe Jackson PSA 9 (MT) sold for $3,333 (eBay; 3/08)
—Christy Mathewson PSA 9 (MT) sold for $665 (Sloate; 1/08)
—Christy Mathewson PSA 9 (MT) sold for $542 (Sloate; 3/07)
—John McGraw PSA 9 (MT) sold for $514 (eBay; 1/08)
—Cy Young PSA 9 (MT) sold for $1,008 (eBay; 9/07)

1913 Fatima Teams T200

		PrFr 1	GD 2	VG 3	VgEx 4	EX 5	ExMt 6	NM 7	NmMt
1	Boston Americans	150	250	350	550	950			
2	Chicago Americans	150	250	300	500	800			
3	Cleveland Americans	500	600	800	1,000	1,800			
4	Detroit Americans	300	600	800	1,200	2,000			
5	New York Americans	400	600	800	1,200				
6	Philadelphia Americans	100	150	300	400	600			
7	St. Louis Americans	300	500	600	1,000	1,500			
8	Washington Americans	200	250	400	500	900			
9	Boston Nationals	600	1,000						
10	Brooklyn Nationals	150	250	300	500	800			
11	Chicago Nationals	120	200	250	400	600			
12	Cincinnati Nationals	100	150	200	400	500			
13	New York Nationals	200	300	400	600	1,200			
14	Philadelphia Nationals	150	200	250	300	500			
15	Pittsburgh Nationals	200	300	400	650	800			
16	St. Louis Nationals	150	250	300	700	1,000			

—Boston Nationals SGC 50 (VgEx) sold for $2,032 (eBay; 5/08)
—Boston Nationals SGC 50 (VgEx) sold for $1,526 (eBay; 2/08)
—Brooklyn Nationals PSA 6 (ExMt) sold for $3,806 (SCP Sotheby's; 11/06)
—Cleveland Americans PSA 8 (NmMt) sold for $13,066 (Mastro; 4/06)
—Cleveland Americans PSA 8 (NmMt) sold for $11,850 (REA; Spring '14)
—Cleveland Americans PSA 7 (NM) sold for $11,816 (SCP Sotheby's; 9/07)
—Detroit Americans PSA 7 (NR-MT) sold for $7,048 (Mastro 4/06)
—New York Nationals PSA 7 (NM) sold for $6,064 (SCP Sotheby's; 9/07)
—New York Nationals PSA 7 (NM) sold for $5,756 (eBay; 11/06)

1914 Boston Garter Color

—Ty Cobb SGC 50 (VgEx) sold for $97,750 (Hunt; 7/07)
—Buck Herzog SGC 30 (Good) sold for $9,988 (REA; 5/08)
—Joe Jackson SGC 70 (EX+) sold for $204,000 (Mastro; 8/07)
—Joe Jackson SGC Authentic sold for $86,976 (Mile High; 2/08)
—Walter Johnson SGC 30 (Good) sold for $55,234 (Goodwin; 3/08)
—Ed Konetchy SGC 50 (VgEx) sold for $21,850 (Hunt; 7/07)
—Rabbit Maranville SGC 60 (EX) sold for $28,750 (Hunt; 7/07)

1914 Cracker Jack

	PrFr 1	GD 2	VG 3	VgEx 4	EX 5	ExMt 6	NM 7	NmMt 8
Otto Knabe	150	500	600	800				
Frank Baker	300	400	800	1,000	1,400	1,800		
Joe Tinker	250	300	800	1,200	1,500	2,200		
Larry Doyle	80	100	150	300	500			
Ward Miller	80	100	200	200	600	800		
Eddie Plank	250	600	900	1,300	2,200			
Eddie Collins	300	500	800	1,000	1,500	2,000		
Rube Oldring	80	100	250	400	1,000			
Artie Hoffman (Hofman)	100	150	200	400	600			
John McInnis	100	150	200	400	500	600		
George Stovall	100	100	300	400	600	800		
Connie Mack MG	150	250	600	1,000	1,500	2,000		
Art Wilson	80	100	250	300	400	400		
Sam Crawford	150	300	800	1,200	2,000	3,000		
Reb Russell	60	100	200	300	600			
Howie Camnitz	80	250	300	400	600	800		
Roger Bresnahan	250	600	1,200	1,500	2,000	2,500		
Roger Bresnahan NNO	1,000	1,500	2,000	2,500	3,500			
Johnny Evers	300	500	1,000	1,500	2,000	2,500		
Chief Bender	150	450	500	1,500	2,000	2,500		
Cy Falkenberg	100	200	250	300	400			
Heinie Zimmerman	60	120	300	400	500			
Joe Wood	400	700	2,000	2,500	3,000			
Charles Comiskey	250	500	800	1,000	1,200	1,500		
George Mullen (Mullin)	100	200	250	400	500	2,000		
Michael Simon	60	200	250	300	400	800		
James Scott	120	200	400	600	800	1,000		
Bill Carrigan	80	300	600	800	1,000			
Jack Barry	100	150	250	300	500			
Vean Gregg	100	250	300	500	600			
Ty Cobb	5,000	6,000	15,000	20,000	30,000	40,000		
Heinie Wagner	60	200	300	500	600	700		
Mordecai Brown	300	400	1,000	1,200	1,500			
Amos Strunk	100	120	250	300	450	400		
Ira Thomas	60	120	150	250	600	1,000		
Harry Hooper	150	250	800	1,500	1,800	2,000		
Ed Walsh	300	500	600	1,000	1,200	1,500		
Grover C. Alexander	1,200	1,500	2,500	4,000				
Red Dooin	120	250	600	800	1,000			
Chick Gandil	800	1,200	2,000	3,000	5,000			
Jimmy Austin	120	250	500	600	1,500			
Tommy Leach	100	200	300	400	1,000			
Al Bridwell	120	250	400	600	800	1,000		
Rube Marquard	400	600	800	1,000	1,500	2,500		
Charles Tesreau	120	250	300	400	600			
Fred Luderus	60	150	200	400	500			
Bob Groom	80	200	250	400	500	600		
Josh Devore	60	120	200	250	300	400		
Harry Lord	60	100	400	500	600	800		
John Miller	60	300	400	500	600			
John Hummell (Hummel)	60	200	300	500	600	800		
Nap Rucker	100	120	150	300	350	400		
Zach Wheat	150	250	700	1,000	1,500	2,000		
Otto Miller	120	250	400	600	800			
Marty O'Toole	120	250	400	600	800	1,000		
Dick Hoblitzel (Hoblitzell)	120	250	400	600	800	1,000		
Clyde Milan	120	250	400	600	800	1,000		
Walter Johnson	1,500	3,000	4,000	6,000	8,000			
Wally Schang	120	250	400	600	800	1,000		
Harry Gessler	80	250	300	600	800	1,000		
Rollie Zeider	100	200	300	500	800	1,000		
Ray Schalk	300	500	600	1,200	1,500	2,000		
Jay Cashion	150	200	400	500	600	1,000		
Babe Adams	100	200	250	400	600	800		
Jimmy Archer	60	120	400	500	600			
Tris Speaker	500	1,000	1,500	1,800	2,000			
Napoleon Lajoie	800	1,200	2,000	3,000	5,000			
Otis Crandall	150	300	400	500	600	800		
Honus Wagner	2,000	2,500	4,000	6,000	10,000			
John McGraw	300	500	800	1,200	2,000	3,000		
Fred Clarke	250	400	600	700	1,200	1,500		
Chief Meyers	80	120	250	400	1,500			
John Boehling	60	200	300	600	1,000			

		PrFr 1	GD 2	VG 3	VgEx 4	EX 5	ExMt 6	NM 7	NmMt 8
73	Max Carey	150	250	450	1,200	2,500	3,000		
74	Frank Owens	60	300	400	1,800	2,000			
75	Miller Huggins	200	300	800	1,000	1,500	2,500		
76	Claude Hendrix	60	100	150	200	300			
77	Hughie Jennings MG	200	300	600	800	1,500	2,500		
78	Fred Merkle	60	300	400	1,000	1,200			
79	Ping Bodie	60	100	400	800	1,000			
80	Ed Ruelbach	60	100	250	300	400			
81	Jim Delahanty	60	120	200	250	300	400		
82	Gavvy Cravath	150	200	400	600	800	1,000		
83	Russ Ford	60	100	150	600	800			
84	Elmer E. Knetzer	60	100	300	400	600			
85	Buck Herzog	80	150	200	250	600			
86	Burt Shotton	60	100	150	200	300			
87	Forrest Cady	100	150	250	300	500			
88	Christy Mathewson	30,000	50,000	80,000	100,000				
89	Lawrence Cheney	120	250	400	1,000	1,500	2,500		
90	Frank Smith	300	500	3,000	4,000	5,000			
91	Roger Peckinpaugh	60	100	600	800	1,000	1,200		
92	Al Demaree	400	800	2,000					
93	Del Pratt	6,000	20,000						
94	Eddie Cicotte	300	500	2,000	2,500				
95	Ray Keating	100	150	250	300				
96	Beals Becker	60	100	2,000	3,000	4,000			
97	Rube Benton	80	100	400	600	800			
98	Frank LaPorte	60	200	400	600	800			
99	Frank Chance	500	800	1,200	2,500	4,000			
100	Thomas Seaton	150	300	500	600	800	1,000		
101	Frank Schulte	60	100	200	400	600			
102	Ray Fisher	60	100	150	400	500	600		
103	Joe Jackson	15,000	25,000	30,000	40,000	60,000			
104	Vic Saier	200	250	400	600	800	1,000		
105	James Lavender	60	100	400	500	800	1,500		
106	Joe Birmingham	120	250	400	1,200	2,000			
107	Tom Downey	80	120	250	400	500	1,200		
108	Sherry Magee	120	250	1,200	2,000	3,000			
109	Fred Blanding	60	100	150	300	600	800		
110	Bob Bescher	60	400	500	600	800			
111	Jim Callahan	60	100	150	200	300			
112	Ed Sweeney	60	100	400	500	600			
113	George Suggs	60	100	150	400	600			
114	George Moriarity (Moriarty)	60	200	300	400	600	1,200		
115	Addison Brennan	60	100	150	200	300	400		
116	Rollie Zeider	80	120	300	400	600	800		
117	Ted Easterly	80	100	300	500	800			
118	Ed Konetchy	120	300	400	500	800			
119	George Perring	60	100	500	800	1,000			
120	Mike Doolan	60	100	200	200	400			
121	Hub Perdue	60	100	400	500	1,500	2,500		
122	Owen Bush	60	100	150	600	800	2,000		
123	Slim Sallee	60	100	150	250	300	400		
124	Earl Moore	200	300	500	800	1,000	1,500		
125	Bert Niehoff	200	300	400	600	800	1,200		
126	Walter Blair	60	100	300	400	600	800		
127	Butch Schmidt	60	100	150	500	800			
128	Steve Evans	60	150	400	500	800	1,000		
129	Ray Caldwell	60	100	120	400	600			
130	Ivy Wingo	100	200	300	1,000				
131	George Baumgardner	60	400	500	600	800	1,000		
132	Les Nunamaker	60	150	200	400	600	800		
133	Branch Rickey MG	400	800	3,000	4,000				
134	Armando Marsans	120	400	500	600	800	1,200		
135	Bill Killefer	250	300	400	500				
136	Rabbit Maranville	400	800	1,200	2,000				
137	William Rariden	120	300	400	600	800			
138	Hank Gowdy	60	100	200	250	300	400		
139	Rebel Oakes	80	150	200	200	600			
140	Danny Murphy	120	300	400	600	800			
141	Cy Barger	100	200	200	800	1,000			
142	Eugene Packard	100	200	300	400	500			
143	Jake Daubert	60	100	800	1,000	1,200			
144	James C. Walsh	250	300	400	600	800			

—Grover Alexander #37 SGC 84 (NM) sold for $6,335 (Mastro; 4/07)
—Grover C. Alexander #37 SGC 60 (EX) sold for $5,500 (Legendary; 8/12)

—Chief Bender #19 SGC 86 (NM+) sold for $4,350 (REA; 4/06)

—Mordecai Brown #32 SGC 7 (Nm) sold for $6,032 (Goodwin; 11/11)

—Del Pratt #93 PSA 4 (VgEx) sold for $17,625 (Mile High; 6/13)

—Frank Chance #99 PSA 8 (NmMt) sold for $8,100 (eBay; 4/08)

—Frank Chance #99 SGC 86 (NM+) sold for $11,600 (REA; 5/05)

—Frank Chance #99 SGC 84 (NM) sold for $9,000 (Mastro; 8/07)

—Ty Cobb #30 PSA 8.5 (NmMt) sold for $106,650 (REA; Spring '14)

—Ty Cobb #30 PSA 8.5 (NmMt) sold for $75,000 (REA; 05/12)

—Ty Cobb #30 PSA 8 (NmMt) sold for $61,810 (SCP Sotheby's; 11/06)

—Ty Cobb #30 SGC 86 (NrMt+) sold for $10,000 (Legendary; 5/10)

—Ty Cobb #30 PSA 5.5 (EX+) sold for $11,042 (SCP; 6/10)

—Ty Cobb #30 GAI 5.5 (EX+) sold for $7,321 (Old Judge; 4/06)

—Charles Comiskey #23 PSA 7 (NM) sold for $2,500 (eBay; 11/05)

—Sam Crawford #14 PSA 8 (NmMt) sold for $6,032 (Mile High; 05/11)

—Sam Crawford #14 SGC 84 (NM) sold for $1,986 (Mastro; 4/07)

—Johnny Evers #18 PSA 8 (NmMt) sold for $6,032 (Mile High; 05/11)

—Johnny Evers #18 PSA 8 (NmMt) sold for $3,977 (Memory Lane; 12/06)

—Joe Jackson #103 PSA 7 (NM) sold for $54,848 (Mile High; 05/11)

—Joe Jackson #103 SGC 7 (NM) sold for $46,575 (Mile High; 10/11)

—Joe Jackson #103 SGC 70 (EX+) sold for $44,057 (Goodwin; 12/12)

—Joe Jackson #103 SGC 70 (EX+) sold for $21,150 (REA; 4/07)

—Joe Jackson #103 PSA 6 (EX) sold for $21,738 (Mile High; 1/07)

—Joe Jackson #103 SGC 60 (EX) sold for $21,738 (Mile High; 1/07)

—Walter Johnson #57 PSA 6 (ExMt) sold for $23,000 (Legendary; 8/10)

—Walter Johnson #57 SGC 80 (ExMt) sold for $5,838 (Goodwin; 11/12)

—Walter Johnson #57 SGC 80 (ExMt) sold for $5,581 (REA; 05/11)

—Walter Johnson #57 SGC 60 (EX) sold for $4,050 (eBay; 12/06)

—Christy Mathewson #88 SGC 9 Mint sold for $35,000 (REA; 05/12)

—Christy Mathewson #88 PSA 5 (EX) sold for $67,798 (Goodwin; 11/12)

—Christy Mathewson #88 GAI 5 (EX) sold for $34,500 (SCP/Sotheby's; 12/04)

—Christy Mathewson #88 SGC 20 (Fair) sold for $18,062 (Goodwin; 12/12)

—John McGraw #69 PSA 7 (NM) solds for $2,969 (Mile High; 1/07)

—Eddie Plank #6 PSA 7 (NM) sold for $3,944 (Mastro; 4/07)

—Eddie Plank #6 SGC 70 (EX+) sold for $3,795 (Hunt; 7/07)

—Del Pratt #93 SGC 80 (ExMt) sold for $24,659 (Goodwin; 12/12)

—Branch Rickey #133 PSA 8 (NmMt) sold for $12,756 (Mastro; 4/07)

—Branch Rickey #133 PSA 5 (EX) sold for $3,659 (Goodwin; 8/07)

—Branch Rickey #133 PSA 5 (EX) sold for $3,598 (Memory Lane; 5/08)

—Tris Speaker #65 SGC 84 (NM) sold for $3,586 (Mastro; 4/07)

—Joe Tinker #3 PSA 7 (NM) sold for $3,974 (eBay; 1/06)

—Honus Wagner #68 SGC 84 (NM) sold for $28,539 (Mile High; 10/12)

—Honus Wagner #68 GAI 7 (NM) sold for $17,250 (SCP Sotheby's; 12/04)

—Honus Wagner #68 PSA 6 (ExMt) sold for $11,100 (eBay; 4/07)

—Honus Wagner #68 GAI 5 (EX) sold for $9,306 (Mastro; 12/06)

1914 Polo Grounds Game WG4

		GD 2	VG 3	VgEx 4	EX 5	ExMt 6	NM 7	NmMt 8	MT 9
1	Jimmy Archer	8	10	12	15	25	40	80	200
2	Frank Baker	20	25	30	40	60	80	150	400
3	Frank Chance	15	20	25	30	50	80	150	400
4	Larry Cheney	8	10	12	15	25	40	80	200
5	Ty Cobb	120	250	300	400	500	600	800	1,500
6	Eddie Collins	20	25	30	40	60	80	150	400
7	Larry Doyle	8	10	12	15	25	40	80	200
8	Art Fletcher	8	10	12	15	25	40	80	200
9	Claude Hendrix	8	10	12	15	25	40	80	200
10	Joe Jackson	300	400	500	600	800	1,400	1,800	2,500
11	Hugh Jennings MG	20	25	30	40	60	80	150	400
12	Nap Lajoie	25	30	40	50	80	175	225	500
13	Jimmy Lavender	8	10	12	15	25	40	80	200
14	Fritz Maisel	8	10	12	15	25	40	80	200
15	Rabbit Maranville	20	25	30	50	60	80	200	400
16	Rube Marquard	20	25	30	40	60	80	150	400
17	Christy Mathewson	50	60	80	100	150	200	400	800
18	John McGraw MG	20	25	30	40	60	100	150	400
19	Stuffy McInnis	8	10	12	15	25	40	80	200
20	Chief Meyers	8	10	12	15	25	40	80	200
21	Red Murray	8	10	12	15	25	40	80	200
22	Eddie Plank	20	25	30	40	60	80	150	400
23	Nap Rucker	8	10	12	15	25	40	80	200
24	Reb Russell	8	10	12	15	25	40	80	200
25	Frank Schulte	8	10	12	15	25	40	80	200
26	Jim Scott	8	10	12	15	25	40	80	200
27	Tris Speaker	25	30	40	50	80	100	250	500

		GD 2	VG 3	VgEx 4	EX 5	ExMt 6	NM 7	NmMt 8	MT 9
28	Honus Wagner	80	100	120	150	250	800	1,000	1,20
29	Ed Walsh	20	25	30	40	60	80	150	40
30	Joe Wood	20	25	30	40	60	100	150	40

—Ty Cobb PSA 10 (Gem) sold for $5,875 (REA; 4/07)

—Joe Jackson PSA 10 (Gem) sold for $7,638 (REA; 4/07)

—Joe Jackson PSA 10 (Gem) sold for $5,288 (REA; 05/11)

—Tris Speaker PSA 10 (Gem) sold for $838 (eBay; 4/08)

1914 Texas Tommy E224

—Nap Lajoie Type I PSA 4 MC (VgEx - Miscut) sold for $6,374 (Memory Lane; 12/07)

—Christy Mathewson Type II PSA 6 (ExMt) sold for $29,586 (Mastro; 12/06)

—Honus Wagner Type II PSA 5 (EX) sold for $22,226 (Mastro; 12/06)

—Honus Wagner Type I PSA 4 (VgEx) sold for $31,564 (Mile High; 1/07)

—Honus Wagner Type II SGC 20 (Fair) sold for $16,450 (REA; 5/08)

1915 American Caramel E106

		PrFr 1	GD 2	VG 3	VgEx 4	EX 5	ExMt 6	NM 7	NmMt
1	Jack Barry	60	150	250	300				
2A	Chief Bender Striped Hat	120	300	600					
2B	Chief Bender White Hat	100	250	400					
3	Bob Bescher	60	150	250	300				
4	Roger Bresnahan	100	250	400	800				
5	Al Bridwell	60	150	250	300				
6	Donie Bush	60	150	250	300				
7A	Hal Chase Portrait	100	200	400					
7B	Hal Chase Catching	100	250	400					
8A	Ty Cobb Batting Front	800	2,500	4,000					
8B	Ty Cobb Batting Side	800	2,500	4,000					
9	Eddie Collins	100	250	400	800				
10	Sam Crawford	150	300	500	800				
11	Ray Demmitt	60	150	250	300				
12	Bill Donovan	60	150	250	300				
13	Red Dooin	60	150	250	300				
14	Mickey Doolan	60	150	250	300				
15	Larry Doyle	60	150	250	300				
16	Clyde Engle	60	150	250	300				
17	Johnny Evers	100	500	600	800				
18	Art Fromme	60	150	250	300				
19A	George Gibson Back	60	150	250	300				
19B	George Gibson Front	60	150	250	300				
20	Topsy Hartzell	60	150	250	300				
21	Fred Jacklitsch	60	150	250	300				
22	Hugh Jennings MG	150	300	500					
23	Otto Knabe	60	150	250	300				
24	Nap Lajoie	250	600	1,000					
25	Hans Lobert	60	150	250	300				
26	Rube Marquard	150	300	500					
27	Christy Mathewson	500	1,200	2,000					
28	John McGraw MG	150	300	500					
29	George McQuillan	60	150	250	300				
30	Dots Miller	60	150	300	400				
31	Danny Murphy	60	150	250	300				
32	Rebel Oakes	60	150	250	300				
33	Eddie Plank	250	600	1,000					
34	Germany Schaefer	60	150	250	300				
35	Tris Speaker	300	800	1,500					
36	Oscar Stanage	60	150	250	300				
37	George Stovall	60	150	250	300				
38	Jeff Sweeney	60	150	250	300				
39A	Joe Tinker Batting	150	300	500					
39B	Joe Tinker Portrait	150	300	600	1,000				
40A	Honus Wagner Batting	1,200	2,500	4,000					
40B	Honus Wagner Throwing	1,200	2,500	4,000					
41	Hooks Wiltse	60	150	250	300				
42	Heinie Zimmerman	60	150	250	300				

—Ty Cobb Batting Front SGC 60 (EX) sold for $14,770 (Mastro; 12/07)

—Eddie Collins PSA 5 (EX) sold for $1,725 (Huggins and Scott; 10/07)

—Nap Lajoie PSA 4 (VgEx) sold for $2,185 (Huggins and Scott; 10/07)

—Christy Mathewson PSA 4 (VgEx) sold for $3,450 (Huggins and Scott; 10/07)

—Eddie Plank SGC 50 (VgEx) sold for $2,963 (Masto; 12/07)

—Tris Speaker SGC 70 (EX+) sold for $5,160 (Mastro; 12/07)

—Tris Speaker PSA 4 (VgEx) sold for $3,450 (Huggins and Scott; 10/07)

—Joe Tinker Batting PSA 5 (EX) sold for $1,093 (Huggins and Scott; 10/07)

—Honus Wagner Batting PSA 5 (EX) sold for $5,880 (Greg Bussineau; 12/12)

—Honus Wagner Throwing PSA 5 (EX) sold for $11,500 (Huggins and Scott; 10/07)

BASEBALL

1915 Cracker Jack

#	Player	PrFr 1	GD 2	VG 3	VgEx 4	EX 5	ExMt 6	NM 7	NmMt 8
1	Otto Knabe	80	100	120	150	250	1,500	3,000	
2	Frank Baker	200	500	800	1,000	1,200	1,500	2,000	6,000
3	Joe Tinker	200	250	300	450	600	800	1,500	8,000
4	Larry Doyle	50	60	80	120	150	250	400	
5	Ward Miller	40	120	250	300	400	500	600	1,500
6	Eddie Plank	600	800	1,200	1,500	2,500	3,000	4,000	20,000
7	Eddie Collins	200	400	600	800	1,000	1,800	2,000	4,000
8	Rube Oldring	40	50	60	150	200	250	300	600
9	Artie Hoffman	40	50	60	150	200	250	300	
10	John McInnis	40	120	150	200	250	300	400	1,000
11	George Stovall	40	50	60	120	150	200	300	500
12	Connie Mack MG	250	500	600	800	1,000	1,200	1,500	4,000
13	Art Wilson	40	80	100	200	250	300	500	800
14	Sam Crawford	250	500	600	800	1,000	1,200	1,500	5,000
15	Reb Russell	40	50	120	120	150	200	300	600
16	Howie Camnitz	40	50	60	150	200	250	300	1,000
17	Roger Bresnahan	150	300	500	600	800	1,000	1,200	2,500
18	Johnny Evers	200	300	400	500	600	800	2,000	5,000
19	Chief Bender	200	400	500	600	800	1,000	1,200	6,000
20	Cy Falkenberg	40	100	120	150	200	250	600	600
21	Heinie Zimmerman	40	80	100	150	200	300	500	1,000
22	Joe Wood	250	300	400	850	1,000	1,200	1,500	2,000
23	Charles Comiskey	250	300	500	600	800	1,000	1,500	8,000
24	George Mullen	40	50	60	120	150	200	300	1,000
25	Michael Simon	40	50	60	100	300	400	500	800
26	James Scott	40	50	60	150	200	500	600	
27	Bill Carrigan	40	50	100	150	200	300	500	
28	Jack Barry	50	100	120	150	300	500		
29	Vean Gregg	40	50	60	150	300	400	600	800
30	Ty Cobb	3,000	6,000	8,000	12,000	15,000	20,000	25,000	30,000
31	Heinie Wagner	40	50	60	100	250	300	500	2,500
32	Mordecai Brown	200	250	500	600	800	1,200	2,500	
33	Amos Strunk	50	100	200	300	500	600	800	2,500
34	Ira Thomas	40	80	120	150	175	200	300	1,000
35	Harry Hooper	150	200	250	400	500	600	1,000	4,000
36	Ed Walsh	200	250	400	500	600	800	1,500	6,000
37	Grover C. Alexander	800	1,000	2,000	2,500	3,000	4,000	6,000	8,000
38	Red Dooin	40	50	60	100	200	250	600	800
39	Chick Gandil	200	300	400	500	600	800	1,200	5,000
40	Jimmy Austin	50	60	80	120	200	250	400	800
41	Tommy Leach	40	50	60	100	120	200	300	800
42	Al Bridwell	40	60	80	150	200	250	300	1,000
43	Rube Marquard	300	400	500	600	800	1,000	2,500	4,000
44	Jeff (Charles) Tesreau	40	50	60	100	200	350	400	1,000
45	Fred Luderus	40	50	60	150	200	250	300	1,000
46	Bob Groom	40	150	200	300	400	500	600	2,000
47	Josh Devore	40	50	60	300	400	500	600	800
48	Steve O'Neill	40	50	80	120	150	200	400	800
49	John Miller	40	50	60	100	120	200	400	1,000
50	John Hummell	40	80	200	250	300	400	500	600
51	Nap Rucker	40	60	80	100	120	200	400	800
52	Zach Wheat	200	250	300	400	1,000	2,000	2,000	4,000
53	Otto Miller	40	50	60	120	150	200	300	450
54	Marty O'Toole	50	60	150	200	300	400	600	800
55	Dick Hoblitzel	40	50	60	100	120	200	300	800
56	Clyde Milan	40	80	100	120	150	200	350	1,000
57	Walter Johnson	2,000	4,000	5,000	6,000	8,000	10,000	12,000	20,000
58	Wally Schang	40	50	60	200	250	300	400	800
59	Harry Gessler	40	50	60	100	120	200	300	800
60	Oscar Dugey	60	150	200	250	300	400	600	800
61	Ray Schalk	200	250	500	600	800	1,000	1,200	4,000
62	Willie Mitchell	40	50	60	100	120	200	400	825
63	Babe Adams	40	50	60	100	120	200	300	925
64	Jimmy Archer	40	100	120	200	250	300	350	750
65	Tris Speaker	600	800	1,000	1,200	2,000	3,000	4,000	5,000
66	Napoleon Lajoie	300	600	800	1,000	1,200	1,500	2,000	8,000
67	Otis Crandall	50	100	200	300	400	500	600	800
68	Honus Wagner	2,500	3,000	4,000	5,000	10,000	12,000	15,000	20,000
69	John McGraw MG	200	250	300	450	500	800	1,200	6,000
70	Fred Clarke	200	400	450	500	600	800	1,300	
71	Chief Meyers	50	60	100	120	150	250	400	1,200
72	John Boehling	40	60	80	120	150	200	300	600
73	Max Carey	200	250	300	400	500	800	1,200	4,000

#	Player	PrFr 1	GD 2	VG 3	VgEx 4	EX 5	ExMt 6	NM 7	NmMt 8
74	Frank Owens	40	50	60	250	400	600	800	1,000
75	Miller Huggins	200	250	300	400	600	800	1,000	2,500
76	Claude Hendrix	40	50	80	100	150	200	400	600
77	Hughie Jennings MG	200	300	400	500	600	800	1,200	3,000
78	Fred Merkle	40	50	60	100	300	400	600	1,000
79	Ping Bodie	40	120	150	200	250	300	400	800
80	Ed Ruelbach	40	50	60	100	200	250	400	800
81	Jim Delahanty	40	50	60	150	200	250	300	
82	Gavvy Cravath	40	50	60	120	150	200	450	1,000
83	Russ Ford	40	50	100	120	150	200	400	
84	Elmer E. Knetzer	50	100	120	150	250	400	500	800
85	Buck Herzog	40	50	60	100	120	300	500	1,000
86	Burt Shotton	40	50	100	200	250	300	350	600
87	Forrest Cady	50	80	120	200	300	500	800	1,200
88	Christy Mathewson	1,200	2,500	3,000	4,000	5,000	6,000	8,000	15,000
89	Lawrence Cheney	50	60	80	120	150	200	400	800
90	Frank Smith	40	50	60	100	120	200	300	1,000
91	Roger Peckinpaugh	40	60	80	120	150		1,000	2,000
92	Al Demaree	80	300	400	500	600	800	1,000	1,500
93	Del Pratt	80	150	200	250	300	400	500	1,200
94	Eddie Cicotte	300	500	800	1,000	1,200	1,500	2,000	4,000
95	Ray Keating	80	250	300	400	500	600	800	1,500
96	Beals Becker	150	250	300	400	500	800	1,200	2,000
97	John (Rube) Benton	40	50	60	200	250	800	1,000	1,200
98	Frank LaPorte	40	50	80	200	250	300	400	600
99	Hal Chase	100	120	200	300	400	500	800	2,500
100	Thomas Seaton	40	50	60	100	120	200	300	600
101	Frank Schulte	40	50	200	300	400	500	600	1,000
102	Ray Fisher	40	100	120	150	200	250	500	800
103	Joe Jackson	10,000	12,000	20,000	25,000	30,000	40,000	50,000	60,000
104	Vic Saier	40	50	60	100	150	200	400	1,200
105	James Lavender	80	150	300	400	500	600	800	1,200
106	Joe Birmingham	40	50	60	120	150	300	400	800
107	Thomas Downey	40	50	60	200	250	300	400	600
108	Sherry Magee	80	100	120	300	400	500	600	1,000
109	Fred Blanding	50	60	120	250	300	400	500	800
110	Bob Bescher	80	150	200	250	300	400	600	2,000
111	Herbie Moran	40	50	120	200	300	400	500	1,000
112	Ed Sweeney	40	50	60	150	200	400	500	1,000
113	George Suggs	40	50	60	200	250	300	400	1,200
114	George Moriarity	40	50	200	300	400	500	600	800
115	Addison Brennan	40	80	100	150	200	400	500	800
116	Rollie Zeider	40	50	60	100	150	250	350	1,000
117	Ted Easterly	40	50	60	100	150	200	300	1,000
118	Ed Konetchy	40	50	250	300	400	500	600	1,000
119	George Perring	40	50	60	200	250	300	400	1,000
120	Mike Doolan	40	200	250	300	400	500	600	1,200
121	Hub Perdue	40	50	60	250	300	400	500	3,000
122	Owen Bush	40	50	60	100	120	200	300	800
123	Slim Sallee	50	80	150	200	250	400	500	600
124	Earl Moore	40	50	60	150	200	250	300	1,000
125	Bert Niehoff	40	120	150	200	250	300	400	2,000
126	Walter Blair	40	150	200	300	400	500	600	1,000
127	Butch Schmidt	40	50	60	100	120	200	300	2,500
128	Steve Evans	50	60	80	250	400	500	600	2,500
129	Ray Caldwell	40	50	60	100	120	200	400	800
130	Ivy Wingo	50	100	120	150	200	250	300	400
131	Geo. Baumgardner	40	100	120	150	200	250	600	4,000
132	Les Nunamaker	60	120	250	300	400	500	800	1,200
133	Branch Rickey MG	250	500	1,000	1,200	1,500	2,000	3,000	5,000
134	Armando Marsans	100	200	250	300	400	500	600	1,500
135	William Killefer	80	150	200	250	300	400	500	1,000
136	Rabbit Maranville	200	250	400	500	800	1,200	2,000	3,000
137	William Rariden	40	50	60	100	120	200	300	1,500
138	Hank Gowdy	40	50	60	100	200	300	400	1,100
139	Rebel Oakes	40	80	150	200	250	300	400	1,500
140	Danny Murphy	50	80	100	120	150	200	400	1,000
141	Cy Barger	40	50	60	150	200	250	300	1,200
142	Eugene Packard	80	150	250	400	500	600	800	1,500
143	Jake Daubert	80	150	200	250	300	400	500	1,000
144	James C. Walsh	40	100	120	150	200	250	300	1,000
145	Ted Cather	40	50	60	100	150	200	300	600
146	George Tyler	40	80	150	250	300	400	500	800
147	Lee Magee	40	50	100	120	150	200	500	800
148	Owen Wilson	40	50	60	200	250	300	400	800
149	Hal Janvrin	40	50	60	100	120	200	350	600
150	Doc Johnston	40	50	100	120	300	400	500	800

		PrFr 1	GD 2	VG 3	VgEx 4	EX 5	ExMt 6	NM 7	NmMt 8
151	George Whitted	40	80	100	150	200	250	400	600
152	George McQuillen	40	50	80	120	150	200	350	1,500
153	Bill James	40	150	200	300	400	500	600	800
154	Dick Rudolph	40	100	120	150	200	250	400	800
155	Joe Connolly	40	50	60	200	250	400	500	800
156	Jean Dubuc	40	50	60	100	120	200	300	1,000
157	George Kaiserling	50	60	80	100	200	300	400	2,000
158	Fritz Maisel	40	150	250	300	400	500	600	1,000
159	Heinie Groh	60	120	250	300	400	500	600	1,200
160	Benny Kauff	50	60	80	120	150	200	300	1,500
161	Edd Roush	250	500	1,000	1,200	1,500	2,000	2,500	4,000
162	George Stallings MG	50	100	200	250	300	400	500	800
163	Bert Whaling	40	50	80	100	120	250	400	800
164	Bob Shawkey	40	50	100	120	150	500	600	1,200
165	Eddie Murphy	50	60	150	200	250	300	400	600
166	Joe Bush	40	50	100	200	250	300	400	1,000
167	Clark Griffith	150	250	300	350	400	600	1,000	4,000
168	Vin Campbell	50	100	120	150	200	250	400	2,500
169	Raymond Collins	40	50	60	100	120	200	300	750
170	Hans Lobert	80	100	120	200	400	500	600	1,000
171	Earl Hamilton	100	120	150	200	250	300	400	800
172	Erskine Mayer	50	100	200	250	300	400	1,000	
173	Tilly Walker	50	100	150	200	300	400	600	3,000
174	Robert Veach	80	100	120	150	200	250	300	2,000
175	Joseph Benz	40	50	60	100	120	200	1,500	2,000
176	Hippo Vaughn	80	100	120	150	300	600		

—Chief Bender #19 PSA 9 (MT) sold for $18,854 (Mastro; 12/07)
—Chief Bender #19 GAI 9 (MT) sold for $8,486 (Mile High; 11/05)
—Roger Bresnahan #17 PSA 9 (MT) sold for $8,932 (Goodwin; 9/12)
—Roger Bresnahan #17 PSA 9 (MT) sold for $6,544 (Mastro; 12/07)
—Mordecai Brown #32 PSA 9 (MT) sold for $40,800 (Mastro; 5/08)
—Mordecai Brown #32 PSA 8 (NmMt) sold for $9,696 (Mastro; 8/07)
—Grover Alexander #37 SGC 92 (NmMt+) sold for $15,405 (REA; 5/13)
—Eddie Cicotte #94 PSA 9 (MT) sold for $10,440 (Bussineau; Fall '13)
—Eddie Cicotte #94 SGC 92 (NmMt+) sold for $7,200 (Mastro; 5/08)
—Fred Clarke PSA 8 (NmMt) sold for $7,337 (SCP; 7/08)
—Ty Cobb #30 SGC 92 (NmMt+) sold for $27,500 (Legendary; 3/10)
—Ty Cobb #30 SGC 92 (NmMt+) sold for $25,000 (REA; 05/12)
—Ty Cobb #30 PSA 8 (NmMt) sold for $39,542 (Mastro; 8/07)
—Ty Cobb #30 SGC 88 (NmMt) sold for $26,286 (Mile High; 6/06)
—Ty Cobb #30 GAI 8 (NmMt) sold for $20,150 (Mile High; 1/07)
—Ty Cobb #30 SGC 88 (NmMt) sold for $19,975 (REA; 4/07)
—Ty Cobb #30 SGC 86 (NrMt+) sold for $17,362 (Mile High; 1/13)
—Ty Cobb #30 SGC 86 (NrMt+) sold for $10,361 (eBay; 9/12)
—Ty Cobb #30 GAI 7.5 (NM+) sold for $12,002 (eBay; 5/06)
—Ty Cobb #30 SGC 7.5 (NM+) sold for $10,000 (REA; 05/12)
—Johnny Evers #18 SGC 96 (MT) sold for $17,003 (Mastro; 8/06)
—Clark Griffith #167 PSA 9 (MT) sold for $14,100 (REA; 4/07)
—Clark Griffith #167 PSA 9 (MT) sold for $8,711 (Mastro; 12/07)
—Joe Jackson #103 SGC 96 (MT) sold for $67,500 (Legendary; 8/10)
—Joe Jackson #103 PSA 8 (NmMt) sold for $60,000 (Memory Lane; Private Sale - 2007)
—Joe Jackson #103 PSA 8 (NmMt) sold for $52,639 (Mastro; 4/06)
—Joe Jackson #103 PSA 8 (NmMt) sold for $41,282 (SCP Sotheby's 5/04)
—Joe Jackson #103 SGC 92 (NmMt+) sold for $38,267 (Goodwin; 9/12)
—Joe Jackson #103 GAI 7.5 (NM+) sold for $17,880 (Memory Lane 12/06)
—Joe Jackson #103 PSA 7 (NM) sold for $24,000 (Mastro; 8/08)
—Joe Jackson #103 PSA 7 (NM) sold for $20,400 (SCP Sotheby's; 6/05)
—Joe Jackson #103 GAI 7 (NM) sold for $16,698 (Memory Lane; 12/06)
—Joe Jackson #103 GAI 7 (NM) sold for $12,076 (Mastro; 2/07)
—Joe Jackson #103 SGC 70 (EX+) sold for $11,488 (Mastro; 12/05)
—Joe Jackson #103 SGC 92 (NmMt+) sold for $38,267 (Goodwin; 10/12)
—Hughie Jennings #77 PSA 9 (MT) sold for $17,100 (Mastro; 12/07)
—Walter Johnson #57 PSA 9 (MT) sold for $41,644 (SCP Sotheby's; 5/04)
—Walter Johnson #57 PSA 9 (MT) sold for $31,998 (SCP Sotheby's; 9/07)
—Walter Johnson #57 SGC 96 (MT) sold for $23,867 (Mile High; 11/10)
—Walter Johnson #57 SGC 96 (MT) sold for $17,925 (Heritage; 8/10)
—Walter Johnson #57 SGC 88 (NmMt) sold for $11,750 (REA; 4/07)
—Walter Johnson #57 SGC 86 (NrMt+) sold for $5,271 (Memory Lane; 5/12)
—Otto Knabe #1 PSA 8 (NmMt) sold for $11,858 (Mastro; 8/07)
—Napoleon Lajoie #66 PSA 9 (MT) sold for $14,864 (Mastro 12/05)
—Napoleon Lajoie #66 PSA 9 (MT) sold for $12,000 (Mastro 5/08)
—Napoleon Lajoie #66 PSA 9 (MT) sold for $9,424 (Mastro 12/07)
—Connie Mack #12 SGC 96 (MT) sold for $12,471 (Goodwin; 11/07)
—Connie Mack #12 PSA 9 (MT) sold for $8,711 (Mastro; 12/07)
—Rabbit Maranville #136 PSA 10 (Gem) sold for $28,770 (Mastro; 12/07)
—Christy Mathewson #88 PSA 9 (MT) sold for $37,781 (Goodwin; 6/06)
—Christy Mathewson #88 SGC 96 (MT) sold for $12,000 (Legendary; 11/10)

—Christy Mathewson #88 SGC 92 (NmMt+) sold for $19,540 (Mastro; 12/06)
—Christy Mathewson #88 SGC 92 (NmMt+) sold for $16,450 (REA; 5/08)
—Christy Mathewson #88 SGC 92 (NmMt+) sold for $14,045 (Mastro; 4/07)
—Christy Mathewson #88 SGC 86 (NM+) sold for $9,494 (Mastro; 4/06)
—Christy Mathewson #88 SGC 92 (NmMt+) sold for $13,920 (Greg Bussineau; 7/12)
—Christy Mathewson #88 SGC 92 (NmMt+) sold for $12,545 (SCP; 9/12)
—Christy Mathewson #88 SGC 86 (NrMt) sold for $5,616 (Goodwin; 7/12)
—Erskine Mayer #172 PSA 9 (MT) sold for $10,237 (Mastro; 12/07)
—Marty O'Toole #54 PSA 10 (Gem) sold for $13,045 (Mastro; 12/07)
—Tris Speaker #65 PSA 9 (MT) sold for $12,131 (Mastro; 12/07)
—Hippo Vaughn #176 PSA 8 (NmMt) sold for $13,045 (Mastro; 12/07)
—Hippo Vaughn #176 PSA 7 (NM) sold for $2,760 (Mastro; 5/08)
—Ed Walsh #36 PSA 9 (MT) sold for $11,596 (Mastro; 12/07)
—Honus Wagner #68 SGC 92 (NmMt+) sold for $14,299 (Mile High; 12/13)
—Honus Wagner #68 SGC 92 (NmMt+) sold for $14,153 (SCP; 11/10)
—Joe Wood #22 SGC 92 (NmMt+) sold for $4,460 (Memory Lane; 5/08)

1916 M101-4 Blank Back

		PrFr 1	GD 2	VG 3	VgEx 4	EX 5	ExMt 6	NM 7	NmMt 8
2	Sam Agnew Red Sox	20	25	30	50	60	80	120	200
8	H. D. Baird C.F.	20	25	30	50	60	80	120	200
9	J. Franklin Baker	60	80	150	200	250	300	400	800
10	Dave Bancroft	60	120	150	200	250	300	550	800
11	Jack Barry	20	25	30	50	60	80	120	200
12	Zinn Beck	20	25	30	50	60	80	120	200
13	Chief Bender	60	80	100	200	250	300	400	800
14	Joe Benz	20	25	30	50	60	80	120	200
15	Bob Bescher	20	25	30	50	60	80	120	200
16	Al Betzel 2nd B.	20	25	30	50	60	80	120	200
17	Mordecai Brown	60	80	100	150	200	250	400	800
18	Eddie Burns	20	25	30	50	60	80	120	200
19	George Burns	20	25	30	50	60	80	120	200
20	Geo. J. Burns	20	25	50	60	80	100	120	200
21	Joe Bush	20	25	30	50	60	80	120	200
22	Donie Bush	20	25	30	50	80	100	120	200
23	Art Butler	20	25	30	50	60	80	120	200
24	Bobbie Byrne	20	25	30	50	60	80	120	200
25	Forrest Cady	20	25	30	50	60	80	120	200
26	Jimmy Callahan	20	25	30	50	60	80	120	200
27	Ray Caldwell	20	25	30	50	60	80	120	200
28	Max Carey	60	80	120	150	200	250	400	800
29	George Chalmers	20	25	30	50	60	80	120	200
30	Ray Chapman	20	25	30	50	60	80	120	200
31	Larry Cheney	20	25	30	50	80	100	120	200
32	Eddie Cicotte	60	80	100	150	200	250	400	800
33	Tom Clarke	20	25	30	50	60	80	120	200
34	Eddie Collins	60	80	100	150	200	250	400	800
35	Shauno Collins	20	25	30	50	60	80	250	300
36	Charles Comiskey	60	80	100	150	200	250	400	800
37	Joe Connolly	20	25	30	50	60	80	120	200
38	Ty Cobb	1,000	1,200	1,500	2,000	2,500	3,000	8,000	
39	Harry Coveleskie (Coveleski)	20	25	30	50	60	80	120	200
40	Gavvy Cravath	20	25	30	50	60	80	120	200
41	Sam Crawford	60	80	100	150	200	250	400	800
42	Jean Dale	20	25	30	50	60	80	120	200
43	Jake Daubert	20	25	30	50	60	80	120	200
44	Charles Deal	20	25	30	50	60	80	120	200
45	Al Demaree	20	25	30	50	60	80	120	200
46	Josh Devore	20	25	30	50	60	80	120	200
47	William Doak	20	25	30	50	60	80	120	200
48	Bill Donovan	20	25	30	50	60	80	120	200
49	Charles Dooin	20	25	30	50	60	80	120	200
50	Mike Doolan	20	25	30	50	60	80	120	200
51	Larry Doyle	20	25	30	50	60	80	120	200
52	Jean Dubuc	20	25	30	50	60	80	120	200
53	Oscar Dugey	20	25	30	50	60	80	120	200
54	Johnny Evers	60	80	100	150	200	250	400	800
55	Urban Faber	50	60	80	120	150	200	300	500
56	Hap Felsch C.F.	40	50	60	700	800	900	1,000	1,200
57	Bill Fischer	20	25	30	50	60	80	120	200
58	Ray Fisher Pitching	20	25	30	50	60	80	120	200
59	Max Flack	20	25	30	50	60	80	150	200
60	Art Fletcher	20	25	30	50	60	80	120	200
61	Eddie Foster	20	25	30	50	60	80	120	200
62	Jacques Fournier	20	25	30	50	60	80	120	200
63	Del Gainer (Gainor)	20	25	30	50	60	80	120	200

#		PrFr 1	GD 2	VG 3	VgEx 4	EX 5	ExMt 6	NM 7	NmMt 8
	Chick Gandil	20	25	30	50	60	80	120	200
	Geo. Gibson (eo Missing)	20	25	30	50	60	80	120	200
2	Clark Griffith	50	60	100	120	150	200	300	500
3	Tom Griffith	20	25	30	50	60	80	120	200
4	Heinie Groh	20	25	30	50	60	80	120	200
	Earl Hamilton	20	25	30	50	60	80	120	200
	Bob Harmon	20	25	30	50	60	80	120	200
	Roy Hartzell Americans	20	25	30	50	80	100	120	200
	Claude Hendrix	20	25	30	50	60	80	120	200
	Olaf Henriksen	20	25	30	50	60	80	120	200
	John Henry	20	25	30	50	60	80	120	200
	Buck Herzog	20	25	30	50	60	80	120	200
2	Hugh High	20	25	30	50	60	80	120	200
3	Dick Hoblitzell	20	25	30	50	60	80	120	200
4	Harry Hooper	50	60	80	120	150	200	300	500
5	Ivan Howard 3rd B.	20	25	30	50	60	80	120	200
6	Miller Huggins	50	60	80	120	150	200	300	500
7	Joe Jackson	2,000	2,500	3,000	4,200	5,000	8,000	10,000	25,000
8	William James	20	25	30	50	60	80	120	200
9	Harold Janvrin	20	25	30	50	60	80	120	200
0	Hughie Jennings	50	60	80	120	150	200	300	500
1	Walter Johnson	200	250	300	500	800	1,000	1,500	
2	Fielder Jones	20	25	30	50	60	80	120	200
3	Joe Judge	20	25	30	50	60	80	120	200
4	Benny Kauff	20	25	30	50	60	80	120	200
5	Wm. Killefer Jr.	20	25	30	50	60	80	120	200
6	Ed. Konetchy	20	25	30	50	60	80	120	200
7	Napoleon Lajoie	100	200	250	300	400	500	600	1,200
8	Jack Lapp	20	25	30	50	60	80	120	200
9	John Lavan	20	25	30	50	60	80	120	200
00	Jimmy Lavender	20	25	30	50	60	80	120	200
01	Nemo Leibold	20	25	30	50	60	80	120	200
02	H. B. Leonard	20	25	30	50	60	80	120	200
03	Duffy Lewis	20	25	30	50	60	80	120	200
04	Hans Lobert	20	25	30	50	60	80	120	200
05	Tom Long	20	25	30	50	60	80	120	200
06	Fred Luderus	20	25	30	50	60	80	120	200
07	Connie Mack	80	100	120	200	250	300	500	1,000
08	Lee Magee L.F.	20	25	30	50	60	80	120	200
09	Sherwood Magee	20	25	30	50	60	80	120	200
10	Al. Mamaux	20	25	30	50	60	80	120	200
11	Leslie Mann L.F.	20	25	30	50	60	80	120	200
12	Rabbit Maranville	60	80	100	150	200	250	400	
13	Rube Marquard	60	80	100	150	200	250	400	800
114	J. Erskine Mayer	20	25	30	50	60	80	120	200
115	George McBride	20	25	30	50	60	80	120	200
116	John J. McGraw	60	80	100	150	200	250	400	800
17	Jack McInnis	20	25	30	80	100	120	150	200
118	Fred Merkle	20	25	30	50	60	200	250	300
119	Chief Meyers	20	25	30	50	60	80	120	200
120	Clyde Milan	20	25	30	50	60	80	120	200
121	John Miller	20	25	30	50	60	80	120	200
122	Otto Miller	20	25	30	50	80	100	120	200
123	Willie Mitchell	20	25	30	50	60	80	120	200
124	Fred Mollwitz	20	25	30	50	60	80	120	200
125	Pat Moran	20	25	30	50	60	80	120	200
126	Ray Morgan	20	25	30	50	60	80	120	200
127	Geo. Moriarty	20	25	30	50	60	80	120	200
128	Guy Morton	20	25	30	50	60	80	250	300
129	Mike Mowrey	20	25	30	50	60	80	120	200
130	Ed. Murphy	20	25	30	50	60	80	120	200
131	Hy Myers	20	25	30	50	60	80	120	200
132	J. A. Niehoff	20	25	30	50	60	80	120	200
133	Rube Oldring	20	25	30	50	60	80	120	200
134	Oliver O'Mara	20	25	30	50	60	80	120	200
135	Steve O'Neill	20	25	30	50	60	80	120	200
136	Dode Paskert C.F.	20	25	30	50	60	80	120	200
137	Roger Peckinpaugh	20	25	30	50	60	80	120	200
138	Wally Pipp	20	25	30	50	60	80	120	200
139	Derril Pratt (Derrill)	20	25	30	50	60	80	120	200
140	Pat Ragan	20	25	30	50	60	80	120	200
145	Bob Roth R.F.	20	25	30	50	60	80	120	200
146	Ed. Rousch R.F. (Roush)	60	80	100	150	200	250	400	800
154	Ray Schalk	50	60	80	120	150	200	300	500
155	Walter Schang	20	25	30	50	60	80	120	200
156	Frank Schulte	20	25	30	50	60	80	120	200
157	Everett Scott	20	25	30	50	60	80	120	200
158	Jim Scott	20	25	30	50	60	80	120	200
159	Tom Seaton	20	25	30	50	60	80	120	200
160	Howard Shanks	20	25	30	50	60	80	120	200
161	Bob Shawkey	20	25	30	50	60	80	120	200
162	Ernie Shore	20	25	30	50	60	80	120	200
163	Burt Shotton	20	25	30	50	60	80	120	200
164	Geo. Sisler 1st B.	60	80	100	150	200	250	400	800
165	J. Carlisle Smith	20	25	30	50	60	80	120	200
166	Fred Snodgrass	20	25	30	50	60	80	120	200
167	Geo. Stallings	20	25	30	50	60	80	120	200
168A	Oscar Stanage Portrait SP	20	25	30	50	60	80	120	200
168B	Oscar Stanage Catching								
169	Charles Stengel	200	250	300	500	600	800	1,200	2,000
170	Milton Stock	20	25	30	50	60	80	120	200
171	Amos Strunk	20	25	30	50	60	80	120	200
172	Billy Sullivan	20	25	30	50	60	80	120	200
173	Jeff Tesreau	20	25	30	50	60	80	120	200
174	Joe Tinker	60	80	100	150	200	250	400	800
175	Fred Toney	20	25	30	50	60	80	120	200
176	Terry Turner 2nd B.	20	25	30	50	60	80	120	200
177	George Tyler	20	25	30	50	60	80	120	200
178	Jim Vaughn	20	25	30	50	60	80	120	200
179	Bob Veach	20	25	30	50	60	80	120	200
180	James Viox 3rd B.	20	25	30	50	60	80	120	200
181	Oscar Vitt	20	25	30	50	60	80	120	200
182	Hans Wagner	900	1,000	1,100	1,200	1,800	2,000	3,000	
183	Clarence Walker Red Sox	20	25	30	50	60	80	120	200
184	Ed. Walsh	60	80	100	150	200	250	400	800
185	W. Wambsganss UER Photo	20	25	30	50	60	80	120	200
186	Buck Weaver 3rd B.	60	80	100	150	200	250	400	800
187	Carl Weilman	20	25	30	50	60	80	120	200
188	Zach Wheat	60	80	100	150	200	250	400	800
189	Geo. Whitted Nationals	20	25	30	50	60	80	120	200
190	Fred Williams	20	25	30	50	60	80	120	200
191	Art Wilson	20	25	30	50	60	80	120	200
192	J. Owen Wilson	20	25	30	50	60	80	120	200
193	Ivy Wingo	20	25	30	50	60	80	120	200
194	Mel Wolfgang	20	25	30	50	60	80	120	200
195	Joe Wood	80	100	120	200	250	300	500	1,000
196	Steve Yerkes	20	25	30	50	60	80	120	200
197	Pep Young	20	25	30	50	60	80	120	200

—Ty Cobb #38 PSA 7 (NM) sold for $10,237 (Mastro; 4/07)
—George Sisler #166 PSA 8 (NmMt) sold for $3,528 (Clean Sweep; 2/08)

1916 M101-4 Sporting News

#		PrFr 1	GD 2	VG 3	VgEx 4	EX 5	ExMt 6	NM 7	NmMt 8
151	Babe Ruth	35,000	50,000	60,000	65,000	90,000	200,000	300,000	

—Joe Jackson SGC 50 (Vg/Ex) sold for $6,422 (Goodwin; 3/12)
—Babe Ruth PSA 6 (ExMt) sold for $54,713 (SCP; 7/08)
—Babe Ruth PSA 1 (Poor) sold for $30,343 (SCP; 5/12)
—Babe Ruth PSA 6 (ExMt) sold for $30,000 (SCP Sotheby's; 6/05)
—Babe Ruth PSA 6 (ExMt) sold for $28,969 (Mastro; 12/05)
—Babe Ruth PSA 3 (VG) sold for $27,500 (Legendary; 3/11)
—Babe Ruth PSA 5 (EX) sold for $26,438 (REA; 4/07)
—Babe Ruth PSA 6 (ExMt) sold for $26,335 (Mastro; 4/06)
—Babe Ruth SGC 70 (EX+) sold for $25,234 (Mastro; 4/07)

1916 M101-5 Blank Back

#		PrFr 1	GD 2	VG 3	VgEx 4	EX 5	ExMt 6	NM 7	NmMt 8
1	Babe Adams *	20	25	30	50	60	80	120	200
2	Sam Agnew Browns	20	25	30	50	60	80	120	200
3	Ed Ainsmith *	20	25	30	50	60	80	120	200
4	Grover Alexander *	100	120	150	650				
5	Leon Ames *	20	25	30	50	60	80	120	200
6	Jimmy Archer *	20	25	30	50	60	80	120	200
7	Jimmy Austin *	20	25	30	50	60	80	120	200
8	J. Franklin Baker *	60	80	100	150	200	250	400	800
9	Dave Bancroft	60	80	100	150	200	250	400	900
10	Jack Barry	20	25	30	50	60	80	175	250
11	Zinn Beck	20	25	30	50	60	80	120	200
12B	Lute Boone *	20	25	30	50	60	80	120	200
13	Joe Benz	20	25	30	50	60	80	120	200
14	Bob Bescher	20	25	30	50	60	80	120	200
15	Al Betzel 3rd B.	20	25	30	50	60	80	120	200
16	Roger Bresnahan	60	80	100	150	200	250	400	800

#	Player	PrFr 1	GD 2	VG 3	VgEx 4	EX 5	ExMt 6	NM 7	NmMt 8
17	Eddie Burns	20	25	30	50	60	80	120	200
18	Geo. J. Burns	20	25	30	50	60	80	120	200
19	Joe Bush Jr.	20	25	30	50	60	80	120	200
20	Owen J. Bush	20	25	30	50	60	80	120	200
21	Art Butler	20	25	30	50	60	80	120	200
22	Bobby Byrne	20	25	30	50	60	80	120	200
23A	Mordecai Brown	60	80	100	150	200	250	1,100	2,000
24	Jimmy Callahan	20	25	30	50	60	80	120	200
25	Ray Caldwell	20	25	30	50	60	80	120	200
26	Max Carey	60	80	100	150	200	250	400	800
27	George Chalmers	20	25	30	50	60	80	120	200
28	Frank Chance	60	80	100	150	200	250	400	800
29	Ray Chapman	20	25	30	50	60	80	120	200
30	Larry Cheney	20	25	30	50	60	80	120	200
31	Eddie Cicotte	60	80	100	150	200	250	400	800
32	Tom Clarke	20	25	30	50	60	80	120	200
33	Eddie Collins	60	80	100	150	200	250	400	800
34	Shauno Collins	20	25	30	50	60	80	120	200
35	Charles Comisky (Comiskey)	60	80	100	150	200	250	400	800
36	Joe Connolly	20	25	30	50	60	80	120	200
37	Luther Cook	20	25	30	50	60	80	120	200
38	Jack Coombs	40	50	60	100	120	150	250	400
39	Dan Costello	20	25	30	50	60	80	120	200
40	Harry Coveleskie (Coveleski)	20	25	30	50	60	80	120	200
41	Gavvy Cravath	20	25	30	50	60	80	120	200
42	Sam Crawford	60	80	100	150	200	250	400	800
43	Jean Dale	20	25	30	50	60	80	120	200
44	Jake Daubert	20	25	30	50	60	80	120	200
45	Geo. A. Davis Jr.	20	25	30	50	60	80	120	200
46	Charles Deal	20	25	30	50	60	80	120	200
47	Al Demaree	20	25	30	50	60	80	120	200
48	William Doak	20	25	30	50	60	80	120	200
49	Bill Donovan	20	25	30	50	60	80	120	200
50	Charles Dooin	20	25	30	50	60	80	120	200
51	Mike Doolan	20	25	30	50	60	80	120	200
52	Larry Doyle	20	25	30	50	60	80	120	200
53	Jean Dubuc	20	25	30	50	60	80	120	200
54	Oscar Dugey	20	25	30	50	60	80	120	200
55	Johnny Evers	60	80	100	150	200	250	400	800
56	Urban Faber	50	60	80	120	150	200	300	500
57	Hap Felsch R.F.	40	50	60	100	120	150	1,000	1,200
58	Bill Fischer	20	25	30	50	60	80	120	200
59	Ray Fisher Hands Over Head	20	25	30	50	60	80	120	200
60	Max Flack	20	25	30	50	60	80	120	200
61	Art Fletcher	20	25	30	50	60	80	120	200
62	Eddie Foster	20	25	30	50	60	80	120	200
63	Jacques Fournier	20	25	30	50	60	80	120	200
64	Del Gainer (Gainor)	20	25	30	50	60	80	120	200
65	Larry Gardner *	20	25	30	50	60	80	120	200
66	Joe Gedeon *	20	25	30	50	60	80	120	200
67	Gus Getz *	20	25	30	50	60	80	120	200
68	Geo. Gibson (eo Not Missing)	20	25	30	50	60	80	120	200
69	Wilbur Good *	20	25	30	50	60	80	120	200
70	Hank Gowdy *	20	25	30	50	60	80	120	200
71	Jack Graney *	20	25	30	50	60	80	120	200
72	Tom Griffith	20	25	30	50	60	80	120	200
73	Heinie Groh	20	25	30	50	60	80	120	200
74	Earl Hamilton	20	25	30	50	60	80	120	200
75	Bob Harmon	20	25	30	50	60	80	120	200
76	Roy Hartzell Am.	20	25	30	50	60	80	120	200
77	Claude Hendrix	20	25	30	50	60	80	120	200
78	Olaf Henriksen	20	25	30	50	60	80	120	200
79	John Henry	20	25	30	50	60	80	120	200
80	Buck Herzog	20	25	30	50	60	80	120	200
81	Hugh High	20	25	30	50	60	80	120	200
82	Dick Hoblitzell	20	25	30	50	60	80	120	200
83	Harry Hooper	50	60	80	120	150	200	300	500
84	Ivan Howard 1st B.	20	25	30	50	60	80	120	200
85	Miller Huggins	50	60	80	120	150	200	300	500
86	Joe Jackson	2,000	2,500	3,000	5,000	6,000	10,000	12,000	20,000
87	William James	20	25	30	50	60	80	120	200
88	Harold Janvrin	20	25	30	50	60	80	120	200
89	Hughie Jennings	50	60	80	120	150	200	300	500
90	Walter Johnson	200	250	300	500	800	1,200	4,200	
91	Fielder Jones	20	25	30	50	60	80	120	200
92	Benny Kauff	20	25	30	50	60	80	120	200
93	Wm. Killefer Jr.	20	25	30	50	60	80	120	200
94	Ed. Konetchy	20	25	30	50	60	80	120	200
95	Napoleon Lajoie	100	120	150	250	300	400	600	1,200
96	Jack Lapp	20	25	30	50	60	80	120	200
97	John Lavan	20	25	30	50	60	80	120	200
98	Jimmy Lavender	20	25	30	50	60	80	120	200
99	Nemo Leibold	20	25	30	50	60	80	120	200
100	H. B. Leonard	20	25	30	50	60	80	120	200
101	Duffy Lewis	20	25	30	50	60	80	120	200
102	Hans Lobert	20	25	30	50	60	80	120	200
103	Tom Long	20	25	30	50	60	80	120	200
104	Fred Luderus	20	25	30	50	60	80	120	200
105	Connie Mack	80	100	120	200	250	300	500	1,000
106	Lee Magee 2nd B.	20	25	30	50	60	80	120	200
107	Al. Mamaux	20	25	30	50	60	80	120	200
108	Leslie Mann C.F.	20	25	30	50	60	80	120	200
109	Rabbit Maranville	60	80	100	150	200	250	400	800
110	Rube Marquard	60	80	100	150	200	425	600	800
111	Armando Marsans	20	25	30	50	60	80	120	200
112	J. Erskine Mayer	20	25	30	50	60	80	120	200
113	George McBride	20	25	30	50	60	80	120	200
114	John J. McGraw	60	80	100	150	200	250	400	800
115	Jack McInnis	20	25	30	50	60	80	120	250
116	Fred Merkle	20	25	30	50	60	80	120	200
117	Chief Meyers	20	25	30	50	60	80	120	200
118	Clyde Milan	20	25	30	50	60	80	120	200
119	Otto Miller	20	25	30	50	60	80	120	200
120	Willie Mitchel (Mitchell)	20	25	30	50	60	80	120	200
121	Fred Mollwitz	20	25	30	50	60	80	120	200
122	J. Herbert Moran	20	25	30	50	60	80	120	200
123	Pat Moran	20	25	30	50	60	80	120	200
124	Ray Morgan	20	25	30	50	60	80	120	200
125	Geo. Moriarty	20	25	30	50	60	80	120	200
126	Guy Morton	20	25	30	50	60	80	120	200
127	Ed. Murphy UER Photo	20	25	30	50	60	80	120	200
128	John Murray	20	25	30	50	60	80	120	200
129	Hy Myers	20	25	30	50	60	80	120	200
130	J. A. Niehoff	20	25	30	50	60	80	120	200
131	Leslie Nunamaker	20	25	30	50	60	80	120	300
132	Rube Oldring	20	25	30	50	60	80	120	200
133	Oliver O'Mara	20	25	30	50	60	80	120	200
134	Steve O'Neill	20	25	30	50	60	80	120	200
135	Dode Paskert C.	20	25	30	50	60	80	120	200
136	Roger Peckinpaugh UER Photo	20	25	30	50	60	80	120	200
137	E. J. Pfeffer	20	25	30	50	60	80	120	200
138	Geo. Pierce (Pearce)	20	25	30	50	60	80	120	200
139	Wally Pipp	20	25	30	50	60	80	120	200
140	Derril Pratt (Derrill)	20	25	30	50	60	80	120	200
141	Bill Rariden *	20	25	30	50	60	80	120	200
142	Eppa Rixey *	50	60	80	120	150	200	300	500
143	Davey Robertson *	20	25	30	50	60	80	120	200
144	Wilbert Robinson *	50	60	80	120	150	475	600	800
145	Bob Roth C.F.	20	25	30	50	60	80	120	200
146	Ed. Roush C.F.	60	80	100	150	200	250	400	800
147	Clarence Rowland *	20	25	30	50	60	80	120	200
148	Nap Rucker *	20	25	30	50	60	80	120	200
149	Dick Rudolph *	20	25	30	50	60	80	120	200
150	Reb Russell *	20	25	30	50	60	80	120	200
151	Babe Ruth *	35,000	50,000	60,000	65,000	80,000	120,000	200,000	
152	Vic Saier *	20	25	30	50	60	80	120	200
153	Slim Sallee *	20	25	30	50	60	80	120	200
154	Germany Schaefer	20	25	30	50	60	80	120	250
155	Ray Schalk	50	60	80	120	150	200	300	500
156	Walter Schang	20	25	30	50	60	80	120	200
157	Chas. Schmidt	20	25	30	50	60	80	120	200
158	Frank Schulte	20	25	30	50	60	80	120	200
159	Jim Scott	20	25	30	50	60	80	120	200
160	Everett Scott	20	25	30	50	60	80	120	200
161	Tom Seaton	20	25	30	50	60	80	120	200
162	Howard Shanks	20	25	30	50	60	80	120	200
163	Bob Shawkey UER Photo	20	25	30	50	60	80	120	200
164	Ernie Shore	20	25	30	50	60	80	120	200
165	Burt Shotton	20	25	30	50	60	80	120	200
166	Geo. Sisler P	60	80	100	150	200	250	1,200	1,600
167	J. Carlisle Smith	20	25	30	50	60	80	120	200
168	Fred Snodgrass	20	25	30	50	60	80	120	200
169	Geo. Stallings	20	25	30	50	60	80	120	200
170	Oscar Stanage UER Photo	20	25	30	50	60	80	120	200

		PrFr 1	GD 2	VG 3	VgEx 4	EX 5	ExMt 6	NM 7	NmMt 8
71	Charles Stengel	200	250	300	500	1,400	1,600	2,000	2,600
72	Milton Stock	20	25	30	50	60	80	120	200
73	Amos Strunk UER Photo	20	25	30	50	60	80	120	200
74	Billy Sullivan	20	25	30	50	60	80	120	200
75	Jeff Tesreau	20	25	30	50	60	80	120	200
76	Jim Thorpe	2,500	3,000	4,000	5,000				
77	Joe Tinker	60	80	100	150	200	250	400	800
78	Fred Toney	20	25	30	50	60	80	120	200
79	Terry Turner 3rd B.	20	25	30	50	60	80	120	200
80	Jim Vaughn	20	25	30	50	60	80	120	200
81	Bob Veach	20	25	30	50	60	80	120	300
82	James Viox 2nd B.	20	25	30	50	60	80	120	200
83	Oscar Vitt	20	25	30	50	60	80	120	200
84	Hans Wagner	600	800	1,000	1,200	1,500	2,000	3,000	
85	Clarence Walker								
	Browns UER Photo	20	25	30	50	60	80	120	200
86A	Zach Wheat	60	80	100	150	200	250	400	800
87	Ed. Walsh	60	80	100	150	200	250	400	800
88	Buck Weaver S.S.	120	150	250	400	600			
89	Carl Weilman	20	25	30	50	60	80	120	200
90	Geo. Whitted Nat'ls	20	25	30	50	60	80	120	200
91	Fred Williams	20	25	30	50	60	80	120	200
92	Art Wilson	20	25	30	50	60	80	120	200
93	J. Owen Wilson	20	25	30	50	60	80	120	200
94	Ivy Wingo	20	25	30	50	60	80	120	200
95	Mel Wolfgang	20	25	30	50	60	80	120	200
96	Joe Wood	80	100	120	200	250	300	500	1,000
97	Steve Yerkes	20	25	30	50	60	80	120	200
98	Rollie Zeider *	20	25	30	50	60	80	120	200
99	Heiny Zimmerman *	20	25	30	50	60	80	120	200
100	Ed. Zwilling *	20	25	30	50	60	80	120	200

—Babe Ruth #151 PSA 7 (NrMt) sold for $200,169 (Goodwin; 1/12)
—Babe Ruth #151 PSA 8 (NmMt) sold for $165,282 (Mile High; 12/05)
—Babe Ruth #151 PSA 8 (NmMt) sold for $120,000 (SCP Sotheby's; 6/05)
—Babe Ruth #151 SGC 5.5 (Ex+) sold for $84,000 (REA; Fall '14)
—George Sisler P #166 PSA 9 (MT) sold for $18,336 (Goodwin; 09/11)
—Jim Thorpe #176 GAI 8 (NmMt) sold for $37,032 (SCP; 7/08)
—Jim Thorpe #176 PSA 8 OC (NmMt OC) sold for $44,063 (REA; 5/08)
—Jim Thorpe #176 SGC 80 (ExMt) sold for $11,596 (Mastro; 12/07)
—Jim Thorpe #176 PSA 6 (ExMt) sold for $11,511 (Goodwin; 03/12)
—Jim Thorpe #176 PSA 5 (EX) sold for $7,870 (eBay; 6/08)
—Jim Thorpe #176 PSA 6 (ExMt) sold for $11,511 (Goodwin; 3/12)

1919-21 W514

		PrFr 1	GD 2	VG 3	VgEx 4	EX 5	ExMt 6	NM 7	NmMt 8
2	Babe Ruth	800	1,000	1,200	1,500	1,800	2,200		
15	Joe Jackson	800	1,000	2,000	2,200	2,500	3,000		
43	Ty Cobb	200	250	300	400	500	800		
56	Rogers Hornsby	100	120	200	250	300	500		
72	Christy Mathewson	120	150	200	250	300	500		
94	Walter Johnson	100	120	300	350	400	600		

—Joe Jackson SGC 96 (MT) sold for $6,552 (Mastro; 8/06)
—Joe Jackson SGC 96 (MT) sold for $4,821 (Mastro; 12/08)
—Joe Jackson PSA 8 (NmMt) sold for $5,280 (Greg Bussineau; 12/12)
—Joe Jackson SGC 88 (NmMt) sold for $5,070 (Mile High; 1/07)
—Walter Johnson SGC 92 (NmMt+) sold for $650 (eBay; 6/08)
—Walter Johnson PSA 7 (NM) sold for $1,700 (Arlington, TX Show, 6/07)
—Christy Mathewson SGC 88 (NmMt) sold for $1,327 (Mastro; 8/06)
—Babe Ruth SGC 84 (NM) sold for $5,558 (Mastro; 8/06)

1921 E121 American Caramel Series of 80

		PrFr 1	GD 2	VG 3	VgEx 4	EX 5	ExMt 6	NM 7	NmMt 8
1A	G.C. Alexander Arms Above	200	250	300	500	800	1,200		
1B	Grover Alexander Arm Forward	200	250	300	500	800	1,200		
11A	Ty Cobb Look Ahead	300	500	600	1,000	1,200			
11B	Ty Cobb Look Right Manager	400	500	600	1,000	1,200			
11C	Ty Cobb Look Right Mgr.	300	500	600	1,000	2,000			
38	Rogers Hornsby	250	300	400	500	1,200			
43A	Walter Johnson Throwing	250	350	500	800	1,000			
43B	Walter Johnson Hands at Chest	250	350	500	800	1,000			
82A	Babe Ruth	2,500	8,000	10,000	12,000	10,000	12,000		
82B	Babe Ruth Babe in Quotations	2,000	4,000	10,000	12,000				
82C	George Ruth	1,500	2,000	25,000					

		PrFr 1	GD 2	VG 3	VgEx 4	EX 5	ExMt 6	NM 7	NmMt 8
94A	Tris Speaker Manager Large	100	120	150	200	400			
94B	Tris Speaker Manager Small	100	120	150	200				
94C	Tris Speaker Mgr.	100	120	150	200	400			

—Ty Cobb Look Right Manager PSA 6 (ExMt) sold for $4,800 (eBay; 6/08)
—Ty Cobb Look Right Mgr. PSA 6 (ExMt) sold for $8,365 (Heritage; 5/08)
—Ty Cobb #11C PSA 8 (NmMt) sold for $9,049 (Goodwin; 8/12)
—Rogers Hornsby PSA 6 (ExMt) sold for $4,706 (eBay; 8/07)
—Babe Ruth SGC 86 (NM+) sold for $31,755 (Goodwin; 3/14)
—Babe Ruth PSA 7 (NM) sold for $23,200 (REA; 4/06)
—Babe Ruth PSA 7 (NM) sold for $22,705 (Heritage; 10/07)
—George Ruth PSA 7 PD (NM - Print Defect) sold for $11,696 (eBay; 1/07)

1921 W551

		PrFr 1	GD 2	VG 3	VgEx 4	EX 5	ExMt 6	NM 7	NmMt 8
4	Ty Cobb	200	250	350	400	500	800		
7	Babe Ruth	200	250	300	800	1,200			

—Ty Cobb PSA 9 (MT) sold for $3,472 (Goodwin; 2/06)
—Ty Cobb SGC 88 (NmMt) sold for $1,066 (Mile High 1/07)
—Babe Ruth PSA 9 (MT) sold for $8,075 (eBay; 2/13)
—Babe Ruth PSA 8 (NmMt) sold for $2,704 (Memory Lane; 5/08)
—Babe Ruth SGC 84 (NM) sold for $1,093 (Huggins and Scott; 10/07)

1922 E120 American Caramel Series of 240

		PrFr 1	GD 2	VG 3	VgEx 4	EX 5	ExMt 6	NM 7	NmMt 8
42	Tris Speaker	100	120	150	300	400	500		
48	Ty Cobb	250	350	600	1,000	1,200	2,000		
71	Babe Ruth	1,500	3,000	5,000	8,000				
110	Walter Johnson	150	200	400	500	800	1,000		
152	Grover C. Alexander	150	200	400	500	600	1,000		
232	Rogers Hornsby	150	200	300	500	600			

—Babe Ruth PSA 5 (EX) sold for $8,183 (Goodwin; 8/07)

1922 E121 American Caramel Series of 120

		PrFr 1	GD 2	VG 3	VgEx 4	EX 5	ExMt 6	NM 7	NmMt 8
2	Grover C. Alexander	120	150	200	350	500	800		
10A	Ty Cobb Batting	500	1,000	1,200	1,500	2,000			
10B	Ty Cobb Throwing	500	1,000	1,200	1,500	2,000			
45	Rogers Hornsby	150	250	450	600	800	1,200		
48	Walter Johnson	200	350	400	600	1,000	1,500		
86A	Babe Ruth Montage	1,000	1,500	3,000	4,000	5,000	6,000		
86B	Babe Ruth Montage (Quotations)	1,000	2,000	3,000	4,000	5,000	6,000		
86C	Babe Ruth Bird	600	1,000	2,000	2,500	4,000	5,000		
86D	Babe Ruth Bird (Quotations)	600	1,000	2,000	2,500	4,000	5,000		
86E	Babe Ruth Holding Ball	1,000	1,500	2,000	3,000	5,000	6,000		
102A	Tris Speaker Large Projection	120	150	200	300	500	800		
102B	Tris Speaker Small Projection	120	150	200	300	500	800		

1922 E122 American Caramel Series of 80

		PrFr 1	GD 2	VG 3	VgEx 4	EX 5	ExMt 6	NM 7	NmMt 8
1	Grover C. Alexander	120	150	200	300	500	800		
11	Ty Cobb	300	400	500	800	1,200	2,000		
30	Rogers Hornsby	120	150	200	300	500	800		
32	Walter Johnson	150	200	250	400	600	1,000		
57	Babe Ruth	1,000	1,500	4,500					
67	Tris Speaker	120	150	200	300	500	800		

1923 W515-1

		PrFr 1	GD 2	VG 3	VgEx 4	EX 5	ExMt 6	NM 7	NmMt 8
3	Babe Ruth	400	500	600	700	800	900	1,100	
47	Babe Ruth	400	500	600	700	800	900	1,100	

—Babe Ruth #47 PSA 8 (NmMt) sold for $1,531 (Clean Sweep; 2/06)

1925 Exhibits

		PrFr 1	GD 2	VG 3	VgEx 4	EX 5	ExMt 6	NM 7	NmMt 8
90	Tyrus Cobb	80	120	200	300	500	800		
97	Lou Gehrig	10,000	25,000	30,000	35,000	80,000			
100	Babe Ruth	800	1,200	1,500	2,500	4,000			

—Lou Gehrig SGC 80 (ExMt) sold for $25,200 (Mastro; 8/07)
—Lou Gehrig #97 PSA 6 (ExMt) sold for $12,000 (Legendary; 8/12)

1927 W560 Black

		GD 2	VG 3	VgEx 4	EX 5	ExMt 6	NM 7	NmMt 8	MT 9
C3	Lou Gehrig	120	150	200	300	400	500	600	1,000
JOK	Babe Ruth	100	120	150	250	300	400	500	800

1932 U.S. Caramel

		PrFr 1	GD 2	VG 3	VgEx 4	EX 5	ExMt 6	NM 7	NmMt 8
1	Eddie Collins	150	200	250	300	400	600	1,200	5,000
2	Paul Waner	150	200	250	300	400	600	1,000	4,000
4	Bill Terry	150	200	250	300	400	600	1,700	
5	Earl Combs	200	250	300	400	500	600	1,000	
6	Bill Dickey	200	250	300	400	500	800	1,200	3,000
7	Joe Cronin	150	200	250	300	400	600	1,000	2,500
8	Chick Hafey	150	200	250	300	400	600	1,000	2,500
10	Rabbit Maranville	150	200	250	300	400	600	1,000	3,000
11	Rogers Hornsby	600	800	1,000	1,200	1,500	2,000	4,000	
12	Mickey Cochrane	200	250	300	400	500	800	1,200	3,000
13	Lloyd Waner	150	200	250	300	400	600	1,000	4,000
14	Ty Cobb	800	1,000	1,200	1,500	2,000	3,000	5,000	12,000
17	Al Simmons	150	200	250	400	500	800	1,200	3,000
18	Tony Lazzeri	200	250	300	400	500	800	1,200	3,000
19	Wally Berger	80	100	120	150	200	300	800	1,200
20	Red Ruffing	150	200	250	300	400	600	1,000	
21	Chuck Klein	150	200	250	300	400	600	1,000	4,500
23	Jimmie Foxx	400	600	800	1,000	1,200	2,500	4,000	5,000
24	Lefty O'Doul	120	150	200	250	350	500	800	1,500
26	Lou Gehrig	2,000	2,500	3,000	5,000	8,000	10,000	15,000	20,000
27	Lefty Grove	500	600	800	1,000	1,200	1,500		
30	Frankie Frisch	200	250	300	400	500	800	1,200	3,000
31	Lefty Gomez	200	250	300	400	500	800	1,200	
32	Babe Ruth	2,000	2,500	5,000	8,000	10,000	12,000	15,000	25,000

—Cards are labeled by most grading companies as a 1932 release, but research indicates the set was most likely released in early 1933.

—Lefty Grove #27 PSA 7 (NM) sold for $3,600 (Mastro; 5/08)

—Rogers Hornsby #11 PSA 8 (NmMt) sold for $12,779 (Memory Lane; 8/06)

1933 DeLong

		PrFr 1	GD 2	VG 3	VgEx 4	EX 5	ExMt 6	NM 7	NmMt 8
1	Marty McManus	40	80	100	150	200	300	800	3,500
2	Al Simmons	100	150	200	250	400	500	1,500	3,500
3	Oscar Melillo	60	80	100	200	300	500	1,000	
4	Bill Terry	80	100	300	400	500	600	1,500	3,000
5	Charlie Gehringer	100	120	200	300	400	600	1,500	4,000
6	Mickey Cochrane	100	200	300	400	500	600	1,500	
7	Lou Gehrig	1,000	2,000	2,500	3,000	5,000	8,000	20,000	60,000
8	Kiki Cuyler	100	120	200	500	600	800	1,500	
9	Bill Urbanski	50	60	80	150	200	300	600	
10	Lefty O'Doul	80	100	150	200	250	▲500	800	3,000
11	Fred Lindstrom	80	100	120	200	500	600	1,500	8,000
12	Pie Traynor	80	150	200	300	500	800	1,500	2,500
13	Rabbit Maranville	120	150	200	400	500	600	1,000	4,000
14	Lefty Gomez	100	150	400	500	600	800	1,000	2,500
15	Riggs Stephenson	60	80	100	150	250	400	1,000	
16	Lon Warneke	60	80	100	200	250	400	1,000	
17	Pepper Martin	80	120	150	200	300	400	1,000	2,000
18	Jimmy Dykes	50	60	120	150	300	400	600	2,000
19	Chick Hafey	80	100	200	250	400	1,000	1,200	20,000
20	Joe Vosmik	50	60	150	200	250	400	1,000	
21	Jimmie Foxx	150	200	300	600	800	1,500	3,000	10,000
22	Chuck Klein	80	100	150	200	400	600	1,200	2,500
23	Lefty Grove	120	150	500	600	800	1,000	1,500	6,000
24	Goose Goslin	120	150	200	300	500	800	2,500	

—Kiki Cuyler #8 PSA 8 (NmMt) sold for $6,355 (Mastro; 4/07)

—Lou Gehrig #7 SGC 92 (NmMt+) sold for $90,648 (Mastro; 4/07)

—Lou Gehrig #7 SGC 88 (NmMt) sold for $55,644 (Mastro; 4/07)

—Lou Gehrig #7 SGC 7.5 (Nm+) sold for $12,925 (REA; 05/11)

—Al Simmons #2 SGC 92 (NmMt+) sold for $5,777 (Mastro; 4/07)

—Joe Vosmik #20 PSA 8 (NmMt) sold for $5,092 (Mile High; 8/07)

—Lon Warneke #16 PSA 8 (NmMt) sold for $6,869 (Mastro; 4/07)

1933 Goudey

		PrFr 1	GD 2	VG 3	VgEx 4	EX 5	ExMt 6	NM 7	NmMt 8
1	Benny Bengough	100	200	250	500	2,000	2,500	8,000	
2	Dazzy Vance	80	100	250	500	800	1,000	7,000	15,000
3	Hugh Critz Batting	25	30	60	100	150	250	1,000	8,000
4	Heinie Schuble	15	40	80	100	150	300	600	
5	Babe Herman	30	80	▲120	▲250	▲300	▲400		
6	Jimmy Dykes	15	50	60	80	100	300	500	
7	Ted Lyons	50	80	120	200	300	400	800	2,000
8	Roy Johnson	15	25	50	80	100	250	500	
9	Dave Harris	15	25	50	80	120	150	300	2,500
10	Glenn Myatt	15	25	50	100	250	400		
11	Billy Rogell	15	30	40	80	120	200	400	1,400
12	George Pipgras	25	40	60	100	150	250	800	
13	Lafayette Thompson	20	30	50	80	120	150	400	3,500
14	Henry Johnson	15	25	50	120	150	200	300	1,200
15	Victor Sorrell	15	25	40	100	120	150	600	
16	George Blaeholder	15	25	40	▲80	150	200	400	1,000
17	Watson Clark	20	30	50	100	120	150	800	
18	Muddy Ruel	15	30	40	80	▲120	150	400	
19	Bill Dickey	80	▲150	300	400	500	600	1,200	4,000
20	Bill Terry Throwing	60	100	150	250	400	500	800	3,000
21	Phil Collins	15	30	40	80	100	120	250	1,500
22	Pie Traynor	60	120	200	300	400	600	1,000	5,000
23	Kiki Cuyler	50	100	150	250	400	500	1,200	3,000
24	Horace Ford	20	30	50	80	120	150	400	
25	Paul Waner	80	150	200	250	400	500	1,500	8,000
26	Chalmer Cissell	25	30	40	80	100	150	400	
27	George Connally	15	25	50	100	▼150	250	300	2,000
28	Dick Bartell	15	30	60	100	120	200	500	
29	Jimmie Foxx	120	250	500	600	1,200	1,500	4,000	18,000
30	Frank Hogan	15	25	40	60	120	200	500	3,000
31	Tony Lazzeri	100	150	250	500	800	1,500	2,000	6,000
32	Bud Clancy	20	30	50	80	120	200	300	2,000
33	Ralph Kress	15	30	50	80	100	200	300	
34	Bob O'Farrell	15	25	40	100	▲150	200	600	
35	Al Simmons	60	100	200	250	400	600	1,200	2,500
36	Tommy Thevenow	20	50	60	100	100	300	1,000	4,000
37	Jimmy Wilson	15	25	30	80	120	150	300	2,000
38	Fred Brickell	15	30	40	▼80	120	150	300	2,500
39	Mark Koenig	15	25	40	80	100	200	800	
40	Taylor Douthit	15	25	50	80	120	150	300	1,000
41	Gus Mancuso Catching	20	25	30	60	100	120	250	800
42	Eddie Collins	50	80	100	200	300	400	800	2,500
43	Lew Fonseca	12	20	40	50	100	120	150	600
44	Jim Bottomley	30	60	▲120	▲150	250	300	600	2,000
45	Larry Benton	15	25	30	▲80	100	150	400	4,000
46	Ethan Allen	20	40	50	80	150	200	400	800
47	Heinie Manush Batting	50	60	▲120	▲150	▲300	▲600	800	4,000
48	Marty McManus	15	25	40	80	100	120	300	
49	Frankie Frisch	50	100	150	200	400	500	1,000	4,000
50	Ed Brandt	15	25	40	80	100	200	300	800
51	Charlie Grimm	15	25	30	▲80	150	300	400	1,200
52	Andy Cohen	15	25	40	80	100	300		
53	Babe Ruth w/Bat Yellow	2,500	5,000	6,000	10,000	20,000	25,000	40,000	60,000
54	Ray Kremer	15	25	40	60	80	100	250	500
55	Pat Malone	12	20	50	60	100	150	600	
56	Red Ruffing	50	100	120	200	250	300	400	1,500
57	Earl Clark	12	▲30	▲40	60	80	120	250	800
58	Lefty O'Doul	15	40	50	120	150	200	300	1,000
59	Bing Miller	12	20	40	50	100	120	200	400
60	Waite Hoyt	30	80	100	150	200	400	500	1,500
61	Max Bishop	12	20	50	60	80	120	150	500
62	Pepper Martin	25	50	60	100	150	200	300	1,000
63	Joe Cronin w/Bat	40	50	100	▲150	250	300	500	2,000
64	Burleigh Grimes	60	80	▲120	150	▲250	▲400	600	1,500
65	Milt Gaston	12	20	40	50	100	120	200	400
66	George Grantham	12	20	25	50	80	120	200	600
67	Guy Bush	12	20	40	60	100	120	200	600
68	Horace Lisenbee	12	20	40	60	80	120	200	400
69	Randy Moore	12	30	30	60	100	120	200	800
70	Floyd (Pete) Scott	12	20	50	60	80	120	200	400
71	Robert J. Burke	12	20	40	80	100	150	200	800
72	Owen Carroll	12	20	25	50	100	120	200	800
73	Jesse Haines	25	60	100	150	200	250	600	1,500

#	Player	PrFr 1	GD 2	VG 3	VgEx 4	EX 5	ExMt 6	NM 7	NmMt 8
74	Eppa Rixey	25	100	120	▲200	250	400	800	1,500
75	Willie Kamm	12	20	25	50	80	100	150	600
76	Mickey Cochrane	40	▲120	▲150	250	300	500	1,000	2,000
77	Adam Comorosky	12	20	30	▲60	▲80	▲100	200	600
78	Jack Quinn	12	20	40	60	100	150	150	600
79	Red Faber	▲50	60	100	150	250	300	500	1,200
80	Clyde Manion	12	20	25	50	100	120	250	800
81	Sam Jones	12	20	50	60	100	120	200	600
82	Dibrell Williams	12	20	25	50	80	100	200	800
83	Pete Jablonowski	12	20	50	60	100	120	200	1,500
84	Glenn Spencer	12	20	40	60	80	200	300	
85	Heinie Sand	12	20	25	50	100	120	250	600
86	Phil Todt	12	20	40	50	80	100	200	800
87	Frank O'Rourke	12	20	40	50	100	120	200	600
88	Russell Rollings	15	25	30	60	80	100	200	800
89	Tris Speaker	100	120	250	400	600	800	1,000	5,000
90	Jess Petty	12	30	40	50	80	100	200	1,000
91	Tom Zachary	12	20	50	60	80	100	200	500
92	Lou Gehrig	▲1,200	2,000	▲3,000	5,000	6,000	8,000	10,000	25,000
93	John Welch	12	25	30	80	100	120	250	500
94	Bill Walker	12	20	40	50	80	120	200	600
95	Alvin Crowder	12	20	50	60	80	120	150	500
96	Willis Hudlin	12	20	25	60	▲100	▲120	▲250	800
97	Joe Morrissey	15	25	40	60	80	100	250	1,200
98	Walter Berger	15	25	30	100	120	150	500	1,500
99	Tony Cuccinello	15	25	30	50	▲80	▲200	250	1,200
100	George Uhle	12	20	30	60	100	120	150	1,000
101	Richard Coffman	12	20	30	▲60	80	120	200	800
102	Travis Jackson	25	60	100	120	150	300	400	1,600
103	Earle Combs	40	80	120	150	250	400	600	2,000
104	Fred Marberry	20	40	50	80	100	120	200	800
105	Bernie Friberg	12	20	40	▲60	100	120	150	400
106	Napoleon Lajoie SP	10,000	15,000	20,000	25,000	30,000	35,000	50,000	75,000
107	Heinie Manush	30	50	100	120	250	300	400	1,500
108	Joe Kuhel	12	20	25	▲60	100	200	250	400
109	Joe Cronin w/Glove	40	60	100	120	200	300	600	1,500
110	Goose Goslin	40	60	100	150	200	250	500	2,000
111	Monte Weaver	12	30	40	▲60	80	150	200	400
112	Fred Schulte	12	20	▲40	80	100	200	250	500
113	Oswald Bluege Portrait	12	20	30	60	80	100	200	800
114	Luke Sewell Fieldin	12	25	50	60	120	200	300	800
115	Cliff Heathcote	12	20	40	50	100	120	200	500
116	Eddie Morgan	12	20	30	50	100	120	200	2,000
117	Rabbit Maranville	30	60	120	150	200	300	500	2,000
118	Val Picinich	20	30	40	80	100	120	200	1,000
119	Rogers Hornsby Fielding	200	300	500	600	1,000	1,200	2,000	12,000
120	Carl Reynolds	15	25	30	50	80	150	300	800
121	Walter Stewart	12	30	40	50	80	120	150	600
122	Alvin Crowder	12	20	25	▲80	▲100	120	200	500
123	Jack Russell	12	20	50	80	100	120	200	500
124	Earl Whitehill	12	20	40	60	100	120	200	1,000
125	Bill Terry	40	60	80	150	250	300	600	2,000
126	Joe Moore Batting	12	20	40	60	100	120	150	500
127	Melvin Ott Portrait	100	250	300	500	1,000	1,200	1,500	2,500
128	Chuck Klein	40	80	120	200	250	400	600	2,000
129	Harold Schumacher Pitching	12	20	40	60	100	150	250	1,000
130	Fred Fitzsimmons Portrait	12	20	30	50	100	120	250	1,200
131	Fred Frankhouse	15	20	40	50	80	150	200	600
132	Jim Elliott	20	30	40	50	100	120	300	1,200
133	Fred Lindstrom	25	40	▲100	150	250	300	400	2,000
134	Sam Rice	30	60	100	120	250	300	600	800
135	Woody English	12	20	25	50	100	120	300	800
136	Flint Rhem	12	20	40	50	100	150	300	800
137	Fred (Red) Lucas	12	20	50	60	120	200	250	800
138	Herb Pennock	60	80	100	150	250	300	600	2,000
139	Ben Cantwell	12	20	50	80	100	120	300	800
140	Bump Hadley	15	25	40	50	100	120	250	1,000
141	Ray Benge	12	20	30	60	80	100	300	1,500
142	Paul Richards	15	25	40	60	80	120	250	1,000
143	Glenn Wright	12	20	60	80	100	120	250	600
144	Babe Ruth Batting DP	2,500	4,000	5,000	8,000	10,000	12,000	35,000	70,000
145	George Walberg	15	25	30	▲60	▲100	▲120	300	800
146	Walter Stewart Pitching	12	20	25	50	60	100	300	1,500
147	Leo Durocher	50	100	120	150	250	500	600	1,500
148	Eddie Farrell	12	20	30	80	100	120	300	
149	Babe Ruth w/Bat Red	3,000	4,000	6,000	8,000	12,000	15,000	30,000	150,000
150	Ray Kolp	12	20	40	80	100	120	200	600
151	Jake Flowers	20	30	50	60	100	150	200	600
152	James (Zack) Taylor	12	20	40	50	100	120	200	800
153	Buddy Myer	12	30	40	50	100	200	400	
154	Jimmie Foxx	250	300	▲600	800	1,000	1,200	2,500	10,000
155	Joe Judge	12	20	40	50	100	120	200	500
156	Danny MacFayden	12	20	25	▲60	60	120	200	600
157	Sam Byrd	25	40	50	100	120	150	200	600
158	Moe Berg	200	300	400	500	600	800	1,000	2,500
159	Oswald Bluege Fielding	12	20	50	60	80	100	200	
160	Lou Gehrig	1,200	1,500	3,000	5,000	6,000	8,000	10,000	50,000
161	Al Spohrer	12	20	40	50	100	120	200	400
162	Leo Mangum	12	20	25	50	100	120	200	1,500
163	Luke Sewell Portrait	12	20	40	50	100	120	200	600
164	Lloyd Waner	50	80	▲150	200	▲300	▲400	800	▲2,000
165	Joe Sewell	50	100	120	200	250	400	500	1,500
166	Sam West	12	20	30	50	100	120	200	1,000
167	Jack Russell	12	20	25	50	100	120	250	800
168	Goose Goslin	40	60	150	250	300	500	600	1,500
169	Al Thomas	12	25	40	60	80	100	200	500
170	Harry McCurdy	12	20	40	50	100	120	200	1,000
171	Charlie Jamieson	15	25	30	60	80	100	250	800
172	Billy Hargrave	12	20	25	50	80	120	200	500
173	Roscoe Holm	12	20	40	60	100	120	200	800
174	Warren (Curley) Ogden	12	20	25	40	60	120	200	800
175	Dan Howley MG	12	20	30	50	80	120	200	600
176	John Ogden	15	25	30	50	80	120	200	800
177	Walter French	12	25	40	50	80	100	200	1,000
178	Jackie Warner	12	20	30	50	80	120	200	1,500
179	Fred Leach	12	20	25	50	60	150	250	500
180	Eddie Moore	12	20	30	50	100	120	200	600
181	Babe Ruth Portrait Green	2,000	4,000	5,000	10,000	12,000	20,000	30,000	70,000
182	Andy High	12	20	40	60	80	100	250	400
183	George Walberg	12	25	40	60	80	120	250	600
184	Charley Berry	12	20	40	80	100	120	300	500
185	Bob Smith	12	20	25	60	100	120	200	600
186	John Schulte	15	25	40	60	100	150	250	800
187	Heinie Manush	25	50	100	150	200	250	500	1,200
188	Rogers Hornsby Pointing	120	250	300	500	600	1,200	1,500	3,500
189	Joe Cronin	50	▲80	▲100	▲200	250	300	▲800	2,500
190	Fred Schulte	12	20	25	50	80	120	200	600
191	Ben Chapman	15	25	40	60	100	150	250	1,000
192	Walter Brown	15	25	40	50	100	150	200	400
193	Lynford Lary	12	20	25	60	120	150	200	1,200
194	Earl Averill	60	80	120	150	200	250	500	1,200
195	Evar Swanson	15	25	30	80	100	120	300	1,500
196	Leroy Mahaffey	12	20	25	60	80	100	300	800
197	Rick Ferrell	25	60	100	150	250	300	500	2,000
198	Jack Burns	12	20	25	50	60	120	200	500
199	Tom Bridges	12	20	50	60	100	150	200	1,000
200	Bill Hallahan	12	30	40	80	100	120	200	400
201	Ernie Orsatti	12	20	40	50	80	150	250	500
202	Gabby Hartnett	50	100	120	250	300	400	800	3,000
203	Lon Warneke	20	30	40	50	80	150	250	800
204	Riggs Stephenson	12	20	25	▲60	100	150	200	400
205	Heinie Meine	12	25	30	60	100	120	200	400
206	Gus Suhr	12	20	25	60	80	100	300	600
207	Melvin Ott w/Bat	100	200	250	500	600	800	1,500	6,000
208	Bernie James	12	20	30	50	100	120	200	400
209	Adolfo Luque	15	25	40	60	80	120	300	1,000
210	Spud Davis	12	30	40	60	100	120	500	800
211	Hack Wilson	80	200	300	▲500	▲600	▲800	1,200	2,500
212	Billy Urbanski	12	20	40	50	100	120	200	400
213	Earl Adams	12	25	▲40	50	100	120	250	1,000
214	John Kerr	12	20	25	40	60	120	200	600
215	Russell Van Atta	12	20	25	30	60	120	200	600
216	Vernon Gomez	80	100	120	250	300	400	500	2,500
217	Frank Crosetti	30	50	80	120	200	250	500	1,500
218	Wes Ferrell	15	25	30	50	100	120	300	800
219	Mule Haas UER	12	20	25	60	150	200	250	800
220	Lefty Grove	150	250	400	500	600	800	1,500	3,000
221	Dale Alexander	12	20	25	60	100	120	300	2,000
222	Charley Gehringer	100	150	250	400	500	600	1,200	4,000
223	Dizzy Dean	250	400	600	800	1,000	1,200	1,500	7,000
224	Frank Demaree	12	20	30	50	100	150	250	600
225	Bill Jurges	12	20	25	50	100	120	250	600
226	Charley Root	15	25	60	100	120	150	250	800
227	Bill Herman	30	50	100	▲200	250	300	600	3,000

		PrFr 1	GD 2	VG 3	VgEx 4	EX 5	ExMt 6	NM 7	NmMt 8
228	Tony Piet	12	20	40	60	80	100	400	600
229	Arky Vaughan	30	50	120	200	250	300	600	3,500
230	Carl Hubbell Pitching	50	120	250	400	500	600	1,200	3,500
231	Joe Moore w/Glove	15	25	30	▲60	100	150		
232	Lefty O'Doul	25	40	60	120	150	200	300	800
233	Johnny Vergez	12	20	40	60	100	150	200	400
234	Carl Hubbell Portrait	100	150	250	300	600	800	1,000	2,000
235	Fred Fitzsimmons Pitching	12	20	25	60	80	100	250	600
236	George Davis	25	40	50	60	100	120	250	1,000
237	Gus Mancuso Fielding	12	20	▲40	▲60	▲100	▲120	200	500
238	Hugh Critz Fielding	12	20	25	60	100	120	200	500
239	Leroy Parmelee	12	20	25	50	100	120	200	600
240	Harold Schumacher	25	40	50	80	120	200	400	2,000

—Dick Bartell #28 PSA 8 (NmMt) sold for $4,249 (Mastro; 8/06)
—Ray Benge #141 PSA 9 (Mint) sold for $5,899 (Goodwin; 8/12)
—Benny Bengough #1 PSA 8 (NmMt) sold for $26,663 (REA; 5/13)
—Benny Bengough #1 PSA 8 (NmMt) sold for $14,864 (Mastro; 12/05)
—Benny Bengough #1 PSA 8 (NmMt) sold for $11,890 (Mile High; 11/10)
—Robert Burke #71 SGC 88 (NmMt) sold for $61,793 (Mile High; 10/12)
—Guy Bush #67 PAA 9 (MT) sold for $9,582 (Mastro; 12/07)
—Chalmer Cissell #26 PSA 8 (NmMt) sold for $7,453 (Memory Lane; 9/07)
—Andy Cohen #52 PSA 8 (NmMt) sold for $38,188 (REA; 4/07)
—Joe Cronin #63 PSA 9 (MT) sold for $12,660 (Goodwin; 10/06)
—Bill Dickey #19 PSA 9 (MT) sold for $17,485 (Mastro; 4/07)
—Jimmy Dykes #6 PSA 8 (NmMt) sold for $6,374 (Memory Lane; 4/07)
—Jimmy Dykes #6 PSA 8 (NmMt) sold for $5,676 (Mastro; 12/06)
—Jimmy Dykes #6 PSA 8 (NmMt) sold for $4,339 (Mastro; 8/07)
—Red Faber #79 PSA 9 (MT) sold for $20,546 (Mastro; 12/06)
—Eddie Farrell #148 PSA 8.5 (NmMt+) sold for $6,302 (Mile High; 05/11)
—Eddie Farrell #148 PSA 8 (NmMt) sold for $15,114 (Mastro; 4/06)
—Eddie Farrell #148 PSA 8 (NmMt) sold for $5,676 (Mastro; 8/07)
—Jimmie Foxx #29 GAI 8 (NmMt) sold for $3,055 (eBay; 1/08)
—Lou Gehrig #92 PSA 10 (Gem) sold for $274,950 (Memory Lane; 9/07)
—Lou Gehrig #92 PSA 9 (MT) sold for $50,000 (Memory Lane; Private Sale - 2007)
—Lou Gehrig #92 SGC 96 (MT) sold for $40,388 (Mastro; 12/06)
—Lou Gehrig #92 PSA 9 (MT) sold for $39,632 (Mile High; 6/06)
—Lou Gehrig #92 PSA 9 (MT) sold for $34,417 (SCP Sotheby's; 11/06)
—Lou Gehrig #92 PSA 8.5 (NmMt+) sold for $29,860 (Goodwin; 9/08)
—Lou Gehrig #92 SGC 92 (NmMt+) sold for $21,405 (Memory Lane; 5/08)
—Lou Gehrig #92 SGC 92 (NmMt+) sold for $17,000 (Legendary; 3/11)
—Lou Gehrig #92 SGC 92 (NmMt+) sold for $14,975 (Lelands; 12/12)
—Lou Gehrig #92 SGC 92 (NmMt+) sold for $13,084 (Goodwin; 7/10)
—Lou Gehrig #92 GAI 8.5 (NmMt+) sold for $7,100 (eBay; 6/07)
—Lou Gehrig #160 PSA 8.5 (NmMt+) sold for $24,068 (Mile High; 11/10)
—Babe Herman #5 PSA 7 (NM) sold for $2,153 (Memory Lane; 12/07)
—Carl Hubbell #230 PSA 9 (MT) sold for $24,898 (Mastro 4/06)
—Carl Hubbell #234 PSA 9 (MT) sold for $14,881 (Mile High; 11/05)
—Roy Johnson #8 PSA 8 (NmMt) sold for $9,382 (Mastro; 4/06)
—Roy Johnson #8 PSA 8 (NmMt) sold for $5,251 (Mastro; 8/07)
—Chuck Klein #128 PSA 9 (MT) sold for $15,352 (SCP Sotheby's; 9/07)
—Nap Lajoie #106 PSA 9 (MT) sold for $123,488 (SCP Sotheby's; 11/06)
—Nap Lajoie #106 PSA 9 (MT) sold for $113,938 (SCP; 6/10)
—Nap Lajoie #106 PSA 9 (MT) sold for $106,705 (Mastro; 4/07)
—Nap Lajoie #106 PSA 9 (MT) sold for $103,137 (Lelands; 12/12)
—Nap Lajoie #106 PSA 9 (MT) sold for $100,000 (REA; 05/12)
—Nap Lajoie #106 (Burdick-Carter) SGC 88 (NmMt) sold for $108,000 (Mastro; 8/07)
—Glenn Myatt #10 PSA 8 (NmMt) sold for $4,339 (Mastro; 12/06)
—Bob O'Farrell #34 PSA 8 (NmMt) sold for $8,460 (Mastro; 12/06)
—Mel Ott Portrait #127 SGC 92 (NmMt+) sold for $5,407 (Mastro; 8/07)
—Leroy Parmelee #239 PSA 9 (MT) sold for $9,582 (Mastro; 12/07)
—Sam Rice #134 PSA 9 (MT) sold for $15,404 (Goodwin; 6/06)
—Muddy Ruel #18 PSA 9 (MT) sold for $10,541 (Mastro; 8/07)
—Babe Ruth #53 SGC 86 (NM+) sold for $21,883 (Goodwin; 7/14)
—Babe Ruth #144 PSA 9 (MT) sold for $75,000 (Memory Lane; Private Sale - 2004)
—Babe Ruth #144 PSA 9 (MT) sold for $74,750 (SCP Sotheby's; 12/04)
—Babe Ruth #144 PSA 9 (MT) sold for $67,797 (Memory Lane; 11/04)
—Babe Ruth #144 GAI 8.5 (NmMt+) sold for $16,698 (Mastro; 12/06)
—Babe Ruth #149 PSA 8.5 (NmMt+) sold for $72,500 (Legendary; 8/10)
—Babe Ruth #181 PSA 9 (MT) sold for $100,000 (Memory Lane; Private Sale - 2006)
—Babe Ruth #181 PSA 9 (MT) sold for $73,624 (19th Century; 6/06)
—Babe Ruth #181 PSA 7.5 (NMt+) sold for $10,073 (REA; 5/13)
—Babe Ruth #181 SGC 86 (NM+) sold for $9,696 (Mastro; 4/07)
—Babe Ruth #181 SGC 86 (NM+) sold for $9,117 (Goodwin; 11/08)
—Babe Ruth #181 SGC 86 (NM+) sold for $7,500 (Mastro; 12/08)
—Heine Schuble #4 PSA 8 (NmMt) sold for $6,991 (Mastro; 12/06)
—Al Simmons #35 PSA 8.5 (NmMt+) sold for $7,299 (Mile High; 05/11)
—Tommy Thevenow #36 PSA 8 (NmMt) sold for $9,860 (REA; 5/05)

—Tommy Thevenow #36 PSA 8 (NmMt) sold for $8,198 (Memory Lane; 9/07)
—Lafayette Thompson #13 PSA 8 (NmMt) sold for $6,375 (Memory Lane; 4/07)
—Paul Waner #25 GAI 8 (NmMt) sold for $1,892 (Memory Lane; 9/07)
—Lonnie Warneke #203 PSA 10 (Gem) sold for $20,575 (Mastro; 4/06)

1933 Sport Kings

		PrFr 1	GD 2	VG 3	VgEx 4	EX 5	ExMt 6	NM 7	NmMt 8
1	Ty Cobb BB	500	1,000	1,200	2,000	3,000	4,000	6,000	12,000
2	Babe Ruth BB	1,200	2,500	3,000	4,000	8,000	10,000	12,000	40,000
42	Carl Hubbell BB	100	150	200	300	500	600	1,000	2,000

—Red Grange #4 PSA 8 (NmMt) sold for $13,394.40 (Mastro; 12/07)
—Red Grange #4 SGC 8 (NmMt) sold for $3,704 (Mile High Auctions; 11/10)
—Carl Hubbell #42 PSA 9 (MT) sold for $7,929 (Mastro; 12/05)
—Babe Ruth #2 SGC 92 (NmMt+) sold for $64,417 (Mastro; 4/07)
—Babe Ruth #2 GAI 7.5 (NM+) sold for $5,541 (Mile High; 8/07)
—Jim Thorpe #6 PSA 8 (NmMt) sold for $7,200.00 (Mastro Auctions; 5/08)
—Ed Wachter #5 PSA 8 (NmMt) sold for $2,100 (Bussineau; 7/13)

1933 Tattoo Orbit

		PrFr 1	GD 2	VG 3	VgEx 4	EX 5	ExMt 6	NM 7	NmMt 8
1	Dale Alexander	30	40	50	100	150	300		
2	Ivy Andrews SP	60	80	100	150	250	400		
3	Earl Averill	60	80	100	150	250	400	600	
4	Dick Bartell	20	30	40	60	100	150	300	
5	Wally Berger	20	30	40	60	100	150	300	
6	George Blaeholder SP	50	60	80	120	200	300		
7	Irving Burns	20	30	40	60	100	150		
8	Guy Bush	20	30	40	80	100	150		
9	Bruce Campbell	20	30	40	60	100	150	300	
10	Chalmers Cissell	20	30	40	60	100	150	200	
11	Watson Clark	20	30	40	80	100	150	120	
12	Mickey Cochrane	100	120	150	250	350	500	1,000	
13	Phil Collins	20	30	40	60	100	150	150	
14	Kiki Cuyler	40	50	60	200	300	400	600	
15	Dizzy Dean	120	150	200	500	600	800	1,500	
16	Jimmy Dykes	20	30	40	60	100	150	300	
17	George Earnshaw	30	40	50	60	100	150	300	
18	Woody English	20	30	40	60	100	150	250	
19	Lou Fonseca	20	30	40	60	100	150	250	
20	Jimmy Foxx	120	150	200	400	500	800	2,000	
21	Burleigh Grimes	40	50	60	100	150	250	600	
22	Charlie Grimm	20	30	40	60	100	150		
23	Lefty Grove	80	100	150	200	300	400	800	
24	Frank Grube	20	30	40	60	100	150	250	
25	George Haas	20	30	40	60	100	150	300	
26	Bump Hadley SP	60	80	100	150	250	400		
27	Chick Hafey	40	50	80	100	175	250	700	
28	Jess Haines	40	50	80	100	150	250	500	
29	Bill Hallahan	20	30	40	60	120	150	300	
30	Mel Harder	20	30	40	60	100	150	300	
31	Gabby Hartnett	40	50	60	100	150	300	800	
32	Babe Herman	20	30	40	60	100	175		
33	Billy Herman	40	50	80	120	200	300		
34	Rogers Hornsby	120	150	200	350	400	600	1,500	
35	Roy Johnson	20	30	40	80	100	150	200	
36	Smead Jolley	20	30	40	60	100	150	300	
37	Billy Jurges	20	30	40	60	100	150	300	
38	Willie Kamm	20	30	40	60	100	150		
39	Mark Koenig	20	30	40	60	100	150	300	
40	Jim Levey	20	30	40	60	100	200		
41	Ernie Lombardi	60	80	100	250	400	600	1,000	
42	Red Lucas	20	30	40	60	100	150	300	
43	Ted Lyons	40	50	60	120	200	250	400	
44	Connie Mack MG	100	120	150	250	300	500	800	
45	Pat Malone	30	40	50	60	100	150	300	
46	Pepper Martin	20	30	40	60	100	150		
47	Marty McManus	20	30	40	60	100	150	300	
48	Lefty O'Doul	20	30	40	60	100	150	450	
49	Dick Porter	20	30	40	60	100	150	300	
50	Carl N. Reynolds	20	30	40	80	100	150	300	
51	Charlie Root	20	30	40	60	100	150	300	
52	Bob Seeds	20	30	40	60	150	200	300	
53	Al Simmons	50	60	100	120	200	300	500	
54	Riggs Stephenson	30	40	50	60	100	150		
55	Lyle Tinning	20	30	40	60	100	150	300	

		PrFr 1	GD 2	VG 3	VgEx 4	EX 5	ExMt 6	NM 7	NmMt 8
	Joe Vosmik	20	30	40	60	100	150	300	
	Rube Walberg	20	30	40	60	100	150	300	
	Paul Waner	40	50	60	100	150	400	600	
	Lon Warneke	20	30	40	60	100	150	300	
	Arthur Whitney	20	30	40	60	80	120	300	

-Dale Alexander PSA 8 (NmMT) sold for $6,142 (Memory Lane; 4/07)
-George Blaeholder PSA 8 (NmMt) sold for $5,353 (eBay; 8/06)
-Kiki Cuyler PSA 8 (NmMt) sold for $6,142 (Memory Lane; 12/06)
-Kiki Cuyler PSA 8 (NmMt) sold for $4,813 (Mile High; 2/08)
-Kiki Cuyler PSA 8 (NmMt) sold for $2,440 (Memory Lane; 5/08)
-Jimmie Foxx PSA 8 (NmMt) sold for $9,815 (Memory Lane; 12/06)
-Lefty Grove PSA 8 (NmMt) sold for $6,703 (Memory Lane; 9/07)
-Connie Mack PSA 8 (NmMt) sold for $6,374 (Memory Lane; 12/06)
-Pepper Martin PSA 8 (NmMt) sold for $6,000 (Memory Lane; 9/07)
-Paul Waner PSA 8 (NmMt) sold for $7,432 (Memory Lane; 12/06)

1934 Goudey

		PrFr 1	GD 2	VG 3	VgEx 4	EX 5	ExMt 6	NM 7	NmMt 8
	Jimmie Foxx	200	300	400	500	600	1,500	2,500	9,600
	Mickey Cochrane	50	100	120	200	250	500	1,000	2,000
	Charlie Grimm	12	15	25	50	60	200	250	1,200
	Woody English	12	15	20	30	60	120	250	1,200
	Ed Brandt	10	12	15	30	80	100	150	
	Dizzy Dean	200	300	500	600	800	1,000	2,000	4,500
	Leo Durocher	20	30	100	120	200	250	500	1,200
	Tony Piet	10	15	25	50	60	150	250	600
	Ben Chapman	10	12	30	40	50	60	150	600
0	Chuck Klein	50	60	80	120	250	250	500	1,500
1	Paul Waner	50	80	100	120	200	250	600	1,500
2	Carl Hubbell	60	100	150	200	250	300	800	2,000
3	Frankie Frisch	40	60	100	150	200	250	500	1,000
4	Willie Kamm	10	12	15	50	80	100	200	600
5	Alvin Crowder	10	12	15	25	60	80	200	600
6	Joe Kuhel	10	12	15	25	60	100	150	500
7	Hugh Critz	10	12	15	60	80	150	200	400
8	Heinie Manush	30	50	60	100	150	200	300	1,200
9	Lefty Grove	150	200	250	400	500	600	800	3,000
0	Frank Hogan	10	12	15	50	60	80	150	600
1	Bill Terry	40	60	80	120	200	300	500	1,500
2	Arky Vaughan	30	40	50	100	150	250	400	1,000
3	Charley Gehringer	50	80	100	150	300	400	800	2,000
4	Ray Benge	10	12	15	60	80	120	250	
5	Roger Cramer	10	12	15	40	60	80	300	500
6	Gerald Walker	10	12	20	25	50	80	150	500
7	Luke Appling	30	50	100	200	250	500	600	
8	Ed Coleman	10	12	15	25	40	60	200	500
9	Larry French	10	12	25	30	▲60	100	150	600
30	Julius Solters	10	12	25	30	60	100	150	500
31	Baxter Jordan	10	12	25	40	60	80	200	500
32	Blondy Ryan	10	12	20	40	60	80	200	650
33	Don Hurst	10	12	15	25	50	80	200	500
34	Chick Hafey	40	60	100	120	200	250	400	1,200
35	Ernie Lombardi	40	60	100	200	250	300	400	1,200
36	Walter Betts	10	12	15	25	60	100	150	500
37	Lou Gehrig	1,200	2,000	3,000	4,000	5,000	8,000	12,000	20,000
38	Oral Hildebrand	20	25	30	50	80	120	200	500
39	Fred Walker	10	12	15	40	60	80	150	500
40	John Stone	10	12	15	30	40	80	150	600
41	George Earnshaw	10	15	25	40	60	80	200	600
42	John Allen	10	12	25	40	60	80	200	600
43	Dick Porter	10	12	15	25	80	100	250	
44	Tom Bridges	10	12	15	25	60	80	200	800
45	Oscar Melillo	10	12	20	40	50	60	150	500
46	Joe Stripp	10	12	15	40	80	100	200	800
47	John Frederick	10	12	15	40	60	80	250	2,000
48	Tex Carleton	15	20	40	50	80	100	300	1,000
49	Sam Leslie	12	15	30	50	80	120	200	600
50	Walter Beck	20	25	30	50	60	80	200	
51	Rip Collins	15	25	30	40	60	120	300	500
52	Herman Bell	12	15	20	50	60	80	150	500
53	George Watkins	12	20	40	60	60	80	150	
54	Wesley Schulmerich	12	15	20	30	50	100	150	500
55	Ed Holley	12	15	40	50	60	80	175	500
56	Mark Koenig	12	15	20	30	50	80	200	400
57	Bill Swift	12	15	20	30	60	100	150	500
58	Earl Grace	12	15	20	30	60	80	▲200	500
59	Joe Mowry	12	15	20	50	60	80	225	600
60	Lynn Nelson	12	15	20	30	50	80	150	500
61	Lou Gehrig	800	2,000	2,500	3,000	6,000	8,000	10,000	15,000
62	Hank Greenberg	300	500	800	1,000	1,200	1,500	2,500	6,000
63	Minter Hayes	15	25	50	60	80	100	120	500
64	Frank Grube	12	20	25	30	80	100	150	
65	Cliff Bolton	15	25	50	60	80	100	200	300
66	Mel Harder	12	15	20	60	80	150	300	600
67	Bob Weiland	12	15	20	50	60	100	200	
68	Bob Johnson	12	15	20	30	80	100	200	1,000
69	John Marcum	12	15	20	40	60	80	150	500
70	Pete Fox	12	15	20	30	50	100	300	800
71	Lyle Tinning	10	12	20	40	50	100	250	800
72	Arndt Jorgens	12	15	20	30	50	120	200	300
73	Ed Wells	20	30	40	60	100	150	250	600
74	Bob Boken	20	30	40	60	100	150	250	600
75	Bill Werber	20	30	50	100	120	150	300	800
76	Hal Trosky	25	60	100	120	200	250	300	800
77	Joe Vosmik	30	40	60	80	120	150	300	800
78	Pinky Higgins	20	30	40	60	120	150	300	800
79	Eddie Durham	20	30	40	60	100	150	250	600
80	Marty McManus	20	30	40	60	200	250	300	800
81	Bob Brown	20	30	40	100	120	150	300	550
82	Bill Hallahan	20	30	40	60	120	200	250	600
83	Jim Mooney	20	30	40	80	120	150	250	600
84	Paul Derringer	20	30	40	60	150	200	400	600
85	Adam Comorosky	20	30	40	60	120	150	250	600
86	Lloyd Johnson	20	30	40	80	100	150	250	600
87	George Darrow	20	30	50	100	120	200	250	600
88	Homer Peel	20	30	50	80	120	200	250	600
89	Linus Frey	50	60	80	100	120	150	250	600
90	KiKi Cuyler	60	100	200	250	300	400	600	1,200
91	Dolph Camilli	20	30	40	60	120	150	250	600
92	Steve Larkin	30	40	50	100	120	150	400	
93	Fred Ostermueller	20	30	40	100	120	200	250	600
94	Red Rolfe	30	60	80	100	120	300	500	1,000
95	Myril Hoag	15	25	40	80	150	200	300	800
96	James DeShong	50	80	100	150	250	400	800	1,500

—Luke Appling #27 SGC 96 (MT) sold for $22,392 (Mastro; 4/06)
—Luke Appling #27 PSA 8 (NmMt) sold for $1,560 (Mastro; 5/08)
—Luke Appling #27 PSA 8 (NmMt) sold for $6,244 (Mastro; 4/07)
—Luke Appling #27 PSA 8 (NmMt) sold for $2,862 (Mastro; 12/05)
—Luke Appling #27 PSA 8 (NmMt) sold for $6,244 (Memory Lane; 11/05)
—Luke Appling #27 PSA 8 (NmMt) sold for $6,244 (Memory Lane; 8/05)
—Ray Benge #24 PSA 8 (NmMt) sold for $5,800 (REA; 5/05)
—Mickey Cochrane #2 SGC 92 (NmMt+) sold for $4,915 (Mastro; 8/07)
—KiKi Cuyler #90 PSA 9 (MT) sold for $8,225 (REA; 4/07)
—Dizzy Dean #6 PSA 9 (MT) sold for $12,650 (SCP Sotheby's; 12/04)
—Leo Durocher #7 SGC 92 (NmMt+) sold for $3,259 (Mastro; 8/07)
—Jimmie Foxx #1 GAI 8 (NmMt) sold for $4,156 (Mile High; 8/07)
—Lou Gehrig #37 SGC 98 (Gem) sold for $125,332 (SCP; 8/13)
—Lou Gehrig #37 SGC 96 (MT) sold for $96,000 (Mastro; 8/07)
—Lou Gehrig #37 SGC 96 (MT) sold for $54,609 (Goodwin; 03/12)
—Lou Gehrig #37 SGC 96 (Mint) sold for $54,609 (Goodwin; 3/12)
—Lou Gehrig #61 PSA 9 (MT) sold for $57,903 (Mastro; 4/06)
—Lou Gehrig #61 PSA 9 (MT) sold for $50,000 (Memory Lane; Private Sale - 2007)
—Lou Gehrig #37 PSA 6.5 (ExMt+) sold for $7,299 (Goodwin; 6/12)
—Hank Greenberg #62 PSA 10 (Gem) sold for $79,069 (Mastro; 12/06)
—Carl Hubbell #12 PSA 9 (MT) sold for $11,488 (Mastro; 8/06)
—Joe Kuhel #16 PSA 9 (MT) sold for $5,836 (Goodwin; 03/12)
—Joe Kuhel #16 PSA 9 (Mint) sold for $5,836 (Goodwin; 3/12)
—Bill Terry #21 SGC 8.5 (NmMtt+) sold for $2,963 (Mastro; 8/07)
—Bob Weiland #67 PSA 9 (MT) sold for $19,665 (Memory Lane; 4/05)

1934-36 Batter-Up

		PrFr 1	GD 2	VG 3	VgEx 4	EX 5	ExMt 6	NM 7	NmMt 8
1	Wally Berger	10	12	15	25	50	100	200	
2	Ed Brandt	10	12	15	25	40	60	150	
3	Al Lopez	15	20	25	40	60	120	250	
4	Dick Bartell	10	12	15	25	40	60	150	
5	Carl Hubbell	30	40	50	80	100	200	400	
6	Bill Terry	25	30	40	60	100	200	400	
7	Pepper Martin	10	12	15	25	40	60	150	
8	Jim Bottomley	15	20	25	40	60	120	250	
9	Tommy Bridges	10	12	15	25	40	60	150	
10	Rick Ferrell	15	20	25	40	60	120	250	

BASEBALL

#	Name	PrFr 1	GD 2	VG 3	VgEx 4	EX 5	ExMt 6	NM 7	NmMt 8
11	Ray Benge	10	12	15	25	40	60	150	
12	Wes Ferrell	10	12	15	25	40	60	150	
13	Chalmer Cissell	10	12	15	25	40	60	150	
14	Pie Traynor	25	30	40	60	100	200	400	
15	Leroy Mahaffey	10	12	15	25	40	60	150	
16	Chick Hafey	15	20	25	40	60	120	250	
17	Lloyd Waner	15	20	25	40	60	120	250	
18	Jack Burns	10	12	15	25	40	60	150	
19	Buddy Myer	10	12	15	25	40	60	150	
20	Bob Johnson	10	12	15	25	40	60	150	
21	Arky Vaughan	15	20	25	40	60	120	250	
22	Red Rolfe	10	12	15	25	40	60	150	
23	Lefty Gomez	25	30	40	80	100	200	500	
24	Earl Averill	25	30	40	60	80	150	250	
25	Mickey Cochrane	25	30	40	60	100	200	400	
26	Van Lingle Mungo	10	12	15	25	40	60	150	
27	Mel Ott	40	50	80	100	200	300	600	
28	Jimmie Foxx	60	80	100	150	250	500	800	
29	Jimmy Dykes	10	12	15	25	40	60	150	
30	Bill Dickey	40	50	80	100	150	250	500	
31	Lefty Grove	40	60	80	100	150	250	500	
32	Joe Cronin	25	30	40	60	100	200	400	
33	Frankie Frisch	25	30	40	60	100	200	400	
34	Al Simmons	25	30	40	60	100	200	400	
35	Rogers Hornsby	60	80	150	200	250	500	800	
36	Ted Lyons	15	20	25	40	60	120	250	
37	Rabbit Maranville	15	20	25	60	60	120	325	
38	Jimmy Wilson	10	12	15	25	40	60	150	
39	Willie Kamm	10	12	15	25	40	60	150	
40	Bill Hallahan	10	12	15	25	40	60	150	
41	Gus Suhr	10	12	15	25	40	60	150	
42	Charley Gehringer	25	30	40	60	150	300	500	
43	Joe Heving	10	12	15	25	40	60	150	
44	Adam Comorosky	10	12	15	25	40	60	150	
45	Tony Lazzeri	25	30	40	60	150	300	500	
46	Sam Leslie	10	12	15	25	40	60	150	
47	Bob Smith	10	12	15	25	40	60	150	
48	Willis Hudlin	10	12	15	25	40	60	150	
49	Carl Reynolds	10	12	15	25	40	60	150	
50	Fred Schulte	10	12	15	25	40	60	150	
51	Cookie Lavagetto	10	12	15	25	40	60	150	
52	Hal Schumacher	10	12	15	25	40	60	150	
53	Roger Cramer	10	12	15	25	40	60	150	
54	Sylvester Johnson	10	12	15	25	40	60	150	
55	Ollie Bejma	10	12	15	25	40	60	150	
56	Sam Byrd	10	12	15	25	40	60	150	
57	Hank Greenberg	80	100	120	200	400	900	1,200	
58	Bill Knickerbocker	10	12	15	25	40	60	150	
59	Bill Urbanski	10	12	15	25	40	60	150	
60	Eddie Morgan	10	12	15	25	40	60	150	
61	Rabbit McNair	10	12	15	25	40	60	150	
62	Ben Chapman	10	12	15	25	40	100		
63	Roy Johnson	10	12	15	25	40	80	150	
64	Dizzy Dean	60	80	120	150	250	500	800	
65	Zeke Bonura	10	12	15	25	40	60	150	
66	Fred Marberry	10	12	15	25	40	60	150	
67	Gus Mancuso	10	12	15	25	40	60	150	
68	Joe Vosmik	10	12	15	25	40	60	150	
69	Earl Grace RC	10	12	15	25	40	60	150	
70	Tony Piet	10	12	15	25	40	60	150	
71	Rollie Hemsley	10	12	15	25	40	60	150	
72	Fred Fitzsimmons	10	12	15	25	50	80	150	
73	Hack Wilson	25	30	40	80	100	250	400	
74	Chick Fullis	10	12	15	25	40	60	150	
75	Fred Frankhouse	10	12	15	25	40	60	150	
76	Ethan Allen	10	12	15	25	40	60	150	
77	Heinie Manush	15	20	25	40	60	120	250	
78	Rip Collins	10	12	15	25	40	60	150	
79	Tony Cuccinello	10	12	15	25	40	60	150	
80	Joe Kuhel	10	12	15	25	40	60	150	
81	Tommy Bridges	20	25	30	100	120	150	250	
82	Clint Brown	20	25	30	50	80	150	250	
83	Albert Blanche	20	25	30	50	80	150	250	
84	Boze Berger	20	25	30	50	80	150	250	
85	Goose Goslin	25	30	40	60	100	200	400	
86	Lefty Gomez	30	40	50	80	120	250	500	
87	Joe Glenn	20	25	30	50	80	150	250	
88	Cy Blanton	20	25	30	50	80	150	250	
89	Tom Carey	20	25	30	50	80	150	250	
90	Ralph Birkofer	20	25	30	50	80	150	250	
91	Fred Gabler	20	25	30	50	80	150	250	
92	Dick Coffman	20	25	30	50	80	150	250	
93	Ollie Bejma	20	25	30	50	80	150	250	
94	Leroy Parmelee	20	25	30	50	80	150	250	
95	Carl Reynolds	20	25	30	50	80	150	250	
96	Ben Cantwell	20	25	30	50	80	150	250	
97	Curtis Davis	20	25	30	50	100	150	250	
98	E. Webb/W. Moses	20	25	30	50	80	150	250	
99	Ray Benge	20	25	30	50	80	150	250	
100	Pie Traynor	25	30	40	60	100	200	400	
101	Phil Cavarretta	20	25	30	50	80	150	250	
102	Pep Young	20	25	30	50	80	150	250	
103	Willis Hudlin	20	25	30	50	80	150	425	
104	Mickey Haslin	20	25	30	50	80	150	250	
105	Ossie Bluege	20	25	30	50	80	150	250	
106	Paul Andrews	20	25	30	50	80	150	250	
107	Ed Brandt	20	25	30	50	80	150	250	
108	Don Taylor	20	25	30	50	80	200	300	
109	Thornton Lee	20	25	30	50	80	150	250	
110	Hal Schumacher	20	25	30	50	80	150	250	
111	F.Hayes/T.Lyons	25	30	40	60	100	250		
112	Odell Hale	20	25	30	50	80	150	250	
113	Earl Averill	25	30	40	60	120	200	400	
114	Italo Chelini	20	25	30	50	80	150	250	
115	I.Andrews/J.Bottomley	25	30	40	60	100	200	400	
116	Bill Walker	20	25	30	50	100	150	250	
117	Bill Dickey	80	100	120	175	250	500	1,000	
118	Gerald Walker	20	25	30	60	80	150	250	
119	Ted Lyons	25	30	40	60	100	200	400	
120	Eldon Auker	20	25	30	50	80	100	250	
121	Bill Hallahan	20	25	30	50	80	150	250	
122	Fred Lindstrom	25	30	40	60	100	200	400	
123	Oral Hildebrand	20	25	30	50	80	150	250	
124	Luke Appling	40	50	100	200	250	300	600	
125	Pepper Martin	20	25	30	50	80	150	250	
126	Rick Ferrell	25	30	40	60	100	200	400	
127	Ival Goodman	20	25	30	50	80	150	250	
128	Joe Kuhel	20	25	30	50	80	150	250	
129	Ernie Lombardi	25	30	40	60	100	200	400	
130	Charley Gehringer	40	50	60	100	150	300	600	
131	Van Lingle Mungo	20	25	30	50	80	150	250	
132	Larry French	20	25	30	50	80	150	250	
133	Buddy Myer	20	25	30	50	80	150	250	
134	Mel Harder	20	25	30	50	100	150	250	
135	Augie Galan	20	25	30	50	80	150	525	
136	Gabby Hartnett	25	30	40	60	100	200	400	
137	Stan Hack	20	25	30	50	80	150	250	
138	Billy Herman	25	30	40	100	120	200	400	
139	Bill Jurges	20	25	30	50	80	150	250	
140	Bill Lee	20	25	30	50	80	150	250	
141	Zeke Bonura	20	25	30	50	80	150	250	
142	Tony Piet	20	25	30	50	80	150	250	
143	Paul Dean	25	30	40	100	150	200	400	
144	Jimmie Foxx	80	100	120	200	300	500	1,000	
145	Joe Medwick	30	50	60	80	120	250	500	
146	Rip Collins	20	25	30	50	80	150	250	
147	Mel Almada	20	25	30	50	80	150	250	
148	Allan Cooke	20	25	30	50	80	150	250	
149	Moe Berg	100	120	150	250	400	600	1,600	
150	Dolph Camilli	20	25	30	50	80	150	250	
151	Oscar Melillo	20	25	30	60	100	150	250	
152	Bruce Campbell	20	25	30	50	80	150	250	
153	Lefty Grove	60	100	120	200	250	400	950	
154	Johnny Murphy	20	25	30	50	80	150	250	
155	Luke Sewell	20	25	30	50	80	150	250	
156	Leo Durocher	25	30	40	60	100	200	400	
157	Lloyd Waner	25	30	40	80	100	200	500	
158	Guy Bush	20	25	30	50	100	150	250	
159	Jimmy Dykes	20	25	30	50	80	150	250	
160	Steve O'Neill	20	25	30	50	80	150	300	
161	General Crowder	20	25	30	50	80	150	250	
162	Joe Cascarella	20	25	30	80	100	150	250	
163	Daniel Hafey	20	25	30	50	80	150	250	
164	Gilly Campbell	20	25	30	50	80	150	250	

		PrFr 1	GD 2	VG 3	VgEx 4	EX 5	ExMt 6	NM 7	NmMt 8
65	Ray Hayworth	20	25	30	50	120	150	275	
66	Frank Demaree	20	25	30	50	80	150	250	
67	John Babich	20	25	30	50	100	150	300	
68	Marvin Owen	20	25	30	50	80	150	250	
69	Ralph Kress	20	25	30	50	80	150	250	
70	Mule Haas	20	25	30	50	80	150	250	
71	Frank Higgins	20	25	50	60	80	150	250	
72	Wally Berger	20	25	30	100	120	150	250	
73	Frankie Frisch	40	50	60	100	150	300	600	
74	Wes Ferrell	20	25	30	50	80	150	250	
75	Pete Fox	20	25	30	50	80	150	250	
76	John Vergez	20	25	30	50	80	150	250	
77	Billy Rogell	20	25	30	50	80	150	300	
78	Don Brennan	20	25	30	50	80	150	250	
79	Jim Bottomley	25	30	40	60	100	200	400	
80	Travis Jackson	25	30	40	60	100	200	400	
81	Red Rolfe	20	25	30	50	80	150	250	
82	Frank Crosetti	25	30	40	60	100	200	400	
83	Joe Cronin	25	30	40	60	100	200	400	
84	Schoolboy Rowe	20	25	30	60	80	150	300	
85	Chuck Klein	30	40	50	150	200	250	500	
86	Lon Warneke	20	25	30	50	80	150	250	
87	Gus Suhr	20	25	30	50	80	150	250	
88	Ben Chapman	20	25	30	50	80	150	275	
89	Clint Brown	20	25	30	50	80	150	250	
90	Paul Derringer	20	25	30	50	80	150	250	
91	John Burns	20	25	30	50	80	150	250	500
92	John Broaca	25	30	40	60	100	200	400	

—Luke Appling #124 PSA 8 (NmMt) sold for $4,200 (Mastro; 5/08)
—John Broaca #192 PSA 8 (NmMt) sold for $2,405 (Mastro; 12/06)
—Dizzy Dean #64 PSA 8.5 (NmMt+) sold for $3,300 (Mastro; 5/08)
—Dizzy Dean #64 PSA 8 (NmMt) sold for $1,892 (Goodwin; 2/06)
—Bill Dickey #117 PSA 8 (NmMt) sold for $2,046 (eBay; 6/08)
—Jimmie Foxx #28 PSA 8 (NmMt) sold for $1,912 (Heritage; 10/07)
—Jimmie Foxx #28 PSA 8 (NmMt) sold for $1,701 (eBay; 4/07)
—Charley Gehringer #130 PSA 8 (NmMt) sold for $1,308 (Madec; 5/07)
—Charley Gehringer #130 PSA 8 (NmMt) sold for $1,143 (eBay; 12/07)
—Charley Gehringer #130 PSA 8 (NmMt) sold for $1,136 (Memory Lane; 5/08)
—Lefty Gomez #23 PSA 8 (NmMt) sold for $914 (eBay; 5/06)
—Carl Hubbell #5 PSA 8 (NmMt) sold for $4,200 (Mastro; 5/08)
—Chuck Klein #185 PSA 9 (MT) sold for $3,151 (eBay; 3/07)
—Bill Terry #6 PSA 8 (NmMt) sold for $1,912 (Mastro; 5/08)
—Pie Traynor #14 PSA 8 (NmMt) sold for $4,481 (Mastro; 5/08)
—Lloyd Waner #157 PSA 8 (NmMt) sold for $1,302 (eBay; 3/06)
—Hack Wilson #73 PSA 8.5 (NmMt+) sold for $4,500 (Mastro; 5/08)

1934-36 Diamond Stars

		PrFr 1	GD 2	VG 3	VgEx 4	EX 5	ExMt 6	NM 7	NmMt 8
1	Lefty Grove	100	250	500	800	1,200	1,500	5,000	20,000
2A	Al Simmons Sox Insignia	30	40	80	100	120	200	500	
2B	Al Simmons No Insignia	30	40	50	80	120	200	600	
3	Rabbit Maranville	30	40	60	100	150	200	500	1,200
4	Buddy Myer	10	12	15	25	80	120	300	800
5	Tom Bridges	10	12	15	25	150	250	350	600
6	Max Bishop	10	12	15	25	60	80	150	500
7	Lew Fonseca	12	15	20	40	50	80	200	850
8	Joe Vosmik	8	10	12	20	35	80	150	300
9	Mickey Cochrane	30	40	80	150	200	400	600	1,200
10A	Roy Mahaffey A's Insignia	8	10	12	20	35	80	200	300
11	Bill Dickey	40	80	80	100	300	400	500	1,200
12A	Dixie Walker 1934 Green Back	8	10	12	20	35	60	120	400
12B	Dixie Walker 1935 Green Back	8	10	12	20	35	60	150	
13	George Blaeholder	12	15	20	30	50	80	200	1,500
14	Bill Terry	30	40	80	150	200	250	600	2,000
15A	Dick Bartell Phillies on Back	10	12	15	25	60	100	250	
16	Lloyd Waner	20	30	60	80	100	250	500	800
17	Frankie Frisch	25	40	50	80	100	300	400	1,000
18	Chick Hafey	20	25	30	80	100	200	300	1,500
19	Van Mungo	15	20	25	60	100	150	300	1,200
20	Shanty Hogan	8	10	12	20	35	60	120	400
21A	Johnny Vergez Giants on back	8	10	12	25	35	100	250	
22	Jimmy Wilson	8	10	12	20	35	60	120	400
23	Bill Hallahan	8	10	12	20	35	60	200	
24	Sparky Adams	8	10	12	20	35	100	120	400
25	Wally Berger	8	10	12	20	35	50	120	300
26	Pepper Martin	12	15	20	60	120	150	200	350

		PrFr 1	GD 2	VG 3	VgEx 4	EX 5	ExMt 6	NM 7	NmMt 8
27	Pie Traynor	25	30	40	80	120	200	350	600
28	Al Lopez	12	15	20	60	100	120	200	650
29	Robert Rolfe	10	12	15	25	40	60	100	300
30A	Heinie Manush W on Sleeve	15	20	25	60	100	120	250	600
31A	Kiki Cuyler Cubs	15	20	25	50	100	150	200	500
31B	Kiki Cuyler Reds	15	20	25	40	100	150	200	500
32	Sam Rice	12	15	20	40	80	120	200	400
33	Schoolboy Rowe	6	8	10	15	30	100	120	250
34	Stanley Hack	6	8	10	15	25	80	150	250
35	Earle Averill	12	15	20	60	80	120	200	400
36A	Earnie Lombardi ERR	20	25	30	80	120	150	350	700
36B	Ernie Lombardi COR	20	25	30	50	80	150	250	
37	Billy Urbanski	6	8	10	20	30	50	100	150
38	Ben Chapman	6	8	10	30	50	60	150	250
39	Carl Hubbell	30	40	50	100	120	200	300	700
40	Blondy Ryan	6	8	10	15	25	40	80	225
41	Harvey Hendrick	6	8	10	15	25	40	80	200
42	Jimmy Dykes	6	8	10	30	60	80	120	400
43	Ted Lyons	12	15	30	40	80	120	200	500
44	Rogers Hornsby	80	100	150	200	250	300	500	1,200
45	Jo Jo White	15	20	25	40	50	60	80	120
46	Red Lucas	6	8	10	15	25	40	80	200
47	Bob Bolton	6	8	10	15	25	60	100	150
48	Rick Ferrell	12	15	20	30	100	150	200	500
49	Buck Jordan	6	8	10	15	25	60	100	200
50	Mel Ott	60	80	120	150	200	300	800	1,000
51	Burgess Whitehead	6	8	10	15	25	80	80	200
52	George Stainback	6	8	10	15	25	40	100	200
53	Oscar Melillo	6	8	10	15	25	40	100	200
54A	Hank Greenburg ERR	120	150	200	500	800	1,200	1,500	
54B	Hank Greenberg COR	80	100	150	200	250	600	800	2,000
55	Tony Cuccinello	12	15	20	30	50	100	150	250
56	Gus Suhr	10	12	15	40	60	80	120	300
57	Cy Blanton	6	8	10	15	25	40	80	200
58	Glenn Myatt	8	10	12	20	30	50	120	300
59	Jim Bottomley	20	25	30	40	80	100	150	500
60	Red Ruffing	20	25	30	60	100	200	250	600
61	Bill Werber	6	8	10	15	25	60	100	300
62	Fred Frankhouse	6	8	10	15	25	60	150	300
63	Stonewall Jackson	15	20	25	40	80	100	150	500
64	Jimmie Foxx	60	80	150	200	300	500	600	1,200
65	Zeke Bonura	6	8	10	15	25	40	80	300
66	Ducky Medwick	60	80	100	120	250	300	350	800
67	Marvin Owen	6	8	10	15	25	80	100	300
68	Sam Leslie	6	8	10	15	25	40	100	250
69	Earl Grace	6	8	10	15	25	40	80	200
70	Hal Trosky	6	8	10	15	50	60	100	500
71	Ossie Bluege	6	8	10	15	25	60	80	200
72	Tony Piet	6	8	10	15	25	40	100	200
73	Fritz Ostermueller	6	8	10	15	30	60	80	200
74	Tony Lazzeri	30	40	50	120	200	300	400	800
75	Irving Burns	10	12	15	25	40	80	120	200
76	Billy Rogell	6	8	10	15	25	50	80	250
77	Charlie Gehringer	40	80	100	120	150	300	400	1,000
78	Joe Kuhel	6	8	10	15	40	60	120	200
79	Willis Hudlin	6	8	10	15	50	80	100	300
80	Lou Chiozza	6	8	10	15	30	60	120	200
81	Bill Delancey	10	12	15	25	40	60	150	300
82A	John Babich Dodgers Insignia	6	8	10	15	25	80	120	200
82B	John Babich No Insignia	6	8	10	15	25	40	80	200
83	Paul Waner	25	30	40	80	150	300	500	800
84	Sam Byrd	12	15	20	30	50	80	100	
85	Julius Solters	12	15	20	40	60	80	150	400
86	Frank Crosetti	20	25	50	60	80	200	300	800
87	Steve O'Neil MG	12	15	20	30	50	80	150	300
88	George Selkirk	12	15	20	40	60	120	150	400
89	Joe Stripp	12	15	20	30	60	120	150	400
90	Ray Hayworth	12	15	20	30	50	80	150	400
91	Bucky Harris MG	25	30	60	80	100	200	400	1,000
92	Ethan Allen	12	15	20	30	50	100	200	400
93	Alvin Crowder	12	15	20	40	80	100	150	400
94	Wes Ferrell	12	15	20	30	60	80	150	500
95	Luke Appling	30	40	50	80	120	300	400	1,200
96	Lew Riggs	12	15	20	50	80	100	250	400
97	Al Lopez	60	80	100	150	250	400	800	2,000
98	Schoolboy Rowe	50	60	80	150	200	300	400	1,500
99	Pie Traynor	60	80	120	150	300	400	800	2,600

		PrFr 1	GD 2	VG 3	VgEx 4	EX 5	ExMt 6	NM 7	NmMt 8
100	Earle Averill	60	80	100	150	250	400	800	1,600
101	Dick Bartell	40	50	60	100	200	400	500	1,000
102	Van Mungo	40	50	60	120	200	300	500	1,500
103	Bill Dickey	150	200	250	300	450	600	1,200	
104	Robert Rolfe	40	50	60	120	150	250	500	1,000
105	Ernie Lombardi	60	80	100	250	350	400	700	2,700
106	Red Lucas	50	60	80	120	200	400	700	1,500
107	Stanley Hack	50	60	80	120	200	300	600	
108	Wallter Berger	50	60	80	300	350	400	800	2,500

—Earle Averill #35 SGC 92 (NmMt+) sold for $2,405 (Mastro; 4/07)
—Wally Berger #108 SGC 92 (NmMt+) sold for $4,468 (Mastro; 4/07)
—Cy Blanton #57 PSA 9 (MT) sold for $11,262 (Mastro; 4/07)
—Bill Dickey #103 PSA 8 (NmMt) sold for $8,529 (Mastro; 12/05)
—Jimmie Foxx #64 PSA 9 (MT) sold for $17,456 (Goodwin; 7/13)
—Charlie Gehringer #77 PSA 9 (MT) sold for $3,779 (Memory Lane; 9/07)
—Charlie Gehringer #77 PSA 9 (MT) sold for $3,004 (eBay; 2/08)
—Charlie Gehringer #77 GAI 9 (MT) sold for $1,554 (Heritage; 5/07)
—Hank Greenberg #54 PSA 9 (MT) sold for $4,163 (Memory Lane; 5/08)
—Hank Greenberg #54 PSA 9 (MT) sold for $3,975 (eBay; 5/07)
—Hank Greenberg #54 PSA 9 (MT) sold for $3,691 (Mastro; 4/07)
—Hank Greenberg #54 SGC 92 (NmMt+) sold for $3,351 (eBay; 4/07)
—Hank Greenburg #54 ERR PSA 8 (NmMt) sold for $6,000 (Mastro; 5/08)
—Rogers Hornsby #44 SGC 96 (MT) sold for $5,142 (Goodwin; 3/08)
—Rogers Hornsby #44 SGC 92 (NmMt+) sold for $2,520 (Mastro; 4/07)
—Rogers Hornsby #44 SGC 92 (NmMt+) sold for $1,837 (Mastro; 12/07)
—Carl Hubbell #39 PSA 9 (MT) sold for $2,460 (Mastro; 5/08)
—Carl Hubbell #39 SGC 92 (NmMt+) sold for $2,022 (Mastro; 4/07)
—Stonewall Jackson #63 SGC 96 (MT) sold for $6,544 (Mastro; 4/07)
—Tony Lazzeri #74 PSA 9 (MT) sold for $5,948 (Mastro; 4/07)
—Al Lopez #28 SGC 96 (MT) sold for $4,774 (Mastro; 4/07)
—Ernie Lombardi #105 SGC 92 (NmMt+) sold for $2,520 (Mastro; 12/07)
—Mel Ott #50 PSA 9 (MT) sold for $3,123 (Memory Lane; 12/07)
—Mel Ott #50 PSA 9 (MT) sold for $3,049 (Mastro; 8/07)
—Mel Ott #50 PSA 9 (MT) sold for $3,010 (eBay; 3/07)
—Mel Ott #50 PSA 9 (MT) sold for $2,850 (eBay; 2/08)
—Red Ruffing #60 SGC 96 (MT) sold for $5,700 (Mastro; 5/08)
—Al Simmons #2 (No Insignia) SGC 88 (NmMt) sold for $4,601 (Old Judge; 11/07)
—Al Simmons #2 (Sox Insignia) PSA 8 (NmMt) sold for $2,400 (Mastro; 5/08)
—Paul Waner #83 PSA 9 (MT) sold for $2,498 (Memory Lane; 5/08)
—Paul Waner #83 PSA 9 (MT) sold for $2,040 (Mastro; 5/08)

1935 Goudey 4-in-1

		PrFr 1	GD 2	VG 3	VgEx 4	EX 5	ExMt 6	NM 7	NmMt 8
1-2	Berry/Burk/Kres/Vance 2C SP	20	25	30	50	80	150	300	
1-4	Berry/Burk/Kres/Vance 4C	15	20	25	40	60	150	6,000	
1-7	Berry/Burk/Kres/Vance 7C	15	20	25	50	60	120	300	
2-8	Burns/Hems/Grub/Weil 8C	15	20	25	40	60	120		
2-9	Burns/Hems/Grub/Weil 9C	15	20	25	40	60	120		
3-8	Campbell/Mey/Good/Kamp 8D	15	20	25	40	60	120		
3-9	Campbell/Mey/Good/Kamp 9D	15	20	25	40	60	120		
4-1	Cochrane/Gehr/Brid/Rog 1D	25	30	40	80	100	250	600	
4-2	Cochrane/Gehr/Brid/Rog 2D	25	30	40	60	100	250	600	
4-6	Cochrane/Gehr/Brid/Rog 6D SP	30	40	50	80	120	300	800	
4-7	Cochrane/Gehr/Brid/Rog 7D SP	40	40	50	80	120	300	800	
5-2	Critz/Bartell/Ott/Manc 2A SP	30	40	50	80	150	250	2,000	
5-4	Critz/Bartell/Ott/Manc 4A	25	30	40	80	120	200	600	
5-7	Critz/Bartell/Ott/Manc 7A	25	30	40	60	120	200	600	
6-1	Cronin/Reyn/Bish/Ciss 1G SP	20	25	30	50	100	250		
6-3	Cronin/Reyn/Bish/Ciss 3E SP	20	25	30	50	100	200		
6-5	Cronin/Reyn/Bish/Ciss 5E SP	20	25	30	50	100	200		
6-6	Cronin/Reyn/Bish/Ciss 6E	15	20	25	40	100	120		
7-8	DeShong/Allen/Rolfe/Walk 8E	15	20	25	40	60	120		
7-9	DeShong/Allen/Rolfe/Walk 9E	15	20	25	40	60	120		
8-1	Earn/Dyk/Sew/Appling 1I	15	20	25	40	60	120	400	
8-2	Earn/Dyk/Sew/Appling 2F	15	20	25	40	60	120	600	
8-6	Earn/Dyk/Sew/Appling 6F SP	20	25	30	50	100	200	500	
8-7	Earn/Dyk/Sew/Appling 7F SP	20	25	30	50	100	200	500	
9-8	Fox/Greenberg/Walk/Rowe 8F	50	60	80	100	250	400	1,000	
9-9	Fox/Greenberg/Walk/Rowe 9F	50	60	80	100	250	400	1,000	
10-1	Frisch/Dean/Ors/Carl 1A	50	80	100	150	200	400	2,000	
10-2	Frisch/Dean/Ors/Carl 2A	50	60	80	120	200	400	1,000	
10-6	Frisch/Dean/Ors/Carl 6A SP	60	80	100	120	250	500	1,500	
10-7	Frisch/Dean/Ors/Carl 7A SP	60	80	100	120	250	500	1,500	
11-1	Grimes/Klein/Cuyl/Eng 1F	25	30	40	80	120	250	600	
11-3	Grimes/Klein/Cuyl/Eng 3D	25	30	40	60	120	250	600	

		PrFr 1	GD 2	VG 3	VgEx 4	EX 5	ExMt 6	NM 7	NmMt 8
11-4	Grimes/Klein/Cuyl/Eng 4D SP	30	40	50	80	150	300	800	
11-5	Grimes/Klein/Cuyl/Eng 5D SP	30	40	50	80	150	300	800	
12-8	Hayes/Lyons/Haas/Bon 8B	15	20	25	40	80	120	300	
12-9	Hayes/Lyons/Haas/Bon 9B	15	20	25	40	60	120	300	
13-8	Herman/Suhr/Padd/Blant 8K	15	20	25	40	60	120		
13-9	Herman/Suhr/Padd/Blant 9K	15	20	25	40	60	120		
14-1	Hudlin/Myatt/Com/Bottomley 1K SP	20	25	30	50	80	150		
14-3	Hudlin/Myatt/Com/Bottomley 3B SP	20	25	30	50	80	150		
14-5	Hudlin/Myatt/Com/Bottomley 5B	15	20	25	40	60	120		
14-6	Hudlin/Myatt/Com/Bottomley 6B	15	20	25	40	60	150		
15-8	Johnson/Cole/Marc/Cramer 8J	15	20	25	40	60	120	300	
15-9	Johnson/Cole/Marc/Cramer 9J	15	20	25	40	60	120	400	
16-1	Kamm/Hild/Averill/Tro 1L	15	20	25	40	80	200	500	
16-2	Kamm/Hild/Averill/Tro 2E	15	20	25	50	60	200	500	
16-6	Kamm/Hild/Averill/Tro 6E SP	20	25	30	50	80	250	600	
16-7	Kamm/Hild/Averill/Tro 7E SP	20	25	30	50	80	250	600	
17-8	Koenig/Fitz/Benge/Zach 8A	15	20	25	40	60	120		
17-8	Koenig/Fitz/Benge/Zach 8M	15	20	25	40	60	120		
18-8	Kuhel/White/Myer/Stone 8H	15	20	25	40	60	120		
18-9	Kuhel/White/Myer/Stone 9H	15	20	25	40	60	120		
19-1	Leslie/Frey/Stripp/Clark 1G	15	20	25	40	80	120		
19-3	Leslie/Frey/Stripp/Clark 3E	15	20	25	40	60	120	300	
19-4	Leslie/Frey/Stripp/Clark 4E SP	20	25	30	50	80	150	400	
19-5	Leslie/Frey/Stripp/Clark 5E	15	20	25	40	60	120	300	
20-1	Mahaffey/Foxx/Will/Hig 1B	30	40	80	100	150	300	800	
20-2	Mahaffey/Foxx/Will/Hig 2B	30	40	50	120	150	300	2,000	
20-6	Mahaffey/Foxx/Will/Hig 6B SP	50	60	80	100	200	400	1,000	
20-7	Mahaffey/Foxx/Will/Hig 7B SP	50	60	80	100	200	400	1,000	
21-1	Manush/Lary/Weav/Had 1C	15	20	25	40	60	120	500	
21-2	Manush/Lary/Weav/Had 2C	15	20	25	60	60	120	500	
21-6	Manush/Lary/Weav/Had 6C SP	20	25	30	50	80	150	600	
21-7	Manush/Lary/Weav/Had 7C SP	20	25	30	50	80	150	600	
22-2	Martin/O'Far/Byrd/Mac 2F SP	20	25	30	50	80	150		
22-4	Martin/O'Far/Byrd/Mac 4F	15	20	25	40	60	120		
22-7	Martin/O'Far/Byrd/Mac 7F	15	20	25	40	60	120		
23-2	Moore/Hogan/Frank/Bran 2E SP	20	25	30	50	80	150	400	
23-4	Moore/Hogan/Frank/Bran 4E	15	20	25	40	60	120		
23-7	Moore/Hogan/Frank/Bran 7E	15	20	25	40	60	120	300	
24-1	Piet/Com/Bottomley/Adam 1H	15	20	25	40	60	120	1,000	
24-3	Piet/Com/Bottomley/Adam 3F	15	20	25	40	60	120	300	
24-4	Piet/Com/Bottomley/Adam 4F SP	20	25	30	50	80	150	400	
24-5	Piet/Com/Bottomley/Adam 5F SP	20	25	30	50	80	150	400	
25-1	Ruel/Simmons/Kam/Coch 1J SP	30	40	50	80	150	300	800	
25-3	Ruel/Simmons/Kam/Coch 3A SP	30	40	50	80	150	300	800	
25-5	Ruel/Simmons/Kam/Coch 5A	25	30	40	60	120	250	600	
25-6	Ruel/Simmons/Kam/Coch 6A	25	30	40	60	120	250	600	
26-2	Ruff/Mal/Lazzeri/Dickey 2D SP	40	50	60	100	200	400	1,000	
26-4	Ruff/Mal/Lazzeri/Dickey 4D	30	40	50	80	200	300	800	
26-7	Ruff/Mal/Lazzeri/Dickey 7D	30	40	50	80	150	300	800	
27-1	Ruth/McM/Bran/Maran 1J	400	500	600	800	1,000	1,500	4,000	
27-3	Ruth/McM/Bran/Maran 3A	300	400	600	800	1,000	1,500	4,000	
27-4	Ruth/McM/Bran/Maran 4A SP	400	500	600	1,000	1,200	2,500	5,000	
27-5	Ruth/McM/Bran/Maran 5A SP	400	500	600	1,000	1,200	2,500	5,000	
28-1	Schuble/Marb/Goslin/Crow 1H SP	20	25	30	50	80	150	500	
28-3	Schuble/Marb/Goslin/Crow 3F SP	20	25	30	50	80	150	400	
28-5	Schuble/Marb/Goslin/Crow 5F	15	20	25	40	80	150	300	
28-6	Schuble/Marb/Goslin/Crow 6F	15	20	25	40	60	120	300	
29-8	Spohrer/Rhem/Cant/Bent 8L	15	20	25	40	60	120		
29-9	Spohrer/Rhem/Cant/Bent 9L	20	25	30	40	60	120		
30-1	Terry/Schu/Man/Jackson 1K	25	30	40	60	120	250		
30-3	Terry/Schu/Man/Jackson 3K	25	30	40	60	120	250		
30-4	Terry/Schu/Man/Jackson 4B SP	30	40	50	80	150	300		
30-5	Terry/Schu/Man/Jackson 5B SP	30	40	50	80	150	300		
31-2	Traynor/Luc/Thev/Wright 2B SP	20	25	30	50	80	150	400	
31-4	Traynor/Luc/Thev/Wright 4B	15	20	25	60	80	150	300	
31-7	Traynor/Luc/Thev/Wright 7B	15	20	25	40	60	120	300	
32-8	Vosmik/Knick/Hard/Stew 8I	15	20	25	40	60	120	500	
32-9	Vosmik/Knick/Hard/Stew 9I	15	20	25	40	60	120	1,200	
33-1	Waner/Bush/Hoyt/Waner 1E	25	30	40	60	100	250	600	
33-3	Waner/Bush/Hoyt/Waner 3C	25	30	40	60	100	250	600	
33-4	Waner/Bush/Hoyt/Waner 5C	25	30	40	60	100	250	600	
33-8	Waner/Bush/Hoyt/Waner 4C SP	30	40	50	80	150	300	1,000	
34-8	Werber/Ferrell/Ferrell/Ost 8G	15	20	25	40	60	200	300	
34-9	Werber/Ferrell/Ferrell/Ost 9G	15	20	25	40	60	250	300	
35-1	West/Melillo/Blae/Coff 1F SP	20	25	30	50	80	150	400	

	PrFr 1	GD 2	VG 3	VgEx 4	EX 5	ExMt 6	NM 7	NmMt 8
-3 West/Melillo/Blae/Coff 3D SP	20	25	30	50	80	150	400	
-5 West/Melillo/Blae/Coff 5D	15	20	25	40	60	120		
-6 West/Melillo/Blae/Coff 6D	15	20	25	40	60	120	300	
-1 Wilson/Allen/Jonnard/Brick 1E SP	20	25	30	50	80	150		
-3 Wilson/Allen/Jonnard/Brick 3C SP	20	25	30	60	80	150		
-5 Wilson/Allen/Jonnard/Brick 5C SP	20	25	30	50	80	150		
-6 Wilson/Allen/Jonnard/Brick 6C	15	20	25	40	60	120		

—Ruffing/Malone/Lazzeri/Dickey #26-4D PSA 8 (NmMt) sold for $6,625 (eBay; 1/08)

1936 Goudey Black and White

	PrFr 1	GD 2	VG 3	VgEx 4	EX 5	ExMt 6	NM 7	NmMt 8
Wally Berger	12	15	20	30	50	60	150	300
Zeke Bonura	10	12	15	25	40	50	120	250
Frenchy Bordagaray	10	12	15	25	40	50	100	250
Bill Brubaker	10	12	15	25	40	50	100	250
Dolph Camilli	10	12	15	25	40	50	100	250
Clyde Castleman	10	12	15	25	40	50	120	
Mickey Cochrane	15	20	30	50	80	100	250	500
Joe Coscarart	10	12	15	25	40	50	100	250
Frank Crosetti	12	15	25	40	60	80	150	400
Kiki Cuyler	12	15	25	40	60	80	150	400
Paul Derringer	10	12	15	25	40	50	120	
Jimmy Dykes	10	12	15	25	40	50	100	250
Rick Ferrell	12	15	25	40	60	80	150	400
Lefty Gomez	15	20	30	50	80	100	200	500
Hank Greenberg	60	80	100	120	200	300	600	
Bucky Harris	12	15	25	40	60	80	150	400
Rollie Hemsley	10	12	15	25	40	50	100	250
Pinky Higgins	10	12	15	25	40	50	100	250
Oral Hildebrand	10	12	15	25	40	50	100	250
Chuck Klein	12	15	25	40	60	100	150	400
Pepper Martin	12	15	25	40	60	80	250	400
Bobo Newsom	10	12	15	25	40	50	100	250
Joe Vosmik	10	12	15	25	40	50	100	250
Paul Waner	12	15	25	40	60	100	150	400
Bill Werber	10	12	15	25	40	50	150	

1936 World Wide Gum

—Joe DiMaggio #51 SGC 84 (NM) sold for $38,400 (Mastro; 5/08)
—Joe DiMaggio #51 SGC 84 (NM) sold for $36,000 (Mastro; 8/07)
—Joe DiMaggio #51 SGC 84 (NM) sold for $22,325 (REA; 5/10)
—Joe DiMaggio #51 SGC 84 (NM) sold for $14,372 (Goodwin; 7/10)
—Joe DiMaggio #51 PSA 5 (EX) sold for $15,275 (REA; 5/09)
—Joe DiMaggio #51 PSA 5 (EX) sold for $11,611 (Goodwin; 9/10)
—Joe DiMaggio #51 SGC 40 (VG) sold for $6,150 (eBay; 6/07)
—Joe DiMaggio #51 PSA 2 (Good) sold for $5,630 (Mastro; 6/07)
—Joe DiMaggio #51 PSA 2 (Good) sold for $4,729 (eBay; 9/06)
—Joe DiMaggio #51 SGC 30 (Good) sold for $4,583 (eBay; 11/06)
—Joe DiMaggio #51 PSA 2 (Good) sold for $4,051 (eBay; 10/07)
—Joe DiMaggio #51 PSA 1 (Poor) sold for $9,400 (REA; 5/08)
—Lou Gehrig #96 SGC 60 (EX) sold for $3,586 (Mastro; 4/07)
—Lou Gehrig #96 SGC 40 (VG) sold for $2,249 (eBay; 1/08)

1938 Goudey Heads-Up

		PrFr 1	GD 2	VG 3	VgEx 4	EX 5	ExMt 6	NM 7	NmMt 8
241	Charley Gehringer	80	100	120	200	400	500	800	3,000
242	Pete Fox	20	30	40	60	100	150	500	800
243	Joe Kuhel	20	30	40	60	100	150	400	800
244	Frank Demaree	20	30	40	60	100	200	300	800
245	Frank Pytlak	20	30	40	60	100	250	400	800
246	Ernie Lombardi	50	80	120	300	400	600	800	1,500
247	Joe Vosmik	20	30	40	80	100	150	300	800
248	Dick Bartell	20	30	40	80	100	200	300	1,000
249	Jimmie Foxx	120	150	200	300	400	600	1,200	4,000
250	Joe DiMaggio	1,000	1,500	2,500	3,000	4,000	5,000	6,000	15,000
251	Bump Hadley	30	40	50	60	100	200	300	800
252	Zeke Bonura	20	30	40	60	100	150	600	800
253	Hank Greenberg	120	150	200	600	800	1,000	1,500	3,000
254	Van Lingle Mungo	20	30	40	60	100	250	400	
255	Moose Solters	20	30	40	60	100	150	300	800
256	Vernon Kennedy	20	30	50	60	80	100	400	800
257	Al Lopez	40	50	60	100	200	300	500	1,200
258	Bobby Doerr	60	100	200	250	300	400	800	2,000
259	Billy Werber	20	30	40	60	100	150	500	800
260	Rudy York	20	30	40	80	150	200	400	1,000
261	Rip Radcliff	20	30	40	50	80	120	300	1,000
262	Joe Medwick	60	80	100	150	300	400	800	2,000
263	Marvin Owen	20	30	40	60	100	150	300	800
264	Bob Feller	250	400	500	600	800	1,500	2,000	5,000
265	Charley Gehringer	80	100	120	200	300	500	800	2,000
266	Pete Fox	40	50	60	100	150	250		
267	Joe Kuhel	20	30	40	60	100	150	300	800
268	Frank Demaree	20	30	40	60	100	150	300	800
269	Frank Pytlak	20	30	40	60	100	150	300	800
270	Ernie Lombardi	50	60	80	200	300	500	600	1,200
271	Joe Vosmik	20	30	40	60	100	150	400	800
272	Dick Bartell	20	30	40	60	100	150	300	800
273	Jimmie Foxx	120	200	250	400	500	800	2,000	4,000
274	Joe DiMaggio	800	1,200	1,400	2,000	2,500	5,000	15,000	20,000
275	Bump Hadley	20	30	40	60	100	150	300	800
276	Zeke Bonura	20	30	40	60	100	200	300	800
277	Hank Greenberg	120	150	200	400	600	1,000	1,500	5,000
278	Van Lingle Mungo	20	30	60	80	100	150	300	800
279	Moose Solters	20	30	40	60	100	150	300	1,200
280	Vernon Kennedy	20	30	40	60	100	150	300	800
281	Al Lopez	40	50	80	100	200	400	500	1,500
282	Bobby Doerr	60	150	200	250	500	600	800	2,000
283	Billy Werber	20	30	40	60	100	150	300	1,000
284	Rudy York	20	30	40	60	150	250	400	1,000
285	Rip Radcliff	20	30	40	60	100	200	300	800
286	Joe Medwick	60	80	100	200	250	400	800	
287	Marvin Owen	20	30	40	60	100	150	400	800
288	Bob Feller	250	300	600	800	1,000	1,500	2,500	

—A complete high-grade SGC set compiled by hobby legend Lionel Carter, including an SGC 98 Greenberg and SGC 96 DiMaggio was sold by Mastro Auctions in April, 2007 for $286,304.
—Joe DiMaggio #274 SGC 8.5 (NmMt+) sold for $19,618 (Goodwin; 3/09)
—Joe DiMaggio #274 PSA 8 (NmMt) sold for $13,066 (Mastro; 4/06)
—Joe DiMaggio #274 SGC 7.5 (Nm+) sold for $9,400 (REA; 05/11)
—Joe DiMaggio #274 PSA 7.5 (Nm+) sold for $7,320 (Greg Bussineau; 12/12)
—Joe DiMaggio #274 SGC 86 (NrMt+) sold for $6,115 (Mile High; 5/12)
—Bob Feller #288 PSA 8 (NmMt) sold for $8,225 (Mastro; 5/08)
—Bob Feller #288 PSA 8 (NmMt) sold for $6,500 (REA; 05/12)
—Bob Feller #288 GAI 8 (NmMt) sold for $4,915 (Mastro; 4/07)
—Jimmie Foxx #249 SGC 96 (MT) sold for $16,652 (Mastro; 4/07)
—Jimmie Foxx #249 SGC 92 (NmMt+) sold for $2,518 (Memory Lane; 9/07)
—Hank Greenberg #277 PSA 9 (MT) sold for $24,898 (Mastro; 6/06)

1939 Play Ball

		PrFr 1	GD 2	VG 3	VgEx 4	EX 5	ExMt 6	NM 7	NmMt 8
1	Jake Powell	12	15	20	25	40	60		
2	Lee Grissom	6	8	10	12	15	25	40	150
3	Red Ruffing	15	25	40	60	100	150	250	500
4	Eldon Auker	6	8	10	12	25	40	80	
5	Luke Sewell	6	8	10	12	15	25	60	100
6	Leo Durocher	15	20	25	30	60	80	150	400
7	Bobby Doerr	20	25	80	120	200	250	400	600
8	Henry Pippen	6	8	10	12	15	25	60	
9	James Tobin	6	8	10	12	15	25	40	
10	James DeShong	6	8	10	12	15	30	40	100
11	Johnny Rizzo	6	8	10	12	15	25	40	100
12	Hershel Martin	6	8	10	12	15	25	40	100
13	Luke Hamlin	6	8	10	12	15	30	50	150
14	Jim Tabor	6	8	10	20	25	30	80	120
15	Paul Derringer	8	10	12	15	20	30	40	120
16	John Peacock	6	8	10	12	15	25	40	100
17	Emerson Dickman	6	8	10	15	15	25	40	100
18	Harry Danning	6	8	10	12	15	25	50	100
19	Paul Dean	12	15	20	25	30	50	120	250
20	Joe Heving	6	6	10	15	25	30	40	
21	Dutch Leonard	8	10	12	15	25	40	60	200
22	Bucky Walters	8	10	12	15	20	30	80	150
23	Burgess Whitehead	6	8	10	20	25	30	40	100
24	Richard Coffman	6	8	10	12	15	25	60	
25	George Selkirk	8	10	12	15	50	60	120	200
26	Joe DiMaggio	500	1,000	1,200	1,500	2,000	2,500	3,000	6,000
27	Fred Ostermueller	6	8	10	12	15	25	40	100
28	Sylvester Johnson	6	8	10	12	15	25	40	100
29	Jack Wilson	6	8	10	12	15	25	40	100
30	Bill Dickey	30	60	80	100	120	150	300	500
31	Sam West	6	8	10	12	15	25	40	100
32	Bob Seeds	6	8	10	12	15	30	80	100

#	Name	PrFr 1	GD 2	VG 3	VgEx 4	EX 5	ExMt 6	NM 7	NmMt 8
33	Del Young	6	8	10	12	15	25	40	100
34	Frank Demaree	6	8	10	12	15	25	40	100
35	Bill Jurges	6	8	10	12	15	25	40	
36	Frank McCormick	6	8	10	12	15	25	40	120
37	Virgil Davis	6	8	10	12	15	25	40	100
38	Billy Myers	6	8	10	12	15	25	40	100
39	Rick Ferrell	12	15	20	25	80	100	150	300
40	James Bagby Jr.	6	8	10	12	15	25	60	
41	Lon Warneke	6	8	10	12	15	25	40	100
42	Arndt Jorgens	6	8	10	12	15	25	40	100
43	Melo Almada	6	8	10	12	15	25	60	
44	Don Heffner	6	8	10	12	15	25	40	
45	Merrill May	6	8	10	12	15	25	40	100
46	Morris Arnovich	6	8	10	12	15	25	40	100
47	Buddy Lewis	6	8	10	12	30	50	80	120
48	Lefty Gomez	25	30	50	80	100	150	200	400
49	Eddie Miller	6	8	10	12	15	25	50	150
50	Charley Gehringer	20	30	60	80	100	120	200	400
51	Mel Ott	20	30	50	150	200	250	300	600
52	Tommy Henrich	6	6	10	15	25	50	100	300
53	Carl Hubbell	25	40	60	80	100	120	200	400
54	Harry Gumpert	6	8	10	12	15	25	40	100
55	Arky Vaughan	12	15	20	25	80	▼100	▲120	▲500
56	Hank Greenberg	40	50	80	150	200	250	▲400	800
57	Buddy Hassett	6	8	10	12	15	25	40	
58	Lou Chiozza	6	8	10	12	15	25	60	
59	Ken Chase	6	8	10	12	15	25	40	100
60	Schoolboy Rowe	8	10	12	15	40	60	80	150
61	Tony Cuccinello	8	12	15	25	30	40	60	100
62	Tom Carey	6	8	10	12	15	25	40	100
63	Emmett Mueller	6	8	10	12	20	25	40	100
64	Wally Moses	6	8	10	15	15	25	40	120
65	Harry Craft	6	8	10	12	20	30	50	100
66	Jimmy Ripple	6	8	10	12	15	25	60	
67	Ed Joost	6	8	10	12	30	50	80	150
68	Fred Sington	6	8	10	12	20	30	50	100
69	Elbie Fletcher	6	8	10	12	15	25	40	150
70	Fred Frankhouse	6	8	10	12	20	30	50	100
71	Monte Pearson	8	10	12	15	25	30	100	150
72	Debs Garms	6	8	10	12	15	25	40	100
73	Hal Schumacher	6	8	10	12	15	25	40	120
74	Cookie Lavagetto	6	8	12	20	30	50	80	1,000
75	Stan Bordagaray	6	8	10	12	15	25	40	100
76	Goody Rosen	6	8	10	12	15	25	50	100
77	Lew Riggs	6	8	10	12	15	30	40	100
78	Julius Solters	6	8	10	12	15	25	40	100
79	Jo Jo Moore	6	8	10	12	15	25	60	150
80	Pete Fox	6	8	10	12	15	25	40	100
81	Babe Dahlgren	8	10	12	15	20	30	50	150
82	Chuck Klein	20	25	30	40	50	100	150	400
83	Gus Suhr	6	8	10	12	15	25	50	
84	Skeeter Newsom	6	8	10	12	15	25	40	120
85	Johnny Cooney	6	8	10	12	15	25	40	100
86	Dolph Camilli	6	8	10	12	20	25	40	120
87	Milburn Shoffner	6	8	10	12	15	25	60	
88	Charlie Keller	12	15	20	25	30	50	80	200
89	Lloyd Waner	15	25	40	60	80	150	250	400
90	Robert Klinger	6	8	10	12	15	25	40	100
91	John Knott	6	8	10	12	15	25	40	100
92	Ted Williams	1,000	2,000	2,500	3,000	5,000	6,000	10,000	25,000
93	Charles Gelbert	6	8	10	12	15	25	40	100
94	Heinie Manush	12	20	30	50	80	120	200	300
95	Whit Wyatt	6	8	10	12	15	25	40	100
96	Babe Phelps	6	8	10	12	15	25	40	100
97	Bob Johnson	8	10	12	15	25	40	60	150
98	Pinky Whitney	6	8	12	20	30	50	80	120
99	Wally Berger	8	10	12	15	20	30	50	120
100	Buddy Myer	6	8	10	12	15	25	40	100
101	Roger Cramer	6	6	10	15	25	40	60	100
102	Lem (Pep) Young	6	8	10	12	15	40	60	100
103	Moe Berg	30	50	80	250	300	400	500	800
104	Tom Bridges	6	8	10	12	15	25	40	120
105	Rabbit McNair	6	8	10	12	20	30	40	100
106	Dolly Stark Umpire	8	10	12	20	30	50	80	250
107	Joe Vosmik	6	8	10	12	15	25	50	100
108	Frank Hayes	6	8	10	12	15	25	40	100
109	Myril Hoag	6	8	10	12	25	40	50	100

#	Name	PrFr 1	GD 2	VG 3	VgEx 4	EX 5	ExMt 6	NM 7	NmMt 8
110	Fred Fitzsimmons	6	8	10	20	30	50	80	12*
111	Van Lingle Mungo	6	8	10	12	20	25	40	10*
112	Paul Waner	15	25	40	60	80	100	120	40*
113	Al Schacht	8	10	12	25	40	40	80	200
114	Cecil Travis	6	8	10	12	25	40	80	
115	Ralph Kress	6	8	10	12	15	25	60	
116	Gene Desautels	10	12	15	20	35	80	150	
117	Wayne Ambler	10	12	15	20	40	60	100	25*
118	Lynn Nelson	10	12	15	20	40	60	100	
119	Will Hershberger	12	15	20	30	50	80	200	50*
120	Rabbit Warstler	10	12	15	20	40	60	150	25*
121	Bill Posedel	10	12	15	20	40	60	150	
122	George McQuinn	10	12	15	20	40	60	100	25*
123	Ray T. Davis	10	12	15	20	40	60	100	25*
124	Walter Brown	10	12	15	20	40	60	100	25*
125	Cliff Melton	10	12	15	20	40	60	120	25*
127	Gil Brack	10	12	15	20	40	60	150	
128	Joe Bowman	10	12	15	20	40	60	100	
129	Bill Swift	10	12	15	20	40	60	150	
130	Bill Brubaker	10	12	15	20	40	80	100	25*
131	Mort Cooper	10	12	15	20	50	80	120	
132	Jim Brown	10	12	15	20	40	80	100	30*
133	Lynn Myers	10	12	15	20	40	60	100	25*
134	Tot Presnell	10	12	15	20	40	60	100	
135	Mickey Owen	12	15	20	30	60	100	120	30*
136	Roy Bell	10	12	15	20	40	60	100	25*
137	Pete Appleton	10	12	15	20	40	60	100	25*
138	George Case	10	12	15	20	40	80	150	
139	Vito Tamulis	10	12	15	20	40	80	100	30*
140	Ray Hayworth	10	12	15	30	40	60	100	
141	Pete Coscarart	10	12	15	20	40	60	100	25*
142	Ira Hutchinson	10	12	15	20	40	60	100	
143	Earl Averill	25	30	40	60	120	200	250	60*
144	Zeke Bonura	10	12	15	20	40	60	120	30*
145	Hugh Mulcahy	10	12	15	20	40	60	150	
146	Tom Sunkel	10	12	15	20	40	60	150	
147	George Coffman	10	12	15	20	40	60	100	25*
148	Bill Trotter	10	12	15	20	40	60	100	25*
149	Max West	10	12	15	20	40	60	100	25*
150	James Walkup	10	12	15	20	40	60	100	25*
151	Hugh Casey	10	12	15	20	40	60	120	40*
152	Roy Weatherly	10	12	15	20	40	60	100	25*
153	Dizzy Trout	12	15	20	30	50	80	150	50*
154	Johnny Hudson	10	12	15	20	40	60	150	
155	Jimmy Outlaw	10	12	15	20	40	60	100	20*
156	Ray Berres	10	12	15	20	40	60	100	
157	Don Padgett	10	12	15	20	40	80	200	
158	Bud Thomas	10	12	15	20	40	80	100	
159	Red Evans	10	12	15	20	40	60	100	25*
160	Gene Moore	10	12	15	20	40	60	150	
161	Lonnie Frey	10	12	15	20	40	60	150	
162	Whitey Moore	25	30	40	60	100	200	400	

—Moe Berg #103 PSA 9 (MT) sold for $4,339 (mastro; 8/07)
—Joe DiMaggio #26 GAI 9.5 (Gem) sold for $13,166 (Mile High; 12/05)
—Joe DiMaggio #26 SGC 96 (MT) sold for $13,200 (SCP Sotheby's; 12/05)
—Joe DiMaggio #26 PSA 9 (MT) sold for $12,906 (Goodwin; 8/07)
—Joe DiMaggio #26 PSA 9 (MT) sold for $11,400 (SCP Sotheby's; 6/05)
—Joe DiMaggio #26 PSA 9 (MT) sold for $10,665 (REA; Spring '14)
—Joe DiMaggio #26 PSA 9 (MT) sold for $9,950 (Memory Lane; 11/04)
—Joe DiMaggio #26 SGC 96 (MT) sold for $9,816 (Mastro; 8/06)
—Joe DiMaggio #26 PSA 9 (MT) sold for $8,923 (Mastro; 12/05)
—Joe DiMaggio #26 GAI 9 (MT) sold for $6,848 (SCP; 7/08)
—Joe DiMaggio #26 SGC 96 (Mint) sold for $6,463 (Huggins and Scott; 6/12)
—Joe DiMaggio #26 SGC 96 (MT) sold for $6,600 (Greg Bussineau; 12/12)
—Joe DiMaggio #26 SGC 92 (NmMt+) sold for $4,705 (eBay; 12/05)
—Joe DiMaggio #26 SGC 92 (NmMt+) sold for $4,521 (Mastro; 12/07)
—Joe DiMaggio #26 SGC 92 (NmMt+) sold for $3,902 (eBay; 6/06)
—Joe DiMaggio #26 GAI 8.5 (NmMt+) sold for $2,291 (Mastro; 12/06)
—Bill Dickey #30 PSA 9 (MT) sold for $3,259 (Mastro; 8/07)
—Bill Dickey #30 PSA 9 (MT) sold for $3,231 (REA; 4/07)
—Whitey Moore #162 PSA 8 (NmMt) sold for $6,192 (Goodwin; 09/11)
—Whitey Moore #162 PSA 8 (NmMt) sold for $4,030 (Goodwin; 3/08)
—Whitey Moore #162 PSA 8 (NmMt) sold for $3,335 (eBay; 2/07)
—Mel Ott #51 PSA 9 (MT) sold for $6,863 (Memory Lane; 8/05)
—Mel Ott #51 PSA 9 (MT) sold for $2,400 (Mastro; 5/08)
—Mel Ott #51 PSA 9 (MT) sold for $2,686 (Memory Lane; 8/05)
—Jake Powell #1 PSA 8 (NmMt) sold for $4,161 (eBay; 12/06)

Dizzy Trout #153 PSA 10 (Gem) sold for $8,529 (Mastro; 8/06)
Lloyd Waner #89 PSA 9 (MT) sold for $1,559 (SCP; 7/08)
Ted Williams #92 GAI 9.5 (Gem) sold for $23,000 (Superior; 3/05)
Ted Williams #92 PSA 9 (MT) sold for $31,720 (Mastro; 8/07)
Ted Williams #92 PSA 9 (MT) sold for $27,025 (Memory Lane; 3/06)
Ted Williams #92 PSA 9 (MT) sold for $23,754 (Memory Lane; 4/07)
Ted Williams #92 PSA 9 (MT) sold for $23,666 (Mastro; 4/07)
Ted Williams #92 PSA 9 (MT) sold for $20,206 (Mastro; 12/06)
Ted Williams #92 GAI 9 (MT) sold for $17,743 (SCP Sotheby's; 11/06)
Ted Williams #92 GAI 9 (MT) sold for $14,887 (Superior; 8/05)
Ted Williams #92 GAI 9 (MT) sold for $5,040 (Mile High; 10/11)
Ted Williams #92 SGC 92 (NmMt+) sold for $9,000 (Mastro; 5/08)
Ted Williams #92 SGC 92 (NmMt+) sold for $8,463 (Mile High; 10/11)
Ted Williams #92 SGC 92 (NmMt+) sold for $6,498 (Goodwin; 3/08)
Ted Williams #92 SGC 92 (NmMt+) sold for $6,462 (REA; 4/07)
Ted Williams #92 GAI 8.5 (NmMt+) sold for $4,915 (Mastro; 4/07)
Ted Williams #92 GAI 8.5 (NmMt+) sold for $4,482 (Memory Lane; 8/06)
Ted Williams #92 GAI 8.5 (NmMt+) sold for $2,760 (Mastro; 5/08)

1940 Play Ball

	PrFr 1	GD 2	VG 3	VgEx 4	EX 5	ExMt 6	NM 7	NmMt 8
Joe DiMaggio	500	800	1,000	1,200	2,000	3,000	8,000	12,000
Art Jorgens	8	10	12	15	20	50	150	
Babe Dahlgren	8	10	12	15	20	25	80	
Tommy Henrich	10	12	15	20	25	60	150	
Monte Pearson	8	10	12	15	20	50	100	
Lefty Gomez	25	60	80	100	120	150	200	600
Bill Dickey	25	30	40	60	150	200	400	800
George Selkirk	8	10	12	15	20	40	150	250
Charlie Keller	10	12	15	20	25	40	80	500
Red Ruffing	20	40	50	60	80	100	150	500
Jake Powell	8	10	12	15	20	25	40	250
Johnny Schulte	8	10	12	15	20	30	40	300
Jack Knott	8	10	12	15	20	30	120	
Rabbit McNair	8	10	12	15	20	40	80	
George Case	8	10	12	15	20	25	50	250
Cecil Travis	8	10	12	15	20	40	60	250
Buddy Myer	8	10	12	15	20	25	60	300
Charlie Gelbert	8	10	12	15	20	25	40	250
Ken Chase	8	10	12	15	20	25	80	
Buddy Lewis	8	10	12	15	20	25	40	250
Rick Ferrell	12	20	30	50	80	100	150	800
Sammy West	8	10	12	15	20	25	60	
Dutch Leonard	8	10	12	25	30	40	60	
Frank Hayes	8	10	12	15	20	25	60	150
Bob Johnson	10	12	15	20	25	50	60	
Wally Moses	8	10	12	15	30	50	60	200
Ted Williams	200	▲500	▲600	800	1,000	2,000	2,500	6,000
Gene Desautels	8	10	12	15	20	30	60	150
Doc Cramer	8	10	12	15	20	25	60	500
Moe Berg	40	50	60	100	200	250	300	600
Jack Wilson	8	10	12	15	20	25	50	250
Jim Bagby	8	10	12	15	20	25	50	250
Fritz Ostermueller	8	10	12	15	20	25	40	120
John Peacock	8	10	12	15	20	25	40	150
Joe Heving	8	10	12	15	20	25	60	150
Jim Tabor	8	10	12	15	20	25	50	150
Emerson Dickman	8	10	12	15	20	25	50	
Bobby Doerr	15	20	25	30	60	100	150	500
Tom Carey	8	10	12	15	20	25	40	150
Hank Greenberg	50	60	80	200	250	400	600	1,200
Charley Gehringer	25	40	60	100	150	250	400	600
Bud Thomas	8	10	12	15	20	25	60	150
Pete Fox	8	10	12	15	20	25	100	200
Dizzy Trout	8	10	12	15	30	40	100	
Red Kress	8	10	12	15	20	25	50	
Earl Averill	15	20	25	40	60	80	150	400
Oscar Vitt RC	8	10	12	15	20	25	50	300
Luke Sewell	8	10	12	15	20	50	60	150
Stormy Weatherly	8	10	12	15	20	25	60	
Hal Trosky	8	10	12	15	20	25	40	250
Don Heffner	8	10	12	15	20	25	40	200
Myril Hoag	8	10	12	15	20	25	40	150
George McQuinn	8	10	12	15	20	25	40	100
Bill Trotter	8	10	12	15	20	25	50	
Slick Coffman	8	10	12	15	20	25	40	150

		PrFr 1	GD 2	VG 3	VgEx 4	EX 5	ExMt 6	NM 7	NmMt 8
56	Eddie Miller RC	8	10	12	15	20	25	60	200
57	Max West	8	10	12	15	20	25	50	100
58	Bill Posedel	8	10	12	15	20	25	50	250
59	Rabbit Warstler	8	10	12	15	20	25	50	100
60	John Cooney	8	10	12	25	30	40	50	150
61	Tony Cuccinello	8	10	12	15	20	25	40	100
62	Buddy Hassett	8	10	12	15	20	25	40	100
63	Pete Coscarart	8	10	12	15	20	25	50	100
64	Van Lingle Mungo	8	10	12	15	20	30	40	150
65	Fred Fitzsimmons	8	10	12	20	30	40	50	100
66	Babe Phelps	8	10	12	15	20	25	40	250
67	Whit Wyatt	8	10	12	15	20	25	40	150
68	Dolph Camilli	8	10	12	20	25	40	60	
69	Cookie Lavagetto	8	10	12	15	20	25	60	
70	Luke Hamlin	8	10	12	15	20	25	80	150
71	Mel Almada	8	10	12	15	20	25	80	
72	Chuck Dressen RC	8	10	12	15	20	25	40	150
73	Bucky Walters	8	10	12	15	25	50	80	200
74	Duke Derringer	8	10	12	15	20	25	80	120
75	Buck McCormick	8	10	12	15	20	25	40	150
76	Lonny Frey	8	10	12	15	20	25	40	300
77	Willard Hershberger	8	10	12	15	• 30	40	60	150
78	Lew Riggs	8	10	12	15	20	30	60	100
79	Harry Craft	8	10	12	15	20	25	60	
80	Billy Myers	8	10	12	15	20	25	40	300
81	Wally Berger	8	10	12	15	20	25	40	250
82	Hank Gowdy CO	8	10	12	15	20	25	50	100
83	Cliff Melton	8	10	12	15	20	25	40	120
84	Jo Jo Moore	8	10	12	15	20	25	50	▲200
85	Hal Schumacher	8	10	12	15	20	25	60	
86	Harry Gumbert	8	10	12	15	20	25	40	100
87	Carl Hubbell	30	40	60	80	120	150	250	600
88	Mel Ott	50	80	100	120	200	200	300	800
89	Bill Jurges	8	10	12	15	20	25	100	250
90	Frank Demaree	8	10	12	15	20	25	40	250
91	Bob Seeds	8	10	12	15	20	25	60	120
92	Whitey Whitehead	8	10	12	15	20	25	60	250
93	Harry Danning	8	10	12	15	20	25	60	
94	Gus Suhr	8	10	12	15	20	25	60	100
95	Hugh Mulcahy	8	10	12	15	20	25	60	300
96	Heinie Mueller	8	10	12	15	20	25	40	150
97	Morry Arnovich	8	10	12	15	20	25	50	250
98	Pinky May	8	10	12	15	20	25	40	250
99	Syl Johnson	8	10	12	15	20	25	50	100
100	Hersh Martin	8	10	12	15	20	25	40	120
101	Del Young	8	10	12	15	25	50	80	120
102	Chuck Klein	15	20	25	40	60	100	150	600
103	Elbie Fletcher	8	10	12	15	20	25	40	100
104	Paul Waner	15	20	25	60	80	100	150	250
105	Lloyd Waner	15	20	80	100	120	150	600	
106	Pep Young	8	10	12	15	20	25	40	120
107	Arky Vaughan	15	20	25	30	40	80	120	400
108	Johnny Rizzo	8	10	12	15	20	25	50	
109	Don Padgett	8	10	12	15	20	25	60	100
110	Tom Sunkel	8	10	12	15	20	25	60	
111	Mickey Owen	8	10	12	15	50	60	80	
112	Jimmy Brown	8	10	12	15	20	40	100	
113	Mort Cooper	8	10	12	15	20	40	150	
114	Lon Warneke	8	10	12	15	20	25	80	250
115	Mike Gonzalez CO	8	10	12	15	20	25	60	250
116	Al Schacht	10	12	15	20	25	80	150	
117	Dolly Stark UMP	8	10	12	20	40	60	80	300
118	Waite Hoyt	15	20	25	40	50	60	150	500
119	Grover C. Alexander	30	40	▲100	▲120	▲150	▲200	250	800
120	Walter Johnson	50	120	150	200	300	500	600	1,200
121	Atley Donald RC	8	10	12	15	20	25	60	
122	Sandy Sundra RC	8	10	12	15	20	40	100	
123	Hildy Hildebrand	8	10	12	15	20	25	40	100
124	Earle Combs	12	15	20	25	60	100	150	200
125	Art Fletcher RC	8	10	12	15	20	25	60	
126	Jake Solters	8	10	12	15	20	25	50	
127	Muddy Ruel	8	10	12	15	20	25	50	120
128	Pete Appleton	8	10	12	15	25	30	40	50	100
129	Bucky Harris MG	15	20	25	30	40	100	120	400
130	Clyde Milan RC	8	10	12	15	20	25	40	120
131	Zeke Bonura	8	10	12	15	20	25	40	100
132	Connie Mack MG	25	30	40	80	▲120	150	400	800

#	Name	PrFr 1	GD 2	VG 3	VgEx 4	EX 5	ExMt 6	NM 7	NmMt 8
133	Jimmie Foxx	80	100	150	250	300	400	500	1,000
134	Joe Cronin	15	20	50	60	80	120	150	
135	Line Drive Nelson	8	10	12	15	20	25	50	100
136	Cotton Pippen	8	10	12	15	20	25	40	100
137	Bing Miller	8	10	12	15	20	25	40	120
138	Beau Bell	8	10	12	15	20	25	60	100
139	Elden Auker	8	10	12	15	20	25	40	120
140	Dick Coffman	8	10	12	15	20	25	40	120
141	Casey Stengel MG	30	40	60	80	150	200	300	800
142	George Kelly RC	15	20	25	30	40	100	150	600
143	Gene Moore	8	10	12	15	20	25	50	150
144	Joe Vosmik	8	10	12	15	20	25	40	300
145	Vito Tamulis	8	10	12	15	20	25	80	150
146	Tot Pressnell	8	10	12	15	20	25	60	150
147	Johnny Hudson	8	10	12	15	20	25	60	150
148	Hugh Casey	8	10	12	15	20	25	100	
149	Pinky Shoffner	8	10	12	15	25	30	40	
150	Whitey Moore	8	10	12	15	30	40	50	150
151	Edwin Joost	8	10	12	25	30	40	50	120
152	Jimmy Wilson	8	10	12	15	25	40	60	120
153	Bill McKechnie MG	15	20	25	30	40	100	120	300
154	Jumbo Brown	8	10	12	15	20	25	40	100
155	Ray Hayworth	8	10	12	15	20	25	50	150
156	Daffy Dean	8	10	12	15	40	50	60	600
157	Lou Chiozza	8	10	12	15	25	60	80	120
158	Travis Jackson	15	20	25	30	60	80	120	400
159	Pancho Snyder	8	10	12	15	20	25	50	450
160	Hans Lobert CO	8	10	12	15	20	25	50	250
161	Debs Garms	8	10	12	15	20	25	40	150
162	Joe Bowman	8	10	12	15	20	40	60	
163	Spud Davis	8	10	12	15	20	25	50	300
164	Ray Berres	8	10	12	15	20	40	60	250
165	Bob Klinger	8	10	12	15	20	25	40	150
166	Bill Brubaker	8	10	12	15	30	40	120	
167	Frankie Frisch MG	15	20	25	50	60	150	250	600
168	Honus Wagner CO	60	100	150	250	300	400	500	1,500
169	Gabby Street	6	10	12	15	25	30	40	100
170	Tris Speaker	25	30	50	60	80	150	200	800
171	Harry Heilmann	15	20	25	60	80	100	150	500
172	Chief Bender	15	20	25	40	50	100	150	400
173	Napoleon Lajoie	30	40	80	100	120	150	200	800
174	Johnny Evers	15	20	25	30	50	80	150	400
175	Christy Mathewson	40	50	100	120	200	250	400	800
176	Heinie Manush	15	20	25	40	60	100	120	400
177	Frank Baker	20	25	30	80	100	120	150	400
178	Max Carey	15	20	25	30	50	60	150	
179	George Sisler	20	25	40	80	100	120	200	500
180	Mickey Cochrane	25	30	40	80	100	120	300	
181	Spud Chandler	10	12	15	20	25	80	300	
182	Knick Knickerbocker	10	12	15	20	25	50	150	400
183	Marvin Breuer	10	12	15	20	25	40	120	200
184	Mule Haas	10	12	15	20	25	40	80	300
185	Joe Kuhel	10	12	15	20	30	50	200	
186	Taft Wright	10	12	15	20	25	50	150	400
187	Jimmy Dykes MG	10	12	15	20	25	50	100	
188	Joe Krakauskas	10	12	15	20	50	60	150	300
189	Jim Bloodworth	10	12	15	20	25	60	200	
190	Charley Berry	10	12	15	30	50	60	100	400
191	John Babich	10	12	15	20	25	40	200	300
192	Dick Siebert	10	12	15	20	25	50	200	400
193	Chubby Dean	10	12	15	20	50	80	120	300
194	Sam Chapman	10	12	15	20	25	40	60	250
195	Dee Miles	10	12	15	20	25	50	150	
196	Red Nonnenkamp	10	12	15	20	40	60	100	300
197	Lou Finney	10	12	15	20	25	40	80	150
198	Denny Galehouse	10	12	15	20	25	40	60	150
199	Pinky Higgins	10	12	15	20	25	40	80	300
200	Soup Campbell	10	12	15	20	25	50	150	
201	Barney McCosky	10	12	15	20	25	40	60	250
202	Al Milnar	10	12	15	20	25	50	80	300
203	Bad News Hale	10	12	15	20	40	80	120	400
204	Harry Eisenstat	10	12	15	60	80	100	120	300
205	Rollie Hemsley	10	12	15	20	25	40	150	
206	Chet Laabs	10	12	15	20		80	200	
207	Gus Mancuso	10	12	15	20	25	40	80	450
208	Lee Gamble	10	12	15	20	25	100	200	
209	Hy Vandenberg	10	12	15	20	25	50	150	
210	Bill Lohrman	10	12	15	20	25	80	120	
211	Pop Joiner	10	12	15	20	25	50	200	450
212	Babe Young	10	12	15	20	30	50	150	
213	John Rucker	10	12	15	20	25	50	80	250
214	Ken O'Dea	10	12	15	20	25	80	150	300
215	Johnnie McCarthy	10	12	15	20	25	50	80	250
216	Joe Marty	10	12	15	20	40	50	60	250
217	Walter Beck	10	12	15	20	30	40	80	250
218	Wally Millies	10	12	15	20	25	50	100	
219	Russ Bauers	10	12	15	20	25	50	100	250
220	Mace Brown	10	12	15	20	25	60	100	300
221	Lee Handley	10	12	15	20	25	60	100	300
222	Max Butcher	10	12	15	20	25	50	100	
223	Hughie Jennings	25	30	40	60	80	100	200	600
224	Pie Traynor	25	30	50	60	80	100	200	1,200
225	Joe Jackson	800	1,200	1,500	2,000	2,500	4,000	5,000	15,000
226	Harry Hooper	25	30	40	50	100	120	250	600
227	Jesse Haines	25	30	40	60		150	200	600
228	Charlie Grimm	10	12	15	20	25	80	100	250
229	Buck Herzog	10	12	15	20	25	80	100	300
230	Red Faber	25	30	40	50	60	120	250	600
231	Dolf Luque	10	12	15	20	50	100	500	
232	Goose Goslin	25	30	40	50	60	150	250	600
233	George Earnshaw	10	12	15	20	25	60	200	
234	Frank Chance	25	30	40	50	100	150	200	600
235	John McGraw	20	30	50	80	120	200	300	800
236	Jim Bottomley	25	30	40	50	80	200	250	600
237	Willie Keeler	30	40	50	60	120	150	400	800
238	Tony Lazzeri	30	40	50	60	80	150	300	600
239	George Uhle	10	12	15	20	25	40	300	500
240	Bill Atwood	15	20	25	30	50	100	300	

—Bill Atwood #240 PSA 8 (NmMt) sold for $2,324 (Memory Lane; 11/05)
—Moe Berg #30 PSA 9 (MT) sold for $2,554 (eBay; 6/08)
—Joe DiMaggio #1 PSA 9 (MT) sold for $34,349 (Goodwin; 11/07)
—Charlie Gelbert #18 SGC 96 (Mint) sold for $5,273 (Goodwin; 3/12)
—Ted Williams #27 PSA 10 (Gem) sold for $60,343 (Goodwin; 6/06)
—Ted Williams #27 GAI 9 (MT) sold for $10,186 (Memory Lane; 8/06)
—Ted Williams #27 GAI 9 (MT) sold for $6,463 (Memory Lane; 9/07)
—Ted Williams #27 GAI 9 (MT) sold for $5,343 (eBay; 2/08)
—Ted Williams #27 GAI 8.5 (NmMt+) sold for $3,331 (Mile High; 8/07)

1941 Double Play

#	Name	PrFr 1	GD 2	VG 3	VgEx 4	EX 5	ExMt 6	NM 7	NmMt 8
1	L.French/V.Page	10	12	15	20	25	40	100	250
3	B.Herman/S.Hack	10	12	15	50	60	80	100	150
5	L.Frey/J.VanderMeer	6	8	10	12	15	25	40	100
7	P.Derringer/B.Walters	6	8	10	12	15	25	40	100
9	F.McCormick/B.Werber	6	8	10	12	15	25	40	100
11	J.Ripple/E.Lombardi	10	12	15	20	25	40	80	
13	A.Kampouris/W.Wyatt	6	8	10	12	15	25	50	100
15	M.Owen/P.Waner	10	12	15	20	40	60	100	150
17	C.Lavagetto/P.Reiser	6	8	10	12	15	25	100	
19	J.Wasdell/D.Camilli	6	8	10	12	15	25	40	100
21	D.Walker/J.Medwick	10	12	15	20	25	80	100	150
23	P.Reese/K.Higbe	40	50	60	120	200	300	400	800
25	H.Danning/C.Melton	6	8	10	12	15	25	40	150
27	H.Gumbert/B.Whitehead	6	8	10	12	15	25	40	100
29	J.Orengo/J.Moore	6	8	10	12	15	50	80	200
31	M.Ott/N.Young	25	30	40	50	80	120	250	400
33	L.Handley/A.Vaughan	10	12	15	20	25	40	60	150
35	B.Klinger/S.Brown	6	8	10	12	15	25	50	100
37	T.Moore/G.Mancuso	6	8	10	12	15	25	40	100
39	J.Mize/E.Slaughter	25	30	40	50	150	200	300	400
41	J.Cooney/S.Sisti	6	8	10	12	15	25	40	100
43	M.West/C.Rowell	6	8	10	12	15	25	40	100
45	D.Litwhiler/M.May	6	8	10	12	15	25	40	100
47	F.Hayes/A.Brancato	6	8	10	12	15	25	40	100
49	B.Johnson/B.Nagel	6	8	10	12	15	25	40	100
51	B.Newsom/H.Greenberg	30	40	80	100	120	150	200	600
53	B.McCosky/C.Gehringer	20	25	30	40	50	80	120	300
55	P.Higgins/D.Bartell	6	8	10	12	15	25	40	100
57	T.Williams/J.Tabor	100	120	150	300	400	500	750	1,500
59	J.Cronin/J.Foxx	40	50	60	80	100	200	300	600
61	L.Gomez/P.Rizzuto	50	60	80	100	300	400	500	800
63	J.DiMaggio/C.Keller	150	200	250	300	350	600	1,000	3,000
65	R.Rolfe/B.Dickey	25	30	40	50	60	100	200	400

	PrFr 1	GD 2	VG 3	VgEx 4	EX 5	ExMt 6	NM 7	NmMt 8
J.Gordon/R.Ruffing	15	20	25	30	40	60	250	400
M.Tresh/L.Appling	10	12	15	20	25	80	150	200
M.Solters/J.Rigney	6	8	10	12	15	25	40	100
B.Meyer/B.Chapman	10	12	15	20	25	40	60	150
C.Travis/G.Case	6	8	10	12	15	25	40	100
J.Krakauskas/B.Feller	30	40	50	60	150	200	325	600
K.Keltner/H.Trosky	6	8	10	12	15	25	40	100
T.Williams/J.Cronin	125	200	200	250	350	500	800	2,000
J.Gordon/C.Keller	30	40	50	60	80	150	200	400
H.Greenberg/R.Ruffing	40	50	80	100	120	150	300	600
H.Trosky/G.Case	6	8	10	12	15	25	40	100
M.Ott/B.Whitehead	25	30	40	50	60	150	225	800
H.Danning/H.Gumbert	6	8	10	12	15	25	40	200
N.Young/C.Melton	6	8	10	12	15	25	40	100
J.Ripple/B.Walters	6	8	10	12	15	25	40	200
S.Hack/B.Klinger	6	8	10	12	30	50	100	120
J.Mize/D.Litwhiler	15	20	25	30	40	80	100	250
D.Dallesandro/A.Galan	8	10	12	15	20	80	50	120
B.Lee/P.Cavarretta	8	10	12	15	20	30	100	120
L.Grove/B.Doerr	40	50	60	100	150	200	250	600
F.Pytlak/D.DiMaggio	15	20	25	30	60	80	100	300
J.Priddy/J.Murphy	8	10	12	15	20	30	80	120
T.Henrich/M.Russo	25	30	40	50	60	80	100	150
F.Crosetti/J.Sturm	10	12	15	20	25	40	60	200
I.Goodman/M.McCormick	8	10	12	15	20	30	50	120
E.Joost/E.Koy	8	10	12	15	20	40	50	120
L.Waner/H.Majeski	20	25	30	40	50	80	120	300
B.Hassett/E.Moore	8	10	12	15	20	30	50	200
N.Etten/J.Rizzo	8	10	12	15	20	40	50	150
S.Chapman/W.Moses	8	10	12	15	20	30	50	120
J.Babich/D.Siebert	8	10	12	15	20	30	50	120
N.Potter/B.McCoy	8	10	12	15	20	30	50	120
C.Campbell/L.Boudreau	20	25	30	40	50	80	120	300
R.Hemsley/M.Harder	8	10	12	15	20	30	60	120
G.Walker/J.Heving	8	10	12	15	20	30	50	200
J.Rucker/A.Adams	8	10	12	15	20	30	60	200
M.Arnovich/C.Hubbell	40	50	60	80	100	150	250	600
L.Riggs/L.Durocher	12	15	20	25	30	40	60	120
F.Fitzsimmons/J.Vosmik	8	10	12	15	20	30	50	120
F.Crespi/J.Brown	8	10	12	15	20	30	50	120
D.Heffner/H.Clift	8	10	12	15	20	30	50	120
D.Garms/E.Fletcher	8	10	12	15	20	30	50	120

—Newsom/Greenberg #51/52 PSA 9 (MT) sold for $2,986 (Mastro; 8/06)
—Reese/Higbe #23/24 PSA 9 (MT) sold for $3,976 (Mastro; 8/06)
—Williams/Tabor #57/58 PSA 9 (MT) sold for $9,595 (Mastro; 8/06)
—Williams/Tabor #57/58 PSA 9 (MT) sold for $9,142 (Memory Lane; 12/07)

1941 Play Ball

	PrFr 1	GD 2	VG 3	VgEx 4	EX 5	ExMt 6	NM 7	NmMt 8
Eddie Miller	20	25	30	40	80	150	300	1,200
Max West	15	20	25	30	50	120	200	1,200
Bucky Walters	12	20	30	50	60	100	200	1,200
Paul Derringer	10	15	20	25	50	80	150	500
Frank (Buck) McCormick	10	15	20	25	60	80	200	600
Carl Hubbell	40	80	100	120	200	300	400	1,000
Harry Danning	6	10	15	20	60	80	100	300
Mel Ott	50	80	120	▲250	▲300	▲400	500	1,200
Pinky May	6	10	15	20	30	80	120	300
Arky Vaughan	25	30	40	50	▲120	▲200	250	800
Debs Garms	10	15	20	25	40	60	150	500
Jimmy Brown	6	10	15	25	30	50	120	300
Jimmie Foxx	120	150	200	250	300	400	1,000	2,000
Ted Williams	400	500	600	1,000	1,200	2,000	3,000	6,000
Joe Cronin	25	40	▲80	▲100	▲150	200	300	800
Hal Trosky	6	10	15	40	80	100	120	300
Roy Weatherly	6	10	15	20	50	50	100	400
Hank Greenberg	80	100	120	200	250	300	600	800
Charley Gehringer	30	40	80	120	150	200	350	1,200
Red Ruffing	25	30	60	80	120	150	250	600
Charlie Keller	20	25	30	40	60	100	150	600
Bob Johnson	6	10	15	30	60	100	150	400
George McQuinn	6	10	15	30	50	80	120	400
Dutch Leonard	6	10	15	30	40	100	120	400
Gene Moore	6	10	15	20	25	60	100	300
Harry Gumpert	6	10	15	20	40	100	150	500
Babe Young	6	10	15	20	60	80	120	500

	PrFr 1	GD 2	VG 3	VgEx 4	EX 5	ExMt 6	NM 7	NmMt 8
28 Joe Marty	6	10	15	20	30	50	150	600
29 Jack Wilson	6	10	15	20	50	80	120	300
30 Lou Finney	6	10	25	30	40	50	150	300
31 Joe Kuhel	6	10	15	20	30	60	200	300
32 Taft Wright	6	10	15	20	30	60	120	500
33 Al Milnar	6	10	15	20	30	50	120	400
34 Rollie Hemsley	6	8	12	20	30	60	100	400
35 Pinky Higgins	6	10	15	20	50	80	150	300
36 Barney McCosky	6	10	15	20	30	50	120	200
37 Bruce Campbell	10	15	20	25	40	80	200	500
38 Atley Donald	6	10	15	20	30	120	150	400
39 Tommy Henrich	20	25	30	50	100	150	300	600
40 John Babich	6	10	15	20	30	60	100	300
41 Blimp Hayes	6	10	15	20	50	80	100	400
42 Wally Moses	6	10	15	20	30	40	120	500
43 Al Brancato	6	10	15	20	50	60	120	400
44 Sam Chapman	6	10	15	20	30	50	100	300
45 Eldon Auker	6	10	15	25	30	50	100	300
46 Sid Hudson	6	10	15	20	30	60	120	500
47 Buddy Lewis	6	10	15	20	30	80	120	500
48 Cecil Travis	6	10	15	20	30	60	200	500
49 Babe Dahlgren	10	15	20	25	40	60	150	400
50 Johnny Cooney	10	15	20	25	40	60	150	500
51 Dolph Camilli	10	20	25	50	80	120	200	400
52 Kirby Higbe	10	15	20	25	50	80	150	400
53 Luke Hamlin	10	15	20	25	40	100	200	400
54 Pee Wee Reese	100	300	400	500	600	800	1,200	4,000
55 Whit Wyatt	6	10	15	25	60	100	200	600
56 Johnny VanderMeer	20	40	50	80	100	120	150	600
57 Moe Arnovich	10	15	20	25	50	100	200	600
58 Frank Demaree	10	15	20	30	40	100	200	800
59 Bill Jurges	10	15	20	25	40	80	120	400
60 Chuck Klein	30	40	60	100	150	250	400	1,000
61 Vince DiMaggio	40	50	60	100	120	200	400	1,200
62 Elbie Fletcher	10	15	20	25	40	60	200	800
63 Dom DiMaggio	40	50	60	200	250	300	500	1,200
64 Bobby Doerr	60	80	100	120	200	250	300	1,000
65 Tommy Bridges	10	15	20	25	50	60	200	800
66 Harland Clift	10	15	25	30	40	80	200	400
67 Walt Judnich	10	15	20	25	40	60	150	400
68 John Knott	10	15	20	25	40	60	100	300
69 George Case	10	15	20	25	40	60	200	600
70 Bill Dickey	60	80	150	200	250	300	500	2,000
71 Joe DiMaggio	600	1,000	1,500	2,500	4,000	6,000	8,000	20,000
72 Lefty Gomez	50	100	120	200	250	600	800	1,500

—Joe Cronin #15 PSA 9 (MT) sold for $3,900 (Mastro; 5/08)
—Joe DiMaggio #71 PSA 9 (MT) sold for $96,075 (Memory Lane; 8/05)
—Joe DiMaggio #71 PSA 9 (MT) sold for $65,493 (Mastro; 8/06)
—Joe DiMaggio #71 SGC 92 (NmMt) sold for $20,206 (Mastro; 12/06)
—Joe DiMaggio #71 GAI 8.5 (NmMt+) sold for $16,372 (Goodwin; 2/06)
—Joe DiMaggio #71 GAI 8.5 (NmMt+) sold for $12,593 (Memory Lane; 12/06)
—Jimmie Foxx #13 GAI 8.5 (NmMt+) sold for $1,833 (Memory Lane; 12/07)
—Hank Greenberg #18 SGC 96 (MT) sold for $5,273 (Goodwin; 03/12)
—Hank Greenberg #18 SGC 96 (MT) sold for $5,105 (Mile High; 05/11)
—Carl Hubbell #6 PSA 9 (MT) sold for $3,600 (Mastro; 5/08)
—Bob Johnson #22 PSA 9 (MT) sold for $5,117 (Mile High; 10/11)
—Charlie Keller #21 PSA 8.5 (NmMt+) sold for $3,525 (eBay; 6/08)
—Chuck Klein #60 PSA 9 (MT) sold for $12,756 (Mastro; 4/07)
—Pee Wee Reese #54 SGC 92 (NmMt+) sold for $5,956 (Mile High; 2/08)
—Ted Williams #14 PSA 9 (MT) sold for $20,724 (Mastro; 12/06)
—Ted Williams #14 GAI 8.5 (NmMt+) sold for $5,724 (Goodwin; 6/06)
—Ted Williams #14 GAI 8.5 (NmMt+) sold for $3,910 (Goodwin; 5/07)
—Ted Williams #14 GAI 8.5 (NmMt+) sold for $3,785 (Memory Lane; 9/07)

1948 Bowman

	GD 2	VG 3	VgEx 4	EX 5	ExMt 6	NM 7	NmMt 8	MT 9
1 Bob Elliott RC	10	20	40	50	100	200	400	2,000
2 Ewell Blackwell RC	6	20	25	40	50	60	250	800
3 Ralph Kiner RC	60	80	120	200	250	300	800	2,000
4 Johnny Mize RC	40	50	60	100	120	200	400	1,200
5 Bob Feller RC	100	120	150	200	250	500	800	2,000
6 Yogi Berra RC	300	400	500	800	1,000	2,000	4,000	8,000
7 Pete Reiser SP RC	10	20	50	80	100	250	500	1,500
8 Phil Rizzuto SP RC	100	120	200	250	300	600	1,200	2,500
9 Walker Cooper RC	5	6	10	40	60	120	200	1,200
10 Buddy Rosar RC	5	6	10	25	30	50	150	800

#	Player	GD 2	VG 3	VgEx 4	EX 5	ExMt 6	NM 7	NmMt 8	MT 9
11	Johnny Lindell RC	5	6	10	25	50	60	200	1,000
12	Johnny Sain RC	6	12	20	40	50	100	250	1,200
13	Willard Marshall SP RC	5	8	12	50	60	100	200	800
14	Allie Reynolds RC	6	12	40	60	80	120	300	1,200
15	Eddie Joost	5	6	10	20	40	80	150	600
16	Jack Lohrke SP RC	5	10	15	30	50	100	400	1,000
17	Enos Slaughter RC	25	50	80	100	150	250	500	1,200
18	Warren Spahn RC	120	150	250	300	500	800	1,800	4,000
19	Tommy Henrich	6	12	30	40	50	100	250	1,000
20	Buddy Kerr SP RC	5	10	15	25	40	120	250	800
21	Ferris Fain RC	5	8	12	30	50	60	150	1,500
22	Floyd Bevens SP RC	5	10	15	50	100	120	250	800
23	Larry Jansen RC	5	6	10	30	40	50	100	500
24	Dutch Leonard SP	5	8	12	20	50	100	250	600
25	Barney McCosky	5	6	10	15	50	60	120	500
26	Frank Shea SP RC	5	10	25	30	60	100	300	
27	Sid Gordon RC	5	6	20	25	50	120	250	1,000
28	Emil Verban SP RC	5	10	15	25	80	100	200	1,200
29	Joe Page SP RC	5	10	30	50	60	120	200	800
30	Whitey Lockman SP RC	6	12	30	50	80	120	250	600
31	Bill McCahan RC	5	6	15	20	25	60	150	500
32	Bill Rigney RC	6	10	15	30	50	80	100	500
33	Bill Johnson RC	5	10	20	30	40	60	150	800
34	Sheldon Jones SP RC	5	15	20	40	60	100	250	800
35	Snuffy Stirnweiss RC	10	15	25	40	80	100	250	1,200
36	Stan Musial RC	400	500	600	1,000	2,000	3,000	12,000	25,000
37	Clint Hartung RC	5	10	15	25	100	120	250	1,400
38	Red Schoendienst RC	60	120	200	250	400	600	1,500	5,000
39	Augie Galan RC	5	10	15	25	40	100	200	1,000
40	Marty Marion RC	15	30	50	80	150	250	500	1,500
41	Rex Barney RC	5	10	15	30	50	150	250	1,000
42	Ray Poat RC	5	10	20	30	50	100	200	1,000
43	Bruce Edwards RC	5	10	15	40	80	150	300	1,000
44	Johnny Wyrostek RC	5	10	25	30	50	120	400	1,000
45	Hank Sauer RC	10	20	30	60	80	200	600	1,500
46	Herman Wehmeier RC	5	10	15	30	50	100	300	2,500
47	Bobby Thomson RC	20	40	60	100	150	300	600	3,000
48	Dave Koslo RC	10	20	30	50	60	200	600	1,800

—Yogi Berra #6 PSA 10 (Gem) sold for $33,583 (Mastro; 4/06)
—Yogi Berra #6 SGC 96 (MT) sold for $5,530 (Mastro; 4/07)
—Yogi Berra #6 GAI 9 (MT) sold for $3,942 (Vintage Authentics; 7/07)
—Bob Feller #5 PSA 10 (Gem) sold for $6,134 (Mastro; 10/03)
—Bob Feller #5 GAI 9 (MT) sold for $1,148 (Mile High; 2/08)
—Marty Marion #40 PSA 10 (Gem) sold for $8,284 (Mastro; 10/05)
—Marty Marion #40 PSA 10 (Gem) sold for $6,683 (Memory Lane; 03/06)
—Johnny Mize #4 PSA 10 (Gem) sold for $3,284 (Memory Lane; 4/05)
—Stan Musial #36 PSA 10 (Gem) (Young Collection) sold for $129,850 (SCP; 5/12)
—Stan Musial #36 PSA 10 (Gem) sold for $50,000 (Memory Lane; Private Sale - 2006)
—Stan Musial #36 PSA 10 (Gem) sold for $28,680 (Heritage; 12/05)
—Stan Musial #36 SGC 96 (MT) sold for $8,923 (Mastro; 8/06)
—Stan Musial #36 GAI 8.5 (NmMt+) sold for $2,443 (Mile High; 2/08)
—Stan Musial #36 GAI 8.5 (NmMt+) sold for $2,275 (eBay; 5/07)
—Phil Rizzuto #8 GAI 9.5 (Gem) sold for $2,675 (Mile Hight; 11/04)
—Phil Rizzuto #8 SGC 8.5 (NmMt+) sold for $1,032 (eBay; 8/07)
—Red Schoendienst #38 PSA 9 (MT) sold for $8,052 (Mile High; 6/06)
—Warren Spahn #18 GAI 9 (MT) sold for $1,290 (Mastro; 4/07)

1949 Bowman

#	Player	GD 2	VG 3	VgEx 4	EX 5	ExMt 6	NM 7	NmMt 8	MT 9
1	Vern Bickford RC	10	15	30	40	60	120	400	
2	Whitey Lockman	5	10	15	20	30	60	150	
3	Bob Porterfield RC	5	6	10	15	20	60	120	
4A	Jerry Priddy NNOF RC	5	6	10	15	20	40	250	
4B	Jerry Priddy NOF	10	15	25	30	50	100	150	
5	Hank Sauer	5	8	12	20	25	50	100	
6	Phil Cavarretta RC	5	8	12	20	25	50	120	
7	Joe Dobson RC	5	6	10	15	20	50	120	
8	Murry Dickson RC	5	6	10	15	20	40	80	
9	Ferris Fain	5	8	12	25	30	50	120	
10	Ted Gray RC	5	6	10	20	30	60	140	
11	Lou Boudreau MG RC	6	10	30	50	60	100	300	
12	Cass Michaels RC	5	6	10	15	20	50	80	
13	Bob Chesnes RC	5	6	10	15	20	50	100	
14	Curt Simmons RC	5	10	15	50	60	80	150	
15	Ned Garver RC	5	6	10	15	20	40	80	
16	Al Kozar RC	5	6	10	15	20	40	80	

#	Player	GD 2	VG 3	VgEx 4	EX 5	ExMt 6	NM 7	NmMt 8	MT
17	Earl Torgeson RC	5	6	10	15	25	50	100	
18	Bobby Thomson	10	15	40	50	80	120	200	
19	Bobby Brown RC	5	10	15	40	50	60	300	
20	Gene Hermanski RC	5	6	10	15	30	50	80	
21	Frank Baumholtz RC	5	6	10	20	25	30	100	
22	Peanuts Lowrey RC	5	6	10	20	25	40	120	
23	Bobby Doerr	20	30	50	80	100	120	250	
24	Stan Musial	200	250	300	400	600	1,000	2,000	8,000
25	Carl Scheib RC	5	6	10	15	20	50	120	
26	George Kell RC	10	50	80	120	200	300	400	
27	Bob Feller	20	100	120	150	250	300	800	1,200
28	Don Kolloway RC	5	6	10	15	30	50	80	
29	Ralph Kiner	25	40	60	▼80	▼100	250	400	
30	Andy Seminick	5	8	12	20	30	50	80	
31	Dick Kokos RC	5	6	10	15	20	50	80	
32	Eddie Yost RC	5	8	12	20	30	50	80	
33	Warren Spahn	50	100	120	200	250	300	600	
34	Dave Koslo	5	6	10	15	20	50	120	
35	Vic Raschi RC	8	12	20	30	60	100	800	
36	Pee Wee Reese	60	80	▲120	150	250	400	800	3,000
37	Johnny Wyrostek	5	6	10	15	20	40	60	
38	Emil Verban	5	6	10	15	20	60	150	
39	Billy Goodman RC	5	6	10	15	40	50	80	
40	George Munger RC	5	6	10	15	20	80	150	
41	Lou Brissie RC	5	6	10	15	20	50	80	
42	Hoot Evers RC	5	6	10	15	20	50	80	
43	Dale Mitchell RC	5	8	15	20	50	60	120	
44	Dave Philley RC	5	6	10	15	20	40	200	
45	Wally Westlake RC	5	6	10	15	20	50	150	
46	Robin Roberts RC	120	250	300	400	500	600	1,000	3,000
47	Johnny Sain	6	10	25	50	60	100	200	
48	Willard Marshall	5	6	10	15	20	50	100	
49	Frank Shea	5	6	10	15	20	50	300	
50	Jackie Robinson RC	1,200	1,500	▲2,500	▲4,000	▲5,000	▲6,000	8,000	30,000
51	Herman Wehmeier	5	6	10	15	20	35	120	
52	Johnny Schmitz RC	5	6	10	15	40	50	100	
53	Jack Kramer RC	5	6	10	15	20	60	100	
54	Marty Marion	6	10	25	30	40	100	300	
55	Eddie Joost	5	6	10	15	30	40	80	
56	Pat Mullin RC	5	6	10	15	20	40	100	
57	Gene Bearden RC	5	8	12	20	25	40	120	
58	Bob Elliott	5	8	12	20	25	50	120	
59	Jack Lohrke	5	6	10	20	25	50	100	
60	Yogi Berra	150	200	250	400	500	800	1,200	3,500
61	Rex Barney	5	8	12	20	25	60	100	
62	Grady Hatton RC	5	6	10	15	20	35	120	
63	Andy Pafko RC	5	10	15	20	50	60	150	
64	Dom DiMaggio	10	15	25	50	100	120	200	
65	Enos Slaughter	20	30	50	80	120	200	300	
66	Elmer Valo RC	5	6	10	15	30	50	80	
67	Alvin Dark RC	5	8	12	20	40	100	150	
68	Sheldon Jones	5	6	10	15	20	30	100	
69	Tommy Henrich	5	10	20	40	50	80	150	
70	Carl Furillo RC	12	20	60	80	120	200	400	
71	Vern Stephens RC	5	6	10	20	40	60	150	
72	Tommy Holmes RC	5	10	15	20	30	80	250	
73	Billy Cox RC	6	10	20	25	40	60	200	
74	Tom McBride RC	5	6	10	15	20	40	80	
75	Eddie Mayo RC	5	6	10	20	25	50	100	
76	Bill Nicholson RC	5	6	10	15	20	60	120	
77	Ernie Bonham RC	5	6	10	15	20	35	80	
78A	Sam Zoldak NNOF RC	5	6	10	15	20	40	80	
78B	Sam Zoldak NOF	10	15	25	30	50	80	400	
79	Ron Northey RC	5	6	10	15	20	50	200	
80	Bill McCahan	5	6	10	15	25	50	120	
81	Virgil Stallcup RC	5	6	10	15	20	40	60	
82	Joe Page	6	10	20	25	40	60	150	
83A	Bob Scheffing NNOF RC	5	6	10	15	20	40	80	
83B	Bob Scheffing NOF	10	15	25	30	50	80	120	
84	Roy Campanella RC	300	400	500	600	1,000	1,200	2,500	8,500
85A	Johnny Mize NNOF	10	20	30	40	80	120	250	1,000
85B	Johnny Mize NOF	15	25	40	60	100	150	400	
86	Johnny Pesky RC	6	10	20	40	60	100	250	
87	Randy Gumpert RC	5	6	10	20	25	50	100	
88A	Bill Salkeld NNOF RC	5	6	10	15	20	35	80	
88B	Bill Salkeld NOF	10	15	25	30	50	80	200	
89	Mizell Platt RC	5	6	10	15	20	40	80	

#	Player	GD 2	VG 3	VgEx 4	EX 5	ExMt 6	NM 7	NmMt 8	MT 9
	Gil Coan RC	5	6	10	15	25	40	100	
	Dick Wakefield RC	5	6	10	15	20	40	80	
	Willie Jones RC	5	8	12	20	25	60	100	
	Ed Stevens RC	5	6	10	15	20	40	120	
	Mickey Vernon RC	5	10	20	25	30	50	200	
	Howie Pollet RC	5	6	10	20	25	50	150	
	Taft Wright	5	6	10	15	20	35	120	
	Danny Litwhiler RC	5	6	10	15	25	35	80	
A	Phil Rizzuto NNOF	20	35	80	100	150	250	500	2,500
B	Phil Rizzuto NOF	30	50	80	150	200	350	600	3,000
	Frank Gustine RC	6	10	15	25	40	60	200	
0	Gil Hodges RC	80	100	120	200	300	400	800	3,500
1	Sid Gordon	5	6	10	15	20	30	120	
2	Stan Spence RC	5	6	10	15	20	50	120	
3	Joe Tipton RC	5	6	15	20	30	50	80	
4	Eddie Stanky RC	5	8	20	25	30	60	150	
5	Bill Kennedy RC	5	6	10	15	20	80	100	
6	Jake Early RC	5	6	10	15	20	35	60	
7	Eddie Lake RC	5	6	10	15	20	35	60	
8	Ken Heintzelman RC	5	6	10	15	30	50	150	
9A	Ed Fitzgerald Script Name RC	5	6	10	15	20	35	80	
9B	Ed Fitzgerald Print Name	10	15	25	30	50	80	250	
0	Early Wynn RC	50	80	120	150	250	500	600	3,000
1	Red Schoendienst	12	20	40	50	▼80	120	250	
2	Sam Chapman	5	6	10	15	20	40	100	
3	Ray LaManno RC	5	6	10	15	25	50	80	
4	Allie Reynolds	6	10	20	25	50	60	150	
5	Dutch Leonard	5	6	10	15	20	50	100	
6	Joe Hatten RC	5	6	10	15	30	60	200	
7	Walker Cooper	5	6	10	15	20	40	150	
8	Sam Mele RC	5	6	10	15	30	40	100	
9	Floyd Baker RC	5	6	10	15	20	30	100	
0	Cliff Fannin RC	5	6	15	20	25	30	100	
1	Mark Christman RC	5	6	10	20	25	40	120	
2	George Vico RC	5	6	10	15	25	40	80	
3	Johnny Blatnick	5	6	10	15	20	40	120	
4A	Danny Murtaugh Script Name RC	5	8	12	20	25	40	80	
4B	Danny Murtaugh Print Name	10	15	25	30	50	80	150	
5	Ken Keltner RC	5	6	10	15	20	40	100	
6A	Al Brazle Script Name RC	5	6	10	15	20	40	100	
6B	Al Brazle Print Name	10	15	25	30	50	80	150	
7A	Hank Majeski Script Name RC	5	6	10	15	20	40	60	
7B	Hank Majeski Print Name	10	15	25	30	50	80	250	
8	Johnny VanderMeer	6	10	30	40	50	80	150	
9	Bill Johnson	5	8	12	20	25	50	150	
0	Harry Walker RC	5	6	10	15	20	60	120	
1	Paul Lehner RC	5	6	10	15	20	30	60	
2A	Al Evans Script Name RC	5	6	10	15	20	40	120	
2B	Al Evans Print Name	10	15	25	30	50	80	100	
3	Aaron Robinson RC	5	6	10	15	20	40	60	
4	Hank Borowy RC	5	6	10	15	20	40	80	
5	Stan Rojek RC	5	6	10	15	20	40	100	
6	Hank Edwards RC	5	6	10	20	25	50	80	
7	Ted Wilks RC	5	6	10	15	20	40	80	
8	Buddy Rosar	5	6	10	15	20	40	80	
9	Hank Arft RC	5	6	10	20	25	50	80	
0	Ray Scarborough RC	5	6	10	15	20	40	60	
1	Tony Lupien RC	5	6	15	20	25	30	100	
2	Eddie Waitkus RC	5	8	12	30	40	50	100	
3A	Bob Dillinger Script Name RC	5	6	10	20	25	100	400	
3B	Bob Dillinger Print Name	10	15	25	30	50	80	200	
4	Mickey Haefner RC	5	6	10	15	20	50	200	
5	Blix Donnelly RC	5	10	15	25	40	100	300	
6	Mike McCormick RC	5	6	10	15	20	80	120	
7	Bert Singleton RC	5	8	12	20	50	120	200	
8	Bob Swift RC	5	8	12	20	30	80	300	
9	Roy Partee RC	5	8	12	20	40	80	250	
0	Allie Clark RC	5	8	12	20	25	50	120	
1	Mickey Harris RC	5	8	12	40	50	120	250	
2	Clarence Maddern RC	5	8	12	20	25	100	200	
3	Phil Masi RC	5	8	12	20	25	150	300	
4	Clint Hartung	5	8	12	20	25	80	150	
5	Mickey Guerra RC	5	8	12	20	40	60	120	
6	Al Zarilla RC	5	8	12	20	25	100	150	
7	Walt Masterson RC	5	8	12	20	25	100	250	
8	Harry Brecheen RC	5	8	12	20	25	80	250	
9	Glen Moulder RC	5	8	12	20	40	50	120	

#	Player	GD 2	VG 3	VgEx 4	EX 5	ExMt 6	NM 7	NmMt 8	MT 9
160	Jim Blackburn RC	5	8	12	20	40	80	200	
161	Jocko Thompson RC	5	8	12	20	25	50	150	
162	Preacher Roe	15	25	80	100	150	200	600	
163	Clyde McCullough RC	5	8	12	20	25	100	200	
164	Vic Wertz RC	12	20	30	50	80	120	400	
165	Snuffy Stirnweiss	5	8	12	20	25	80	250	
166	Mike Tresh RC	5	8	30	40	50	150	600	
167	Babe Martin RC	5	8	12	30	40	60	150	
168	Doyle Lade RC	5	8	12	20	30	80	150	
169	Jeff Heath RC	5	8	12	20	40	100	200	
170	Bill Rigney	5	8	12	20	25	80	400	
171	Dick Fowler RC	5	8	12	20	40	100	300	
172	Eddie Pellagrini RC	5	8	12	20	25	50	200	
173	Eddie Stewart RC	5	8	12	20	30	50	150	
174	Terry Moore RC	10	20	30	50	80	150	600	
175	Luke Appling	15	25	60	80	200	250	500	
176	Ken Raffensberger RC	5	8	20	25	30	80	100	
177	Stan Lopata RC	5	8	12	20	25	60	200	
178	Tommy Brown RC	5	10	15	25	40	100	250	
179	Hugh Casey RC	5	12	25	50	60	150	400	
180	Connie Berry	5	8	12	20	40	150	300	
181	Gus Niarhos RC	5	8	12	30	40	80	300	
182	Hal Peck RC	5	8	12	25	30	60	200	
183	Lou Stringer RC	5	8	12	25	40	50	150	
184	Bob Chipman RC	5	8	12	20	25	50	100	
185	Pete Reiser	5	8	12	40	60	100	200	
186	Buddy Kerr	5	8	12	20	40	60	120	
187	Phil Marchildon RC	5	8	12	20	25	60	120	
188	Karl Drews RC	5	8	12	20	40	150	500	
189	Earl Wooten RC	5	8	12	20	50	200	400	
190	Jim Hearn RC	5	8	25	30	40	100	150	
191	Joe Haynes RC	5	8	12	20	25	50	120	
192	Harry Gumbert RC	5	8	12	20	25	50	100	
193	Ken Trinkle RC	5	8	12	20	25	80	200	
194	Ralph Branca RC	10	15	25	40	120	200	300	
195	Eddie Bockman RC	5	8	12	20	25	60	150	
196	Fred Hutchinson RC	5	8	12	20	25	50	120	
197	Johnny Lindell	5	8	12	30	40	120		
198	Steve Gromek RC	5	8	12	20	25	50	250	
199	Tex Hughson RC	5	8	12	20	30	60	120	
200	Jess Dobernic RC	5	8	12	20	25	50	150	
201	Sibby Sisti RC	5	8	12	20	25	80	150	
202	Larry Jansen	5	8	12	20	25	50	150	
203	Barney McCosky	5	8	12	20	25	50	150	
204	Bob Savage RC	5	8	12	20	25	60	200	
205	Dick Sisler RC	5	8	12	20	25	80	150	
206	Bruce Edwards	5	8	12	20	40	150		
207	Johnny Hopp RC	10	15	25	40	50	150	500	
208	Dizzy Trout	5	8	12	30	40	60	150	
209	Charlie Keller	15	30	40	50	100	120	300	
210	Joe Gordon RC	8	12	30	50	80	150	300	
211	Boo Ferriss RC	10	20	30	80	200	250	400	
212	Ralph Hamner RC	5	8	12	20	40	50	150	
213	Red Barrett RC	5	8	12	20	25	60	150	
214	Richie Ashburn RC	250	400	500	600	800	1,000	2,500	
215	Kirby Higbe	5	8	12	20	25	80		
216	Schoolboy Rowe	5	8	12	50	60	100	500	
217	Marino Pieretti RC	5	8	12	20	50	80	120	
218	Dick Kryhoski RC	10	15	30	40	50	80	150	
219	Virgil Trucks RC	5	8	12	20	25	50	200	
220	Johnny McCarthy	5	8	12	20	25	200	400	
221	Bob Muncrief RC	5	8	12	20	25	50	150	
222	Alex Kellner RC	5	8	12	20	40	60	120	
223	Bobby Hofman RC	5	8	12	20	25	60	200	
224	Satchel Paige RC	1,200	1,500	2,000	2,500	4,000	5,000	10,000	20,000
225	Jerry Coleman RC	10	15	25	40	60	120	400	
226	Duke Snider RC	500	600	800	1,000	1,200	2,000	3,000	10,000
227	Fritz Ostermueller RC	5	8	12	20	50	60	120	
228	Jackie Mayo RC	5	8	12	20	25	50	200	
229	Ed Lopat RC	10	25	40	50	80	120	300	
230	Augie Galan	5	8	12	20	30	50	120	
231	Earl Johnson RC	5	8	12	20	40	100	120	
232	George McQuinn RC	5	8	12	20	40	60	150	
233	Larry Doby RC	200	250	400	500	800	1,000	2,000	
234	Rip Sewell RC	5	8	12	20	40	80	200	
235	Jim Russell RC	5	8	12	25	30	60	150	
236	Fred Sanford RC	5	8	12	20	30	50	150	

		GD 2	VG 3	VgEx 4	EX 5	ExMt 6	NM 7	NmMt 8	MT 9
237	Monte Kennedy RC	5	8	12	20	30	80	150	
238	Bob Lemon RC	150	200	250	400	500	600	1,500	
239	Frank McCormick	5	8	12	20	25	80	150	
240	Babe Young	10	20	30	50	100	200		

—Yogi Berra #60 SGC 96 (MT) sold for $2,711 (Memory Lane; 8/06)
—Yogi Berra #60 BVG 9 (MT) sold for $921 (eBay; 4/08)
—Yogi Berra #60 GAI 9 (MT) sold for $874 (eBay; 3/08)
—Roy Campanella #84 PSA 10 (Gem) (Young Collection) sold for $44,428 (SCP; 5/12)
—Roy Campanella #84 PSA 10 (Gem) sold for $37,950 (Memory Lane; 3/06)
—Roy Campanella #84 SGC 96 (MT) sold for $3,437 (Goodwin; 2/07)
—Larry Doby #233 PSA 9 (MT) sold for $10,024 (Goodwin; 3/08)
—Larry Doby #233 PSA 9 (MT) sold for $5,824 (Goodwin; 3/09)
—Larry Doby #233 PSA 9 (Mint) sold for $5,180 (Memory Lane; 8/12)
—Bob Feller GAI 9 (MT) sold for $1,227 (Mastro; 4/06)
—Gil Hodges #100 GAI 9 (MT) sold for $686 (Mastro; 6/07)
—Sheldon Jones #68 PSA 10 (Gem) sold for $5,899 (Mile High; 5/12)
—Bob Lemon #PSA 9 (MT) sold for $10,555 (Goodwin; 3/09)
—Stan Musial #24 GAI 8.5 (NmMt+) sold for $1,075 (eBay; 12/06)
—Stan Musial #24 GAI 8.5 (NmMt+) sold for $1,021 (eBay; 1/08)
—Pee Wee Reese #36 PSA 10 (Gem) sold for $7,398 (Memory Lane; 4/05)
—Phil Rizzuto NNOF #98 PSA 10 (Gem) sold for $7,223 (Memory Lane; 4/05)
—Phil Rizzuto NNOF #98 SGC 96 (MT) sold for $1,706 (Goodwin; 2/07)
—Phil Rizzuto NNOF #98 GAI 9 (MT) sold for $1,375 (eBay; 10/06)
—Satchel Paige #224 GAI 9 (MT) sold for $5,212 (eBay; 2/06)
—Satchel Paige #224 PSA 8.5 (NmMt+) sold for $6,498 (Goodwin; 5/08)
—Satchel Paige #224 PSA 8.5 (NmMt+) sold for $3,280 (Memory Lane; 8/05)
—Satchel Paige #224 GAI 8 (NmMt) sold for $1,514 (eBay; 12/07)
—Jackie Robinson #50 SGC 98 (GemMt) sold for $32,500 (Mastro; 12/08)
—Jackie Robinson #50 SGC 96 (MT) sold for $11,586 (Mile High; 6/06)
—Jackie Robinson #50 GAI 9 (MT) sold for $4,692 (Goodwin; 6/06)
—Jackie Robinson #50 GAI 9 (MT) sold for $4,632 (Madec; 11/07)
—Jackie Robinson #50 SGC 92 (NmMt+) sold for $10,073 (REA; Fall '13)
—Jackie Robinson #50 SGC 92 (NmMt+) sold for $4,325 (Goodwin; 8/07)
—Jackie Robinson #50 GAI 8.5 (NmMt+) sold for $3,280 (Memory Lane; 8/05)
—Jackie Robinson #50 SGC 88 (NmMt) sold for $4,263 (Memory Lane; 3/06)
—Jackie Robinson #50 GAI 8 (NmMt) sold for $1,669 (Mastro; 12/07)
—Jackie Robinson #50 GAI 8 (NmMt) sold for $1,495 (eBay; 6/06)
—Duke Snider #226 PSA 10 (Gem) sold for $57,575 (Memory Lane; 4/07)
—Duke Snider #226 GAI 9.5 (Gem) sold for $6,600 (eBay; 9/06)
—Duke Snider #226 GAI 9.5 (Gem) sold for $4,153 (Mastro; 4/07)
—Duke Snider #226 GAI 9.5 (Gem) sold for $4,112 (REA; 4/07)
—Duke Snider #226 GAI 9.5 (Gem) sold for $3,251 (eBay; 5/07)
—Duke Snider #226 SGC 96 (MT) sold for $14,373 (Mastro; 8/06)
—Duke Snider #226 PSA 9 (MT) sold for $10,920 (Memory Lane; 4/05)
—Warren Spahn #33 PSA 9 (MT) sold for $5,785 (Mile High; 6/06)
—Babe Young #240 PSA 8 (NmMt) sold for $1,447 (Mile High; 2/08)
—Babe Young #240 PSA 8 (NmMt) sold for $1,187 (Memory Lane; 9/07)

1949 Leaf

		PrFr 1	GD 2	VG 3	VgEx 4	EX 5	ExMt 6	NM 7	NmMt 8
1	Joe DiMaggio	500	600	800	1,000	1,500	2,000	5,000	10,000
3	Babe Ruth	800	1,000	1,200	1,500	2,500	4,000	6,000	8,000
4	Stan Musial	300	500	800	1,000	1,200	3,000	8,000	20,000
5	Virgil Trucks SP RC	80	120	200	300	400	500		
8	Satchel Paige SP RC	3,000	5,000	10,000	15,000	20,000	25,000	80,000	
10	Paul Trout	5	10	15	20	25	80	150	400
11	Phil Rizzuto	60	80	100	120	200	300	600	1,200
13	Casimer Michaels SP RC	60	100	250	400	500	600	1,500	
14	Billy Johnson	5	10	15	20	40	60	150	
17	Frank Overmire RC	5	10	15	20	25	40	100	300
19	John Wyrostek SP	60	100	150	250	400	600	1,200	
20	Hank Sauer SP	100	200	300	400	500	800	1,200	
22	Al Evans RC	5	10	15	20	40	60	100	400
26	Sam Chapman	5	10	15	20	25	40	100	400
27	Mickey Harris RC	5	10	15	20	25	50	100	300
28	Jim Hegan RC	5	10	15	30	40	60	150	600
29	Elmer Valo RC	5	10	15	20	25	50	100	300
30	Billy Goodman SP RC	60	100	150	250	400	600	1,500	
31	Lou Brissie RC	5	10	15	20	25	40	100	300
32	Warren Spahn	120	200	250	400	600	800	1,500	3,000
33	Harry Lowrey SP RC	60	100	150	250	400	600	1,000	
36	Al Zarilla SP	100	150	200	300	400	600		
38	Ted Kluszewski RC	20	40	80	100	200	250	300	800
39	Ewell Blackwell	10	15	25	40	60	80	150	400
42A	Kent Peterson Black Cap RC	5	10	15	20	25	50	150	
42B	Kent Peterson Red Cap	60	100	150	150	400	600		

		PrFr 1	GD 2	VG 3	VgEx 4	EX 5	ExMt 6	NM 7	NmMt
43	Eddie Stevens SP RC	100	120	150	250	400	600		
45	Ken Keltner SP RC	60	150	200	250	400	600		
46	Johnny Mize	10	15	20	50	80	150	200	80
47	George Vico RC	5	10	20	25	30	40	120	60
48	Johnny Schmitz SP RC	100	120	150	250	400	600	1,000	
49	Del Ennis RC	5	10	15	20	25	50	100	40
50	Dick Wakefield RC	5	10	15	20	40	60	100	30
51	Alvin Dark SP RC	100	150	250	400	600	1,000		
53	John VanderMeer	10	15	25	40	60	100	150	1,00
54	Bobby Adams SP RC	100	150	200	300	400	600	1,000	
55	Tommy Henrich SP	100	250	300	400	600	800	1,500	
56	Larry Jensen	5	10	15	20	25	60	100	30
57	Bob McCall RC	5	10	15	25	30	40	100	40
59	Luke Appling	10	15	40	60	80	120	200	60
61	Jake Early RC	5	10	15	20	25	40	100	40
62	Eddie Joost SP	60	100	150	400	400	600	1,000	1,50
63	Barney McCosky SP	60	100	150	250	400	600	1,000	
65	Bob Elliott	5	10	15	20	25	40	100	30
66	Orval Grove SP RC	60	200	250	300	400	600		
68	Ed Miller SP	60	100	150	250	500	600		
70	Honus Wagner	80	120	200	250	300	500	800	1,20
72	Hank Edwards RC	5	10	15	20	25	40	100	30
73	Pat Seerey RC	5	10	15	20	25	120	250	60
75	Dom DiMaggio SP	100	200	300	500	800	1,200		
76	Ted Williams	300	500	600	800	1,200	1,500	2,000	8,00
77	Roy Smalley RC	5	10	15	20	25	50	120	40
78	Walter Evers SP RC	80	100	200	250	600	800	1,000	
79	Jackie Robinson RC	1,200	2,000	3,000	4,000	6,000	12,000	15,000	25,00
81	George Kurowski SP RC	80	120	200	300	500	800		
82	Johnny Lindell	5	10	15	20	40	60	120	30
83	Bobby Doerr	10	15	25	60	100	120	250	60
84	Sid Hudson	5	10	20	25	30	40	100	30
85	Dave Philley SP RC	60	100	150	250	500	600	1,200	
86	Ralph Weigel RC	5	10	15	30	40	50	100	40
88	Frank Gustine SP RC	80	120	200	300	600	800	1,500	
91	Ralph Kiner SP	15	25	80	100	150	250	400	1,00
93	Bob Feller SP	800	1,000	1,200	1,500	2,000	2,500		
95	George Stirnweiss	5	10	15	20	25	40	100	30
97	Marty Marion	6	10	20	25	40	100	200	50
98	Hal Newhouser SP RC	300	400	500	1,000	1,500	2,200		
102A	Gene Hermanski ERR	150	250	400	600	1,200			
102B	Gene Hermanski COR RC	10	15	25	40	50	80	200	60
104	Edward Stewart SP RC	100	120	150	250	400	600		
106	Lou Boudreau MG RC	10	15	25	40	80	120	200	60
108	Matthew Batts SP RC	60	120	150	250	400	600	1,000	1,50
111	Gerald Priddy RC	5	10	15	20	25	40	100	30
113	Emil Leonard SP	60	100	150	400	400	600	1,500	
117	Joe Gordon RC	5	10	15	60	80	100	150	60
120	George Kell SP RC	150	250	400	800	1,000	1,200	3,000	
121	Johnny Pesky SP RC	100	150	200	300	500	800		
123	Cliff Fannin SP RC	60	100	200	250	400	600	1,200	
125	Andy Pafko RC	5	10	15	20	25	100	120	80
127	Enos Slaughter SP	300	400	500	600	1,000	1,200	2,000	
128	Warren Rosar	5	10	15	20	25	40	100	30
129	Kirby Higbe SP	100	120	150	200	300	600		
131	Sid Gordon SP	60	200	250	300	400	600		
133	Tommy Holmes SP RC	100	150	200	400	600	800		
136A	Cliff Aberson Full Sleeve RC	5	10	15	20	120	150	200	
136B	Cliff Aberson Short Sleeve	15	25	40	60	100	150	1,000	
137	Harry Walker SP RC	60	120	150	200	400	800		
138	Larry Doby SP RC	300	400	600	1,200	1,500	2,500	4,000	
139	Johnny Hopp RC	5	10	15	30	40	60	100	30
142	Danny Murtaugh SP RC	60	100	150	200	250	500		
143	Dick Sisler SP RC	60	120	150	400	400	600	1,000	2,00
144	Bob Dillinger SP RC	60	100	150	250	400	600	1,200	
146	Harold Reiser SP	80	120	200	300	800	800		
149	Henry Majeski SP RC	60	100	150	250	400	1,000		
153	Floyd Baker SP RC	100	150	200	300	500	800		
158	Harry Brecheen SP RC	100	250	300	400	800	1,500		
159	Mizell Platt RC	6	10	20	25	35	50	120	50
160	Bob Scheffing SP RC	60	120	150	250	400	800		
161	Vernon Stephens SP RC	100	150	300	400	500	800		
163	Fred Hutchinson SP RC	100	150	200	300	500	800		
165	Dale Mitchell SP RC	100	150	200	300	400	600	2,000	
168	Phil Cavaretta SP RC	100	150	250	500	800	1,000		

—Short Prints from this set often have PSA popualtions of five or fewer copies in NmMt condition.
—Though values for Common & Minor Star Short Prints in NmMt condition can fluctuate wildly on occasion, most sell between $4,000-$8,000 per.

Bobby Adams #54 PSA 8 (NmMt) sold for $3,850 (eBay; 9/07)
Cliff Alberson Full Sleeve PSA 8 (NmMt) sold for $2,025 (eBay; 9/07)
Cliff Alberson Full Sleeve PSA 8 (NmMt) sold for $1,459 (Mile High; 2/08)
Cliff Alberson Full Sleeve PSA 8 (NmMt) sold for $1,095 (Mile High; 2/08)
Floyd Baker #153 PSA 8 (NmMt) sold for $4,623 (eBay; 9/07)
Floyd Baker #153 PSA 8 (NmMt) sold for $3,952 (Mile High; 1/07)
Floyd Baker #153 PSA 7 (NM) sold for $3,081 (Mile High; 1/07)
Floyd Baker #153 PSA 7 (NM) sold for $2,015 (eBay; 9/07)
Harry Brecheen #158 PSA 7 (NM) sold for $13,011 (Memory Lane; 12/06)
Harry Brecheen #158 PSA 7 (NM) sold for $12,159 (Memory Lane; 8/06)
Harry Brecheen #158 PSA 7 (NM) sold for $9,900 (eBay; 9/07)
Harry Brecheen #158 PSA 7 (NM) sold for $8,833 (Goodwin; 11/11)
Lou Brissie #31 PSA 9 (MT) sold for $7,184 (Memory Lane; 4/07)
Phil Cavaretta #168 PSA 7 (NM) sold for $7,550 (Memory Lane; 8/06)
Phil Cavaretta #168 PSA 7 (NM) sold for $4,797 (eBay; 12/07)
Phil Cavaretta #168 PSA 7 (NM) sold for $4,593 (Goodwin; 3/08)
Alvin Dark #51 PSA 8 (NmMt) sold for $7,170 (Heritage; 10/07)
Alvin Dark #51 PSA 7 (NM) sold for $3,884 Heritage; 10/07)
Alvin Dark #51 PSA 7 (NM) sold for $3,362 (Mile High; 6/06)
Alvin Dark #51 PSA 7 (NM) sold for $1,526 (Memory Lane; 9/07)
Dom DiMaggio #75 PSA 8 (NmMt) sold for $15,535 (Heritage; 10/07)
Joe DiMaggio #1 GAI 9.5 (Gem) sold for $43,180 (Goodwin; 5/07)
Joe DiMaggio #1 PSA 9 (MT) sold for $53,084 (Mastro; 6/05)
Larry Doby #138 PSA 8 (NmMt) sold for $4,165 (eBay; 9/07)
Larry Doby #138 PSA 8 (NmMt) sold for $3,936 (Mile High; 2/08)
Walter Evers #78 PSA 8 (NmMt) sold for $2,468 (Mile High; 2/08)
Walter Evers #78 PSA 8 (NmMt) sold for $1,793 (eBay; 10/07)
Bob Feller #101 PSA 8 (NmMt) sold for $24,612 (Memory Lane; 12/06)
Bob Feller #101 PSA 7 (NM) sold for $18,606 (Mile High; 1/07)
Bob Feller #101 PSA 7 (NM) sold for $6,038 (Goodwin; 12/07)
Billy Goodman #30 PSA 8 (NmMt) sold for $7,699 (Mile High; 6/06)
Billy Goodman #30 PSA 8 (NmMt) sold for $2,646 (Mastro; 8/07)
Sid Gordon #131 SGC 86 (NM+) sold for $1,227 (Mile High; 2/08)
Sid Gordon #131 PSA 7 (NM) sold for $4,292 (SCP Sotheby's; 11/06)
Orval Grove #66 PSA 8 (NmMt) sold for $5,777 (Mastro; 4/07)
Orval Grove #66 PSA 7 (NM) sold for $2,025 (eBay; 9/07)
Frank Gustine #88 PSA 8 (NmMt) sold for $3,300 (Mastro; 5/08)
Frank Gustine #88 PSA 8 (NmMt) sold for $2,079 (Mile High; 1/07)
Tommy Henrich #55 PSA 8 (NmMt) sold for $4,055 (Memory Lane; 4/07)
Tommy Henrich #55 PSA 8 (NmMt) sold for $3,195 (eBay; 9/07)
Gene Hermansk Error PSA 8 (NmMt) sold for $3,994 (Mile High; 8/07)
Gene Hermansk Error PSA 7 (NM) sold for $5,555 (eBay; 9/07)
Fred Hutchinson #163 PSA 8 (NmMt) sold for $13,789 (Mile High; 1/07)
Fred Hutchinson #163 PSA 7 (NM) sold for $2,706 (eBay; 9/07)
George Kell #120 PSA 8 (NmMt) sold for $15,782 (Mile High; 1/07)
George Kell #120 PSA 8 (NmMt) sold for $11,448 (Memory Lane; 5/08)
Ken Keltner #45 PSA 7 (NM) sold for $4,817 (eBay; 9/07)
Ken Keltner #45 PSA 7 (NM) sold for $4,050 (eBay; 4/08)
Ted Kluszewski #38 SGC 96 (MT) sold for $7,199 (Mastro; 4/07)
George Kurowski #81 PSA 7 (NM) sold for $5,457 (Mile High; 1/07)
George Kurowski #81 PSA 7 (NM) sold for $1,505 (eBay; 9/07)
Emil Leonard #113 SGC 92 (NmMt+) sold for $2,225 (eBay; 9/07)
Harry Lowrey #33 PSA 8 (NmMt) sold for $5,260 (Mile High; 1/07)
Harry Lowrey #33 PSA 8 (NmMt) sold for $2,911 (Mastro; 8/07)
Harry Lowrey #33 PSA 8 (NmMt) sold for $2,726 (eBay; 9/07)
Barney McCosky #63 PSA 8 (NmMt) sold for $4,163 (Memory Lane; 12/06)
Barney McCosky #63 PSA 8 (NmMt) sold for $2,646 (Mastro; 8/07)
Barney McCosky #63 PSA 8 (NmMt) sold for $2,009 (eBay; 9/07)
Ed Miller #68 PSA 8 (NmMt) sold for $10,251 (Mile High; 8/07)
Ed Miller #68 PSA 8 (NmMt) sold for $7,800 (Mastro; 5/08)
Ed Miller #68 PSA 8 (NmMt) sold for $5,295 (Mile High; 1/08)
Ed Miller #68 PSA 7 (NM) sold for $2,591 (Goodwin; 3/08)
Ed Miller #68 PSA 7 (NM) sold for $2,025 (eBay; 9/07)
Ed Miller #68 PSA 7 (NM) sold for $810 (eBay; 2/08)
Dale Mitchell #165 PSA 8 (NmMt) sold for $7,365 (Mile High; 8/07)
Dale Mitchell #165 PSA 8 (NmMt) sold for $5,400 (Mastro; 5/08)
Dale Mitchell #165 PSA 8 (NmMt) sold for $3,136 (Mile High; 2/08)
Dale Mitchell #165 PSA 8 (NmMt) sold for $2,995 (eBay; 9/07)
Stan Musial #4 GAI 8 (NmMt) sold for $2,520 (Mastro; 12/06)
Hal Newhouser Proof #98A SGC 1 (Poor) sold for $84,000 (Huggins and Scott; 3/09)
Hal Newhouser #98 PSA 8 (NmMt) sold for $7,638 (REA; 4/07)
Hal Newhouser #98 PSA 7 (NM) sold for $6,523 (Mile High; 1/07)
Hal Newhouser #98 PSA 7 (NM) sold for $2,727 (eBay; 4/08)
Satchel Paige #8 PSA 8 (NmMt) sold for $89,087 (Goodwin; 8/07)
Satchel Paige #8 PSA 8 (NmMt) sold for $50,556 (Mastro; 6/05)
Satchel Paige #8 PSA 8 (NmMt) sold for $39,100 (Superior; 8/03)
Satchel Paige #8 GAI 8 (NmMt) sold for $27,706 (Mile High; 1/07)
Satchel Paige #8 GAI 8 (NmMt) sold for $20,400 (Mastro; 8/07)

Johnny Pesky #121 PSA 7 (NM) sold for $2,950 (eBay; 9/07)
Kent Peterson Black Cap #42 PSA 8 (NmMt) sold for $2,911 (Mastro; 12/06)
Kent Peterson Black Cap #42 PSA 8 (NmMt) sold for $1,490 (Mastro; 8/07)
Kent Peterson Black Cap #42 PSA 8 (NmMt) sold for $522 (Mile High; 2/08)
Kent Peterson Black Cap #42 PSA 8 (NmMt) sold for $504 (Mile High; 2/08)
Kent Peterson Red Cap #42 PSA 7 (NM) sold for $4,365 (Memory Lane; 12/07)
Dave Philley #85 PSA 8 (NmMt) sold for $7,614 (SCP Sotheby's; 11/06)
Dave Philley #85 PSA 8 (NmMt) sold for $3,095 (eBay; 9/07)
Harold Reiser #146 PSA 8 (NmMt) sold for $3,121 (eBay; 9/07)
Harold Reiser #146 PSA 7 (NM) sold for $5,930 (Mile High; 1/07)
Harold Reiser #146 PSA 7 (NM) sold for $1,847 (Memory Lane; 9/07)
Phil Rizzuto #11 SGC 96 (MT) sold for $5,484 (Goodwin; 10/12)
Jackie Robinson #79 PSA 9 (MT) sold for $45,000 (Memory Lane; Private - 2006)
Jackie Robinson #79 PSA 9 (MT) sold for $39,547 (Mastro; 10/05)
Jackie Robinson #79 PSA 9 (MT) sold for $33,657 (Mastro; 6/05)
Jackie Robinson #79 GAI 9 (MT) sold for $8,100 (eBay; 7/06)
Jackie Robinson #79 SGC 92 (NmMt+) sold for $13,035 (REA; 5/13)
Jackie Robinson #79 SGC 92 (NmMt+) sold for $11,850 (REA; Spring '14)
Jackie Robinson #79 SGC 92 (NmMt+) sold for $7,883 (eBay; 2/08)
Jackie Robinson #79 SGC 88 (NmMt) sold for $15,859 (Mastro; 4/07)
Jackie Robinson #79 GAI 8 (NmMt) sold for $6,021 (Memory Lane; 12/06)
Babe Ruth #3 SGC 96 (MT) sold for $48,066 (Mastro; 4/07)
Babe Ruth #3 PSA 9 (MT) sold for $28,536 (Mastro; 4/04)
Babe Ruth #3 SGC 96 (MT) sold for $22,987 (Mastro; 1/04)
Babe Ruth #3 PSA 9 (MT) sold for $18,975 (Superior; 3/04)
Hank Sauer #20 PSA 8 (NmMt) sold for $4,743 (Mile High; 8/07)
Johnny Schmitz #48 PSA 8 (NmMt) sold for $4,208 (Mile High; 1/07)
Johnny Schmitz #48 PSA 8 (NmMt) sold for $3,285 (Mile High; 2/08)
Johnny Schmitz #48 PSA 8 (NmMt) sold for $3,203 (Mastro; 8/07)
Johnny Schmitz #48 PSA 8 (NmMt) sold for $2,247 (eBay; 10/07)
Enos Slaughter #127 PSA 8 (NmMt) sold for $12,756 (Mastro; 12/06)
Enos Slaughter #127 PSA 8 (NmMt) sold for $3,436 (Memory Lane; 9/07)
Enos Slaughter #127 PSA 8 (NmMt) sold for $2,751 (Mile High; 2/08)
Enos Slaughter #127 GAI 8 (NmMt) sold for $1,837 (Mastro; 4/07)
Enos Slaughter #127 SGC 84 (NM) sold for $1,043 (Mile High; 2/08)
Warren Spahn #32 GAI 9 (MT) sold for $5,999 (Mastro; 4/04)
Warren Spahn #32 SGC 92 (NmMt+) sold for $3,586 (Mastro; 4/07)
Vernon Stephens #161 PSA 8 (NmMt) sold for $3,047 (Memory Lane; 9/07)
Vernon Stephens #161 PSA 7 (NM) sold for $2,348 (eBay; 9/07)
Vernon Stephens #161 PSA 7 (NM) sold for $2,324 (Memory Lane; 3/06)
Eddie Stevens #43 PSA 7 (NM) sold for $2,706 (eBay; 9/07)
Edward Stewart #104 PSA 8 (NmMt) sold for $4,375 (Mile High; 2/08)
Edward Stewart #104 PSA 7 (NM) sold for $4,364 (Memory Lane; 8/06)
Edward Stewart #104 PSA 7 (NM) sold for $1,258 (eBay; 9/07)
Virgil Trucks #5 PSA 7 (NM) sold for $4,292 (SCP Sotheby's; 11/06)
Virgil Trucks #5 PSA 7 (NM) sold for $2,550 (eBay; 9/07)
Honus Wagner #70 SGC 96 (MT) sold for $3,100 (eBay; 9/04)
Honus Wagner #70 SGC 92 (NmMt+) sold for $6,355 (Mastro; 4/07)
Harry Walker #137 PSA 8 (NmMt) sold for $10,237 (Mastro; 12/06)
Harry Walker #137 SGC 88 (NmMt) sold for $3,614 (Mastro; 8/06)
Harry Walker #137 SGC 88 (NmMt) sold for $1,147 (Memory Lane; 12/07)
Harry Walker #137 PSA 7 (NM) sold for $2,025 (eBay; 9/07)
Ted Williams #76 PSA 9 (MT) sold for $17,400 (REA; 4/06)
Ted Williams #76 PSA 9 (MT) sold for $17,261 (Mile High; 12/05)
Ted Williams #76 PSA 9 (MT) sold for $15,639 (Leland's; 2/05)
Ted Williams #76 PSA 9 (MT) sold for $15,180 (Mastro; 12/06)
Ted Williams #76 PSA 9 (MT) sold for $14,700 (eBay; 9/04)
Ted Williams #76 PSA 9 (MT) sold for $14,524 (Mastro; 8/07)
Ted Williams #76 GAI 9 (MT) sold for $6,244 (Memory Lane; 5/08)
Ted Williams #76 SGC 92 (NmMt+) sold for $13,045 (Mastro; 4/07)
Ted Williams #76 SGC 92 (NmMt+) sold for $8,911 (Memory Lane; 5/08)
Ted Williams #76 SGC 92 (NmMt+) sold for $6,932 (Goodwin; 5/08)
Ted Williams #76 SGC 8.5 (NmMt+) sold for $5,253 (Mile High; 10/11)
Ted Williams #76 GAI 8.5 (NmMt+) sold for $3,550 (eBay; 5/06)
John Wyrostek #19 PSA 8 (NmMt) sold for $15,008 (Mile High; 1/07)
Al Zarilla #36 PSA 7 (NM) sold for $3,389 (Mile High; 1/07)
Al Zarilla #36 PSA 7 (NM) sold for $2,865 (Memory Lane; 4/07)
Al Zarilla #36 PSA 7 (NM) sold for $1,575 (eBay; 9/07)

1950 Bowman

		GD 2	VG 3	VgEx 4	EX 5	ExMt 6	NM 7	NmMt 8	MT 9
1	Mel Parnell RC	15	25	50	100	350			
2	Vern Stephens	10	15	25	40	80	100	1,000	
3	Dom DiMaggio	10	15	50	80	120	250	1,200	
4	Gus Zernial RC	5	10	15	25	50	80	500	
5	Bob Kuzava RC	5	8	12	25	30	80	250	
6	Bob Feller	60	▲100	150	200	250	600	2,000	

#	Player	GD 2	VG 3	VgEx 4	EX 5	ExMt 6	NM 7	NmMt 8	MT 9
7	Jim Hegan	5	10	15	40	60	200	400	
8	George Kell	10	15	50	60	80	150	400	
9	Vic Wertz	5	10	15	25	40	120		
10	Tommy Henrich	10	30	40	50	100	150	1,000	
11	Phil Rizzuto	40	60	100	150	300	400	1,200	
12	Joe Page	8	12	18	40	50	100	300	
13	Ferris Fain	5	10	15	30	40	200	300	
14	Alex Kellner	5	8	12	20	30	60	100	
15	Al Kozar	5	8	12	20	30	100	200	
16	Roy Sievers RC	8	12	40	50	100	200	500	
17	Sid Hudson	5	8	12	20	30	60	200	
18	Eddie Robinson RC	5	8	12	20	30	80	300	
19	Warren Spahn	40	80	100	200	250	500	1,200	
20	Bob Elliott	5	10	15	25	40	100	200	
21	Pee Wee Reese	30	60	100	150	250	300	1,000	
22	Jackie Robinson	▲600	▲800	1,000	▲1,500	▲3,000	5,000	8,000	15,000
23	Don Newcombe RC	40	50	60	120	250	400	800	
24	Johnny Schmitz	5	8	12	20	30	50	150	
25	Hank Sauer	5	10	15	25	40	80	300	
26	Grady Hatton	5	8	12	30	50	60	250	
27	Herman Wehmeier	5	8	12	20	30	50	120	
28	Bobby Thomson	20	30	40	50	80	200	300	
29	Eddie Stanky	5	10	15	25	40	80	300	
30	Eddie Waitkus	5	10	15	25	50	80	200	
31	Del Ennis	8	12	20	30	80	100	500	
32	Robin Roberts	25	50	80	120	200	400	1,200	
33	Ralph Kiner	25	30	50	100	150	400	500	2,000
34	Murry Dickson	5	10	15	25	40	250	500	
35	Enos Slaughter	25	30	50	60	80	250	500	
36	Eddie Kazak RC	8	12	20	30	50	100	1,200	
37	Luke Appling	10	15	40	80	100	200	500	
38	Bill Wight RC	5	8	12	20	30	50	120	
39	Larry Doby	30	50	60	100	150	300	1,000	
40	Bob Lemon	10	15	50	60	80	200	500	
41	Hoot Evers	5	8	12	20	30	60	150	
42	Art Houtteman RC	5	8	12	20	40	60	150	
43	Bobby Doerr	30	40	60	100	120	200	400	
44	Joe Dobson	5	8	12	20	30	50	150	
45	Al Zarilla	5	8	12	20	30	50	200	
46	Yogi Berra	100	150	250	300	600	1,000	2,500	
47	Jerry Coleman	5	10	25	30	50	80	250	
48	Lou Brissie	5	8	12	20	25	50	150	
49	Elmer Valo	5	8	12	20	30	80	250	
50	Dick Kokos	5	8	12	20	30	60	100	
51	Ned Garver	5	10	15	25	40	60	250	
52	Sam Mele	5	8	12	20	30	60	150	
53	Clyde Vollmer RC	5	8	12	20	30	80	100	
54	Gil Coan	5	8	12	20	30	50	120	
55	Buddy Kerr	5	8	12	20	30	50	150	
56	Del Crandall RC	5	10	25	40	50	100	200	
57	Vern Bickford	5	8	12	20	30	50	200	
58	Carl Furillo	10	15	25	60	80	120	300	800
59	Ralph Branca	5	10	15	25	80	100	300	
60	Andy Pafko	5	20	30	40	50	80	200	
61	Bob Rush RC	5	8	12	20	30	60	100	
62	Ted Kluszewski	10	15	25	60	80	120	400	
63	Ewell Blackwell	5	8	25	30	40	60	250	
64	Alvin Dark	5	10	15	25	50	80	200	
65	Dave Koslo	5	8	12	20	30	50	150	
66	Larry Jansen	5	8	12	20	30	50	200	
67	Willie Jones	5	10	15	25	40	100	500	
68	Curt Simmons	5	10	15	25	40	80	200	
69	Wally Westlake	5	8	12	20	30	50	100	
70	Bob Chesnes	5	8	12	20	30	40	200	
71	Red Schoendienst	10	15	50	60	80	120	400	
72	Howie Pollet	5	8	12	20	30	50	200	
73	Willard Marshall	5	8	12	20	30	60	400	
74	Johnny Antonelli RC	5	10	15	25	40	50	200	
75	Roy Campanella	30	60	100	120	▲250	300	800	4,000
76	Rex Barney	5	5	8	12	15	30	500	
77	Duke Snider	50	60	80	120	250	300	1,000	5,000
78	Mickey Owen	5	5	8	20	25	40	100	
79	Johnny VanderMeer	5	10	15	25	50	120	200	
80	Howard Fox RC	5	5	8	12	15	25	80	
81	Ron Northey	5	6	10	12	15	30	150	
82	Whitey Lockman	5	8	12	15	20	40	150	
83	Sheldon Jones	5	5	8	12	25	50	60	
84	Richie Ashburn	25	30	50	80	120	200	500	
85	Ken Heintzelman	5	5	8	12	15	40	150	
86	Stan Rojek	5	6	10	15	25	40	100	
87	Bill Werle RC	5	5	8	12	20	30	80	
88	Marty Marion	5	8	12	20	50	60	300	
89	George Munger	5	5	8	12	15	40	120	
90	Harry Brecheen	5	5	8	12	15	40	120	
91	Cass Michaels	5	5	8	12	15	40	100	
92	Hank Majeski	5	6	10	12	15	30	150	
93	Gene Bearden	5	5	8	12	25	30	150	
94	Lou Boudreau MG	8	12	20	30	50	100	150	7
95	Aaron Robinson	5	5	8	12	15	25	80	
96	Virgil Trucks	5	5	8	12	30	40	200	
97	Maurice McDermott RC	5	5	8	12	15	25	300	
98	Ted Williams	200	300	400	500	800	1,200	5,000	10,00
99	Billy Goodman	5	8	12	20	25	40	150	
100	Vic Raschi	5	10	15	25	40	60	200	
101	Bobby Brown	5	10	15	25	40	80	200	
102	Billy Johnson	5	5	8	12	15	60	120	
103	Eddie Joost	5	5	8	12	25	30	60	
104	Sam Chapman	5	6	10	15	20	30	200	
105	Bob Dillinger	5	5	8	12	15	30	80	
106	Cliff Fannin	5	5	8	12	15	40	150	
107	Sam Dente RC	5	5	8	12	15	40	150	
108	Ray Scarborough	5	5	8	12	25	50	200	
109	Sid Gordon	5	5	8	12	15	40	150	
110	Tommy Holmes	5	5	8	20	25	50	60	
111	Walker Cooper	5	5	8	12	15	25	60	
112	Gil Hodges	12	20	60	80	120	200	500	1,00
113	Gene Hermanski	5	5	8	12	15	40	100	
114	Wayne Terwilliger RC	5	5	8	12	25	50	120	
115	Roy Smalley	5	6	10	12	30	50	80	
116	Virgil Stallcup	5	5	8	12	15	25	80	
117	Bill Rigney	5	5	8	12	15	40	80	
118	Clint Hartung	5	6	10	12	25	30	250	
119	Dick Sisler	5	5	8	12	15	60	80	
120	John Thompson	5	5	8	12	15	25	80	
121	Andy Seminick	5	5	8	12	15	80	150	
122	Johnny Hopp	5	5	8	12	15	25	80	
123	Dino Restelli RC	5	6	10	12	15	40	120	
124	Clyde McCullough	5	5	8	12	15	25	80	
125	Del Rice RC	5	5	8	12	15	40	80	
126	Al Brazle	5	5	8	12	15	25	50	
127	Dave Philley	5	6	10	12	20	30	100	
128	Phil Masi	5	5	12	15	20	50	60	
129	Joe Gordon	5	6	10	25	50	80	250	
130	Dale Mitchell	5	5	8	12	15	50	150	
131	Steve Gromek	5	5	12	15	20	40	80	
132	Mickey Vernon	5	5	8	12	15	40	150	
133	Don Kolloway	5	5	8	12	25	30	80	
134	Paul Trout	5	5	8	12	25	30	80	
135	Pat Mullin	5	5	8	12	15	25	▲80	
136	Buddy Rosar	5	6	10	12	15	30	200	
137	Johnny Pesky	5	8	12	20	60	100	120	
138	Allie Reynolds	5	10	25	30	50	60	150	
139	Johnny Mize	8	20	30	50	60	150	300	
140	Pete Suder RC	5	5	8	12	15	30	50	
141	Joe Coleman RC	5	5	8	25	30	50	80	
142	Sherman Lollar RC	5	8	12	20	25	50	250	
143	Eddie Stewart	5	5	8	12	15	25	50	
144	Al Evans	5	5	8	12	15	25	120	
145	Jack Graham RC	5	5	8	12	15	40	80	
146	Floyd Baker	5	6	10	12	15	30	100	
147	Mike Garcia RC	5	8	12	20	25	40	120	
148	Early Wynn	8	12	30	50	▲80	100	300	
149	Bob Swift	5	5	8	12	15	25	120	
150	George Vico	5	5	8	12	15	25	50	
151	Fred Hutchinson	5	5	8	12	25	30	100	
152	Ellis Kinder RC	5	5	8	12	25	30	100	
153	Walt Masterson	5	5	8	12	15	25	80	
154	Gus Niarhos	5	5	8	12	25	30	150	
155	Frank Shea	5	5	8	12	15	30	100	
156	Fred Sanford	5	5	8	12	20	50	80	
157	Mike Guerra	5	5	8	20	25	30	80	
158	Paul Lehner	5	5	8	12	15	30	▼60	
159	Joe Tipton	5	5	8	15	20	30	60	
160	Mickey Harris	5	5	8	12	15	40	100	

		GD 2	VG 3	VgEx 4	EX 5	ExMt 6	NM 7	NmMt 8	MT 9
61	Sherry Robertson RC	5	5	8	12	20	25	60	
62	Eddie Yost	5	5	8	12	20	30	80	
63	Earl Torgeson	5	5	8	12	25	30	60	
64	Sibby Sisti	5	5	8	12	15	40	80	
65	Bruce Edwards	5	6	10	12	20	30	120	
66	Joe Hatton	5	5	8	12	15	40	80	
67	Preacher Roe	5	10	20	25	40	60	200	1,000
68	Bob Scheffing	5	5	8	20	25	30	80	
69	Hank Edwards	5	5	8	12	15	25	100	
70	Dutch Leonard	5	5	8	12	25	40	60	
71	Harry Gumbert	5	5	8	12	15	25	60	
72	Peanuts Lowrey	5	5	8	12	25	25	80	
73	Lloyd Merriman RC	5	5	8	20	25	30	80	
74	Hank Thompson RC	6	10	15	25	40	60	150	
75	Monte Kennedy	5	5	8	12	15	40	50	
76	Sylvester Donnelly	5	5	8	12	30	60	80	
77	Hank Borowy	5	5	8	12	15	30	60	
78	Ed Fitzgerald	5	5	8	12	15	40	100	
79	Chuck Diering RC	5	5	8	12	20	25	80	
80	Harry Walker	5	5	8	20	25	30	60	
81	Marino Pieretti	5	5	8	12	15	50	100	
82	Sam Zoldak	5	5	8	12	15	40	100	
83	Mickey Haefner	5	5	8	12	20	25	50	
84	Randy Gumpert	5	5	8	12	15	25	100	
85	Howie Judson RC	5	5	8	12	30	50	80	
86	Ken Keltner	5	5	8	12	15	30	120	
87	Lou Stringer	5	5	8	12	15	30	60	
88	Earl Johnson	5	5	8	12	25	50	60	
89	Owen Friend RC	5	6	10	15	20	30	80	
90	Ken Wood RC	5	6	10	15	20	30	100	
91	Dick Starr RC	5	5	8	12	15	30	60	
92	Bob Chipman	5	5	8	12	15	25	60	
93	Pete Reiser	5	8	12	20	25	40	120	
94	Billy Cox	5	8	12	20	30	50	120	600
95	Phil Cavarretta	5	8	12	20	25	40	100	
96	Doyle Lade	5	5	8	12	15	30	80	
97	Johnny Wyrostek	5	5	8	12	20	30	80	
98	Danny Litwhiler	5	5	8	12	15	25	50	
99	Jack Kramer	5	5	8	12	15	40	120	
100	Kirby Higbe	5	5	8	15	20	25	80	
101	Pete Castiglione RC	5	5	8	15	20	40	80	
102	Cliff Chambers RC	5	5	8	12	20	50	80	
103	Danny Murtaugh	5	5	8	12	15	30	60	
104	Granny Hamner RC	5	8	12	20	40	50	100	
105	Mike Goliat RC	5	5	8	12	15	30	80	
106	Stan Lopata	5	5	8	12	25	30	120	
107	Max Lanier RC	5	5	8	12	20	30	80	
108	Jim Hearn	5	5	8	12	15	40	80	
109	Johnny Lindell	5	5	8	12	15	25	100	
110	Ted Gray	5	5	8	12	15	40	80	
111	Charlie Keller	5	8	12	20	25	80	120	
112	Jerry Priddy	5	5	8	15	20	25	60	
113	Carl Scheib	5	5	8	12	20	30	80	
114	Dick Fowler	5	5	8	12	25	30	60	
115	Ed Lopat	5	10	15	25	40	60	150	
116	Bob Porterfield	5	5	8	12	15	40	100	
117	Casey Stengel MG	10	15	50	60	100	120	400	1,000
118	Cliff Mapes RC	5	5	8	30	40	50	80	
119	Hank Bauer RC	8	25	30	50	60	120	250	800
120	Leo Durocher MG	5	10	30	40	60	100	200	800
121	Don Mueller RC	5	8	12	20	25	50	100	
122	Bobby Morgan RC	5	5	8	12	25	50	120	
123	Jim Russell	5	5	8	12	15	40	80	
124	Jack Banta RC	5	5	8	12	15	30	80	
125	Eddie Sawyer MG RC	5	5	8	20	25	50	100	
126	Jim Konstanty RC	5	8	12	20	50	60	150	
127	Bob Miller RC	5	5	8	12	20	30	80	
128	Bill Nicholson	5	5	8	12	20	40	60	
129	Frankie Frisch MG	6	10	15	25	40	80	▲200	
130	Bill Serena RC	5	5	8	12	15	30	60	
131	Preston Ward RC	5	5	8	12	25	40	60	
132	Al Rosen RC	5	10	40	50	60	80	200	
133	Allie Clark	5	5	8	20	25	40	60	
134	Bobby Shantz RC	5	10	15	25	40	60	250	
135	Harold Gilbert RC	5	5	8	15	20	50	80	
136	Bob Cain RC	5	5	8	12	20	25	100	
137	Bill Salkeld	5	5	8	12	15	25	60	

		GD 2	VG 3	VgEx 4	EX 5	ExMt 6	NM 7	NmMt 8	MT 9
238	Nippy Jones RC	5	5	8	12	20	30	60	
239	Bill Howerton RC	5	5	8	12	15	30	100	
240	Eddie Lake	5	5	8	12	15	50	80	
241	Neil Berry RC	5	5	8	12	30	40	80	
242	Dick Kryhoski	5	5	8	12	25	30	100	
243	Johnny Groth RC	5	5	8	12	15	25	100	
244	Dale Coogan RC	5	5	8	12	15	▲40	80	
245	Al Papai RC	5	5	8	12	40	60	100	
246	Walt Dropo RC	5	10	12	20	25	80	100	
247	Irv Noren RC	5	5	8	20	30	40	250	
248	Sam Jethroe RC	5	10	15	25	50	80	200	
249	Snuffy Stirnweiss	5	5	8	12	15	30	100	
250	Ray Coleman RC	5	5	8	12	15	50	80	
251	Les Moss RC	5	5	8	12	25	30	150	
252	Billy DeMars RC	5	6	10	30	40	100	400	

—Richie Ashburn #84 PSA 9 (MT) sold for $2,760 (Mastro; 5/08)
—Yogi Berra #46 GAI 8 (NmMt) sold for $832 (Mastro; 2/07)
—Bob Feller #6 PSA 9 (MT) sold for $9,028 (Superior; 4/03)
—Jim Hegan #7 PSA 9 (MT) sold for $6,613 (Memory Lane; 3/06)
—Jim Hegan #7 PSA 8 (NmMt) sold for $3,001 (eBay; 6/06)
—Don Newcombe #23 BVG 9 (MT) sold for $1,125 (eBay; 2/08)
—Mel Parnell #1 PSA 8 (NmMt) sold for $13,532 (Goodwin; 6/06)
—Mel Parnell #1 PSA 8 (NmMt) sold for $10,199 (Memory Lane; 9/07)
—Mel Parnell #1 PSA 7 (NM) sold for $2,115 (eBay; 4/07)
—Pee Wee Reese #21 GAI 9 (MT) sold for $2,988 (Mastro; 2/05)
—Pee Wee Reese #21 GAI 9 (MT) sold for $1,720 (Memory Lane; 9/07)
—Phil Rizzuto #11 PSA 9 (MT) sold for $3,351 (Memory Lane; 9/07)
—Jackie Robinson #22 PSA 8.5 (NmMt+) sold for $5,969 (Mile High; 1/13)
—Jackie Robinson #22 GAI 8 (NmMt) sold for $1,892 (Mile High; 8/07)
—Jackie Robinson #22 GAI 8 (NmMt) sold for $1,684 (Mile High; 2/08)
—Enos Slaughter #35 PSA 9 (MT) sold for $1,526 (Memory Lane; 4/07)
—Warren Spahn #19 GAI 9 (MT) sold for $1,390 (Goodwin; 10/06)
—Vic Wertz #9 PSA 8 (NmMt) sold for $1,400 (Goodwin; 6/06)
—Vic Wertz #9 SGC 88 (NmMt) sold for $761 (eBay; 2/08)
—Ted Williams #98 PSA 9 (MT) sold for $21,076 (Mile High; 2/08)
—Ted Williams #98 SGC 92 (NmMt+) sold for $4,500 (eBay; 5/07)
—Ted Williams #98 SGC 92 (NmMt+) sold for $3,614 (Goodwin; 3/08)
—Early Wynn #148 PSA 10 (Gem) sold for $10,630 (Mastro; 4/04)
—Early Wynn #148 PSA 9 (MT) sold for $3,000 (eBay; 6/04)

1950-51 Toleteros

—Joshua Gibson SGC 88 (NmMt) sold for $42,000 (Mastro; 8/07)
—Joshua Gibson #JG PSA 7 (NrMt) sold for $27,631 (Mile High; 1/12)
—Joshua Gibson PSA 7 (NM) sold for $26,995 (Lelands; 12/05)
—Joshua Gibson SGC 6 (ExMt) sold for $21,600 (Mastro; 8/08)
—Joshua Gibson SGC 80 (ExMt) sold for $20,315 (Heritage; 10/07)
—Joshua Gibson SGC 60 (EX) sold for $18,800 (REA; 5/08)
—Joshua Gibson SGC 60 (EX) sold for $17,925 (Heritage; 10/07)
—Joshua Gibson SGC 50 (VgEx) sold for $24,851 (Mastro; 4/07)
—Joshua Gibson #JG PSA 4 (VgEx) sold for $18,330 (Goodwin; 9/13)
—Joshua Gibson #JG PSA 4 (Vg/Ex) sold for $9,076 (Legendary; 6/12)
—Joshua Gibson SGC 40 (VG) sold for $14,617 (Leland's ; 6/08)
—Joshua Gibson SGC 40 (VG) sold for $11,448 (Memory Lane; 12/07)

1951 Bowman

		GD 2	VG 3	VgEx 4	EX 5	ExMt 6	NM 7	NmMt 8	MT 9
1	Whitey Ford RC	250	400	600	▲1,200	▲1,500	3,000	15,000	
2	Yogi Berra	100	120	▲250	300	500	600	3,000	6,000
3	Robin Roberts	10	30	40	60	100	200	▲500	2,000
4	Del Ennis	12	15	40	50	80	120	250	1,000
5	Dale Mitchell	5	5	8	12	20	30	120	
6	Don Newcombe	10	20	30	50	80	200	500	
7	Gil Hodges	12	30	50	60	100	150	400	4,000
8	Paul Lehner	5	5	8	12	20	40	80	1,000
9	Sam Chapman	5	5	8	25	30	80	250	500
10	Red Schoendienst	12	20	30	40	80	120	300	1,200
11	George Munger	5	5	8	12	20	30	80	500
12	Hank Majeski	5	5	8	20	25	40	60	600
13	Eddie Stanky	5	5	8	12	20	50	100	2,800
14	Alvin Dark	5	5	8	12	25	60	100	1,500
15	Johnny Pesky	5	5	8	12	50	50	250	1,000
16	Maurice McDermott	5	5	8	12	20	40	100	500
17	Pete Castiglione	5	5	8	12	20	40	80	500
18	Gil Coan	5	5	8	12	20	120	200	
19	Sid Gordon	5	5	8	12	25	50	100	1,200

#	Player	GD 2	VG 3	VgEx 4	EX 5	ExMt 6	NM 7	NmMt 8	MT 9
20	Del Crandall	5	5	8	12	20	30	80	800
21	Snuffy Stirnweiss	5	5	8	12	20	40	150	500
22	Hank Sauer	5	5	8	12	20	150	200	
23	Hoot Evers	5	5	8	12	25	60	100	800
24	Ewell Blackwell	5	5	8	20	30	40	80	
25	Vic Raschi	8	12	20	25	30	60	150	800
26	Phil Rizzuto	15	60	80	100	150	▼250	500	3,000
27	Jim Konstanty	5	6	10	25	30	40	150	
28	Eddie Waitkus	5	5	8	12	20	100	500	400
29	Allie Clark	5	8	12	15	25	40	80	500
30	Bob Feller	30	50	60	100	200	250	600	4,500
31	Roy Campanella	60	80	120	200	250	400	1,000	8,000
32	Duke Snider	50	80	100	150	200	400	800	
33	Bob Hooper RC	5	5	8	12	40	60	80	
34	Marty Marion MG	5	8	12	20	30	50	200	1,500
35	Al Zarilla	5	5	8	12	20	40	80	
36	Joe Dobson	5	5	8	12	20	40	100	
37	Whitey Lockman	5	5	8	12	20	50	120	
38	Al Evans	5	5	8	12	20	40	100	800
39	Ray Scarborough	5	6	10	15	20	50	80	500
40	Gus Bell RC	5	6	10	15	40	60	120	1,000
41	Eddie Yost	5	5	8	12	25	40	80	700
42	Vern Bickford	5	5	8	12	20	40	80	400
43	Billy DeMars	5	5	8	12	20	▲40	80	500
44	Roy Smalley	5	5	8	12	20	40	100	500
45	Art Houtteman	5	5	8	12	20	40	100	
46	George Kell	12	20	30	▲50	60	120	250	1,000
47	Grady Hatton	5	5	8	12	20	40	80	500
48	Ken Raffensberger	5	5	8	12	20	40	80	600
49	Jerry Coleman	5	5	8	12	20	60	150	600
50	Johnny Mize	15	25	30	40	50	100	250	1,200
51	Andy Seminick	5	5	8	15	20	40	100	500
52	Dick Sisler	5	5	8	12	20	60	100	1,000
53	Bob Lemon	5	25	30	40	50	100	200	1,000
54	Ray Boone RC	5	6	10	15	25	50	120	
55	Gene Hermanski	5	5	8	12	30	40	150	
56	Ralph Branca	5	10	25	30	50	80	250	
57	Alex Kellner	5	5	8	12	20	30	80	500
58	Enos Slaughter	20	25	30	40	50	100	250	800
59	Randy Gumpert	5	5	8	12	20	30	80	600
60	Chico Carrasquel RC	5	8	20	30	40	50	150	2,200
61	Jim Hearn	5	5	8	12	20	40	80	800
62	Lou Boudreau MG	10	15	30	40	50	80	200	1,000
63	Bob Dillinger	5	5	8	12	20	30	100	
64	Bill Werle	5	5	8	12	20	▲40	100	
65	Mickey Vernon	5	8	12	20	30	50	120	600
66	Bob Elliott	5	5	8	12	20	30	60	1,000
67	Roy Sievers	5	5	8	12	20	30	100	2,500
68	Dick Kokos	5	5	8	12	20	30	80	
69	Johnny Schmitz	5	5	8	12	20	50	80	
70	Ron Northey	5	5	8	12	20	40	100	1,200
71	Jerry Priddy	5	5	8	12	20	25	60	
72	Lloyd Merriman	5	5	8	12	20	50	60	500
73	Tommy Byrne RC	5	6	10	15	25	100		
74	Billy Johnson	5	5	8	12	20	30	150	1,200
75	Russ Meyer RC	5	5	8	25	30	50	100	1,000
76	Stan Lopata	5	5	8	12	20	▲50	▼100	400
77	Mike Goliat	5	5	8	12	20	50	80	250
78	Early Wynn	8	12	20	50	60	100	200	550
79	Jim Hegan	5	5	8	12	25	40	120	800
80	Pee Wee Reese	40	50	80	100	120	250	400	10,000
81	Carl Furillo	8	12	20	25	50	100	200	1,000
82	Joe Tipton	5	5	8	12	25	40	60	1,200
83	Carl Scheib	5	5	8	12	20	30	80	400
84	Barney McCosky	5	5	8	12	20	30	100	800
85	Eddie Kazak	5	5	8	12	20	30	60	400
86	Harry Brecheen	5	6	10	15	25	40	80	800
87	Floyd Baker	5	5	8	12	20	30	60	500
88	Eddie Robinson	5	5	8	12	20	40	80	▼300
89	Hank Thompson	5	5	8	12	25	40	120	400
90	Dave Koslo	5	5	8	12	20	30	80	
91	Clyde Vollmer	5	5	8	12	25	40	100	1,000
92	Vern Stephens	5	5	8	20	30	40	60	500
93	Danny O'Connell RC	5	5	8	12	20	40	60	500
94	Clyde McCullough	5	6	10	15	25	30	80	600
95	Sherry Robertson	5	5	8	12	20	40	80	1,200
96	Sandy Consuegra RC	5	5	8	12	20	30	100	400

#	Player	GD 2	VG 3	VgEx 4	EX 5	ExMt 6	NM 7	NmMt 8	MT 9
97	Bob Kuzava	5	5	8	12	20	30	80	50
98	Willard Marshall	5	5	8	12	20	30	80	40
99	Earl Torgeson	5	5	8	12	20	40	80	50
100	Sherm Lollar	5	5	8	20	30	50	120	
101	Owen Friend	5	5	8	12	20	40	80	1,00
102	Dutch Leonard	5	5	8	12	20	100		50
103	Andy Pafko	6	10	15	25	40	60	150	1,00
104	Virgil Trucks	5	5	8	12	30	50	150	80
105	Don Kolloway	5	5	8	12	20	30	60	1,20
106	Pat Mullin	5	5	8	12	20	30	80	50
107	Johnny Wyrostek	5	5	8	12	20	30	80	50
108	Virgil Stallcup	5	5	8	12	20	30	100	
109	Allie Reynolds	8	12	20	30	40	100	200	1,50
110	Bobby Brown	5	8	12	20	▲40	60	100	80
111	Curt Simmons	5	5	8	25	30	50	120	1,00
112	Willie Jones	5	5	8	12	20	50	100	50
113	Bill Nicholson	5	5	8	12	20	30	100	50
114	Sam Zoldak	5	5	8	12	20	30	80	
115	Steve Gromek	5	5	8	12	20	40	80	2,00
116	Bruce Edwards	5	5	8	12	20	30	120	
117	Eddie Miksis RC	5	5	15	12	20	250		
118	Preacher Roe	8	20	25	30	40	60	200	80
119	Eddie Joost	5	5	8	12	20	40	80	
120	Joe Coleman	5	5	8	12	20	30	80	40
121	Gerry Staley RC	5	5	8	12	20	40	80	50
122	Joe Garagiola RC	8	12	40	50	80	▼100	250	80
123	Howie Judson	5	5	8	12	20	30	80	1,00
124	Gus Niarhos	5	5	8	12	20	30	60	40
125	Bill Rigney	5	5	12	15	20	30	80	50
126	Bobby Thomson	8	12	20	30	60	100	▼250	1,00
127	Sal Maglie RC	5	10	25	30	50	60	250	
128	Ellis Kinder	5	5	8	12	25	50	120	40
129	Matt Batts	5	5	8	12	20	30	120	50
130	Tom Saffell RC	5	5	8	12	20	30	60	60
131	Cliff Chambers	5	5	8	12	20	30	60	50
132	Cass Michaels	5	5	8	12	20	30	60	80
133	Sam Dente	5	5	8	12	25	30	60	40
134	Warren Spahn	40	60	80	100	▲200	250	▲800	4,00
135	Walker Cooper	5	5	8	20	25	40	100	
136	Ray Coleman	5	5	8	12	20	30	80	50
137	Dick Starr	5	5	8	12	20	30	100	
138	Phil Cavarretta	5	5	8	12	30	40	▲100	50
139	Doyle Lade	5	5	8	12	20	40	60	
140	Eddie Lake	5	5	8	12	20	30	80	4,00
141	Fred Hutchinson	5	5	8	12	20	▲50	80	50
142	Aaron Robinson	5	5	8	12	20	40	80	50
143	Ted Kluszewski	5	10	30	40	60	100	200	1,50
144	Herman Wehmeier	5	5	8	12	20	30	80	50
145	Fred Sanford	5	5	8	12	20	40	80	50
146	Johnny Hopp	5	6	10	15	25	30	120	50
147	Ken Heintzelman	5	5	8	12	20	30	60	50
148	Granny Hamner	5	5	8	12	20	40	▲100	
149	Bubba Church RC	5	5	8	12	20	40	60	50
150	Mike Garcia	5	5	8	12	20	50	100	40
151	Larry Doby	15	25	60	80	100	150	300	2,50
152	Cal Abrams RC	5	6	10	15	25	30	80	1,20
153	Rex Barney	5	5	8	12	20	40	80	
154	Pete Suder	5	6	10	15	20	30	60	50
155	Lou Brissie	5	5	8	12	20	30	60	40
156	Del Rice	5	5	8	12	25	30	60	60
157	Al Brazle	5	6	10	15	20	25	60	40
158	Chuck Diering	5	5	8	12	20	30	60	1,00
159	Eddie Stewart	5	5	8	15	20	40	60	40
160	Phil Masi	5	5	8	12	20	30	60	80
161	Wes Westrum RC	5	5	8	12	▲25	40	60	
162	Larry Jansen	5	5	8	12	20	40	80	
163	Monte Kennedy	5	5	8	▲20	▲25	30	60	50
164	Bill Wight	5	5	8	12	20	30	60	50
165	Ted Williams	200	250	300	500	600	1,000	2,500	8,0
166	Stan Rojek	5	5	8	12	20	40	80	40
167	Murry Dickson	5	5	8	12	20	30	60	50
168	Sam Mele	5	5	8	12	20	30	80	50
169	Sid Hudson	5	5	8	12	20	30	80	2,50
170	Sibby Sisti	5	5	8	12	20	30	80	
171	Buddy Kerr	5	5	8	12	20	30	80	40
172	Ned Garver	5	5	8	12	20	30	100	
173	Hank Arft	5	5	8	12	20	30	60	50

#	Player	GD 2	VG 3	VgEx 4	EX 5	ExMt 6	NM 7	NmMt 8	MT 9
174	Mickey Owen	5	5	8	12	20	30	80	
175	Wayne Terwilliger	5	5	8	12	20	40	60	400
176	Vic Wertz	5	5	8	12	25	40	80	800
177	Charlie Keller	5	5	8	12	20	30	▼60	600
178	Ted Gray	5	5	8	12	20	30	60	400
179	Danny Litwhiler	5	5	8	12	20	30	80	400
180	Howie Fox	5	5	8	12	20	30	80	500
181	Casey Stengel MG	15	25	50	60	100	150	300	2,000
182	Tom Ferrick RC	5	5	8	12	20	30	120	1,000
183	Hank Bauer	5	10	15	25	30	▲80	150	2,000
184	Eddie Sawyer MG	5	5	8	12	20	50	80	500
185	Jimmy Bloodworth	5	5	8	12	20	30	60	600
186	Richie Ashburn	15	25	50	60	100	▼120	300	1,200
187	Al Rosen	5	8	12	20	50	80	200	
188	Roberto Avila RC	5	8	12	20	50	100	500	
189	Erv Palica RC	5	5	8	25	30	40	100	
190	Joe Hatten	5	5	8	12	20	50	80	2,500
191	Billy Hitchcock RC	5	5	8	12	20	25	80	600
192	Hank Wyse RC	5	5	8	12	20	30	60	400
193	Ted Wilks	5	5	8	12	20	30	80	400
194	Peanuts Lowrey	5	6	10	15	25	30	60	
195	Paul Richards MG	5	5	8	12	25	30	60	800
196	Billy Pierce RC	5	8	12	20	30	50	150	600
197	Bob Cain	5	5	8	12	20	30	100	2,500
198	Monte Irvin RC	15	25	100	120	200	▲500	1,200	
199	Sheldon Jones	5	5	8	12	25	30	▼80	
200	Jack Kramer	5	5	8	12	20	50	60	400
201	Steve O'Neill MG RC	5	5	8	12	20	30	80	500
202	Mike Guerra	5	5	8	12	20	30	100	400
203	Vern Law RC	6	10	15	25	40	50	150	600
204	Vic Lombardi RC	5	5	8	20	25	30	60	500
205	Mickey Grasso RC	5	5	8	12	20	40	60	800
206	Conrado Marrero RC	5	5	8	12	20	30	80	1,500
207	Billy Southworth MG RC	5	5	8	12	40	50	120	▲800
208	Blix Donnelly	5	5	8	12	20	30	80	
209	Ken Wood	5	5	8	12	25	30	60	600
210	Les Moss	5	5	8	12	20	30	100	500
211	Hal Jeffcoat RC	5	5	8	12	20	30	60	2,500
212	Bob Rush	5	5	8	12	25	30	▲80	500
213	Neil Berry	5	5	8	12	20	30	120	600
214	Bob Swift	5	5	8	12	20	30	100	300
215	Ken Peterson	5	5	8	12	▲25	30	80	400
216	Connie Ryan RC	5	5	8	12	20	30	100	
217	Joe Page	5	5	15	20	25	40	▲100	
218	Ed Lopat	5	10	15	25	30	▲50	100	1,200
219	Gene Woodling RC	5	8	15	25	40	60	150	1,500
220	Bob Miller	5	6	10	15	25	30	80	500
221	Dick Whitman RC	5	5	8	12	20	30	60	500
222	Thurman Tucker RC	5	5	8	12	20	30	60	400
223	Johnny VanderMeer	5	8	12	20	30	50	150	800
224	Billy Cox	5	5	8	12	20	40	120	500
225	Dan Bankhead RC	5	5	8	20	40	50	▲120	600
226	Jimmie Dykes MG	5	5	8	12	20	30	50	1,200
227	Bobby Shantz	5	5	8	12	25	30	80	2,000
228	Cloyd Boyer RC	5	5	8	12	20	30	60	500
229	Bill Howerton	5	5	8	12	20	30	80	500
230	Max Lanier	5	5	8	12	20	30	60	400
231	Luis Aloma RC	5	6	10	15	25	30	80	400
232	Nellie Fox RC	40	100	120	150	250	300	▲1,000	4,000
233	Leo Durocher MG	10	15	25	30	50	100	200	800
234	Clint Hartung	5	5	8	12	20	30	60	400
235	Jack Lohrke	5	5	8	20	25	40	60	400
236	Buddy Rosar	5	5	8	12	20	30	50	400
237	Billy Goodman	5	5	8	12	20	40	60	1,500
238	Pete Reiser	5	6	10	15	20	40	80	1,000
239	Bill MacDonald RC	5	5	8	12	20	30	50	800
240	Joe Haynes	5	5	8	12	20	30	60	400
241	Irv Noren	5	5	8	12	20	30	60	500
242	Sam Jethroe	5	5	8	12	20	30	100	500
243	Johnny Antonelli	5	5	8	12	20	30	100	400
244	Cliff Fannin	5	5	8	12	20	30	60	600
245	John Berardino RC	5	6	10	15	25	50	60	3,000
246	Bill Serena	5	5	8	12	20	40	60	500
247	Bob Ramazzotti RC	5	5	8	12	20	30	60	800
248	Johnny Klippstein RC	5	5	8	12	20	30	80	600
249	Johnny Groth	5	5	8	12	20	30	50	400
250	Hank Borowy	5	5	8	12	20	30	60	400
251	Willard Ramsdell RC	5	5	8	12	20	30	80	400
252	Dixie Howell RC	5	5	8	12	20	30	80	500
253	Mickey Mantle RC	▲6,000	▲8,000	▲12,000	15,000	25,000	40,000	150,000	
254	Jackie Jensen RC	12	20	40	80	80	120	400	5,000
255	Milo Candini RC	5	8	12	25	30	60	200	800
256	Ken Silvestri RC	5	8	12	20	30	60	200	
257	Birdie Tebbetts RC	5	8	12	20	30	50	120	
258	Luke Easter RC	5	10	15	25	40	60	250	800
259	Chuck Dressen MG	5	8	12	20	30	80	200	800
260	Carl Erskine RC	15	25	40	80	120	150	350	2,500
261	Wally Moses	5	8	12	20	30	50	120	600
262	Gus Zernial	5	8	12	20	30	50	150	600
263	Howie Pollet	5	8	12	20	30	60	120	
264	Don Richmond RC	5	8	12	20	30	50	150	
265	Steve Bilko RC	5	8	15	20	50	120	200	1,200
266	Harry Dorish RC	5	8	12	20	30	60	100	
267	Ken Holcombe RC	5	8	12	20	30	50	100	800
268	Don Mueller	5	8	12	20	30	50	120	2,000
269	Ray Noble RC	5	8	12	20	30	60	120	800
270	Willard Nixon RC	5	8	12	20	30	60	200	800
271	Tommy Wright RC	5	10	15	25	40	80	400	
272	Billy Meyer MG RC	5	8	12	20	50	80	300	
273	Danny Murtaugh	5	8	12	20	40	60	500	
274	George Metkovich RC	5	8	12	20	40	60	250	
275	Bucky Harris MG	5	10	15	50	60	100	250	
276	Frank Quinn RC	5	8	12	20	30	60	200	800
277	Roy Hartsfield RC	5	8	12	15	30	50	120	600
278	Norman Roy RC	5	8	12	20	30	60	120	
279	Jim Delsing RC	5	8	12	20	30	50	120	600
280	Frank Overmire	5	8	12	20	30	80	400	
281	Al Widmar RC	5	8	12	20	30	50	120	
282	Frankie Frisch MG	5	10	15	25	80	100	300	
283	Walt Dubiel RC	5	8	12	20	50	60	120	600
284	Gene Bearden	5	8	12	20	30	50	120	
285	Johnny Lipon RC	5	8	12	20	30	50	120	600
286	Bob Usher RC	5	8	12	20	30	60	250	
287	Jim Blackburn RC	5	8	12	20	30	50	150	600
288	Bobby Adams	5	8	12	20	30	50	150	600
289	Cliff Mapes	5	8	12	20	30	50	150	
290	Bill Dickey CO	10	15	25	80	120	200	400	
291	Tommy Henrich CO	8	12	20	40	80	100	300	1,500
292	Eddie Pellagrini	5	8	12	25	30	50	100	800
293	Ken Johnson RC	5	8	12	20	30	50	200	600
294	Jocko Thompson	5	8	12	20	30	50	120	1,200
295	Al Lopez MG RC	20	30	40	50	60	100	200	1,500
296	Bob Kennedy RC	5	8	12	20	30	100	120	600
297	Dave Philley	5	8	12	20	30	50	100	
298	Joe Astroth RC	5	8	12	20	30	60	200	
299	Clyde King RC	5	8	12	20	40	50	150	
300	Hal Rice RC	5	8	12	20	30	50	200	5,000
301	Tommy Glaviano RC	5	8	12	20	30	40	150	1,200
302	Jim Busby RC	5	8	12	20	40	60	150	1,500
303	Marv Rotblatt RC	5	8	12	20	30	60	150	800
304	Al Gettell RC	5	8	12	20	30	50	150	600
305	Willie Mays RC	▲2,500	▲3,000	▲5,000	6,000	▲12,000	20,000	80,000	
306	Jimmy Piersall RC	12	20	60	80	100	200	500	1,200
307	Walt Masterson	5	8	12	20	40	100	120	800
308	Ted Beard RC	5	8	15	20	30	50	150	
309	Mel Queen RC	5	8	12	20	50	60	150	
310	Erv Dusak RC	5	8	12	20	30	60	150	1,300
311	Mickey Harris	5	8	12	20	30	50	100	800
312	Gene Mauch RC	15	25	30	40	60	100	200	
313	Ray Mueller RC	5	8	12	20	30	50	100	2,800
314	Johnny Sain	8	12	20	25	60	120	300	1,200
315	Zack Taylor MG	5	8	12	20	40	60	120	
316	Duane Pillette RC	5	8	12	15	30	60	150	600
317	Forrest Burgess RC	5	10	15	25	60	120	250	
318	Warren Hacker RC	5	8	12	20	30	50	120	800
319	Red Rolfe MG	5	10	15	25	40	60	200	800
320	Hal White RC	5	8	12	20	30	80	120	
321	Earl Johnson	5	8	12	20	30	50	150	1,700
322	Luke Sewell MG	5	9	15	25	40	100	250	
323	Joe Adcock RC	8	12	20	30	60	120	400	

		GD 2	VG 3	VgEx 4	EX 5	ExMt 6	NM 7	NmMt 8	MT 9
324	Johnny Pramesa RC	9	15	25	40	80	150	500	3,500

—Several PSA 10 Commons & Minor Stars sold between $5,500 and $8,000 per in the August, 2007 Mastro auction.

—Listed pricing for Commons & Minor Stars in Mint condition refers to cards carrying PSA populations of five or more copies.

—Commons & Minor Stars in Mint condition with PSA populations of 1-4 copies typically command between $1,000-$5,000 per.

—Joe Adcock #323 PSA 9 (MT) sold for $3,420 (Mastro; 3/06)

— Yogi Berra #2 GAI 8.5 (NmMt+) sold for $1,517 (Mastro; 8/07)

— Yogi Berra #2 GAI 8 (NmMt) sold for $1,086 (eBay; 9/07)

—Ralph Branca #56 PSA 9 (MT) sold for $8,250 (eBay; 5/08)

—Tommy Byrne #73 PSA 8 (NmMt) sold for $2,269 (Mile High; 2/08)

—Tommy Byrne #73 PSA 8 (NmMt) sold for $705 (eBay; 11/06)

—Tommy Byrne #73 PSA 8 (NmMt) sold for $334 (eBay; 9/07)

—Bill Dickey #290 PSA 9 (MT) sold for $4,400 (Mile High; 6/06)

—Whitey Ford #1 PSA 9 (MT) sold for $75,000 (Memory Lane; Private 2007)

—Whitey Ford #1 GAI 9 (MT) sold for $12,325 (Memory Lane; 9/06)

—Whitey Ford #1 GAI 8.5 (NmMt+) sold for $4,050 (eBay; 3/08)

—Nellie Fox #232 PSA 10 (Gem) (Young Collection) sold for $13,344 (SCP; 5/12)

—Nellie Fox #232 PSA 10 (Gem) sold for $4,506 (Mastro; 6/05)

—Nellie Fox #232 GAI 9 (MT) sold for $681 (eBay; 10/06)

—Monte Irvin #198 PSA 9 (MT) sold for $6,479 (Memory Lane; 5/08)

—Monte Irvin #198 PSA 9 (MT) sold for $5,142 (Goodwin; 11/07)

—Vern Law #203 PSA 10 (Gem) (Young Collection) sold for $6,991 (SCP; 5/12)

—Bob Lemon #53 PSA 10 (Gem) sold for $12,000 (Mastro; 5/08)

—Mickey Mantle #253 PSA 10 (Gem) sold for $600,000 (Memory Lane-Private 2/08)

—Mickey Mantle #253 (Lionel Carter) SGC 96 (MT) sold for $162,412 (Mastro; 4/07)

—Mickey Mantle #253 PSA 9 (MT) sold for $135,000 (Memory Lane - Private 2007)

—Mickey Mantle #253 SGC 96 (MT) sold for $127,810 (Mile High; 10/13)

—Mickey Mantle #253 PSA 9 (MT) sold for $93,206 (Mastro; 8/07)

—Mickey Mantle #253 SGC 96 (MT) sold for $75,100 (BMW via eBay; 5/03)

—Mickey Mantle #253 PSA 9 (MT) sold for $67,048 (Goodwin; 2/06)

—Mickey Mantle #253 PSA 9 (MT) sold for $45,960 (Mastro; 4/03)

—Mickey Mantle #253 PSA 9 (MT) sold for $41,718 (Mastro; 4/04)

—Mickey Mantle #253 PSA 9 (MT) sold for $40,726 (Mastro; 8/04)

—Mickey Mantle #253 GAI 9 (MT) sold for $25,850 (Memory Lane; 12/07)

—Mickey Mantle #253 SGC 92 (NmMt+) sold for $32,037 (Mile High; 11/10)

—Mickey Mantle #253 SGC 92 (NmMt+) sold for $28,680 (Heritage; 5/08)

—Mickey Mantle #253 GAI 8.5 (NmMt+) sold for $23,250 (Mile High; 6/06)

—Mickey Mantle #253 GAI 8.5 (NmMt+) sold for $22,738 (Mile High; 5/04)

—Mickey Mantle #253 GAI 8.5 (NmMt+) sold for $16,838 (Mastro; 1/05)

—Mickey Mantle #253 GAI 8.5 (NmMt+) sold for $16,730 (Heritage; 10/05)

—Mickey Mantle #253 SGC 92 (NmMt+) sold for $15,307 (Mastro; 88/04)

—Willie Mays #305 PSA 9 (MT) sold for $93,413 (Memory Lane; 4/07)

—Willie Mays #305 PSA 9 (MT) sold for $85,775 (Memory Lane; 5/08)

—Willie Mays #305 PSA 9 (MT) sold for $85,000 (Memory Lane; Private Sale - 2007)

—Willie Mays #305 PSA 9 (MT) sold for $78,832 (SCP Sotheby's; 9/07)

—Willie Mays #305 PSA 9 (MT) sold for $50,556 (Mastro; 12/03)

—Willie Mays #305 PSA 9 (MT) sold for $46,000 (Superior; 3/04)

—Willie Mays #305 GAI 9 (MT) sold for $45,960 (Mastro; 10/03)

—Willie Mays #305 GAI 9 (MT) sold for $32,683 (Mastro; 4/06)

—Willie Mays #305 GAI 9 (MT) sold for $26,290 (Heritage; 12/05)

—Willie Mays #305 SGC 92 (NmMt+) sold for $30,822 (Goodwin; 12/14)

—Willie Mays #305 SGC 92 (NmMt+) sold for $22,730 (Mile High; 4/14)

—Willie Mays #305 PSA 8.5 (NmMt+) sold for $14,400 (Mastro; 5/08)

—Willie Mays #305 BVG 8.5 (NmMt+) sold for $10,064 (Mile High; 2/08)

—Willie Mays #305 BVG 8 (NmMt) sold for $6,226 (SCP Sotheby's; 9/07)

—Don Newcombe #6 PSA 10 (Gem) sold for $6,533 (Leland's; 2/05)

—Allie Reynolds #109 PSA 10 (Gem) sold for $5,787 (Leland's; 2/05)

—Duke Snider #32 PSA 10 (Gem) sold for $14,471 (Mastro; 12/05)

—Duke Snider #32 PSA 9 (MT) sold for $7,365 (Memory Lane; 9/07)

—Duke Snider #32 PSA 9 (MT) sold for $3,600 (Mastro; 5/08)

—Warren Spahn #134 GAI 9 (MT) sold for $4,619 (Goodwin; 8/07)

—Warren Spahn #134 GAI 9 (MT) sold for $1,767 (Mile High; 2/08)

—Ted Williams #165 GAI 9 (MT) sold for $3,300 (SCP Sotheby's; 6/06)

—Ted Williams #165 GAI 8.5 (NmMt+) sold for $2,771 (Mile High; 1/07)

—Ted Williams #165 GAI 8.5 (NmMt+) sold for $2,610 (REA; 6/05)

—Ted Williams #165 GAI 8.5 (NmMt+) sold for $2,463 (Memory Lane; 10/05)

—Ted Williams #165 GAI 8.5 (NmMt+) sold for $1,920 (Vintage Authentics; 7/07)

—Ted Williams #165 GAI 8.5 (NmMt+) sold for $1,884 (eBay; 5/06)

—Sam Zoldak #114 PSA 10 (Gem) sold for $6,610 (eBay; 9/12)

1951 Topps Blue Backs

		GD 2	VG 3	VgEx 4	EX 5	ExMt 6	NM 7	NmMt 8	MT
1	Eddie Yost	5	10	15	80	100	200	250	40
2	Hank Majeski	5	30	40	50	60	80	100	20
3	Richie Ashburn	50	80	120	200	250	300	400	60
4	Del Ennis	40	50	60	80	100	120	150	25
5	Johnny Pesky	5	8	25	60	80	50	100	25
6	Red Schoendienst	12	20	30	40	50	80	150	30
7	Gerry Staley RC	5	8	12	15	20	30	60	15
8	Dick Sisler	5	8	12	15	20	30	80	20
9	Johnny Sain	8	12	20	25	30	50	100	20
10	Joe Page	10	15	25	40	50	60	150	25
11	Johnny Groth	5	8	12	40	50	60	60	20
12	Sam Jethroe	5	10	15	20	50	60	80	20
13	Mickey Vernon	5	8	12	15	30	60	80	15
14	George Munger	5	8	12	15	20	60	100	20
15	Eddie Joost	10	15	25	30	40	60	120	20
16	Murry Dickson	5	8	12	15	20	30	80	15
17	Roy Smalley	5	8	12	15	20	60	120	15
18	Ned Garver	5	8	12	15	20	30	100	20
19	Phil Masi	5	8	12	15	20	30	60	15
20	Ralph Branca	5	10	15	20	25	40	100	25
21	Billy Johnson	5	8	12	15	20	30	60	15
22	Bob Kuzava	5	8	12	15	50	60	80	15
23	Dizzy Trout	5	10	15	20	25	40	120	20
24	Sherman Lollar	5	8	12	15	20	60	80	25
25	Sam Mele	5	8	12	15	20	50	60	10
26	Chico Carrasquel RC	5	8	12	15	20	30	150	20
27	Andy Pafko	5	8	12	15	20	30	80	15
28	Harry Brecheen	5	8	12	15	20	30	60	15
29	Granville Hamner	5	8	12	15	20	30	80	15
30	Enos Slaughter	15	25	40	50	60	100	150	40
31	Lou Brissie	5	8	12	15	20	30	60	15
32	Bob Elliott	5	10	15	20	25	40	80	20
33	Don Lenhardt RC	5	8	12	15	20	30	100	15
34	Earl Torgeson	5	8	12	15	20	30	60	25
35	Tommy Byrne RC	6	10	15	25	40	50	60	15
36	Cliff Fannin	5	8	12	40	50	60	100	20
37	Bobby Doerr	12	20	30	60	80	100	250	40
38	Irv Noren	5	8	12	15	20	30	80	20
39	Ed Lopat	5	10	15	20	25	40	80	20
40	Vic Wertz	5	8	12	15	20	30	120	15
41	Johnny Schmitz	5	8	12	15	20	30	80	15
42	Bruce Edwards	5	8	12	15	20	30	100	20
43	Willie Jones	5	8	12	15	20	30	100	20
44	Johnny Wyrostek	5	8	12	15	20	30	80	25
45	Billy Pierce RC	5	10	15	20	25	40	100	20
46	Gerry Priddy	5	8	12	15	20	30	60	15
47	Herman Wehmeier	5	8	12	15	20	30	80	15
48	Billy Cox	5	10	15	20	25	50	80	20
49	Hank Sauer	5	10	15	20	60	80	150	
50	Johnny Mize	12	20	30	40	80	100	150	30
51	Eddie Waitkus	5	25	30	40	50	60	300	
52	Sam Chapman	5	10	50	60	80	100	300	40

—Eddie Waitkus #51 PSA 9 (MT) sold for $2,550 (eBay; 6/07)

1951 Topps Connie Mack's All-Stars

		PrFr 1	GD 2	VG 3	VgEx 4	EX 5	ExMt 6	NM 7	NmMt
1	Grover C. Alexander	100	150	250	300	500	600		
2	Mickey Cochrane	80	100	150	250	300	400		
3	Eddie Collins	80	100	200	250	400	600		
4	Jimmy Collins	60	80	120	200	250	450		
5	Lou Gehrig	300	400	600	1,200	1,500	2,000		
6	Walter Johnson	200	250	400	500	600	800		
7	Connie Mack	100	120	200	300	400	800		
8	Christy Mathewson	150	200	300	400	800	1,000		
9	Babe Ruth	350	500	800	1,200	2,000	2,800		
10	Tris Speaker	80	250	300	400	500	600		
11	Honus Wagner	150	250	300	450	600	800		

—Lou Gehrig #5 PSA 8 (NmMt) sold for $16,816 (Mastro; 8/07)

—Babe Ruth #9 SGC 92 (NmMt+) sold for $10,157 (Heritage; 4/10)

—Babe Ruth #9 SGC 92 (NmMt+) sold for $8,927 (Memory Lane; 5/12)

—Babe Ruth #9 PSA 7 (NM) sold for $11,596 (Mastro; 8/07)

—Honus Wagner #11 PSA 8 (NmMt) sold for $4,474 (Mastro; 8/06)

—Honus Wagner #11 PSA 8 (NmMt) sold for $3,691 (Mastro; 12/07)

951 Topps Major League All-Stars

Yogi Berra #1 PSA 6 (ExMt) sold for $3,224 (SCP Sotheby's; 9/07)
-Yogi Berra #1 PSA 5 (EX) sold for $2,256 (eBay; 6/06)
-George Kell #5 PSA 4 (VgEx) sold for $679 (Goodwin; 11/07)
-George Kell #5 PSA 4 (VgEx) sold for $355 (eBay; 1/08)
-Bob Lemon #8 PSA 7 (NM) sold for $3,523 (Mastro; 8/07)
-Bob Lemon #8 PSA 7 (NM) sold for $2,223 (eBay; 5/06)
-Phil Rizzuto #9 PSA 8 (NmMt) sold for $10,780 (Mastro; 8/07)

951 Topps Red Backs

	GD 2	VG 3	VgEx 4	EX 5	ExMt 6	NM 7	NmMt 8	MT 9
Yogi Berra	40	50	100	120	200	250	300	1,000
Sid Gordon	5	5	8	10	12	20	120	250
Ferris Fain	5	5	8	10	12	20	60	120
Vern Stephens	5	5	8	10	40	50	120	200
Phil Rizzuto	15	25	30	50	60	80	150	400
Allie Reynolds	8	12	20	30	50	60	100	200
Howie Pollet	5	5	8	10	12	20	50	100
Early Wynn	10	15	25	30	40	50	100	▲2,500
Roy Sievers	5	5	8	10	12	20	60	100
Mel Parnell	5	5	8	10	12	20	60	150
Gene Hermanski	5	5	8	10	12	20	80	120
Jim Hegan	5	6	10	15	25	30	50	100
Dale Mitchell	5	5	8	10	12	20	50	100
Wayne Terwilliger	5	5	8	10	12	40	50	120
Ralph Kiner	6	10	25	30	50	60	▲100	150
Preacher Roe	5	5	8	10	12	40	80	100
Gus Bell RC	5	5	8	12	20	30	50	100
Jerry Coleman	5	5	8	12	25	30	100	120
Dick Kokos	5	5	8	12	15	20	40	100
Dom DiMaggio	5	8	25	30	40	50	120	200
Larry Jansen	5	5	8	10	12	25	50	250
Bob Feller	15	25	40	60	80	100	150	350
Ray Boone RC	5	5	8	10	12	20	80	150
Hank Bauer	5	8	12	15	30	50	100	200
Cliff Chambers	5	5	8	10	12	20	50	100
Luke Easter RC	5	5	8	10	12	20	▲50	150
Wally Westlake	5	5	8	10	12	20	50	100
Elmer Valo	5	5	8	10	12	20	40	120
Bob Kennedy RC	5	5	8	10	12	20	40	80
Warren Spahn	20	30	60	80	100	120	▼150	300
Gil Hodges	8	12	30	40	50	80	120	600
Henry Thompson	5	5	8	10	12	20	40	200
William Werle	5	5	8	10	12	20	50	150
Grady Hatton	5	5	8	10	12	20	50	100
Al Rosen	5	6	10	25	30	50	80	150
Gus Zernial Chicago	5	10	15	20	30	50	100	500
Gus Zernial Philadelphia	5	6	10	12	15	25	80	400
Wes Westrum RC	5	5	8	10	12	20	50	200
Duke Snider	12	20	50	60	80	120	150	300
Ted Kluszewski	5	8	30	40	50	60	100	150
Mike Garcia	5	5	8	12	20	30	50	150
Whitey Lockman	5	5	6	10	15	25	60	120
Ray Scarborough	5	5	8	10	12	20	50	100
Maurice McDermott	5	5	8	20	25	30	60	120
Sid Hudson	5	5	8	12	20	30	60	100
Andy Seminick	5	5	8	10	12	20	50	150
Billy Goodman	5	6	10	15	25	30	60	100
Tommy Glaviano RC	5	5	8	10	12	20	40	100
Eddie Stanky	5	5	8	10	12	20	200	250
Al Zarilla	5	5	8	10	12	40	60	200
Monte Irvin RC	30	40	50	60	80	100	120	250
Eddie Robinson	5	5	8	10	12	30	40	200
Tommy Holmes Boston	5	10	15	20	30	60		
Tommy Holmes Hartford	5	8	12	15	20	80		

1952 Berk Ross

	GD 2	VG 3	VgEx 4	EX 5	ExMt 6	NM 7	NmMt 8	MT 9
COMMON CARD	5	6	10	15	20	30	80	
Richie Ashburn	6	10	15	25	40	60	200	
Hank Bauer	5	6	10	15	20	30	80	
Yogi Berra	25	40	60	80	150	250	500	
Ewell Blackwell	5	6	10	15	20	30	200	

		GD 2	VG 3	VgEx 4	EX 5	ExMt 6	NM 7	NmMt 8	MT 9
5	Bobby Brown	5	6	10	15	20	30	80	
6	Jim Busby	5	6	10	15	20	30	100	
7	Roy Campanella	12	20	30	60	80	200	650	
8	Chico Carrasquel	5	6	10	15	20	30	250	
9	Jerry Coleman	5	6	10	15	20	30	80	
10	Joe Collins	5	6	10	15	20	30	80	
11	Alvin Dark	5	6	10	15	20	30	550	
12	Dom DiMaggio	5	6	10	15	20	400	1,000	
13	Joe DiMaggio	150	200	250	300	500	700	1,000	
14	Larry Doby	10	15	25	40	60	100	300	
15	Bobby Doerr	5	8	12	20	40	100	200	
16	Bob Elliott	5	6	10	15	20	30	80	
17	Del Ennis	5	6	10	15	20	30	80	
18	Ferris Fain	5	6	10	15	20	30	100	
19	Bob Feller	10	15	25	40	100	120	400	
20	Nellie Fox	6	10	15	25	40	60	150	
21	Ned Garver	5	6	10	15	20	30	120	
22	Clint Hartung	5	6	10	15	20	30	80	
23	Jim Hearn	5	6	10	15	20	30		
24	Gil Hodges	6	10	15	25	40	60	400	
25	Monte Irvin	5	8	12	20	30	50		
26	Larry Jansen	5	6	10	15	20	30	150	
27	Sheldon Jones	5	6	10	15	20	2,000		
28	George Kell	5	6	10	15	20	30	600	
29	Monte Kennedy	5	6	10	15	20	30		
30	Ralph Kiner	5	8	12	20	30	50		
31	Dave Koslo	5	6	10	15	20	80		
32	Bob Kuzava	5	6	10	15	20	30		
33	Bob Lemon	5	6	10	15	20	60		
34	Whitey Lockman	5	6	10	15	20	30		
35	Ed Lopat	5	6	10	15	20	30	80	
36	Sal Maglie	5	6	10	15	20	30		
37	Mickey Mantle	400	450	600	1,200	3,000	5,000		
38	Billy Martin	8	12	20	30	50	80	200	
39	Willie Mays	100	125	175	250	500	750	1,500	
40	Gil McDougald	12	20	30	50	80	200	500	
41	Minnie Minoso	5	6	10	15	20	30		
42	Johnny Mize	5	8	12	20	30	50	120	
43	Tom Morgan	5	6	10	15	20	30		
44	Don Mueller	5	6	10	15	20	30	80	
45	Stan Musial	25	40	80	100	250	400	1,200	
46	Don Newcombe	5	6	10	15	20	30	200	
47	Ray Noble	5	6	10	15	20	30		
48	Joe Ostrowski	5	6	10	15	20	30		
49	Mel Parnell	5	6	10	15	20	30	80	
50	Vic Raschi	5	6	10	15	20	30	80	
51	Pee Wee Reese	10	15	25	40	100	250	400	
52	Allie Reynolds	5	6	10	20	30	50	200	
53	Bill Rigney	5	6	10	15	20	30	150	
54A	Phil Rizzuto Bunting	10	15	25	40	60	80	300	
54B	Phil Rizzuto Swinging	10	15	25	40	80	100		
55	Robin Roberts	5	8	12	20	30	50	200	
56	Eddie Robinson	5	6	10	15	20	30		
57	Jackie Robinson	120	150	200	250	600	1,000	1,500	
58	Preacher Roe	5	6	10	50	60	80	400	
59	Johnny Sain	5	6	10	15	20	120		
60	Red Schoendienst	5	8	12	20	30	50	120	
61	Duke Snider	15	25	40	60	100	200	700	
62	George Spencer	5	6	10	15	20	30	80	
63	Eddie Stanky	5	6	10	15	20	30	100	
64	Hank Thompson	5	6	10	15	20	30	80	
65	Bobby Thomson	5	6	10	15	20	1,000		
66	Vic Wertz	5	6	10	15	20	30	80	
67	Wally Westlake	5	6	10	15	20	30		
68	Wes Westrum	5	6	10	15	20	30		
69	Ted Williams	100	120	200	300	500	800	1,800	
70	Gene Woodling	5	6	10	15	20	30	150	
71	Gus Zernial	5	6	10	15	20	30	80	

—Joe DiMaggio PSA 9 (MT) sold for $6,974 (Goodwin; 11/07)
—Joe DiMaggio PSA 9 (MT) sold for $5,948 (Mastro; 12/06)
—Mickey Mantle PSA 9 (MT) sold for $9,999 (Mile High; 6/06)
—Willie Mays PSA 9 (MT) sold for $5,899 (Goodwin; 03/12)
—Willie Mays PSA 8.5 (NmMt+) sold for $3,271 (Memory Lane; 5/08)
—Jackie Robinson PSA 9 (MT) sold for $5,407 (Mastro; 12/06)

1952 Bowman

#	Player	GD 2	VG 3	VgEx 4	EX 5	ExMt 6	NM 7	NmMt 8	MT 9
1	Yogi Berra	100	▲150	200	500	600	800	4,000	18,000
2	Bobby Thomson	20	▼25	▼30	▼40	▼50	150	500	
3	Fred Hutchinson	5	5	8	10	25	50	120	400
4	Robin Roberts	12	20	30	60	80	150	300	1,200
5	Minnie Minoso RC	15	25	60	80	100	250	500	1,200
6	Virgil Stallcup	5	5	8	10	30	40	150	
7	Mike Garcia	5	8	12	20	30	50	200	
8	Pee Wee Reese	25	50	60	100	120	200	500	2,500
9	Vern Stephens	6	10	15	25	40	50	120	
10	Bob Hooper	5	5	8	10	15	30	80	
11	Ralph Kiner	10	25	30	40	60	120	300	1,000
12	Max Surkont RC	5	5	8	10	25	40	60	
13	Cliff Mapes	5	5	8	10	15	40	80	250
14	Cliff Chambers	5	5	8	12	20	40	100	400
15	Sam Mele	5	5	8	12	20	40	80	400
16	Turk Lown RC	5	5	8	10	15	25	100	
17	Ed Lopat	5	10	15	20	40	60	▼120	800
18	Don Mueller	5	5	8	10	15	25	120	
19	Bob Cain	5	8	12	20	30	40	80	
20	Willie Jones	5	5	8	10	15	50	80	250
21	Nellie Fox	15	25	30	▼50	80	120	400	2,500
22	Willard Ramsdell	5	5	8	10	25	60	80	400
23	Bob Lemon	5	10	25	30	50	80	250	1,000
24	Carl Furillo	8	20	25	30	50	▼80	200	1,000
25	Mickey McDermott	5	5	8	12	20	25	100	
26	Eddie Joost	5	5	8	12	20	40	100	800
27	Joe Garagiola	10	15	25	30	▼40	80	150	600
28	Roy Hartsfield	5	5	10	15	25	50	150	400
29	Ned Garver	5	5	8	12	20	40	120	
30	Red Schoendienst	12	20	30	50	▼60	100	300	1,000
31	Eddie Yost	5	6	10	15	25	50	120	
32	Eddie Miksis	5	5	8	12	20	30	60	400
33	Gil McDougald RC	12	20	30	50	60	▼80	250	1,000
34	Alvin Dark	5	8	12	20	30	50	150	500
35	Granny Hamner	5	6	10	15	25	30	120	
36	Cass Michaels	5	5	8	10	20	50	100	
37	Vic Raschi	5	8	12	15	25	▼50	200	
38	Whitey Lockman	5	5	8	10	15	▼30	120	
39	Vic Wertz	5	6	10	12	20	30	120	
40	Bubba Church	5	6	10	15	25	30	80	
41	Chico Carrasquel	5	6	10	12	20	30	80	500
42	Johnny Wyrostek	5	5	8	12	20	30	100	
43	Bob Feller	40	50	60	100	150	250	▼80	2,000
44	Roy Campanella	50	60	80	120	200	300	▼800	2,500
45	Johnny Pesky	10	15	25	40	50	80	250	
46	Carl Scheib	5	5	8	10	25	30	60	
47	Pete Castiglione	5	5	8	10	25	30	60	400
48	Vern Bickford	5	5	8	12	20	30	80	
49	Jim Hearn	5	5	8	10	15	25	60	
50	Gerry Staley	5	6	10	15	25	40	80	
51	Gil Coan	5	6	10	15	25	40	80	400
52	Phil Rizzuto	30	40	50	80	120	200	400	2,000
53	Richie Ashburn	12	20	▲50	▲60	▲100	150	▼300	1,500
54	Billy Pierce	5	6	10	12	20	50	100	
55	Ken Raffensberger	5	5	8	10	15	40	60	
56	Clyde King	5	5	8	10	30	40	100	400
57	Clyde Vollmer	5	5	8	15	20	40	80	
58	Hank Majeski	5	5	8	10	25	40	100	
59	Murry Dickson	5	5	8	10	15	40	60	250
60	Sid Gordon	5	5	8	10	25	40	60	
61	Tommy Byrne	5	5	8	12	20	25	100	300
62	Joe Presko RC	5	5	8	10	15	40	80	400
63	Irv Noren	5	5	8	10	15	50	80	400
64	Roy Smalley	5	5	8	10	40	80	120	400
65	Hank Bauer	5	10	20	▼30	▼40	100	250	800
66	Sal Maglie	5	5	10	15	25	50	120	400
67	Johnny Groth	5	5	8	10	20	25	80	300
68	Jim Busby	5	5	8	10	15	40	120	
69	Joe Adcock	5	5	8	10	15	40	▼80	400
70	Carl Erskine	5	10	15	20	40	80	▼150	
71	Vern Law	5	6	10	12	20	30	▼80	
72	Earl Torgeson	5	6	10	15	25	40	200	300
73	Jerry Coleman	6	10	15	25	40	50	250	600

#	Player	GD 2	VG 3	VgEx 4	EX 5	ExMt 6	NM 7	NmMt 8	MT
74	Wes Westrum	5	5	8	10	30	40	100	
75	George Kell	12	20	30	40	50	100	▼200	1,00
76	Del Ennis	5	6	10	15	25	▲50	150	40
77	Eddie Robinson	5	5	8	10	15	40	80	30
78	Lloyd Merriman	5	5	8	10	25	30	80	40
79	Lou Brissie	5	5	8	10	15	30	100	40
80	Gil Hodges	15	25	50	60	100	150	400	3,00
81	Billy Goodman	5	6	10	12	20	30	100	25
82	Gus Zernial	5	5	8	10	20	50	100	
83	Howie Pollet	5	5	8	10	20	30	60	
84	Sam Jethroe	6	10	15	25	30	50	120	
85	Marty Marion CO	5	6	10	12	25	50	120	
86	Cal Abrams	5	5	8	10	25	50	100	40
87	Mickey Vernon	5	6	10	15	25	30	100	40
88	Bruce Edwards	5	5	6	10	15	30	80	30
89	Billy Hitchcock	5	5	8	12	20	25	60	30
90	Larry Jansen	5	5	8	10	25	50	150	
91	Don Kolloway	5	5	8	10	15	40	100	30
92	Eddie Waitkus	5	5	8	10	▲25	60	100	40
93	Paul Richards MG	5	5	8	12	20	30	120	40
94	Luke Sewell MG	5	6	10	15	20	40	80	400
95	Luke Easter	5	8	12	20	40	50	150	50
96	Ralph Branca	5	8	12	▲25	▼30	80	150	80
97	Willard Marshall	5	5	8	10	15	50	▼60	
98	Jimmie Dykes MG	5	5	8	10	15	40	80	50
99	Clyde McCullough	5	5	8	10	15	25	80	50
100	Sibby Sisti	5	5	8	15	25	30	40	
101	Mickey Mantle	1,000	1,200	▲2,500	3,000	▲5,000	6,000	20,000	30,00
102	Peanuts Lowrey	5	5	8	10	15	50	60	40
103	Joe Haynes	5	5	8	10	15	25	120	40
104	Hal Jeffcoat	5	5	8	10	15	25	▲60	30
105	Bobby Brown	8	12	20	30	40	60	150	
106	Randy Gumpert	5	5	8	10	20	30	80	50
107	Del Rice	5	6	10	15	25	40	100	30
108	George Metkovich	5	5	8	10	15	30	100	
109	Tom Morgan RC	5	8	12	15	30	▼50	150	
110	Max Lanier	5	5	8	10	20	50	60	
111	Hoot Evers	5	5	8	10	15	50	100	
112	Smoky Burgess	5	8	12	20	25	80	150	50
113	Al Zarilla	5	5	8	12	20	30	120	40
114	Frank Hiller RC	5	5	8	10	20	40	120	50
115	Larry Doby	10	15	40	50	▼60	100	300	
116	Duke Snider	40	60	80	100	200	300	600	3,00
117	Bill Wight	5	5	8	10	15	25	60	
118	Ray Murray RC	5	5	8	12	20	30	120	30
119	Bill Howerton	5	5	8	10	25	30	50	25
120	Chet Nichols RC	5	5	8	10	15	60	80	30
121	Al Corwin RC	5	5	8	10	20	40	▼60	50
122	Billy Johnson	5	5	8	10	15	25	▼60	400
123	Sid Hudson	5	5	8	10	15	50	▼60	25
124	Birdie Tebbetts	5	8	12	20	25	50	120	25
125	Howie Fox	5	5	8	10	15	25	80	250
126	Phil Cavarretta	5	5	8	10	15	50	100	40
127	Dick Sisler	5	5	8	10	15	50	▲120	40
128	Don Newcombe	12	20	30	50	60	▲120	▼250	1,20
129	Gus Niarhos	5	5	8	10	15	25	100	
130	Allie Clark	5	5	8	10	15	25	80	
131	Bob Swift	5	5	8	10	15	40	80	
132	Dave Cole RC	5	6	10	15	25	50	80	
133	Dick Kryhoski	5	6	10	15	25	40	60	
134	Al Brazle	5	5	8	10	15	25	50	
135	Mickey Harris	5	5	8	10	15	40	150	
136	Gene Hermanski	5	5	8	10	15	25	100	
137	Stan Rojek	5	5	8	10	15	25	100	30
138	Ted Wilks	5	5	8	10	15	25	120	50
139	Jerry Priddy	5	5	8	10	15	25	80	250
140	Ray Scarborough	5	5	8	10	25	50	80	
141	Hank Edwards	5	6	10	15	25	40	60	
142	Early Wynn	10	15	25	30	50	80	250	1,000
143	Sandy Consuegra	5	5	8	10	15	40	100	40
144	Joe Hatton	5	6	10	15	25	40	80	40
145	Johnny Mize	15	25	30	50	60	150	300	90
146	Leo Durocher MG	8	12	40	40	50	80	300	80
147	Marlin Stuart RC	5	5	8	20	25	60	120	
148	Ken Heintzelman	5	5	8	10	30	40	100	
149	Howie Judson	5	5	8	10	25	30	80	40
150	Herman Wehmeier	5	5	8	10	20	50	80	35

	GD 2	VG 3	VgEx 4	EX 5	ExMt 6	NM 7	NmMt 8	MT 9
Al Rosen	5	8	12	15	40	50	150	900
Billy Cox	5	6	10	12	20	30	150	400
Fred Hatfield RC	5	5	8	10	30	50	80	
Ferris Fain	5	5	8	10	15	30	80	
Billy Meyer MG	5	5	8	12	20	50	80	300
Warren Spahn	30	50	60	100	120	▲300	▼500	1,500
Jim Delsing	5	5	8	10	15	40	80	400
Bucky Harris MG	5	8	12	20	30	60	200	600
Dutch Leonard	5	5	8	10	15	30	120	250
Eddie Stanky	5	6	10	15	20	40	120	400
Jackie Jensen	5	10	15	30	40	80	150	750
Monte Irvin	8	12	30	50	80	200	400	800
Johnny Lipon	5	5	8	10	15	25	60	
Connie Ryan	5	6	10	15	25	30	100	
Saul Rogovin RC	5	5	8	10	25	40	100	700
Bobby Adams	5	5	8	10	15	40	50	250
Bobby Avila	5	6	10	12	20	50	100	400
Preacher Roe	5	10	15	20	40	80	200	600
Walt Dropo	5	6	10	12	20	50	120	400
Joe Astroth	5	5	8	10	15	25	80	
Mel Queen	5	5	8	10	25	30	80	
Ebba St.Claire RC	5	5	8	10	25	30	150	300
Gene Bearden	5	5	8	10	40	50	100	300
Mickey Grasso	5	5	8	12	20	25	60	300
Randy Jackson RC	5	6	10	15	25	50	100	300
Harry Brecheen	5	5	8	10	30	50	100	400
Gene Woodling	5	8	12	20	30	60	150	500
Dave Williams RC	5	5	8	10	15	25	80	400
Pete Suder	5	5	8	10	15	30	60	250
Ed Fitzgerald	5	5	8	10	15	30	150	
Joe Collins RC	5	6	10	15	25	40	200	
Dave Koslo	5	5	8	12	20	25	▼60	
Pat Mullin	5	6	10	15	25	40	▼60	
Curt Simmons	5	5	8	10	15	▲30	80	800
Eddie Stewart	5	5	8	10	15	25	60	300
Frank Smith RC	5	5	8	10	15	40	100	
Jim Hegan	5	5	8	10	15	40	100	
Chuck Dressen MG	5	5	8	10	15	30	150	500
Jimmy Piersall	5	6	10	15	40	60	120	500
Dick Fowler	5	5	8	10	15	25	60	
Bob Friend RC	5	12	20	25	30	50	120	800
John Cusick RC	5	5	8	10	15	25	▼50	400
Bobby Young RC	5	5	8	10	20	50	▼50	300
Bob Porterfield	5	5	8	10	25	40	▼50	300
Frank Baumholtz	5	6	10	15	25	50	▼60	300
Stan Musial	150	150	▲300	▲400	500	800	1,500	4,000
Charlie Silvera RC	5	6	10	15	25	40	▼80	800
Chuck Diering	5	5	8	10	15	50	100	
Ted Gray	5	5	8	10	25	30	▼60	
Ken Silvestri	5	5	8	10	20	40	50	200
Ray Coleman	5	5	8	10	15	25	▼60	
Harry Perkowski RC	5	5	8	12	20	25	▼60	300
Steve Gromek	5	6	10	15	25	30	60	250
Andy Pafko	5	6	10	12	40	50	100	500
Walt Masterson	5	5	8	10	25	40	▼60	400
Elmer Valo	5	5	8	10	15	40	▼60	400
George Strickland RC	5	5	8	10	15	50	80	500
Walker Cooper	5	5	8	10	15	30	100	400
Dick Littlefield RC	5	5	8	10	15	40	50	
Archie Wilson RC	5	6	10	15	20	30	▼80	400
Paul Minner RC	5	5	8	10	15	25	▼60	
Solly Hemus RC	5	6	10	15	25	40	▼60	300
Monte Kennedy	5	5	8	10	15	25	60	300
Ray Boone	5	6	10	15	25	50	▼60	300
Sheldon Jones	5	5	8	12	20	30	▼100	
Matt Batts	5	5	8	10	15	25	100	300
Casey Stengel MG	15	30	40	100	120	200	▼250	600
Willie Mays	400	500	600	▲1,000	1,500	2,500	8,000	
Neil Berry	5	8	12	15	25	100	120	
Russ Meyer	5	8	12	15	25	80	▼150	
Lou Kretlow RC	5	8	12	15	25	50	▼60	
Dixie Howell	5	8	12	15	25	40	120	
Harry Simpson RC	5	8	12	15	25	50	▼80	
Johnny Schmitz	5	8	12	15	30	60	▼80	
Del Wilber RC	5	8	15	20	25	80	120	800
Alex Kellner	5	8	12	15	25	50	200	300
Clyde Sukeforth CO RC	5	8	12	25	40	50	100	800

		GD 2	VG 3	VgEx 4	EX 5	ExMt 6	NM 7	NmMt 8	MT 9
228	Bob Chipman	6	10	15	20	25	80	200	500
229	Hank Arft	5	8	12	15	25	50	▼60	
230	Frank Shea	5	8	12	15	25	40	▼150	
231	Dee Fondy RC	5	8	12	15	25	40	80	
232	Enos Slaughter	12	20	30	50	80	120	250	1,200
233	Bob Kuzava	8	12	20	30	50	100	120	800
234	Fred Fitzsimmons CO	5	8	12	15	50	80	80	600
235	Steve Souchock RC	6	10	15	20	25	60	150	600
236	Tommy Brown	5	8	12	15	25	80	150	400
237	Sherm Lollar	5	10	15	20	30	80	150	
238	Roy McMillan RC	5	10	15	20	30	80	150	800
239	Dale Mitchell	8	12	20	25	40	▼60	▼200	
240	Billy Loes RC	5	15	20	25	50	80	▼100	600
241	Mel Parnell	5	10	15	25	50	100	▼150	
242	Everett Kell RC	5	8	12	20	40	100	120	
243	George Munger	5	8	12	15	25	100	150	
244	Lew Burdette RC	10	15	25	50	60	120	500	1,000
245	George Schmees RC	5	8	12	15	25	80	250	
246	Jerry Snyder RC	5	8	12	15	30	50	200	
247	Johnny Pramesa	6	10	15	20	25	40	▼100	600
248	Bill Werle	5	8	12	15	25	40	100	
249	Hank Thompson	5	8	12	▼20	▼25	▼30	▼80	400
250	Ike Delock RC	5	8	12	15	25	50	100	500
251	Jack Lohrke	5	8	12	15	25	60	120	
252	Frank Crosetti CO	12	30	40	60	150	300	600	

—Listed pricing for Mint Commons & Minor Stars refers to cards carrying PSA populations of six or more copies.

—Mint Commons & Minor Stars with PSA populations of 3-5 copies typically command between $300-$600 per

—Mint Commons & Minor Stars with PSA populations of 2 copies typically command between $500-$800 per and 1 of 1's can sell upwards of $2,000 per.

—Yogi Berra #1 PSA 9 (MT) sold for $12,013 (Memory Lane; 8/05)

—Yogi Berra #1 GAI 9 (MT) sold for $3,910 (Mile High; 1/07)

—Yogi Berra #1 GAI 9 (MT) sold for $3,554 (Memory Lane; 9/07)

—Yogi Berra #1 SGC 92 (NmMt+) sold for $4,157 (Memory Lane; 5/08)

—Yogi Berra #1 SGC 92 (NmMt+) sold for $3,614 (Mastro; 4/06)

—Larry Doby #115 PSA 9 (MT) sold for $2,933 (Superior; 8/03)

—Mickey Mantle #101 GAI 10 (Perfect) sold for $42,288 (Mile High; 5/04)

—Mickey Mantle #101 GAI 10 (Perfect) sold for $20,125 (Memory Lane; 3/06)

—Mickey Mantle #101 PSA 10 (Gem) sold for $69,000 (Mastro; 5/08)

—Mickey Mantle #101 PSA 10 (Gem) sold for $43,125 (REA; 5/04)

—Mickey Mantle #101 SGC 92 (NmMt+) sold for $5,581 (REA; 5/08)

—Willie Mays #218 PSA 9 (MT) sold for $30,674 (Mastro; 4/07)

—Willie Mays #218 GAI 9 (MT) sold for $7,594 (Mastro; 1/05)

—Willie Mays #218 GAI 8.5 (NmMt+) sold for $4,930 (Memory Lane; 3/06)

—Willie Mays #218 GAI 8.5 (NmMt+) sold for $4,573 (Memory Lane; 5/08)

—Willie Mays #218 GAI 8 (NmMt) sold for $1,979 (Mastro; 8/06)

—Stan Musial #196 SGC 92 (NmMt+) sold for $871 (eBay; 1/08)

—Warren Spahn #156 SGC 98 (Gem) sold for $6,274 (Heritage; 10/05)

—Warren Spahn #156 SGC 98 (Gem) sold for $3,978 (Mastro; 4/04)

—Warren Spahn #156 GAI 9 (MT) sold for $976 (eBay; 2/08)

—Casey Stengel #217 PSA 9 (MT) sold for $5,118 (Mastro; 6/07)

—Casey Stengel #217 PSA 9 (MT) sold for $3,978 (Mastro; 12/03)

—Casey Stengel #217 PSA 9 (MT) sold for $2,448 (Mastro; 8/07)

—Casey Stengel #217 PSA 9 (MT) sold for $1,313 (eBay; 10/07)

—Casey Stengel #217 PSA 9 (MT) sold for $1,081 (eBay; 12/07)

—Willie Mays #218 SGC 96 (Mint) sold for $20,037 (Goodwin; 7/12)

1952 Red Man

		GD 2	VG 3	VgEx 4	EX 5	ExMt 6	NM 7	NmMt 8	MT 9
AL1	Casey Stengel MG	15	25	40	60	150			
AL2	Bobby Avila	8	12	20	30	50	100	300	
AL3	Yogi Berra	25	40	100	120	200	300	1,000	
AL4	Gil Coan	8	12	20	30	50	100		
AL5	Dom DiMaggio	10	15	25	40	60	120	400	
AL6	Larry Doby	10	15	25	40	60	120	400	
AL7	Ferris Fain	8	12	20	30	50	100		
AL8	Bob Feller	20	30	50	100	150	250		
AL9	Nellie Fox	10	15	25	40	60	120	400	
AL10	Johnny Groth	8	12	20	30	50	120	300	
AL11	Jim Hegan	8	12	20	30	50	100	300	
AL12	Eddie Joost	8	12	20	30	50	100	300	
AL13	George Kell	10	15	25	50	60	120	500	
AL14	Gil McDougald	10	15	25	40	60	120	400	
AL15	Minnie Minoso	8	12	20	30	50	100	300	
AL16	Billy Pierce	8	12	20	30	50	100	300	
AL17	Bob Porterfield	8	12	20	30	100	175	300	

	GD 2	VG 3	VgEx 4	EX 5	ExMt 6	NM 7	NmMt 8	MT 9
AL18 Eddie Robinson	8	12	20	30	50	100		
AL19 Saul Rogovin	8	12	20	30	50	100	300	
AL20 Bobby Shantz	8	12	20	30	50	120	600	
AL21 Vern Stephens	8	12	20	30	50	100	300	
AL22 Vic Wertz	8	12	20	30	50	100	300	
AL23 Ted Williams	125	200	300	600	1,000	2,500	8,000	
AL24 Early Wynn	10	15	25	40	100	120	400	
AL25 Eddie Yost	8	12	20	30	50	120	300	
AL26 Gus Zernial	8	12	20	30	50	120	325	
NL1 Leo Durocher MG	10	15	25	40	80	120		
NL2 Richie Ashburn	12	20	30	50	80	250	500	
NL3 Ewell Blackwell	8	12	20	30	50	100	300	
NL4 Cliff Chambers	8	12	20	30	50	100	300	
NL5 Murry Dickson	8	12	20	30	50	100	300	
NL6 Sid Gordon	8	12	20	30	50	100		
NL7 Granny Hamner	8	12	20	30	50	100	350	
NL8 Jim Hearn	8	12	20	30	50	100	300	
NL9 Monte Irvin	10	15	25	40	60	120	600	
NL10 Larry Jansen	8	12	20	30	50	100	300	
NL11 Willie Jones	8	12	20	30	50	120	300	
NL12 Ralph Kiner	10	15	25	40	60	150	400	
NL13 Whitey Lockman	8	12	20	30	50	100	300	
NL14 Sal Maglie	8	12	20	30	50	100	300	
NL15 Willie Mays	50	100	200	250	500	800	2,000	
NL16 Stan Musial	80	100	150	250	600	800	2,500	
NL17 Pee Wee Reese	20	30	50	100	150	350	800	
NL18 Robin Roberts	15	25	40	60	100	150	400	
NL19 Red Schoendienst	10	15	25	40	80	120	400	
NL20 Enos Slaughter	10	15	25	40	60	200	500	
NL21 Duke Snider	25	40	60	120	200	400	1,600	
NL22 Warren Spahn	12	20	30	50	80	250	800	
NL23 Eddie Stanky	8	12	20	30	50	100	300	
NL24 Bobby Thomson	8	12	20	30	50	100		
NL25 Earl Torgeson	8	12	20	30	50	150	300	
NL26 Wes Westrum	8	12	20	30	50	100	300	

—Prices reference cards with tabs

—Bob Feller # AL8 PSA 9 (MT) sold for $4,692 (Memory Lane; 12/06)

1952 Topps

	GD 2	VG 3	VgEx 4	EX 5	ExMt 6	NM 7	NmMt 8	MT 9
1 Andy Pafko	200	300	500	1,200	5,000			
1A Andy Pafko Black	200	300	▼500	800	2,000			
2 Pete Runnels RC	25	40	80	250	500			
2A Pete Runnels Black RC	25	40	60	120	500			
3 Hank Thompson	12	20	40	80	120	400	2,500	
3A Hank Thompson Black	12	20	30	50	80	700	3,000	
4 Don Lenhardt	12	20	50	60	▼150	250	800	
4A Don Lenhardt Black	8	12	20	40	120	250	600	
5 Larry Jansen	12	20	40	60	120	250	800	
5A Larry Jansen Black	12	20	40	60	100	250	800	
6 Grady Hatton	8	12	50	60	100	200	800	
6A Grady Hatton Black	8	12	20	40	80	200	1,500	
7 Wayne Terwilliger	8	15	40	▲60	120	400		
7A Wayne Terwilliger Black	8	12	20	40	120	350	1,000	
8 Fred Marsh RC	8	12	30	50	▼100	200	600	
8A Fred Marsh Black	8	12	20	40	80	200	500	
9 Bobby Hogue RC	15	25	50	80	200	500		
9A Bobby Hogue Black	15	25	40	80	150	400		
10 Al Rosen	25	30	80	100	300	600	2,000	
10A Al Rosen Black	20	30	50	80	200	500	4,000	
11 Phil Rizzuto	80	100	150	▲300	400	1,000		
11A Phil Rizzuto Black	40	80	120	250	500	600		
12 Monty Basgall RC	8	12	▲40	60	200	400		
12A Monty Basgall Black	8	12	20	50	100	250		
13 Johnny Wyrostek	12	20	30	50	▲100	200	600	
13A Johnny Wyrostek Black	8	12	20	40	50	200	300	
14 Bob Elliott	8	12	30	50	100	200	500	
14A Bob Elliott Black	8	12	20	40	60	200	500	
15 Johnny Pesky	25	▲50	▲60	100	120	250	1,000	
15A Johnny Pesky Black	12	20	40	80	120	300	1,000	
16 Gene Hermanski	12	20	30	50	100	200		
16A Gene Hermanski Black	10	15	25	40	100	200	800	
17 Jim Hegan	15	20	40	80	100	250		
17A Jim Hegan Black	8	12	20	40	100	300	1,200	
18 Merrill Combs RC	8	12	20	50	100	400		
18A Merrill Combs Black	8	12	20	40	80	200		

	GD 2	VG 3	VgEx 4	EX 5	ExMt 6	NM 7	NmMt 8	M
19 Johnny Bucha RC	15	25	40	80	150	400		
19A Johnny Bucha Black	10	15	25	40	120	400	1,500	
20 Billy Loes SP RC	15	25	60	120	300			
20A Billy Loes Black	15	25	60	150	250			
21 Ferris Fain	8	20	30	50	100	250		
21A Ferris Fain Black	8	12	20	50	120	150	500	
22 Dom DiMaggio	40	50	60	▼150	250	500		
22A Dom DiMaggio Black	15	30	40	80	200	600		
23 Billy Goodman	10	15	25	50	100	250	500	
23A Billy Goodman Black	8	12	20	40	80	150	500	
24 Luke Easter	10	15	40	60	100	250	600	
24A Luke Easter Black	10	15	25	40	80	150	600	
25 Johnny Groth	12	20	25	▲50	80	250	1,000	
25A Johnny Groth Black	8	12	20	40	50	200	1,000	
26 Monte Irvin	25	40	60	100	200	300		
26A Monte Irvin Black	15	25	40	60	100	400		
27 Sam Jethroe	10	15	30	50	100	120	500	
27A Sam Jethroe Black	8	12	20	40	80	250		
28 Jerry Priddy	12	20	30	50	▲100	200	500	
28A Jerry Priddy Black	8	12	20	40	80	100	400	
29 Ted Kluszewski	30	40	▲60	100	200	500	3,000	
29A Ted Kluszewski Black	15	25	40	60	150	500	2,000	
30 Mel Parnell	25	30	40	▲80	150	400	1,200	
30A Mel Parnell Black	10	15	25	60	100	400	2,000	
31 Gus Zernial	12	20	50	60	150	300		
31A Gus Zernial Black	10	15	25	60	100	250	800	
32 Eddie Robinson	20	25	40	80	150	400		
32A Eddie Robinson Black	8	12	20	150	100	400		
33 Warren Spahn	80	100	120	200	300	600	3,000	
33A Warren Spahn Black	25	40	120	150	200	600	1,200	
34 Elmer Valo	8	20	25	50	▲100	200	400	
34A Elmer Valo Black	8	12	20	40	80	200	400	
35 Hank Sauer	20	30	50	80	100	250		
35A Hank Sauer Black	10	15	25	60	100	300	800	
36 Gil Hodges	▲60	▼80	100	▲200	400	600	2,500	
36A Gil Hodges Black	25	40	120	150	250	500		
37 Duke Snider	80	100	200	250	▼400	▼600	2,500	
37A Duke Snider Black	50	80	120	200	300	600	2,000	
38 Wally Westlake	8	20	30	50	60	150	500	
38A Wally Westlake Black	8	12	20	40	60	150	500	
39 Dizzy Trout	12	20	30	▲60	100	250		
39A Dizzy Trout Black	8	12	20	40	50	300		
40 Irv Noren	8	12	▲30	60	120	300	800	
40A Irv Noren Black	8	12	20	40	50	400		
41 Bob Wellman RC	8	20	30	50	100	250		
41A Bob Wellman Black	8	12	20	50	100	500		
42 Lou Kretlow RC	10	15	30	80	120	400		
42A Lou Kretlow Black	10	15	25	40	120	400		
43 Ray Scarborough	15	25	30	60	100	250		
43A Ray Scarborough Black	8	12	20	40	150	250	1,000	
44 Con Dempsey RC	12	20	30	50	200	1,200		
44A Con Dempsey Black	8	12	20	50	60	200	1,000	
45 Eddie Joost	12	20	40	50	100	250		
45A Eddie Joost Black	8	12	20	50	100	120	1,200	
46 Gordon Goldsberry RC	12	20	30	50	100	250		
46A Gordon Goldsberry Black	8	12	20	40	100	400		
47 Willie Jones	8	12	40	50	100	150		
47A Willie Jones Black	8	12	20	40	120	200	1,000	
48A Joe Page Error Sain Bio Black	200	300	600	900	1,000	1,500	5,000	
48B Joe Page Correct Bio Black	12	20	30	100	150	400		
48C Joe Page Correct Bio Red	12	20	30	60	120	250		
49A John Sain Error Page Bio Black	250	300	500	1,000	1,500			
49B John Sain Correct Bio Black	15	25	40	60	200	500		
49C John Sain Correct Bio Red	15	25	40	60	150	800		
50 Marv Rickert RC	12	20	30	60	150	250		
50A Marv Rickert Black	8	12	20	40	100	150		
51 Jim Russell	10	15	25	50	120	250		
51A Jim Russell Black	8	12	20	40	150	200		
52 Don Mueller	10	15	30	50	120	150		
52A Don Mueller Black	8	12	20	40	60	500		
53 Chris Van Cuyk RC	12	20	30	▲60	▲80	250		
53A Chris Van Cuyk Black	8	12	20	40	80	200		
54 Leo Kiely RC	10	15	25	▲50	80	▲150	400	
54A Leo Kiely Black	8	12	20	40	60	120	400	
55 Ray Boone	12	20	40	50	100	200	600	
55A Ray Boone Black	8	12	20	40	80	200		
56 Tommy Glaviano	10	15	30	50	80	200		

#	Player	GD 2	VG 3	VgEx 4	EX 5	ExMt 6	NM 7	NmMt 8	MT 9
6A	Tommy Glaviano Black	8	12	20	40	50	120	600	
7	Ed Lopat	20	30	40	▲60	100	250	600	
7A	Ed Lopat Black	12	25	30	50	100	200	500	
8	Bob Mahoney RC	15	25	40	50	80	200	400	
8A	Bob Mahoney Black	8	12	20	40	50	120	400	
9	Robin Roberts	30	50	80	120	200	500	2,500	
9A	Robin Roberts Black	30	50	80	120	200	400	1,800	
	Sid Hudson	12	20	30	50	100	250	800	
0A	Sid Hudson Black	8	12	20	40	60	300		
1	Tookie Gilbert	8	12	25	50	80	200		
1A	Tookie Gilbert Black	8	12	20	40	80	300	800	
2	Chuck Stobbs RC	8	12	25	50	100	200		
2A	Chuck Stobbs Black	8	12	20	40	60	200	1,000	
3	Howie Pollet	8	12	25	▲50	▲120	150	800	
3A	Howie Pollet Black	8	12	20	40	80	200	500	
4	Roy Sievers	10	15	30	▲50	80	▲200	400	
4A	Roy Sievers Black	8	12	20	40	80	100	600	
5	Enos Slaughter	40	50	▲80	100	200	400	3,000	
5A	Enos Slaughter Black	20	30	50	80	200	300	1,500	
6	Preacher Roe	25	30	▲50	60	120	250	1,500	
6A	Preacher Roe Black	12	20	30	80	120	150	800	
7	Allie Reynolds	12	30	40	80	120	250	500	
7A	Allie Reynolds Black	12	20	30	50	120	200	800	
8	Cliff Chambers	12	20	30	40	80	200	400	
8A	Cliff Chambers Black	8	12	20	40	60	120	400	
9	Virgil Stallcup	8	12	25	50	100	▲250	500	
9A	Virgil Stallcup Black	8	12	20	40	50	200	800	
0	Al Zarilla	8	12	30	50	100	250		
0A	Al Zarilla Black	8	12	20	40	50	800		
1	Tom Upton RC	8	12	30	60	100	300	1,000	
1A	Tom Upton Black	8	12	20	40	60	300	2,500	
2	Karl Olson RC	8	12	25	▼60	200	500		
2A	Karl Olson Black	8	12	20	80	120	1,500		
3	Bill Werle	8	12	20	60	100	300		
3A	Bill Werle Black	8	12	20	40	50	400	2,000	
4	Andy Hansen RC	10	15	30	50	100	250	500	
4A	Andy Hansen Black	8	12	20	40	60	200		
5	Wes Westrum	15	20	30	50	150	250		
5A	Wes Westrum Black	8	12	20	40	120	300		
6	Eddie Stanky	10	15	40	50	120	200	1,000	
6A	Eddie Stanky Black	10	15	25	40	150	200		
7	Bob Kennedy	12	20	40	50	100	250		
7A	Bob Kennedy Black	8	12	20	40	100	200		
8	Ellis Kinder	20	25	40	50	100	▼250	800	
8A	Ellis Kinder Black	8	12	20	40	50	250		
9	Gerald Staley	8	20	25	50	120	600		
9A	Gerald Staley Black	8	12	20	40	80	800		
0	Herman Wehmeier	12	20	50	60	300	1,000		
0A	Herman Wehmeier Black	10	15	30	60				
1	Vern Law	8	12	30	40	80	150	800	
2	Duane Pillette	10	15	25	30	50	100	250	
3	Billy Johnson	6	10	25	30	60	80	250	
4	Vern Stephens	6	10	25	30	50	100	300	1,000
5	Bob Kuzava	6	10	25	40	50	100	250	
6	Ted Gray	10	15	25	30	50	100	200	
7	Dale Coogan	8	12	25	30	50	80	200	
8	Bob Feller	60	100	120	200	300	500	1,200	3,000
9	Johnny Lipon	6	12	25	30	50	100	300	
0	Mickey Grasso	6	10	25	30	40	100	400	
1	Red Schoendienst	30	40	60	80	▼150	400	800	
2	Dale Mitchell	10	15	25	30	60	150	500	
3	Al Sima RC	6	15	20	30	40	80	250	
4	Sam Mele	8	12	25	30	60	80	250	1,000
5	Ken Holcombe	6	10	25	30	▲60	80	150	1,000
6	Willard Marshall	10	15	25	40	50	80	250	
7	Earl Torgeson	8	12	25	40	50	80	250	
8	Bill Pierce	10	15	25	40	50	100	400	
9	Gene Woodling	10	15	▲40	▲50	100	150	400	
00	Del Rice	8	12	20	30	60	100	250	
01	Max Lanier	6	20	25	30	50	80	200	
02	Bill Kennedy	6	10	25	30	50	100	300	
03	Cliff Mapes	12	15	20	25	50	80	250	
04	Don Kolloway	10	15	25	30	▲50	80	250	
05	Johnny Pramesa	6	10	25	▲40	50	100	200	1,000
06	Mickey Vernon	6	10	25	40	50	100	400	1,000
07	Connie Ryan	6	10	15	30	50	80	250	
08	Jim Konstanty	10	15	25	40	▲60	100	300	

#	Player	GD 2	VG 3	VgEx 4	EX 5	ExMt 6	NM 7	NmMt 8	MT 9
109	Ted Wilks	10	15	25	30	▲60	80	250	
110	Dutch Leonard	8	12	25	40	50	100	400	1,200
111	Peanuts Lowrey	12	15	20	40	50	100	250	
112	Hank Majeski	6	10	25	40	50	80	250	
113	Dick Sisler	6	10	25	40	50	100	250	1,000
114	Willard Ramsdell	6	10	15	30	50	80	250	
115	George Munger	8	12	25	30	40	80	200	1,000
116	Carl Scheib	8	12	25	30	50	80	300	
117	Sherm Lollar	8	12	25	30	50	100	250	
118	Ken Raffensberger	8	12	25	30	50	80	250	
119	Mickey McDermott	6	10	25	30	50	80	250	
120	Bob Chakales RC	6	10	25	40	50	100	250	
121	Gus Niarhos	10	15	25	▲40	▲50	80	250	
122	Jack Jensen	12	25	40	60	100	200	400	
123	Eddie Yost	8	12	20	30	50	100	▼250	1,000
124	Monte Kennedy	6	10	20	30	50	100	250	1,000
125	Bill Rigney	6	10	15	30	50	80	250	
126	Fred Hutchinson	10	15	25	40	50	80	250	1,000
127	Paul Minner RC	6	10	15	30	50	100	250	
128	Don Bollweg RC	15	25	30	50	80	120	500	
129	Johnny Mize	30	50	80	150	300	600		
130	Sheldon Jones	8	12	25	40	60	80	250	
131	Morrie Martin RC	8	12	25	30	50	80	250	
132	Clyde Kluttz RC	10	15	25	40	50	100	250	
133	Al Widmar	10	15	25	40	50	80	250	
134	Joe Tipton	10	15	25	30	50	80	250	
135	Dixie Howell	6	10	30	40	50	100	400	
136	Johnny Schmitz	10	15	25	50	▼60	120		
137	Roy McMillan RC	10	15	30	40	60	100	300	
138	Bill MacDonald	10	15	25	30	50	80	250	
139	Ken Wood	6	10	15	25	50	80	250	
140	Johnny Antonelli	8	20	25	40	50	100	800	
141	Clint Hartung	6	10	25	30	50	100	250	
142	Harry Perkowski RC	12	20	25	40	60	120	600	
143	Les Moss	6	10	25	40	50	100	250	
144	Ed Blake RC	8	12	20	30	50	80	250	
145	Joe Haynes	6	10	15	30	50	100	300	
146	Frank House RC	6	10	15	50	60	100	250	
147	Bob Young RC	10	15	25	40	50	120	250	
148	Johnny Klippstein	8	12	20	▲40	50	80	250	
149	Dick Kryhoski	8	12	20	40	50	60	250	
150	Ted Beard	6	10	15	50	60	▲100	250	
151	Wally Post RC	6	10	15	50	80	150		
152	Al Evans	6	10	25	▲50	▲60	120	500	
153	Bob Rush	8	12	25	30	50	100	300	
154	Joe Muir RC	8	12	25	30	60	▼80	300	
155	Frank Overmire	6	10	25	40	50	100	400	
156	Frank Hiller RC	6	10	25	30	40	100	300	
157	Bob Usher	6	10	15	50	60	80	250	
158	Eddie Waitkus	6	10	25	40	60	100	300	
159	Saul Rogovin RC	10	15	25	50	60	100	250	
160	Owen Friend	6	10	30	40	60	100	300	
161	Bud Byerly RC	6	10	15	30	80	▲300		
162	Del Crandall	10	15	30	50	80	250		
163	Stan Rojek	6	10	20	30	50	150	500	
164	Walt Dubiel	10	15	30	40	50	100	400	
165	Eddie Kazak	6	10	15	40	60	200		
166	Paul LaPalme RC	6	10	25	30	40	100	250	
167	Bill Howerton	6	10	15	30	60	80	250	
168	Charlie Silvera RC	12	25	30	50	80	100	300	
169	Howie Judson	6	10	15	50	60	150		
170	Gus Bell	10	15	30	50	80	120	1,200	
171	Ed Erautt RC	6	10	15	50	80	200		
172	Eddie Miksis	6	10	25	50	60	250		
173	Roy Smalley	6	10	25	50	60	250		
174	Clarence Marshall RC	6	10	15	40	60	120	1,000	
175	Billy Martin RC	120	150	200	300	▲500	800	5,000	
176	Hank Edwards	6	10	15	50	60	80	400	
177	Bill Wight	6	10	15	25	60	150	300	
178	Cass Michaels	6	10	15	50	60	100	400	
179	Frank Smith RC	6	10	15	25	50	120	400	
180	Charlie Maxwell RC	12	20	60	80	400	500		
181	Bob Swift	10	15	25	50	100	250		
182	Billy Hitchcock	6	12	20	30	50	60	250	
183	Erv Dusak	6	10	25	30	50	100	300	
184	Bob Ramazzotti	8	12	20	40	50	100	250	1,200
185	Bill Nicholson	12	25	30	40	100	150	400	

#	Name	GD 2	VG 3	VgEx 4	EX 5	ExMt 6	NM 7	NmMt 8	MT 9
186	Walt Masterson	8	12	25	30	60	100	400	
187	Bob Miller	6	10	15	40	60	100	400	
188	Clarence Podbielan RC	8	12	25	50	60	▲120	300	1,000
189	Pete Reiser	15	25	40	50	100	200		
190	Don Johnson RC	6	10	15	30	60	100	500	
191	Yogi Berra	150	▲250	▲300	500	800	2,000	10,000	
192	Myron Ginsberg RC	12	20	30	50	60	150		
193	Harry Simpson RC	8	12	30	40	80	150	600	
194	Joe Hatton	6	10	25	40	50	100	300	
195	Orestes Minoso RC	40	60	80	120	250	400	1,000	3,000
196	Solly Hemus RC	6	10	25	40	50	100	250	1,000
197	George Strickland RC	6	10	15	30	50	100	250	
198	Phil Haugstad RC	6	10	25	40	50	80	250	
199	George Zuverink RC	6	10	15	50	60	100	300	
200	Ralph Houk RC	12	20	50	60	80	250	400	
201	Alex Kellner	6	10	25	40	60	60	250	
202	Joe Collins RC	12	20	30	50	80	120	600	
203	Curt Simmons	8	12	25	40	▲60	80	250	
204	Ron Northey	8	12	25	40	50	80	250	
205	Clyde King	8	12	25	40	50	100	300	1,000
206	Joe Ostrowski RC	6	10	15	40	60	100	250	1,500
207	Mickey Harris	6	10	15	25	50	100	250	1,000
208	Marlin Stuart RC	8	12	25	30	50	100	250	
209	Howie Fox	8	12	25	40	60	80	250	
210	Dick Fowler	6	10	15	30	50	80	250	1,000
211	Ray Coleman	8	12	25	30	60	80		
212	Ned Garver	6	10	20	40	80	100		
213	Nippy Jones	6	20	25	40	50	80	250	
214	Johnny Hopp	8	12	30	40	50	120	250	1,200
215	Hank Bauer	12	20	30	60	▲100	150	400	
216	Richie Ashburn	40	50	100	120	200	300	600	3,000
217	Snuffy Stirnweiss	10	15	25	40	50	80	250	1,000
218	Clyde McCullough	8	12	20	30	50	60	200	
219	Bobby Shantz	8	12	25	40	60	120	300	
220	Joe Presko RC	6	10	15	▲40	50	80	▼200	
221	Granny Hamner	6	10	15	40	60	100	400	
222	Hoot Evers	10	15	25	40	60	80	250	1,000
223	Del Ennis	8	12	20	25	60	100	250	
224	Bruce Edwards	6	10	25	30	50	80	250	
225	Frank Baumholtz	10	15	25	40	50	80	250	1,000
226	Dave Philley	8	12	20	40	50	80	250	
227	Joe Garagiola	12	20	40	60	80	200	400	1,500
228	Al Brazle	6	10	15	25	50	80	250	1,200
229	Gene Bearden	6	10	15	30	50	100	250	
230	Matt Batts	15	20	25	40	60	80	250	
231	Sam Zoldak	6	10	15	30	50	100	300	
232	Billy Cox	12	20	▲40	50	80	150	400	
233	Bob Friend RC	10	15	25	50	60	▼120	400	
234	Steve Souchock RC	10	15	25	30	80	100	200	
235	Walt Dropo	6	10	15	30	▲60	100	250	
236	Ed Fitzgerald	10	15	25	40	50	100	250	1,000
237	Jerry Coleman	10	15	25	50	80	150	400	
238	Art Houtteman	8	12	20	30	50	100	200	
239	Rocky Bridges RC	12	20	30	40	60	120	250	
240	Jack Phillips RC	8	12	20	30	50	100	250	1,000
241	Tommy Byrne	12	20	30	40	60	150	800	
242	Tom Poholsky RC	10	15	25	30	60	100	300	
243	Larry Doby	40	50	60	100	120	300	1,200	
244	Vic Wertz	8	12	25	30	50	100	300	
245	Sherry Robertson	6	10	15	40	50	120	250	
246	George Kell	12	20	50	80	100	250	600	
247	Randy Gumpert	6	10	20	40	50	100	250	
248	Frank Shea	6	10	25	40	60	150	400	
249	Bobby Adams	6	10	30	40	50	80	300	
250	Carl Erskine	15	25	▼40	▼60	▲120	250	800	
251	Chico Carrasquel	12	20	30	60	150	250		
252	Vern Bickford	15	25	30	50	60	120	300	
253	Johnny Berardino	12	20	30	50	▲80	120	300	
254	Joe Dobson	8	12	30	40	60	120	▼250	
255	Clyde Vollmer	12	20	40	50	60	100	300	
256	Pete Suder	8	12	25	50	60	100	250	1,000
257	Bobby Avila	15	25	40	50	80	100	250	1,000
258	Steve Gromek	12	20	40	50	60	120	300	1,000
259	Bob Addis RC	10	15	30	40	50	100	▼250	
260	Pete Castiglione	8	12	25	40	50	150	500	
261	Willie Mays	1,200	▲2,000	2,500	4,000	6,000	12,000	40,000	
262	Virgil Trucks	10	15	40	60	80	120	500	
263	Harry Brecheen	8	12	30	40	80	120	300	1,000
264	Roy Hartsfield	▲8	12	20	40	50	100	250	1,000
265	Chuck Diering	8	12	30	40	50	100	300	
266	Murry Dickson	8	12	25	40	50	150	300	1,000
267	Sid Gordon	8	12	30	40	60	120	300	
268	Bob Lemon	25	50	▲80	100	150	300	600	3,500
269	Willard Nixon	8	25	30	40	50	120	300	
270	Lou Brissie	15	25	40	60	80	120	400	
271	Jim Delsing	8	12	30	40	▲80	120	400	1,000
272	Mike Garcia	10	25	30	60	80	150	500	
273	Erv Palica	10	15	25	▲50	60	250	300	
274	Ralph Branca	30	50	80	100	120	250	800	
275	Pat Mullin	8	12	20	50	80	150	400	
276	Jim Wilson RC	10	15	25	40	60	100	▼250	
277	Early Wynn	50	60	▲120	▲150	250	300	500	2,500
278	Allie Clark	12	20	30	40	▲80	120	250	
279	Eddie Stewart	8	12	30	40	60	100	250	1,500
280	Cloyd Boyer	12	20	40	100	150	250	500	
281	Tommy Brown SP	15	25	40	60	100	150	300	
282	Birdie Tebbetts SP	10	15	50	60	100	120	300	2,000
283	Phil Masi SP	8	12	30	50	60	100	250	1,200
284	Hank Arft SP	8	25	30	50	60	100	250	1,000
285	Cliff Fannin SP	8	12	40	50	▲100	▲120	250	
286	Joe DeMaestri SP RC	8	12	30	50	60	80	250	1,000
287	Steve Bilko SP	8	12	50	60	80	150	400	1,000
288	Chet Nichols SP RC	10	15	25	▼50	80	120	250	
289	Tommy Holmes MG	20	30	50	80	150	250	400	1,500
290	Joe Astroth SP	8	12	30	50	80	100	300	
291	Gil Coan SP	12	20	40	50	80	120	300	1,000
292	Floyd Baker SP	8	12	40	50	60	120	300	1,200
293	Sibby Sisti SP	8	12	30	50	60	100	250	
294	Walker Cooper SP	8	12	30	50	80	120	250	800
295	Phil Cavarretta	10	15	50	80	100	150	▼300	1,200
296	Red Rolfe MG	10	15	▼60	▼80	▼100	250	500	1,200
297	Andy Seminick SP	10	15	25	50	100	120	200	1,000
298	Bob Ross SP RC	8	12	20	40	100	150	300	1,000
299	Ray Murray SP RC	10	15	25	50	60	100	250	1,200
300	Barney McCosky SP	12	20	40	60	100	150	300	1,200
301	Bob Porterfield	12	20	40	60	80	120	400	
302	Max Surkont RC	8	12	20	▼40	▼60	100	250	1,000
303	Harry Dorish	8	12	20	40	60	100	300	1,000
304	Sam Dente	10	15	25	50	80	120	300	
305	Paul Richards MG	10	15	40	60	80	100	300	
306	Lou Sleater RC	10	15	30	50	60	120	300	1,000
307	Frank Campos RC	15	▲40	▲50	100	120	200	300	
308	Luis Aloma	10	15	30	60	80	120	250	
309	Jim Busby	10	15	25	50	100	120	300	1,200
310	George Metkovich	15	25	40	80	150	250	600	
311	Mickey Mantle DP	20,000	25,000	▲50,000	60,000	120,000	250,000	500,000	
312	Jackie Robinson DP	1,200	2,000	2,500	4,000	5,000	10,000	30,000	
313	Bobby Thomson DP	120	150	200	250	400	800	1,200	3,000
314	Roy Campanella	800	1,000	1,200	2,000	2,500	3,000	6,000	
315	Leo Durocher MG	150	200	250	400	800	1,000	2,500	
316	Davey Williams RC	120	150	200	300	400	600		
317	Connie Marrero	100	150	200	300	400	800		
318	Harold Gregg RC	100	150	250	300	400	500	800	
319	Al Walker RC	120	150	250	300	400	600		
320	John Rutherford RC	150	200	250	400	800	3,000		
321	Joe Black RC	200	250	300	400	500	800	1,500	
322	Randy Jackson RC	120	150	200	300	400	600	1,000	2,500
323	Bubba Church	100	150	200	250	400	500	1,000	
324	Warren Hacker	100	150	200	250	300	500	1,000	2,500
325	Bill Serena	100	150	200	250	300	500	1,000	
326	George Shuba RC	120	200	250	300	400	1,000		
327	Al Wilson RC	100	150	200	▼250	▼300	800	1,000	
328	Bob Borkowski RC	100	▼120	▼150	▼200	▼300	▼400	▼600	
329	Ike Delock RC	120	150	200	250	300	500	800	
330	Turk Lown RC	120	200	250	300	400	500	800	
331	Tom Morgan RC	150	200	250	300	400	600	2,000	
332	Tony Bartirome RC	1,000	1,200	1,500	2,000	2,500	6,000	8,000	
333	Pee Wee Reese	500	600	800	1,200	1,500	2,000	5,000	
334	Wilmer Mizell RC	100	150	250	300	400	600	1,000	2,500
335	Ted Lepcio RC	100	▼150	▼200	300	400	600	1,000	
336	Dave Koslo	120	150	200	250	300	600	1,200	
337	Jim Hearn	100	150	200	250	300	500	1,000	
338	Sal Yvars RC	▲120	▲200	250	300	400	500	800	
339	Russ Meyer	50	80	150	300	400	500	800	2,500

	GD 2	VG 3	VgEx 4	EX 5	ExMt 6	NM 7	NmMt 8	MT 9
Bob Hooper	100	120	250	300	400	500	1,000	
Hal Jeffcoat	120	150	200	250	300	500		
Clem Labine RC	150	200	300	400	500	600	1,000	3,000
Dick Gernert RC	120	150	200	250	400	500	800	
Ewell Blackwell	120	200	250	300	500	600	1,500	3,000
Sammy White RC	120	150	200	250	400	500	800	2,500
George Spencer RC	100	150	200	250	300	600	1,000	
Joe Adcock	120	▲200	▲250	300	400	800	1,800	3,000
Robert Kelly RC	100	▼150	▼200	▼250	400	500	1,000	
Bob Cain	100	150	250	300	400	500		
Cal Abrams	100	▲200	▲250	300	400	600	1,000	
Alvin Dark	120	200	250	300	500	600	1,000	5,500
Karl Drews	100	200	250	300	400	500	1,000	3,000
Bob Del Greco RC	100	150	200	250	400	600	800	3,500
Fred Hatfield RC	80	120	200	300	400	600	1,000	
Bobby Morgan	100	200	250	300	400	600		
Toby Atwell RC	120	150	250	300	400	500	1,000	
Smoky Burgess	120	200	300	400	500	800	2,000	
John Kucab RC	100	120	▼150	▼200	300	500	800	
Dee Fondy RC	100	150	200	250	▼400	600	800	
George Crowe RC	150	200	250	300	400	600	1,500	
Bill Posedel CO	80	100	200	250	300	500	800	
Ken Heintzelman	120	150	200	300	400	500	1,000	
Dick Rozek RC	80	100	200	250	400	600	1,000	1,200
Clyde Sukeforth CO RC	100	150	200	250	300	500	800	
Cookie Lavagetto CO	150	250	300	400	500	▲800	1,200	3,000
Dave Madison RC	120	150	200	250	300	400	800	
Ben Thorpe RC	80	120	200	250	300	400	1,000	
Ed Wright RC	80	120	200	250	400	500	1,500	
Dick Groat RC	200	300	400	500	600	800	1,500	5,000
Billy Hoeft RC	150	200	250	500	600	800	1,000	
Bobby Hofman	120	150	200	250	300	400	800	
Gil McDougald RC	150	▼250	400	600	800	1,200	2,500	5,000
Jim Turner CO RC	150	300	400	600	800	1,000		
Al Benton RC	100	200	250	300	400	500	1,000	2,500
John Merson RC	80	150	200	250	400	500	800	2,500
Faye Throneberry RC	100	120	200	300	400	600	1,200	
Chuck Dressen MG	120	150	200	250	400	600		
Leroy Fusselman RC	150	200	250	400	500	800	1,200	
Joe Rossi RC	100	150	200	250	300	600		
Clem Koshorek RC	120	150	200	250	300	500	1,000	
Milton Stock CO RC	100	120	150	300	400	500	800	
Sam Jones RC	120	200	250	300	400	600	1,200	
Del Wilber RC	100	150	250	300	400	600	1,500	2,500
Frank Crosetti CO	200	▼250	▼300	▼400	▼500	800	2,000	5,000
Herman Franks CO RC	100	150	200	300	400	500	1,000	
Ed Yuhas RC	120	150	200	300	400	600	800	
Billy Meyer MG	100	150	200	250	400	600	800	2,500
Bob Chipman	120	200	250	300	400	800		
Ben Wade RC	120	150	250	300	400	500	1,500	
Glenn Nelson RC	120	150	200	250	300	600	1,000	
Ben Chapman CO UER	120	200	250	300	400	600	1,000	
Hoyt Wilhelm RC	500	600	1,000	1,200	1,500	2,500	4,000	8,000
Ebba St.Claire RC	80	200	250	300	400	500	1,200	
Billy Herman CO	120	200	400	500	600	800		
Jake Pitler CO	100	250	300	400	500	600		
Dick Williams RC	200	250	300	500	600	1,000		
Forrest Main RC	80	150	200	250	300	▼400	2,000	
Hal Rice	120	▲200	▲250	400	500	800		
Jim Fridley RC	120	150	250	300	500	800		
Bill Dickey CO	500	600	800	1,000	1,200	1,500	4,000	
Bob Schultz RC	80	200	250	300	400	400	800	3,600
Earl Harrist RC	100	120	200	300	400	500	800	
Bill Miller RC	200	250	300	400	500	600		
Dick Brodowski RC	50	80	250	400	500	600	1,000	
Eddie Pellagrini	100	150	200	400	500	600	1,000	
Joe Nuxhall RC	250	400	500	600	1,000	1,500	2,500	
Eddie Mathews RC	2,500	4,000	5,000	6,000	8,000	20,000	60,000	

—Monty Basgall #12 (Red) PSA 8 (NmMt) sold for $1,437 (Goodwin; 6/06)
—Yogi Berra #191 GAI 9 (MT) sold for $10,186 (Memory Lane; 11/05)
—Yogi Berra #191 PSA 8.5 (NmMt+) sold for $17,775 (REA; 5/13)
—Yogi Berra #191 PSA 8.5 (NmMt+) sold for $14,220 (REA; Spring '14)
—Johnny Bucha #19 (Red) PSA 8 (NmMt) sold for $2,622 (eBay; 3/08)
—Bud Byerly #161 PSA 8 (NmMt) sold for $4,627 (Goodwin; 9/07)
—Bud Byerly #161 PSA 8 (NmMt) sold for $2,855 (Goodwin; 11/04)
—Bob Cain #349 PSA 8 (NmMt) sold for $1,737 (Memory Lane; 4/07)
—Bob Cain #349 PSA 8 (NmMt) sold for $1,446 (Mastro; 3/06)

—Roy Campanella #314 PSA 9 (MT) sold for $9,882 (Mastro; 8/04)
—Frank Campos #307 (Black Star) PSA 8 (NmMt) sold for $34,717 (Goodwin; 5/07)
—Frank Campos #307 (Black Star) PSA 8 (NmMt) sold for $25,726 (SCP; 11/10)
—Frank Campos #307 (Black Star) PSA 8 (NmMt) sold for $21,256 (Mastro; 12/07)
—Frank Campos Black Star #307A PSA 8 (NmMt) sold for $10,207 (Goodwin; 8/12)
—Frank Campos #307 (Black Star) SGC 86 (NrMt+) sold for $19,975 (REA; 4/07)
—Frank Campos #307 (Black Star) PSA 6 (ExMt) sold for $8,935 (Goodwin; 11/07)
—Frank Campos #307 (Black Star) SGC 50 (VG) sold for $4,038 (eBay; 5/06)
—Chico Carrasquel #251 SGC 92 (NmMt+) sold for $1,297 (Goodwin; 12/05)
—Chico Carrasquel #251 PSA 8 (NmMt) sold for $2,015 (Goodwin; 10/04)
—Bob Chipman #388 PSA 8 (NmMt) sold for $7,531 (Goodwin; 10/06)
—Bob Chipman #388 PSA 8 (NmMt) sold for $4,265 (Mastro; 10/05)
—Ray Coleman #211 PSA 8 (NmMt) sold for $1,647 (Madec; 5/07)
— George Crowe #360 PSA 8.5 (NmMt+) sold for $5,207 (Mile High; 10/11)
—Con Dempsey #44 PSA 9 (MT) sold for $9,265 (Goodwin; 03/12)
—Con Dempsey #44 PSA 9 (Mint) sold for $9,265 (Goodwin; 3/12)
—Bill Dickey #400 PSA 9 (MT) sold for $7,846 (Mile High; 12/05)
—Dom DiMaggio #22 (Red) PSA 8 (NmMt) sold for $5,536 (Madec; 11/07)
—Dom DiMaggio #22 (Black) PSA 8 (NmMt) sold for $3,764 (Mastro; 3/06)
—Larry Doby #243 PSA 8 (NmMt) sold for $18,854 (Mastro; 12/07)
—Larry Doby #243 PSA 9 (MT) sold for $11,693 (Mastro; 12/03)
—Larry Doby #243 SGC 96 (MT) sold for $3,287 (Mastro; 1/05)
— Chuck Dressen MG #377 PSA 9 (MT) sold for $15,439 (Goodwin; 12/11)
—Ed Erautt #171 PSA 8 (NmMt) sold for $1,647 (Memory Lane; 8/06)
—Bob Feller #88 PSA 9 (MT) sold for $2,643 (REA; 4/07)
— Jim Fridley #399 PSA 8 (NmMt) sold for $1,796 (Mile High; 8/07)
—Myron Ginsberg #192 PSA 8 (NmMt) sold for $1,628 (eBay; 1/08)
—Gene Hermanski #16 (Red) PSA 8 (NmMt) sold for $6,434 (Goodwin; 6/06)
—Gene Hermanski #16 (Red) PSA 8 (NmMt) sold for $3,531 (Madec; 5/07)
—Gil Hodges #36 (Red) PSA 9 (MT) sold for $5,969 (Mile High; 10/12)
—Gil Hodges #36 (Black) PSA 8 (NmMt) sold for $5,141 (Goodwin; 8/08)
—Robert Hogue #9 PSA 8 (NmMt) sold for $11,919 (Goodwin; 8/08)
—Howie Judson #169 PSA 8 (NmMt) sold for $624 (eBay; 9/06)
—Eddie Kazak #165 PSA 8 (NmMt) sold for $1,365 (Mastro; 12/05)
—Eddie Kazak #165 PSA 8 (NmMt) sold for $770 (eBay; 5/07)
—Eddie Kazak #165 PSA 8 (NmMt) sold for $579 (eBay; 11/07)
—Bob Kennedy #77 (Black) PSA 8 (NmMt) sold for $1,437 (eBay; 8/07)
—Ted Kluszewski #29 (Red) PSA 9 (MT) sold for $13,753 (Memory Lane; 11/04)
—Lou Kretlow #42 PSA 8 (NmMt) sold for $19,200 (Goodwin; 08/08)
—Ted Lepcio #335 PSA 9 (MT) sold for $11,712 (Mile High; 6/06)
—Billy Loes #20 (Red) PSA 8 (NmMt) sold for $4,141 (Mastro; 3/06)
—Billy Loes #20 (Red) PSA 8 (NmMt) sold for $2,552 (eBay; 12/07)
—Billy Loes #20 (Red) PSA 8 (NmMt) sold for $2,505 (Mile High; 11/04)
—Billy Loes #20 (Red) PSA 7 (NM) sold for $2,826 (Goodwin; 5/08)
—Billy Loes #20 (Red) PSA 7 (NM) sold for $2,766 (Madec; 5/08)
—Mickey Mantle #311 PSA 9 (MT) sold for $282,588 (Memory Lane; 12/06)
—Mickey Mantle #311 PSA 9 (MT) sold for $225,000 (Memory Lane; Private 2006)
—Mickey Mantle #311 PSA 8.5 (NmMt+) sold for $272,550 (REA; 5/13)
—Mickey Mantle #311 PSA 8 (NmMt) sold for $486,100 (eBay; 11/15)
—Mickey Mantle #311 PSA 8 (NmMt) sold for $268,644 (SCP; 12/14)
—Mickey Mantle #311 PSA 8 (NmMt) sold for $112,800 (Memory Lane; 5/08)
—Mickey Mantle #311 PSA 8 (NmMt) sold for $98,177 (Goodwin; 8/08)
—Mickey Mantle #311 BGS 8 (NmMt) sold for $81,348 (Goodwin; 9/13)
—Mickey Mantle #311 PSA 8 (NmMt) sold for $75,198 (Mile High; 5/12)
—Mickey Mantle #311 PSA 8 (NmMt) sold for $66,687 (Mastro; 12/06)
—Mickey Mantle #311 PSA 8 (NmMt) sold for $65,493 (Mastro; 8/06)
—Mickey Mantle #311 PSA 8 (NmMt) sold for $65,000 (Mastro; 12/08)
—Mickey Mantle #311 PSA 8 (NmMt) sold for $60,000 (Legendary; 8/10)
—Mickey Mantle #311 PSA 8 (NmMt) sold for $51,000 (SCP; 6/05;)
—Mickey Mantle #311 PSA 8 (NmMt) sold for $49,424 (Mastro; 4/07)
—Mickey Mantle #311 GAI 8 (NmMt) sold for $30,000 (SCP; 11/10)
—Mickey Mantle #311 GAI 8 (NmMt) sold for $27,180 (Mile High; 10/12)
— Mickey Mantle #311 SGC 86 (NrMt+) sold for $54,038 (Mile High; 05/11)
—Mickey Mantle #311 PSA 7.5 (NM+) sold for $37,453 (Mile High; 6/10)
—Connie Marrero #317 PSA 8 (NmMt) sold for $2,391 (Mile High; 5/07)
—Billy Martin #175 PSA 9 (MT) sold for $8,080 (Mastro; 6/05)
—Morrie Martin #131 PSA 8 (NmMt) sold for $981 (Memory Lane; 4/07)
—Morrie Martin #131 PSA 8 (NmMt) sold for $956 (Mile High; 8/07)
—Eddie Mathews #407 GAI 7.5 (NmMt+) sold for $11,294 (Goodwin; 5/07)
—Charley Maxwell #180 PSA 9 (MT) sold for $10,779 (Goodwin; Mastro; 2/06)
—Charley Maxwell #180 PSA 8 (NmMt) sold for $3,909 (Mastro; 12/05)
—Charley Maxwell #180 PSA 8 (NmMt) sold for $3,697 (Goodwin; 2/07)
—Charley Maxwell #180 PSA 8 (NmMt) sold for $3,001 (Mile High; 1/07)
—Willie Mays #261 PSA 9 (MT) sold for $478,000 (Heritage; 5/16)
—Willie Mays #261 PSA 9 (MT) sold for $382,400 (Heritage; 8/16)
—Willie Mays #261 PSA 9 (MT) sold for $310,700 (Heritage; 11/16)
—Willie Mays #261 PSA 9 (MT) sold for $40,000 (Memory Lane; Private Sale - 2007)

—Willie Mays #261 SGC 96 (MT) sold for $32,400 (Mastro; 8/08)
—Willie Mays #261 PSA 9 (MT) sold for $24,851 (Mastro; 4/07)
—Willie Mays #244 PSA 8 (NmMt) sold for $12,684 (Bussineau; 7/13)
—Bill Miller #403 PSA 9 (MT) sold for $20,546 (Mastro; 12/06)
—Bill Miller #403 PSA 8 (NmMt) sold for $5,223 (Memory Lane; 5/08)
—Irv Noren #40 (Black) PSA 8 (NmMt) sold for $2,247 (eBay; 12/07)
—Andy Pafko #1 PSA 10 (Gem) sold for $250,000 (Memory Lane; Private Sale - 2007)
—Andy Pafko #1 (Black) PSA 8 (NmMt) sold for $95,170 (Memory Lane; 9/07)
—Andy Pafko #1 (Black) PSA 8 (NmMt) sold for $81,137 (Goodwin; 8/08)
—Andy Pafko #1 PSA 8 (NmMt) sold for $80,000 (Memory Lane; Private Sale - 2007)
—Andy Pafko #1 (Black) PSA 8 (NmMt) sold for $46,772 (SCP; 11/10)
—Andy Pafko #1 (Black) PSA 8 (NmMt) sold for $45,000 (Legendary; 8/10)
—Andy Pafko #1 (Black) PSA 7 (NM) sold for $19,519 (Memory Lane; 12/07)
—Andy Pafko #1 (Red) PSA 7 (NM) sold for $18,639 (Mile High; 8/07)
—Andy Pafko #1 (Black) PSA 7 (NM) sold for $14,197 (Mastro; 12/06)
—Andy Pafko #1 PSA 7 (NrMt) sold for $14,100 (Huggins and Scott; 8/12)
—Andy Pafko #1 (Red) SGC 84 (NM) sold for $13,739 (Mastro; 4/06)
—Andy Pafko #1 (Red) PSA 7 (NM) sold for $12,100 (eBay; 4/07)
—Andy Pafko #1 (Red) BVG 7 (NM) sold for $5,079 (Heritage; 5/08)
—Andy Pafko #1 (Black) BVG 6.5 (ExMt+) sold for $4,102 (eBay; 5/08)
—Joe Page #48 (Error - Black) PSA 8 (NmMt) sold for $16,350 (Goodwin; 8/08)
—Joe Page #48 (Correct Bio - Black) PSA 8 (NmMt) sold for $1,913 (Mile High; 8/07)
—Joe Page #48 (Correct Bio - Black) PSA 7 (NM) sold for $740 (eBay; 2/08)
—Joe Page #48 (Correct Bio - Black) PSA 7 (NM) sold for $310 (Goodwin; 3/08)
—Wally Post #151 PSA 8 (NmMt) sold for $1,530 (Memory Lane; 12/06)
—Wally Post #151 PSA 8 (NmMt) sold for $446 (Mile High; 8/07)
—Jake Pitler CO #395 PSA 9 (MT) sold for $13,894 (Goodwin; 11/12)
—Pete Reiser #189 PSA 8 (NmMt) sold for $1,136 (eBay; 1/06)
—Pete Reiser #189 PSA 8 (NmMt) sold for $811 (Memory Lane; 12/07)
—Pete Reiser #189 PSA 8 (NmMt) sold for $406 (eBay; 5/07)
—Hal Rice #398 PSA 8 (NmMt) sold for $3,877 (Mastro; 10/05)
—Hal Rice #398 PSA 8 (NmMt) sold for $2,391 (Mile High; 8/07)
—Phil Rizzuto #11 PSA 8 (NmMt) sold for $6,412 (Madec; 5/08)
—Phil Rizzuto #11 PSA 8 (NmMt) sold for $4,306 (eBay; 10/08)
—Eddie Robinson #32 (Black) PSA 8 (NmMt) sold for $2,299 (Memory Lane; 4/05)
—Eddie Robinson #32 (Red) PSA 8 (NmMt) sold for $3,603 (eBay; 7/06)
—Jackie Robinson #312 PSA 9 (MT) sold for $23,843 (Mastro; 12/05)
—Jackie Robinson #312 GAI 8.5 (NmMt+) sold for $6,599 (Mastro; 8/04)
—Joe Rossi #379 PSA 8 (NmMt) sold for $1,804 (eBay; 12/07)
—James E. Runnels #2 (Black) PSA 8 (NmMt) sold for $49,636 (Goodwin; 8/08)
—James E. Runnels #2 PSA 8 (NmMt) sold for $10,798 (Goodwin; 8/08)
—James E. Runnels #2 (Black) PSA 7 (NM) sold for $6,034 (Goodwin; 2/06)
—James E. Runnels #2 (Red) PSA 7 (NM) sold for $2,559 (Goodwin; 6/06)
—James E. Runnels #2 (Red) PSA 7 (NM) sold for $2,104 (Mile High; 8/07)
—Jim Russell #51 (Red) PSA 8 (NmMt) sold for $2,603 (eBay; 3/07)
—Jim Russell #51 (Red) PSA 8 (NmMt) sold for $2,355 (Goodwin; 3/08)
—Jim Russell #51 (Red) PSA 8 (NmMt) sold for $985 (eBay; 7/06)
—John Rutherford #320 PSA 8 (NmMt) sold for $10,322 (Goodwin; 8/08)
—John Rutherford #320 PSA 8 (NmMt) sold for $5,558 (Mastro; 10/05)
—John Rutherford #320 PSA 8 (NmMt) sold for $4,392 (Mile High; 6/06)
—Johnny Sain #49 (Correct Bio - Red) PSA 8 (NmMt) sold for $3,717 (eBay; 11/07)
—Johnny Sain #49 (Correct Bio - Black) PSA 8 (NmMt) sold for $13,344 (Goodwin; 8/08)
—Johnny Sain #49 (Page Bio-Black) PSA 8 (NmMt) sold for $16,867 (Mem Lane; 4/07)
—Johnny Sain #49 (Page Bio - Black) PSA 8 (NmMt) sold for $15,542 (Goodwin; 3/04)
—Johnny Sain #49 (Page Bio - Black) PSA 8 (NmMt) sold for $14,864 (Goodwin; 8/08)
—Johnny Sain #49 (Page Bio - Black) PSA 7 (NM) sold for $2,135 (Goodwin; 5/07)
—Ray Scarborough PSA 8 (NmMt) sold for $11,193 (Goodwin; 8/08)
—Red Schoendienst #91 PSA 9 (MT) sold for $4,061 (eBay; 6/04)
—George Shuba #326 PSA 8 (NmMt) sold for $16,626 (Goodwin; 8/08)
—George Shuba #326 PSA 8 (NmMt) sold for $4,480 (Memory Lane; 9/06)
—George Shuba #326 PSA 8 (NmMt) sold for $3,450 (Mastro; 10/05)
—Roy Smalley #173 PSA 8 (NmMt) sold for $1,164 (eBay; 4/07)
—Roy Smalley #173 PSA 8 (NmMt) sold for $677 (eBay; 1/08)
—Warren Spahn (Black) #33 PSA 8.5 (NmMt+) sold for $3,598 (Memory Lane; 5/08)
—Gerald Staley #79 (Red) PSA 8 (NmMt) sold for $1,926 (eBay; 7/06)
—Wayne Terwilliger #7 PSA 8 (NmMt) sold for $15,866 (Goodwin; 8/08)
—Bobby Thompson #313 PSA 10 (Gem) sold for $10,443 (Mastro; 10/05)
—Bobby Thompson #313 PSA 10 (Gem) sold for $9,775 (Superior; 8/03)
—Jim Turner #373 PSA 8 (NmMt) sold for $4,276 (Goodwin; 6/06)
—Herman Wehmeier #80 (Red) PSA 8 (NmMt) sold for $4,957 (Mastro; 6/05)
—Herman Wehmeier #80 (Red) PSA 8 (NmMt) sold for $4,715 (Superior (4/03)
—Herman Wehmeier #80 (Red) PSA 8 (NmMt) sold for $4,376 (Mastro; 4/04)
—Herman Wehmeier #80 (Red) GAI 8 (NmMt) sold for $1,511 (Goodwin; 6/06)
—Herman Wehmeier #80 (Red) GAI 8 (NmMt) sold for $1,367 (Mastro; 6/05)
—Herman Wehmeier #80 (Red) GAI 8 (NmMt) sold for $1,327 (Mile High; 6/03)
—Herman Wehmeier #80 (Black) PSA 7 (NM) sold for $2,312 (Memory Lane; 12/07)
—Bob Wellman #41 (Red) PSA 8 (NmMt) sold for $2,475 (eBay; 10/06)

—Hoyt Wilhelm #392 PSA 10 (Gem) (Young Collection) sold for $23,352 (SCP; 5/12)
—Wes Westrum #75 PSA 8 (NmMt) sold for $11,919 (Goodwin; 08/08)
—Davey Williams #316 PSA 8 (NmMt) sold for $2,913 (Goodwin; 11/07)
—Davey Williams #316 PSA 8 (NmMt) sold for $1,502 (Mile High; 6/06)
—Al Zarilla #70 (Black) PSA 8 (NmMt) sold for $3,203 (eBay; 11/07)
—Gus Zernial #31 PSA 8 (NmMt) sold for $11,027 (Goodwin; 8/08)

1953 Bowman Black and White

		PrFr 1	GD 2	VG 3	VgEx 4	EX 5	ExMt 6	NM 7	NmMt
1	Gus Bell	8	12	20	30	40	100	500	
2	Willard Nixon	5	6	10	15	20	30	80	20
3	Bill Rigney	5	6	10	15	20	30	80	20
4	Pat Mullin	5	6	10	15	20	30	60	20
5	Dee Fondy	5	6	10	15	20	30	60	30
6	Ray Murray	5	6	10	15	20	30	80	20
7	Andy Seminick	5	6	10	15	20	30	60	20
8	Pete Suder	5	6	10	15	20	30	60	20
9	Walt Masterson	5	6	10	15	40	60	150	
10	Dick Sisler	5	8	12	20	25	40	80	20
11	Dick Gernert	5	6	10	15	20	30	60	20
12	Randy Jackson	5	6	10	15	20	30	80	20
13	Joe Tipton	5	6	10	15	30	40	60	20
14	Bill Nicholson	5	8	12	20	25	40	100	30
15	Johnny Mize	10	15	25	50	60	100	200	35
16	Stu Miller RC	5	8	12	20	25	502	80	30
17	Virgil Trucks	5	8	12	20	30	50	100	50
18	Billy Hoeft	5	6	10	15	50	60	80	20
19	Paul LaPalme	5	6	10	15	30	40	60	20
20	Eddie Robinson	5	6	10	15	20	30	60	20
21	Clarence Podbielan	5	6	10	15	20	30	60	20
22	Matt Batts	5	6	10	15	20	30	60	20
23	Wilmer Mizell	5	6	10	15	20	50	100	20
24	Del Wilber	5	6	10	15	20	40	80	20
25	Johnny Sain	8	12	20	30	50	60	150	60
26	Preacher Roe	8	12	20	30	50	60	150	30
27	Bob Lemon	10	15	25	40	50	120	200	60
28	Hoyt Wilhelm	10	15	25	50	80	120	200	40
29	Sid Hudson	5	8	12	20	30	60	100	20
30	Walker Cooper	5	6	10	15	20	30	60	20
31	Gene Woodling	8	12	20	30	40	80	300	50
32	Rocky Bridges	5	6	10	15	20	30	60	20
33	Bob Kuzava	5	8	12	20	25	50	120	25
34	Ebba St.Claire	5	6	10	15	20	30	100	20
35	Johnny Wyrostek	5	6	10	15	20	30	60	20
36	Jimmy Piersall	8	12	20	30	40	80	150	50
37	Hal Jeffcoat	5	8	12	20	25	40	100	50
38	Dave Cole	5	6	10	15	20	30	60	30
39	Casey Stengel MG	50	80	150	200	300	400	600	
40	Larry Jansen	5	8	12	20	25	60		
41	Bob Ramazzotti	5	6	10	15	20	30	60	20
42	Howie Judson	5	6	10	15	20	30	60	20
43	Hal Bevan RC	5	6	10	15	20	40	80	50
44	Jim Delsing	5	6	10	20	25	30	80	25
45	Irv Noren	6	10	15	25	30	50	100	60
46	Bucky Harris MG	8	12	20	30	40	80	120	50
47	Jack Lohrke	5	8	12	20	30	60	150	40
48	Steve Ridzik RC	5	6	10	15	20	50	150	
49	Floyd Baker	5	6	10	15	20	30	80	30
50	Dutch Leonard	5	6	10	15	20	30	60	25
51	Lew Burdette	5	8	12	20	25	50	200	40
52	Ralph Branca	8	12	20	30	40	60	200	
53	Morrie Martin	5	6	10	15	20	30	80	25
54	Bill Miller	5	6	10	15	20	30	120	25
55	Don Johnson	5	6	10	15	25	80		
56	Roy Smalley	8	12	20	30	40	80		
57	Andy Pafko	5	8	12	20	25	40	80	40
58	Jim Konstanty	5	8	12	20	25	40	80	50
59	Duane Pillette	5	6	8	12	20	40	80	20
60	Billy Cox	8	12	20	30	40	80	250	
61	Tom Gorman RC	5	6	10	15	20	30	100	30
62	Keith Thomas RC	5	6	10	15	20	60	150	
63	Steve Gromek	5	6	10	15	20	60		
64	Andy Hansen	10	15	25	40	60	300		

—Gus Bell #1 PSA 8 (NmMt) sold for $986 (Memory Lane; 11/05)
—Ralph Branca #52 PSA 8 (NmMt) sold for $812 (Memory Lane; 8/06)
—Ralph Branca #52 PSA 8 (NmMt) sold for $580 (eBay; 2/08)

—Billy Cox #60 PSA 8 (NmMt) sold for $1,080 (Goodwin; 6/06)
—Dick Gernert #11 PSA 9 (MT) sold for $2,132 (Madec; 11/07)
—Andy Hansen #64 PSA 7 (NM) sold for $520 (eBay; 12/06)
—Larry Jansen #40 PSA 8 (NmMt) sold for $4,053 (Madec; 11/07)
—Larry Jansen #40 PSA 7 (NM) sold for $369 (eBay; 10/07)
—Don Johnson #55 PSA 8 (NmMt) sold for $636 (eBay; 10/07)
—Don Johnson #55 PSA 7 (NM) sold for $400 (eBay; 11/06)
—Bob Lemon #27 PSA 9 (MT) sold for $2,796 (Mastro; 1/05)
—Walt Masterson #9 PSA 9 (MT) sold for $4,614 (Memory Lane; 4/07)
—Walt Masterson #9 PSA 8 (NmMt) sold for $766 (eBay; 4/07)
—Walt Masterson #9 PSA 8 (NmMt) sold for $405 (eBay; 11/07)
—Johnny Mize #15 SGC 96 (MT) sold for $2,469 (Mastro; 1/05)
—Irv Noren #45 PSA 9 (MT) sold for $3,202 (Memory Lane; 3/06)
—Roy Smalley #56 PSA 8 (NmMt) sold for $2,413 (eBay; 10/06)
—Casey Stengel #39 PSA 8 (NmMt) sold for $4,470 (eBay;9/07)
—Casey Stengel #39 SGC 88 (NmMt) sold for $1,422 (Memory Lane; 12/07)

1953 Bowman Color

		GD 2	VG 3	VgEx 4	EX 5	ExMt 6	NM 7	NmMt 8	MT 9
1	Davey Williams	10	15	25	50	120	500	800	
2	Vic Wertz	6	10	15	20	30	80	250	1,000
3	Sam Jethroe	6	10	15	25	80	120	1,000	
4	Art Houtteman	6	8	12	20	30	60	200	800
5	Sid Gordon	5	8	12	20	40	60	150	600
6	Joe Ginsberg	5	8	12	20	50	80	150	800
7	Harry Chiti RC	5	8	12	20	40	50	150	800
8	Al Rosen	8	12	20	50	60	100	250	800
9	Phil Rizzuto	25	50	60	100	150	300	800	
10	Richie Ashburn	20	30	50	60	▼100	200	400	2,000
11	Bobby Shantz	6	10	15	30	50	80	150	1,000
12	Carl Erskine	6	10	15	25	50	100	250	
13	Gus Zernial	5	8	12	25	40	60	150	1,000
14	Billy Loes	8	12	20	▼25	▼30	▼60	200	
15	Jim Busby	5	8	12	20	30	▼50	150	800
16	Bob Friend	6	10	15	25	40	▲60	150	600
17	Gerry Staley	5	8	12	20	30	60	300	
18	Nellie Fox	15	25	40	50	100	150	300	▲2,000
19	Alvin Dark	5	8	12	20	30	50	150	800
20	Don Lenhardt	5	8	12	20	30	50	120	800
21	Joe Garagiola	10	15	25	▼30	▼40	▼60	▼200	1,000
22	Bob Porterfield	5	8	12	20	40	60	150	800
23	Herman Wehmeier	6	10	15	25	40	60	150	800
24	Jackie Jensen	10	15	25	30	40	80	250	
25	Hoot Evers	5	8	12	20	40	60	200	800
26	Roy McMillan	6	10	15	25	40	80	200	600
27	Vic Raschi	8	12	20	30	50	100	300	1,500
28	Smoky Burgess	5	8	12	20	40	60	250	1,000
29	Bobby Avila	5	8	12	20	40	60	250	600
30	Phil Cavarretta	5	8	12	20	40	60	200	1,000
31	Jimmy Dykes MG	5	8	12	20	30	50	200	800
32	Stan Musial	100	150	▲250	▲400	▼500	▼800	▲2,500	4,000
33	Pee Wee Reese	150	250	300	400	600	1,000	2,000	5,000
34	Gil Coan	5	8	12	20	30	50	▼150	600
35	Maurice McDermott	5	8	12	20	30	60	▼120	600
36	Minnie Minoso	12	20	40	50	80	120	400	1,200
37	Jim Wilson	5	8	12	20	30	50	150	600
38	Harry Byrd RC	5	8	12	20	30	50	150	
39	Paul Richards MG	6	10	15	25	40	80	150	800
40	Larry Doby	12	20	30	60	100	250	1,000	2,000
41	Sammy White	6	10	15	25	30	50	150	800
42	Tommy Brown	5	8	12	20	30	60	150	
43	Mike Garcia	6	10	15	25	40	60	200	1,000
44	Bauer/Berra/Mantle	120	200	250	400	600	1,000	▼2,000	8,000
45	Walt Dropo	5	8	12	20	30	80	150	600
46	Roy Campanella	50	60	80	120	200	400	800	4,000
47	Ned Garver	6	10	15	30	50	60	200	600
48	Hank Sauer	6	10	15	25	60	120	300	
49	Eddie Stanky MG	5	8	12	20	40	80	150	1,000
50	Lou Kretlow	5	8	12	20	40	60	200	800
51	Monte Irvin	12	20	30	40	80	200	300	1,200
52	Marty Marion MG	6	10	15	25	40	▼60	▼150	
53	Del Rice	6	10	15	25	40	60	200	
54	Chico Carrasquel	5	8	12	20	30	80	200	800
55	Leo Durocher MG	10	15	25	40	80	▼120	300	1,000
56	Bob Cain	5	8	12	25	40	60	▼150	
57	Lou Boudreau MG	12	20	30	▼50	▼60	▼100	250	1,000

		GD 2	VG 3	VgEx 4	EX 5	ExMt 6	NM 7	NmMt 8	MT 9
58	Willard Marshall	6	10	15	25	40	80	120	800
59	Mickey Mantle	▲600	800	1,200	2,000	2,500	5,000	12,000	15,000
60	Granny Hamner	5	8	12	30	40	60	200	800
61	George Kell	15	25	30	40	80	120	300	
62	Ted Kluszewski	15	25	40	50	80	150	300	
63	Gil McDougald	10	15	25	50	100	150	400	
64	Curt Simmons	6	10	15	25	50	200	1,500	
65	Robin Roberts	12	20	30	60	150	400	600	
66	Mel Parnell	6	10	15	25	40	▼150	800	
67	Mel Clark RC	6	10	15	25	30	▼60	400	
68	Allie Reynolds	10	15	30	60	100	▼150	▼600	
69	Charlie Grimm MG	8	12	20	30	40	150	250	
70	Clint Courtney RC	5	8	12	30	40	150	300	
71	Paul Minner	5	8	12	20	40	60	400	
72	Ted Gray	5	8	12	20	50	60	200	
73	Billy Pierce	6	10	15	25	40	120	250	1,000
74	Don Mueller	5	8	12	20	40	100	250	
75	Saul Rogovin	5	8	12	20	30	60	200	
76	Jim Hearn	5	8	12	20	30	100	200	800
77	Mickey Grasso	5	8	12	25	30	60	200	
78	Carl Furillo	8	12	30	40	80	150	500	
79	Ray Boone	6	10	15	30	50	150	300	1,000
80	Ralph Kiner	12	20	30	50	80	250	500	1,200
81	Enos Slaughter	12	25	50	60	▼100	▼200	600	
82	Joe Astroth	5	8	12	20	50	60	200	
83	Jack Daniels RC	5	8	12	20	50	80	300	800
84	Hank Bauer	12	20	25	40	▼60	150	250	1,200
85	Solly Hemus	8	12	20	30	50	60	250	800
86	Harry Simpson	5	8	12	25	50	120	250	
87	Harry Perkowski	5	8	12	25	50	80	250	800
88	Joe Dobson	5	8	12	20	30	50	120	800
89	Sandy Consuegra	6	10	15	25	50	100	300	
90	Joe Nuxhall	6	10	20	30	40	120	300	
91	Steve Souchock	5	8	12	20	30	50	200	600
92	Gil Hodges	40	50	▼60	100	200	▼300	800	3,500
93	P.Rizzuto/B.Martin	50	60	100	120	200	▼400	1,000	6,000
94	Bob Addis	5	8	12	20	40	120	400	
95	Wally Moses CO	6	10	15	25	40	60	200	
96	Sal Maglie	6	10	15	25	40	200	400	
97	Eddie Mathews	50	80	100	200	250	500	1,200	4,000
98	Hector Rodriguez RC	6	10	15	25	60	200		
99	Warren Spahn	50	60	120	▲200	300	500	1,500	4,000
100	Bill Wight	5	8	12	50	60	80	300	
101	Red Schoendienst	10	15	30	60	100	200	500	
102	Jim Hegan	5	8	12	20	40	250	400	
103	Del Ennis	8	12	20	30	50	250		
104	Luke Easter	10	15	25	50	200			
105	Eddie Joost	6	10	15	25	40	120	500	
106	Ken Raffensberger	5	8	12	25	30	120	400	
107	Alex Kellner	5	8	12	25	40	80	200	
108	Bobby Adams	5	8	12	20	30	50	200	800
109	Ken Wood	6	10	15	30	40	150	400	
110	Bob Rush	5	8	20	25	30	80	300	
111	Jim Dyck RC	5	8	12	20	50	120	400	
112	Toby Atwell	8	12	20	30	80	200		
113	Karl Drews	8	12	20	30	100	300		
114	Bob Feller	60	80	150	250	500	800	▲2,500	5,000
115	Cloyd Boyer	12	20	30	50	▼80	300	600	
116	Eddie Yost	12	20	30	50	80	250	800	
117	Duke Snider	100	150	200	250	500	1,000	2,500	10,000
118	Billy Martin	40	80	100	200	300	600	3,000	6,000
119	Dale Mitchell	10	15	40	60	80	150		
120	Marlin Stuart	10	15	25	80	120	250		
121	Yogi Berra	120	150	250	400	600	1,200	3,000	10,000
122	Bill Serena	10	15	25	40	60	200	500	
123	Johnny Lipon	10	15	25	40	100	200	500	2,500
124	Chuck Dressen MG	12	20	30	80	150	250	600	3,000
125	Fred Hatfield	10	15	25	40	80	250	800	
126	Al Corwin	10	15	25	40	60	250	1,200	
127	Dick Kryhoski	10	15	25	40	60	250	800	
128	Whitey Lockman	10	15	25	50	200	600		
129	Russ Meyer	10	15	40	50	100	300		
130	Cass Michaels	8	12	20	40	60	300	800	2,000
131	Connie Ryan	8	12	25	50	60	200	800	
132	Fred Hutchinson	8	12	20	30	100	300	800	1,200
133	Willie Jones	8	12	20	30	60	250	400	2,000
134	Johnny Pesky	10	15	25	50	120	200	1,000	

		GD 2	VG 3	VgEx 4	EX 5	ExMt 6	NM 7	NmMt 8	MT 9
135	Bobby Morgan	8	12	20	30	60	200		
136	Jim Brideweser RC	8	12	20	40	100	250	600	
137	Sam Dente	8	12	20	30	100	250	600	2,500
138	Bubba Church	8	12	20	40	60	200	500	
139	Pete Runnels	8	12	20	50	100	150	1,200	
140	Al Brazle	8	12	20	30	▼60	▼150	500	
141	Frank Shea	8	12	20	30	80	200	600	1,500
142	Larry Miggins RC	8	12	20	40	50	250	1,200	
143	Al Lopez MG	10	15	25	80	100	300	2,000	
144	Warren Hacker	10	15	25	40	50	150	1,000	
145	George Shuba	20	30	40	50	100			
146	Early Wynn	25	40	50	80	120	400	1,000	2,500
147	Clem Koshorek	6	10	15	25	▼50	200	500	1,500
148	Billy Goodman	10	▼20	▼25	▼30	120	300		
149	Al Corwin	8	12	20	50	60	150	▲600	
150	Carl Scheib	8	12	20	30	50	100	300	
151	Joe Adcock	10	15	25	60	100	200	1,000	
152	Clyde Vollmer	8	12	20	30	50	200	400	
153	Whitey Ford	60	120	150	250	500	1,200	10,000	
154	Turk Lown	8	12	20	▲40	▲80	300	▲1,000	
155	Allie Clark	10	15	25	30	60	250	600	
156	Max Surkont	8	12	20	50	60	300	600	
157	Sherm Lollar	10	15	25	50	80	150	500	2,000
158	Howard Fox	8	12	20	30	▼60	250	1,000	
159	Mickey Vernon	10	15	25	60	100	250	1,200	
160	Cal Abrams	12	20	50	60	250	600	800	

—A complete set with each card uniformly graded PSA 8 (NmMt), except for #153 Ford PSA 7, sold for $ 94,000 (REA; 4/07)
—Toby Atwell #112 PSA 8 (NmMt) sold for $2,550 (eBay; 6/04)
—Toby Atwell #112 PSA 8 (NmMt) sold for $1,052 (Mile High; 8/07)
—Toby Atwell #112 PSA 8 (NmMt) sold for $443 (Memory Lane; 9/07)
—Toby Atwell #112 PSA 8 (NmMt) sold for $277 (eBay; 7/07)
—Yogi Berra #121 SGC 92 (NmMt+) sold for $3,697 (Goodwin; 3/08)
—Yogi Berra #121 GAI 8.5 (NmMt+) sold for $2,766 (Mile High; 8/07)
—Yogi Berra #121 GAI 8 (NmMt) sold for $1,892 (Memory Lane; 12/07)
—Yogi Berra #121 GAI 8 (NmMt) sold for $1,417 (eBay; 5/07)
—Karl Drews #113 PSA 8 (NmMt) sold for $2,646 (Mastro; 12/06)
—Karl Drews #113 PSA 8 (NmMt) sold for $2,368 (Memory Lane; 9/07)
—Luke Easter #103 PSA 8 (NmMt) sold for $908 (eBay; 8/07)
—Luke Easter #103 PSA 8 (NmMt) sold for $788 (eBay; 9/04)
—Luke Easter #103 PSA 8 (NmMt) sold for $618 (eBay; 7/07)
—Luke Easter #103 PSA 7 (NM) sold for $465 (eBay; 11/07)
—Carl Erskine #12 PSA 9 (MT) sold for $2,911 (Memory Lane; 8/06)
—Del Ennis #103 PSA 8 (NmMt) sold for $891 (Goodwin; 6/06)
—Del Ennis #103 PSA 8 (NmMt) sold for $713 (Memory Lane; 4/07)
—Bob Feller #114 GAI 9 (MT) sold for $2,960 (eBay; 3/08)
—Bob Feller #114 GAI 8.5 (NmMt+) sold for $2,300 (Memory Lane; 3/06)
—Bob Feller #114 SGC 86 (NM+) sold for $1,339 (Goodwin; 2/06)
—Whitey Ford #153 PSA 9 (MT) sold for $75,000 (Memory Lane; Private - 2007)
—Whitey Ford #153 PSA 9 (MT) sold for $24,019 (Memory Lane; 8/05)
—Whitey Ford #153 SGC 96 (MT) sold for $9,202 (Mastro; 8/03)
—Whitey Ford #153 BVG 8.5 (NmMt+) sold for $2,949 (4/07)
—Billy Goodman #148 PSA 8 (NmMt) sold for $2,260 (eBay; 7/06)
—Billy Goodman #148 PSA 8 (NmMt) sold for $1,093 (eBay; 7/06)
—Ted Kluszewski #62 PSA 9 (MT) sold for $7,550 (Memory Lane; 8/05)
—Ted Kluszewski #62 PSA 9 (MT) sold for $5,808 (Memory Lane; 3/06)
—Dick Kryhoski #127 PSA 9 (MT) sold for $6,406 (Memory Lane; 11/04)
—Dick Kryhoski #127 PSA 8 (NmMt) sold for $1,736 (Mile High; 8/07)
—Dick Kryhoski #127 PSA 8 (NmMt) sold for $1,336 (Mile High; 1/08)
—Dick Kryhoski #127 PSA 8 (NmMt) sold for $913 (Memory Lane; 9/07)
—Whitey Lockman #128 PSA 8 (NmMt) sold for $1,782 (Goodwin; 6/06)
—Whitey Lockman #128 PSA 8 (NmMt) sold for $1,494 (Memory Lane; 8/06)
—Whitey Lockman #128 PSA 8 (NmMt) sold for $1,180 (eBay; 5/08)
—Mickey Mantle #59 PSA 10 (Gem) sold for $115,000 (Memory Lane; Private - 2007)
—Mickey Mantle #59 GAI 9.5 (Gem) sold for $9,843 (Mile High; 6/06)
—Mickey Mantle #59 BVG 9 (MT) sold for $5,400 (eBay; 11/07)
—Mickey Mantle #59 SGC 92 (NmMt+) sold for $4,605 (eBay; 8/07)
—Mickey Mantle #59 GAI 8 (NmMt) sold for $2,375 (eBay; 4/07)
—Mickey Mantle #59 GAI 8 (NmMt) sold for $2,317 (Mastro; 12/07)
—Eddie Mathews #97 GAI 8.5 (NmMt+) sold for $1,106 (Mile High; 1/07)
—Gil McDougald #63 PSA 9 (MT) sold for $3,553 (Mastro; 4/03)
—Gil McDougald #63 PSA 9 (MT) sold for $2,468 (Goodwin; 10/06)
—Russ Meyer #129 PSA 8 (NmMt) sold for $2,799 (Memory Lane; 9/07)
—Dale Mitchell #119 PSA 8 (NmMt) sold for $949 (Memory Lane; 3/06)
—Bobby Morgan #135 PSA 8 (NmMt) sold for $2,102 (Memory Lane; 5/08)
—Stan Musial #32 GAI 9 (MT) sold for $1,912 (Heritage; 10/07)
—Stan Musial #32 GAI 8.5 (NmMt+) sold for $2,239 (Memory Lane; 3/06)

—Stan Musial #32 GAI 8.5 (NmMt+) sold for $1,515 (eBay; 3/08)
—Johnny Pesky #134 PSA 8 (NmMt) sold for $873 (Memory Lane; 3/06)
—Johnny Pesky #134 PSA 8 (NmMt) sold for $628 (eBay; 7/07)
—Pee Wee Reese #33 GAI 8.5 (NmMt+) sold for $1,684 (Mile High; 2/08)
—Pee Wee Reese #33 GAI 8.5 (NmMt+) sold for $1,604 (Memory Lane; 4/07)
—Pee Wee Reese #33 SGC 88 (NmMt) sold for $1,009 (eBay; 10/07)
—Allie Reynolds #68 PSA 9 (MT) sold for $6,441 (Mile High; 6/06)
—Phil Rizzuto #9 PSA 9 (MT) sold for $8,537 (Mile High; 6/06)
—Phil Rizzuto #9 GAI 8.5 (NmMt+) sold for $670 (eBay; 2/07)
—Robin Roberts #65 PSA 9 (MT) sold for $7,031 (Memory Lane; 4/05)
—Robin Roberts #65 PSA 9 (MT) sold for $2,911 (Madec; 5/07)
—Robin Roberts #65 PSA 8.5 (NmMt+) sold for $826 (eBay; 4/08)
—Hector Rodriguez #98 PSA 9 (MT) sold for $1,741 (Memory Lane; 8/06)
—Hector Rodriguez #98 PSA 8 (NmMt) sold for $1,100 (Mile High; 6/06)
—Hector Rodriguez #98 PSA 8 (NmMt) sold for $785 (Memory Lane; 4/07)
—George Shuba #145 PSA 8 (NmMt) sold for $1,010 (eBay; 7/06)
—George Shuba #145 PSA 7 (NM) sold for $888 (eBay; 4/08)
—Enos Slaughter #81 GAI 9 (MT) sold for $1,390 (Mile High; 12/05)
—Duke Snider #117 GAI 8.5 (NmMt+) sold for $3,163 (19th Century; 6/06)
—Duke Snider #117 SGC 88 (NmMt) sold for $1,730 (eBay; 2/08)
—Warren Spahn #99 GAI 8 (NmMt) sold for $511 (eBay; 2/07)
—Mickey Vernon #159 (PSA 8 (NmMt) sold for $1,273 (Mile High; 8/07)
—Davey Williams #1 GAI 8.5 (NmMt+) sold for $411 (eBay; 11/07)
—Davey Williams #1 GAI 8 (NmMt) sold for $434 (eBay; 6/06)
—Bauer/Berra/Mantle #44 GAI 9 (MT) sold for $2,683 (eBay; 3/08)
—Bauer/Berra/Mantle #44 GAI 8.5 (NmMt+) sold for $1,375 (eBay; 8/07)
—P.Rizzuto/B.Martin #93 GAI 9 (MT) sold for $3,200 (eBay; 10/06)
—P.Rizzuto/B.Martin #93 GAI 9 (MT) sold for $1,237 (eBay; 3/08)
—P.Rizzuto/B.Martin #93 GAI 8.5 (NmMt+) sold for $936 (eBay; 11/06)

1953 Red Man

		GD 2	VG 3	VgEx 4	EX 5	ExMt 6	NM 7	NmMt 8	MT 9
AL1	Casey Stengel MG	10	15	25	80	100	150		
AL2	Hank Bauer	8	12	20	30	50	100	300	
AL3	Yogi Berra	15	25	50	100	120	250	1,000	
AL4	Walt Dropo	6	10	15	25	40	80	200	
AL5	Nellie Fox	10	15	25	40	60	120	500	
AL6	Jackie Jensen	8	12	20	30	50	100		
AL7	Eddie Joost	6	10	15	25	40	80	200	
AL8	George Kell	10	15	25	40	60	120	500	
AL9	Dale Mitchell	6	10	15	25	40	80	200	
AL10	Phil Rizzuto	15	25	40	60	100	250	800	
AL11	Eddie Robinson	6	10	15	25	40	80		
AL12	Gene Woodling	8	12	20	30	50	100	300	
AL13	Gus Zernial	6	10	15	25	40	80		
AL14	Early Wynn	10	15	25	40	60	120	300	
AL15	Joe Dobson	6	10	15	25	40	80	200	
AL16	Billy Pierce	6	10	15	25	40	80	200	
AL17	Bob Lemon	10	15	25	40	60	120	500	
AL18	Johnny Mize	10	15	25	40	60	120	500	
AL19	Bob Porterfield	6	10	15	25	40	80	250	
AL20	Bobby Shantz	6	10	15	25	40	80		
AL21	Mickey Vernon	6	10	15	25	40	80	200	
AL22	Dom DiMaggio	8	12	20	30	50	100	250	
AL23	Gil McDougald	8	12	20	30	50	100	300	
AL24	Al Rosen	8	12	20	30	50	100	300	
AL25	Mel Parnell	6	10	15	25	40	80	200	
AL26	Bobby Avila	6	10	15	25	40	80	200	
NL1	Charlie Dressen MG	6	10	15	25	40	80		
NL2	Bobby Adams	6	10	15	25	40	80	200	
NL3	Richie Ashburn	10	15	25	40	60	120	500	
NL4	Joe Black	8	12	20	30	60	100	300	
NL5	Roy Campanella	15	25	50	100	120	250	1,200	
NL6	Ted Kluszewski	10	15	25	40	60	120	500	
NL7	Whitey Lockman	6	10	15	25	40	80	300	
NL8	Sal Maglie	6	10	15	25	40	80	200	
NL9	Andy Pafko	6	10	15	25	40	80	200	
NL10	Pee Wee Reese	15	25	40	80	100	200	800	
NL11	Robin Roberts	10	15	25	40	60	120	600	
NL12	Red Schoendienst	10	15	25	40	60	120	500	
NL13	Enos Slaughter	10	15	25	40	60	120	500	
NL14	Duke Snider	15	25	50	80	120	250	1,200	
NL15	Ralph Kiner	8	12	20	30	50	100	300	
NL16	Hank Sauer	6	10	15	25	40	150	200	
NL17	Del Ennis	6	10	15	25	40	80	350	
NL18	Granny Hamner	6	10	15	25	40	80	200	

	GD 2	VG 3	VgEx 4	EX 5	ExMt 6	NM 7	NmMt 8	MT 9
.19 Warren Spahn	15	25	40	60	100	200	800	
.20 Wes Westrum	6	10	15	25	40	80	400	
.21 Hoyt Wilhelm	10	15	25	40	60	120	500	
.22 Murry Dickson	6	10	15	25	40	80	250	
.23 Warren Hacker	6	10	15	25	40	80	200	
.24 Gerry Staley	6	10	15	25	40	80		
.25 Bobby Thomson	8	12	20	30	50	100	300	
.26 Stan Musial	30	50	100	250	350	500		

Prices reference cards with tabs.

-Yogi Berra #AL3 PSA 9 (MT) sold for $3,658 (Memory Lane; 5/08)
-Roy Campanella #NL5 PSA 9 (MT) sold for $2,445 (Memory Lane; 8/06)
-Jackie Jensen #AL6 PSA 9 (NmMt) sold for $766 (Mile High; 2/08)
-Gil McDougald #AL23 PSA 9 (MT) sold for $1,380 (Huggins and Scott; 4/08)
-Johnny Mize #AL18 PSA 9 (MT) sold for $1,495 (Huggins and Scott; 4/08)
-Stan Musial #NL26 PSA 8 (NmMt) sold for $2,480 (eBay; 9/06)
-Pee Wee Reese #NL10 PSA 9 (MT) sold for $3,248 (Memory Lane; 8/06)
-Phil Rizzuto #AL10 PSA 9 (MT) sold for $2,454 (Mile High; 1/07)
-Bobby Shantz #AL20 PSA 8 (NmMt) sold for $696 (Mile High; 2/08)
-Duke Snider #NL14 BVG 9 (MT) sold for $1,355 (eBay; 1/0/)
-Casey Stengel #AL1 PSA 8 (NmMt) sold for $1,741 (Memory Lane; 8/06)
-Casey Stengel #AL1 PSA 8 (NmMt) sold for $737 (eBay; 3/08)

1953 Topps

	GD 2	VG 3	VgEx 4	EX 5	ExMt 6	NM 7	NmMt 8	MT 9
COMMON DP (221-280)			15	25	40	60	200	1,200
Jackie Robinson DP	▲300	400	500	800	1,200	4,000	8,000	10,000
Luke Easter DP	6	10	15	25	40	100	250	
George Crowe	6	10	15	25	60	100	300	
Ben Wade	6	10	15	30	50	100	300	
Joe Dobson	5	8	12	20	50	50	200	1,200
Sam Jones	8	12	20	40	50	80	200	800
Bob Borkowski DP	5	6	10	15	30	50	120	1,000
Clem Koshorek DP	6	8	12	20	40	50	150	1,000
Joe Collins	6	15	20	40	80	200		
0 Smoky Burgess SP	10	15	25	40	80	150	600	
1 Sal Yvars	6	10	15	30	50	100	250	
2 Howie Judson DP	5	6	10	25	30	60	150	
3 Conrado Marrero DP	5	6	10	30	40	50	150	
4 Clem Labine DP	10	15	25	40	50	100	600	
5 Bobo Newsom DP RC	6	10	15	25	40	50	120	
6 Harry Lowrey DP	5	6	10	25	30	50	200	1,500
7 Billy Hitchcock	5	8	12	25	30	80	200	1,500
8 Ted Lepcio DP	5	6	10	15	30	▼60	150	1,200
9 Mel Parnell DP	5	8	12	20	50	▼50	150	800
20 Hank Thompson	6	10	15	25	50	80	200	1,800
21 Billy Johnson	5	8	12	25	30	50	150	1,200
22 Howie Fox	6	10	15	30	50	60	200	
23 Toby Atwell DP	5	6	10	15	40	50	150	1,000
24 Ferris Fain	6	10	15	25	40	80	200	1,200
25 Ray Boone	6	10	15	30	50	80	250	
26 Dale Mitchell DP	6	10	15	30	50	60	▲200	
27 Roy Campanella DP	▲60	80	100	150	▼250	400	600	2,000
28 Eddie Pellagrini	5	8	12	20	40	80	200	1,000
29 Hal Jeffcoat	5	8	12	25	40	60	150	1,200
30 Willard Nixon	5	8	12	25	50	80	400	1,200
31 Ewell Blackwell	8	12	20	40	50	100	300	
32 Clyde Vollmer	6	10	15	25	30	60	200	
33 Bob Kennedy DP	5	6	10	15	25	60	120	800
34 George Shuba	6	10	15	25	50	60	300	
35 Irv Noren DP	8	12	20	25	30	80	120	1,200
36 Johnny Groth DP	5	6	10	15	40	50	150	800
37 Eddie Mathews DP	▲50	▲80	▲100	120	200	▲500	800	2,500
38 Jim Hearn DP	6	10	15	25	40	60	120	1,200
39 Eddie Miksis	5	8	12	20	40	60	150	1,200
40 John Lipon	5	8	12	20	40	80	200	1,200
41 Enos Slaughter	15	25	50	60	100	250	500	
42 Gus Zernial DP	6	10	15	25	30	50	150	1,200
43 Gil McDougald	8	12	40	50	80	250		
44 Ellis Kinder SP	8	12	20	30	60	250		
45 Grady Hatton DP	5	6	15	20	30	60	150	
46 Johnny Klippstein DP	5	6	10	15	40	200		
47 Bubba Church DP	5	8	12	25	30	60	150	
48 Bob Del Greco DP	5	6	10	25	30	60	120	
49 Faye Throneberry DP	6	10	15	30	40	60	150	1,200
50 Chuck Dressen DP	10	15	25	30	50	80	200	1,200
51 Frank Campos DP	6	10	15	25	40	50	150	1,200

	GD 2	VG 3	VgEx 4	EX 5	ExMt 6	NM 7	NmMt 8	MT 9
52 Ted Gray DP	5	6	10	15	30	60	100	1,500
53 Sherm Lollar DP	6	10	15	25	30	80	120	800
54 Bob Feller DP	50	60	▲100	120	200	300	1,000	4,000
55 Maurice McDermott DP	5	6	10	15	30	50	200	
56 Gerry Staley DP	6	10	15	25	50	80	120	1,200
57 Carl Scheib	6	10	15	25	30	50	120	
58 George Metkovich	5	8	12	20	40	60	200	1,200
59 Karl Drews DP	6	10	15	25	40	50	120	1,000
60 Cloyd Boyer DP	5	6	20	25	30	60	200	
61 Early Wynn SP	10	15	50	80	100	200	600	
62 Monte Irvin DP	15	30	40	60	100	250	800	
63 Gus Niarhos DP	5	6	10	25	30	60	120	1,000
64 Dave Philley	5	8	12	20	40	50	200	
65 Earl Harrist	10	15	25	30	60	80	200	1,500
66 Orestes Minoso	12	20	40	50	100	120	300	1,200
67 Roy Sievers DP	5	6	10	15	30	60	150	800
68 Del Rice	5	8	12	20	40	60	150	1,200
69 Dick Brodowski	5	8	12	25	30	80	150	1,000
70 Ed Yuhas	5	8	12	20	40	60	150	1,200
71 Tony Bartirome	6	10	15	25	40	80	200	
72 Fred Hutchinson SP	10	15	25	40	60	200	600	
73 Eddie Robinson	5	8	12	20	30	60	150	800
74 Joe Rossi	6	10	15	25	30	60	▲200	1,400
75 Mike Garcia	6	10	15	25	40	80	150	1,200
76 Pee Wee Reese	50	60	100	120	200	400	700	4,000
77 Johnny Mize DP	10	15	40	50	100	200	400	1,200
78 Al Schoendienst	10	15	50	80	100	200	1,000	
79 Johnny Wyrostek	6	10	15	25	40	▲80	▼200	1,200
80 Jim Hegan	10	15	25	40	50	80	150	1,200
81 Joe Black SP	10	15	25	50	100	200	600	
82 Mickey Mantle	▲2,000	▲2,500	3,000	5,000	▲10,000	12,000	30,000	
83 Howie Pollet	6	10	15	30	40	100	500	
84 Bob Hooper DP	5	6	10	15	30	50	150	1,000
85 Bobby Morgan DP	6	10	15	25	50	120		
86 Billy Martin	40	60	80	120	200	300	1,000	4,000
87 Ed Lopat	8	12	20	50	60	150	400	
88 Willie Jones DP	5	6	10	15	50	150	1,200	
89 Chuck Stobbs DP	5	6	10	20	30	50	150	
90 Hank Edwards DP	5	6	10	25	60	150		
91 Ebba St.Claire DP	5	6	10	15	25	80	400	1,200
92 Paul Minner DP	5	6	10	30	40	100	300	
93 Hal Rice DP	8	12	20	30	60	120		
94 Bill Kennedy DP	5	6	10	15	25	▲60	200	1,200
95 Willard Marshall DP	6	10	15	25	40	▼60	250	
96 Virgil Trucks	6	10	15	40	50	100	800	
97 Don Kolloway DP	5	8	12	20	40	60	200	
98 Cal Abrams DP	5	6	▲20	▲25	30	▼50	250	1,200
99 Dave Madison	6	10	15	30	▼40	▼60	200	
100 Bill Miller	6	10	25	30	50	200	600	
101 Ted Wilks	6	10	15	25	50	200	1,200	
102 Connie Ryan DP	6	10	15	30	40	250	600	
103 Joe Astroth DP	5	8	12	25	40	60	200	1,200
104 Yogi Berra	60	100	120	250	400	600	2,000	12,000
105 Joe Nuxhall DP	10	20	30	50	150	500		
106 Johnny Antonelli	6	10	15	40	60	▲100	250	
107 Danny O'Connell DP	5	6	10	15	30	80	400	
108 Bob Porterfield DP	5	6	15	25	30	50	120	1,400
109 Alvin Dark	8	12	30	40	60	▼120	600	
110 Herman Wehmeier DP	5	6	10	15	30	50	150	1,200
111 Hank Sauer DP	6	10	15	25	▼40	100	150	1,800
112 Ned Garver DP	5	6	10	20	30	80	250	
113 Jerry Priddy	5	8	12	20	60	100	400	
114 Phil Rizzuto	50	60	100	120	250	400	1,000	
115 George Spencer	5	8	25	30	50	60	250	
116 Frank Smith DP	5	6	10	15	30	60	250	
117 Sid Gordon DP	5	6	10	15	▲30	80	300	
118 Gus Bell DP	5	8	12	25	40	▼100	200	1,200
119 Johnny Sain SP	10	15	25	50	100	150	600	
120 Davey Williams	8	12	20	25	50	60	500	
121 Walt Dropo	6	10	15	40	50	150	300	
122 Elmer Valo	8	12	20	30	50	80	250	
123 Tommy Byrne DP	6	10	15	25	▼30	▼60	150	1,200
124 Sibby Sisti DP	5	6	10	15	30	60	200	
125 Dick Williams DP	12	20	25	30	60	150	500	
126 Bill Connelly DP RC	5	6	10	25	30	50	300	
127 Clint Courtney DP RC	5	6	10	25	40	60	150	
128 Wilmer Mizell DP	5	6	10	30	50	100	400	

#	Player	GD 2	VG 3	VgEx 4	EX 5	ExMt 6	NM 7	NmMt 8	MT 9
129	Keith Thomas RC	5	8	12	20	50	80	300	
130	Turk Lown DP	8	12	20	30	50	150	800	
131	Harry Byrd DP RC	6	8	12	20	40	50	120	
132	Tom Morgan	8	12	25	40	60	200	600	
133	Gil Coan	5	8	12	20	40	80	200	
134	Rube Walker	8	12	20	40	60	100	800	
135	Al Rosen DP	6	10	15	30	60	120	500	
136	Ken Heintzelman DP	5	6	10	25	50	100	150	
137	John Rutherford DP	8	12	25	30	40	▼60	400	
138	George Kell	12	20	40	50	80	150	▲400	
139	Sammy White	5	8	12	20	50	80	200	
140	Tommy Glaviano	5	8	25	30	40	150		
141	Allie Reynolds DP	10	25	30	50	▼60	▼150		
142	Vic Wertz	8	12	20	▼30	▼40	80	500	
143	Billy Pierce	8	12	20	40	60	150	500	
144	Bob Schultz DP	5	6	10	25	40	60	250	
145	Harry Dorish DP	5	8	12	25	30	50	150	
146	Granville Hamner	6	10	15	30	60	150		
147	Warren Spahn	40	60	100	150	200	▼400	1,200	
148	Mickey Grasso	5	8	12	20	40	100	200	
149	Dom DiMaggio DP	12	20	40	50	60	150	400	
150	Harry Simpson DP	5	8	12	20	▼30	60	200	
151	Hoyt Wilhelm	15	25	▼40	▼50	100	250	500	
152	Bob Adams DP	5	6	10	25	30	▼60	400	
153	Andy Seminick DP	6	10	15	25	40	80	300	
154	Dick Groat	12	20	30	50	100	600		
155	Dutch Leonard	6	10	15	▲30	▼40	100	250	
156	Jim Rivera DP RC	5	6	12	20	▼25	50	▲120	1,200
157	Bob Addis DP	6	10	15	30	40	100		
158	Johnny Logan RC	6	10	15	25	▲50	100	400	1,200
159	Wayne Terwilliger DP	6	10	15	30	40	200	600	
160	Bob Young	5	8	12	20	40	80	150	1,200
161	Vern Bickford DP	5	6	10	30	50	150	300	
162	Ted Kluszewski	10	15	40	80	100	▲200	400	
163	Fred Hatfield DP	5	6	10	15	30	▼60	300	1,500
164	Frank Shea DP	5	6	15	25	50	120		
165	Billy Hoeft	5	8	12	40	50	200	400	
166	Billy Hunter RC	5	6	10	25	▲40	50	▲200	
167	Art Schult RC	5	6	10	▼25	▼40	▼60	200	1,200
168	Willard Schmidt RC	6	10	15	25	40	60	120	
169	Dizzy Trout	5	6	10	25	40	▼60	250	1,200
170	Bill Werle	6	10	15	25	30	50	200	1,200
171	Bill Glynn RC	5	6	10	25	30	▼50	200	
172	Rip Repulski RC	5	6	10	15	50	100	800	
173	Preston Ward	8	12	20	25	30	60	120	1,200
174	Billy Loes	6	10	25	30	40	60	400	
175	Ron Kline RC	6	10	15	25	50	100		
176	Don Hoak RC	6	10	15	30	40	60	200	1,800
177	Jim Dyck RC	5	6	10	20	25	40	100	
178	Jim Waugh RC	5	6	10	25	30	60	200	1,500
179	Gene Hermanski	5	6	10	30	50	▼60	250	
180	Virgil Stallcup	5	8	12	25	30	60	▼150	1,200
181	Al Zarilla	5	6	10	15	30	▼50	250	1,200
182	Bobby Hofman	5	6	10	20	30	50	120	
183	Stu Miller RC	5	6	15	25	30	80	300	
184	Hal Brown RC	6	10	15	25	40	60	250	1,200
185	Jim Pendleton RC	6	10	15	25	30	50	120	
186	Charlie Bishop RC	5	6	10	15	30	50	200	1,200
187	Jim Fridley	5	6	15	25	30	50	200	1,200
188	Andy Carey RC	8	12	20	40	60	100	400	
189	Ray Jablonski RC	5	6	10	25	40	60	150	1,200
190	Dixie Walker CO	5	6	10	25	40	60	200	
191	Ralph Kiner	20	30	▼40	▼50	120	250	500	
192	Wally Westlake	5	6	15	20	▲30	80	200	1,200
193	Mike Clark RC	6	10	15	25	30	50	200	
194	Eddie Kazak	6	10	15	25	40	50	150	
195	Ed McGhee RC	5	6	10	15	25	50	150	
196	Bob Keegan RC	5	6	10	20	25	▼50	150	1,200
197	Del Crandall	5	6	10	25	40	▼60	200	
198	Forrest Main	6	10	15	25	30	50	150	
199	Marion Fricano RC	5	8	12	20	25	50	200	
200	Gordon Goldsberry	5	8	12	20	40	60	150	1,200
201	Paul LaPalme	6	10	15	25	40	50	300	
202	Carl Sawatski RC	5	8	12	▲30	40	50	200	1,200
203	Cliff Fannin	5	6	10	30	40	60	250	
204	Dick Bokelman RC	5	6	10	15	30	50	150	2,000
205	Vern Benson RC	6	10	15	25	▼30	60	250	

#	Player	GD 2	VG 3	VgEx 4	EX 5	ExMt 6	NM 7	NmMt 8	MT 9
206	Ed Bailey RC	5	6	10	15	▲40	60	200	
207	Whitey Ford	50	60	100	120	250	▼400	800	4,000
208	Jim Wilson	5	6	10	20	25	60	120	1,200
209	Jim Greengrass RC	5	6	10	20	30	60	200	1,200
210	Bob Cerv RC	10	15	25	40	60	150	600	
211	J.W. Porter RC	8	12	20	25	30	▼50	150	150
212	Jack Dittmer RC	6	10	15	25	▼30	60		
213	Ray Scarborough	6	10	15	30	50	100	400	
214	Bill Bruton RC	5	6	10	25	30	60	150	
215	Gene Conley RC	6	10	15	25	50	80	400	
216	Jim Hughes RC	8	12	20	30	40	80	300	
217	Murray Wall RC	6	10	15	25	50	60	250	
218	Les Fusselman	5	6	20	25	50	120	200	
219	Pete Runnels	5	8	12	30	30	60	200	
220	Satchel Paige	250	400	500	600	1,000	2,000	5,000	12,000
221	Bob Milliken RC	8	12	20	60	80	200	500	
222	Vic Janowicz DP RC	15	25	50	60	80	250		
223	Johnny O'Brien DP RC	6	10	15	40	50	100	300	
224	Lou Sleater DP	6	10	25	30	80	100	400	
225	Bobby Shantz	12	20	30	60	120	150	400	
226	Ed Erautt	8	12	20	50	60	100	400	
227	Morris Martin	8	12	20	50	60	150	400	
228	Hal Newhouser	30	50	60	100	150	400	800	
229	Rocky Krsnich RC	8	12	20	50	80	200	500	
230	Johnny Lindell DP	10	15	25	50	60	100	500	1,200
231	Solly Hemus DP	6	10	15	30	60	100	500	
232	Dick Kokos	10	15	30	60	100	150	400	
233	Al Aber RC	8	12	20	30	80	250	600	
234	Ray Murray DP	6	10	25	40	50	100	250	1,200
235	John Hetki DP RC	6	10	15	40	50	150	400	
236	Harry Perkowski DP	8	12	20	50	80	150	800	
237	Clarence Podbielan DP	6	10	15	40	60	120	500	
238	Cal Hogue DP RC	10	15	25	50	80	150	500	
239	Jim Delsing	8	12	20	▼50	▼60	120	400	
240	Freddie Marsh	10	15	25	50	80	250	500	
241	Al Sima DP	6	10	25	30	40	80	200	2,000
242	Charlie Silvera	10	30	40	50	60	200	500	
243	Carlos Bernier DP RC	10	15	30	50	60	▲120	500	
244	Willie Mays	▲800	1,000	▲1,500	2,500	▲4,000	▲6,000		
245	Bill Norman CO	10	15	25	50	100	200		
246	Roy Face DP RC	10	15	50	100	120	250	800	
247	Mike Sandlock DP RC	8	20	25	30	50	100	300	
248	Gene Stephens DP RC	6	10	15	30	60	100	250	
249	Eddie O'Brien RC	8	12	25	40	80	120	250	1,200
250	Bob Wilson RC	8	12	20	40	80	250	600	
251	Sid Hudson	12	20	80	60	200	250		
252	Henry Foiles RC	10	15	25	60	80	200	600	
254	Preacher Roe DP	10	15	50	60	100	300	500	
255	Dixie Howell	20	30	50	100	120	200	800	
256	Les Peden RC	10	15	25	50	80	200	500	
257	Bob Boyd RC	15	25	40	100	120	200	400	
258	Jim Gilliam RC	100	120	150	250	400	600	2,500	
259	Roy McMillan DP	6	10	30	40	60	▲200		
260	Sam Calderone RC	12	20	30	50	100	300		
262	Bob Oldis RC	8	12	20	60	80	300	600	
263	Johnny Podres RC	60	100	120	250	400	1,000	2,000	
264	Gene Woodling DP	10	15	30	60	80	200	600	
265	Jackie Jensen	12	20	50	80	100	250	500	
266	Bob Cain	8	12	20	50	80	200	600	
269	Duane Pillette	12	20	40	50	100	250	500	
270	Vern Stephens	10	15	30	80	100	150	400	
272	Bill Antonello RC	10	15	40	50	▼80	300	500	
273	Harvey Haddix RC	20	50	100	120	250	500		
274	John Riddle CO	10	15	25	100	150	500		
276	Ken Raffensberger	15	25	50	60	150	300	800	
277	Don Lund RC	8	12	20	50	60	120	150	500
278	Willie Miranda RC	15	25	50	120	200	▼600		
279	Joe Coleman DP	10	15	25	40	60	120	400	
280	Milt Bolling RC	40	80	120	200	300			

—Bob Addis #157 PSA 8 (NmMt) sold for $1,601 (Goodwin; 12/05)
—Bob Addis #157 PSA 8 (NmMt) sold for $578 (eBay; 3/07)
—Milt Bolling #274 PSA 8 (NmMt) sold for $2,768 (Memory Lane; 12/07)
—Milt Bolling #274 SGC 88 (NmMt) sold for $1,793 (Heritage; 5/08)
—Milt Bolling #274 SGC 88 (NmMt) sold for $1,325 (eBay; 5/07)
—Milt Bolling #274 PSA 7 (NM) sold for $925 (eBay; 11/07)

Milt Bolling #274 PSA 7 (NM) sold for $699 (eBay; 4/08)
Milt Bolling #274 PSA 7 (NM) sold for $580 (eBay; 4/08)
Sam Calderone #260 PSA 8 (NmMt) sold for $2,213 (eBay; 12/06)
Sam Calderone #260 PSA 8 (NmMt) sold for $1,737 (Memory Lane; 9/07)
Sam Calderone #260 PSA 8 (NmMt) sold for $1,593 (eBay; 10/06)
Roy Campanella #27 PSA 10 (Gem) sold for $9,746 (Mastro; 4/03)
Joe Collins #9 PSA 8 (NmMt) sold for $1,683 (Memory Lane; 12/07)
Joe Collins #9 PSA 8 (NmMt) sold for $811 (eBay; 8/06)
Dom DiMaggio #149 PSA 9 (MT) sold for $3,897 (Mile High; 6/06)
Whitey Ford #207 GAI 9.5 (Gem) sold for $7,208 (Memory Lane; 10/05)
Jim Gilliam #258 PSA 9 (MT) sold for $8,384 (Memory Lane; 9/07)
Tommy Glaviano #140 PSA 8 (NmMt) sold for $1,427 (eBay; 6/06)
Tommy Glaviano #140 PSA 8 (NmMt) sold for $1,149 (Memory Lane; 9/07)
Tommy Glaviano #140 PSA 8 (NmMt) sold for $632 (Mile High; 2/08)
Dick Groat #154 PSA 8 (NmMt) sold for $1,754 (Superior; 3/04)
Dick Groat #154 PSA 8 (NmMt) sold for $1,411 (Goodwin; 10/04)
Dick Groat #154 PSA 8 (NmMt) sold for $942 (Goodwin; 10/05)
Harvey Haddix #273 PSA 8 (NmMt) sold for $1,141 (eBay; 7/06)
Harvey Haddix #273 PSA 8 (NmMt) sold for $981 (Memory Lane; 9/07)
Granville Hamner #146 PSA 8 (NmMt) sold for $635 (Madec; 5/07)
Sid Hudson #251 PSA 8 (NmMt) sold for $1,737 (Memory Lane; 12/07)
Sid Hudson #251 PSA 8 (NmMt) sold for $689 (eBay; 5/07)
Sid Hudson #251 PSA 8 (NmMt) sold for $557 (eBay; 12/07)
Vic Janowicz #222 PSA 8 (NmMt) sold for $1,914 (eBay; 11/06)
George Kell #138 PSA 9 (MT) sold for $3,884 (Memory Lane; 11/05)
Ellis Kinder #44 PSA 8 (NmMt) sold for $1,119 (Goodwin; 10/05)
Ellis Kinder #44 PSA 8 (NmMt) sold for $877 (eBay; 12/06)
Johnny Klippstein #46 PSA 8 (NmMt) sold for $912 (eBay; 11/06)
Ted Kluszewski #162 PSA 9 (MT) sold for $2,954 (Memory Lane; 4/07)
Mickey Mantle #82 PSA 9 (MT) sold for $80,000 (Memory Lane; Private Sale - 2007)
Mickey Mantle #82 SGC 96 (MT) sold for $18,997 (Mastro; 4/04)
Mickey Mantle #82 SGC 92 (NmMt+) sold for $28,800 (Mastro; 8/08)
Mickey Mantle #82 SGC 92 (NmMt+) sold for $16,450 (REA; 4/07)
Mickey Mantle #82 SGC 92 (NmMt+) sold for $15,535 (Heritage; 5/08)
Mickey Mantle #82 PSA 8.5 (NmMt+) sold for $23,640 (Greg Bussineau; 7/12)
Mickey Mantle #82 GAI 8.5 (NmMt+) sold for $11,936 (Memory Lane; 11/04)
Mickey Mantle #82 SGC 84 (NM) sold for $2,125 (eBay; 4/07)
Eddie Mathews #37 GAI 9 (MT) sold for $1,392 (Memory Lane; 8/06)
Willie Mays #244 PSA 9 (MT) sold for $135,000 (Memory Lane; Private Sale - 2007)
Willie Mays #244 SGC 96 (MT) sold for $31,342 (Mastro; 4/04)
Willie Mays #244 GAI 9 (MT) sold for $22,370 (Madec; 5/06)
Willie Mays #244 GAI 9 (MT) sold for $20,169 (Mile High; 6/05)
Willie Mays #244 GAI 9 (MT) sold for $13,375 (Mastro; 4/07)
Willie Mays #244 GAI 8.5 (NmMt+) sold for $8,418 (Memory Lane; 3/06)
Willie Mays #244 GAI 8.5 (NmMt+) sold for $6,868 (Memory Lane; 5/08)
Willie Mays #244 PSA 8 (NmMt) sold for $17,915 (SCP; 7/08)
Willie Mays #244 SGC 88 (NmMt) sold for $13,045 (Mastro; 12/06)
Willie Mays #244 PSA 8 (NmMt) sold for $8,935 (Mile High; 2/08)
Willie Mays #244 PSA 8 (NmMt) sold for $8,388 (Mile High; 2/08)
Willie Mays #244 PSA 8 (NmMt) sold for $8,050 (eBay; 11/06)
Willie Mays #244 GAI 8 (NmMt) sold for $4,915 (Mastro; 4/07)
Gil McDougald #43 PSA 8 (NmMt) sold for $1,992 (Memory Lane; 8/06)
Roy McMillan #259 PSA 8 (NmMt) sold for $1,227 (Goodwin; 6/06)
Roy McMillan #259 PSA 8 (NmMt) sold for $891 (Memory Lane; 4/07)
Roy McMillan #259 PSA 8 (NmMt) sold for $447 (eBay; 5/07)
Roy McMillan #259 PSA 8 (NmMt) sold for $371 (eBay; 1/07)
Willie Miranda #278 PSA 8 (NmMt) sold for $3,653 (eBay; 9/07)
Bobby Morgan #85 PSA 8 (NmMt) sold for $1,009 (eBay; 10/04)
Bill Norman #245 PSA 8 (NmMt) sold for $2,310 (Goodwin; 6/06)
Bill Norman #245 PSA 8 (NmMt) sold for $1,413 (eBay; 7/06)
Bill Norman #245 PSA 8 (NmMt) sold for $929 (Memory Lane; 8/06)
Bill Norman #245 PSA 8 (NmMt) sold for $465 (eBay; 8/07)
Joe Nuxhall #105 PSA 8 (NmMt) sold for $1,613 (eBay; 12/06)
Joe Nuxhall #105 PSA 8 (NmMt) sold for $1,149 (Memory Lane; 4/07)
Satchel Paige #220 GAI 9.5 (Gem) sold for $15,990 (Memory Lane; 10/05)
Johnny Podres #263 PSA 9 (MT) sold for $4,915 (Mastro; 12/06)
Johnny Podres #263 GAI 8 (NmMt) sold for $949 (Memory Lane; 8/06)
Allie Reynolds #141 PSA 8 (NmMt) sold for $864 (Memory Lane; 9/07)
Allie Reynolds #141 PSA 8 (NmMt) sold for $848 (Mile High; 6/06)
Allie Reynolds #141 PSA 8 (NmMt) sold for $420 (eBay; 11/03)
Hal Rice #93 PSA 9 (MT) sold for $3,646 (Memroy Lane; 8/06)
Hal Rice #93 PSA 8 (NmMt) sold for $1,264 (Memory Lane; 4/07)
Hal Rice #93 PSA 8 (NmMt) sold for $669 (Goodwin; 6/06)
Hal Rice #93 PSA 8 (NmMt) sold for $590 (Memory Lane; 9/07)
Hal Rice #93 PSA 8 (NmMt) sold for $344 (eBay; 1/08)

John Riddle #274 PSA 8 (NmMt) sold for $1,009 (Goodwin; 10/05)
John Riddle #274 PSA 8 (NmMt) sold for $566 (eBay; 5/07)
Phil Rizzuto #114 GAI 9 (MT) sold for $2,040 (Mastro; 12/03)
Jackie Robinson #1 GAI 8.5 (NmMt+) sold for $6,087 (Memory Lane; 12/07)
Jackie Robinson #1 GAI 8 (NmMt) sold for $1,517 (Mastro; 12/06)
Frank Shea #164 PSA 8 (NmMt) sold for $710 (eBay; 5/07)
Early Wynn #61 PSA 9 (MT) sold for $2,520 (Mastro; 5/08)

1954 Bowman

#	Name	GD 2	VG 3	VgEx 4	EX 5	ExMt 6	NM 7	NmMt 8	MT 9
1	Phil Rizzuto	30	40	50	80	120	250	800	
2	Jackie Jensen	5	6	10	15	25	60	300	
3	Marion Fricano	5	5	5	6	10	20	120	
4	Bob Hooper	5	5	5	6	10	15	60	300
5	Billy Hunter	5	5	5	6	10	15	50	
6	Nellie Fox	10	20	25	40	60	100	300	
7	Walter Dropo	5	5	6	10	15	40	80	
8	Jim Busby	5	5	5	6	10	25	80	
9	Dave Williams	5	5	5	6	10	30	60	
10	Carl Erskine	5	5	8	25	30	50	120	
11	Sid Gordon	5	5	5	6	10	20	50	350
12A	Roy McMillan 551/1290 At Bat	5	5	5	6	10	15	50	250
12B	Roy McMillan 557/1296 At Bat	5	5	6	10	15	25	150	
13	Paul Minner	5	5	5	6	10	20	50	300
14	Gerry Staley	5	5	5	6	10	25	50	
15	Richie Ashburn	6	15	20	50	60	80	200	
16	Jim Wilson	5	5	5	6	10	25	80	
17	Tom Gorman	5	5	5	6	10	25	50	350
18	Hoot Evers	5	5	5	6	10	30	80	300
19	Bobby Shantz	5	5	5	6	10	20	50	
20	Art Houtteman	5	5	5	6	10	25	50	300
21	Vic Wertz	5	5	5	6	10	25	60	
22A	Sam Mele 213/1661 Putouts	5	5	5	6	10	15	50	350
22B	Sam Mele 217/1665 Putouts	5	5	6	10	15	25	200	
23	Harvey Kuenn RC	5	5	8	12	20	40	100	500
24	Bob Porterfield	5	5	5	6	10	25	50	
25A	Wes Westrum 1.000/.987	5	5	6	10	15	30		
25B	Wes Westrum .982/.986	5	5	8	12	20	40		
26A	Billy Cox 1.000/.960	5	5	6	10	15	30	150	
26B	Billy Cox .972/.960	5	5	8	12	20	40	150	
27	Dick Cole RC	5	5	5	6	10	30	60	250
28A	Jim Greengrass Addison, NJ	5	5	5	6	10	15	50	250
28B	Jim Greengrass Addison, NY	5	5	5	6	10	15	50	
29	Johnny Klippstein	5	5	5	8	15	20	50	350
30	Del Rice	5	5	5	6	10	25	30	300
31	Smoky Burgess	5	5	5	6	15	30	50	300
32	Del Crandall	5	5	5	8	12	20	60	300
33A	Vic Raschi No Trade	5	5	8	12	20	50	150	
33B	Vic Raschi Traded to St.Louis	5	6	10	15	25	80	600	
34	Sammy White	5	5	5	6	10	25	50	400
35A	Eddie Joost Quiz Answer is 8	5	5	5	6	10	15	50	300
35B	Eddie Joost Quiz Answer is 33	5	5	6	10	15	25		
36	George Strickland	5	5	5	6	15	25	50	250
37	Dick Kokos	5	5	5	6	10	20	50	250
38A	Minnie Minoso .895/.961	5	5	8	12	20	30	80	500
38B	Minnie Minoso .963/.963	5	6	10	15	25	40	250	
39	Ned Garver	5	5	5	6	10	20	50	300
40	Gil Coan	5	5	5	6	10	25	50	
41A	Alvin Dark .986/960	5	5	5	6	10	25	80	400
41B	Alvin Dark .968/.960	5	5	6	10	15	30		
42	Billy Loes	5	5	5	6	10	30	80	400
43A	Bob Friend 20 Shutouts in Quiz	5	5	5	6	10	25	80	
43B	Bob Friend 16 Shutouts in Quiz	5	5	6	10	15	40	120	
44	Harry Perkowski	5	5	5	6	10	25	50	300
45	Ralph Kiner	5	8	25	30	40	80	150	
46	Rip Repulski	5	5	5	6	20	25	50	300
47A	Granny Hamner .970/.953	5	5	5	6	10	15	60	300
47B	Granny Hamner .953/.951	5	5	8	12	20	30	120	
48	Jack Dittmer	5	5	5	6	10	25	80	
49	Harry Byrd	5	5	5	6	20	25	60	
50	George Kell	5	5	15	25	40	50	150	400
51	Alex Kellner	5	5	5	6	10	25	60	300
52	Joe Ginsberg	5	5	5	6	10	20	50	350
53A	Don Lenhardt .969/.984	5	5	5	6	10	15	50	300
53B	Don Lenhardt .966/.983	5	5	5	6	10	25	60	
54	Chico Carrasquel	5	5	5	6	10	25	50	300

#	Player	GD 2	VG 3	VgEx 4	EX 5	ExMt 6	NM 7	NmMt 8	MT 9
55	Jim Delsing	5	5	5	6	12	25	50	250
56	Maurice McDermott	5	5	5	6	10	20	50	
57	Hoyt Wilhelm	5	6	10	25	40	60	120	500
58	Pee Wee Reese	15	30	50	60	100	150	250	1,500
59	Bob Schultz	5	5	5	6	10	25	50	300
60	Fred Baczewski RC	5	5	5	6	15	25	50	250
61A	Eddie Miksis .954/.962	5	5	5	6	10	15	50	300
61B	Eddie Miksis .954/.961	5	5	6	10	15	25	120	
62	Enos Slaughter	5	8	20	30	40	60	120	600
63	Earl Torgeson	5	5	5	6	10	15	50	250
64	Eddie Mathews	10	25	40	50	80	200	400	1,500
65	Mickey Mantle	▲500	▲600	▲1,000	▲1,200	▲2,500	3,000	8,000	25,000
66A	Ted Williams	600	1,000	▲1,500	2,000	2,500	4,000	8,000	
66B	Jimmy Piersall	6	10	15	25	60	100	250	
67A	Carl Scheib .306 Pct. Two Lines	5	5	5	8	12	40	200	
67B	Carl Scheib .306 Pct. One Line	5	5	6	10	15	60	300	
67C	Carl Scheib .300 Pct.	5	5	5	8	15	50	200	
68	Bobby Avila	5	5	5	8	12	30	80	
69	Clint Courtney	5	5	5	6	10	15	50	300
70	Willard Marshall	5	5	5	6	10	20	50	250
71	Ted Gray	5	5	5	6	15	30	50	300
72	Eddie Yost	5	5	5	6	10	30	50	300
73	Don Mueller	5	5	5	6	10	20	50	300
74	Jim Gilliam	5	6	10	20	25	60	120	500
75	Max Surkont	5	5	5	6	10	20	50	
76	Joe Nuxhall	5	5	5	8	12	40	60	250
77	Bob Rush	5	5	5	6	10	25	50	300
78	Sal Yvars	5	5	5	6	10	25	50	300
79	Curt Simmons	5	5	5	6	10	25	50	
80A	Johnny Logan 106 Runs	5	5	5	6	10	25	60	
80B	Johnny Logan 100 Runs	5	5	6	10	15	25	150	
81A	Jerry Coleman 1.000/.975	5	5	8	12	20	40	500	
81B	Jerry Coleman .952/.975	5	6	10	15	25	60	500	
82A	Bill Goodman .965/.986	5	5	6	10	15	30	80	400
82B	Bill Goodman .972/.985	5	5	8	12	20	40	120	
83	Ray Murray	5	5	5	6	10	30	50	300
84	Larry Doby	5	8	25	40	50	80	▼200	600
85A	Jim Dyck .926/.956	5	5	5	6	10	15	60	
85B	Jim Dyck .947/.960	5	5	5	6	10	15	25	100
86	Harry Dorish	5	5	5	6	10	25	50	300
87	Don Lund	5	5	5	6	10	20	50	300
88	Tom Umphlett RC	5	5	5	6	10	15	50	
89	Willie Mays	▲150	200	250	▼300	600	▲1,500	3,000	4,000
90	Roy Campanella	15	40	50	▲80	▲120	200	600	800
91	Cal Abrams	5	5	5	6	10	25	50	300
92	Ken Raffensberger	5	5	5	6	10	15	50	300
93A	Bill Serena .983/.966	5	5	5	6	10	15	60	300
93B	Bill Serena .977/.966	5	5	6	10	15	25	120	
94A	Solly Hemus 476/1343	5	5	5	6	10	15	50	300
94B	Solly Hemus 477/1343	5	5	6	10	15	25	150	
95	Robin Roberts	5	8	20	30	▲50	80	120	600
96	Joe Adcock	5	5	8	12	20	30	100	
97	Gil McDougald	5	6	10	15	25	40	120	500
98	Ellis Kinder	5	5	5	6	20	25	60	400
99A	Peter Suder .985/.974	5	5	5	6	10	15	50	300
99B	Peter Suder .978/.974	5	5	6	10	15	40	200	
100	Mike Garcia	5	5	5	6	20	25	50	
101	Don Larsen RC	6	20	25	30	50	60	▼200	600
102	Billy Pierce	5	5	5	8	20	40	60	300
103A	Stephen Souchock 144/1192	5	5	5	6	10	15	50	250
103B	Stephen Souchock 147/1195	5	5	6	10	15	25	120	
104	Frank Shea	5	5	5	6	10	25	50	300
105A	Sal Maglie Quiz Answer is 8	5	5	5	8	12	25	150	
105B	Sal Maglie Quiz Answer is 1904	5	5	8	12	20	30		
106	Clem Labine	5	5	8	12	20	30	80	400
107	Paul LaPalme	5	5	5	6	10	25	50	300
108	Bobby Adams	5	5	5	6	10	20	50	300
109	Roy Smalley	5	5	5	6	15	30	50	300
110	Red Schoendienst	5	6	15	25	30	50	100	
111	Murry Dickson	5	5	5	6	20	25	50	
112	Andy Pafko	5	5	5	6	20	30	60	
113	Allie Reynolds	5	8	15	25	30	50	120	600
114	Willard Nixon	5	5	5	6	10	15	50	300
115	Don Bollweg	5	5	5	6	10	25	50	250
116	Luke Easter	5	5	5	8	12	30	100	
117	Dick Kryhoski	5	5	5	6	25	30	50	350
118	Bob Boyd	5	5	5	6	10	15	50	350

#	Player	GD 2	VG 3	VgEx 4	EX 5	ExMt 6	NM 7	NmMt 8	MT
119	Fred Hatfield	5	5	5	6	10	15	40	35
120	Mel Hoderlein RC	5	5	5	6	10	20	50	20
121	Ray Katt RC	5	5	5	6	10	60		
122	Carl Furillo	5	6	20	25	30	50	150	60
123	Toby Atwell	5	5	5	6	10	15	50	35
124A	Gus Bell 15/27 Errors	5	5	5	6	10	15	50	45
124B	Gus Bell 11/26 Errors	5	6	10	15	25	120		
125	Warren Hacker	5	5	5	6	10	15	50	25
126	Cliff Chambers	5	5	5	6	10	25	50	40
127	Del Ennis	5	5	5	6	20	25	50	
128	Ebba St.Claire	5	5	5	6	10	30	50	35
129	Hank Bauer	5	6	10	40	50	100	1,200	
130	Milt Bolling	5	5	5	10	12	40	150	
131	Joe Astroth	5	5	5	6	10	25	200	
132	Bob Feller	10	15	50	60	100	200	600	
133	Duane Pillette	5	5	5	6	10	15	50	
134	Luis Aloma	5	5	5	6	10	25	60	
135	Johnny Pesky	5	5	5	8	12	30	80	
136	Clyde Vollmer	5	5	5	6	10	15	60	30
137	Al Corwin	5	5	5	6	10	80		
138A	Gil Hodges .993/.991	10	15	25	40	60	100	600	
138B	Gil Hodges .992/.991	10	15	25	40	60	100	600	
139A	Preston Ward .961/.992	5	5	5	6	10	40	300	
139B	Preston Ward .990/.992	5	5	6	10	15	60		
140A	Saul Rogovin 7-12 W-L 2 K's	5	8	12	20	30	80		
140B	Saul Rogovin 7-12 W-L 62 K's	5	8	12	20	30			
140C	Saul Rogovin 8-12 W-L	5	8	12	20	30	80	150	
141	Joe Garagiola	5	6	10	25	40	60	150	
142	Al Brazle	5	5	5	6	10	20	60	
143	Willie Jones	5	5	5	6	10	40	150	35
144	Ernie Johnson RC	5	5	8	12	20	30	250	
145A	Billy Martin .985/.983	10	15	25	40	60	100	400	
145B	Billy Martin .983/.982	10	15	25	40	60	120	400	
146	Dick Gernert	5	5	5	6	10	25	60	30
147	Joe DeMaestri	5	5	5	6	10	25	80	
148	Dale Mitchell	5	5	6	10	15	30	100	
149	Bob Young	5	5	5	6	10	25	200	
150	Cass Michaels	5	5	5	6	10	25	120	
151	Pat Mullin	5	5	5	6	10	25	150	
152	Mickey Vernon	5	6	10	15	25	100		
153A	Whitey Lockman 100/331	5	6	10	15	25			
153B	Whitey Lockman 102/333	5	8	12	20	30			
154	Don Newcombe	5	6	10	15	50	150	500	
155	Frank Thomas RC	5	5	6	10	15	40	120	
156A	Rocky Bridges 320/467	5	5	5	6	10	40	150	
156B	Rocky Bridges 328/475	5	5	6	10	15	40	300	
157	Omar Lown	5	5	5	6	10	40	250	
158	Stu Miller	5	5	5	6	10	30	400	
159	John Lindell	5	5	5	6	10	50	450	
160	Danny O'Connell	5	5	5	6	15	150		
161	Yogi Berra	40	60	80	100	200	250	500	1,400
162	Ted Lepcio	5	5	5	6	20	25	60	300
163A	Dave Philley No Trade 152 Games	5	5	6	10	15	40	120	
163B	Dave Philley Traded 152 Games	5	5	8	12	20	50	150	
163C	Dave Philley Traded 157 Games	5	6	10	15	25	50	150	
164	Early Wynn	5	8	20	25	40	60	150	
165	Johnny Groth	5	5	5	6	10	30	50	250
166	Sandy Consuegra	5	5	5	6	10	15	50	
167	Billy Hoeft	5	5	5	6	10	25	60	350
168	Ed Fitzgerald	5	5	5	6	10	25	60	
169	Larry Jansen	5	5	5	6	10	25	60	350
170	Duke Snider	25	▲50	▲80	▲100	150	200	400	1,000
171	Carlos Bernier	5	5	5	6	10	25	50	250
172	Andy Seminick	5	5	5	6	10	20	50	250
173	Dee Fondy	5	5	5	6	10	25	50	300
174A	Pete Castiglione .966/.959	5	5	5	6	10	15	60	300
174B	Pete Castiglione .970/.959	5	5	5	8	12	25	80	
175	Mel Clark	5	5	5	6	10	20	60	350
176	Vern Bickford	5	5	5	6	10	25	80	350
177	Whitey Ford	▲30	40	▲60	80	100	▲200	400	2,000
178	Del Wilber	5	5	5	6	10	15	50	
179A	Morris Martin 44 ERA	5	5	5	6	10	15	50	
179B	Morris Martin 4.44 ERA	5	5	5	8	12	25	80	
180	Joe Tipton	5	5	5	6	10	25	50	250
181	Les Moss	5	5	5	6	10	25	50	350
182	Sherm Lollar	5	5	5	12	15	25	50	
183	Matt Batts	5	5	5	6	10	25	50	300

		GD 2	VG 3	VgEx 4	EX 5	ExMt 6	NM 7	NmMt 8	MT 9
4	Mickey Grasso	5	5	5	6	20	25	60	
5A	Daryl Spencer .941/.944 RC	5	5	5	6	10	15	50	300
5B	Daryl Spencer .933/.936	5	5	6	10	15	25		
6	Russ Meyer	5	5	8	12	20	30	80	
7	Vern Law	5	5	5	8	25	30	80	
8	Frank Smith	5	5	5	6	15	20	50	350
9	Randy Jackson	5	5	5	6	10	25	50	350
0	Joe Presko	5	5	5	6	10	25	50	350
1	Karl Drews	5	5	5	6	10	25	50	250
2	Lew Burdette	5	5	8	12	20	30	120	500
3	Eddie Robinson	5	6	10	15	25	120	200	
4	Sid Hudson	5	5	5	6	20	30	100	
5	Bob Cain	5	5	5	6	20	25	50	250
6	Bob Lemon	5	8	20	25	30	60	100	500
7	Lou Kretlow	5	5	5	6	10	25	50	250
8	Virgil Trucks	5	5	5	6	20	25	40	300
9	Steve Gromek	5	5	5	6	10	30	60	250
0	Conrado Marrero	5	5	5	6	10	25	60	300
1	Bob Thomson	5	5	8	12	20	40	175	
2	George Shuba	5	5	6	10	15	40	120	
3	Vic Janowicz	5	5	5	8	12	30	100	
4	Jack Collum RC	5	5	5	6	10	15	60	300
5	Hal Jeffcoat	5	5	5	6	10	30	50	
6	Steve Bilko	5	5	5	6	20	25	60	250
7	Stan Lopata	5	5	5	6	10	25	50	250
8	Johnny Antonelli	5	5	5	6	10	15	60	300
9	Gene Woodling	5	6	10	15	25	60	200	
10	Jimmy Piersall	5	6	10	25	40	60	120	
11	Al Robertson RC	5	5	5	6	10	15	60	350
12A	Owen Friend .964/.957	5	5	5	6	10	25	80	300
12B	Owen Friend .967/.958	5	5	6	10	15	30	100	350
13	Dick Littlefield	5	5	5	6	10	25	50	350
14	Ferris Fain	5	5	8	12	20	60	250	
15	Johnny Bucha	5	5	5	6	10	15	60	300
16A	Jerry Snyder .988/.988	5	5	5	6	10	25	80	300
16B	Jerry Snyder .968/.968	5	5	5	6	10	25	80	
17A	Henry Thompson .956/.951	5	5	6	10	25	60	350	
17B	Henry Thompson .958/.952	5	5	8	12	30	80	450	
18	Preacher Roe	5	6	10	15	25	60	150	
19	Hal Rice	5	5	5	6	10	25	80	350
20	Hobie Landrith RC	5	5	5	6	10	15	60	
21	Frank Baumholtz	5	5	5	6	10	25	50	400
22	Memo Luna RC	5	5	5	6	10	30	80	250
23	Steve Ridzik	5	5	5	6	10	20	80	250
24	Bill Bruton	5	6	10	15	25	80	300	

—Listed pricing for Mint cards typically references cards with PSA populations of 6 or more copies.
—Mint Commons & Minor Stars w/PSA populations of 5 or fewer copies sell as follows: 3-5 copies - $300-$350, 2 copies - $350-$500, 1 copy - $1,000-$1,500 per.
—Hank Bauer #129 PSA 9 (MT) sold for $3,191 (Goodwin; 10/06)
—Yogi Berra #161 PSA 10 (Gem) sold for $6,149 (Memory Lane; 8/06)
—Bill Bruton #224 PSA 9 (MT) sold for $2,704 (Memory Lane; 5/08)
—Roy Campanella #90 GAI 9.5 (Gem) sold for $1,348 (Memory Lane; 4/05)
—Al Corwin #137 PSA 8 (NmMt) sold for $1,485 (Leland's; 2/05)
—Al Corwin #137 PSA 8 (NmMt) sold for $364 (eBay; 8/07)
—Bob Feller PSA 9 (MT) sold for $6,159 (Memory Lane; 5/08)
—Whitey Ford #177 SGC 96 (MT) sold for $861 (Memory Lane; 4/07)
—Ralph Kiner #45 PSA 9 (MT) sold for $2,901 (Goodwin; 2/07)
—Don Larsen #101 GAI 9 (MT) sold for $378 (Mile High; 1/07)
—Whitey Lockman #153 (100/331) PSA 8 (NmMt) sold for $870 (eBay; 6/07)
—Whitey Lockman #153 (100/331) PSA 7 (NM) sold for $482 (eBay; 11/07)
—Whitey Lockman #153 (102/333) PSA 9 (MT) sold for $2,849 (eBay; 5/08)
—Whitey Lockman #153 (102/333) PSA 8 (NmMt) sold for $594 (Mile High; 8/07)
—Mickey Mantle #65 GAI 9 (MT) sold for $9,273 (Goodwin; 2/06)
—Mickey Mantle #65 SGC 92 (NmMt+) sold for $6,375 (eBay; 7/06)
—Mickey Mantle #65 SGC 92 (NmMt+) sold for $4,462 (Mile High; 1/07)
—Mickey Mantle #65 GAI 8 (NmMt) sold for $1,700 (eBay; 8/06)
—Mickey Mantle #65 GAI 8 (NmMt) sold for $1,153 (eBay; 12/07)
—Billy Martin #145 GAI 9 (MT) sold for $672 (Memory Lane; 11/05)
—Willie Mays #89 GAI 9 (MT) sold for $3,827 (Memory Lane; 8/06)
—Don Newcombe #154 PSA 9 (MT) sold for $4,138 (Memory Lane; 3/06)
—Don Newcombe #154 PSA 9 (MT) sold for $3,631 (Mile High; 8/07)
—Don Newcombe #154 PSA 9 (MT) sold for $2,158 (Memory Lane; 5/08)
—Don Newcombe #154 PSA 9 (MT) sold for $1,439 (Memory Lane; 8/06)
—Danny O'Connell #160 PSA 8 (NmMt) sold for $2,137 (Goodwin; 10/04)
—Danny O'Connell #160 PSA 8 (NmMt) sold for $1,367 (Mastro; 12/04)
—Danny O'Connell #160 PSA 8 (NmMt) sold for $1,025 (eBay; 11/06)
—Danny O'Connell #160 PSA 8 (NmMt) sold for $742 (eBay; 9/06)
—Danny O'Connell #160 PSA 8 (NmMt) sold for $713 (Memory Lane; 12/06)
—Danny O'Connell #160 PSA 8 (NmMt) sold for $698 (eBay; 10/07)
—Pee Wee Reese #58 PSA 10 (Gem) sold for $5,533 (Memory Lane; 9/07)
—Pee Wee Reese #58 PSA 10 (Gem) sold for $4,347 (Mile High; 8/07)
—Pee Wee Reese #58 GAI 9.5 (Gem) sold for $1,264 (Memory Lane; 4/05)
—Phil Rizzuto #1 PSA 9 (MT) sold for $3,266 (Goodwin; 6/06)
—Phil Rizzuto #1 PSA 9 (MT) sold for $2,557 (eBay; 7/06)
—Phil Rizzuto #1 PSA 9 (MT) sold for $2,028 (Mile High; 8/07)
—Phil Rizzuto #1 GAI 8.5 (NmMt+) sold for $560 (eBay; 5/07)
—Phil Rizzuto #1 GAI 8 (NmMt) sold for $305 (eBay; 12/06)
—Saul Rogovin #140 (7-12 W-L, 2 K's) PSA 8 (NmMt) sold for $956 (Mile High; 8/07)
—Saul Rogovin #140 (7-12 W-L, 2 K's) PSA 8 (NmMt) sold for $505 (eBay; 7/06)
—Carl Scheib #67 (.306 Pct. One Line) PSA 9 (MT) sold for $1,825 (eBay; 5/08)
—Duke Snider #170 PSA 10 (Gem) sold for $9,359 (Memory Lane; 8/05)
—Duke Snider #170 PSA 10 (Gem) sold for $8,201 (Mile High; 1/07)
—Duke Snider #170 GAI 9 (MT) sold for $759 (Memory Lane; 3/06)
—Daryl Spencer #185 (.933/.936) PSA 8 (NmMt) sold for $390 (Mile High; 2/08)
—Daryl Spencer #185 (.933/.936) PSA 8 (NmMt) sold for $288 (Mile High; 2/08)
—Henry Thompson #217 (.958/.952) PSA 9 (MT) sold for $3,631 (Mile High; 8/07)
—Mickey Vernon #152 PSA 8 (NmMt) sold for $786 (eBay; 6/07)
—Mickey Vernon #152 PSA 8 (NmMt) sold for $649 (Memory Lane; 12/07)
—Mickey Vernon #152 PSA 8 (NmMt) sold for $526 (Mile High; 8/07)
—Mickey Vernon #152 PSA 8 (NmMt) sold for $427 (eBay; 3/07)
—Preston Ward #139 (.990/.992) PSA 8 (NmMt) sold for $310 (Goodwin; 3/08)
—Wes Westrum #25 (.982/.986) PSA 8 (NmMt) sold for $1,157 (Mile High; 8/07)
—Wes Westrum #25 (.982/.986) PSA 8 (NmMt) sold for $578 (eBay; 1/08)
—Wes Westrum #25 (.982/.986) PSA 8 (NmMt) sold for $565 (eBay; 9/07)
—Ted Williams #66A PSA 9 (MT) sold for $35,952 (Mastro; 4/06)
—Ted Williams #66A SGC 92 (NmMt+) sold for $11,600 (REA; 4/06)
—Ted Williams #66A SGC 92 (NmMt+) sold for $7,080 (Greg Bussineau; 7/12)
—Ted Williams #66A SGC 92 (NmMt+) sold for $6,382 (Mile High; 10/12)
—Ted Williams #66A GAI 8.5 (NmMt+) sold for $6,083 (Mastro; 12/06)
—Ted Williams #66A GAI 8 (NmMt) sold for $4,175 (Memory Lane; 8/06)
—Ted Williams #66A SGC 86 (NM+) sold for $4,055 (Memory Lane; 4/07)
—Ted Williams #66A GAI 7.5 (NM+) sold for $2,780 (Memory Lane; 4/05)

1954 Braves Johnston Cookies

		GD 2	VG 3	VgEx 4	EX 5	ExMt 6	NM 7	NmMt 8	MT 9
	COMMON CARD	5	8	12	15	20	30	60	200
1	Del Crandall	5	8	12	15	20	30	100	
3	Jim Pendleton	5	8	12	15	20	40	60	
4	Danny O'Connell	5	8	12	15	20	30	100	200
5	Hank Aaron	250	300	350	600	1,200	2,500	3,000	
6	Jack Dittmer	5	8	12	15	20	30	80	
9	Joe Adcock	5	8	12	15	20	30	60	
10	Bob Buhl	5	8	12	15	20	30	80	200
11	Phil Paine	5	8	12	15	20	30	100	200
12	Ben Johnson	5	8	12	15	20	30	60	
13	Sibbi Sisti	5	8	12	15	20	30	60	
15	Charles Gorin	5	8	12	15	20	30	60	
16	Chet Nichols	5	8	12	15	20	30	60	
17	Dave Jolly	5	8	12	15	20	30	120	
19	Jim Wilson	5	8	12	15	20	30	100	
20	Ray Crone	5	8	12	15	20	30		
21	Warren Spahn	15	25	35	50	100	150	350	
22	Gene Conley	5	8	12	15	20	30	80	
23	Johnny Logan	5	8	12	15	20	30		
24	Charlie White	5	8	12	15	20	30	120	
27	George Metkovich	5	8	12	15	20	30	80	
28	Johnny Cooney CO	5	8	12	15	20	30	60	
29	Paul Burris	5	8	12	15	20	30	60	200
31	Bucky Walters CO	5	8	12	15	20	30	60	200
32	Ernie Johnson	5	8	12	15	20	30	60	
33	Lou Burdette	5	8	12	15	20	30	100	
34	Bobby Thomson SP	50	75	100	150	300	400		
35	Bob Keely	5	8	12	15	20	30		
38	Bill Bruton	5	8	12	15	20	30	60	
40	Charlie Grimm MG	5	8	12	15	20	30	60	200
41	Eddie Mathews	15	25	35	50	80	300		
42	Sam Calderone	5	8	12	15	20	30	60	200
47	Joey Jay	5	8	12	15	20	30	80	
48	Andy Pafko	5	8	12	15	20	30	100	
49	Dr. Charles Lacks (Unnumbered)	5	8	12	15	20	30	60	
50	Joseph F. Taylor (Unnumbered)	5	8	12	15	20	30	80	

—Eddie Mathews #41 PSA 9 (MT) sold for $584 (SCP Sotheby's; 6/06)
—Warren Spahn #21 PSA 9 (MT) sold for $686 (Memory Lane; 12/06)

1954 Dan-Dee

		GD 2	VG 3	VgEx 4	EX 5	ExMt 6	NM 7	NmMt 8	MT 9
1	Bobby Avila	10	15	25	40	60	150	450	
2	Hank Bauer	15	25	40	80	150	250	600	
3	Walker Cooper SP	30	150	300	350	400	450		
4	Larry Doby	20	30	50	80	120	250	800	
5	Luke Easter	10	15	25	120	150	250	300	
6	Bob Feller	30	100	150	200	250	400	1,500	
7	Bob Friend	10	15	25	40	150	200	400	
8	Mike Garcia	10	15	25	40	60	150	300	
9	Sid Gordon	10	15	25	40	60	150	500	
10	Jim Hegan	10	15	25	40	60	150	300	
11	Gil Hodges	30	100	120	150	200	300	1,200	
12	Art Houtteman	10	15	25	40	60	150	400	
13	Monte Irvin	15	25	40	80	100	300	500	
14	Paul LaPalme	10	15	25	60	80	300	400	
15	Bob Lemon	15	25	40	60	100	225	500	
16	Al Lopez MG	10	15	25	40	60	200		
17	Mickey Mantle	500	1,000	1,200	1,500	2,500	3,000	7,000	
18	Dale Mitchell	10	15	25	40	80	150	300	
19	Phil Rizzuto	25	60	100	120	150	400		
20	Curt Roberts	10	15	25	40	60	150	500	
21	Al Rosen	12	20	30	50	60	175	400	
22	Red Schoendienst	15	25	40	80	120	250	600	
23	Paul Smith SP	30	50	80	120	200	300	800	
24	Duke Snider	50	100	120	200	375	600	1,500	
25	George Strickland	10	15	25	40	60	150	300	
26	Max Surkont	10	15	25	40	60	150	500	
27	Frank Thomas	12	20	30	50	80	200	500	
28	Wally Westlake	10	15	25	40	60	150	300	
29	Early Wynn	15	25	40	60	150	225	500	

—Walker Cooper PSA 8 (NmMt) sold for $696 (Mile High; 2/08)
—Bob Feller PSA 9 (MT) sold for $5,034 (Goodwin; 5/08)
—Bob Feller PSA 9 (MT) sold for $4,157 (Memory Lane; 12/07)
—Mickey Mantle PSA 9 (MT) sold for $28,200 (Memory Lane; 12/07)
—Mickey Mantle PSA 9 (MT) sold for $15,405 (REA; Spring '14)
—Mickey Mantle PSA 9 (MT) sold for $16,286 (Mile High; 10/13)
—Mickey Mantle PSA 9 OC (MT w/OC Qualifier) sold for $2,032 (Heritage; 10/07)
— Mickey Mantle #17 PSA 8.5 (NmMt+) sold for $9,037 (Goodwin; 12/11)
—Mickey Mantle #17 PSA 8.5 (NmMt+) sold for $6,840 (Greg Bussineau; 12/12)
—Mickey Mantle SGC 92 (NmMt+) sold for $4,406 (REA; 4/07)
—Mickey Mantle #17 PSA 8.5 (NmMt+) sold for $6,791 (Memory Lane; 5/12)
—Dale Mitchell PSA 9 (MT) sold for $3,825 (Memory Lane; 12/07)
—Dale Mitchell PSA 9 (MT) sold for $1,659 (Mile High; 2/08)
—Duke Snider SGC 92 (NmMt+) sold for $1,920 (Mastro; 5/08)
—Duke Snider SGC 92 (NmMt+) sold for $1,836 (eBay; 2/08)

1954 Red Heart

		GD 2	VG 3	VgEx 4	EX 5	ExMt 6	NM 7	NmMt 8	MT 9
	COMMON CARD	5	8	12	20	30	50	120	500
1	Richie Ashburn SP	15	25	40	60	100	150	500	
2	Frank Baumholtz SP	5	8	12	20	30	100	150	
3	Gus Bell	5	8	12	20	30	50	250	700
4	Billy Cox	5	8	12	20	40	50	150	500
5	Alvin Dark	5	8	12	20	30	50	150	
6	Carl Erskine SP	10	15	25	40	120	200	500	
7	Ferris Fain	5	8	12	20	30	50	200	
8	Dee Fondy	5	8	12	20	30	150	200	
9	Nellie Fox	12	20	30	50	80	200	250	
10	Jim Gilliam	6	10	15	25	40	80	150	800
11	Jim Hegan SP	5	8	12	20	30	80	225	
12	George Kell	6	10	15	25	40	60	150	
13	Ralph Kiner SP	8	12	20	30	50	150	300	
14	Ted Kluszewski SP	8	12	20	100	120	150	300	1,000
15	Harvey Kuenn	5	8	12	20	30	50	150	500
16	Bob Lemon SP	8	12	20	30	50	100	400	
17	Sherman Lollar	5	8	12	20	30	50	135	
18	Mickey Mantle	300	400	500	800	1,000	1,200	3,000	4,000
19	Billy Martin	8	12	20	30	100	150	400	1,000
20	Gil McDougald SP	6	10	15	25	50	80	250	800
21	Roy McMillan	5	8	12	20	30	60	120	500
22	Minnie Minoso	6	10	15	25	40	80	300	600
23	Stan Musial SP	80	150	200	250	400	800	2,000	7,000
24	Billy Pierce	5	8	12	20	30	50	200	600

		GD 2	VG 3	VgEx 4	EX 5	ExMt 6	NM 7	NmMt 8	MT
25	Al Rosen SP	6	10	15	25	40	100	300	
26	Hank Sauer	5	8	12	20	30	50	150	500
27	Red Schoendienst SP	12	20	30	50	100	200	300	
28	Enos Slaughter	6	10	15	25	40	150	250	800
29	Duke Snider	15	25	40	100	100	250	800	
30	Warren Spahn	10	15	25	40	60	120	350	
31	Sammy White	5	8	12	20	30	50	250	700
32	Eddie Yost	5	8	12	20	30	50	250	500
33	Gus Zernial	5	8	12	20	30	100	300	

—Richie Ashburn #1 SGC 92 (NmMt+) sold for $565 (eBay; 2/08)
—Stan Musial #23 PSA 8.5 (NmMt+) sold for $1,485 (eBay; 4/08)

1954 Red Man

		GD 2	VG 3	VgEx 4	EX 5	ExMt 6	NM 7	NmMt 8	MT 9
AL1	Bobby Avila	5	8	12	20	30	60	250	
AL2	Jim Busby	5	8	12	20	30	60	150	
AL3	Nellie Fox	10	15	25	40	60	120	400	
AL4	George Kell Boston	10	15	25	40	60	120	400	
AL4	George Kell Chicago	12	20	30	50	80	150		
AL5	Sherman Lollar	5	8	12	20	30	60	150	
AL6	Sam Mele Baltimore	6	10	15	25	40	80	200	
AL6	Sam Mele Chicago	10	15	25	40	60	120		
AL7	Minnie Minoso	6	10	15	25	40	80		
AL8	Mel Parnell	5	8	12	20	30	60	150	
AL9	Dave Philley Cleveland	6	10	15	25	40	80	200	
AL9	Dave Philley Philadelphia	10	15	25	40	60	120	300	
AL10	Billy Pierce	5	8	12	20	30	60	150	
AL11	Jimmy Piersall	6	10	15	25	40	80	200	
AL12	Al Rosen	6	10	15	25	40	80	200	
AL13	Mickey Vernon	5	8	12	20	30	60	150	
AL14	Sammy White	5	8	12	20	30	60	150	
AL15	Gene Woodling	6	10	15	25	40	80	200	
AL16	Whitey Ford	15	25	40	60	80	200	500	
AL17	Phil Rizzuto	12	20	30	50	80	150	500	
AL18	Bob Porterfield	5	8	12	20	30	60	150	
AL19	Chico Carrasquel	5	8	12	20	30	60	150	
AL20	Yogi Berra	15	25	40	80	100	200	600	
AL21	Bob Lemon	6	10	15	25	40	80	200	
AL22	Ferris Fain	5	8	12	20	30	60	150	
AL23	Hank Bauer	6	10	15	25	40	80	200	
AL24	Jim Delsing	5	8	12	20	30	60	150	
AL25	Gil McDougald	6	10	15	25	40	80	250	
NL1	Richie Ashburn	10	15	25	40	60	120	400	
NL2	Billy Cox	6	10	15	25	40	80	200	
NL3	Del Crandall	5	8	12	20	30	60	150	
NL4	Carl Erskine	6	10	15	25	40	80	250	
NL5	Monte Irvin	6	10	15	25	40	80	200	
NL6	Ted Kluszewski	8	12	20	30	50	100	250	
NL7	Don Mueller	5	8	12	20	30	60	175	
NL8	Andy Pafko	5	8	12	20	30	60	150	
NL9	Del Rice	5	8	12	20	30	60	150	
NL10	Red Schoendienst	6	10	15	25	40	80	250	
NL11	Warren Spahn	12	20	30	50	80	150		
NL12	Curt Simmons	5	8	12	20	30	60	150	
NL13	Roy Campanella	15	25	40	80	150	250	800	
NL14	Jim Gilliam	6	10	15	25	40	80	250	
NL15	Pee Wee Reese	12	20	30	50	80	150	500	
NL16	Duke Snider	12	20	30	80	100	200	600	
NL17	Rip Repulski	5	8	12	20	30	60	150	
NL18	Robin Roberts	6	10	15	25	40	80	225	
NL19	Enos Slaughter	12	20	30	50	80	150	500	
NL19	Gus Bell	10	15	25	40	60	120	400	
NL20	Johnny Logan	5	8	12	20	30	60	150	
NL21	John Antonelli	5	8	12	20	30	60	150	
NL22	Gil Hodges	10	15	25	40	60	150	400	
NL23	Eddie Mathews	12	20	30	50	100	150	400	
NL24	Lew Burdette	5	8	12	20	30	60	150	
NL25	Willie Mays	30	50	100	120	250	400	1,200	

—Prices reference cards with tabs.
—Whitey Ford #AL16 PSA 9 (MT) sold for $1,684 (Mastro; 8/06)
—Gil Hodges #NL22 PSA 9 (MT) sold for $1,785 (Goodwin; 6/06)
—Eddie Mathews #NL23 PSA 9 (MT) sold for $1,530 (Mastro; 8/06)
—Robin Roberts #NL18 PSA 9 (MT) sold for $1,799 (Mile High; 2/08)
—Al Rosen #AL12 PSA 9 (MT) sold for $1,973 (Goodwin; 8/07)

954 Topps

	GD 2	VG 3	VgEx 4	EX 5	ExMt 6	NM 7	NmMt 8	MT 9
Ted Williams	150	200	250	500	800	2,500	6,000	
Gus Zernial	5	5	8	12	20	50	250	
Monte Irvin	12	25	30	50	80	100	400	
Hank Sauer	5	6	10	25	30	60	100	
Ed Lopat	5	6	10	20	30	50	250	
Pete Runnels	5	5	8	12	30	40	120	800
Ted Kluszewski	6	10	20	30	40	80	200	1,500
Bob Young	5	5	8	20	25	40	100	800
Harvey Haddix	5	6	10	15	30	40	100	800
Jackie Robinson	150	200	▲300	400	▲600	1,000	3,000	
Paul Leslie Smith RC	5	5	8	12	20	40	60	400
Del Crandall	5	6	10	15	30	50	100	1,200
Billy Martin	25	▲40	▲50	60	100	200	400	
Preacher Roe	5	6	▲20	▲25	▲30	50	▲200	
Al Rosen	5	6	10	25	40	50	150	800
Vic Janowicz	5	6	10	15	25	50	100	
Phil Rizzuto	25	40	50	60	100	150	400	2,000
Walt Dropo	5	6	10	15	30	50	80	600
Johnny Lipon	5	5	8	12	25	30	80	800
Warren Spahn	25	▲50	▲60	80	120	▲250	600	1,500
Bobby Shantz	5	6	10	15	25	50	100	
Jim Greengrass	5	5	8	12	20	40	120	
Luke Easter	5	5	8	12	30	40	100	1,000
Granny Hamner	5	5	8	25	30	50	60	
Harvey Kuenn RC	5	12	15	25	40	60	150	
Ray Jablonski	5	5	8	12	25	40	150	
Ferris Fain	5	6	10	15	25	40	60	
Paul Minner	5	5	8	12	20	30	60	800
Jim Hegan	5	5	8	12	20	30	120	1,000
Eddie Mathews	25	40	50	80	120	250	500	2,000
Johnny Klippstein	5	5	8	12	25	30	▲80	800
Duke Snider	30	50	60	100	120	250	500	2,500
Johnny Schmitz	5	5	8	12	20	40	80	800
Jim Rivera	5	5	8	20	25	30	80	
Jim Gilliam	6	10	15	25	50	60	200	
Hoyt Wilhelm	6	10	25	40	60	80	250	1,500
Whitey Ford	30	50	60	▼80	150	250	500	3,500
Eddie Stanky MG	5	6	10	20	25	40	80	
Sherm Lollar	5	5	8	12	20	50	100	
Mel Parnell	5	5	12	15	20	40	60	600
Willie Jones	5	5	8	12	25	30	60	600
Don Mueller	5	5	8	12	20	40	80	600
Dick Groat	5	6	10	15	25	50	100	
Ned Garver	5	5	8	12	25	50	120	
Richie Ashburn	10	▲25	30	50	80	120	250	1,500
Ken Raffensberger	5	5	8	12	25	40	120	
Ellis Kinder	5	5	8	15	20	30	80	400
Billy Hunter	5	5	8	20	25	▲40	▲100	600
Ray Murray	5	5	8	12	20	25	60	
Yogi Berra	60	80	100	120	200	400	800	3,500
Johnny Lindell	5	6	10	20	25	60	150	
Vic Power RC	5	8	12	30	40	60	200	
Jack Dittmer	5	6	10	15	30	60	200	
Vern Stephens	5	8	12	20	40	60	150	
Phil Cavarretta MG	6	10	15	25	40	80	150	1,200
Willie Miranda	5	6	10	15	25	60	100	
Luis Aloma	5	6	10	15	30	50	100	600
Bob Wilson	5	6	10	15	25	50	80	600
Gene Conley	5	8	12	20	30	80	150	
Frank Baumholtz	5	6	10	15	30	50	150	
Bob Cain	5	6	10	15	30	40	120	1,200
Eddie Robinson	6	10	20	25	50	120	150	1,200
Johnny Pesky	5	8	20	40	50	80	200	800
Hank Thompson	5	6	10	30	40	120	800	
Bob Swift CO	5	6	10	15	25	60	120	
Ted Lepcio	5	6	10	15	25	40	80	
Jim Willis RC	5	6	10	20	25	40	100	600
Sam Calderone	5	6	10	25	30	50	100	1,200
Bud Podbielan	5	6	10	15	25	50	80	1,000
Larry Doby	10	30	50	80	120	150	600	1,500
Frank Smith	5	6	10	15	25	50	100	
Preston Ward	5	6	10	20	40	60	250	1,200
Wayne Terwilliger	5	6	10	15	25	50	120	

		GD 2	VG 3	VgEx 4	EX 5	ExMt 6	NM 7	NmMt 8	MT 9
74	Bill Taylor RC	5	6	10	15	25	50	120	
75	Fred Haney MG RC	5	6	20	30	50	120	500	
76	Bob Scheffing CO	5	5	8	12	20	40	120	800
77	Ray Boone	5	6	10	15	25	40	80	500
78	Ted Kazanski RC	5	5	8	12	20	50	120	
79	Andy Pafko	5	6	10	20	30	50	200	
80	Jackie Jensen	5	8	15	25	40	60	250	1,200
81	Dave Hoskins RC	5	5	8	20	25	50	60	600
82	Milt Bolling	5	5	15	20	25	50	80	600
83	Joe Collins	5	6	15	25	30	50	100	800
84	Dick Cole RC	5	5	8	12	25	40	100	
85	Bob Turley RC	5	8	25	30	40	50	100	1,000
86	Billy Herman CO	5	8	15	25	60	60	120	700
87	Roy Face	5	6	10	15	25	40	▲120	500
88	Matt Batts	5	5	8	12	30	40	80	600
89	Howie Pollet	5	5	8	12	20	40	60	600
90	Willie Mays	▲150	200	250	500	▲800	1,500	3,000	9,000
91	Bob Oldis	5	5	8	12	25	30	80	600
92	Wally Westlake	5	5	8	25	40	40	80	600
93	Sid Hudson	5	5	8	12	20	40	100	800
94	Ernie Banks RC	400	500	800	1,000	▲2,500	5,000	12,000	40,000
95	Hal Rice	5	5	8	12	20	40	80	
96	Charlie Silvera	5	6	10	15	30	50	100	900
97	Hal Lane RC	5	5	8	12	20	50	120	500
98	Joe Black	5	6	10	30	40	80	250	
99	Bobby Hofman	5	5	8	12	20	50	80	
100	Bob Keegan	5	5	8	25	30	50	100	
101	Gene Woodling	6	10	15	25	60	120	500	2,500
102	Gil Hodges	15	25	40	▲80	100	150	500	
103	Jim Lemon RC	5	5	8	25	30	40	100	500
104	Mike Sandlock	5	5	8	12	25	40	50	600
105	Andy Carey	5	6	10	25	40	80	200	
106	Dick Kokos	5	5	8	12	▲30	▼50	150	
107	Duane Pillette	5	5	8	12	20	40	80	800
108	Thornton Kipper RC	5	5	8	12	25	30	80	800
109	Bill Bruton	5	5	8	15	30	40	120	
110	Harry Dorish	5	5	8	12	20	25	60	400
111	Jim Delsing	5	5	8	12	25	40	100	600
112	Bill Renna RC	5	5	8	12	20	40	60	600
113	Bob Boyd	5	5	8	12	20	40	60	600
114	Dean Stone RC	5	5	8	12	25	40	80	
115	Rip Repulski	5	5	8	12	25	50	150	
116	Steve Bilko	5	5	8	12	30	100	150	
117	Solly Hemus	5	5	8	12	20	40	▲100	350
118	Carl Scheib	5	5	8	12	20	30	80	
119	Johnny Antonelli	5	5	8	12	20	50	80	600
120	Roy McMillan	5	5	8	12	20	40	100	
121	Clem Labine	5	6	20	25	30	100	400	
122	Johnny Logan	5	6	10	20	25	40	100	
123	Bobby Adams	5	5	8	12	30	40	80	800
124	Marion Fricano	5	5	8	12	20	30	100	800
125	Harry Perkowski	5	5	8	12	20	40	120	
126	Ben Wade	5	5	8	25	60	400		
127	Steve O'Neill MG	5	5	8	12	30	40	60	400
128	Hank Aaron RC	▲1,500	▲2,000	2,500	4,000	5,000	▲10,000	▲30,000	250,000
129	Forrest Jacobs RC	5	5	8	12	20	40	100	500
130	Hank Bauer	6	10	20	40	50	100	800	
131	Reno Bertoia RC	5	5	8	15	25	30	60	400
132	Tommy Lasorda RC	60	120	150	200	250	400	▲600	▲3,000
133	Del Baker CO	5	5	8	12	25	40	60	400
134	Cal Hogue	5	5	8	12	20	50	200	800
135	Joe Presko	5	5	8	12	20	40	100	
136	Connie Ryan	5	5	8	12	20	40	80	400
137	Wally Moon RC	6	10	25	30	60	80	150	800
138	Bob Borkowski	5	5	8	12	20	30	60	400
139	J.O'Brien/E.O'Brien	6	10	25	50	100	150	400	1,500
140	Tom Wright	5	5	8	12	20	30	50	300
141	Joey Jay RC	5	6	10	15	30	60	250	1,000
142	Tom Poholsky	5	5	8	12	20	40	60	500
143	Rollie Hemsley CO	5	5	8	12	25	40	60	600
144	Bill Werle	5	5	8	12	20	40	60	400
145	Elmer Valo	5	5	8	12	20	30	80	400
146	Don Johnson	5	5	12	15	20	40	60	400
147	Johnny Riddle CO	5	5	8	12	20	50	60	
148	Bob Trice RC	5	5	8	12	25	50	80	600
149	Al Robertson	5	5	8	12	20	40	60	400
150	Dick Kryhoski	5	5	8	12	30	60	100	800

#	Player	GD 2	VG 3	VgEx 4	EX 5	ExMt 6	NM 7	NmMt 8	MT 9
151	Alex Grammas RC	5	5	8	20	25	40	100	1,000
152	Michael Blyzka RC	5	5	8	12	25	40	80	
153	Rube Walker	5	6	10	15	40	50	120	600
154	Mike Fornieles RC	5	5	8	20	30	50	80	
155	Bob Kennedy	5	5	8	12	20	50	150	
156	Joe Coleman	5	6	10	15	25	50	150	
157	Don Lenhardt	5	5	8	12	40	80	250	
158	Peanuts Lowrey	5	5	8	12	30	50	100	600
159	Dave Philley	5	5	8	12	30	50	120	
160	Ralph Kress CO	5	5	8	30	40	50	150	
161	John Hetki	5	5	8	12	20	40	100	800
162	Herman Wehmeier	5	5	8	12	30	50	100	
163	Frank House	5	5	8	12	20	50	100	
164	Stu Miller	5	6	10	15	25	50	120	
165	Jim Pendleton	5	5	8	12	30	60	120	
166	Johnny Podres	6	10	20	30	50	80	250	
167	Don Lund	5	5	8	12	20	60	150	
168	Morrie Martin	5	5	8	12	20	30	60	
169	Jim Hughes	5	5	8	12	25	80	200	
170	Dusty Rhodes RC	5	6	10	20	30	80	200	
171	Leo Kiely	5	5	8	12	20	50	100	
172	Hal Brown RC	5	5	8	12	20	50	▲150	1,200
173	Jack Harshman RC	5	5	8	12	20	40	100	600
174	Tom Qualters RC	5	5	8	12	40	50	200	1,200
175	Frank Leja RC	5	5	8	25	60	80	800	
176	Robert Keely CO	5	5	8	12	▲30	40	80	600
177	Bob Milliken	5	5	8	12	15	40	60	500
178	Bill Glynn UER	5	5	8	12	20	40	80	400
179	Gair Allie RC	5	5	8	20	25	40	60	400
180	Wes Westrum	5	5	8	12	20	40	100	600
181	Mel Roach RC	5	5	8	12	25	30	60	400
182	Chuck Harmon RC	5	5	8	20	30	200	600	
183	Earle Combs CO	5	5	8	20	40	50	100	
184	Ed Bailey	5	5	8	20	25	40	80	500
185	Chuck Stobbs	5	5	8	12	20	30	80	500
186	Karl Olson	5	5	8	12	30	40	80	400
187	Heinie Manush CO	5	6	10	25	30	50	100	600
188	Dave Jolly RC	5	5	8	12	30	40	80	400
189	Bob Ross	5	5	8	12	20	30	80	500
190	Ray Herbert RC	5	5	8	25	30	50	120	
191	Dick Schofield RC	5	6	10	25	30	60	80	1,000
192	Ellis Deal CO	5	5	8	12	20	30	60	400
193	Johnny Hopp CO	5	5	8	12	30	50	60	600
194	Bill Sarni RC	5	5	8	12	25	40	▲60	600
195	Billy Consolo RC	5	5	8	12	20	50	120	
196	Stan Jok RC	5	5	8	12	20	▲50	60	800
197	Lynwood Rowe CO	5	6	10	25	30	60	100	600
198	Carl Sawatski	5	5	8	12	25	40	60	600
199	Glenn (Rocky) Nelson	5	5	8	12	20	30	80	500
200	Larry Jansen	5	5	8	25	30	80	250	1,000
201	Al Kaline RC	300	400	500	600	1,000	▲2,000	5,000	40,000
202	Bob Purkey RC	5	6	10	15	25	40	80	650
203	Harry Brecheen CO	5	5	8	12	▲25	40	120	1,200
204	Angel Scull RC	5	5	8	12	25	40	100	400
205	Johnny Sain	6	10	15	25	▲50	60	120	800
206	Ray Crone RC	5	5	8	12	25	40	80	
207	Tom Oliver CO RC	5	5	8	12	20	40	100	
208	Grady Hatton	5	5	8	12	30	40	50	400
209	Chuck Thompson RC	5	5	8	12	20	40	▼400	
210	Bob Buhl RC	5	5	8	12	30	40	80	600
211	Don Hoak	5	5	8	15	30	50	120	800
212	Bob Micelotta RC	5	5	8	12	20	40	60	400
213	Johnny Fitzpatrick CO RC	5	5	8	12	30	50	▲200	
214	Arnie Portocarrero RC	5	5	8	12	25	30	60	600
215	Ed McGhee	5	5	8	12	20	30	80	400
216	Al Sima	5	5	8	12	20	30	60	800
217	Paul Schreiber CO RC	5	5	8	20	25	40	80	500
218	Fred Marsh	5	5	8	12	20	30	60	400
219	Chuck Kress RC	5	5	8	12	25	40	80	800
220	Ruben Gomez RC	5	5	8	12	25	40	60	300
221	Dick Brodowski	5	5	8	12	25	40	60	400
222	Bill Wilson RC	5	5	8	12	20	40	50	800
223	Joe Haynes CO	5	5	8	12	▲30	40	80	800
224	Dick Weik RC	5	5	8	12	20	40	100	
225	Don Liddle RC	5	5	8	12	25	40	80	400
226	Jehosie Heard RC	5	5	8	12	30	40	80	300
227	Buster Mills CO RC	5	6	10	15	40	200		

#	Player	GD 2	VG 3	VgEx 4	EX 5	ExMt 6	NM 7	NmMt 8	MT
228	Gene Hermanski	5	5	15	20	25	40	60	40
229	Bob Talbot RC	5	5	8	12	20	40	60	40
230	Bob Kuzava	5	6	10	20	30	50	100	50
231	Roy Smalley	5	5	8	12	20	50	120	
232	Lou Limmer RC	5	5	8	12	20	30	50	40
233	Augie Galan CO	5	5	8	12	20	40	60	
234	Jerry Lynch RC	5	5	8	12	25	40	100	
235	Vern Law	5	5	8	20	25	60	120	60
236	Paul Penson RC	5	5	8	20	25	50	120	
237	Mike Ryba CO RC	5	5	8	12	30	50	80	50
238	Al Aber	5	5	8	12	20	40	60	80
239	Bill Skowron RC	15	25	40	60	80	120	400	1,50
240	Sam Mele	5	6	10	15	25	50	100	
241	Robert Miller RC	5	5	8	20	30	50	80	
242	Curt Roberts RC	5	5	8	12	20	40	▲100	60
243	Ray Blades CO RC	5	5	8	12	25	60	100	
244	Leroy Wheat RC	5	5	8	12	25	40	60	60
245	Roy Sievers	5	5	8	12	30	200	600	
246	Howie Fox	5	5	8	12	25	40	120	80
247	Ed Mayo CO	5	5	8	12	25	80	80	80
248	Al Smith RC	5	5	8	12	20	50	200	1,200
249	Wilmer Mizell	5	5	8	12	30	60	100	
250	Ted Williams	▲200	▲250	▲300	▲500	▲800	2,000	8,000	15,00

—Hank Aaron #128 PSA 10 (Gem) (Young Collection) sold for $357,594 (SCP; 5/12)
—Hank Aaron #128 PSA 10 (Gem) sold for $110,000 (Memory Lane; Private Sale - 2006)
—Hank Aaron #128 PSA 10 (Gem) sold for $78,434 (Mastro; 8/04)
—Hank Aaron #128 GAI 9.5 (Gem) sold for $7,530 (Mastro; 12/06)
—Hank Aaron #128 SGC 96 (MT) sold for $16,117 (Memory Lane; 4/07)
—Hank Aaron #128 SGC 96 (MT) sold for $15,251 (Mastro; 4/07)
—Hank Aaron #128 GAI 9 (MT) sold for $4,673 (Mastro; 4/07)
—Hank Aaron #128 SGC 92 (NmMt+) sold for $21,856 (Goodwin; 12/14)
—Hank Aaron #128 SGC 92 (NmMt+) sold for $17,775 (Huggins and Scott; 8/14)
—Hank Aaron #128 PSA 8.5 sold for $9,718 (Goodwin; 1/13)
—Hank Aaron #128 SGC 92 (NmMt+) sold for $7,475 (Hunt; 3/08)
—Hank Aaron #128 SGC 92 (NmMt+) sold for $6,407 (Mastro; 8/06)
—Hank Aaron #128 GAI 8.5 (NmMt+) sold for $3,271 (eBay; 9/06)
—Hank Aaron #128 GAI 8 (NmMt) sold for $3,181 (Mile High; 6/06)
—Hank Aaron #128 BVG 7.5 (NM+) sold for $2,136 (eBay; 3/07)
—Ernie Banks #94 PSA 10 (Gem) (Young Collection) sold for $142,836 (SCP; 5/12)
—Ernie Banks #94 PSA 10 (Gem) sold for $33,657 (Mastro; 12/05)
—Ernie Banks #94 GAI 9 (MT) sold for $4,649 (eBay; 2/07)
—Ernie Banks #94 GAI 9 (MT) sold for $4,112 (Goodwin; 8/07)
—Ernie Banks #94 SGC 92 (NmMt+) sold for $5,750 (Hunt; 9/06)
—Ernie Banks #94 GAI 8.5 (NmMt+) sold for $3,521 (Madec; 5/07)
—Ernie Banks #94 GAI 8.5 (NmMt+) sold for $2,437 (Memory Lane; 12/07)
—Ernie Banks #94 GAI 8 (NmMt) sold for $1,717 (Goodwin; 6/06)
—Ernie Banks #94 GAI 8 (NmMt) sold for $1,220 (Mastro; 6/07)
—Yogi Berra #50 GAI 8.5 (NmMt+) sold for $610 (eBay; 4/07)
— Bob Borkowski #138 PSA 10 (Gem) sold for $68,112 (Mile High; 10/11)
—Gil Hodges #102 PSA 9 (MT) sold for $1,606 (Mastro; 8/06)
—Gil Hodges #102 SGC 92 (NmMt+) sold for $690 (Mastro; 8/06)
—Al Kaline #201 PSA 10 (Gem) (Young Collection) sold for $88,688 (SCP; 5/12)
—Al Kaline #201 SGC 92 (NmMt+) sold for $2,875 (eBay; 11/06)
—Al Kaline #201 PSA 8.5 (NmMt+) sold for $3,000 (Mastro; 5/08)
—Al Kaline #201 PSA 8.5 (NmMt+) sold for $2,329 (eBay; 4/08)
—Al Kaline #201 SGC 88 (NmMt) sold for $1,361 (Lelands; 11/07)
—Al Kaline #201 GAI 8 (NmMt) sold for $749 (eBay; 10/06)
—Willie Mays #90 GAI 8.5 (NmMt+) sold for $1,224 (Memory Lane; 3/06)
—Willie Mays #90 GAI 8 (NmMt) sold for $855 (eBay; 12/07)
—Willie Mays #90 GAI 8 (NmMt) sold for $644 (eBay; 1/08)
—Willie Mays #90 GAI 8 (NmMt) sold for $610 (eBay; 5/07)
—Buster Mills #227 PSA 8 (NmMt) sold for $1,850 (eBay; 9/04)
—Buster Mills #227 PSA 8 (NmMt) sold for $1,404 (Goodwin; 2/06)
—Buster Mills #227 PSA 8 (NmMt) sold for $1,045 (Memory Lane; 4/07)
—Buster Mills #227 PSA 8 (NmMt) sold for $752 (Goodwin; 11/07)
—Buster Mills #227 PSA 8 (NmMt) sold for $713 (Memory Lane; 9/07)
—Buster Mills #227 PSA 8 (NmMt) sold for $677 (eBay; 12/07)
—Buster Mills #227 PSA 8 (NmMt) sold for $575 (Mile High; 2/08)
—Buster Mills #227 PSA 8 (NmMt) sold for $383 (eBay; 6/08)
—Buster Mills #227 PSA 8 (NmMt) sold for $364 (eBay; 6/08)
—Buster Mills #227 PSA 8 (NmMt) sold for $252 (eBay; 5/07)
—Johnny Podres #166 PSA 9 (MT) sold for $6,775 (Memory Lane; 4/07)
—Bill Skowron #239 PSA 10 (Gem) (Young Collection) sold for $9,799 (SCP; 5/12)
—Ben Wade #126 PSA 8 (NmMt) sold for $2,355 (Goodwin; 11/07)
—Ben Wade #126 PSA 8 (NmMt) sold for $2,243 (Mile High; 2/08)
—Ben Wade #126 PSA 8 (NmMt) sold for $1,980 (Goodwin; 5/08)
—Ben Wade #126 PSA 8 (NmMt) sold for $1,892 (Memory Lane; 9/07)

Ben Wade #126 PSA 8 (NmMt) sold for $1,651 (eBay; 11/06)
Ben Wade #126 PSA 8 (NmMt) sold for $1,611 (eBay; 11/03)
Ted Williams #1 PSA 9 (MT) sold for $16,698 (Mastro; 12/06)
Ted Williams #1 PSA 9 (MT) sold for $16,100 (Superior; 3/03)
Ted Williams #1 SGC 96 (MT) sold for $13,302 (Mastro; 12/03)
Ted Williams #1 SGC 96 (Mint) sold for $12,000 (Greg Bussineau; 4/12)
Ted Williams #1 PSA 8.5 (NmMt+) sold for $5,314 (Memory Lane; 8/12)
Ted Williams #250 GAI 8.5 (NmMt+) sold for $1,892 (Mastro; 4/07)
Ted Williams #250 GAI 8 (NmMt) sold for $2,672 (eBay; 1/08)

954 Wilson Franks

	PrFr 1	GD 2	VG 3	VgEx 4	EX 5	ExMt 6	NM 7	NmMt 8
Roy Campanella	300	400	500	600	700	2,000	3,000	
Del Ennis	100	150	200	400	300	500		
Carl Erskine	80	120	150	200	400	450	800	
Ferris Fain	80	120	150	200	300	400		
Bob Feller	150	250	300	450	600	800	1,500	
Nellie Fox	150	250	300	500	600	1,000		
Johnny Groth	80	120	150	200	400			
Stan Hack MG	80	120	175	300				
Gil Hodges	150	250	300	500	600	1,200		
Ray Jablonski	200	300	475	550	650			
Harvey Kuenn	80	120	150	250				
Roy McMillan	60	100	120	200	250	300	500	
Andy Pafko	60	100	120	150	200	400	500	
Paul Richards MG	60	100	150	250				
Hank Sauer	60	100	120	150	200	600	650	
Red Schoendienst	100	150	250	300	500			
Enos Slaughter	100	150	200	250	300	500		
Vern Stephens	60	100	120	150	200	300	500	
Sammy White	60	100	120	150	200	300	500	
Ted Williams	1,300	1,800	3,000	5,000	6,000	10,000		

-Roy Campanella #1 PSA 8 (NmMt) sold for $6,268 (Memory Lane; 8/12)
-Del Ennis PSA 7 (NM) sold for $3,450 (Huggins and Scott; 10/07)
-Carl Erskine PSA 8 (NmMt) sold for $8,625 (Huggins and Scott; 10/07)
-Ferris Fain PSA 7 (NM) sold for $3,450 (Huggins and Scott; 10/07)
-Bob Feller PSA 8 (NmMt) sold for $5,175 (Huggins and Scott; 10/07)
-Stan Hack PSA 8 (NmMt) sold for $6,900 (Huggins and Scott; 10/07)
-Gil Hodges SGC 88 (NmMt) sold for $5,400 (Hunt; 11/08)
-Gil Hodges PSA 7 (NM) sold for $4,888 (Huggins and Scott; 10/07)
-Ray Jablonski PSA 8 (NmMt) sold for $6,900 (Huggins and Scott; 10/07)
-Andy Pafko PSA 8 (NmMt) sold for $2,875 (Huggins and Scott; 10/07)
-Hank Sauer PSA 8 (NmMt) sold for $6,325 (Huggins and Scott; 10/07)
-Red Schoendienst PSA 7 (NM) sold for $1,840 (Huggins and Scott; 10/07)
-Enos Slaughter PSA 7 (NM) sold for $3,000 (Mastro; 2/08)
-Vern Stephens PSA 8 (NmMt) sold for $7,475 (Huggins and Scott; 10/07)
-Ted Williams #20 SGC 88 (NmMt) sold for $54,000 (Mastro; 11/08)
-Ted Williams #20 SGC 86 (NM+) sold for $19,278 (Mastro; 4/07)
-Ted Williams #20 SGC 84 (NM) sold for $15,275 (REA; 5/08)
-Ted Williams #20 SGC 84 (NrMt) sold for $11,228 (Goodwin; 8/12)
-Ted Williams #20 PSA 7 (NrMt) sold for $17,261 (Memory Lane; 8/12)
-Ted Williams #20 GAI 7 (NM) sold for $10,6665 (Memory Lane; 5/08)

1955 Bowman

#	Player	GD 2	VG 3	VgEx 4	EX 5	ExMt 6	NM 7	NmMt 8	MT 9
1	Hoyt Wilhelm	6	15	30	50	80	120	500	
2	Alvin Dark	5	5	6	8	15	25	60	
3	Joe Coleman	5	5	6	8	12	20	80	
4	Eddie Waitkus	5	5	5	6	10	15	50	
5	Jim Robertson	5	5	5	6	10	15	50	
6	Pete Suder	5	5	5	6	10	30	100	
7	Gene Baker RC	5	5	5	6	10	25	100	
8	Warren Hacker	5	5	5	6	10	30	80	
9	Gil McDougald	5	8	12	15	25	60	120	500
10	Phil Rizzuto	20	30	40	50	▲80	100	250	800
11	Bill Bruton	5	5	6	8	12	25	50	
12	Andy Pafko	5	5	6	8	12	20	50	300
13	Clyde Vollmer	5	5	5	6	20	25	50	250
14	Gus Keriazakos RC	5	5	5	6	10	15	40	
15	Frank Sullivan RC	5	5	5	6	20	25	50	300
16	Jimmy Piersall	5	5	6	15	30	50	120	300
17	Del Ennis	5	5	6	8	20	25	80	
18	Stan Lopata	5	5	6	8	15	25	50	350
19	Bobby Avila	5	5	6	8	12	20	150	
20	Al Smith	5	5	6	10	30	50	250	
21	Don Hoak	5	5	6	8	15	25	80	250
22	Roy Campanella	25	30	40	60	100	150	300	
23	Al Kaline	12	20	50	80	100	150	300	2,500
24	Al Aber	5	5	5	6	10	15	40	
25	Minnie Minoso	5	8	12	15	30	60	120	
26	Virgil Trucks	5	5	5	6	10	20	▲60	
27	Preston Ward	5	5	5	6	10	20	80	350
28	Dick Cole	5	5	5	6	10	25	50	
29	Red Schoendienst	5	8	12	30	40	80	100	400
30	Bill Sarni	5	5	5	6	10	20	60	
31	Johnny Temple RC	5	5	6	8	25	30	50	
32	Wally Post	5	5	6	8	12	30	50	250
33	Nellie Fox	6	10	15	30	50	80	200	
34	Clint Courtney	5	5	5	6	10	25	60	350
35	Bill Tuttle RC	5	5	5	6	10	25	40	
36	Wayne Belardi RC	5	5	5	6	10	20	60	
37	Pee Wee Reese	10	15	50	60	80	120	250	
38	Early Wynn	5	8	15	20	30	60	120	600
39	Bob Darnell RC	5	5	6	8	25	40	200	400
40	Vic Wertz	5	5	6	8	20	25	100	
41	Mel Clark	5	5	5	6	10	20	50	
42	Bob Greenwood RC	5	5	6		15	25	50	300
43	Bob Buhl	5	5	6		12	30	50	400
44	Danny O'Connell	5	5	5	6	10	25	50	200
45	Tom Umphlett	5	5	6		10	25	60	300
46	Mickey Vernon	5	5	6	8	12	20	200	
47	Sammy White	5	5	5	6	15	20	50	300
48A	Milt Bolling ERR Frank on Back	5	5	6	8	12	40	100	
48B	Milt Bolling COR Milt on Back	5	5	6	8	12	25		
49	Jim Greengrass	5	5	5	6	12	25	50	
50	Hobie Landrith	5	5	5	6	10	15	50	250
51	Elvin Tappe RC	5	5	6		15	25	40	250
52	Hal Rice	5	5	5	6	10	25	40	250
53	Alex Kellner	5	5	5	6	12	20	50	300
54	Don Bollweg	5	5	5	6	10	30	60	300
55	Cal Abrams	5	5	5	6	10	▲30	50	200
56	Billy Cox	5	5	5	6	20	25	50	
57	Bob Friend	5	5	6	8	12	30	80	
58	Frank Thomas	5	5	6	8	15	25	50	
59	Whitey Ford	25	30	40	50	▲100	150	250	2,000
60	Enos Slaughter	5	8	▼20	▼25	▼30	▼60	120	500
61	Paul LaPalme	5	5	5	6	10	30	50	
62	Royce Lint RC	5	5	5	6	10	25	60	
63	Irv Noren	5	5	6	8	12	20	50	300
64	Curt Simmons	5	5	6	8	20	25	60	
65	Don Zimmer RC	6	10	25	30	50	100	200	500
66	George Shuba	5	5	6	8	12	25		
67	Don Larsen	5	8	12	25	40	80	200	
68	Elston Howard RC	10	15	25	50	80	150	400	800
69	Billy Hunter	5	5	6	8	12	40	150	
70	Lew Burdette	5	5	6	10	20	40	100	
71	Dave Jolly	5	5	5	6	10	40	50	300
72	Chet Nichols	5	5	5	6	10	20	80	
73	Eddie Yost	5	5	6	8	12	25	80	400
74	Jerry Snyder	5	5	5	6	10	30	50	
75	Brooks Lawrence RC	5	5	6		25	30	150	300
76	Tom Poholsky	5	5	5	6	10	30	150	
77	Jim McDonald RC	5	5	5	6	10	15	60	
78	Gil Coan	5	5	5	6	10	25	80	300
79	Willie Miranda	5	5	5	6	10	30	80	
80	Lou Limmer	5	5	5	6	10	20	200	
81	Bobby Morgan	5	5	5	6	10	20	80	
82	Lee Walls RC	5	5	6		20	30	80	300
83	Max Surkont	5	5	5	6	10	20	100	400
84	George Freese RC	5	5	5	6	10	30	80	
85	Cass Michaels	5	5	5	6	10	25	60	
86	Ted Gray	5	5	5	6	10	25	80	
87	Randy Jackson	5	5	5	6	10	15	60	300
88	Steve Bilko	5	5	5	6	12	25		300
89	Lou Boudreau MG	5	12	20	25	40	▲60	120	
90	Art Ditmar RC	5	5	5	6	15	20	60	
91	Dick Marlowe RC	5	5	5	6	12	25	120	
92	George Zuverink	5	5	5	6	10	30	50	
93	Andy Seminick	5	5	5	6	10	25	80	
94	Hank Thompson	5	5	6	8	12	30	80	
95	Sal Maglie	5	5	8	10	30	40	100	
96	Ray Narleski RC	5	5	5	6	25	30	150	

#	Player	GD 2	VG 3	VgEx 4	EX 5	ExMt 6	NM 7	NmMt 8	MT 9
97	Johnny Podres	5	8	12	▲25	▼30	60	120	
98	Jim Gilliam	5	6	10	12	30	60	200	
99	Jerry Coleman	5	5	6	8	30	50	100	
100	Tom Morgan	5	5	6	8	20	30	200	
101A	Don Johnson ERR Ernie on Front	5	5	6	8	12	40	150	
101B	Don Johnson COR Don on Front	5	5	6	8	12	25	60	
102	Bobby Thomson	5	5	8	10	25	30	80	
103	Eddie Mathews	10	15	30	50	100	150	▲500	
104	Bob Porterfield	5	5	5	6	15	20	60	
105	Johnny Schmitz	5	5	5	6	10	30	60	
106	Del Rice	5	5	5	6	20	25	120	400
107	Solly Hemus	5	5	5	6	10	15	80	
108	Lou Kretlow	5	5	5	6	10	15	80	
109	Vern Stephens	5	5	5	6	10	25	100	250
110	Bob Miller	5	5	5	6	10	15	50	
111	Steve Ridzik	5	5	5	6	10	30	60	
112	Granny Hamner	5	5	5	6	12	25	100	
113	Bob Hall RC	5	5	5	6	10	15	60	
114	Vic Janowicz	5	5	6	8	15	20	120	
115	Roger Bowman RC	5	5	5	6	20	25	50	
116	Sandy Consuegra	5	5	5	6	10	15	60	
117	Johnny Groth	5	5	5	6	10	15	50	
118	Bobby Adams	5	5	5	6	10	15	100	
119	Joe Astroth	5	5	5	6	15	25	80	
120	Ed Burtschy RC	5	5	5	6	10	15	50	
121	Rufus Crawford RC	5	5	5	6	15	30	60	
122	Al Corwin	5	5	5	6	10	20	100	
123	Marv Grissom RC	5	5	5	6	15	25	40	
124	Johnny Antonelli	5	5	5	6	20	25	60	
125	Paul Giel RC	5	5	5	6	20	25	60	
126	Billy Goodman	5	5	5	6	15	20	60	
127	Hank Majeski	5	5	5	6	20	30	100	
128	Mike Garcia	5	5	6	8	12	30	80	
129	Hal Naragon RC	5	5	5	6	10	20	60	
130	Richie Ashburn	12	15	25	30	50	100	300	
131	Willard Marshall	5	5	5	6	10	15	50	
132A	Harvey Kueen ERR	5	5	8	10	15	25	100	
132B	Harvey Kuenn COR	5	8	12	15	25	40		
133	Charles King RC	5	5	5	12	15	25	60	300
134	Bob Feller	25	30	40	60	80	150	500	
135	Lloyd Merriman	5	5	5	6	10	15	50	
136	Rocky Bridges	5	5	5	6	10	20	80	
137	Bob Talbot	5	5	5	6	10	15	100	350
138	Davey Williams	5	5	6	8	20	25	80	
139	B.Shantz/B.Shantz	5	5	6	8	20	40	200	
140	Bobby Shantz	5	5	6	8	12	30	120	
141	Wes Westrum	5	5	5	6	10	25	60	
142	Rudy Regalado RC	5	5	5	6	10	15	100	
143	Don Newcombe	5	8	20	30	50	60	200	
144	Art Houtteman	5	5	5	6	10	25	80	
145	Bob Nieman RC	5	5	5	6	10	20		
146	Don Liddle	5	5	5	6	12	30	150	
147	Sam Mele	5	5	5	6	10	20	100	
148	Bob Chakales	5	5	5	6	20	25	60	300
149	Cloyd Boyer	5	5	5	6	20	30	50	300
150	Billy Klaus RC	5	5	5	6	10	15	50	
151	Jim Brideweser	5	5	5	6	10	15	60	
152	Johnny Klippstein	5	5	5	6	10	20	100	
153	Eddie Robinson	5	5	6	8	20	50		
154	Frank Lary RC	5	5	6	8	15	40		
155	Gerry Staley	5	5	5	6	10	20	150	
156	Jim Hughes	5	5	8	10	25	30	100	
157A	Ernie Johnson ERR Don on Front	5	5	6	8	12	40	225	
157B	Ernie Johnson COR Ernie on Front	5	5	6	8	12	25		
158	Gil Hodges	8	12	30	40	50	80	250	
159	Harry Byrd	5	5	5	6	10	15	50	
160	Bill Skowron	6	10	15	20	40	100	200	
161	Matt Batts	5	5	5	6	10	15	60	300
162	Charlie Maxwell	5	5	5	6	10	15	150	350
163	Sid Gordon	5	5	5	6	10	25	40	400
164	Toby Atwell	5	5	5	6	20	25	60	
165	Maurice McDermott	5	5	5	6	10	30	50	
166	Jim Busby	5	5	5	6	10	15	50	
167	Bob Grim RC	5	5	8	10	20	30	80	
168	Yogi Berra	40	50	▲80	100	150	300	600	
169	Carl Furillo	5	8	12	15	40	50	150	800
170	Carl Erskine	5	6	15	20	40	50	200	

#	Player	GD 2	VG 3	VgEx 4	EX 5	ExMt 6	NM 7	NmMt 8	MT 9
171	Robin Roberts	6	10	25	40	50	60	150	
172	Willie Jones	5	5	5	6	10	25	60	300
173	Chico Carrasquel	5	5	5	6	10	25	80	250
174	Sherm Lollar	5	5	6	8	20	30	60	400
175	Wilmer Shantz RC	5	5	5	6	20	25	60	
176	Joe DeMaestri	5	5	5	6	10	30	100	
177	Willard Nixon	5	5	5	6	20	25	60	350
178	Tom Brewer RC	5	5	5	6	25	30	60	
179	Hank Aaron	▲100	▲120	150	250	400	800	3,000	
180	Johnny Logan	5	5	6	8	20	50	80	
181	Eddie Miksis	5	5	5	6	15	30	50	
182	Bob Rush	5	5	5	6	10	30	50	
183	Ray Katt	5	5	5	6	15	20	50	300
184	Willie Mays	▲80	100	150	250	500	1,200	4,000	
185	Vic Raschi	5	5	5	6	10	15	50	
186	Alex Grammas	5	5	5	6	10	15	100	
187	Fred Hatfield	5	5	5	6	10	25	60	
188	Ned Garver	5	5	5	6	10	30	80	
189	Jack Collum	5	5	5	6	10	15	50	
190	Fred Baczewski	5	5	5	6	10	30	50	
191	Bob Lemon	5	8	12	25	30	40	150	500
192	George Strickland	5	5	5	6	20	30	150	
193	Howie Judson	5	5	5	6	20	25	60	300
194	Joe Nuxhall	5	5	6	8	20	30	50	
195A	Erv Palica No Trade	5	5	6	8	12	20	80	
195B	Erv Palica Trade	6	10	15	20	30	50	150	
196	Russ Meyer	5	5	6	8	12	50	100	
197	Ralph Kiner	6	10	20	25	30	100	150	600
198	Dave Pope RC	5	5	5	6	10	15	80	
199	Vern Law	5	5	5	6	10	25	60	
200	Dick Littlefield	5	5	5	6	10	20	60	
201	Allie Reynolds	5	6	10	20	25	50	100	400
202	Mickey Mantle	▲300	400	▲600	▲1,000	▲1,500	2,500	8,000	12,000
203	Steve Gromek	5	5	5	6	10	15	50	
204A	Frank Bolling ERR Milt on Back RC	5	5	6	8	12	40		
204B	Frank Bolling COR Frank on Back	5	5	6	8	12	25		
205	Rip Repulski	5	5	5	6	10	20	100	
206	Ralph Beard RC	5	5	5	6	20	25	60	
207	Frank Shea	5	5	5	6	10	30	80	
208	Ed Fitzgerald	5	5	5	6	10	40	80	300
209	Smoky Burgess	5	5	6	8	12	20	80	
210	Earl Torgeson	5	5	5	6	25	30	200	
211	Sonny Dixon RC	5	5	5	6	10	50	60	
212	Jack Dittmer	5	5	5	6	10	15	50	
213	George Kell	5	6	10	20	25	60	120	
214	Billy Pierce	5	5	6	8	20	30	60	300
215	Bob Kuzava	5	5	5	6	10	15	40	
216	Preacher Roe	5	5	8	10	25	40	100	
217	Del Crandall	5	5	6	8	20	30	100	
218	Joe Adcock	5	5	6	8	20	▲50	100	
219	Whitey Lockman	5	5	5	6	12	30	50	
220	Jim Hearn	5	5	5	6	10	30	50	
221	Hector Brown	5	5	5	6	10	15	50	
222	Russ Kemmerer RC	5	5	5	6	10	40	60	
223	Hal Jeffcoat	5	5	5	6	10	25	100	350
224	Dee Fondy	5	5	5	6	20	30	100	
225	Paul Richards MG	5	6	10	12	25	60	300	
226	Bill McKinley UMP	5	6	10	12	20	80	250	
227	Frank Baumholtz	5	5	8	10	30	50	100	
228	John Phillips RC	5	5	8	10	15	40	100	
229	Jim Brosnan RC	5	5	8	10	15	40	150	500
230	Al Brazle	5	5	8	10	15	25	100	
231	Jim Konstanty	5	6	10	12	20	50	200	500
232	Birdie Tebbetts MG	6	10	15	20	30	60	300	
233	Bill Serena	5	5	8	10	15	40	300	
234	Dick Bartell CO	5	5	6	8	10	25	40	120
235	Joe Paparella UMP	5	6	10	12	30	40	120	
236	Murry Dickson	5	5	8	10	30	40	250	
237	Johnny Wyrostek	5	5	8	10	15	40	80	
238	Eddie Stanky MG	5	6	10	12	20	30	250	500
239	Edwin Rommel UMP	5	6	10	12	30	60	120	
240	Billy Loes	5	8	12	15	50	100		
241	Johnny Pesky	5	6	10	12	20	40		
242	Ernie Banks	80	120	▲200	300	400	1,000	3,000	
243	Gus Bell	5	5	8	10	15	60	100	500
244	Duane Pillette	5	5	8	10	15	60	200	
245	Bill Miller	5	5	8	10	15	40	100	400

	GD 2	VG 3	VgEx 4	EX 5	ExMt 6	NM 7	NmMt 8	MT 9
Hank Bauer	8	12	20	40	60	80	200	500
Dutch Leonard CO	5	5	8	10	20	40	120	400
Harry Dorish	5	5	8	10	15	40	150	
Billy Gardner RC	5	5	8	10	15	40	400	
Larry Napp UMP	5	6	10	12	40	60	250	
Stan Jok	5	5	8	10	20	25	80	
Roy Smalley	5	5	8	10	15	25	100	400
Jim Wilson	5	5	8	10	15	40	250	
Bennett Flowers RC	5	5	8	10	25	40	120	400
Pete Runnels	5	5	8	10	15	50	100	
Owen Friend	5	5	8	10	25	50	100	
Tom Alston RC	5	5	8	10	15	50	80	400
John Stevens UMP	5	6	10	12	25	30	100	
Don Mossi RC	5	8	12	15	25	50	120	500
Edwin Hurley UMP	5	6	10	12	20	40	150	
Walt Moryn RC	5	6	10	12	25	80	250	
Jim Lemon	5	5	8	20	25	30	100	
Eddie Joost	5	5	8	20	25	40	80	
Bill Henry RC	5	5	8	10	30	50	200	
Al Barlick UMP	8	12	20	40	50	60	250	
Mike Fornieles	5	5	8	10	15	25	200	
Jim Honochick UMP	6	10	15	25	30	50	120	500
Roy Lee Hawes RC	5	5	8	10	25	40	120	
Joe Amalfitano RC	5	8	12	15	50	60	120	
Chico Fernandez RC	5	6	10	12	50	60	250	
Bob Hooper	5	5	8	10	15	25	100	500
John Flaherty UMP	5	6	10	12	20	40	150	
Bubba Church	5	5	8	10	15	25	100	
Jim Delsing	5	5	8	25	30	50	150	
William Grieve UMP	5	6	10	12	20	40	120	
Ike Delock	5	5	8	10	15	50	120	
Ed Runge UMP	5	6	10	25	30	50	150	
Charlie Neal RC	8	12	20	40	50	100	600	
Hank Soar UMP	5	6	15	20	25	50	150	
Clyde McCullough	5	5	8	10	20	50	400	
Charles Berry UMP	5	6	10	12	25	30	120	
Phil Cavarretta MG	5	8	12	15	25	80	250	
Nestor Chylak UMP	8	12	20	40	80	80	500	
Bill Jackowski UMP	5	6	10	12	20	50	200	
Walt Dropo	5	5	8	15	20	80	100	
Frank Secory UMP	5	6	10	12	25	60	150	400
Ron Mrozinski RC	5	5	8	10	25	60	250	
Dick Smith RC	5	5	8	10	15	60	200	
Arthur Gore UMP	5	6	10	12	20	120	150	400
Hershell Freeman RC	5	5	8	10	15	25	100	
Frank Dascoli UMP	5	6	10	12	20	60	120	
Marv Blaylock RC	5	5	8	10	25	60	300	500
Thomas Gorman UMP	5	6	10	12	30	50	100	
Wally Moses CO	5	5	8	10	15	25	80	500
Lee Ballanfant UMP	5	6	10	12	20	▲60	100	
Bill Virdon RC	6	10	15	30	40	80	200	
Dusty Boggess UMP	5	6	10	12	20	80	250	
Charlie Grimm	5	5	8	10	30	40		
Lon Warneke UMP	5	6	10	12	20	80	200	
Tommy Byrne	5	8	12	20	40	120		
William Engeln UMP	5	6	10	12	30	30	150	
Frank Malzone RC	5	8	12	15	50	80	300	
Jocko Conlan UMP	8	12	20	25	80	120	300	1,000
Harry Chiti	5	5	8	10	15	30	150	
Frank Umont UMP	5	6	10	12	25	30	250	
Bob Cerv	5	8	15	20	60	100	400	
Babe Pinelli UMP	5	6	10	12	30	100	120	
Al Lopez MG	6	10	25	30	40	100	150	
Hal Dixon UMP	5	6	10	12	20	50	100	
Ken Lehman RC	5	5	8	10	15	80		
Lawrence Goetz UMP	5	6	10	12	25	30	100	
Bill Wight	5	5	8	10	20	40	120	
Augie Donatelli UMP	5	8	12	15	25	50	120	
Dale Mitchell	5	6	10	25	30	150		
Cal Hubbard UMP	6	10	15	40	▼60	100	250	
Marion Fricano	5	5	8	10	15	25	100	
William Summers UMP	5	6	10	12	30	▲60		
Sid Hudson	5	5	8	10	15	40	120	
Al Schroll RC	5	5	8	10	20	40		
George Susce RC	8	12	20	30	50	120		

-Listed pricing for Mint cards typically references cards with PSA populations of 6 or more copies.
-Mint Commons & Minor Stars (1-224) w/PSA populations of 5 or fewer copies sell as follows: 4-5 copies -

$300, 3 copies - $350, 2 copies - $400-$500 and 1 copy - $400-$600 per.
-Mint Commons & Minor Stars (225-320) w/PSA populations of 5 or fewer copies sell as follows: 3-5 copies - $400, 2 copies - $500-$600 and 1 copy - $500-$800 per.
—Hank Aaron #179 GAI 9.5 (Gem) sold for $3,697 (Goodwin; 3/08)
—Hank Aaron #179 GAI 9.5 (Gem) sold for $888 (eBay; 5/08)
—Hank Aaron #179 PSA 9 (MT) sold for $4,915 (Mastro; 12/06)
—Hank Aaron #179 GAI 9 (MT) sold for $3,148 (Mile High; 1/07)
—Hank Aaron #179 GAI 9 (MT) sold for $2,875 (Memory Lane; 11/05)
—Hank Aaron #179 GAI 9 (MT) sold for $2,839 (Memory Lane; 4/07)
—Hank Aaron #179 GAI 9 (MT) sold for $2,550 (eBay; 10/06)
—Hank Aaron #179 GAI 9 (MT) sold for $921 (eBay; 11/07)
—Ernie Banks #242 GAI 9.5 (Gem) sold for $3,163 (Memory Lane; 11/05)
—Ernie Banks #242 GAI 9 (MT) sold for $1,939 (Memory Lane; 4/07)
—Ernie Banks #242 GAI 9 (MT) sold for $1,898 (Memory Lane; 3/06)
—Ernie Banks #242 GAI 9 (MT) sold for $1,834 (Madec; 11/07)
—Ernie Banks #242 GAI 9 (MT) sold for $1,725 (eBay; 10/06)
—Ernie Banks #242 GAI 9 (MT) sold for $1,084 (eBay; 11/07)
—Ernie Banks #242 GAI 9 (MT) sold for $1,036 (eBay; 2/07)
—Ernie Banks #242 GAI 9 (MT) sold for $789 (eBay; 6/08)
—Yogi Berra #168 GAI 9 (MT) sold for $1,746 (Memory Lane; 8/05)
—Frank Bolling COR #204 PSA 8 (NmMt) sold for $228 (12/06)
—Tommy Byrne #300 PSA 8 (NmMt) sold for $698 (eBay; 11/05)
—Tommy Byrne #300 PSA 8 (NmMt) sold for $587 (eBay; 4/07)
—Roy Campanella #22 PSA 9 (MT) sold for $3,403 (Memory Lane; 8/06)
—Roy Campanella #22 GAI 9 (MT) sold for $416 (eBay; 7/06)
—Alvin Dark #2 PSA 8 (NmMt) sold for $361 (eBay; 9/04)
—Bob Feller #134 PSA 9 (MT) sold for $1,779 (Memory Lane; 12/06)
—Bob Feller #134 GAI 9 (MT) sold for $408 (eBay; 1/08)
—Whitey Ford #59 GAI 9 (MT) sold for $569 (Memory Lane; 9/07)
—Charlie Grimm #298 PSA 8 (NmMt) sold for $700 (eBay; 8/06)
—Charlie Grimm #298 PSA 8 (NmMt) sold for $381 (Goodwin; 2/07)
—Gil Hodges #158 PSA 9 (MT) sold for $2,263 (Memory Lane; 11/05)
—Gil Hodges #158 GAI 9 (MT) sold for $620 (Goodwin; 10/05)
—Gil Hodges #158 GAI 9 (MT) sold for $306 (eBay; 5/07)
—Elston Howard #68 GAI 9 (MT) sold for $329 (eBay; 11/07)
—Elston Howard #68 GAI 9 (MT) sold for $187 (eBay; 1/08)
—Al Kaline #23 GAI 9 (MT) sold for $403 (eBay; 5/07)
—Al Kaline #23 GAI 9 (MT) sold for $375 (eBay; 11/07)
—Al Kaline #23 GAI 9 (MT) sold for $253 (eBay; 2/08)
—Al Kaline #23 GAI 9 (MT) sold for $223 (eBay; 1/08)
—Ken Lehman #310 PSA 8 (NmMt) sold for $449 (eBay; 3/07)
—Ken Lehman #310 PSA 8 (NmMt) sold for $313 (eBay; 1/06)
—Ken Lehman #310 PSA 8 (NmMt) sold for $118 (eBay; 2/04)
—Billy Loes #240 PSA 9 (MT) sold for $1,497 (Memory Lane; 11/05)
—Billy Loes #240 PSA 8 (NmMt) sold for $461 (eBay; 8/06)
—Billy Loes #240 PSA 8 (NmMt) sold for $332 (eBay; 9/06)
—Mickey Mantle #202 PSA 10 (Gem) sold for $14,400 (SCP Sotheby's; 12/05)
—Mickey Mantle #202 GAI 9 (MT) sold for $3,877 (Goodwin; 10/06)
—Mickey Mantle #202 GAI 9 (MT) sold for $2,800 (eBay; 11/07)
—Mickey Mantle #202 GAI 9 (MT) sold for $2,551 (eBay; 9/06)
—Mickey Mantle #202 GAI 9 (MT) sold for $2,475 (eBay; 2/07)
—Mickey Mantle #202 GAI 9 (MT) sold for $1,894 (Goodwin; 3/08)
—Mickey Mantle #202 SGC 92 (NmMt+) sold for $2,868 (Heritage; 5/08)
—Mickey Mantle #202 BVG 8.5 (NmMt+) sold for $2,000 (eBay; 3/07)
—Mickey Mantle #202 GAI 8.5 (NmMt+) sold for $1,746 (eBay; 12/06)
—Mickey Mantle #202 GAI 8.5 (NmMt+) sold for $1,648 (Madec; 5/08)
—Mickey Mantle #202 GAI 8 (NmMt) sold for $1,225 (eBay; 5/07)
—Mickey Mantle #202 GAI 8 (NmMt) sold for $1,150 (eBay; 11/07)
—Willie Mays #184 GAI 9.5 (Gem) sold for $4,175 (Memory Lane; 11/05)
—Willie Mays #184 GAI 9.5 (Gem) sold for $3,055 (Goodwin; 3/08)
—Willie Mays #184 GAI 9.5 (Gem) sold for $1,892 (Mastro; 8/07)
—Willie Mays #184 GAI 9.5 (Gem) sold for $1,347 (eBay; 5/08)
—Willie Mays #184 PSA 9 (MT) sold for $17,658 (Goodwin; 10/06)
—Willie Mays #184 PSA 9 (MT) sold for $5,016 (Mastro; 4/04)
—Willie Mays #184 PSA 9 (MT) sold for $4,140 (Superior; 7/03)
—Willie Mays #184 GAI 9 (MT) sold for $2,778 (Mile High; 6/05)
—Willie Mays #184 GAI 9 (MT) sold for $2,530 (Memory Lane; 3/06)
—Willie Mays #184 GAI 9 (MT) sold for $2,133 (Memory Lane; 4/07)
—Willie Mays #184 GAI 9 (MT) sold for $1,528 (eBay; 1/07)
—Willie Mays #184 GAI 9 (MT) sold for $1,526 (eBay; 12/06)
—Willie Mays #184 GAI 9 (MT) sold for $1,517 (eBay; 9/07)
—Willie Mays #184 GAI 9 (MT) sold for $1,513 (eBay; 5/08)
—Willie Mays #184 GAI 9 (MT) sold for $1,390 (Mastro; 4/06)
—Willie Mays #184 GAI 9 (MT) sold for $1,336 (eBay; 5/07)
—Willie Mays #184 GAI 9 (MT) sold for $921 (eBay; 11/07)
—Willie Mays #184 PSA 8.5 (NmMt+) sold for $1,726 (eBay; 4/08)
—Dale Mitchell #314 PSA 8 (NmMt) sold for $632 (eBay; 9/06)

—Dale Mitchell #314 PSA 8 (NmMt) sold for $306 (eBay; 5/07)
—Don Newcombe #143 PSA 9 (MT) sold for $1,996 (Mile High; 6/06)
—Don Newcombe #143 PSA 9 (MT) sold for $1,208 (Superior; 7/03)
—Bob Nieman #145 PSA 8 (NmMt) sold for $394 (eBay; 6/06)
—Bob Nieman #145 PSA 8 (NmMt) sold for $312 (eBay; 2/07)
—Johnny Pesky #241 PSA 8 (NmMt) sold for $811 (eBay; 8/06)
—Johnny Pesky #241 PSA 8 (NmMt) sold for $294 (eBay; 9/04)
—Johnny Podres #97 PSA 9 (MT) sold for $2,263 (Memory Lane; 11/05)
—Pee Wee Reese #37 PSA 9 (MT) sold for $1,915 (Memory Lane; 8/06)
—Pee Wee Reese #37 PSA 9 (MT) sold for $1,216 (Goodwin; 8/07)
—Pee Wee Reese #37 GAI 9 (MT) sold for $559 (eBay; 7/06)
—Allie Reynolds #201 PSA 10 sold for $2,458 (Goodwin; 5/07)
—Phil Rizzuto #10 PSA 10 (Gem) sold for $4,907 (Goodwin; 5/07)
—Eddie Robinson #153 PSA 8 (NmMt) sold for $520 (eBay; 8/06)
—Al Schroll #319 PSA 8 (NmMt) sold for $340 (eBay; 8/06)
—Al Schroll #319 PSA 8 (NmMt) sold for $215 (eBay; 4/07)
—Al Schroll #319 PSA 8 (NmMt) sold for $210 (eBay; 3/07)
—George Shuba #66 PSA 8 (NmMt) sold for $360 (eBay; 1/06)
—George Shuba #66 PSA 8 (NmMt) sold for $287 (eBay; 1/07)
—Bill Summers #317 PSA 8 (NmMt) sold for $561 (eBay; 8/06)
—Bill Summers #317 PSA 8 (NmMt) sold for $255 (eBay; 1/08)
—George Susce #320 PSA 8 (NmMt) sold for $895 (Mile High; 12/05)
—George Susce #320 PSA 8 (NmMt) sold for $236 (eBay; 4/07)
—Hoyt Wilhelm #1 SGC 96 (MT) sold for $4,780 (Heritage; 5/08)
—Hoyt Wilhelm #1 PSA 9 (MT) sold for $4,067 (Goodwin; 3/08)
—Hoyt Wilhelm #1 GAI 9 (MT) sold for $1,601 (Mile High; 12/05)
—Hoyt Wilhelm #1 GAI 8.5 (NmMt+) sold for $407 (Memory Lane; 3/06)

1955 Red Man

		GD 2	VG 3	VgEx 4	EX 5	ExMt 6	NM 7	NmMt 8	MT 9
AL1	Ray Boone	5	8	12	20	35	100	200	
AL2	Jim Busby	5	8	12	20	35	60	200	
AL3	Whitey Ford	12	20	30	50	80	120	500	
AL4	Nellie Fox	8	12	20	30	50	80	250	
AL5	Bob Grim	5	8	12	20	35	80	200	500
AL6	Jack Harshman	5	8	12	20	35	80	200	500
AL7	Jim Hegan	5	8	12	20	35	60	200	
AL8	Bob Lemon	8	12	20	30	50	80	250	
AL9	Irv Noren	5	8	12	20	35	60	200	
AL10	Bob Porterfield	5	8	12	20	35	60	200	
AL11	Al Rosen	5	8	12	20	35	60	200	
AL12	Mickey Vernon	5	8	12	20	35	60	200	
AL13	Vic Wertz	5	8	12	20	35	60	200	
AL14	Early Wynn	8	12	20	30	50	80	250	
AL15	Bobby Avila	5	8	12	20	35	60	200	
AL16	Yogi Berra	20	30	40	60	120	150	600	
AL17	Joe Coleman	5	8	12	20	35	60	200	500
AL18	Larry Doby	8	12	20	30	50	80	200	
AL19	Jackie Jensen	5	8	12	20	35	60	200	
AL20	Pete Runnels	5	8	12	20	35	60		
AL21	Jimmy Piersall	5	8	12	20	35	60	200	
AL22	Hank Bauer	5	8	12	20	35	60	200	800
AL23	Chico Carrasquel	5	8	12	20	35	60	200	
AL24	Minnie Minoso	5	8	12	20	35	60	200	
AL25	Sandy Consuegra	5	8	12	20	35	60	200	500
NL1	Richie Ashburn	10	15	25	40	60	100	400	
NL2	Del Crandall	5	8	12	20	35	60	200	500
NL3	Gil Hodges	10	15	25	40	80	100	400	
NL4	Brooks Lawrence	5	8	12	20	35	60	200	500
NL5	Johnny Logan	5	8	12	20	35	60	200	500
NL6	Sal Maglie	5	8	12	20	35	60	200	
NL7	Willie Mays	40	60	80	120	300	400	1,200	
NL8	Don Mueller	5	8	12	20	35	60	200	
NL9	Bill Sarni	5	8	12	20	35	60	200	500
NL10	Warren Spahn	12	20	30	50	80	120	500	
NL11	Hank Thompson	5	8	12	20	35	60	200	
NL12	Hoyt Wilhelm	8	12	20	30	50	80	250	
NL13	John Antonelli	5	8	12	20	35	60	200	
NL14	Carl Erskine	5	8	12	20	35	60	200	
NL15	Granny Hamner	5	8	12	20	35	60	200	
NL16	Ted Kluszewski	8	12	20	30	50	80	250	
NL17	Pee Wee Reese	12	20	30	50	80	120	500	
NL18	Red Schoendienst	8	12	20	30	50	80	250	
NL19	Duke Snider	20	30	40	60	100	150	600	
NL20	Frank Thomas	5	8	12	20	35	60	200	
NL21	Ray Jablonski	5	8	12	20	35	60	200	

		GD 2	VG 3	VgEx 4	EX 5	ExMt 6	NM 7	NmMt 8	MT
NL22	Dusty Rhodes	5	8	12	20	35	80	300	
NL23	Gus Bell	5	8	12	20	35	60	200	5
NL24	Curt Simmons	5	8	12	20	35	60		
NL25	Marv Grissom	5	8	12	20	35	80	250	

—Prices reference cards with tabs.
—Duke Snider #NL19 SGC 96 (MT) sold for $1,800 (Mastro; 5/08)
—Duke Snider #NL19 SGC 96 (MT) sold for $1,433 (eBay; 2/08)

1955 Topps

		GD 2	VG 3	VgEx 4	EX 5	ExMt 6	NM 7	NmMt 8	MT
1	Dusty Rhodes	5	15	20	30	60	150	300	4,00
2	Ted Williams	120	200	250	▲400	600	1,200	5,000	10,00
3	Art Fowler RC	5	5	8	12	30	100	800	
4	Al Kaline	40	50	80	100	200	▼300	1,200	
5	Jim Gilliam	5	8	15	40	50	150	500	
6	Stan Hack MG RC	5	5	8	12	25	50	100	
7	Jim Hegan	5	5	6	15	50	200	1,000	
8	Hal Smith RC	5	5	6	10	40	80	600	
9	Bob Miller	5	5	6	10	15	30	100	1,20
10	Bob Keegan	5	5	6	10	25	100	800	
11	Ferris Fain	5	5	8	12	25	▲80	▲400	
12	Jake Thies RC	5	5	6	10	15	30	100	6
13	Fred Marsh	5	5	6	10	20	40	80	50
14	Jim Finigan RC	5	5	6	10	25	50	150	
15	Jim Pendleton	5	5	6	10	15	50	80	4
16	Roy Sievers	5	5	6	10	30	100	250	
17	Bobby Hofman	5	5	6	10	15	40	60	60
18	Russ Kemmerer RC	5	5	6	10	25	50	100	
19	Billy Herman CO	5	5	8	30	50	100	500	
20	Andy Carey	5	6	10	15	30	150	1,200	
21	Alex Grammas	5	5	6	15	20	50	100	
22	Bill Skowron	5	6	20	25	40	60	200	1,00
23	Jack Parks RC	5	5	6	10	30	60	600	
24	Hal Newhouser	5	8	25	30	50	120	1,000	
25	Johnny Podres	6	10	25	40	50	150	1,500	
26	Dick Groat	5	10	15	25	50	200	1,200	
27	Billy Gardner RC	5	5	6	10	25	40	80	
28	Ernie Banks	50	60	▲120	▲200	250	400	1,200	8,00
29	Herman Wehmeier	5	5	6	10	20	60	120	
30	Vic Power	5	5	8	15	25	100	250	
31	Warren Spahn	25	50	60	80	100	300	1,000	
32	Ed McGhee RC	5	5	6	10	25	50	250	
33	Tom Qualters	5	5	6	10	25	80	400	
34	Wayne Terwilliger	5	5	6	10	25	50	300	
35	Dave Jolly	5	5	6	20	25	40	80	40
36	Leo Kiely	5	5	6	10	25	40	250	
37	Joe Cunningham RC	5	5	8	12	25	50	100	1,00
38	Bob Turley	5	5	8	25	30	50	120	1,20
39	Bill Glynn	5	5	6	10	25	80	250	
40	Don Hoak	5	6	20	30	40	60	300	
41	Chuck Stobbs	5	5	12	15	25	50	80	60
42	Windy McCall RC	5	5	6	10	20	30	60	65
43	Harvey Haddix	5	5	6	10	25	50	▲100	50
44	Harold Valentine RC	5	5	6	10	25	40	80	
45	Hank Sauer	5	5	8	12	25	30	100	
46	Ted Kazanski	5	5	6	20	25	30	100	60
47	Hank Aaron	▲150	▲250	▲300	500	600	▲1,500	4,000	15,00
48	Bob Kennedy	5	5	6	10	25	30	60	
49	J.W. Porter	10	12	15	20	25	60	400	
50	Jackie Robinson	200	250	300	400	▲600	1,200	4,000	10,00
51	Jim Hughes	5	5	8	12	25	60	80	
52	Bill Tremel RC	5	5	6	10	15	40	80	50
53	Bill Taylor	5	5	6	10	15	30	100	60
54	Lou Limmer	5	5	6	15	25	40	80	80
55	Rip Repulski	5	5	6	10	25	50	100	
56	Ray Jablonski	5	5	6	15	25	50	120	80
57	Billy O'Dell RC	5	5	6	10	15	40	80	
58	Jim Rivera	5	5	6	10	25	60	400	
59	Gair Allie	5	5	6	10	15	40	120	
60	Dean Stone	5	5	6	10	15	30	80	80
61	Spook Jacobs	5	5	8	12	20	50	100	
62	Thornton Kipper	5	5	6	10	30	50	100	
63	Joe Collins	5	5	6	20	40	150		
64	Gus Triandos RC	5	5	8	12	25	60	250	
65	Ray Boone	5	5	6	10	30	50	150	
66	Ron Jackson RC	5	5	6	10	25	50	250	

	GD 2	VG 3	VgEx 4	EX 5	ExMt 6	NM 7	NmMt 8	MT 9
Wally Moon	5	5	6	20	30	50	100	
Jim Davis RC	5	5	6	10	25	30	100	600
Ed Bailey	5	5	6	10	25	40	80	
Al Rosen	5	6	10	25	40	80	300	
Ruben Gomez	5	5	6	25	30	40	80	400
Karl Olson	5	5	6	10	20	60	150	
Jack Shepard RC	5	5	6	10	15	40	80	600
Bob Borkowski	5	5	6	10	20	50	80	500
Sandy Amoros RC	5	8	20	25	30	80	200	
Howie Pollet	5	5	6	10	15	40	80	400
Arnie Portocarrero	5	5	6	10	25	40	300	
Gordon Jones RC	5	5	6	10	30	50	300	
Danny Schell RC	5	5	6	15	20	40	▲100	600
Bob Grim RC	5	5	8	20	40	80	250	1,500
Gene Conley	5	5	6	10	30	60	300	
Chuck Harmon	5	5	6	10	25	▼50	120	600
Tom Brewer RC	5	5	6	15	20	60	200	
Camilo Pascual RC	5	5	8	20	30	60	300	
Don Mossi RC	5	5	6	10	25	50	80	1,200
Bill Wilson	5	5	10	12	20	30	80	
Frank House	5	5	6	10	20	40	80	800
Bob Skinner RC	5	5	6	15	20	50	100	
Joe Frazier RC	5	5	6	10	25	60	250	
Karl Spooner RC	5	5	20	25	30	60	80	
Milt Bolling	5	5	6	▲20	25	50	100	650
Don Zimmer RC	6	10	▲40	50	80	▲200	800	
Steve Bilko	5	5	6	10	25	▲50	80	
Reno Bertoia	5	5	6	10	25	50	100	600
Preston Ward	5	5	6	10	20	40	100	600
Chuck Bishop	5	5	6	10	15	30	80	600
Carlos Paula RC	5	5	6	10	20	40	80	600
John Riddle CO	5	5	6	10	20	30	60	800
Frank Leja	5	5	6	10	20	40	150	
Monte Irvin	6	10	30	40	▼50	250		
Johnny Gray RC	5	5	6	10	25	60	200	
Wally Westlake	5	5	6	10	20	40	80	1,200
Chuck White RC	5	5	6	15	20	40	80	500
Jack Harshman	5	5	6	10	20	30	80	800
Chuck Diering	5	5	6	10	20	50	100	
Frank Sullivan RC	5	5	6	15	30	60		
Curt Roberts	5	5	6	15	20	40	80	500
Rube Walker	5	5	8	20	30	50	▲120	800
Ed Lopat	5	6	20	25	30	80	400	
Gus Zernial	5	5	8	12	20	▼40	120	
Bob Milliken	5	5	8	12	30	50	100	
Nelson King RC	5	5	6	10	30	40	80	500
Harry Brecheen CO	5	5	6	15	25	40	80	600
Lou Ortiz RC	5	5	6	10	20	40	100	500
Ellis Kinder	5	5	6	15	20	40	80	500
Tom Hurd RC	5	5	6	10	15	30	80	800
Mel Roach RC	5	5	6	10	15	40	60	1,000
Bob Purkey	5	5	6	10	25	40	80	600
Bob Lennon RC	5	5	6	10	25	40	100	
Ted Kluszewski	5	12	25	30	50	100	250	2,000
Bill Renna	5	5	6	10	20	40	▲100	500
Carl Sawatski	5	5	6	10	15	50	80	600
Sandy Koufax RC	400	500	600	1,000	1,500	4,000	12,000	100,000
Harmon Killebrew RC	▲100	▲120	150	250	▼400	800	2,500	12,000
Ken Boyer RC	6	10	40	60	80	120	500	
Dick Hall RC	5	5	6	10	15	40	80	600
Dale Long RC	5	5	6	10	20	40	80	500
Ted Lepcio	5	5	6	10	25	30	80	600
Elvin Tappe	5	5	6	15	20	40	80	600
Mayo Smith MG RC	5	5	6	10	▲25	40	80	400
Grady Hatton	5	5	6	10	15	40	80	500
Bob Trice	5	5	6	20	25	40	120	400
Dave Hoskins	5	5	6	10	25	50	100	
Joey Jay	5	5	6	10	20	40	100	600
Johnny O'Brien	5	5	6	10	30	40	80	
Bunky Stewart RC	5	5	6	10	20	30	100	600
Harry Elliott RC	5	5	6	10	12	30	50	150
Ray Herbert	5	5	6	15	20	40	100	600
Steve Kraly RC	5	5	6	12	20	▲50	100	800
Mel Parnell	5	5	6	10	25	50	80	
Tom Wright	5	5	6	10	20	40	100	600
Jerry Lynch	5	5	6	15	20	40	▲80	500
Dick Schofield	5	5	8	12	30	50	150	1,200

		GD 2	VG 3	VgEx 4	EX 5	ExMt 6	NM 7	NmMt 8	MT 9
144	Joe Amalfitano RC	5	5	8	12	20	50	100	
145	Elmer Valo	5	5	6	10	25	50	100	800
146	Dick Donovan RC	5	5	6	10	25	40	100	500
147	Hugh Pepper RC	5	5	6	10	20	40	100	
148	Hal Brown	5	5	6	10	20	30	100	500
149	Ray Crone	5	5	6	10	20	40	80	400
150	Mike Higgins MG	5	5	6	10	25	40	100	700
151	Red Kress CO	5	5	6	10	30	50	120	700
152	Harry Agganis RC	10	15	40	60	100	250	600	
153	Bud Podbielan	5	5	10	20	40	50	100	600
154	Willie Miranda	5	5	8	12	25	50	100	
155	Eddie Mathews	40	60	80	100	150	300	600	2,000
156	Joe Black	6	10	25	50	50	150	500	1,000
157	Robert Miller	5	5	8	25	30	50	100	600
158	Tom Carroll RC	5	6	10	15	40	80	250	800
159	Johnny Schmitz	5	5	8	12	25	50	120	
160	Ray Narleski RC	5	5	8	12	40	60	100	
161	Chuck Tanner RC	5	6	10	15	60	80	250	
162	Joe Coleman	5	6	10	20	30	60	250	
163	Faye Throneberry	5	6	10	15	40	100	250	
164	Roberto Clemente RC	1,000	1,200	1,500	3,000	5,000	10,000	30,000	
165	Don Johnson	5	6	10	15	40	80	200	
166	Hank Bauer	10	15	40	50	80	150	500	
167	Tom Casagrande RC	5	6	10	15	50	100	300	
168	Duane Pillette	5	6	10	25	40	80	250	800
169	Bob Oldis	5	8	12	20	40	60	200	800
170	Jim Pearce DP RC	5	5	8	12	25	60	120	
171	Dick Brodowski	5	6	25	30	40	80	120	800
172	Frank Baumholtz DP	5	5	8	15	30	60	120	600
173	Bob Kline RC	5	6	10	15	30	60	200	
174	Rudy Minarcin RC	5	6	10	25	30	50	120	600
176	Norm Zauchin RC	5	8	12	25	60	250	600	
177	Jim Robertson	5	6	10	25	30	80	150	1,000
178	Bobby Adams	5	6	10	30	40	100	200	
179	Jim Bolger RC	5	6	10	30	▲60	120	250	
180	Clem Labine	6	10	15	50	80	150	400	
181	Roy McMillan	5	8	12	30	50	100	250	
182	Humberto Robinson RC	5	6	10	15	40	100	200	
183	Tony Jacobs RC	5	6	15	20	60	120	800	
184	Harry Perkowski DP	5	5	8	12	25	▼50	150	600
185	Don Ferrarese RC	5	6	10	15	50	60	200	800
187	Gil Hodges	25	40	60	100	150	250	800	3,500
188	Charlie Silvera DP	5	6	10	25	30	50	200	
189	Phil Rizzuto	50	60	80	100	150	▲400	600	
190	Gene Woodling	5	8	12	40	60	100	300	
191	Ed Stanky MG	5	8	12	25	50	100	250	
192	Jim Delsing	6	10	15	25	60	200	500	
193	Johnny Sain	10	15	20	40	60	120	300	
194	Willie Mays	150	▲250	▲400	500	▲1,000	2,000	6,000	
195	Ed Roebuck RC	6	10	15	50	60	▲400	1,000	
196	Gale Wade RC	5	6	10	25	50	120	250	
197	Al Smith	6	10	15	30	60	120	400	
198	Yogi Berra	▲80	100	120	250	400	600	1,500	7,000
199	Bert Hamric RC	5	6	10	25	50	100	200	
200	Jackie Jensen	6	10	25	50	60	120	400	
201	Sherman Lollar	6	10	15	25	80	200	1,000	
202	Jim Owens RC	5	6	10	15	80	250	800	
204	Frank Smith	5	6	10	30	60	120	500	
205	Gene Freese RC	6	10	15	60	100	250	1,200	
206	Pete Daley RC	5	6	15	30	60	200	500	
207	Bill Consolo	6	10	15	25	100	250	1,000	
208	Ray Moore RC	5	8	12	20	60	250	500	
210	Duke Snider	80	100	▲200	300	500	1,000	5,000	

—A complete set with each card uniformly graded PSA 7 (NM) sold for $19,975 (REA; 4/07)
—Hank Aaron #47 SGC 96 (MT) sold for $4,870 (Mastro; 4/06)
—Hank Aaron #47 SGC 92 (NmMt+) sold for $1,512 (Memory Lane; 5/08)
—Hank Aaron #47 SGC 92 (NmMt+) sold for $1,459 (Mastro; 4/06)
—Hank Aaron #47 SGC 92 (NmMt+) sold for $1,434 (Heritage; 10/07)
—Harry Agganis #152 PSA 9 (MT) sold for $2,156 (Mile High; 1/07)
—Yogi Berra #198 SGC 92 (NmMt+) sold for $1,025 (eBay; 3/07)
—Roberto Clemente #164 PSA 10 (Gem) (Young Collection) sold for $432,690 (SCP; 5/12)
—Roberto Clemente #164 PSA 9 (MT) sold for $478,000 (Heritage; 2/16)
—Roberto Clemente #164 PSA 9 (MT) sold for $310,700 (Heritage; 7/15)
—Roberto Clemente #164 PSA 9 (MT) sold for $36,312 (Mastro; 4/06)
—Roberto Clemente #164 PSA 9 (MT) sold for $18,997 (Mile High; 10/04)
—Roberto Clemente #164 PSA 9 (MT) sold for $18,046 (Mile High; 6/05)
—Roberto Clemente #164 PSA 9 (MT) sold for $17,500 (eBay; 6/04)

—Roberto Clemente #164 PSA 9 (MT) sold for $13,508 (SCP; 8/03)
—Roberto Clemente #164 PSA 8.5 (NmMt+) sold for $14,457 (Madec; 5/08)
—Roberto Clemente #164 BVG 8.5 (NmMt+) sold for $4,807 (eBay; 5/08)
—Roberto Clemente #164 BVG 8.5 (NmMt+) sold for $4,300 (eBay; 10/06)
—Joe Collins #63 PSA 8 (NmMt) sold for $1,305 (Memory Lane; 5/08)
—Joe Collins #63 PSA 8 (NmMt) sold for $1,264 (eBay; 5/08)
—Joe Collins #63 PSA 8 (NmMt) sold for $874 (eBay; 2/08)
—Joe Collins #63 PSA 8 (NmMt) sold for $798 (eBay; 2/07)
—Joe Collins #63 PSA 8 (NmMt) sold for $380 (eBay; 10/06)
—Bill Consolo #207 PSA 9 (MT) sold for $5,465 (Memory Lane; 8/06)
—Art Fowler #3 PSA 9 (MT) sold for $4,833 (Mile High; 1/07)
—Jim Hegan #7 PSA 9 (MT) sold for $2,275 (eBay; 6/06)
—Monte Irvin #100 PSA 8 (NmMt) sold for $4,365 (Memory Lane; 9/07)
—Monte Irvin #100 PSA 8 (NmMt) sold for $3,818 (Goodwin; 8/07)
—Monte Irvin #100 PSA 8 (NmMt) sold for $3,365 (eBay; 9/07)
—Monte Irvin #100 PSA 8 (NmMt) sold for $3,232 (eBay; 1/08)
—Monte Irvin #100 PSA 8 (NmMt) sold for $2,900 (eBay; 11/06)
—Monte Irvin #100 PSA 8 (NmMt) sold for $2,732 (eBay; 8/07)
—Monte Irvin #100 PSA 8 (NmMt) sold for $2,550 (eBay; 5/07)
—Monte Irvin #100 PSA 8 (NmMt) sold for $2,349 (Memory Lane; 5/08)
—Monte Irvin #100 PSA 8 (NmMt) sold for $1,826 (eBay; 4/08)
—Monte Irvin #100 PSA 8 (NmMt) sold for $1,715 (Madec; 5/08)
—Monte Irvin #100 PSA 8 (NmMt) sold for $1,525 (eBay; 6/08)
—Spook Jacobs #61 PSA 9 (MT) sold for $4,459 (Madec; 5/08)
—Bob Keegan #10 PSA 9 (MT) sold for $7,184 (Madec; 5/08)
—Harmon Killebrew #124 PSA 10 (Gem) (Young Collection) sold for $59,135 (SCP; 5/12)
—Sandy Koufax #123 GAI 10 (Perfect) sold for $35,931 (Mile High; 8/07)
—Sandy Koufax #123 PSA 10 (Gem) (Memory Lane; Private 2006) sold for $100,000
—Sandy Koufax #123 GAI 9.5 (Gem) sold for $16,213 (Goodwin; 8/07)
—Sandy Koufax #123 SGC 96 (Mint) sold for $27,009 (Goodwin; 11/08)
—Sandy Koufax #123 SGC 92 (NmMt+) sold for $3,976 (Mastro; 8/06)
—Sandy Koufax #123 SGC 92 (NmMt+) sold for $3,049 (Mastro; 4/07)
—Sandy Koufax #123 BVG 8 (NmMt) sold for $2,081 (eBay; 3/08)
—Sandy Koufax #123 BVG 8 (NmMt) sold for $2,040 (eBay; 3/08)
—Sandy Koufax #123 BVG 8 (NmMt) sold for $1,907 (eBay; 1/08)
—Sandy Koufax #123 SGC 88 (NmMt) sold for $1,847 (eBay; 2/08)
—Willie Mays #194 SGC 92 (NmMt+) sold for $2,195 (Madec; 5/08)
—Wally Moon #67 PSA 9 (MT) sold for $4,086 (Madec; 5/08)
—Dusty Rhodes #1 SGC 92 (NmMt+) sold for $492 (Madec; 5/06)
—Phil Rizzuto #189 PSA 9 (MT) sold for $2,143 (Superior; 8/03)
—Jackie Robinson #50 PSA 10 (Gem) sold for $44,318 (Memory Lane; 4/07)
—Jackie Robinson #50 SGC 92 (NmMt+) sold for $1,767 (Mastro; 4/06)
—Roy Sievers #16 PSA 9 (MT) sold for $4,289 (Memory Lane; 5/08)
—Duke Snider #210 PSA 9 (MT) sold for $12,650 (Superior; 7/03)
—Warren Spahn #31 PSA 9 (MT) sold for $8,695 (Leland's; 12/04)
—Warren Spahn #31 PSA 9 (MT) sold for $4,177 (Leland's; 12/05)
—Warren Spahn #31 PSA 9 (MT) sold for $4,096 (Mastro; 4/03)
—Frank Sullivan #106 PSA 8 (NmMt) sold for $728 (eBay; 8/07)
—Frank Sullivan #106 PSA 8 (NmMt) sold for $632 (eBay; 1/08)
—Frank Sullivan #106 PSA 8 (NmMt) sold for $482 (eBay; 11/07)
—Frank Sullivan #106 PSA 8 (NmMt) sold for $211 (eBay; 10/06)
—Ted Williams #2 SGC 92 (NmMt+) sold for $5,295 (Mastro; 8/06)

1955 Topps Double Header

		GD 2	VG 3	VgEx 4	EX 5	ExMt 6	NM 7	NmMt 8	MT 9
1	A.Rosen/C.Diering	15	25	40	80	150	1,200		
3	M.Irvin/R.Kemmerer	8	12	20	30	50	100	250	
5	T.Kazanski/G.Jones	5	8	12	20	40	80	150	
7	B.Taylor/B.O'Dell	5	8	12	20	40	80	100	
9	J.Porter/T.Kipper	5	8	12	20	40,	60	150	
11	C.Roberts/A.Portocarrero	5	8	12	20	40	60	200	
13	W.Westlake/F.House	5	8	12	20	40	60	100	
15	R.Walker/L.Limmer	5	8	12	20	40	80	150	
17	D.Stone/C.White	5	8	12	20	40	60	100	
19	K.Spooner/J.Hughes	5	8	12	20	40	60	150	
21	B.Skowron/F.Sullivan	6	10	15	25	40	80	250	
23	J.Shepard/S.Hack	5	8	12	20	40	60	150	
25	J.Robinson/D.Hoak	40	60	80	250	300	500	1,200	
27	D.Rhodes/J.Davis	5	8	12	20	50	60	150	
29	V.Power/E.Bailey	5	8	12	20	40	60	150	
31	H.Pollet/E.Banks	20	30	50	100	250	300	400	
33	J.Pendleton/G.Conley	5	8	12	20	40	100	300	
35	K.Olson/A.Carey	5	8	12	20	50	60	225	
37	W.Moon/J.Cunningham	5	8	12	20	40	60	150	
39	F.Marsh/V.Thies	5	8	12	20	40	60	150	
41	E.Lopat/H.Haddix	5	8	12	20	40	100	150	

		GD 2	VG 3	VgEx 4	EX 5	ExMt 6	NM 7	NmMt 8	MT
43	L.Kiely/C.Stobbs	5	8	12	20	40	60	150	
45	A.Kaline/H.Valentine	20	30	50	100	60	300		
47	F.Jacobs/J.Gray	5	8	12	20	60	80	250	
49	R.Jackson/J.Finigan	5	8	12	20	60	80	225	
51	R.Jablonski/B.Keegan	5	8	12	20	60	80	150	
53	B.Herman/S.Amoros	6	10	15	25	80	100	300	
55	C.Harmon/B.Skinner	5	8	12	20	40	60	150	
57	D.Hall/B.Grim	5	8	12	20	40	80	200	
59	B.Glynn/B.Miller	5	8	12	20	40	60	150	
61	B.Gardner/J.Hetki	5	8	12	20	40	60	150	
63	B.Borkowski/B.Turley	5	8	12	20	40	60	150	
65	J.Collins/J.Harshman	5	8	12	20	40	60	200	
67	J.Hegan/J.Parks	5	8	12	20	40	60	150	
69	T.Williams/M.Smith	80	100	120	300	400	600	2,500	
71	G.Allie/G.Hatton	5	8	12	20	30	80	150	
73	J.Lynch/H.Brecheen	5	8	12	20	30	80	150	
75	T.Wright/V.Stewart	5	8	12	20	40	80		
77	D.Hoskins/W.McGhee	5	8	12	20	40	60	150	
79	R.Sievers/A.Fowler	5	8	12	20	40	80	150	
81	D.Schell/G.Triandos	5	8	12	20	60	80	200	
83	J.Frazier/D.Mossi	5	8	12	20	40	60		
85	E.Valo/H.Brown	5	8	12	20	40	80		
87	B.Kennedy/W.McCall	5	8	12	20	60	80		
89	R.Gomez/J.Rivera	5	8	12	20	40	60	300	
91	L.Ortiz/M.Bolling	5	8	12	20	40	60	150	
93	C.Sawatski/E.Tappe	5	8	12	20	40	60	150	
95	D.Jolly/B.Hofman	5	8	12	20	40	60	150	
97	P.Ward/D.Zimmer	5	8	12	20	40	80	150	
99	B.Renna/D.Groat	5	8	12	20	30	60	200	
101	B.Wilson/B.Tremel	5	8	12	20	30	80	150	
103	H.Sauer/C.Pascual	5	8	12	20	60	120	200	
105	H.Aaron/R.Herbert	50	80	150	200	250	600	1,800	
107	A.Grammas/T.Qualters	5	8	12	20	30	80	150	
109	H.Newhouser/C.Bishop	8	12	20	30	50	100	250	
111	H.Killebrew/J.Podres	15	25	40	100	200	300	600	
113	R.Boone/B.Purkey	5	8	12	20	30	60	150	
115	D.Long/F.Fain	5	8	12	20	30	60	150	
117	S.Bilko/B.Milliken	5	8	12	20	30	80	150	
119	M.Parnell/T.Hurd	5	8	12	20	30	80	250	
121	T.Kluszewski/J.Owens	10	15	25	40	80	120	500	
123	G.Zernial/B.Trice	5	8	12	20	30	60		
125	R.Repulski/T.Lepcio	5	8	12	20	50	60	150	
127	W.Spahn/T.Brewer	15	25	50	60	100	300		
129	J.Gilliam/E.Kinder	6	10	15	25	80	200		
131	H.Wehmeier/W.Terwilliger	5	8	12	20	100	120		

—H.Aaron/R.Herbert #105-106 PSA 9 (MT) sold for $16,465 (Madec; 11/07)
—A.Kaline/H.Valentine #45-46 PSA 8 (NmMt) sold for $1,328 (eBay; 4/08)
—A.Kaline/H.Valentine #45-46 SGC 88 (NmMt) sold for $795 (eBay; 9/06)
—W.Spahn/T.Brewer #127-128 PSA 8 (NmMt) sold for $1,428 (Madec; 11/07)
—W.Spahn/T.Brewer #127-128 SGC 88 (NmMt) sold for $427 (eBay; 5/08)
—H.Wehmeier/W.Terwilliger #131-132 PSA 8 (NmMt) sold for $1,287 (Madec; 11/07)
—H.Wehmeier/W.Terwilliger #131-132 PSA 8 (NmMt) sold for $443 (Memory Lane; 5/08)

1956 Topps

		GD 2	VG 3	VgEx 4	EX 5	ExMt 6	NM 7	NmMt 8	MT
1	Will Harridge PRES	12	15	30	40	80	200	800	
2	Warren Giles PRES DP	8	10	20	40	50	▲100	200	
3	Elmer Valo	5	5	6	10	30	50	200	50
4	Carlos Paula	5	5	6	10	25	60	120	
5	Ted Williams	120	▲200	250	300	500	▲1,000	2,500	6,00
6	Ray Boone	5	6	8	12	25	40	60	50
7	Ron Negray RC	5	5	6	10	15	30	60	
8	Walter Alston MG RC	6	8	10	20	40	80	150	
9	Ruben Gomez DP	5	5	6	10	20	25	50	50
10	Warren Spahn	20	30	50	60	100	150	400	
11A	Chicago Cubs TC Center	10	12	15	25	40	100	350	
11B	Chicago Cubs TC Dated 55	12	15	20	30	60	150		
11C	Chicago Cubs TC Left	10	12	15	25	40	135	600	
12	Andy Carey	5	6	8	12	20	40	100	40
13	Roy Face	5	6	8	12	20	50	80	50
14	Ken Boyer DP	5	6	8	20	30	50	100	1,00
15	Ernie Banks DP	50	60	80	▲120	▲200	400	1,200	5,00
16	Hector Lopez RC	5	5	6	10	20	30	60	50
17	Gene Conley	5	5	6	10	15	25	60	50
18	Dick Donovan	5	5	6	15	20	30	50	40
19	Chuck Diering DP	5	5	6	10	15	25	50	50

	GD 2	VG 3	VgEx 4	EX 5	ExMt 6	NM 7	NmMt 8	MT 9
Al Kaline	30	40	50	80	120	250	600	4,000
Joe Collins DP	5	5	6	10	20	40	60	400
Jim Finigan	5	5	6	10	15	30	60	
Fred Marsh	5	5	6	10	15	30	50	400
Dick Groat	5	6	8	12	25	50	100	500
Ted Kluszewski	8	10	12	30	50	80	250	800
Grady Hatton	5	5	6	10	15	30	60	500
Nelson Burbrink DP RC	5	5	6	10	15	25	50	400
Bobby Hofman	5	5	6	15	20	30	50	400
Jack Harshman	5	5	6	15	25	30	60	
Jackie Robinson DP	▲200	▲250	▲300	▲400	▲500	▲1,000	2,500	12,000
Hank Aaron DP	100	120	200	250	▲400	600	1,500	6,000
Frank House	5	5	6	10	15	30	60	400
Roberto Clemente	150	▲250	▲300	▲500	600	1,000	4,000	10,000
Tom Brewer DP	5	5	6	10	15	25	50	
Al Rosen	5	6	8	25	30	50	80	
Rudy Minarcin	5	5	6	10	20	40	80	
Alex Grammas	5	5	6	20	25	30	50	400
Bob Kennedy	5	5	6	10	20	25	50	300
Don Mossi	5	5	6	10	25	30	60	400
Bob Turley	5	6	12	20	30	50	100	600
Hank Sauer	5	6	8	12	20	30	60	
Sandy Amoros	5	6	8	25	50	60	120	
Ray Moore	5	5	6	10	15	25	60	
Windy McCall	5	5	6	15	25	30	60	500
Gus Zernial	5	5	6	10	20	30	80	600
Gene Freese DP	5	5	6	10	20	25	50	300
Art Fowler	5	5	6	10	20	25	60	400
Jim Hegan	5	5	8	12	15	25	60	500
Pedro Ramos RC	5	5	6	10	20	30	60	300
Dusty Rhodes DP	5	5	6	10	20	25	60	
Ernie Oravetz RC	5	5	6	10	20	30	80	500
Bob Grim DP	5	6	8	12	▲30	40	80	
Arnie Portocarrero	5	5	6	10	15	30	60	
Bob Keegan	5	5	6	10	15	25	60	
Wally Moon	5	5	6	10	25	40	▼50	500
Dale Long	5	5	6	10	20	40	80	
Duke Maas RC	5	5	6	10	15	25	50	400
Ed Roebuck	5	5	6	15	20	40	80	500
Jose Santiago RC	5	5	6	10	15	30	60	400
Mayo Smith MG DP	5	5	6	10	20	30	50	400
Bill Skowron	8	10	12	20	40	80	300	
Hal Smith	5	5	6	10	15	30	50	500
Roger Craig RC	5	6	20	25	40	60	120	800
Luis Arroyo RC	5	5	6	10	20	30	60	400
Johnny O'Brien	5	5	6	10	25	30	60	600
Bob Speake DP RC	5	5	6	10	15	25	60	300
Vic Power	5	6	8	12	20	30	80	400
Chuck Stobbs	5	5	6	10	15	25	▼50	500
Chuck Tanner	5	5	6	10	15	40	80	400
Jim Rivera	5	5	6	15	20	50	60	800
Frank Sullivan	5	5	6	10	20	40	60	500
A Philadelphia Phillies TC Center	6	8	10	15	25	50		
B Philadelphia Phillies TC Dated 5510	12	15	25	80	100	600		
C Philadelphia Phillies TC Left DP	6	8	10	15	25	80	750	
Wayne Terwilliger	5	5	6	15	20	30	50	300
Jim King RC	5	5	6	10	20	30	50	400
Roy Sievers DP	5	5	6	10	15	25	60	400
Ray Crone	5	5	6	10	▲25	50	60	500
Harvey Haddix	5	6	8	20	25	30	60	400
Herman Wehmeier	5	5	6	10	20	25	60	500
Sandy Koufax	▲100	120	▲200	250	300	▲600	1,200	4,000
Gus Triandos DP	5	5	6	10	15	25	50	
Wally Westlake	5	5	6	10	15	25	50	400
Bill Renna DP	5	5	6	10	▲20	▲30	50	
Karl Spooner	5	6	8	12	25	40	60	500
Babe Birrer RC	5	5	6	10	20	30	50	250
A Cleveland Indians TC Center	8	10	12	20	30	60	250	
B Cleveland Indians TC Dated 55	12	15	20	30	50	100	450	
C Cleveland Indians TC Left	8	10	12	20	30	60	400	
Ray Jablonski DP	5	5	6	10	15	30	50	250
Dean Stone	5	5	6	10	20	30	50	500
Johnny Kucks RC	5	6	10	15	20	50	80	
Norm Zauchin	5	5	6	12	25	30	50	300
A Cincinnati Reds TC Center	8	10	12	20	40	80	300	
B Cincinnati Reds TC Dated 55	12	15	20	30	50	135	600	
C Cincinnati Reds TC Left	8	10	12	20	40	100	600	

		GD 2	VG 3	VgEx 4	EX 5	ExMt 6	NM 7	NmMt 8	MT 9
91	Gail Harris RC	5	5	6	10	20	25	60	
92	Bob (Red) Wilson	5	5	6	10	20	40	50	500
93	George Susce	5	5	6	10	20	30	80	
94	Ron Kline	5	5	6	10	15	25	60	300
95A	Milwaukee Braves TC Center	10	12	15	25	40	150	600	
95B	Milwaukee Braves TC Dated 55	12	15	20	40	100	250	1,000	
95C	Milwaukee Braves TC Left	10	12	15	25	50	200	600	
96	Bill Tremel	5	5	6	10	25	30	50	500
97	Jerry Lynch	5	5	6	10	20	30	60	
98	Camilo Pascual	5	5	6	10	20	25	80	500
99	Don Zimmer	6	8	15	30	40	60	▼120	1,000
100A	Baltimore Orioles TC Center	10	12	15	25	60	200		
100B	Baltimore Orioles TC Dated 55	12	15	20	30	80	400	600	
100C	Baltimore Orioles TC Left	10	12	15	25	60	300		
101	Roy Campanella	40	50	60	▼100	150	300	600	
102	Jim Davis	5	5	6	10	20	25	60	400
103	Willie Miranda	5	5	6	10	25	▲50	80	
104	Bob Lennon	5	5	6	10	15	30	60	400
105	Al Smith	5	5	6	20	25	30	50	
106	Joe Astroth	5	5	20	25	30	40	▼50	500
107	Eddie Mathews	12	25	50	▼60	▼80			1,500
108	Laurin Pepper	5	5	6	25	30	40	▼80	400
109	Enos Slaughter	8	12	15	25	50	80	▼150	1,200
110	Yogi Berra	50	60	▲100	120	200	▲400	800	3,000
111	Boston Red Sox TC	8	10	12	25	40	80	200	
112	Dee Fondy	5	10	15	20	25	30	50	400
113	Phil Rizzuto	25	30	60	80	▲120	200	400	1,200
114	Jim Owens	5	5	6	10	20	25	80	300
115	Jackie Jensen	5	6	8	25	30	40	80	500
116	Eddie O'Brien	5	5	6	10	15	25	60	500
117	Virgil Trucks	5	5	6	10	25	40	100	
118	Nellie Fox	20	25	30	40	60	100	250	800
119	Larry Jackson RC	5	5	6	10	15	30	50	400
120	Richie Ashburn	10	15	25	50	60	100	200	1,000
121	Pittsburgh Pirates TC	10	12	20	60	100	200	500	1,500
122	Willard Nixon	5	6	10	15	25	40	50	300
123	Roy McMillan	5	5	6	10	20	40	80	500
124	Don Kaiser	5	5	6	10	25	40	80	500
125	Minnie Minoso	6	8	25	30	▲50	100	200	
126	Jim Brady RC	5	5	6	10	25	50	100	500
127	Willie Jones	5	5	6	10	25	30	60	1,800
128	Eddie Yost	5	5	6	10	20	50	150	400
129	Jake Martin RC	5	5	6	20	25	30	50	400
130	Willie Mays	100	150	200	300	▲500	600	2,000	8,000
131	Bob Roselli RC	5	5	6	10	15	30	60	
132	Bobby Avila	5	5	6	10	25	40	60	
133	Ray Narleski	5	5	6	10	15	30	50	400
134	St. Louis Cardinals TC	8	10	12	25	40	60	200	
135	Mickey Mantle	500	▲800	1,000	▲1,500	2,500	4,000	12,000	50,000
136	Johnny Logan	5	5	6	10	15	25	60	
137	Al Silvera RC	5	5	6	10	15	40	50	
138	Johnny Antonelli	5	5	6	12	20	40	60	300
139	Tommy Carroll	5	6	8	12	30	50	80	
140	Herb Score RC	8	10	30	40	50	80	150	
141	Joe Frazier	5	5	6	10	▲25	▲30	60	400
142	Gene Baker	5	5	6	15	20	30	50	300
143	Jim Piersall	5	6	8	12	25	40	80	
144	Leroy Powell RC	5	5	6	10	15	40	60	300
145	Gil Hodges	15	25	40	50	60	150	300	1,500
146	Washington Nationals TC	8	10	30	40	80	100	250	
147	Earl Torgeson	5	5	6	10	20	30	60	400
148	Alvin Dark	5	6	8	12	▲30	40	60	300
149	Dixie Howell	5	5	6	10	25	30	60	
150	Duke Snider	30	40	50	80	120	250	500	2,000
151	Spook Jacobs	5	5	6	10	15	30	▼60	▼250
152	Billy Hoeft	5	5	6	20	25	30	60	400
153	Frank Thomas	5	5	6	10	20	40	100	
154	Dave Pope	5	5	6	10	15	40	50	300
155	Harvey Kuenn	5	6	8	15	40	50	80	500
156	Wes Westrum	5	5	6	10	30	40	50	
157	Dick Brodowski	5	5	6	10	15	25	50	500
158	Wally Post	5	5	6	10	20	30	60	400
159	Clint Courtney	5	5	6	10	15	40	250	
160	Billy Pierce	5	6	15	20	25	40	80	
161	Joe DeMaestri	5	6	10	15	25	40	60	400
162	Dave (Gus) Bell	5	5	6	10	20	30	80	
163	Gene Woodling	5	5	6	20	25	30	60	400

#	Name	GD 2	VG 3	VgEx 4	EX 5	ExMt 6	NM 7	NmMt 8	MT 9
164	Harmon Killebrew	25	50	60	▲100	▼120	▼200	▼600	
165	Red Schoendienst	6	10	20	30	60	100	150	1,000
166	Brooklyn Dodgers TC	25	40	60	80	100	300	500	
167	Harry Dorish	5	5	6	10	15	25	60	300
168	Sammy White	5	5	6	10	25	30	50	500
169	Bob Nelson RC	5	5	6	15	20	40	50	500
170	Bill Virdon	5	6	8	12	20	30	60	500
171	Jim Wilson	5	5	6	10	25	30	50	
172	Frank Torre RC	5	5	6	25	30	40	60	300
173	Johnny Podres	6	8	25	30	50	60	150	
174	Glen Gorbous RC	5	5	6	20	25	30	80	500
175	Del Crandall	5	5	6	10	15	30	50	500
176	Alex Kellner	5	5	6	10	15	30	50	300
177	Hank Bauer	6	10	15	25	40	60	150	
178	Joe Black	5	6	8	12	20	30	80	
179	Harry Chiti	5	5	6	10	25	30	60	
180	Robin Roberts	8	12	25	40	50	80	▼200	800
181	Billy Martin	12	25	40	60	100	150	300	1,000
182	Paul Minner	5	5	6	20	25	40	60	500
183	Stan Lopata	5	5	6	10	20	30	60	
184	Don Bessent RC	5	5	6	10	25	50	100	
185	Bill Bruton	5	5	6	20	25	40	120	
186	Ron Jackson	5	5	6	10	20	40	60	500
187	Early Wynn	8	10	20	30	▼50	120	300	
188	Chicago White Sox TC	10	12	20	30	80	200	500	
189	Ned Garver	5	5	6	10	20	30	▼60	300
190	Carl Furillo	8	12	20	25	40	80	200	
191	Frank Lary	5	5	6	10	20	50	100	500
192	Smoky Burgess	5	5	6	10	20	▲50	80	400
193	Wilmer Mizell	5	5	6	10	20	60	100	
194	Monte Irvin	8	12	25	40	60	80	300	800
195	George Kell	6	8	▲20	25	40	50	150	600
196	Tom Poholsky	5	5	6	10	20	50	100	
197	Granny Hamner	5	5	6	10	25	▲40	100	500
198	Ed Fitzgerald	5	5	6	10	25	30	100	
199	Hank Thompson	5	5	6	10	25	40	100	
200	Bob Feller	30	▲50	60	▲100	▲120	200	500	1,000
201	Rip Repulski	5	5	6	10	20	30	60	500
202	Jim Hearn	5	5	6	10	20	25	50	400
203	Bill Tuttle	5	5	6	10	20	30	60	
204	Art Swanson RC	5	6	10	15	25	40	80	400
205	Whitey Lockman	5	5	6	10	25	40	100	500
206	Erv Palica	5	5	6	10	15	30	60	300
207	Jim Small RC	5	5	6	10	25	30	60	500
208	Elston Howard	10	12	25	40	60	100	250	1,000
209	Max Surkont	5	5	6	10	15	30	50	500
210	Mike Garcia	5	5	6	10	25	30	▼60	
211	Murry Dickson	5	5	6	10	25	40	60	400
212	Johnny Temple	5	5	6	10	20	40	60	100
213	Detroit Tigers TC	8	10	12	30	50	120	500	
214	Bob Rush	5	5	6	10	25	40	80	400
215	Tommy Byrne	5	5	6	20	25	40	100	
216	Jerry Schoonmaker RC	5	6	10	15	25	40	80	500
217	Billy Klaus	5	5	6	10	20	30	80	300
218	Joe Nuxhall	5	5	6	10	25	50	100	600
219	Lew Burdette	5	5	6	10	30	60	250	
220	Del Ennis	5	5	6	10	25	40	80	
221	Bob Friend	5	5	6	10	25	40	▼60	▼300
222	Dave Philley	5	5	6	10	25	30	60	
223	Randy Jackson	5	6	10	15	25	50	100	
224	Bud Podbielan	5	5	6	10	15	30	80	
225	Gil McDougald	6	10	15	30	▲50	60	150	500
226	New York Giants TC	10	15	25	30	60	100	400	1,000
227	Russ Meyer	5	5	6	10	15	40	80	500
228	Mickey Vernon	5	5	6	10	30	50	120	
229	Harry Brecheen CO	5	5	6	10	25	50	80	400
230	Chico Carrasquel	5	5	6	10	▲25	30	60	600
231	Bob Hale RC	5	5	6	10	25	40	80	500
232	Toby Atwell	5	5	6	10	25	50	120	
233	Carl Erskine	6	8	10	25	30	80	150	800
234	Pete Runnels	5	5	6	12	30	40	60	500
235	Don Newcombe	8	15	30	40	50	100	300	
236	Kansas City Athletics TC	6	8	10	15	30	50	200	
237	Jose Valdivielso RC	5	5	6	10	15	40	100	
238	Walt Dropo	5	5	6	▲10	25	40	80	500
239	Harry Simpson	5	5	6	10	15	30	60	
240	Whitey Ford	▲30	▲40	▲60	80	120	250	600	2,500

#	Name	GD 2	VG 3	VgEx 4	EX 5	ExMt 6	NM 7	NmMt 8	MT 9
241	Don Mueller	5	5	6	10	15	30	120	5
242	Hershell Freeman	5	5	6	10	25	40	120	
243	Sherm Lollar	5	5	6	10	15	40	▼60	5
244	Bob Buhl	5	6	10	15	25	60	100	5
245	Billy Goodman	5	6	10	15	25	40	100	5
246	Tom Gorman	5	5	6	10	25	30	80	4
247	Bill Sarni	5	5	6	10	15	30	80	4
248	Bob Porterfield	5	5	6	10	25	40	80	5
249	Johnny Klippstein	5	5	6	10	20	50	▼80	
250	Larry Doby	8	12	30	40	60	80	300	1,2
251	New York Yankees TC	30	50	60	100	200	600	2,500	3,5
252	Vern Law	5	5	6	10	25	40	100	
253	Irv Noren	6	8	10	15	50	120	500	
254	George Crowe	5	5	6	10	25	60	200	
255	Bob Lemon	8	10	12	20	50	60	150	1,0
256	Tom Hurd	5	5	6	10	25	40	80	5
257	Bobby Thomson	5	5	6	10	30	40	150	
258	Art Ditmar	5	5	6	10	15	50	100	
259	Sam Jones	5	5	6	10	15	40	100	
260	Pee Wee Reese	20	40	50	100	▼120	250	600	
261	Bobby Shantz	5	5	6	10	25	40	100	5
262	Howie Pollet	5	5	6	20	25	30	80	5
263	Bob Miller	5	5	6	10	15	40	120	
264	Ray Monzant RC	5	5	6	10	25	▼30	▼40	4
265	Sandy Consuegra	5	5	6	10	15	25	60	
266	Don Ferrarese	5	5	6	10	25	30	80	
267	Bob Nieman	5	5	6	10	15	30	50	4
268	Dale Mitchell	5	6	8	15	60	200	800	
269	Jack Meyer RC	5	5	6	10	15	30	60	5
270	Billy Loes	5	6	8	12	▲30	40	80	5
271	Foster Castleman RC	5	5	6	10	25	60	150	
272	Danny O'Connell	5	5	6	10	20	30	60	2
273	Walker Cooper	5	5	6	10	20	30	50	5
274	Frank Baumholtz	5	5	6	10	15	30	60	5
275	Jim Greengrass	5	5	6	8	12	20	60	4
276	George Zuverink	5	5	6	10	30	100	150	
277	Daryl Spencer	5	5	6	10	20	30	100	5
278	Chet Nichols	5	5	6	10	15	30	60	5
279	Johnny Groth	5	5	6	15	25	30	50	2
280	Jim Gilliam	8	10	12	25	40	100	200	6
281	Art Houtteman	5	5	6	10	25	30	60	4
282	Warren Hacker	5	5	8	12	20	40	50	3
283	Hal R.Smith RC	5	6	10	15	20	30	50	
284	Ike Delock	5	5	6	10	20	30	60	5
285	Eddie Miksis	5	5	6	10	15	30	60	4
286	Bill Wight	5	5	6	15	20	25	60	
287	Bobby Adams	5	5	6	10	20	▲40	50	3
288	Bob Cerv	8	10	12	20	40	80	120	6
289	Hal Jeffcoat	5	5	6	10	25	30	50	3
290	Curt Simmons	5	5	8	12	20	40	60	4
291	Frank Kellert RC	5	5	6	15	25	30	80	4
292	Luis Aparicio RC	30	50	60	100	▲200	300	1,000	
293	Stu Miller	5	6	8	12	30	50	80	8
294	Ernie Johnson	5	5	6	10	20	30	60	4
295	Clem Labine	5	6	10	15	30	50	100	6
296	Andy Seminick	5	5	6	10	20	30	80	5
297	Bob Skinner	5	5	6	10	20	40	60	5
298	Johnny Schmitz	5	5	6	10	15	30	60	2
299	Charlie Neal	6	10	15	25	40	▼50	100	6
300	Vic Wertz	5	6	10	20	25	30	80	8
301	Marv Grissom	5	5	6	10	20	30	80	3
302	Eddie Robinson	5	6	8	12	25	40	300	5
303	Jim Dyck	5	5	6	10	15	30	60	
304	Frank Malzone	5	6	8	12	25	50	100	
305	Brooks Lawrence	5	5	6	10	20	30	60	5
306	Curt Roberts	5	5	6	10	20	50	120	6
307	Hoyt Wilhelm	8	12	20	30	40	60	200	8
308	Chuck Harmon	5	5	6	10	15	50	120	5
309	Don Blasingame RC	5	6	8	12	25	40	80	4
310	Steve Gromek	5	5	6	10	15	30	50	3
311	Hal Naragon	5	5	6	15	25	40	80	
312	Andy Pafko	5	6	8	12	25	30	100	4
313	Gene Stephens	5	5	6	10	20	40	60	5
314	Hobie Landrith	5	6	8	10	20	30	80	3
315	Milt Bolling	5	5	6	10	20	30	60	2
316	Jerry Coleman	5	6	8	20	25	40	120	8
317	Al Aber	5	5	6	10	20	25	50	

	GD 2	VG 3	VgEx 4	EX 5	ExMt 6	NM 7	NmMt 8	MT 9
Fred Hatfield	5	5	6	10	15	30	80	
Jack Crimian RC	5	6	10	15	25	30	80	
Joe Adcock	5	6	8	12	▲30	40	80	600
Jim Konstanty	5	6	8	15	30	40	60	500
Karl Olson	5	5	8	12	20	30	50	
Willard Schmidt	5	5	6	10	15	30	50	300
Rocky Bridges	5	6	10	15	25	40	80	
Don Liddle	5	5	6	10	15	30	80	400
Connie Johnson RC	5	5	6	10	15	60	250	
Bob Wiesler RC	5	5	6	10	15	25	50	300
Preston Ward	5	5	6	20	25	40	80	
Lou Berberet RC	5	5	6	10	20	40	60	400
Jim Busby	5	5	6	10	20	40	60	400
Dick Hall	5	5	6	10	15	30	60	400
Don Larsen	10	25	30	50	80	150	500	
Rube Walker	5	6	8	12	20	50	120	500
Bob Miller	5	6	10	15	30	80	120	800
Don Hoak	5	5	6	10	20	25	60	400
Ellis Kinder	5	5	6	20	25	40	80	
Bobby Morgan	5	5	6	10	25	30	100	
Jim Delsing	5	5	6	10	20	40	80	
Rance Pless RC	5	5	6	10	20	60	300	
Mickey McDermott	8	10	20	30	40	150	400	
Checklist 1/3	30	40	60	100	150	300	800	
Checklist 2/4	30	40	60	100	150	300	800	2,000

Hank Aaron #31 SGC 92 (NmMt+) sold for $545 (eBay; 11/06)
Luis Aparicio #292 PSA 10 (Gem) (Young Collection) sold for $11,028 (SCP; 5/12)
Luis Aparicio #292 PSA 9 (MT) sold for $5,142 (Goodwin; 3/08)
Luis Aparicio #292 PSA 9 (MT) sold for $5,111 (eBay; 11/07)
Luis Aparicio #292 PSA 9 (MT) sold for $4,745 (eBay; 4/08)
Ernie Banks #15 SGC 96 (MT) sold for $2,875 (eBay; 11/06)
Yogi Berra #110 PSA 10 (Gem) sold for $14,052 (Mile High; 2/08)
Boston Red Sox TC #111 PSA 10 (Gem) sold for $6,000 (Legendary; 5/12)
Brooklyn Dodgers TC #166 PSA 9 (MT) sold for $3,912 (Goodwin; 6/06)
Brooklyn Dodgers TC #166 PSA 9 (MT) sold for $2,276 (eBay; 2/08)
Brooklyn Dodgers TC #166 PSA 9 (MT) sold for $2,231 (Mile High; 1/07)
Roy Campanella #101 SGC 96 (MT) sold for $1,359 (eBay; 1/07)
Chicago Cubs TC D'55 #11 PSA 9 (MT) sold for $3,725 (Memory Lane; 9/07)
Chicago Cubs TC D'55 #11 PSA 8 (NmMt) sold for $1,720 (eBay; 2/08)
Chicago Cubs TC D'55 #11 PSA 8 (NmMt) sold for $1,658 (Mile High; 6/06)
Chicago Cubs TC D'55 #11 PSA 8 (NmMt) sold for $1,235 (eBay; 2/08)
Chicago Cubs TC D'55 #11 PSA 8 (NmMt) sold for $623 (eBay; 11/06)
Chicago Cubs TC D'55 #11 PSA 8 (NmMt) sold for $595 (eBay; 2/08)
Chicago Cubs TC D'55 #11 PSA 8 (NmMt) sold for $590 (eBay; 6/07)
Chicago White Sox TC #188 PSA 9 (MT) sold for $4,138 (Memory Lane; 11/05)
Roberto Clemente #33 SGC 8.5 (NmMt+) sold for $1,581 (Mile High; 8/07)
Roberto Clemente #33 BVG 8.5 (NmMt+) sold for $800 (eBay; 9/06)
Carl Furillo #190 PSA 10 (Gem) sold for $5,414 (Mile High; 2/08)
Carl Furillo #190 PSA 9 (MT) sold for $3,636 (Mile High; 6/06)
Carl Furillo #190 PSA 9 (MT) sold for $2,617 (eBay; 6/07)
Warren Giles #2 PSA 9 (MT) sold for $3,553 (Mastro; 2/05)
Will Harridge #1 PSA 9 (MT) sold for $4,454 (Mile High; 1/07)
Will Harridge #1 PSA 9 (MT) sold for $4,379 (Memory Lane; 11/04)
Elston Howard #208 PSA 10 (Gem) sold for $2,185 (Superior; 7/03)
Monte Irvin #194 PSA 10 (Gem) sold for $5,157 (Memory Lane; 8/06)
Harmon Killebrew #164 PSA 9 (MT) sold for $5,460 (Greg Bussineau; 12/12)
Harmon Killebrew #164 PSA 9 (MT) sold for $3,574 (Memory Lane; 4/07)
Sandy Koufax #79 PSA 8.5 (NmMt+) sold for $1,561 (eBay; 3/08)
Don Larsen #332 PSA 9 (MT) sold for $2,608 (Goodwin; 6/06)
Don Larsen #332 PSA 9 (MT) sold for $1,956 (Memory Lane; 12/06)
Mickey Mantle #135 PSA 10 (Gem) sold for $382,400 (Heritage; 8/16)
Mickey Mantle #135 PSA 10 (Gem) sold for $50,000 (Memory Lane; Private 2006)
Mickey Mantle #135 BVG 9 (MT) sold for $6,450 (eBay; 2/07)
Mickey Mantle #135 PSA 8.5 (NmMt+) sold for $5,678 (eBay; 5/08)
Mickey Mantle #135 SGC 92 (NmMt+) sold for $4,481 (Heritage; 5/08)
Mickey Mantle #135 PSA 8.5 (NmMt+) sold for $3,884 (Heritage; 5/08)
Mickey Mantle #135 (White Back) PSA 8 (NmMt) sold for $5,538 (Goodwin; 5/08)
Eddie Mathews #107 PSA 10 (Gem) sold for $6,324 (Goodwin; 66/06)
Willie Mays #130 BVG 9 (MT) sold for $2,027 (eBay; 1/07)
Willie Mays #130 BVG 9 (MT) sold for $1,825 (eBay; 12/06)
Willie Mays #130 BVG 8.5 (NmMt+) sold for $923 (eBay; 11/07)
Willie Mays #130 SGC 92 (NmMt+) sold for $680 (eBay; 1/08)
Milwaukee Braves TC Left #95 PSA 9 MT sold for $3,386 (Memory Lane; 9/07)
Milwaukee Braves TC Left #95 PSA 9 MT sold for $2,175 (eBay; 2/07)
Rudy Minarcin #36 PSA 10 (Gem) sold for $5,106 (Memory Lane; 8/12)
New York Yankees TC #251 PSA 10 (Gem) sold for $18,067 (Goodwin; 8/07)
Pee Wee Reese #260 PSA 9 (MT) sold for $3,174 (Mile High; 6/05)
Pee Wee Reese #260 PSA 9 (MT) sold for $2,769 (Memory Lane; 9/07)
Pee Wee Reese #260 PSA 9 (MT) sold for $2,267 (Memory Lane; 12/07)
Rip Repulski #201 PSA 10 (Gem) sold for $2,228 (eBay; 1/13)
Jackie Robinson #30 BVG 8.5 (NmMt) sold for $561 (eBay; 10/06)
Warren Spahn #10 PSA 10 (Gem) sold for $6,463 (REA; 5/08)
Warren Spahn #10 PSA 9 (MT) sold for $2,032 (Memory Lane; 12/07)
Ted Williams #5 PSA 10 (Gem) sold for $32,666 (Goodwin; 8/07)
Early Wynn #187 PSA 9 (MT) sold for $1,779 (Memory Lane; 5/08)
Checklist 1/3 PSA 9 (MT) sold for $4,853 (Madec; 5/07)

1957 Topps

		GD 2	VG 3	VgEx 4	EX 5	ExMt 6	NM 7	NmMt 8	MT 9
1	Ted Williams	100	▲150	200	250	▼400	1,000	2,500	8,000
2	Yogi Berra	40	50	80	100	150	250	500	3,000
3	Dale Long	5	5	6	10	25	30	100	
4	Johnny Logan	5	6	8	12	25	40	250	
5	Sal Maglie	6	8	10	15	30	60	120	800
6	Hector Lopez	5	5	5	8	15	25	100	
7	Luis Aparicio	6	10	▲25	▲30	▲40	60	150	1,000
8	Don Mossi	5	5	5	8	20	25	100	
9	Johnny Temple	5	5	6	8	12	25	100	500
10	Willie Mays	60	100	150	250	300	▲800	2,500	4,000
11	George Zuverink	5	5	5	6	15	20	50	400
12	Dick Groat	5	5	6	10	15	40	120	
13	Wally Burnette RC	5	5	5	6	10	15	40	
14	Bob Nieman	5	5	5	6	10	25	80	
15	Robin Roberts	8	10	12	25	40	100	400	1,200
16	Walt Moryn	5	5	5	8	12	25	60	400
17	Billy Gardner	5	5	5	6	10	25	50	
18	Don Drysdale RC	60	80	100	150	250	500	▲2,000	15,000
19	Bob Wilson	5	5	5	6	10	20	50	400
20	Hank Aaron	60	100	▲200	▲250	300	600	2,500	10,000
21	Frank Sullivan	5	5	5	6	10	20	50	300
22	Jerry Snyder	5	5	5	6	10	20	80	400
23	Sherm Lollar	5	5	5	6	10	25	50	
24	Bill Mazeroski RC	12	40	▲60	80	100	200	500	2,500
25	Whitey Ford	20	30	50	80	100	200	1,000	5,000
26	Bob Boyd	5	5	5	6	10	20	50	
27	Ted Kazanski	5	5	5	6	10	25	▲50	300
28	Gene Conley	5	5	5	8	15	30	200	
29	Whitey Herzog RC	5	6	8	25	30	60	120	600
30	Pee Wee Reese	30	40	50	60	▲100	120	400	1,200
31	Ron Northey	5	5	5	6	10	25	50	
32	Hershell Freeman	5	5	5	6	10	20	50	250
33	Jim Small	5	5	5	6	10	30	80	
34	Tom Sturdivant RC	5	5	5	8	12	25	60	250
35	Frank Robinson RC	100	▲150	▲200	▲300	400	600	2,500	
36	Bob Grim	5	5	6	10	15	40	100	
37	Frank Torre	5	5	5	8	20	30	80	
38	Nellie Fox	8	10	12	25	30	▼60	250	800
39	Al Worthington RC	5	5	5	6	12	25	50	
40	Early Wynn	5	6	8	15	25	60	▼150	1,000
41	Hal W. Smith	5	5	5	6	10	15	50	250
42	Dee Fondy	5	5	5	6	10	25	50	250
43	Connie Johnson	5	5	5	6	10	25	40	250
44	Joe DeMaestri	5	5	5	6	10	20	50	
45	Carl Furillo	6	8	10	20	40	60	200	
46	Robert J. Miller	5	5	5	6	10	20	▼40	150
47	Don Blasingame	5	5	5	6	10	25	60	500
48	Bill Bruton	5	5	5	8	12	▲25	80	400
49	Daryl Spencer	5	5	5	6	10	25	60	
50	Herb Score	5	6	8	20	30	40	100	
51	Clint Courtney	5	5	5	8	12	25	50	
52	Lee Walls	5	5	5	6	15	25	50	300
53	Clem Labine	5	5	5	8	20	30	60	250
54	Elmer Valo	5	5	5	8	15	25	60	400
55	Ernie Banks	▲50	▲60	▲80	100	150	300	500	4,000
56	Dave Sisler RC	5	5	5	6	10	25	80	
57	Jim Lemon	5	5	5	6	10	25	50	400
58	Ruben Gomez	5	5	5	8	12	25	50	
59	Dick Williams	5	5	5	6	10	25	50	250
60	Billy Hoeft	5	5	5	6	10	20	60	
61	Dusty Rhodes	5	5	5	6	25	30	80	
62	Billy Martin	10	12	25	▲40	50	100	300	1,200
63	Ike Delock	5	5	5	6	12	25	50	300
64	Pete Runnels	5	5	5	6	10	25	50	250

#	Player	GD 2	VG 3	VgEx 4	EX 5	ExMt 6	NM 7	NmMt 8	MT 9
65	Wally Moon	5	5	5	8	12	30	80	
66	Brooks Lawrence	5	5	5	6	10	25	60	
67	Chico Carrasquel	5	5	5	6	10	30	60	
68	Ray Crone	5	5	5	6	15	25	250	
69	Roy McMillan	5	5	5	8	20	25	100	
70	Richie Ashburn	6	8*	10	30	50	▼60	▼120	500
71	Murry Dickson	5	5	5	6	12	25	40	300
72	Bill Tuttle	5	5	5	6	10	25	50	250
73	George Crowe	5	5	5	6	15	25	50	
74	Vito Valentinetti RC	5	5	5	6	15	20	▼40	400
75	Jimmy Piersall	5	5	5	8	12	25	60	400
76	Roberto Clemente	60	100	120	200	250	500	1,200	6,000
77	Paul Foytack RC	5	5	5	8	12	20	60	
78	Vic Wertz	5	5	5	8	12	25	80	400
79	Lindy McDaniel RC	5	5	5	6	10	20	50	500
80	Gil Hodges	10	20	30	40	50	100	250	1,500
81	Herman Wehmeier	5	5	5	6	10	20	40	250
82	Elston Howard	6	8	10	15	30	50	▼120	800
83	Lou Skizas RC	5	5	5	6	10	20	40	400
84	Moe Drabowsky RC	5	5	5	8	12	▲30	50	300
85	Larry Doby	6	▲12	▲20	▲25	50	100	300	
86	Bill Sarni	5	5	5	6	10	20	60	400
87	Tom Gorman	5	5	5	6	12	25	▼40	300
88	Harvey Kuenn	5	5	5	8	12	30	80	500
89	Roy Sievers	5	5	5	6	10	25	60	
90	Warren Spahn	12	25	30	50	80	120	250	1,000
91	Mack Burk RC	5	5	5	6	10	▲20	50	
92	Mickey Vernon	5	5	5	8	15	25	50	
93	Hal Jeffcoat	5	5	5	6	10	20	40	
94	Bobby Del Greco	5	5	5	6	10	15	60	400
95	Mickey Mantle	250	400	500	800	1,200	2,500	8,000	40,000
96	Hank Aguirre RC	5	5	5	6	10	25	60	300
97	New York Yankees TC	15	20	25	50	80	120	250	1,000
98	Alvin Dark	5	5	5	8	12	25	60	200
99	Bob Keegan	5	5	5	6	10	25	120	400
100	League Presidents	5	6	8	12	25	50	200	
101	Chuck Stobbs	5	5	5	6	10	20	50	
102	Ray Boone	5	5	5	8	20	30	50	400
103	Joe Nuxhall	5	5	6	10	15	30	100	
104	Hank Foiles	5	5	5	6	10	25	50	
105	Johnny Antonelli	5	5	5	8	12	25	60	
106	Ray Moore	5	5	5	6	10	25	50	
107	Jim Rivera	5	5	5	6	10	20	50	200
108	Tommy Byrne	5	5	5	8	25	50	150	
109	Hank Thompson	5	5	5	6	10	25	50	250
110	Bill Virdon	5	5	5	8	12	25	50	250
111	Hal R. Smith	5	5	5	6	10	20	50	
112	Tom Brewer	5	5	5	6	10	25	80	
113	Wilmer Mizell	5	5	5	6	10	20	50	400
114	Milwaukee Braves TC	5	6	8	12	25	40	120	500
115	Jim Gilliam	6	8	10	15	30	50	▲150	
116	Mike Fornieles	5	5	5	6	10	25	50	400
117	Joe Adcock	5	6	8	12	15	50	▼120	
118	Bob Porterfield	5	5	5	6	10	25	40	
119	Stan Lopata	5	5	5	6	10	25	50	
120	Bob Lemon	5	6	8	25	30	50	150	1,500
121	Clete Boyer RC	5	6	8	20	25	60	120	
122	Ken Boyer	5	6	8	12	▲25	40	120	
123	Steve Ridzik	5	5	5	6	10	25	60	
124	Dave Philley	5	5	5	6	10	15	50	
125	Al Kaline	25	30	40	60	▼80	▼120	▼300	2,500
126	Bob Wiesler	5	5	5	6	10	25	50	1,000
127	Bob Buhl	5	5	6	10	15	25	80	
128	Ed Bailey	5	5	5	8	12	30	80	
129	Saul Rogovin	5	5	5	6	10	25	50	250
130	Don Newcombe	5	6	8	25	30	60	150	700
131	Milt Bolling	5	5	5	6	10	20	50	300
132	Art Ditmar	5	5	5	8	12	30	50	300
133	Del Crandall	5	5	6	10	15	30	100	600
134	Don Kaiser	5	5	5	6	10	20	40	350
135	Bill Skowron	5	6	8	12	40	50	120	600
136	Jim Hegan	5	5	5	6	10	25	50	200
137	Bob Rush	5	5	5	6	10	20	50	300
138	Minnie Minoso	5	6	8	20	25	50	120	500
139	Lou Kretlow	5	5	5	6	10	25	50	200
140	Frank Thomas	5	5	5	6	10	25	50	400
141	Al Aber	5	5	5	6	10	15	40	400
142	Charley Thompson	5	5	5	6	10	20	40	
143	Andy Pafko	5	5	5	6	20	25	60	
144	Ray Narleski	5	5	5	6	10	25	40	
145	Al Smith	5	5	5	6	10	25	50	
146	Don Ferrarese	5	5	5	6	10	25	50	
147	Al Walker	5	5	6	10	20	30	100	
148	Don Mueller	5	5	5	6	10	20	50	
149	Bob Kennedy	5	5	5	8	12	25	80	
150	Bob Friend	5	5	5	8	12	20	▼40	
151	Willie Miranda	5	5	5	6	10	20	40	
152	Jack Harshman	5	5	5	6	10	20	40	
153	Karl Olson	5	5	5	6	10	15	40	
154	Red Schoendienst	5	6	8	20	30	50	150	
155	Jim Brosnan	5	5	5	6	10	25	60	
156	Gus Triandos	5	5	5	6	10	25	50	
157	Wally Post	5	5	5	8	12	25	60	
158	Curt Simmons	5	5	5	8	12	20	60	
159	Solly Drake RC	5	5	5	6	10	20	50	
160	Billy Pierce	5	5	6	10	15	25	80	
161	Pittsburgh Pirates TC	5	5	6	20	25	50	200	
162	Jack Meyer	5	5	5	6	10	25	50	
163	Sammy White	5	5	5	6	10	20	50	
164	Tommy Carroll	5	5	6	10	15	30	60	
165	Ted Kluszewski	12	15	30	50	80	120	400	3,
166	Roy Face	5	5	5	8	15	25	80	
167	Vic Power	5	5	5	8	12	20	50	
168	Frank Lary	5	5	5	8	12	20	50	
169	Herb Plews RC	5	5	5	6	10	25	40	
170	Duke Snider	20	40	50	60	100	120	500	
171	Boston Red Sox TC	6	8	10	15	25	80	150	
172	Gene Woodling	5	5	5	8	12	30	50	
173	Roger Craig	5	5	5	▲15	▲20	25	▼50	
174	Willie Jones	5	5	5	6	10	20	50	
175	Don Larsen	8	10	12	30	40	▼80	150	
176A	Gene Bakep ERR (Baker)	150	200	250	300	400			
176B	Gene Baker COR	5	5	5	6	10	15	80	
177	Eddie Yost	5	5	5	8	15	40	120	
178	Don Bessent	5	5	5	8	15	50	200	
179	Ernie Oravetz	5	5	5	6	10	20	40	
180	Gus Bell	5	5	5	6	25	40	100	
181	Dick Donovan	5	5	5	6	10	25	40	
182	Hobie Landrith	5	5	5	6	10	25	50	
183	Chicago Cubs TC	5	5	6	10	25	40	100	
184	Tito Francona RC	5	5	5	8	12	▼40	150	
185	Johnny Kucks	5	5	6	10	15	25	60	
186	Jim King	5	5	5	6	10	25	50	
187	Virgil Trucks	5	5	5	6	10	20	40	
188	Felix Mantilla RC	5	5	5	6	10	25	▼50	
189	Willard Nixon	5	5	5	6	10	20	40	
190	Randy Jackson	5	5	5	8	12	30	50	
191	Joe Margoneri RC	5	5	5	6	10	20	50	
192	Jerry Coleman	5	5	5	8	12	30	80	
193	Del Rice	5	5	5	6	10	20	50	
194	Hal Brown	5	5	5	6	10	25	50	
195	Bobby Avila	5	5	5	6	10	25	50	
196	Larry Jackson	5	5	5	6	15	25	60	
197	Hank Sauer	5	5	5	6	15	25	50	
198	Detroit Tigers TC	5	5	6	10	15	50	100	
199	Vern Law	5	5	5	6	10	20	50	
200	Gil McDougald	5	6	8	12	25	30	100	
201	Sandy Amoros	5	5	6	10	25	50	150	
202	Dick Gernert	5	5	5	6	10	30	40	
203	Hoyt Wilhelm	5	6	15	20	25	50	120	
204	Kansas City Athletics TC	5	5	6	10	25	40	80	
205	Charlie Maxwell	5	5	5	8	12	25	80	
206	Willard Schmidt	5	5	5	6	10	20	40	
207	Gordon (Billy) Hunter	5	5	5	6	10	15	50	
208	Lew Burdette	5	5	5	8	15	40	80	
209	Bob Skinner	5	5	5	6	10	25	50	
210	Roy Campanella	25	40	50	60	100	150	300	1,
211	Camilo Pascual	5	5	5	6	10	25	50	
212	Rocky Colavito RC	25	30	50	60	▲100	▲150	250	1,
213	Les Moss	5	5	5	6	10	25	40	
214	Philadelphia Phillies TC	5	5	6	6	15	30	80	
215	Enos Slaughter	5	6	8	25	▲40	▲60	120	
216	Marv Grissom	5	5	5	6	10	25	▼40	
217	Gene Stephens	5	5	5	6	10	25	50	

#	Player	GD 2	VG 3	VgEx 4	EX 5	ExMt 6	NM 7	NmMt 8	MT 9
218	Ray Jablonski	5	5	5	6	10	25	40	150
219	Tom Acker RC	5	5	5	6	10	15	40	250
220	Jackie Jensen	5	5	6	10	15	30	80	500
221	Dixie Howell	5	5	6	10	20	40	250	
222	Alex Grammas	5	5	5	6	10	15	▼40	250
223	Frank House	5	5	5	6	10	25	50	300
224	Marv Blaylock	5	5	5	6	10	25	50	250
225	Harry Simpson	5	5	5	6	10	25	40	200
226	Preston Ward	5	5	5	6	10	20	50	200
227	Gerry Staley	5	5	5	6	10	25	40	300
228	Smoky Burgess	5	5	5	8	12	25	60	250
229	George Susce	5	5	5	6	10	25	50	250
230	George Kell	5	6	8	20	25	40	100	400
231	Solly Hemus	5	5	5	6	10	25	40	250
232	Whitey Lockman	5	5	5	6	10	25	50	200
233	Art Fowler	5	5	5	6	10	25	50	200
234	Dick Cole	5	5	5	6	10	15	40	300
235	Tom Poholsky	5	5	5	6	10	25	50	300
236	Joe Ginsberg	5	5	5	6	10	25	40	250
237	Foster Castleman	5	5	5	6	10	25	40	250
238	Eddie Robinson	5	5	5	6	10	25	50	250
239	Tom Morgan	5	5	5	6	10	20	40	300
240	Hank Bauer	6	8	10	15	▲50	60	▼250	
241	Joe Lonnett RC	5	5	5	6	10	20	40	300
242	Charlie Neal	5	5	5	8	15	30	50	300
243	St. Louis Cardinals TC	5	5	6	10	15	30	80	250
244	Billy Loes	5	5	5	6	10	20	40	300
245	Rip Repulski	5	5	5	6	10	15	50	300
246	Jose Valdivielso	5	5	5	6	10	20	40	250
247	Turk Lown	5	5	5	6	10	25	40	250
248	Jim Finigan	5	5	5	6	10	20	50	200
249	Dave Pope	5	5	5	6	10	25	50	300
250	Eddie Mathews	12	25	30	50	60	▼100	▼300	1,500
251	Baltimore Orioles TC	5	5	6	10	25	60	100	300
252	Carl Erskine	5	5	5	8	25	50	100	600
253	Gus Zernial	5	5	5	6	15	20	50	200
254	Ron Negray	5	5	5	6	10	20	40	250
255	Charlie Silvera	5	5	5	6	10	25	50	200
256	Ron Kline	5	5	5	6	10	25	40	250
257	Walt Dropo	5	5	5	6	10	20	40	200
258	Steve Gromek	5	5	5	6	15	25	50	300
259	Eddie O'Brien	5	5	5	6	10	20	40	300
260	Del Ennis	5	5	5	8	12		60	300
261	Bob Chakales	5	5	5	6	10	20	▼40	300
262	Bobby Thomson	5	5	5	20	25	40	80	
263	George Strickland	5	5	5	6	10	15	50	300
264	Bob Turley	5	5	6	10	15	30	100	400
265	Harvey Haddix DP	5	6	8	12	25	60	150	
266	Ken Kuhn DP RC	5	5	6	10	25	40	100	
267	Danny Kravitz RC	5	5	6	10	15	30	80	
268	Jack Collum	5	5	6	10	20	40	80	
269	Bob Cerv	5	5	6	10	25	40	▼80	
270	Washington Senators TC	8	10	12	20	40	120	600	
271	Danny O'Connell DP	5	5	6	10	15	60	150	
272	Bobby Shantz	6	8	10	25	40	50	100	600
273	Jim Davis	5	5	6	10	15	30	100	500
274	Don Hoak	5	5	6	10	15	40	80	
275	Cleveland Indians TC	8	10	12	30	40	100	150	
276	Jim Pyburn RC	5	5	6	10	15	50	300	
277	Johnny Podres DP	8	10	12	25	50	80	200	800
278	Fred Hatfield DP	5	5	6	10	15	40	60	
279	Bob Thurman RC	5	5	6	10	20	50	250	
280	Alex Kellner	5	5	6	20	25	50	250	
281	Gail Harris	5	5	6	10	15	30	60	
282	Jack Dittmer DP	5	6	8	12	20	30	80	
283	Wes Covington DP RC	5	6	8	12	20	60	200	1,000
284	Don Zimmer	8	10	12	30	40	80	150	1,500
285	Ned Garver	5	5	6	10	15	30	100	400
286	Bobby Richardson RC	25	30	50	▼60	▲120	200	500	
287	Sam Jones	5	5	6	10	30	50	150	
288	Ted Lepcio	5	5	6	10	15	40	80	
289	Jim Bolger DP	5	5	6	10	15	25	50	
290	Andy Carey DP	6	8	10	25	30	120	500	
291	Windy McCall	5	5	6	10	20	50	250	
292	Billy Klaus	5	5	6	10	15	60	200	
293	Ted Abernathy RC	5	5	6	10	15	30	▼50	
294	Rocky Bridges DP	5	5	6	10	30	40	80	
295	Joe Collins DP	6	8	10	15	40	80	200	
296	Johnny Klippstein	5	5	6	10	15	30	80	
297	Jack Crimian	5	5	6	10	25	30	150	
298	Irv Noren DP	5	5	6	10	20	50	600	
299	Chuck Harmon	5	5	6	10	25	40	200	
300	Mike Garcia	5	6	8	12	30	120	1,000	
301	Sammy Esposito DP RC	5	5	6	10	15	40	▲100	400
302	Sandy Koufax DP	80	120	200	250	300	800	2,500	
303	Billy Goodman	5	6	8	15	40	120	400	
304	Joe Cunningham	5	5	6	10	15	30	60	500
305	Chico Fernandez	5	5	6	10	25	40	100	
306	Darrell Johnson DP RC	5	6	8	20	30	40	80	400
307	Jack D. Phillips DP	5	5	6	10	25	50	500	
308	Dick Hall	5	5	6	10	15	30	80	
309	Jim Busby DP	5	5	6	10	20	40	120	
310	Max Surkont DP	5	5	6	10	25	100	2,000	
311	Al Pilarcik DP RC	5	5	6	10	15	30	▼60	500
312	Tony Kubek DP RC	20	30	50	60	▲100	150	300	1,000
313	Mel Parnell	5	5	6	10	25	50	150	
314	Ed Bouchee DP RC	5	5	6	10	25	50	100	
315	Lou Berberet DP	5	5	6	10	15	30	80	
316	Billy O'Dell	5	5	6	10	15	40	100	
317	New York Giants TC	10	12	15	30	60	120	250	
318	Mickey McDermott	5	5	6	10	25	40	100	
319	Gino Cimoli RC	5	5	6	10	30	80	▲1,000	
320	Neil Chrisley RC	5	5	6	10	20	30	80	400
321	John (Red) Murff RC	5	5	6	10	25	40	100	
322	Cincinnati Reds TC	8	10	12	20	50	100	400	
323	Wes Westrum	5	5	6	10	15	30	100	
324	Brooklyn Dodgers TC	20	25	50	60	▲100	200	400	2,500
325	Frank Bolling	5	5	6	10	20	▼30	100	
326	Pedro Ramos	5	5	6	10	15	30	▼80	
327	Jim Pendleton	5	5	6	10	15	30	▲100	
328	Brooks Robinson RC	250	300	400	500	▼600	▲1,200	3,000	20,000
329	Chicago White Sox TC	8	10	12	20	▲50	80	250	
330	Jim Wilson	5	5	6	10	20	25	60	
331	Ray Katt	5	5	6	10	25	40	150	
332	Bob Bowman RC	5	5	6	10	20	30	80	
333	Ernie Johnson	5	5	6	10	30	▲50	250	
334	Jerry Schoonmaker	5	5	6	10	20	30	100	
335	Granny Hamner	5	5	6	10	25	40	600	
336	Haywood Sullivan RC	5	5	6	10	20	30	80	
337	Rene Valdes RC	5	6	8	12	25	50	100	600
338	Jim Bunning RC	25	60	80	100	150	250	500	2,000
339	Bob Speake	5	5	6	10	25	30	80	400
340	Bill Wight	5	5	6	10	25	60	200	
341	Don Gross RC	5	5	6	10	15	30	100	
342	Gene Mauch	5	5	6	10	20	50	200	
343	Taylor Phillips RC	5	5	6	10	25	100	500	
344	Paul LaPalme	5	5	6	10	15	40	100	
345	Paul Smith	5	5	6	10	15	50	60	250
346	Dick Littlefield	5	5	6	10	15	30	120	500
347	Hal Naragon	5	5	6	10	15	▲50	300	
348	Jim Hearn	5	5	6	10	20	30	80	
349	Nelson King	5	5	6	10	20	40	100	
350	Eddie Miksis	5	5	6	10	25	50	400	
351	Dave Hillman RC	5	5	6	10	15	50	80	400
352	Ellis Kinder	5	5	6	10	20	50	150	
353	Cal Neeman RC	5	5	5	6	10	25	50	300
354	Rip Coleman RC	5	5	5	6	10	25	50	
355	Frank Malzone	5	5	6	8	12	25	50	250
356	Faye Throneberry	5	5	6	10	30	50		
357	Earl Torgeson	5	5	6	10	25	50		
358	Jerry Lynch	5	5	6	10	20	50		
359	Tom Cheney RC	5	5	6	10	20	50		
360	Johnny Groth	5	5	5	6	10	20	▼40	250
361	Curt Barclay RC	5	5	6	12	25	80		
362	Roman Mejias RC	5	5	6	10	25	50		
363	Eddie Kasko RC	5	5	6	10	20	50	400	
364	Cal McLish RC	5	5	5	6	10	25	50	300
365	Ozzie Virgil RC	5	5	6	10	30	60	400	
366	Ken Lehman	5	5	6	8	12	20	50	
367	Ed Fitzgerald	5	5	5	6	10	20	40	
368	Bob Purkey	5	5	5	6	10	15	40	
369	Milt Graff RC	5	5	5	6	10	25	60	
370	Warren Hacker	5	5	5	6	10	15	50	400
371	Bob Lennon	5	5	5	6	10	20	40	

#	Name	GD 2	VG 3	VgEx 4	EX 5	ExMt 6	NM 7	NmMt 8	MT 9
372	Norm Zauchin	5	5	5	6	10	25	40	250
373	Pete Whisenant RC	5	5	5	6	10	20	50	350
374	Don Cardwell RC	5	5	5	6	10	20	50	
375	Jim Landis RC	5	5	5	8	12	20	▼60	
376	Don Elston RC	5	5	5	8	12	30	60	
377	Andre Rodgers RC	5	5	5	6	10	25	60	
378	Elmer Singleton	5	5	5	6	10	25	50	
379	Don Lee RC	5	5	5	6	10	25	50	
380	Walker Cooper	5	5	5	6	10	20	50	
381	Dean Stone	5	5	5	6	10	25	50	
382	Jim Brideweser	5	5	5	6	10	20	50	400
383	Juan Pizarro RC	5	5	5	6	10	40	80	
384	Bobby G. Smith RC	5	5	5	6	10	25	60	
385	Art Houtteman	5	5	5	6	10	20	40	
386	Lyle Luttrell RC	5	5	5	6	10	25	40	400
387	Jack Sanford RC	5	5	5	6	10	25	50	
388	Pete Daley	5	5	5	6	10	25	50	400
389	Dave Jolly	5	5	5	6	10	20	50	
390	Reno Bertoia	5	5	5	6	10	25	50	200
391	Ralph Terry RC	5	6	8	12	30	60	150	500
392	Chuck Tanner	5	5	5	6	10	30	200	
393	Raul Sanchez RC	5	5	5	6	10	25	50	
394	Luis Arroyo	5	5	5	6	10	20	50	500
395	Bubba Phillips	5	5	5	6	10	25	60	
396	Casey Wise RC	5	5	5	6	10	25	50	400
397	Roy Smalley	5	5	5	6	10	25	50	400
398	Al Cicotte RC	5	5	5	8	12	▼30	100	
399	Billy Consolo	5	5	5	6	10	20	50	200
400	Dodgers Sluggers	30	40	50	80	▼120	▼250	800	
401	Earl Battey RC	5	5	5	8	12	20	50	300
402	Jim Pisoni RC	5	5	5	6	10	20	50	
403	Dick Hyde RC	5	5	5	6	10	25	80	
404	Harry Anderson RC	5	5	5	6	10	20	60	
405	Duke Maas	5	5	5	6	15	25	50	400
406	Bob Hale	5	5	5	8	15	30	120	
407	Yankees Power Hitters	100	150	200	250	400	800	▼3,000	
CC1	Contest May 4th	15	20	25	40	60	150		
CC2	Contest May 25th	15	20	25	40	60	150		
CC3	Contest June 22nd	20	25	30	50	100	200		
CC4	Contest July 19th	20	25	30	50	80	250		
NNO	Checklist 1/2 Bazooka	60	80	100	150	200	400		
NNO	Checklist 1/2 Big Blony	60	80	100	135	200	600		
NNO	Checklist 2/3 Bazooka	60	80	100	150	250			
NNO	Checklist 2/3 Big Blony	60	80	100	200				
NNO	Checklist 3/4 Bazooka	150	200	250	400	600			
NNO	Checklist 3/4 Big Blony	120	150	200	300	500			
NNO	Checklist 4/5 Bazooka	200	300	400	500				
NNO	Checklist 4/5 Big Blony	300	400	500	800				
NNO	Lucky Penny Card	50	60	80	120	200			

—Sandy Amoros #201 PSA 9 (MT) sold for $3,551 (eBay; 10/07)
—Richie Ashburn #70 PSA 10 (Gem) sold for $5,100 (Mastro; 5/08)
—Gene Bakep #176 (Error) PSA 7 (NM) sold for $460 (eBay; 3/08)
—Ernie Banks #55 PSA 10 (Gem) sold for $10,073 (REA; Spring '14)
—Ernie Banks #55 PSA 10 (Gem) sold for $7,345 (Mastro; 6/05)
—Ernie Banks #55 PSA 8.5 (NmMt+) sold for $10,665 (REA; Spring '14)
—Jim Bunning #338 PSA 9 (MT) sold for $3,525 (REA; 4/07)
—Jim Bunning #338 PSA 8.5 (NmMt+) sold for $631 (eBay; 3/08)
—Roy Campanella #210 PSA 10 (Gem) sold for $3,113 (Mastro; 12/05)
—Roberto Clemente #76 PSA 10 (Gem) sold for $17,455 (Mile High; 5/04)
—Roberto Clemente #76 SGC 96 (MT) sold for $2,039 (Mastro; 8/06)
—Rocky Colavito #212 PSA 10 (Gem) (Young Collection) sold for $7,352 (SCP; 5/12)
—Rocky Colavito #212 PSA 10 (Gem) sold for $5,407 (Mastro; 4/07)
—Dodgers Sluggers #400 PSA 9 (MT) sold for $7,199 (Mastro; 4/07)
—Dodgers Sluggers #400 PSA 9 (MT) sold for $6,484 (Mastro; 8/06)
—Dodgers Sluggers #400 PSA 9 (MT) sold for $3,944 (Mastro; 8/07)
—Whitey Ford #25 PSA 9 (MT) sold for $3,580 (Memory Lane; 8/06)
—Whitey Ford #25 PSA 9 (MT) sold for $2,711 (Memory Lane; 11/05)
—Al Kaline #125 BVG 9 (MT) sold for $1,025 (eBay; 3/07)
—Sandy Koufax #302 PSA 9 (MT) sold for $78,086 (Madec; 10/06)
—Sandy Koufax #302 PSA 9 (MT) sold for $44,111 (Mastro; 8/06)
—Sandy Koufax #302 PSA 9 (MT) sold for $21,256 (Mastro; 8/07)
—Sandy Koufax #302 BVG 9 (MT) sold for $3,697 (Goodwin; 2/07)
—Sandy Koufax #302 SGC 92 (NmMt+) sold for $3,243 (Memory Lane; 5/08)
—Sandy Koufax #302 SGC 92 (NmMt+) sold for $2,126 (eBay; 6/08)
—Mickey Mantle #95 PSA 10 (Gem) sold for $36,225 (Memory Lane; 3/06)
—Mickey Mantle #95 BVG 8.5 (NmMt+) sold for $2,581 (eBay; 1/08)
—Mickey Mantle #95 BVG 8.5 (NmMt+) sold for $2,470 (eBay; 11/07)

—Willie Mays #10 PSA 8.5 (NmMt+) sold for $1,617 (Memory Lane; 5/08)
—Willie Mays #10 PSA 8.5 (NmMt+) sold for $1,589 (eBay; 6/08)
—Bill Mazeroski #24 PSA 10 (Gem) sold for $21,762 (Mile High; 12/14)
—Bill Mazeroski #24 PSA 10 (Gem) sold for $13,898 (Memory Lane; 4/05)
—Bobby Richardson #286 PSA 9 (MT) sold for $5,117 (Goodwin; 03/12)
—Bobby Richardson #286 PSA 9 (MT) sold for $3,439 (Memory Lane; 9/07)
—Bobby Richardson #286 PSA 9 (MT) sold for $3,300 (Mastro; 5/08)
—Bobby Richardson #286 PSA 9 (MT) sold for $2,318 (eBay; 3/08)
—Bobby Richardson #286 PSA 9 (MT) sold for $2,302 (eBay; 1/08)
—Bobby Richardson #286 PSA 9 (Mint) sold for $5,117 (Goodwin; 3/12)
—Brooks Robinson #328 PSA 10 (Gem) (Young Collection) sold for $47,251 (SCP; 5/12)
—Brooks Robinson #328 SGC 92 (NmMt+) sold for $995 (Mastro; 8/06)
—Brooks Robinson #328 SGC 92 (NmMt+) sold for $568 (eBay; 4/07)
—Frank Robinson #35 PSA 9 (MT) sold for $10,695 (Goodwin; 8/07)
—Frank Robinson #35 PSA 9 (MT) sold for $9,582 (Mastro; 12/06)
—Frank Robinson RC #35 PSA 9 (MT) sold for $6,840 (Greg Bussineau; 12/12)
—Frank Robinson #35 PSA 9 (MT) sold for $6,748 (eBay; 1/08)
—Frank Robinson #35 PSA 9 (MT) sold for $6,706 (Memory Lane; 9/07)
—Frank Robinson #35 PSA 9 (Mint) sold for $9,718 (Mile High; 5/12)
—Frank Robinson #35 SGC 96 (MT) sold for $4,096 (Mastro; 12/05)
—Frank Robinson #35 BVG 9 (MT) sold for $2,181 (eBay; 10/06)
—Frank Robinson #35 BVG 8.5 (NmMt+) sold for $986 (eBay; 3/07)
—Frank Robinson #35 BVG 8.5 (NmMt+) sold for $935 (eBay; 10/06)
—Frank Robinson #35 BVG 8.5 (NmMt+) sold for $898 (eBay; 12/07)
—Duke Snider #170 PSA 10 (Gem) sold for $8,210 (Memory Lane; 11/04)
—Duke Snider #170 PSA 9 (MT) sold for $4,734 (Mile High; 8/07)
—Duke Snider #170 PSA 9 (MT) sold for $3,504 (eBay; 5/08)
—Duke Snider #170 PSA 9 (MT) sold for $2,426 (Mastro; 12/05)
—Warren Spahn #90 PSA 10 (Gem) sold for $11,860 (Memory Lane; 9/07)
—Warren Spahn #90 PSA 10 (Gem) sold for $4,375 (Mastro; 10/05)
—Haywood Sullivan #336 PSA 9 (MT) sold for $3,348 (Madec; 5/08)
—Ted Williams #1 SGC 92 (NmMt+) sold for $2,375 (eBay; 3/08)
—Ted Williams #1 BVG 8.5 (NmMt+) sold for $1,550 (eBay; 5/07)
—Ted Williams #1 BVG 8.5 (NmMt+) sold for $1,525 (eBay; 6/07)
—Yankees Power Hitters #407 PSA 9 (MT) sold for $7,361 (Mastro; 12/06)
—Checklist 1/2 Bazooka PSA 8 (NmMt) sold for $1,536 (eBay; 11/07)
—Checklist 1/2 Big Blony PSA 9 (MT) sold for $4,922 (Goodwin; 3/08)
—Checklist 1/2 Big Blony PSA 8 (NmMt) sold for $1,700 (eBay; 10/07)
—Checklist 1/2 Big Blony PSA 8 (NmMt) sold for $1,675 (eBay; 8/07)
—Checklist 2/3 Bazooka PSA 8 (NmMt) sold for $4,328 (Goodwin; 3/08)
—Checklist 2/3 Bazooka PSA 7 (NM) sold for $1,716 (eBay; 4/07)
—Checklist 2/3 Big Blony PSA 7 (NM) sold for $1,009 (eBay; 6/07)
—Checklist 2/3 Big Blony PSA 6 (ExMt) sold for $710 (eBay; 4/07)
—Checklist 3/4 Bazooka PSA 8 (NmMt) sold for $3,616 (Mastro; 12/05)
—Checklist 3/4 Big Blony PSA 8 (NmMt) sold for $7,207 (Goodwin; 3/08)
—Contest May 4 PSA 8 (NmMt) sold for $1,224 (eBay; 8/07)
—Contest May 4 PSA 8 (NmMt) sold for $1,187 (Memory Lane; 5/08)
—Contest May 25 PSA 8 (NmMt) sold for $2,637 (Goodwin; 3/08)
—Contest May 25 PSA 8 (NmMt) sold for $1,306 (eBay; 8/06)
—Contest May 25 PSA 8 (NmMt) sold for $912 (eBay; 2/07)
—Contest May 25 PSA 8 (NmMt) sold for $816 (eBay; 11/07)
—Contest June 22 PSA 8 (NmMt) sold for $1,437 (Goodwin; 5/07)
—Contest June 22 PSA 8 (NmMt) sold for $920 (Goodwin; 3/08)
—Contest June 22 PSA 8 (NmMt) sold for $686 (eBay; 4/08)
—Contest July 19 PSA 8 (NmMt) sold for $1,470 (Memory Lane; 9/07)
—Contest July 19 PSA 8 (NmMt) sold for $1,470 (Memory Lane; 4/07)
—Lucky Penny Card PSA 8 (NmMt) sold for $1,227 (Goodwin; 3/08)
—Lucky Penny Card PSA 7 (NM) sold for $677 (eBay; 9/07)

1958 Hires Root Beer

#	Name	GD 2	VG 3	VgEx 4	EX 5	ExMt 6	NM 7	NmMt 8	MT
10	Richie Ashburn	8	12	20	30	50	150	1,000	
11	Chico Carrasquel	5	5	8	12	20	30	60	
12	Dave Philley	5	5	8	12	20	30	60	
13	Don Newcombe	5	8	12	20	30	50	100	
14	Wally Post	5	5	8	12	20	30	60	
15	Rip Repulski	5	5	8	12	20	30	60	
16	Chico Fernandez	5	5	8	12	20	30	60	
17	Larry Doby	6	10	15	25	40	60	120	
18	Hector Brown	5	5	8	12	20	30	60	
19	Danny O'Connell	5	5	8	12	20	30	60	
20	Granny Hamner	5	5	8	12	20	30	60	
21	Dick Groat	5	5	8	12	20	30	60	
22	Ray Narleski	5	5	8	12	20	30	60	
23	Pee Wee Reese	8	12	20	30	50	120	150	
24	Bob Friend	5	5	8	12	20	30	60	

	GD 2	VG 3	VgEx 4	EX 5	ExMt 6	NM 7	NmMt 8	MT 9
Willie Mays	40	60	80	200	400	800	1,000	
Bob Nieman	5	5	8	12	20	30	60	
Frank Thomas	5	5	8	12	20	30	60	
Curt Simmons	5	5	8	12	20	30	60	
Stan Lopata	5	5	8	12	20	30	60	
Bob Skinner	5	5	8	12	20	30	60	
Ron Kline	5	5	8	12	20	30	80	
Willie Miranda	5	5	8	12	20	30	60	
Bobby Avila	5	5	8	12	20	30	60	
Clem Labine	5	6	10	15	25	40	80	
Ray Jablonski	5	5	8	12	20	30	60	
Bill Mazeroski	6	10	15	25	80	120	150	
Billy Gardner	5	5	8	50	80	120	250	
Pete Runnels	5	5	8	12	20	30	60	
Jack Sanford	5	5	8	12	20	30	60	
Dave Sisler	5	5	8	12	20	30	60	
Don Zimmer	5	8	12	20	30	50	100	
Johnny Podres	5	8	12	20	30	50	100	
Dick Farrell	5	5	8	12	20	30	60	
Hank Aaron	40	60	80	150	550	700	1,500	
Bill Virdon	5	5	8	12	20	30	60	
Bobby Thomson	5	8	12	20	30	50	120	
Willard Nixon	5	5	8	12	20	30	60	
Billy Loes	5	5	8	12	20	30	60	
Hank Sauer	5	5	8	12	20	30	100	
Johnny Antonelli	5	5	8	12	20	30	60	
Daryl Spencer	5	5	8	12	20	30	60	
Ken Lehman	5	5	8	12	20	30	60	
Sammy White	5	5	8	12	20	30	60	
Charley Neal	5	5	8	12	20	30	60	
Don Drysdale	8	12	20	30	50	80	300	
Jackie Jensen	5	5	8	12	20	30	60	
Ray Katt	5	5	8	12	20	30	120	
Frank Sullivan	5	5	8	12	20	30	60	
Roy Face	5	5	8	12	20	30	80	
Willie Jones	5	5	8	12	20	30	60	
Duke Snider	15	25	60	80	100	150	300	
Whitey Lockman	5	5	8	12	20	30	80	
Gino Cimoli	5	5	8	12	20	30	60	
Marv Grissom	5	5	8	12	20	30	60	
Gene Baker	5	5	8	12	20	30	60	
George Zuverink	5	5	8	12	20	30	60	
Ted Kluszewski	6	10	15	25	40	80	150	
Jim Busby	5	5	8	12	20	30	60	
Curt Barclay	5	5	8	12	20	30	80	
Hank Foiles	5	5	8	12	20	30	60	
Gene Stephens	5	5	8	12	20	30	80	
Al Worthington	5	5	8	12	20	30	60	
Al Walker	5	5	8	12	20	30	60	
Bob Boyd	5	5	8	12	20	30	60	
Al Pilarcik	5	5	8	12	20	30	60	

Prices reference cards without tabs. Cards w/tabs generally sell for 2.5X to 3X listed price.

Hank Aaron #44 (w/tab) PSA 8 (NmMt) sold for $2,604 (Memory Lane; 2/07)
Richie Ashburn #10 (w/tab) PSA 8 (NmMt) sold for $3,607 (Memory Lane; 9/07)
Don Drysdale #55 (w/tab) PSA 9 (MT) sold for $3,721 (Memory Lane; 2/07)
Don Drysdale #55 (w/tab) PSA 9 (MT) sold for $1,784 (Memory Lane; 12/07)
Don Drysdale #55 (w/tab) PSA 8 (NmMt) sold for $2,604 (Memory Lane; 12/06)
Don Drysdale #55 (w/tab) PSA 8 (NmMt) sold for $850 (eBay; 1/08)
Jackie Jensen #56 (w/tab) PSA 8 (NmMt) sold for $949 (Memory Lane; 12/07)
Willie Mays #25 (w/tab) PSA 8 (NmMt) sold for $7,432 (Memory Lane; 12/06)

1958 Topps

	GD 2	VG 3	VgEx 4	EX 5	ExMt 6	NM 7	NmMt 8	MT 9
Ted Williams	100	120	150	250	400	600	2,500	
Bob Lemon	5	6	10	15	25	40	200	
Bob Lemon YT	10	15	25	40	80			
Alex Kellner	5	5	5	8	20	40	60	
Hank Foiles	5	5	5	8	12	20	60	
Willie Mays	▲60	80	100	150	300	600	5,000	
George Zuverink	5	5	5	8	12	40	60	250
Dale Long	5	5	5	8	12	50	120	
Eddie Kasko	5	5	5	8	12	30	200	
Eddie Kasko YN	6	10	15	25	60	200		
Hank Bauer	5	6	10	25	30	50	120	
Lou Burdette	5	5	8	12	30	60	150	
Jim Rivera	5	5	6	10	15	40	400	

	GD 2	VG 3	VgEx 4	EX 5	ExMt 6	NM 7	NmMt 8	MT 9
11B	Jim Rivera YT	6	10	15	25	50	150		
12	George Crowe	5	5	5	8	12	20	50	
13A	Billy Hoeft	5	5	5	8	12	30	250	
13B	Billy Hoeft YN	6	10	15	25	40	80		
14	Rip Repulski	5	5	5	8	12	30	60	200
15	Jim Lemon	5	5	5	8	12	30	▼40	
16	Charlie Neal	5	5	6	10	30	50	300	
17	Felix Mantilla	5	5	5	8	15	50	250	
18	Frank Sullivan	5	5	5	8	12	20	50	
19	San Francisco Giants TC	5	6	10	15	50	100	400	
20A	Gil McDougald	5	6	10	15	25	40	200	
20B	Gil McDougald YN	10	15	25	40	60	400	600	
21	Curt Barclay	5	5	5	8	12	25	60	
22	Hal Naragon	5	5	5	8	12	30	60	
23A	Bill Tuttle	5	5	5	8	12	30		
23B	Bill Tuttle YN	6	10	15	30	40	150		
24A	Hobie Landrith	5	5	5	8	12	25	80	
24B	Hobie Landrith YN	6	10	15	30	60	100		
25	Don Drysdale	8	25	30	40	80	200	600	
26	Ron Jackson	5	5	5	8	12	20	50	300
27	Bud Freeman	5	5	5	8	12	25	40	300
28	Jim Busby	5	5	5	8	12	30	50	400
29	Ted Lepcio	5	5	5	8	12	20	60	
30A	Hank Aaron	20	50	80	150	200	400	800	
30B	Hank Aaron YN	50	120	150	200	300	500	2,500	
31	Tex Clevenger RC	5	5	5	8	12	25	50	300
32A	J.W. Porter	5	5	5	8	12	40	150	
32B	J.W. Porter YN	6	10	15	25	40	120	400	
33A	Cal Neeman	5	5	5	8	12	20	50	
33B	Cal Neeman YT	6	10	15	25	40	150	500	
34	Bob Thurman	5	5	5	8	12	20	50	250
35A	Don Mossi	5	5	5	10	15	25	150	
35B	Don Mossi YT	6	10	15	25	40	80	300	
36	Ted Kazanski	5	5	5	8	12	25	50	
37	Mike McCormick RC	5	5	6	10	25	60		
38	Dick Gernert	5	5	5	8	20	30	50	
39	Bob Martyn RC	5	5	5	8	12	20	100	250
40	George Kell	5	5	8	20	30	50	100	
41	Dave Hillman	5	5	5	8	12	25	30	300
42	John Roseboro RC	6	10	15	25	50	100	600	
43	Sal Maglie	5	5	6	10	25	50	80	250
44	Washington Senators TC	5	5	6	10	50	120	800	
45	Dick Groat	5	5	6	10	15	40	50	
46A	Lou Sleater	5	5	5	8	12	25	250	
46B	Lou Sleater YN	6	10	15	25	40	150	500	
47	Roger Maris RC	▲120	▲200	250	300	500	800	2,500	15,000
48	Chuck Harmon	5	5	5	8	12	20	40	400
49	Smoky Burgess	5	5	6	10	15	40	100	
50A	Billy Pierce	5	5	5	8	12	20	50	
50B	Billy Pierce YT	6	10	15	25	40	80	250	
51	Del Rice	5	5	5	8	12	20	▼120	
52A	Roberto Clemente	40	60	100	150	200	500	200	800
52B	Roberto Clemente YT	50	80	100	200	300	800	400	
53A	Morrie Martin	5	5	5	8	12	20	100	
53B	Morrie Martin YN	6	10	15	25	40	80	300	
54	Norm Siebern RC	5	5	6	10	15	40	120	400
55	Chico Carrasquel	5	5	5	8	12	20	50	500
56	Bill Fischer RC	5	5	5	8	12	20	30	250
57A	Tim Thompson	5	5	5	8	12	20	50	
57B	Tim Thompson YN	6	10	15	25	40	100	400	
58A	Art Schult	5	5	5	8	12	20	80	
58B	Art Schult YT	12	20	30	60	100	120	100	
59	Dave Sisler	5	5	5	8	12	50	150	
60A	Del Ennis	5	5	5	8	12	20	50	
60B	Del Ennis YN	6	10	15	25	40	80	300	
61A	Darrell Johnson	5	5	6	10	15	25	100	
61B	Darrell Johnson YN	6	10	15	25	40	100		
62	Joe DeMaestri	5	5	5	8	12	20	50	250
63	Joe Nuxhall	5	5	5	8	12	30	40	
64	Joe Lonnett	5	5	5	8	12	40	120	
65A	Von McDaniel RC	5	5	5	8	12	25	135	
65B	Von McDaniel YN	6	10	15	25	50	100		
66	Lee Walls	5	5	5	8	12	20	50	500
67	Joe Ginsberg	5	5	5	8	12	20	80	
68	Daryl Spencer	5	5	5	8	12	25	80	
69	Wally Burnette	5	5	5	8	12	20	40	
70A	Al Kaline	10	15	25	40	100	150	300	1,000

#	Player	GD 2	VG 3	VgEx 4	EX 5	ExMt 6	NM 7	NmMt 8	MT 9
70B	Al Kaline YN	20	30	80	120	200	300	1,000	
71	Los Angeles Dodgers TC	6	10	15	40	60	200	500	
72	Bud Byerly	5	5	5	8	12	20	60	
73	Pete Daley	5	5	5	8	25	30	120	
74	Roy Face	5	5	5	10	15	25	60	500
75	Gus Bell	5	5	5	8	12	30	40	
76A	Dick Farrell RC	5	5	5	8	12	20	80	
76B	Dick Farrell YT	6	10	15	25	80	200		
77A	Don Zimmer	5	5	6	10	15	40	100	
77B	Don Zimmer YT	10	15	25	40	60	250	1,000	
78A	Ernie Johnson	5	5	5	8	12	250	400	
78B	Ernie Johnson YN	6	10	15	25	50	150		
79A	Dick Williams	5	5	5	8	12	25	50	
79B	Dick Williams YT	6	10	15	25	50	100	300	
80	Dick Drott RC	5	5	5	8	12	20	40	250
81A	Steve Boros RC	5	5	5	8	12	30	200	
81B	Steve Boros YT	6	10	15	25	60	150		
82	Ron Kline	5	5	5	8	12	15	40	
83	Bob Hazle RC	5	5	5	8	12	30	120	
84	Billy O'Dell	5	5	5	8	12	20	40	300
85A	Luis Aparicio	5	6	10	15	25	40	200	
85B	Luis Aparicio YT	15	25	40	60	100	250		
86	Valmy Thomas RC	5	5	5	8	12	20	40	250
87	Johnny Kucks	5	5	6	10	15	▲100	200	
88	Duke Snider	6	25	30	50	60	120	400	
89	Billy Klaus	5	5	5	8	12	30	200	
90	Robin Roberts	5	6	10	20	60	80	200	
91	Chuck Tanner	5	5	6	10	15	50	250	
92A	Clint Courtney	5	5	5	8	12	20	40	500
92B	Clint Courtney YN	5	6	10	15	25	40	200	
93	Sandy Amoros	5	5	5	8	20	30	80	
94	Bob Skinner	5	5	5	8	12	25	40	300
95	Frank Bolling	5	5	5	8	12	20	50	
96	Joe Durham RC	5	5	5	8	12	20	40	800
97A	Larry Jackson	5	5	5	8	12	20	100	400
97B	Larry Jackson YN	6	10	15	25	60	80	675	
98A	Billy Hunter	5	5	5	8	12	20	50	
98B	Billy Hunter YN	6	10	15	25	40	100		
99	Bobby Adams	5	5	5	8	12	20	40	400
100A	Early Wynn	5	5	8	12	20	40	100	500
100B	Early Wynn YT	10	15	25	40	60	100	200	
101A	Bobby Richardson	5	8	12	20	30	60	150	
101B	Bobby Richardson YN	10	15	25	40	80	120		
102	George Strickland	5	5	5	8	12	30	50	
103	Jerry Lynch	5	5	5	8	12	20	50	400
104	Jim Pendleton	5	5	5	8	12	30	▼60	
105	Billy Gardner	5	5	5	8	12	40	250	
106	Dick Schofield	5	5	5	8	12	20	40	300
107	Ossie Virgil	5	5	6	10	15	60	250	
108A	Jim Landis	5	5	5	8	12	25	80	
108B	Jim Landis YT	6	10	15	25	40	100	400	
109	Herb Plews	5	5	5	8	12	30	50	300
110	Johnny Logan	5	5	6	10	15	50	100	
111	Stu Miller	5	5	5	6	10	25	50	
112	Gus Zernial	5	5	5	6	10	25	40	300
113	Jerry Walker RC	5	5	5	6	10	15	40	
114	Irv Noren	5	5	5	6	10	25	40	
115	Jim Bunning	5	5	8	20	▲30	40	100	400
116	Dave Philley	5	5	5	6	10	15	60	
117	Frank Torre	5	5	5	6	10	25	50	300
118	Harvey Haddix	5	5	5	6	10	25	50	300
119	Harry Chiti	5	5	5	6	10	15	30	200
120	Johnny Podres	5	5	6	10	25	30	60	400
121	Eddie Miksis	5	5	5	6	10	15	30	500
122	Walt Moryn	5	5	5	6	10	15	40	150
123	Dick Tomanek RC	5	5	5	8	12	20	40	250
124	Bobby Usher	5	5	5	6	10	15	30	200
125	Alvin Dark	5	5	5	6	10	15	40	300
126	Stan Palys RC	5	5	5	6	10	15	40	
127	Tom Sturdivant	5	5	5	6	10	25	50	300
128	Willie Kirkland RC	5	5	5	6	10	15	40	275
129	Jim Derrington RC	5	5	5	6	10	15	50	
130	Jackie Jensen	5	5	5	8	12	25	60	250
131	Bob Henrich RC	5	5	5	6	10	20	40	500
132	Vern Law	5	5	5	6	10	20	40	150
133	Russ Nixon RC	5	5	5	6	10	15	40	400
134	Philadelphia Phillies TC	5	5	6	10	25	50	60	300

#	Player	GD 2	VG 3	VgEx 4	EX 5	ExMt 6	NM 7	NmMt 8	M
135	Mike Drabowsky	5	5	5	6	10	15	40	4
136	Jim Finigan	5	5	5	6	10	30	40	3
137	Russ Kemmerer	5	5	5	6	10	15	40	
138	Earl Torgeson	5	5	5	6	10	15	40	4
139	George Brunet RC	5	5	5	6	10	15	30	3
140	Wes Covington	5	5	5	6	10	15	40	
141	Ken Lehman	5	5	5	6	10	15	50	4
142	Enos Slaughter	5	8	12	25	30	50	120	2
143	Billy Muffett RC	5	5	5	6	10	15	30	2
144	Bobby Morgan	5	5	5	6	10	15	40	4
146	Dick Gray RC	5	5	5	6	10	25	50	2
147	Don McMahon RC	5	5	5	6	10	15	40	
148	Billy Consolo	5	5	5	6	10	15	40	
149	Tom Acker	5	5	5	6	10	15	30	2
150	Mickey Mantle	250	300	▲500	600	1,000	▲2,500	6,000	
151	Buddy Pritchard RC	5	5	5	6	15	60	250	
152	Johnny Antonelli	5	5	5	6	10	15	40	4
153	Les Moss	5	5	5	6	10	15	40	3
154	Harry Byrd	5	5	5	6	10	15	80	
155	Hector Lopez	5	5	5	6	10	20	40	2
156	Dick Hyde	5	5	5	6	10	15	60	
157	Dee Fondy	5	5	5	6	10	15	30	4
158	Cleveland Indians TC	5	5	6	10	25	50	120	
159	Taylor Phillips	5	5	5	6	10	15	30	3
160	Don Hoak	5	5	5	6	10	25	30	2
161	Don Larsen	5	5	6	10	25	50	100	5
162	Gil Hodges	5	15	20	25	40	60	120	6
163	Jim Wilson	5	5	5	6	10	15	30	1
164	Bob Taylor RC	5	5	5	6	10	30	200	
165	Bob Nieman	5	5	5	6	10	15	40	
166	Danny O'Connell	5	5	5	6	10	15	30	2
167	Frank Baumann RC	5	5	5	6	10	15	30	1
168	Joe Cunningham	5	5	5	6	10	15	50	
169	Ralph Terry	5	5	5	8	12	20	60	
170	Vic Wertz	5	5	5	6	10	20	40	2
171	Harry Anderson	5	5	5	6	10	15	40	
172	Don Gross	5	5	5	6	10	15	50	
173	Eddie Yost	5	5	5	6	10	15	50	4
174	Kansas City Athletics TC	5	5	6	10	15	50	100	
175	Marv Throneberry RC	5	5	8	12	50	60	150	
176	Bob Buhl	5	5	5	6	10	25	50	
177	Al Smith	5	5	5	6	10	25	50	3
178	Ted Kluszewski	5	5	8	12	25	50	80	6
179	Willie Miranda	5	5	5	6	10	15	40	
180	Lindy McDaniel	5	5	5	6	10	15	30	2
181	Willie Jones	5	5	5	6	10	15	30	3
182	Joe Caffie RC	5	5	5	6	10	15	50	4
183	Dave Jolly	5	5	5	6	10	15	40	3
184	Elvin Tappe	5	5	5	6	10	20	50	
185	Ray Boone	5	5	5	6	10	20	40	
186	Jack Meyer	5	5	5	6	10	25	60	2
187	Sandy Koufax	50	60	100	120	200	400	800	5,0
188	Milt Bolling	5	5	5	6	10	15	40	
189	George Susce	5	5	5	6	10	15	40	
190	Red Schoendienst	5	5	6	10	25	50	100	
191	Art Ceccarelli RC	5	5	5	6	10	15	80	
192	Milt Graff	5	5	5	6	10	20	40	3
193	Jerry Lumpe RC	5	5	5	8	12	30	50	5
194	Roger Craig	5	5	5	6	10	30	60	
195	Whitey Lockman	5	5	5	6	10	15	60	
196	Mike Garcia	5	5	5	6	10	20	30	2
197	Haywood Sullivan	5	5	5	6	10	15	40	2
198	Bill Virdon	5	5	5	6	10	25	60	
199	Don Blasingame	5	5	5	6	10	15	60	
200	Bob Keegan	5	5	5	6	10	25	40	
201	Jim Bolger	5	5	5	6	10	20	30	
202	Woody Held RC	5	5	5	6	10	15	30	3
203	Al Walker	5	5	5	6	10	15	30	3
204	Leo Kiely	5	5	5	6	10	15	60	
205	Johnny Temple	5	5	5	6	10	25	40	
206	Bob Shaw RC	5	5	5	6	10	15	60	
207	Solly Hemus	5	5	5	6	15	30	300	
208	Cal McLish	5	5	5	6	10	25	60	
209	Bob Anderson RC	5	5	5	6	10	25	50	
210	Wally Moon	5	5	5	6	10	25	80	
211	Pete Burnside RC	5	5	5	6	10	15	30	
212	Bubba Phillips	5	5	5	6	10	20	100	

	GD 2	VG 3	VgEx 4	EX 5	ExMt 6	NM 7	NmMt 8	MT 9
Red Wilson	5	5	5	6	10	15	40	
Willard Schmidt	5	5	5	6	10	20	40	
Jim Gilliam	5	5	5	8	20	30	80	
St. Louis Cardinals TC	5	5	6	10	25	60	120	
Jack Harshman	5	5	5	6	10	15	60	
Dick Rand RC	5	5	5	6	10	25	100	
Camilo Pascual	5	5	5	6	10	15	40	
Tom Brewer	5	5	5	6	10	20	40	300
Jerry Kindall RC	5	5	5	6	10	15	40	300
Bud Daley RC	5	5	5	6	10	20	30	350
Andy Pafko	5	5	5	8	25	40	100	
Bob Grim	5	5	5	8	12	25	50	300
Billy Goodman	5	5	5	6	10	25	50	
Bob Smith RC	5	5	5	6	10	15	40	150
Gene Stephens	5	5	5	6	10	15	40	
Duke Maas	5	5	5	6	10	15	40	300
Frank Zupo RC	5	5	5	6	10	20	40	300
Richie Ashburn	10	12	15	20	30	60	150	
Lloyd Merritt RC	5	5	5	6	10	25	50	
Reno Bertoia	5	5	5	6	10	15	40	300
Mickey Vernon	5	5	5	6	20	25	50	
Carl Sawatski	5	5	5	6	10	20	50	400
Tom Gorman	5	5	5	6	10	15	40	300
Ed Fitzgerald	5	5	5	6	10	15	50	
Bill Wight	5	5	5	6	10	15	50	250
Bill Mazeroski	5	8	20	25	40	80	400	
Chuck Stobbs	5	5	5	6	10	25	80	
Bill Skowron	5	5	8	12	20	50	150	600
Dick Littlefield	5	5	5	6	10	15	50	
Johnny Klippstein	5	5	5	6	10	20	60	400
Larry Raines RC	5	5	5	6	10	25	50	400
Don Demeter RC	5	5	5	6	10	15	50	
Frank Lary	5	5	5	6	10	25	50	300
New York Yankees TC	10	20	40	60	80	300	1,200	
Casey Wise	5	5	5	6	10	20	50	
Herman Wehmeier	5	5	5	6	10	25	80	
Ray Moore	5	5	5	6	10	15	60	
Roy Sievers	5	5	5	6	10	25	50	300
Warren Hacker	5	5	5	6	10	15	50	
Bob Trowbridge RC	5	5	5	6	10	20	▼60	
Don Mueller	5	5	5	6	10	25	40	300
Alex Grammas	5	5	5	6	10	15	50	
Bob Turley	5	5	6	10	30	40	120	
Chicago White Sox TC	5	5	6	10	40	▲80	400	
Hal Smith	5	5	5	6	10	15	70	
Carl Erskine	5	5	5	8	20	40	80	400
Al Pilarcik	5	5	5	6	10	25	50	400
Frank Malzone	5	5	5	6	10	30	60	
Turk Lown	5	5	5	6	10	15	60	400
Johnny Groth	5	5	5	6	10	15	60	400
Eddie Bressoud RC	5	5	5	6	10	25	40	
Jack Sanford	5	5	5	6	10	15	40	200
Pete Runnels	5	5	5	6	10	25	120	
Connie Johnson	5	5	5	6	10	15	40	
Sherm Lollar	5	5	5	6	10	20	60	400
Granny Hamner	5	5	5	6	10	15	60	
Paul Smith	5	5	5	6	10	15	40	300
Warren Spahn	8	25	30	40	80	120	500	
Billy Martin	5	6	10	20	▲30	60	100	800
Ray Crone	5	5	5	6	10	15	50	200
Hal Smith	5	5	5	6	10	15	40	200
Rocky Bridges	5	5	5	6	10	15	40	400
Elston Howard	5	5	8	25	40	▼60	300	
Bobby Avila	5	5	5	6	10	15	50	
Virgil Trucks	5	5	5	6	10	25	80	300
Mack Burk	5	5	5	6	10	15	40	
Bob Boyd	5	5	5	6	10	25	50	300
Jim Piersall	5	5	5	8	12	50	100	
Sammy Taylor RC	5	5	5	6	10	15	60	
Paul Foytack	5	5	5	6	10	15	30	200
Ray Shearer RC	5	5	5	6	10	30	120	300
Ray Katt	5	5	5	6	10	15	40	300
Frank Robinson	15	20	40	50	100	150	500	
Gino Cimoli	5	5	5	6	10	30	120	
Sam Jones	5	5	5	6	10	25	150	400
Harmon Killebrew	12	25	40	50	80	150	300	2,000
Series Hurling Rivals	5	5	5	10	15	60	400	

	GD 2	VG 3	VgEx 4	EX 5	ExMt 6	NM 7	NmMt 8	MT 9
290 Dick Donovan	5	5	5	6	10	15	40	400
291 Don Landrum RC	5	5	5	6	10	25	100	
292 Ned Garver	5	5	5	6	10	15	50	200
293 Gene Freese	5	5	5	6	10	15	50	300
294 Hal Jeffcoat	5	5	5	6	10	15	60	
295 Minnie Minoso	5	5	12	15	20	50	100	400
296 Ryne Duren RC	5	6	10	15	40	150	500	
297 Don Buddin RC	5	5	5	6	10	15	50	
298 Jim Hearn	5	5	5	6	10	15	50	
299 Harry Simpson	5	5	5	6	10	20	80	300
300 League Presidents	5	5	6	10	15	30	80	
301 Randy Jackson	5	5	5	6	10	20	60	300
302 Mike Baxes RC	5	5	5	6	10	25	150	
303 Neil Chrisley	5	5	5	6	10	25	40	300
304 Tigers Big Bats	5	6	10	15	50	80	200	
305 Clem Labine	5	5	5	6	10	25	60	300
306 Whammy Douglas RC	5	5	5	6	10	15	40	500
307 Brooks Robinson	30	40	50	60	100	250	500	
308 Paul Giel	5	5	5	6	10	15	40	
309 Gail Harris	5	5	5	6	10	15	40	400
310 Ernie Banks	10	30	60	▲100	▲120	▲250	500	3,000
311 Bob Purkey	5	5	5	6	10	15	60	
312 Boston Red Sox TC	5	5	8	25	30	150	800	
313 Bob Rush	5	5	5	6	10	30	80	
314 Dodgers Boss and Power	5	8	12	20	40	80	200	
315 Bob Friend	5	5	5	6	10	15	▼80	400
316 Tito Francona	5	5	5	6	10	25	80	400
317 Albie Pearson RC	5	5	5	6	10	15	100	
318 Frank House	5	5	5	6	10	15	50	
319 Lou Skizas	5	5	5	6	10	15	50	400
320 Whitey Ford	10	25	40	50	80	150	400	1,500
321 Sluggers Supreme	10	15	30	50	60	120	300	2,000
322 Harding Peterson RC	5	5	5	6	10	15	60	
323 Elmer Valo	5	5	5	6	10	25	80	
324 Hoyt Wilhelm	5	5	8	12	25	50	120	600
325 Joe Adcock	5	5	5	6	15	25	100	300
326 Bob Miller	5	5	5	6	10	15	40	
327 Chicago Cubs TC	5	5	8	12	25	80	400	
328 Ike Delock	5	5	5	6	10	30	60	
329 Bob Cerv	5	5	5	6	10	25	50	250
330 Ed Bailey	5	5	5	6	10	15	50	
331 Pedro Ramos	5	5	5	6	10	15	100	400
332 Jim King	5	5	5	6	10	20	60	
333 Andy Carey	5	5	5	8	12	25	60	600
334 Mound Aces	5	5	5	6	10	20	60	
335 Ruben Gomez	5	5	5	6	10	15	25	60	
336 Bert Hamric	5	5	5	6	10	15	40	
337 Hank Aguirre	5	5	5	6	10	15	40	200
338 Walt Dropo	5	5	5	6	10	15	60	400
339 Fred Hatfield	5	5	5	6	10	15	40	
340 Don Newcombe	5	5	5	10	30	50	120	
341 Pittsburgh Pirates TC	5	5	8	12	25	60	400	
342 Jim Brosnan	5	5	5	6	10	▼25	▼60	
343 Orlando Cepeda RC	10	50	60	100	▲150	250	600	2,500
344 Bob Porterfield	5	5	5	6	10	15	50	300
345 Jim Hegan	5	5	5	6	10	15	50	
346 Steve Bilko	5	5	5	6	10	20	80	
347 Don Rudolph RC	5	5	5	6	10	20	40	
348 Chico Fernandez	5	5	5	6	10	20	60	400
349 Murry Dickson	5	5	5	6	10	20		
350 Ken Boyer	5	5	8	12	20	60	200	
351 Braves Fence Busters	10	30	40	60	80	▼150	400	2,000
352 Herb Score	5	5	5	8	20	40	100	
353 Stan Lopata	5	5	5	6	10	15	60	
354 Art Ditmar	5	5	5	8	12	25	100	400
355 Bill Bruton	5	5	5	8	12	60	250	500
356 Bob Malkmus RC	5	5	5	6	10	15	60	
357 Danny McDevitt RC	5	5	5	6	10	20	80	
358 Gene Baker	5	5	5	6	10	15	50	
359 Billy Loes	5	5	5	6	10	15	50	
360 Roy McMillan	5	5	5	6	10	25	50	250
361 Mike Fornieles	5	5	5	6	10	15	50	
362 Ray Jablonski	5	5	5	6	10	15	80	
363 Don Elston	5	5	5	6	10	20	50	300
364 Earl Battey	5	5	5	6	10	15	50	200
365 Tom Morgan	5	5	5	6	10	15	40	
366 Gene Green RC	5	5	5	6	10	15	60	

#	Player	GD 2	VG 3	VgEx 4	EX 5	ExMt 6	NM 7	NmMt 8	MT 9
367	Jack Urban RC	5	5	5	6	10	15	40	300
368	Rocky Colavito	8	12	30	40	50	80	300	1,500
369	Ralph Lumenti RC	5	5	5	6	10	15	50	200
370	Yogi Berra	25	40	60	100	120	200	600	2,000
371	Marty Keough RC	5	5	5	6	10	15	40	
372	Don Cardwell	5	5	5	6	10	15	60	
373	Joe Pignatano RC	5	5	5	6	10	20	80	400
374	Brooks Lawrence	5	5	5	6	10	40	120	
375	Pee Wee Reese	20	25	30	40	50	▲100	200	800
376	Charley Rabe RC	5	5	5	6	10	15	80	300
377A	Milwaukee Braves TC Alpha	5	5	8	12	20	30	120	
377B	Milwaukee Braves TC Num	10	15	25	40	80			
378	Hank Sauer	5	5	5	15	20	25	50	400
379	Ray Herbert	5	5	5	6	10	15	50	300
380	Charlie Maxwell	5	5	5	6	10	25	60	400
381	Hal Brown	5	5	5	6	10	15	60	
382	Al Cicotte	5	5	5	6	10	25	50	300
383	Lou Berberet	5	5	5	6	10	15	30	
384	John Goryl RC	5	5	5	6	10	25	50	
385	Wilmer Mizell	5	5	5	6	10	20	50	250
386	Birdie's Young Sluggers	5	5	8	20	25	50	200	
387	Wally Post	5	5	5	6	10	20	60	300
388	Billy Moran RC	5	5	5	6	10	15	30	300
389	Bill Taylor	5	5	5	6	10	15	30	250
390	Del Crandall	5	5	5	6	15	25	50	400
391	Dave Melton RC	5	5	5	6	10	15	60	
392	Bennie Daniels RC	5	5	5	6	15	80	400	
393	Tony Kubek	5	5	15	20	30	40	100	400
394	Jim Grant RC	5	5	5	6	20	30	150	
395	Willard Nixon	5	5	5	6	10	15	80	
396	Dutch Dotterer RC	5	5	5	6	10	15	30	250
397A	Detroit Tigers TC Alpha	5	5	6	10	15	25	80	
397B	Detroit Tigers TC Num	10	15	25	40	60			
398	Gene Woodling	5	5	5	6	10	15	60	
399	Marv Grissom	5	5	5	6	10	15	40	300
400	Nellie Fox	6	10	15	20	30	▼50	150	500
401	Don Bessent	5	5	5	6	10	15	30	300
402	Bobby Gene Smith	5	5	5	6	10	15	50	
403	Steve Korcheck RC	5	5	5	6	10	15	30	300
404	Curt Simmons	5	5	5	6	10	15	40	
405	Ken Aspromonte RC	5	5	5	6	10	25	40	250
406	Vic Power	5	5	5	6	10	15	40	
407	Carlton Willey RC	5	5	5	6	10	20	30	250
408A	Baltimore Orioles TC Alpha	5	5	6	10	15	25	80	
408B	Baltimore Orioles TC Num	10	15	25	40	80			
409	Frank Thomas	5	5	5	8	15	80	600	
410	Murray Wall	5	5	5	6	10	15	30	
411	Tony Taylor RC	5	5	5	6	10	20	40	300
412	Gerry Staley	5	5	5	6	10	▲20	40	
413	Jim Davenport RC	5	5	5	6	10	15	40	
414	Sammy White	5	5	5	6	10	25	40	
415	Bob Bowman	5	5	5	6	10	15	30	200
416	Foster Castleman	5	5	5	6	10	25	50	
417	Carl Furillo	5	5	6	10	25	30	100	400
418	World Series Batting Foes	60	▲120	▲150	200	300	600	2,500	20,000
419	Bobby Shantz	5	5	5	8	12	25	120	500
420	Vada Pinson RC	6	10	12	25	40	60	200	
421	Dixie Howell	5	5	5	6	10	15	40	
422	Norm Zauchin	5	5	5	6	10	15	80	
423	Phil Clark RC	5	5	5	6	10	15	30	
424	Larry Doby	5	5	8	20	30	50	150	
425	Sammy Esposito	5	5	5	6	10	15	40	
426	Johnny O'Brien	5	5	5	6	10	15	40	250
427	Al Worthington	5	5	5	6	15	20	60	300
428A	Cincinnati Reds TC Alpha	5	5	6	10	15	25	120	
428B	Cincinnati Reds TC Num	8	12	20	30	50	80		
429	Gus Triandos	5	5	5	6	10	40	100	
430	Bobby Thomson	5	5	5	8	12	30	50	250
431	Gene Conley	5	5	5	6	20	100	250	
432	John Powers RC	5	5	5	6	10	15	50	
433A	Pancho Herrera COR RC	5	5	5	6	10	15	60	300
434	Harvey Kuenn	5	5	5	8	12	30	50	
435	Ed Roebuck	5	5	5	6	10	20	40	250
436	Rival Fence Busters	12	25	40	50	▼60	150	600	
437	Bob Speake	5	5	5	6	10	15	50	400
438	Whitey Herzog	5	5	5	6	10	30	50	300
439	Ray Narleski	5	5	5	6	10	25	50	
440	Eddie Mathews	10	15	25	50	▼60	250	500	
441	Jim Marshall RC	5	5	5	6	10	25	60	
442	Phil Paine RC	5	5	5	6	10	15	30	
443	Billy Harrell SP RC	5	5	5	6	10	30	150	
444	Danny Kravitz	5	5	5	6	10	15	30	3
445	Bob Smith RC	5	5	5	6	10	15	40	5
446	Carroll Hardy SP RC	5	5	5	6	10	25	60	
447	Ray Monzant	5	5	5	6	10	15	40	
448	Charley Lau RC	5	5	5	8	12	30	200	
449	Gene Fodge RC	5	5	5	6	10	20	30	6
450	Preston Ward SP	5	5	5	6	10	40	50	
451	Joe Taylor RC	5	5	5	6	10	25	50	
452	Roman Mejias	5	5	5	6	10	15	30	2
453	Tom Qualters	5	5	5	6	10	15	40	1
454	Harry Hanebrink RC	5	5	5	6	10	20	40	4
455	Hal Griggs RC	5	5	5	6	10	15	30	
456	Dick Brown RC	5	5	5	6	10	15	30	1
457	Milt Pappas RC	5	5	5	8	20	25	80	
458	Julio Becquer RC	5	5	5	6	10	15	40	
459	Ron Blackburn RC	5	5	5	6	10	15	40	2
460	Chuck Essegian RC	5	5	5	6	10	15	40	3
461	Ed Mayer RC	5	5	5	6	10	15	30	3
462	Gary Geiger SP RC	5	5	5	8	20	30	100	
463	Vito Valentinetti	5	5	5	6	10	15	60	
464	Curt Flood RC	8	20	25	30	50	80	250	
465	Arnie Portocarrero	5	5	5	6	10	15	50	4
466	Pete Whisenant	5	5	5	6	10	15	50	4
467	Glen Hobbie RC	5	5	5	6	10	15	40	2
468	Bob Schmidt RC	5	5	5	6	10	15	40	4
469	Don Ferrarese	5	5	5	6	10	15	30	3
470	R.C. Stevens RC	5	5	5	6	10	15	40	3
471	Lenny Green RC	5	5	5	6	10	20	40	
472	Joey Jay	5	5	5	6	10	60	120	
473	Bill Renna	5	5	5	6	10	15	30	4
474	Roman Semproch RC	5	5	5	6	10	30	50	
475	All-Star Managers	5	6	25	30	40	60	300	
476	Stan Musial AS TP	5	20	30	40	50	80	200	1,0
477	Bill Skowron AS	5	5	15	20	30	50	80	6
478	Johnny Temple AS	5	5	5	6	10	15	50	4
479	Nellie Fox AS	5	5	▲15	▲20	25	40	80	6
480	Eddie Mathews AS	5	8	▲25	▲30	▲40	60	200	
481	Frank Malzone AS	5	5	5	6	10	25	100	
482	Ernie Banks AS	5	20	30	▲50	50	80	150	1,0
483	Luis Aparicio AS	5	5	6	10	25	40	80	
484	Frank Robinson AS	5	15	20	▲30	▲50	▲60	150	▲1,5
485	Ted Williams AS	40	50	60	▲100	120	▲200	400	1,5
486	Willie Mays AS	20	25	▲50	▲60	100	▲250	500	3,0
487	Mickey Mantle AS TP	60	80	100	120	200	300	600	2,5
488	Hank Aaron AS	8	30	40	50	80	150	400	5,0
489	Jackie Jensen AS	5	5	5	6	10	50	150	
490	Ed Bailey AS	5	5	5	6	10	15	80	
491	Sherm Lollar AS	5	5	5	6	10	15	60	
492	Bob Friend AS	5	5	5	▲20	▲25	▲30	120	
493	Bob Turley AS	5	5	5	6	25	50	120	
494	Warren Spahn AS	5	15	20	30	40	60	250	1,5
495	Herb Score AS	5	5	6	10	25	50	300	
NNO	Contest Card July 8th	5	8	12	20	30	150		
NNO	Felt Emblem Insert	5	8	12	20	30	60	500	

—Hank Aaron #30 (White) PSA 9 (MT) sold for $4,974 (Mastro; 4/07)
—Hank Aaron #30 (White) PSA 9 (MT) sold for $4,522 (Mastro; 12/06)
—Hank Aaron #30 (White) SGC 92 (NmMt+) sold for $1,700 (Madec; 10/06)
—Hank Aaron #30 (White) GAI 8.5 (NmMt) sold for $1,669 (Mastro; 8/07)
—Hank Aaron #30 (Yellow) GAI 8 (NmMt) sold for $1,680 (Mastro; 5/08)
—Hank Aaron #30 (Yellow) BVG 8 (NmMt) sold for $1,336 (eBay; 1/08)
—Hank Aaron #30 (Yellow) BVG 8 (NmMt) sold for $1,250 (eBay; 3/07)
—Hank Aaron AS #488 GAI 9 (MT) sold for $1,030 (eBay; 3/08)
—Hank Aaron AS #488 GAI 9 (MT) sold for $843 (eBay; 1/08)
—Hank Aaron AS #488 GAI 9 (MT) sold for $586 (eBay; 2/08)
—Luis Aparicio #85 (White) PSA 9 (MT) sold for $1,779 (Memory Lane; 9/07)
—Luis Aparicio #85 (Yellow) PSA 8 (NmMt) sold for $1,417 (eBay; 5/08)
—Luis Aparicio #85 (Yellow) PSA 8 (NmMt) sold for $1,282 (Goodwin; 11/04)
—Luis Aparicio #85 (Yellow) PSA 8 (NmMt) sold for $1,121 (eBay; 9/07)
—Luis Aparicio #85 (Yellow) PSA 8 (NmMt) sold for $1,077 (eBay; 10/06)
—Richie Ashburn #230 PSA 9 (MT) sold for $1,578 (Mile High; 1/07)
—Ernie Banks AS #482 GAI 9 (MT) sold for $404 (eBay; 12/07)
—Yogi Berra #370 PSA 10 (Gem) sold for $7,365 (Memory Lane; 12/06)
—Gus Bell #75 PSA 10 (Gem) sold for $7,114 (eBay; 10/12)

Steve Boros #81 (Yellow) PSA 8 (NmMt) sold for $2,750 (eBay; 6/06)
Steve Boros #81 (Yellow) PSA 8 (NmMt) sold for $1,606 (Mile High; 2/08)
Steve Boros #81 (Yellow) PSA 8 (NmMt) sold for $1,050 (eBay; 1/08)
Boston Red Sox TC #312 PSA 9 (MT) sold for $3,169 (eBay; 3/08)
Roberto Clemente #52 (White) GAI 9.5 (Gem) sold for $3,614 (Mastro; 10/05)
Roberto Clemente #52 (White) GAI 9 (MT) sold for $1,777 (Mile High; 1/07)
Roberto Clemente #52 (White) GAI 8.5 (NmMt) sold for $559 (eBay; 10/07)
Roberto Clemente #52 (Yellow) PSA 9 (MT) sold for $18,262 (Goodwin; 11/07)
Roberto Clemente #52 (Yellow) GAI 9 (MT) sold for $4,482 (Memory Lane; 3/06)
Roberto Clemente #52 (Yellow) BVG 8.5 (NmMt+) sold for $2,494 (eBay; 4/08)
Roberto Clemente #52 (Yellow) BVG 8.5 (NmMt+) sold for $2,075 (eBay; 10/07)
Detroit Tigers TC #397 (Numerical) PSA 7 (NM) sold for $625 (eBay; 11/07)
Detroit Tigers TC #397 (Numerical) PSA 7 (NM) sold for $503 (eBay; 6/08)
Murry Dickson #349 PSA 8 (NmMt) sold for $1,584 (eBay; 10/06)
Murry Dickson #349 PSA 8 (NmMt) sold for $1,025 (eBay; 1/07)
Murry Dickson #349 PSA 8 (NmMt) sold for $192 (eBay; 11/07)
Murry Dickson #349 PSA 8 (NmMt) sold for $79 (eBay; 12/07)
Dodgers Boss and Power #314 PSA 9 (MT) sold for $1,324 (Superior; 3/04)
Don Drysdale #25 GAI 9 (MT) sold for $1,1011 (Memory Lane; 3/06)
Curt Flood #464 PSA 9 (MT) sold for $4,106 (Memory Lane; 3/06)
Curt Flood #464 PSA 9 (MT) sold for $1,036 (eBay; 11/07)
P.Herrer ERR (No a) #433 PSA 8 (NmMt) sold for $25,461 (Mile High; 8/07)
P.Herrer ERR (No a) #433 PSA 8 OC (NmMt OC) sold for $7,207 (Goodwin; 5/08)
P.Herrer ERR (No a) #433 PSA 7 (NM) sold for $7,250 (Mile High; 1/07)
P.Herrer ERR (No a) #433 PSA 7 (NM) sold for $7,222 (eBay; 8/07)
P.Herrer ERR (No a) #433 SGC 80 (ExMt) sold for $4,715 (Hunt; 3/08)
P.Herrer ERR (No a) #433 SGC 50 (VgEx) sold for $1,422 (eBay; 3/08)
P.Herrer ERR (No a) #433 GAI 3.5 (VG+) sold for $1,900 (Huggins & Scott; 10/05)
P.Herrer ERR (No a) #433 SGC 30 (Good) sold for $1,080 (eBay; 1/08)
Billy Hoeft #13 (Yellow) PSA 8 (NmMt) sold for $920 (eBay; 7/07)
Billy Hoeft #13 (Yellow) PSA 8 (NmMt) sold for $712 (eBay; 6/06)
Billy Hoeft #13 (Yellow) PSA 8 (NmMt) sold for $484 (eBay; 10/07)
Elston Howard #275 PSA 9 (MT) sold for $2,706 (eBay; 12/06)
Elston Howard #275 PSA 9 (MT) sold for $1,925 (eBay; 6/07)
Billy Hunter #98 (Yellow) PSA 9 (MT) sold for $2,873 (Memory Lane; 5/08)
Billy Hunter #98 (Yellow) PSA 8 (NmMt) sold for $1,825 (eBay; 6/06)
Darrell Johnson #61 (Yellow) PSA 8 (NmMt) sold for $1,009 (eBay; 6/06)
Darrell Johnson #61 (Yellow) PSA 8 (NmMt) sold for $626 (eBay; 1/06)
Darrell Johnson #61 (Yellow) PSA 8 (NmMt) sold for $571 (eBay; 9/07)
Ernie Johnson #78 (Yellow) PSA 9 (MT) sold for $4,750 (eBay; 5/08)
Ernie Johnson #78 (Yellow) PSA 9 (MT) sold for $3,755 (eBay; 3/08)
Al Kaline #70 (Yellow) PSA 9 (MT) sold for $3,202 (Madec; 10/06)
Al Kaline #70 (Yellow) PSA 9 (MT) sold for $3,055 (eBay; 2/08)
Al Kaline #70 (Yellow) BVG 8.5 (NmMt+) sold for $734 (eBay; 10/07)
Eddie Kasko #8 (Yellow) PSA 9 (MT) sold for $2,280 (Mastro; 5/08)
Eddie Kasko #8 (Yellow) PSA 8 (NmMt) sold for $2,255 (Mile High; 8/07)
Harmon Killebrew #288 GAI 9 (MT) sold for $525 (eBay; 12/07)
Harmon Killebrew #288 GAI 9 (MT) sold for $510 (Mastro; 2/08)
Sandy Koufax #187 PSA 10 (Gem) sold for $40,000 (Memory Lane; Private 2007)
Sandy Koufax #187 GAI 9.5 (Gem) sold for $2,662 (Goodwin; 10/05)
Sandy Koufax #187 GAI 9 (MT) sold for $1,988 (Madec; 5/07)
Hobie Landrith #24 (Yellow) PSA 8 (NmMt) sold for $682 (Mile High; 6/06)
Hobie Landrith #24 (Yellow) PSA 8 (NmMt) sold for $407 (eBay; 10/07)
Bob Lemon #2 (White) PSA 9 (MT) sold for $3,728 (Mile High; 8/07)
Bob Lemon #2 (White) PSA 9 (MT) sold for $2,842 (Memory Lane; 5/08)
Bob Lemon #2 (White) PSA 9 (MT) sold for $1,617 (Memory Lane; 9/07)
Bob Lemon #2 (Yellow) PSA 8 (NmMt) sold for $13,544 (Mile High; 2/08)
Bob Lemon #2 (Yellow) PSA 8 (NmMt) sold for $10,600 (eBay; 11/07)
Bob Lemon #2 (Yellow) PSA 7 (NM) sold for $734 (eBay; 8/07)
Bob Lemon #2 (Yellow) PSA 7 (NM) sold for $572 (eBay; 1/07)
Bob Lemon #2 (Yellow) PSA 7 (NM) sold for $338 (eBay; 6/06)
Los Angeles Dodgers TC #71 PSA 9 (MT) sold for $2,107 (Memory Lane; 8/06)
Mickey Mantle #150 PSA 9 (MT) sold for $16,213 (Mile High; 2/08)
Mickey Mantle #150 PSA 9 (MT) sold for $15,692 (Memory Lane; Winter '13)
Mickey Mantle #150 PSA 9 (MT) sold for $15,405 (REA; Spring '14)
Mickey Mantle #150 PSA 9 (MT) sold for $13,458 (Memory Lane; 8/12)
Mickey Mantle #150 PSA 9 (MT) sold for $13,062 (Mile High; 4/14)
Mickey Mantle #150 PSA 9 (MT) sold for $12,866 (SCP; 8/13)
Mickey Mantle #150 PSA 9 (MT) sold for $12,440 (Mile High; 5/12)
Mickey Mantle #150 PSA 9 (MT) sold for $11,741 (Goodwin; 11/07)
Mickey Mantle #150 SGC 96 (MT) sold for $9,219 (Mile High; 1/07)
Mickey Mantle #150 PSA 9 (MT) sold for $7,638 (REA; 05/11)
Mickey Mantle #150 PSA 9 (MT) sold for $7,530 (Mastro; 12/06)
Mickey Mantle #150 SGC 92 (NmMt+) sold for $3,738 (eBay; 11/06)
Mickey Mantle #150 SGC 92 (NmMt+) sold for $3,123 (Memory Lane; 5/08)
Mickey Mantle #150 SGC 92 (NmMt+) sold for $3,049 (Mastro; 8/07)
Mickey Mantle #150 SGC 92 (NmMt+) sold for $2,685 (Goodwin; 5/07)

—Mickey Mantle #150 GAI 8.5 (NmMt+) sold for $2,133 (Mile High; 1/07)
—Mickey Mantle #150 GAI 8.5 (NmMt+) sold for $2,064 (Memory Lane; 12/07)
—Mickey Mantle #150 GAI 8 (NmMt) sold for $1,516 (Mile High; 2/08)
—Mickey Mantle #150 GAI 8 (NmMt) sold for $1,391 (eBay; 4/07)
—Mickey Mantle AS #487 GAI 9 (MT) sold for $1,405 (Madec; 5/07)
—Milwaukee Braves TC #377 (Num) PSA 8 (NmMt) sold for $2,077 (Goodwin; 10/04)
—Roger Maris #47 GAI 9.5 (Gem) sold for $5,037 (Memory Lane; 5/08)
—Roger Maris #47 GAI 9.5 (Gem) sold for $2,629 (Heritage; 5/07)
—Roger Maris #47 GAI 9.5 (Gem) sold for $2,390 (Heritage; 10/06)
—Roger Maris #47 SGC 96 (MT) sold for $3,556 (eBay; 5/08)
—Roger Maris #47 GAI 9 (MT) sold for $2,704 (Goodwin; 8/07)
—Roger Maris #47 GAI 9 (MT) sold for $2,398 (eBay; 5/08)
—Roger Maris #47 GAI 9 (MT) sold for $2,032 (Heritage; 5/08)
—Roger Maris #47 GAI 9 (MT) sold for $2,031 (eBay; 2/07)
—Roger Maris #47 GAI 9 (MT) sold for $1,825 (eBay; 7/06)
—Roger Maris #47 BVG 8.5 (NmMt+) sold for $1,132 (eBay; 5/08)
—Roger Maris #47 GAI 8.5 (NmMt+) sold for $910 (eBay; 11/07)
—Roger Maris #47 GAI 8.5 (NmMt+) sold for $710 (eBay; 8/06)
—Bob Martyn RC #39 PSA 10 (Gem) sold for $2,560 (eBay; 9/12)
—Morrie Martin #53 (Yellow) PSA 9 (MT) sold for $2,606 (eBay; 4/08)
—Eddie Mathews #440 PSA 9 (MT) sold for $4,573 (Memory Lane; 9/07)
—Eddie Mathews #440 PSA 9 (MT) sold for $3,363 (Memory Lane; 3/06)
—Eddie Mathews AS #480 PSA 9 (MT) sold for $2,385 (Memory Lane; 8/06)
—Eddie Mathews AS #480 PSA 9 (MT) sold for $1,180 (Mastro; 6/06)
—Willie Mays #5 PSA 9 (MT) sold for $12,169 (Goodwin; 6/06)
—Willie Mays #5 GAI 8.5 (NmMt+) sold for $1,013 (Mastro; 8/06)
—Willie Mays #5 GAI 8.5 (NmMt+) sold for $812 (eBay; 12/07)
—Mike McCormick RC #37 PSA 9 (MT) sold for $5,609 (eBay; 8/12)
—Mike McCormick #37 PSA 8 (NmMt) sold for $1,035 (eBay; 7/06)
—Von McDaniel #65 (Yellow) PSA 8 (NmMt) sold for $721 (Goodwin; 10/04)
—Gil McDougald #20 (Yellow) PSA 8 (NmMt) sold for $2,084 (eBay; 7/06)
—Gil McDougald #20 (Yellow) PSA 8 (NmMt) sold for $1,780 (Mile High; 2/08)
—Gil McDougald #20 (Yellow) PSA 8 (NmMt) sold for $705 (eBay; 8/07)
—Gil McDougald #20 (Yellow) PSA 8 (NmMt) sold for $456 (eBay; 2/06)
—Milwaukee Braves #377 (Numerical) PSA 8 (NmMt) sold for $1,281 (eBay; 11/07)
—Milwaukee Braves #377 (Numerical) PSA 7 (NM) sold for $317 (eBay; 11/07)
—Don Mossi #35 (Yellow) PSA 9 (MT) sold for $4,775 (eBay; 5/08)
—Don Mossi #35 (Yellow) PSA 9 (MT) sold for $3,605 (eBay; 3/08)
—New York Yankees TC #246 PSA 8 (NmMt) sold for $1,679 (eBay; 10/06)
—New York Yankees TC #246 PSA 8 (NmMt) sold for $1,226 (eBay; 5/07)
—New York Yankees TC #246 PSA 8 (NmMt) sold for $540 (eBay; 12/07)
—Pee Wee Reese #375 PSA 10 (Gem) sold for $2,839 (Memory Lane; 12/06)
—Bobby Richardson #101 (White) PSA 9 (MT) sold for $1,870 (Memory Lane; 8/06)
—Bobby Richardson #101 (Yellow) PSA 9 (MT) sold for $3,608 (Memory Lane; 6/06)
—Bobby Richardson #101 (Yellow) PSA 8 (NmMt) sold for $1,078 (Mile High; 8/07)
—Bobby Richardson #101 (Yellow) PSA 8 (NmMt) sold for $588 (eBay; 11/07)
—Bobby Richardson #101 (Yellow) PSA 8 (NmMt) sold for $548 (eBay; 10/06)
—Rival Fence Busters #436 PSA 9 (MT) sold for $3,614 (Mastro; 4/06)
—Jim Rivera #11 (Yellow) PSA 8 (NmMt) sold for $2,357 (Mile High; 6/06)
—Jim Rivera #11 (Yellow) PSA 8 (NmMt) sold for $788 (eBay; 2/08)
—Robin Roberts #90 PSA 9 (MT) sold for $4,836 (eBay; 02/12)
—Brooks Robinson #307 PSA 9 (MT) sold for $3,920 (Mile High; 8/07)
—Brooks Robinson #307 PSA 9 (MT) sold for $2,011 (Goodwin; 6/06)
—John Roseboro #42 PSA 9 (MT) sold for $1,634 (Goodwin; 10/06)
—Herb Score AS #495 PSA 9 (MT) sold for $2,727 (Mile High; 6/06)
—Series Hurling Rivals #289 PSA 8 (NmMt) sold for $1,625 (eBay; 7/06)
—Series Hurling Rivals #289 PSA 8 (NmMt) sold for $1,225 (eBay; 7/07)
—Series Hurling Rivals #289 PSA 8 (NmMt) sold for $898 (eBay; 10/07)
—Series Hurling Rivals #289 PSA 8 (NmMt) sold for $637 (eBay; 9/07)
—Duke Snider #88 PSA 9 (MT) sold for $7,550 (Madec; 5/07)
—Duke Snider #88 PSA 9 (MT) sold for $3,551 (eBay; 10/05)
—Duke Snider #88 PSA 9 (MT) sold for $3,384 (Mastro; 6/05)
—Warren Spahn #270 PSA 9 (MT) sold for $2,349 (Memory Lane; 9/07)
—Bobby Thomson #430 PSA 10 (Gem) sold for $4,893 (eBay; 12/12)
—Bobby Thomson #430 PSA 10 (Gem) sold for $3,000 (Legendary; 11/12)
—Marv Throneberry #175 PSA 9 (MT) sold for $2,238 (Memory Lane; 12/06)
—Tigers Big Bats #304 PSA 9 (MT) sold for $1,606 (Mile High; 2/08)
—Bob Turley AS #493 PSA 9 (MT) sold for $3,005 (eBay; 4/08)
—Bill Tuttle #23 (White) PSA 8 (NmMt) sold for $865 (eBay; 1/07)
—Bill Tuttle #23 (White) PSA 8 (NmMt) sold for $669 (eBay; 8/06)
—Bill Tuttle #23 (White) PSA 8 (NmMt) sold for $338 (eBay; 11/07)
—Bill Tuttle #23 (White) PSA 8 (NmMt) sold for $198 (eBay; 6/07)
—Bill Tuttle #23 (Yellow) PSA 8 (NmMt) sold for $1,187 (eBay; 2/08)
—Ted Williams #1 PSA 9 (MT) sold for $24,308 (Goodwin; 11/07)
—Ted Williams #1 PSA 9 (MT) sold for $23,573 (Goodwin; 5/08)
—Ted Williams #1 PSA 9 (MT) sold for $17,500 (Memory Lane; 8/06)
—Ted Williams #1 PSA 9 (MT) sold for $7,223 (Mile High; 6/05)

—Ted Williams #1 GAI 9 (MT) sold for $3,554 (Mile High; 1/07)
—Ted Williams #1 SGC 92 (NmMt+) sold for $3,944 (Mastro; 4/07)
—Ted Williams #1 SGC 92 (NmMt+) sold for $3,124 (Goodwin; 3/08)
—Ted Williams #1 GAI 8.5 (NmMt+) sold for $1,725 (eBay; 6/06)
—Ted Williams #1 GAI 8.5 (NmMt+) sold for $1,524 (Mile High; 8/07)
—Ted Williams AS #485 PSA 10 (Gem) sold for $8,512 (eBay; 9/06)
—Ted Williams AS #485 PSA 10 (Gem) sold for $7,763 (Superior; 3/04)
—Ted Williams AS #485 GAI 9 (MT) sold for $721 (eBay; 1/08)
—Tigers Big Bats #304 PSA 9 (MT) sold for $2,317 (Memory Lane; 8/06)
—World Series Batting Foes #418 GAI 9 (MT) sold for $3,355 (Mastro; 12/06)
—World Series Batting Foes #418 BVG 8.5 (NmMt+) sold for $936 (eBay; 3/07)
—World Series Batting Foes #418 GAI 8.5 (NmMt+) sold for $919 (Memory Lane; 11/05)
—Early Wynn #100 (Yellow) PSA 9 (MT) sold for $2,544 (Mile High; 6/06)
—Contest Card July 8 PSA 8 (NmMt) sold for $1,303 (eBay; 4/08)

1959 Fleer Ted Williams

#		GD 2	VG 3	VgEx 4	EX 5	ExMt 6	NM 7	NmMt 8	MT 9
1	The Early Years	6	10	15	25	60	100	400	
2	Ted's Idol Babe Ruth	8	12	20	80	100	150	300	600
3	Practice Makes Perfect	5	5	5	8	12	20	80	150
4	Learns Fine Points	5	5	5	8	12	20	50	200
5	Ted's Fame Spreads	5	5	5	8	12	20	40	120
6	Ted Turns Professional	5	5	6	10	15	25	50	250
7	From Mound to Plate	5	5	5	8	12	20	40	150
8	1937 First Full Season	5	5	5	8	20	30	50	250
9	First Step to the Majors w/Collins	5	5	6	10	15	25	50	200
10	Gunning as Pastime	5	5	5	8	12	20	40	200
11	First Spring Training w/Foxx	5	5	8	12	20	50	120	200
12	Burning Up Minors	5	5	5	8	12	20	40	200
13	1939 Shows Will Stay	5	5	5	8	12	20	40	150
14	Outstanding Rookie '39	5	5	5	8	12	25	60	200
15	Licks Sophomore Jinx	5	5	5	8	12	20	40	120
16	Williams' Greatest Year	5	5	5	8	15	30	50	120
17	How Ted Hit .400	5	6	10	15	25	50	100	300
18	1941 All Star Hero	5	5	5	8	12	20	40	120
19	Ted Wins Triple Crown	5	5	5	8	12	20	40	150
20	On to Naval Training	5	5	5	8	12	20	40	150
21	Honors for Williams	5	5	5	8	12	20	40	
22	1944 Ted Solos	5	5	5	8	12	20	40	150
23	Williams Wins His Wings	5	5	5	8	12	20	40	175
24	1945 Sharpshooter	5	5	5	8	12	20	25	100
25	1945 Ted Discharged	5	5	5	8	12	20	40	100
26	Off to Flying Start	5	5	5	8	12	20	30	150
27	7/9/46 One Man Show	5	5	5	8	12	30	50	150
28	The Williams Shift	5	5	5	8	12	20	40	120
29	Ted Hits for Cycle	5	5	5	8	12	20	40	120
30	Beating The Williams Shift	5	5	5	8	12	20	50	80
31	Sox Lose Series	5	5	5	8	12	25	40	100
32	Most Valuable Player	5	5	5	8	15	20	40	150
33	Another Triple Crown	5	5	5	8	12	20	40	80
34	Runs Scored Record	5	5	5	8	12	20	40	150
35	Sox Miss Pennant	5	5	5	8	12	20	40	100
36	Banner Year for Ted	5	5	5	8	12	20	40	150
37	1949 Sox Miss Again	5	5	5	8	12	20	40	100
38	1949 Power Rampage	5	5	5	8	12	20	40	100
39	1950 Great Start	5	5	5	8	12	20	40	100
40	Ted Crashes into Wall	5	5	5	8	12	20	50	250
41	1950 Ted Recovers	5	5	5	8	12	20	25	120
42	Williams/Tom Yawkey	5	5	5	8	12	20	40	120
43	Double Play Lead	5	5	5	8	12	20	40	120
44	Back to Marines	5	5	5	8	12	20	40	150
45	Farewell to Baseball	5	5	5	8	12	20	40	100
46	Ready for Combat	5	5	5	8	12	20	30	
47	Ted Crash Lands Jet	5	5	5	8	12	20	40	100
48	1953 Ted Returns	5	5	5	8	12	20	40	100
49	Smash Return	5	5	5	8	12	20	40	100
50	1954 Spring Injury	5	5	5	8	12	20	30	150
51	Ted is Patched Up	5	5	5	8	12	20	25	150
52	1954 Ted's Comeback	5	5	5	8	12	30	50	100
53	Comeback is Success	5	5	5	8	12	20	40	120
54	Ted Hooks Big One	5	5	5	8	12	20	40	80
55	Retirement No Go	5	5	5	8	12	20	40	150
56	2,000th Hit 8/11/55	5	5	5	8	12	20	30	120
57	Ted Reaches 400th Homer	5	5	5	8	12	20	40	
58	Williams Hits .388	5	5	5	8	12	20	40	100
59	Hot September for Ted	5	5	5	8	12	20	40	120
60	More Records for Ted	5	5	5	8	12	20	40	10
61	1957 Outfielder Ted	5	5	5	8	12	20	40	17
62	1958 Sixth Batting Title	5	5	5	8	12	20	40	10
63	All-Star Record w/facsimile Auto	5	6	10	15	25	50	100	10
64	Daughter and Daddy	5	5	5	8	12	20	40	10
65	1958 August 30	5	5	5	8	12	20	40	8
66	1958 Powerhouse	5	5	5	8	12	20	40	10
67	Two Famous Fishermen w/Snead	5	5	8	12	20	30	60	12
68	Ted Signs for 1959 SP	200	250	325	500	600	1,000	1,200	2,00
69	A Future Ted Williams	5	5	5	8	12	20	25	10
70	Ted Williams and Jim Thorpe	5	5	8	12	20	40	50	20
71	Hitting Fundamental 1	5	5	5	8	12	20	25	12
72	Hitting Fundamental 2	5	5	5	8	12	20	40	12
73	Hitting Fundamental 3	5	5	5	8	12	20	30	12
74	Here's How	5	5	5	8	12	20	40	20
75	Williams' Value to Sox w/Ruth	5	5	8	12	20	50	80	30
76	On Base Record	5	5	5	8	12	20	40	10
77	Ted Relaxes	5	5	5	8	12	20	25	15
78	Honors for Williams	5	5	5	8	12	20	40	17
79	Where Ted Stands	5	5	5	8	12	20	50	25
80	Ted's Goals for 1959	5	5	8	10	15	25	50	150

—The Early Years #1 PSA 10 (Gem) sold for $9,799 (Mastro; 12/06)
—The Early Years #1 PSA 9 (MT) sold for $4,201 (Goodwin; 6/06)
—The Early Years #1 PSA 9 (MT) sold for $3,873 (Madec; 10/06)
—The Early Years #1 PSA 9 (MT) sold for $2,289 (Memory Lane; 2/07)
—The Early Years #1 GAI 9 (MT) sold for $1,086 (Mastro; 6/06)
—Ted's Idol Babe Ruth #2 PSA 9 (MT) sold for $1,550 (eBay; 2/07)
—Ted's Idol Babe Ruth #2 PSA 9 (MT) sold for $780 (eBay; 12/07)
—Ted's Idol Babe Ruth #2 PSA 9 (MT) sold for $682 (eBay; 6/08)
—Ted Signs for 1959 #68 SGC 96 (MT) sold for $3,175 (Mastro; 6/07)
—Ted Signs for 1959 #68 GAI 9 (MT) sold for $1,231 (Mastro; 12/06)
—Ted Signs for 1959 #68 GAI 8.5 (NmMt+) sold for $634 (eBay; 1/08)
—Ted Relaxes #77 PSA 10 (Gem) sold for $985 (eBay; 12/07)

1959 Topps

#		GD 2	VG 3	VgEx 4	EX 5	ExMt 6	NM 7	NmMt 8	MT
1	Ford Frick COMM	6	10	25	40	100	200	600	
2	Eddie Yost	5	5	5	5	8	25	100	50
3	Don McMahon	5	5	5	6	10	20	60	
4	Albie Pearson	5	5	6	10	15	25	60	40
5	Dick Donovan	5	5	5	5	8	15	40	40
6	Alex Grammas	5	5	5	5	8	15	30	30
7	Al Pilarcik	5	5	5	5	8	15	40	25
8	Philadelphia Phillies CL	6	10	25	50	100	150	400	
9	Paul Giel	5	5	5	5	8	20	60	
10	Mickey Mantle	200	250	400	600	▲1,000	2,000	6,000	8,50
11	Billy Hunter	5	5	5	5	8	25	80	150
12	Vern Law	5	5	5	8	12	50	80	40
13	Dick Gernert	5	5	5	5	8	15	50	30
14	Pete Whisenant	5	5	5	5	8	15	50	15
15	Dick Drott	5	5	5	5	8	30	▼50	
16	Joe Pignatano	5	5	5	5	8	15	40	40
17	Danny's All-Stars	5	5	5	8	12	25	50	
18	Jack Urban	5	5	5	5	8	15	30	20
19	Eddie Bressoud	5	5	5	5	8	15	30	30
20	Duke Snider	6	10	25	▲40	50	80	250	1,20
21	Connie Johnson	5	5	5	5	8	15	40	25
22	Al Smith	5	5	5	5	8	25	30	
23	Murry Dickson	5	5	6	10	15	25	▲80	30
24	Red Wilson	5	5	5	5	8	15	30	20
25	Don Hoak	5	5	5	5	8	12	40	
26	Chuck Stobbs	5	5	5	5	8	15	40	20
27	Andy Pafko	5	5	5	5	8	12	40	30
28	Al Worthington	5	5	5	5	8	15	25	20
29	Jim Bolger	5	5	5	5	8	15	30	15
30	Nellie Fox	5	5	8	12	30	50	120	50
31	Ken Lehman	5	5	5	5	8	15	30	15
32	Don Buddin	5	5	5	5	8	15	▲50	30
33	Ed Fitzgerald	5	5	5	5	10	30	60	
34	Pitchers Beware	5	5	6	10	15	50	120	40
35	Ted Kluszewski	5	5	5	8	▲25	40	80	40
36	Hank Aguirre	5	5	5	5	8	30	50	25
37	Gene Green	5	5	5	5	8	15	50	
38	Morrie Martin	5	5	5	5	8	30	60	40
39	Ed Bouchee	5	5	5	5	8	25	40	
40A	Warren Spahn 1931 Clear	3	10	15	25	40	60	150	

		GD 2	VG 3	VgEx 4	EX 5	ExMt 6	NM 7	NmMt 8	MT 9
B	Warren Spahn 1931 Obscured 3	8	12	20	30	50	120	400	
C	Warren Spahn 1921	6	10	15	25	40	100	250	
	Bob Martyn	5	5	5	5	8	15	40	150
	Murray Wall	5	5	5	5	8	15	30	200
	Steve Bilko	5	5	5	5	8	25	40	250
	Vito Valentinetti	5	5	5	5	8	15	40	120
	Andy Carey	5	5	6	10	15	50	150	
	Bill R. Henry	5	5	5	5	8	15	40	
	Jim Finigan	5	5	5	5	8	30	120	
	Baltimore Orioles CL	5	5	6	10	15	40	100	400
	Bill Hall RC	5	5	5	5	8	15	50	250
	Willie Mays	40	60	100	▲150	250	400	▲1,000	6,000
	Rip Coleman	5	5	5	5	8	15	50	
	Coot Veal RC	5	5	5	5	8	15	80	300
	Stan Williams RC	5	5	5	8	12	20	50	300
	Mel Roach	5	5	5	5	8	15	40	250
	Tom Brewer	5	5	5	5	8	15	30	150
	Carl Sawatski	5	5	5	5	8	25	80	400
	Al Cicotte	5	5	5	5	8	15	30	300
	Eddie Miksis	5	5	5	5	8	15	40	150
	Irv Noren	5	5	5	5	8	15	30	350
	Bob Turley	5	5	6	10	15	30	90	
	Dick Brown	5	5	5	5	10	30	60	
	Tony Taylor	5	5	5	5	8	20	40	200
	Jim Hearn	5	5	5	5	8	15	40	150
	Joe DeMaestri	5	5	5	5	8	15	30	150
	Frank Torre	5	5	5	5	8	20	50	300
	Joe Ginsberg	5	5	5	5	8	15	30	250
	Brooks Lawrence	5	5	5	5	8	15	30	150
	Dick Schofield	5	5	5	5	8	20	40	
	San Francisco Giants CL	5	6	10	15	25	60	120	500
	Harvey Kuenn	5	5	5	5	8	25	40	300
	Don Bessent	5	5	5	6	10	15	40	150
	Bill Renna	5	5	5	5	8	15	40	150
	Ron Jackson	5	5	5	5	8	15	40	200
	Directing the Power	5	5	5	8	12	30	80	
	Sam Jones	5	5	5	5	8	15	30	400
	Bobby Richardson	5	5	8	20	30	60	120	500
	John Goryl	5	5	5	5	8	25	80	
	Pedro Ramos	5	5	5	5	8	15	▲30	200
	Harry Chiti	5	5	5	5	8	15	25	150
	Minnie Minoso	5	6	10	15	25	50	100	
	Hal Jeffcoat	5	5	5	5	8	25	40	200
	Bob Boyd	5	5	5	5	8	15	40	
	Bob Smith	5	5	5	5	8	15	30	200
	Reno Bertoia	5	5	5	5	8	25	40	300
	Harry Anderson	5	5	5	5	8	15	30	300
	Bob Keegan	5	5	5	5	8	15	30	250
	Danny O'Connell	5	5	5	5	8	15	30	150
	Herb Score	5	5	5	8	12	25	50	
	Billy Gardner	5	5	5	5	8	15	50	250
	Bill Skowron	5	5	8	12	20	50	120	
	Herb Moford RC	5	5	5	5	8	15	40	200
	Dave Philley	5	5	5	5	8	30	80	
	Julio Becquer	5	5	5	5	8	20	60	250
	Chicago White Sox CL	5	5	6	10	25	50	100	400
	Carl Willey	5	5	5	5	8	15	▲50	250
	Lou Berberet	5	5	5	5	8	15	25	120
	Jerry Lynch	5	5	5	5	8	15	40	
	Arnie Portocarrero	5	5	5	5	8	15	25	300
	Ted Kazanski	5	5	5	5	8	15	40	200
	Bob Cerv	5	5	5	5	8	15	40	150
	Alex Kellner	5	5	5	5	8	15	30	200
	Felipe Alou RC	5	5	5	12	30	80	100	500
	Billy Goodman	5	5	5	5	8	25	50	
	Del Rice	5	5	8	12	50	▼80	250	
	Lee Walls	5	5	5	5	8	20	150	
	Hal Woodeshick RC	5	5	5	5	8	30	60	
	Norm Larker RC	5	5	5	5	8	15	40	250
	Zack Monroe RC	5	5	5	5	8	20	100	
	Bob Schmidt	5	5	5	5	8	25	120	
	George Witt RC	5	5	5	5	8	15	30	200
	Cincinnati Redlegs CL	5	5	6	10	60	▲300		
	Billy Consolo	5	5	5	5	8	12	40	250
	Taylor Phillips	5	5	5	5	6	12	30	
	Earl Battey	5	5	5	5	8	20	50	
	Mickey Vernon	5	5	5	5	8	40	200	

		GD 2	VG 3	VgEx 4	EX 5	ExMt 6	NM 7	NmMt 8	MT 9
116	Bob Allison RS RC	5	5	5	6	10	30	▼60	400
117	John Blanchard RS RC	5	5	5	6	10	30	50	400
118	John Buzhardt RS RC	5	5	5	5	6	12	30	150
119	Johnny Callison RS RC	5	5	5	6	10	40	80	
120	Chuck Coles RS RC	5	5	5	5	6	15	▲50	200
121	Bob Conley RS RC	5	5	5	5	6	12	50	250
122	Bennie Daniels RS	5	5	5	5	6	20	30	150
123	Don Dillard RS RC	5	5	5	5	6	12	25	200
124	Dan Dobbek RS RC	5	5	5	5	6	12	40	200
125	Ron Fairly RS RC	5	5	5	6	10	25	60	500
126	Eddie Haas RS RC	5	5	5	5	6	12	30	250
127	Kent Hadley RS RC	5	5	5	5	6	12	30	200
128	Bob Hartman RS RC	5	5	5	5	6	12	50	
129	Frank Herrera RS	5	5	5	5	6	20	40	250
130	Lou Jackson RS RC	5	5	5	5	6	▲20	▼60	
131	Deron Johnson RS RC	5	5	5	8	12	25	80	
132	Don Lee RS	5	5	5	5	6	12	40	250
133	Bob Lillis RS RC	5	5	5	5	6	15	40	120
134	Jim McDaniel RS RC	5	5	5	5	6	25	40	
135	Gene Oliver RS RC	5	5	5	5	6	20	30	200
136	Jim O'Toole RS RC	5	5	5	5	6	12	50	
137	Dick Ricketts RS RC	5	5	5	5	6	20	40	200
138	John Romano RS RC	5	5	5	5	6	20	40	
139	Ed Sadowski RS RC	5	5	5	5	6	15	50	150
140	Charlie Secrest RS RC	5	5	5	5	6	12	30	250
141	Joe Shipley RS RC	5	5	5	5	6	12	30	200
142	Dick Stigman RS RC	5	5	5	5	6	15	50	
143	Willie Tasby RS RC	5	5	5	5	6	12	30	200
144	Jerry Walker RS	5	5	5	5	6	12	▲50	250
145	Dom Zanni RS RC	5	5	5	5	6	15	30	200
146	Jerry Zimmerman RS RC	5	5	5	5	6	20	50	
147	Cubs Clubbers	5	5	6	20	25	50	100	300
148	Mike McCormick	5	5	5	5	6	12	40	250
149	Jim Bunning	5	5	10	20	25	50	150	
150	Stan Musial	▼30	▼40	▼50	80	100	200	500	2,000
151	Bob Malkmus	5	5	5	5	6	12	30	150
152	Johnny Klippstein	5	5	5	5	6	12	30	200
153	Jim Marshall	5	5	5	5	6	12	40	250
154	Ray Herbert	5	5	5	5	6	12	25	250
155	Enos Slaughter	5	5	6	10	25	50	120	500
156	Ace Hurlers	5	5	5	8	20	30	80	300
157	Felix Mantilla	5	5	5	5	6	12	30	150
158	Walt Dropo	5	5	5	5	6	15	30	200
159	Bob Shaw	5	5	5	5	6	25	60	300
160	Dick Groat	5	5	5	5	8	25	60	250
161	Frank Baumann	5	5	5	5	6	12	40	
162	Bobby G. Smith	5	5	5	5	6	12	30	150
163	Sandy Koufax	40	▲60	▲80	100	150	300	1,000	6,000
164	Johnny Groth	5	5	5	5	6	12	40	250
165	Bill Bruton	5	5	5	5	6	12	40	250
166	Destruction Crew	5	5	6	20	25	50	80	500
167	Duke Maas	5	5	5	5	6	10	25	120
168	Carroll Hardy	5	5	5	5	6	12	30	120
169	Ted Abernathy	5	5	5	5	6	15	40	250
170	Gene Woodling	5	5	5	5	6	12	40	150
171	Willard Schmidt	5	5	5	5	6	12	40	
172	Kansas City Athletics CL	5	5	5	8	12	25	80	300
173	Bill Monbouquette RC	5	5	5	5	6	20	60	300
174	Jim Pendleton	5	5	5	5	6	15	40	300
175	Dick Farrell	5	5	5	5	6	12	30	150
176	Preston Ward	5	5	5	5	6	12	30	150
177	John Briggs RC	5	5	5	5	6	12	30	200
178	Ruben Amaro RC	5	5	5	8	20	40	300	
179	Don Rudolph	5	5	5	5	8	25	60	
180	Yogi Berra	30	50	60	80	100	200	500	2,000
181	Bob Porterfield	5	5	5	6	15	25	150	
182	Milt Graff	5	5	5	5	6	20	120	
183	Stu Miller	5	5	5	5	6	40	150	
184	Harvey Haddix	5	5	5	5	6	20	30	200
185	Jim Busby	5	5	5	5	6	12	40	200
186	Mudcat Grant	5	5	5	5	8	15	30	250
187	Bubba Phillips	5	5	5	5	6	12	20	
188	Juan Pizarro	5	5	5	5	6	12	40	250
189	Neil Chrisley	5	5	5	5	6	12	60	
190	Bill Virdon	5	5	5	5	8	15	50	450
191	Russ Kemmerer	5	5	5	5	6	12	30	150
192	Charlie Beamon RC	5	5	5	5	6	12	30	300

#	Player	GD 2	VG 3	VgEx 4	EX 5	ExMt 6	NM 7	NmMt 8	MT 9
193	Sammy Taylor	5	5	5	5	6	12	30	200
194	Jim Brosnan	5	5	5	5	6	15	25	150
195	Rip Repulski	5	5	5	5	8	40	100	
196	Billy Moran	5	5	5	5	6	12	40	200
197	Ray Semproch	5	5	5	5	6	20	100	
198	Jim Davenport	5	5	5	5	6	20	80	
199	Leo Kiely	5	5	5	5	6	30	200	
200	Warren Giles NL PRES	5	5	5	8	12	25	60	300
201	Tom Acker	5	5	5	5	6	15	60	
202	Roger Maris	30	▲50	60	80	▲120	250	500	2,500
203	Ossie Virgil	5	5	5	5	6	12	30	250
204	Casey Wise	5	5	5	5	6	15	80	
205	Don Larsen	5	5	8	12	25	30	100	
206	Carl Furillo	5	5	6	10	15	30	80	400
207	George Strickland	5	5	5	5	6	12	50	150
208	Willie Jones	5	5	5	5	6	12	25	250
209	Lenny Green	5	5	5	5	6	12	40	200
210	Ed Bailey	5	5	5	5	6	12	40	200
211	Bob Blaylock RC	5	5	5	5	6	12	40	300
212	Fence Busters	15	20	25	40	60	100	200	1,000
213	Jim Rivera	5	5	5	5	6	20	30	200
214	Marcelino Solis RC	5	5	5	5	6	12	50	
215	Jim Lemon	5	5	5	5	6	25	30	200
216	Andre Rodgers	5	5	5	5	6	12	40	250
217	Carl Erskine	5	5	5	6	10	25	60	200
218	Roman Mejias	5	5	5	5	6	20	40	250
219	George Zuverink	5	5	5	5	6	15	60	150
220	Frank Malzone	5	5	5	5	6	20	40	
221	Bob Bowman	5	5	5	5	6	40	200	
222	Bobby Shantz	5	5	5	10	25	40	400	
223	St. Louis Cardinals CL	5	5	6	10	15	100	250	
224	Claude Osteen RC	5	5	6	10	10	20	50	400
225	Johnny Logan	5	5	5	5	8	25	80	300
226	Art Ceccarelli	5	5	5	5	6	12	30	200
227	Hal W. Smith	5	5	5	5	6	20	40	200
228	Don Gross	5	5	5	5	6	12	25	200
229	Vic Power	5	5	5	5	8	30	100	
230	Bill Fischer	5	5	5	5	6	12	30	150
231	Ellis Burton RC	5	5	5	5	6	15	60	250
232	Eddie Kasko	5	5	5	5	6	15	50	250
233	Paul Foytack	5	5	5	5	6	15	40	200
234	Chuck Tanner	5	5	5	5	6	12	30	120
235	Valmy Thomas	5	5	5	5	6	12	25	150
236	Ted Bowsfield RC	5	5	5	5	6	12	30	200
237	Run Preventers	5	5	6	10	15	30	100	
238	Gene Baker	5	5	5	5	6	40	100	400
239	Bob Trowbridge	5	5	5	5	6	12	30	150
240	Hank Bauer	5	5	5	8	12	30	60	
241	Billy Muffett	5	5	5	5	6	12	30	150
242	Ron Samford RC	5	5	5	5	6	12	25	150
243	Marv Grissom	5	5	5	5	6	12	25	150
244	Dick Gray	5	5	5	5	6	12	30	250
245	Ned Garver	5	5	5	5	6	12	25	250
246	J.W. Porter	5	5	5	5	6	12	25	150
247	Don Ferrarese	5	5	5	5	6	12	25	200
248	Boston Red Sox CL	5	5	6	10	25	40	80	300
249	Bobby Adams	5	5	5	5	6	15	40	
250	Billy O'Dell	5	5	5	6	10	70	300	
251	Clete Boyer	5	5	6	10	25	30	▲100	500
252	Ray Boone	5	5	5	5	8	15	50	250
253	Seth Morehead RC	5	5	5	5	6	20	30	150
254	Zeke Bella RC	5	5	5	5	6	20	30	150
255	Del Ennis	5	5	5	5	6	12	30	200
256	Jerry Davie RC	5	5	5	5	6	12	30	150
257	Leon Wagner RC	5	5	5	5	8	15	50	200
258	Fred Kipp RC	5	5	5	5	8	15	50	250
259	Jim Pisoni	5	5	5	5	6	20	40	300
260	Early Wynn	5	5	5	8	25	50	100	500
261	Gene Stephens	5	5	5	5	6	12	25	300
262	Hitters Foes	10	12	15	25	30	50	100	400
263	Bud Daley	5	5	5	5	6	12	30	250
264	Chico Carrasquel	5	5	5	5	6	12	60	250
265	Ron Kline	5	5	5	5	6	12	25	120
266	Woody Held	5	5	5	5	8	25	50	
267	John Romonosky RC	5	5	5	5	6	12	30	200
268	Tito Francona	5	5	5	5	6	12	40	200
269	Jack Meyer	5	5	5	5	6	12	25	150

#	Player	GD 2	VG 3	VgEx 4	EX 5	ExMt 6	NM 7	NmMt 8	MT 9
270	Gil Hodges	5	5	8	20	30	50	100	55
271	Orlando Pena RC	5	5	5	5	6	25	60	
272	Jerry Lumpe	5	5	5	5	8	15	50	
273	Joey Jay	5	5	5	5	6	25	30	10
274	Jerry Kindall	5	5	5	5	6	12	25	12
275	Jack Sanford	5	5	5	5	6	15	50	20
276	Pete Daley	5	5	5	5	6	12	25	15
277	Turk Lown	5	5	5	5	6	12	30	20
278	Chuck Essegian	5	5	5	5	6	12	30	25
279	Ernie Johnson	5	5	5	5	6	12	25	12
280	Frank Bolling	5	5	5	5	6	12	175	40
281	Walt Craddock RC	5	5	5	5	6	12	30	20
282	R.C. Stevens	5	5	5	6	12	30	200	
283	Russ Heman RC	5	5	5	5	6	12	25	15
284	Steve Korcheck	5	5	5	5	6	12	30	20
285	Joe Cunningham	5	5	5	5	6	20	200	25
286	Dean Stone	5	5	5	5	6	20	250	
287	Don Zimmer	5	5	5	8	20	25	100	
288	Dutch Dotterer	5	5	5	5	6	12	30	20
289	Johnny Kucks	5	5	5	5	8	20	40	25
290	Wes Covington	5	5	5	5	6	12	40	20
291	Pitching Partners	5	5	5	5	8	15	30	20
292	Dick Williams	5	5	5	5	6	12	25	20
293	Ray Moore	5	5	5	5	6	20	80	
294	Hank Foiles	5	5	5	5	6	12	25	12
295	Billy Martin	5	12	15	20	25	50	100	
296	Ernie Broglio RC	5	5	5	5	6	12	20	15
297	Jackie Brandt RC	5	5	5	5	6	12	30	25
298	Tex Clevenger	5	5	5	5	6	12	25	15
299	Billy Klaus	5	5	5	5	6	12	40	25
300	Richie Ashburn	5	5	8	25	30	▲80	300	
301	Earl Averill Jr. RC	5	5	5	5	6	12	25	15
302	Don Mossi	5	5	5	5	6	25	50	
303	Marty Keough	5	5	5	5	6	12	30	25
304	Chicago Cubs CL	5	5	5	8	▲30	40	80	50
305	Curt Raydon RC	5	5	5	5	6	12	25	20
306	Jim Gilliam	5	5	5	6	10	25	▲50	25
307	Curt Barclay	5	5	5	5	6	20	40	
308	Norm Siebern	5	5	5	5	6	25	50	
309	Sal Maglie	5	5	5	5	8	15	40	30
310	Luis Aparicio	5	10	12	15	30	50	200	
311	Norm Zauchin	5	5	5	5	6	15	25	25
312	Don Newcombe	5	5	5	5	8	25	50	30
313	Frank House	5	5	5	5	6	12	30	20
314	Don Cardwell	5	5	5	5	6	12	25	15
315	Joe Adcock	5	5	5	5	6	15	30	20
316A	Ralph Lumenti Option	5	5	5	5	6	12	30	
316B	Ralph Lumenti No Option ERR	12	20	30	50	80			
317	NL Hitting Kings	10	20	30	40	50	80	150	80
318	Rocky Bridges	5	5	5	5	6	20	25	20
319	Dave Hillman	5	5	5	5	6	15	50	25
320	Bob Skinner	5	5	5	6	10	20	60	25
321A	Bob Giallombardo Option RC	5	5	5	5	6	20	30	
321B	Bob Giallombardo No Option ERR	10	15	25	40	80	120		
322A	Harry Hanebrink Trade	5	5	5	5	6	15	80	
322B	Harry Hanebrink No Trade ERR	40	60	100	150	250			
323	Frank Sullivan	5	5	5	5	6	12	25	15
324	Don Demeter	5	5	5	5	6	15	60	30
325	Ken Boyer	5	5	5	6	20	30	80	
326	Marv Throneberry	5	5	5	5	6	25	50	30
327	Gary Bell RC	5	5	5	5	5	20	30	15
328	Lou Skizas	5	5	5	5	6	15	30	25
329	Detroit Tigers CL	5	5	6	10	15	50	60	20
330	Gus Triandos	5	5	5	5	6	25	250	
331	Steve Boros	5	5	5	5	6	12	30	25
332	Ray Monzant	5	5	5	5	6	12	25	12
333	Harry Simpson	5	5	5	5	6	12	40	25
334	Glen Hobbie	5	5	5	5	6	12	25	15
335	Johnny Temple	5	5	5	5	6	15	50	30
336A	Billy Loes Trade	5	5	5	5	6	12	40	30
336B	Billy Loes No Trade ERR	12	20	30	50	120	300		
337	George Crowe	5	5	5	5	6	20	40	20
338	Sparky Anderson RC	5	6	25	30	▼40	▼60	120	50
339	Roy Face	5	5	5	5	6	12	25	20
340	Roy Sievers	5	5	5	5	6	20	50	30
341	Tom Qualters	5	5	5	5	6	12	40	25
342	Ray Jablonski	5	5	5	5	6	12	25	15

#	Player	GD 2	VG 3	VgEx 4	EX 5	ExMt 6	NM 7	NmMt 8	MT 9
343	Billy Hoeft	5	5	5	5	6	15	50	150
344	Russ Nixon	5	5	5	5	6	12	30	250
345	Gil McDougald	5	5	5	8	25	30	80	
346	Batter Bafflers	5	5	5	5	8	20	30	200
347	Bob Buhl	5	5	5	5	8	20	80	
348	Ted Lepcio	5	5	5	5	6	12	25	150
349	Hoyt Wilhelm	5	5	5	6	25	40	100	300
350	Ernie Banks	25	30	50	60	100	▲200	300	1,000
351	Earl Torgeson	5	5	5	5	6	15	40	
352	Robin Roberts	8	10	12	15	25	40	100	500
353	Curt Flood	5	5	5	6	10	30	80	200
354	Pete Burnside	5	5	5	5	6	12	30	200
355	Jimmy Piersall	5	5	5	5	8	25	80	
356	Bob Mabe RC	5	5	5	5	6	12	25	150
357	Dick Stuart RC	5	5	5	5	8	15	30	150
358	Ralph Terry	5	5	5	5	6	12	40	300
359	Bill White RC	5	5	5	12	25	50	80	250
360	Al Kaline	10	25	30	50	60	100	250	1,800
361	Willard Nixon	5	5	5	5	6	12	25	120
362A	Dolan Nichols Option RC	5	5	5	5	6	12	30	
362B	Dolan Nichols No Option ERR	12	20	30	50	80	275		
363	Bobby Avila	5	5	5	6	10	30	150	
364	Danny McDevitt	5	5	5	5	6	12	30	150
365	Gus Bell	5	5	5	5	6	12	▲30	200
366	Humberto Robinson	5	5	5	5	6	15	40	200
367	Cal Neeman	5	5	5	5	6	12	25	200
368	Don Mueller	5	5	5	5	6	25	40	200
369	Dick Tomanek	5	5	5	5	6	12	25	250
370	Pete Runnels	5	5	5	5	6	20	30	
371	Dick Brodowski	5	5	5	5	6	12	25	150
372	Jim Hegan	5	5	5	5	8	30	400	
373	Herb Plews	5	5	5	5	6	12	30	
374	Art Ditmar	5	5	5	5	8	25	100	
375	Bob Nieman	5	5	5	5	6	15	25	250
376	Hal Naragon	5	5	5	5	6	12	25	120
377	John Antonelli	5	5	5	5	6	12	25	150
378	Gail Harris	5	5	5	5	6	12	25	120
379	Bob Miller	5	5	5	5	6	12	25	120
380	Hank Aaron	50	▲80	▲100	120	150	400	▲1,000	6,000
381	Mike Baxes	5	5	5	5	6	12	25	150
382	Curt Simmons	5	5	5	5	6	12	30	120
383	Words of Wisdom	5	5	5	8	20	40	100	300
384	Dave Sisler	5	5	5	5	6	12	25	150
385	Sherm Lollar	5	5	5	5	6	12	25	120
386	Jim Delsing	5	5	5	5	6	12	30	250
387	Don Drysdale	5	8	20	40	50	80	120	500
388	Bob Will RC	5	5	5	5	6	12	25	120
389	Joe Nuxhall	5	5	5	5	6	25	50	150
390	Orlando Cepeda	5	10	12	15	30	60	100	400
391	Milt Pappas	5	5	5	5	6	15	30	200
392	Whitey Herzog	5	5	5	5	6	20	30	120
393	Frank Lary	5	5	5	5	6	15	30	150
394	Randy Jackson	5	5	5	5	6	12	25	150
395	Elston Howard	5	6	12	20	25	40	80	300
396	Bob Rush	5	5	5	5	6	12	25	250
397	Washington Senators CL	5	5	5	6	10	20	40	150
398	Wally Post	5	5	5	5	6	12	25	120
399	Larry Jackson	5	5	5	5	6	12	25	120
400	Jackie Jensen	5	5	5	5	8	30	60	400
401	Ron Blackburn	5	5	5	5	6	12	30	120
402	Hector Lopez	5	5	5	5	6	12	25	120
403	Clem Labine	5	5	5	5	6	12	30	200
404	Hank Sauer	5	5	5	5	6	12	30	200
405	Roy McMillan	5	5	5	5	6	12	25	120
406	Solly Drake	5	5	5	5	6	12	25	120
407	Moe Drabowsky	5	5	5	5	6	15	25	120
408	Keystone Combo	5	5	5	8	25	40	80	300
409	Gus Zernial	5	5	5	5	6	12	25	100
410	Billy Pierce	5	5	5	5	8	15	40	200
411	Whitey Lockman	5	5	5	5	6	12	25	120
412	Stan Lopata	5	5	5	5	6	12	25	150
413	Camilo Pascual	5	5	5	5	6	12	30	200
414	Dale Long	5	5	5	5	6	12	25	120
415	Bill Mazeroski	5	5	5	20	25	50	80	250
416	Haywood Sullivan	5	5	20	25	30	50	▲100	500
417	Virgil Trucks	5	5	5	5	6	15	30	100
418	Gino Cimoli	5	5	5	5	6	12	25	120
419	Milwaukee Braves CL	5	5	5	6	10	25	60	200
420	Rocky Colavito	5	5	5	20	30	50	80	300
421	Herman Wehmeier	5	5	5	5	6	12	25	120
422	Hobie Landrith	5	5	5	5	6	12	25	150
423	Bob Grim	5	5	5	5	6	15	25	120
424	Ken Aspromonte	5	5	5	5	6	12	25	80
425	Del Crandall	5	5	5	5	6	▲20	30	120
426	Gerry Staley	5	5	5	5	6	▲15	30	120
427	Charlie Neal	5	5	5	5	8	25	50	300
428	Buc Hill Aces	5	5	5	5	6	20	25	150
429	Bobby Thomson	5	5	5	5	8	20	40	150
430	Whitey Ford	6	20	30	40	60	100	250	800
431	Whammy Douglas	5	5	5	5	6	12	30	200
432	Smoky Burgess	5	5	5	5	6	20	40	200
433	Billy Harrell	5	5	5	5	6	12	25	120
434	Hal Griggs	5	5	5	5	6	12	20	80
435	Frank Robinson	10	20	▲30	▲50	60	▲100	200	1,000
436	Granny Hamner	5	5	5	5	6	15	25	120
437	Ike Delock	5	5	5	5	6	12	25	120
438	Sammy Esposito	5	5	5	5	6	12	25	150
439	Brooks Robinson	15	20	25	40	60	100	200	1,000
440	Lew Burdette	5	5	5	5	8	30	60	250
441	John Roseboro	5	5	5	5	8	25	50	300
442	Ray Narleski	5	5	5	5	6	15	40	
443	Daryl Spencer	5	5	5	5	8	25	120	
444	Ron Hansen RC	5	5	5	5	6	12	30	150
445	Cal McLish	5	5	5	5	8	60	450	
446	Rocky Nelson	5	5	5	5	6	12	30	150
447	Bob Anderson	5	5	5	5	6	12	25	150
448	Vada Pinson	5	5	5	6	20	40	60	250
449	Tom Gorman	5	5	5	5	6	12	80	250
450	Eddie Mathews	8	20	30	40	60	200	600	
451	Jimmy Constable RC	5	5	5	5	6	12	30	250
452	Chico Fernandez	5	5	5	5	6	15	30	120
453	Les Moss	5	5	5	5	6	12	30	150
454	Phil Clark	5	5	5	5	6	12	40	250
455	Larry Doby	5	5	5	8	25	40	150	800
456	Jerry Casale RC	5	5	5	5	6	12	30	200
457	Los Angeles Dodgers CL	5	5	5	8	30	50	80	500
458	Gordon Jones	5	5	5	5	6	12	25	200
459	Bill Tuttle	5	5	5	5	6	15	30	120
460	Bob Friend	5	5	5	5	8	20	40	
461	Mickey Mantle BT	30	40	50	60	▲100	200	▲400	1,200
462	Rocky Colavito BT	5	5	5	6	20	25	▲60	250
463	Al Kaline BT	5	5	5	20	30	40	80	250
464	Willie Mays BT	12	25	30	50	60	▲100	200	600
465	Roy Sievers BT	5	5	5	5	6	15	50	300
466	Billy Pierce BT	5	5	5	5	6	15	50	300
467	Hank Aaron BT	12	15	20	40	50	60	120	600
468	Duke Snider BT	5	5	10	15	20	25	60	300
469	Ernie Banks BT	5	6	10	20	30	40	100	300
470	Stan Musial BT	5	10	12	15	30	60	120	600
471	Tom Sturdivant	5	5	5	5	8	25	120	
472	Gene Freese	5	5	5	5	6	20	80	250
473	Mike Fornieles	5	5	5	5	6	15	30	
474	Moe Thacker RC	5	5	5	5	6	15	50	250
475	Jack Harshman	5	5	5	5	6	15	100	
476	Cleveland Indians CL	5	5	5	6	20	25	100	300
477	Barry Latman RC	5	5	5	5	6	20	25	150
478	Roberto Clemente	50	60	80	120	150	▲400	600	5,000
479	Lindy McDaniel	5	5	5	5	6	25	200	300
480	Red Schoendienst	5	5	5	15	25	40	100	300
481	Charlie Maxwell	5	5	5	5	6	25	120	
482	Russ Meyer	5	5	5	5	6	12	30	250
483	Clint Courtney	5	5	5	5	6	12	25	150
484	Willie Kirkland	5	5	5	5	6	12	40	200
485	Ryne Duren	5	5	5	5	8	20	60	250
486	Sammy White	5	5	5	5	6	12	25	120
487	Hal Brown	5	5	5	5	6	12	80	300
488	Walt Moryn	5	5	5	5	6	12	60	150
489	John Powers	5	5	5	5	6	12	40	
490	Frank Thomas	5	5	5	5	6	20	30	
491	Don Blasingame	5	5	5	5	6	12	30	250
492	Gene Conley	5	5	5	5	6	12	25	150
493	Jim Landis	5	5	5	5	6	12	25	200
494	Don Pavletich RC	5	5	5	6	15	30	300	
495	Johnny Podres	5	5	5	6	10	30	50	250

#	Name	GD 2	VG 3	VgEx 4	EX 5	ExMt 6	NM 7	NmMt 8	MT 9
496	Wayne Terwilliger	5	5	5	5	6	25	30	250
497	Hal R. Smith	5	5	5	5	6	15	30	150
498	Dick Hyde	5	5	5	5	6	12	50	250
499	Johnny O'Brien	5	5	5	5	6	15	60	
500	Vic Wertz	5	5	5	5	10	30	300	
501	Bob Tiefenauer RC	5	5	5	5	6	12	25	250
502	Alvin Dark	5	5	5	5	6	15	40	200
503	Jim Owens	5	5	5	5	6	15	80	
504	Ossie Alvarez RC	5	5	5	5	6	20	80	250
505	Tony Kubek	5	5	6	10	25	50	120	400
506	Bob Purkey	5	5	5	5	6	15	60	200
507	Bob Hale	5	5	5	6	25	30	60	
508	Art Fowler	5	5	5	8	25	30	100	
509	Norm Cash RC	15	▲25	▲40	50	60	100	300	
510	New York Yankees CL	12	20	50	60	▲100	200	400	1,200
511	George Susce	5	5	5	6	25	30	80	300
512	George Altman RC	5	5	5	6	10	40	80	300
513	Tommy Carroll	5	5	5	6	10	20	40	200
514	Bob Gibson RC	250	300	400	500	▲800	▲1,200	2,500	15,000
515	Harmon Killebrew	25	30	▲60	▲80	100	250	500	5,000
516	Mike Garcia	5	5	6	10	15	30	80	300
517	Joe Koppe RC	5	5	5	6	10	25	60	
518	Mike Cuellar RC	5	5	6	25	40	50	120	600
519	Infield Power	5	5	6	10	20	50	350	
520	Don Elston	5	5	5	6	10	40	60	250
521	Gary Geiger	5	5	5	6	20	30	50	
522	Gene Snyder RC	5	5	5	6	20	50	60	250
523	Harry Bright RC	5	5	5	6	10	25	40	300
524	Larry Osborne RC	5	5	5	6	10	25	60	
525	Jim Coates RC	5	5	6	10	15	40	100	400
526	Bob Speake	5	5	5	6	10	20	60	
527	Solly Hemus	5	5	5	6	10	25	60	250
528	Pittsburgh Pirates CL	5	8	12	20	50	100	150	600
529	George Bamberger RC	5	5	5	6	25	30	80	250
530	Wally Moon	5	5	8	12	30	50	120	
531	Ray Webster RC	5	5	5	6	10	25	50	200
532	Mark Freeman RC	5	5	5	6	10	20	50	250
533	Darrell Johnson	5	5	6	10	15	50	80	
534	Faye Throneberry	5	5	5	6	10	25	100	400
535	Ruben Gomez	5	5	5	6	20	30	60	250
536	Danny Kravitz	5	5	5	6	10	20	50	
537	Rodolfo Arias RC	5	5	5	6	10	30	100	500
538	Chick King	5	5	5	6	25	30	80	400
539	Gary Blaylock RC	5	5	5	6	10	40	200	400
540	Willie Miranda	5	5	5	6	20	30	60	
541	Bob Thurman	5	5	5	6	10	20	60	200
542	Jim Perry RC	5	5	8	12	20	40	100	500
543	Corsair Trio	5	15	40	50	60	100	200	1,000
544	Lee Tate RC	5	5	5	6	10	25	50	200
545	Tom Morgan	5	5	5	6	10	30	40	
546	Al Schroll	5	5	5	6	10	20	50	250
547	Jim Baxes RC	5	5	5	8	12	40	120	
548	Elmer Singleton	5	5	5	8	25	50	300	
549	Howie Nunn RC	5	5	5	6	10	30	50	200
550	Roy Campanella Courage	10	25	40	60	100	200	600	1,500
551	Fred Haney AS MG	5	5	5	8	12	25	80	400
552	Casey Stengel AS MG	5	6	10	15	25	60	150	
553	Orlando Cepeda AS	5	15	20	25	40	60	150	
554	Bill Skowron AS	5	6	10	15	30	40	250	
555	Bill Mazeroski AS	5	5	8	12	40	50	100	400
556	Nellie Fox AS	5	6	10	20	25	50	150	
557	Ken Boyer AS	5	5	8	25	30	50	100	500
558	Frank Malzone AS	5	5	5	6	15	30	80	250
559	Ernie Banks AS	5	20	30	40	60	100	250	2,000
560	Luis Aparicio AS	5	6	10	15	30	50	200	
561	Hank Aaron AS	30	40	▲60	▲80	100	150	400	
562	Al Kaline AS	5	8	12	30	▲50	80	200	600
563	Willie Mays AS	25	40	50	60	100	150	400	1,200
564	Mickey Mantle AS	100	120	150	200	▲300	400	1,200	3,000
565	Wes Covington AS	5	5	5	6	10	40	80	250
566	Roy Sievers AS	5	5	5	6	10	40	80	300
567	Del Crandall AS	5	5	5	6	20	30	135	
568	Gus Triandos AS	5	5	5	6	10	30	120	200
569	Bob Friend AS	5	5	5	6	10	80	200	
570	Bob Turley AS	5	5	6	10	15	40	150	
571	Warren Spahn AS	5	8	12	20	50	80	150	1,000
572	Billy Pierce AS	5	5	8	30	100	250		

—Hank Aaron #380 PSA 10 (Gem) sold for $27,126 (Goodwin; 11/12)
—Hank Aaron #380 BVG 8.5 (NmMt+) sold for $415 (eBay; 6/07)
—Hank Aaron AS #561 PSA 9 (MT) sold for $4,802 (Memory Lane; 8/05)
—Hank Aaron AS #561 PSA 9 (MT) sold for $3,819 (Leland's; 12/05)
—Hank Aaron AS #561 PSA 9 (MT) sold for $2,390 (Heritage; 10/07)
—Luis Aparicio AS #560 PSA 9 (MT) sold for $1,662 (eBay; 2/08)
—Ernie Banks #350 PSA 10 (Gem) sold for $12,757 (Mile High; 2/08)
—Roy Campanella Courage #550 PSA 10 (Gem) sold for $4,923 (Memory Lane; 11/05)
—Roy Campanella Courage #550 PSA 10 (Gem) sold for $4,506 (Mastro; 6/05)
—Andy Carey #45 PSA 9 (MT) sold for $5,809 (Memory Lane; 5/08)
—Norm Cash #509 PSA 10 (Gem) (Young Collection) sold for $6,544 (SCP; 5/12)
—Norm Cash #509 SGC 96 (MT) sold for $4,081 (eBay; 1/08)
—Norm Cash #509 PSA 9 (MT) sold for $3,383 (eBay; 10/07)
—Norm Cash #509 PSA 9 (MT) sold for $2,235 (Memory Lane; 2/07)
—Norm Cash #509 BVG 9 (MT) sold for $712 (eBay; 10/07)
—Norm Cash #509 BVG 9 (MT) sold for $567 (eBay; 1/08)
—Orlando Cepeda #390 PSA 10 (Gem) sold for $5,269 (Memory Lane; 9/07)
—Corsair Trio #543 PSA 10 (Gem) sold for $3,162 (eBay; 5/04)
—Roberto Clemente #478 SGC 92 (NmMt+) sold for $448 (eBay; 11/07)
—Roberto Clemente #478 BVG 8.5 (NmMt+) sold for $416 (eBay; 11/07)
—Roberto Clemente #478 SGC 92 (NmMt+) sold for $415 (eBay; 2/08)
—Roberto Clemente #478 BVG 8.5 (NmMt+) sold for $409 (eBay; 2/08)
—Ford Frick #1 PSA 8.5 (NmMt+) sold for $2,032 (Memory Lane; 5/08)
—Ford Frick #1 PSA 8.5 (NmMt+) sold for $1,764 (eBay; 6/08)
—Bob Gibson #514 PSA 10 (Gem) (Young Collection) sold for $53,759 (SCP; 5/12)
—Bob Gibson #514 PSA 10 (Gem) sold for $32,450 (SCP; 7/08)
—Bob Gibson #514 PSA 10 (Gem) sold for $19,055 (Memory Lane; 12/06)
—Bob Gibson #514 PSA 9 (MT) sold for $10,461 (Goodwin; 5/08)
—Bob Gibson #514 PSA 9 (MT) sold for $7,365 (Memory Lane; 9/07)
—Bob Gibson #514 PSA 9 (MT) sold for $6,702 (Goodwin; 11/07)
—Bob Gibson #514 PSA 9 (MT) sold for $5,701 (Madec; 11/07)
—Bob Gibson #514 PSA 9 (MT) sold for $5,205 (Memory Lane; 5/08)
—Bob Gibson #514 PSA 9 (MT) sold for $4,376 (eBay; 11/07)
—Bob Gibson #514 PSA 9 (MT) sold for $3,944 (Mastro; 12/06)
—Bob Gibson #514 PSA 8.5 (NmMt+) sold for $1,524 (eBay; 5/08)
—Bob Hale #507 PSA 9 (MT) sold for $2,453 (eBay; 5/08)
—Harry Hanebrink #322 (No Trade) PSA 8 (NmMt) sold for $2,025 (eBay; 5/07)
—Harry Hanebrink #322 (No Trade) PSA 6 (ExMt) sold for $250 (eBay; 4/08)
—Fred Haney AS MG #551 PSA 10 (GemMt) sold for $3,780 (Andy Madec; 11/08)
—Elston Howard #395 PSA 10 (Gem) sold for $4,158 (eBay; 8/12)
—Billy Loes #336 (No Trade) PSA 8 (NmMt) sold for $2,826 (Mile High; 2/08)
—Ralph Lumenti #316 (No Option) PSA 8 (NmMt) sold for $787 (eBay; 2/07)
—Ralph Lumenti #316 (No Option) PSA 8 (NmMt) sold for $688 (eBay; 4/07)
—Ralph Lumenti #316 (No Option) PSA 7 (NM) sold for $408 (eBay; 6/08)
—Ralph Lumenti #316 (No Option) PSA 7 (NM) sold for $170 (eBay; 10/07)
—Mickey Mantle #10 BVG 8.5 (NmMt+) sold for $2,504 (eBay; 4/08)
—Mickey Mantle #10 BVG 8.5 (NmMt+) sold for $2,438 (eBay; 12/07)
—Mickey Mantle AS #564 PSA 10 (Gem) sold for $6,600 (SCP Sotheby's; 6/05)
—Eddie Mathews #450 PSA 9 (MT) sold for $3,523 (Mastro; 12/06)
—Willie Mays #50 PSA 10 (Gem) sold for $12,232 (Mastro; 4/04)
—Willie Mays #50 BVG 8.5 (NmMt+) sold for $926 (eBay; 1/07)
—Willie Mays #50 SGC 92 (NmMt+) sold for $481 (eBay; 5/06)
—Dolan Nichols #362 (No Option) PSA 8 (NmMt) sold for $899 (eBay; 5/08)
—Orlando Pena #271 PSA 9 (MT) sold for $3,348 (Madec; 11/07)
—Billy Pierce AS #572 PSA 9 (MT) sold for $8,993 (Memory Lane; 9/07)
—Billy Pierce AS #572 PSA 8 (NmMt) sold for $3,618 (eBay; 4/07)
—Billy Pierce AS #572 PSA 8 (NmMt) sold for $3,010 (eBay; 11/07)
—Billy Pierce AS #572 PSA 8 (NmMt) sold for $2,938 (eBay; 6/08)
—Frank Robinson #435 PSA 10 (Gem) sold for $6,654 (Mile High; 6/06)
—Run Preventers #237 PSA 10 (Gem) sold for $5,282 (Memory Lane; 5/08)
—Bill Skowron #90 PSA 9 (MT) sold for $2,544 (Memory Lane; 12/06)
—Bill Skowron AS #554 PSA 9 (MT) sold for $4,097 (Memory Lane; 12/06)
—Duke Snider #20 PSA 10 (Gem) sold for $4,210 (Memory Lane; 4/05)
—Warren Spahn 1921 #40C PSA 10 (Gem) sold for $4,613 (eBay; 9/12)

1960 Fleer

#	Name	GD 2	VG 3	VgEx 4	EX 5	ExMt 6	NM 7	NmMt 8	MT 9
1	Napoleon Lajoie DP	6	6	8	12	25	40	150	
2	Christy Mathewson	5	5	5	8	15	30	60	
3	Babe Ruth	10	50	60	80	100	150	300	600
4	Carl Hubbell	5	5	5	5	8	15	40	200
5	Grover C. Alexander	5	5	5	5	8	15	60	700
6	Walter Johnson DP	5	5	5	8	15	25	40	150
7	Chief Bender	5	5	5	6	12	20	175	
8	Roger Bresnahan	8	8	8	8	10	20	30	135
9	Mordecai Brown	8	8	8	8	10	20	30	350

		GD 2	VG 3	VgEx 4	EX 5	ExMt 6	NM 7	NmMt 8	MT 9
0	Tris Speaker	5	5	5	5	6	12	30	200
1	Arky Vaughan DP	5	5	5	5	6	12	25	
2	Zach Wheat	6	6	6	6	8	15	25	150
3	George Sisler	6	6	6	6	8	15	20	120
4	Connie Mack	5	5	5	5	10	20	40	
5	Clark Griffith	5	5	5	5	6	12	40	
6	Lou Boudreau DP	5	5	5	5	6	12	25	
7	Ernie Lombardi	6	6	6	6	8	15	25	80
8	Heinie Manush	6	6	6	6	8	15	30	200
9	Marty Marion	5	5	5	5	6	12	25	
0	Eddie Collins DP	5	5	5	5	6	12	25	80
1	Rabbit Maranville DP	6	6	6	6	8	15	20	200
2	Joe Medwick	5	5	5	5	6	12	25	100
3	Ed Barrow	5	5	5	5	6	12	25	
4	Mickey Cochrane	5	5	5	5	6	12	30	
5	Jimmy Collins	5	5	5	5	6	12	30	300
6	Bob Feller DP	6	6	6	10	20	30	50	150
7	Luke Appling	5	5	5	5	6	12	25	120
8	Lou Gehrig	6	12	40	50	60	80	120	400
29	Gabby Hartnett	6	6	6	6	8	15	20	80
30	Chuck Klein	5	5	5	5	6	12	20	100
31	Tony Lazzeri DP	6	6	6	6	8	15	40	135
32	Al Simmons	6	6	6	6	8	15	40	120
33	Wilbert Robinson	6	6	6	6	8	15	40	150
34	Sam Rice	5	5	5	5	6	12	20	150
35	Herb Pennock	5	5	5	5	6	12	20	200
36	Mel Ott DP	5	5	5	8	12	20	40	150
37	Lefty O'Doul	5	5	5	5	6	12	20	200
38	Johnny Mize	6	6	8	12	15	25	30	135
39	Bing Miller	6	6	6	6	8	15	20	120
40	Joe Tinker	5	5	5	5	6	12	20	120
41	Frank Baker DP	5	5	5	5	6	12	40	200
42	Ty Cobb	5	5	6	12	50	60	120	300
43	Paul Derringer	5	5	5	5	6	12	30	150
44	Cap Anson	5	5	5	5	10	20	40	200
45	Jim Bottomley	5	5	5	5	6	12	25	150
46	Eddie Plank DP	6	6	6	6	8	15	25	100
47	Cy Young	6	6	6	6	8	30	50	200
48	Hack Wilson	5	5	5	5	6	20	25	50
49	Ed Walsh	5	5	5	5	6	12	20	100
50	Frank Chance	6	6	6	6	8	15	20	100
51	Dazzy Vance DP	6	6	6	6	8	15	20	150
52	Bill Terry	5	5	5	5	6	12	25	120
53	Jimmie Foxx	6	6	6	8	15	30	60	150
54	Lefty Gomez	8	8	8	8	10	20	25	120
55	Branch Rickey	6	6	6	6	8	15	25	175
56	Ray Schalk DP	5	5	5	5	6	12	25	150
57	Johnny Evers	5	5	5	5	6	12	25	100
58	Charley Gehringer	6	6	6	6	8	25	30	150
59	Burleigh Grimes	6	6	6	6	10	20	25	150
60	Lefty Grove	6	6	6	6	8	15	40	150
61	Rube Waddell DP	5	5	5	5	6	12	25	
62	Honus Wagner	6	6	8	12	30	50	80	300
63	Red Ruffing	5	5	5	5	8	15	30	80
64	Kenesaw M. Landis	5	5	5	5	6	12	20	150
65	Harry Heilmann	6	6	6	6	8	15	25	150
66	John McGraw DP	5	5	5	5	6	12	20	150
67	Hughie Jennings	5	5	5	5	6	12	20	150
68	Hal Newhouser	5	5	5	5	6	12	25	200
69	Waite Hoyt	5	5	5	5	6	12	25	150
70	Bobo Newsom	6	6	6	6	8	15	25	
71	Earl Averill DP	6	6	6	6	8	15	40	250
72	Ted Williams	25	40	50	60	80	120	250	500
73	Warren Giles	5	5	5	5	6	12	25	150
74	Ford Frick	5	5	5	5	6	12	30	250
75	Kiki Cuyler	5	5	5	5	6	12	20	625
76	Paul Waner DP	5	5	5	5	6	12	25	225
77	Pie Traynor	5	5	5	5	6	12	40	200
78	Lloyd Waner	5	5	5	5	6	12	30	200
79	Ralph Kiner	5	5	5	5	6	15	80	

—Lou Boudreau #16 PSA 9 (MT) sold for $416 (Goodwin; 2/07)
—Mickey Cochrane #24 PSA 9 (MT) sold for $1,526 (eBay; 2/07)
—Jimmie Foxx #53 PSA 10 (Gem) sold for $3,376 (Madec; 55/08)
—Ralph Kiner #79 PSA 9 (MT) sold for $899 (eBay; 3/07)
—Ralph Kiner #79 PSA 9 (MT) sold for $494 (eBay; 11/07)
—Ralph Kiner #79 PSA 9 (MT) sold for $458 (eBay; 2/08)
—Ralph Kiner #79 PSA 9 (MT) sold for $415 (eBay; 5/08)
—Connie Mack #14 PSA 9 (MT) sold for $622 (eBay; 12/06)
—Connie Mack #14 PSA 9 (MT) sold for $303 (eBay; 3/08)
—Arky Vaughn #11 PSA 9 (MT) sold for $505 (eBay; 2/07)
—Rube Waddell #61 PSA 9 (MT) sold for $290 (eBay; 1/08)

1960 Leaf

		GD 2	VG 3	VgEx 4	EX 5	ExMt 6	NM 7	NmMt 8	MT 9
27	Brooks Robinson	5	8	12	20	▲60	100	150	
37	Duke Snider	5	6	10	15	40	50	100	
125	Sparky Anderson	8	12	20	30	50	250	400	
128	Orlando Cepeda	6	10	15	25	40	60	120	
144	Jim Bunning	6	10	15	25	40	60	135	

—Luis Aparicio #1 PSA 9 (MT) sold for $1,694 (Mile High; 1/07)
—Luis Aparicio #1 PSA 8 (NmMt) sold for $185 (eBay; 7/07)

1960 Topps

		GD 2	VG 3	VgEx 4	EX 5	ExMt 6	NM 7	NmMt 8	MT 9
1	Early Wynn	5	5	12	25	50	150	▲600	
2	Roman Mejias	5	5	5	6	10	50	150	
3	Joe Adcock	5	5	6	10	15	25	40	
4	Bob Purkey	5	5	5	6	10	20	30	100
5	Wally Moon	5	5	5	5	6	15	50	
6	Lou Berberet	5	5	5	5	5	20		
7	Master and Mentor	5	15	20	25	30	40	80	500
8	Bud Daley	5	5	5	5	5	15	25	150
9	Faye Throneberry	5	5	5	5	8	15	40	
10	Ernie Banks	20	30	50	60	100	▲250	500	
11	Norm Siebern	5	5	5	6	10	15	30	150
12	Milt Pappas	5	5	5	6	10	15	30	150
13	Wally Post	5	5	5	8	12	20	30	
14	Jim Grant	5	5	6	10	15	25	200	
15	Pete Runnels	5	5	5	5	5	15	25	150
16	Ernie Broglio	5	5	5	6	10	15	30	120
17	Johnny Callison	5	5	5	8	12	20	30	150
18	Los Angeles Dodgers CL	5	6	10	15	25	60	250	
19	Felix Mantilla	5	5	5	5	8	25	120	
20	Roy Face	5	5	5	8	12	20	30	200
21	Dutch Dotterer	5	5	5	5	8	25	200	
22	Rocky Bridges	5	5	5	5	5	15	25	150
23	Eddie Fisher RC	5	5	5	6	10	15	80	
24	Dick Gray	5	5	5	5	5	15	40	150
25	Roy Sievers	5	5	5	5	5	15	30	
26	Wayne Terwilliger	5	5	5	5	8	30	200	
27	Dick Drott	5	5	5	5	8	40	120	
28	Brooks Robinson	6	12	25	▼30	▲60	100	250	2,500
29	Clem Labine	5	5	5	6	10	15	30	
30	Tito Francona	5	5	5	8	12	30	80	150
31	Sammy Esposito	5	5	5	5	5	15	25	150
32	Sophomore Stalwarts	5	5	5	5	6	15	50	200
33	Tom Morgan	5	5	5	5	8	25	120	300
34	Sparky Anderson	5	5	8	12	20	30	150	
35	Whitey Ford	8	25	▲40	▲50	60	100	▼200	800
36	Russ Nixon	5	5	5	6	10	15	25	150
37	Bill Bruton	5	5	5	5	5	15	25	
38	Jerry Casale	5	5	5	5	5	15	80	
39	Earl Averill Jr.	5	5	5	8	12	20	25	150
40	Joe Cunningham	5	5	5	6	10	15	25	150
41	Barry Latman	5	5	5	5	5	15	30	
42	Hobie Landrith	5	5	5	5	8	15	25	
43	Washington Senators CL	5	5	5	5	8	15	250	400
44	Bobby Locke RC	5	5	5	5	10	20	250	400
45	Roy McMillan	5	5	5	5	6	12	25	150
46	Jack Fisher RC	5	5	5	5	5	15	40	150
47	Don Zimmer	5	5	5	8	15	25	40	250
48	Hal W. Smith	5	5	5	5	5	15	30	175
49	Curt Raydon	5	5	5	5	5	15	60	200
50	Al Kaline	20	25	30	▲50	▲60	120	400	
51	Jim Coates	5	5	5	5	10	20	40	200
52	Dave Philley	5	5	5	5	5	15	120	
53	Jackie Brandt	5	5	5	5	5	15	25	150
54	Mike Fornieles	5	5	5	5	5	15	25	150
55	Bill Mazeroski	5	5	8	25	30	▲60	250	800
56	Steve Korcheck	5	5	5	5	5	15	25	150

BASEBALL

#	Player	GD 2	VG 3	VgEx 4	EX 5	ExMt 6	NM 7	NmMt 8	MT 9
57	Win Savers	5	5	5	5	8	15	60	150
58	Gino Cimoli	5	5	5	5	5	15	30	200
59	Juan Pizarro	5	5	5	5	8	15	25	100
60	Gus Triandos	5	5	5	5	5	15	25	120
61	Eddie Kasko	5	5	5	5	5	15	30	150
62	Roger Craig	5	5	5	5	6	15	30	150
63	George Strickland	5	5	5	5	5	15	25	100
64	Jack Meyer	5	5	5	5	5	15	60	120
65	Elston Howard	5	5	5	8	20	40	80	350
66	Bob Trowbridge	5	5	5	5	5	15	40	150
67	Jose Pagan RC	5	5	5	6	10	15	30	120
68	Dave Hillman	5	5	5	5	5	15	25	120
69	Billy Goodman	5	5	5	5	5	15	20	
70	Lew Burdette	5	5	5	6	10	15	30	200
71	Marty Keough	5	5	5	5	5	15	25	150
72	Detroit Tigers CL	5	5	6	10	15	60	120	400
73	Bob Gibson	15	25	40	50	▲100	150	500	4,000
74	Walt Moryn	5	5	5	5	5	15	25	100
75	Vic Power	5	5	5	5	6	15	40	150
76	Bill Fischer	5	5	5	5	5	15	30	150
77	Hank Foiles	5	5	5	5	5	15	25	120
78	Bob Grim	5	5	5	5	5	15	150	250
79	Walt Dropo	5	5	5	5	5	15	25	
80	Johnny Antonelli	5	5	5	5	6	15	25	120
81	Russ Snyder RC	5	5	5	5	5	15	25	150
82	Ruben Gomez	5	5	5	5	6	15	30	120
83	Tony Kubek	5	5	6	15	20	50	300	
84	Hal R. Smith	5	5	5	5	5	15	30	100
85	Frank Lary	5	5	5	5	5	15	25	100
86	Dick Gernert	5	5	5	5	5	25	80	120
87	John Romanosky	5	5	5	5	5	15	25	
88	John Roseboro	5	5	5	5	6	15	30	
89	Hal Brown	5	5	5	8	12	20	50	
90	Bobby Avila	5	5	5	6	10	15	40	
91	Bennie Daniels	5	5	5	5	5	25	80	120
92	Whitey Herzog	5	5	6	10	15	25	30	150
93	Art Schult	5	5	5	6	10	15	25	100
94	Leo Kiely	5	5	5	5	8	20	120	
95	Frank Thomas	5	5	5	6	10	15	25	175
96	Ralph Terry	5	5	5	5	8	20	50	300
97	Ted Lepcio	5	5	5	5	5	15	50	200
98	Gordon Jones	5	5	5	5	5	15	80	
99	Lenny Green	5	5	5	6	10	20	25	200
100	Nellie Fox	5	10	15	▲25	▲40	▲50	100	500
101	Bob Miller RC	5	5	5	5	5	15	25	150
102	Kent Hadley	5	5	6	10	15	25	100	
103	Dick Farrell	5	5	5	5	5	15	50	150
104	Dick Schofield	5	5	5	5	5	15	50	200
105	Larry Sherry RC	5	5	5	5	8	15	25	
106	Billy Gardner	5	5	5	5	5	15	150	
107	Carlton Willey	5	5	5	5	5	15	25	
108	Pete Daley	5	5	5	5	5	15	25	100
109	Clete Boyer	5	5	6	10	20	40	120	400
110	Cal McLish	5	5	5	5	5	15	100	
111	Vic Wertz	5	5	5	5	8	30	400	
112	Jack Harshman	5	5	5	5	8	20		
113	Bob Skinner	5	5	5	5	5	15	40	100
114	Ken Aspromonte	5	5	5	5	5	15	150	
115	Fork and Knuckler	5	5	5	6	10	15	30	200
116	Jim Rivera	5	5	5	8	12	30	600	
117	Tom Borland RS	5	5	5	5	5	15	25	100
118	Bob Bruce RS RC	5	5	5	5	5	15	25	150
119	Chico Cardenas RS RC	5	5	5	5	10	25	30	120
120	Duke Carmel RS RC	5	5	5	5	8	15	25	
121	Camilo Carreon RS RC	5	5	5	5	5	15	25	120
122	Don Dillard RS	5	5	5	5	5	15	20	100
123	Dan Dobbek RS	5	5	5	5	5	15	25	150
124	Jim Donohue RS RC	5	5	5	5	5	15	25	100
125	Dick Ellsworth RS RC	5	5	5	5	5	15	25	150
126	Chuck Estrada RS RC	5	5	5	6	10	15	25	200
127	Ron Hansen RS	5	5	5	5	5	15	25	100
128	Bill Harris RS RC	5	5	5	5	5	15	25	100
129	Bob Hartman RS	5	5	5	5	5	15	25	100
130	Frank Herrera RS	5	5	5	5	5	15	25	150
131	Ed Hobaugh RS RC	5	5	5	5	5	15	25	100
132	Frank Howard RS RC	5	10	12	15	▲30	▲50	120	
133	Julian Javier RS RC	5	5	5	5	6	15	30	120
134	Deron Johnson RS	5	5	5	5	6	15	30	120
135	Ken Johnson RS RC	5	5	5	5	5	15	25	100
136	Jim Kaat RS RC	5	12	15	20	40	▲80	▲250	
137	Lou Klimchock RS RC	5	5	5	5	5	15	25	120
138	Art Mahaffey RS RC	5	5	5	5	5	15	25	100
139	Carl Mathias RS RC	5	5	5	5	5	15	25	120
140	Julio Navarro RS RC	5	5	5	5	5	10	25	100
141	Jim Proctor RS RC	5	5	5	5	5	15	25	120
142	Bill Short RS RC	5	5	5	5	6	15	30	250
143	Al Spangler RS RC	5	5	5	5	5	15	25	150
144	Al Stieglitz RS RC	5	5	5	5	6	15	40	150
145	Jim Umbricht RS RC	5	5	5	5	8	15	25	200
146	Ted Wieand RS RC	5	5	5	5	5	15	25	100
147	Bob Will RS	5	5	5	6	10	15	40	150
148	Carl Yastrzemski RS RC	80	100	▲150	200	250	500	1,500	15,000
149	Bob Nieman	5	5	5	5	5	10	20	120
150	Billy Pierce	5	5	5	5	6	20	▲50	175
151	San Francisco Giants CL	5	5	5	5	25	30	400	800
152	Gail Harris	5	5	5	5	5	15	30	150
153	Bobby Thomson	5	5	5	5	6	15	30	200
154	Jim Davenport	5	5	5	6	10	15	120	
155	Charlie Neal	5	5	5	5	6	20	30	200
156	Art Ceccarelli	5	5	5	5	5	10	25	120
157	Rocky Nelson	5	5	5	5	5	15	30	150
158	Wes Covington	5	5	5	5	5	15	30	
159	Jim Piersall	5	5	5	8	12	20	60	120
160	Rival All-Stars	30	40	50	60	100	120	250	800
161	Ray Narleski	5	5	5	5	5	15	25	200
162	Sammy Taylor	5	5	5	5	5	15	40	
163	Hector Lopez	5	5	5	5	20	25	200	250
164	Cincinnati Reds CL	5	5	5	8	12	20	40	150
165	Jack Sanford	5	5	5	5	5	15	25	100
166	Chuck Essegian	5	5	5	5	5	12	25	
167	Valmy Thomas	5	5	5	5	5	15	25	120
168	Alex Grammas	5	5	5	5	5	15	25	125
169	Jake Striker RC	5	5	5	5	5	15	25	150
170	Del Crandall	5	5	5	8	12	40	150	
171	Johnny Groth	5	5	5	5	5	12	25	100
172	Willie Kirkland	5	5	5	5	5	15	20	150
173	Billy Martin	5	5	10	12	▲25	30	80	250
174	Cleveland Indians CL	5	5	5	5	6	25	40	200
175	Pedro Ramos	5	5	5	5	5	15	25	120
176	Vada Pinson	5	5	6	10	15	25	300	
177	Johnny Kucks	5	5	5	5	5	15	100	
178	Woody Held	5	5	5	6	10	15	25	100
179	Rip Coleman	5	5	5	5	5	15	25	100
180	Harry Simpson	5	5	5	5	6	15	25	120
181	Billy Loes	5	5	5	5	8	15	25	120
182	Glen Hobbie	5	5	5	5	5	15	25	150
183	Eli Grba RC	5	5	5	5	5	15	30	200
184	Gary Geiger	5	5	5	5	5	15	25	100
185	Jim Owens	5	5	5	5	5	15	100	150
186	Dave Sisler	5	5	5	5	5	15	25	
187	Jay Hook RC	5	5	5	5	5	15	25	150
188	Dick Williams	5	5	5	5	5	15	25	100
189	Don McMahon	5	5	5	5	5	15	25	150
190	Gene Woodling	5	5	5	5	5	15	25	
191	Johnny Klippstein	5	5	5	6	10	15	60	
192	Danny O'Connell	5	5	5	5	5	15	25	100
193	Dick Hyde	5	5	5	5	5	15	25	100
194	Bobby Gene Smith	5	5	5	5	5	20	80	
195	Lindy McDaniel	5	5	5	5	5	15	25	100
196	Andy Carey	5	5	5	5	6	30	60	
197	Ron Kline	5	5	5	5	5	15	40	120
198	Jerry Lynch	5	5	5	5	5	15	25	100
199	Dick Donovan	5	5	5	5	5	15	40	200
200	Willie Mays	50	60	80	100	200	300	1,000	4,000
201	Larry Osborne	5	5	5	5	5	15	25	100
202	Fred Kipp	5	5	5	5	5	15	25	150
203	Sammy White	5	5	5	5	5	15	25	
204	Ryne Duren	5	6	10	15	25	50		
205	Johnny Logan	5	5	5	5	5	20	25	200
206	Claude Osteen	5	5	5	5	5	15	40	
207	Bob Boyd	5	5	5	5	5	15	25	80
208	Chicago White Sox CL	5	5	5	5	8	15	80	200
209	Ron Blackburn	5	5	5	5	5	15	25	150
210	Harmon Killebrew	6	12	20	30	▲60	80	200	

Player	GD 2	VG 3	VgEx 4	EX 5	ExMt 6	NM 7	NmMt 8	MT 9
Taylor Phillips	5	5	5	5	5	15	25	150
Walter Alston MG	5	5	6	10	20	25	50	150
Chuck Dressen MG	5	5	5	5	5	15	50	
Jimmy Dykes MG	5	5	5	5	8	15	20	
Bob Elliott MG	5	5	5	5	5	15	25	100
Joe Gordon MG	5	5	5	5	6	20	30	120
Charlie Grimm MG	5	5	5	5	5	15	25	120
Solly Hemus MG	5	5	5	5	5	15	25	150
Fred Hutchinson MG	5	5	5	5	5	20	30	120
Billy Jurges MG	5	5	5	5	8	80	300	
Cookie Lavagetto MG	5	5	5	5	5	15	25	120
Al Lopez MG	5	5	5	5	15	30	60	250
Danny Murtaugh MG	5	5	8	12	20	100		
Paul Richards MG	5	5	5	5	5	15	200	500
Bill Rigney MG	5	5	5	5	5	15	25	120
Eddie Sawyer MG	5	5	5	5	5	15	40	150
Casey Stengel MG	5	5	8	12	30	50	150	
Ernie Johnson	5	5	5	5	6	15	30	200
Joe M. Morgan RC	5	5	5	5	5	15	20	100
Mound Magicians	5	5	10	12	20	50	100	300
Hal Naragon	5	5	5	5	5	15	25	120
Jim Busby	5	5	5	5	5	10	15	175
Don Elston	5	5	5	5	5	15	25	120
Don Demeter	5	5	5	5	5	20	25	120
Gus Bell	5	5	5	5	5	15	30	
Dick Ricketts	5	5	5	5	5	15	25	150
Elmer Valo	5	5	5	5	10	30	250	
Danny Kravitz	5	5	5	5	5	15	25	200
Joe Shipley	5	5	5	5	5	15	80	
Luis Aparicio	5	5	15	20	30	50	150	500
Albie Pearson	5	5	5	5	5	15	25	150
St. Louis Cardinals CL	5	5	5	5	8	30	100	
Bubba Phillips	5	5	5	5	5	15	25	100
Hal Griggs	5	5	5	5	5	15	25	150
Eddie Yost	5	5	5	5	6	15	80	
Lee Maye RC	5	5	5	5	8	20	▲80	200
Gil McDougald	5	5	5	6	10	25	50	250
Del Rice	5	5	5	5	5	15	25	120
Earl Wilson RC	5	5	5	5	5	15	30	120
Stan Musial	30	40	50	▲80	100	150	▼400	2,000
Bob Malkmus	5	5	5	5	5	15	25	120
Ray Herbert	5	5	5	5	5	15	25	150
Eddie Bressoud	5	5	5	5	5	15	25	100
Arnie Portocarrero	5	5	5	5	5	15	25	150
Jim Gilliam	5	5	5	5	8	15	50	200
Dick Brown	5	5	5	5	5	15	50	150
Gordy Coleman RC	5	5	6	10	15	25	150	150
Dick Groat	5	5	5	8	12	25	50	250
George Altman	5	5	5	5	5	15	25	120
Power Plus	5	5	5	8	12	25	60	250
Pete Burnside	5	5	5	5	5	15	60	
Hank Bauer	5	5	5	5	8	15	300	
Darrell Johnson	5	5	5	5	5	15	25	120
Robin Roberts	5	5	6	12	25	40	80	
Rip Repulski	5	5	5	5	5	15	20	100
Joey Jay	5	5	5	5	5	20	▲30	150
Jim Marshall	5	5	5	5	5	15	30	120
Al Worthington	5	5	5	5	5	15	25	200
Gene Green	5	5	5	5	5	15	25	120
Bob Turley	5	5	5	5	8	25	30	200
Julio Becquer	5	5	5	5	5	15	15	150
Fred Green RC	5	5	5	5	5	15	30	120
Neil Chrisley	5	5	5	5	5	15	30	
Tom Acker	5	5	5	5	5	15	30	
Curt Flood	5	5	5	8	12	30	50	200
Ken McBride RC	5	5	5	5	5	15	25	100
Harry Bright	5	5	5	5	5	15	25	100
Stan Williams	5	5	5	5	5	15	25	120
Chuck Tanner	5	5	5	5	5	15	25	150
Frank Sullivan	5	5	5	5	5	15	25	120
Ray Boone	5	5	5	6	10	15	40	
Joe Nuxhall	5	5	5	5	6	15	40	200
Johnny Blanchard	5	5	5	5	8	15	40	
Don Gross	5	5	5	5	5	20	60	150
Harry Anderson	5	5	5	5	5	20	25	120
Ray Semproch	5	5	8	12	20	30	150	
Felipe Alou	5	5	5	8	12	40	400	

#	Player	GD 2	VG 3	VgEx 4	EX 5	ExMt 6	NM 7	NmMt 8	MT 9
288	Bob Mabe	5	5	5	5	5	15	30	
289	Willie Jones	5	5	5	6	10	15	25	200
290	Jerry Lumpe	5	5	5	5	5	15	50	
291	Bob Keegan	5	5	5	6	10	15	25	
292	Dodger Backstops	5	5	5	5	6	15	80	150
293	Gene Conley	5	5	5	5	5	15	40	150
294	Tony Taylor	5	5	5	5	5	25	40	150
295	Gil Hodges	5	10	12	15	30	40	80	500
296	Nelson Chittum RC	5	5	5	5	5	15	30	
297	Reno Bertoia	5	5	5	5	5	15	25	150
298	George Witt	5	5	5	5	5	15	50	150
299	Earl Torgeson	5	5	5	5	5	15	40	200
300	Hank Aaron	▲50	▲80	100	▲200	250	500	2,000	
301	Jerry Davie	5	5	5	5	5	15	25	
302	Philadelphia Phillies CL	5	5	5	8	12	20	40	
303	Billy O'Dell	5	5	5	5	5	15	25	120
304	Joe Ginsberg	5	5	5	5	6	15	200	300
305	Richie Ashburn	5	5	6	15	25	40	100	300
306	Frank Baumann	5	5	5	5	5	15	25	120
307	Gene Oliver	5	5	5	5	5	15	25	120
308	Dick Hall	5	5	5	5	5	15	30	100
309	Bob Hale	5	5	5	5	5	15	50	120
310	Frank Malzone	5	5	5	8	12	20	80	
311	Raul Sanchez	5	5	5	5	5	15	30	200
312	Charley Lau	5	5	5	5	5	15	25	150
313	Turk Lown	5	5	5	5	5	15	25	120
314	Chico Fernandez	5	5	5	5	5	15	25	100
315	Bobby Shantz	5	5	6	15	20	25	60	300
316	Willie McCovey ASR RC	60	80	▲120	150	250	500	2,000	12,000
317	Pumpsie Green ASR RC	5	5	5	6	10	▲50	▲100	
318	Jim Baxes ASR	5	5	5	5	5	15	60	
319	Joe Koppe ASR	5	5	5	5	5	15	50	150
320	Bob Allison ASR	5	5	5	5	6	15	50	500
321	Ron Fairly ASR	5	5	5	5	5	20	60	200
322	Willie Tasby ASR	5	5	5	5	8	15	40	▲250
323	John Romano ASR	5	5	5	5	5	15	40	200
324	Jim Perry ASR	5	5	5	6	10	25	200	
325	Jim O'Toole ASR	5	5	5	6	10	20	30	
326	Roberto Clemente	50	▲80	100	120	200	▲400	1,000	8,000
327	Ray Sadecki RC	5	5	5	5	5	15	25	100
328	Earl Battey	5	5	5	5	5	15	50	200
329	Zack Monroe	5	5	5	5	6	15	30	150
330	Harvey Kuenn	5	5	5	5	8	30	40	
331	Henry Mason RC	5	5	5	5	5	15	25	100
332	New York Yankees CL	5	8	25	30	50	80	150	400
333	Danny McDevitt	5	5	5	6	10	15	120	250
334	Ted Abernathy	5	5	5	6	10	15	25	100
335	Red Schoendienst	5	5	6	10	25	30	80	250
336	Ike Delock	5	5	5	5	5	15	25	100
337	Cal Neeman	5	5	5	5	5	15	100	
338	Ray Monzant	5	5	5	5	5	15	25	120
339	Harry Chiti	5	5	5	5	5	15	25	200
340	Harvey Haddix	5	5	5	5	8	20	80	150
341	Carroll Hardy	5	5	5	5	5	15	40	150
342	Casey Wise	5	5	5	6	10	15	30	200
343	Sandy Koufax	40	50	60	100	120	200	500	2,500
344	Clint Courtney	5	5	5	5	5	15	25	120
345	Don Newcombe	5	5	5	6	10	25	50	120
346	J.C. Martin RC	5	5	5	5	5	15	40	150
347	Ed Bouchee	5	5	5	5	5	15	25	120
348	Barry Shetrone RC	5	5	5	5	5	15	25	150
349	Moe Drabowsky	5	5	5	5	8	15	30	120
350	Mickey Mantle	▲250	▲300	▲400	500	800	2,000	5,000	18,000
351	Don Nottebart RC	5	5	5	5	5	15	40	200
352	Cincy Clouters	5	5	5	6	10	40	60	500
353	Don Larsen	5	5	5	6	▲25	▲30	50	250
354	Bob Lillis	5	5	5	5	6	15	80	120
355	Bill White	5	5	5	5	8	40	120	200
356	Joe Amalfitano	5	5	5	5	5	15	25	
357	Al Schroll	5	5	5	5	5	15	25	250
358	Joe DeMaestri	5	5	5	5	8	20	150	
359	Buddy Gilbert RC	5	5	5	5	5	15	25	120
360	Herb Score	5	5	5	5	5	15	80	150
361	Bob Oldis	5	5	5	8	12	20	150	200
362	Russ Kemmerer	5	5	5	5	5	15	100	
363	Gene Stephens	5	5	5	6	15	25	40	120
364	Paul Foytack	5	5	5	5	5	15	25	200

#	Player	GD 2	VG 3	VgEx 4	EX 5	ExMt 6	NM 7	NmMt 8	MT 9
365	Minnie Minoso	5	5	5	10	15	40	60	175
366	Dallas Green RC	5	5	5	15	20	30	60	300
367	Bill Tuttle	5	5	5	5	5	15	40	
368	Daryl Spencer	5	5	5	5	5	15	25	150
369	Billy Hoeft	5	5	5	5	5	15	25	200
370	Bill Skowron	5	5	8	12	25	50		
371	Bud Byerly	5	5	5	5	5	15	25	150
372	Frank House	5	5	5	5	5	15	25	120
373	Don Hoak	5	5	5	5	5	20	50	120
374	Bob Buhl	5	5	5	6	10	15	▲40	200
375	Dale Long	5	5	5	6	10	25	▼60	
376	John Briggs	5	5	5	5	5	10	25	225
377	Roger Maris	40	50	60	80	100	▲200	400	1,500
378	Stu Miller	5	5	5	5	5	15	25	150
379	Red Wilson	5	5	5	8	12	20	60	150
380	Bob Shaw	5	5	5	5	5	10	25	
381	Milwaukee Braves CL	5	5	5	5	8	15	50	150
382	Ted Bowsfield	5	5	5	5	5	10	25	
383	Leon Wagner	5	5	5	5	5	10	25	120
384	Don Cardwell	5	5	5	5	5	10	80	150
385	Charlie Neal WS1	5	5	5	5	8	40	50	300
386	Charlie Neal WS2	5	5	5	5	6	15	40	250
387	Carl Furillo WS3	5	5	5	5	12	15	40	300
388	Gil Hodges WS4	5	5	8	10	12	40	120	500
389	L.Aparcio/M.Wills WS 5	5	5	5	12	25	50	100	
390	Scrambling After Ball WS6	5	5	5	5	8	20	60	250
391	Champs Celebrate WS	5	5	5	5	10	50	250	
392	Tex Clevenger	5	5	5	5	5	15	25	100
393	Smoky Burgess	5	5	5	5	8	30	80	200
394	Norm Larker	5	5	5	5	6	15	30	150
395	Hoyt Wilhelm	5	5	5	8	20	▲40	60	200
396	Steve Bilko	5	5	5	5	6	15	50	150
397	Don Blasingame	5	5	5	5	5	10	40	200
398	Mike Cuellar	5	5	5	8	12	20	30	120
399	Young Hill Stars	5	5	5	5	6	20	50	200
400	Rocky Colavito	5	6	10	15	25	60	120	800
401	Bob Duliba RC	5	5	5	8	12	20	80	
402	Dick Stuart	5	5	5	5	8	20	50	
403	Ed Sadowski	5	5	5	5	5	10	25	100
404	Bob Rush	5	5	5	5	5	10	25	100
405	Bobby Richardson	5	8	12	20	25	80	120	
406	Billy Klaus	5	5	5	5	5	10	25	150
407	Gary Peters RC	5	5	5	5	6	12	40	150
408	Carl Furillo	5	5	5	5	6	25	40	150
409	Ron Samford	5	5	5	5	5	15	25	100
410	Sam Jones	5	5	5	5	5	15	25	120
411	Ed Bailey	5	5	5	5	5	15	25	120
412	Bob Anderson	5	5	5	5	5	15	40	
413	Kansas City Athletics CL	5	5	5	10	15	25	30	100
414	Don Williams RC	5	5	5	5	8	25	60	
415	Bob Cerv	5	5	5	5	8	12	25	100
416	Humberto Robinson	5	5	5	5	5	10	25	150
417	Chuck Cottier RC	5	5	5	6	10	15	25	100
418	Don Mossi	5	5	5	5	5	10	30	
419	George Crowe	5	5	5	5	8	20	60	200
420	Eddie Mathews	12	20	25	30	50	80	200	1,000
421	Duke Maas	5	5	5	5	8	15	40	175
422	John Powers	5	5	5	5	5	10	30	100
423	Ed Fitzgerald	5	5	5	5	5	10	25	120
424	Pete Whisenant	5	5	5	5	5	10	25	150
425	Johnny Podres	5	5	5	5	6	20	30	150
426	Ron Jackson	5	5	5	5	5	15	25	120
427	Al Grunwald RC	5	5	5	5	5	15	30	250
428	Al Smith	5	5	5	5	5	15	30	175
429	American League Kings	5	5	5	6	15	25	80	
430	Art Ditmar	5	5	5	5	8	15	40	200
431	Andre Rodgers	5	5	5	5	5	10	40	200
432	Chuck Stobbs	5	5	5	5	5	10	25	200
433	Irv Noren	5	5	5	5	5	10	25	150
434	Brooks Lawrence	5	5	5	5	5	10	25	
435	Gene Freese	5	5	5	5	5	10	25	150
436	Marv Throneberry	5	5	5	5	5	10	25	150
437	Bob Friend	5	5	5	5	6	20	25	150
438	Jim Coker RC	5	5	5	5	8	25	150	300
439	Tom Brewer	5	5	5	5	5	15	25	120
440	Jim Lemon	5	5	5	5	5	15	40	150
441	Gary Bell	5	5	5	6	10	15	30	300
442	Joe Pignatano	5	5	5	5	6	20	120	30
443	Charlie Maxwell	5	5	5	5	6	15	30	15
444	Jerry Kindall	5	5	5	5	6	15	30	12
445	Warren Spahn	5	8	30	40	60	80	200	50
446	Ellis Burton	5	5	5	5	6	40	800	
447	Ray Moore	5	5	5	5	6	20	100	
448	Jim Gentile RC	5	5	6	10	20	50	120	
449	Jim Brosnan	5	5	5	6	10	12	25	15
450	Orlando Cepeda	5	12	20	25	▲50	100	400	80
451	Curt Simmons	5	6	10	15	25	80	500	
452	Ray Webster	5	5	5	5	6	20	60	
453	Vern Law	5	5	5	5	8	25	50	30
454	Hal Woodeshick	5	5	5	5	6	15	50	
455	Baltimore Coaches	5	5	5	5	6	15	40	25
456	Red Sox Coaches	5	5	5	8	12	30	120	
457	Cubs Coaches	5	5	5	5	6	15	30	
458	White Sox Coaches	5	5	5	6	10	25	30	150
459	Reds Coaches	5	5	5	5	6	15	40	150
460	Indians Coaches	5	5	5	5	6	20	50	150
461	Tigers Coaches	5	5	5	6	10	30	50	
462	Athletics Coaches	5	5	5	6	10	15	25	150
463	Dodgers Coaches	5	5	5	5	8	15	80	300
464	Braves Coaches	5	5	5	5	6	15	40	
465	Yankees Coaches	5	5	6	10	25	30	60	250
466	Phillies Coaches	5	5	5	5	6	15	30	200
467	Pirates Coaches	5	5	5	8	12	20	30	200
468	Cardinals Coaches	5	5	5	5	8	20	60	150
469	Giants Coaches	5	5	5	5	6	15	100	250
470	Senators Coaches	5	5	5	6	10	15	40	150
471	Ned Garver	5	5	5	5	6	20	400	
472	Alvin Dark	5	5	5	5	6	12	30	120
473	Al Cicotte	5	5	5	5	6	20	60	
474	Haywood Sullivan	5	5	5	5	6	12	30	200
475	Don Drysdale	6	10	25	30	▲60	80	▲200	400
476	Lou Johnson RC	5	5	5	5	8	25	80	
477	Don Ferrarese	5	5	5	5	6	15	120	
478	Frank Torre	5	5	5	5	6	15	25	500
479	Georges Maranda RC	5	5	5	5	6	15	40	120
480	Yogi Berra	20	40	50	80	100	200	500	1,000
481	Wes Stock RC	5	5	5	5	8	12	30	120
482	Frank Bolling	5	5	5	5	5	20	30	120
483	Camilo Pascual	5	5	5	5	6	20	30	120
484	Pittsburgh Pirates CL	5	5	8	12	20	50	100	800
485	Ken Boyer	5	5	6	10	15	30	80	200
486	Bobby Del Greco	5	5	5	5	6	15	30	200
487	Tom Sturdivant	5	5	5	5	6	12	30	100
488	Norm Cash	5	5	8	12	25	80		
489	Steve Ridzik	5	6	10	15	25	40	300	
490	Frank Robinson	20	25	30	40	60	100	250	
491	Mel Roach	5	5	5	5	6	12	80	
492	Larry Jackson	5	5	5	5	6	12	30	120
493	Duke Snider	15	▲30	▲40	▲50	60	100	300	800
494	Baltimore Orioles CL	5	5	5	8	12	40	80	
495	Sherm Lollar	5	5	5	5	8	15	120	
496	Bill Virdon	5	5	5	5	25	30	500	
497	John Tsitouris	5	5	5	8	12	20	80	
498	Al Pilarcik	5	5	5	5	8	25	400	
499	Johnny James RC	5	5	5	5	8	20	50	
500	Johnny Temple	5	5	5	6	10	15	30	250
501	Bob Schmidt	5	5	5	5	6	15	120	
502	Jim Bunning	5	5	8	20	25	60	200	
503	Don Lee	5	5	5	5	6	15	30	
504	Seth Morehead	5	5	5	5	6	15	▲40	200
505	Ted Kluszewski	5	5	6	10	25	60	120	250
506	Lee Walls	5	5	5	5	6	15	25	200
507	Dick Stigman	5	5	5	5	8	20	▲50	200
508	Billy Consolo	5	5	5	5	8	30	50	
509	Tommy Davis RC	5	5	8	12	50	150	500	
510	Gerry Staley	5	5	5	5	8	15	40	200
511	Ken Walters RC	5	5	5	5	8	25	120	500
512	Joe Gibbon RC	5	5	5	5	8	30	▲100	200
513	Chicago Cubs CL	5	6	10	15	30	50	80	300
514	Steve Barber RC	5	5	5	5	8	20	60	
515	Stan Lopata	5	5	5	5	6	20	100	120
516	Marty Kutyna RC	5	5	5	5	8	25	120	
517	Charlie James RC	5	5	5	5	8	25	40	250
518	Tony Gonzalez RC	5	5	5	5	8	25	60	150

#	Player	GD 2	VG 3	VgEx 4	EX 5	ExMt 6	NM 7	NmMt 8	MT 9
9	Ed Roebuck	5	5	5	5	15	20	50	
0	Don Buddin	5	5	5	5	8	30	50	200
1	Mike Lee RC	5	5	5	8	12	25	40	150
2	Ken Hunt RC	5	5	6	10	25	50	100	
3	Clay Dalrymple RC	5	5	5	5	8	20	40	200
4	Bill Henry	5	5	5	5	8	25	50	120
5	Marv Breeding RC	5	5	5	8	12	15	50	250
6	Paul Giel	5	5	5	6	10	30	60	
7	Jose Valdivielso	5	5	5	5	8	15	40	100
8	Ben Johnson RC	5	5	5	6	10	60	150	
9	Norm Sherry RC	5	5	5	6	10	40	50	200
0	Mike McCormick	5	5	5	5	8	30	80	400
1	Sandy Amoros	5	5	5	10	25	40	250	
2	Mike Garcia	5	5	5	5	8	25	50	
3	Lu Clinton RC	5	5	5	6	10	20	30	200
4	Ken MacKenzie RC	5	5	5	6	10	15	50	300
5	Whitey Lockman	5	5	5	6	10	15	60	200
6	Wynn Hawkins RC	5	5	5	6	10	15	50	150
7	Boston Red Sox CL	5	5	6	10	15	50	80	300
8	Frank Barnes RC	5	5	5	6	10	20	40	120
9	Gene Baker	5	5	5	6	25	100	400	
0	Jerry Walker	5	5	5	6	10	20	50	120
1	Tony Curry RC	5	5	5	6	10	25	40	120
2	Ken Hamlin RC	5	5	5	5	8	20	▲50	150
3	Elio Chacon RC	5	5	5	5	12	25	60	
4	Bill Monbouquette	5	5	5	5	8	25	50	
5	Carl Sawatski	5	5	5	5	8	25	40	
6	Hank Aguirre	5	5	5	5	8	20	80	
7	Bob Aspromonte RC	5	5	5	5	8	20	50	150
8	Don Mincher RC	5	5	5	5	8	15	40	300
9	John Buzhardt	5	5	5	5	8	15	40	120
50	Jim Landis	5	5	5	8	12	25	50	150
51	Ed Rakow RC	5	5	5	5	8	15	50	
52	Walt Bond RC	5	5	5	5	8	▲25	40	150
53	Bill Skowron AS	5	5	8	25	30	40	80	400
54	Willie McCovey AS	15	20	30	40	▲80	▲120	200	800
55	Nellie Fox AS	5	5	8	12	25	50	100	400
56	Charlie Neal AS	5	5	5	8	12	30	60	250
57	Frank Malzone AS	5	5	6	10	15	40	150	300
58	Eddie Mathews AS	5	6	25	30	40	60	120	
59	Luis Aparicio AS	5	5	6	20	30	▲50	60	300
60	Ernie Banks AS	6	20	25	40	▲80	▲120	▲200	500
61	Al Kaline AS	5	20	25	30	50	60	120	500
62	Joe Cunningham AS	5	5	5	5	8	20	80	150
63	Mickey Mantle AS	100	120	▲200	▲250	▲300	▲400	500	2,000
64	Willie Mays AS	15	▲50	▲60	▲80	▲120	▲200	400	
65	Roger Maris AS	15	30	50	▲80	100	150	300	
66	Hank Aaron AS	12	40	▲60	80	100	▲200	300	1,200
67	Sherm Lollar AS	5	5	5	5	8	25	60	150
68	Del Crandall AS	5	5	6	10	15	40	50	250
69	Camilo Pascual AS	5	5	5	6	10	30	100	
70	Don Drysdale AS	5	6	10	25	60	80	250	800
71	Billy Pierce AS	5	5	5	5	15	30	60	200
72	Johnny Antonelli AS	5	5	8	12	20	40	100	

—Hank Aaron #300 PSA 9 (MT) sold for $19,805 (Memory Lane; 5/08)
—Hank Aaron #300 PSA 9 (MT) sold for $10,018 (Goodwin; 3/07)
—Hank Aaron #300 PSA 8.5 (NmMt+) sold for $2,492 (eBay; 08/12)
—Ernie Banks #10 PSA 9 (MT) sold for $4,386 (eBay; 12/12)
—Lou Berberet #6 PSA 8 (NmMt) sold for $863 (eBay; 3/08)
—Lou Berberet #6 PSA 8 (NmMt) sold for $371 (eBay; 3/08)
—Lou Berberet #6 PSA 8 (NmMt) sold for $316 (eBay; 4/08)
—Lou Berberet #6 PSA 8 (NmMt) sold for $182 (eBay; 4/08)
—Norm Cash #388 PSA 8 (NmMt) sold for $713 (eBay; 1/08)
—Norm Cash #388 PSA 8 (NmMt) sold for $699 (eBay; 2/08)
—Norm Cash #388 PSA 8 (NmMt) sold for $650 (eBay; 1/08)
—Norm Cash #388 PSA 8 (NmMt) sold for $486 (eBay; 3/08)
—Norm Cash #388 PSA 8 (NmMt) sold for $369 (eBay; 6/07)
—Norm Cash #388 PSA 8 (NmMt) sold for $306 (eBay; 6/07)
—Norm Cash #388 PSA 8 (NmMt) sold for $305 (eBay; 5/07)
—Roberto Clemente #326 BVG 9 (MT) sold for $818 (eBay; 5/08)
—Roberto Clemente #326 BVG 8.5 (NmMt+) sold for $586 (eBay; 3/07)
—Roberto Clemente #326 BVG 8.5 (NmMt+) sold for $418 (eBay; 11/07)
—Dodgers Team #18 PSA 9 (MT) sold for $3,079 (Memory Lane; 9/07)
—Dodgers Team #18 PSA 9 (MT) sold for $693 (Mastro; 10/05)
—Ryne Duren #204 PSA 8 (NmMt) sold for $614 (eBay; 6/08)
—Ryne Duren #204 PSA 8 (NmMt) sold for $405 (eBay; 10/07)
—Ryne Duren #204 PSA 8 (NmMt) sold for $372 (eBay; 6/06)
—Ryne Duren #204 PSA 8 (NmMt) sold for $204 (eBay; 10/06)
—Jack Harshman #112 PSA 8 (NmMt) sold for $1,004 (eBay; 3/08)
—Jack Harshman #112 PSA 8 (NmMt) sold for $510 (eBay; 3/08)
—Jack Harshman #112 PSA 8 (NmMt) sold for $184 (eBay; 4/07)
—Jack Harshman #112 PSA 8 (NmMt) sold for $128 (eBay; 10/07)
—Jim Kaat #136 PSA 9 (MT) sold for $4,037 (eBay; 6/08)
—Jim Kaat #136 PSA 9 (MT) sold for $1,158 (eBay; 1/08)
—Al Kaline #50 PSA 9 (MT) sold for $5,970 (eBay; 10/07)
—Al Kaline #50 PSA 9 (MT) sold for $932 (Mastro; 12/05)
—Harmon Killebrew #210 PSA 9 (MT) sold for $1,776 (eBay; 11/07)
—Harmon Killebrew #210 PSA 9 (MT) sold for $1,659 (Mile High; 2/08)
—Tony Kubek #83 PSA 9 (MT) sold for $1,446 (Mile High; 2/08)
—Tony Kubek #83 PSA 9 (MT) sold for $488 (eBay; 10/07)
—Tony Kubek #83 PSA 8.5 (NmMt+) sold for $692 (eBay; 3/08)
—Mickey Mantle #350 PSA 8.5 (NmMt+) sold for $3,270 (Greg Bussineau; 12/12)
—Mickey Mantle AS #563 PSA 10 (Gem) sold for $5,801 (eBay; 10/06)
—Roger Maris #377 PSA 10 (Gem) sold for $11,882 (Memory Lane; 9/07)
—Roger Maris #377 PSA 10 (Gem) sold for $3,346 (Mile High; 1/07)
—Roger Maris AS #565 PSA 9 (MT) sold for $4,911 (eBay; 4/08)
—Roger Maris AS #565 PSA 9 (MT) sold for $3,976 (Goodwin; 11/07)
—Eddie Mathews #420 PSA 9 (MT) sold for $1,784 (Memory Lane; 9/07)
—Eddie Mathews #420 PSA 9 (MT) sold for $685 (eBay; 12/07)
—Willie Mays #200 PSA 10 (Gem) sold for $8,983 (Mastro; 8/04)
—Willie Mays #200 PSA 10 (Gem) sold for $8,710 (Mile High; 6/05)
—Willie Mays AS #564 PSA 9 (MT) sold for $2,440 (Goodwin; 3/07)
—Willie Mays AS #564 PSA 9 (MT) sold for $1,145 (Leland's; 12/04)
—Willie McCovey #316 BVG 9 (MT) sold for $2,265 (eBay; 11/07)
—Mound Magicians #230 PSA 10 (Gem) sold for $5,515 (eBay; 6/08)
—Danny Murtaugh #223 PSA 8 (NmMt) sold for $809 (eBay; 2/08)
—Danny Murtaugh #223 PSA 8 (NmMt) sold for $388 (eBay; 6/07)
—Danny Murtaugh #223 PSA 8 (NmMt) sold for $327 (eBay; 6/07)
—Danny Murtaugh #223 PSA 8 (NmMt) sold for $305 (eBay; 6/07)
—Danny Murtaugh #223 PSA 8 (NmMt) sold for $202 (eBay; 8/07)
—Danny Murtaugh #223 PSA 8 (NmMt) sold for $157 (eBay; 11/07)
—Steve Ridzik #489 PSA 8 (NmMt) sold for $312 (eBay; 1/07)
—Steve Ridzik #489 PSA 8 (NmMt) sold for $138 (eBay; 5/07)
—Rival All-Stars #160 PSA 10 (Gem) sold for $5,533 (Memory Lane; 12/06)
—Frank Robinson #490 PSA 9 (MT) sold for $569 (Goodwin; 5/08)
—Bill Skowron #370 PSA 8 (NmMt) sold for $522 (eBay; 2/08)
—Bill Skowron #370 PSA 8 (NmMt) sold for $288 (eBay; 3/08)
—Bill Skowron #370 PSA 8 (NmMt) sold for $237 (eBay; 3/08)
—Bill Skowron #370 PSA 8 (NmMt) sold for $214 (eBay; 4/08)
—Early Wynn #1 PSA 9 (MT) sold for $3,065 (eBay; 2/08)
—Early Wynn #1 PSA 9 (MT) sold for $1,680 (Mastro; 5/08)
—Carl Yastrzemski #148 PSA 10 (Gem) (Young Collection) sold for $83,813 (SCP; 5/12)

1961 Fleer

#	Player	GD 2	VG 3	VgEx 4	EX 5	ExMt 6	NM 7	NmMt 8	MT 9
1	Baker/Cobb/Wheat CL	5	6	10	15	30	80	250	
2	Grover C. Alexander	5	5	5	5	6	15	60	
3	Nick Altrock	5	5	5	5	5	12	30	
4	Cap Anson	5	5	5	5	5	10	30	
5	Earl Averill	5	5	5	5	5	8	25	
6	Frank Baker	5	5	5	5	5	8	20	
7	Dave Bancroft	5	5	5	5	8	10	30	60
8	Chief Bender	5	5	5	5	5	8	15	80
9	Jim Bottomley	5	5	5	5	5	8	15	60
10	Roger Bresnahan	5	5	5	5	5	5	25	
11	Mordecai Brown	5	5	5	5	5	8	20	
12	Max Carey	5	5	5	5	5	8	40	
13	Jack Chesbro	5	5	5	5	5	10	20	60
14	Ty Cobb	5	6	10	20	50	60	80	250
15	Mickey Cochrane	5	5	5	5	5	10	20	60
16	Eddie Collins	5	5	5	5	8	15	60	
17	Earle Combs	5	5	5	5	5	8	30	
18	Charles Comiskey	5	5	5	5	5	10	30	
19	Kiki Cuyler	5	5	5	5	5	8	15	50
20	Paul Derringer	5	5	5	5	5	8	20	100
21	Howard Ehmke	5	5	5	5	5	8	15	50
22	Billy Evans UMP	5	5	5	5	5	10	20	50
23	Johnny Evers	5	5	5	5	5	8	15	50
24	Red Faber	5	5	5	5	5	8	15	50
25	Bob Feller	5	5	5	6	10	20	40	200
26	Wes Ferrell	5	5	5	5	5	10	20	50
27	Lew Fonseca	5	5	5	5	5	8	15	60
28	Jimmie Foxx	5	5	5	6	10	15	50	120

#	Name	GD 2	VG 3	VgEx 4	EX 5	ExMt 6	NM 7	NmMt 8	MT 9
29	Ford Frick	5	5	5	5	5	8	15	80
30	Frankie Frisch	5	5	5	6	10	20	25	60
31	Lou Gehrig	8	10	30	40	60	80	120	250
32	Charley Gehringer	5	5	5	5	5	8	15	50
33	Warren Giles	5	5	5	5	5	10	25	
34	Lefty Gomez	5	5	5	5	5	10	20	60
35	Goose Goslin	5	5	5	5	5	8	15	60
36	Clark Griffith	5	5	5	5	5	8	15	60
37	Burleigh Grimes	5	5	5	5	5	8	15	50
38	Lefty Grove	5	5	5	5	5	10	25	50
39	Chick Hafey	5	5	5	5	5	8	15	60
40	Jesse Haines	5	5	5	5	8	10	20	50
41	Gabby Hartnett	5	5	5	5	5	8	15	60
42	Harry Heilmann	5	5	5	5	5	8	15	60
43	Rogers Hornsby	5	5	5	6	10	15	40	150
44	Waite Hoyt	5	5	5	5	5	8	15	60
45	Carl Hubbell	5	5	5	5	8	15	25	80
46	Miller Huggins	5	5	5	5	8	15	25	80
47	Hughie Jennings	5	5	5	5	5	8	15	50
48	Ban Johnson	5	5	5	5	5	10	20	50
49	Walter Johnson	5	5	5	8	12	25	40	150
50	Ralph Kiner	5	5	5	8	10	20	40	60
51	Chuck Klein	5	5	5	5	8	10	20	60
52	Johnny Kling	5	5	5	5	5	8	15	50
53	Kenesaw M. Landis	5	5	5	5	5	8	15	50
54	Tony Lazzeri	5	5	5	5	5	8	15	60
55	Ernie Lombardi	5	5	5	5	5	8	15	50
56	Dolf Luque	5	5	5	5	5	8	15	60
57	Heinie Manush	5	5	5	8	10	15	25	50
58	Marty Marion	5	5	5	5	5	8	15	60
59	Christy Mathewson	5	5	8	10	15	25	50	300
60	John McGraw	5	5	5	5	8	10	20	50
61	Joe Medwick	5	5	5	5	5	8	15	50
62	Bing Miller	5	5	5	5	5	5	15	50
63	Johnny Mize	5	5	5	5	5	8	15	50
64	John Mostil	5	5	5	5	5	8	15	50
65	Art Nehf	5	5	5	8	10	15	25	
66	Hal Newhouser	5	5	5	5	5	8	15	50
67	Bobo Newsom	5	5	5	5	5	8	15	50
68	Mel Ott	5	5	5	8	10	15	25	60
69	Allie Reynolds	5	5	5	5	5	8	15	50
70	Sam Rice	5	5	5	5	8	10	20	50
71	Eppa Rixey	5	5	5	5	5	8	15	50
72	Edd Roush	5	5	5	8	10	15	25	60
73	Schoolboy Rowe	5	5	5	5	5	8	20	50
74	Red Ruffing	5	5	5	5	5	10	20	50
75	Babe Ruth	25	30	80	100	120	▲250	▲300	600
76	Joe Sewell	5	5	5	5	5	12	30	
77	Al Simmons	5	5	5	5	5	8	15	50
78	George Sisler	5	5	5	5	5	8	15	50
79	Tris Speaker	5	5	5	8	10	15	25	50
80	Fred Toney	5	5	5	8	10	15	25	60
81	Dazzy Vance	5	5	5	5	5	8	25	
82	Jim Vaughn	5	5	5	8	10	15	25	60
83	Ed Walsh	5	5	5	8	10	15	25	60
84	Lloyd Waner	5	5	5	8	10	15	25	60
85	Paul Waner	5	5	5	8	10	15	25	80
86	Zack Wheat	5	5	5	5	5	8	15	100
87	Hack Wilson	5	5	5	5	5	10	25	80
88	Jimmy Wilson	5	5	5	5	5	8	20	100
89	G.Sisler/P.Traynor CL	8	10	15	25	40	80	150	
90	Babe Adams	5	5	5	5	5	10	25	
91	Dale Alexander	5	5	5	5	5	10	30	
92	Jim Bagby	5	5	5	5	5	10		
93	Ossie Bluege	5	5	5	5	5	10	20	
94	Lou Boudreau	5	5	5	5	5	10	50	
95	Tommy Bridges	5	5	5	5	5	10	80	
96	Donie Bush	5	5	5	5	5	10	20	120
97	Dolph Camilli	5	5	5	5	5	10	25	150
98	Frank Chance	5	5	5	5	5	10	40	60
99	Jimmy Collins	5	5	5	5	5	10	25	
100	Stan Coveleskie	5	5	5	5	5	10	150	
101	Hugh Critz	5	5	5	5	5	10	20	60
102	Alvin Crowder	5	5	5	5	5	10	20	60
103	Joe Dugan	5	5	5	5	5	10	20	60
104	Bibb Falk	5	5	5	5	5	10	25	60
105	Rick Ferrell	5	5	5	5	8	15	30	80

#	Name	GD 2	VG 3	VgEx 4	EX 5	ExMt 6	NM 7	NmMt 8	MT
106	Art Fletcher	5	5	5	5	5	10	20	150
107	Dennis Galehouse	5	5	5	5	5	10	20	60
108	Chick Galloway	5	5	5	5	5	10	20	60
109	Mule Haas	5	5	5	5	5	10	20	150
110	Stan Hack	5	5	5	5	5	10	20	150
111	Bump Hadley	5	5	5	8	10	15	30	60
112	Billy Hamilton	5	5	5	5	5	10	20	
113	Joe Hauser	5	5	5	8	10	15	30	60
114	Babe Herman	5	5	5	8	10	15	30	60
115	Travis Jackson	5	5	5	5	5	10	50	
116	Eddie Joost	5	5	5	5	5	10	20	80
117	Addie Joss	5	5	5	8	10	20	40	80
118	Joe Judge	5	5	5	5	5	10	20	
119	Joe Kuhel	5	5	5	8	10	15	30	60
120	Napoleon Lajoie	5	5	5	6	10	20	40	
121	Dutch Leonard	5	5	5	5	5	10	40	
122	Ted Lyons	5	5	8	10	15	30	60	
123	Connie Mack	5	5	5	5	8	15	60	150
124	Rabbit Maranville	5	5	5	5	5	10	20	
125	Fred Marberry	5	5	5	5	5	10	20	100
126	Joe McGinnity	5	5	5	5	5	10	20	60
127	Oscar Melillo	5	5	5	8	12	20	40	80
128	Ray Mueller	5	5	5	5	5	10	20	60
129	Kid Nichols	5	5	5	5	5	10	20	60
130	Lefty O'Doul	5	5	5	5	5	10	20	60
131	Bob O'Farrell	5	5	5	5	5	10	20	60
132	Roger Peckinpaugh	5	5	5	5	5	10	20	80
133	Herb Pennock	5	5	5	5	12	25	50	
134	George Pipgras	5	5	5	5	5	10	100	200
135	Eddie Plank	5	5	5	8	12	25	25	80
136	Ray Schalk	5	5	5	5	5	10	20	60
137	Hal Schumacher	5	5	5	5	5	10	20	60
138	Luke Sewell	5	5	5	5	5	10	20	60
139	Bob Shawkey	5	5	5	5	5	10	20	60
140	Riggs Stephenson	5	5	5	5	5	15	20	60
141	Billy Sullivan	5	5	5	5	5	10	20	60
142	Bill Terry	5	5	5	5	8	12	40	100
143	Joe Tinker	5	5	5	5	5	10	20	60
144	Pie Traynor	5	5	5	5	5	10	40	
145	Hal Trosky	5	5	5	5	5	10	30	200
146	George Uhle	5	5	5	5	5	10	20	60
147	Johnny VanderMeer	5	5	5	5	5	10	20	60
148	Arky Vaughan	5	5	5	5	5	10	40	80
149	Rube Waddell	5	5	5	5	5	10	100	150
150	Honus Wagner	5	8	12	20	40	60	100	300
151	Dixie Walker	5	5	5	5	5	10	60	
152	Ted Williams	15	25	40	80	100	120	300	800
153	Cy Young	5	5	8	15	25	50	80	250
154	Ross Youngs	5	5	5	6	12	30	150	

—Jim Bagby #92 PSA 8 (NmMt) sold for $152 (eBay; 5/08)
—Frank Chance #98 PSA 10 (Gem) sold for $200 (eBay; 11/06)
—Charles Comiskey #18 PSA 9 (MT) sold for $273 (eBay; 10/06)
—Carl Hubbell #45 PSA 10 (Gem) sold for $320 (eBay; 2/08)
—Ralph Kiner #50 PSA 10 (Gem) sold for $406 (Mile High; 1/07)

1961 Golden Press

#	Name	VG 3	VgEx 4	EX 5	ExMt 6	NM 7	NmMt 8	MT 9	Gem 9.5/10
1	Mel Ott	5	5	6	10	40	80	250	
2	Grover C. Alexander	5	5	5	8	15	50	250	
3	Babe Ruth	10	12	40	50	100	150	500	
4	Hank Greenberg	5	5	5	5	8	15	50	200
5	Bill Terry	5	5	5	5	8	15	40	250
6	Carl Hubbell	5	5	5	5	10	20	40	
7	Rogers Hornsby	5	5	6	10	15	25	80	
8	Dizzy Dean	5	5	5	12	20	40	80	
9	Joe DiMaggio	8	10	12	20	35	120	200	
10	Charlie Gehringer	5	5	5	5	8	15	40	250
11	Gabby Hartnett	5	5	5	5	8	15	40	
12	Mickey Cochrane	5	5	5	5	8	15	40	
13	George Sisler	5	5	5	5	8	15	40	200
14	Joe Cronin	5	5	5	5	8	30	40	200
15	Pie Traynor	5	5	5	5	8	15	40	150
16	Lou Gehrig	8	10	12	20	35	80	250	
17	Lefty Grove	5	5	5	5	8	15	40	250
18	Chief Bender	5	5	5	5	8	15	40	200
19	Frankie Frisch	5	5	5	5	8	15	40	200

	VG 3	VgEx 4	EX 5	ExMt 6	NM 7	NmMt 8	MT 9	Gem 9.5/10
Al Simmons	5	5	5	8	15	40		200
Home Run Baker	5	5	5	5	8	15	50	200
Jimmy Foxx	5	5	6	10	15	40	60	
John McGraw	5	5	5	5	8	15	40	200
Christy Mathewson	5	5	6	10	15	25	60	
Ty Cobb	6	8	10	15	25	80	120	300
Dazzy Vance	5	5	5	5	8	15	40	
Bill Dickey	5	5	5	5	8	15	40	
Eddie Collins	5	5	5	5	8	40		120
Walter Johnson	5	5	8	12	25	60		250
Tris Speaker	5	5	6	10	15	25		150
Nap Lajoie	5	5	5	8	12	40		120
Honus Wagner	8	10	10	25	60	80		200
Cy Young	5	5	8	12	25	30		300

Dizzy Dean #8 PSA 10 (Gem) sold for $1,543 (eBay; 3/07)
Dizzy Dean #8 PSA 10 (Gem) sold for $1,311 (eBay; 12/07)
Joe DiMaggio #9 PSA 10 (Gem) sold for $3,839 (eBay; 3/07)
Jimmie Foxx #22 PSA 10 (Gem) sold for $1,156 (eBay; 5/08)
Christy Mathewson #24 PSA 10 (Gem) sold for $2,207 (eBay; 2/08)
Babe Ruth #3 GAI 9.5 (Gem) sold for $278 (eBay; 7/07)
Babe Ruth #3 GAI 9.5 (Gem) sold for $205 (eBay; 1/08)
Babe Ruth #3 GAI 9.5 (Gem) sold for $150 (eBay; 5/08)

961 Topps

	GD 2	VG 3	VgEx 4	EX 5	ExMt 6	NM 7	NmMt 8	MT 9
Dick Groat	5	5	6	10	25	40	150	300
Roger Maris	40	60	80	100	▲200	300	600	7,000
John Buzhardt	5	5	5	5	5	10	20	80
Lenny Green	5	5	5	5	5	10	20	80
John Romano	5	5	5	5	5	10	25	
Ed Roebuck	5	5	5	5	8	12	20	80
Chicago White Sox TC	5	5	5	5	6	12	30	100
Dick Williams	5	5	5	5	6	12	40	▼120
Bob Purkey	5	5	5	5	5	10	20	60
Brooks Robinson	5	6	25	30	40	60	100	500
Curt Simmons	5	5	5	5	5	10	25	80
Moe Thacker	5	5	5	5	5	10	20	50
Chuck Cottier	5	5	5	5	5	10	20	60
Don Mossi	5	5	5	5	5	10	20	50
Willie Kirkland	5	5	5	5	5	10	30	
Billy Muffett	5	5	5	5	5	10	20	80
Checklist 1	5	5	5	5	6	12	25	100
Jim Grant	5	5	5	5	5	10	20	80
Clete Boyer	5	5	5	8	12	40	100	
Robin Roberts	5	5	5	8	15	25	50	150
Zoilo Versalles RC	5	5	5	5	6	12	30	100
Clem Labine	5	5	5	5	6	12	25	80
Don Demeter	5	5	5	5	6	12	25	150
Ken Johnson	5	5	5	5	5	10	20	80
Reds Heavy Artillery	5	5	5	8	12	25	50	120
Wes Stock	5	5	5	5	5	10	20	100
Jerry Kindall	5	5	5	5	5	10	25	80
Hector Lopez	5	5	5	5	8	12	30	150
Don Nottebart	5	5	5	5	5	10	20	60
Nellie Fox	5	5	6	10	25	30	60	250
Bob Schmidt	5	5	5	5	5	10	20	80
Ray Sadecki	5	5	5	5	5	10	20	80
Gary Geiger	5	5	5	5	5	10	20	50
Wynn Hawkins	5	5	5	5	5	10	15	50
Ron Santo RC	15	30	40	▲60	▲100	120	300	1,000
Jack Kralick RC	5	5	5	5	5	10	20	60
Charley Maxwell	5	5	5	5	6	12	30	100
Bob Lillis	5	5	5	5	5	10	20	40
Leo Posada RC	5	5	5	5	5	10	20	60
Bob Turley	5	5	5	5	8	15	50	120
NL Batting Leaders	5	5	8	20	25	▲50	▲80	250
AL Batting Leaders	5	5	5	6	10	15	30	100
NL Home Run Leaders	5	5	15	20	25	40	80	300
AL Home Run Leaders	15	25	40	50	60	120	200	800
NL ERA Leaders	5	5	5	5	8	15	30	80
AL ERA Leaders	5	5	5	5	6	12	25	120
NL Pitching Leaders	5	5	5	5	8	20	40	300
AL Pitching Leaders	5	5	5	6	10	15	25	100
NL Strikeout Leaders	5	5	6	10	20	30	80	300
AL Strikeout Leaders	5	5	5	5	8	15	40	200
Detroit Tigers TC	5	5	5	5	6	12	30	150

		GD 2	VG 3	VgEx 4	EX 5	ExMt 6	NM 7	NmMt 8	MT 9
52	George Crowe	5	5	5	5	5	10	20	60
53	Russ Nixon	5	5	5	5	5	10	20	80
54	Earl Francis RC	5	5	5	5	5	10	20	150
55	Jim Davenport	5	5	5	5	5	10	20	60
56	Russ Kemmerer	5	5	5	5	5	10	20	100
57	Marv Throneberry	5	5	5	5	6	12	20	80
58	Joe Schaffernoth RC	5	5	5	5	5	10	20	80
59	Jim Woods	5	5	5	5	5	10	20	80
60	Woody Held	5	5	5	5	5	10	20	80
61	Ron Piche RC	5	5	5	5	5	10	20	120
62	Al Pilarcik	5	5	5	5	5	10	20	60
63	Jim Kaat	5	5	6	10	15	25	40	250
64	Alex Grammas	5	5	5	5	5	10	20	60
65	Ted Kluszewski	5	5	5	5	8	20	40	200
66	Bill Henry	5	5	5	5	5	10	20	80
67	Ossie Virgil	5	5	5	5	5	12	50	
68	Deron Johnson	5	5	5	5	8	12	20	60
69	Earl Wilson	5	5	5	5	5	10	25	80
70	Bill Virdon	5	5	5	5	8	15	50	150
71	Jerry Adair	5	5	5	5	5	10	15	80
72	Stu Miller	5	5	5	5	5	10	20	100
73	Al Spangler	5	5	5	5	5	10	20	80
74	Joe Pignatano	5	5	5	5	5	10	20	80
75	Lindy Shows Larry	5	5	5	5	6	12	25	80
76	Harry Anderson	5	5	5	5	5	10	20	60
77	Dick Stigman	5	5	5	5	5	10	20	80
78	Lee Walls	5	5	5	5	5	10	20	80
79	Joe Ginsberg	5	5	5	5	5	10	20	80
80	Harmon Killebrew	5	15	20	25	30	60	150	
81	Tracy Stallard RC	5	5	5	5	5	10	20	80
82	Joe Christopher RC	5	5	5	5	5	10	20	80
83	Bob Bruce	5	5	5	5	5	10	20	80
84	Lee Maye	5	5	5	5	5	10	20	100
85	Jerry Walker	5	5	5	5	5	10	20	50
86	Los Angeles Dodgers TC	5	5	6	10	15	25	40	250
87	Joe Amalfitano	5	5	5	5	5	10	20	60
88	Richie Ashburn	6	8	10	12	15	25	40	120
89	Billy Martin	5	5	8	12	▲25	40	100	
90	Gerry Staley	5	5	5	5	5	10	20	100
91	Walt Moryn	5	5	5	5	5	10	20	100
92	Hal Naragon	5	5	5	5	5	10	20	80
93	Tony Gonzalez	5	5	5	5	5	10	20	100
94	Johnny Kucks	5	5	5	5	5	10	20	80
95	Norm Cash	5	5	5	5	6	25	40	120
96	Billy O'Dell	5	5	5	5	6	12	80	100
97	Jerry Lynch	5	5	5	5	5	10	15	50
98A	Checklist 2 Red	5	5	5		15	60	150	
98B	Checklist 2 Yellow w/White 98	5	5	5	6	12	50		
98C	Checklist 2 Yellow w/Black 98	5	5	5	12	30			
99	Don Buddin	5	5	5	5	5	10	20	80
100	Harvey Haddix	5	5	5	5	6	12	20	80
101	Bubba Phillips	5	5	5	5	5	10	20	100
102	Gene Stephens	5	5	5	5	5	10	20	80
103	Ruben Amaro	5	5	5	5	5	10	20	120
104	John Blanchard	5	5	5	5	8	15	25	80
105	Carl Willey	5	5	5	5	6	10	15	80
106	Whitey Herzog	5	5	5	5	5	10	20	80
107	Seth Morehead	5	5	5	5	5	10	20	80
108	Dan Dobbek	5	5	5	5	5	10	20	100
109	Johnny Podres	5	5	5	5	6	12	▲30	100
110	Vada Pinson	5	5	5	8	12	30	50	
111	Jack Meyer	5	5	5	5	5	10	20	150
112	Chico Fernandez	5	5	5	5	5	10	20	
113	Mike Fornieles	5	5	5	5	5	10	80	
114	Hobie Landrith	5	5	5	5	5	12	30	
115	Johnny Antonelli	5	5	5	5	5	10	25	
116	Joe DeMaestri	5	5	5	5	6	12	25	120
117	Dale Long	5	5	5	5	5	10	20	120
118	Chris Cannizzaro RC	5	5	5	5	5	10	25	
119	A's Big Armor	5	5	5	5	6	12	100	200
120	Eddie Mathews	12	15	20	25	30	40	80	400
121	Eli Grba	5	5	5	5	5	10	25	
122	Chicago Cubs TC	5	5	5	5	6	12	30	
123	Billy Gardner	5	5	5	5	5	10	30	
124	J.C. Martin	5	5	5	5	5	10	20	
125	Steve Barber	5	5	5	5	5	10	20	100
126	Dick Stuart	5	5	5	8	12	20	100	400

#	Name	GD 2	VG 3	VgEx 4	EX 5	ExMt 6	NM 7	NmMt 8	MT 9
127	Ron Kline	5	5	5	5	5	10	20	80
128	Rip Repulski	5	5	5	5	5	12	60	
129	Ed Hobaugh	5	5	5	5	5	8	15	50
130	Norm Larker	5	5	5	5	5	10	20	100
131	Paul Richards MG	5	5	5	5	5	10	20	
132	Al Lopez MG	5	5	5	5	6	25	▼60	
133	Ralph Houk MG	5	5	8	12	20	▼40	▼400	
134	Mickey Vernon MG	5	5	5	5	6	12	25	150
135	Fred Hutchinson MG	5	5	5	5	8	15	30	
136	Walter Alston MG	5	5	5	5	8	20	60	
137	Chuck Dressen MG	5	5	5	5	6	15	150	
138	Danny Murtaugh MG	5	5	5	5	5	12	30	
139	Solly Hemus MG	5	5	5	5	5	12	25	
140	Gus Triandos	5	5	5	5	6	12	25	500
141	Billy Williams RC	10	25	▼40	▼50	60	120	300	2,500
142	Luis Arroyo	5	5	5	5	6	12	25	100
143	Russ Snyder	5	5	5	6	10	15	60	
144	Jim Coker	5	5	5	5	5	10	20	100
145	Bob Buhl	5	5	5	5	6	12	25	150
146	Marty Keough	5	5	5	5	5	10	20	150
147	Ed Rakow	5	5	5	5	5	10	20	100
148	Julian Javier	5	5	5	5	6	15	50	
149	Bob Oldis	5	5	5	5	5	10	20	100
150	Willie Mays	▲30	40	50	▲80	100	200	500	2,500
151	Jim Donohue	5	5	5	5	5	10	30	
152	Earl Torgeson	5	5	5	5	5	10	20	100
153	Don Lee	5	5	5	5	5	12	80	
154	Bobby Del Greco	5	5	5	5	5	10	50	150
155	Johnny Temple	5	5	5	5	8	12	20	
156	Ken Hunt	5	5	5	5	6	12	25	
157	Cal McLish	5	5	5	5	5	10	20	200
158	Pete Daley	5	5	5	5	5	10	20	100
159	Baltimore Orioles TC	5	5	5	5	6	12	25	250
160	Whitey Ford	▲15	▲20	▲25	▲30	▲50	80	400	
161	Sherman Jones RC	5	5	5	5	5	10	20	150
162	Jay Hook	5	5	5	5	5	10	20	120
163	Ed Sadowski	5	5	5	5	5	10	20	100
164	Felix Mantilla	5	5	5	5	5	10	20	100
165	Gino Cimoli	5	5	5	5	5	10	25	100
166	Danny Kravitz	5	5	5	5	5	10	20	80
167	San Francisco Giants TC	5	5	5	5	6	12	60	100
168	Tommy Davis	5	5	5	6	10	15	50	120
169	Don Elston	5	5	5	5	5	10	20	80
170	Al Smith	5	5	5	5	5	12	40	
171	Paul Foytack	5	5	5	5	5	12	80	
172	Don Dillard	5	5	5	5	5	8	15	100
173	Beantown Bombers	5	5	5	5	6	25	50	
174	Ray Semproch	5	5	5	5	5	10	25	
175	Gene Freese	5	5	5	5	6	15	60	
176	Ken Aspromonte	5	5	5	5	5	10	20	80
177	Don Larsen	5	5	5	5	8	12	60	250
178	Bob Nieman	5	5	5	5	5	10	20	100
179	Joe Koppe	5	5	5	5	5	10	20	
180	Bobby Richardson	5	5	6	12	20	50	▼100	600
181	Fred Green	5	5	5	5	5	10	20	150
182	Dave Nicholson RC	5	5	5	5	5	10	150	
183	Andre Rodgers	5	5	5	5	5	10	20	120
184	Steve Bilko	5	5	5	5	5	10	15	80
185	Herb Score	5	5	5	5	6	25	60	
186	Elmer Valo	5	5	5	5	5	10	30	
187	Billy Klaus	5	5	5	5	5	10	20	100
188	Jim Marshall	5	5	5	5	5	10	20	
189A	Checklist 3 Copyright at 263	5	5	5	5	6	12	25	
189B	Checklist 3 Copyright at 264	5	5	5	5	8	15		
190	Stan Williams	5	5	5	5	5	8	15	60
191	Mike de la Hoz RC	5	5	5	5	5	10	20	
192	Dick Brown	5	5	5	5	5	10	25	
193	Gene Conley	5	5	5	5	5	10	20	80
194	Gordy Coleman	5	5	5	5	5	10	20	80
195	Jerry Casale	5	5	5	5	5	10	30	
196	Ed Bouchee	5	5	5	5	5	10	20	100
197	Dick Hall	5	5	5	5	5	10	20	80
198	Carl Sawatski	5	5	5	5	5	10	20	80
199	Bob Boyd	5	5	5	5	5	10	20	80
200	Warren Spahn	5	10	20	30	40	50	120	600
201	Pete Whisenant	5	5	5	5	5	10	15	120
202	Al Neiger RC	5	5	5	5	8	10	15	100

#	Name	GD 2	VG 3	VgEx 4	EX 5	ExMt 6	NM 7	NmMt 8	MT
203	Eddie Bressoud	5	5	5	5	5	10	20	8
204	Bob Skinner	5	5	5	5	6	12	40	17
205	Billy Pierce	5	5	5	5	5	10	20	8
206	Gene Green	5	5	5	5	5	10	20	6
207	Dodger Southpaws	5	6	10	25	40	60	120	60
208	Larry Osborne	5	5	5	5	5	10	20	8
209	Ken McBride	5	5	5	5	5	10	20	6
210	Pete Runnels	5	5	5	5	5	10	30	15
211	Bob Gibson	10	15	25	▲40	50	▲80	150	60
212	Haywood Sullivan	5	5	5	5	5	10	20	8
213	Bill Stafford RC	5	5	6	10	15	25	30	10
214	Danny Murphy RC	5	5	5	5	5	10	25	12
215	Gus Bell	5	5	5	5	5	10	25	8
216	Ted Bowsfield	5	5	5	5	5	10	20	8
217	Mel Roach	5	5	5	5	5	10	20	10
218	Hal Brown	5	5	5	5	5	10	20	10
219	Gene Mauch MG	5	5	5	5	5	10	20	8
220	Alvin Dark MG	5	5	5	5	6	12	20	8
221	Mike Higgins MG	5	5	5	5	8	15	12	
222	Jimmy Dykes MG	5	5	5	5	5	10	20	8
223	Bob Scheffing MG	5	5	5	5	6	12	30	10
224	Joe Gordon MG	5	5	5	5	5	12	25	8
225	Bill Rigney MG	5	5	5	5	5	10	25	8
226	Cookie Lavagetto MG	5	5	5	5	5	10	25	10
227	Juan Pizarro	5	5	5	5	5	10	20	8
228	New York Yankees TC	12	15	25	30	40	50	150	60
229	Rudy Hernandez RC	5	5	5	5	5	10	20	8
230	Don Hoak	5	5	5	5	5	12	40	200
231	Dick Drott	5	5	5	5	5	10	20	
232	Bill White	5	5	5	5	8	15	50	
233	Joey Jay	5	5	5	5	5	10	20	100
234	Ted Lepcio	5	5	5	5	5	12	60	15
235	Camilo Pascual	5	5	5	5	5	10	25	8
236	Don Gile RC	5	5	5	5	5	10	20	100
237	Billy Loes	5	5	5	5	5	10	20	80
238	Jim Gilliam	5	5	5	5	6	12	25	100
239	Dave Sisler	5	5	5	5	5	10	20	60
240	Ron Hansen	5	5	5	5	5	12	60	150
241	Al Cicotte	5	5	5	5	5	10	20	60
242	Hal Smith	5	5	5	12	25	50	100	150
243	Frank Lary	5	5	5	5	5	10	60	150
244	Chico Cardenas	5	5	5	5	5	10	25	100
245	Joe Adcock	5	5	5	5	6	15	25	
246	Bob Davis RC	5	5	5	5	5	10	20	80
247	Billy Goodman	5	5	5	5	8	15	80	
248	Ed Keegan RC	5	5	5	5	5	10	15	60
249	Cincinnati Reds TC	5	5	5	8	12	20	50	250
250	Buc Hill Aces	5	5	5	5	6	12	50	150
251	Bill Bruton	5	5	5	5	5	12	40	
252	Bill Short	5	5	5	5	5	10	25	200
253	Sammy Taylor	5	5	5	5	5	8	15	80
254	Ted Sadowski RC	5	5	5	5	8	10	20	80
255	Vic Power	5	5	5	6	8	12	25	100
256	Billy Hoeft	5	5	5	6	8	12	25	100
257	Carroll Hardy	5	5	5	6	8	12	25	100
258	Jack Sanford	5	5	6	8	10	15	30	120
259	John Schaive RC	5	5	5	5	5	10	20	80
260	Don Drysdale	5	8	▲25	▲30	▲40	▲60	100	400
261	Charlie Lau	5	5	5	5	5	10	20	80
262	Tony Curry	5	5	5	5	5	10	20	80
263	Ken Hamlin	5	5	5	5	5	10	20	80
264	Glen Hobbie	5	5	5	5	5	10	20	
265	Tony Kubek	5	6	8	12	25	60	150	
266	Lindy McDaniel	5	5	5	5	8	15	80	
267	Norm Siebern	5	5	5	5	5	10	20	120
268	Ike Delock	5	5	5	5	5	10	20	80
269	Harry Chiti	5	5	5	5	5	10	20	80
270	Bob Friend	5	5	5	5	8	12	40	200
271	Jim Landis	5	5	5	5	5	10	20	100
272	Tom Morgan	5	5	5	5	5	10	20	80
273A	Checklist 4 Copyright at 336	5	5	5	5	8	15		
273B	Checklist 4 Copyright at 339	5	5	5	5	6	12	30	
274	Gary Bell	5	5	5	5	5	8	15	100
275	Gene Woodling	5	5	5	5	5	10	25	60
276	Ray Rippelmeyer RC	5	5	5	5	5	10	20	80
277	Hank Foiles	5	5	5	5	5	10	20	60
278	Don McMahon	5	5	5	5	5	10	20	80

	GD 2	VG 3	VgEx 4	EX 5	ExMt 6	NM 7	NmMt 8	MT 9
279 Jose Pagan	5	5	5	5	5	12	40	
280 Frank Howard	5	6	8	10	12	20	60	120
281 Frank Sullivan	5	5	6	10	15	25	60	
282 Faye Throneberry	5	5	5	5	5	10	20	100
283 Bob Anderson	5	5	5	5	5	10	20	60
284 Dick Gernert	5	5	5	5	5	8	15	60
285 Sherm Lollar	5	5	5	5	6	12	25	80
286 George Witt	5	5	5	5	5	10	20	120
287 Carl Yastrzemski	10	40	▲60	▲80	100	150	400	1,500
288 Albie Pearson	5	5	5	5	5	10	25	
289 Ray Moore	5	5	5	5	5	10	25	
290 Stan Musial	10	25	▲40	50	80	▲120	250	1,000
291 Tex Clevenger	5	5	5	5	5	12	50	
292 Jim Baumer RC	5	5	5	5	5	10	25	100
293 Tom Sturdivant	5	5	5	5	5	12	60	
294 Don Blasingame	5	5	5	5	6	15	80	
295 Milt Pappas	5	5	5	5	5	10	25	100
296 Wes Covington	5	5	5	5	6	20	40	80
297 Kansas City Athletics TC	5	5	5	5	6	12	30	
298 Jim Golden RC	5	5	5	5	5	10	20	100
299 Clay Dalrymple	5	5	5	5	5	10	20	200
300 Mickey Mantle	▲200	▲250	▲300	▲400	▲600	▲1,200	3,000	20,000
301 Chet Nichols	5	5	5	5	5	15	80	150
302 Al Heist RC	5	5	5	5	5	10	60	
303 Gary Peters	5	5	5	5	5	12	30	150
304 Rocky Nelson	5	5	5	5	6	12	25	100
305 Mike McCormick	5	5	5	5	6	12	25	150
306 Bill Virdon WS1	5	5	5	5	15	80	500	
307 Mickey Mantle WS2	30	40	50	60	80	120	250	800
308 Bobby Richardson WS3	5	5	5	5	12	40	120	
309 Gino Cimoli WS4	5	5	5	5	12	30	80	
310 Roy Face WS5	5	5	5	5	8	40	200	500
311 Whitey Ford WS6	5	5	6	10	15	30	60	500
312 Bill Mazeroski WS7	5	6	10	15	50	100	400	
313 The Winners Celebrate WS	5	5	6	10	15	25	80	
314 Bob Miller	5	5	5	5	5	10	20	80
315 Earl Battey	5	5	5	5	5	10	50	100
316 Bobby Gene Smith	5	5	5	5	5	10	25	
317 Jim Brewer RC	5	5	5	5	5	10	20	60
318 Danny O'Connell	5	5	5	5	5	10	20	100
319 Valmy Thomas	5	5	5	5	5	10	20	100
320 Lou Burdette	5	5	5	5	6	12	50	150
321 Marv Breeding	5	5	5	5	5	10	20	80
322 Bill Kunkel RC	5	5	5	5	5	10	20	
323 Sammy Esposito	5	5	5	5	5	10	20	
324 Hank Aguirre	5	5	5	5	6	10	30	300
325 Wally Moon	5	5	5	5	6	12	30	250
326 Dave Hillman	5	5	5	5	5	10	20	100
327 Matty Alou RC	5	5	6	8	20	25	60	150
328 Jim O'Toole	5	5	5	5	5	10	25	80
329 Julio Becquer	5	5	5	5	5	10	20	100
330 Rocky Colavito	5	8	10	15	20	40	60	500
331 Ned Garver	5	5	5	5	5	10	30	
332 Dutch Dotterer	5	5	5	5	5	10	20	50
333 Fritz Brickell RC	5	5	5	5	6	12	25	100
334 Walt Bond	5	5	5	5	5	10	20	80
335 Frank Bolling	5	5	5	5	5	10	20	120
336 Don Mincher	5	5	5	5	5	10	30	80
337 Al's Aces	5	5	5	5	8	20	80	
338 Don Landrum	5	5	5	5	5	15	80	
339 Gene Baker	5	5	5	5	5	10	20	80
340 Vic Wertz	5	5	5	5	5	▲20	▲25	80
341 Jim Owens	5	5	5	5	5	10	20	100
342 Clint Courtney	5	5	5	5	6	12	40	100
343 Earl Robinson RC	5	5	5	5	5	10	20	80
344 Sandy Koufax	30	▲50	▲60	▲80	100	▼150	400	1,500
345 Jimmy Piersall	5	5	5	5	8	30	60	250
346 Howie Nunn	5	5	5	5	5	10	20	80
347 St. Louis Cardinals TC	5	5	5	5	6	12	30	100
348 Steve Boros	5	5	5	5	6	12	50	200
349 Danny McDevitt	5	5	6	10	15	25	40	
350 Ernie Banks	8	10	30	40	50	80	200	800
351 Jim King	5	5	5	5	5	10	30	
352 Bob Shaw	5	5	5	5	6	12	40	
353 Howie Bedell RC	5	5	5	5	5	10	20	100
354 Billy Harrell	5	5	5	5	5	10	20	
355 Bob Allison	5	5	5	6	8	40	60	

	GD 2	VG 3	VgEx 4	EX 5	ExMt 6	NM 7	NmMt 8	MT 9
356 Ryne Duren	5	5	5	5	8	25	80	300
357 Daryl Spencer	5	5	5	5	5	10	20	80
358 Earl Averill Jr.	5	5	5	5	8	12	30	100
359 Dallas Green	5	5	5	5	6	12	25	120
360 Frank Robinson	5	10	▲30	▲40	▲50	▲60	100	400
361A Checklist 5 Black Topps	5	5	5	5	6	12	50	200
361B Checklist 5 Yelllow Topps	5	5	5	5	8	15	120	
362 Frank Funk RC	5	5	5	5	5	10	20	
363 John Roseboro	5	5	5	5	6	12	25	80
364 Moe Drabowsky	5	5	5	5	5	10	25	60
365 Jerry Lumpe	5	5	5	5	5	10	30	
366 Eddie Fisher	5	5	5	5	5	8	20	80
367 Jim Rivera	5	5	5	5	5	10	25	150
368 Bennie Daniels	5	5	5	5	5	10	30	200
369 Dave Philley	5	5	5	5	5	10	80	100
370 Roy Face	5	5	5	5	6	12	40	250
371 Bill Skowron SP	5	6	10	15	30	50	80	200
372 Bob Hendley RC	5	5	5	5	5	10	20	
373 Boston Red Sox TC	5	5	5	5	8	15	40	
374 Paul Giel	5	5	5	5	5	10	20	80
375 Ken Boyer	5	5	5	8	10	25	80	
376 Mike Roarke RC	5	5	5	5	5	10	25	100
377 Ruben Gomez	5	5	5	5	6	12	25	80
378 Wally Post	5	5	5	5	6	12	25	80
379 Bobby Shantz	5	5	5	5	8	15	50	200
380 Minnie Minoso	5	5	5	5	6	12	40	150
381 Dave Wickersham RC	5	5	5	5	6	12	25	
382 Frank Thomas	5	5	5	5	5	20	40	120
383 Frisco First Liners	5	5	5	5	8	25	80	
384 Chuck Essegian	5	5	5	5	5	10	20	80
385 Jim Perry	5	5	5	5	5	10	25	50
386 Joe Hicks	5	5	5	5	5	10	20	100
387 Duke Maas	5	5	5	5	6	12	25	100
388 Roberto Clemente	▲30	▲50	▲60	80	▲120	▲250	▼500	1,500
389 Ralph Terry	5	5	5	5	15	40	150	
390 Del Crandall	5	5	5	5	5	10	25	80
391 Winston Brown RC	5	5	5	5	5	10	20	80
392 Reno Bertoia	5	5	5	5	5	10	20	80
393 Batter Bafflers	5	5	5	5	6	12	25	120
394 Ken Walters	5	5	5	5	5	10	60	80
395 Chuck Estrada	5	5	5	5	5	▲20	30	
396 Bob Aspromonte	5	5	5	5	6	12	40	80
397 Hal Woodeshick	5	5	5	5	5	10	20	80
398 Hank Bauer	5	5	5	5	6	12	40	
399 Cliff Cook RC	5	5	5	5	5	10	20	80
400 Vern Law	5	5	5	5	6	12	40	150
401 Babe Ruth 60th HR	10	25	40	50	▲100	▲120	250	600
402 Don Larsen Perfect SP	5	6	10	15	25	40	▼80	200
403 26 Inning Tire	5	5	5	5	6	15	30	100
404 Rogers Hornsby .424	5	5	5	8	12	20	50	120
405 Lou Gehrig Streak	8	10	25	30	50	60	100	250
406 Mickey Mantle 565 HR	8	30	40	50	60	100	200	▼500
407 Jack Chesbro Wins 41	5	5	6	10	12	20	30	200
408 Christy Mathewson K's SP	6	8	12	15	20	30	50	
409 Walter Johnson Shutout	5	5	6	10	20	25	80	
410 Harvey Haddix 12 Perfect	5	5	5	6	8	20	▲30	80
411 Tony Taylor	5	5	5	5	5	10	20	▼50
412 Larry Sherry	5	5	5	5	5	10	25	100
413 Eddie Yost	5	5	5	5	5	10	25	100
414 Dick Donovan	5	5	5	5	5	10	20	80
415 Hank Aaron	40	60	80	100	200	300	▲800	3,000
416 Dick Howser RC	5	5	5	5	6	20	80	200
417 Juan Marichal SP RC	30	50	60	100	▲150	250	400	2,500
418 Ed Bailey	5	5	5	5	5	10	20	60
419 Tom Borland	5	5	5	5	6	12	40	
420 Ernie Broglio	5	5	5	5	5	10	20	80
421 Ty Cline SP RC	5	5	5	8	12	20	30	120
422 Bud Daley	5	5	5	5	5	10	20	350
423 Charlie Neal SP	5	5	5	8	12	25	40	100
424 Turk Lown	5	5	5	5	6	12	25	
425 Yogi Berra	20	30	50	60	100	200	400	2,000
426 Milwaukee Braves TC UER 463	5	5	5	5	8	15	40	150
427 Dick Ellsworth	5	5	5	5	5	10	25	80
428 Ray Barker SP RC	5	5	5	5	8	30	40	80
429 Al Kaline	6	10	15	25	40	80	200	
430 Bill Mazeroski SP	6	10	15	▼20	▼25	60	▼100	500
431 Chuck Stobbs	5	5	5	5	5	10	30	100

#	Player	GD 2	VG 3	VgEx 4	EX 5	ExMt 6	NM 7	NmMt 8	MT 9
432	Coot Veal	5	5	5	5	5	10	30	60
433	Art Mahaffey	5	5	5	5	5	10	20	80
434	Tom Brewer	5	5	5	5	5	10	20	80
435	Orlando Cepeda	5	5	6	10	25	▼30	80	
436	Jim Maloney SP RC	5	5	5	8	12	50	100	250
437A	Checklist 6 440 is Louis	5	5	5	5	6	12	60	100
437B	Checklist 6 440 is Luis	5	5	5	5	6	12	25	150
438	Curt Flood	5	5	5	10	15	25	40	
439	Phil Regan RC	5	5	5	5	8	15	30	100
440	Luis Aparicio	5	5	6	10	20	30	60	120
441	Dick Bertell RC	5	5	5	5	10	20	60	
442	Gordon Jones	5	5	5	5	10	20	100	
443	Duke Snider	5	6	20	▼25	▼30	50	120	400
444	Joe Nuxhall	5	5	5	5	6	12	25	80
445	Frank Malzone	5	5	5	5	6	10	25	200
446	Bob Taylor	5	5	5	5	8	20	50	
447	Harry Bright	5	5	5	5	6	12	20	
448	Del Rice	5	5	5	5	6	12	25	60
449	Bob Bolin RC	5	5	5	5	6	12	25	80
450	Jim Lemon	5	5	5	5	6	12	40	120
451	Power for Ernie	5	5	5	5	8	15	30	100
452	Bob Allen RC	5	5	5	5	6	10	▲25	80
453	Dick Schofield	5	5	5	5	6	12	25	80
454	Pumpsie Green	5	5	5	5	6	12	30	80
455	Early Wynn	5	5	6	8	12	25	50	200
456	Hal Bevan	5	5	5	5	6	12	25	100
457	Johnny James	5	5	5	5	8	15	40	150
458	Willie Tasby	5	5	5	5	6	10	20	60
459	Terry Fox RC	5	5	5	5	6	12	25	80
460	Gil Hodges	5	5	6	15	25	40	60	250
461	Smoky Burgess	5	5	5	5	8	15	50	120
462	Lou Klimchock	5	5	5	5	6	12	20	80
463	Jack Fisher	5	5	6	8	10	25	100	150
464	Lee Thomas RC	5	5	5	5	6	12	40	120
465	Roy McMillan	5	5	5	5	6	12	30	100
466	Ron Moeller RC	5	5	5	5	6	12	25	80
467	Cleveland Indians TC	5	5	5	5	8	20	40	150
468	John Callison	5	5	5	5	6	20	40	80
469	Ralph Lumenti	5	5	5	5	6	12	20	80
470	Roy Sievers	5	5	5	5	12	15	25	
471	Phil Rizzuto MVP	5	6	12	20	30	50	150	
472	Yogi Berra MVP SP	12	20	30	50	60	100	250	1,500
473	Bob Shantz MVP	5	5	5	5	6	12	30	
474	Al Rosen MVP	5	5	5	5	6	20	40	150
475	Mickey Mantle MVP	80	100	120	▲200	▲250	300	▲800	2,000
476	Jackie Jensen MVP	5	5	5	5	10	20	50	100
477	Nellie Fox MVP	5	5	5	8	15	50	60	300
478	Roger Maris MVP	10	25	40	50	60	▼80	250	1,000
479	Jim Konstanty MVP	5	5	5	5	6	25	60	
480	Roy Campanella MVP	6	8	20	25	40	60	▼120	800
481	Hank Sauer MVP	5	5	5	5	10	15	20	120
482	Willie Mays MVP	6	25	▲40	▲50	▲60	80	250	1,000
483	Don Newcombe MVP	5	5	5	5	12	25	50	100
484	Hank Aaron MVP	10	▲30	▲40	50	60	▲100	200	600
485	Ernie Banks MVP	8	12	20	30	50	▲80	200	1,000
486	Dick Groat MVP	5	5	5	8	12	20	50	300
487	Gene Oliver	5	5	5	5	6	12	25	100
488	Joe McClain RC	5	5	5	5	6	12	20	60
489	Walt Dropo	5	5	5	5	8	25	60	
490	Jim Bunning	5	5	5	8	15	25	60	300
491	Philadelphia Phillies TC	5	5	5	5	8	20	40	120
492A	Ron Fairly White	5	5	5	5	8	15	60	
493	Don Zimmer	5	5	5	5	12	25	30	150
494	Tom Cheney	5	5	5	6	10	20	50	200
495	Elston Howard	5	5	6	10	25	40	80	250
496	Ken MacKenzie	5	5	5	5	6	12	30	100
497	Willie Jones	5	5	5	5	6	12	30	80
498	Ray Herbert	5	5	5	5	6	12	50	100
499	Chuck Schilling RC	5	5	5	5	10	12	25	80
500	Harvey Kuenn	5	5	5	5	15	25	40	
501	John DeMerit RC	5	5	5	5	6	25	40	100
502	Choo Choo Coleman RC	5	5	5	5	6	12	30	100
503	Tito Francona	5	5	5	5	6	12	30	100
504	Billy Consolo	5	5	5	5	6	20	60	
505	Red Schoendienst	5	5	6	8	20	25	50	400
506	Willie Davis RC	5	6	8	12	20	30	80	
507	Pete Burnside	5	5	5	6	8	10	25	60

#	Player	GD 2	VG 3	VgEx 4	EX 5	ExMt 6	NM 7	NmMt 8	MT 9
508	Rocky Bridges	5	5	5	5	6	12	25	
509	Camilo Carreon	5	5	5	5	6	12	40	
510	Art Ditmar	5	5	5	5	8	15	▲40	
511	Joe M. Morgan	5	5	5	5	6	15	30	10
512	Bob Will	5	5	5	5	6	12	30	1
513	Jim Brosnan	5	5	5	5	6	12	25	
514	Jake Wood RC	5	5	5	5	6	12	25	8
515	Jackie Brandt	5	5	5	8	12	20	40	6
516A	Checklist 7	5	5	5	5	8	15	100	
516B	Checklist 7#((C on front fully above Braves cap)								
517	Willie McCovey	6	15	20	25	40	▲80	150	6
518	Andy Carey	5	5	5	5	6	12	25	8
519	Jim Pagliaroni RC	5	5	5	5	6	12	30	10
520	Joe Cunningham	5	5	5	8	12	20	80	
521	Brother Battery	5	5	5	8	12	20	30	
522	Dick Farrell	5	5	5	8	12	20	25	
523	Joe Gibbon	5	6	10	15	40	80	300	
524	Johnny Logan	5	6	10	15	40	50	50	30
525	Ron Perranoski RC	6	10	15	25	30	50	80	20
526	R.C. Stevens	5	5	8	12	20	40	80	
527	Gene Leek RC	5	5	8	12	20	30	60	15
528	Pedro Ramos	5	6	8	12	20	50	80	
529	Bob Roselli	5	5	6	15	20	50	80	12
530	Bob Malkmus	5	5	8	12	20	30	60	
531	Jim Coates	6	10	15	40	50	80	150	
532	Bob Hale	5	5	6	10	15	40	50	
533	Jack Curtis RC	5	5	8	12	20	40	60	
534	Eddie Kasko	5	5	8	12	20	30	100	60
535	Larry Jackson	5	8	12	20	30	50	60	
536	Bill Tuttle	5	5	6	8	12	40	60	10
537	Bobby Locke	5	5	8	12	20	40	50	15
538	Chuck Hiller RC	5	5	8	15	20	50	80	250
539	Johnny Klippstein	5	5	8	12	25	30	60	20
540	Jackie Jensen	5	6	8	12	25	30	60	20
541	Rollie Sheldon RC	6	10	15	25	50	100	150	
542	Minnesota Twins TC	6	10	15	25	40	80	150	80
543	Roger Craig	5	6	8	25	30	50	80	250
544	George Thomas RC	5	6	8	12	25	50	60	150
545	Hoyt Wilhelm	5	10	30	40	60	80	120	300
546	Marty Kutyna	5	5	8	12	20	50	60	
547	Leon Wagner	5	8	12	20	30	40	60	150
548	Ted Wills	5	6	10	15	25	50	120	
549	Hal R. Smith	5	5	6	10	15	40	50	80
550	Frank Baumann	5	5	8	12	20	30	50	150
551	George Altman	5	5	8	12	20	40	60	150
552	Jim Archer RC	5	6	8	12	25	40	60	
553	Bill Fischer	5	5	8	12	20	50	80	
554	Pittsburgh Pirates TC	15	20	50	60	80	120	250	
555	Sam Jones	5	6	10	15	25	50	100	250
556	Ken R. Hunt RC	5	5	8	12	20	30	50	
557	Jose Valdivielso	5	5	8	12	20	30	80	150
558	Don Ferrarese	5	5	8	12	20	40	60	100
559	Jim Gentile	15	20	30	50	80	200	600	
560	Barry Latman	5	5	8	12	20	50	50	120
561	Charley James	5	5	8	12	20	30	50	120
562	Bill Monbouquette	5	5	8	12	20	40	50	
563	Bob Cerv	10	15	30	50	80	120	500	
564	Don Cardwell	5	5	8	12	20	50	80	
565	Felipe Alou	5	6	8	12	30	50	100	150
566	Paul Richards AS MG	5	5	8	12	20	40	50	150
567	Danny Murtaugh AS MG	5	5	8	12	20	40	100	250
568	Bill Skowron AS	5	5	8	12	30	60	80	250
569	Frank Herrera AS	5	5	8	12	25	30	80	250
570	Nellie Fox AS	5	6	8	12	40	60	80	150
571	Bill Mazeroski AS	5	8	12	40	50	60	120	300
572	Brooks Robinson AS	6	10	15	25	60	80	150	400
573	Ken Boyer AS	8	8	12	30	40	50	60	120
574	Luis Aparicio AS	6	8	12	20	30	60	80	150
575	Ernie Banks AS	8	12	30	60	80	100	200	600
576	Roger Maris AS	25	30	60	80	120	200	250	600
577	Hank Aaron AS	20	25	▼50	▲100	120	200	300	500
578	Mickey Mantle AS	150	200	250	300	400	500	800	2,000
579	Willie Mays AS	20	30	50	80	120	200	300	1,200
580	Al Kaline AS	6	10	15	40	50	80	150	400
581	Frank Robinson AS	25	30	40	50	60	80	150	400
582	Earl Battey AS	5	5	8	25	30	40	60	120
583	Del Crandall AS	5	5	8	12	20	40	80	200

		GD 2	VG 3	VgEx 4	EX 5	ExMt 6	NM 7	NmMt 8	MT 9
84	Jim Perry AS	5	5	8	12	25	40	80	200
85	Bob Friend AS	5	6	8	12	25	40	80	200
86	Whitey Ford AS	8	12	20	40	60	80	120	500
89	Warren Spahn AS	6	10	15	40	80	100	200	500

–AL Home Run Leaders #44 PSA 10 (Gem) sold for $5,251 (Mastro; 4/07)
–AL Strikeout Leaders #50 PSA 10 (Gem) sold for $1,227 (Mile High; 2/08)
–Hank Aaron AS #577 PSA 10 (Gem) sold for $7,691 (Mastro; 8/07)
–Ernie Banks #350 PSA 10 (Gem) sold for $2,244 (Mastro; 6/04)
–Ernie Banks AS #575 PSA 10 (Gem) sold for $1,433 (Mastro; 12/05)
–Yogi Berra #425 BVG 8.5 (NmMt+) sold for $229 (eBay; 6/07)
–Roy Campanella MVP #480 PSA 9 (MT) sold for $625 (Memory Lane; 12/06)
–Bob Cerv #563 PSA 9 (MT) sold for $2,424 (eBay; 4/08)
–Roberto Clemente #387 PSA 10 (Gem) sold for $12,773 (Goodwin; 3/08)
–Roberto Clemente #387 PSA 10 (Gem) sold for $7,938 (Mile High; 5/04)
–Willie Davis #506 PSA 9 (MT) sold for $506 (eBay; 2/07)
–Don Drysdale #260 PSA 10 (Gem) sold for $3,472 (Mile High; 1/07)
–Don Drysdale #260 PSA 10 (Gem) sold for $2,669 (Mastro; 4/04)
–Whitey Ford #160 PSA 9 (MT) sold for $3,518 (Mile High; 05/11)
–Lou Gehrig Streak #405 PSA 10 (Gem) sold for $2,397 (Leland's; 2/05)
–Jim Gentile #559 PSA 9 (MT) sold for $2,035 (Memory Lane; 2/07)
–Jim Gentile #559 PSA 9 (MT) sold for $1,429 (eBay; 2/08)
–Dick Groat #1 PSA 10 (Gem) sold for $4,915 (Mastro; 8/07)
–Ralph Houk #133 PSA 9 (MT) sold for $589 (eBay; 9/04)
–Al Kaline #429 PSA 9 (MT) sold for $4,053 (Madec; 11/07)
–Al Kaline #429 PSA 9 (MT) sold for $1,737 (Memory Lane; 9/07)
–Al Kaline #429 PSA 9 (MT) sold for $671 (eBay; 4/05)
–Mickey Mantle 565 HR #406 PSA 10 (Gem) sold for $4,365 (Memory Lane; 10/05)
–Mickey Mantle AS #578 PSA 10 (Gem) sold for $15,799 (Memory Lane; 5/08)
–Mickey Mantle AS #578 PSA 10 (Gem) sold for $10,572 (Memory Lane; 10/05)
–Juan Marichal #417 PSA 10 (Gem) sold for $4,591 (Memory Lane; 12/05)
–Juan Marichal #417 PSA 10 (Gem) sold for $3,686 (Memory Lane; 2/07)
–Juan Marichal #417 PSA 10 (Gem) sold for $3,028 (Superior; 3/04)
–Roger Maris #2 SGC 96 (MT) sold for $4,400 (eBay; 6/07)
–Billy Martin #89 PSA 9 (MT) sold for $434 (Madec; 5/07)
–Juan Marichal SP #417 PSA 10 (Gem) (Young Collection) sold for $7,691 (SCP; 5/12)
–Willie Mays AS #150 PSA 10 (Gem) sold for $15,140 (eBay; 10/08)
–Bill Mazeroski WS7 #312 PSA 10 (Gem) sold for $2,426 (Mastro; 12/04)
–Bill Mazeroski WS7 #312 PSA 9 (MT) sold for $756 (eBay; 3/05)
–Bill Mazeroski WS7 #312 PSA 9 (MT) sold for $718 (eBay; 8/07)
–Bill Mazeroski WS7 #312 PSA 9 (MT) sold for $650 (eBay; 2/07)
–Stan Musial #290 PSA 10 (Gem) sold for $4,096 (Mastro; 6/05)
–Stan Musial #290 PSA 10 (Gem) sold for $2,704 (Memory Lane; 12/06)
–NL Batting Leaders #41 PSA 10 (Gem) sold for $11,065 (Mastro; 4/07)
–NL Strikeout Leaders #49 PSA 9 (MT) sold for $890 (eBay; 4/07)
–NL Strikeout Leaders #49 PSA 9 (MT) sold for $595 (eBay; 4/08)
–NL Strikeout Leaders #49 PSA 9 (MT) sold for $328 (eBay; 1/08)
–Pittsburgh Pirates TC #554 PSA 9 (MT) sold for $2,102 (Memory Lane; 9/07)
–Pittsburgh Pirates TC #554 PSA 9 (MT) sold for $1,140 (eBay; 3/04)
–Phil Rizzuto MVP #471 PSA 9 (MT) sold for $1,707 (eBay; 2/08)
–Phil Rizzuto MVP #471 PSA 9 (MT) sold for $1,186 (Mile High; 1/07)
–Phil Rizzuto MVP #471 PSA 9 (MT) sold for $568 (Memory Lane; 9/07)
–Phil Rizzuto MVP #471 PSA 9 (MT) sold for $458 (eBay; 12/06)
–Brooks Robinson AS #572 PSA 10 (Gem) sold for $2,592 (Memory Lane; 12/05)
–Ron Santo #35 PSA 10 (Gem) (Young Collection) sold for $5,948 (SCP; 5/12)
–Rollie Sheldon #541 SGC 96 (MT) sold for $777 (Heritage; 10/05)
–Rollie Sheldon #541 PSA 9 (MT) sold for $689 (eBay; 4/08)
–Duke Snider #443 PSA 10 (Gem) sold for $1,655 (Mastro; 12/04)
–Warren Spahn #200 PSA 9 (MT) sold for $532 (eBay; 8/07)
–Ralph Terry #389 PSA 9 (MT) sold for $899 (eBay; 12/07)
–Ralph Terry #389 PSA 9 (MT) sold for $787 (eBay; 1/05)
–Billy Williams #141 PSA 10 (Gem) (Young Collection) sold for $6,738 (SCP; 5/12)

1962 Topps

		GD 2	VG 3	VgEx 4	EX 5	ExMt 6	NM 7	NmMt 8	MT 9
1	Roger Maris	50	60	▲100	120	250	600	3,000	
2	Jim Brosnan	5	5	5	8	15	30	100	
3	Pete Runnels	5	5	6	10	15	25	450	
4	John DeMerit	5	5	5	5	6	12	25	
5	Sandy Koufax	30	40	50	80	120	300	1,500	
6	Marv Breeding	5	5	5	5	6	25	300	
7	Frank Thomas	5	5	5	5	6	15	60	
8	Ray Herbert	5	5	5	5	6	20	60	
9	Jim Davenport	5	5	5	5	6	15	40	
10	Roberto Clemente	40	50	60	100	120	300	▲1,500	5,000
11	Tom Morgan	5	5	5	5	6	12	25	
12	Harry Craft MG	5	5	5	5	6	15	80	
13	Dick Howser	5	5	5	5	6	12	30	
14	Bill White	5	5	5	5	8	15	120	
15	Dick Donovan	5	5	5	5	6	12	25	
16	Darrell Johnson	5	5	5	5	6	12	25	
17	Johnny Callison	5	5	5	5	8	15	150	
18	Managers Dream	50	60	▲100	▲120	150	300	1,200	
19	Ray Washburn RC	5	5	5	5	6	12	25	
20	Rocky Colavito	5	6	8	12	20	30	60	
21	Jim Kaat	5	5	6	8	12	20	40	200
22A	Checklist 1 ERR 121-176	5	5	5	5	6	12	25	150
22B	Checklist 1 COR 33-88	5	5	5	8	12	25	100	
23	Norm Larker	5	5	5	5	6	12	20	80
24	Detroit Tigers TC	5	5	5	5	8	15	30	300
25	Ernie Banks	8	15	30	50	60	▲150	400	4,000
26	Chris Cannizzaro	8	12	25	5	6	12	30	
27	Chuck Cottier	5	5	5	5	6	12	25	
28	Minnie Minoso	5	5	5	6	20	30	80	
29	Casey Stengel MG	5	5	6	8	20	40	80	
30	Eddie Mathews	12	15	10	25	40	60	300	
31	Tom Tresh RC	5	5	6	10	20	30	80	400
32	John Roseboro	5	5	5	5	8	15	80	
33	Don Larsen	5	5	5	5	8	15	30	200
34	Johnny Temple	5	5	5	5	6	12	25	200
35	Don Schwall RC	5	5	5	5	8	20	50	400
36	Don Leppert RC	5	5	5	5	6	12	25	
37	Tribe Hill Trio	5	5	5	5	8	15	30	
38	Gene Stephens	5	5	5	5	6	12	80	
39	Joe Koppe	5	5	5	5	6	12	▼25	200
40	Orlando Cepeda	5	5	8	12	25	100	300	
41	Cliff Cook	5	5	5	5	6	12	25	
42	Jim King	5	5	5	5	6	12	25	
43	Los Angeles Dodgers TC	5	5	5	6	10	20	40	325
44	Don Taussig RC	5	5	5	5	6	12	25	250
45	Brooks Robinson	8	15	20	30	▼50	80	▼300	
46	Jack Baldschun RC	5	5	5	6	8	15	30	
47	Bob Will	5	5	5	5	6	12	25	
48	Ralph Terry	5	5	5	6	10	25	50	
49	Hal Jones RC	5	5	5	5	6	12	25	
50	Stan Musial	20	30	40	60	80	120	▼250	2,000
51	AL Batting Leaders	5	5	5	5	8	20	60	
52	NL Batting Leaders	5	12	15	20	25	50	80	500
53	AL Home Run Leaders	10	30	40	▲60	▲80	120	400	800
54	NL Home Run Leaders	5	5	6	20	25	40	80	600
55	AL ERA Leaders	5	5	5	5	8	15	30	200
56	NL ERA Leaders	5	5	5	5	8	15	40	300
57	AL Win Leaders	5	5	6	10	15	25	50	300
58	NL Win Leaders	5	5	5	6	10	25	80	
59	AL Strikout Leaders	5	5	5	5	8	20	30	250
60	NL Strikeout Leaders	5	5	6	8	30	40	100	575
61	St. Louis Cardinals TC	5	5	5	5	8	15	40	250
62	Steve Boros	5	5	5	5	6	12	25	
63	Tony Cloninger RC	5	5	5	5	6	12	25	350
64	Russ Snyder	5	5	5	5	6	12	25	250
65	Bobby Richardson	5	5	5	12	15	50	120	
66	Cuno Barragan RC	5	5	5	5	6	12	25	150
67	Harvey Haddix	5	5	5	5	8	15	30	
68	Ken Hunt	5	5	5	5	6	12	30	
69	Phil Ortega RC	5	5	5	5	6	12	25	150
70	Harmon Killebrew	5	8	20	▲30	▲40	80	400	4,000
71	Dick LeMay RC	5	5	5	5	6	12	25	200
72	Bob's Pupils	5	5	5	5	6	12	30	300
73	Nellie Fox	5	5	12	15	25	50	250	500
74	Bob Lillis	5	5	5	5	6	12	25	
75	Milt Pappas	5	5	5	5	6	20	80	
76	Howie Bedell	5	5	5	5	6	12	25	
77	Tony Taylor	5	5	5	5	6	25	60	
78	Gene Green	5	5	5	5	6	12	50	150
79	Ed Hobaugh	5	5	5	5	6	12	25	200
80	Vada Pinson	5	5	5	5	8	▲20	50	250
81	Jim Pagliaroni	5	5	5	5	6	12	25	
82	Deron Johnson	5	5	5	5	6	15	25	200
83	Larry Jackson	5	5	5	5	6	12	40	
84	Lenny Green	5	5	5	5	6	20	100	
85	Gil Hodges	5	5	5	10	20	30	100	
86	Donn Clendenon RC	5	5	5	5	8	15	40	250
87	Mike Roarke	5	5	5	5	6	12	30	
88	Ralph Houk MG	5	5	5	5	8	15	60	

#	Player	GD 2	VG 3	VgEx 4	EX 5	ExMt 6	NM 7	NmMt 8	MT 9
89	Barney Schultz RC	5	5	5	5	6	12	25	175
90	Jimmy Piersall	5	5	5	5	8	20	30	
91	J.C. Martin	5	5	5	5	6	12	200	
92	Sam Jones	5	5	5	5	6	25	30	
93	John Blanchard	5	5	5	5	8	▲50	▲500	
94	Jay Hook	5	5	5	5	6	12	25	250
95	Don Hoak	5	5	5	5	6	15	50	
96	Eli Grba	5	5	5	5	6	12	25	
97	Tito Francona	5	5	5	5	6	12	40	
98	Checklist 2	5	5	5	5	6	12	25	100
99	Boog Powell RC	5	6	20	25	30	50	120	
100	Warren Spahn	12	15	20	▲30	40	100	400	
101	Carroll Hardy	5	5	5	5	6	12	25	150
102	Al Schroll	5	5	5	5	6	12	25	
103	Don Blasingame	5	5	5	5	6	12	80	
104	Ted Savage RC	5	5	5	6	10	15	30	120
105	Don Mossi	5	5	5	5	6	15	25	
106	Carl Sawatski	5	5	5	6	10	15	25	150
107	Mike McCormick	5	5	5	5	6	20	30	
108	Willie Davis	5	5	5	5	8	20	30	
109	Bob Shaw	5	5	5	5	6	12	30	
110	Bill Skowron	5	5	5	6	10	40	▲200	500
111	Dallas Green	5	5	5	5	8	30	135	
112	Hank Foiles	5	5	5	5	6	12	30	
113	Chicago White Sox TC	5	5	5	5	8	15	50	200
114	Howie Koplitz RC	5	5	5	5	6	12	30	200
115	Bob Skinner	5	5	5	5	10	50	▲200	
116	Herb Score	5	5	5	5	8	40	▼10	
117	Gary Geiger	5	5	5	5	6	15	120	
118	Julian Javier	5	5	5	6	12	60	300	
119	Danny Murphy	5	5	5	5	6	12	30	200
120	Bob Purkey	5	5	5	5	6	25	200	
121	Billy Hitchcock MG	5	5	5	5	6	15	40	
122	Norm Bass RC	5	5	5	5	6	20	30	
123	Mike de la Hoz	5	5	5	5	6	12	40	
124	Bill Pleis RC	5	5	5	5	6	12	30	
125	Gene Woodling	5	5	5	5	6	12	▲30	
126	Al Cicotte	5	5	5	5	6	12	30	200
127	Pride of A's	5	5	5	5	8	15	40	200
128	Art Fowler	5	5	5	5	6	12	40	
129A	Lee Walls Face Right, Plain Jsy	5	5	5	5	6	15	80	
129B	Lee Walls Face Left, Striped Jsy	5	5	5	8	12	30	100	
130	Frank Bolling	5	5	5	5	6	30	250	
131	Pete Richert RC	5	5	5	5	6	10	40	
132A	Los Angeles Angels TC No Inset	5	5	5	5	8	15	40	
132B	Los Angeles Angels TC With Inset	5	5	6	10	15	25	60	
133	Felipe Alou	5	5	5	5	8	15	50	300
134A	Billy Hoeft Blue Sky	5	5	6	10	15	60		
135	Babe as a Boy	5	5	8	12	25	50	250	800
136	Babe Joins Yanks	5	5	6	10	30	50	100	
137	Babe with Mgr. Huggins	5	5	15	20	25	30	▲100	800
138	The Famous Slugger	5	5	6	10	40	50	120	800
139A1	Babe Hits 60 (Pole)	5	6	10	30	50	100		
139A2	Babe Hits 60 (No Pole)	5	6	10	30	50	80		1,000
139B	Hal Reniff Portrait	5	5	5	8	15	50	250	
139C	Hal Reniff Pitching	6	10	15	25	40	100	400	
140	Gehrig and Ruth	5	8	12	40	50	80	250	800
141	Twilight Years	10	12	15	25	30	40	120	600
142	Coaching the Dodgers	5	5	8	15	40	50	120	800
143	Greatest Sports Hero	5	15	20	25	30	40	100	600
144	Farewell Speech	5	5	8	25	30	60	150	800
145	Barry Latman	5	5	5	5	8	15	30	150
146	Don Demeter	5	5	5	5	6	12	25	
147A	Bill Kunkel Portrait	5	5	5	8	12	20	100	
147B	Bill Kunkel Pitching	5	5	5	10	15	25	100	
148	Wally Post	5	5	5	5	12	20	60	400
149	Bob Duliba	5	5	5	5	6	12	25	200
150	Al Kaline	10	20	25	30	50	80	400	2,700
151	Johnny Klippstein	5	5	5	5	6	12	30	150
152	Mickey Vernon MG	5	5	5	6	10	15	30	150
153	Pumpsie Green	5	5	5	5	8	15	30	225
154	Lee Thomas	5	5	5	5	6	25	60	
155	Stu Miller	5	5	5	5	6	12	40	150
156	Merritt Ranew RC	5	5	5	5	6	20	40	150
157	Wes Covington	5	5	5	5	8	15	30	
158	Milwaukee Braves TC	5	5	5	5	8	15	30	200
159	Hal Reniff RC	5	5	5	6	12	40	200	

#	Player	GD 2	VG 3	VgEx 4	EX 5	ExMt 6	NM 7	NmMt 8	M
160	Dick Stuart	5	5	5	5	8	30	200	
161	Frank Baumann	5	5	5	5	6	25	30	
162	Sammy Drake RC	5	5	5	5	8	15	40	2
163	Hot Corner Guardians	5	5	5	8	12	20	80	3
164	Hal Naragon	5	5	5	5	6	12	25	1
165	Jackie Brandt	5	5	5	5	6	15	50	
166	Don Lee	5	5	5	5	6	12	50	4
167	Tim McCarver RC	5	5	20	25	▲40	50	150	6
168	Leo Posada	5	5	5	5	6	12	25	
169	Bob Cerv	5	5	5	5	6	10	40	120
170	Ron Santo	5	5	15	25	30	60	200	9
171	Dave Sisler	5	5	5	5	8	15	40	
172	Fred Hutchinson MG	5	5	5	5	6	12	30	15
173	Chico Fernandez	5	5	5	5	6	12	100	
174A	Carl Willey w/o Cap	5	5	5	8	12	30	175	
174B	Carl Willey w/Cap	5	6	10	15	25	60	150	
175	Frank Howard	5	5	5	5	20	25	80	
176A	Eddie Yost Portrait	5	5	5	5	6	15	100	
176B	Eddie Yost Batting	5	5	8	12	20	40	150	
177	Bobby Shantz	5	5	5	5	8	15	40	
178	Camilo Carreon	5	5	5	5	6	12	40	
179	Tom Sturdivant	5	5	5	5	6	12	40	
180	Bob Allison	5	5	5	5	8	30	60	25
181	Paul Brown RC	5	5	5	5	6	12	25	10
182	Bob Nieman	5	5	5	5	6	15	150	
183	Roger Craig	5	5	5	5	8	15	30	20
184	Haywood Sullivan	5	5	5	5	6	12	40	15
185	Roland Sheldon	5	5	5	5	8	15	50	
186	Mack Jones RC	5	5	5	5	6	12	80	
187	Gene Conley	5	5	5	5	8	15	30	20
188	Chuck Hiller	5	5	5	5	6	10	15	25
189	Dick Hall	5	5	5	5	6	12	80	
190A	Wally Moon No Cap	5	5	5	5	8	30	200	
190B	Wally Moon w/Cap	5	5	6	10	15	50	250	
191	Jim Brewer	5	5	5	8	12	20	40	
192A	Checklist 3 192 No Comma	5	5	5	5	6	12	30	
192B	Checklist 3 192 with Comma	5	5	5	5	6	12	40	15
193	Eddie Kasko	5	5	5	5	6	12	30	
194	Dean Chance RC	5	5	5	6	10	50	200	
195	Joe Cunningham	5	5	5	5	6	12	50	
196	Terry Fox	5	5	5	5	6	15	120	
197	Daryl Spencer	5	5	5	5	6	15	60	300
198	Johnny Keane MG	5	5	5	5	6	12	30	
199	Gaylord Perry RC	25	40	50	60	100	▲250	1,000	
200	Mickey Mantle	▲150	200	250	▲500	▲800	1,500	8,000	20,000
201	Ike Delock	5	5	5	5	6	12	60	
202	Carl Warwick RC	5	5	5	5	6	12	25	150
203	Jack Fisher	5	5	5	5	6	12	25	
204	Johnny Weekly RC	5	5	5	5	6	12	25	200
205	Gene Freese	5	5	5	5	6	12	30	
206	Washington Senators TC	5	5	5	5	8	25	30	200
207	Pete Burnside	5	5	5	5	6	15	120	
208	Billy Martin	5	5	8	12	30	40	120	
209	Jim Fregosi RC	5	5	5	8	12	▲50	▲100	1,000
210	Roy Face	5	5	5	5	8	25	80	
211	Midway Masters	5	5	5	5	8	15	40	250
212	Jim Owens	5	5	5	5	6	12	30	
213	Richie Ashburn	5	5	5	10	15	30	100	300
214	Dom Zanni	5	5	5	5	6	15	40	
215	Woody Held	5	5	5	5	6	12	40	
216	Ron Kline	5	5	5	5	6	12	40	200
217	Walter Alston MG	5	5	5	5	8	25	50	
218	Joe Torre RC	15	20	▲50	▲60	100	250	600	
219	Al Downing RC	5	5	8	12	20	40	80	
220	Roy Sievers	5	5	5	5	6	12	30	
221	Bill Short	5	5	5	5	6	15	200	
222	Jerry Zimmerman	5	5	5	5	6	12	25	
223	Alex Grammas	5	5	5	5	6	12	50	
224	Don Rudolph	5	5	5	5	6	15	60	
225	Frank Malzone	5	5	5	5	8	15	100	
226	San Francisco Giants TC	5	5	5	5	8	15	50	300
227	Bob Tiefenauer	5	5	5	5	6	12	25	200
228	Dale Long	5	5	5	5	6	12	40	
229	Jesus McFarlane RC	5	5	5	5	6	12	30	
230	Camilo Pascual	5	5	5	5	6	15	60	
231	Ernie Bowman RC	5	5	5	5	6	12	25	
232	Yanks Win Opener WS1	5	5	5	6	10	25	60	300

#		GD 2	VG 3	VgEx 4	EX 5	ExMt 6	NM 7	NmMt 8	MT 9
233	Joey Jay WS2	5	8	12	20	30	60	200	
234	Roger Maris WS3	5	5	8	30	40	60	150	400
235	Whitey Ford WS4	5	5	5	6	25	60	80	
236	Yanks Crush Reds WS5	5	6	10	15	25	40	250	
237	Yanks Celebrate WS	5	5	6	8	12	40	100	400
238	Norm Sherry	5	5	5	5	6	12	25	
239	Cecil Butler RC	5	5	5	5	6	12	25	
240	George Altman	5	5	5	5	6	12	40	
241	Johnny Kucks	5	5	5	5	6	12	40	
242	Mel McGaha MG RC	5	5	5	5	6	12	30	
243	Robin Roberts	5	5	6	10	25	40	100	900
244	Don Gile	5	5	5	5	6	12	25	200
245	Ron Hansen	5	5	5	5	6	12	25	150
246	Art Ditmar	5	5	5	5	6	12	25	
247	Joe Pignatano	5	5	5	5	8	15	30	200
248	Bob Aspromonte	5	5	5	5	6	12	25	200
249	Ed Keegan	5	5	5	5	6	12	30	
250	Norm Cash	5	5	5	6	10	25	60	
251	New York Yankees TC	5	8	12	30	50	60	200	700
252	Earl Francis	5	5	5	5	6	12	60	200
253	Harry Chiti CO	5	5	5	5	6	12	25	
254	Gordon Windhorn RC	5	5	5	5	6	12	50	250
255	Juan Pizarro	5	5	5	5	6	10	30	
256	Elio Chacon	5	5	5	5	6	15	60	
257	Jack Spring RC	5	5	5	5	6	12	25	200
258	Marty Keough	5	5	5	5	6	10	25	150
259	Lou Klimchock	5	5	5	5	6	12	30	150
260	Billy Pierce	5	5	5	5	6	12	40	
261	George Alusik RC	5	5	5	5	6	12	25	
262	Bob Schmidt	5	5	5	5	6	12	25	150
263	The Right Pitch	5	5	5	5	6	12	40	200
264	Dick Ellsworth	5	5	5	5	6	10	20	
265	Joe Adcock	5	5	5	5	8	20	150	
266	John Anderson RC	5	5	5	5	6	20	80	150
267	Dan Dobbek	5	5	5	5	6	10	20	
268	Ken McBride	5	5	5	5	6	12	30	
269	Bob Oldis	5	5	5	5	6	12	25	200
270	Dick Groat	5	5	5	5	8	15	60	250
271	Ray Rippelmeyer	5	5	5	5	6	12	30	
272	Earl Robinson	5	5	5	5	6	12	30	
273	Gary Bell	5	5	5	5	6	12	40	
274	Sammy Taylor	5	5	5	5	6	12	25	
275	Norm Siebern	5	5	5	5	6	12	40	250
276	Hal Kolstad RC	5	5	5	5	6	12	25	200
277	Checklist 4	5	5	5	5	15	20	25	
278	Ken Johnson	5	5	5	5	6	12	50	
279	Hobie Landrith	5	5	5	5	6	12	25	
280	Johnny Podres	5	5	5	5	8	20	80	
281	Jake Gibbs RC	5	5	6	8	12	25	60	
282	Dave Hillman	5	5	5	5	6	12	25	200
283	Charlie Smith RC	5	5	5	5	6	15	30	
284	Ruben Amaro	5	5	5	5	6	20	250	
285	Curt Simmons	5	5	5	5	8	30	200	
286	Al Lopez MG	5	5	5	5	8	25	50	250
287	George Witt	5	5	6	10	15	100		
288	Billy Williams	5	6	▲20	▲40	50	▲150	800	
289	Mike Krsnich RC	5	5	5	6	8	15	50	
290	Jim Gentile	5	5	5	5	8	30	300	
291	Hal Stowe RC	5	5	5	8	12	20	200	
292	Jerry Kindall	5	5	5	5	6	12	40	250
293	Bob Miller	5	5	5	5	6	15	60	
294	Philadelphia Phillies TC	5	5	5	5	8	15	30	
295	Vern Law	5	5	5	5	8	50	400	
296	Ken Hamlin	5	5	5	5	6	15	80	
297	Ron Perranoski	5	5	5	5	6	25	200	
298	Bill Tuttle	5	5	5	5	6	30	300	
299	Don Wert RC	5	5	5	5	6	40	300	
300	Willie Mays	▲50	▲60	▲80	120	250	1,000	2,000	6,000
301	Galen Cisco RC	5	5	5	5	8	25	400	
302	Johnny Edwards RC	5	5	5	5	6	15	60	
303	Frank Torre	5	5	5	5	6	25	50	
304	Dick Farrell	5	5	5	5	6	25	40	
305	Jerry Lumpe	5	5	5	5	6	12	80	
306	Redbird Rippers	5	5	5	5	6	15	80	
307	Jim Grant	5	5	5	5	6	25	60	
308	Neil Chrisley	5	5	5	5	6	15	80	300
309	Moe Morhardt RC	5	5	5	5	6	15	60	

#		GD 2	VG 3	VgEx 4	EX 5	ExMt 6	NM 7	NmMt 8	MT 9
310	Whitey Ford	15	25	30	40	50	100	400	1,800
311	Tony Kubek IA	5	5	5	8	20	50	150	
312	Warren Spahn IA	5	5	5	8	20	50	100	
313	Roger Maris IA	8	12	20	40	60	100	300	
314	Rocky Colavito IA	5	5	5	5	25	30	60	
315	Whitey Ford IA	5	6	10	15	30	40	80	500
316	Harmon Killebrew IA	5	5	15	20	25	50	150	
317	Stan Musial IA	5	6	10	15	25	50	120	400
318	Mickey Mantle IA	30	40	60	80	100	250	1,200	3,000
319	Mike McCormick IA	5	5	5	5	6	12	50	
320	Hank Aaron	25	50	▲80	100	150	400	1,500	10,000
321	Lee Stange RC	5	5	5	5	8	15	40	
322	Alvin Dark MG	5	5	5	5	6	15	100	
323	Don Landrum	5	5	5	5	8	60		
324	Joe McClain	5	5	5	5	6	15	80	
325	Luis Aparicio	5	5	5	8	25	40	400	
326	Tom Parsons RC	5	5	5	5	8	15	80	
327	Ozzie Virgil	5	5	5	5	6	15	40	
328	Ken Walters	5	5	5	5	6	12	25	200
329	Bob Bolin	5	5	5	5	6	15	300	
330	John Romano	5	5	5	5	6	25	60	
331	Moe Drabowsky	5	5	5	5	8	15	100	400
332	Don Buddin	5	5	5	5	6	15	80	
333	Frank Cipriani RC	5	5	5	5	6	12	30	
334	Boston Red Sox TC	5	5	5	8	20	30	60	
335	Bill Bruton	5	5	5	5	8	25	60	
336	Billy Muffett	5	5	5	5	6	30	120	
337	Jim Marshall	5	5	5	5	8	40	300	
338	Billy Gardner	5	5	5	5	6	15	60	250
339	Jose Valdivielso	5	5	5	5	6	12	60	200
340	Don Drysdale	5	15	▲25	▲30	▼40	▼60	400	1,000
341	Mike Hershberger RC	5	5	5	5	6	15	30	250
342	Ed Rakow	5	5	5	5	6	12	60	
343	Albie Pearson	5	5	5	5	8	25	200	
344	Ed Bauta RC	5	5	5	5	6	15	60	
345	Chuck Schilling	5	5	5	5	6	15	50	300
346	Jack Kralick	5	5	5	5	6	12	25	
347	Chuck Hinton RC	5	5	5	5	6	12	30	
348	Larry Burright RC	5	5	5	5	6	15	120	
349	Paul Foytack	5	5	5	8	12	100		
350	Frank Robinson	6	10	20	▲40	▲80	▲300	3,000	
351	Braves Backstops	5	5	5	5	6	30	100	
352	Frank Sullivan	5	5	5	5	6	30	150	
353	Bill Mazeroski	5	5	8	25	40	50	400	
354	Roman Mejias	5	5	5	5	6	12	40	150
355	Steve Barber	5	5	5	5	6	15	100	
356	Tom Haller RC	5	5	5	5	6	15	120	
357	Jerry Walker	5	5	5	5	6	12	30	
358	Tommy Davis	5	5	5	5	8	25	50	200
359	Bobby Locke	5	5	5	5	6	30	250	
360	Yogi Berra	15	40	50	60	80	▲150	▼400	1,500
361	Bob Hendley	5	5	5	5	6	15	150	
362	Ty Cline	5	5	5	5	6	15	60	
363	Bob Roselli	5	5	5	5	6	15	40	
364	Ken Hunt	5	5	5	5	6	12	40	
365	Charlie Neal	5	5	5	5	8	40	250	
366	Phil Regan	5	5	5	5	6	12	40	
367	Checklist 5	5	5	5	5	6	25	30	300
368	Bob Tillman RC	5	5	5	5	6	12	25	
369	Ted Bowsfield	5	5	5	5	6	12	30	
370	Ken Boyer	5	5	5	8	12	50	200	
371	Earl Battey	5	5	5	5	6	15	100	
372	Jack Curtis	5	5	5	5	6	12	25	200
373	Al Heist	5	5	5	5	6	12	25	325
374	Gene Mauch MG	5	5	5	5	6	25	60	200
375	Ron Fairly	5	5	5	5	8	25	30	300
376	Bud Daley	5	5	5	5	8	12	40	
377	John Orsino RC	5	5	5	5	6	12	25	
378	Bennie Daniels	5	5	5	5	6	12	30	
379	Chuck Essegian	5	5	5	5	6	12	25	250
380	Lew Burdette	5	5	5	5	8	20	80	200
381	Chico Cardenas	5	5	5	5	6	12	40	
382	Dick Williams	5	5	5	5	6	25	40	
383	Ray Sadecki	5	5	5	5	8	15	30	250
384	Kansas City Athletics TC	5	5	5	6	10	▼15	▼20	▼60
385	Early Wynn	5	5	5	5	6	12	25	400
386	Don Mincher	5	5	5	5	6	12	25	

#	Player	GD 2	VG 3	VgEx 4	EX 5	ExMt 6	NM 7	NmMt 8	MT 9
387	Lou Brock RC	50	▲100	▲120	150	250	500	▲2,000	15,000
388	Ryne Duren	5	5	5	5	8	15	150	
389	Smoky Burgess	5	5	5	5	8	25	80	
390	Orlando Cepeda AS	5	5	5	5	20	30	80	
391	Bill Mazeroski AS	5	5	5	15	25	50		200
392	Ken Boyer AS	5	5	5	5	8	15	120	
393	Roy McMillan AS	5	5	5	5	6	12	40	
394	Hank Aaron AS	6	15	30	40	60	80	300	
395	Willie Mays AS	5	8	30	40	50	80	200	800
396	Frank Robinson AS	5	5	5	6	25	40	100	1,200
397	John Roseboro AS	5	5	5	5	6	12	25	200
398	Don Drysdale AS	5	5	10	12	15	30	60	300
399	Warren Spahn AS	5	5	12	15	20	40	60	300
400	Elston Howard	5	6	10	15	30	80	150	
401	AL and NL Homer Kings	6	10	25	30	40	100	250	1,000
402	Gino Cimoli	5	5	5	5	6	12	30	
403	Chet Nichols	5	5	5	5	6	12	25	150
404	Tim Harkness RC	5	5	5	5	6	12	30	250
405	Jim Perry	5	5	5	5	6	15	100	
406	Bob Taylor	5	5	5	5	6	12	40	200
407	Hank Aguirre	5	5	5	5	6	12	30	
408	Gus Bell	5	5	5	5	6	25	50	
409	Pittsburgh Pirates TC	5	5	5	5	8	15	30	200
410	Al Smith	5	5	5	5	6	12	40	
411	Danny O'Connell	5	5	5	5	6	12	25	200
412	Charlie James	5	5	5	5	6	12	25	
413	Matty Alou	5	5	5	5	8	30	120	
414	Joe Gaines RC	5	5	5	5	6	12	25	150
415	Bill Virdon	5	5	5	5	6	12	50	
416	Bob Scheffing MG	5	5	5	5	6	12	30	200
417	Joe Azcue RC	5	5	5	5	6	12	40	
418	Andy Carey	5	5	5	5	6	12	25	
419	Bob Bruce	5	5	5	5	6	12	25	
420	Gus Triandos	5	5	5	5	6	15	120	
421	Ken MacKenzie	5	5	5	5	6	12	25	
422	Steve Bilko	5	5	5	5	6	12	30	200
423	Rival League Relief Aces	5	5	5	5	8	15	50	
424	Al McBean RC	5	5	5	5	6	12	30	300
425	Carl Yastrzemski	15	25	50	60	100	200	▼600	1,200
426	Bob Farley RC	5	5	5	5	8	20	40	200
427	Jake Wood	5	5	5	5	6	12	30	200
428	Joe Hicks	5	5	5	5	6	12	40	
429	Billy O'Dell	5	5	5	5	6	15	40	
430	Tony Kubek	5	6	10	15	20	60	250	
431	Bob Rodgers RC	5	5	5	5	6	25	40	200
432	Jim Pendleton	5	5	5	5	6	12	25	
433	Jim Archer	5	5	5	5	6	12	25	
434	Clay Dalrymple	5	5	5	5	6	15	50	
435	Larry Sherry	5	5	5	5	8	30	250	
436	Felix Mantilla	5	5	5	5	6	20	25	
437	Ray Moore	5	5	5	5	6	12	30	250
438	Dick Brown	5	5	5	5	6	12	25	250
439	Jerry Buchek RC	5	5	5	5	6	20	30	150
440	Joey Jay	5	5	5	5	6	12	25	250
441	Checklist 6	5	5	5	5	15	30	300	
442	Wes Stock	5	5	5	5	6	12	25	
443	Del Crandall	5	5	5	5	8	15	30	200
444	Ted Wills	5	5	5	5	6	12	25	
445	Vic Power	5	5	5	5	8	25	80	
446	Don Elston	5	5	5	5	6	12	25	200
447	Willie Kirkland	5	5	5	5	8	15	30	
448	Joe Gibbon	5	5	5	5	8	15	25	
449	Jerry Adair	5	5	5	5	8	15	50	▲300
450	Jim O'Toole	5	5	5	5	8	25	60	
451	Jose Tartabull RC	5	5	5	5	15	20	30	350
452	Earl Averill Jr.	5	5	5	5	8	20	▼80	
453	Cal McLish	5	5	5	5	8	25	80	
454	Floyd Robinson RC	5	5	5	5	8	20	120	
455	Luis Arroyo	5	5	5	5	20	25	50	
456	Joe Amalfitano	5	5	5	5	8	15	30	
457	Lou Clinton	5	5	5	5	8	15	30	200
458A	Bob Buhl M on Cap	5	5	5	5	8	30	150	
458B	Bob Buhl Plain Cap	5	6	10	15	25	40	120	
459	Ed Bailey	5	5	5	5	10	25	120	200
460	Jim Bunning	5	6	8	12	20	60	100	
461	Ken Hubbs RC	5	5	6	10	15	▲30	▼80	600
462A	Willie Tasby W on Cap	5	5	5	5	8	30	150	

#	Player	GD 2	VG 3	VgEx 4	EX 5	ExMt 6	NM 7	NmMt 8	MT 9
462B	Willie Tasby Plain Cap	5	6	10	15	25	40	80	2
463	Hank Bauer MG	5	5	5	6	10	20	25	2
464	Al Jackson RC	5	5	5	5	8	50	300	
465	Cincinnati Reds TC	5	5	5	5	8	15	50	3
466	Norm Cash AS	5	5	5	6	15	30	120	
467	Chuck Schilling AS	5	5	5	5	8	30	40	2
468	Brooks Robinson AS	5	5	5	6	▲30	40	80	4
469	Luis Aparicio AS	5	5	5	6	15	25	50	3
470	Al Kaline AS	5	6	8	12	50	60	300	
471	Mickey Mantle AS	50	▲100	▲120	▲150	▲250	▲400	1,200	10,0
472	Rocky Colavito AS	5	5	5	6	20	25	50	4
473	Elston Howard AS	5	5	5	6	10	30	80	3
474	Frank Lary AS	5	5	5	5	8	25	60	3
475	Whitey Ford AS	5	8	12	20	40	50	100	
476	Baltimore Orioles TC	5	5	5	5	8	25	50	3
477	Andre Rodgers	5	5	5	5	8	15	40	
478	Don Zimmer	5	5	5	6	15	30	100	3
479	Joel Horlen RC	5	5	5	5	8	20	40	
480	Harvey Kuenn	5	5	5	5	8	20	40	10
481	Vic Wertz	5	5	5	5	8	15	30	20
482	Sam Mele MG	5	5	5	5	8	15	30	1
483	Don McMahon	5	5	5	5	8	15	40	
484	Dick Schofield	5	5	5	5	8	15	80	
485	Pedro Ramos	5	5	5	5	8	25	30	
486	Jim Gilliam	5	5	5	6	10	20	80	
487	Jerry Lynch	5	5	5	5	8	20	40	25
488	Hal Brown	5	5	5	5	8	25	60	
489	Julio Gotay RC	5	5	5	5	8	15	40	32
490	Clete Boyer	5	8	12	20	25	30	120	
491	Leon Wagner	5	5	5	6	10	25	50	
492	Hal W. Smith	5	5	5	5	12	20	30	15
493	Danny McDevitt	5	5	5	5	8	15	50	
494	Sammy White	5	5	5	5	8	15	50	
495	Don Cardwell	5	5	5	5	8	20	40	
496	Wayne Causey RC	5	5	5	5	8	15	40	15
497	Ed Bouchee	5	5	5	5	8	25	50	25
498	Jim Donohue	5	5	5	5	8	25	30	15
499	Zoilo Versalles	5	5	5	5	8	15	100	25
500	Duke Snider	6	10	25	30	50	100	300	1,20
501	Claude Osteen	5	5	5	5	15	20	30	20
502	Hector Lopez	5	5	5	6	10	20	80	25
503	Danny Murtaugh MG	5	5	5	5	12	20	40	
504	Eddie Bressoud	5	5	5	5	8	15	40	
505	Juan Marichal	5	8	15	25	40	80	150	
506	Charlie Maxwell	5	5	5	5	8	25	50	
507	Ernie Broglio	5	5	5	5	8	25	50	
508	Gordy Coleman	5	5	5	5	6	25	40	
509	Dave Giusti RC	5	5	5	5	8	25	50	
510	Jim Lemon	5	5	6	10	15	25	40	
511	Bubba Phillips	5	5	5	5	8	15	80	
512	Mike Fornieles	5	5	6	8	12	30	50	15
513	Whitey Herzog	5	5	5	10	12	25	50	300
514	Sherm Lollar	5	5	5	6	10	25	80	
515	Stan Williams	5	5	5	5	8	15	30	25
516A	Checklist 7 White Boxes	5	5	5	5	8	15	30	
516B	Checklist 7 Yellow Boxes	5	5	5	5	8			
517	Dave Wickersham	5	5	5	5	8	15	50	
518	Lee Maye	5	5	5	5	8	15	40	15
519	Bob Johnson RC	5	5	5	5	8	15	60	
520	Bob Friend	5	5	5	5	8	25	120	
521	Jacke Davis RC	5	5	5	5	8	25	50	20
522	Lindy McDaniel	5	5	5	5	8	15	30	
523	Russ Nixon SP	5	5	5	8	12	20	60	
524	Howie Nunn SP	5	5	5	8	12	40	60	
525	George Thomas	5	5	5	6	8	15	30	15
526	Hal Woodeshick SP	5	5	5	6	8	25	60	200
527	Dick McAuliffe RC	5	5	6	10	15	40	100	
528	Turk Lown	5	5	5	6	10	25	40	800
529	John Schaive SP	5	5	5	8	12	25	60	120
530	Bob Gibson SP	10	20	80	100	150	300	1,500	
531	Bobby G. Smith	5	5	5	5	10	18	40	
532	Dick Stigman	5	5	6	6	10	15	40	
533	Charley Lau SP	5	5	6	10	15	25	60	250
534	Tony Gonzalez SP	5	6	8	10	20	30	60	500
535	Ed Roebuck	5	5	6	8	20	25	40	250
536	Dick Gernert	5	5	6	8	12	20	50	300
537	Cleveland Indians TC	5	5	5	6	25	30	50	150

	GD 2	VG 3	VgEx 4	EX 5	ExMt 6	NM 7	NmMt 8	MT 9
Jack Sanford	5	5	5	6	8	20	40	150
Billy Moran	5	5	5	6	8	25	40	150
Jim Landis SP	5	5	6	8	12	30	50	
Don Nottebart SP	5	5	5	8	12	30	40	150
Dave Philley	5	5	5	6	8	20	50	
Bob Allen SP	5	5	5	8	25	30	60	200
Willie McCovey SP	12	20	60	▲100	▲150	200	500	1,000
Hoyt Wilhelm SP	8	10	15	30	50	100	300	
Moe Thacker SP	5	5	6	8	15	30	60	200
Don Ferrarese	5	5	6	8	12	20	40	200
Bobby Del Greco	5	5	6	8	12	20	30	200
Bill Rigney MG SP	5	5	5	8	12	30	80	
Art Mahaffey SP	5	5	6	10	15	40	60	250
Harry Bright	5	5	6	8	12	20	40	200
Chicago Cubs TC SP	5	6	8	12	40	50	100	400
Jim Coates	5	5	5	8	12	30	50	250
Bubba Morton SP RC	5	6	8	12	20	40	80	250
John Buzhardt SP	5	5	5	8	100	20	120	
Al Spangler	5	5	5	6	6	15	50	250
Bob Anderson SP	5	5	5	8	25	30	50	120
John Goryl	5	5	5	6	8	25	40	100
Mike Higgins MG	5	5	5	6	8	25	50	
Chuck Estrada SP	5	5	5	8	12	25	40	200
Gene Oliver SP	5	5	5	8	10	40	80	200
Bill Henry	5	5	5	6	8	20	40	120
Ken Aspromonte	5	5	5	6	6	15	30	80
Bob Grim	5	5	5	6	10	20	50	150
Jose Pagan	5	5	5	6	8	25	40	150
Marty Kutyna SP	5	5	5	8	10	30	50	200
Tracy Stallard SP	5	5	5	8	10	30	40	200
Jim Golden	5	5	5	6	10	20	60	150
Ed Sadowski SP	5	5	5	8	12	30	50	
Bill Stafford SP	5	5	6	25	40	50	150	
Billy Klaus SP	5	5	5	8	10	30	60	200
Bob G.Miller SP	5	5	5	8	12	25	60	350
Johnny Logan	5	5	5	6	10	20	40	250
Dean Stone	5	5	5	8	10	20	50	150
Red Schoendienst SP	8	12	20	40	50	80	150	
Russ Kemmerer SP	5	5	5	8	12	30	80	200
Dave Nicholson SP	5	5	5	8	12	40	60	300
Jim Duffalo RC	5	5	5	8	8	25	40	350
Jim Schaffer SP RC	5	5	5	8	12	25	120	
Bill Monbouquette	5	5	6	10	15	25	40	250
Mel Roach	5	5	5	6	8	20	40	
Ron Piche	5	6	8	10	12	25	40	150
Larry Osborne	5	6	8	10	12	25	40	150
Minnesota Twins TC SP	5	8	12	20	40	80	100	
Glen Hobbie SP	5	5	5	8	12	20	50	
Sammy Esposito SP	5	5	5	8	12	25	60	200
Frank Funk SP	5	5	5	8	12	30	60	200
Birdie Tebbetts MG	5	5	5	8	12	20	50	150
Bob Turley	5	5	8	12	40	50	80	300
Curt Flood	5	5	6	10	15	60	150	500
Sam McDowell SP RC	25	40	50	▲80	▲100	▲120	300	
Jim Bouton SP RC	8	12	20	▼60	▼80	▼100	▼120	500
Bob Veale SP RC	5	8	40	60	80	100	200	
Bob Uecker SP RC	8	12	20	150	▲250	300	500	
Rookie Infielders SP	5	8	12	20	50	80	120	250
Joe Pepitone SP RC	10	15	40	60	100	120	250	
Rookie Infielders SP	5	8	12	20	80	100	250	
Rookie Outfielders SP	15	25	▲60	▲80	100	250	1,200	

—Hank Aaron #320 PSA 8.5 (NmMt+) sold for $1,627 (eBay; 6/08)
—Hank Aaron AS #394 SGC 96 (MT) sold for $1,490 (eBay; 5/08)
—Hank Aaron AS #394 SGC 96 (MT) sold for $1,140 (Mastro; 5/08)
—Richie Ashburn #213 PSA 10 (Gem) sold for $4,674 (Mile High; 2/08)
—Ernie Banks #25 SGC 96 (MT) sold for $660 (Mastro; 5/08)
—Lou Brock #387 PSA 10 (Gem) (Young Collection) sold for $32,545 (SCP; 5/12)
—Lou Brock #387 BVG 8.5 (NmMt+) sold for $645 (eBay; 2/07)
—Rocky Colavito #20 PSA 9 (MT) sold for $1,330 (eBay; 5/08)
—Rocky Colavito #20 PSA 9 (MT) sold for $1,275 (eBay; 3/07)
—Paul Foytack #349 PSA 8 (NmMt) sold for $1,619 (eBay; 4/08)
—Paul Foytack #349 PSA 8 (NmMt) sold for $1,304 (eBay; 1/08)
—Paul Foytack #349 PSA 8 (NmMt) sold for $1,206 (Goodwin; 11/07)
—Paul Foytack #349 PSA 8 (NmMt) sold for $714 (eBay; 4/07)
—Paul Foytack #349 BVG 8 (NmMt) sold for $360 (eBay; 11/07)
—Bob Gibson #530 PSA 9 (MT) sold for $2,218 (Goodwin; 3/08)
—Bob Gibson #530 SGC 96 (MT) sold for $1,195 (Heritage; 5/08)

—Bob Gibson #530 SGC 96 (MT) sold for $840 (Mastro; 5/08)
—Gil Hodges #85 PSA 9 (MT) sold for $1,086 (Mile High; 2/08)
—Billy Hoeft #134 (Blue Sky) PSA 8 (NmMt) sold for $612 (eBay; 4/07)
—Billy Hoeft #134 (Blue Sky) PSA 8 (NmMt) sold for $405 (eBay; 2/08)
—Billy Hoeft #134 (Blue Sky) PSA 8 (NmMt) sold for $262 (eBay; 11/07)
—Billy Hoeft #134 (Green Sky) PSA 8 (NmMt) sold for $446 (eBay; 4/08)
—Billy Hoeft #134 (Green Sky) PSA 8 (NmMt) sold for $416 (eBay; 3/08)
—Al Kaline #150 PSA 9 (MT) sold for $2,026 (eBay; 3/04)
—Al Kaline #150 PSA 9 (MT) sold for $1,725 (eBay; 3/07)
—Al Kaline #150 SGC 96 (MT) sold for $823 (eBay; 2/08)
—Al Kaline AS #470 PSA 9 (MT) sold for $1,847 (Memory Lane; 12/07)
—Al Kaline AS #470 PSA 9 (MT) sold for $1,507 (eBay; 3/08)
—Harmon Killebrew #70 SGC 96 (MT) sold for $570 (Mastro; 5/08)
—Sandy Koufax #5 PSA 9 (MT) sold for $66,789 (Madec; 10/06)
—Sandy Koufax #5 PSA 9 (MT) sold for $25,751 (Madec; 5/07)
—Sandy Koufax #5 PSA 9 (MT) sold for $21,046 (Mastro; 8/06)
—Sandy Koufax #5 SGC 96 (MT) sold for $11,448 (Memory Lane; 5/08)
—Sandy Koufax #5 SGC 96 (MT) sold for $11,309 (Goodwin; 9/13)
—Sandy Koufax #5 PSA 9 (MT) sold for $9,116 (SCP Sotheby's; 11/06)
—Sandy Koufax #5 SGC 96 (MT) sold for $4,320 (Mile High; 10/11)
—Tony Kubek #430 PSA 9 (MT) sold for $1,053 (eBay; 2/07)
—Don Landrum #323 PSA 8 (NmMt) sold for $2,000 (eBay; 1/08)
—Don Landrum #323 PSA 8 (NmMt) sold for $1,359 (eBay; 3/08)
—Don Landrum #323 PSA 8 (NmMt) sold for $1,221 (eBay; 5/07)
—Don Landrum #323 PSA 8 (NmMt) sold for $754 (eBay; 1/07)
—Manager's Dream #18 PSA 9 (MT) sold for $7,555 (Memory Lane; 12/06)
—Manager's Dream #18 PSA 9 (MT) sold for $5,175 (eBay; 6/08)
—Manager's Dream #18 PSA 9 (MT) sold for $4,560 (Mastro; 12/03)
—Manager's Dream #18 PSA 9 (MT) sold for $4,167 (eBay; 3/05)
—Mickey Mantle IA #318 SGC 96 (MT) sold for $1,680 (Mastro; 5/08)
—Juan Marichal #505 PSA 9 (MT) sold for $3,151 (Memory Lane; 5/08)
—Eddie Mathews #30 PSA 9 (MT) sold for $2,591 (Goodwin; 5/08)
—Eddie Mathews #30 PSA 9 (MT) sold for $1,821 (eBay; 3/07)
—Juan Marichal #505 PSA 9 (MT) sold for $3,505 (eBay; 12/12)
—Roger Maris #1 PSA 9 (Mint) sold for $27,171 (Mile High; 12/13)
—Roger Maris #1 SGC 92 (NmMt+) sold for $2,065 (Mile High; 10/12)
—Roger Maris IA #313 PSA 9 (MT) sold for $1,609 (eBay; 3/07)
—Roger Maris IA #313 PSA 9 (MT) sold for $1,547 (Mile High; 6/06)
—Roger Maris IA #313 PSA 9 (MT) sold for $1,056 (Madec; 5/07)
—Roger Maris WS3 #234 PSA 10 (Gem) sold for $4,691 (Mastro; 4/07)
—Willie Mays #300 PSA 10 (Gem) sold for $11,120 (Mastro; 8/04)
—Willie Mays #300 PSA 10 (Gem) sold for $10,454 (Mastro; 12/03)
—Tim McCarver #167 PSA 10 (Gem) sold for $3,418 (eBay; 5/08)
—Joe Pepitone #596 PSA 9 (MT) sold for $1,866 (eBay; 6/08)
—Gaylord Perry #199 PSA 9 (MT) sold for $3,876 (Mastro; 12/06)
—Gaylord Perry #199 PSA 9 (MT) sold for $2,646 (Mastro; 4/07)
—Gaylord Perry #199 PSA 9 (MT) sold for $2,485 (eBay; 1/08)
—Gaylord Perry #199 PSA 9 (MT) sold for $2,310 (Goodwin; 11/08)
—Gaylord Perry #199 PSA 9 (MT) sold for $2,040 (Mastro; 5/08)
—Boog Powell #99 PSA 9 (MT) sold for $666 (eBay; 6/04)
—Boog Powell #99 PSA 9 (MT) sold for $636 (eBay; 1/08)
—Brooks Robinson #45 SGC 96 (MT) sold for $1,350 (Mile High; 2/08)
—Frank Robinson #350 PSA 9 (MT) sold for $3,951 (eBay; 3/07)
—Babe Ruth Hits 60 #139 (No Pole) PSA 9 (MT) sold for $1,475 (eBay; 3/07)
—Ron Santo #170 PSA 10 (Gem) sold for $5,899 (Goodwin; 09/11)
—Warren Spahn #100 PSA 9 (MT) sold for $1,129 (Mastro; 6/05)
—Joe Torre #218 PSA 10 (Gem) (Young Collection) sold for $10,780 (SCP; 5/12)
—Joe Torre #218 PSA 9 (MT) sold for $2,212 (eBay; 3/08)
—Joe Torre #218 PSA 9 (MT) sold for $1,633 (Leland's; 10/05)
—Joe Torre #218 PSA 9 (MT) sold for $1,590 (Superior; 3/04)
—Bob Uecker #594 PSA 9 (MT) sold for $1,729 (eBay; 5/08)
—Billy Williams #288 PSA 9 (MT) sold for $2,069 (eBay; 3/07)
—George Witt #287 PSA 8 (NmMt) sold for $3,614 (Goodwin; 11/07)
—George Witt #287 PSA 8 (NmMt) sold for $3,385 (eBay; 4/08)

1963 Fleer

		GD 2	VG 3	VgEx 4	EX 5	ExMt 6	NM 7	NmMt 8	MT 9
1	Steve Barber	5	5	8	12	30	80	250	
2	Ron Hansen	5	5	5	6	12	25	60	
3	Milt Pappas	5	5	5	10	12	30	80	200
4	Brooks Robinson	8	20	25	40	50	80	120	600
5	Willie Mays	25	40	50	100	120	200	500	2,500
6	Lou Clinton	5	5	5	6	20	25	40	200
7	Bill Monbouquette	5	5	5	6	12	20	30	150
8	Carl Yastrzemski	8	12	20	40	50	100	200	600
9	Ray Herbert	5	5	5	6	12	20	30	150

#	Player	GD 2	VG 3	VgEx 4	EX 5	ExMt 6	NM 7	NmMt 8	MT 9
10	Jim Landis	5	5	5	6	12	20	40	150
11	Dick Donovan	5	5	5	6	12	20	40	
12	Tito Francona	5	5	5	6	12	20	40	
13	Jerry Kindall	5	5	5	6	12	20	30	200
14	Frank Lary	5	5	5	6	12	20	40	150
15	Dick Howser	5	5	5	6	10	15	30	120
16	Jerry Lumpe	5	5	5	6	12	20	30	200
17	Norm Siebern	5	5	5	6	10	15	30	
18	Don Lee	5	5	5	6	12	20	40	150
19	Albie Pearson	5	5	5	6	12	20	40	200
20	Bob Rodgers	5	5	5	6	12	20	40	150
21	Leon Wagner	5	5	5	6	12	25	50	150
22	Jim Kaat	5	5	6	15	20	25	50	250
23	Vic Power	5	5	5	6	12	20	40	200
24	Rich Rollins	5	5	5	6	10	15	40	200
25	Bobby Richardson	5	5	8	12	20	30	50	400
26	Ralph Terry	5	5	5	8	15	25	50	150
27	Tom Cheney	5	5	5	6	12	20	40	150
28	Chuck Cottier	5	5	5	6	10	15	30	100
29	Jimmy Piersall	5	5	6	8	12	15	40	200
30	Dave Stenhouse	5	5	5	6	12	20	30	200
31	Glen Hobbie	5	5	5	6	10	15	30	150
32	Ron Santo	5	6	10	15	40	50	80	300
33	Gene Freese	5	5	5	6	12	20	40	200
34	Vada Pinson	5	5	6	10	15	25	50	150
35	Bob Purkey	5	5	5	6	10	15	40	200
36	Joe Amalfitano	5	5	5	6	12	25	40	150
37	Bob Aspromonte	5	5	5	6	10	25	30	200
38	Dick Farrell	5	5	5	6	10	15	30	120
39	Al Spangler	5	5	5	6	10	15	30	150
40	Tommy Davis	5	5	6	10	15	25	50	250
41	Don Drysdale	6	8	30	40	50	80	120	500
42	Sandy Koufax	25	50	60	100	120	200	400	2,000
43	Maury Wills RC	12	20	30	50	80	120	200	700
44	Frank Bolling	5	5	5	6	12	20	25	200
45	Warren Spahn	6	10	15	30	40	50	100	250
46	Joe Adcock SP	12	30	40	50	60	100	250	1,000
47	Roger Craig	5	5	5	6	12	25	40	150
48	Al Jackson	5	5	6	8	15	25	50	200
49	Rod Kanehl	5	5	5	8	15	25	50	200
50	Ruben Amaro	5	5	5	8	15	25	50	150
51	Johnny Callison	5	5	5	8	15	25	60	200
52	Clay Dalrymple	5	5	5	6	12	20	50	150
53	Don Demeter	5	5	5	6	12	20	40	250
54	Art Mahaffey	5	5	5	6	12	20	40	250
55	Smoky Burgess	5	5	5	6	10	25	60	200
56	Roberto Clemente	30	50	80	100	120	200	300	1,200
57	Roy Face	5	5	5	6	12	25	40	200
58	Vern Law	5	5	5	8	15	25	40	200
59	Bill Mazeroski	5	5	8	12	20	50	60	
60	Ken Boyer	5	5	6	10	15	25	50	
61	Bob Gibson	6	8	25	▲50	▲60	▲80	120	500
62	Gene Oliver	5	5	5	6	12	20	40	150
63	Bill White	5	5	6	10	25	40	50	200
64	Orlando Cepeda	5	5	8	12	20	50	100	400
65	Jim Davenport	5	5	5	6	12	25	50	
66	Billy O'Dell	5	5	6	10	15	30	120	
NNO	Checklist SP	75	100	150	200	250	400	600	800

—Joe Adcock #46 PSA 10 (Gem) sold for $6,700 (Mastro; 6/06)
—Joe Adcock #46 GAI 9 (MT) sold for $520 (Mastro; 12/06)
—Joe Adcock #46 GAI 9 (MT) sold for $300 (eBay; 2/07)
—Joe Adcock #46 GAI 8.5 (NmMt+) sold for $239 (eBay; 4/07)
—Steve Barber #1 PSA 9 (MT) sold for $2,426 (Mastro; 12/05)
—Steve Barber #1 PSA 9 (MT) sold for $1,821 (Mastro; 6/05)
—Steve Barber #1 PSA 9 (MT) sold for $1,650 (eBay; 5/07)
—Ken Boyer #60 PSA 9 (MT) sold for $515 (eBay; 8/07)
—Roberto Clemente #56 SGC 96 (MT) sold for $1,206 (Mastro; 8/06)
—Roberto Clemente #56 GAI 9 (MT) sold for $693 (Mastro; 10/05)
—Roberto Clemente #56 GAI 9 (MT) sold for $667 (eBay; 11/06)
—Roberto Clemente #56 GAI 9 (MT) sold for $666 (eBay; 11/07)
—Roberto Clemente #56 GAI 9 (MT) sold for $505 (eBay; 11/06)
—Don Drysdale #41 PSA 10 (Gem) sold for $1,851 (Mile High; 6/05)
—Don Drysdale #41 PSA 10 (Gem) sold for $1,655 (Mastro; 6/05)
—Don Drysdale #41 GAI 9.5 (Gem) sold for $675 (Memory Lane; 11/04)
—Bob Gibson #61 GAI 9.5 (Gem) sold for $477 (Mastro; 12/04)
—Ron Hansen #2 PSA 9 (MT) sold for $521 (eBay; 11/07)
—Sandy Koufax #42 PSA 10 (Gem) sold for $25,503 (Mile High; 2/08)

—Sandy Koufax #42 SGC 96 (MT) sold for $1,036 (eBay; 5/07)
—Willie Mays #5 GAI 9 (MT) sold for $715 (Mile High; 12/05)
—Willie Mays #5 GAI 8.5 (NmMt+) sold for $250 (eBay; 2/08)
—Willie Mays #5 GAI 8.5 (NmMt+) sold for $205 (eBay; 6/07)
—Willie Mays #5 GAI 8.5 (NmMt+) sold for $204 (eBay; 11/07)
—Bill Mazeroski #59 PSA 9 (MT) sold for $910 (eBay; 5/07)
—Billy O'Dell #66 PSA 9 (MT) sold for $1,025 (eBay; 5/07)
—Billy O'Dell #66 PSA 9 (MT) sold for $949 (Memory Lane; 12/07)
—Ron Santo #32 PSA 9 (MT) sold for $799 (eBay; 2/07)
—Ron Santo #32 PSA 9 (MT) sold for $683 (Goodwin; 3/08)
—Warren Spahn #45 PSA 10 (Gem) sold for $2,550 (eBay; 12/03)
—Carl Yastrzemski #8 GAI 9.5 (Gem) sold for $578 (Mastro; 12/04)
—Checklist #NNO SGC 92 (NmMt+) sold for $560 (eBay; 11/07)

1963 Topps

#	Player	GD 2	VG 3	VgEx 4	EX 5	ExMt 6	NM 7	NmMt 8	M
1	NL Batting Leaders	5	6	10	15	25	100	800	
2	AL Batting Leaders	6	25	30	40	50	80	150	
3	NL Home Run Leaders	5	8	12	20	50	80	400	
4	AL Home Run Leaders	5	5	6	10	25	50	80	
5	NL ERA Leaders	5	6	10	15	25	50	200	
6	AL ERA Leaders	5	5	8	12	20	30	60	
7	NL Pitching Leaders	5	5	5	8	12	30	80	
8	AL Pitching Leaders	5	5	6	6	10	20	40	
9	NL Strikeout Leaders	5	6	10	20	30	40	▼60	
10	AL Strikeout Leaders	5	5	5	8	12	30	80	
11	Lee Walls	5	5	6	8	12	20	40	
12	Steve Barber	5	5	5	5	10	20		
13	Philadelphia Phillies TC	5	5	5	8	15	120		
14	Pedro Ramos	5	5	8	15	30	60	120	
15	Ken Hubbs NPO	5	5	5	5	8	30	80	
16	Al Smith	5	5	5	5	5	10	20	
17	Ryne Duren	5	5	5	5	5	10	50	
18	Buc Blasters	8	6	8	30	▲50	▲80	▼150	1,0
19	Pete Burnside	5	5	5	5	5	10	20	
20	Tony Kubek	5	5	6	10	15	30	100	
21	Marty Keough	5	5	5	5	8	20	200	
22	Curt Simmons	5	5	5	5	6	20	80	
23	Ed Lopat MG	5	5	5	5	5	10	30	
24	Bob Bruce	5	5	5	5	5	10	20	
25	Al Kaline	10	20	25	30	40	▲80	250	
26	Ray Moore	5	5	5	5	5	10	40	
27	Choo Choo Coleman	5	5	5	5	6	15	80	
28	Mike Fornieles	5	5	5	5	5	10	50	
29A	1962 Rookie Stars	5	5	5	5	8	15	30	
29B	1963 Rookie Stars	5	5	5	5	5	10	25	
30	Harvey Kuenn	5	5	5	5	8	12	60	
31	Cal Koonce RC	5	5	5	5	5	10	25	
32	Tony Gonzalez	5	5	5	5	5	10	20	
33	Bo Belinsky	5	5	5	5	5	10	20	1
34	Dick Schofield	5	5	6	10	15	25	400	
35	John Buzhardt	5	5	5	5	5	10	25	
36	Jerry Kindall	5	5	5	5	5	10	30	
37	Jerry Lynch	5	5	5	5	5	10	40	
38	Bud Daley	5	5	5	5	6	12	25	1
39	Los Angeles Angels TC	5	5	5	5	6	12	25	1
40	Vic Power	5	5	5	5	6	15	60	
41	Charley Lau	5	5	5	5	5	12	25	
42	Stan Williams	5	5	6	8	12	25	50	
43	Veteran Masters	5	5	5	8	12	20	100	
44	Terry Fox	5	5	5	5	5	10	30	
45	Bob Aspromonte	5	5	5	5	5	10	20	1
46	Tommie Aaron RC	5	5	5	5	5	10	30	
47	Don Lock RC	5	5	6	8	12	25	50	1
48	Birdie Tebbetts MG	5	5	5	5	5	10	30	
49	Dal Maxvill RC	5	5	5	6	10	20	40	
50	Billy Pierce	5	5	5	5	5	10	50	1
51	George Alusik	5	5	5	5	5	10	20	1
52	Chuck Schilling	5	5	5	5	5	10	25	
53	Joe Moeller RC	5	5	5	5	5	10	30	12
54A	Dave DeBusschere 1962	5	5	5	5	8	15	30	35
54B	Dave DeBusschere 1963 RC	5	5	5	5	6	25	60	
55	Bill Virdon	5	5	5	6	10	20	40	
56	Dennis Bennett RC	5	5	5	5	5	10	40	
57	Billy Moran	5	5	5	6	10	20	40	8
58	Bob Will	5	5	5	6	10	20	40	

	GD 2	VG 3	VgEx 4	EX 5	ExMt 6	NM 7	NmMt 8	MT 9
Craig Anderson	5	5	5	5	5	10	20	150
Elston Howard	5	5	5	8	12	60	80	
Ernie Bowman	5	5	6	8	15	30	60	
Bob Hendley	5	5	5	5	5	10	20	80
Cincinnati Reds TC	5	5	5	5	6	12	50	325
Dick McAuliffe	5	5	5	5	8	15	50	
Jackie Brandt	5	5	5	5	5	10	20	100
Mike Joyce RC	5	5	5	5	5	10	25	
Ed Charles	5	5	5	5	5	10	20	
Friendly Foes	5	5	6	15	25	30	80	2,000
Bud Zipfel RC	5	5	5	5	5	10	20	
Jim O'Toole	5	5	5	5	8	15	30	
Bobby Wine RC	5	5	5	5	5	10	20	150
Johnny Romano	5	5	5	5	5	10	40	
Bobby Bragan MG RC	5	5	5	5	5	10	20	100
Denny Lemaster RC	5	5	5	5	5	10	20	120
Bob Allison	5	5	5	5	8	15	50	
Earl Wilson	5	5	5	5	6	12	40	
Al Spangler	5	5	5	5	5	10	20	
Marv Throneberry	5	5	5	6	8	15	50	150
Checklist 1	5	5	5	6	8	15	50	120
Jim Gilliam	5	5	5	5	6	15	30	
Jim Schaffer	5	5	5	5	5	10	20	
Ed Rakow	5	5	5	5	5	10	20	
Charley James	5	5	5	5	5	10	20	100
Ron Kline	5	5	5	5	5	15	60	
Tom Haller	5	5	5	5	5	10	30	80
Charley Maxwell	5	5	5	5	5	10	20	300
Bob Veale	5	5	5	5	5	10	30	
Ron Hansen	5	5	5	5	5	10	20	150
Dick Stigman	5	5	5	5	5	12	80	
Gordy Coleman	5	5	5	5	5	10	30	
Dallas Green	5	5	5	5	5	10	20	120
Hector Lopez	5	5	5	5	6	20	25	
Galen Cisco	5	5	5	5	5	10	20	80
Bob Schmidt	5	5	5	5	5	10	25	
Larry Jackson	5	5	5	5	5	10	30	80
Lou Clinton	5	5	5	5	5	10	40	
Bob Duliba	5	5	5	5	5	10	20	150
George Thomas	5	5	5	5	5	10	20	
Jim Umbricht	5	5	5	5	5	10	20	
Joe Cunningham	5	5	5	5	8	20	150	
Joe Gibbon	5	5	5	5	5	12	30	
Checklist 2 Red/Yellow	5	5	5	5	5	10	25	
Checklist 2 White/Red	5	5	5	5	5	10	25	120
Chuck Essegian	5	5	5	5	5	10	20	200
Lew Krausse RC	5	5	5	5	5	10	30	150
Ron Fairly	5	5	5	5	8	20	120	250
Bobby Bolin	5	5	5	5	5	10	20	120
Jim Hickman	5	5	5	5	5	10	50	
Hoyt Wilhelm	5	5	5	5	20	25	40	200
Lee Maye	5	5	5	5	5	12	30	
Rich Rollins	5	5	5	5	5	10	20	
Al Jackson	5	5	5	5	5	10	20	
Dick Brown	5	5	5	5	5	10	30	80
Don Landrum	5	5	5	5	5	10	20	
Dan Osinski RC	5	5	5	5	5	15	30	150
Carl Yastrzemski	8	20	30	50	60	100	250	
Jim Brosnan	5	5	5	5	5	10	20	80
Jacke Davis	5	5	5	5	5	10	30	
Sherm Lollar	5	5	5	5	5	10	20	
Bob Lillis	5	5	5	5	5	10	20	120
Roger Maris	30	40	▲60	▲80	▲100	▼150	600	
Jim Hannan RC	5	5	5	5	5	10	20	
Julio Gotay	5	5	5	5	5	10	25	150
Frank Howard	5	5	5	5	8	25	100	150
Dick Howser	5	5	5	5	5	10	20	120
Robin Roberts	5	5	5	15	20	30	100	
Bob Uecker	5	8	12	40	50	100	150	
Bill Tuttle	5	5	5	5	5	10	20	
Matty Alou	5	5	5	5	6	12	25	100
Gary Bell	5	5	5	5	5	10	20	
Dick Groat	5	5	5	5	6	12	25	150
Washington Senators TC	5	5	5	5	6	12	50	150
Jack Hamilton	5	5	5	5	5	10	20	60
Gene Freese	5	5	5	5	5	10	25	150
Bob Scheffing MG	5	5	5	5	5	10	30	150

		GD 2	VG 3	VgEx 4	EX 5	ExMt 6	NM 7	NmMt 8	MT 9
135	Richie Ashburn	5	5	6	10	▲25	30	80	
136	Ike Delock	5	5	5	5	5	10	20	150
137	Mack Jones	5	5	5	5	5	10	20	80
138	Pride of NL	6	20	25	40	50	80	200	600
139	Earl Averill Jr.	5	5	5	5	5	10	20	100
140	Frank Lary	5	5	5	6	10	15	50	200
141	Manny Mota RC	5	5	5	5	6	12	50	150
142	Whitey Ford WS1	5	5	5	12	20	25	120	500
143	Jack Sanford WS2	5	5	5	5	6	30	50	175
144	Roger Maris WS3	5	5	6	20	25	30	200	
145	Chuck Hiller WS4	5	5	5	5	6	12	40	150
146	Tom Tresh WS5	5	5	5	5	8	15	120	
147	Billy Pierce WS6	5	5	5	5	5	12	50	
148	Ralph Terry WS7	5	5	5	5	8	20	150	
149	Marv Breeding	5	5	5	5	5	12	40	
150	Johnny Podres	5	5	5	6	10	15	25	400
151	Pittsburgh Pirates TC	5	5	5	5	6	12	40	150
152	Ron Nischwitz	5	5	5	5	5	10	20	150
153	Hal Smith	5	5	5	5	5	10	20	100
154	Walter Alston MG	5	5	5	5	6	12	30	150
155	Bill Stafford	5	5	5	5	6	15	120	
156	Roy McMillan	5	5	5	5	5	10	20	
157	Diego Segui RC	5	5	5	5	5	10	30	80
158	Tommy Harper RC	5	5	5	8	12	20	40	150
159	Jim Pagliaroni	5	5	5	5	5	10	30	
160	Juan Pizarro	5	5	5	5	5	10	20	120
161	Frank Torre	5	5	5	5	6	12	25	100
162	Minnesota Twins TC	5	5	5	5	8	25	80	
163	Don Larsen	5	5	5	5	6	12	30	135
164	Bubba Morton	5	5	5	5	5	10	20	200
165	Jim Kaat	5	5	5	5	10	20	25	150
166	Johnny Keane MG	5	5	5	5	5	12	40	
167	Jim Fregosi	5	5	5	5	6	12	40	150
168	Russ Nixon	5	5	5	5	5	12	40	
169	Gaylord Perry	5	5	15	20	25	40	100	300
170	Joe Adcock	5	5	5	5	6	12	30	100
171	Steve Hamilton RC	5	5	5	5	5	10	20	80
172	Gene Oliver	5	5	5	5	5	10	20	
173	Bomber's Best	30	40	50	▼60	▼80	▲200	500	1,000
174	Larry Burright	5	5	5	5	5	12	40	
175	Bob Buhl	5	5	5	5	5	10	25	
176	Jim King	5	5	5	5	5	10	25	
177	Bubba Phillips	5	5	5	5	5	10	20	120
178	Johnny Edwards	5	5	5	5	5	10	20	150
179	Ron Piche	5	5	5	5	5	10	20	150
180	Bill Skowron	5	5	5	5	6	12	25	120
181	Sammy Esposito	5	5	5	5	5	10	20	80
182	Albie Pearson	5	5	5	5	5	10	20	80
183	Joe Pepitone	5	5	5	5	8	20	40	150
184	Vern Law	5	5	5	5	5	15	50	200
185	Chuck Hiller	5	5	5	5	5	10	20	150
186	Jerry Zimmerman	5	5	5	5	5	10	20	
187	Willie Kirkland	5	5	5	5	5	10	20	200
188	Eddie Bressoud	5	5	5	5	5	10	20	
189	Dave Giusti	5	5	5	5	5	10	25	150
190	Minnie Minoso	5	5	5	5	8	25	150	
191	Checklist 3	5	5	5	5	5	12	30	150
192	Clay Dalrymple	5	5	5	5	5	10	20	80
193	Andre Rodgers	5	5	5	5	5	10	20	150
194	Joe Nuxhall	5	5	5	5	6	12	40	
195	Manny Jimenez	5	5	5	5	5	10	20	
196	Doug Camilli	5	5	5	5	5	10	20	120
197	Roger Craig	5	5	5	5	5	10	20	200
198	Lenny Green	5	5	5	5	5	10	20	100
199	Joe Amalfitano	5	5	5	5	5	10	20	
200	Mickey Mantle	150	250	300	▲500	600	▲1,200	4,000	12,000
201	Cecil Butler	5	5	5	5	5	20	25	150
202	Boston Red Sox TC	5	5	5	5	6	12	40	150
203	Chico Cardenas	5	5	5	5	5	10	20	80
204	Don Nottebart	5	5	5	5	5	10	25	150
205	Luis Aparicio	5	5	5	8	20	25	50	200
206	Ray Washburn	5	5	5	5	5	10	20	200
207	Ken Hunt	5	5	5	5	5	10	20	150
208	1963 Rookie Stars	5	5	5	5	5	8	▲60	100
209	Hobie Landrith	5	5	5	5	5	10	20	200
210	Sandy Koufax	40	50	80	▲120	150	400	1,000	4,000
211	Fred Whitfield RC	5	5	5	5	5	10	30	

BASEBALL

#	Player	GD 2	VG 3	VgEx 4	EX 5	ExMt 6	NM 7	NmMt 8	MT 9
212	Glen Hobbie	5	5	5	5	5	10	25	150
213	Billy Hitchcock MG	5	5	5	5	5	10	20	100
214	Orlando Pena	5	5	5	5	5	10	20	80
215	Bob Skinner	5	5	5	5	5	10	20	100
216	Gene Conley	5	5	5	5	5	10	30	100
217	Joe Christopher	5	5	5	5	5	10	60	
218	Tiger Twirlers	5	5	5	5	6	20	80	120
219	Chuck Cottier	5	5	5	5	5	10	25	60
220	Camilo Pascual	5	5	5	5	6	12	60	
221	Cookie Rojas RC	5	5	5	8	12	20	60	
222	Chicago Cubs TC	5	5	5	8	12	20	100	
223	Eddie Fisher	5	5	5	5	5	10	20	80
224	Mike Roarke	5	5	5	5	5	12	60	
225	Joey Jay	5	5	5	5	5	10	25	
226	Julian Javier	5	5	5	5	5	10	40	150
227	Jim Grant	5	5	5	8	12	20	60	
228	Tony Oliva RC	10	25	30	40	▲60	▼120	500	
229	Willie Davis	5	5	5	5	6	12	40	150
230	Pete Runnels	5	5	5	5	5	10	50	
231	Eli Grba	5	5	5	5	5	10	20	80
232	Frank Malzone	5	5	5	5	5	10	50	120
233	Casey Stengel MG	5	5	6	10	20	25	80	200
234	Dave Nicholson	5	5	5	5	5	10	20	80
235	Billy O'Dell	5	5	5	5	5	10	20	80
236	Bill Bryan RC	5	5	5	5	5	12	40	
237	Jim Coates	5	5	5	5	5	25	120	
238	Lou Johnson	5	5	5	5	5	10	20	100
239	Harvey Haddix	5	5	5	5	6	12	40	100
240	Rocky Colavito	5	5	6	10	15	30	100	
241	Billy Smith RC	5	5	5	5	5	10	30	80
242	Power Plus	8	12	40	50	▲80	120	▲300	1,500
243	Don Leppert	5	5	5	5	5	10	20	▼50
244	John Tsitouris	5	5	5	5	5	10	30	100
245	Gil Hodges	5	5	5	8	20	30	100	200
246	Lee Stange	5	5	5	5	5	10	20	150
247	New York Yankees TC	6	10	15	40	60	120	600	
248	Tito Francona	5	5	5	5	5	10	40	200
249	Leo Burke RC	5	5	5	5	5	10	20	100
250	Stan Musial	15	25	50	60	100	150	▲400	2,000
251	Jack Lamabe	5	5	5	5	5	10	20	200
252	Ron Santo	5	5	6	10	▲30	50	▲120	500
253	1963 Rookie Stars	5	5	5	5	5	10	▲40	120
254	Mike Hershberger	5	5	5	5	5	10	40	150
255	Bob Shaw	5	5	5	5	5	10	20	80
256	Jerry Lumpe	5	5	5	5	5	12	40	
257	Hank Aguirre	5	5	5	5	5	10	20	100
258	Alvin Dark MG	5	5	5	5	5	10	25	80
259	Johnny Logan	5	5	5	5	5	10	20	300
260	Jim Gentile	5	5	5	5	6	12	40	
261	Bob Miller	5	5	5	5	5	15	80	
262	Ellis Burton	5	5	5	5	5	12	40	
263	Dave Stenhouse	5	5	5	5	5	10	30	100
264	Phil Linz	5	5	5	5	6	15	80	
265	Vada Pinson	5	5	5	5	6	12	60	
266	Bob Allen	5	5	5	5	5	10	30	150
267	Carl Sawatski	5	5	5	5	5	10	20	100
268	Don Demeter	5	5	5	5	5	10	30	
269	Don Mincher	5	5	5	5	5	10	20	200
270	Felipe Alou	5	5	5	5	6	20	50	200
271	Dean Stone	5	5	5	5	5	10	40	
272	Danny Murphy	5	5	5	5	5	10	50	150
273	Sammy Taylor	5	5	5	5	5	10	30	80
274	Checklist 4	5	5	5	5	5	10	25	150
275	Eddie Mathews	5	10	20	30	40	▲60	120	500
276	Barry Shetrone	5	5	5	5	5	10	20	80
277	Dick Farrell	5	5	5	5	5	12	40	
278	Chico Fernandez	5	5	5	5	5	10	30	150
279	Wally Moon	5	5	5	5	6	12	50	
280	Bob Rodgers	5	5	5	5	5	10	30	150
281	Tom Sturdivant	5	5	5	5	5	10	20	80
282	Bobby Del Greco	5	5	5	5	5	10	25	80
283	Roy Sievers	5	5	5	5	5	15	300	300
284	Dave Sisler	5	5	5	5	5	12	40	150
285	Dick Stuart	5	5	5	5	5	30	100	
286	Stu Miller	5	5	5	5	5	10	50	200
287	Dick Bertell	5	5	5	5	5	10	20	120
288	Chicago White Sox TC	5	5	5	5	8	15	50	120

#	Player	GD 2	VG 3	VgEx 4	EX 5	ExMt 6	NM 7	NmMt 8	MT 9
289	Hal Brown	5	5	5	5	6	20	200	
290	Bill White	5	5	5	5	6	12	40	
291	Don Rudolph	5	5	5	5	6	15	80	
292	Pumpsie Green	5	5	5	5	6	12	50	
293	Bill Pleis	5	5	5	5	5	12	100	
294	Bill Rigney MG	5	5	5	5	5	10	40	
295	Ed Roebuck	5	5	5	5	5	10	40	
296	Doc Edwards	5	5	5	5	5	10	20	
297	Jim Golden	5	5	5	5	5	10	40	
298	Don Dillard	5	5	5	5	5	10	100	
299	1963 Rookie Stars	5	5	5	5	6	15	120	
300	Willie Mays	50	60	80	▲120	200	400	800	3...
301	Bill Fischer	5	5	5	5	5	10	40	
302	Whitey Herzog	5	5	5	5	5	50	200	
303	Earl Francis	5	5	5	5	5	10	25	
304	Harry Bright	5	5	5	5	5	10	30	
305	Don Hoak	5	5	5	5	5	12	80	
306	Star Receivers	5	5	5	5	8	30	100	
307	Chet Nichols	5	5	5	5	5	10	50	
308	Camilo Carreon	5	5	5	5	5	10	40	
309	Jim Brewer	5	5	5	5	5	15	100	
310	Tommy Davis	5	5	5	5	8	40	150	
311	Joe McClain	5	5	5	5	5	10	40	
312	Houston Colts TC	5	5	5	5	8	25	30	100
313	Ernie Broglio	5	5	5	5	5	15	50	
314	John Goryl	5	5	5	5	5	15	60	
315	Ralph Terry	5	5	5	5	8	20	200	
316	Norm Sherry	5	5	5	5	5	10	50	
317	Sam McDowell	5	5	6	10	15	25	30	
318	Gene Mauch MG	5	5	5	5	5	10	25	
319	Joe Gaines	5	5	5	5	5	12	80	
320	Warren Spahn	8	12	20	50	60	100	300	
321	Gino Cimoli	5	5	5	5	5	10	40	
322	Bob Turley	5	5	5	5	5	10	40	
323	Bill Mazeroski	5	5	6	20	40	60	300	
324	Vic Davalillo RC	5	5	5	5	8	25	120	
325	Jack Sanford	5	5	6	10	15	25	100	
326	Hank Foiles	5	5	5	5	5	10	80	
327	Paul Foytack	5	5	5	5	5	10	40	
328	Dick Williams	5	5	5	5	8	25	300	
329	Lindy McDaniel	5	5	5	5	5	10	30	
330	Chuck Hinton	5	5	5	5	5	10	30	
331	Series Foes	5	5	5	5	8	30	60	
332	Joel Horlen	5	5	5	5	5	10	40	
333	Carl Warwick	5	5	5	5	5	15	120	
334	Wynn Hawkins	5	5	5	5	5	10	50	
335	Leon Wagner	5	5	5	5	5	15	120	
336	Ed Bauta	5	5	5	5	5	10	60	
337	Los Angeles Dodgers TC	5	5	8	12	20	30	200	
338	Russ Kemmerer	5	5	5	5	5	12	40	
339	Ted Bowsfield	5	5	5	5	5	10	25	
340	Yogi Berra	12	30	50	60	100	250	1,500	
341	Jack Baldschun	5	5	5	5	5	15	60	
342	Gene Woodling	5	5	5	6	10	15	25	
343	Johnny Pesky MG	5	5	5	5	8	15	80	
344	Don Schwall	5	5	5	5	5	10	30	
345	Brooks Robinson	10	15	25	30	50	80	250	
346	Billy Hoeft	5	5	5	5	5	10	30	
347	Joe Torre	5	5	6	10	15	60	120	
348	Vic Wertz	5	5	5	5	5	10	50	
349	Zoilo Versalles	5	5	5	5	5	10	60	
350	Bob Purkey	5	5	5	5	5	10	40	
351	Al Luplow	5	5	5	8	12	20	80	
352	Ken Johnson	5	5	5	5	5	10	40	
353	Billy Williams	5	6	20	25	50	60	150	
354	Dom Zanni	5	5	5	5	5	15	80	
355	Dean Chance	5	5	5	5	8	15	80	
356	John Schaive	5	5	5	5	5	10	200	
357	George Altman	5	5	5	5	5	10	20	
358	Milt Pappas	5	5	5	5	5	10	60	
359	Haywood Sullivan	5	5	5	5	5	10	60	
360	Don Drysdale	10	15	25	40	50	100	250	
361	Clete Boyer	5	5	6	10	25	50	120	
362	Checklist 5						15	100	
363	Dick Radatz	5	5	5	5	6	20	80	
364	Howie Goss	5	5	5	5	5	10	25	
365	Jim Bunning	5	5	5	8	20	50	120	

Player	GD 2	VG 3	VgEx 4	EX 5	ExMt 6	NM 7	NmMt 8	MT 9
Tony Taylor	5	5	5	5	5	10	60	150
Tony Cloninger	5	5	5	5	5	10	30	120
Ed Bailey	5	5	5	5	5	10	40	150
Jim Lemon	5	5	5	5	5	12	50	
Dick Donovan	5	5	5	5	5	10	30	150
Rod Kanehl	5	5	5	5	5	10	20	100
Don Lee	5	5	5	5	5	10	20	100
Jim Campbell RC	5	5	5	5	5	10	20	80
Claude Osteen	5	5	5	5	5	10	25	120
Ken Boyer	5	5	5	8	15	50	100	150
John Wyatt RC	5	5	5	5	5	10	20	80
Baltimore Orioles TC	5	5	5	5	20	25	40	150
Bill Henry	5	5	5	5	5	10	20	80
Bob Anderson	5	5	5	5	5	10	20	120
Ernie Banks	12	20	50	▼60	100	200	500	2,500
Frank Baumann	5	5	5	5	5	10	25	100
Ralph Houk MG	5	5	5	8	25	30	150	400
Pete Richert	5	5	5	5	5	10	100	
Bob Tillman	5	5	5	5	5	10	40	
Art Mahaffey	5	5	5	5	5	10	20	150
1963 Rookie Stars	5	5	5	5	5	12	50	
Al McBean	5	5	5	5	5	10	40	120
Jim Davenport	5	5	5	5	5	12	25	80
Frank Sullivan	5	5	5	5	5	10	20	100
Hank Aaron	25	60	▲100	120	200	400	1,000	4,000
Bill Dailey RC	5	5	5	5	5	10	20	150
Tribe Thumpers	5	5	5	5	6	12	50	250
Ken MacKenzie	5	5	5	5	5	15	50	
Tim McCarver	5	5	5	5	15	25	50	120
Don McMahon	5	5	5	5	5	10	20	120
Joe Koppe	5	5	5	5	5	10	20	120
Kansas City Athletics TC	5	5	5	5	8	15	50	120
Boog Powell	5	5	6	10	40	50	120	
Dick Ellsworth	5	5	5	5	5	10	40	100
Frank Robinson	10	25	30	40	80	100	200	1,500
Jim Bouton	5	5	6	10	25	50	120	1,200
Mickey Vernon MG	5	5	5	5	6	12	25	150
Ron Perranoski	5	5	5	5	5	10	30	100
Bob Oldis	5	5	5	5	5	10	20	150
Floyd Robinson	5	5	5	5	5	10	20	80
Howie Koplitz	5	5	5	5	5	12	30	
1963 Rookie Stars	5	5	5	5	5	10	40	
Billy Gardner	5	5	5	5	5	10	50	
Roy Face	5	5	5	5	6	12	30	
Earl Battey	5	5	5	5	5	10	30	200
Jim Constable	5	5	5	5	5	10	20	
Dodgers Big Three	8	12	20	30	60	▲120	200	800
Jerry Walker	5	5	5	5	5	10	20	150
Ty Cline	5	5	5	5	5	10	20	
Bob Gibson	6	10	25	50	60	150	400	1,000
Alex Grammas	5	5	5	5	5	10	20	
San Francisco Giants TC	5	5	5	5	5	25	100	
John Orsino	5	5	5	5	5	10	20	150
Tracy Stallard	5	5	5	5	5	10	20	80
Bobby Richardson	5	▲15	▲20	▲25	▲30	▼40	▲100	▼200
Tom Morgan	5	5	5	5	5	10	30	
Fred Hutchinson MG	5	5	5	5	5	10	20	135
Ed Hobaugh	5	5	5	5	5	10	25	100
Charlie Smith	5	5	5	5	5	10	20	100
Smoky Burgess	5	5	5	5	6	12	30	150
Barry Latman	5	5	5	5	5	10	20	120
Bernie Allen	5	5	5	5	5	10	25	80
Carl Boles RC	5	5	5	5	5	10	25	
Lew Burdette	5	5	5	5	6	12	40	
Norm Siebern	5	5	5	5	5	10	20	
Checklist 6 White/Red	5	5	5	5	5	15	100	
Checklist 6 Black/Orange	5	5	5	5	8	15	40	200
Roman Mejias	5	5	5	5	5	10	20	100
Denis Menke	5	5	5	6	10	15	40	80
John Callison	5	5	5	5	6	12	60	200
Woody Held	5	5	5	5	5	10	20	120
Tim Harkness	5	5	5	5	5	10	20	120
Bill Bruton	5	5	5	5	5	10	20	
Wes Stock	5	5	5	5	5	10	20	80
Don Zimmer	5	5	5	5	6	12	30	120
Juan Marichal	5	8	12	25	▲40	60	120	400
Lee Thomas	5	5	5	5	5	10	25	

#	Player	GD 2	VG 3	VgEx 4	EX 5	ExMt 6	NM 7	NmMt 8	MT 9
442	J.C. Hartman RC	5	5	5	5	5	10	30	150
443	Jimmy Piersall	5	5	5	5	6	20	60	
444	Jim Maloney	5	5	5	5	5	10	30	120
445	Norm Cash	5	5	5	8	12	30	40	
446	Whitey Ford	8	12	30	40	50	▼80	300	
447	Felix Mantilla	5	5	5	6	10	15	40	80
448	Jack Kralick	5	5	5	6	10	15	30	120
449	Jose Tartabull	5	5	5	6	10	20	50	
450	Bob Friend	5	5	5	6	10	15	30	80
451	Cleveland Indians TC	5	5	6	10	15	25	50	
452	Barney Schultz	5	5	5	6	10	15	40	150
453	Jake Wood	5	5	5	6	10	15	30	
454A	Art Fowler White Card No.	5	5	5	6	10	60	100	200
454B	Art Fowler Orange Card No.	5	5	5	6	10	15	25	120
455	Ruben Amaro	5	5	5	6	10	15	80	
456	Jim Coker	5	5	5	6	10	15	50	100
457	Tex Clevenger	5	5	5	8	12	20	60	200
458	Al Lopez MG	5	5	5	8	20	30	80	
459	Dick LeMay	5	5	5	6	10	15	40	120
460	Del Crandall	5	5	5	8	12	20	60	
461	Norm Bass	5	5	5	6	10	15	40	100
462	Wally Post	5	5	5	6	10	15	50	150
463	Joe Schaffernoth	5	5	5	6	10	15	30	100
464	Ken Aspromonte	5	5	5	6	10	25	60	
465	Chuck Estrada	5	5	5	6	10	20	40	100
466	Bill Freehan SP RC	5	6	10	15	50	60	200	300
467	Phil Ortega	5	5	5	6	10	15	50	
468	Carroll Hardy	5	5	5	6	10	15	30	200
469	Jay Hook	5	5	5	8	12	30	60	
470	Tom Tresh SP	5	6	10	15	30	80	120	400
471	Ken Retzer	5	5	5	6	10	15	30	80
472	Lou Brock	10	25	40	60	100	150	400	
473	New York Mets TC	6	10	15	25	40	50	150	800
474	Jack Fisher	5	5	5	6	10	15	40	100
475	Gus Triandos	5	5	5	8	12	20	50	
476	Frank Funk	5	5	5	6	10	15	50	120
477	Donn Clendenon	5	5	5	8	12	25	60	
478	Paul Brown	5	5	5	6	10	25	80	150
479	Ed Brinkman RC	5	5	5	6	10	15	50	
480	Bill Monbouquette	5	5	5	6	10	40	80	150
481	Bob Taylor	5	5	5	6	10	15	40	100
482	Felix Torres	5	5	5	6	10	15	30	80
483	Jim Owens	5	5	5	6	10	15	30	275
484	Dale Long SP	5	5	6	10	25	30	60	550
485	Jim Landis	5	5	5	6	10	15	25	100
486	Ray Sadecki	5	5	5	6	10	20	40	80
487	John Roseboro	5	5	5	8	12	20	40	250
488	Jerry Adair	5	5	5	6	10	30	40	150
489	Paul Toth RC	5	5	5	6	10	15	30	120
490	Willie McCovey	10	15	40	50	80	120	250	700
491	Harry Craft MG	5	5	5	6	10	25	40	60
492	Dave Wickersham	5	5	5	6	10	15	30	150
493	Walt Bond	5	5	5	6	10	15	50	120
494	Phil Regan	5	5	5	6	10	15	▲30	100
495	Frank Thomas SP	5	5	6	10	15	40	150	
496	1963 Rookie Stars	5	5	60	80	100	▼120	600	
497	Bennie Daniels	5	5	5	6	10	15	30	120
498	Eddie Kasko	5	5	5	6	10	15	30	100
499	J.C. Martin	5	5	5	6	10	15	40	100
500	Harmon Killebrew SP	15	25	40	60	▼80	150	400	1,500
501	Joe Azcue	5	5	5	6	10	15	100	
502	Daryl Spencer	5	5	5	6	10	15	40	80
503	Milwaukee Braves TC	5	5	6	8	12	30	60	120
504	Bob Johnson	5	5	5	6	10	15	40	100
505	Curt Flood	5	5	6	10	25	50	200	250
506	Gene Green	5	5	5	6	10	15	40	
507	Roland Sheldon	5	5	5	8	20	25	50	100
508	Ted Savage	5	5	5	6	10	15	40	200
509A	Checklist 7 Copyright Centered	5	5	5	8	12	20	30	
509B	Checklist 7 Copyright to Right	5	5	5	8	12	20	40	
510	Ken McBride	5	5	5	6	10	15	30	100
511	Charlie Neal	5	5	5	8	12	20	50	
512	Cal McLish	5	5	5	6	10	15	50	
513	Gary Geiger	5	5	5	6	10	15	50	150
514	Larry Osborne	5	5	5	6	10	15	40	100
515	Don Elston	5	5	5	6	10	15	25	100
516	Purnell Goldy RC	5	5	5	6	10	30	60	

#	Name	GD 2	VG 3	VgEx 4	EX 5	ExMt 6	NM 7	NmMt 8	MT 9
517	Hal Woodeshick	5	5	5	6	10	15	50	
518	Don Blasingame	5	5	5	6	10	15	30	80
519	Claude Raymond RC	5	5	5	6	10	25	40	150
520	Orlando Cepeda	5	6	10	25	30	80	300	500
521	Dan Pfister	5	5	5	6	10	15	25	100
522	1963 Rookie Stars	5	5	5	8	12	20	80	
523	Bill Kunkel	5	5	5	5	8	25	60	
524	St. Louis Cardinals TC	5	5	5	8	12	20	50	200
525	Nellie Fox	5	5	6	10	40	50	▼60	300
526	Dick Hall	5	5	5	5	8	20	80	
527	Ed Sadowski	5	5	5	5	6	20	30	80
528	Carl Willey	5	5	5	5	12	30	80	
529	Wes Covington	5	5	5	5	6	12	60	
530	Don Mossi	5	5	5	5	6	12	60	100
531	Sam Mele MG	5	5	5	5	6	12	25	120
532	Steve Boros	5	5	5	5	6	12	40	100
533	Bobby Shantz	5	5	5	5	6	25	30	80
534	Ken Walters	5	5	5	5	6	12	30	
535	Jim Perry	5	5	5	5	8	15	50	
536	Norm Larker	5	5	5	5	6	12	40	
537	Pete Rose RC	▲600	▲800	▲1,000	1,000	▲1,500	2,500	6,000	75,000
538	George Brunet	5	5	5	5	6	12	25	100
539	Wayne Causey	5	5	5	5	6	12	25	100
540	Roberto Clemente	20	60	▲120	150	▲250	400	800	2,000
541	Ron Moeller	5	5	5	5	6	12	30	80
542	Lou Klimchock	5	5	5	5	6	12	25	100
543	Russ Snyder	5	5	5	5	6	12	25	100
544	Rusty Staub RC	5	6	10	30	▼50	100	250	600
545	Jose Pagan	5	5	5	5	6	12	40	100
546	Hal Reniff	5	5	5	5	8	20	40	
547	Gus Bell	5	5	5	5	6	12	30	135
548	Tom Satriano RC	5	5	5	5	6	12	100	
549	1963 Rookie Stars	5	5	5	5	8	15	120	
550	Duke Snider	10	15	25	40	50	60	120	800
551	Billy Klaus	5	5	5	5	6	12	25	80
552	Detroit Tigers TC	5	5	6	10	▲25	40	100	750
553	Willie Stargell RC	100	120	150	200	300	500	1,200	6,000
554	Hank Fischer RC	5	5	5	5	8	15	40	150
555	John Blanchard	5	5	5	6	10	30	50	
556	Al Worthington	5	5	5	5	6	12	40	100
557	Cuno Barragan	5	5	5	5	6	12	25	575
558	Ron Hunt RC	5	5	5	6	10	50	80	150
559	Danny Murtaugh MG	5	5	5	5	6	12	60	
560	Ray Herbert	5	5	5	5	6	15	30	80
561	Mike De La Hoz	5	5	5	5	6	12	50	
562	Dave McNally RC	5	5	8	12	20	60	120	300
563	Mike McCormick	5	5	5	5	6	12	30	80
564	George Banks RC	5	5	5	5	8	15	40	
565	Larry Sherry	5	5	5	5	6	30	60	
566	Cliff Cook	5	5	5	5	6	12	40	100
567	Jim Duffalo	5	5	5	5	6	12	50	
568	Bob Sadowski	5	5	5	5	6	12	30	150
569	Luis Arroyo	5	5	5	5	8	25	60	200
570	Frank Bolling	5	5	5	5	6	12	40	
571	Johnny Klippstein	5	5	5	5	6	12	25	50
572	Jack Spring	5	5	5	5	6	12	25	60
573	Coot Veal	5	5	5	5	6	25	60	150
574	Hal Kolstad	5	5	5	5	8	15	60	
575	Don Cardwell	5	5	5	5	8	15	60	200
576	Johnny Temple	5	5	5	5	8	25	50	200

—Hank Aaron #390 PSA 10 (Gem) sold for $5,856 (eBay; 5/04)
—Hank Aaron #390 SGC 96 (MT) sold for $1,227 (Mile High; 2/08)
—Hank Aaron #390 SGC 92 (NmMt+) sold for $520 (Leland's; 12/04)
—AL Strikeout Leaders #10 PSA 8 (NmMt) sold for $501 (eBay; 6/07)
—AL Strikeout Leaders #10 PSA 8 (NmMt) sold for $260 (eBay; 12/07)
—AL Strikeout Leaders #10 PSA 8 (NmMt) sold for $87 (eBay; 11/06)
—Luis Aparicio #205 PSA 10 (Gem) sold for $1,026 (eBay; 6/07)
—Richie Ashburn #135 PSA 9 (MT) sold for $1,446 (Mile High; 2/08)
—Yogi Berra #340 PSA 9 (MT) sold for $8,772 (Mile High; 2/08)
—Yogi Berra #340 PSA 9 (MT) sold for $8,246 (Mastro Classic; 10/07)
—Yogi Berra #340 SGC 8.5 (NmMt+) sold for $3,157 (Mile High; 2/08)
—Yogi Berra #340 PSA 8.5 (NmMt+) sold for $1,941 (eBay; 5/08)
—Lou Brock #472 PSA 9 (MT) sold for $3,191 (Goodwin; 11/07)
—Lou Brock #472 SGC 96 (MT) sold for $913 (eBay; 11/06)
—Norm Cash #445 PSA 9 (MT) sold for $1,878 (Goodwin; 8/07)
—Roberto Clemente #540 PSA 10 (Gem) sold for $6,275 (Mastro; 4/04)
—Roberto Clemente #540 BVG 8.5 (NmMt+) sold for $699 (eBay; 3/07)

—Roberto Clemente #540 BVG 8.5 (NmMt+) sold for $572 (eBay; 1/06)
—Whitey Ford #446 PSA 9 (MT) sold for $1,187 (Memory Lane; 12/07)
—Whitey Ford #446 PSA 9 (MT) sold for $468 (eBay; 2/08)
—Al Kaline #25 PSA 9 (MT) sold for $7,816 (Madec; 5/07)
—Mickey Mantle #200 PSA 10 (Gem) sold for $20,282 (Leland's; 10/05)
—Mickey Mantle #200 PSA 10 (Gem) sold for $16,800 (SCP Sotheby's; 12/05)
—Roger Maris #120 PSA 9 (MT) sold for $2,670 (Mile High; 05/11)
—Roger Maris #120 PSA 9 (MT) sold for $2,235 (eBay; 5/08)
—Roger Maris #120 PSA 9 (MT) sold for $2,177 (eBay; 01/12)
—Roger Maris #120 PSA 9 (MT) sold for $2,040 (Memory Lane; 11/04)
—Roger Maris #120 PSA 9 (MT) sold for $1,854 (Mastro; 12/03)
—Roger Maris WS3 #144 PSA 9 (MT) sold for $1,263 (Goodwin; 3/08)
—Stan Musial #250 SGC 92 (NmMt+) sold for $323 (Leland's; 12/04)
—New York Yankees TC #247 PSA 9 (MT) sold for $2,405 (Mastro; 10/05)
—New York Yankees TC #247 PSA 9 (MT) sold for $961 (eBay; 3/07)
—NL Batting Leaders #1 PSA 9 (MT) sold for $3,976 (Goodwin; 3/08)
—NL ERA Leaders #5 PSA 9 (MT) sold for $2,368 (Memory Lane; 12/07)
—NL ERA Leaders #5 PSA 9 (MT) sold for $1,118 (eBay; 2/08)
—NL Home Run Leaders #3 PSA 9 (MT) sold for $3,884 (Madec; 11/06)
—NL Home Run Leaders #3 PSA 9 (MT) sold for $2,032 (Memory Lane; 5/08)
—NL Home Run Leaders #3 PSA 9 (MT) sold for $1,255 (eBay; 2/08)
—Tony Oliva #228 PSA 9 (MT) sold for $3,050 (eBay; 9/07)
—Tony Oliva #228 PSA 9 (MT) sold for $2,944 (eBay; 2/08)
—Pride of NL #138 PSA 10 (Gem) sold for $6,991 (Mastro; 4/07)
—Pride of NL #138 PSA 10 (Gem) sold for $4,050 (eBay; 1/04)
—Brooks Robinson #345 SGC 92 (NmMt+) sold for $210 (eBay; 3/07)
—Pete Rose #537 PSA 10 (Gem) sold for $717,000 (Heritage; 8/16)
—Pete Rose #537 PSA 10 (Gem) (Young Collection) sold for $157,366 (SCP; 5/12)
—Pete Rose #537 SGC 98 (Gem) sold for $19,975 (REA; 5/10)
—Pete Rose #537 GAI 9.5 (Gem) sold for $19,263 (Mastro; 8/04)
—Pete Rose #537 BVG 9 (MT) sold for $8,000 (eBay; 3/07)
—Pete Rose #537 SGC 96 (MT) sold for $6,600 (eBay; 1/05)
—Pete Rose #537 BVG 9 (MT) sold for $6,000 (eBay; 4/08)
—Pete Rose #537 BVG 9 (MT) sold for $5,206 (eBay; 2/07)
—Pete Rose #537 BVG 9 (MT) sold for $4,494 (eBay; 12/06)
—Pete Rose RC #537 PSA 8.5 (NmMt+) sold for $5,005 (eBay; 12/12)
—Pete Rose #537 PSA 8.5 (NmMt+) sold for $3,660 (Goodwin; 11/11)
—Pete Rose #537 PSA 8.5 (NmMt+) sold for $3,475 (eBay; 5/08)
—Pete Rose #537 SGC 92 (NmMt+) sold for $2,938 (REA; 5/08)
—Pete Rose #537 SGC 92 (NmMt+) sold for $2,580 (Leland's; 12/04)
—Pete Rose #537 SGC 92 (NmMt+) sold for $2,032 (eBay; 2/06)
—Pete Rose #537 SGC 92 (NmMt+) sold for $2,040 (Mastro; 12/05)
—Pete Rose #537 SGC 92 (NmMt+) sold for $1,833 (Memory Lane; 5/08)
—Pete Rose #537 BVG 8.5 (NmMt+) sold for $1,826 (eBay; 1/07)
—Pete Rose #537 SGC 92 (NmMt+) sold for $1,525 (eBay; 5/08)
—Pete Rose #537 SGC 88 (NmMt) sold for $1,950 (eBay; 5/07)
—Pete Rose #537 BVG 8 (NmMt) sold for $1,477 (Mastro; 2/07)
—Pete Rose #537 BVG 8 (NmMt) sold for $1,325 (eBay; 3/07)
—Pete Rose #537 SGC 88 (NmMt) sold for $1,286 (Goodwin; 2/06)
—Pete Rose #537 BVG 8 (NmMt) sold for $1,237 (eBay; 10/07)
—Warren Spahn #320 PSA 9 (MT) sold for $670 (eBay; 1/08)
—Warren Spahn #320 SGC 96 (MT) sold for $621 (eBay; 3/07)
—Willie Stargell #553 PSA 10 (Gem) (Young Collection) sold for $12,131 (SCP; 5/12)
—Willie Stargell #553 SGC 96 (MT) sold for $1,109 (eBay; 11/07)
—Billy Williams #353 PSA 9 (MT) sold for $1,549 (eBay; 10/07)
—Billy Williams #353 PSA 9 (MT) sold for $813 (eBay; 4/08)
—Billy Williams #353 SGC 96 (MT) sold for $419 (eBay; 4/08)
—Carl Yastrzemski #115 PSA 9 (MT) sold for $1,916 (eBay; 4/08)

1963 Topps Peel-Offs

#	Name	GD 2	VG 3	VgEx 4	EX 5	ExMt 6	NM 7	NmMt 8	MT
1	Hank Aaron	5	8	10	12	20	100	200	3
2	Luis Aparicio	5	5	5	5	5	10	20	6
3	Richie Ashburn	5	5	5	5	8	12	40	
4	Bob Aspromonte	5	5	5	5	5	8	15	
5	Ernie Banks	5	5	5	6	10	15	50	
6	Ken Boyer	5	5	5	5	5	8	15	5
7	Jim Bunning	5	5	5	5	5	10	25	
8	Johnny Callison	5	5	5	5	5	8	15	5
9	Roberto Clemente	5	8	12	15	25	100	250	
10	Orlando Cepeda	5	5	5	5	5	10	20	6
11	Rocky Colavito	5	5	5	5	8	12	80	
12	Tommy Davis	5	5	5	5	8	8	15	
13	Dick Donovan	5	5	5	5	5	8	15	6
14	Don Drysdale	5	5	5	5	8	12	40	8
15	Dick Farrell	5	5	5	5	5	8	15	5

	GD 2	VG 3	VgEx 4	EX 5	ExMt 6	NM 7	NmMt 8	MT 9
Jim Gentile	5	5	5	5	5	8	15	
Ray Herbert	5	5	5	5	5	8	15	50
Chuck Hinton	5	5	5	5	5	8	15	
Ken Hubbs	5	5	5	5	5	10	30	60
Al Jackson	5	5	5	5	5	8	15	50
Al Kaline	5	5	5	6	10	15	150	
Harmon Killebrew	5	5	5	6	10	15	60	80
Sandy Koufax	5	8	12	15	60	80	200	
Jerry Lumpe	5	5	5	5	8	12	30	
Art Mahaffey	5	5	5	5	5	8	15	
Mickey Mantle	15	20	25	80	100	120	500	
Willie Mays	5	5	8	10	15	30	60	
Bill Mazeroski	5	5	5	5	8	12	80	150
Bill Monbouquette	5	5	5	5	5	8	15	50
Stan Musial	5	5	8	10	15	50	80	
Camilo Pascual	5	5	5	5	5	8	15	
Bob Purkey	5	5	5	5	5	8	15	60
Bobby Richardson	5	5	5	5	5	10	40	60
Brooks Robinson	5	5	5	6	10	15	50	100
Floyd Robinson	5	5	5	5	5	8	15	60
Frank Robinson	5	5	5	6	10	15	50	
Bob Rodgers	5	5	5	5	5	8	15	60
Johnny Romano	5	5	5	5	5	8	15	
Jack Sanford	5	5	5	5	5	8	15	
Norm Siebern	5	5	5	5	5	8	15	50
Warren Spahn	5	5	5	6	10	15	50	100
Dave Stenhouse	5	5	5	5	5	8	15	
Ralph Terry	5	5	5	5	5	8	15	
Lee Thomas	5	5	5	5	5	8	15	60
Bill White	5	5	5	5	5	8	15	
Carl Yastrzemski	5	5	8	10	40	60	200	

andy Koufax #23 PSA 9 (MT) sold for $238 (eBay; 10/07)

64 Topps

	GD 2	VG 3	VgEx 4	EX 5	ExMt 6	NM 7	NmMt 8	MT 9
NL ERA Leaders	5	5	8	12	30	▼50	250	
AL ERA Leaders	5	5	5	6	10	15	120	
NL Pitching Leaders	5	5	8	12	20	120		
AL Pitching Leaders	5	5	5	8	12	40	100	500
NL Strikeout Leaders	5	5	6	10	12	30	60	400
AL Strikeout Leaders	5	5	5	5	8	30	80	300
NL Batting Leaders	5	6	10	15	25	50	100	600
AL Batting Leaders	5	5	6	10	25	40	500	
NL Home Run Leaders	5	6	10	30	50	60	150	500
AL Home Run Leaders	5	5	5	6	10	15	80	500
NL RBI Leaders	5	5	6	15	25	30	80	500
AL RBI Leaders	5	5	5	6	10	15	100	600
Hoyt Wilhelm	5	5	5	5	20	25	100	400
D.Nen RC/N.Willhite RC	5	5	5	5	5	8	15	100
Zoilo Versalles	5	5	5	5	6	15	40	
John Boozer	5	5	5	5	5	8	15	50
Willie Kirkland	5	5	5	5	5	8	15	50
Billy O'Dell	5	5	5	5	5	8	15	50
Don Wert	5	5	5	5	5	8	15	100
Bob Friend	5	5	5	5	5	▲15	20	
Yogi Berra MG	6	20	25	40	50	80	150	600
Jerry Adair	5	5	5	5	5	8	20	150
Chris Zachary RC	5	5	5	5	5	8	30	100
Carl Sawatski	5	5	5	5	5	8	15	50
Bill Monbouquette	5	5	5	5	5	8	25	80
Gino Cimoli	5	5	5	5	5	8	15	50
New York Mets TC	5	5	5	5	8	15	30	100
Claude Osteen	5	5	5	5	5	15	50	80
Lou Brock	5	15	30	40	60	100	250	800
Ron Perranoski	5	5	5	5	5	8	20	80
Dave Nicholson	5	5	5	5	5	8	15	800
Dean Chance	5	5	5	5	5	10	20	80
S.Ellis/M.Queen	5	5	5	5	5	8	25	
Jim Perry	5	5	5	5	5	10	50	80
Eddie Mathews	5	6	10	30	50	100	250	800
Hal Reniff	5	5	5	5	6	15	50	
Smoky Burgess	5	5	5	5	5	15	40	
Jim Wynn RC	5	5	5	5	6	▲30	▲60	100
Hank Aguirre	5	5	5	5	5	8	15	50
Dick Groat	5	5	5	5	8	25	60	
Friendly Foes	5	5	5	8	12	20	40	

	GD 2	VG 3	VgEx 4	EX 5	ExMt 6	NM 7	NmMt 8	MT 9
42 Moe Drabowsky	5	5	5	5	5	8	20	
43 Roy Sievers	5	5	5	5	5	10	20	100
44 Duke Carmel	5	5	5	5	5	8	15	100
45 Milt Pappas	5	5	5	5	5	8	15	100
46 Ed Brinkman	5	5	5	5	5	8	15	50
47 J.Alou RC/R.Herbel	5	5	5	5	5	10	20	80
48 Bob Perry RC	5	5	5	5	5	8	25	120
49 Bill Henry	5	5	5	5	5	8	20	
50 Mickey Mantle	120	150	▲250	300	▲500	▲1,000	▲3,000	6,000
51 Pete Richert	5	5	5	5	5	8	20	50
52 Chuck Hinton	5	5	5	5	5	8	15	50
53 Denis Menke	5	5	5	5	5	8	25	80
54 Sam Mele MG	5	5	5	5	5	8	15	60
55 Ernie Banks	10	25	30	▲50	▲80	120	▲300	▲1,200
56 Hal Brown	5	5	5	5	5	8	15	60
57 Tim Harkness	5	5	5	5	5	8	15	80
58 Don Demeter	5	5	5	5	5	8	25	
59 Ernie Broglio	5	5	5	5	5	8	25	100
60 Frank Malzone	5	5	5	5	5	10	30	80
61 Angel Backstops	5	5	5	5	5	8	15	50
62 Ted Savage	5	5	5	5	5	8	15	50
63 John Orsino	5	5	5	5	5	8	15	50
64 Ted Abernathy	5	5	5	5	5	8	25	
65 Felipe Alou	5	5	5	5	5	10	20	80
66 Eddie Fisher	5	5	5	5	5	8	20	
67 Detroit Tigers TC	5	5	5	5	6	12	25	200
68 Willie Davis	5	5	5	6	10	15	60	50
69 Clete Boyer	5	5	5	5	15	60	200	
70 Joe Torre	5	5	5	8	12	30	▲100	250
71 Jack Spring	5	5	5	5	6	12	30	100
72 Chico Cardenas	5	5	5	5	5	15	50	
73 Jimmie Hall RC	5	5	5	5	5	15	50	100
74 B.Priddy RC/T.Butters	5	5	5	5	5	8	25	100
75 Wayne Causey	5	5	5	5	5	8	25	
76 Checklist 1	5	5	5	5	5	10	20	80
77 Jerry Walker	5	5	5	5	5	8	25	100
78 Merritt Ranew	5	5	5	5	5	8	15	50
79 Bob Heffner RC	5	5	5	5	5	8	25	100
80 Vada Pinson	5	5	5	5	5	10	80	150
81 All-Star Vets	5	5	5	8	12	20	60	200
82 Jim Davenport	5	5	5	5	5	10	20	80
83 Gus Triandos	5	5	5	5	5	8	15	80
84 Carl Willey	5	5	5	5	5	8	15	50
85 Pete Ward	5	5	5	5	5	8	15	50
86 Al Downing	5	5	5	5	5	10	30	150
87 St. Louis Cardinals TC	5	5	5	5	5	10	20	100
88 John Roseboro	5	5	5	5	5	10	20	100
89 Boog Powell	5	5	5	5	5	10	▲80	200
90 Earl Battey	5	5	5	5	5	8	15	150
91 Bob Bailey	5	5	5	5	5	8	25	
92 Steve Ridzik	5	5	5	5	5	8	25	100
93 Gary Geiger	5	5	5	5	5	8	25	
94 J.Britton RC/L.Maxie RC	5	5	5	5	5	8	20	
95 George Altman	5	5	5	5	5	8	15	50
96 Bob Buhl	5	5	5	5	5	8	15	100
97 Jim Fregosi	5	5	5	5	5	10	20	60
98 Bill Bruton	5	5	5	5	5	10	20	120
99 Al Stanek RC	5	5	5	5	5	8	25	80
100 Elston Howard	5	5	5	8	12	20	40	200
101 Walt Alston MG	5	5	5	5	5	10	20	80
102 Checklist 2	5	5	5	5	5	8	15	50
103 Curt Flood	6	10	15	25	40	100	300	
104 Art Mahaffey	5	5	5	5	5	8	15	120
105 Woody Held	5	5	5	5	5	8	15	60
106 Joe Nuxhall	5	5	5	5	5	10	25	
107 B.Howard RC/F.Kruetzer RC	5	5	5	5	5	8	15	50
108 John Wyatt	5	5	5	5	5	8	25	
109 Rusty Staub	5	5	5	5	8	25	30	150
110 Albie Pearson	5	5	5	5	5	12	25	
111 Don Elston	5	5	5	5	5	8	15	50
112 Bob Tillman	5	5	5	5	5	8	15	50
113 Grover Powell RC	5	5	5	5	5	8	15	50
114 Don Lock	5	5	5	5	5	8	30	60
115 Frank Bolling	5	5	5	5	5	8	15	80
116 J.Ward RC/T.Oliva	5	5	5	8	▲15	▲50	60	300
117 Earl Francis	5	5	5	5	5	8	15	80
118 John Blanchard	5	5	5	5	6	20	50	

#	Player	GD 2	VG 3	VgEx 4	EX 5	ExMt 6	NM 7	NmMt 8	MT 9
119	Gary Kolb RC	5	5	5	5	5	8	15	50
120	Don Drysdale	▼10	▼12	▼15	▼20	▼25	50	100	400
121	Pete Runnels	5	5	5	5	5	10	40	
122	Don McMahon	5	5	5	5	5	8	15	50
123	Jose Pagan	5	5	5	5	5	8	15	50
124	Orlando Pena	5	5	5	5	5	8	15	50
125	Pete Rose	80	100	▲150	200	300	600	2,000	5,000
126	Russ Snyder	5	5	5	5	5	8	15	50
127	A.Gatewood RC/D.Simpson	5	5	5	5	5	8	15	50
128	Mickey Lolich RC	5	5	6	10	25	40	120	400
129	Amado Samuel	5	5	5	5	5	8	15	50
130	Gary Peters	5	5	5	5	5	8	20	100
131	Steve Boros	5	5	5	5	5	8	15	50
132	Milwaukee Braves TC	5	5	5	5	5	10	20	70
133	Jim Grant	5	5	5	5	5	8	25	80
134	Don Zimmer	5	5	5	5	5	10	25	80
135	Johnny Callison	5	5	5	5	5	10	▲25	80
136	Sandy Koufax WS1	6	10	15	25	40	80	400	
137	Willie Davis WS2	5	5	5	5	8	15	40	150
138	Ron Fairly WS3	5	5	5	5	8	15	40	120
139	Frank Howard WS4	5	5	5	5	8	15	50	650
140	Dodgers Celebrate WS	5	5	5	5	8	15	30	120
141	Danny Murtaugh MG	5	5	5	5	5	8	25	50
142	John Bateman	5	5	5	5	5	10	30	120
143	Bubba Phillips	5	5	5	5	5	8	15	50
144	Al Worthington	5	5	5	5	5	8	15	50
145	Norm Siebern	5	5	5	5	5	8	15	80
146	T.John RC/B.Chance RC	5	10	12	▲20	30	50	100	500
147	Ray Sadecki	5	5	5	5	5	8	30	120
148	J.C. Martin	5	5	5	5	5	10	40	100
149	Paul Foytack	5	5	5	5	5	8	15	50
150	Willie Mays	▲40	▲50	▲60	▲100	▲150	250	▲600	▼2,500
151	Kansas City Athletics TC	5	5	5	5	5	10	20	80
152	Denny Lemaster	5	5	5	5	5	8	15	50
153	Dick Williams	5	5	5	5	5	8	25	50
154	Dick Tracewski RC	5	5	5	5	5	10	20	60
155	Duke Snider	5	5	8	15	30	50	100	250
156	Bill Dailey	5	5	5	5	5	8	15	60
157	Gene Mauch MG	5	5	5	5	5	8	15	100
158	Ken Johnson	5	5	5	5	5	8	15	50
159	Charlie Dees RC	5	5	5	5	5	8	50	80
160	Ken Boyer	5	5	5	5	8	20	60	200
161	Dave McNally	5	5	5	5	5	10	25	60
162	Hitting Area	5	5	5	5	5	8	30	
163	Donn Clendenon	5	5	5	5	5	10	20	80
164	Bud Daley	5	5	5	5	5	8	15	50
165	Jerry Lumpe	5	5	5	5	5	8	15	50
166	Marty Keough	5	5	5	5	5	8	15	50
167	M.Brumley RC/L.Piniella RC	5	5	12	15	30	50	100	800
168	Al Weis	5	5	5	5	5	8	15	60
169	Del Crandall	5	5	5	5	5	10	20	80
170	Dick Radatz	5	5	5	5	5	15	40	100
171	Ty Cline	5	5	5	5	5	8	15	50
172	Cleveland Indians TC	5	5	5	5	5	10	20	80
173	Ryne Duren	5	5	5	5	5	8	15	60
174	Doc Edwards	5	5	5	5	5	8	15	50
175	Billy Williams	5	5	6	15	40	60	200	
176	Tracy Stallard	5	5	5	5	5	8	15	50
177	Harmon Killebrew	5	6	10	25	30	50	200	1,000
178	Hank Bauer MG	5	5	5	5	5	10	20	60
179	Carl Warwick	5	5	5	5	5	8	20	50
180	Tommy Davis	5	5	5	5	5	10	25	80
181	Dave Wickersham	5	5	5	5	5	8	15	50
182	Sox Sockers	5	5	5	8	15	30	60	250
183	Ron Taylor	5	5	5	5	5	8	15	450
184	Al Luplow	5	5	5	5	5	8	15	50
185	Jim O'Toole	5	5	5	5	5	8	15	50
186	Roman Mejias	5	5	5	5	5	8	25	
187	Ed Roebuck	5	5	5	5	5	8	15	50
188	Checklist 3	5	5	5	5	5	8	25	80
189	Bob Hendley	5	5	5	5	5	8	15	175
190	Bobby Richardson	5	5	5	6	10	20	80	300
191	Clay Dalrymple	5	5	5	5	5	8	15	50
192	J.Boccabella RC/B.Cowan RC	5	5	5	5	8	15	50	
193	Jerry Lynch	5	5	5	5	5	8	15	120
194	John Goryl	5	5	5	5	5	8	15	50
195	Floyd Robinson	5	5	5	5	5	8	15	50

#	Player	GD 2	VG 3	VgEx 4	EX 5	ExMt 6	NM 7	NmMt 8
196	Jim Gentile	5	5	5	5	5	8	20
197	Frank Lary	5	5	5	5	5	8	15
198	Len Gabrielson	5	5	5	5	6	12	30
199	Joe Azcue	5	5	5	5	5	8	15
200	Sandy Koufax	30	40	▲60	80	120	▲200	400
201	S.Bowens RC/W.Bunker RC	5	5	5	5	5	8	15
202	Galen Cisco	5	5	5	5	5	8	25
203	John Kennedy RC	5	5	5	5	5	8	20
204	Matty Alou	5	5	5	6	10	15	40
205	Nellie Fox	5	5	5	8	20	25	40
206	Steve Hamilton	5	5	5	5	5	8	30
207	Fred Hutchinson MG	5	5	5	5	5	8	15
208	Wes Covington	5	5	5	5	5	10	30
209	Bob Allen	5	5	5	5	6	12	30
210	Carl Yastrzemski	6	20	25	30	50	100	200
211	Jim Coker	5	5	5	5	5	8	15
212	Pete Lovrich	5	5	5	5	5	8	15
213	Los Angeles Angels TC	5	5	5	5	5	10	20
214	Ken McMullen	5	5	5	5	5	8	25
215	Ray Herbert	5	5	5	5	5	8	25
216	Mike de la Hoz	5	5	5	5	5	8	15
217	Jim King	5	5	5	5	5	8	15
218	Hank Fischer	5	5	5	5	5	8	15
219	Young Aces	5	5	5	5	5	10	30
220	Dick Ellsworth	5	5	5	5	5	8	15
221	Bob Saverine	5	5	5	5	5	8	15
222	Billy Pierce	5	5	5	5	5	8	25
223	George Banks	5	5	5	5	5	8	15
224	Tommie Sisk	5	5	5	5	5	8	15
225	Roger Maris	20	25	40	50	80	120	250
226	J.Grote RC/L.Yellen RC	5	5	5	5	5	8	15
227	Barry Latman	5	5	5	5	5	8	15
228	Felix Mantilla	5	5	5	5	5	8	15
229	Charley Lau	5	5	5	5	5	8	15
230	Brooks Robinson	5	12	15	25	40	50	100
231	Dick Calmus RC	5	5	5	5	5	8	15
232	Al Lopez MG	5	5	5	5	5	10	20
233	Hal Smith	5	5	5	5	5	8	15
234	Gary Bell	5	5	5	5	5	10	20
235	Ron Hunt	5	5	5	5	5	8	15
236	Bill Faul	5	5	5	5	5	8	15
237	Chicago Cubs TC	5	5	5	5	5	10	25
238	Roy McMillan	5	5	5	5	5	8	20
239	Herm Starrette RC	5	5	5	5	5	8	25
240	Bill White	5	5	5	5	5	8	15
241	Jim Owens	5	5	5	5	5	8	15
242	Harvey Kuenn	5	5	5	5	5	8	15
243	R.Allen RC/J.Hernstein	5	12	20	25	30	50	200
244	Tony LaRussa RC	5	5	8	12	30	50	80
245	Dick Stigman	5	5	5	5	5	8	15
246	Manny Mota	5	5	5	5	5	10	20
247	Dave DeBusschere	5	5	5	5	5	10	40
248	Johnny Pesky MG	5	5	5	5	5	10	30
249	Doug Camilli	5	5	5	5	5	8	20
250	Al Kaline	20	25	30	40	50	60	100
251	Choo Choo Coleman	5	5	5	5	5	10	20
252	Ken Aspromonte	5	5	5	5	5	8	25
253	Wally Post	5	5	5	5	5	8	25
254	Don Hoak	5	5	5	5	5	8	15
255	Lee Thomas	5	5	5	5	5	8	15
256	Johnny Weekly	5	5	5	5	5	8	25
257	San Francisco Giants TC	5	5	5	5	5	8	25
258	Garry Roggenburk	5	5	5	5	5	10	20
259	Harry Bright	5	5	5	5	5	10	20
260	Frank Robinson	6	8	20	25	40	60	▲150
261	Jim Hannan	5	5	5	5	5	8	15
262	M.Shannon RC/H.Fanok	5	5	5	5	8	15	50
263	Chuck Estrada	5	5	5	5	5	8	15
264	Jim Landis	5	5	5	5	5	8	15
265	Jim Bunning	5	5	5	8	12	20	50
266	Gene Freese	5	5	5	5	5	8	15
267	Wilbur Wood RC	5	5	5	5	6	12	25
268	Bill's Got It	5	5	5	5	6	12	40
269	Ellis Burton	5	5	5	5	5	8	15
270	Rich Rollins	5	5	5	5	5	8	15
271	Bob Sadowski	5	5	5	5	5	8	15
272	Jake Wood	5	5	5	5	5	8	15

Name	GD 2	VG 3	VgEx 4	EX 5	ExMt 6	NM 7	NmMt 8	MT 9
Mel Nelson	5	5	5	5	5	8	15	50
Checklist 4	5	5	5	5	5	8	25	50
John Tsitouris	5	5	5	5	5	10	30	100
Jose Tartabull	5	5	5	5	5	8	20	50
Ken Retzer	5	5	5	5	5	10	30	100
Bobby Shantz	5	5	5	5	5	8	25	50
Joe Koppe	5	5	5	5	5	8	15	50
Juan Marichal	5	5	8	12	30	40	100	350
J.,Gibbs/T.Metcalf RC	5	5	5	5	5	10	25	120
Bob Bruce	5	5	5	5	5	8	15	50
Tom McCraw RC	5	5	5	5	5	8	15	50
Dick Schofield	5	5	5	5	5	8	15	80
Robin Roberts	5	5	5	8	12	20	40	100
Don Landrum	5	5	5	5	5	8	15	50
Tony Conigliaro RC	5	8	12	15	50	60	▲150	400
Al Moran	5	5	5	5	5	8	15	50
Frank Funk	5	5	5	5	5	8	15	50
Bob Allison	5	5	5	5	5	10	20	80
Phil Ortega	5	5	5	5	5	8	15	50
Mike Roarke	5	5	5	5	5	8	15	50
Philadelphia Phillies TC	5	5	5	5	5	10	20	120
Ken L. Hunt	5	5	5	5	5	8	15	30
Roger Craig	5	5	5	5	5	8	25	100
Ed Kirkpatrick	5	5	5	5	5	8	15	50
Ken MacKenzie	5	5	5	5	5	8	15	50
Harry Craft MG	5	5	5	5	5	8	15	50
Bill Stafford	5	5	5	5	5	12	60	100
Hank Aaron	25	50	80	100	150	250	600	3,000
Larry Brown RC	5	5	5	5	5	8	15	50
Dan Pfister	5	5	5	5	5	8	15	60
Jim Campbell	5	5	5	5	5	8	15	50
Bob Johnson	5	5	5	5	5	8	15	50
Jack Lamabe	5	5	5	5	5	8	15	50
Giant Gunners	5	6	10	30	40	50	▼80	▲500
Joe Gibbon	5	5	5	5	5	8	15	50
Gene Stephens	5	5	5	5	5	8	15	50
Paul Toth	5	5	5	5	6	12	30	100
Jim Gilliam	5	5	5	5	6	12	30	50
Tom W. Brown RC	5	5	5	5	5	8	15	50
F.Fisher RC/F.Gladding RC	5	5	5	5	5	8	15	50
Chuck Hiller	5	5	5	5	5	8	15	50
Jerry Buchek	5	5	5	5	5	8	15	50
Bo Belinsky	5	5	5	5	5	8	15	50
Gene Oliver	5	5	5	5	5	8	15	50
Al Smith	5	5	5	5	5	8	15	50
Minnesota Twins TC	5	5	5	5	6	12	25	120
Paul Brown	5	5	5	5	5	8	15	50
Rocky Colavito	5	5	5	8	12	20	50	300
Bob Lillis	5	5	5	5	5	8	15	50
George Brunet	5	5	5	5	5	8	15	50
John Buzhardt	5	5	5	5	5	8	15	50
Casey Stengel MG	5	5	10	12	25	30	50	250
Hector Lopez	5	5	5	5	5	10	30	80
Ron Brand RC	5	5	5	5	5	8	15	50
Don Blasingame	5	5	5	5	5	8	15	50
Bob Shaw	5	5	5	5	5	8	15	50
Russ Nixon	5	5	5	5	5	8	15	60
Tommy Harper	5	5	5	5	8	20	60	120
AL Bombers	50	60	80	100	▲150	200	500	1,200
Ray Washburn	5	5	5	5	6	12	30	150
Billy Moran	5	5	5	5	5	8	15	50
Lew Krausse	5	5	5	5	5	8	15	50
Don Mossi	5	5	5	5	5	10	25	80
Andre Rodgers	5	5	5	5	5	8	15	50
A.Ferrara RC/J.Torborg RC	5	5	5	5	5	8	25	50
Jack Kralick	5	5	5	5	5	8	15	50
Walt Bond	5	5	5	5	5	8	15	50
Joe Cunningham	5	5	5	5	5	8	15	50
Jim Roland	5	5	5	5	5	8	15	50
Willie Stargell	5	6	25	40	50	100	200	800
Washington Senators TC	5	5	5	5	5	10	20	80
Phil Linz	5	5	5	5	5	10	25	80
Frank Thomas	5	5	5	5	5	10	25	80
Joey Jay	5	5	5	5	5	8	15	50
Bobby Wine	5	5	5	5	5	8	15	50
Ed Lopat MG	5	5	5	5	5	10	20	50
Art Fowler	5	5	5	5	5	8	15	50

#	Name	GD 2	VG 3	VgEx 4	EX 5	ExMt 6	NM 7	NmMt 8	MT 9
350	Willie McCovey	5	6	20	25	30	50	100	400
351	Dan Schneider	5	5	5	5	5	8	15	50
352	Eddie Bressoud	5	5	5	5	5	8	15	50
353	Wally Moon	5	5	5	5	5	10	60	80
354	Dave Giusti	5	5	5	5	5	8	15	50
355	Vic Power	5	5	5	5	5	10	25	50
356	B.McCool RC/C.Ruiz	5	5	5	5	5	8	15	50
357	Charley James	5	5	5	5	5	8	15	60
358	Ron Kline	5	5	5	5	5	8	15	50
359	Jim Schaffer	5	5	5	5	5	8	15	50
360	Joe Pepitone	5	5	5	5	8	25	40	100
361	Jay Hook	5	5	5	5	5	8	15	50
362	Checklist 5	5	5	5	5	5	15	20	60
363	Dick McAuliffe	5	5	5	5	5	15	25	50
364	Joe Gaines	5	5	5	5	5	8	15	50
365	Cal McLish	5	5	5	5	5	8	15	50
366	Nelson Mathews	5	5	5	5	5	8	15	50
367	Fred Whitfield	5	5	5	5	5	8	15	50
368	F.Ackley RC/D.Buford RC	5	5	5	5	5	8	20	100
369	Jerry Zimmerman	5	5	5	5	5	8	15	50
370	Hal Woodeshick	5	5	5	5	5	8	15	50
371	Frank Howard	5	5	5	10	15	30	60	150
372	Howie Koplitz	5	5	5	5	5	10	25	60
373	Pittsburgh Pirates TC	5	5	5	5	6	15	60	100
374	Bobby Bolin	5	5	5	5	5	10	20	60
375	Ron Santo	5	5	6	20	30	60	250	600
376	Dave Morehead	5	5	5	5	5	10	25	60
377	Bob Skinner	5	5	5	5	5	10	20	60
378	W.Woodward RC/J.Smith	5	5	5	5	5	10	25	60
379	Tony Gonzalez	5	5	5	5	5	15	30	120
380	Whitey Ford	6	10	15	30	60	80	150	500
381	Bob Taylor	5	5	5	5	5	10	30	60
382	Wes Stock	5	5	5	5	5	20	30	60
383	Bill Rigney MG	5	5	5	5	5	15	25	60
384	Ron Hansen	5	5	5	5	5	15	40	80
385	Curt Simmons	5	5	5	5	6	12	30	150
386	Lenny Green	5	5	5	5	5	10	25	60
387	Terry Fox	5	5	5	5	5	10	25	80
388	J.O'Donoghue RC/G.Williams	5	5	5	5	5	10	25	80
389	Jim Umbricht	5	5	5	5	5	10	20	60
390	Orlando Cepeda	5	5	8	12	25	50	100	250
391	Sam McDowell	5	5	5	5	6	15	25	80
392	Jim Pagliaroni	5	5	5	5	5	10	25	60
393	Casey Teaches	5	5	5	6	15	20	30	120
394	Bob Miller	5	5	5	5	5	10	20	60
395	Tom Tresh	5	5	5	5	6	10	30	100	150
396	Dennis Bennett	5	5	5	5	5	10	20	60
397	Chuck Cottier	5	5	5	5	5	10	25	60
398	B.Haas/D.Smith	5	5	5	5	6	15	60	80
399	Jackie Brandt	5	5	5	5	5	10	25	120
400	Warren Spahn	5	8	12	30	▲50	60	150	400
401	Charlie Maxwell	5	5	5	5	5	15	80	100
402	Tom Sturdivant	5	5	5	5	5	10	20	60
403	Cincinnati Reds TC	5	5	5	5	6	12	60	150
404	Tony Martinez	5	5	5	5	5	10	20	60
405	Ken McBride	5	5	5	5	5	10	20	60
406	Al Spangler	5	5	5	5	5	10	25	100
407	Bill Freehan	5	5	5	8	12	25	50	150
408	J.Stewart RC/F.Burdette RC	5	5	5	5	5	10	25	60
409	Bill Fischer	5	5	5	5	5	10	20	60
410	Dick Stuart	5	5	5	5	5	10	30	60
411	Lee Walls	5	5	5	5	5	10	20	60
412	Ray Culp	5	5	6	8	12	20	50	80
413	Johnny Keane MG	5	5	5	5	5	10	20	60
414	Jack Sanford	5	5	5	5	5	15	30	100
415	Tony Kubek	5	8	12	20	25	40	60	250
416	Lee Maye	5	5	5	5	5	10	40	80
417	Don Cardwell	5	5	5	5	5	10	25	60
418	D.Knowles RC/B.Narum RC	5	5	5	5	5	10	30	60
419	Ken Harrelson RC	5	5	5	5	6	20	40	100
420	Jim Maloney	5	5	5	5	5	20	25	30	60
421	Camilo Carreon	5	5	5	5	5	5	10	60
422	Jack Fisher	5	5	5	5	5	10	25	60
423	Tops in NL	12	20	50	80	100	150	300	800
424	Dick Bertell	5	5	5	5	5	10	20	60
425	Norm Cash	5	5	5	8	12	20	40	100
426	Bob Rodgers	5	5	5	5	5	10	30	50

#	Player	GD 2	VG 3	VgEx 4	EX 5	ExMt 6	NM 7	NmMt 8	MT 9
427	Don Rudolph	5	5	5	5	5	10	20	60
428	A.Skeen RC/P.Smith RC	5	5	5	5	5	10	25	60
429	Tim McCarver	5	5	5	5	20	25	60	250
430	Juan Pizarro	5	5	5	5	5	20		
431	George Alusik	5	5	5	5	5	10	20	60
432	Ruben Amaro	5	5	5	5	5	10	25	60
433	New York Yankees TC	5	6	15	20	30	50	120	400
434	Don Nottebart	5	5	5	5	5	10	20	60
435	Vic Davalillo	5	5	5	5	8	30	80	400
436	Charlie Neal	5	5	5	5	6	12	30	80
437	Ed Bailey	5	5	5	5	5	10	30	80
438	Checklist 6	5	5	5	5	8	15	30	100
439	Harvey Haddix	5	5	5	5	6	15	60	80
440	Roberto Clemente	15	60	▲100	120	▼200	400	▲1,000	2,000
441	Bob Duliba	5	5	5	5	5	10	20	60
442	Pumpsie Green	5	5	5	5	6	15	40	100
443	Chuck Dressen MG	5	5	5	5	6	20	30	80
444	Larry Jackson	5	5	5	5	5	10	20	150
445	Bill Skowron	5	5	5	5	6	12	30	80
446	Julian Javier	5	5	6	10	15	25	150	
447	Ted Bowsfield	5	5	5	5	5	10	20	60
448	Cookie Rojas	5	5	5	5	6	20	25	80
449	Deron Johnson	5	5	5	5	8	12	25	80
450	Steve Barber	5	5	5	5	8	20	50	100
451	Joe Amalfitano	5	5	5	5	5	10	20	60
452	G.Garrido RC/J.Hart RC	5	5	5	5	8	15	40	80
453	Frank Baumann	5	5	5	5	5	15	40	80
454	Tommie Aaron	5	5	5	5	6	12	25	60
455	Bernie Allen	5	5	5	5	5	10	25	60
456	W.Parker RC/J.Werhas RC	5	5	5	5	6	20	50	100
457	Jesse Gonder	5	5	5	5	5	10	25	60
458	Ralph Terry	5	5	5	5	6	25	50	300
459	P.Charton RC/D.Jones RC	5	5	5	5	5	10	20	60
460	Bob Gibson	5	8	25	30	50	100	200	800
461	George Thomas	5	5	5	5	5	15	40	80
462	Birdie Tebbetts MG	5	5	5	5	5	15	40	100
463	Don Leppert	5	5	5	5	5	10	25	80
464	Dallas Green	5	5	5	8	15	20	80	120
465	Mike Hershberger	5	5	5	5	5	15	100	
466	D.Green RC/A.Monteagudo RC	5	5	5	5	6	20	60	80
467	Bob Aspromonte	5	5	5	5	5	10	20	60
468	Gaylord Perry	5	6	10	25	40	60	120	500
469	F.Norman RC/S.Slaughter RC	5	5	5	5	6	20	50	120
470	Jim Bouton	5	5	5	8	12	▲30	▼50	120
471	Gates Brown RC	5	5	5	8	12	20	50	
472	Vern Law	5	5	5	5	6	20	40	80
473	Baltimore Orioles TC	5	5	5	10	60	80	800	
474	Larry Sherry	5	5	5	5	5	12	60	100
475	Ed Charles	5	5	5	5	5	10	20	60
476	R.Carty RC/D.Kelley RC	5	5	5	5	10	40	120	200
477	Mike Joyce	5	5	5	5	5	15	50	50
478	Dick Howser	5	5	5	5	5	10	30	120
479	D.Bakenhaster RC/J.Lewis RC	5	5	5	5	5	10	25	60
480	Bob Purkey	5	5	5	5	5	10	25	60
481	Chuck Schilling	5	5	5	5	5	10	30	80
482	J.Briggs RC/D.Cater RC	5	5	5	5	10	20	80	▲150
483	Fred Valentine RC	5	5	5	5	5	10	20	60
484	Bill Pleis	5	5	5	5	5	10	20	60
485	Tom Haller	5	5	5	5	5	10	20	60
486	Bob Kennedy MG	5	5	5	5	5	10	25	60
487	Mike McCormick	5	5	5	5	6	25	40	
488	P.Mikkelsen RC/B.Meyer RC	5	5	5	5	6	12	30	800
489	Julio Navarro	5	5	5	5	5	10	40	60
490	Ron Fairly	5	5	5	5	6	12	40	80
491	Ed Rakow	5	5	5	5	5	10	30	60
492	J.Beauchamp RC/M.White RC	5	5	5	5	5	10	25	60
493	Don Lee	5	5	5	5	5	10	20	40
494	Al Jackson	5	5	5	5	5	10	25	60
495	Bill Virdon	5	5	5	5	6	15	50	120
496	Chicago White Sox TC	5	5	5	5	6	12	25	80
497	Jeff Long RC	5	5	5	5	5	10	20	60
498	Dave Stenhouse	5	5	5	5	5	10	20	60
499	C.Slamon RC/G.Seyfried RC	5	5	5	5	▲8	▲15	30	100
500	Camilo Pascual	5	5	5	5	6	40	100	
501	Bob Veale	5	5	5	5	5	10	150	
502	B.Knoop RC/B.Lee RC	5	5	5	5	5	10	20	60
503	Earl Wilson	5	5	5	5	5	10	40	100

#	Player	GD 2	VG 3	VgEx 4	EX 5	ExMt 6	NM 7	NmMt 8	MT 9
504	Claude Raymond	5	5	5	5	5	10	25	
505	Stan Williams	5	5	5	5	12	25	80	1
506	Bobby Bragan MG	5	5	5	5	5	10	30	1
507	Johnny Edwards	5	5	5	5	5	10	25	
508	Diego Segui	5	5	5	5	5	10	25	
509	G.Alley RC/O.McFarlane RC	5	5	5	5	8	25	100	4
510	Lindy McDaniel	5	5	5	5	6	12	30	
511	Lou Jackson	5	5	5	5	5	10	25	
512	W.Horton RC/J.Sparma RC	5	5	6	10	15	25	80	3
513	Don Larsen	5	5	5	5	8	15	60	1
514	Jim Hickman	5	5	5	5	8	12	50	1
515	Johnny Romano	5	5	5	5	5	10	60	
516	J.Arrigo RC/D.Siebler RC	5	5	5	5	5	10	30	
517A	Checklist 7 Incorrect Numbering	5	5	6	10	15	25	40	1
517B	Checklist 7 Correct Numbering	5	5	6	10	15	50	40	1
518	Carl Bouldin	5	5	5	5	5	10	20	
519	Charlie Smith	5	5	5	5	5	10	20	
520	Jack Baldschun	5	5	5	5	5	10	40	1
521	Tom Satriano	5	5	5	5	5	15	60	1
522	Bob Tiefenauer	5	5	5	5	5	10	25	
523	Lou Burdette	5	5	5	5	5	15	50	1
524	J.Dickson RC/B.Klaus RC	5	5	5	5	8	15	40	
525	Al McBean	5	5	5	5	5	15	30	
526	Lou Clinton	5	5	5	5	8	20	30	
527	Larry Bearnarth	5	5	5	5	5	15	40	1
528	D.Duncan RC/T.Reynolds RC	5	5	5	5	8	15	30	
529	Alvin Dark MG	5	5	5	5	8	15	30	
530	Leon Wagner	5	5	5	5	8	15	50	1
531	Los Angeles Dodgers TC	5	5	8	12	20	40	120	4
532	B.Bloomfield RC/J.Nossek RC	5	5	5	5	8	15	60	1
533	Johnny Klippstein	5	5	5	5	8	15	30	
534	Gus Bell	5	5	5	5	8	15	40	
535	Phil Regan	5	5	5	5	8	20	30	
536	L.Elliot/J.Stephenson RC	5	5	5	5	8	15	30	
537	Dan Osinski	5	5	5	5	8	15	30	
538	Minnie Minoso	5	5	6	10	15	60	150	
539	Roy Face	5	5	5	5	8	15	40	1
540	Luis Aparicio	5	6	10	15	25	60	500	
541	P.Roof/P.Niekro RC	10	15	50	100	120	200	400	1,0
542	Don Mincher	5	5	5	5	8	15	30	1
543	Bob Uecker	5	6	10	15	50	60	120	4
544	S.Hertz RC/J.Hoerner RC	5	5	5	5	8	15	40	
545	Max Alvis	5	5	5	5	8	15	40	
546	Joe Christopher	5	5	5	5	8	15	50	1
547	Gil Hodges MG	5	8	10	15	20	40	50	2*
548	W.Schurr RC/P.Speckenbach RC	5	5	5	5	8	15	25	
549	Joe Moeller	5	5	5	5	5	15	30	
550	Ken Hubbs MEM	5	6	10	15	25	50	100	30
551	Billy Hoeft	5	5	5	5	8	15	40	
552	T.Kelley RC/S.Siebert RC	5	5	8	10	15	20	25	12
553	Jim Brewer	5	5	5	5	8	15	30	
554	Hank Foiles	5	5	5	5	8	15	25	
555	Lee Stange	5	5	5	5	8	15	25	1
556	S.Dillon RC/R.Locke RC	5	5	5	5	8	15	50	
557	Leo Burke	5	5	5	5	8	15	25	
558	Don Schwall	5	5	5	5	8	15	40	
559	Dick Phillips	5	5	5	5	8	15	30	
560	Dick Farrell	5	5	5	5	8	15	30	
561	D.Bennett RC/R.Wise RC	5	5	8	10	15	25	60	1
562	Pedro Ramos	5	5	5	8	10	20	40	
563	Dal Maxvill	5	5	5	5	8	25	60	12
564	J.McCabe RC/J.McNertney RC	5	5	5	5	8	15	40	8
565	Stu Miller	5	5	5	5	8	15	30	
566	Ed Kranepool	5	5	5	6	10	20	40	1
567	Jim Kaat	5	5	5	6	10	30	60	12
568	P.Gagliano RC/C.Peterson RC	5	5	5	5	8	▼12	▼25	
569	Fred Newman	5	5	5	5	8	20	25	
570	Bill Mazeroski	5	6	10	15	30	60	▼80	25
571	Gene Conley	5	5	5	5	8	15	30	
572	D.Gray RC/D.Egan	5	5	5	5	8	15	50	
573	Jim Duffalo	5	5	5	5	8	15	20	
574	Manny Jimenez	5	5	5	5	8	15	25	
575	Tony Cloninger	5	5	5	5	8	15	30	
576	J.Hinsley RC/B.Wakefield RC	5	5	8	12	20	40		2
577	Gordy Coleman	5	5	5	5	8	15	60	2
578	Glen Hobbie	5	5	5	5	8	15	30	
579	Boston Red Sox TC	5	5	8	12	20	30	50	3

	GD 2	VG 3	VgEx 4	EX 5	ExMt 6	NM 7	NmMt 8	MT 9
Johnny Podres	5	5	5	6	10	25	40	100
P.Gonzalez/A.Moore RC	5	5	5	8	15	50	200	
Rod Kanehl	5	5	5	5	8	20	40	80
Tito Francona	5	5	5	5	8	20	50	200
Joel Horlen	5	5	5	5	10	25	60	50
Tony Taylor	5	5	5	5	8	25	80	
Jimmy Piersall	5	5	5	5	8	25	60	150
Bennie Daniels	5	5	5	6	10	25	60	

AL Batting Leaders #8 PSA 9 (MT) sold for $1,730 (Madec; 11/07)
AL Batting Leaders #8 PSA 9 (MT) sold for $1,334 (Superior; 3/04)
AL Batting Leaders #8 PSA 9 (MT) sold for $841 (eBay; 9/07)
Hank Aaron #300 PSA 10 (Gem) sold for $6,558 (eBay; 12/06)
Lou Brock #29 PSA 10 (Gem) sold for $3,081 (Mile High; 1/07)
Gates Brown #471 PSA 9 (MT) sold for $782 (eBay; 2/08)
Gates Brown #471 PSA 9 (MT) sold for $707 (eBay; 9/07)
Tony Conigliaro #287 PSA 10 (Gem) sold for $5,625 (eBay; 10/07)
Chicago Cubs TC #237 PSA 10 (Gem) sold for $2,670 (Greg Bussineau; 12/12)
Giant Gunners #306 PSA 10 (Gem) sold for $3,683 (eBay; 5/08)
Sandy Koufax WS1 #136 PSA 10 (Gem) sold for $3,676 (Mastro; 8/04)
Sandy Koufax WS1 #136 PSA 9 (MT) sold for $2,551 (eBay; 12/06)
Sandy Koufax WS1 #136 PSA 9 (MT) sold for $2,544 (Memory Lane; 12/07)
Tony LaRussa #244 PSA 10 (Gem) sold for $1,999 (eBay; 6/08)
Mickey Mantle #50 PSA 10 (Gem) sold for $26,995 (Leland's; 12/04)
Mickey Mantle #50 BVG 8.5 (NmMt+) sold for $998 (eBay; 3/07)
Minnie Minoso #538 PSA 9 (MT) sold for $1,1170 (Madec; 5/08)
New York Mets TC #27 PSA 10 (Gem) sold for $1,446 (Mile High; 2/08)
New York Yankees TC #433 PSA 10 (Gem) sold for $1,962 (Memory Lane; 2/07)
NL ERA Leaders #1 PSA 9 (MT) sold for $2,368 (Memory Lane; 12/07)
NL ERA Leaders #1 PSA 9 (MT) sold for $2,013 (eBay; 5/08)
NL Pitching Leaders #3 PSA 8 (NmMt) sold for $910 (eBay; 4/07)
NL Pitching Leaders #3 PSA 8 (NmMt) sold for $612 (eBay; 4/08)
NL Pitching Leaders #3 PSA 8 (NmMt) sold for $518 (eBay; 5/08)
Juan Pizarro #430 PSA 8 (NmMt) sold for $566 (eBay; 10/07)
Juan Pizarro #430 PSA 8 (NmMt) sold for $135 (eBay; 3/07)
Juan Pizarro #430 PSA 8 (NmMt) sold for $131 (eBay; 4/07)
Juan Pizarro #430 PSA 8 (NmMt) sold for $42 (eBay; 10/07)
Juan Pizarro #430 PSA 8 (NmMt) sold for $34 (eBay; 11/06)
Juan Pizarro #430 PSA 8 (NmMt) sold for $31 (eBay; 10/06)
P.Roof/P.Niekro #541 PSA 10 (Gem) (Young Collection) sold for $8,711 (SCP; 5/12)
Willie Stargell #342 PSA 10 (Gem) sold for $2,900 (eBay; 3/04)
Willie Stargell #342 PSA 10 (Gem) sold for $1,626 (Mastro; 6/07)
Tops in NL #423 SGC 96 (MT) sold for $905 (Goodwin; 10/06)
Billy Williams #175 PSA 9 (MT) sold for $1,558 (Madec; 5/08)

1964 Topps Giants

	VG 3	VgEx 4	EX 5	ExMt 6	NM 7	NmMt 8	MT 9	Gem 9.5/10
Gary Peters	5	5	5	5	8	30	120	
Ken Johnson	5	5	5	5	8	25	100	
Sandy Koufax SP	15	25	▲80	▼100	150	▼300	2,500	
Bob Bailey	5	5	5	5	8	15	60	
Milt Pappas	5	5	5	5	8	15	30	400
Ron Hunt	5	5	5	5	8	15	40	250
Whitey Ford	5	5	6	20	25	▲40	▲80	
Roy McMillan	5	5	5	5	8	20	40	300
Rocky Colavito	5	5	5	5	8	15	60	300
Jim Bunning	5	5	5	6	10	30	200	300
Roberto Clemente	15	20	30	▲50	60	120	500	
Al Kaline	5	5	5	6	20	▼25	60	400
Nellie Fox	5	5	5	6	10	▲30	40	400
Tony Gonzalez	5	5	5	5	8	30	80	
Jim Gentile	5	5	5	5	8	40	60	
Dean Chance	5	5	5	5	8	20	60	
Dick Ellsworth	5	5	5	5	8	15	40	
Jim Fregosi	5	5	5	6	15	50		
Dick Groat	5	5	5	5	8	15	50	350
Chuck Hinton	5	5	5	5	8	15	40	450
Elston Howard	5	5	5	6	15	80	150	
Dick Farrell	5	5	5	5	8	15	40	150
Albie Pearson	5	5	5	5	8	15	30	150
Frank Howard	5	5	5	5	8	15	40	300
Mickey Mantle	50	60	80	100	120	200	500	
Joe Torre	5	5	5	5	8	15	40	500
Eddie Brinkman	5	5	5	5	8	40	60	
Bob Friend SP	5	5	8	15	30	40	120	
Frank Robinson	5	5	5	6	▼25	▲60	200	▲1,200
Bill Freehan	5	5	5	6	15	50	300	

	VG 3	VgEx 4	EX 5	ExMt 6	NM 7	NmMt 8	MT 9	Gem 9.5/10
31 Warren Spahn	5	5	5	6	▲20	30	▲50	300
32 Camilo Pascual	5	5	5	5	8	15	30	300
33 Pete Ward	5	5	5	5	8	15	30	
34 Jim Maloney	5	5	5	5	8	40	60	275
35 Dave Wickersham	5	5	5	5	8	15	60	500
36 Johnny Callison	5	5	5	5	8	15	30	225
37 Juan Marichal	5	5	5	6	10	20	50	
38 Harmon Killebrew	5	5	5	6	20	30	60	400
39 Luis Aparicio	5	5	5	6	10	20	60	
40 Dick Radatz	5	5	5	5	8	15	30	200
41 Bob Gibson	6	8	12	▲30	▲40	▼50	150	
42 Dick Stuart SP	5	5	6	10	25	50	80	
43 Tommy Davis	5	5	5	5	8	15	60	200
44 Tony Oliva	5	5	5	6	10	20	40	400
45 Wayne Causey SP	5	5	5	25	30	40	100	
46 Max Alvis	5	5	5	5	8	15	40	
47 Galen Cisco SP	5	5	6	25	30	40	100	
48 Carl Yastrzemski	5	5	6	▼20	▼25	▲50	100	
49 Hank Aaron	5	6	20	50	60	▲100	200	
50 Brooks Robinson	5	5	5	▲15	25	40	▲150	600
51 Willie Mays SP	12	20	60	80	▼100	200	▼500	
52 Billy Williams	5	5	5	6	10	25	200	
53 Juan Pizarro	5	5	8	12	20	30		250
54 Leon Wagner	5	5	5	5	8	15	30	250
55 Orlando Cepeda	5	5	5	8	12	20	25	200
56 Vada Pinson	5	5	5	5	8	15	30	400
57 Ken Boyer	5	6	10	15	25	200		
58 Ron Santo	5	5	6	10	15	20	100	
59 John Romano	5	5	5	5	8	20	80	
60 Bill Skowron SP	5	6	15	30	40	150		

—Hank Aaron #49 PSA 10 (Gem) sold for $3,000 (eBay; 12/07)
—Hank Aaron #49 PSA 10 (Gem) sold for $1,679 (Memory Lane; 5/08)
—Ken Boyer #57 PSA 9 (MT) sold for $904 (eBay; 8/07)
—Ken Boyer #57 PSA 9 (MT) sold for $856 (eBay; 3/07)
—Ken Boyer #57 PSA 9 (MT) sold for $814 (eBay; 8/07)
—Ken Boyer #57 PSA 9 (MT) sold for $565 (eBay; 7/07)
—Roberto Clemente #11 PSA 10 (Gem) sold for $2,886 (Mastro; 2/07)
—Bill Freehan #30 PSA 10 (Gem) sold for $2,030 (eBay; 1/13)
—Jim Fregosi #18 PSA 9 (MT) sold for $460 (eBay; 11/07)
—Jim Fregosi #18 PSA 9 (MT) sold for $233 (eBay; 3/07)
—Elston Howard #21 PSA 10 (Gem) sold for $785 (eBay; 12/06)
—Elston Howard #21 PSA 10 (Gem) sold for $765 (eBay; 4/07)
—Elston Howard #21 PSA 10 (Gem) sold for $329 (eBay; 3/08)
—Sandy Koufax #3 PSA 10 (Gem) sold for $32,891 (Mastro; 9/07)
—Mickey Mantle #25 PSA 10 (Gem) sold for $5,777 (Mastro; 4/07)
—John Romano #59 PSA 10 Gem) sold for $696 (eBay; 8/07)
—Ron Santo #58 PSA 10 (Gem) sold for $414 (eBay; 1/08)
—Bill Skowron #60 PSA 9 (MT) sold for $800 (eBay; 11/07)
—Bill Skowron #60 PSA 9 (MT) sold for $501 (eBay; 7/07)
—Bill Skowron #60 PSA 9 (MT) sold for $355 (eBay; 3/07)
—Dick Stuart #42 PSA 10 (Gem) sold for $556 (eBay; 5/07)
—Carl Yastrzemski #48 PSA 10 (Gem) sold for $754 (eBay; 2/08)

1964 Topps Stand-Ups

	GD 2	VG 3	VgEx 4	EX 5	ExMt 6	NM 7	NmMt 8	MT 9
1 Hank Aaron	20	30	40	80	150	200	600	2,500
2 Hank Aguirre	5	5	5	5	20	25	50	300
3 George Altman	5	5	5	5	10	30	200	
4 Max Alvis	5	5	6	10	15	25	60	
5 Bob Aspromonte	5	5	5	5	10	15	50	300
6 Jack Baldschun SP	5	5	8	12	20	200		
7 Ernie Banks	8	12	20	40	80	150	300	
8 Steve Barber	5	5	5	5	10	20	300	
9 Earl Battey	5	5	5	5	10	20	200	
10 Ken Boyer	5	5	5	8	15	30	120	
11 Ernie Broglio	5	5	5	8	12	20	100	
12 John Callison	5	5	5	8	12	20	100	
13 Norm Cash SP	6	10	15	25	40	120	300	
14 Wayne Causey	5	5	5	5	10	15	80	
15 Orlando Cepeda	5	5	8	15	60	200		
16 Ed Charles	5	5	5	10	15	40	250	
17 Roberto Clemente	25	50	60	150	200	350	600	
18 Donn Clendenon SP	5	5	8	12	20	30	80	300
19 Rocky Colavito	5	5	5	8	15	20	80	
20 Ray Culp SP	5	5	8	12	20	40	200	
21 Tommy Davis	5	5	5	5	10	20	120	

BASEBALL

		GD 2	VG 3	VgEx 4	EX 5	ExMt 6	NM 7	NmMt 8	MT 9
22	Don Drysdale SP	10	15	40	50	100	120	300	
23	Dick Ellsworth	5	5	5	5	10	15	40	250
24	Dick Farrell	5	5	5	5	10	15	40	300
25	Jim Fregosi	5	5	5	5	10	20	200	
26	Bob Friend	5	5	5	5	10	15	100	
27	Jim Gentile	5	5	5	5	10	15	60	
28	Jesse Gonder SP	5	5	8	12	20	100	200	
29	Tony Gonzalez SP	5	5	8	12	20	100	200	
30	Dick Groat	5	5	5	6	12	25	200	
31	Woody Held	5	5	5	5	10	15	120	
32	Chuck Hinton	5	5	5	5	10	15	40	400
33	Elston Howard	5	5	5	8	15	30	120	
34	Frank Howard SP	5	8	12	20	30	80	150	
35	Ron Hunt	5	5	5	5	10	20		
36	Al Jackson	5	5	5	5	10	15	80	
37	Ken Johnson	5	5	5	5	10	20	120	
38	Al Kaline	10	15	25	40	80	100	200	
39	Harmon Killebrew	5	8	12	20	30	100	200	
40	Sandy Koufax	20	30	40	100	150	200	600	
41	Don Lock SP	5	5	8	12	20	40	100	
42	Jerry Lumpe SP	5	5	8	12	20	40	200	
43	Jim Maloney	5	5	5	5	10	15	80	
44	Frank Malzone	5	5	5	5	10	15	80	
45	Mickey Mantle	80	120	200	250	400	800	1,500	5,000
46	Juan Marichal SP	8	12	20	30	50	100	250	800
47	Eddie Mathews SP	10	15	25	40	60	120	300	1,200
48	Willie Mays	25	40	50	80	150	300	1,500	
49	Bill Mazeroski	5	5	5	10	15	50	150	
50	Ken McBride	5	5	5	5	10	15	50	
51	Willie McCovey SP	8	12	20	30	50	200	400	
52	Claude Osteen	5	5	5	5	10	20	60	
53	Jim O'Toole	5	5	5	5	10	15	50	
54	Camilo Pascual	5	5	5	5	10	15	80	
55	Albie Pearson SP	5	5	8	12	20	35	70	
56	Gary Peters	5	5	5	5	10	15	100	
57	Vada Pinson	5	5	5	5	10	20	100	
58	Juan Pizarro	5	5	5	5	10	15	40	150
59	Boog Powell	5	5	5	8	15	30	120	
60	Bobby Richardson	5	5	5	8	15	30	150	300
61	Brooks Robinson	6	10	15	25	60	100	250	700
62	Floyd Robinson	5	5	5	5	10	30	80	
63	Frank Robinson	6	10	15	25	80	100	400	
64	Ed Roebuck SP	5	5	8	12	20	35	100	
65	Rich Rollins	5	5	5	5	10	20		
66	John Romano	5	5	5	5	10	15	50	200
67	Ron Santo SP	6	10	15	25	50	200	350	
68	Norm Siebern	5	5	5	5	10	15	80	
69	Warren Spahn SP	10	15	25	40	60	150	350	1,200
70	Dick Stuart SP	5	8	12	20	30	80	200	
71	Lee Thomas	5	5	5	8	12	20	50	
72	Joe Torre	5	5	8	12	20	60	250	
73	Pete Ward	5	5	5	5	10	15	120	
74	Bill White SP	5	6	10	15	25	50	135	400
75	Billy Williams SP	8	12	20	30	50	300	500	
76	Hal Woodeshick SP	5	5	8	12	30	50		
77	Carl Yastrzemski SP	25	40	80	200	250	500	1,000	

—Jack Baldschun PSA 8 (NmMt) sold for $1,739 (Goodwin; 8/07)
—Ernie Banks PSA 8 (MT) sold for $2,440 (Goodwin; 11/07)
—Roberto Clemente PSA 9 (MT) sold for $2,055 (eBay; 6/08)
—Roberto Clemente SGC 92 (NmMt+) sold for $598 (Heritage; 10/07)
—Roberto Clemente SGC 88 (NmMt) sold for $406 (eBay; 10/07)
—Roberto Clemente GAI 8 (NmMt) sold for $256 (eBay; 12/07)
—Don Drysdale PSA 9 (MT) sold for $1,847 (Memory Lane; 5/08)
—Dick Farrell PSA 9 (MT) sold for $1,863 (Mile High; 1/07)
—Dick Farrell PSA 9 (MT) sold for $1,391 (Memory Lane; 5/08)
—Ron Hunt PSA 8 (NmMt) sold for $307 (Goodwin; 8/07)
—Ron Hunt PSA 8 (NmMt) sold for $220 (eBay; 10/06)
—Sandy Koufax PSA 9 (MT) sold for $10,802 (Memory Lane; 5/08)
—Sandy Koufax PSA 9 (MT) sold for $10,049 (Madec; 10/06)
—Sandy Koufax PSA 8.5 (NmMt+) sold for $1,244 (eBay; 3/08)
—Mickey Mantle SGC 92 (NmMt+) sold for $1,680 (Mastro; 5/08)
—Mickey Mantle SGC 88 (NmMt) sold for $1,329 (American Memorabilia; 9/07)
—Willie Mays PSA 9 (MT) sold for $4,163 (Memory Lane; 5/08)
—Bill Mazeroski PSA 9 (MT) sold for $5,316 (Mile High; 1/07)
—Rich Rollins PSA 8 (NmMt) sold for $371 (Goodwin; 8/07)
—Rich Rollins PSA 8 (NmMt) sold for $300 (eBay; 1/08)
—Hal Woodeshick PSA 8 (NmMt) sold for $378 (Goodwin; 8/07)
—Hal Woodeshick PSA 8 (NmMt) sold for $224 (Madec; 5/07)

1965 Topps

		GD 2	VG 3	VgEx 4	EX 5	ExMt 6	NM 7	NmMt 8	MT
	COMMON SP (371-598)	5	5	5	5	8	15	25	
1	AL Batting Leaders	5	5	8	12	20	30	120	5
2	NL Batting Leaders	5	6	10	15	50	80	150	7
3	AL Home Run Leaders	6	▲30	40	50	60	80	120	6
4	NL Home Run Leaders	5	5	6	10	20	50	120	6
5	AL RBI Leaders	6	10	15	25	60	80	▲200	5
6	NL RBI Leaders	5	5	5	8	20	▲40	▲80	5
7	AL ERA Leaders	5	5	5	5	5	10	30	1
8	NL ERA Leaders	5	6	10	25	30	60	120	5
9	AL Pitching Leaders	5	5	5	6	10	20	80	1
10	NL Pitching Leaders	5	5	5	8	12	20	50	1
11	AL Strikeout Leaders	5	5	5	6	10	25	100	3
12	NL Strikeout Leaders	5	5	8	12	20	60	3	
13	Pedro Ramos	5	5	5	5	5	10	25	
14	Len Gabrielson	5	5	5	5	8	30	200	
15	Robin Roberts	5	5	5	6	20	25	50	1
16	Joe Morgan DP RC	30	▲50	▲60	80	▲150	250	600	2,5
17	Johnny Romano	5	5	5	5	5	8	20	
18	Bill McCool	5	5	5	5	5	8	20	
19	Gates Brown	5	5	5	6	10	25	80	
20	Jim Bunning	5	5	5	5	8	25	50	3
21	Don Blasingame	5	5	5	5	8	15	100	
22	Charlie Smith	5	5	8	12	20	30	250	
23	Bob Tiefenauer	5	5	5	5	5	8	20	
24	Minnesota Twins TC	5	5	5	5	8	20	80	1
25	Al McBean	5	5	5	5	5	8	40	
26	Bobby Knoop	5	5	5	5	5	8	25	
27	Dick Bertell	5	5	5	5	5	8	20	
28	Barney Schultz	5	5	5	5	5	8	20	
29	Felix Mantilla	5	5	5	5	5	8	20	
30	Jim Bouton	5	5	5	5	8	15	50	1
31	Mike White	5	5	5	5	5	8	20	1
32	Herman Franks MG	5	5	5	5	5	8	20	
33	Jackie Brandt	5	5	5	5	5	8	20	
34	Cal Koonce	5	5	5	5	5	8	20	
35	Ed Charles	5	5	5	5	5	8	20	
36	Bobby Wine	5	5	5	5	5	8	20	
37	Fred Gladding	5	5	5	5	5	8	20	
38	Jim King	5	5	5	5	5	8	20	
39	Gerry Arrigo	5	5	5	5	5	8	20	
40	Frank Howard	5	5	5	5	8	15	50	12
41	B.Howard/M.Staehle RC	5	5	5	5	5	8	20	
42	Earl Wilson	5	5	5	5	5	10	30	
43	Mike Shannon	5	5	5	5	5	8	20	
44	Wade Blasingame RC	5	5	5	5	6	10	40	
45	Roy McMillan	5	5	5	5	5	8	20	
46	Bob Lee	5	5	5	5	8	15	25	2
47	Tommy Harper	5	5	5	5	5	8	20	
48	Claude Raymond	5	5	5	5	5	8	20	5
49	C.Blefary RC/J.Miller	5	5	5	5	5	8	20	5
50	Juan Marichal	5	10	12	15	25	▲60	120	5
51	Bill Bryan	5	5	5	5	5	8	20	
52	Ed Roebuck	5	5	5	5	5	8	25	15
53	Dick McAuliffe	5	5	5	5	5	10	30	2
54	Joe Gibbon	5	5	5	5	5	8	20	
55	Tony Conigliaro	5	6	10	15	25	50	80	
56	Ron Kline	5	5	5	5	5	8	20	6
57	St. Louis Cardinals TC	5	5	5	5	5	10	25	
58	Fred Talbot RC	5	5	5	5	5	8	20	6
59	Nate Oliver	5	5	5	5	5	8	20	15
60	Jim O'Toole	5	5	5	5	5	8	20	12
61	Chris Cannizzaro	5	5	5	5	5	8	25	
62	Jim Kaat DP	5	5	5	6	10	15	30	7
63	Ty Cline	5	5	5	5	5	8	20	
64	Lou Burdette	5	5	5	5	5	8	20	
65	Tony Kubek	5	5	6	10	15	30	100	2
66	Bill Rigney MG	5	5	5	5	5	8	20	
67	Harvey Haddix	5	5	5	5	5	10	25	15
68	Del Crandall	5	5	5	5	5	8	20	
69	Bill Virdon	5	5	5	5	5	8	25	
70	Bill Skowron	5	5	5	5	5	10	25	
71	John O'Donoghue	5	5	5	5	5	8	40	
72	Tony Gonzalez	5	5	5	5	5	8	20	

Left section

Player	GD 2	VG 3	VgEx 4	EX 5	ExMt 6	NM 7	NmMt 8	MT 9
Dennis Ribant RC	5	5	5	5	5	8	20	60
Rico Petrocelli RC	5	5	5	8	25	30	50	120
Deron Johnson	5	5	5	5	5	8	20	150
Sam McDowell	5	5	5	5	6	10	40	120
Doug Camilli	5	5	5	5	5	10	30	60
Dal Maxvill	5	5	5	5	5	8	20	60
Checklist 1 Cannizzaro	5	5	5	5	5	8	150	
Checklist 1 C.Cannizzaro	5	5	5	5	5	8	30	
Turk Farrell	5	5	5	5	5	8	20	60
Don Buford	5	5	5	5	5	8	20	50
S.Alomar RC/J.Braun RC	5	5	5	5	5	10	25	150
George Thomas	5	5	5	5	5	8	20	100
Ron Herbel	5	5	5	5	5	8	20	80
Willie Smith RC	5	5	5	5	5	8	25	120
Buster Narum	5	5	5	5	5	8	20	60
Nelson Mathews	5	5	5	5	5	8	20	60
Jack Lamabe	5	5	5	5	5	8	20	80
Mike Hershberger	5	5	5	5	5	8	25	80
Rich Rollins	5	5	5	5	5	8	20	60
Chicago Cubs TC	5	5	5	5	5	8	50	80
Dick Howser	5	5	5	5	5	10	40	
Jack Fisher	5	5	5	5	5	8	20	80
Charlie Lau	5	5	5	5	5	8	60	
Bill Mazeroski DP	5	5	5	5	5	15	40	150
Sonny Siebert	5	5	5	5	6	15	150	
Pedro Gonzalez	5	5	5	5	5	8	20	50
Bob Miller	5	5	5	5	5	8	30	60
Gil Hodges MG	5	5	5	5	8	15	40	150
Ken Boyer	5	5	5	6	10	30	80	
Fred Newman	5	5	5	5	5	8	20	60
Steve Boros	5	5	5	5	5	8	20	80
Harvey Kuenn	5	5	5	5	5	8	20	60
Checklist 2	5	5	5	5	5	8	20	80
Chico Salmon	5	5	5	5	5	8	20	50
Gene Oliver	5	5	5	5	5	8	20	50
P.Corrales RC/C.Shockley RC	5	5	5	5	5	8	40	150
Don Mincher	5	5	5	5	5	8	20	80
Walt Bond	5	5	5	5	5	10	60	150
Ron Santo	5	5	8	12	25	50	100	400
Lee Thomas	5	5	5	5	5	8	20	60
Derrell Griffith RC	5	5	5	5	5	8	20	60
Steve Barber	5	5	5	5	5	8	20	60
Jim Hickman	5	5	5	5	5	10	40	175
Bobby Richardson	5	5	8	12	20	60	150	
D.Dowling RC/B.Tolan RC	5	5	5	5	5	8	20	50
Wes Stock	5	5	5	5	5	8	25	100
Hal Lanier RC	5	5	5	5	5	8	20	60
John Kennedy	5	5	5	5	5	8	20	60
Frank Robinson	5	10	25	40	▲60	▲100	200	2,000
Gene Alley	5	5	5	5	5	8	20	60
Bill Pleis	5	5	5	5	5	8	20	60
Frank Thomas	5	5	5	5	5	8	20	80
Tom Satriano	5	5	5	5	5	8	20	80
Juan Pizarro	5	5	5	5	5	8	20	60
Los Angeles Dodgers TC	5	5	5	5	8	15	40	150
Frank Lary	5	5	5	5	5	8	25	
Vic Davalillo	5	5	5	5	5	8	20	60
Bennie Daniels	5	5	5	5	5	8	20	50
Al Kaline	6	15	20	25	40	▲60	▲120	600
Johnny Keane MG	5	5	5	5	5	8	40	
Cards Take Opener WS1	5	5	5	5	8	15	80	150
Mel Stottlemyre WS2	5	5	5	5	5	10	40	250
Mickey Mantle WS3	15	25	50	60	80	120	200	600
Ken Boyer WS4	5	5	5	5	8	20	60	150
Tim McCarver WS5	5	5	5	5	5	10	30	80
Jim Bouton WS6	5	5	5	5	5	10	30	100
Bob Gibson WS7	5	5	5	5	8	20	40	200
Cards Celebrate WS	5	5	5	5	5	10	30	100
Dean Chance	5	5	5	5	5	8	20	60
Charlie James	5	5	5	5	5	8	20	60
Bill Monbouquette	5	5	5	5	5	8	20	80
J.Gelnar RC/J.May RC	5	5	5	5	5	8	20	60
Ed Kranepool	5	5	5	5	5	8	30	60
Luis Tiant RC	5	5	6	▲25	30	60	100	400
Ron Hansen	5	5	5	5	5	8	20	60
Dennis Bennett	5	5	5	5	5	8	20	60
Willie Kirkland	5	5	5	5	5	8	25	80

Right section

#	Player	GD 2	VG 3	VgEx 4	EX 5	ExMt 6	NM 7	NmMt 8	MT 9
149	Wayne Schurr	5	5	5	5	5	8	20	50
150	Brooks Robinson	5	8	20	▲40	▲50	60	120	500
151	Kansas City Athletics TC	5	5	5	5	5	10	25	80
152	Phil Ortega	5	5	5	5	5	8	20	50
153	Norm Cash	5	5	5	▲20	▲25	▲30	▲40	150
154	Bob Humphreys RC	5	5	5	5	5	8	20	50
155	Roger Maris	10	15	40	50	80	100	▲250	1,000
156	Bob Sadowski	5	5	5	5	5	8	20	50
157	Zoilo Versalles	5	5	5	5	5	10	40	100
158	Dick Sisler	5	5	5	5	5	8	20	60
159	Jim Duffalo	5	5	5	5	5	8	20	80
160	Roberto Clemente	25	50	80	100	▲150	▲300	800	6,000
161	Frank Baumann	5	5	5	5	5	8	20	80
162	Russ Nixon	5	5	5	5	5	8	20	60
163	Johnny Briggs	5	5	5	5	5	8	20	60
164	Al Spangler	5	5	5	5	5	8	25	80
165	Dick Ellsworth	5	5	5	5	5	8	20	50
166	G.Culver RC/T.Agee RC	5	5	5	5	5	8	20	50
167	Bill Wakefield	5	5	5	5	5	8	20	50
168	Dick Green	5	5	5	5	5	8	25	50
169	Dave Vineyard RC	5	5	5	5	5	8	20	50
170	Hank Aaron	25	50	60	100	120	250	500	2,500
171	Jim Roland	5	5	5	5	5	8	20	80
172	Jimmy Piersall	5	5	5	5	5	10	30	80
173	Detroit Tigers TC	5	5	5	5	6	12	25	60
174	Joey Jay	5	5	5	5	5	8	20	60
175	Bob Aspromonte	5	5	5	5	5	8	20	80
176	Willie McCovey	5	5	15	25	▲40	60	120	400
177	Pete Mikkelsen	5	5	5	5	5	10	25	100
178	Dalton Jones	5	5	5	5	5	8	20	60
179	Hal Woodeshick	5	5	5	5	5	8	20	50
180	Bob Allison	5	5	5	5	5	8	30	100
181	D.Loun RC/J.McCabe	5	5	5	5	5	8	20	50
182	Mike de la Hoz	5	5	5	5	5	8	20	50
183	Dave Nicholson	5	5	5	5	5	8	20	50
184	John Boozer	5	5	5	5	5	8	20	60
185	Max Alvis	5	5	5	5	5	8	20	60
186	Billy Cowan	5	5	5	5	5	8	25	100
187	Casey Stengel MG	5	5	15	20	25	30	60	200
188	Sam Bowens	5	5	5	5	5	8	20	50
189	Checklist 3	5	5	5	5	6	10	25	60
190	Bill White	5	5	5	5	8	15	40	100
191	Phil Regan	5	5	5	5	5	8	20	100
192	Jim Coker	5	5	5	5	5	8	20	60
193	Gaylord Perry	5	5	15	20	25	30	▲60	▲150
194	B.Kelso RC/R.Reichardt RC	5	5	5	5	5	8	20	50
195	Bob Veale	5	5	5	5	5	8	20	60
196	Ron Fairly	5	5	5	5	5	12	40	120
197	Diego Segui	5	5	5	5	5	8	20	60
198	Smoky Burgess	5	5	5	5	8	12	40	150
199	Bob Heffner	5	5	5	5	5	8	20	60
200	Joe Torre	5	5	5	6	10	▲30	100	300
201	S.Valdespino RC/C.Tovar RC	5	5	5	5	5	8	25	
202	Leo Burke	5	5	5	5	5	8	20	60
203	Dallas Green	5	5	5	5	5	8	40	60
204	Russ Snyder	5	5	5	5	5	8	20	50
205	Warren Spahn	5	5	6	15	25	50	▲100	250
206	Willie Horton	5	5	5	5	8	20	120	150
207	Pete Rose	40	50	60	100	150	250	800	5,000
208	Tommy John	5	5	5	8	12	30	120	150
209	Pittsburgh Pirates TC	5	5	5	5	5	20	120	
210	Jim Fregosi	5	5	5	5	5	8	20	80
211	Steve Ridzik	5	5	5	5	5	8	20	80
212	Ron Brand	5	5	5	5	5	8	20	60
213	Jim Davenport	5	5	5	5	5	8	30	100
214	Bob Purkey	5	5	5	5	5	8	20	300
215	Pete Ward	5	5	5	5	5	8	25	200
216	Al Worthington	5	5	5	5	5	8	20	80
217	Walter Alston MG	5	5	5	5	5	10	30	80
218	Dick Schofield	5	5	5	5	8	15	60	150
219	Bob Meyer	5	5	5	5	5	8	25	100
220	Billy Williams	5	5	6	10	50	80	150	
221	John Tsitouris	5	5	5	5	5	8	20	50
222	Bob Tillman	5	5	5	5	5	8	20	60
223	Dan Osinski	5	5	5	6	10	15	30	80
224	Bob Chance	5	5	5	5	5	8	20	60
225	Bo Belinsky	5	5	5	5	5	8	20	60

#	Player	GD 2	VG 3	VgEx 4	EX 5	ExMt 6	NM 7	NmMt 8	MT 9
226	E.Jimenez RC/J.Gibbs	5	5	5	5	8	10	40	100
227	Bobby Klaus	5	5	5	5	5	8	20	80
228	Jack Sanford	5	5	5	5	5	8	20	60
229	Lou Clinton	5	5	5	5	5	8	20	60
230	Ray Sadecki	5	5	5	5	5	8	20	60
231	Jerry Adair	5	5	5	5	5	8	20	80
232	Steve Blass RC	5	5	5	5	5	8	30	100
233	Don Zimmer	5	5	5	5	5	10	25	100
234	Chicago White Sox TC	5	5	5	5	5	10	25	100
235	Chuck Hinton	5	5	5	5	5	8	20	60
236	Denny McLain RC	5	5	20	25	40	60	100	600
237	Bernie Allen	5	5	5	5	5	8	20	80
238	Joe Moeller	5	5	5	5	5	8	40	80
239	Doc Edwards	5	5	5	5	5	8	20	80
240	Bob Bruce	5	5	5	5	5	8	25	50
241	Mack Jones	5	5	5	5	5	8	20	60
242	George Brunet	5	5	5	5	5	8	25	
243	T.Davidson RC/T.Helms RC	5	5	5	5	5	10	30	100
244	Lindy McDaniel	5	5	5	5	5	8	20	50
245	Joe Pepitone	5	5	5	6	10	30	250	
246	Tom Butters	5	5	5	5	5	8	20	80
247	Wally Moon	5	5	5	5	5	10	25	80
248	Gus Triandos	5	5	5	5	5	8	20	80
249	Dave McNally	5	5	5	5	5	10	25	100
250	Willie Mays	30	▲60	80	100	200	300	600	2,500
251	Billy Herman MG	5	5	5	5	5	8	20	80
252	Pete Richert	5	5	5	5	5	8	20	80
253	Danny Cater	5	5	5	5	5	8	20	100
254	Roland Sheldon	5	5	5	5	5	10	40	200
255	Camilo Pascual	5	5	5	5	5	10	40	200
256	Tito Francona	5	5	5	5	5	10	25	200
257	Jim Wynn	5	5	5	5	6	15	50	
258	Larry Bearnarth	5	5	5	5	5	8	20	150
259	J.Northrup RC/R.Oyler RC	5	5	5	5	8	15	40	250
260	Don Drysdale	5	15	20	25	50	60	▼100	600
261	Duke Carmel	5	5	5	5	5	10	50	150
262	Bud Daley	5	5	5	5	5	8	20	60
263	Marty Keough	5	5	5	5	5	8	20	60
264	Bob Buhl	5	5	5	5	5	8	25	80
265	Jim Pagliaroni	5	5	5	5	5	8	20	120
266	Bert Campaneris RC	5	5	5	6	25	30	▼80	200
267	Washington Senators TC	5	5	5	5	5	10	25	150
268	Ken McBride	5	5	5	5	5	8	20	80
269	Frank Bolling	5	5	5	5	5	8	20	80
270	Milt Pappas	5	5	5	5	5	8	20	60
271	Don Wert	5	5	5	5	5	12	60	250
272	Chuck Schilling	5	5	5	5	5	8	20	150
273	Checklist 4	5	5	5	5	5	8	20	60
274	Lum Harris MG RC	5	5	5	5	5	8	20	60
275	Dick Groat	5	5	5	5	5	15	80	150
276	Hoyt Wilhelm	5	5	5	6	10	30	50	250
277	Johnny Lewis	5	5	5	5	5	8	60	150
278	Ken Retzer	5	5	5	5	5	8	30	80
279	Dick Tracewski	5	5	5	5	5	8	20	80
280	Dick Stuart	5	5	5	5	5	8	25	100
281	Bill Stafford	5	5	5	5	5	12	30	150
282	Masanori Murakami RC	5	5	6	10	20	50	60	250
283	Fred Whitfield	5	5	5	5	5	8	25	80
284	Nick Willhite	5	5	5	5	5	8	20	80
285	Ron Hunt	5	5	5	5	5	10	80	150
286	J.Dickson/A.Monteagudo	5	5	5	5	5	8	20	60
287	Gary Kolb	5	5	5	5	5	8	25	80
288	Jack Hamilton	5	5	5	5	5	8	20	50
289	Gordy Coleman	5	5	5	5	5	8	30	150
290	Wally Bunker	5	5	5	5	5	8	25	120
291	Jerry Lynch	5	5	5	5	5	10	40	
292	Larry Yellen	5	5	5	5	5	10	40	150
293	Los Angeles Angels TC	5	5	5	5	6	12	30	100
294	Tim McCarver	5	5	5	5	8	30	80	150
295	Dick Radatz	5	5	5	5	5	8	20	60
296	Tony Taylor	5	5	5	5	5	8	30	100
297	Dave DeBusschere	5	5	5	5	5	20	30	200
298	Jim Stewart	5	5	5	5	5	10	30	150
299	Jerry Zimmerman	5	5	5	5	5	8	30	120
300	Sandy Koufax	20	50	60	100	▲200	▲300	▼500	4,000
301	Birdie Tebbetts MG	5	5	5	5	5	10	30	150
302	Al Stanek	5	5	5	5	5	8	20	50

#	Player	GD 2	VG 3	VgEx 4	EX 5	ExMt 6	NM 7	NmMt 8	MT
303	John Orsino	5	5	5	5	5	8	20	6
304	Dave Stenhouse	5	5	5	5	5	8	20	5
305	Rico Carty	5	5	5	5	10	60	100	
306	Bubba Phillips	5	5	5	5	6	15	80	12
307	Barry Latman	5	5	5	5	5	8	20	5
308	C.Jones RC/T.Parsons	5	5	5	5	8	15	80	12
309	Steve Hamilton	5	5	5	5	5	10	50	
310	Johnny Callison	5	5	5	5	8	15	40	20
311	Orlando Pena	5	5	5	5	5	8	20	10
312	Joe Nuxhall	5	5	5	5	5	10	25	10
313	Jim Schaffer	5	5	5	5	5	8	25	8
314	Sterling Slaughter	5	5	5	5	5	8	30	6
315	Frank Malzone	5	5	5	5	5	10	25	10
316	Cincinnati Reds TC	5	5	5	5	8	15	60	30
317	Don McMahon	5	5	5	5	5	8	20	20
318	Matty Alou	5	5	5	5	8	15	80	10
319	Ken McMullen	5	5	5	5	5	8	20	6
320	Bob Gibson	6	10	30	40	▲60	100	250	1,20
321	Rusty Staub	5	5	5	5	10	20	50	10
322	Rick Wise	5	5	5	5	5	8	25	8
323	Hank Bauer MG	5	5	5	5	5	10	40	
324	Bobby Locke	5	5	5	5	5	8	20	6
325	Donn Clendenon	5	5	5	5	5	10	30	6
326	Dwight Siebler	5	5	5	5	5	8	60	12
327	Denis Menke	5	5	5	5	5	8	30	8
328	Eddie Fisher	5	5	5	5	5	8	25	12
329	Hawk Taylor RC	5	5	5	5	5	8	20	8
330	Whitey Ford	5	8	25	30	50	80	150	60
331	A.Ferrara/J.Purdin RC	5	5	5	5	5	15	25	10
332	Ted Abernathy	5	5	5	5	5	8	25	
333	Tom Reynolds	5	5	5	5	5	8	20	6
334	Vic Roznovsky RC	5	5	5	5	5	8	30	
335	Mickey Lolich	5	5	5	5	6	10	25	50
336	Woody Held	5	5	5	5	5	8	30	15
337	Mike Cuellar	5	5	5	5	6	10	15	30
338	Philadelphia Phillies TC	5	5	5	5	5	10	30	12
339	Ryne Duren	5	5	5	5	6	10	20	60
340	Tony Oliva	5	6	10	25	50	100	200	
341	Bob Bolin	5	5	5	5	5	8	30	10
342	Bob Rodgers	5	5	5	5	5	8	25	10
343	Mike McCormick	5	5	5	5	5	8	25	8
344	Wes Parker	5	5	5	5	5	8	25	10
345	Floyd Robinson	5	5	5	5	5	8	20	8
346	Bobby Bragan MG	5	5	5	5	5	8	25	10
347	Roy Face	5	5	5	5	5	10	25	10
348	George Banks	5	5	5	5	5	8	30	6
349	Larry Miller RC	5	5	5	5	5	10	40	10
350	Mickey Mantle	▲200	▲250	300	500	800	1,200	4,000	20,00
351	Jim Perry	5	5	5	5	5	10	40	6
352	Alex Johnson RC	5	5	5	5	5	8	60	12
353	Jerry Lumpe	5	5	5	5	5	8	15	50
354	B.Ott RC/J.Warner RC	5	5	5	5	5	8	20	6
355	Vada Pinson	5	5	5	5	5	10	50	12
356	Bill Spanswick	5	5	5	5	5	8	20	10
357	Carl Warwick	5	5	5	5	5	8	20	8
358	Albie Pearson	5	5	5	5	5	8	20	6
359	Ken Johnson	5	5	5	5	5	8	20	8
360	Orlando Cepeda	5	5	6	20	25	60	150	40
361	Checklist 5	5	5	5	5	5	8	25	5
362	Don Schwall	5	5	5	5	8	15	40	
363	Bob Johnson	5	5	5	5	5	8	20	8
364	Galen Cisco	5	5	5	5	5	8	20	6
365	Jim Gentile	5	5	5	5	5	8	20	8
366	Dan Schneider	5	5	5	5	5	8	20	8
367	Leon Wagner	5	5	5	5	5	10	60	80
368	K.Berry RC/J.Gibson RC	5	5	5	5	5	8	20	6
369	Phil Linz	5	6	10	15	25	40	120	
370	Tommy Davis	5	5	5	5	5	15	50	80
371	Frank Kreutzer	5	5	5	5	5	10	25	10
372	Clay Dalrymple	5	5	5	5	5	10	20	60
373	Curt Simmons	5	5	5	5	5	10	20	60
374	J.Cardenal RC/D.Simpson	5	5	5	5	5	10	20	60
375	Dave Wickersham	5	5	5	5	5	10	20	50
376	Jim Landis	5	5	5	5	5	10	20	60
377	Willie Stargell	5	15	20	25	▼40	100	150	500
378	Chuck Estrada	5	5	5	5	5	10	20	60
379	San Francisco Giants TC	5	5	5	5	6	12	30	100

Player	GD 2	VG 3	VgEx 4	EX 5	ExMt 6	NM 7	NmMt 8	MT 9
Rocky Colavito	5	5	6	10	15	40	50	200
Al Jackson	5	5	5	5	5	10	30	80
J.C. Martin	5	5	5	5	5	10	20	60
Felipe Alou	5	5	5	5	8	20	80	
Johnny Klippstein	5	5	5	5	5	10	20	50
Carl Yastrzemski	6	▲25	▲30	▲50	60	100	▼150	▲800
P.Jaeckel RC/F.Norman	5	5	5	5	5	10	20	50
Johnny Podres	5	5	5	6	10	15	25	80
John Blanchard	5	5	5	8	12	20	80	250
Don Larsen	5	5	5	6	10	15	25	50
Bill Freehan	5	5	5	6	10	15	60	
Mel McGaha MG	5	5	5	5	5	10	20	100
Bob Friend	5	5	5	5	5	20	30	80
Ed Kirkpatrick	5	5	5	5	5	10	15	40
Jim Hannan	5	5	5	5	5	10	20	50
Jim Ray Hart	5	5	5	5	6	12	25	80
Frank Bertaina RC	5	5	5	5	5	12	50	
Jerry Buchek	5	5	5	5	5	10	20	40
D.Neville RC/A.Shamsky RC	5	5	5	5	6	12	25	60
Ray Herbert	5	5	5	5	5	10	25	60
Harmon Killebrew	5	12	15	▲30	▲60	▲100	150	600
Carl Willey	5	5	5	5	5	10	20	60
Joe Amalfitano	5	5	5	5	6	12	30	200
Boston Red Sox TC	5	5	5	6	10	15	30	150
Stan Williams	5	5	5	5	5	10	20	60
John Roseboro	5	5	5	5	5	12	50	150
Ralph Terry	5	5	5	5	6	12	30	80
Lee Maye	5	5	5	5	5	10	20	80
Larry Sherry	5	5	5	6	10	15	25	80
J.Beauchamp RC/L.Dierker RC	5	5	5	6	10	15	30	120
Luis Aparicio	5	5	6	10	15	50	60	250
Roger Craig	5	5	5	5	5	10	30	50
Bob Bailey	5	5	5	5	5	10	30	80
Hal Reniff	5	5	5	5	6	12	30	100
Al Lopez MG	5	5	5	6	10	15	25	▲80
Curt Flood	5	5	5	6	10	40	60	150
Jim Brewer	5	5	5	5	5	10	25	60
Ed Brinkman	5	5	5	5	5	10	20	40
Johnny Edwards	5	5	5	5	5	10	20	60
Ruben Amaro	5	5	5	5	5	10	30	60
Larry Jackson	5	5	5	5	5	10	40	80
G.Dotter RC/J.Ward	5	5	5	5	5	10	20	50
Aubrey Gatewood	5	5	5	5	5	10	20	50
Jesse Gonder	5	5	5	5	5	10	25	60
Gary Bell	5	5	5	5	5	10	20	60
Wayne Causey	5	5	5	5	5	10	25	60
Milwaukee Braves TC	5	5	5	5	6	12	50	100
Bob Saverine	5	5	5	5	5	10	20	40
Bob Shaw	5	5	5	5	5	10	50	150
Don Demeter	5	5	5	5	5	10	20	60
Gary Peters	5	5	5	5	6	12	30	80
N.Briles RC/W.Spiezio RC	5	5	5	5	6	12	40	120
Jim Grant	5	5	5	5	5	10	25	80
John Bateman	5	5	5	5	6	12	30	150
Dave Morehead	5	5	5	5	5	10	30	60
Willie Davis	5	5	5	6	10	25	40	60
Don Elston	5	5	5	5	5	10	20	60
Chico Cardenas	5	5	5	5	5	10	25	60
Harry Walker MG	5	5	5	5	6	10	30	50
Moe Drabowsky	5	5	5	5	5	10	25	60
Tom Tresh	5	5	5	5	6	10	15	50
Denny Lemaster	5	5	5	5	5	10	20	60
Vic Power	5	5	5	5	5	10	20	80
Checklist 6	5	5	5	5	5	12	25	80
Bob Hendley	5	5	5	5	5	10	20	80
Don Lock	5	5	5	5	5	10	20	60
Art Mahaffey	5	5	5	5	5	10	25	100
Julian Javier	5	5	5	5	6	20	40	150
Lee Stange	5	5	5	5	5	10	25	60
J.Hinsley/G.Kroll RC	5	5	5	5	6	12	30	80
Elston Howard	5	5	6	15	20	50	100	200
Jim Owens	5	5	5	5	5	10	20	50
Gary Geiger	5	5	5	5	5	10	20	40
W.Crawford RC/J.Werhas	5	5	5	5	6	12	20	60
Ed Rakow	5	5	5	5	5	10	20	50
Norm Siebern	5	5	5	5	5	20	60	
Bill Henry	5	5	5	5	5	10	30	120

#	Player	GD 2	VG 3	VgEx 4	EX 5	ExMt 6	NM 7	NmMt 8	MT 9
457	Bob Kennedy MG	5	5	5	5	5	10	25	100
458	John Buzhardt	5	5	5	5	5	10	25	40
459	Frank Kostro	5	5	5	5	5	10	20	60
460	Richie Allen	5	5	8	15	30	80	120	400
461	C.Carroll RC/P.Niekro	5	10	25	30	60	80	120	400
462	Lew Krausse	5	5	5	5	5	10	25	150
463	Manny Mota	5	5	5	5	6	15	25	60
464	Ron Piche	5	5	5	5	5	10	20	50
465	Tom Haller	5	5	5	5	5	10	20	80
466	P.Craig RC/D.Nen	5	5	5	5	5	10	20	50
467	Ray Washburn	5	5	5	5	5	10	20	80
468	Larry Brown	5	5	5	5	5	10	25	60
469	Don Nottebart	5	5	5	5	5	10	20	50
470	Yogi Berra P/CO	8	20	25	40	50	80	120	400
471	Billy Hoeft	5	5	5	5	5	10	30	
472	Don Pavletich	5	5	5	5	5	10	20	80
473	P.Blair RC/D.Johnson RC	5	5	5	6	10	20	50	150
474	Cookie Rojas	5	5	5	5	6	12	40	60
475	Clete Boyer	5	5	6	10	15	25	40	60
476	Billy O'Dell	5	5	5	5	5	10	20	50
477	Steve Carlton RC	60	80	100	120	200	300	600	▲2,500
478	Wilbur Wood	5	5	5	5	6	12	25	60
479	Len Harrelson	5	5	5	5	5	10	25	50
480	Joel Horlen	5	5	5	5	5	10	25	80
481	Cleveland Indians TC	5	5	5	5	6	12	30	60
482	Bob Priddy	5	5	5	5	5	10	30	80
483	George Smith RC	5	5	5	5	5	10	25	120
484	Ron Perranoski	5	5	5	5	6	12	30	250
485	Nellie Fox	5	5	5	8	15	25	40	100
486	T.Egan/P.Rogan RC	5	5	5	5	5	10	20	50
487	Woody Woodward	5	5	5	5	5	5	10	60
488	Ted Wills	5	5	5	5	6	12	40	150
489	Gene Mauch MG	5	5	5	5	6	12	40	80
490	Earl Battey	5	5	5	5	5	12	25	80
491	Tracy Stallard	5	5	5	5	5	10	20	60
492	Gene Freese	5	5	5	5	5	10	25	50
493	B.Roman RC/B.Brubaker RC	5	5	5	5	5	10	20	60
494	Jay Ritchie RC	5	5	5	5	5	10	30	50
495	Joe Christopher	5	5	5	5	5	10	25	60
496	Joe Cunningham	5	5	5	5	5	5	25	80
497	K.Henderson RC/J.Hiatt RC	5	5	5	5	5	10	20	80
498	Gene Stephens	5	5	5	5	5	10	20	30
499	Stu Miller	5	5	5	5	6	12	30	40
500	Eddie Mathews	5	8	20	25	50	100	200	1,000
501	R.Gagliano RC/J.Rittwage RC	5	5	5	5	5	10	20	50
502	Don Cardwell	5	5	5	5	5	10	20	80
503	Phil Gagliano	5	5	5	5	5	10	20	50
504	Jerry Grote	5	5	5	5	6	12	25	60
505	Ray Culp	5	5	5	5	5	12	25	100
506	Sam Mele MG	5	5	5	5	5	10	25	80
507	Sammy Ellis	5	5	5	5	5	10	30	60
508	Checklist 7	5	5	5	5	6	12	30	50
509	B.Guindon RC/G.Vezendy RC	5	5	5	5	5	10	25	60
510	Ernie Banks	8	30	40	50	▼80	120	400	1,200
511	Ron Locke	5	5	5	5	5	10	25	60
512	Cap Peterson	5	5	5	5	5	10	20	60
513	New York Yankees TC	5	6	20	25	40	50	80	300
514	Joe Azcue	5	5	5	5	5	10	20	50
515	Vern Law	5	5	5	5	6	12	25	80
516	Al Weis	5	5	5	5	5	10	20	50
517	P.Schaal RC/J.Warner	5	5	5	5	5	10	20	50
518	Ken Rowe	5	5	5	5	5	10	20	60
519	Bob Uecker	5	5	20	30	50	60	100	200
520	Tony Cloninger	5	5	5	5	5	10	25	60
521	D.Bennett/M.Steevens RC	5	5	5	5	5	10	20	80
522	Hank Aguirre	5	5	5	5	5	10	20	50
523	Mike Brumley SP	5	5	5	5	6	10	15	100
524	Dave Giusti SP	5	5	5	5	6	10	15	60
525	Eddie Bressoud	5	5	5	5	5	10	20	50
526	J.Odom/J.Hunter SP RC	10	15	▲50	60	100	▲200	300	1,500
527	Jeff Torborg SP	5	5	5	5	6	10	15	25
528	George Altman	5	5	5	5	5	10	20	80
529	Jerry Fosnow SP RC	5	5	5	5	6	10	15	200
530	Jim Maloney	5	5	5	5	5	10	25	80
531	Chuck Hiller	5	5	5	5	5	10	20	80
532	Hector Lopez	5	5	5	5	5	10	20	50
533	R.Swoboda RC/T.McGraw RC SP	5	8	20	25	30	▼40	▲80	150

#	Player	GD 2	VG 3	VgEx 4	EX 5	ExMt 6	NM 7	NmMt 8	MT 9
534	John Herrnstein	5	5	5	5	5	10	20	50
535	Jack Kralick SP	5	5	5	6	10	20	40	80
536	Andre Rodgers SP	5	5	5	6	10	15	25	120
537	Lopez/Roof/May RC	5	5	5	5	5	10	25	60
538	Chuck Dressen MG SP	5	5	5	6	10	15	25	80
539	Herm Starrette	5	5	5	5	5	10	20	50
540	Lou Brock SP	5	8	30	40	50	80	▲150	500
541	G.Bollo RC/B.Locker RC	5	5	5	5	5	10	20	40
542	Lou Klimchock	5	5	5	5	5	10	20	60
543	Ed Connolly SP RC	5	5	5	6	10	15	25	100
544	Howie Reed RC	5	5	5	5	5	10	25	60
545	Jesus Alou SP	5	5	6	10	15	25	50	200
546	Davis/Hed/Bark/Weav RC	5	5	5	5	6	12	25	50
547	Jake Wood SP	5	5	5	6	10	15	40	150
548	Dick Stigman	5	5	5	5	5	10	20	60
549	R.Pena RC/G.Beckert RC	5	5	5	6	10	15	50	80
550	Mel Stottlemyre SP RC	5	6	10	25	50	80	100	600
551	New York Mets TC SP	5	5	5	8	12	30	40	100
552	Julio Gotay	5	5	5	5	5	10	20	80
553	Coombs/Ratliff/McClure RC	5	5	5	5	5	10	20	50
554	Chico Ruiz SP	5	5	5	6	10	15	50	80
555	Jack Baldschun SP	5	5	6	10	25	50	100
556	Red Schoendienst SP	5	5	5	8	12	30	50	120
557	Jose Santiago RC	5	5	5	5	5	10	20	50
558	Tommie Sisk	5	5	5	5	5	10	20	60
559	Ed Bailey SP	5	5	5	6	10	15	25	100
560	Boog Powell SP	5	5	6	8	20	30	50	200
561	Dab/Kek/Valle/Lefebvre RC	5	5	5	5	6	20	30	100
562	Billy Moran	5	5	5	5	5	10	20	50
563	Julio Navarro	5	5	5	5	5	10	20	50
564	Mel Nelson	5	5	5	5	5	10	20	60
565	Ernie Broglio SP	5	5	5	6	10	25	40	150
566	Blanco RC/Mosch RC/Lopez RC	5	5	5	6	10	15	30	80
567	Tommie Aaron	5	5	5	5	5	10	30	80
568	Ron Taylor SP	5	5	5	6	10	25	50	150
569	Gino Cimoli SP	5	5	5	6	10	15	25	60
570	Claude Osteen SP	5	5	5	6	10	15	40	150
571	Ossie Virgil SP	5	5	5	6	10	15	30	80
572	Baltimore Orioles TC SP	5	5	5	8	20	25	40	100
573	Jim Lonborg SP RC	5	5	6	10	15	30	50	200
574	Roy Sievers	5	5	5	5	6	20	25	60
575	Jose Pagan	5	5	5	5	8	12	25	60
576	Terry Fox SP	5	5	5	6	10	15	30	150
577	Knowles/Buschhorn RC/Schein RC	5	5	5	6	10	15	25	80
578	Camilo Carreon SP	5	5	5	6	10	15	25	60
579	Dick Smith SP	5	5	5	6	10	15	40	
580	Jimmie Hall SP	5	5	5	6	10	15	25	60
581	Tony Perez SP RC	25	▲50	▲60	80	100	200	400	2,000
582	Bob Schmidt SP	5	5	5	8	12	25	30	100
583	Wes Covington SP	5	5	5	6	10	15	25	50
584	Harry Bright	5	5	5	5	5	10	20	50
585	Hank Fischer	5	5	5	5	5	10	20	60
586	Tom McCraw SP	5	5	5	6	10	15	30	120
587	Joe Sparma	5	5	5	5	5	10	15	100
588	Lenny Green	5	5	5	5	5	10	25	80
589	F.Linzy RC/B.Schroder RC	5	5	5	5	6	20	30	150
590	John Wyatt	5	5	5	5	5	10	25	80
591	Bob Skinner SP	5	5	5	6	10	15	30	100
592	Frank Bork SP RC	5	5	5	6	10	15	30	80
593	J.Sullivan RC/J.Moore RC SP	5	5	5	6	10	15	30	
594	Joe Gaines	5	5	5	5	5	10	25	100
595	Don Lee	5	5	5	5	5	10	15	60
596	Don Landrum SP	5	5	5	6	10	15	25	80
597	Nossek/Sevcik/Reese RC	5	6	8	15	30	80	150	
598	Al Downing SP	5	5	8	12	20	50	120	600

—AL RBI Leaders #5 PSA 10 (Gem) sold for $3,957 (Memory Lane; 2/07)
—Ernie Banks #510 PSA 10 (Gem) sold for $2,988 (Mastro; 8/04)
—Yogi Berra #470 PSA 10 (Gem) sold for $5,558 (Mile High; 2/08)
—Yogi Berra #470 PSA 10 (Gem) sold for $3,700 (Memory Lane; 11/04)
—Lou Brock #540 PSA 10 (Gem) sold for $3,351 (Memory Lane; 12/06)
—Lou Brock #540 PSA 10 (Gem) sold for $2,969 (Leland's; 12/04)
—Bert Campaneris #266 PSA 10 (Gem) sold for $1,447 (Superior; 3/04)
—Steve Carlton #477 PSA 10 (Gem) (Young Collection) sold for $12,756 (SCP; 5/12)
—Steve Carlton #477 PSA 10 (Gem) sold for $9,778 (eBay; 11/06)
—Steve Carlton #477 BVG 9 (MT) sold for $560 (eBay; 12/07)
—Norm Cash #153 PSA 10 (Gem) sold for $1,920 (Mastro; 5/08)

—Roberto Clemente #160 SGC 96 (MT) sold for $806 (Mile High; 2/08)
—Tony Congiliaro #55 PSA 10 (Gem) sold for $1,737 (Memory Lane; 12/06)
—Bill Freehan #390 PSA 9 (MT) sold for $587 (eBay; 1/08)
—Len Gabrielson #14 PSA 9 (MT) sold for $2,862 (Mile High; 10/12)
—Len Gabrielson #14 PSA 9 (MT) sold for $2,238 (Memory Lane; 12/06)
—Jim Hunter #526 PSA 10 (Gem) (Young Collection) sold for $11,596 (SCP; 5/12)
—Jim Hunter #526 SGC 96 (MT) sold for $525 (Superior; 12/05)
—Jim Hunter #526 SGC 96 (MT) sold for $285 (Goodwin; 6/06)
—Sandy Koufax #300 SGC 96 (MT) sold for $1,837 (Mastro; 4/07)
—Sandy Koufax #300 BVG 9 (MT) sold for $941 (eBay; 4/04)
—Mets Rookies #308 PSA 10 (Gem) sold for $4,065 (eBay; 3/08)
—Mickey Mantle WS3 #134 PSA 10 (Gem) sold for $5,547 (eBay; 6/08)
—Mickey Mantle WS3 #134 PSA 10 (Gem) sold for $3,287 (Mastro; 8/04)
—Roger Maris #155 PSA 10 (Gem) sold for $6,706 (Memory Lane; 4/07)
—Eddie Mathews #500 SGC 96 (MT) sold for $247 (eBay; 5/07)
—Willie Mays #250 PSA 10 (Gem) sold for $6,567 (Memory Lane; 6/05)
—Willie Mays #250 PSA 10 (Gem) sold for $6,544 (Mastro; 4/07)
—Mets Rookies #308 PSA 10 (Gem) sold for $2,569 (Mile High; 2/08)
—Joe Morgan #16 PSA 10 (Gem) (Young Collection) sold for $8,897 (SCP; 5/12)
—Joe Morgan #16 BVG 9.5 (Gem) sold for $3,423 (eBay; 4/08)
—New York Mets TC #551 PSA 10 (Gem) sold for $2,591 (Mile High; 2/08)
—NL ERA Leaders #8 PSA 10 (Gem) sold for $24,541 (Mastro; 4/07)
—NL ERA Leaders #8 PSA 10 (Gem) sold for $18,725 (Madec; 11/07)
—NL ERA Leaders #8 SGC 98 (MT) sold for $2,693 (Mastro; 4/07)
—NL RBI Leaders #6 PSA 10 (Gem) sold for $4,610 (eBay; 2/08)
—NL Strikeout Leaders #12 PSA 10 (Gem) sold for $2,000 (eBay; 10/12)
—Tony Oliva #340 PSA 9 (MT) sold for $3,055 (eBay; 08/12)
—Tony Oliva #340 PSA 9 (MT) sold for $760 (eBay; 11/06)
—Tony Oliva #340 PSA 9 (MT) sold for $453 (eBay; 12/06)
—Tony Perez #581 PSA 10 (Gem) sold for $15,099 (eBay; 10/07)
—Tony Perez SP #581 PSA 10 (Gem) (Young Collection) sold for $7,919 (SCP; 5/12)
—Pittsburgh Pirates TC #209 PSA 9 (MT) sold for $688 (eBay; 9/07)
—Frank Robinson #120 SGC 96 (MT) sold for $516 (Memory Lane; 12/07)
—Pete Rose #207 PSA 10 (Gem) sold for $5,518 (Mastro; 6/05)
—Charlie Smith #22 PSA 9 (MT) sold for $2,062 (Mile High; 2/08)
—Warren Spahn #205 PSA 10 (Gem) sold for $3,524 (Mastro; 10/05)
—Warren Spahn #205 PSA 10 (Gem) sold for $2,500 (eBay; 12/06)
—Warren Spahn #205 PSA 10 (Gem) sold for $1,945 (Mile High; 2/08)
—Willie Stargell #377 PSA 10 (Gem) sold for $6,047 (Goodwin; 3/08)
—Casey Stengel #187 PSA 10 (Gem) sold for $3,136 (Mile High; 2/08)
—Luis Tiant #145 PSA 10 (Gem) sold for $4,800 (Mastro; 2/08)
—Luis Tiant #145 PSA 10 (Gem) sold for $1,367 (Mastro; 8/04)
—Tom Tresh #440 PSA 9 (MT) sold for $571 (eBay; 3/08)
—Billy Williams #220 PSA 9 (MT) sold for $809 (eBay; 12/06)
—Billy Williams #220 PSA 9 (MT) sold for $518 (eBay; 3/05)
—Billy Williams #220 PSA 9 (MT) sold for $357 (eBay; 10/07)

1965 Topps Embossed

#	Player	GD 2	VG 3	VgEx 4	EX 5	ExMt 6	NM 7	NmMt 8	MT
8	Sandy Koufax	6	10	15	30	50	60	150	
11	Mickey Mantle	25	30	50	60	100	150	800	
19	Roberto Clemente	5	6	10	25	50	100	300	
27	Willie Mays	5	5	8	12	25	40		
59	Hank Aaron	5	5	8	20	40	80	120	

—Hank Aaron #59 PSA 9 (MT) sold for $474 (eBay; 3/07)
—Carl Yastrzemski #1 PSA 8 (NmMt) sold for $734 (eBay; 4/08)

1966 Topps

#	Player	GD 2	VG 3	VgEx 4	EX 5	ExMt 6	NM 7	NmMt 8	MT
1	Willie Mays	30	50	60	120	250	600	2,000	5,00
2	Ted Abernathy	5	5	5	5	5	12	30	
3	Sam Mele MG	5	5	5	5	5	10	50	
4	Ray Culp	5	5	5	5	5	10	30	
5	Jim Fregosi	5	5	5	5	5	20	30	
6	Chuck Schilling	5	5	5	5	8	20	20	
7	Tracy Stallard	5	5	5	5	5	8	20	
8	Floyd Robinson	5	5	5	5	8	15	6	
9	Clete Boyer	5	5	5	5	8	15	50	
10	Tony Cloninger	5	5	5	5	5	10	25	15
11	B.Alyea RC/P.Craig	5	5	5	5	5	8	25	
12	John Tsitouris	5	5	5	5	5	8	25	
13	Lou Johnson	5	5	5	5	5	8	25	
14	Norm Siebern	5	5	5	5	5	8	20	6
15	Vern Law	5	5	5	5	5	8	15	6
16	Larry Brown	5	5	5	5	5	8	15	5

	GD 2	VG 3	VgEx 4	EX 5	ExMt 6	NM 7	NmMt 8	MT 9
John Stephenson	5	5	5	5	5	8	15	100
Roland Sheldon	5	5	5	5	5	8	20	
San Francisco Giants TC	5	5	5	5	5	10	40	
Willie Horton	5	5	5	5	6	15	50	
Don Nottebart	5	5	5	5	5	8	15	50
Joe Nossek	5	5	5	5	5	8	20	60
Jack Sanford	5	5	5	5	5	8	20	100
Don Kessinger RC	5	5	5	5	5	12	40	
Pete Ward	5	5	5	5	5	8	30	
Ray Sadecki	5	5	5	5	5	8	25	60
D.Knowles/A.Etchebarren RC	5	5	5	5	5	10	30	80
Phil Niekro	5	5	5	8	12	25	50	
Mike Brumley	5	5	5	5	5	8	25	60
Pete Rose DP	25	30	▲50	▲60	80	150	▲500	3,000
Jack Cullen	5	5	5	5	5	10	25	
Adolfo Phillips RC	5	5	5	5	5	8	15	80
Jim Pagliaroni	5	5	5	5	5	8	15	50
Checklist 1	5	5	5	5	5	8	25	
Ron Swoboda	5	5	5	5	8	15	40	
Jim Hunter DP	5	5	6	15	20	30	80	500
Billy Herman MG	5	5	5	5	5	8	15	50
Ron Nischwitz	5	5	5	5	5	8	20	80
Ken Henderson	5	5	5	5	5	8	20	100
Jim Grant	5	5	5	5	5	8	15	80
Don LeJohn RC	5	5	5	5	5	8	20	100
Aubrey Gatewood	5	5	5	5	5	8	25	100
A Don Landrum Full Button	5	5	5	5	6	12	40	
B Don Landrum Partial Button	5	5	6	10	15	25		
C Don Landrum No Button	5	5	5	5	6	12	40	
B.Davis/T.Kelley	5	5	5	5	5	8	20	70
Jim Gentile	5	5	5	5	5	8	15	60
Howie Koplitz	5	5	5	5	5	8	15	50
J.C. Martin	5	5	5	5	5	8	20	80
Paul Blair	5	5	5	5	5	10	40	
Woody Woodward	5	5	5	5	5	8	15	
Mickey Mantle DP	▲120	▲150	200	250	500	1,000	2,500	12,000
Gordon Richardson RC	5	5	5	5	5	8	20	60
Power Plus	5	5	5	5	5	10	20	100
Bob Duliba	5	5	5	5	5	8	20	
Jose Pagan	5	5	5	5	5	8	20	100
Ken Harrelson	5	5	5	5	5	8	30	100
Sandy Valdespino	5	5	5	5	5	8	30	
Jim Lefebvre	5	5	5	5	5	8	20	100
Dave Wickersham	5	5	5	5	5	8	15	60
Cincinnati Reds TC	5	5	5	5	5	10	40	80
Curt Flood	5	5	5	5	5	10	40	
Bob Bolin	5	5	5	5	5	8	15	60
A Merritt Ranew Sold Line	5	5	5	5	5	8	25	80
B Merritt Ranew No Sold Line	5	6	10	15	25	40		
Jim Stewart	5	5	5	5	5	8	20	60
Bob Bruce	5	5	5	5	5	8	25	80
Leon Wagner	5	5	5	5	5	8	20	60
Al Weis	5	5	5	5	5	8	15	50
C.Jones/D.Selma RC	5	5	5	5	5	10	40	120
Hal Reniff	5	5	5	5	5	8	20	300
Ken Hamlin	5	5	5	5	5	8	20	60
Carl Yastrzemski	5	6	25	30	▲60	▲80	200	800
Frank Carpin RC	5	5	5	5	5	8	25	120
Tony Perez	8	12	25	30	50	▲100	250	
Jerry Zimmerman	5	5	5	5	5	8	20	60
Don Mossi	5	5	5	5	5	8	15	60
Tommy Davis	5	5	5	5	5	8	60	
Red Schoendienst MG	5	5	5	5	8	15	30	
Johnny Orsino	5	5	5	5	5	8	15	50
Frank Linzy	5	5	5	5	5	8	15	60
Joe Pepitone	5	5	5	5	6	12	30	
Richie Allen	5	5	5	5	8	20	60	
Ray Oyler	5	5	5	5	5	8	30	100
Bob Hendley	5	5	5	5	5	8	15	60
Albie Pearson	5	5	5	5	5	8	20	60
J.Beauchamp/D.Kelley	5	5	5	5	5	8	15	50
Eddie Fisher	5	5	5	5	5	8	20	60
John Bateman	5	5	5	5	5	8	20	80
Dan Napoleon	5	5	5	5	5	8	20	100
Fred Whitfield	5	5	5	5	5	8	20	60
Ted Davidson	5	5	5	5	5	8	20	60
Luis Aparicio DP	5	5	5	5	8	▲30	40	200

	GD 2	VG 3	VgEx 4	EX 5	ExMt 6	NM 7	NmMt 8	MT 9
91A Bob Uecker Trade Line	5	5	6	10	15	50	200	
91B Bob Uecker No Trade Line	12	20	30	50	60	150		
92 New York Yankees TC	5	5	6	10	15	25	100	
93 Jim Lonborg DP	5	5	5	5	5	8	20	60
94 Matty Alou	5	5	5	5	5	8	25	80
95 Pete Richert	5	5	5	5	5	8	15	50
96 Felipe Alou	5	5	5	5	5	10	30	
97 Jim Merritt RC	5	5	5	5	5	8	25	100
98 Don Demeter	5	5	5	5	5	10	30	
99 Buc Belters	5	5	5	5	8	20	40	
100 Sandy Koufax DP	▲30	▲50	▲60	▲80	100	200	500	5,000
101A Checklist 2 Spahn 115 ERR	5	5	5	5	5	8	30	
101B Cheklist 2 Henry 115 COR	5	5	5	5	5	8	30	
102 Ed Kirkpatrick	5	5	5	5	5	8	20	100
103A Dick Groat Trade Line	5	5	5	5	5	10	25	60
103B Dick Groat No Trade Line	5	6	10	15	25	40		
104A Alex Johnson Trade Line	5	5	5	5	5	8	20	100
104B Alex Johnson No Trade Line	5	6	10	15	25	40		
105 Milt Pappas	5	5	5	5	5	12	40	
106 Rusty Staub	5	5	5	5	5	10	30	
107 L.Stahl RC/R.Tompkins RC	5	5	5	5	5	8	20	100
108 Bobby Klaus	5	5	5	5	5	8	25	
109 Ralph Terry	5	5	5	5	5	8	25	200
110 Ernie Banks	5	▲25	▲30	▲40	60	100	250	1,200
111 Gary Peters	5	5	5	5	5	12	40	100
112 Manny Mota	5	5	5	5	5	8	30	
113 Hank Aguirre	5	5	5	5	5	8	20	60
114 Jim Gosger	5	5	5	5	5	8	20	80
115 Bill Henry	5	5	5	5	5	8	25	
116 Walter Alston MG	5	5	5	5	5	10	30	
117 Jake Gibbs	5	5	5	5	5	10	40	
118 Mike McCormick	5	5	5	5	5	8	20	60
119 Art Shamsky	5	5	5	5	5	8	20	60
120 Harmon Killebrew	5	6	▲15	20	30	▲50	100	800
121 Ray Herbert	5	5	5	5	5	8	25	100
122 Joe Gaines	5	5	5	5	5	8	25	
123 F.Bork/J.May	5	5	5	5	5	8	20	
124 Tug McGraw	5	5	5	5	5	10	25	
125 Lou Brock	5	6	10	25	50	60	250	600
126 Jim Palmer UER RC	25	30	50	60	100	200	600	3,000
127 Ken Berry	5	5	5	5	5	8	25	120
128 Jim Landis	5	5	5	5	5	8	25	100
129 Jack Kralick	5	5	5	5	5	8	30	100
130 Joe Torre	5	5	5	5	8	25	40	120
131 California Angels TC	5	5	5	5	5	10	20	80
132 Orlando Cepeda	5	5	5	5	15	25	60	200
133 Don McMahon	5	5	5	5	5	8	20	60
134 Wes Parker	5	5	5	5	5	10	25	60
135 Dave Morehead	5	5	5	5	5	8	20	
136 Woody Held	5	5	5	5	5	8	20	80
137 Pat Corrales	5	5	5	5	5	8	20	
138 Roger Repoz RC	5	5	5	5	5	12	50	
139 B.Browne RC/D.Young RC	5	5	5	5	5	8	15	50
140 Jim Maloney	5	5	5	5	5	12	60	
141 Tom McCraw	5	5	5	5	5	8	15	60
142 Don Dennis RC	5	5	5	5	5	8	20	
143 Jose Tartabull	5	5	5	5	5	8	25	
144 Don Schwall	5	5	5	5	5	8	15	100
145 Bill Freehan	5	5	5	5	8	15	40	
146 George Altman	5	5	5	5	5	8	25	60
147 Lum Harris MG	5	5	5	5	5	8	20	100
148 Bob Johnson	5	5	5	5	5	8	20	100
149 Dick Nen	5	5	5	5	5	8	20	
150 Rocky Colavito	5	5	6	10	15	25	80	400
151 Gary Wagner RC	5	5	5	5	5	8	25	60
152 Frank Malzone	5	5	5	5	5	8	20	
153 Rico Carty	5	5	5	5	5	10	25	80
154 Chuck Hiller	5	5	5	5	5	8	25	
155 Marcelino Lopez	5	5	5	5	5	8	15	50
156 DP Combo	5	5	5	5	5	8	20	100
157 Rene Lachemann	5	5	5	5	5	8	25	60
158 Jim Brewer	5	5	5	5	5	8	15	60
159 Chico Ruiz	5	5	5	5	5	8	20	60
160 Whitey Ford	5	15	20	30	▲50	▲60	150	600
161 Jerry Lumpe	5	5	5	5	5	10	30	80
162 Lee Maye	5	5	5	5	5	8	20	120
163 Tito Francona	5	5	5	5	5	8	25	80

#	Name	GD 2	VG 3	VgEx 4	EX 5	ExMt 6	NM 7	NmMt 8	MT 9
164	T.Agee/M.Staehle	5	5	5	5	5	10	25	80
165	Don Lock	5	5	5	5	5	8	15	50
166	Chris Krug RC	5	5	5	5	5	8	20	60
167	Boog Powell	5	5	5	5	5	20	50	
168	Dan Osinski	5	5	5	5	5	8	20	60
169	Duke Sims RC	5	5	5	5	5	8	20	
170	Cookie Rojas	5	5	5	5	5	10	25	
171	Nick Willhite	5	5	5	5	5	8	40	80
172	New York Mets TC	5	5	5	5	8	15	30	60
173	Al Spangler	5	5	5	5	5	8	15	60
174	Ron Taylor	5	5	5	5	5	8	15	80
175	Bert Campaneris	5	5	5	5	5	10	40	
176	Jim Davenport	5	5	5	5	5	8	20	100
177	Hector Lopez	5	5	5	5	5	10	30	80
178	Bob Tillman	5	5	5	5	5	8	25	100
179	D.Aust RC/B.Tolan	5	5	5	5	5	10	30	
180	Vada Pinson	5	5	5	5	5	10	25	80
181	Al Worthington	5	5	5	5	5	8	20	50
182	Jerry Lynch	5	5	5	5	5	8	20	60
183A	Checklist 3 Large Print	5	5	5	5	5	8	20	60
183B	Checklist 3 Small Print	5	5	5	5	5	8	25	60
184	Denis Menke	5	5	5	5	5	8	20	50
185	Bob Buhl	5	5	5	5	5	8	25	
186	Ruben Amaro	5	5	5	5	5	15	50	
187	Chuck Dressen MG	5	5	5	6	10	15	50	100
188	Al Luplow	5	5	5	5	5	8	25	60
189	John Roseboro	5	5	5	5	5	10	20	80
190	Jimmie Hall	5	5	5	5	5	8	15	60
191	Darrell Sutherland RC	5	5	5	5	5	8	15	60
192	Vic Power	5	5	5	5	5	8	20	60
193	Dave McNally	5	5	5	5	5	10	20	200
194	Washington Senators TC	5	5	5	5	5	10	20	80
195	Joe Morgan	15	20	25	30	▲50	100	▲250	1,500
196	Don Pavletich	5	5	5	5	5	8	25	
197	Sonny Siebert	5	5	5	5	5	8	15	80
198	Mickey Stanley RC	5	5	5	5	8	15	50	120
199	ChiSox Clubbers	5	5	5	5	5	10	20	60
200	Eddie Mathews	5	5	15	25	30	40	100	400
201	Jim Dickson	5	5	5	5	5	8	15	50
202	Clay Dalrymple	5	5	5	5	5	5	30	
203	Jose Santiago	5	5	5	5	5	8	15	50
204	Chicago Cubs TC	5	5	5	5	5	10	20	60
205	Tom Tresh	5	5	5	5	8	15	50	250
206	Al Jackson	5	5	5	5	5	8	15	50
207	Frank Quilici RC	5	5	5	5	5	8	15	50
208	Bob Miller	5	5	5	5	5	8	20	50
209	F.Fisher/J.Hiller RC	5	5	5	5	5	10	20	150
210	Bill Mazeroski	5	5	5	8	12	25	50	120
211	Frank Kreutzer	5	5	5	5	5	8	20	100
212	Ed Kranepool	5	5	5	5	5	10	25	
213	Fred Newman	5	5	5	5	5	8	15	50
214	Tommy Harper	5	5	5	5	5	10	20	80
215	NL Batting Leaders	20	25	40	50	80	150	▲400	
216	AL Batting Leaders	5	6	10	15	25	40	250	
217	NL Home Run Leaders	5	6	10	15	20	50	▲100	400
218	AL Home Run Leaders	5	5	5	6	10	20	60	200
219	NL RBI Leaders	5	5	8	12	25	40	100	
220	AL RBI Leaders	5	5	5	5	8	15	60	
221	NL ERA Leaders	5	5	6	10	15	30	120	
222	AL ERA Leaders	5	5	5	5	8	15	50	
223	NL Pitching Leaders	5	15	20	25	30	40	100	
224	AL Pitching Leaders	5	5	5	5	8	20	120	
225	NL Strikeout Leaders	5	12	15	20	30	50	80	400
226	AL Strikeout Leaders	5	5	5	5	8	15	50	
227	Russ Nixon	5	5	5	5	5	8	20	80
228	Larry Dierker	5	5	5	5	5	8	15	60
229	Hank Bauer MG	5	5	5	5	5	8	20	60
230	Johnny Callison	5	5	5	5	5	10	30	100
231	Floyd Weaver	5	5	5	5	5	8	20	60
232	Glenn Beckert	5	5	5	5	5	8	25	80
233	Dom Zanni	5	5	5	5	5	8	20	100
234	R.Beck RC/R.White RC	5	5	5	5	5	10	40	150
235	Don Cardwell	5	5	5	5	5	8	15	50
236	Mike Hershberger	5	5	5	5	5	8	15	50
237	Billy O'Dell	5	5	5	5	5	8	20	60
238	Los Angeles Dodgers TC	5	5	5	5	8	15	40	200
239	Orlando Pena	5	5	5	5	5	8	15	120

#	Name	GD 2	VG 3	VgEx 4	EX 5	ExMt 6	NM 7	NmMt 8	MT
240	Earl Battey	5	5	5	5	5	8	20	1
241	Dennis Ribant	5	5	5	5	5	8	20	
242	Jesus Alou	5	5	5	5	5	8	20	1
243	Nelson Briles	5	5	5	5	5	8	15	
244	C.Harrison RC//S.Jackson	5	5	5	5	5	8	15	
245	John Buzhardt	5	5	5	5	5	8	15	
246	Ed Bailey	5	5	5	5	5	8	15	
247	Carl Warwick	5	5	5	5	5	8	15	
248	Pete Mikkelsen	5	5	5	5	5	8	15	
249	Bill Rigney MG	5	5	5	5	5	8	20	
250	Sammy Ellis	5	5	5	5	5	8	20	6
251	Ed Brinkman	5	5	5	5	5	8	20	5
252	Denny Lemaster	5	5	5	5	5	8	15	
253	Don Wert	5	5	5	5	5	8	15	12
254	Fergie Jenkins RC	25	30	40	50	80	150	300	1,5
255	Willie Stargell	5	6	10	15	▲40	50	120	1,00
256	Lew Krausse	5	5	5	5	5	8	20	6
257	Jeff Torborg	5	5	5	5	5	8	20	8
258	Dave Giusti	5	5	5	5	5	8	15	5
259	Boston Red Sox TC	5	5	5	5	6	12	30	30
260	Bob Shaw	5	5	5	5	5	8	20	
261	Ron Hansen	5	5	5	5	5	8	15	5
262	Jack Hamilton	5	5	5	5	5	8	15	5
263	Tom Egan	5	5	5	5	5	8	15	5
264	A.Kosco RC/T.Uhlaender RC	5	5	5	5	5	8	20	6
265	Stu Miller	5	5	5	5	5	8	20	6
266	Pedro Gonzalez	5	5	5	5	5	8	15	5
267	Joe Sparma	5	5	5	5	5	8	15	5
268	John Blanchard	5	5	5	5	5	8	15	8
269	Don Heffner MG	5	5	5	5	5	8	20	8
270	Claude Osteen	5	5	5	5	5	10	20	6
271	Hal Lanier	5	5	5	5	5	8	20	6
272	Jack Baldschun	5	5	5	5	5	8	15	5
273	Astro Aces	5	5	5	5	5	10	25	12
274	Buster Narum	5	5	5	5	5	8	20	6
275	Tim McCarver	5	5	5	5	6	12	30	10
276	Jim Bouton	5	5	5	5	5	10	20	6
277	George Thomas	5	5	5	5	5	8	15	5
278	Cal Koonce	5	5	5	5	5	8	15	6
279A	Checklist 4 Black Cap	5	5	5	5	5	10	20	12
279B	Checklist 4 Red Cap	5	5	5	5	5	8	25	
280	Bobby Knoop	5	5	5	5	5	8	15	5
281	Bruce Howard	5	5	5	5	5	8	20	6
282	Johnny Lewis	5	5	5	5	5	8	15	6
283	Jim Perry	5	5	5	5	5	8	20	8
284	Bobby Wine	5	5	5	5	5	5	40	
285	Luis Tiant	5	5	5	5	5	10	40	8
286	Gary Geiger	5	5	5	5	5	8	20	20
287	Jack Aker RC	5	5	5	5	5	8	40	10
288	Don Sutton RC	15	25	▲40	▼50	80	120	400	1,50
289	Larry Sherry	5	5	5	5	5	8	20	8
290	Ron Santo	5	5	6	10	15	40	120	25
291	Moe Drabowsky	5	5	5	5	5	10	30	
292	Jim Coker	5	5	5	5	5	8	25	6
293	Mike Shannon	5	5	5	5	8	15	30	
294	Steve Ridzik	5	5	5	5	5	8	20	6
295	Jim Ray Hart	5	5	5	5	5	8	25	8
296	Johnny Keane MG	5	5	5	5	5	10	25	
297	Jim Owens	5	5	5	5	5	8	15	6
298	Rico Petrocelli	5	5	5	8	12	30	100	30
299	Lou Burdette	5	5	5	8	10	20	40	
300	Roberto Clemente	20	50	60	100	120	250	800	3,00
301	Greg Bollo	5	5	5	5	5	8	20	6
302	Ernie Bowman	5	5	5	5	5	8	40	
303	Cleveland Indians TC	5	5	5	5	5	8	25	8
304	John Herrnstein	5	5	5	5	5	8	20	6
305	Camilo Pascual	5	5	5	5	5	8	25	150
306	Ty Cline	5	5	5	5	5	8	20	60
307	Clay Carroll	5	5	5	5	5	8	40	
308	Tom Haller	5	5	5	5	5	8	40	
309	Diego Segui	5	5	5	5	5	8	25	60
310	Frank Robinson	5	20	25	30	40	60	120	800
311	T.Helms/D.Simpson	5	5	5	5	5	8	25	60
312	Bob Saverine	5	5	5	5	5	8	20	60
313	Chris Zachary	5	5	5	5	5	8	25	100
314	Hector Valle	5	5	5	5	5	8	20	150
315	Norm Cash	5	5	5	8	12	25	150	

#	Player	GD 2	VG 3	VgEx 4	EX 5	ExMt 6	NM 7	NmMt 8	MT 9
316	Jack Fisher	5	5	5	5	5	8	20	120
317	Dalton Jones	5	5	5	5	5	8	15	60
318	Harry Walker MG	5	5	5	5	5	8	30	80
319	Gene Freese	5	5	5	5	5	8	25	100
320	Bob Gibson	15	20	30	40	50	100	200	1,000
321	Rick Reichardt	5	5	5	5	5	8	20	100
322	Bill Faul	5	5	5	5	5	8	15	60
323	Ray Barker	5	5	5	5	5	12	40	120
324	John Boozer	5	5	5	5	5	8	20	
325	Vic Davalillo	5	5	5	5	5	8	25	
326	Atlanta Braves TC	5	5	5	5	5	10	30	
327	Bernie Allen	5	5	5	5	5	8	20	60
328	Jerry Grote	5	5	5	5	5	10	25	
329	Pete Charton	5	5	5	5	5	8	20	60
330	Ron Fairly	5	5	5	5	5	20	60	
331	Ron Herbel	5	5	5	5	5	12	40	100
332	Bill Bryan	5	5	5	5	5	8	25	100
333	J.Coleman RC/J.French RC	5	5	5	5	5	8	20	80
334	Marty Keough	5	5	5	5	5	10	30	150
335	Juan Pizarro	5	5	5	5	5	8	20	60
336	Gene Alley	5	5	5	5	5	10	30	80
337	Fred Gladding	5	5	5	5	5	8	20	60
338	Dal Maxvill	5	5	5	5	5	8	30	100
339	Del Crandall	5	5	5	5	5	10	20	80
340	Dean Chance	5	5	5	5	5	8	20	100
341	Wes Westrum MG	5	5	5	5	5	10	25	60
342	Bob Humphreys	5	5	5	5	5	8	25	
343	Joe Christopher	5	5	5	5	5	8	15	60
344	Steve Blass	5	5	5	5	5	8	15	120
345	Bob Allison	5	5	5	5	5	10	120	
346	Mike de la Hoz	5	5	5	5	5	8	20	50
347	Phil Regan	5	5	5	5	5	8	20	60
348	Baltimore Orioles TC	5	5	5	5	6	12	120	150
349	Cap Peterson	5	5	5	5	5	8	20	60
350	Mel Stottlemyre	5	5	5	5	8	40	120	
351	Fred Valentine	5	5	5	5	5	8	20	
352	Bob Aspromonte	5	5	5	5	5	8	25	80
353	Al McBean	5	5	5	5	5	8	20	120
354	Smoky Burgess	5	5	5	5	5	10	25	80
355	Wade Blasingame	5	5	5	5	5	8	20	60
356	O.Johnson RC/K.Sanders RC	5	5	5	5	5	12	80	100
357	Gerry Arrigo	5	5	5	5	5	8	20	60
358	Charlie Smith	5	5	5	5	5	8	15	60
359	Johnny Briggs	5	5	5	5	5	8	20	100
360	Ron Hunt	5	5	5	5	5	10	30	200
361	Tom Satriano	5	5	5	5	5	8	20	60
362	Gates Brown	5	5	5	5	6	15	40	100
363	Checklist 5	5	5	5	5	5	8	25	
364	Nate Oliver	5	5	5	5	5	8	20	60
365	Roger Maris	25	30	40	50	▲100	120	250	1,200
366	Wayne Causey	5	5	5	5	5	8	25	
367	Mel Nelson	5	5	5	5	5	8	25	100
368	Charlie Lau	5	5	5	5	5	8	20	60
369	Jim King	5	5	5	5	5	8	15	60
370	Chico Cardenas	5	5	5	5	5	8	40	60
371	Lee Stange	5	5	5	5	6	10	15	50
372	Harvey Kuenn	5	5	5	5	8	12	20	50
373	J.Hiatt/D.Estelle	5	5	5	5	6	10	15	60
374	Bob Locker	5	5	5	5	6	10	15	50
375	Donn Clendenon	5	5	5	5	6	10	20	60
376	Paul Schaal	5	5	5	5	6	10	20	50
377	Turk Farrell	5	5	5	5	6	10	20	60
378	Dick Tracewski	5	5	5	5	8	12	30	80
379	St. Louis Cardinals TC	5	5	5	5	8	12	25	100
380	Tony Conigliaro	5	5	5	8	15	25	80	200
381	Hank Fischer	5	5	5	5	6	10	20	60
382	Phil Roof	5	5	5	5	6	10	20	60
383	Jackie Brandt	5	5	5	5	6	10	15	50
384	Al Downing	5	5	5	5	8	12	20	80
385	Ken Boyer	5	5	5	6	10	15	40	80
386	Gil Hodges MG	5	5	5	8	12	20	40	120
387	Howie Reed	5	5	5	5	6	10	15	50
388	Don Mincher	5	5	5	5	6	10	20	
389	Jim O'Toole	5	5	5	5	6	10	20	60
390	Brooks Robinson	5	6	10	25	40	60	120	600
391	Chuck Hinton	5	5	5	5	6	10	20	120
392	B.Hands RC/R.Hundley RC	5	5	5	6	10	15	40	200
393	George Brunet	5	5	5	5	6	10	15	50
394	Ron Brand	5	5	5	5	6	10	15	50
395	Len Gabrielson	5	5	5	5	6	10	15	60
396	Jerry Stephenson	5	5	5	5	6	10	20	100
397	Bill White	5	5	5	5	8	12	20	60
398	Danny Cater	5	5	5	5	6	10	20	60
399	Ray Washburn	5	5	5	5	6	10	25	60
400	Zoilo Versalles	5	5	5	5	6	10	25	50
401	Ken McMullen	5	5	5	5	6	12	20	50
402	Jim Hickman	5	5	5	5	6	10	20	100
403	Fred Talbot	5	5	5	5	6	10	15	50
404	Pittsburgh Pirates TC	5	5	8	12	20	25	50	150
405	Elston Howard	5	5	5	6	10	15	120	250
406	Joey Jay	5	5	5	5	6	10	20	80
407	John Kennedy	5	5	5	5	6	10	15	50
408	Lee Thomas	5	5	5	5	6	10	15	50
409	Billy Hoeft	5	5	5	5	6	10	15	60
410	Al Kaline	5	15	20	25	40	60	▼150	
411	Gene Mauch MG	5	5	5	5	6	10	15	60
412	Sam Bowens	5	5	5	5	6	10	20	50
413	Johnny Romano	5	5	5	5	6	10	20	60
414	Dan Coombs	5	5	5	5	6	10	15	50
415	Max Alvis	5	5	5	5	6	10	20	80
416	Phil Ortega	5	5	5	5	6	10	15	60
417	J.McGlothlin RC/E.Sukla RC	5	5	5	5	6	10	15	50
418	Phil Gagliano	5	5	5	5	6	10	15	50
419	Mike Ryan	5	5	5	5	6	10	20	
420	Juan Marichal	5	5	6	10	25	40	100	500
421	Roy McMillan	5	5	5	5	6	10	20	
422	Ed Charles	5	5	5	5	6	10	15	50
423	Ernie Broglio	5	5	5	5	6	10	20	60
424	L.May RC/D.Osteen RC	5	5	6	15	20	40	120	
425	Bob Veale	5	5	5	5	6	10	20	100
426	Chicago White Sox TC	5	5	5	5	8	12	50	300
427	John Miller	5	5	5	5	6	10	15	80
428	Sandy Alomar	5	5	5	5	6	10	15	60
429	Bill Monbouquette	5	5	5	5	8	12	30	
430	Don Drysdale	5	8	12	20	30	▲60	100	600
431	Walt Bond	5	5	5	5	6	10	20	
432	Bob Heffner	5	5	5	5	6	10	15	50
433	Alvin Dark MG	5	5	5	5	6	10	15	50
434	Willie Kirkland	5	5	5	5	6	10	15	50
435	Jim Bunning	5	5	5	8	15	40	120	
436	Julian Javier	5	5	5	5	6	10	60	200
437	Al Stanek	5	5	5	5	6	10	15	50
438	Willie Smith	5	5	5	5	6	10	15	60
439	Pedro Ramos	5	5	5	5	8	12	20	60
440	Deron Johnson	5	5	5	5	6	10	25	100
441	Tommie Sisk	5	5	5	5	6	10	15	50
442	E.Barnowski RC/E.Watt RC	5	5	5	5	8	25	200	
443	Bill Wakefield	5	5	5	5	6	10	20	60
444	Checklist 6 R.Sox	5	5	5	5	6	10	30	60
445	Jim Kaat	5	5	5	6	10	15	25	100
446	Mack Jones	5	5	5	5	6	10	20	50
447	Dick Ellsworth (Hubbs Photo)	5	5	5	5	8	20	30	200
448	Eddie Stanky MG	5	5	5	5	8	12	20	80
449	Joe Moeller	5	5	5	5	10	25	80	
450	Tony Oliva	5	5	6	10	40	50	100	400
451	Barry Latman	5	5	5	5	8	12	20	60
452	Joe Azcue	5	5	5	5	8	12	20	60
453	Ron Kline	5	5	5	5	8	12	20	60
454	Jerry Buchek	5	5	5	5	8	12	20	60
455	Mickey Lolich	5	5	5	6	10	25	40	150
456	D.Brandon RC/J.Foy RC	5	5	5	5	8	20	25	80
457	Joe Gibbon	5	5	5	5	8	12	20	80
458	Manny Jiminez	5	5	5	5	8	12	20	60
459	Bill McCool	5	5	5	5	8	12	20	60
460	Curt Blefary	5	5	5	6	10	25	30	60
461	Roy Face	5	5	5	6	10	15	20	60
462	Bob Rodgers	5	5	5	5	8	12	20	60
463	Philadelphia Phillies TC	5	5	5	5	8	12	30	100
464	Larry Bearnarth	5	5	5	5	8	12	25	60
465	Don Buford	5	5	5	5	8	15	25	60
466	Ken Johnson	5	5	5	5	8	12	20	50
467	Vic Roznovsky	5	5	5	5	8	12	20	60
468	Johnny Podres	5	5	5	6	10	15	40	80
469	Bobby Murcer RC	6	8	12	20	40	500	100	

#	Player	GD 2	VG 3	VgEx 4	EX 5	ExMt 6	NM 7	NmMt 8	MT 9
470	Sam McDowell	5	5	5	6	10	15	60	100
471	Bob Skinner	5	5	5	5	10	25	60	
472	Terry Fox	5	5	5	5	10	25	100	
473	Rich Rollins	5	5	5	5	8	12	20	80
474	Dick Schofield	5	5	5	5	8	12	20	80
475	Dick Radatz	5	5	5	5	8	12	25	60
476	Bobby Bragan MG	5	5	5	5	8	12	20	50
477	Steve Barber	5	5	5	5	8	12	30	60
478	Tony Gonzalez	5	5	5	5	8	20	50	150
479	Jim Hannan	5	5	5	5	8	12	20	60
480	Dick Stuart	5	5	5	5	8	12	20	100
481	Bob Lee	5	5	5	5	8	12	20	80
482	J.Boccabella/D.Dowling	5	5	5	6	15	50	2,001	
483	Joe Nuxhall	5	5	5	5	8	12	60	100
484	Wes Covington	5	5	5	5	8	12	25	80
485	Bob Bailey	5	5	5	5	8	12	25	80
486	Tommy John	5	5	5	6	10	25	50	120
487	Al Ferrara	5	5	5	5	8	12	25	60
488	George Banks	5	5	5	5	8	12	20	100
489	Curt Simmons	5	5	5	5	8	12	20	60
490	Bobby Richardson	5	6	10	15	25	40	80	200
491	Dennis Bennett	5	5	5	5	8	12	25	60
492	Kansas City Athletics TC	5	5	5	5	8	12	25	60
493	Johnny Klippstein	5	5	5	5	8	12	20	60
494	Gordy Coleman	5	5	5	5	8	12	25	80
495	Dick McAuliffe	5	5	5	6	10	15	25	120
496	Lindy McDaniel	5	5	5	5	8	12	25	60
497	Chris Cannizzaro	5	5	5	5	8	12	20	60
498	L.Walker RC/W.Fryman RC	5	5	5	5	8	12	25	80
499	Wally Bunker	5	5	5	5	8	12	60	100
500	Hank Aaron	40	50	60	100	▲150	250	800	3,000
501	John O'Donoghue	5	5	5	5	8	12	20	50
502	Lenny Green	5	5	5	5	8	12	20	60
503	Steve Hamilton	5	5	5	6	10	15	40	150
504	Grady Hatton MG	5	5	5	5	8	12	20	50
505	Jose Cardenal	5	5	5	5	8	12	30	60
506	Bo Belinsky	5	5	5	6	10	15	25	60
507	Johnny Edwards	5	5	5	5	8	20	100	
508	Steve Hargan RC	5	5	5	5	8	12	20	80
509	Jake Wood	5	5	5	5	10	25	80	
510	Hoyt Wilhelm	5	5	5	8	12	20	40	150
511	B.Barton RC/T.Fuentes RC	5	5	5	6	15	40	200	
512	Dick Stigman	5	5	5	5	8	12	20	40
513	Camilo Carreon	5	5	5	8	12	30	80	
514	Hal Woodeshick	5	5	5	5	8	12	20	80
515	Frank Howard	5	5	5	6	10	15	40	120
516	Eddie Bressoud	5	5	5	5	8	12	30	200
517A	Checklist 7 529 is White Sox	5	5	5	6	10	15	40	
517B	Checklist 7 529 is W.Sox	5	5	5	6	10	15	50	
518	H.Hippauf RC/A.Umbach RC	5	5	5	8	20	30	120	
519	Bob Friend	5	5	5	5	8	15	80	120
520	Jim Wynn	5	5	5	6	10	15	50	60
521	John Wyatt	5	5	5	5	8	12	20	60
522	Phil Linz	5	5	5	5	8	12	20	60
523	Bob Sadowski	5	5	5	6	10	15	40	100
524	O.Brown RC/D.Mason RC SP	5	5	8	12	50	60	100	500
525	Gary Bell SP	5	5	6	10	15	25	100	250
526	Minnesota Twins TC SP	8	12	20	30	100	120	200	400
527	Julio Navarro	5	5	5	8	20	50	80	250
528	Jesse Gonder SP	5	5	6	10	30	50	80	100
529	Elia/Higgins/Voss RC	5	5	5	6	10	15	40	80
530	Robin Roberts	5	8	12	20	50	60	100	▲200
531	Joe Cunningham	5	5	5	6	10	25	30	60
532	Aurelio Monteagudo SP	5	5	6	10	15	40	60	150
533	Jerry Adair SP	5	5	6	10	15	30	60	150
534	D.Eilers RC/R.Gardner RC	5	5	5	6	15	25	50	60
535	Willie Davis SP	5	6	10	15	40	100	120	300
536	Dick Egan	5	5	5	6	10	15	30	60
537	Herman Franks MG	5	5	8	12	20	25	80	
538	Bob Allen SP	5	5	5	8	15	40	50	100
539	B.Heath RC/C.Sembera RC	5	5	5	8	12	50	100	
540	Denny McLain SP	15	25	50	80	100	120	200	500
541	Gene Oliver SP	5	6	10	15	25	40	60	100
542	George Smith	5	5	5	6	10	15	30	60
543	Roger Craig SP	5	8	10	15	25	50	60	150
544	Cardinals Rookies SP RC	5	8	12	20	30	250	500	
545	Dick Green SP	5	5	6	10	20	30	60	150

#	Player	GD 2	VG 3	VgEx 4	EX 5	ExMt 6	NM 7	NmMt 8	MT 9
546	Dwight Siebler	5	5	5	8	12	40	50	100
547	Horace Clarke SP RC	6	10	15	100	120	200	400	600
548	Gary Kroll SP	5	5	6	10	15	25	50	100
549	A.Closter RC/C.Cox RC	5	5	5	6	10	25	40	100
550	Willie McCovey SP	8	25	60	80	100	150	250	800
551	Bob Purkey SP	5	5	6	10	30	50	60	150
552	Birdie Tebbetts MG SP	5	5	6	10	15	60	100	150
553	P.Garrett RC/J.Warner	5	5	5	8	12	30	40	100
554	Jim Northrup SP	5	6	10	15	25	40	80	200
555	Ron Perranoski SP	5	8	12	20	40	120	250	
556	Mel Queen SP	5	5	10	15	50	100	200	
557	Felix Mantilla SP	5	5	8	12	20	60	80	250
558	Grilli/Magrini/Scott RC	5	5	8	12	25	50	80	250
559	Roberto Pena SP	5	5	8	12	20	50	▲120	
560	Joel Horlen	5	5	5	6	10	25	50	150
561	Choo Choo Coleman SP	50	60	80	100	120	150	▲250	
562	Russ Snyder	5	6	10	15	60	100	400	
563	P.Cimino RC/C.Tovar RC	5	5	5	8	12	50	100	200
564	Bob Chance	5	5	6	10	30	40	80	200
565	Jimmy Piersall SP	5	6	10	15	40	50	80	500
566	Mike Cuellar SP	5	8	12	20	30	50	80	200
567	Dick Howser SP	5	5	6	10	40	60	80	300
568	P.Lindblad RC/R.Stone RC	5	5	5	6	10	15	40	100
569	Orlando McFarlane SP	5	5	6	10	15	40	80	120
570	Art Mahaffey SP	5	5	6	10	15	60	120	
571	Dave Roberts SP	5	5	6	10	20	30	50	100
572	Bob Priddy	5	5	5	5	10	20	30	60
573	Derrell Griffith	5	5	5	6	10	25	40	60
574	B.Hepler RC/B.Murphy RC	5	5	5	6	10	30	50	80
575	Earl Wilson	5	5	5	8	12	20	50	100
576	Dave Nicholson SP	5	5	8	12	30	50	60	400
577	Jack Lamabe SP	5	5	6	10	15	40	50	100
578	Chi Chi Olivo SP RC	5	5	6	10	15	25	60	120
579	Bertaina/Brabender/Johnson RC	5	5	8	10	25	40	60	200
580	Billy Williams SP	5	8	12	30	▲60	100	250	800
581	Tony Martinez	5	5	5	6	10	20	40	60
582	Garry Roggenburk	5	5	5	6	10	15	30	80
583	Detroit Tigers TC SP	12	20	30	100	120	150	300	600
584	F.Fernandez RC/F.Peterson RC	5	5	6	10	20	40	50	150
585	Tony Taylor	5	5	5	6	10	50	60	
586	Claude Raymond SP	5	5	6	10	15	80	80	200
587	Dick Bertell	5	5	5	6	10	15	40	80
588	C.Dobson RC/K.Suarez RC	5	5	5	6	10	50	60	80
589	Lou Klimchock SP	5	6	10	15	25	60	100	200
590	Bill Skowron SP	5	6	10	40	50	80	100	250
591	Grant Jackson SP RC	30	120	150	200	250	400	▼500	
592	Andre Rodgers	5	5	5	6	10	20	50	80
593	Doug Camilli SP	5	5	6	10	15	25	50	150
594	Chico Salmon	5	5	6	10	20	100	100	
595	Larry Jackson	5	5	5	8	12	20	40	80
596	N.Colbert RC/G.Sims RC SP	5	6	10	15	25	50	80	300
597	John Sullivan	5	5	5	8	12	40	60	150
598	Gaylord Perry SP	20	25	60	100	200	250	400	1,000

—AL Batting Leaders #216 PSA 9 (MT) sold for $1,500 (eBay; 12/07)
—AL Pitching Leaders #224 PSA 9 (MT) sold for $709 (eBay; 2/08)
—AL RBI Leaders #220 PSA 9 (MT) sold for $634 (eBay; 4/08)
—AL RBI Leaders #220 PSA 9 (MT) sold for $609 (eBay; 7/07)
—Richie Allen #80 PSA 9 (MT) sold for $620 (eBay; 4/08)
—Buc Belters #99 PSA 9 (MT) sold for $504 (Goodwin; 3/08)
—Cardinals Rookies #544 PSA 9 (MT) sold for $725 (eBay; 1/07)
—Cardinals Rookies #544 PSA 8 (NmMt) sold for $802 (eBay; 3/08)
—Cardinals Rookies #544 PSA 8 (NmMt) sold for $510 (eBay; 7/07)
—Cardinals Rookies #544 PSA 8 (NmMt) sold for $207 (Goodwin; 5/07)
—Norm Cash #315 PSA 9 (MT) sold for $515 (eBay; 8/07)
—Norm Cash #315 PSA 9 (MT) sold for $504 (eBay; 2/07)
—Choo Choo Coleman #561 PSA 9 (MT) sold for $696 (Mile High; 2/08)
—Don Demeter #98 PSA 9 (MT) sold for $812 (eBay; 1/08)
—Don Dennis #142 PSA 9 (MT) sold for $639 (eBay; 4/08)
—Don Drysdale #430 PSA 9 (MT) sold for $2,263 (Madec; 5/07)
—Fergie Jenkins #254 PSA 10 (Gem) sold for $4,774 (Mastro; 12/06)
—Jake Gibbs #117 PSA 9 (MT) sold for $616 (eBay; 3/08)
—Alex Johnson #104 (No Trade) PSA 8 (NmMt) sold for $284 (eBay; 1/08)
—Al Kaline #410 PSA 9 (MT) sold for $1,492 (eBay; 8/07)
—Al Kaline #410 PSA 9 (MT) sold for $1,326 (eBay; 7/07)
—Al Kaline #410 PSA 9 (MT) sold for $1,000 (eBay; 7/07)
—Mickey Mantle #50 BVG 8.5 (NmMt) sold for $904 (eBay; 8/07)
—Mickey Mantle #50 BVG 8.5 (NmMt+) sold for $826 (eBay; 3/07)

Mickey Mantle #50 BVG 8.5 (NmMt+) sold for $712 (Mile High; 6/05)
Roger Maris #365 SGC 96 (MT) sold for $924 (Mastro; 12/06)
Willie Mays #1 SGC 92 (NmMt+) sold for $1,227 (Mastro; 8/06)
Willie McCovey #550 PSA 10 (Gem) sold for $1,825 (eBay; 1/04)
Willie McCovey #550 PSA 10 (Gem) sold for $950 (Mastro; 12/05)
Sam Mele #3 PSA 9 (MT) sold for $504 (eBay; 6/07)
Joe Moeller #449 PSA 9 (MT) sold for $825 (eBay; 10/07)
Bobby Murcer #469 PSA 9 (MT) sold for 4458 (Goodwin; 5/08)
New York Yankees TC #92 PSA 9 (MT) sold for $1,026 (eBay; 8/07)
New York Yankees TC #92 PSA 9 (MT) sold for $557 (eBay; 6/08)
NL Batting Leaders #215 PSA 9 (MT) sold for $427 (Goodwin; 5/07)
NL ERA Leaders #221 PSA 9 (MT) sold for $2,559 (eBay; 8/07)
NL ERA Leaders #221 PSA 9 (MT) sold for $1,737 (Memory Lane; 12/07)
NL ERA Leaders #221 PSA 9 (MT) sold for $873 (Memory Lane; 8/06)
NL ERA Leaders #221 PSA 9 (MT) sold for $659 (eBay; 5/08)
NL RBI Leaders #219 PSA 9 (MT) sold for $609 (Memory Lane; 5/08)
Joe Pepitone #79 PSA 9 (MT) sold for $604 (eBay; 5/08)
Joe Pepitone #79 PSA 9 (MT) sold for $525 (eBay; 6/07)
Ron Perranoski #555 PSA 9 (MT) sold for $1,009 (eBay; 12/06)
Pete Rose #30 PSA 8.5 (NmMt+) sold for $611 (eBay; 6/08)
Mel Stottlemyre #350 PSA 9 (MT) sold for $504 (eBay; 7/07)
Mel Stottlemyre #350 PSA 9 (MT) sold for $449 (eBay; 5/07)
Don Sutton #288 PSA 10 (Gem) (Young Collection) sold for $7,919 (SCP; 5/12)
Don Sutton #288 PSA 10 (Gem) sold for $5,371 (eBay; 1/08)
Don Sutton #288 PSA 10 (Gem) sold for $5,160 (Mastro; 4/07)
Billy Williams #580 PSA 10 (Gem) sold for $2,600 (eBay; 9/04)
Don Sutton #288 PSA 10 (Gem) sold for $5,160 (Mastro; 4/07)
Bob Uecker #91 (No Trade Line) PSA 9 (MT) sold for $2,024 (eBay; 9/07)
Bob Uecker #91 (No Trade Line) PSA 8 (NmMt) sold for $420 (eBay; 5/08)
Billy Williams #580 PSA 10 (Gem) sold for $2,600 (eBay; 9/04)

1966 Topps Rub-Offs

	GD 2	VG 3	VgEx 4	EX 5	ExMt 6	NM 7	NmMt 8	MT 9
Hank Aaron	5	5	6	10	20			
Roberto Clemente	5	6	10	15	25			
Sandy Koufax	5	6	10	15	25	40	80	150
Mickey Mantle	10	15	25	40	80	100	120	300
Willie Mays	5	5	6	10	15	25	100	150
Pete Rose	5	5	8	12	20	30	50	120
Carl Yastrzemski	5	5	5	6	10	15	60	80

-Roberto Clemente #18 PSA 10 (Gem) sold for $7,014 (eBay; 1/13)
-Roberto Clemente PSA 7 (NM) sold for $128 (eBay; 11/07)
-Sandy Koufax PSA 10 (Gem) sold for $1,737 (Memory Lane; 12/07)
-Sandy Koufax PSA 10 (Gem) sold for $1,275 (eBay; 12/06)
-Mickey Mantle PSA 10 (Gem) sold for $861 (eBay; 1/07)
-Mickey Mantle PSA 10 (Gem) sold for $853 (Memory Lane; 5/08)
-Pete Rose PSA 10 (Gem) sold for $504 (eBay; 2/08)
-Pete Rose PSA 10 (Gem) sold for $494 (eBay; 4/07)

1967 Topps

		GD 2	VG 3	VgEx 4	EX 5	ExMt 6	NM 7	NmMt 8	MT 9
	The Champs	5	5	6	15	40	60	150	1,000
	Jack Hamilton	5	5	5	5	5	8	40	
	Duke Sims	5	5	5	6	10	25	150	
	Hal Lanier	5	5	5	5	5	8	30	200
	Whitey Ford	5	5	8	20	▲40	50	100	400
	Dick Simpson	5	5	5	5	5	8	50	200
	Don McMahon	5	5	5	5	5	8	20	200
	Chuck Harrison	5	5	5	5	5	8	20	80
	Ron Hansen	5	5	5	5	5	8	15	80
0	Matty Alou	5	5	5	5	6	15	100	200
1	Barry Moore RC	5	5	5	5	5	8	20	80
2	J.Campanis RC/B.Singer	5	5	5	5	5	8	40	80
3	Joe Sparma	5	5	5	5	6	15	60	200
4	Phil Linz	5	5	5	5	5	8	25	300
5	Earl Battey	5	5	5	5	5	8	15	60
6	Bill Hands	5	5	5	5	6	15	50	
7	Jim Gosger	5	5	5	5	5	8	15	80
8	Gene Oliver	5	5	5	5	5	8	20	100
9	Jim McGlothlin	5	5	5	5	5	8	20	60
0	Orlando Cepeda	5	5	5	6	▲30	60	▲200	1,000
1	Dave Bristol MG RC	5	5	5	5	6	15	80	200
2	Gene Brabender	5	5	5	5	5	8	20	50
3	Larry Elliot	5	5	5	5	5	8	25	100
4	Bob Allen	5	5	5	5	5	8	20	80

		GD 2	VG 3	VgEx 4	EX 5	ExMt 6	NM 7	NmMt 8	MT 9
25	Elston Howard	5	5	5	5	5	10	25	80
26A	Bob Priddy No Trade Line	5	6	10	15	25	60	25	
26B	Bob Priddy Trade Line	5	5	5	5	6	15	60	150
27	Bob Saverine	5	5	5	5	5	8	15	80
28	Barry Latman	5	5	5	5	5	8	20	100
29	Tom McCraw	5	5	5	5	5	8	20	80
30	Al Kaline DP	5	5	▲20	25	30	40	100	600
31	Jim Brewer	5	5	5	5	5	8	15	80
32	Bob Bailey	5	5	5	5	6	20	100	
33	S.Bando RC/R.Schwartz RC	5	5	5	5	6	15	100	
34	Pete Cimino	5	5	5	5	5	8	15	80
35	Rico Carty	5	5	5	5	5	8	25	120
36	Bob Tillman	5	5	5	5	5	10	20	200
37	Rick Wise	5	5	5	5	6	15	100	250
38	Bob Johnson	5	5	5	5	5	8	30	100
39	Curt Simmons	5	5	5	5	5	8	15	80
40	Rick Reichardt	5	5	5	5	5	8	15	100
41	Joe Hoerner	5	5	5	5	6	15	60	150
42	New York Mets TC	5	5	5	5	6	15	40	300
43	Chico Salmon	5	5	5	5	6	15	50	400
44	Joe Nuxhall	5	5	5	5	5	8	25	100
45	Roger Maris Cardinals	5	8	25	40	▲60	100	150	
46	Lindy McDaniel	5	5	5	5	5	8	15	60
47	Ken McMullen	5	5	5	5	5	8	15	80
48	Bill Freehan	5	5	5	5	8	15	30	300
49	Roy Face	5	5	5	5	5	10	15	150
50	Tony Oliva	5	5	5	5	8	15	80	150
51	D.Adlesh RC/W.Bales RC	5	5	5	5	5	8	15	60
52	Dennis Higgins	5	5	5	5	5	8	30	100
53	Clay Dalrymple	5	5	5	5	5	8	15	80
54	Dick Green	5	5	5	5	5	8	25	150
55	Don Drysdale	5	5	12	20	▲40	60	120	600
56	Jose Tartabull	5	5	5	5	5	8	50	150
57	Pat Jarvis RC	5	5	5	5	5	8	25	100
58A	Paul Schaal Green Bat	5	5	6	10	15	25	60	250
58B	Paul Schaal Natural Bat	5	5	5	5	5	8	15	80
59	Ralph Terry	5	5	5	5	5	8	15	80
60	Luis Aparicio	5	5	5	5	8	30	50	
61	Gordy Coleman	5	5	5	5	5	8	15	50
62	Frank Robinson CL1	5	5	5	5	8	15	80	
63	Cards Clubbers	5	5	5	8	12	30	100	
64	Fred Valentine	5	5	5	5	5	8	15	80
65	Tom Haller	5	5	5	5	5	8	15	50
66	Manny Mota	5	5	5	5	5	8	15	60
67	Ken Berry	5	5	5	5	5	8	15	120
68	Bob Buhl	5	5	5	5	5	8	25	100
69	Vic Davalillo	5	5	5	5	5	8	60	200
70	Ron Santo	5	5	▲10	▲15	▲20	25	▲80	200
71	Camilo Pascual	5	5	5	5	5	8	15	100
72	G.Korince RC/T.Matchick RC	5	5	5	5	6	20	80	400
73	Rusty Staub	5	5	5	6	15	▼40	150	
74	Wes Stock	5	5	5	5	5	8	20	100
75	George Scott	5	5	5	5	5	10	25	100
76	Jim Barbieri RC	5	5	5	5	5	8	15	80
77	Dooley Womack	5	5	5	5	5	8	15	80
78	Pat Corrales	5	5	5	5	5	8	15	80
79	Bubba Morton	5	5	5	5	5	8	15	100
80	Jim Maloney	5	5	5	5	6	12	25	150
81	Eddie Stanky MG	5	5	5	5	5	8	15	50
82	Steve Barber	5	5	5	5	6	15	120	
83	Ollie Brown	5	5	5	5	5	8	25	100
84	Tommie Sisk	5	5	5	5	5	8	15	50
85	Johnny Callison	5	5	5	5	6	15	80	200
86A	Mike McCormick No Trade Line	5	6	10	15	25	40		
86B	Mike McCormick Trade Line	5	5	5	5	5	8	25	150
87	George Altman	5	5	5	5	5	8	15	50
88	Mickey Lolich	5	5	5	5	5	10	25	
89	Felix Millan RC	5	5	5	5	5	8	15	60
90	Jim Nash RC	5	5	5	5	6	25	80	
91	Johnny Lewis	5	5	5	5	5	10	20	60
92	Ray Washburn	5	5	5	5	5	8	25	150
93	S.Bahnsen RC/B.Murcer	5	5	5	5	8	30	40	200
94	Ron Fairly	5	5	5	5	5	8	15	60
95	Sonny Siebert	5	5	5	5	6	12	25	100
96	Art Shamsky	5	5	5	5	5	8	15	60
97	Mike Cuellar	5	5	5	5	5	10	20	80
98	Rich Rollins	5	5	5	5	6	15	40	135

#	Player	GD 2	VG 3	VgEx 4	EX 5	ExMt 6	NM 7	NmMt 8	MT 9
99	Lee Stange	5	5	5	5	5	8	20	150
100	Frank Robinson DP	5	5	15	20	▲40	50	120	300
101	Ken Johnson	5	5	5	5	5	8	15	50
102	Philadelphia Phillies TC	5	5	5	5	5	8	15	50
103A	Mickey Mantle CL2 DP D.McAuliffe	5	5	6	10	15	25	60	200
103B	Mickey Mantle CL2 DP D McAuliffe	5	5	5	8	12	20	30	
104	Minnie Rojas RC	5	5	5	5	5	8	25	100
105	Ken Boyer	5	5	5	5	6	12	40	200
106	Randy Hundley	5	5	5	5	6	12	25	150
107	Joel Horlen	5	5	5	5	5	8	20	80
108	Alex Johnson	5	5	5	5	5	10	30	300
109	Tribe Thumpers	5	5	5	5	5	10	30	60
110	Jack Aker	5	5	5	5	5	8	15	50
111	John Kennedy	5	5	5	5	5	8	40	150
112	Dave Wickersham	5	5	5	5	5	8	20	100
113	Dave Nicholson	5	5	5	5	5	8	15	80
114	Jack Baldschun	5	5	5	5	5	8	15	150
115	Paul Casanova RC	5	5	5	5	6	15	60	200
116	Herman Franks MG	5	5	5	5	5	8	15	60
117	Darrell Brandon	5	5	5	5	5	8	15	120
118	Bernie Allen	5	5	5	5	5	8	15	80
119	Wade Blasingame	5	5	5	5	5	8	15	50
120	Floyd Robinson	5	5	5	5	5	8	20	80
121	Eddie Bressoud	5	5	5	5	5	8	25	120
122	George Brunet	5	5	5	5	5	8	15	60
123	J.Price RC/L.Walker	5	5	5	5	5	8	15	120
124	Jim Stewart	5	5	5	5	5	8	15	100
125	Moe Drabowsky	5	5	5	5	6	15	30	100
126	Tony Taylor	5	5	5	5	6	15	50	150
127	John O'Donoghue	5	5	5	5	5	8	30	120
128A	Ed Spiezio RC	5	5	5	5	5	8	25	120
129	Phil Roof	5	5	5	5	5	8	15	50
130	Phil Regan	5	5	5	5	5	10	25	120
131	New York Yankees TC	5	5	5	15	20	▼30	▲800	200
132	Ozzie Virgil	5	5	5	5	5	8	20	100
133	Ron Kline	5	5	5	5	5	8	15	60
134	Gates Brown	5	5	5	5	6	12	60	
135	Deron Johnson	5	5	5	5	6	15	40	120
136	Carroll Sembera	5	5	5	5	5	8	40	120
137	R.Clark RC/J.Ollum	5	5	5	5	5	8	15	60
138	Dick Kelley	5	5	5	5	5	8	20	80
139	Dalton Jones	5	5	5	5	5	10	20	100
140	Willie Stargell	5	12	15	25	40	60	150	1,000
141	John Miller	5	5	5	5	5	10	50	100
142	Jackie Brandt	5	5	5	5	5	8	15	80
143	Sox Sockers	5	5	5	5	5	10	25	150
144	Bill Hepler	5	5	5	5	5	8	30	
145	Larry Brown	5	5	5	5	6	15	40	200
146	Steve Carlton	5	6	20	40	50	80	200	1,200
147	Tom Egan	5	5	5	5	5	8	15	80
148	Adolfo Phillips	5	5	5	5	5	8	15	80
149	Joe Moeller	5	5	5	5	5	8	50	100
150	Mickey Mantle	▲120	▲150	200	250	▲400	600	▲1,500	12,000
151	Moe Drabowsky WS1	5	5	5	5	5	10	40	200
152	Jim Palmer WS2	5	5	8	20		100		250
153	Paul Blair WS3	5	5	5	5	5	10	30	80
154	B.Robinson/D.McNally WS4	5	5	5	5	6	12	30	
155	Orioles Celebrate WS	5	5	5	5	6	12	50	80
156	Ron Herbel	5	5	5	5	5	8	20	100
157	Danny Cater	5	5	5	5	5	8	15	100
158	Jimmie Coker	5	5	5	5	5	8	15	80
159	Bruce Howard	5	5	5	5	5	8	15	80
160	Willie Davis	5	5	5	5	5	10	20	80
161	Dick Williams MG	5	5	5	5	6	15	50	250
162	Billy O'Dell	5	5	5	5	5	8	20	80
163	Vic Roznovsky	5	5	5	5	6	20	50	200
164	Dwight Siebler	5	5	5	5	5	8	20	100
165	Cleon Jones	5	5	5	5	6	12	30	200
166	Eddie Mathews	5	5	6	10	▲25	▲30	50	200
167	J.Coleman RC/T.Cullen RC	5	5	5	5	5	8	25	150
168	Ray Culp	5	5	5	5	5	8	20	80
169	Horace Clarke	5	5	5	5	6	12	25	150
170	Dick McAuliffe	5	5	5	5	6	15	60	
171	Cal Koonce	5	5	5	5	5	8	20	60
172	Bill Heath	5	5	5	5	5	8	20	80
173	St. Louis Cardinals TC	5	5	5	5	6	12	30	120
174	Dick Radatz	5	5	5	5	5	8	15	
175	Bobby Knoop	5	5	5	5	5	8	15	
176	Sammy Ellis	5	5	5	5	5	8	30	12
177	Tito Fuentes	5	5	5	5	5	8	15	
178	John Buzhardt	5	5	5	5	5	8	20	
179	C.Vaughan RC/C.Epshaw RC	5	5	5	5	5	8	20	12
180	Curt Blefary	5	5	5	5	5	8	20	16
181	Terry Fox	5	5	5	5	5	8	25	15
182	Ed Charles	5	5	5	5	5	8	20	20
183	Jim Pagliaroni	5	5	5	5	5	8	15	
184	George Thomas	5	5	5	5	5	8	30	25
185	Ken Holtzman RC	5	5	5	5	6	10	40	10
186	Mets Maulers	5	5	5	5	6	15	70	25
187	Pedro Ramos	5	5	5	5	5	8	15	8
188	Ken Harrelson	5	5	5	5	5	8	25	12
189	Chuck Hinton	5	5	5	5	6	15	40	12
190	Turk Farrell	5	5	5	5	5	8	20	13
191A	Willie Mays CL3 214 is Tom	5	5	5	5	5	10	30	15
191B	Willie Mays CL3 214 is Dick	5	5	5	5	5	10	25	8
192	Fred Gladding	5	5	5	5	5	8	15	13
193	Jose Cardenal	5	5	5	5	5	8	15	6
194	Bob Allison	5	5	5	5	6	10	25	6
195	Al Jackson	5	5	5	5	5	8	30	20
196	Johnny Romano	5	5	5	5	5	12	150	
197	Ron Perranoski	5	5	5	5	5	10	20	8
198	Chuck Hiller	5	5	5	5	5	8	20	8
199	Billy Hitchcock MG	5	5	5	5	5	8	15	5
200	Willie Mays	15	40	▲60	80	100	200	▲400	1,50
201	Hal Reniff	5	5	5	5	5	10	25	15
202	Johnny Edwards	5	5	5	5	5	8	15	5
203	Al McBean	5	5	5	5	5	8	15	6
204	M.Epstein RC/T.Phoebus RC	5	5	5	5	5	8	20	8
205	Dick Groat	5	5	5	5	5	10	20	5
206	Dennis Bennett	5	5	5	5	5	8	20	6
207	John Orsino	5	5	5	5	5	8	15	8
208	Jack Lamabe	5	5	5	5	5	8	15	5
209	Joe Nossek	5	5	5	5	5	8	15	8
210	Bob Gibson	5	5	▼20	▼30	▼40	▲100	150	80
211	Minnesota Twins TC	5	5	5	5	5	8	15	6
212	Chris Zachary	5	5	5	5	5	8	15	5
213	Jay Johnstone RC	5	5	5	5	5	8	15	5
214	Tom Kelley	5	5	5	5	5	8	15	5
215	Ernie Banks	5	▲25	30	▲50	▲60	▲100	▲200	▼8
216	Bengal Belters	5	5	6	10	▲20	▲50	▲100	25
217	Rob Gardner	5	5	5	5	5	8	15	8
218	Wes Parker	5	5	5	5	6	15	40	200
219	Clay Carroll	5	5	5	5	5	8	15	5
220	Jim Ray Hart	5	5	5	5	5	8	15	60
221	Woody Fryman	5	5	5	5	5	8	15	5
222	D.Osteen/L.May	5	5	5	5	5	8	25	50
223	Mike Ryan	5	5	5	5	5	10	60	50
224	Walt Bond	5	5	5	5	5	8	15	50
225	Mel Stottlemyre	5	5	5	5	6	12	40	150
226	Julian Javier	5	5	5	5	5	8	15	60
227	Paul Lindblad	5	5	5	5	5	8	15	80
228	Gil Hodges MG	5	5	5	5	6	12	25	100
229	Larry Jackson	5	5	5	5	5	8	20	120
230	Boog Powell	5	5	5	5	5	10	▲40	
231	John Bateman	5	5	5	5	5	8	15	50
232	Don Buford	5	5	5	5	5	8	20	100
233	AL ERA Leaders	5	5	5	5	5	8	25	100
234	NL ERA Leaders	5	5	6	20	25	30	60	200
235	AL Pitching Leaders	5	5	5	5	5	10	25	200
236	NL Pitching Leaders	5	6	10	15	25	50	80	300
237	AL Strikeout Leaders	5	5	5	5	5	10	40	100
238	NL Strikeout Leaders	5	12	15	20	25	25	50	200
239	AL Batting Leaders	5	5	5	5	5	8	15	400
240	NL Batting Leaders	5	5	5	5	5	10	50	100
241	AL RBI Leaders	5	5	5	5	5	8	25	50
242	NL RBI Leaders	5	5	▲20	25	▲50	60	▲120	500
243	AL Home Run Leaders	5	5	5	5	5	8	25	40
244	NL Home Run Leaders	5	5	15	20	30	50	100	400
245	Curt Flood	5	5	5	5	6	12	40	150
246	Jim Perry	5	5	5	5	5	10	25	120
247	Jerry Lumpe	5	5	5	5	5	8	20	100
248	Gene Mauch MG	5	5	5	5	5	8	20	100
249	Nick Willhite	5	5	5	5	5	8	15	50

No.	Player	GD 2	VG 3	VgEx 4	EX 5	ExMt 6	NM 7	NmMt 8	MT 9
250	Hank Aaron	25	▲50	▲60	80	100	▲250	▲500	▲4,000
251	Woody Held	5	5	5	5	5	8	30	80
252	Bob Bolin	5	5	5	5	5	8	20	50
253	B.Davis/G.Gil RC	5	5	5	5	5	8	15	50
254	Milt Pappas	5	5	5	5	5	8	15	50
255	Frank Howard	5	5	5	5	5	10	30	60
256	Bob Hendley	5	5	5	5	5	8	15	50
257	Charlie Smith	5	5	5	5	5	8	15	100
258	Lee Maye	5	5	5	5	5	8	15	50
259	Don Dennis	5	5	5	5	5	8	15	50
260	Jim Lefebvre	5	5	5	5	5	8	20	80
261	John Wyatt	5	5	5	5	5	8	15	50
262	Kansas City Athletics TC	5	5	5	5	5	8	20	60
263	Hank Aguirre	5	5	5	5	5	8	15	50
264	Ron Swoboda	5	5	5	5	5	10	25	
265	Lou Burdette	5	5	5	5	5	8	15	50
266	Pitt Power	5	5	5	5	8	15	40	150
267	Don Schwall	5	5	5	5	5	8	15	50
268	Johnny Briggs	5	5	5	5	5	8	15	60
269	Don Nottebart	5	5	5	5	5	8	20	80
270	Zoilo Versalles	5	5	5	5	5	8	15	80
271	Eddie Watt	5	5	5	5	5	8	20	80
272	B.Connors RC/D.Dowling	5	5	5	5	5	8	15	50
273	Dick Lines RC	5	5	5	5	5	8	15	120
274	Bob Aspromonte	5	5	5	5	5	8	20	80
275	Fred Whitfield	5	5	5	5	5	8	30	100
276	Bruce Brubaker	5	5	5	5	5	8	15	50
277	Steve Whitaker RC	5	5	5	5	5	10	20	▼60
278	Jim Kaat CL4	5	5	5	6	10	15	25	250
279	Frank Linzy	5	5	5	5	5	8	15	60
280	Tony Conigliaro	5	5	5	8	12	40	60	250
281	Bob Rodgers	5	5	5	5	5	8	15	100
282	John Odom	5	5	5	5	5	8	15	60
283	Gene Alley	5	5	5	5	5	8	15	100
284	Johnny Podres	5	5	5	5	6	10	20	80
285	Lou Brock	5	5	20	30	40	60	120	800
286	Wayne Causey	5	5	5	5	5	8	15	60
287	G.Goosen RC/B.Shirley	5	5	5	5	5	8	30	100
288	Denny Lemaster	5	5	5	5	5	8	20	50
289	Tom Tresh	5	5	5	5	5	10	25	50
290	Bill White	5	5	5	5	5	10	20	100
291	Jim Hannan	5	5	5	5	5	8	15	80
292	Don Pavletich	5	5	5	5	5	10	20	100
293	Ed Kirkpatrick	5	5	5	5	5	8	15	50
294	Walter Alston MG	5	5	5	5	5	10	50	120
295	Sam McDowell	5	5	5	5	5	10	▲50	150
296	Glenn Beckert	5	5	5	5	5	10	40	80
297	Dave Morehead	5	5	5	5	5	8	20	50
298	Ron Davis RC	5	5	5	5	5	8	15	50
299	Norm Siebern	5	5	5	5	6	15	40	200
300	Jim Kaat	5	5	5	5	8	15	50	150
301	Jesse Gonder	5	5	5	5	5	10	20	80
302	Baltimore Orioles TC	5	5	5	5	5	8	25	80
303	Gil Blanco	5	5	5	5	5	8	25	120
304	Phil Gagliano	5	5	5	5	5	8	20	80
305	Earl Wilson	5	5	5	5	5	12	25	80
306	Bud Harrelson RC	5	5	5	8	12	20	50	60
307	Jim Beauchamp	5	5	5	5	5	8	15	50
308	Al Downing	5	5	5	5	5	8	40	80
309	Hurlers Beware	5	5	5	5	10	25	80	150
310	Gary Peters	5	5	5	5	5	8	20	80
311	Ed Brinkman	5	5	5	5	5	8	15	60
312	Don Mincher	5	5	5	5	5	8	15	60
313	Bob Lee	5	5	5	5	5	8	20	80
314	M.Andrews RC/R.Smith RC	5	5	5	5	6	12	50	300
315	Billy Williams	5	5	5	6	30	▼40	80	300
316	Jack Kralick	5	5	5	5	5	15	50	200
317	Cesar Tovar	5	5	5	5	5	8	20	80
318	Dave Giusti	5	5	5	5	5	8	15	100
319	Paul Blair	5	5	5	6	10	15	40	100
320	Gaylord Perry	5	5	5	8	12	20	60	150
321	Mayo Smith MG	5	5	5	5	5	10	20	120
322	Jose Pagan	5	5	5	5	5	8	15	50
323	Mike Hershberger	5	5	5	5	5	8	15	60
324	Hal Woodeshick	5	5	5	5	5	8	30	200
325	Chico Cardenas	5	5	5	5	5	8	15	50
326	Bob Uecker	5	5	5	8	25	50	80	300
327	California Angels TC	5	5	5	5	5	8	20	40
328	Clete Boyer	5	5	5	5	5	10	25	60
329	Charlie Lau	5	5	5	5	5	8	15	30
330	Claude Osteen	5	5	5	5	5	8	15	▼50
331	Joe Foy	5	5	5	5	5	8	40	100
332	Jesus Alou	5	5	5	5	5	8	15	60
333	Fergie Jenkins	5	5	5	8	25	▲50	80	250
334	Twin Terrors	5	5	5	5	8	▲25	50	200
335	Bob Veale	5	5	5	5	5	8	15	60
336	Joe Azcue	5	5	5	5	5	8	15	60
337	Joe Morgan	5	5	6	20	25	▲40	60	250
338	Bob Locker	5	5	5	5	5	8	15	80
339	Chico Ruiz	5	5	5	5	5	8	25	80
340	Joe Pepitone	5	5	5	5	6	12	40	80
341	D.Dietz RC/B.Sorrell	5	5	5	5	5	8	15	60
342	Hank Fischer	5	5	5	5	5	8	20	60
343	Tom Satriano	5	5	5	5	5	8	15	50
344	Ossie Chavarria RC	5	5	5	5	5	8	20	50
345	Stu Miller	5	5	5	5	5	8	25	▼50
346	Jim Hickman	5	5	5	5	5	8	15	50
347	Grady Hatton MG	5	5	5	5	5	8	15	50
348	Tug McGraw	5	5	5	5	5	10	30	80
349	Bob Chance	5	5	5	5	5	8	15	80
350	Joe Torre	5	5	5	5	▲25	30	50	150
351	Vern Law	5	5	5	5	6	15	60	200
352	Ray Oyler	5	5	5	5	5	10	20	80
353	Bill McCool	5	5	5	5	5	8	15	50
354	Chicago Cubs TC	5	5	5	5	5	6	12	30
355	Carl Yastrzemski	6	▼25	▼30	▼40	▼60	150	300	1,200
356	Larry Jaster RC	5	5	5	5	5	8	15	50
357	Bill Skowron	5	5	5	5	5	10	20	50
358	Ruben Amaro	5	5	5	5	5	8	15	60
359	Dick Ellsworth	5	5	5	5	5	8	15	50
360	Leon Wagner	5	5	5	5	5	10	20	100
361	Roberto Clemente CL5	5	5	5	10	20	25	40	120
362	Darold Knowles	5	5	5	5	5	8	30	200
363	Davey Johnson	5	5	5	5	6	12	▲80	150
364	Claude Raymond	5	5	5	5	5	8	15	60
365	John Roseboro	5	5	5	5	5	10	20	60
366	Andy Kosco	5	5	5	5	5	8	15	50
367	B.Kelso/D.Wallace RC	5	5	5	5	5	8	15	40
368	Jack Hiatt	5	5	5	5	5	8	15	60
369	Jim Hunter	5	5	15	20	25	40	60	300
370	Tommy Davis	5	5	5	5	5	10	20	50
371	Jim Lonborg	5	5	5	5	6	20	100	600
372	Mike de la Hoz	5	5	5	5	5	8	20	100
373	D.Josephson RC/F.Klages RC DP	5	5	5	5	5	8	20	100
374A	Mel Queen Partial Line	5	5	6	10	15	25		
374B	Mel Queen Complete Line DP	5	5	5	5	6	15	60	350
375	Jake Gibbs	5	5	5	5	5	8	30	80
376	Don Lock DP	5	5	5	5	5	8	30	200
377	Luis Tiant	5	5	5	5	8	20	80	400
378	Detroit Tigers TC	5	5	5	5	8	20	60	
379	Jerry May DP	5	5	5	5	5	8	15	80
380	Dean Chance DP	5	5	5	5	5	10	25	100
381	Dick Schofield DP	5	5	5	5	5	8	15	60
382	Dave McNally	5	5	5	6	10	15	80	250
383	Ken Henderson DP	5	5	5	5	5	8	30	80
384	J.Cosman RC/D.Hughes RC	5	5	5	5	5	8	15	100
385	Jim Fregosi	5	5	5	5	5	8	20	80
386	Dick Selma DP	5	5	5	5	5	10	30	120
387	Cap Peterson DP	5	5	5	5	5	8	15	80
388	Arnold Earley DP	5	5	5	5	5	8	30	300
389	Alvin Dark MG DP	5	5	5	5	5	8	15	50
390	Jim Wynn DP	5	5	5	5	5	8	20	60
391	Wilbur Wood DP	5	5	5	5	5	10	25	100
392	Tommy Harper DP	5	5	5	5	6	15	40	150
393	Jim Bouton DP	5	5	5	5	5	8	12	50
394	Jake Wood DP	5	5	5	5	8	12	30	200
395	Chris Short RC	5	5	5	5	5	10	▲50	150
396	Atlanta Aces	5	5	5	5	8	20	80	200
397	Willie Smith DP	5	5	5	5	5	8	30	80
398	Jeff Torborg	5	5	5	5	5	8	15	50
399	Al Worthington DP	5	5	5	5	6	15	60	250
400	Roberto Clemente DP	12	50	60	100	120	250	600	2,500
401	Jim Coates	5	5	5	5	5	8	15	80
402A	G.Jackson/B.Wilson Partial	5	5	6	10	15			

#	Player	GD 2	VG 3	VgEx 4	EX 5	ExMt 6	NM 7	NmMt 8	MT 9
402B	G.Jackson B.Wilson Complete RC DP	5	5	5	5	6	15	40	125
403	Dick Nen	5	5	5	5	6	15	30	500
404	Nelson Briles	5	5	5	5	5	8	30	
405	Russ Snyder	5	5	5	5	5	8	15	60
406	Lee Elia DP	5	5	5	5	5	8	20	100
407	Cincinnati Reds TC	5	5	5	5	5	▲20	▲40	120
408	Jim Northrup DP	5	5	5	5	8	20	60	300
409	Ray Sadecki	5	5	5	5	5	8	15	120
410	Lou Johnson DP	5	5	5	5	5	8	30	100
411	Dick Howser DP	5	5	5	5	5	10	25	80
412	N.Miller RC/D.Rader RC	5	5	5	5	5	10	40	80
413	Jerry Grote	5	5	5	5	6	12	40	120
414	Casey Cox	5	5	5	5	5	8	30	50
415	Sonny Jackson	5	5	5	5	5	8	25	150
416	Roger Repoz	5	5	5	5		10	30	150
417A	Bob Bruce ERR Rbaves	5	5	6	10	15	25	120	
417B	Bob Bruce COR Braves DP	5	5	5	5	5	8	40	200
418	Sam Mele MG	5	5	5	5	6	15	50	150
419	Don Kessinger DP	5	5	5	5	5	8	25	80
420	Denny McLain	5	5	5	5	8	25	60	200
421	Dal Maxvill DP	5	5	5	5	5	12	35	175
422	Hoyt Wilhelm	5	5	5	5	6	20	40	120
423	Fence Busters	5	6	10	30	60	100	200	
424	Pedro Gonzalez	5	5	5	5	6	15	50	135
425	Pete Mikkelsen	5	5	5	5	6	15	50	150
426	Lou Clinton	5	5	5	5	5	10	25	200
427A	Ruben Gomez Partial	5	5	6	10	25			
427B	Ruben Gomez Complete DP	5	5	5	5	6	15	40	
428	T.Hutton RC/G.Michael RC DP	5	5	5	5	6	15	50	165
429	Garry Roggenburk DP	5	5	5	5	6	15	80	
430	Pete Rose	10	40	50	60	100	200	400	2,500
431	Ted Uhlaender	5	5	5	5	5	8	25	120
432	Jimmie Hall DP	5	5	5	5	5	8	15	100
433	Al Luplow DP	5	5	5	5	5	8	30	150
434	Eddie Fisher DP	5	5	5	5	5	8	20	80
435	Mack Jones DP	5	5	5	5	5	8	15	80
436	Pete Ward	5	5	5	5	5	10	30	100
437	Washington Senators TC	5	5	5	5	5	8	15	80
438	Chuck Dobson	5	5	5	5	5	8	15	80
439	Byron Browne	5	5	5	5	5	8	25	100
440	Steve Hargan	5	5	5	5	5	8	15	60
441	Jim Davenport	5	5	5	5	5	10	20	80
442	B.Robinson RC/J.Verbanic RC DP	5	5	6	10	15	40	200	
443	Tito Francona DP	5	5	5	5	5	8	25	100
444	George Smith	5	5	5	5	5	10	20	80
445	Don Sutton	5	5	▲15	▲20	▲25	▲50	▲120	500
446	Russ Nixon DP	5	5	5	5	5	8	20	120
447A	Bo Belinsky Partial	5	5	6	10	15			
447B	Bo Belinsky Complete DP	5	5	5	5	5	8	25	250
448	Harry Walker MG DP	5	5	5	5	6	15	40	300
449	Orlando Pena	5	5	5	5	5	8	25	150
450	Richie Allen	5	5	5	5	8	15	80	150
451	Fred Newman DP	5	5	5	5	5	8	15	60
452	Ed Kranepool	5	5	5	5	6	15	40	150
453	Aurelio Monteagudo DP	5	5	5	5	5	8	40	250
454A	Juan Marichal CL6 No Left Ear DP	5	5	5	5	5	8	30	150
454B	Juan Marichal CL6 Left Ear DP	5	5	5	5	5	8	30	150
455	Tommie Agee	5	5	5	5	5	10	30	150
456	Phil Niekro UER ERA incorrect as .288	5	5	5	▲25	▲30	▲40	60	200
457	Andy Etchebarren DP	5	5	5	10	25	50	200	300
458	Lee Thomas	5	5	5	5	5	10	20	60
459	D.Bosman RC/P.Craig	5	5	5	5	5	10	20	80
460	Harmon Killebrew	6	10	15	▲30	▼40	▲100	150	▲600
461	Bob Miller	5	5	5	5	6	15	60	120
462	Bob Barton	5	5	5	5	5	10	40	100
463	Hill Aces	5	5	5	5	6	12	40	120
464	Dan Coombs	5	5	5	5	5	10	30	80
465	Willie Horton	5	5	5	5	8	30	100	250
466	Bobby Wine	5	5	5	5	▲20	▲25	▲60	300
467	Jim O'Toole	5	5	5	5	5	10	20	80
468	Ralph Houk MG	5	5	5	5	6	15	40	150
469	Len Gabrielson	5	5	5	5	5	10	20	80
470	Bob Shaw	5	5	5	5	5	10	60	
471	Rene Lachemann	5	5	5	5	5	10	40	80
472	J.Gelnar/G.Spriggs RC	5	5	5	5	8	25	60	

#	Player	GD 2	VG 3	VgEx 4	EX 5	ExMt 6	NM 7	NmMt 8	MT
473	Jose Santiago	5	5	5	5	5	10	50	10
474	Bob Tolan	5	5	5	5	▲10	▲25	▼50	▼12
475	Jim Palmer	5	8	25	30	50	80	200	
476	Tony Perez SP	6	10	30	40	60	120	250	1,00
477	Atlanta Braves TC	5	5	5	5	6	30	50	15
478	Bob Humphreys	5	5	5	5	5	10	25	8
479	Gary Bell	5	5	5	5	5	12	60	15
480	Willie McCovey	5	12	20	25	40	50	100	30
481	Leo Durocher MG	5	5	5	5	8	30	▲60	12
482	Bill Monbouquette	5	5	5	10	15	30	80	
483	Jim Landis	5	5	5	5	5	10	20	20
484	Jerry Adair	5	5	5	5	5	10	40	
485	Tim McCarver	5	5	5	25	30	80	250	
486	R.Reese RC/B.Whitby RC	5	5	5	5	5	10	50	10
487	Tommie Reynolds	5	5	5	5	5	10	30	10
488	Gerry Arrigo	5	5	5	5	5	10	25	8
489	Doug Clemens RC	5	5	5	5	5	10	50	15
490	Tony Cloninger	5	5	5	5	5	10	30	8
491	Sam Bowens	5	5	5	5	5	10	20	8
492	Pittsburgh Pirates TC	5	5	6	10	15	80	150	
493	Phil Ortega	5	5	5	5	5	10	25	15
494	Bill Rigney MG	5	5	5	5	5	10	20	8
495	Fritz Peterson	5	5	5	5	6	15	60	
496	Orlando McFarlane	5	5	5	5	5	10	20	5
497	Ron Campbell RC	5	5	5	5	6	25	80	200
498	Larry Dierker	5	5	5	5	5	10	40	100
499	G.Culver/J.Vidal RC	5	5	5	5	5	10	20	80
500	Juan Marichal	5	5	▲10	▲25	▲40	50	80	200
501	Jerry Zimmerman	5	5	5	5	6	15	50	
502	Derrell Griffith	5	5	5	5	5	10	30	100
503	Los Angeles Dodgers TC	5	5	5	8	12	20	40	150
504	Orlando Martinez RC	5	5	5	5	5	10	20	120
505	Tommy Helms	5	5	5	8	12	40	120	400
506	Smoky Burgess	5	5	5	5	5	10	30	100
507	E.Barnowski/L.Haney RC	5	5	5	5	5	10	20	80
508	Dick Hall	5	5	5	5	15	30	80	120
509	Jim King	5	5	5	5	5	10	25	100
510	Bill Mazeroski	5	5	5	8	▼20	▲40	50	200
511	Don Wert	5	5	5	5	6	15	30	150
512	Red Schoendienst MG	5	5	6	10	15	40	100	250
513	Marcelino Lopez	5	5	5	5	5	10	25	100
514	John Werhas	5	5	5	5	10	20	50	100
515	Bert Campaneris	5	5	5	8	10	20	50	120
516	San Francisco Giants TC	5	5	5	5	6	30	100	200
517	Fred Talbot	5	5	5	5	5	10	25	
518	Denis Menke	5	5	5	5	5	10	20	80
519	Ted Davidson	5	5	5	5	5	10	30	100
520	Max Alvis	5	5	5	5	5	10	25	80
521	Bird Bombers	5	5	5	5	6	30	100	200
522	John Stephenson	5	5	5	5	5	10	▲30	80
523	Jim Merritt	5	5	5	5	5	10	▲40	80
524	Felix Mantilla	5	5	5	5	6	15	50	150
525	Ron Hunt	5	5	5	5	5	10	20	80
526	P.Dobson RC/G.Korince RC	5	5	5	6	15	40	175	
527	Dennis Ribant	5	5	5	5	6	15	30	100
528	Rico Petrocelli	5	5	8	12	20	60	120	300
529	Gary Wagner	5	5	5	5	5	10	▲50	▼200
530	Felipe Alou	5	5	5	5	6	25	50	200
531	Brooks Robinson CL7 DP	5	5	6	10	20	▲100	300	1,200
532	Jim Hicks RC	5	5	5	5	5	10	30	80
533	Jack Fisher	5	5	5	5	6	15	80	300
534	Hank Bauer MG DP	5	5	5	6	10	25	40	150
535	Donn Clendenon	5	8	12	20	60	100	200	600
536	J.Niekro RC/P.Popovich RC	5	8	12	60	100	▲150	120	600
537	Chuck Estrada DP	5	5	5	6	10	15	30	80
538	J.C. Martin	5	5	6	10	15	30	50	120
539	Dick Egan DP	5	5	5	6	10	15	30	100
540	Norm Cash	6	10	15	25	60	100	▲200	400
541	Joe Gibbon	5	5	6	10	15	40	50	100
542	R.Monday RC/T.Pierce RC DP	5	5	5	6	25	30	60	▲120
543	Dan Schneider	5	5	6	10	15	25	50	250
544	Cleveland Indians TC	5	6	10	15	80	100	150	300
545	Jim Grant	5	5	8	12	30	50	▲100	300
546	Woody Woodward	5	5	5	10	15	40	50	200
547	R.Gibson RC/B.Rohr RC DP	5	5	5	6	10	20	60	100
548	Tony Gonzalez DP	5	5	5	6	10	15	30	100
549	Jack Sanford	5	5	6	10	15	30	50	

	GD 2	VG 3	VgEx 4	EX 5	ExMt 6	NM 7	NmMt 8	MT 9
Vada Pinson DP	5	5		8	25	▲50	60	300
Doug Camilli DP	5	5	5	6	10	20	25	60
Ted Savage	5	5	6	10	30	50	80	150
M.Hegan RC/T.Tillotson	5	5	8	12	50	60	100	300
Andre Rodgers DP	5	5	5	6	10	15	50	
Don Cardwell	5	5	6	10	30	50	80	100
Al Weis DP	5	5	5	10	15	25	30	80
Al Ferrara	5	5	6	10	15	30	80	150
M.Belanger RC/B.Dillman RC	6	10	25	80	100	120	250	800
Dick Tracewski DP	5	5	5	6	10	25	30	120
Jim Bunning	10	40	50	80	100	150	250	600
Sandy Alomar	5	6	10	15	50	60	▲120	200
Steve Blass DP	5	5	5	6	10	30	50	300
Joe Adcock MG	5	5	8	12	20	60	80	200
A.Harris RC/A.Pointer RC DP	5	5	5	6	10	20	▲40	80
Lew Krausse	5	5	6	10	15	25	50	120
Gary Geiger DP	5	5	5	6	▲12	▲20	▲30	100
Steve Hamilton	5	6	10	15	25	50	120	150
John Sullivan	5	5	8	12	40	50	100	150
Rod Carew DP RC	150	▲250	▲300	▲400	500	800	1,500	10,000
Maury Wills	10	15	25	60	80	100	▲300	1,000
Larry Sherry	5	5	8	12	20	50	80	
Don Demeter	5	8	12	20	30	100	250	
Chicago White Sox TC	5	5	8	15	20	50	80	150
Jerry Buchek	5	5	6	10	15	60	100	120
Dave Boswell RC	5	5	6	10	15	60	100	200
R.Hernandez RC/N.Gigon RC	5	8	12	20	40	100	200	250
Bill Short	5	5	8	12	20	50	80	
John Boccabella	5	5	6	10	15	40	▲80	150
Bill Henry	5	5	6	10	15	25	50	120
Rocky Colavito	12	20	100	120	150	200	300	500
Tom Seaver RC	▲500	▲600	▲800	▲1,000	▲1,200	1,500	2,500	10,000
Jim Owens DP	5	5	5	6	10	15	25	150
Ray Barker	5	6	10	15	25	60	80	
Jimmy Piersall	5	5	6	10	25	50	60	150
Wally Bunker	5	5	6	10	15	60	▲120	
Manny Jimenez	5	5	8	12	20	40	▲120	300
D.Shaw RC/G.Sutherland RC	5	8	12	20	80	100	120	200
Johnny Klippstein DP	5	5	5	6	10	15	40	150
Dave Ricketts DP	5	5	5	6	10	15	50	150
Pete Richert	5	5	6	10	15	25	60	150
Ty Cline	5	5	6	10	25	40	60	120
J.Shellenback RC/R.Willis RC	8	12	20	30	80	150	200	
Wes Westrum MG	5	5	8	12	40	50	80	150
Dan Osinski	5	6	10	15	25	50	100	300
Cookie Rojas	5	6	10	15	25	60	120	200
Galen Cisco DP	5	5	5	6	10	25	100	400
Ted Abernathy	5	5	6	10	15	50	80	120
W.Williams RC/E.Stroud RC	5	5	6	10	25	40	60	100
Bob Duliba DP	5	5	5	6	10	15	30	80
Brooks Robinson	80	100	▲200	▲250	400	500	▲1,000	3,000
Bill Bryan DP	5	5	5	6	10	15	40	
Juan Pizarro	5	5	8	12	50	60	100	200
T.Talton RC/R.Webster RC	5	5	6	10	25	30	50	300
Boston Red Sox TC	12	20	80	100	120	200	300	
Mike Shannon	10	15	25	60	150	200	250	400
Ron Taylor	5	5	8	12	40	60	100	
Mickey Stanley	8	12	25	50	100	120	300	
R.Nye RC/J.Upham RC DP	5	5	5	6	10	15	40	
Tommy John	8	12	20	60	▼80	120	▲300	1,500

-AL HR Leaders #243 PSA 10 (Gem) sold for $1,024 (eBay; 1/05)
-Luis Aparicio #60 PSA 9 (MT) sold for $610 (eBay; 11/06)
-Luis Aparicio #60 PSA 9 (MT) sold for $556 (Mile High; 12/05)
-Sal Bando #33 PSA 9 (MT) sold for $307 (eBay; 1/07)
-Bengal Belters #216 PSA 9 (MT) sold for $931 (eBay; 4/08)
-Boston Red Sox TC #604 PSA 9 (MT) sold for $1,247 (eBay; 4/08)
-Jim Bouton #393 PSA 9 (MT) sold for $485 (eBay; 12/06)
-Jim Bouton #393 PSA 9 (MT) sold for $449 (eBay; 1/07)
-Gates Brown #134 PSA 9 (MT) sold for $683 (eBay; 1/08)
-Gates Brown #134 PSA 9 (MT) sold for $515 (eBay; 4/08)
-Wally Bunker #585 PSA 9 (MT) sold for $797 (eBay; 9/07)
-Wally Bunker #585 PSA 9 (MT) sold for $570 (eBay; 1/08)
-Rod Carew #569 PSA 10 (Gem) (Young Collection) sold for $95,294 (Mile High; 12/14)
-Rod Carew #569 PSA 10 (Gem) (Young Collection) sold for $40,388 (SCP; 5/12)
-Rod Carew #569 BVG 8.5 (NmMt+) sold for $607 (eBay; 11/07)
-Rod Carew #569 BVG 8.5 (NmMt+) sold for $517 (eBay; 5/07)
-Orlando Cepeda #20 PSA 9 (MT) sold for $2,649 (eBay; 11/07)
-Orlando Cepeda #20 PSA 9 (MT) sold for $1,929 (eBay; 4/08)
-Tony Coningliaro #280 PSA 9 (MT) sold for $4,710 (Madec; 11/08)
-Fence Busters #423 PSA 9 (MT) sold for $2,094 (Madec;11/07)
-Whitey Ford #5 SGC 96 (MT) sold for $407 (eBay; 6/07)
-Ruben Gomez #427 (Partial Line) PSA 8 (NmMt) sold for $590 (eBay; 6/07)
-Ruben Gomez #427 (Partial Line) PSA 7 (NM) sold for $160 (eBay; 5/07)
-Elston Howard #25 PSA 10 (Gem) sold for $1,315 (eBay; 6/07)
-Mickey Mantle #150 PSA 10 (Gem) sold for $68,676 (Mile High; 10/13)
-Mickey Mantle CL2 #103 (D McAuliffe) PSA 8 (NmMt) sold for $582 (eBay; 4/08)
-Mickey Mantle CL2 #103 (D McAuliffe) PSA 8 (NmMt) sold for $510 (eBay; 6/08)
-Roger Maris #45 (Cardinals) PSA 9 (MT) sold for $1,813 (eBay; 1/08)
-Roger Maris #45 (Cardinals) PSA 9 (MT) sold for $1,305 (eBay; 12/07)
-Roger Maris #45 (Cardinals) PSA 9 (MT) sold for $614 (eBay; 4/08)
-Roger Maris #45 (Yankees) SGC Authentic sold for $1,912 (Heritage; 5/08)
-Roger Maris #45 (Yankees) PSA Authentic sold for $1,495 (Huggins and Scott; 4/08)
-Roger Maris #45 (Yankees) PSA Authentic sold for $1,242 (Mastro; 12/04)
-Eddie Mathews #166 PSA 10 (Gem) sold for $1,530 (eBay; 2/06)
-Mets Maulers #186 PSA 10 (Gem) sold for $3,851 (Leland's; 12/04)
-Mets Maulers #186 PSA 10 (Gem) sold for $2,569 (Mile High; 2/08)
-Dick McAuliffe #170 PSA 9 (MT) sold for $1,324 (eBay; 12/07)
-Mike McCormick #86 (No Trade Line) PSA 8 (NmMt) sold for $391 (eBay; 6/08)
-Bill Monbouquette #482 PSA 9 (MT) sold for $626 (eBay; 1/08)
-Jim Nash #90 PSA 9 (MT) sold for $1,000 (eBay; 1/08)
-Jim Nash #90 PSA 9 (MT) sold for $566 (eBay; 4/08)
-New York Yankees TC #131 PSA 10 (Gem) sold for $1,200 (eBay; 12/07)
-Phil Niekro #456 PSA 10 (Gem) sold for $1,880 (eBay; 2/07)
-Jim Palmer #475 PSA 9 (MT) sold for $1,393 (eBay; 12/07)
-Jim Palmer #475 PSA 9 (MT) sold for $615 (eBay; 4/08)
-Pirates Rookies #472 PSA 9 (MT) sold for $899 (eBay; 2/08)
-Pittsburgh Pirates TC #492 PSA 9 (MT) sold for $1,000 (eBay; 1/08)
-Pittsburgh Pirates TC #492 PSA 9 (MT) sold for $779 (eBay; 3/08)
-Mel Queen #374 (Partial Line) PSA 9 (MT) sold for $1,292 (eBay; 6/07)
-Brooks Robinson #600 SGC 92 (NmMt+) sold for $633 (Regency Superior; 6/07)
-Gary Roggenburk #429 PSA 9 (MT) sold for $3,683 (eBay; 10/07)
-Tom Seaver #581 PSA 10 (Gem) (Young Collection) sold for $24,450 (SCP; 5/12)
-Tom Seaver #581 PSA 10 (Gem) sold for $20,573 (Mile High; 2/08)
-Tom Seaver #581 BVG 9 (MT) sold for $2,026 (eBay; 1/05)
-Tom Seaver #581 PSA 8.5 (NmMt+) sold for $1,142 (eBay; 4/08)
-Tom Seaver #581 PSA 8.5 (NmMt+) sold for $1,027 (eBay; 3/08)
-Tom Seaver #581 BVG 8.5 (NmMt+) sold for $956 (eBay; 11/07)
-Tom Seaver #581 BVG 8.5 (NmMt+) sold for $876 (eBay; 12/06)
-J.Shellenback/R.Willis #592 PSA 9 (MT) sold for $2,000 (eBay; 1/08)
-J.Shellenback/R.Willis #592 PSA 9 (MT) sold for $1,385 (eBay; 9/07)
-Mickey Stanley #607 PSA 9 (MT) sold for $2,500 (eBay; 4/08)
-Mickey Stanley #607 PSA 9 (MT) sold for $2,224 (eBay; 12/07)
-Mickey Stanley #607 PSA 9 (MT) sold for $2,132 (eBay; 2/08)
-Willie Stargell #140 PSA 10 (Gem) sold for $2,405 (Mastro; 10/05)
-Willie Stargell #140 PSA 10 (Gem) sold for $1,626 (eBay; 5/07)
-Don Sutton #445 PSA 10 (Gem) sold for $1,227 (Leland's; 10/05)
-Tigers Rookies #526 PSA 9 (MT) sold for $660 (eBay; 9/07)
-Maury Wills #570 PSA 9 (MT) sold for $2,345 (eBay; 4/08)
-Carl Yastrzemski #355 PSA 10 (Gem) sold for $4,339 (Mastro; 12/06)

1967 Topps Who Am I

		GD 2	VG 3	VgEx 4	EX 5	ExMt 6	NM 7	NmMt 8	MT 9
12	Babe Ruth	15	50	60	80	100	20	400	
22	Mickey Mantle	40	50	60	100	150	400	600	
33	Willie Mays	15	20	30	50	80	120	300	
41	Sandy Koufax	15	20	30	80	100	150	400	

-Willie Mays #33 PSA 9 (MT) sold for $913 (Memory Lane; 5/08)

1968 Topps

		GD 2	VG 3	VgEx 4	EX 5	ExMt 6	NM 7	NmMt 8	MT 9
1	NL Batting Leaders	5	5	6	15	25	▲50	80	
2	AL Batting Leaders	5	5	5	8	30	60	150	
3	NL RBI Leaders	5	5	20	25	40	60	200	
4	AL RBI Leaders	5	5	5	6	10	30	60	200
5	NL Home Run Leaders	5	5	6	10	30	50	▲250	
6	AL Home Run Leaders	5	5	5	6	10	▲60		200
7	NL ERA Leaders	5	5	5	5	6	15	25	250
8	AL ERA Leaders	5	5	5	5	8	15		50
9	NL Pitching Leaders	5	5	5	6	10	30		200
10A	AL Pitching Leaders ERR Lonborg	5	5	5	6	15	80		
10B	AL Pitching Leaders COR Lonborg	5	5	5	6	15	120		
11	NL Strikeout Leaders	5	5	5	6	10	30		80

#	Player	GD 2	VG 3	VgEx 4	EX 5	ExMt 6	NM 7	NmMt 8	MT 9
12	AL Strikeout Leaders#(Jim Lonborg Sam McDowell#(Dean Chance	5	5	5	5	6	10	40	200
13	Chuck Hartenstein RC	5	5	5	5	5	5	15	120
14	Jerry McNertney	5	5	5	5	5	5	10	30
15	Ron Hunt	5	5	5	5	5	6	12	30
16	L.Piniella/R.Scheinblum	5	5	5	5	6	10	30	300
17	Dick Hall	5	5	5	5	5	5	10	25
18	Mike Hershberger	5	5	5	5	5	5	10	30
19	Juan Pizarro	5	5	5	5	5	6	20	150
20	Brooks Robinson	5	5	6	10	30	50	80	200
21	Ron Davis	5	5	5	5	5	8	25	80
22	Pat Dobson	5	5	5	5	6	15	50	250
23	Chico Cardenas	5	5	5	5	5	6	15	40
24	Bobby Locke	5	5	5	5	5	5	10	60
25	Julian Javier	5	5	5	5	5	6	20	80
26	Darrell Brandon	5	5	5	5	5	5	10	60
27	Gil Hodges MG	5	5	5	▲15	▲20	▲25	▲30	60
28	Ted Uhlaender	5	5	5	5	5	5	10	25
29	Joe Verbanic	5	5	5	5	5	5	10	30
30	Joe Torre	5	5	5	5	10	20	▲60	150
31	Ed Stroud	5	5	5	5	5	5	15	50
32	Joe Gibbon	5	5	5	5	5	5	10	25
33	Pete Ward	5	5	5	5	5	5	15	80
34	Al Ferrara	5	5	5	5	5	5	10	50
35	Steve Hargan	5	5	5	5	5	5	10	30
36	B.Moose RC/B.Robertson RC	5	5	5	5	5	6	12	30
37	Billy Williams	5	5	5	15	20	40	50	100
38	Tony Pierce	5	5	5	5	5	5	10	25
39	Cookie Rojas	5	5	5	5	5	6	15	80
40	Denny McLain	5	5	5	6	15	30	50	120
41	Julio Gotay	5	5	5	5	5	5	12	40
42	Larry Haney	5	5	5	5	5	5	15	100
43	Gary Bell	5	5	5	5	5	5	10	25
44	Frank Kostro	5	5	5	5	5	5	10	25
45	Tom Seaver DP	5	6	15	▲50	60	▲120	▲300	1,000
46	Dave Ricketts	5	5	5	5	5	5	10	25
47	Ralph Houk MG	5	5	5	5	5	6	12	30
48	Ted Davidson	5	5	5	5	5	5	20	60
49A	Ed Brinkman White Team	5	5	5	5	5	5	10	25
49B	Ed Brinkman Yellow Team	8	12	20	30	100	150	450	
50	Willie Mays	25	30	50	60	100	200	400	1,500
51	Bob Locker	5	5	5	5	5	5	10	60
52	Hawk Taylor	5	5	5	5	5	5	10	25
53	Gene Alley	5	5	5	5	5	5	10	25
54	Stan Williams	5	5	5	5	5	5	10	25
55	Felipe Alou	5	5	5	5	5	6	12	30
56	D.Leonhard RC/D.May RC	5	5	5	5	5	5	20	100
57	Dan Schneider	5	5	5	5	5	5	10	25
58	Eddie Mathews	5	5	5	8	20	40	60	250
59	Don Lock	5	5	5	5	5	5	10	25
60	Ken Holtzman	5	5	5	5	5	6	12	30
61	Reggie Smith	5	5	5	5	5	6	12	30
62	Chuck Dobson	5	5	5	5	5	5	10	25
63	Dick Kenworthy RC	5	5	5	5	5	5	25	60
64	Jim Merritt	5	5	5	5	5	5	10	25
65	John Roseboro	5	5	5	5	5	5	10	30
66A	Casey Cox White Team	5	5	5	5	5	5	10	25
66B	Casey Cox Yellow Team	8	12	20	30	50	80	120	
67	Checklist 1/Kaat	5	5	5	5	5	6	20	30
68	Ron Willis	5	5	5	5	5	5	10	120
69	Tom Tresh	5	5	5	5	5	8	15	50
70	Bob Veale	5	5	5	5	5	10	60	150
71	Vern Fuller RC	5	5	5	5	5	5	10	30
72	Tommy John	5	5	5	5	5	6	15	30
73	Jim Ray Hart	5	5	5	5	5	5	15	80
74	Milt Pappas	5	5	5	5	5	6	15	60
75	Don Mincher	5	5	5	5	5	6	20	80
76	J.Britton/R.Reed RC	5	5	5	5	5	8	25	150
77	Don Wilson RC	5	5	5	5	5	5	10	30
78	Jim Northrup	5	5	5	5	5	8	15	60
79	Ted Kubiak RC	5	5	5	5	5	5	10	25
80	Rod Carew	5	6	10	15	30	▲150	▲250	800
81	Larry Jackson	5	5	5	5	5	5	10	30
82	Sam Bowens	5	5	5	5	5	5	10	50
83	John Stephenson	5	5	5	5	5	5	10	25
84	Bob Tolan	5	5	5	5	5	5	10	60
85	Gaylord Perry	5	5	5	5	6	15	25	60

#	Player	GD 2	VG 3	VgEx 4	EX 5	ExMt 6	NM 7	NmMt 8	MT
86	Willie Stargell	5	5	10	12	25	40	80	250
87	Dick Williams MG	5	5	5	5	5	5	10	25
88	Phil Regan	5	5	5	5	5	5	10	25
89	Jake Gibbs	5	5	5	5	5	5	12	30
90	Vada Pinson	5	5	5	5	5	5	10	30
91	Jim Ollom RC	5	5	5	5	5	5	10	25
92	Ed Kranepool	5	5	5	5	5	6	12	40
93	Tony Cloninger	5	5	5	5	5	5	10	25
94	Lee Maye	5	5	5	5	5	5	10	25
95	Bob Aspromonte	5	5	5	5	5	6	12	30
96	F.Coggins RC/D.Nold	5	5	5	5	5	5	15	120
97	Tom Phoebus	5	5	5	5	5	5	10	25
98	Gary Sutherland	5	5	5	5	5	5	10	25
99	Rocky Colavito	5	5	5	5	5	8	25	▲50
100	Bob Gibson	5	5	6	10	▲50	▲60	150	400
101	Glenn Beckert	5	5	5	5	5	6	12	50
102	Jose Cardenal	5	5	5	5	5	5	30	100
103	Don Sutton	5	5	5	5	10	15	30	100
104	Dick Dietz	5	5	5	5	5	5	10	25
105	Al Downing	5	5	5	5	5	6	15	30
106	Dalton Jones	5	5	5	5	5	5	10	25
107A	Checklist 2/Marichal Wide Mesh	5	5	5	5	5	12	30	150
107B	Checklist 2/Marichal Fine Mesh	5	5	5	5	5	12	30	200
108	Don Pavletich	5	5	5	5	5	5	10	25
109	Bert Campaneris	5	5	5	5	5	5	15	40
110	Hank Aaron	6	20	25	60	100	150	300	1,000
111	Rich Reese	5	5	5	5	5	5	10	25
112	Woody Fryman	5	5	5	5	5	5	10	40
113	T.Matchick/D.Patterson RC	5	5	5	5	6	10	25	100
114	Ron Swoboda	5	5	5	5	5	8	15	40
115	Sam McDowell	5	5	5	5	5	6	12	40
116	Ken McMullen	5	5	5	5	5	5	10	25
117	Larry Jaster	5	5	5	5	5	5	10	25
118	Mark Belanger	5	5	5	5	5	5	12	40
119	Ted Savage	5	5	5	5	5	5	10	25
120	Mel Stottlemyre	5	5	5	5	5	6	15	40
121	Jimmie Hall	5	5	5	5	5	5	10	30
122	Gene Mauch MG	5	5	5	5	5	5	15	80
123	Jose Santiago	5	5	5	5	5	5	10	25
124	Nate Oliver	5	5	5	5	5	5	10	40
125	Joel Horlen	5	5	5	5	5	5	10	40
126	Bobby Etheridge RC	5	5	5	5	5	5	20	80
127	Paul Lindblad	5	5	5	5	5	6	15	80
128	T.Dukes RC/A.Harris	5	5	5	5	5	8	30	150
129	Mickey Stanley	5	5	5	5	5	8	20	60
130	Tony Perez	5	5	5	5	▲25	40	120	250
131	Frank Bertaina	5	5	5	5	5	5	10	25
132	Bud Harrelson	5	5	5	5	5	8	15	40
133	Fred Whitfield	5	5	5	5	5	5	10	25
134	Pat Jarvis	5	5	5	5	5	5	10	25
135	Paul Blair	5	5	5	5	5	8	20	135
136	Randy Hundley	5	5	5	5	5	5	15	60
137	Minnesota Twins TC	5	5	5	5	5	6	15	40
138	Ruben Amaro	5	5	5	5	5	5	10	30
139	Chris Short	5	5	5	5	5	5	10	30
140	Tony Conigliaro	5	5	5	5	6	15	25	120
141	Dal Maxvill	5	5	5	5	5	6	12	50
142	B.Bradford RC/B.Voss	5	5	5	5	5	5	10	40
143	Pete Cimino	5	5	5	5	5	5	15	80
144	Joe Morgan	5	5	10	12	20	30	60	150
145	Don Drysdale	5	5	6	12	25	40	60	120
146	Sal Bando	5	5	5	5	5	6	12	60
147	Frank Linzy	5	5	5	5	5	5	10	40
148	Dave Bristol MG	5	5	5	5	5	5	10	25
149	Bob Saverine	5	5	5	5	5	5	10	25
150	Roberto Clemente	10	30	50	▲80	100	▲200	500	2,500
151	Lou Brock WS1	5	5	5	5	6	20	▲40	▲60
152	Carl Yastrzemski WS2	5	5	5	6	10	25	▲60	150
153	Nelson Briles WS3	5	5	5	5	5	5	10	30
154	Bob Gibson WS4	5	5	5	5	5	20	30	60
155	Jim Lonborg WS5	5	5	5	5	5	6	12	30
156	Rico Petrocelli WS6	5	5	5	5	5	6	12	40
157	St. Louis Wins It WS7	5	5	5	5	5	6	20	40
158	Cardinals Celebrate WS (GD2 VG3 VgEx4 EX5 ExMt6 NM7 NmMt8 MT)	5	5	5	5	5	12	25	50
159	Don Kessinger	5	5	5	5	5	8	15	80
160	Earl Wilson	5	5	5	5	5	8	12	100
161	Norm Miller	5	5	5	5	5	5	30	120

		GD 2	VG 3	VgEx 4	EX 5	ExMt 6	NM 7	NmMt 8	MT 9
	H.Gilson RC/M.Torrez RC	5	5	5	5	5	6	12	40
	Gene Brabender	5	5	5	5	5	5	10	60
	Ramon Webster	5	5	5	5	5	5	10	50
	Tony Oliva	5	5	5	5	8	15	60	225
	Claude Raymond	5	5	5	5	5	6	20	80
	Elston Howard	5	5	5	5	5	8	25	60
	Los Angeles Dodgers TC	5	5	5	5	8	12	30	
	Bob Bolin	5	5	5	5	5	5	10	50
	Jim Fregosi	5	5	5	5	5	6	12	40
	Don Nottebart	5	5	5	5	5	5	10	30
	Walt Williams	5	5	5	5	5	8	25	135
	John Boozer	5	5	5	5	5	5	10	50
	Bob Tillman	5	5	5	5	5	5	10	30
	Maury Wills	5	5	5	5	5	8	20	150
	Bob Allen	5	5	5	5	5	5	10	50
	N.Ryan RC/J.Koosman RC	▲300	▲400	▲500	▲600	1,000	1,500	4,000	30,000
	Don Wert	5	5	5	5	6	15	60	250
	Bill Stoneman RC	5	5	5	5	5	5	10	30
	Curt Flood	5	5	5	5	5	8	15	40
	Jerry Zimmerman	5	5	5	5	5	5	15	50
	Dave Giusti	5	5	5	5	5	5	10	25
	Bob Kennedy MG	5	5	5	5	5	5	12	120
	Lou Johnson	5	5	5	5	5	5	10	30
	Tom Haller	5	5	5	5	5	5	10	60
	Eddie Watt	5	5	5	5	5	5	10	30
	Sonny Jackson	5	5	5	5	5	5	10	40
	Cap Peterson	5	5	5	5	5	5	10	60
	Bill Landis RC	5	5	5	5	5	5	10	50
	Bill White	5	5	5	5	5	6	15	50
	Dan Frisella RC	5	5	5	5	5	5	12	80
2A	Checklist 3/Yaz Spec. BB	5	5	5	5	8	12	40	
2B	Checklist 3/Yaz Spec. BB Play Card	5	5	5	5	5	8	12	30
3	Jack Hamilton	5	5	5	5	5	5	15	100
4	Don Buford	5	5	5	5	5	5	12	50
5	Joe Pepitone	5	5	5	5	5	6	12	50
6	Gary Nolan RC	5	5	5	5	6	10	25	135
7	Larry Brown	5	5	5	5	5	5	10	40
8	Roy Face	5	5	5	5	5	6	12	50
9	R.Rodriguez RC/D.Osteen	5	5	5	5	5	5	15	100
00	Orlando Cepeda	5	5	5	10	▲25	▲30	80	150
01	Mike Marshall RC	5	5	5	5	5	8	15	120
02	Adolfo Phillips	5	5	5	5	5	5	10	25
03	Dick Kelley	5	5	5	5	5	5	10	25
04	Andy Etchebarren	5	5	5	5	5	5	10	25
05	Juan Marichal	5	5	5	8	12	30	▲50	150
06	Cal Ermer MG RC	5	5	5	5	5	5	10	25
07	Carroll Sembera	5	5	5	5	5	5	10	25
08	Willie Davis	5	5	5	5	5	5	10	25
09	Tim Cullen	5	5	5	5	5	5	10	25
10	Gary Peters	5	5	5	5	5	5	10	25
11	J.C. Martin	5	5	5	5	5	5	10	25
12	Dave Morehead	5	5	5	5	5	5	10	25
13	Chico Ruiz	5	5	5	5	5	5	10	30
14	S.Bahnsen/F.Fernandez	5	5	5	5	5	6	15	175
15	Jim Bunning	5	5	5	5	5	8	25	50
16	Bubba Morton	5	5	5	5	5	5	10	25
17	Dick Farrell	5	5	5	5	5	5	10	25
18	Ken Suarez	5	5	5	5	5	5	10	30
19	Rob Gardner	5	5	5	5	5	5	10	40
20	Harmon Killebrew	5	5	15	25	30	▲50	80	▲200
221	Atlanta Braves TC	5	5	5	5	5	6	12	30
222	Jim Hardin RC	5	5	5	5	5	5	10	25
223	Ollie Brown	5	5	5	5	5	5	15	
224	Jack Aker	5	5	5	5	5	5	12	50
225	Richie Allen	5	5	5	5	5	8	15	60
226	Jimmie Price	5	5	5	5	5	8	15	40
227	Joe Hoerner	5	5	5	5	5	5	10	50
228	J.Billingham RC/J.Fairey RC	5	5	5	5	5	6	12	40
229	Fred Klages	5	5	5	5	5	5	10	25
230	Pete Rose	15	25	40	50	60	150	300	1,000
231	Dave Baldwin RC	5	5	5	5	5	5	10	25
232	Denis Menke	5	5	5	5	5	5	10	25
233	George Scott	5	5	5	5	5	6	12	40
234	Bill Monbouquette	5	5	5	5	5	5	10	30
235	Ron Santo	5	5	5	8	12	25	40	150
236	Tug McGraw	5	5	5	5	5	8	30	50
237	Alvin Dark MG	5	5	5	5	5	6	15	

		GD 2	VG 3	VgEx 4	EX 5	ExMt 6	NM 7	NmMt 8	MT 9
238	Tom Satriano	5	5	5	5	5	6	20	200
239	Bill Henry	5	5	5	5	5	5	10	25
240	Al Kaline	5	15	20	25	40	50	▲120	500
241	Felix Millan	5	5	5	5	5	5	10	25
242	Moe Drabowsky	5	5	5	5	5	8	20	100
243	Rich Rollins	5	5	5	5	5	5	10	60
244	John Donaldson RC	5	5	5	5	5	5	10	25
245	Tony Gonzalez	5	5	5	5	5	5	10	40
246	Fritz Peterson	5	5	5	5	5	6	12	80
247	Johnny Bench RC	60	▲100	▲120	150	▲250	400	800	4,000
248	Fred Valentine	5	5	5	5	5	5	10	25
249	Bill Singer	5	5	5	5	5	5	10	25
250	Carl Yastrzemski	5	▲20	▲25	▲30	▲50	▲60	▲120	400
251	Manny Sanguillen RC	5	5	5	5	5	8	40	200
252	California Angels TC	5	5	5	5	5	6	12	40
253	Dick Hughes	5	5	5	5	5	5	10	40
254	Cleon Jones	5	5	5	5	5	8	20	100
255	Dean Chance	5	5	5	5	5	5	10	30
256	Norm Cash	5	5	6	10	15	30	50	150
257	Phil Niekro	5	5	5	5	▲20	▲25	40	100
258	J.Arcia RC/B.Schlesinger	5	5	5	5	5	5	15	80
259	Ken Boyer	5	5	5	6	10	▲30		100
260	Jim Wynn	5	5	5	5	5	6	12	40
261	Dave Duncan	5	5	5	5	5	5	10	30
262	Rick Wise	5	5	5	5	5	5	10	30
263	Horace Clarke	5	5	5	5	5	6	15	
264	Ted Abernathy	5	5	5	5	5	5	10	50
265	Tommy Davis	5	5	5	5	5	6	15	120
266	Paul Popovich	5	5	5	5	5	5	10	50
267	Herman Franks MG	5	5	5	5	5	5	10	40
268	Bob Humphreys	5	5	5	5	5	5	15	50
269	Bob Tiefenauer	5	5	5	5	5	5	10	40
270	Matty Alou	5	5	5	5	5	6	15	120
271	Bobby Knoop	5	5	5	5	5	5	15	80
272	Ray Culp	5	5	5	5	5	5	10	25
273	Dave Johnson	5	5	5	5	5	6	12	40
274	Mike Cuellar	5	5	5	5	5	6	12	40
275	Tim McCarver	5	5	5	5	8	12	▲40	150
276	Jim Roland	5	5	5	5	5	5	10	40
277	Jerry Buchek	5	5	5	5	5	5	12	40
278	Checklist 4/Cepeda	5	5	5	5	5	8	25	80
279	Bill Hands	5	5	5	5	5	5	15	60
280	Mickey Mantle	120	150	200	250	▲400	500	▲1,200	▲5,000
281	Jim Campanis	5	5	5	5	5	5	15	150
282	Rick Monday	5	5	5	5	5	6	15	165
283	Mel Queen	5	5	5	5	5	5	10	25
284	Johnny Briggs	5	5	5	5	5	5	10	40
285	Dick McAuliffe	5	5	5	5	6	10	25	▲80
286	Cecil Upshaw	5	5	5	5	5	5	15	80
287	M.Abarbanel RC/C.Carlos RC	5	5	5	5	5	5	10	25
288	Dave Wickersham	5	5	5	5	5	5	10	25
289	Woody Held	5	5	5	5	5	5	10	25
290	Willie McCovey	5	10	12	20	30	50	80	200
291	Dick Lines	5	5	5	5	5	5	10	40
292	Art Shamsky	5	5	5	5	5	5	10	25
293	Bruce Howard	5	5	5	5	5	5	10	25
294	Red Schoendienst MG	5	5	5	5	5	10	30	100
295	Sonny Siebert	5	5	5	5	5	5	10	40
296	Byron Browne	5	5	5	5	5	5	10	40
297	Russ Gibson	5	5	5	5	5	5	10	25
298	Jim Brewer	5	5	5	5	5	5	10	30
299	Gene Michael	5	5	5	5	5	5	10	25
300	Rusty Staub	5	5	5	5	5	8	12	40	100
301	G.Mitterwald RC/R.Renick RC	5	5	5	5	5	5	10	40
302	Gerry Arrigo	5	5	5	5	5	5	10	25
303	Dick Green	5	5	5	5	5	5	10	25
304	Sandy Valdespino	5	5	5	5	5	5	10	25
305	Minnie Rojas	5	5	5	5	5	5	10	25
306	Mike Ryan	5	5	5	5	5	5	10	30
307	John Hiller	5	5	5	5	5	8	25	120
308	Pittsburgh Pirates TC	5	5	5	5	5	8	20	80
309	Ken Henderson	5	5	5	5	5	6	12	50
310	Luis Aparicio	5	5	5	5	6	10	25	60
311	Jack Lamabe	5	5	5	5	5	5	10	25
312	Curt Blefary	5	5	5	5	5	6	15	60
313	Al Weis	5	5	5	5	5	6	12	30
314	B.Rohr/G.Spriggs	5	5	5	5	5	5	15	120

#	Player	GD 2	VG 3	VgEx 4	EX 5	ExMt 6	NM 7	NmMt 8	MT 9
315	Zoilo Versalles	5	5	5	5	5	5	10	30
316	Steve Barber	5	5	5	5	5	6	12	30
317	Ron Brand	5	5	5	5	5	5	10	25
318	Chico Salmon	5	5	5	5	5	5	10	30
319	George Culver	5	5	5	5	5	5	10	25
320	Frank Howard	5	5	5	5	5	6	12	50
321	Leo Durocher MG	5	5	5	5	5	6	▲40	60
322	Dave Boswell	5	5	5	5	5	5	10	40
323	Deron Johnson	5	5	5	5	5	5	10	30
324	Jim Nash	5	5	5	5	5	5	10	50
325	Manny Mota	5	5	5	5	5	8	25	120
326	Dennis Ribant	5	5	5	5	5	8	15	100
327	Tony Taylor	5	5	5	5	5	6	12	50
328	C.Vinson RC/J.Weaver RC	5	5	5	5	5	5	10	30
329	Duane Josephson	5	5	5	5	5	5	10	30
330	Roger Maris	▲15	▲20	▲30	▲40	▲50	▲60	100	300
331	Dan Osinski	5	5	5	5	5	5	10	40
332	Doug Rader	5	5	5	5	5	6	12	50
333	Ron Herbel	5	5	5	5	5	5	10	40
334	Baltimore Orioles TC	5	5	5	5	5	6	12	40
335	Bob Allison	5	5	5	5	5	5	12	50
336	John Purdin	5	5	5	5	5	5	10	25
337	Bill Robinson	5	5	5	5	5	6	12	40
338	Bob Johnson	5	5	5	5	5	5	10	25
339	Rich Nye	5	5	5	5	5	5	10	25
340	Max Alvis	5	5	5	5	5	5	10	25
341	Jim Lemon MG	5	5	5	5	5	5	10	25
342	Ken Johnson	5	5	5	5	5	5	10	30
343	Jim Gosger	5	5	5	5	5	5	10	25
344	Donn Clendenon	5	5	5	5	5	6	12	40
345	Bob Hendley	5	5	5	5	5	6	12	30
346	Jerry Adair	5	5	5	5	5	5	10	30
347	George Brunet	5	5	5	5	5	5	10	25
348	L.Colton RC/D.Thoenen RC	5	5	5	5	5	5	10	30
349	Ed Spiezio	5	5	5	5	5	5	10	25
350	Hoyt Wilhelm	5	5	5	5	5	8	25	80
351	Bob Barton	5	5	5	5	5	5	10	25
352	Jackie Hernandez RC	5	5	5	5	5	5	10	25
353	Mack Jones	5	5	5	5	5	6	12	30
354	Pete Richert	5	5	5	5	5	5	10	25
355	Ernie Banks	6	10	20	30	50	60	100	300
356A	Checklist 5/Holtzman Center	5	5	5	5	5	8	25	
356B	Checklist 5/Holtzman Right	5	5	5	5	5	8	20	80
357	Len Gabrielson	5	5	5	5	5	5	10	40
358	Mike Epstein	5	5	5	5	5	5	10	30
359	Joe Moeller	5	5	5	5	5	5	10	30
360	Willie Horton	5	5	5	5	8	15	40	150
361	Harmon Killebrew AS	5	5	5	5	▲20	▲25	▲50	100
362	Orlando Cepeda AS	5	5	5	5	5	6	▲25	60
363	Rod Carew AS	5	5	5	5	6	25	▲50	100
364	Joe Morgan AS	5	5	5	5	6	20	▲30	▲80
365	Brooks Robinson AS	5	5	5	5	15	▲25	▲50	100
366	Ron Santo AS	5	5	5	5	5	10	15	80
367	Jim Fregosi AS	5	5	5	5	5	5	10	25
368	Gene Alley AS	5	5	5	5	5	5	15	80
369	Carl Yastrzemski AS	5	5	▲15	▲20	25	30	▲60	100
370	Hank Aaron AS	5	10	20	25	30	50	80	250
371	Tony Oliva AS	5	5	5	5	5	6	25	▲60
372	Lou Brock AS	5	5	5	6	▲15	▲20	▲40	▲100
373	Frank Robinson AS	5	5	5	5	8	▲25	▲50	100
374	Roberto Clemente AS	10	20	25	30	50	80	150	600
375	Bill Freehan AS	5	5	5	5	5	8	25	80
376	Tim McCarver AS	5	5	5	5	5	6	12	40
377	Joel Horlen AS	5	5	5	5	5	5	10	25
378	Bob Gibson AS	5	5	5	5	8	20	50	100
379	Gary Peters AS	5	5	5	5	5	6	15	30
380	Ken Holtzman AS	5	5	5	5	5	6	15	30
381	Boog Powell	5	5	5	5	6	10	25	100
382	Ramon Hernandez	5	5	5	5	5	5	10	60
383	Steve Whitaker	5	5	5	5	5	6	15	30
384	B.Henry/H.McRae RC	5	5	5	5	5	8	20	120
385	Jim Hunter	5	6	5	8	20	25	50	120
386	Greg Goossen	5	5	5	5	5	5	12	30
387	Joe Foy	5	5	5	5	5	6	15	30
388	Ray Washburn	5	5	5	5	5	5	10	25
389	Jay Johnstone	5	5	5	5	5	5	10	40
390	Bill Mazeroski	5	5	1	10	15	25	▲40	▲100

#	Player	GD 2	VG 3	VgEx 4	EX 5	ExMt 6	NM 7	NmMt 8	MT
391	Bob Priddy	5	5	5	5	5	5	10	2
392	Grady Hatton MG	5	5	5	5	5	5	20	12
393	Jim Perry	5	5	5	5	5	5	10	2
394	Tommie Aaron	5	5	5	5	5	5	10	2
395	Camilo Pascual	5	5	5	5	5	6	15	6
396	Bobby Wine	5	5	5	5	5	5	10	2
397	Vic Davalillo	5	5	5	5	5	5	15	2
398	Jim Grant	5	5	5	5	5	5	10	2
399	Ray Oyler	5	5	5	5	5	8	20	6
400A	Mike McCormick Yellow Team	5	5	5	5	5	5	10	2
401	Mets Team	5	5	5	5	5	6	20	4
402	Mike Hegan	5	5	5	5	5	5	10	2
403	John Buzhardt	5	5	5	5	5	5	10	2
404	Floyd Robinson	5	5	5	5	5	5	10	2
405	Tommy Helms	5	5	5	5	5	6	15	8
406	Dick Ellsworth	5	5	5	5	5	5	10	6
407	Gary Kolb	5	5	5	5	5	5	10	2
408	Steve Carlton	5	6	10	12	▲30	50	▲80	20
409	F.Peters RC/R.Stone	5	5	5	5	5	5	10	2
410	Ferguson Jenkins	5	5	6	10	15	30	80	30
411	Ron Hansen	5	5	5	5	5	5	10	2
412	Clay Carroll	5	5	5	5	5	5	10	25
413	Tom McCraw	5	5	5	5	5	5	10	2
414	Mickey Lolich	5	5	5	6	10	30	150	
415	Johnny Callison	5	5	5	5	5	6	12	4
416	Bill Rigney MG	5	5	5	5	5	5	10	2
417	Willie Crawford	5	5	5	5	5	5	10	25
418	Eddie Fisher	5	5	5	5	5	5	10	25
419	Jack Hiatt	5	5	5	5	5	5	12	4
420	Cesar Tovar	5	5	5	5	5	5	8	25
421	Ron Taylor	5	5	5	5	5	6	25	100
422	Rene Lachemann	5	5	5	5	5	5	10	25
423	Fred Gladding	5	5	5	5	5	5	10	25
424	Chicago White Sox TC	5	5	5	5	5	6	20	80
425	Jim Maloney	5	5	5	5	5	6	12	40
426	Hank Allen	5	5	5	5	5	5	10	25
427	Dick Calmus	5	5	5	5	5	5	10	25
428	Vic Roznovsky	5	5	5	5	5	5	10	60
429	Tommie Sisk	5	5	5	5	5	5	10	25
430	Rico Petrocelli	5	5	5	5	6	10	30	150
431	Dooley Womack	5	5	5	5	5	6	12	60
432	B.Davis/J.Vidal	5	5	5	5	5	5	10	50
433	Bob Rodgers	5	5	5	5	5	5	10	25
434	Ricardo Joseph RC	5	5	5	5	5	5	10	80
435	Ron Perranoski	5	5	5	5	5	6	12	50
436	Hal Lanier	5	5	5	5	5	5	10	60
437	Don Cardwell	5	5	5	5	5	8	40	120
438	Lee Thomas	5	5	5	5	5	5	10	25
439	Lum Harris MG	5	5	5	5	5	5	10	25
440	Claude Osteen	5	5	5	5	5	5	10	30
441	Alex Johnson	5	5	5	5	5	8	30	135
442	Dick Bosman	5	5	5	5	5	5	10	50
443	Joe Azcue	5	5	5	5	5	5	10	25
444	Jack Fisher	5	5	5	5	5	5	10	25
445	Mike Shannon	5	5	5	5	5	8	15	50
446	Ron Kline	5	5	5	5	5	5	10	40
447	G.Korince/F.Lasher RC	5	5	5	5	5	8	30	200
448	Gary Wagner	5	5	5	5	5	5	10	25
449	Gene Oliver	5	5	5	5	5	5	15	60
450	Jim Kaat	5	5	5	5	6	10	20	▲60
451	Al Spangler	5	5	5	5	5	5	10	25
452	Jesus Alou	5	5	5	5	5	6	12	60
453	Sammy Ellis	5	5	5	5	5	8	30	250
454A	Checklist 6/F.Rob Cap Complete	5	5	5	5	5	6	12	60
454B	Checklist 6/F.Rob Cap Partial	5	5	5	5	5	6	12	60
455	Rico Carty	5	5	5	5	5	6	15	80
456	John O'Donoghue	5	5	5	5	5	5	10	25
457	Jim Lefebvre	5	5	5	5	5	5	10	30
458	Lew Krausse	5	5	5	5	5	5	10	25
459	Dick Simpson	5	5	5	5	5	5	10	25
460	Jim Lonborg	5	5	5	5	5	6	15	30
461	Chuck Hiller	5	5	5	5	5	5	10	25
462	Barry Moore	5	5	5	5	5	5	10	25
463	Jim Schaffer	GD 2	VG 3	VgEx 4	EX 5	ExMt 6	NM 7	NmMt 8	25
		5	5	5	5	5	5	10	25
464	Don McMahon	5	5	5	5	5	8	40	135
465	Tommie Agee	5	5	5	5	5	6	30	50
466	Bill Dillman	5	5	5	5	5	5	10	25

	GD 2	VG 3	VgEx 4	EX 5	ExMt 6	NM 7	NmMt 8	MT 9
Dick Howser	5	5	5	5	5	6	25	40
Larry Sherry	5	5	5	5	5	5	10	25
Ty Cline	5	5	5	5	5	5	10	30
Bill Freehan	5	5	5	6	10	15	▲50	▲80
Orlando Pena	5	5	5	5	5	5	10	25
Walter Alston MG	5	5	5	5	5	6	20	40
Al Worthington	5	5	5	5	5	5	10	25
Paul Schaal	5	5	5	5	5	5	6	15
Joe Niekro	5	5	5	5	5	6	▲20	30
Woody Woodward	5	5	5	5	5	5	10	25
Philadelphia Phillies TC	5	5	5	5	5	5	10	30
Dave McNally	5	5	5	5	5	8	15	50
Phil Gagliano	5	5	5	5	5	5	10	25
Manager's Dream	8	25	40	50	60	▲100	120	300
John Wyatt	5	5	5	5	5	5	10	25
Jose Pagan	5	5	5	5	5	5	10	25
Darold Knowles	5	5	5	5	5	5	10	30
Phil Roof	5	5	5	5	5	5	8	20
Ken Berry	5	5	5	5	5	5	10	25
Cal Koonce	5	5	5	5	5	6	15	30
Lee May	5	5	5	25	30	50	60	250
Dick Tracewski	5	5	5	6	8	10	20	80
Wally Bunker	5	5	5	5	5	5	10	25
Super Stars	50	60	▲120	▲150	200	250	500	1,000
Denny Lemaster	5	5	5	5	5	5	10	25
Jeff Torborg	5	5	5	5	5	5	10	80
Jim McGlothlin	5	5	5	5	5	5	6	15
Ray Sadecki	5	5	5	5	5	5	6	15
Leon Wagner	5	5	5	5	5	8	60	120
Steve Hamilton	5	5	5	5	5	5	15	50
St. Louis Cardinals TC	5	5	5	5	8	12	40	80
Bill Bryan	5	5	5	5	5	8	40	80
Steve Blass	5	5	5	5	5	5	10	25
Frank Robinson	5	5	6	20	30	60	100	250
John Odom	5	5	5	5	6	15	▲120	250
Mike Andrews	5	5	5	5	5	5	10	30
Al Jackson	5	5	5	5	6	8	12	50
Russ Snyder	5	5	5	5	5	5	10	40
Joe Sparma	5	5	5	6	25	50	▼60	120
Clarence Jones RC	5	5	5	5	5	5	10	25
Wade Blasingame	5	5	5	5	5	5	10	25
Duke Sims	5	5	5	5	5	5	10	25
Dennis Higgins	5	5	5	5	5	5	10	25
Ron Fairly	5	5	5	5	5	6	20	30
Bill Kelso	5	5	5	5	5	6	8	20
Grant Jackson	5	5	5	5	5	5	10	25
Hank Bauer MG	5	5	5	5	5	6	12	30
Al McBean	5	5	5	5	5	5	10	25
Russ Nixon	5	5	5	5	5	5	10	25
Pete Mikkelsen	5	5	5	5	5	5	10	25
Diego Segui	5	5	5	5	5	5	10	25
8A Checklist 7/Boyer ERR AL	5	5	5	5	5	5	15	25
8B Checklist 7/Boyer COR ML	5	5	5	5	5	5	10	25
19 Jerry Stephenson	5	5	5	5	5	5	10	25
20 Lou Brock	5	5	20	25	40	▼50	80	200
21 Don Shaw	5	5	5	5	5	5	10	25
22 Wayne Causey	5	5	5	5	5	5	10	25
23 John Tsitouris	5	5	5	5	5	6	30	60
24 Andy Kosco	5	5	5	5	5	6	12	80
25 Jim Davenport	5	5	5	5	5	5	10	50
26 Bill Denehy	5	5	5	5	5	6	15	80
27 Tito Francona	5	5	5	5	5	5	10	50
28 Detroit Tigers TC	5	6	10	20	50	60	100	300
29 Bruce Von Hoff RC	5	5	5	5	5	6	20	80
30 Bird Belters	5	5	8	30	40	50	100	200
31 Chuck Hinton	5	5	5	5	5	5	10	30
32 Luis Tiant	5	5	5	5	▲8	▲12	▲30	▲50
33 Wes Parker	5	5	5	5	5	8	25	60
34 Bob Miller	5	5	5	5	5	5	12	40
35 Danny Cater	5	5	5	5	5	5	12	20
36 Bill Short	5	5	5	5	6	8	10	25
37 Norm Siebern	5	5	5	5	5	5	20	30
38 Manny Jimenez	5	5	5	5	5	5	10	30
39 J.Ray RC/M.Ferraro RC	5	5	5	5	5	5	10	50
40 Nelson Briles	5	5	5	5	5	5	▲25	40
41 Sandy Alomar	5	5	5	5	5	5	10	25
42 John Boccabella	5	5	5	5	5	5	10	25

		GD 2	VG 3	VgEx 4	EX 5	ExMt 6	NM 7	NmMt 8	MT 9
543	Bob Lee	5	5	5	5	5	5	12	40
544	Mayo Smith MG	5	5	5	8	12	20	30	80
545	Lindy McDaniel	5	5	5	5	5	5	20	40
546	Roy White	5	5	5	5	5	10	25	60
547	Dan Coombs	5	5	5	5	5	5	10	25
548	Bernie Allen	5	5	5	5	5	5	10	25
549	C.Motton RC/R.Nelson RC	5	5	5	5	5	5	10	40
550	Clete Boyer	5	5	5	5	5	6	12	40
551	Darrell Sutherland	5	5	5	5	5	5	10	25
552	Ed Kirkpatrick	5	5	5	5	5	5	10	40
553	Hank Aguirre	5	5	5	5	5	5	10	25
554	Oakland Athletics TC	5	5	5	5	5	8	25	▲120
555	Jose Tartabull	5	5	5	5	5	5	10	25
556	Dick Selma	5	5	5	5	5	6	30	80
557	Frank Quilici	5	5	5	5	5	6	15	50
558	Johnny Edwards	5	5	5	5	5	5	10	50
559	C.Taylor RC/L.Walker	5	5	5	5	5	6	15	100
560	Paul Casanova	5	5	5	5	5	5	10	40
561	Lee Elia	5	5	5	5	5	5	10	25
562	Jim Bouton	5	5	5	5	▲10	▲25	▲30	60
563	Ed Charles	5	5	5	5	5	6	20	100
564	Eddie Stanky MG	5	5	5	5	5	8	40	150
565	Larry Dierker	5	5	5	5	5	5	15	40
566	Ken Harrelson	5	5	5	5	5	8	25	40
567	Clay Dalrymple	5	5	5	5	5	6	15	60
568	Willie Smith	5	5	5	5	5	5	10	25
569	I.Murrell RC/L.Rohr RC	5	5	5	5	5	5	15	80
570	Rick Reichardt	5	5	5	5	5	5	10	25
571	Tony LaRussa	5	5	5	5	5	8	30	60
572	Don Bosch RC	5	5	5	5	5	5	12	30
573	Joe Coleman	5	5	5	5	5	5	10	25
574	Cincinnati Reds TC	5	5	5	5	5	6	25	50
575	Jim Palmer	5	6	10	25	30	40	60	200
576	Dave Adlesh	5	5	5	5	5	5	10	25
577	Fred Talbot	5	5	5	5	5	5	10	25
578	Orlando Martinez	5	5	5	5	5	5	10	25
579	L.Hisle RC/M.Lum RC	5	5	5	5	6	10	40	60
580	Bob Bailey	5	5	5	5	5	6	20	50
581	Garry Roggenburk	5	5	5	5	5	5	10	25
582	Jerry Grote	5	5	5	5	5	5	▲20	50
583	Gates Brown	5	5	5	8	15	30	80	200
584	Larry Shepard MG RC	5	5	5	5	5	5	10	30
585	Wilbur Wood	5	5	5	5	5	5	10	30
586	Jim Pagliaroni	5	5	5	5	5	5	10	40
587	Roger Repoz	5	5	5	5	5	5	10	25
588	Dick Schofield	5	5	5	5	5	5	12	30
589	R.Clark/M.Ogier RC	5	5	5	5	5	6	15	100
590	Tommy Harper	5	5	5	5	5	5	10	30
591	Dick Nen	5	5	5	5	5	5	10	25
592	John Bateman	5	5	5	5	5	5	10	25
593	Lee Stange	5	5	5	5	5	5	10	25
594	Phil Linz	5	5	5	5	5	5	10	30
595	Phil Ortega	5	5	5	5	5	5	10	40
596	Charlie Smith	5	5	5	5	5	5	10	30
597	Bill McCool	5	5	5	5	5	5	20	50
598	Jerry May	5	5	5	5	5	8	20	100

—Hank Aaron #110 PSA 10 (Gem) sold for $10,213 (Mile High; 2/08)
—Hank Aaron #110 SGC 96 (MT) sold for $450 (eBay; 12/06)
—Hank Aaron AS #370 PSA 10 (Gem) sold for $1,679 (Memory Lane; 4/07)
—AL Batting Leaders #2 PSA 9 (MT) sold for $1,694 (eBay; 4/08)
—AL Batting Leaders #2 PSA 9 (MT) sold for $1,285 (eBay; 4/08)
—AL Batting Leaders #2 PSA 9 (MT) sold for $1,190 (eBay; 6/08)
—AL Batting Leaders #2 PSA 9 (MT) sold for $679 (eBay; 6/07)
—AL Batting Leaders #2 PSA 9 (MT) sold for $611 (eBay; 7/07)
—AL Pitching Leaders #10 (Lonborg) PSA 9 (MT) sold for $1,009 (eBay; 6/08)
—AL Pitching Leaders #10 (Lonborg) PSA 9 (MT) sold for $824 (eBay; 2/08)
—AL Pitching Leaders #10 (Lonberg) PSA 9 (MT) sold for $760 (eBay; 4/08)
—Ernie Banks #355 PSA 10 (Gem) sold for $1,938 (Madec; 11/07)
—Ernie Banks #355 PSA 10 (Gem) sold for $1,599 (Mastro; 6/06)
—Ernie Banks #355 PSA 10 (Gem) sold for $1,424 (eBay; 5/07)
—Ernie Banks #355 PSA 10 (Gem) sold for $603 (eBay; 1/07)
—Johnny Bench #247 PSA 10 (Gem) (Young Collection) sold for $8,711 (SCP; 5/12)
—Johnny Bench #247 PSA 10 (Gem) sold for $6,096 (Memory Lane; 12/07)
—Johnny Bench #247 PSA 10 (Gem) sold for $5,765 (Goodwin; 5/08)
—Johnny Bench #247 PSA 10 (Gem) sold for $4,655 (Mastro; 12/04)
—Johnny Bench #247 PSA 10 (Gem) sold for $4,376 (Mastro; 12/04)
—Johnny Bench #247 SGC 96 (MT) sold for $774 (eBay; 12/06)

—Lou Brock #520 PSA 10 (Gem) sold for $855 (eBay; 11/07)
—Rod Carew #80 PSA 10 (Gem) sold for $2,607 (eBay; 02/12)
—Rod Carew AS #363 PSA 10 (Gem) sold for $921 (eBay; 3/08)
—Steve Carlton #408 PSA 10 (Gem) sold for $1,108 (Memory Lane; 9/07)
—Steve Carlton #408 PSA 10 (Gem) sold for $1,016 (eBay; 4/08)
—Steve Carlton #408 PSA 10 (Gem) sold for $900 (eBay; 8/07)
—Steve Carlton #408 PSA 10 (Gem) sold for $899 (eBay; 1/08)
—Steve Carlton #408 PSA 10 (Gem) sold for $721 (Madec; 10/06)
—Steve Carlton #408 PSA 10 (Gem) sold for $688 (eBay; 6/08)
—Norm Cash #256 PSA 10 (Gem) sold for $2,476 (eBay; 4/07)
—Orlando Cepeda AS #362 PSA 10 (Gem) sold for $1,307 (eBay; 3/08)
—Detroit Tigers TC #528 PSA 10 (Gem) sold for $987 (Mastro; 10/06)
—Pat Dobson #22 PSA 10 (Gem) sold for $1,809 (eBay; 2/08)
—Don Drysdale #145 PSA 10 (Gem) sold for $572 (Mastro; 4/07)
—Don Drysdale #145 PSA 10 (Gem) sold for $476 (Mile High; 2/08)
—Don Drysdale #145 PSA 10 (Gem) sold for $399 (eBay; 4/08)
—Don Drysdale #145 PSA 10 (Gem) sold for $385 (eBay; 8/07)
—Don Drysdale #145 PSA 10 (Gem) sold for $335 (eBay; 3/08)
—Don Drysdale #145 PSA 10 (Gem) sold for $309 (eBay; 5/08)
—Don Drysdale #145 PSA 10 (Gem) sold for $296 (eBay; 5/08)
—Bob Gibson #100 PSA 10 (Gem) sold for $2,080 (Memory Lane; 12/06)
—Bob Gibson #100 PSA 10 (Gem) sold for $1,767 (Mile High; 2/08)
—Bob Gibson #100 PSA 10 (Gem) sold for $1,295 (eBay; 4/08)
—Bob Gibson #100 PSA 10 (Gem) sold for $1,100 (Mastro; 12/08)
—Bob Gibson #100 PSA 10 (Gem) sold for $1,018 (eBay; 5/08)
—Bob Gibson #100 PSA 10 (Gem) sold for $924 (Mastro; 12/07)
—Mickey Lolich #414 PSA 10 (Gem) sold for $4,550 (eBay; 11/07)
—Mickey Lolich #414 PSA 9 (MT) sold for $1,230 (eBay; 4/08)
—Mickey Lolich #414 PSA 9 (MT) sold for $1,225 (eBay; 5/07)
—Managers Dream #480 PSA 10 (Gem) sold for $2,244 (Andy Madec; 3/03)
—Managers Dream #480 PSA 10 (Gem) sold for $1,789 (Mastro; 2/07)
—Managers Dream #480 PSA 10 (Gem) sold for $914 (eBay; 3/08)
—Mickey Mantle #280 PSA 10 (Gem) sold for $9,889 (eBay; 1/07)
—Mickey Mantle #280 PSA 10 (Gem) sold for $8,733 (Madec; 11/07)
—Mickey Mantle #280 PSA 10 (Gem) sold for $6,451 (Superior; 3/03)
—Mickey Mantle #280 PSA 10 (Gem) sold for $7,373 (Mile High; 2/08)
—Mickey Mantle #280 PSA 10 (Gem) sold for $7,216 (Mile High; 6/05)
—Mickey Mantle #280 PSA 10 (Gem) sold for $4,957 (Mastro; 5/05)
—Juan Marichal #205 PSA 10 (Gem) sold for $1,235 (eBay; 2/08)
—Roger Maris #330 PSA 10 (Gem) sold for $3,191 (Mile High; 2/08)
—Roger Maris #330 PSA 10 (Gem) sold for $2,185 (Mastro; 12/07)
—Roger Maris #330 PSA 10 (Gem) sold for $1,500 (eBay; 5/07)
—Roger Maris #330 PSA 10 (Gem) sold for $1,231 (Mastro; 10/05)
—Mike McCormick #400 (White) PSA 9 (MT) sold for $5,956 (Goodwin; 5/08)
—Mike McCormick #400 (White) PSA 7 (NM) sold for $850 (eBay; 4/08)
—Mike McCormick #400 (White) PSA 7 (NM) sold for $811 (eBay; 12/07)
—Mike McCormick #400 (White) PSA 6 (ExMt) sold for $403 (eBay; 3/08)
—Mike McCormick #400 (White) PSA 4 (VG) sold for $335 (Madec; 11/07)
—Mike McCormick #400 (White) PSA 4 (VG) sold for $172 (eBay; 6/08)
—Willie McCovey #290 PSA 10 (Gem) sold for $905 (Mile High; 2/08)
—Willie McCovey #290 PSA 10 (Gem) sold for $820 (eBay; 2/08)
—Willie McCovey #290 PSA 10 (Gem) sold for $609 (Memory Lane; 4/07)
—Denny McLain #40 PSA 10 (Gem) sold for $804 (eBay; 4/08)
—Denny McLain #40 PSA 10 (Gem) sold for $785 (eBay; 1/07)
—Denny McLain #40 PSA 10 (Gem) sold for $740 (Mile High; 2/08)
—Joe Morgan #144 PSA 10 (Gem) sold for $1,505 (eBay; 11/07)
—Phil Niekro #257 PSA 10 (Gem) sold for $897 (Mile High; 2/08)
—NL Batting Leaders #1 PSA 9 (MT) sold for $1,469 (Mile High; 2/08)
—NL Batting Leaders #1 PSA 9 (MT) sold for $1,444 (eBay; 4/08)
—NL Batting Leaders #1 PSA 9 (MT) sold for $611 (eBay; 6/07)
—NL Batting Leaders #1 PSA 9 (MT) sold for $611 (eBay; 4/07)
—NL Batting Leaders #1 PSA 9 (MT) sold for $456 (eBay; 1/07)
—NL Home Run Leaders #5 PSA 9 (MT) sold for $1,010 (eBay; 10/07)
—NL RBI Leaders #3 PSA 9 (MT) sold for $2,046 (eBay; 12/07)
—NL RBI Leaders #3 PSA 9 (MT) sold for $788 (eBay; 4/07)
—NL RBI Leaders #3 SGC 96 (MT) sold for $293 (eBay; 11/07)
—NL RBI Leaders #3 SGC 96 (MT) sold for $194 (eBay; 6/07)
—Jim Northrup #78 PSA 10 (Gem) sold for $1,677 (eBay; 3/08)
—Jim Palmer #575 PSA 10 (Gem) sold for $2,310 (Mile High; 11/03)
—Gaylord Perry #85 PSA 10 (Gem) sold for $809 (eBay; 5/07)
—Lou Piniella #16 PSA 10 (Gem) sold for $1,152 (eBay; 4/08)
—Brooks Robinson #20 PSA 10 (Gem) sold for $3,329 (eBay; 4/07)
—Brooks Robinson #20 PSA 10 (Gem) sold for $2,529 (eBay; 4/08)
—Frank Robinson #500 PSA 10 (Gem) sold for $2,025 (eBay; 7/07)
—Nolan Ryan #177 PSA 10 (Gem) sold for $612,360 (Heritage; 8/27)
—Nolan Ryan #177 SGC 98 (Gem) sold for $43,502 (Mastro; 8/06)
—Nolan Ryan #177 BVG 9 (MT) sold for $4,105 (eBay; 9/07)

—Nolan Ryan #177 BVG 9 (MT) sold for $3,755 (eBay; 3/08)
—Nolan Ryan #177 PSA 8.5 (NmMt+) sold for $3,281 (eBay; 5/08)
—Manny Sanguillen #251 PSA 10 (Gem) sold for $1,194 (eBay; 4/08)
—Tom Seaver #45 SGC 96 (MT) sold for $320 (eBay; 2/08)
—Joe Sparma #505 PSA 10 (Gem) sold for $851 (eBay; 12/06)
—Willie Stargell #86 PSA 10 (Gem) sold for $763 (Mastro; 12/07)
—Super Stars #490 PSA 10 (Gem) sold for $4,6691 (Mastro; 4/07)
—Super Stars #490 PSA 10 (Gem) sold for $3,076 (Mastro; 12/05)
—Super Stars #490 PSA 10 (Gem) sold for $1,843 (Lelands; 12/04)
—Don Wert #178 PSA 10 (Gem) sold for $2,710 (Memory Lane; 4/07)
—Billy Williams #37 PSA 10 (Gem) sold for $995 (eBay; 11/06)
—Carl Yastrzemski #250 PSA 10 (Gem) sold for $3,028 (eBay; 5/07)
—Checklist 3/Yaz #192 (Spec.BB) PSA 10 (Gem) sold for $1,045 (eBay; 4/08)
—Checklist 3/Yaz #192 (Spec.BB Play) PSA 9 (MT) sold for $551 (eBay; 4/08)

1968 Topps 3-D

—Roberto Clemente PSA 10 (Gem) sold for $40,197 (Lelands; 11/08)
—Roberto Clemente PSA 10 (Gem) sold for $30,343 (Mastro; 12/06)
—Roberto Clemente PSA 10 (Gem) sold for $30,000 (REA; 05/12)
—Roberto Clemente PSA 9 (MT) sold for $25,061 (Mile High; 11/10)
—Roberto Clemente SGC 96 (MT) sold for $15,569 (SCP; 5/12)
—Roberto Clemente PSA 9 (MT) sold for $25,000 (REA; 05/12)
—Roberto Clemente SGC 96 (MT) sold for $17,163 (Mile High; 6/10)
—Roberto Clemente PSA 8 (NmMt) sold for $15,120 (eBay; 1/08)
—Roberto Clemente #1 PSA 6 (ExMt) sold for $8,000 (Legendary; 5/12)
—Roberto Clemente SGC 60 (EX) sold for $12,548 (Heritage; 9/04)
—Willie Davis PSA 10 (Gem) sold for $2,974 (Memory Lane; 4/07)
—Willie Davis PSA 9 (MT) sold for $734 (eBay; 1/08)
—Ron Fairly PSA 9 (MT) sold for $840 (eBay; 1/08)
—Ron Fairly PSA 2 (Good) sold for $315 (eBay; 1/08)
—Curt Flood PSA 9 (MT) sold for $4,059 (eBay; 1/08)
—Jim Lonborg PSA 8 (NmMt) sold for $2,522 (eBay; 1/08)
—Jim Maloney PSA 9 (MT) sold for $804 (eBay; 1/08)
—Jim Maloney PSA 6 (ExMt) sold for $452 (eBay; 1/08)
—Tony Perez PSA 5 (EX) sold for $740 (eBay; 1/08)
—Tony Perez PSA 5 (EX) sold for $710 (eBay; 2/08)
—Boog Powell PSA 2 (Good) sold for $2,282 (eBay; 1/08)
—Bill Robinson PSA 8 (NmMt) sold for $1,257 (eBay; 1/08)
—Bill Robinson PSA 6 (ExMt) sold for $456 (eBay; 5/08)
—Rusty Staub PSA 8 (NmMt) sold for $5,665 (eBay; 1/08)
—Mel Stottlemyre PSA 6 (ExMt) sold for $5,110 (eBay; 1/08)
—Ron Swoboda PSA 8 (NmMt) sold for $3,192 (eBay; 1/08)

1968 Topps Game

		GD 2	VG 3	VgEx 4	EX 5	ExMt 6	NM 7	NmMt 8	MT
1	Matty Alou	5	5	5	5	6	10	50	
2	Mickey Mantle	20	40	50	60	80	120	200	60
3	Carl Yastrzemski	5	5	5	5	6	30	40	20
4	Hank Aaron	5	5	5	6	25	▲40	60	20
5	Harmon Killebrew	5	5	5	8	▲20	▲25	50	15
6	Roberto Clemente	5	20	25	30	40	▲60	80	30
7	Frank Robinson	5	5	6	8	▲20	▲25	▲60	10
8	Willie Mays	5	5	▲15	▲30	▲40	50	100	20
9	Brooks Robinson	5	5	5	5	20	25	40	15
10	Tommy Davis	5	5	5	5	5	6	15	5
11	Bill Freehan	5	5	5	5	5	8	20	6
12	Claude Osteen	5	5	5	5	5	6	20	12
13	Gary Peters	5	5	5	5	5	6	15	6
14	Jim Lonborg	5	5	5	5	5	6	15	8
15	Steve Hargan	5	5	5	5	5	6	15	6
16	Dean Chance	5	5	5	5	5	6	15	5
17	Mike McCormick	5	5	5	5	5	6	15	5
18	Tim McCarver	5	5	5	5	5	6	15	5
19	Ron Santo	5	5	5	5	5	8	20	8
20	Tony Gonzalez	5	5	5	5	5	6	15	10
21	Frank Howard	5	5	5	5	5	8	20	10
22	George Scott	5	5	5	5	5	6	30	20
23	Richie Allen	5	5	5	5	5	6	15	10
24	Jim Wynn	5	5	5	5	5	8	25	8
25	Gene Alley	5	5	5	5	5	6	15	8
26	Rick Monday	5	5	5	5	5	8	25	12
27	Al Kaline	5	5	5	5	15	▲30	30	125
28	Rusty Staub	5	5	5	5	5	6	25	6
29	Rod Carew	5	5	5	6	▲15	▲20	30	▲150
30	Pete Rose	5	6	▲20	▲30	▲40	50	80	150

	GD 2	VG 3	VgEx 4	EX 5	ExMt 6	NM 7	NmMt 8	MT 9
Joe Torre	5	5	5	5	5	8	20	80
Orlando Cepeda	5	5	5	5	5	8	20	120
Jim Fregosi	5	5	5	5	6	10	40	300

Hank Aaron #4 PSA 10 (Gem) sold for $576 (eBay; 1/08)
Matty Alou #1 PSA 9 (MT) sold for $367 (eBay; 4/08)
Willie Mays #8 PSA 10 (Gem) sold for $2,375 (Memory Lane; 5/08)
Willie Mays #8 PSA 10 (Gem) sold for $1,026 (eBay; 3/07)
Ron Santo #19 PSA 10 (Gem) sold for $382 (eBay; 10/07)
Ron Santo #19 PSA 10 (Gem) sold for $370 (eBay; 1/07)
Carl Yastrzemski #3 PSA 10 (Gem) sold for $675 (eBay; 4/08)

1969 Topps

#		GD 2	VG 3	VgEx 4	EX 5	ExMt 6	NM 7	NmMt 8	MT 9
1	AL Batting Leaders	5	5	6	10	25	30	80	150
2	NL Batting Leaders	5	5	5	8	20	40	▲120	250
3	AL RBI Leaders	5	5	5	5	5	8	20	30
4	NL RBI Leaders	5	5	5	5	5	8	15	80
5	AL Home Run Leaders	5	5	5	5	5	8	25	60
6	NL Home Run Leaders	5	5	5	5	6	▲15	▲60	▲100
7	AL ERA Leaders	5	5	5	5	5	6	12	25
8	NL ERA Leaders	5	5	5	5	6	10	20	120
9	AL Pitching Leaders	5	5	5	5	5	6	25	60
10	NL Pitching Leaders	5	5	5	5	5	8	25	50
11	AL Strikeout Leaders	5	5	5	5	5	6	12	30
12	NL Strikeout Leaders	5	5	5	5	6	10	25	50
13	Mickey Stanley	5	5	5	5	6	10	25	50
14	Al McBean	5	5	5	5	5	5	10	25
15	Boog Powell	5	5	5	6	10	15	25	60
16	C.Gutierrez RC/R.Robertson RC	5	5	5	5	5	5	25	40
17	Mike Marshall	5	5	5	5	5	6	12	25
18	Dick Schofield	5	5	5	5	5	5	10	25
19	Ken Suarez	5	5	5	5	5	6	12	30
20	Ernie Banks	8	▲15	▲20	▲40	50	60	▲120	300
21	Jose Santiago	5	5	5	5	5	8	20	150
22	Jesus Alou	5	5	5	5	5	6	12	30
23	Lew Krausse	5	5	5	5	5	8	20	40
24	Walt Alston MG	5	5	5	5	5	8	20	40
25	Roy White	5	5	5	5	6	15	40	150
26	Clay Carroll	5	5	5	5	5	5	10	25
27	Bernie Allen	5	5	5	5	5	5	10	25
28	Mike Ryan	5	5	5	5	5	8	15	25
29	Dave Morehead	5	5	5	5	5	5	10	25
30	Bob Allison	5	5	5	5	5	8	15	30
31	G.Gentry RC/A.Otis RC	5	5	5	5	5	8	20	40
32	Sammy Ellis	5	5	5	5	5	8	15	60
33	Wayne Causey	5	5	5	5	5	8	15	25
34	Gary Peters	5	5	5	5	5	8	15	80
35	Joe Morgan	5	5	5	12	25	30	40	250
36	Luke Walker	5	5	5	5	5	5	15	25
37	Curt Motton	5	5	5	5	5	8	15	50
38	Zoilo Versalles	5	5	5	5	5	8	15	30
39	Dick Hughes	5	5	5	5	5	5	10	25
40	Mayo Smith MG	5	5	5	6	10	15	25	100
41	Bob Barton	5	5	5	5	5	5	12	40
42	Tommy Harper	5	5	5	5	5	5	10	30
43	Joe Niekro	5	5	5	5	5	8	20	
44	Danny Cater	5	5	5	5	5	5	15	30
45	Maury Wills	5	5	5	5	5	6	15	30
46	Fritz Peterson	5	5	5	5	5	8	15	40
47A	Paul Popovich No C/Thick Airbrush	5	5	5	5	5	5	10	25
47B	Paul Popovich No C/Light Airbrush	5	5	5	5	5	5	10	25
47C	Paul Popovich C on Helmet	5	5	5	6	10	15	25	
48	Brant Alyea	5	5	5	5	5	8	20	120
49A	S.Jones/E.Rodriguez ERR	5	5	5	6	10	30	40	
49B	S.Jones RC/E.Rodriguez RC	5	5	5	5	5	5	10	25
50	Roberto Clemente	▲30	▲40	▲50	60	100	▲150	300	1,500
51	Woody Fryman	5	5	5	5	5	5	10	25
52	Mike Andrews	5	5	5	5	5	6	15	60
53	Sonny Jackson	5	5	5	5	5	5	10	25
54	Cisco Carlos	5	5	5	5	5	8	60	175
55	Jerry Grote	5	5	5	5	5	8	15	30
56	Rich Reese	5	5	5	5	5	8	40	60
57	Checklist 1/McLain	5	5	5	5	5	8	15	30
58	Fred Gladding	5	5	5	5	5	5	10	25
59	Jay Johnstone	5	5	5	5	5	6	15	80
60	Nelson Briles	5	5	5	5	6	15	25	200
61	Jimmie Hall	5	5	5	5	5	5	10	30
62	Chico Salmon	5	5	5	5	5	5	10	25
63	Jim Hickman	5	5	5	5	6	25	40	150
64	Bill Monbouquette	5	5	5	5	5	5	10	25
65	Willie Davis	5	5	5	5	5	8	15	120
66	M.Adamson RC/M.Rettenmund RC	5	5	5	5	5	5	10	50
67	Bill Stoneman	5	5	5	5	5	5	12	60
68	Dave Duncan	5	5	5	5	5	8	20	200
69	Steve Hamilton	5	5	5	5	5	8	30	300
70	Tommy Helms	5	5	5	5	6	10	50	120
71	Steve Whitaker	5	5	5	5	5	8	40	100
72	Ron Taylor	5	5	5	5	6	10	40	200
73	Johnny Briggs	5	5	5	5	5	5	10	25
74	Preston Gomez MG	5	5	5	5	5	5	10	25
75	Luis Aparicio	5	5	5	5	5	▲12	▲30	▲50
76	Norm Miller	5	5	5	5	5	5	10	80
77A	Ron Perranoski No LA on Cap	5	5	5	5	5	8	20	50
77B	Ron Perranoski LA on Cap	5	5	5	6	10	15	25	150
78	Tom Satriano	5	5	5	5	5	5	20	80
79	Milt Pappas	5	5	5	5	5	5	12	25
80	Norm Cash	5	5	5	8	12	20	25	120
81	Mel Queen	5	5	5	5	5	5	12	25
82	R.Hebner RC/A.Oliver RC	5	5	5	5	8	▲40	50	250
83	Mike Ferraro	5	5	5	5	5	6	15	100
84	Bob Humphreys	5	5	5	5	5	5	10	25
85	Lou Brock	6	10	12	25	▼40	100	▲800	
86	Pete Richert	5	5	5	5	5	5	5	50
87	Horace Clarke	5	5	5	5	5	10	30	200
88	Rich Nye	5	5	5	5	5	5	10	25
89	Russ Gibson	5	5	5	5	5	5	10	30
90	Jerry Koosman	5	5	5	5	8	15	40	200
91	Alvin Dark MG	5	5	5	5	5	5	10	25
92	Jack Billingham	5	5	5	5	5	5	12	30
93	Joe Foy	5	5	5	5	5	6	40	
94	Hank Aguirre	5	5	5	5	5	5	15	40
95	Johnny Bench	15	50	60	▲120	▲150	250	500	▲2,000
96	Denny Lemaster	5	5	5	5	5	5	10	30
97	Buddy Bradford	5	5	5	5	5	5	12	40
98	Dave Giusti	5	5	5	5	5	5	12	60
99A	D.Morris RC/G.Nettles RC No Loop	5	5	5	5	8	12	20	200
99B	D.Morris/G.Nettles Black Loop	5	5	5	5	8	12	20	60
100	Hank Aaron	20	25	▲50	▲60	80	▲200	▲500	3,000
101	Daryl Patterson	5	5	5	5	5	5	12	50
102	Jim Davenport	5	5	5	5	5	6	15	150
103	Roger Repoz	5	5	5	5	5	5	10	30
104	Steve Blass	5	5	5	5	5	6	15	50
105	Rick Monday	5	5	5	5	5	5	8	50
106	Jim Hannan	5	5	5	5	5	5	25	50
107A	Checklist 2 Gibson ERR 161 is Jim	5	5	5	5	5	6	20	40
107B	Checklist 2 Gibson COR 161 is John	5	5	5	5	5	6	20	50
108	Tony Taylor	5	5	5	5	5	8	30	135
109	Jim Lonborg	5	5	5	5	6	10	25	60
110	Mike Shannon	5	5	5	5	6	15	30	150
111	John Morris RC	5	5	5	5	5	5	15	80
112	J.C. Martin	5	5	5	5	6	10	25	50
113	Dave May	5	5	5	5	5	5	12	50
114	A.Closter/J.Cumberland RC	5	5	5	5	5	6	25	100
115	Bill Hands	5	5	5	5	5	5	25	120
116	Chuck Harrison	5	5	5	5	8	12	40	60
117	Jim Fairey	5	5	5	5	5	5	15	30
118	Stan Williams	5	5	5	5	5	5	10	25
119	Doug Rader	5	5	5	5	5	5	10	40
120	Pete Rose	5	25	▲40	▲50	60	100	200	1,000
121	Joe Grzenda RC	5	5	5	5	5	8	25	
122	Ron Fairly	5	5	5	5	5	6	12	40
123	Wilbur Wood	5	5	5	5	5	5	10	25
124	Hank Bauer MG	5	5	5	5	5	5	10	40
125	Ray Sadecki	5	5	5	5	5	5	10	30
126	Dick Tracewski	5	5	5	5	5	6	15	50
127	Kevin Collins	5	5	5	5	6	15	50	200
128	Tommie Aaron	5	5	5	5	5	5	10	30
129	Bill McCool	5	5	5	5	5	5	10	40
130	Carl Yastrzemski	5	10	20	25	▲50	▲80	▼250	2,000

#	Player	VG 3	VgEx 4	EX 5	ExMt 6	NM 7	NmMt 8	MT 9	Gem 9.5/10
131	Chris Cannizzaro	5	5	5	5	5	6	20	80
132	Dave Baldwin	5	5	5	5	5	5	15	40
133	Johnny Callison	5	5	5	5	6	15	60	150
134	Jim Weaver	5	5	5	5	5	5	10	40
135	Tommy Davis	5	5	5	5	5	8	20	60
136	S.Huntz RC/M.Torrez	5	5	5	5	5	6	15	50
137	Wally Bunker	5	5	5	5	5	6	15	30
138	John Bateman	5	5	5	5	5	6	15	80
139	Andy Kosco	5	5	5	5	5	6	20	
140	Jim Lefebvre	5	5	5	5	5	6	12	50
141	Bill Dillman	5	5	5	5	8	12	30	135
142	Woody Woodward	5	5	5	5	5	5	10	25
143	Joe Nossek	5	5	5	5	5	6	20	
144	Bob Hendley	5	5	5	5	6	10	60	100
145	Max Alvis	5	5	5	5	5	8	25	60
146	Jim Perry	5	5	5	5	5	8	25	60
147	Leo Durocher MG	5	5	5	5	5	6	20	60
148	Lee Stange	5	5	5	5	5	5	15	40
149	Ollie Brown	5	5	5	5	5	5	10	25
150	Denny McLain	5	5	5	5	8	25	50	300
151A	Clay Dalrymple Orioles	5	5	5	5	5	8	20	50
151B	Clay Dalrymple Phillies	5	5	5	6	10	15	60	
152	Tommie Sisk	5	5	5	5	5	8	30	80
153	Ed Brinkman	5	5	5	5	5	6	25	60
154	Jim Britton	5	5	5	5	5	5	10	40
155	Pete Ward	5	5	5	5	5	5	30	60
156	H.Gilson/L.McFadden RC	5	5	5	5	5	6	15	25
157	Bob Rodgers	5	5	5	5	5	6	25	80
158	Joe Gibbon	5	5	5	5	5	5	10	50
159	Jerry Adair	5	5	5	5	5	5	15	40
160	Vada Pinson	5	5	5	5	5	6	15	60
161	John Purdin	5	5	5	5	5	6	20	60
162	Bob Gibson WS1	5	5	5	5	10	20	80	300
163	Willie Horton WS2	5	5	5	5	5	6	30	50
164	T.McCarver w/Maris WS3	5	5	5	5	5	8	20	50
165	Lou Brock WS4	5	5	5	5	6	10	40	100
166	Al Kaline WS5	5	5	5	10	15	30	▲80	400
167	Jim Northrup WS6	5	5	5	5	5	5	15	60
168	M.Lolich/B.Gibson WS7	5	5	5	6	10	15	30	100
169	Tigers Celebrate WS	5	5	5	5	6	15	40	150
170	Frank Howard	5	5	5	5	5	6	15	60
171	Glenn Beckert	5	5	5	5	8	12	20	200
172	Jerry Stephenson	5	5	5	5	5	5	15	50
173	B.Christian RC/G.Nyman RC	5	5	5	5	5	5	15	60
174	Grant Jackson	5	5	5	5	5	5	15	40
175	Jim Bunning	5	5	5	5	6	10	25	100
176	Joe Azcue	5	5	5	5	5	5	10	80
177	Ron Reed	5	5	5	5	5	5	10	40
178	Ray Oyler	5	5	5	5	6	15	30	
179	Don Pavletich	5	5	5	5	5	5	10	25
180	Willie Horton	5	5	5	5	8	12	40	300
181	Mel Nelson	5	5	5	5	5	8	20	60
182	Bill Rigney MG	5	5	5	5	5	8	40	150
183	Don Shaw	5	5	5	5	5	5	15	50
184	Roberto Pena	5	5	5	5	5	5	12	50
185	Tom Phoebus	5	5	5	5	5	8	25	60
186	Johnny Edwards	5	5	5	5	5	6	15	80
187	Leon Wagner	5	5	5	5	5	6	15	150
188	Rick Wise	5	5	5	5	5	5	10	60
189	J.Lahoud RC/J.Thibodeau RC	5	5	5	5	5	6	15	80
190	Willie Mays	12	30	50	80	100	▲250	▲400	2,000
191	Lindy McDaniel	5	5	5	5	8	25	250	
192	Jose Pagan	5	5	5	5	8	25	50	
193	Don Cardwell	5	5	5	5	5	8	15	80
194	Ted Uhlaender	5	5	5	5	5	5	15	50
195	John Odom	5	5	5	5	5	5	12	25
196	Lum Harris MG	5	5	5	5	5	6	12	40
197	Dick Selma	5	5	5	5	5	5	15	40
198	Willie Smith	5	5	5	5	5	8	20	100
199	Jim French	5	5	5	5	5	5	15	40
200	Bob Gibson	5	5	20	30	▲60	▼80	▲250	800
201	Russ Snyder	5	5	5	5	5	8	20	80
202	Don Wilson	5	5	5	5	5	6	20	50
203	Dave Johnson	5	5	5	5	5	6	12	40
204	Jack Hiatt	5	5	5	5	5	6	15	80
205	Rick Reichardt	5	5	5	5	5	6	20	60
206	L.Hisle/B.Lersch RC	5	5	5	5	5	6	12	25

#	Player	VG 3	VgEx 4	EX 5	ExMt 6	NM 7	NmMt 8	MT 9	Gem 9.5
207	Roy Face	5	5	5	5	6	15	30	15
208A	Donn Clendenon Houston	5	5	5	5	5	8	40	1
208B	Donn Clendenon Expos	5	5	6	10	15	40	100	4
209	Larry Haney	5	5	5	5	5	6	15	
210	Felix Millan	5	5	5	5	5	8	25	1
211	Galen Cisco	5	5	5	5	5	6	20	20
212	Tom Tresh	5	5	5	6	10	15	40	2
213	Gerry Arrigo	5	5	5	5	5	5	15	
214	Checklist 3	5	5	5	5	5	8	20	6
215	Rico Petrocelli	5	5	5	5	8	12	30	2
216	Don Sutton DP	5	5	5	5	8	15	30	1
217	John Donaldson	5	5	5	5	5	8	20	1
218	John Roseboro	5	5	5	5	5	8	20	4
219	Fred Patek RC	5	5	5	5	5	6	15	6
220	Sam McDowell	5	5	5	5	6	10	80	20
221	Art Shamsky	5	5	5	5	6	15	60	3
222	Duane Josephson	5	5	5	5	5	6	15	6
223	Tom Dukes	5	5	5	5	5	6	15	5
224	B.Harrelson RC/S.Kealey RC	5	5	5	5	5	6	10	3
225	Don Kessinger	5	5	5	5	6	15	40	
226	Bruce Howard	5	5	5	5	5	8	30	8
227	Frank Johnson RC	5	5	5	5	5	5	10	5
228	Dave Leonhard	5	5	5	5	5	6	12	2
229	Don Lock	5	5	5	5	5	8	30	10
230	Rusty Staub	5	5	5	5	5	6	15	17
231	Pat Dobson	5	5	5	5	5	8	30	12
232	Dave Ricketts	5	5	5	5	6	15	30	15
233	Steve Barber	5	5	5	5	5	12	30	8
234	Dave Bristol MG	5	5	5	5	5	6	15	6
235	Jim Hunter	5	5	5	8	15	30	60	
236	Manny Mota	5	5	5	5	5	8	40	
237	Bobby Cox RC	5	5	15	25	60	80	▼100	▲30
238	Ken Johnson	5	5	5	5	5	6	25	1
239	Bob Taylor	5	5	5	5	5	8	60	20
240	Ken Harrelson	5	5	5	5	6	10	50	15
241	Jim Brewer	5	5	5	5	5	5	12	4
242	Frank Kostro	5	5	5	5	5	6	10	6
243	Ron Kline	5	5	5	5	6	15	25	
244	R.Fosse RC/G.Woodson RC	5	5	5	5	5	8	25	10
245	Ed Charles	5	5	5	5	8	25	60	
246	Joe Coleman	5	5	5	5	5	6	20	5
247	Gene Oliver	5	5	5	5	5	6	15	6
248	Bob Priddy	5	5	5	5	8	12	40	
249	Ed Spiezio	5	5	5	5	5	6	15	8
250	Frank Robinson	5	5	8	20	40	80	▲200	1,00
251	Ron Herbel	5	5	5	5	5	5	10	3
252	Chuck Cottier	5	5	5	5	5	8	20	8
253	Jerry Johnson RC	5	5	5	5	5	5	20	4
254	Joe Schultz MG RC	5	5	5	5	5	6	15	40
255	Steve Carlton	5	15	20	25	▲40	50	▲120	40
256	Gates Brown	5	5	5	6	10	15	60	120
257	Jim Ray	5	5	5	5	5	5	10	4
258	Jackie Hernandez	5	5	5	5	5	6	30	
259	Bill Short	5	5	5	5	5	6	20	100
260	Reggie Jackson RC	80	100	120	200	300	600	▼2,000	▲25,00
261	Bob Johnson	5	5	5	5	5	5	10	2
262	Mike Kekich	5	5	5	5	8	40	150	
263	Jerry May	5	5	5	5	5	8	30	10
264	Bill Landis	5	5	5	5	5	5	10	40
265	Chico Cardenas	5	5	5	5	6	25	50	
266	T.Hutton/A.Foster RC	5	5	5	5	5	12	40	
267	Vicente Romo RC	5	5	5	5	6	10	40	15
268	Al Spangler	5	5	5	5	6	15	30	60
269	Al Weis	5	5	5	5	8	30	60	200
270	Mickey Lolich	5	5	5	6	10	25	60	300
271	Larry Stahl	5	5	5	5	5	8	20	80
272	Ed Stroud	5	5	5	5	5	5	10	25
273	Ron Willis	5	5	5	5	6	15	100	250
274	Clyde King MG	5	5	5	5	5	5	25	60
275	Vic Davalillo	5	5	5	5	5	8	30	60
276	Gary Wagner	5	5	5	5	5	5	15	40
277	Rod Hendricks RC	5	5	5	5	6	10	30	100
278	Gary Geiger	5	5	5	5	5	5	20	120
279	Roger Nelson	5	5	5	5	5	5	12	50
280	Alex Johnson	5	5	5	5	5	6	15	80
281	Ted Kubiak	5	5	5	5	5	6	15	80
282	Pat Jarvis	5	5	5	5	5	5	25	120

	VG 3	VgEx 4	EX 5	ExMt 6	NM 7	NmMt 8	MT 9	Gem 9.5/10
Sandy Alomar	5	5	5	5	5	8	25	80
J.Robertson RC/M.Wegener RC	5	5	5	5	5	5	12	50
Don Mincher	5	5	5	5	5	6	20	
Dock Ellis RC	5	5	5	5	8	12	100	200
Jose Tartabull	5	5	5	5	5	8	25	
Ken Holtzman	5	5	5	5	8	20	80	
Bart Shirley	5	5	5	5	5	5	20	100
Jim Kaat	5	5	5	5	6	10	60	200
Vern Fuller	5	5	5	5	5	8	30	120
Al Downing	5	5	5	5	6	15	40	120
Dick Dietz	5	5	5	5	5	6	15	50
Jim Lemon MG	5	5	5	5	5	12	50	
Tony Perez	5	5	5	6	▲30	▲40	▲60	▲200
Andy Messersmith RC	5	5	5	5	5	6	25	120
Deron Johnson	5	5	5	5	5	8	30	100
Dave Nicholson	5	5	5	5	5	6	15	60
Mark Belanger	5	5	5	5*	6	10	30	
Felipe Alou	5	5	5	5	8	15	60	
Darrell Brandon	5	5	5	5	5	5	10	30
Jim Pagliaroni	5	5	5	5	5	8	30	120
Cal Koonce	5	5	5	5	5	6	15	100
B.Davis/C.Gaston RC	5	5	5	5	5	6	12	30
Dick McAuliffe	5	5	5	5	6	10	30	
Jim Grant	5	5	5	5	5	5	15	80
Gary Kolb	5	5	5	5	5	5	20	80
Wade Blasingame	5	5	5	5	5	6	20	
Walt Williams	5	5	5	5	5	5	10	30
Tom Haller	5	5	5	5	5	5	10	50
Sparky Lyle RC	5	5	5	5	5	8	50	150
Lee Elia	5	5	5	5	6	15	25	
Bill Robinson	5	5	5	5	8	25	80	
Checklist 4/Drysdale	5	5	5	5	8	12	30	150
Eddie Fisher	5	5	5	5	5	8	30	100
Hal Lanier	5	5	5	5	5	6	15	60
Bruce Look RC	5	5	5	5	5	5	12	50
Jack Fisher	5	5	5	5	5	5	10	30
Ken McMullen	5	5	5	5	5	5	10	50
Dal Maxvill	5	5	5	5	5	6	15	80
Jim McAndrew RC	5	5	5	5	5	8	25	80
Jose Vidal	5	5	5	5	5	5	10	25
Larry Miller	5	5	5	5	5	5	10	40
L.Cain RC/D.Campbell RC	5	5	5	5	5	6	12	40
Jose Cardenal	5	5	5	5	5	6	12	40
Gary Sutherland	5	5	5	5	5	6	40	100
Willie Crawford	5	5	5	5	5	5	10	25
Joel Horlen	5	5	5	5	5	8	30	120
Rick Joseph	5	5	5	5	5	5	10	25
Tony Conigliaro	5	5	5	5	8	12	30	120
G.Garrido/T.House RC	5	5	5	5	5	5	10	40
Fred Talbot	5	5	5	5	5	5	15	50
Ivan Murrell	5	5	5	5	5	5	10	40
Phil Roof	5	5	5	5	5	5	15	50
Bill Mazeroski	5	5	5	6	10	20	40	150
Jim Roland	5	5	5	5	5	6	15	80
Marty Martinez RC	5	5	5	5	5	5	10	25
Del Unser RC	5	5	5	5	5	5	15	50
S.Mingori RC/J.Pena RC	5	5	5	5	5	5	10	25
Dave McNally	5	5	5	5	5	8	20	100
Dave Adlesh	5	5	5	5	5	6	15	40
Bubba Morton	5	5	5	5	5	8	25	120
Dan Frisella	5	5	5	5	5	8	20	60
Tom Matchick	5	5	5	5	5	5	10	40
Frank Linzy	5	5	5	5	5	5	10	60
Wayne Comer RC	5	5	5	5	5	6	20	50
Randy Hundley	5	5	5	5	8	25	50	
Steve Hargan	5	5	5	5	5	5	10	25
Dick Williams MG	5	5	5	5	5	5	15	60
Richie Allen	5	5	5	5	8	25	200	
Carroll Sembera	5	5	5	5	5	5	10	30
Paul Schaal	5	5	5	5	5	5	10	25
Jeff Torborg	5	5	5	5	5	5	12	60
Nate Oliver	5	5	5	5	5	5	10	30
Phil Niekro	5	5	5	5	▲20	▲25	30	100
Frank Quilici	5	5	5	5	5	6	15	60
Carl Taylor	5	5	5	5	5	6	15	60
G.Lauzerique RC/R.Rodriguez	5	5	5	5	5	5	10	25
Dick Kelley	5	5	5	5	5	5	15	60

		VG 3	VgEx 4	EX 5	ExMt 6	NM 7	NmMt 8	MT 9	Gem 9.5/10
360	Jim Wynn	5	5	5	5	5	6	12	30
361	Gary Holman RC	5	5	5	5	5	5	10	25
362	Jim Maloney	5	5	5	5	5	5	15	40
363	Russ Nixon	5	5	5	5	5	5	10	25
364	Tommie Agee	5	5	5	5	6	10	20	150
365	Jim Fregosi	5	5	5	5	5	6	15	40
366	Bo Belinsky	5	5	5	5	5	5	15	25
367	Lou Johnson	5	5	5	5	5	6	20	40
368	Vic Roznovsky	5	5	5	5	5	5	10	30
369	Bob Skinner MG	5	5	5	5	5	5	12	40
370	Juan Marichal	5	5	5	6	12	▲40	50	▲400
371	Sal Bando	5	5	5	5	5	8	20	80
372	Adolfo Phillips	5	5	5	5	5	8	25	
373	Fred Lasher	5	5	5	5	5	5	12	40
374	Bob Tillman	5	5	5	5	5	5	10	40
375	Harmon Killebrew	5	6	12	15	30	40	▲100	500
376	M.Fiore RC/J.Rooker RC	5	5	5	5	5	5	15	40
377	Gary Bell	5	5	5	5	5	5	15	50
378	Jose Herrera RC	5	5	5	5	5	5	10	30
379	Ken Boyer	5	5	5	5	5	8	15	40
380	Stan Bahnsen	5	5	5	5	8	20	30	120
381	Ed Kranepool	5	5	5	8	12	30	100	300
382	Pat Corrales	5	5	5	5	5	5	15	40
383	Casey Cox	5	5	5	5	5	5	15	40
384	Larry Shepard MG	5	5	5	5	5	5	20	30
385	Orlando Cepeda	5	5	5	5	8	15	30	100
386	Jim McGlothlin	5	5	5	5	5	5	12	80
387	Bobby Klaus	5	5	5	5	5	5	10	60
388	Tom McCraw	5	5	5	5	5	5	25	60
389	Dan Coombs	5	5	5	5	5	5	25	60
390	Bill Freehan	5	5	5	6	10	25	50	150
391	Ray Culp	5	5	5	5	5	8	20	80
392	Bob Burda RC	5	5	5	5	5	6	15	60
393	Gene Brabender	5	5	5	5	5	6	15	40
394	L.Piniella/M.Staehle	5	5	5	5	8	12	40	
395	Chris Short	5	5	5	5	5	6	15	50
396	Jim Campanis	5	5	5	5	5	5	10	40
397	Chuck Dobson	5	5	5	5	5	6	15	60
398	Tito Francona	5	5	5	5	6	25	100	
399	Bob Bailey	5	5	5	5	5	5	15	40
400	Don Drysdale	5	5	15	20	25	▲40	▲60	300
401	Jake Gibbs	5	5	5	5	5	6	15	40
402	Ken Boswell RC	5	5	5	8	12	20	50	120
403	Bob Miller	5	5	5	5	5	5	12	40
404	V.LaRose RC/G.Ross RC	5	5	5	5	5	5	20	80
405	Lee May	5	5	5	5	5	6	30	100
406	Phil Ortega	5	5	5	5	5	5	10	40
407	Tom Egan	5	5	5	5	5	5	10	60
408	Nate Colbert	5	5	5	5	5	5	10	40
409	Bob Moose	5	5	5	5	5	6	15	40
410	Al Kaline	5	12	15	20	25	50	100	
411	Larry Dierker	5	5	5	5	5	5	10	50
412	Checklist 5/Mantle DP	6	8	20	25	30	60	80	200
413	Roland Sheldon	5	5	5	5	5	6	15	50
414	Duke Sims	5	5	5	5	5	5	10	40
415	Ray Washburn	5	5	5	5	5	6	20	125
416	Willie McCovey AS	5	5	5	5	8	15	60	300
417	Ken Harrelson AS	5	5	5	5	5	5	20	
418	Tommy Helms AS	5	5	5	5	5	6	25	100
419	Rod Carew AS	5	5	5	5	6	15	20	500
420	Ron Santo AS	5	5	5	5	5	8	20	60
421	Brooks Robinson AS	5	5	5	6	10	15	40	150
422	Don Kessinger AS	5	5	5	5	5	6	20	
423	Bert Campaneris AS	5	5	5	5	5	6	25	80
424	Pete Rose AS	8	10	12	15	25	▲50	▲100	250
425	Carl Yastrzemski AS	5	5	5	12	▲25	▲30	50	350
426	Curt Flood AS	5	5	5	5	8	25	100	300
427	Tony Oliva AS	5	5	5	5	5	8	50	175
428	Lou Brock AS	5	5	5	6	10	25	40	
429	Willie Horton AS	5	5	5	5	6	15	25	150
430	Johnny Bench AS	5	5	6	▲25	▲50	60	100	400
431	Bill Freehan AS	5	5	5	5	8	20	60	200
432	Bob Gibson AS	5	5	5	6	▲15	▲20	▲60	350
433	Denny McLain AS	5	5	5	5	6	15	50	150
434	Jerry Koosman AS	5	5	5	5	6	15	40	150
435	Sam McDowell AS	5	5	5	5	5	6	30	80
436	Gene Alley	5	5	5	5	5	6	15	100

#	Player	VG 3	VgEx 4	EX 5	ExMt 6	NM 7	NmMt 8	MT 9	Gem 9.5/10
437	Luis Alcaraz RC	5	5	5	5	5	6	15	80
438	Gary Waslewski RC	5	5	5	5	5	6	15	40
439	E.Herrmann RC/D.Lazar RC	5	5	5	5	5	5	12	50
440A	Willie McCovey	5	5	6	10	15	25	120	
440B	Willie McCovey WL	12	20	30	40	60	150	500	
441A	Dennis Higgins	5	5	5	5	5	5	15	30
441B	Dennis Higgins WL	5	8	12	20	30	80	200	
442	Ty Cline	5	5	5	5	5	5	15	40
443	Don Wert	5	5	5	5	12	20	30	
444A	Joe Moeller	5	5	5	5	5	5	15	30
444B	Joe Moeller WL	5	8	12	20	30	60		
445	Bobby Knoop	5	5	5	5	5	5	15	50
446	Claude Raymond	5	5	5	5	5	6	15	80
447A	Ralph Houk MG	5	5	5	5	5	8	25	100
447B	Ralph Houk MG WL	6	10	15	25	40	80	250	
448	Bob Tolan	5	5	5	5	5	5	15	
449	Paul Lindblad	5	5	5	5	5	8	20	80
450	Billy Williams	5	6	8	12	20	40	100	
451A	Rich Rollins	5	5	5	5	6	15	100	
451B	Rich Rollins WL	5	8	12	20	30	60		
452A	Al Ferrara	5	5	5	5	5	5	15	80
452B	Al Ferrara WL	5	8	12	20	30	80	200	
453	Mike Cuellar	5	5	5	5	6	10	25	150
454A	L.Colton/D.Money RC	5	5	5	5	5	5	15	30
454B	L.Colton/D.Money WL	5	8	12	20	30	150	350	
455	Sonny Siebert	5	5	5	5	5	6	15	60
456	Bud Harrelson	5	5	5	5	8	20	80	
457	Dalton Jones	5	5	5	5	5	6	15	60
458	Curt Blefary	5	5	5	5	5	6	20	
459	Dave Boswell	5	5	5	5	5	8	30	80
460	Joe Torre	5	5	5	5	8	12	30	
461A	Mike Epstein	5	5	5	5	5	6	20	
461B	Mike Epstein WL	5	8	12	20	30	100	200	
462	Red Schoendienst MG	5	5	5	5	6	15	50	
463	Dennis Ribant	5	5	5	5	5	5	10	50
464A	Dave Marshall RC	5	5	5	5	5	8	25	
464B	Dave Marshall WL	5	8	12	20	30	120		
465	Tommy John	5	5	5	5	8	12	30	150
466	John Boccabella	5	5	5	6	10	15	60	150
467	Tommie Reynolds	5	5	5	5	5	6	20	150
468A	B.Dal Canton RC/B.Robertson	5	5	5	5	5	5	15	30
468B	B.Dal Canton/B.Robertson WL	5	8	12	20	30	60	200	
469	Chico Ruiz	5	5	5	5	5	8	60	100
470A	Mel Stottlemyre	5	5	5	5	8	12	25	200
470B	Mel Stottlemyre WL	6	10	15	25	40	80	250	
471A	Ted Savage	5	5	5	5	5	5	12	50
471B	Ted Savage WL	5	8	12	20	30	60	200	
472	Jim Price	5	5	5	5	5	8	25	120
473A	Jose Arcia	5	5	5	5	5	5	15	30
473B	Jose Arcia WL	5	8	12	20	50	60	200	
474	Tom Murphy RC	5	5	5	5	5	6	15	100
475	Tim McCarver	5	5	5	6	15	50	200	
476A	K.Brett RC/G.Moses	5	5	5	5	5	12	40	
476B	K.Brett/G.Moses WL	5	8	12	20	30	60		
477	Jeff James RC	5	5	5	5	5	5	15	100
478	Don Buford	5	5	5	5	5	5	15	100
479	Richie Scheinblum	5	5	5	5	5	6	20	60
480	Tom Seaver	6	20	25	30	▼50	▲120	400	
481	Bill Melton RC	5	5	5	5	5	6	15	50
482A	Jim Gosger	5	5	5	5	5	5	15	50
482B	Jim Gosger WL	5	8	12	20	30	100	200	
483	Ted Abernathy	5	5	5	5	6	20	150	
484	Joe Gordon MG	5	5	5	5	5	6	20	100
485A	Gaylord Perry	5	5	5	5	8	12	40	300
485B	Gaylord Perry WL	6	10	15	25	40	150	300	
486A	Paul Casanova	5	5	5	5	5	5	15	50
486B	Paul Casanova WL	5	8	12	20	30	100		
487	Denis Menke	5	5	5	5	5	6	25	
488	Joe Sparma	5	5	5	5	5	8	25	80
489	Clete Boyer	5	5	5	5	6	15	50	
490	Matty Alou	5	5	5	5	5	6	20	100
491A	J.Crider RC/G.Mitterwald	5	5	5	5	5	5	15	50
491B	J.Crider/G.Mitterwald WL	5	8	12	20	30	60	250	
492	Tony Cloninger	5	5	5	5	5	5	15	60
493A	Wes Parker	5	5	5	5	5	8	15	80
493B	Wes Parker WL	8	12	20	30	50	100	400	
494	Ken Berry	5	5	5	5	5	8	40	100

#	Player	VG 3	VgEx 4	EX 5	ExMt 6	NM 7	NmMt 8	MT 9	Gem 9.5/10
495	Bert Campaneris	5	5	5	5	6	10	40	1
496	Larry Jaster	5	5	5	5	5	6	15	1
497	Julian Javier	5	5	5	5	5	6	15	
498	Juan Pizarro	5	5	5	5	5	6	15	
499	D.Bryant RC/S.Shea RC	5	5	5	5	5	6	12	
500A	Mickey Mantle	80	100	150	200	300	600	2,000	15,0
500B	Mickey Mantle WL	300	350	450	650	850	3,000	9,000	
501A	Tony Gonzalez	5	5	5	5	5	6	25	
501B	Tony Gonzalez WL	6	10	15	25	40	100	200	
502	Minnie Rojas	5	5	5	5	5	12	30	
503	Larry Brown	5	5	5	5	5	6	15	1
504	Checklist 6/B.Robinson	5	5	5	5	5	6	20	
505A	Bobby Bolin	5	5	5	5	5	5	15	
505B	Bobby Bolin WL	5	8	12	20	50	60		
506	Paul Blair	5	5	5	5	5	8	30	
507	Cookie Rojas	5	5	5	5	5	6	15	
508	Moe Drabowsky	5	5	5	5	5	6	15	
509	Manny Sanguillen	5	5	5	5	6	10	25	1
510	Rod Carew	5	5	20	25	40	50	▲120	▼5
511A	Diego Segui	5	5	5	5	5	5	10	1
511B	Diego Segui WL	5	8	12	20	30	60	200	1.
512	Cleon Jones	5	5	6	10	15	30	150	40
513	Camilo Pascual	5	5	5	5	5	5	12	
514	Mike Lum	5	5	5	5	5	5	10	
515	Dick Green	5	5	5	5	5	5	12	
516	Earl Weaver MG RC	5	5	5	6	30	50		25
517	Mike McCormick	5	5	5	5	5	5	10	
518	Fred Whitfield	5	5	5	5	5	5	10	
519	J.Kenney RC/L.Boehmer RC	5	5	5	5	5	5	10	
520	Bob Veale	5	5	5	5	5	5	10	
521	George Thomas	5	5	5	5	5	5	15	
522	Joe Hoerner	5	5	5	5	5	5	20	
523	Bob Chance	5	5	5	5	5	5	10	
524	J.Laboy RC/F.Wicker RC	5	5	5	5	5	5	10	
525	Earl Wilson	5	5	5	5	5	5	12	
526	Hector Torres RC	5	5	5	5	5	5	10	
527	Al Lopez MG	5	5	5	5	5	5	12	
528	Claude Osteen	5	5	5	5	5	5	12	
529	Ed Kirkpatrick	5	5	5	5	5	5	10	
530	Cesar Tovar	5	5	5	5	5	5	10	
531	Dick Farrell	5	5	5	5	5	5	10	
532	Bird Hill Aces	5	5	5	5	5	5	12	
533	Nolan Ryan	60	100	120	150	200	▲400	▼600	4,00
534	Jerry McNertney	5	5	5	5	5	5	10	
535	Phil Regan	5	5	5	5	5	6	12	
536	D.Breeden RC/D.Roberts RC	5	5	5	5	5	5	10	
537	Mike Paul RC	5	5	5	5	5	5	10	
538	Charlie Smith	5	5	5	5	5	5	10	
539	Ted Shows How	5	5	5	6	20	25	30	10
540	Curt Flood	5	5	5	5	5	8	20	8
541	Joe Verbanic	5	5	5	5	5	5	10	
542	Bob Aspromonte	5	5	5	5	5	5	10	
543	Fred Newman	5	5	5	5	5	5	10	3
544	M.Kilkenny RC/R.Woods RC	5	5	5	5	5	5	10	
545	Willie Stargell	5	5	5	▲20	▲25	▲40	▲60	12
546	Jim Nash	5	5	5	5	5	5	10	3
547	Billy Martin MG	5	5	5	5	5	5	25	8
548	Bob Locker	5	5	5	5	5	5	10	2
549	Ron Brand	5	5	5	5	5	5	10	2
550	Brooks Robinson	5	5	6	20	30	40	60	25
551	Wayne Granger RC	5	5	5	5	5	5	10	2
552	T.Sizemore RC/B.Sudakis RC	5	5	5	5	5	5	12	5
553	Ron Davis	5	5	5	5	5	5	10	
554	Frank Bertaina	5	5	5	5	5	5	10	3
555	Jim Ray Hart	5	5	5	5	5	5	10	2
556	A's Stars	5	5	5	5	5	5	15	2
557	Frank Fernandez	5	5	5	5	5	5	10	3
558	Tom Burgmeier RC	5	5	5	5	5	5	15	3
559	J.Hague RC/J.Hicks	5	5	5	5	5	5	10	2
560	Luis Tiant	5	5	5	5	5	8	20	4
561	Ron Clark	5	5	5	5	5	5	10	
562	Bob Watson RC	5	5	5	5	5	5	▲20	▲3
563	Marty Pattin RC	5	5	5	5	5	5	10	2
564	Gil Hodges MG	5	5	5	5	6	25	50	10
565	Hoyt Wilhelm	5	5	5	5	5	12	25	▲6
566	Ron Hansen	5	5	5	5	5	5	10	2
567	E.Jimenez/J.Shellenback	5	5	5	5	5	5	10	

	VG 3	VgEx 4	EX 5	ExMt 6	NM 7	NmMt 8	MT 9	Gem 9.5/10
Cecil Upshaw	5	5	5	5	5	5	10	40
Billy Harris	5	5	5	5	5	5	10	40
Ron Santo	5	5	6	15	20	40	50	150
Cap Peterson	5	5	5	5	5	5	10	25
Giants Heroes	5	5	5	8	15	25	50	120
Jim Palmer	5	5	5	▲25	▲30	▲40	60	200
George Scott	5	5	5	5	5	6	12	30
Bill Singer	5	5	5	5	5	5	10	25
R.Stone/B.Wilson	5	5	5	5	5	5	10	25
Mike Hegan	5	5	5	5	5	5	10	25
Don Bosch	5	5	5	5	5	5	10	25
Dave Nelson RC	5	5	5	5	5	5	10	25
Jim Northrup	5	5	5	5	5	6	12	30
Gary Nolan	5	5	5	5	5	6	12	30
Checklist 7/Oliva White Circle	5	5	5	5	5	6	15	40
Checklist 7/Oliva Red Circle	5	5	5	5	5	6	15	40
Clyde Wright RC	5	5	5	5	5	5	15	30
Don Mason	5	5	5	5	5	5	10	25
Ron Swoboda	5	5	5	5	5	5	15	40
Tim Cullen	5	5	5	5	5	5	10	25
Joe Rudi RC	5	5	5	5	5	6	30	60
Bill White	5	5	5	5	5	5	10	25
Joe Pepitone	5	5	5	5	5	8	20	50
Rico Carty	5	5	5	5	5	8	20	60
Mike Hedlund	5	5	5	5	5	6	12	30
R.Robles RC/A.Santorini RC	5	5	5	5	5	6	12	40
Don Nottebart	5	5	5	5	5	6	12	30
Dooley Womack	5	5	5	5	5	6	12	25
Lee Maye	5	5	5	5	5	6	12	30
Chuck Hartenstein	5	5	5	5	5	6	12	30
Rollie Fingers RC	10	25	30	▲50	▲60	100	150	600
Ruben Amaro	5	5	5	5	5	6	15	100
John Boozer	5	5	5	5	5	6	12	25
Tony Oliva	5	5	5	8	15	▲50	▲60	200
Tug McGraw SP	5	5	5	5	6	15	50	▲100
Distaso/Young/Qualls RC	5	5	5	5	6	10	40	100
Joe Keough RC	5	5	5	5	5	6	12	40
Bobby Etheridge	5	5	5	5	5	6	12	40
Dick Ellsworth	5	5	5	5	5	6	20	60
Gene Mauch MG	5	5	5	5	5	6	12	20
Dick Bosman	5	5	5	5	5	6	12	30
Dick Simpson	5	5	5	5	5	6	12	30
Phil Gagliano	5	5	5	5	6	15	50	120
Jim Hardin	5	5	5	5	5	5	10	25
Didier/Hriniak/Niebauer RC	5	5	5	5	5	6	12	30
Jack Aker	5	5	5	5	5	6	12	30
Jim Beauchamp	5	5	5	5	5	6	12	30
T.Griffin RC/S.Guinn RC	5	5	5	5	5	6	12	40
Len Gabrielson	5	5	5	5	5	6	12	30
Don McMahon	5	5	5	5	5	8	20	30
Jesse Gonder	5	5	5	5	5	6	15	60
Ramon Webster	5	5	5	5	5	6	15	80
Butler/Kelly/Rios RC	5	5	5	5	5	5	12	30
Dean Chance	5	5	5	5	6	15	30	80
Bill Voss	5	5	5	5	5	6	12	40
Dan Osinski	5	5	5	5	5	6	12	40
Hank Allen	5	5	5	5	5	6	12	40
Chaney/Dyer/Harmon RC	5	5	5	5	5	8	15	30
Mack Jones	5	5	5	5	5	6	12	40
Gene Michael	5	5	5	5	5	8	25	50
George Stone RC	5	5	5	5	5	8	25	60
Conigliaro/O'Brien/Wenz RC	5	5	5	5	5	6	▲20	40
Jack Hamilton	5	5	5	5	5	6	12	30
Bobby Bonds RC	5	5	8	▲20	30	50	▼80	200
John Kennedy	5	5	5	5	5	6	12	30
Jon Warden RC	5	5	5	5	5	6	15	50
Harry Walker MG	5	5	5	5	5	6	12	30
Andy Etchebarren	5	5	5	5	5	6	15	30
George Culver	5	5	5	5	5	6	12	30
Woody Held	5	5	5	5	5	6	12	40
DaVanon/Reberger/Kirby RC	5	5	5	5	5	6	12	30
Ed Sprague RC	5	5	5	5	5	6	10	25
Barry Moore	5	5	5	5	5	6	12	25
Ferguson Jenkins	5	5	8	15	30	40	▲80	▲200
Darwin/Miller/Dean RC	5	5	5	5	5	6	12	30
John Hiller	5	5	5	5	5	8	20	50
Billy Cowan	5	5	5	5	5	8	40	50

		VG 3	VgEx 4	EX 5	ExMt 6	NM 7	NmMt 8	MT 9	Gem 9.5/10
644	Chuck Hinton	5	5	5	5	5	6	12	30
645	George Brunet	5	5	5	5	5	6	12	30
646	D.McGinn RC/C.Morton RC	5	5	5	5	5	6	12	30
647	Dave Wickersham	5	5	5	5	5	6	12	40
648	Bobby Wine	5	5	5	5	5	6	12	40
649	Al Jackson	5	5	5	5	6	10	25	80
650	Ted Williams MG	5	5	5	▲20	25	50	60	250
651	Gus Gil	5	5	5	5	5	6	15	100
652	Eddie Watt	5	5	5	5	5	6	12	30
653	Aurelio Rodriguez RC	5	5	5	5	5	6	15	50
654	May/Secrist/Morales RC	5	5	5	5	5	6	15	40
655	Mike Hershberger	5	5	5	5	5	8	40	100
656	Dan Schneider	5	5	5	5	5	6	10	25
657	Bobby Murcer	5	5	5	6	12	30	40	120
658	Hall/Burbach/Miles RC	5	5	5	5	5	6	12	30
659	Johnny Podres	5	5	5	5	6	10	12	30
660	Reggie Smith	5	5	5	5	6	10	25	100
661	Jim Merritt	5	5	5	5	5	6	12	30
662	Drago/Spriggs/Oliver RC	5	5	5	5	5	8	30	
663	Dick Radatz	5	5	5	5	5	8	25	50
664	Ron Hunt	5	5	5	5	5	10	20	120

—Ernie Banks #20 PSA 10 (Gem) sold for $1,321 (Mile High; 5/04)
—Johnny Bench #95 PSA 10 (Gem) sold for $2,911 (Mastro; 10/05)
—Johnny Bench #95 PSA 10 (Gem) sold for $2,749 (Mile High; 10/11)
—Johnny Bench #95 PSA 10 (Gem) sold for $2,132 (Mastro; 5/06)
—Lou Brock #85 PSA 9 (MT) sold for $4,850 (eBay; 5/06)
—Steve Carlton #255 PSA 10 (Gem) sold for $3,823 (eBay; 09/12)
—Paul Casanova #486 (White) PSA 8 (NmMt) sold for $449 (eBay; 8/07)
—Paul Casanova #486 (White) PSA 8 (NmMt) sold for $209 (eBay; 2/08)
—Ed Charles #245 PSA 9 (MT) sold for $654 (Mile High; 2/08)
—Roberto Clemente #50 PSA 10 (Gem) sold for $6,950 (eBay; 5/07)
—Roberto Clemente #50 PSA 10 (Gem) sold for $4,281 (Mile High; 5/04)
—Rollie Fingers #597 PSA 10 (Gem) (Young Collection) sold for $5,329 (SCP; 5/12)
—Rollie Fingers #597 PSA 10 (Gem) sold for $1,026 (Mastro; 12/05)
—Bob Gibson #200 PSA 10 (Gem) sold for $4,162 (Memory Lane; 12/06)
—Bob Gibson #200 PSA 10 (Gem) sold for $3,585 (eBay; 4/08)
—Steve Hamilton #69 PSA 9 (MT) sold for $459 (eBay; 5/08)
—Bud Harrelson #456 PSA 9 (MT) sold for $565 (eBay; 3/07)
—Bud Harrelson #456 PSA 9 (MT) sold for $202 (eBay; 4/07)
—Bud Harrelson #456 PSA 9 (MT) sold for $124 (eBay; 5/07)
—Jim Hunter #235 PSA 9 (MT) sold for $510 (eBay; 3/07)
—Jim Hunter #235 PSA 9 (MT) sold for $277 (eBay; 8/07)
—Jim Hunter #235 PSA 9 (MT) sold for $203 (eBay; 3/07)
—Reggie Jackson #260 PSA 10 (Gem) (Young Collection) sold for $115,242 (SCP; 5/12)
—Reggie Jackson #260 BVG 9 (MT) sold for $2,905 (eBay; 2/08)
—Reggie Jackson #260 PSA 8.5 (NmMt+) sold for $1,075 (eBay; 5/08)
—Al Kaline #410 PSA 10 (Gem) sold for $1,945 (Mastro; 8/06)
—Al Kaline #410 PSA 9 (MT) sold for $1,222 (eBay; 6/07)
—Al Kaline #410 PSA 9 (MT) sold for $1,033 (eBay; 4/08)
—Al Kaline #410 PSA 9 (MT) sold for $734 (eBay; 11/07)
—Al Kaline #410 PSA 9 (MT) sold for $686 (eBay; 8/07)
—Jerry Koosman #90 PSA 10 (Gem) sold for $1,086 (Mile High; 2/08)
—Mickey Mantle #500 SGC 96 (MT) sold for $2,580 (Memory Lane; 4/07)
—Mickey Mantle #500 (White) PSA 9 (MT) sold for $17,292 (Memory Lane; 4/07)
—Dave Marshall WL #464B PSA 8 (NmMt) sold for $3,029 (eBay; 08/12)
—Willie McCovey #440 (White) PSA 9 (MT) sold for $560 (eBay; 2/08)
—Willie McCovey #440 (Yellow) PSA 9 (MT) sold for $1,126 (eBay; 11/06)
—Joe Moeller #444 (White) PSA 9 (MT) sold for $1,956 (Memory Lane; 5/08)
—Joe Moeller #444 (White) PSA 9 (MT) sold for $799 (eBay; 4/07)
—Joe Moeller #444 (White) PSA 8 (NmMt) sold for $454 (eBay; 8/07)
—Graig Nettles #99 (Black Loop) PSA 9 (MT) sold for $1,053 (eBay; 9/07)
—Graig Nettles #99 (Black Loop) PSA 8.5 (NmMt+) sold for $360 (eBay; 4/08)
—Joe Niekro #43 PSA 9 (MT) sold for $1,111 (eBay; 12/06)
—Joe Niekro #43 PSA 9 (MT) sold for $510 (eBay; 2/07)
—Phil Niekro #355 PSA 10 (Gem) sold for $903 (eBay; 4/08)
—Gaylord Perry #485 (White) PSA 9 (MT) sold for $3,466 (Memory Lane; 5/08)
—Fritz Peterson #46 PSA 9 (MT) sold for $427 (eBay; 10/07)
—Fritz Peterson #46 PSA 9 (MT) sold for $342 (eBay; 10/06)
—Red Sox Rookies #476 (White) PSA 8 (NmMt) sold for $860 (eBay; 1/07)
—Bill Robinson #313 PSA 9 (MT) sold for $1,480 (eBay; 12/07)
—Bill Robinson #313 PSA 9 (MT) sold for $785 (Memory Lane; 5/08)
—Brooks Robinson #550 PSA 10 (Gem) sold for $1,530 (Memory Lane; 11/04)
—Frank Robinson #250 PSA 9 (MT) sold for $6,433 (Mile High; 8/07)
—Frank Robinson #250 PSA 9 (MT) sold for $2,036 (eBay; 10/06)
—Frank Robinson #250 PSA 9 (MT) sold for $1,014 (eBay; 5/08)

—Frank Robinson #250 PSA 9 (MT) sold for $908 (eBay; 8/07)
—Minnie Rojas #502 PSA 9 (MT) sold for $561 (eBay; 5/08)
—Pete Rose #120 PSA 10 (Gem) sold for $10,600 (eBay; 2/07)
—Pete Rose AS #424 PSA 9 (MT) sold for $472 (eBay; 2/07)
—Pete Rose AS #424 PSA 9 (MT) sold for $375 (eBay; 1/08)
—Pete Rose AS #424 PSA 9 (MT) sold for $308 (eBay; 8/07)
—Royals Rookies #49 (Rodriquez ERR) PSA 9 (MT) sold for $495 (eBay; 2/08)
—Nolan Ryan #533 PSA 10 (Gem) sold for $20,100 (Mile High; 10/12)
—Tom Satriano #78 PSA 9 (MT) sold for $640 (eBay; 4/08)
—Red Schoendienst #462 PSA 9 (MT) sold for $819 (eBay; 5/08)
—Red Schoendienst #462 PSA 9 (MT) sold for $530 (eBay; 2/08)
—Tom Seaver #480 PSA 9 (MT) sold for $6,933 (Mile High; 05/11)
—Tom Seaver #480 PSA 9 (MT) sold for $3,936 (eBay; 11/12)
—Tom Seaver #480 PSA 9 (MT) sold for $2,900 (eBay; 1/13)
—Tom Seaver #480 PSA 9 (MT) sold for $1,095 (Mile High; 2/08)
—Willie Stargell #545 PSA 10 (Gem) sold for $1,001 (eBay; 1/07)
—Ted Williams #650 PSA 10 (Gem) sold for $2,032 (Memory Lane; 5/08)
—Ted Williams #650 PSA 10 (Gem) sold for $1,056 (Madec; 5/0)

1969 Topps Decals

		VG 3	VgEx 4	EX 5	ExMt 6	NM 7	NmMt 8	MT 9	Gem 9.5/10
1	Hank Aaron	5	5	8	12	20	30	100	
2	Richie Allen	5	5	5	5	6	10	30	
3	Felipe Alou	5	5	5	5	5	10	40	
4	Matty Alou	5	5	5	5	5	10	30	
5	Luis Aparicio	5	5	5	5	6	10	40	60
6	Roberto Clemente	5	6	10	15	25	40	200	
7	Donn Clendenon	5	5	5	5	5	10	30	
8	Tommy Davis	5	5	5	5	5	8	15	40
9	Don Drysdale	5	5	5	6	10	15	25	50
10	Joe Foy	5	5	5	5	5	8	15	30
11	Jim Fregosi	5	5	5	5	5	8	15	60
12	Bob Gibson	5	5	5	5	8	12	50	120
13	Tony Gonzalez	5	5	5	5	5	10	40	
14	Tom Haller	5	5	5	5	5	8	15	
15	Ken Harrelson	5	5	5	5	5	8	20	
16	Tommy Helms	5	5	5	5	5	8	15	40
17	Willie Horton	5	5	5	5	5	8	15	50
18	Frank Howard	5	5	5	5	5	8	15	
19	Reggie Jackson	5	5	8	12	25	60	100	500
20	Ferguson Jenkins	5	5	5	5	6	10	40	80
21	Harmon Killebrew	5	5	5	6	10	15	50	100
22	Jerry Koosman	5	5	5	5	5	8	15	40
23	Mickey Mantle	30	50	80	100	120	200	500	
24	Willie Mays	5	5	▲20	▲25	▲30	40	100	500
25	Tim McCarver	5	5	5	5	5	8	15	
26	Willie McCovey	5	5	5	6	10	15	40	
27	Sam McDowell	5	5	5	5	5	8	15	▲50
28	Denny McLain	5	5	5	5	5	8	15	▲100
29	Dave McNally	5	5	5	5	5	8	15	▲100
30	Don Mincher	5	5	5	5	5	8	15	
31	Rick Monday	5	5	5	5	5	8	15	
32	Tony Oliva	5	5	5	5	5	8	25	40
33	Camilo Pascual	5	5	5	5	5	10	40	
34	Rick Reichardt	5	5	5	5	5	8	15	40
35	Frank Robinson	5	5	5	6	10	15	30	50
36	Pete Rose	5	5	6	25	30	40	80	200
37	Ron Santo	5	5	5	5	8	12	30	▲100
38	Tom Seaver	5	5	5	8	12	50	80	
39	Dick Selma	5	5	5	5	5	8	15	40
40	Chris Short	5	5	5	5	5	8	15	40
41	Rusty Staub	5	5	5	5	5	10	40	
42	Mel Stottlemyre	5	5	5	5	5	10	30	
43	Luis Tiant	5	5	5	5	5	8	15	40
44	Pete Ward	5	5	5	5	5	10	40	
45	Hoyt Wilhelm	5	5	5	5	5	8	15	30
46	Maury Wills	5	5	5	5	5	8	15	30
47	Jim Wynn	5	5	5	5	5	10	40	
48	Carl Yastrzemski	5	5	5	20	25	30	50	250

—Hank Aaron #1 PSA 10 (Gem) sold for $378 (Memory Lane; 4/07)
—Reggie Jackson #19 PSA 10 (Gem) sold for $378 (Memory Lane; 4/07)
—Tom Seaver #38 PSA 10 (Gem) sold for $202 (eBay; 7/07)

1969 Topps Deckle Edge

		GD 2	VG 3	VgEx 4	EX 5	ExMt 6	NM 7	NmMt 8	M
1	Brooks Robinson	5	5	5	6	10	20	80	
2	Boog Powell	5	5	5	5	8	15	50	
3	Ken Harrelson	5	5	5	5	6	12	60	
4	Carl Yastrzemski	5	5	5	6	10	50	80	
5	Jim Fregosi	5	5	5	5	6	15	80	
6	Luis Aparicio	5	5	5	5	8	20	80	
7	Luis Tiant	5	5	5	5	6	12	50	
8	Denny McLain	5	5	5	5	8	20	60	
9	Willie Horton	5	5	5	5	6	12	60	
10	Bill Freehan	5	5	5	5	6	12	80	
11A	Hoyt Wilhelm	5	5	5	5	8	15		
11B	Jim Wynn	5	5	5	6	10	30	80	
12	Rod Carew	5	5	5	6	10	20	80	
13	Mel Stottlemyre	5	5	5	5	6	12	50	
14	Rick Monday	5	5	5	5	6	12	30	
15	Tommy Davis	5	5	5	5	6	12	60	
16	Frank Howard	5	5	5	5	6	12	80	
17	Felipe Alou	5	5	5	5	6	15	150	
18	Don Kessinger	5	5	5	5	6	12	50	
19	Ron Santo	5	5	5	5	8	15	50	
20	Tommy Helms	5	5	5	5	6	12	80	
21	Pete Rose	5	5	8	10	40	50	200	
22A	Rusty Staub	5	5	5	5	6	12		
22B	Joe Foy	5	5	5	8	12	30	150	
23	Tom Haller	5	5	5	5	6	15	60	
24	Maury Wills	5	5	5	5	6	12	50	
25	Jerry Koosman	5	5	5	5	6	12	30	
26	Richie Allen	5	5	5	5	8	15	120	
27	Roberto Clemente	5	8	25	40	50	60	400	
28	Curt Flood	5	5	5	5	6	12	50	
29	Bob Gibson	5	5	5	6	10	50	175	
30	Al Ferrara	5	5	5	5	6	12	40	
31	Willie McCovey	5	5	5	6	10	20	50	
32	Juan Marichal	5	5	5	5	8	15	150	
33	Willie Mays	5	6	15	40	50	100		

—Bob Gibson #29 PSA 9 (MT) sold for $327 (eBay; 5/07)
—Denny McLain #8 PSA 9 (MT) sold for $272 (eBay; 12/06)
—Luis Tiant #7 PSA 9 (MT) sold for $404 (eBay; 5/07)
—Willie Mays #33 PSA 8 (NmMt) sold for $534 (eBay; 5/07)
—Willie Mays #33 PSA 8 (NmMt) sold for $192 (eBay; 12/06)

1969 Topps Super

		VG 3	VgEx 4	EX 5	ExMt 6	NM 7	NmMt 8	MT 9	Gem 9.5/
1	Dave McNally	12	20	30	50	80	200		
2	Frank Robinson	10	15	25	60	80	100	250	5
3	Brooks Robinson	15	25	40	60	100	200	500	
4	Ken Harrelson	5	5	6	10	15	30	80	1
5	Carl Yastrzemski	20	30	50	80	120	300	400	
6	Ray Culp	5	5	6	10	15	30	50	1
7	Jim Fregosi	5	5	6	10	15	30	80	1
8	Rick Reichardt	5	5	6	10	15	30	50	1
9	Vic Davalillo	5	5	6	10	15	30	50	2
10	Luis Aparicio	8	12	20	30	50	80	150	2
11	Pete Ward	5	5	6	10	15	30	80	1
12	Joel Horlen	5	5	6	10	15	30	100	
13	Luis Tiant	5	5	6	10	15	30	80	2
14	Sam McDowell	5	5	8	12	20	40	100	4
15	Jose Cardenal	5	5	6	10	15	30	50	3
16	Willie Horton	5	5	6	10	15	30	80	1
17	Denny McLain	5	8	12	20	30	50	120	1
18	Bill Freehan	5	5	6	10	15	30	50	1
19	Harmon Killebrew	12	20	30	50	80	150	250	6
20	Tony Oliva	5	8	12	20	30	50	120	2
21	Dean Chance	5	5	6	10	15	30	50	4
22	Joe Foy	5	5	6	10	15	30	50	1
23	Roger Nelson	5	5	6	10	15	30	100	1
24	Mickey Mantle	200	250	400	500	900	1,200	▲3,000	
25	Mel Stottlemyre	5	5	6	10	15	30	120	1
26	Roy White	5	5	6	10	15	40	80	3
27	Rick Monday	5	5	6	10	15	30	50	1
28	Reggie Jackson	40	60	100	150	250	600	▲1,500	
29	Bert Campaneris	5	5	6	10	15	30	50	1

BASEBALL

	VG 3	VgEx 4	EX 5	ExMt 6	NM 7	NmMt 8	MT 9	Gem 9.5/10
Frank Howard	5	5	6	10	15	30	80	150
Camilo Pascual	5	5	6	10	15	30	50	120
Tommy Davis	5	5	6	10	15	30	80	250
Don Mincher	5	5	6	10	15	30	100	150
Hank Aaron	25	40	60	100	150	200	▲800	800
Felipe Alou	5	5	6	10	15	30	60	100
Joe Torre	5	6	10	15	25	80	120	200
Ferguson Jenkins	6	10	15	25	40	60	120	300
Ron Santo	6	10	15	25	40	60	200	250
Billy Williams	6	10	15	25	40	60	200	
Tommy Helms	5	5	6	10	15	30	60	
Pete Rose	30	50	80	120	200	300	800	1,200
Joe Morgan	10	15	25	40	60	250	400	300
Jim Wynn	5	5	6	10	15	30	60	120
Curt Blefary	5	5	6	10	15	30	50	100
Willie Davis	5	5	6	10	15	30	60	200
Don Drysdale	10	15	25	40	60	100	150	500
Tom Haller	5	5	6	10	15	30	60	120
Rusty Staub	5	5	6	10	15	30	60	120
Maury Wills	5	5	6	10	15	30	60	
Cleon Jones	5	6	10	15	25	40	150	200
Jerry Koosman	5	5	6	10	15	30	60	▲400
Tom Seaver	25	40	60	100	150	300	600	
Richie Allen	5	5	6	10	15	30	60	400
Chris Short	5	5	6	10	15	30	100	150
Cookie Rojas	5	5	6	10	15	30	60	150
Matty Alou	5	5	6	10	15	30	120	150
Steve Blass	5	5	6	10	15	50	80	150
Roberto Clemente	50	80	120	200	300	800	▲1,500	
Curt Flood	5	5	6	10	15	30	100	200
Bob Gibson	12	20	30	50	80	150	▲400	
Tim McCarver	5	6	10	15	25	40	80	250
Dick Selma	5	5	6	10	15	30	50	150
Ollie Brown	5	5	6	10	15	30	60	120
Juan Marichal	10	15	25	40	60	150	250	
Willie Mays	30	50	80	120	200	600	1,000	
Willie McCovey	12	20	30	50	80	250	500	

ank Aaron #34 PSA 10 (Gem) sold for $2,214 (Memory Lane; 4/07)
oberto Clemente #58 PSA 10 (Gem) sold for $4,162 (Memory Lane; 12/06)
on Drysdale #46 PSA 10 (Gem) sold for $1,028 (Goodwin; 11/07)
on Drysdale #46 PSA 10 (Gem) sold for $290 (SCP Sotheby's; 1/08)
ob Gibson #60 PSA 10 (Gem) sold for $910 (eBay; 3/07)
eggie Jackson #28 PSA 10 (Gem) sold for $3,957 (Memory Lane; 12/06)
eggie Jackson #28 PSA 10 (Gem) sold for $1,564 (Memory Lane; 12/07)
ickey Mantle #24 PSA 10 (Gem) sold for $6,868 (Memory Lane; 5/08)
ickey Mantle #24 PSA 10 (Gem) sold for $4,025 (Huggins and Scott; 10/07)
uan Marichal #64 PSA 10 (Gem) sold for $1,125 (eBay; 7/07)
ave McNally #1 PSA 9 (MT) sold for $666 (eBay; 3/08)

970 Kellogg's

	VG 3	VgEx 4	EX 5	ExMt 6	NM 7	NmMt 8	MT 9	Gem 9.5/10
Ed Kranepool	4	4	4	5	10	15	70	250
Pete Rose	4	4	10	12	15	20	60	250
Cleon Jones	4	4	4	4	5	8	15	100
Willie McCovey	4	4	4	5	6	10	20	100
Mel Stottlemyre	4	4	4	4	5	8	12	30
Frank Howard	4	4	4	4	5	8	12	50
Tom Seaver	4	4	6	8	10	15	30	120
Don Sutton	4	4	4	5	6	10	20	80
Jim Wynn	4	4	4	4	5	8	12	40
Jim Maloney	4	4	4	4	5	8	12	40
Tommie Agee	4	4	4	4	5	8	15	100
Willie Mays	4	4	10	12	15	20	50	150
Juan Marichal	4	4	4	5	6	10	25	60
Dave McNally	4	4	4	4	5	8	15	40
Frank Robinson	4	4	5	6	8	12	25	80
Carlos May	4	4	4	4	5	8	100	
Bill Singer	4	4	4	4	5	8	50	250
Rick Reichardt	4	4	4	4	5	8	150	
Boog Powell	4	4	4	4	5	8	25	
Gaylord Perry	4	4	4	5	6	10	30	120
Brooks Robinson	4	4	6	8	10	15	80	250
Luis Aparicio	4	4	4	5	6	10	20	80
Joel Horlen	4	4	4	4	5	8	12	80
Mike Epstein	4	4	4	4	5	8	15	
Tom Haller	4	4	4	4	5	8	50	

#		VG 3	VgEx 4	EX 5	ExMt 6	NM 7	NmMt 8	MT 9	Gem 9.5/10
26	Willie Crawford	4	4	4	4	5	8	12	
27	Roberto Clemente	4	8	25	30	40	80	120	500
28	Matty Alou	4	4	4	4	5	8	15	120
29	Willie Stargell	4	4	4	6	8	25	60	200
30	Tim Cullen	4	4	4	4	5	8	80	200
31	Randy Hundley	4	4	4	4	5	8	15	50
32	Reggie Jackson	4	4	6	8	10	15	40	150
33	Rich Allen	4	4	4	4	5	8	15	175
34	Tim McCarver	4	4	4	4	5	8	25	50
35	Ray Culp	4	4	4	4	5	8	12	50
36	Jim Fregosi	4	4	4	4	5	8	12	100
37	Billy Williams	4	4	4	5	6	10	25	80
38	Johnny Odom	4	4	4	4	5	8	12	80
39	Bert Campaneris	4	4	4	4	5	8	12	60
40	Ernie Banks	4	4	6	8	10	15	50	120
41	Chris Short	4	4	4	4	5	8	15	60
42	Ron Santo	4	4	4	5	6	10	20	
43	Glenn Beckert	4	4	4	4	5	8	12	40
44	Lou Brock	4	4	4	5	6	10	20	60
45	Larry Hisle	4	4	4	4	5	8	15	50
46	Reggie Smith	4	4	4	4	5	8	15	200
47	Rod Carew	4	4	4	5	6	10	20	80
48	Curt Flood	4	4	4	4	5	8	15	
49	Jim Lonborg	4	4	4	4	5	8	15	200
50	Sam McDowell	4	4	4	4	5	8	15	60
51	Sal Bando	4	4	4	4	5	8	30	60
52	Al Kaline	4	4	5	6	8	12	25	80
53	Gary Nolan	4	4	4	4	5	8	20	120
54	Rico Petrocelli	4	4	4	4	5	8	12	50
55	Ollie Brown	4	4	4	4	5	8	30	
56	Luis Tiant	4	4	4	4	5	8	12	80
57	Bill Freehan	4	4	4	4	5	8	15	150
58	Johnny Bench	4	4	6	8	10	15	50	200
59	Joe Pepitone	4	4	4	4	5	8	20	80
60	Bobby Murcer	4	4	5	6	8	12	40	100
61	Harmon Killebrew	4	4	5	6	8	12	25	120
62	Don Wilson	4	4	4	4	5	8	12	40
63	Tony Oliva	4	4	4	4	5	8	15	60
64	Jim Perry	4	4	4	4	5	8	12	30
65	Mickey Lolich	4	4	4	4	5	8	15	30
66	Jose Laboy	4	4	4	4	5	8	12	40
67	Dean Chance	4	4	4	4	5	8	12	40
68	Ken Harrelson	4	4	4	4	5	8	12	50
69	Willie Horton	4	4	4	4	5	8	25	60
70	Wally Bunker	4	4	4	4	5	8	12	50
71A	Bob Gibson ERR 1959 IP Blank	4	4	4	5	6	10	20	
71B	Bob Gibson COR 1959 IP 76	4	4	5	6	8	12	60	120
72	Joe Morgan	4	4	4	5	6	10	25	150
73	Denny McLain	4	4	4	4	5	8	15	80
74	Tommy Harper	4	4	4	4	5	8	15	80
75	Don Mincher	4	4	4	4	5	8	20	300

—Roberto Clemente #27 PSA 10 (Gem) sold for $1,604 (eBay; 2/08)
—Roberto Clemente #27 PSA 10 (Gem) sold for $1,469 (eBay; 6/08)
—Willie Mays #12 PSA 10 (Gem) sold for $665 (eBay; 2/08)
—Willie Mays #12 PSA 10 (Gem) sold for $280 (eBay; 6/08)

1970 Topps

#		VG 3	VgEx 4	EX 5	ExMt 6	NM 7	NmMt 8	NmMt+ 8.5	MT 9
1	New York Mets TC	5	10	20	25	50	100		
2	Diego Segui	4	8	15	20	40	80		
3	Darrel Chaney	4	4	8	10	20	50		
4	Tom Egan	4	4	4	5	10	20	25	50
5	Wes Parker	4	4	8	10	20	40	80	100
6	Grant Jackson	4	4	4	5	10	20	25	50
7	G.Boyd RC/R.Nagelson RC	4	6	12	15	30	80		
8	Jose Martinez RC	4	4	4	5	10	20	25	50
9	Checklist 1	4	8	15	20	40	80		
10	Carl Yastrzemski	6	15	20	30	▲50	▲100	150	400
11	Nate Colbert	4	4	4	5	10	20	25	50
12	John Hiller	4	4	5	6	12	25	30	80
13	Jack Hiatt	4	6	12	15	30	60		
14	Hank Allen	4	4	4	4	6	12	15	30
15	Larry Dierker	4	4	4	5	10	20	25	80
16	Charlie Metro MG RC	4	4	4	5	10	20	25	100
17	Hoyt Wilhelm	4	4	6	8	15	50		
18	Carlos May	4	4	6	8	15	30		

#	Player	VG 3	VgEx 4	EX 5	ExMt 6	NM 7	NmMt 8	NmMt+ 8.5	MT 9
19	John Boccabella	4	4	4	5	10	20	25	80
20	Dave McNally	4	4	4	5	10	20		
21	V.Blue RC/G.Tenace RC	4	6	12	15	30	100		
22	Ray Washburn	4	4	4	4	6	15	15	30
23	Bill Robinson	4	4	4	4	8	15	20	
24	Dick Selma	4	4	4	4	5	15	15	25
25	Cesar Tovar	4	4	4	5	10	20	30	50
26	Tug McGraw	6	12	20	25	30	40	150	250
27	Chuck Hinton	4	4	4	5	10	12	25	50
28	Billy Wilson	4	4	4	4	6	12	15	40
29	Sandy Alomar	4	4	4	4	6	12	15	30
30	Matty Alou	4	4	4	5	10	20	25	
31	Marty Pattin	4	4	4	5	10	20	30	50
32	Harry Walker MG	4	4	4	4	6	12	15	30
33	Don Wert	4	4	4	4	6	12	15	25
34	Willie Crawford	4	4	4	4	5	10	12	25
35	Joel Horlen	4	4	4	4	5	10	12	25
36	D.Breeden/B.Carbo RC	4	4	4	4	5	10	12	25
37	Dick Drago	4	4	4	4	6	15	20	30
38	Mack Jones	4	4	4	4	5	10	12	25
39	Mike Nagy RC	4	4	4	5	10	20	25	100
40	Richie Allen	4	4	6	8	15	30		
41	George Lauzerique	4	4	4	4	8	15	20	
42	Tito Fuentes	4	4	4	5	10	12	25	
43	Jack Aker	4	4	4	4	8	30	40	50
44	Roberto Pena	4	4	6	8	15	30	40	80
45	Dave Johnson	4	4	5	6	12	25	30	60
46	Ken Rudolph RC	4	4	4	4	6	12	15	60
47	Bob Miller	4	4	4	5	10	12	25	
48	Gil Garrido	4	4	4	4	6	12	15	40
49	Tim Cullen	4	4	4	4	5	10	12	25
50	Tommie Agee	4	8	15	20	40	50		
51	Bob Christian	4	4	4	4	8	15	20	40
52	Bruce Dal Canton	4	4	5	6	12	25	60	100
53	John Kennedy	4	4	5	6	8	12	30	60
54	Jeff Torborg	4	4	4	5	10	20	25	80
55	John Odom	4	4	4	6	10	15	40	80
56	J.Lis RC/S.Reid RC	4	4	4	4	5	10	12	25
57	Pat Kelly	4	4	4	4	5	10	12	30
58	Dave Marshall	4	4	4	5	10	12	30	
59	Dick Ellsworth	4	4	4	4	8	20	30	
60	Jim Wynn	4	4	4	4	6	12	15	60
61	NL Batting Leaders	12	15	▲30	▲40	60	150	200	500
62	AL Batting Leaders	6	12	25	30	50	60	150	300
63	NL RBI Leaders	4	4	8	10	20	40	60	
64	AL RBI Leaders	4	4	8	10	15	25	50	150
65	NL Home Run Leaders	4	8	12	15	20	▲50	▲60	120
66	AL Home Run Leaders	4	4	6	8	15	30		
67	NL ERA Leaders	4	4	8	10	20	50		
68	AL ERA Leaders	4	6	12	15	25	30	80	150
69	NL Pitching Leaders	4	5	6	8	12	30	60	120
70	AL Pitching Leaders	4	5	10	12	25	50		
71	NL Strikeout Leaders	4	5	10	12	20	25	80	150
72	AL Strikeout Leaders	4	4	8	10	20	40	50	150
73	Wayne Granger	4	4	4	5	10	20	25	60
74	G.Washburn RC/W.Wolf	4	4	4	4	6	12	15	30
75	Jim Kaat	4	4	5	6	12	20	25	100
76	Carl Taylor	4	4	8	10	20	40	50	
77	Frank Linzy	4	5	10	12	25	50	60	150
78	Joe Lahoud	4	4	5	6	12	15	20	60
79	Clay Kirby	4	4	4	4	6	12	15	30
80	Don Kessinger	4	4	4	4	8	20	30	
81	Dave May	4	4	4	4	6	12	15	60
82	Frank Fernandez	4	4	4	4	8	15	20	30
83	Don Cardwell	4	4	4	4	8	15	20	40
84	Paul Casanova	4	4	6	8	15	30	40	120
85	Max Alvis	4	4	4	4	5	10	12	50
86	Lum Harris MG	4	4	4	4	8	15	20	60
87	Steve Renko RC	4	4	4	4	8	15	20	50
88	M.Fuentes RC/D.Baney RC	4	4	4	4	6	12	15	30
89	Juan Rios	4	4	4	5	10	25	30	60
90	Tim McCarver	4	4	6	8	15	30	40	80
91	Rich Morales	4	4	4	4	8	15	20	50
92	George Culver	4	4	4	4	6	12	15	20
93	Rick Renick	4	4	4	4	6	12	15	40
94	Freddie Patek	4	4	5	6	12	25	30	60
95	Earl Wilson	4	4	4	4	8	15	20	40

#	Player	VG 3	VgEx 4	EX 5	ExMt 6	NM 7	NmMt 8	NmMt+ 8.5	MT 9
96	L.Lee RC/J.Reuss RC	4	4	6	8	15	30	50	
97	Joe Moeller	4	4	4	4	8	15	20	
98	Gates Brown	4	4	4	4	6	15	20	
99	Bobby Pfeil RC	4	4	6	8	15	30		
100	Mel Stottlemyre	4	4	4	4	8	15	20	
101	Bobby Floyd	4	4	4	4	8	15	20	
102	Joe Rudi	4	4	4	4	8	15	20	
103	Frank Reberger	4	4	4	4	6	12	15	
104	Gerry Moses	4	4	4	4	8	15	25	
105	Tony Gonzalez	4	4	4	4	6	12	15	
106	Darold Knowles	4	4	4	5	10	20	25	
107	Bobby Etheridge	4	4	4	4	6	12	20	
108	Tom Burgmeier	4	4	4	5	10	20	25	
109	G.Jestadt RC/C.Morton	4	4	4	4	8	15	20	
110	Bob Moose	4	4	4	4	5	10	12	
111	Mike Hegan	4	4	6	8	15	30		
112	Dave Nelson	4	4	4	4	8	15	20	
113	Jim Ray	4	4	4	4	8	15	20	
114	Gene Michael	4	6	8	10	20	30	40	
115	Alex Johnson	6	12	25	30	50	60	200	
116	Sparky Lyle	4	4	5	6	12	25	30	
117	Don Young	4	4	4	4	8	15	20	
118	George Mitterwald	4	4	4	6	10	15	20	
119	Chuck Taylor RC	4	4	4	4	8	15	20	
120	Sal Bando	4	4	5	6	12	25	30	
121	F.Beene RC/T.Crowley RC	4	4	8	10	20	40	50	
122	George Stone	4	4	4	4	6	12	15	
123	Don Gutteridge MG RC	4	4	6	8	15	30	40	
124	Larry Jaster	4	4	4	4	5	10	12	
125	Deron Johnson	4	4	8	10	20	80		
126	Marty Martinez	4	6	12	15	30	60	80	2
127	Joe Coleman	4	4	4	4	5	10	12	
128A	Checklist 2 R Perranoski	4	4	5	6	12	25		
128B	Checklist 2 R. Perranoski	4	4	5	6	12	30		
129	Jimmie Price	4	4	4	4	6	15	20	
130	Ollie Brown	4	4	4	5	10	20	25	
131	R.Lamb RC/B.Stinson RC	4	4	4	5	10	20	25	
132	Jim McGlothlin	4	4	4	4	8	20	25	
133	Clay Carroll	4	4	6	8	15	30	40	
134	Danny Walton RC	4	4	4	4	5	10	12	
135	Dick Dietz	4	6	12	15	30	60	80	1
136	Steve Hargan	4	4	4	4	6	10	12	
137	Art Shamsky	4	5	10	12	25	30	40	2
138	Joe Foy	4	4	6	8	15	30	40	1
139	Rich Nye	4	4	4	4	5	10	12	
140	Reggie Jackson	▲25	▲30	▲40	50	80	250	500	1,5
141	D.Cash RC/J.Jeter RC	4	4	4	5	10	20	25	
142	Fritz Peterson	4	4	8	10	20	40	50	1
143	Phil Gagliano	4	4	4	5	10	20	25	
144	Ray Culp	4	5	10	12	20	25	30	
145	Rico Carty	4	4	4	5	10	20	25	
146	Danny Murphy	4	4	4	5	10	20	25	
147	Angel Hermoso RC	4	4	4	4	6	12	15	
148	Earl Weaver MG	4	4	8	10	20	25	30	
149	Billy Champion RC	4	4	4	5	10	20	25	
150	Harmon Killebrew	5	10	15	▲30	▲40	▲100	120	▼3
151	Dave Roberts	4	4	4	4	6	12	15	
152	Ike Brown RC	4	4	4	4	6	12	15	
153	Gary Gentry	4	4	4	5	10	12		
154	J.Miles/J.Dukes RC	4	4	5	6	12	30	40	
155	Denis Menke	4	4	4	4	8	15	20	
156	Eddie Fisher	4	4	4	4	5	10	12	
157	Manny Mota	4	4	5	6	12	15	20	
158	Jerry McNertney	4	4	4	5	10	20	25	
159	Tommy Helms	4	4	4	4	6	12	15	
160	Phil Niekro	4	5	10	12	20	▲50	▲60	▲2
161	Richie Scheinblum	4	4	4	6	12	25	30	
162	Jerry Johnson	4	4	4	5	10	12	15	
163	Syd O'Brien	4	4	4	4	8	15	20	
164	Ty Cline	4	4	4	4	6	10	8	
165	Ed Kirkpatrick	4	4	4	5	10	12	15	
166	Al Oliver	4	4	5	6	12	25		
167	Bill Burbach	4	4	4	5	10	12	15	
168	Dave Watkins RC	4	4	5	6	12	25	30	
169	Tom Hall	4	4	4	4	8	15	20	
170	Billy Williams	4	5	10	12	▲30	▲40	▲50	1
171	Jim Nash	4	4	4	5	10	12	15	

	VG 3	VgEx 4	EX 5	ExMt 6	NM 7	NmMt 8	NmMt+ 8.5	MT 9
G.Hill RC/R.Garr RC	4	4	4	4	6	12	15	80
Jim Hicks	4	4	5	6	10	12	15	60
Ted Sizemore	4	4	5	6	10	12	15	60
Dick Bosman	4	4	4	4	8	15	20	80
Jim Ray Hart	4	4	8	10	20	25	30	120
Jim Northrup	4	4	4	5	10	15	20	80
Denny Lemaster	4	4	4	5	10	20	25	50
Ivan Murrell	4	4	5	6	12	25	30	60
Tommy John	4	4	6	8	15	25	40	60
Sparky Anderson MG	4	4	4	5	10	30	40	
Dick Hall	4	4	4	4	8	15	20	80
Jerry Grote	4	4	4	4	6	12	15	30
Ray Fosse	4	4	8	10	20	25	30	100
Don Mincher	4	4	4	4	8	15	20	30
Rick Joseph	4	4	5	6	12	15	20	60
Mike Hedlund	4	4	4	4	5	10	12	20
Manny Sanguillen	4	4	6	8	15	30	40	150
Thurman Munson RC	40	50	60	100	150	400	800	2,000
Joe Torre	4	4	8	10	30	60	80	200
Vicente Romo	4	4	4	4	8	15	20	60
Jim Qualls	4	4	5	6	12	25	30	60
Mike Wegener	4	4	4	4	8	15	20	40
Chuck Manuel RC	4	4	4	4	5	10	12	80
Tom Seaver NLCS1	4	4	8	10	20	50	60	150
Ken Boswell NLCS2	4	8	15	20	25	80	100	200
Nolan Ryan NLCS3	4	6	12	20	50	80	100	300
Mets Celebrate NLCS w/Ryan	4	6	12	▲25	30	80	100	500
Mike Cuellar ALCS1	4	4	6	8	15	30		
Boog Powell ALCS2	4	8	15	20	40	80		
B.Powell/A.Etchebarren ALCS3	4	4	8	10	20	25	50	150
Orioles Celebrate ALCS	4	4	4	5	10	25	25	50
Rudy May	4	4	4	4	8	15	20	40
Len Gabrielson	4	4	4	4	6	12	15	30
Bert Campaneris	4	4	6	8	15	30	40	150
Clete Boyer	4	4	4	4	6	12	15	30
N.McRae RC/B.Reed RC	4	4	5	6	12	25	30	60
Fred Gladding	4	4	4	4	5	10	12	25
Ken Suarez	4	4	4	4	5	10	12	25
Juan Marichal	6	8	10	15	25	40		
Ted Williams MG	4	4	10	20	30	50	80	200
Al Santorini	4	4	4	4	6	12	15	25
Andy Etchebarren	4	4	4	4	6	12	15	50
Ken Boswell	4	4	4	5	10	20	25	120
Reggie Smith	4	4	4	4	6	15	20	60
Chuck Hartenstein	4	4	4	4	6	12	15	60
Ron Hansen	4	4	4	4	6	12	15	40
Ron Stone	4	4	4	4	5	10	12	30
Jerry Kenney	4	4	4	4	6	20	25	30
Steve Carlton	4	8	15	20	▲30	▲50	80	200
Ron Brand	4	4	4	4	6	12	25	50
Jim Rooker	4	4	4	5	10	20	25	50
Nate Oliver	4	4	4	5	8	15	20	40
Steve Barber	4	4	4	4	5	10	12	50
Lee May	4	4	4	4	8	20	25	80
Ron Perranoski	4	4	4	4	8	15	20	50
J.Mayberry RC/B.Watkins RC	4	4	4	4	8	15		
Aurelio Rodriguez	4	4	4	4	5	10	12	25
Rich Robertson	4	4	4	4	8	20	25	40
Brooks Robinson	4	8	▲15	20	30	60	80	300
Luis Tiant	4	4	5	6	12	15	20	80
Bob Didier	4	4	4	4	8	60	30	
Lew Krausse	4	4	4	4	5	10	12	50
Tommy Dean	4	4	4	4	8	20	25	
Mike Epstein	4	4	4	4	8	15	20	100
Bob Veale	4	4	4	5	10	20	25	50
Russ Gibson	4	4	4	4	6	12	15	30
Jose Laboy	4	4	4	4	5	10	12	50
Ken Berry	4	4	4	5	10	20	25	100
Ferguson Jenkins	4	5	10	12	25	40	50	120
A.Fitzmorris RC/S.Northey RC	4	4	5	6	12	25	30	60
Walt Alston MG	4	4	4	4	8	15	20	60
Joe Sparma	4	4	4	5	10	20	25	100

	VG 3	VgEx 4	EX 5	ExMt 6	NM 7	NmMt 8	NmMt+ 8.5	MT 9
A Checklist 3 Red Bat	4	4	5	6	12	40		
3 Checklist 3 Brown Bat	4	8	15	20	40	80		
Leo Cardenas	4	4	4	5	10	12	15	60
Jim McAndrew	4	4	8	10	20	40	50	100
Lou Klimchock	4	4	4	4	8	15	20	80

		VG 3	VgEx 4	EX 5	ExMt 6	NM 7	NmMt 8	NmMt+ 8.5	MT 9
248	Jesus Alou	4	4	4	4	8	15	20	40
249	Bob Locker	4	4	4	4	8	15	20	100
250	Willie McCovey	4	8	15	20	50	80	100	500
251	Dick Schofield	4	4	4	5	10	20	25	30
252	Lowell Palmer RC	4	4	4	5	10	20	25	50
253	Ron Woods	4	4	4	4	8	15		
254	Camilo Pascual	4	4	4	4	6	12	15	30
255	Jim Spencer RC	4	4	4	4	5	10	12	25
256	Vic Davalillo	4	4	4	5	10	20	25	50
257	Dennis Higgins	4	4	4	5	10	20	25	60
258	Paul Popovich	4	4	4	4	6	12	15	30
259	Tommie Reynolds	4	4	4	4	8	15	20	60
260	Claude Osteen	4	4	4	4	6	12	15	30
261	Curt Motton	4	4	4	4	8	25	40	60
262	J.Morales RC/J.Williams RC	4	4	4	5	10	30	40	50
263	Duane Josephson	4	4	4	5	10	20		
264	Rich Hebner	4	4	4	5	10	80		
265	Randy Hundley	4	4	4	4	5	10	12	25
266	Wally Bunker	4	4	4	4	5	10	12	25
267	H.Hill RC/P.Ratliff	4	4	4	5	10	20		
268	Claude Raymond	4	4	4	4	6	8	12	
269	Cesar Guiterrez	4	4	4	4	5	10	12	15
270	Chris Short	4	4	4	4	6	12	15	30
271	Greg Goossen	4	4	4	5	10	12	15	25
272	Hector Torres	4	4	4	4	8	15		
273	Ralph Houk MG	4	4	4	5	10	20		
274	Gerry Arrigo	4	4	4	4	8	10	12	20
275	Duke Sims	4	4	4	4	8	15	20	40
276	Ron Hunt	4	4	4	4	6	12	15	
277	Paul Doyle RC	4	4	4	4	6	10	12	15
278	Tommie Aaron	4	4	4	4	5	10	12	20
279	Bill Lee RC	4	4	4	8	10	20	40	80
280	Donn Clendenon	4	5	10	12	25	50		
281	Casey Cox	4	4	4	4	6	12	15	30
282	Steve Huntz	4	4	4	4	6	12	15	30
283	Angel Bravo RC	4	4	4	4	4	6	8	12
284	Jack Baldschun	4	4	4	4	5	10	12	25
285	Paul Blair	4	4	4	4	5	10	12	25
286	Bill Buckner RC	4	4	4	▲15	▲20	▲40	▲50	80
287	Fred Talbot	4	4	4	4	8	10	12	50
288	Larry Hisle	4	4	4	4	4	8	10	15
289	Gene Brabender	4	4	6	8	15	30	40	80
290	Rod Carew	6	10	▲20	25	▲40	80	80	400
291	Leo Durocher MG	4	4	4	4	6	12	15	30
292	Eddie Leon RC	4	4	4	4	5	10	12	25
293	Bob Bailey	4	4	4	4	5	10	12	25
294	Jose Azcue	4	4	4	4	5	10	12	25
295	Cecil Upshaw	4	4	4	4	4	8	10	15
296	Woody Woodward	4	4	4	4	5	10	12	50
297	Curt Blefary	4	4	4	4	5	10	12	20
298	Ken Henderson	4	4	4	4	5	10	12	20
299	Buddy Bradford	4	4	4	4	6	12	15	30
300	Tom Seaver	8	▲20	▲25	▲30	▲50	80	150	400
301	Chico Salmon	4	4	4	4	6	12	15	30
302	Jeff James	4	4	4	4	5	10	12	25
303	Brant Alyea	4	4	4	4	6	12	15	30
304	Bill Russell RC	4	4	4	4	8	20	25	▲60
305	Don Buford WS1	4	4	4	4	6	12	15	30
306	Donn Clendenon WS2	4	4	4	4	8	20	25	60
307	Tommie Agee WS3	4	8	15	20	40	60	80	200
308	J.C. Martin WS4	4	4	5	6	12	25	30	80
309	Jerry Koosman WS5	4	4	4	4	5	10	12	25
310	Mets Celebrate WS	4	4	4	5	10	30	40	80
311	Dick Green	4	4	4	4	4	8	10	15
312	Mike Torrez	4	4	4	5	10	15	20	50
313	Mayo Smith MG	4	4	4	4	5	10	12	25
314	Bill McCool	4	4	4	4	6	12	15	25
315	Luis Aparicio	4	4	4	5	10	25	30	50
316	Skip Guinn	4	4	4	4	5	10	12	25
317	B.Conigliaro/L.Alvarado RC	4	4	4	4	4	8	15	
318	Willie Smith	4	4	4	4	6	12	15	30
319	Clay Dalrymple	4	4	4	4	5	10	12	20
320	Jim Maloney	4	4	4	5	10	30		
321	Lou Piniella	4	4	4	4	8	15	20	80
322	Luke Walker	4	4	4	4	4	8	10	15
323	Wayne Comer	4	4	4	4	6	12	15	40
324	Tony Taylor	4	4	4	4	6	12	15	30

#	Player	VG 3	VgEx 4	EX 5	ExMt 6	NM 7	NmMt 8	NmMt+ 8.5	MT 9
325	Dave Boswell	4	4	4	4	8	15	20	40
326	Bill Voss	4	4	4	4	4	8	10	15
327	Hal King RC	4	4	4	4	5	10	12	25
328	George Brunet	4	4	4	4	4	8	10	15
329	Chris Cannizzaro	4	4	4	4	6	12	15	80
330	Lou Brock	4	4	5	20	25	40	50	100
331	Chuck Dobson	4	4	4	4	6	12	15	30
332	Bobby Wine	4	4	4	4	4	8	10	15
333	Bobby Murcer	4	4	5	6	12	25	30	100
334	Phil Regan	4	4	4	4	5	10	12	30
335	Bill Freehan	4	4	4	4	8	15	20	50
336	Del Unser	4	4	4	4	8	15		
337	Mike McCormick	4	4	4	4	6	12	15	30
338	Paul Schaal	4	4	4	4	6	12	15	30
339	Johnny Edwards	4	4	4	4	5	10	12	25
340	Tony Conigliaro	6	12	25	30	50	80	150	150
341	Bill Sudakis	4	4	4	4	6	12	15	30
342	Wilbur Wood	4	4	4	4	5	10	12	20
343A	Checklist 4 Red Bat	4	4	6	8	15	50		
343B	Checklist 4 Brown Bat	4	4	5	6	12	25		
344	Marcelino Lopez	4	4	4	4	6	12	15	50
345	Al Ferrara	4	4	4	4	4	8	10	15
346	Red Schoendienst MG	4	4	4	4	8	15		
347	Russ Snyder	4	4	4	4	5	10	12	25
348	M.Jorgensen RC/J.Hudson RC	4	4	4	4	8	15	20	40
349	Steve Hamilton	4	4	4	4	6	12	15	30
350	Roberto Clemente	▲30	▲40	50	60	120	300	▼800	2,000
351	Tom Murphy	4	4	4	4	6	12	15	30
352	Bob Barton	4	4	4	4	5	10	12	20
353	Stan Williams	4	4	4	4	6	12	15	30
354	Amos Otis	4	4	4	5	10	20	25	50
355	Doug Rader	4	4	4	4	5	10	12	25
356	Fred Lasher	4	4	4	4	4	8	10	15
357	Bob Burda	4	4	4	4	6	12	15	30
358	Pedro Borbon RC	4	4	4	4	5	10	12	25
359	Phil Roof	4	4	4	4	6	12	15	30
360	Curt Flood	4	4	4	4	8	15	20	60
361	Ray Jarvis	4	4	4	4	5	10	12	25
362	Joe Hague	4	4	4	4	5	10	12	25
363	Tom Shopay RC	4	4	4	4	5	10	12	25
364	Dan McGinn	4	4	4	4	5	10	12	20
365	Zoilo Versalles	4	4	4	4	5	10	12	80
366	Barry Moore	4	4	4	4	5	10	12	25
367	Mike Lum	4	4	4	4	5	10	12	30
368	Ed Herrmann	4	4	4	4	6	12	15	30
369	Alan Foster	4	4	4	4	8	15		
370	Tommy Harper	4	4	4	4	8	15	20	40
371	Rod Gaspar RC	4	4	4	4	5	10	12	25
372	Dave Giusti	4	4	4	4	6	12	15	30
373	Roy White	4	4	4	5	10	20	25	100
374	Tommie Sisk	4	4	4	4	6	12	15	30
375	Johnny Callison	4	4	4	4	8	15	20	80
376	Lefty Phillips MG RC	4	4	4	4	8	15	20	25
377	Bill Butler	4	4	4	4	8	15		
378	Jim Davenport	4	4	4	4	6	12	15	30
379	Tom Tischinski RC	4	4	5	6	12	25		
380	Tony Perez	4	5	10	12	30	100		
381	B.Brooks RC/M.Olivo RC	4	4	4	4	6	12	15	25
382	Jack DiLauro RC	4	4	4	4	5	10	12	50
383	Mickey Stanley	4	4	4	5	10	20	25	120
384	Gary Neibauer	4	4	4	4	8	15		
385	George Scott	4	4	5	6	12	25	30	60
386	Bill Dillman	4	4	4	4	6	12	15	50
387	Baltimore Orioles TC	4	4	8	10	20	30		
388	Byron Browne	4	4	4	4	6	12	15	30
389	Jim Shellenback	4	4	4	4	6	15	20	30
390	Willie Davis	4	4	4	4	8	20	25	80
391	Larry Brown	4	4	4	4	6	12	15	30
392	Walt Hriniak	4	4	4	4	8	15		
393	John Gelnar	4	4	4	4	6	12	15	50
394	Gil Hodges MG	4	5	10	12	25	50		
395	Walt Williams	4	4	4	4	8	15	20	80
396	Steve Blass	4	4	5	6	12	25	30	100
397	Roger Repoz	4	4	4	4	8	15		
398	Bill Stoneman	4	4	4	4	6	12	15	25
399	New York Yankees TC	4	6	12	15	20	30	40	150
400	Denny McLain	4	6	12	15	30	80	150	250

#	Player	VG 3	VgEx 4	EX 5	ExMt 6	NM 7	NmMt 8	NmMt+ 8.5	M
401	J.Harrell RC/B.Williams RC	4	4	4	5	10	20	25	
402	Ellie Rodriguez	4	4	4	4	6	12	15	
403	Jim Bunning	4	4	5	6	12	25	30	
404	Rich Reese	4	4	4	4	6	12	15	
405	Bill Hands	4	4	4	4	5	20	25	
406	Mike Andrews	4	4	4	4	6	12	15	
407	Bob Watson	4	4	4	4	6	12	15	
408	Paul Lindblad	4	4	6	8	15	30	40	1
409	Bob Tolan	4	4	4	4	5	10	12	
410	Boog Powell	4	4	5	6	12	25	30	1
411	Los Angeles Dodgers TC	4	4	4	4	6	12	15	
412	Larry Burchart	4	4	6	8	15	30	40	
413	Sonny Jackson	4	4	4	4	6	12	15	
414	Paul Edmondson RC	4	4	4	4	5	10	12	
415	Julian Javier	4	4	4	5	10	20	25	
416	Joe Verbanic	4	4	4	4	6	12	15	
417	John Bateman	4	4	4	4	8	15		
418	John Donaldson	4	4	5	6	12	25	30	
419	Ron Taylor	4	4	6	8	15	30	40	1
420	Ken McMullen	4	4	4	4	8	15	20	
421	Pat Dobson	4	4	5	6	12	25	30	
422	Kansas City Royals TC	4	4	4	4	5	10	12	
423	Jerry May	4	6	12	15	30	60	80	1
424	Mike Kilkenny	4	4	6	8	15	30	40	1
425	Bobby Bonds	4	5	10	10	20	25	60	1
426	Bill Rigney MG	4	4	6	8	15	30	40	
427	Fred Norman	4	4	4	4	6	12	15	
428	Don Buford	4	4	4	4	6	12	15	
429	R.Bobb RC/J.Cosman	4	4	4	5	10	20	25	
430	Andy Messersmith	4	4	4	4	8	80		
431	Ron Swoboda	4	4	4	4	6	12	15	
432A	Checklist 5 Yellow Letters	4	4	5	6	12	40		
432B	Checklist 5 White Letters	4	4	5	6	12	25		
433	Ron Bryant RC	4	4	4	4	8	15	20	
434	Felipe Alou	4	4	4	4	6	12	15	1
435	Nelson Briles	4	4	4	4	6	12	15	
436	Philadelphia Phillies TC	4	4	4	4	6	12	15	
437	Danny Cater	4	4	4	4	6	12	15	
438	Pat Jarvis	4	4	4	4	6	12	15	1
439	Lee Maye	4	4	4	4	5	10	12	
440	Bill Mazeroski	4	4	6	15	25	30	50	
441	John O'Donoghue	4	4	4	4	5	10	12	
442	Gene Mauch MG	4	4	4	5	10	20	25	
443	Al Jackson	4	4	4	4	5	10	12	
444	B.Farmer RC/J.Matias RC	4	4	4	4	6	12	15	1
445	Vada Pinson	4	4	5	6	12	25	40	1
446	Billy Grabarkewitz RC	4	4	4	4	5	10	12	
447	Lee Stange	4	4	4	4	6	20	25	
448	Houston Astros TC	4	4	4	4	5	10	12	
449	Jim Palmer	4	6	10	12	25	50	60	2
450	Willie McCovey AS	6	8	10	▲20	25	▲60	▲80	
451	Boog Powell AS	4	4	6	8	15	50		
452	Felix Millan AS	4	4	4	5	10	20	25	
453	Rod Carew AS	4	6	8	10	20	▲40	100	2
454	Ron Santo AS	4	4	5	6	12	50		
455	Brooks Robinson AS	4	5	10	▲20	30	150		
456	Don Kessinger AS	4	4	4	5	10	20	25	
457	Rico Petrocelli AS	4	4	6	8	15	30	50	
458	Pete Rose AS	8	12	15	25	▲80	300		
459	Reggie Jackson AS	4	10	12	▲25	60	250		
460	Matty Alou AS	4	6	12	15	30	100		
461	Carl Yastrzemski AS	4	10	20	30	60	250		
462	Hank Aaron AS	12	▲25	▲30	50	80	500		
463	Frank Robinson AS	4	4	▲20	▲25	30	50	60	3
464	Johnny Bench AS	10	20	25	▲40	100	400		
465	Bill Freehan AS	4	6	12	15	30	60	80	1
466	Juan Marichal AS	4	6	12	15	30	60	80	
467	Denny McLain AS	4	4	5	6	12	50		
468	Jerry Koosman AS	4	6	12	15	30	80		
469	Sam McDowell AS	4	8	15	20	40	200		
470	Willie Stargell	4	▲12	▲15	20	50	120		
471	Chris Zachary	4	4	4	4	6	12	15	
472	Atlanta Braves TC	4	4	4	4	5	10	12	
473	Don Bryant	4	4	4	4	8	15		1
474	Dick Kelley	4	4	4	4	6	12	15	
475	Dick McAuliffe	4	4	5	6	12	25	30	
476	Don Shaw	4	4	4	5	10	20	25	

	VG 3	VgEx 4	EX 5	ExMt 6	NM 7	NmMt 8	NmMt+ 8.5	MT 9
A.Severinsen RC/R.Freed RC	4	4	5	6	12	25	60	100
Bobby Heise RC	4	4	4	4	8	20		
Dick Woodson RC	4	4	5	6	12	25		
Glenn Beckert	4	4	6	8	15	30	40	200
Jose Tartabull	4	4	4	5	10	20	30	60
Tom Hilgendorf RC	4	4	4	4	6	12	15	25
Gail Hopkins RC	4	4	4	4	8	15		
Gary Nolan	5	6	8	10	20	80	100	150
Jay Johnstone	4	5	6	8	10	20	25	60
Terry Harmon	4	4	4	5	6	12	40	
Cisco Carlos	4	4	4	4	8	15		
J.C. Martin	4	4	6	8	15	30	40	80
Eddie Kasko MG	4	4	4	5	10	20	25	50
Bill Singer	4	4	4	5	10	20	25	100
Graig Nettles	4	4	4	8	15	30	40	120
K.Lampard RC/S.Spinks RC	4	4	4	4	6	12	15	30
Lindy McDaniel	4	4	4	4	8	20	25	50
Larry Stahl	4	4	4	4	8	15	20	60
Dave Morehead	4	4	4	5	10	20	25	50
Steve Whitaker	4	4	4	5	10	20	25	
Eddie Watt	4	4	8	10	20	40	50	100
Al Weis	4	4	4	4	5	10	12	60
Skip Lockwood	4	4	5	6	12	25	30	120
Hank Aaron	25	▲40	▲50	60	▲120	250	400	▼1,000
Chicago White Sox TC	4	4	4	4	8	15	20	60
Rollie Fingers	4	4	4	▲25	▲30	50	60	150
Dal Maxvill	4	4	4	4	8	15	20	100
Don Pavletich	4	4	4	4	6	12	15	80
Ken Holtzman	4	4	5	6	12	25	30	150
Ed Stroud	4	4	4	5	10	20	25	80
Pat Corrales	6	8	10	12	25	40		
Joe Niekro	4	4	4	4	8	15	30	50
Montreal Expos TC	4	4	4	5	10	20	25	
Tony Oliva	6	8	10	12	25	120		
Joe Hoerner	4	4	4	4	8	15	20	80
Billy Harris	4	4	4	4	6	12	15	50
Preston Gomez MG	4	4	4	4	5	10	12	25
Steve Hovley RC	4	4	4	4	5	10	12	25
Don Wilson	4	4	4	5	10	20	25	60
J.Ellis RC/J.Lyttle RC	4	5	10	12	25	50		
Joe Gibbon	4	4	4	4	5	10	12	25
Bill Melton	4	4	4	5	10	20	25	
Don McMahon	4	4	4	4	8	15		
Willie Horton	8	10	12	15	30	80		
Cal Koonce	5	6	8	10	20	40		
California Angels TC	4	4	5	6	12	25	30	60
Jose Pena	4	4	5	6	12	100		
Alvin Dark MG	4	4	4	4	6	12	15	25
Jerry Adair	4	4	4	8	15	30	50	80
Ron Herbel	4	4	4	5	10	20	25	
Don Bosch	4	4	4	4	8	15	20	40
Elrod Hendricks	4	4	5	6	12	25	30	200
Bob Aspromonte	4	4	4	4	6	12	15	30
Bob Gibson	6	20	25	30	40	80	120	400
Ron Clark	4	4	4	5	10	20	25	
Danny Murtaugh MG	4	4	5	6	12	25	30	80
Buzz Stephen RC	4	4	4	4	8	15	20	50
Minnesota Twins TC	4	4	5	6	12	25	30	60
Andy Kosco	4	4	4	4	8	15	20	25
Mike Kekich	4	5	10	12	25	50		
Joe Morgan	4	4	10	15	▲30	50	60	250
Bob Humphreys	4	4	4	5	10	20	25	60
D.Doyle RC/L.Bowa RC	6	8	15	20	30	60		
Gary Peters	4	4	6	8	15	30	40	
Bill Heath	4	4	4	4	5	10	12	40
Checklist 6 Brown Bat	4	4	4	8	15	30	40	80
Checklist 6 Gray Bat	4	4	5	6	12	25		
Clyde Wright	4	4	4	5	10	60	80	
Cincinnati Reds TC	4	4	5	6	12	25	30	150
Ken Harrelson	4	4	4	5	10	50	60	100
Ron Reed	4	4	4	4	6	12	15	30
Rick Monday	4	4	4	5	10	20	25	100
Howie Reed	4	4	4	4	5	10	12	40
St. Louis Cardinals TC	4	4	4	4	6	20	30	100
Frank Howard	4	4	4	4	8	▲40	▲50	▲60
Dock Ellis	4	4	4	5	10	20	25	30
O'Riley/Paepke/Rico RC	4	4	4	4	8	15	20	60

		VG 3	VgEx 4	EX 5	ExMt 6	NM 7	NmMt 8	NmMt+ 8.5	MT 9
553	Jim Lefebvre	4	4	4	4	5	10	12	25
554	Tom Timmermann RC	4	4	4	4	5	10	12	30
555	Orlando Cepeda	4	5	15	20	30	80	100	200
556	Dave Bristol MG	4	4	4	4	6	12	15	40
557	Ed Kranepool	4	5	10	12	25	50	60	150
558	Vern Fuller	4	4	4	4	5	10	12	25
559	Tommy Davis	4	4	4	4	5	12	15	80
560	Gaylord Perry	4	4	6	12	25	30	50	100
561	Tom McCraw	4	4	4	4	6	12	15	30
562	Ted Abernathy	4	4	4	4	5	10	12	20
563	Boston Red Sox TC	4	4	5	6	12	25	30	50
564	Johnny Briggs	4	4	4	5	6	12	15	25
565	Jim Hunter	4	5	10	20	25	▲50	60	120
566	Gene Alley	4	4	4	4	6	15	20	25
567	Bob Oliver	4	4	4	4	5	10	12	20
568	Stan Bahnsen	4	4	4	4	5	15	20	25
569	Cookie Rojas	4	4	4	4	5	15	20	25
570	Jim Fregosi	4	4	4	4	6	12	15	30
571	Jim Brewer	4	4	4	4	5	10	12	30
572	Frank Quilici	4	4	4	4	4	8	10	15
573	Corkins/Robles/Slocum RC	4	4	4	4	6	10	12	20
574	Bobby Bolin	4	4	4	4	6	10	12	25
575	Cleon Jones	4	4	4	4	5	▲30	▲40	▲50
576	Milt Pappas	4	4	4	4	5	10	12	25
577	Bernie Allen	4	4	4	4	5	10	12	25
578	Tom Griffin	4	4	4	4	8	15	20	30
579	Detroit Tigers TC	4	4	4	4	8	30	▲50	100
580	Pete Rose	12	30	50	60	100	▲300	500	800
581	Tom Satriano	4	4	4	4	6	12	15	25
582	Mike Paul	4	4	4	4	5	10	12	25
583	Hal Lanier	4	4	4	4	5	10	12	25
584	Al Downing	4	4	4	4	6	12	15	50
585	Rusty Staub	4	4	4	6	12	25	30	80
586	Rickey Clark RC	4	4	6	8	15	30	40	80
587	Jose Arcia	4	4	4	4	5	10	12	25
588A	Checklist 7 666 is Adolfo	4	4	5	6	12	25		
588B	Checklist 7 666 is Adolpho	4	4	5	6	12	25		
589	Joe Keough	4	4	4	4	5	10	12	20
590	Mike Cuellar	4	4	5	6	12	25	30	80
591	Mike Ryan	4	4	4	4	5	10	12	25
592	Daryl Patterson	4	4	4	4	5	10	12	20
593	Chicago Cubs TC	4	4	4	5	10	20	25	40
594	Jake Gibbs	4	4	4	4	8	15	20	80
595	Maury Wills	4	5	6	12	▲25	▲40	▲50	120
596	Mike Hershberger	4	4	4	4	4	8	15	25
597	Sonny Siebert	4	4	4	4	5	10	12	25
598	Joe Pepitone	4	4	4	4	6	12	15	25
599	Stelmaszek/Martin/Such RC	4	4	4	4	5	12	15	25
600	Willie Mays	▲30	▲50	▲60	80	▲150	200	400	1,000
601	Pete Richert	4	4	4	4	5	10	12	20
602	Ted Savage	4	4	4	4	5	10	12	25
603	Ray Oyler	4	4	4	4	5	10	12	25
604	Cito Gaston	4	4	4	4	5	10	12	25
605	Rick Wise	4	4	4	4	5	10	12	25
606	Chico Ruiz	4	4	4	4	5	10	12	25
607	Gary Waslewski	4	4	4	4	4	8	10	15
608	Pittsburgh Pirates TC	4	4	4	5	10	20	25	80
609	Buck Martinez RC	4	4	4	4	8	15	20	30
610	Jerry Koosman	4	4	5	6	8	15	20	40
611	Norm Cash	4	5	6	12	15	30	40	200
612	Jim Hickman	4	4	4	4	8	15	20	50
613	Dave Baldwin	4	4	4	4	5	15	20	25
614	Mike Shannon	4	4	4	4	6	12	15	60
615	Mark Belanger	4	4	4	4	6	15	20	30
616	Jim Merritt	4	4	4	4	5	12	15	25
617	Jim French	4	4	4	4	4	8	10	15
618	Billy Wynne RC	4	4	4	4	5	10	12	25
619	Norm Miller	4	4	4	4	5	10	12	25
620	Jim Perry	4	4	4	4	5	12	15	▲50
621	McQueen/Evans/Kester RC	4	4	5	10	25	40	50	▲200
622	Don Sutton	4	4	6	12	20	30	50	120
623	Horace Clarke	4	4	4	4	5	10	12	25
624	Clyde King MG	4	4	4	4	4	8	10	15
625	Dean Chance	4	4	4	5	10	12	15	20
626	Dave Ricketts	4	4	4	4	5	10	12	30
627	Gary Wagner	4	4	4	4	5	10	12	25
628	Wayne Garrett RC	4	4	4	5	10	20	25	200

		VG 3	VgEx 4	EX 5	ExMt 6	NM 7	NmMt 8	NmMt+ 8.5	MT 9
629	Merv Rettenmund	4	4	4	4	8	15	20	40
630	Ernie Banks	12	20	40	▼50	80	▲150	▲200	400
631	Oakland Athletics TC	4	4	6	8	15	30	40	80
632	Gary Sutherland	4	4	4	4	5	10	12	20
633	Roger Nelson	4	4	4	4	4	8	10	15
634	Bud Harrelson	5	10	20	25	50	100		
635	Bob Allison	4	4	4	5	20	25	30	50
636	Jim Stewart	4	4	4	4	6	15	20	50
637	Cleveland Indians TC	4	4	4	4	8	25	30	50
638	Frank Bertaina	4	4	4	5	10	30	40	
639	Dave Campbell	4	4	4	4	6	20	25	50
640	Al Kaline	6	25	▼25	▼30	▼40	▲100	100	250
641	Al McBean	4	4	4	4	6	15	25	30
642	Garrett/Lund/Tatum RC	4	4	4	4	8	25	30	40
643	Jose Pagan	4	4	4	5	10	20	25	80
644	Gerry Nyman	4	4	4	5	10	20	25	▲80
645	Don Money	4	4	4	5	10	20	30	40
646	Jim Britton	4	4	4	4	6	12	20	40
647	Tom Matchick	4	4	4	4	6	15	20	50
648	Larry Haney	4	4	4	4	6	15	20	30
649	Jimmie Hall	4	4	4	4	6	15	20	30
650	Sam McDowell	4	4	4	6	12	25	30	▲60
651	Jim Gosger	4	4	4	4	10	20	25	40
652	Rich Rollins	4	4	4	5	10	15	30	60
653	Moe Drabowsky	4	4	4	4	6	12	25	40
654	Oscar Gamble RC	4	4	10	20	50	100	150	300
655	John Roseboro	4	4	4	6	12	25	30	60
656	Jim Hardin	4	4	4	4	8	20	25	50
657	San Diego Padres TC	4	4	4	4	6	20	25	40
658	Ken Tatum RC	4	4	4	4	6	20	25	50
659	Pete Ward	4	4	5	10	20	40	50	80
660	Johnny Bench	12	60	80	120	▲200	300	400	800
661	Jerry Robertson	4	4	4	6	12	25	40	60
662	Frank Lucchesi MG RC	4	4	4	6	12	25	30	80
663	Tito Francona	4	4	4	4	6	20	25	60
664	Bob Robertson	4	4	4	6	12	25	30	100
665	Jim Lonborg	4	4	4	5	10	20	25	50
666	Adolpho Phillips	4	4	4	5	10	20	25	50
667	Bob Meyer	4	4	4	4	8	25	30	50
668	Bob Tillman	4	4	4	4	8	15		
669	Johnson/Lazar/Scott RC	4	4	4	4	8	25	30	80
670	Ron Santo	4	8	15	30	▲50	▲120	100	500
671	Jim Campanis	4	4	4	4	5	8	12	30
672	Leon McFadden	4	4	4	4	6	15	20	40
673	Ted Uhlaender	4	4	4	4	6	20	25	30
674	Dave Leonhard	4	4	4	4	6	12	15	40
675	Jose Cardenal	4	4	4	4	6	15	20	30
676	Washington Senators TC	4	4	5	6	10	15	25	100
677	Woodie Fryman	4	4	4	4	6	15	20	30
678	Dave Duncan	4	4	4	4	8	15	20	40
679	Ray Sadecki	4	4	4	4	6	20	25	80
680	Rico Petrocelli	4	5	10	12	25	30	60	120
681	Bob Garibaldi RC	4	4	4	5	10	20	25	100
682	Dalton Jones	4	4	4	5	10	20	25	50
683	Geishart/McRae/Simpson RC	4	6	12	15	40	50	100	300
684	Jack Fisher	4	4	4	4	6	15	20	50
685	Tom Haller	4	4	4	5	10	20	25	50
686	Jackie Hernandez	4	4	4	4	6	12	15	50
687	Bob Priddy	4	4	4	4	6	12	15	40
688	Ted Kubiak	4	4	4	4	8	15	20	40
689	Frank Tepedino RC	4	4	4	5	10	25	30	60
690	Ron Fairly	4	4	5	6	12	25	30	80
691	Joe Grzenda	4	4	4	4	6	12	15	30
692	Duffy Dyer	4	4	5	6	12	25	30	100
693	Bob Johnson	4	4	4	4	6	15	20	40
694	Gary Ross	4	4	4	4	6	20	25	40
695	Bobby Knoop	4	4	4	4	8	25	30	80
696	San Francisco Giants TC	4	4	5	6	12	30	50	50
697	Jim Hannan	4	4	4	4	8	25	30	60
698	Tom Tresh	4	6	12	15	30	40	80	250
699	Hank Aguirre	4	4	4	4	6	15	20	40
700	Frank Robinson	6	25	30	50	60	80	150	400
701	Jack Billingham	4	4	4	4	8	15	20	80
702	Johnson/Klimkowski/Zepp RC	4	4	5	6	25	80	100	300
703	Lou Marone	4	4	4	4	6	15	20	150
704	Frank Baker RC	4	4	5	6	12	25	30	80
705	Tony Cloninger	4	4	4	4	6	20	25	50

		VG 3	VgEx 4	EX 5	ExMt 6	NM 7	NmMt 8	NmMt+ 8.5	M
706	John McNamara MG RC	4	4	4	4	6	12	15	
707	Kevin Collins	4	4	4	4	8	15	20	
708	Jose Santiago	4	4	4	4	6	12	15	
709	Mike Fiore	4	4	4	4	6	15	20	
710	Felix Millan	4	4	4	4	5	15	20	
711	Ed Brinkman	4	4	4	4	6	20	25	
712	Nolan Ryan	100	▲150	200	250	500	1,000		2,5
713	Seattle Pilots TC	5	6	12	15	30	60	80	1
714	Al Spangler	4	4	4	6	12	25	30	
715	Mickey Lolich	4	8	15	20	40	50	80	3
716	Campisi/Cleveland/Guzman RC	4	4	4	4	8	25	30	
717	Tom Phoebus	4	4	4	4	8	20	25	
718	Ed Spiezio	4	4	4	4	6	15	20	
719	Jim Roland	4	4	4	4	6	20	25	
720	Rick Reichardt	4	4	5	6	12	40	60	

—Hank Aaron AS #462 PSA 9 (MT) sold for $2,005 (Mile High; 05/11)
—Hank Aaron AS #462 PSA 9 (MT) sold for $1,580 (Goodwin; 5/07)
—AL Home Run Leaders #66 PSA 9 (MT) sold for $1,105 (eBay; 4/08)
—AL Home Run Leaders #66 PSA 9 (MT) sold for $754 (eBay; 5/08)
—AL Pitching Leaders #70 PSA 9 (MT) sold for $787 (eBay; 12/07)
—V.Blue/G.Tenace #21 PSA 9 (MT) sold for $960 (eBay; 11/07)
—V.Blue/G.Tenace #21 PSA 9 (MT) sold for $730 (eBay; 7/07)
—V.Blue/G.Tenace #21 PSA 9 (MT) sold for $329 (eBay; 4/07)
—Johnny Bench #660 PSA 10 (Gem) sold for $3,553 (Mastro; 12/04)
—Johnny Bench #660 PSA 10 (Gem) sold for $3,480 (eBay; 8/07)
—Johnny Bench AS #464 PSA 9 (MT) sold for $1,217 (eBay; 9/07)
—Johnny Bench AS #464 PSA 9 (MT) sold for $1,075 (eBay; 2/07)
—Lou Brock #330 PSA 10 (Gem) sold for $431 (eBay; 4/07)
—Steve Carlton #220 PSA 10 (Gem) sold for $956 (Heritage; 10/07)
—Cincinnati Reds TC #544 PSA 10 (Gem) sold for $954 (Mile High; 8/07)
—Roberto Clemente #350 PSA 10 (Gem) sold for $5,829 (Mile High; 5/04)
—Gil Hodges #394 PSA 9 (MT) sold for $660 (eBay; 10/07)
—Gil Hodges #394 PSA 9 (MT) sold for $575 (Mile High; 2/08)
—Gil Hodges #394 PSA 9 (MT) sold for $307 (eBay; 12/06)
—Al Kaline #640 PSA 10 (Gem) sold for $2,325 (eBay; 3/07)
—Al Kaline #640 PSA 10 (Gem) sold for $1,356 (Superior; 3/05)
—Harmon Killebrew #150 PSA 10 (Gem) sold for $1,803 (eBay; 3/07)
—Jerry Koosman AS #468 PSA 9 (MT) sold for $610 (eBay; 10/07)
—Juan Marichal #210 PSA 10 (Gem) sold for $1,187 (Memory Lane; 4/07)
—Juan Marichal #210 PSA 9 (MT) sold for $405 (eBay; 4/07)
—Willie McCovey #250 PSA 10 (Gem) sold for $2,500 (eBay; 10/06)
—Willie McCovey AS #450 PSA 10 (Gem) sold for $1,986 (Mastro; 12/07)
—Denny McLain #400 PSA 10 (Gem) sold for $4,700 (REA; 4/07)
—Denny McLain AS #467 PSA 9 (MT) sold for $411 (eBay; 5/07)
—Mets Celebrate #198 PSA 10 (Gem) sold for $1,010 (eBay; 2/07)
—Mets Celebrate #198 PSA 9 (MT) sold for $278 (eBay; 9/07)
—Joe Morgan #537 PSA 10 (Gem) sold for $1,276 (Mile High; 6/06)
—Joe Morgan #537 PSA 10 (Gem) sold for $955 (eBay; 12/06)
—Thurman Munson #189 PSA 10 (Gem) (Young Collection) sold for $13,045 (SCP; 5/12)
—Thurman Munson #189 PSA 10 (Gem) sold for $9,582 (Mastro; 8/07)
—Thurman Munson #189 BVG 8.5 (NmMt+) sold for $305 (eBay; 3/07)
—New York Mets TC #1 PSA 10 (Gem) sold for $2,851 (Mile High; 2/08)
—New York Mets TC #1 PSA 9 (MT) sold for $995 (Mile High; 2/08)
—New York Mets TC #1 PSA 9 (MT) sold for $936 (eBay; 3/07)
—Gary Neibauer #384 PSA 9 (MT) sold for $428 (eBay; 1/08)
—NL ERA Leaders #67 PSA 9 (MT) sold for $459 (eBay; 4/08)
—Tony Oliva #510 PSA 10 (Gem) sold for $956 (Mile High; 8/07)
—Jim Palmer #449 PSA 10 (Gem) sold for $2,200 (eBay; 1/07)
—Jim Palmer #449 PSA 10 (Gem) sold for $1,880 (REA; 5/08)
—Jose Pena #523 PSA 9 (MT) sold for $359 (eBay; 1/08)
—Tony Perez #380 PSA 9 (MT) sold for $815 (eBay; 5/07)
—Boog Powell ALCS2 #200 PSA 9 (MT) sold for $873 (Madec; 10/06)
—Boog Powell ALCS2 #200 PSA 9 (MT) sold for $201 (eBay; 5/07)
—Brooks Robinson AS #455 PSA 9 (MT) sold for $485 (eBay; 11/06)
—Pete Rose #580 PSA 10 (Gem) sold for $5,100 (eBay; 12/06)
—Pete Rose #580 PSA 10 (Gem) sold for $3,686 (Memory Lane; 5/08)
—Pete Rose #580 PSA 10 (Gem) sold for $3,355 (Mastro; 4/07)
—Pete Rose #580 PSA 10 (Gem) sold for $2,499 (Mile High; 05/11)
—Pete Rose #580 PSA 10 (Gem) sold for $2,133 (eBay; 6/08)
—Pete Rose #580 PSA 10 (Gem) sold for $1,673 (Heritage; 5/08)
—Pete Rose AS #458 PSA 9 (MT) sold for $1,911 (Memory Lane; 12/06)
—Pete Rose AS #458 PSA 9 (MT) sold for $1,478 (eBay; 01/12)
—Nolan Ryan #712 PSA 10 (Gem) sold for $7,050 (Mastro; 12/04)
—Nolan Ryan #712 SGC 96 (MT) sold for $950 (eBay; 5/07)
—Nolan Ryan #712 GAI 9 (MT) sold for $526 (eBay; 2/08)
—Nolan Ryan #712 BVG 8.5 (NmMt+) sold for $606 (eBay; 8/07)
—Nolan Ryan NLCS3 #197 PSA 10 (Gem) sold for $3,250 (eBay; 7/07)

n Santo AS #464 PSA 9 (MT) sold for $333 (eBay; 11/06)
m Seaver #300 PSA 10 (Gem) sold for $10,645 (Memory Lane; 5/13)
llie Stargell #470 PSA 10 (Gem) sold for $2,335 (eBay; 10/06)
llie Stargell #470 PSA 10 (Gem) sold for $1,987 (Mastro; 11/06)
ly Williams #170 PSA 10 (Gem) sold for $572 (Leland's; 12/06)
arl Yastrzemski AS #461 PSA 9 (MT) sold for $1,992 (Madec; 5/07)
arl Yastrzemski AS #461 PSA 9 (MT) sold for $916 (eBay; 1/08)
arl Yastrzemski AS #461 SGC 9 (MT) sold for $405 (eBay; 1/07)

70 Topps Super

	GD 2	VG 3	VgEx 4	EX 5	ExMt 6	NM 7	NmMt 8	MT 9
Claude Osteen SP	4	4	6	12	15	30	60	
Sal Bando SP	4	4	4	4	4	8	60	100
Luis Aparicio SP	4	4	4	4	4	8	20	150
Harmon Killebrew	4	4	4	4	5	10	20	60
Tom Seaver SP	4	4	5	10	12	25	80	120
Larry Dierker	4	4	4	4	4	8	15	40
Bill Freehan	4	4	4	6	8	15	60	120
Johnny Bench	4	4	4	5	6	12	100	150
Tommy Harper	4	4	4	4	4	8	15	30
Sam McDowell	4	4	4	4	5	10	20	50
Lou Brock	4	4	4	4	5	10	25	100
Roberto Clemente	4	5	10	20	60	80	120	500
Willie McCovey	4	4	4	4	5	15	50	80
Rico Petrocelli	4	4	4	4	4	8	15	50
Phil Niekro	4	4	4	4	4	8	15	50
Frank Howard	4	4	4	4	4	8	15	80
Denny McLain	4	4	4	4	4	8	15	40
Willie Mays	4	4	6	30	40	60	120	250
Willie Stargell	4	4	4	4	5	10	40	120
Joel Horlen	4	4	4	4	4	8	15	30
Ron Santo	4	4	4	4	5	10	20	60
Dick Bosman	4	4	4	4	4	8	15	50
Tim McCarver	4	4	4	4	4	8	15	60
Hank Aaron	4	4	5	10	12	25	▲120	200
Andy Messersmith	4	4	4	4	4	8	15	40
Tony Oliva	4	4	4	4	4	8	15	120
Mel Stottlemyre	4	4	4	4	4	8	15	40
Reggie Jackson	4	4	6	15	50	60	80	200
Carl Yastrzemski	4	4	4	5	6	30	60	150
Jim Fregosi	4	4	4	4	4	8	15	60
Vada Pinson	4	4	4	4	4	8	15	60
Lou Piniella	4	4	4	4	4	8	15	40
Bob Gibson	4	4	4	4	5	10	20	100
Pete Rose	4	4	5	10	12	25	60	250
Jim Wynn	4	4	4	4	4	8	15	30
Ollie Brown SP	4	4	4	5	6	12	25	100
Frank Robinson SP	4	4	5	25	40	50	80	150
Boog Powell SP	4	6	12	50	60	80	200	
Willie Davis SP	4	4	4	6	8	15	30	80
Billy Williams SP	4	4	4	8	10	20	60	
Rusty Staub	4	4	4	5	6	12	25	80
Tommie Agee	4	4	4	5	6	12	25	80

ill Freehan #7 PSA 9 (MT) sold for $133 (eBay; 11/06)
ob Gibson #33 PSA 10 (Gem) sold for $304 (eBay; 2/08)
illy Williams #40 PSA 9 (MT) sold for $179 (eBay; 11/06)

971 Kellogg's

	GD 2	VG 3	VgEx 4	EX 5	ExMt 6	NM 7	NmMt 8	MT 9
Wayne Simpson 119 SO	4	4	4	5	6	12	120	
Wayne Simpson 120 SO	4	4	4	5	6	12	25	
Tom Seaver	4	4	8	10	20	40	80	200
Jim Perry 2238 IP	4	4	4	4	5	10	20	40
Jim Perry 2239 IP	4	4	4	4	6	12	25	
Bob Robertson 94 RBI	4	4	6	8	15	30	60	150
Bob Robertson 95 RBI	4	4	4	6	12	25	50	
Roberto Clemente	4	5	10	20	50	80	150	400
Gaylord Perry 2014 IP	4	4	4	8	10	20	40	100
Gaylord Perry 2015 IP	4	4	4	8	10	20	40	100
Felipe Alou Oakland NL	4	4	4	4	6	12	20	40
Felipe Alou Oakland AL	4	4	4	8	10	20	40	60
Denis Menke	4	4	4	8	10	20	40	60
Don Kessinger 1970, 849 Hits	4	4	4	5	6	12	25	60
Don Kessinger 1970, 850 Hits	4	4	4	5	6	12	25	50
Willie Mays	4	4	4	8	15	30	60	150

	GD 2	VG 3	VgEx 4	EX 5	ExMt 6	NM 7	NmMt 8	MT 9
11	Jim Hickman	4	4	4	4	5	10	20	60
12	Tony Oliva	4	4	4	5	10	20	40	60
13	Manny Sanguillen	4	4	4	4	5	12	25	60
14A	Frank Howard Washington NL	4	4	4	6	12	25	50	80
14B	Frank Howard Washington AL	4	4	4	8	10	20	40	
15	Frank Robinson	4	4	4	6	8	15	30	150
16	Willie Davis	4	4	4	4	5	10	20	40
17	Lou Brock	4	4	4	6	8	15	30	100
18	Cesar Tovar	4	4	4	4	5	10	20	50
19	Luis Aparicio	4	4	4	4	6	12	25	80
20	Boog Powell	4	4	4	5	6	12	25	50
21A	Dick Selma 584 SO	4	4	4	4	5	10	20	40
21B	Dick Selma 587 SO	4	4	4	5	6	12	25	50
22	Danny Walton	4	4	4	4	5	10	20	60
23	Carl Morton	4	4	4	4	5	10	20	40
24A	Sonny Siebert 1054 SO	4	4	4	4	5	10	20	40
24B	Sonny Siebert 1055 SO	4	4	4	6	8	15	30	50
25	Jim Merritt	4	4	4	4	5	10	20	40
26A	Jose Cardenal 828 Hits	4	4	4	4	5	10	20	40
26B	Jose Cardenal 829 Hits	4	4	4	5	6	12	25	50
27	Don Mincher	4	4	4	4	5	10	20	40
28B	Clyde Wright No 1970, Cal	4	4	4	4	5	10	20	50
28C	Clyde Wright 1970, Cal	4	4	4	4	5	10	20	60
29	Les Cain	4	4	4	5	6	12	25	50
30	Danny Cater	4	4	4	4	5	10	20	60
31	Don Sutton	4	4	4	5	6	12	25	60
32	Chuck Dobson	4	4	4	4	5	10	20	60
33	Willie McCovey	4	4	4	6	12	25	50	120
34	Mike Epstein	4	4	4	4	5	10	50	70
35A	Paul Blair 386 Runs	4	4	4	4	5	10	20	100
35B	Paul Blair 385 Runs	4	4	4	5	6	12	25	
36B	Gary Nolan 1970, 577 SO	4	4	4	4	5	10	20	50
36C	Gary Nolan 1970, 581 SO	4	4	4	4	5	10	20	100
37	Sam McDowell	4	4	4	5	6	12	25	60
38	Amos Otis	4	4	4	4	5	10	20	50
39A	Ray Fosse 69 RBI	4	4	4	4	5	10	20	40
39B	Ray Fosse 70 RBI	4	4	4	5	6	12	25	50
40	Mel Stottlemyre	4	4	4	5	6	12	25	50
41	Clarence Gaston	4	4	4	4	5	10	20	50
42	Dick Dietz	4	4	4	4	5	10	20	50
43	Roy White	4	4	4	4	5	10	20	50
44	Al Kaline	4	4	4	8	10	20	40	120
45	Carlos May	4	4	4	4	5	10	20	60
46A	Tommie Agee 313 RBI	4	4	4	5	6	12	25	100
46B	Tommie Agee 314 RBI	4	4	6	12	25	50	100	
47	Tommy Harper	4	4	4	4	5	10	20	40
48	Larry Dierker	4	4	4	4	5	10	20	60
49	Mike Cuellar	4	4	4	5	6	12	25	50
50	Ernie Banks	4	4	4	8	10	20	40	100
51	Bob Gibson	4	4	4	6	8	15	30	120
52	Reggie Smith	4	4	4	4	5	10	20	60
53A	Matty Alou 273 RBI	4	4	4	4	5	10	20	100
53B	Matty Alou 274 RBI	4	4	4	5	6	12	25	
54A	Alex Johnson No 1970, Angels	4	4	4	4	5	10	20	50
54B	Alex Johnson No 1970, Cal	4	4	4	4	5	10	20	100
55	Harmon Killebrew	4	4	4	8	10	20	40	100
56	Bill Grabarkewitz	4	4	4	4	5	10	20	40
57	Richie Allen	4	4	4	5	6	12	25	50
58	Tony Perez	4	4	4	8	15	30	60	100
59A	Dave McNally 1065 SO	4	4	4	5	6	12	25	80
59B	Dave McNally 1067 SO	4	5	10	20	40	80	150	
60A	Jim Palmer 564 SO	4	4	4	6	8	15	30	120
60B	Jim Palmer 567 SO	4	4	4	8	10	20	40	
61	Billy Williams	4	4	4	8	10	20	40	80
62	Joe Torre	4	4	4	6	8	15	30	80
63A	Jim Northrup 2773 AB	4	4	4	4	5	10	20	
63B	Jim Northrup 2772 AB	4	4	6	12	25	50	100	
64A	Jim Fregosi No 1970, Angels	4	4	4	6	8	15	30	
64C	Jim Fregosi 1970, Cal, 1326 Hits	4	4	4	4	5	10	20	40
64D	Jim Fregosi 1970, Cal, 1327 Hits	4	4	4	5	6	12	25	
65	Pete Rose	4	4	8	15	30	60	200	300
66B	Bud Harrelson 1970, 112 RBI	4	4	4	5	6	12	25	50
66C	Bud Harrelson 1970, 113 RBI	4	4	4	5	6	12	25	60
67	Tony Taylor	4	4	4	4	5	10	20	50
68	Willie Stargell	4	4	4	8	10	20	50	100
69	Tony Horton	4	4	4	4	5	10	20	100
70A	Claude Osteen No 1970, No #	4	4	4	6	8	15	30	

#		GD 2	VG 3	VgEx 4	EX 5	ExMt 6	NM 7	NmMt 8	MT 9
70C	Claude Osteen 1970, No. 70	4	4	4	4	5	10	20	60
71	Glenn Beckert	4	4	4	8	10	20	40	80
72	Nate Colbert	4	4	4	4	5	10	20	60
73B	Rick Monday 1970, 1705 AB	4	4	4	4	5	10	20	
73C	Rick Monday 1970, 1704 AB	4	4	4	6	8	15	30	
74A	Tommy John 444 BB	4	4	4	8	10	20	40	80
74B	Tommy John 443 BB	4	4	4	6	8	15	30	
75	Chris Short	4	4	4	8	10	20	40	150

—Richie Allen #57 PSA 10 (Gem) sold for $515 (eBay; 3/08)
—Lou Brock #17 PSA 10 (Gem) sold for $664 (eBay; 5/08)
—Willie McCovey #33 PSA 10 (Gem) sold for $335 (eBay; 3/08)
—Claude Osteen #70 (No 1970, No #) PSA 9 (MT) sold for $504 (eBay; 5/08)
—Wayne Simpson #1 (120 SO) PSA 9 (MT) sold for $459 (eBay; 4/08)

1971 O-Pee-Chee

—Bert Blyleven #26 PSA 8 (NmMt) sold for $1,305 (eBay; 4/08)
—Willie Mays #600 PSA 9 (MT) sold for $3,505 (eBay; 3/08)
—Thurman Munson #5 PSA 8 (NmMt) sold for $2,012 (eBay; 3/08)
—Pete Rose #100 SGC 96 (MT) sold for $2,386 (eBay; 09/12)

1971 Topps

#		VG 3	VgEx 4	EX 5	ExMt 6	NM 7	NmMt 8	NmMt+ 8.5	MT 9
1	Baltimore Orioles TC	5	10	20	25	50	150		
2	Dock Ellis	4	4	8	10	20	60		
3	Dick McAuliffe	4	5	10	12	25	60		
4	Vic Davalillo	4	4	6	8	15	30	50	200
5	Thurman Munson	▲30	▲50	▲60	120	400	3,000		
6	Ed Spiezio	4	4	4	8	15	30	100	325
7	Jim Holt RC	4	4	5	6	12	60	80	150
8	Mike McQueen	4	4	4	5	10	20	25	200
9	George Scott	5	10	20	25	50	100	120	200
10	Claude Osteen	4	5	10	12	25	50		
11	Elliott Maddox RC	4	4	6	8	15	30	80	200
12	Johnny Callison	4	5	10	12	25	60		
13	C.Brinkman RC/D.Moloney RC	4	4	4	4	8	30	40	120
14	Dave Concepcion RC	4	5	15	30	60	200	300	600
15	Andy Messersmith	4	4	8	10	20	60	80	275
16	Ken Singleton RC	4	4	6	8	15	30		
17	Billy Sorrell	4	4	4	4	8	15	40	120
18	Norm Miller	4	4	4	4	8	20	100	150
19	Skip Pitlock RC	4	4	4	4	8	30	100	120
20	Reggie Jackson	10	▲20	▲50	▲60	200	1,200		
21	Dan McGinn	4	4	4	5	10	20		
22	Phil Roof	4	4	4	6	12	25	50	175
23	Oscar Gamble	4	4	8	10	20	40		
24	Rich Hand RC	4	4	4	4	4	8	25	
25	Cito Gaston	4	4	8	10	30	80		
26	Bert Blyleven RC	8	25	30	▲60	▲200	800		
27	F.Cambria RC/G.Clines RC	4	4	6	8	25	30		
28	Ron Klimkowski	4	5	10	12	25	80		
29	Don Buford	4	4	4	4	8	20	40	175
30	Phil Niekro	4	4	▲12	▲15	20	▲80		
31	Eddie Kasko MG	4	4	5	6	12	30		
32	Jerry DaVanon	4	4	6	8	15	30	50	200
33	Del Unser	4	4	6	8	15	30		
34	Sandy Vance RC	4	8	15	20	40	100		
35	Lou Piniella	4	4	5	10	20	40		
36	Dean Chance	4	4	8	10	20	40		
37	Rich McKinney RC	4	4	8	10	20	40		
38	Jim Colborn RC	4	4	4	5	10	20	40	500
39	L.LaGrow RC/G.Lamont RC	4	4	5	6	12	30	60	400
40	Lee May	4	4	8	10	20	40	60	150
41	Rick Austin RC	4	4	4	4	8	15	30	
42	Boots Day	4	4	4	4	8	15	40	150
43	Steve Kealey	4	4	4	4	8	15	25	100
44	Johnny Edwards	4	4	5	6	12	25	30	150
45	Jim Hunter	4	4	5	▲15	▲25	▲60	120	400
46	Dave Campbell	4	4	4	4	8	15	40	500
47	Johnny Jeter	4	4	4	4	8	15	40	150
48	Dave Baldwin	4	4	4	4	8	15	25	150
49	Don Money	4	6	12	15	30	60		
50	Willie McCovey	4	10	15	25	40	100	300	500
51	Steve Kline RC	4	4	4	5	10	20	40	150
52	O.Brown RC/E.Williams RC	4	4	4	4	8	15	25	200

#		VG 3	VgEx 4	EX 5	ExMt 6	NM 7	NmMt 8	NmMt+ 8.5	MT 9
53	Paul Blair	4	4	6	8	15	30	50	2
54	Checklist 1	4	6	12	15	30	60		
55	Steve Carlton	4	4	▲20	▲25	▲50	100		
56	Duane Josephson	4	4	6	8	15	30		
57	Von Joshua RC	4	4	4	5	10	20		
58	Bill Lee	4	4	6	8	15	40		
59	Gene Mauch MG	4	4	4	4	8	20	40	1
60	Dick Bosman	4	8	15	20	40	100		
61	AL Batting Leaders	4	6	12	15	30	80		
62	NL Batting Leaders	4	4	6	8	15	30	50	1
63	AL RBI Leaders	4	4	5	6	12	25		
64	NL RBI Leaders	4	4	8	15	30	60	120	4
65	AL Home Run Leaders	4	5	10	12	25	50	60	3
66	NL Home Run Leaders	4	4	6	12	▲40	▲100	▲120	3
67	AL ERA Leaders	4	4	8	10	20	40	80	2
68	NL ERA Leaders	4	4	8	10	20	50	80	2
69	AL Pitching Leaders	4	4	8	10	20	50		
70	NL Pitching Leaders	4	4	6	12	25	80	100	2
71	AL Strikeout Leaders	4	4	6	8	15	30	60	3
72	NL Strikeout Leaders	4	4	8	10	20	40	80	4
73	George Brunet	4	4	4	4	8	15	40	1
74	P.Hamm RC/J.Nettles RC	4	4	4	5	10	20		
75	Gary Nolan	4	4	4	5	10	50	80	1
76	Ted Savage	4	4	5	6	12	30		
77	Mike Compton RC	4	4	4	5	10	25		
78	Jim Spencer	4	4	4	4	8	15		
79	Wade Blasingame	4	6	12	15	30	50		
80	Bill Melton	4	4	4	5	10	20		
81	Felix Millan	4	4	4	5	10	20		
82	Casey Cox	4	4	5	6	12	25		
83	T.Foli RC/R.Bobb RC	4	8	15	20	40	120		
84	Marcel Lachemann RC	4	4	5	6	12	30		
85	Billy Grabarkewitz	4	4	5	6	12	50	40	3
86	Mike Kilkenny	4	4	4	4	8	20		
87	Jack Heidemann RC	4	4	4	5	10	20		
88	Hal King	4	4	4	4	8	15	40	2
89	Ken Brett	4	4	6	8	15	40		
90	Joe Pepitone	4	4	4	5	10	25	50	2
91	Bob Lemon MG	4	4	4	6	12	25		
92	Fred Wenz	4	6	12	15	30	80		
93	N.McRae/D.Riddleberger	4	4	4	5	10	25		
94	Don Hahn RC	4	4	4	5	10	20		
95	Luis Tiant	4	4	8	10	20	40		
96	Joe Hague	4	4	6	8	15	30		
97	Floyd Wicker	4	4	4	4	8	15	50	1
98	Joe Decker RC	4	4	4	4	8	15		
99	Mark Belanger	4	4	4	5	10	30	80	4
100	Pete Rose	25	30	40	60	200	▲1,200		
101	Les Cain	4	4	4	5	10	20		
102	K.Forsch RC/L.Howard RC	4	4	4	5	10	25	60	2
103	Rich Severson RC	4	4	4	4	8	15		
104	Dan Frisella	4	4	6	8	15	30		3
105	Tony Conigliaro	4	4	6	8	15	25		2
106	Tom Dukes	4	4	4	4	8	15	40	1
107	Roy Foster RC	4	8	15	20	40	80	40	1
108	John Cumberland	4	4	4	4	8	15	50	2
109	Steve Hovley	4	4	4	5	10	20	40	1
110	Bill Mazeroski	4	4	4	8	▲25	▲60	100	3
111	L.Colson RC/B.Mitchell RC	4	8	15	20	40	80		
112	Manny Mota	4	4	5	6	12	25	80	2
113	Jerry Crider	4	4	4	4	8	20	40	1
114	Billy Conigliaro	4	6	12	15	40	60		
115	Donn Clendenon	4	4	6	8	15	30		
116	Ken Sanders	4	4	4	4	6	20	40	1
117	Ted Simmons RC	4	4	8	▲30	▲100	▲400	▲500	▲6
118	Cookie Rojas	4	4	4	4	8	15	20	
119	Frank Lucchesi MG	4	4	4	4	8	20	40	1
120	Willie Horton	4	4	4	5	10	25	50	2
121	J.Dunegan/R.Skidmore RC	4	4	4	5	10	20		
122	Eddie Watt	4	4	8	10	20	40	80	2
123A	Checklist 2 Bottom Right	4	5	10	12	25	50		
123B	Checklist 2 Centered	4	6	12	15	30	60		
124	Don Gullett RC	4	4	4	8	15	20	50	2
125	Ray Fosse	4	4	4	5	10	20	50	1
126	Danny Coombs	4	4	4	4	8	15	40	1
127	Danny Thompson RC	4	4	4	6	12	25		
128	Frank Johnson	4	4	4	5	10	20	25	20

	VG 3	VgEx 4	EX 5	ExMt 6	NM 7	NmMt 8	NmMt+ 8.5	MT 9
Aurelio Monteagudo	4	4	4	5	10	20		
Denis Menke	4	4	4	5	10	20	40	120
Curt Blefary	4	5	10	12	25	50		
Jose Laboy	4	5	10	12	25	50		
Mickey Lolich	4	5	10	20	40	80		
Jose Arcia	4	4	4	5	10	30		
Rick Monday	5	10	20	25	50	100		
Duffy Dyer	4	4	4	5	10	20	40	275
Marcelino Lopez	4	4	8	10	20	40		
J.Lis/W.Montanez RC	5	10	20	25	50	100		
Paul Casanova	4	4	4	4	8	15		
Gaylord Perry	4	4	5	10	25	80		
Frank Quilici	4	4	5	10	20	40		
Mack Jones	4	4	5	10	20	40		
Steve Blass	4	4	4	5	10	30		
Jackie Hernandez	4	4	4	5	10	20	50	200
Bill Singer	4	4	4	6	12	25		
Ralph Houk MG	4	4	6	8	15	50		
Bob Priddy	4	4	4	4	8	15		
John Mayberry	4	4	8	10	20	50		
Mike Hershberger	4	4	4	5	10	20		
Sam McDowell	4	4	4	8	15	30	50	150
Tommy Davis	4	4	4	5	10	20		
L.Allen RC/W.Llenas RC	4	4	4	5	10	20		
Gary Ross	4	6	12	15	30	60		
Cesar Gutierrez	4	4	4	4	8	20	40	150
Ken Henderson	4	4	4	5	10	20	40	120
Bart Johnson	4	6	12	15	30	100		
Bob Bailey	4	4	4	4	8	15	40	120
Jerry Reuss	4	4	4	6	12	25	60	150
Jarvis Tatum	4	4	4	4	8	15	50	150
Tom Seaver	4	▲20	▲25	▲30	▲100	250		
Coin Checklist	4	4	4	6	▲20	▲25	40	120
Jack Billingham	4	4	4	4	8	15		
Buck Martinez	4	4	4	6	12	25		
F.Duffy RC/M.Wilcox RC	4	4	4	8	15	30		
Cesar Tovar	4	4	6	8	15	30		
Joe Hoerner	4	4	5	6	12	25		
Tom Grieve RC	4	4	4	4	5	20	60	200
Bruce Dal Canton	4	4	6	8	15	30	40	150
Ed Herrmann	4	4	5	6	12	25		
Mike Cuellar	4	4	4	8	15	30	60	250
Bobby Wine	4	5	10	12	25	50		
Duke Sims	4	4	5	6	12	25	60	275
Gil Garrido	4	5	10	12	25	80		
Dave LaRoche RC	4	4	4	5	10	20		
Jim Hickman	4	4	4	5	10	25	30	400
B.Montgomery RC/D.Griffin RC	4	4	8	10	20	50		
Hal McRae	4	4	4	5	10	25	50	200
Dave Duncan	4	4	4	5	10	80	100	200
Mike Corkins	4	4	4	4	8	15	40	120
Al Kaline	4	15	20	▲30	60	300	400	3,000
Hal Lanier	4	4	4	5	10	20		
Al Downing	4	4	4	5	10	20	50	150
Gil Hodges MG	4	4	6	8	15	30		
Stan Bahnsen	4	4	4	4	8	20	100	250
Julian Javier	4	4	8	10	20	40		
Bob Spence RC	4	4	4	4	8	15		
Ted Abernathy	4	4	4	4	8	15	40	150
Bobby Valentine RC	4	4	6	10	15	40		
George Mitterwald	4	4	4	5	10	50	60	150
Bob Tolan	4	4	6	12	25	50		
Mike Andrews	4	4	4	5	10	25		
Billy Wilson	4	4	4	8	15	30		
Bob Grich RC	4	4	6	8	15	30		
Mike Lum	4	4	4	8	15	30	40	120
Boog Powell ALCS	4	4	4	8	15	40		
Dave McNally ALCS	4	4	4	6	12	25		
Jim Palmer ALCS	4	4	8	15	30	200		
Orioles Celebrate ALCS	4	6	12	15	30	120		
Ty Cline NLCS	5	10	20	25	50	120		
Bobby Tolan NLCS	4	6	12	15	30	100		
Ty Cline NLCS	4	4	5	10	20	40	80	150
Reds Celebrate NLCS	4	4	5	10	20	80		
Larry Gura RC	4	4	4	6	12	25	50	250
B.Smith RC/G.Kopacz RC	4	4	4	4	8	20		
Gerry Moses	4	4	4	8	15	40	120	

	VG 3	VgEx 4	EX 5	ExMt 6	NM 7	NmMt 8	NmMt+ 8.5	MT 9
206 Checklist 3 Orange Helmet	4	4	4	8	▲25	▲30	50	150
207 Alan Foster	4	4	4	5	10	30		
208 Billy Martin MG	4	4	5	6	12	30	80	300
209 Steve Renko	4	4	4	4	8	15		
210 Rod Carew	4	12	20	25	▲50	200	250	1,000
211 Phil Hennigan RC	4	4	4	4	8	15	40	120
212 Rich Hebner	4	4	4	4	8	25	40	120
213 Frank Baker RC	4	4	4	5	10	25		
214 Al Ferrara	4	4	4	4	8	15	40	150
215 Diego Segui	4	4	4	5	10	25	40	250
216 R.Cleveland/L.Melendez RC	4	5	10	12	25	50		
217 Ed Stroud	4	4	4	5	10	20	40	120
218 Tony Cloninger	4	4	4	5	10	20	40	150
219 Elrod Hendricks	4	4	4	4	8	15	40	150
220 Ron Santo	6	12	25	30	50	150		
221 Dave Morehead	4	4	4	5	10	20	50	150
222 Bob Watson	4	4	4	5	10	30		
223 Cecil Upshaw	4	4	4	5	10	20	40	120
224 Alan Gallagher RC	4	4	4	4	8	15		
225 Gary Peters	4	4	8	10	20	40	100	200
226 Bill Russell	4	4	8	10	20	40		
227 Floyd Weaver	4	4	4	8	15	40	40	100
228 Wayne Garrett	4	4	4	6	12	25	80	300
229 Jim Hannan	4	4	8	10	20	40	60	250
230 Willie Stargell	4	8	20	25	50	120	200	1,000
231 V.Colbert RC/J.Lowenstein RC	4	4	4	8	15	60		
232 John Strohmayer RC	4	4	5	6	12	30	40	150
233 Larry Bowa	4	4	5	10	20	40		
234 Jim Lyttle	4	4	4	8	15	100		
235 Nate Colbert	4	4	4	5	10	20		
236 Bob Humphreys	4	4	4	5	10	20	40	150
237 Cesar Cedeno RC	4	4	4	15	30	60		
238 Chuck Dobson	4	4	4	6	12	25	50	120
239 Red Schoendienst MG	4	4	8	15	25	60	150	
240 Clyde Wright	4	4	4	5	10	20	40	150
241 Dave Nelson	4	4	4	4	8	15	50	150
242 Jim Ray	4	4	4	5	10	20	40	120
243 Carlos May	4	4	5	10	20	40	60	250
244 Bob Tillman	4	4	4	5	10	20	40	100
245 Jim Kaat	4	4	4	8	15	30	60	200
246 Tony Taylor	5	10	20	25	50	100		
247 J.Cram RC/P.Splittorff RC	4	4	4	5	10	20	50	150
248 Hoyt Wilhelm	4	4	8	10	20	80	15	300
249 Chico Salmon	4	4	4	5	10	20		
250 Johnny Bench	10	25	50	60	▲200	1,000		
251 Frank Reberger	4	4	4	5	10	20		
252 Eddie Leon	4	4	5	10	20	30	50	150
253 Bill Sudakis	4	4	8	10	20	120		
254 Cal Koonce	4	4	4	5	10	20		
255 Bob Robertson	4	4	4	6	12	25	40	150
256 Tony Gonzalez	4	4	4	5	10	20	30	120
257 Nelson Briles	4	4	4	4	8	20		
258 Dick Green	5	10	20	25	50	200		
259 Dave Marshall	4	4	4	4	8	15		
260 Tommy Harper	4	4	8	10	20	100		
261 Darold Knowles	4	4	4	4	8	20	120	
262 J.Williams/D.Robinson RC	4	4	4	5	10	20	30	150
263 John Ellis	4	8	15	20	40	80		
264 Joe Morgan	4	8	15	25	50	200		
265 Jim Northrup	4	4	4	5	10	40	60	200
266 Bill Stoneman	4	4	4	8	15	40	120	
267 Rich Morales	4	4	4	5	10	20	40	200
268 Philadelphia Phillies TC	4	4	4	6	12	20	40	150
269 Gail Hopkins	4	4	4	5	10	20		
270 Rico Carty	5	6	12	15	30	200		
271 Bill Zepp	4	4	4	5	10	20	40	200
272 Tommy Helms	4	4	5	10	20	40	60	120
273 Pete Richert	4	4	8	15	40	100	150	
274 Ron Slocum	4	4	4	8	15	50		
275 Vada Pinson	5	10	20	25	50	100		
276 M.Davison RC/G.Foster RC	4	5	10	30	50	▲120		
277 Gary Waslewski	4	8	15	20	40	100		
278 Jerry Grote	4	5	10	12	25	80		
279 Lefty Phillips MG	4	4	4	5	10	20		
280 Ferguson Jenkins	4	6	12	20	▲50	▲150		
281 Danny Walton	4	4	4	8	15	30		
282 Jose Pagan	4	4	5	6	12	30	60	150

#	Player	VG 3	VgEx 4	EX 5	ExMt 6	NM 7	NmMt 8	NmMt+ 8.5	MT 9
283	Dick Such	4	4	4	6	12	25	40	150
284	Jim Gosger	4	4	4	4	8	15	40	150
285	Sal Bando	4	4	4	5	10	20	80	350
286	Jerry McNertney	4	4	4	5	10	20	40	100
287	Mike Fiore	5	10	20	25	50	60		
288	Joe Moeller	4	5	10	12	25	80		
289	Chicago White Sox TC	4	4	4	5	10	20		
290	Tony Oliva	4	6	12	25	50	80		
291	George Culver	4	4	4	4	8	15	40	150
292	Jay Johnstone	4	4	4	5	10	20		
293	Pat Corrales	4	4	4	4	8	15	40	100
294	Steve Dunning RC	6	12	25	30	60	80		
295	Bobby Bonds	4	4	5	6	12	50	60	200
296	Tom Timmermann	4	4	5	6	12	25	50	200
297	Johnny Briggs	4	4	4	6	12	25	50	175
298	Jim Nelson RC	4	4	4	6	12	25	40	150
299	Ed Kirkpatrick	4	6	12	15	30	60		
300	Brooks Robinson	8	15	30	50	120	800		
301	Earl Wilson	4	4	4	5	10	20	80	200
302	Phil Gagliano	4	4	5	6	12	25		
303	Lindy McDaniel	4	4	4	8	15	50		
304	Ron Brand	4	4	4	4	8	15	80	300
305	Reggie Smith	4	4	8	10	20	40		
306	Jim Nash	4	4	4	4	8	20	40	100
307	Don Wert	4	4	4	4	8	15		
308	St. Louis Cardinals TC	4	4	5	6	12	25	40	120
309	Dick Ellsworth	4	6	12	15	30	60		
310	Tommie Agee	4	4	5	10	20	40	50	175
311	Lee Stange	4	4	4	5	10	20	40	120
312	Harry Walker MG	4	4	4	5	10	20		
313	Tom Hall	4	4	4	4	8	15	40	300
314	Jeff Torborg	4	4	8	15	30	60		
315	Ron Fairly	4	4	4	4	8	15	40	150
316	Fred Scherman RC	4	4	4	5	10	20	40	100
317	J.Driscoll RC/A.Mangual	4	4	4	5	10	20		
318	Rudy May	4	4	5	6	12	25	60	200
319	Ty Cline	4	4	4	5	10	20	50	120
320	Dave McNally	4	4	6	8	15	100		
321	Tom Matchick	4	4	4	4	8	15	40	120
322	Jim Beauchamp	4	4	5	6	12	25		
323	Billy Champion	4	4	4	4	8	15		
324	Graig Nettles	4	4	5	10	20	60	200	575
325	Juan Marichal	4	4	▲20	▲25	30	▲80		
326	Richie Scheinblum	4	4	4	4	8	15	40	120
327	Boog Powell WS	4	4	4	8	15	30		
328	Don Buford WS	4	4	5	10	20	50	100	250
329	Frank Robinson WS	4	4	5	6	12	30	60	200
330	Reds Stay Alive WS	4	4	4	5	10	25	60	300
331	Brooks Robinson WS	4	4	4	8	15	30	60	200
332	Orioles Celebrate WS	4	4	6	12	25	50		
333	Clay Kirby	4	4	4	6	12	25		
334	Roberto Pena	4	4	5	6	12	60		
335	Jerry Koosman	4	4	4	8	15	30	80	200
336	Detroit Tigers TC	4	4	4	6	12	25	50	200
337	Jesus Alou	4	4	6	8	15	60		
338	Gene Tenace	4	4	4	6	12	60		
339	Wayne Simpson	4	4	4	5	10	20	60	300
340	Rico Petrocelli	4	4	4	6	12	25		
341	Steve Garvey RC	15	▲40	▲50	▲60	80	250	500	2,500
342	Frank Tepedino	4	4	4	5	10	25		
343	E.Acosta RC/M.May RC	4	4	4	5	10	20	50	100
344	Ellie Rodriguez	4	4	4	4	8	15	50	120
345	Joel Horlen	4	4	4	5	10	20	40	100
346	Lum Harris MG	4	4	6	8	15	50		
347	Ted Uhlaender	4	4	4	4	8	15	30	80
348	Fred Norman	4	4	4	5	10	20		
349	Rich Reese	4	4	5	10	20	40		
350	Billy Williams	4	5	10	15	▲40	▲100		
351	Jim Shellenback	12	25	50	60	120	400		
352	Denny Doyle	4	4	5	10	20	50		
353	Carl Taylor	4	4	4	5	10	20	40	150
354	Don McMahon	4	4	4	5	10	20		
355	Bud Harrelson w/Ryan	4	4	8	10	20	60		
356	Bob Locker	4	4	4	4	8	15	40	100
357	Cincinnati Reds TC	4	4	6	8	15	40	60	250
358	Danny Cater	4	4	8	15	30	40	100	150
359	Ron Reed	4	4	4	4	8	15	40	120
360	Jim Fregosi	4	4	5	6	12	80		
361	Don Sutton	4	4	4	8	▲20	▲50		
362	M.Adamson/R.Freed	4	4	4	5	10	25		
363	Mike Nagy	4	4	4	8	15	60		
364	Tommy Dean	4	4	4	4	8	15	40	
365	Bob Johnson	4	4	8	10	20	40		
366	Ron Stone	4	4	4	5	10	20		
367	Dalton Jones	4	4	4	4	8	25		
368	Bob Veale	4	4	4	5	10	20	50	
369	Checklist 4	4	4	6	10	20	30		
370	Joe Torre	4	5	10	12	25	100	120	3
371	Jack Hiatt	4	4	4	4	8	15	50	
372	Lew Krausse	4	4	4	5	10	20	40	
373	Tom McCraw	4	5	10	12	25	60		
374	Clete Boyer	4	4	4	5	10	20		
375	Steve Hargan	4	4	4	5	10	20	40	
376	C.Mashore RC/E.McAnally RC	4	4	4	4	8	15	40	
377	Greg Garrett	4	4	4	8	15	30		
378	Tito Fuentes	4	4	4	4	8	100	150	2
379	Wayne Granger	4	5	10	12	25	50		
380	Ted Williams MG	4	5	15	▲25	40	100		
381	Fred Gladding	4	4	4	8	15	80		
382	Jake Gibbs	5	10	20	25	50	100		
383	Rod Gaspar	4	4	4	8	15	30		
384	Rollie Fingers	6	12	25	50	100	500		
385	Maury Wills	4	4	4	8	15	120		
386	Boston Red Sox TC	4	4	4	8	15	30	50	
387	Ron Herbel	4	4	4	4	8	15	40	
388	Al Oliver	4	4	4	8	15	30		
389	Ed Brinkman	4	4	4	4	8	20		
390	Glenn Beckert	4	6	12	15	30	60		
391	S.Brye RC/C.Nash RC	4	4	4	6	12	25		
392	Grant Jackson	4	4	5	6	12	40		
393	Merv Rettenmund	4	4	4	8	15	40		
394	Clay Carroll	4	4	4	8	15	30	50	3
395	Roy White	4	6	12	15	30	60	60	2
396	Dick Schofield	4	4	4	5	10	25		
397	Alvin Dark MG	4	4	4	5	10	40		
398	Howie Reed	4	8	15	20	40	100		
399	Jim French	4	4	4	5	10	25	40	1
400	Hank Aaron	30	40	50	80	▲150	400	500	4,0
401	Tom Murphy	4	4	4	4	8	15	40	1
402	Los Angeles Dodgers TC	4	4	4	8	15	30	50	2
403	Joe Coleman	4	4	5	6	12	25		
404	B.Harris RC/R.Metzger RC	4	4	4	6	12	20	100	2
405	Leo Cardenas	4	4	4	4	8	15	80	1
406	Ray Sadecki	4	4	4	4	8	15	50	4
407	Joe Rudi	4	4	8	10	20	40	80	2
408	Rafael Robles	4	4	4	6	12	25		
409	Don Pavletich	4	4	4	5	10	50		
410	Ken Holtzman	4	4	4	5	10	20	60	1
411	George Spriggs	4	4	4	4	8	25		
412	Jerry Johnson	4	4	4	5	10	20		
413	Pat Kelly	4	4	8	10	20	40		
414	Woodie Fryman	4	4	4	4	8	20	40	2
415	Mike Hegan	4	4	4	4	10	20	40	
416	Gene Alley	4	4	4	5	10	20	50	1
417	Dick Hall	4	4	4	8	15	30		
418	Adolfo Phillips	4	4	4	6	12	25		
419	Ron Hansen	4	4	4	5	10	20		
420	Jim Merritt	4	4	4	6	12	25	40	1
421	John Stephenson	4	4	4	4	8	15	40	1
422	Frank Bertaina	4	5	10	12	25	50		
423	D.Saunders/T.Marting RC	4	4	4	5	10	25	50	1
424	Roberto Rodriguez	4	4	4	4	8	15		
425	Doug Rader	4	4	4	5	10	20	50	1
426	Chris Cannizzaro	4	4	4	6	12	40	1	
427	Bernie Allen	4	4	4	4	8	15	40	2
428	Jim McAndrew	4	4	4	6	12	25		
429	Chuck Hinton	4	4	8	10	20	40		
430	Wes Parker	4	4	4	5	10	20	50	2
431	Tom Burgmeier	4	4	4	5	10	20		
432	Bob Didier	4	4	4	5	10	20		
433	Skip Lockwood	4	4	4	4	8	25		
434	Gary Sutherland	8	15	30	40	60	120		
435	Jose Cardenal	4	4	4	6	12	25	40	15
436	Wilbur Wood	4	4	4	5	10	25		

Name	VG 3	VgEx 4	EX 5	ExMt 6	NM 7	NmMt 8	NmMt+ 8.5	MT 9
Danny Murtaugh MG	4	4	4	5	6	12	25	
Mike McCormick	4	4	4	5	10	20		
Greg Luzinski RC	4	4	8	10	25	50	80	200
Bert Campaneris	4	4	4	6	12	25	50	250
Milt Pappas	4	4	4	5	10	20		
California Angels TC	4	4	4	5	10	20	40	120
Rich Robertson	4	4	4	4	8	20	40	120
Jimmie Price	4	4	4	4	8	60	100	150
Art Shamsky	4	4	8	10	20	50	100	375
Bobby Bolin	4	4	4	5	10	20	50	150
Cesar Geronimo RC	4	4	5	10	20	50		
Dave Roberts	4	4	4	4	8	15	40	120
Brant Alyea	4	4	4	4	8	20	40	200
Bob Gibson	4	15	20	40	▲80	200	350	1,200
Joe Keough	4	4	4	4	8	15	40	120
John Boccabella	4	4	4	4	8	20	40	120
Terry Crowley	4	4	4	6	12	25	50	300
Mike Paul	4	4	4	5	10	20	40	200
Don Kessinger	4	4	4	5	10	25	60	400
Bob Meyer	4	4	4	4	8	15	40	120
Willie Smith	4	4	4	5	10	20	50	120
R.Lolich RC/D.Lemonds RC	4	4	4	4	8	15	40	120
Jim Lefebvre	4	4	8	10	20	120	150	200
Fritz Peterson	4	4	4	6	12	25	40	120
Jim Ray Hart	4	4	4	4	8	15		
Washington Senators TC	4	4	4	6	12	25	50	200
Tom Kelley	4	4	4	4	8	15	50	80
Aurelio Rodriguez	4	4	4	4	6	12	40	100
Tim McCarver	4	4	4	5	10	20	60	120
Ken Berry	4	4	4	5	10	20	50	350
Al Santorini	4	4	4	5	10	20	40	120
Frank Fernandez	4	4	4	4	8	15	40	100
Bob Aspromonte	4	4	4	5	10	20	60	100
Bob Oliver	4	4	4	5	10	20	40	150
Tom Griffin	4	4	4	5	10	20	40	150
Ken Rudolph	4	4	4	5	10	20		
Gary Wagner	4	8	15	20	40	50		
Jim Fairey	4	4	4	4	8	15	40	100
Ron Perranoski	4	4	4	5	10	20	80	250
Dal Maxvill	4	4	5	6	12	40		
Earl Weaver MG	4	4	4	6	12	▲30	80	200
Bernie Carbo	4	5	10	12	25	80	120	200
Dennis Higgins	4	4	4	4	8	15	40	120
Manny Sanguillen	4	4	6	8	15	30	60	150
Daryl Patterson	4	4	4	4	6	12	40	120
San Diego Padres TC	4	4	4	4	8	20	40	120
Gene Michael	4	4	4	4	8	20	40	200
Don Wilson	4	4	4	6	12	25		
Ken McMullen	4	4	4	4	8	15	40	120
Steve Huntz	4	4	4	4	8	15	60	150
Paul Schaal	4	4	4	6	12	25	40	100
Jerry Stephenson	4	4	6	8	15	40		
Luis Alvarado	4	4	4	4	8	20	40	200
Deron Johnson	4	5	10	12	25	50		
Jim Hardin	4	4	4	5	10	25		
Ken Boswell	4	6	12	15	30	60	100	150
Dave May	4	4	4	5	10	20	40	100
R.Garr/R.Kester	4	4	4	5	10	20	40	200
Felipe Alou	4	4	5	6	12	30	50	150
Woody Woodward	4	4	6	8	15	30	80	200
Horacio Pina RC	4	4	4	4	8	20		
John Kennedy	4	4	4	5	10	20		
Checklist 5	4	4	4	6	12	25	80	500
Jim Perry	4	4	4	5	10	20	120	200
Andy Etchebarren	4	4	6	8	15	30	120	400
Chicago Cubs TC	4	4	8	10	20	50	150	450
Gates Brown	4	4	5	10	20	50	60	200
Ken Wright RC	4	4	4	5	10	20		
Ollie Brown	4	4	4	4	8	15		
Bobby Knoop	4	4	4	4	8	20	80	120
George Stone	4	4	4	5	10	20	40	120
Roger Repoz	4	4	4	4	8	15	50	120
Jim Grant	4	4	4	4	8	15		
Ken Harrelson	4	4	4	4	8	20	40	150
Chris Short w/Rose	4	4	4	8	15	30		
D.Mills RC/M.Garman RC	4	4	4	4	8	15	40	100
Nolan Ryan	40	50	▲80	120	▲250	600		

#	Name	VG 3	VgEx 4	EX 5	ExMt 6	NM 7	NmMt 8	NmMt+ 8.5	MT 9
514	Ron Woods	4	4	4	5	10	20		
515	Carl Morton	4	4	4	8	15	30		
516	Ted Kubiak	4	4	4	6	12	25	40	150
517	Charlie Fox MG RC	4	4	4	4	8	15	25	200
518	Joe Grzenda	4	4	4	4	8	20	40	100
519	Willie Crawford	4	4	6	8	15	80		
520	Tommy John	4	4	5	10	25	50	80	450
521	Leron Lee	4	4	4	5	10	20	40	150
522	Minnesota Twins TC	4	4	4	5	10	▲40	50	200
523	John Odom	4	4	4	5	10	20	50	120
524	Mickey Stanley	4	4	5	6	12	40	50	200
525	Ernie Banks	10	25	50	▲80	▲150	▲500		
526	Ray Jarvis	4	4	4	4	8	15	40	100
527	Cleon Jones	4	4	4	8	15	80	120	250
528	Wally Bunker	4	4	4	4	8	15	40	120
529	Hernandez/Buckner/Perez RC	4	4	6	15	30	▲80	100	200
530	Carl Yastrzemski	15	20	25	30	50	▲150		
531	Mike Torrez	4	4	4	5	10	20	50	150
532	Bill Rigney MG	4	4	4	4	8	15	40	100
533	Mike Ryan	4	4	4	6	12	25	40	120
534	Luke Walker	4	4	4	4	8	15	40	80
535	Curt Flood	4	4	5	10	20	25	60	150
536	Claude Raymond	8	15	30	40	100			
537	Tom Egan	4	4	4	4	8	15	40	100
538	Angel Bravo	4	4	5	6	12	25		
539	Larry Brown	10	20	40	50	100	200		
540	Larry Dierker	4	4	4	4	15	20	40	100
541	Bob Burda	4	5	10	12	25	50		
542	Bob Miller	4	4	4	4	8	25		
543	New York Yankees TC	4	4	5	10	25	40		400
544	Vida Blue	4	8	15	25	▲80	150	200	300
545	Dick Dietz	4	4	4	5	10	20	40	150
546	John Matias	4	4	4	4	8	15	40	150
547	Pat Dobson	4	4	4	8	15	25	50	200
548	Don Mason	4	4	4	4	8	15	40	120
549	Jim Brewer	12	25	40	60	80	500		
550	Harmon Killebrew	4	6	20	30	▲80	100	250	600
551	Frank Linzy	6	12	25	30	60	150	200	250
552	Buddy Bradford	4	4	4	4	8	20	40	100
553	Kevin Collins	4	4	4	5	10	20		
554	Lowell Palmer	4	4	4	6	12	25		
555	Walt Williams	4	4	5	10	12	25	40	250
556	Jim McGlothlin	4	4	4	5	10	20	40	120
557	Tom Satriano	4	4	8	10	20	120	150	500
558	Hector Torres	4	4	4	4	8	15	40	150
559	Cox/Gogolewsk/Jones RC	4	4	6	12	25	50	60	150
560	Rusty Staub	4	4	5	6	12	50	80	200
561	Syd O'Brien	4	4	8	10	20	60		
562	Dave Giusti	4	4	4	8	15	30		
563	San Francisco Giants TC	4	4	4	8	15	30		
564	Al Fitzmorris	6	12	25	30	60	150		
565	Jim Wynn	4	4	4	8	▲20	25		
566	Tim Cullen	4	4	4	4	8	15	40	250
567	Walt Alston MG	4	4	4	5	20	▲30	50	150
568	Sal Campisi	4	4	6	8	15	40		
569	Ivan Murrell	4	4	4	4	8	15	30	
570	Jim Palmer	4	5	20	25	50	120	200	1,000
571	Ted Sizemore	4	4	4	6	12	25	40	120
572	Jerry Kenney	4	4	4	8	15	30	50	120
573	Ed Kranepool	4	6	12	15	30	80	120	300
574	Jim Bunning	4	4	6	8	▲30	▲50	80	200
575	Bill Freehan	4	5	10	12	25	120		
576	Garrett/Davis/Jestadt RC	4	4	4	5	10	40	50	500
577	Jim Lonborg	8	15	30	40	80	150		
578	Ron Hunt	4	4	4	4	8	15	40	100
579	Marty Pattin	4	4	12	15	20	100	150	200
580	Tony Perez	6	12	15	50	60	250	300	500
581	Roger Nelson	4	4	6	8	15	100	120	300
582	Dave Cash	4	4	6	12	25	50		
583	Ron Cook RC	4	4	4	5	10	20		
584	Cleveland Indians TC	4	4	4	4	8	20	40	120
585	Willie Davis	4	8	15	30	60	250		
586	Dick Woodson	4	4	4	8	15	30		
587	Sonny Jackson	4	4	4	4	8	20		
588	Tom Bradley RC	4	8	15	20	30	80		
589	Bob Barton	4	4	4	5	10	20	40	150
590	Alex Johnson	4	4	4	6	12	25	50	120

#	Player	VG 3	VgEx 4	EX 5	ExMt 6	NM 7	NmMt 8	NmMt+ 8.5	MT 9
591	Jackie Brown RC	4	4	4	6	12	25	40	150
592	Randy Hundley	4	4	8	10	20	40	60	250
593	Jack Aker	4	4	4	4	8	15	40	120
594	Chlupsa/Stinson/Hrabosky RC	4	4	6	12	25	50		
595	Dave Johnson	4	4	4	6	12	25	60	300
596	Mike Jorgensen	6	12	25	30	60	100		
597	Ken Suarez	4	4	4	6	12	25		
598	Rick Wise	4	4	4	4	8	20	40	120
599	Norm Cash	4	4	4	8	15	30	60	150
600	Willie Mays	12	▲50	▲60	100	250	800		
601	Ken Tatum	4	4	4	4	8	15	40	120
602	Marty Martinez	4	4	4	4	8	15	25	150
603	Pittsburgh Pirates TC	4	4	6	12	25	50	80	200
604	John Gelnar	4	4	6	8	15	40		
605	Orlando Cepeda	4	4	6	12	25	80		
606	Chuck Taylor	4	4	4	5	10	20	50	120
607	Paul Ratliff	4	4	4	4	8	15		
608	Mike Wegener	15	25	30	40	50	200		
609	Leo Durocher MG	4	4	8	10	25	80		
610	Amos Otis	4	4	6	8	20	50	60	▲500
611	Tom Phoebus	4	4	6	8	15	30	50	120
612	Camilli/Ford/Mingori RC	4	4	5	6	12	25		
613	Pedro Borbon	4	4	4	5	10	20	40	300
614	Billy Cowan	4	4	5	6	12	30	40	150
615	Mel Stottlemyre	4	4	6	12	25	50		
616	Larry Hisle	4	4	4	4	8	15	40	100
617	Clay Dalrymple	4	4	8	10	20	40	60	150
618	Tug McGraw	4	4	4	6	12	▲40	50	200
619A	Checklist 6 No Copyright No Line	4	4	5	6	12	50		
619B	Checklist 6 Copyright w/Line	4	4	5	6	12	50		
620	Frank Howard	4	4	4	6	▲25	▲30	50	150
621	Ron Bryant	4	4	4	4	8	15	40	150
622	Joe Lahoud	4	4	5	6	12	25	40	200
623	Pat Jarvis	4	4	4	5	10	20		
624	Oakland Athletics TC	4	4	5	10	20	60	100	250
625	Lou Brock	4	8	25	40	▲60	200	300	2,500
626	Freddie Patek	4	4	4	6	15	30		
627	Steve Hamilton	4	4	4	5	10	20	40	150
628	John Bateman	4	4	6	8	15	60		
629	John Hiller	4	4	4	6	12	25	50	200
630	Roberto Clemente	50	80	▲120	200	400	1,500		
631	Eddie Fisher	4	4	4	5	10	20	50	120
632	Darrel Chaney	4	4	4	5	10	20	40	120
633	Brooks/Koegel/Northey RC	4	4	4	4	8	20	40	120
634	Phil Regan	4	8	15	20	40	300		
635	Bobby Murcer	15	30	60	80	100	600		
636	Denny Lemaster	4	4	8	10	20	60	80	150
637	Dave Bristol MG	4	4	5	10	20	25	50	200
638	Stan Williams	4	4	4	6	12	25	40	
639	Tom Haller	4	5	10	12	40	120		
640	Frank Robinson	4	8	25	▲40	60	200	200	1,200
641	New York Mets TC	4	4	4	5	20	30	50	200
642	Jim Roland	4	4	5	6	12	25	50	150
643	Rick Reichardt	4	4	4	6	12	25	40	120
644	Jim Stewart SP	10	20	30	40	50	100		
645	Jim Maloney SP	4	6	12	15	25	60		
646	Bobby Floyd SP	8	15	20	25	30	60		
647	Juan Pizarro	4	6	12	15	30	60		
648	Folkers/Martinez/Matlack RC	6	12	25	30	▲50	▲120		
649	Sparky Lyle SP	12	20	25	30	▲100	▼200		
650	Richie Allen SP	8	12	20	50	100	400		
651	Jerry Robertson SP	5	10	12	15	50	80		
652	Atlanta Braves TC	4	4	8	10	25	50	80	300
653	Russ Snyder SP	4	8	15	20	30	80		
654	Don Shaw SP	4	4	6	10	20	▲50		
655	Mike Epstein SP	4	5	10	20	▲50	150		
656	Gerry Nyman SP	5	8	10	15	25	80		
657	Jose Azcue	4	4	4	8	15	25		
658	Paul Lindblad SP	4	4	6	10	25	50		
659	Byron Browne SP	4	5	10	12	25	50		
660	Ray Culp	4	4	4	8	15	30		
661	Chuck Tanner MG SP	4	4	8	10	20	50		
662	Mike Hedlund SP	12	15	20	30	50	300		
663	Marv Staehle	4	5	10	12	25	50		
664	Reynolds/Reynolds/Reynolds RC	6	10	20	30	▲80	200		
665	Ron Swoboda SP	4	6	12	25	▲50	250		
666	Gene Brabender SP	4	4	6	12	25	60		
667	Pete Ward	4	4	6	12	30	80		
668	Gary Neibauer	4	4	4	5	12	30		
669	Ike Brown SP	5	10	20	25	40	150		
670	Bill Hands	4	4	4	8	15	40		
671	Bill Voss SP	5	10	20	25	30	150		
672	Ed Crosby SP RC	4	4	6	12	25	40		
673	Gerry Janeski SP RC	4	8	15	20	50	120		
674	Montreal Expos TC	4	4	5	6	12	30	80	200
675	Dave Boswell	4	4	4	6	12	30	60	200
676	Tommie Reynolds	4	6	8	10	15	40		
677	Jack DiLauro SP	4	4	4	6	20	40		
678	George Thomas	4	4	5	8	15	30		
679	Don O'Riley	4	4	5	6	12	25	60	200
680	Don Mincher SP	4	4	6	12	25	50		
681	Bill Butler	4	4	4	5	10	20		
682	Terry Harmon	4	4	4	6	20	40		
683	Bill Burbach SP	4	4	4	8	20	30		
684	Curt Motton	4	4	4	8	15	40		
685	Moe Drabowsky	6	10	20	30	40	60		
686	Chico Ruiz SP	4	4	8	10	20	40		
687	Ron Taylor SP	4	4	6	12	25	50		
688	Sparky Anderson MG SP	4	8	15	▼30	▲60	100		
689	Frank Baker	8	10	20	25	40	50		
690	Bob Moose	4	4	4	8	15	30		
691	Bobby Heise	4	4	5	5	20	25		
692	Haydel/Moret/Twitchell RC	4	4	5	10	40	50	60	200
693	Jose Pena SP	4	5	10	20	40	150		
694	Rick Renick SP	4	4	6	12	20	50		
695	Joe Niekro	4	4	5	8	15	30		40
696	Jerry Morales	4	4	6	8	15	30		
697	Rickey Clark SP	4	4	4	8	20	50		
698	Milwaukee Brewers TC SP	4	4	8	20	30	50		
699	Jim Britton	4	4	5	10	20	30		
700	Boog Powell SP	5	15	30	40	80	200		
701	Bob Garibaldi	4	4	4	8	15	30		
702	Milt Ramirez RC	4	4	4	8	15	40		
703	Mike Kekich	4	4	4	8	15	25		
704	J.C. Martin SP	4	15	20	25	50	100		
705	Dick Selma SP	4	4	5	6	12	50		
706	Joe Foy SP	4	6	12	15	30	80		
707	Fred Lasher	4	4	8	10	20	40		
708	Russ Nagelson SP	4	8	15	20	40	120		
709	Baker/Baylor/Paciorek SP RC	10	50	60	80	▲150	400		
710	Sonny Siebert	4	4	5	10	30	40	150	25
711	Larry Stahl SP	4	5	10	12	20	40		
712	Jose Martinez	4	4	4	10	20	30		
713	Mike Marshall SP	4	4	8	10	20	60		
714	Dick Williams MG SP	4	4	6	20	30	80		
715	Horace Clarke SP	4	4	6	12	25	50		
716	Dave Leonhard	4	4	5	6	12	30	60	25
717	Tommie Aaron SP	4	4	5	15	30	50		
718	Billy Wynne	4	5	10	12	25	60		
719	Jerry May SP	4	4	4	6	15	40		
720	Matty Alou	4	4	4	12	15	30		
721	John Morris	4	4	5	6	20	25	60	25
722	Houston Astros TC SP	6	12	25	25	50	150		
723	Vicente Romo SP	4	6	12	15	50	120		
724	Tom Tischinski SP	4	5	10	12	30	40		
725	Gary Gentry SP	4	4	6	12	25	80		
726	Paul Popovich	4	4	6	8	15	30	80	20
727	Ray Lamb SP	4	4	5	10	20	50		
728	Redmond/Lampard/Williams RC	4	4	5	10	20	30	60	12
729	Dick Billings RC	4	4	5	8	25	30		
730	Jim Rooker	4	4	5	10	20	40		
731	Jim Qualls SP	10	20	40	50	▲100	200		
732	Bob Reed	4	4	4	5	10	20	60	15
733	Lee Maye SP	12	15	20	25	40	300		
734	Rob Gardner SP	4	4	8	15	40	50		
735	Mike Shannon SP	4	4	6	12	25	60		
736	Mel Queen SP	4	4	5	8	15	▲40		
737	Preston Gomez MG SP	4	6	12	15	20	50		
738	Russ Gibson SP	4	4	8	10	25	30		
739	Barry Lersch SP	4	4	6	8	15	40	80	20
740	Luis Aparicio SP	4	5	10	25	▲50	100	120	50
741	Skip Guinn	4	4	4	6	12	30		
742	Kansas City Royals TC	4	4	5	10	20	40	60	15
743	John O'Donoghue SP	8	15	25	40	60	▲150		

	VG 3	VgEx 4	EX 5	ExMt 6	NM 7	NmMt 8	NmMt+ 8.5	MT 9
Chuck Manuel SP	4	4	8	10	30	50	80	200
Sandy Alomar SP	8	15	25	30	60	80		
Andy Kosco	4	4	4	5	10	30	60	250
Severinsen/Spinks/Moore RC	4	4	5	6	25	50	60	350
John Purdin SP	8	12	15	20	50	400		
Ken Szotkiewicz RC	5	8	12	20	30	100		
Denny McLain SP	12	20	25	30	60	200		
Al Weis SP	10	12	15	20	40	120		
Dick Drago	4	4	8	10	25	50		

-Hank Aaron #400 PSA 10 (Gem) sold for $5,605 (Memory Lane; 11/04)
-Hank Aaron #400 PSA 10 (Gem) sold for $4,700 (REA; 4/07)
-Hank Aaron #400 GAI 9 (MT) sold for $810 (eBay; 8/07)
-Hank Aaron #400 GAI 9 (MT) sold for $765 (eBay; 8/07)
-AL Batting Leaders #61 PSA 9 (MT) sold for $988 (eBay; 5/07)
-AL Pitching Leaders #69 PSA 9 (MT) sold for $640 (eBay; 2/08)
-AL RBI Leaders #63 PSA 9 (MT) sold for $566 (eBay; 1/08)
-AL RBI Leaders #63 PSA 9 (MT) sold for $410 (eBay; 1/08)
-Baker/Baylor/Paciorek #709 GAI 9.5 (Gem) sold for $2,602 (eBay; 4/07)
-Baker/Baylor/Paciorek #709 SGC 92 (NmMt+) sold for $717 (eBay; 3/08)
-Ernie Banks #525 PSA 10 (Gem) sold for $5,999 (Mastro 4/03)
-Johnny Bench #250 PSA 9 (MT) sold for $1,554 (eBay; 3/07)
-Bert Blyleven #26 PSA 10 (Gem) (Young Collection) sold for $15,052 (SCP; 5/12)
-Bert Blyleven RC #26 PSA 9 (MT) sold for $3,080 (eBay; 1/13)
-Bert Blyleven #26 SGC 96 (MT) sold for $1,217 (eBay; 3/08)
-Bert Blyleven #26 PSA 8.5 (NmMt+) sold for $661 (eBay; 4/08)
-Ken Boswell #492 PSA 10 (Gem) sold for $1,058 (Mile High; 2/08)
-Steve Carlton #55 PSA 9 (MT) sold for $1,526 (eBay; 7/07)
-Orlando Cepeda #605 PSA 9 (MT) sold for $764 (eBay; 4/08)
-Orlando Cepeda #605 PSA 9 (MT) sold for $487 (eBay; 11/07)
-Orlando Cepeda #605 PSA 9 (MT) sold for $332 (eBay; 5/08)
-Roberto Clemente #630 GAI 9.5 (Gem) sold for $1,375 (eBay; 12/07)
-Roberto Clemente #630 PSA 9 (MT) sold for $4,700 (REA; 05/11)
-Roberto Clemente #630 PSA 9 (MT) sold for $4,652 (Mile High; 05/11)
-Roberto Clemente #630 SGC 96 (MT) sold for $2,064 (Memory Lane; 9/07)
-Roberto Clemente #630 PSA 9 (MT) sold for $3,781 (Goodwin; 2/07)
-Willie Davis #585 PSA 9 (MT) sold for $1,600 (eBay; 4/07)
-Dock Ellis #2 PSA 8 (NmMt) sold for $329 (eBay; 6/08)
-Dock Ellis #2 PSA 8 (NmMt) sold for $307 (eBay; 4/08)
-John Ellis #263 PSA 9 (MT) sold for $961 (eBay; 12/06)
-George Foster #276 PSA 9 (MT) sold for $2,222 (eBay; 6/08)
-George Foster #276 PSA 9 (MT) sold for $471 (eBay; 12/06)
-Bill Freehan #575 PSA 9 (MT) sold for $760 (eBay; 12/06)
-Steve Garvey #341 PSA 10 (Gem) (Young Collection) sold for $25,393 (SCP; 5/12)
-Steve Garvey #341 SGC 96 (MT) sold for $1,720 (eBay; 3/08)
-Steve Garvey #341 SGC 92 (NmMt+) sold for $510 (eBay; 12/07)
-Cito Gaston #25 PSA 9 (MT) sold for $1,533 (eBay; 3/08)
-Bob Grich #193 PSA 10 (Gem) sold for $4,570 (eBay; 3/08)
-Bob Grich #193 PSA 9 (MT) sold for $896 (eBay; 11/07)
-Gil Hodges #183 PSA 10 (Gem) sold for $1,767 (Mile High; 2/08)
-Gil Hodges #183 PSA 9 (MT) sold for $709 (eBay; 2/07)
-Indians Rookies #231 PSA 9 (MT) sold for $1,754 (eBay; 5/08)
-Reggie Jackson #20 GAI 9.5 (Gem) sold for $2,035 (Mile High; 6/05)
-Reggie Jackson #20 BVG 9 (MT) sold for $810 (eBay; 7/07)
-Fergie Jenkins #280 PSA 9 (MT) sold for $566 (eBay; 9/07)
-Tommy John #520 PSA 10 (Gem) sold for $1,085 (eBay; 02/12)
-Sparky Lyle #649 PSA 9 (MT) sold for $1,175 (eBay; 4/07)
-Juan Marichal #325 PSA 9 (MT) sold for $461 (eBay; 1/07)
-John Mayberry #148 PSA 9 (MT) sold for $1,480 (eBay; 2/08)
-John Mayberry #148 PSA 9 (MT) sold for $941 (eBay; 4/08)
-Willie Mays #600 SGC 96 (MT) sold for $3,658 (Memory Lane; 5/08)
-Willie Mays #600 PSA 9 (MT) sold for $3,158 (eBay; 4/08)
-Willie Mays #600 PSA 9 (MT) sold for $3,123 (Memory Lane; 9/07)
-Willie Mays #600 PSA 9 (MT) sold for $3,000 (eBay; 10/12)
-Willie Mays #600 SGC 96 (MT) sold for $2,498 (eBay; 5/08)
-Bill Mazeroski #110 PSA 9 (MT) sold for $2,550 (eBay; 3/08)
-Mets Rookies #648 PSA 10 (Gem) sold for $4,509 (eBay; 3/08)
-Mets Rookies #648 PSA 10 (Gem) sold for $1,928 (Mile High; 2/08)
-Joe Morgan #264 PSA 9 (MT) sold for $1,025 (eBay; 12/06)
-Thurman Munson #5 PSA 9 (MT) sold for $11,596 (Mastro; 4/07)
-Thurman Munson #5 PSA 9 (MT) sold for $8,460 (Mastro; 12/06)
-Thurman Munson #5 BVG 9 (MT) sold for $4,010 (eBay; 4/08)
-Thurman Munson #5 BGS 9 (MT) sold for $2,111 (eBay; 11/11)
-Thurman Munson #5 GAI 9 (MT) sold for $1,930 (eBay; 9/07)
-Thurman Munson #5 BVG 9 (MT) sold for $1,880 (eBay; 2/08)
-Thurman Munson #5 BVG 9 (MT) sold for $1,520 (eBay; 2/08)
-Thurman Munson #5 SGC 92 (NmMt+) sold for $1,791 (eBay; 1/08)
-Thurman Munson #5 SGC 92 (NmMt+) sold for $1,000 (eBay; 5/08)

-Phil Niekro #30 PSA 9 (MT) sold for $595 (eBay; 3/07)
-NL Pitching Leaders #70 PSA 9 (MT) sold for $561 (eBay; 10/07)
-NL Strikeout Leaders #72 PSA 10 (Gem) sold for $1,459 (Mile High; 2/08)
-Orioles Celebrate #198 PSA 9 (MT) sold for $1,125 (eBay; 6/07)
-Jim Palmer #570 PSA 10 (Gem) sold for $1,317 (Memory Lane; 6/05)
-Gaylord Perry #140 PSA 9 (MT) sold for $1,535 (eBay; 5/08)
-Boog Powell #700 PSA 9 (MT) sold for $1,410 (eBay; 10/06)
-Boog Powell ALCS #195 PSA 9 (MT) sold for $1,273 (eBay; 2/08)
-Boog Powell ALCS #195 PSA 9 (MT) sold for $463 (eBay; 11/06)
-Jim Qualls #731 PSA 9 (MT) sold for $1,235 (eBay; 2/08)
-Claude Raymond #536 PSA 8 (NmMt) sold for $1,311 (eBay; 6/08)
-Claude Raymond #536 PSA 9 (NmMt) sold for $636 (eBay; 12/06)
-Rick Renick #694 PSA 9 (MT) sold for $986 (eBay; 6/08)
-Brooks Robinson #300 PSA 9 (MT) sold for $4,051 (eBay; 11/11)
-Brooks Robinson #300 PSA 9 (MT) sold for $3,454 (eBay; 1/13)
-Brooks Robinson #300 PSA 9 (MT) sold for $3,160 (eBay; 02/12)
-Pete Rose #100 PSA 10 (Gem) sold for $7,345 (Mastro 4/05)
-Pete Rose #100 PSA 9 (MT) sold for $7,199 (Mastro; 12/06)
-Pete Rose #100 PSA 9 (MT) sold for $5,407 (Mastro 4/07)
-Pete Rose #100 BVG 9 (MT) sold for $4,225 (eBay; 4/08)
-Pete Rose #100 BVG 9 (MT) sold for $2,575 (eBay; 7/07)
-Pete Rose #100 BVG 9 (MT) sold for $1,853 (Goodwin; 2/07)
-Pete Rose #100 GAI 9 (MT) sold for $1,339 (eBay; 4/08)
-Pete Rose #100 BVG 8.5 (NmMt+) sold for $410 (eBay; 1/08)
-Pete Rose #100 BVG 8.5 (NmMt+) sold for $384 (eBay; 12/07)
-Nolan Ryan #513 GAI 9.5 (Gem) sold for $2,714 (Mile High; 3/09)
-Nolan Ryan #513 GAI 9.5 (Gem) sold for $1,321 (Madec; 5/08)
-Nolan Ryan #513 GAI 9.5 (Gem) sold for $1,089 (eBay; 10/07)
-Nolan Ryan #513 PSA 9 (MT) sold for $6,846 (Mile High; 2/08)
-Nolan Ryan #513 PSA 9 (MT) sold for $5,700 (Madec; 12/08)
-Nolan Ryan #513 PSA 9 (MT) sold for $1,109 (Mastro; 2/07)
-Nolan Ryan #513 BVG 8.5 (NmMt+) sold for $1,025 (eBay; 8/07)
-Nolan Ryan #513 8.5 (NmMt+) sold for $551 (eBay; 5/08)
-Tom Seaver #160 PSA 10 (Gem) sold for $6,270 (Mile High; 5/04)
-Tom Seaver #160 PSA 9 (MT) sold for $5,700 (eBay; 11/11)
-Jim Shellenback #351 PSA 8.5 (NmMt+) sold for $625 (eBay; 4/08)
-Ken Singleton #16 PSA 10 (Gem) sold for $6,100 (eBay; 10/07)
-Jerry Stephenson #488 PSA 9 (MT) sold for $959 (eBay; 1/08)
-Don Sutton #361 PSA 9 (MT) sold for $760 (eBay; 6/07)
-Don Sutton #361 PSA 9 (MT) sold for $329 (eBay; 4/08)
-Danny Walton #281 PSA 9 (MT) sold for $1,128 (eBay; 2/08)
-Al Weis #751 PSA 9 (MT) sold for $913 (eBay; 3/07)
-Al Weis #751 PSA 9 (MT) sold for $740 (Mile High; 2/08)
-Billy Williams #350 PSA 9 (MT) sold for $1,028 (eBay; 5/08)
-Billy Williams #350 PSA 9 (MT) sold for $611 (eBay; 2/07)
-Ted Williams #380 PSA 9 (MT) sold for $761 (eBay; 12/06)
-Maury Wills #385 PSA 9 (MT) sold for $2,025 (eBay; 10/07)
-Yankees Rookies #111 PSA 9 (MT) sold for $1,031 (eBay; 2/08)
-Carl Yastrzemski #530 GAI 10 (Perfect) sold for $682 (eBay; 3/08)
-Carl Yastrzemski #530 GAI 9.5 (Gem) sold for $350 (eBay; 3/08)
-Carl Yastrzemski #530 PSA 9 (MT) sold for $840 (eBay; 3/08)

1971 Topps Greatest Moments

		GD 2	VG 3	VgEx 4	EX 5	ExMt 6	NM 7	NmMt 8	MT 9
1	Thurman Munson DP	25	50	100	200	350			
2	Hoyt Wilhelm	5	10	20	40	250			
3	Rico Carty	4	8	15	30	150	400	500	
4	Carl Morton DP	5	10	20	40	80	150		
5	Sal Bando DP	4	5	10	50	60	80	200	
6	Bert Campaneris DP	4	4	8	15	40	120		
7	Jim Kaat	5	10	20	40	100	200	250	
8	Harmon Killebrew	10	20	40	80	250			
9	Brooks Robinson	6	12	25	50	100	400	1,000	
10	Jim Perry	4	8	15	30	300			
11	Tony Oliva	8	15	30	60	150	250	300	
12	Vada Pinson	8	15	30	60	120	300	500	
13	Johnny Bench	12	25	50	100	200	600	800	
14	Tony Perez	8	15	30	80	150	500		
15	Pete Rose DP	10	20	40	80	200	400	600	
16	Jim Fregosi DP	4	6	10	25	50			
17	Alex Johnson DP	4	5	10	20	40			
18	Clyde Wright DP	4	4	5	10	20			
19	Al Kaline DP	5	10	20	80	100	200	400	
20	Denny McLain	5	10	20	40	80	150	300	
21	Jim Northrup	4	8	15	30	60	120	400	
22	Bill Freehan	4	6	12	25	50	▲120	400	

		GD 2	VG 3	VgEx 4	EX 5	ExMt 6	NM 7	NmMt 8	MT 9
23	Mickey Lolich	4	8	15	30	60	120	250	
24	Bob Gibson DP	5	10	20	40	100	250	400	
25	Tim McCarver DP	4	5	10	20	40	120	200	
26	Orlando Cepeda DP	4	8	15	30	80	200	250	
27	Lou Brock DP	6	12	25	50	100			
28	Nate Colbert DP	4	5	10	25	40	80	150	
29	Maury Wills	5	10	20	40	120	150		
30	Wes Parker	4	8	15	30	80	150	250	
31	Jim Wynn	4	6	12	25	100	120	200	
32	Larry Dierker	4	8	15	30	60	200		
33	Bill Melton	4	5	10	20	40	80		
34	Joe Morgan	5	10	20	40	120	150		
35	Rusty Staub	4	8	15	30	60	150	250	
36	Ernie Banks DP	5	10	50	60	250	300	400	
37	Billy Williams	6	12	25	50	100	200	400	
38	Lou Piniella	4	8	15	30	80	150	250	
39	Rico Petrocelli DP	4	5	10	20	50	100	250	
40	Carl Yastrzemski DP	5	10	20	50	200	300	800	
41	Willie Mays DP	8	15	30	60	150	400	800	
42	Tommy Harper	4	8	15	30	60	120	250	
43	Jim Bunning DP	4	6	12	25	50	100	200	
44	Fritz Peterson	4	6	12	25	50	150	200	
45	Roy White	4	6	12	25	80	400		
46	Bobby Murcer	5	10	20	100	300	500	800	
47	Reggie Jackson	20	40	80	150	600			
48	Frank Howard	4	6	12	25	150			
49	Dick Bosman	4	6	12	25	50	150	200	
50	Sam McDowell DP	4	5	10	30	40	▲100	250	
51	Luis Aparicio DP	4	6	12	25	50	100	250	
52	Willie McCovey DP	4	8	15	30	80	120	350	
53	Joe Pepitone	6	12	25	50	100	175		
54	Jerry Grote	5	10	20	40	80	150	300	
55	Bud Harrelson	6	12	25	80	150			

—Lou Brock #27 PSA 7 (NM) sold for $452 (eBay; 6/07)
—Lou Brock #27 PSA 7 (NM) sold for $415 (eBay; 4/08)
—Bert Campaneris #6 PSA 8 (NmMt) sold for $405 (eBay; 5/07)
—Orlando Cepeda #26 PSA 9 (MT) sold for $924 (Mastro; 8/07)
—Nate Colbert #28 PSA 9 (MT) sold for $630 (Mastro; 8/07)
—Tommy Harper #42 PSA 9 (MT) sold for $3,523 (Mastro; 12/06)
—Bud Harrelson #55 PSA 7 (NM) sold for $434 (eBay; 6/08)
—Bud Harrelson #55 PSA 7 (NM) sold for $353 (eBay; 9/07)
—Frank Howard #48 PSA 7 (NM) sold for $350 (eBay; 5/08)
—Reggie Jackson #47 PSA 7 (NM) sold for $745 (eBay; 11/07)
—Alex Johnson #17 PSA 7 (NM) sold for $341 (eBay; 6/07)
—Harmon Killebrew #8 PSA 9 (MT) sold for $7,691 (Mastro; 12/06)
—Harmon Killebrew #8 PSA 8 (NmMt) sold for $1,095 (Mastro; 12/06)
—Harmon Killebrew #8 PSA 7 (NM) sold for $610 (eBay; 2/08)
—Mickey Lolich #23 PSA 9 (MT) sold for $1,118 (Mastro; 8/07)
—Willie Mays #41 PSA 9 (MT) sold for $5,407 (Mastro; 9/07)
—Tim McCarver #25 PSA 9 (MT) sold for $1,231 (Mastro; 8/07)
—Willie McCovey #52 PSA 9 (MT) sold for $1,139 (Mastro; 8/07)
—Carl Morton #4 PSA 8 (NmMt) sold for $566 (eBay; 1/07)
—Thurman Munson #1 PSA 7 (NM) sold for $3,050 (eBay; 11/07)
—Bobby Murcer #46 PSA 8 (NmMt) sold for $540 (Mile High; 1/07)
—Bobby Murcer #46 PSA 8 (NmMt) sold for $530 (eBay; 3/08)
—Rico Petrocelli #39 PSA 9 (MT) sold for $694 (Mastro; 8/07)
—Vada Pinson #12 PSA 9 (MT) sold for $3,523 (Mastro; 12/06)
—Brooks Robinson #9 PSA 9 (MT) sold for $5,777 (Mastro; 12/06)
—Pete Rose #15 PSA 9 (MT) sold for $4,915 (Mastro; 4/07)
—Pete Rose #15 PSA 9 (MT) sold for $3,049 (Mastro; 12/07)
—Hoyt Wilhelm #2 PSA 7 (NM) sold for $500 (eBay; 5/08)
—Clyde Wright #18 PSA 7 (NM) sold for $314 (eBay; 1/07)

1971 Topps Super

		GD 2	VG 3	VgEx 4	EX 5	ExMt 6	NM 7	NmMt 8	MT 9
1	Reggie Smith	4	4	4	4	4	6	12	50
2	Gaylord Perry	4	4	4	4	4	6	12	80
3	Ted Savage	4	4	4	4	4	5	10	20
4	Donn Clendenon	4	4	4	4	4	6	12	25
5	Boog Powell	4	4	4	4	4	6	12	30
6	Tony Perez	4	4	4	4	4	6	12	60
7	Dick Bosman	4	4	4	4	4	5	10	20
8	Alex Johnson	4	4	4	4	4	5	10	25
9	Rusty Staub	4	4	4	4	4	8	15	100
10	Mel Stottlemyre	4	4	4	4	4	5	10	60
11	Tony Oliva	4	4	4	4	4	6	12	40

		GD 2	VG 3	VgEx 4	EX 5	ExMt 6	NM 7	NmMt 8	MT
12	Bill Freehan	4	4	4	4	4	5	10	20
13	Fritz Peterson	4	4	4	4	4	5	10	20
14	Wes Parker	4	4	4	4	4	5	10	25
15	Cesar Cedeno	4	4	4	4	4	5	10	20
16	Sam McDowell	4	4	4	4	4	5	10	20
17	Frank Howard	4	4	4	4	4	5	10	20
18	Dave McNally	4	4	4	4	4	5	10	20
19	Rico Petrocelli	4	4	4	4	4	5	10	20
20	Pete Rose	4	4	6	12	15	80	200	400
21	Luke Walker	4	4	4	4	4	5	10	20
22	Nate Colbert	4	4	4	4	4	5	10	20
23	Luis Aparicio	4	4	4	4	4	8	15	
24	Jim Perry	4	4	4	4	4	5	10	40
25	Lou Brock	4	4	4	5	6	12	25	150
26	Roy White	4	4	4	4	4	5	10	20
27	Claude Osteen	4	4	4	4	4	5	10	25
28	Carl Morton	4	4	4	4	4	5	10	20
29	Rico Carty	4	4	4	4	4	5	10	20
30	Larry Dierker	4	4	4	4	4	5	10	80
31	Bert Campaneris	4	4	4	4	4	6	12	80
32	Johnny Bench	4	4	4	8	10	20	60	300
33	Felix Millan	4	4	4	4	4	6	12	150
34	Tim McCarver	4	4	4	4	4	5	10	120
35	Ron Santo	4	4	4	5	6	12	40	120
36	Tommie Agee	4	4	4	4	4	5	10	40
37	Roberto Clemente	5	10	15	30	100	150	300	500
38	Reggie Jackson	4	4	8	15	20	40	60	200
39	Clyde Wright	4	4	4	4	4	5	10	80
40	Rich Allen	4	4	4	4	4	5	10	20
41	Curt Flood	4	4	4	4	4	5	10	50
42	Ferguson Jenkins	4	4	4	4	4	6	12	60
43	Willie Stargell	4	4	4	4	4	8	20	120
44	Hank Aaron	4	4	6	12	40	50	100	200
45	Amos Otis	4	4	4	4	4	5	10	40
46	Willie McCovey	4	4	4	5	6	12	25	60
47	Bill Melton	4	4	4	4	4	5	10	25
48	Bob Gibson	4	4	6	10	20	30	60	120
49	Carl Yastrzemski	4	4	4	5	6	12	80	300
50	Glenn Beckert	4	4	4	4	4	5	10	25
51	Ray Fosse	4	4	4	4	4	5	10	20
52	Cito Gaston	4	4	4	4	4	5	10	20
53	Tom Seaver	4	4	4	6	8	40	100	150
54	Al Kaline	4	4	4	5	6	12	80	150
55	Jim Northrup	4	4	4	4	4	5	10	80
56	Willie Mays	4	5	10	25	50	60	100	400
57	Sal Bando	4	4	4	4	4	5	10	50
58	Deron Johnson	4	4	4	4	4	5	10	40
59	Brooks Robinson	4	4	4	5	6	12	25	100
60	Harmon Killebrew	4	4	4	8	10	20	40	100
61	Joe Torre	4	4	4	4	4	6	12	60
62	Lou Piniella	4	4	4	4	4	5	10	30
63	Tommy Harper	4	4	4	4	4	6	12	30

—Carl Yastrzemski #49 PSA 10 (Gem) sold for $2,003 (eBay; 7/07)

1972 Kellogg's

		VG 3	VgEx 4	EX 5	ExMt 6	NM 7	NmMt 8	MT 9	Gem 9.5/10
1A	Tom Seaver ERA 2.85	4	4	4	4	8	15	135	
1B	Tom Seaver ERA 2.81	4	4	4	4	6	12	100	
2	Amos Otis	4	4	4	4	4	4	10	60
3A	Willie Davis Runs 842	4	4	4	4	4	4	10	
3B	Willie Davis Runs 841	4	4	4	4	4	4	10	60
4	Wilbur Wood	4	4	4	4	4	4	10	40
5	Bill Parsons	4	4	4	4	4	4	10	
6	Pete Rose	4	4	4	4	8	15	40	
7A	Willie McCovey HR 360	4	4	4	4	4	6	15	
7B	Willie McCovey HR 370	4	4	4	4	4	6	15	
8	Ferguson Jenkins	4	4	4	4	4	6	15	30
9A	Vida Blue ERA 2.35	4	4	4	4	4	4	15	
9B	Vida Blue ERA 2.31	4	4	4	4	4	4	10	60
10	Joe Torre	4	4	4	4	4	4	10	
11	Merv Rettenmund	4	4	4	4	4	4	10	
12	Bill Melton	4	4	4	4	4	4	10	
13A	Jim Palmer Games 170	4	4	4	4	4	6	25	
13B	Jim Palmer Games 168	4	4	4	4	4	6	15	60
14	Doug Rader	4	4	4	4	4	4	20	30
15B	Dave Roberts NL Leader	4	4	4	4	4	4	10	60

		VG 3	VgEx 4	EX 5	ExMt 6	NM 7	NmMt 8	MT 9	Gem 9.5/10
	Bobby Murcer	4	4	4	4	4	6	15	80
	Wes Parker	4	4	4	4	4	4	10	25
A	Joe Coleman BB 394	4	4	4	4	4	4	10	
B	Joe Coleman BB 393	4	4	4	4	4	4	10	25
	Manny Sanguillen	4	4	4	4	4	4	10	60
	Reggie Jackson	4	4	4	4	5	10	25	
	Ralph Garr	4	4	4	4	4	4	10	50
	Jim Hunter	4	4	4	4	4	6	15	
	Rick Wise	4	4	4	4	4	4	10	
	Glenn Beckert	4	4	4	4	4	4	10	25
	Tony Oliva	4	4	4	4	4	4	10	50
6A	Bob Gibson SO 2577	4	4	4	4	4	6	15	
6B	Bob Gibson SO 2578	4	4	4	4	4	6	15	
7A	Mike Cuellar ERA 3.80	4	4	4	4	4	4	25	
7B	Mike Cuellar ERA 3.08	4	4	4	4	4	4	10	
8	Chris Speier	4	4	4	4	4	4	10	
9A	Dave McNally ERA 3.18	4	4	4	4	4	4	10	
9B	Dave McNally ERA 3.15	4	4	4	4	4	4	10	
0	Leo Cardenas	4	4	4	4	4	4	10	
1A	Bill Freehan Runs 497	4	4	4	4	4	4	10	
2A	Bud Harrelson Hits 634	4	4	4	4	4	4	10	
2B	Bud Harrelson Hits 624	4	4	4	4	4	4	10	
3B	Sam McDowell Less than 225	4	4	4	4	4	4	10	50
4B	Claude Osteen ERA 3.51	4	4	4	4	4	4	10	
5	Reggie Smith	4	4	4	4	4	4	10	25
6	Sonny Siebert	4	4	4	4	4	4	10	25
7	Lee May	4	4	4	4	4	4	10	60
8	Mickey Lolich	4	4	4	4	4	4	10	
9A	Cookie Rojas 2B 149	4	4	4	4	4	4	10	
9B	Cookie Rojas 2B 150	4	4	4	4	4	4	10	30
0A	Dick Drago Poyals	4	4	4	4	4	4	10	
0B	Dick Drago Royals	4	4	4	4	4	4	10	25
1	Nate Colbert	4	4	4	4	4	4	10	25
2	Andy Messersmith	4	4	4	4	4	4	10	25
3B	Dave Johnson Avg .264	4	4	4	4	4	4	10	60
4	Steve Blass	4	4	4	4	4	4	10	
5	Bob Robertson	4	4	4	4	4	4	10	
6A	Billy Williams Missed Only 1	4	4	4	4	4	6	15	
6B	Billy Williams Phrase Omitted	4	4	4	4	4	6	15	40
7	Juan Marichal	4	4	4	4	4	6	15	60
8	Lou Brock	4	4	4	4	4	6	15	
9	Roberto Clemente	4	4	6	8	15	30	100	300
0	Mel Stottlemyre	4	4	4	4	4	4	10	25
1	Don Wilson	4	4	4	4	4	4	10	30
2A	Sal Bando RBI 355	4	4	4	4	4	4	10	
2B	Sal Bando RBI 356	4	4	4	4	4	4	10	
3A	Willie Stargell 2B 197	4	4	4	4	4	6	60	
3B	Willie Stargell 2B 196	4	4	4	4	4	6	20	50
4A	Willie Mays RBI 1855	4	4	4	4	8	15	80	
4B	Willie Mays RBI 1856	4	4	4	4	8	15	50	

—Reggie Jackson #20 PSA 10 (Gem) sold for $110 (eBay; 2/08)
—Pete Rose #6 PSA 10 (Gem) sold for $182 (eBay; 2/08)

1972 Kellogg's ATG

		VG 3	VgEx 4	EX 5	ExMt 6	NM 7	NmMt 8	MT 9	Gem 9.5/10
1	Walter Johnson	4	4	4	4	5	10	30	
2	Rogers Hornsby	4	4	4	4	4	8	15	60
3	John McGraw	4	4	4	4	4	8	15	40
4	Mickey Cochrane	4	4	4	4	4	8	15	
5	George Sisler	4	4	4	4	4	8	15	60
6	Babe Ruth	4	4	4	4	8	15	30	200
7	Lefty Grove	4	4	4	4	4	8	15	
8	Pie Traynor	4	4	4	4	4	8	15	60
9	Honus Wagner	4	4	4	4	6	12	25	100
10	Eddie Collins	4	4	4	4	4	8	15	50
11	Tris Speaker	4	4	4	4	4	8	15	60
12	Cy Young	4	4	4	4	5	10	20	60
13	Lou Gehrig	4	4	4	4	6	12	25	100
14	Babe Ruth	4	4	4	4	8	15	50	120
15	Ty Cobb	4	4	4	4	6	12	25	

—Mickey Cochrane #4 PSA 10 (Gem) sold for $304 (eBay; 4/08)

1972 Topps

		VG 3	VgEx 4	EX 5	ExMt 6	NM 7	NmMt 8	NmMt+ 8.5	MT 9
1	Pittsburgh Pirates TC	4	5	10	20	40	100	150	250
2	Ray Culp	4	5	10	12	25	80	100	200
3	Bob Tolan	4	4	4	4	8	15	20	30
4	Checklist 1-132	4	4	4	4	6	12	20	200
5	John Bateman	4	4	4	4	6	12	20	80
6	Fred Scherman	4	4	4	4	5	10	12	30
7	Enzo Hernandez	4	4	4	4	5	10	12	20
8	Ron Swoboda	4	4	4	4	8	15	20	150
9	Stan Williams	4	4	4	4	5	10	12	25
10	Amos Otis	4	4	4	4	5	10	12	25
11	Bobby Valentine	4	4	4	4	5	10	12	25
12	Jose Cardenal	4	4	4	4	5	10	15	40
13	Joe Grzenda	4	4	4	4	6	12	40	150
14	Koegel/Anderson/Twitchell RC	4	4	4	4	8	15		
15	Walt Williams	4	4	4	4	5	10	12	30
16	Mike Jorgensen	4	4	4	4	5	10	15	80
17	Dave Duncan	4	4	4	4	5	10	12	50
18A	Juan Pizarro Yellow	4	4	4	4	5	10	15	60
18B	Juan Pizarro Green	4	4	4	4	5	10	15	60
19	Billy Cowan	4	4	4	4	5	10	12	20
20	Don Wilson	4	4	4	4	5	10	12	20
21	Atlanta Braves TC	4	4	4	4	5	10	12	20
22	Rob Gardner	4	4	5	6	12	25	40	250
23	Ted Kubiak	4	4	4	4	5	10	12	80
24	Ted Ford	4	4	4	4	5	10	12	40
25	Bill Singer	4	4	4	4	5	10	12	50
26	Andy Etchebarren	4	4	4	4	6	12	20	60
27	Bob Johnson	4	4	4	4	5	10	12	200
28	Gebhard/Brye/Haydel RC	4	4	4	4	5	10	12	25
29A	Bill Bonham Yellow RC	4	4	4	4	5	10	15	50
29B	Bill Bonham Green	4	4	4	4	5	10	15	40
30	Rico Petrocelli	4	4	4	4	8	15	20	30
31	Cleon Jones	4	4	4	4	5	10	12	25
32	Cleon Jones IA	4	4	4	5	10	20	30	100
33	Billy Martin MG	4	4	4	6	12	25	30	150
34	Billy Martin IA	4	4	4	4	8	15	25	120
35	Jerry Johnson	4	4	4	4	5	10	12	20
36	Jerry Johnson IA	4	4	4	4	8	15	25	100
37	Carl Yastrzemski	6	10	▲20	▲25	▲30	▲60	▲80	200
38	Carl Yastrzemski IA	4	4	▲12	▲15	20	▲30	40	100
39	Bob Barton	4	4	4	4	5	10	12	25
40	Bob Barton IA	4	5	10	12	30	50	100	200
41	Tommy Davis	4	4	4	4	5	10	12	25
42	Tommy Davis IA	4	4	4	4	5	10	12	25
43	Rick Wise	4	4	4	4	5	10	12	25
44	Rick Wise IA	4	4	4	4	8	15	25	150
45A	Glenn Beckert Yellow	4	4	4	4	5	10	12	25
45B	Glenn Beckert Green	4	4	4	4	5	10	12	60
46	Glenn Beckert IA	4	4	4	4	5	10	12	60
47	John Ellis	4	4	4	4	5	10	12	60
48	John Ellis IA	4	4	4	4	8	15	25	120
49	Willie Mays	15	▲25	▲30	▲50	▲80	120	200	500
50	Willie Mays IA	12	15	20	25	60	200		
51	Harmon Killebrew	4	4	5	15	▲30	40	50	120
52	Harmon Killebrew IA	4	4	4	5	10	20	30	100
53	Bud Harrelson	4	4	4	4	5	10	15	40
54	Bud Harrelson IA	4	4	4	4	6	12	20	100
55	Clyde Wright	4	4	4	4	5	10	12	40
56	Rich Chiles RC	4	4	4	4	5	10	12	20
57	Bob Oliver	4	4	4	4	5	10	12	25
58	Ernie McAnally	4	4	4	4	5	10	12	20
59	Fred Stanley RC	4	4	4	4	5	10	12	25
60	Manny Sanguillen	4	4	4	4	5	10	12	30
61	Burt Hooten RC	4	4	4	4	5	10	15	60
62	Angel Mangual	4	4	4	4	5	10	12	25
63	Duke Sims	4	4	4	4	5	10	12	20
64	Pete Broberg RC	4	4	4	4	5	10	12	30
65	Cesar Cedeno	4	4	4	4	5	10	12	25
66	Ray Corbin RC	4	4	4	4	5	10	12	20
67	Red Schoendienst MG	4	4	4	4	6	12	20	30
68	Jim York RC	4	4	4	4	5	10	12	40
69	Roger Freed	4	4	4	4	6	12	20	150
70	Mike Cuellar	4	4	4	4	5	10	15	25

#	Player	VG 3	VgEx 4	EX 5	ExMt 6	NM 7	NmMt 8	NmMt+ 8.5	MT 9
71	California Angels TC	4	4	4	4	5	10	12	25
72	Bruce Kison RC	4	4	4	4	6	12	15	25
73	Steve Huntz	4	4	4	4	5	10	12	20
74	Cecil Upshaw	4	4	4	4	5	10	12	30
75	Bert Campaneris	4	4	4	4	8	15	20	30
76	Don Carrithers RC	4	4	4	4	5	10	12	40
77	Ron Theobald RC	4	4	4	4	5	10	12	25
78	Steve Arlin RC	4	4	4	4	5	10	12	30
79	C.Fisk RC/C.Cooper RC	25	30	40	50	80	▲250	300	1,200
80	Tony Perez	4	4	5	6	12	25	30	100
81	Mike Hedlund	4	4	4	4	5	10	12	20
82	Ron Woods	4	4	4	4	5	10	12	60
83	Dalton Jones	4	4	4	4	5	10	12	20
84	Vince Colbert	4	4	4	4	5	10	12	30
85	NL Batting Leaders	4	4	4	4	6	12	20	200
86	AL Batting Leaders	4	4	4	4	6	12	20	80
87	NL RBI Leaders	4	4	4	6	12	25	30	100
88	AL RBI Leaders	4	4	4	4	8	15	25	80
89	NL Home Run Leaders	4	4	4	8	20	30	40	100
90	AL Home Run Leaders	4	4	4	4	6	12	15	40
91	NL ERA Leaders	4	4	4	4	6	12	20	50
92	AL ERA Leaders	4	4	4	4	6	12	15	30
93	NL Pitching Leaders	4	4	4	4	8	15	30	100
94	NL Pitching Leaders	4	4	4	4	8	15	25	150
95	NL Strikeout Leaders	4	4	4	5	10	20	25	120
96	AL Strikeout Leaders	4	4	4	4	8	15	25	80
97	Tom Kelley	4	4	4	4	4	6	8	12
98	Chuck Tanner MG	4	4	4	4	5	10	12	30
99	Ross Grimsley RC	4	4	4	4	5	10	12	50
100	Frank Robinson	4	4	6	10	20	30	40	100
101	J.R. Richard RC	4	4	4	4	6	12	15	50
102	Lloyd Allen	4	4	4	4	5	10	15	200
103	Checklist 133-263	4	4	4	4	5	10	12	20
104	Toby Harrah RC	4	4	4	4	5	10	15	40
105	Gary Gentry	4	4	4	4	5	10	12	20
106	Milwaukee Brewers TC	4	4	4	4	5	10	12	20
107	Jose Cruz RC	4	4	4	4	5	10	12	25
108	Gary Waslewski	4	4	4	4	5	10	12	30
109	Jerry May	4	4	4	4	5	10	12	20
110	Ron Hunt	4	4	4	4	5	10	12	120
111	Jim Grant	4	4	4	4	5	10	12	20
112	Greg Luzinski	4	4	4	4	5	10	12	25
113	Rogelio Moret	4	4	4	4	6	12	15	80
114	Bill Buckner	4	4	4	6	12	25	30	60
115	Jim Fregosi	4	4	4	4	5	10	12	20
116	Ed Farmer RC	4	4	4	4	5	10	12	20
117A	Cleo James Yellow RC	4	4	4	4	5	10	15	80
117B	Cleo James Green	4	4	4	4	8	15	25	250
118	Skip Lockwood	4	4	4	4	5	10	12	30
119	Marty Perez	4	4	4	4	5	10	12	25
120	Bill Freehan	4	4	4	4	6	12	20	50
121	Ed Sprague	4	4	4	4	5	10	12	20
122	Larry Biittner RC	4	4	4	4	5	10	12	50
123	Ed Acosta	4	4	4	4	5	10	12	60
124	Closter/Torres/Hambright RC	4	4	4	4	5	10	12	20
125	Dave Cash	4	4	4	4	8	15	25	80
126	Bart Johnson	4	4	4	4	5	10	12	20
127	Duffy Dyer	4	4	4	4	5	10	12	30
128	Eddie Watt	4	4	4	4	5	10	12	25
129	Charlie Fox MG	4	4	4	4	5	10	12	25
130	Bob Gibson	4	6	10	20	30	▲80	▲100	300
131	Jim Nettles	4	4	4	4	5	10	12	20
132	Joe Morgan	4	4	4	8	▲15	▲40	▲50	200
133	Joe Keough	4	4	4	4	5	10	12	60
134	Carl Morton	4	4	4	4	5	10	12	20
135	Vada Pinson	4	4	4	4	5	10	12	60
136	Darrel Chaney	4	4	4	4	5	10	12	20
137	Dick Williams MG	4	4	4	4	8	15	20	60
138	Mike Kekich	4	4	4	4	8	15	25	300
139	Tim McCarver	4	4	4	4	6	12	15	40
140	Pat Dobson	4	4	4	4	5	10	12	25
141	Capra/Stanton/Matlack RC	4	4	4	4	5	10	12	25
142	Chris Chambliss RC	4	4	4	4	6	12	15	30
143	Garry Jestadt	4	4	4	4	5	10	12	100
144	Marty Pattin	4	5	10	12	25	30		
145	Don Kessinger	4	4	4	4	5	10	12	20
146	Steve Kealey	4	4	4	4	5	10	12	20

#	Player	VG 3	VgEx 4	EX 5	ExMt 6	NM 7	NmMt 8	NmMt+ 8.5	MT 9
147	Dave Kingman RC	4	4	4	▲15	▲20	30	40	120
148	Dick Billings	4	4	4	4	5	10	12	20
149	Gary Neibauer	4	4	4	4	5	10	15	50
150	Norm Cash	4	6	12	15	30	60		
151	Jim Brewer	4	4	4	4	8	15	20	150
152	Gene Clines	4	4	4	4	5	10	12	20
153	Rick Auerbach RC	4	4	4	4	5	10	12	30
154	Ted Simmons	4	4	4	4	5	10	12	200
155	Larry Dierker	4	4	4	4	5	10	12	25
156	Minnesota Twins TC	4	4	4	4	5	10	12	25
157	Don Gullett	4	4	4	4	5	10	12	30
158	Jerry Kenney	4	4	4	4	5	10	12	25
159	John Boccabella	4	4	4	4	4	8	10	15
160	Andy Messersmith	4	4	4	4	5	10	12	25
161	Brock Davis	4	4	4	4	5	10	15	40
162	Bell/Porter/Reynolds RC	4	4	4	4	5	10	12	30
163	Tug McGraw	4	4	4	4	5	10	12	40
164	Tug McGraw IA	4	4	4	4	5	10	12	100
165	Chris Speier RC	4	4	4	4	5	10	12	25
166	Chris Speier IA	4	4	4	4	5	10	12	25
167	Deron Johnson	4		4	4	5	10	12	20
168	Deron Johnson IA	4	4	4	4	8	15	20	80
169	Vida Blue	4	4	4	4	6	12	15	100
170	Vida Blue IA	6	12	25	30	60	120	135	400
171	Darrell Evans	4	4	4	4	5	10	12	25
172	Darrell Evans IA	4	4	4	4	5	10	12	80
173	Clay Kirby	4	4	4	4	5	10	12	20
174	Clay Kirby IA	4	4	4	4	5	10	12	40
175	Tom Haller	4	4	4	4	5	10	12	20
176	Tom Haller IA	4	4	4	4	5	10	12	40
177	Paul Schaal	4	4	4	4	5	10	12	20
178	Paul Schaal IA	4	4	6	8	15	30	50	250
179	Dock Ellis	4	4	4	4	5	10	12	100
180	Dock Ellis IA	4	4	4	4	6	12	15	80
181	Ed Kranepool	4	4	4	4	6	12	15	25
182	Ed Kranepool IA	4	4	4	5	10	20	25	120
183	Bill Melton	4	4	4	4	5	10	12	40
184	Bill Melton IA	4	4	4	4	5	10	12	25
185	Ron Bryant	4	4	4	4	5	10	12	20
186	Ron Bryant IA	4	4	4	4	5	10	12	20
187	Gates Brown	4	4	4	4	5	10	12	20
188	Frank Lucchesi MG	4	4	4	4	5	10	12	20
189	Gene Tenace	4	4	4	4	6	12	15	25
190	Dave Giusti	4	4	4	4	5	10	12	50
191	Jeff Burroughs RC	4	4	4	4	6	12	20	100
192	Chicago Cubs TC	4	4	4	4	5	10	12	60
193	Kurt Bevacqua RC	4	4	4	4	5	10	12	40
194	Fred Norman	4	4	4	4	5	10	12	20
195	Orlando Cepeda	4	4	4	5	▲12	▲30	▲40	80
196	Mel Queen	4	4	4	4	5	10	12	20
197	Johnny Briggs	4	4	4	4	5	10	12	20
198	Charlie Hough RC	4	4	4	4	8	20	30	150
199	Mike Fiore	4	4	4	4	5	10	12	20
200	Lou Brock	4	4	5	10	15	▲40	50	150
201	Phil Roof	4	4	4	4	5	10	12	20
202	Scipio Spinks	4	4	4	4	5	10	12	20
203	Ron Blomberg RC	4	4	4	4	5	10	12	25
204	Tommy Helms	4	4	4	4	5	10	12	80
205	Dick Drago	4	4	4	4	5	10	12	20
206	Dal Maxvill	4	4	4	4	5	10	12	20
207	Tom Egan	4	4	4	4	5	10	12	20
208	Milt Pappas	4	4	4	4	6	12	15	25
209	Joe Rudi	4	4	4	4	5	10	12	100
210	Denny McLain	4	4	4	4	5	10	12	30
211	Gary Sutherland	4	4	4	4	5	10	12	25
212	Grant Jackson	4	4	4	4	5	10	12	20
213	Parker/Kusnyer/Silverio RC	4	4	4	4	5	10	12	40
214	Mike McQueen	4	4	4	4	5	10	12	20
215	Alex Johnson	4	4	4	4	5	10	12	20
216	Joe Niekro	4	4	4	4	6	12	15	20
217	Roger Metzger	4	4	4	4	5	10	12	30
218	Eddie Kasko MG	4	4	4	4	5	10	12	100
219	Rennie Stennett RC	4	4	4	4	6	12	20	80
220	Jim Perry	4	4	4	4	5	10	12	20
221	NL Playoffs Bucs	4	4	4	4	8	15	20	120
222	AL Playoffs B.Robinson	4	4	4	4	6	12	15	40
223	Dave McNally WS1	4	4	4	4	8	15	25	100

#	Player	VG 3	VgEx 4	EX 5	ExMt 6	NM 7	NmMt 8	NmMt+ 8.5	MT 9
	D.Johnson/M.Belanger WS2	4	4	4	6	12	25	30	350
	Manny Sanguillen WS3	4	4	4	4	6	12	15	80
	Roberto Clemente WS4	4	4	5	10	30	50	60	200
	Nellie Briles WS5	4	4	4	4	5	10	12	25
	F.Robinson/M.Sanguillen WS6	4	6	12	15	30	60	100	250
	Steve Blass WS7	4	4	4	5	10	20	30	200
	Pirates Celebrate WS	4	5	6	12	25	50	80	200
	Casey Cox	4	4	4	4	5	10	12	80
	Arnold/Barr/Rader RC	4	4	4	4	5	10	12	20
	Jay Johnstone	4	4	4	4	5	10	12	25
	Ron Taylor	4	4	4	4	5	10	12	50
	Merv Rettenmund	4	4	4	4	5	10	12	20
	Jim McGlothlin	4	4	4	4	5	10	12	20
	New York Yankees TC	4	4	4	4	6	12	15	30
	Leron Lee	4	4	4	4	5	10	12	20
	Tom Timmermann	4	4	4	4	6	12	20	150
	Richie Allen	4	4	4	4	5	10	12	30
	Rollie Fingers	4	4	4	5	▲12	▲25	▲30	▲80
	Don Mincher	4	4	4	4	5	10	12	40
	Frank Linzy	4	4	4	4	5	10	12	80
	Steve Braun RC	4	4	4	4	5	10	12	20
	Tommie Agee	4	4	4	4	6	12	15	80
	Tom Burgmeier	4	4	4	4	5	10	12	20
	Milt May	4	4	4	4	5	10	12	20
	Tom Bradley	4	4	4	4	5	10	12	20
	Harry Walker MG	4	4	4	4	5	10	12	20
	Boog Powell	4	4	5	6	12	25	30	100
	Checklist 264-394	4	4	4	4	6	12	15	80
	Ken Reynolds	4	4	4	4	5	10	12	20
	Sandy Alomar	4	4	4	4	5	10	12	25
	Boots Day	4	4	4	4	5	10	12	20
	Jim Lonborg	4	4	4	4	5	10	12	25
	George Foster	4	4	4	4	6	12	15	40
	Foor/Hosley/Jata RC	4	4	4	4	6	12	20	60
	Randy Hundley	4	4	4	4	5	10	12	20
	Sparky Lyle	4	4	4	4	5	10	12	20
	Ralph Garr	4	4	4	4	5	10	12	20
	Steve Mingori	4	4	4	4	5	10	12	20
	San Diego Padres TC	4	4	4	4	5	10	12	40
	Felipe Alou	4	6	12	15	30	80	100	200
	Tommy John	4	4	4	4	6	12	15	30
	Wes Parker	4	4	4	4	5	10	12	20
	Bobby Bolin	4	4	4	4	5	10	12	20
	Dave Concepcion	4	4	4	5	10	20	25	100
	D.Anderson RC/C.Floethe RC	4	4	4	4	4	8	10	15
	Don Hahn	4	4	4	4	5	10	12	20
	Jim Palmer	4	4	4	▲15	20	▲50	▲60	▲80
	Ken Rudolph	4	4	4	4	5	10	12	20
	Mickey Rivers RC	4	4	4	4	5	10	12	25
	Bobby Floyd	4	4	4	4	5	10	12	20
	Al Severinsen	4	4	4	4	4	8	10	15
	Cesar Tovar	4	4	4	4	5	10	12	25
	Gene Mauch MG	4	4	4	4	4	8	10	15
	Elliott Maddox	4	4	4	4	5	10	12	25
	Dennis Higgins	4	4	4	4	5	10	12	20
	Larry Brown	4	4	4	4	5	10	12	20
	Willie McCovey	4	4	4	8	15	▲40	50	▲120
	Bill Parsons RC	4	4	4	4	5	10	12	20
	Houston Astros TC	4	4	4	4	5	10	12	20
	Darrell Brandon	4	4	4	4	5	10	12	20
	Ike Brown	4	4	4	4	5	10	12	20
	Gaylord Perry	4	4	4	4	8	15	20	40
	Gene Alley	4	4	4	4	5	10	12	25
	Jim Hardin	4	4	4	4	5	10	12	20
	Johnny Jeter	4	4	4	4	5	10	12	20
	Syd O'Brien	4	4	4	4	4	8	10	15
	Sonny Siebert	4	4	4	4	5	10	12	20
	Hal McRae	4	4	4	4	5	10	12	30
	Hal McRae IA	8	15	30	40	80	100		
	Dan Frisella	4	4	4	4	8	15	25	120
	Dan Frisella IA	4	4	4	4	5	10	12	30
	Dick Dietz	4	4	4	4	5	10	12	50
	Dick Dietz IA	4	5	10	12	25	50	60	200
	Claude Osteen	4	4	4	4	5	10	12	25
	Claude Osteen IA	4	4	4	5	10	20	25	80
299	Hank Aaron	15	▲25	▲50	▲60	100	250	400	1,200
300	Hank Aaron IA	12	15	20	30	80	250		

#	Player	VG 3	VgEx 4	EX 5	ExMt 6	NM 7	NmMt 8	NmMt+ 8.5	MT 9
301	George Mitterwald	4	4	4	4	5	10	12	40
302	George Mitterwald IA	4	4	4	4	5	10	12	50
303	Joe Pepitone	4	4	4	4	5	10	12	25
304	Joe Pepitone IA	4	4	4	4	5	10	12	30
305	Ken Boswell	4	4	4	4	5	10	12	20
306	Ken Boswell IA	4	4	5	6	12	25	30	100
307	Steve Renko	4	4	4	4	5	10	12	20
308	Steve Renko IA	4	4	4	5	10	20	25	60
309	Roberto Clemente	25	▲40	▲60	80	100	▲250	▲300	600
310	Roberto Clemente IA	4	4	▲25	▲30	40	100	200	300
311	Clay Carroll	4	4	4	4	5	10	12	20
312	Clay Carroll IA	4	4	4	4	6	12	15	100
313	Luis Aparicio	4	4	4	5	10	▲30	▲40	80
314	Luis Aparicio IA	4	4	4	4	6	12	15	40
315	Paul Splittorff	4	4	4	4	5	10	12	25
316	Bibby/Roque/Guzman RC	4	4	4	4	5	10	12	20
317	Rich Hand	4	4	4	4	5	10	12	20
318	Sonny Jackson	4	4	4	4	4	8	10	15
319	Aurelio Rodriguez	4	4	4	4	5	10	12	25
320	Steve Blass	4	4	4	4	8	15	20	100
321	Joe Lahoud	4	4	4	4	5	10	12	25
322	Jose Pena	4	4	4	4	8	15	25	80
323	Earl Weaver MG	4	4	4	4	6	15	20	80
324	Mike Ryan	4	4	4	4	5	10	12	20
325	Mel Stottlemyre	4	4	4	4	5	10	12	20
326	Pat Kelly	4	4	4	4	4	8	10	15
327	Steve Stone RC	4	4	4	4	5	10	12	60
328	Boston Red Sox TC	4	4	4	4	8	15	25	150
329	Roy Foster	4	4	4	4	5	10	12	20
330	Jim Hunter	4	4	6	8	15	30	40	200
331	Stan Swanson RC	4	4	4	4	5	10	12	20
332	Buck Martinez	4	4	4	4	5	10	12	20
333	Steve Barber	4	4	4	4	5	10	12	20
334	Fahey/Mason Ragland RC	4	4	4	4	5	10	12	20
335	Bill Hands	4	4	4	4	5	10	12	20
336	Marty Martinez	4	4	4	4	6	12	20	120
337	Mike Kilkenny	4	4	4	4	5	10	12	20
338	Bob Grich	4	4	4	4	5	10	12	25
339	Ron Cook	4	4	4	4	5	10	12	20
340	Roy White	4	4	4	4	8	15	20	30
341	Joe Torre KP	4	4	4	4	5	10	12	20
342	Wilbur Wood KP	4	4	4	4	5	10	12	50
343	Willie Stargell KP	4	4	4	4	6	12	15	50
344	Dave McNally KP	4	4	4	4	5	10	12	50
345	Rick Wise KP	4	4	4	4	5	10	12	20
346	Jim Fregosi KP	4	4	5	6	8	15	20	100
347	Tom Seaver KP	4	4	4	4	8	15	20	50
348	Sal Bando KP	4	4	5	4	8	15	20	100
349	Al Fitzmorris	4	4	4	4	5	10	12	25
350	Frank Howard	4	4	4	4	5	10	12	25
351	House/Kester/Britton	4	4	4	4	5	10	12	20
352	Dave LaRoche	4	4	4	4	5	10	12	20
353	Art Shamsky	4	4	4	4	5	10	12	20
354	Tom Murphy	4	4	4	4	5	10	12	20
355	Bob Watson	4	4	4	4	4	8	10	15
356	Gerry Moses	4	4	4	4	5	10	12	20
357	Woody Fryman	4	4	4	4	5	10	12	20
358	Sparky Anderson MG	4	4	4	5	10	20	25	50
359	Don Pavletich	4	4	4	4	5	10	12	20
360	Dave Roberts	4	4	4	4	5	10	12	20
361	Mike Andrews	4	4	4	4	5	10	12	20
362	New York Mets TC	4	4	4	4	6	12	15	40
363	Ron Klimkowski	4	4	4	4	5	10	12	20
364	Johnny Callison	4	4	4	4	5	10	12	30
365	Dick Bosman	4	4	4	4	5	10	12	20
366	Jimmy Rosario RC	4	4	4	4	8	15	25	100
367	Ron Perranoski	4	4	4	4	5	10	12	25
368	Danny Thompson	4	4	4	4	4	8	10	15
369	Jim Lefebvre	4	4	4	4	6	12	15	30
370	Don Buford	4	4	4	4	5	10	12	30
371	Denny Lemaster	4	4	4	4	5	10	12	20
372	L.Clemons RC/M.Montgomery RC4	4	4	4	4	5	10	12	20
373	John Mayberry	4	4	4	4	4	8	10	40
374	Jack Heidemann	4	4	4	4	5	10	12	20
375	Reggie Cleveland	4	4	4	4	4	8	10	15
376	Andy Kosco	4	4	4	4	5	10	12	25
377	Terry Harmon	4	4	6	8	15	30		

#	Name	VG 3	VgEx 4	EX 5	ExMt 6	NM 7	NmMt 8	NmMt+ 8.5	MT 9
378	Checklist 395-525	4	4	4	4	4	10	12	20
379	Ken Berry	4	4	4	4	5	10	12	30
380	Earl Williams	4	4	4	4	5	10	12	20
381	Chicago White Sox TC	4	4	4	4	5	10	12	25
382	Joe Gibbon	4	4	4	4	5	10	12	25
383	Brant Alyea	4	4	4	4	5	10	12	25
384	Dave Campbell	4	4	4	4	5	10	12	20
385	Mickey Stanley	4	4	4	4	8	15	20	80
386	Jim Colborn	4	4	4	4	5	10	12	20
387	Horace Clarke	4	4	4	4	5	10	12	25
388	Charlie Williams RC	4	4	4	4	4	8	10	15
389	Bill Rigney MG	4	4	4	4	5	10	12	20
390	Willie Davis	4	4	4	4	5	10	12	30
391	Ken Sanders	4	4	4	4	5	10	12	20
392	F.Cambria/R.Zisk RC	4	4	4	4	6	12	15	30
393	Curt Motton	4	4	4	4	5	10	12	20
394	Ken Forsch	4	4	4	4	5	10	12	20
395	Matty Alou	4	4	8	15	30	60	80	200
396	Paul Lindblad	4	4	4	4	5	10	12	30
397	Philadelphia Phillies TC	4	4	4	4	8	15	20	80
398	Larry Hisle	4	4	4	5	10	20	25	200
399	Milt Wilcox	4	4	4	4	8	15	20	40
400	Tony Oliva	4	4	4	6	12	25	30	100
401	Jim Nash	4	4	4	4	8	15	20	50
402	Bobby Heise	4	4	4	4	5	10	15	80
403	John Cumberland	4	4	4	4	5	10	12	20
404	Jeff Torborg	4	4	4	4	5	10	12	40
405	Ron Fairly	4	4	4	4	6	12	20	50
406	George Hendrick RC	4	4	4	4	5	10	15	40
407	Chuck Taylor	4	4	4	4	5	10	12	50
408	Jim Northrup	4	4	4	5	10	20	25	50
409	Frank Baker	4	4	4	4	5	10	15	50
410	Ferguson Jenkins	4	4	4	5	10	▲30	▲40	60
411	Bob Montgomery	4	4	4	4	8	15	20	80
412	Dick Kelley	4	4	4	4	8	15	20	40
413	D.Eddy/D.Lemonds	4	4	4	4	8	15	20	60
414	Bob Miller	4	4	4	4	8	15	20	40
415	Cookie Rojas	4	4	4	4	6	12	15	40
416	Johnny Edwards	4	4	4	4	5	10	12	25
417	Tom Hall	4	4	4	4	5	10	12	20
418	Tom Shopay	4	4	4	4	5	10	12	20
419	Jim Spencer	4	4	4	4	5	10	12	40
420	Steve Carlton	4	4	6	8	25	40	50	150
421	Ellie Rodriguez	4	4	4	4	5	10	12	25
422	Ray Lamb	4	4	4	4	5	10	12	20
423	Oscar Gamble	4	4	4	4	5	10	12	20
424	Bill Gogolewski	4	4	4	4	5	10	12	20
425	Ken Singleton	4	4	4	5	10	20	25	80
426	Ken Singleton IA	4	4	4	4	8	15	20	40
427	Tito Fuentes	4	4	4	6	12	25	30	50
428	Tito Fuentes IA	4	4	4	4	5	10	12	25
429	Bob Robertson	4	4	4	5	10	20	25	50
430	Bob Robertson IA	4	4	4	4	8	15	20	30
431	Cito Gaston	4	4	4	4	5	10	12	20
432	Cito Gaston IA	4	4	4	4	5	10	12	20
433	Johnny Bench	4	20	▲30	▲40	▲60	150	200	▼600
434	Johnny Bench IA	4	4	12	20	50	100	120	600
435	Reggie Jackson	10	20	25	30	50	100	200	600
436	Reggie Jackson IA	4	5	8	15	30	80	100	300
437	Maury Wills	4	4	4	4	6	12	15	50
438	Maury Wills IA	4	4	5	10	20	40	50	300
439	Billy Williams	4	4	4	5	10	50	60	80
440	Billy Williams IA	4	4	4	4	6	12	15	40
441	Thurman Munson	10	15	▲25	▲30	40	80	100	250
442	Thurman Munson IA	4	4	6	12	▲25	40	60	200
443	Ken Henderson	4	6	12	25	50	60		
444	Ken Henderson IA	4	4	4	4	5	10	12	20
445	Tom Seaver	4	12	25	30	40	▲150	▲200	600
446	Tom Seaver IA	4	4	6	▲20	25	40	80	300
447	Willie Stargell	4	4	5	10	▲30	50	60	200
448	Willie Stargell IA	4	4	6	8	15	50	60	300
449	Bob Lemon MG	4	4	4	4	8	15	20	40
450	Mickey Lolich	4	4	4	5	10	20	25	50
451	Tony LaRussa	4	4	4	4	8	15	20	50
452	Ed Herrmann	4	4	4	4	5	10	12	25
453	Barry Lersch	4	4	4	4	8	15	20	40
454	Oakland Athletics TC	4	4	4	5	10	20	25	80

#	Name	VG 3	VgEx 4	EX 5	ExMt 6	NM 7	NmMt 8	NmMt+ 8.5	MT
455	Tommy Harper	4	4	4	4	5	10	12	3
456	Mark Belanger	4	4	4	5	10	20	25	▲5
457	Fast/Thomas/Ivie RC	4	4	4	4	6	12	20	15
458	Aurelio Monteagudo	4	4	4	4	5	10	12	2
459	Rick Renick	4	4	4	4	5	10	12	2
460	Al Downing	4	4	4	4	5	10	12	5
461	Tim Cullen	4	4	4	4	5	10	12	2
462	Rickey Clark	4	4	4	4	5	10	12	2
463	Bernie Carbo	4	4	4	8	15	30	40	8
464	Jim Roland	4	4	4	4	5	10	12	2
465	Gil Hodges MG	4	4	5	10	20	40		
466	Norm Miller	4	4	4	4	5	10	12	2
467	Steve Kline	4	4	4	4	5	10	15	12
468	Richie Scheinblum	4	4	4	4	5	10	12	2
469	Ron Herbel	4	4	4	4	5	10	12	2
470	Ray Fosse	4	4	4	4	5	10	12	5
471	Luke Walker	4	4	4	4	5	10	12	20
472	Phil Gagliano	4	4	4	4	5	10	12	20
473	Dan McGinn	4	4	4	4	5	10	12	2
474	Baylor/Harrison/Oates RC	4	4	10	15	20	25	30	60
475	Gary Nolan	4	4	4	4	5	10	12	2
476	Lee Richard RC	4	4	4	4	5	10	12	2
477	Tom Phoebus	4	4	4	4	5	10	12	20
478	Checklist 526-656	4	4	4	4	5	10	12	120
479	Don Shaw	4	4	4	4	5	10	12	20
480	Lee May	4	4	4	4	5	10	12	20
481	Billy Conigliaro	4	4	4	4	4	8	10	15
482	Joe Hoerner	4	4	4	4	8	15	20	40
483	Ken Suarez	4	4	4	4	5	10	12	20
484	Lum Harris MG	4	4	4	4	5	10	12	20
485	Phil Regan	4	4	4	4	5	10	12	40
486	John Lowenstein	4	4	4	4	8	15	20	40
487	Detroit Tigers TC	4	4	4	4	8	15	20	40
488	Mike Nagy	4	4	4	4	5	10	12	20
489	T.Humphrey RC/K.Lampard	4	4	4	5	10	20	25	250
490	Dave McNally	4	4	4	6	12	15		120
491	Lou Piniella KP	4	4	4	4	5	10	12	25
492	Mel Stottlemyre KP	4	4	4	4	6	12	15	25
493	Bob Bailey KP	4	4	5	6	12	25	30	50
494	Willie Horton KP	4	4	4	4	6	12	15	30
495	Bill Melton KP	4	4	4	4	8	15	20	40
496	Bud Harrelson KP	4	4	4	5	10	20	25	100
497	Jim Perry KP	4	4	4	4	5	10	15	50
498	Brooks Robinson KP	4	4	4	4	8	15	20	80
499	Vicente Romo	4	4	4	4	5	10	12	20
500	Joe Torre	4	4	4	5	10	20	25	120
501	Pete Hamm	4	4	4	4	8	15	20	40
502	Jackie Hernandez	4	4	4	4	5	10	12	20
503	Gary Peters	4	4	4	4	8	15	20	50
504	Ed Spiezio	4	4	4	4	5	10	12	120
505	Mike Marshall	4	4	4	4	5	10	12	30
506	Ley/Moyer/Tidrow RC	4	4	4	4	8	15	20	80
507	Fred Gladding	4	4	4	4	5	10	12	25
508	Elrod Hendricks	4	4	4	4	5	10	12	60
509	Don McMahon	4	4	4	4	5	10	12	25
510	Ted Williams MG	4	4	6	20	▲30	60	80	200
511	Tony Taylor	4	4	4	4	5	10	12	25
512	Paul Popovich	4	4	4	4	5	10	12	80
513	Lindy McDaniel	4	4	4	4	5	10	12	30
514	Ted Sizemore	4	4	4	4	5	10	15	50
515	Bert Blyleven	4	4	4	4	6	12	15	120
516	Oscar Brown	4	4	4	4	5	10	12	20
517	Ken Brett	4	4	4	4	8	20	25	60
518	Wayne Garrett	8	15	30	40	80	100		
519	Ted Abernathy	4	4	4	4	6	12	20	120
520	Larry Bowa	4	4	4	4	6	12	20	150
521	Alan Foster	4	4	4	4	5	10	12	60
522	Los Angeles Dodgers TC	4	4	4	4	5	10	15	60
523	Chuck Dobson	4	4	4	4	5	10	15	60
524	E.Armbrister RC/M.Behney RC	4	5	10	12	25	80		
525	Carlos May	4	4	8	10	20	40		
526	Bob Bailey	4	4	4	4	5	10	15	40
527	Dave Leonhard	4	4	4	4	5	10	15	100
528	Ron Stone	4	4	4	4	5	12	15	40
529	Dave Nelson	4	4	4	4	5	10	12	20
530	Don Sutton	4	4	4	6	12	▲40	▲50	▲80
531	Freddie Patek	4	4	4	4	5	10	12	20

	VG 3	VgEx 4	EX 5	ExMt 6	NM 7	NmMt 8	NmMt+ 8.5	MT 9
Fred Kendall RC	5	10	20	25	50	150		
Ralph Houk MG	4	6	12	15	30	60	100	250
Jim Hickman	4	4	4	4	5	10	12	20
Ed Brinkman	4	4	4	4	5	10	12	25
Doug Rader	4	4	4	4	5	10	12	150
Bob Locker	4	4	4	4	5	10	12	30
Charlie Sands RC	4	4	4	4	5	10	12	80
Terry Forster RC	4	4	4	4	5	10	12	20
Felix Millan	4	4	4	4	6	12	15	30
Roger Repoz	4	4	4	4	5	10	12	20
Jack Billingham	4	4	4	4	8	15	20	40
Duane Josephson	4	4	4	4	5	10	12	20
Ted Martinez	4	4	4	4	5	10	12	30
Wayne Granger	4	4	4	4	5	10	12	20
Joe Hague	4	4	4	4	5	10	12	20
Cleveland Indians TC	4	4	4	4	5	10	12	20
Frank Reberger	4	4	4	4	5	10	12	20
Dave May	4	4	4	4	5	10	12	50
Brooks Robinson	4	10	12	20	30	50	80	150
Ollie Brown	4	4	4	4	6	12	15	40
Ollie Brown IA	4	4	4	4	6	12	15	40
Wilbur Wood	4	4	4	4	5	10	12	20
Wilbur Wood IA	4	4	4	4	5	10	12	20
Ron Santo	4	4	5	6	25	▲50	▲60	100
Ron Santo IA	4	4	8	10	20	40	50	120
John Odom	4	4	4	4	5	10	12	20
John Odom IA	4	4	4	4	5	10	15	50
Pete Rose	10	▲30	▲40	50	80	150	250	600
Pete Rose IA	10	20	25	25	50	80	100	500
Leo Cardenas	4	4	4	4	5	10	12	25
Leo Cardenas IA	4	4	4	4	5	10	12	20
Ray Sadecki	4	4	4	4	6	12	20	150
Ray Sadecki IA	4	4	4	4	5	10	12	30
Reggie Smith	4	4	4	4	8	15	20	100
Reggie Smith IA	4	4	4	4	5	10	12	30
Juan Marichal	4	6	12	15	30	40	80	200
Juan Marichal IA	4	4	5	10	30	40	50	150
Ed Kirkpatrick	4	4	4	4	5	10	12	20
Ed Kirkpatrick IA	4	4	4	4	5	10	15	80
Nate Colbert	4	4	4	4	5	10	12	20
Nate Colbert IA	4	4	4	4	6	12	20	120
Fritz Peterson	4	4	4	4	5	10	12	20
Fritz Peterson IA	4	4	4	4	5	10	15	40
Al Oliver	4	4	4	4	5	15	20	30
Leo Durocher MG	4	4	4	5	15	25	30	80
Mike Paul	4	4	4	4	5	10	12	20
Billy Grabarkewitz	4	4	4	4	5	10	12	20
Doyle Alexander RC	4	4	4	4	6	20	25	30
Lou Piniella	4	4	4	4	8	15	20	30
Wade Blasingame	4	4	4	4	5	10	12	25
Montreal Expos TC	5	8	10	15	60	120		
Darold Knowles	4	4	4	4	5	10	12	20
Jerry McNertney	4	4	4	4	5	10	12	20
George Scott	4	4	4	4	6	12	15	60
Denis Menke	4	4	4	4	5	10	12	25
Billy Wilson	4	4	4	4	5	10	12	20
Jim Holt	4	4	4	4	5	10	12	120
Hal Lanier	4	4	4	4	5	10	12	30
Graig Nettles	4	4	4	5	8	12	20	40
Paul Casanova	4	4	4	4	5	10	12	20
Lew Krausse	4	4	4	4	5	10	12	20
Rich Morales	4	4	4	4	5	10	12	20
Jim Beauchamp	4	4	4	4	5	10	12	20
Nolan Ryan	40	50	60	80	100	250	500	1,200
Manny Mota	4	4	4	4	8	15	20	80
Jim Magnuson RC	4	4	4	4	5	10	12	20
Hal King	4	4	4	4	5	10	12	30
Billy Champion	4	4	4	4	5	10	12	20
Al Kaline	6	8	12	25	30	▲60	80	200
George Stone	4	4	4	4	5	10	12	20
Dave Bristol MG	4	4	4	4	5	10	15	60
Jim Ray	4	4	4	4	5	10	12	20
604A Checklist 657-787 Copyright on Right	4	4	5	4	6	8	12	30
604B Checklist 657-787 Copyright on Left	4	4	4	4	6	12	15	30
Nelson Briles	4	4	4	4	5	10	12	50

		VG 3	VgEx 4	EX 5	ExMt 6	NM 7	NmMt 8	NmMt+ 8.5	MT 9
606	Luis Melendez	4	4	4	4	5	10	12	20
607	Frank Duffy	4	4	4	4	5	10	12	20
608	Mike Corkins	4	4	4	4	5	10	12	20
609	Tom Grieve	4	4	4	4	5	10	12	25
610	Bill Stoneman	4	4	4	4	5	10	12	25
611	Rich Reese	4	4	4	4	5	10	12	20
612	Joe Decker	4	4	4	4	6	12	15	60
613	Mike Ferraro	4	4	4	4	5	10	12	20
614	Ted Uhlaender	4	4	4	4	5	10	12	50
615	Steve Hargan	4	4	4	4	5	10	12	20
616	Joe Ferguson RC	4	4	4	4	6	12	15	40
617	Kansas City Royals TC	4	4	4	4	8	12	20	20
618	Rich Robertson	4	4	4	4	5	10	12	20
619	Rich McKinney	4	4	4	5	10	20	25	250
620	Phil Niekro	4	4	5	8	20	50	60	350
621	Commish Award	4	4	4	4	5	10	12	50
622	MVP Award	4	4	4	4	6	12	15	30
623	Cy Young Award	4	4	4	4	6	15	30	40
624	Minor Lg POY Award	4	4	4	4	8	15		
625	Rookie of the Year	4	4	4	4	5	15	20	50
626	Babe Ruth Award	4	6	8	10	15	25	40	60
627	Moe Drabowsky	4	4	5	6	12	25		
628	Terry Crowley	4	4	4	4	5	10	12	25
629	Paul Doyle	4	4	4	4	5	10	12	25
630	Rich Hebner	4	4	4	4	6	12	15	30
631	John Strohmayer	4	4	4	4	5	10	12	30
632	Mike Hegan	4	4	4	4	5	10	15	60
633	Jack Hiatt	4	4	4	4	5	10	12	25
634	Dick Woodson	4	4	4	4	5	10	12	25
635	Don Money	4	4	4	4	5	15	20	50
636	Bill Lee	4	4	4	4	5	10	20	60
637	Preston Gomez MG	4	4	4	4	5	10	12	30
638	Ken Wright	4	4	4	4	5	10	15	40
639	J.C. Martin	4	4	4	4	5	10	12	40
640	Joe Coleman	4	4	4	4	5	10	12	25
641	Mike Lum	4	4	4	6	12	25	30	80
642	Dennis Riddleberger RC	4	4	4	4	5	10	12	20
643	Russ Gibson	4	4	4	4	5	10	12	60
644	Bernie Allen	4	4	4	4	5	10	12	60
645	Jim Maloney	4	4	4	4	6	12	20	50
646	Chico Salmon	4	4	4	4	5	10	12	200
647	Bob Moose	4	4	4	4	6	12	15	60
648	Jim Lyttle	4	4	4	4	5	10	12	25
649	Pete Richert	4	4	4	4	5	10	12	20
650	Sal Bando	4	4	4	4	5	20	40	80
651	Cincinnati Reds TC	4	4	4	4	6	15	20	100
652	Marcelino Lopez	4	4	4	4	5	10	12	20
653	Jim Fairey	4	4	4	4	5	10	12	30
654	Horacio Pina	4	4	4	4	5	10	12	60
655	Jerry Grote	4	8	15	20	40	80		
656	Rudy May	4	4	4	4	5	10	12	25
657	Bobby Wine	4	4	4	4	8	25	30	40
658	Steve Dunning	4	4	8	10	20	50	60	300
659	Bob Aspromonte	4	4	4	4	8	15	20	50
660	Paul Blair	4	4	4	6	15	20	40	60
661	Bill Virdon MG	4	4	4	6	8	15	50	100
662	Stan Bahnsen	4	4	4	4	5	10	20	80
663	Fran Healy RC	4	4	5	8	15	25	40	50
664	Bobby Knoop	4	4	4	4	8	15	25	40
665	Chris Short	4	4	5	6	12	25	30	50
666	Hector Torres	4	4	4	5	10	25	30	50
667	Ray Newman RC	4	4	5	6	12	25	30	120
668	Texas Rangers TC	4	5	8	10	20	30	50	60
669	Willie Crawford	4	4	4	4	5	10	20	50
670	Ken Holtzman	4	5	10	12	25	50		
671	Donn Clendenon	4	4	4	5	10	30	25	50
672	Archie Reynolds	4	4	4	5	10	20	25	30
673	Dave Marshall	4	5	10	12	25	50		
674	John Kennedy	4	4	4	5	10	20	30	80
675	Pat Jarvis	4	4	4	4	8	20	25	30
676	Danny Cater	4	4	5	6	12	25	30	150
677	Ivan Murrell	4	4	4	4	8	15	20	50
678	Steve Luebber RC	4	4	4	4	8	15	30	40
679	B.Fenwick RC/B.Stinson	4	4	4	4	8	15	25	30
680	Dave Johnson	4	4	4	5	10	25	30	50
681	Bobby Pfeil	4	4	4	5	10	25	25	100
682	Mike McCormick	4	4	4	5	10	20	30	80

#		VG 3	VgEx 4	EX 5	ExMt 6	NM 7	NmMt 8	NmMt+ 8.5	MT 9
683	Steve Hovley	4	4	6	8	15	25		
684	Hal Breeden RC	4	4	4	4	8	15	20	30
685	Joel Horlen	4	4	4	4	8	15	20	30
686	Steve Garvey	4	8	15	30	▲60	100	150	600
687	Del Unser	4	5	6	8	12	25		
688	St. Louis Cardinals TC	4	4	5	8	12	25	30	50
689	Eddie Fisher	4	4	4	4	8	▲25	▲30	50
690	Willie Montanez	4	4	4	6	12	30		50
691	Curt Blefary	4	4	4	5	10	20	30	100
692	Curt Blefary IA	4	4	4	5	10	30	40	120
693	Alan Gallagher	4	5	8	12	20	30		
694	Alan Gallagher IA	4	4	5	6	12	25	30	75
695	Rod Carew	5	15	40	▲80	▲100	150	250	600
696	Rod Carew IA	5	8	15	30	40	60	120	500
697	Jerry Koosman	4	4	5	6	12	25	30	80
698	Jerry Koosman IA	4	4	8	10	20	50		
699	Bobby Murcer	4	4	8	15	50	80	100	150
700	Bobby Murcer IA	4	4	8	10	30	50	60	200
701	Jose Pagan	4	4	4	4	8	20	25	50
702	Jose Pagan IA	4	4	5	8	12	40	60	100
703	Doug Griffin	4	4	4	4	8	25	30	40
704	Doug Griffin IA	4	4	4	5	10	25	30	150
705	Pat Corrales	4	4	4	15	20	25	30	50
706	Pat Corrales IA	4	4	4	6	12	25	30	80
707	Tim Foli	4	4	4	5	10	20	25	40
708	Tim Foli IA	6	12	25	30	60	150		
709	Jim Kaat	4	4	4	6	12	40	50	60
710	Jim Kaat IA	4	4	6	8	25	30	40	80
711	Bobby Bonds	4	4	5	6	12	30	40	50
712	Bobby Bonds IA	4	4	5	6	12	30	40	60
713	Gene Michael	4	4	8	10	20	40	50	200
714	Gene Michael IA	4	4	8	15	30	50	80	300
715	Mike Epstein	4	4	6	8	15	30	40	100
716	Jesus Alou	4	4	5	6	12	30		
717	Bruce Dal Canton	4	4	4	5	10	25	30	100
718	Del Rice MG	4	4	4	4	8	15	20	60
719	Cesar Geronimo	4	4	4	5	10	30	40	80
720	Sam McDowell	4	4	4	4	10	30	40	50
721	Eddie Leon	4	4	4	4	8	15	20	30
722	Bill Sudakis	4	4	4	5	10	20	30	80
723	Al Santorini	4	4	8	10	20	40	60	350
724	Curtis/Hinton/Scott RC	4	4	8	10	20	40	50	60
725	Dick McAuliffe	4	4	4	4	8	25	30	60
726	Dick Selma	4	4	4	4	8	15	20	30
727	Jose Laboy	4	4	4	5	10	20	25	40
728	Gail Hopkins	4	4	4	6	12	30	40	250
729	Bob Veale	4	4	4	5	10	20	25	50
730	Rick Monday	4	4	6	8	15	40	50	120
731	Baltimore Orioles TC	4	5	6	8	15	30	40	60
732	George Culver	4	4	4	4	8	15	20	50
733	Jim Ray Hart	4	4	4	4	8	25	30	50
734	Bob Burda	4	4	4	8	15	30	40	200
735	Diego Segui	4	4	4	4	8	25	30	40
736	Bill Russell	4	4	4	5	8	20	25	50
737	Len Randle RC	4	4	6	8	15	30	60	300
738	Jim Merritt	4	4	4	4	8	20	25	30
739	Don Mason	4	4	4	4	8	15	20	40
740	Rico Carty	4	4	6	8	15	30	40	150
741	Hutton/Milner/Miller RC	4	4	4	8	15	30	40	50
742	Jim Rooker	4	4	4	4	8	15	20	40
743	Cesar Gutierrez	4	4	4	4	12	20	25	30
744	Jim Slaton RC	4	4	4	4	8	15	20	40
745	Julian Javier	4	4	4	5	10	20	25	80
746	Lowell Palmer	4	4	4	4	8	20	25	50
747	Jim Stewart	4	4	4	4	8	25	30	60
748	Phil Hennigan	4	4	4	4	8	15	20	30
749	Walt Alston MG	4	4	5	10	20	25	40	60
750	Willie Horton	4	4	4	6	12	25	30	60
751	Steve Carlton TR	4	4	20	25	40	60	80	250
752	Joe Morgan TR	4	5	25	30	50	100	120	600
753	Denny McLain TR	4	4	4	12	15	40	50	60
754	Frank Robinson TR	4	4	8	25	50	60	80	200
755	Jim Fregosi TR	4	4	4	10	20	30	50	100
756	Rick Wise TR	4	4	4	5	10	30	40	60
757	Jose Cardenal TR	4	6	12	15	30	80	120	450
758	Gil Garrido	4	4	4	5	10	25	40	120
759	Chris Cannizzaro	4	4	4	5	10	25	30	40

#		VG 3	VgEx 4	EX 5	ExMt 6	NM 7	NmMt 8	NmMt+ 8.5	MT
760	Bill Mazeroski	4	4	15	25	50	100	120	15
761	Oglivie/Cey/Williams RC	8	10	30	50	60	100	150	▲25
762	Wayne Simpson	4	4	4	4	10	20	30	4
763	Ron Hansen	4	4	4	5	10	20	25	10
764	Dusty Baker	4	4	5	6	25	30	40	15
765	Ken McMullen	4	4	4	4	8	15	20	4
766	Steve Hamilton	4	4	5	6	12	25	40	35
767	Tom McCraw	4	4	4	5	10	30	40	6
768	Denny Doyle	4	4	4	4	8	25	30	4
769	Jack Aker	4	4	4	4	8	20	25	4
770	Jim Wynn	4	4	4	4	10	30	40	15
771	San Francisco Giants TC	4	4	4	5	10	25	30	4
772	Ken Tatum	4	4	4	4	8	20	25	3
773	Ron Brand	4	4	4	4	8	20	25	4
774	Luis Alvarado	4	4	4	4	8	20	25	4
775	Jerry Reuss	4	4	4	6	10	20	25	5
776	Bill Voss	4	4	4	5	10	20	30	10
777	Hoyt Wilhelm	4	4	4	12	20	25	40	6
778	Rick Dempsey RC	4	4	8	10	20	30	50	10
779	Tony Cloninger	4	4	4	4	8	25	30	4
780	Dick Green	4	4	4	4	8	15	20	4
781	Jim McAndrew	4	4	4	5	8	15	20	5
782	Larry Stahl	4	5	6	8	15	30	40	15
783	Les Cain	4	4	4	5	10	25	30	4
784	Ken Aspromonte	4	4	4	5	10	30	40	5
785	Vic Davalillo	4	4	8	10	20	30	40	5
786	Chuck Brinkman	4	5	6	8	15	30	40	10
787	Ron Reed	4	5	10	12	25	50	120	20

—Hank Aaron #299 PSA 10 (Gem) sold for $20,655 (Mile High; 10/13)
—Hank Aaron IA #300 PSA 9 (MT) sold for $1,832 (eBay; 5/07)
—Hank Aaron IA #300 PSA 9 (MT) sold for $1,725 (eBay; 1/07)
—Hank Aaron IA #300 PSA 9 (MT) sold for $1,600 (eBay; 11/06)
—Hank Aaron IA #300 PSA 9 (MT) sold for $1,128 (eBay; 6/08)
—Johnny Bench #433 PSA 10 (Gem) sold for $2,325 (eBay; 5/07)
—Johnny Bench #433 BVG 9 (MT) sold for $238 (eBay; 12/06)
—Lou Brock #200 PSA 10 (Gem) sold for $754 (eBay; 2/08)
—Steve Carlton Traded #751 PSA 10 (Gem) sold for $1,122 (eBay; 12/06)
—Norm Cash #150 PSA 9 (MT) sold for $885 (eBay; 4/08)
—Norm Cash #150 PSA 9 (MT) sold for $764 (eBay; 4/08)
—Norm Cash #150 PSA 9 (MT) sold for $325 (eBay; 6/08)
—Norm Cash #150 PSA 9 (MT) sold for $321 (eBay; 6/08)
—Orlando Cepeda #195 PSA 10 (Gem) sold for $917 (eBay; 2/08)
—Roberto Clemente #309 PSA 10 (Gem) sold for $3,888 (eBay; 09/12)
—Roberto Clemente #309 PSA 10 (Gem) sold for $3,007 (eBay; 2/08)
—C.Fisk/C.Cooper #79 PSA 10 (Gem) (Young Collection) sold for $10,855 (SCP; 5/12)
—C.Fisk/C.Cooper #79 PSA 10 (Gem) sold for $7,855 (eBay; 2/08)
—C.Fisk/C.Cooper #79 PSA 10 (Gem) sold for $6,100 (eBay; 2/07)
—C.Fisk/C.Cooper #79 BVG 9 (MT) sold for $766 (eBay; 1/07)
—C.Fisk/C.Cooper #79 GAI 9 (MT) sold for $219 (eBay; 12/06)
—C.Fisk/C.Cooper #79 GAI 9 (MT) sold for $214 (eBay; 2/08)
—Rollie Fingers #241 PSA 10 (Gem) sold for $610 (eBay; 5/08)
—Tim Foli IA #705 PSA 9 (MT) sold for $556 (eBay; 12/07)
—Tim Foli IA #705 PSA 9 (MT) sold for $500 (eBay; 10/07)
—Tim Foli IA #705 PSA 9 (MT) sold for $432 (eBay; 6/08)
—Steve Garvey #686 PSA 10 (Gem) sold for $2,003 (eBay; 1/13)
—Jerry Grote #655 PSA 9 (MT) sold for $507 (eBay; 8/07)
—Ken Henderson #443 PSA 9 (MT) sold for $1,233 (eBay; 1/08)
—Ken Henderson #443 PSA 9 (MT) sold for $825 (eBay; 6/08)
—Gil Hodges #465 PSA 9 (MT) sold for $405 (eBay; 4/08)
—Ken Holtzman #670 PSA 9 (MT) sold for $569 (eBay; 2/08)
—Ken Holtzman #670 PSA 9 (MT) sold for $510 (eBay; 11/06)
—Steve Hovley #683 PSA 9 (MT) sold for $504 (eBay; 3/08)
—Jim Hunter #330 PSA 10 (Gem) sold for $3,050 (eBay; 1/07)
—Reggie Jackson #435 BVG 9 (MT) sold for $325 (eBay; 1/07)
—Reggie Jackson IA #436 PSA 10 (Gem) sold for $1,825 (eBay; 3/08)
—Al Kaline #600 PSA 10 (Gem) sold for $1,992 (Madec; 5/07)
—Al Kaline #600 PSA 10 (Gem) sold for $1,802 (eBay; 5/08)
—Al Kaline #600 PSA 10 (Gem) sold for $1,650 (eBay; 5/07)
—Harmon Killebrew IA #52 PSA 10 (Gem) sold for $1,004 (eBay; 2/08)
—Harmon Killebrew IA #52 PSA 10 (Gem) sold for $997 (eBay; 5/07)
—Juan Marichal #567 PSA 10 (Gem) sold for $1,815 (eBay; 10/06)
—Dave Marshall #673 PSA 9 (MT) sold for $910 (eBay; 12/07)
—Dave Marshall #673 PSA 9 (MT) sold for $580 (eBay; 10/07)
—Dave Marshall #673 PSA 9 (MT) sold for $504 (eBay; 8/07)
—Dave Marshall #673 PSA 9 (MT) sold for $411 (eBay; 3/08)
—Willie Mays #49 GAI 9.5 (Gem) sold for $380 (eBay; 11/07)
—Willie Mays #49 GAI 9.5 (Gem) sold for $207 (eBay; 3/08)

Willie Mays #49 GAI 9 (MT) sold for $260 (eBay; 8/07)
Willie Mays #49 BVG 9 (MT) sold for $225 (eBay; 8/07)
Willie Mays #49 BVG 9 (MT) sold for $225 (eBay; 5/07)
Willie Mays IA #50 PSA 10 (Gem) sold for $8,104 (eBay; 3/08)
Willie Mays IA #50 PSA 9 (MT) sold for $710 (eBay; 4/08)
Willie Mays IA #50 PSA 9 (MT) sold for $609 (Memory Lane; 5/08)
Willie Mays IA #50 PSA 9 (MT) sold for $528 (eBay; 6/08)
Willie McCovey #280 PSA 10 (Gem) sold for $811 (eBay; 6/07)
Joe Morgan Traded #752 PSA 10 (Gem) sold for $1,030 (eBay; 9/07)
Joe Morgan Traded #752 PSA 10 (Gem) sold for $887 (eBay; 6/07)
Thurman Munson IA #442 GAI 9.5 (Gem) sold for $176 (eBay; 11/07)
Bobby Murcer IA #700 PSA 10 (Gem) sold for $1,169 (eBay; 3/07)
Oglivie/Cey/Williams #761 PSA 10 (Gem) sold for $2,504 (eBay; 4/08)
Jim Palmer #270 PSA 10 (Gem) sold for $510 (eBay; 7/07)
Jim Palmer #270 PSA 10 (Gem) sold for $443 (eBay; 5/08)
Tony Perez #80 PSA 10 (Gem) sold for $474 (eBay; 2/08)
Tony Perez #80 PSA 10 (Gem) sold for $434 (eBay; 8/07)
Gaylord Perry #285 PSA 10 (Gem) sold for $504 (Mile High; 2/08)
Gaylord Perry #285 PSA 10 (Gem) sold for $320 (eBay; 6/08)
Reds Rookies #524 PSA 9 (MT) sold for $680 (eBay; 5/07)
Reds Rookies #524 PSA 9 (MT) sold for $665 (eBay; 12/07)
Reds Rookies #524 PSA 9 (MT) sold for $455 (eBay; 3/07)
Reds Rookies #524 PSA 9 (MT) sold for $248 (eBay; 4/08)
Frank Robinson #100 PSA 10 (Gem) sold for $1,207 (eBay; 2/08)
Frank Robinson #100 PSA 10 (Gem) sold for $859 (eBay; 11/06)
Frank Robinson #100 PSA 10 (Gem) sold for $660 (eBay; 3/08)
Frank Robinson #100 GAI 9.5 (Gem) sold for $208 (eBay; 1/07)
Frank Robinson Traded #754 PSA 10 (Gem) sold for $1,275 (eBay; 11/06)
Frank Robinson Traded #754 PSA 10 (Gem) sold for $1,006 (Mile High; 5/04)
Pete Rose #559 PSA 10 (Gem) sold for $5,937 (Memory Lane; 5/08)
Pete Rose #559 BVG 9 (MT) sold for $355 (eBay; 12/06)
Pete Rose #559 GAI 9 (MT) sold for $295 (eBay; 1/07)
Pete Rose IA #560 PSA 10 (Gem) sold for $2,750 (eBay; 1/08)
Pete Rose IA #560 GAI 9 (MT) sold for $270 (eBay; 12/07)
Nolan Ryan #595 PSA 10 (Gem) sold for $9,355 (eBay; 3/07)
Nolan Ryan #595 PSA 10 (Gem) sold for $7,109 (Mile High; 6/06)
Tom Seaver KP #347 PSA 10 (Gem) sold for $1,175 (eBay; 2/07)
Don Sutton #530 PSA 10 (Gem) sold for $1,524 (eBay; 7/07)
Carl Yastrzemski #37 PSA 10 (Gem) sold for $1,834 (eBay; 2/08)
Carl Yastrzemski IA #38 PSA 10 (Gem) sold for $2,011 (eBay; 8/07)

1973 Kellogg's

	VG 3	VgEx 4	EX 5	ExMt 6	NM 7	NmMt 8	MT 9	Gem 9.5/10
Amos Otis	4	4	4	4	4	5	8	40
Ellie Rodriguez	4	4	4	4	4	5	8	25
Mickey Lolich	4	4	4	4	4	5	8	25
Tony Oliva	4	4	4	4	4	5	8	20
Don Sutton	4	4	4	4	4	5	8	20
Pete Rose	4	4	4	4	6	12	25	100
Steve Carlton	4	4	4	4	4	5	10	25
Bobby Bonds	4	4	4	4	4	5	8	20
Wilbur Wood	4	4	4	4	4	5	8	25
Billy Williams	4	4	4	4	4	5	10	25
Steve Blass	4	4	4	4	4	5	8	25
Jon Matlack	4	4	4	4	4	5	8	25
Cesar Cedeno	4	4	4	4	4	5	8	40
Bob Gibson	4	4	4	4	4	5	10	30
Sparky Lyle	4	4	4	4	4	5	8	60
Nolan Ryan	4	4	4	5	10	20	50	120
Jim Palmer	4	4	4	4	4	5	10	25
Ray Fosse	4	4	4	4	4	5	8	20
Bobby Murcer	4	4	4	4	4	5	10	25
Jim Hunter	4	4	4	4	4	5	10	25
Tug McGraw	4	4	4	4	4	5	8	25
Reggie Jackson	4	4	4	4	4	8	15	40
Bill Stoneman	4	4	4	4	4	5	8	60
Lou Piniella	4	4	4	4	4	5	8	50
Willie Stargell	4	4	4	4	4	5	10	25
Dick Allen	4	4	4	4	4	5	10	25
Carlton Fisk	4	4	4	4	4	6	50	60
Ferguson Jenkins	4	4	4	4	4	5	10	60
Phil Niekro	4	4	4	4	4	5	10	25
Gary Nolan	4	4	4	4	4	5	8	25
Joe Torre	4	4	4	4	4	5	8	20
Bobby Tolan	4	4	4	4	4	5	8	20
Nate Colbert	4	4	4	4	4	5	8	60

	VG 3	VgEx 4	EX 5	ExMt 6	NM 7	NmMt 8	MT 9	Gem 9.5/10
34 Joe Morgan	4	4	4	4	4	5	10	25
35 Bert Blyleven	4	4	4	4	4	5	8	20
36 Joe Rudi	4	4	4	4	4	5	8	25
37 Ralph Garr	4	4	4	4	4	5	8	40
38 Gaylord Perry	4	4	4	4	4	5	10	50
39 Bobby Grich	4	4	4	4	4	5	8	40
40 Lou Brock	4	4	4	4	4	5	10	150
41 Pete Broberg	4	4	4	4	4	5	8	25
42 Manny Sanguillen	4	4	4	4	4	5	8	20
43 Willie Davis	4	4	4	4	4	5	8	20
44 Dave Kingman	4	4	4	4	4	5	8	20
45 Carlos May	4	4	4	4	4	5	8	20
46 Tom Seaver	4	4	4	4	4	8	15	30
47 Mike Cuellar	4	4	4	4	4	5	8	60
48 Joe Coleman	4	4	4	4	4	5	8	20
49 Claude Osteen	4	4	4	4	4	5	8	25
50 Steve Kline	4	4	4	4	4	5	8	20
51 Rod Carew	4	4	4	4	4	5	10	50
52 Al Kaline	4	4	4	4	4	6	15	30
53 Larry Dierker	4	4	4	4	4	5	8	20
54 Ron Santo	4	4	4	4	4	5	10	25

1973 O-Pee-Chee

		GD 2	VG 3	VgEx 4	EX 5	ExMt 6	NM 7	NmMt 8	MT 9
615	Mike Schmidt RC	60	80	100	150	250	300	600	2,000

—Rich Gossage #174 BVG 9.5 (Gem) sold for $610 (eBay; 1/08)
—Rich Gossage #174 PSA 9 (MT) sold for $389 (eBay; 5/08)
—Mike Schmidt #615 PSA 10 (Gem) sold for $8,711 (Mastro; 9/07)
—Mike Schmidt #615 GAI 9.5 (Gem) sold for $620 (eBay; 6/08)

1973 Topps

		VG 3	VgEx 4	EX 5	ExMt 6	NM 7	NmMt 8	NmMt+ 8.5	MT 9
1	Ruth/Aaron/Mays HR	20	25	30	60	80	150	200	600
2	Rich Hebner	4	4	4	4	4	8	10	30
3	Jim Lonborg	4	4	4	4	4	6	8	20
4	John Milner	4	4	4	4	4	6	8	60
5	Ed Brinkman	4	4	4	4	4	6	8	20
6	Mac Scarce RC	4	4	4	4	4	6	8	20
7	Texas Rangers TC	4	4	4	4	4	6	8	20
8	Tom Hall	4	4	4	4	4	6	8	15
9	Johnny Oates	4	4	4	4	4	6	8	15
10	Don Sutton	4	4	4	4	5	10	12	40
11	Chris Chambliss	4	4	4	4	4	8	10	30
12A	Don Zimmer MG Podres w/o Ear	4	4	4	4	4	6	8	20
12B	Don Zimmer MG Podres w/Ear	4	4	4	4	4	6	8	20
13	George Hendrick	4	4	4	4	4	6	8	20
14	Sonny Siebert	4	4	4	4	4	6	8	20
15	Ralph Garr	4	4	4	4	4	6	8	20
16	Steve Braun	4	4	4	4	4	6	8	20
17	Fred Gladding	4	4	4	4	4	6	8	25
18	Leroy Stanton	4	4	4	4	4	6	8	40
19	Tim Foli	4	4	4	4	4	6	8	12
20	Stan Bahnsen	4	4	4	4	4	6	8	20
21	Randy Hundley	4	4	4	4	4	6	8	20
22	Ted Abernathy	4	4	4	4	4	6	8	20
23	Dave Kingman	4	4	4	4	4	6	10	40
24	Al Santorini	4	4	4	4	4	6	8	20
25	Roy White	4	4	4	4	4	8	10	30
26	Pittsburgh Pirates TC	4	4	4	4	4	6	8	20
27	Bill Gogolewski	4	4	4	4	4	6	8	20
28	Hal McRae	4	4	4	4	4	8	10	25
29	Tony Taylor	4	4	4	4	4	6	8	20
30	Tug McGraw	4	4	4	4	4	8	10	25
31	Buddy Bell RC	4	4	4	4	8	15	20	120
32	Fred Norman	4	4	4	4	4	6	8	20
33	Jim Breazeale RC	4	4	4	4	4	6	8	20
34	Pat Dobson	4	4	4	4	4	6	8	20
35	Willie Davis	4	4	4	4	4	6	8	20
36	Steve Barber	4	4	4	4	4	6	8	20
37	Bill Robinson	4	4	4	4	4	6	8	20
38	Mike Epstein	4	4	4	4	4	6	8	20
39	Dave Roberts	4	4	4	4	4	6	8	20
40	Reggie Smith	4	4	4	4	4	8	10	50
41	Tom Walker RC	4	4	4	4	4	6	8	25
42	Mike Andrews	4	4	4	4	4	6	8	12

#	Player	VG 3	VgEx 4	EX 5	ExMt 6	NM 7	NmMt 8	NmMt+ 8.5	MT 9
43	Randy Moffitt RC	4	4	4	4	4	6	8	20
44	Rick Monday	4	4	4	4	4	6	8	30
45	Ellie Rodriguez	4	4	4	4	4	6	8	20
46	Lindy McDaniel	4	4	4	4	4	6	8	20
47	Luis Melendez	4	4	4	4	4	6	8	20
48	Paul Splittorff	4	4	4	4	4	6	8	50
49A	Frank Quilici MG Solid	4	4	4	4	4	6	8	40
49B	Frank Quilici MG Natural	4	4	4	4	4	6	8	20
50	Roberto Clemente	▲25	▲30	▲50	▲60	▲100	200	300	800
51	Chuck Seelbach RC	4	4	4	4	4	6	8	20
52	Denis Menke	4	4	4	4	4	6	8	20
53	Steve Dunning	4	4	4	4	4	6	8	20
54	Checklist 1-132	4	4	4	4	8	20	25	40
55	Jon Matlack	4	4	4	4	4	6	8	20
56	Merv Rettenmund	4	4	4	4	4	6	8	20
57	Derrel Thomas	4	4	4	4	4	6	8	20
58	Mike Paul	4	4	4	4	4	6	8	15
59	Steve Yeager RC	4	4	4	4	5	10	12	30
60	Ken Holtzman	4	4	4	4	4	6	8	30
61	Batting Leaders	4	4	4	4	4	8	10	30
62	Home Run Leaders	4	4	4	4	4	8	10	25
63	RBI Leaders	4	4	4	4	5	10	12	50
64	Stolen Base Leaders	4	4	4	4	4	8	10	25
65	ERA Leaders	4	4	4	4	4	8	10	25
66	Victory Leaders	4	4	4	4	4	8	10	25
67	Strikeout Leaders	4	4	8	12	20	▲80	▲100	▲120
68	Leading Firemen	4	4	4	4	4	8	10	25
69	Phil Gagliano	4	4	4	4	4	6	8	20
70	Milt Pappas	4	4	4	4	4	6	8	15
71	Johnny Briggs	4	4	4	4	4	6	8	12
72	Ron Reed	4	4	4	4	4	6	8	15
73	Ed Herrmann	4	4	4	4	4	5	6	10
74	Billy Champion	4	4	4	4	4	5	6	10
75	Vada Pinson	4	4	4	4	4	6	8	20
76	Doug Rader	4	4	4	4	4	6	8	15
77	Mike Torrez	4	4	4	4	4	6	8	20
78	Richie Scheinblum	4	4	4	4	4	6	8	12
79	Jim Willoughby RC	4	4	4	4	4	6	8	12
80	Tony Oliva	4	4	4	4	5	10	12	250
81A	W.Lockman MG w/Banks Solid	4	4	4	4	4	8	10	60
81B	W.Lockman MG w/Banks Natural	4	4	4	4	4	8	10	25
82	Fritz Peterson	4	4	4	4	4	6	8	20
83	Leron Lee	4	4	4	4	4	6	8	15
84	Rollie Fingers	4	4	5	6	12	25	30	150
85	Ted Simmons	4	4	4	4	4	8	10	30
86	Tom McCraw	4	4	4	4	4	6	8	15
87	Ken Boswell	4	4	4	4	4	6	8	20
88	Mickey Stanley	4	4	4	4	4	6	8	20
89	Jack Billingham	4	4	4	4	4	6	8	20
90	Brooks Robinson	4	4	4	20	25	▲50	▲60	120
91	Los Angeles Dodgers TC	4	4	4	4	4	8	10	25
92	Jerry Bell	4	4	4	4	4	6	8	20
93	Jesus Alou	4	4	4	4	4	6	8	20
94	Dick Billings	4	4	4	4	4	6	8	20
95	Steve Blass	4	4	4	4	4	6	8	20
96	Doug Griffin	4	4	4	4	4	6	8	20
97	Willie Montanez	4	4	4	4	4	6	8	20
98	Dick Woodson	4	4	4	4	4	6	8	20
99	Carl Taylor	4	4	4	4	4	6	8	20
100	Hank Aaron	▲25	▲30	▲40	▲50	60	▲150	200	500
101	Ken Henderson	4	4	4	4	4	6	8	20
102	Rudy May	4	4	4	4	4	6	8	20
103	Celerino Sanchez RC	4	4	4	4	4	6	8	20
104	Reggie Cleveland	4	4	4	4	4	6	8	12
105	Carlos May	4	4	4	4	4	6	8	20
106	Terry Humphrey	4	4	4	4	4	6	8	20
107	Phil Hennigan	4	4	4	4	4	6	8	20
108	Bill Russell	4	4	4	4	4	8	10	25
109	Doyle Alexander	4	4	4	4	4	6	8	20
110	Bob Watson	4	4	4	4	4	6	8	20
111	Dave Nelson	4	4	4	4	4	6	8	20
112	Gary Ross	4	4	4	4	4	6	8	20
113	Jerry Grote	4	4	4	4	4	5	6	10
114	Lynn McGlothen RC	4	4	4	4	4	6	8	12
115	Ron Santo	4	4	4	4	8	15	20	30
116A	Ralph Houk MG Solid	4	4	4	4	4	6	8	120
116B	Ralph Houk MG Natural	4	4	4	4	4	6	8	20

#	Player	VG 3	VgEx 4	EX 5	ExMt 6	NM 7	NmMt 8	NmMt+ 8.5	MT 9
117	Ramon Hernandez	4	4	4	4	4	6	8	
118	John Mayberry	4	4	4	4	4	6	8	
119	Larry Bowa	4	4	4	4	4	8	10	
120	Joe Coleman	4	4	4	4	4	6	8	
121	Dave Rader	4	4	4	4	4	6	8	
122	Jim Strickland	4	4	4	4	4	6	8	
123	Sandy Alomar	4	4	4	4	4	8	10	
124	Jim Hardin	4	4	4	4	4	6	8	
125	Ron Fairly	4	4	4	4	4	6	8	
126	Jim Brewer	4	4	4	4	4	6	8	
127	Milwaukee Brewers TC	4	4	4	4	4	6	8	
128	Ted Sizemore	4	4	4	4	4	6	8	6
129	Terry Forster	4	4	4	4	4	8	10	
130	Pete Rose	12	15	▲30	▲40	▲50	▲100	▲200	▲60
131A	Eddie Kasko MG Popowski w/oEar	4	4	4	4	4	60	80	40
131B	Eddie Kasko MG Popowski w/Ear	4	4	4	4	4	6	8	
132	Matty Alou	4	4	4	4	4	6	8	
133	Dave Roberts RC	4	4	4	4	4	6	8	
134	Milt Wilcox	4	4	4	4	4	6	8	
135	Lee May	4	4	4	4	4	6	8	
136A	Earl Weaver MG Orange	4	4	4	4	5	10	12	6
136B	Earl Weaver MG Brown	4	4	4	4	4	8	10	40
137	Jim Beauchamp	4	4	4	4	4	6	8	
138	Horacio Pina	4	4	4	4	4	6	8	
139	Carmen Fanzone RC	4	4	4	4	4	6	8	
140	Lou Piniella	4	4	4	4	4	8	10	
141	Bruce Kison	4	4	4	4	4	6	8	15
142	Thurman Munson	4	▲12	▲15	25	▲40	80	120	50
143	John Curtis	4	4	4	4	4	6	8	
144	Marty Perez	4	4	4	4	4	8	10	
145	Bobby Bonds	4	4	4	4	4	8	10	8
146	Woodie Fryman	4	4	4	4	4	15	20	
147	Mike Anderson	4	4	4	4	4	6	8	2
148	Dave Goltz RC	4	4	4	4	4	6	8	2
149	Ron Hunt	4	4	4	4	4	6	8	2
150	Wilbur Wood	4	4	4	4	4	8	10	2
151	Wes Parker	4	4	4	4	4	8	10	2
152	Dave May	4	4	4	4	4	6	8	2
153	Al Hrabosky	4	4	4	4	4	8	10	2
154	Jeff Torborg	4	4	4	4	4	6	8	20
155	Sal Bando	4	4	4	4	4	8	10	3
156	Cesar Geronimo	4	4	4	4	4	6	8	5
157	Denny Riddleberger	4	4	4	4	4	6	8	200
158	Houston Astros TC	4	4	4	4	4	6	8	2
159	Cito Gaston	4	4	4	4	4	6	8	20
160	Jim Palmer	4	4	4	4	8	30	40	200
161	Ted Martinez	4	4	4	4	4	6	8	20
162	Pete Broberg	4	4	4	4	4	6	8	12
163	Vic Davalillo	4	4	4	4	4	8	10	
164	Monty Montgomery	4	4	4	4	4	6	8	20
165	Luis Aparicio	4	4	4	4	5	15	20	30
166	Terry Harmon	4	4	4	4	4	6	8	20
167	Steve Stone	4	4	4	4	4	6	8	20
168	Jim Northrup	4	4	4	4	4	8	10	25
169	Ron Schueler RC	4	4	4	4	4	6	8	250
170	Harmon Killebrew	4	4	6	15	▲30	▲40	50	200
171	Bernie Carbo	4	4	4	4	4	6	8	25
172	Steve Kline	4	4	4	4	4	6	8	20
173	Hal Breeden	4	4	4	5	10	40		
174	Rich Gossage RC	10	12	20	▲30	50	120	200	500
175	Frank Robinson	4	4	▲10	▲12	▲25	▲40	▲50	100
176	Chuck Taylor	4	4	4	4	4	6	8	20
177	Bill Plummer RC	4	4	4	4	4	6	8	20
178	Don Rose RC	4	4	4	4	4	6	8	80
179A	Dick Williams MG Hoscheit w/Ear	4	4	4	4	4	6	8	30
179B	Dick Williams MG Hoscheit w/o Ear	4	4	4	4	4	6	8	20
180	Ferguson Jenkins	4	4	4	4	5	10	12	50
181	Jack Brohamer RC	4	4	4	4	4	6	8	25
182	Mike Caldwell RC	4	4	4	4	4	8	10	30
183	Don Buford	4	4	4	4	4	8	10	
184	Jerry Koosman	4	4	4	4	4	8	10	25
185	Jim Wynn	4	4	4	4	4	8	10	25
186	Bill Fahey	4	4	4	4	4	6	8	40
187	Luke Walker	4	4	4	4	4	6	8	15
188	Cookie Rojas	4	4	4	4	4	6	8	20
189	Greg Luzinski	4	4	4	4	4	8	10	50

#	Player	VG 3	VgEx 4	EX 5	ExMt 6	NM 7	NmMt 8	NmMt+ 8.5	MT 9
190	Bob Gibson	4	5	8	▲20	▲25	▲50	▲60	▲200
191	Detroit Tigers TC	4	4	4	4	4	8	10	50
192	Pat Jarvis	4	4	4	4	4	6	8	25
193	Carlton Fisk	8	10	12	25	30	60	80	▲250
194	Jorge Orta RC	4	4	4	4	4	6	8	50
195	Clay Carroll	4	4	4	4	4	15	20	100
196	Ken McMullen	4	4	4	4	4	6	8	20
197	Ed Goodson RC	4	4	4	4	4	6	8	25
198	Horace Clarke	4	4	4	4	4	6	8	30
199	Bert Blyleven	4	4	4	4	4	8	10	60
200	Billy Williams	4	4	4	4	6	20	25	80
201	George Hendrick ALCS	4	4	4	4	4	8	10	30
202	George Foster NLCS	4	4	4	4	4	15	20	150
203	Gene Tenace WS1	4	4	4	4	4	8	10	25
204	A's Two Straight WS2	4	4	4	4	4	8	10	30
205	Tony Perez WS3	4	4	4	4	4	8	10	30
206	Gene Tenace WS4	4	4	4	4	4	8	10	40
207	Blue Moon Odom WS5	4	4	4	4	4	8	10	50
208	Johnny Bench WS6	4	4	4	5	8	12	20	25
209	Bert Campaneris WS7	4	4	4	4	4	8	10	30
210	A's Win WS	4	4	4	4	4	6	8	80
211	Balor Moore	4	4	4	4	4	6	8	40
212	Joe Lahoud	4	4	4	4	4	6	8	20
213	Steve Garvey	4	4	5	6	12	25	30	▲100
214	Dave Hamilton RC	4	4	4	4	4	6	8	25
215	Dusty Baker	4	4	4	4	4	8	10	25
216	Toby Harrah	4	4	4	4	4	6	8	20
217	Don Wilson	4	4	4	6	12	25	30	900
218	Aurelio Rodriguez	4	4	4	4	4	6	8	25
219	St. Louis Cardinals TC	4	4	4	4	4	8	10	80
220	Nolan Ryan	15	▲25	▲30	40	80	250	600	▲1,500
221	Fred Kendall	4	4	4	4	4	6	8	20
222	Rob Gardner	4	4	4	4	5	10	12	25
223	Bud Harrelson	4	4	4	4	5	10	12	60
224	Bill Lee	4	4	4	4	4	8	10	30
225	Al Oliver	4	4	4	4	4	8	10	25
226	Ray Fosse	4	4	4	4	4	6	8	20
227	Wayne Twitchell	4	4	4	4	4	12	15	60
228	Bobby Darwin	4	4	4	4	4	6	8	20
229	Roric Harrison	4	4	4	4	4	6	8	60
230	Joe Morgan	4	4	8	▲20	30	100		
231	Bill Parsons	4	4	4	4	4	6	8	20
232	Ken Singleton	4	4	4	4	4	8	10	25
233	Ed Kirkpatrick	4	4	4	4	4	6	8	25
234	Bill North RC	4	4	4	4	4	6	8	50
235	Jim Hunter	4	4	5	6	12	25	30	60
236	Tito Fuentes	4	4	4	4	4	6	8	15
237A	Eddie Mathews MG Burdette w/Ear	4	4	4	4	5	10	12	700
237B	Eddie Mathews MG Burdette w/o Ear	4.	4	4	4	5	10	12	300
238	Tony Muser RC	4	4	4	4	4	6	8	20
239	Pete Richert	4	4	4	4	5	10	15	
240	Bobby Murcer	4	4	4	4	8	15	20	50
241	Dwain Anderson	4	4	4	4	5	10	12	20
242	George Culver	4	4	4	4	4	6	8	20
243	California Angels TC	4	4	4	4	4	6	8	25
244	Ed Acosta	4	4	4	4	4	6	8	20
245	Carl Yastrzemski	4	8	▲20	▲25	40	120		
246	Ken Sanders	4	4	4	4	4	6	8	20
247	Del Unser	4	4	4	4	5	10	15	
248	Jerry Johnson	4	4	4	4	4	6	8	20
249	Larry Biittner	4	4	4	4	4	6	8	20
250	Manny Sanguillen	4	4	4	4	4	8	10	50
251	Roger Nelson	4	4	4	4	4	6	8	15
252A	Charlie Fox MG Orange	4	4	4	4	4	6	8	60
252B	Charlie Fox MG Brown	4	4	4	4	4	6	8	80
253	Mark Belanger	4	4	4	4	4	8	10	25
254	Bill Stoneman	4	4	4	4	4	6	8	12
255	Reggie Jackson	5	8	15	20	30	60	▲100	▲1,000
256	Chris Zachary	4	4	4	4	4	6	8	15
257A	Yogi Berra MG Orange	4	4	4	4	5	15	20	80
257B	Yogi Berra MG Brown	4	4	4	4	5	15	20	60
258	Tommy John	4	4	4	4	4	8	10	50
259	Jim Holt	4	4	4	4	5	10	15	
260	Gary Nolan	4	4	4	4	4	6	8	20
261	Pat Kelly	4	4	4	4	4	6	8	25
262	Jack Aker	4	4	4	4	4	6	8	20

#	Player	VG 3	VgEx 4	EX 5	ExMt 6	NM 7	NmMt 8	NmMt+ 8.5	MT 9
263	George Scott	4	4	4	4	4	6	8	20
264	Checklist 133-264	4	4	4	4	8	60	80	100
265	Gene Michael	4	4	4	4	4	6	8	50
266	Mike Lum	4	4	4	4	4	6	8	25
267	Lloyd Allen	4	4	4	4	4	6	8	20
268	Jerry Morales	4	4	4	4	4	6	8	20
269	Tim McCarver	4	4	4	4	4	8	10	25
270	Luis Tiant	4	4	4	4	4	8	10	25
271	Tom Hutton	4	4	4	4	4	6	8	20
272	Ed Farmer	4	4	4	4	4	6	8	25
273	Chris Speier	4	4	4	4	4	6	8	20
274	Darold Knowles	4	4	4	4	4	6	8	25
275	Tony Perez	4	4	4	4	8	60	80	200
276	Joe Lovitto RC	4	4	4	4	4	6	8	20
277	Bob Miller	4	4	4	4	4	6	8	20
278	Baltimore Orioles TC	4	4	4	4	6	12	15	100
279	Mike Strahler	4	4	4	4	4	6	8	50
280	Al Kaline	4	4	4	▲15	25	50	60	▲200
281	Mike Jorgensen	4	4	4	4	4	6	8	80
282	Steve Hovley	4	4	4	4	4	6	8	80
283	Ray Sadecki	4	4	4	4	4	6	8	120
284	Glenn Borgmann RC	4	4	4	4	4	6	8	20
285	Don Kessinger	4	4	4	4	4	6	8	120
286	Frank Linzy	4	4	4	4	4	6	8	20
287	Eddie Leon	4	4	4	4	4	6	8	20
288	Gary Gentry	4	4	4	4	4	6	8	120
289	Bob Oliver	4	4	4	4	4	6	8	25
290	Cesar Cedeno	4	4	4	4	4	8	10	50
291	Rogelio Moret	4	4	4	4	4	6	8	15
292	Jose Cruz	4	4	4	4	4	8	10	25
293	Bernie Allen	4	4	4	4	4	6	8	20
294	Steve Arlin	4	4	4	4	4	6	8	20
295	Bert Campaneris	4	4	4	4	4	6	8	25
296	Sparky Anderson MG	4	4	4	4	6	12	15	60
297	Walt Williams	4	4	4	4	4	6	8	20
298	Ron Bryant	4	4	4	4	4	6	8	50
299	Ted Ford	4	4	4	4	4	6	8	30
300	Steve Carlton	5	6	8	10	25	50	80	200
301	Billy Grabarkewitz	4	4	4	4	4	6	8	15
302	Terry Crowley	4	4	4	4	4	6	8	100
303	Nelson Briles	4	4	4	4	4	6	8	25
304	Duke Sims	4	4	4	4	4	6	8	20
305	Willie Mays	▲30	▲40	▲50	▲60	▲80	▲200	250	600
306	Tom Burgmeier	4	4	4	4	4	6	8	40
307	Boots Day	4	4	4	4	4	6	8	20
308	Skip Lockwood	4	4	4	4	4	6	8	30
309	Paul Popovich	4	4	4	4	4	6	8	20
310	Dick Allen	4	4	4	5	10	20	25	150
311	Joe Decker	4	4	4	4	4	6	8	20
312	Oscar Brown	4	4	4	4	4	6	8	20
313	Jim Ray	4	4	4	4	4	6	8	25
314	Ron Swoboda	4	4	4	4	4	6	8	25
315	John Odom	4	4	4	4	4	6	8	40
316	San Diego Padres TC	4	4	4	4	4	6	8	30
317	Danny Cater	4	4	4	4	4	6	8	20
318	Jim McGlothlin	4	4	4	4	4	6	8	20
319	Jim Spencer	4	4	4	4	4	6	8	50
320	Lou Brock	4	4	5	10	20	▲40	▲50	100
321	Rich Hinton	4	4	4	4	4	6	8	20
322	Garry Maddox RC	4	4	4	4	4	8	10	80
323	Billy Martin MG	4	4	4	4	6	12	15	80
324	Al Downing	4	4	4	4	4	6	8	50
325	Boog Powell	4	4	5	6	8	15	20	50
326	Darrell Brandon	4	4	4	4	4	6	8	25
327	John Lowenstein	4	4	4	4	4	6	8	30
328	Bill Bonham	4	4	4	4	4	6	8	80
329	Ed Kranepool	4	4	4	4	4	6	8	20
330	Rod Carew	4	4	5	15	25	50	80	500
331	Carl Morton	4	4	4	4	4	6	8	25
332	John Felske RC	4	4	4	4	4	6	8	25
333	Gene Clines	4	4	4	4	4	6	8	60
334	Freddie Patek	4	4	4	4	4	6	8	30
335	Bob Tolan	4	4	4	4	4	6	8	25
336	Tom Bradley	4	4	4	4	4	6	8	20
337	Dave Duncan	4	4	4	4	4	6	8	20
338	Checklist 265-396	4	4	4	4	8	15	20	100
339	Dick Tidrow	4	4	4	4	4	6	8	80

#	Player	VG 3	VgEx 4	EX 5	ExMt 6	NM 7	NmMt 8	NmMt+ 8.5	MT 9
340	Nate Colbert	4	4	4	4	4	6	8	20
341	Jim Palmer KP	4	4	4	4	4	8	10	30
342	Sam McDowell KP	4	4	4	4	4	6	8	50
343	Bobby Murcer KP	4	4	4	4	4	6	8	20
344	Jim Hunter KP	4	4	4	4	4	8	10	25
345	Chris Speier KP	4	4	4	4	4	6	8	30
346	Gaylord Perry KP	4	4	4	4	4	8	10	30
347	Kansas City Royals TC	4	4	4	4	4	6	8	100
348	Rennie Stennett	4	4	4	4	4	6	8	60
349	Dick McAuliffe	4	4	4	4	4	6	8	25
350	Tom Seaver	5	▲15	▲20	▲25	▲30	▲80	▲100	250
351	Jimmy Stewart	4	4	4	4	4	6	8	25
352	Don Stanhouse RC	4	4	4	4	4	6	8	20
353	Steve Brye	4	4	4	4	4	6	8	20
354	Billy Parker	4	4	4	4	4	6	8	20
355	Mike Marshall	4	4	4	4	4	8	10	150
356	Chuck Tanner MG	4	4	4	4	4	6	8	50
357	Ross Grimsley	4	4	4	4	4	6	8	15
358	Jim Nettles	4	4	4	4	4	6	8	15
359	Cecil Upshaw	4	4	4	4	4	6	8	30
360	Joe Rudi	4	4	4	4	4	8	10	50
361	Fran Healy	4	4	4	4	4	6	8	25
362	Eddie Watt	4	4	4	4	4	6	8	25
363	Jackie Hernandez	4	4	4	4	4	6	8	60
364	Rick Wise	4	4	4	4	4	6	8	25
365	Rico Petrocelli	4	4	4	4	4	8	10	25
366	Brock Davis	4	4	4	4	4	6	8	20
367	Burt Hooton	4	4	4	4	4	6	8	25
368	Bill Buckner	4	4	4	4	4	8	10	50
369	Lerrin LaGrow	4	4	4	4	4	6	8	20
370	Willie Stargell	5	6	8	10	▲25	40	50	150
371	Mike Kekich	4	4	4	4	4	6	8	20
372	Oscar Gamble	4	4	4	4	4	6	8	20
373	Clyde Wright	4	4	4	4	4	6	8	50
374	Darrell Evans	4	4	4	4	4	8	10	25
375	Larry Dierker	4	4	4	4	4	6	8	20
376	Frank Duffy	4	4	4	4	4	6	8	25
377	Gene Mauch MG	4	4	4	4	4	6	8	30
378	Len Randle	4	4	4	4	4	6	8	80
379	Cy Acosta RC	4	4	4	4	4	6	8	40
380	Johnny Bench	12	15	20	25	▲50	100	120	▲1,000
381	Vicente Romo	4	4	4	4	4	6	8	120
382	Mike Hegan	4	4	4	4	4	20	25	
383	Diego Segui	4	4	4	4	4	6	8	30
384	Don Baylor	4	4	4	4	4	8	10	50
385	Jim Perry	4	4	4	4	6	12	15	50
386	Don Money	4	4	4	4	4	6	8	20
387	Jim Barr	4	4	4	4	4	6	8	20
388	Ben Oglivie	4	4	4	4	4	8	10	30
389	New York Mets TC	4	4	4	4	8	15	20	60
390	Mickey Lolich	4	4	4	4	4	8	10	25
391	Lee Lacy RC	4	4	4	4	4	8	10	25
392	Dick Drago	4	4	4	4	4	6	8	40
393	Jose Cardenal	4	4	4	4	4	6	8	20
394	Sparky Lyle	4	4	4	4	5	10	12	30
395	Roger Metzger	4	4	4	4	4	6	8	20
396	Grant Jackson	4	4	4	4	4	6	8	80
397	Dave Cash	4	4	4	4	4	6	8	50
398	Rich Hand	4	4	4	4	4	6	8	20
399	George Foster	4	4	4	4	5	10	12	200
400	Gaylord Perry	4	5	6	8	15	30	40	▲150
401	Clyde Mashore	4	4	4	4	4	6	8	20
402	Jack Hiatt	4	4	4	4	4	6	8	20
403	Sonny Jackson	4	4	4	4	4	6	8	20
404	Chuck Brinkman	4	4	4	4	4	6	8	30
405	Cesar Tovar	4	4	4	4	4	6	8	20
406	Paul Lindblad	4	4	4	4	4	6	8	80
407	Felix Millan	4	4	4	4	4	6	8	20
408	Jim Colborn	4	4	4	4	4	6	8	20
409	Ivan Murrell	4	4	4	4	4	6	8	20
410	Willie McCovey	4	4	5	6	20	30	40	▼120
411	Ray Corbin	4	4	4	4	4	6	8	40
412	Manny Mota	4	4	4	4	4	6	8	30
413	Tom Timmermann	4	4	4	4	4	6	8	20
414	Ken Rudolph	4	4	4	4	4	6	8	20
415	Marty Pattin	4	4	4	4	4	6	8	20
416	Paul Schaal	4	4	4	4	4	6	8	30

#	Player	VG 3	VgEx 4	EX 5	ExMt 6	NM 7	NmMt 8	NmMt+ 8.5	MT 9
417	Scipio Spinks	4	4	4	4	4	6	8	2
418	Bob Grich	4	4	4	4	4	8	10	
419	Casey Cox	4	4	4	4	4	6	8	5
420	Tommie Agee	4	4	4	4	4	6	8	12
421A	Bobby Winkles MG Orange RC	4	4	4	4	4	6	8	3
421B	Bobby Winkles MG Brown	4	4	4	4	4	6	8	10
422	Bob Robertson	4	4	4	4	4	6	8	3
423	Johnny Jeter	4	4	4	4	4	6	8	2
424	Denny Doyle	4	4	4	4	4	6	8	6
425	Alex Johnson	4	4	4	4	4	6	8	2
426	Dave LaRoche	4	4	4	4	4	6	8	2
427	Rick Auerbach	4	4	4	4	4	6	8	3
428	Wayne Simpson	4	4	4	4	4	6	8	6
429	Jim Fairey	4	4	4	4	4	6	8	2
430	Vida Blue	4	4	4	4	8	15	20	5
431	Gerry Moses	4	4	4	4	4	6	8	6
432	Dan Frisella	4	4	4	4	4	6	8	6
433	Willie Horton	4	4	4	4	5	10	12	5
434	San Francisco Giants TC	4	4	4	4	4	6	8	2
435	Rico Carty	4	4	4	4	4	6	8	2
436	Jim McAndrew	4	4	4	4	4	6	8	30
437	John Kennedy	4	4	4	4	4	6	8	2
438	Enzo Hernandez	4	4	4	4	4	6	8	2
439	Eddie Fisher	4	4	4	4	4	6	8	20
440	Glenn Beckert	4	4	4	4	4	6	8	8
441	Gail Hopkins	4	4	4	4	4	6	8	100
442	Dick Dietz	4	4	4	4	4	6	8	20
443	Danny Thompson	4	4	4	4	4	6	8	20
444	Ken Brett	4	4	4	4	4	6	8	25
445	Ken Berry	4	4	4	4	4	6	8	20
446	Jerry Reuss	4	4	4	4	4	6	8	50
447	Joe Hague	4	4	4	4	4	6	8	25
448	John Hiller	4	4	4	4	4	6	8	20
449A	Ken Aspromonte MG Spahn Ear Pointed	4	4	4	4	4	8	10	25
449B	Ken Aspromonte MG Spahn Ear Round	4	4	4	4	4	8	10	40
450	Joe Torre	4	4	4	4	8	15	20	30
451	John Vukovich RC	4	4	4	4	4	6	8	20
452	Paul Casanova	4	4	4	4	4	6	8	25
453	Checklist 397-528	4	4	4	4	8	15	20	150
454	Tom Haller	4	4	4	4	4	6	8	20
455	Bill Melton	4	4	4	4	4	6	8	25
456	Dick Green	4	4	4	4	4	6	8	30
457	John Strohmayer	4	4	4	4	4	6	8	25
458	Jim Mason	4	4	4	4	4	6	8	20
459	Jimmy Howarth RC	4	4	4	4	4	6	8	20
460	Bill Freehan	4	4	4	4	4	8	10	80
461	Mike Corkins	4	4	4	4	4	6	8	20
462	Ron Blomberg	4	4	4	4	4	6	8	20
463	Ken Tatum	4	4	4	4	4	6	8	20
464	Chicago Cubs TC	4	4	4	4	4	8	10	80
465	Dave Giusti	4	4	4	4	4	6	8	20
466	Jose Arcia	4	4	4	4	4	8	10	
467	Mike Ryan	4	4	4	4	4	6	8	15
468	Tom Griffin	4	4	4	4	4	6	8	40
469	Dan Monzon RC	4	4	4	4	4	6	8	20
470	Mike Cuellar	4	4	4	4	8	15	20	120
471	Ty Cobb LDR	4	4	4	12	15	30	60	250
472	Lou Gehrig LDR	4	4	6	12	25	30	40	120
473	Hank Aaron LDR	4	5	10	20	30	60	100	350
474	Babe Ruth LDR	12	15	20	25	30	60	100	200
475	Ty Cobb LDR	4	4	4	15	25	50	60	150
476	Walter Johnson LDR	4	4	4	4	8	15	20	80
477	Cy Young LDR	4	4	5	6	12	40		
478	Walter Johnson LDR	4	4	4	5	10	20	25	100
479	Hal Lanier	4	4	4	4	4	6	8	20
480	Juan Marichal	4	4	4	6	12	30	40	120
481	Chicago White Sox TC	4	4	4	4	4	6	8	50
482	Rick Reuschel RC	4	4	4	4	5	10	12	80
483	Dal Maxvill	4	4	4	4	4	6	8	25
484	Ernie McAnally	4	4	4	4	4	6	8	20
485	Norm Cash	4	4	4	4	5	10	12	40
486A	Danny Ozark MG Orange RC	4	4	4	4	4	6	8	60
486B	Danny Ozark MG Brown	4	4	4	4	4	6	8	25
487	Bruce Dal Canton	4	4	4	4	4	6	8	30
488	Dave Campbell	4	4	4	4	4	8	10	25

	VG 3	VgEx 4	EX 5	ExMt 6	NM 7	NmMt 8	NmMt+ 8.5	MT 9
Jeff Burroughs	4	4	4	4	4	8	10	25
Claude Osteen	4	4	4	4	4	6	8	20
Bob Montgomery	4	4	4	4	4	6	8	20
Pedro Borbon	4	4	4	4	4	6	8	25
Duffy Dyer	4	4	4	4	4	6	8	20
Rich Morales	4	4	4	4	4	6	8	20
Tommy Helms	4	4	4	4	4	6	8	20
Ray Lamb	4	4	4	4	4	6	8	100
A Red Schoendienst MG Orange	4	4	4	4	4	8	10	60
B Red Schoendienst MG Brown	4	4	4	4	4	8	10	25
Graig Nettles	4	4	4	4	8	15	20	200
Bob Moose	4	4	4	4	4	6	8	80
Oakland Athletics TC	4	4	4	4	4	8	10	20
Larry Gura	4	4	4	4	4	6	8	20
Bobby Valentine	4	4	4	4	4	8	10	25
Phil Niekro	4	4	4	4	8	15	20	▲120
Earl Williams	4	4	4	4	4	6	8	50
Bob Bailey	4	4	4	4	4	6	8	20
Bart Johnson	4	4	4	4	4	6	8	20
Darrel Chaney	4	4	4	4	4	6	8	25
Gates Brown	4	4	4	4	4	6	8	20
Jim Nash	4	4	4	4	4	6	8	20
Amos Otis	4	4	4	4	4	8	10	40
Sam McDowell	4	4	4	4	4	8	10	40
Dalton Jones	4	4	4	4	4	6	8	20
Dave Marshall	4	4	4	4	4	6	8	20
Jerry Kenney	4	4	4	4	4	6	8	25
Andy Messersmith	4	4	4	4	4	8	10	15
Danny Walton	4	4	4	4	5	10	12	20
7A Bill Virdon MG Mazeroski w/o Ear	4	4	4	4	4	6	8	60
7B Bill Virdon MG Mazeroski w/Ear	4	4	4	4	4	6	8	60
Bob Veale	4	4	4	4	4	6	8	20
Johnny Edwards	4	4	4	4	4	6	8	15
Mel Stottlemyre	4	4	4	4	6	12	15	25
Atlanta Braves TC	4	4	4	4	4	6	8	20
Leo Cardenas	4	4	4	4	4	6	8	20
Wayne Granger	4	4	4	4	4	6	8	20
Gene Tenace	4	4	4	4	4	8	10	200
Jim Fregosi	4	4	4	4	4	8	10	25
Ollie Brown	4	4	4	4	4	6	8	25
Dan McGinn	4	4	4	4	4	6	8	25
Paul Blair	4	4	4	4	4	8	10	100
Milt May	4	4	4	4	5	10	12	25
Jim Kaat	4	4	6	12	25	30	60	100
Ron Woods	4	4	4	4	5	10	12	30
Steve Mingori	4	4	4	4	5	10	12	25
Larry Stahl	4	4	4	4	5	10	12	25
Dave Lemonds	4	4	4	4	8	15	25	
Johnny Callison	4	4	4	4	6	12	15	100
Philadelphia Phillies TC	4	4	4	4	6	12	15	40
Bill Slayback RC	4	4	4	4	5	10	12	30
Jim Ray Hart	4	4	4	4	5	10	12	50
Tom Murphy	4	4	4	4	5	10	12	80
Cleon Jones	4	4	4	4	6	12	15	50
Bob Bolin	4	4	4	4	5	10	12	25
Pat Corrales	4	4	4	4	5	10	12	40
Alan Foster	4	4	4	4	5	10	12	25
Von Joshua	4	4	4	4	5	10	12	25
Orlando Cepeda	4	4	4	8	12	20	30	80
Jim York	4	4	4	4	5	10	12	25
Bobby Heise	5	6	8	10	20	40	50	
Don Durham RC	4	4	4	4	5	10	12	80
Whitey Herzog MG	4	4	4	4	30	80		
Dave Johnson	4	4	4	4	10	25		
Mike Kilkenny	4	4	4	4	8	15	25	
J.C. Martin	4	4	4	4	5	10	12	40
Mickey Scott	4	4	4	4	8	15	25	
Dave Concepcion	4	4	5	8	15	▲40	50	150
Bill Hands	4	4	4	4	5	10	12	400
New York Yankees TC	5	6	8	10	15	20	50	120
Bernie Williams	4	4	4	4	5	10	12	50
Jerry May	4	4	4	4	5	10	12	40
Barry Lersch	4	4	4	4	5	10	12	50
Frank Howard	5	4	6	8	10	20	30	
Jim Geddes RC	4	4	4	4	8	25	30	
Wayne Garrett	4	4	4	4	5	10	12	50
Larry Haney	4	4	4	4	5	10	12	120

	VG 3	VgEx 4	EX 5	ExMt 6	NM 7	NmMt 8	NmMt+ 8.5	MT 9
564 Mike Thompson RC	4	4	4	4	5	10	12	25
565 Jim Hickman	4	4	4	4	5	10	12	50
566 Lew Krausse	4	4	4	4	5	10	12	80
567 Bob Fenwick	4	4	4	4	5	10	12	40
568 Ray Newman	4	4	4	4	5	10	12	30
569 Walt Alston MG	4	4	4	5	6	12	25	120
570 Bill Singer	4	4	4	4	5	10	12	25
571 Rusty Torres	4	4	4	4	6	12	15	25
572 Gary Sutherland	4	4	4	4	6	12	15	30
573 Fred Beene	4	4	4	4	5	10	12	80
574 Bob Didier	4	4	4	5	10	20	25	200
575 Dock Ellis	4	4	4	4	5	10	12	60
576 Montreal Expos TC	4	4	4	4	4	8	10	15
577 Eric Soderholm RC	4	4	4	4	5	10	12	25
578 Ken Wright	4	4	4	4	5	10	12	60
579 Tom Grieve	4	4	4	4	5	10	12	25
580 Joe Pepitone	4	4	4	4	6	12	15	40
581 Steve Kealey	4	4	4	4	8	15	25	
582 Darrell Porter	4	4	4	4	8	15	20	40
583 Bill Grief	4	4	4	4	5	10	12	25
584 Chris Arnold	4	4	4	4	8	15	20	150
585 Joe Niekro	4	4	4	4	5	10	12	50
586 Bill Sudakis	4	4	4	4	5	10	12	80
587 Rich McKinney	4	4	4	4	5	10	12	50
588 Checklist 529-660	4	8	15	20	60	120	150	400
589 Ken Forsch	4	4	4	4	5	10	12	80
590 Deron Johnson	4	4	5	6	12	25	30	200
591 Mike Hedlund	4	4	4	4	5	10	12	25
592 John Boccabella	4	4	4	4	5	10	12	60
593 Jack McKeon MG RC	4	4	4	4	8	100	120	300
594 Vic Harris RC	4	4	4	4	8	15	25	
595 Don Gullett	4	4	4	4	5	10	12	80
596 Boston Red Sox TC	4	4	4	4	8	15	20	▲150
597 Mickey Rivers	4	4	4	4	6	12	15	40
598 Phil Roof	4	4	4	4	5	10	12	60
599 Ed Crosby	4	4	4	4	5	10	12	100
600 Dave McNally	4	4	4	4	6	30	40	100
601 Rookie Catchers	4	4	4	5	10	20	25	150
602 Rookie Pitchers	4	4	4	4	8	15	20	250
603 Rookie Third Basemen	4	4	4	4	8	40	60	450
604 Rookie Pitchers	4	4	4	4	6	12	20	100
605 Rookie First Basemen	4	4	4	5	10	▲25	▲30	100
606 Gary Matthews RC	4	4	4	5	10	20	25	100
607 Rookie Shortstops	4	4	4	5	10	20	30	100
608 Rookie Pitchers	4	4	4	8	15	30	40	500
609 Davey Lopes RC	4	5	10	12	25	50		
610 Rookie Pitchers	4	4	4	5	10	20	25	120
611 Rookie Outfielders	4	4	4	5	10	20	25	60
612 Rookie Pitchers	4	4	4	4	6	12	15	40
613 Bob Boone RC	8	10	12	15	20	30	50	100
614 Dwight Evans RC	10	12	15	20	50	▲120	▲150	400
615 Mike Schmidt RC	80	100	120	200	300	600	1,200	3,000
616 Rookie Pitchers	4	4	4	5	10	25	30	150
617 Rich Chiles	4	4	4	4	5	10	12	50
618 Andy Etchebarren	4	4	4	4	5	10	12	50
619 Billy Wilson	4	4	4	4	5	10	12	20
620 Tommy Harper	4	4	4	4	6	12	15	100
621 Joe Ferguson	4	4	4	4	5	10	20	50
622 Larry Hisle	4	4	4	5	8	15	20	200
623 Steve Renko	4	4	4	4	8	15	20	50
624 Leo Durocher MG	4	4	4	5	8	20	25	50
625 Angel Mangual	4	4	4	5	8	15	20	25
626 Bob Barton	4	4	4	4	5	10	12	50
627 Luis Alvarado	4	4	4	4	6	12	15	25
628 Jim Slaton	4	4	4	4	5	10	12	50
629 Cleveland Indians TC	4	4	4	4	5	10	12	25
630 Denny McLain	4	4	4	5	8	15	25	80
631 Tom Matchick	4	4	4	4	5	10	12	100
632 Dick Selma	4	4	4	4	5	10	12	80
633 Ike Brown	4	4	4	4	5	10	12	80
634 Alan Closter	4	4	4	4	5	10	12	40
635 Gene Alley	4	4	4	4	5	10	12	80
636 Rickey Clark	4	4	4	4	5	10	12	25
637 Norm Miller	4	4	4	4	5	10	12	25
638 Ken Reynolds	4	4	4	4	5	10	12	50
639 Willie Crawford	4	4	4	4	5	10	12	30
640 Dick Bosman	4	4	4	4	5	10	12	25

		VG 3	VgEx 4	EX 5	ExMt 6	NM 7	NmMt 8	NmMt+ 8.5	MT 9
641	Cincinnati Reds TC	4	5	6	8	15	60	80	150
642	Jose Laboy	4	4	4	4	5	10	12	30
643	Al Fitzmorris	4	4	4	4	5	10	12	80
644	Jack Heidemann	4	4	4	4	5	10	12	25
645	Bob Locker	4	4	4	4	5	10	12	250
646	Del Crandall MG	4	4	4	4	6	12	15	50
647	George Stone	4	4	4	4	5	10	12	25
648	Tom Egan	4	4	4	5	8	15	20	50
649	Rich Folkers	4	4	4	4	5	10	12	60
650	Felipe Alou	4	4	4	4	8	15	20	80
651	Don Carrithers	4	4	4	4	5	10	12	25
652	Ted Kubiak	4	4	4	4	5	10	12	25
653	Joe Hoerner	4	4	8	10	20	25		
654	Minnesota Twins TC	4	5	6	8	15	30	40	150
655	Clay Kirby	4	4	4	4	5	10	12	150
656	John Ellis	4	4	4	4	5	10	12	50
657	Bob Johnson	4	4	4	4	5	10	12	60
658	Elliott Maddox	4	4	4	4	5	10	12	60
659	Jose Pagan	4	4	4	4	5	10	12	25
660	Fred Scherman	4	4	6	10	15	40	60	100

—Hank Aaron #100 BVG 9.5 (Gem) sold for $688 (eBay; 2/08)
—Hank Aaron LDR #473 PSA 9 (MT) sold for $273 (eBay; 3/07)
—Luis Aparicio #165 PSA 10 (Gem) sold for $825 (eBay; 10/07)
—Roberto Clemente #50 PSA 10 (Gem) sold for $6,120 (eBay; 4/08)
—Dwight Evans #614 PSA 10 (Gem) sold for $371 (eBay; 7/07)
—Carlton Fisk #193 PSA 10 (Gem) sold for $1,292 (eBay; 8/07)
—Carlton Fisk #193 PSA 10 (Gem) sold for $986 (eBay; 6/07)
—Bob Gibson #190 PSA 10 (Gem) sold for $2,903 (eBay; 3/08)
—Rich Gossage #174 PSA 10 (Gem) sold for $3,222 (eBay; 1/08)
—Woodie Fryman #146 PSA 9 (MT) sold for $208 (eBay; 3/07)
—Frank Howard #560 PSA 9 (MT) sold for $208 (eBay; 4/07)
—Frank Howard #560 PSA 9 (MT) sold for $177 (eBay; 8/07)
—Ferguson Jenkins #180 PSA 10 (Gem) sold for $747 (Mile High; 2/08)
—Davey Lopes #609 PSA 10 (Gem) sold for $1,426 (eBay; 3/08)
—Davey Lopes #609 PSA 10 (Gem) sold for $1,260 (eBay; 1/07)
—Willie McCovey #410 PSA 10 (Gem) sold for $1,160 (eBay; 6/08)
—Joe Morgan #230 PSA 9 (MT) sold for $871 (eBay; 11/07)
—Joe Morgan #230 PSA 9 (MT) sold for $640 (eBay; 2/08)
—Joe Morgan #230 PSA 9 (MT) sold for $530 (eBay; 5/07)
—Joe Morgan #230 PSA 9 (MT) sold for $387 (eBay; 4/07)
—Brooks Robinson #90 PSA 10 (Gem) sold for $832 (eBay; 8/07)
—Pete Rose #130 PSA 10 (Gem) sold for $12,704 (eBay; 10/08)
—Nolan Ryan #220 PSA 10 (Gem) sold for $10,573 (Memory Lane; 8/12)
—Mike Schmidt #615 PSA 10 (Gem) (Young Collection) sold for $15,766 (SCP; 5/12)
—Mike Schmidt #615 PSA 10 (Gem) sold for $11,305 (eBay; 3/08)
—Mike Schmidt #615 PSA 10 (Gem) sold for $7,188 (Superior 12/05)
—Mike Schmidt #615 PSA 10 (Gem) sold for $4,692 (Mastro 10/05)
—Mike Schmidt #615 SGC 96 (MT) sold for $2,178 (Mile High; 2/08)
—Mike Schmidt #615 SGC 96 (MT) sold for $1,240 (eBay; 2/08)
—Strikeout Leaders #67 PSA 10 (Gem) sold for $1,887 (Madec; 11/07)
—Carl Yastrzemski #245 PSA 9 (MT) sold for $1,100 (eBay; 5/08)
—Carl Yastrzemski #245 PSA 9 (MT) sold for $988 (eBay; 12/06)
—Carl Yastrzemski #245 PSA 9 (MT) sold for $836 (eBay; 1/07)
—Carl Yastrzemski #245 PSA 9 (MT) sold for $810 (eBay; 5/07)
—Carl Yastrzemski #245 PSA 9 (MT) sold for $761 (eBay; 3/07)
—Carl Yastrzemski #245 PSA 9 (MT) sold for $734 (eBay; 9/07)
—Carl Yastrzemski #245 PSA 9 (MT) sold for $610 (eBay; 6/08)

1974 Kellogg's

		VG 3	VgEx 4	EX 5	ExMt 6	NM 7	NmMt 8	MT 9	Gem 9.5/10
1	Bob Gibson	4	4	4	4	4	5		
2	Rick Monday	4	4	4	4	4	5		
3	Joe Coleman	4	4	4	4	4	5	10	25
4	Bert Campaneris	4	4	4	4	4	8	15	50
5	Carlton Fisk	4	4	4	4	4	8	15	80
6	Jim Palmer	4	4	4	4	4	5	10	30
7A	Ron Santo Cubs	4	4	4	4	5	10	20	
7B	Ron Santo White Sox	4	4	4	4	4	8	15	
8	Nolan Ryan	4	4	4	5	10	20	40	200
9	Greg Luzinski	4	4	4	4	4	5	10	40
10A	Buddy Bell 134 Runs	4	4	4	4	4	5	10	
10B	Buddy Bell 135 Runs	4	4	4	4	4	5	10	
11	Bob Watson	4	4	4	4	4	5	10	25
12	Bill Singer	4	4	4	4	4	5	10	20
13	Dave May	4	4	4	4	4	5	10	20
14	Jim Brewer	4	4	4	4	4	5	10	25

		VG 3	VgEx 4	EX 5	ExMt 6	NM 7	NmMt 8	MT 9	Gem 9.5
15	Manny Sanguillen	4	4	4	4	4	5	10	
16	Jeff Burroughs	4	4	4	4	4	5	10	
17	Amos Otis	4	4	4	4	4	5	10	
18	Ed Goodson	4	4	4	4	4	5	10	
19	Nate Colbert	4	4	4	4	4	5	10	
20	Reggie Jackson	4	4	4	4	4	8	15	
21	Ted Simmons	4	4	4	4	4	5	10	
22	Bobby Murcer	4	4	4	4	4	5	10	
23	Willie Horton	4	4	4	4	4	5	10	
24	Orlando Cepeda	4	4	4	4	4	5	10	
25	Ron Hunt	4	4	4	4	4	5	10	
26	Wayne Twitchell	4	4	4	4	4	5	10	
27	Ron Fairly	4	4	4	4	4	5	10	
28	Johnny Bench	4	4	4	4	4	8	15	
29	John Mayberry	4	4	4	4	4	5	10	
30	Rod Carew	4	4	4	4	4	5	10	
31	Ken Holtzman	4	4	4	4	4	5	10	
32	Billy Williams	4	4	4	4	4	5	10	3
33	Dick Allen	4	4	4	4	4	5	10	4
34A	Wilbur Wood SO 959	4	4	4	4	4	5	10	
34B	Wilbur Wood SO 960	4	4	4	4	4	5		2
35	Danny Thompson	4	4	4	4	4	5	10	2
36	Joe Morgan	4	4	4	4	4	5	10	3
37	Willie Stargell	4	4	4	4	4	5	10	3
38	Pete Rose	4	4	4	4	5	10	20	8
39	Bobby Bonds	4	4	4	4	4	5	10	2
40	Chris Speier	4	4	4	4	4	5	10	2
41	Sparky Lyle	4	4	4	4	4	5	10	2
42	Cookie Rojas	4	4	4	4	4	5	10	2
43	Tommy Davis	4	4	4	4	4	5	10	2
44	Jim Hunter	4	4	4	4	4	5	10	3
45	Willie Davis	4	4	4	4	4	5	10	3
46	Bert Blyleven	4	4	4	4	4	5	10	2
47	Pat Kelly	4	4	4	4	4	5	10	2
48	Ken Singleton	4	4	4	4	4	5	10	2
49	Manny Mota	4	4	4	4	4	5	10	2
50	Dave Johnson	4	4	4	4	4	5	10	2
51	Sal Bando	4	4	4	4	4	5	10	2
52	Tom Seaver	4	4	4	4	4	8	15	4
53	Felix Millan	4	4	4	4	4	5	10	2
54	Ron Blomberg	4	4	4	4	4	5	10	2

—Bob Gibson #1 PSA 10 (Gem) sold for $144 (eBay; 4/08)

1974 Topps

		GD 2	VG 3	EX 5	ExMt 6	NM 7	NmMt 8	NmMt+ 8.5	MT
1	Hank Aaron 715	4	4	20	40	▲100	200	250	1,50
2	Aaron Special 54-57	4	4	15	20	25	60	80	15
3	Aaron Special 58-61	4	4	15	20	25	50	60	12
4	Aaron Special 62-65	4	4	12	15	20	50	60	12
5	Aaron Special 66-69	4	4	15	20	25	40	50	12
6	Aaron Special 70-73	4	4	5	8	20	40	50	12
7	Jim Hunter	4	4	4	6	12	25	30	15
8	George Theodore RC	4	4	4	4	8	15	20	12
9	Mickey Lolich	4	4	4	4	4	5	6	2
10	Johnny Bench	4	4	15	20	30	60	80	30
11	Jim Bibby	4	4	4	4	4	5	6	1
12	Dave May	4	4	4	4	4	5	6	1
13	Tom Hilgendorf	4	4	4	4	4	5	6	1
14	Paul Popovich	4	4	4	4	4	8	10	4
15	Joe Torre	4	4	4	4	4	6	8	2
16	Baltimore Orioles TC	4	4	4	4	4	6	10	150
17	Doug Bird RC	4	4	4	4	4	5	6	1
18	Gary Thomasson RC	4	4	4	4	4	5	6	1
19	Gerry Moses	4	4	4	4	4	5	6	2
20	Nolan Ryan	12	15	25	30	50	100	250	600
21	Bob Gallagher RC	4	4	4	4	4	5	6	1
22	Cy Acosta	4	4	4	4	4	5	6	2
23	Craig Robinson RC	4	4	4	4	4	5	6	1
24	John Hiller	4	4	4	4	4	5	6	1
25	Ken Singleton	4	4	4	4	4	5	6	1
26	Bill Campbell RC	4	4	4	4	4	5	6	2
27	George Scott	4	4	4	4	4	5	6	1
28	Manny Sanguillen	4	4	4	4	4	5	6	1
29	Phil Niekro	4	4	4	4	4	8	10	80
30	Bobby Bonds	4	4	4	4	4	5	6	1
31	Preston Gomez MG	4	4	4	4	4	5	6	2

	GD 2	VG 3	EX 5	ExMt 6	NM 7	NmMt 8	NmMt+ 8.5	MT 9
Johnny Grubb SD RC	4	4	4	4	4	5	6	15
Johnny Grubb WASH	4	4	5	6	12	25	30	100
Don Newhauser RC	4	4	4	4	4	5	6	15
Andy Kosco	4	4	4	4	4	5	6	15
Gaylord Perry	4	4	4	4	4	6	8	20
St. Louis Cardinals TC	4	4	4	4	4	5	6	15
Dave Sells RC	4	4	4	4	4	5	6	15
Don Kessinger	4	4	4	4	4	5	6	15
Ken Suarez	4	4	4	4	4	5	6	20
Jim Palmer	4	4	4	4	12	▲40	▲50	150
Bobby Floyd	4	4	4	4	4	5	6	15
Claude Osteen	4	4	4	4	4	5	6	15
Jim Wynn	4	4	4	4	4	5	6	15
Mel Stottlemyre	4	4	4	4	4	5	6	15
Dave Johnson	4	4	4	4	4	5	6	15
Pat Kelly	4	4	4	4	4	5	6	15
Dick Ruthven RC	4	4	4	4	4	5	6	20
Dick Sharon RC	4	4	4	4	4	5	6	15
Steve Renko	4	4	4	4	4	5	6	15
Rod Carew	4	4	4	▲15	▲20	▲30	▲40	100
Bobby Heise	4	4	4	4	4	5	6	15
Al Oliver	4	4	4	4	4	5	6	20
Fred Kendall SD	4	4	4	4	4	5	6	60
Fred Kendall WASH	4	4	5	6	12	25	30	120
Elias Sosa RC	4	4	4	4	4	5	6	20
Frank Robinson	4	4	4	4	12	25	30	60
New York Mets TC	4	4	4	4	4	5	6	15
Darold Knowles	4	4	4	4	4	5	6	15
Charlie Spikes	4	4	4	4	4	5	6	25
Ross Grimsley	4	4	4	4	4	5	6	15
Lou Brock	4	4	4	5	12	▲30	▲40	▲80
Luis Aparicio	4	4	4	4	5	10	15	60
Bob Locker	4	4	4	4	4	5	6	15
Bill Sudakis	4	4	4	4	4	5	6	10
Doug Rau	4	4	4	4	4	5	6	15
Amos Otis	4	4	4	4	4	8	10	100
Sparky Lyle	4	4	4	4	4	5	6	30
Tommy Helms	4	4	4	4	4	5	6	15
Grant Jackson	4	4	4	4	4	5	6	25
Del Unser	4	4	4	4	4	8	12	80
Dick Allen	4	4	4	4	4	8	10	25
Dan Frisella	4	4	4	4	4	5	6	15
Aurelio Rodriguez	4	4	4	4	4	5	6	15
Mike Marshall	4	4	4	4	4	5	6	15
Minnesota Twins TC	4	4	4	4	4	5	6	15
Jim Colborn	4	4	4	4	4	5	6	15
Mickey Rivers	4	4	4	4	4	5	6	25
Rich Troedson SD	4	4	4	4	4	5	6	25
Rich Troedson WASH	4	4	5	6	12	25	30	80
Charlie Fox MG	4	4	4	4	4	5	6	20
Gene Tenace	4	4	4	4	4	5	6	15
Tom Seaver	4	4	10	▲25	30	50	60	▲200
Frank Duffy	4	4	4	4	4	5	6	15
Dave Giusti	4	4	4	4	4	5	6	15
Orlando Cepeda	4	4	4	4	8	12	15	50
Rick Wise	4	4	4	4	4	5	6	15
Joe Morgan	4	4	4	5	▲15	25	30	100
Joe Ferguson	4	4	4	4	4	5	6	15
Fergie Jenkins	4	4	4	4	6	12	15	30
Freddie Patek	4	4	4	4	4	5	6	15
Jackie Brown	4	4	4	4	4	5	6	120
Bobby Murcer	4	4	4	4	5	10	15	60
Ken Forsch	4	4	4	4	4	5	6	15
Paul Blair	4	4	4	4	4	5	6	20
Rod Gilbreath RC	4	4	4	4	4	5	6	15
Detroit Tigers TC	4	4	4	4	4	8	10	25
Steve Carlton	4	4	4	8	▲20	25	30	▲250
Jerry Hairston RC	4	4	4	4	4	5	6	15
Bob Bailey	4	4	4	4	4	5	6	15
Bert Blyleven	4	4	4	4	4	6	8	25
Del Crandall MG	4	4	4	4	4	5	6	15
Willie Stargell	4	4	4	6	12	▲30	▲40	100
Bobby Valentine	4	4	4	4	4	5	6	25
Bill Greif SD	4	4	4	4	4	6	10	40
Bill Greif WASH	4	4	4	4	8	15	20	50
Sal Bando	4	4	4	4	4	5	6	15
Ron Bryant	4	4	4	4	4	5	6	15

		GD 2	VG 3	EX 5	ExMt 6	NM 7	NmMt 8	NmMt+ 8.5	MT 9
105	Carlton Fisk	5	6	10	12	25	50	60	300
106	Harry Parker RC	4	4	4	4	4	5	6	15
107	Alex Johnson	4	4	4	4	4	5	6	15
108	Al Hrabosky	4	4	4	4	4	5	6	15
109	Bob Grich	4	4	4	4	4	5	6	20
110	Billy Williams	4	4	4	4	5	10	15	200
111	Clay Carroll	4	4	4	4	6	12	15	300
112	Davey Lopes	4	4	4	4	4	6	8	20
113	Dick Drago	4	4	4	4	4	5	6	25
114	California Angels TC	4	4	4	4	4	5	6	15
115	Willie Horton	4	4	4	4	4	5	6	15
116	Jerry Reuss	4	4	4	4	4	5	6	50
117	Ron Blomberg	4	4	4	4	4	5	6	20
118	Bill Lee	4	4	4	4	4	5	6	15
119	Danny Ozark MG	4	4	4	4	4	5	6	20
120	Wilbur Wood	4	4	4	4	5	10	12	20
121	Larry Lintz RC	4	4	4	4	4	5	6	15
122	Jim Holt	4	4	4	4	4	5	6	15
123	Nelson Briles	4	4	4	4	4	5	6	15
124	Bobby Coluccio RC	4	4	4	4	4	5	6	50
125A	Nate Colbert SD	4	4	4	4	4	6	10	60
125B	Nate Colbert WASH	4	4	5	6	12	25	30	80
126	Checklist 1-132	4	4	4	4	4	6	8	25
127	Tom Paciorek	4	4	4	4	4	5	6	15
128	John Ellis	4	4	4	4	4	5	6	15
129	Chris Speier	4	4	4	4	4	5	6	15
130	Reggie Jackson	8	10	15	20	30	60	200	▲800
131	Bob Boone	4	4	4	4	4	5	6	15
132	Felix Millan	4	4	4	4	4	8	10	200
133	David Clyde RC	4	4	4	4	4	5	6	15
134	Denis Menke	4	4	4	4	4	5	6	15
135	Roy White	4	4	4	4	4	6	10	80
136	Rick Reuschel	4	4	4	4	4	5	6	15
137	Al Bumbry	4	4	4	4	4	5	6	15
138	Eddie Brinkman	4	4	4	4	4	5	6	15
139	Aurelio Monteagudo	4	4	4	4	4	5	6	15
140	Darrell Evans	4	4	4	4	4	5	6	15
141	Pat Bourque	4	4	4	4	4	5	6	15
142	Pedro Garcia	4	4	4	4	4	5	6	20
143	Dick Woodson	4	4	4	4	4	5	6	15
144	Walter Alston MG	4	4	4	4	4	6	8	20
145	Dock Ellis	4	4	4	4	4	5	6	15
146	Ron Fairly	4	4	4	4	4	5	6	20
147	Bart Johnson	4	4	4	4	4	5	6	20
148A	Dave Hilton SD	4	4	4	4	4	5	6	15
148B	Dave Hilton WASH	4	4	5	6	12	25	30	100
149	Mac Scarce	4	4	4	4	4	5	6	15
150	John Mayberry	4	4	4	4	4	5	6	40
151	Diego Segui	4	4	4	4	4	5	6	15
152	Oscar Gamble	4	4	4	4	4	5	6	15
153	Jon Matlack	4	4	4	4	4	5	6	15
154	Houston Astros TC	4	4	4	4	4	5	6	15
155	Bert Campaneris	4	4	4	4	4	5	6	15
156	Randy Moffitt	4	4	4	4	4	5	6	15
157	Vic Harris	4	4	4	4	4	5	6	15
158	Jack Billingham	4	4	4	4	4	5	6	15
159	Jim Ray Hart	4	4	4	4	4	5	6	15
160	Brooks Robinson	4	4	4	▲15	▲20	▲30	▲40	▲100
161	Ray Burris RC	4	4	4	4	4	5	6	15
162	Bill Freehan	4	4	4	4	4	5	6	15
163	Ken Berry	4	4	4	4	4	5	6	15
164	Tom House	4	4	4	4	4	5	6	20
165	Willie Davis	4	4	4	4	4	5	6	60
166	Jack McKeon MG	4	4	4	4	4	5	6	20
167	Luis Tiant	4	4	4	4	4	5	6	15
168	Danny Thompson	4	4	4	4	4	5	6	15
169	Steve Rogers RC	4	4	4	4	4	5	6	15
170	Bill Melton	4	4	4	4	4	5	6	60
171	Eduardo Rodriguez RC	4	4	4	4	4	5	6	15
172	Gene Clines	4	4	4	4	4	5	6	20
173A	Randy Jones SD RC	4	4	4	4	4	6	10	200
173B	Randy Jones WASH	4	4	6	8	15	30	40	120
174	Bill Robinson	4	4	4	4	4	5	6	20
175	Reggie Cleveland	4	4	4	4	4	5	6	15
176	John Lowenstein	4	4	4	4	4	5	6	15
177	Dave Roberts	4	4	4	4	4	5	6	15
178	Garry Maddox	4	4	4	4	4	5	6	15

No.	Player	GD 2	VG 3	EX 5	ExMt 6	NM 7	NmMt 8	NmMt+ 8.5	MT 9
179	Yogi Berra MG	4	4	4	4	5	10	15	100
180	Ken Holtzman	4	4	4	4	4	5	6	15
181	Cesar Geronimo	4	4	4	4	4	5	6	20
182	Lindy McDaniel	4	4	4	4	4	5	6	12
183	Johnny Oates	4	4	4	4	4	5	6	15
184	Texas Rangers TC	4	4	4	4	4	5	6	15
185	Jose Cardenal	4	4	4	4	4	5	6	15
186	Fred Scherman	4	4	4	4	4	5	6	15
187	Don Baylor	4	4	4	4	4	5	6	15
188	Rudy Meoli RC	4	4	4	4	4	5	6	15
189	Jim Brewer	4	4	4	4	4	5	6	15
190	Tony Oliva	4	4	4	4	6	12	15	40
191	Al Fitzmorris	4	4	4	4	4	5	6	15
192	Mario Guerrero	4	4	4	4	4	5	6	10
193	Tom Walker	4	4	4	4	4	5	6	20
194	Darrell Porter	4	4	4	4	4	5	6	15
195	Carlos May	4	4	4	4	4	5	6	20
196	Jim Fregosi	4	4	4	4	4	5	6	15
197A	Vicente Romo SD	4	4	4	4	4	5	6	50
197B	Vicente Romo WASH	4	4	5	6	12	25	30	100
198	Dave Cash	4	4	4	4	4	5	6	15
199	Mike Kekich	4	4	4	4	4	5	6	25
200	Cesar Cedeno	4	4	4	4	4	5	6	20
201	Batting Leaders	4	4	4	4	8	25	30	60
202	Home Run Leaders	4	4	4	4	6	12	15	40
203	RBI Leaders	4	4	4	4	6	▲20	▲25	▲150
204	Stolen Base Leaders	4	4	4	4	4	5	6	15
205	Victory Leaders	4	4	4	4	4	5	6	15
206	ERA Leaders	4	4	4	4	6	12	15	50
207	Strikeout Leaders	4	4	4	5	▲25	▲50	▲60	120
208	Leading Firemen	4	4	4	4	4	5	6	15
209	Ted Sizemore	4	4	4	4	4	5	6	15
210	Bill Singer	4	4	4	4	4	5	6	15
211	Chicago Cubs TC	4	4	4	4	4	5	6	15
212	Rollie Fingers	4	4	4	4	6	12	15	30
213	Dave Rader	4	4	4	4	4	6	8	120
214	Billy Grabarkewitz	4	4	4	4	4	5	6	15
215	Al Kaline	4	4	4	▲15	▲20	▲50	▲60	▲300
216	Ray Sadecki	4	4	4	4	4	5	6	15
217	Tim Foli	4	4	4	4	4	5	6	15
218	Johnny Briggs	4	4	4	4	4	5	6	20
219	Doug Griffin	4	4	4	4	4	5	6	20
220	Don Sutton	4	4	4	4	4	6	8	25
221	Chuck Tanner MG	4	4	4	4	4	5	6	30
222	Ramon Hernandez	4	4	4	4	4	5	6	20
223	Jeff Burroughs	4	4	4	4	4	5	6	15
224	Roger Metzger	4	4	4	4	4	5	6	15
225	Paul Splittorff	4	4	4	4	4	5	6	20
226A	San Diego Padres TC SD	4	4	4	4	4	6	8	60
226B	San Diego Padres TC WASH	4	4	5	8	15	30	40	300
227	Mike Lum	4	4	4	4	4	5	6	15
228	Ted Kubiak	4	4	4	4	4	5	6	15
229	Fritz Peterson	4	4	4	4	4	5	6	200
230	Tony Perez	4	4	4	4	8	15	20	80
231	Dick Tidrow	4	4	4	4	4	5	6	15
232	Steve Brye	4	4	4	4	4	5	6	25
233	Jim Barr	4	4	4	4	4	5	6	30
234	John Milner	4	4	4	4	4	5	6	12
235	Dave McNally	4	4	4	4	4	6	8	20
236	Red Schoendienst MG	4	4	4	4	4	6	8	20
237	Ken Brett	4	4	4	4	4	5	6	20
238	F.Healy w/Munson	4	4	4	4	4	5	6	80
239	Bill Russell	4	4	4	4	4	5	6	20
240	Joe Coleman	4	4	4	4	4	5	6	15
241A	Glenn Beckert SD	4	4	4	4	4	5	6	25
241B	Glenn Beckert WASH	4	4	5	6	12	25	30	150
242	Bill Gogolewski	4	4	4	4	4	5	6	15
243	Bob Oliver	4	4	4	4	4	5	6	15
244	Carl Morton	4	4	4	4	4	5	6	15
245	Cleon Jones	4	4	4	4	4	5	6	25
246	Oakland Athletics TC	4	4	4	4	4	5	6	15
247	Rick Miller	4	4	4	4	4	5	6	15
248	Tom Hall	4	4	4	4	4	5	6	15
249	George Mitterwald	4	4	4	4	4	5	6	50
250A	Willie McCovey SD	4	4	4	4	8	25	30	80
250B	Willie McCovey WASH	4	4	8	10	20	50	60	200
251	Graig Nettles	4	4	4	4	6	12	15	120

No.	Player	GD 2	VG 3	EX 5	ExMt 6	NM 7	NmMt 8	NmMt+ 8.5	MT 9
252	Dave Parker RC	6	8	12	▲20	▲30	▲60	▲80	▲2…
253	John Boccabella	4	4	4	4	4	5	6	
254	Stan Bahnsen	4	4	4	4	4	5	6	
255	Larry Bowa	4	4	4	4	4	5	6	
256	Tom Griffin	4	4	4	4	4	5	6	
257	Buddy Bell	4	4	4	4	4	5	6	
258	Jerry Morales	4	4	4	4	4	5	6	
259	Bob Reynolds	4	4	4	4	4	5	6	2
260	Ted Simmons	4	4	4	4	4	6	8	2
261	Jerry Bell	4	4	4	4	4	5	6	
262	Ed Kirkpatrick	4	4	4	4	4	5	6	
263	Checklist 133-264	4	4	4	4	4	8		8
264	Joe Rudi	4	4	4	4	4	5		5
265	Tug McGraw	4	4	4	4	4	5	6	
266	Jim Northrup	4	4	4	4	4	5	6	
267	Andy Messersmith	4	4	4	4	4	5	6	
268	Tom Grieve	4	4	4	4	4	5	6	
269	Bob Johnson	4	4	4	4	4	5	6	
270	Ron Santo	4	4	4	4	4	8	10	5
271	Bill Hands	4	4	4	4	4	5	6	
272	Paul Casanova	4	4	4	4	4	5	6	
273	Checklist 265-396	4	4	4	4	4	8	10	10
274	Fred Beene	4	4	4	4	4	5	6	
275	Ron Hunt	4	4	4	4	4	5	6	
276	Bobby Winkles MG	4	4	4	4	4	5	6	
277	Gary Nolan	4	4	4	4	4	8	10	12
278	Cookie Rojas	4	4	4	4	4	5	6	
279	Jim Crawford RC	4	4	4	4	4	5	6	
280	Carl Yastrzemski	4	4	12	15	20	▲40	50	▲12…
281	San Francisco Giants TC	4	4	4	4	4	5	6	
282	Doyle Alexander	4	4	4	4	4	5	6	
283	Mike Schmidt	4	4	▲25	▲30	▲50	▲100	200	30…
284	Dave Duncan	4	4	4	4	4	5	6	
285	Reggie Smith	4	4	4	4	4	5	6	
286	Tony Muser	4	4	4	4	4	5	6	
287	Clay Kirby	4	4	4	4	4	5	6	
288	Gorman Thomas RC	4	4	4	4	4	5	6	
289	Rick Auerbach	4	4	4	4	4	5	6	10
290	Vida Blue	4	4	4	4	4	5	6	3
291	Don Hahn	4	4	4	4	4	5	6	
292	Chuck Seelbach	4	4	4	4	4	5	6	
293	Milt May	4	4	4	4	4	5	6	
294	Steve Foucault RC	4	4	4	4	4	5	6	
295	Rick Monday	4	4	4	4	4	5	6	
296	Ray Corbin	4	4	4	4	4	5	6	
297	Hal Breeden	4	4	4	4	4	5	6	
298	Roric Harrison	4	4	4	4	4	5	6	
299	Gene Michael	4	4	4	4	4	5	6	
300	Pete Rose	10	12	▲25	▲30	40	80	100	50…
301	Bob Montgomery	4	4	4	4	4	5	6	
302	Rudy May	4	4	4	4	4	5	6	
303	George Hendrick	4	4	4	4	4	5	6	
304	Don Wilson	4	4	4	4	4	5	6	1
305	Tito Fuentes	4	4	4	4	4	5	6	15
306	Earl Weaver MG	4	4	4	4	4	5	6	1
307	Luis Melendez	4	4	4	4	4	5	6	1
308	Bruce Dal Canton	4	4	4	4	4	5	6	1
309A	Dave Roberts SD	4	4	4	4	4	5	6	2
309B	Dave Roberts WASH	4	4	6	8	15	60	80	12
310	Terry Forster	4	4	4	4	4	5	6	
311	Jerry Grote	4	4	4	4	4	6	8	5
312	Deron Johnson	4	4	4	4	4	5	6	6
313	Barry Lersch	4	4	4	4	4	5	6	15
314	Milwaukee Brewers TC	4	4	4	4	4	5	6	1
315	Ron Cey	4	4	4	4	4	5	6	15
316	Jim Perry	4	4	4	4	4	5	6	15
317	Richie Zisk	4	4	4	4	4	5	6	4
318	Jim Merritt	4	4	4	4	4	5	6	15
319	Randy Hundley	4	4	4	4	4	5	6	20
320	Dusty Baker	4	4	4	4	4	6	8	20
321	Steve Braun	4	4	4	4	4	5	6	300
322	Ernie McAnally	4	4	4	4	4	5	6	15
323	Richie Scheinblum	4	4	4	4	4	5	6	150
324	Steve Kline	4	4	4	4	4	5	6	15
325	Tommy Harper	6	6	4	4	4	5	6	15
326	Sparky Anderson MG	4	4	4	4	4	8	10	80
327	Tom Timmermann	4	4	4	4	4	5	6	20

	GD 2	VG 3	EX 5	ExMt 6	NM 7	NmMt 8	NmMt+ 8.5	MT 9
Skip Jutze	4	4	4	4	4	5	6	15
Mark Belanger	4	4	4	4	4	5	6	15
Juan Marichal	4	4	4	4	8	15	20	▲60
C.Fisk/J.Bench AS	4	4	4	4	10	▲30	40	80
D.Allen/H.Aaron AS	4	4	4	5	10	▲25	▲30	60
R.Carew/J.Morgan AS	4	4	4	5	10	20	25	150
B.Robinson/R.Santo AS	4	4	4	4	4	8	10	30
B.Campaneris/C.Speier AS	4	4	4	4	4	5	6	15
B.Murcer/P.Rose AS	4	4	4	4	8	15	20	80
A.Otis/C.Cedeno AS	4	4	4	4	4	5	6	15
R.Jackson/B.Williams AS	4	4	4	4	6	15	20	25
J.Hunter/R.Wise AS	4	4	4	4	4	6	8	50
Thurman Munson	4	4	5	12	25	▲50	▲60	▲120
Dan Driessen RC	4	4	4	4	4	5	6	15
Jim Lonborg	4	4	4	4	4	5	6	15
Kansas City Royals TC	4	4	4	4	4	5	6	15
Mike Caldwell	4	4	4	4	4	5	6	100
Bill North	4	4	4	4	4	5	6	15
Ron Reed	4	4	4	4	4	5	6	15
Sandy Alomar	4	4	4	4	4	5	6	20
Pete Richert	4	4	4	4	4	5	6	15
John Vukovich	4	4	4	4	4	5	6	20
Bob Gibson	4	4	4	6	20	▲40	▲50	100
Dwight Evans	4	4	4	4	6	12	15	40
Bill Stoneman	4	4	4	4	4	5	6	80
Rich Coggins	4	4	4	4	4	5	6	25
Whitey Lockman MG	4	4	4	4	4	5	6	15
Dave Nelson	4	4	4	4	4	5	6	50
Jerry Koosman	4	4	4	4	4	5	6	12
Buddy Bradford	4	4	4	4	4	5	6	15
Dal Maxvill	4	4	4	4	4	5	6	80
Brent Strom	4	4	4	4	4	5	6	15
Greg Luzinski	4	4	4	4	4	5	6	15
Don Carrithers	4	4	4	4	4	5	6	60
Hal King	4	4	4	4	4	5	6	15
New York Yankees TC	4	4	4	4	4	6	8	25
Cito Gaston SD	4	4	4	4	8	15	20	200
Cito Gaston WASH	4	4	12	15	30	60	80	450
Steve Busby	4	4	4	4	4	5	6	15
Larry Hisle	4	4	4	4	4	5	6	15
Norm Cash	4	4	4	4	4	8	10	20
Manny Mota	4	4	4	4	4	5	6	15
Paul Lindblad	4	4	4	4	4	8	10	60
Bob Watson	4	4	4	4	4	5	6	15
Jim Slaton	4	4	4	4	4	5	6	15
Ken Reitz	4	4	4	4	4	5	6	15
John Curtis	4	4	4	4	4	5	6	15
Marty Perez	4	4	4	4	4	5	6	25
Earl Williams	4	4	4	4	4	5	6	15
Jorge Orta	4	4	4	4	4	5	6	10
Ron Woods	4	4	4	4	4	5	6	15
Burt Hooton	4	4	4	4	4	5	6	20
Billy Martin MG	4	4	4	4	6	8	6	25
Bud Harrelson	4	4	4	4	4	5	6	15
Charlie Sands	4	4	4	4	4	5	6	15
Bob Moose	4	4	4	4	4	5	6	15
Philadelphia Phillies TC	4	4	4	4	4	5	6	120
Chris Chambliss	4	4	4	4	4	5	6	15
Don Gullett	4	4	4	4	4	5	6	15
Gary Matthews	4	4	4	4	4	5	6	15
Rich Morales SD	4	4	4	4	4	5	6	20
Rich Morales WASH	4	4	8	10	20	40	60	100
Phil Roof	4	4	4	4	4	5	6	25
Gates Brown	4	4	4	4	4	5	6	15
Lou Piniella	4	4	4	4	4	5	6	15
Billy Champion	4	4	4	4	4	5	6	15
Dick Green	4	4	4	4	4	5	6	15
Orlando Pena	4	4	4	4	4	5	6	15
Ken Henderson	4	4	4	4	4	5	6	25
Doug Rader	4	4	4	4	4	5	6	15
Tommy Davis	4	4	4	4	4	5	6	15
George Stone	4	4	4	4	4	5	6	20
Duke Sims	4	4	4	4	4	5	6	15
Mike Paul	4	4	4	4	4	5	6	20
Harmon Killebrew	4	4	4	5	15	▲30	▲40	100
Elliott Maddox	4	4	4	4	4	5	6	15
Jim Rooker	4	4	4	4	4	5	6	15

		GD 2	VG 3	EX 5	ExMt 6	NM 7	NmMt 8	NmMt+ 8.5	MT 9
403	Darrell Johnson MG	4	4	4	4	4	5	6	15
404	Jim Howarth	4	4	4	4	4	5	6	15
405	Ellie Rodriguez	4	4	4	4	4	5	6	25
406	Steve Arlin	4	4	4	4	4	5	6	25
407	Jim Wohlford	4	4	4	4	4	5	6	15
408	Charlie Hough	4	4	4	4	4	5	6	15
409	Ike Brown	4	4	4	4	4	5	6	20
410	Pedro Borbon	4	4	4	4	4	5	6	15
411	Frank Baker	4	4	4	4	4	5	6	12
412	Chuck Taylor	4	4	4	4	4	5	6	15
413	Don Money	4	4	4	4	4	5	6	15
414	Checklist 397-528	4	4	4	4	5	10	12	50
415	Gary Gentry	4	4	4	4	4	5	6	15
416	Chicago White Sox TC	4	4	4	4	4	5	6	12
417	Rich Folkers	4	4	4	4	4	5	6	20
418	Walt Williams	4	4	4	4	4	5	6	15
419	Wayne Twitchell	4	4	4	4	4	5	6	15
420	Ray Fosse	4	4	4	4	4	5	6	15
421	Dan Fife RC	4	4	4	4	4	5	6	15
422	Gonzalo Marquez	4	4	4	4	4	5	6	15
423	Fred Stanley	4	4	4	4	4	5	6	15
424	Jim Beauchamp	4	4	4	4	4	5	6	15
425	Pete Broberg	4	4	4	4	4	5	6	15
426	Rennie Stennett	4	4	4	4	4	5	6	20
427	Bobby Bolin	4	4	4	4	4	5	6	15
428	Gary Sutherland	4	4	4	4	4	5	6	15
429	Dick Lange RC	4	4	4	4	4	5	6	15
430	Matty Alou	4	4	4	4	4	6	8	80
431	Gene Garber RC	4	4	4	4	4	5	6	15
432	Chris Arnold	4	4	4	4	4	5	6	15
433	Lerrin LaGrow	4	4	4	4	4	5	6	15
434	Ken McMullen	4	4	4	4	4	5	6	15
435	Dave Concepcion	4	4	4	4	4	8	10	50
436	Don Hood RC	4	4	4	4	4	5	6	15
437	Jim Lyttle	4	4	4	4	4	5	6	15
438	Ed Herrmann	4	4	4	4	4	5	6	15
439	Norm Miller	4	4	4	4	4	5	6	15
440	Jim Kaat	4	4	4	4	4	8	12	200
441	Tom Ragland	4	4	4	4	4	5	6	15
442	Alan Foster	4	4	4	4	4	5	6	25
443	Tom Hutton	4	4	4	4	4	5	6	15
444	Vic Davalillo	4	4	4	4	4	5	6	15
445	George Medich	4	4	4	4	4	5	6	15
446	Len Randle	4	4	4	4	4	5	6	15
447	Frank Quilici MG	4	4	4	4	4	5	6	15
448	Ron Hodges RC	4	4	4	4	4	5	6	15
449	Tom McCraw	4	4	4	4	4	5	6	15
450	Rich Hebner	4	4	4	4	4	5	6	20
451	Tommy John	4	4	4	4	4	5	6	15
452	Gene Hiser	4	4	4	4	4	5	6	25
453	Balor Moore	4	4	4	4	4	5	6	15
454	Kurt Bevacqua	4	4	4	4	4	5	6	40
455	Tom Bradley	4	4	4	4	4	5	6	20
456	Dave Winfield RC	15	20	30	▲50	60	150	300	800
457	Chuck Goggin RC	4	4	4	4	4	5	6	15
458	Jim Ray	4	4	4	4	4	5	6	15
459	Cincinnati Reds TC	4	4	4	4	4	8	10	30
460	Boog Powell	4	4	4	4	5	10	12	30
461	John Odom	4	4	4	4	4	5	6	50
462	Luis Alvarado	4	4	4	4	4	5	6	15
463	Pat Dobson	4	4	4	4	4	5	6	15
464	Jose Cruz	4	4	4	4	4	5	6	15
465	Dick Bosman	4	4	4	4	4	5	6	20
466	Dick Billings	4	4	4	4	4	5	6	10
467	Winston Llenas	4	4	4	4	4	5	6	15
468	Pepe Frias	4	4	4	4	4	5	6	12
469	Joe Decker	4	4	4	4	4	5	6	15
470	Reggie Jackson ALCS	4	4	4	4	4	12	20	30
471	Jon Matlack NLCS	4	4	4	4	4	5	6	15
472	Darold Knowles WS1	4	4	4	4	4	5	6	15
473	Willie Mays WS	6	8	12	15	20	▲50	▲60	▲100
474	Bert Campaneris WS3	4	4	4	4	4	8	10	150
475	Rusty Staub WS4	4	4	4	4	4	5	6	12
476	Cleon Jones WS5	4	4	4	4	4	5	6	12
477	Reggie Jackson WS	4	4	4	4	4	10	15	25
478	Bert Campaneris WS7	4	4	4	4	4	5	6	12
479	A's Celebrate WS	4	4	4	4	4	5	6	15

#	Player	GD 2	VG 3	EX 5	ExMt 6	NM 7	NmMt 8	NmMt+ 8.5	MT 9
480	Willie Crawford	4	4	4	4	4	5	6	50
481	Jerry Terrell RC	4	4	4	4	4	5	6	15
482	Bob Didier	4	4	4	4	4	5	6	15
483	Atlanta Braves TC	4	4	4	4	4	5	6	10
484	Carmen Fanzone	4	4	4	4	4	5	6	15
485	Felipe Alou	4	4	4	4	4	5	6	10
486	Steve Stone	4	4	4	4	4	5	6	15
487	Ted Martinez	4	4	4	4	4	5	6	20
488	Andy Etchebarren	4	4	4	4	4	5	6	15
489	Danny Murtaugh MG	4	4	4	4	4	5	6	15
490	Vada Pinson	4	4	4	4	4	6	8	40
491	Roger Nelson	4	4	4	4	4	5	6	15
492	Mike Rogodzinski RC	4	4	4	4	6	12	15	100
493	Joe Hoerner	4	4	4	4	4	5	6	20
494	Ed Goodson	4	4	4	4	4	5	6	15
495	Dick McAuliffe	4	4	4	4	4	5	6	15
496	Tom Murphy	4	4	4	4	4	5	6	15
497	Bobby Mitchell	4	4	4	4	4	5	6	15
498	Pat Corrales	4	4	4	4	4	5	6	15
499	Rusty Torres	4	4	4	4	4	5	6	20
500	Lee May	4	4	4	4	4	5	6	12
501	Eddie Leon	4	4	4	4	4	5	6	20
502	Dave LaRoche	4	4	4	4	4	5	6	15
503	Eric Soderholm	4	4	4	4	4	5	6	15
504	Joe Niekro	4	4	4	4	4	5	6	15
505	Bill Buckner	4	4	4	4	4	5	6	15
506	Ed Farmer	4	4	4	4	4	5	6	15
507	Larry Stahl	4	4	4	4	4	5	6	15
508	Montreal Expos TC	4	4	4	4	4	5	6	15
509	Jesse Jefferson	4	4	4	4	4	5	6	15
510	Wayne Garrett	4	4	4	4	4	5	6	10
511	Toby Harrah	4	4	4	4	4	5	6	15
512	Joe Lahoud	4	4	4	4	4	5	6	15
513	Jim Campanis	4	4	4	4	4	5	6	15
514	Paul Schaal	4	4	4	4	4	5	6	15
515	Willie Montanez	4	4	4	4	4	5	6	20
516	Horacio Pina	4	4	4	4	4	5	6	15
517	Mike Hegan	4	4	4	4	4	5	6	15
518	Derrel Thomas	4	4	4	4	4	5	6	15
519	Bill Sharp RC	4	4	4	4	4	5	6	15
520	Tim McCarver	4	4	4	4	4	5	6	15
521	Ken Aspromonte MG	4	4	4	4	4	5	6	15
522	J.R. Richard	4	4	4	4	4	5	6	15
523	Cecil Cooper	4	4	4	4	4	5	6	15
524	Bill Plummer	4	4	4	4	4	5	6	15
525	Clyde Wright	4	4	4	4	4	5	6	15
526	Frank Tepedino	4	4	4	4	4	5	6	15
527	Bobby Darwin	4	4	4	4	4	5	6	20
528	Bill Bonham	4	4	4	4	4	5	6	15
529	Horace Clarke	4	4	4	4	4	5	6	15
530	Mickey Stanley	4	4	4	4	4	5	6	15
531	Gene Mauch MG	4	4	4	4	4	5	6	15
532	Skip Lockwood	4	4	4	4	4	5	6	15
533	Mike Phillips RC	4	4	4	4	4	5	6	25
534	Eddie Watt	4	4	4	4	4	5	6	15
535	Bob Tolan	4	4	4	4	4	5	6	15
536	Duffy Dyer	4	4	4	4	4	5	6	15
537	Steve Mingori	4	4	4	4	4	5	6	15
538	Cesar Tovar	4	4	4	4	4	5	6	15
539	Lloyd Allen	4	4	4	4	4	5	6	15
540	Bob Robertson	4	4	4	4	4	5	6	15
541	Cleveland Indians TC	4	4	4	4	4	5	6	15
542	Goose Gossage	4	4	4	4	8	15	20	50
543	Danny Cater	4	4	4	4	4	5	6	15
544	Ron Schueler	4	4	4	4	4	5	6	15
545	Billy Conigliaro	4	4	4	4	4	5	6	15
546	Mike Corkins	4	4	4	4	4	5	6	15
547	Glenn Borgmann	4	4	4	4	4	5	6	15
548	Sonny Siebert	4	4	4	4	4	5	6	15
549	Mike Jorgensen	4	4	4	4	4	5	6	15
550	Sam McDowell	4	4	4	4	4	5	6	15
551	Von Joshua	4	4	4	4	4	5	6	20
552	Denny Doyle	4	4	4	4	4	5	6	15
553	Jim Willoughby	4	4	4	4	4	5	6	15
554	Tim Johnson RC	4	4	4	4	4	5	6	15
555	Woodie Fryman	4	4	4	4	4	5	6	15
556	Dave Campbell	4	4	4	4	4	5	6	15

#	Player	GD 2	VG 3	EX 5	ExMt 6	NM 7	NmMt 8	NmMt+ 8.5	M
557	Jim McGlothlin	4	4	4	4	4	5	6	
558	Bill Fahey	4	4	4	4	4	5	6	
559	Darrel Chaney	4	4	4	4	4	5	6	
560	Mike Cuellar	4	4	4	4	4	5	6	
561	Ed Kranepool	4	4	4	4	4	5	6	
562	Jack Aker	4	4	4	4	4	5	6	
563	Hal McRae	4	4	4	4	4	5	6	
564	Mike Ryan	4	4	4	4	4	5	6	
565	Milt Wilcox	4	4	4	4	4	5	6	
566	Jackie Hernandez	4	4	4	4	4	5	6	
567	Boston Red Sox TC	4	4	4	4	4	5	6	
568	Mike Torrez	4	4	4	4	4	5	6	
569	Rick Dempsey	4	4	4	4	4	5	6	
570	Ralph Garr	4	4	4	4	4	5	6	
571	Rich Hand	4	4	4	4	4	5	6	
572	Enzo Hernandez	4	4	4	4	4	5	6	
573	Mike Adams RC	4	4	4	4	4	5	6	
574	Bill Parsons	4	4	4	4	4	5	6	
575	Steve Garvey	4	4	4	5	10	25	30	3
576	Scipio Spinks	4	4	4	4	4	5	6	
577	Mike Sadek RC	4	4	4	4	4	5	6	
578	Ralph Houk MG	4	4	4	4	4	5	6	
579	Cecil Upshaw	4	4	4	4	4	5	6	
580	Jim Spencer	4	4	4	4	4	5	6	
581	Fred Norman	4	4	4	4	4	5	6	
582	Bucky Dent RC	4	4	4	4		20	40	2
583	Marty Pattin	4	4	4	4	4	5	6	
584	Ken Rudolph	4	4	4	4	4	5	6	
585	Merv Rettenmund	4	4	4	4	4	5	6	
586	Jack Brohamer	4	4	4	4	4	5	6	
587	Larry Christenson RC	4	4	4	4	4	5	6	
588	Hal Lanier	4	4	4	4	4	5	6	
589	Boots Day	4	4	4	4	4	5	6	
590	Roger Moret	4	4	4	4	4	5	6	
591	Sonny Jackson	4	4	4	4	4	5	6	
592	Ed Bane RC	4	4	4	4	4	5	6	
593	Steve Yeager	4	4	4	4	4	5	6	
594	Leroy Stanton	4	4	4	4	4	5	6	
595	Steve Blass	4	4	4	4	4	5	6	
596	Rookie Pitchers	4	4	4	4	4	5	6	
597	Rookie Infielders	4	4	4	4	4	6	8	
598	Ken Griffey RC	8	10	15	20	25	40	50	
599A	Rookie Pitchers WASH	4	4	4	4	8	15	20	
599B	Rookie Pitchers SD Large	4	4	4	4	8	15	20	1
599C	Rookie Pitchers SD Small	4	5	20	25				
600	Bill Madlock RC	4	4	4	5	10	▲30	40	
601	Rookie Outfielders	4	4	4	4	5	10	15	
602	Rookie Pitchers	4	4	4	4	4	5	6	1
603	Rookie Catchers	4	4	4	4	4	5	6	
604	A.Thornton RC/F.White RC	4	4	4	4	8	15	25	▲
605	Frank Tanana RC	4	4	4	4	4	8	10	
606	Rookie Outfielders	4	4	4	4	4	5	6	
607	Rookie Shortstops	4	4	4	4	4	5	6	
608A	Rookie Pitchers ERR Apodaco	4	4	4	4	4	8	10	
608B	Rookie Pitchers COR Apodaca	4	4	4	4	5	10	12	
609	Rico Petrocelli	4	4	4	4	4	5	6	
610	Dave Kingman	4	4	4	4	4	6	8	
611	Rich Stelmaszek	4	4	4	4	4	5	6	
612	Luke Walker	4	4	4	4	4	5	6	
613	Dan Monzon	4	4	4	4	4	5	6	
614	Adrian Devine RC	4	4	4	4	4	5	6	
615	Johnny Jeter	4	4	4	4	4	5	6	
616	Larry Gura	4	4	4	4	4	5	6	
617	Ted Ford	4	4	4	4	4	5	6	
618	Jim Mason	4	4	4	4	4	5	6	
619	Mike Anderson	4	4	4	4	4	5	6	
620	Al Downing	4	4	4	4	4	5	6	
621	Bernie Carbo	4	4	4	4	4	5	6	
622	Phil Gagliano	4	4	4	4	4	5	6	
623	Celerino Sanchez	4	4	4	4	4	5	6	
624	Bob Miller	4	4	4	4	4	5	6	
625	Ollie Brown	4	4	4	4	4	5	6	
626	Pittsburgh Pirates TC	4	4	4	4	4	5	6	
627	Carl Taylor	4	4	4	4	4	5	6	
628	Ivan Murrell	4	4	4	4	4	5	6	
629	Rusty Staub	4	4	4	4	4	8	10	
630	Tommie Agee	4	4	4	4	4	5	6	

	GD 2	VG 3	EX 5	ExMt 6	NM 7	NmMt 8	NmMt+ 8.5	MT 9
Steve Barber	4	4	4	4	4	5	6	15
George Culver	4	4	4	4	4	5	6	30
Dave Hamilton	4	4	4	4	4	5	6	15
Eddie Mathews MG	4	4	4	4	4	6	8	20
Johnny Edwards	4	4	4	4	4	5	6	15
Dave Goltz	4	4	4	4	4	5	6	15
Checklist 529-660	4	4	4	4	4	8	10	50
Ken Sanders	4	4	4	4	4	5	6	15
Joe Lovitto	4	4	4	4	4	5	6	15
Milt Pappas	4	4	4	4	4	5	6	15
Chuck Brinkman	4	4	4	4	4	5	6	15
Terry Harmon	4	4	4	4	4	5	6	15
Los Angeles Dodgers TC	4	4	4	4	4	5	6	15
Wayne Granger	4	4	4	4	4	5	6	15
Ken Boswell	4	4	4	4	4	5	6	300
George Foster	4	4	4	4	6	12	15	25
Juan Beniquez RC	4	4	4	4	4	5	6	15
Terry Crowley	4	4	4	4	4	5	6	15
Fernando Gonzalez RC	4	4	4	4	4	5	6	15
Mike Epstein	4	4	4	4	4	5	6	15
Leron Lee	4	4	4	4	4	5	6	15
Gail Hopkins	4	4	4	4	4	5	6	15
Bob Stinson	4	4	4	4	4	5	6	100
Jesus Alou ERR No Position	4	4	4	4	4	6	8	25
Jesus Alou COR Outfield	4	4	4	4	4	5	6	40
Mike Tyson RC	4	4	4	4	4	5	6	15
Adrian Garrett	4	4	4	4	4	5	6	15
Jim Shellenback	4	4	4	4	4	5	6	20
Lee Lacy	4	4	4	4	4	5	6	15
Joe Lis	4	4	4	6	8	15	20	150
Larry Dierker	4	4	4	4	4	5	6	15

ank Aaron 715 #1 BVG 9 (MT) sold for $442 (eBay; 8/07)
ank Aaron 715 #1 PSA 10 (Gem) sold for $9,677 (Memory Lane; 5/12)
Fisk/J.Bench AS #331 PSA 10 (Gem) sold for $660 (eBay; 5/07)
ob Gibson #350 PSA 10 (Gem) sold for $510 (eBay; 3/07)
ob Gibson #350 PSA 10 (Gem) sold for $309 (eBay; 9/07)
ob Gibson #350 PSA 10 (Gem) sold for $256 (eBay; 6/07)
ob Gibson #350 PSA 10 (Gem) sold for $230 (eBay; 2/08)
ome Run Leaders #202 PSA 10 (Gem) sold for $1,844 (eBay; 10/07)
an Marichal #330 PSA 10 (Gem) sold for $462 (eBay; 8/07)
an Marichal #330 PSA 10 (Gem) sold for $277 (eBay; 4/08)
illie McCovey #250 (Washington) PSA 10 (Gem) sold for $2,137 (eBay; 2/07)
urman Munson #340 PSA 10 (Gem) sold for $3,000 (eBay; 5/07)
urman Munson #340 PSA 10 (Gem) sold for $2,911 (Mastro; 12/07)
ave Parker #252 PSA 10 (Gem) sold for $2,028 (eBay; 01/12)
ookie Pitchers #599 (Small Print) PSA 8 (NmMt) sold for $362 (eBay; 7/07)
ookie Pitchers #599 (Small Print) PSA 8 (NmMt) sold for $300 (eBay; 10/07)
ookie Pitchers #599 (Small Print) PSA 8 (NmMt) sold for $217 (eBay; 1/08)
rank Robinson #55 PSA 10 (Gem) sold for $1,028 (eBay; 01/12)
olan Ryan #20 PSA 10 (Gem) sold for $4,151 (eBay; 1/07)
olan Ryan #20 PSA 10 (Gem) sold for $2,346 (Mile High; 5/04)
ike Schmidt #283 PSA 10 (Gem) sold for $9,775 (Huggins and Scott; 4/08)
m Seaver #80 PSA 10 (Gem) sold for $1,380 (eBay; 01/12)
m Seaver #80 PSA 10 (Gem) sold for $1,034 (eBay; 11/06)
m Seaver #80 PSA 10 (Gem) sold for $763 (eBay; 9/07)
ave Winfield #456 PSA 10 (Gem) (Young Collection) sold for $5,020 (SCP; 5/12)
ave Winfield #456 PSA 10 (Gem) sold for $3,850 (eBay; 12/07)
ave Winfield #456 PSA 10 (Gem) sold for $3,605 (eBay; 9/07)
ave Winfield #456 BVG 9 (MT) sold for $518 (eBay; 9/07)
ave Winfield #456 SGC 96 (MT) sold for $504 (eBay; 1/08)
arl Yastrzemski #280 PSA 10 (Gem) sold for $3,051 (eBay; 11/06)

74 Topps Traded

	GD 2	VG 3	EX 5	ExMt 6	NM 7	NmMt 8	NmMt+ 8.5	MT 9
Craig Robinson	4	4	4	4	4	5	6	
Claude Osteen	4	4	4	4	4	5	6	
Jim Wynn	4	4	4	4	5	10	12	
Bobby Heise	4	4	4	4	4	5	6	20
Ross Grimsley	4	4	4	4	4	6	8	
Bob Locker	4	4	4	4	4	6	8	25
Bill Sudakis	4	4	4	4	4	6	8	
Mike Marshall	4	4	4	4	5	10	12	
Nelson Briles	4	4	4	4	4	6	8	80
Aurelio Monteagudo	4	4	4	4	4	5	6	
Diego Segui	4	4	4	4	4	5	6	
Willie Davis	4	4	4	4	4	6	8	25

	GD 2	VG 3	EX 5	ExMt 6	NM 7	NmMt 8	NmMt+ 8.5	MT 9
175T Reggie Cleveland	4	4	4	4	4	5	6	20
182T Lindy McDaniel	4	4	4	4	4	5	6	20
186T Fred Scherman	4	4	4	4	4	5	6	
249T George Mitterwald	4	4	4	4	4	5	6	15
262T Ed Kirkpatrick	4	4	4	4	4	5	6	15
269T Bob Johnson	4	4	4	4	4	6	8	25
270T Ron Santo	4	4	4	4	8	10	12	25
313T Barry Lersch	4	4	4	4	4	6	8	25
319T Randy Hundley	4	4	4	4	4	8	10	40
330T Juan Marichal	4	4	4	4	5	10	12	25
348T Pete Richert	4	4	4	4	4	5	6	20
373T John Curtis	4	4	4	4	4	6	8	
390T Lou Piniella	4	4	4	4	5	10	12	40
428T Gary Sutherland	4	4	4	4	4	8	10	40
454T Kurt Bevacqua	4	4	4	4	4	6	8	25
458T Jim Ray	4	4	4	4	4	6	8	25
485T Felipe Alou	4	4	4	4	4	6	8	
486T Steve Stone	4	4	4	4	4	8	10	
496T Tom Murphy	4	4	4	4	4	6	8	15
516T Horacio Pina	4	4	4	4	4	5	6	15
534T Eddie Watt	4	4	4	4	4	6	8	25
538T Cesar Tovar	4	4	4	4	4	5	6	15
544T Ron Schueler	4	4	4	4	4	6	8	20
579T Cecil Upshaw	4	4	4	4	4	6	8	15
585T Merv Rettenmund	4	4	4	4	4	5	6	20
612T Luke Walker	4	4	4	4	4	5	6	
616T Larry Gura	4	4	4	4	4	6	8	
618T Jim Mason	4	4	4	4	4	5	6	80
630T Tommie Agee	4	4	4	4	4	6	8	120
648T Terry Crowley	4	4	4	4	4	6	8	25
649T Fernando Gonzalez	4	4	4	4	4	5	6	20
NNO Traded Checklist	4	4	4	8	15	30	100	

1975 Kellogg's

	VG 3	VgEx 4	EX 5	ExMt 6	NM 7	NmMt 8	MT 9	Gem 9.5/10
1 Roy White	4	4	4	4	4	8		
2 Ross Grimsley	4	4	4	4	4	6	12	
3 Reggie Smith	4	4	4	4	4	6	40	
4A Bob Grich 1973 Work	4	4	4	4	4	6	12	
4B Bob Grich Because	4	4	4					
5 Greg Gross	4	4	4	4	4	6	12	
6 Bob Watson	4	4	4	4	4	6	12	
7 Johnny Bench	4	4	4	4	8	15	50	
8 Jeff Burroughs	4	4	4	4	4	6	12	
9 Elliott Maddox	4	4	4	4	4	6	12	
10 Jon Matlack	4	4	4	4	4	6	25	
11 Pete Rose	4	4	6	8	15	30	80	
12 Lee Stanton	4	4	4	4	4	6	15	
13 Bake McBride	4	4	4	4	4	6	12	40
14 Jorge Orta	4	4	4	4	4	6	12	25
15 Al Oliver	4	4	4	4	4	6	12	50
16 John Briggs	4	4	4	4	4	6	12	
17 Steve Garvey	4	4	4	4	4	8	15	50
18 Brooks Robinson	4	4	4	4	5	10	20	
19 John Hiller	4	4	4	4	4	6	12	
20 Lynn McGlothen	4	4	4	4	4	6	12	
21 Cleon Jones	4	4	4	4	4	6	12	
22 Fergie Jenkins	4	4	4	4	4	8	15	
23 Bill North	4	4	4	4	4	6	12	
24 Steve Busby	4	4	4	4	4	6	12	
25 Richie Zisk	4	4	4	4	4	6	12	25
26 Nolan Ryan	4	4	6	8	15	30	80	
27 Joe Morgan	4	4	4	4	5	10	20	60
28 Joe Rudi	4	4	4	4	4	6	12	
29 Jose Cardenal	4	4	4	4	4	6	12	40
30 Andy Messersmith	4	4	4	4	4	6	12	
31 Willie Montanez	4	4	4	4	4	6	12	25
32 Bill Buckner	4	4	4	4	4	6	12	40
33 Rod Carew	4	4	4	4	5	10	25	
34 Lou Piniella	4	4	4	4	4	6	12	
35 Ralph Garr	4	4	4	4	4	6	12	
36 Mike Marshall	4	4	4	4	4	6	12	
37 Garry Maddox	4	4	4	4	4	6	12	40
38 Dwight Evans	4	4	4	4	4	8	20	
39 Lou Brock	4	4	4	4	5	10	100	
40 Ken Singleton	4	4	4	4	4	6	12	60

#	Player	VG 3	VgEx 4	EX 5	ExMt 6	NM 7	NmMt 8	MT 9	Gem 9.5/10
41	Steve Braun	4	4	4	4	4	6	12	
42	Rich Allen	4	4	4	4	4	8	15	40
43	John Grubb	4	4	4	4	4	6	12	25
44A	Jim Hunter Oakland	4	4	4	4	4	8	15	
44B	Jim Hunter New York	4	4	4	4	4	8		40
45	Gaylord Perry	4	4	4	4	4	8	15	
46	George Hendrick	4	4	4	4	4	6	12	
47	Sparky Lyle	4	4	4	4	4	6	20	
48	Dave Cash	4	4	4	4	4	6	12	
49	Luis Tiant	4	4	4		4	6	12	40
50	Cesar Geronimo	4	4	4	4	4	6	12	25
51	Carl Yastrzemski	4	4	4	4	8	15	40	
52	Ken Brett	4	4	4	4	4	6	12	25
53	Hal McRae	4	4	4	4	4	6	12	
54	Reggie Jackson	4	4	4	4	8	15	30	
55	Rollie Fingers	4	4	4	4	5	10		
56	Mike Schmidt	4	4	4	4	8	15	50	
57	Richie Hebner	4	4	4	4	5	10		

—Johnny Bench #7 PSA 10 (Gem) sold for $103 (eBay; 2/08)
—Rod Carew #33 PSA 10 (Gem) sold for $158 (eBay; 2/08)
—Jim Hunter (Oakland) #44 PSA 10 (Gem) sold for $311 (eBay; 4/08)
—Reggie Jackson #54 PSA 10 (Gem) sold for $102 (eBay; 5/08)
—Pete Rose #11 PSA 10 (Gem) sold for $504 (eBay; 2/08)
—Mike Schmidt #56 PSA 10 (Gem) sold for $504 (eBay; 4/08)

1975 O-Pee-Chee

—George Brett #228 PSA 10 (Gem) sold for $7,184 (Memory Lane; 4/07)
—George Brett #228 PSA 10 (Gem) sold for $5,216 (eBay; 1/08)
—George Brett #228 PSA 10 (Gem) sold for $3,350 (eBay; 3/06)
—Nolan Ryan #500 PSA 9 (MT) sold for $1,679 (Memory Lane; 5/08)
—Robin Yount #223 PSA 9 (MT) sold for $521 (eBay; 11/06)

1975 Topps

#	Player	VG 3	VgEx 4	EX 5	ExMt 6	NM 7	NmMt 8	NmMt+ 8.5	MT 9
1	Hank Aaron HL	12	15	25	30	50	▲200	▲250	800
2	Lou Brock HL	4	4	4	5	10	50	80	400
3	Bob Gibson HL	4	4	4	5	10	40	50	250
4	Al Kaline HL	4	4	4	8	15	30	40	200
5	Nolan Ryan HL	4	8	12	15	20	50	100	300
6	Mike Marshall HL	4	4	5	6	12	25	80	400
7	Ryan/Busby/Bosman HL	4	4	4	5	10	25	30	100
8	Rogelio Moret	4	4	4	4	5	10	12	25
9	Frank Tepedino	4	4	4	4	5	10	12	25
10	Willie Davis	4	4	4	4	5	10	12	25
11	Bill Melton	4	4	4	4	5	10	12	25
12	David Clyde	4	4	4	4	5	10	12	25
13	Gene Locklear RC	4	4	4	4	6	12	15	30
14	Milt Wilcox	4	4	4	4	5	10	12	30
15	Jose Cardenal	4	4	4	4	6	12	20	120
16	Frank Tanana	4	6	12	15	30	60	80	250
17	Dave Concepcion	4	4	4	4	8	15	20	40
18	Detroit Tigers CL/Houk	4	4	4	4	6	12	15	50
19	Jerry Koosman	4	4	4	4	5	10	12	25
20	Thurman Munson	4	4	8	▲15	30	▲60	▲80	200
21	Rollie Fingers	4	4	4	4	8	15	20	150
22	Dave Cash	4	4	4	4	6	12	15	60
23	Bill Russell	4	4	4	4	6	12	20	80
24	Al Fitzmorris	4	4	4	4	5	10	12	25
25	Lee May	4	4	4	4	4	8	10	15
26	Dave McNally	4	4	4	4	5	10	12	30
27	Ken Reitz	4	4	4	4	5	10	15	60
28	Tom Murphy	4	4	4	4	5	10	12	25
29	Dave Parker	4	4	4	4	8	15	20	100
30	Bert Blyleven	4	4	4	6	12	25	30	400
31	Dave Rader	4	4	4	4	5	10	12	25
32	Reggie Cleveland	4	4	4	4	5	10	12	60
33	Dusty Baker	4	4	4	4	6	12	15	60
34	Steve Renko	4	4	4	4	4	8	10	15
35	Ron Santo	4	4	4	4	6	12	15	30
36	Joe Lovitto	4	4	4	4	8	15	20	50
37	Dave Freisleben	4	4	4	4	5	10	15	120
38	Buddy Bell	4	4	4	4	5	10	12	25
39	Andre Thornton	4	4	4	4	5	10	12	50
40	Bill Singer	4	4	4	4	5	10	12	25
41	Cesar Geronimo	4	4	4	4	8	15	20	80

#	Player	VG 3	VgEx 4	EX 5	ExMt 6	NM 7	NmMt 8	NmMt+ 8.5	M
42	Joe Coleman	4	4	4	4	5	10	12	
43	Cleon Jones	4	4	4	4	6	12	15	
44	Pat Dobson	4	4	4	4	5	10	12	
45	Joe Rudi	4	4	4	4	6	12	15	
46	Philadelphia Phillies CL/Ozark	4	4	4	4	5	10	12	
47	Tommy John	4	4	4	4	8	20	25	
48	Freddie Patek	4	4	4	4	5	10	12	
49	Larry Dierker	4	4	4	4	5	10	12	
50	Brooks Robinson	4	4	4	6	15	▲50	▲60	
51	Bob Forsch RC	4	4	4	4	6	12	15	
52	Darrell Porter	4	4	4	4	5	10	12	
53	Dave Giusti	4	4	5	6	12	25	40	
54	Eric Soderholm	4	4	4	4	6	12	15	
55	Bobby Bonds	4	4	4	4	6	12	20	
56	Rick Wise	4	4	5	6	12	25	40	
57	Dave Johnson	4	4	4	4	5	10	12	
58	Chuck Taylor	4	4	4	4	5	10	12	
59	Ken Henderson	4	4	4	4	5	10	12	
60	Fergie Jenkins	4	4	4	4	8	15	20	
61	Dave Winfield	6	8	10	▲20	▲25	50	60	
62	Fritz Peterson	4	4	4	4	5	10	12	
63	Steve Swisher RC	4	4	4	4	5	10	12	
64	Dave Chalk	4	4	4	4	5	10	12	
65	Don Gullett	4	4	4	6	12	25	30	
66	Willie Horton	4	4	4	4	6	12	15	
67	Tug McGraw	4	4	4	4	6	12	15	
68	Ron Blomberg	4	4	4	4	5	10	12	
69	John Odom	4	4	4	4	5	10	12	
70	Mike Schmidt	8	10	12	15	25	60	100	
71	Charlie Hough	4	4	4	4	6	12	15	
72	Kansas City Royals CL/McKeon	4	4	4	4	5	10	12	
73	J.R. Richard	4	4	4	4	6	12	15	
74	Mark Belanger	4	4	4	4	6	12	20	
75	Ted Simmons	4	4	4	4	8	15	60	
76	Ed Sprague	4	4	4	4	5	10	12	
77	Richie Zisk	4	4	4	4	5	10	15	
78	Ray Corbin	4	4	4	4	5	10	12	
79	Gary Matthews	4	4	4	4	6	12	15	
80	Carlton Fisk	4	5	5	10	▲25	30	40	
81	Ron Reed	4	4	4	4	5	10	12	
82	Pat Kelly	4	4	4	4	8	15	25	
83	Jim Merritt	4	4	4	4	5	10	12	
84	Enzo Hernandez	4	4	4	4	4	8	10	
85	Bill Bonham	4	4	4	4	6	12	15	
86	Joe Lis	4	4	4	4	8	15	20	
87	George Foster	4	4	4	6	12	25	30	
88	Tom Egan	4	4	4	4	5	10	12	
89	Jim Ray	4	4	4	4	4	8	10	
90	Rusty Staub	4	4	4	4	8	25	30	
91	Dick Green	4	4	4	4	5	10	12	
92	Cecil Upshaw	4	4	4	4	5	10	12	
93	Davey Lopes	4	4	4	4	6	12	15	
94	Jim Lonborg	4	4	4	4	5	10	12	
95	John Mayberry	4	4	4	4	5	10	12	
96	Mike Cosgrove RC	4	4	4	4	5	10	12	
97	Earl Williams	4	4	4	4	5	10	12	
98	Rich Folkers	4	4	4	4	5	10	12	
99	Mike Hegan	4	4	4	4	5	10	12	
100	Willie Stargell	4	4	5	6	12	25	40	
101	Montreal Expos CL/Mauch	4	4	4	5	10	20	40	
102	Joe Decker	4	4	4	4	5	10	12	
103	Rick Miller	4	5	10	12	25	50	60	
104	Bill Madlock	4	4	4	5	10	20	25	
105	Buzz Capra	4	4	4	4	5	10	12	
106	Mike Hargrove RC	4	4	4	4	8	15	25	
107	Jim Barr	4	4	4	4	5	10	12	
108	Tom Hall	4	4	4	4	5	10	12	
109	George Hendrick	4	4	4	4	5	10	12	
110	Wilbur Wood	4	4	4	4	5	10	12	
111	Wayne Garrett	4	4	4	4	6	12	15	
112	Larry Hardy RC	4	4	4	4	5	10	12	
113	Elliott Maddox	4	4	4	4	5	10	12	
114	Dick Lange	4	4	4	4	5	10	12	
115	Joe Ferguson	4	4	4	4	5	10	12	
116	Lerrin LaGrow	4	4	4	4	5	10	12	
117	Baltimore Orioles CL/Weaver	4	4	5	10	20	40	50	
118	Mike Anderson	4	4	4	4	5	10	12	

Name	VG 3	VgEx 4	EX 5	ExMt 6	NM 7	NmMt 8	NmMt+ 8.5	MT 9
Tommy Helms	4	4	4	4	4	8	10	15
Steve Busby	4	4	4	4	5	10	15	100
Bill North	4	4	4	4	5	10	12	25
Al Hrabosky	4	4	4	4	6	12	15	25
Johnny Briggs	4	4	4	4	5	10	12	25
Jerry Reuss	4	4	4	4	5	10	12	25
Ken Singleton	4	4	4	4	6	12	20	150
Checklist 1-132	4	4	4	4	5	10	15	50
Glenn Borgmann	4	4	4	4	6	12	15	120
Bill Lee	4	4	4	4	6	12	15	30
Rick Monday	4	4	4	5	10	20	25	150
Phil Niekro	4	4	4	4	8	15	20	50
Toby Harrah	4	4	4	4	5	10	12	50
Randy Moffitt	4	4	4	4	5	10	15	60
Dan Driessen	4	5	6	12	25	50	60	200
Ron Hodges	4	4	4	4	5	10	12	60
Charlie Spikes	4	4	4	4	5	10	12	60
Jim Mason	4	4	4	4	5	10	12	60
Terry Forster	4	4	4	4	6	12	15	30
Del Unser	4	4	4	4	4	8	10	15
Horacio Pina	4	4	4	4	5	10	15	100
Steve Garvey	4	4	4	6	12	25	30	100
Mickey Stanley	4	4	4	4	5	10	15	80
Bob Reynolds	4	4	4	4	5	10	12	25
Cliff Johnson RC	4	4	4	4	5	10	15	150
Jim Wohlford	4	4	4	4	5	10	12	30
Ken Holtzman	4	4	4	4	5	10	12	25
San Diego Padres CL/McNamara	4	4	4	4	5	10	12	25
Pedro Garcia	4	4	4	4	5	10	12	25
Jim Rooker	4	4	4	4	5	10	12	20
Tim Foli	4	4	4	4	5	10	12	20
Bob Gibson	4	4	8	10	20	▲80	100	500
Steve Brye	4	4	4	4	5	10	12	30
Mario Guerrero	4	4	4	4	5	10	12	25
Rick Reuschel	4	4	4	4	5	10	12	30
Mike Lum	4	4	4	4	4	8	10	15
Jim Bibby	4	4	4	4	5	10	12	25
Dave Kingman	4	4	4	4	5	10	12	50
Pedro Borbon	4	4	4	4	5	10	12	20
Jerry Grote	4	4	4	4	5	10	12	25
Steve Arlin	4	4	4	4	5	10	12	25
Graig Nettles	4	4	4	4	8	15	20	30
Stan Bahnsen	4	4	4	4	5	10	12	25
Willie Montanez	4	4	4	4	5	10	12	25
Jim Brewer	4	4	4	4	5	10	12	25
Mickey Rivers	4	4	4	4	6	12	15	30
Doug Rader	4	4	4	4	5	10	12	25
Woodie Fryman	4	4	4	4	5	10	12	25
Rich Coggins	4	4	4	4	5	10	12	25
Bill Greif	4	4	4	4	5	10	15	150
Cookie Rojas	4	4	4	4	5	10	12	40
Bert Campaneris	4	4	4	4	6	12	15	80
Ed Kirkpatrick	4	4	4	4	5	10	15	80
Boston Red Sox CL/Johnson	4	4	4	4	8	15	20	40
Steve Rogers	4	4	4	4	5	10	15	80
Bake McBride	4	4	4	4	5	10	12	25
Don Money	4	4	4	4	5	10	15	150
Burt Hooton	4	4	4	4	5	10	12	30
Vic Correll RC	4	4	4	4	5	10	12	25
Cesar Tovar	4	4	4	6	12	25	30	150
Tom Bradley	4	4	4	4	5	10	12	25
Joe Morgan	4	4	4	6	12	▲40	▲50	▲100
Fred Beene	4	4	4	4	5	10	12	25
Don Hahn	4	4	4	4	5	10	12	80
Mel Stottlemyre	4	4	4	4	8	15	20	40
Jorge Orta	4	4	4	4	5	10	12	40
Steve Carlton	4	4	4	6	15	▲30	40	200
Willie Crawford	4	4	4	4	5	10	12	25
Denny Doyle	4	4	4	4	5	10	15	40
Tom Griffin	4	4	4	4	5	10	12	25
Y.Berra/Campanella MVP	4	4	4	4	6	12	15	50
B.Shantz/H.Sauer MVP	4	4	4	4	5	10	12	50
Al Rosen/Campanella MVP	4	4	4	4	8	15	20	80
Y.Berra/W.Mays MVP	4	4	4	5	10	20	25	400
Y.Berra/Campanella MVP	4	4	4	4	6	12	15	40
M.Mantle/D.Newcombe MVP	4	4	4	6	20	25	30	100
M.Mantle/H.Aaron MVP	4	4	4	6	8	20	50	150
196 J.Jensen/E.Banks MVP	4	4	4	4	6	20	25	200
197 N.Fox/E.Banks MVP	4	4	4	4	5	10	12	25
198 R.Maris/D.Groat MVP	4	4	4	4	6	12	15	60
199 R.Maris/F.Robinson MVP	4	4	4	4	6	12	15	40
200 M.Mantle/M.Wills MVP	4	4	4	6	12	30	40	200
201 E.Howard/S.Koufax MVP	4	4	4	4	5	10	12	20
202 B.Robinson/K.Boyer MVP	4	4	4	4	6	12	20	100
203 Z.Versailes/W.Mays MVP	4	4	4	4	6	12	15	40
204 F.Robinson/B.Clemente MVP	4	4	4	5	10	20	30	80
205 C.Yastrzemski/O.Cepeda MVP	4	4	4	4	6	12	15	50
206 D.McLain/B.Gibson MVP	4	4	4	4	6	12	15	25
207 H.Killebrew/W.McCovey MVP	4	4	4	4	6	12	15	40
208 B.Powell/J.Bench MVP	4	4	4	4	6	12	50	275
209 V.Blue/J.Torre MVP	4	4	4	4	5	10	12	30
210 D.Allen/J.Bench MVP	4	4	4	4	8	15	20	100
211 R.Jackson/P.Rose MVP	4	4	4	4	8	15	25	100
212 J.Burroughs/S.Garvey MVP	4	4	4	4	5	10	12	40
213 Oscar Gamble	4	4	4	4	6	12	15	25
214 Harry Parker	4	4	4	4	5	10	12	25
215 Bobby Valentine	4	4	4	4	6	12	20	50
216 San Francisco Giants CL/Westrum	4	4	4	4	6	12	15	25
217 Lou Piniella	4	4	4	4	6	12	15	40
218 Jerry Johnson	4	4	4	4	4	8	10	15
219 Ed Herrmann	4	4	4	4	5	60	80	150
220 Don Sutton	4	4	4	4	6	12	15	40
221 Aurelio Rodriguez	4	4	4	4	5	10	12	25
222 Dan Spillner RC	4	4	4	4	5	10	12	25
223 Robin Yount RC	10	25	30	50	100	250	500	1,200
224 Ramon Hernandez	4	4	4	4	5	10	12	25
225 Bob Grich	4	4	4	4	6	12	20	80
226 Bill Campbell	4	4	4	4	5	10	12	25
227 Bob Watson	4	4	4	4	5	10	12	25
228 George Brett RC	50	60	80	100	150	400	600	▲3,000
229 Barry Foote	4	4	4	4	5	10	12	60
230 Jim Hunter	4	4	4	4	8	15	20	80
231 Mike Tyson	4	4	4	4	5	10	12	25
232 Diego Segui	4	4	4	4	4	8	10	15
233 Billy Grabarkewitz	4	4	4	4	5	10	12	50
234 Tom Grieve	4	4	4	4	5	10	10	15
235 Jack Billingham	4	4	4	4	5	10	12	40
236 California Angels CL/Williams	4	4	4	4	5	10	12	60
237 Carl Morton	4	4	4	4	4	8	10	15
238 Dave Duncan	4	4	4	4	5	10	15	80
239 George Stone	4	4	4	4	4	8	10	15
240 Garry Maddox	4	4	4	4	6	12	15	30
241 Dick Tidrow	4	4	4	4	5	10	12	25
242 Jay Johnstone	4	4	4	4	5	10	12	25
243 Jim Kaat	4	4	4	4	6	12	15	30
244 Bill Buckner	4	4	4	4	6	12	15	40
245 Mickey Lolich	4	4	4	4	6	12	15	60
246 St. Louis Cardinals CL/Schoen	4	4	4	4	5	10	12	50
247 Enos Cabell	4	4	4	4	5	10	12	25
248 Randy Jones	4	4	4	4	6	12	15	30
249 Danny Thompson	4	4	4	4	5	10	15	60
250 Ken Brett	4	4	4	5	10	20	30	200
251 Fran Healy	4	4	4	4	6	12	20	60
252 Fred Scherman	4	4	4	4	5	10	12	30
253 Jesus Alou	4	4	4	4	8	15	25	100
254 Mike Torrez	4	4	4	4	8	15	20	40
255 Dwight Evans	4	4	4	4	8	15	20	80
256 Billy Champion	4	4	4	4	5	10	15	40
257 Checklist: 133-264	4	4	4	4	5	10	15	40
258 Dave LaRoche	4	4	4	4	5	10	12	25
259 Len Randle	4	4	4	5	10	20	30	100
260 Johnny Bench	4	5	12	25	30	60	100	▲300
261 Andy Hassler RC	4	4	4	4	5	10	12	25
262 Rowland Office RC	4	4	4	4	5	10	15	30
263 Jim Perry	4	4	4	4	5	10	15	40
264 John Milner	4	4	4	4	5	10	12	25
265 Ron Bryant	4	4	4	4	5	10	12	25
266 Sandy Alomar	4	4	4	4	6	12	15	30
267 Dick Ruthven	4	4	4	4	5	10	12	25
268 Hal McRae	4	4	4	4	6	12	20	150
269 Doug Rau	4	4	4	4	5	10	12	25
270 Ron Fairly	4	4	4	4	6	12	15	30
271 Gerry Moses	4	4	4	4	5	10	12	25
272 Lynn McGlothen	4	4	4	4	5	10	12	25

#	Player	VG 3	VgEx 4	EX 5	ExMt 6	NM 7	NmMt 8	NmMt+ 8.5	MT 9
273	Steve Braun	4	4	4	4	5	10	12	30
274	Vicente Romo	4	4	4	4	5	10	12	25
275	Paul Blair	4	4	4	4	6	12	15	30
276	Chicago White Sox CL/Tanner	4	4	4	4	5	10	12	30
277	Frank Taveras	4	4	4	4	5	10	12	50
278	Paul Lindblad	4	4	4	4	5	10	12	25
279	Milt May	4	4	4	4	4	8	10	15
280	Carl Yastrzemski	6	8	10	12	20	30	40	120
281	Jim Slaton	4	4	4	4	5	10	12	25
282	Jerry Morales	4	4	4	4	5	10	12	25
283	Steve Foucault	4	4	4	4	5	10	12	25
284	Ken Griffey Sr.	4	4	4	5	10	20	25	120
285	Ellie Rodriguez	4	4	4	4	5	10	12	25
286	Mike Jorgensen	4	4	4	4	5	10	12	25
287	Roric Harrison	4	4	4	4	4	8	10	15
288	Bruce Ellingsen RC	4	4	4	4	4	8	10	15
289	Ken Rudolph	4	4	4	4	4	8	10	15
290	Jon Matlack	4	4	4	4	5	10	12	80
291	Bill Sudakis	4	4	4	4	5	10	12	25
292	Ron Schueler	4	4	4	4	5	10	12	25
293	Dick Sharon	4	4	4	4	5	10	12	25
294	Geoff Zahn RC	4	4	4	4	5	10	12	25
295	Vada Pinson	4	4	4	4	5	10	12	50
296	Alan Foster	4	4	4	4	5	10	12	25
297	Craig Kusick RC	4	4	5	6	12	25	30	60
298	Johnny Grubb	4	4	4	4	5	10	12	25
299	Bucky Dent	4	4	4	4	5	10	12	20
300	Reggie Jackson	4	4	6	12	▲30	80	100	500
301	Dave Roberts	4	4	4	4	5	10	12	500
302	Rick Burleson RC	4	4	4	4	8	15	25	150
303	Grant Jackson	4	4	4	4	4	8	10	15
304	Pittsburgh Pirates CL/Murtaugh	4	4	4	4	5	10	12	30
305	Jim Colborn	4	4	4	4	5	10	12	25
306	Batting Leaders	4	4	4	4	6	12	15	30
307	Home Run Leaders	4	4	4	4	6	12	15	30
308	RBI Leaders	4	4	4	4	6	12	15	60
309	Stolen Base Leaders	4	4	4	4	6	12	15	80
310	Victory Leaders	4	4	4	4	6	12	15	50
311	ERA Leaders	4	4	4	4	6	12	15	30
312	Strikeout Leaders	4	4	4	5	12	▲30	▲40	▲80
313	Leading Firemen	4	4	4	4	6	12	15	50
314	Buck Martinez	4	4	4	4	5	10	12	25
315	Don Kessinger	4	4	4	4	5	10	12	100
316	Jackie Brown	4	4	4	4	5	10	12	25
317	Joe Lahoud	4	4	4	4	5	10	12	25
318	Ernie McAnally	4	4	4	4	4	8	10	15
319	Johnny Oates	4	4	4	4	5	10	12	25
320	Pete Rose	4	6	10	25	40	60	80	▲300
321	Rudy May	4	4	4	4	5	10	12	20
322	Ed Goodson	4	4	4	4	5	10	15	50
323	Fred Holdsworth	4	4	4	4	4	8	10	15
324	Ed Kranepool	4	4	4	4	4	8	10	15
325	Tony Oliva	4	4	4	4	6	12	15	40
326	Wayne Twitchell	4	4	4	4	5	10	12	40
327	Jerry Hairston	4	4	4	4	4	8	10	15
328	Sonny Siebert	4	4	4	4	4	8	10	15
329	Ted Kubiak	4	4	4	4	5	10	12	25
330	Mike Marshall	4	4	4	4	6	12	15	25
331	Cleveland Indians CL/Robinson	4	4	4	4	6	12	15	60
332	Fred Kendall	4	4	4	4	5	10	12	25
333	Dick Drago	4	4	4	4	5	10	12	25
334	Greg Gross RC	4	4	4	4	4	8	10	15
335	Jim Palmer	4	4	4	6	12	25	30	400
336	Rennie Stennett	4	4	4	5	10	20	25	100
337	Kevin Kobel	4	4	4	4	5	10	12	25
338	Rich Stelmaszek	4	4	4	4	5	10	12	80
339	Jim Fregosi	4	4	4	4	5	10	12	25
340	Paul Splittorff	4	4	4	4	6	12	20	150
341	Hal Breeden	4	4	4	4	4	8	10	15
342	Leroy Stanton	4	4	4	4	4	8	10	15
343	Danny Frisella	4	4	4	4	8	15	25	80
344	Ben Oglivie	4	4	4	4	6	12	15	30
345	Clay Carroll	4	4	4	4	5	10	12	25
346	Bobby Darwin	4	4	4	4	5	10	12	25
347	Mike Caldwell	4	4	4	4	5	10	12	25
348	Tony Muser	4	4	4	4	5	10	12	25
349	Ray Sadecki	4	4	4	4	5	10	12	25

#	Player	VG 3	VgEx 4	EX 5	ExMt 6	NM 7	NmMt 8	NmMt+ 8.5	MT 9
350	Bobby Murcer	4	4	4	4	6	12	15	
351	Bob Boone	4	4	4	4	5	10	12	
352	Darold Knowles	4	4	4	4	5	10	12	
353	Luis Melendez	4	4	4	4	5	10	12	
354	Dick Bosman	4	4	4	4	5	10	12	
355	Chris Cannizzaro	4	4	4	4	4	8	10	
356	Rico Petrocelli	4	4	4	4	6	12	15	
357	Ken Forsch	4	4	4	4	5	10	12	
358	Al Bumbry	4	4	4	4	6	12	15	
359	Paul Popovich	4	4	4	4	5	10	12	
360	George Scott	4	4	4	4	5	10	12	
361	Los Angeles Dodgers CL/Alston	4	4	4	4	6	12	15	
362	Steve Hargan	4	4	4	4	5	10	12	
363	Carmen Fanzone	4	4	4	4	5	10	12	
364	Doug Bird	4	4	4	4	5	10	12	
365	Bob Bailey	4	4	4	4	5	10	12	
366	Ken Sanders	4	4	4	4	5	10	12	
367	Craig Robinson	4	4	4	4	5	10	12	
368	Vic Albury	4	4	4	4	5	10	12	
369	Merv Rettenmund	4	4	4	4	5	10	12	
370	Tom Seaver	8	10	12	▲20	25	50	60	▲20
371	Gates Brown	4	4	4	4	6	12	15	
372	John D'Acquisto	4	4	4	4	5	10	15	
373	Bill Sharp	4	4	4	4	4	8	10	
374	Eddie Watt	4	4	4	4	4	8	10	
375	Roy White	4	4	4	4	5	10	12	
376	Steve Yeager	4	4	4	4	6	12	15	
377	Tom Hilgendorf	4	4	4	4	5	10	12	
378	Derrel Thomas	4	4	4	4	5	10	15	
379	Bernie Carbo	4	4	4	4	5	10	12	
380	Sal Bando	4	4	4	4	6	12	20	25
381	John Curtis	4	4	4	4	5	10	12	
382	Don Baylor	4	4	4	4	5	10	12	
383	Jim York	4	4	4	4	5	10	12	
384	Milwaukee Brewers CL/Crandall	4	4	4	4	5	10	12	
385	Dock Ellis	4	4	4	4	4	8	10	
386	Checklist: 265-396	4	4	4	4	5	10	12	
387	Jim Spencer	4	4	4	4	5	10	12	
388	Steve Stone	4	4	4	4	5	10	12	
389	Tony Solaita RC	4	4	4	4	5	10	12	
390	Ron Cey	4	4	4	4	5	10	12	
391	Don DeMola RC	4	4	4	4	5	10	12	
392	Bruce Bochte RC	4	4	4	4	5	10	12	12
393	Gary Gentry	4	4	4	4	4	8	10	
394	Larvell Blanks	4	4	4	4	5	10	12	
395	Bud Harrelson	4	4	4	4	5	10	12	
396	Fred Norman	4	4	4	4	6	12	15	10
397	Bill Freehan	4	4	4	4	6	12	15	
398	Elias Sosa	4	4	4	4	4	8	10	
399	Terry Harmon	4	4	4	4	5	10	12	
400	Dick Allen	4	4	4	4	6	12	15	
401	Mike Wallace	4	4	4	4	5	10	12	
402	Bob Tolan	4	4	4	4	6	12	25	5
403	Tom Buskey RC	4	4	4	4	5	10	12	
404	Ted Sizemore	4	4	4	4	5	10	12	
405	John Montague RC	4	4	4	4	6	12	20	25
406	Bob Gallagher	4	4	4	4	5	10	12	
407	Herb Washington RC	4	4	4	4	8	15	30	15
408	Clyde Wright	4	4	4	4	5	10	12	
409	Bob Robertson	4	4	4	4	5	10	15	
410	Mike Cuellar	4	4	4	4	6	12	20	
411	George Mitterwald	4	4	4	4	5	10	12	
412	Bill Hands	4	4	4	4	5	10	12	
413	Marty Pattin	4	4	4	4	5	10	12	
414	Manny Mota	4	4	4	4	5	10	12	
415	John Hiller	4	4	4	4	5	10	12	
416	Larry Lintz	4	4	4	4	5	10	12	
417	Skip Lockwood	4	4	4	4	5	10	15	12
418	Leo Foster	4	4	4	4	5	10	12	
419	Dave Goltz	4	4	4	4	5	10	12	
420	Larry Bowa	4	4	4	4	6	12	15	
421	New York Mets CL/Berra	4	4	4	4	6	12	15	
422	Brian Downing	4	4	4	4	5	10	12	
423	Clay Kirby	4	4	4	4	5	10	12	
424	John Lowenstein	4	4	4	4	5	10	12	
425	Tito Fuentes	4	4	4	4	5	10	12	
426	George Medich	4	4	4	4	5	10	12	

	VG 3	VgEx 4	EX 5	ExMt 6	NM 7	NmMt 8	NmMt+ 8.5	MT 9
Clarence Gaston	4	4	4	4	5	10	15	40
Dave Hamilton	4	4	4	4	5	10	12	60
Jim Dwyer RC	4	4	4	4	5	10	12	25
Luis Tiant	4	4	4	4	6	12	15	60
Rod Gilbreath	4	4	4	4	5	10	12	25
Ken Berry	4	4	4	4	5	10	12	25
Larry Demery RC	4	4	4	4	5	10	15	40
Bob Locker	4	4	4	4	5	10	15	50
Dave Nelson	4	4	4	4	5	10	15	50
Ken Frailing	4	4	4	4	5	10	15	60
Al Cowens RC	4	4	4	4	6	12	15	30
Don Carrithers	4	4	4	4	8	15	25	80
Ed Brinkman	4	4	4	4	5	10	12	25
Andy Messersmith	4	4	4	4	6	12	15	60
Bobby Heise	4	4	4	4	6	12	15	50
Maximino Leon RC	4	4	4	4	6	12	15	80
Minnesota Twins CL/Quilici	4	4	4	4	5	10	12	25
Gene Garber	4	4	4	4	5	10		40
Felix Millan	4	4	4	4	6	12	15	100
Bart Johnson	4	4	4	4	6	12	15	100
Terry Crowley	4	4	4	4	5	10	12	50
Frank Duffy	4	4	4	4	4	8	10	15
Charlie Williams	4	4	4	4	5	10	12	25
Willie McCovey	4	4	4	5	▲20	▲30	▲40	▲60
Rick Dempsey	4	4	4	4	5	10	12	25
Angel Mangual	4	4	4	4	6	12	15	50
Claude Osteen	4	4	4	4	5	10	12	25
Doug Griffin	4	4	4	4	5	10	12	25
Don Wilson	4	4	4	4	5	10	12	25
Bob Coluccio	4	4	4	4	5	10	12	25
Mario Mendoza RC	4	4	4	4	5	10	12	25
Ross Grimsley	4	4	4	4	8	15	25	150
1974 AL Championships	4	4	4	4	8	15		
1974 NL Championships	4	4	4	4	6	12	20	150
Reggie Jackson WS1	4	4	4	4	6	12	15	40
W.Alston/J.Ferguson WS2	4	4	4	4	6	12	15	30
Rollie Fingers WS3	4	4	4	4	6	12	15	30
A's Batter WS4	4	4	4	4	6	12	15	50
Joe Rudi WS5	4	4	4	4	6	12	15	30
A's Do it Again WS	4	4	4	4	6	12	15	150
Ed Halicki RC	4	4	4	4	5	10	15	150
Bobby Mitchell	4	4	4	4	5	10	12	25
Tom Dettore RC	4	4	4	4	5	10	12	25
Jeff Burroughs	4	4	4	4	6	12	15	30
Bob Stinson	4	4	4	4	5	10	15	150
Bruce Dal Canton	4	4	4	4	5	10	15	80
Ken McMullen	4	4	4	4	6	12	15	25
Luke Walker	4	4	4	4	5	10	12	25
Darrell Evans	4	4	5	5	10	20		
Ed Figueroa RC	4	4	4	4	5	10	15	40
Tom Hutton	4	4	4	4	5	10	15	80
Tom Burgmeier	4	4	4	4	5	10	12	25
Ken Boswell	4	4	4	4	5	10	12	25
Carlos May	4	4	4	4	5	10	12	25
Will McEnaney RC	4	4	8	15	30	60	80	800
Tom McCraw	4	4	4	4	5	10	12	25
Steve Ontiveros	4	4	4	4	5	10	12	50
Glenn Beckert	4	4	4	4	5	10	15	50
Sparky Lyle	4	4	4	4	8	15	20	200
Ray Fosse	4	4	4	4	5	10	12	30
Houston Astros CL/Gomez	4	4	4	4	5	10	12	40
Bill Travers RC	4	4	4	4	6	12	15	30
Cecil Cooper	4	4	4	4	6	12	20	80
Reggie Smith	4	4	4	4	6	12	20	100
Doyle Alexander	4	4	4	4	5	10	12	20
Rich Hebner	4	4	4	4	5	10	12	40
Don Stanhouse	4	4	4	4	4	8	10	15
Pete LaCock RC	4	4	4	4	5	10	15	50
Nelson Briles	4	4	4	4	5	10	12	25
Pepe Frias	4	4	4	4	5	10	12	25
Jim Nettles	4	4	4	4	5	10	15	50
Al Downing	4	4	4	4	5	10	12	25
Marty Perez	4	4	4	6	12	25	30	120
Nolan Ryan	5	15	25	▲50	80	▲300	800	2,500
Bill Robinson	4	4	4	4	5	10	12	25
Pat Bourque	4	4	4	4	4	8	10	15
Fred Stanley	4	4	4	4	5	10	15	200

	VG 3	VgEx 4	EX 5	ExMt 6	NM 7	NmMt 8	NmMt+ 8.5	MT 9
504 Buddy Bradford	4	4	4	4	6	12	20	50
505 Chris Speier	4	4	4	4	5	10	15	50
506 Leron Lee	4	4	4	4	5	10	12	25
507 Tom Carroll RC	4	4	4	4	5	10	12	25
508 Bob Hansen RC	4	4	4	4	5	10	12	50
509 Dave Hilton	4	4	4	4	5	10	12	25
510 Vida Blue	4	4	4	4	8	15	20	100
511 Texas Rangers CL/Martin	4	4	4	4	4	8	10	15
512 Larry Milbourne RC	4	4	4	4	5	10	12	80
513 Dick Pole	4	4	4	4	5	10	15	80
514 Jose Cruz	4	4	4	4	6	12	20	100
515 Manny Sanguillen	4	4	4	4	6	12	15	40
516 Don Hood	4	4	4	4	5	10	12	25
517 Checklist: 397-528	4	4	4	4	5	10	12	30
518 Leo Cardenas	4	4	4	4	5	10	12	25
519 Jim Todd RC	4	4	4	4	5	10	12	50
520 Amos Otis	4	4	4	4	6	12	20	200
521 Dennis Blair RC	4	4	4	4	5	10	15	80
522 Gary Sutherland	4	4	4	4	5	10	12	25
523 Tom Paciorek	4	4	4	4	5	10	15	50
524 John Doherty RC	4	4	4	4	5	10	12	25
525 Tom House	4	4	4	4	5	10	12	25
526 Larry Hisle	4	4	4	4	5	10	15	30
527 Mac Scarce	4	4	4	4	5	10	15	50
528 Eddie Leon	4	4	4	4	5	10	12	50
529 Gary Thomasson	4	4	4	4	5	10	15	60
530 Gaylord Perry	4	4	4	4	8	15	30	150
531 Cincinnati Reds CL/Anderson	4	4	4	6	12	20	30	80
532 Gorman Thomas	4	4	4	4	5	10	15	30
533 Rudy Meoli	4	4	4	4	5	10	12	25
534 Alex Johnson	4	4	4	4	6	12	15	60
535 Gene Tenace	4	4	4	4	6	12	15	40
536 Bob Moose	4	4	4	5	10	20	25	300
537 Tommy Harper	4	4	4	4	5	10	12	25
538 Duffy Dyer	4	4	4	4	5	10	15	60
539 Jesse Jefferson	4	4	4	4	6	12	15	30
540 Lou Brock	4	4	4	6	12	20	30	80
541 Roger Metzger	4	4	4	4	5	10	12	25
542 Pete Broberg	4	4	4	4	5	10	12	25
543 Larry Biittner	4	4	4	4	5	10	12	25
544 Steve Mingori	4	4	4	4	5	10	15	80
545 Billy Williams	4	4	4	4	8	15	20	50
546 John Knox	4	4	4	4	4	8	10	15
547 Von Joshua	4	4	5	6	12	25	30	120
548 Charlie Sands	4	4	4	4	5	10	15	80
549 Bill Butler	4	4	4	4	5	10	12	30
550 Ralph Garr	4	4	4	4	5	10	15	50
551 Larry Christenson	4	4	4	4	6	12	20	275
552 Jack Brohamer	4	4	4	4	4	8	10	15
553 John Boccabella	4	4	4	4	5	10	15	30
554 Rich Gossage	4	4	4	5	10	20	25	80
555 Al Oliver	4	4	4	4	6	12	20	150
556 Tim Johnson	4	4	4	4	5	10	15	60
557 Larry Gura	4	4	4	4	5	10	12	25
558 Dave Roberts	4	4	4	4	5	10	12	25
559 Bob Montgomery	4	4	4	4	5	10	12	25
560 Tony Perez	4	4	4	4	6	12	15	40
561 Oakland Athletics CL/Dark	4	4	4	4	6	12	15	50
562 Gary Nolan	4	4	4	4	5	10	12	25
563 Wilbur Howard	4	4	4	4	4	8	10	15
564 Tommy Davis	4	6	12	15	30	60	90	500
565 Joe Torre	4	4	4	4	6	12	20	60
566 Ray Burris	4	4	4	4	5	10	12	25
567 Jim Sundberg RC	4	4	4	4	6	12	15	40
568 Dale Murray RC	4	4	4	4	5	10	12	50
569 Frank White	4	4	4	4	5	10	15	20
570 Jim Wynn	4	4	4	4	6	12	15	50
571 Dave Lemanczyk RC	4	4	4	4	5	10	12	25
572 Roger Nelson	4	4	4	4	5	10	12	25
573 Orlando Pena	4	4	4	4	4	8	10	15
574 Tony Taylor	4	4	4	4	5	10	60	30
575 Gene Clines	4	4	4	4	5	10	15	50
576 Phil Roof	4	4	4	4	5	10	12	25
577 John Morris	4	4	4	4	5	10	12	25
578 Dave Tomlin RC	4	4	4	4	5	10	12	25
579 Skip Pitlock	4	4	4	4	5	10	12	25
580 Frank Robinson	4	4	4	5	12	▲40	▲50	150

#	Name	VG 3	VgEx 4	EX 5	ExMt 6	NM 7	NmMt 8	NmMt+ 8.5	MT 9
581	Darrel Chaney	4	4	4	4	8	15	20	40
582	Eduardo Rodriguez	4	4	4	4	5	10	12	40
583	Andy Etchebarren	4	4	4	5	10	20	40	350
584	Mike Garman	4	4	4	4	5	10	15	80
585	Chris Chambliss	4	4	4	4	8	15	20	60
586	Tim McCarver	4	4	4	4	6	12	15	60
587	Chris Ward RC	4	4	4	4	4	8	10	15
588	Rick Auerbach	4	4	4	4	5	10	15	80
589	Atlanta Braves CL/King	4	4	4	4	5	10	12	30
590	Cesar Cedeno	4	4	4	4	6	12	20	80
591	Glenn Abbott	4	4	4	4	5	10	12	25
592	Balor Moore	4	4	4	4	5	10	12	20
593	Gene Lamont	4	4	4	4	4	8	10	15
594	Jim Fuller	4	4	4	4	5	10	12	25
595	Joe Niekro	4	4	4	4	6	12	15	60
596	Ollie Brown	4	4	4	4	5	10	12	60
597	Winston Llenas	4	4	4	4	5	10	12	25
598	Bruce Kison	4	4	4	4	5	10	12	30
599	Nate Colbert	4	4	4	4	5	10	12	25
600	Rod Carew	4	4	5	10	20	40	50	300
601	Juan Beniquez	4	4	6	8	15	30	60	400
602	John Vukovich	4	4	4	4	8	15	20	50
603	Lew Krausse	4	4	4	4	6	12	15	100
604	Oscar Zamora RC	4	4	4	4	6	12	15	30
605	John Ellis	4	4	4	4	5	10	12	25
606	Bruce Miller RC	4	4	4	4	5	10	12	25
607	Jim Holt	4	4	4	4	6	12	15	40
608	Gene Michael	4	4	4	4	5	10	15	60
609	Elrod Hendricks	4	4	4	4	5	10	15	40
610	Ron Hunt	4	4	4	4	5	10	12	25
611	New York Yankees CL/Virdon	4	4	4	4	6	12	15	50
612	Terry Hughes	4	4	4	4	6	15	15	150
613	Bill Parsons	4	4	4	4	5	10	12	25
614	Rookie Pitchers	4	4	4	4	5	10	12	25
615	Rookie Pitchers	4	4	4	4	6	12	15	40
616	Jim Rice RC	4	6	25	30	50	100	150	500
617	Rookie Infielders	4	4	4	4	6	12	15	50
618	Rookie Pitchers	4	4	4	4	6	12	15	120
619	Rookie Outfielders	4	4	4	4	5	10	12	25
620	Gary Carter RC	4	▲15	▲20	30	50	100	200	500
621	Rookie Pitchers	4	4	4	4	6	12	15	30
622	Fred Lynn RC	4	4	5	12	25	40	50	120
623	K.Hernandez/P.Garner RC	4	4	4	8	25	▲50	▲60	150
624	Rookie Pitchers	4	4	4	4	5	10	15	60
625	Boog Powell	4	4	4	5	10	20	25	250
626	Larry Haney	4	4	4	4	5	10	12	25
627	Tom Walker	4	4	4	4	5	10	15	30
628	Ron LeFlore RC	4	4	4	4	8	15	30	100
629	Joe Hoerner	4	4	4	4	4	8	10	15
630	Greg Luzinski	4	4	4	4	6	12	15	25
631	Lee Lacy	4	4	4	4	6	12	20	80
632	Morris Nettles RC	4	4	4	4	5	10	12	25
633	Paul Casanova	4	4	4	4	5	10	15	60
634	Cy Acosta	4	4	4	4	6	12	20	120
635	Chuck Dobson	4	4	4	4	5	10	12	25
636	Charlie Moore	4	4	4	4	5	10	12	25
637	Ted Martinez	4	4	4	4	5	10	15	250
638	Chicago Cubs CL/Marshall	4	4	8	10	20	40	50	250
639	Steve Kline	4	4	4	4	5	10	15	80
640	Harmon Killebrew	4	4	5	10	20	30	40	200
641	Jim Northrup	4	4	4	4	6	12	15	50
642	Mike Phillips	4	4	4	4	8	15	40	350
643	Brent Strom	4	4	4	4	5	10	15	100
644	Bill Fahey	4	4	4	4	4	8	10	15
645	Danny Cater	4	4	4	4	5	10	15	40
646	Checklist: 529-660	4	4	4	4	5	10	15	40
647	Claudell Washington RC	4	4	5	6	12	150	200	500
648	Dave Pagan RC	4	4	4	4	5	10	12	60
649	Jack Heidemann	4	4	4	4	8	15	20	80
650	Dave May	4	4	4	4	5	10	15	50
651	John Morlan RC	4	5	10	12	25	50	60	80
652	Lindy McDaniel	4	4	4	4	5	10	15	50
653	Lee Richard	4	4	4	4	4	8	10	15
654	Jerry Terrell	4	4	4	4	5	10	15	30
655	Rico Carty	4	4	4	4	5	10	15	30
656	Bill Plummer	4	4	4	4	6	12	15	30
657	Bob Oliver	4	4	4	4	5	10	15	60

#	Name	VG 3	VgEx 4	EX 5	ExMt 6	NM 7	NmMt 8	NmMt+ 8.5
658	Vic Harris	4	4	4	5	10	20	25
659	Bob Apodaca	4	4	4	4	8	15	20
660	Hank Aaron	4	8	25	▲50	60	250	

—Hank Aaron #660 PSA 9 (MT) sold for $1,494 (eBay; 2/08)
—Hank Aaron #660 PSA 9 (MT) sold for $1,342 (eBay; 3/08)
—Hank Aaron #660 PSA 9 (MT) sold for $605 (eBay; 3/07)
—Johnny Bench #260 PSA 10 (Gem) sold for $1,857 (eBay; 8/07)
—Johnny Bench #260 GAI 9.5 (Gem) sold for $134 (eBay; 10/07)
—George Brett #228 PSA 10 (Gem) (Young Collection) sold for $11,596 (SCP; 5/12)
—George Brett #228 PSA 10 (Gem) sold for $8,775 (eBay; 2/08)
—George Brett #228 PSA 10 (Gem) sold for $7,207 (Mile High; 2/08)
—George Brett #228 PSA 10 (Gem) sold for $6,749 (eBay; 9/07)
—George Brett #228 PSA 10 (Gem) sold for $3,230 (Mastro; 4/05)
—Rod Carew #600 PSA 10 (Gem) sold for $2,956 (eBay; 5/08)
—Gary Carter #620 PSA 10 (Gem) (Young Collection) sold for $9,144 (SCP; 5/12)
—Gary Carter #620 PSA 10 (Gem) sold for $6,933 (Mile High; 1/13)
—Gary Carter #620 PSA 10 (Gem) sold for $4,060 (eBay; 09/12)
—Gary Carter #620 PSA 10 (Gem) sold for $3,736 (eBay; 11/12)
—Gary Carter #620 BVG 9 (MT) sold for $280 (eBay; 5/07)
—Gary Carter #620 BVG 9 (MT) sold for $230 (eBay; 2/07)
—Darrell Evans #475 PSA 9 (MT) sold for $296 (eBay; 3/07)
—Darrell Evans #475 PSA 9 (MT) sold for $242 (eBay; 2/08)
—Carlton Fisk #80 PSA 10 (Gem) sold for $2,003 (eBay; 44/08)
—Steve Garvey #140 PSA 10 (Gem) sold for $819 (eBay; 5/08)
—Steve Garvey #140 PSA 10 (Gem) sold for $562 (eBay; 2/07)
—Bob Gibson HL #3 PSA 10 (Gem) sold for $895 (eBay; 1/07)
—K.Hernandez/P.Garner #623 PSA 10 (Gem) sold for $1,378 (eBay; 2/08)
—K.Hernandez/P.Garner #623 PSA 10 (Gem) sold for $810 (eBay; 10/06)
—K.Hernandez/P.Garner #623 PSA 10 (Gem) sold for $661 (eBay; 5/07)
—Reggie Jackson #300 PSA 10 (Gem) sold for $1,526 (Memory Lane; 12/05)
—Al Kaline HL #4 PSA 10 (Gem) sold for $1,026 (eBay; 11/06)
—Larry Lintz #416 PSA 10 (Gem) sold for $2,958 (eBay; 08/12)
—Fred Lynn #622 PSA 10 (Gem) sold for $1,880 (eBay; 10/07)
—Joe Morgan #180 PSA 10 (Gem) sold for $616 (eBay; 5/08)
—Jim Rice #616 PSA 10 (Gem) (Young Collection) sold for $5,676 (SCP; 5/12)
—Jim Rice #616 BVG 9 (MT) sold for $345 (eBay; 2/07)
—Jim Rice #616 BVG 9 (MT) sold for $218 (eBay; 4/07)
—Jim Rice #616 SGC 96 (MT) sold for $179 (eBay; 4/07)
—Brooks Robinson #50 PSA 10 (Gem) sold for $1,675 (eBay; 11/06)
—Brooks Robinson #50 PSA 10 (Gem) sold for $1,133 (eBay; 02/12)
—Frank Robinson #580 PSA 10 (Gem) sold for $1,682 (eBay; 02/12)
—Pete Rose #320 PSA 10 (Gem) sold for $2,803 (Memory Lane; 9/06)
—Pete Rose #320 PSA 10 (Gem) sold for $2,328 (eBay; 08/12)
—Nolan Ryan #500 PSA 10 (Gem) sold for $29,247 (Mile High; 8/07)
—Nolan Ryan #500 BVG 9.5 (Gem) sold for $9,000 (eBay; 11/07)
—Nolan Ryan #500 SGC 96 (MT) sold for $861 (Memory Lane; 5/08)
—Nolan Ryan #500 BVG 9 (MT) sold for $704 (eBay; 8/07)
—Nolan Ryan #500 GAI 9 (MT) sold for $356 (eBay; 2/08)
—Nolan Ryan HL #5 PSA 10 (Gem) sold for $706 (eBay; 2/07)
—Mike Schmidt #70 PSA 10 (Gem) sold for $5,591 (Mile High; 8/07)
—Tom Seaver #370 PSA 10 (Gem) sold for $655 (eBay; 3/07)
—Ted Simmons #75 PSA 9 (MT) sold for $409 (eBay; 8/07)
—Willie Stargell #100 PSA 10 (Gem) sold for $1,199 (eBay; 4/08)
—Strikeout Leaders #312 PSA 10 (Gem) sold for $1,105 (Memory Lane; 4/07)
—Strikeout Leaders #312 PSA 10 (Gem) sold for $898 (eBay; 2/07)
—Strikeout Leaders #312 PSA 10 (Gem) sold for $456 (eBay; 2/07)
—Strikeout Leaders #312 PSA 10 (Gem) sold for $404 (eBay; 6/07)
—Don Sutton #220 PSA 10 (Gem) sold for $1,030 (eBay; 5/08)
—Carl Yastrzemski #280 PSA 10 (Gem) sold for $921 (eBay; 5/08)
—Carl Yastrzemski #280 PSA 10 (Gem) sold for $289 (eBay; 2/07)
—Carl Yastrzemski #280 PSA 10 (Gem) sold for $273 (eBay; 2/07)
—Robin Yount #223 PSA 10 (Gem) (Young Collection) sold for $22,602 (SCP; 5/12)
—Robin Yount #223 PSA 10 (Gem) sold for $19,799 (Mile High; 4/14)
—Robin Yount #223 PSA 10 (Gem) sold for $3,682 (Mile High; 8/07)
—Robin Yount #223 BVG 9.5 (Gem) sold for $2,650 (eBay; 12/07)

1975 Topps Mini

#	Name	GD 2	VG 3	VgEx 4	EX 5	ExMt 6	NM 7	NmMt 8
1	Hank Aaron HL	4	4	4	12	25	50	200
2	Lou Brock HL	4	4	4	4	5	10	25
3	Bob Gibson HL	4	4	4	4	8	15	30
4	Al Kaline HL	4	4	5	8	10	20	50
5	Nolan Ryan HL	6	8	10	12	15	25	60
6	Mike Marshall HL	4	4	4	4	4	6	12
7	Ryan/Busby/Bosman HL	4	4	4	4	6	20	25
8	Rogelio Moret	4	4	4	4	4	5	10

	GD 2	VG 3	VgEx 4	EX 5	ExMt 6	NM 7	NmMt 8	MT 9
Frank Tepedino	4	4	4	4	4	5	10	30
Willie Davis	4	4	4	4	4	5	10	25
Bill Melton	4	4	4	4	4	5	10	25
David Clyde	4	4	4	4	4	5	10	
Gene Locklear	4	4	4	4	4	5	10	25
Milt Wilcox	4	4	4	4	4	5	10	60
Jose Cardenal	4	4	4	4	4	5	10	50
Frank Tanana	4	4	4	6	8	15	80	
Dave Concepcion	4	4	4	5	6	12	25	
Detroit Tigers CL/Houk	4	4	4	4	4	8	15	50
Jerry Koosman	4	4	4	4	4	6	12	30
Thurman Munson	5	6	8	10	12	25	50	250
Rollie Fingers	4	4	4	4	4	8	25	150
Dave Cash	4	4	4	4	4	5	10	25
Bill Russell	4	4	4	4	4	6	12	60
Al Fitzmorris	4	4	4	4	4	5	10	25
Lee May	4	4	4	4	4	5	10	100
Dave McNally	4	4	4	4	4	6	12	40
Ken Reitz	4	4	4	4	4	5	10	150
Tom Murphy	4	4	4	4	4	6	12	50
Dave Parker	4	4	4	4	4	8	15	60
Bert Blyleven	4	4	8	15	20	40	80	
Dave Rader	4	4	4	4	4	8	15	
Reggie Cleveland	4	4	4	4	4	5	10	30
Dusty Baker	4	4	4	4	4	6	12	60
Steve Renko	4	4	4	4	4	5	10	25
Ron Santo	4	4	4	4	4	6	12	25
Joe Lovitto	4	4	4	4	4	5	10	25
Dave Freisleben	4	4	4	4	4	5	10	50
Buddy Bell	4	4	4	4	4	6	12	50
Andre Thornton	4	4	4	4	4	8	15	60
Bill Singer	4	4	4	4	4	5	10	25
Cesar Geronimo	4	4	4	4	4	6	12	
Joe Coleman	4	4	4	4	4	5	10	25
Cleon Jones	4	4	4	4	4	6	12	30
Pat Dobson	4	4	4	4	4	8	15	
Joe Rudi	4	4	4	4	4	6	12	30
Philadelphia Phillies CL/Ozark	4	4	4	4	4	6	12	30
Tommy John	4	4	4	4	4	8	15	
Freddie Patek	4	4	4	4	4	8	15	
Larry Dierker	4	4	4	4	4	5	10	25
Brooks Robinson	4	4	5	6	10	25	80	800
Bob Forsch	4	4	4	4	4	5	10	25
Darrell Porter	4	4	4	4	4	5	10	25
Dave Giusti	4	4	4	5	6	12	60	
Eric Soderholm	4	4	4	4	5	6	12	30
Bobby Bonds	4	4	4	6	8	15	30	
Rick Wise	4	4	4	4	4	8	15	
Dave Johnson	4	4	4	4	4	5	10	40
Chuck Taylor	4	4	4	6	8	15	30	
Ken Henderson	4	4	4	4	4	5	10	25
Fergie Jenkins	4	4	4	4	4	12	20	100
Dave Winfield	4	4	4	5	10	25	30	300
Fritz Peterson	4	4	4	4	4	5	10	100
Steve Swisher	4	4	4	4	4	8	15	
Dave Chalk	4	4	4	4	4	8	15	135
Don Gullett	4	4	4	4	4	6	12	80
Willie Horton	4	4	4	4	4	6	12	80
Tug McGraw	4	4	4	4	4	6	12	30
Ron Blomberg	4	4	4	4	4	5	10	25
John Odom	4	4	4	4	4	6	12	40
Mike Schmidt	4	4	6	12	15	25	60	600
Charlie Hough	4	4	4	4	4	6	12	30
Kansas City Royals CL/McKeon	4	4	4	4	4	6	12	40
J.R. Richard	4	4	4	4	4	6	12	30
Mark Belanger	4	4	4	5	6	8	15	80
Ted Simmons	4	4	4	8	10	12	25	120
Ed Sprague	4	4	4	4	4	8	15	
Richie Zisk	4	4	4	4	4	8	15	
Ray Corbin	4	4	4	4	4	5	10	25
Gary Matthews	4	4	4	4	4	6	12	30
Carlton Fisk	4	4	4	5	10	20	50	120
Ron Reed	4	4	4	4	4	8	15	
Pat Kelly	4	4	4	4	4	5	10	100
Jim Merritt	4	4	4	4	4	5	10	25
Enzo Hernandez	4	4	4	4	4	5	10	50
Bill Bonham	4	4	4	4	4	5	10	50

		GD 2	VG 3	VgEx 4	EX 5	ExMt 6	NM 7	NmMt 8	MT 9
86	Joe Lis	4	4	4	5	6	12	25	
87	George Foster	4	4	4	4	4	6	12	50
88	Tom Egan	4	4	4	4	4	5	10	25
89	Jim Ray	4	4	4	4	4	5	10	25
90	Rusty Staub	4	4	4	4	5	10	20	200
91	Dick Green	4	4	4	6	8	15	30	
92	Cecil Upshaw	4	4	4	4	4	6	12	30
93	Davey Lopes	4	4	4	4	4	6	12	30
94	Jim Lonborg	4	4	4	4	4	8	15	60
95	John Mayberry	4	4	4	4	4	5	10	40
96	Mike Cosgrove	4	4	4	4	6	8	15	30
97	Earl Williams	4	4	4	4	4	5	10	60
98	Rich Folkers	4	4	4	4	4	5	10	25
99	Mike Hegan	4	5	10	20	25	50	100	
100	Willie Stargell	4	4	4	4	5	20	25	80
101	Montreal Expos CL/Mauch	4	4	4	5	6	12	25	
102	Joe Decker	4	4	4	4	4	5	10	25
103	Rick Miller	4	4	4	4	4	8	15	
104	Bill Madlock	4	4	4	5	6	12	25	200
105	Buzz Capra	4	4	4	4	4	5	10	30
106	Mike Hargrove	4	4	4	4	4	6	12	40
107	Jim Barr	4	4	4	4	4	5	10	25
108	Tom Hall	4	4	4	4	4	5	10	25
109	George Hendrick	4	4	4	4	4	8	15	
110	Wilbur Wood	4	4	4	4	4	5	10	25
111	Wayne Garrett	4	4	4	4	4	8	15	
112	Larry Hardy	4	4	4	4	4	5	10	25
113	Elliott Maddox	4	4	4	4	4	5	10	25
114	Dick Lange	4	4	4	4	4	5	10	25
115	Joe Ferguson	4	4	4	4	4	5	10	25
116	Lerrin LaGrow	4	4	4	4	4	5	10	100
117	Baltimore Orioles CL/Weaver	4	4	4	4	4	6	12	50
118	Mike Anderson	4	4	4	4	4	5	10	25
119	Tommy Helms	4	4	4	4	4	5	10	25
120	Steve Busby	4	4	4	4	4	6	12	100
121	Bill North	4	4	4	4	4	5	10	30
122	Al Hrabosky	4	4	4	4	4	8	15	
123	Johnny Briggs	4	4	4	4	4	5	10	25
124	Jerry Reuss	4	4	4	4	4	5	10	25
125	Ken Singleton	4	4	4	5	6	12	50	
126	Checklist 1-132	4	4	4	4	4	6	12	50
127	Glenn Borgmann	4	4	4	4	5	10	80	
128	Bill Lee	4	4	4	4	4	6	12	40
129	Rick Monday	4	4	4	4	4	6	12	50
130	Phil Niekro	4	4	4	4	4	6	12	100
131	Toby Harrah	4	4	4	6	8	15	30	
132	Randy Moffitt	4	4	4	4	4	5	10	25
133	Dan Driessen	4	4	4	5	6	12	80	
134	Ron Hodges	4	4	4	4	4	5	10	25
135	Charlie Spikes	4	4	4	4	4	5	10	50
136	Jim Mason	4	4	4	5	6	12	25	
137	Terry Forster	4	4	4	4	4	6	12	40
138	Del Unser	4	4	4	4	4	5	10	25
139	Horacio Pina	4	4	4	4	5	6	12	25
140	Steve Garvey	4	4	4	8	10	20	50	
141	Mickey Stanley	4	4	4	4	4	8	15	
142	Bob Reynolds	4	4	4	4	4	5	10	30
143	Cliff Johnson	4	4	4	4	5	10	50	
144	Jim Wohlford	4	4	4	4	4	5	10	25
145	Ken Holtzman	4	4	4	4	4	5	10	30
146	San Diego Padres CL/McNamara	4	4	4	4	4	6	12	40
147	Pedro Garcia	4	4	4	4	4	5	10	25
148	Jim Rooker	4	4	4	4	4	5	10	25
149	Tim Foli	4	4	4	4	4	8	15	
150	Bob Gibson	4	5	8	10	20	25	60	300
151	Steve Brye	4	4	4	4	4	5	10	25
152	Mario Guerrero	4	4	4	4	4	5	10	80
153	Rick Reuschel	4	4	4	4	4	5	10	30
154	Mike Lum	4	4	4	4	4	6	12	30
155	Jim Bibby	4	4	4	4	4	5	10	80
156	Dave Kingman	4	4	4	4	4	6	12	60
157	Pedro Borbon	4	4	4	4	4	8	30	
158	Jerry Grote	4	4	4	4	4	8	15	175
159	Steve Arlin	4	4	4	4	4	5	10	25
160	Graig Nettles	4	4	4	4	4	6	12	120
161	Stan Bahnsen	4	4	4	6	8	15	30	
162	Willie Montanez	4	4	4	4	4	8	15	

#	Player	GD 2	VG 3	VgEx 4	EX 5	ExMt 6	NM 7	NmMt 8	MT 9
163	Jim Brewer	4	4	4	4	4	8	15	
164	Mickey Rivers	4	4	4	4	4	8	15	
165	Doug Rader	4	4	4	4	4	5	10	25
166	Woodie Fryman	4	4	4	4	4	5	10	25
167	Rich Coggins	4	4	4	4	4	5	10	25
168	Bill Greif	4	4	5	10	12	25	60	
169	Cookie Rojas	4	4	4	4	4	8	15	50
170	Bert Campaneris	4	4	4	5	6	12	25	
171	Ed Kirkpatrick	4	4	4	4	4	5	10	30
172	Boston Red Sox CL/Johnson	4	4	4	4	4	6	12	50
173	Steve Rogers	4	4	4	5	6	12	25	
174	Bake McBride	4	4	4	4	4	6	12	30
175	Don Money	4	4	4	4	4	5	10	40
176	Burt Hooton	4	4	4	4	4	5	10	60
177	Vic Correll	4	4	4	4	4	5	10	80
178	Cesar Tovar	4	4	4	4	4	5	10	100
179	Tom Bradley	4	4	4	4	4	6	12	25
180	Joe Morgan	4	4	4	5	8	15	40	120
181	Fred Beene	4	4	4	4	4	5	10	25
182	Don Hahn	4	4	4	4	4	5	10	50
183	Mel Stottlemyre	4	4	4	4	4	8	15	80
184	Jorge Orta	4	4	4	4	4	5	10	25
185	Steve Carlton	4	4	4	5	6	15	30	80
186	Willie Crawford	4	4	4	4	4	5	10	25
187	Denny Doyle	4	4	4	5	6	12	40	
188	Tom Griffin	4	4	4	4	4	5	10	25
189	Y.Berra/Campanella MVP	4	4	4	4	4	6	15	30
190	B.Shantz/H.Sauer MVP	4	4	4	4	4	6	12	30
191	Al Rosen/Campanella MVP	4	4	4	4	4	6	12	30
192	Y.Berra/W.Mays MVP	4	4	4	4	4	8	25	80
193	Y.Berra/Campanella MVP	4	4	4	4	4	5	10	25
194	M.Mantle/D.Newcombe MVP	4	4	4	5	5	20	30	80
195	M.Mantle/H.Aaron MVP	6	8	10	12	15	20	40	250
196	J.Jensen/E.Banks MVP	4	4	4	4	4	6	12	60
197	N.Fox/E.Banks MVP	4	4	4	4	4	5	10	50
198	R.Maris/D.Groat MVP	4	4	4	4	4	8	15	40
199	R.Maris/F.Robinson MVP	4	4	4	4	4	8	10	25
200	M.Mantle/M.Wills MVP	4	4	4	5	6	12	30	80
201	E.Howard/S.Koufax MVP	4	4	4	4	4	6	12	40
202	B.Robinson/K.Boyer MVP	4	4	4	4	4	6	12	80
203	Z.Versalles/W.Mays MVP	4	4	4	4	4	8	15	25
204	F.Robinson/B.Clemente MVP	4	4	4	5	10	20		100
205	C.Yastrzemski/O.Cepeda MVP	4	4	4	4	8	15		50
206	D.McLain/B.Gibson MVP	4	4	4	4	4	6	12	40
207	H.Killebrew/W.McCovey MVP	4	4	4	4	4	6	12	30
208	B.Powell/J.Bench MVP	4	4	4	4	4	6	12	60
209	V.Blue/J.Torre MVP	4	4	4	4	4	6	12	60
210	R.Allen/J.Bench MVP	4	4	4	4	5	10	20	50
211	R.Jackson/P.Rose MVP	4	4	4	4	5	10	20	150
212	J.Burroughs/S.Garvey MVP	4	4	4	4	4	6	12	50
213	Oscar Gamble	4	4	4	4	4	4	8	15
214	Harry Parker	4	4	4	4	4	5	10	25
215	Bobby Valentine	4	4	4	4	4	6	12	40
216	San Francisco Giants CL/Westrum	4	4	4	4	4	6	12	40
217	Lou Piniella	4	4	4	4	4	6	12	40
218	Jerry Johnson	4	4	4	4	4	5	10	25
219	Ed Herrmann	4	4	4	4	4	8	15	
220	Don Sutton	4	4	4	5	6	12	25	80
221	Aurelio Rodriguez	4	4	4	4	4	5	10	25
222	Dan Spillner	4	4	4	4	5	10	20	
223	Robin Yount	4	5	25	50	60	100	200	1,000
224	Ramon Hernandez	4	4	4	4	4	5	10	25
225	Bob Grich	4	4	4	4	4	8	15	
226	Bill Campbell	4	4	4	4	4	8	15	
227	Bob Watson	4	4	4	4	4	8	15	150
228	George Brett	5	10	50	60	100	150	300	1,500
229	Barry Foote	4	4	4	4	4	5	10	
230	Jim Hunter	4	4	4	4	4	8	25	80
231	Mike Tyson	4	4	4	4	4	5	10	25
232	Diego Segui	4	4	4	5	6	12	25	100
233	Billy Grabarkewitz	4	4	4	6	8	15	30	
234	Tom Grieve	4	4	4	4	4	5	10	25
235	Jack Billingham	4	4	4	4	4	6	12	30
236	California Angels CL/Williams	4	4	4	4	4	6	12	60
237	Carl Morton	4	4	4	4	4	8	15	
238	Dave Duncan	4	4	4	4	4	5	10	80
239	George Stone	4	4	4	4	4	5	10	25
240	Garry Maddox	4	4	4	4	4	6	12	4
241	Dick Tidrow	4	4	4	4	4	5	10	5
242	Jay Johnstone	4	4	4	4	4	5	10	3
243	Jim Kaat	4	4	6	12	15	30	60	
244	Bill Buckner	4	4	4	4	4	8	15	
245	Mickey Lolich	4	4	4	4	5	10	20	30
246	St. Louis Cardinals CL/Schoen	4	4	5	10	20	40	80	15
247	Enos Cabell	4	4	4	4	4	5	10	2
248	Randy Jones	4	4	4	4	4	8	15	
249	Danny Thompson	4	4	4	4	4	8	15	
250	Ken Brett	4	4	4	4	4	8	15	6
251	Fran Healy	4	4	4	4	4	8	15	
252	Fred Scherman	4	4	4	4	4	5	10	2
253	Jesus Alou	4	8	15	30	40	80	150	
254	Mike Torrez	4	4	4	4	4	5	10	3
255	Dwight Evans	4	4	4	4	4	6	12	5
256	Billy Champion	4	4	4	4	4	8	15	
257	Checklist: 133-264	4	4	4	4	4	6	12	4
258	Dave LaRoche	4	4	4	4	4	8	15	10
259	Len Randle	4	4	4	4	4	8	15	
260	Johnny Bench	4	4	5	10	12	30	60	30
261	Andy Hassler	4	4	4	4	4	5	10	2
262	Rowland Office	4	4	4	4	4	8	15	10
263	Jim Perry	4	4	4	4	4	5	10	2
264	John Milner	4	4	4	4	4	8	15	
265	Ron Bryant	4	4	4	4	4	5	10	2
266	Sandy Alomar	4	4	4	4	4	6	12	4
267	Dick Ruthven	4	4	4	4	4	5	10	2
268	Hal McRae	4	4	4	4	4	8	15	12
269	Doug Rau	4	4	4	4	4	5	10	2
270	Ron Fairly	4	4	4	4	4	6	12	5
271	Gerry Moses	4	4	4	4	4	8	15	
272	Lynn McGlothen	4	4	4	4	4	5	10	2
273	Steve Braun	4	4	4	4	4	5	10	2
274	Vicente Romo	4	4	4	4	4	5	10	2
275	Paul Blair	4	4	4	4	4	6	12	5
276	Chicago White Sox CL/Tanner	4	4	4	4	4	6	12	4
277	Frank Taveras	4	4	4	4	4	8	15	
278	Paul Lindblad	4	4	4	4	4	8	15	
279	Milt May	4	4	4	4	4	5	10	2
280	Carl Yastrzemski	8	10	15	20	25	30	50	25
281	Jim Slaton	4	4	4	4	4	5	10	2
282	Jerry Morales	4	4	4	4	4	5	10	2
283	Steve Foucault	4	4	4	4	4	5	10	2
284	Ken Griffey Sr.	4	4	4	4	4	8	25	6
285	Ellie Rodriguez	4	4	4	4	4	5	10	2
286	Mike Jorgensen	4	4	4	4	4	5	10	2
287	Roric Harrison	4	4	4	4	4	8	15	5
288	Bruce Ellingsen	4	4	4	4	4	5	10	2
289	Ken Rudolph	4	4	4	4	4	8	15	5
290	Jon Matlack	4	4	4	4	4	8	15	
291	Bill Sudakis	4	4	4	4	4	5	10	2
292	Ron Schueler	4	4	4	4	4	5	10	2
293	Dick Sharon	4	4	4	4	4	5	10	2
294	Geoff Zahn	4	4	4	4	4	5	10	2
295	Vada Pinson	4	4	4	4	4	6	12	12
296	Alan Foster	4	4	4	4	4	8	15	
297	Craig Kusick	4	4	4	4	4	5	50	
298	Johnny Grubb	4	4	4	4	4	5	10	2
299	Bucky Dent	4	4	4	4	4	6	12	4
300	Reggie Jackson	4	4	4	6	12	25	50	40
301	Dave Roberts	4	4	6	12	15	30	60	
302	Rick Burleson	6	12	15	30	40	80	150	
303	Grant Jackson	4	4	4	4	4	8	15	10
304	Pittsburgh Pirates CL/Murtaugh	4	4	4	4	4	6	12	8
305	Jim Colborn	4	4	4	4	4	5	10	2
306	Batting Leaders	4	4	4	4	4	6	12	3
307	Home Run Leaders	4	4	4	4	4	6	12	6
308	RBI Leaders	4	4	4	4	4	6	12	3
309	Stolen Base Leaders	4	4	4	4	4	6	12	4
310	Victory Leaders	4	4	4	4	4	8	15	
311	ERA Leaders	4	4	4	4	4	6	12	3
312	Strikeout Leaders	4	4	4	4	6	8	15	25
313	Leading Firemen	4	4	4	4	4	6	12	4
314	Buck Martinez	4	4	4	4	4	8	15	
315	Don Kessinger	4	4	5	10	12	25	50	
316	Jackie Brown	4	4	4	4	4	5	10	

	GD 2	VG 3	VgEx 4	EX 5	ExMt 6	NM 7	NmMt 8	MT 9
Joe Lahoud	4	4	4	4	4	5	10	80
Ernie McAnally	4	4	4	4	4	5	10	25
Johnny Oates	4	4	4	4	4	8	15	
Pete Rose	10	12	15	20	25	40	▲80	500
Rudy May	4	4	4	4	4	5	10	25
Ed Goodson	4	4	4	4	4	8	15	
Fred Holdsworth	4	4	4	4	4	5	10	50
Ed Kranepool	4	4	4	4	4	6	12	30
Tony Oliva	4	4	4	4	4	6	12	50
Wayne Twitchell	4	4	4	4	4	8	60	
Jerry Hairston	4	4	4	4	4	5	10	20
Sonny Siebert	4	4	4	4	4	5	10	25
Ted Kubiak	4	4	4	4	4	5	10	25
Mike Marshall	4	4	4	4	4	6	12	40
Cleveland Indians CL/Robinson	4	4	4	4	4	8	15	
Fred Kendall	4	4	4	4	4	5	10	25
Dick Drago	4	4	4	4	4	5	10	30
Greg Gross	4	4	4	4	4	5	10	25
Jim Palmer	4	4	4	4	8	▲20	30	300
Rennie Stennett	4	4	4	8	10	20	40	
Kevin Kobel	4	4	4	4	4	8	15	
Rich Stelmaszek	4	4	4	4	4	8	15	
Jim Fregosi	4	4	4	5	6	12	50	
Paul Splittorff	4	4	4	4	4	8	15	
Hal Breeden	4	4	4	4	4	5	10	25
Leroy Stanton	4	4	4	4	4	5	10	25
Danny Frisella	4	4	4	4	4	8	15	
Ben Oglivie	4	4	4	5	6	12	25	
Clay Carroll	4	4	4	4	4	6	12	80
Bobby Darwin	4	4	4	4	4	8	15	
Mike Caldwell	4	4	4	4	4	5	10	25
Tony Muser	4	4	4	4	4	5	10	25
Ray Sadecki	4	4	4	4	4	5	10	25
Bobby Murcer	4	4	4	4	4	8	15	80
Bob Boone	4	4	4	4	4	6	12	30
Darold Knowles	4	4	4	4	4	5	10	50
Luis Melendez	4	4	4	4	4	5	10	25
Dick Bosman	4	4	4	4	4	5	10	50
Chris Cannizzaro	4	4	4	4	4	5	10	25
Rico Petrocelli	4	4	4	4	4	6	12	40
Ken Forsch	4	4	4	4	4	5	10	25
Al Bumbry	4	4	4	4	4	5	10	30
Paul Popovich	4	4	4	4	4	5	10	25
George Scott	4	4	4	4	4	5	10	30
Los Angeles Dodgers CL/Alston	4	4	4	4	4	6	12	30
Steve Hargan	4	4	4	4	4	8	15	
Carmen Fanzone	4	4	4	4	4	5	10	25
Doug Bird	4	4	4	4	4	8	15	
Bob Bailey	4	4	4	4	4	5	10	25
Ken Sanders	4	4	4	4	4	8	15	
Craig Robinson	4	4	4	4	4	5	10	25
Vic Albury	4	4	4	4	4	5	10	25
Merv Rettenmund	4	4	4	4	4	8	15	
Tom Seaver	4	4	4	5	12	25	▲40	100
Gates Brown	4	4	5	10	12	25	60	
John D'Acquisto	4	4	4	4	4	8	15	
Bill Sharp	4	4	4	4	4	5	10	25
Eddie Watt	4	4	4	4	4	5	10	25
Roy White	4	4	4	4	4	8	15	
Steve Yeager	4	4	4	4	4	8	15	
Tom Hilgendorf	4	4	4	4	4	5	10	25
Derrel Thomas	4	4	4	4	4	5	10	60
Bernie Carbo	4	4	4	4	4	5	10	60
Sal Bando	4	4	4	8	10	20	50	
John Curtis	4	4	4	4	4	5	10	25
Don Baylor	4	4	4	4	4	6	12	40
Jim York	4	4	4	4	4	5	10	25
Milwaukee Brewers CL/Crandall	4	4	4	4	4	6	12	60
Dock Ellis	4	4	4	4	4	5	10	25
Checklist: 265-396	4	4	4	4	4	6	12	30
Jim Spencer	4	4	4	4	4	5	10	25
Steve Stone	4	4	4	4	4	5	10	25
Tony Solaita	4	4	4	4	4	5	10	25
Ron Cey	4	4	4	5	6	12	25	
Don DeMola	4	4	4	4	4	5	10	25
Bruce Bochte	4	4	4	6	8	15	30	
Gary Gentry	4	4	4	4	4	5	10	25

		GD 2	VG 3	VgEx 4	EX 5	ExMt 6	NM 7	NmMt 8	MT 9
394	Larvell Blanks	4	4	4	4	4	5	10	25
395	Bud Harrelson	4	4	4	4	4	5	10	30
396	Fred Norman	4	4	4	4	4	5	10	25
397	Bill Freehan	4	4	4	4	4	6	12	40
398	Elias Sosa	4	4	4	4	4	5	10	25
399	Terry Harmon	4	4	4	4	4	5	10	25
400	Dick Allen	4	4	4	4	4	8	15	
401	Mike Wallace	4	4	4	4	4	8	15	
402	Bob Tolan	4	4	4	5	6	12	25	
403	Tom Buskey	4	4	4	4	4	5	10	25
404	Ted Sizemore	4	4	4	4	4	5	10	25
405	John Montague	4	4	4	8	10	20	40	
406	Bob Gallagher	4	4	4	4	4	5	10	25
407	Herb Washington	4	4	4	4	4	6	12	120
408	Clyde Wright	4	4	4	4	4	5	10	25
409	Bob Robertson	4	4	4	4	4	8	15	
410	Mike Cuellar	4	4	4	4	4	8	15	
411	George Mitterwald	4	4	4	4	4	5	10	25
412	Bill Hands	4	4	4	4	4	5	10	25
413	Marty Pattin	4	4	4	4	4	5	10	25
414	Manny Mota	4	4	4	4	4	5	10	50
415	John Hiller	4	4	4	4	4	5	10	30
416	Larry Lintz	4	4	4	4	4	5	10	25
417	Skip Lockwood	4	4	4	8	10	20	40	
418	Leo Foster	4	4	4	4	4	5	10	25
419	Dave Goltz	4	4	4	4	4	5	10	25
420	Larry Bowa	4	4	4	4	4	6	12	30
421	New York Mets CL/Berra	4	4	4	4	4	8	15	
422	Brian Downing	4	4	4	4	4	6	12	40
423	Clay Kirby	4	4	4	4	4	5	10	30
424	John Lowenstein	4	4	4	4	4	5	10	25
425	Tito Fuentes	4	4	4	4	4	4	8	15
426	George Medich	4	4	4	4	4	5	10	50
427	Clarence Gaston	4	4	4	4	4	5	10	30
428	Dave Hamilton	4	4	4	4	4	5	10	25
429	Jim Dwyer	4	4	4	4	4	5	10	25
430	Luis Tiant	4	4	4	4	4	6	12	100
431	Rod Gilbreath	4	4	4	4	4	8	15	
432	Ken Berry	4	4	4	4	4	5	10	25
433	Larry Demery	4	4	4	4	4	8	15	
434	Bob Locker	4	4	4	4	4	5	10	25
435	Dave Nelson	4	4	4	4	4	5	10	150
436	Ken Frailing	4	4	4	4	4	5	10	40
437	Al Cowens	4	4	4	4	4	5	10	25
438	Don Carrithers	4	4	4	4	4	5	10	60
439	Ed Brinkman	4	4	4	4	4	5	10	25
440	Andy Messersmith	4	4	4	4	4	5	10	60
441	Bobby Heise	4	4	4	4	4	5	10	80
442	Maximino Leon	4	4	4	4	4	5	10	20
443	Minnesota Twins CL/Quilici	4	4	4	4	4	6	12	40
444	Gene Garber	4	4	4	4	4	5	10	20
445	Felix Millan	4	4	4	4	4	8	15	
446	Bart Johnson	4	4	4	4	4	8	15	
447	Terry Crowley	4	4	4	4	4	5	10	25
448	Frank Duffy	4	4	4	4	4	5	10	25
449	Charlie Williams	4	4	4	4	4	5	10	50
450	Willie McCovey	5	6	8	10	12	15	▲30	50
451	Rick Dempsey	4	4	4	4	4	5	10	25
452	Angel Mangual	4	4	4	4	4	5	10	25
453	Claude Osteen	4	4	4	4	4	8	15	
454	Doug Griffin	4	4	4	4	4	5	10	25
455	Don Wilson	4	4	4	4	4	5	10	25
456	Bob Coluccio	4	4	4	4	4	5	10	25
457	Mario Mendoza	4	4	4	4	4	5	10	25
458	Ross Grimsley	4	5	10	20	25	50	100	
459	1974 AL Championships	4	4	5	10	12	25	50	
460	1974 NL Championships	4	4	4	8	10	20	40	
461	Reggie Jackson WS1	4	4	4	4	4	8	15	50
462	W.Alston/J.Ferguson WS2	4	4	4	4	4	6	12	40
463	Rollie Fingers WS3	4	4	4	5	6	12	25	
464	A's Batter WS4	4	4	4	4	4	8	15	
465	Joe Rudi WS5	4	4	4	4	4	5	10	20
466	A's Do it Again WS	4	4	4	4	4	6	12	40
467	Ed Halicki	4	4	4	5	6	12	25	
468	Bobby Mitchell	4	4	4	4	4	8	15	
469	Tom Dettore	4	4	4	4	4	5	10	25
470	Jeff Burroughs	4	4	4	4	4	5	10	50

#	Player	GD 2	VG 3	VgEx 4	EX 5	ExMt 6	NM 7	NmMt 8	MT 9
471	Bob Stinson	4	4	4	4	4	5	10	150
472	Bruce Dal Canton	4	4	4	4	4	5	10	40
473	Ken McMullen	4	4	4	4	4	5	10	25
474	Luke Walker	4	4	4	4	4	5	10	25
475	Darrell Evans	4	4	4	4	4	8	15	
476	Ed Figueroa	4	4	4	4	4	8	15	
477	Tom Hutton	4	4	4	4	4	8	15	
478	Tom Burgmeier	4	4	4	4	4	5	10	40
479	Ken Boswell	4	4	4	4	4	5	10	25
480	Carlos May	4	4	4	4	4	5	10	120
481	Will McEnaney	4	4	4	4	5	10	20	
482	Tom McCraw	4	4	4	4	4	8	15	
483	Steve Ontiveros	4	4	4	4	5	6	12	25
484	Glenn Beckert	4	4	4	4	4	5	10	25
485	Sparky Lyle	4	4	4	4	4	6	12	40
486	Ray Fosse	4	4	4	4	4	5	10	25
487	Houston Astros CL/Gomez	4	4	4	4	4	8	15	40
488	Bill Travers	4	4	4	4	4	5	10	40
489	Cecil Cooper	4	4	4	4	4	8	15	
490	Reggie Smith	4	4	4	4	4	8	15	
491	Doyle Alexander	4	4	4	4	4	5	10	25
492	Rich Hebner	4	4	4	4	4	8	15	50
493	Don Stanhouse	4	4	4	4	4	5	10	30
494	Pete LaCock	4	4	4	4	4	5	10	25
495	Nelson Briles	4	4	4	4	4	5	10	30
496	Pepe Frias	4	4	4	4	4	5	10	25
497	Jim Nettles	4	4	4	4	4	5	10	25
498	Al Downing	4	4	4	4	4	5	10	25
499	Marty Perez	4	4	4	4	4	8	15	
500	Nolan Ryan	4	6	12	25	30	60	250	1,000
501	Bill Robinson	4	4	4	4	4	5	10	60
502	Pat Bourque	4	4	4	4	4	5	10	25
503	Fred Stanley	4	5	10	20	25	50	100	
504	Buddy Bradford	4	4	4	4	4	8	15	
505	Chris Speier	4	4	4	4	4	8	15	
506	Leron Lee	4	4	4	4	4	5	10	25
507	Tom Carroll	4	4	4	4	4	5	10	25
508	Bob Hansen	4	4	4	4	4	5	10	80
509	Dave Hilton	4	4	4	4	4	5	10	25
510	Vida Blue	4	4	4	4	4	8	15	60
511	Texas Rangers CL/Martin	4	4	4	4	4	6	12	30
512	Larry Milbourne	4	4	4	8	10	20	100	
513	Dick Pole	4	4	4	4	4	8	15	
514	Jose Cruz	4	4	4	6	8	15	30	
515	Manny Sanguillen	4	4	4	4	4	8	15	
516	Don Hood	4	4	4	4	4	5	10	25
517	Checklist: 397-528	4	4	4	4	4	8	15	
518	Leo Cardenas	4	4	4	4	4	5	10	25
519	Jim Todd	4	4	4	4	4	8	15	100
520	Amos Otis	4	4	4	4	4	5	10	50
521	Dennis Blair	4	4	4	4	4	5	10	30
522	Gary Sutherland	4	4	4	4	4	5	10	25
523	Tom Paciorek	4	4	4	4	4	5	10	80
524	John Doherty	4	4	4	4	4	5	10	25
525	Tom House	4	4	4	4	4	8	15	
526	Larry Hisle	4	4	4	4	4	5	10	25
527	Mac Scarce	4	4	4	4	4	8	15	
528	Eddie Leon	4	4	4	4	4	5	10	25
529	Gary Thomasson	4	4	4	4	4	5	10	25
530	Gaylord Perry	4	4	4	4	5	10	20	150
531	Cincinnati Reds CL/Anderson	4	4	4	4	6	12	25	50
532	Gorman Thomas	4	4	4	4	4	6	12	40
533	Rudy Meoli	4	4	4	4	4	5	10	25
534	Alex Johnson	4	4	4	4	4	6	12	40
535	Gene Tenace	4	4	4	4	4	8	15	
536	Bob Moose	4	4	4	4	4	5	10	40
537	Tommy Harper	4	4	4	4	4	8	15	
538	Duffy Dyer	4	4	4	4	4	5	10	40
539	Jesse Jefferson	4	4	4	4	4	8	15	
540	Lou Brock	4	4	4	4	▲10	▲15	▲30	80
541	Roger Metzger	4	4	4	4	4	5	10	25
542	Pete Broberg	4	4	4	4	4	8	15	
543	Larry Biittner	4	4	4	4	4	5	10	25
544	Steve Mingori	4	4	4	5	6	12	25	
545	Billy Williams	4	4	4	4	4	8	15	200
546	John Knox	4	4	4	4	4	5	10	25
547	Von Joshua	4	4	4	4	4	5	10	50
548	Charlie Sands	4	4	4	4	4	5	10	
549	Bill Butler	4	4	4	4	4	5	10	
550	Ralph Garr	4	4	4	4	4	5	10	
551	Larry Christenson	4	4	4	4	4	8	15	
552	Jack Brohamer	4	4	4	4	4	5	10	
553	John Boccabella	4	4	4	4	4	5	10	
554	Goose Gossage	4	4	4	4	4	8	15	
555	Al Oliver	4	4	4	4	4	6	12	
556	Tim Johnson	4	4	4	4	4	8	15	
557	Larry Gura	4	4	4	4	4	5	10	
558	Dave Roberts	4	4	4	4	4	5	10	
559	Bob Montgomery	4	4	4	4	4	5	10	
560	Tony Perez	4	4	4	4	5	10	20	
561	Oakland Athletics CL/Dark	4	4	4	5	6	12	25	
562	Gary Nolan	4	4	4	4	4	8	15	
563	Wilbur Howard	4	4	4	4	4	5	10	
564	Tommy Davis	4	4	4	4	8	15	150	
565	Joe Torre	4	4	4	4	4	6	12	
566	Ray Burris	4	4	4	4	4	5	10	
567	Jim Sundberg	4	4	4	4	4	6	12	
568	Dale Murray	4	4	4	4	4	5	10	
569	Frank White	4	4	4	4	4	6	12	
570	Jim Wynn	4	4	4	4	4	6	12	
571	Dave Lemanczyk	4	4	4	4	4	5	10	
572	Roger Nelson	4	4	4	4	4	8	15	
573	Orlando Pena	4	4	4	4	4	5	10	
574	Tony Taylor	4	4	4	4	4	8	15	
575	Gene Clines	4	4	4	4	4	5	10	
576	Phil Roof	4	4	4	4	4	5	10	
577	John Morris	4	4	4	4	4	5	10	
578	Dave Tomlin	4	4	4	4	4	5	10	
579	Skip Pitlock	4	4	4	4	4	5	10	
580	Frank Robinson	4	4	8	10	12	20	30	
581	Darrel Chaney	4	4	4	4	4	5	10	
582	Eduardo Rodriguez	4	4	4	4	4	5	10	
583	Andy Etchebarren	4	4	4	5	6	12	25	
584	Mike Garman	4	4	4	4	4	5	10	
585	Chris Chambliss	4	4	4	4	4	6	12	
586	Tim McCarver	4	4	4	4	4	8	15	
587	Chris Ward	4	4	4	4	4	5	10	
588	Rick Auerbach	4	4	4	4	4	8	15	
589	Atlanta Braves CL/King	4	4	4	4	4	8	15	
590	Cesar Cedeno	4	4	4	5	6	12	25	
591	Glenn Abbott	4	4	4	4	4	5	10	
592	Balor Moore	4	4	4	4	4	5	10	
593	Gene Lamont	4	4	4	4	4	5	10	
594	Jim Fuller	4	4	4	4	4	5	10	
595	Joe Niekro	4	4	4	4	4	6	12	
596	Ollie Brown	4	4	4	4	4	8	15	
597	Winston Llenas	4	4	4	4	4	5	10	
598	Bruce Kison	4	4	4	4	4	5	10	
599	Nate Colbert	4	4	4	4	4	5	10	
600	Rod Carew	4	4	4	4	8	25	40	
601	Juan Beniquez	4	4	4	4	4	8	15	
602	John Vukovich	4	4	4	4	4	5	10	
603	Lew Krausse	4	4	5	10	12	25	50	
604	Oscar Zamora	4	4	4	4	4	5	10	
605	John Ellis	4	4	4	4	4	5	10	
606	Bruce Miller	4	4	4	4	4	6	12	
607	Jim Holt	4	4	4	4	4	8	15	
608	Gene Michael	4	4	4	4	4	5	10	
609	Elrod Hendricks	4	4	4	4	4	5	10	
610	Ron Hunt	4	4	4	4	4	5	10	
611	New York Yankees CL/Virdon	4	4	4	4	4	8	15	
612	Terry Hughes	4	4	4	4	4	5	10	
613	Bill Parsons	4	4	4	4	4	5	10	
614	Rookie Pitchers	4	4	4	4	4	5	10	
615	Rookie Pitchers	4	4	4	4	4	6	12	
616	Jim Rice	4	4	5	10	30	40	80	
617	Rookie Infielders	4	4	4	4	4	6	12	
618	Rookie Pitchers	4	4	4	4	4	6	12	
619	Rookie Outfielders	4	4	4	4	4	5	10	
620	Gary Carter	4	4	5	10	25	50	80	
621	Rookie Pitchers	4	4	4	4	4	6	12	
622	Fred Lynn	4	4	4	4	8	15	25	
623	K.Hernandez/P.Garner	4	4	4	4	8	15	40	
624	Rookie Pitchers	4	4	4	5	6	12	25	

	GD 2	VG 3	VgEx 4	EX 5	ExMt 6	NM 7	NmMt 8	MT 9
Boog Powell	4	4	4	4	6	12	25	200
Larry Haney	4	4	4	8	10	20	40	
Tom Walker	4	4	4	4	4	5	10	25
Ron LeFlore	4	4	4	4	4	5	10	40
Joe Hoerner	4	4	4	4	4	5	10	40
Greg Luzinski	4	4	4	4	4	6	12	30
Lee Lacy	4	4	4	4	4	8	15	
Morris Nettles	4	4	4	4	4	5	10	25
Paul Casanova	4	4	4	4	4	5	10	50
Cy Acosta	4	4	4	4	4	8	15	40
Chuck Dobson	4	4	4	4	4	5	10	25
Charlie Moore	4	4	4	4	4	5	10	20
Ted Martinez	4	4	4	4	4	8	15	
Chicago Cubs CL/Marshall	4	4	4	8	10	20	40	
Steve Kline	4	4	4	4	4	5	10	25
Harmon Killebrew	4	4	4	6	8	25	30	200
Jim Northrup	4	4	4	4	4	6	12	30
Mike Phillips	4	4	4	4	4	8	15	
Brent Strom	4	4	4	4	4	5	10	25
Bill Fahey	4	4	4	4	4	5	10	25
Danny Cater	4	4	4	4	4	5	10	25
Checklist: 529-660	4	4	4	4	4	8	15	
Claudell Washington	4	4	5	10	12	25		
Dave Pagan	4	4	4	4	4	5	10	25
Jack Heidemann	4	4	4	4	4	8	15	
Dave May	4	4	4	4	4	5	10	60
John Morlan	4	4	4	4	4	8	15	
Lindy McDaniel	4	4	4	4	4	5	10	60
Lee Richard	4	4	4	4	4	5	10	20
Jerry Terrell	4	4	4	4	4	5	10	60
Rico Carty	4	4	4	4	4	5	10	25
Bill Plummer	4	4	4	4	4	5	10	25
Bob Oliver	4	4	4	4	4	8	15	
Vic Harris	4	4	4	4	4	5	10	25
Bob Apodaca	4	4	4	4	4	8	15	150
Hank Aaron	8	10	12	25	40	▲60	▲200	800

957 MVP's #195 PSA 10 (Gem) sold for $685 (eBay; 3/07)
959 MVP's #197 PSA 10 (Gem) sold for $810 (eBay; 7/07)
1974 NL Championship #460 PSA 9 (MT) sold for $809 (eBay; 11/07)
Hank Aaron HL #1 PSA 10 (Gem) sold for $1,236 (eBay; 5/07)
Jesus Alou #253 PSA 9 (MT) sold for $584 (eBay; 1/08)
George Brett #228 PSA 10 (Gem) (Young Collection) sold for $5,948 (SCP; 5/12)
Lou Brock #540 PSA 10 (Gem) sold for $2,279 (eBay; 5/08)
Gary Carter #620 PSA 10 (Gem) sold for $4,035 (eBay; 7/07)
Gary Carter #620 PSA 10 (Gem) sold for $3,315 (eBay; 09/12)
Gary Carter #620 PSA 10 (Gem) sold for $3,050 (eBay; 12/07)
Gary Carter #620 PSA 10 (Gem) sold for $2,895 (eBay; 1/08)
Gary Carter #620 PSA 10 (Gem) sold for $2,504 (eBay; 4/08)
Gary Carter #620 BVG 9.5 (Gem) sold for $1,000 (eBay; 12/07)
Steve Garvey #140 PSA 9 (MT) sold for $910 (eBay; 11/07)
Steve Garvey #140 PSA 9 (MT) sold for $504 (eBay; 4/08)
Bill Grief #168 PSA 9 (MT) sold for $570 (eBay; 5/08)
Bob Gibson HL #3 PSA 9 (MT) sold for $504 (eBay; 1/08)
K.Hernandez/P.Garner #623 PSA 10 (Gem) sold for $3,049 (eBay; 5/08)
Home Run Leaders #307 PSA 10 (Gem) sold for $781 (eBay; 5/07)
Reggie Jackson #300 PSA 10 (Gem) sold for $4,404 (eBay; 2/08)
Fred Lynn #622 PSA 10 (Gem) sold for $532 (eBay; 7/07)
Ron Reed #81 PSA 9 (MT) sold for $581 (eBay; 6/08)
Jim Rice #616 PSA 10 (Gem) sold for $2,817 (eBay; 4/07)
Nolan Ryan HL #5 BVG 9.5 (Gem) sold for $205 (eBay; 11/07)
Ryan/Busby/Bosman HL #7 PSA 10 (Gem) sold for $785 (eBay; 3/08)
Ryan/Busby/Bosman HL #7 PSA 10 (Gem) sold for $767 (eBay; 5/08)
Willie Stargell #100 PSA 10 (Gem) sold for $691 (eBay; 11/07)
Frank Tanana #16 PSA 9 (MT) sold for $508 (eBay; 1/08)
Bob Tolan #402 PSA 9 (MT) sold for $504 (eBay; 5/08)
Claudell Washington #647 PSA 8 (NmMt) sold for $414 (eBay; 5/08)
Claudell Washington #647 PSA 8 (NmMt) sold for $174 (eBay; 3/08)
Claudell Washington #647 PSA 8 (NmMt) sold for $158 (eBay; 12/07)
Carl Yastrzemski #280 PSA 10 (Gem) sold for $4,265 (eBay; 2/08)
Robin Yount #223 PSA 10 (Gem) sold for $2,568 (eBay; 3/07)
Robin Yount #223 BVG 9 (MT) sold for $290 (eBay; 2/08)
1965 MVP's #203 PSA 10 (Gem) sold for $2,001 (eBay; 6/08)
1974 NL Championships #460 PSA 9 (MT) sold for $502 (eBay; 5/08)

1976 Kellogg's

		VG 3	VgEx 4	EX 5	ExMt 6	NM 7	NmMt 8	MT 9	Gem 9.5/10
1	Steve Hargan SP	4	4	4	4	8	15	30	
2	Claudell Washington SP	4	4	4	4	6	12	25	60
3	Don Gullett SP	4	4	4	4	6	12	25	120
4	Randy Jones	4	4	4	4	4	4	8	20
5	Jim Hunter	4	4	4	4	4	5	10	25
6A	Clay Carroll Reds Logo	4	4	4	4	4	4	8	
6B	Clay Carroll White Sox Logo	4	4	4	4	4	4	8	
7	Joe Rudi	4	4	4	4	4	4	8	20
8	Reggie Jackson	4	4	4	4	4	8	15	50
9	Felix Millan	4	4	4	4	4	4	8	25
10	Jim Rice	4	4	4	4	4	6	12	40
11	Bert Blyleven	4	4	4	4	4	4	8	25
12	Ken Singleton	4	4	4	4	4	4	8	25
13	Don Sutton	4	4	4	4	4	5	10	25
14	Joe Morgan	4	4	4	4	4	5	10	25
15	Dave Parker	4	4	4	4	4	5	10	60
16	Dave Cash	4	4	4	4	4	4	8	25
17	Ron LeFlore	4	4	4	4	4	4	8	25
18	Greg Luzinski	4	4	4	4	4	4	8	25
19	Dennis Eckersley	4	4	4	4	4	8	15	60
20	Bill Madlock	4	4	4	4	4	4	8	25
21	George Scott	4	4	4	4	4	4	8	3
22	Willie Stargell	4	4	4	4	4	5	10	25
23	Al Hrabosky	4	4	4	4	4	4	8	25
24	Carl Yastrzemski	4	4	4	4	4	8	15	40
25A	Jim Kaat White Sox Logo	4	4	4	4	4	4	8	30
25B	Jim Kaat Phillies Logo	4	4	4	4	4	4	8	
26	Marty Perez	4	4	4	4	4	4	8	15
27	Bob Watson	4	4	4	4	4	4	8	25
28	Eric Soderholm	4	4	4	4	4	4	8	25
29	Bill Lee	4	4	4	4	4	4	8	20
30A	Frank Tanana 1975 ERA 2.63	4	4	4	4	4	4	8	25
31	Fred Lynn	4	4	4	4	4	5	10	40
32A	Tom Seaver Pct. 552 No Decimal	4	4	4	4	4	8	15	40
32B	Tom Seaver Pct. .552 w/Decimal	4	4	4	4	4	4	8	
33	Steve Busby	4	4	4	4	4	4	8	25
34	Gary Carter	4	4	4	4	4	5	10	25
35	Rick Wise	4	4	4	4	4	4	8	15
36	Johnny Bench	4	4	4	4	4	8	15	60
37	Jim Palmer	4	4	4	4	4	5	10	25
38	Bobby Murcer	4	4	4	4	4	4	8	25
39	Von Joshua	4	4	4	4	4	4	8	25
40	Lou Brock	4	4	4	4	4	5	10	25
41A	Mickey Rivers No Last Line	4	4	4	4	4	4	8	25
42	Manny Sanguillen	4	4	4	4	4	4	8	25
43	Jerry Reuss	4	4	4	4	4	4	8	15
44	Ken Griffey	4	4	4	4	4	4	8	15
45B	Jorge Orta AB 1616	4	4	4	4	4	4	8	15
46	John Mayberry	4	4	4	4	4	4	8	25
47A	Vida Blue Struck Out More	4	4	4	4	4	4	8	20
47B	Vida Blue Pitched More	4	4	4	4	4	4	8	25
48	Rod Carew	4	4	4	4	4	5	10	25
49B	Jon Matlack ER 86	4	4	4	4	4	4	8	25
50	Boog Powell	4	4	4	4	4	4	8	20
51B	Mike Hargrove AB 934	4	4	4	4	4	4	8	25
52A	Paul Lindblad ERA 2.73	4	4	4	4	4	4	8	20
53	Thurman Munson	4	4	4	4	4	8	15	50
54	Steve Garvey	4	4	4	4	4	5	10	25
55	Pete Rose	4	4	4	4	5	10	20	60
56A	Greg Gross Games 334	4	4	4	4	4	4	8	25
57	Ted Simmons	4	4	4	4	4	4	8	25

1976 Topps

		VG 3	VgEx 4	EX 5	ExMt 6	NM 7	NmMt 8	NmMt+ 8.5	MT 9
1	Hank Aaron RB	8	10	12	20	25	50	100	250
2	Bobby Bonds RB	4	4	4	4	4	6	15	80
3	Mickey Lolich RB	4	4	4	4	4	6	10	200
4	Dave Lopes RB	4	4	4	4	4	6	8	25
5	Tom Seaver RB	4	4	4	4	5	▲20	▲25	30
6	Rennie Stennett RB	4	4	4	4	4	6	8	200
7	Jim Umbarger RC	4	4	4	4	4	6	8	150
8	Tito Fuentes	4	4	4	4	4	5	8	50

#	Player	VG 3	VgEx 4	EX 5	ExMt 6	NM 7	NmMt 8	NmMt+ 8.5	MT 9
9	Paul Lindblad	4	4	4	4	4	5	6	15
10	Lou Brock	4	4	4	4	8	15	20	50
11	Jim Hughes	4	4	4	4	4	6	8	60
12	Richie Zisk	4	4	4	4	4	6	8	25
13	John Wockenfuss RC	4	4	4	4	4	5	6	15
14	Gene Garber	4	4	4	4	4	5	6	10
15	George Scott	4	4	4	4	4	5	6	20
16	Bob Apodaca	4	4	4	4	4	5	6	10
17	New York Yankees CL/Martin	4	4	4	4	4	6	8	25
18	Dale Murray	4	4	4	4	4	5	6	12
19	George Brett	10	12	25	30	80	400	500	
20	Bob Watson	4	4	4	4	4	5	6	15
21	Dave LaRoche	4	4	4	4	4	5	8	30
22	Bill Russell	4	4	4	4	4	5	6	15
23	Brian Downing	4	4	4	4	4	5	8	25
24	Cesar Geronimo	4	4	4	4	4	5	6	20
25	Mike Torrez	4	4	4	4	4	5	6	15
26	Andre Thornton	4	4	4	4	4	5	6	10
27	Ed Figueroa	4	4	4	4	4	5	6	15
28	Dusty Baker	4	4	4	4	4	6	8	20
29	Rick Burleson	4	4	4	4	4	5	6	15
30	John Montefusco RC	4	4	4	4	4	6	8	20
31	Len Randle	4	4	4	4	4	5	6	12
32	Danny Frisella	4	4	4	4	4	6	8	20
33	Bill North	4	4	4	4	4	5	6	20
34	Mike Garman	4	4	4	4	4	5	6	15
35	Tony Oliva	4	4	4	4	4	25	30	400
36	Frank Taveras	4	4	4	4	4	5	8	40
37	John Hiller	4	4	4	4	4	5	6	10
38	Garry Maddox	4	4	4	4	4	5	6	15
39	Pete Broberg	4	4	4	4	4	5	6	15
40	Dave Kingman	4	4	4	4	4	6	8	20
41	Tippy Martinez RC	4	4	4	4	4	5	6	30
42	Barry Foote	4	4	4	4	4	5	6	10
43	Paul Splittorff	4	4	4	4	4	5	6	15
44	Doug Rader	4	4	4	4	4	5	6	10
45	Boog Powell	4	4	4	4	4	6	8	40
46	Los Angeles Dodgers CL/Alston	4	4	4	4	4	5	6	15
47	Jesse Jefferson	4	4	4	4	4	6	8	60
48	Dave Concepcion	4	4	4	4	4	8	10	50
49	Dave Duncan	4	4	4	4	4	5	6	15
50	Fred Lynn	4	4	4	4	5	10	15	50
51	Ray Burris	4	4	4	4	4	6	8	40
52	Dave Chalk	4	4	4	4	4	5	6	10
53	Mike Beard RC	4	4	4	4	4	5	6	15
54	Dave Rader	4	4	4	4	4	5	6	15
55	Gaylord Perry	4	4	4	4	4	10	12	100
56	Bob Tolan	4	4	4	4	4	5	6	10
57	Phil Garner	4	4	4	4	4	5	6	15
58	Ron Reed	4	4	4	4	4	5	6	15
59	Larry Hisle	4	4	4	4	4	5	6	10
60	Jerry Reuss	4	4	4	4	4	5	6	15
61	Ron LeFlore	4	4	4	4	4	5	6	15
62	Johnny Oates	4	4	4	4	4	5	6	15
63	Bobby Darwin	4	4	4	4	4	5	6	15
64	Jerry Koosman	4	4	4	4	4	5	6	15
65	Chris Chambliss	4	4	4	4	4	5	6	40
66	Gus/Buddy Bell FS	4	4	4	4	4	5	6	15
67	Bob/Ray Boone FS	4	4	4	4	4	5	6	15
68	Joe/Joe Jr. Coleman FS	4	4	4	4	4	5	6	15
69	Jim/Mike Hegan FS	4	4	4	4	4	5	6	15
70	Roy/Roy Jr. Smalley FS	4	4	4	4	4	5	6	30
71	Steve Rogers	4	4	4	4	4	5	6	15
72	Hal McRae	4	4	4	4	4	5	6	15
73	Baltimore Orioles CL/Weaver	4	4	4	4	4	5	6	12
74	Oscar Gamble	4	4	4	4	4	5	6	15
75	Larry Dierker	4	4	4	4	4	5	8	25
76	Willie Crawford	4	4	4	4	4	6	8	50
77	Pedro Borbon	4	4	4	4	4	5	6	20
78	Cecil Cooper	4	4	4	4	4	5	6	25
79	Jerry Morales	4	4	4	4	4	5	6	15
80	Jim Kaat	4	4	4	4	4	6	8	20
81	Darrell Evans	4	4	4	4	4	5	6	15
82	Von Joshua	4	4	4	4	4	5	6	10
83	Jim Spencer	4	4	4	4	4	5	6	10
84	Brent Strom	4	4	4	4	4	5	6	10
85	Mickey Rivers	4	4	4	4	4	5	6	20

#	Player	VG 3	VgEx 4	EX 5	ExMt 6	NM 7	NmMt 8	NmMt+ 8.5	M
86	Mike Tyson	4	4	4	4	4	5	6	
87	Tom Burgmeier	4	4	4	4	4	5	6	
88	Duffy Dyer	4	4	4	4	4	5	6	
89	Vern Ruhle	4	4	4	4	4	5	6	
90	Sal Bando	4	4	4	4	4	5	6	
91	Tom Hutton	4	4	4	4	4	5	6	
92	Eduardo Rodriguez	4	4	4	4	4	5	6	
93	Mike Phillips	4	4	4	4	4	5	6	
94	Jim Dwyer	4	4	4	4	4	5	6	
95	Brooks Robinson	4	4	4	4	▲20	▲30	▲40	▲
96	Doug Bird	4	4	4	4	4	5	6	
97	Wilbur Howard	4	4	4	4	4	5	6	
98	Dennis Eckersley RC	4	12	25	▲40	60	150	200	1,0
99	Lee Lacy	4	4	4	4	4	5	8	
100	Jim Hunter	4	4	4	4	8	15	25	1
101	Pete LaCock	4	4	4	4	4	5	6	
102	Jim Willoughby	4	4	4	4	4	5	6	
103	Biff Pocoroba RC	4	4	4	4	4	5	6	
104	Cincinnati Reds CL/Anderson	4	4	4	4	5	10	12	
105	Gary Lavelle	4	4	4	4	4	5	6	
106	Tom Grieve	4	4	4	4	4	5	6	
107	Dave Roberts	4	4	4	4	4	5	6	
108	Don Kirkwood RC	4	4	4	4	4	5	6	
109	Larry Lintz	4	4	4	4	4	5	6	
110	Carlos May	4	4	4	4	4	5	6	
111	Danny Thompson	4	4	4	4	4	5	6	
112	Kent Tekulve RC	4	4	4	4	4	8	10	
113	Gary Sutherland	4	4	4	4	4	5	6	
114	Jay Johnstone	4	4	4	4	4	5	6	
115	Ken Holtzman	4	4	4	4	4	5	6	
116	Charlie Moore	4	4	4	4	4	5	6	
117	Mike Jorgensen	4	4	4	4	4	5	6	
118	Boston Red Sox CL/Johnson	4	4	4	4	4	5	6	
119	Checklist 1-132	4	4	4	4	4	6	8	
120	Rusty Staub	4	4	4	4	4	5	6	
121	Tony Solaita	4	4	4	4	4	5	6	
122	Mike Cosgrove	4	4	4	4	4	5	6	
123	Walt Williams	4	4	4	4	4	5	6	
124	Doug Rau	4	4	4	4	4	5	6	
125	Don Baylor	4	4	4	4	4	6	8	
126	Tom Dettore	4	4	4	4	4	6	8	2
127	Larvell Blanks	4	4	4	4	4	5	6	
128	Ken Griffey Sr.	4	4	4	4	4	6	8	
129	Andy Etchebarren	4	4	4	4	4	5	6	
130	Luis Tiant	4	4	4	4	4	6	8	
131	Bill Stein RC	4	4	4	4	4	5	6	
132	Don Hood	4	4	4	4	4	5	6	
133	Gary Matthews	4	4	4	4	4	5	6	
134	Mike Ivie	4	4	4	4	4	5	8	
135	Bake McBride	4	4	4	4	4	5	6	
136	Dave Goltz	4	4	4	4	4	5	6	
137	Bill Robinson	4	4	4	4	4	5	8	
138	Lerrin LaGrow	4	4	4	4	4	5	6	
139	Gorman Thomas	4	4	4	4	4	5	6	
140	Vida Blue	4	4	4	4	4	6	8	
141	Larry Parrish RC	4	4	4	4	4	6	8	
142	Dick Drago	4	4	4	4	4	5	8	
143	Jerry Grote	4	4	4	4	4	5	6	
144	Al Fitzmorris	4	4	4	4	4	5	6	
145	Larry Bowa	4	4	4	4	4	6	8	
146	George Medich	4	4	4	4	4	5	6	
147	Houston Astros CL/Virdon	4	4	4	4	4	5	6	
148	Stan Thomas RC	4	4	4	4	4	5	6	
149	Tommy Davis	4	4	4	4	4	5	6	
150	Steve Garvey	4	4	4	4	5	10	15	5
151	Bill Bonham	4	4	4	4	4	5	6	
152	Leroy Stanton	4	4	4	4	4	6	8	
153	Buzz Capra	4	4	4	4	4	5	6	
154	Bucky Dent	4	4	4	4	4	6	8	
155	Jack Billingham	4	4	4	4	4	5	6	
156	Rico Carty	4	4	4	4	4	5	6	
157	Mike Caldwell	4	4	4	4	4	5	8	
158	Ken Reitz	4	4	4	4	4	5	6	
159	Jerry Terrell	4	4	4	4	4	5	6	
160	Dave Winfield	6	8	10	12	15	25	40	12
161	Bruce Kison	4	4	4	4	4	6	8	1
162	Jack Pierce RC	4	4	4	4	4	5	6	1

BASEBALL

Player	VG 3	VgEx 4	EX 5	ExMt 6	NM 7	NmMt 8	NmMt+ 8.5	MT 9
Jim Slaton	4	4	4	4	4	6	8	100
Pepe Mangual	4	4	4	4	4	5	6	15
Gene Tenace	4	4	4	4	4	5	6	15
Skip Lockwood	4	4	4	4	4	5	6	12
Freddie Patek	4	4	4	4	4	5	6	10
Tom Hilgendorf	4	4	4	4	4	5	8	25
Graig Nettles	4	4	4	4	4	8	10	30
Rick Wise	4	4	4	4	4	5	8	25
Greg Gross	4	4	4	4	4	5	6	15
Texas Rangers CL/Lucchesi	4	4	4	4	4	5	6	12
Steve Swisher	4	4	4	4	4	5	6	15
Charlie Hough	4	4	4	4	4	6	8	40
Ken Singleton	4	4	4	4	4	5	6	15
Dick Lange	4	4	4	4	4	6	8	80
Marty Perez	4	4	4	4	4	5	6	15
Tom Buskey	4	4	4	4	4	5	6	15
George Foster	4	4	4	4	4	8	10	25
Goose Gossage	4	4	4	4	4	8	10	25
Willie Montanez	4	4	4	4	4	5	6	15
Harry Rasmussen	4	4	4	4	4	5	8	25
Steve Braun	4	4	4	4	4	5	6	25
Bill Greif	4	4	4	4	4	5	6	15
Dave Parker	4	4	4	4	4	12	15	25
Tom Walker	4	4	4	4	4	5	6	15
Pedro Garcia	4	4	4	4	4	5	6	15
Fred Scherman	4	4	4	4	4	5	6	10
Claudell Washington	4	4	4	4	4	5	6	10
Jon Matlack	4	4	4	4	4	5	6	15
NL Batting Leaders	4	4	4	4	4	5	6	15
AL Batting Leaders	4	4	4	4	4	6	8	20
NL Home Run Leaders	4	4	4	4	4	10	12	15
AL Home Run Leaders	4	4	4	4	4	6	8	20
NL RBI Leaders	4	4	4	4	4	6	8	15
AL RBI Leaders	4	4	4	4	4	5	6	15
NL Stolen Base Leaders	4	4	4	4	4	6	8	15
AL Stolen Base Leaders	4	4	4	4	4	6	8	20
NL Victory Leaders	4	4	4	4	4	6	8	20
AL Victory Leaders	4	4	4	4	4	6	8	20
NL ERA Leaders	4	4	4	4	4	6	8	20
AL ERA Leaders	4	4	4	4	4	6	8	15
NL Strikeout Leaders	4	4	4	4	4	6	8	20
AL Strikeout Leaders	4	4	4	4	4	5	6	15
NL/AL Leading Firemen	4	4	4	4	4	5	6	20
Manny Trillo	4	4	4	4	4	8	10	80
Andy Hassler	4	4	4	4	4	5	6	15
Mike Lum	4	4	4	4	4	5	6	12
Alan Ashby RC	4	4	4	4	4	5	6	15
Lee May	4	4	4	4	4	5	6	15
Clay Carroll	4	4	4	4	4	5	6	15
Pat Kelly	4	4	4	4	4	5	6	10
Dave Heaverlo RC	4	4	4	4	4	5	6	15
Eric Soderholm	4	4	4	4	4	5	6	15
Reggie Smith	4	4	4	4	4	5	6	15
Montreal Expos CL/Kuehl	4	4	4	4	4	5	6	10
Dave Freisleben	4	4	4	4	4	5	6	15
John Knox	4	4	4	4	4	5	8	25
Tom Murphy	4	4	4	4	4	5	6	25
Manny Sanguillen	4	4	4	4	4	5	6	20
Jim Todd	4	4	4	4	4	5	6	10
Wayne Garrett	4	4	4	4	4	5	6	10
Ollie Brown	4	4	4	4	4	5	6	15
Jim York	4	4	4	4	4	5	6	15
Roy White	4	4	4	4	4	5	6	20
Jim Sundberg	4	4	4	4	4	5	6	15
Oscar Zamora	4	4	4	4	4	5	6	15
John Hale RC	4	4	4	4	4	5	6	15
Jerry Remy RC	4	4	4	4	4	5	6	60
Carl Yastrzemski	8	10	12	15	▲25	▲40	▲50	120
Tom House	4	4	4	4	4	5	6	15
Frank Duffy	4	4	4	4	4	5	6	15
Grant Jackson	4	4	4	4	4	5	6	15
Mike Sadek	4	4	4	4	4	5	6	15
Bert Blyleven	4	4	4	4	4	6	8	60
Kansas City Royals CL/Herzog	4	4	4	4	4	5	6	15
Dave Hamilton	4	4	4	4	4	5	6	15
Larry Biittner	4	4	4	4	4	5	6	10
John Curtis	4	4	4	4	4	5	6	15

#	Player	VG 3	VgEx 4	EX 5	ExMt 6	NM 7	NmMt 8	NmMt+ 8.5	MT 9
240	Pete Rose	5	6	15	30	40	100	150	800
241	Hector Torres	4	4	4	4	4	5	6	15
242	Dan Meyer	4	4	4	4	4	5	6	10
243	Jim Rooker	4	4	4	4	4	5	6	10
244	Bill Sharp	4	4	4	4	4	5	6	25
245	Felix Millan	4	4	4	4	4	5	6	15
246	Cesar Tovar	4	4	4	4	4	5	6	15
247	Terry Harmon	4	4	4	4	4	5	6	15
248	Dick Tidrow	4	4	4	4	4	5	6	15
249	Cliff Johnson	4	4	4	4	4	5	6	15
250	Fergie Jenkins	4	4	4	4	4	6	8	25
251	Rick Monday	4	4	4	4	4	5	6	15
252	Tim Nordbrook RC	4	4	4	4	4	5	6	15
253	Bill Buckner	4	4	4	4	4	5	6	15
254	Rudy Meoli	4	4	4	4	4	5	8	10
255	Fritz Peterson	4	4	4	4	4	5	6	10
256	Rowland Office	4	4	4	4	4	5	6	15
257	Ross Grimsley	4	4	4	4	4	5	6	15
258	Nyls Nyman	4	4	4	4	4	5	6	10
259	Darrel Chaney	4	4	4	4	4	5	6	15
260	Steve Busby	4	4	4	4	4	5	6	15
261	Gary Thomasson	4	4	4	4	4	5	6	40
262	Checklist 133-264	4	4	4	4	4	6	8	40
263	Lyman Bostock RC	4	4	4	4	4	8	10	40
264	Steve Renko	4	4	4	4	4	5	6	4
265	Willie Davis	4	4	4	4	4	5	6	50
266	Alan Foster	4	4	4	4	4	5	8	25
267	Aurelio Rodriguez	4	4	4	4	4	5	6	15
268	Del Unser	4	4	4	4	4	5	8	25
269	Rick Austin	4	4	4	4	4	5	6	15
270	Willie Stargell	4	4	4	4	8	15	20	60
271	Jim Lonborg	4	4	4	4	4	5	6	15
272	Rick Dempsey	4	4	4	4	4	5	6	15
273	Joe Niekro	4	4	4	4	4	5	6	15
274	Tommy Harper	4	4	4	4	4	5	6	15
275	Rick Manning RC	4	4	4	4	4	5	6	20
276	Mickey Scott	4	4	4	4	4	5	6	25
277	Chicago Cubs CL/Marshall	4	4	4	4	4	5	6	15
278	Bernie Carbo	4	4	4	4	4	5	6	80
279	Roy Howell RC	4	4	4	4	4	5	6	15
280	Burt Hooton	4	4	4	4	4	5	6	15
281	Dave May	4	4	4	4	4	5	6	15
282	Dan Osborn RC	4	4	4	4	4	5	6	10
283	Merv Rettenmund	4	4	4	4	4	5	6	12
284	Steve Ontiveros	4	4	4	4	4	5	6	15
285	Mike Cuellar	4	4	4	4	4	5	8	100
286	Jim Wohlford	4	4	4	4	4	5	6	15
287	Pete Mackanin	4	4	4	4	4	5	6	15
288	Bill Campbell	4	4	4	4	4	5	6	15
289	Enzo Hernandez	4	4	4	4	4	5	6	15
290	Ted Simmons	4	4	4	4	4	8	10	50
291	Ken Sanders	4	4	4	4	4	5	6	10
292	Leon Roberts	4	4	4	4	4	5	6	15
293	Bill Castro RC	4	4	4	4	4	5	6	15
294	Ed Kirkpatrick	4	4	4	4	4	5	8	60
295	Dave Cash	4	4	4	4	4	5	6	100
296	Pat Dobson	4	4	4	4	4	5	6	10
297	Roger Metzger	4	4	4	4	4	5	6	10
298	Dick Bosman	4	4	4	4	4	5	6	12
299	Champ Summers RC	4	4	4	4	4	5	6	15
300	Johnny Bench	8	10	12	25	30	▲60	80	▲250
301	Jackie Brown	4	4	4	4	4	5	6	15
302	Rick Miller	4	4	4	4	4	6	8	40
303	Steve Foucault	4	4	4	4	4	5	6	15
304	California Angels CL/Williams	4	4	4	4	4	5	6	10
305	Andy Messersmith	4	4	4	4	4	5	6	15
306	Rod Gilbreath	4	4	4	4	4	5	6	10
307	Al Bumbry	4	4	4	4	4	5	6	15
308	Jim Barr	4	4	4	4	4	5	8	80
309	Bill Melton	4	4	4	4	4	5	6	15
310	Randy Jones	4	4	4	4	4	5	6	10
311	Cookie Rojas	4	4	4	4	4	5	6	15
312	Don Carrithers	4	4	4	4	4	5	6	15
313	Dan Ford RC	4	4	4	4	4	5	6	150
314	Ed Kranepool	5	4	4	4	4	5	6	15
315	Al Hrabosky	4	4	4	4	4	8	10	200
316	Robin Yount	4	6	10	▲15	▲20	▲30	40	80

#	Name	VG 3	VgEx 4	EX 5	ExMt 6	NM 7	NmMt 8	NmMt+ 8.5	MT 9
317	John Candelaria RC	4	4	4	4	4	8	10	30
318	Bob Boone	4	4	4	4	4	6	8	25
319	Larry Gura	4	4	4	4	4	5	6	15
320	Willie Horton	4	4	4	4	4	6	8	60
321	Jose Cruz	4	4	4	4	4	5	6	15
322	Glenn Abbott	4	4	4	4	4	5	6	15
323	Rob Sperring RC	4	4	4	4	4	5	6	25
324	Jim Bibby	4	4	4	4	4	5	6	12
325	Tony Perez	4	4	4	4	4	8	10	40
326	Dick Pole	4	4	4	4	4	5	6	15
327	Dave Moates RC	4	4	4	4	4	5	6	10
328	Carl Morton	4	4	4	4	4	5	6	15
329	Joe Ferguson	4	4	4	4	4	5	8	15
330	Nolan Ryan	10	12	▲20	25	30	▲80	150	500
331	San Diego Padres CL/McNamara	4	4	4	4	4	5	6	15
332	Charlie Williams	4	4	4	4	4	5	6	15
333	Bob Coluccio	4	4	4	4	4	5	6	10
334	Dennis Leonard	4	4	4	4	4	5	6	15
335	Bob Grich	4	4	4	4	4	5	6	15
336	Vic Albury	4	4	4	4	4	5	6	10
337	Bud Harrelson	4	4	4	4	4	5	6	20
338	Bob Bailey	4	4	4	4	4	5	6	10
339	John Denny	4	4	4	4	4	5	6	15
340	Jim Rice	4	4	6	12	15	50	60	200
341	Lou Gehrig ATG	4	4	4	4	5	25	30	40
342	Rogers Hornsby ATG	4	4	4	4	4	6	8	30
343	Pie Traynor ATG	4	4	4	4	4	6	8	80
344	Honus Wagner ATG	4	4	4	4	5	12	15	30
345	Babe Ruth ATG	4	4	4	20	25	40	50	100
346	Ty Cobb ATG	4	4	4	4	6	25	30	40
347	Ted Williams ATG	8	10	12	15	20	20	30	50
348	Mickey Cochrane ATG	4	4	4	4	4	6	8	20
349	Walter Johnson ATG	4	4	4	4	4	6	8	▲40
350	Lefty Grove ATG	4	4	4	4	4	6	10	60
351	Randy Hundley	4	4	4	4	4	5	6	10
352	Dave Giusti	4	4	4	4	4	5	6	12
353	Sixto Lezcano RC	4	4	4	4	4	5	6	10
354	Ron Blomberg	4	4	4	4	4	5	6	20
355	Steve Carlton	4	4	4	4	8	15	20	50
356	Ted Martinez	4	4	4	4	4	5	6	15
357	Ken Forsch	4	4	4	4	4	6	8	30
358	Buddy Bell	4	4	4	4	4	5	6	15
359	Rick Reuschel	4	4	4	4	4	5	6	15
360	Jeff Burroughs	4	4	4	4	4	5	6	15
361	Detroit Tigers CL/Houk	4	4	4	4	4	5	6	15
362	Will McEnaney	4	4	4	4	4	5	6	15
363	Dave Collins RC	4	4	4	4	4	5	6	10
364	Elias Sosa	4	4	4	4	4	5	6	15
365	Carlton Fisk	4	4	4	5	10	25	30	100
366	Bobby Valentine	4	4	4	4	4	5	6	15
367	Bruce Miller	4	4	4	4	4	5	6	15
368	Wilbur Wood	4	4	4	4	4	5	8	25
369	Frank White	4	4	4	4	4	5	6	20
370	Ron Cey	4	4	4	4	4	6	8	20
371	Elrod Hendricks	4	4	4	4	4	5	6	15
372	Rick Baldwin RC	4	4	4	4	4	5	6	12
373	Johnny Briggs	4	4	4	4	8	15	25	
374	Dan Warthen RC	4	4	4	4	4	5	6	15
375	Ron Fairly	4	4	4	4	4	5	6	10
376	Rich Hebner	4	4	4	4	4	5	6	15
377	Mike Hegan	4	4	4	4	4	5	6	20
378	Steve Stone	4	4	4	4	4	5	6	15
379	Ken Boswell	4	4	4	4	4	5	6	15
380	Bobby Bonds	4	4	4	4	4	6	8	25
381	Denny Doyle	4	4	4	4	4	5	8	25
382	Matt Alexander RC	4	4	4	4	4	5	6	15
383	John Ellis	4	4	4	4	4	6	8	50
384	Philadelphia Phillies CL/Ozark	4	4	4	4	4	5	6	15
385	Mickey Lolich	4	4	4	4	4	6	8	30
386	Ed Goodson	4	4	4	4	4	5	6	15
387	Mike Miley RC	4	4	4	4	4	5	6	15
388	Stan Perzanowski RC	4	4	4	4	4	5	6	15
389	Glenn Adams RC	4	4	4	4	4	5	6	25
390	Don Gullett	4	4	4	4	4	5	6	20
391	Jerry Hairston	4	4	4	4	4	5	6	15
392	Checklist 265-396	4	4	4	4	4	6	8	
393	Paul Mitchell RC	4	4	4	4	4	5	6	15

#	Name	VG 3	VgEx 4	EX 5	ExMt 6	NM 7	NmMt 8	NmMt+ 8.5	M
394	Fran Healy	4	4	4	4	4	5	6	
395	Jim Wynn	4	4	4	4	4	5	6	
396	Bill Lee	4	4	4	4	4	5	6	
397	Tim Foli	4	4	4	4	4	5	6	
398	Dave Tomlin	4	4	4	4	4	5	6	
399	Luis Melendez	4	4	4	4	4	5	6	
400	Rod Carew	4	4	4	▲6	▲15	20	25	▲1
401	Ken Brett	4	4	4	4	4	5	6	
402	Don Money	4	4	4	4	4	5	6	
403	Geoff Zahn	4	4	4	4	4	5	6	
404	Enos Cabell	4	4	4	4	4	5	6	
405	Rollie Fingers	4	4	4	4	4	6	8	
406	Ed Herrmann	4	4	4	4	4	5	6	
407	Tom Underwood	4	4	4	4	4	5	6	
408	Charlie Spikes	4	4	4	4	4	5	6	
409	Dave Lemanczyk	4	4	4	4	4	5	6	
410	Ralph Garr	4	4	4	4	4	5	8	
411	Bill Singer	4	4	4	4	4	5	6	
412	Toby Harrah	4	4	4	4	4	5	6	
413	Pete Varney RC	4	4	4	4	4	5	6	
414	Wayne Garland	4	4	4	4	4	5	6	
415	Vada Pinson	4	4	4	4	4	5	6	
416	Tommy John	4	4	4	4	4	5	6	
417	Gene Clines	4	4	4	4	4	5	6	
418	Jose Morales RC	4	4	4	4	4	5	6	
419	Reggie Cleveland	4	4	4	4	4	5	6	
420	Joe Morgan	4	4	4	5	▲15	▲30	▲40	▲
421	Oakland Athletics CL	4	4	4	4	4	5	6	
422	Johnny Grubb	4	4	4	4	4	5	8	
423	Ed Halicki	4	4	4	4	4	5	6	
424	Phil Roof	4	4	4	4	4	5	6	
425	Rennie Stennett	4	4	4	4	4	5	8	6
426	Bob Forsch	4	4	4	4	4	5	6	
427	Kurt Bevacqua	4	4	4	4	4	5	6	
428	Jim Crawford	4	4	4	4	4	5	6	
429	Fred Stanley	4	4	4	4	4	5	6	
430	Jose Cardenal	4	4	4	4	4	5	6	
431	Dick Ruthven	4	4	4	4	4	5	6	1
432	Tom Veryzer	4	4	4	4	4	5	6	2
433	Rick Waits RC	4	4	4	4	4	5	6	1
434	Morris Nettles	4	4	4	4	4	5	6	1
435	Phil Niekro	4	4	4	4	4	8	10	2
436	Bill Fahey	4	4	4	4	4	5	6	1
437	Terry Forster	4	4	4	4	4	5	6	
438	Doug DeCinces	4	4	4	4	4	5	6	2
439	Rick Rhoden	4	4	4	4	4	5	6	1
440	John Mayberry	4	4	4	4	4	5	6	12
441	Gary Carter	4	4	4	6	12	25	30	5
442	Hank Webb	4	4	4	4	4	5	6	
443	San Francisco Giants CL	4	4	4	4	4	5	6	
444	Gary Nolan	4	4	4	4	4	5	6	
445	Rico Petrocelli	4	4	4	4	4	6	8	3
446	Larry Haney	4	4	4	4	4	5	8	1
447	Gene Locklear	4	4	4	4	4	5	6	1
448	Tom Johnson	4	4	4	4	4	5	6	1
449	Bob Robertson	4	4	4	4	4	6	8	4
450	Jim Palmer	4	4	4	4	8	15	▲25	▲6
451	Buddy Bradford	4	4	4	4	4	5	8	1
452	Tom Hausman RC	4	4	4	4	4	5	6	1
453	Lou Piniella	4	4	4	4	5	10	12	5
454	Tom Griffin	4	4	4	4	4	5	6	2
455	Dick Allen	4	4	4	4	4	6	8	2
456	Joe Coleman	4	4	4	4	4	5	6	1
457	Ed Crosby	4	4	4	4	4	5	6	1
458	Earl Williams	4	4	4	4	4	5	6	1
459	Jim Brewer	4	4	4	4	4	5	8	2
460	Cesar Cedeno	4	4	4	4	4	5	6	1
461	NL/AL Champs	4	4	4	4	4	5	6	2
462	1975 WS/Reds Champs	4	4	4	4	5	10	12	3
463	Steve Hargan	4	4	4	4	4	5	6	1
464	Ken Henderson	4	4	4	4	4	5	6	1
465	Mike Marshall	4	4	4	4	4	5	6	3
466	Bob Stinson	4	4	4	4	4	5	6	1
467	Woodie Fryman	4	4	4	4	4	5	6	1
468	Jesus Alou	4	4	4	4	4	5	6	1
469	Rawly Eastwick	4	4	4	4	4	5	6	1
470	Bobby Murcer	4	4	4	4	4	5	6	3

	VG 3	VgEx 4	EX 5	ExMt 6	NM 7	NmMt 8	NmMt+ 8.5	MT 9
Jim Burton	4	4	4	4	4	5	6	15
Bob Davis RC	4	4	4	4	4	5	6	15
Paul Blair	4	4	4	4	4	5	6	15
Ray Corbin	4	4	4	4	4	5	6	15
Joe Rudi	4	4	4	4	4	6	8	80
Bob Moose	4	4	4	4	4	5	6	15
Cleveland Indians CL/Robinson	4	4	4	4	4	5	6	10
Lynn McGlothen	4	4	4	4	4	5	6	15
Bobby Mitchell	4	4	4	4	4	5	6	15
Mike Schmidt	4	4	12	▲20	▲25	▲50	▲60	250
Rudy May	4	4	4	4	4	5	6	25
Tim Hosley	4	4	4	4	4	5	6	15
Mickey Stanley	4	4	4	4	4	5	6	15
Eric Raich RC	4	4	4	4	4	5	6	10
Mike Hargrove	4	4	4	4	4	5	6	15
Bruce Dal Canton	4	4	4	4	4	5	6	15
Leron Lee	4	4	4	4	4	5	6	15
Claude Osteen	4	4	4	4	4	5	6	15
Skip Jutze	4	4	4	4	4	5	6	10
Frank Tanana	4	4	4	4	4	5	6	15
Terry Crowley	4	4	4	4	4	5	6	15
Marty Pattin	4	4	4	4	4	5	6	12
Derrel Thomas	4	4	4	4	4	5	6	10
Craig Swan	4	4	4	4	4	5	6	15
Nate Colbert	4	4	4	4	4	5	6	10
Juan Beniquez	4	4	4	4	4	5	6	20
Joe McIntosh RC	4	4	4	4	4	5	6	15
Glenn Borgmann	4	4	4	4	4	5	6	10
Mario Guerrero	4	4	4	4	4	5	6	15
Reggie Jackson	4	4	4	8	30	50	60	250
Billy Champion	4	4	4	4	4	5	6	15
Tim McCarver	4	4	4	4	4	6	8	20
Elliott Maddox	4	4	4	4	4	5	6	10
Pittsburgh Pirates CL/Murtaugh	4	4	4	4	4	5	6	20
Mark Belanger	4	4	4	4	4	5	6	15
George Mitterwald	4	4	4	4	4	5	6	15
Ray Bare RC	4	4	4	4	4	5	6	15
Duane Kuiper RC	4	4	4	4	4	5	6	15
Bill Hands	4	4	4	4	4	5	6	15
Amos Otis	4	4	4	4	4	5	6	15
Jamie Easterley	4	4	4	4	4	5	6	15
Ellie Rodriguez	4	4	4	4	4	5	6	15
Bart Johnson	4	4	4	4	4	5	6	15
Dan Driessen	4	4	4	4	4	5	6	15
Steve Yeager	4	4	4	4	4	5	6	15
Wayne Granger	4	4	4	4	4	5	6	15
John Milner	4	4	4	4	4	5	6	15
Doug Flynn RC	4	4	4	4	4	5	6	60
Steve Brye	4	4	4	4	4	5	6	15
Willie McCovey	4	4	4	4	4	▲20	▲30	▲50
Jim Colborn	4	4	4	4	4	5	6	10
Ted Sizemore	4	4	4	4	4	5	6	10
Bob Montgomery	4	4	4	4	4	5	6	15
Pete Falcone RC	4	4	4	4	4	5	6	15
Billy Williams	4	4	4	4	4	6	8	30
Checklist 397-528	4	4	4	4	4	6	8	12
Mike Anderson	4	4	4	4	4	5	6	10
Dock Ellis	4	4	4	4	4	5	6	15
Deron Johnson	4	4	4	4	4	5	6	20
Don Sutton	4	4	4	4	4	6	8	25
New York Mets CL/Frazier	4	4	4	4	4	5	6	12
Milt May	4	4	4	4	4	5	6	10
Lee Richard	4	4	4	4	4	5	6	15
Stan Bahnsen	4	4	4	4	4	5	6	10
Dave Nelson	4	4	4	4	4	5	8	25
Mike Thompson	4	4	4	4	4	5	6	10
Tony Muser	4	4	4	4	4	5	6	10
Pat Darcy	4	4	4	4	4	5	6	15
John Balaz RC	4	4	4	4	4	5	6	15
Bill Freehan	4	4	4	4	4	5	6	20
Steve Mingori	4	4	4	4	4	5	8	25
Keith Hernandez	4	4	4	4	4	8	10	40
Wayne Twitchell	4	4	4	4	4	5	6	15
Pepe Frias	4	4	4	4	4	5	6	15
Sparky Lyle	4	4	4	4	4	5	6	15
Dave Rosello	4	4	4	4	4	5	6	10
Roric Harrison	4	4	4	4	4	5	6	15

	VG 3	VgEx 4	EX 5	ExMt 6	NM 7	NmMt 8	NmMt+ 8.5	MT 9
548 Manny Mota	4	4	4	4	4	5	6	15
549 Randy Tate RC	4	4	4	4	4	5	6	15
550 Hank Aaron	15	20	25	▲40	▲60	150	250	1,000
551 Jerry DaVanon	4	4	4	4	4	5	6	15
552 Terry Humphrey	4	4	4	4	4	5	6	15
553 Randy Moffitt	4	4	4	4	4	5	6	15
554 Ray Fosse	4	4	4	4	4	5	6	15
555 Dyar Miller	4	4	4	4	4	5	6	15
556 Minnesota Twins CL/Mauch	4	4	4	4	4	5	6	15
557 Dan Spillner	4	4	4	4	4	5	6	15
558 Clarence Gaston	4	4	4	4	4	5	6	15
559 Clyde Wright	4	4	4	4	4	5	6	15
560 Jorge Orta	4	4	4	4	4	5	6	15
561 Tom Carroll	4	4	4	4	4	5	8	40
562 Adrian Garrett	4	4	4	4	4	5	6	15
563 Larry Demery	4	4	4	4	4	5	6	15
564 Kurt Bevacqua GUM	4	4	4	4	4	5	6	50
565 Tug McGraw	4	4	4	4	4	5	6	15
566 Ken McMullen	4	4	4	4	4	5	6	15
567 George Stone	4	4	4	4	4	5	6	15
568 Rob Andrews RC	4	4	4	4	4	5	6	15
569 Nelson Briles	4	4	4	4	4	5	6	15
570 George Hendrick	4	4	4	4	4	5	6	15
571 Don DeMola	4	4	4	4	4	5	6	10
572 Rich Coggins	4	4	4	4	4	5	6	15
573 Bill Travers	4	4	4	4	4	5	8	25
574 Don Kessinger	4	4	4	4	4	5	6	10
575 Dwight Evans	4	4	4	4	4	5	8	25
576 Maximino Leon	4	4	4	4	4	5	6	15
577 Marc Hill	4	4	4	4	4	5	6	15
578 Ted Kubiak	4	4	4	4	4	5	6	25
579 Clay Kirby	4	4	4	4	4	5	6	15
580 Bert Campaneris	4	4	4	4	4	5	6	15
581 St. Louis Cardinals CL/Schoendienst	4	4	4	4	4	5	6	20
582 Mike Kekich	4	4	4	4	4	5	6	15
583 Tommy Helms	4	4	4	4	4	5	8	40
584 Stan Wall RC	4	4	4	4	4	5	6	15
585 Joe Torre	4	4	4	4	8	15	25	120
586 Ron Schueler	4	4	4	4	4	5	6	15
587 Leo Cardenas	4	4	4	4	4	5	6	10
588 Kevin Kobel	4	4	4	4	4	5	6	15
589 Rookie Pitchers	4	4	4	4	4	8	10	30
590 Rookie Outfielders	4	4	4	4	4	8	10	25
591 Rookie Pitchers	4	4	4	4	4	6	8	25
592 Willie Randolph RC	4	4	4	4	12	25	30	▲60
593 Rookie Pitchers	4	4	4	4	4	6	8	25
594 Rookie Catchers and Outfielders	4	4	4	4	4	5	6	15
595 Rookie Pitchers	4	4	4	4	4	5	6	15
596 Rookie Infielders	4	4	4	4	4	5	6	15
597 Rookie Pitchers	4	4	4	4	4	5	6	15
598 Rookie Outfielders	4	4	4	4	4	5	6	15
599 Ron Guidry RC	4	4	6	12	15	30	40	250
600 Tom Seaver	8	10	12	15	25	30	30	▲100
601 Ken Rudolph	4	4	4	4	4	5	6	15
602 Doug Konieczny	4	4	4	4	4	5	6	15
603 Jim Holt	4	4	4	4	4	5	6	15
604 Joe Lovitto	4	4	4	4	4	5	6	15
605 Al Downing	4	4	4	4	4	5	6	15
606 Milwaukee Brewers CL/Grammas	4	4	4	4	4	5	6	15
607 Rich Hinton	4	4	4	4	4	5	6	15
608 Vic Correll	4	4	4	4	4	5	6	15
609 Fred Norman	4	4	4	4	4	5	8	25
610 Greg Luzinski	4	4	4	4	4	6	15	60
611 Rich Folkers	4	4	4	4	4	5	6	15
612 Joe Lahoud	4	4	4	4	4	5	6	10
613 Tim Johnson	4	4	4	4	4	6	8	40
614 Fernando Arroyo RC	4	4	4	4	4	5	8	25
615 Mike Cubbage	4	4	4	4	4	5	6	15
616 Buck Martinez	4	4	4	4	4	5	6	10
617 Darold Knowles	4	4	4	4	4	5	6	12
618 Jack Brohamer	4	4	4	4	4	5	6	15
619 Bill Butler	4	4	4	4	4	6	8	80
620 Al Oliver	4	4	4	4	4	6	6	15
621 Tom Hall	4	4	4	4	4	5	6	25
622 Rick Auerbach	4	4	4	4	4	5	6	10
623 Bob Allietta RC	4	4	4	4	4	5	6	15

		VG 3	VgEx 4	EX 5	ExMt 6	NM 7	NmMt 8	NmMt+ 8.5	MT 9
624	Tony Taylor	4	4	4	4	4	6	8	60
625	J.R. Richard	4	4	4	4	4	8	10	30
626	Bob Sheldon	4	4	4	4	4	5	6	10
627	Bill Plummer	4	4	4	4	4	5	6	15
628	John D'Acquisto	4	4	4	4	4	5	6	10
629	Sandy Alomar	4	4	4	4	4	6	8	30
630	Chris Speier	4	4	4	4	4	5	6	15
631	Atlanta Braves CL/Bristol	4	4	4	4	4	5	6	12
632	Rogelio Moret	4	4	4	4	4	5	6	15
633	John Stearns RC	4	4	4	4	4	5	6	15
634	Larry Christenson	4	4	4	4	4	5	8	60
635	Jim Fregosi	4	4	4	4	4	5	6	15
636	Joe Decker	4	4	4	4	4	5	6	15
637	Bruce Bochte	4	4	4	4	4	5	6	10
638	Doyle Alexander	4	4	4	4	4	5	6	15
639	Fred Kendall	4	4	4	4	4	5	6	15
640	Bill Madlock	4	4	4	4	4	8	10	20
641	Tom Paciorek	4	4	4	4	4	5	6	15
642	Dennis Blair	4	4	4	4	4	5	6	10
643	Checklist 529-660	4	4	4	4	4	6	8	15
644	Tom Bradley	4	4	4	4	4	5	6	15
645	Darrell Porter	4	4	4	4	4	5	6	15
646	John Lowenstein	4	4	4	4	4	5	6	15
647	Ramon Hernandez	4	4	4	4	4	6	15	150
648	Al Cowens	4	4	4	4	4	6	8	
649	Dave Roberts	4	4	4	4	4	5	6	15
650	Thurman Munson	4	4	5	8	▲25	▲40	▲50	100
651	John Odom	4	4	4	4	4	5	6	30
652	Ed Armbrister	4	4	4	4	4	5	6	15
653	Mike Norris RC	4	4	4	4	4	5	6	15
654	Doug Griffin	4	4	4	4	4	5	6	15
655	Mike Vail RC	4	4	4	4	4	5	8	25
656	Chicago White Sox CL/Tanner	4	4	4	4	4	5	6	15
657	Roy Smalley RC	4	4	4	4	4	5	8	25
658	Jerry Johnson	4	4	4	4	4	5	6	10
659	Ben Oglivie	4	4	4	4	4	6	8	20
660	Davey Lopes	4	4	4	4	4	6	10	50

—Hank Aaron RB #1 PSA 10 (Gem) sold for $755 (eBay; 7/07)
—Hank Aaron RB #1 PSA 10 (Gem) sold for $711 (eBay; 1/07)
—Johnny Bench #300 PSA 10 (Gem) sold for $653 (eBay; 4/08)
—Johnny Bench #300 PSA 10 (Gem) sold for $644 (eBay; 9/07)
—Johnny Bench #300 PSA 10 (Gem) sold for $616 (eBay; 8/07)
—Johnny Bench #300 PSA 10 (Gem) sold for $611 (eBay; 10/07)
—Bobby Bonds RB #2 PSA 10 (Gem) sold for $415 (eBay; 5/07)
—George Brett #19 PSA 9 (MT) sold for $3,685 (eBay; 12/12)
—George Brett #19 PSA 9 (MT) sold for $3,200 (eBay; 11/12)
—George Brett #19 PSA 9 (MT) sold for $1,775 (eBay; 12/07)
—George Brett #19 PSA 9 (MT) sold for $1,635 (eBay; 10/07)
—George Brett #19 PSA 9 (MT) sold for $1,513 (eBay; 6/07)
—George Brett #19 PSA 9 (MT) sold for $1,187 (Mile High 5/04)
—Johnny Briggs #373 PSA 9 (MT) sold for $225 (eBay; 6/07)
—Lou Brock #10 PSA 10 (Gem) sold for $535 (eBay; 10/07)
—Rod Carew #400 PSA 10 (Gem) sold for $797 (Madec; 11/07)
—Rod Carew #400 PSA 10 (Gem) sold for $493 (Madec; 5/08)
—Steve Carlton #355 PSA 10 (Gem) sold for $487 (eBay; 8/07)
—Steve Carlton #355 PSA 10 (Gem) sold for $434 (eBay; 12/06)
—Steve Carlton #355 PSA 10 (Gem) sold for $425 (eBay; 6/07)
—Steve Carlton #355 BVG 9.5 (Gem) sold for $125 (eBay; 7/07)
—Gary Carter #441 PSA 10 (Gem) sold for $324 (eBay; 11/07)
—Ty Cobb ATG #346 PSA 10 (Gem) sold for $266 (eBay; 6/07)
—Dennis Eckersley #98 PSA 10 (Gem) (Young Collection) sold for $6,684 (SCP; 5/12)
—Dennis Eckersley #98 PSA 10 (Gem) sold for $4,157 (eBay; 1/08)
—Dennis Eckersley #98 GAI 10 (MT) sold for $214 (eBay; 2/07)
—Carlton Fisk #365 PSA 10 (Gem) sold for $500 (eBay; 10/06)
—Lou Gehrig ATG #341 PSA 10 (Gem) sold for $164 (eBay; 11/07)
—Jim Hunter #100 BVG 9.5 (Gem) sold for $128 (eBay; 11/07)
—Walter Johnson ATG #349 PSA 10 (Gem) sold for $430 (eBay; 6/07)
—Joe Morgan #420 PSA 10 (Gem) sold for $360 (eBay; 10/07)
—Joe Morgan #420 PSA 10 (Gem) sold for $316 (eBay; 10/06)
—Joe Morgan #420 PSA 10 (Gem) sold for $223 (eBay; 2/08)
—Joe Morgan #420 PSA 10 (Gem) sold for $203 (eBay; 4/07)
—Joe Morgan #420 PSA 10 (Gem) sold for $186 (eBay; 11/06)
—Joe Morgan #420 PSA 10 (Gem) sold for $182 (eBay; 10/07)
—Joe Morgan #420 PSA 10 (Gem) sold for $179 (eBay; 3/07)
—Joe Morgan #420 PSA 10 (Gem) sold for $179 (eBay; 12/06)
—Joe Morgan #420 PSA 10 (Gem) sold for $154 (eBay; 12/06)
—Thurman Munson #650 BVG 9.5 (Gem) sold for $242 (eBay; 1/07)

—Jim Palmer #450 PSA 10 (Gem) sold for $306 (eBay; 10/06)
—Jim Palmer #450 PSA 10 (Gem) sold for $187 (eBay; 8/07)
—Jim Palmer #450 PSA 10 (Gem) sold for $178 (eBay; 11/07)
—Jim Palmer #450 PSA 10 (Gem) sold for $170 (eBay; 9/07)
—Jim Palmer #450 PSA 10 (Gem) sold for $138 (eBay; 6/07)
—Willie Randolph #592 PSA 10 (Gem) sold for $440 (eBay; 12/07)
—Willie Randolph #592 PSA 10 (Gem) sold for $380 (eBay; 7/07)
—Jim Rice #340 PSA 10 (Gem) sold for $1,009 (eBay; 10/06)
—Brooks Robinson #95 PSA 10 (Gem) sold for $239 (eBay; 11/06)
—Brooks Robinson #95 PSA 10 (Gem) sold for $212 (eBay; 11/07)
—Brooks Robinson #95 PSA 10 (Gem) sold for $189 (eBay; 3/08)
—Brooks Robinson #95 PSA 10 (Gem) sold for $170 (eBay; 6/07)
—Brooks Robinson #95 PSA 10 (Gem) sold for $144 (eBay; 1/07)
—Brooks Robinson #95 PSA 10 (Gem) sold for $143 (eBay; 5/07)
—Nolan Ryan #330 PSA 10 (Gem) sold for $8,100 (eBay; 4/07)
—Nolan Ryan #330 PSA 10 (Gem) sold for $3,119 (eBay; 08/12)
—Nolan Ryan #330 PSA 10 (Gem) sold for $2,984 (eBay; 11/12)
—Nolan Ryan #330 SGC 96 (MT) sold for $154 (eBay; 12/06)
—Tom Seaver #600 PSA 10 (Gem) sold for $434 (eBay; 11/07)
—Tom Seaver #600 PSA 10 (Gem) sold for $306 (eBay; 8/07)
—Ted Williams ATG #347 PSA 10 (Gem) sold for $163 (eBay; 11/07)
—Dave Winfield #160 PSA 10 (Gem) sold for $394 (eBay; 6/07)
—Carl Yastrzemski #230 PSA 10 (Gem) sold for $1,000 (eBay; 7/07)
—Carl Yastrzemski #230 PSA 10 (Gem) sold for $400 (eBay; 10/07)
—Carl Yastrzemski #230 BVG 9.5 (Gem) sold for $280 (eBay; 5/08)
—Robin Yount #316 PSA 10 (Gem) sold for $515 (eBay; 1/08)
—Robin Yount #316 PSA 10 (Gem) sold for $474 (eBay; 11/07)
—Robin Yount #316 PSA 10 (Gem) sold for $292 (eBay; 3/08)
—Robin Yount #316 PSA 10 (Gem) sold for $229 (eBay; 6/07)
—Robin Yount #316 BVG 9.5 (Gem) sold for $114 (eBay; 10/06)

1976 Topps Traded

		GD 2	VG 3	VgEx 4	EX 5	ExMt 6	NM 7	NmMt 8	MT
27T	Ed Figueroa	4	4	4	4	4	4	5	2
28T	Dusty Baker	4	4	4	4	4	4	8	4
44T	Doug Rader	4	4	4	4	4	4	5	1
58T	Ron Reed	4	4	4	4	4	4	5	1
74T	Oscar Gamble	4	4	4	4	4	4	6	2
80T	Jim Kaat	4	4	4	4	4	4	8	2
83T	Jim Spencer	4	4	4	4	4	4	5	1
85T	Mickey Rivers	4	4	4	4	4	4	5	2
99T	Lee Lacy	4	4	4	4	4	4	5	10
120T	Rusty Staub	4	4	4	4	4	4	6	2
127T	Larvell Blanks	4	4	4	4	4	4	5	8
146T	George Medich	4	4	4	4	4	4	5	1
158T	Ken Reitz	4	4	4	4	4	4	5	2
208T	Mike Lum	4	4	4	4	4	4	5	2
211T	Clay Carroll	4	4	4	4	4	4	5	2
231T	Tom House	4	4	4	4	4	4	5	2
250T	Fergie Jenkins	4	4	4	4	4	5	10	5
259T	Darrel Chaney	4	4	4	4	4	4	5	2
292T	Leon Roberts	4	4	4	4	4	4	5	1
296T	Pat Dobson	4	4	4	4	4	4	5	2
309T	Bill Melton	4	4	4	4	4	4	5	1
338T	Bob Bailey	4	4	4	4	4	4	5	2
380T	Bobby Bonds	4	4	4	4	4	4	8	2
383T	John Ellis	4	4	4	4	4	4	5	1
385T	Mickey Lolich	4	4	4	4	4	4	6	2
401T	Ken Brett	4	4	4	4	4	4	5	1
410T	Ralph Garr	4	4	4	4	4	4	5	1
411T	Bill Singer	4	4	4	4	4	4	5	1
428T	Jim Crawford	4	4	4	4	4	4	5	8
434T	Morris Nettles	4	4	4	4	4	4	5	1
464T	Ken Henderson	4	4	4	4	4	4	5	1
497T	Joe McIntosh	4	4	4	4	4	4	5	1
524T	Pete Falcone	4	4	4	4	4	4	5	2
527T	Mike Anderson	4	4	4	4	4	4	5	1
528T	Dock Ellis	4	4	4	4	4	4	5	2
532T	Milt May	4	4	4	4	4	4	5	
554T	Ray Fosse	4	4	4	4	4	4	5	
579T	Clay Kirby	4	4	4	4	4	4	5	15
583T	Tommy Helms	4	4	4	4	4	4	5	1
592T	Willie Randolph	4	4	4	4	4	6	12	2
618T	Jack Brohamer	4	4	4	4	4	4	5	15
632T	Rogelio Moret	4	4	4	4	4	4	5	20
649T	Dave Roberts	4	4	4	4	4	4	5	1
NNO	Traded Checklist	4	4	4	4	4	4	6	2

877 Topps

#	Player	VgEx 4	EX 5	ExMt 6	NM 7	NmMt 8	NmMt+ 8.5	MT 9	Gem 9.5/10
1	Batting Leaders	4	4	4	4	8	12	50	
2	Home Run Leaders	4	4	4	4	6	8	25	
3	RBI Leaders	4	4	4	4	5	6	15	100
4	Stolen Base Leaders	4	4	4	4	5	6	15	
5	Victory Leaders	4	4	4	4	5	6	15	
6	Strikeout Leaders	4	4	4	6	25	30	50	
7	ERA Leaders	4	4	4	4	6	8	50	
8	Leading Firemen	4	4	4	4	5	6	15	
9	Doug Rader	4	4	4	4	5	6	15	
10	Reggie Jackson	10	12	15	25	▲50	▲60	150	
11	Rob Dressler	4	4	4	4	5	6	15	
12	Larry Haney	4	4	4	4	5	6	15	
13	Luis Gomez RC	4	4	4	4	5	6	15	
14	Tommy Smith	4	4	4	4	6	8	20	
15	Don Gullett	4	4	4	4	5	6	15	
16	Bob Jones RC	4	4	4	4	5	6	15	
17	Steve Stone	4	4	4	4	5	8		
18	Cleveland Indians CL/Robinson	4	4	4	4	5	6	15	
19	John D'Acquisto	4	4	4	4	5	6	15	
20	Graig Nettles	4	4	4	4	6	8	25	100
21	Ken Forsch	4	4	4	4	5	6	15	
22	Bill Freehan	4	4	4	4	5	6	15	60
23	Dan Driessen	4	4	4	4	5	6	15	60
24	Carl Morton	4	4	4	4	5	6	60	50
25	Dwight Evans	4	4	4	4	6	10		
26	Ray Sadecki	4	4	4	4	5	6	15	100
27	Bill Buckner	4	4	4	4	5	6	15	
28	Woodie Fryman	4	4	4	4	5	6	15	50
29	Bucky Dent	4	4	4	4	6	8	30	
30	Greg Luzinski	4	4	4	4	6	8	15	100
31	Jim Todd	4	4	4	4	5	6	15	
32	Checklist 1-132	4	4	4	4	5	6	15	
33	Wayne Garland	4	4	4	4	5	6	15	50
34	California Angels CL/Sherry	4	4	4	4	5	6	30	50
35	Rennie Stennett	4	4	4	4	5	6	15	
36	John Ellis	4	4	4	4	5	6	15	
37	Steve Hargan	4	4	4	4	5	6	15	100
38	Craig Kusick	4	4	4	4	5	6	15	50
39	Tom Griffin	4	4	4	4	5	6	15	
40	Bobby Murcer	4	4	4	4	5	6	15	
41	Jim Kern	4	4	4	4	5	6	15	50
42	Jose Cruz	4	4	4	4	5	6	20	50
43	Ray Bare	4	4	4	4	5	6	15	
44	Bud Harrelson	4	4	4	4	5	6	15	50
45	Rawly Eastwick	4	4	4	4	5	6	20	
46	Buck Martinez	4	4	4	4	5	6	15	50
47	Lynn McGlothen	4	4	4	4	5	6	15	50
48	Tom Paciorek	4	4	4	4	5	6	15	
49	Grant Jackson	4	4	4	4	5	6	15	
50	Ron Cey	4	4	4	4	5	6	15	
51	Milwaukee Brewers CL/Grammas	4	4	4	4	5	6	15	100
52	Ellis Valentine	4	4	4	4	5	6	15	
53	Paul Mitchell	4	4	4	4	5	6	15	
54	Sandy Alomar	4	4	4	4	5	6	15	
55	Jeff Burroughs	4	4	4	4	5	8		
56	Rudy May	4	4	4	4	5	6	100	
57	Marc Hill	4	4	4	4	5	6	15	
58	Chet Lemon	4	4	4	4	5	6	20	
59	Larry Christenson	4	4	4	4	5	6	15	
60	Jim Rice	4	4	4	4	8	10	30	
61	Manny Sanguillen	4	4	4	4	5	6	15	
62	Eric Raich	4	4	4	4	5	6	15	50
63	Tito Fuentes	4	4	4	4	5	6	10	50
64	Larry Biittner	4	4	4	4	5	6	15	50
65	Skip Lockwood	4	4	4	4	5	6	15	50
66	Roy Smalley	4	4	4	4	5	6	15	50
67	Joaquin Andujar RC	4	4	4	4	5	6	15	120
68	Bruce Bochte	4	4	4	4	5	6	15	60
69	Jim Crawford	4	4	4	4	5	6	15	
70	Johnny Bench	8	10	15	20	▲30	▲40	100	
71	Dock Ellis	4	4	4	4	5	6	15	80
72	Mike Anderson	4	4	4	4	5	6	15	50
73	Charlie Williams	4	4	4	4	5	6	15	
74	Oakland Athletics CL/McKeon	4	4	4	4	5	6	15	
75	Dennis Leonard	4	4	4	4	5	6	50	
76	Tim Foli	4	4	4	4	5	6	15	
77	Dyar Miller	4	4	4	4	5	6	15	
78	Bob Davis	4	4	4	4	5	6	15	
79	Don Money	4	4	4	4	5	6	15	
80	Andy Messersmith	4	4	4	4	5	6	15	
81	Juan Beniquez	4	4	4	4	5	8		
82	Jim Rooker	4	4	4	4	5	6	15	50
83	Kevin Bell RC	4	4	4	4	5	6	60	
84	Ollie Brown	4	4	4	4	5	6	15	
85	Duane Kuiper	4	4	4	4	5	6	20	
86	Pat Zachry	4	4	4	4	5	6	60	
87	Glenn Borgmann	4	4	4	4	5	6	15	50
88	Stan Wall	4	4	4	4	5	6	15	50
89	Butch Hobson RC	4	4	4	4	6	8	60	
90	Cesar Cedeno	4	4	4	4	5	6	15	50
91	John Verhoeven RC	4	4	4	4	5	6	15	50
92	Dave Rosello	4	4	4	4	5	6	15	
93	Tom Poquette	4	4	4	4	5	6	15	50
94	Craig Swan	4	4	4	4	5	6	15	
95	Keith Hernandez	4	4	4	4	8	12	40	
96	Lou Piniella	4	4	4	4	5	6	15	60
97	Dave Heaverlo	4	4	4	4	5	6	15	
98	Milt May	4	4	4	4	5	6	20	
99	Tom Hausman	4	4	4	4	5	6	15	
100	Joe Morgan	4	4	4	8	15	20	50	
101	Dick Bosman	4	4	4	4	5	6	15	
102	Jose Morales	4	4	4	4	5	6	15	50
103	Mike Bacsik RC	4	4	4	4	5	8		
104	Omar Moreno RC	4	4	4	4	5	6	15	
105	Steve Yeager	4	4	4	4	5	6	15	
106	Mike Flanagan	4	4	4	4	5	6	12	
107	Bill Melton	4	4	4	4	5	6	10	50
108	Alan Foster	4	4	4	4	5	6	15	
109	Jorge Orta	4	4	4	4	5	6	15	
110	Steve Carlton	4	4	4	5	▲15	▲25	▲30	300
111	Rico Petrocelli	4	4	4	4	5	6	15	100
112	Bill Greif	4	4	4	4	5	6	15	
113	Toronto Blue Jays CL/Hartsfield	4	4	4	4	5	6	15	
114	Bruce Dal Canton	4	4	4	4	5	6	15	
115	Rick Manning	4	4	4	4	5	6	15	
116	Joe Niekro	4	4	4	4	5	6	15	
117	Frank White	4	4	4	4	5	6	15	
118	Rick Jones RC	4	4	4	4	5	6	15	
119	John Stearns	4	4	4	4	5	6	15	100
120	Rod Carew	4	4	10	12	▲25	▲30	▲50	
121	Gary Nolan	4	4	4	4	5	6	15	
122	Ben Oglivie	4	4	4	4	5	6	15	
123	Fred Stanley	4	4	4	4	5	6	15	
124	George Mitterwald	4	4	4	4	5	6	15	50
125	Bill Travers	4	4	4	4	5	6	15	
126	Rod Gilbreath	4	4	4	4	5	6	15	
127	Ron Fairly	4	4	4	4	5	6	15	50
128	Tommy John	4	4	4	4	5	6	15	
129	Mike Sadek	4	4	4	4	5	6	15	50
130	Al Oliver	4	4	4	4	5	6	15	
131	Orlando Ramirez RC	4	4	4	4	5	6	15	
132	Chip Lang RC	4	4	4	4	5	6	15	
133	Ralph Garr	4	4	4	4	5	6	15	
134	San Diego Padres CL/McNamara	4	4	4	4	5	6	15	
135	Mark Belanger	4	4	4	4	5	6	40	
136	Jerry Mumphrey RC	4	4	4	4	5	6	10	
137	Jeff Terpko RC	4	4	4	4	5	6	15	50
138	Bob Stinson	4	4	4	4	5	6	15	
139	Fred Norman	4	4	4	4	5	6	10	50
140	Mike Schmidt	4	4	8	12	25	30	80	
141	Mark Littell	4	4	4	4	5	6	150	
142	Steve Dillard RC	4	4	4	4	5	6	15	50
143	Ed Herrmann	4	4	4	4	5	6	15	50
144	Bruce Sutter RC	4	5	12	▲30	50	60	120	1,200
145	Tom Veryzer	4	4	4	4	5	6	15	
146	Dusty Baker	4	4	4	4	5	6	15	
147	Jackie Brown	4	4	4	4	5	6	15	
148	Fran Healy	4	4	4	4	5	6	15	
149	Mike Cubbage	4	4	4	4	5	6	250	
150	Tom Seaver	4	4	5	▲20	50	60	▲500	

#	Player	VgEx 4	EX 5	ExMt 6	NM 7	NmMt 8	NmMt+ 8.5	MT 9	Gem 9.5/10
151	Johnny LeMaster	4	4	4	4	5	6	15	
152	Gaylord Perry	4	4	4	4	6	8	20	
153	Ron Jackson RC	4	4	4	5	6		15	50
154	Dave Giusti	4	4	4	4	5	6	15	
155	Joe Rudi	4	4	4	4	5	6	15	60
156	Pete Mackanin	4	4	4	4	5	6	15	
157	Ken Brett	4	4	4	4	5	6	15	
158	Ted Kubiak	4	4	4	4	5	6	15	
159	Bernie Carbo	4	4	4	4	5	6	15	
160	Will McEnaney	4	4	4	4	5	6	25	80
161	Garry Templeton RC	4	4	4	4	8	10	20	
162	Mike Cuellar	4	4	4	4	5	6	15	
163	Dave Hilton	4	4	4	4	5	6	15	
164	Tug McGraw	4	4	4	4	5	6	15	
165	Jim Wynn	4	4	4	4	5	6	15	50
166	Bill Campbell	4	4	4	4	5	6	15	
167	Rich Hebner	4	4	4	4	5	6	15	50
168	Charlie Spikes	4	4	4	4	5	6	15	50
169	Darold Knowles	4	4	4	4	5	6	15	50
170	Thurman Munson	5	10	▲25	▲30	60	80	300	
171	Ken Sanders	4	4	4	4	5	6	15	50
172	John Milner	4	4	4	4	5	6	15	50
173	Chuck Scrivener RC	4	4	4	4	5	6	15	
174	Nelson Briles	4	4	4	4	5	6	15	50
175	Butch Wynegar RC	4	4	4	4	5	6	15	
176	Bob Robertson	4	4	4	4	5	6	15	
177	Bart Johnson	4	4	4	4	5	6	15	
178	Bombo Rivera RC	4	4	4	4	5	6	15	
179	Paul Hartzell RC	4	4	4	4	5	6	10	
180	Dave Lopes	4	4	4	4	5	6	20	
181	Ken McMullen	4	4	4	4	5	6	15	
182	Dan Spillner	4	4	4	4	5	6	15	
183	St. Louis Cardinals CL/V.Rapp	4	4	4	4	5	6	15	100
184	Bo McLaughlin RC	4	4	4	4	5	6	15	
185	Sixto Lezcano	4	4	4	4	5	6	10	50
186	Doug Flynn	4	4	4	4	5	6	15	
187	Dick Pole	4	4	4	4	5	8		
188	Bob Tolan	4	4	4	4	5	6	10	
189	Rick Dempsey	4	4	4	4	5	6	10	
190	Ray Burris	4	4	4	4	5	6	10	100
191	Doug Griffin	4	4	4	4	5	6	10	
192	Clarence Gaston	4	4	4	4	5	6	15	50
193	Larry Gura	4	4	4	4	5	6	10	50
194	Gary Matthews	4	4	4	4	5	6	15	
195	Ed Figueroa	4	4	4	4	5	6	15	50
196	Len Randle	4	4	4	4	5	6	15	
197	Ed Ott	4	4	4	4	5	6	15	50
198	Wilbur Wood	4	4	4	4	5	6	15	
199	Pepe Frias	4	4	4	4	5	6		
200	Frank Tanana	4	4	4	4	5	6	20	60
201	Ed Kranepool	4	4	4	4	5	6	30	
202	Tom Johnson	4	4	4	4	5	6	15	
203	Ed Armbrister	4	4	4	4	5	6	15	50
204	Jeff Newman RC	4	4	4	4	5	6	60	
205	Pete Falcone	4	4	4	4	5	6	15	50
206	Boog Powell	4	4	4	4	5	6	10	150
207	Glenn Abbott	4	4	4	4	5	8		
208	Checklist 133-264	4	4	4	4	5	6	25	80
209	Rob Andrews	4	4	4	4	5	6	15	
210	Fred Lynn	4	4	4	5	10	12	30	
211	San Francisco Giants CL/Altobelli	4	4	4	4	5	6	15	50
212	Jim Mason	4	4	4	4	5	6	10	
213	Maximino Leon	4	4	4	4	5	6	15	50
214	Darrell Porter	4	4	4	4	5	6	10	
215	Butch Metzger	4	4	4	4	5	6	15	
216	Doug DeCinces	4	4	4	4	5	6	15	
217	Tom Underwood	4	4	4	4	5	6	15	
218	John Wathan RC	4	4	4	4	5	6	15	
219	Joe Coleman	4	4	4	4	5	6	15	
220	Chris Chambliss	4	4	4	4	6	8	20	
221	Bob Bailey	4	4	4	4	5	6	15	
222	Francisco Barrios RC	4	4	4	4	5	6	15	
223	Earl Williams	4	4	4	4	5	6	15	
224	Rusty Torres	4	4	4	4	5	6	15	
225	Bob Apodaca	4	4	4	4	5	6	15	
226	Leroy Stanton	4	4	4	4	5	6	15	
227	Joe Sambito RC	4	4	4	4	5	6	15	

#	Player	VgEx 4	EX 5	ExMt 6	NM 7	NmMt 8	NmMt+ 8.5	MT 9	Gem 9.5/
228	Minnesota Twins CL/Mauch	4	4	4	4	5	6	15	
229	Don Kessinger	4	4	4	4	5	6	15	
230	Vida Blue	4	4	4	4	6	8	25	
231	George Brett RB	4	4	4	5	▲15	▲20	25	
232	Minnie Minoso RB	4	4	4	4	5	6	15	1
233	Jose Morales RB	4	4	4	4	5	6	12	
234	Nolan Ryan RB	8	10	12	20	25	30	50	
235	Cecil Cooper	4	4	4	4	5	6	10	
236	Tom Buskey	4	4	4	4	5	6	15	
237	Gene Clines	4	4	4	4	5	6	15	
238	Tippy Martinez	4	4	4	4	5	6	10	
239	Bill Plummer	4	4	4	4	5	6	15	
240	Ron LeFlore	4	4	4	4	6	8	20	12
241	Dave Tomlin	4	4	4	4	5	6	15	
242	Ken Henderson	4	4	4	4	5	6	15	
243	Ron Reed	4	4	4	4	5	6	15	5
244	John Mayberry	4	4	4	4	5	6	15	
245	Rick Rhoden	4	4	4	4	5	6	15	5
246	Mike Vail	4	4	4	4	5	6	15	6
247	Chris Knapp RC	4	4	4	4	5	6	15	
248	Wilbur Howard	4	4	4	4	5	6	15	5
249	Pete Redfern RC	4	4	4	4	5	6	15	
250	Bill Madlock	4	4	4	4	5	6	10	20
251	Tony Muser	4	4	4	4	5	6	10	5
252	Dale Murray	4	4	4	4	5	6	15	
253	John Hale	4	4	4	4	5	6	25	
254	Doyle Alexander	4	4	4	4	5	6	10	
255	George Scott	4	4	4	4	5	8		
256	Joe Hoerner	4	4	4	4	5	6	15	6
257	Mike Miley	4	4	4	4	5	6	15	
258	Luis Tiant	4	4	4	4	6	8	15	
259	New York Mets CL/Frazier	4	4	4	4	5	6	15	
260	J.R. Richard	4	4	4	4	5	6	15	10
261	Phil Garner	4	4	4	4	5	6	15	
262	Al Cowens	4	4	4	4	5	6	15	5
263	Mike Marshall	4	4	4	4	6	8	20	
264	Tom Hutton	4	4	4	4	5	6	15	
265	Mark Fidrych RC	4	5	10	20	30	40	250	
266	Derrel Thomas	4	4	4	4	5	6	15	8
267	Ray Fosse	4	4	4	4	5	6	15	
268	Rick Sawyer RC	4	4	4	4	5	6	15	5
269	Joe Lis	4	4	4	4	5	6	25	5
270	Dave Parker	4	4	4	4	6	8	50	
271	Terry Forster	4	4	4	4	5	6	15	
272	Lee Lacy	4	4	4	4	5	6	15	
273	Eric Soderholm	4	4	4	4	5	6	15	6
274	Don Stanhouse	4	4	4	4	5	6	15	5
275	Mike Hargrove	4	4	4	4	5	6	15	
276	Chris Chambliss ALCS	4	4	4	4	5	6	15	
277	Pete Rose NLCS	4	4	4	4	8	10	25	200
278	Danny Frisella	4	4	4	4	5	6	15	50
279	Joe Wallis	4	4	4	4	5	6	15	
280	Jim Hunter	4	4	5	10	20	30	150	
281	Roy Staiger	4	4	4	4	5	6	15	
282	Sid Monge	4	4	4	4	5	6	15	50
283	Jerry DaVanon	4	4	4	4	5	6	15	
284	Mike Norris	4	4	4	4	5	6	15	50
285	Brooks Robinson	4	4	4	▲20	▲25	▲30	▲60	
286	Johnny Grubb	4	4	4	4	5	6	15	
287	Cincinnati Reds CL/Anderson	4	4	4	4	6	8	50	
288	Bob Montgomery	4	4	4	4	5	6	15	
289	Gene Garber	4	4	4	4	5	6	60	
290	Amos Otis	4	4	4	4	5	6	15	120
291	Jason Thompson RC	4	4	4	4	6	8	50	
292	Rogelio Moret	4	4	4	4	5	6	15	
293	Jack Brohamer	4	4	4	4	5	6	15	
294	George Medich	4	4	4	4	5	6	15	
295	Gary Carter	4	4	5	10	20	25	30	200
296	Don Hood	4	4	4	4	5	6	10	50
297	Ken Reitz	4	4	4	4	5	6	15	
298	Charlie Hough	4	4	4	4	5	6	15	
299	Otto Velez	4	4	4	4	5	6	10	
300	Jerry Koosman	4	4	4	4	5	6	15	
301	Toby Harrah	4	4	4	4	6	8	25	
302	Mike Garman	4	4	4	4	5	6	15	50
303	Gene Tenace	4	4	4	4	5	6	15	
304	Jim Hughes	4	4	4	4	5	6	15	

	VgEx 4	EX 5	ExMt 6	NM 7	NmMt 8	NmMt+ 8.5	MT 9	Gem 9.5/10
Mickey Rivers	4	4	4	4	5	6	15	
Rick Waits	4	4	4	4	5	6	15	
Gary Sutherland	4	4	4	4	5	6	10	50
Gene Pentz RC	4	4	4	4	5	6	15	
Boston Red Sox CL/Zimmer	4	4	4	6	12	15	25	
Larry Bowa	4	4	4	4	5	6	15	100
Vern Ruhle	4	4	4	4	5	6	15	
Rob Belloir RC	4	4	4	4	5	6	15	
Paul Blair	4	4	4	4	5	6	15	
Steve Mingori	4	4	4	4	5	6	15	50
Dave Chalk	4	4	4	4	5	8		
Steve Rogers	4	4	4	4	5	6	15	
Kurt Bevacqua	4	4	4	4	5	6	10	
Duffy Dyer	4	4	4	4	5	6	15	
Goose Gossage	4	4	4	4	8	12	40	
Ken Griffey Sr.	4	4	4	4	6	8	20	
Dave Goltz	4	4	4	4	5	6	15	
Bill Russell	4	4	4	4	5	6	15	
Larry Lintz	4	4	4	4	5	6	15	
John Curtis	4	4	4	4	5	6	15	50
Mike Ivie	4	4	4	4	5	6	20	
Jesse Jefferson	4	4	4	4	5	6	15	
Houston Astros CL/Virdon	4	4	4	4	5	6	15	120
Tommy Boggs RC	4	4	4	4	5	6	15	100
Ron Hodges	4	4	4	4	5	6	15	
George Hendrick	4	4	4	4	5	6	15	
Jim Colborn	4	4	4	4	5	6	15	50
Elliott Maddox	4	4	4	4	5	6	15	
Paul Reuschel RC	4	4	4	4	5	6	20	50
Bill Stein	4	4	4	4	5	6	15	
Bill Robinson	4	4	4	4	5	6	15	
Denny Doyle	4	4	4	4	5	6	15	50
Ron Schueler	4	4	4	4	5	6	10	
Dave Duncan	4	4	4	4	5	6	15	
Adrian Devine	4	4	4	4	5	6	15	120
Hal McRae	4	4	4	4	5	6	15	60
Joe Kerrigan RC	4	4	4	4	5	6	15	80
Jerry Remy	4	4	4	4	5	6	15	50
Ed Halicki	4	4	4	4	5	6	15	50
Brian Downing	4	4	4	4	5	8		
Reggie Smith	4	4	4	4	5	6	15	50
Bill Singer	4	4	4	4	5	8		
George Foster	4	4	4	4	8	10	25	
Brent Strom	4	4	4	4	5	6	15	60
Jim Holt	4	4	4	4	5	6	15	
Larry Dierker	4	4	4	4	5	6	15	
Jim Sundberg	4	4	4	4	5	6	15	
Mike Phillips	4	4	4	4	5	6	15	
Stan Thomas	4	4	4	4	5	6	15	
Pittsburgh Pirates CL/Tanner	4	4	4	4	5	6	15	
Lou Brock	4	4	4	5	10	15	30	
Checklist 265-396	4	4	4	4	5	6	15	
Tim McCarver	4	4	4	4	5	6	15	
Tom House	4	4	4	4	5	6	15	
Willie Randolph	4	4	4	4	6	8	20	
Rick Monday	4	4	4	4	5	6	15	
Eduardo Rodriguez	4	4	4	4	5	6	15	
Tommy Davis	4	4	4	4	5	6	15	80
Dave Roberts	4	4	4	4	5	6	15	
Vic Correll	4	4	4	4	5	6	15	50
Mike Torrez	4	4	4	4	5	6	20	50
Ted Sizemore	4	4	4	4	5	6	15	50
Dave Hamilton	4	4	4	4	5	6	15	
Mike Jorgensen	4	4	4	4	5	6	15	
Terry Humphrey	4	4	4	4	5	6	15	50
John Montefusco	4	4	4	4	5	6	15	50
Kansas City Royals CL/Herzog	4	4	4	4	5	6	15	50
Rich Folkers	4	4	4	4	5	6	10	
Bert Campaneris	4	4	4	4	5	6	10	
Kent Tekulve	4	4	4	4	6	8	25	
Larry Hisle	4	4	4	4	5	6	15	
Nino Espinosa RC	4	4	4	4	5	6	15	
Dave McKay	4	4	4	4	5	6	10	50
Jim Umbarger	4	4	4	4	5	6	15	50
Larry Cox RC	4	4	4	4	5	6	15	
Lee May	4	4	4	4	5	6	15	80
Bob Forsch	4	4	4	4	5	6	15	50

		VgEx 4	EX 5	ExMt 6	NM 7	NmMt 8	NmMt+ 8.5	MT 9	Gem 9.5/10
382	Charlie Moore	4	4	4	4	5	6	15	60
383	Stan Bahnsen	4	4	4	4	5	8		
384	Darrel Chaney	4	4	4	4	5	6	15	50
385	Dave LaRoche	4	4	4	4	5	6	15	
386	Manny Mota	4	4	4	4	5	6	20	
387	New York Yankees CL/Martin	4	4	4	6	20	25	200	
388	Terry Harmon	4	4	4	4	5	8		
389	Ken Kravec RC	4	4	4	4	5	6	15	50
390	Dave Winfield	4	4	4	▲20	▲25	▲30	40	
391	Dan Warthen	4	4	4	4	5	6	15	50
392	Phil Roof	4	4	4	4	5	6	15	
393	John Lowenstein	4	4	4	4	5	6	15	
394	Bill Laxton RC	4	4	4	4	5	6	15	50
395	Manny Trillo	4	4	4	4	5	6	20	
396	Tom Murphy	4	4	4	4	5	6	15	50
397	Larry Herndon RC	4	4	4	4	5	6	15	
398	Tom Burgmeier	4	4	4	4	5	6	15	
399	Bruce Boisclair RC	4	4	4	4	5	6	20	
400	Steve Garvey	4	4	5	10	20	25	60	
401	Mickey Scott	4	4	4	4	5	6	20	
402	Tommy Helms	4	4	4	4	5	6	15	
403	Tom Grieve	4	4	4	4	5	6	15	
404	Eric Rasmussen RC	4	4	4	4	5	6	15	
405	Claudell Washington	4	4	4	4	5	6	15	
406	Tim Johnson	4	4	4	4	5	6	10	50
407	Dave Freisleben	4	4	4	4	5	6	15	
408	Cesar Tovar	4	4	4	4	5	6	15	50
409	Pete Broberg	4	4	4	4	5	6	15	100
410	Willie Montanez	4	4	4	4	5	6	15	
411	J.Morgan/J.Bench WS	4	4	4	4	6	8	20	
412	Johnny Bench WS	4	4	4	4	6	8	20	
413	Cincy Wins WS	4	4	4	4	5	6	15	60
414	Tommy Harper	4	4	4	4	5	6	15	50
415	Jay Johnstone	4	4	4	4	5	6	15	
416	Chuck Hartenstein	4	4	4	4	5	6	25	
417	Wayne Garrett	4	4	4	4	5	6	15	
418	Chicago White Sox CL/Lemon	4	4	4	4	6	8	30	
419	Steve Swisher	4	4	4	4	5	6	15	
420	Rusty Staub	4	4	4	4	5	6	30	
421	Doug Rau	4	4	4	4	5	6	15	
422	Freddie Patek	4	4	4	4	5	6	15	
423	Gary Lavelle	4	4	4	4	5	6	15	
424	Steve Brye	4	4	4	4	5	6	15	50
425	Joe Torre	4	4	4	4	6	8	20	60
426	Dick Drago	4	4	4	4	5	6	15	50
427	Dave Rader	4	4	4	4	5	6	15	
428	Texas Rangers CL/Lucchesi	4	4	4	4	5	6	15	
429	Ken Boswell	4	4	4	4	5	6	15	
430	Fergie Jenkins	4	4	4	4	5	8	10	
431	Dave Collins	4	4	4	4	5	8		
432	Buzz Capra	4	4	4	4	5	6	10	
433	Nate Colbert TBC	4	4	4	4	5	6	15	
434	Carl Yastrzemski TBC	4	4	4	4	5	6	10	
435	Maury Wills TBC	4	4	4	4	5	6	15	
436	Bob Keegan TBC	4	4	4	4	5	6	15	
437	Ralph Kiner TBC	4	4	4	4	5	6	15	
438	Marty Perez	4	4	4	4	5	6	15	50
439	Gorman Thomas	4	4	4	4	5	6	15	
440	Jon Matlack	4	4	4	4	5	6	15	60
441	Larvell Blanks	4	4	4	4	5	6	15	50
442	Atlanta Braves CL/Bristol	4	4	4	4	5	6	20	
443	Lamar Johnson	4	4	4	4	5	6	15	120
444	Wayne Twitchell	4	4	4	4	5	6	15	50
445	Ken Singleton	4	4	4	4	5	6	15	100
446	Bill Bonham	4	4	4	4	5	6	15	
447	Jerry Turner	4	4	4	4	5	6	15	
448	Ellie Rodriguez	4	4	4	4	5	6	15	50
449	Al Fitzmorris	4	4	4	4	5	6	15	
450	Pete Rose	8	10	12	20	▲50	▲60	100	2,500
451	Checklist 397-528	4	4	4	4	5	6	15	80
452	Mike Caldwell	4	4	4	4	5	6	15	
453	Pedro Garcia	4	4	4	4	5	6	15	
454	Andy Etchebarren	4	4	4	4	5	6	15	
455	Rick Wise	4	4	4	4	5	6	25	
456	Leon Roberts	4	4	4	4	5	8		
457	Steve Luebber	4	4	4	4	5	8		
458	Leo Foster	4	4	4	4	5	6	15	

#	Player	VgEx 4	EX 5	ExMt 6	NM 7	NmMt 8	NmMt+ 8.5	MT 9	Gem 9.5/10
459	Steve Foucault	4	4	4	4	5	6	15	50
460	Willie Stargell	4	4	5	6	12	15	50	
461	Dick Tidrow	4	4	4	4	5	6	15	120
462	Don Baylor	4	4	4	4	6	8	20	
463	Jamie Quirk	4	4	4	4	5	6	15	
464	Randy Moffitt	4	4	4	4	5	6	15	
465	Rico Carty	4	4	4	4	5	6	15	
466	Fred Holdsworth	4	4	4	4	5	6	15	
467	Philadelphia Phillies CL/Ozark	4	4	4	4	5	6	15	50
468	Ramon Hernandez	4	4	4	4	5	6	15	
469	Pat Kelly	4	4	4	4	5	6	15	
470	Ted Simmons	4	4	4	4	5	6	20	200
471	Del Unser	4	4	4	4	5	6	15	
472	Rookie Pitchers	4	4	4	4	5	6	15	
473	Andre Dawson RC	15	20	▲30	40	▲80	120	250	2,500
474	Rookie Shortstops	4	4	4	4	5	6	15	60
475	Rookie Pitchers	4	4	4	5	10	15		
476	Dale Murphy RC	15	20	25	▲40	▲60	80	▲200	1,000
477	Rookie Infielders	4	4	4	4	5	6	15	60
478	Rookie Pitchers	4	4	4	4	5	6	15	60
479	Rookie Outfielders	4	4	4	4	5	6	15	
480	Carl Yastrzemski	4	4	5	▲25	▲30	▲40	80	
481	Roger Metzger	4	4	4	4	5	6	15	
482	Tony Solaita	4	4	4	4	5	6	25	
483	Richie Zisk	4	4	4	4	5	6	15	
484	Burt Hooton	4	4	4	4	5	6	15	
485	Roy White	4	4	4	4	5	6	15	60
486	Ed Bane	4	4	4	4	5	6	15	50
487	Rookie Pitchers	4	4	4	4	5	6	15	60
488	J.Clark RC/L.Mazzilli RC	4	4	4	6	12	15	30	
489	Rookie Pitchers	4	4	4	4	6	8	20	60
490	Rookie Shortstops	4	4	4	4	5	6	25	
491	Dennis Martinez RC	4	4	4	5	10	12	25	150
492	Rookie Outfielders	4	4	4	4	5	6	15	
493	Rookie Pitchers	4	4	4	4	5	6	15	
494	Rookie Infielders	4	4	4	4	5	6	15	
495	Al Hrabosky	4	4	4	4	5	6	80	
496	Gary Thomasson	4	4	4	4	5	6	30	50
497	Clay Carroll	4	4	4	4	5	6	15	50
498	Sal Bando	4	4	4	4	5	6	15	
499	Pablo Torrealba	4	4	4	4	5	6	15	
500	Dave Kingman	4	4	4	4	6	8	40	
501	Jim Bibby	4	4	4	4	5	6	15	50
502	Randy Hundley	4	4	4	4	5	6	15	50
503	Bill Lee	4	4	4	4	5	6	15	50
504	Los Angeles Dodgers CL/Lasorda	4	4	4	4	5	6	10	60
505	Oscar Gamble	4	4	4	4	5	6	15	
506	Steve Grilli	4	4	4	4	5	6	15	50
507	Mike Hegan	4	4	4	4	5	6	15	50
508	Dave Pagan	4	4	4	4	5	8		
509	Cookie Rojas	4	4	4	4	5	6	15	50
510	John Candelaria	4	4	4	4	5	6	20	
511	Bill Fahey	4	4	4	4	5	6	15	50
512	Jack Billingham	4	4	4	4	5	6	15	
513	Jerry Terrell	4	4	4	4	5	6	15	
514	Cliff Johnson	4	4	4	4	5	6	15	
515	Chris Speier	4	4	4	4	5	6	15	
516	Bake McBride	4	4	4	4	5	6	15	
517	Pete Vuckovich RC	4	4	4	4	5	6	100	
518	Chicago Cubs CL/Franks	4	4	4	4	6	8	12	
519	Don Kirkwood	4	4	4	4	5	6	15	
520	Garry Maddox	4	4	4	4	5	6	15	
521	Bob Grich	4	4	4	4	5	6	20	
522	Enzo Hernandez	4	4	4	4	5	6	15	
523	Rollie Fingers	4	4	4	4	6	8	20	
524	Rowland Office	4	4	4	4	5	6	15	
525	Dennis Eckersley	4	4	4	6	15	20	▲40	300
526	Larry Parrish	4	4	4	4	5	6	15	80
527	Dan Meyer	4	4	4	4	5	6	15	
528	Bill Castro	4	4	4	4	5	6	15	50
529	Jim Essian RC	4	4	4	4	5	6	15	
530	Rick Reuschel	4	4	4	4	5	6	15	
531	Lyman Bostock	4	4	4	4	5	6	50	80
532	Jim Willoughby	4	4	4	4	5	6	15	100
533	Mickey Stanley	4	4	4	4	5	6	15	
534	Paul Splittorff	4	4	4	4	5	6	15	
535	Cesar Geronimo	4	4	4	4	5	6	15	60

#	Player	VgEx 4	EX 5	ExMt 6	NM 7	NmMt 8	NmMt+ 8.5	MT 9	Gem 9.5
536	Vic Albury	4	4	4	4	5	6	12	
537	Dave Roberts	4	4	4	4	5	6	15	
538	Frank Taveras	4	4	4	4	5	6	15	
539	Mike Wallace	4	4	4	4	5	6	10	
540	Bob Watson	4	4	4	4	5	6	15	
541	John Denny	4	4	4	4	5	6	15	
542	Frank Duffy	4	4	4	4	5	6	15	
543	Ron Blomberg	4	4	4	4	5	6	15	
544	Gary Ross	4	4	4	4	5	6	15	
545	Bob Boone	4	4	4	4	5	6	15	
546	Baltimore Orioles CL/Weaver	4	4	4	4	5	6	15	
547	Willie McCovey	4	4	4	5	10	12	25	
548	Joel Youngblood RC	4	4	4	4	5	6	15	
549	Jerry Royster	4	4	4	4	5	8		
550	Randy Jones	4	4	4	4	6	8	30	
551	Bill North	4	4	4	4	5	6	15	
552	Pepe Mangual	4	4	4	4	5	6	15	
553	Jack Heidemann	4	4	4	4	5	6	15	
554	Bruce Kimm RC	4	4	4	4	5	6	15	
555	Dan Ford	4	4	4	4	5	6	15	
556	Doug Bird	4	4	4	4	5	6	15	
557	Jerry White	4	4	4	4	5	6	15	
558	Elias Sosa	4	4	4	4	5	6	15	
559	Alan Bannister RC	4	4	4	4	5	6	15	
560	Dave Concepcion	4	4	4	4	6	8	30	
561	Pete LaCock	4	4	4	4	6	8	20	
562	Checklist 529-660	4	4	4	4	5	6	15	6
563	Bruce Kison	4	4	4	4	5	6	15	12
564	Alan Ashby	4	4	4	4	5	6	15	
565	Mickey Lolich	4	4	4	4	6	8	20	8
566	Rick Miller	4	4	4	4	5	6	15	8
567	Enos Cabell	4	4	4	4	5	6	15	
568	Carlos May	4	4	4	4	5	6	15	
569	Jim Lonborg	4	4	4	4	5	6	15	
570	Bobby Bonds	4	4	4	4	6	8	20	
571	Darrell Evans	4	4	4	4	5	6	15	10
572	Ross Grimsley	4	4	4	4	5	6	10	5
573	Joe Ferguson	4	4	4	4	5	6	15	
574	Aurelio Rodriguez	4	4	4	4	5	6	15	5
575	Dick Ruthven	4	4	4	4	5	8		
576	Fred Kendall	4	4	4	4	5	6	15	
577	Jerry Augustine RC	4	4	4	4	5	6	10	
578	Bob Randall RC	4	4	4	4	5	6	15	
579	Don Carrithers	4	4	4	4	5	6	15	50
580	George Brett	12	15	20	25	▲50	▲60	120	1,500
581	Pedro Borbon	4	4	4	4	5	6	15	5
582	Ed Kirkpatrick	4	4	4	4	5	6	50	
583	Paul Lindblad	4	4	4	4	5	6	15	
584	Ed Goodson	4	4	4	4	5	6	10	
585	Rick Burleson	4	4	4	4	5	6	15	
586	Steve Renko	4	4	4	4	5	6	15	
587	Rick Baldwin	4	4	4	4	5	6	15	
588	Dave Moates	4	4	4	4	5	6	15	
589	Mike Cosgrove	4	4	4	4	5	6	15	50
590	Buddy Bell	4	4	4	4	5	6	10	50
591	Chris Arnold	4	4	4	4	5	6	15	
592	Dan Briggs RC	4	4	4	4	5	6	15	
593	Dennis Blair	4	4	4	4	5	6	15	
594	Biff Pocoroba	4	4	4	4	5	6	15	
595	John Hiller	4	4	4	4	5	6	15	50
596	Jerry Martin RC	4	4	4	4	5	8		
597	Seattle Mariners CL/Johnson	4	4	4	4	5	6	15	50
598	Sparky Lyle	4	4	4	4	6	8	20	
599	Mike Tyson	4	4	4	4	5	6	15	
600	Jim Palmer	4	4	4	8	15	20	100	
601	Mike Lum	4	4	4	4	5	6	15	
602	Andy Hassler	4	4	4	4	5	6	100	
603	Willie Davis	4	4	4	4	5	8		
604	Jim Slaton	4	4	4	4	5	6	15	
605	Felix Millan	4	4	4	4	5	6	10	
606	Steve Braun	4	4	4	4	5	6	15	
607	Larry Demery	4	4	4	4	5	6	15	
608	Roy Howell	4	4	4	4	5	6	15	
609	Jim Barr	4	4	4	4	5	6	20	
610	Jose Cardenal	4	4	4	4	5	8		
611	Dave Lemanczyk	4	4	4	4	5	6	15	
612	Barry Foote	4	4	4	4	5	6	15	

	VgEx 4	EX 5	ExMt 6	NM 7	NmMt 8	NmMt+ 8.5	MT 9	Gem 9.5/10
Reggie Cleveland	4	4	4	4	5	6	15	80
Greg Gross	4	4	4	4	5	6	15	50
Phil Niekro	4	4	4	4	8	10	40	
Tommy Sandt RC	4	4	4	4	5	6	15	80
Bobby Darwin	4	4	4	4	5	6	15	50
Pat Dobson	4	4	4	4	5	6	15	50
Johnny Oates	4	4	4	4	5	6	15	
Don Sutton	4	4	4	4	8	10	25	
Detroit Tigers CL/Houk	4	4	4	4	6	8	20	
Jim Wohlford	4	4	4	4	5	8		
Jack Kucek	4	4	4	4	5	8		
Hector Cruz	4	4	4	4	5	6	15	
Ken Holtzman	4	4	4	4	5	6	15	80
Al Bumbry	4	4	4	4	5	6	15	150
Bob Myrick RC	4	4	4	4	5	6	15	50
Mario Guerrero	4	4	4	4	5	6	15	80
Bobby Valentine	4	4	4	4	5	8		
Bert Blyleven	4	4	4	4	6	8	80	
Brett Brothers	4	4	4	5	10	15	80	
Forsch Brothers	4	4	4	4	5	8		
May Brothers	4	4	4	4	5	6	15	
Reuschel Brothers	4	4	4	4	5	6	20	
Robin Yount	4	4	6	12	▲50	▲60	350	
Santo Alcala	4	4	4	4	5	6	15	50
Alex Johnson	4	4	4	4	5	6	15	
Jim Kaat	4	4	4	4	5	6	15	80
Jerry Morales	4	4	4	4	5	6	15	
Carlton Fisk	4	4	6	▲20	▲25	▲30	▲100	
Dan Larson RC	4	4	4	4	5	6	15	50
Willie Crawford	4	4	4	4	5	6	15	50
Mike Pazik	4	4	4	4	5	8		
Matt Alexander	4	4	4	4	5	6	15	
Jerry Reuss	4	4	4	4	5	6	15	
Andres Mora RC	4	4	4	4	5	6	15	
Montreal Expos CL/Williams	4	4	4	4	5	6	15	
Jim Spencer	4	4	4	4	5	6	15	
Dave Cash	4	4	4	4	5	6	15	50
Nolan Ryan	▲15	▲20	▲25	▲40	60	120	400	
Von Joshua	4	4	4	4	5	6	40	
Tom Walker	4	4	4	4	5	6	15	50
Diego Segui	4	4	4	4	5	6	15	50
Ron Pruitt RC	4	4	4	4	5	6	15	
Tony Perez	4	4	4	6	12	15	40	
Ron Guidry	4	4	5	10	20	25		
Mick Kelleher RC	4	4	4	4	5	6	15	
Marty Pattin	4	4	4	4	5	8		
Merv Rettenmund	4	4	4	4	5	6	15	
Willie Horton	4	4	4	4	6	8	25	

—Batting Leaders #1 PSA 10 (Gem) sold for $297 (eBay; 3/07)
—Johnny Bench #70 PSA 10 (Gem) sold for $504 (eBay; 9/07)
—Johnny Bench #70 PSA 10 (Gem) sold for $425 (eBay; 9/07)
—George Brett RB #231 PSA 10 (Gem) sold for $192 (Mile High; 2/08)
—Dwight Evans #25 PSA 9 (MT) sold for $305 (eBay; 4/07)
—Dwight Evans #25 PSA 9 (MT) sold for $285 (eBay; 4/08)
—Dwight Evans #25 PSA 9 (MT) sold for $107 (eBay; 5/08)
—Carlton Fisk #640 PSA 10 (Gem) sold for $205 (eBay; 11/06)
—Ron Guidry #656 PSA 9 (MT) sold for $169 (eBay; 6/07)
—Home Run Leaders #2 PSA 10 (Gem) sold for $515 (eBay; 3/07)
—Home Run Leaders #2 PSA 10 (Gem) sold for $355 (eBay; 7/07)
—Reggie Jackson #10 PSA 10 (Gem) sold for $790 (eBay; 7/07)
—Reggie Jackson #10 PSA 10 (Gem) sold for $577 (eBay; 4/07)
—Ron LeFlore #240 PSA 10 (Gem) sold for $288 (eBay; 5/08)
—Joe Morgan #100 PSA 10 (Gem) sold for $543 (Madec; 11/07)
—Joe Morgan #100 PSA 10 (Gem) sold for $479 (eBay; 2/08)
—Jim Palmer #600 PSA 10 (Gem) sold for $256 (eBay; 3/07)
—Jim Rice #60 PSA 10 (Gem) sold for $407 (eBay; 11/07)
—Jim Rice #60 PSA 10 (Gem) sold for $338 (eBay; 7/08)
—Brooks Robinson #285 PSA 10 (Gem) sold for $300 (eBay; 1/07)
—Brooks Robinson #285 PSA 10 (Gem) sold for $262 (eBay; 7/08)
—Brooks Robinson #285 PSA 10 (Gem) sold for $135 (eBay; 5/08)
—Nolan Ryan #650 PSA 10 (Gem) sold for $3,203 (Mastro; 12/07)
—Nolan Ryan #650 PSA 10 (Gem) sold for $2,655 (eBay; 5/07)
—Nolan Ryan #650 PSA 10 (Gem) sold for $2,475 (eBay; 9/07)
—Nolan Ryan #650 BVG 9.5 (Gem) sold for $1,035 (eBay; 9/07)
—Nolan Ryan #650 BVG 9.5 (Gem) sold for $1,005 (eBay; 3/08)
—Nolan Ryan RB #234 BVG 9.5 (Gem) sold for $139 (eBay; 10/06)
—Tom Seaver #150 PSA 10 (Gem) sold for $1,368 (eBay; 02/12)

—Mike Schmidt #140 PSA 10 (Gem) sold for $525 (eBay; 5/07)
—Willie Stargell #460 PSA 10 (Gem) sold for $293 (eBay; 2/08)
—Dave Winfield #390 PSA 10 (Gem) sold for $371 (eBay; 5/08)
—Dave Winfield #390 PSA 10 (Gem) sold for $180 (eBay; 11/06)
—World Series Games 1-2 #411 PSA 10 (Gem) sold for $261 (eBay; 10/07)
—World Series Games 3-4 #412 PSA 10 (Gem) sold for $180 (eBay; 8/07)
—Carl Yastrzemski #480 PSA 10 (Gem) sold for $456 (eBay; 2/07)
—Robin Yount #635 PSA 10 (Gem) sold for $1,813 (eBay; 01/12)

1977 Topps Cloth Stickers

		VG 3	VgEx 4	EX 5	ExMt 6	NM 7	NmMt 8	MT 9	Gem 9.5/10
1	Alan Ashby	4	4	4	4	5	6	12	80
2	Buddy Bell SP	4	4	4	4	5	6	12	
3	Johnny Bench	4	4	5	6	8	12	25	100
4	Vida Blue	4	4	4	4	5	6	12	
5	Bert Blyleven	4	4	4	4	5	6	12	40
6	Steve Braun SP	4	4	4	4	5	6	12	
7	George Brett	4	5	6	8	10	25	40	
8	Lou Brock	4	4	4	4	5	6	15	40
9	Jose Cardenal	4	4	4	4	5	6	12	
10	Rod Carew SP	4	4	4	5	6	10	25	100
11	Steve Carlton	4	4	4	4	5	8	15	80
12	Dave Cash	4	4	4	4	5	6	12	40
13	Cesar Cedeno SP	4	4	4	4	5	6	12	40
14	Ron Cey	4	4	4	4	5	6	15	50
15	Mark Fidrych	4	4	4	4	8	10	30	100
16	Dan Ford	4	4	4	4	5	6	12	30
17	Wayne Garland	4	4	4	4	5	6	12	50
18	Ralph Garr	4	4	4	4	5	6	12	40
19	Steve Garvey	4	4	4	4	5	8	15	50
20	Mike Hargrove	4	4	4	4	5	6	12	40
21	Jim Hunter	4	4	4	4	5	8	15	
22	Reggie Jackson	4	4	5	6	8	15	25	150
23	Randy Jones	4	4	4	4	5	6	15	
24	Dave Kingman SP	4	4	4	4	5	6	12	40
25	Bill Madlock	4	4	4	4	5	6	12	30
26	Lee May SP	4	4	4	4	5	6	12	40
27	John Mayberry	4	4	4	4	5	6	12	30
28	Andy Messersmith	4	4	4	4	5	6	12	50
29	Willie Montanez	4	4	4	4	5	6	12	30
30	John Montefusco SP	4	4	4	4	5	6	12	
31	Joe Morgan	4	4	4	4	5	8	15	50
32	Thurman Munson	4	4	5	6	8	12	50	100
33	Bobby Murcer	4	4	4	4	5	6	12	
34	Al Oliver SP	4	4	4	4	5	6	12	50
35	Dave Pagan	4	4	4	4	5	6	12	50
36	Jim Palmer SP	4	4	4	4	5	8	15	200
37	Tony Perez	4	4	4	4	5	8	15	40
38	Pete Rose SP	8	10	12	15	20	▲40	120	
39	Joe Rudi	4	4	4	4	5	6	12	
40	Nolan Ryan SP	8	10	15	20	25	50	120	
41	Mike Schmidt	4	4	5	6	8	12	50	250
42	Tom Seaver	4	4	4	5	6	10	25	
43	Ted Simmons	4	4	4	4	5	6	12	50
44	Bill Singer	4	4	4	4	5	6	12	
45	Willie Stargell	4	4	4	4	5	8	30	40
46	Rusty Staub	4	4	4	4	5	6	12	100
47	Don Sutton	4	4	4	4	5	8	15	60
48	Luis Tiant	4	4	4	4	5	6	12	30
49	Bill Travers	4	4	4	4	5	6	12	
50	Claudell Washington	4	4	4	4	5	6	12	
51	Bob Watson	4	4	4	4	5	6	12	
52	Dave Winfield	4	4	4	4	8	15	30	100
53	Carl Yastrzemski	4	4	4	4	8	15	30	120
54	Robin Yount	4	4	4	4	5	10	25	100
55	Richie Zisk	4	4	4	4	5	6	12	40

1978 Kellogg's

		VG 3	VgEx 4	EX 5	ExMt 6	NM 7	NmMt 8	MT 9	Gem 9.5/10
1	Steve Carlton	4	4	4	4	4	5	10	30
2	Bucky Dent	4	4	4	4	4	4	8	25
3	Mike Schmidt	4	4	4	4	4	8	15	50
4	Ken Griffey	4	4	4	4	4	4	8	25
5	Al Cowens	4	4	4	4	4	4	8	25
6	George Brett	4	4	5	10	20	40	80	

#	Player	VG 3	VgEx 4	EX 5	ExMt 6	NM 7	NmMt 8	MT 9	Gem 9.5/10
7	Lou Brock	4	4	4	4	4	5	10	30
8	Goose Gossage	4	4	4	4	4	4	8	30
9	Tom Johnson	4	4	4	4	4	4	8	30
10	George Foster	4	4	4	4	4	4	8	30
11	Dave Winfield	4	4	4	4	4	5	10	30
12	Dan Meyer	4	4	4	4	4	4	8	25
13	Chris Chambliss	4	4	4	4	4	4	8	25
14	Paul Dade	4	4	4	4	4	4	8	
15	Jeff Burroughs	4	4	4	4	4	4	8	
16	Jose Cruz	4	4	4	4	4	4	8	
17	Mickey Rivers	4	4	4	4	4	4	8	
18	John Candelaria	4	4	4	4	4	4	8	50
19	Ellis Valentine	4	4	4	4	4	4	8	25
20	Hal McRae	4	4	4	4	4	4	8	
21	Dave Rozema	4	4	4	4	4	4	8	
22	Lenny Randle	4	4	4	4	4	4	8	
23	Willie McCovey	4	4	4	4	4	5	10	
24	Ron Cey	4	4	4	4	4	4	8	30
25	Eddie Murray	4	4	4	5	10	20	40	
26	Larry Bowa	4	4	4	4	4	4	8	25
27	Tom Seaver	4	4	4	4	4	6	12	
28	Garry Maddox	4	4	4	4	4	4	8	
29	Rod Carew	4	4	4	4	4	5	10	
30	Thurman Munson	4	4	4	4	5	10	20	
31	Garry Templeton	4	4	4	4	4	4	8	30
32	Eric Soderholm	4	4	4	4	4	4	8	
33	Greg Luzinski	4	4	4	4	4	4	8	25
34	Reggie Smith	4	4	4	4	4	4	8	25
35	Dave Goltz	4	4	4	4	4	4	8	25
36	Tommy John	4	4	4	4	4	4	8	25
37	Ralph Garr	4	4	4	4	4	4	8	
38	Alan Bannister	4	4	4	4	4	4	8	25
39	Bob Bailor	4	4	4	4	4	4	8	
40	Reggie Jackson	4	4	4	4	4	8	15	50
41	Cecil Cooper	4	4	4	4	4	4	8	30
42	Burt Hooton	4	4	4	4	4	4	8	25
43	Sparky Lyle	4	4	4	4	4	4	8	30
44	Steve Ontiveros	4	4	4	4	4	4	8	25
45	Rick Reuschel	4	4	4	4	4	4	8	25
46	Lyman Bostock	4	4	4	4	4	4	8	
47	Mitchell Page	4	4	4	4	4	4	8	25
48	Bruce Sutter	4	4	4	4	4	4	8	
49	Jim Rice	4	4	4	4	4	4	8	25
50	Ken Forsch	4	4	4	4	4	4	8	25
51	Nolan Ryan	4	4	4	4	8	15	30	100
52	Dave Parker	4	4	4	4	4	4	8	30
53	Bert Blyleven	4	4	4	4	4	4	8	25
54	Frank Tanana	4	4	4	4	4	4	8	25
55	Ken Singleton	4	4	4	4	4	4	8	25
56	Mike Hargrove	4	4	4	4	4	4	8	
57	Don Sutton	4	4	4	4	4	4	8	30

1978 O-Pee-Chee

#	Player	GD 2	VG 3	VgEx 4	EX 5	ExMt 6	NM 7	NmMt 8	MT 9
154	Eddie Murray RC	4	4	4	8	15	50	100	▲400

—Milt May #115 PSA 10 (Gem) sold for $4,546 (eBay; 10/12)
—Eddie Murray #154 PSA 10 (Gem) sold for $6,244 (Mastro; 4/07)
—Eddie Murray #154 PSA 10 (Gem) sold for $2,385 (Mile High; 10/12)

1978 Tigers Burger King

#	Player	GD 2	VG 3	VgEx 4	EX 5	ExMt 6	NM 7	NmMt 8	MT 9
8	Jack Morris *	4	4	4	5	6	8	15	
13	Lou Whitaker *	4	4	4	5	6	8	15	
15	Alan Trammell *	4	4	5	6	8	15	30	120

—Cards produced by Topps and feature same design as basic 1978 Topps set (but photos are different).

1978 Topps

#	Player	VgEx 4	EX 5	ExMt 6	NM 7	NmMt 8	NmMt+ 8.5	MT 9	Gem 9.5/10
1	Lou Brock RB	4	4	4	4	8	10	25	500
2	Sparky Lyle RB	4	4	4	4	8	10	15	
3	Willie McCovey RB	4	4	4	4	8	10	15	
4	Brooks Robinson RB	4	8	10	20	40	50	80	
5	Pete Rose RB	4	4	4	6	12	15	30	150
6	Nolan Ryan RB	8	10	12	15	20	25	40	
7	Reggie Jackson RB	4	4	4	5	10	12	20	
8	Mike Sadek	4	4	4	4	4	5	8	
9	Doug DeCinces	4	4	4	4	4	5	8	
10	Phil Niekro	4	4	4	5	6		10	20
11	Rick Manning	4	4	4	4	4	5	8	
12	Don Aase	4	4	4	4	4	5	8	
13	Art Howe RC	4	4	4		8	10	15	
14	Lerrin LaGrow	4	4	4	4	4	5	8	
15	Tony Perez DP	4	4	4	5	6		10	8
16	Roy White	4	4	4	5	6		10	8
17	Mike Krukow	4	4	4	4	4	5	8	
18	Bob Grich	4	4	4	4	4	5	8	
19	Darrell Porter	4	4	4	4	4	5	8	4
20	Pete Rose DP	8	10	12	15	20	25	30	30
21	Steve Kemp	4	4	4	4	4	5	8	
22	Charlie Hough	4	4	4	4	4	5	8	4
23	Bump Wills	4	4	4	4	4	5	8	4
24	Don Money DP	4	4	4	4	4	5	8	4
25	Jon Matlack	4	4	4	4	4	5	8	5
26	Rich Hebner	4	4	4	4	4	5	8	
27	Geoff Zahn	4	4	4	4	4	5	8	5
28	Ed Ott	4	4	4	4	4	5	8	5
29	Bob Lacey RC	4	4	4	4	4	5	8	
30	George Hendrick	4	4	4	4	4	5	8	4
31	Glenn Abbott	4	4	4	4	4	5	8	5
32	Garry Templeton	4	4	4	4	4	5	8	
33	Dave Lemanczyk	4	4	4	4	4	5	8	5
34	Willie McCovey	4	4	4	5	10	12	50	
35	Sparky Lyle	4	4	4	4	8	10	15	
36	Eddie Murray RC	20	25	30	50	▲120	250	▲800	20,000
37	Rick Waits	4	4	4	4	4	5	8	5
38	Willie Montanez	4	4	4	4	8	10	15	
39	Floyd Bannister RC	4	4	4	4	4	5	8	
40	Carl Yastrzemski	4	4	4	12	▲25	▲30	▲80	
41	Burt Hooton	4	4	4	4	4	5	8	4
42	Jorge Orta	4	4	4	4	4	5	8	5
43	Bill Atkinson RC	4	4	4	4	4	5	8	60
44	Toby Harrah	4	4	4	4	4	5	8	
45	Mark Fidrych	4	4	4	4	8	10	15	200
46	Al Cowens	4	4	4	4	4	5	8	
47	Jack Billingham	4	4	4	4	4	5	8	40
48	Don Baylor	4	4	4	4	5	6	10	50
49	Ed Kranepool	4	4	4	4	4	5	8	40
50	Rick Reuschel	4	4	4	4	4	5	8	60
51	Charlie Moore DP	4	4	4	4	4	5	8	40
52	Jim Lonborg	4	4	4	4	4	5	8	
53	Phil Garner DP	4	4	4	4	4	5	8	40
54	Tom Johnson	4	4	4	4	4	5	8	50
55	Mitchell Page RC	4	4	4	4	4	5	8	50
56	Randy Jones	4	4	4	4	4	5	8	
57	Dan Meyer	4	4	4	4	4	5	8	40
58	Bob Forsch	4	4	4	4	4	5	8	40
59	Otto Velez	4	4	4	4	4	5	8	50
60	Thurman Munson	4	4	5	10	20	25	50	
61	Larvell Blanks	4	4	4	4	4	5	8	40
62	Jim Barr	4	4	4	4	4	5	8	40
63	Don Zimmer MG	4	4	4	4	4	5	8	40
64	Gene Pentz	4	4	4	4	4	5	8	
65	Ken Singleton	4	4	4	4	4	5	8	40
66	Chicago White Sox CL	4	4	4	4	8	10	80	
67	Claudell Washington	4	4	4	4	4	5	8	40
68	Steve Foucault DP	4	4	4	4	4	5	8	40
69	Mike Vail	4	4	4	4	4	5	8	40
70	Goose Gossage	4	4	4	4	8	10	15	250
71	Terry Humphrey	4	4	4	4	4	5	8	
72	Andre Dawson	4	4	4	8	15	20	30	300
73	Andy Hassler	4	4	4	4	8	10	15	
74	Checklist 1-121	4	4	4	4	4	5	8	60
75	Dick Ruthven	4	4	4	4	4	5	8	50
76	Steve Ontiveros	4	4	4	4	4	5	8	50
77	Ed Kirkpatrick	4	4	4	4	4	5	8	60
78	Pablo Torrealba	4	4	4	4	4	5	8	60
79	Darrell Johnson MG DP	4	4	4	4	4	5	8	60
80	Ken Griffey Sr.	4	4	4	4	5	6	10	80
81	Pete Redfern	4	4	4	4	4	5	8	40
82	San Francisco Giants CL	4	4	4	4	8	10	15	
83	Bob Montgomery	4	4	4	4	4	5	8	100
84	Kent Tekulve	4	4	4	4	4	5	8	40

#	Player	VgEx 4	EX 5	ExMt 6	NM 7	NmMt 8	NmMt+ 8.5	MT 9	Gem 9.5/10
85	Ron Fairly	4	4	4	4	4	5	8	50
86	Dave Tomlin	4	4	4	4	4	5	8	40
87	John Lowenstein	4	4	4	4	8	10	15	
88	Mike Phillips	4	4	4	4	4	5	8	60
89	Ken Clay RC	4	4	4	4	8	10	15	120
90	Larry Bowa	4	4	4	4	4	5	8	40
91	Oscar Zamora	4	4	4	4	8	10	15	
92	Adrian Devine	4	4	4	4	4	5	8	40
93	Bobby Cox DP	4	4	4	4	4	5	8	40
94	Chuck Scrivener	4	4	4	4	4	5	8	
95	Jamie Quirk	4	4	4	4	4	5	8	40
96	Baltimore Orioles CL	4	4	4	8	15	20	30	40
97	Stan Bahnsen	4	4	4	4	8	10	15	
98	Jim Essian	4	4	4	4	4	5	8	
99	Willie Hernandez RC	4	4	5	10	20	25	40	80
100	George Brett	6	8	10	▲25	▲30	40	200	
101	Sid Monge	4	4	4	4	8	10	15	
102	Matt Alexander	4	4	4	4	8	10	15	
103	Tom Murphy	4	4	5	10	20	25	40	
104	Lee Lacy	4	4	4	4	4	5	8	40
105	Reggie Cleveland	4	4	4	4	4	5	8	40
106	Bill Plummer	4	4	4	4	8	10	15	
107	Ed Halicki	4	4	4	4	4	5	8	
108	Von Joshua	4	4	4	4	4	5	8	40
109	Joe Torre MG	4	4	4	4	5	6	12	50
110	Richie Zisk	4	4	4	6	12	15	25	
111	Mike Tyson	4	4	4	4	8	10	15	
112	Houston Astros CL	4	4	4	4	8	10	15	
113	Don Carrithers	4	4	4	4	4	5	8	
114	Paul Blair	4	4	4	4	5	6	10	
115	Gary Nolan	4	4	4	4	8	10	15	
116	Tucker Ashford RC	4	4	4	4	4	5	8	60
117	John Montague	4	4	4	4	4	5	8	40
118	Terry Harmon	4	4	4	4	4	5	8	40
119	Dennis Martinez	4	4	4	4	4	5	8	40
120	Gary Carter	4	4	4	4	8	10	15	350
121	Alvis Woods	4	4	4	4	8	10	15	60
122	Dennis Eckersley	4	4	4	4	8	10	15	100
123	Manny Trillo	4	4	4	4	4	5	8	40
124	Dave Rozema RC	4	4	4	4	4	5	8	40
125	George Scott	4	4	4	4	8	10	15	
126	Paul Moskau RC	4	4	4	4	4	5	10	40
127	Chet Lemon	4	4	4	4	4	5	8	40
128	Bill Russell	4	4	4	4	4	5	8	40
129	Jim Colborn	4	4	4	4	4	5	8	40
130	Jeff Burroughs	4	4	4	4	4	5	8	
131	Bert Blyleven	4	4	4	4	5	6	10	80
132	Enos Cabell	4	4	4	4	4	5	8	
133	Jerry Augustine	4	4	4	4	4	5	8	
134	Steve Henderson RC	4	4	4	4	4	5	8	100
135	Ron Guidry DP	4	4	4	4	8	10	15	100
136	Ted Sizemore	4	4	4	4	4	5	8	40
137	Craig Kusick	4	4	4	4	8	10	10	
138	Larry Demery	4	4	4	4	4	5	8	60
139	Wayne Gross	4	4	4	4	4	5	8	40
140	Rollie Fingers	4	4	4	4	5	6	10	100
141	Ruppert Jones	4	4	4	4	8	10	15	
142	John Montefusco	4	4	4	4	4	5	8	
143	Keith Hernandez	4	4	4	4	4	5	8	40
144	Jesse Jefferson	4	4	4	4	4	5	8	40
145	Rick Monday	4	4	4	4	4	5	8	
146	Doyle Alexander	4	4	4	4	4	5	8	40
147	Lee Mazzilli	4	4	4	4	4	5	8	40
148	Andre Thornton	4	4	4	4	8	10	15	
149	Dale Murray	4	4	4	4	4	5	8	40
150	Bobby Bonds	4	4	4	4	4	5	8	
151	Milt Wilcox	4	4	4	4	4	5	8	
152	Ivan DeJesus RC	4	4	4	4	4	5	8	60
153	Steve Stone	4	4	4	4	4	5	8	60
154	Cecil Cooper DP	4	4	4	4	4	5	8	
155	Butch Hobson	4	4	4	4	4	5	8	40
156	Andy Messersmith	4	4	4	4	4	5	8	100
157	Pete LaCock DP	4	4	4	4	4	5	8	40
158	Joaquin Andujar	4	4	4	5	10	20	25	40
159	Lou Piniella	4	4	4	4	4	5	6	10
160	Jim Palmer	4	4	4	4	8	10	15	200
161	Bob Boone	4	4	4	4	4	5	8	60

#	Player	VgEx 4	EX 5	ExMt 6	NM 7	NmMt 8	NmMt+ 8.5	MT 9	Gem 9.5/10
162	Paul Thormodsgard RC	4	4	4	4	4	5	8	50
163	Bill North	4	4	4	4	4	5	8	
164	Bob Owchinko RC	4	4	4	4	4	5	8	60
165	Rennie Stennett	4	8	10	20	40	50	80	
166	Carlos Lopez	4	4	4	4	4	5	8	40
167	Tim Foli	4	4	4	4	4	5	8	
168	Reggie Smith	4	4	4	4	4	5	8	
169	Jerry Johnson	4	4	4	4	8	10	15	50
170	Lou Brock	4	4	4	4	8	10	15	80
171	Pat Zachry	4	4	4	4	4	5	8	40
172	Mike Hargrove	4	4	4	4	8	10	15	
173	Robin Yount	4	4	10	12	▲20	▲25	▲30	300
174	Wayne Garland	4	4	4	4	4	5	8	60
175	Jerry Morales	4	4	4	4	4	5	8	60
176	Milt May	4	4	4	4	4	5	8	50
177	Gene Garber DP	4	4	4	4	4	5	8	40
178	Dave Chalk	4	4	4	4	8	10	15	
179	Dick Tidrow	4	4	4	4	6	8	12	80
180	Dave Concepcion	4	4	4	4	5	6	10	80
181	Ken Forsch	4	4	4	4	4	5	8	
182	Jim Spencer	4	4	4	4	4	5	8	60
183	Doug Bird	4	4	4	4	8	10		60
184	Checklist 122-242	4	4	4	4	4	5	8	60
185	Ellis Valentine	4	4	4	4	4		10	100
186	Bob Stanley DP RC	4	4	4	4	4	5	8	
187	Jerry Royster DP	4	4	4	4	4	5	8	40
188	Al Bumbry	4	4	4	4	4	5	8	
189	Tom Lasorda MG DP	4	4	4	4	8	10	15	100
190	John Candelaria	4	4	4	4	4	5	8	80
191	Rodney Scott RC	4	4	4	4	4	5	8	
192	San Diego Padres CL	4	4	4	4	4	5	8	
193	Rich Chiles	4	4	4	4	4	5	8	
194	Derrel Thomas	4	4	4	4	4	5	8	60
195	Larry Dierker	4	4	4	4	4	5	8	
196	Bob Bailor	4	4	4	4	8	10	15	150
197	Nino Espinosa	4	4	4	4	4	5	8	
198	Ron Pruitt	4	4	4	4	4	5	8	40
199	Craig Reynolds	4	4	4	4	4	5	8	60
200	Reggie Jackson	4	4	5	20	▲40	▲50	120	
201	Batting Leaders	4	4	4	4	5	6	10	80
202	Home Run Leaders DP	4	4	4	4	6	8	12	100
203	RBI Leaders	4	4	4	4	4	5	8	50
204	Stolen Base Leaders DP	4	4	4	4	4	5	8	60
205	Victory Leaders	4	4	4	4	6	8	12	50
206	Strikeout Leaders DP	4	4	4	5	▲15	▲20	▲30	150
207	ERA Leaders DP	4	4	4	4	4	5	8	40
208	Leading Firemen	4	4	4	4	6	8	12	
209	Dock Ellis	4	4	4	4	4	5	8	60
210	Jose Cardenal	4	4	4	4	4	5	8	
211	Earl Weaver MG DP	4	4	4	4	5	6	10	60
212	Mike Caldwell	4	4	4	4	4	5	8	
213	Alan Bannister	4	4	4	4	4	5	8	60
214	California Angels CL	4	4	4	4	4	5	8	200
215	Darrell Evans	4	4	4	4	4	5	8	50
216	Mike Paxton RC	4	4	4	4	4	5	8	40
217	Rod Gilbreath	4	4	4	4	4	5	8	60
218	Marty Pattin	4	4	4	4	4	5	8	40
219	Mike Cubbage	4	4	4	4	4	5	8	60
220	Pedro Borbon	4	4	4	4	4	5	8	60
221	Chris Speier	4	4	5	10	20	25	40	
222	Jerry Martin	4	4	4	4	4	5	8	40
223	Bruce Kison	4	4	4	4	4	5	8	60
224	Jerry Tabb RC	4	4	4	4	4	5	8	40
225	Don Gullett DP	4	4	4	4	5	6	10	50
226	Joe Ferguson	4	4	4	4	4	5	8	60
227	Al Fitzmorris	4	4	4	4	4	5	8	40
228	Manny Mota DP	4	4	4	4	4	5	8	40
229	Leo Foster	4	4	4	4	4	5	8	40
230	Al Hrabosky	4	4	4	4	4	5	8	
231	Wayne Nordhagen RC	4	4	4	4	8	10	15	
232	Mickey Stanley	4	4	4	4	4	5	8	60
233	Dick Pole	4	4	4	4	4	5	8	
234	Herman Franks MG	4	4	4	4	8	10	15	40
235	Tim McCarver	4	4	4	4	8	10	15	
236	Terry Whitfield	4	4	4	4	4	5	8	
237	Rich Dauer	4	4	4	4	8	10	15	50
238	Juan Beniquez	4	4	4	4	4	5	8	40

#	Player	VgEx 4	EX 5	ExMt 6	NM 7	NmMt 8	NmMt+ 8.5	MT 9	Gem 9.5/10
239	Dyar Miller	4	4	4	4	4	5	8	40
240	Gene Tenace	4	4	4	4	4	5	8	50
241	Pete Vuckovich	4	4	4	4	4	5	8	40
242	Barry Bonnell DP RC	4	4	4	4	4	5	8	
243	Bob McClure	4	4	4	4	4	5	8	60
244	Montreal Expos CL DP	4	4	4	4	4	5	8	40
245	Rick Burleson	4	4	5	10	20	25	250	
246	Dan Driessen	4	4	4	4	4	5	8	
247	Larry Christenson	4	4	4	4	4	5	8	40
248	Frank White DP	4	4	4	4	4	5	8	40
249	Dave Goltz DP	4	4	4	4	4	5	8	40
250	Graig Nettles DP	4	4	4	5	10	12	20	100
251	Don Kirkwood	4	4	4	4	4	5	8	40
252	Steve Swisher DP	4	4	4	4	4	5	8	40
253	Jim Kern	4	4	4	4	4	5	8	40
254	Dave Collins	4	4	4	4	4	5	8	50
255	Jerry Reuss	4	4	4	4	4	5	8	40
256	Joe Altobelli MG RC	4	4	4	6	12	15	25	80
257	Hector Cruz	4	4	4	4	4	5	8	60
258	John Hiller	4	4	4	4	8	10	15	200
259	Los Angeles Dodgers CL	4	4	5	10	20	25	40	
260	Bert Campaneris	4	4	4	4	4	5	8	40
261	Tim Hosley	4	4	4	4	4	5	8	40
262	Rudy May	4	4	4	4	4	5	8	60
263	Danny Walton	4	4	4	4	8	10	15	
264	Jamie Easterly	4	4	4	4	8	10	15	60
265	Sal Bando DP	4	4	4	4	4	5	8	40
266	Bob Shirley RC	4	4	4	4	4	5	8	40
267	Doug Ault	4	4	4	4	4	5	8	50
268	Gil Flores RC	4	4	4	4	4	5	8	
269	Wayne Twitchell	4	4	4	4	4	5	8	40
270	Carlton Fisk	4	4	4	4	8	10	20	200
271	Randy Lerch DP	4	4	4	4	4	5	8	40
272	Royle Stillman	4	4	4	4	8	10	15	60
273	Fred Norman	4	4	4	4	4	5	8	40
274	Freddie Patek	4	4	4	4	4	5	8	40
275	Dan Ford	4	4	4	4	4	5	8	
276	Bill Bonham DP	4	4	4	4	4	5	8	40
277	Bruce Boisclair	4	4	4	4	4	5	8	60
278	Enrique Romo RC	4	4	4	4	4	5	8	40
279	Bill Virdon MG	4	4	4	4	8	10	15	80
280	Buddy Bell	4	4	4	4	4	5	8	40
281	Eric Rasmussen DP	4	4	4	4	4	5	8	60
282	New York Yankees CL	4	6	8	15	30	40	200	
283	Omar Moreno	4	4	4	4	4	5	8	
284	Randy Moffitt	4	4	4	4	4	5	8	
285	Steve Yeager DP	4	4	4	4	4	5	8	40
286	Ben Oglivie	4	4	4	4	4	5	8	50
287	Kiko Garcia	4	4	4	4	4	5	8	60
288	Dave Hamilton	4	4	4	4	4	5	8	40
289	Checklist 243-363	4	4	4	4	4	5	8	40
290	Willie Horton	4	4	4	4	4	5	8	
291	Gary Ross	4	4	4	4	4	5	8	
292	Gene Richards	4	4	4	4	4	5	8	40
293	Mike Willis	4	4	4	4	4	5	8	40
294	Larry Parrish	4	4	4	4	4	5	8	50
295	Bill Lee	4	4	4	4	4	5	8	50
296	Biff Pocoroba	4	4	4	4	4	5	8	40
297	Warren Brusstar DP RC	4	4	4	4	4	5	8	40
298	Tony Armas	4	4	4	4	8	10	15	
299	Whitey Herzog MG	4	4	4	4	4	5	8	
300	Joe Morgan	4	4	4	5	10	12	20	200
301	Buddy Schultz RC	4	4	4	4	4	5	8	60
302	Chicago Cubs CL	4	4	4	4	8	10	50	
303	Sam Hinds RC	4	4	4	4	4	5	8	40
304	John Milner	4	4	4	4	4	5	8	80
305	Rico Carty	4	4	4	4	4	5	8	40
306	Joe Niekro	4	4	4	4	4	5	8	
307	Glenn Borgmann	4	4	4	4	4	5	8	40
308	Jim Rooker	4	4	4	4	4	5	8	40
309	Cliff Johnson	4	4	4	4	5	6	10	60
310	Don Sutton	4	4	4	4	5	6	10	100
311	Jose Baez DP RC	4	4	4	4	4	5	8	40
312	Greg Minton	4	4	4	4	4	5	8	80
313	Andy Etchebarren	4	4	4	4	4	5	8	
314	Paul Lindblad	4	4	4	4	4	5	8	
315	Mark Belanger	4	4	4	4	4	5	8	50
316	Henry Cruz DP	4	4	4	4	4	5	8	
317	Dave Johnson	4	4	4	4	4	5	8	
318	Tom Griffin	4	4	4	4	4	5	8	
319	Alan Ashby	4	4	4	4	8	10	15	
320	Fred Lynn	4	4	4	4	6	8	12	
321	Santo Alcala	4	4	4	4	4	5	8	
322	Tom Paciorek	4	4	4	4	5	6	10	
323	Jim Fregosi DP	4	4	4	4	4	5	8	
324	Vern Rapp MG RC	4	4	4	4	4	5	8	
325	Bruce Sutter	4	4	4	4	8	10	15	1
326	Mike Lum DP	4	4	4	4	4	5	8	
327	Rick Langford DP RC	4	4	4	4	4	5	8	
328	Milwaukee Brewers CL	4	4	5	10	20	25	40	
329	John Verhoeven	4	4	4	4	4	5	8	
330	Bob Watson	4	8	10	20	40	50	250	
331	Mark Littell	4	4	4	4	4	5	8	
332	Duane Kuiper	4	4	4	4	4	5	8	
333	Jim Todd	4	4	4	4	8	10	15	
334	John Stearns	4	4	4	4	4	5	8	6
335	Bucky Dent	4	4	4	4	8	10	15	10
336	Steve Busby	4	4	4	4	4	5	8	6
337	Tom Grieve	4	4	4	4	4	5	8	5
338	Dave Heaverlo	4	4	4	4	8	10	15	
339	Mario Guerrero	4	4	4	4	4	5	8	
340	Bake McBride	4	4	4	4	4	5	8	5
341	Mike Flanagan	4	4	4	4	4	5	15	10
342	Aurelio Rodriguez	4	4	4	4	4	5	8	6
343	John Wathan DP	4	4	4	4	4	5	8	2
344	Sam Ewing RC	4	4	4	4	8	10	15	
345	Luis Tiant	4	4	4	4	4	5	8	5
346	Larry Biittner	4	4	4	4	8	10	15	
347	Terry Forster	5	10	12	25	50	60	100	
348	Del Unser	4	4	4	4	4	5	8	
349	Rick Camp DP	4	4	4	4	8	10	15	
350	Steve Garvey	4	4	4	4	8	10	15	10
351	Jeff Torborg	4	4	4	4	8	10	15	6
352	Tony Scott RC	4	4	4	4	4	5	8	4
353	Doug Bair RC	4	4	4	4	4	5	8	
354	Cesar Geronimo	4	4	4	4	4	5	8	15
355	Bill Travers	4	4	4	4	4	5	8	4
356	New York Mets CL	4	4	4	4	8	10	20	5
357	Tom Poquette	4	4	4	4	4	5	8	
358	Mark Lemongello	4	4	4	4	4	5	8	4
359	Marc Hill	4	4	4	4	4	5	8	
360	Mike Schmidt	6	8	10	12	▲20	25	40	500
361	Chris Knapp	4	4	4	4	8	10	15	60
362	Dave May	4	4	4	4	4	5	8	40
363	Bob Randall	4	4	4	4	6	8	12	
364	Jerry Turner	4	4	4	4	4	5	8	
365	Ed Figueroa	4	4	4	4	8	10	10	
366	Larry Milbourne DP	4	4	4	4	8	10	15	
367	Rick Dempsey	4	4	4	4	4	5	8	40
368	Balor Moore	4	4	4	4	4	5	8	
369	Tim Nordbrook	4	4	4	4	8	10	15	
370	Rusty Staub	4	4	4	4	8	10	15	40
371	Ray Burris	4	4	4	4	4	5	8	
372	Brian Asselstine	4	4	4	4	4	5	8	40
373	Jim Willoughby	4	4	4	4	8	10	15	
374A	Jose Morales	4	4	4	4	4	5	8	
375	Tommy John	4	4	4	4	4	5	8	50
376	Jim Wohlford	4	4	4	4	8	10	15	60
377	Manny Sarmiento	4	4	4	4	4	5	8	60
378	Bobby Winkles MG	4	4	4	4	4	5	8	40
379	Skip Lockwood	4	4	4	4	8	10	15	60
380	Ted Simmons	4	4	4	4	5	6	10	50
381	Philadelphia Phillies CL	4	4	4	4	4	5	8	40
382	Joe Lahoud	4	4	4	4	4	5	8	60
383	Mario Mendoza	4	4	4	4	4	5	8	40
384	Jack Clark	4	4	4	4	5	6	10	80
385	Tito Fuentes	4	4	4	4	5	6	10	
386	Bob Gorinski RC	4	4	4	4	8	10	15	
387	Ken Holtzman	4	4	4	4	5	6	10	
388	Bill Fahey DP	4	4	4	4	4	5	8	40
389	Julio Gonzalez RC	4	4	4	4	4	5	8	
390	Oscar Gamble	4	4	4	4	4	5	8	
391	Larry Haney	4	4	4	4	4	5	8	40
392	Billy Almon	4	4	4	4	4	5	8	40

#	Player	VgEx 4	EX 5	ExMt 6	NM 7	NmMt 8	NmMt+ 8.5	MT 9	Gem 9.5/10
393	Tippy Martinez	4	4	4		4	5	8	
394	Roy Howell DP	4	4	4		4	5	8	40
395	Jim Hughes	4	4	4	5	10	12	20	
396	Bob Stinson DP	4	4	4		4	5	8	40
397	Greg Gross	4	4	4		4	5	8	
398	Don Hood	4	4	4		4	5	8	40
399	Pete Mackanin	4	4	4		4	5	8	
400	Nolan Ryan	12	15	20	▲30	60	80	800	
401	Sparky Anderson MG	4	4	4	4	5	6	10	80
402	Dave Campbell	4	4	5	10	20	25	40	
403	Bud Harrelson	4	4	4		4	4	8	40
404	Detroit Tigers CL	4	4	4	4	5	6	10	80
405	Rawly Eastwick	4	4	4		4	5	8	
406	Mike Jorgensen	4	4	4		4	5	8	
407	Odell Jones RC	4	4	4		4	5	8	40
408	Joe Zdeb RC	4	4	4		4	5	8	
409	Ron Schueler	4	4	4		4	5	8	
410	Bill Madlock	4	4	4		4	5	8	
411	Mickey Rivers ALCS	4	4	4	4	5	6	10	80
412	Davey Lopes NLCS	4	4	4	4	8	10	15	120
413	Reggie Jackson WS	4	4	4	5	10	12	25	
414	Darold Knowles DP	4	4	4		4	5	8	
415	Ray Fosse	4	4	4		4	5	8	
416	Jack Brohamer	4	4	4		4	5	8	
417	Mike Garman DP	4	4	4		4	5	8	40
418	Tony Muser	4	4	4		4	5	8	60
419	Jerry Garvin RC	4	4	4	4	8	10	15	
420	Greg Luzinski	4	4	4		4	5	8	60
421	Junior Moore RC	4	4	4		4	5	8	40
422	Steve Braun	4	4	4		4	5	8	40
423	Dave Rosello	4	4	4		4	5	8	60
424	Boston Red Sox CL	4	4	4	4	8	10	15	60
425	Steve Rogers DP	4	4	4		4	5	8	40
426	Fred Kendall	4	4	4		4	5	8	60
427	Mario Soto RC	4	4	4		4	5	8	100
428	Joel Youngblood	4	4	4		4	5	8	60
429	Mike Barlow RC	4	4	4		4	5	8	50
430	Al Oliver	4	4	4		4	5	8	
431	Butch Metzger	4	4	4		4	5	8	
432	Terry Bulling RC	4	4	4		4	5	8	
433	Fernando Gonzalez	4	4	4		4	5	8	
434	Mike Norris	4	4	4		4	5	8	100
435	Checklist 364-484	4	4	4		4	5	8	60
436	Vic Harris DP	4	4	4		4	5	8	60
437	Bo McLaughlin	4	4	4		4	5	8	60
438	John Ellis	4	4	4		4	4.5	8	40
439	Ken Kravec	4	4	4		4	4	8	40
440	Dave Lopes	4	4	4		4	5	8	
441	Larry Gura	4	4	4		4	5	8	40
442	Elliott Maddox	4	4	4		4	5	8	
443	Darrel Chaney	4	4	4	4	4	5	8	
444	Roy Hartsfield MG	4	4	5	10	20	25	40	
445	Mike Ivie	4	4	4		4	5	8	40
446	Tug McGraw	4	4	4		4	5	8	60
447	Leroy Stanton	4	4	4		4	5	8	40
448	Bill Castro	4	4	4		4	5	8	60
449	Tim Blackwell DP RC	4	4	4		4	5	8	40
450	Tom Seaver	4	4	4	5	▲20	▲25	▲30	200
451	Minnesota Twins CL	4	4	4	4	8	10	15	
452	Jerry Mumphrey	4	4	4		4	5	8	60
453	Doug Flynn	4	4	4		4	5	8	40
454	Dave LaRoche	4	4	4		4	5	8	40
455	Bill Robinson	4	4	4		4	5	8	50
456	Vern Ruhle	4	4	5	10	20	25	50	
457	Bob Bailey	4	4	4		4	5	8	
458	Jeff Newman	4	4	4		4	5	8	40
459	Charlie Spikes	4	4	4		4	5	8	40
460	Jim Hunter	4	4	4	4	8	10	15	120
461	Rob Andrews DP	4	4	4		4	5	8	
462	Rogelio Moret	4	4	4		4	5	8	40
463	Kevin Bell	4	4	4		4	5	8	
464	Jerry Grote	4	4	4		4	5	8	
465	Hal McRae	4	4	4		4	5	8	
466	Dennis Blair	4	6	8	15	30	40	60	
467	Alvin Dark MG	4	4	4		4	5	8	50
468	Warren Cromartie RC	4	4	4		4	5	8	40
469	Rick Cerone	4	4	4		4	5	8	40

#	Player	VgEx 4	EX 5	ExMt 6	NM 7	NmMt 8	NmMt+ 8.5	MT 9	Gem 9.5/10
470	J.R. Richard	4	4	4		4	5	8	50
471	Roy Smalley	4	4	4		4	5	8	
472	Ron Reed	4	4	4		4	5	8	40
473	Bill Buckner	4	4	4		4	5	8	40
474	Jim Slaton	4	4	4		4	5	8	40
475	Gary Matthews	4	4	4		4	5	8	40
476	Bill Stein	4	4	4		4	5	8	40
477	Doug Capilla RC	4	4	4		4	5	8	
478	Jerry Remy	4	4	4		4	5	8	60
479	St. Louis Cardinals CL	4	4	4		4	5	8	
480	Ron LeFlore	4	4	4		4	5	8	40
481	Jackson Todd RC	4	4	4		4	8	10	
482	Rick Miller	4	4	4		4	8	10	15
483	Ken Macha RC	4	4	4		4	5	8	
484	Jim Norris RC	4	4	4		4	8	10	15
485	Chris Chambliss	4	4	4		4	5	10	60
486	John Curtis	4	4	4		4	5	8	60
487	Jim Tyrone	4	4	4		4	5	8	
488	Dan Spillner	4	4	4		4	5	8	40
489	Rudy Meoli	4	4	5	10	20	25	40	
490	Amos Otis	4	4	4		4	5	8	50
491	Scott McGregor	4	4	4	4	5	6	10	60
492	Jim Sundberg	4	4	4		4	5	8	50
493	Steve Renko	4	4	4		4	5		40
494	Chuck Tanner MG	4	4	4		4	5	8	40
495	Dave Cash	4	4	4		4	5	8	60
496	Jim Clancy DP RC	4	4	4		4	5	8	40
497	Glenn Adams	4	4	4		4	5	8	40
498	Joe Sambito	4	4	4		4	5	8	40
499	Seattle Mariners CL	4	4	4		4	5	8	40
500	George Foster	4	4	4		4	8	15	150
501	Dave Roberts	4	4	4		4	5	8	60
502	Pat Rockett RC	4	4	4		4	5	8	60
503	Ike Hampton RC	4	4	4		4	5	8	
504	Roger Freed	4	4	4		6	12	15	25
505	Felix Millan	4	4	4		4	5	8	
506	Ron Blomberg	4	4	5	10	20	25	40	
507	Willie Crawford	4	4	4		4	5	8	
508	Johnny Oates	4	4	4		8	15	20	30
509	Brent Strom	4	4	4		8	10	15	
510	Willie Stargell	4	4	4		8	10	15	100
511	Frank Duffy	4	4	4		4	5	8	40
512	Larry Herndon	4	4	4		8	10	15	
513	Barry Foote	4	4	4		4	5	8	
514	Rob Sperring	4	4	4		4	5	8	60
515	Tim Corcoran RC	4	4	4		8	10	15	
516	Gary Beare RC	4	4	4		8	10	15	
517	Andres Mora	4	4	4		8	10	15	
518	Tommy Boggs DP	4	4	4		4	5	8	50
519	Brian Downing	4	4	4		4	5	8	
520	Larry Hisle	4	4	4		4	5	8	80
521	Steve Staggs RC	4	4	4		4	5	8	60
522	Dick Williams MG	4	4	4		8	10		80
523	Donnie Moore RC	4	4	4		4	5	8	
524	Bernie Carbo	4	4	4		4	5	8	40
525	Jerry Terrell	4	4	4		8	10	15	60
526	Cincinnati Reds CL	4	5	6	12	25	30		150
527	Vic Correll	4	4	4		4	5	8	
528	Rob Picciolo RC	4	4	4		4	5	8	100
529	Paul Hartzell	4	4	4		4	5	8	40
530	Dave Winfield	4	4	4	6	12	15	30	200
531	Tom Underwood	4	4	4		8	10	15	
532	Skip Jutze	4	4	4		4	5	8	
533	Sandy Alomar	4	4	4		8	10	15	
534	Wilbur Howard	4	4	5	10	20	25	40	
535	Checklist 485-605	4	4	4		4	5	8	
536	Roric Harrison	4	4	4		4	5	8	
537	Bruce Bochte	4	4	4		8	10		40
538	Johnny LeMaster	4	4	4		8	10		
539	Vic Davalillo DP	4	4	4		4	5	8	50
540	Steve Carlton	4	4	4		8	10	15	200
541	Larry Cox	4	4	4		4	5	8	
542	Tim Johnson	4	4	4		8	10	15	
543	Larry Harlow DP RC	4	4	4		4	5	8	50
544	Len Randle DP	4	4	4		4	5	8	40
545	Bill Campbell	4	4	4		4	5	8	40
546	Ted Martinez	4	4	4		4	5	8	40

#	Player	VgEx 4	EX 5	ExMt 6	NM 7	NmMt 8	NmMt+ 8.5	MT 9	Gem 9.5/10
547	John Scott	4	4	4	4	4	5	8	40
548	Billy Hunter MG DP	4	4	4	4	4	5	8	40
549	Joe Kerrigan	4	4	4	4	4	5	8	
550	John Mayberry	4	4	4	4	4	5	8	50
551	Atlanta Braves CL	4	4	4	4	4	5	8	
552	Francisco Barrios	4	4	4	4	4	5	8	50
553	Terry Puhl RC	4	4	4	4	4	5	8	80
554	Joe Coleman	4	4	4	4	4	5	8	
555	Butch Wynegar	4	4	4	4	8	10	15	
556	Ed Armbrister	4	4	4	4	8	10	15	
557	Tony Solaita	4	4	4	4	4	5	8	40
558	Paul Mitchell	4	4	4	4	4	5	8	
559	Phil Mankowski	4	4	5	10	20	25	80	
560	Dave Parker	4	4	6	12	25	30	120	
561	Charlie Williams	4	4	4	4	4	5	8	
562	Glenn Burke RC	4	4	5	10	20	25	60	
563	Dave Rader	4	5	6	12	25	30	50	
564	Mick Kelleher	4	4	4	4	4	5	8	60
565	Jerry Koosman	4	4	4	4	4	5	8	50
566	Merv Rettenmund	4	4	4	4	4	5	8	60
567	Dick Drago	4	4	4	4	4	5	8	
568	Tom Hutton	4	4	4	4	4	5	8	60
569	Lary Sorensen RC	4	4	4	4	4	5	8	
570	Dave Kingman	4	4	4	4	5	6	10	60
571	Buck Martinez	4	4	4	4	4	5	8	40
572	Rick Wise	4	4	5	10	20	25	40	
573	Luis Gomez	4	4	4	6	12	15	25	
574	Bob Lemon MG	4	4	4	6	12	15	25	
575	Pat Dobson	4	4	4	4	4	5	8	40
576	Sam Mejias	4	4	4	4	8	10	100	
577	Oakland Athletics CL	4	4	4	4	4	5	8	40
578	Buzz Capra	4	4	4	4	4	5	8	
579	Rance Mulliniks RC	4	4	4	4	4	5	8	
580	Rod Carew	4	4	4	8	15	20	80	
581	Lynn McGlothen	4	4	4	4	4	5	8	40
582	Fran Healy	4	4	4	4	8	10	15	
583	George Medich	4	4	4	4	4	5	8	40
584	John Hale	4	4	4	4	8	10	15	60
585	Woodie Fryman DP	4	4	4	4	4	5	8	40
586	Ed Goodson	4	4	4	4	8	10	15	60
587	John Urrea RC	4	4	4	4	4	5	8	
588	Jim Mason	4	4	4	4	4	5	8	
589	Bob Knepper RC	4	4	4	4	4	5	8	
590	Bobby Murcer	4	4	4	5	10	12	20	
591	George Zeber RC	4	4	4	4	5	6	10	80
592	Bob Apodaca	4	4	4	4	8	10	15	
593	Dave Skaggs RC	4	4	4	4	4	5	8	60
594	Dave Freisleben	4	4	4	4	4	5	8	50
595	Sixto Lezcano	4	4	4	4	4	5	8	40
596	Gary Wheelock	4	4	4	4	4	5	8	40
597	Steve Dillard	4	4	4	4	8	10	15	
598	Eddie Solomon	4	4	4	4	4	5	8	
599	Gary Woods	4	4	4	4	4	5	8	
600	Frank Tanana	4	4	4	4	4	5	8	
601	Gene Mauch MG	4	4	4	4	8	10	15	
602	Eric Soderholm	4	4	4	4	4	5	8	80
603	Will McEnaney	4	4	4	4	4	5	8	
604	Earl Williams	4	4	4	4	4	5	8	40
605	Rick Rhoden	4	4	4	4	4	5	8	50
606	Pittsburgh Pirates CL	4	4	4	4	8	10	15	
607	Fernando Arroyo	4	4	4	4	8	10	15	
608	Johnny Grubb	4	4	4	4	8	10	15	
609	John Denny	4	4	4	4	8	10	60	
610	Garry Maddox	4	4	4	4	8	10	15	50
611	Pat Scanlon RC	4	4	4	4	4	5	8	
612	Ken Henderson	4	4	4	4	4	5	8	
613	Marty Perez	4	4	4	4	4	5	8	40
614	Joe Wallis	4	4	4	4	4	5	8	
615	Clay Carroll	4	4	4	4	4	5	8	
616	Pat Kelly	4	4	4	4	4	5	8	
617	Joe Nolan RC	4	4	4	4	4	5	8	
618	Tommy Helms	4	4	4	4	8	10	60	60
619	Thad Bosley DP RC	4	4	4	4	4	5	8	
620	Willie Randolph	4	4	4	4	8	10	15	100
621	Craig Swan DP	4	4	4	4	4	5	8	40

#	Player	VgEx 4	EX 5	ExMt 6	NM 7	NmMt 8	NmMt+ 8.5	MT 9	Gem 9.5
622	Champ Summers	4	4	4	4	4	5	8	
623	Eduardo Rodriguez	4	4	4	4	4	5	8	
624	Gary Alexander DP	4	4	4	4	4	5	8	
625	Jose Cruz	4	4	4	4	4	5	8	
626	Toronto Blue Jays CL DP	4	4	4	4	4	5	8	
627	David Johnson	4	4	4	4	4	5	8	
628	Ralph Garr	4	4	4	4	4	5	8	
629	Don Stanhouse	4	4	4	4	4	5	8	
630	Ron Cey	4	6	8	15	30	40	60	
631	Danny Ozark MG	4	4	4	4	4	5	8	
632	Rowland Office	4	4	4	4	4	5	8	
633	Tom Veryzer	4	4	4	4	4	5	8	
634	Len Barker	4	4	4	4	4	5	8	
635	Joe Rudi	4	4	4	4	4	5	8	
636	Jim Bibby	4	4	4	4	8	10	15	
637	Duffy Dyer	4	4	4	4	4	5	8	
638	Paul Splittorff	4	4	4	4	4	5	8	
639	Gene Clines	4	4	4	4	4	5	8	
640	Lee May DP	4	4	4	4	4	5	8	6
641	Doug Rau	4	4	4	4	4	5	8	
642	Denny Doyle	4	4	5	10	20	25	120	
643	Tom House	4	4	4	4	4	5	8	
644	Jim Dwyer	4	4	4	4	4	5	8	
645	Mike Torrez	4	4	4	4	8	10	15	
646	Rick Auerbach DP	4	4	4	4	4	5	8	5
647	Steve Dunning	4	4	4	4	4	5	8	4
648	Gary Thomasson	4	4	4	4	4	5	8	4
649	Moose Haas RC	4	4	4	4	4	5	8	
650	Cesar Cedeno	4	4	4	4	4	5	8	
651	Doug Rader	4	4	4	4	8	10	15	
652	Checklist 606-726	4	4	4	4	5	6	10	5
653	Ron Hodges DP	4	4	4	4	4	5	8	4
654	Pepe Frias	4	4	4	4	4	5	8	
655	Lyman Bostock	4	4	4	4	4	5	8	4
656	Dave Garcia MG RC	4	4	4	4	4	5	8	
657	Bombo Rivera	4	4	4	4	4	5	8	
658	Manny Sanguillen	4	4	4	4	4	5	8	
659	Texas Rangers CL	4	4	4	4	4	5	8	4
660	Jason Thompson	4	4	4	4	4	5	8	6
661	Grant Jackson	4	4	4	4	4	5	8	4
662	Paul Dade RC	4	4	4	4	4	5	8	
663	Paul Reuschel	4	4	4	4	4	5	8	4
664	Fred Stanley	4	4	4	6	12	15	25	
665	Dennis Leonard	4	4	4	4	8	10	15	
666	Billy Smith RC	4	4	4	4	4	5	8	8
667	Jeff Byrd RC	4	4	4	4	4	5	8	60
668	Dusty Baker	4	4	4	4	4	5	8	
669	Pete Falcone	4	4	4	4	4	5	8	6
670	Jim Rice	4	4	4	6	12	15	25	175
671	Gary Lavelle	4	4	4	4	4	5	8	
672	Don Kessinger	4	4	4	4	4	5	8	
673	Steve Brye	4	4	4	4	8	10	60	
674	Ray Knight RC	4	4	4	4	5	6	10	80
675	Jay Johnstone	4	4	4	4	8	10	15	80
676	Bob Myrick	4	4	4	4	4	5	8	40
677	Ed Herrmann	4	4	4	4	4	5	8	
678	Tom Burgmeier	4	4	4	4	4	5	8	40
679	Wayne Garrett	4	4	4	4	4	5	8	40
680	Vida Blue	4	4	4	4	4	5	8	50
681	Rob Belloir	4	4	4	4	8	10	15	
682	Ken Brett	4	4	4	4	8	10	15	
683	Mike Champion	4	4	4	4	4	5	8	60
684	Ralph Houk MG	4	4	4	4	8	10	15	60
685	Frank Taveras	4	4	4	4	4	5	8	60
686	Gaylord Perry	4	4	4	4	5	6	10	
687	Julio Cruz RC	4	4	4	4	4	5	8	
688	George Mitterwald	4	4	4	4	4	5	8	
689	Cleveland Indians CL	4	4	4	4	8	10	15	
690	Mickey Rivers	5	10	12	25	50	60	120	
691	Ross Grimsley	4	4	4	4	4	5	8	
692	Ken Reitz	4	4	4	4	4	5	8	60
693	Lamar Johnson	4	4	4	4	8	10	15	
694	Elias Sosa	4	4	4	4	4	5	8	40
695	Dwight Evans	4	4	4	6	12	15	25	

	VgEx 4	EX 5	ExMt 6	NM 7	NmMt 8	NmMt+ 8.5	MT 9	Gem 9.5/10
Steve Mingori	4	4	4	4	4	5	8	40
Roger Metzger	4	4	4	4	4	5	8	40
Juan Bernhardt	4	4	4	4	4	5	8	40
Jackie Brown	4	4	4	4	4	5	8	40
Johnny Bench	4	4	4	8	▲25	▲30	60	600
Rookie Pitchers	4	4	4	4	4	5	8	
Rookie Catchers	4	4	4	4	8	10	15	60
Jack Morris DP RC	4	6	▲15	▲20	▲25	▲30	40	▲1,000
Lou Whitaker RC	8	10	20	25	▲40	▲50	▲120	1,000
Rookie Outfielders	4	4	4	4	4	5	8	
Rookie 1st Basemen	4	4	4	4	5	6	10	60
P.Molitor RC/A.Trammell RC	20	30	▲50	60	120	▲200	▲1,000	12,000
D.Murphy/L.Parrish RC	4	4	6	12	20	25	40	450
Rookie Pitchers	4	4	4	4	4	5	8	40
Rookie Outfielders	4	8	10	20	40	50	80	
Rookie Pitchers	4	4	4	4	4	5	8	60
Bobby Valentine	4	4	4	4	4	5	8	
Bob Davis	4	4	4	4	4	5	8	
Mike Anderson	4	4	4	4	4	5	8	60
Jim Kaat	4	4	4	4	5	6	10	
Clarence Gaston	4	4	4	4	4	5	8	
Nelson Briles	4	4	4	4	8	10	15	
Ron Jackson	4	4	4	4	4	5	8	60
Randy Elliott RC	4	4	4	4	8	10	15	
Fergie Jenkins	4	4	4	5	10	12	20	250
Billy Martin MG	4	4	4	4	8	8	15	100
Pete Broberg	4	4	4	4	4	5	8	60
John Wockenfuss	4	4	4	4	8	10	15	60
Kansas City Royals CL	4	4	5	10	20	25	40	
Kurt Bevacqua	4	4	5	10	20	25	50	
Wilbur Wood	4	4	4	6	8	12	50	

George Brett #100 PSA 10 (Gem) sold for $1,229 (eBay; 8/07)
Lou Brock RB #1 PSA 10 (Gem) sold for $120 (eBay; 3/07)
Reggie Jackson RB #7 PSA 10 (Gem) sold for $283 (eBay; 7/07)
Reggie Jackson RB #7 PSA 10 (Gem) sold for $261 (eBay; 10/07)
Reggie Jackson WS #413 PSA 10 (Gem) sold for $254 (eBay; 9/07)
Sparky Lyle RB #2 PSA 10 (Gem) sold for $114 (eBay; 3/07)
P.Molitor/A.Trammell #707 BVG 9.5 (Gem) sold for $1,155 (eBay; 4/07)
P.Molitor/A.Trammell #707 GAI 9.5 (Gem) sold for $360 (eBay; 4/07)
Jack Morris #703 BVG 9.5 (Gem) sold for $210 (eBay; 5/08)
Thurman Munson #60 PSA 10 (Gem) sold for $592 (eBay; 9/07)
Thurman Munson #60 PSA 10 (Gem) sold for $566 (eBay; 7/07)
Thurman Munson #60 PSA 10 (Gem) sold for $524 (eBay; 3/08)
Eddie Murray #36 BVG 9.5 (Gem) sold for $1,875 (eBay; 11/07)
Eddie Murray #36 BVG 9.5 (Gem) sold for $1,775 (eBay; 7/07)
Eddie Murray #36 BVG 9.5 (Gem) sold for $1,390 (eBay; 12/07)
Eddie Murray #36 BVG 9.5 (Gem) sold for $1,030 (eBay; 8/07)
Eddie Murray #36 BVG 9.5 (Gem) sold for $923 (eBay; 2/08)
Eddie Murray #36 GAI 9.5 (Gem) sold for $523 (eBay; 9/07)
Nolan Ryan RB #6 PSA 10 (Gem) sold for $585 (eBay; 10/07)
Jackson Todd #481 PSA 9 (MT) sold for $364 (eBay; 4/08)
Jackson Todd #481 PSA 9 (MT) sold for $305 (eBay; 3/07)
Carl Yastrzemski #40 PSA 10 (Gem) sold for $416 (eBay; 4/07)

1979 Kellogg's

	VG 3	VgEx 4	EX 5	ExMt 6	NM 7	NmMt 8	MT 9	Gem 9.5/10
Bruce Sutter	4	4	4	4	4	5	10	30
Ted Simmons	4	4	4	4	4	4	8	
Ross Grimsley	4	4	4	4	4	4	8	
Wayne Nordhagen	4	4	4	4	4	4	8	25
3 Jim Palmer Pct .650	4	4	4	4	4	5	10	
John Henry Johnson	4	4	4	4	4	5	10	
Jason Thompson	4	4	4	4	4	4	8	
Pat Zachry	4	4	4	4	4	4	8	25
Dennis Eckersley	4	4	4	4	4	5	10	
0B Paul Splittorff IP 1666	4	4	4	4	4	4	8	25
1B Ron Guidry Hits 396	4	4	4	4	4	5	10	
2 Jeff Burroughs	4	4	4	4	4	4	8	
Rod Carew	4	4	4	4	4	5	10	
4A Buddy Bell No Trade	4	4	4	4	4	4	8	
5 Jim Rice	4	4	4	4	4	5	10	
6 Garry Maddox	4	4	4	4	4	4	8	
7 Willie McCovey	4	4	4	4	4	5	10	40

	VG 3	VgEx 4	EX 5	ExMt 6	NM 7	NmMt 8	MT 9	Gem 9.5/10
18 Steve Carlton	4	4	4	4	4	5	10	
19B J.R. Richard Stats Begin 1971	4	4	4	4	4	4	8	
20 Paul Molitor	4	4	4	4	4	8	15	
21B Dave Parker Avg. 318	4	4	4	4	4	4	10	
22A Pete Rose 1978 3B 3	4	4	4	4	5	10	20	80
23B Vida Blue Runs 818	4	4	4	4	4	4	8	
24 Richie Zisk	4	4	4	4	4	4	8	
25B Darrell Porter 2B 111	4	4	4	4	4	4	8	25
26A Dan Driessen Games 742	4	4	4	4	4	4	8	
27B Geoff Zahn 1978 Minnesota	4	4	4	4	4	8	15	
28 Phil Niekro	4	4	4	4	4	5	10	
29 Tom Seaver	4	4	4	4	4	8	15	
30 Fred Lynn	4	4	4	4	4	5	10	
31 Bill Bonham	4	4	4	4	4	4	8	
32 George Foster	4	4	4	4	4	5	10	
34B John Candelaria Age 25	4	4	4	4	4	4	8	
35 Bob Knepper	4	4	4	4	4	4	8	25
36 Fred Patek	4	4	4	4	4	4	8	
37 Chris Chambliss	4	4	4	4	4	4	8	25
38B Bob Forsch 1977 Games 35	4	4	4	4	4	4	8	
40 Jack Clark	4	4	4	4	4	4	8	
41B Dwight Evans 1978 Hits 123	4	4	4	4	4	5	10	
42 Lee Mazzilli	4	4	4	4	4	4	8	
43 Mario Guerrero	4	4	4	4	4	4	8	25
44 Larry Bowa	4	4	4	4	4	4	8	
45A Carl Yastrzemski AB 9930 SP	4	4	4	4	5	10	20	
45B Carl Yastrzemski AB 9929	4	4	4	4	4	8	15	
46B Reggie Jackson 1978 Games 1394	4	4	4	4	4	8	15	
47 Rick Reuschel	4	4	4	4	4	4	8	
48B Mike Flanagan 1976 SO 56	4	4	4	4	4	4	8	
49A Gaylord Perry 1973 Hits 315	4	4	4	4	4	5	10	
50 George Brett	4	4	4	4	4	8	15	
51B Craig Reynolds In Those	4	4	4	4	4	4	8	
52 Dave Lopes	4	4	4	4	4	4	8	
53B Bill Almon 2B 41	4	4	4	4	4	4	8	
54 Roy Howell	4	4	4	4	4	4	8	
55 Frank Tanana	4	4	4	4	4	4	8	25
56B Doug Rau 1978 Pct. .625	4	4	4	4	4	8	15	
58 Jon Matlack	4	4	4	4	4	4	8	
59B Ron Jackson The Twins	4	4	4	4	4	4	8	
60 Jim Sundberg	4	4	4	4	4	5	10	

1979 Ogden A's TCMA

	VG 3	VgEx 4	EX 5	ExMt 6	NM 7	NmMt 8	MT 9	Gem 9.5/10
9 Rickey Henderson	4	6	8	12	20	120	300	

1979 O-Pee-Chee

	GD 2	VG 3	VgEx 4	EX 5	ExMt 6	NM 7	NmMt 8	MT 9
51 Nolan Ryan	4	4	4	4	8	15	30	200
52 Ozzie Smith RC	4	5	15	20	40	▲100	▲250	800

Nolan Ryan #51 BVG 9.5 (Gem) sold for $280 (eBay; 1/07)
Ozzie Smith #52 PSA 10 (Gem) sold for $7,271 (eBay; 5/07)
Ozzie Smith #52 PSA 10 (Gem) sold for $3,819 (REA; 4/07)
Ozzie Smith #52 PSA 10 (Gem) sold for $2,790 (eBay; 5/08)
Steve Stone #115 PSA 10 (Gem) sold for $3,174 (eBay; 1/13)

1979 Topps

	VgEx 4	EX 5	ExMt 6	NM 7	NmMt 8	NmMt+ 8.5	MT 9	Gem 9.5/10
1 Batting Leaders	4	4	4	6	12	15	25	
2 Home Run Leaders	4	6	8	15	30	40	60	
3 RBI Leaders	4	4	4	4	8	10	15	
4 Stolen Base Leaders	4	4	4	4	5	6	10	
5 Victory Leaders	4	4	4	4	5	6	10	
6 Strikeout Leaders	4	4	4	4	8	10	20	100
7 ERA Leaders	4	4	5	10	20	25	40	
8 Leading Firemen	4	4	4	4	5	6	10	
9 Dave Campbell	4	4	4	4	5	6	10	
10 Lee May	4	4	4	4	4	5	10	
11 Marc Hill	4	4	4	4	8	10	15	
12 Dick Drago	4	4	4	4	4	5	10	
13 Paul Dade	4	4	4	4	8	10	15	
14 Rafael Landestoy RC	4	4	4	4	5	6	10	

#	Player	VgEx 4	EX 5	ExMt 6	NM 7	NmMt 8	NmMt+ 8.5	MT 9	Gem 9.5/10
15	Ross Grimsley	4	4	4	4	5	6	10	
16	Fred Stanley	4	4	4	4	5	6	10	
17	Donnie Moore	4	4	4	4	5	6	10	
18	Tony Solaita	4	4	4	4	5	6	10	
19	Larry Gura DP	4	4	4	4	5	6	10	
20	Joe Morgan DP	4	4	4	5	10	12	20	150
21	Kevin Kobel	4	4	4	4	5	6	10	
22	Mike Jorgensen	4	4	4	4	5	6	10	
23	Terry Forster	4	4	4	4	5	6	10	
24	Paul Molitor	8	10	12	25	30	40	200	
25	Steve Carlton	4	4	4	4	8	10	20	200
26	Jamie Quirk	4	4	4	4	8	10	50	
27	Dave Goltz	4	4	4	4	8	10	15	
28	Steve Brye	4	4	4	6	10	15		
29	Rick Langford	4	4	4	4	8	10	15	
30	Dave Winfield	6	8	10	20	40	50	80	
31	Tom House DP	4	4	4	4	8	10	15	
32	Jerry Mumphrey	4	4	4	4	5	6	10	
33	Dave Rozema	4	4	4	4	5	6	10	
34	Rob Andrews	4	4	4	4	8	10	15	
35	Ed Figueroa	4	4	4	4	5	6	50	
36	Alan Ashby	4	4	4	4	8	10	15	
37	Joe Kerrigan DP	4	4	4	4	5	6	10	
38	Bernie Carbo	4	4	4	4	8	10	15	40
39	Dale Murphy	4	4	4	8	15	20	40	
40	Dennis Eckersley	4	4	4	8	15	20	60	
41	Minnesota Twins CL/Mauch	4	4	4	4	8	10	15	
42	Ron Blomberg	4	4	4	4	5	6	10	50
43	Wayne Twitchell	4	4	4	4	5	6	10	
44	Kurt Bevacqua	4	4	4	4	5	6	10	
45	Al Hrabosky	4	4	4	4	5	6	10	
46	Ron Hodges	4	4	4	4	8	10	15	
47	Fred Norman	4	4	4	4	5	6	10	
48	Merv Rettenmund	4	4	4	4	5	6	10	
49	Vern Ruhle	4	4	4	4	5	6	10	
50	Steve Garvey DP	4	4	4	4	8	10	15	200
51	Ray Fosse DP	4	4	4	4	5	6	10	
52	Randy Lerch	4	4	4	4	5	6	10	
53	Mick Kelleher	4	4	4	4	8	10	15	
54	Dell Alston DP	4	4	4	4	5	6	10	40
55	Willie Stargell	4	5	10	20	40	50	400	
56	John Hale	4	4	4	4	5	6	10	
57	Eric Rasmussen	4	4	4	6	10	15		
58	Bob Randall DP	4	4	4	4	5	6	10	40
59	John Denny DP	4	4	4	4	5	6	10	40
60	Mickey Rivers	4	4	4	4	6	8	12	50
61	Bo Diaz	4	4	4	4	5	6	10	
62	Randy Moffitt	4	4	4	4	5	6	10	
63	Jack Brohamer	4	4	4	4	5	6	10	
64	Tom Underwood	4	4	4	4	8	10	15	
65	Mark Belanger	4	4	4	4	5	6	10	80
66	Detroit Tigers CL/Moss	4	4	4	4	8	10	15	
67	Jim Mason DP	4	4	4	4	5	6	10	
68	Joe Niekro DP	4	4	4	4	5	6	10	
69	Elliott Maddox	4	4	4	4	5	6	10	
70	John Candelaria	4	4	4	4	8	10	15	50
71	Brian Downing	4	4	4	4	5	6	10	
72	Steve Mingori	4	4	4	4	5	6	10	
73	Ken Henderson	4	4	4	4	8	10	15	
74	Shane Rawley RC	4	4	4	4	8	10	15	
75	Steve Yeager	4	4	4	4	5	6	10	
76	Warren Cromartie	4	4	4	4	5	6	10	
77	Dan Briggs DP	4	4	4	4	8	10	15	
78	Elias Sosa	4	4	4	4	8	10	15	
79	Ted Cox	4	4	4	4	8	10	15	
80	Jason Thompson	4	4	4	4	5	6	10	
81	Roger Erickson RC	4	4	4	4	5	6	10	40
82	New York Mets CL/Torre	4	4	4	5	10	12	50	
83	Fred Kendall	4	4	4	4	8	10	15	
84	Greg Minton	4	4	4	4	8	10	15	
85	Gary Matthews	4	4	4	4	5	6	10	
86	Rodney Scott	4	4	4	4	5	6	10	
87	Pete Falcone	4	4	4	4	5	6	10	

#	Player	VgEx 4	EX 5	ExMt 6	NM 7	NmMt 8	NmMt+ 8.5	MT 9	Gem 9.5
88	Bob Molinaro RC	4	4	4	4	5	6	10	
89	Dick Tidrow	4	4	4	4	5	6	10	
90	Bob Boone	4	4	4	4	8	10	15	
91	Terry Crowley	4	4	4	4	8	10	60	
92	Jim Bibby	4	4	4	4	8	10	15	
93	Phil Mankowski	4	4	4	4	5	6	10	
94	Len Barker	4	4	4	4	5	6	10	
95	Robin Yount	4	4	4	5	12	15	30	
96	Cleveland Indians CL/Torborg	4	4	4	4	5	6	10	
97	Sam Mejias	4	4	4	6	10	15		
98	Ray Burris	4	4	4	4	5	6	10	
99	John Wathan	4	4	4	4	5	6	10	
100	Tom Seaver DP	4	4	4	4	8	10	20	3
101	Roy Howell	4	4	4	4	5	6	10	
102	Mike Anderson	4	4	4	6	10	15		
103	Jim Todd	4	4	4	4	5	6	10	
104	Johnny Oates DP	4	4	4	4	5	6	10	
105	Rick Camp DP	4	4	4	6	10	15		
106	Frank Duffy	4	4	4	4	5	6	10	
107	Jesus Alou DP	4	4	4	4	5	6	10	
108	Eduardo Rodriguez	4	4	4	4	5	6	10	
109	Joel Youngblood	4	4	4	4	5	6	10	
110	Vida Blue	4	4	4	4	5	6	10	
111	Roger Freed	4	4	4	4	8	10	15	
112	Philadelphia Phillies CL/Ozark	4	4	4	4	8	10	15	
113	Pete Redfern	4	4	4	4	8	10	15	
114	Cliff Johnson	4	4	4	4	8	10	15	
115	Nolan Ryan	8	10	15	▲25	▲40	▲100	▲150	
116	Ozzie Smith RC	25	30	40	80	▲200	500	▲1,200	
117	Grant Jackson	4	4	4	4	5	6	10	
118	Bud Harrelson	4	4	4	4	8	10	15	
119	Don Stanhouse	4	4	4	4	8	10	15	
120	Jim Sundberg	4	4	4	4	5	6	10	
121	Checklist 1-121 DP	4	4	4	4	5	6	10	
122	Mike Paxton	4	4	4	4	5	6	10	
123	Lou Whitaker	4	4	4	4	8	10	15	
124	Dan Schatzeder	4	4	4	4	8	10	15	
125	Rick Burleson	4	4	4	4	5	6	10	
126	Doug Bair	4	4	4	4	5	6	10	
127	Thad Bosley	4	4	4	4	5	6	10	5
128	Ted Martinez	4	4	4	4	8	10	15	
129	Marty Pattin DP	4	4	4	4	5	6	10	
130	Bob Watson DP	4	4	4	4	5	6	10	4
131	Jim Clancy	4	4	4	4	5	6	10	
132	Rowland Office	4	4	4	4	5	6	10	4
133	Bill Castro	4	4	4	4	8	10	15	
134	Alan Bannister	4	4	4	4	5	6	10	
135	Bobby Murcer	4	4	4	4	5	6	10	8
136	Jim Kaat	4	4	4	4	6	8	12	
137	Larry Wolfe DP RC	4	4	4	4	5	6	10	
138	Mark Lee RC	4	4	4	4	8	10	15	
139	Luis Pujols RC	4	4	4	4	5	6	10	
140	Don Gullett	4	4	4	4	5	6	10	
141	Tom Paciorek	4	4	4	4	5	6	10	
142	Charlie Williams	4	4	4	4	5	6	10	
143	Tony Scott	4	4	4	4	8	10	15	
144	Sandy Alomar	4	4	4	4	8	10	15	
145	Rick Rhoden	4	4	4	4	5	6	10	
146	Duane Kuiper	4	4	4	4	5	6	10	4
147	Dave Hamilton	4	4	4	4	5	6	10	
148	Bruce Boisclair	4	4	4	4	5	6	10	
149	Manny Sarmiento	4	4	4	4	5	6	10	
150	Wayne Cage	4	4	4	4	8	10	15	
151	John Hiller	4	4	4	4	5	6	10	
152	Rick Cerone	4	4	4	4	5	6	10	40
153	Dennis Lamp	4	4	4	4	5	6	10	
154	Jim Gantner DP	4	4	4	4	5	6	10	
155	Dwight Evans	4	4	4	4	5	6	10	120
156	Buddy Solomon RC	4	4	4	4	5	6	10	
157	U.L. Washington	4	4	4	6	10	15		
158	Joe Sambito	4	4	4	4	8	10	15	
159	Roy White	4	4	4	4	8	10	15	
160	Mike Flanagan	4	4	4	4	5	6	10	

Player	VgEx 4	EX 5	ExMt 6	NM 7	NmMt 8	NmMt+ 8.5	MT 9	Gem 9.5/10
Barry Foote	4	4	4	4	5	6	10	
Tom Johnson	4	4	4	4	5	6	10	
Glenn Burke	4	4	4	4	5	6	10	
Mickey Lolich	4	4	4	4	8	10	15	
Frank Taveras	4	4	4	4	5	6	10	
Leon Roberts	4	4	4	4	5	6	10	
Roger Metzger DP	4	4	5	10	20	25	40	80
Dave Freisleben	4	4	4	6	10	15		
Bill Nahorodny	4	4	4	4	8	10	15	
Don Sutton	4	4	4	4	5	6	10	
Gene Clines	4	4	4	4	5	6	10	
Mike Bruhert RC	4	4	4	4	8	10	15	
John Lowenstein	4	4	4	4	5	6	10	
Rick Auerbach	4	4	4	4	5	6	10	
George Hendrick	4	4	4	4	5	6	10	
Aurelio Rodriguez	4	4	4	4	8	10	15	40
Ron Reed	4	4	4	4	5	6	10	
Alvis Woods	4	4	4	4	5	6	10	
Jim Beattie DP RC	4	4	4	4	5	6	10	40
Larry Hisle	4	4	4	4	8	10	15	
Mike Garman	4	4	4	4	5	6	10	
Tim Johnson	4	4	4	4	5	6	10	
Paul Splittorff	4	4	4	4	8	10	15	
Darrel Chaney	4	4	4	4	5	6	10	
Mike Torrez	4	4	4	4	5	6	10	
Eric Soderholm	4	4	4	4	5	6	10	
Mark Lemongello	4	4	4	6	10	15		
Pat Kelly	4	4	4	4	5	6	10	
Ed Whitson RC	4	4	4	4	5	6	10	
Ron Cey	4	4	4	4	6	8	12	
Mike Norris	4	4	4	4	5	6	10	
St. Louis Cardinals CL/Boyer	4	4	4	4	8	10	15	
Glenn Adams	4	4	4	4	5	6	10	
Randy Jones	4	4	4	4	5	6	10	
Bill Madlock	4	4	4	4	8	10	15	
Steve Kemp DP	4	4	4	4	5	6	10	40
Bob Apodaca	4	4	4	4	5	6	10	40
Johnny Grubb	4	4	4	4	5	6	10	
Larry Milbourne	4	4	4	4	5	6	10	
Johnny Bench DP	4	4	4	5	15	20	▲30	150
Mike Edwards RB	4	4	4	4	5	6	10	
Ron Guidry RB	4	4	4	4	5	6	10	
J.R. Richard RB	4	4	4	4	5	6	10	
Pete Rose RB	4	4	4	5	12	15	20	150
John Stearns RB	4	4	4	4	5	6	10	
Sammy Stewart RB	4	4	4	4	5	6	10	40
Dave Lemanczyk	4	4	4	4	5	6	10	
Clarence Gaston	4	4	4	4	5	6	10	
Reggie Cleveland	4	4	4	4	5	6	10	
Larry Bowa	4	4	4	4	5	6	10	40
Dennis Martinez	4	4	4	4	5	6	10	
Carney Lansford RC	4	4	4	4	8	10	15	
Bill Travers	4	4	4	6	10	15		
Boston Red Sox CL/Zimmer	4	4	4	4	5	6	10	
Willie McCovey	4	4	4	6	12	15	25	
Wilbur Wood	4	4	4	4	5	6	10	
Steve Dillard	4	4	4	4	5	6	10	
Dennis Leonard	4	4	4	4	5	6	10	
Roy Smalley	4	4	4	4	5	6	10	40
Cesar Geronimo	4	4	4	4	5	6	10	
Jesse Jefferson	4	4	4	6	10	15		
Bob Beall RC	4	4	4	4	5	6	10	40
Kent Tekulve	4	4	4	4	5	6	10	
Dave Revering	4	4	4	4	5	6	10	
Goose Gossage	4	4	4	4	8	10	15	60
Ron Pruitt	4	4	4	4	8	10	15	
Steve Stone	4	4	4	4	5	6	10	
Vic Davalillo	4	4	4	4	5	6	10	
Doug Flynn	4	4	4	4	5	6	10	
Bob Forsch	4	4	5	4	5	6	10	
John Wockenfuss	4	4	4	4	5	6	10	
Jimmy Sexton RC	4	4	4	4	5	6	10	
Paul Mitchell	4	4	4	4	5	6	10	

Card	Player	VgEx 4	EX 5	ExMt 6	NM 7	NmMt 8	NmMt+ 8.5	MT 9	Gem 9.5/10
234	Toby Harrah	4	4	4	4	5	6	10	40
235	Steve Rogers	4	4	4	4	5	6	10	
236	Jim Dwyer	4	4	6	10	15			
237	Billy Smith	4	4	4	4	8	10	15	
238	Balor Moore	4	4	4	4	5	6	10	
239	Willie Horton	4	4	4	4	5	6	10	
240	Rick Reuschel	4	4	4	4	8	10	15	
241	Checklist 122-242 DP	4	4	4	4	8	10	15	
242	Pablo Torrealba	4	4	4	4	8	10	15	
243	Buck Martinez DP	4	4	4	4	5	6	10	40
244	Pittsburgh Pirates CL/Tanner	4	4	4	4	8	10	15	
245	Jeff Burroughs	4	4	4	4	5	6	10	40
246	Darrell Jackson RC	4	4	4	4	8	10	15	
247	Tucker Ashford DP	4	4	4	4	5	6	10	40
248	Pete LaCock	4	4	4	4	5	6	10	
249	Paul Thormodsgard	4	4	4	4	8	10	15	
250	Willie Randolph	4	4	4	4	5	6	10	100
251	Jack Morris	4	4	4	4	5	6	10	
252	Bob Stinson	4	4	4	4	5	6	10	
253	Rick Wise	4	4	4	4	5	6	10	
254	Luis Gomez	4	4	4	4	8	10	15	
255	Tommy John	4	4	4	4	5	6	10	60
256	Mike Sadek	4	4	4	4	5	6	10	
257	Adrian Devine	4	4	4	4	8	10	15	
258	Mike Phillips	4	4	4	6	10	15		
259	Cincinnati Reds CL/Anderson	4	4	4	4	5	6	10	
260	Richie Zisk	4	4	4	4	5	6	10	
261	Mario Guerrero	4	4	4	4	5	6	10	
262	Nelson Briles	4	4	4	4	5	6	10	
263	Oscar Gamble	4	4	4	4	5	6	10	40
264	Don Robinson RC	4	4	4	4	5	6	10	40
265	Don Money	4	4	4	4	5	6	10	
266	Jim Willoughby	4	4	4	4	5	6	10	
267	Joe Rudi	4	4	4	4	5	6	10	
268	Julio Gonzalez	4	4	4	4	5	6	10	
269	Woodie Fryman	4	4	4	4	5	6	10	
270	Butch Hobson	4	4	4	4	8	10	15	
271	Rawly Eastwick	4	4	4	4	5	6	10	
272	Tim Corcoran	4	4	4	4	5	6	10	
273	Jerry Terrell	4	4	4	6	10	15		
274	Willie Norwood	4	4	4	4	5	6	10	
275	Junior Moore	4	4	4	4	5	6	10	
276	Jim Colborn	4	4	4	4	8	10	15	
277	Tom Grieve	4	4	4	4	5	6	10	40
278	Andy Messersmith	4	4	4	4	5	6	10	
279	Jerry Grote DP	4	4	4	4	5	6	10	
280	Andre Thornton	4	4	4	4	5	6	10	
281	Vic Correll DP	4	4	4	4	5	6	10	
282	Toronto Blue Jays CL/Hartsfield	4	4	4	4	8	10	15	
283	Ken Kravec	4	4	4	4	5	6	10	
284	Johnnie LeMaster	4	4	4	6	10	15		
285	Bobby Bonds	4	4	4	4	5	6	10	
286	Duffy Dyer	4	4	4	4	5	6	10	
287	Andres Mora	4	4	4	4	8	10	15	
288	Milt Wilcox	4	4	4	4	5	6	10	
289	Jose Cruz	4	4	4	4	5	6	10	
290	Dave Lopes	4	4	4	4	5	6	10	
291	Tom Griffin	4	4	4	4	5	6	10	
292	Don Reynolds RC	4	4	4	4	5	6	10	40
293	Jerry Garvin	4	4	4	4	5	6	10	
294	Pepe Frias	4	4	4	4	8	10	15	
295	Mitchell Page	4	4	4	4	8	10	15	
296	Preston Hanna RC	4	4	4	4	5	6	10	
297	Ted Sizemore	4	4	4	4	5	6	10	40
298	Rich Gale RC	4	4	4	6	10	15		
299	Steve Ontiveros	4	4	4	4	5	6	10	
300	Rod Carew	4	4	4	5	10	12	25	200
301	Tom Hume	4	4	4	4	5	6	10	
302	Atlanta Braves CL/Cox	4	4	5	8	12	20		
303	Lary Sorensen DP	4	4	4	4	5	6	10	
304	Steve Swisher	4	4	4	4	5	6	10	
305	Willie Montanez	4	4	4	4	5	6	10	50
306	Floyd Bannister	4	4	4	4	5	6	10	

#	Name	VgEx 4	EX 5	ExMt 6	NM 7	NmMt 8	NmMt+ 8.5	MT 9	Gem 9.5/10
307	Larvell Blanks	4	4	4	4	5	6	10	
308	Bert Blyleven	4	4	4	4	8	10	15	
309	Ralph Garr	4	4	4	4	5	6	10	
310	Thurman Munson	4	4	5	10	15	20	50	
311	Gary Lavelle	4	4	4	4	5	6	10	
312	Bob Robertson	4	4	4	4	5	6	10	
313	Dyar Miller	4	4	4	4	5	6	10	
314	Larry Harlow	4	4	4	4	5	6	10	
315	Jon Matlack	4	4	4	4	5	6	10	
316	Milt May	4	4	4	4	5	6	10	
317	Jose Cardenal	4	4	4	4	5	6	10	
318	Bob Welch RC	4	4	4	4	8	10	25	
319	Wayne Garrett	4	4	4	6	10	15		
320	Carl Yastrzemski	4	4	4	6	15	20	▲60	
321	Gaylord Perry	4	4	4	4	6	8	12	
322	Danny Goodwin RC	4	4	4	4	8	10	60	
323	Lynn McGlothen	4	4	4	4	5	6	10	
324	Mike Tyson	4	4	4	4	5	6	10	40
325	Cecil Cooper	4	4	5	8	12	20		
326	Pedro Borbon	4	4	4	4	5	6	10	
327	Art Howe DP	4	4	4	4	8	10	15	
328	Oakland Athletics CL/McKeon	4	4	4	4	5	6	10	
329	Joe Coleman	4	4	4	4	8	10	15	
330	George Brett	6	8	10	12	25	30	100	
331	Mickey Mahler	4	4	4	4	8	10	50	
332	Gary Alexander	4	4	4	4	5	6	10	
333	Chet Lemon	4	4	4	4	5	6	10	
334	Craig Swan	4	4	4	4	8	10	15	
335	Chris Chambliss	4	4	4	4	6	8	12	
336	Bobby Thompson RC	4	4	4	4	5	6	10	
337	John Montague	4	4	4	4	5	6	10	
338	Vic Harris	4	4	4	4	8	10	15	
339	Ron Jackson	4	4	4	4	5	6	10	
340	Jim Palmer	4	4	4	6	12	15	80	
341	Willie Upshaw RC	4	4	4	4	8	10	15	
342	Dave Roberts	4	4	4	4	5	6	10	
343	Ed Glynn	4	4	4	4	5	6	10	40
344	Jerry Royster	4	4	4	4	8	10	15	
345	Tug McGraw	4	4	4	4	5	6	10	50
346	Bill Buckner	4	4	4	4	5	6	10	
347	Doug Rau	4	4	4	4	5	6	10	
348	Andre Dawson	4	4	4	5	10	12	20	
349	Jim Wright RC	4	4	4	4	5	6	10	
350	Garry Templeton	4	4	4	4	5	6	10	
351	Wayne Nordhagen DP	4	4	4	4	5	6	10	
352	Steve Renko	4	4	4	4	5	6	10	
353	Checklist 243-363	4	4	4	4	5	6	10	
354	Bill Bonham	4	4	4	4	5	6	10	
355	Lee Mazzilli	4	4	4	4	5	6	10	40
356	San Francisco Giants CL/Altobelli	4	4	5	8	12	20		
357	Jerry Augustine	4	4	4	4	5	6	10	
358	Alan Trammell	4	4	4	4	8	10	15	
359	Dan Spillner DP	4	4	4	4	5	6	10	40
360	Amos Otis	4	4	4	4	5	6	10	
361	Tom Dixon RC	4	4	4	4	8	10	15	
362	Mike Cubbage	4	4	4	4	8	10	15	
363	Craig Skok RC	4	4	4	4	5	6	10	
364	Gene Richards	4	4	4	6	10	15		
365	Sparky Lyle	4	4	4	4	5	6	10	120
366	Juan Bernhardt	4	4	4	4	5	6	10	
367	Dave Skaggs	4	4	4	6	10	15		
368	Don Aase	4	4	4	4	5	6	10	
369A	Bump Wills ERR Blue Jays	4	4	4	4	8	10	15	
369B	Bump Wills COR Rangers	4	4	4	4	6	8	12	
370	Dave Kingman	4	4	4	4	5	6	10	
371	Jeff Holly RC	4	4	4	4	5	6	10	
372	Lamar Johnson	4	4	4	4	5	6	10	
373	Lance Rautzhan	4	4	4	4	5	6	10	
374	Ed Herrmann	4	4	4	4	5	6	10	
375	Bill Campbell	4	4	4	4	5	6	10	40
376	Gorman Thomas	4	4	4	4	5	6	10	
377	Paul Moskau	4	4	4	4	8	10	15	
378	Rob Picciolo DP	4	4	4	4	5	6	10	
379	Dale Murray	4	4	4	4	5	6	10	
380	John Mayberry	4	4	4	4	5	6	10	
381	Houston Astros CL/Virdon	4	4	4	4	8	10	15	
382	Jerry Martin	4	4	4	4	5	6	10	
383	Phil Garner	4	4	4	4	5	6	10	
384	Tommy Boggs	4	4	4	4	5	6	10	
385	Dan Ford	4	4	4	4	5	6	10	
386	Francisco Barrios	4	4	4	4	5	6	10	
387	Gary Thomasson	4	4	4	4	8	10	15	
388	Jack Billingham	4	4	4	6	10	15		
389	Joe Zdeb	4	4	4	4	8	10	15	
390	Rollie Fingers	4	4	4	5	50	80	100	
391	Al Oliver	4	4	4	4	5	6	10	
392	Doug Ault	4	4	4	4	5	6	10	
393	Scott McGregor	4	4	4	4	8	10	15	
394	Randy Stein RC	4	4	4	4	5	6	10	
395	Dave Cash	4	4	4	4	5	6	10	
396	Bill Plummer	4	4	4	4	5	6	10	
397	Sergio Ferrer RC	4	4	4	4	5	6	10	
398	Ivan DeJesus	4	4	4	4	5	6	10	
399	David Clyde	4	4	4	4	8	10	15	
400	Jim Rice	4	4	4	5	10	12	25	
401	Ray Knight	4	4	4	4	5	6	10	
402	Paul Hartzell	4	4	4	4	5	6	10	
403	Tim Foli	4	4	4	4	8	10	15	
404	Chicago White Sox CL/Kessinger	4	4	4	4	5	6	10	
405	Butch Wynegar DP	4	4	4	4	5	6	10	4
406	Joe Wallis DP	4	4	4	4	5	6	10	
407	Pete Vuckovich	4	4	4	4	5	6	10	
408	Charlie Moore DP	4	4	4	4	5	6	10	4
409	Willie Wilson RC	4	4	4	8	15	20	50	
410	Darrell Evans	4	4	4	4	5	6	10	
411	G.Sisler/T.Cobb ATL	4	4	4	4	5	6	10	4
412	H.Wilson/H.Aaron ATL	4	4	4	4	6	8	12	6
413	R.Maris/H.Aaron ATL	4	4	4	4	8	10	15	6
414	R.Hornsby/T.Cobb ATL	4	4	4	4	5	6	10	4
415	L.Brock/L.Brock ATL	4	4	4	4	5	6	10	4
416	J.Chesbro/C.Young ATL	4	4	4	4	5	6	10	4
417	N.Ryan/W.Johnson ATL DP	4	4	5	8	▲12	▲15	20	▲10
418	D.Leonard/W.Johnson ATL DP	4	4	4	4	5	6	10	4
419	Dick Ruthven	4	4	4	4	5	6	10	
420	Ken Griffey Sr.	4	4	4	4	5	6	10	
421	Doug DeCinces	4	4	4	4	5	6	10	
422	Ruppert Jones	4	4	4	4	8	10	15	
423	Bob Montgomery	4	4	4	4	5	6	10	
424	California Angels CL/Fregosi	4	4	4	4	5	6	10	
425	Rick Manning	4	4	4	4	5	6	10	
426	Chris Speier	4	4	4	4	5	6	10	
427	Andy Replogle RC	4	4	4	4	8	10	15	
428	Bobby Valentine	4	4	4	4	5	6	10	
429	John Urrea DP	4	4	4	4	5	6	10	4
430	Dave Parker	4	4	4	4	8	10	15	12
431	Glenn Borgmann	4	4	4	4	5	6	10	
432	Dave Heaverlo	4	4	4	4	5	6	10	
433	Larry Biittner	4	4	4	4	8	10	15	
434	Ken Clay	4	4	4	4	5	6	10	4
435	Gene Tenace	4	4	4	4	5	6	10	
436	Hector Cruz	4	4	4	4	8	10	15	
437	Rick Williams RC	4	4	4	4	8	10	15	
438	Horace Speed RC	4	4	4	4	5	6	10	
439	Frank White	4	4	4	4	5	6	10	
440	Rusty Staub	4	4	4	4	5	6	10	5
441	Lee Lacy	4	4	4	4	5	6	10	
442	Doyle Alexander	4	4	4	4	5	6	10	
443	Bruce Bochte	4	4	4	6	10	15		
444	Aurelio Lopez RC	4	4	4	4	8	10	15	
445	Steve Henderson	4	4	4	4	5	6	10	
446	Jim Lonborg	4	4	4	4	5	6	10	
447	Manny Sanguillen	4	4	4	4	5	6	10	
448	Moose Haas	4	4	4	4	5	6	10	
449	Bombo Rivera	4	4	4	4	8	10	15	
450	Dave Concepcion	4	4	4	4	8	10	60	
451	Kansas City Royals CL/Herzog	4	4	4	4	8	10	15	

	VgEx 4	EX 5	ExMt 6	NM 7	NmMt 8	NmMt+ 8.5	MT 9	Gem 9.5/10
Jerry Morales	4	4	4	4	5	6	10	40
Chris Knapp	4	4	4	4	8	10	15	
Len Randle	4	4	4	4	5	6	10	
Bill Lee DP	4	4	4	4	5	6	10	50
Chuck Baker RC	4	4	4	4	5	6	10	40
Bruce Sutter	4	4	4	5	10	12	20	
Jim Essian	4	4	4	4	5	6	10	
Sid Monge	4	4	4	4	5	6	10	
Graig Nettles	4	4	4	4	6	8	12	
Jim Barr DP	4	4	4	4	5	6	10	40
Otto Velez	4	4	4	4	5	6	10	
Steve Comer RC	4	4	4	4	8	10	15	
Joe Nolan	4	4	4	4	5	6	10	
Reggie Smith	4	4	4	4	5	6	10	
Mark Littell	4	4	4	4	5	6	10	
Don Kessinger DP	4	4	4	4	5	6	10	
Stan Bahnsen DP	4	4	4	4	5	6	10	
Lance Parrish	4	4	4	4	5	6	10	
Garry Maddox DP	4	4	4	4	5	6	10	40
Joaquin Andujar	4	4	4	4	8	10	15	
Craig Kusick	4	4	4	4	5	6	10	
Dave Roberts	4	4	4	4	5	6	10	
Dick Davis RC	4	4	4	4	8	10	15	
Dan Driessen	4	4	4	4	8	10	15	
Tom Poquette	4	4	4	4	8	10	15	
Bob Grich	4	4	4	4	5	6	10	
Juan Beniquez	4	4	4	4	8	10	15	
San Diego Padres CL/Craig	4	4	4	4	5	6	10	
Fred Lynn	4	4	4	4	5	6	10	150
Skip Lockwood	4	4	4	4	5	6	10	50
Craig Reynolds	4	4	4	4	5	6	10	
Checklist 364-484 DP	4	4	4	4	5	6	10	
Rick Waits	4	4	4	4	8	10	15	
Bucky Dent	4	4	4	4	5	6	10	50
Bob Knepper	4	4	4	4	8	10	15	
Miguel Dilone	4	4	4	4	5	6	10	
Bob Owchinko	4	4	4	4	5	6	10	
Larry Cox	4	4	4	4	5	6	10	40
Al Cowens	4	4	4	4	8	10	15	
Tippy Martinez	4	4	4	6	10	15		
Bob Bailor	4	4	4	4	5	6	10	40
Larry Christenson	4	4	4	4	5	6	10	40
Jerry White	4	4	4	4	5	6	10	
Tony Perez	4	4	4	4	5	6	10	
Barry Bonnell DP	4	4	4	4	5	6	10	
Glenn Abbott	4	4	4	4	5	6	10	
Rich Chiles	4	4	4	6	10	15		
Texas Rangers CL/Corrales	4	4	4	4	8	10	15	
Ron Guidry	4	4	4	4	8	10	15	80
Junior Kennedy RC	4	4	4	6	10	15		
Steve Braun	4	4	4	4	5	6	10	
Terry Humphrey	4	4	4	4	8	10	15	
Larry McWilliams RC	4	4	4	4	5	6	10	
Ed Kranepool	4	4	4	4	5	6	10	
John D'Acquisto	4	4	4	4	5	6	10	
Tony Armas	4	4	4	4	5	6	10	40
Charlie Hough	4	4	4	4	5	6	10	
Mario Mendoza	4	4	4	4	5	6	10	40
Ted Simmons	4	4	4	4	5	6	10	
Paul Reuschel DP	4	4	4	4	5	6	10	
Jack Clark	4	4	4	4	5	6	10	
Dave Johnson	4	4	4	4	5	6	10	
Mike Proly RC	4	4	4	4	8	10	15	
Enos Cabell	4	4	4	4	5	6	10	
Champ Summers DP	4	4	4	4	5	6	10	40
Al Bumbry	4	4	5		12	20		
Jim Umbarger	4	4	4	4	5	6	10	
Ben Oglivie	4	4	5		12	20		
Gary Carter	4	4	4	5	10	12	20	
Sam Ewing	4	4	4	4	8	10	15	
Ken Holtzman	4	4	4	4	5	6	10	
John Milner	4	4	4	4	5	6	10	
Tom Burgmeier	4	4	4	4	5	6	10	40

		VgEx 4	EX 5	ExMt 6	NM 7	NmMt 8	NmMt+ 8.5	MT 9	Gem 9.5/10
525	Freddie Patek	4	4	4	4	5	6	10	100
526	Los Angeles Dodgers CL/Lasorda	4	4	4	4	5	6	10	
527	Lerrin LaGrow	4	4	4	6	10	15		
528	Wayne Gross DP	4	4	4	4	5	6	10	
529	Brian Asselstine	4	4	4	4	5	6	10	
530	Frank Tanana	4	4	4	4	8	10	15	
531	Fernando Gonzalez	4	4	4	4	8	10	15	
532	Buddy Schultz	4	4	4	4	5	6	10	
533	Leroy Stanton	4	4	4	4	5	6	10	
534	Ken Forsch	4	4	4	4	8	10	15	
535	Ellis Valentine	4	4	4	4	5	6	10	60
536	Jerry Reuss	4	4	4	4	8	10	15	
537	Tom Veryzer	4	4	4	4	5	6	10	
538	Mike Ivie DP	4	4	4	4	5	6	10	
539	John Ellis	4	4	4	4	5	6	10	40
540	Greg Luzinski	4	4	4	4	6	8	12	
541	Jim Slaton	4	4	4	4	8	10	15	
542	Rick Bosetti	4	4	4	4	5	6	10	
543	Kiko Garcia	4	4	4	6	10	15		
544	Fergie Jenkins	4	4	4	4	8	10	15	
545	John Stearns	4	4	4	4	5	6	10	
546	Bill Russell	4	4	4	4	5	6	10	
547	Clint Hurdle	4	4	4	4	5	6	10	
548	Enrique Romo	4	4	4	4	8	10	15	
549	Bob Bailey	4	4	4	4	5	6	10	
550	Sal Bando	4	4	4	4	5	6	10	40
551	Chicago Cubs CL/Franks	4	4	4	8	15	20	30	
552	Jose Morales	4	4	4	4	5	6	10	
553	Denny Walling	4	4	4	4	8	10	15	
554	Matt Keough	4	4	4	4	8	10	15	
555	Biff Pocoroba	4	4	4	4	5	6	10	
556	Mike Lum	4	4	4	4	5	6	10	
557	Ken Brett	4	4	4	4	8	10	15	
558	Jay Johnstone	4	4	4	4	5	6	10	
559	Greg Pryor RC	4	4	4	4	8	10	15	
560	John Montefusco	4	4	4	4	5	6	10	
561	Ed Ott	4	4	4	4	5	6	10	40
562	Dusty Baker	4	4	4	4	5	6	10	
563	Roy Thomas	4	4	4	4	8	10	15	
564	Jerry Turner	4	4	4	6	10	15		
565	Rico Carty	4	4	4	4	5	6	10	
566	Nino Espinosa	4	4	4	4	5	6	10	
567	Richie Hebner	4	4	4	4	5	6	10	
568	Carlos Lopez	4	4	4	4	8	10	15	
569	Bob Sykes	4	4	4	4	8	10	15	
570	Cesar Cedeno	4	4	4	4	8	10	15	
571	Darrell Porter	4	4	4	4	5	6	10	
572	Rod Gilbreath	4	4	4	4	5	6	10	40
573	Jim Kern	4	4	4	4	5	6	10	
574	Claudell Washington	4	4	4	4	5	6	10	
575	Luis Tiant	4	4	4	4	5	6	10	
576	Mike Parrott RC	4	4	4	4	8	10	15	40
577	Milwaukee Brewers CL/Bamberger	4	4	4	4	5	6	10	
578	Pete Broberg	4	4	4	4	5	6	10	
579	Greg Gross	4	4	4	4	5	6	10	40
580	Ron Fairly	4	4	4	4	5	6	10	
581	Darold Knowles	4	4	4	4	5	6	10	
582	Paul Blair	4	4	4	4	5	6	10	
583	Julio Cruz	4	4	4	4	5	6	10	40
584	Jim Rooker	4	4	4	4	8	10	60	
585	Hal McRae	4	4	4	4	5	6	10	
586	Bob Horner RC	4	4	4	6	12	15	25	
587	Ken Reitz	4	4	4	4	5	6	10	
588	Tom Murphy	4	4	4	4	5	6	10	
589	Terry Whitfield	4	4	4	4	5	6	10	40
590	J.R. Richard	4	4	4	4	5	6	10	
591	Mike Hargrove	4	4	4	4	5	6	10	
592	Mike Krukow	4	4	4	4	5	6	10	
593	Rick Dempsey	4	4	4	4	8	10	15	
594	Bob Shirley	4	4	4	4	5	6	10	
595	Phil Niekro	4	4	4	5	10	12	20	
596	Jim Wohlford	4	4	4	4	5	6	10	
597	Bob Stanley	4	4	4	4	5	6	10	

		VgEx 4	EX 5	ExMt 6	NM 7	NmMt 8	NmMt+ 8.5	MT 9	Gem 9.5/10
598	Mark Wagner	4	4	4	4	5	6	10	
599	Jim Spencer	4	4	4	4	8	10	15	
600	George Foster	4	4	4	4	8	10	15	
601	Dave LaRoche	4	4	4	4	5	6	10	
602	Checklist 485-605	4	4	4	4	8	10	15	
603	Rudy May	4	4	4	4	5	6	10	
604	Jeff Newman	4	4	4	4	5	6	10	40
605	Rick Monday DP	4	4	4	4	5	6	10	
606	Montreal Expos CL/Williams	4	4	4	4	5	6	10	
607	Omar Moreno	4	4	4	4	5	6	10	
608	Dave McKay	4	4	4	4	5	6	10	
609	Silvio Martinez RC	4	4	4	4	5	6	10	
610	Mike Schmidt	4	4	8	10	15	20	▲40	400
611	Jim Norris	4	4	4	6	10	15		
612	Rick Honeycutt RC	4	4	4	4	5	6	10	
613	Mike Edwards RC	4	4	4	4	8	10	15	
614	Willie Hernandez	4	4	4	4	5	6	10	
615	Ken Singleton	4	4	4	4	5	6	10	
616	Billy Almon	4	4	4	4	5	6	10	
617	Terry Puhl	4	4	4	4	5	6	10	
618	Jerry Remy	4	4	4	4	5	6	10	
619	Ken Landreaux RC	4	4	5		12	20		
620	Bert Campaneris	4	4	4	4	5	6	10	
621	Pat Zachry	4	4	4	4	5	6	10	
622	Dave Collins	4	4	4	4	5	6	10	80
623	Bob McClure	4	4	4	4	5	6	10	
624	Larry Herndon	4	4	4	4	8	10	15	
625	Mark Fidrych	4	4	4	4	5	6	10	
626	New York Yankees CL/Lemon	4	4	4	4	8	10	20	60
627	Gary Serum RC	4	4	4	4	8	10	15	
628	Del Unser	4	4	4	4	5	6	10	
629	Gene Garber	4	4	4	4	8	10	15	
630	Bake McBride	4	4	4	4	5	6	10	
631	Jorge Orta	4	4	4	4	5	6	10	
632	Don Kirkwood	4	4	4	4	5	6	10	
633	Rob Wilfong DP RC	4	4	4	4	5	6	10	
634	Paul Lindblad	4	4	4	4	5	6	10	
635	Don Baylor	4	4	4	4	5	6	10	
636	Wayne Garland	4	4	4	4	8	10	15	
637	Bill Robinson	4	4	4	4	5	6	10	
638	Al Fitzmorris	4	4	4	6	10	15		
639	Manny Trillo	4	4	4	4	5	6	10	
640	Eddie Murray	4	4	4	12	20	25	60	600
641	Bobby Castillo RC	4	4	4	6	10			
642	Wilbur Howard DP	4	4	4	4	5	6	10	
643	Tom Hausman	4	4	4	4	5	6	10	40
644	Manny Mota	4	4	4	4	5	6	10	80
645	George Scott DP	4	4	4	4	5	6	10	50
646	Rick Sweet	4	4	4	4	5	6	10	40
647	Bob Lacey	4	4	4	4	5	6	10	
648	Lou Piniella	4	4	4	4	6	8	12	
649	John Curtis	4	4	4	4	5	6	▲10	
650	Pete Rose	10	12	15	20	30	40	▲250	
651	Mike Caldwell	4	4	4	4	8	10	15	
652	Stan Papi RC	4	4	4	4	8	10	15	
653	Warren Brusstar DP	4	4	4	4	5	6	10	
654	Rick Miller	4	4	4	4	5	6	10	
655	Jerry Koosman	4	4	4	4	5	6	10	40
656	Hosken Powell RC	4	4	4	4	5	6	10	
657	George Medich	4	4	4	4	8	10	15	
658	Taylor Duncan RC	4	4	4	4	8	10	15	
659	Seattle Mariners CL/Johnson	4	4	4	4	8	10	15	
660	Ron LeFlore DP	4	4	4	4	5	6	10	
661	Bruce Kison	4	4	4	4	8	10	15	
662	Kevin Bell	4	4	4	4	5	6	10	
663	Mike Vail	4	4	4	4	5	6	10	
664	Doug Bird	4	4	4	4	5	6	10	
665	Lou Brock	4	4	4	6	12	15	25	
666	Rich Dauer	4	4	4	4	5	6	10	
667	Don Hood	4	4	4	4	5	6	10	
668	Bill North	4	4	4	4	8	10	15	
669	Checklist 606-726	4	4	4	4	5	6	10	
670	Jim Hunter DP	4	4	4	4	6	8	12	80

		VgEx 4	EX 5	ExMt 6	NM 7	NmMt 8	NmMt+ 8.5	MT 9	Gem 9.5
671	Joe Ferguson DP	4	4	4	4	5	6	10	
672	Ed Halicki	4	4	4	4	5	6	10	
673	Tom Hutton	4	4	4	4	5	6	10	
674	Dave Tomlin	4	4	4	4	5	6	10	
675	Tim McCarver	4	4	4	4	5	6	10	
676	Johnny Sutton RC	4	4	4	4	5	6	10	
677	Larry Parrish	4	4	4	4	5	6	10	
678	Geoff Zahn	4	4	4	4	5	6	10	
679	Derrel Thomas	4	4	4	4	5	6	10	
680	Carlton Fisk	4	4	4	5	10	12	25	2
681	John Henry Johnson RC	4	4	4	4	5	6	10	
682	Dave Chalk	4	4	4	4	5	6	10	
683	Dan Meyer DP	4	4	4	4	5	6	10	
684	Jamie Easterly DP	4	4	4	4	5	6	10	
685	Sixto Lezcano	4	4	4	4	5	6	10	
686	Ron Schueler DP	4	4	4	4	5	6	10	
687	Rennie Stennett	4	4	4	4	5	6	10	
688	Mike Willis	4	4	4	4	8	10	15	
689	Baltimore Orioles CL/Weaver	4	4	4	4	5	6	10	
690	Buddy Bell DP	4	4	4	4	5	6	10	
691	Dock Ellis DP	4	4	4	4	5	6	10	
692	Mickey Stanley	4	4	4	4	5	6	10	
693	Dave Rader	4	4	4	4	5	6	10	
694	Burt Hooton	4	4	4	4	5	6	10	
695	Keith Hernandez	4	4	4	4	6	8	12	
696	Andy Hassler	4	4	4	4	8	10	15	
697	Dave Bergman	4	4	4	4	8	10	15	
698	Bill Stein	4	4	4	4	5	6	10	
699	Hal Dues RC	4	4	4	4	5	6	10	
700	Reggie Jackson DP	4	4	4	▲12	▲20	▲25	▲50	▲5
701	Corey/Flinn/Stewart RC	4	4	4	4	5	6	10	
702	Finch/Hancock/Ripley RC	4	4	4	4	5	6	10	
703	Anderson/Frost/Slater RC	4	4	4	4	5	6	10	
704	Baumgarten/Colbern/Squires RC	4	4	4	4	5	6	10	
705	Griffin/Norrid/Oliver RC	4	4	4	4	5	6	10	
706	Stegman/Tobik/Young RC	4	4	4	4	5	6	10	
707	Bass/Gaudet/McGilberry RC	4	4	4	4	5	6	10	
708	Bass/Romero/Yost RC	4	4	4	4	5	6	10	
709	Perlozzo/Sofield/Stanfield RC	4	4	4	4	5	6	10	
710	Doyle/Heath/Rajisch RC	4	4	4	4	5	6	10	
711	Murphy/Robinson/Wirth RC	4	4	4	4	5	6	10	
712	Anderson/Biercevicz/McLaughlin RC	4	4	4	4	4	5	6	
713	Darwin/Putnam/Sample RC	4	4	4	4	5	6	10	
714	Cruz/Kelly/Whitt RC	4	4	4	4	5	6	10	6
715	Benedict/Hubbard/Whisenton RC	4	4	4	4	5	6	10	
716	Geisel/Pagel/Thompson RC	4	4	4	4	5	6	10	
717	LaCoss/Oester/Spilman RC	4	4	4	4	5	6	10	
718	Bochy/Fischlin/Pisker RC	4	4	4	4	▲25	▲30	▲50	15
719	Guerrero/Law/Simpson RC	4	4	4	4	6	8	12	5
720	Fry/Pirtle/Sanderson RC	4	4	4	4	5	6	10	
721	Berenguer/Bernard/Norman RC	4	4	4	4	5	6	10	4
722	Morrison/Smith/Wright RC	4	4	4	4	5	6	10	5
723	Berra/Cotes/Wiltbank RC	4	4	4	4	5	6	10	4
724	Bruno/Frazier/Kennedy RC	4	4	4	4	5	6	10	4
725	Beswick/Mura/Perkins RC	4	4	4	4	5	6	10	4
726	Johnston/Strain/Tamargo RC	4	4	4	4	5		10	4

—Andre Dawson #348 PSA 10 (Gem) sold for $302 (eBay; 2/07)
—George Brett #330 PSA 10 (Gem) sold for $1,500 (eBay; 9/07)
—George Brett #330 PSA 10 (Gem) sold for $589 (eBay; 11/06)
—George Brett #330 PSA 10 (Gem) sold for $500 (eBay; 8/07)
—Andre Dawson #348 PSA 10 (Gem) sold for $484 (eBay; 9/07)
—Thurman Munson #310 PSA 10 (Gem) sold for $255 (eBay; 5/07)
—Dale Murphy #39 PSA 10 (Gem) sold for $316 (eBay; 5/07)
—Jim Rice #400 PSA 10 (Gem) sold for $308 (eBay; 1/08)
—Pete Rose #650 PSA 10 (Gem) sold for $1,875 (eBay; 5/07)
—Nolan Ryan #115 PSA 10 (Gem) sold for $3,051 (eBay; 3/07)
—Nolan Ryan #115 BVG 9.5 (Gem) sold for $760 (eBay; 1/08)
—Ozzie Smith #116 PSA 10 (Gem) sold for $20,852 (Mile High; 1/12)
—Ozzie Smith #116 PSA 10 (Gem) (Young Collection) sold for $19,567 (SCP; 5/12)
—Ozzie Smith #116 PSA 10 (Gem) sold for $4,096 (Mastro; 12/06)
—Ozzie Smith #116 PSA 10 (Gem) sold for $4,000 (eBay; 8/07)
—Ozzie Smith #116 PSA 10 (Gem) sold for $3,795 (Mile High; 3/03)
—Ozzie Smith #116 PSA 10 (Gem) sold for $3,663 (Mile High; 11/03)

zzie Smith #116 BVG 9.5 (Gem) sold for $1,755 (eBay; 10/07)
zzie Smith #116 BVG 9.5 (Gem) sold for $1,007 (eBay; 4/07)
zzie Smith #116 GAI 9.5 (Gem) sold for $351 (eBay; 9/07)
ou Whitaker #123 PSA 10 (Gem) sold for $304 (eBay; 12/07)
arl Yastrzemski #320 PSA 10 (Gem) sold for $200 (eBay; 11/06)
obin Yount #95 PSA 10 (Gem) sold for $200 (eBay; 12/06)

80 Topps

	VgEx 4	EX 5	ExMt 6	NM 7	NmMt 8	NmMt+ 8.5	MT 9	Gem 9.5/10
L.Brock/C.Yastrzemski HL	4	4	4	6	12	20	40	
Willie McCovey HL	4	4	4	5	6		10	100
Manny Mota HL	4	4	4	4	5	6	10	
Pete Rose HL	4	4	4	4	8	10	20	
Garry Templeton HL	4	4	4	4	5	6	10	50
Del Unser HL	4	4	4	4	5	6	10	
Mike Lum	4	4	4	4	5	6	10	40
Craig Swan	4	4	4	4	5	6	10	40
Steve Braun	4	4	4	4	5	6	10	
Dennis Martinez	4	4	4	6	12	15	25	30
Jimmy Sexton	4	4	4	4	5	6	10	25
John Curtis DP	4	4	4	4	5	6	10	40
Ron Pruitt	4	4	4	4	5	6	10	
Dave Cash	4	4	4	4	5	6	10	
Bill Campbell	4	4	4	4	5	6	10	40
Jerry Narron RC	4	4	4	4	5	10	20	50
Bruce Sutter	4	4	4	8	15	15	20	80
Ron Jackson	4	4	4	4	5	6	10	
Balor Moore	4	4	4	4	5	6	10	40
Dan Ford	4	4	4	4	5	6	10	
Manny Sarmiento	4	4	4	4	5	6	10	
Pat Putnam	4	4	4	4	5	6	10	
Derrel Thomas	4	4	4	4	5	6	10	
Jim Slaton	4	4	4	4	5	6	10	25
Lee Mazzilli	4	4	4	4	6	8	12	
Marty Pattin	4	4	4	6	12	15	25	
Del Unser	4	4	4	4	5	6	10	40
Bruce Kison	4	4	4	4	5	6	10	
Mark Wagner	4	4	4	4	5	6	10	
Vida Blue	4	4	4	4	5	6	10	40
Jay Johnstone	4	4	4	4	5	6	10	40
Julio Cruz DP	4	4	4	4	5	6	10	40
Tony Scott	4	4	4	4	5	6	10	
Jeff Newman DP	4	4	4	4	5	6	10	40
Luis Tiant	4	4	4	4	5	6	10	80
Rusty Torres	4	4	4	4	5	6	10	
Kiko Garcia	4	4	4	4	5	6	10	
Dan Spillner DP	4	4	4	4	5	6	10	40
Rowland Office	4	4	4	4	5	6	10	
Carlton Fisk	4	4	4	4	8	10	15	80
Texas Rangers CL/Corrrales	4	4	4	4	5	6	10	
David Palmer RC	4	4	4	4	5	6	10	40
Bombo Rivera	4	4	4	4	5	6	10	
Bill Fahey	4	4	4	4	5	6	10	
Frank White	4	4	4	4	5	6	30	
Rico Carty	4	4	4	4	5	6	10	
Bill Bonham DP	4	4	4	4	5	6	10	
Rick Miller	4	4	4	4	5	6	10	
Mario Guerrero	4	4	4	4	5	6	10	
J.R. Richard	4	4	4	4	5	6	10	40
Joe Ferguson DP	4	4	4	4	5	6	10	40
Warren Brusstar	4	4	4	4	5	6	10	
Ben Oglivie	4	4	4	4	5	6	10	40
Dennis Lamp	4	4	4	4	5	6	10	
Bill Madlock	4	4	4	4	5	6	10	40
Bobby Valentine	4	4	4	4	5	6	10	
Pete Vuckovich	4	4	4	4	5	6	10	50
Doug Flynn	4	4	4	4	5	6	10	40
Eddy Putman RC	4	4	4	4	5	6	10	
Bucky Dent	4	4	4	4	5	6	10	40
Gary Serum	4	4	4	4	5	6	10	
Mike Ivie	4	4	4	4	5	6	10	40
Bob Stanley	4	4	4	4	5	6	10	
Joe Nolan	4	4	4	4	5	6	10	
Al Bumbry	4	4	4	4	5	6	10	
Kansas City Royals CL/Frey	4	4	4	4	8	10	15	
Doyle Alexander	4	4	4	4	6	8	12	

		VgEx 4	EX 5	ExMt 6	NM 7	NmMt 8	NmMt+ 8.5	MT 9	Gem 9.5/10
68	Larry Harlow	4	4	4	4	6	8	12	
69	Rick Williams	4	4	4	4	5	6	10	
70	Gary Carter	4	4	4	4	6	8	20	100
71	John Milner DP	4	4	4	4	5	6	10	
72	Fred Howard DP RC	4	4	4	4	5	6	10	25
73	Dave Collins	4	4	4	4	5	6	10	
74	Sid Monge	4	4	4	4	5	6	10	
75	Bill Russell	4	4	4	4	6	8	15	25
76	John Stearns	4	4	4	4	5	6	10	40
77	Dave Stieb RC	4	4	4	4	6	10	15	150
78	Ruppert Jones	4	4	4	4	5	6	10	
79	Bob Owchinko	4	4	4	4	5	6	10	
80	Ron LeFlore	4	4	4	4	5	6	10	
81	Ted Sizemore	4	4	4	4	5	8	12	
82	Houston Astros CL/Virdon	4	4	4	4	8	10	15	
83	Steve Trout RC	4	4	4	4	5	6	10	25
84	Gary Lavelle	4	4	4	4	5	6	10	40
85	Ted Simmons	4	4	4	5	10	12	20	200
86	Dave Hamilton	4	4	4	4	5	6	10	40
87	Pepe Frias	4	4	4	4	5	6	10	
88	Ken Landreaux	4	4	4	4	5	6	10	
89	Don Hood	4	4	4	4	5	6	15	60
90	Manny Trillo	4	4	4	4	5	6	10	
91	Rick Dempsey	4	4	4	4	5	6	10	40
92	Rick Rhoden	4	4	4	4	5	6	10	
93	Dave Roberts DP	4	4	4	4	5	6	10	25
94	Neil Allen RC	4	4	4	4	5	6	10	40
95	Cecil Cooper	4	4	4	4	5	6	10	30
96	Oakland Athletics CL/Marshall	4	4	4	4	5	6	10	50
97	Bill Lee	4	4	4	4	5	6	10	40
98	Jerry Terrell	4	4	4	4	5	6	10	
99	Victor Cruz	4	4	4	4	5	6	10	25
100	Johnny Bench	4	4	4	4	8	15	25	150
101	Aurelio Lopez	4	4	4	4	5	6	10	
102	Rich Dauer	4	4	4	4	5	6	15	
103	Bill Caudill RC	4	4	4	4	5	6	10	
104	Manny Mota	4	4	4	4	5	8	15	40
105	Frank Tanana	4	4	4	4	5	6	10	40
106	Jeff Leonard RC	4	4	4	4	6	8	12	
107	Francisco Barrios	4	4	4	4	5	6	10	
108	Bob Horner	4	4	4	4	5	6	10	30
109	Bill Travers	4	4	4	4	5	6	10	
110	Fred Lynn DP	4	4	4	5	8	10	15	60
111	Bob Knepper	4	4	4	4	5	6	10	
112	Chicago White Sox CL/LaRussa	4	4	4	4	6	8	12	
113	Geoff Zahn	4	4	4	4	5	6	10	40
114	Juan Beniquez	4	4	4	4	5	6	10	
115	Sparky Lyle	4	4	4	4	5	6	10	
116	Larry Cox	4	4	4	4	5	6	10	40
117	Dock Ellis	4	4	4	4	5	6	10	40
118	Phil Garner	4	4	4	4	5	6	10	40
119	Sammy Stewart	4	4	4	4	5	6	10	
120	Greg Luzinski	4	4	4	4	5	6	10	30
121	Checklist 1-121	4	4	4	4	5	8	15	
122	Dave Rosello DP	4	4	4	4	5	6	10	25
123	Lynn Jones RC	4	4	4	4	5	6	10	40
124	Dave Lemanczyk	4	4	4	4	5	6	10	
125	Tony Perez	4	4	4	4	5	10	20	50
126	Dave Tomlin	4	4	4	4	5	6	10	
127	Gary Thomasson	4	4	4	4	5	6	10	
128	Tom Burgmeier	4	4	4	4	5	8	12	
129	Craig Reynolds	4	4	4	4	5	6	10	40
130	Amos Otis	4	4	4	4	5	6	10	
131	Paul Mitchell	4	4	4	4	5	6	10	60
132	Biff Pocoroba	4	4	4	4	5	6	10	40
133	Jerry Turner	4	4	4	4	5	6	10	
134	Matt Keough	4	4	4	4	5	6	10	
135	Bill Buckner	4	4	4	4	5	6	10	25
136	Dick Ruthven	4	4	4	4	5	6	10	
137	John Castino RC	4	4	4	4	5	6	10	
138	Ross Baumgarten	4	4	4	4	5	6	12	
139	Dane Iorg RC	4	4	4	4	5	6	10	30
140	Rich Gossage	4	4	4	4	5	6	30	100

#	Player	VgEx 4	EX 5	ExMt 6	NM 7	NmMt 8	NmMt+ 8.5	MT 9	Gem 9.5/10
141	Gary Alexander	4	4	4	4	5	6	10	
142	Phil Huffman RC	4	4	4	4	5	6	10	40
143	Bruce Bochte DP	4	4	4	4	5	6	10	25
144	Steve Comer	4	4	4	4	5	6	10	
145	Darrell Evans	4	4	4	4	5	6	10	
146	Bob Welch	4	4	4	4	5	6	10	
147	Terry Puhl	4	4	4	4	5	6	10	
148	Manny Sanguillen	4	4	4	4	5	6	10	40
149	Tom Hume	4	4	4	4	5	6	10	
150	Jason Thompson	4	4	4	4	5	6	10	40
151	Tom Hausman DP	4	4	4	4	5	6	10	
152	John Fulgham RC	4	4	4	4	5	6	10	40
153	Tim Blackwell	4	4	4	4	5	6	10	
154	Lary Sorensen	4	4	4	4	5	6	10	
155	Jerry Remy	4	4	4	4	5	6	10	
156	Tony Brizzolara RC	4	4	4	4	5	6	10	
157	Willie Wilson DP	4	4	4	4	5	6	10	40
158	Rob Picciolo DP	4	4	4	4	5	6	10	
159	Ken Clay	4	4	4	4	5	6	10	30
160	Eddie Murray	4	4	4		▲12	▲15	▲25	200
161	Larry Christenson	4	4	4	4	5	6	10	40
162	Bob Randall	4	4	4	4	5	6	10	
163	Steve Swisher	4	4	4	4	5	6	10	25
164	Greg Pryor	4	4	4	4	6	8	12	
165	Omar Moreno	4	4	4	4	5	6	10	20
166	Glenn Abbott	4	4	4	4	5	6	10	
167	Jack Clark	4	4	4	4	5	6	10	40
168	Rick Waits	4	4	4	4	5	6	10	40
169	Luis Gomez	4	4	4	4	5	6	10	40
170	Burt Hooton	4	4	4	4	5	6	10	40
171	Fernando Gonzalez	4	4	4	4	5	6	10	
172	Ron Hodges	4	4	4	4	5	6	10	40
173	John Henry Johnson	4	4	4	4	5	6	10	
174	Ray Knight	4	4	4	4	5	6	10	25
175	Rick Reuschel	4	4	4	4	6	8	12	
176	Champ Summers	4	4	4	4	5	6	10	
177	Dave Heaverlo	4	4	4	4	5	6	10	40
178	Tim McCarver	4	4	4	4	5	6	10	40
179	Ron Davis RC	4	4	4	4	6	8	12	50
180	Warren Cromartie	4	4	4	4	5	6	10	40
181	Moose Haas	4	4	4	4	5	6	10	40
182	Ken Reitz	4	4	4	4	5	8	15	40
183	Jim Anderson DP	4	4	4	4	5	6	10	15
184	Steve Renko DP	4	4	4	4	5	6	10	
185	Hal McRae	4	4	4	4	5	6	10	40
186	Junior Moore	4	4	4	4	5	6	10	
187	Alan Ashby	4	4	4	4	5	6	10	
188	Terry Crowley	4	4	4	4	5	6	10	40
189	Kevin Kobel	4	4	4	4	5	8	12	
190	Buddy Bell	4	4	4	4	5	6	10	50
191	Ted Martinez	4	4	4	4	5	6	10	
192	Atlanta Braves CL/Cox	4	4	4	4	5	6	10	
193	Dave Goltz	4	4	4	4	5	6	10	
194	Mike Easler	4	4	4	4	5	10	20	
195	John Montefusco	4	4	4	4	5	6	10	
196	Lance Parrish	4	4	4	4	5	8	12	
197	Byron McLaughlin	4	4	4	4	5	6	10	20
198	Dell Alston DP	4	4	4	4	5	6	10	
199	Mike LaCoss	4	4	4	4	5	6	10	
200	Jim Rice	4	4	5	10	12	15	20	150
201	Batting Leaders	4	4	4	4	5	6	10	40
202	Home Run Leaders	4	4	4	4	6	8	12	80
203	RBI Leaders	4	4	4	4	5	6	10	30
204	Stolen Base Leaders	4	4	4	4	5	10	20	40
205	Victory Leaders	4	4	4	4	5	6	10	25
206	Strikeout Leaders	4	4	4	4	8	12	15	100
207	ERA Leaders	4	4	4	5	10	12	20	40
208	Wayne Cage	4	4	4	4	5	6	10	30
209	Von Joshua	4	4	4	4	5	6	10	25
210	Steve Carlton	4	4	4	5	8	10	15	200
211	Dave Skaggs DP	4	4	4	4	5	6	10	
212	Dave Roberts	4	4	4	4	5	6	10	30
213	Mike Jorgensen DP	4	4	4	4	5	6	10	40
214	California Angels CL/Fregosi	4	4	4	4	8	10	15	
215	Sixto Lezcano	4	4	4	4	5	6	10	
216	Phil Mankowski	4	4	4	4	5	6	10	
217	Ed Halicki	4	4	4	4	5	6	10	
218	Jose Morales	4	4	4	4	5	6	10	
219	Steve Mingori	4	4	4	4	5	6	10	
220	Dave Concepcion	4	4	4	4	5	6	10	
221	Joe Cannon RC	4	4	4	4	5	6	10	
222	Ron Hassey RC	4	4	4	4	5	6	10	
223	Bob Sykes	4	4	4	4	5	6	10	
224	Willie Montanez	4	4	4	4	5	6	10	
225	Lou Piniella	4	4	4	4	5	6	10	
226	Bill Stein	4	4	4	4	5	6	10	
227	Len Barker	4	4	4	4	5	6	10	
228	Johnny Oates	4	4	4	4	5	6	10	
229	Jim Bibby	4	4	4	4	8	10	20	
230	Dave Winfield	4	4	4	4	8	10	15	
231	Steve McCatty	4	4	4	4	5	6	10	
232	Alan Trammell	4	4	4	5	10	12	20	
233	LaRue Washington RC	4	4	4	4	5	6	10	
234	Vern Ruhle	4	4	4	4	5	6	10	
235	Andre Dawson	4	4	4	4	8	10	15	
236	Marc Hill	4	4	4	4	5	6	10	
237	Scott McGregor	4	4	4	4	5	6	10	
238	Rob Wilfong	4	4	4	4	5	6	10	
239	Don Aase	4	4	4	4	5	6	10	
240	Dave Kingman	4	4	4	4	5	6	10	
241	Checklist 122-242	4	4	4	4	5	6	10	
242	Lamar Johnson	4	4	4	4	5	6	10	
243	Jerry Augustine	4	4	4	4	5	6	10	
244	St. Louis Cardinals CL/Boyer	4	4	4	4	5	8	12	
245	Phil Niekro	4	4	4	4	6	8	12	
246	Tim Foli DP	4	4	4	4	5	6	10	
247	Frank Riccelli	4	4	4	4	5	6	10	
248	Jamie Quirk	4	4	4	4	5	6	10	
249	Jim Clancy	4	4	4	4	5	6	10	
250	Jim Kaat	4	4	4	4	5	6	10	
251	Kip Young	4	4	4	4	5	6	10	
252	Ted Cox	4	4	4	4	5	6	10	
253	John Montague	4	4	4	4	6	8	12	
254	Paul Dade DP	4	4	4	4	5	6	10	
255	Dusty Baker DP	4	4	4	4	5	6	10	
256	Roger Erickson	4	4	4	4	5	6	10	
257	Larry Herndon	4	4	4	4	5	6	10	
258	Paul Moskau	4	4	4	4	5	6	10	
259	New York Mets CL/Torre	4	4	4	4	6	8	12	
260	Al Oliver	4	4	4	4	5	6	10	
261	Dave Chalk	4	4	4	4	5	6	10	
262	Benny Ayala	4	4	4	4	5	6	10	
263	Dave LaRoche DP	4	4	4	4	5	6	10	
264	Bill Robinson	4	4	4	4	5	6	10	
265	Robin Yount	4	4	4	4	8	12	25	
266	Bernie Carbo	4	4	4	4	5	6	10	
267	Dan Schatzeder	4	4	4	4	5	6	10	
268	Rafael Landestoy	4	4	4	4	5	6	10	
269	Dave Tobik	4	4	4	4	5	6	10	
270	Mike Schmidt DP	4	4	4	5	10	12	20	
271	Dick Drago DP	4	4	4	4	5	6	10	
272	Ralph Garr	4	4	4	4	5	6	10	
273	Eduardo Rodriguez	4	4	4	4	5	6	10	
274	Dale Murphy	4	4	4	4	6	8	15	
275	Jerry Koosman	4	4	4	4	5	6	10	
276	Tom Veryzer	4	4	4	4	5	6	10	
277	Rick Bosetti	4	4	4	4	5	6	10	
278	Jim Spencer	4	4	4	4	5	6	10	
279	Rob Andrews	4	4	4	4	5	6	10	
280	Gaylord Perry	4	4	4	4	5	6	10	
281	Paul Blair	4	4	4	4	5	6	10	
282	Seattle Mariners CL/Johnson	4	4	4	4	8	10	15	
283	John Ellis	4	4	4	4	5	6	10	
284	Larry Murray DP RC	4	4	4	4		6	10	
285	Don Baylor	4	4	4	4	5	10	20	
286	Darold Knowles DP	4	4	4	4	5	6	10	
287	John Lowenstein	4	4	4	4	5	6	10	

	VgEx 4	EX 5	ExMt 6	NM 7	NmMt 8	NmMt+ 8.5	MT 9	Gem 9.5/10
Dave Rozema	4	4	4	4	5	6	10	40
Bruce Bochy	4	4	4	4	5	6	10	
Steve Garvey	4	4	4	4	6	8	12	120
Randy Scarberry RC	4	4	4	4	5	6	10	
Dale Berra	4	4	4	4	5	6	10	
Elias Sosa	4	4	4	4	5	6	10	
Charlie Spikes	4	4	4	4	5	8	15	
Larry Gura	4	4	4	4	5	6	10	30
Dave Rader	4	4	4	4	5	6	10	
Tim Johnson	4	4	4	4	5	6	10	40
Ken Holtzman	4	4	4	4	5	6	10	40
Steve Henderson	4	4	4	4	5	6	10	40
Ron Guidry	4	4	4	4	5	6	10	40
Mike Edwards	4	4	4	4	5	6	10	
Los Angeles Dodgers CL/Lasorda	4	4	4	4	6	8	12	50
Bill Castro	4	4	4	4	5	6	10	30
Butch Wynegar	4	4	4	4	5	6	10	40
Randy Jones	4	4	4	4	5	6	10	
Denny Walling	4	4	4	4	5	6	10	25
Rick Honeycutt	4	4	4	4	5	6	10	
Mike Hargrove	4	4	4	4	5	6	10	
Larry McWilliams	4	4	4	4	5	6	10	
Dave Parker	4	4	4	6	12	15	25	150
Roger Metzger	4	4	4	4	5	8	15	
Mike Barlow	4	4	4	4	5	6	10	
Johnny Grubb	4	4	4	4	5	6	10	
Tim Stoddard RC	4	4	4	4	5	6	10	40
Steve Kemp	4	4	4	4	5	6	10	
Bob Lacey	4	4	4	4	5	6	10	
Mike Anderson DP	4	4	4	4	5	6	10	40
Jerry Reuss	4	4	4	4	5	6	10	
Chris Speier	4	4	4	4	5	6	10	25
Dennis Eckersley	4	4	4	4	8	10	15	80
Keith Hernandez	4	4	4	4	5	8	15	40
Claudell Washington	4	4	4	4	5	6	10	
Mick Kelleher	4	4	4	4	5	6	10	25
Tom Underwood	4	4	4	4	5	6	10	40
Dan Driessen	4	4	4	4	5	6	10	
Bo McLaughlin	4	4	4	4	5	6	10	40
Ray Fosse DP	4	4	4	4	5	6	10	40
Minnesota Twins CL/Mauch	4	4	4	4	5	6	10	40
Bert Roberge RC	4	4	4	4	5	6	10	
Al Cowens	4	4	4	4	5	6	10	
Richie Hebner	4	4	4	4	5	6	10	
Enrique Romo	4	4	4	4	5	6	10	
Jim Norris DP	4	4	4	4	5	6	10	25
Jim Beattie	4	4	4	4	5	6	10	40
Willie McCovey	4	4	4	4	8	12	20	120
George Medich	4	4	4	4	5	6	10	
Carney Lansford	4	4	4	4	5	6	10	40
John Wockenfuss	4	4	4	4	5	6	10	
John D'Acquisto	4	4	4	4	5	6	10	
Ken Singleton	4	4	4	4	5	6	10	
Jim Essian	4	4	4	4	5	6	10	40
Odell Jones	4	4	4	4	5	6	10	
Mike Vail	4	4	4	4	5	6	10	
Randy Lerch	4	4	4	4	5	6	10	
Larry Parrish	4	4	4	4	5	6	10	25
Buddy Solomon	4	4	4	4	5	6	10	
Harry Chappas RC	4	4	4	4	5	6	10	
Checklist 243-363	4	4	4	4	5	12	25	
Jack Brohamer	4	4	4	4	5	6	10	
George Hendrick	4	4	4	4	5	6	10	
Bob Davis	4	4	4	4	5	6	10	
Dan Briggs	4	4	4	4	5	6	10	40
Andy Hassler	4	4	4	4	5	6	10	40
Rick Auerbach	4	4	4	4	5	6	10	25
Gary Matthews	4	4	4	4	5	6	10	40
San Diego Padres CL/Coleman	4	4	4	4	5	6	10	40
Bob McClure	4	4	4	4	5	6	10	40
Lou Whitaker	4	4	4	4	5	6	10	50
Randy Moffitt	4	4	4	4	5	6	10	25
Darrell Porter DP	4	4	4	4	5	6	10	25
Wayne Garland	4	4	4	4	5	10	20	40
Danny Goodwin	4	4	4	4	5	6	10	

	VgEx 4	EX 5	ExMt 6	NM 7	NmMt 8	NmMt+ 8.5	MT 9	Gem 9.5/10
363 Wayne Gross	4	4	4	4	5	6	10	25
364 Ray Burris	4	4	4	4	5	6	10	
365 Bobby Murcer	4	4	4	4	5	6	10	100
366 Rob Dressler	4	4	4	4	5	6	10	
367 Billy Smith	4	4	4	4	5	6	10	
368 Willie Aikens RC	4	4	4	4	5	6	10	
369 Jim Kern	4	4	4	4	5	6	10	
370 Cesar Cedeno	4	4	4	4	5	6	10	40
371 Jack Morris	4	4	4	4	5	6	10	
372 Joel Youngblood	4	4	4	4	5	6	10	
373 Dan Petry DP RC	4	4	4	4	5	6	10	50
374 Jim Gantner	4	4	4	4	5	6	10	
375 Ross Grimsley	4	4	4	4	5	6	10	40
376 Gary Allenson RC	4	4	4	4	5	8	15	
377 Junior Kennedy	4	4	4	4	5	6	10	
378 Jerry Mumphrey	4	4	4	4	5	6	10	
379 Kevin Bell	4	4	4	4	5	6	10	40
380 Garry Maddox	4	4	4	4	5	6	10	
381 Chicago Cubs CL/Gomez	4	4	4	5	10	12	20	
382 Dave Freisleben	4	4	4	4	5	6	10	
383 Ed Ott	4	4	4	4	5	6	10	40
384 Joey McLaughlin RC	4	4	4	4	5	6	10	
385 Enos Cabell	4	4	4	4	5	6	10	
386 Darrell Jackson	4	4	4	4	5	12	25	40
387A Fred Stanley Yellow Name	4	4	4	4	6	8	12	50
388 Mike Paxton	4	4	4	4	5	6	10	
389 Pete LaCock	4	4	4	4	5	6	10	
390 Fergie Jenkins	4	4	4	4	5	6	10	50
391 Tony Armas DP	4	4	4	4	5	6	10	
392 Milt Wilcox	4	4	4	4	5	6	10	
393 Ozzie Smith	8	10	12	15	15	20	▲30	200
394 Reggie Cleveland	4	4	4	4	5	6	10	40
395 Ellis Valentine	4	4	4	4	5	6	10	
396 Dan Meyer	4	4	4	4	5	6	10	
397 Roy Thomas DP	4	4	4	4	5	6	10	40
398 Barry Foote	4	4	4	4	5	6	10	
399 Mike Proly DP	4	4	4	4	5	6	10	
400 George Foster	4	4	4	4	6	8	15	
401 Pete Falcone	4	4	4	4	8	10	15	
402 Merv Rettenmund	4	4	4	4	5	6	10	20
403 Pete Redfern DP	4	4	4	4	5	6	10	
404 Baltimore Orioles CL/Weaver	4	4	4	4	5	8	12	40
405 Dwight Evans	4	4	4	4	5	8	15	
406 Paul Molitor	4	4	4	4	8	10	15	80
407 Tony Solaita	4	4	4	4	5	6	10	40
408 Bill North	4	4	4	4	5	6	10	40
409 Paul Splittorff	4	4	4	4	5	6	10	40
410 Bobby Bonds	4	4	4	4	6	8	12	
411 Frank LaCorte	4	4	4	4	5	6	10	40
412 Thad Bosley	4	4	4	4	5	6	10	
413 Allen Ripley	4	4	4	4	5	6	10	30
414 George Scott	4	4	4	4	5	6	10	40
415 Bill Atkinson	4	4	4	4	5	6	10	30
416 Tom Brookens RC	4	4	4	4	5	6	10	
417 Craig Chamberlain DP RC	4	4	4	4	5	6	10	25
418 Roger Freed DP	4	4	4	4	5	6	10	20
419 Vic Correll	4	4	4	4	5	6	10	40
420 Butch Hobson	4	4	4	4	6	8	12	
421 Doug Bird	4	4	4	4	5	6	10	40
422 Larry Milbourne	4	4	4	4	5	6	10	
423 Dave Frost	4	4	4	4	5	6	10	40
424 New York Yankees CL/Howser	4	4	4	5	10	12	20	80
425 Mark Belanger	4	4	4	4	5	6	10	40
426 Grant Jackson	4	4	4	4	5	6	10	
427 Tom Hutton DP	4	4	4	4	5	6	10	30
428 Pat Zachry	4	4	4	4	5	6	10	
429 Duane Kuiper	4	4	4	4	5	6	10	25
430 Larry Hisle DP	4	4	4	4	5	6	10	40
431 Mike Krukow	4	4	4	4	5	6	10	40
432 Willie Norwood	4	4	4	4	5	6	10	
433 Rich Gale	4	4	4	4	5	6	10	40
434 Johnnie LeMaster	4	4	4	4	5	6	10	40
435 Don Gullett	4	4	4	4	5	6	10	
436 Billy Almon	4	4	4	4	5	6	10	40
437 Joe Niekro	4	4	4	4	5	6	10	

#	Player	VgEx 4	EX 5	ExMt 6	NM 7	NmMt 8	NmMt+ 8.5	MT 9	Gem 9.5/10
438	Dave Revering	4	4	4	4	5	6	10	
439	Mike Phillips	4	4	4	4	5	6	10	
440	Don Sutton	4	4	4	4	5	6	10	40
441	Eric Soderholm	4	4	4	4	5	6	10	40
442	Jorge Orta	4	4	4	4	5	6	10	40
443	Mike Parrott	4	4	4	4	5	6	10	
444	Alvis Woods	4	4	4	4	5	6	10	
445	Mark Fidrych	4	4	4	4	6	8	12	50
446	Duffy Dyer	4	4	4	4	5	6	10	
447	Nino Espinosa	4	4	4	4	5	6	10	
448	Jim Wohlford	4	4	4	4	5	6	10	25
449	Doug Bair	4	4	4	4	5	6	10	
450	George Brett	4	4	4	5	20	25	▲40	600
451	Cleveland Indians CL/Garcia	4	4	4	4	6	8	12	
452	Steve Dillard	4	4	4	4	5	6	10	
453	Mike Bacsik	4	4	4	4	5	6	10	
454	Tom Donohue RC	4	4	4	4	5	6	10	40
455	Mike Torrez	4	4	4	4	5	6	10	
456	Frank Taveras	4	4	4	4	5	6	10	
457	Bert Blyleven	4	4	4	4	5	10	20	30
458	Billy Sample	4	4	4	4	5	6	10	30
459	Mickey Lolich DP	4	4	4	4	5	6	10	80
460	Willie Randolph	4	4	4	5	10	12	20	
461	Dwayne Murphy	4	4	4	4	5	6	10	
462	Mike Sadek DP	4	4	4	4	5	6	10	
463	Jerry Royster	4	4	4	4	5	6	10	40
464	John Denny	4	4	4	4	5	6	10	40
465	Rick Monday	4	4	4	4	5	6	10	40
466	Mike Squires	4	4	4	8	15	20	30	
467	Jesse Jefferson	4	4	4	4	5	6	10	
468	Aurelio Rodriguez	4	4	4	4	5	6	10	40
469	Randy Niemann DP RC	4	4	4	4	5	6	10	40
470	Bob Boone	4	4	4	4	5	6	10	30
471	Hosken Powell DP	4	4	4	4	5	6	10	25
472	Willie Hernandez	4	4	4	4	5	6	10	40
473	Bump Wills	4	4	4	4	5	6	10	40
474	Steve Busby	4	4	4	4	5	6	10	40
475	Cesar Geronimo	4	4	4	4	5	6	10	
476	Bob Shirley	4	4	4	4	5	6	10	40
477	Buck Martinez	4	4	4	4	5	6	10	
478	Gil Flores	4	4	4	4	5	6	10	
479	Montreal Expos CL/Williams	4	4	4	4	8	10	15	50
480	Bob Watson	4	4	4	4	5	6	10	40
481	Tom Paciorek	4	4	4	4	5	6	10	40
482	Rickey Henderson RC	▲40	▲50	▲60	▲80	▲120	200	500	6,000
483	Bo Diaz	4	4	4	4	5	6	10	
484	Checklist 364-484	4	4	4	4	5	6	10	30
485	Mickey Rivers	4	4	4	4	5	6	10	40
486	Mike Tyson DP	4	4	4	4	5	6	10	25
487	Wayne Nordhagen	4	4	4	4	5	6	10	
488	Roy Howell	4	4	4	4	5	6	10	40
489	Preston Hanna DP	4	4	4	4	5	15	30	
490	Lee May	4	4	4	4	5	6	10	
491	Steve Mura DP	4	4	4	4	5	6	10	
492	Todd Cruz RC	4	4	4	4	5	6	10	40
493	Jerry Martin	4	4	4	4	5	6	10	
494	Craig Minetto RC	4	4	4	4	5	6	10	
495	Bake McBride	4	4	4	4	5	6	10	
496	Silvio Martinez	4	4	4	4	5	6	10	
497	Jim Mason	4	4	4	4	5	6	10	
498	Danny Darwin	4	4	4	4	5	6	10	500
499	San Francisco Giants CL/Bristol	4	4	4	4	8	10	15	50
500	Tom Seaver	4	4	4	6	8	10	15	150
501	Rennie Stennett	4	4	4	4	5	6	10	
502	Rich Wortham DP RC	4	4	4	4	5	6	10	25
503	Mike Cubbage	4	4	4	4	5	6	10	40
504	Gene Garber	4	4	4	4	5	6	10	
505	Bert Campaneris	4	4	4	4	5	6	10	
506	Tom Buskey	4	4	4	4	5	6	10	
507	Leon Roberts	4	4	4	4	5	6	10	
508	U.L. Washington	4	4	4	4	5	6	10	
509	Ed Glynn	4	4	4	4		6	10	
510	Ron Cey	4	4	4	4	5	6	10	40
511	Eric Wilkins RC	4	4	4	4	5	6	10	40
512	Jose Cardenal	4	4	4	4	5	6	10	40

#	Player	VgEx 4	EX 5	ExMt 6	NM 7	NmMt 8	NmMt+ 8.5	MT 9	Gem 9.5/10
513	Tom Dixon DP	4	4	4	4	5	6	10	
514	Steve Ontiveros	4	4	4	4	5	6	10	
515	Mike Caldwell	4	4	4	4	5	6	10	
516	Hector Cruz	4	4	4	4	5	6	10	
517	Don Stanhouse	4	4	4	4	5	6	10	
518	Nelson Norman RC	4	4	4	4	5	6	10	
519	Steve Nicosia RC	4	4	4	4	5	6	10	
520	Steve Rogers	4	4	4	4	5	6	10	
521	Ken Brett	4	4	4	4	5	6	10	
522	Jim Morrison	4	4	4	4	5	6	10	
523	Ken Henderson	4	4	4	4	5	6	10	
524	Jim Wright DP	4	4	4	4	5	6	10	
525	Clint Hurdle	4	4	4	4	5	6	10	
526	Philadelphia Phillies CL/Green	4	4	4	6	12	20	50	
527	Doug Rau DP	4	4	4	4	5	6	10	
528	Adrian Devine	4	4	4	4	5	6	10	
529	Jim Barr	4	4	4	4	5	6	10	
530	Jim Sundberg DP	4	4	4	4	5	6	10	
531	Eric Rasmussen	4	4	4	4	5	6	10	
532	Willie Horton	4	4	4	4	5	6	10	
533	Checklist 485-605	4	4	4	4	8	10	15	
534	Andre Thornton	4	4	4	4	5	6	10	
535	Bob Forsch	4	4	4	4	5	6	10	
536	Lee Lacy	4	4	4	4	5	6	10	
537	Alex Trevino RC	4	4	4	4	5	6	10	
538	Joe Strain	4	4	4	4	5	6	10	
539	Rudy May	4	4	4	4	5	6	10	
540	Pete Rose	5	6	8	10	15	20	30	
541	Miguel Dilone	4	4	4	4	5	12	25	
542	Joe Coleman	4	4	4	4	5	6	10	
543	Pat Kelly	4	4	4	4	5	6	10	
544	Rick Sutcliffe RC	4	4	4	4	6	8	12	
545	Jeff Burroughs	4	4	4	4	5	6	10	
546	Rick Langford	4	4	4	4	5	6	10	
547	John Wathan	4	4	4	4	5	6	10	
548	Dave Rajsich	4	4	4	4	5	6	10	
549	Larry Wolfe	4	4	5	10	20	25	40	
550	Ken Griffey Sr.	4	4	4	4	5	6	10	
551	Pittsburgh Pirates CL/Tanner	4	4	5	10	12	15	25	
552	Bill Nahorodny	4	4	4	4	5	6	10	
553	Dick Davis	4	4	4	4	5	6	10	
554	Art Howe	4	4	4	4	5	6	10	
555	Ed Figueroa	4	4	4	4	5	6	10	
556	Joe Rudi	4	4	4	4	5	6	10	
557	Mark Lee	4	4	4	4	5	6	10	
558	Alfredo Griffin	4	4	4	4	5	6	10	
559	Dale Murray	4	4	4	4	5	6	10	
560	Dave Lopes	4	4	4	4	5	6	10	
561	Eddie Whitson	4	4	4	4	5	6	10	
562	Joe Wallis	4	4	4	4	5	6	10	
563	Will McEnaney	4	4	4	4	5	6	10	
564	Rick Manning	4	4	4	4	5	6	10	
565	Dennis Leonard	4	4	4	4	5	6	10	
566	Bud Harrelson	4	4	4	4	5	6	10	
567	Skip Lockwood	4	4	4	4	5	6	10	
568	Gary Roenicke RC	4	4	4	4	5	6	10	
569	Terry Kennedy	4	4	4	4	5	6	10	
570	Roy Smalley	4	4	4	6	12	15	25	
571	Joe Sambito	4	4	4	4	5	6	10	
572	Jerry Morales DP	4	4	4	4	5	6	10	
573	Kent Tekulve	4	4	4	4	5	6	10	
574	Scot Thompson	4	4	4	4	5	6	10	
575	Ken Kravec	4	4	4	4	5	6	10	
576	Jim Dwyer	4	4	4	4	5	6	10	
577	Toronto Blue Jays CL/Matlick	4	4	4	4	5	6	10	
578	Scott Sanderson	4	4	4	4	5	6	10	
579	Charlie Moore	4	4	4	4	5	6	10	
580	Nolan Ryan	5	5	12	20	▲30	40	120	1,5
581	Bob Bailor	4	4	4	4	5	6	10	
582	Brian Doyle	4	4	4	4	5	6	10	
583	Bob Stinson	4	4	4	4	6	8	12	
584	Kurt Bevacqua	4	4	4	4	5	6	10	
585	Al Hrabosky	4	4	4	4	5	6	10	
586	Mitchell Page	4	4	4	4	5	6	10	
587	Garry Templeton	4	4	4	4	5	6	10	
588	Greg Minton	4	4	4	4	5	6	10	
589	Chet Lemon	4	4	4	4	5	6	10	

	VgEx 4	EX 5	ExMt 6	NM 7	NmMt 8	NmMt+ 8.5	MT 9	Gem 9.5/10
Jim Palmer	4	4	4	8	15	20	40	
Rick Cerone	4	4	4	4	5	6	10	
Jon Matlack	4	4	4	4	5	6	10	
Jesus Alou	4	4	4	4	5	6	10	40
Dick Tidrow	4	4	4	4	5	6	10	
Don Money	4	4	4	4	5	6	10	40
Rick Matula RC	4	4	4	4	5	6	10	
Tom Poquette	4	4	4	4	5	6	10	
Fred Kendall DP	4	4	4	4	5	6	10	20
Mike Norris	4	4	4	4	5	6	10	
Reggie Jackson	4	4	4	6	12	15	25	150
Buddy Schultz	4	4	4	4	5	6	10	
Brian Downing	4	4	4	4	5	6	10	
Jack Billingham DP	4	4	4	4	5	6	10	40
Glenn Adams	4	4	4	4	5	6	10	40
Terry Forster	4	4	4	4	5	6	10	
Cincinnati Reds CL/McNamara	4	4	4	5	10	15	30	50
Woodie Fryman	4	4	4	4	5	6	10	40
Alan Bannister	4	4	4	4	5	6	10	40
Ron Reed	4	4	4	4	5	6	10	
Willie Stargell	4	4	4	6	12	15	25	
Jerry Garvin DP	4	4	4	4	5	6	10	40
Cliff Johnson	4	4	4	4	5	6	10	
Randy Stein	4	4	4	4	5	6	10	40
John Hiller	4	4	4	4	5	6	10	40
Doug DeCinces	4	4	4	4	5	6	10	
Gene Richards	4	4	4	4	5	6	10	40
Joaquin Andujar	4	4	4	4	5	6	10	
Bob Montgomery DP	4	4	4	4	5	6	10	30
Sergio Ferrer	4	4	4	4	5	6	10	
Richie Zisk	4	4	4	4	6	8	12	
Bob Grich	4	4	4	4	5	6	10	
Mario Soto	4	4	4	4	5	6	10	40
Gorman Thomas	4	4	4	4	5	8	12	30
Lerrin LaGrow	4	4	4	4	5	6	10	40
Chris Chambliss	4	4	4	4	6	8	12	40
Detroit Tigers CL/Anderson	4	4	4	6	12	15	25	
Pedro Borbon	4	4	4	4	5	6	10	
Doug Capilla	4	4	4	4	5	6	10	
Jim Todd	4	4	4	4	5	6	10	40
Larry Bowa	4	4	4	4	5	6	10	40
Mark Littell	4	4	4	4	5	6	10	25
Barry Bonnell	4	4	4	4	5	6	10	40
Bob Apodaca	4	4	4	4	5	6	10	40
Glenn Borgmann DP	4	4	4	4	5	6	10	40
John Candelaria	4	4	4	4	5	10	20	
Toby Harrah	4	4	4	4	5	6	10	40
Joe Simpson	4	4	4	4	5	6	10	
Mark Clear RC	4	4	4	4	5	6	10	
Larry Biittner	4	4	4	4	5	8	15	
Mike Flanagan	4	4	4	4	5	6	10	
Ed Kranepool	4	4	4	4	5	6	10	
Ken Forsch DP	4	4	4	4	5	6	10	40
John Mayberry	4	4	4	4	5	6	10	
Charlie Hough	4	4	4	4	5	6	10	40
Rick Burleson	4	4	4	4	5	6	10	
Checklist 606-726	4	4	4	4	5	6	10	40
Milt May	4	4	4	4	5	6	10	40
Roy White	4	4	4	4	5	6	10	60
Tom Griffin	4	4	4	4	5	6	10	
Joe Morgan	4	4	4	4	6	8	12	100
Rollie Fingers	4	4	4	4	5	6	10	50
Mario Mendoza	4	4	4	4	5	6	10	
Stan Bahnsen	4	4	4	4	5	6	10	25
Bruce Boisclair DP	4	4	4	4	5	6	10	
Tug McGraw	4	4	4	4	5	6	10	40
Larvell Blanks	4	4	4	4	5	6	10	40
Dave Edwards RC	4	4	4	4	5	6	10	
Chris Knapp	4	4	4	4	5	6	10	60
Milwaukee Brewers CL/Bamberger	4	4	4	4	5	6	10	40
Rusty Staub	4	4	4	4	5	6	10	25
Corey/Ford/Krenchiki RC	4	4	4	4	5	6	10	
Finch/O'Berry/Rainey RC	4	4	4	4	5	8	15	
Botting/Clark/Thon RC	4	4	4	4	5	8	15	
Colbern/Hoffman/Robinson RC	4	4	4	4	5	6	10	40
Andersen/Cuellar/Wihtol RC	4	4	4	4	5	6	10	
Chris/Greene/Robbins RC	4	4	4	4	5	6	10	

	VgEx 4	EX 5	ExMt 6	NM 7	NmMt 8	NmMt+ 8.5	MT 9	Gem 9.5/10
667 Mart/Pasch/Quisenberry RC	4	4	4	4	8	10	15	60
668 Boitano/Mueller/Sakata RC	4	4	4	4	5	6	10	25
669 Graham/Sofield/Ward RC	4	4	4	4	5	6	10	40
670 Brown/Gulden/Jones RC	4	4	4	4	5	6	10	
671 Bryant/Kingman/Morgan RC	4	4	4	4	5	6	10	
672 Beamon/Craig/Vasquez RC	4	4	4	4	5	6	10	
673 Allard/Gleaton/Mahlberg RC	4	4	4	4	5	6	10	
674 Edge/Kelly/Wilborn RC	4	4	4	4	5	6	10	
675 Benedict/Bradford/Miller RC	4	4	4	4	5	6	10	40
676 Geisel/Macko/Pagel RC	4	4	4	4	5	6	10	40
677 DeFreites/Pastore/Spilman RC	4	4	4	4	5	6	10	
678 Baldwin/Knicely/Ladd RC	4	4	4	4	5	6	10	
679 Beckwith/Hatcher/Patterson RC	4	4	4	4	5	6	10	
680 Bernazard/Miller/Tamargo RC	4	4	4	4	8	10	15	
681 Norman/Orosco/Scott RC	4	4	4	4	6	8	12	
682 Aviles/Noles/Saucier RC	4	4	4	4	6	8	12	
683 Boyland/Lois/Saferight RC	4	4	4	4	5	8	15	
684 Frazier/Herr/O'Brien RC	4	4	4	4	5	8	15	
685 Flannery/Greer/Wilhelm RC	4	4	4	4	5	6	10	25
686 Johnston/Littlejohn/Nastu RC	4	4	4	4	5	6	10	
687 Mike Heath DP	4	4	4	4	5	6	10	40
688 Steve Stone	4	4	4	4	5	6	10	
689 Boston Red Sox CL/Zimmer	4	4	4	4	8	10	15	60
690 Tommy John	4	4	4	4	5	6	10	40
691 Ivan DeJesus	4	4	4	4	5	6	10	
692 Rawly Eastwick DP	4	4	4	4	5	6	10	
693 Craig Kusick	4	4	4	4	5	6	10	40
694 Jim Rooker	4	4	4	4	5	6	10	40
695 Reggie Smith	4	4	4	4	5	6	10	
696 Julio Gonzalez	4	4	4	4	5	6	10	
697 David Clyde	4	4	4	4	5	6	10	
698 Oscar Gamble	4	4	4	4	5	6	10	
699 Floyd Bannister	4	4	4	4	5	6	10	
700 Rod Carew DP	4	4	4	4	6	8	12	120
701 Ken Oberkfell RC	4	4	4	4	5	6	10	
702 Ed Farmer	4	4	4	4	5	6	10	
703 Otto Velez	4	4	4	4	5	6	10	
704 Gene Tenace	4	4	4	4	5	6	10	40
705 Freddie Patek	4	4	4	4	5	6	10	
706 Tippy Martinez	4	4	4	6	12	15	25	
707 Elliott Maddox	4	4	4	4	5	6	10	
708 Bob Tolan	4	4	4	4	5	6	10	
709 Pat Underwood RC	4	4	4	4	5	6	10	
710 Graig Nettles	4	4	4	5	10	15	20	50
711 Bob Galasso RC	4	4	4	4	5	6	10	25
712 Rodney Scott	4	4	4	4	5	6	10	
713 Terry Whitfield	4	4	4	4	5	6	10	40
714 Fred Norman	4	4	4	4	5	6	10	
715 Sal Bando	4	4	4	4	5	6	10	40
716 Lynn McGlothen	4	4	4	4	5	6	10	30
717 Mickey Klutts DP	4	4	4	4	5	6	10	50
718 Greg Gross	4	4	4	4	5	6	10	
719 Don Robinson	4	4	4	4	5	6	10	40
720 Carl Yastrzemski DP	4	4	5	10	12	15	20	120
721 Paul Hartzell	4	4	4	4	5	6	10	40
722 Jose Cruz	4	4	4	4	5	6	10	40
723 Shane Rawley	4	4	4	4	5	6	10	
724 Jerry White	4	4	4	4	5	6	10	50
725 Rick Wise	4	4	4	4	5	6	10	25
726 Steve Yeager	4	4	4	4	5	6	10	

—Brock/Yastrzemski HL #1 PSA 10 (Gem) sold for $118 (eBay; 12/06)
—Rickey Henderson #482 BVG 9.5 (Gem) sold for $1,698 (eBay; 10/07)
—Rickey Henderson #482 GAI 9.5 (Gem) sold for $1,378 (eBay; 5/08)
—Rickey Henderson #482 GAI 9.5 (Gem) sold for $555 (eBay; 1/08)
—Rickey Henderson #482 BVG 9 (MT) sold for $661 (eBay; 6/07)
—Rickey Henderson #482 BVG 9 (MT) sold for $484 (eBay; 6/07)
—Rickey Henderson #482 BVG 9 (MT) sold for $325 (eBay; 6/07)
—Rickey Henderson #482 BVG 9 (MT) sold for $281 (eBay; 5/07)
—Rickey Henderson #482 BVG 9 (MT) sold for $226 (eBay; 2/07)
—Rickey Henderson #482 SGC 96 (MT) sold for $138 (eBay; 7/07)
—Rickey Henderson #482 GAI 9 (MT) sold for $109 (eBay; 4/07)
—Rickey Henderson #482 SGC 96 (MT) sold for $109 (eBay; 4/07)
—Mets Rookies #681 PSA 10 (Gem) sold for $187 (eBay; 3/08)
—Jim Palmer #590 PSA 10 (Gem) sold for $350 (eBay; 5/07)
—Jim Palmer #590 PSA 10 (Gem) sold for $205 (eBay; 12/06)
—Willie Randolph #460 PSA 10 (Gem) sold for $435 (eBay; 6/08)
—Robin Yount #265 PSA 10 (Gem) sold for $209 (eBay; 11/06)

BASEBALL
1981 - Present

1981 Rochester Red Wings TCMA

		NmMt 8	NmMt+ 8.5	MT 9	Gem 9.5/10
15	Cal Ripken Jr.	250	300	350	700

1981 Topps

		NmMt 8	NmMt+ 8.5	MT 9	Gem 9.5/10
180	Pete Rose	▲15	▲20	40	1,500
240	Nolan Ryan	20	25	60	1,500
254	Ozzie Smith	▲10	▲15	▲20	80
261	Rickey Henderson	▲20	▲25	50	500
302	F.Valenzuela/M.Scioscia RC	25	30	▲120	
315	Kirk Gibson RC	25	30	100	1,500
347	Harold Baines RC	8	10	15	400
479	Tim Raines RC	15	20	25	250

—Harold Baines #347 PSA 10 (Gem) sold for $260 (eBay; 1/04)
—Rickey Henderson #261 PSA 10 (Gem) sold for $355 (eBay; 02/13)
—Pete Rose #180 PSA 10 (Gem) sold for $2,567 (eBay; 3/13)
—Pete Rose #180 PSA 10 (Gem) sold for $1,870 (eBay; 7/13)
—Nolan Ryan #240 PSA 10 (Gem) sold for $924 (eBay; 9/12)
—Nolan Ryan #240 PSA 10 (Gem) sold for $791 (eBay; 11/12)

1981 Topps Traded

		NmMt 8	NmMt+ 8.5	MT 9	Gem 9.5/10
727	Danny Ainge XRC	6	10	15	150
816	Tim Raines	25	30	60	600
850	Fernando Valenzuela	25	30	60	

—Tim Raines #816 PSA 10 (Gem) sold for $408 (eBay; 3/13)
—Tim Raines #816 BGS 9.5 (Gem) sold for $302 (eBay; 2/13)
—Tim Raines #816 BGS 9.5 (Gem) sold for $258 (eBay; 4/13)
—Fernando Valenzuela #850 PSA 10 (Gem) sold for $660 (eBay; 4/13)

1982 Anchorage Glacier Pilots McGwire

		NmMt 8	NmMt+ 8.5	MT 9	Gem 9.5/10
1	Mark McGwire	30	40	50	500

—Mark McGwire #1 PSA 10 (Gem) sold for $400 (eBay; 12/12)

1982 Donruss

		NmMt 8	NmMt+ 8.5	MT 9	Gem 9.5/10
168	Pete Rose	6	8	12	60
405	Cal Ripken RC	30	40	60	250
419	Nolan Ryan	5	6	10	40

—Cal Ripken #405 BGS 10 (Pristine) sold for $2,026 (eBay; 5/13)

1982 Fleer

		NmMt 8	NmMt+ 8.5	MT 9	Gem 9.5/10
176	Cal Ripken RC	▲30	▲40	60	800
229	Nolan Ryan	10	15	25	40

1982 Topps

		NmMt 8	NmMt+ 8.5	MT 9	Gem 9.5/10
21	Cal Ripken RC	▼30	▼40	▲100	600
90	Nolan Ryan	▲15	▲20	25	300
780	Pete Rose	10	12	20	120

—Rickey Henderson #610 PSA 8 (NmMt) sold for $1,305 (eBay; 10/12)
—Lee Smith #458 PSA 10 (Gem) sold for $257 (eBay; 3/09)

1982 Topps Traded

		NmMt 8	NmMt+ 8.5	MT 9	Gem 9.5/10
98T	Cal Ripken	150	200	▲300	1,500
109T	Ozzie Smith	20	25	40	120

1983 Donruss

		NmMt 8	NmMt+ 8.5	MT 9	Gem 9.5/10
42	Pete Rose	5	8	15	40
118	Nolan Ryan	6	8	12	30
277	Ryne Sandberg RC	▲20	▲25	▲40	250
279	Cal Ripken	6	8	▲20	80
525	Julio Franco RC	6	8	12	40
586	Wade Boggs RC	15	20	▲30	80
598	Tony Gwynn RC	20	25	▲40	120

1983 Fleer

		NmMt 8	NmMt+ 8.5	MT 9	Gem 9.5/10
70	Cal Ripken	6	8	▲20	▲80
171	Pete Rose	5	6	12	40
179	Wade Boggs RC	▲20	▲25	▲30	▲80
360	Tony Gwynn RC	20	25	▲40	120
463	Nolan Ryan	5	6	10	80
507	Ryne Sandberg RC	20	25	30	100

1983 Topps

		NmMt 8	NmMt+ 8.5	MT 9	Gem 9.5/10
83	Ryne Sandberg RC	30	40	▲60	500
100	Pete Rose	8	10	15	50
163	Cal Ripken	12	15	▲25	120
180	Rickey Henderson	6	8	12	50
360	Nolan Ryan	10	12	▲25	120
482	Tony Gwynn RC	▲30	▲40	100	800
498	Wade Boggs RC	▲25	30	▲80	600

—Ryne Sandberg #83 BGS 10 (Pristine) sold for $1,100 (Goodwin; 6/13)

1984 Donruss

		NmMt 8	NmMt+ 8.5	MT 9	Gem 9.5/10
41	Joe Carter RC	▲20	▲25	▲50	120
60	Nolan Ryan	10	12	▲25	80
61	Pete Rose	8	10	▲20	60
68	Darryl Strawberry RC	▲25	▲30	▲40	120
106	Cal Ripken	▲12	▲15	▲25	50
248	Don Mattingly RC	▲60	▲80	▲200	1,000
311	Ryne Sandberg	8	10	25	60

1984 Fleer

		NmMt 8	NmMt+ 8.5	MT 9	Gem 9.5/10
17	Cal Ripken	10	12	20	50
46	Pete Rose	5	6	10	30
131	Don Mattingly RC	▲30	▲50	▲60	250
239	Nolan Ryan	5	6	▲20	60
504	Ryne Sandberg	6	8	15	40
599	Darryl Strawberry	5	6	▲25	50

1984 Fleer Update

		NmMt 8	NmMt+ 8.5	MT 9	Gem 9.5/10
27	Roger Clemens XRC	▲200	▲250	▲300	800
43	Dwight Gooden XRC	50	60	100	250
93	Kirby Puckett XRC	150	200	250	500
102	Pete Rose	12	15	25	80

—Roger Clemens #27 BGS 10 (Pristine) sold for $1,300 (eBay; 11/13)

1984 Pawtucket Red Sox TCMA

		NmMt 8	NmMt+ 8.5	MT 9	Gem 9.5/10
22	Roger Clemens	80	100	700	

1984 Topps

		NmMt 8	NmMt+ 8.5	MT 9	Gem 9.5/10
8	Don Mattingly RC	25	30	▲60	250
182	Darryl Strawberry RC	8	10	15	50
300	Pete Rose	6	8	12	50
470	Nolan Ryan	8	10	15	100
490	Cal Ripken	6	8	12	50
596	Ryne Sandberg	5	6	12	60

1984 Topps Traded Tiffany

		NmMt 8	NmMt+ 8.5	MT 9	Gem 9.5/10
104T	Bret Saberhagen	12	15	25	80

1985 Donruss

		NmMt 8	NmMt+ 8.5	MT 9	Gem 9.5/10
60	Nolan Ryan	8	10	▲20	80
169	Cal Ripken	5	6	15	50
190	Dwight Gooden RC	5	6	12	50
254	Pete Rose Expos	6	8	15	50
273	Roger Clemens RC	25	30	▲50	250
438	Kirby Puckett RC	▲25	▲30	▲50	250
581	Orel Hershiser RC	5	6	10	80
641	Pete Rose	5	6	12	60

—Roger Clemens #273 BGS 10 (Pristine) sold for $3,940 (eBay; 2/05)
—Roger Clemens #273 BGS 10 (Pristine) sold for $2,580 (eBay; 4/05)
—Roger Clemens #273 BGS 10 (Pristine) sold for $2,560 (eBay; 8/05)

1985 Fleer

		NmMt 8	NmMt+ 8.5	MT 9	Gem 9.5/10
155	Roger Clemens RC	▲25	▲30	50	400
187	Cal Ripken	5	6	15	50
286	Kirby Puckett RC	20	25	▲50	250
359	Nolan Ryan	5	6	10	100
550	Pete Rose	6	8	12	40

1985 Modesto A's Chong

		NmMt 8	NmMt+ 8.5	MT 9	Gem 9.5/10
17B	Mark McGwire COR	8	10	15	30

1985 Topps

		NmMt 8	NmMt+ 8.5	MT 9	Gem 9.5/10
30	Cal Ripken	5	6	12	600
181	Roger Clemens RC	▲20	▲25	▲50	120
401	Mark McGwire OLY RC	▲30	▲40	▲80	400
493	Orel Hershiser RC	6	8	12	40
536	Kirby Puckett RC	▲25	▲30	40	300
600	Pete Rose	5	6	12	50
620	Dwight Gooden RC	10	12	20	80
760	Nolan Ryan	8	10	20	120

—Cal Ripken #30 PSA 10 (Gem) sold for $305 (eBay; 11/05)

1986 Donruss

		NmMt 8	NmMt+ 8.5	MT 9	Gem 9.5/10
28	Fred McGriff RC	▲20	▲25	▲40	60
33A	Andres Galarraga RC	5	6	8	25
37	Paul O'Neill RC	5	5	10	30
39	Jose Canseco RC	▲30	▲40	▲60	250
258	Nolan Ryan	5	6	12	50
512	Cecil Fielder RC	8	10	15	

—Fred McGriff #28 BGS 10 (Pristine) sold for $690 (eBay; 03/09)

1986 Donruss Rookies

		NmMt 8	NmMt+ 8.5	MT 9	Gem 9.5/10
11	Barry Bonds XRC	▲15	▲20	25	120
22	Jose Canseco	5	5	8	25
32	Will Clark XRC	5	5	6	25
38	Bo Jackson XRC	5	6	▲25	50

1986 Fleer Update

		NmMt 8	NmMt+ 8.5	MT 9	Gem 9.5/10
14	Barry Bonds XRC	12	15	25	150
20	Jose Canseco	5	6	12	40
25	Will Clark XRC	10	12	25	80

1986 Pittsfield Cubs ProCards

		NmMt 8	NmMt+ 8.5	MT 9	Gem 9.5/10
14	Greg Maddux	150	200	250	500
18	Rafael Palmeiro	40	50	80	100

1986 Sportflics Rookies

		NmMt 8	NmMt+ 8.5	MT 9	Gem 9.5/10
34	Barry Larkin	5	8	15	50

86 Topps Traded

	NmMt 8	NmMt+ 8.5	MT 9	Gem 9.5/10
Barry Bonds XRC	15	20	25	120
Jose Canseco XRC	5	6	10	25
Will Clark XRC	5	5	8	30
Bo Jackson XRC	10	12	▲25	80

86 Topps Traded Tiffany

	NmMt 8	NmMt+ 8.5	MT 9	Gem 9.5/10
Barry Bonds	300	400	600	2,000
Jose Canseco	12	20	▲60	300
Will Clark	10	12	40	120
Bo Jackson	200	▲250	500	3,000

87 Bellingham Mariners Team Issue

	NmMt 8	NmMt+ 8.5	MT 9	Gem 9.5/10
Ken Griffey Jr.	50	60	80	200

—Ken Griffey Jr. #15 BGS 10 (Pristine) sold for $7,990 (eBay; 5/03)

87 Donruss

	NmMt 8	NmMt+ 8.5	MT 9	Gem 9.5/10
Bo Jackson RC	10	12	15	30
Greg Maddux RC	12	15	20	80
Rafael Palmeiro RC	5	6	10	25
Mark McGwire	5	6	15	40
Will Clark RC	5	5	8	20
Jamie Moyer RC	5	5	6	25
Barry Bonds RC	▲12	▲15	▲20	60
Barry Larkin RC	6	8	12	30
David Cone RC	5	5	6	25

—Barry Bonds #361 BGS 10 (Pristine) sold for $920 (eBay; 11/05)
—Barry Bonds #361 BGS 10 (Pristine) sold for $850 (eBay; 12/05)
—Barry Bonds #361 BGS 10 (Pristine) sold for $790 (eBay; 10/05)
—Jamie Moyer #315 BGS 10 (Pristine) sold for $215 (eBay; 11/03)
—Rafael Palmeiro #43 BGS 10 (Pristine) sold for $690 (eBay; 8/05)

87 Fleer

	NmMt 8	NmMt+ 8.5	MT 9	Gem 9.5/10
Barry Larkin RC	6	8	▲20	50
Will Clark RC	5	6	12	30
Bo Jackson RC	10	12	▲20	50
Barry Bonds RC	12	15	▲25	100

—Barry Bonds #604 BGS 10 (Pristine) sold for $1,800 (eBay; 9/04)

87 Topps

	NmMt 8	NmMt+ 8.5	MT 9	Gem 9.5/10
Bo Jackson RC	5	5	8	30
Barry Bonds RC	▲12	▲15	20	60
Mark McGwire	5	6	10	20
Will Clark RC	5	5	6	20
Rafael Palmeiro RC	5	6	10	20
Barry Larkin RC	4	10	15	30

—Barry Bonds #302 BGS 10 (Pristine) sold for $760 (eBay; 8/05)

88 Cape Cod Prospects P and L Promotions

	NmMt 8	NmMt+ 8.5	MT 9	Gem 9.5/10
Frank Thomas	20	25	30	80

—Frank Thomas #126 BGS 10 (Pristine) sold for $280 (eBay; 1/04)

88 Fleer Glossy

	NmMt 8	NmMt+ 8.5	MT 9	Gem 9.5/10
Edgar Martinez			▲50	200
Tom Glavine	6	8	▲20	50

88 Fleer Update

	NmMt 8	NmMt+ 8.5	MT 9	Gem 9.5/10
David Wells XRC	5	5	8	20
John Smoltz XRC	6	8	15	120
Craig Biggio XRC	6	8	12	50
Roberto Alomar XRC	5	5	8	20

88 Fleer Update Glossy

	NmMt 8	NmMt+ 8.5	MT 9	Gem 9.5/10
John Smoltz	20	25	30	150
Craig Biggio	12	15	25	100

88 San Bernardino Spirit Cal League Cards

	NmMt 8	NmMt+ 8.5	MT 9	Gem 9.5/10
Ken Griffey Jr.	30	40	60	5,000

1988 Score Rookie/Traded

	NmMt 8	NmMt+ 8.5	MT 9	Gem 9.5/10
80T Mark Grace XRC	8	10	12	25
103T Craig Biggio XRC	12	15	20	50
105T Roberto Alomar XRC	10	12	15	40

1988 Score Rookie/Traded Glossy

	NmMt 8	NmMt+ 8.5	MT 9	Gem 9.5/10
80T Mark Grace	8	10	12	30
103T Craig Biggio	60	80	80	400
105T Roberto Alomar	25	30	50	400

1989 Bowman

	NmMt 8	NmMt+ 8.5	MT 9	Gem 9.5/10
142 Gary Sheffield RC	5	5	5	40
220 Ken Griffey Jr. RC	10	10	▲25	80
266 John Smoltz RC	6	8	12	25

—Ken Griffey Jr. #41T BGS 10 (Pristine) sold for $3,505 (eBay; 8/05)

1989 Donruss

	NmMt 8	NmMt+ 8.5	MT 9	Gem 9.5/10
31 Gary Sheffield RC	5	5	5	5
33 Ken Griffey Jr. RC	▲15	▲20	▲30	150
42 Randy Johnson RC	5	5	8	30
561 Craig Biggio RC	5	5	10	20
635 Curt Schilling RC	5	5	10	25
642 John Smoltz RC	5	5	6	20

—Ken Griffey Jr. #33 BGS 10 (Pristine) sold for $440 (eBay; 11/05)
—Gary Sheffield #31 BGS 10 (Pristine) sold for $1,500 (eBay; 9/03)

1989 Fleer

	NmMt 8	NmMt+ 8.5	MT 9	Gem 9.5/10
196 Gary Sheffield RC	5	5	6	30
353 Craig Biggio RC	5	6	10	40
381 Randy Johnson RC	6	8	12	40
548 Ken Griffey Jr. RC	12	12	▲20	60
602 John Smoltz RC	5	5	10	30
616A Bill Ripken ERR	15	20	▲60	▲150
Rick Face written#(on knob of bat				

1989 Score Rookie/Traded

	NmMt 8	NmMt+ 8.5	MT 9	Gem 9.5/10
77T Randy Johnson	5	5	5	25
100T Ken Griffey Jr. RC	6	8	15	30

1989 Topps

	NmMt 8	NmMt+ 8.5	MT 9	Gem 9.5/10
49 Craig Biggio RC	5	5	6	30
343 Gary Sheffield RC	6	8	10	20
382 John Smoltz RC	6	8	10	30
647 Randy Johnson RC	6	8	10	30

1989 Topps Traded

	NmMt 8	NmMt+ 8.5	MT 9	Gem 9.5/10
41T Ken Griffey Jr. RC	12	15	20	▲50
57T Randy Johnson	4	5	8	15
104T Kenny Rogers RC	5	5	8	15
122T Omar Vizquel RC	5	5	5	25

1989 Upper Deck

	NmMt 8	NmMt+ 8.5	MT 9	Gem 9.5/10
1 Ken Griffey Jr. RC	▲60	▲60	▲120	500
13 Gary Sheffield RC	5	6	▲12	15
17 John Smoltz RC	8	10	▲15	25
25 Randy Johnson RC	12	15	20	50
273 Craig Biggio RC	6	8	10	25
787 Omar Vizquel RC	5	5	10	25

—Randy Johnson #25 BGS 10 (Pristine) sold for $264 (eBay; 4/09)

1990 Leaf

	NmMt 8	NmMt+ 8.5	MT 9	Gem 9.5/10
220 Sammy Sosa RC	10	▲12	▲15	50
237 John Olerud RC	4	5	8	25
245 Ken Griffey Jr.	8	8	12	50
297 David Justice RC	6	8	12	20
300 Frank Thomas RC	▲25	▲30	40	200
325 Larry Walker RC	12	15	▲20	100

—Sammy Sosa #220 BGS 10 (Pristine) sold for $2,525 (eBay; 11/05)
—Frank Thomas #300 BGS 10 (Pristine) sold for $1,049 (eBay; 7/13)

1990 Topps

	NmMt 8	NmMt+ 8.5	MT 9	Gem 9.5/10
331 Juan Gonzalez RC	5	5	6	15
414A FrankThomas NNOF	2,000	2,500	4,500	
414B Frank Thomas RC	5	6	10	30
692 Sammy Sosa RC	5	5	5	25
701 Bernie Williams RC	5	5	6	25
757 Larry Walker RC	5	5	6	20
USA1 George Bush PRES	1,500	2,000		

1991 Bowman

	NmMt 8	NmMt+ 8.5	MT 9	Gem 9.5/10
68 Jim Thome RC	8	12	15	60
183 Jeff Bagwell RC	5	6	10	60
272 Ivan Rodriguez RC	6	8	12	60
569 Chipper Jones RC	12	12	20	60

1991 Fleer Update

	NmMt 8	NmMt+ 8.5	MT 9	Gem 9.5/10
62 Ivan Rodriguez RC	5	5	8	25
87 Jeff Bagwell RC	5	6	10	20

1991 Stadium Club

	NmMt 8	NmMt+ 8.5	MT 9	Gem 9.5/10
388 Jeff Bagwell RC	8	10	15	25
576 Luis Gonzalez RC	5	6	10	50

1991 Topps

	NmMt 8	NmMt+ 8.5	MT 9	Gem 9.5/10
333 Chipper Jones RC	▲15	▲20	▲25	▲50

1991 Upper Deck

	NmMt 8	NmMt+ 8.5	MT 9	Gem 9.5/10
55 Chipper Jones RC	▲10	▲12	▲15	▲40
65 Mike Mussina RC	4	5	8	15
567 Luis Gonzalez RC	4	4	5	10
755 Jeff Bagwell RC	5	5	8	20
SP1 Michael Jordan	25	30	40	150

—Chipper Jones RC #55 BGS 10 (Pristine) sold for $260 (eBay; 3/13)
—Chipper Jones RC #55 BGS 10 (Pristine) sold for $255 (eBay; 3/13)

1991 Upper Deck Final Edition

	NmMt 8	NmMt+ 8.5	MT 9	Gem 9.5/10
2F Pedro Martinez RC	8	10	12	▲50
17F Jim Thome RC	10	12	▼15	40
55F Ivan Rodriguez RC	5	5	6	20

—Pedro Martinez #2F BGS 10 (Pristine) sold for $455 (eBay; 8/05)
—Ivan Rodriguez #55F SGC 100 (Pristine) sold for $85 (eBay; 7/05)
—Ivan Rodriguez #55F BGS 10 (Pristine) sold for $65 (eBay; 7/05)
—Ivan Rodriguez #55F BGS 10 (Pristine) sold for $60 (eBay; 5/05)
—Jim Thome #17F BGS 10 (Pristine) sold for $220 (eBay; 2/05)

1992 Bowman

	NmMt 8	NmMt+ 8.5	MT 9	Gem 9.5/10
11 Trevor Hoffman RC	25	30	▼40	120
28 Chipper Jones	12	15	20	▼40
82 Pedro Martinez	▲12	▲15	▲20	▲80
127 Carlos Delgado RC	6	8	12	50
298 Garret Anderson RC	5	6	10	30
302 Mariano Rivera RC	▼60	▼80	150	500
460 Jim Thome	6	8	10	30
461 Mike Piazza RC	25	30	40	▲150
532 Manny Ramirez RC	8	8	12	30
676 Manny Ramirez FOIL	4	5	10	20

—Pedro Martinez #82 BGS 10 (Pristine) sold for $820 (eBay; 8/05)
—Pedro Martinez #82 BGS 10 (Pristine) sold for $505 (eBay; 10/05)
—Mike Piazza #461 BGS 10 (Pristine) sold for $535 (eBay; 12/05)
—Mike Piazza #461 BGS 10 (Pristine) sold for $360 (eBay; 10/05)
—Manny Ramirez #532 BGS 10 (Pristine) sold for $1003 (eBay; 11/05)
—Manny Ramirez #532 BGS 10 (Pristine) sold for $635 (eBay; 11/05)
—Manny Ramirez #532 BGS 10 (Pristine) sold for $625 (eBay; 1/09)
—Manny Ramirez #532 BGS 10 (Pristine) sold for $535 (eBay; 11/05)

1992 Fleer Update

	NmMt 8	NmMt+ 8.5	MT 9	Gem 9.5/10
92 Mike Piazza RC	60	80	100	250
104 Jeff Kent RC	15	20	30	150

1992 Front Row Draft Picks

	NmMt 8	NmMt+ 8.5	MT 9	Gem 9.5/10
55 Derek Jeter	▲25	▲30	40	200

1992 Little Sun High School Prospects

	NmMt 8	NmMt+ 8.5	MT 9	Gem 9.5/10
2 Derek Jeter	100	120	200	400

1992 Upper Deck Minors

		NmMt 8	NmMt+ 8.5	MT 9	Gem 9.5/10
5	Derek Jeter FDP	15	20	30	100

1993 Bowman

		NmMt 8	NmMt+ 8.5	MT 9	Gem 9.5/10
103	Andy Pettitte RC	10	12	25	▼80
327	Mariano Rivera	25	30	40	120
511	Derek Jeter RC	▲30	▲40	▲100	▲500

1993 Pinnacle

		NmMt 8	NmMt+ 8.5	MT 9	Gem 9.5/10
457	Derek Jeter RC	▲40	▲50	▲100	▲500

1993 Select

		NmMt 8	NmMt+ 8.5	MT 9	Gem 9.5/10
360	Derek Jeter RC	▲20	▲25	40	▲300

1993 SP

		NmMt 8	NmMt+ 8.5	MT 9	Gem 9.5/10
273	Johnny Damon FOIL RC	10	12	20	200
279	Derek Jeter FOIL RC	▲800	▲1,000	2,500	8,000

—Derek Jeter #279 PSA 10 (Gem Mt) sold for $32,816 (Small Traditions; 9/14)
—Derek Jeter #279 PSA 10 (Gem Mt) sold for $30,000 (Heritage; 2/15)
—Derek Jeter #279 PSA 9 (Mint) priced at $1,500

1993 Stadium Club Murphy

		NmMt 8	NmMt+ 8.5	MT 9	Gem 9.5/10
93	Nomar Garciaparra USA	5	6	15	30
117	Derek Jeter RC	▲120	▲150	▲300	▲600

—Derek Jeter RC #117 BGS 10 (Pristine) sold for $1,267 (eBay; 10/12)

1993 Topps

		NmMt 8	NmMt+ 8.5	MT 9	Gem 9.5/10
98	Derek Jeter RC	▲25	▲30	▲50	200
799	Jim Edmonds RC	5	5	8	25

—Derek Jeter #98 BGS 10 (Pristine) sold for $2,669 (Small Traditions; 6/13)

1993 Topps Inaugural Marlins

		NmMt 8	NmMt+ 8.5	MT 9	Gem 9.5/10
98	Derek Jeter	100	150	▲250	▲1,200

1993 Topps Inaugural Rockies

		NmMt 8	NmMt+ 8.5	MT 9	Gem 9.5/10
98	Derek Jeter	120	150	▲400	▲1,500

1993 Topps Traded

		NmMt 8	NmMt+ 8.5	MT 9	Gem 9.5/10
19T	Todd Helton USA RC	6	8	▲12	▲50

—Todd Helton #19T BGS 10 (Pristine) sold for $470 (eBay; 6/05)

1993 Upper Deck

		NmMt 8	NmMt+ 8.5	MT 9	Gem 9.5/10
449	Derek Jeter RC	▲20	▲25	▲50	250

1994 Appleton Foxes Fleer/ProCards

		NmMt 8	NmMt+ 8.5	MT 9	Gem 9.5/10
1063	Alex Rodriguez	8	8	12	40

1994 Bowman

		NmMt 8	NmMt+ 8.5	MT 9	Gem 9.5/10
38	Jorge Posada RC	8	10	20	100
94	Edgar Renteria RC	5	6	8	25
104	Torii Hunter RC	8	10	15	40
232	Derrek Lee RC	8	10	15	20
433	Jermaine Dye RC	5	6	10	20
594	Paul LoDuca RC	5	5	8	15

1994 Bowman's Best

		NmMt 8	NmMt+ 8.5	MT 9	Gem 9.5/10
B19	Billy Wagner RC	5	5	8	12
B29	Jorge Posada RC	10	12	20	40
B63	Edgar Renteria RC	6	6	8	12

1994 Flair

		NmMt 8	NmMt+ 8.5	MT 9	Gem 9.5/10
340	Alex Rodriguez RC	12	12	15	50

—Alex Rodriguez #340 BGS 10 (Pristine) sold for $620 (eBay; 12/05)
—Alex Rodriguez #340 BGS 10 (Pristine) sold for $515 (eBay; 11/05)

1994 Flair Wave of the Future

		NmMt 8	NmMt+ 8.5	MT 9	Gem 9.5/10
B8	Alex Rodriguez	8	10	▲15	40

—Alex Rodriugez #B8 BGS 10 (Pristine) sold for $145 (eBay; 6/05)

1994 Fleer Update

		NmMt 8	NmMt+ 8.5	MT 9	Gem 9.5/10
86	Alex Rodriguez RC	8	12	15	50

1994 Leaf Limited Rookies Phenoms

		NmMt 8	NmMt+ 8.5	MT 9	Gem 9.5/10
10	Alex Rodriguez	80	120	120	800

1994 Score Rookie/Traded

		NmMt 8	NmMt+ 8.5	MT 9	Gem 9.5/10
HC1	Alex Rodriguez CU	120	150	250	

—Alex Rodriguez #HC1 BGS 9.5 (Gem) sold for $3,855 (eBay; 11/05)
—Alex Rodriguez #HC1 PSA 10 (Gem) sold for $1,525 (eBay; 11/05)

1994 SP

		NmMt 8	NmMt+ 8.5	MT 9	Gem 9.5/10
10	Derrek Lee FOIL RC	10	12	50	150
15	Alex Rodriguez FOIL RC	▲50	▲60	150	600

1994 SP Holoviews

		NmMt 8	NmMt+ 8.5	MT 9	Gem 9.5/10
33	Alex Rodriguez	15	20	25	150

1994 SP Holoviews Die Cuts

		NmMt 8	NmMt+ 8.5	MT 9	Gem 9.5/10
16	Michael Jordan	120	150	200	800
33	Alex Rodriguez	200	200	250	1,000

1994 Upper Deck

		NmMt 8	NmMt+ 8.5	MT 9	Gem 9.5/10
19	Michael Jordan RC	20	25	30	60
24	Alex Rodriguez RC	12	15	20	60
298	Alex Rodriguez UDCA	5	6	10	30
A298	Alex Rodriguez AU	100	100	120	300

—Alex Rodriguez AU #A298 BGS 10 (Pristine) sold for $3,305 (eBay; 4/09)

1995 Bowman's Best

		NmMt 8	NmMt+ 8.5	MT 9	Gem 9.5/10
B2	Vladimir Guerrero RC	30	40	60	500
B3	Bob Abreu RC	6	8	10	40
B7	Andruw Jones RC	8	12	25	60
B10	Richie Sexson RC	8	10	15	40
B73	Bartolo Colon RC	8	10	12	50
B74	Chris Carpenter RC	8	10	12	20
B87	Scott Rolen RC	8	10	20	25
X5	C.Beltran/J.Gonzalez UER	5	6	8	20

—Andruw Jones #B7 BGS 10 (Pristine) sold for $1,225 (eBay; 5/05)
—Andruw Jones #B7 BGS 10 (Pristine) sold for $865 (eBay; 8/05)
—Scott Rolen #B87 BGS 10 (Pristine) sold for $510 (eBay; 12/05)

1997 Bowman

		NmMt 8	NmMt+ 8.5	MT 9	Gem 9.5/10
194	Adrian Beltre RC	15	20	40	300
196	Kerry Wood RC	5	6	8	15
308	Roy Halladay RC	15	20	50	300
411	Miguel Tejada RC	8	10	15	30
424	Vernon Wells RC	5	5	6	10
438	Lance Berkman RC	5	6	10	20

1997 Bowman Chrome

		NmMt 8	NmMt+ 8.5	MT 9	Gem 9.5/10
182	Adrian Beltre RC	30	40	50	150
183	Kerry Wood RC	5	6	▲12	30
192	Eric Chavez RC	5	5	6	15
212	Roy Halladay RC	50	60	100	400
214	Aramis Ramirez RC	5	6	10	15
273	Miguel Tejada RC	5	5	10	20
284	Vernon Wells RC	6	8	10	30
287	Jon Garland RC	6	8	12	40

—Eric Chavez #192 BGS 10 (Pristine) sold for $205 (eBay; 8/05)

1997 Bowman's Best

		NmMt 8	NmMt+ 8.5	MT 9	Gem 9.5/10
114	Miguel Tejada RC	6	8	12	25
117	Adrian Beltre RC	12	20	25	60
134	Roy Halladay RC	▼15	▼20	▼25	120
154	Kerry Wood RC	5	5	8	20

1997 Fleer

		NmMt 8	NmMt+ 8.5	MT 9	Gem 9.5/10
512	David Arias-Ortiz RC	50	60	80	150

1997 Ultra

		NmMt 8	NmMt+ 8.5	MT 9	Gem 9.5/10
518	David Arias-Ortiz RC	80	80	▲150	600

1998 Bowman Chrome

		NmMt 8	NmMt+ 8.5	MT 9	Gem 9.5/10
85	Mike Lowell RC	5	6	10	15
91	Kevin Millwood RC	5	5	8	12
134	Troy Glaus RC	4	5	8	12
181	Jimmy Rollins RC	5	6	10	40
185	Magglio Ordonez RC	6	6	8	15
221	Orlando Hernandez RC	5	6	8	25
428	Carlos Lee RC	8	10	15	25

1999 Bowman Chrome

		NmMt 8	NmMt+ 8.5	MT 9	Gem 9.5/10
175	Pat Burrell RC	4	5	8	12
200	Austin Kearns RC	8	10	15	25
344	C.C. Sabathia RC	8	10	15	100
350	Alfonso Soriano RC	5	6	10	20
355	Mark Mulder RC	5	6	10	20
364	Rafael Furcal RC	5	6	10	20
369	Adam Dunn RC	6	6	10	15
375	Tim Hudson RC	5	5	10	30
400	Matt Holliday RC	5	5	8	20
421	David Eckstein RC	6	8	12	25
431	Josh Hamilton RC	6	8	15	20
440	Carl Crawford RC	4	5	8	12

—Matt Holliday #400 BGS 10 (Pristine) sold for $100 (eBay; 10/05)
—Wily Mo Pena #401 BGS 10 (Pristine) sold for $150 (eBay; 1/05)

1999 Bowman's Best

		NmMt 8	NmMt+ 8.5	MT 9	Gem 9.5/10
151	Pat Burrell RC	5	5	5	20
160	Austin Kearns RC	5	5	5	20
169	Alfonso Soriano RC	5	6	10	25
171	C.C. Sabathia RC	5	6	12	40
172	Matt Holliday RC	6	8	12	30

1999 Finest

		NmMt 8	NmMt+ 8.5	MT 9	Gem 9.5/10
131	Pat Burrell RC	5	5	6	25
133	Austin Kearns RC	5	5	5	20
286	Alfonso Soriano RC	8	10	15	30
294	C.C. Sabathia RC	6	8	12	30

1999 Fleer Tradition Update

		NmMt 8	NmMt+ 8.5	MT 9	Gem 9.5/10
U3	Pat Burrell RC	5	5	8	20
U5	Alfonso Soriano RC	5	6	10	25
U42	Eric Gagne RC	5	5	8	25
U122	Josh Beckett RC	10	12	15	25

1999 Topps Traded Autographs

		NmMt 8	NmMt+ 8.5	MT 9	Gem 9.5/10
T33	C.C. Sabathia	30	40	50	120
T50	Adam Dunn	15	20	25	50
T51	Austin Kearns	6	8	10	25
T65	Alfonso Soriano	25	30	50	80
T66	Josh Hamilton	50	60	100	200

1999 Topps Chrome Traded

		NmMt 8	NmMt+ 8.5	MT 9	Gem 9.5/10
T8	Mark Mulder RC	5	5	6	10
T33	C.C. Sabathia RC	6	6	12	50
T44	Pat Burrell	5	5	6	10
T50	Adam Dunn	5	5	8	20
T65	Alfonso Soriano RC	6	6	10	15
T66	Josh Hamilton RC	6	8	10	15
T75	Carl Crawford RC	5	6	8	15

1999 Ultimate Victory

		NmMt 8	NmMt+ 8.5	MT 9	Gem 9.5/10
136	Alfonso Soriano SP RC	8	10	12	20
137	Tim Hudson SP RC	6	8	12	20
138	Josh Beckett SP RC	8	10	15	25
141	Pat Burrell SP RC	6	8	12	20
145	Rick Ankiel SP RC	6	8	12	20

2000 Bowman Draft

		NmMt 8	NmMt+ 8.5	MT 9	Gem 9.5/10
4	Barry Zito	5	5	6	12
69	Mark Buehrle RC	5	5	8	12
86	Adrian Gonzalez RC	6	8	12	15

	NmMt 8	NmMt+ 8.5	MT 9	Gem 9.5/10
Adam Wainwright RC	5	5	6	12
Grady Sizemore RC	5	5	6	10

00 Bowman Chrome

	NmMt 8	NmMt+ 8.5	MT 9	Gem 9.5/10
Francisco Rodriguez RC	6	8	20	40
Roy Oswalt RC	8	10	12	25
Barry Zito RC	10	12	15	20

00 Bowman Chrome Draft

	NmMt 8	NmMt+ 8.5	MT 9	Gem 9.5/10
Barry Zito	5	5	10	30
Mark Buehrle RC	6	6	8	15
Adrian Gonzalez RC	8	10	12	15
Adam Wainwright RC	5	6	10	20

00 SPx

	NmMt 8	NmMt+ 8.5	MT 9	Gem 9.5/10
Roy Oswalt/1600 RC	15	20	30	50
Barry Zito AU/1500 RC	12	15	25	200

00 Topps Traded

	NmMt 8	NmMt+ 8.5	MT 9	Gem 9.5/10
Carlos Zambrano RC	4	5	6	10
Francisco Rodriguez RC	8	10	15	40
Miguel Cabrera RC	25	30	50	120
Mike Young RC	5	5	8	12

00 Topps Traded Autographs

	NmMt 8	NmMt+ 8.5	MT 9	Gem 9.5/10
Carlos Zambrano	12	15	25	150
Francisco Rodriguez	15	20	25	60
Miguel Cabrera	800	1,000	1,200	3,000
Mike Young	40	50	100	250

00 Topps Chrome Traded

	NmMt 8	NmMt+ 8.5	MT 9	Gem 9.5/10
Carlos Zambrano RC	5	5	5	10
Francisco Rodriguez RC	5	5	12	10
Miguel Cabrera RC	60	80	100	300
Mike Young RC	6	8	12	25
Adrian Gonzalez RC	5	6	10	20
Adam Wainwright RC	5	8	12	30

01 Bowman

	NmMt 8	NmMt+ 8.5	MT 9	Gem 9.5/10
Albert Pujols RC	50	60	▲120	500

01 Bowman Autographs

	NmMt 8	NmMt+ 8.5	MT 9	Gem 9.5/10
Albert Pujols	300	400	▲800	▲1,200

—ert Pujols #AP BGS 10 (Pristine) sold for $3,240 (eBay; 3/05)
—ert Pujols #AP BGS 10 (Pristine) sold for $1,302 (eBay; 5/09)
—ert Pujols #AP BGS 10 (Pristine) sold for $1,0768 (eBay; 4/12)

01 Bowman Draft

	NmMt 8	NmMt+ 8.5	MT 9	Gem 9.5/10
9 Chase Utley RC	10	12	15	80
4 Ichiro Suzuki RC	12	15	30	150
8 Bobby Crosby RC	5	5	10	30

01 Bowman Chrome

	NmMt 8	NmMt+ 8.5	MT 9	Gem 9.5/10
Travis Hafner RC	8	10	12	50
Wilson Betemit RC	8	10	15	30
Jose Reyes RC	10	10	12	40
Justin Morneau RC	8	10	12	15
Jake Peavy RC	15	20	25	40
Albert Pujols AU RC	2,500	3,000	7,000	15,000
Ichiro Suzuki English RC	100	120	200	300
Ichiro Suzuki Japan RC	200		200	300

—ert Pujols #340 BGS 10 (Pristine) sold for $12,100 (eBay; 3/05)
—ert Pujols #340 BGS 10 (Pristine) sold for $11,000 (eBay; 4/05)

01 Bowman Heritage

	NmMt 8	NmMt+ 8.5	MT 9	Gem 9.5/10
Travis Hafner RC	5	5	20	30
Chase Utley RC	10	12	25	40
Albert Pujols SP RC	40	50	▲80	250
Ichiro Suzuki SP RC	12	15	25	120

2001 Bowman's Best

	NmMt 8	NmMt+ 8.5	MT 9	Gem 9.5/10
162 Ichiro Suzuki RC	40	50	120	300
166 Justin Morneau RC	5	6	10	25
174 Albert Pujols RC	80	100	▲250	500

2001 Donruss Rookies

	NmMt 8	NmMt+ 8.5	MT 9	Gem 9.5/10
R97 Albert Pujols UPD	20	25	40	80

2001 Donruss Elite

	NmMt 8	NmMt+ 8.5	MT 9	Gem 9.5/10
156 Albert Pujols SP RC	150	200	200	600
195 Ichiro Suzuki SP RC	50	60	150	400
206 Victor Martinez/410 XRC	30	40	120	200
250 Mark Teixeira/543 XRC	20	25	50	200

—Albert Pujols #156 PSA 10 (Gem) sold for $1,325 (eBay; 4/05)
—Albert Pujols #156 PSA 10 (Gem) sold for $910 (eBay; 11/05)

2001 E-X

	NmMt 8	NmMt+ 8.5	MT 9	Gem 9.5/10
105 Ichiro Suzuki/1999 RC	30	40	100	200
131 Albert Pujols/499 RC	150	200	250	600

2001 Finest

	NmMt 8	NmMt+ 8.5	MT 9	Gem 9.5/10
134 Jose Reyes PROS RC	20	25	30	50

2001 Fleer Authority

	NmMt 8	NmMt+ 8.5	MT 9	Gem 9.5/10
101 Ichiro Suzuki RC	15	30	40	200
102 Albert Pujols RC	25	25	60	200
146 Mark Teixeira RC	5	5	8	20

2001 Fleer Platinum

	NmMt 8	NmMt+ 8.5	MT 9	Gem 9.5/10
301 Albert Pujols/1500 RC	25	30	50	150

2001 Fleer Premium

	NmMt 8	NmMt+ 8.5	MT 9	Gem 9.5/10
233 Albert Pujols RC	30	40	60	300

—Ichiro Suzuki #231 BGS 9.5 (Gem) sold for $420 (eBay; 5/05)
—Ichiro Suzuki #231 PSA 10 (Gem) sold for $220 (eBay; 11/05)

2001 Fleer Tradition

	NmMt 8	NmMt+ 8.5	MT 9	Gem 9.5/10
451 Albert Pujols RC	20	25	40	80

2001 Fleer Triple Crown

	NmMt 8	NmMt+ 8.5	MT 9	Gem 9.5/10
309 Albert Pujols/2999 RC	30	30	60	150

2001 Leaf Rookies and Stars

	NmMt 8	NmMt+ 8.5	MT 9	Gem 9.5/10
205 Albert Pujols RC	100	120	150	300
221 Mark Teixeira RC	20	25	40	100
273 Mark Prior RC	20	25	50	120

—Ichiro Suzuki #251 BGS 9.5 (Gem) sold for $310 (eBay; 5/05)

2001 SP Authentic

	NmMt 8	NmMt+ 8.5	MT 9	Gem 9.5/10
91 Ichiro Suzuki FW RC	150	200	500	▲1,000
95 Travis Hafner FW RC	30	40	50	200
126 Albert Pujols FW RC	150	200	400	▲1,500
211 Mark Prior FW RC	12	15	30	50
212 Mark Teixeira FW RC	15	20	25	50
234 Brian Roberts FW RC				

—Mark Prior #211 BGS 10 (Pristine) sold for $250 (eBay; 9/05)
—Brian Roberts #234 BGS 10 (Pristine) sold for $145 (eBay; 8/05)
—Mark Teixeira #212 BGS 10 (Pristine) sold for $475 (eBay; 10/05)
—Mark Teixeira #212 BGS 10 (Pristine) sold for $420 (eBay; 4/05)
—Mark Teixeira #212 BGS 10 (Pristine) sold for $375 (eBay; 7/05)
—Mark Teixeira #212 BGS 10 (Pristine) sold for $370 (eBay; 8/05)
—Mark Teixeira #212 BGS 10 (Pristine) sold for $350 (eBay; 10/05)
—Mark Teixeira #212 BGS 10 (Pristine) sold for $340 (eBay; 9/05)

2001 SPx

	NmMt 8	NmMt+ 8.5	MT 9	Gem 9.5/10
150 Ichiro Suzuki Jsy AU RC	1,000	1,200	2,000	4,000
206 Albert Pujols YS AU RC	400	500	600	1,200
207 Mark Teixeira YS AU RC	12	15	20	40
208 Mark Prior YS AU RC	10	12	20	40

—Mark Prior #208 BGS 10 (Pristine) sold for $1,580 (eBay; 2/05)

2001 Sweet Spot

	NmMt 8	NmMt+ 8.5	MT 9	Gem 9.5/10
62 Ichiro Suzuki SB RC	100	120	150	300
121 Albert Pujols SB RC	50	60	100	250
138 Mark Teixeira SB RC	10	12	15	30
139 Mark Prior SB RC	5	6	8	12

2001 Topps

	NmMt 8	NmMt+ 8.5	MT 9	Gem 9.5/10
726 Ichiro Suzuki RC	▲25	▲30	▲60	250

2001 Topps Traded

	NmMt 8	NmMt+ 8.5	MT 9	Gem 9.5/10
T99 I.Suzuki/A.Pujols ROY	▲40	▲50	▲80	250
T235 Justin Morneau RC	6	8	15	60
T242 Jose Reyes RC	8	10	15	40
T247 Albert Pujols RC	40	50	▲100	300

2001 Topps Chrome

	NmMt 8	NmMt+ 8.5	MT 9	Gem 9.5/10
596 Albert Pujols RC	50	50	▲120	▲400

2001 Topps Chrome Traded

	NmMt 8	NmMt+ 8.5	MT 9	Gem 9.5/10
T99 I.Suzuki/A.Pujols ROY	40	50	60	300
T214 Hank Blalock RC	5	6	15	80
T235 Justin Morneau RC	5	6	10	15
T242 Jose Reyes RC	8	10	15	30
T247 Albert Pujols	25	50	▲150	400
T266 Ichiro Suzuki RC	50	60	100	250

2001 Topps Gallery

	NmMt 8	NmMt+ 8.5	MT 9	Gem 9.5/10
135 Albert Pujols RC	30	30	▲50	100
151A Ichiro Suzuki English RC	12	15	25	60
151B Ichiro Suzuki Japan RC	12	15	25	60

2001 Topps Stars

	NmMt 8	NmMt+ 8.5	MT 9	Gem 9.5/10
198 Albert Pujols RC	20	25	▲50	100

2001 UD Reserve

	NmMt 8	NmMt+ 8.5	MT 9	Gem 9.5/10
181 Ichiro Suzuki SP RC	15	20	30	50
204 Albert Pujols SP RC	60	80	100	250

2001 Upper Deck Ovation

	NmMt 8	NmMt+ 8.5	MT 9	Gem 9.5/10
76 Ichiro Suzuki WP RC	12	15	120	150

2001 Upper Deck Pros and Prospects

	NmMt 8	NmMt+ 8.5	MT 9	Gem 9.5/10

2001 Upper Deck Victory

	NmMt 8	NmMt+ 8.5	MT 9	Gem 9.5/10
564 Ichiro Suzuki RC	6	8	12	25

—Ichiro Suzuki #564 BGS 10 (Pristine) sold for $100 (eBay; 3/05)
—Ichiro Suzuki #564 BGS 10 (Pristine) sold for $95 (eBay; 7/05)

2001 Upper Deck Vintage

	NmMt 8	NmMt+ 8.5	MT 9	Gem 9.5/10
346 Ichiro Suzuki RC	6	8	15	40

2002 Bowman Chrome

	NmMt 8	NmMt+ 8.5	MT 9	Gem 9.5/10
165 Rich Harden SP RC	5	8	10	15
348 Jose Bautista SP RC	12	15	25	60
385 David Wright AU A RC	60	80	100	200
391 Joe Mauer AU A RC	60	80	120	300

2002 Bowman Chrome Draft

	NmMt 8	NmMt+ 8.5	MT 9	Gem 9.5/10
6 Zack Greinke RC	10	12	20	30
16 Nick Swisher RC	5	5	6	15
17 Cole Hamels RC	6	8	12	40
23 Jeff Francoeur RC	5	5	6	15
25 Matt Cain RC	8	10	15	▼20
44 Joey Votto RC	▼40	▼50	▼60	▲250
71 Curtis Granderson RC	10	12	15	25
99 B.J. Upton RC	5	5	8	12

—Cole Hamels #17 BGS 10 (Pristine) sold for $370 (eBay; 4/04)
—Dallas McPherson #112 BGS 10 (Pristine) sold for $210 (eBay; 9/05)
—Jeremy Reed #59 BGS 10 (Pristine) sold for $300 (eBay; 4/05)

2002 Bowman's Best

		NmMt 8	NmMt+ 8.5	MT 9	Gem 9.5/10
110	Joe Mauer AU A RC	40	50	60	100
168	Francisco Liriano AU A RC	10	12	15	30

2002 Topps

		NmMt 8	NmMt+ 8.5	MT 9	Gem 9.5/10
622	Joe Mauer RC	5	6	15	60

2002 Upper Deck Prospect Premieres

		NmMt 8	NmMt+ 8.5	MT 9	Gem 9.5/10
12	Jon Lester XRC	6	8	20	40
14	Curtis Granderson XRC	5	5	8	12
25	Francisco Liriano XRC	5	5	8	12
92	Prince Fielder AU XRC	20	20	25	30
93	Zack Greinke AU XRC	30	40	50	80
95	Scott Kazmir AU XRC	6	8	12	20
96	B.J. Upton AU XRC	6	8	12	20

2002 USA Baseball National Team

		NmMt 8	NmMt+ 8.5	MT 9	Gem 9.5/10
17	Dustin Pedroia	8	10	15	30

2003 Bowman Chrome

		NmMt 8	NmMt+ 8.5	MT 9	Gem 9.5/10
331	Brian McCann AU A RC	12	15	20	50
334	Hanley Ramirez AU A RC	15	20	40	80
336	Kevin Youkilis AU A RC	10	12	15	40

2003 Bowman Chrome Draft

		NmMt 8	NmMt+ 8.5	MT 9	Gem 9.5/10
51	Jon Papelbon RC	5	6	10	20
124	Robinson Cano RC	15	20	▼25	▼100
138	Ryan Howard RC	8	10	▼12	▼20
171	Nick Markakis AU RC	40	50	60	100

2003 Bowman Heritage Signs of Greatness

		NmMt 8	NmMt+ 8.5	MT 9	Gem 9.5/10
RC	Robinson Cano	▼50	▼60	▼100	▼250

2003 SP Authentic

		NmMt 8	NmMt+ 8.5	MT 9	Gem 9.5/10
181	Hid Matsui FW AU RC	275	300	350	450
215	Delmon Young FW RC	12	15	20	60

2003 SPx

		NmMt 8	NmMt+ 8.5	MT 9	Gem 9.5/10
161	Hideki Matsui AU Jsy RC	150	200	250	400
382	Delm Young AU Jsy RC	20	25	30	60

—Delmon Young #382 BGS 10 (Pristine) sold for $2,805 (eBay; 8/05)

2003 Upper Deck Prospect Premieres

		NmMt 8	NmMt+ 8.5	MT 9	Gem 9.5/10
7	Adam Jones XRC	6	8	12	30
9	Andre Ethier XRC	8	10	15	30
16	Carlos Quentin XRC	6	8	12	25
17	Chad Billingsley XRC	6	8	12	25
21	Conor Jackson XRC	5	6	10	25
34	Jarrod Saltalamacchia XRC	5	6	10	25
43	Lastings Milledge XRC	5	6	10	25
73	Brandon Wood XRC	5	6	10	25
84	Nick Markakis XRC	5	6	10	25
90	Delmon Young XRC	8	10	15	30

—Conor Jackson #21 BGS 10 (Pristine) sold for $410 (eBay; 6/05)

2003 Upper Deck Prospect Premieres Autographs

		NmMt 8	NmMt+ 8.5	MT 9	Gem 9.5/10
P7	Adam Jones	50	60	80	200

2003 USA Baseball National Team

		NmMt 8	NmMt+ 8.5	MT 9	Gem 9.5/10
5	Justin Verlander	10	12	25	60

2004 Bowman Signs of the Future

		NmMt 8	NmMt+ 8.5	MT 9	Gem 9.5/10
JV	Joey Votto A	150	150	200	500

2004 Bowman Chrome

		NmMt 8	NmMt+ 8.5	MT 9	Gem 9.5/10
301	Yadier Molina RC	25	30	60	150
345	Felix Hernandez AU RC	80	▼80	▼100	▲200

2004 Bowman Chrome Draft

		NmMt 8	NmMt+ 8.5	MT 9	Gem 9.5/10
166	Matt Bush AU RC	10	12	15	25
170	Homer Bailey AU RC	10	12	15	25
172	Neil Walker AU RC	10	12	15	25
174	Philip Hughes AU RC	8	10	12	20

2004 Bowman Chrome Draft AFLAC

		NmMt 8	NmMt+ 8.5	MT 9	Gem 9.5/10
5	Andrew McCutchen	12	15	25	40

2004 Bowman Heritage

		NmMt 8	NmMt+ 8.5	MT 9	Gem 9.5/10
30	Yadier Molina FY RC	10	12	▲50	▲200

2004 Bowman Sterling

		NmMt 8	NmMt+ 8.5	MT 9	Gem 9.5/10
DW	David Wright AU Jsy	15	20	25	40
FH	Felix Hernandez FY RC	12	15	20	25

—Robinson Cano #RC BGS 10 (Pristine) sold for $230 (eBay; 6/05)
—Felix Hernandez #FH BGS 10 (Pristine) sold for $155 (eBay; 11/05)
—Felix Hernandez #FH BGS 10 (Pristine) sold for $150 (eBay; 10/05)

2004 Bowman's Best

		NmMt 8	NmMt+ 8.5	MT 9	Gem 9.5/10
FH	Felix Hernandez FY AU RC	30	30	40	150
YM	Yadier Molina FY AU RC	200	200	300	500

2004 SP Prospects

		NmMt 8	NmMt+ 8.5	MT 9	Gem 9.5/10
339	Hunter Pence AU 600/RC	30	40	50	120
340	Dustin Pedroia AU 400/RC	50	60	200	400

2004 Topps

		NmMt 8	NmMt+ 8.5	MT 9	Gem 9.5/10
324	Yadier Molina FY RC	12	15	50	100

2004 Topps Traded

		NmMt 8	NmMt+ 8.5	MT 9	Gem 9.5/10
T144	Felix Hernandez FY RC	5	6	10	30

2004 Topps Chrome

		NmMt 8	NmMt+ 8.5	MT 9	Gem 9.5/10
219	Yadier Molina FY RC	12	15	▲120	200

2004 Topps Chrome Traded

		NmMt 8	NmMt+ 8.5	MT 9	Gem 9.5/10
T144	Felix Hernandez FY RC	8	10	15	50

2004 Topps Cracker Jack

		NmMt 8	NmMt+ 8.5	MT 9	Gem 9.5/10
204	Yadier Molina RC	8	10	20	40

2005 BBM Japan Rookie Edition

		NmMt 8	NmMt+ 8.5	MT 9	Gem 9.5/10
12	Yu Darvish	20	25	30	50

2005 Bowman Chrome

		NmMt 8	NmMt+ 8.5	MT 9	Gem 9.5/10
171	Ian Kinsler RC	5	5	5	40
316	Carlos Gonzalez RC	6	8	8	20
331	Justin Verlander AU RC	120	150	▲300	▲500
349	Matthew Kemp AU RC	30	40	60	100

—Tadahito Iguchi #301 BGS 10 (Pristine) sold for $90 (eBay; 10/050)
—Chuck James #298 BGS 10 (Pristine) sold for $165 (eBay; 10/05)
—Chris Young #318 BGS 10 (Pristine) sold for $90 (eBay; 11/05)

2005 Bowman Chrome Draft

		NmMt 8	NmMt+ 8.5	MT 9	Gem 9.5/10
32	Jay Bruce FY RC	5	6	▼8	▼12
63	Andrew McCutchen FY RC	8	▲15	▲20	▲40
105	Troy Tulowitzki FY RC	5	6	10	25
129	Justin Verlander FY	8	10	15	30
167	Jered Weaver AU A RC	15	20	25	50
168	Ryan Braun AU B RC	30	40	50	80
178	Ryan Zimmerman AU B RC	25	30	▲50	80

2005 Bowman Sterling

		NmMt 8	NmMt+ 8.5	MT 9	Gem 9.5/10
AM	Andrew McCutchen AU Jsy D RC	40	40	50	120
DP	Dustin Pedroia AU Jsy A	30	40	50	100
JB	Jay Bruce AU Jsy D RC	8	10	12	30
JV	J.Verlander AU Jsy A RC	▲120	▲150	▲200	▲300

		NmMt 8	NmMt+ 8.5	MT 9	Gem 9.5/1
RB	Ryan Braun AU A RC	15	20	25	60
RM	Russ Martin AU Jsy F RC	8	10	12	30
RZ	Ryan Zimmerman RC	6	8	10	25
TT	Troy Tulowitzki RC	10	12	15	30

2005 SP Authentic

		NmMt 8	NmMt+ 8.5	MT 9	Gem 9.5/1
137	Justin Verlander AU RC	80	100	120	400
152	Nelson Cruz AU RC	50	60	80	120
159	Prince Fielder AU RC	25	30	40	100

2005 SPx

		NmMt 8	NmMt+ 8.5	MT 9	Gem 9.5/1
135	Justin Verlander AU RC	60	80	100	200
147	Nelson Cruz AU RC	30	40	50	100
153	Prince Fielder AU RC	20	25	30	60
169	Ubaldo Jimenez AU RC	15	20	25	50
173	Ryan Zimmerman AU RC	40	50	60	120

2005 Topps

		NmMt 8	NmMt+ 8.5	MT 9	Gem 9.5/1
677	Justin Verlander FY RC	▲60	▲80	▲100	▲300

2005 Topps Chrome

		NmMt 8	NmMt+ 8.5	MT 9	Gem 9.5/10
214	Ian Kinsler FY RC	6	8	10	25
242	Justin Verlander FY AU RC	80	100	▲250	▲400

2005 Topps Chrome Update

		NmMt 8	NmMt+ 8.5	MT 9	Gem 9.5/1
169	Matthew Kemp FY RC	5	6	8	20
198	Ryan Braun FY RC	8	10	15	25
202	Jacoby Ellsbury FY RC	8	10	15	25
208	Ryan Zimmerman FY RC	8	10	12	15
222	Jay Bruce FY AU A RC	12	15	20	40
234	A.McCutchen FY AU B RC	50	60	80	120

2005-06 USA Baseball Junior National Team

		NmMt 8	NmMt+ 8.5	MT 9	Gem 9.5/1
86	Clayton Kershaw	8	10	15	60

2005-06 USA Baseball National Team

		NmMt 8	NmMt+ 8.5	MT 9	Gem 9.5/1
56	Max Scherzer	8	12	25	100

2006 Bowman Chrome Prospects

		NmMt 8	NmMt+ 8.5	MT 9	Gem 9.5/1
BC1	Alex Gordon	5	5	8	15
BC122	Elvis Andrus	5	5	8	15
BC129	Hunter Pence	5	5	8	15
BC221	Alex Gordon AU	20	25	30	50
BC223	Justin Upton AU	25	30	40	60
BC239	Jon Lester AU	40	50	60	100
BC242	Jose Bautista AU	15	20	25	40

2006 Bowman Chrome Draft Draft Picks

		NmMt 8	NmMt+ 8.5	MT 9	Gem 9.5/1
66	Evan Longoria AU	30	40	50	100
84	Clayton Kershaw AU	▼300	▼400	▼500	▼800

2006 Bowman Heritage Prospects

		NmMt 8	NmMt+ 8.5	MT 9	Gem 9.5/1
85	Clayton Kershaw	15	25	30	150

2006 Bowman Sterling Prospects

		NmMt 8	NmMt+ 8.5	MT 9	Gem 9.5/1
CHH	Chad Huffman AU B	15	20	25	40
CK	Clayton Kershaw AU A	200	250	300	400
CW	Colton Willems AU B	15	20	25	40
EL	Evan Longoria AU B	15	20	25	60
JU	Justin Upton AU B	15	20	25	40

2006-07 USA Baseball

		NmMt 8	NmMt+ 8.5	MT 9	Gem 9.5/1
45	Matt Harvey	6	8	12	50

2007 Bowman Draft Draft Picks

		NmMt 8	NmMt+ 8.5	MT 9	Gem 9.5/1
BDPP54	Jason Heyward	5	6	20	30

007 Bowman Draft Future's Game Prospects

	NmMt 8	NmMt+ 8.5	MT 9	Gem 9.5/10
P77 Clayton Kershaw	10	12	25	60

007 Bowman Chrome

	NmMt 8	NmMt+ 8.5	MT 9	Gem 9.5/10
Daisuke Matsuzaka RC	6	8	15	25
Tim Lincecum RC	5	6	10	15

007 Bowman Chrome Prospects

	NmMt 8	NmMt+ 8.5	MT 9	Gem 9.5/10
31 Daniel Murphy	10	12	20	50
38 Tim Lincecum AU	20	25	30	▲60
48 Hunter Pence AU	10	12	15	25
49 Dellin Betances AU	15	20	25	40
—Tommy Hanson #BC162 BGS 10 (Pristine) sold for $332 (eBay; 4/09)				

007 Bowman Chrome Draft

	NmMt 8	NmMt+ 8.5	MT 9	Gem 9.5/10
3 Justin Upton RC	6	8	12	30
11 Tim Lincecum RC	8	10	15	40
54 Mark Reynolds RC	5	6	10	20

007 Bowman Chrome Draft Draft Picks

	NmMt 8	NmMt+ 8.5	MT 9	Gem 9.5/10
P54 Jason Heyward	5	5	8	15
P55 David Price	5	5	8	15
P61 Madison Bumgarner	8	10	▲20	▲40
—David Price #BDPP55 BGS 10 (Pristine) sold for $96 (eBay; 5/09)				

007 Bowman Chrome Draft Future's Game Prospects

	NmMt 8	NmMt+ 8.5	MT 9	Gem 9.5/10
P77 Clayton Kershaw	15	20	20	100

007 Bowman Sterling

	NmMt 8	NmMt+ 8.5	MT 9	Gem 9.5/10
Ryan Braun AU (RC)	15	20	25	40
Tim Lincecum AU RC	15	20	25	50

007 Bowman Sterling Prospects

	NmMt 8	NmMt+ 8.5	MT 9	Gem 9.5/10
Clayton Kershaw Jsy AU	120	150	200	250
David Price AU	20	25	30	40
Evan Longoria Jsy AU	12	15	20	30
Joey Votto Jsy AU	25	30	40	60
3 Madison Bumgarner AU	60	80	100	150
Steve Pearce Jsy AU	15	20	25	40

007 Bowman's Best

	NmMt 8	NmMt+ 8.5	MT 9	Gem 9.5/10
Tim Lincecum AU RC UER	30	40	50	100

007 Donruss Elite Extra Edition

	NmMt 8	NmMt+ 8.5	MT 9	Gem 9.5/10
Jake Arrieta AU/949	100	120	150	300
Jason Heyward AU/750	20	25	30	50
Madison Bumgarner AU/794	50	60	80	120
Matt Wieters AU/799	12	15	20	40
Mike Moustakas AU/999	10	12	15	50
Chris Davis AU/374	20	25	30	100
Austin Jackson AU/794	15	20	25	50

007 SPx

	NmMt 8	NmMt+ 8.5	MT 9	Gem 9.5/10
Tim Lincecum AU RC	40	50	60	150
Ryan Braun AU (RC)	15	20	25	50
Daisuke Matsuzaka AU RC	30	40	50	120

007 Topps

	NmMt 8	NmMt+ 8.5	MT 9	Gem 9.5/10
Derek Jeter w/Mantle#/Bush	12	15	20	150

007 Topps AFLAC

	NmMt 8	NmMt+ 8.5	MT 9	Gem 9.5/10
Tim Beckham	60	80	120	200

007 Upper Deck Goudey Sport Royalty

	NmMt 8	NmMt+ 8.5	MT 9	Gem 9.5/10
Kevin Durant	15	20	40	100

2008 Bowman Chrome Prospects

	NmMt 8	NmMt+ 8.5	MT 9	Gem 9.5/10
BCP111 David Price AU	20	25	30	50
BCP120 Madison Bumgarner AU	100	120	150	250
BCP121 Jason Heyward AU	12	15	20	30
—Matt Laporta AU #BCP113 BGS 10 (Pristine) sold for $267 (eBay; 5/09)				
—Matt Laporta AU #BCP113 BGS 10 (Pristine) sold for $179 (eBay; 4/09)				

2008 Bowman Chrome Draft

	NmMt 8	NmMt+ 8.5	MT 9	Gem 9.5/10
BDP26a Clayton Kershaw RC	12	15	30	80
BDP26b Clayton Kershaw AU	300	400	500	800
BDP33 Max Scherzer RC	12	15	25	100

2008 Bowman Chrome Draft Prospects

	NmMt 8	NmMt+ 8.5	MT 9	Gem 9.5/10
BDPP115 Michael Stanton AU	500	600	700	1,000
BDPP128 Buster Posey AU	150	200	250	400

2008 Bowman Sterling

	NmMt 8	NmMt+ 8.5	MT 9	Gem 9.5/10
EL Evan Longoria AU RC	15	20	25	30

2008 Bowman Sterling Prospects

	NmMt 8	NmMt+ 8.5	MT 9	Gem 9.5/10
BP Buster Posey AU	60	80	100	150
CB Charlie Blackmon AU	20	25	30	50
JA Jake Arrieta Jsy AU	20	25	30	50

2008 Playoff Contenders

	NmMt 8	NmMt+ 8.5	MT 9	Gem 9.5/10
63 Buster Posey AU	60	80	100	150
66 Chris Davis AU	15	20	25	50
117 Rick Porcello AU	10	12	15	30

2008 SPx

	NmMt 8	NmMt+ 8.5	MT 9	Gem 9.5/10
150 Max Scherzer AU RC	120	150	200	500

2008 Topps Update

	NmMt 8	NmMt+ 8.5	MT 9	Gem 9.5/10
UH240 Clayton Kershaw RC	60	80	100	▲250
UH280 Max Scherzer RC	▲50	▲60	▲80	▲200

2008 Topps Allen and Ginter

	NmMt 8	NmMt+ 8.5	MT 9	Gem 9.5/10
72 Clayton Kershaw RC	10	12	20	40
297 Max Scherzer RC	8	10	▲20	▲30

2008 Topps Chrome

	NmMt 8	NmMt+ 8.5	MT 9	Gem 9.5/10
193 Evan Longoria RC	6	8	12	25

2008 Upper Deck Goudey

	NmMt 8	NmMt+ 8.5	MT 9	Gem 9.5/10
75 Clayton Kershaw RC	10	12	20	40

2009 Bowman AFLAC

	NmMt 8	NmMt+ 8.5	MT 9	Gem 9.5/10
BH Bryce Harper	120	150	200	400
KB2 Kris Bryant	60	80	100	250

2009 Bowman Chrome Prospects

	NmMt 8	NmMt+ 8.5	MT 9	Gem 9.5/10
BCP101 Freddie Freeman AU	120	150	200	▲400
BCP108 Carlos Santana AU	15	20	25	40
BCP121 Charlie Blackmon AU	50	60	80	120

2009 Bowman Chrome WBC Prospects

	NmMt 8	NmMt+ 8.5	MT 9	Gem 9.5/10
BCW1 Yu Darvish	6	8	10	20
BCW12 Aroldis Chapman	4	5	8	20
BCW30 Masahiro Tanaka	8	10	15	30
BCW49 Yoennis Cespedes	5	6	10	25

2009 Bowman Chrome Draft Prospects

	NmMt 8	NmMt+ 8.5	MT 9	Gem 9.5/10
BDPP81 Randal Grichuk AU	12	15	20	30
BDPP82 A.J. Pollock AU	12	15	20	30
BDPP85 Steve Matz AU	20	25	50	80
BDPP86 Zack Wheeler AU	25	30	40	60
BDPP89 Mike Trout AU	▲5,000	▲6,000	▲8,000	▲12,000

2009 Bowman Chrome Draft WBC Prospects

	NmMt 8	NmMt+ 8.5	MT 9	Gem 9.5/10
BDPW2 Yu Darvish	6	8	12	30

2009 Bowman Sterling Prospects

	NmMt 8	NmMt+ 8.5	MT 9	Gem 9.5/10
MT Mike Trout AU	1,000	1,200	1,500	▲3,000

2009 Donruss Elite Extra Edition

	NmMt 8	NmMt+ 8.5	MT 9	Gem 9.5/10
57 Mike Trout AU/495	500	1,000	▲1,500	▲4,000

2009 Donruss Elite Extra Edition Signature Turn of the Century

	NmMt 8	NmMt+ 8.5	MT 9	Gem 9.5/10
6 Nolan Arenado AU/844	50	60	100	200
57 Mike Trout AU/149	300	400	500	1,000
90 Randal Grichuk AU/50	50	60	80	150
150 Aroldis Chapman AU/149	40	50	60	120

2009 Topps Chrome

	NmMt 8	NmMt+ 8.5	MT 9	Gem 9.5/10
NNO1 Tommy Hanson AU RC	12	15	20	25

2009 Topps Chrome World Baseball Classic

	NmMt 8	NmMt+ 8.5	MT 9	Gem 9.5/10
W37 Masahiro Tanaka	25	30	40	150

2009 TRISTAR Prospects Plus

	NmMt 8	NmMt+ 8.5	MT 9	Gem 9.5/10
20 Michael Trout	15	20	30	80

Team Future Watch Jersey Autographs

	NmMt 8	NmMt+ 8.5	MT 9	Gem 9.5/10
30 Bryce Harper/899	120	150	200	250

2009 Upper Deck Signature Stars USA Star Prospects

	NmMt 8	NmMt+ 8.5	MT 9	Gem 9.5/10
USA8 Bryce Harper	12	15	20	60

2010 Bowman

	NmMt 8	NmMt+ 8.5	MT 9	Gem 9.5/10
200 Jason Heyward RC	5	6	10	15
208 Buster Posey RC	8	10	15	25

2010 Bowman Prospects

	NmMt 8	NmMt+ 8.5	MT 9	Gem 9.5/10
BP1a Stephen Strasburg	6	8	12	25
BP1b Stephen Strasburg AU	80	80	100	150

2010 Bowman Draft

	NmMt 8	NmMt+ 8.5	MT 9	Gem 9.5/10
BDP1 Stephen Strasburg RC	5	6	10	20

2010 Bowman Draft Prospects

	NmMt 8	NmMt+ 8.5	MT 9	Gem 9.5/10
BDPP47 Russell Wilson	5	6	12	25
BDPP80 Manny Machado	8	10	15	30
BDPP84 Matt Harvey	4	5	10	20

2010 Bowman Chrome

	NmMt 8	NmMt+ 8.5	MT 9	Gem 9.5/10
198B Mike Stanton RC	10	12	▼20	▲60
200A Jason Heyward AU	10	12	15	25
205A Stephen Strasburg RC	10	12	20	40
205B Stephen Strasburg AU	▼40	▼50	▼60	120
—Stephen Strasburg AU #205B BGS 10 (Pristine) sold for $1,009 (eBay; 05/12)				

2010 Bowman Chrome 18U USA Baseball

	NmMt 8	NmMt+ 8.5	MT 9	Gem 9.5/10
18BC8 Bryce Harper	50	60	80	150

2010 Bowman Chrome Prospects

	NmMt 8	NmMt+ 8.5	MT 9	Gem 9.5/10
BCP1 Stephen Strasburg	5	6	10	15
BCP91B Nolan Arenado AU	250	300	400	600
BCP100B Starlin Castro AU	12	15	20	30
BCP101B Anthony Rizzo AU	100	120	150	250
BCP105B Julio Teheran AU	10	12	15	25
BCP113B Josh Donaldson AU	40	50	60	100
BCP117B Wil Myers AU	20	25	30	50
BCP137 Jose Altuve	▼20	▼25	▼40	▼120
BCP165 J.D. Martinez	12	15	25	100

		NmMt 8	NmMt+ 8.5	MT 9	Gem 9.5/10
BCP195B	Kyle Seager AU	10	12	15	25
BCP196B	Jason Kipnis AU	12	15	20	30
BCP199B	Aroldis Chapman AU	20	25	▼20	▼40
BCP203B	Max Kepler AU	10	12	15	25
BCP205B	Miguel Sano AU	▼20	▼25	▼30	▼50
BCP207B	Gary Sanchez AU	120	150	200	300

2010 Bowman Chrome Draft

		NmMt 8	NmMt+ 8.5	MT 9	Gem 9.5/10
BDP1A	Stephen Strasburg RC	5	6	10	50
BDP1B	Stephen Strasburg AU	150	200	250	400
BDP30	Mike Stanton RC	8	10	30	60
BDP61	Buster Posey RC	5	6	10	50

2010 Bowman Chrome Draft Prospect Autographs

		NmMt 8	NmMt+ 8.5	MT 9	Gem 9.5/10
BDPP71	Mike Foltynewicz	15	20	25	40
BDPP74	Aaron Sanchez	20	25	30	50
BDPP75	Noah Syndergaard	60	80	100	150
BDPP78	Christian Yelich	▼300	▼400	▼500	▼800
BDPP80	Manny Machado	▼200	▼250	▼300	▼400
BDPP84	Matt Harvey	30	40	50	80
BDPP92	Chris Sale	100	120	150	250

2010 Bowman Chrome Draft Prospects

		NmMt 8	NmMt+ 8.5	MT 9	Gem 9.5/10
BDPP47	Russell Wilson	6	8	12	25
BDPP80	Manny Machado	12	15	25	50
BDPP108	Corey Seager	12	15	25	50

2010 Bowman Platinum

		NmMt 8	NmMt+ 8.5	MT 9	Gem 9.5/10
1	Stephen Strasburg RC	5	6	8	25
18	Buster Posey RC	6	8	15	50
73	Madison Bumgarner RC	6	8	12	25
86	Mike Stanton RC	6	8	15	60

2010 Bowman Platinum Prospect Autographs Refractors

		NmMt 8	NmMt+ 8.5	MT 9	Gem 9.5/10
ACH	Aroldis Chapman	20	25	30	50
FF	Freddie Freeman	25	30	40	60
JDM	J.D. Martinez	60	80	100	150
MS	Miguel Sano	15	20	25	40
MT	Mike Trout	400	500	600	▲1,500
PG	Paul Goldschmidt	30	40	50	80

2010 Bowman Platinum Prospects

		NmMt 8	NmMt+ 8.5	MT 9	Gem 9.5/10
PP5	Mike Trout	▲60	▲80	▲100	▲250

2010 Bowman Sterling Prospect Autographs

		NmMt 8	NmMt+ 8.5	MT 9	Gem 9.5/10
AC	Aroldis Chapman	12	15	20	30
CS	Chris Sale	▼15	▼20	▼25	▼50
CY	Christian Yelich	100	120	▲200	▲300

2010 Bowman Sterling Rookie Autographs

		NmMt 8	NmMt+ 8.5	MT 9	Gem 9.5/10
1	Stephen Strasburg	40	50	▲80	▲120

2010 Donruss Elite Extra Edition

		NmMt 8	NmMt+ 8.5	MT 9	Gem 9.5/10
103	Chris Sale AU/655	30	40	80	120
113	Noah Syndergaard AU/809	50	60	80	120
132	Manny Machado AU/425	60	80	100	150
147	Christian Yelich AU/815	40	50	▲150	▲250
191	Paul Goldschmidt AU/820	60	80	▲150	▲200

2010 Donruss Elite Extra Edition Franchise Futures Signatures

		NmMt 8	NmMt+ 8.5	MT 9	Gem 9.5/10
34	Gary Sanchez/669	100	120	150	250
46	Matt Harvey/149	80	100	120	200

2010 Topps

		NmMt 8	NmMt+ 8.5	MT 9	Gem 9.5/10
2	Buster Posey RC	12	15	20	▲60
105	Madison Bumgarner RC	6	8	12	30
661A	Stephen Strasburg				
	Million Card Giveaway	15	20	25	40

2010 Topps Red Hot Rookie Redemption

		NmMt 8	NmMt+ 8.5	MT 9	Gem 9.5/10
RHR8	Stephen Strasburg	15	20	25	50

2010 Topps 206

		NmMt 8	NmMt+ 8.5	MT 9	Gem 9.5/10
55	Stephen Strasburg RC	6	8	12	30

2010 Topps Allen and Ginter

		NmMt 8	NmMt+ 8.5	MT 9	Gem 9.5/10
6	Madison Bumgarner RC	4	5	20	40
294	Buster Posey RC	8	10	20	30

2010 Topps Chrome

		NmMt 8	NmMt+ 8.5	MT 9	Gem 9.5/10
212	Stephen Strasburg RC	5	6	10	20

2010 Topps Chrome Rookie Autographs

		NmMt 8	NmMt+ 8.5	MT 9	Gem 9.5/10
190	Mike Stanton	100	120	150	250
195	Starlin Castro	15	20	25	40
212	Stephen Strasburg	25	30	▲80	▲120

2010 Topps Chrome Wrapper Redemption Refractors

		NmMt 8	NmMt+ 8.5	MT 9	Gem 9.5/10
221	Buster Posey	12	15	▲50	▲80

2010 Topps Pro Debut

		NmMt 8	NmMt+ 8.5	MT 9	Gem 9.5/10
181	Mike Trout	100	120	▲300	▲500

2010 Upper Deck

		NmMt 8	NmMt+ 8.5	MT 9	Gem 9.5/10
28	Buster Posey RC	10	12	20	50

2011 Bowman Bowman's Best Prospects

		NmMt 8	NmMt+ 8.5	MT 9	Gem 9.5/10
BBP1	Bryce Harper	8	10	25	▲60
BBP9	Mike Trout	▲30	▲50	▲100	▲200
BBP51	Bryce Harper	8	10	12	▲50
BBP55	Manny Machado	5	6	10	25

2011 Bowman Prospect Autographs

		NmMt 8	NmMt+ 8.5	MT 9	Gem 9.5/10
MM	Manny Machado	▼40	▼50	▼60	▼100

2011 Bowman Prospects

		NmMt 8	NmMt+ 8.5	MT 9	Gem 9.5/10
BP1A	Bryce Harper	5	6	12	30
BP1B	Bryce Harper AU	250	300	400	500

2011 Bowman Chrome

		NmMt 8	NmMt+ 8.5	MT 9	Gem 9.5/10
175	Mike Trout RC	80	100	▲400	▲800

2011 Bowman Chrome Bryce Harper Retail Exclusive

		NmMt 8	NmMt+ 8.5	MT 9	Gem 9.5/10
BCE1G	Bryce Harper Gold	15	20	25	50
BCE1R	Bryce Harper Red	6	8	12	25
BCE1S	Bryce Harper Silver	6	8	12	25

2011 Bowman Chrome Prospect Autographs

		NmMt 8	NmMt+ 8.5	MT 9	Gem 9.5/10
BCP92	J.D. Martinez	▼60	▼80	▼100	▼150
BCP99	Paul Goldschmidt	▼100	▼120	▼150	▼250
BCP102	Eric Thames	15	20	25	40
BCP104	Ben Gamel	15	20	25	40
BCP111B	Bryce Harper	▼300	▼400	▼500	▼1,000
BCP131	Jean Segura	25	30	40	60
BCP163	Khris Davis	▼20	▼25	▼30	▼80
BCP175	Brett Lawrie	25	30	40	60
BCP178	Starling Marte	15	20	25	40

—Bryce Harper #BCP111B BGS 10 (Pristine) sold for $1,335 (eBay; 8/12)
—Bryce Harper #BCP111B BGS 10 (Pristine) sold for $1,200 (eBay; 9/12)

2011 Bowman Chrome Prospects

		NmMt 8	NmMt+ 8.5	MT 9	Gem 9.5/10
BCP1	Bryce Harper	15	▲30	▲40	▲60
BCP111	Bryce Harper	15	20	▼25	▼60

2011 Bowman Chrome Rookie Autographs

		NmMt 8	NmMt+ 8.5	MT 9	Gem 9.5/10
197	Aroldis Chapman	15	20	25	40
205	Freddie Freeman	40	50	60	100
220	Chris Sale	30	40	50	80

2011 Bowman Chrome Draft

		NmMt 8	NmMt+ 8.5	MT 9	Gem 9.5/10
11	Jose Altuve RC	20	25	40	▲80
101	Mike Trout RC	▲150	▲200	▲250	▲600

2011 Bowman Chrome Draft Prospects

		NmMt 8	NmMt+ 8.5	MT 9	Gem 9.5/10
BDPP18	Dylan Bundy	5	6	10	20
BDPP29	Jose Fernandez	6	8	12	25

2011 Bowman Chrome Draft Prospect Autographs

		NmMt 8	NmMt+ 8.5	MT 9	Gem 9.5/10
BN	Brandon Nimmo	30	40	50	80
BSN	Blake Snell	60	80	100	150
BSW	Blake Swihart	15	20	25	40
DB	Dylan Bundy	20	25	30	50
DV	Daniel Vogelbach	▼12	▼15	▼20	▼25
FL	Francisco Lindor	250	300	400	600
GS	George Springer	100	120	150	250
JBA	Javier Baez	150	200	250	400
JF	Jose Fernandez	15	20	25	▲60
JP	Joe Panik	20	25	30	50
KW	Kolten Wong	15	20	25	40
MF	Michael Fulmer	30	40	50	80
SGR	Sonny Gray	25	30	40	60
TB	Trevor Bauer	15	20	25	40
TS	Trevor Story	40	50	▲80	▲150

2011 Bowman Draft

		NmMt 8	NmMt+ 8.5	MT 9	Gem 9.5/10
101	Mike Trout RC	▲120	▲150	▲200	▲300

2011 Bowman Draft Bryce Harper Green Border Autograph

		NmMt 8	NmMt+ 8.5	MT 9	Gem 9.5/10
BH	Bryce Harper	250	300	400	500

2011 Bowman Platinum Prospect Autograph Refractors

		NmMt 8	NmMt+ 8.5	MT 9	Gem 9.5/10
BH	Bryce Harper	▼150	▼200	▼250	▼300
MH	Matt Harvey	15	20	25	40
MM	Manny Machado	▼40	▼50	▼60	▼100

2011 Bowman Sterling

		NmMt 8	NmMt+ 8.5	MT 9	Gem 9.5/10
15	Jose Altuve RC	60	80	▲120	▲150
22	Mike Trout RC	200	250	▲800	▲1,200
27	Paul Goldschmidt RC	30	40	50	80

2011 Bowman Sterling Prospect Autographs

		NmMt 8	NmMt+ 8.5	MT 9	Gem 9.5/10
BS	Blake Snell	15	20	25	40
FL	Francisco Lindor	50	60	80	120
GS	George Springer	30	40	50	▲100
JB	Javier Baez	50	60	80	120
JF	Jose Fernandez	12	15	20	30
TS	Trevor Story	25	30	40	60

2011 Bowman Sterling Rookie Autographs

		NmMt 8	NmMt+ 8.5	MT 9	Gem 9.5/10
4	Anthony Rizzo	40	50	60	▼80
6	Eric Hosmer	30	40	50	80
7	Freddie Freeman	15	20	25	40
13	Mike Moustakas	20	25	30	50

2011 Donruss Elite Extra Edition Prospects

		NmMt 8	NmMt+ 8.5	MT 9	Gem 9.5/10
P4	Dylan Bundy AU/435	50	60	80	100

2011 Finest

		NmMt 8	NmMt+ 8.5	MT 9	Gem 9.5/10
94	Mike Trout RC	▲120	▲150	▲200	▲400

2011 Finest Rookie Autographs Refractors

		NmMt 8	NmMt+ 8.5	MT 9	Gem 9.5/10
84	Mike Trout	▲1,000	▲2,000	▲2,500	▲3,000

2011 Playoff Contenders

	NmMt 8	NmMt+ 8.5	MT 9	Gem 9.5/10
Mike Trout RC	25	25	▲80	▲150

2011 Topps Update

	NmMt 8	NmMt+ 8.5	MT 9	Gem 9.5/10
47 Paul Goldschmidt RC	▼15	▼20	▼25	60
55 Anthony Rizzo RC	15	20	25	50
132 Jose Altuve RC	40	50	50	100
175 Mike Trout RC	▲500	▲500	▲600	▲1,200
186 J.D. Martinez RC	▼15	▼20	▼25	60

2011 Topps Chrome Rookie Autographs

	NmMt 8	NmMt+ 8.5	MT 9	Gem 9.5/10
Eric Hosmer	40	50	60	100
Freddie Freeman	50	60	▲100	▲200
Craig Kimbrel	30	40	50	80
Chris Sale	30	40	50	80

2011 Topps Heritage Minors

	NmMt 8	NmMt+ 8.5	MT 9	Gem 9.5/10
Mike Trout	25	30	▲100	▲200

2011 Topps Pro Debut

	NmMt 8	NmMt+ 8.5	MT 9	Gem 9.5/10
Joc Pederson	5	6	10	15
Bryce Harper	20	25	40	60
Mike Trout	30	50	▲150	▲300

2011 USA Baseball Autographs

	NmMt 8	NmMt+ 8.5	MT 9	Gem 9.5/10
Joey Gallo	30	40	50	80

2012 Bowman

	NmMt 8	NmMt+ 8.5	MT 9	Gem 9.5/10
9A Yu Darvish RC	8	10	15	30

2012 Bowman Prospects

	NmMt 8	NmMt+ 8.5	MT 9	Gem 9.5/10
10 Bryce Harper	6	8	▲15	▼25

2012 Bowman Chrome

	NmMt 8	NmMt+ 8.5	MT 9	Gem 9.5/10
Yu Darvish RC	8	10	15	25
4 Bryce Harper RC	15	20	▼25	50

2012 Bowman Chrome Prospect Autographs

	NmMt 8	NmMt+ 8.5	MT 9	Gem 9.5/10
Avisail Garcia	15	20	25	40
James Paxton	30	40	50	80
Marcell Ozuna	25	30	40	60
Nomar Mazara	40	50	60	100
Ronald Guzman	15	20	25	40
Rougned Odor	▼15	▼20	▼25	▼30
Jorge Soler	25	30	40	60
CP18 Brandon Drury	25	30	40	60
CP66 Jackie Bradley Jr.	30	40	50	80
CP79 Josh Bell	▼60	▼80	▼100	▼150
CP86 Gerrit Cole	25	30	40	60
CP88 Anthony Rendon	40	50	▲120	▲200
CP98 Greg Bird	▼15	▼20	▼25	▼60
CP104 Joc Pederson	30	40	50	80
CP105 Xander Bogaerts	100	120	150	250
CP108 Carlos Martinez	15	20	25	40

2012 Bowman Chrome Prospects

	NmMt 8	NmMt+ 8.5	MT 9	Gem 9.5/10
CP10 Bryce Harper	12	15	25	40
CP105 Xander Bogaerts	8	10	15	25
CP120 Jorge Soler	8	10	15	25
CP182 Gregory Polanco	10	12	20	30
CP217 Manny Machado	8	10	15	25

2012 Bowman Chrome Rookie Autographs

	NmMt 8	NmMt+ 8.5	MT 9	Gem 9.5/10
Bryce Harper	200	250	300	500
Yu Darvish	120	150	200	300
9 Yu Darvish	120	150	200	300
1 Matt Moore	15	20	25	40

2012 Bowman Chrome Draft

	NmMt 8	NmMt+ 8.5	MT 9	Gem 9.5/10
10 Bryce Harper RC	15	20	▼25	▼30
50 Yu Darvish RC	5	6	10	25

2012 Bowman Chrome Draft Draft Pick Autographs

	NmMt 8	NmMt+ 8.5	MT 9	Gem 9.5/10
AA Albert Almora	25	30	40	60
AR Addison Russell	40	50	60	100
CS Corey Seager	▼150	▼200	▼250	▼300
DD David Dahl	30	40	50	80
JG Joey Gallo	80	100	120	200
LB Lewis Brinson	25	30	40	60
MH Mitch Haniger	20	25	30	50
MS Marcus Stroman	20	25	30	50
MW Michael Wacha	15	20	25	40
MZ Mike Zunino	15	20	25	40

2012 Bowman Chrome Draft Rookie Autographs

	NmMt 8	NmMt+ 8.5	MT 9	Gem 9.5/10
BH Bryce Harper	200	250	300	500
YD Yu Darvish EXCH	120	150	200	300

2012 Bowman Draft

	NmMt 8	NmMt+ 8.5	MT 9	Gem 9.5/10
10 Bryce Harper RC	8	10	20	30
50 Yu Darvish RC	5	6	10	25

2012 Bowman Platinum

	NmMt 8	NmMt+ 8.5	MT 9	Gem 9.5/10
9 Yu Darvish RC	8	10	15	25
16 Mike Trout	12	▲25	▲30	▲40
56 Bryce Harper RC	15	20	▼25	50

2012 Bowman Platinum Prospect Autographs

	NmMt 8	NmMt+ 8.5	MT 9	Gem 9.5/10
AR Anthony Rendon	15	20	25	40
GB Greg Bird	30	40	60	100
YC Yoenis Cespedes	25	30	50	80
YD Yu Darvish	60	80	120	200

2012 Bowman Sterling Prospect Autographs

	NmMt 8	NmMt+ 8.5	MT 9	Gem 9.5/10
AR Addison Russell	10	12	15	25
CS Corey Seager	▼25	▼30	▼40	▼60
FL Francisco Lindor	▼25	▼30	▼40	▼60
JGA Joey Gallo	10	12	15	25

2012 Elite Extra Edition

	NmMt 8	NmMt+ 8.5	MT 9	Gem 9.5/10
101 Carlos Correa AU/470	100	120	150	250
102 Byron Buxton AU/599	20	25	30	60
113 Corey Seager AU/330	50	60	80	120

2012 Finest

	NmMt 8	NmMt+ 8.5	MT 9	Gem 9.5/10
35 Yu Darvish RC	6	8	15	30
73 Bryce Harper RC	20	25	25	50

2012 Panini Prizm

	NmMt 8	NmMt+ 8.5	MT 9	Gem 9.5/10
151 Yu Darvish RC	4	5	6	15
152 Bryce Harper RC	5	6	10	40
179 Matt Harvey RC	5	6	10	15

2012 Panini Prizm Rookie Autographs

	NmMt 8	NmMt+ 8.5	MT 9	Gem 9.5/10
RMH Matt Harvey	30	40	50	100

2012 Topps

	NmMt 8	NmMt+ 8.5	MT 9	Gem 9.5/10
660A Yu Darvish RC	5	6	10	30

2012 Topps Update

	NmMt 8	NmMt+ 8.5	MT 9	Gem 9.5/10
US183 Bryce Harper RC	25	30	▼40	▼80
US299A Bryce Harper	10	12	20	30

2012 Topps Allen and Ginter

	NmMt 8	NmMt+ 8.5	MT 9	Gem 9.5/10
4 Yu Darvish RC	8	10	15	25
12 Bryce Harper RC	10	12	15	40

2012 Topps Archives

	NmMt 8	NmMt+ 8.5	MT 9	Gem 9.5/10
119 Yu Darvish RC	5	6	10	25

2012 Topps Chrome

	NmMt 8	NmMt+ 8.5	MT 9	Gem 9.5/10
151A Yu Darvish Arm Back RC	6	8	12	25
196A Bryce Harper Hitting RC	8	10	15	50

2012 Topps Chrome Rookie Autographs

	NmMt 8	NmMt+ 8.5	MT 9	Gem 9.5/10
BH Bryce Harper	250	300	400	600
151 Yu Darvish	60	80	100	150
180 Yoenis Cespedes	30	40	50	80

2012 Topps Heritage

	NmMt 8	NmMt+ 8.5	MT 9	Gem 9.5/10
207 Mike Trout	▲80	▲100	▲120	▲400
H650 Bryce Harper RC	400	500	600	800

2012 USA Baseball

2013 Bowman

	NmMt 8	NmMt+ 8.5	MT 9	Gem 9.5/10
215 Manny Machado RC	5	6	10	20

2013 Bowman Prospects

	NmMt 8	NmMt+ 8.5	MT 9	Gem 9.5/10
BP1 Byron Buxton	5	6	10	30
BP100 Carlos Correa	10	12	15	25

2013 Bowman Top 100 Prospects

	NmMt 8	NmMt+ 8.5	MT 9	Gem 9.5/10
BTP58 Yasiel Puig	15	20	25	50

2013 Bowman Chrome

	NmMt 8	NmMt+ 8.5	MT 9	Gem 9.5/10
78 Yasiel Puig RC	5	6	12	20
147 Didi Gregorius RC	4	5	8	15
205 Manny Machado RC	5	6	12	30

2013 Bowman Chrome Cream of the Crop Mini Refractors

	NmMt 8	NmMt+ 8.5	MT 9	Gem 9.5/10
LAD3 Yasiel Puig	12	15	20	40

2013 Bowman Chrome Prospect Autographs

	NmMt 8	NmMt+ 8.5	MT 9	Gem 9.5/10
AMO Adalberto Mondesi	30	40	50	80
BB Byron Buxton	60	80	▼80	▼120
CC Carlos Correa	▼150	▼200	▼250	▼400
DC Dylan Cozens	15	20	25	40
JA Jorge Alfaro	15	20	25	40
JB Jose Berrios	20	25	30	50
LM Lance McCullers	15	20	25	40
MAJ Miguel Andujar	▼50	▼60	▼80	▼200
MO Matt Olson	20	25	▲40	▲60
YP Yasiel Puig	100	120	150	250

2013 Bowman Chrome Prospects

	NmMt 8	NmMt+ 8.5	MT 9	Gem 9.5/10
BCP100 Carlos Correa	8	10	15	▼25

2013 Bowman Chrome Rookie Autographs

	NmMt 8	NmMt+ 8.5	MT 9	Gem 9.5/10
EG Evan Gattis	30	40	50	80
HJR Hyun-Jin Ryu	80	100	120	200
MM Manny Machado	40	50	60	100
WM Wil Myers	30	40	50	80

2013 Bowman Chrome Draft

	NmMt 8	NmMt+ 8.5	MT 9	Gem 9.5/10
1 Yasiel Puig RC	6	8	10	20

2013 Bowman Chrome Draft Draft Pick Autographs

	NmMt 8	NmMt+ 8.5	MT 9	Gem 9.5/10
AJ Aaron Judge	600	800	1,000	1,500
AM Austin Meadows	40	50	60	100
CF Clint Frazier	60	80	100	150
CSA Cord Sandberg	20	25	30	50
DS Dominic Smith	25	30	40	60
KB Kris Bryant	400	500	600	1,000
RMC Ryan McMahon	15	20	25	40

2013 Bowman Chrome Draft Draft Picks

	NmMt 8	NmMt+ 8.5	MT 9	Gem 9.5/10
BDPP19 Aaron Judge	▼30	▼40	▼50	150

2013 Bowman Chrome Draft Top Prospects

	NmMt 8	NmMt+ 8.5	MT 9	Gem 9.5/10
TP10 Carlos Correa	8	10	15	20

2013 Bowman Chrome Mini

	NmMt 8	NmMt+ 8.5	MT 9	Gem 9.5/10
311 Aaron Judge	25	30	40	60

2013 Bowman Draft

	NmMt 8	NmMt+ 8.5	MT 9	Gem 9.5/10
1 Yasiel Puig RC	5	6	10	20

2013 Bowman Draft Draft Picks

	NmMt 8	NmMt+ 8.5	MT 9	Gem 9.5/10
BDPP19 Aaron Judge	20	25	30	50

2013 Bowman Draft Top Prospects

	NmMt 8	NmMt+ 8.5	MT 9	Gem 9.5/10
TP10 Carlos Correa	6	8	12	25

2013 Bowman Platinum Prospect Autographs

	NmMt 8	NmMt+ 8.5	MT 9	Gem 9.5/10
AR Addison Russell	15	20	25	40
BB Byron Buxton	20	25	30	50
CC Carlos Correa	80	100	120	200

2013 Bowman Sterling

	NmMt 8	NmMt+ 8.5	MT 9	Gem 9.5/10
32 Yasiel Puig RC	10	12	25	40

2013 Bowman Sterling Prospect Autographs

	NmMt 8	NmMt+ 8.5	MT 9	Gem 9.5/10
AJ Aaron Judge	150	200	250	400
BB Byron Buxton	15	20	25	40
CC Carlos Correa	30	40	50	80
JU Julio Urias	15	20	25	40
NS Noah Syndergaard	15	20	25	40

2013 Bowman Sterling Prospects

	NmMt 8	NmMt+ 8.5	MT 9	Gem 9.5/10
11 Kris Bryant	40	50	100	150

2013 Elite Extra Edition

	NmMt 8	NmMt+ 8.5	MT 9	Gem 9.5/10
102 Kris Bryant AU/324	120	150	200	300
107 Austin Meadows AU/322	15	20	25	40
111 J.P. Crawford AU/411	15	20	25	40
116 Alex Gonzalez AU/420	15	20	25	40
122 Aaron Judge AU/599	150	200	250	400
158 Cody Bellinger AU/673	150	200	250	400
185 Rosell Herrera AU/174 EXCH	20	25	30	50

2013 Elite Extra Edition Franchise Futures Signatures

	NmMt 8	NmMt+ 8.5	MT 9	Gem 9.5/10
71 Gleyber Torres/250	100	120	150	250

2013 Finest

	NmMt 8	NmMt+ 8.5	MT 9	Gem 9.5/10
80 Manny Machado RC	5	5	8	25
91 Yasiel Puig RC	5	6	10	20

2013 Topps

	NmMt 8	NmMt+ 8.5	MT 9	Gem 9.5/10
270A Manny Machado RC	5	6	10	25

2013 Topps Allen and Ginter

	NmMt 8	NmMt+ 8.5	MT 9	Gem 9.5/10
44 Yasiel Puig RC	6	8	15	30

2013 Topps Chrome

	NmMt 8	NmMt+ 8.5	MT 9	Gem 9.5/10
12 Manny Machado RC	8	12	20	50
78 Nolan Arenado RC	12	20	▼30	80
138A Yasiel Puig RC	6	8	12	25

2013 Topps Chrome Rookie Autographs

	NmMt 8	NmMt+ 8.5	MT 9	Gem 9.5/10
CY Christian Yelich	▼100	▼150	▼200	▼300
GC Gerrit Cole	15	20	25	40
YP Yasiel Puig	120	150	200	300
12 Manny Machado	80	100	120	200
25 Hyun-Jin Ryu	25	30	40	60
32 Jose Fernandez	30	40	50	80
65 Didi Gregorius	15	20	25	40
78 Nolan Arenado	100	120	150	250
125 Dylan Bundy	15	20	25	40
128 Anthony Rendon	25	30	40	60

2013 Topps Heritage

	NmMt 8	NmMt+ 8.5	MT 9	Gem 9.5/10
201 Manny Machado RC / Dylan Bundy RC	6	8	12	40
H519 Nolan Arenado RC	8	10	40	100
H536 Christian Yelich RC	12	▲60	▲100	▲120
H584 Yasiel Puig RC	6	8	12	▼20
H596 Gerrit Cole RC	12	15	20	50

2013 Topps Pro Debut

	NmMt 8	NmMt+ 8.5	MT 9	Gem 9.5/10
35A Yasiel Puig	6	8	12	30

2013 Topps Update

	NmMt 8	NmMt+ 8.5	MT 9	Gem 9.5/10
US250A Yasiel Puig RC	5	6	10	20
US259 Nolan Arenado RC	▲15	▲20	25	▲60
US290 Christian Yelich RC	▲30	▲40	▲50	▲120

2014 Bowman Prospects

	NmMt 8	NmMt+ 8.5	MT 9	Gem 9.5/10
BP17 Jose Abreu	5	6	10	15
BP25 Kris Bryant	8	10	15	40
BP73 Jacob deGrom	10	12	20	50

2014 Bowman Chrome Fire Die-Cut Refractors

	NmMt 8	NmMt+ 8.5	MT 9	Gem 9.5/10
FDCKB Kris Bryant	12	15	40	50

2014 Bowman Chrome Mini

	NmMt 8	NmMt+ 8.5	MT 9	Gem 9.5/10
MCKB Kris Bryant	8	10	12	25

2014 Bowman Chrome Prospect Autographs

	NmMt 8	NmMt+ 8.5	MT 9	Gem 9.5/10
BCAPED Edwin Diaz	15	20	25	40
BCAPFR Franmil Reyes	25	30	40	60
BCAPJAB Jose Abreu	▼25	▼30	▼40	▼50
BCAPJHA Josh Hader	20	25	30	50
BCAPJMC Jeff McNeil	30	40	▲60	▲150
BCAPJU Julio Urias	▼20	▼25	▼30	▼50
BCAPKB Kris Bryant	▼150	▼200	▼250	▼400
BCAPKM Ketel Marte	40	50	60	100
BCAPMB Mookie Betts	400	500	600	1,000
BCAPMMA Manuel Margot	15	20	25	40

2014 Bowman Chrome Prospects

	NmMt 8	NmMt+ 8.5	MT 9	Gem 9.5/10
BCP17 Jose Abreu	5	6	10	15
BCP25 Kris Bryant	10	12	▼15	30
BCP73 Jacob deGrom	10	12	20	50
BCP109 Mookie Betts	10	10	15	60

2014 Bowman Chrome Rookie Autographs

	NmMt 8	NmMt+ 8.5	MT 9	Gem 9.5/10
BCARJA Jose Abreu	25	30	▲50	▲80
BCARJS Jonathan Schoop	20	25	30	50

2014 Bowman Chrome Draft

	NmMt 8	NmMt+ 8.5	MT 9	Gem 9.5/10
CDP2 Kyle Schwarber	6	8	20	50
CDP122 Rhys Hoskins	10	12	20	50

2014 Bowman Chrome Draft Draft Pick Autographs

	NmMt 8	NmMt+ 8.5	MT 9	Gem 9.5/10
BCAAN Aaron Nola	▼40	▼50	▼60	▼80
BCAAV Alex Verdugo	40	50	60	100
BCABZ Bradley Zimmer	20	25	30	50
BCADC Dylan Cease	25	30	40	60
BCAJF Jack Flaherty	20	25	▲50	▲80
BCAJS Justus Sheffield	12	15	20	30
BCAKF Kyle Freeland	15	20	25	40
BCAKS Kyle Schwarber	60	80	100	150
BCAMCH Matt Chapman	50	60	80	▲150
BCAMH Monte Harrison	25	30	40	60
BCAMIC Michael Chavis	80	100	120	200
BCAMK Michael Kopech	50	60	80	120
BCAMC Michael Conforto	30	40	50	80
BCATT Trea Turner	40	50	60	100

2014 Bowman Chrome Draft Top Prospects

	NmMt 8	NmMt+ 8.5	MT 9	Gem 9.5/10
CTP33 Eloy Jimenez	12	15	▼25	▼40
CTP39 Aaron Judge	12	15	20	40
CTP62 Kris Bryant	8	10	12	25

2014 Bowman Draft

	NmMt 8	NmMt+ 8.5	MT 9	Gem 9.5/10
DP2 Kyle Schwarber	8	10	15	30

2014 Bowman Draft Top Prospects

	NmMt 8	NmMt+ 8.5	MT 9	Gem 9.5/10
TP37 Rafael Devers	6	8	12	25
TP39 Aaron Judge	▲10	▲12	▲20	▲40
TP62 Kris Bryant	8	10	15	25

2014 Bowman Platinum Prospect Autographs

	NmMt 8	NmMt+ 8.5	MT 9	Gem 9.5/10
APCCO Carlos Correa	▼25	▼30	▼40	▼60
APCFR Clint Frazier	20	25	30	50
APCT Chris Taylor	20	25	30	50
APJBA Javier Baez	40	50	60	100
APKB Kris Bryant	250	300	350	500

2014 Bowman Sterling Prospect Autographs

	NmMt 8	NmMt+ 8.5	MT 9	Gem 9.5/10
BSPACC Carlos Correa	30	40	50	80
BSPACF Clint Frazier	▼12	▼15	▼20	▼30
BSPAFL Francisco Lindor	20	25	30	50
BSPAGS Gary Sanchez	60	80	100	150
BSPAJBA Javier Baez	30	40	50	80
BSPAKSC Kyle Schwarber	15	20	25	40
BSPALS Luis Severino	15	20	25	40
BSPAMIC Michael Chavis	25	30	40	60

2014 Topps Update

	NmMt 8	NmMt+ 8.5	MT 9	Gem 9.5/10
US26A Mookie Betts RC	30	40	50	120
US50A Jacob deGrom RC	5	5	8	20

2014 Topps Chrome Rookie Autographs

	NmMt 8	NmMt+ 8.5	MT 9	Gem 9.5/10
45 Jose Ramirez	50	60	80	120
GS George Springer	30	40	50	80
JA Jose Abreu	15	20	25	40

2014 Topps Heritage

	NmMt 8	NmMt+ 8.5	MT 9	Gem 9.5/10
H519 Randal Grichuk RC	8	10	15	30
H549 Jacob deGrom RC	10	15	30	▼50
H558 Mookie Betts RC	60	80	100	200
H590 Jose Ramirez RC	10	12	▼15	▼25

2015 Bowman Chrome

	NmMt 8	NmMt+ 8.5	MT 9	Gem 9.5/10
110 Carlos Correa RC	10	10	12	25
200 Kris Bryant RC	10	12	15	30

2015 Bowman Chrome Prospect Autographs

	NmMt 8	NmMt+ 8.5	MT 9	Gem 9.5/10
BCAPAMR Amed Rosario	25	30	40	60
BCAPAR Alex Reyes	25	30	40	60
BCAPBB Bobby Bradley	▼12	▼15	▼20	▲60
BCAPBH Brent Honeywell	15	20	25	40
BCAPCBE Cody Bellinger	300	400	▲600	▲1,000
BCAPDG Dermis Garcia	20	25	30	50
BCAPDGE Domingo German	60	80	100	150
BCAPGT Gleyber Torres	250	▲400	▲500	▲800
BCAPJM Jorge Mateo	15	20	25	40
BCAPLS Luis Severino	▼30	▼40	▼50	▼80
BCAPOA Orlando Arcia	15	20	25	40
BCAPOAL Ozhaino Albies	80	100	120	▲250
BCAPRD Rafael Devers	100	120	▲200	▲300
BCAPTH Teoscar Hernandez	15	20	25	40
BCAPTT Touki Toussaint	20	25	30	50
BCAPWA Willy Adames	25	30	40	60

2015 Bowman Chrome Rookie Autographs

		NmMt 8	NmMt+ 8.5	MT 9	Gem 9.5/10
RBB	Byron Buxton	20	25	30	50
RCW	Christian Walker	20	25	30	50
RFL	Francisco Lindor	40	50	60	100
RJB	Javier Baez	50	60	80	120
RJP	Joc Pederson	15	20	25	40
RJPE	Joc Pederson	15	20	25	40
RJS	Jorge Soler	15	20	25	40
RJSO	Jorge Soler	15	20	25	40
RKB	Kris Bryant	200	250	300	500
RNS	Noah Syndergaard	50	60	80	120

2015 Bowman Chrome Draft

	NmMt 8	NmMt+ 8.5	MT 9	Gem 9.5/10
Aaron Judge	10	12	20	▼30
Andrew Benintendi	10	12	15	▼20

2015 Bowman Chrome Draft Draft Pick Autographs

		NmMt 8	NmMt+ 8.5	MT 9	Gem 9.5/10
AB	Andrew Benintendi	▼60	▼80	▼100	▼150
ARI	Austin Riley	50	60	▲100	▲150
BR	Brendan Rodgers	60	80	100	150
DS	Dansby Swanson	25	30	▲50	▲80
IH	Ian Happ	▼15	▼20	▼25	▼40
KHA	Ke'Bryan Hayes	25	30	40	60
KT	Kyle Tucker	60	80	100	150
MS	Michael Soroka	50	60	▲100	▲150
RMO	Ryan Mountcastle	30	40	50	80
WB	Walker Buehler	80	100	▲150	▲250

2015 Bowman's Best

	NmMt 8	NmMt+ 8.5	MT 9	Gem 9.5/10
Kris Bryant RC	12	15	20	30

2015 Bowman's Best Best of '15 Autographs

		NmMt 8	NmMt+ 8.5	MT 9	Gem 9.5/10
5ANB	Andrew Benintendi	30	40	50	80
5BR	Brendan Rodgers	15	20	25	40
5DS	Dansby Swanson	15	20	25	40
5FL	Francisco Lindor	50	60	80	120

2015 Finest

	NmMt 8	NmMt+ 8.5	MT 9	Gem 9.5/10
Kris Bryant SP RC	100	120	150	250

2015 Stadium Club

	NmMt 8	NmMt+ 8.5	MT 9	Gem 9.5/10
Kris Bryant RC	12	15	20	60

2015 Topps

	NmMt 8	NmMt+ 8.5	MT 9	Gem 9.5/10
6A Kris Bryant RC	10	12	20	60

2015 Topps Update

	NmMt 8	NmMt+ 8.5	MT 9	Gem 9.5/10
78 Kris Bryant RC	10	12	20	40
242 Kris Bryant	10	12	20	40

2015 Topps Update Chrome

	NmMt 8	NmMt+ 8.5	MT 9	Gem 9.5/10
174 Carlos Correa RC	10	12	25	60

2015 Topps Allen and Ginter

	NmMt 8	NmMt+ 8.5	MT 9	Gem 9.5/10
Kris Bryant RC	10	12	20	40

2015 Topps Chrome

	NmMt 8	NmMt+ 8.5	MT 9	Gem 9.5/10
2 Kris Bryant RC	15	20	25	▼50
5 Carlos Correa SP RC	▼20	▼25	▼30	▼60

2015 Topps Chrome Rookie Autographs

		NmMt 8	NmMt+ 8.5	MT 9	Gem 9.5/10
BBN	Byron Buxton	25	30	40	60
CC	Carlos Correa	100	120	150	250
FL	Francisco Lindor	80	100	120	200

		NmMt 8	NmMt+ 8.5	MT 9	Gem 9.5/10
ARJB	Javier Baez	40	50	60	100
ARJK	Jung-ho Kang	25	30	40	60
ARKB	Kris Bryant	250	300	400	600

2016 Bowman Prospects

		NmMt 8	NmMt+ 8.5	MT 9	Gem 9.5/10
BP55	Vladimir Guerrero Jr.	10	12	30	▼60

2016 Bowman Chrome Prospect Autographs

		NmMt 8	NmMt+ 8.5	MT 9	Gem 9.5/10
BCAPOC	Oneal Cruz	40	50	60	100
BCAPWC	Willie Calhoun	15	20	25	40
CPAAB	Alex Bregman	150	200	▲300	▲500
CPABR	Brendan Rodgers	40	50	60	100
CPADAS	Dansby Swanson	50	60	80	120
CPADC	Daz Cameron	25	30	40	60
CPAFT	Fernando Tatis Jr.	250	300	▲600	▲1,000
CPAHB	Harrison Bader	▼15	▼20	▼25	▼40
CPAJS	Juan Soto	300	400	▲800	▲1,200
CPAMC	Mike Clevinger	15	20	25	40
CPAPD	Paul DeJong	30	40	50	80
CPATM	Trey Mancini	15	20	30	50
CPATO	Tyler O'Neill	25	30	40	60
CPAVG	Vladimir Guerrero Jr.	▼500	▼600	▼800	▼1,200
CPAVR	Victor Robles	120	▼120	▼150	▼250
CPAWC	Willson Contreras	▼25	▼30	▼40	▼80
CPAYM	Yoan Moncada	▼80	▼100	▼120	▼400
CPACF	Clint Frazier	12	15	25	30
CPACHR	Christian Arroyo	15	20	25	40
CPACP	Chris Paddack	50	60	80	120
CPAEJ	Eloy Jimenez	250	300	400	600
CPAFM	Francisco Mejia	25	30	40	60
CPAGT	Gleyber Torres	80	100	120	200
CPAJC	Jazz Chisholm	50	60	80	120
CPAJG	Jason Groome	25	30	40	60
CPAJS	Jesus Sanchez	50	60	80	120
CPAKM	Kevin Maitan	50	60	80	▼100
CPALA	Lazarito Armenteros	25	30	40	60
CPALGU	Lourdes Gurriel Jr.	40	50	60	100
CPALT	Leody Taveras	15	20	25	40
CPAMK	Michael Kopech	20	25	25	50
CPAMK	Mitch Keller	25	30	40	60
CPAMM	Mickey Moniak	30	40	50	80
CPAMS	Magneuris Sierra	15	20	25	40
CPANS	Nick Senzel	120	150	200	300
CPARA	Ronald Acuna	500	600	800	1,200
CPASS	Sixto Sanchez	25	30	40	60
CPATM	Triston McKenzie	20	25	30	50
CPAWJ	Wander Javier	25	30	40	60
CPAYD	Yusniel Diaz	25	30	40	60

2016 Bowman Chrome Prospects

		NmMt 8	NmMt+ 8.5	MT 9	Gem 9.5/10
BCP17	Fernando Tatis Jr.	15	20	30	100
BCP55	Vladimir Guerrero Jr.	▼40	▼50	▼60	▼120
BCP182	Cody Bellinger	10	12	▲25	50
BCP236	Gleyber Torres	15	20	25	50

2016 Bowman Chrome Rookie Autographs

		NmMt 8	NmMt+ 8.5	MT 9	Gem 9.5/10
CRAAN	Aaron Nola	25	30	40	60
CRAGB	Greg Bird	25	30	40	60
CRAMS	Miguel Sano#(White jersey)	15	20	25	40
BCARJBE	Jose Berrios	15	20	25	40

2016 Bowman Chrome Draft

		NmMt 8	NmMt+ 8.5	MT 9	Gem 9.5/10
BDC74	Bo Bichette	20	25	30	50
BDC92	Pete Alonso	▲25	▲30	▲50	▲100
BDC143	Gleyber Torres	8	10	▲25	▲50

2016 Topps Chrome

		NmMt 8	NmMt+ 8.5	MT 9	Gem 9.5/10
143	Gary Sanchez RC	8	10	10	20
150	Corey Seager RC	6	8	10	30

2016 Topps Chrome Rookie Autographs

		NmMt 8	NmMt+ 8.5	MT 9	Gem 9.5/10
RAALA	Albert Almora	25	30	40	60
RAAN	Aaron Nola	20	25	30	50
RABS	Blake Snell	15	20	25	40
RACS	Corey Seager	▼50	▼60	▼80	▼120
RADL	Dae-Ho Lee	15	20	25	40
RAGB	Greg Bird	20	25	30	50
RAJU	Julio Urias	15	20	25	40
RAKSC	Kyle Schwarber	30	40	50	80
RALS	Luis Severino	20	25	30	50
RAMC	Michael Conforto	25	30	40	60
RAMS	Miguel Sano	15	20	25	40
RATS	Trevor Story	25	30	40	60
RATTU	Trea Turner	▼25	▼30	▼40	▼60

2016 Topps Transcendent

		NmMt 8	NmMt+ 8.5	MT 9	Gem 9.5/10
12	Kris Bryant	100	120	150	250

2017 Bowman

	NmMt 8	NmMt+ 8.5	MT 9	Gem 9.5/10
32 Aaron Judge RC	6	8	15	30

2017 Bowman Chrome Prospect Autographs

		NmMt 8	NmMt+ 8.5	MT 9	Gem 9.5/10
CPAAH	Austin Hays	25	30	40	60
CPABR	Blake Rutherford	25	30	40	60

2017 Bowman Chrome Prospects

		NmMt 8	NmMt+ 8.5	MT 9	Gem 9.5/10
BCP32	Vladimir Guerrero Jr.	8	10	15	30
BCP127	Ronald Acuna	▲15	▲20	▲40	▲100
BCP180	Juan Soto	10	12	▲25	▲50

2017 Bowman Chrome Rookie Autographs

		NmMt 8	NmMt+ 8.5	MT 9	Gem 9.5/10
BCARAB	Alex Bregman	30	40	50	80
BCARCB	Cody Bellinger	150	200	250	400
BCARYM	Yoan Moncada	40	50	60	100
CRAAB	Alex Bregman	30	40	50	80
CRAABE	Andrew Benintendi	40	50	60	100
CRAAJ	Aaron Judge	250	300	400	600
CRADS	Dansby Swanson	30	40	50	80
CRAYM	Yoan Moncada	60	80	100	150

2017 Bowman Chrome Draft

		NmMt 8	NmMt+ 8.5	MT 9	Gem 9.5/10
BDC39	Ronald Acuna	10	12	▲25	▲50
BDC95	Jo Adell	10	12	15	30
BDC150	Vladimir Guerrero Jr.	8	10	15	▼25
BDC162	Juan Soto	8	10	▲20	▲40

2017 Bowman Chrome Draft Autographs

		NmMt 8	NmMt+ 8.5	MT 9	Gem 9.5/10
CDAAB	Austin Beck	30	40	50	80
CDAAH	Adam Haseley	25	30	40	60
CDABM	Brendan McKay	▼20	▼25	▼30	▼60
CDABR	Brent Rooker	20	25	30	50
CDABT	Bubba Thompson	25	30	40	60
CDADW	Drew Waters	50	60	80	▼100
CDAHR	Heliot Ramos	50	60	▲100	▲150
CDAJA	Jo Adell	▲500	▲600	▲800	▲1,200
CDAKH	Keston Hiura	60	80	▲150	▲250
CDAKW	Kyle Wright	25	30	40	60
CDAMG	MacKenzie Gore	50	60	80	120
CDAMV	Mark Vientos	40	50	60	100
CDANPE	Nate Pearson	20	25	30	50
CDAPS	Pavin Smith	▼12	▼15	▼20	▼30
CDARL	Royce Lewis	100	120	▲250	▲400
CDATL	Tristen Lutz	▼12	▼15	▼20	▼30

2017 Bowman Chrome Mega Box Prospects Refractors

	NmMt 8	NmMt+ 8.5	MT 9	Gem 9.5/10
BCP31 Shohei Otani UER#(Ohtani)	150	200	250	400

2017 Bowman Platinum

		NmMt 8	NmMt+ 8.5	MT 9	Gem 9.5/10
76	Cody Bellinger RC	10	12	15	30
91	Aaron Judge RC	10	12	15	30

2017 Bowman Platinum Top Prospects Autographs

		NmMt 8	NmMt+ 8.5	MT 9	Gem 9.5/10
TPAR	Amed Rosario	30	30	50	100
TPEJ	Eloy Jimenez	50	50	60	100
TPGT	Gleyber Torres	60	60	80	120

	NmMt 8	NmMt+ 8.5	MT 9	Gem 9.5/10
TPIH Ian Happ	30	30	40	60
TPJG Jason Groome	15	20	25	40
TPJS Juan Soto	250	250	300	500
TPKM Kevin Maitan	80	80	100	150
TPMM Mickey Moniak	15	20	25	40
TPNS Nick Senzel	50	50	60	100

2017 Bowman's Best Best of '17 Autographs

	NmMt 8	NmMt+ 8.5	MT 9	Gem 9.5/10
B17RA Ronald Acuna	120	150	200	300
B17RL Royce Lewis	20	25	40	60

2017 Donruss Optic

		NmMt 8	NmMt+ 8.5	MT 9	Gem 9.5/10
38	Aaron Judge RR RC	8	10	20	40

2017 Finest

		NmMt 8	NmMt+ 8.5	MT 9	Gem 9.5/10
2	Aaron Judge RC	12	15	20	40

2017 Topps Allen and Ginter

		NmMt 8	NmMt+ 8.5	MT 9	Gem 9.5/10
172	Aaron Judge RC	10	12	15	30

2017 Topps Archives

		NmMt 8	NmMt+ 8.5	MT 9	Gem 9.5/10
62	Aaron Judge RC	15	20	40	▼100

2017 Topps Chrome

		NmMt 8	NmMt+ 8.5	MT 9	Gem 9.5/10
79	Cody Bellinger RC	12	15	20	40
169A	Aaron Judge RC	15	20	20	30

2017 Topps Chrome Rookie Autographs

	NmMt 8	NmMt+ 8.5	MT 9	Gem 9.5/10
RAAB Alex Bregman	50	60	80	120
RAABE Andrew Benintendi	50	60	80	120
RAAJ Aaron Judge	150	200	250	400
RACB Cody Bellinger	120	150	▲300	▲400
RAYM Yoan Moncada	50	60	80	120

2018 Bowman

		NmMt 8	NmMt+ 8.5	MT 9	Gem 9.5/10
49	Shohei Ohtani RC	8	12	25	80

2018 Bowman Chrome

		NmMt 8	NmMt+ 8.5	MT 9	Gem 9.5/10
1	Shohei Ohtani RC	10	12	15	30
40	Ronald Acuna Jr. RC	12	15	20	50

2018 Bowman Chrome Prospect Autographs

	NmMt 8	NmMt+ 8.5	MT 9	Gem 9.5/10
CPAAG Andres Gimenez	▼15	▼20	▼25	▼40
CPABMC Brendan McKay	25	30	40	60
CPACP Cristian Pache	100	120	150	250
CPACW Colton Welker	30	40	50	80
CPADP DJ Peters	25	30	40	60
CPAEF Estevan Florial	100	120	150	250
CPAEPA Eric Pardinho	25	30	40	60
CPAHG Hunter Greene	60	80	100	150
CPAJHI Jordan Hicks	20	25	30	50
CPAKR Keibert Ruiz	40	50	60	100
CPALR Luis Robert	150	200	▲400	▲600
CPAMGO MacKenzie Gore	15	20	25	40
CPARL Royce Lewis	80	100	120	200
CPASMU Sean Murphy	15	20	▲40	▲60
CPAYA Yordan Alvarez	200	250	▲500	▲800
BCPAAF Antoni Flores	30	40	▼20	80
BCPABM Brandon Marsh	20	25	30	50
BCPACK Carter Kieboom	60	80	100	150
BCPADM Dustin May	15	20	25	40
BCPAJLO Jonathan Loaisiga	25	30	40	60
BCPAKR Kristian Robinson	120	150	200	300
BCPALGA Luis Garcia	60	80	100	150
BCPALSA LoLo Sanchez	25	30	40	60
BCPALU Luis Urias	30	40	50	80
BCPARW Russell Wilson	250	300	400	600

	NmMt 8	NmMt+ 8.5	MT 9	Gem 9.5/10
BCPASB Shane Bieber	15	20	25	40
BCPATF Tyler Freeman	25	30	40	60
BCPAWCO William Contreras	25	30	40	60

2018 Bowman Chrome Prospects

		NmMt 8	NmMt+ 8.5	MT 9	Gem 9.5/10
BCP21	Luis Robert				50
BCP52	Juan Soto	10	12	15	30

2018 Bowman Chrome Rookie Autographs

	NmMt 8	NmMt+ 8.5	MT 9	Gem 9.5/10
BCRAGT Gleyber Torres	50	60	▲100	▲150
BCRAOA Ozzie Albies	25	30	40	60
BCRARA Ronald Acuna	150	200	▲300	▲500
BCRARD Rafael Devers	30	40	50	80
BCRASO Shohei Ohtani#(Batting	400	500	600	1,000
BCRAVR Victor Robles	40	50	60	100
CRAMA Miguel Andujar	▼20	▼25	▼30	▼50
CRARD Rafael Devers	30	40	50	80
CRARH Rhys Hoskins	▼80	▼100	▼120	▼300
CRASO Shohei Ohtani#(Pitching	500	600	800	1,200
CRAVR Victor Robles	40	50	60	100
CRAWB Walker Buehler	40	50	60	100

2018 Bowman Chrome Draft Autographs

	NmMt 8	NmMt+ 8.5	MT 9	Gem 9.5/10
CDAAB Alec Bohm	▲60	▲80	▲100	▲200
CDAAS Anthony Seigler	25	30	40	60
CDAAT Alek Thomas	30	40	50	80
CDABT Brice Turang	25	30	40	60
CDACM Casey Mize	50	60	▲120	▲200
CDACR Cole Roederer	▼25	▼30	▼40	▼60
CDAGL Grant Lavigne	▼20	▼25	▼30	120
CDAJA Jordyn Adams	▼25	▼30	▼40	▼60
CDAJG Jordan Groshans	60	80	100	150
CDAJI Jonathan India	▼30	▼40	▼50	▼80
CDAJK Jarred Kelenic	▲100	▲150	▲250	▲400
CDANG Nolan Gorman	150	200	250	400
CDANH Nico Hoerner	60	80	100	150
CDANM Nick Madrigal	▼40	▼50	▼60	▼100
CDATC Triston Casas	50	60	▲100	▲150
CDATL Trevor Larnach	▼30	▼40	▼50	▼80

2018 Bowman Platinum Top Prospect Autographs

	NmMt 8	NmMt+ 8.5	MT 9	Gem 9.5/10
TOP2 Ronald Acuna	120	150	200	300
TOP3 Gleyber Torres	60	80	100	150
TOP4 Hunter Greene	40	50	60	100
TOP5 Royce Lewis	30	40	50	80
TOP8 Luis Robert	20	25	30	50
TOP11 Jo Adell	30	40	50	80
TOP21 Cristian Pache	20	25	30	50

2018 Bowman's Best

		NmMt 8	NmMt+ 8.5	MT 9	Gem 9.5/10
1	Shohei Ohtani RC	15	20	25	30
29	Juan Soto RC	12	15	20	25
50	Gleyber Torres RC	20	25	30	40
51	Ronald Acuna Jr. RC	20	25	30	40

2018 Bowman's Best Best of '18 Autographs

	NmMt 8	NmMt+ 8.5	MT 9	Gem 9.5/10
B18AJ Aaron Judge	100	120	150	250
B18EF Estevan Florial	30	40	50	80
B18FT Fernando Tatis Jr.	80	100	120	200
B18JAD Jo Adell	30	40	50	80
B18JSO Juan Soto	120	150	200	300
B18KB Kris Bryant	80	100	120	200
B18MT Mike Trout	250	300	400	600
B18NG Nolan Gorman	▼30	▼40	▼50	▼80
B18RA Ronald Acuna Jr.	100	120	150	250
B18SO Shohei Ohtani	250	300	400	600
B18YA Yordan Alvarez	40	50	▲150	▲250

2018 Diamond Kings

		NmMt 8	NmMt+ 8.5	MT 9	Gem 9.5/10
73	Shohei Ohtani RC	8	10	12	15
76	Shohei Ohtani RC	8	10	12	20

2018 Donruss Optic

		NmMt 8	NmMt+ 8.5	MT 9	Gem 9.5/10
56	Shohei Ohtani RR RC	8	10	15	25
63	Ronald Acuna Jr. RR RC	8	10	12	40

2018 Finest

		NmMt 8	NmMt+ 8.5	MT 9	Gem 9.5/10
100	Shohei Ohtani RC	8	10	▲15	▼25

2018 Topps Update

	NmMt 8	NmMt+ 8.5	MT 9	Gem 9.5/10
US200 Gleyber Torres RC	25	30	40	80
US250 Ronald Acuna Jr. RC	30	40	50	100

2018 Topps Allen and Ginter

		NmMt 8	NmMt+ 8.5	MT 9	Gem 9.5/10
207	Ronald Acuna Jr. RC	10	12	15	30
240	Gleyber Torres RC	8	10	12	25

2018 Topps Chrome

		NmMt 8	NmMt+ 8.5	MT 9	Gem 9.5/10
31	Gleyber Torres RC	20	25	30	40
150	Shohei Ohtani RC	8	10	▲15	30
193	Ronald Acuna RC	10	12	25	50

2018 Topps Chrome Rookie Autographs

	NmMt 8	NmMt+ 8.5	MT 9	Gem 9.5/10
RAAUM Austin Meadows	15	20	25	40
RACF Clint Frazier	15	20	25	40
RAGT Gleyber Torres	50	60	▲150	▲250
RAMA Miguel Andujar	30	40	50	80
RAOA Ozzie Albies	30	40	50	80
RARA Ronald Acuna	200	250	300	500
RARD Rafael Devers	25	30	40	60
RARH Rhys Hoskins	40	50	60	100
RASO Shohei Ohtani	300	400	500	800
RAVR Victor Robles	30	40	50	80
RAWB Walker Buehler	30	40	▲60	▲100

2018 Topps Chrome Update

	NmMt 8	NmMt+ 8.5	MT 9	Gem 9.5/10
HMT1 Shohei Ohtani RC	8	10	▲15	▼30
HMT9 Gleyber Torres RC	15	20	25	80
HMT19 Walker Buehler RC	12	15	20	30
HMT25 Ronald Acuna Jr. RC	10	12	▲25	50
HMT26 Gleyber Torres RC	8	10	12	30
HMT55 Juan Soto RC	20	▼25	▼30	▼60

2018 Topps Gypsy Queen

		NmMt 8	NmMt+ 8.5	MT 9	Gem 9.5/10
89	Shohei Ohtani RC	10	12	15	30

2018 Topps Heritage

		NmMt 8	NmMt+ 8.5	MT 9	Gem 9.5/10
502	Juan Soto RC	10	12	20	60
580	Ronald Acuna Jr. RC	10	12	20	▼40
600	Shohei Ohtani RC	8	10	▲20	▼40
603	Gleyber Torres RC	12	15	20	40

2018 Topps Heritage Real One Autographs

	NmMt 8	NmMt+ 8.5	MT 9	Gem 9.5/10
ROASO Shohei Ohtani	1,000	1,200	1,600	3,000

2018 Topps Living

		NmMt 8	NmMt+ 8.5	MT 9	Gem 9.5/10
1	Aaron Judge/13,256*	20	30	▼30	▼60
4	Rhys Hoskins/5446*	15	20	▼25	120
7	Shohei Ohtani/20,966*	8	10	15	40
10	Derek Jeter/10,692*	10	12	20	40
19	Ronald Acuna/46,809*	8	10	▲20	40
34	Gleyber Torres/28,550*	8	10	▲15	▲30
43	Juan Soto/28,572*	10	12	15	▼30
49	Miguel Andujar/12,794*	10	12	15	30
53	Walker Buehler/7503*	10	12	15	30
73	Cody Bellinger/5273*	8	10	12	25
80	Victor Robles/6104*	10	12	15	30
94	Christian Yelich/5025*	10	12	15	30

2018 Topps Opening Day

		NmMt 8	NmMt+ 8.5	MT 9	Gem 9.5/10
200	Shohei Ohtani RC	8	10	15	30

BASKETBALL
1933 -1989/90

933 Sport Kings

	PrFr 1	GD 2	VG 3	VgEx 4	EX 5	ExMt 6	NM 7	NmMt 8
Nat Holman BK	60	80	100	175	400	600		
Ed Wachter BK	40	50	60	80	175	275		
Joe Lapchick BK	100	125	175	300	500	800	1,200	2,400
Eddie Burke BK	60	80	100	175	250	350		

Red Grange #4 PSA 8 (NmMt) sold for $13,394.40 (Mastro Auctions; 12/07)
Red Grange #4 SGC 8 (NmMt) sold for $3,704 (Mile High Auctions; 11/10)
Carl Hubbell #42 PSA 9 (MT) sold for $7,929 (Mastro; 12/05)
Babe Ruth #2 SGC 92 (NmMt+) sold for $64,417 (Mastro; 4/07)
Babe Ruth #2 GAI 7.5 (NM+) sold for $5,541 (Mile High; 8/07)
Jim Thorpe #6 PSA 8 (NmMt) sold for $7,200.00 (Mastro Auctions; 5/08)
Ed Wachter #5 PSA 8 (NmMt) sold for $2,100 (Bussineau; 7/13)

948 Bowman

	PrFr 1	GD 2	VG 3	VgEx 4	EX 5	ExMt 6	NM 7	NmMt 8
Ernie Calverley RC	15	30	40	50	80	100	250	500
Ralph Hamilton	10	15	20	25	40	50	80	200
Gale Bishop	10	12	20	30	50	60	100	200
Fred Lewis RC	10	12	20	30	40	60	80	150
Single Cut Off Post	10	12	20	30	40	50	80	200
Bob Feerick RC	10	12	20	30	40	60	120	200
John Logan	10	12	15	20	40	50	60	120
Mel Riebe	10	12	20	30	40	60	80	200
Andy Phillip RC	15	20	30	60	80	125	300	600
Bob Davies RC	15	30	60	80	100	125	200	450
Single Cut With	10	12	20	25	40	60	80	200
Kenny Sailors RC	10	12	20	30	50	80	120	350
Paul Armstrong	10	12	20	25	40	50	75	200
Howard Dallmar RC	10	15	30	35	40	80	100	150
Bruce Hale RC	10	12	25	30	40	50	80	200
Sid Hertzberg	10	12	20	25	40	50	80	200
Single Cut Using	10	12	20	25	40	50	80	225
Red Rocha	10	12	25	30	40	50	120	200
Eddie Ehlers	10	12	20	30	40	50	80	200
Ellis (Gene) Vance	10	12	15	20	30	50	80	200
Fuzzy Levane RC	10	12	25	30	40	80	100	150
Earl Shannon	10	12	20	25	30	50	80	200
Double Cut Off Post	10	12	20	25	30	50	80	200
Leo(Crystal) Klier	10	12	20	25	40	50	80	150
George Senesky	10	12	20	25	40	60	80	200
Price Brookfield	10	12	25	30	40	50	80	200
John Norlander	10	12	25	30	40	60	80	200
Don Putman	10	12	20	30	40	60	80	150
Double Post	10	12	25	30	40	50	80	200
Jack Garfinkel	10	12	20	25	40	60	120	▲250
Chuck Gilmur	10	12	15	20	30	40	80	250
Red Holzman RC	25	30	60	80	100	150	250	500
Jack Smiley	10	12	20	25	30	50	80	▲250
Joe Fulks RC	20	30	40	60	100	▼150	400	600
Screen Play	10	12	20	30	40	50	80	250
Hal Tidrick	10	12	20	25	40	60	▲120	400
Don (Swede) Carlson	10	25	40	50	60	100	250	525
Buddy Jeanette CO RC	20	40	80	100	200	300	450	800
Ray Kuka	15	25	40	60	80	100	200	400
Stan Miasek	15	20	30	50	60	80	200	400

	PrFr 1	GD 2	VG 3	VgEx 4	EX 5	ExMt 6	NM 7	NmMt 8
41 Double Screen With	15	25	40	60	100	125	200	375
42 George Nostrand	20	30	50	60	80	100	120	500
43 Chuck Halbert RC	20	30	40	60	80	100	200	▼400
44 Arnie Johnson	10	12	25	40	60	80	120	400
45 Bob Doll	15	25	30	40	60	100	150	500
46 Bones McKinney RC	15	25	40	50	75	150	225	400
47 Out Of Bounds	10	12	25	40	60	125	200	350
48 Ed Sadowski	20	30	50	75	100	150	250	500
49 Bob Kinney	15	25	40	50	80	150	300	
50 Charles (Hawk) Black	10	15	30	40	60	80	150	500
51 Jack Dwan	15	30	50	80	150	250	300	600
52 Connie Simmons RC	20	30	50	60	100	125	200	400
53 Out Of Bounds Play	15	25	40	50	100	150	200	300
54 Bud Palmer RC	15	25	40	60	100	150	250	600
55 Max Zaslofsky RC	30	50	60	80	100	150	400	800
56 Lee Roy Robbins	15	25	40	60	100	200	250	600
57 Arthur Spector	15	25	▲50	▲80	100	150	200	400
58 Arnie Risen RC	25	40	60	80	200	250	300	700
59 Out Of Bounds Play	10	12	20	30	50	100	200	350
60 Ariel Maughan	10	12	25	40	60	80	▲200	▲500
61 Dick O'Keefe	15	25	40	50	60	60	100	400
62 Herman Schaefer	10	15	30	40	50	100	200	400
63 John Mahnken	20	25	50	60	80	120	200	400
64 Tommy Byrnes	10	15	30	40	60	100	200	450
65 Held Ball Play	15	25	40	60	80	150	200	500
66 Jim Pollard RC	30	60	100	200	300	400	▲850	2,000
67 Lee Mogus	12	20	30	50	80	120	150	500
68 Lee Knorek	12	20	30	40	50	80	300	700
69 George Mikan RC	1,200	1,500	2,500	3,500	5,000	6,000	8,000	25,000
70 Walter Budko	10	12	30	50	60	150	200	400
71 Guards Down Play	20	30	50	60	100	150	400	600
72 Carl Braun RC	50	80	150	200	250	300	600	1,500

—Max Zaslofsky #55 PSA 9 (MT) sold for $2,953 (Mile High; 1/10)
—Jim Pollard #66 PSA 9 (MT) sold for $8,520 (Greg Bussineau; Fall 2012
—Jim Pollard #66 PSA 8 (NmMt) sold for $1,704 (Memory Lane; 5/13)
—Jim Pollard #66 PSA 8 (NmMt) sold for $1,059 (eBay; 12/12)
—George Mikan #69 PSA 10 (Gem Mt) sold for $403,664 (SCP; 12/15)
—George Mikan #69 SGC 96 (Mint) sold for $35,850 (Heritage; 11/15)
—George Mikan #69 PSA 7 (NM) sold for $4,877 (Mile High; 6/10)

1957-58 Topps

	PrFr 1	GD 2	VG 3	VgEx 4	EX 5	ExMt 6	NM 7	NmMt 8
1 Nat Clifton DP RC	35	50	60	100	200	400	1,500	
2 George Yardley DP RC	10	15	25	40	70	200	400	4,000
3 Neil Johnston DP RC	10	12	20	25	40	60	350	2,000
4 Carl Braun DP	10	12	20	25	30	50	150	700
5 Bill Sharman DP RC	15	25	30	50	80	150	400	1,000
6 George King DP RC	8	10	15	25	30	50	125	400
7 Kenny Sears DP RC	10	12	20	25	30	50	150	500
8 Dick Ricketts DP RC	10	12	20	30	40	50	150	400
9 Jack Nichols DP	8	10	15	20	50	60	150	400
10 Paul Arizin DP RC	20	25	30	40	60	100	300	800
11 Chuck Noble DP	10	12	20	25	30	60	100	400
12 Slater Martin DP RC	15	30	50	60	80	150	300	1,000
13 Dolph Schayes DP RC	15	25	30	40	60	120	400	1,000
14 Dick Atha DP	8	10	15	20	30	60	125	400
15 Frank Ramsey DP RC	15	25	40	50	80	150	400	600

#	Name	PrFr 1	GD 2	VG 3	VgEx 4	EX 5	ExMt 6	NM 7	NmMt 8
16	Dick McGuire DP RC	10	15	25	30	40	100	250	650
17	Bob Cousy DP RC	▲100	▲200	▲300	▲400	500	800	2,000	5,000
18	Larry Foust DP RC	8	10	15	25	30	60	150	450
19	Tom Heinsohn RC	50	60	80	100	150	300	800	2,000
20	Bill Thieben DP	8	10	15	20	30	60	300	1,500
21	Don Meineke DP RC	8	10	15	25	40	60	100	600
22	Tom Marshall	10	12	20	25	40	50	100	450
23	Dick Garmaker	10	12	20	25	30	50	150	600
24	Bob Pettit QP RC	20	35	50	60	100	150	400	1,200
25	Jim Krebs DP RC	10	12	20	25	40	60	120	500
26	Gene Shue DP RC	10	15	25	30	40	50	100	500
27	Ed Macauley DP RC	12	20	25	30	60	120	300	1,000
28	Vern Mikkelsen RC	12	20	30	50	80	120	400	2,000
29	Willie Naulls RC	10	12	15	20	40	60	200	500
30	Walter Dukes DP RC	10	15	25	30	40	60	120	250
31	Dave Piontek DP	8	10	15	20	30	50	100	300
32	John (Red) Kerr RC	15	25	40	50	60	80	200	600
33	Larry Costello DP RC	10	12	20	25	30	60	150	450
34	Woody Sauldsberry DP RC	10	15	25	30	40	50	125	400
35	Ray Felix RC	10	12	20	25	30	40	150	500
36	Ernie Beck	8	10	20	30	40	60	200	3,000
37	Cliff Hagan RC	12	20	30	50	60	100	200	600
38	Guy Sparrow DP	10	12	20	25	30	50	100	400
39	Jim Loscutoff RC	10	15	25	30	60	100	300	1,200
40	Arnie Risen DP	10	15	25	30	50	100	200	600
41	Joe Graboski	10	12	20	25	40	80	120	500
42	Maurice Stokes DP RC	12	20	25	40	60	100	200	500
43	Rod Hundley DP RC	12	20	30	40	80	100	▲250	500
44	Tom Gola DP RC	15	25	30	▲50	▲80	▲120	400	1,500
45	Med Park RC	10	12	20	40	60	80	150	450
46	Mel Hutchins DP	8	10	20	30	40	60	300	700
47	Larry Friend DP	8	10	15	20	30	50	80	800
48	Len Rosenbluth DP RC	10	15	25	30	40	60	120	500
49	Walt Davis	10	12	20	25	30	40	150	600
50	Richie Regan RC	10	12	20	25	40	50	150	450
51	Frank Selvy DP RC	12	20	25	30	40	60	150	450
52	Art Spoelstra DP	8	10	15	20	30	▲60	120	400
53	Bob Hopkins RC	8	10	15	20	30	50	150	600
54	Earl Lloyd RC	12	20	30	50	60	120	200	450
55	Phil Jordan DP	8	10	15	20	30	50	100	400
56	Bob Houbregs DP RC	10	12	20	25	30	50	150	500
57	Lou Tsioropoulos DP	10	12	20	30	40	80	120	400
58	Ed Conlin RC	10	12	20	30	40	60	125	700
59	Al Bianchi RC	10	12	20	25	40	50	150	800
60	George Dempsey RC	10	12	15	20	30	60	120	300
61	Chuck Share	8	10	12	20	30	60	150	500
62	Harry Gallatin DP RC	10	15	25	40	80	120	400	600
63	Bob Harrison	10	15	25	40	50			150
64	Bob Burrow DP	8	10	15	25	30	60	125	400
65	Win Wilfong DP	8	10	15	25	40	60	125	300
66	Jack McMahon DP RC	8	10	15	25	40	60	150	450
67	Jack George	8	10	15	20	30	40	200	400
68	Charlie Tyra DP	10	12	20	25	30	60	125	500
69	Ron Sobie	10	12	20	25	30	60	150	450
70	Jack Coleman	10	12	20	25	30	50	125	450
71	Jack Twyman DP RC	12	20	30	50	60	150	400	800
72	Paul Seymour RC	10	12	20	25	40	60	120	550
73	Jim Paxson DP RC	10	12	20	30	40	60	120	400
74	Bob Leonard RC	10	12	20	40	60	100	200	500
75	Andy Phillip	12	20	25	30	40	80	400	700
76	Joe Holup	10	12	20	30	50	60	150	400
77	Bill Russell RC	1,000	1,200	▲2,000	▲2,500	3,000	▲5,000	25,000	35,000
78	Clyde Lovellette DP RC	15	25	40	50	80	125	250	900
79	Ed Fleming DP	10	12	20	25	40	100	300	
80	Dick Schnittker RC	15	20	30	40	80	125	500	3,500

—Nat Clifton #1 PSA 8 (NMMT) sold for $3,081 (eBay; 12/10)
—Tom Heinsohn #19 PSA 8 (NMMT) sold for $822 (Mile High; 6/10)
—Phil Jordan #55 PSA 9 (MT) sold for $2,225 (eBay; 2/12)
—Bob Houbregs #56 PSA 9 (MT) sold for $4,062 (eBay; 4/12)
—Lou Tsioropoluos #57 PSA 9 (MT) sold for $3,950 (eBay; 4/12)
—Jack McMahon #66 PSA 9 (MT) sold for $2,948 (eBay; 4/12)
—Bill Russell #77 PSA 7 (NM) sold for $2,218 (Mile High; 10/09)
—Bill Russell #77 SGC 70 (EX+) sold for $1,304 (Huggins & Scott; 4/13)
—Clyde Lovellette #78 PSA 8 (NMMT) sold for $910 (Mile High; 6/10)
—Ed Flemming #79 PSA 8 (NMMT) sold for $4,057 (eBay; 3/12)
—Dick Schnittker #80 PSA 8 (NMMT) sold for $2,901 (Goodwin; 6/10)

1961-62 Fleer

#	Name	GD 2	VG 3	VgEx 4	EX 5	ExMt 6	NM 7	NmMt 8	MT 9
1	Al Attles RC	10	30	50	60	120	500	1,200	▲4,000
2	Paul Arizin	10	15	30	60	100	250	1,000	2,000
3	Elgin Baylor RC	60	120	150	300	400	▼800	4,000	30,000
4	Walt Bellamy RC	10	15	30	60	80	300	1,000	6,000
5	Arlen Bockhorn	5	8	10	20	30	50	250	1,500
6	Bob Boozer RC	5	8	15	20	30	100	400	2,000
7	Carl Braun	5	8	10	15	30	60	150	800
8	Wilt Chamberlain RC	800	1,000	▲1,500	▲2,000	3,500	5,000	20,000	45,000
9	Larry Costello	5	8	10	20	25	50	80	500
10	Bob Cousy	40	50	60	100	150	300	500	1,500
11	Walter Dukes	5	8	12	15	30	80	120	700
12	Wayne Embry RC	5	8	10	15	30	80	150	
13	Dave Gambee	5	8	12	20	30	40	120	500
14	Tom Gola	5	8	10	15	40	60	125	600
15	Sihugo Green RC	5	8	12	15	25	50	100	500
16	Hal Greer RC	10	15	50	60	80	120	300	1,200
17	Richie Guerin RC	5	8	10	20	40	80	150	500
18	Cliff Hagan	8	12	20	25	40	60	200	650
19	Tom Heinsohn	10	15	30	50	80	120	250	800
20	Bailey Howell RC	8	12	20	25	50	100	200	1,000
21	Rod Hundley	8	12	15	20	40	60	120	800
22	K.C. Jones RC	15	40	50	60	100	150	500	1,800
23	Sam Jones RC	15	30	60	100	150	200	400	2,000
24	Phil Jordan	5	8	12	15	30	50	120	1,000
25	John/Red Kerr	5	8	12	15	30	80	150	800
26	Rudy LaRusso RC	5	8	10	15	30	60	120	600
27	George Lee	5	8	10	20	25	50	120	550
28	Bob Leonard	5	8	12	20	30	60	150	450
29	Clyde Lovellette	5	8	12	20	40	80	150	850
30	John McCarthy	5	6	8	10	15	40	100	400
31	Tom Meschery RC	5	10	15	30	50	100	300	800
32	Willie Naulls	5	10	15	30	50	100	250	1,000
33	Don Ohl RC	5	10	15	20	30	60	300	1,800
34	Bob Pettit	10	20	30	40	60	120	300	1,800
35	Frank Ramsey	5	10	15	20	50	100	250	1,800
36	Oscar Robertson RC	120	200	400	600	800	2,000	5,000	30,000
37	Guy Rodgers RC	8	10	20	40	80	120	200	800
38	Bill Russell	80	100	150	200	400	600	1,500	5,000
39	Dolph Schayes	5	10	15	20	40	60	150	800
40	Frank Selvy	5	8	10	15	30	60	150	1,000
41	Gene Shue	5	10	15	20	30	60	150	800
42	Jack Twyman	8	12	20	25	30	60	100	900
43	Jerry West RC	100	350	400	500	800	2,000	5,000	20,000
44	Len Wilkens RC	15	25	50	80	100	200	500	1,800
45	Paul Arizin IA	6	8	10	15	25	40	100	800
46	Elgin Baylor IA	10	15	40	60	100	150	250	1,200
47	Wilt Chamberlain IA	80	120	150	200	300	400	800	2,000
48	Larry Costello IA	5	8	12	15	20	50	100	550
49	Bob Cousy IA	15	25	40	60	80	150	250	800
50	Walter Dukes IA	5	8	10	15	20	40	80	500
51	Tom Gola IA	5	8	12	15	25	50	100	500
52	Richie Guerin IA	5	8	10	15	30	40	80	525

	GD 2	VG 3	VgEx 4	EX 5	ExMt 6	NM 7	NmMt 8	MT 9
Cliff Hagan IA	8	10	15	20	30	50	120	500
Tom Heinsohn IA	10	15	25	30	50	80	150	550
Bailey Howell IA	5	8	12	15	40	60	▼100	600
John/Red Kerr IA	8	12	20	25	30	50	100	500
Rudy LaRusso IA	5	8	10	15	30	50	100	
Clyde Lovellette IA	5	10	15	20	25	60	120	600
Bob Pettit IA	8	12	20	30	40	80	150	700
Frank Ramsey IA	5	8	12	15	25	50	100	600
Oscar Robertson IA	25	40	60	100	120	200	400	2,000
Bill Russell IA	25	60	80	150	200	300	800	2,200
Dolph Schayes IA	5	8	15	20	40	60	125	800
Gene Shue IA	5	8	12	20	25	50	200	
Jack Twyman IA	5	10	15	20	25	60	120	500
Jerry West IA	40	60	80	120	200	350	500	4,000

gin Baylor #3 PSA 9 (Mint) sold for $3,730 (eBay, 2/10)

ilt Chamberlain #8 PSA 9 (Mint) sold for $7,240 (eBay, 4/12)

ayne Embry #12 PSA 9 (MT) sold for $1,118 (SCP; 4/13)

am Jones #23 PSA 10 (Gem Mt) sold for $10,157 (Heritage; 8/16)

erry West #43 PSA 9 (Mint) sold for $6,932 (Goodwin; 2/11)

erry West #43 PSA 8.5 (NmMt+) sold for $17,788 (Goodwin; 8/16)

en Wilkens #44 PSA 10 (Gem Mt) sold for $10,157 (Heritage; 8/16)

369-70 Topps

	GD 2	VG 3	VgEx 4	EX 5	ExMt 6	NM 7	NmMt 8	MT 9
Wilt Chamberlain	50	120	200	▲300	500	800	2,500	10,000
Gail Goodrich RC	5	10	15	20	40	60	225	1,500
Cazzie Russell RC	5	8	10	12	30	60	120	450
Darrall Imhoff RC	5	8	10	12	15	20	50	350
Bailey Howell	5	5	8	10	12	20	60	200
Lucius Allen RC	5	8	10	15	25	30	80	
Tom Boerwinkle RC	5	5	6	8	12	30	120	
Jimmy Walker RC	5	5	8	10	15	25	80	
John Block RC	5	5	6	8	10	15	60	425
Nate Thurmond RC	5	10	15	25	40	80	200	700
Gary Gregor	5	5	8	10	15	20	40	400
Gus Johnson RC	5	10	15	20	25	50	120	
Luther Rackley	5	5	6	8	10	20	50	
Jon McGlocklin RC	5	5	12	15	20	50	125	250
Connie Hawkins RC	5	8	12	15	40	80	200	600
Johnny Egan	5	5	6	8	10	15	40	150
Jim Washington	5	5	6	8	10	15	30	150
Dick Barnett RC	5	6	8	10	▲20	▲80	▲150	300
Tom Meschery	5	5	8	10	15	20	50	
John Havlicek RC	30	50	60	100	150	300	800	10,000
Eddie Miles	5	5	8	10	12	15	40	200
Walt Wesley	5	8	10	12	20	40	80	225
Rick Adelman RC	5	5	8	10	15	30	60	250
Al Attles	5	5	8	10	12	25	50	300
Lew Alcindor RC	250	300	400	600	1,200	2,500	8,000	40,000
Jack Marin RC	5	5	8	10	12	25	50	225
Walt Hazzard RC	5	8	10	12	15	25	50	350
Connie Dierking	5	5	8	12	15	20	30	
Keith Erickson RC	5	8	10	12	15	30	50	300
Bob Rule RC	5	8	10	12	15	25	40	175
Dick Van Arsdale RC	5	8	10	12	15	25	50	350
Archie Clark RC	5	8	10	12	15	30	50	300
Terry Dischinger RC	5	5	6	8	10	20	50	200
Henry Finkel RC	5	5	6	8	10	15	40	175
Elgin Baylor	8	12	20	30	40	60	200	1,000
Ron Williams	5	5	6	8	10	20	50	125
Loy Petersen	5	5	6	8	10	20	50	300
Guy Rodgers	5	8	10	12	15	20	50	250
Toby Kimball	5	5	6	8	12	25	50	125
Billy Cunningham RC	5	10	15	20	30	50	150	750

	GD 2	VG 3	VgEx 4	EX 5	ExMt 6	NM 7	NmMt 8	MT 9
41 Joe Caldwell RC	5	8	12	15	25	50		
42 Leroy Ellis RC	5	5	8	10	12	20	50	200
43 Bill Bradley RC	8	12	20	40	50	80	220	1,200
44 Len Wilkens	5	10	15	20	30	40	100	800
45 Jerry Lucas RC	5	10	15	20	30	50	120	650
46 Neal Walk RC	5	8	10	12	15	20	40	200
47 Emmette Bryant RC	5	8	10	12	20	40	80	525
48 Bob Kauffman RC	5	5	8	10	12	20	50	200
49 Mel Counts RC	5	5	8	10	12	20	40	200
50 Oscar Robertson	5	10	15	25	80	100	400	1,000
51 Jim Barnett RC	5	5	8	10	12	20	50	350
52 Don Smith	5	5	6	8	10	15	30	350
53 Jim Davis	5	5	8	10	12	20	40	350
54 Wally Jones RC	5	5	6	8	10	20	40	300
55 Dave Bing RC	5	10	15	20	40	50	150	800
56 Wes Unseld RC	5	8	12	20	40	60	200	800
57 Joe Ellis	5	5	8	12	15	20	40	
58 John Tresvant	5	5	6	8	10	20	40	500
59 Larry Siegfried RC	5	5	6	8	10	20	50	200
60 Willis Reed RC	5	8	12	40	60	100	250	1,500
61 Paul Silas RC	5	8	12	15	20	80	400	
62 Bob Weiss RC	5	8	12	15	20	25	80	300
63 Willie McCarter	5	5	6	8	10	12	30	200
64 Don Kojis RC	5	5	6	8	10	20	30	125
65 Lou Hudson RC	5	10	15	20	25	40	100	500
66 Jim King	5	5	6	8	10	12	40	200
67 Luke Jackson RC	5	5	6	8	12	20	60	200
68 Len Chappell RC	5	5	6	8	10	15	25	50
69 Ray Scott	5	5	6	8	10	12	15	40
70 Jeff Mullins RC	5	5	6	8	10	12	25	60
71 Howie Komives	5	5	6	8	12	15	35	200
72 Tom Sanders RC	5	8	10	15	20	40	150	600
73 Dick Snyder	5	5	6	8	10	20	35	
74 Dave Stallworth RC	5	5	6	8	10	15	30	60
75 Elvin Hayes RC	5	10	20	30	50	80	200	1,500
76 Art Harris	5	5	6	8	10	20	50	200
77 Don Ohl	5	5	6	8	12	20	40	
78 Bob Love RC	5	8	12	20	25	40	100	400
79 Tom Van Arsdale RC	5	8	10	12	15	30	150	
80 Earl Monroe RC	5	10	20	40	60	120	250	800
81 Greg Smith	5	5	6	8	10	15	30	325
82 Don Nelson RC	8	12	20	25	30	50	100	600
83 Happy Hairston RC	5	5	8	10	15	30	50	300
84 Hal Greer	5	8	10	12	20	40	150	550
85 Dave DeBusschere RC	5	10	15	20	40	60	200	
86 Bill Bridges RC	5	5	8	10	12	25	50	200
87 Herm Gilliam RC	5	5	6	8	10	12	25	50
88 Jim Fox	5	5	6	8	10	20	50	550
89 Bob Boozer	5	5	6	8	15	20	100	
90 Jerry West	12	25	30	60	80	120	250	1,000
91 Chet Walker RC	5	10	15	20	25	40	80	400
92 Flynn Robinson RC	5	8	12	15	20	25	60	400
93 Clyde Lee	5	5	6	8	12	20	40	175
94 Kevin Loughery RC	5	5	8	10	15	25	50	250
95 Walt Bellamy	5	5	10	15	20	30	60	
96 Art Williams	5	5	8	10	15	20	40	
97 Adrian Smith RC	5	5	8	10	15	20	50	225
98 Walt Frazier RC	5	15	30	50	80	200	500	3,000
99 Checklist 1-99	40	60	100	250	500	800	2,500	10,000

—Rick Adelman #23 PSA 10 (Gem MT) sold for $2,025 (eBay; 3/12)

—Lew Alcindor #25 PSA 10 (Gem MT) sold for $501,900 (Heritage; 8/16)

—Lew Alcindor #25 BSG 10 (Pristine) sold for $12,245 (eBay; 3/11)

—John Havlicek #20 PSA 10 (Gem MT) sold for $25,273 (Mile High; 12/13)

—John Havlicek #20 PSA 9 (MT) sold for $3,696 (Mile High; 10/09)

1970-71 Topps

#	Player	GD 2	VG 3	VgEx 4	EX 5	ExMt 6	NM 7	NmMt 8	MT 9
1	Alcind/West/Hayes LL	5	5	10	12	30	50	200	
2	West/Alcin/Hayes LL SP	5	5	10	12	30	60	250	800
3	Green/Imhof/Hudson LL	5	5	8	10	12	15	30	125
4	Rob/Walker/Mull LL SP	5	5	8	10	12	200	500	
5	Hayes/Uns/Alcindor LL	5	5	8	10	20	30	50	200
6	Wilkens/Fraz/Hask LL SP	5	5	10	12	15	30	80	
7	Bill Bradley	5	5	10	12	20	40	60	300
8	Ron Williams	5	5	5	8	10	12	▲30	
9	Otto Moore	5	5	6	8	10	12	20	40
10	John Havlicek SP	5	10	15	25	80	150	350	500
11	George Wilson RC	5	5	5	8	10	12	20	50
12	John Trapp	5	5	5	8	10	12	20	50
13	Pat Riley RC	5	10	15	25	40	60	250	900
14	Jim Washington	5	5	5	5	6	8	20	75
15	Bob Rule	5	5	5	6	8	10	15	200
16	Bob Weiss	5	5	5	8	10	12	100	
17	Neil Johnson	5	5	5	8	10	15	60	
18	Walt Bellamy	5	5	5	6	8	12	▲40	150
19	McCoy McLemore	5	5	5	6	8	15	60	
20	Earl Monroe	5	5	8	10	15	20	40	150
21	Wally Anderzunas	5	5	5	6	8	12	50	
22	Guy Rodgers	5	5	5	8	10	12	60	
23	Rick Roberson	5	5	6	8	10	12	50	
24	Checklist 1-110	5	5	8	10	12	20	60	300
25	Jimmy Walker	5	5	5	5	6	8	20	50
26	Mike Riordan RC	5	5	6	8	10	12	25	150
27	Henry Finkel	5	5	5	5	6	10	▲20	▲80
28	Joe Ellis	5	5	5	8	10	20	60	
29	Mike Davis	5	5	5	5	6	8	12	60
30	Lou Hudson	5	5	8	10	12	15	25	80
31	Lucius Allen SP	5	5	8	10	12	80	150	
32	Toby Kimball SP	5	5	6	15	20	30	150	
33	Luke Jackson SP	5	5	6	8	10	15	80	250
34	Johnny Egan	5	5	6	8	10	15	80	200
35	Leroy Ellis SP	5	5	8	10	30	150	300	
36	Jack Marin SP	5	5	6	8	12	20	60	
37	Joe Caldwell SP	5	5	6	8	12	25	80	
38	Keith Erickson	5	5	6	8	10	12	20	80
39	Don Smith	5	5	5	5	6	10	▲40	
40	Flynn Robinson	5	5	5	6	8	10	20	▲100
41	Bob Boozer	5	5	5	5	6	10	20	
42	Howie Komives	5	5	5	5	6	8	12	40
43	Dick Barnett	5	5	6	8	10	12	15	100
44	Stu Lantz RC	5	5	6	8	10	12	15	80
45	Dick Van Arsdale	5	5	6	8	10	12	25	150
46	Jerry Lucas	5	5	8	10	12	15	40	200
47	Don Chaney RC	5	5	8	10	12	15	40	150
48	Ray Scott	5	5	5	5	6	10	20	60
49	Dick Cunningham SP	5	5	5	6	20	50	350	
50	Wilt Chamberlain	20	30	40	60	80	120	300	800
51	Kevin Loughery	5	5	5	6	8	10	20	70
52	Stan McKenzie	5	5	5	6	8	10	15	60
53	Fred Foster	5	5	5	6	8	10	15	40
54	Jim Davis	5	5	5	6	8	10	12	40
55	Walt Wesley	5	5	5	6	8	10	15	50
56	Bill Hewitt	5	5	5	6	8	10	12	50
57	Darrall Imhoff	5	5	5	6	8	10	15	35
58	John Block	5	5	5	6	8	10	15	
59	Al Attles SP	5	5	6	8	12	▼30	200	
60	Chet Walker	5	5	6	8	10	15	20	100
61	Luther Rackley	5	5	5	6	8	10	15	60
62	Jerry Chambers SP RC	5	5	5	8	12	30	100	200
63	Bob Dandridge RC	5	5	6	8	15	40	100	450

#	Player	GD 2	VG 3	VgEx 4	EX 5	ExMt 6	NM 7	NmMt 8	MT 9
64	Dick Snyder	5	5	5	5	6	8	12	40
65	Elgin Baylor	5	5	10	12	15	30	60	250
66	Connie Dierking	5	5	5	5	8	10	15	50
67	Steve Kuberski RC	5	5	5	6	10	20		
68	Tom Boerwinkle	5	5	5	8	10	15	60	
69	Paul Silas	5	5	6	8	15	20	30	200
70	Elvin Hayes	5	5	10	15	20	30	60	200
71	Bill Bridges	5	5	5	6	8	10	20	75
72	Wes Unseld	5	5	8	10	20	60	250	
73	Herm Gilliam	5	5	5	6	8	20	80	
74	Bobby Smith SP RC	5	5	6	8	10	60	150	
75	Lew Alcindor	8	12	30	60	▲150	▲200	400	1,200
76	Jeff Mullins	5	5	5	6	8	10	12	70
77	Happy Hairston	5	5	5	6	8	10	20	60
78	Dave Stallworth SP	5	5	6	8	15	25	80	300
79	Fred Hetzel	5	5	5	6	8	10	15	50
80	Len Wilkens SP	5	5	10	12	30	60	120	
81	Johnny Green RC	5	5	6	8	10	15	25	
82	Erwin Mueller	5	5	5	5	6	8	12	
83	Wally Jones	5	5	5	8	10	15	70	
84	Bob Love	5	5	6	8	10	12	20	100
85	Dick Garrett RC	5	5	5	5	6	10	15	50
86	Don Nelson SP	5	8	12	15	20	30	80	250
87	Neal Walk SP	5	5	6	8	10	30	100	
88	Larry Siegfried	5	5	5	6	8	10	15	80
89	Gary Gregor	5	5	5	5	6	8	12	50
90	Nate Thurmond	5	5	6	8	10	20	100	200
91	John Warren	5	5	6	8	10	12	20	150
92	Gus Johnson	5	5	6	8	10	12	30	150
93	Gail Goodrich	5	5	8	10	15	20	30	100
94	Dorrie Murrey	5	5	5	5	6	10	15	60
95	Cazzie Russell SP	5	8	12	15	20	60	300	
96	Terry Dischinger	5	5	5	5	6	8	12	50
97	Norm Van Lier SP RC	5	5	10	12	20	120	450	
98	Jim Fox	5	5	5	5	6	10	15	60
99	Tom Meschery	5	5	5	5	6	8	12	100
100	Oscar Robertson	5	5	10	25	30	50	100	450
101A	Checklist 111-175	5	5	8	12	20	25	60	
101B	Checklist 111-175	5	10	15	20	25	30	40	150
102	Rich Johnson	5	5	5	5	6	8	12	75
103	Mel Counts	5	5	5	6	8	10	15	100
104	Bill Hosket SP RC	5	▲10	▲15	▲40	▲50	▲80	200	
105	Archie Clark	5	5	5	6	8	10	20	80
106	Walt Frazier AS	5	5	8	10	12	15	60	125
107	Jerry West AS	5	5	10	12	15	25	50	225
108	Billy Cunningham AS SP	5	5	8	10	15	20	120	
109	Connie Hawkins AS	5	5	6	8	10	12	40	
110	Willis Reed AS	5	5	6	8	12	15	30	150
111	Nate Thurmond AS	5	5	6	8	12	15	25	80
112	John Havlicek AS	5	5	10	15	20	25	60	400
113	Elgin Baylor AS	5	5	8	10	12	15	25	150
114	Oscar Robertson AS	5	5	8	10	12	20	50	200
115	Lou Hudson AS	5	5	5	6	8	10	▲100	▲200
116	Emmette Bryant	5	5	5	▲6	▲8	▲10	▲30	60
117	Greg Howard	5	5	5	5	6	8	15	50
118	Rick Adelman	5	5	6	8	10	12	15	50
119	Barry Clemens	5	5	5	5	6	8	20	60
120	Walt Frazier	5	5	10	12	20	40	60	300
121	Jim Barnes RC	5	5	5	5	6	8	15	60
122	Bernie Williams	5	5	5	5	6	10	15	125
123	Pete Maravich RC	80	150	200	300	500	600	1,200	8,000
124	Matt Guokas RC	5	5	6	8	10	12	20	80
125	Dave Bing	5	5	8	10	12	15	25	120
126	John Tresvant	5	5	5	6	8	10	15	30
127	Shaler Halimon	5	5	5	6	8	10	15	50
128	Don Ohl	5	5	5	5	6	8	12	50

	GD 2	VG 3	VgEx 4	EX 5	ExMt 6	NM 7	NmMt 8	MT 9
Fred Carter RC	5	5	6	8	10	12	20	60
Connie Hawkins	5	5	10	12	15	20	30	120
Jim King	5	5	5	5	6	8	15	50
Ed Manning RC	5	5	6	8	10	12	20	80
Adrian Smith	5	5	5	5	6	8	15	30
Walt Hazzard	5	5	6	8	10	12	20	150
Dave DeBusschere	5	5	8	10	12	30	40	▲250
Don Kojis	5	5	5	5	6	10	15	50
Calvin Murphy RC	5	8	12	15	20	40	80	400
Nate Bowman	5	5	5	5	6	8	12	40
Jon McGlocklin	5	5	5	6	8	12	25	60
Billy Cunningham	5	5	8	10	12	25	60	200
Willie McCarter	5	5	5	5	6	8	12	50
Jim Barnett	5	5	5	5	6	8	12	60
Jo Jo White RC	5	5	8	10	12	25	60	120
Clyde Lee	5	5	5	5	8	10	15	30
Tom Van Arsdale	5	5	5	8	10	15	25	100
Len Chappell	5	5	5	5	6	8	12	30
Lee Winfield	5	5	5	5	6	8	15	50
Jerry Sloan RC	5	5	6	15	20	30	50	200
Art Harris	5	5	5	5	6	10	20	60
Willis Reed	5	5	8	15	20	25	40	150
Art Williams	5	5	5	5	6	8	12	50
Don May	5	5	5	5	6	8	12	50
Loy Petersen	5	5	5	5	6	10	25	70
Dave Gambee	5	5	5	5	6	8	12	50
Hal Greer	5	5	6	8	12	20	40	80
Dave Newmark	5	5	5	5	6	10	25	60
Jimmy Collins	5	5	5	5	6	8	15	50
Bill Turner	5	5	5	5	6	8	15	50
Eddie Miles	5	5	5	5	6	8	15	50
Jerry West	5	5	10	15	50	60	100	600
Fred Crawford	5	5	5	5	6	8	15	40
Tom Sanders	5	5	6	8	10	15	40	125
Dale Schlueter	5	5	5	5	6	8	12	50
Clem Haskins RC	5	5	8	10	12	15	20	50
Greg Smith	5	5	5	5	6	8	15	50
Rod Thorn RC	5	5	6	8	10	12	25	80
Playoff G1/W.Reed	5	5	8	10	12	20	50	100
Playoff G2/D.Garnett	5	5	5	6	8	10	25	150
Playoff G3/DeBussch	5	5	8	10	12	15	30	
Playoff G4/J.West	5	8	12	15	20	30	50	250
Playoff G5/Bradley	5	5	8	10	12	15	25	
Playoff G6/Wilt	5	8	12	15	20	30	50	120
Playoff G7/Frazier	5	5	8	10	15	20	80	
Knicks Celebrate	5	6	10	12	15	30	80	125

Wally Anderzunas #21 PSA 10 (Gem MT) sold for $2,615 (eBay; 9/12)

Al Attles #59 PSA 9 (Mint) sold for $459 (eBay; 9/12)

Connie Hawkins #130 PSA 10 (Gem MT) sold for 1,502 (eBay; 6/11)

Pete Maravich #123 PSA 8 (NMMT) sold for $470 (Goodwin; 9/11)

Pete Maravich #123 PSA 9 (MT) sold for $2,987 (eBay; 12/11)

Oscar Robertson #114 PSA 10 (Gem MT) sold for $3,232 (Goodwin; 2012)

1971-72 Topps

	GD 2	VG 3	VgEx 4	EX 5	ExMt 6	NM 7	NmMt 8	MT 9
Oscar Robertson	4	5	10	15	30	80	200	800
Bill Bradley	4	5	8	10	12	20	40	▲200
Jim Fox	4	4	4	4	5	▲8	▲20	▲80
John Johnson RC	4	4	4	4	5	6	8	30
Luke Jackson	4	4	4	4	5	6	8	40
Don May DP	4	4	4	4	5	6	10	40
Kevin Loughery	4	4	4	4	5	6	8	40
Terry Dischinger	4	4	4	4	4	5	8	20
Neal Walk	4	4	4	4	5	6	▲20	▲50
Elgin Baylor	4	5	10	15	20	30	50	350
Rick Adelman	4	4	4	4	5	6	15	50
12 Clyde Lee	4	4	4	4	5	6	10	50
13 Jerry Chambers	4	4	4	4	5	6	15	30
14 Fred Carter	4	4	4	4	5	6	12	80
15 Tom Boerwinkle DP	4	4	4	4	5	6	8	50
16 John Block	4	4	4	4	5	6	50	
17 Dick Barnett	4	4	4	4	5	6	12	40
18 Henry Finkel	4	4	4	4	5	6	15	
19 Norm Van Lier	4	4	4	4	5	8	12	60
20 Spencer Haywood RC	4	5	12	20	25	50	150	300
21 George Johnson	4	4	4	4	5	6	20	40
22 Bobby Lewis	4	4	4	4	5	6	12	40
23 Bill Hewitt	4	4	4	4	5	6	8	40
24 Walt Hazzard	4	4	4	4	5	8	15	50
25 Happy Hairston	4	4	4	4	5	▲10	▲40	▲80
26 George Wilson	4	4	4	4	5	▲8	▲25	60
27 Lucius Allen	4	4	4	4	5	6	▲20	▲40
28 Jim Washington	4	4	4	4	5	8	12	60
29 Nate Archibald RC	4	5	12	20	25	60	150	700
30 Willis Reed	4	4	4	8	15	20	60	200
31 Erwin Mueller	4	4	4	4	5	8	15	75
32 Art Harris	4	4	4	4	5	6	8	40
33 Pete Cross	4	4	4	4	5	6	10	40
34 Geoff Petrie RC	4	4	4	4	5	8	20	50
35 John Havlicek	4	5	8	12	20	30	50	200
36 Larry Siegfried	4	4	4	4	5	▲8	▲20	▲80
37 John Tresvant DP	4	4	4	4	5	6	8	50
38 Ron Williams	4	4	4	4	5	6	10	40
39 Lamar Green DP	4	4	4	4	5	6	8	25
40 Bob Rule DP	4	4	4	4	5	6	▲20	▲40
41 Jim McMillian RC	4	4	4	5	8	12	20	50
42 Wally Jones	4	4	4	4	6	10	15	50
43 Bob Boozer	4	4	4	4	5	6	15	65
44 Eddie Miles	4	4	4	4	5	6	8	40
45 Bob Love DP	4	4	4	4	5	6	10	30
46 Claude English	4	4	4	4	5	6	10	60
47 Dave Cowens RC	4	5	10	12	30	40	▼60	300
48 Emmette Bryant	4	4	4	4	5	6	8	40
49 Dave Stallworth	4	4	4	4	5	12	30	125
50 Jerry West	5	8	12	15	30	▲60	100	350
51 Joe Ellis	4	4	4	4	5	6	8	40
52 Walt Wesley DP	4	4	4	4	5	6	8	25
53 Howie Komives	4	4	4	4	5	6	12	40
54 Paul Silas	4	4	4	4	5	8	12	50
55 Pete Maravich DP	6	12	20	30	50	80	150	400
56 Gary Gregor	4	4	4	4	5	6	8	40
57 Sam Lacey RC	4	4	4	4	5	8	10	50
58 Calvin Murphy DP	4	4	4	5	6	10	15	40
59 Bob Dandridge	4	4	4	4	5	8	▲20	60
60 Hal Greer	4	4	4	4	5	10	15	80
61 Keith Erickson	4	4	4	4	6	10	20	120
62 Joe Cooke	4	4	4	4	5	8	12	35
63 Bob Lanier RC	4	5	8	12	20	40	▼80	500
64 Don Kojis	4	4	4	4	5	6	10	30
65 Walt Frazier	4	4	6	8	15	40	80	200
66 Chet Walker DP	4	4	4	4	5	6	8	25
67 Dick Garrett	4	4	4	4	5	6	▲20	50
68 John Trapp	4	4	4	4	5	6	8	50
69 Jo Jo White	4	4	4	4	6	10	20	75
70 Wilt Chamberlain	8	15	40	50	60	100	250	700
71 Dave Sorenson	4	4	4	4	5	8	15	80
72 Jim King	4	4	4	4	5	6	15	60
73 Cazzie Russell	4	4	4	4	5	8	15	70
74 Jon McGlocklin	4	4	4	4	5	6	8	40
75 Tom Van Arsdale	4	4	4	4	5	6	8	50
76 Dale Schlueter	4	4	4	4	5	6	8	40
77 Gus Johnson DP	4	4	4	4	5	8	12	40
78 Dave Bing	4	4	4	5	6	10	40	200

#	Player	GD 2	VG 3	VgEx 4	EX 5	ExMt 6	NM 7	NmMt 8	MT 9
		4	4	6	8	10	12	20	70
79	Billy Cunningham	4	4	6	8	10	12	20	70
80	Len Wilkens	4	4	4	8	10	12	40	150
81	Jerry Lucas DP	4	4	4	4	5	6	15	25
82	Don Chaney	4	4	4	4	5	8	15	60
83	McCoy McLemore	4	4	4	4	5	6	10	60
84	Bob Kauffman DP	4	4	4	4	5	6	8	20
85	Dick Van Arsdale	4	4	4	4	5	8	10	
86	Johnny Green	4	4	4	4	5	6	8	50
87	Jerry Sloan	4	4	4	6	8	12	20	▲80
88	Luther Rackley DP	4	4	4	4	5	6	8	20
89	Shaler Halimon	4	4	4	4	5	6	8	
90	Jimmy Walker	4	4	4	4	5	6	10	40
91	Rudy Tomjanovich RC	4	4	6	8	12	15	30	150
92	Levi Fontaine	4	4	4	4	5	6	10	20
93	Bobby Smith	4	4	4	4	5	6	▲20	60
94	Bob Arnzen	4	4	4	4	5	6	12	30
95	Wes Unseld DP	4	4	4	5	6	10	12	40
96	Clem Haskins DP	4	4	4	4	5	8	10	20
97	Jim Davis	4	4	4	4	5	6	8	
98	Steve Kuberski	4	4	4	4	5	6	8	100
99	Mike Davis DP	4	4	4	4	5	6	10	40
100	Lew Alcindor	8	12	20	40	60	100	300	900
101	Willie McCarter	4	4	4	4	5	6	8	40
102	Charlie Paulk	4	4	4	4	5	6	8	50
103	Lee Winfield	4	4	4	4	5	6	15	75
104	Jim Barnett	4	4	4	4	5	6	8	20
105	Connie Hawkins DP	4	4	4	5	6	15	25	80
106	Archie Clark DP	4	4	4	4	5	6	8	20
107	Dave DeBusschere	4	4	5	6	10	20	40	60
108	Stu Lantz DP	4	4	4	4	5	6	8	40
109	Don Smith	4	4	4	4	5	8	15	60
110	Lou Hudson	4	4	4	4	5	8	10	50
111	Leroy Ellis	4	4	4	4	5	6	25	
112	Jack Marin	4	4	4	4	5	6	15	60
113	Matt Guokas	4	4	4	4	5	6	15	80
114	Don Nelson	4	4	6	8	10	15	20	80
115	Jeff Mullins DP	4	4	4	4	5	6	10	40
116	Walt Bellamy	4	4	5	6	8	12	25	60
117	Bob Quick	4	4	4	5	6	8	20	120
118	John Warren	4	4	4	4	5	6	20	60
119	Barry Clemens	4	4	4	4	5	6	12	60
120	Elvin Hayes DP	4	4	6	8	10	12	20	50
121	Gail Goodrich	4	4	4	5	6	12	40	100
122	Ed Manning	4	4	4	4	5	6	8	40
123	Herm Gilliam DP	4	4	4	4	5	6	8	20
124	Dennis Awtrey RC	4	4	4	4	5	8	15	50
125	John Hummer DP	4	4	4	4	5	6	8	20
126	Mike Riordan	4	4	4	4	5	6	15	
127	Mel Counts	4	4	4	4	5	6	8	20
128	Bob Weiss DP	4	4	4	4	5	6	8	20
129	Greg Smith DP	4	4	4	4	5	6	8	20
130	Earl Monroe	4	4	6	8	10	15	25	100
131	Nate Thurmond DP	4	4	4	4	5	10	15	40
132	Bill Bridges DP	4	4	4	4	5	6	8	30
133	Playoffs G1/Alcindor	4	4	5	6	8	10	30	75
134	NBA Playoffs G2	4	4	4	4	6	12	20	60
135	NBA Playoffs G3	4	4	4	4	5	8	12	75
136	Playoffs G4/Oscar	4	4	4	4	5	8	20	50
137	NBA Champs/Oscar	4	4	6	8	10	15	20	50
138	Alcind/Hayes/Havl LL	4	4	4	8	10	30	80	
139	Alcind/Havl/Hayes LL	4	4	4	8	10	20	60	
140	Green/Alcind/Wilt LL	4	5	8	10	12	20	60	175
141	Walker/Oscar/Williams LL	4	4	4	4	5	8	10	
142	Wilt/Hayes/Alcind LL	4	4	4	6	12	20	60	150
143	Van Lier/Oscar/West LL	4	4	6	8	10	12	30	100
144A	NBA Checklist 1-144	4	4	6	8	10	12	15	60
144B	NBA Checklist 1-144	4	4	6	8	10	12	15	60

#	Player	GD 2	VG 3	VgEx 4	EX 5	ExMt 6	NM 7	NmMt 8	MT 9
		4	4	5	6	8	10	15	50
145	ABA Checklist 145-233	4	4	5	6	8	10	15	50
146	Issel/Brisker/Scott LL	4	4	4	8	10	15	25	60
147	Issel/Barry/Brisker LL	4	4	6	8	10	15	25	80
148	ABA 2pt FG Pct Leaders	4	4	4	4	8	8	12	50
149	Barry/Carrier/Keller LL	4	4	6	8	10	12	20	80
150	ABA Rebound Leaders	4	4	4	4	5	10	15	80
151	ABA Assist Leaders	4	4	5	6	8	15	30	75
152	Larry Brown RC	5	8	12	15	20	30	50	225
153	Bob Bedell	4	4	4	4	5	6	10	
154	Merv Jackson	4	4	4	4	5	6	10	50
155	Joe Caldwell	4	4	4	5	6	8	12	60
156	Billy Paultz RC	4	4	4	5	6	10	▲30	▲80
157	Les Hunter	4	4	4	4	5	6	8	35
158	Charlie Williams	4	4	4	4	5	6	10	40
159	Stew Johnson	4	4	4	4	6	12	25	50
160	Mack Calvin RC	4	4	4	4	5	12	40	150
161	Don Sidle	4	4	4	5	6	8	10	50
162	Mike Barrett	4	4	4	4	5	6	10	65
163	Tom Workman	4	4	4	4	5	6	10	50
164	Joe Hamilton	4	4	4	4	5	6	12	50
165	Zelmo Beaty RC	4	4	4	10	20	60	150	
166	Dan Hester	4	4	4	4	5	6	12	40
167	Bob Verga	4	4	4	4	5	6	12	50
168	Wilbert Jones	4	4	4	4	5	8	20	100
169	Skeeter Swift	4	4	4	4	5	6	12	50
170	Rick Barry RC	6	10	15	20	60	80	150	800
171	Billy Keller RC	4	4	4	4	5	8	15	60
172	Ron Franz	4	4	4	4	5	6	10	60
173	Roland Taylor RC	4	4	4	4	5	6	10	60
174	Julian Hammond	4	4	4	4	5	8	12	30
175	Steve Jones RC	4	4	4	5	6	10	12	40
176	Gerald Govan	4	4	4	4	5	8	25	
177	Darrell Carrier RC	4	4	4	4	5	6	12	50
178	Ron Boone RC	4	4	4	4	5	10	20	50
179	George Peeples	4	4	4	4	5	6	8	50
180	John Brisker	4	4	4	4	5	6	10	40
181	Doug Moe RC	4	4	4	5	6	10	20	60
182	Ollie Taylor	4	4	4	4	5	6	8	40
183	Bob Netolicky RC	4	4	4	4	5	6	12	50
184	Sam Robinson	4	4	4	4	5	6	8	50
185	James Jones	4	4	4	4	5	6	8	40
186	Julius Keye	4	4	4	4	5	6	8	40
187	Wayne Hightower	4	4	4	4	8	10	15	40
188	Warren Armstrong RC	4	4	4	6	10	20	50	
189	Mike Lewis	4	4	4	4	5	6	10	50
190	Charlie Scott RC	4	4	6	12	40	60	200	400
191	Jim Ard	4	4	4	4	5	6	10	50
192	George Lehmann	4	4	4	4	5	6	10	30
193	Ira Harge	4	4	4	4	5	6	10	40
194	Willie Wise RC	4	4	4	4	5	10	20	80
195	Mel Daniels RC	4	4	6	15	40	80	200	400
196	Larry Cannon	4	4	4	4	5	6	10	60
197	Jim Eakins	4	4	4	4	5	8	15	60
198	Rich Jones	4	4	4	5	6	8	10	60
199	Bill Melchionni RC	4	4	4	4	5	8	10	40
200	Dan Issel RC	4	5	10	15	20	40	80	▼300
201	George Stone	4	4	4	4	5	6	12	75
202	George Thompson	4	4	4	4	5	6	8	
203	Craig Raymond	4	4	4	4	5	8	20	100
204	Freddie Lewis RC	4	4	4	4	5	6	8	50
205	George Carter	4	4	4	4	5	6	10	40
206	Lonnie Wright	4	4	4	4	5	6	8	40
207	Cincy Powell	4	4	4	4	5	6	10	50
208	Larry Miller	4	4	4	5	6	8	12	30
209	Sonny Dove	4	4	4	5	6	8	10	50
210	Byron Beck RC	4	4	4	5	6	8	15	70
211	John Beasley	4	4	4	4	5	8	15	100

	GD 2	VG 3	VgEx 4	EX 5	ExMt 6	NM 7	NmMt 8	MT 9
Lee Davis	4	4	4	4	5	6	8	30
Rick Mount RC	4	4	4	6	10	15	40	80
Walt Simon	4	4	4	4	5	6	10	30
Glen Combs	4	4	4	4	5	6	8	30
Neil Johnson	4	4	4	4	5	6	12	
Manny Leaks	4	4	4	4	5	8	15	50
Chuck Williams	4	4	4	4	5	6	10	50
Warren Davis	4	4	4	4	5	6	12	100
Donnie Freeman RC	4	4	5	6	8	10	15	80
Randy Mahaffey	4	4	4	4	5	6	8	50
John Barnhill	4	4	4	4	5	6	12	30
Al Cueto	4	4	4	4	5	6	8	40
Louie Dampier RC	4	4	4	12	20	80	100	500
Roger Brown RC	4	4	5	12	20	50	100	300
Joe DePre	4	4	4	4	5	6	10	30
Ray Scott	4	4	4	4	5	6	12	50
Arvesta Kelly	4	4	4	4	5	6	10	40
Vann Williford	4	4	4	4	5	6	▲20	
Larry Jones	4	4	4	4	5	8	12	50
Gene Moore	4	4	4	4	5	6	▲15	40
Ralph Simpson RC	4	4	4	4	5	6	10	
Red Robbins RC	4	4	4	4	10	30	60	▼200

scar Robertson #1 PSA 9 (MT) sold for $1,219 (eBay; 4/12)

te Maravich #55 PSA 10 (Gem MT) sold for $2,397 (Mile High; 6/10)

te Maravich #55 PSA 10 (Gem MT) sold for $1,937 (eBay; 4/12)

alt Frazier #65 PSA 10 (Gem MT) sold for $640 (eBay; 1/13)

ew Alcindor #100 PSA 10 (Gem MT) sold for $3,070 (eBay; 4/12)

ck Barry #170 PSA 10 (Gem MT) sold for $2,117 (eBay; 4/12)

871-72 Topps Trios

	GD 2	VG 3	VgEx 4	EX 5	ExMt 6	NM 7	NmMt 8	MT 9
Hudson/Rule/Murphy	5	5	6	10	12	15	50	250
Jones/Wise/Issel SP	5	5	8	12	15	20	60	250
Wesley/White/Dand	5	5	6	10	12	15	50	
Calvin/Brown/Verga SP	5	5	6	10	12	20	40	200
Thurm/Monroe/Hay	5	5	6	10	15	25	80	225
Melch/Daniels/Freem SP	5	5	6	10	12	20	40	125
DeBuss/Lanier/Van Ars	5	5	8	12	15	20	60	250
Cald/Dampier/Lewis SP	5	5	8	12	20	30	80	
Greer/Green/Hayes	5	5	8	12	20	40	150	425
Barry/Jones/Keye SP	5	5	8	12	15	25	60	
Walker/May/Clark	5	5	6	10	12	15	40	200
Cannon/Beaty/Scott SP	5	5	6	10	12	15	60	175
Hairston/Ellis/Sloan	5	5	6	10	12	15	60	150
Jones/Carter/Brisk SP	5	5	8	12	15	20	60	250
Maravich/Kauf/Hav	8	12	20	25	40	80	200	500
ABA Team DP	5	5	6	10	12	20	50	275
ABA Team SP	5	5	8	15	20	30	60	
ABA Team SP	5	5	8	15	20	40	80	
Frazier/Van Arsd/Bing	5	5	8	15	20	25	60	300
Love/Williams/Cowens	5	5	6	12	15	20	75	325
West/Reed/Walker	5	8	10	25	30	40	175	
Rober/Unsel/Smith SP	5	5	8	15	25	50	150	
Hawk/Mullins/Alcin	5	8	10	25	30	60	80	425
Cunn/Bellamy/Petrie SP	5	5	8	12	15	30	70	225
Cham/Johns/Van L SP	5	8	10	20	35	50	100	
NBA Team QP	5	5	6	10	12	15	30	100

ABA Team SP #24 A PSA 10 (Gem MT) sold for $1,137 (eBay; 4/07)

Cannon/Beaty/Scott #16A PSA 10 (Gem MT) sold for $750 (eBay; 12/06)

Walker/May/Clark #16 PSA 10 (Gem MT) sold for $1,425 (eBay; 3/07)

1972-73 Icee Bear

	VG 3	VgEx 4	EX 5	ExMt 6	NM 7	NmMt 8	MT 9	Gem 9.5/10
Kareem Abdul-Jabbar	4	6	10	15	25	40	60	
Dennis Awtrey	4	4	4	4	6	12	15	40
Tom Boerwinkle	4	4	8	10	15	20	60	

		VG 3	VgEx 4	EX 5	ExMt 6	NM 7	NmMt 8	MT 9	Gem 9.5/10
4	Austin Carr SP	4	4	5	6	8	▲15	▲30	120
5	Wilt Chamberlain	12	20	30	40	50	80	250	
6	Archie Clark SP	4	6	8	12	20	▼30	80	
7	Dave DeBusschere	4	4	4	8	12	20	40	100
8	Walt Frazier SP	4	6	8	10	12	20	40	200
9	John Havlicek	4	6	8	10	15	30	150	
10	Connie Hawkins	4	5	6	8	12	15	25	100
11	Bob Love	4	4	4	5	6	12	35	125
12	Jerry Lucas	4	5	6	8	10	15	75	150
13	Pete Maravich SP	8	15	25	40	50	80	250	
14	Calvin Murphy	4	4	4	5	6	12	40	80
15	Oscar Robertson	4	5	6	10	12	20	50	
16	Jerry Sloan	4	4	4	5	6	▲20	▲50	80
17	Wes Unseld	4	4	4	5	6	12	40	
18	Dick Van Arsdale	4	4	4	5	6	12	35	
19	Jerry West	5	8	12	20	30	50	100	
20	Sidney Wicks	4	4	5	6	8	12	25	

—Pete Maravich #13 PSA 10 (Gem MT) sold for $1,084 (eBay; 4/12)

—Oscar Robertson #15 PSA 10 (Gem MT) sold for $810 (eBay; 4/07)

—Jerry West #19 PSA 10 (Gem MT) sold for $802 (eBay; 7/07)

—Sidney Wicks #20 PSA 10 (Gem MT) sold for $356 (eBay; 11/06)

1972-73 Topps

		VG 3	VgEx 4	EX 5	ExMt 6	NM 7	NmMt 8	MT 9	Gem 9.5/10
1	Wilt Chamberlain	12	20	40	50	100	▲200	400	700
2	Stan Love	4	4	4	5	6	▲20	40	
3	Geoff Petrie	4	5	6	8	10	12	25	
4	Curtis Perry RC	4	4	4	5	6	10	25	
5	Pete Maravich	12	15	20	40	50	100	300	
6	Gus Johnson	4	4	4	5	6	10	20	100
7	Dave Cowens	4	6	8	10	20	40	60	
8	Randy Smith RC	4	5	6	8	10	20	25	225
9	Matt Guokas	4	4	4	5	6	8	15	
10	Spencer Haywood	4	4	5	6	8	12	40	150
11	Jerry Sloan	4	4	5	6	8	20	30	125
12	Dave Sorenson	4	4	4	5	6	8	15	
13	Howie Komives	4	4	4	5	6	8	15	
14	Joe Ellis	4	4	4	5	6	8	15	
15	Jerry Lucas	4	4	5	6	8	▲25	50	
16	Stu Lantz	4	4	4	5	6	8	15	100
17	Bill Bridges	4	4	4	5	6	8	15	
18	Leroy Ellis	4	4	4	5	6	8	20	
19	Art Williams	4	4	4	5	6	8	15	125
20	Sidney Wicks RC	4	4	5	6	8	15	50	300
21	Wes Unseld	4	4	5	6	8	15	50	
22	Jim Washington	4	4	4	5	6	8	20	
23	Fred Hilton	4	4	4	5	6	10	50	
24	Curtis Rowe RC	4	4	4	5	6	8	15	120
25	Oscar Robertson	4	4	10	15	30	60	200	800
26	Larry Steele RC	4	4	4	5	6	8	15	30
27	Charlie Davis	4	4	4	5	6	8	15	60
28	Nate Thurmond	4	4	4	5	6	8	12	30
29	Fred Carter	4	4	4	5	6	8	15	80
30	Connie Hawkins	4	4	5	6	8	10	15	75
31	Calvin Murphy	4	4	4	5	6	8	12	30
32	Phil Jackson RC	6	12	20	40	80	▼120	500	
33	Lee Winfield	4	4	4	5	6	8	15	
34	Jim Fox	4	4	4	5	6	8	20	100
35	Dave Bing	4	4	5	6	8	12	30	250
36	Gary Gregor	4	4	4	5	6	8	20	
37	Mike Riordan	4	4	4	5	6	8	30	100
38	George Trapp	4	4	5	6	8	12	25	
39	Mike Davis	4	4	4	5	6	8	15	
40	Bob Rule	4	4	4	5	6	8	15	100
41	John Block	4	4	5	6	8	10	20	
42	Bob Dandridge	4	4	4	6	8	10	35	

#	Player	VG 3	VgEx 4	EX 5	ExMt 6	NM 7	NmMt 8	MT 9	Gem 9.5/10
43	John Johnson	4	4	4	5	6	8	20	
44	Rick Barry	5	8	10	12	15	40	250	
45	Jo Jo White	4	4	4	6	8	15	50	100
46	Cliff Meely	4	4	5	6	8	12	40	
47	Charlie Scott	4	4	4	5	6	8	25	
48	Johnny Green	4	4	4	5	6	8	25	125
49	Pete Cross	4	4	4	5	6	8	15	
50	Gail Goodrich	4	4	6	8	10	15	50	
51	Jim Davis	4	4	4	5	6	8	15	100
52	Dick Barnett	4	4	4	5	6	8	15	100
53	Bob Christian	4	4	4	5	6	8	15	100
54	Jon McGlocklin	4	4	4	5	8	12	30	150
55	Paul Silas	4	4	4	5	6	10	25	100
56	Hal Greer	4	4	4	5	6	10	20	
57	Barry Clemens	4	4	4	5	6	▲10	▲25	
58	Nick Jones	4	4	4	5	8	12	30	150
59	Cornell Warner	4	4	4	5	6	8	15	100
60	Walt Frazier	4	4	6	12	30	60	200	
61	Dorie Murrey	4	4	4	5	6	8	15	100
62	Dick Cunningham	4	4	4	5	6	8	20	100
63	Sam Lacey	4	4	4	5	6	8	▲20	▲80
64	John Warren	4	4	4	5	6	8	15	100
65	Tom Boerwinkle	4	4	4	5	6	8	15	100
66	Fred Foster	4	4	4	5	6	8	20	
67	Mel Counts	4	4	4	5	6	10	20	80
68	Toby Kimball	4	4	4	5	6	8	15	
69	Dale Schlueter	4	4	4	5	6	8	15	100
70	Jack Marin	4	4	4	5	6	8	15	125
71	Jim Barnett	4	4	4	5	6	8	15	
72	Clem Haskins	4	4	4	5	6	8	15	
73	Earl Monroe	4	5	6	8	10	▲25	60	
74	Tom Sanders	4	4	4	5	6	10	20	
75	Jerry West	5	8	10	15	40	80	150	
76	Elmore Smith RC	4	4	4	5	6	10	20	200
77	Don Adams	4	4	4	5	6	8	15	80
78	Wally Jones	4	4	4	5	6	8	15	
79	Tom Van Arsdale	4	4	4	5	6	8	15	80
80	Bob Lanier	5	8	10	15	20	25	50	200
81	Len Wilkens	4	4	4	5	8	12	50	
82	Neal Walk	4	4	4	5	6	8	15	
83	Kevin Loughery	4	4	4	5	6	8	15	80
84	Stan McKenzie	4	4	4	5	6	8	15	
85	Jeff Mullins	4	4	4	5	6	8	15	80
86	Otto Moore	4	4	4	5	6	8	20	80
87	John Tresvant	4	4	4	5	6	8	15	
88	Dean Meminger RC	4	4	4	5	▲8	▲20	▲80	
89	Jim McMillian	4	4	4	5	6	8	15	
90	Austin Carr RC	4	4	5	6	8	15	60	
91	Clifford Ray RC	4	4	4	5	6	10	20	
92	Don Nelson	4	4	4	5	6	10	20	
93	Mahdi Abdul-Rahman	4	4	4	5	6	8	15	100
94	Willie Norwood	4	4	4	5	6	8	20	
95	Dick Van Arsdale	4	4	4	5	6	8	20	125
96	Don May	4	4	4	5	6	10	30	
97	Walt Bellamy	4	4	5	6	8	10	50	
98	Garfield Heard RC	4	4	5	6	8	12	50	
99	Dave Wohl	4	4	4	5	6	8	15	
100	Kareem Abdul-Jabbar	6	15	25	40	60	200	300	500
101	Ron Knight	4	4	4	5	▲8	▲25	▲50	
102	Phil Chenier RC	4	4	5	6	8	10	20	
103	Rudy Tomjanovich	4	4	5	6	8	12	15	
104	Flynn Robinson	4	4	4	5	6	8	40	
105	Dave DeBusschere	4	4	5	6	8	12	50	
106	Dennis Layton	4	4	4	5	6	8	20	
107	Bill Hewitt	4	4	4	5	6	10	30	
108	Dick Garrett	4	4	4	5	6	8	20	

#	Player	VG 3	VgEx 4	EX 5	ExMt 6	NM 7	NmMt 8	MT 9	Gem 9.5/10
109	Walt Wesley	4	4	4	5	6	8	15	
110	John Havlicek	5	8	10	15	20	40	100	400
111	Norm Van Lier	4	4	4	5	6	8	15	
112	Cazzie Russell	4	4	4	5	6	8	20	100
113	Herm Gilliam	4	4	4	5	6	8	15	
114	Greg Smith	4	4	4	5	6	8	25	100
115	Nate Archibald	4	4	5	6	10	30	120	
116	Don Kojis	4	4	4	5	6	8	15	
117	Rick Adelman	4	4	4	5	6	8	20	100
118	Luke Jackson	4	4	4	5	6	8	20	
119	Lamar Green	4	4	4	5	6	8	15	60
120	Archie Clark	4	4	4	5	6	8	25	
121	Happy Hairston	4	4	4	5	6	8	20	
122	Bill Bradley	4	6	8	10	15	25	60	
123	Ron Williams	4	4	4	5	6	8	20	
124	Jimmy Walker	4	4	4	5	6	8	15	
125	Bob Kauffman	4	4	4	5	6	8	▲30	100
126	Rick Roberson	4	4	4	5	6	8	25	
127	Howard Porter RC	4	4	4	5	6	8	20	
128	Mike Newlin RC	4	4	4	5	6	8	20	125
129	Willis Reed	4	5	6	8	15	30	▲100	
130	Lou Hudson	4	4	4	5	6	8	20	
131	Don Chaney	4	4	4	5	8	10	25	
132	Dave Stallworth	4	4	4	5	6	8	15	
133	Charlie Yelverton	4	4	4	5	6	8	15	
134	Ken Durrett	4	6	10	15	30	200	400	
135	John Brisker	4	4	4	5	6	8	15	
136	Dick Snyder	4	4	4	5	6	8	50	
137	Jim McDaniels	4	4	4	5	6	8	50	
138	Clyde Lee	4	4	4	5	6	8	70	
139	Dennis Awtrey	4	4	4	5	6	8	40	
140	Keith Erickson	4	4	4	5	6	10	60	
141	Bob Weiss	4	4	4	5	8	15	120	
142	Butch Beard RC	4	4	4	5	6	10	75	
143	Terry Dischinger	4	4	4	8	20	50	100	
144	Pat Riley	5	8	10	15	20	▲30	80	
145	Lucius Allen	4	4	4	5	6	8	40	
146	John Mengelt RC	4	4	4	5	8	25	150	
147	John Hummer	4	4	4	5	6	8	40	
148	Bob Love	4	5	6	8	10	15	75	
149	Bobby Smith	4	4	4	5	8	15	100	
150	Elvin Hayes	4	4	6	10	12	20	50	
151	Nate Williams	4	4	4	5	6	8	80	
152	Chet Walker	4	4	4	5	10	25	100	
153	Steve Kuberski	4	4	4	5	6	8	20	
154	Playoffs G1/Monroe	4	4	4	5	8	20		
155	NBA Playoffs G2	4	4	4	5	10	20	125	
156	NBA Playoffs G3	4	4	4	6	12	25	80	
157	NBA Playoffs G4	4	4	4	5	6	10	60	
158	Playoffs G5/J.West	4	4	5	6	20	60	225	
159	Champs Lakers/Wilt	4	5	6	8	12	20	80	
160	NBA Checklist 1-176	4	5	6	10	12	40	175	
161	John Havlicek AS	4	5	6	8	10	30	75	
162	Spencer Haywood AS	4	4	4	5	6	8	50	
163	Kareem Abdul-Jabbar AS	5	8	10	15	40	80		
164	Jerry West AS	5	8	10	12	20	40	450	
165	Walt Frazier AS	4	4	5	6	8	15	60	
166	Bob Love AS	4	4	4	5	8	30	100	
167	Billy Cunningham AS	4	4	5	6	8	15	30	
168	Wilt Chamberlain AS	5	10	15	20	30	60	200	
169	Nate Archibald AS	4	4	5	6	8	20	50	
170	Archie Clark AS	4	4	5	6	6	8	70	
171	Jabbar/Havl/Arch LL	4	6	8	10	12	30	200	
172	Jabbar/Arch/Havl LL	4	5	6	8	10	30	100	
173	Wilt/Jabbar/Bell LL	4	6	8	10	15	25	80	
174	Marin/Murphy/Goodr LL	4	4	4	5	6	8	50	

	VG 3	VgEx 4	EX 5	ExMt 6	NM 7	NmMt 8	MT 9	Gem 9.5/10
Wilt/Jabbar/Unseld LL	5	8	10	12	15	▲30	150	
Wilkens/West/Arch LL	4	4	6	8	10	20	225	
Roland Taylor	4	4	4	5	6	8	20	
Art Becker	4	4	4	5	6	10	30	
Mack Calvin	4	4	4	5	6	8	30	
Artis Gilmore RC	5	8	12	20	40	▼80	▼300	
Collis Jones	4	4	4	5	6	12	125	
John Roche RC	4	4	4	5	6	8	100	
George McGinnis RC	4	6	8	20	60	300	1,000	
Johnny Neumann	4	4	4	5	6	8	15	
Willie Wise	4	4	4	5	6	8	25	
Bernie Williams	4	4	4	5	6	8	40	
Byron Beck	4	4	4	5	6	8	15	
Larry Miller	4	4	4	5	6	8	40	
Cincy Powell	4	4	4	5	6	8	60	
Donnie Freeman	4	4	4	5	6	12	60	
John Baum	4	4	4	5	6	12	20	
Billy Keller	4	4	4	5	6	8	15	125
Wilbert Jones	4	4	4	5	6	8	75	
Glen Combs	4	4	4	5	6	8	15	
Julius Erving RC	100	150	200	300	600	1,200	6,000	
Al Smith	4	4	4	5	6	8	50	
George Carter	4	4	4	5	6	8	15	
Louie Dampier	4	4	4	6	8	10	20	
Rich Jones	4	4	4	5	6	8	15	
Mel Daniels	4	4	4	5	8	12	30	
Gene Moore	4	4	4	5	6	8	15	100
Randy Denton	4	4	4	5	6	8	50	
Larry Jones	4	4	4	5	6	8	15	
Jim Ligon	4	4	4	5	10	50	150	
Warren Jabali	4	4	4	5	6	8	15	
Joe Caldwell	4	4	4	6	8	10	25	100
Darrell Carrier	4	4	4	5	6	8	15	
Gene Kennedy	4	4	4	5	6	8	60	
Ollie Taylor	4	4	4	5	6	8	20	
Roger Brown	4	4	4	5	6	8	40	
George Lehmann	4	4	4	5	8	12	30	
Red Robbins	4	4	4	5	6	8	30	
Jim Eakins	4	4	4	5	8	15	30	
Willie Long	4	4	4	5	6	8	15	
Billy Cunningham	4	4	4	6	8	15	80	
Steve Jones	4	4	4	5	6	8	15	
Les Hunter	4	4	4	5	6	8	50	
Billy Paultz	4	4	4	5	6	8	30	
Freddie Lewis	4	4	4	6	10	15	30	125
Zelmo Beaty	4	4	4	5	6	10	25	
George Thompson	4	4	4	5	6	8	15	
Neil Johnson	4	4	4	5	6	8	30	80
Dave Robisch RC	4	4	4	5	6	8	50	
Walt Simon	4	4	4	5	6	8	30	125
Bill Melchionni	4	4	4	5	6	8	30	
Wendell Ladner RC	4	4	4	6	10	60		
Joe Hamilton	4	4	4	5	6	10	30	
Bob Netolicky	4	4	4	5	6	8	15	
James Jones	4	4	4	5	6	8	15	
Dan Issel	4	5	8	10	12	20	60	
Charlie Williams	4	4	4	5	6	8	▲25	
Willie Sojourner	4	4	4	5	6	8	15	
Merv Jackson	4	4	4	6	8	12	30	
Mike Lewis	4	4	4	5	6	8	15	125
Ralph Simpson	4	4	4	5	6	8	15	125
Darnell Hillman	4	4	5	8	10	12	40	
Rick Mount	4	4	4	5	10	50		
Gerald Govan	4	4	4	5	6	10	40	
Ron Boone	4	4	5	6	8	10	30	
Tom Washington	4	4	4	5	6	8	15	

#		VG 3	VgEx 4	EX 5	ExMt 6	NM 7	NmMt 8	MT 9	Gem 9.5/10
241	ABA Playoffs G1	4	4	4	5	6	8	20	100
242	Playoffs G2/Barry	4	4	4	6	15	50		150
243	Playoffs G3/McGinnis	4	4	4	6	8		160	
244	Playoffs G4/Barry	4	4	4	6	8		30	
245	ABA Playoffs G5	4	4	4	6	10		25	
246	ABA Playoffs G6	4	4	4	6	8		20	
247	ABA Champs: Pacers	4	4	4	6	6	8	30	
248	ABA Checklist 177-264	4	5	10	12	20	30	200	
249	Dan Issel AS	4	4	4	6	10	20	40	
250	Rick Barry AS	4	4	4	6	10	25	100	
251	Artis Gilmore AS	4	4	4	6	10	25	80	
252	Donnie Freeman AS	4	4	4	5	6	10	40	150
253	Bill Melchionni AS	4	4	4	5	6	10	25	
254	Willie Wise AS	4	4	4	5	8	15	60	
255	Julius Erving AS	8	12	20	30	50	100	300	
256	Zelmo Beaty AS	4	4	4	5	6	10	25	
257	Ralph Simpson AS	4	4	4	6	10	50		
258	Charlie Scott AS	4	4	4	5	6	10	60	150
259	Scott/Barry/Issel LL	4	4	4	6	8	12	50	
260	Gilmore/Wash/Jones LL	4	4	4	6	8	12	100	
261	ABA 3pt FG Pct.	4	4	4	5	6	10	100	
262	Barry/Calvin/Jones LL	4	4	4	6	8	15	150	
263	Gilmore/Erving/Dan LL	4	5	10	12	15	40	150	
264	Melch/Brown/Damp LL!	4	4	4	6	10	60	150	

—Kareem Abdul-Jabbar #100 PSA 10 (Gem MT) sold for $2,040 (eBay; 1/11)

—Artis Gilmore #180 PSA 10 (Gem MT) sold for $618 (Goodwin; 11/12)

—Julius Erving #195 BGS 9.5 (Gem MT) sold for $3,057 (eBay; 8/12)

—Julius Erving #195 BGS 9.5 (Gem MT) sold for $2,638 (eBay; 1/13)

1973-74 Topps

#		GD 2	VG 3	VgEx 4	EX 5	ExMt 6	NM 7	NmMt 8	MT 9
	COM. NBA CARD (1-176)	4	4	4	4	4	4	5	15
1	Nate Archibald		4	4	5	6	8	10	100
4	Jim McMillian		4	4	4	5	6	8	20
5	Nate Thurmond		4	4	4	5	8	15	30
10	Walt Frazier		4	4	6	10	12	40	200
13	Calvin Murphy		4	4	4	5	6	8	120
20	John Havlicek		4	4	5	8	10	20	80
21	Pat Riley		4	4	5	8	10	12	20	50
30	Dave DeBusschere	4	4	4	4	5	6	▲15	▲30
34	Leroy Ellis		4	4	4	5	8	15	50
40	Dave Cowens		4	4	6	8	10	20	100
41	Cazzie Russell		4	4	4	5	6	10	20
43	Connie Hawkins		4	4	4	5	6	10	50
45	Chet Walker		4	4	4	5	6	10	25
50	Kareem Abdul-Jabbar	4	5	8	10	15	30	50	220
53	Kevin Porter RC		4	4	4	5	6	8	20
57	Don Chaney		4	4	4	5	6	12	40
60	Bob Love		4	4	4	5	6	12	25
64	Western Semis/Wilt	4	4	4	5	6	12	30	80
65	NBA Western Semis		4	4	4	5	6	8	30
68	Knicks Champs/Frazier		4	4	4	5	6	8	25
70	Oscar Robertson	4	4	5	8	10	15	30	100
71	Phil Jackson	4	4	5	8	10	12	20	50
80	Wilt Chamberlain	4	4	8	15	30	40	100	300
82	Bill Bradley	4	4	4	6	8	10	12	30
86	Dick Snyder	4	4	4	4	4	4	5	50
90	Rick Barry		4	4	4	6	10	25	120
95	Elvin Hayes	4	4	4	5	6	8	20	80
100	Jerry West	4	4	6	8	12	25	40	150
103	Fred Brown RC	4	4	4	4	6	8	20	100
105	Willis Reed	4	4	4	4	5	8	12	30
119	Steve Bracey	4	4	4	4	4	4	5	20
120	Spencer Haywood	4	4	4	4	4	6	8	30
121	NBA Checklist 1-176	4	4	4	6	8	10	12	30
122	Jack Marin	4	4	4	4	6	8	20	

		GD 2	VG	VgEx 4	EX 5	ExMt 6	NM 7	NmMt 8	MT 9
125	Jerry Lucas	4	4	4	4	4	8	10	20
126	Paul Westphal RC	4	4	▲6	▲8	12	15	50	150
130	Pete Maravich	5	8	12	15	20	30	50	220
131	Don May	4	4	4	4	4	4	5	20
134	Dick Cunningham	4	4	4	4	4	8	10	40
135	Bob McAdoo RC	4	5	8	10	15	25	60	400
142	Earl Monroe	4	4	4	4	5	8	12	50
143	Clyde Lee	4	4	4	4	4	4	5	60
144	Rick Roberson	4	4	4	4	4	4	5	40
145	Rudy Tomjanovich	4	4	4	4	6	8	12	25
147	Art Williams	4	4	4	4	4	4	5	20
153	Arch/Jabbar/Hayw LL	4	4	4	4	6	8	15	60
154	Arch/Jabbar/Hayw LL	4	4	4	4	6	10	15	60
155	Wilt/Guokas/Jabbar LL	4	4	5	8	10	15	20	40
156	Barry/Murphy/Newlin LL	4	4	4	4	4	6	8	50
157	Wilt/Thurm/Cowens LL	4	4	4	4	6	8	12	50
158	Arch/Wilkens/Bing LL	4	4	4	4	4	6	8	40
165	Len Wilkens	4	4	4	4	6	8	12	20
168	Jo Jo White	4	4	4	4	4	6	8	20
170	Dave Bing	4	4	4	4	4	6	8	20
175	Geoff Petrie	4	4	4	4	4	6	8	20
176	Wes Unseld	4	4	4	4	4	8	10	40
190	Ralph Simpson AS2	4	4	4	4	4	4	8	50
200	Billy Cunningham	4	4	4	4	4	6	8	30
201	John Roche	4	4	4	4	4	6	8	20
202	ABA Western Semis	4	4	4	4	4	6	8	20
203	ABA Western Semis	4	4	4	4	4	6	8	20
204	ABA Eastern Semis	4	4	4	4	4	6	8	20
205	ABA Eastern Semis	4	4	4	4	4	6	8	30
206	ABA Western Finals	4	4	4	4	4	6	8	20
207	Eastern Finals/Gilmore	4	4	4	4	4	6	8	20
208	ABA Championship	4	4	4	4	4	6	8	20
210	Dan Issel	4	4	4	4	6	8	12	30
222	Don Buse RC	4	4	4	4	6	8	12	
234	Erving/McG/Issel LL	4	4	4	4	6	10	25	60
240	Julius Erving	4	6	10	15	20	40	▲80	300
242	ABA Checklist 177-264	4	4	4	6	8	12	20	40
243	Johnny Neumann	4	4	4	4	4	6	8	20
250	Artis Gilmore	4	4	4	4	5	8	12	30
263	Les Hunter	4	4	4	4	4	6	8	20
264	Billy Keller	4	4	4	4	4	6	8	30

1974-75 Topps

		GD 2	VG 3	VgEx 4	EX 5	ExMt 6	NM 7	NmMt 8	MT 9
	COM. NBA CARD (1-176)	4	4	4	4	4	4	5	15
1	Kareem Abdul-Jabbar	4	5	8	12	20	50	150	1,000
6	Jim Chones	4	4	4	4	4	6	8	20
10	Pete Maravich	4	5	8	12	25	40	60	250
25	Earl Monroe	4	4	4	4	4	6	8	20
27	Jo Jo White	4	4	4	4	4	6	8	25
28	Rudy Tomjanovich	4	4	4	4	5	8	12	20
30	Elvin Hayes	4	4	4	4	5	8	15	40
31	Pat Riley	4	4	4	4	5	8	12	25
39	Bill Walton RC	5	8	15	40	50	80	150	650
50	Rick Barry	4	4	4	4	5	8	15	100
51	Jerry Sloan	4	4	4	4	4	6	15	30
55	Oscar Robertson	4	4	4	4	8	12	30	80
64	Paul Westphal	4	4	4	4	4	6	8	25
70	Spencer Haywood	4	4	4	4	4	6	10	60
80	Bob McAdoo	4	4	4	4	5	8	▲15	30
81	Hawks TL/Maravich/Bell	4	4	4	4	4	8	15	40
82	Celtics TL/Havlicek	4	4	4	4	4	8	12	40
83	Buffalo Braves TL	4	4	4	4	4	6	8	20
84	Bulls TL/Love/Walker	4	4	4	4	4	6	8	20
87	Warriors TL/Barry	4	4	4	4	4	6	8	40
91	Bucks TL/Jabbar/Oscar	4	4	4	5	6	12	15	30

		VG 3	VgEx 4	EX 5	ExMt 6	NM 7	NmMt 8	MT 9	Gem 9.5/10
92	New Orleans Jazz	4	4	4	4	4	6	8	25
93	Knicks TL/Fraz/Brad/DeB	4	4	4	4	4	6	8	20
100	John Havlicek	4	4	4	5	8	12	40	▲450
105	Nate Thurmond	4	4	4	4	4	6	8	50
113	Bill Bradley	4	4	4	5	8	15	40	
120	Gail Goodrich	4	4	4	4	4	6	10	20
123	Jeff Mullins	4	4	4	4	4	6	8	40
129	Doug Collins RC	4	4	4	6	8	15	30	60
131	Bob Lanier	4	4	4	4	4	6	10	80
132	Phil Jackson	4	4	4	4	8	12	15	40
135	Ernie DiGregorio RC	4	4	4	4	5	10	15	30
141	NBA Checklist 1-176	4	4	4	4	6	10	15	30
144	McAd/Jabbar/Marav LL	4	4	4	4	8	12	30	80
145	McAd/Marav/Jabbar LL	4	4	4	4	8	15	40	
146	McAd/Jabbar/Tomjan LL	4	4	4	4	6	8	25	50
148	Hayes/Cowens/McAd LL	4	4	4	4	4	6	10	20
150	Walt Frazier	4	4	4	4	4	8	20	60
155	Dave Cowens	4	4	4	4	6	8	15	150
170	Nate Archibald	4	4	4	4	6	8	10	
175	Sidney Wicks	4	4	4	4	4	6	8	30
176	Jerry West	4	4	5	8	10	20	30	150
178	George Carter	4	4	4	4	4	6	8	25
180	Artis Gilmore	4	4	4	4	4	6	10	40
186	James Silas RC	4	4	4	4	4	6	8	30
187	Caldwell Jones RC	4	4	4	4	4	6	8	30
190	Dan Issel	4	4	4	4	5	8	10	
196	George Gervin RC	4	5	12	15	30	80	250	1,000
200	Julius Erving	4	5	10	15	20	50	100	500
203	ABA Checklist 177-264	4	4	4	4	6	10	15	
207	Erving/McG/Issel LL	4	4	4	4	6	10	20	60
220	George McGinnis	4	4	4	4	4	6	8	30
224	Colonels TL/Issel	4	4	4	4	4	6	8	30
226	Nets TL/Erving	4	4	4	4	8	10	15	40
227	Spurs TL/Gervin	4	4	4	4	4	8	12	40
248	ABA Div. Finals	4	4	4	4	6	10	12	
249	ABA Championships/Dr.J.	4	4	4	4	8	15	▲40	80
250	Wilt Chamberlain CO	4	4	6	15	30	40	60	200
257	George Karl RC	4	4	4	5	8	12	15	40

1975-76 Topps

		GD 2	VG 3	VgEx 4	EX 5	ExMt 6	NM 7	NmMt 8	MT 9
	COM. NBA CARD (1-220)	4	4	4	4	4	4	5	15
1	McAd/Barry/Jabbar LL	4	4	4	6	8	12	20	60
2	Nelson/Beard/Tomj LL	4	4	4	4	4	6	8	40
3	Barry/Murphy/Bradley LL	4	4	4	4	6	8	10	30
4	Unseld/Cowens/Lacey LL	4	4	4	4	4	6	8	30
7	Tom Van Arsdale	4	4	4	4	4	6	8	30
9	Jerry Sloan	4	4	4	4	4	6	8	▲30
10	Bob McAdoo	4	4	4	4	6	8	10	60
20	Billy Cunningham	4	4	4	4	4	6	8	30
30	Bob Lanier	4	4	4		6	8	▲12	▲50
34	Cazzie Russell	4	4	4	4	4	6	8	25
37	Bill Bradley	4	4	4	4	6	12	15	50
38	Fred Carter	4	4	4	4	4	6	8	20
42	Rowland Garrett	4	4	4	4	4	4	5	25
50	Keith/Jamaal Wilkes RC	4	4	4	4	10	40	100	400
55	Walt Frazier	4	4	5	6	12	15	▲40	▲120
57	Nate Hawthorne	4	4	4	4	4	4	5	25
60	Elvin Hayes	4	4	4	4	4	8	12	30
61	Checklist 1-110	4	4	4	4	6	8	12	
63	Randy Smith	4	4	4	4	4	6	8	60
65	Charlie Scott	4	4	4	4	4	6	20	▲60
67	Rick Adelman	4	4	4	4	4	6	8	20
70	Rudy Tomjanovich	4	4	4	4	4	6	10	20
71	Pat Riley	4	4	4	4	4	6	10	20
73	Earl Monroe	4	4	4	4	4	8	12	30

	GD 2	VG 3	VgEx 4	EX 5	ExMt 6	NM 7	NmMt 8	MT 9
Allan Bristow RC	4	4	4	4	4	6	8	20
Pete Maravich DP	4	4	6	10	15	20	▲50	200
Bill Walton	4	4	6	8	12	15	▲40	▲120
John Havlicek	4	4	4	4	8	12	30	80
Nate Thurmond	4	4	4	4	4	6	8	40
Kareem Abdul-Jabbar	4	4	4	8	12	40	100	400
Mike Bantom	4	4	4	4	4	4	5	40
Kevin Stacom RC	4	4	4	4	4	4	5	25
Rick Barry	4	4	4	4	4	6	10	30
Austin Carr	4	4	4	4	4	6	8	25
Gail Goodrich	4	4	4	4	▲6	▲8	▲20	▲80
Phil Jackson	4	4	4	4	4	6	12	40
Wes Unseld	4	4	4	4	4	6	8	30
Kareem Abdul-Jabbar TL	4	4	4	4	6	8	12	40
Pete Maravich TL	4	4	4	4	6	10	25	80
John Drew RC	4	4	4	4	4	▲8	▲15	▲60
Jo Jo White	4	4	4	4	4	▲8	▲15	▲60
Brian Winters RC	4	4	4	4	4	6	8	20
Leonard Robinson RC	4	4	4	4	4	▲8	▲15	▲60
Campy Russell RC	4	4	4	4	▲6	▲10	▲20	▲80
Dave Cowens	4	4	4	4	6	10	12	30
Zelmo Beaty	4	4	4	4	4	6	8	25
Checklist 111-220 DP	4	4	4	4	4	8	12	40
Connie Hawkins DP	4	4	4	4	4	6	8	30
Spencer Haywood	4	4	4	4	4	6	8	▲30
Atlanta Hawks	4	4	4	4	4	6	8	20
Celtics Team CL	4	4	4	4	4	6	8	20
Bulls Team CL	4	4	4	4	4	6	8	25
Milwaukee Bucks	4	4	4	4	4	6	8	30
New York Knicks	4	4	4	4	4	6	8	30
Sonics Team/B.Russell	4	4	4	4	6	10	20	60
McGin/Erving/Boone LL	4	4	4	4	4	6	10	▲30
Jones/Gilmore/Malone LL	4	4	4	4	4	6	15	30
ABA Rebounds Leaders	4	4	4	4	4	6	8	30
George Gervin	4	4	5	8	12	20	25	60
Kevin Joyce RC	4	4	4	4	4	6	8	40
Artis Gilmore	4	4	4	4	4	6	8	25
Moses Malone RC	4	5	12	15	30	60	120	400
Checklist 221-330	4	4	4	4	4	8	15	25
Dan Issel	4	4	4	4	5	8	10	50
Julius Erving TL	4	4	5	6	10	15	20	40
Fly Williams RC	4	4	4	4	4	6	8	20
Red Robbins	4	4	4	4	4	6	8	25
Bobby Jones RC	4	4	4	6	10	15	40	150
Julius Erving	4	5	10	12	15	30	50	125
Billy Shepherd	4	4	4	4	4	6	8	20
Maurice Lucas RC	4	4	4	4	6	8	10	40
George Karl	4	4	4	4	4	6	8	20
Artis Gilmore PO	4	4	4	4	4	6	8	20
Denver Nuggets	4	4	4	4	4	6	8	50
Memphis Sounds	4	4	4	4	4	6	8	20
San Diego Sails	4	4	4	4	4	6	8	40

-Pete Maravich #75 PSA 10 (Gem MT) sold for $1,732 (Memory Lane; 7/12)
-Moses Malone #254 PSA 10 (Gem MT) sold for $1,540 (eBay; 4/12)
-Maurice Lucas #302 PSA 10 (Gem MT) sold for $248 (eBay; 1/13)

1976-77 Topps

	VG 3	VgEx 4	EX 5	ExMt 6	NM 7	NmMt 8	MT 9	Gem 9.5/10
COMMON CARD (1-144)	4	4	4	4	5	8	20	
Julius Erving	10	15	25	40	80	100	500	
Paul Silas	4	4	4	4	5	8	25	
Keith Erickson	4	4	4	4	▲6	▲25	60	
Wes Unseld	4	4	4	5	6	8	60	200
Jim McMillian	4	4	4	4	5	8	60	
Bob Lanier	4	4	4	5	6	12	30	100
Junior Bridgeman RC	4	4	4	4	5	8	30	

		VG 3	VgEx 4	EX 5	ExMt 6	NM 7	NmMt 8	MT 9	Gem 9.5/10
13	Billy Keller	4	4	4	4	6	8	60	200
20	Nate Archibald	4	4	4	5	6	8	25	
22	Ralph Simpson	4	4	4	4	5	8	25	
23	Campy Russell	4	4	4	4	▲8	▲50	▲80	
24	Charlie Scott	4	4	4	4	6	10	60	
25	Artis Gilmore	4	4	4	4	8	15	80	
26	Dick Van Arsdale	4	4	4	4	5	8	50	
29	Chris Ford	4	4	4	4	6	10	25	
30	Dave Cowens	4	4	6	8	12	▲30	80	
34	Lucius Allen	4	4	4	6	8	12	60	
36	Henry Bibby	4	4	4	4	5	8	80	
38	Doug Collins	4	4	4	6	10	12	80	
39	Garfield Heard	4	4	4	4	5	8	30	
40	Randy Smith	4	4	4	4	5	8	25	
42	Dave Twardzik	4	4	4	4	5	8	25	
43	Bill Bradley	4	4	6	8	12	15	25	100
44	Calvin Murphy	4	4	4	4	6	10	25	175
46	Brian Winters	4	4	4	4	5	8	50	
48	Checklist 1-144	5	8	12	15	20	25	80	
49	Bird Averitt	4	4	4	4	5	8	40	
50	Rick Barry	4	4	4	8	12	20	80	
53	Austin Carr	4	4	4	4	5	8	80	
56	Mike Riordan	4	4	4	4	5	8	25	
57	Bill Walton	4	4	6	10	15	30	▲60	
58	Eric Money RC	4	4	4	4	5	8	30	
60	Pete Maravich	6	10	15	20	25	50	150	600
61	John Shumate RC	4	4	4	5	8	12	30	200
64	Walt Frazier	4	4	6	10	15	200		
65	Elmore Smith	4	4	6	8	15	80		
66	Rudy Tomjanovich	4	4	4	4	6	12	25	
67	Sam Lacey	4	4	4	4	6	10	30	125
68	George Gervin	4	5	8	10	15	30	80	200
69	Gus Williams RC	4	5	8	10	20	40	80	125
70	George McGinnis	4	4	4	4	5	8	30	
71	Len Elmore	4	4	4	4	5	8	25	
75	Alvan Adams RC	4	4	4	5	6	12	25	
76	Dave Bing	4	4	4	5	6	10	30	225
77	Phil Jackson	4	4	6	8	12	40	90	
82	Ernie DiGregorio	4	4	4	4	8	12	60	
90	John Havlicek	4	4	6	8	12	20	35	300
91	Kevin Kunnert	4	4	4	4	5	10	50	
92	Jimmy Walker	4	4	4	4	6	10	20	
93	Billy Cunningham	4	4	4	6	8	15	80	
94	Dan Issel	4	4	4	5	6	8	25	500
98	Earl Monroe	4	4	4	5	10	20	100	
100	Kareem Abdul-Jabbar	5	8	10	20	▲40	▲80	200	
101	Moses Malone	4	5	8	12	20	40	100	250
106	Otto Moore	4	4	4	4	5	8	25	60
107	Maurice Lucas	4	4	4	4	5	8	25	60
108	Norm Van Lier	4	4	4	4	5	8	25	
109	Clifford Ray	4	4	4	4	5	8	40	
110	David Thompson RC	8	10	20	30	▲50	▲100	▲400	
114	Bobby Smith	4	4	4	4	5	8	25	150
115	Jo Jo White	4	4	4	4	5	8	40	
118	Curtis Rowe	4	4	4	4	5	8	25	
120	Elvin Hayes	4	4	4	5	8	▲30	▲60	
123	Jerry Sloan	4	4	4	4	5	10	40	200
124	Billy Knight	4	4	4	4	5	10	80	
126	K. Abdul-Jabbar AS	4	4	6	10	20	30	80	350
127	Julius Erving AS	4	4	6	10	20	40	80	250
128	George McGinnis AS	4	4	4	4	8	12	30	
130	Pete Maravich AS	4	4	6	10	▲25	▲50	▲100	
131	Dave Cowens AS	4	4	4	4	6	8	60	
132	Rick Barry AS	4	4	4	5	6	10	80	300
133	Elvin Hayes AS	4	4	4	4	6	10	40	200
134	James Silas AS	4	4	4	4	5	8	30	

#	Player	VG 3	VgEx 4	EX 5	ExMt 6	NM 7	NmMt 8	MT 9	Gem 9.5/10
139	Mike Newlin	4	4	4	4	5	8	80	
140	Bob McAdoo	4	4	4	6	8	30	80	
141	Mike Gale	4	4	4	4	5	8	25	
142	Scott Wedman	4	4	4	4	5	8	30	125
143	Lloyd Free RC	4	4	8	20	30	200	400	
144	Bobby Jones	4	4	4	6	10	12	80	

—David Thompson #110 PSA 10 (Gem MT) sold for $404 (eBay; 12/12)

1977-78 Topps

#	Player	VG 3	VgEx 4	EX 5	ExMt 6	NM 7	NmMt 8	MT 9	Gem 9.5/10
	COMMON CARD (1-132)	4	4	4	4	4	5	10	
1	Kareem Abdul-Jabbar	4	▲6	▲8	▲12	▲15	30	80	
6	Earl Monroe	4	4	4	4	6	8	15	40
7	Leonard Gray	4	4	4	4	4	5	15	
9	Jim Brewer	4	4	4	4	4	5	15	
10	Paul Westphal	4	4	4	4	6	10	15	30
11	Bob Gross RC	4	4	4	4	4	5	15	
15	Rudy Tomjanovich	4	4	4	4	6	8	12	
16	Kevin Porter	4	4	4	4	4	5	20	
18	Lloyd Free	4	4	4	4	4	5	15	50
20	Pete Maravich	4	4	6	10	15	40	150	
23	Kevin Grevey RC	4	4	4	4	6	8	12	
28	Larry Kenon	4	4	4	4	4	5	15	
29	Checklist 1-132	4	4	4	4	4	8	15	
33	Keith/Jamaal Wilkes	4	4	4	4	4	5	15	
35	Jo Jo White	4	4	4	4	4	5	15	
36	Scott May RC	4	4	4	4	6	8	25	
40	Elvin Hayes	4	4	4	4	6	8	15	
41	Dan Issel	4	4	4	4	6	10	20	
42	Ricky Sobers	4	4	4	4	4	5	12	
43	Don Ford	4	4	4	4	4	5	12	
45	Bob McAdoo	4	4	4	4	6	8	20	
49	Sam Lacey	4	4	4	4	4	5	12	
50	George McGinnis	4	4	4	4	4	5	12	30
56	Adrian Dantley RC	4	4	6	8	12	30	100	
57	Jim Chones	4	4	4	4	4	5	20	
58	John Lucas RC	4	4	4	4	6	8	20	
59	Cazzie Russell	4	4	4	4	4	8	12	
60	David Thompson	4	4	4	4	6	20	50	
61	Bob Lanier	4	4	4	4	6	8	15	
65	Doug Collins	4	4	4	4	6	8	12	
66	Tom McMillen RC	4	4	4	4	6	8	12	
68	Mike Bantom	4	4	4	4	4	5	12	
70	John Havlicek	4	4	6	8	10	12	20	
71	Marvin Webster RC	4	4	4	4	4	5	12	
73	George Gervin	4	4	4	4	8	12	20	
75	Wes Unseld	4	4	4	4	6	8	30	
78	Richard Washington RC	4	4	4	4	4	5	50	
84	Kevin Kunnert	4	4	4	4	4	5	12	
85	Lou Hudson	4	4	4	4	4	5	12	
87	Lucius Allen	4	4	4	4	4	5	30	
88	Spencer Haywood	4	4	4	4	6	8	20	
93	Tom Henderson	4	4	4	4	4	5	15	
100	Julius Erving	4	6	8	12	15	40	60	800
103	Billy Paultz	4	4	4	4	5	10	25	
105	Calvin Murphy	4	4	4	4	6	8	20	
107	Jim McMillian	4	4	4	4	4	5	12	20
111	Robert Parish RC	8	10	15	20	25	40	250	
113	Bruce Seals	4	4	4	4	8	10	20	
116	Steve Mix	4	4	4	4	4	5	12	25
120	Bill Walton	4	4	4	6	8	12	20	400
124	Moses Malone	4	4	4	4	6	8	10	25
127	Nate Archibald	4	4	4	4	6	8	15	30

#	Player	VG 3	VgEx 4	EX 5	ExMt 6	NM 7	NmMt 8	MT 9	Gem 9.5/10
128	Mitch Kupchak RC	4	4	4	4	6	8	12	
129	Walt Frazier	4	4	4	4	6	8	15	
130	Rick Barry	4	4	4	6	10	20	60	
131	Ernie DiGregorio	4	4	4	4	5	15		
132	Darryl Dawkins RC	4	4	6	10	15	30	60	

1978-79 Topps

#	Player	VG 3	VgEx 4	EX 5	ExMt 6	NM 7	NmMt 8	MT 9	Gem 9.5/10
	COMMON CARD (1-132)	4	4	4	4	5	6	10	
1	Bill Walton	4	4	4	5	8	10	20	80
5	Bob McAdoo	4	4	4	4	6	8	12	30
7	Wes Unseld	4	4	4	4	6	8	12	60
9	Austin Carr	4	4	4	4	5	6	12	40
10	Walter Davis RC	4	4	4	6	8	10	20	
14	Bobby Jones	4	4	4	4	5	8	12	30
20	George Gervin	4	4	4	6	8	10	60	
25	Elvin Hayes	4	4	4	4	6	8	15	
27	James Edwards RC	4	4	4	4	4	8	12	
28	Howard Porter	4	4	4	4	5	6	15	
29	Quinn Buckner RC	4	4	4	4	6	8	30	
32	Campy Russell	4	4	4	4	5	6	15	50
39	Gus Williams	4	4	4	4	6	8	15	
40	Dave Cowens	4	4	4	4	6	8	12	60
42	Wilbert Jones	4	4	4	4	5	6	15	
43	Charlie Scott	4	4	4	4	5	8	20	
45	Earl Monroe	4	4	4	4	6	8	12	
51	Louie Dampier	4	4	4	4	5	8	12	40
61	Dave Bing	4	4	4	4	6	10	15	
63	Norm Nixon RC	4	4	4	6	10	30	50	
67	Checklist 1-132	4	4	4	4	6	10	15	60
75	Bernard King RC	4	4	4	6	12	25	100	300
78	Dennis Johnson RC	4	4	6	8	12	25	60	
79	Scott Wedman	4	4	4	4	6	8	12	40
80	Pete Maravich	4	4	4	6	15	▲25	50	200
81	Dan Issel	4	4	4	4	6	8	12	
83	Walt Frazier	4	4	4	4	6	10	15	
85	Jo Jo White	4	4	4	4	5	10	15	
86	Robert Parish	4	4	4	4	6	10	15	40
95	Gail Goodrich	4	4	4	4	5	6	15	
100	David Thompson	4	4	4	4	6	8	12	50
110	Kareem Abdul-Jabbar	4	4	6	8	10	15	30	300
117	Jack Sikma RC	4	4	4	4	6	8	20	40
126	Marques Johnson RC	4	4	4	4	6	8	12	50
128	Cedric Maxwell RC	4	4	4	4	6	8	12	50
130	Julius Erving	4	4	4	6	10	20	40	200
132	Adrian Dantley	4	4	4	4	6	8	20	

1979-80 Topps

#	Player	GD 2	VG 3	VgEx 4	EX 5	ExMt 6	NM 7	NmMt 8	MT 9
	COMMON CARD (1-132)	4	4	4	4	4	4	5	10
1	George Gervin	4	4	4	4	5	8	15	80
3	Henry Bibby	4	4	4	4	4	4	5	12
6	Dennis Johnson	4	4	4	4	4	5	8	25
10	Kareem Abdul-Jabbar	4	4	4	4	6	10	20	40
13	Kevin Porter	4	4	4	4	4	4	5	15
14	Bernard King	4	4	4	4	4	5	6	40
17	Dan Issel	4	4	4	4	4	5	6	15
20	Julius Erving	4	4	4	4	6	▲12	▲25	120
23	Cedric Maxwell	4	4	4	4	4	4	5	20
25	Artis Gilmore	4	4	4	4	4	4	5	15
31	Alex English RC	4	4	4	6	10	20	40	150
32	Gail Goodrich	4	4	4	4	4	4	8	12
33	Caldwell Jones	4	4	4	4	4	4	5	12
41	Rudy Tomjanovich	4	4	4	4	4	5	6	12
42	Foots Walker	4	4	4	4	4	4	5	20
44	Reggie Theus RC	4	4	4	4	4	5	8	25
45	Bill Walton	4	4	4	4	4	4	6	25
54	Adrian Dantley	4	4	4	4	4	5	6	20
58	Bob Lanier	4	4	4	4	4	5	10	15
60	Pete Maravich	4	4	4	5	10	12	▲25	150
62	Robert Reid RC	4	4	4	4	4	4	10	30

	GD 2	VG 3	VgEx 4	EX 5	ExMt 6	NM 7	NmMt 8	MT 9
Mychal Thompson RC	4	4	4	4	4	5	6	12
Doug Collins	4	4	4	4	4	5	6	10
Wes Unseld	4	4	4	4	4	5	6	10
Bobby Wilkerson	4	4	4	4	4	4	6	12
Tim Bassett	4	4	4	4	4	4	6	15
Bob McAdoo	4	4	4	4	4	4	5	12
Robert Parish	4	4	4	4	4	6	10	15
Moses Malone	4	4	4	4	4	5	8	25
Checklist 1-132	4	4	4	4	4	5	6	12
Darryl Dawkins	4	4	4	4	4	5	6	12
Bob Dandridge AS2	4	4	4	4	4	4	6	15
Bobby Jones	4	4	4	4	4	5	8	50

80-81 Topps

	GD 2	VG 3	VgEx 4	EX 5	ExMt 6	NM 7	NmMt 8	MT 9
Bird/Erving/Magic	▲120	▲200	▲250	300	400	▲600	▲1,500	5,000
Maravich/Free/Johnson	4	4	5	6	8	12	20	100
40 Rick Robey	4	4	4	4	4	4	6	12
74 John Roche TL	4	4	4	4	4	8	10	40
Bird/Marques/Sikma	4	5	6	10	15	30	40	60
Bridgeman/Bird/Brewer	4	4	4	8	10	20	30	50
Cheeks/Johnson/Boone	4	4	4	6	8	15	30	120
Bird/Cartwright/Drew	4	5	6	12	25	25	40	120
May/Bird/Sikma	4	4	4	6	10	15	▲30	▲80
Long/Johnson/Boone	4	4	4	6	10	15	20	60
95 Wayne Cooper	4	4	4	4	4	4	4	6
108 Calvin Murphy	4	4	4	4	4	4	4	8
111 Rudy Tomjanovich	4	4	4	4	4	4	4	8
118/Archibald TL/Hayes	4	4	4	4	4	6	8	15
Kloft/Erving/Johnson	4	4	6	10	20	▲40	▲80	▲200
Brown/Bird/Brewer	4	4	4	6	10	20	25	▲50

—rd/Erving/Magic #6 BGS 10 (Pristine) sold for $60,667 (SCP; 8/13)

—rd/Erving/Magic #6 PSA 10 (Gem MT) sold for $14,467 (eBay; 9/12)

981-82 Topps

	VG 3	VgEx 4	EX 5	ExMt 6	NM 7	NmMt 8	MT 9	Gem 9.5/10
Larry Bird	4	4	6	10	▲20	30	▲120	1,000
Robert Parish	4	4	4	4	4	5	8	50
Moses Malone	4	4	4	4	4	5	8	30
Kareem Abdul-Jabbar	4	4	4	4	▲6	▲10	▲25	150
Magic Johnson	4	4	6	10	15	25	▲120	▼600
Julius Erving	4	4	4	4	▲5	▲10	25	
Lionel Hollins	4	4	4	4	4	4	8	50
George Gervin	4	4	4	4	4	6	15	40
Celtics TL/Bird/Arch	4	4	4	4	4	6	12	150
Lakers TL/Jabbar	4	4	4	4	4	6	8	40
76ers TL/Erving	4	4	4	4	4	6	8	50
Kevin McHale RC	4	4	4	6	20	25	100	600
Larry Bird SA	4	4	4	5	8	15	30	
Julius Erving SA	4	4	4	4	6	8	25	100
Alex English	4	4	4	4	4	4	8	50
Jim Paxson RC	4	4	4	4	4	4	5	15
Kareem Abdul-Jabbar SA	4	4	4	4	4	4	12	25
Magic Johnson SA	4	4	4	4	6	10	25	
Bill Laimbeer RC	4	4	4	4	5	10	30	

—arry Bird #4 PSA 10 (Gem MT) sold for $518 (Mile High; 5/11)

—Magic Johnson #21 PSA 10 (Gem MT) sold for $285 (Mile High; 5/11)

983 Star All-Star Game

	VgEx 4	EX 5	ExMt 6	NM 7	NmMt 8	NmMt+ 8.5	MT 9	Gem 9.5/10
Larry Bird	5	6	10	15	20	30	40	100
Isiah Thomas	5	5	6	10	15	20	25	50
Kareem Abdul-Jabbar	5	5	5	8	12	20	30	60
Magic Johnson	5	6	10	15	20	30	40	100
Julius Erving MVP	5	5	6	10	12	20	30	60

1983-84 Star

		VgEx 4	EX 5	ExMt 6	NM 7	NmMt 8	NmMt+ 8.5	MT 9	Gem 9.5/10
1	Julius Erving SP !	6	8	10	15	25	30	60	
2	Maurice Cheeks SP	5	5	5	5	8	15	30	
13	Magic Johnson SP !	10	12	15	30	50	60	100	
14	Kareem Abdul-Jabbar SP	5	6	8	12	25	40	50	
21	Kurt Rambis SP XRC	5	5	6	10	15	20	30	
22	Byron Scott SP XRC	5	5	6	10	15	20	40	
25	James Worthy SP XRC	5	6	8	15	40	60	120	200
27	Danny Ainge SP XRC	5	6	8	12	25	40	50	
35	Robert Parish SP !	5	5	6	10	15	20	30	
49	Mark Aguirre SP XRC	5	6	8	12	30	60	80	
51	Pat Cummings SP	5	5	5	6	10	15	25	
52	Brad Davis SP XRC	5	6	8	12	15	25	40	80
94	Isiah Thomas XRC	20	25	50	60	120	150	▲300	700
100	Clyde Drexler XRC	30	40	80	125	150	200	300	600
263	Dominique Wilkins XRC	30	40	80	125	220	300	450	

—Larry Bird #26 BGS 9.5 (Gem MT) sold for $487 (eBay; 4/13)

—Clyde Drexler #100 BGS 10 (Pristine) sold for $1,549 (Memory Lane; 5/13)

1983-84 Star All-Rookies

		VgEx 4	EX 5	ExMt 6	NM 7	NmMt 8	NmMt+ 8.5	MT 9	Gem 9.5/10
8	Dominique Wilkins !	5	5	5	8	12	20	40	120
10	James Worthy	5	5	5	6	8	12	20	50

1984-85 Star

		VG 3	VgEx 4	EX 5	ExMt 6	NM 7	NmMt 8	NmMt+ 8.5	MT 9
1	Larry Bird	10	15	25	40	50			
101	Michael Jordan XRC	800	1,200	1,500	▲3,000	4,000	7,000	10,000	
195	Michael Jordan OLY !	40	50	75	▲350	▲400	▲1,000		
202	Charles Barkley XRC	40	50	60	80	150	200	300	500
204	Julius Erving	5	8	10	15	20	30	40	▲70
235	John Stockton XRC	30	40	50	60	80	200	250	300
237	Hakeem Olajuwon XRC !	40	50	60	80	220	300	400	700
288	Michael Jordan SPEC !	▲80	▲150	▲250	▲300	400	▲800		

—Michael Jordan #101 BGS 9.5 (Gem Mt) sold for $52,500 (Beckett Auctions; 3/15)

—Michael Jordan #101 BGS 9 (Mint) sold for $9,531 (eBay; 3/13)

—Michael Jordan #101 BGS 9 (Mint) sold for $6,102 (eBay; 2/14)

—Michael Jordan #101 BGS 8.5 (NMMT+) sold for $3,200 (eBay; 9/11)

—Michael Jordan #101 BGS 8.5 (NMMT+) sold for $2,225 (eBay; 9/11)

—Charles Barkley #202 BGS 9.5 (Gem MT) sold for $1,038 (eBay; 10/12)

—Hakeem Olajuwon #237 BGS 9 (Mint) sold for $1,825 (eBay; 4/13)

1984-85 Star Court Kings 5x7

		VgEx 4	EX 5	ExMt 6	NM 7	NmMt 8	NmMt+ 8.5	MT 9	Gem 9.5/10
26	Michael Jordan	▲150	▲300	▲400	▲500	600	800	1,200	
47	Hakeem Olajuwon	8	10	15	25	▲40	▲60	▲200	

1985 Star Gatorade Slam Dunk

		VgEx 4	EX 5	ExMt 6	NM 7	NmMt 8	NmMt+ 8.5	MT 9	Gem 9.5/10
NNO	Charles Barkley SP	10	15	20	30	50	80	125	

1985-86 Star

		VgEx 4	EX 5	ExMt 6	NM 7	NmMt 8	NmMt+ 8.5	MT 9	Gem 9.5/10
106	Clyde Drexler !	8	10	15	20	30	40	50	100
117	Michael Jordan !	120	150	200	250	400	600	800	1,200
144	John Stockton	10	15	25	40	60	70	80	200
166	Patrick Ewing XRC	40	50	60	▲100	▲150	200	300	800

1985-86 Star All-Rookie Team

		VgEx 4	EX 5	ExMt 6	NM 7	NmMt 8	NmMt+ 8.5	MT 9	Gem 9.5/10
1	Hakeem Olajuwon	6	8	10	15	30	40	▲100	
2	Michael Jordan	60	80	100	200	400	500	800	
8	John Stockton	6	8	10	15	30	40	100	

1986 Star Michael Jordan

	VgEx 4	EX 5	ExMt 6	NM 7	NmMt 8	NmMt+ 8.5	MT 9	Gem 9.5/10
COMMON CARD (1-10)	20	25	50	80	100	150	250	500

1986-87 Fleer

		VgEx 4	EX 5	ExMt 6	NM 7	NmMt 8	NmMt+ 8.5	MT 9	Gem 9.5/10
1	Kareem Abdul-Jabbar	4	5	8	20	50	80	200	700
2	Alvan Adams	4	4	4	6	25	30	▼120	▼800
3	Mark Aguirre RC	4	4	4	5	25	30	▼50	▼400
4	Danny Ainge RC	4	4	5	10	▼20	▼25	▼40	120
5	John Bagley RC	4	4	4	8	15	20	30	150
6	Thurl Bailey RC	4	4	4	8	15	20	30	80
7	Charles Barkley RC	10	25	60	80	120	150	350	800
8	Benoit Benjamin RC	4	4	4	5	15	20	30	300
9	Larry Bird	4	6	8	25	50	60	150	600
10	Otis Birdsong	4	4	4	6	15	20	60	400
11	Rolando Blackman RC	4	4	6	10	25	30	120	300
12	Manute Bol RC	4	4	4	10	30	40	▲120	▲300
13	Sam Bowie RC	4	4	4	6	15	20	40	80
14	Joe Barry Carroll	4	4	4	6	10	15	25	80
15	Tom Chambers RC	4	4	4	6	12	15	30	80
16	Maurice Cheeks	4	4	4	6	10	15	30	80
17	Michael Cooper	4	4	4	4	15	20	25	100
18	Wayne Cooper	4	4	4	4	12	15	25	50
19	Pat Cummings	4	4	4	4	12	15	30	80
20	Terry Cummings RC	4	4	4	6	10	15	25	100
21	Adrian Dantley	4	4	4	5	15	20	30	150
22	Brad Davis RC	4	4	5	10	25	30	60	300
23	Walter Davis	4	4	4	6	15	20	25	80
24	Darryl Dawkins	4	4	4	4	15	20	25	80
25	Larry Drew	4	4	4	6	10	15	25	80
26	Clyde Drexler RC	6	10	12	30	50	60	▼120	400
27	Joe Dumars RC	4	5	6	12	25	30	60	300
28	Mark Eaton RC	4	4	4	6	15	20	30	80
29	James Edwards	4	4	4	4	6	12	25	60
30	Alex English	4	4	4	4	20	25	30	100
31	Julius Erving	4	6	8	15	30	40	80	400
32	Patrick Ewing RC	10	15	30	40	▼60	100	▼200	600
33	Vern Fleming RC	4	4	4	10	20	25	40	225
34	Sleepy Floyd RC	4	4	4	6	20	25	40	120
35	World B. Free	4	4	4	6	▼12	▼15	▼25	▼60
36	George Gervin	4	4	4	6	12	15	25	80
37	Artis Gilmore	4	4	4	6	12	15	25	80
38	Mike Gminski	4	4	4	4	10	15	25	150
39	Rickey Green	4	4	4	4	10	12	25	100
40	Sidney Green	4	4	4	4	15	20	25	80
41	David Greenwood	4	4	4	4	15	20	25	60
42	Darrell Griffith	4	4	4	4	15	20	25	100
43	Bill Hanzlik	4	4	4	4	10	15	30	300
44	Derek Harper RC	4	4	4	8	20	25	80	250
45	Gerald Henderson	4	4	4	5	10	15	25	100
46	Roy Hinson	4	4	4	4	12	15	25	80
47	Craig Hodges RC	4	4	4	4	15	20	25	150
48	Phil Hubbard	4	4	4	4	15	20	25	60
49	Jay Humphries RC	4	4	4	4	10	15	25	60
50	Dennis Johnson	4	4	4	5	▼10	▼15	▲30	100
51	Eddie Johnson RC	4	4	4	5	10	15	25	60
52	Frank Johnson RC	4	4	4	4	10	15	25	120
53	Magic Johnson	4	8	15	25	60	80	120	500
54	Marques Johnson	4	4	4	5	15	20	50	400
55	Steve Johnson	4	4	4	8	20	25	100	300
56	Vinnie Johnson	4	4	4	4	15	20	60	300
57	Michael Jordan RC	1,000	1,200	1,500	▲2,200	▲3,000	▲3,500	7,000	15,000
58	Clark Kellogg RC	4	4	4	5	10	15	25	100
59	Albert King	4	4	4	4	15	20	25	60
60	Bernard King	4	4	4	6	20	25	40	60
61	Bill Laimbeer	4	4	4	6	▼12	▼15	▼40	▲150
62	Allen Leavell	4	4	4	4	15	20	25	120
63	Fat Lever RC	4	4	4	4	10	12	30	▲200
64	Alton Lister	4	4	4	4	15	20	40	300
65	Lewis Lloyd	4	4	4	4	10	20	100	500
66	Maurice Lucas	4	4	4	4	10	15	120	500
67	Jeff Malone RC	4	4	4	8	15	20	100	300
68	Karl Malone RC	▲10	▲15	25	50	60	80	200	600
69	Moses Malone	4	4	4	5	10	20	25	120
70	Cedric Maxwell	4	4	4	4	15	20	25	150
71	Rodney McCray RC	4	4	4	5	10	15	25	200
72	Xavier McDaniel RC	4	4	4	5	10	15	30	150
73	Kevin McHale	4	4	4	8	20	25	50	150
74	Mike Mitchell	4	4	4	4	10	12	25	200
75	Sidney Moncrief	4	4	4	5	15	20	30	▲200
76	Johnny Moore	4	4	4	8	20	50	150	600
77	Chris Mullin RC	4	6	10	25	▼50	▼80	▼250	600
78	Larry Nance RC	4	4	4	8	▲20	▲30	▲50	300
79	Calvin Natt	4	4	4	5	15	20	25	120
80	Norm Nixon	4	4	4	5	10	12	30	60
81	Charles Oakley RC	4	4	4	▲8	▲15	▲20	▲40	▲100
82	Hakeem Olajuwon RC	8	12	25	60	▲100	▲120	▲300	600
83	Louis Orr	4	4	4	5	10	15	25	80
84	Robert Parish	4	4	4	6	15	20	30	150
85	Jim Paxson	4	4	4	4	15	20	25	100
86	Sam Perkins RC	4	4	4	5	15	20	30	200
87	Ricky Pierce RC	4	4	4	5	12	15	30	125
88	Paul Pressey RC	4	4	4	4	10	20	60	250
89	Kurt Rambis RC	4	4	4	5	10	20	50	250
90	Robert Reid	4	4	4	5	12	15	25	60
91	Doc Rivers RC	4	4	4	10	20	25	30	▲120
92	Alvin Robertson RC	4	4	4	4	10	12	25	80
93	Cliff Robinson	4	4	4	4	10	12	25	80
94	Tree Rollins	4	4	4	4	15	20	25	100
95	Dan Roundfield	4	4	4	4	15	20	25	60
96	Jeff Ruland	4	4	4	5	15	20	25	125
97	Ralph Sampson RC	4	4	4	5	▼12	▼15	▼40	▲120
98	Danny Schayes RC	4	4	4	4	15	20	30	120
99	Byron Scott RC	4	4	4	8	25	▲40	120	250
100	Purvis Short	4	4	4	6	15	20	30	100
101	Jerry Sichting	4	4	4	4	12	15	25	150
102	Jack Sikma	4	4	4	4	15	20	25	60
103	Derek Smith	4	4	4	4	10	12	25	80
104	Larry Smith	4	4	4	4	10	15	25	100
105	Rory Sparrow	4	4	4	4	10	15	25	80
106	Steve Stipanovich	4	4	4	4	12	15	25	80
107	Terry Teagle	4	4	4	4	10	15	30	80
108	Reggie Theus	4	4	4	5	10	20	30	60
109	Isiah Thomas RC	6	8	10	25	50	60	150	600
110	LaSalle Thompson RC	4	4	4	6	25	30	60	200
111	Mychal Thompson	4	4	4	4	12	15	30	200
112	Sedale Threatt RC	4	4	4	5	12	15	25	80
113	Wayman Tisdale RC	4	4	4	6	▼12	▼15	▼25	60
114	Andrew Toney	4	4	4	4	15	20	30	80
115	Kelly Tripucka RC	4	4	4	4	15	20	25	60
116	Mel Turpin	4	4	4	4	15	20	25	60
117	Kiki Vandeweghe	4	4	4	8	10	15	25	120
118	Jay Vincent	4	4	4	4	10	15	30	100
119	Bill Walton	4	4	4	8	▲25	▲30	50	▲150
120	Spud Webb RC	4	6	10	20	40	50	▼100	300
121	Dominique Wilkins RC	6	12	25	40	100	120	400	1,000
122	Gerald Wilkins RC	4	4	4	5	▼12	▼15	▼30	200
123	Buck Williams RC	4	4	4	5	12	15	30	120
124	Gus Williams	4	4	4	4	15	20	25	80
125	Herb Williams RC	4	4	4	4	15	20	25	▲80
126	Kevin Willis RC	4	4	4	6	12	15	40	100
127	Randy Wittman	4	4	4	6	15	20	25	80
128	Al Wood	4	4	4	4	15	20	25	120
129	Mike Woodson	4	4	4	4	10	15	30	60
130	Orlando Woolridge RC	4	4	6	▼8	▼15	▼20	▼50	200
131	James Worthy RC	4	5	10	20	50	80	▼200	600
132	Checklist 1-132	4	5	10	25	80	120	400	▲1,000

—Charles Barkley #7 PSA 10 (Gem MT) sold for $455 (eBay; 10/11)

—Magic Johnson #53 PSA 10 (Gem MT) sold for $346 (Mile High; 5/11)

—Michael Jordan #57 BGS 10 (Pristine) sold for $8,025 (eBay; 10/12)

—Michael Jordan #57 in PSA 10 (Gem MT) typically sell for $14,000-$18,000

—Michael Jordan #57 BGS 9.5 (Gem MT) sold for $6,500 (eBay; 10/11)

—Karl Malone #68 PSA 10 (Gem MT) sold for $471 (Mile High; 5/11)

—Hakeem Olajuwon #82 PSA 10 (Gem MT) sold for $510 (Mile High; 5/11)

—Dominique Wilkins #121 BGS 10 (Pristine) sold for $3,859 (eBay; 4/14)

36-87 Fleer Stickers

	VgEx 4	EX 5	ExMt 6	NM 7	NmMt 8	NmMt+ 8.5	MT 9	Gem 9.5/10
Kareem Abdul-Jabbar	6	8	15	▲40	80	150	1,000	2,000
Larry Bird	4	4	10	20	40	50	120	1,500
Adrian Dantley	4	4	4	6	15	20	50	400
Alex English	4	4	4	6	25	30	50	300
Julius Erving	4	▲8	▲10	▲20	▼50	▼80	120	1,000
Patrick Ewing	4	▲6	▲8	▲20	▲25	▲30	80	600
Magic Johnson	4	4	8	20	40	50	80	1,000
Michael Jordan	80	200	250	▲350	▲600	▲700	▲2,000	8,000
Hakeem Olajuwon	4	4	8	12	30	50	100	1,000
Isiah Thomas	▲6	▲6	▲8	▲12	30	60	120	1,500
Dominique Wilkins	4	6	12	15	50	80	300	1,500

87-88 Fleer

	VgEx 4	EX 5	ExMt 6	NM 7	NmMt 8	NmMt+ 8.5	MT 9	Gem 9.5/10
Kareem Abdul-Jabbar	4	4	4	6	▲12	15	30	350
Alvan Adams	4	4	4	5	10	15	25	
Mark Aguirre	4	4	4	4	8	8	15	
Danny Ainge	4	4	4	6	12	15	35	
John Bagley	4	4	4	5	▲8	▲12	▲50	
Thurl Bailey	4	4	4	4	6	8	15	
Greg Ballard	4	4	4	5	8	10	▲60	
Gene Banks	4	4	4	6	10	15	25	
Charles Barkley	4	4	4	8	20	25	40	
Benoit Benjamin	4	4	4	5	8	10	20	
Larry Bird	4	4	8	12	20	25	125	
Rolando Blackman	4	4	4	4	4	8	12	40
Manute Bol	4	4	4	5	6	15	30	
Tony Brown	4	4	4	5	10	15	25	
Michael Cage RC	4	4	4	5	6	15	40	150
Joe Barry Carroll	4	4	4	4	6	8	12	
Bill Cartwright	4	4	4	4	6	8	20	
Terry Catledge RC	4	4	4	5	10	15	25	
Tom Chambers	4	4	4	4	8	8	25	
Maurice Cheeks	4	4	4	4	6	8	15	50
Michael Cooper	4	4	4	4	6	8	15	
Dave Corzine	4	4	4	5	8	10	20	
Terry Cummings	4	4	4	4	6	8	15	
Adrian Dantley	4	4	4	4	6	8	15	
Brad Daugherty RC	4	4	4	5	6	8	▲20	100
Walter Davis	4	4	4	4	6	8	15	
Johnny Dawkins RC	4	4	4	5	10	15	20	60
James Donaldson	4	4	4	4	5	8	10	
Larry Drew	4	4	4	4	5	8	10	30
Clyde Drexler	4	4	4	8	10	15	25	
Joe Dumars	4	4	4	5	6	8	10	40
Mark Eaton	4	4	4	4	6	8	15	
Dale Ellis RC	4	4	4	5	8	12	50	
Alex English	4	4	4	4	6	8	12	
Julius Erving	4	4	4	8	12	15	25	150
Mike Evans	4	4	4	4	6	8	10	
Patrick Ewing	4	4	4	4	8	12	20	
Vern Fleming	4	4	4	4	5	8	10	25
Sleepy Floyd	4	4	4	4	6	8	12	
Artis Gilmore	4	4	4	4	6	8	12	40
Mike Gminski	4	4	4	4	6	8	15	30
A.C. Green RC	4	4	4	4	6	8	12	80
Rickey Green	4	4	4	4	5	8	10	
Sidney Green	4	4	4	4	5	8	10	
David Greenwood	4	4	4	4	5	8	10	40
Darrell Griffith	4	4	4	4	6	8	12	40
Bill Hanzlik	4	4	4	4	6	8	20	
Derek Harper	4	4	4	4	6	8	10	40
Ron Harper RC	4	4	4	4	6	10	20	100
Gerald Henderson	4	4	4	4	4	5	6	

		VgEx 4	EX 5	ExMt 6	NM 7	NmMt 8	NmMt+ 8.5	MT 9	Gem 9.5/10
51	Roy Hinson	4	4	4	4	6	8	30	
52	Craig Hodges	4	4	4	4	6	8	30	
53	Phil Hubbard	4	4	4	4	6	8	12	
54	Dennis Johnson	4	4	4	4	6	8	12	60
55	Eddie Johnson	4	4	4	4	6	8	10	25
56	Magic Johnson	4	4	10	12	15	▲25	▲50	400
57	Steve Johnson	4	4	4	4	6	8	12	
58	Vinnie Johnson	4	4	4	5	8	10	12	50
59	Michael Jordan	20	25	60	120	200	250	500	2,000
60	Jerome Kersey RC	4	4	4	4	8	10	12	50
61	Bill Laimbeer	4	4	4	5	8	10	12	
62	Lafayette Lever	4	4	4	4	6	8	10	
63	Cliff Levingston RC	4	4	4	4	6	8	12	
64	Alton Lister	4	4	4	6	8	12	25	
65	John Long	4	4	4	5	8	10	12	
66	John Lucas	4	4	4	5	8	10	12	
67	Jeff Malone	4	4	4	4	6	8	10	
68	Karl Malone	4	4	6	10	15	18	25	60
69	Moses Malone	4	4	4	6	8	10	80	
70	Cedric Maxwell	4	4	4	4	6	8	50	
71	Tim McCormick	4	4	4	4	4	6	8	
72	Rodney McCray	4	4	4	4	6	8	10	25
73	Xavier McDaniel	4	4	4	4	6	8	10	25
74	Kevin McHale	4	4	4	4	6	8	10	50
75	Nate McMillan RC	4	4	4	4	6	10	15	
76	Sidney Moncrief	4	4	4	4	6	8		
77	Chris Mullin	4	4	4	4	6	8	12	60
78	Larry Nance	4	4	4	4	5	6	10	100
79	Charles Oakley	4	4	4	4	5	8	12	30
80	Hakeem Olajuwon	4	4	4	8	10	15	25	150
81	Robert Parish	4	4	4	5	10	12	15	100
82	Jim Paxson	4	4	4	4	6	8	12	
83	John Paxson RC	4	4	4	4	6	8	12	60
84	Sam Perkins	4	4	4	4	6	8	10	50
85	Chuck Person RC	4	4	4	4	5	6	8	60
86	Jim Petersen	4	4	4	4	4	6	8	25
87	Ricky Pierce	4	4	4	4	6	8	10	25
88	Ed Pinckney RC	4	4	4	4	8	10	15	
89	Terry Porter RC	4	4	4	4	8	12	15	50
90	Paul Pressey	4	4	4	4	6	8	10	25
91	Robert Reid	4	4	4	4	5	8	10	25
92	Doc Rivers	4	4	4	4	4	6	8	50
93	Alvin Robertson	4	4	4	4	4	6	8	30
94	Tree Rollins	4	4	4	4	4	6	8	25
95	Ralph Sampson	4	4	4	4	6	8	10	30
96	Mike Sanders	4	4	4	5	8	10	12	60
97	Detlef Schrempf RC	4	4	4	6	8	10	▲20	50
98	Byron Scott	4	4	4	4	6	8	12	25
99	Jerry Sichting	4	4	4	4	6	8	10	25
100	Jack Sikma	4	4	4	4	6	8	10	40
101	Larry Smith	4	4	4	4	6	8	10	25
102	Rory Sparrow	4	4	4	4	6	8	25	
103	Steve Stipanovich	4	4	4	4	6	8	25	
104	Jon Sundvold	4	4	4	4	6	8	10	25
105	Reggie Theus	4	4	4	4	6	8	10	30
106	Isiah Thomas	4	4	4	4	6	8	15	40
107	LaSalle Thompson	4	4	4	4	6	8	25	
108	Mychal Thompson	4	4	4	4	6	8	10	25
109	Otis Thorpe RC	4	4	4	8	10	15	40	
110	Sedale Threatt	4	4	4	4	4	6	8	25
111	Wayman Tisdale	4	4	4	5	8	10	15	
112	Kelly Tripucka	4	4	4	4	4	5	6	30
113	Trent Tucker RC	4	4	4	4	4	6	8	25
114	Terry Tyler	4	4	4	4	6	8	10	30
115	Darnell Valentine	4	4	4	4	4	6	8	25
116	Kiki Vandeweghe	4	4	4	4	6	8	25	
117	Darrell Walker RC	4	4	4	4	6	8	25	

		VgEx 4	EX 5	ExMt 6	NM 7	NmMt 8	NmMt+ 8.5	MT 9	Gem 9.5/10
118	Dominique Wilkins	4	4	4	4	8	10	20	50
119	Gerald Wilkins	4	4	4	4	6	8	10	25
120	Buck Williams	4	4	4	4	6	8	10	25
121	Herb Williams	4	4	4	4	6	8	10	25
122	John Williams RC	4	4	4	6	10	15	25	
123	Hot Rod Williams RC	4	4	4	4	6	8	10	
124	Kevin Willis	4	4	4	4	4	6	10	25
125	David Wingate RC	4	4	4	4	6	8	10	30
126	Randy Wittman	4	4	4	6	8	10	12	25
127	Leon Wood	4	4	4	4	4	6	8	30
128	Mike Woodson	4	4	4	5	8	10	15	50
129	Orlando Woolridge	4	4	4	4	4	6	8	40
130	James Worthy	4	4	4	4	10	12	25	150
131	Danny Young RC	4	4	4	6	8	10	12	
132	Checklist 1-132	4	4	4	5	8	10	15	80

1987-88 Fleer Stickers

		VgEx 4	EX 5	ExMt 6	NM 7	NmMt 8	NmMt+ 8.5	MT 9	Gem 9.5/10
1	Magic Johnson	4	4	4	6	8	▲15	▲50	
2	Michael Jordan	6	8	15	40	▲100	150	▲400	8,000
3	Hakeem Olajuwon	4	4	4	6	12	▲20	▲40	
4	Larry Bird	4	4	4	6	8	12	40	1,000
5	Kevin McHale	4	4	4	4	8	12	25	
6	Charles Barkley	4	4	4	▲6	▲10	▲15	30	
7	Dominique Wilkins	4	4	4	4	▲10	▲15	▲40	1,200
8	Kareem Abdul-Jabbar	4	4	6	8	12	15	25	
9	Mark Aguirre	4	4	4	4	8	10	20	
10	Chuck Person	4	4	4	4	8	10	30	
11	Alex English	4	4	4	4	8	▲15	▼150	

—Larry Bird #4 BGS 9.5 (Gem MT) sold for $650 (eBay; 10/11)

1988-89 Fleer

		VgEx 4	EX 5	ExMt 6	NM 7	NmMt 8	NmMt+ 8.5	MT 9	Gem 9.5/10
	COMMON CARD (1-132)	4	4	4	4	4	6	8	20
1	Antoine Carr RC	4	4	4	4	6	8	10	50
5	Dominique Wilkins	4	4	4	4	6	8	10	30
8	Danny Ainge	4	4	4	4	6	8	12	25
9	Larry Bird	4	4	4	6	▼8	▼10	15	50
11	Kevin McHale	4	4	4	4	6	8	10	30
13	Muggsy Bogues RC	4	4	4	4	6	8	▲12	40
14	Dell Curry RC	4	4	4	4	6	8	10	▲30
16	Horace Grant RC	4	4	4	4	▼8	▼10	20	60
17	Michael Jordan	5	10	25	40	50	60	120	600
20	Scottie Pippen RC	4	5	10	20	30	40	80	600
25	Mark Price RC	4	4	4	5	6	8	12	▲60
32	Roy Tarpley RC	4	4	4	4	6	8	10	▲60
33	Michael Adams RC	4	4	4	4	6	8	10	▲50
39	Adrian Dantley	4	4	4	4	5	▼6	10	▲30
40	Joe Dumars	4	4	4	4	4	6	▲12	▲30
43	Dennis Rodman RC	4	4	4	8	10	20	▲60	500
44	John Salley RC	4	4	4	▲10	▲15	▲30	▲60	
45	Isiah Thomas	4	4	4	4	6	▲10	▲20	▲50
53	Hakeem Olajuwon	4	4	4	5	6	8	12	30
57	Reggie Miller RC	4	4	8	15	20	25	60	600
58	Chuck Person	4	4	4	4	▲6	▲8	▲12	▼30
61	Benoit Benjamin	4	4	4	4	4	5	8	30
64	Kareem Abdul-Jabbar	4	4	4	4	6	▼8	▼12	▲30
67	Magic Johnson	4	4	4	5	8	10	15	▲100
70	James Worthy	4	4	4	4	6	8	10	25
76	Jack Sikma	4	4	4	4	6	8	10	▲30
80	Patrick Ewing	4	4	4	4	6	▼8	15	40
82	Mark Jackson RC	4	4	4	4	6	8	10	25
83	Kenny Walker RC	4	4	4	4	4	6	10	▲40
84	Gerald Wilkins	4	4	4	4	6	8	10	25
85	Charles Barkley	4	4	4	4	▼6	▼8	20	60
86	Maurice Cheeks	4	4	4	4	4	▼6	10	25
88	Cliff Robinson	4	4	4	4	5	6	10	25
92	Clyde Drexler	4	4	4	4	5	8	12	
93	Kevin Duckworth RC	4	4	4	4	5	8	12	30
94	Steve Johnson	4	4	4	4	4	5	▲12	▲50
98	Reggie Theus	4	4	4	4	4	5	6	25
99	Otis Thorpe	4	4	4	4	4	5	8	▲40
100	Kenny Smith RC	4	4	4	4	5	▼6	10	▲50

		VgEx 4	EX 5	ExMt 6	NM 7	NmMt 8	NmMt+ 8.5	MT 9	Gem 9.5/10
102	Walter Berry RC	4	4	4	4	4	5	6	25
103	Frank Brickowski RC	4	4	4	4	4	6	▼8	25
105	Alvin Robertson	4	4	4	4	4	5	6	25
106	Tom Chambers	4	4	4	4	5	6	▼8	▼25
108	Xavier McDaniel	4	4	4	4	4	5	6	25
112	Mark Eaton	4	4	4	4	4	5	6	25
114	Karl Malone	4	4	4	5	▼6	▼8	12	▼40
115	John Stockton RC	4	5	6	10	20	25	▲50	200
116	Bernard King	4	4	4	4	5	6	10	80
118	Moses Malone	4	4	4	4	4	5	8	40
120	Michael Jordan AS	4	5	10	25	▲50	▲60	▲125	600
123	Magic Johnson AS	4	4	4	4	5	8	10	40
124	Larry Bird AS	4	4	4	4	5	8	▼10	40
125	Dominique Wilkins AS	4	4	4	4	4	5	▲10	▲40
126	Hakeem Olajuwon AS	4	4	4	4	5	6	8	30
127	John Stockton AS	4	4	4	4	6	8	12	60
129	Charles Barkley AS	4	4	4	4	▲6	▲8	▲10	▲40
130	Patrick Ewing AS	4	4	4	4	5	6	8	30
132	Checklist 1-132	4	4	4	4	4	5	6	60

—Dennis Rodman #43 PSA 10 (Gem MT) sold for $200 (eBay; 9/11)

—Reggie Miller #57 PSA 10 (Gem MT) sold for $222 (eBay; 10/11)

1988-89 Fleer Stickers

		VgEx 4	EX 5	ExMt 6	NM 7	NmMt 8	NmMt+ 8.5	MT 9	Gem 9.5/10
1	Mark Aguirre	4	4	4	4	▲10			
2	Larry Bird	4	4	4	5	8	12	▲40	
3	Clyde Drexler	4	4	4	5	10	▲15	▲150	
4	Alex English	4	4	4	4	6	8		
5	Patrick Ewing	4	4	4	5	8	12	30	
6	Magic Johnson	4	4	4	5	▲10	▲15	▲50	
7	Michael Jordan	4	▲8	▲20	▲30	60	▲100	▲450	
8	Karl Malone	4	4	4	4	▲8	10	▲30	
9	Kevin McHale	4	4	4	4	6	10	40	
10	Isiah Thomas	4	4	4	4	6	10	15	
11	Dominique Wilkins	4	4	4	4	6	10	▲40	

—Clyde Drexler #3 PSA 10 (Gem MT) sold for $475 (eBay; 12/06)

—Magic Johnson #6 PSA 10 (Gem MT) sold for $763 (eBay; 4/13)

1989-90 Fleer

		VgEx 4	EX 5	ExMt 6	NM 7	NmMt 8	NmMt+ 8.5	MT 9	Gem 9.5/10
4	Moses Malone	4	4	4	4	6	8	10	12
12	Robert Parish	4	4	4	4	6	8	10	15
19	Bill Cartwright UER	4	4	4	4	6	8	10	▲20
21	Michael Jordan	4	4	5	6	15	20	40	150
22	John Paxson	4	4	4	4	5	6	8	▲20
23	Scottie Pippen	4	4	4	4	6	8	12	▲40
28	Larry Nance	4	4	4	4	6	8	10	15
48	Bill Laimbeer	4	4	4	4	6	8	10	15
49	Dennis Rodman	4	4	4	4	6	8	10	20
55	Chris Mullin	4	4	4	4	4	6	8	14
56	Mitch Richmond RC	4	4	4	4	6	8	15	60
61	Hakeem Olajuwon	4	4	4	4	6	8	12	▲30
65	Reggie Miller	4	4	4	4	6	8	12	20
77	Magic Johnson	4	4	4	6	8	10	12	▲60
100	Patrick Ewing	4	4	4	4	6	8	10	25
113	Charles Barkley	4	4	4	4	6	8	15	40
121	Jeff Hornacek RC	4	4	4	4	8	10	12	20
163	Malone/Stockton/Eaton AS	4	4	4	4	6	8	10	15

1989-90 Fleer Stickers

		VgEx 4	EX 5	ExMt 6	NM 7	NmMt 8	NmMt+ 8.5	MT 9	Gem 9.5/10
3	Michael Jordan	4	5	6	8	20	40	80	800
10	Larry Bird	4	4	4	4	6	8		

—Michael Jordan #3 BGS 10 (Pristine) sold for $2,985 (Mile High; 1/10)

1989-90 Hoops

		VgEx 4	EX 5	ExMt 6	NM 7	NmMt 8	NmMt+ 8.5	MT 9	Gem 9.5/10
21	Michael Jordan AS	4	4	4	4	4	6	15	▲40
138	David Robinson SP RC	4	4	4	8	10	▲30	▼120	
150	Larry Bird	4	4	4	4	4	6	15	
200	Michael Jordan	4	4	4	▲6	▲8	▲20	▲40	
310	David Robinson IA	4	4	4	4	6	20	▲50	
351	Steve Kerr RC	4	4	4	4	6	10	25	

BASKETBALL

1990/91 - Present

1990-91 Fleer

		NmMt 8	NmMt+ 8.5	MT 9	Gem 9.5/10
	Larry Bird	4	6	12	20
6	Michael Jordan	6	10	▲25	▲150
3	Magic Johnson	4	4	8	15
01	Glen Rice RC	4	4	8	15
39	Charles Barkley UER	4	4	8	15
72	David Robinson	4	4	6	20
78	Shawn Kemp RC	6	10	15	25
89	John Stockton	4	4	6	15

1990-91 Fleer All-Stars

		NmMt 8	NmMt+ 8.5	MT 9	Gem 9.5/10
	Charles Barkley	4	4	6	30
	Larry Bird	4	▲6	▲12	30
	Hakeem Olajuwon	4	4	6	30
	Magic Johnson	4	4	8	50
	Michael Jordan	10	12	30	150
0	David Robinson	4	4	10	30
2	Patrick Ewing	4	4	6	20

1990-91 Fleer Rookie Sensations

		NmMt 8	NmMt+ 8.5	MT 9	Gem 9.5/10
	David Robinson	8	10	20	60
	Tim Hardaway	6	8	12	40

1990-91 Fleer Update

		NmMt 8	NmMt+ 8.5	MT 9	Gem 9.5/10
J92	Gary Payton RC	5	8	12	40

1990-91 Hoops

		NmMt 8	NmMt+ 8.5	MT 9	Gem 9.5/10
5	Michael Jordan AS SP	4	8	20	50
65	Michael Jordan	8	10	▲20	80
205	Mark Jackson/Lyle and Erik Menendez in background	▲25	▲30	▲60	
248	Drazen Petrovic RC	4	4	15	30
391	Gary Payton RC	4	4	10	30

1990-91 SkyBox

		NmMt 8	NmMt+ 8.5	MT 9	Gem 9.5/10
41	Michael Jordan	8	10	15	40
268	Shawn Kemp RC	4	4	10	30
365	Gary Payton RC	4	6	12	30

1991-92 Fleer

		NmMt 8	NmMt+ 8.5	MT 9	Gem 9.5/10
29	Michael Jordan	8	10	▲20	▲80
211	Michael Jordan AS	8	10	30	40

1991-92 Fleer Pro-Visions

		NmMt 8	NmMt+ 8.5	MT 9	Gem 9.5/10
2	Michael Jordan	4	6	15	▲50

1991-92 Hoops

		NmMt 8	NmMt+ 8.5	MT 9	Gem 9.5/10
30	Michael Jordan	4	6	12	25
253	Michael Jordan AS	4	6	12	30
455	Michael Jordan SC	4	▲8	▲20	▲40
579	Michael Jordan USA	5	8	▲15	▲60

1991-92 Hoops All-Star MVP's

		NmMt 8	NmMt+ 8.5	MT 9	Gem 9.5/10
9	Michael Jordan	10	15	20	80

1991-92 Hoops Slam Dunk

		NmMt 8	NmMt+ 8.5	MT 9	Gem 9.5/10
4	Michael Jordan	12	15	30	100

1991-92 SkyBox

		NmMt 8	NmMt+ 8.5	MT 9	Gem 9.5/10
39	Michael Jordan	5	8	15	40
534	Michael Jordan USA	6	8	15	40
572	Michael Jordan SAL	6	8	12	30

1991-92 Upper Deck

		NmMt 8	NmMt+ 8.5	MT 9	Gem 9.5/10
34	M.Johnson/M.Jordan CC	4	5	8	25
44	Michael Jordan	4	5	10	25
48	Michael Jordan AS CL	4	5	8	25
452	Michael Jordan AS	4	4	6	20

1991-92 Upper Deck Award Winner Holograms

		NmMt 8	NmMt+ 8.5	MT 9	Gem 9.5/10
AW1	Michael Jordan	8	12	20	50
AW4	Michael Jordan	8	12	20	50

1992 Classic

		NmMt 8	NmMt+ 8.5	MT 9	Gem 9.5/10
1	Shaquille O'Neal	8	10	15	25

1992 Classic Gold

		NmMt 8	NmMt+ 8.5	MT 9	Gem 9.5/10
1	Shaquille O'Neal	8	12	25	40

1992-93 Fleer

		NmMt 8	NmMt+ 8.5	MT 9	Gem 9.5/10
32	Michael Jordan	▲8	12	▲30	▲60
238	Michael Jordan LL	▲6	▲8	12	30
298	Shaquille O'Neal SD	4	6	12	40
401	Shaquille O'Neal RC	6	8	20	40

1992-93 Fleer All-Stars

		NmMt 8	NmMt+ 8.5	MT 9	Gem 9.5/10
6	Michael Jordan	▲50	60	250	1,200

1992-93 Fleer Team Leaders

		NmMt 8	NmMt+ 8.5	MT 9	Gem 9.5/10
4	Michael Jordan	200	250	450	

1992-93 Fleer Total D

		NmMt 8	NmMt+ 8.5	MT 9	Gem 9.5/10
5	Michael Jordan	120	150	400	

1992-93 Hoops

		NmMt 8	NmMt+ 8.5	MT 9	Gem 9.5/10
30	Michael Jordan	▲6	▲8	▲15	▲40
442	Shaquille O'Neal RC	6	8	10	20

1992-93 Hoops Draft Redemption

		NmMt 8	NmMt+ 8.5	MT 9	Gem 9.5/10
A	Shaquille O'Neal	▼20	▼25	40	120
B	Alonzo Mourning	6	8	12	30

1992-93 Hoops Magic's All-Rookies

		NmMt 8	NmMt+ 8.5	MT 9	Gem 9.5/10
1	Shaquille O'Neal	▼15	▼25	40	120
2	Alonzo Mourning	▼8	▼10	▼20	

1992-93 Hoops Supreme Court

		NmMt 8	NmMt+ 8.5	MT 9	Gem 9.5/10
SC1	Michael Jordan	8	10	20	50

1992-93 SkyBox

		NmMt 8	NmMt+ 8.5	MT 9	Gem 9.5/10
31	Michael Jordan	6	10	20	60
314	Michael Jordan MVP	4	5	10	25
382	Shaquille O'Neal SP RC	6	8	10	30

1992-93 SkyBox Draft Picks

		NmMt 8	NmMt+ 8.5	MT 9	Gem 9.5/10
DP1	Shaquille O'Neal	▼12	▼15	30	▲60

1992-93 SkyBox Olympic Team

		NmMt 8	NmMt+ 8.5	MT 9	Gem 9.5/10
USA11	Michael Jordan	8	12	30	80

1992-93 Stadium Club

		NmMt 8	NmMt+ 8.5	MT 9	Gem 9.5/10
1	Michael Jordan	8	10	20	50
201	Shaquille O'Neal MC	5	8	12	25
210	Michael Jordan MC	8	10	15	25
247	Shaquille O'Neal RC	8	10	15	40

1992-93 Stadium Club Beam Team

		NmMt 8	NmMt+ 8.5	MT 9	Gem 9.5/10
1	Michael Jordan	60	80	150	500
3	Shawn Kemp	6	10	15	40
11	John Stockton	4	10	20	50
21	Shaquille O'Neal	60	80	120	500

1992-93 Topps

		NmMt 8	NmMt+ 8.5	MT 9	Gem 9.5/10
115	Michael Jordan AS	4	5	8	20
141	Michael Jordan	4	5	10	25
205	Michael Jordan 50P	4	5	10	25
362	Shaquille O'Neal RC	8	10	12	30

1992-93 Topps Gold

		NmMt 8	NmMt+ 8.5	MT 9	Gem 9.5/10
141	Michael Jordan	8	12	25	60
362	Shaquille O'Neal	12	15	30	100

1992-93 Ultra

		NmMt 8	NmMt+ 8.5	MT 9	Gem 9.5/10
27	Michael Jordan	6	10	▼20	▲50
328	Shaquille O'Neal RC	6	8	12	30

1992-93 Ultra All-NBA

		NmMt 8	NmMt+ 8.5	MT 9	Gem 9.5/10
4	Michael Jordan	15	20	25	▲60

1992-93 Ultra All-Rookies

		NmMt 8	NmMt+ 8.5	MT 9	Gem 9.5/10
6	Alonzo Mourning	5	6	10	20
7	Shaquille O'Neal	▼8	▼12	▼20	50

1992-93 Ultra Award Winners

		NmMt 8	NmMt+ 8.5	MT 9	Gem 9.5/10
1	Michael Jordan	▼12	▼15	25	60

1992-93 Ultra Rejectors

		NmMt 8	NmMt+ 8.5	MT 9	Gem 9.5/10
4	Shaquille O'Neal	8	10	▲25	▲50

1992-93 Upper Deck

		NmMt 8	NmMt+ 8.5	MT 9	Gem 9.5/10
1	Shaquille O'Neal SP RC	20	25	40	300
1B	Shaquille O'Neal TRADE	10	15	20	60
23	Michael Jordan	▲6	10	▲25	▲50
67	Michael Jordan MVP	4	4	6	15
453A	M.Jordan FACE 85 ERR	15	25	40	
474	Shaquille O'Neal TP	4	6	10	25

1992-93 Upper Deck All-Division

		NmMt 8	NmMt+ 8.5	MT 9	Gem 9.5/10
AD1	Shaquille O'Neal	6	8	10	30
AD9	Michael Jordan	6	12	20	40

1992-93 Upper Deck Award Winner Holograms

		NmMt 8	NmMt+ 8.5	MT 9	Gem 9.5/10
AW9	Michael Jordan	▼8	▼12	▼25	50

1992-93 Upper Deck 15000 Point Club

		NmMt 8	NmMt+ 8.5	MT 9	Gem 9.5/10
PC4	Michael Jordan	12	20	30	100

1992-93 Upper Deck Rookie Standouts

		NmMt 8	NmMt+ 8.5	MT 9	Gem 9.5/10
RS15	Shaquille O'Neal	10	15	20	50

1992-93 Upper Deck Team MVPs

		NmMt 8	NmMt+ 8.5	MT 9	Gem 9.5/10
TM1	Michael Jordan CL	▼12	▼15	25	50
TM5	Michael Jordan	15	20	30	60

1993-94 Finest

		NmMt 8	NmMt+ 8.5	MT 9	Gem 9.5/10
1	Michael Jordan	20	25	▲60	150
189	Anfernee Hardaway RC	8	10	▲15	60
212	Chris Webber RC	8	10	▲20	▼80

1993-94 Finest Refractors

		NmMt 8	NmMt+ 8.5	MT 9	Gem 9.5/10
1	Michael Jordan	400	▲600	▲900	▲3,000
3	Shaquille O'Neal SP !	60	80	120	
189	Anfernee Hardaway	80	120	200	500
212	Chris Webber SP !	120	150	200	

1993-94 Fleer

		NmMt 8	NmMt+ 8.5	MT 9	Gem 9.5/10
28	Michael Jordan	4	6	▲15	▲50
224	Michael Jordan LL	4	5	8	20

1993-94 Fleer All-Stars

		NmMt 8	NmMt+ 8.5	MT 9	Gem 9.5/10
5	Michael Jordan	20	30	80	

1993-94 Fleer Living Legends

		NmMt 8	NmMt+ 8.5	MT 9	Gem 9.5/10
4	Michael Jordan	25	40	150	500

1993-94 Fleer NBA Superstars

		NmMt 8	NmMt+ 8.5	MT 9	Gem 9.5/10
7	Michael Jordan	8	10	20	50

1993-94 Fleer Sharpshooters

		NmMt 8	NmMt+ 8.5	MT 9	Gem 9.5/10
3	Michael Jordan	12	15	30	100

1993-94 Hoops

		NmMt 8	NmMt+ 8.5	MT 9	Gem 9.5/10
28	Michael Jordan	4	5	▲12	30
257	Michael Jordan AS	4	5	8	20

1993-94 Hoops Fifth Anniversary Gold

		NmMt 8	NmMt+ 8.5	MT 9	Gem 9.5/10
28	Michael Jordan	▲12	▲20	▲40	

1993-94 Hoops Draft Redemption

		NmMt 8	NmMt+ 8.5	MT 9	Gem 9.5/10
LP1	Chris Webber	10	15	30	100
LP3	Anfernee Hardaway	10	15	20	35

1993-94 Hoops Supreme Court

		NmMt 8	NmMt+ 8.5	MT 9	Gem 9.5/10
SC11	Michael Jordan	6	12	20	40

1993-94 SkyBox Premium

		NmMt 8	NmMt+ 8.5	MT 9	Gem 9.5/10
14	Michael Jordan PO	6	▼8	▼12	20
45	Michael Jordan	6	12	15	▲25
227	Chris Webber RC	4	6	10	20

1993-94 SkyBox Premium Center Stage

		NmMt 8	NmMt+ 8.5	MT 9	Gem 9.5/10
CS1	Michael Jordan	15	▲25	50	▲200

1993-94 SkyBox Premium Draft Picks

		NmMt 8	NmMt+ 8.5	MT 9	Gem 9.5/10
DP1	Chris Webber	8	10	▼12	25

1993-94 SkyBox Premium Dynamic Dunks

		NmMt 8	NmMt+ 8.5	MT 9	Gem 9.5/1
D4	Michael Jordan	▲25	30	▲60	▲400

1993-94 SkyBox Premium Showdown Serie

		NmMt 8	NmMt+ 8.5	MT 9	Gem 9.5/1
SS11	C.Drexler/M.Jordan	4	▲6	▲10	▲25

1993-94 Stadium Club

		NmMt 8	NmMt+ 8.5	MT 9	Gem 9.5/1
169	Michael Jordan	5	8	12	30

1993-94 Stadium Club First Day Issue

		NmMt 8	NmMt+ 8.5	MT 9	Gem 9.5/1
1	Michael Jordan TD	80	100	▲120	300

1993-94 Stadium Club Beam Team

		NmMt 8	NmMt+ 8.5	MT 9	Gem 9.5/1
4	Michael Jordan	40	60	150	

1993-94 Topps

		NmMt 8	NmMt+ 8.5	MT 9	Gem 9.5/1
224	Chris Webber RC	5	8	20	

1993-94 Ultra

		NmMt 8	NmMt+ 8.5	MT 9	Gem 9.5/1
30	Michael Jordan	▲6	▼8	▼12	▲35

1993-94 Ultra All-Defensive

		NmMt 8	NmMt+ 8.5	MT 9	Gem 9.5/1
2	Michael Jordan	60	80	150	300

1993-94 Ultra All-NBA

		NmMt 8	NmMt+ 8.5	MT 9	Gem 9.5/1
2	Michael Jordan	12	20	30	100

1993-94 Ultra Famous Nicknames

		NmMt 8	NmMt+ 8.5	MT 9	Gem 9.5/1
7	Michael Jordan	15	20	40	150

1993-94 Ultra Inside/Outside

		NmMt 8	NmMt+ 8.5	MT 9	Gem 9.5/1
4	Michael Jordan	▲10	▲20	▲30	

1993-94 Ultra Power In The Key

		NmMt 8	NmMt+ 8.5	MT 9	Gem 9.5/1
2	Michael Jordan	▲60	80	▲220	

1993-94 Ultra Scoring Kings

		NmMt 8	NmMt+ 8.5	MT 9	Gem 9.5/1
5	Michael Jordan	200	300	500	1,200
8	Shaquille O'Neal	20	30	50	

1993-94 Upper Deck

		NmMt 8	NmMt+ 8.5	MT 9	Gem 9.5/1
23A	Michael Jordan	5	10	15	30

1993-94 Upper Deck All-NBA

		NmMt 8	NmMt+ 8.5	MT 9	Gem 9.5/1
AN4	Michael Jordan	8	10	15	100
AN15	Michael Jordan CL	8	10	15	100

1993-94 Upper Deck SE Behind the Glass

		NmMt 8	NmMt+ 8.5	MT 9	Gem 9.5/1
G11	Michael Jordan	20	40	200	500

93-94 Upper Deck SE Die Cut All-Stars

	NmMt 8	NmMt+ 8.5	MT 9	Gem 9.5/10
Shaquille O'Neal	20	30	60	

94-95 Emotion

	NmMt 8	NmMt+ 8.5	MT 9	Gem 9.5/10
Jason Kidd RC	▼4	▼5	8	15
Michael Jordan	10	15	▼25	60

94-95 Emotion N-Tense

	NmMt 8	NmMt+ 8.5	MT 9	Gem 9.5/10
Michael Jordan	▲40	▲60	▲120	200
Shaquille O'Neal	8	12	15	30

94-95 Finest

	NmMt 8	NmMt+ 8.5	MT 9	Gem 9.5/10
Grant Hill CB	4	6	10	30
Grant Hill RC	10	15	25	50
Jason Kidd RC	10	12	20	50
Michael Jordan	25	30	▲50	▲200

94-95 Finest Refractors

	NmMt 8	NmMt+ 8.5	MT 9	Gem 9.5/10
Grant Hill	100	150	300	600
Jason Kidd	80	150	300	600
Michael Jordan	200	250	400	800

94-95 Flair

	NmMt 8	NmMt+ 8.5	MT 9	Gem 9.5/10
Michael Jordan	8	12	25	60

94-95 SP

	NmMt 8	NmMt+ 8.5	MT 9	Gem 9.5/10
Jason Kidd FOIL RC	5	8	15	50
Grant Hill FOIL RC	6	12	25	100
RM.Jordan Red	8	15	40	100

94-95 SP Die Cuts

	NmMt 8	NmMt+ 8.5	MT 9	Gem 9.5/10
Jason Kidd	10	15	25	

94-95 SP Championship Playoff Heroes

	NmMt 8	NmMt+ 8.5	MT 9	Gem 9.5/10
Michael Jordan	8	15	25	50

94-95 SP Championship Playoff Heroes Die Cuts

	NmMt 8	NmMt+ 8.5	MT 9	Gem 9.5/10
Michael Jordan	50	60	120	300

94-95 Topps

	NmMt 8	NmMt+ 8.5	MT 9	Gem 9.5/10
Jason Kidd RC	4	4	4	15
Grant Hill RC	4	4	4	15

94-95 Upper Deck

	NmMt 8	NmMt+ 8.5	MT 9	Gem 9.5/10
Grant Hill RC	4	4	6	25
Jason Kidd RC	4	4	6	25

1995-96 Collector's Choice

	NmMt 8	NmMt+ 8.5	MT 9	Gem 9.5/10
Kevin Garnett RC	4	4	6	12

1995-96 E-XL

		NmMt 8	NmMt+ 8.5	MT 9	Gem 9.5/10
10	Michael Jordan	5	8	20	50
49	Kevin Garnett RC	4	5	8	20

1995-96 E-XL Blue

		NmMt 8	NmMt+ 8.5	MT 9	Gem 9.5/10
10	Michael Jordan	10	15	25	60
49	Kevin Garnett RC	6	10	15	25

1995-96 E-XL Natural Born Thrillers

		NmMt 8	NmMt+ 8.5	MT 9	Gem 9.5/10
1	Michael Jordan	150	250	400	▲800

1995-96 E-XL No Boundaries

		NmMt 8	NmMt+ 8.5	MT 9	Gem 9.5/10
1	Michael Jordan	▲40	▲50	▲100	▲250

1995-96 Finest

		NmMt 8	NmMt+ 8.5	MT 9	Gem 9.5/10
115	Kevin Garnett RC	25	30	60	250
229	Michael Jordan	20	25	40	▼120

1995-96 Finest Refractors

		NmMt 8	NmMt+ 8.5	MT 9	Gem 9.5/10
229	Michael Jordan	200	250	400	1,000

1995-96 Finest Hot Stuff

		NmMt 8	NmMt+ 8.5	MT 9	Gem 9.5/10
HS1	Michael Jordan	20	30	50	200

1995-96 Finest Mystery

		NmMt 8	NmMt+ 8.5	MT 9	Gem 9.5/10
M1	Michael Jordan	▲20	25	40	120

1995-96 Finest Veteran/Rookie

		NmMt 8	NmMt+ 8.5	MT 9	Gem 9.5/10
RV5	K.Garnett/T.Gugliotta	25	30	40	
RV20	J.Caffey/M.Jordan	50	80	120	300

1995-96 Flair

		NmMt 8	NmMt+ 8.5	MT 9	Gem 9.5/10
15	Michael Jordan	6	8	20	80
206	Kevin Garnett RC	8	12	15	40

1995-96 Flair Anticipation

		NmMt 8	NmMt+ 8.5	MT 9	Gem 9.5/10
2	Michael Jordan	80	120	▲200	▲400

1995-96 Flair Class of '95

		NmMt 8	NmMt+ 8.5	MT 9	Gem 9.5/10
R2	Kevin Garnett	8	15	20	30

1995-96 Flair Hot Numbers

		NmMt 8	NmMt+ 8.5	MT 9	Gem 9.5/10
4	Michael Jordan	300	400	600	▲900
11	Shaquille O'Neal	25	30	60	120

1995-96 Flair New Heights

		NmMt 8	NmMt+ 8.5	MT 9	Gem 9.5/10
4	Michael Jordan	60	100	▲175	300

1995-96 Flair Wave of the Future

		NmMt 8	NmMt+ 8.5	MT 9	Gem 9.5/10
3	Kevin Garnett	8	10	15	40

1995-96 Fleer

		NmMt 8	NmMt+ 8.5	MT 9	Gem 9.5/10
22	Michael Jordan	▲6	▲8	▲10	40

1995-96 Fleer Flair Hardwood Leaders

		NmMt 8	NmMt+ 8.5	MT 9	Gem 9.5/10
4	Michael Jordan	▲15	▲20	25	▲60

1995-96 Hoops Hot List

		NmMt 8	NmMt+ 8.5	MT 9	Gem 9.5/10
1	Michael Jordan	▲60	▲80	▲120	▲300

1995-96 Hoops SkyView

		NmMt 8	NmMt+ 8.5	MT 9	Gem 9.5/10
SV1	Michael Jordan	120	150	250	500

1995-96 Metal

		NmMt 8	NmMt+ 8.5	MT 9	Gem 9.5/10
167	Kevin Garnett RC	5	6	8	20
212	Michael Jordan NB	4	8	15	40

1995-96 Metal Maximum Metal

		NmMt 8	NmMt+ 8.5	MT 9	Gem 9.5/10
4	Michael Jordan	25	40	80	200

1995-96 Metal Scoring Magnets

		NmMt 8	NmMt+ 8.5	MT 9	Gem 9.5/10
4	Michael Jordan	▲100	▲150	▲200	▲400

1995-96 Metal Slick Silver

		NmMt 8	NmMt+ 8.5	MT 9	Gem 9.5/10
3	Michael Jordan	30	50	80	200

1995-96 SkyBox Premium Larger Than Life

		NmMt 8	NmMt+ 8.5	MT 9	Gem 9.5/10
L1	Michael Jordan	▲80	▲150	▲400	

1995-96 SkyBox Premium Meltdown

		NmMt 8	NmMt+ 8.5	MT 9	Gem 9.5/10
M1	Michael Jordan	▲200	▲250	400	

1995-96 SP

		NmMt 8	NmMt+ 8.5	MT 9	Gem 9.5/10
23	Michael Jordan	4	6	15	50
159	Kevin Garnett RC	8	10	12	30
163	Arvydas Sabonis RC	4	5	15	50

1995-96 SP All-Stars

		NmMt 8	NmMt+ 8.5	MT 9	Gem 9.5/10
AS2	Michael Jordan	15	20	30	50
AS28	Kevin Garnett	6	8	10	30

1995-96 SP All-Stars Gold

		NmMt 8	NmMt+ 8.5	MT 9	Gem 9.5/10
AS2	Michael Jordan	70	80	150	

1995-96 SP Holoviews

		NmMt 8	NmMt+ 8.5	MT 9	Gem 9.5/10
PC5	Michael Jordan	30	40	60	150

1995-96 Stadium Club

		NmMt 8	NmMt+ 8.5	MT 9	Gem 9.5/10
1	Michael Jordan	5	8	12	40
343	Kevin Garnett RC	5	10	15	40

1995-96 Stadium Club Beam Team

		NmMt 8	NmMt+ 8.5	MT 9	Gem 9.5/10
BT14	Michael Jordan	100	150	300	800

1995-96 Stadium Club Warp Speed

		NmMt 8	NmMt+ 8.5	MT 9	Gem 9.5/10
WS1	Michael Jordan	60	80	200	400

1995-96 Topps

		NmMt 8	NmMt+ 8.5	MT 9	Gem 9.5/10
237	Kevin Garnett RC	4	5	8	20

1995-96 Topps Draft Redemption

		NmMt 8	NmMt+ 8.5	MT 9	Gem 9.5/10
5	Kevin Garnett	50	60	100	200

1995-96 Topps Power Boosters

		NmMt 8	NmMt+ 8.5	MT 9	Gem 9.5/10
277	Michael Jordan	▲60	▲80	150	250

1995-96 Topps Spark Plugs

		NmMt 8	NmMt+ 8.5	MT 9	Gem 9.5/10
SP2	Michael Jordan	12	15	40	100

1995-96 Topps Top Flight

		NmMt 8	NmMt+ 8.5	MT 9	Gem 9.5/10
TF1	Michael Jordan	▲15	▲20	▲50	▲150

1995-96 Ultra

		NmMt 8	NmMt+ 8.5	MT 9	Gem 9.5/10
274	Kevin Garnett RC	6	10	12	▲25

1995-96 Ultra Gold Medallion

		NmMt 8	NmMt+ 8.5	MT 9	Gem 9.5/10
25	Michael Jordan	▲60	80	120	300

1995-96 Ultra Double Trouble

		NmMt 8	NmMt+ 8.5	MT 9	Gem 9.5/10
3	Michael Jordan	8	12	25	60

1995-96 Upper Deck

		NmMt 8	NmMt+ 8.5	MT 9	Gem 9.5/10
23	Michael Jordan	5	8	15	40
273	Kevin Garnett RC	6	10	15	25

1995-96 Upper Deck Special Edition

		NmMt 8	NmMt+ 8.5	MT 9	Gem 9.5/10
100	Michael Jordan	15	30	60	150

1996 Score Board Rookies Die Cuts

		NmMt 8	NmMt+ 8.5	MT 9	Gem 9.5/10
13	Kobe Bryant	20	25	40	

1996 SPx

		NmMt 8	NmMt+ 8.5	MT 9	Gem 9.5/10
8	Michael Jordan	12	15	30	▲120
R1	Michael Jordan RB	12	20	30	80

1996 SPx Gold

		NmMt 8	NmMt+ 8.5	MT 9	Gem 9.5/10
8	Michael Jordan	50	80	100	200

1996 SPx Holoview Heroes

		NmMt 8	NmMt+ 8.5	MT 9	Gem 9.5/10
H1	Michael Jordan	20	30	60	200

1996-97 Bowman's Best

		NmMt 8	NmMt+ 8.5	MT 9	Gem 9.5/10
80	Michael Jordan	8	12	25	50
R1	Allen Iverson RC	6	10	15	30
R5	Ray Allen RC	5	6	12	20
R18	Steve Nash RC	5	8	12	20
R23	Kobe Bryant RC	15	20	40	80

1996-97 Bowman's Best Atomic Refractors

		NmMt 8	NmMt+ 8.5	MT 9	Gem 9.5/10
80	Michael Jordan	150	300	500	800
R1	Allen Iverson	60	80	100	
R18	Steve Nash	60	80	100	200
R23	Kobe Bryant	300	450	700	1,500

1996-97 Bowman's Best Refractors

		NmMt 8	NmMt+ 8.5	MT 9	Gem 9.5/10
80	Michael Jordan	80	120	250	
R1	Allen Iverson	30	40	50	
R5	Ray Allen	25	30	40	
R18	Steve Nash	30	40	50	
R23	Kobe Bryant	120	150	300	

1996-97 Bowman's Best Honor Roll

		NmMt 8	NmMt+ 8.5	MT 9	Gem 9.5/10
HR2	M.Jordan/H.Olajuwon	30	40	60	100

1996-97 Bowman's Best Picks

		NmMt 8	NmMt+ 8.5	MT 9	Gem 9.5/10
BP10	Kobe Bryant	25	30	60	

1996-97 Bowman's Best Picks Atomic Refractors

		NmMt 8	NmMt+ 8.5	MT 9	Gem 9.5/10
BP10	Kobe Bryant	300	350	500	

1996-97 Bowman's Best Picks Refractors

		NmMt 8	NmMt+ 8.5	MT 9	Gem 9.5/10
BP10	Kobe Bryant	100	120	200	

1996-97 Bowman's Best Shots

		NmMt 8	NmMt+ 8.5	MT 9	Gem 9.5/10
BS6	Michael Jordan	15	20	40	80

1996-97 Bowman's Best Shots Atomic Refractors

		NmMt 8	NmMt+ 8.5	MT 9	Gem 9.5/10
BS6	Michael Jordan	100	200	300	400

1996-97 Bowman's Best Shots Refractors

		NmMt 8	NmMt+ 8.5	MT 9	Gem 9.5/10
BS6	Michael Jordan	40	50	80	200

1996-97 Collector's Choice

		NmMt 8	NmMt+ 8.5	MT 9	Gem 9.5/10
267	Kobe Bryant RC	5	8	12	30
301	Allen Iverson RC	4	4	4	10

1996-97 E-X2000

		NmMt 8	NmMt+ 8.5	MT 9	Gem 9.5/10
9	Michael Jordan	20	25	50	200
30	Kobe Bryant RC	40	60	200	1,000
37	Ray Allen RC	15	20	30	
53	Allen Iverson RC	10	15	40	

1996-97 E-X2000 Credentials

		NmMt 8	NmMt+ 8.5	MT 9	Gem 9.5/10
9	Michael Jordan	4,000	5,000	6,000	
30	Kobe Bryant	2,500	4,000	5,000	
53	Allen Iverson	200	300	400	

1996-97 E-X2000 A Cut Above

		NmMt 8	NmMt+ 8.5	MT 9	Gem 9.5/1
5	Michael Jordan	1,500	2,000	2,500	

1996-97 E-X2000 Net Assets

		NmMt 8	NmMt+ 8.5	MT 9	Gem 9.5/10
8	Michael Jordan	100	200	350	500

1996-97 E-X2000 Star Date 2000

		NmMt 8	NmMt+ 8.5	MT 9	Gem 9.5/1
3	Kobe Bryant	30	40	60	150
7	Allen Iverson	5	8	12	40

1996-97 Finest

		NmMt 8	NmMt+ 8.5	MT 9	Gem 9.5/10
22	Ray Allen B RC	8	12	15	30
50	Michael Jordan B	10	12	20	50
69	Allen Iverson B RC	6	8	20	30
74	Kobe Bryant B RC	25	30	40	100
75	Steve Nash B RC	10	12	15	30
127	Michael Jordan S	15	20	30	
269	Kobe Bryant G	80	120	150	300
291	Michael Jordan G	60	80	150	300

1996-97 Finest Refractors

		NmMt 8	NmMt+ 8.5	MT 9	Gem 9.5/10
22	Ray Allen B	35	50	60	
50	Michael Jordan B	100	150	250	
69	Allen Iverson B	50	60	100	
74	Kobe Bryant B	350	400	700	3,000
75	Steve Nash B	50	60	100	
127	Michael Jordan S	100	150	250	400
269	Kobe Bryant G	500	800	1,200	2,000
291	Michael Jordan G	800	1,000	1,500	3,000

1996-97 Flair Showcase Row 2

		NmMt 8	NmMt+ 8.5	MT 9	Gem 9.5/1
3	Allen Iverson RC	5	6	10	25
23	Michael Jordan	10	15	30	60
31	Kobe Bryant RC	15	20	30	80

1996-97 Flair Showcase Row 1

		NmMt 8	NmMt+ 8.5	MT 9	Gem 9.5/1
23	Michael Jordan	15	30	50	
31	Kobe Bryant	20	25	50	100

1996-97 Flair Showcase Row 0

		NmMt 8	NmMt+ 8.5	MT 9	Gem 9.5/1
23	Michael Jordan	80	120	250	500
31	Kobe Bryant	40	60	100	250
35	Ray Allen	6	8	12	30

1996-97 Flair Showcase Class of '96

		NmMt 8	NmMt+ 8.5	MT 9	Gem 9.5/1
4	Kobe Bryant	12	25	50	100
10	Allen Iverson	5	10	15	35
15	Steve Nash	5	10	15	25

1996-97 Flair Showcase Hot Shots

	NmMt 8	NmMt+ 8.5	MT 9	Gem 9.5/10
Michael Jordan	1,000	1,500	3,000	4,000

1996-97 Fleer

	NmMt 8	NmMt+ 8.5	MT 9	Gem 9.5/10
Kobe Bryant RC	15	15	25	50
Allen Iverson RC	4	4	8	20
Steve Nash RC	4	4	8	25

1996-97 Fleer Decade of Excellence

	NmMt 8	NmMt+ 8.5	MT 9	Gem 9.5/10
Michael Jordan	15	30	60	100

1996-97 Fleer Game Breakers

	NmMt 8	NmMt+ 8.5	MT 9	Gem 9.5/10
M.Jordan/S.Pippen	50	80	120	

1996-97 Fleer Lucky 13

	NmMt 8	NmMt+ 8.5	MT 9	Gem 9.5/10
Allen Iverson	5	10	15	30
Ray Allen	5	10	15	25
Kobe Bryant	15	30	40	150

1996-97 Fleer Rookie Sensations

	NmMt 8	NmMt+ 8.5	MT 9	Gem 9.5/10
Kobe Bryant	50	60	100	200
Allen Iverson	20	25	30	

1996-97 Fleer Total O

	NmMt 8	NmMt+ 8.5	MT 9	Gem 9.5/10
Michael Jordan	60	80	200	300

1996-97 Hoops

	NmMt 8	NmMt+ 8.5	MT 9	Gem 9.5/10
Kobe Bryant RC	10	15	25	40
Allen Iverson RC	4	4	6	12
Steve Nash RC	4	6	10	40

1996-97 Hoops Hot List

	NmMt 8	NmMt+ 8.5	MT 9	Gem 9.5/10
Michael Jordan	30	60	120	250

1996-97 Hoops Rookies

	NmMt 8	NmMt+ 8.5	MT 9	Gem 9.5/10
Kobe Bryant	15	20	20	100

1996-97 Hoops Superfeats

	NmMt 8	NmMt+ 8.5	MT 9	Gem 9.5/10
Michael Jordan	15	20	40	100

1996-97 Metal

	NmMt 8	NmMt+ 8.5	MT 9	Gem 9.5/10
Michael Jordan	6	10	20	50
Kobe Bryant FF RC	12	15	20	50
Kobe Bryant	6	10	20	40
Allen Iverson RC	4	5	8	30
Michael Jordan MS	6	10	20	50

1996-97 Metal Cyber-Metal

	NmMt 8	NmMt+ 8.5	MT 9	Gem 9.5/10
Kobe Bryant	15	25	40	80

1996-97 Metal Decade of Excellence

	NmMt 8	NmMt+ 8.5	MT 9	Gem 9.5/10
Michael Jordan	30	40	60	100

1996-97 Metal Freshly Forged

		NmMt 8	NmMt+ 8.5	MT 9	Gem 9.5/10
3	Kobe Bryant	20	25	40	100

1996-97 Metal Maximum Metal

		NmMt 8	NmMt+ 8.5	MT 9	Gem 9.5/10
4	Michael Jordan	200	250	400	600

1996-97 Metal Metal Edge

		NmMt 8	NmMt+ 8.5	MT 9	Gem 9.5/10
15	Kobe Bryant	15	25	40	

1996-97 Metal Molten Metal

		NmMt 8	NmMt+ 8.5	MT 9	Gem 9.5/10
18	Michael Jordan	300	350	400	600

1996-97 Metal Net-Rageous

		NmMt 8	NmMt+ 8.5	MT 9	Gem 9.5/10
5	Michael Jordan	450	600	800	2,000

1996-97 Metal Platinum Portraits

		NmMt 8	NmMt+ 8.5	MT 9	Gem 9.5/10
5	Michael Jordan	150	250	400	600

1996-97 Metal Steel Slammin'

		NmMt 8	NmMt+ 8.5	MT 9	Gem 9.5/10
6	Michael Jordan	80	100	200	400

1996-97 SkyBox Premium

		NmMt 8	NmMt+ 8.5	MT 9	Gem 9.5/10
16	Michael Jordan	4	6	10	30
55	Kobe Bryant RC	5	8	15	50
85	Allen Iverson RC	4	4	6	15
91	Steve Nash RC	4	6	10	25
203	Kobe Bryant ROO	6	10	20	40

1996-97 SkyBox Premium Rubies

		NmMt 8	NmMt+ 8.5	MT 9	Gem 9.5/10
55	Kobe Bryant	400	500	700	2,000
203	Kobe Bryant ROO	150	250	400	

1996-97 SkyBox Premium Golden Touch

		NmMt 8	NmMt+ 8.5	MT 9	Gem 9.5/10
5	Michael Jordan	400	500	800	1,500

1996-97 SkyBox Premium New Edition

		NmMt 8	NmMt+ 8.5	MT 9	Gem 9.5/10
3	Kobe Bryant	60	80	150	500

1996-97 SkyBox Premium Rookie Prevue

		NmMt 8	NmMt+ 8.5	MT 9	Gem 9.5/10
R3	Kobe Bryant	30	40	50	

1996-97 SP

		NmMt 8	NmMt+ 8.5	MT 9	Gem 9.5/10
134	Kobe Bryant RC	15	20	20	50
136	Ray Allen RC	4	5	10	20
141	Allen Iverson RC	5	6	10	25
142	Steve Nash RC	6	10	12	20

1996-97 SP Holoviews

		NmMt 8	NmMt+ 8.5	MT 9	Gem 9.5/10
PC5	Michael Jordan	30	40	80	200
PC18	Kobe Bryant	40	60	120	300

1996-97 Stadium Club

		NmMt 8	NmMt+ 8.5	MT 9	Gem 9.5/10
101	Michael Jordan	6	10	15	40

1996-97 Stadium Club Rookie Showcase

		NmMt 8	NmMt+ 8.5	MT 9	Gem 9.5/10
RS11	Kobe Bryant	25	30	40	80

1996-97 Stadium Club Rookies 1

		NmMt 8	NmMt+ 8.5	MT 9	Gem 9.5/10
R5	Ray Allen	4	6	10	20
R12	Kobe Bryant	15	20	30	50

1996-97 Stadium Club Rookies 2

		NmMt 8	NmMt+ 8.5	MT 9	Gem 9.5/10
R9	Kobe Bryant	10	15	25	50

1996-97 Stadium Club Top Crop

		NmMt 8	NmMt+ 8.5	MT 9	Gem 9.5/10
TC9	M.Jordan/G.Payton	20	30	80	200

1996-97 Topps

		NmMt 8	NmMt+ 8.5	MT 9	Gem 9.5/10
138	Kobe Bryant RC	15	20	25	80
139	Michael Jordan	4	6	10	25
171	Allen Iverson RC	4	5	8	15
182	Steve Nash RC	4	5	10	30

1996-97 Topps NBA at 50

		NmMt 8	NmMt+ 8.5	MT 9	Gem 9.5/10
138	Kobe Bryant	30	60	120	400

1996-97 Topps Draft Redemption

		NmMt 8	NmMt+ 8.5	MT 9	Gem 9.5/10
1	Allen Iverson	20	30	50	150
5	Ray Allen	15	25	50	
13	Kobe Bryant	120	150	200	400

1996-97 Topps Holding Court Refractors

		NmMt 8	NmMt+ 8.5	MT 9	Gem 9.5/10
HC2	Michael Jordan	60	100	200	300

1996-97 Topps Pro Files

		NmMt 8	NmMt+ 8.5	MT 9	Gem 9.5/10
PF3	Michael Jordan	8	12	25	60

1996-97 Topps Season's Best

		NmMt 8	NmMt+ 8.5	MT 9	Gem 9.5/10
SB1	Michael Jordan	10	20	40	100
SB18	Michael Jordan	10	20	40	100

1996-97 Topps Youthquake

		NmMt 8	NmMt+ 8.5	MT 9	Gem 9.5/10
YQ1	Allen Iverson	8	12	20	60
YQ15	Kobe Bryant	25	30	60	200

1996-97 Topps Chrome

		NmMt 8	NmMt+ 8.5	MT 9	Gem 9.5/10
138	Kobe Bryant RC	400	500	▲700	▲1,500
139	Michael Jordan	20	30	50	200
171	Allen Iverson RC	25	40	60	200
182	Steve Nash RC	25	30	50	120
217	Ray Allen RC	20	30	50	125

1996-97 Topps Chrome Refractors

		NmMt 8	NmMt+ 8.5	MT 9	Gem 9.5/10
138	Kobe Bryant	3,500	4,000	▲8,000	▲12,000
139	Michael Jordan	800	1,000	2,000	4,000
171	Allen Iverson	400	500	1,000	2,000
182	Steve Nash	300	350	500	
217	Ray Allen	300	400	1,000	

1996-97 Topps Chrome Youthquake

		NmMt 8	NmMt+ 8.5	MT 9	Gem 9.5/10
YQ1	Allen Iverson	12	15	40	80
YQ9	Ray Allen	10	15	30	
YQ15	Kobe Bryant	60	80	120	250

1996-97 UD3

		NmMt 8	NmMt+ 8.5	MT 9	Gem 9.5/10
5	Ray Allen RC	4	6	10	20
14	Allen Iverson RC	4	4	6	15
15	Steve Nash RC	4	6	10	20
19	Kobe Bryant RC	15	20	25	50
43	Kobe Bryant	10	12	20	60

1996-97 Ultra

		NmMt 8	NmMt+ 8.5	MT 9	Gem 9.5/10
52	Kobe Bryant RC	12	15	25	100
60	Ray Allen RC	4	6	10	25
82	Allen Iverson RC	5	8	20	40
87	Steve Nash RC	5	6	10	25

1996-97 Ultra Gold Medallion

		NmMt 8	NmMt+ 8.5	MT 9	Gem 9.5/10
G52	Kobe Bryant	40	50	120	

1996-97 Ultra All-Rookies

		NmMt 8	NmMt+ 8.5	MT 9	Gem 9.5/10
3	Kobe Bryant	20	25	30	250

1996-97 Ultra Court Masters

		NmMt 8	NmMt+ 8.5	MT 9	Gem 9.5/10
2	Michael Jordan	350	500	700	1,000

1996-97 Ultra Fresh Faces

		NmMt 8	NmMt+ 8.5	MT 9	Gem 9.5/10
3	Kobe Bryant	40	50	80	400

1996-97 Ultra Full Court Trap

		NmMt 8	NmMt+ 8.5	MT 9	Gem 9.5/10
1	Michael Jordan	20	30	50	300

1996-97 Ultra Scoring Kings

		NmMt 8	NmMt+ 8.5	MT 9	Gem 9.5/10
4	Michael Jordan	150	200	400	1,000

1996-97 Upper Deck

		NmMt 8	NmMt+ 8.5	MT 9	Gem 9.5/10
16	Michael Jordan	5	8	12	25
58	Kobe Bryant RC	10	15	20	40
91	Allen Iverson RC	4	4	6	15
280	Steve Nash RC	4	5	12	30

1996-97 Upper Deck Fast Break Connections

		NmMt 8	NmMt+ 8.5	MT 9	Gem 9.5/10
FB23	Michael Jordan	15	20	25	50

1996-97 Upper Deck Rookie Exclusives

		NmMt 8	NmMt+ 8.5	MT 9	Gem 9.5/10
R1	Allen Iverson	4	6	10	25
R7	Ray Allen	4	6	8	20
R10	Kobe Bryant	8	10	20	50

1996-97 Upper Deck Smooth Grooves

		NmMt 8	NmMt+ 8.5	MT 9	Gem 9.5/10
SG8	Michael Jordan	40	50	100	200

1996-97 Z-Force

		NmMt 8	NmMt+ 8.5	MT 9	Gem 9.5/10
142	Kobe Bryant RC	12	15	25	50

1996-97 Z-Force Slam Cam

		NmMt 8	NmMt+ 8.5	MT 9	Gem 9.5/10
SC5	Michael Jordan	400	500	800	1,500

1996-97 Z-Force Zebut

		NmMt 8	NmMt+ 8.5	MT 9	Gem 9.5/10
3	Kobe Bryant	25	30	50	250

1996-97 Z-Force Zebut Z-peat

		NmMt 8	NmMt+ 8.5	MT 9	Gem 9.5/10
3	Kobe Bryant	250	300	400	

1997 SPx

		NmMt 8	NmMt+ 8.5	MT 9	Gem 9.5/10
22	Kobe Bryant	15	20	30	150

1997 SPx Gold

		NmMt 8	NmMt+ 8.5	MT 9	Gem 9.5/10
22	Kobe Bryant	50	60	80	

1997-98 Bowman's Best

		NmMt 8	NmMt+ 8.5	MT 9	Gem 9.5/10
60	Michael Jordan	4	6	10	25
96	Michael Jordan BP	4	5	8	25
106	Tim Duncan RC	4	5	10	30
111	Tracy McGrady RC	4	4	5	15

1997-98 Bowman's Best Atomic Refractors

		NmMt 8	NmMt+ 8.5	MT 9	Gem 9.5/10
60	Michael Jordan	150	200	300	500
106	Tim Duncan	150	200	350	500
111	Tracy McGrady	20	30	50	120

1997-98 Bowman's Best Refractors

		NmMt 8	NmMt+ 8.5	MT 9	Gem 9.5/10
60	Michael Jordan	40	60	120	250
106	Tim Duncan	50	80	120	200
111	Tracy McGrady	10	12	15	40

1997-98 Bowman's Best Mirror Image Atomic Refractors

		NmMt 8	NmMt+ 8.5	MT 9	Gem 9.5/10
MI1	Jordan/Mercer Marbury/Payton	50	60	80	150

1997-98 Bowman's Best Techniques

		NmMt 8	NmMt+ 8.5	MT 9	Gem 9.5/10
T2	Michael Jordan	10	15	30	60

1997-98 Bowman's Best Techniques Atomic Refractors

		NmMt 8	NmMt+ 8.5	MT 9	Gem 9.5/10
T2	Michael Jordan	120	200	300	500
T4	Kobe Bryant	25	40	60	90

1997-98 Bowman's Best Techniques Refractors

		NmMt 8	NmMt+ 8.5	MT 9	Gem 9.5/10
T2	Michael Jordan	40	60	100	200

1997-98 Collector's Choice StarQuest

		NmMt 8	NmMt+ 8.5	MT 9	Gem 9.5/1
83	Michael Jordan	40	50	60	80

1997-98 E-X2001

		NmMt 8	NmMt+ 8.5	MT 9	Gem 9.5/1
9	Michael Jordan	15	30	60	
75	Tim Duncan RC	10	20	30	60
79	Tracy McGrady RC	6	8	10	50

1997-98 E-X2001 Jambalaya

		NmMt 8	NmMt+ 8.5	MT 9	Gem 9.5/1
6	Michael Jordan	6,000	8,000	10,000	
12	Kobe Bryant	1,200	1,500	2,500	4,000

1997-98 Finest

		NmMt 8	NmMt+ 8.5	MT 9	Gem 9.5/1
101	Tim Duncan B RC	8	10	20	50
103	Chauncey Billups B RC	5	6	8	20
107	Tracy McGrady B RC	5	6	8	15
137	Kobe Bryant S	8	10	15	25
154	Michael Jordan G	50	60	80	120
262	Kobe Bryant B	4	8	10	25
271	Michael Jordan B	6	8	12	25
287	Michael Jordan S	12	15	25	50
294	Tracy McGrady S	4	6	10	20
306	Tim Duncan S	6	8	12	25
316	Tracy McGrady G	8	12	15	25
325	Tim Duncan G	25	30	40	60

1997-98 Finest Embossed

		NmMt 8	NmMt+ 8.5	MT 9	Gem 9.5/1
154	Michael Jordan G	60	100	150	250
287	Michael Jordan S	10	15	25	80

1997-98 Finest Refractors

		NmMt 8	NmMt+ 8.5	MT 9	Gem 9.5/1
101	Tim Duncan B	60	80	120	300
107	Tracy McGrady B	25	40	50	80
137	Kobe Bryant S	30	40	50	
154	Michael Jordan G	500	600	1,000	
271	Michael Jordan B	50	60	80	150
287	Michael Jordan S	150	200	300	500

1997-98 Flair Showcase Row 3

		NmMt 8	NmMt+ 8.5	MT 9	Gem 9.5/1
1	Michael Jordan	10	15	20	50
5	Tim Duncan RC	8	10	15	25

1997-98 Flair Showcase Row 2

		NmMt 8	NmMt+ 8.5	MT 9	Gem 9.5/1
5	Tim Duncan	6	8	12	30
18	Kobe Bryant	8	10	15	

1997-98 Flair Showcase Row 1

		NmMt 8	NmMt+ 8.5	MT 9	Gem 9.5/1
1	Michael Jordan	60	100	150	300
5	Tim Duncan	15	20	25	80
18	Kobe Bryant	15	20	25	

1997-98 Flair Showcase Row 0

	NmMt 8	NmMt+ 8.5	MT 9	Gem 9.5/10
Kobe Bryant	100	125	175	350

1997-98 Fleer

	NmMt 8	NmMt+ 8.5	MT 9	Gem 9.5/10
Michael Jordan	4	5	8	30
Tim Duncan RC	4	5	8	40
Tracy McGrady RC	4	4	5	15

1997-98 Fleer Tiffany Collection

	NmMt 8	NmMt+ 8.5	MT 9	Gem 9.5/10
Michael Jordan	100	150	300	600

1997-98 Fleer Decade of Excellence

	NmMt 8	NmMt+ 8.5	MT 9	Gem 9.5/10
Michael Jordan	25	40	80	200

1997-98 Fleer Soaring Stars

	NmMt 8	NmMt+ 8.5	MT 9	Gem 9.5/10
Michael Jordan	▲12	▲15	▲40	▲80

1997-98 Fleer Thrill Seekers

	NmMt 8	NmMt+ 8.5	MT 9	Gem 9.5/10
Michael Jordan	300	500	800	1,500

1997-98 Hoops

	NmMt 8	NmMt+ 8.5	MT 9	Gem 9.5/10
Tim Duncan RC	4	4	6	15
Tracy McGrady RC	4	4	4	12

1997-98 Hoops Frequent Flyer Club

	NmMt 8	NmMt+ 8.5	MT 9	Gem 9.5/10
Michael Jordan	30	40	80	200

1997-98 Hoops Frequent Flyer Club Upgrade

	NmMt 8	NmMt+ 8.5	MT 9	Gem 9.5/10
Michael Jordan	150	200	400	600

1997-98 Hoops HOOPerstars

	NmMt 8	NmMt+ 8.5	MT 9	Gem 9.5/10
Michael Jordan	125	200	300	500

1997-98 Metal Universe

	NmMt 8	NmMt+ 8.5	MT 9	Gem 9.5/10
Michael Jordan	80	100	200	500
Tracy McGrady RC	4	5	8	20
Tim Duncan RC	4	6	10	25

1997-98 Metal Universe Planet Metal

	NmMt 8	NmMt+ 8.5	MT 9	Gem 9.5/10
Michael Jordan	150	200	350	600

1997-98 Metal Universe Titanium

	NmMt 8	NmMt+ 8.5	MT 9	Gem 9.5/10
Michael Jordan	400	500	800	1,500
Kobe Bryant	100	125	200	400

1997-98 Metal Universe Championship

	NmMt 8	NmMt+ 8.5	MT 9	Gem 9.5/10
Tracy McGrady RC	4	5	8	20
Tim Duncan RC	4	6	10	25

1997-98 Metal Universe Championship Championship Galaxy

	NmMt 8	NmMt+ 8.5	MT 9	Gem 9.5/10
Michael Jordan	750	800	1,000	2,000

1997-98 SkyBox Premium

		NmMt 8	NmMt+ 8.5	MT 9	Gem 9.5/10
79	Tracy McGrady RC	4	6	10	20
112	Tim Duncan RC	4	8	12	25

1997-98 SkyBox Premium Competitive Advantage

		NmMt 8	NmMt+ 8.5	MT 9	Gem 9.5/10
CA2	Kobe Bryant	30	40	80	200
CA3	Michael Jordan	200	300	500	800

1997-98 SkyBox Premium Premium Players

		NmMt 8	NmMt+ 8.5	MT 9	Gem 9.5/10
1	Michael Jordan	600	700	800	
3	Kobe Bryant	60	125	200	

1997-98 SP Authentic

		NmMt 8	NmMt+ 8.5	MT 9	Gem 9.5/10
128	Tim Duncan RC	15	20	30	100
166	Tracy McGrady FW RC	12	20	40	100

1997-98 SPx

		NmMt 8	NmMt+ 8.5	MT 9	Gem 9.5/10
37	Tim Duncan RC	10	12	15	120
42	Tracy McGrady RC	10	12	15	25

1997-98 Stadium Club

		NmMt 8	NmMt+ 8.5	MT 9	Gem 9.5/10
201	Tim Duncan RC	4	5	10	30
217	Tracy McGrady RC	4	4	8	15

1997-98 Stadium Club Hardcourt Heroics

		NmMt 8	NmMt+ 8.5	MT 9	Gem 9.5/10
H1	Michael Jordan	30	40	80	200

1997-98 Stadium Club Hardwood Hopefuls

		NmMt 8	NmMt+ 8.5	MT 9	Gem 9.5/10
HH4	Tim Duncan	6	8	10	30

1997-98 Stadium Club Triumvirate

		NmMt 8	NmMt+ 8.5	MT 9	Gem 9.5/10
T1B	Michael Jordan	200	250	400	700
T9B	Michael Jordan	200	250	400	700

1997-98 Topps

		NmMt 8	NmMt+ 8.5	MT 9	Gem 9.5/10
115	Tim Duncan RC	4	5	8	40
123	Michael Jordan	4	5	8	20
125	Tracy McGrady RC	4	4	6	20

1997-98 Topps Draft Redemption

		NmMt 8	NmMt+ 8.5	MT 9	Gem 9.5/10
DP1	Tim Duncan	30	40	80	150

1997-98 Topps Generations

		NmMt 8	NmMt+ 8.5	MT 9	Gem 9.5/10
G2	Michael Jordan	40	80	150	250

1997-98 Topps Generations Refractors

		NmMt 8	NmMt+ 8.5	MT 9	Gem 9.5/10
G2	Michael Jordan	120	200	400	600
G24	Kobe Bryant	40	50	80	

1997-98 Topps Rock Stars

		NmMt 8	NmMt+ 8.5	MT 9	Gem 9.5/10
RS1	Michael Jordan	50	100	150	250

1997-98 Topps Rock Stars Refractors

		NmMt 8	NmMt+ 8.5	MT 9	Gem 9.5/10
RS1	Michael Jordan	200	300	500	700

1997-98 Topps Chrome

		NmMt 8	NmMt+ 8.5	MT 9	Gem 9.5/10
115	Tim Duncan RC	30	40	80	200
123	Michael Jordan	10	15	30	60
125	Tracy McGrady RC	6	8	15	40
171	Kobe Bryant	6	8	20	
181	Chauncey Billups RC	8	10	12	30

1997-98 Topps Chrome Refractors

		NmMt 8	NmMt+ 8.5	MT 9	Gem 9.5/10
51	CL/Bulls - Team of the 90s	150	250	400	600
115	Tim Duncan	600	800	1,000	2,200
123	Michael Jordan	300	400	600	1,000
125	Tracy McGrady	125	150	300	500
171	Kobe Bryant	100	150	300	500

1997-98 Topps Chrome Destiny Refractors

		NmMt 8	NmMt+ 8.5	MT 9	Gem 9.5/10
D5	Kobe Bryant	20	25	40	
D8	Tim Duncan	25	30	60	100

1997-98 Topps Chrome Season's Best

		NmMt 8	NmMt+ 8.5	MT 9	Gem 9.5/10
SB6	Michael Jordan	25	40	60	150

1997-98 Topps Chrome Season's Best Refractors

		NmMt 8	NmMt+ 8.5	MT 9	Gem 9.5/10
SB6	Michael Jordan	60	80	200	350

1997-98 Topps Chrome Topps 40

		NmMt 8	NmMt+ 8.5	MT 9	Gem 9.5/10
T5	Michael Jordan	12	25	40	120

1997-98 Topps Chrome Topps 40 Refractors

		NmMt 8	NmMt+ 8.5	MT 9	Gem 9.5/10
T5	Michael Jordan	60	80	150	300

1997-98 Ultra

		NmMt 8	NmMt+ 8.5	MT 9	Gem 9.5/10
131	Tim Duncan RC	15	30	120	
138	Tracy McGrady RC	12	15	50	

1997-98 Ultra Gold Medallion

		NmMt 8	NmMt+ 8.5	MT 9	Gem 9.5/10
131	Tim Duncan	15	30	60	250

1997-98 Ultra Big Shots

		NmMt 8	NmMt+ 8.5	MT 9	Gem 9.5/10
1	Michael Jordan	15	20	30	80

1997-98 Ultra Court Masters

		NmMt 8	NmMt+ 8.5	MT 9	Gem 9.5/10
CM1	Michael Jordan	400	600	1,000	1,500

1997-98 Ultra Star Power

		NmMt 8	NmMt+ 8.5	MT 9	Gem 9.5/10
SP1	Michael Jordan	12	20	40	120

1997-98 Ultra Star Power Plus

		NmMt 8	NmMt+ 8.5	MT 9	Gem 9.5/10
SPP1	Michael Jordan	150	250	350	500

1997-98 Ultra Stars

		NmMt 8	NmMt+ 8.5	MT 9	Gem 9.5/10
1	Michael Jordan	600	800	1,200	2,200

1997-98 Upper Deck

		NmMt 8	NmMt+ 8.5	MT 9	Gem 9.5/10
114	Tim Duncan RC	4	6	10	30
300	Tracy McGrady RC	4	5	8	25

1997-98 Upper Deck Game Jerseys

		NmMt 8	NmMt+ 8.5	MT 9	Gem 9.5/10
GJ13	Michael Jordan	3,000	5,000	8,000	

1997-98 Upper Deck Rookie Discovery 1

		NmMt 8	NmMt+ 8.5	MT 9	Gem 9.5/10
R1	Tim Duncan	5	6	10	25

1997-98 Z-Force

		NmMt 8	NmMt+ 8.5	MT 9	Gem 9.5/10
111	Tim Duncan RC	4	4	6	20

1997-98 Z-Force Big Men on Court

		NmMt 8	NmMt+ 8.5	MT 9	Gem 9.5/10
2	Kobe Bryant	350	400	600	800
9	Michael Jordan	1,500	2,000	3,000	

1997-98 Z-Force Slam Cam

		NmMt 8	NmMt+ 8.5	MT 9	Gem 9.5/10
1	Kobe Bryant	12	15	20	40
5	Michael Jordan	30	50	80	200

1998-99 Black Diamond

		NmMt 8	NmMt+ 8.5	MT 9	Gem 9.5/10
22	Michael Jordan	4	5	10	30
92	Dirk Nowitzki RC	12	15	20	50
101	Paul Pierce RC	10	12	15	25
120	Vince Carter RC	10	12	15	25

1998-99 Black Diamond Double Diamond

		NmMt 8	NmMt+ 8.5	MT 9	Gem 9.5/10
92	Dirk Nowitzki	15	25	40	80

1998-99 Bowman's Best

		NmMt 8	NmMt+ 8.5	MT 9	Gem 9.5/10
105	Vince Carter RC	6	8	10	15
109	Dirk Nowitzki RC	10	12	15	40
110	Paul Pierce RC	8	10	12	25

1998-99 Bowman's Best Refractors

		NmMt 8	NmMt+ 8.5	MT 9	Gem 9.5/10
109	Dirk Nowitzki	50	80	150	300

1998-99 Bowman's Best Autographs Refractors

		NmMt 8	NmMt+ 8.5	MT 9	Gem 9.5/10
A9	Vince Carter	150	250	400	

1998-99 E-X Century

		NmMt 8	NmMt+ 8.5	MT 9	Gem 9.5/10
68	Dirk Nowitzki RC	8	10	15	50
82	Paul Pierce RC	10	12	15	30
89	Vince Carter RC	10	12	15	25

1998-99 E-X Century Dunk 'N Go Nuts

		NmMt 8	NmMt+ 8.5	MT 9	Gem 9.5/10
6	Kobe Bryant	120	150	300	500
15	Michael Jordan	600	800	1,000	2,000

1998-99 Finest

		NmMt 8	NmMt+ 8.5	MT 9	Gem 9.5/10
81	Michael Jordan	6	8	15	40
230	Vince Carter RC	6	8	10	15
234	Dirk Nowitzki RC	8	10	15	30
235	Paul Pierce RC	6	8	10	15

1998-99 Finest No Protectors

		NmMt 8	NmMt+ 8.5	MT 9	Gem 9.5/10
234	Dirk Nowitzki	15	20	25	40

1998-99 Finest Refractors

		NmMt 8	NmMt+ 8.5	MT 9	Gem 9.5/10
230	Vince Carter	30	40	60	120
234	Dirk Nowitzki	40	50	80	200

1998-99 Finest Arena Stars

		NmMt 8	NmMt+ 8.5	MT 9	Gem 9.5/10
AS19	Michael Jordan	100	150	200	400

1998-99 Flair Showcase Row 3

		NmMt 8	NmMt+ 8.5	MT 9	Gem 9.5/10
16	Dirk Nowitzki RC	8	12	15	30
25	Vince Carter RC	6	8	10	15
29	Paul Pierce RC	6	10	12	25

1998-99 Flair Showcase takeit2.net

		NmMt 8	NmMt+ 8.5	MT 9	Gem 9.5/10
5	Kobe Bryant	120	150	300	400
13	Michael Jordan	▲1,000	▲1,200	▲2,000	3,000

1998-99 Fleer Electrifying

		NmMt 8	NmMt+ 8.5	MT 9	Gem 9.5/10
1	Kobe Bryant	20	30	50	100
6	Michael Jordan	200	300	500	700

1998-99 Fleer Lucky 13

		NmMt 8	NmMt+ 8.5	MT 9	Gem 9.5/10
5	Vince Carter	50	60	100	250

1998-99 Fleer Brilliants

		NmMt 8	NmMt+ 8.5	MT 9	Gem 9.5/10
105	Vince Carter RC	6	8	12	25
109	Dirk Nowitzki RC	10	20	30	60

1998-99 Metal Universe Linchpins

		NmMt 8	NmMt+ 8.5	MT 9	Gem 9.5/10
8	Michael Jordan	1,000	1,500	2,500	

1998-99 SkyBox Molten Metal

		NmMt 8	NmMt+ 8.5	MT 9	Gem 9.5/10
35	Dirk Nowitzki RC	8	10	12	30
91	Paul Pierce RC	6	8	10	25
134	Vince Carter RC	8	10	12	20

1998-99 SkyBox Molten Metal Xplosion

		NmMt 8	NmMt+ 8.5	MT 9	Gem 9.5/10
141	Michael Jordan	150	200	250	400

1998-99 SkyBox Premium

		NmMt 8	NmMt+ 8.5	MT 9	Gem 9.5/10
234	Vince Carter RC	6	8	12	25
255	Dirk Nowitzki RC	8	12	15	40

1998-99 SkyBox Premium 3D's

		NmMt 8	NmMt+ 8.5	MT 9	Gem 9.5/10
4	Michael Jordan	400	600	800	1,500

1998-99 SkyBox Thunder Noyz Boyz

		NmMt 8	NmMt+ 8.5	MT 9	Gem 9.5/10
9	Michael Jordan	1,500	2,000	3,000	4,000

1998-99 SP Authentic

		NmMt 8	NmMt+ 8.5	MT 9	Gem 9.5/10
95	Vince Carter RC	120	150	200	300
97	Jason Williams RC	10	15	30	60
99	Dirk Nowitzki RC	120	150	200	300
100	Paul Pierce RC	30	40	80	150

1998-99 SP Authentic First Class

		NmMt 8	NmMt+ 8.5	MT 9	Gem 9.5/10
FC1	Michael Jordan	12	15	30	100

1998-99 SP Authentic Sign of the Times Gol

		NmMt 8	NmMt+ 8.5	MT 9	Gem 9.5/10
MJ	Michael Jordan	10,000	12,000	15,000	25,000

1998-99 SP Authentic Sign of the Times Sil

		NmMt 8	NmMt+ 8.5	MT 9	Gem 9.5/10
VC	Vince Carter	80	100	200	350

1998-99 SPx Finite

		NmMt 8	NmMt+ 8.5	MT 9	Gem 9.5/10
215	Vince Carter RC	20	30	40	100
219	Dirk Nowitzki RC	30	50	80	200

1998-99 SPx Finite Radiance

		NmMt 8	NmMt+ 8.5	MT 9	Gem 9.5/10
215	Vince Carter	30	40	50	

1998-99 Stadium Club

		NmMt 8	NmMt+ 8.5	MT 9	Gem 9.5/10
62	Michael Jordan	5	10	15	25
105	Vince Carter RC	15	20	25	40
109	Dirk Nowitzki RC	20	25	30	50

1998-99 Topps

		NmMt 8	NmMt+ 8.5	MT 9	Gem 9.5/1
154	Dirk Nowitzki RC	5	6	12	25
199	Vince Carter RC	4	5	10	20

1998-99 Topps Draft Redemption

		NmMt 8	NmMt+ 8.5	MT 9	Gem 9.5/1
9	Dirk Nowitzki	15	30	60	150

1998-99 Topps East/West

		NmMt 8	NmMt+ 8.5	MT 9	Gem 9.5/1
EW5	M.Jordan/K.Bryant	20	40	60	120

1998-99 Topps East/West Refractors

		NmMt 8	NmMt+ 8.5	MT 9	Gem 9.5/1
EW5	M.Jordan/K.Bryant	150	250	350	500

1998-99 Topps Gold Label

		NmMt 8	NmMt+ 8.5	MT 9	Gem 9.5/10
GL1	Michael Jordan	12	20	30	60

1998-99 Topps Legacies

		NmMt 8	NmMt+ 8.5	MT 9	Gem 9.5/1
L15	Michael Jordan	80	120	150	300

98-99 Topps Roundball Royalty

	NmMt 8	NmMt+ 8.5	MT 9	Gem 9.5/10
Michael Jordan	40	60	80	200

98-99 Topps Roundball Royalty Refractors

	NmMt 8	NmMt+ 8.5	MT 9	Gem 9.5/10
Michael Jordan	250	300	400	800

98-99 Topps Chrome

	NmMt 8	NmMt+ 8.5	MT 9	Gem 9.5/10
Paul Pierce RC	8	10	20	100
Dirk Nowitzki RC	20	40	80	300
Vince Carter RC	8	10	30	100

98-99 Topps Chrome Refractors

	NmMt 8	NmMt+ 8.5	MT 9	Gem 9.5/10
Paul Pierce	100	150	250	500
Dirk Nowitzki	500	700	1,000	4,000
Vince Carter	300	400	500	800

98-99 Topps Chrome Back 2 Back

	NmMt 8	NmMt+ 8.5	MT 9	Gem 9.5/10
Michael Jordan	10	12	15	40

98-99 Topps Chrome Champion Spirit

	NmMt 8	NmMt+ 8.5	MT 9	Gem 9.5/10
Michael Jordan	10	15	20	60

98-99 UD Ionix

	NmMt 8	NmMt+ 8.5	MT 9	Gem 9.5/10
Vince Carter RC	6	8	12	25
Dirk Nowitzki RC	8	10	15	40
Paul Pierce RC	6	8	12	25

98-99 UD Ionix Warp Zone

	NmMt 8	NmMt+ 8.5	MT 9	Gem 9.5/10
Michael Jordan	150	200	300	400

98-99 Ultra

	NmMt 8	NmMt+ 8.5	MT 9	Gem 9.5/10
Michael Jordan	5	6	10	25
Vince Carter RC	6	8	12	50
Dirk Nowitzki RC	10	12	20	50

98-99 Upper Deck

	NmMt 8	NmMt+ 8.5	MT 9	Gem 9.5/10
Vince Carter RC	8	10	12	30
Dirk Nowitzki RC	10	15	20	60

98-99 Upper Deck Game Jerseys

	NmMt 8	NmMt+ 8.5	MT 9	Gem 9.5/10
20 Michael Jordan	1,000	2,000	3,000	

98-99 Upper Deck Ovation

	NmMt 8	NmMt+ 8.5	MT 9	Gem 9.5/10
Vince Carter RC	8	10	12	20
Dirk Nowitzki RC	10	12	15	30
Paul Pierce RC	8	10	12	20

98-99 Upper Deck Ovation Gold

	NmMt 8	NmMt+ 8.5	MT 9	Gem 9.5/10
Dirk Nowitzki	25	30	60	120

1999-00 SPx

		NmMt 8	NmMt+ 8.5	MT 9	Gem 9.5/10
92	Steve Francis AU/500 RC	20	30	60	
93	Baron Davis AU/500 RC	30	40	80	

1999-00 Upper Deck Retro Inkredible

		NmMt 8	NmMt+ 8.5	MT 9	Gem 9.5/10
JW	Jerry West	30	40	60	120

2000-01 Ultimate Collection

		NmMt 8	NmMt+ 8.5	MT 9	Gem 9.5/10
8	Michael Jordan	30	50	100	200

2001-02 SP Authentic

		NmMt 8	NmMt+ 8.5	MT 9	Gem 9.5/10
90	Michael Jordan	8	10	15	25
138	Tony Parker AU RC	25	60	80	125

2001-02 SPx

		NmMt 8	NmMt+ 8.5	MT 9	Gem 9.5/10
90	Michael Jordan	15	20	25	40
91A	Tony Parker JSY AU RC	30	40	60	120
91B	Tony Parker JSY AU RC	30	40	60	
91C	Tony Parker JSY AU RC	30	40	60	
140	Pau Gasol RC	8	10	18	25

2001-02 Topps Chrome

		NmMt 8	NmMt+ 8.5	MT 9	Gem 9.5/10
95	Michael Jordan	10	12	20	50
131	Pau Gasol RC	5	8	15	30
155	Tony Parker RC	6	10	15	40

2001-02 Topps Chrome Refractors

		NmMt 8	NmMt+ 8.5	MT 9	Gem 9.5/10
131	Pau Gasol	20	25	60	250
155	Tony Parker	50	60	120	300

2001-02 Topps Chrome Fast and Furious

		NmMt 8	NmMt+ 8.5	MT 9	Gem 9.5/10
FF5	Michael Jordan	12	15	20	40

2001-02 Topps Chrome Fast and Furious Refractors

		NmMt 8	NmMt+ 8.5	MT 9	Gem 9.5/10
FF5	Michael Jordan	40	60	100	150

2001-02 Topps Pristine

		NmMt 8	NmMt+ 8.5	MT 9	Gem 9.5/10
75	Pau Gasol C RC	5	6	8	15
108	Tony Parker C RC	6	8	10	20

2001-02 Topps Pristine Refractors

		NmMt 8	NmMt+ 8.5	MT 9	Gem 9.5/10
108	Tony Parker	15	20	25	40

2001-02 Ultimate Collection

		NmMt 8	NmMt+ 8.5	MT 9	Gem 9.5/10
64	Tony Parker RC	20	25	35	60

2001-02 Upper Deck

		NmMt 8	NmMt+ 8.5	MT 9	Gem 9.5/10
403	Michael Jordan	8	10	12	25

2002-03 Bowman Signature Edition

		NmMt 8	NmMt+ 8.5	MT 9	Gem 9.5/10
SEEG	Manu Ginobili AU RC	60	100	150	
SEYM	Yao Ming AU RC	40	60	100	

2002-03 Finest

		NmMt 8	NmMt+ 8.5	MT 9	Gem 9.5/10
100	Michael Jordan	6	8	12	30
169	Yao Ming AU RC	50	60	100	
173	Amare Stoudemire AU RC	8	12	30	
178	LeBron James XRC	120	150	300	500
180	Carmelo Anthony XRC	8	10	15	25
182	Dwyane Wade XRC	12	15	20	50

2002-03 Finest Refractors

		NmMt 8	NmMt+ 8.5	MT 9	Gem 9.5/10
100	Michael Jordan	150	200	300	500
178	LeBron James	700	800	1,200	3,000
182	Dwyane Wade	80	100	130	

2002-03 Hoops Hot Prospects

		NmMt 8	NmMt+ 8.5	MT 9	Gem 9.5/10
81	Yao Ming JSY RC	40	50	60	

2002-03 SP Authentic

		NmMt 8	NmMt+ 8.5	MT 9	Gem 9.5/10
99	Michael Jordan	6	8	12	20
143	Yao Ming AU RC	40	60	100	200
172	M.Ginobili AU RC	60	80	150	250

2002-03 SP Game Used

		NmMt 8	NmMt+ 8.5	MT 9	Gem 9.5/10
142	Manu Ginobili RC	15	20	30	80

2002-03 SPx

		NmMt 8	NmMt+ 8.5	MT 9	Gem 9.5/10
125	A.Stoudemire JSY AU RC	10	15	25	60
132	Yao Ming JSY AU RC	60	80	100	250
155	Manu Ginobili RC	8	12	20	50

2002-03 Topps Chrome

		NmMt 8	NmMt+ 8.5	MT 9	Gem 9.5/10
124A	Manu Ginobili RC	8	10	15	40
124B	Manu Ginobili RC	8	10	15	40
146A	Yao Ming RC	12	15	20	30
146B	Yao Ming RC	12	15	20	30

2002-03 Topps Chrome Refractors

		NmMt 8	NmMt+ 8.5	MT 9	Gem 9.5/10
10	Michael Jordan	80	120	200	350
124A	Manu Ginobili	40	60	100	200
124B	Manu Ginobili	40	60	100	200
146A	Yao Ming	80	100	150	
146B	Yao Ming	80	100	150	

2002-03 Topps Chrome Coast to Coast

		NmMt 8	NmMt+ 8.5	MT 9	Gem 9.5/10
CC8	Michael Jordan	10	15	20	50

2002-03 Topps Chrome Coast to Coast Refractors

		NmMt 8	NmMt+ 8.5	MT 9	Gem 9.5/10
CC8	Michael Jordan	40	60	100	200

2002-03 Topps Chrome Zone Busters

		NmMt 8	NmMt+ 8.5	MT 9	Gem 9.5/10
ZB13	Michael Jordan	10	12	15	30

2002-03 Topps Chrome Zone Busters Refractors

		NmMt 8	NmMt+ 8.5	MT 9	Gem 9.5/10
ZB13	Michael Jordan	30	50	80	150

2002-03 Topps Pristine

		NmMt 8	NmMt+ 8.5	MT 9	Gem 9.5/10
4	Michael Jordan	6	8	15	40
52	Yao Ming U	10	12	15	30

2002-03 Ultimate Collection

		NmMt 8	NmMt+ 8.5	MT 9	Gem 9.5/10
79	Yao Ming AU RC	150	250	400	600

2002-03 Ultimate Collection Signatures

		NmMt 8	NmMt+ 8.5	MT 9	Gem 9.5/10
BRS	Bill Russell	150	175	225	300
KBS	Kobe Bryant	150	175	225	400
LBS	Larry Bird	125	140	160	225
MJS	Michael Jordan	800	1,000	1,500	2,500
YMS	Yao Ming	60	80	150	400

2002-03 Ultra

		NmMt 8	NmMt+ 8.5	MT 9	Gem 9.5/10
181	Yao Ming RC	12	15	20	40
204	Manu Ginobili RC	8	10	15	30

2002-03 Upper Deck

		NmMt 8	NmMt+ 8.5	MT 9	Gem 9.5/10
210	Yao Ming RC	6	8	15	40
392	Manu Ginobili RC	6	8	15	40

2002-03 Upper Deck Inspirations

		NmMt 8	NmMt+ 8.5	MT 9	Gem 9.5/10
156	LeBron James XRC	400	500	800	2,000

2003-04 Bazooka

		NmMt 8	NmMt+ 8.5	MT 9	Gem 9.5/10
223A	LeBron James RC	12	20	40	100
223B	LeBron James RC	12	20	40	100
252A	Dwyane Wade Dribble RC	5	5	6	15
252B	Dwyane Wade Layup RC	5	5	6	15
276	LeBron James BAZ	15	20	40	100
280	Dwyane Wade BAZ	6	8	10	20

2003-04 Bazooka Comics

		NmMt 8	NmMt+ 8.5	MT 9	Gem 9.5/10
15	LeBron James	8	10	15	60

2003-04 Black Diamond

		NmMt 8	NmMt+ 8.5	MT 9	Gem 9.5/10
148	Dwyane Wade RC	10	15	25	40
184	LeBron James RC	150	200	300	600
186	Carmelo Anthony RC	10	15	20	40

2003-04 Bowman

		NmMt 8	NmMt+ 8.5	MT 9	Gem 9.5/10
123	LeBron James RC	60	80	120	300
140	Carmelo Anthony RC	6	8	15	25
149	Dwyane Wade AU RC	100	125	150	400

2003-04 Bowman Chrome

		NmMt 8	NmMt+ 8.5	MT 9	Gem 9.5/10
123	LeBron James RC	120	150	250	500
140	Carmelo Anthony RC	10	15	20	25
149	Dwyane Wade AU RC	120	150	200	300

2003-04 Bowman Chrome Refractors

		NmMt 8	NmMt+ 8.5	MT 9	Gem 9.5/10
123	LeBron James	600	800	1,200	3,000

2003-04 Bowman Chrome Refractors Gold

		NmMt 8	NmMt+ 8.5	MT 9	Gem 9.5/10
123	LeBron James	5,000	6,000	8,000	15,000
140	Carmelo Anthony	175	200	300	

2003-04 Bowman Chrome X-fractors

		NmMt 8	NmMt+ 8.5	MT 9	Gem 9.5/10
123	LeBron James	1,500	2,000	3,000	6,000

2003-04 E-X

		NmMt 8	NmMt+ 8.5	MT 9	Gem 9.5/10
73	Carmelo Anthony RC	10	15	25	40
90	Dwyane Wade RC	25	30	40	60
102	LeBron James RC	300	450	600	800

2003-04 E-X Buzzer Beaters Autographs

		NmMt 8	NmMt+ 8.5	MT 9	Gem 9.5/10
10	Dwyane Wade/299	80	100	125	

2003-04 Exquisite Collection

		NmMt 8	NmMt+ 8.5	MT 9	Gem 9.5/10
74	D.Wade JSY AU RC	6,000	▲8,000	▲13,000	
76	C.Anthony JSY AU RC	2,000	2,500	▲4,000	

2003-04 Finest

		NmMt 8	NmMt+ 8.5	MT 9	Gem 9.5/10
133	LeBron James RC	500	700	800	2,000
158	Dwyane Wade AU RC	80	100	150	
163	Carmelo Anthony AU RC	40	50	80	150
173	Dwight Howard XRC	10	12	15	25

2003-04 Finest Refractors

		NmMt 8	NmMt+ 8.5	MT 9	Gem 9.5/10
133	LeBron James	1,500	2,000	3,000	
163	Carmelo Anthony JSY AU	60	80	100	

2003-04 Flair

		NmMt 8	NmMt+ 8.5	MT 9	Gem 9.5/10
94	LeBron James RC	300	400	500	

2003-04 Fleer Focus

		NmMt 8	NmMt+ 8.5	MT 9	Gem 9.5/10
137	LeBron James RC	200	300	400	800
148	Dwyane Wade RC	10	12	20	40

2003-04 Fleer Mystique

		NmMt 8	NmMt+ 8.5	MT 9	Gem 9.5/10
99	LeBron James RC	150	250	400	600
119	Dwyane Wade RC	12	15	30	60

2003-04 Fleer Mystique Die Cut

		NmMt 8	NmMt+ 8.5	MT 9	Gem 9.5/10
99	LeBron James	200	300	500	800
119	Dwyane Wade	15	25	40	80

2003-04 Fleer Showcase

		NmMt 8	NmMt+ 8.5	MT 9	Gem 9.5/10
130	LeBron James RC	150	250	400	600

2003-04 Fleer Showcase Legacy

		NmMt 8	NmMt+ 8.5	MT 9	Gem 9.5/10
130	LeBron James	600	700	1,000	3,000

2003-04 Fleer Tradition

		NmMt 8	NmMt+ 8.5	MT 9	Gem 9.5/10
261	LeBron James RC	40	60	80	200
263	Carmelo Anthony RC	4	5	8	15
265	Dwyane Wade RC	6	10	12	20
291	James/Darko/Melo	12	15	30	60
300	LeBron/Melo/Wade	40	60	80	200

2003-04 Fleer Tradition Draft Day Rookie

		NmMt 8	NmMt+ 8.5	MT 9	Gem 9.5/1
300	James/Melo/Wade	60	80	125	

2003-04 Hoops Hot Prospects Cream of the Cro

		NmMt 8	NmMt+ 8.5	MT 9	Gem 9.5/1
1	LeBron James	20	25	30	80
8	Carmelo Anthony	5	6	10	15

2003-04 SkyBox Autographics

		NmMt 8	NmMt+ 8.5	MT 9	Gem 9.5/1
77	LeBron James RC	100	150	250	500

2003-04 SkyBox LE Sky's the Limit

		NmMt 8	NmMt+ 8.5	MT 9	Gem 9.5/1
16	LeBron James	30	40	60	120

2003-04 SP Authentic

		NmMt 8	NmMt+ 8.5	MT 9	Gem 9.5/1
148	LeBron James AU RC	6,000	8,000	10,000	15,000
150	Carmelo Anthony AU RC	80	100	120	200
152	Dwyane Wade AU RC	150	200	300	600

2003-04 SP Authentic Limited

		NmMt 8	NmMt+ 8.5	MT 9	Gem 9.5/1
152	Dwyane Wade AU	600	700	800	1,000

2003-04 SP Authentic Signatures

		NmMt 8	NmMt+ 8.5	MT 9	Gem 9.5/10
DYA	Dwyane Wade	60	100	150	300
LJA	LeBron James SP	1,000	1,200	1,500	5,000

2003-04 SP Game Used

		NmMt 8	NmMt+ 8.5	MT 9	Gem 9.5/1
107	LeBron James RC	200	250	400	800
109	Carmelo Anthony RC	10	12	25	
111	Dwyane Wade RC	20	25	40	120

2003-04 SP Signature Edition

		NmMt 8	NmMt+ 8.5	MT 9	Gem 9.5/10
101	LeBron James RC	200	300	450	800

2003-04 SP Signature Edition Rookie INKorporated

		NmMt 8	NmMt+ 8.5	MT 9	Gem 9.5/10
LJ	LeBron James	4,000	5,000	6,000	10,000

2003-04 SP Signature Edition Signatures

		NmMt 8	NmMt+ 8.5	MT 9	Gem 9.5/10
DY	Dwyane Wade	80	100	120	200
KB	Kobe Bryant	150	175	250	400
LJ	LeBron James	1,000	1,500	2,000	4,000

2003-04 SPx

		NmMt 8	NmMt+ 8.5	MT 9	Gem 9.5/10
9	Michael Jordan	8	10	12	40
151	LeBron James JSY AU RC	3,000	4,000	6,000	10,000
153	Carmelo Anthony JSY AU RC	50	60	100	200
155	Dwyane Wade JSY AU RC	60	80	120	250

03-04 SPx Spectrum

	NmMt 8	NmMt+ 8.5	MT 9	Gem 9.5/10
LeBron James JSY AU	5,000	6,000	8,000	12,000

03-04 Sweet Shot

	NmMt 8	NmMt+ 8.5	MT 9	Gem 9.5/10
LeBron James RC	150	250	400	700
Dwyane Wade RC	12	15	20	30

03-04 Topps

	NmMt 8	NmMt+ 8.5	MT 9	Gem 9.5/10
LeBron James RC	▲100	▲120	▲200	▲400
Carmelo Anthony RC	4	6	8	25
Dwyane Wade RC	8	10	20	40

03-04 Topps First Edition

	NmMt 8	NmMt+ 8.5	MT 9	Gem 9.5/10
LeBron James	150	250	400	600

03-04 Topps Collection

	NmMt 8	NmMt+ 8.5	MT 9	Gem 9.5/10
LeBron James RC	80	120	200	400

03-04 Topps Chrome

	NmMt 8	NmMt+ 8.5	MT 9	Gem 9.5/10
Lebron James RC	▲450	▲500	▲800	▲1,200
Carmelo Anthony RC	12	15	20	40
Dwyane Wade RC	12	20	40	80

03-04 Topps Chrome Refractors

	NmMt 8	NmMt+ 8.5	MT 9	Gem 9.5/10
LeBron James	1,500	2,000	3,000	5,000
Carmelo Anthony	30	40	50	150
Dwyane Wade	80	100	200	300

03-04 Topps Chrome Refractors Black

	NmMt 8	NmMt+ 8.5	MT 9	Gem 9.5/10
LeBron James	2,500	3,000	6,000	
Carmelo Anthony	60	80	150	250
Dwyane Wade	200	300	500	800

03-04 Topps Chrome Refractors Gold

	NmMt 8	NmMt+ 8.5	MT 9	Gem 9.5/10
Lebron James	8,000	10,000	12,000	
Carmelo Anthony	200	300	500	1,200
Dwyane Wade	1,000	2,000	3,000	

03-04 Topps Chrome X-Fractors

	NmMt 8	NmMt+ 8.5	MT 9	Gem 9.5/10
LeBron James	5,000	6,000	8,000	
Dwyane Wade	300	400	600	1,000

LeBron James #111 BGS 10 (Pristine) sold for $5,200 (eBay; 3/14)

2003-04 Topps Chrome Autographs

	NmMt 8	NmMt+ 8.5	MT 9	Gem 9.5/10
CA Carmelo Anthony A	40	50	100	200
DW Dwyane Wade A	100	125	150	350

2003-04 Topps Contemporary Collection

	NmMt 8	NmMt+ 8.5	MT 9	Gem 9.5/10
LeBron James RC	200	250	400	700
Dwyane Wade RC	20	25	30	60

2003-04 Topps Jersey Edition

	NmMt 8	NmMt+ 8.5	MT 9	Gem 9.5/10
DW Dwyane Wade SS RC	25	30	35	
LJ LeBron James SS RC	300	500	700	1,000

2003-04 Topps Pristine

	NmMt 8	NmMt+ 8.5	MT 9	Gem 9.5/10
101 LeBron James C RC	40	60	120	250
102 LeBron James U	80	100	150	300
103 LeBron James R	100	120	200	400
107 Carmelo Anthony C RC	6	8	15	20
108 Carmelo Anthony U	8	10	20	25
109 Carmelo Anthony R	10	12	25	30
113 Dwyane Wade C RC	10	12	15	25
114 Dwyane Wade U	12	15	20	30
115 Dwyane Wade R	15	20	25	40

2003-04 Topps Pristine Refractors

	NmMt 8	NmMt+ 8.5	MT 9	Gem 9.5/10
102 LeBron James U	200	300	500	600
103 LeBron James R	450	600	800	1,200
107 Carmelo Anthony C	12	15	30	40
108 Carmelo Anthony U	20	25	50	80
109 Carmelo Anthony R	25	30	60	100
113 Dwyane Wade C	25	30	40	60
114 Dwyane Wade U	30	50	60	120
115 Dwyane Wade R	40	60	100	150

2003-04 Topps Pristine Minis

	NmMt 8	NmMt+ 8.5	MT 9	Gem 9.5/10
PM21 LeBron James	30	50	80	200
PM23 Carmelo Anthony	6	8	15	25

2003-04 Topps Pristine Personal Endorsements

	NmMt 8	NmMt+ 8.5	MT 9	Gem 9.5/10
DWA Dwyane Wade C	50	60	80	120

2003-04 Topps Rookie Matrix

	NmMt 8	NmMt+ 8.5	MT 9	Gem 9.5/10
AJF Carmelo/LeBron/Ford	8	10	15	30
BAJ Bosh/Carmelo/LeBron	15	25	30	40
JAW LeBron/Carmelo/Wade	20	25	40	80
JKA LeBron/Kaman/Carmelo	12	15	20	30
JMA LeBron/Darko/Carmelo	15	20	25	40
MJW Darko/LeBron/Wade	12	15	20	30
WJB Wade/LeBron/Bosh	40	60	80	250

2003-04 Topps Rookie Matrix Rookie Frames

	NmMt 8	NmMt+ 8.5	MT 9	Gem 9.5/10
111 LeBron James	25	30	50	

2003-04 UD Top Prospects

	NmMt 8	NmMt+ 8.5	MT 9	Gem 9.5/10
3 LeBron James	6	8	10	30
55 LeBron James	6	8	10	30
60 LeBron James	6	8	10	30

2003-04 UD Top Prospects Signs of Success

	NmMt 8	NmMt+ 8.5	MT 9	Gem 9.5/10
SSCA Carmelo Anthony	40	50	60	120
SSLJ LeBron James	800	1,000	1,500	2,500

2003-04 Ultimate Collection

	NmMt 8	NmMt+ 8.5	MT 9	Gem 9.5/10
127 LeBron James AU RC	10,000	12,000	25,000	50,000
129 Carmelo Anthony AU RC	100	120	150	250
130 Chris Bosh AU RC	40	60	80	120
131 Dwyane Wade AU RC	200	300	400	600

2003-04 Ultimate Collection Signatures

	NmMt 8	NmMt+ 8.5	MT 9	Gem 9.5/10
CA Carmelo Anthony	50	80	100	200
DY Dwyane Wade	60	80	100	150
LJ LeBron James	3,500	4,000	5,000	6,000
MJ Michael Jordan	1,800	2,000	3,000	5,000

2003-04 Ultra

	NmMt 8	NmMt+ 8.5	MT 9	Gem 9.5/10
171 LeBron James L13 RC	200	300	400	600

2003-04 Ultra Gold Medallion

	NmMt 8	NmMt+ 8.5	MT 9	Gem 9.5/10
171 LeBron James L13	80	100	200	600

2003-04 Ultra Platinum Medallion

	NmMt 8	NmMt+ 8.5	MT 9	Gem 9.5/10
171 LeBron James L13	500	700	1,200	2,500

2003-04 Ultra Roundball Discs

	NmMt 8	NmMt+ 8.5	MT 9	Gem 9.5/10
31 LeBron James	12	20	50	120

2003-04 Upper Deck

	NmMt 8	NmMt+ 8.5	MT 9	Gem 9.5/10
301 LeBron James RC	40	60	120	300
303 Carmelo Anthony RC	5	6	12	25
305 Dwyane Wade RC	8	12	15	30

2003-04 Upper Deck Air Academy

	NmMt 8	NmMt+ 8.5	MT 9	Gem 9.5/10
AA3 LeBron James	10	15	30	60

2003-04 Upper Deck Black Diamond Rookies F/X

	NmMt 8	NmMt+ 8.5	MT 9	Gem 9.5/10
BD1 LeBron James	150	250	400	600

2003-04 Upper Deck SE Die Cut Future All-Stars

	NmMt 8	NmMt+ 8.5	MT 9	Gem 9.5/10
E11 Dwyane Wade	12	15	30	60
E15 LeBron James	150	200	300	500

2003-04 Upper Deck Finite

	NmMt 8	NmMt+ 8.5	MT 9	Gem 9.5/10
242 LeBron James RC	800	1,000	2,000	

2003-04 Upper Deck Finite Elements Jerseys

	NmMt 8	NmMt+ 8.5	MT 9	Gem 9.5/10
FJ18 LeBron James	80	120	200	400

2003-04 Upper Deck Finite Signatures

	NmMt 8	NmMt+ 8.5	MT 9	Gem 9.5/10
CA Carmelo Anthony	60	80	100	150
DW Dwyane Wade	80	100	200	300

2003-04 Upper Deck Hardcourt

		NmMt 8	NmMt+ 8.5	MT 9	Gem 9.5/10
132	LeBron James RC	200	250	400	800

2003-04 Upper Deck Legends

		NmMt 8	NmMt+ 8.5	MT 9	Gem 9.5/10
131	Dwyane Wade RC	20	25	50	100
133	Carmelo Anthony RC	10	12	25	50
135	LeBron James RC	80	120	250	400

2003-04 Upper Deck Legends Legendary Signatures

		NmMt 8	NmMt+ 8.5	MT 9	Gem 9.5/10
MJ	Michael Jordan SP	600	700	800	2,000

2003-04 Upper Deck MVP

		NmMt 8	NmMt+ 8.5	MT 9	Gem 9.5/10
201	LeBron James RC	20	30	50	100
203	Carmelo Anthony RC	4	4	8	15
205	Dwyane Wade RC	5	6	12	25

2003-04 Upper Deck MVP Rising to the Occasion

		NmMt 8	NmMt+ 8.5	MT 9	Gem 9.5/10
RO2	LeBron James	10	12	20	50

2003-04 Upper Deck Rookie Exclusives

		NmMt 8	NmMt+ 8.5	MT 9	Gem 9.5/10
1	LeBron James RC	10	15	30	60
5	Dwyane Wade RC	4	6	8	20

2003-04 Upper Deck Rookie Exclusives Jerseys

		NmMt 8	NmMt+ 8.5	MT 9	Gem 9.5/10
J1	LeBron James	80	120	200	

2003-04 Upper Deck Standing O

		NmMt 8	NmMt+ 8.5	MT 9	Gem 9.5/10
85	LeBron James RC	25	40	80	200

2003-04 Upper Deck Triple Dimensions Reflections

		NmMt 8	NmMt+ 8.5	MT 9	Gem 9.5/10
10	LeBron James	25	30	60	100

2003-04 Upper Deck Victory

		NmMt 8	NmMt+ 8.5	MT 9	Gem 9.5/10
100	Michael Jordan	4	6	10	20
101	Lebron James SP RC	15	25	40	100
103	Carmelo Anthony RC	4	6	10	15

2004-05 Bowman Chrome

		NmMt 8	NmMt+ 8.5	MT 9	Gem 9.5/10
129	Dwight Howard RC	5	6	10	20

2004-05 Exquisite Collection

		NmMt 8	NmMt+ 8.5	MT 9	Gem 9.5/10
90	Dwight Howard JSY AU RC	400	500	600	1,000

2004-05 Finest

		NmMt 8	NmMt+ 8.5	MT 9	Gem 9.5/10
159	Dwight Howard RC	15	20	25	60
194	Chris Paul XRC	15	20	40	60

2004-05 Finest Refractors Red

		NmMt 8	NmMt+ 8.5	MT 9	Gem 9.5/10
194	Chris Paul	40	50	60	100

2004-05 Finest X-Fractors

		NmMt 8	NmMt+ 8.5	MT 9	Gem 9.5/10
159	Dwight Howard	20	30	50	100
194	Chris Paul	30	40	50	70

2004-05 Fleer Tradition

		NmMt 8	NmMt+ 8.5	MT 9	Gem 9.5/10
221	Dwight Howard RC	4	5	6	12

2004-05 SP Authentic

		NmMt 8	NmMt+ 8.5	MT 9	Gem 9.5/10
14	LeBron James	6	8	12	30
186	Dwight Howard AU RC	15	20	40	60

2004-05 SP Authentic Limited

		NmMt 8	NmMt+ 8.5	MT 9	Gem 9.5/10
186	Dwight Howard AU	40	60	80	150

2004-05 SP Authentic Signatures

		NmMt 8	NmMt+ 8.5	MT 9	Gem 9.5/10
DH	Dwight Howard	20	25	30	80

2004-05 SP Game Used SIGnificance

		NmMt 8	NmMt+ 8.5	MT 9	Gem 9.5/10
MJ	Michael Jordan	400	500	700	

2004-05 SPx

		NmMt 8	NmMt+ 8.5	MT 9	Gem 9.5/10
147	Dwight Howard JSY AU RC	20	30	50	100

2004-05 Topps

		NmMt 8	NmMt+ 8.5	MT 9	Gem 9.5/10
221	Dwight Howard RC	4	5	8	15

2004-05 Topps Chrome

		NmMt 8	NmMt+ 8.5	MT 9	Gem 9.5/10
23	LeBron James	30	40	60	150
166	Dwight Howard RC	5	6	10	25

2004-05 Topps Chrome Refractors

		NmMt 8	NmMt+ 8.5	MT 9	Gem 9.5/10
23	LeBron James	200	250	400	600
166	Dwight Howard	10	12	25	40

2004-05 Topps Chrome Refractors Black

		NmMt 8	NmMt+ 8.5	MT 9	Gem 9.5/10
23	LeBron James	500	600	800	1,200

2004-05 Topps Pristine

		NmMt 8	NmMt+ 8.5	MT 9	Gem 9.5/10
101	Dwight Howard C RC	4	5	8	20

2004-05 Ultimate Collection

		NmMt 8	NmMt+ 8.5	MT 9	Gem 9.5/10
127	Dwight Howard AU RC	30	40	60	100

2004-05 Upper Deck

		NmMt 8	NmMt+ 8.5	MT 9	Gem 9.5/10
224	Dwight Howard SP RC	4	5	8	20

2004-05 Upper Deck Trilogy

		NmMt 8	NmMt+ 8.5	MT 9	Gem 9.5/10
141	Dwight Howard RC	8	10	20	40

2005-06 Bowman

		NmMt 8	NmMt+ 8.5	MT 9	Gem 9.5/1
111	Chris Paul RC	6	8	10	20

2005-06 Bowman Chrome

		NmMt 8	NmMt+ 8.5	MT 9	Gem 9.5/1
111	Chris Paul RC	6	8	12	30

2005-06 Bowman Chrome Refractors

		NmMt 8	NmMt+ 8.5	MT 9	Gem 9.5/1
111	Chris Paul	30	40	80	150

2005-06 Exquisite Collection

		NmMt 8	NmMt+ 8.5	MT 9	Gem 9.5/1
5	Michael Jordan	275	300	400	
46	Chris Paul JSY AU RC/99	1,500	2,000	3,000	

2005-06 Finest

		NmMt 8	NmMt+ 8.5	MT 9	Gem 9.5/1
106	Chris Paul RC	8	10	15	40

2005-06 Finest Refractors

		NmMt 8	NmMt+ 8.5	MT 9	Gem 9.5/1
106	Chris Paul	12	20	40	80

2005-06 Greats of the Game

		NmMt 8	NmMt+ 8.5	MT 9	Gem 9.5/1
113	Chris Paul AU RC	80	100	200	

2005-06 SP Authentic

		NmMt 8	NmMt+ 8.5	MT 9	Gem 9.5/10
94	Chris Paul AU RC	50	60	120	200

2005-06 SP Game Used

		NmMt 8	NmMt+ 8.5	MT 9	Gem 9.5/10
149	Chris Paul RC	10	12	20	40

2005-06 SPx

		NmMt 8	NmMt+ 8.5	MT 9	Gem 9.5/10
153	Chris Paul JSY AU RC	60	80	150	250

2005-06 Topps

		NmMt 8	NmMt+ 8.5	MT 9	Gem 9.5/10
224	Chris Paul RC	5	6	8	20

2005-06 Topps Chrome

		NmMt 8	NmMt+ 8.5	MT 9	Gem 9.5/10
168	Chris Paul RC	10	15	30	80

2005-06 Topps Chrome Refractors

		NmMt 8	NmMt+ 8.5	MT 9	Gem 9.5/10
168	Chris Paul	100	120	200	400

2005-06 Topps Chrome Refractors Black

		NmMt 8	NmMt+ 8.5	MT 9	Gem 9.5/10
168	Chris Paul	120	150	250	400

2005-06 Topps Chrome X-Fractors

		NmMt 8	NmMt+ 8.5	MT 9	Gem 9.5/10
168	Chris Paul	200	300	500	700

2005-06 Topps Style

		NmMt 8	NmMt+ 8.5	MT 9	Gem 9.5/10
154	Chris Paul RC	6	8	12	25

05-06 Ultimate Collection

	NmMt 8	NmMt+ 8.5	MT 9	Gem 9.5/10
Chris Paul AU RC	100	150	200	350

05-06 Ultimate Collection Rookie Autographs Gold

	NmMt 8	NmMt+ 8.5	MT 9	Gem 9.5/10
Chris Paul	250	300	400	600

05-06 Ultimate Collection Signatures

	NmMt 8	NmMt+ 8.5	MT 9	Gem 9.5/10
P Chris Paul	60	80	125	200

05-06 Upper Deck

	NmMt 8	NmMt+ 8.5	MT 9	Gem 9.5/10
Chris Paul SP RC	8	10	20	30

05-06 Upper Deck Rookie Debut

	NmMt 8	NmMt+ 8.5	MT 9	Gem 9.5/10
Chris Paul RC	5	6	8	15

05-06 Upper Deck Slam

	NmMt 8	NmMt+ 8.5	MT 9	Gem 9.5/10
Chris Paul RC	5	6	8	20

05-06 Upper Deck Trilogy

	NmMt 8	NmMt+ 8.5	MT 9	Gem 9.5/10
Chris Paul RC	10	12	25	40

05-06 Upper Deck Trilogy Auto Focus

	NmMt 8	NmMt+ 8.5	MT 9	Gem 9.5/10
Chris Paul	50	80	100	150

006-07 Bowman Chrome

	NmMt 8	NmMt+ 8.5	MT 9	Gem 9.5/10
Rajon Rondo B AU RC	12	15	30	80

006-07 E-X

	NmMt 8	NmMt+ 8.5	MT 9	Gem 9.5/10
Michael Jordan	20	25	60	120
LeBron James	12	15	30	80
LaMarcus Aldridge				
199 AU RC	15	25	40	60

006-07 Exquisite Collection

	NmMt 8	NmMt+ 8.5	MT 9	Gem 9.5/10
Rajon Rondo JSY AU RC	150	200	300	

006-07 Finest

	NmMt 8	NmMt+ 8.5	MT 9	Gem 9.5/10
Rajon Rondo RC	5	6	8	15
LaMarcus Aldridge RC	6	8	10	20
2 Kevin Durant XRC	80	100	150	250

006-07 Finest Refractors

	NmMt 8	NmMt+ 8.5	MT 9	Gem 9.5/10
LeBron James	40	40	60	120
2 Kevin Durant	100	125	200	350

006-07 Finest Refractors Black

	NmMt 8	NmMt+ 8.5	MT 9	Gem 9.5/10
2 Kevin Durant	150	250	400	600

2006-07 Finest Refractors Blue

	NmMt 8	NmMt+ 8.5	MT 9	Gem 9.5/10
102 Kevin Durant	100	150	250	400

2006-07 Finest Refractors Silver

	NmMt 8	NmMt+ 8.5	MT 9	Gem 9.5/10
102 Kevin Durant	100	150	250	400

2006-07 Fleer

	NmMt 8	NmMt+ 8.5	MT 9	Gem 9.5/10
27 Michael Jordan	6	10	20	40

2006-07 Fleer 1986-87 20th Anniversary

	NmMt 8	NmMt+ 8.5	MT 9	Gem 9.5/10
57 Michael Jordan	50	80	120	300
71 LeBron James	30	40	80	150

2006-07 SP Authentic

	NmMt 8	NmMt+ 8.5	MT 9	Gem 9.5/10
111 Rajon Rondo AU RC	10	12	25	50

2006-07 Topps

	NmMt 8	NmMt+ 8.5	MT 9	Gem 9.5/10
241A LaMarcus Aldridge RC	4	5	8	20
241B LaMarcus Aldridge Draft RC	4	5	8	20

2006-07 Topps Chrome

	NmMt 8	NmMt+ 8.5	MT 9	Gem 9.5/10
183 LaMarcus Aldridge RC	6	8	15	25
201 Rajon Rondo RC	4	6	10	20

2006-07 Topps Chrome Autographs Refractors Black

	NmMt 8	NmMt+ 8.5	MT 9	Gem 9.5/10
201 Rajon Rondo C	20	25	30	80

2006-07 Ultimate Collection

	NmMt 8	NmMt+ 8.5	MT 9	Gem 9.5/10
209 Rajon Rondo AU RC	15	20	30	60

2007 Topps McDonald's All-American

	NmMt 8	NmMt+ 8.5	MT 9	Gem 9.5/10
BG Blake Griffin	8	10	15	40

2007-08 Bowman Chrome

	NmMt 8	NmMt+ 8.5	MT 9	Gem 9.5/10
111 Kevin Durant RC	60	80	150	300

2007-08 Bowman Chrome Refractors

	NmMt 8	NmMt+ 8.5	MT 9	Gem 9.5/10
111 Kevin Durant	200	300	500	800

2007-08 Bowman Chrome Refractors Black

	NmMt 8	NmMt+ 8.5	MT 9	Gem 9.5/10
111 Kevin Durant	400	600	800	1,500

2007-08 Bowman Chrome Refractors Gold

	NmMt 8	NmMt+ 8.5	MT 9	Gem 9.5/10
111 Kevin Durant	800	900	1,500	3,000

2007-08 Bowman Elevation

	NmMt 8	NmMt+ 8.5	MT 9	Gem 9.5/10
71 Kevin Durant RC	15	25	40	80

2007-08 Bowman Sterling

	NmMt 8	NmMt+ 8.5	MT 9	Gem 9.5/10
KD Kevin Durant RC	20	25	40	80

2007-08 Bowman Sterling Refractors

	NmMt 8	NmMt+ 8.5	MT 9	Gem 9.5/10
KD Kevin Durant/399	100	150	250	400

2007-08 Finest

	NmMt 8	NmMt+ 8.5	MT 9	Gem 9.5/10
71 Kevin Durant RC	20	25	50	80
101 Derrick Rose XRC	40	60	80	100
104 Russell Westbrook XRC	80	100	200	300
105 Kevin Love XRC	20	30	40	60

2007-08 Finest Refractors

	NmMt 8	NmMt+ 8.5	MT 9	Gem 9.5/10
71 Kevin Durant	80	100	200	300

2007-08 Fleer

	NmMt 8	NmMt+ 8.5	MT 9	Gem 9.5/10
212 Kevin Durant RC	8	10	25	60

2007-08 Fleer 1986-87 Rookies

	NmMt 8	NmMt+ 8.5	MT 9	Gem 9.5/10
143 Kevin Durant	30	40	80	200

2007-08 Fleer Rookie Sensations

	NmMt 8	NmMt+ 8.5	MT 9	Gem 9.5/10
RS2 Kevin Durant	8	10	20	50

2007-08 Fleer Rookie Sensations Glossy

	NmMt 8	NmMt+ 8.5	MT 9	Gem 9.5/10
RS2 Kevin Durant	15	25	50	80

2007-08 Fleer Hot Prospects

	NmMt 8	NmMt+ 8.5	MT 9	Gem 9.5/10
123 Kevin Durant JSY AU RC	300	350	500	1,000

2007-08 Fleer Hot Prospects Notable Newcomers

	NmMt 8	NmMt+ 8.5	MT 9	Gem 9.5/10
1 Kevin Durant	10	15	25	40

2007-08 SP Authentic

	NmMt 8	NmMt+ 8.5	MT 9	Gem 9.5/10
152 Kevin Durant JSY AU/299 RC	3,000	4,000	5,000	10,000

2007-08 SP Authentic Profiles

	NmMt 8	NmMt+ 8.5	MT 9	Gem 9.5/10
AP13 Kevin Durant	10	15	25	50

2007-08 SP Authentic Retail Rookie Autographs

	NmMt 8	NmMt+ 8.5	MT 9	Gem 9.5/10
152 Kevin Durant/399	800	1,000	2,000	4,000

2007-08 SP Game Used

	NmMt 8	NmMt+ 8.5	MT 9	Gem 9.5/10
142 Kevin Durant RC	30	40	60	150

2007-08 SP Rookie Edition

	NmMt 8	NmMt+ 8.5	MT 9	Gem 9.5/10
61 Kevin Durant RC	10	12	25	60
106 Kevin Durant 96-97	15	20	25	60

2007-08 SP Rookie Edition Rookie Autographs

	NmMt 8	NmMt+ 8.5	MT 9	Gem 9.5/10
61 Kevin Durant	200	250	400	600

2007-08 SP Rookie Threads

		NmMt 8	NmMt+ 8.5	MT 9	Gem 9.5/10
49	Kevin Durant JSY AU RC	450	600	800	1,500

2007-08 SPx

		NmMt 8	NmMt+ 8.5	MT 9	Gem 9.5/10
101	Kevin Durant JSY AU RC	500	600	1,000	3,000

2007-08 SPx Endorsements

		NmMt 8	NmMt+ 8.5	MT 9	Gem 9.5/10
KD	Kevin Durant	200	250	400	500

2007-08 SPx Super Scripts

		NmMt 8	NmMt+ 8.5	MT 9	Gem 9.5/10
KD	Kevin Durant	125	175	225	400

2007-08 Stadium Club

		NmMt 8	NmMt+ 8.5	MT 9	Gem 9.5/10
102	Kevin Durant RC	25	40	60	125

2007-08 Stadium Club Chrome Rookie Refractors

		NmMt 8	NmMt+ 8.5	MT 9	Gem 9.5/10
102	Kevin Durant	60	80	200	300

2007-08 Topps

		NmMt 8	NmMt+ 8.5	MT 9	Gem 9.5/10
112	Kevin Durant RC	20	20	25	60

2007-08 Topps 1957-58 Variations

		NmMt 8	NmMt+ 8.5	MT 9	Gem 9.5/10
112	Kevin Durant	20	25	30	60

2007-08 Topps Rookie Set

		NmMt 8	NmMt+ 8.5	MT 9	Gem 9.5/10
2	Kevin Durant	8	10	25	40

2007-08 Topps Chrome

		NmMt 8	NmMt+ 8.5	MT 9	Gem 9.5/10
131	Kevin Durant RC	80	150	250	400

2007-08 Topps Chrome Refractors

		NmMt 8	NmMt+ 8.5	MT 9	Gem 9.5/10
131	Kevin Durant	800	1,000	1,200	2,000

2007-08 Topps Chrome Refractors Orange

		NmMt 8	NmMt+ 8.5	MT 9	Gem 9.5/10
131	Kevin Durant	1,000	1,500	3,000	5,000

2007-08 Topps Echelon

		NmMt 8	NmMt+ 8.5	MT 9	Gem 9.5/10
74	Kevin Durant RC	40	60	150	300

2007-08 Ultra SE

		NmMt 8	NmMt+ 8.5	MT 9	Gem 9.5/10
232	Kevin Durant L13 RC	30	40	60	100

2007-08 Upper Deck

		NmMt 8	NmMt+ 8.5	MT 9	Gem 9.5/10
234	Kevin Durant SP RC	15	20	40	80

2007-08 Upper Deck First Edition

		NmMt 8	NmMt+ 8.5	MT 9	Gem 9.5/10
202	Kevin Durant RC	15	20	35	60

2007-08 Upper Deck NBA Rookie Box Set

		NmMt 8	NmMt+ 8.5	MT 9	Gem 9.5/10
11	Kevin Durant	8	10	15	40

2008-09 Bowman

		NmMt 8	NmMt+ 8.5	MT 9	Gem 9.5/10
111	Derrick Rose RC	6	8	10	20
114	Russell Westbrook RC	10	15	30	60
115	Kevin Love RC	5	6	8	15

2008-09 Bowman Chrome

		NmMt 8	NmMt+ 8.5	MT 9	Gem 9.5/10
111	Derrick Rose RC	12	15	20	40
114	Russell Westbrook RC	30	40	60	100
115	Kevin Love RC	10	12	20	30

2008-09 Bowman Chrome Refractors

		NmMt 8	NmMt+ 8.5	MT 9	Gem 9.5/10
111	Derrick Rose	40	50	60	120
114	Russell Westbrook	80	100	150	250

2008-09 Bowman Chrome X-Fractors

		NmMt 8	NmMt+ 8.5	MT 9	Gem 9.5/10
114	Russell Westbrook	100	200	300	400

2008-09 Exquisite Collection

		NmMt 8	NmMt+ 8.5	MT 9	Gem 9.5/10
61	Kevin Love JSY AU RC	100	120	200	400
92	Derrick Rose JSY AU/99 RC	500	700	1,000	
93	R.Westbrook JSY AU RC	1,500	2,000	3,500	

2008-09 Fleer

		NmMt 8	NmMt+ 8.5	MT 9	Gem 9.5/10
201	Derrick Rose RC	6	8	10	15
204	Russell Westbrook RC	8	10	15	30

2008-09 Fleer 1986-87 Rookies

		NmMt 8	NmMt+ 8.5	MT 9	Gem 9.5/10
86R163	Derrick Rose	6	8	10	20
86R166	Russell Westbrook	15	20	30	100
86R167	Kevin Love	4	5	8	12

2008-09 SkyBox

		NmMt 8	NmMt+ 8.5	MT 9	Gem 9.5/10
201	Derrick Rose RC	6	8	10	20
204	Russell Westbrook RC	20	25	50	80

2008-09 SP Authentic

		NmMt 8	NmMt+ 8.5	MT 9	Gem 9.5/10
126	Kevin Love JSY AU/299 RC	40	50	80	150
130	D.Rose JSY AU/299 RC	100	150	300	400
139	R.Westbrook JSY AU/299 RC	250	300	500	800

2008-09 SP Authentic Destination Stardom

		NmMt 8	NmMt+ 8.5	MT 9	Gem 9.5/10
DS1	Derrick Rose	10	15	20	40

2008-09 SP Authentic Profiles

		NmMt 8	NmMt+ 8.5	MT 9	Gem 9.5/10
AP46	Derrick Rose	6	6	8	15
AP49	Russell Westbrook	6	10	15	30
AP50	Kevin Love	4	5	6	12

2008-09 SP Rookie Threads

		NmMt 8	NmMt+ 8.5	MT 9	Gem 9.5/1
67	Russell Westbrook				
	JSY AU RC	100	150	250	400
95	Derrick Rose JSY AU RC	150	200	250	300

2008-09 SPx

		NmMt 8	NmMt+ 8.5	MT 9	Gem 9.5/1
111	Derrick Rose JSY AU RC	30	50	80	150
114	Russell Westbrook				
	JSY AU RC	120	150	250	400
121	Derrick Rose JSY AU RC	30	50	80	150
124	Russell Westbrook				
	JSY AU RC	120	150	250	400
125	Kevin Love JSY AU RC	15	20	40	100

2008-09 Topps

		NmMt 8	NmMt+ 8.5	MT 9	Gem 9.5/10
196	Derrick Rose RC	4	5	8	15
199	Russell Westbrook RC	10	12	25	60

2008-09 Topps 1958-59 Variations

		NmMt 8	NmMt+ 8.5	MT 9	Gem 9.5/10
196	Derrick Rose	4	6	8	20
199	Russell Westbrook	8	12	20	40

2008-09 Topps Chrome

		NmMt 8	NmMt+ 8.5	MT 9	Gem 9.5/10
181	Derrick Rose RC	8	10	15	30
184	Russell Westbrook RC	40	60	100	250

2008-09 Topps Chrome Refractors

		NmMt 8	NmMt+ 8.5	MT 9	Gem 9.5/10
184	Russell Westbrook	150	200	300	600
221	Derrick Rose AU A	200	250	400	500
224	Russell Westbrook AU A	700	800	1,000	1,500
225	Kevin Love AU A	75	100	150	200

2008-09 Topps Chrome Refractors Gold

		NmMt 8	NmMt+ 8.5	MT 9	Gem 9.5/10
181	Derrick Rose	175	200	400	
184	Russell Westbrook	1,000	1,200	1,500	2,500

2008-09 Topps Chrome Refractors Orange

		NmMt 8	NmMt+ 8.5	MT 9	Gem 9.5/10
184	Russell Westbrook	300	400	500	800

2008-09 Topps Signature

		NmMt 8	NmMt+ 8.5	MT 9	Gem 9.5/10
TSDR	Derrick Rose RC	5	8	12	20
TSRW	Russell Westbrook RC	10	15	25	50

2008-09 Topps Signature Autographs

		NmMt 8	NmMt+ 8.5	MT 9	Gem 9.5/10
TSADR	Derrick Rose/649	25	30	60	80
TSARW	Russell Westbrook/184	150	200	300	500

2008-09 Upper Deck

		NmMt 8	NmMt+ 8.5	MT 9	Gem 9.5/10
259	Derrick Rose RC	6	8	10	20
262	Russell Westbrook RC	8	12	20	40

008-09 Upper Deck First Edition

	NmMt 8	NmMt+ 8.5	MT 9	Gem 9.5/10
Derrick Rose	4	4	6	12
Russell Westbrook	10	12	15	40

008-09 Upper Deck MVP

	NmMt 8	NmMt+ 8.5	MT 9	Gem 9.5/10
Derrick Rose RC	4	4	6	10
Russell Westbrook RC	8	10	15	40

008-09 Upper Deck Radiance

	NmMt 8	NmMt+ 8.5	MT 9	Gem 9.5/10
C Derrick Rose AU RC	30	50	80	300
C Russell Westbrook AU RC	150	200	300	500

009-10 Absolute Memorabilia

	NmMt 8	NmMt+ 8.5	MT 9	Gem 9.5/10
4 Stephen Curry				
JSY AU/499 RC	350	500	800	2,000
6 James Harden				
JSY AU/499 RC	▲125	150	▲300	▲500
2 Blake Griffin JSY AU/499 RC	▼25	▼30	▼60	▼120

009-10 Adrenalyn XL

	NmMt 8	NmMt+ 8.5	MT 9	Gem 9.5/10
Stephen Curry RC	▼12	▼20	▼40	▼80

009-10 Bowman 48

	NmMt 8	NmMt+ 8.5	MT 9	Gem 9.5/10
1 Blake Griffin RC	▼6	▼8	15	▼25
4 James Harden RC	▲25	▲40	▲60	▲150
6 Stephen Curry RC	▼100	▼150	▼250	▼400

009-10 Certified

	NmMt 8	NmMt+ 8.5	MT 9	Gem 9.5/10
1 Blake Griffin JSY AU RC	▼25	▼30	▼60	▼100
3 James Harden JSY AU RC	▲80	▲120	▲200	▲400
6 Stephen Curry JSY AU RC	200	▼300	▼500	800

009-10 Classics

	NmMt 8	NmMt+ 8.5	MT 9	Gem 9.5/10
1 Blake Griffin AU/499 RC	▼30	▼40	▼80	150
3 James Harden AU/499 RC	150	200	300	▲450
6 Stephen Curry AU/499 RC	600	800	1,000	2,000

009-10 Court Kings

	NmMt 8	NmMt+ 8.5	MT 9	Gem 9.5/10
*9 Stephen Curry AU RC	300	450	600	1,000
45 James Harden AU RC	80	120	200	▲400
50 Blake Griffin AU RC	▼25	▼40	▼60	▼100

2009-10 Crown Royale

	NmMt 8	NmMt+ 8.5	MT 9	Gem 9.5/10
03 Stephen Curry AU/399 RC	800	1,000	1,500	3,000
04 James Harden AU/599 RC	150	250	400	600
08 Blake Griffin AU/399 RC	▼30	▼50	▼80	150

2009-10 Donruss Elite

	NmMt 8	NmMt+ 8.5	MT 9	Gem 9.5/10
51 Blake Griffin AU RC	▼25	▼40	▼60	▼120
53 James Harden/479 AU RC	80	120	▲200	▲400
66 Stephen Curry AU RC	▼250	▼350	500	800

2009-10 Exquisite Collection

	NmMt 8	NmMt+ 8.5	MT 9	Gem 9.5/10
43 Blake Griffin RC	▼100	▼120	▼200	300
45 James Harden AU RC	500	700	1,000	2,000
64 Stephen Curry AU RC	2,000	2,500	4,000	8,000
72 Stephen Curry AU	2,000	2,500	4,000	8,000
73 Ricky Rubio AU	80	100	120	250
74 James Harden AU	500	600	1,000	2,000

2009-10 Limited

	NmMt 8	NmMt+ 8.5	MT 9	Gem 9.5/10
151 Blake Griffin JSY AU RC	▼20	▼25	▼50	100
156 Stephen Curry JSY AU RC	▼300	▼450	▼600	▼1,000

2009-10 Panini

	NmMt 8	NmMt+ 8.5	MT 9	Gem 9.5/10
303 James Harden RC	6	8	12	30
307 Stephen Curry RC	▼12	▼20	▼30	▼60
353 James Harden RC	6	8	12	30
357 Stephen Curry RC	▼12	▼20	▼30	▼60
372 Stephen Curry RC	▼12	▼20	▼30	▼60
400 James Harden RC	6	8	12	30

2009-10 Playoff Contenders

	NmMt 8	NmMt+ 8.5	MT 9	Gem 9.5/10
101 Blake Griffin SP AU RC	▼25	▼30	▼60	▼120
103 James Harden SP AU RC	▲120	▲200	300	▲500
106 Stephen Curry SP AU RC	400	600	800	1,500

2009-10 Playoff National Treasures

	NmMt 8	NmMt+ 8.5	MT 9	Gem 9.5/10
201 Blake Griffin JSY AU RC	▼600	▼800	▼1,000	
203 James Harden JSY AU RC	5,000	6,000	8,000	12,000
206 Stephen Curry JSY AU RC	20,000	25,000	30,000	50,000

2009-10 Prestige

	NmMt 8	NmMt+ 8.5	MT 9	Gem 9.5/10
157 Stephen Curry RC	25	30	40	60
207 Stephen Curry RC	25	30	40	60
230 Stephen Curry Davidson RC	15	20	30	50

2009-10 Rookies and Stars

	NmMt 8	NmMt+ 8.5	MT 9	Gem 9.5/10
131 Blake Griffin AU/449 RC	▼20	▼30	▼50	▼100
133 James Harden AU/449 RC	80	100	▲200	▲400
136 Stephen Curry AU/449 RC	400	▲600	▲800	▲2,000

2009-10 Studio

	NmMt 8	NmMt+ 8.5	MT 9	Gem 9.5/10
129 Stephen Curry RC	▼15	▼20	40	▼80

2009-10 Topps

	NmMt 8	NmMt+ 8.5	MT 9	Gem 9.5/10
319 James Harden RC	▲50	60	100	200
321 Stephen Curry RC	120	▼150	▼250	▼500

2009-10 Topps Chrome

	NmMt 8	NmMt+ 8.5	MT 9	Gem 9.5/10
96 Blake Griffin RC	▼40	60	▲100	▲200
97 Ricky Rubio RC	15	20	25	50
99 James Harden RC	250	300	500	800
101 Stephen Curry RC	800	1,000	1,500	3,000

2009-10 Topps Chrome Refractors

	NmMt 8	NmMt+ 8.5	MT 9	Gem 9.5/10
96 Blake Griffin	80	100	200	300
101 Stephen Curry	3,000	4,000	5,000	8,000

2009-10 Upper Deck

	NmMt 8	NmMt+ 8.5	MT 9	Gem 9.5/10
227 James Harden SP RC	10	15	25	60
234 Stephen Curry SP RC	▼25	▼30	▼60	▼120

2009-10 Upper Deck Draft Edition

	NmMt 8	NmMt+ 8.5	MT 9	Gem 9.5/10
34 Stephen Curry SP	15	20	40	80
40 James Harden	10	15	30	60

2009-10 Upper Deck First Edition

	NmMt 8	NmMt+ 8.5	MT 9	Gem 9.5/10
188 James Harden RC	10	15	25	60
196 Stephen Curry RC	50	60	100	200

2010-11 Classics

	NmMt 8	NmMt+ 8.5	MT 9	Gem 9.5/10
164 Paul George/449 AU RC	▲50	60	▲120	▲300

2010-11 Donruss

	NmMt 8	NmMt+ 8.5	MT 9	Gem 9.5/10
237 Paul George RC	▲8	▲10	▲20	▲50

2010-11 Limited

	NmMt 8	NmMt+ 8.5	MT 9	Gem 9.5/10
183 Paul George JSY AU RC	50	60	120	200

2010-11 Panini Gold Standard

	NmMt 8	NmMt+ 8.5	MT 9	Gem 9.5/10
222 Paul George AU RC	▲60	▲80	▲150	▲400

2010-11 Panini Threads

	NmMt 8	NmMt+ 8.5	MT 9	Gem 9.5/10
33 Paul George AU RC	▲50	60	▲120	▲250

2010-11 Playoff National Treasures

	NmMt 8	NmMt+ 8.5	MT 9	Gem 9.5/10
201 John Wall JSY AU/99 RC	600	700	800	1,500
210 Paul George JSY AU/99 RC	1,000	1,500	3,000	4,000

2010-11 Rookies and Stars

	NmMt 8	NmMt+ 8.5	MT 9	Gem 9.5/10
140 Paul George AU/455 RC	▲40	▲50	▲100	▲200
170 John Wall AU/454 RC	▼15	▼20	▼40	80

2010-11 Totally Certified

	NmMt 8	NmMt+ 8.5	MT 9	Gem 9.5/10
151 John Wall/599 JSY AU RC	▼20	▼25	▼50	▼80
173 Paul George/599 JSY AU RC	▲40	▲60	▲100	▲200

2011-12 Exquisite Collection

	NmMt 8	NmMt+ 8.5	MT 9	Gem 9.5/10
64 Klay Thompson AU	▼200	▼250	400	600
65 Kawhi Leonard AU	400	500	700	1,000

2011-12 Limited 2011 Draft Pick Redemptions Autographs

	NmMt 8	NmMt+ 8.5	MT 9	Gem 9.5/10
XRCG Klay Thompson	40	60	100	200
XRCN Kawhi Leonard	80	100	▲150	250

2011-12 Panini Gold Standard 2011 Draft Pick Redemptions Autographs

		NmMt 8	NmMt+ 8.5	MT 9	Gem 9.5/10
KI	Kyrie Irving	60	80	100	200
KL	Kawhi Leonard	▲100	▲150	▲250	▲400
KT	Klay Thompson	50	60	80	200

2011-12 SP Authentic

		NmMt 8	NmMt+ 8.5	MT 9	Gem 9.5/10
27	Kawhi Leonard	▲12	▲15	▲30	60

2011-12 SP Authentic Autographs

		NmMt 8	NmMt+ 8.5	MT 9	Gem 9.5/10
23	Klay Thompson	50	60	▲100	▲200
27	Kawhi Leonard	▲150	▲200	▲400	500

2012-13 Absolute

		NmMt 8	NmMt+ 8.5	MT 9	Gem 9.5/10
151	Kyrie Irving AU/199 RC	▼50	▼80	120	▼220
165	Anthony Davis AU/199 RC	▼120	200	▲300	400
200	Kawhi Leonard AU/399 RC	120	200	300	500

2012-13 Elite

		NmMt 8	NmMt+ 8.5	MT 9	Gem 9.5/10
215	Kawhi Leonard RC	30	40	60	120
257	Damian Lillard RC	12	15	30	60

2012-13 Hoops

		NmMt 8	NmMt+ 8.5	MT 9	Gem 9.5/10
223	Kyrie Irving RC	5	6	8	▼15
236	Kawhi Leonard RC	6	8	15	40
275	Anthony Davis RC	6	8	15	40
280	Damian Lillard RC	5	6	▼8	▼20

2012-13 Hoops Autographs

		NmMt 8	NmMt+ 8.5	MT 9	Gem 9.5/10
232	Klay Thompson	40	50	▲80	▲150
236	Kawhi Leonard	80	100	▲200	400
275	Anthony Davis	120	150	▲250	▲400

2012-13 Immaculate Collection

		NmMt 8	NmMt+ 8.5	MT 9	Gem 9.5/10
112	Kawhi Leonard JSY AU RC	1,500	2,500	4,000	
134	Anthony Davis JSY AU RC	1,500	2,500	4,000	

2012-13 Limited

		NmMt 8	NmMt+ 8.5	MT 9	Gem 9.5/10
155	Kyrie Irving AU/199 RC	▼30	▼50	▼80	▼150
156	Anthony Davis AU/199 RC	120	150	200	300
174	Kawhi Leonard AU/349 RC	100	120	▲200	300
190	Klay Thompson AU/299 RC	▲40	▲60	▲100	▲200

2012-13 Panini Contenders

		NmMt 8	NmMt+ 8.5	MT 9	Gem 9.5/10
201	Anthony Davis AU RC	150	▲250	▲400	▲600
203	Bradley Beal AU RC	▲20	▲30	▲60	▲120
250	Kyrie Irving AU RC	60	80	120	200
254	Jimmy Butler AU RC	▲20	▲30	▲50	▲100
263	Kawhi Leonard AU RC	▲200	▲250	▲400	▲800
271	Klay Thompson AU RC	▲60	▲100	▲150	▲300

2012-13 Panini Gold Standard

		NmMt 8	NmMt+ 8.5	MT 9	Gem 9.5/10
227	Kyrie Irving JSY AU RC	60	80	150	250
228	Anthony Davis JSY AU RC	▲150	▲250	▲400	▲600
259	Kawhi Leonard JSY AU RC	150	250	400	600

2012-13 Panini National Treasures

		NmMt 8	NmMt+ 8.5	MT 9	Gem 9.5/10
100	Damian Lillard RC	60	80	150	300
101	Kyrie Irving JSY AU 199 RC	1,000	1,500	3,000	4,000
110	Klay Thompson JSY AU 199 RC	1,000	1,500	2,000	3,000
114	Kawhi Leonard JSY AU 199 RC	5,000	6,000	9,000	▲15,000
127	Jimmy Butler JSY AU 199 RC	250	400	600	800
151	Anthony Davis JSY AU 199 RC	▲5,000	▲6,000	▲9,000	▲15,000
153	Bradley Beal JSY AU/199 RC	▲500	▲600	▲800	▲1,500
201	Damian Lillard JSY AU/99	600	800	1,000	2,000

2012-13 Panini Prizm

		NmMt 8	NmMt+ 8.5	MT 9	Gem 9.5/10
1	LeBron James	12	15	30	120
201	Kyrie Irving RC	15	20	40	80
203	Klay Thompson RC	▲15	▲20	▲40	▲100
205	Jimmy Butler RC	▲6	▲8	▲15	30
209	Kawhi Leonard RC	▲80	▲120	▲200	▲400
225	Kemba Walker RC	12	15	30	100
236	Anthony Davis RC	▲60	▲100	▲150	▲300
238	Bradley Beal RC	8	10	▲20	▲50
245	Damian Lillard RC	12	▲20	▲40	▲80
282	Draymond Green RC	8	▼10	20	40

2012-13 Panini Prizm Prizms

		NmMt 8	NmMt+ 8.5	MT 9	Gem 9.5/10
201	Kyrie Irving	▼200	300	400	800
203	Klay Thompson	▲200	▲300	▲500	▲800
209	Kawhi Leonard	▲800	▲1,000	▲2,000	▲3,000
236	Anthony Davis	▲800	▲1,000	▲2,000	▲3,000
245	Damian Lillard	▲150	▲250	▲400	600

2012-13 Panini Threads

		NmMt 8	NmMt+ 8.5	MT 9	Gem 9.5/10
151	Kyrie Irving AU RC	60	80	120	200
159	Klay Thompson AU RC	50	60	▲100	200
163	Kawhi Leonard AU RC	80	▲120	▲200	▲400
201	Anthony Davis AU RC	▼80	120	▲200	▲400

2012-13 Select

		NmMt 8	NmMt+ 8.5	MT 9	Gem 9.5/10
150	Damian Lillard RC	6	▲12	▲20	▲40
151	Kyrie Irving AU/149 RC	50	60	100	200
152	Anthony Davis AU/149 RC	100	▲150	▲250	400
178	Kawhi Leonard AU/199	100	120	200	400
246	Klay Thompson JSY AU/199 RC	60	80	150	▲250

		NmMt 8	NmMt+ 8.5	MT 9	Gem 9.5/10
250	Kawhi Leonard JSY AU/249 RC	▲150	▲200	▲300	▲500
270	Anthony Davis JSY AU/149 RC	150	200	▲300	▲500

2012-13 Totally Certified

		NmMt 8	NmMt+ 8.5	MT 9	Gem 9.5/10
11	Kawhi Leonard RC	▲15	▲20	▲40	▲80
12	Kyrie Irving RC	▼6	▼10	▼12	▼30
29	Anthony Davis RC	15	20	40	80
70	Damian Lillard RC	▼6	10	12	▲30

2013-14 Elite

		NmMt 8	NmMt+ 8.5	MT 9	Gem 9.5/10
229	Giannis Antetokounmpo RC	80	100	200	▲400

2013-14 Hoops

		NmMt 8	NmMt+ 8.5	MT 9	Gem 9.5/10
275	Giannis Antetokounmpo RC	25	40	60	120

2013-14 Immaculate Collection

		NmMt 8	NmMt+ 8.5	MT 9	Gem 9.5/10
131	Giannis Antetokounmpo JSY AU RC	6,000	8,000	10,000	15,000

2013-14 Panini Crusade

		NmMt 8	NmMt+ 8.5	MT 9	Gem 9.5/10
122	Giannis Antetokounmpo RC	20	25	40	100

2013-14 Panini Gold Standard

		NmMt 8	NmMt+ 8.5	MT 9	Gem 9.5/10
231	Giannis Antetokounmpo JSY AU RC	800	1,000	1,500	2,500

2013-14 Panini Preferred

		NmMt 8	NmMt+ 8.5	MT 9	Gem 9.5/10
380	Giannis Antetokounmpo SL JSY AU/99	1,000	1,200	2,000	3,000

2013-14 Panini Prizm

		NmMt 8	NmMt+ 8.5	MT 9	Gem 9.5/10
276	Victor Oladipo RC	6	8	15	40
290	Giannis Antetokounmpo RC	▼150	▼200	400	600

2013-14 Panini Prizm Autographs

		NmMt 8	NmMt+ 8.5	MT 9	Gem 9.5/10
13	Victor Oladipo	40	60	100	200
33	Giannis Antetokounmpo	▲600	▲800	▲1,200	2,000

2013-14 Panini Signatures '14 Draft X-Change

		NmMt 8	NmMt+ 8.5	MT 9	Gem 9.5/10
1	Andrew Wiggins#(Pick 1	8	10	20	40
3	Joel Embiid#(Pick 3	10	15	30	120

2013-14 Panini Spectra

		NmMt 8	NmMt+ 8.5	MT 9	Gem 9.5/10
120	Giannis Antetokounmpo JSY AU RC	450	600	800	1,200

2013-14 Prestige

	NmMt 8	NmMt+ 8.5	MT 9	Gem 9.5/10
Giannis Antetokounmpo RC	15	25	40	80

2013-14 Select

	NmMt 8	NmMt+ 8.5	MT 9	Gem 9.5/10
Giannis Antetokounmpo RC	30	50	80	150

2014-15 Immaculate Collection

	NmMt 8	NmMt+ 8.5	MT 9	Gem 9.5/10
Joel Embiid JSY AU RC	600	800	1,000	3,000

2014-15 Panini National Treasures

	NmMt 8	NmMt+ 8.5	MT 9	Gem 9.5/10
Andrew Wiggins JSY AU/99 RC		800	1,000	2,000
500				
Joel Embiid JSY AU/99 RC	2,000	2,500	4,000	6,000

2014-15 Panini Prizm

	NmMt 8	NmMt+ 8.5	MT 9	Gem 9.5/10
Andrew Wiggins RC	5	6	▲12	▲30
3 Joel Embiid RC	15	20	40	80

2014-15 Panini Prizm Prizms

	NmMt 8	NmMt+ 8.5	MT 9	Gem 9.5/10
Andrew Wiggins	40	60	100	250
3 Joel Embiid	200	300	400	600

2014-15 Panini Spectra

	NmMt 8	NmMt+ 8.5	MT 9	Gem 9.5/10
2 Andrew Wiggins JSY AU RC	▲15	▲20	▲40	▲80
3 Joel Embiid JSY AU RC	80	120	200	400

2014-15 Select

	NmMt 8	NmMt+ 8.5	MT 9	Gem 9.5/10
Joel Embiid CON RC	5	6	▼12	▼30
0 Andrew Wiggins CON RC	4	5	6	15

2015-16 Hoops

	NmMt 8	NmMt+ 8.5	MT 9	Gem 9.5/10
51 Kristaps Porzingis RC	5	6	8	15
58 Devin Booker RC	6	8	12	25
39 Karl-Anthony Towns RC	5	6	10	20

2015-16 Immaculate Collection

	NmMt 8	NmMt+ 8.5	MT 9	Gem 9.5/10
01 Karl-Anthony Towns JSY AU/99 RC	600	800	1,000	
21 Devin Booker JSY AU/99 RC	800	1,200	2,000	

2015-16 Panini Prizm

	NmMt 8	NmMt+ 8.5	MT 9	Gem 9.5/10
308 Devin Booker RC	▲15	▲25	▲50	▲120
328 Karl-Anthony Towns RC	▲12	▲15	▲30	▲80
335 Nikola Jokic RC	▲12	▲20	▲40	▲100
348 Kristaps Porzingis RC	▲10	▲12	▲25	▲50

2015-16 Panini Prizm Prizms Silver

	NmMt 8	NmMt+ 8.5	MT 9	Gem 9.5/10
308 Devin Booker	150	200	400	600
328 Karl-Anthony Towns	100	150	250	▲400
335 Nikola Jokic	120	200	300	500
348 Kristaps Porzingis	▼80	▼100	200	300

2015-16 Panini Prizm Autographs

	NmMt 8	NmMt+ 8.5	MT 9	Gem 9.5/10
88 Devin Booker	60	80	150	250
91 Karl-Anthony Towns	60	80	150	250
98 Kristaps Porzingis	30	50	80	150

2015-16 Panini Spectra

	NmMt 8	NmMt+ 8.5	MT 9	Gem 9.5/10
101 Karl-Anthony Towns JSY AU RC	40	60	100	200
105 Kristaps Porzingis JSY AU RC	30	40	60	120
112 Devin Booker JSY AU RC	40	60	100	200

2016-17 Absolute Memorabilia

	NmMt 8	NmMt+ 8.5	MT 9	Gem 9.5/10
200 Ben Simmons RC	▼12	▼15	▼30	▼60

2016-17 Donruss Optic

	NmMt 8	NmMt+ 8.5	MT 9	Gem 9.5/10
151 Ben Simmons RC	8	10	12	30
152 Brandon Ingram RC	5	6	10	25
171 Pascal Siakam RC	5	6	12	25

2016-17 Limited

	NmMt 8	NmMt+ 8.5	MT 9	Gem 9.5/10
145 Ben Simmons SP RC	▼40	▼60	▼100	250

2016-17 Panini National Treasures

	NmMt 8	NmMt+ 8.5	MT 9	Gem 9.5/10
53 Ben Simmons RC	2,000	2,500	4,000	6,000
122 B.Ingram JSY AU/99 RC	2,000	2,500	4,000	
148 Pascal Siakam JSY AU/99 RC	1,000	1,500	2,000	

2016-17 Panini Prizm

	NmMt 8	NmMt+ 8.5	MT 9	Gem 9.5/10
1 Ben Simmons RC	▲25	▲40	▲60	▲120
44 Jaylen Brown RC	5	6	10	20
131 Brandon Ingram RC	▲8	▲12	▲25	▲60
175 Jamal Murray RC	▲8	▲12	▲20	▲50
220 Pascal Siakam RC	▲15	▲25	▲40	▲100
236 Dejounte Murray RC	8	10	20	50

2016-17 Panini Prizm Prizms Silver

	NmMt 8	NmMt+ 8.5	MT 9	Gem 9.5/10
1 Ben Simmons	▼300	▼400	▼600	▼1,000
131 Brandon Ingram	100	150	250	400
220 Pascal Siakam	100	150	250	500

2016-17 Panini Spectra

	NmMt 8	NmMt+ 8.5	MT 9	Gem 9.5/10
60 Ben Simmons RC	▼20	▼30	▼60	▼100

2016-17 Select

	NmMt 8	NmMt+ 8.5	MT 9	Gem 9.5/10
60 Ben Simmons RC	▼6	▼8	▼15	▼40

2017-18 Donruss Optic Holo

	NmMt 8	NmMt+ 8.5	MT 9	Gem 9.5/10
188 Donovan Mitchell RR	25	40	60	120
196 De'Aaron Fox RR	20	30	50	100
198 Jayson Tatum RR	25	40	60	150

2017-18 Panini National Treasures

	NmMt 8	NmMt+ 8.5	MT 9	Gem 9.5/10
103 Jayson Tatum JSY AU RC	3,000	4,000	5,000	7,000

	NmMt 8	NmMt+ 8.5	MT 9	Gem 9.5/10
105 De'Aaron Fox JSY AU RC	1,000	1,500	▲3,000	▲4,000
113 Donovan Mitchell JSY AU RC	3,000	4,000	5,000	▲7,000
126 Kyle Kuzma JSY AU RC	1,000	1,500	2,000	3,000

2017-18 Panini Prizm

	NmMt 8	NmMt+ 8.5	MT 9	Gem 9.5/10
16 Jayson Tatum RC	6	▲10	▲15	▲40
24 De'Aaron Fox RC	▲10	▲12	▲20	▲40
117 Donovan Mitchell RC	▲10	12	▲25	▲60

2017-18 Panini Prizm Prizms Silver

	NmMt 8	NmMt+ 8.5	MT 9	Gem 9.5/10
16 Jayson Tatum	80	100	200	300
24 De'Aaron Fox	50	60	120	200
117 Donovan Mitchell	80	100	200	300

2017-18 Panini Prizm Autographs

	NmMt 8	NmMt+ 8.5	MT 9	Gem 9.5/10
16 Jayson Tatum	120	200	300	400
117 Donovan Mitchell	150	250	400	600
247 Lauri Markkanen	40	60	100	200

2018-19 Absolute Memorabilia

	NmMt 8	NmMt+ 8.5	MT 9	Gem 9.5/10
58 Luka Doncic RC	80	100	200	400

2018-19 Donruss Optic

	NmMt 8	NmMt+ 8.5	MT 9	Gem 9.5/10
177 Luka Doncic RR RC	▲30	▲40	▲60	▲150
198 Trae Young RR RC	6	10	15	40

2018-19 Donruss Optic Holo

	NmMt 8	NmMt+ 8.5	MT 9	Gem 9.5/10
177 Luka Doncic RR	500	600	1,000	2,500
198 Trae Young RR	150	200	300	500

2018-19 Hoops

	NmMt 8	NmMt+ 8.5	MT 9	Gem 9.5/10
250 Trae Young RC	5	6	8	20
268 Luka Doncic RC	▲8	▲12	▲20	▲60

2018-19 Panini Contenders

	NmMt 8	NmMt+ 8.5	MT 9	Gem 9.5/10
122 Luka Doncic AU RC	400	600	800	1,200
142 Trae Young AU RC	100	150	250	400

2018-19 Panini Contenders Draft Picks

	NmMt 8	NmMt+ 8.5	MT 9	Gem 9.5/10
126 Luka Doncic AU RC	250	300	500	800

2018-19 Panini Prizm

	NmMt 8	NmMt+ 8.5	MT 9	Gem 9.5/10
78 Trae Young RC	6	8	15	40
280 Luka Doncic RC	▲40	▲60	▲100	▲220

2018-19 Panini Prizm Prizms Silver

	NmMt 8	NmMt+ 8.5	MT 9	Gem 9.5/10
78 Trae Young	100	150	300	500
280 Luka Doncic	400	600	800	1,500

2000 Ultra WNBA

	NmMt 8	NmMt+ 8.5	MT 9	Gem 9.5/10
21 Becky Hammon RC	8	12	25	60

2016 WNBA

	NmMt 8	NmMt+ 8.5	MT 9	Gem 9.5/10
95 Breanna Stewart RC	60	80	120	

FOOTBALL

1888 - 1979

1888 Goodwin Champions N162

		PrFr 1	GD 2	VG 3	VgEx 4	EX 5	ExMt 6	NM 7	NmMt 8
12	Harry Beecher (Football)	1,500	3,000	6,000					

—Ed Andrews PSA 7 (NM) sold for $6,600 (Mastro; 5/08)
—Ed Andrews PSA 7 (NM) sold for $3,884 (Heritage; 10/07)
—Cap Anson PSA 7 (NM) sold for $25,831 (Memory Lane; 5/08)
—Cap Anson PSA 7 (NM) sold for $23,184 (Goodwin; 3/09)
—Cap Anson PSA 7 (NM) sold for $10,443 (Mastro; 12/05)
—Cap Anson SGC 80 (ExMt) sold for $13,698 (Mastro; 4/07)
—Dan Brouthers PSA 7 (NM) sold for $11,596 (Mastro; 4/07)
—Dan Brouthers PSA 7 (NM) sold for $6,600 (Mastro; 5/08)
—Fred Dunlap PSA 7.5 (NM+) sold for $9,000 (mastro; 5/08)
—Tim Keefe PSA 8 (NmMt) sold for $18,448 (Goodwin; 11/07)
—Tim Keefe PSA 7 (NM) sold for $13,394 (Mastro; 4/07)
—Tim Keefe SGC 80 (ExMt) sold for $7,050 (REA; 5/08)
—Tim Keefe PSA 6 (ExMt) sold for $3,680 (Superior; 3/05)
—King Kelly PSA 8 (NmMt) sold for $66,337 (SCP; 7/08)
—King Kelly PSA 8 (NmMt) sold for $18,975 (SCP Sotheby's 8/03)
—King Kelly PSA 7 (NM) sold for $12,000 (Mastro; 5/08)

1894 Mayo

—George Adee #2 PSA 8 (NM/MT) sold for $2400 (Legendary; 8/12)
—H.W.Barnett #4 PSA 8 (NM/MT) sold for $2100 (Legendary; 8/12)
—Anson Beard #6 SGC 5 (EXC) sold for $1057.5 (Huggins&Scott; 10/12)
—Charles Brewer #7 SGC 7.5 (Near MT+) sold for $1600 (Legendary; 8/12)
—H.D.Brown #8 PSA 8 (NM/MT) sold for $2200 (Legendary; 8/12)
—C.D. Burt #9 PSA 6 (EX-MT) sold for $1300 (Legendary; 8/12)
—Frank Butterworth #10 SGC 7 (Near MT) sold for $950 (Legendary; 8/12)
—Anonymous John Dunlop SGC 1 (Poor) sold for $12,659 (Goodiwn; 7/09)
—Anonymous John Dunlop #35 PSA 1 (Poor) sold for $9000 (Legendary; 8/12)
—Madison Gonterman #13 PSA 7 (Near MT) sold for $1000 (Legendary; 8/12)
—George Gray PSA 5 (Ex) sold for $1,035 (Huggins&Scott; 4/08)
—George Gray #14 PSA 7 (Near MT) sold for $900 (Legendary; 8/12)
—John Greenway SGC 4 (VgEx) sold for $794 (Memory Lane; 8/06)
—Frank Hinkey PSA 6 (ExMt) sold for $1,645 (Robert Edward Auction; 4/07)
—Augustus Holly #18 SGC 4 (VgEx) sold for $655 (Memory Lane; 8/06)
—Langdon Lea #19 PSA 7 (Near MT) sold for $1200 (Legendary; 8/12)
—William Mackie #20 PSA 7 (Near MT) sold for $1400 (Legendary; 8/12)
—Tom Manahan #21 PSA 7 (Near MT) sold for $2000 (Legendary; 8/12)
—Fred Murphy #24 PSA 7 (Near MT) sold for $950 (Legendary; 8/12)
—Neilson Poe #25 PSA 3 (VG) sold for $1,406 (Barry Sloate Auction; 9/07)
—Neilson Poe #25 PSA 7 (Near MT) sold for $3750 (Legendary; 8/12)
—Dudley Riggs #26 PSA 8 (NM/MT) sold for $2300 (Legendary; 8/12)
—Phillip Stillman #27 PSA 8 (NM/MT) sold for $2200 (Legendary; 8/12)
—Knox Taylor #28 PSA 8 (NM/MT) sold for $2500 (Legendary; 8/12)
—T.Trenchard #30 SGC 7 (Near MT) sold for $2100 (Legendary; 8/12)
—William Ward #31 PSA 7 (Near MT) sold for $1600 (Legendary; 8/12)
—Bert Waters #32 PSA 8 (NM/MT) sold for $2200 (Legendary; 8/12)
—A. Wheeler #33 PSA 7 (Near MT) sold for $1300 (Legendary; 8/12)
—Edgar Wrightington #34 PSA 7 (Near MT) sold for $1200 (Legendary; 8/12)

1933 Sport Kings

		PrFr 1	GD 2	VG 3	VgEx 4	EX 5	ExMt 6	NM 7	NmMt 8
4	Red Grange RC FB	250	300	400	550	700	1,200	2,500	
6	Jim Thorpe RC FB	300	400	500	600	900	1,500	2,500	
35	Knute Rockne RC FB		200	250	450	600	800	1,200	4,000

—Red Grange #4 PSA 8 (NmMt) sold for $13,394.40 (Mastro Auctions; 12/07)
—Red Grange #4 SGC 8 (NmMt) sold for $3,704 (Mile High Auctions; 11/10)
—Carl Hubbell #42 PSA 9 (MT) sold for $7,929 (Mastro; 12/05)
—Babe Ruth #2 SGC 92 (NmMt+) sold for $64,417 (Mastro; 4/07)
—Babe Ruth #2 GAI 7.5 (NM+) sold for $5,541 (Mile High; 8/07)
—Jim Thorpe #6 PSA 8 (NmMt) sold for $7,200.00 (Mastro Auctions; 5/08)
—Ed Wachter #5 PSA 8 (NmMt) sold for $2,100 (Bussineau; 7/13)

1935 National Chicle

		PrFr 1	GD 2	VG 3	VgEx 4	EX 5	ExMt 6	NM 7	NmMt 8
1A	Dutch Clark RC	150	200	250	400	600	1,000	2,500	3,500
2A	Bo Molenda RC	30	50	60	100	150	250	600	3,000
3A	George Kenneally RC	30	50	60	100	150	200	800	1,500
4A	Ed Matesic RC	30	50	60	100	125	200	600	1,500
5A	Glenn Presnell RC	30	50	60	100	150	225	500	1,800
6A	Pug Rentner RC	30	50	60	100	125	200	400	1,000
7A	Ken Strong RC	60	80	125	200	350	400	1,000	2,500
8A	Jim Zyntell RC	30	50	60	100	125	175	400	900
9A	Knute Rockne CO	250	350	450	600	1,200	2,000	4,000	8,000
10A	Cliff Battles RC	80	120	150	250	400	600	1,000	2,500
11A	Turk Edwards RC	80	120	150	250	400	600	1,200	4,000
12A	Tom Hupke RC	30	50	60	100	125	175	400	900
13A	Homer Griffiths RC	30	50	60	100	125	175	400	900
14A	Phil Sarboe RC	30	50	60	100	125	175	400	900
15A	Ben Ciccone RC	30	50	60	100	125	175	400	900
16A	Ben Smith RC	30	50	60	100	125	175	400	900
17A	Tom Jones RC	30	50	60	100	125	175	400	900
18A	Mike Mikulak RC	30	50	60	100	125	200	400	900
19	Ralph Kercheval RC	30	50	60	100	125	200	400	900
20A	Warren Heller RC	30	50	60	100	125	175	400	900
21A	Cliff Montgomery RC	30	50	60	100	125	175	400	900
22A	Shipwreck Kelly RC	30	50	60	100	125	175	400	900
23A	Beattie Feathers RC	40	60	90	150	200	300	600	1,200
24A	Clarke Hinkle RC	120	150	200	350	500	700	1,500	3,500
25	Dale Burnett RC	175	250	300	400	500	750	1,200	
26	John Dell Isola RC	175	250	400	400	500	750	1,200	
27	Bull Tosi RC	▲300	600	900	1,500	2,500	4,000	12,000	
28	Stan Kostka RC	175	250	300	500	600	750	1,200	
29	Jim MacMurdo RC	175	250	300	400	500	750	1,200	
30	Ernie Caddel RC	175	250	300	400	500	750	1,200	
31	Nic Niccola RC	175	250	300	400	500	1,200	1,500	
32	Swede Johnston RC	175	250	300	400	500	750	1,200	
33	Ernie Smith RC	175	250	300	400	500	750	2,000	
34	Bronko Nagurski RC	3,000	3,500	4,000	▲10,000	▲15,000	▲20,000	25,000	
35	Luke Johnsos RC	175	250	300	400	600	1,000	1,500	
36	Bernie Masterson RC	175	250	300	450	600	1,000	3,000	

—Dale Burnett #25 PSA 8 (NmMt) sold for $2,550 (eBay; 1/05)
—Ernie Caddel #30 SGC 96 (Mint) sold for $5,000 (Robert Edward; 5/09)
—Ernie Caddel #30 PSA 8 (NmMt) sold for $2,360 (Love of the Game Winter; 2/14)
—John Dell Isola #26 SGC 96 (Mint) sold for $3,500 (Robert Edward; 5/09)
—John Dell Isola #26 PSA 8 (NmMt) sold for $1,912 (Heritage; 10/06)
—Beattie Feathers #23 PSA 9 (Mint) sold for $2,496 (Mile High; 11/09)
—Homer Griffiths #13 PSA 9 (Mint) sold for $1,912 (Heritage; 10/06)
—Warren Heller #20 PSA 9 (Mint) sold for $3,287 (Mastro; 12/03)
—Luke Johnsos #35 PSA 8 (NmMt) sold for $2,988 (Mastro; 4/04)
—Swede Johnston #32 PSA 8 (NmMt) sold for $2,490 (Heritage; 5/06)
—Swede Johnston #32 PSA 8 (NmMt) sold for $2,950 (Love of the Game Winter; 2/14)
—Tom Jones #17 PSA 9 (Mint) sold for $3,884 (Heritage; 5/06)
—Shipwreck Kelly #22 PSA 9 (Mint) sold for $1,400 (Robert Edward; 5/09)
—Ralph Kercheval #19 PSA 9 (Mint) sold for $2,495 (eBay; 6/04)
—Stan Kostka #28 PSA 8 (NmMt) sold for $3,300 (Mastro; 5/08)
—Bernie Masterson #36 PSA 8 (NmMt) sold for $14,340 (Heritage; 5/06)
—Jim MacMurdo #36 PSA 8 (NmMt) sold for $3,650 (Memory Lane; 6/08)
—Jim MacMurdo #36 PSA 8 (NmMt) sold for $2,478 (Love of the Game Winter; 2/14)
—Mike Mikulak #18 PSA 9 (Mint) sold for $4,050 (eBay; 11/07)
—Mike Mikulak #18 SGC 96 (Mint) sold for $1,526 (eBay; 5/05)
—Bronko Nagurski #34 SGC 96 (Mint) private sale $240,000 (SGC reported; 7/06)
—Bronko Nagurski #34 SGC 96 (Mint) sold for $80,000 (eBay; 6/03)
—Bronko Nagurski #34 PSA 8 (NmMt) sold for $58,417 (Memory Lane; 12/06)
—Bronko Nagurski #34 PSA 8 (NmMt) sold for $66,354 (SCP Auctions; 7/08)
—Bronko Nagurski #34 PSA 7 (NmMt) sold for $23,148 (Memory Lane; 5/13)
—Nic Niccola #31 PSA 9 (Mint) sold for $7,200 (Mastro; 4/08)
—Nic Niccola #31 PSA 8 (NmMt) sold for $2,616 (eBay; 4/07)
—Nic Niccola #31 PSA 8 (NmMt) sold for $4,050 (eBay; 3/05)

...ute Rockne #9 SGC 8.5 (NmMt+) sold for $6,019 (Mastro; 12/07)
...ute Rockne #9 PSA 8 (NmMt) sold for $6,114 (SCP Auctions; 7/08)
...n Strong #7 PSA 9 (Mint) sold for $11,352 (Heritage; 5/06)
...ll Tosi #27 PSA 8 (NmMt) sold for $5,826 (Mastro; 4/04)
...m Zyntell #8 PSA 9 (Mint) sold for $2,987 (Heritage; 5/06)

48 Bowman

	PrFr 1	GD 2	VG 3	VgEx 4	EX 5	ExMt 6	NM 7	NmMt 8
Joe Tereshinski RC	20	30	25	30	40	100	200	700
Larry Olsonoski	6	8	10	15	25	35	▲60	250
Johnny Lujack SP RC	30	50	80	125	175	250	450	1,000
Ray Poole	5	6	8	12	20	30	50	150
Bill DeCorrevont RC	6	8	10	15	25	35	50	175
Paul Briggs SP	10	15	25	30	50	75	100	250
Steve Van Buren RC	20	30	40	60	100	150	300	800
Kenny Washington RC	10	15	20	40	50	60	120	▼150
Nolan Luhn SP	10	15	25	30	60	100	175	400
Chris Iversen	5	6	8	12	20	30	50	▼150
Jack Wiley	6	8	10	15	25	35	50	175
Charley Conerly SP RC	30	50	▲80	100	150	200	350	500
Hugh Taylor RC	5	6	8	12	20	30	50	150
Frank Seno	6	8	10	15	25	35	50	150
Gil Bouley SP	10	15	25	30	50	75	100	300
Tommy Thompson RC	5	6	8	12	20	30	50	200
Charley Trippi RC	10	15	20	30	50	75	125	400
Vince Banonis SP	10	15	25	30	50	75	100	350
Art Faircloth	5	6	8	12	20	30	50	150
Clyde Goodnight	6	8	10	15	25	35	50	150
Bill Chipley SP	10	15	25	30	50	75	100	300
Sammy Baugh RC	60	100	125	175	250	▼400	▼800	1,500
Don Kindt	6	8	10	15	25	35	50	175
John Koniszewski SP	10	15	25	30	50	75	150	300
Pat McHugh	5	6	8	12	20	30	50	200
Bob Waterfield RC	20	30	40	60	80	125	250	500
Tony Compagno SP	10	15	25	30	50	75	100	350
Paul Governali RC	5	6	8	12	20	30	50	175
Pat Harder RC	8	12	15	20	35	50	80	200
Vic Lindskog SP	10	15	25	30	50	75	150	300
Salvatore Rosato	5	6	8	12	20	30	50	175
John Mastrangelo	6	8	10	15	25	▲40	50	175
Fred Gehrke SP	10	15	25	30	50	75	100	300
Bosh Pritchard	5	6	8	12	20	30	50	175
Mike Micka	6	8	10	15	25	35	50	175
Bulldog Turner SP RC	30	50	60	100	150	250	600	2,000
Len Younce	5	6	8	12	20	30	50	175
Pat West	6	8	10	15	25	35	50	175
Russ Thomas SP	10	15	25	30	40	50	60	350
James Peebles	5	6	8	12	20	30	50	150
Bob Skoglund	6	8	10	15	25	35	50	175
Walt Stickle SP	10	15	25	30	50	75	100	300
Whitey Wistert RC	5	6	8	12	20	30	60	175
Paul Christman RC	8	12	15	20	35	50	80	200
Jay Rhodemyre SP	10	15	25	30	50	75	100	350
Tony Minisi	5	6	8	12	20	30	50	150
Bob Mann	6	8	10	15	25	35	50	175
Mal Kutner SP RC	10	15	25	30	50	75	100	300
Dick Poillon	5	6	8	12	20	30	50	175
Charles Cherundolo	6	8	10	15	25	35	50	175
Gerald Cowhig SP	10	15	25	30	40	75	100	300
Neill Armstrong RC	5	6	8	12	20	30	50	200
Frank Maznicki	6	8	10	15	25	35	50	175
John Sanchez SP	10	15	25	30	50	75	100	300
Frank Reagan	5	6	8	12	20	30	60	200
Jim Hardy	6	8	10	15	25	35	80	150
John Badaczewski SP	10	15	25	30	50	75	100	350
Robert Nussbaumer	5	6	8	12	20	30	50	175
Marvin Pregulman	6	8	10	15	25	35	50	125
Elbie Nickel SP RC	12	20	30	40	75	100	150	350
Alex Wojciechowicz RC	20	30	40	60	80	100	300	600
Walt Schlinkman	6	8	10	15	25	35	50	175
Pete Pihos SP RC	30	50	60	▲125	▲200	250	350	1,200
Joseph Sulaitis	5	6	8	12	20	30	50	125
Mike Holovak RC	6	8	10	15	25	35	50	175
Cy Souders SP	10	15	25	30	50	75	100	300
Paul McKee	5	6	8	12	20	30	50	150
Bill Blackburn	6	8	10	15	25	35	50	175
Frank Minini SP	10	15	25	30	50	75	▲125	300
Jack Ferrante	5	6	8	12	20	30	50	175

	PrFr 1	GD 2	VG 3	VgEx 4	EX 5	ExMt 6	NM 7	NmMt 8
71 Les Horvath RC	6	10	12	▲25	30	50	125	200
72 Ted Fritsch Sr. SP RC	12	20	30	35	60	▼80	200	350
73 Tex Coulter RC	5	6	8	12	20	30	50	200
74 Boley Dancewicz RC	6	8	10	15	25	35	50	▼150
75 Dante Mangani SP	10	15	25	30	50	75	100	300
76 James Hefti	5	6	8	12	20	30	50	▼150
77 Paul Sarringhaus	6	8	10	15	25	35	50	175
78 Joe Scott SP	10	15	25	30	50	75	100	200
79 Bucko Kilroy RC	5	6	8	12	20	30	80	300
80 Bill Dudley RC	12	20	30	50	80	100	▲150	▲350
81 Mar.Goldberg SP RC	10	15	25	40	60	100	225	400
82 John Cannady	5	6	8	12	20	30	50	175
83 Perry Moss	6	8	10	15	25	35	50	200
84 Harold Crisler SP RC	10	15	25	30	50	75	100	400
85 Bill Gray	5	6	8	12	20	30	50	175
86 John Clement	5	6	8	12	20	30	50	175
87 Dan Sandifer SP	10	15	25	30	50	75	100	300
88 Ben Kish	5	6	8	12	20	30	50	175
89 Herbert Banta	6	8	10	15	25	35	50	175
90 Bill Garnaas SP	10	15	25	30	50	100	150	
91 Jim White RC	8	12	15	25	50	80	150	200
92 Frank Barzilauskas	6	8	10	15	25	35	50	175
93 Vic Sears SP	10	15	25	30	50	75	125	300
94 John Adams	5	6	8	12	20	30	50	250
95 George McAfee RC	15	25	35	50	80	100	▼150	500
96 Ralph Heywood SP	10	15	25	30	40	50	150	300
97 Joe Muha	5	6	8	12	20	30	50	175
98 Fred Enke	6	8	10	15	25	35	50	175
99 Harry Gilmer SP RC	25	40	50	100	150	200	300	500
100 Bill Miklich	5	6	8	12	20	30	60	125
101 Joe Gottlieb	5	6	8	12	20	35	60	200
102 Bud Angsman SP RC	10	15	25	30	50	75	100	400
103 Tom Farmer	5	6	8	12	20	30	50	
104 Bruce Smith RC	12	20	30	40	100	200	400	800
105 Bob Cifers SP	10	15	25	30	50	75	100	400
106 Ernie Steele	5	6	8	12	25	60	150	
107 Sid Luckman RC	25	40	50	100	▲150	175	400	800
108 Buford Ray SP RC	30	50	60	▲150	225	350	500	1,200

—Bud Angsman #102 PSA 9 (Mint) sold for $1,478.56 (Ebay; 1/14)
—Sammy Baugh #22 SGC 9 (Mint) sold for $2640 (Ebay; 9/14)
—Sammy Baugh #22 PSA 9 (Mint) sold for $6917 (Ebay; 4/15)
—John Cannady #82 PSA 9 (Mint) sold for $1,477.98 (Goodwin; 8/12)
—John Clement #86 PSA 9 (Mint) sold for $464 (eBay; 6/12)
—Paul Christman #44 PSA 9 (Mint) sold for $1,533 (eBay; 2/14)
—Harold Crisler #84 PSA 9 (MT) sold for $1,475 (REA; 4/07)
—Gerald Cowhig SP #51 PSA 9 (Mint) sold for $1633 (eBay; 8/12)
—Bill Dudley #80 PSA 9 (MT) sold for $3,285 (Goodwin; 7/09)
—Boley Dancewicz #74 PSA 9 (MT) sold for $1,170 (eBay; 8/08)
—Art Faircloth #19 PSA 9 (MT) sold for $810 (REA; 4/07)
—Harry Gilmer #99 PSA 8.5 (NmMt+) sold for $3,253.50 (Ebay; 3/14)
—Jim Hardy #56 PSA 9 (MT) sold for $761 (eBay; 11/07)
—John Mastrangelo #32 PSA 9 (Mint) sold for $1,076 (Memory Lane; 8/12)
— Mar. Goldberg #81 PSA 9 (Mint) sold for $3,546.95 (Ebay; 2/14)
—Marvin Pregulman #59 PSA 9 (MT) sold for $1,261 (Goodwin;01/13)
—Frank Reagan #55 PSA 9 (MT) sold for $895 (REA; 4/07)
—John Sanchez #54 PSA 9 (MT) sold for $961 (eBay; 11/07)
—Ernie Steele #54 PSA 8 (NmMt) sold for $1,075 (eBay; 11/07)
—Joe Tereshinski #1 PSA 9 (MT) sold for $2,448 (Mastro; 12/06)
—Charley Trippi #17 PSA 9 (MT) sold for $1,853 (Goodwin; 2/10)
—Charley Trippi #17 PSA 9 (MT) sold for $1,373 (eBay; 4/07)
—Charley Trippi #17 PSA 9 (MT) sold for $1,229 (eBay; 9/14)
—Bob Waterfield #26 PSA 9 (MT) sold for $1,833 (Memory Lane; 12/06)
—Pat West #38 PSA 9 (MT) sold for $1,767 (Goodwin; 2/10)
—Alex Wojciechowicz #38 PSA 9 (MT) sold for $2,042 (Mile High; 11/10)

1948 Leaf

	PrFr 1	GD 2	VG 3	VgEx 4	EX 5	ExMt 6	NM 7	NmMt 8
1A Sid Luckman Yell.Bkgrd RC	100	125	200	250	450	1,600		
2 Steve Suhey	6	10	12	20	30	50	150	
3A BulldogTurner Red Bkgrd RC	20	35	40	60	100	250	600	
3C Bulldog Turner Wht.Bkgrd RC	20	30	40	60	125	200		
4A Doak Walker RC	30	50	75	135	175	800	1,600	
5A Levi Jackson Blu Jsy RC	6	10	12	20	30	50	150	
5B Levi Jackson Wht Jsy RC	10	15	20	30	50	75		
6A Bobby Layne Yell.Pants RC	80	125	150	225	300	700	4,000	
6B Bobby Layne Red Pants RC	100	125	150	225	400	600		
7A Bill Fischer Red Bkgrd RC	6	10	12	20	30	50	350	
7C Bill Fischer Wht.Bkgrd RC	10	15	20	30	50	75		

FOOTBALL

		PrFr 1	GD 2	VG 3	VgEx 4	EX 5	ExMt 6	NM 7	NmMt 8
8A	Vince Banonis Blk Name RC	6	10	12	20	30	50	150	
8B	Vince Banonis Wht Name RC	10	15	20	30	50	75		
9A	Tommy Thompson Yell.#'s RC	6	10	12	20	30	60	250	
9B	Tommy Thompson Blu #'s RC	10	15	20	30	50	75		
10A	Perry Moss	6	10	15	30	50	75	200	
11A	Terry Brennan RC	6	10	12	20	30	50	150	
12A	Bill Swiacki Blk Name RC	6	10	12	20	30	50	150	
12B	Bill Swiacki Wht Name RC	10	15	20	30	50	75		
13A	Johnny Lujack RC	25	40	50	75	100	200	600	
13B	Johnny Lujack RC ERR	125	200	300	400	500	750		
14A	Mal Kutner BL RC	6	10	12	20	30	50	150	
14B	Mal Kutner WL RC	10	15	20	30	50	75		
15	Charlie Justice RC	10	15	20	35	60	90	350	
16A	Pete Pihos Yell.#'s RC	20	30	35	60	100	175	600	
16B	Pete Pihos Blu #'s RC	30	50	60	80	100	300		
17A	Ken Washington Blk Name RC	6	10	12	20	30	50	150	
17B	Ken Washington Wht Name RC	10	15	20	30	50	80		
18A	Harry Gilmer RC	6	10	12	20	30	50	150	
19A	George McAfee RC	15	25	30	50	100	250	600	
19B	Gorgeous George McAfee RC	80	60	80	100	200	350		
20A	George Taliaferro Yell.Bkgrd RC	6	10	12	20	30	80	150	
20B	George Taliaferro Wht.Bkgrd RC	10	15	20	30	50	75		
21	Paul Christman RC	6	10	12	20	35	60	150	
22A	Steve Van Buren Green Jsy RC	30	50	60	100	150	300	1,000	
22B	Steve Van Buren Yell.Jsy RC	40	60	90	150	250	400		
22C	S.Van Buren Grn Jsy Blu Sck RC	80	100	125	175	300			
23A	Ken Kavanaugh YS RC	6	10	12	20	30	50	150	
24A	Jim Martin Red Bkgrd RC	6	10	12	20	30	75	175	
24C	Jim Martin Wht.Bkgrd RC	10	15	20	30	50	75		
25A	Bud Angsman Blk Name RC	6	10	12	20	30	50	150	
25B	Bud Angsman Wht Name RC	10	15	20	30	50	75		
26A	Bob Waterfield Blk Name RC	30	50	60	100	175	300	1,000	
26B	Bob Waterfield Wht.Name RC	40	60	90	150	250	450		
27A	Fred Davis Yell.Bkgrd	6	10	12	20	30	50	600	
27B	Fred Davis Wht.Bkgrd	10	15	20	30	50	75		
28A	Whitey Wistert Yell.Jsy RC	8	12	15	30	40	100	250	
28B	Whitey Wistert Green Jsy RC	12	20	25	40	60	150		
29	Charley Trippi RC	10	15	20	40	▲125	225	500	2,000
30A	P.Governali RC dark tan hlmt	6	10	12	20	30	50	150	
31A	Tom McWilliams Maroon Jsy RC	6	10	12	20	30	50	150	
31B	Tom McWilliams Red Jsy RC	10	15	20	30	50	75		
32A	Leroy Zimmerman	6	10	12	20	30	50	150	
33	Pat Harder RC	6	10	12	20	▲60	▲80	150	
34A	Sammy Baugh RC maroon	100	125	200	300	500	1,500	8,000	
35A	Ted Fritsch Sr. RC	6	10	12	20	40	80	300	
36	Bill Dudley RC	12	20	35	60	100	200	600	
37A	George Connor RC	10	15	25	35	80	150	400	
38A	F.Dancewicz RC green num	6	10	12	20	30	50	150	
39	Billy Dewell	6	10	12	20	30	50	150	
40A	John Nolan RC green numbr	6	10	12	20	30	50	150	
41A	H.Szulborski Orng Pants RC	6	10	12	20	30	50	150	
41B	Harry Szulborski Yell.Pants RC	10	15	20	30	50	75		
42	Tex Coulter RC	6	10	12	20	30	50	200	
43A	R.Nussbaumer Maroon RC	6	10	12	20	30	50	200	
43B	R.Nussbaumer Red Jsy RC	10	15	20	30	50	75		
44	Bob Mann	6	10	12	25	30	40	150	
45A	Jim White RC	20	30	35	60	80	125	400	
46A	Jack Jacobs Jsy # RC	6	10	12	20	30	50	300	
46B	Jack Jacobs No Jsy # RC	12	20	25	40	60	100		
47A	John Clement RC brown FB	6	10	12	20	30	50	150	
48	Frank Reagan	6	10	12	20	30	50	200	
49	Frank Tripucka RC	8	12	15	25	40	100	300	
50	John Rauch RC	20	30	40	60	120	200	800	
51A	Mike Dimitro	20	30	40	60	120	200	800	
52A	Nomellini Blu Bkg Maroon RC	125	150	200	300	500	1,000	2,000	
52B	Nomellini Blu Bkg Red Jsy RC	100	125	150	250	500	1,200		
53	Charley Conerly RC	100	125	150	250	400	800		
54A	Chuck Bednarik Yell Bkgrd RC	150	225	350	500	800	2,000	3,500	
55	Chick Jagade	20	30	40	60	120	250		
56A	Bob Folsom RC	20	30	40	60	120	▲300		
57	Gene Rossides RC	20	30	40	60	80	300		
58	Art Weiner	20	30	40	60	120	200	800	
59	Alex Sarkistian	20	30	40	60	100	200	800	
60	Dick Harris Texas	20	30	40	60	100	250		
61	Len Younce	20	30	40	60	120	150		
62	Gene Derricotte	20	30	40	60	100	200		
63A	Roy Rebel Steiner Red Jsy RC	20	30	40	60	120	250		
64A	Frank Seno	20	30	40	60	100	250		
65A	Bob Hendren RC	20	30	40	60	120	200	600	

		PrFr 1	GD 2	VG 3	VgEx 4	EX 5	ExMt 6	NM 7	NmMt 8
66A	Jack Cloud Blue Bkgrd RC	20	30	40	60	120	200	600	
67	Harrell Collins	20	30	40	50	120	200	800	
68A	Clyde LeForce Red Bkgrd RC	20	30	40	60	100	200	400	
69	Larry Joe	20	30	40	60	100	200	300	
70	Phil O'Reilly	20	30	40	60	100	150		
71	Paul Campbell	20	30	40	60	120	150	500	
72A	Ray Evans	20	30	40	60	120	400	800	
73A	Jackie Jensen Red Bkgrd RC	60	80	100	175	250	400	800	
74	Russ Steger	20	30	40	60	100	120	400	
75	Tony Minisi	20	30	40	60	120	200	500	
76A	Clayton Tonnemaker	20	30	40	60	120	200	1,000	
77A	George Savitsky Grn Strps RC	20	30	40	60	120	200	800	
78	Clarence Self	20	30	40	60	120	250	400	
79	Rod Franz	20	30	40	60	120	200	800	
80A	Jim Youle Red Bkgrd RC	20	30	40	60	120	250		
81A	B.Bye Yell.Pants Maroon Jsy RC	20	30	40	60	120	200	800	
82	Fred Enke	20	30	40	60	100	200	500	
83A	Fred Folger Gray Jsy RC	20	30	40	60	120	250		
84	Jug Girard RC	20	30	40	100	120	200	400	
85	Joe Scott	20	30	40	60	100	150	200	
86A	Bob Demoss	20	30	60	80	150	400	1,000	
87	Dave Templeton	20	30	40	60	120	200	800	
88A	Herb Siegert	20	30	40	60	120	200	800	
89A	Bucky O'Conner RC blu jsy	20	30	40	60	120	200	800	
90	Joe Whisler	20	30	40	60	120	250	500	
91	Leon Hart RC	60	80	100	200	300	500		
92	Earl Banks	20	30	40	60	100	250	800	
93A	Frank Aschenbrenner	20	30	40	60	120	200	800	
94	John Goldsberry RC	20	30	40	60	100	250		
95	Porter Payne	20	30	40	60	100	150	800	
96A	Pete Perini	20	30	40	60	120	250		
97A	Jay Rhodemyre	20	30	40	60	120	250		
98A	Al DiMarco RC	30	50	60	100	200	300		

—Al DiMarco #98A PSA 7 (NrMt) sold for $5,121 (eBay; 7/13)
—Sammy Baugh #34 SGC 9 (NmMt) sold for $37,950 (Hunt; 3/08)
—Sammy Baugh #34 SGC 9 (NmMt) sold for $14,998(eBay; 01/13)
—Sammy Baugh #34 PSA 8 (NmMt) sold for $12,925 (REA; 4/07)
—Sammy Baugh #34 SGC 8 (NmMt) sold for $9121 (eBay; 9/14)
—Sammy Baugh #34 PSA 8 (NmMt) sold for $7,000 (Legendary; 8/13)
—Sammy Baugh #34 SGC 8.5 (NmMt) sold for $12,000 (Hunt; 3/09)
—Sammy Baugh #34 PSA 8 (NmMt) sold for $8,833 (Goodwin; 2/11)
—Sammy Baugh #34 PSA 8 (NmMt) sold for $8,495 (Mile High; 5/11)
—Sammy Baugh #34 PSA 8 (NmMt) sold for $4,500 (Mastro; 5/08)
—Sammy Baugh #34 PSA 8 (NmMt) sold for $7,000 (Legendary; 8/13)
—Chuck Bednarik YB #54A PSA 8 (NmMt) sold for $38,561 (Goodwin; 11/07)
—Chuck Bednarik YB #54A PSA 7 (NrMt) sold for $8,159 (Ebay; 11/13)
—Terry Brennan #11 SGC 9 (Mt) sold for $2,990 (Hunt; 3/08)
—Paul Campbell #71 PSA 8.5 (NmMt+) sold for $9,112 (Goodwin; 9/09)
—Paul Christman #21 PSA 8 (NmMt) sold for $3,815 (REA; 4/07)
—John Clement #47 PSA 8 (NmMt) sold for $1,277 (eBay; 2/09)
—Jack Cloud Blue Bkgrd #66A PSA 8 (NmMt) sold for $1,012 (eBay; 4/12)
—Charley Conerly RC #53 PSA 8 (NM/MT) sold for $11227.65 (Goodwin; 9/12)
—Charley Conerly RC #53 PSA 7 (NM) sold for $3080 (eBay; 6/16)
—George Connor #37 SGC 8 (NmMt) sold for $2,185 (Hunt; 3/08)
—George Connor #37 PSA 8 (NmMt) sold for $2,450 (eBay; 11/07)
—George Connor #37 PSA 8 (NmMt) sold for $1,367 (Goodwin; 2/11)
—Frank Dancewicz #38A PSA 9 (Mt) sold for $3,327 (Goodwin; 9/11)
—Bill Dudley #36 PSA 8 (NmMt) sold for $4,150 (eBay; 11/06)
—Bill Dudley #36 PSA 8 (NMMT) sold for $3163.07 (eBay; 6/12)
—Bill Dudley #36 SGC 8 (NmMt) sold for $2,226 (Mile High; 11/09)
—Fred Enke #82 PSA 8 (NmMt) sold for $2,851 (Goodwin; 11/07)
—Ray Evans #72 PSA 8 (NM/MT) sold for $2805.99 (eBay; 6/12)
—Ted Fritsch #35 SGC 8.5 (NmMt+) sold for $1,840 (Hunt; 3/08)
—Jug Girard #84 PSA 8 (NmMt) sold for $1,828 (eBay; 4/11)
—John Goldsberry #94 PSA 7.5 (NrMt+) sold for $1,928 (eBay; 10/11)
—Jug Girard RC #84 PSA 8 (NM/MT) sold for $1488.69 (Goodwin; 2/12)
—Pat Harder #33 PSA 9 (Mt) sold for $1,979 (Goodwin; 11/09)
—Pat Harder #33 SGC 8.5 (NmMt+) sold for $1,092 (Hunt; 3/08)
—Bob Hendren #65 PSA 9 (Mt) sold for $2,021 (eBay; 11/07)
—Bob Hendren #65 PSA 8 (NmMt) sold for $1,012 (eBay; 4/12)
—Jack Jacobs #46A PSA 9 (Mt) sold for $5,362 (Goodwin; 2/11)
—Jack Jacobs #46A SGC 8.5 (NmMt+) sold for $1,955 (Hunt; 3/08)
—Levi Jackson BL JSY #5A PSA 8.5 (NmMt+) sold for $1,626 (Goodwin; 11/12)
—Jackie Jensen RB #73A PSA 8.5 (NmMt+) sold for $15,114 (Goodwin; 9/09)
—Jackie Jensen RB #73A PSA 8 (NmMt) sold for $3,862 (Mile High; 6/10)
—Charlie Justice #15 PSA 8.5 (NmMt+) sold for $5,295 (Goodwin; 6/10)
—Charlie Justice #15 SGC 8 (NmMt) sold for $5,142 (Goodwin; 3/08)
—Sid Luckman YB #1A PSA 8 (NmMt) sold for $71,836 (Goodwin; 9/09)
—Sid Luckman YB #1A PSA 7 (NrMt) sold for $11,239 (Goodwin; 2/10)

d Luckman YB #1A PSA 7 (NmMt) sold for $5605 (eBay; 10/14)
d Luckman YB #1A PSA 7 (Near MT) sold for $5483.52 (Goodwin; 6/12)
d Luckman YB #1A PSA 7 (NrMT) sold for $9,717 (Goodwin;01/13)
d Luckman YB #1A PSA 7 (NrMT) sold for $6,933 (Goodwin;06/13)
hnny Lujack #13 PSA 9 (Mt) sold for $10,701 (Goodwin; 5/08)
hnny Lujack #13 SGC 9 (Mt) sold for $8,912 (Hunt; 3/08)
hnny Lujack #13 SGC 8 (NmMt) sold for $2,760 (Hunt; 3/08)
ob Mann #44 SGC 9 (Mt) sold for $3,105 (Hunt; 3/08)
erry Moss #10 PSA 9 (Mt) sold for $4,027 (Goodwin; 2/11)
eorge McAfee #19A PSA 8 (NmMt) sold for $1,980 (Goodwin; 2/10)
eorge McAfee #19A PSA 8 (NmMt) sold for $1,504 (Goodwin; 2/11)
eo Nomellini Blu Bkg Maroon RC #52A PSA 8 (NM/MT) sold for $10539.83 (Memory Lane; 5/12)
orter Payne #95 PSA 8 (NmMt) sold for $5,052 (Goodwin; 2/09)
ete Perini #96 PSA 7 (NrMT) sold for $1,057 (eBay; 9/07)
ete Pihos #16A PSA 8.5 (NmMt+) sold for $4,813 (Goodwin; 6/10)
rank Reagan #48 PSA 8 (NmMt) sold for $1,955 (eBay; 11/07)
larence Self #78 PSA 7 (NM) sold for $1,780 (eBay; 1/07)
uss Steger #74 PSA 8 (NmMt) sold for $6,846 (Goodwin; 2/10)
oy Steiner #63 PSA 9 (Mt) sold for $19,160 (Goodwin; 9/09)
ill Swiacki #12A PSA 9 (Mt) sold for $4,922 (Goodwin; 5/08)
ill Swiacki #12A SGC 9 (Mt) sold for $3,680 (Hunt; 3/08)
arry Szulborski #41A SGC 9 (Mt) sold for $2,185 (Hunt; 3/08)
ave Templeton #87 PSA 8 (NmMt) sold for $6,223 (Goodwin; 9/09)
harley Trippi #29 SGC 8 (NmMt) sold for $3,220 (Hunt; 3/08)
harley Trippi #29 PSA 8 (NmMt) sold for $2,427 (Mile High; 11/10)
harley Trippi #29 PSA 8 (NmMt) sold for $1,275 (eBay; 4/11)
ulldog Turner RB #3A PSA 9 (Mint) sold for $7,207 (Goodwin; 2/09)
ulldog Turner RB #3A PSA 8 (NmMt) sold for $2,196 (eBay; 4/11)
ulldog Turner RB #3A PSA 8 (NmMt) sold for $2,140 (Goodwin; 11/09)
ulldog Turner RB #3A PSA 8 (NmMt) sold for $2,070 (Hunt; 3/08)
Steve Van Buren #22A PSA 7.5 (NrMt+) sold for $3,176 (Goodwin; 2/11)
Steve Van Buren Green Jsy RC #22A PSA 8 (NM/MT) sold for $3427.07 (eBay; 6/12)
Doak Walker #4 SGC 8.5 (NmMt+) sold for $6,325 (Hunt; 3/08)
Doak Walker #4 PSA 8 (NmMt) sold for $9,382 (Goodwin; 6/10)
Doak Walker #4 PSA 8 (NmMt) sold for $8,139 (Goodwin; 11/07)
Doak Walker #4 PSA 8 (NmMt) sold for $6,489 (Goodwin; 2/11)
Bob Waterfield #26A PSA 8.5 (NmMt+) sold for $31,598 (Goodwin; 2/10)
Bob Waterfield Blk Name RC #26A PSA 8 (NM/MT) sold for $2811.97 (Goodwin; 6/12)
Jim Youle Red Bkgrd RC #80A PSA 7.5 (Near MT+) sold for $1090 (eBay; 6/12)

949 Leaf

	PrFr 1	GD 2	VG 3	VgEx 4	EX 5	ExMt 6	NM 7	NmMt 8
Bob Hendren	10	15	20	30	50	80	175	
Joe Scott	6	10	12	20	30	50	200	
Frank Reagan	6	10	12	20	30	80		
John Rauch	6	10	12	20	30	50	120	
Bill Fischer	6	10	12	20	30	50	120	
Elmer Bud Angsman	6	10	10	15	5	40	100	350
Billy Dewell	6	10	12	20	30	50	120	
Tommy Thompson QB	6	10	12	20	30	50	120	
Sid Luckman	20	30	▲60	100	125	250	350	500
Charley Trippi	8	12	15	25	35	▲80	200	
Bob Mann	6	10	12	20	30	80		
Paul Christman	6	10	12	20	▲50	▲60	▲125	
Bill Dudley	8	12	15	50	60	200	300	
Clyde LeForce	6	10	12	20	30	50	120	
Sammy Baugh	50	80	100	150	250	400	600	2,000
Pete Pihos	10	15	20	30	50	80	175	600
Tex Coulter	6	10	12	20	30	50	120	
Mal Kutner	6	10	12	30	40	50	120	350
Whitey Wistert	6	10	12	▲25	30	50	120	
Ted Fritsch Sr.	6	10	12	20	40	50	120	
Vince Banonis	6	10	12	20	30	60	120	
Jim White	6	10	12	20	30	50	120	
George Connor	8	12	15	25	40	60	125	400
George McAfee	8	12	15	40	50	60	200	
Frank Tripucka	8	12	15	25	40	80	250	
Fred Enke	6	10	12	20	30	80		
Charley Conerly	10	15	25	40	60	100		
Ken Kavanaugh	6	10	12	20	30	50	120	350
Bob Demoss	6	10	12	20	30	60	120	
Johnny Lujack	10	15	25	40	80	120	175	600
Jim Youle	6	10	12	20	30	80		
Harry Gilmer	6	10	12	20	30	50	120	
Robert Nussbaumer	6	10	12	20	30	50	120	
Bobby Layne	25	50	▲80	▲100	125	225	400	
Herb Siegert	6	10	12	20	30	50	120	350
Tony Minisi	6	10	12	20	30	80		

	PrFr 1	GD 2	VG 3	VgEx 4	EX 5	ExMt 6	NM 7	NmMt 8
79	Steve Van Buren	15	25	40	60	80	200	300	800
81	Perry Moss	6	10	12	20	30	50	120	
89	Bob Waterfield	12	20	30	50	75	125	225	600
90	Jack Jacobs	6	10	12	20	30	50	120	
95	Kenny Washington	8	12	15	20	40	60	120	
101	Pat Harder	6	10	12	20	30	50	120	
110	Bill Swiacki	6	10	12	20	30	50	120	
118	Fred Davis	6	10	12	20	30	50	120	350
126	Jay Rhodemyre	6	10	12	20	30	50	120	
127	Frank Seno	6	10	12	20	30	50	120	
134	Chuck Bednarik	20	30	50	100	120	200	350	
144	George Savitsky	6	10	12	20	30	150		
150	Bulldog Turner	25	40	50	90	125	200	300	400

Chuck Bednarik #134 SGC 8.5 (NmMt+) sold for $1,526 (Memory Lane; 5/08)
Bob Demoss #52 PSA 8 (NmMt) sold for $1,440 (eBay; 2/08)
Bob Hendren #1 PSA 8 (NmMt) sold for $1,930 (eBay; 4/07)
Bob Mann #17 PSA 8 (NmMt) sold for $1,295 (eBay; 12/07)
Frank Tripucka #43 PSA 8 (NmMt) sold for $822 (Goodwin; 11/07)

1950 Bowman

		GD 2	VG 3	VgEx 4	EX 5	ExMt 6	NM 7	NmMt 8	MT 9
1	Doak Walker	40	50	▲80	100	175	800	▲6,300	
2	John Greene	8	10	12	20	30	80	150	
3	Bob Nowasky	8	10	12	20	25	50	125	
4	Jonathan Jenkins	8	10	12	20	25	50	125	
5	Y.A.Tittle RC	▲80	100	150	250	350	600	2,500	
6	Lou Groza RC	25	30	40	100	200	250	600	
7	Alex Agase RC	8	10	12	20	25	40	150	
8	Mac Speedie RC	8	10	12	20	30	60	250	
9	Tony Canadeo RC	25	35	80	100	150	400	1,000	
10	Larry Craig	8	10	12	20	25	125	250	
11	Ted Fritsch Sr.	8	10	12	20	25	40	100	
12	Joe Golding	8	10	12	20	25	40	100	
13	Martin Ruby	8	10	12	20	25	40	125	
14	George Taliaferro	8	10	12	20	25	40	100	
15	Tank Younger RC	10	12	15	30	40	60	200	1,000
16	Glenn Davis RC	20	25	40	50	75	100	▼250	
17	Bob Waterfield	20	25	30	50	75	125	300	
18	Val Jansante	8	10	12	20	25	50	100	
19	Joe Geri	8	10	12	20	25	40	100	
20	Jerry Nuzum	8	10	12	20	25	40	100	
21	Elmer Bud Angsman	8	10	12	20	25	40	100	
22	Billy Dewell	8	10	12	20	25	40	100	
23	Steve Van Buren	15	20	25	35	60	100	300	
24	Cliff Patton	8	10	12	20	30	60	150	500
25	Bosh Pritchard	8	10	12	20	25	40	100	
26	Johnny Lujack	15	20	25	35	60	100	200	600
27	Sid Luckman	20	25	30	50	75	135	350	1,200
28	Bulldog Turner	10	12	15	25	40	80	250	
29	Bill Dudley	10	12	15	25	▲50	80	175	
30	Hugh Taylor	8	10	12	20	25	40	100	
31	George Thomas	8	10	12	20	25	40	100	
32	Ray Poole	8	10	12	20	25	40	100	
33	Travis Tidwell	8	10	12	20	25	40	100	
34	Gail Bruce	8	10	12	20	25	40	100	
35	Joe Perry RC	40	50	60	90	135	225	600	2,500
36	Frankie Albert RC	8	10	12	20	25	40	75	▲200
37	Bobby Layne	30	50	60	75	125	150	400	
38	Leon Hart	8	10	12	20	30	50	175	
39	Bob Hoernschemeyer RC	8	10	12	20	25	50	200	
40	Dick Barwegan RC	8	10	12	20	25	50	150	
41	Adrian Burk RC	8	10	12	20	25	40	100	500
42	Barry French	8	10	12	20	25	40	100	
43	Marion Motley RC	40	60	80	150	250	400	1,200	
44	Jim Martin	8	10	12	20	25	40	100	500
45	Otto Graham RC	150	250	350	450	700	1,500	3,000	1,500
46	Al Baldwin	8	10	12	20	25	40	100	800
47	Larry Coutre	8	10	12	20	25	40	100	
48	John Rauch	8	10	12	20	25	40	100	
49	Sam Tamburo	8	10	12	20	25	40	100	500
50	Mike Swistowicz	8	10	12	20	25	40	100	
51	Tom Fears RC	25	30	40	60	90	175	400	1,800
52	Elroy Hirsch RC	40	50	60	100	200	300	800	3,000
53	Dick Huffman	8	10	12	20	25	40	100	400
54	Bob Gage	8	10	12	20	25	40	100	
55	Buddy Tinsley	8	10	12	20	25	40	100	
56	Bill Blackburn	8	10	12	20	25	40	80	
57	John Cochran	8	10	12	20	25	40	100	

#	Player	GD 2	VG 3	VgEx 4	EX 5	ExMt 6	NM 7	NmMt 8	MT 9
58	Bill Fischer	8	10	12	20	25	40	100	
59	Whitey Wistert	8	10	12	20	25	40	100	
60	Clyde Scott	8	10	12	20	25	40	100	
61	Walter Barnes	8	10	12	20	25	40	100	
62	Bob Perina	8	10	12	20	25	40	100	
63	Bill Wightkin	8	10	12	20	25	40	100	
64	Bob Goode	8	10	12	20	25	40	100	500
65	Al Demao	8	10	12	20	25	40	100	
66	Harry Gilmer	8	10	12	20	25	40	100	
67	Bill Austin	8	10	12	20	25	40	100	
68	Joe Scott	8	10	12	20	25	40	100	
69	Tex Coulter	8	10	12	20	25	40	100	500
70	Paul Salata	8	10	12	20	25	40	100	
71	Emil Sitko RC	8	10	12	20	25	40	100	
72	Bill Johnson C	8	10	12	20	25	40	100	
73	Don Doll RC	8	10	12	20	25	40	100	
74	Dan Sandifer	8	10	12	20	25	40	100	
75	John Panelli	8	10	12	20	25	40	100	
76	Bill Leonard	8	10	12	20	25	40	100	
77	Bob Kelly	8	10	12	20	25	40	100	400
78	Dante Lavelli RC	25	30	40	60	100	175	600	
79	Tony Adamle	8	10	12	20	25	40	100	
80	Dick Wildung	8	10	12	20	25	40	100	
81	Tobin Rote RC	10	12	15	25	40	60	300	
82	Paul Burris	8	10	12	20	25	40	100	
83	Lowell Tew	8	10	12	20	25	40	100	
84	Barney Poole	8	10	12	20	25	40	100	
85	Fred Naumetz	8	10	12	20	25	40	▲150	
86	Dick Hoerner	8	10	12	20	25	40	100	
87	Bob Reinhard	8	10	12	20	25	40	100	
88	Howard Hartley RC	8	10	12	20	25	40	100	
89	Darrell Hogan RC	8	10	12	20	25	40	100	
90	Jerry Shipkey	8	10	12	20	25	40	100	
91	Frank Tripucka	8	10	12	20	25	40	100	
92	Buster Ramsey RC	8	10	12	20	25	40	100	
93	Pat Harder	8	10	12	20	25	40	100	500
94	Vic Sears	8	10	12	20	25	40	100	
95	Tommy Thompson QB	8	10	12	20	25	40	100	
96	Bucko Kilroy	8	10	12	20	25	40	▼100	
97	George Connor	10	12	15	25	35	100	150	
98	Fred Morrison	8	10	12	20	25	40	100	
99	Jim Keane RC	8	10	12	20	25	40	100	
100	Sammy Baugh	50	60	75	100	175	300	600	
101	Harry Ulinski	8	10	12	20	25	40	100	
102	Frank Spaniel	8	10	12	20	25	40	100	
103	Charley Conerly	15	20	25	50	60	100	225	1,000
104	Dick Hensley	8	10	12	20	25	40	100	500
105	Eddie Price	8	10	12	20	25	40	100	400
106	Ed Carr	8	10	12	20	25	40	100	
107	Leo Nomellini	12	15	20	30	50	75	200	▲1,000
108	Verl Lillywhite	8	10	12	20	25	40	100	
109	Wallace Triplett	8	10	12	20	25	50	100	
110	Joe Watson	8	10	12	20	25	40	100	400
111	Cloyce Box RC	8	10	12	20	25	40	100	400
112	Billy Stone	8	10	12	20	25	40	100	
113	Earl Murray	8	10	12	20	25	40	100	
114	Chet Mutryn RC	8	10	12	20	25	40	100	
115	Ken Carpenter	8	10	12	20	25	40	100	400
116	Lou Rymkus RC	8	10	12	20	25	40	100	
117	Dub Jones RC	8	10	12	20	40	60	▼300	
118	Clayton Tonnemaker	8	10	12	20	25	50	100	
119	Walt Schlinkman	8	10	12	20	25	40	200	
120	Billy Grimes	8	10	12	20	25	40	100	
121	George Ratterman RC	8	10	12	20	25	50	100	
122	Bob Mann	8	10	12	20	25	40	125	
123	Buddy Young RC	8	10	12	30	40	50	120	600
124	Jack Zilly	8	10	12	20	25	40	100	500
125	Tom Kalmanir	8	10	12	20	25	40	100	
126	Frank Sinkovitz	8	10	12	20	25	40	100	
127	Elbert Nickel	8	10	12	20	25	40	100	
128	Jim Finks RC	12	15	20	30	▲60	75	▲300	
129	Charley Trippi	12	15	20	30	50	75	200	
130	Tom Wham	8	10	12	20	25	40	100	
131	Ventan Yablonski	8	10	12	20	25	40	150	
132	Chuck Bednarik	20	25	30	80	100	125	350	
133	Joe Muha	8	10	12	20	25	40	125	
134	Pete Pihos	12	15	20	30	60	100	175	400
135	Washington Serini	8	10	12	20	25	40	125	
136	George Gulyanics	8	10	12	20	25	40	150	

#	Player	GD 2	VG 3	VgEx 4	EX 5	ExMt 6	NM 7	NmMt 8	MT 9
137	Ken Kavanaugh	8	10	12	20	25	40	150	
138	Howie Livingston	8	10	12	20	25	40	100	
139	Joe Tereshinski	8	10	12	20	30	40	200	
140	Jim White	10	15	40	100	200	300	600	
141	Gene Roberts	8	10	12	20	25	40	150	
142	Bill Swiacki	8	10	12	20	25	40	125	
143	Norm Standlee	8	10	12	20	25	40	200	
144	Knox Ramsey RC	25	40	60	80	150	300	1,200	

—Chuck Bednarik #132 PSA 9 (MT) sold for $1,410 (eBay; 4/11)
—Chuck Bednarik #132 SGC 98 (Gem MT) sold for $1,004 (eBay; 7/09)
—Tony Canadeo #9 PSA 8.5 (NmMt+) sold for $1,214 (Mile High; 3/09)
—Glenn Davis #16 PSA 9 (MT) sold for $1,526 (Memory Lane; 12/07)
—Jim Finks RC #128 PSA 9 (Mint) sold for $810.94 (eBay; 5/12)
—Otto Graham #45 PSA 8.5 (NmMt+) sold for $1,853 (Goodwin; 5/08)
—John Greene #2 PSA 9 (Mint) sold for $1,278 (eBay; 12/12)
—Lou Groza #6 PSA 10 (Gem Mt) sold for $4,918 (eBay; 01/13)
—Lou Groza #6 PSA 9 (Mint) sold for $1,444 (eBay; 11/12)
—Lou Groza #6 PSA 9 (Mint) sold for $1,700 (Memory; 05/13)
—Lou Groza #6 PSA 9 (Mint) sold for $4,030 (eBay; 09/16)
—Howard Hartley #88 PSA 9 (Mint) sold for $1,229 (eBay; 08/13)
—Elroy Hirsch #52 PSA 10 (Gem Mt) sold for $4,481 (Legendary; 8/11)
—Elroy Hirsch #52 PSA 9 (MT) sold for $3,976 (Goodwin; 2/09)
—Elroy Hirsch #52 PSA 9 (MT) sold for $2,700 (Mastro; 3/05)
—Dub Jones #117 PSA 9 (MT) sold for $791.27 (eBay; 1/14)
—Johnny Lujack #26 PSA 9 (MT) sold for $1,218 (Memory Lane; 12/07)
—Marion Motley #43 PSA 9 (MT) sold for $6,600 (Mastro; 12/08)
—Marion Motley #43 PSA 9 (MT) sold for $2,030 (eBay; 4/11)
—Marion Motley #43 PSA 9 (MT) sold for $2,221 (eBay; 2/12)
—Vic Sears #94 PSA 9 (Mint) sold for $1076.5 (eBay; 7/12)
—Mac Speedie #8 PSA 10 (Gem MT) sold for $3,471 (Mile High; 1/07)
—Billy Stone #112 PSA 9 (MT) sold for $718 (eBay; 11/07)
—George Taliaferro #14 PSA 9 (MT) sold for $1596 (eBay; 08/13)
—Y.A. Tittle #5 SGC 9 (MT) sold for $4,200 (Mastro; 5/08)
—Steve Van Buren #23 PSA 9 (MT) sold for $1,108 (Mastro, 2/07)
—Doak Walker #1 PSA 8 (NmMt) sold for $3,585 (Legendary, 8/11)
—Doak Walker #1 SGC 8.5 (NmMt+) sold for $2,839 (Memory Lane, 5/08)
—Bob Waterfield #17 PSA 9 (MT) sold for $997 (eBay, 11/07)
—Bob Waterfield #17 PSA 9 (Mint) sold for $983.55 (eBay; 9/12)

1949 Topps Felt Backs

#	Player	PrFr 1	GD 2	VG 3	VgEx 4	EX 5	ExMt 6	NM 7	NmMt 8
1	Lou Allen	10	15	25	40	60			
2	Morris Bailey	10	15	25	40	50	80		
3	George Bell	10	15	25					
4	Lindy Berry HOR	10	15	25	40	60			
5B	Mike Boldin Yel	25	30	50	60	80	125		
6B	Bernie Botula Yel	25	30	50	60	80	125		
7	Bob Bowlby	10	15	25	40	50	80		
8	Bob Bucher	10	15	25	40	50	80		
9B	Al Burnett Yel	25	30	50	60	80			
10	Don Burson	10	15	25	40	50	80		
11	Paul Campbell	10	15	25	40	50	80		
12	Herb Carey	10	15	25	40	50	80		
13B	Bimbo Cecconi Yel	25	30	50	60	80	125		
14	Bill Chauncey	10	15	25	40	60			
15	Dick Clark	10	15	25	40	50	80		
16	Tom Coleman	10	15	25	40	50	80		
17	Billy Conn	10	15	25	40	60			
18	John Cox	10	15	25	40	60			
19	Lou Creekmur RC	50	60	100	150	300			
20	Richard Glen Davis RC	15	20	30	50	75			
21	Warren Davis	10	15	25	40	50	80		
22	Bob Deuber	10	15	25	40	50	80		
23	Ray Dooney	10	15	25	40	50	80		
24	Tom Dublinski	15	20	30	50	75			
25	Jeff Fleischman	10	15	25	40	50	80		
26	Jack Friedland	10	15	25	40	60			
27	Bob Fuchs	10	15	25	40	60			
28	Arnold Galiffa RC	15	20	30	50	60	100		
29	Dick Gilman	10	15	25	40	50	80		
30A	Frank Gitschier Brn	25	30	50	60	80	125		
30B	Frank Gitschier Yel	25	30	50	60	80	125		
31	Gene Glick	10	15	25	40	50	80		
32	Bill Gregus	10	15	25	40	50	80		
33	Harold Hagan	10	15	25	40	50	80		
34	Charles Hall	10	15	25	40	60			
35A	Leon Hart Brn	50	60	100	150	200	350		
35B	Leon Hart Yel	50	60	100	150	200	350		

	PrFr 1	GD 2	VG 3	VgEx 4	EX 5	ExMt 6	NM 7	NmMt 8
Bob Hester Yel	25	30	50	60	80	150		
George Hughes	10	15	25	40	60			
Levi Jackson	15	20	30	50	60	100		
Jack Jensen Brn	60	80	135	175	250	500		
Jack Jensen Yel	60	80	135	175	250	500		
Charlie Justice	30	40	60	80	100			
Gary Kerkorian	10	15	25	40	60			
Bernie Krueger	10	15	25	40	50	80		
Bill Kuhn	10	15	25	40	60			
Dean Laun	10	15	25	40	60			
Chet Leach	10	15	25	40	50	80		
Bobby Lee Yel	25	30	50	60	80			
Roger Lehew	10	15	25	40	50	80		
Glenn Lippman	10	15	25	40	50	80		
Melvin Lyle	10	15	25	40	50	80		
Len Makowski	10	15	25	40	50	80		
Al Malekoff Yel	25	30	50	60	80			
Jim Martin Yel	30	40	60	80	100			
Frank Mataya	10	15	25	40	60			
Ray Mathews Yel RC	30	40	60	80	100	150		
Dick McKissack Yel	25	30	50	60	80	125		
Frank Miller	10	15	25	40	50	80		
John Miller Yel	25	30	50	60	80	125		
Ed Modzelewski RC	15	20	30	50	80	125		
Don Mouser	10	15	25	40	60			
James Murphy	10	15	25	40	60			
Ray Nagle Brn	25	30	50	60	80	150		
Ray Nagle Yel	25	30	50	60	80	150		
Leo Nomellini	60	80	125	200	350	500		
James O'Day	10	15	25	40				
Joe Paterno RC	400	500	800	1,200	1,500	3,500		
Andy Pavich	10	15	25	40	50	80		
Pete Perini Brn	25	30	50	60	80			
Pete Perini Yel	25	30	50	60	80			
Jim Powers	10	15	25	40	60			
Dave Rakestraw	10	15	25	40	50	80		
Herb Rich	10	15	25	40	50	80		
Fran Rogel RC	10	15	25	40	60			
Darrell Royal Brn RC	175	225	350					
Darrell Royal Yel RC	150	200	300	500				
Steve Sawle	10	15	25	40	50	80		
Nick Sebek	10	15	25	40	60			
Herb Seidell	10	15	25	40	50	80		
Charles Shaw Yel	25	30	50	60	80			
Emil Sitko Brn RC	25	30	50	60	80	125		
Emil Sitko Yel RC	25	30	50	60	80	125		
Butch Songin RC	15	20	30	50	80	100		
Mariano Stalloni Brn	25	30	50	60	80			
Mariano Stalloni Yel	25	30	50	60	80			
Ernie Stautner RC	60	80	125	200	300	400		
Don Stehley	10	15	25	40	60			
Gil Stevenson	10	15	25	40	50	80		
Bishop Strickland	10	15	25	40	50	80		
Harry Szulborski	10	15	25	40	60			
Wally Teninga Brn	25	30	50	60	80			
Wally Teninga Yel	25	30	50	60	80			
Clayton Tonnemaker	10	15	25	40	50	80		
Dan Towler Brn RC	60	80	125	175	250			
Dan Towler RC Yel	60	80	125	175	250			
Bert Turek Brn	25	30	50	60	80			
Bert Turek Yel	25	30	50	60	80			
Harry Ulinski	10	15	25	40	60			
Leon Van Billingham	10	15	25	40	60			
Langdon Viracola	10	15	25	40	60			
Leo Wagner	10	15	25	40	50	80		
Doak Walker Brn	150	200	300					
Doak Walker Yel	125	150	250	350	500			
Jim Ward	10	15	25	40	60			
Art Weiner	10	15	25	40	50	80		
Dick Weiss	10	15	25	40	50	80		
Froggie Williams	10	15	25	40	50	80		
Robert (Red) Wilson	10	15	25	40	50	80		
Roger Red Wilson	10	15	25	40	60	80		
Carl Wren	10	15	25	40				
Pete Zinaich Brn	25	30	50	60	80	125		
Pete Zinaich Yel	25	30	50	60	80	125		

—Len Makowski PSA 8 (NmMt) sold for $1,035 (Huggins&Scott; 4/08)
—Joe Paterno PSA 7 (NrMt) sold for $5,215 (eBay; 10/11)
—Joe Paterno PSA 7 (NrMt) sold for $2,714.51 (eBay; 11/13)

—Joe Paterno RC #64 PSA 8 (NM/MT) sold for $9124.8 (SCP; 5/12)
—Darrell Royal Yel PSA 5 (NmMt) sold for $1,265 (Huggins&Scott; 4/08)
—Wally Teninga Yel PSA 7 (NM) sold for $431 (Huggins&Scott; 4/08)
—Dan Towler Yel PSA 8 (NmMt) sold for $1,305 (eBay; 12/08)
—Bert Turek Yel PSA 7 (NM) sold for $431 (Huggins&Scott; 4/08)
—Doak Walker Brn SGC 6 (ExNm) sold for $700 (eBay; 1/08)

1951 Bowman

		GD 2	VG 3	VgEx 4	EX 5	ExMt 6	NM 7	NmMt 8	MT 9
1	Weldon Humble RC	12	20	25	40	60	▼100	800	
2	Otto Graham	▲40	50	60	100	200	250	600	
3	Mac Speedie	5	8	10	15	25	40	▼200	
4	Norm Van Brocklin RC	60	100	125	175	250	450	1,200	
5	Woodley Lewis RC	5	8	10	15	20	30	100	
6	Tom Fears	6	10	12	20	40	80	150	
7	George Musacco	5	8	10	15	20	30	100	
8	George Taliaferro	5	8	10	15	20	30	100	
9	Barney Poole	5	8	10	15	20	30	150	
10	Steve Van Buren	8	12	15	25	40	80	▼200	
11	Whitey Wistert	5	8	10	15	20	40	100	
12	Chuck Bednarik	10	15	20	▲40	60	100	200	
13	Bulldog Turner	6	10	12	▲30	▲40	▲80	175	
14	Bob Williams	5	8	10	15	20	30	100	
15	Johnny Lujack	8	12	15	▲30	40	▲80	150	
16	Roy Rebel Steiner	5	8	10	15	20	▲40	100	
17	Jug Girard	5	8	10	15	20	30	100	
18	Bill Neal	5	8	10	15	20	▲40	100	
19	Travis Tidwell	5	8	10	15	20	30	100	
20	Tom Landry RC	125	150	200	250	400	500	1,200	4,000
21	Arnie Weinmeister RC	8	12	15	40	80	135	350	
22	Joe Geri	5	8	10	15	20	30	100	
23	Bill Walsh C RC	6	10	12	18	30	50	120	
24	Fran Rogel	5	8	10	15	20	30	100	
25	Doak Walker	8	12	20	30	50	75	150	
26	Leon Hart	5	8	10	15	25	40	120	
27	Thurman McGraw	5	8	10	15	20	30	100	
28	Buster Ramsey	5	8	10	15	20	30	▼80	
29	Frank Tripucka	5	8	10	15	20	40	▼80	
30	Don Paul DB	5	8	10	15	20	30	80	
31	Alex Loyd	5	8	10	15	25	40	100	
32	Y.A. Tittle	20	30	35	60	100	135	450	1,500
33	Verl Lillywhite	5	8	10	15	20	▲50	100	
34	Sammy Baugh	30	40	80	100	125	200	400	
35	Chuck Drazenovich	5	8	10	15	20	30	100	
36	Bob Goode	5	8	10	15	20	30	100	
37	Horace Gillom RC	5	8	10	15	20	30	100	
38	Lou Rymkus	5	8	10	15	20	30	100	
39	Ken Carpenter	5	8	10	15	20	50	250	
40	Bob Waterfield	10	15	20	30	50	75	200	
41	Vitamin Smith RC	5	8	10	15	20	30	80	
42	Glenn Davis	8	12	15	25	40	60	200	
43	Dan Edwards	5	8	10	15	25	40	200	
44	John Rauch	5	8	10	15	20	30	100	
45	Zollie Toth	5	8	10	15	20	40	250	
46	Pete Pihos	8	12	15	25	40	60	200	
47	Russ Craft	5	8	10	15	20	30	100	
48	Walter Barnes	5	8	10	15	20	30	80	
49	Fred Morrison	5	8	10	15	20	30	100	
50	Ray Bray	5	8	10	15	20	30	80	350
51	Ed Sprinkle RC	5	8	10	15	20	35	120	
52	Floyd Reid	5	8	10	15	20	30	100	
53	Billy Grimes	5	8	10	15	20	40	150	
54	Ted Fritsch Sr.	5	8	10	15	20	40	200	
55	Al DeRogatis	5	8	10	15	20	30	100	
56	Charley Conerly	10	15	20	30	50	75	200	800
57	Jon Baker	5	8	10	15	20	30	100	
58	Tom McWilliams	5	8	10	15	20	30	100	
59	Jerry Shipkey	5	8	10	15	20	30	100	
60	Lynn Chandnois RC	5	8	10	15	20	30	100	
61	Don Doll	5	8	10	15	20	30	100	
62	Lou Creekmur	8	12	15	25	40	125	400	
63	Bob Hoernschemeyer	5	8	10	15	20	30	100	
64	Tom Wham	5	8	10	15	20	30	100	
65	Bill Fischer	5	8	10	15	20	40	100	
66	Robert Nussbaumer	5	8	10	15	20	30	▼80	
67	Gordy Soltau RC	5	8	10	15	20	30	100	
68	Visco Grgich	5	8	10	15	20	30	100	
69	John Strzykalski RC	5	8	10	15	20	30	100	

FOOTBALL

		GD 2	VG 3	VgEx 4	EX 5	ExMt 6	NM 7	NmMt 8	MT 9
70	Pete Stout	5	8	10	15	20	30	100	
71	Paul Lipscomb	5	8	10	15	20	30	100	
72	Harry Gilmer	5	8	10	15	25	40	120	
73	Dante Lavelli	8	12	15	25	50	▼100	▼500	
74	Dub Jones	5	8	10	15	20	30	300	
75	Lou Groza	10	15	20	30	50	100	300	
76	Elroy Hirsch	10	15	20	30	60	▲100	300	
77	Tom Kalmanir	5	8	10	15	20	▲40	100	
78	Jack Zilly	5	8	10	15	20	30	100	
79	Bruce Alford	5	8	10	15	20	30	100	
80	Art Weiner	5	8	10	15	20	30	100	
81	Brad Ecklund	5	8	10	15	20	40	200	
82	Bosh Pritchard	5	8	10	15	20	30	100	
83	John Green	5	8	10	15	20	30	100	
84	Ebert Van Buren	5	8	10	15	20	30	80	
85	Julie Rykovich	5	8	10	15	20	30	100	
86	Fred Davis	5	8	10	15	20	30	80	
87	John Hoffman RC	5	8	10	15	20	30	100	
88	Tobin Rote	5	8	10	15	20	30	100	
89	Paul Burris	5	8	10	15	20	30	100	
90	Tony Canadeo	6	10	12	30	40	125	▲400	
91	Emlen Tunnell RC	15	25	30	50	80	200	600	
92	Otto Schnellbacher RC	5	8	10	15	20	30	100	
93	Ray Poole	5	8	10	15	20	30	100	
94	Darrell Hogan	5	8	10	15	20	30	80	
95	Frank Sinkovitz	5	8	10	15	20	30	100	
96	Ernie Stautner	12	20	25	50	80	150	500	
97	Elmer Bud Angsman	5	8	10	15	20	30	100	
98	Jack Jennings	5	8	10	15	20	30	100	
99	Jerry Groom	5	8	10	15	20	30	100	
100	John Prchlik	5	8	10	15	20	30	100	
101	J. Robert Smith	5	8	10	15	20	30	100	
102	Bobby Layne	20	30	35	50	80	135	▲350	
103	Frankie Albert	5	8	10	15	25	40	120	
104	Gail Bruce	5	8	10	15	20	30	100	
105	Joe Perry	10	15	20	30	50	80	200	
106	Leon Heath	5	8	10	15	20	30	100	
107	Ed Quirk	5	8	10	15	20	30	100	
108	Hugh Taylor	5	8	10	15	20	30	▼100	
109	Marion Motley	12	20	25	▲60	▲100	135	500	
110	Tony Adamle	5	8	10	15	20	▲40	120	
111	Alex Agase	5	8	10	15	20	30	100	
112	Tank Younger	5	8	10	15	25	50	▲150	
113	Bob Boyd	5	8	10	15	20	30	100	
114	Jerry Williams	5	8	10	15	20	30	100	
115	Joe Golding	5	8	10	15	20	30	100	
116	Sherman Howard	5	8	10	15	20	30	100	
117	John Wozniak	5	8	10	15	20	50	▼150	
118	Frank Reagan	5	8	10	15	20	30	175	
119	Vic Sears	5	8	10	15	20	30	100	
120	Clyde Scott	5	8	10	15	20	30	100	
121	George Gulyanics	5	8	10	15	20	40	100	
122	Bill Wightkin	5	8	10	15	20	30	100	
123	Chuck Hunsinger	5	8	10	15	20	30	100	
124	Jack Cloud	5	8	10	15	20	30	100	
125	Abner Wimberly	5	8	10	15	30	40	200	
126	Dick Wildung	5	8	10	15	20	50	▲200	
127	Eddie Price	5	8	10	15	20	30	150	
128	Joe Scott	5	8	10	15	20	30	100	
129	Jerry Nuzum	5	8	10	15	20	30	100	
130	Jim Finks	5	8	10	15	25	▼60	150	
131	Bob Gage	5	8	10	15	20	30	100	
132	Bill Swiacki	5	8	10	15	20	30	100	
133	Joe Watson	5	8	10	15	20	30	100	
134	Ollie Cline	5	8	10	15	20	30	100	
135	Jack Lininger	5	8	10	15	20	50	175	
136	Fran Polsfoot	5	8	10	15	20	50	125	
137	Charley Trippi	6	10	12	20	30	60	250	
138	Ventan Yablonski	5	8	10	15	20	30	150	
139	Emil Sitko	5	8	10	15	20	40	125	
140	Leo Nomellini	8	12	15	25	40	60	250	
141	Norm Standlee	5	8	10	15	20	30	100	
142	Eddie Saenz	5	8	10	15	20	30	▼125	
143	Al Demao	5	8	10	15	20	30	120	
144	Bill Dudley	20	40	60	100	▼100	200	1,500	

—Sammy Baugh #34 SGC 96 (MT) sold for $1,440 (Mastro; 5/08)
—Chuck Bednarik #12 PSA 9 (MT) sold for $897 (eBay; 2/10)
—Tony Canadeo #12 PSA 9 (MT) sold for $1,780 (Mile High; 6/10)
—Lou Creekmur #34 PSA 9 (MT) sold for $2,640 (Mastro; 7/08)

—Al DeRogatis #55 PSA 9 (Mint) sold for $747.5 (eBay: 7/12)
—Bill Dudley #144 PSA 9 (MT) sold for $6,087 (Memory Lane; 5/08)
—Bill Dudley #144 PSA 9 (MT) sold for $3,245 (Mile High; 1/07)
—Dan Edwards #43 PSA 9 (MT) sold for $1,225 (eBay; 3/08)
—Elroy Hirsch #76 PSA 9 (MT) sold for $2,520 (eBay; 11/06)
—Weldon Humble #1 PSA 9 (MT) sold for $3,386 (Memory Lane; 12/06)
—Tom Landry #20 PSA 10 (Gem MT) sold for $16,286 (Mile High; 11/10)
—Tom Landry #20 PSA 10 (Gem MT) sold for $22,130 (eBay; 7/16)
—Tom Landry #20 PSA 9 (MT) sold for $5,407 (Mastro; 12/07)
—Tom Landry #20 PSA 9 (Gem MT) sold for $4483 (eBay; 10/14)
—Bobby Layne #102 PSA 9 (MT) sold for $1,350 (eBay; 2/10)
—Woodley Lewis #5 PSA 9 (MT) sold for $1,187 (Memory Lane; 5/08)
—Floyd Reid #52 PSA 9 (MT) sold for $1,148 (eBay; 8/07)
—Ernie Stautner #96 PSA 9 (MT) sold for $3,976 (Goodwin; 2/10)
—Ernie Stautner #96 PSA 9 (MT) sold for $3,900 (eBay; 4/09)
—Ernie Stautner #96 SGC 9 (MT) sold for $1,136 (Mile High; 10/09)
—Norm Van Brocklin #4 PSA 9 (MT) sold for $8063 (eBay, 11/14)
—Norm Van Brocklin #4 SGC 9 (MT) sold for $2,250 (eBay; 11/09)
—Norm Van Brocklin #4 SGC 8.5 (NmMt+) sold for $1,560 (Mastro; 5/08)
—Norm Van Brocklin #4 SGC 8.5 (NmMt+) sold for $2,554.95 (eBay; 2/14)
—Steve Van Buren #10 PSA 9 (MT) sold for $1,614 (eBay; 11/07)
—Arnie Weinmeister #21 PSA 9 (MT) sold for $1,242 (Mile High; 5/11)
—Arnie Weinmeister #21 PSA 9 (MT) sold for $1,481 (eBay; 2/14)

1951 Topps Magic

		PrFr 1	GD 2	VG 3	VgEx 4	EX 5	ExMt 6	NM 7	NmMt 8
1	Jimmy Monahan RC	5	6	8	12	25	50		
2	Bill Wade RC	8	10	12	20	40	75		
3	Bill Reichardt	5	5	5	10	20	40		
4	Babe Parilli RC	8	10	20	20	40	75	350	
5	Billie Burkhalter	5	5	5	10	20	40		
6	Ed Weber	5	5	5	10	20	40		
7	Tom Scott	5	5	6	12	25	50		
8	Frank Guthridge	5	5	5	10	20	40	150	
9	John Karras	5	5	5	10	20	40		
10	Vic Janowicz RC	15	25	40	60	125	200	1,000	
11	Lloyd Hill	5	5	5	10	20	40	150	
12	Jim Weatherall RC	5	5	6	12	25	50	100	
13	Howard Hansen	5	5	5	10	20	40		
14	Lou D'Achille	5	5	5	10	20	40		
15	Johnny Turco	5	5	5	10	20	40		
16	Jerrell Price	5	5	5	10	20	40		
17	John Coatta	5	5	5	10	20	40		
18	Bruce Patton	5	5	5	10	20	40		
19	Marion Campbell RC	6	8	12	20	35	60		
20	Blaine Earon	5	5	5	10	20	40		
21	Dewey McConnell	5	5	5	10	20	40		
22	Ray Beck	5	5	5	10	20	40		
23	Jim Prewett	5	5	5	10	30	40	150	
24	Bob Steele	5	5	5	10	20	40	150	
25	Art Betts	5	5	5	10	20	40		
26	Walt Trillhaase	5	5	5	10	30	40		
27	Gil Bartosh	5	5	5	10	20	40		
28	Bob Bestwick	5	5	5	10	20	40		
29	Tom Rushing	5	5	5	10	20	30	100	
30	Bert Rechichar RC	6	8	10	15	30	40	50	
31	Bill Owens	5	5	5	10	20	40		
32	Mike Goggins	5	5	5	10	20	40		
33	John Petitbon	5	5	5	10	20	40		
34	Byron Townsend	5	5	5	10	30	40	150	
35	Ed Rotticci	5	5	5	10	20	40		
36	Steve Wadiak	5	5	5	10	20	40		
37	Bobby Marlow RC	5	5	6	12	25	50		
38	Bill Fuchs	5	5	5	10	20	40		
39	Ralph Staub	5	5	5	10	20	40		
40	Bill Vesprini	5	5	5	10	20	40		
41	Zack Jordan	5	5	5	10	20	40		
42	Bob Smith RC	5	5	6	12	25	50		
43	Charles Hanson	5	5	5	10	20	40		
44	Glenn Smith	5	5	5	10	20	40		
45	Armand Kitto	5	5	5	10	20	40		
46	Vinnie Drake	5	5	5	10	20	40	150	
47	Bill Putich RC	5	5	5	10	20	40		
48	George Young RC	6	8	10	15	30	50		
49	Don McRae	5	5	5	10	20	40		
50	Frank Smith RC	5	5	5	10	20	40		
51	Dick Hightower	5	5	5	10	20	40		
52	Clyde Pickard	5	5	5	10	30	40		

	PrFr 1	GD 2	VG 3	VgEx 4	EX 5	ExMt 6	NM 7	NmMt 8
Bob Reynolds HB	5	5	6	12	25	50		
Dick Gregory	5	5	5	10	20	40		
Dale Samuels	5	5	5	10	20	40		
Gale Galloway	5	5	5	10	20	40		
Vic Pujo		5	5	10	20	40		
Dave Waters	5	5	5	10	20	40		
Joe Ernest	5	5	5	10	20	40		
Elmer Costa	5	5	5	10	20	40		
Nick Liotta	5	5	5	10	20	40		
John Dottley	5	5	5	10	20	40		
Hi Faubion	5	5	5	10	20	40		
David Harr	5	5	5	10	20	40		
Bill Matthews	5	5	5	10	20	40		
Carroll McDonald	5	5	5	10	20	40		
Dick Dewing	5	5	5	10	20	40		
Joe Johnson RB	5	5	5	10	20	40		
Arnold Burwitz	5	5	5	10	20	40		
Ed Dobrowolski	5	5	5	10	20	40		
Joe Dudeck	5	5	5	10	20	40		
Johnny Bright RC	5	5	6	12	25	50		
Harold Loehlein	5	5	5	10	20	35		
Lawrence Hairston	5	5	5	10	20	40		
Bob Carey RC	5	5	6	12	25	50		

Bill Wade #2 PSA 7 (NrMt) sold for $565 (eBay; 10/07)
Bob Carey #75 PSA 7 (NrMt) sold for $1,260 (eBay; 11/07)

1952 Bowman Large

		GD 2	VG 3	VgEx 4	EX 5	ExMt 6	NM 7	NmMt 8	MT 9
1	Norm Van Brocklin SP	60	125	150	250	400	800	2,800	
2	Otto Graham	▲60	▲80	▲100	135	175	500	1,400	
3	Doak Walker	10	15	20	35	80	150	500	
4	Steve Owen CO RC	10	15	20	35	60	150	500	
5	Frankie Albert	6	10	12	20	40	60	200	
6	Laurie Niemi RC	5	8	12	20	40	60	175	
7	Chuck Hunsinger	5	8	12	20	40	80	200	
8	Ed Modzelewski	6	10	12	20	40	60	250	
9	Joe Spencer SP RC	15	25	30	50	75	300		
10	Chuck Bednarik SP	60	80	100	150	350	500	1,200	
11	Barney Poole	5	8	12	20	40	60	225	
12	Charley Trippi	10	15	18	30	60	▼100	350	
13	Tom Fears	10	15	20	35	50	125	300	
14	Paul Brown CO RC	30	50	60	100	200	350	1,000	
15	Leon Hart	8	12	15	25	40	▲100	200	
16	Frank Gifford RC	100	150	200	250	500	1,000	2,500	6,000
17	Y.A. Tittle	40	60	80	125	175	300	800	
18	Charlie Justice SP	30	50	60	100	▲200	400	1,500	
19	George Connor SP	30	50	60	100	150	225	500	
20	Lynn Chandnois	5	8	12	20	40	60	225	
21	Billy Howton RC	6	10	12	30	40	100	400	
22	Kenneth Snyder RC	5	8	12	20	40	60	225	
23	Gino Marchetti RC	30	50	80	200	250	400	2,000	
24	John Karras	5	8	12	20	40	60	225	
25	Tank Younger	6	10	12	20	40	80	350	
26	Tommy Thompson LB RC	5	8	12	20	40	150	600	
27	Bob Miller SP RC	80	▲150	200	250	350	500		
28	Kyle Rote SP RC	30	50	60	100	150	300	600	
29	Hugh McElhenny RC	40	60	80	125	300	450	1,500	
30	Sammy Baugh	50	80	100	150	200	500	1,200	
31	Jim Dooley RC	6	10	12	20	40	60	300	
32	Ray Mathews	5	8	12	20	40	60	▲200	
33	Fred Cone RC	5	8	12	20	40	60	▲225	
34	Al Pollard RC	5	8	12	20	40	80	400	
35	Brad Ecklund	5	8	12	20	40	60	250	
36	John Hancock SP RC	100	150	200	250	400	800		
37	Elroy Hirsch SP	40	50	80	125	175	250	600	
38	Keever Jankovich RC	5	8	12	20	25	60	175	
39	Emlen Tunnell	12	20	25	40	▲80	125	400	
40	Steve Dowden RC	5	8	12	20	40	60	200	
41	Claude Hipps RC	5	8	12	20	40	60	200	
42	Norm Standlee	5	8	12	20	40	60	150	
43	Dick Todd CO RC	5	8	12	20	40	80	200	
44	Babe Parilli	6	10	12	25	50	▲150	400	
45	Steve Van Buren SP	50	60	80	200	300	500		
46	Art Donovan SP RC	60	100	125	200	250	500	1,200	
47	Bill Fischer	5	8	12	20	40	60	175	
48	George Halas CO RC	40	60	80	200	250	400	800	
49	Jerrell Price	5	8	12	20	40	60	100	
50	John Sandusky RC	5	8	12	20	40	80	250	

		GD 2	VG 3	VgEx 4	EX 5	ExMt 6	NM 7	NmMt 8	MT 9
51	Ray Beck	5	8	12	20	40	60	175	
52	Jim Martin	6	10	12	20	30	80	200	
53	Joe Bach CO RC	5	8	12	20	40	60	175	
54	Glen Christian SP RC	15	25	30	50	125	400		
55	Andy Davis SP RC	15	25	30	50	80	150	400	
56	Tobin Rote	6	10	12	50	80	100	350	
57	Wayne Millner CO RC	15	25	30	50	80	250	1,000	
58	Zollie Toth	5	8	12	20	40	60	150	
59	Jack Jennings	5	8	12	20	40	60	175	
60	Bill McColl RC	5	8	12	20	40	60	200	
61	Les Richter RC	10	15	20	35	50	250	400	
62	Walt Michaels RC	6	10	12	20	30	80	▲350	
63	Charley Conerly SP	200	300	350	400	700	1,000	2,500	
64	Howard Hartley SP	15	20	25	50	75	125	400	
65	Jerome Smith RC	5	8	12	20	40	60	300	
66	James Clark RC	5	8	12	20	40	60	300	
67	Dick Logan RC	5	8	12	20	40	80	250	
68	Wayne Robinson RC	5	8	12	20	40	60	300	
69	James Hammond RC	5	8	12	20	40	80	350	
70	Gene Schroeder RC	5	8	12	20	50	60	300	
71	Tex Coulter	6	10	12	20	40	60	250	
72	John Schweder SP RC	125	150	200	450	550	1,200		
73	Vitamin Smith SP	30	50	60	100	125	225	500	
74	Joe Campanella RC	8	12	15	25	40	80	250	
75	Joe Kuharich CO RC	8	12	15	25	40	80	250	
76	Herman Clark RC	8	12	15	25	40	80	250	
77	Dan Edwards	8	12	15	25	40	80	250	
78	Bobby Layne	40	60	80	100	125	150	600	
79	Bob Hoernschemeyer	8	12	15	25	40	80	200	
80	John Carr Blount RC	8	12	15	25	40	60	200	
81	John Kastan SP RC	30	50	60	100	150	250	500	
82	Harry Minarik SP RC	30	50	60	100	▼125	225	500	
83	Joe Perry	15	25	30	50	75	150	450	
84	Buddy Parker CO RC	8	12	15	25	40	▼80	▼150	
85	Andy Robustelli RC	25	40	50	90	150	300	800	
86	Dub Jones	8	12	15	25	40	80	400	
87	Mal Cook RC	8	12	15	25	40	80	200	
88	Billy Stone	8	12	15	25	40	80	200	
89	George Taliaferro	8	12	15	25	40	80	200	
90	Thomas Johnson SP RC	30	50	60	100	150	400	800	
91	Leon Heath SP	20	30	40	60	▼80	150	300	
92	Pete Pihos	12	20	25	40	75	125	300	
93	Fred Benners RC	8	12	15	25	40	80	200	
94	George Tarasovic RC	12	20	25	30	40	80	250	
95	Buck Shaw CO RC	8	12	15	25	40	80	250	
96	Bill Wightkin	8	12	15	25	40	80	250	
97	John Wozniak	8	12	15	25	40	80	200	
98	Bobby Dillon RC	8	12	15	25	40	100	500	
99	Joe Stydahar SP RC	200	300	350	600	800	1,000	3,000	
100	Dick Alban SP RC	30	50	60	100	150	250	600	
101	Arnie Weinmeister	10	15	18	30	40	▲100	400	
102	Bobby Cross RC	8	12	15	25	40	80	350	
103	Don Paul DB	8	12	15	25	40	▼80	400	
104	Buddy Young	10	15	18	30	40	80	250	
105	Lou Groza	20	30	40	▼60	100	200	600	
106	Ray Pelfrey RC	8	12	15	30	80	100	350	
107	Maurice Nipp RC	8	12	15	25	40	80	400	
108	Hubert Johnston SP RC	200	250	300	500	600	800	2,500	
109	Vol.Quinlan SP RC	20	30	40	60	100	175	450	
110	Jack Simmons RC	8	12	15	25	40	80	120	
111	George Ratterman	8	12	15	25	40	80	200	
112	John Badaczewski RC	8	12	15	25	40	80	200	
113	Bill Reichardt	8	12	15	25	40	80	200	
114	Art Weiner	8	12	15	25	40	80	200	
115	Keith Flowers RC	8	12	15	25	40	80	200	
116	Russ Craft	8	12	15	25	40	80	150	
117	Jim O'Donahue SP RC	30	50	60	100	135	250	800	
118	Darrell Hogan SP	20	30	40	60	100	150	500	
119	Frank Ziegler RC	8	12	15	25	40	80	150	
120	Dan Towler	10	15	18	30	40	▲100	250	
121	Fred Williams RC	8	12	15	25	40	80	200	
122	Jimmy Phelan CO RC	8	12	15	25	40	80	200	
123	Eddie Price	8	12	15	▲40	▲50	100	▲250	
124	Chet Ostrowski RC	8	12	15	25	40	80	200	
125	Leo Nomellini	12	20	▲40	▲50	60	150	450	
126	Steve Romanik SP RC	50	75	80	200	300	400	2,000	
127	Ollie Matson SP RC	100	125	150	200	400	800	3,400	
128	Dante Lavelli	12	20	25	40	75	▲200	350	
129	Jack Christiansen RC	30	50	60	100	175	400	1,000	

		GD 2	VG 3	VgEx 4	EX 5	ExMt 6	NM 7	NmMt 8	MT 9
130	Dom Moselle RC	8	12	15	25	40	80	▲500	
131	John Rapacz RC	8	12	15	25	50	125	300	
132	Chuck Ortmann UER RC	8	12	15	25	40	80	200	
133	Bob Williams	8	12	15	25	40	80	200	
134	Chuck Ulrich RC	8	12	15	25	40	125	300	
135	Gene Ronzani CO SP RC	200	450	500	600	700	1,200	3,000	
136	Bert Rechichar SP	25	40	50	100	200	250	600	
137	Bob Waterfield	15	25	50	80	100	200	600	
138	Bobby Walston RC	8	12	15	25	40	125	200	
139	Jerry Shipkey	8	12	15	25	40	100	600	
140	Yale Lary RC	30	50	60	100	175	400	1,000	
141	Gordy Soltau	8	12	15	25	40	100	200	
142	Tom Landry	125	150	200	250	500	800	1,500	5,000
143	John Papit RC	8	12	15	25	40	80	200	
144	Jim Lansford SP RC	400	500	800	1,500	2,000	▲4,400	10,000	

—Dick Alban #5 PSA 10 (Gem) sold for $3,273 (Memory Lane; 5/13)
—Dick Alban #100 PSA 9 (MT) sold for $1,790 (Mile High; 6/13)
—Frankie Albert #5 PSA 9 (MT) sold for $1,055 (eBay; 12/12)
—Lou Groza #105 PSA 9 (MT) sold for $1,100 (eBay; 11/07)
—Otto Graham #2 PSA 9 (MT) sold for $5,467 (eBay; 5/13)
—Leon Hart #15 PSA 9 (MT) sold for $1,055 (eBay; 1/08)
—George Halas #48 PSA 9 (MT) sold for $3,550 (eBay; 1/07)
—Jim Lansford #144 PSA 8 (NmMt) sold for $10,321 (Andy Madec; 11/09)
—Jim Lansford #144 PSA 9 (Mint) sold for $17,920 (Memory Lane; 5/13)
—Dante Lavelli #128 PSA 9 (MT) sold for $1,446.40 (eBay; 2/14)
—Bobby Layne #78 PSA 9 (MT) sold for $2,247 (Mile High; 6/13)
—Yale Lary #140 PSA 9 (MT) sold for $4,517 (Memory Lane; 5/13)
—Gino Marchetti #23 PSA 9 (Mint) sold for $2,272 (Mile High; 11/10)
—Ray Matthews #32 PSA 9 (Mint) sold for $1,353 (Mile High; 6/13)
—Ollie Matson #127 PSA 7.5 (NrMt+) sold for $1,361 (Mile High; 3/09)
—Leo Nomellini #125 PSA 9 (Mint) sold for $1,375 (eBay; 11/13)
—Joe Perry #83 PSA 10 (Gem) sold for $4,357 (Memory Lane; 5/13)
—Kyle Rote #28 PSA 9 (MT) sold for $2,151 (Legendary; 3/11)
—Joe Spencer #9 PSA 8 (NmMt) sold for $3,912 (Mile High; 6/13)
—John Schweder SP RC #72 SGC 8 (NM/MT) sold for $2249.1 (Goodwin; 9/12)
—Y.A. Tittle #17 PSA 9 (MT) sold for $2,278 (Mastro; 12/06)
—Charley Trippi #12 PSA 9 (MT) sold for $1,243 (eBay; 02/13)
—Chuck Ulrich #134 PSA 9 (MT) sold for $1,620 (REA; 4/07)
—Steve Van Buren #45 PSA 8 (NmMt) sold for $2,140 (eBay; 4/07)
—Steve Van Buren #45 PSA 8 (NmMt) sold for $2,804 (Memory Lane; 5/13)

1952 Bowman Small

		GD 2	VG 3	VgEx 4	EX 5	ExMt 6	NM 7	NmMt 8	MT 9
1	Norm Van Brocklin	50	60	100	150	350	500	2,500	
2	Otto Graham	25	40	▲60	▲100	▲150	300	550	
3	Doak Walker	8	12	15	25	60	100	300	
4	Steve Owen CO RC	10	15	20	30	60	80	300	
5	Frankie Albert	6	10	12	18	25	50	125	
6	Laurie Niemi	6	8	10	15	25	50	150	
7	Chuck Hunsinger	6	8	10	15	25.	50	200	
8	Ed Modzelewski	6	10	12	18	25	60	300	
9	Joe Spencer	6	8	10	15	25	50	300	
10	Chuck Bednarik	10	15	20	30	50	80	300	
11	Barney Poole	6	8	10	15	25	50	125	
12	Charley Trippi	8	12	15	25	40	80	200	
13	Tom Fears	8	12	15	25	35	60	225	
14	Paul Brown CO RC	20	35	50	60	125	250	800	
15	Leon Hart	6	10	12	18	25	50	150	
16	Frank Gifford RC	50	60	150	200	350	600	1,000	3,000
17	Y.A.Tittle	20	30	40	60	100	175	500	
18	Charlie Justice	8	12	15	20	30	50	300	
19	George Connor	6	10	12	18	30	50	150	
20	Lynn Chandnois	6	8	10	15	25	50	125	
21	Billy Howton RC	6	10	12	18	25	50	400	
22	Kenneth Snyder	6	8	10	15	25	50	175	
23	Gino Marchetti RC	25	40	50	75	125	250	550	
24	John Karras	6	8	10	15	25	50	100	
25	Tank Younger	6	10	12	18	25	50	250	
26	Tommy Thompson LB	6	8	10	15	25	60		
27	Bob Miller RC	6	8	10	15	25	50	250	
28	Kyle Rote RC	10	15	20	30	50	100	500	
29	Hugh McElhenny RC	25	40	50	75	125	300	800	
30	Sammy Baugh	30	40	50	80	100	200	500	
31	Jim Dooley RC	6	8	10	15	25	50	125	
32	Ray Mathews	6	8	10	15	25	50	150	
33	Fred Cone	6	8	10	15	25	50	150	
34	Al Pollard	6	8	10	15	25	50	125	
35	Brad Ecklund	6	8	10	15	25	50	125	

		GD 2	VG 3	VgEx 4	EX 5	ExMt 6	NM 7	NmMt 8	MT 9
36	John Lee Hancock	6	8	10	15	25	50	125	
37	Elroy Hirsch	10	15	20	30	60	80	250	
38	Keever Jankovich	6	8	10	15	25	60	300	
39	Emlen Tunnell	8	12	15	20	30	60	225	
40	Steve Dowden	6	8	10	15	30	50	125	
41	Claude Hipps	6	8	10	15	25	50	125	
42	Norm Standlee	6	8	10	15	25	50	125	
43	Dick Todd CO	6	8	10	15	25	50	125	
44	Babe Parilli	6	10	12	18	30	60	400	
45	Steve Van Buren	10	15	20	30	50	75	400	
46	Art Donovan RC	25	40	60	75	▼125	350	800	
47	Bill Fischer	6	8	10	15	25	50	125	
48	George Halas CO RC	30	50	80	100	150	300	700	
49	Jerrell Price	6	8	10	15	25	50	125	
50	John Sandusky RC	6	8	10	15	25	100	150	
51	Ray Beck	6	8	10	15	25	50	125	
52	Jim Martin	6	8	10	15	25	50	200	
53	Joe Bach CO	6	8	10	15	25	50	125	
54	Glen Christian	6	8	10	15	25	75	200	
55	Andy Davis	6	8	10	15	25	50		
56	Tobin Rote	6	10	12	20	30	75		
57	Wayne Millner CO RC	8	12	15	30	▲100	150	300	
58	Zollie Toth	6	8	10	15	25	50	175	
59	Jack Jennings	6	8	10	15	25	50	125	
60	Bill McColl	6	8	10	15	25	50	125	
61	Les Richter RC	12	15	25	40	60	175	500	
62	Walt Michaels RC	6	8	10	15	25	50	250	
63	Charley Conerly	10	15	20	30	50	▲80		
64	Howard Hartley	6	8	10	15	25	50	125	
65	Jerome Smith	6	8	10	15	25	50	150	
66	James Clark	6	8	10	15	25	50	▼250	
67	Dick Logan	6	8	10	15	25	50	150	
68	Wayne Robinson	6	8	10	15	25	50	200	
69	James Hammond	6	8	10	15	25	50	125	
70	Gene Schroeder	6	8	10	15	25	50	125	
71	Tex Coulter	6	8	10	15	25	50	100	
72	John Schweder	6	8	10	15	25	125		
73	Vitamin Smith	8	12	15	25	40	225		
74	Joe Campanella RC	6	10	12	20	30	60	400	
75	Joe Kuharich CO RC	6	10	12	18	30	80	200	
76	Herman Clark	6	10	12	18	30	60	300	
77	Dan Edwards	6	10	12	18	30	60	300	
78	Bobby Layne	20	30	40	60	100	175	500	
79	Bob Hoernschemeyer	6	10	12	18	30	60	300	
80	John Carr Blount	6	10	12	18	30	60	▼250	
81	John Kastan RC	6	10	12	18	30	60	300	
82	Harry Minarik	6	10	12	18	30	60		
83	Joe Perry	10	15	20	30	50	75	450	
84	Buddy Parker CO RC	6	10	12	18	30	60	250	
85	Andy Robustelli RC	15	25	30	60	100	▲200	500	
86	Dub Jones	6	10	12	18	▲40	60	350	
87	Mal Cook	6	10	12	18	30	60		
88	Billy Stone	8	12	15	25	40	60	350	
89	George Taliaferro	6	10	12	18	▲40	60	300	
90	Thomas Johnson RC	6	10	12	18	40	80	300	
91	Leon Heath	6	10	12	▲25	50	100	600	
92	Pete Pihos	8	12	15	25	35	60	300	
93	Fred Benners	6	10	12	▲40	100			
94	George Tarasovic	6	10	12	18	30	60	300	
95	Buck Shaw CO RC	6	10	12	18	▲50	60	200	
96	Bill Wightkin	6	10	12	18	30	60	300	
97	John Wozniak	6	10	12	18	30	60	300	
98	Bobby Dillon RC	6	10	12	18	▲50	60	400	
99	Joe Stydahar CO RC	40	60	▼60	125	200	400	2,000	
100	Dick Alban RC	6	10	12	18	30	60	300	
101	Arnie Weinmeister	8	12	15	20	35	60	300	
102	Bobby Cross	6	10	12	18	30	60	250	
103	Don Paul DB	6	10	12	18	30	60	250	
104	Buddy Young	8	12	15	20	35	60	300	
105	Lou Groza	10	15	20	30	60	100	300	
106	Ray Pelfrey	6	10	12	18	30	80	600	
107	Maurice Nipp	6	10	12	18	30	60	300	
108	Hubert Johnston	6	10	12	18	30	60	400	
109	Volney Quinlan RC	8	12	15	25	40	80		
110	Jack Simmons	6	10	12	18	30	60	250	
111	George Ratterman	6	10	12	18	30	60	250	
112	John Badaczewski	6	10	12	18	50	60	300	
113	Bill Reichardt	6	10	12	18	30	60	300	
114	Art Weiner	6	10	12	18	30	60	250	

	GD 2	VG 3	VgEx 4	EX 5	ExMt 6	NM 7	NmMt 8	MT 9
Keith Flowers	6	10	12	18	30	60	400	
Russ Craft	6	10	12	18	30	60	250	
Jim O'Donahue RC	6	10	12	18	30	80	300	
Darrell Hogan	8	12	15	25	40			
Frank Ziegler	6	10	12	18	30	60	▲1,000	
Dan Towler	8	12	15	20	30	60	300	
Fred Williams	6	10	12	18	30	60	▼300	
Jimmy Phelan CO	6	10	12	18	30	▼50	250	
Eddie Price	6	10	12	18	30	60	300	
Chet Ostrowski	6	10	12	18	30	60	150	
Leo Nomellini	10	15	20	30	50	100	300	
Steve Romanik	6	10	12	18	30	60	▼250	
Ollie Matson RC	18	30	40	80	200	500		
Dante Lavelli	10	15	20	30	50	75	300	
Jack Christiansen RC	12	20	25	35	60	150	400	
Dom Moselle	6	10	12	18	30	60	800	
John Rapacz	6	10	12	18	30	60	250	
Chuck Ortmann	6	10	12	18	30	60	250	
Bob Williams	6	10	12	18	30	60	250	
Chuck Ulrich	6	10	12	18	30	100	300	
Gene Ronzani CO RC	6	10	12	18	30	60	300	
Bert Rechichar	6	10	12	18	30	60	500	
Bob Waterfield	10	15	20	30	60	100	600	
Bobby Walston RC	6	10	12	18	40	▼50	400	
Jerry Shipkey	6	10	12	18	30	60	300	
Yale Lary RC	12	20	25	40	125	300	600	
Gordy Soltau	6	10	12	18	30	60	500	
Tom Landry	50	60	100	150	250	400	1,000	
John Papit	6	10	12	18	30	60	▼200	
Jim Lansford RC	25	40	50	75	150	▼200	1,200	

—Mal Cook #87 PSA 8 (NmMt) sold for $2,223 (Mile High; 5/11)
—Mal Cook #87 PSA 8 (NmMt) sold for $1683 (eBay; 12/12)
—Art Donovan #46 PSA 8.5 (NmMt+) sold for $1,367 (Mile High; 11/10)
—Art Donovan #46 PSA 8.5 (NmMt+) sold for $2,310 (Greg Bussineau Fall; Fall 2013)
—Frank Gifford #16 PSA 9 (Mint) sold for $8,500 (eBay; 10/11)
—Frank Gifford #16 PSA 9 (Mint) sold for $3658 (eBay; 11/12)
—Frank Gifford #16 PSA 9 (Mint) sold for $3480 (Memory Lane; 5/13)
—Frank Gifford #16 SGC 8.5 (NmMt+) sold for $1,826 (Mile High; 3/09)
—Darrell Hogan #118 PSA 8 (NmMt) sold for $1,034 (Mile High; 5/11)
—Tom Landry #142 SGC 9 (Mint) sold for $1209 (Memory Lane; 8/12)
—Ollie Matson #118 PSA 8 (NmMt) sold for $999 (Mile High; 5/11)
—Ollie Matson #118 PSA 8 (NmMt) sold for $1,079 (eBay; 12/12)
—Hugh McElhenny #29 PSA 8.5 (NmMt+) sold for $1,969 (Mile High; 11/10)
—Jim O'Donahue #117 PSA 8.5 (NmMt+) sold for $1,099 (Mile High; 5/11)
—Steve Owen #4 PSA 9 (Mint) sold for $1,115 (Mile High; 3/09)
—Buddy Parker #84 PSA 9 (Mint) sold for $1,206 (eBay; 5/09)
—Volney Quinlan #109 PSA 8 (NmMt) sold for $1,034 (Mile High; 5/11)
—Zollie Toth #58 PSA 9 (Mint) sold for $1,015 (eBay; 2/09)
—Emlen Tunnell #39 PSA 9 (Mint) sold for $1106 (eBay; 11/14)
—Chuck Ulrich #134 PSA 9 (Mint) sold for $1,002 (Mile High; 10/09)
—Norm Van Brocklin #1 PSA 8.5 (NmMt+) sold for $2,153 (Goodwin; 5/08)
—Bob Williams #133 PSA 9 (Mint) sold for $1,015 (eBay; 2/09)

1953 Bowman

	GD 2	VG 3	VgEx 4	EX 5	ExMt 6	NM 7	NmMt 8	MT 9
Eddie LeBaron RC	15	30	25	50	100	300	2,000	
John Dottley	8	10	12	15	25	60	200	
Babe Parilli	8	10	12	15	25	60	200	
Bucko Kilroy	8	10	12	15	25	80	300	
Joe Tereshinski	8	10	12	15	25	60	175	
Doak Walker	15	20	25	35	60	▲125	350	
Fran Polsfoot	8	10	12	15	25	60	150	
Sisto Averno RC	8	10	12	15	25	60	175	
Marion Motley	20	30	35	60	100	▼250	▼1,000	
Pat Brady RC	8	10	12	15	25	60	175	
Norm Van Brocklin	25	35	40	60	90	150	500	
Bill McColl	8	10	12	15	25	60	175	
Jerry Groom	8	10	12	15	25	60	175	
Al Pollard	8	10	12	15	25	60	175	
Dante Lavelli	10	12	15	20	40	80	300	
Eddie Price	8	10	12	15	25	60	175	
Charley Trippi	10	12	15	20	35	60	250	
Elbert Nickel	8	10	12	15	25	60	175	
George Taliaferro	8	10	12	15	25	60	175	
Charley Conerly	15	20	25	35	60	80	250	
Bobby Layne	20	30	35	50	75	150	300	
Elroy Hirsch	15	20	25	35	60	100	400	1,000
Jim Finks	8	10	12	15	25	80	250	

	GD 2	VG 3	VgEx 4	EX 5	ExMt 6	NM 7	NmMt 8	MT 9
24 Chuck Bednarik	15	20	25	35	60	100	400	
25 Kyle Rote	8	10	12	15	25	▲80	150	
26 Otto Graham	25	35	▲60	▲80	100	▲300	800	
27 Harry Gilmer	8	10	12	15	25	60	175	
28 Tobin Rote	8	10	12	15	30	60	200	
29 Billy Stone	8	10	12	15	30	60	125	
30 Buddy Young	8	10	12	15	30	60	200	
31 Leon Hart	8	10	12	15	30	80	300	
32 Hugh McElhenny	12	15	15	30	50	100	450	
33 Dale Samuels	8	10	12	15	30	60		
34 Lou Creekmur	10	12	15	20	30	60		
35 Tom Catlin RC	8	10	12	20	35	80	300	
36 Tom Fears	10	12	15	20	50	100	150	
37 George Connor	8	10	12	15	25	60	175	
38 Bill Walsh C	8	10	12	15	25	60	250	
39 Leo Sanford SP RC	10	12	15	20	35	100	300	
40 Horace Gillom	8	10	12	15	25	60		
41 John Schweder SP	10	12	15	20	35	80	350	
42 Tom O'Connell RC	8	10	12	15	25	60	175	
43 Frank Gifford SP	60	80	100	125	250	300	1,000	
44 Frank Continetti SP RC	10	12	15	20	35	60	250	
45 John Olszewski SP RC	10	12	15	20	35	60	250	
46 Dub Jones	8	10	12	15	25	100	▼200	
47 Don Paul LB SP RC	10	12	15	20	35	100	500	
48 Gerald Weatherly RC	8	10	12	15	25	60	175	
49 Fred Bruney SP RC	10	12	15	20	50	100	450	
50 Jack Scarbath RC	8	10	12	15	25	60	200	
51 John Karras	8	10	12	15	25	60	200	
52 Al Conway RC	8	10	12	15	25	60	125	
53 Emlen Tunnell SP	20	30	35	50	75	125	600	
54 Gern Nagler SP RC	10	12	15	20	35	60	250	
55 Kenneth Snyder SP	10	12	15	20	35	60	250	
56 Y.A.Tittle	25	35	40	60	100	200	600	
57 John Rapacz SP	10	12	15	20	35	100	350	
58 Harley Sewell SP RC	10	12	15	25	40	80	250	
59 Don Bingham RC	8	10	12	15	25	60	150	
60 Darrell Hogan	8	10	12	15	25	60	200	
61 Tony Curcillo RC	8	10	12	15	25	60	175	
62 Ray Renfro SP RC	10	12	15	25	60	80	300	
63 Leon Heath	8	10	12	15	25	60	200	
64 Tex Coulter SP	10	12	15	20	35	60	250	
65 Dewayne Douglas RC	8	10	12	15	25	60		
66 J. Robert Smith SP	10	12	15	20	35	80	300	
67 Bob McChesney SP RC	10	12	15	20	35	60	200	
68 Dick Alban SP	10	12	15	20	35	60	250	
69 Andy Kozar RC	8	10	12	15	25	60	175	
70 Merwin Hodel SP RC	10	12	15	20	35	60	250	
71 Thurman McGraw	8	10	12	15	25	60	150	
72 Cliff Anderson RC	8	10	12	15	25	60	150	
73 Pete Pihos	10	12	15	20	35	60	250	
74 Julie Rykovich	8	10	12	15	25	60	200	
75 John Kreamcheck SP RC	10	12	15	20	35	60	250	
76 Lynn Chandnois	8	10	12	15	25	60	125	
77 Cloyce Box SP	10	12	15	20	35	80	300	
78 Ray Mathews	8	10	12	15	25	60	175	
79 Bobby Walston	8	10	12	15	25	60	200	
80 Jim Dooley	8	10	12	15	25	60	175	
81 Pat Harder SP	10	12	15	20	35	80	400	
82 Jerry Shipkey	8	10	12	15	25	60	175	
83 Bobby Thomason RC	8	10	12	15	25	60	175	
84 Hugh Taylor	8	10	12	15	25	60	175	
85 George Ratterman	8	10	12	15	25	60	175	
86 Don Stonesifer RC	8	10	12	15	25	60	175	
87 John Williams SP RC	10	12	15	20	35	60	250	
88 Leo Nomellini	10	12	15	25	40	100	400	
89 Frank Ziegler	8	10	12	15	25	60	175	
90 Don Paul DB UER	8	10	12	15	25	60	200	
91 Tom Dublinski	8	10	12	15	25	60	150	
92 Ken Carpenter	8	10	12	15	25	60	250	
93 Ted Marchibroda RC	8	10	12	15	25	50	80	250
94 Chuck Drazenovich	8	10	12	15	25	60	200	
95 Lou Groza SP	25	35	40	60	100	▲150	600	
96 William Cross SP RC	20	25	25	35	60	▲300	800	

—Chuck Bednarik #24 PSA 9 (Mint) sold for $1,510 (eBay; 10/08)
—Cloyce Box #77 PSA 9 (Mint) sold for $1,015 (eBay; 7/07)
—Cloyce Box #77 PSA 9 (Mint) sold for $686 (Mastro; 6/07)
—Lou Creekmur #34 PSA 8 (NmMt) sold for $1,220 (eBay; 3/07)
—William Cross #96 PSA 9 (Mint) sold for $1,975 (Mile High; 12/10)
—William Cross #96 PSA 9 (Mint) sold for $2,247 (Mile High; 6/13)

—Frank Gifford #43 SGC 8.5 (NmMt+) sold for $2,160 (Mastro; 5/08)
—Frank Gifford #43 PSA 8.5 (NmMt+) sold for $1,821 (Mile High; 5/08)
—Horace Gillom #40 PSA 8 (NmMt) sold for $1,983 (Goodwin; 11/12)
—Hugh McElhenny #32 PSA 9 (Mint) sold for $1,617.55 (eBay; 10/13)
—Marion Motley #9 PSA 9 (Mint) sold for $2,775 (eBay; 7/07)
—Marion Motley #9 PSA 9 (Mint) sold for $1,378 (Mastro; 12/06)
—Dale Samuels #33 PSA 9 (NmMt) sold for $1,353 (Goodwin; 11/12)
—Don Stonesifer #86 PSA 9 (Mint) sold for $831 (Mastro; 2/07)
—Charley Trippi #86 PSA 9 (Mint) sold for $1,313 (eBay; 1/08)

1954 Bowman

#	Player	GD 2	VG 3	VgEx 4	EX 5	ExMt 6	NM 7	NmMt 8	MT 9
1	Ray Mathews	6	8	10	12	30	▼100	▼250	1,000
2	John Huzvar	5	5	6	8	12	20	40	
3	Jack Scarbath	5	5	6	8	12	20	40	200
4	Doug Atkins RC	12	15	20	25	50	100	400	800
5	Bill Stits	5	5	6	8	12	20	40	
6	Joe Perry	8	10	12	15	18	30	75	350
7	Kyle Rote	6	8	10	12	15	25	60	
8	Norm Van Brocklin	10	12	15	20	30	50	125	600
9	Pete Pihos	6	8	10	12	15	30	75	
10	Babe Parilli	5	5	6	8	12	20	40	
11	Zeke Bratkowski RC	6	8	10	12	15	30	60	300
12	Ollie Matson	8	10	12	15	18	30	75	350
13	Pat Brady	5	5	6	8	12	20	40	200
14	Fred Enke	5	5	6	8	12	20	80	200
15	Harry Ulinski	5	5	6	8	12	20	40	
16	Bob Garrett	5	5	6	8	12	20	80	200
17	Bill Bowman	5	5	6	8	12	20	80	
18	Leo Rucka	5	5	6	8	12	20	50	
19	John Cannady	5	5	6	8	12	20	40	200
20	Tom Fears	8	10	12	15	18	30	80	▼200
21	Norm Willey	5	5	6	8	12	20	40	
22	Floyd Reid	5	5	6	8	12	20	40	200
23	George Blanda RC	30	50	80	100	150	300	600	1,500
24	Don Doheney	5	5	6	8	12	20	40	200
25	John Schweder	5	5	6	8	12	20	40	200
26	Bert Rechichar	5	5	6	8	12	20	40	200
27	Harry Dowda	5	5	6	8	12	20	40	
28	John Sandusky	5	5	6	8	12	20	40	200
29	Les Bingaman RC	6	8	10	12	15	25	50	250
30	Joe Arenas	5	5	6	8	12	20	40	200
31	Ray Wietecha RC	5	5	6	8	12	20	40	200
32	Elroy Hirsch	8	10	12	15	20	40	100	
33	Harold Giancanelli	5	5	6	8	12	20	40	
34	Billy Howton	5	5	6	8	12	▲30	80	▲250
35	Fred Morrison	5	5	6	8	12	20	40	200
36	Bobby Cavazos	5	5	6	8	12	20	40	
37	Darrell Hogan	5	5	6	8	12	20	40	200
38	Buddy Young	5	5	6	8	12	20	40	200
39	Charlie Justice	6	8	10	12	15	25	60	300
40	Otto Graham	15	20	25	30	50	100	225	800
41	Doak Walker	10	12	15	20	25	50	120	
42	Y.A. Tittle	10	12	15	20	40	60	175	800
43	Buford Long	5	5	6	8	12	20	40	200
44	Volney Quinlan	5	5	6	8	12	20	40	200
45	Bobby Thomason	5	5	6	8	12	20	50	200
46	Fred Cone	5	5	6	8	12	20	40	
47	Gerald Weatherly	5	5	6	8	12	20	40	200
48	Don Stonesifer	5	5	6	8	12	20	40	
49A	L. Chandnois ERR Chadnois back	5	5	6	8	12	20	40	
49B	Lynn Chandnois COR	5	5	6	8	12	20	40	
50	George Taliaferro	5	5	6	8	12	20	40	200
51	Dick Alban	5	5	6	8	12	20	60	200
52	Lou Groza	10	12	15	20	25	40	100	500
53	Bobby Layne	10	12	15	20	40	▼60	120	600
54	Hugh McElhenny	10	12	15	20	25	40	75	▼400
55	Frank Gifford	15	20	25	35	60	100	200	1,000
56	Leon McLaughlin	5	5	6	8	12	20	40	
57	Chuck Bednarik	10	12	15	20	25	40	100	
58	Art Hunter	5	5	6	8	12	20	40	
59	Bill McColl	5	5	6	8	12	20	40	200
60	Charley Trippi	8	10	12	15	18	30	75	
61	Jim Finks	6	8	10	12	15	25	60	250
62	Bill Lange G	5	5	6	8	12	20	40	
63	Laurie Niemi	5	5	6	8	12	20	40	200
64	Ray Renfro	5	5	6	8	12	20	40	
65	Dick Chapman SP	8	10	12	15	25	30	80	

#	Player	GD 2	VG 3	VgEx 4	EX 5	ExMt 6	NM 7	NmMt 8	MT 9
66	Bob Hantla SP	8	10	12	15	20	30	120	
67	Ralph Starkey SP	8	10	12	15	20	30	80	250
68	Don Paul LB SP	8	10	12	15	20	30	100	
69	Kenneth Snyder SP	8	10	12	15	20	30	▼50	250
70	Tobin Rote SP	8	10	12	15	20	30	120	
71	Art DeCarlo SP	8	10	12	15	20	30	▼60	250
72	Tom Keane SP	8	10	12	15	20	30	80	
73	Hugh Taylor SP	8	10	12	15	20	30	120	
74	Warren Lahr SP RC	8	10	12	15	20	60	150	
75	Jim Neal SP	8	10	12	15	20	30	80	250
76	Leo Nomellini SP	15	20	25	30	50	80	125	800
77	Dick Yelvington SP	8	10	12	15	20	30	80	250
78	Les Richter SP	8	10	12	15	20	30	80	250
79	Bucko Kilroy SP	8	10	12	15	20	30	▼80	
80	John Martinkovic SP	8	10	12	15	20	30	120	250
81	Dale Dodrill SP RC	8	10	12	15	20	30	150	
82	Ken Jackson SP	8	10	12	15	20	30	150	
83	Paul Lipscomb SP	8	10	12	15	20	40	100	
84	John Bauer SP	8	10	12	15	20	30	80	
85	Lou Creekmur SP	12	15	20	25	35	50	▼80	400
86	Eddie Price SP	8	10	12	15	20	30	80	250
87	Kenneth Farragut SP	8	10	12	15	20	30	80	250
88	Dave Hanner SP RC	8	10	12	15	20	40	200	250
89	Don Boll SP	8	10	12	15	20	30	150	
90	Chet Hanulak SP	8	10	12	15	20	40	125	300
91	Thurman McGraw SP	8	10	12	15	20	30	100	150
92	Don Heinrich SP RC	8	10	12	15	20	30	100	
93	Dan McKown SP	8	10	12	15	20	30	100	
94	Bob Fleck SP	8	10	12	15	30	60	100	250
95	Jerry Hilgenberg SP	8	10	12	15	20	50	▼80	200
96	Bill Walsh C SP	8	10	12	15	20	30	80	250
97A	Tom Finnin ERR	15	20	25	40	60	100	300	
97B	Tom Finnan COR	5	5	6	8	12	20	40	200
98	Paul Barry	5	5	6	8	12	20	40	200
99	Chick Jagade	5	5	6	8	12	20	40	200
100	Jack Christiansen	6	8	10	12	15	30	60	▲400
101	Gordy Soltau	5	5	6	8	12	20	40	200
102A	Emlen Tunnell ERR Tunnel	10	12	15	20	40	75	200	500
102B	Emlen Tunnell COR	6	8	10	12	15	25	75	300
102C	Emlen Tunnell COR	6	8	10	12	15	25	75	300
103	Stan West	5	5	6	8	12	20	40	
104	Jerry Williams	5	5	6	8	12	▲30	40	
105	Veryl Switzer	5	5	6	8	12	20	30	150
106	Billy Stone	5	5	6	8	12	20	40	200
107	Jerry Watford	5	5	6	8	12	20	40	200
108	Elbert Nickel	5	5	6	8	12	20	40	200
109	Ed Sharkey	5	5	6	8	12	20	40	200
110	Steve Meilinger	5	5	6	8	12	20	40	200
111	Dante Lavelli	6	8	10	12	15	25	60	300
112	Leon Hart	6	8	10	12	15	25	50	
113	Charley Conerly	8	10	12	15	18	30	100	300
114	Richard Lemmon	5	5	6	8	12	20	40	
115	Al Carmichael	5	5	6	8	12	20	50	
116	George Connor	6	8	10	12	15	25	60	
117	John Olszewski	5	5	6	8	12	20	40	150
118	Ernie Stautner	8	10	12	15	20	30	100	
119	Ray Smith	5	5	6	8	12	20	80	
120	Neil Worden	5	5	6	8	12	20	40	
121	Jim Dooley	5	5	6	8	12	20	60	200
122	Arnold Galiffa	5	5	6	8	12	20	60	200
123	Kline Gilbert	5	5	6	8	12	20	40	200
124	Bob Hoernschemeyer	5	5	6	8	12	20	50	
125	Wilford White RC	6	8	10	12	15	30	100	250
126	Art Spinney	5	5	6	8	12	20	40	
127	Joe Koch	5	5	6	8	12	50	100	200
128	John Lattner RC	12	15	20	25	50	150	800	

—George Connor #116 PSA 9 (Mt) sold for $411 (eBay; 11/14)
—Doak Walker #41 PSA 9 (Mt) sold for $1,023 (eBay; 2/10)
—Jerry Watford #107 PSA 10 (Gem) sold for $790 (eBay; 7/07)

1955 Bowman

#	Player	GD 2	VG 3	VgEx 4	EX 5	ExMt 6	NM 7	NmMt 8	MT 9
1	Doak Walker	10	12	15	25	50	120	400	1,800
2	Mike McCormack RC	8	10	12	18	30	60	200	600
3	John Olszewski	5	5	6	8	12	20	40	250
4	Dorne Dibble RC	5	5	6	8	12	20	40	250
5	Lindon Crow RC	5	5	6	8	12	20	40	
6	Hugh Taylor UER	5	5	6	8	12	20	40	250

	GD 2	VG 3	VgEx 4	EX 5	ExMt 6	NM 7	NmMt 8	MT 9
Frank Gifford	10	12	15	25	40	60	150	800
Alan Ameche RC	8	10	12	15	25	50	125	800
Don Stonesifer	5	5	6	8	12	25	60	
Pete Pihos	6	8	10	12	18	30	60	
Bill Austin	5	5	6	8	12	20	40	250
Dick Alban	5	5	6	8	12	20	40	250
Bobby Walston	5	5	6	8	12	20	50	250
Len Ford RC	8	10	12	15	25	50	125	
Jug Girard	5	5	6	8	12	20	40	
Charley Conerly	8	10	12	15	20	30	60	400
Volney Peters RC	5	5	6	8	12	20	40	▲300
Max Boydston RC	5	5	6	8	12	20	40	
Leon Hart	6	8	10	12	15	25	50	
Bert Rechichar	5	5	6	8	12	20	40	250
Lee Riley RC	5	5	6	8	12	20	40	250
Johnny Carson RC	5	5	6	8	12	20	40	200
Harry Thompson	5	5	6	8	12	20	40	250
Ray Wietecha	5	5	6	8	12	20	40	250
Ollie Matson	8	10	12	15	20	35	75	
Eddie LeBaron	6	8	10	12	18	30	75	400
Jack Simmons	5	5	6	8	12	20	40	
Jack Christiansen	6	8	10	12	18	30	60	
Bucko Kilroy	5	5	6	8	12	20	50	
Tom Keane	5	5	6	8	12	20	50	
Dave Leggett RC	5	5	6	8	12	20	40	
Norm Van Brocklin	8	10	12	15	25	50	150	1,000
Harlon Hill RC	5	5	6	8	12	25	60	200
Robert Haner RC	5	5	6	8	12	20	40	200
Veryl Switzer	5	5	6	8	12	20	40	250
Dick Stanfel RC	6	8	10	12	18	30	200	
Lou Groza	8	10	12	15	20	35	75	500
Tank Younger	6	8	10	12	15	25	50	300
Dick Flanagan RC	5	5	6	8	12	20	40	200
Jim Dooley	5	5	6	8	12	20	40	250
Ray Collins RC	5	5	6	8	12	20	40	250
John Henry Johnson RC	8	10	12	15	30	60	▼150	1,200
Tom Fears	6	8	10	12	18	30	60	
Joe Perry	8	10	12	15	25	35	75	
Gene Brito RC	5	5	6	8	12	20	40	
Bill Johnson C	5	5	6	8	12	20	40	
Dan Towler	6	8	10	12	15	25	50	
Dick Moegle RC	5	5	6	8	12	20	40	200
Kline Gilbert	5	5	6	8	12	20	40	200
Les Gobel RC	5	5	6	8	12	20	40	▼125
Ray Krouse RC	5	5	6	8	12	20	40	250
Pat Summerall RC	12	15	18	30	50	75	120	400
Ed Brown RC	6	8	10	12	20	30	50	
Lynn Chandnois	5	5	6	8	12	20	40	200
Joe Heap RC	5	5	6	8	12	20	40	200
John Hoffman	5	5	6	8	12	20	40	
Howard Ferguson RC	5	5	6	8	12	20	100	300
Bobby Watkins RC	5	5	6	8	12	20	40	
Charlie Ane RC	5	5	6	8	12	20	40	250
Ken MacAfee E RC	5	5	6	8	12	20	▼40	
Ralph Guglielmi RC	5	5	6	8	12	20	40	
George Blanda	10	12	15	25	35	60	150	600
Kenneth Snyder	5	5	6	8	12	20	50	
Chet Ostrowski	5	5	6	8	12	20	40	
Buddy Young	8	10	12	15	20	30	80	
Gordy Soltau	5	6	8	10	15	30	80	
Eddie Bell RC	5	6	8	10	15	30	80	200
Ben Agajanian RC	6	8	10	12	15	30	50	200
Tom Dahms RC	5	6	8	10	15	30	▼60	
Jim Ringo RC	15	20	30	35	50	125	1,000	
Bobby Layne	15	20	25	30	40	75	200	800
Y.A.Tittle	15	▲30	▲40	▲50	▲60	100	200	
Bob Gaona RC	5	6	8	10	15	30	▲100	
Tobin Rote	6	8	10	12	15	30	▲100	
Hugh McElhenny	10	12	15	20	25	35	100	400
John Kreamcheck	5	6	8	10	15	30	▼60	
Al Dorow RC	6	8	10	12	15	30	▼60	
Bill Wade	8	10	12	15	20	30	▼60	
Dale Dodrill	5	6	8	10	15	30	80	200
Chuck Drazenovich	5	6	8	10	15	30	80	
Billy Wilson RC	6	8	10	12	15	30	50	200
Les Richter	6	8	10	12	15	30	80	
Pat Brady	5	6	8	10	15	30	80	

	GD 2	VG 3	VgEx 4	EX 5	ExMt 6	NM 7	NmMt 8	MT 9
84	Bob Hoernschemeyer	6	8	10	12	15	30	80	200
85	Joe Arenas	5	6	8	10	15	30	60	200
86	Len Szafaryn UER RC	5	6	8	10	15	30	100	
87	Rick Casares RC	10	12	15	20	25	35	80	
88	Leon McLaughlin	5	6	8	10	15	30	60	200
89	Charley Toogood RC	5	6	8	10	15	50	250	
90	Tom Bettis RC	5	6	8	10	15	50	125	
91	John Sandusky	5	6	8	10	15	30	80	250
92	Bill Wightkin	5	6	8	10	15	30	80	250
93	Darrel Brewster RC	5	6	8	10	15	30	80	
94	Marion Campbell	8	10	12	15	20	30	60	350
95	Floyd Reid	5	6	8	10	15	30	80	
96	Chick Jagade	5	6	8	10	15	30	60	250
97	George Taliaferro	5	6	8	10	15	25	150	
98	Carlton Massey RC	5	6	8	10	15	30	▲250	
99	Fran Rogel	5	6	8	10	15	25	150	
100	Alex Sandusky RC	5	6	8	10	15	30	125	
101	Bob St.Clair RC	15	20	25	30	60	200	600	
102	Al Carmichael	5	6	8	10	15	30	200	
103	Carl Taseff RC	5	6	8	10	15	30	▼125	
104	Leo Nomellini	10	12	15	20	25	35	100	
105	Tom Scott	5	6	8	10	15	30	100	
106	Ted Marchibroda	8	10	12	15	20	30	80	
107	Art Spinney	5	6	8	10	15	30	80	
108	Wayne Robinson	5	6	8	10	15	30	80	
109	Jim Ricca RC	5	6	8	10	15	30	50	
110	Lou Ferry RC	5	6	8	10	15	30	80	
111	Roger Zatkoff RC	5	6	8	10	15	30	120	
112	Lou Creekmur	8	10	12	15	20	35	80	
113	Kenny Konz RC	5	6	8	10	15	▲50	80	
114	Doug Eggers RC	5	6	8	10	15	30	▼60	
115	Bobby Thomason	5	6	8	10	15	30	80	
116	Bill McPeak RC	5	6	8	10	15	30	100	
117	William Brown RC	5	6	8	10	15	30	80	
118	Royce Womble RC	5	6	8	10	15	30	60	200
119	Frank Gatski RC	10	12	15	30	40	100	225	
120	Jim Finks	8	10	12	15	20	35	80	
121	Andy Robustelli	10	12	15	20	25	40	125	
122	Bobby Dillon	5	6	8	10	15	30	80	
123	Leo Sanford	5	6	8	10	15	30	60	250
124	Elbert Nickel	6	8	10	12	15	30	80	
125	Wayne Hansen RC	5	6	8	10	15	50	▼60	200
126	Buck Lansford RC	5	6	8	10	15	30	80	
127	Gern Nagler	5	6	8	10	15	25	60	200
128	Jim Salsbury RC	5	6	8	10	15	30	80	
129	Dale Atkeson RC	5	6	8	10	15	30	150	
130	John Schweder	5	6	8	10	15	30	100	
131	Dave Hanner	6	8	10	12	15	30	100	
132	Eddie Price	5	6	8	10	15	30	80	250
133	Vic Janowicz	10	12	15	20	25	35	125	300
134	Ernie Stautner	10	12	15	20	25	35	135	
135	James Parmer RC	5	6	8	10	15	25	120	
136	Emlen Tunnell UER	10	12	15	20	25	▲50	▲200	
137	Kyle Rote	8	10	12	15	25	60	1,200	
138	Norm Willey	5	6	8	10	15	30	135	
139	Charley Trippi	10	12	15	20	25	40	150	
140	Billy Howton	6	8	10	12	15	▲40	100	
141	Bobby Clatterbuck RC	5	6	8	10	15	30	▼60	
142	Bob Boyd	5	6	8	10	15	30	150	
143	Bob Toneff RC	6	8	10	12	20	30	▼200	
144	Jerry Helluin RC	5	6	8	10	15	30	120	
145	Adrian Burk	5	6	8	10	15	30	150	
146	Walt Michaels	6	8	10	12	15	30	▼80	
147	Zollie Toth	5	6	8	10	15	30	80	
148	Frank Varrichione RC	5	6	8	10	15	30	150	
149	Dick Bielski RC	5	6	8	10	15	30	80	300
150	George Ratterman	6	8	10	12	15	30	200	
151	Mike Jarmoluk RC	5	6	8	10	15	40	400	
152	Tom Landry	▲60	▲80	▲100	▲125	150	350	1,000	
153	Ray Renfro	6	8	10	12	15	30	▲100	
154	Zeke Bratkowski	6	8	10	12	15	30	80	
155	Jerry Norton RC	5	6	8	10	15	30	80	
156	Maurice Bassett RC	5	6	8	10	20	30	60	300
157	Volney Quinlan	5	6	8	10	15	40	100	
158	Chuck Bednarik	10	12	15	20	25	40	300	
159	Don Colo RC	5	6	8	10	18	▲60	350	
160	L.G. Dupre RC	6	8	12	20	40	60	300	

—Joe Arenas #85 PSA 9 (Mint) sold for $568.5 (eBay: 4/12)
—Len Ford #14 PSA 9 (Mint) sold for $921 (eBay: 11/14)
—Tom Fears #43 PSA 9 (MT) sold for $990 (Mastro: 10/06)
—Frank Gatski #119 PSA 9 (MT) sold for $940 (eBay: 10/12)
—Les Richter #82 PSA 9 (MT) sold for $714 (eBay: 10/07)
—Y.A.Tittle #72 PSA 9 (Mint) sold for $569.5 (eBay: 5/12)

1955 Topps All American

		GD 2	VG 3	VgEx 4	EX 5	ExMt 6	NM 7	NmMt 8	MT 9
1	Herman Hickman RC	30	35	40	60	80	▼125	250	2,000
2	John Kimbrough RC	5	6	8	12	25	50	150	
3	Ed Weir RC	5	6	8	12	25	80	500	
4	Erny Pinckert RC	5	6	8	12	20	50	125	
5	Bobby Grayson RC	5	6	8	12	20	40	125	500
6	Nile Kinnick UER RC	30	35	40	60	100	175	500	1,500
7	Andy Bershak RC	5	6	8	12	20	40	125	500
8	George Cafego RC	5	6	8	12	20	40	125	400
9	Tom Hamilton SP RC	6	8	10	15	30	50	125	600
10	Bill Dudley	8	10	12	20	35	60	120	500
11	Bobby Dodd SP RC	6	8	10	15	30	60	▼125	400
12	Otto Graham	35	40	50	75	100	200	400	1,500
13	Aaron Rosenberg	5	6	8	12	20	40	125	500
14A	Gaynell Tinsley ERR RC	30	35	40	60	100	250	800	
14B	Gaynell Tinsley COR RC	6	8	10	18	30	80	200	
15	Ed Kaw SP	6	8	10	15	25	40	100	600
16	Knute Rockne	50	60	80	125	200	300	600	1,500
17	Bob Reynolds	6	8	10	15	25	80	▼150	
18	Pudge Heffelfinger SP RC	6	8	10	15	30	50	120	400
19	Bruce Smith	8	10	12	20	40	80	250	800
20	Sammy Baugh	40	50	60	100	125	200	▼300	1,500
21A	W.White RC SP ERR	60	80	100	150	250	400	800	
21B	W.White RC SP COR	15	20	25	40	75	150	250	1,000
22	Brick Muller RC	5	6	8	12	20	40	125	
23	Dick Kazmaier RC	5	6	8	20	25	40	150	
24	Ken Strong	10	12	15	20	35	80	400	800
25	Casimir Myslinski SP RC	6	8	10	15	25	▼50	120	
26	Larry Kelley SP RC	6	8	10	15	25	50	120	750
27	Red Grange UER	50	80	100	150	200	300	600	2,000
28	Mel Hein SP RC	12	15	20	35	60	100	▼250	
29	Leo Nomellini SP	12	15	20	35	50	80	150	1,000
30	Wes Fesler RC	5	6	8	12	20	40	125	500
31	George Sauer Sr. RC	5	6	8	12	20	50	▼125	500
32	Hank Foldberg RC	8	10	12	18	40	60	▼125	
33	Bob Higgins RC	5	6	8	12	20	40	125	500
34	Davey O'Brien RC	10	12	15	25	40	80	150	500
35	Tom Harmon SP RC	15	20	25	40	75	125	250	1,200
36	Turk Edwards SP	10	12	15	25	40	60	200	800
37	Jim Thorpe	100	125	150	225	350	600	1,500	
38	Amos A. Stagg RC	12	15	18	25	50	100	300	1,600
39	Jerome Holland RC	5	6	8	12	20	40	125	1,200
40	Donn Moomaw RC	5	6	8	12	20	40	125	500
41	Joseph Alexander SP RC	6	8	10	15	30	50	175	
42	Eddie Tryon SP RC	6	8	10	15	25	50	100	750
43	George Savitsky RC	5	6	8	12	20	40	125	500
44	Ed Garbisch RC	5	6	8	12	20	40	100	500
45	Elmer Oliphant RC	5	6	8	12	35	80	200	
46	Arnold Lassman RC	5	6	8	12	20	40	125	
47	Bo McMillin RC	5	6	8	20	30	40	▼125	500
48	Ed Widseth RC	5	6	8	12	25	50	200	
49	Don Gordon Zimmerman RC	5	6	8	12	20	40	125	500
50	Ken Kavanaugh RC	5	6	8	12	20	40	175	500
51	Duane Purvis SP RC	6	8	10	15	25	50	120	
52	Johnny Lujack	15	20	25	35	50	100	200	1,000
53	John F. Green RC	5	6	8	12	20	40	125	600
54	Edwin Dooley SP RC	6	8	10	15	30	50	150	500
55	Frank Merritt SP RC	6	8	10	15	25	40	100	600
56	Ernie Nevers RC	25	30	35	50	75	125	400	
57	Vic Hanson SP RC	6	8	10	15	25	40	125	500
58	Ed Franco RC	5	6	8	12	20	40	125	500
59	Doc Blanchard RC	12	15	20	30	50	100	250	
60	Dan Hill RC	5	6	8	12	20	40	100	
61	Charles Brickley SP RC	6	8	10	15	25	40	125	600
62	Harry Newman RC	6	8	10	20	30	50	150	600
63	Charlie Justice	8	10	12	18	30	50	125	600
64	Benny Friedman RC	8	10	15	25	35	80	200	
65	Joe Donchess SP RC	6	8	10	15	25	40	120	
66	Bruiser Kinard RC	8	10	15	25	35	80	150	600
67	Frankie Albert	8	10	12	18	30	50	225	600

		GD 2	VG 3	VgEx 4	EX 5	ExMt 6	NM 7	NmMt 8	MT 9
68	Four Horsemen SP RC	80	125	200	250	400	600	1,500	5,000
69	Frank Sinkwich RC	8	10	12	20	40	100	700	
70	Bill Daddio RC	5	6	8	12	20	40	125	
71	Bobby Wilson	6	8	10	15	25	40	175	500
72	Chub Peabody RC	5	6	8	12	20	50	150	
73	Paul Governali RC	5	6	8	12	25	50	125	500
74	Gene McEver RC	5	6	8	12	20	40	125	500
75	Hugh Gallarneau RC	5	6	8	12	20	40	125	500
76	Angelo Bertelli RC	6	8	10	20	40	100	200	
77	Bowden Wyatt SP RC	6	8	10	15	25	40	125	750
78	Jay Berwanger RC	8	10	12	20	30	60	150	1,000
79	Pug Lund RC	6	8	10	15	25	40	125	
80	Bennie Oosterbaan RC	6	8	10	15	25	50	250	
81	Cotton Warburton RC	6	8	10	15	25	80	400	
82	Alex Wojciechowicz	8	10	12	20	35	60	400	
83	Ted Coy SP RC	6	8	10	18	30	50	125	750
84	Ace Parker SP RC	12	15	18	35	60	100	300	
85	Sid Luckman	35	40	50	60	80	120	300	
86	Albie Booth SP RC	6	8	10	18	30	50	125	
87	Adolph Schultz SP	6	8	10	15	25	40	175	700
88	Ralph Kercheval	5	6	8	12	20	40	125	600
89	Marshall Goldberg	6	8	10	15	25	50·	100	600
90	Charlie O'Rourke RC	5	6	8	12	25	100	800	
91	Bob Odell UER RC	5	6	8	12	20	40	▼125	600
92	Biggie Munn RC	6	8	10	12	20	50	125	500
93	Willie Heston SP RC	8	10	12	18	35	60	150	750
94	Joe Bernard SP RC	8	10	12	18	30	60	125	
95	Chris Cagle SP RC	8	10	12	20	30	60	120	500
96	Bill Hollenback SP	8	10	12	18	30	60	150	750
97	Don Hutson SP RC	60	80	125	150	225	400	1,000	5,500
98	Beattie Feathers SP	20	25	30	40	60	100	200	1,000
99	Don Whitmire SP RC	8	10	12	18	30	60	200	750
100	Fats Henry SP RC	20	25	30	60	120	300	800	2,500

—Joe Bernard #94 PSA 9 (MT) sold for $960 (eBay: 12/06)
—Otto Graham #12 PSA 10 (Gem Mt) sold for $4,900 (eBay: 11/09)
—Mel Hein SP RC #28 PSA 9 (Mint) sold for $1,478 (Memory Lane; 8/12)
—Mel Hein SP RC #28 PSA 9 (Mint) sold for $1,422 (Robert Edward; Fall 2013)
—Fats Henry SP RC #100 PSA 9 (Mint) sold for $4,444 (Robert Edward; Fall 2013)
—Four Horsemen #68 GAI 9 (Mint) sold for $2,082 (Mastro; 4/07)
—Sid Luckman #85 PSA 9 (MT) sold for $2,805 (eBay; 7/08)
—Sid Luckman #85 SGC 9 (Mint) sold for $1504.16 (Goodwin; 2/12)
—Ernie Nevers #56 PSA 9 (MT) sold for $1,549 (eBay; 2/14)
—Charlie O'Rourke #90 PSA 9 (MT) sold for $1,075 (Legendary; 5/11)
—Knute Rockne #16 PSA 10 (Gem Mint) sold for $4680 (SCP; 5/12)
—Jim Thorpe #37 PSA 9 (MT) sold for $11,860 (Memory Lane; 4/07)
—Jim Thorpe #37 PSA 9 (Mint) sold for $6791 (Memory Lane; 5/12)
—Jim Thorpe #37 PSA 8.5 (NrMt) sold for $1946 (eBay; 8/13)

1956 Topps

		GD 2	VG 3	VgEx 4	EX 5	ExMt 6	NM 7	NmMt 8	MT 9
1	Johnny Carson SP	10	12	15	30	60	200	2,000	
2	Gordy Soltau	5	5	5	8	12	▲50	80	200
3	Frank Varrichione	5	5	5	8	12	40	100	200
4	Eddie Bell	5	5	5	8	12	20	40	200
5	Alex Webster RC	5	6	8	10	15	25	▲80	250
6	Norm Van Brocklin	8	10	12	20	30	40	125	450
7	Green Bay Packers	8	10	12	18	30	50	100	600
8	Lou Creekmur	5	6	8	10	15	25	60	300
9	Lou Groza	6	8	10	15	20	35	100	550
10	Tom Bienemann SP RC	5	6	8	10	18	25	40	100
11	George Blanda	8	10	12	20	30	50	100	300
12	Alan Ameche	5	6	8	10	15	25	60	150
13	Vic Janowicz SP	8	10	25	40	50	60	500	
14	Dick Moegle	5	5	5	8	12	20	▼60	
15	Fran Rogel	5	5	5	8	12	20	40	
16	Harold Giancanelli	5	5	5	8	12	20	40	200
17	Emlen Tunnell	5	6	8	10	15	25	60	
18	Tank Younger	5	6	8	10	15	25	50	250
19	Billy Howton	5	5	5	8	12	20	40	200
20	Jack Christiansen	5	6	8	10	15	25	60	350
21	Darrel Brewster	5	5	5	8	12	20	40	
22	Chicago Cardinals SP	12	15	18	30	50	80	100	200
23	Ed Brown	5	5	5	8	12	20	40	125
24	Joe Campanella	5	5	5	8	12	20	40	125
25	Leon Heath SP	6	8	10	15	25	50	300	
26	San Francisco 49ers	5	6	8	10	15	25	80	
27	Dick Flanagan RC	5	5	5	8	12	20	40	
28	Chuck Bednarik	6	8	10	15	20	35	100	500

	GD 2	VG 3	VgEx 4	EX 5	ExMt 6	NM 7	NmMt 8	MT 9
Kyle Rote	5	6	8	10	15	25	50	250
Les Richter	5	5	5	8	12	20	40	
Howard Ferguson	5	5	5	8	12	20	40	200
Dorne Dibble	5	5	5	8	12	20	40	
Kenny Konz	5	5	5	8	12	20	50	500
Dave Mann SP RC	5	6	8	10	18	80	500	
Rick Casares	5	6	8	10	15	25	50	300
Art Donovan	8	10	12	18	25	40	80	400
Chuck Drazenovich SP	6	8	10	15	25	40	350	
Joe Arenas	5	5	5	8	12	20	125	400
Lynn Chandnois	5	5	5	8	12	20	30	300
Philadelphia Eagles	5	6	8	10	15	25	60	300
Roosevelt Brown RC	8	10	12	18	30	50	▼200	600
Tom Fears	6	8	10	15	20	35	80	400
Gary Knafelc RC	5	5	5	8	12	20	40	250
Joe Schmidt RC	8	10	12	20	30	80	300	600
Cleveland Browns	5	6	8	10	15	25	80	400
Len Teeuws SP RC	6	8	10	15	25	40	300	
Bill George RC	8	10	12	18	30	60	150	600
Baltimore Colts	5	6	8	10	15	25	60	150
Eddie LeBaron SP	10	12	15	25	40	175	600	
Hugh McElhenny	8	10	12	18	25	35	100	400
Ted Marchibroda	5	6	8	10	15	25	60	250
Adrian Burk	5	5	5	8	12	20	40	200
Frank Gifford	10	12	15	25	35	60	150	500
Charley Toogood	5	5	5	8	12	20	40	200
Tobin Rote	5	5	5	8	12	20	40	200
Bill Stits	5	5	5	8	12	20	60	
Don Colo	5	5	5	8	12	20	40	
Ollie Matson SP	12	15	18	30	50	60	250	500
Harlon Hill	5	5	5	8	12	20	40	
Lenny Moore RC	15	20	40	50	▲100	175	800	
Wash.Redskins SP	12	15	18	30	60	100	250	
Billy Wilson	5	5	5	8	12	20	60	
Pittsburgh Steelers	5	6	8	10	15	25	60	300
Bob Pellegrini RC	5	5	5	8	12	20	40	
Ken MacAfee E	5	5	5	8	12	20	40	
Willard Sherman RC	5	5	5	8	12	20	40	200
Roger Zatkoff	5	5	5	8	12	20	40	
Dave Middleton RC	5	5	5	8	12	20	40	200
Ray Renfro	5	5	5	8	12	20	50	
Don Stonesifer SP	8	10	12	20	30	150	400	
Stan Jones RC	8	10	12	18	30	60	300	
Jim Mutscheller RC	5	5	5	8	12	30	50	
Volney Peters SP	6	8	10	15	25	50	500	1,000
Leo Nomellini	6	8	10	12	18	30	80	300
Ray Mathews	5	5	5	8	12	20	50	200
Dick Bielski	5	5	5	8	12	20	40	
Charley Conerly	6	8	10	15	20	35	▲100	350
Elroy Hirsch	8	10	12	18	25	35	100	
Bill Forester RC	5	5	5	8	12	20	50	200
Jim Doran RC	5	5	5	8	12	20	40	200
Fred Morrison	5	5	5	8	12	20	40	
Jack Simmons SP	6	8	10	15	20	30	60	250
Bill McColl	5	5	5	8	12	20	40	125
Bert Rechichar	5	5	5	8	12	20	40	125
Joe Scudero SP RC	6	8	10	15	20	40	300	
Y.A.Tittle	8	10	12	20	30	50	175	600
Ernie Stautner	6	8	10	12	18	30	90	
Norm Willey	5	5	5	8	12	20	40	
Bob Schnelker RC	5	5	5	8	12	20	40	200
Dan Towler	5	6	8	10	15	25	60	
John Martinkovic	5	5	5	8	12	20	40	200
Detroit Lions	5	6	8	10	15	25	60	300
George Ratterman	5	5	5	8	12	20	40	
Chuck Ulrich SP	6	8	10	15	20	40	200	
Bobby Watkins	5	5	5	8	12	20	40	200
Buddy Young	5	6	8	10	15	25	50	250
Billy Wells SP RC	6	8	10	15	20	40	250	
Bob Toneff	5	5	5	8	12	20	50	200
Bill McPeak	5	5	5	8	12	20	50	200
Bobby Thomason	5	5	5	8	12	30	40	400
Roosevelt Grier RC	12	15	25	30	40	60	175	500
Ron Waller RC	5	5	5	8	12	20	40	200
Bobby Dillon	5	5	5	8	12	20	50	300
Leon Hart	5	6	8	10	15	25	60	250
Mike McCormack	5	6	8	10	15	25	80	400
John Olszewski SP	6	8	10	15	25	50	500	
Bill Wightkin	5	6	8	10	15	40	80	300

		GD 2	VG 3	VgEx 4	EX 5	ExMt 6	NM 7	NmMt 8	MT 9
108	George Shaw RC	5	8	12	25	60			250
109	Dale Atkeson SP	6	8	10	15	30	175	1,600	
110	Joe Perry	6	8	10	15	20	35	75	
111	Dale Dodrill	5	5	5	8	12	20	50	
112	Tom Scott	5	5	5	8	12	20	40	
113	New York Giants	5	6	8	10	15	50	80	600
114	Los Angeles Rams	5	6	8	10	15	25	60	
115	Al Carmichael	5	5	5	8	12	20	50	
116	Bobby Layne	8	10	15	25	30	50	150	500
117	Ed Modzelewski	5	5	5	8	12	20	40	
118	Lamar McHan RC SP	6	8	10	15	20	20	50	250
119	Chicago Bears	5	6	8	10	15	60	150	500
120	Billy Vessels RC	5	8	10	25	35	60	150	500
NNO	Checklist SP NNO	50	60	100	200	300	500	1,000	
C1	Contest Card 1	20	25	30	50	100	175		
C2	Contest Card 2	25	30	40	75	150	225		
C3	Contest Card 3	25	30	40	75				
CA	Contest Card A	25	30	40	75	150	250		
CB	Contest Card B	25	30	40	75	150	250	400	

—George Blanda #11 PSA 10 (Gem) sold for $940 (eBay; 3/07)
—Stan Jones #71 SGC 9 (Mint) sold for $987 (Mile High; 10/09)
—Dick Moegle #14 PSA 10 (Gem) sold for $1,485 (eBay; 3/07)
—Lenny Moore #60 PSA 9 (Mint) sold for $3,385 (eBay; 12/07)
—Lenny Moore #60 PSA 9 (Mint) sold for $2,201 (eBay; 7/13)
—Lenny Moore #60 PSA 9 (Mint) sold for $5,730 (eBay; 7/16)
—Volney Peters SP #73 PSA 9 (Mint) sold for $1480 (eBay: 9/12)

1957 Topps

		GD 2	VG 3	VgEx 4	EX 5	ExMt 6	NM 7	NmMt 8	MT 9
1	Eddie LeBaron	6	8	10	15	25	60	175	800
2	Pete Retzlaff RC	5	5	6	10	15	30	150	
3	Mike McCormack	5	5	10	15	25	60		
4	Lou Baldacci	5	5	5	8	12	20	40	
5	Gino Marchetti	5	6	8	12	20	40	80	300
6	Leo Nomellini	5	6	8	12	20	30	60	400
7	Bobby Watkins	5	5	5	8	12	20	40	
8	Dave Middleton	5	5	5	8	12	20	40	250
9	Bobby Dillon	5	5	5	8	12	20	50	300
10	Les Richter	5	5	5	8	12	20	40	
11	Roosevelt Brown	5	6	8	12	20	30	60	
12	Lavern Torgeson RC	5	5	5	8	12	20	50	
13	Dick Bielski	5	5	5	8	12	20	40	
14	Pat Summerall	5	6	8	12	20	30	80	
15	Jack Butler RC	5	5	10	20	35	60	175	300
16	John Henry Johnson	5	5	6	10	15	30	80	
17	Art Spinney	5	5	5	8	12	20	40	
18	Bob St. Clair	5	5	6	10	15	25	50	350
19	Perry Jeter	5	5	5	8	12	20	40	
20	Lou Creekmur	5	5	6	10	15	25	50	400
21	Dave Hanner	5	5	5	8	12	20	40	300
22	Norm Van Brocklin	6	8	10	15	25	35	75	600
23	Don Chandler RC	5	5	6	10	15	25	50	500
24	Al Dorow	5	5	5	8	12	20	35	250
25	Tom Scott	5	5	5	8	12	20	40	
26	Ollie Matson	5	6	8	12	20	25	60	
27	Fran Rogel	5	5	5	8	12	20	40	
28	Lou Groza	6	8	10	15	20	30	75	500
29	Billy Vessels	5	5	5	8	12	30	150	
30	Y.A.Tittle	8	10	12	18	30	50	100	400
31	George Blanda	6	8	10	15	30	50	125	300
32	Bobby Layne	8	10	12	18	30	50	125	400
33	Billy Howton	5	5	5	8	12	20	30	
34	Bill Wade	5	5	6	10	15	25	50	300
35	Emlen Tunnell	5	6	8	10	15	25	50	
36	Leo Elter	5	5	5	8	12	20	35	250
37	Clarence Peaks RC	5	5	5	8	12	20	40	400
38	Don Stonesifer	5	5	5	8	12	20	40	
39	George Tarasovic	5	5	5	8	12	20	40	
40	Darrel Brewster	5	5	5	8	12	20	40	
41	Bert Rechichar	5	5	5	8	12	20	35	250
42	Billy Wilson	5	5	5	8	12	20	40	200
43	Ed Brown	5	5	5	8	12	20	50	250
44	Gene Gedman	5	5	5	8	12	20	35	250
45	Gary Knafelc	5	5	5	8	12	20	35	250
46	Elroy Hirsch	6	8	10	15	25	35	▲100	600
47	Don Heinrich	5	5	5	8	12	20	40	
48	Gene Brito	5	5	5	8	12	20	35	200
49	Chuck Bednarik	6	8	10	15	20	30	75	

#	Name	GD 2	VG 3	VgEx 4	EX 5	ExMt 6	NM 7	NmMt 8	MT 9
50	Dave Mann	5	5	5	8	12	20	40	
51	Bill McPeak	5	5	5	8	12	20	40	
52	Kenny Konz	5	5	5	8	12	20	40	
53	Alan Ameche	5	5	6	10	15	25	80	600
54	Gordy Soltau	5	5	5	8	12	20	35	350
55	Rick Casares	5	5	5	8	12	20	40	
56	Charlie Ane	5	5	5	8	12	20	40	
57	Al Carmichael	5	5	5	8	12	20	40	
58A	W.Sherman ERR no pos/team	60	80	100	150	200	350	600	
58B	Willard Sherman COR	5	5	5	8	12	20	35	250
59	Kyle Rote	5	5	5	10	15	30	50	500
60	Chuck Drazenovich	5	5	5	8	12	20	35	300
61	Bobby Walston	5	5	5	8	12	20	35	250
62	John Olszewski	5	5	5	8	12	20	35	250
63	Ray Mathews	5	5	5	8	12	20	35	350
64	Maurice Bassett	5	5	5	8	12	20	35	250
65	Art Donovan	6	8	10	15	20	30	60	350
66	Joe Arenas	5	5	5	8	12	20	35	250
67	Harlon Hill	5	5	5	8	12	20	35	250
68	Yale Lary	5	5	5	10	15	25	▲60	
69	Bill Forester	5	5	5	8	12	20	35	250
70	Bob Boyd	5	5	5	8	12	20	35	250
71	Andy Robustelli	5	6	8	12	20	30	60	
72	Sam Baker RC	5	5	5	8	12	20	35	250
73	Bob Pellegrini	5	5	5	8	12	20	40	
74	Leo Sanford	5	5	5	8	12	20	100	
75	Sid Watson	5	5	5	8	12	20	60	250
76	Ray Renfro	5	5	5	8	12	20	35	250
77	Carl Taseff	5	5	5	8	12	20	50	
78	Clyde Conner	5	5	5	8	12	20	35	250
79	J.C. Caroline	5	5	5	8	12	20	25	50
80	Howard Cassady RC	5	5	6	10	15	25	60	400
81	Tobin Rote	5	5	5	8	12	30	40	
82	Ron Waller	5	5	5	8	12	20	35	250
83	Jim Patton RC	5	5	5	8	12	20	50	300
84	Volney Peters	5	5	5	8	12	20	40	250
85	Dick Lane RC	10	12	15	40	50	120	600	
86	Royce Womble	5	5	5	8	12	20	35	200
87	Duane Putnam RC	5	5	5	8	12	20	35	250
88	Frank Gifford	8	10	12	20	35	60	150	400
89	Steve Meilinger	5	6	8	12	20	30	100	
90	Buck Lansford	5	6	8	12	20	30	150	
91	Lindon Crow DP	5	5	5	8	12	25	60	
92	Ernie Stautner DP	5	6	8	12	30	40	200	
93	Preston Carpenter DP RC	5	5	5	8	15	40	80	
94	Raymond Berry RC	40	60	80	150	300	600	▼5,000	
95	Hugh McElhenny	6	8	10	15	30	60	200	
96	Stan Jones	6	8	10	15	25	35	175	
97	Dorne Dibble	5	6	8	12	20	40	120	
98	Joe Scudero DP	5	5	5	8	12	30	120	
99	Eddie Bell	5	6	8	12	20	30	100	
100	Joe Childress DP	5	5	5	8	12	30	150	
101	Elbert Nickel	5	6	8	12	20	40	350	
102	Walt Michaels	5	6	8	12	20	30	▼100	
103	Jim Mutscheller DP	5	5	5	8	12	25	250	
104	Earl Morrall RC	8	10	12	25	40	120	500	
105	Larry Strickland	5	6	8	12	20	30	135	
106	Jack Christiansen	5	6	8	12	20	30	100	
107	Fred Cone DP	5	5	5	8	12	25	60	
108	Bud McFadin RC	5	6	8	12	20	30	250	
109	Charley Conerly	6	8	10	15	20	50	150	600
110	Tom Runnels DP	5	5	5	8	12	20	60	
111	Ken Keller DP	5	5	5	8	12	20	60	
112	James Root	5	6	8	12	20	40	150	
113	Ted Marchibroda DP	5	5	6	10	15	30	135	
114	Don Paul DB	5	5	6	10	15	35	125	
115	George Shaw	5	6	8	12	20	40	200	
116	Dick Moegle	5	6	8	12	20	50	100	
117	Don Bingham	5	6	8	12	20	60	175	
118	Leon Hart	5	6	8	12	20	125	250	
119	Bart Starr RC	250	400	500	800	1,200	2,000	10,000	
120	Paul Miller DP	5	5	5	8	12	20	80	
121	Alex Webster	5	6	8	12	20	30	200	
122	Ray Wietecha DP	5	5	5	8	12	20	120	
123	Johnny Carson	5	6	8	12	20	40	135	
124	Tom. McDonald DP RC	8	10	12	25	40	100	400	
125	Jerry Tubbs RC	5	6	8	12	20	30	80	
126	Jack Scarbath	5	6	8	12	30	40	80	
127	Ed Modzelewski DP	5	5	5	8	20	100	400	

#	Name	GD 2	VG 3	VgEx 4	EX 5	ExMt 6	NM 7	NmMt 8	MT 9
128	Lenny Moore	8	10	12	18	35	80	175	
129	Joe Perry DP	5	6	8	12	25	35	100	
130	Bill Wightkin	5	6	8	12	20	30	80	
131	Jim Doran	5	6	8	12	20	30	80	
132	Howard Ferguson	5	6	8	12	20	30	300	
133	Tom Wilson	5	6	8	12	20	30	135	
134	Dick James	5	6	8	12	20	40	150	
135	Jimmy Harris	5	6	8	12	20	30	100	
136	Chuck Ulrich	6	8	10	20	40	60	200	
137	Lynn Chandnois	5	6	8	12	20	30	80	
138	Johnny Unitas DP RC	200	250	400	500	1,000	▼2,000	▼8,000	15,000
139	Jim Ridlon DP	5	5	5	8	12	20	60	
140	Zeke Bratkowski DP	5	5	5	10	30	135	1,000	
141	Ray Krouse	5	6	8	12	20	30	150	
142	John Martinkovic	5	6	8	12	20	50	250	
143	Jim Cason DP	5	5	5	8	12	20	60	
144	Ken MacAfee E	5	6	8	12	20	50	200	
145	Sid Youngelman RC	5	6	8	12	20	40	150	
146	Paul Larson	5	6	8	12	▲30	40	150	
147	Len Ford	6	8	10	15	30	▲80	▲250	
148	Bob Toneff DP	5	5	5	8	12	20	60	
149	Ronnie Knox DP	5	5	5	8	12	20	60	
150	Jim David RC	5	6	8	12	20	40	150	
151	Paul Hornung RC	80	120	150	250	400	▼1,000	6,000	
152	Tank Younger	5	6	8	12	20	40	250	
153	Bill Svoboda DP	5	5	5	8	12	20	200	
154	Fred Morrison	6	8	10	15	80	150	1,500	
CL1	Checklist Card SP/(Bazooka back)	175	250	300	400	600	1,200		
CL2	Checklist Blony SP	175	250	300	400	800			

—Alan Ameche #12 PSA 9 (Mint) sold for $681 (Mile High; 11/10)
—Raymond Berry #94 PSA 8.5 (NmMt+) sold for $3,862 (Mile High; 6/10)
—Raymond Berry #94 PSA 8.5 (NmMt+) sold for $9,009 (eBay; 8/16)
—Jack Christiansen #106 PSA 9 (Mint) sold for $528 (eBay; 6/12)
—Jack Christiansen #106 PSA 9 (Mint) sold for $1,097.50 (eBay; 11/13)
—Charlie Conerly #109 PSA 9 (Mint) sold for $1,497 (Andy Madec; 5/07)
—Howard Ferguson #132 PSA 9 (Mint) sold for $901 (eBay; 12/13)
—Paul Hornung #151 PSA 9 (Mint) sold for $6,552 (Mile High; 6/10)
—Paul Hornung #151 PSA 9 (Mint) sold for $7,300 (Goodwin; 6/13)
—Dick Lane #85 SGC 9 (Mint) sold for $1,833 (Mile High; 10/09)
—Dick Lane #85 SGC 9 (Mint) sold for $825 (Goodwin; 2/11)
—Ollie Matson #26 PSA 9 (Mint) sold for $737 (eBay; 11/14)
—Hugh McElhenny #95 PSA 9 (Mint) sold for $761.5 (eBay; 5/12)
—Walt Michaels #102 PSA 9 (Mint) sold for $715 (eBay; 1/08)
—Dave Middleton #8 PSA 10 (Gem Mt) sold for $904 (Mile High; 10/09)
—Lenny Moore #128 PSA 9 (Mt) sold for $2,949 (eBay; 9/12)
—Pete Retzlaff #2 PSA 9 (Mint) sold for $1,260 (eBay; 3/07)
—Andy Robustelli #71 PSA 9 (Mint) sold for $897 (eBay; 1/08)
—George Shaw #115 PSA 9 (Mint) sold for $810 (eBay; 4/05)
—Willard Sherman ERR #58A SGC 9 (Mint) sold for $1,684 (Mile High; 3/09)
—Bart Starr RC #119 SGC 9 (Mint) sold for $10280.41 (Mile High; 5/12)
—Johnny Unitas #138 PSA 9 (Mint) sold for $15,457 (Goodwin; 11/09)
—Johnny Unitas DP RC #138 PSA 9 (Mint) sold for $27205.78 (Mile High; 1/12)
—Johnny Unitas #138 SGC 8.5 (NmMt+) sold for $2,954 (Mile High; 3/09)
—Johnny Unitas #138 PSA 8.5 (NmMt+) sold for $7,626.71 (Mile High; Dec 2013)
—Royce Womble #86 PSA 10 (Gem Mint) sold for $954 (Ebay; 1/14)

1958 Topps

#	Name	GD 2	VG 3	VgEx 4	EX 5	ExMt 6	NM 7	NmMt 8	MT 9
1	Gene Filipski RC	5	5	6	10	18	40	125	
2	Bobby Layne	6	8	10	15	20	40	150	
3	Joe Schmidt	5	5	6	10	15	30	100	
4	Bill Barnes	5	5	5	8	12	25	80	
5	Milt Plum RC	5	6	8	10	15	30	150	
6	Billy Howton	5	5	5	8	12	30	200	
7	Howard Cassady	5	5	5	8	12	30	80	
8	Jim Dooley	5	5	5	8	12	25	125	
9	Cleveland Browns	5	5	5	8	12	25	250	
10	Lenny Moore	5	6	8	12	20	50	250	
11	Darrel Brewster	5	5	5	8	12	25	100	
12	Alan Ameche	5	6	8	10	12	30	100	
13	Jim David	5	5	5	8	12	25	80	
14	Jim Mutscheller	5	5	5	8	12	25	80	
15	Andy Robustelli	5	6	8	10	15	30	80	
16	Gino Marchetti	5	5	6	10	15	40	150	
17	Ray Renfro	5	5	5	8	12	30	200	500
18	Yale Lary	5	6	8	10	12	30	80	
19	Gary Glick	5	5	5	8	12	30	120	
20	Jon Arnett RC	5	6	8	10	12	30	60	500

	GD 2	VG 3	VgEx 4	EX 5	ExMt 6	NM 7	NmMt 8	MT 9
Bob Boyd	5	5	5	8	12	25	80	
Johnny Unitas	30	40	50	75	125	300	1,500	
Zeke Bratkowski	5	5	5	8	12	25	80	
Sid Youngelman	5	5	5	8	12	25	80	
Leo Elter	5	5	5	8	12	25	100	
Kenny Konz	5	5	5	8	12	25	80	
Washington Redskins	5	5	6	8	12	25	80	
Carl Brettschneider	5	5	5	8	12	25	80	
Chicago Bears	5	5	6	8	12	30	120	
Alex Webster	5	5	5	8	12	25	80	
Al Carmichael	5	5	5	8	12	25	80	
Bobby Dillon	5	5	5	8	12	30	100	
Steve Meilinger	5	5	5	8	12	25	80	
Sam Baker	5	5	5	8	12	25	60	
Chuck Bednarik	5	6	8	12	18	30	100	
Bert Vic Zucco	5	5	5	8	12	25	80	
George Tarasovic	5	5	5	8	12	25	80	
Bill Wade	5	6	8	10	12	30	80	
Dick Stanfel	5	5	5	8	12	40	200	
Jerry Norton	5	5	5	8	12	25	80	
San Francisco 49ers	5	5	6	8	12	25	60	
Emlen Tunnell	5	5	6	10	15	30	80	
Jim Doran	5	5	5	8	12	25	80	
Ted Marchibroda	5	6	8	10	12	30	200	
Chet Hanulak	5	5	5	8	12	25	80	
Dale Dodrill	5	5	5	8	12	25	80	
Johnny Carson	5	5	5	8	12	25	80	
Dick Deschaine	5	5	5	8	12	25	80	
Billy Wells	5	5	5	8	12	25	80	
Larry Morris	5	5	5	8	12	25	80	
Jack McClairen	5	5	5	8	12	25	80	
Lou Groza	5	6	8	12	18	30	80	
Rick Casares	5	5	5	8	12	25	100	
Don Chandler	5	5	5	8	12	30	120	
Duane Putnam	5	5	5	8	12	25	80	
Gary Knafelc	5	5	5	8	12	25	80	
Earl Morrall	5	5	6	10	15	30	80	
Ron Kramer RC	5	5	5	8	12	25	400	
Mike McCormack	5	6	8	10	12	30	80	
Gern Nagler	5	5	5	8	12	25	80	
New York Giants	5	5	6	8	12	25	80	
Jim Brown RC	300	400	▲600	700	1,000	2,000	10,000	20,000
Joe Marconi RC	5	5	5	8	12	25	80	
R.C. Owens RC	5	5	5	8	12	25	80	
Jimmy Carr RC	5	5	5	8	12	30	80	
Bart Starr	20	30	40	80	100	200	600	
Tom Wilson	5	5	5	8	12	30	80	
Lamar McHan	5	5	5	8	12	25	100	
Chicago Cardinals	5	5	6	8	12	30	100	
Jack Christiansen	5	6	8	10	12	30	80	
Don McIlhenny RC	5	5	5	8	12	25	80	
Ron Waller	5	5	5	8	12	35	80	
Frank Gifford	8	10	12	20	30	50	150	
Bert Rechichar	5	5	5	8	12	25	225	
John Henry Johnson	5	5	6	10	15	30	350	
Jack Butler	5	5	5	8	20	30	80	
Frank Varrichione	5	5	5	8	12	30	80	
Ray Mathews	5	5	5	8	12	30	80	
Marv Matuszak	5	5	5	8	12	25	80	
Harlon Hill	5	5	5	8	12	25	80	
Lou Creekmur	5	6	8	10	12	30	100	
Woodley Lewis	5	5	5	8	12	25	100	
Don Heinrich	5	5	5	8	12	25	80	
Charley Conerly	5	6	8	12	18	30	80	
Los Angeles Rams	5	5	6	8	12	25	80	
Y.A.Tittle	5	6	8	12	20	40	125	
Bobby Walston	5	5	5	8	12	25	80	
Earl Putman	5	5	5	8	12	30	100	
Leo Nomellini	5	6	8	12	18	30	80	
Sonny Jurgensen RC	15	20	40	50	80	150	500	2,000
Don Paul DB	5	5	5	8	12	30	80	
Paige Cothren	5	5	5	8	12	25	80	
Joe Perry	5	6	8	12	18	30	80	
Tobin Rote	5	5	5	8	12	25	80	
Billy Wilson	5	5	5	8	12	25	80	
Green Bay Packers	5	6	8	12	25	50	300	
Lavern Torgeson	5	5	5	8	12	25	80	
Milt Davis	5	5	5	8	12	25	80	
Larry Strickland	5	5	5	8	12	30	150	

		GD 2	VG 3	VgEx 4	EX 5	ExMt 6	NM 7	NmMt 8	MT 9
100	Matt Hazeltine RC	5	5	5	8	12	30	200	
101	Walt Yowarsky	5	5	5	8	12	30	125	
102	Roosevelt Brown	5	6	8	10	12	30	▲400	
103	Jim Ringo	5	6	8	10	15	30	80	400
104	Joe Krupa	5	5	5	8	12	25	80	
105	Les Richter	5	5	5	8	12	25	80	
106	Art Donovan	5	6	8	12	18	30	100	
107	John Olszewski	5	5	5	8	12	30	125	
108	Ken Keller	5	5	5	8	12	25	80	
109	Philadelphia Eagles	5	5	6	8	15	30	200	
110	Baltimore Colts	5	5	5	8	12	25	80	
111	Dick Bielski	5	5	5	8	12	25	80	
112	Eddie LeBaron	5	6	8	10	12	30	80	400
113	Gene Brito	5	5	5	8	12	25	80	
114	Willie Galimore RC	5	5	5	8	12	30	300	
115	Detroit Lions	5	5	5	8	12	25	100	
116	Pittsburgh Steelers	5	5	6	8	12	25	80	300
117	L.G. Dupre	5	5	5	8	12	25	80	
118	Babe Parilli	5	5	5	8	12	25	100	
119	Bill George	5	5	6	10	15	30	80	
120	Raymond Berry	6	8	10	15	25	50	150	
121	Jim Podoley	5	5	5	8	12	25	100	
122	Hugh McElhenny	5	6	8	12	18	30	80	
123	Ed Brown	5	5	5	8	12	30	100	
124	Dick Moegle	5	5	5	8	12	30	80	
125	Tom Scott	5	5	5	8	12	25	60	250
126	Tommy McDonald	5	5	6	10	15	30	80	
127	Ollie Matson	5	6	8	12	18	30	100	
128	Preston Carpenter	5	5	5	8	12	25	80	
129	George Blanda	5	6	8	12	20	40	250	
130	Gordy Soltau	5	5	5	8	12	30	80	
131	Dick Nolan RC	5	5	5	8	12	30	80	
132	Don Bosseler RC	5	6	8	12	20	50	350	1,200
NNO	Free Felt Initial Card	5	6	10	15	30	80		

—Chuck Bednarik #35 PSA 9 (Mint) sold for $700 (eBay; 12/07)
—George Blanda #129 PSA 9 (Mint) sold for $1,277 (Andy Madec; 5/07)
—Gene Brito #113 PSA 9 (Mint) sold for $713 (eBay; 12/12)
—Jim Brown #62 PSA 9 (Mint) sold for $29,257 (Mile High; 11/10)
—Jim Brown #62 SGC 8.5 (NmMt+) sold for $4,474 (Mile High; 3/09)
—Jim Brown #62 PSA 8.5 (NmMt+) sold for $5,377 (eBay; 4/12)
—Rick Casares #53 PSA 9 (Mint) sold for $1,230 (Greg Bussineau; Fall 2013)
—Jack Christiansen #70 PSA 9 (Mint) sold for $630 (eBay 11/14)
—Paige Cothran #28 PSA 10 (Gem Mt) sold for $908 (Mile High; 11/10)
—Bobby Dillon #32 PSA 9 (Mint) sold for $570 (eBay; 10/13)
—Lou Groza #52 PSA 9 (Mint) sold for $831 (Mastro; 2/07)
—Sonny Jurgensen #90 PSA 9 (Mint) sold for $2,180 (eBay; 12/07)
—Bobby Layne #2 PSA 9 (Mint) sold for $1,055 (Andy Madec; 5/07)
—Ted Marchibroda #44 PSA 9 (Mint) sold for $725 (eBay; 9/07)
—Earl Morrall #57 PSA 9 (Mint) sold for $410 (eBay; 6/06)
—Don Owens #47 PSA 10 (Gem Mt) sold for $1,634 (Goodwin; 6/10)
—Babe Parilli #118 PSA 9 (Mint) sold for $549 (eBay 11/14)
—Duane Putnam #55 PSA 10 (Gem Mt) sold for $1,030 (eBay; 3/07)
—Bart Starr #66 PSA 10 (Gem Mint) sold for $9036.86 (Mile High; 1/12)
—Y.A. Tittle #86 PSA 9 (Mint) sold for $1,055 (Andy Madec; 5/07)
—Johnny Unitas #22 PSA 9 (Mint) sold for $5,105 (eBay; 9/08)
—Johnny Unitas #22 PSA 9 (Mint) sold for $7852.81 (Mile High; 1/12)
—Johnny Unitas #22 PSA 9 (Mint) sold for $9239 (eBay; 8/13)
—Johnny Unitas #22 PSA 9 (Mint) sold for $ 4,737 (eBay; 11/13)
—Johnny Unitas #22 PSA 8.5 (Mint) sold for $ 1806 (eBay; 11/14)

1959 Topps

		GD 2	VG 3	VgEx 4	EX 5	ExMt 6	NM 7	NmMt 8	MT 9
1	Johnny Unitas	30	35	50	▲80	150	300	1,800	
2	Gene Brito	5	5	5	6	10	15	60	
3	Detroit Lions CL	5	5	6	8	12	20	60	175
4	Max McGee RC	5	6	8	10	20	50	80	400
5	Hugh McElhenny	5	6	8	12	20	50	200	
6	Joe Schmidt	5	5	6	8	12	40	175	
7	Kyle Rote	5	5	5	8	12	25	80	
8	Clarence Peaks	5	5	5	6	10	15	30	
9	Steelers Pennant	5	5	5	6	10	15	30	125
10	Jim Brown	30	40	80	100	125	150	500	3,000
11	Ray Mathews	5	5	5	6	10	15	30	125
12	Bobby Dillon	5	5	5	6	10	15	30	125
13	Joe Childress	5	5	5	6	10	15	40	125
14	Terry Barr RC	5	5	5	6	10	15	30	125
15	Del Shofner RC	5	5	5	6	10	15	50	125
16	Bob Pellegrini UER	5	5	5	6	10	15	▲30	125

FOOTBALL

#	Player	GD 2	VG 3	VgEx 4	EX 5	ExMt 6	NM 7	NmMt 8	MT 9
17	Baltimore Colts CL	5	5	6	8	12	20	35	
18	Preston Carpenter	5	5	5	6	10	15	30	
19	Leo Nomellini	5	5	6	8	12	20	40	150
20	Frank Gifford	8	10	12	15	25	40	80	250
21	Charlie Ane	5	5	5	6	10	15	30	125
22	Jack Butler	5	5	5	6	10	25	30	125
23	Bart Starr	15	20	25	40	60	150	300	1,500
24	Cardinals Pennant	5	5	5	6	10	20	60	125
25	Bill Barnes	5	5	5	6	10	15	30	125
26	Walt Michaels	5	5	5	6	10	15	30	125
27	Clyde Conner UER	5	5	5	6	10	15	60	125
28	Paige Cothren	5	5	5	6	10	15	30	125
29	Roosevelt Grier	5	5	6	8	12	20	50	150
30	Alan Ameche	5	5	6	8	12	25	60	200
31	Philadelphia Eagles CL	5	5	6	8	12	20	35	100
32	Dick Nolan	5	5	5	6	10	15	30	
33	R.C. Owens	5	5	5	6	10	15	30	125
34	Dale Dodrill	5	5	5	6	10	15	30	
35	Gene Gedman	5	5	5	6	10	15	30	125
36	Gene Lipscomb RC	5	5	6	8	12	20	60	400
37	Ray Renfro	5	5	5	6	10	15	30	150
38	Browns Pennant	5	5	5	6	10	20	50	125
39	Bill Forester	5	5	5	6	10	15	40	125
40	Bobby Layne	6	8	10	12	18	30	60	250
41	Pat Summerall	5	5	6	8	12	20	60	200
42	Jerry Mertens RC	5	5	5	6	10	15	30	125
43	Steve Myhra RC	5	5	5	6	10	15	30	125
44	John Henry Johnson	5	5	6	8	12	20	35	125
45	Woodley Lewis UER	5	5	5	6	10	15	30	
46	Green Bay Packers CL	5	5	6	8	12	30	60	200
47	Don Owens UER RC	5	5	5	6	10	15	30	125
48	Ed Beatty RC	5	5	5	6	10	15	30	125
49	Don Chandler	5	5	5	6	10	15	40	125
50	Ollie Matson	5	5	6	8	12	20	40	175
51	Sam Huff RC	12	15	20	25	40	▲80	150	600
52	Tom Miner RC	5	5	5	6	10	15	30	125
53	Giants Pennant	5	5	5	6	10	15	30	125
54	Kenny Konz	5	5	5	6	10	15	30	125
55	Raymond Berry	5	6	8	10	15	25	60	300
56	Howard Ferguson UER	5	5	5	6	10	15	30	125
57	Chuck Ulrich	5	5	5	6	10	15	30	125
58	Bob St.Clair	5	5	5	6	8	12	50	150
59	Don Burroughs RC	5	5	5	6	10	15	30	100
60	Lou Groza	5	5	6	8	12	25	50	125
61	San Francisco 49ers CL	5	5	6	8	12	20	35	100
62	Andy Nelson RC	5	5	5	6	10	15	30	125
63	Harold Bradley RC	5	5	5	6	10	15	40	
64	Dave Hanner	5	5	5	6	10	15	30	150
65	Charley Conerly	5	6	8	10	15	25	60	
66	Gene Cronin RC	5	5	5	6	10	15	30	100
67	Duane Putnam	5	5	5	6	10	15	30	
68	Colts Pennant	5	5	5	6	10	15	80	250
69	Ernie Stautner	5	5	6	8	12	20	50	150
70	Jon Arnett	5	5	5	6	10	15	30	100
71	Ken Panfil RC	5	5	5	6	10	15	50	125
72	Matt Hazeltine	5	5	5	6	10	15	30	125
73	Harley Sewell	5	5	5	6	10	15	30	125
74	Mike McCormack	5	5	6	8	12	20	120	
75	Jim Ringo	5	5	6	8	12	25	80	300
76	Los Angeles Rams CL	5	5	6	8	12	20	50	120
77	Bob Gain RC	5	5	5	6	10	15	60	
78	Buzz Nutter RC	5	5	5	6	10	15	40	125
79	Jerry Norton	5	5	5	6	10	15	30	125
80	Joe Perry	5	5	6	8	12	20	40	150
81	Carl Brettschneider	5	5	5	6	10	15	30	100
82	Paul Hornung	10	12	15	20	50	100	▼150	800
83	Eagles Pennant	5	5	5	6	10	15	30	125
84	Les Richter	5	5	5	6	10	15	40	
85	Howard Cassady	5	5	5	6	10	15	30	125
86	Art Donovan	5	5	6	8	12	20	50	200
87	Jim Patton	5	5	5	6	10	15	30	120
88	Pete Retzlaff	5	5	5	6	10	15	30	100
89	Jim Mutscheller	5	5	5	5	8	12	50	125
90	Zeke Bratkowski	5	5	5	5	8	12	25	
91	Washington Redskins CL	5	5	5	5	8	12	25	100
92	Art Hunter	5	5	5	5	8	12	25	100
93	Gern Nagler	5	5	5	5	8	12	25	100
94	Chuck Weber RC	5	5	5	5	8	12	30	100
95	Lew Carpenter RC	5	5	5	5	8	12	25	100
96	Stan Jones	5	5	5	6	10	15	30	150

#	Player	GD 2	VG 3	VgEx 4	EX 5	ExMt 6	NM 7	NmMt 8	MT 9
97	Ralph Guglielmi UER	5	5	5	5	8	12	25	100
98	Packers Pennant	5	5	5	5	8	12	25	100
99	Ray Wietecha	5	5	5	5	8	12	25	100
100	Lenny Moore	5	6	8	10	15	25	50	200
101	Jim Ray Smith UER RC	5	5	6	8	10	20	80	250
102	Abe Woodson RC	5	5	5	5	8	12	25	100
103	Alex Karras RC	8	10	12	15	25	50	100	250
104	Chicago Bears CL	5	5	5	5	8	12	25	80
105	John David Crow RC	5	6	8	10	15	25	50	150
106	Joe Fortunato RC	5	5	5	5	8	12	25	100
107	Babe Parilli	5	5	5	5	8	12	25	100
108	Proverb Jacobs RC	5	5	5	5	8	12	30	100
109	Gino Marchetti	5	5	6	8	12	20	50	200
110	Bill Wade	5	5	5	5	8	12	25	
111	49ers Pennant	5	5	5	5	8	12	25	80
112	Karl Rubke RC	5	5	5	5	8	12	25	100
113	Dave Middleton UER	5	5	5	5	8	12	25	80
114	Roosevelt Brown	5	5	5	6	10	15	30	125
115	John Olszewski	5	5	5	5	8	12	25	80
116	Jerry Kramer RC	6	8	10	12	30	▲100	▲250	400
117	King Hill RC	5	5	5	5	8	12	25	80
118	Chicago Cardinals CL	5	5	5	5	8	12	25	80
119	Frank Varrichione	5	5	5	5	8	12	25	80
120	Rick Casares	5	5	5	5	8	12	25	
121	George Strugar RC	5	5	5	5	8	12	25	80
122	Bill Glass RC	5	5	5	5	8	12	25	80
123	Don Bosseler	5	5	5	5	8	12	25	80
124	John Reger RC	5	5	5	5	8	12	25	
125	Jim Ninowski RC	5	5	5	5	8	12	50	100
126	Rams Pennant	5	5	5	5	8	12	25	100
127	Willard Sherman	5	5	5	5	8	12	25	100
128	Bob Schnelker	5	5	5	5	8	12	25	80
129	Ollie Spencer RC	5	5	5	5	8	12	25	100
130	Y.A.Tittle	6	8	10	12	20	30	60	200
131	Yale Lary	5	5	5	6	10	15	30	100
132	Jim Parker RC	6	8	10	12	20	40	150	600
133	New York Giants CL	5	5	5	5	8	12	25	80
134	Jim Schrader RC	5	5	5	5	8	12	25	
135	M.C. Reynolds RC	5	5	5	5	8	12	25	100
136	Mike Sandusky RC	5	5	5	5	8	12	25	80
137	Ed Brown	5	5	5	5	8	12	25	150
138	Al Barry RC	5	5	5	5	8	12	25	100
139	Lions Pennant	5	5	5	5	8	12	25	80
140	Bobby Mitchell RC	6	8	10	12	20	▲40	▲100	600
141	Larry Morris	5	5	5	5	8	12	25	100
142	Jim Phillips RC	5	5	5	5	8	12	25	100
143	Jim David	5	5	5	5	8	12	25	80
144	Joe Krupa	5	5	5	5	8	12	25	100
145	Willie Galimore	5	5	5	5	8	12	25	80
146	Pittsburgh Steelers CL	5	5	5	5	8	12	25	80
147	Andy Robustelli	5	5	6	8	12	20	40	200
148	Billy Wilson	5	5	5	5	8	12	25	100
149	Leo Sanford	5	5	5	5	8	12	25	100
150	Eddie LeBaron	5	5	5	6	10	15	30	125
151	Bill McColl	5	5	5	5	8	12	25	100
152	Buck Lansford UER	5	5	5	5	8	12	25	100
153	Bears Pennant	5	5	5	5	8	12	25	100
154	Leo Sugar RC	5	5	5	5	8	12	25	100
155	Jim Taylor UER RC	8	10	12	15	▲50	60	125	600
156	Lindon Crow	5	5	5	5	8	12	100	
157	Jack McClairen	5	5	5	5	8	12	25	100
158	Vince Costello UER RC	5	5	5	5	8	12	25	100
159	Stan Wallace RC	5	5	5	5	8	12	25	80
160	Mel Triplett RC	5	5	5	5	8	12	25	80
161	Cleveland Browns CL	5	5	5	5	8	12	25	80
162	Dan Currie RC	5	5	5	5	8	15	40	200
163	L.G. Dupre UER	5	5	5	5	8	12	25	80
164	John Morrow UER RC	5	5	5	5	8	12	25	100
165	Jim Podoley	5	5	5	5	8	12	25	80
166	Bruce Bosley RC	5	5	5	5	8	12	25	100
167	Harlon Hill	5	5	5	5	8	12	25	100
168	Redskins Pennant	5	5	5	5	8	12	25	100
169	Junior Wren RC	5	5	5	5	8	12	40	125
170	Tobin Rote	5	5	5	5	8	12	25	100
171	Art Spinney	5	5	5	5	8	12	25	100
172	Chuck Drazenovich UER	5	5	5	5	8	12	25	80
173	Bobby Joe Conrad RC	5	5	5	5	8	12	25	80
174	Jesse Richardson RC	5	5	5	5	8	12	25	100
175	Sam Baker	5	5	5	5	8	12	25	80
176	Tom Tracy RC	5	5	6	8	12	20	50	150

n Arnett #70 PSA 10 (Gem Mint) sold for $1330 (eBay; 11/14)
Beatty RC #48 PSA 10 (Gem Mint) sold for $870 (Bussineau; 4/12)
k Butler #22 PSA 10 (Gem Mint) sold for $1050 (Bussineau; 4/12)
e Childress #13 PSA 10 (Gem Mint) sold for $628 (eBay 11/14)
rley Conerly #65 PSA 9 (Mint) sold for $2,006 (eBay; 1/09)
le Dodrill #34 PSA 10 (Gem Mint) sold for $870 (Bussineau; 4/12)
rlon Hill #103 PSA 10 (Gem Mint) sold for $1,280 (eBay; 3/11)
ex Karras #103 PSA 10 (Gem) sold for $1,740 (eBay; 1/06)
an Jones #96 PSA 10 (Gem) sold for $1630 (eBay; 11/14)
bby Layne #40 PSA 10 (Gem Mint) sold for $3150 (Bussineau; 4/12)
die LeBaron #150 PSA 10 (Gem Mint) sold for $1590 (Bussineau; 4/12)
y Mathews #11 PSA 10 (Gem Mint) sold for $810 (Bussineau; 4/12)
n Owens UER RC #47 PSA 10 (Gem Mint) sold for $810 (Bussineau; 4/12)
n Panfil RC #71 PSA 10 (Gem Mint) sold for $990 (Bussineau; 4/12)
n Patton RC #87 PSA 10 (Gem Mint) sold for $740 (ebay; 11/14)
b Pellegrini UER #16 PSA 10 (Gem Mint) sold for $930 (Bussineau; 4/12)
ane Putnam #67 PSA 10 (Gem Mint) sold for $1,210 (eBay; 1/14)
y Renfro #37 PSA 10 (Gem Mint) sold for $1685 (eBay; 4/12)
l Shofner RC #15 PSA 10 (Gem Mint) sold for $1170 (Bussineau; 4/12)
rt Starr #23 PSA 10 (Gem Mint) sold for $7260 (Bussineau; 4/12)
rt Starr #23 PSA 9 (Mint) sold for $802 (eBay; 11/14)
A. Tittle #130 PSA 10 (Gem Mint) sold for $3,200 (Mastro; 4/07)
ly Wilson#148 PSA 10 (Gem Mint) sold for $1,366 (eBay; 10/12)
dskins Pennant #168 PSA 10 (Gem) sold for $2,129.50 (eBay; 2/14)

60 Fleer

	GD 2	VG 3	VgEx 4	EX 5	ExMt 6	NM 7	NmMt 8	MT 9
Harvey White RC	4	4	4	5	8	20	175	
Tom Corky Tharp	4	4	4	5	6	20	175	
Dan McGrew	4	4	4	5	6	20	200	
Bob White	4	4	4	5	6	20	200	
Dick Jamieson	4	4	4	5	6	15	150	
Sam Salerno	4	4	4	5	6	15	100	
Sid Gillman CO RC	5	6	8	12	15	30	175	
Ben Preston	4	4	4	5	6	10	25	100
George Blanch	4	4	4	5	6	10	50	
Bob Stransky	4	4	4	5	6	10	30	150
Fran Curci	4	4	4	5	6	10	30	
George Shirkey	4	4	4	5	6	10	25	100
Paul Larson	4	4	4	5	6	10	25	100
John Stolte	4	4	4	5	6	10	30	
Serafino Fazio RC	4	4	4	5	6	10	30	
Tom Dimitroff	4	4	4	5	6	10	25	
Elbert Dubenion RC	4	5	6	8	10	15	40	
Hogan Wharton	4	4	4	5	6	10	25	100
Tom O'Connell	4	4	4	5	6	10	25	80
Sammy Baugh CO	10	12	15	20	25	40	60	150
Tony Sardisco	4	4	4	5	6	10	25	100
Alan Cann	4	4	4	5	6	10	25	100
Mike Hudock	4	4	4	5	6	10	30	
Bill Atkins	4	4	4	5	6	10	25	100
Charlie Jackson	4	4	4	5	6	10	25	80
Frank Tripucka	4	4	4	5	8	12	30	▼100
Tony Teresa	4	4	4	5	6	10	25	100
Joe Amstutz	4	4	4	5	6	10	25	100
Bob Fee RC	4	4	4	5	6	10	30	
Jim Baldwin	4	4	4	5	6	10	25	100
Jim Yates	4	4	4	5	6	10	25	100
Don Flynn	4	4	4	5	6	10	25	80
Ken Adamson	4	4	4	5	6	10	25	100
Ron Drzewiecki	4	4	4	5	6	10	25	80
J.W. Slack	4	4	4	5	6	10	25	80
Bob Yates	4	4	4	5	6	10	30	80
Gary Cobb	4	4	4	5	6	10	30	80
Jacky Lee RC	4	4	4	5	6	10	25	80
Jack Spikes RC	4	4	4	5	6	10	30	
Jim Padgett	4	4	4	5	6	10	30	100
Jack Larscheid RC	4	4	4	5	6	10	25	100
Bob Reifsnyder RC	4	4	4	5	6	10	30	
Fran Rogel	4	4	4	5	6	10	25	100
Ray Moss	4	4	4	5	6	10	25	80
Tony Banfield RC	4	4	4	5	6	10	25	100
George Herring	4	4	4	5	6	10	30	100
Willie Smith RC	4	4	4	5	6	10	25	100
Buddy Allen	4	4	4	5	6	10	35	100
Bill Brown LB	4	4	4	5	6	10	25	80
Ken Ford RC	4	4	4	5	6	10	25	100
Billy Kinard	4	4	4	5	6	10	25	100

		GD 2	VG 3	VgEx 4	EX 5	ExMt 6	NM 7	NmMt 8	MT 9
52	Buddy Mayfield	4	4	4	5	6	10	25	100
53	Bill Krisher	4	4	4	5	6	10	25	100
54	Frank Bernardi	4	4	4	5	6	10	30	
55	Lou Saban CO RC	4	4	4	5	6	10	25	100
56	Gene Cockrell	4	4	4	5	6	10	25	80
57	Sam Sanders	4	4	4	5	6	10	25	100
58	George Blanda	12	15	18	20	30	40	80	250
59	Sherrill Headrick RC	4	4	4	5	6	10	25	100
60	Carl Larpenter	4	4	4	5	6	10	30	
61	Gene Prebola	4	4	4	5	6	10	25	100
62	Dick Chorovich	4	4	4	5	6	10	25	100
63	Bob McNamara	4	4	4	5	6	10	30	
64	Tom Saidock	4	4	4	5	6	10	30	
65	Willie Evans	4	4	4	5	6	10	25	100
66	Billy Cannon RC	5	6	8	10	20	30	125	250
67	Sam McCord	4	4	4	5	6	10	25	100
68	Mike Simmons	4	4	4	5	6	10	25	80
69	Jim Swink RC	4	4	4	5	6	10	25	80
70	Don Hitt	4	4	4	5	6	10	25	80
71	Gerhard Schwedes	4	4	4	5	6	10	30	
72	Thurlow Cooper	4	4	4	5	6	10	30	
73	Abner Haynes RC	5	6	8	10	12	30	40	
74	Billy Shoemake	4	4	4	5	6	10	30	
75	Marv Lasater	4	4	6	10	15	40	100	
76	Paul Lowe RC	5	6	8	10	12	20	200	
77	Bruce Hartman	4	4	4	5	6	10	60	135
78	Blanche Martin	4	4	6	10	15	40	100	
79	Gene Grabosky	4	4	4	5	6	10	30	
80	Lou Rymkus CO	4	4	4	5	6	10	30	80
81	Chris Burford RC	4	4	4	5	8	25	125	
82	Don Allen	4	4	4	5	6	10	150	
83	Bob Nelson C	4	4	4	5	6	10	125	
84	Jim Woodard	4	4	4	5	6	20		
85	Tom Rychlec	4	4	4	5	6	10	25	100
86	Bob Cox	4	4	4	5	6	10	20	80
87	Jerry Cornelison	4	4	4	5	6	10	25	100
88	Jack Work	4	4	4	5	6	10	25	100
89	Sam DeLuca	4	4	4	5	6	10	25	100
90	Rommie Loudd	4	4	4	5	6	10	30	
91	Teddy Edmondson	4	4	4	5	6	10	25	80
92	Buster Ramsey CO	4	4	4	5	6	10	25	80
93	Doug Asad	4	4	4	5	6	10	25	80
94	Jimmy Harris	4	4	4	5	6	10	25	
95	Larry Cundiff	4	4	4	5	6	10	25	80
96	Richie Lucas RC	4	4	4	5	8	12	30	150
97	Don Norwood	4	4	4	5	6	10	25	80
98	Larry Grantham RC	4	4	4	5	8	12	30	100
99	Bill Mathis RC	4	4	4	5	8	12	30	150
100	Mel Branch RC	4	4	4	5	6	10	25	100
101	Marvin Terrell	4	4	4	5	6	10	25	100
102	Charlie Flowers	4	4	4	5	6	10	25	80
103	John McMullan	4	4	4	5	6	10	25	80
104	Charlie Kaaihue	4	4	4	5	6	10	25	100
105	Joe Schaffer	4	4	4	5	6	10	30	
106	Al Day	4	4	4	5	6	10	30	
107	Johnny Carson	4	4	4	5	6	10	30	
108	Alan Goldstein	4	4	4	5	6	10	25	100
109	Doug Cline	4	4	4	5	6	10	30	
110	Al Carmichael	4	4	4	5	6	10	25	100
111	Bob Dee	4	4	4	5	6	10	30	
112	John Bredice	4	4	4	5	6	10	30	
113	Don Floyd	4	4	4	5	6	10	25	100
114	Ronnie Cain	4	4	4	5	6	10	30	
115	Stan Flowers	4	4	4	5	6	10	25	100
116	Hank Stram CO RC	10	12	15	20	30	40	100	350
117	Bob Dougherty	4	4	4	5	6	10	25	100
118	Ron Mix RC	10	12	15	15	25	60	150	800
119	Roger Ellis	4	4	4	5	6	10	25	100
120	Elvin Caldwell	4	4	4	5	6	10	30	100
121	Bill Kimber	4	4	4	5	6	10	30	
122	Jim Matheny	4	4	4	5	6	10	25	80
123	Curley Johnson RC	4	4	4	5	6	10	40	
124	Jack Kemp RC	30	40	50	60	80	100	175	600
125	Ed Denk	4	4	4	5	6	10	25	80
126	Jerry McFarland	4	4	4	5	6	10	30	
127	Dan Lanphear	4	4	4	5	6	15	80	
128	Paul Maguire RC	5	6	8	10	12	20	40	▼100
129	Ray Collins	4	4	4	5	6	10	20	100
130	Ron Burton RC	4	4	4	5	8	12	30	

		GD 2	VG 3	VgEx 4	EX 5	ExMt 6	NM 7	NmMt 8	MT 9
131	Eddie Erdelatz CO	4	4	4	5	6	10	30	100
132	Ron Beagle RC	4	4	4	5	6	10	40	250

—Jack Kemp RC #124 PSA 10 (Gem Mint) sold for $2850 (eBay: 4/12)
—Paul Maguire #128 PSA 10 (Gem) sold for $2,505 (eBay; 4/08)

1960 Topps

		GD 2	VG 3	VgEx 4	EX 5	ExMt 6	NM 7	NmMt 8	MT 9
1	Johnny Unitas	20	▲30	▲40	▲50	100	300	1,200	15,000
2	Alan Ameche	4	4	4	6	10	15	300	
3	Lenny Moore	5	5	6	8	12	25	60	
4	Raymond Berry	5	5	6	8	12	25	▼50	250
5	Jim Parker	4	4	5	6	10	20	40	▼125
6	George Preas	4	4	4	4	6	12	60	
7	Art Spinney	4	4	4	4	6	12	50	
8	Bill Pellington RC	4	4	4	4	6	12	40	
9	Johnny Sample RC	4	4	4	4	6	12	40	
10	Gene Lipscomb	4	4	4	4	6	12	25	120
11	Baltimore Colts	4	4	4	4	6	12	80	200
12	Ed Brown	4	4	4	4	6	12	30	120
13	Rick Casares	4	4	4	4	6	12	40	
14	Willie Galimore	4	4	4	4	6	12	135	
15	Jim Dooley	4	4	4	4	6	12	40	
16	Harlon Hill	4	4	4	4	6	12	30	120
17	Stan Jones	4	4	4	4	6	12	25	150
18	Bill George	4	4	4	4	6	12	30	150
19	Erich Barnes RC	4	4	4	4	6	12	40	120
20	Doug Atkins	4	4	5	6	10	20	60	
21	Chicago Bears	4	4	4	4	6	12	30	120
22	Milt Plum	4	4	4	4	6	12	25	120
23	Jim Brown	20	25	40	▲80	100	125	400	800
24	Sam Baker	4	4	4	4	6	12	60	
25	Bobby Mitchell	5	5	6	8	12	25	50	250
26	Ray Renfro	4	4	4	4	6	12	20	120
27	Billy Howton	4	4	4	4	6	12	40	120
28	Jim Ray Smith	4	4	4	4	6	12	30	120
29	Jim Shofner RC	4	4	4	4	6	12	50	
30	Bob Gain	4	4	4	4	6	12	40	
31	Cleveland Browns	4	4	6	10	15	40	100	
32	Don Heinrich	4	4	4	4	6	12	40	120
33	Ed Modzelewski	4	4	4	4	6	12	40	
34	Fred Cone	4	4	4	4	6	20	40	120
35	L.G. Dupre	4	4	4	4	6	12	25	120
36	Dick Bielski	4	4	4	4	6	12	30	120
37	Charlie Ane	4	4	4	4	6	12	60	
38	Jerry Tubbs	4	4	4	5	8	15	50	200
39	Doyle Nix	4	4	4	4	6	12	20	200
40	Ray Krouse	4	4	4	4	6	12	40	
41	Earl Morrall	4	4	4	5	10	15	60	
42	Howard Cassady	4	4	4	4	6	12	40	
43	Dave Middleton	4	4	4	4	6	12	25	120
44	Jim Gibbons RC	4	4	4	4	6	12	20	175
45	Darris McCord	4	4	4	4	6	12	50	
46	Joe Schmidt	4	4	5	6	10	20	40	
47	Terry Barr	4	4	4	4	6	12	60	
48	Yale Lary	4	4	4	4	6	12	40	
49	Gil Mains	4	4	4	4	6	12	25	120
50	Detroit Lions	4	4	4	4	6	12	40	
51	Bart Starr	10	12	15	▲30	▲50	80	200	800
52	Jim Taylor	4	4	5	6	10	20	50	200
53	Lew Carpenter	4	4	4	4	6	12	40	
54	Paul Hornung	8	10	12	20	30	50	100	400
55	Max McGee	4	4	5	6	10	25	125	
56	Forrest Gregg RC	8	10	12	20	30	50	200	1,000
57	Jim Ringo	4	4	5	6	10	20	40	▼150
58	Bill Forester	4	4	4	4	6	12	40	200
59	Dave Hanner	4	4	4	4	6	12	60	
60	Green Bay Packers	4	4	5	6	10	20	80	
61	Bill Wade	4	4	4	4	6	12	20	120
62	Frank Ryan RC	4	4	4	5	8	15	30	250
63	Ollie Matson	5	5	6	8	12	25	60	200
64	Jon Arnett	4	4	4	4	6	12	20	120
65	Del Shofner	4	4	4	4	6	12	20	120
66	Jim Phillips	4	4	4	4	6	12	20	120
67	Art Hunter	4	4	4	4	6	12	40	
68	Les Richter	4	4	4	4	6	12	50	
69	Lou Michaels RC	4	4	4	4	6	12	80	
70	John Baker	4	4	4	4	6	12	40	200
71	Los Angeles Rams	4	4	4	4	6	12	40	
72	Charley Conerly	4	4	5	6	10	20	40	150
73	Mel Triplett	4	4	4	4	6	12	40	
74	Frank Gifford	6	8	10	15	25	▲60	100	250
75	Alex Webster	4	4	4	4	6	12	40	150
76	Bob Schnelker	4	4	4	4	6	12	20	120
77	Pat Summerall	5	5	6	8	12	25	60	
78	Roosevelt Brown	4	4	4	4	6	12	30	150
79	Jim Patton	4	4	4	4	6	12	20	120
80	Sam Huff	5	5	6	8	12	25	50	200
81	Andy Robustelli	4	4	5	6	10	20	40	150
82	New York Giants	4	4	4	4	6	12	40	
83	Clarence Peaks	4	4	4	4	6	12	40	
84	Bill Barnes	4	4	4	4	6	12	30	120
85	Pete Retzlaff	4	4	4	4	6	12	20	120
86	Bobby Walston	4	4	4	4	6	12	40	
87	Chuck Bednarik	4	4	5	6	10	20	50	200
88	Bob Pellegrini	4	4	4	4	6	12	20	120
89	Tom Brookshier RC	4	4	4	4	6	15	200	
90	Marion Campbell	4	4	4	4	6	12	30	120
91	Jesse Richardson	4	4	4	4	6	12	20	120
92	Philadelphia Eagles	4	4	4	4	6	12	30	120
93	Bobby Layne	6	8	10	12	18	30	60	250
94	John Henry Johnson	4	4	6	10	15	40	120	
95	Tom Tracy	4	4	4	4	6	12	40	
96	Preston Carpenter	4	4	4	4	6	12	20	120
97	Frank Varrichione	4	4	4	4	6	12	40	
98	John Nisby	4	4	4	4	6	12	40	
99	Dean Derby	4	4	4	4	6	12	40	
100	George Tarasovic	4	4	4	4	6	12	25	120
101	Ernie Stautner	4	4	5	6	10	20	60	200
102	Pittsburgh Steelers	4	4	4	4	6	12	40	
103	King Hill	4	4	4	4	6	12	20	120
104	Mal Hammack	4	4	4	4	6	12	80	175
105	John David Crow	4	4	4	6	10	30	120	
106	Bobby Joe Conrad	4	4	4	4	6	12	20	120
107	Woodley Lewis	4	4	4	4	6	12	20	120
108	Don Gillis	4	4	4	4	6	12	20	120
109	Carl Brettschneider	4	4	4	4	6	12	20	120
110	Leo Sugar	4	4	4	4	6	12	60	
111	Frank Fuller	4	4	4	4	6	12	60	300
112	St. Louis Cardinals	4	4	4	4	6	12	20	120
113	Y.A.Tittle	6	8	10	12	20	30	75	300
114	Joe Perry	4	4	4	6	10	20	60	500
115	J.D.Smith RC	4	4	4	4	6	12	40	
116	Hugh McElhenny	4	4	5	6	10	20	40	200
117	Billy Wilson	4	4	4	4	6	12	25	150
118	Bob St.Clair	4	4	4	4	6	12	30	150
119	Matt Hazeltine	4	4	4	4	6	12	20	120
120	Abe Woodson	4	4	4	4	6	12	20	120
121	Leo Nomellini	4	4	5	6	10	20	40	
122	San Francisco 49ers	4	4	4	4	6	12	50	150
123	Ralph Guglielmi	4	4	4	4	6	12	40	
124	Don Bosseler	4	4	4	4	6	12	20	120
125	John Olszewski	4	4	4	4	6	12	20	120
126	Bill Anderson	4	4	4	4	6	12	20	120
127	Joe Walton RC	4	4	4	4	6	12	25	120
128	Jim Schrader	4	4	4	4	6	12	20	120
129	Ralph Felton	4	4	4	4	6	12	20	120
130	Gary Glick	4	4	4	4	6	20	200	
131	Bob Toneff	4	4	4	4	6	12	40	
132	Redskins Team	5	5	6	8	12	30	50	200

—Cleveland Browns #31 PSA 9 (Mint) sold for $903.5 (eBay: 4/12)
—Forrest Gregg #56 PSA 9 (Mint) sold for $840 (eBay; 3/07)
—John Henry Johnson #94 PSA 9 (Mint) sold for $405.83 (eBay; 4/12)
—Leo Nomellini #121 PSA 10 (Gem Mt) sold for $1,327 (Goodwin; 12/10)
—Bart Starr #51 PSA 10 (Gem Mt) sold for $2400 (Mastro; 12/08)

1961 Fleer

		GD 2	VG 3	VgEx 4	EX 5	ExMt 6	NM 7	NmMt 8	MT 9
1	Ed Brown	4	5	6	8	12	20	40	
2	Rick Casares	4	5	5	5	6	10	60	
3	Willie Galimore	4	5	5	5	6	10	40	
4	Jim Dooley	4	5	5	5	6	10	25	100
5	Harlon Hill	4	5	5	5	6	10	30	
6	Stan Jones	4	5	5	5	8	12	80	
7	J.C. Caroline	4	5	5	5	6	10	30	
8	Joe Fortunato	4	5	5	5	6	10	30	250
9	Doug Atkins	4	5	5	6	8	▲12	25	150

	GD 2	VG 3	VgEx 4	EX 5	ExMt 6	NM 7	NmMt 8	MT 9
Milt Plum	4	5	5	5	6	10	20	175
Jim Brown	25	40	50	80	100	150	300	1,500
Bobby Mitchell	4	5	6	8	10	15	50	300
Ray Renfro	4	5	5	5	6	10	20	120
Gern Nagler	4	5	5	5	6	10	30	
Jim Shofner	4	5	5	5	6	10	20	100
Vince Costello	4	5	5	5	6	10	20	125
Galen Fiss RC	4	5	5	5	6	10	20	100
Walt Michaels	4	5	5	5	6	10	30	
Bob Gain	4	5	5	5	6	10	30	
Mal Hammack	4	5	5	5	6	10	20	100
Frank Mestnik RC	4	5	5	5	6	10	20	100
Bobby Joe Conrad	4	5	5	5	6	10	30	
John David Crow	4	5	5	5	6	10	20	100
Sonny Randle RC	4	5	5	5	6	10	25	100
Don Gillis	4	5	5	5	6	10	30	
Jerry Norton	4	5	5	5	6	10	20	80
Bill Stacy RC	4	5	5	5	6	10	50	200
Leo Sugar	4	5	5	5	6	10	20	100
Frank Fuller	4	5	5	5	6	10	20	100
Johnny Unitas	12	20	25	50	60	80	300	600
Alan Ameche	4	5	5	6	8	12	30	150
Lenny Moore	4	6	8	10	12	20	40	▲300
Raymond Berry	4	6	8	10	12	20	40	200
Jim Mutscheller	4	5	5	5	6	10	20	100
Jim Parker	4	5	5	6	8	12	25	150
Bill Pellington	4	5	5	5	6	10	20	100
Gino Marchetti	4	5	6	8	10	15	25	150
Gene Lipscomb	4	5	6	6	8	12	35	150
Art Donovan	4	6	8	10	12	25	▲60	250
Eddie LeBaron	4	5	5	5	6	10	20	120
Don Meredith RC	25	▲60	▲80	▲100	▲125	150	350	800
Don McIlhenny	4	5	5	5	6	10	20	100
L.G. Dupre	4	5	5	5	6	10	40	100
Fred Dugan RC	4	5	5	5	6	10	20	100
Billy Howton	4	5	5	5	6	10	30	100
Duane Putnam	4	5	5	5	6	10	20	100
Gene Cronin	4	5	5	5	6	15	20	100
Jerry Tubbs	4	5	5	5	6	10	40	100
Clarence Peaks	4	5	5	5	6	10	20	100
Ted Dean RC	4	5	5	5	6	10	20	100
Tommy McDonald	4	5	5	6	8	12	30	
Bill Barnes	4	5	5	5	6	10	40	
Pete Retzlaff	4	5	5	5	6	10	20	100
Bobby Walston	4	5	5	5	6	10	40	
Chuck Bednarik	4	5	6	8	10	15	30	200
Maxie Baughan RC	4	5	5	5	20	60	80	175
Bob Pellegrini	4	5	5	5	6	10	20	100
Jesse Richardson	4	5	5	5	6	10	30	
John Brodie RC	8	12	15	20	30	50	150	500
J.D. Smith RB	4	5	5	5	6	10	20	100
Ray Norton RC	4	5	5	5	6	10	40	400
Monty Stickles RC	4	5	5	5	6	10	30	
Bob St.Clair	4	5	5	6	8	12	30	150
Dave Baker RC	4	5	5	5	6	10	30	
Abe Woodson	4	5	5	5	6	10	20	100
Matt Hazeltine	4	5	5	5	6	10	30	120
Leo Nomellini	4	5	6	8	10	15	30	
Charley Conerly	4	5	6	8	10	18	30	300
Kyle Rote	4	5	5	6	8	12	30	
Jack Stroud RC	4	5	5	5	6	10	20	100
Roosevelt Brown	4	5	5	6	8	12	25	150
Jim Patton	4	5	5	5	6	10	80	
Erich Barnes	4	5	5	5	6	10	20	100
Sam Huff	4	6	8	10	12	20	60	250
Andy Robustelli	4	5	6	8	10	15	25	120
Dick Modzelewski RC	4	5	5	5	6	10	50	120
Roosevelt Grier	4	5	5	6	8	15	40	
Earl Morrall	4	5	5	6	8	12	25	150
Jim Ninowski	4	5	5	5	6	10	25	100
Nick Pietrosante RC	4	5	5	5	6	10	20	100
Howard Cassady	4	5	5	5	6	10	25	100
Jim Gibbons	4	5	5	5	6	10	20	100
Gail Cogdill RC	4	5	5	5	6	10	20	100
Dick Lane	4	5	5	6	8	12	35	
Yale Lary	4	5	5	6	8	12	35	
Joe Schmidt	4	5	5	6	8	12	25	150
Darris McCord	4	5	5	5	6	10	40	
Bart Starr	12	20	25	35	50	75	150	600

	GD 2	VG 3	VgEx 4	EX 5	ExMt 6	NM 7	NmMt 8	MT 9
89	Jim Taylor	6	10	12	18	30	50	125	350
90	Paul Hornung	8	12	15	25	35	60	▼125	500
91	Tom Moore RC	4	5	5	5	6	8	12	30	150
92	Boyd Dowler RC	4	5	6	8	10	15	60	250
93	Max McGee	4	5	5	6	8	12	40	
94	Forrest Gregg	4	5	5	6	8	15	40	250
95	Jerry Kramer	4	5	6	8	10	15	40	
96	Jim Ringo	4	5	5	6	8	12	40	
97	Bill Forester	4	5	5	5	6	10	40	100
98	Frank Ryan	4	5	5	5	6	10	40	
99	Ollie Matson	4	5	6	8	10	15	30	175
100	Jon Arnett	4	5	5	5	6	10	20	100
101	Dick Bass RC	4	5	5	5	6	10	20	100
102	Jim Phillips	4	5	5	5	6	10	20	100
103	Del Shofner	4	5	5	5	6	10	20	100
104	Art Hunter	4	5	5	5	6	10	30	
105	Lindon Crow	4	5	5	5	6	10	20	100
106	Les Richter	4	5	5	5	6	10	20	100
107	Lou Michaels	4	5	5	5	6	10	20	100
108	Ralph Guglielmi	4	5	5	5	6	10	20	100
109	Don Bosseler	4	5	5	5	6	10	30	
110	John Olszewski	4	5	5	5	6	10	20	100
111	Bill Anderson	4	5	5	5	6	10	20	100
112	Joe Walton	4	5	5	5	6	10	20	100
113	Jim Schrader	4	5	5	5	6	10	20	100
114	Gary Glick	4	5	5	5	6	10	30	
115	Ralph Felton	4	5	5	5	6	10	20	100
116	Bob Toneff	4	5	5	5	6	10	20	100
117	Bobby Layne	5	8	10	15	25	40	80	200
118	John Henry Johnson	4	5	5	6	8	12	30	
119	Tom Tracy	4	5	5	5	6	10	20	▼60
120	Jimmy Orr RC	4	5	5	6	8	20	40	150
121	John Nisby	4	5	5	5	6	10	20	100
122	Dean Derby	4	5	5	5	6	10	20	100
123	John Reger	4	5	5	5	6	10	20	100
124	George Tarasovic	4	5	5	5	6	10	20	100
125	Ernie Stautner	4	5	6	8	10	15	30	
126	George Shaw	4	5	5	5	6	15	60	250
127	Hugh McElhenny	4	5	6	8	10	15	30	175
128	Dick Haley RC	4	5	5	5	6	10	30	120
129	Dave Middleton	4	5	5	5	6	10	30	
130	Perry Richards RC	4	5	5	5	6	10	20	100
131	Gene Johnson DB RC	4	5	5	5	6	10	20	
132	Don Joyce RC	4	5	5	5	6	10	25	175
133	Johnny Green RC	4	5	5	5	6	10	25	80
134	Wray Carlton RC	4	5	5	5	6	10	20	80
135	Richie Lucas	4	5	5	5	6	10	20	80
136	Elbert Dubenion	4	5	5	5	6	10	20	80
137	Tom Rychlec	4	5	5	5	6	10	20	60
138	Mack Yoho RC	4	5	5	5	6	10	20	60
139	Phil Blazer RC	4	5	5	5	6	10	25	80
140	Dan McGrew	4	5	5	5	6	10	20	60
141	Bill Atkins	4	5	5	5	6	10	20	50
142	Archie Matsos RC	4	5	5	5	6	10	20	60
143	Gene Grabosky	4	5	5	5	6	10	20	50
144	Frank Tripucka	4	5	5	6	8	12	25	80
145	Al Carmichael	4	5	5	5	6	10	20	60
146	Bob McNamara	4	5	5	5	6	10	20	60
147	Lionel Taylor RC	4	5	5	6	8	10	20	30	120
148	Eldon Danehauer RC	4	5	5	5	6	10	20	60
149	Willie Smith	4	5	5	5	6	10	20	60
150	Carl Larpenter	4	5	5	5	6	10	20	60
151	Ken Adamson	4	5	5	5	6	10	20	60
152	Goose Gonsoulin UER RC	4	5	5	6	8	12	25	60
153	Joe Young RC	4	5	5	5	6	10	20	60
154	Gordy Holz RC	4	5	5	5	6	10	20	50
155	Jack Kemp	12	20	25	30	40	60	100	200
156	Charlie Flowers	4	5	5	5	6	10	20	60
157	Paul Lowe	4	5	5	6	8	12	25	80
158	Don Norton RC	4	5	5	5	6	10	20	80
159	Howard Clark RC	4	5	5	5	6	10	20	60
160	Paul Maguire	4	5	5	6	8	10	15	30	100
161	Ernie Wright RC	4	5	5	5	6	10	60	
162	Ron Mix	4	5	6	8	10	15	40	100
163	Fred Cole RC	4	5	5	5	6	10	20	60
164	Jim Sears RC	4	5	5	5	6	10	20	60
165	Volney Peters	4	5	5	5	6	10	20	60
166	George Blanda	6	10	12	18	30	50	▼60	100
167	Jacky Lee	4	5	5	5	6	10	20	60

#	Name	GD 2	VG 3	VgEx 4	EX 5	ExMt 6	NM 7	NmMt 8	MT 9
168	Bob White	4	5	5	5	6	10	20	60
169	Doug Cline	4	5	5	5	6	10	20	60
170	Dave Smith RB RC	4	5	5	5	6	10	20	40
171	Billy Cannon	4	5	6	8	10	15	40	80
172	Bill Groman RC	4	5	5	5	6	10	20	▼60
173	Al Jamison RC	4	5	5	5	6	10	20	40
174	Jim Norton RC	4	5	5	5	6	10	20	40
175	Dennit Morris RC	4	5	5	5	6	10	20	60
176	Don Floyd	4	5	5	5	6	15	20	60
177	Butch Songin	4	5	5	5	6	10	20	60
178	Billy Lott RC	4	5	5	5	6	10	20	80
179	Ron Burton	4	5	5	6	8	12	25	80
180	Jim Colclough RC	4	5	5	5	6	10	25	
181	Charley Leo RC	4	5	5	5	6	10	20	60
182	Walt Cudzik RC	4	5	5	5	6	10	20	60
183	Fred Bruney	4	5	5	5	6	10	20	60
184	Ross O'Hanley RC	4	5	5	5	6	10	20	60
185	Tony Sardisco	4	5	5	5	6	10	20	60
186	Harry Jacobs RC	4	5	5	5	6	10	20	80
187	Bob Dee	4	5	5	5	6	10	20	60
188	Tom Flores RC	5	8	10	15	18	30	60	▲200
189	Jack Larscheid	4	5	5	5	6	10	20	60
190	Dick Christy RC	4	5	5	5	6	10	20	40
191	Alan Miller RC	4	5	5	5	6	10	20	60
192	James Smith	4	5	5	5	6	10	20	60
193	Gerald Burch RC	4	5	5	5	6	10	20	60
194	Gene Prebola	4	5	5	5	6	10	20	60
195	Alan Goldstein	4	5	5	5	6	10	20	60
196	Don Manoukian RC	4	5	5	5	6	10	20	80
197	Jim Otto RC	10	15	20	30	50	75	120	300
198	Wayne Crow	4	5	5	5	6	10	20	80
199	Cotton Davidson RC	4	5	5	5	6	10	20	80
200	Randy Duncan RC	4	5	5	5	6	10	25	
201	Jack Spikes	4	5	5	5	6	10	20	80
202	Johnny Robinson RC	4	6	8	10	12	20	50	150
203	Abner Haynes	4	5	6	8	10	15	30	100
204	Chris Burford	4	5	5	5	6	10	20	80
205	Bill Krisher	4	5	5	5	6	10	20	60
206	Marvin Terrell	4	5	5	5	6	10	20	60
207	Jimmy Harris	4	5	5	5	6	10	20	80
208	Mel Branch	4	5	5	5	6	10	20	80
209	Paul Miller	4	5	5	5	6	10	25	
210	Al Dorow	4	5	5	5	6	10	25	
211	Dick Jamieson	4	5	5	5	6	10	25	
212	Pete Hart RC	4	5	5	5	6	10	20	60
213	Bill Shockley RC	4	5	5	5	6	10	20	60
214	Dewey Bohling RC	4	5	5	5	6	10	20	60
215	Don Maynard RC	12	20	25	35	50	75	125	350
216	Bob Mischak RC	4	5	5	5	6	10	20	80
217	Mike Hudock	4	5	5	5	6	10	20	80
218	Bob Reifsnyder	4	5	5	5	6	10	25	
219	Tom Saidock	4	5	5	5	6	10	25	
220	Sid Youngelman	4	5	6	8	10	20	40	800

—Billy Cannon #171 PSA 10 (Gem Mt) sold for $653 (Mile High; 1/07)
—Jerry Kramer #95 PSA 9 (MT) sold for $899 (ebay; 11/07)
—Dick Lane #84 PSA 10 (Gem Mt) sold for $643 (eBay; 5/11)
—Paul Maguire #160 PSA 10 (Gem Mt) sold for $715 (eBay; 3/07)
—Jim Otto #197 PSA 10 (Gem Mt) sold for $2,843 (eBay; 2/08)
—Jim Otto #197 PSA 10 (Gem Mt) sold for $2,500 (eBay; 4/11)
—Jim Otto #197 PSA 10 (Gem Mt) sold for $2,251 (eBay; 11/09)
—Jim Otto #197 PSA 10 (Gem Mint) sold for $1,080 (Bussineau; 7/12)
—Jim Otto #197 PSA 10 (Gem Mint) sold for $1,206 (eBay; 2/14)
—Gern Nagler #14 PSA 10 (Gem Mt) sold for $755 (eBay; 6/06)

1961 Nu-Card

#	Name	VG 3	VgEx 4	EX 5	ExMt 6	NM 7	NmMt 8	MT 9	Gem 9.5/10
	COMMON CARD (101-180)	4	4	5	5	6	10	20	
101	Bob Ferguson	4	4	5	5	8	12	30	
105	Vern Von Sydow	4	4	5	5	6	10	20	80
112	Don Purcell	4	4	5	5	6	10	20	80
116	Bobby Iles	4	4	5	5	6	10	25	
117	John Hadl	6	8	10	12	20	30	60	
118	Charlie Mitchell	4	4	5	5	6	10	25	
120	Bill King	4	4	5	5	6	10	25	
121	Mike Lucci	4	4	5	5	8	12	25	
128	Gary Collins	4	4	5	6	10	15	25	
130	Bobby Dodd Flor.	4	4	5	5	8	12	25	
131	Curtis McClinton	4	4	5	6	10	15	30	

#	Name	VG 3	VgEx 4	EX 5	ExMt 6	NM 7	NmMt 8	MT 9	Gem 9
135	Larry Libertore	4	4	5	5	6	10	20	80
136	Stan Sczurek	4	4	5	5	6	10	20	80
138	Jesse Bradford	4	4	5	5	6	10	15	80
140	Walter Doleschal	4	4	5	5	6	10	20	80
142	Pat Trammell	4	4	5	5	8	12	25	80
143	Ernie Davis	10	12	15	20	35	60	120	
148	Roger Kochman	4	4	5	5	6	10	20	
150	Sherwyn Torson	4	4	5	5	6	10	25	
151	Russ Hepner	4	4	5	5	6	10	20	80
155	Ken Bolin	4	4	5	5	6	10	20	80
159	Dan Celoni G	4	4	5	5	6	10	20	80
166	Roman Gabriel	6	8	10	12	20	30	80	
169	Charles Rieves	4	4	5	5	6	10	20	80
172	Galen Hall	4	4	5	5	8	12	25	
174	Don Kasso	4	4	5	5	6	15		
175	Bill Miller	4	4	5	5	6	10	20	80
178	Mel Melin UER (misspelled Mellin)	4	4	5	5	6	10	15	80
179	Tom Vassell	4	4	5	5	6	10	25	

—Ernie Davis #143 PSA 10 (Gem) sold for $420 (eBay; 2/07)

1961 Topps

#	Name	GD 2	VG 3	VgEx 4	EX 5	ExMt 6	NM 7	NmMt 8	MT 9
1	Johnny Unitas	20	25	30	40	60	150	350	1,200
2	Lenny Moore	4	4	5	8	12	25	50	
3	Alan Ameche	4	4	5	5	10	15	60	
4	Raymond Berry	4	4	5	8	12	25	50	
5	Jim Mutscheller	4	4	5	5	6	12	20	100
6	Jim Parker	4	4	5	5	8	15	35	
7	Gino Marchetti	4	4	5	6	10	20	40	175
8	Gene Lipscomb	4	4	5	5	8	12	50	
9	Baltimore Colts	4	4	5	5	6	12	60	
10	Bill Wade	4	4	5	5	6	12	25	
11	Johnny Morris RC	4	4	5	5	8	12	30	150
12	Rick Casares	4	4	5	5	6	12	35	
13	Harlon Hill	4	4	5	5	6	12	25	
14	Stan Jones	4	4	5	5	8	12	25	120
15	Doug Atkins	4	4	5	5	8	15	40	150
16	Bill George	4	4	5	5	8	12	25	120
17	J.C. Caroline	4	4	5	5	6	12	20	100
18	Chicago Bears	4	4	5	5	6	12	20	150
19	Eddie LeBaron IA	4	4	5	6	10	20	100	
20	Eddie LeBaron	4	4	5	5	6	12	50	
21	Don McIlhenny	4	4	5	5	6	12	40	
22	L.G. Dupre	4	4	5	5	6	12	40	125
23	Jim Doran	4	4	5	5	6	12	35	
24	Billy Howton	4	4	5	5	6	12	40	
25	Buzz Guy	4	4	5	6	12	15	60	
26	Jack Patera RC	4	4	5	5	6	12	40	120
27	Tom Franckhauser RC	4	4	5	5	6	12	40	
28	Cowboys Team	4	5	6	10	15	25	80	
29	Jim Ninowski	4	4	5	5	6	12	25	
30	Dan Lewis RC	4	4	5	5	6	12	20	100
31	Nick Pietrosante RC	4	4	5	5	6	12	25	
32	Gail Cogdill RC	4	4	5	5	6	12	40	
33	Jim Gibbons	4	4	5	5	6	12	25	
34	Jim Martin	4	4	5	5	6	12	20	100
35	Alex Karras	4	5	6	10	15	25	60	
36	Joe Schmidt	4	4	5	5	8	15	40	
37	Detroit Lions	4	4	5	5	6	12	25	
38	Paul Hornung IA	4	5	6	10	15	25	150	
39	Bart Starr	10	12	15	25	50	80	200	600
40	Paul Hornung	6	8	10	15	25	50	100	400
41	Jim Taylor	6	8	10	15	25	40	125	450
42	Max McGee	4	4	5	5	8	12	50	150
43	Boyd Dowler RC	4	4	5	6	10	25	100	
44	Jim Ringo	4	4	5	5	8	15	50	300
45	Hank Jordan RC	6	8	10	20	30	60	300	
46	Bill Forester	4	4	5	5	6	12	30	100
47	Green Bay Packers	4	5	6	10	15	25	60	200
48	Frank Ryan	4	4	5	5	6	12	20	100
49	Jon Arnett	4	4	5	5	6	12	20	100
50	Ollie Matson	4	4	5	6	10	20	40	150
51	Jim Phillips	4	4	5	5	6	12	30	100
52	Del Shofner	4	4	5	5	6	12	25	
53	Art Hunter	4	4	5	5	6	12	25	
54	Gene Brito	4	4	5	5	6	12	25	
55	Lindon Crow	4	4	5	5	6	12	25	
56	Los Angeles Rams	4	4	5	5	6	12	20	100

	GD 2	VG 3	VgEx 4	EX 5	ExMt 6	NM 7	NmMt 8	MT 9
Johnny Unitas IA	5	6	8	12	20	35	150	
Y.A.Tittle	5	6	8	12	18	30	80	250
John Brodie RC	6	8	10	15	25	40	80	350
J.D. Smith	4	4	5	5	6	12	25	
R.C. Owens	4	4	5	5	6	12	20	100
Clyde Conner	4	4	5	5	6	12	25	
Bob St.Clair	4	4	5	5	8	12	25	
Leo Nomellini	4	4	5	6	10	20	50	
Abe Woodson	4	4	5	5	6	12	20	100
San Francisco 49ers	4	4	5	5	6	12	20	100
Checklist 1	4	5	6	10	15	40	80	
Milt Plum	4	4	5	5	6	12	20	100
Ray Renfro	4	4	5	5	6	12	30	120
Bobby Mitchell	4	5	6	8	15	30	80	200
Jim Brown	20	30	50	60	100	200	400	1,500
Mike McCormack	4	4	5	5	8	12	30	
Jim Ray Smith	4	4	5	5	6	12	25	
Sam Baker	4	4	5	5	6	12	25	
Walt Michaels	4	4	5	5	6	12	20	100
Cleveland Browns	4	4	5	5	6	15	25	100
Jim Brown IA	8	10	12	15	30	60	225	400
George Shaw	4	4	5	5	6	12	25	
Hugh McElhenny	4	4	5	6	10	20	40	200
Clancy Osborne	4	4	5	5	6	12	30	
Dave Middleton	4	4	5	5	6	12	30	
Frank Youso	4	4	5	6	12	15	50	
Don Joyce	4	4	5	5	6	12	30	
Ed Culpepper	4	4	5	5	6	12	30	
Charley Conerly	4	4	5	6	10	20	40	150
Mel Triplett	4	4	5	5	6	12	20	100
Kyle Rote	4	4	5	5	6	12	20	100
Roosevelt Brown	4	4	5	5	8	12	25	
Ray Wietecha	4	4	5	5	6	12	20	100
Andy Robustelli	4	4	5	5	8	15	50	
Sam Huff	4	4	5	6	10	20	30	125
Jim Patton	4	4	5	5	6	12	20	100
New York Giants	4	4	5	5	6	12	50	
Charley Conerly IA	4	4	5	6	10	20	50	
Sonny Jurgensen	4	5	6	10	15	25	60	250
Tommy McDonald	4	4	5	5	8	20	40	
Bill Barnes	4	4	5	5	6	12	20	100
Bobby Walston	4	4	5	5	6	12	25	
Pete Retzlaff	4	4	5	5	6	12	25	
Jim McCusker	4	4	5	5	6	12	25	
Chuck Bednarik	4	4	5	6	10	20	50	175
Tom Brookshier	4	4	5	5	6	12	20	100
Philadelphia Eagles	4	4	5	5	6	12	30	100
Bobby Layne	5	6	8	12	18	30	50	
John Henry Johnson	4	4	5	5	8	12	25	120
Tom Tracy	4	4	5	5	6	12	60	
Buddy Dial RC	4	4	5	5	6	12	25	
Jimmy Orr RC	4	4	5	6	10	20	50	120
Mike Sandusky	4	4	5	5	6	12	20	100
John Reger	4	4	5	5	6	12	20	100
Junior Wren	4	4	5	5	6	12	20	100
Pittsburgh Steelers	4	4	5	5	6	15	30	150
Bobby Layne IA	4	4	5	8	12	25	50	
John Roach	4	4	5	5	6	12	20	100
Sam Etcheverry RC	4	4	5	5	6	12	20	100
John David Crow	4	4	5	5	6	12	25	
Mal Hammack	4	4	5	5	6	12	25	
Sonny Randle RC	4	4	5	5	6	12	80	
Leo Sugar	4	4	5	5	6	12	25	
Jerry Norton	4	4	5	5	6	12	20	100
St. Louis Cardinals	4	4	5	5	6	12	25	
Checklist 2	5	6	8	12	20	50	100	
Ralph Guglielmi	4	4	5	5	6	12	25	
Dick James	4	4	5	5	6	12	20	100
Don Bosseler	4	4	5	5	6	12	20	100
Joe Walton	4	4	5	5	6	12	20	100
Bill Anderson	4	4	5	5	6	12	20	100
Vince Promuto RC	4	4	5	5	6	12	50	
Bob Toneff	4	4	5	5	6	12	20	100
John Paluck	4	4	5	5	6	12	25	
Washington Redskins	4	4	5	5	6	12	60	
Milt Plum IA	4	4	5	5	6	12	30	
Abner Haynes IA	4	4	5	5	8	12	25	100
Mel Branch	4	4	5	5	6	12	20	80
Jerry Cornelison	4	4	5	5	6	12	20	80

		GD 2	VG 3	VgEx 4	EX 5	ExMt 6	NM 7	NmMt 8	MT 9
136	Bill Krisher	4	4	5	5	6	12	20	80
137	Paul Miller	4	4	5	5	6	12	20	80
138	Jack Spikes	4	4	5	5	6	12	20	80
139	Johnny Robinson RC	4	4	5	8	8	12	25	100
140	Cotton Davidson RC	4	4	5	5	6	12	20	80
141	Dave Smith RB	4	4	5	5	6	12	20	80
142	Bill Groman	4	4	5	5	6	12	20	80
143	Rich Michael	4	4	5	5	6	12	20	80
144	Mike Dukes	4	4	5	5	6	12	20	50
145	George Blanda	4	4	5	8	12	25	50	150
146	Billy Cannon	4	4	5	5	6	12	20	80
147	Dennit Morris	4	4	5	5	6	12	20	50
148	Jacky Lee	4	4	5	5	6	12	20	80
149	Al Dorow	4	4	5	5	6	12	20	80
150	Don Maynard RC	10	12	15	20	30	60	100	250
151	Art Powell RC	4	4	5	8	8	12	25	150
152	Sid Youngelman	4	4	5	5	6	12	20	80
153	Bob Mischak	4	4	5	5	6	12	20	80
154	Larry Grantham	4	4	5	5	6	12	20	80
155	Tom Saidock	4	4	5	5	6	12	20	80
156	Roger Donnahoo	4	4	5	5	6	12	20	
157	Laverne Torczon	4	4	5	5	6	12	20	
158	Archie Matsos RC	4	4	5	5	6	12	20	80
159	Elbert Dubenion	4	4	5	5	6	12	20	80
160	Wray Carlton RC	4	4	5	5	6	12	20	80
161	Rich McCabe	4	4	5	5	6	12	20	80
162	Ken Rice	4	4	5	5	6	12	20	80
163	Art Baker RC	4	4	5	5	6	12	20	80
164	Tom Rychlec	4	4	5	5	6	12	20	80
165	Mack Yoho	4	4	5	5	6	12	25	100
166	Jack Kemp	12	20	25	35	40	50	100	300
167	Paul Lowe	4	4	5	5	6	12	20	80
168	Ron Mix	4	4	5	6	10	15	30	
169	Paul Maguire	4	4	5	5	6	12	20	60
170	Volney Peters	4	4	5	5	6	12	20	
171	Ernie Wright RC	4	4	5	5	6	12	20	135
172	Ron Nery RC	4	4	5	5	6	12	20	80
173	Dave Kocourek RC	4	4	5	5	6	12	20	100
174	Jim Colclough	4	4	5	5	6	12	20	80
175	Babe Parilli	4	4	5	5	6	12	20	80
176	Billy Lott	4	4	5	5	6	12	20	80
177	Fred Bruney	4	4	5	5	6	12	20	80
178	Ross O'Hanley	4	4	5	5	6	12	20	80
179	Walt Cudzik	4	4	5	5	6	10	20	80
180	Charley Leo	4	4	5	5	6	10	20	80
181	Bob Dee	4	4	5	5	6	12	20	80
182	Jim Otto RC	8	20	25	30	40	45	100	250
183	Eddie Macon	4	4	5	5	6	10	20	80
184	Dick Christy	4	4	5	5	6	10	20	80
185	Alan Miller RC	4	4	5	5	6	10	20	80
186	Tom Flores RC	5	6	8	10	20	30	50	200
187	Joe Cannavino	4	4	5	5	6	10	20	80
188	Don Manoukian	4	4	5	5	6	10	20	80
189	Bob Coolbaugh	4	4	5	5	6	10	20	
190	Lionel Taylor RC	4	4	5	5	8	12	30	
191	Bud McFadin	4	4	5	5	6	12	20	80
192	Goose Gonsoulin RC	4	4	5	5	6	12	20	100
193	Frank Tripucka	4	4	5	5	6	10	20	80
194	Gene Mingo RC	4	4	5	5	6	10	30	100
195	Eldon Danenhauer	4	4	5	5	6	12	20	80
196	Bob McNamara	4	4	5	5	6	12	20	80
197	Dave Rolle	4	4	5	5	6	12	20	80
198	Checklist 3	6	8	10	20	40	50	100	250

—Alan Ameche #2 PSA 9 (MT) sold for $610 (eBay; 2/07)
—Joe Cannavino #187 PSA 10 (Gem Mt) sold for $611 (Mile High; 3/09)
—Paul Hornung IA #38 PSA 9 (MT) sold for $770 (eBay; 4/07)
—Don Joyce #83 PSA 10 (Gem Mint) sold for $464 (eBay; 4/12)
—Jim Parker #6 PSA 9 (Mint) sold for $1,583.50 (eBay; 2/14)
—Vince Promuto #128 PSA 9 (Mint) sold for $725 (eBay; 11/14)

1962 Fleer

		GD 2	VG 3	VgEx 4	EX 5	ExMt 6	NM 7	NmMt 8	MT 9
1	Billy Lott	5	5	5	8	15	35	125	
2	Ron Burton	5	5	5	8	12	18	80	
3	Gino Cappelletti RC	5	5	5	10	15	20	60	
4	Babe Parilli	5	5	5	8	12	18	40	
5	Jim Colclough	5	5	5	8	10	15	40	
6	Tony Sardisco	5	5	5	6	10	15	40	

#	Player	GD 2	VG 3	VgEx 4	EX 5	ExMt 6	NM 7	NmMt 8	MT 9
7	Walt Cudzik	5	5	5	6	10	15	40	
8	Bob Dee	5	5	5	6	10	15	40	
9	Tommy Addison RC	5	5	5	6	10	15	40	
10	Harry Jacobs	5	5	5	6	10	15	40	150
11	Ross O'Hanley	5	5	5	6	10	15	40	
12	Art Baker	5	5	5	6	10	15	40	
13	Johnny Green	5	5	5	6	10	15	40	120
14	Elbert Dubenion	5	5	5	8	12	18	40	
15	Tom Rychlec	5	5	5	6	10	15	80	
16	Billy Shaw RC	15	20	25	60	80	200	500	
17	Ken Rice	5	5	5	6	10	15	40	
18	Bill Atkins	5	5	5	6	10	15	40	
19	Richie Lucas	5	5	5	6	10	15	40	150
20	Archie Matsos	5	5	5	6	10	15	40	
21	Laverne Torczon	5	5	5	6	10	15	40	
22	Warren Rabb RC UER	5	5	5	6	10	15	40	
23	Jack Spikes	5	5	5	6	10	15	40	
24	Cotton Davidson	5	5	5	6	10	15	40	
25	Abner Haynes	5	5	5	8	12	20	50	
26	Jimmy Saxton	5	5	5	6	10	15	40	
27	Chris Burford	5	5	5	6	10	15	40	
28	Bill Miller	5	5	5	6	10	15	40	
29	Sherrill Headrick	5	5	5	6	10	15	40	
30	E.J.Holub RC	5	5	5	6	10	15	40	
31	Jerry Mays RC	5	5	5	8	12	18	40	
32	Mel Branch	5	5	5	6	10	15	40	
33	Paul Rochester RC	5	5	5	6	10	15	40	
34	Frank Tripucka	5	5	5	8	12	18	50	250
35	Gene Mingo	5	5	5	6	10	15	40	
36	Lionel Taylor	5	5	5	8	12	20	50	200
37	Ken Adamson	5	5	5	6	10	15	40	▼125
38	Eldon Danenhauer	5	5	5	6	10	15	40	
39	Goose Gonsoulin	5	5	5	8	12	18	40	
40	Gordy Holz	5	5	5	6	10	15	40	100
41	Bud McFadin	5	5	5	6	10	15	40	150
42	Jim Stinnette	5	5	5	6	10	15	40	
43	Bob Hudson RC	5	5	5	6	10	15	40	
44	George Herring	5	5	5	6	10	15	40	
45	Charley Tolar RC	5	5	5	6	10	15	40	150
46	George Blanda	10	12	15	20	30	50	100	400
47	Billy Cannon	5	5	5	8	12	20	60	
48	Charlie Hennigan RC	5	5	5	8	12	20	▼60	
49	Bill Groman	5	5	5	6	10	15	40	
50	Al Jamison	5	5	5	6	10	15	40	
51	Tony Banfield	5	5	5	6	10	15	40	
52	Jim Norton	5	5	5	6	10	15	40	
53	Dennit Morris	5	5	5	6	10	15	40	120
54	Don Floyd	5	5	5	6	10	15	40	
55	Ed Husmann	5	5	5	6	10	15	40	
56	Robert Brooks	5	5	5	6	10	15	40	100
57	Al Dorow	5	5	5	6	10	15	40	
58	Dick Christy	5	5	5	6	10	15	40	
59	Don Maynard	10	12	15	20	30	50	80	500
60	Art Powell	5	5	5	8	12	18	40	
61	Mike Hudock	5	5	5	6	10	15	40	150
62	Bill Mathis	5	5	5	6	10	15	40	150
63	Butch Songin	5	5	5	6	10	15	40	
64	Larry Grantham	5	5	5	6	10	15	40	
65	Nick Mumley	5	5	5	6	10	15	40	
66	Tom Saidock	5	5	5	6	10	15	40	
67	Alan Miller	5	5	5	6	10	15	40	
68	Tom Flores	5	5	5	8	12	20	50	
69	Bob Coolbaugh	5	5	5	6	10	15	40	150
70	George Fleming	5	5	5	6	10	15	40	
71	Wayne Hawkins RC	5	5	5	6	10	25	40	
72	Jim Otto	6	8	10	15	25	40	120	
73	Wayne Crow	5	5	5	6	10	15	40	
74	Fred Williamson RC	5	6	8	20	60	100	150	
75	Tom Louderback	5	5	5	6	10	15	100	
76	Volney Peters	5	5	5	6	10	15	50	
77	Charley Powell	5	5	5	6	10	15	40	225
78	Don Norton	5	5	5	6	10	15	40	
79	Jack Kemp	15	20	30	40	60	60	125	600
80	Paul Lowe	5	5	5	8	12	18	40	
81	Dave Kocourek	5	5	5	6	10	15	40	
82	Ron Mix	5	5	5	8	12	20	50	400
83	Ernie Wright	5	5	5	8	12	20	40	
84	Dick Harris	5	5	5	6	10	15	40	
85	Bill Hudson	5	5	5	6	10	15	40	
86	Ernie Ladd RC	5	5	6	12	30	40	60	300
87	Earl Faison RC	5	5	6	10	20	60	100	
88	Ron Nery	5	5	5	6	15	30	100	

—Gordy Holz #40 PSA 10 (Gem) sold for $500 (eBay; 6/06)
—Bill Hudson #85 PSA 10 (Gem Mt) sold for $987 (Mile High, 10/09)
—Al Jamison #50 PSA 10 (Gem Mt) sold for $1,265 (eBay; 3/07)
—Ron Mix #82 PSA 9 (MT) sold for $1,275 (eBay; 2/07)
—Babe Parilli #4 PSA 10 (Gem Mt) sold for $1,053 (eBay; 11/12)
—Warren Rabb #22 PSA 10 (Gem Mt) sold for $987 (Mile High; 10/09)
—Billy Shaw #16 PSA 9 (MT) sold for $4275 (eBay; 11/07)
—Jack Spikes #23 PSA 10 (Gem) sold for $930 (eBay; 4/06)
—LaVerne Torczon #21 PSA 10 (Gem) sold for $905 (eBay; 1/06)

1962 Topps

#	Player	GD 2	VG 3	VgEx 4	EX 5	ExMt 6	NM 7	NmMt 8	MT 9
1	Johnny Unitas	30	35	60	100	150	500	3,000	
2	Lenny Moore	6	8	10	12	20	80	300	
3	Alex Hawkins SP RC	4	5	6	8	12	60	200	
4	Joe Perry	4	5	6	8	20	150	500	
5	Raymond Berry SP	10	12	15	20	30	50	200	
6	Steve Myhra	4	4	5	6	12	25	80	
7	Tom Gilburg SP	4	5	6	8	12	30	150	
8	Gino Marchetti	4	5	6	8	15	50	125	
9	Bill Pellington	4	4	5	6	12	40	125	
10	Andy Nelson	4	4	5	6	12	25	80	
11	Wendell Harris SP	4	5	6	8	12	30	135	
12	Baltimore Colts	4	4	5	6	12	30	100	
13	Bill Wade SP	4	5	6	8	12	30	135	
14	Willie Galimore	4	4	5	6	12	25	150	
15	Johnny Morris SP	4	5	6	8	12	30	100	
16	Rick Casares	4	4	5	6	12	40	100	
17	Mike Ditka RC	50	▲150	▲200	▲300	500	1,000	2,500	
18	Stan Jones	4	4	5	6	12	40	100	
19	Roger LeClerc	4	4	5	6	12	25	100	
20	Angelo Coia	4	4	5	6	12	25	100	
21	Doug Atkins	4	5	6	8	15	25	125	
22	Bill George	4	4	5	6	12	25	350	
23	Richie Petitbon RC	4	4	5	6	12	25	350	
24	Ronnie Bull SP RC	5	6	8	10	15	50	150	
25	Chicago Bears	4	4	5	6	12	25	100	
26	Howard Cassady	4	4	5	6	12	25	80	
27	Ray Renfro SP	4	5	6	8	12	30	175	
28	Jim Brown	25	30	50	100	150	400	3,000	
29	Rich Kreitling	4	4	5	6	12	25	135	
30	Jim Ray Smith	4	4	5	6	12	25	80	
31	John Morrow	4	4	5	6	12	25	150	
32	Lou Groza	5	6	8	10	15	30	150	
33	Bob Gain	4	4	5	6	12	25	150	
34	Bernie Parrish	4	4	5	6	12	30	150	
35	Jim Shofner	4	4	5	6	12	40	150	
36	Ernie Davis SP RC	30	60	▼80	125	200	350	750	
37	Cleveland Browns	4	4	5	6	12	35	150	
38	Eddie LeBaron	4	4	5	6	12	25	80	
39	Don Meredith SP	25	30	40	60	80	150	300	
40	J.W. Lockett SP	4	5	6	8	12	30	100	
41	Don Perkins RC	8	10	12	20	60	250	500	
42	Billy Howton	4	4	8	10	20	50	250	
43	Dick Bielski	4	4	5	6	15	25	80	
44	Mike Connelly RC	4	4	5	6	12	40	120	
45	Jerry Tubbs SP	4	5	6	8	12	50	120	
46	Don Bishop SP	4	4	5	6	15	40	200	
47	Dick Moegle	4	4	5	6	12	40	150	
48	Bobby Plummer SP	4	5	6	8	20	60	120	
49	Cowboys Team	6	8	10	12	25	40	150	
50	Milt Plum	4	4	5	6	12	25	80	
51	Dan Lewis	4	4	5	6	12	30	100	
52	Nick Pietrosante SP	4	4	5	6	12	30	125	
53	Gail Cogdill	4	4	5	6	12	25	80	
54	Jim Gibbons	4	4	5	6	12	25	120	
55	Jim Martin	4	4	5	6	12	40	100	
56	Yale Lary	4	4	5	6	12	40	100	
57	Darris McCord	4	4	5	6	12	25	80	
58	Alex Karras	6	8	10	12	20	40	120	
59	Joe Schmidt	4	5	6	8	15	40	100	
60	Dick Lane	4	4	5	6	12	40	120	
61	John Lomakoski SP	4	5	6	8	12	30	100	
62	Detroit Lions SP	6	8	10	12	18	30	125	
63	Bart Starr SP	20	25	35	50	75	150	600	

	GD 2	VG 3	VgEx 4	EX 5	ExMt 6	NM 7	NmMt 8	MT 9
Paul Hornung SP	15	20	25	35	60	100	400	
Tom Moore SP	5	6	8	10	15	60	300	
Jim Taylor SP	12	15	20	25	35	80	250	
Max McGee SP	5	6	8	10	20	50	120	
Jim Ringo SP	5	6	8	10	18	30	120	
Fuzzy Thurston SP RC	8	10	12	15	30	60	175	
Forrest Gregg	4	5	6	8	15	40	150	
Boyd Dowler	4	4	5	6	12	40	200	
Hank Jordan SP	6	8	10	12	20	60	120	
Bill Forester SP	4	5	6	8	12	30	120	
Earl Gros SP	4	5	6	8	12	100	150	
Packers Team SP	10	12	15	18	30	60	225	
Checklist SP	6	8	10	20	50	125	250	
Zeke Bratkowski SP	4	5	6	8	12	50	250	
Jon Arnett SP	4	5	6	8	12	30	100	
Ollie Matson SP	10	12	15	18	25	40	100	
Dick Bass SP	4	5	6	8	12	80	225	
Jim Phillips	4	4	5	6	12	30	80	
Carroll Dale RC	4	4	5	6	12	30	100	
Frank Varrichione	4	4	5	6	12	25	100	
Art Hunter	4	4	5	6	12	60	300	
Danny Villanueva RC	4	4	5	6	12	25	80	
Les Richter SP	4	5	6	8	12	30	100	
Lindon Crow	4	4	5	6	12	25	80	
Roman Gabriel SP RC	12	15	20	40	60	120	250	
Los Angeles Rams SP	6	8	10	12	18	40	150	
Fran Tarkenton SP RC	40	▲80	100	150	250	600	4,000	
Jerry Reichow SP	4	5	6	8	12	30	100	
Hugh McElhenny SP	8	10	12	15	25	40	200	
Mel Triplett SP	4	5	6	8	12	40	150	
Tommy Mason SP RC	5	6	8	12	30	150	350	
Dave Middleton SP	4	5	6	8	12	60	120	
Frank Youso SP	4	5	6	8	12	30	100	
Mike Mercer SP	4	5	6	8	12	40	400	
Rip Hawkins SP	4	5	6	8	15	100	400	
Cliff Livingston SP	4	5	6	8	12	30	120	
Roy Winston SP RC	4	5	6	8	12	40	▲125	
Vikings Team SP	8	10	12	15	20	80	150	
Y.A. Tittle	10	12	15	20	30	60	150	
Joe Walton	4	4	5	6	12	40	100	
Frank Gifford	12	15	20	25	35	80	200	
Alex Webster	4	4	5	6	12	25	100	
Del Shofner	4	4	5	6	12	40	150	
Don Chandler	4	4	5	6	12	25	80	
Andy Robustelli	4	5	6	8	15	25	100	
Jim Katcavage RC	4	4	5	6	12	25	80	
Sam Huff SP	10	12	15	18	25	80	300	
Erich Barnes	4	4	5	6	12	25	100	
Jim Patton	4	4	5	6	12	30	125	
Jerry Hillebrand SP	4	5	6	8	12	40	100	
New York Giants	4	4	5	6	12	25	80	
Sonny Jurgensen	10	12	15	18	30	50	175	
Tommy McDonald	4	5	6	8	15	25	80	
Ted Dean SP	4	5	6	12	25	40	250	
Clarence Peaks	4	4	5	6	12	25	80	
Bobby Walston	4	4	5	6	12	25	125	
Pete Retzlaff SP	4	5	6	8	12	30	▼80	
Jim Schrader SP	4	5	6	8	12	30	200	
J.D. Smith T	4	4	5	6	12	25	125	
King Hill	4	4	5	6	12	30	80	
Maxie Baughan	4	4	5	6	12	25	80	
Pete Case SP	4	5	6	8	12	30	100	
Philadelphia Eagles	4	4	5	6	12	25	100	
Bobby Layne	10	12	15	18	30	40	150	
Tom Tracy	4	4	5	6	12	40	100	
John Henry Johnson	4	4	5	6	12	30	80	
Buddy Dial SP	4	5	6	8	12	35	120	
Preston Carpenter	4	4	5	6	20	40	225	
Lou Michaels SP	4	5	6	8	12	30	100	
Gene Lipscomb SP	5	6	8	10	15	40	150	
Ernie Stautner SP	6	8	10	12	25	80	150	
John Reger SP	4	5	6	8	12	30	100	
Myron Pottios RC	4	4	5	6	12	40	300	
Bob Ferguson SP	4	5	6	8	12	40	150	
Pittsburgh Steelers SP	6	8	10	12	20	50	135	
Sam Etcheverry	4	4	5	6	12	25	80	
John David Crow SP	4	5	6	8	15	30	175	
Bobby Joe Conrad SP	4	5	6	8	12	30	100	
Prentice Gautt SP RC	4	5	6	8	12	▼80	250	

		GD 2	VG 3	VgEx 4	EX 5	ExMt 6	NM 7	NmMt 8	MT 9
143	Frank Mestnik	4	4	5	6	12	25	80	
144	Sonny Randle	4	4	5	6	12	25	100	
145	Gerry Perry	4	4	5	6	12	25	150	
146	Jerry Norton	4	4	5	6	12	25	80	
147	Jimmy Hill	4	4	5	6	12	35	175	
148	Bill Stacy	4	4	5	6	12	25	80	
149	Fate Echols SP	4	5	6	8	12	30	100	
150	St. Louis Cardinals	4	4	5	6	12	25	120	
151	Billy Kilmer RC	10	12	15	20	35	60	150	
152	John Brodie	6	8	10	12	20	40	350	
153	J.D. Smith RB	4	4	5	6	12	30	120	
154	C.R. Roberts SP	4	5	6	8	12	40	100	
155	Monty Stickles	4	4	5	6	12	30	80	
156	Clyde Conner	4	4	5	6	12	30	80	
157	Bob St.Clair	4	4	5	6	12	30	80	
158	Tommy Davis RC	4	4	5	6	12	40	80	
159	Leo Nomellini	4	5	6	8	15	40	80	
160	Matt Hazeltine	4	4	5	6	20	25	120	
161	Abe Woodson	4	4	5	6	12	25	80	
162	Dave Baker	4	4	5	6	12	30	100	
163	San Francisco 49ers	4	4	5	6	12	30	200	
164	Norm Snead SP RC	10	12	15	20	30	150	350	
165	Dick James	4	4	5	6	12	80	200	
166	Bobby Mitchell	4	5	6	8	15	30	200	
167	Sam Horner	4	4	5	6	12	25	80	
168	Bill Barnes	4	4	5	6	12	25	80	
169	Bill Anderson	4	4	5	6	12	25	80	
170	Fred Dugan	4	4	5	6	12	25	80	
171	John Aveni SP	4	5	6	8	12	30	100	
172	Bob Toneff	4	4	5	6	12	50	250	
173	Jim Kerr	4	4	5	6	12	100	300	
174	Leroy Jackson SP	4	4	5	8	12	40	150	
175	Washington Redskins	4	4	5	6	15	50	200	
176	Checklist	15	20	25	40	60	125	800	

—Raymond Berry SP #5 PSA 9 (Mint) sold for $2384.76 (Goodwin; 8/12)
—Dick Bielski #43 PSA 9 (Mint) sold for $957.5 (eBay: 7/12)
—Jim Brown #28 PSA 9 (MT) sold for $10,540 (Mastro; 12/06)
—Jim Brown #28 PSA 8.5 (NmMt+) sold for $2,714 (Mile High; 3/09)
—Ronnie Bull #24 PSA 9 (Mt) sold for $1185 (eBay; 11/14)
—Mike Ditka #17 PSA 9 (Mt) sold for $9,132 (eBay; 02/13)
—Bill Forester #73 PSA 9 (MT) sold for $615 (eBay; 1/07)
—Rip Hawkins #98 PSA 9 (MT) sold for $1,459 (Goodwin; 11/09)
—Matt Hazeltine #160 PSA 9 (MT) sold for $1,631 (eBay; 2/14)
—Jim Kerr #173 PSA 9 (Mint) sold for $813.49 (eBay; 8/12)
—Dick Lane #60 PSA 9 (MT) sold for $925 (eBay; 4/07)
—Max Mcgee #67 PSA 9 (MT) sold for $1,240 (eBay; 2/13)
—Hugh McElhenny #92 PSA 9 (MT) sold for $715 (eBay; 9/05)
—Lenny Moore #1 PSA 9 (MT) sold for $635 (eBay; 6/06)
—Johnny Morris #15 PSA 9 (MT) sold for $390 (eBay; 9/05)
—Bernie Parrish #34 PSA 9 (MT) sold for $510 (eBay; 1/06)
—Don Perkins RC #41 PSA 9 (Mint) sold for $890.5 (eBay; 6/12)

1963 Fleer

		GD 2	VG 3	VgEx 4	EX 5	ExMt 6	NM 7	NmMt 8	MT 9
1	Larry Garron RC	4	5	6	10	15	30	250	
2	Babe Parilli	4	5	5	6	10	20	80	
3	Ron Burton	4	5	5	8	12	20	60	
4	Jim Colclough	4	5	5	6	10	15	150	
5	Gino Cappelletti	4	5	5	8	12	20	40	150
6	Charles Long SP RC	25	35	40	50	60	80	100	450
7	Billy Neighbors RC	4	5	5	6	10	20	60	
8	Dick Felt	4	5	5	6	10	15	30	120
9	Tommy Addison	4	5	5	6	10	15	40	
10	Nick Buoniconti RC	12	20	25	35	75	200	400	1,200
11	Larry Eisenhauer RC	4	5	5	6	10	20	35	200
12	Bill Mathis	4	5	5	6	10	15	40	
13	Lee Grosscup RC	4	5	5	6	10	15	30	120
14	Dick Christy	4	5	5	6	10	15	30	150
15	Don Maynard	6	10	12	18	30	50	▼80	300
16	Alex Kroll RC	4	5	5	6	10	15	30	150
17	Bob Mischak	4	5	5	6	10	15	30	100
18	Dainard Paulson	4	5	5	6	10	15	40	
19	Lee Riley	4	5	5	6	10	15	30	100
20	Larry Grantham	4	5	5	6	10	15	25	150
21	Hubert Bobo	4	5	5	6	10	15	30	150
22	Nick Mumley	4	5	5	6	10	15	30	150
23	Cookie Gilchrist RC	10	12	15	30	40	60	100	300
24	Jack Kemp	15	25	30	50	75	100	150	350

#	Player	GD 2	VG 3	VgEx 4	EX 5	ExMt 6	NM 7	NmMt 8	MT 9
25	Wray Carlton	4	5	5	6	10	15	40	100
26	Elbert Dubenion	4	5	5	6	10	15	60	
27	Ernie Warlick RC	4	5	5	6	10	15	30	120
28	Billy Shaw	4	5	6	10	15	25	50	150
29	Ken Rice	4	5	5	6	10	15	30	100
30	Booker Edgerson	4	5	5	6	10	15	30	150
31	Ray Abruzzese	4	5	5	6	10	15	30	120
32	Mike Stratton RC	4	5	6	10	15	30	60	150
33	Tom Sestak RC	4	5	5	6	10	20	▼50	
34	Charley Tolar	4	5	5	6	10	15	40	
35	Dave Smith RB	4	5	5	6	10	15	40	
36	George Blanda	10	12	15	20	35	50	100	300
37	Billy Cannon	4	5	6	10	15	25	40	150
38	Charlie Hennigan	4	5	5	6	10	15	30	150
39	Bob Talamini RC	4	5	5	6	10	15	30	120
40	Jim Norton	4	5	5	6	10	15	25	120
41	Tony Banfield	4	5	5	6	10	15	50	100
42	Doug Cline	4	5	5	6	10	15	40	
43	Don Floyd	4	5	5	6	10	15	40	
44	Ed Husmann	4	5	5	6	10	15	40	
45	Curtis McClinton RC	4	5	6	10	15	25	40	200
46	Jack Spikes	4	5	5	6	10	15	30	150
47	Len Dawson RC	50	80	100	250	300	500	600	2,000
48	Abner Haynes	4	5	6	10	15	25	40	200
49	Chris Burford	4	5	5	6	10	15	30	120
50	Fred Arbanas RC	4	5	5	8	12	20	40	150
51	Johnny Robinson	4	5	5	6	10	15	40	100
52	E.J. Holub	4	5	5	6	10	15	120	150
53	Sherrill Headrick	4	5	5	6	10	15	30	100
54	Mel Branch	4	5	5	6	10	15	30	120
55	Jerry Mays	4	5	5	6	10	15	30	▲150
56	Cotton Davidson	4	5	5	6	10	15	40	100
57	Clem Daniels RC	4	5	6	10	20	30	50	
58	Bo Roberson RC	4	5	5	6	10	15	40	150
59	Art Powell	4	5	5	8	12	20	30	150
60	Bob Coolbaugh	4	5	5	6	10	15	40	100
61	Wayne Hawkins	4	5	5	6	10	20	30	100
62	Jim Otto	4	6	8	12	18	30	80	
63	Fred Williamson	4	5	6	10	15	25	50	
64	Bob Dougherty SP	20	30	35	80	100	125	150	300
65	Dalva Allen	4	5	5	6	10	15	30	80
66	Chuck McMurtry	4	5	5	6	10	15	60	
67	Gerry McDougall RC	4	5	5	6	10	15	30	100
68	Tobin Rote	4	5	5	6	10	20	40	120
69	Paul Lowe	4	5	5	8	12	20	50	200
70	Keith Lincoln RC	5	8	10	15	25	40	100	250
71	Dave Kocourek	4	5	5	6	10	18	40	250
72	Lance Alworth RC	50	80	100	250	500	600	1,000	2,200
73	Ron Mix	4	5	6	10	15	25	100	300
74	Charley McNeil RC	4	5	5	6	10	15	30	150
75	Emil Karas	4	5	5	6	10	15	40	▼80
76	Ernie Ladd	4	5	6	10	15	25	40	120
77	Earl Faison	4	5	5	6	10	15	30	▼80
78	Jim Stinnette	4	5	5	6	10	15	30	150
79	Frank Tripucka	4	5	5	8	12	20	35	150
80	Don Stone	4	5	5	6	10	15	30	100
81	Bob Scarpitto	4	5	5	6	10	15	40	
82	Lionel Taylor	4	5	5	8	12	20	40	150
83	Jerry Tarr	4	5	5	6	10	15	30	100
84	Eldon Danenhauer	4	5	5	6	10	15	25	150
85	Goose Gonsoulin	4	5	5	6	10	15	25	100
86	Jim Fraser	4	5	5	6	10	15	30	▼80
87	Chuck Gavin	4	5	5	6	10	15	30	100
88	Bud McFadin	4	5	6	10	15	25	80	
NNO	Checklist SP	60	100	150	200	250	400	1,200	

—Checklist SP #NNO PSA 9 (Mint) sold for $2,747 (Mile High; 10/09)
—Checklist SP #NNO PSA 9 (Mint) sold for $2,182 (Goodwin; 2/11)
—Earl Faison #77 PSA 10 (Gem Mt) sold for $561 (eBay; 11/14)
—Larry Garron RC #1 PSA 9 (Mint) sold for $1042.03 (eBay; 8/12)
—Ron Mix #73 PSA 10 (Gem Mt) sold for $1,618 (eBay; 6/07)
—Ron Mix #73 PSA 10 (Gem Mt) sold for $1,010 (eBay; 1/06)

1963 Topps

#	Player	GD 2	VG 3	VgEx 4	EX 5	ExMt 6	NM 7	NmMt 8	MT 9
1	Johnny Unitas	20	25	35	60	75	200	550	
2	Lenny Moore	4	5	6	10	15	30	100	
3	Jimmy Orr	4	5	5	6	10	40	80	
4	Raymond Berry	4	5	6	10	15	30	60	
5	Jim Parker	4	5	5	8	12	▲30	60	
6	Alex Sandusky	4	5	5	6	10	15	40	
7	Dick Szymanski RC	4	5	5	6	10	15	40	
8	Gino Marchetti	4	5	5	8	12	20	40	
9	Billy Ray Smith RC	4	5	5	6	10	15	40	
10	Bill Pellington	4	5	5	6	10	30	60	
11	Bob Boyd DB RC	4	5	5	6	10	40	80	
12	Baltimore Colts SP	4	5	5	8	12	40	100	
13	Frank Ryan SP	4	5	5	8	10	▲60	100	
14	Jim Brown SP	30	40	80	100	125	250	800	6,000
15	Ray Renfro SP	4	5	5	8	10	20	40	
16	Rich Kreitling SP	4	5	5	8	10	15	40	
17	Mike McCormack SP	4	5	5	8	12	40	60	
18	Jim Ray Smith SP	4	5	5	8	10	15	40	
19	Lou Groza SP	4	5	6	10	15	25	120	
20	Bill Glass SP	4	5	5	8	10	15	40	
21	Galen Fiss SP	4	5	5	6	10	40	80	
22	Don Fleming SP RC	4	5	5	8	10	40	150	
23	Bob Gain SP	4	5	5	8	10	40	100	
24	Cleveland Browns SP	4	5	5	8	12	80	200	
25	Milt Plum	4	5	5	6	10	30	80	
26	Dan Lewis	4	5	5	6	10	15	40	
27	Nick Pietrosante	4	5	5	6	10	15	50	
28	Gail Cogdill	4	5	5	6	10	15	40	
29	Harley Sewell	4	5	5	6	10	15	40	
30	Jim Gibbons	4	5	5	6	10	15	40	
31	Carl Brettschneider	4	5	5	6	10	15	40	
32	Dick Lane	4	5	5	8	12	20	40	
33	Yale Lary	4	5	5	8	12	20	40	
34	Roger Brown RC	4	5	5	6	10	15	40	
35	Joe Schmidt	4	5	5	8	12	40	80	
36	Detroit Lions SP	4	5	5	8	12	20	40	
37	Roman Gabriel	4	5	6	8	12	30	100	
38	Zeke Bratkowski	4	5	5	6	10	15	30	
39	Dick Bass	4	5	5	6	10	15	40	
40	Jon Arnett	4	5	5	6	10	15	40	300
41	Jim Phillips	4	5	5	6	10	15	30	
42	Frank Varrichione	4	5	5	6	10	15	40	
43	Danny Villanueva	4	5	5	6	10	15	40	
44	Deacon Jones RC	8	12	20	30	40	125	600	1,500
45	Lindon Crow	4	5	5	6	10	15	40	
46	Marlin McKeever	4	5	5	6	10	15	30	
47	Ed Meador RC	4	5	5	6	10	40	80	
48	Los Angeles Rams	4	5	5	6	10	15	40	
49	Y.A.Tittle SP	6	10	12	20	30	50	175	
50	Del Shofner SP	4	5	5	8	10	15	80	
51	Alex Webster SP	4	5	5	8	10	20	40	
52	Phil King SP	4	5	5	8	10	15	40	
53	Jack Stroud SP	4	5	5	8	10	40	50	
54	Darrell Dess SP	4	5	5	8	10	15	20	
55	Jim Katcavage SP	4	5	5	8	10	15	40	
56	Roosevelt Grier SP	4	5	5	8	12	20	60	225
57	Erich Barnes SP	4	5	5	8	10	15	40	
58	Jim Patton SP	4	5	5	8	10	15	30	150
59	Sam Huff SP	4	5	6	10	15	30	120	
60	New York Giants	4	5	5	6	10	15	40	
61	Bill Wade	4	5	5	6	10	40	100	
62	Mike Ditka	10	15	20	30	40	80	400	1,000
63	Johnny Morris	4	5	5	6	10	15	40	
64	Roger LeClerc	4	5	5	6	10	15	40	
65	Roger Davis RC	4	5	5	6	10	15	40	
66	Joe Marconi	4	5	5	6	10	15	40	
67	Herman Lee	4	5	5	6	10	15	40	
68	Doug Atkins	4	5	5	8	12	20	40	
69	Joe Fortunato	4	5	5	6	10	15	40	
70	Bill George	4	5	5	8	12	20	40	
71	Richie Petitbon	4	5	5	6	10	40	80	
72	Bears Team SP	4	5	5	8	12	40	80	
73	Eddie LeBaron SP	4	5	5	8	12	40	80	
74	Don Meredith SP	8	12	15	25	35	75	200	
75	Don Perkins SP	4	5	5	8	12	20	80	
76	Amos Marsh SP	4	5	5	8	10	15	40	
77	Billy Howton SP	4	5	5	8	10	40	150	
78	Andy Cvercko SP	4	5	5	8	10	15	50	
79	Sam Baker SP	4	5	5	8	10	40	80	
80	Jerry Tubbs SP	4	5	5	8	10	20	40	
81	Don Bishop SP	4	5	5	6	10	15	50	
82	Bob Lilly SP RC	35	▲80	▲100	▲150	▲200	300	800	
83	Jerry Norton SP	4	5	5	8	10	40	120	

	GD 2	VG 3	VgEx 4	EX 5	ExMt 6	NM 7	NmMt 8	MT 9
Cowboys Team SP	4	5	6	10	15	30	80	350
Checklist 1	4	5	6	10	15	30	80	
Bart Starr	10	15	20	35	50	100	500	
Jim Taylor	5	6	8	12	18	35	100	
Boyd Dowler	4	5	5	8	12	25	60	
Forrest Gregg	4	5	5	8	12	25	60	400
Fuzzy Thurston	4	5	6	12	20	30	60	
Jim Ringo	4	5	5	8	12	20	50	
Ron Kramer	4	5	5	6	10	15	40	
Hank Jordan	4	5	5	8	12	20	50	
Bill Forester	4	5	5	6	10	15	40	
Willie Wood RC	6	10	12	20	30	60	150	1,000
Ray Nitschke RC	20	25	40	60	100	250	800	▲4,200
Green Bay Packers	4	5	6	10	20	30	60	
Fran Tarkenton	8	12	15	25	35	60	200	
Tommy Mason	4	5	5	6	10	15	40	
Mel Triplett	4	5	5	6	10	15	40	
Jerry Reichow	4	5	5	6	10	15	40	
Frank Youso	4	5	5	6	10	15	40	
Hugh McElhenny	4	5	6	8	12	20	50	
Gerald Huth	4	5	5	6	10	15	40	
Ed Sharockman	4	5	5	6	10	15	40	
Rip Hawkins	4	5	5	6	10	15	40	
Jim Marshall RC	5	8	10	20	25	▲50	100	
Jim Prestel	4	5	5	6	10	15	40	
Minnesota Vikings	4	5	5	6	10	15	40	
Sonny Jurgensen SP	5	8	10	15	25	50	200	
Timmy Brown SP RC	4	5	5	8	12	25	100	
Tommy McDonald SP	4	5	6	10	15	40	175	
Clarence Peaks SP	4	5	5	8	10	15	40	
Pete Retzlaff SP	4	5	5	8	10	15	40	
Jim Schrader SP	4	5	5	8	10	15	40	
Jim McCusker SP	4	5	5	8	10	15	40	
Don Burroughs SP	4	5	5	8	10	15	40	
Maxie Baughan SP	4	5	5	8	10	20	40	
Riley Gunnels SP	4	5	5	8	10	15	40	
Jimmy Carr SP	4	5	5	8	10	40	135	
Philadelphia Eagles SP	4	5	5	8	12	20	60	
Ed Brown SP	4	5	5	8	12	60		
John H. Johnson SP	4	5	6	10	15	40	150	
Buddy Dial SP	4	5	5	8	10	40	120	
Bill Red Mack SP	4	5	5	8	10	15	50	
Preston Carpenter SP	4	5	5	8	10	40	100	
Ray Lemek SP	4	5	5	8	10	20	40	
Buzz Nutter SP	4	5	5	8	10	40	150	
Ernie Stautner SP	4	5	6	10	15	25	80	
Lou Michaels SP	4	5	5	8	10	40	135	
Clendon Thomas SP RC	4	5	5	8	10	20	50	
Tom Bettis SP	4	5	5	8	10	40	135	
Pittsburgh Steelers SP	4	5	5	8	12	40	100	
John Brodie	4	5	6	8	12	40	135	
J.D. Smith	4	5	5	6	10	15	30	
Billy Kilmer	4	5	5	8	12	20	40	
Bernie Casey RC	4	5	5	6	10	15	40	
Tommy Davis	4	5	5	6	10	15	40	
Ted Connolly	4	5	5	6	10	15	30	
Bob St.Clair	4	5	5	8	12	20	40	
Abe Woodson	4	5	5	6	10	15	30	100
Matt Hazeltine	4	5	5	6	10	15	40	
Leo Nomellini	4	5	5	8	12	20	40	▲350
Dan Colchico	4	5	5	6	10	15	40	
San Francisco 49ers SP	4	5	5	8	12	30		
Charlie Johnson RC	4	5	6	8	12	20	40	
John David Crow	4	5	5	6	10	15	40	400
Bobby Joe Conrad	4	5	5	6	10	15	40	
Sonny Randle	4	5	5	6	10	15	25	100
Prentice Gautt	4	5	5	6	10	15	40	
Taz Anderson	4	5	5	6	10	15	30	100
Ernie McMillan RC	4	5	5	6	10	15	40	
Jimmy Hill	4	5	5	6	10	15	40	150
Bill Koman	4	5	5	6	10	15	40	100
Larry Wilson RC	4	5	5	8	12	▲40	100	
Don Owens	4	5	5	6	10	15	40	
St. Louis Cardinals SP	4	5	5	8	12	20	50	
Norm Snead SP	4	5	5	8	12	20	100	
Bobby Mitchell SP	4	5	6	10	15	30	60	
Bill Barnes SP	4	5	5	8	10	15	40	
Fred Dugan SP	4	5	5	8	10	15	40	
Don Bosseler SP	4	5	5	8	10	15	40	300

		GD 2	VG 3	VgEx 4	EX 5	ExMt 6	NM 7	NmMt 8	MT 9
163	John Nisby SP	4	5	5	8	10	15	40	
164	Riley Mattson SP	4	5	5	8	10	40	100	
165	Bob Toneff SP	4	5	5	8	10	40	100	
166	Rod Breedlove SP	4	5	5	8	10	40	150	
167	Dick James SP	4	5	5	8	10	40	100	
168	Claude Crabb SP	4	5	5	8	10	50	250	
169	Washington Redskins SP	4	5	5	8	12	40	200	
170	Checklist 2 UER	6	10	12	20	30	50	80	

—Raymond Berry #4 PSA 10 (Gem Mint) sold for $3,235 (eBay:11/13)
—John Brodie #134 PSA 9 (Mint) sold for $1117.89 (eBay: 7/12)
—Mike Ditka #62 PSA 9 (MT) sold for $2,247 (eBay; 12/07)
—Mike Ditka #62 SGC 9 (MT) sold for $1,095 (eBay; 10/09)
—Mike Ditka #62 PSA 9 (MT) sold for $995 (Mile High; 10/09)
—Mike Ditka #62 PSA 9 (MT) sold for $1,503 (eBay; 60/16)
—Boyd Dowler #88 PSA 9 (Mint) sold for $865.49 (eBay: 4/12)
—Forrest Gregg #89 PSA 9 (MT) sold for $570 (eBay; 2/07)
—Rosey Grier #56 PSA 10 (Gem Mt) sold for $1,194 (Mile High; 10/09)
—Sam Huff #59 PSA 9 (MT) sold for $1,580 (eBay; 4/12)
—Sam Huff SP #59 PSA 9 (Mint) sold for $1580.49 (eBay; 4/12)
—Deacon Jones #44 PSA 9 (MT) sold for $2869 (Mile High; 6/10)
—Deacon Jones #44 PSA 9 (MT) sold for $2,505 (eBay; 4/08)
—Deacon Jones #44 PSA 9 (MT) sold for $2,250 (eBay; 10/11)
—Deacon Jones #44 PSA 9 (MT) sold for $1415 (eBay; 11/14)
—Deacon Jones #44 PSA 9 (MT) sold for $1,312 (eBay; 10/12)
—Deacon Jones #44 PSA 9 (MT) sold for $968 (eBay; 12/12)
—Deacon Jones #44 PSA 9 (MT) sold for $1,216 (eBay; 3/14)
—Sonny Jurgensen #110 PSA 9 (MT) sold for $1,085 (Mastro; 10/06)
—Rich Kreitling #16 PSA 10 (Gem Mint) sold for $1,789 (Memory Lane; Winter 2013)
—Dick Lane #32 PSA 9 (MT) sold for $1230 (eBay; 6/13)
—Dan Lewis #26 PSA 10 (Gem Mt) sold for $1,108 (Mastro; 6/07)
—Bob Lilly #26 PSA 9 (Mt) sold for $7050 (eBay; 11/14)
—Bob Lilly #26 PSA 8.5 (NmMt+) sold for $1,095 (Mile High; 10/09)
—Gino Marchetti #8 PSA 9 (Mint) sold for $1528 (eBay; 11/14)
—Gino Marchetti #8 PSA 9 (MT) sold for $590.77 (eBay; 7/12)
—Jim Marshall RC #107 PSA 9 (Mint) sold for $767 (eBay; 11/13)
—Riley Mattson SP #164 PSA 9 (Mint) sold for $613.49 (eBay; 7/12)
—Mike McCormack SP #17 PSA 9 (Mint) sold for $901.5 (eBay; 4/12)
—Marlin McKeever #46 PSA 10 (Gem Mint) sold for $1681.5 (eBay; 4/12)
—Minnesota Vikings #109 PSA 9 (Mint) sold for $630 (Bussineau; 4/12)
—Lenny Moore #2 PSA 9 (Mint) sold for $2998 (eBay; 6/13)
—Jim Parker #5 PSA 10 (GemMt) sold for $1033 (eBay; 11/14)
—Jim Ray Smith SP #18 PSA 9 (Mint) sold for $913.5 (eBay; 5/12)
—Ernie Stautner #129 PSA 9 (MT) sold for $1,013 (eBay; 2/10)
—Bart Starr #86 PSA 9 (MT) sold for $1,578 (Mile High; 1/07)
—Fran Tarkenton #98 PSA 9 (Mint) sold for $3750 (Bussineau; 4/12)
—Fuzzy Thurston #90 PSA 9 (Mint) sold for $703.89 (eBay; 6/12)
—Johnny Unitas #1 PSA 9 (MT) sold for $4,340 (Mastro; 4/07)
—Washington Redskins SP #169 PSA 9 (Mint) sold for $902.49 (eBay; 8/12)
—Larry Wilson #551 PSA 9 (Mint) sold for $995 (eBay; 5/11)
—Willie Wood #95 PSA 9 (MT) sold for $903 (eBay; 2/10)
—Willie Wood #95 PSA 9 (MT) sold for $961.5 (eBay; 4/12)

1964 Philadelphia

		GD 2	VG 3	VgEx 4	EX 5	ExMt 6	NM 7	NmMt 8	MT 9
1	Raymond Berry	4	5	5	8	12	20	50	100
2	Tom Gilburg	4	5	5	8	8	20	50	
3	John Mackey RC	4	5	6	10	40	80	200	800
4	Gino Marchetti	4	5	5	8	12	18	40	125
5	Jim Martin	4	5	5	8	12	20	120	
6	Tom Matte RC	4	5	5	6	10	15	40	120
7	Jimmy Orr	4	5	5	8	12	20	80	
8	Jim Parker	4	5	6	10	15	25	80	
9	Bill Pellington	4	5	5	8	12	20	80	
10	Alex Sandusky	4	5	5	8	12	20	80	
11	Dick Szymanski	4	5	5	8	12	20	80	
12	Johnny Unitas	5	10	15	20	35	50	120	400
13	Baltimore Colts Team	4	5	5	5	8	20	60	
14	Colts Play/Don Shula	4	6	8	12	20	35	50	80
15	Doug Atkins	4	5	5	8	12	18	30	100
16	Ronnie Bull	4	5	5	8	20	50	100	
17	Mike Ditka	4	6	8	20	30	40	80	400
18	Joe Fortunato	4	5	5	8	12	20	60	
19	Willie Galimore	4	5	5	8	12	20	80	
20	Joe Marconi	4	5	5	8	12	20	80	
21	Bennie McRae RC	4	5	5	8	12	20	50	
22	Johnny Morris	4	5	5	8	12	20	80	
23	Richie Petitbon	4	5	5	8	12	30	80	
24	Mike Pyle	4	5	5	8	12	20	80	

FOOTBALL

#	Player	GD 2	VG 3	VgEx 4	EX 5	ExMt 6	NM 7	NmMt 8	MT 9
25	Roosevelt Taylor RC	4	5	5	5	8	12	20	80
26	Bill Wade	4	5	5	5	8	12	20	80
27	Chicago Bears Team	4	5	5	5	8	12	20	80
28	Bears Play/George Halas	4	5	5	8	12	18	30	100
29	Johnny Brewer	4	5	5	5	8	12	20	80
30	Jim Brown	15	30	▲50	60	▲100	125	300	▼2,000
31	Gary Collins RC	4	5	5	5	8	20	50	
32	Vince Costello	4	5	5	5	8	12	20	60
33	Galen Fiss	4	5	5	5	8	12	40	80
34	Bill Glass	4	5	5	5	8	12	20	60
35	Ernie Green RC	4	5	5	5	8	15	150	250
36	Rich Kreitling	4	5	5	5	8	12	20	
37	John Morrow	4	5	5	5	8	12	20	100
38	Frank Ryan	4	5	5	5	8	12	20	80
39	Charlie Scales RC	4	5	5	5	8	12	20	80
40	Dick Schafrath RC	4	5	5	5	8	12	40	80
41	Cleveland Browns Team	4	5	5	5	8	12	30	100
42	Cleveland Browns Play	4	5	5	5	8	12	20	80
43	Don Bishop	4	5	5	5	8	12	20	80
44	Frank Clarke RC	4	5	5	5	8	12	20	80
45	Mike Connelly	4	5	5	5	8	12	20	80
46	Lee Folkins	4	5	5	5	8	12	20	80
47	Cornell Green RC	4	5	5	5	8	12	40	150
48	Bob Lilly	4	6	8	12	20	40	100	400
49	Amos Marsh	4	5	5	5	8	12	30	
50	Tommy McDonald	4	5	5	8	12	18	30	400
51	Don Meredith	6	8	10	15	25	35	80	500
52	Pettis Norman RC	4	5	5	5	8	12	25	200
53	Don Perkins	4	5	5	6	10	15	25	120
54	Guy Reese	4	5	5	5	8	12	25	80
55	Dallas Cowboys Team	4	5	5	5	8	12	50	
56	Cowboys Play/Landry	4	5	5	8	12	20	30	150
57	Terry Barr	4	5	5	5	8	12	20	80
58	Roger Brown	4	5	5	5	8	12	20	60
59	Gail Cogdill	4	5	5	5	8	12	20	80
60	John Gordy	4	5	5	5	8	12	20	60
61	Dick Lane	4	5	5	6	10	15	25	100
62	Yale Lary	4	5	5	6	10	15	25	
63	Dan Lewis	4	5	5	5	8	12	20	50
64	Darris McCord	4	5	5	5	8	12	20	
65	Earl Morrall	4	5	5	5	8	12	20	80
66	Joe Schmidt	4	5	5	5	8	12	18	50
67	Pat Studstill RC	4	5	5	5	8	15	30	80
68	Wayne Walker RC	4	5	5	5	8	15	30	100
69	Detroit Lions Team	4	5	5	5	8	12	20	80
70	Detroit Lions Play	4	5	5	5	8	12	20	80
71	Herb Adderley RC	4	6	8	12	20	40	▲100	300
72	Willie Davis DE RC	4	6	8	12	20	40	60	300
73	Forrest Gregg	4	5	5	8	12	18	30	80
74	Paul Hornung	4	6	8	12	20	35	80	250
75	Hank Jordan	4	5	5	8	12	18	30	100
76	Jerry Kramer	4	5	5	8	12	18	30	100
77	Tom Moore	4	5	5	5	8	12	20	200
78	Jim Ringo	4	5	5	8	12	18	30	120
79	Bart Starr	8	12	15	25	60	80	250	500
80	Jim Taylor	4	5	6	10	15	25	50	175
81	Jesse Whittenton RC	4	5	5	5	8	12	20	80
82	Willie Wood	4	5	5	8	12	18	40	150
83	Green Bay Packers Team	4	5	5	8	12	18	40	300
84	Packers Play/Lombardi	4	6	8	12	20	35	60	200
85	Jon Arnett	4	5	5	5	8	12	25	80
86	Pervis Atkins RC	4	5	5	5	8	12	20	80
87	Dick Bass	4	5	5	5	8	12	20	80
88	Carroll Dale	4	5	5	6	10	15	25	120
89	Roman Gabriel	4	5	5	8	12	18	40	200
90	Ed Meador	4	5	5	5	8	12	20	80
91	Merlin Olsen RC	5	8	12	25	35	60	100	300
92	Jack Pardee RC	4	5	5	6	10	15	25	100
93	Jim Phillips	4	5	5	5	8	12	20	60
94	Carver Shannon	4	5	5	5	8	12	20	50
95	Frank Varrichione	4	5	5	5	8	12	20	60
96	Danny Villanueva	4	5	5	5	8	12	20	50
97	Los Angeles Rams Team	4	5	5	5	8	12	20	80
98	Los Angeles Rams Play	4	5	5	5	8	12	20	60
99	Grady Alderman RC	4	5	5	5	8	12	25	120
100	Larry Bowie	4	5	5	5	8	12	20	
101	Bill Brown RC	4	5	5	6	10	15	30	
102	Paul Flatley RC	4	5	5	5	8	12	20	
103	Rip Hawkins	4	5	5	5	8	12	20	50
104	Jim Marshall	4	5	5	8	12	18	30	150
105	Tommy Mason	4	5	5	5	8	12	20	60
106	Jim Prestel	4	5	5	5	8	12	20	80
107	Jerry Reichow	4	5	5	5	8	12	20	80
108	Ed Sharockman	4	5	5	5	8	12	20	80
109	Fran Tarkenton	4	6	8	12	30	40	60	200
110	Mick Tingelhoff RC	4	5	5	6	10	30	80	600
111	Minnesota Vikings Team	4	5	5	5	8	12	25	80
112	Vikings Play/Van Brocklin	4	5	5	5	8	12	20	80
113	Erich Barnes	4	5	5	5	8	12	20	80
114	Roosevelt Brown	4	5	5	6	10	15	25	100
115	Don Chandler	4	5	5	5	8	12	20	80
116	Darrell Dess	4	5	5	5	8	12	20	60
117	Frank Gifford	4	6	8	12	20	35	60	200
118	Dick James	4	5	5	5	8	12	20	80
119	Jim Katcavage	4	5	5	5	8	12	20	80
120	John Lovetere	4	5	5	5	8	12	20	50
121	Dick Lynch RC	4	5	5	5	8	12	20	80
122	Jim Patton	4	5	5	5	8	12	20	80
123	Del Shofner	4	5	5	5	8	12	20	60
124	Y.A.Tittle	4	5	5	8	12	20	50	200
125	New York Giants Team	4	5	5	5	8	12	40	50
126	New York Giants Play	4	5	5	5	8	12	20	80
127	Sam Baker	4	5	5	5	8	12	20	60
128	Maxie Baughan	4	5	5	5	8	12	20	60
129	Timmy Brown	4	5	5	5	8	12	20	60
130	Mike Clark	4	5	5	5	8	12	20	80
131	Irv Cross RC	4	5	5	5	8	12	30	60
132	Ted Dean	4	5	5	5	8	12	20	60
133	Ron Goodwin	4	5	5	5	8	12	20	80
134	King Hill	4	5	5	5	8	12	20	80
135	Clarence Peaks	4	5	5	5	8	12	20	80
136	Pete Retzlaff	4	5	5	5	8	12	20	80
137	Jim Schrader	4	5	5	5	8	12	60	
138	Norm Snead	4	5	5	5	8	12	20	80
139	Philadelphia Eagles Team	4	5	5	5	8	12	25	80
140	Philadelphia Eagles Play	4	5	5	5	8	12	20	80
141	Gary Ballman RC	4	5	5	5	8	12	20	
142	Charley Bradshaw RC	4	5	5	5	8	12	20	50
143	Ed Brown	4	5	5	5	8	12	20	80
144	John Henry Johnson	4	5	5	6	10	15	25	80
145	Joe Krupa	4	5	5	5	8	12	30	
146	Bill Mack	4	5	5	5	8	12	20	
147	Lou Michaels	4	5	5	5	8	12	20	50
148	Buzz Nutter	4	5	5	5	8	12	20	
149	Myron Pottios	4	5	5	5	8	12	20	50
150	John Reger	4	5	5	5	8	12	50	
151	Mike Sandusky	4	5	5	5	8	12	20	80
152	Clendon Thomas	4	5	5	5	8	12	20	
153	Pittsburgh Steelers Team	4	5	5	5	8	12	40	175
154	Pittsburgh Steelers Play	4	5	5	5	8	12	20	40
155	Kermit Alexander RC	4	5	5	5	8	12	20	80
156	Bernie Casey	4	5	5	5	8	12	20	80
157	Dan Colchico	4	5	5	5	8	12	20	80
158	Clyde Conner	4	5	5	5	8	12	20	50
159	Tommy Davis	4	5	5	5	8	12	20	80
160	Matt Hazeltine	4	5	5	5	8	12	20	80
161	Jim Johnson RC	4	5	6	10	15	35	80	500
162	Don Lisbon RC	4	5	5	5	8	12	20	100
163	Lamar McHan	4	5	5	5	8	12	20	100
164	Bob St.Clair	4	5	5	6	10	15	25	80
165	J.D. Smith	4	5	5	5	8	12	20	100
166	Abe Woodson	4	5	5	5	8	12	20	60
167	San Francisco 49ers Team	4	5	5	5	8	12	20	80
168	San Francisco 49ers Play	4	5	5	5	8	12	20	60
169	Garland Boyette	4	5	5	5	8	12	20	60
170	Bobby Joe Conrad	4	5	5	5	8	12	20	80
171	Bob DeMarco RC	4	5	5	5	8	12	20	80
172	Ken Gray RC	4	5	5	5	8	12	20	80
173	Jimmy Hill	4	5	5	5	8	12	20	60
174	Charlie Johnson	4	5	5	5	8	12	20	50
175	Ernie McMillan	4	5	5	5	8	12	20	80
176	Dale Meinert	4	5	5	5	8	12	20	60
177	Luke Owens	4	5	5	5	8	12	20	80
178	Sonny Randle	4	5	5	5	8	12	20	80
179	Joe Robb	4	5	5	5	8	12	20	80
180	Bill Stacy	4	5	5	5	8	12	20	50
181	St. Louis Cardinals Team	4	5	5	5	8	12	20	80
182	St. Louis Cardinals Play	4	5	5	5	8	12	20	50

	GD 2	VG 3	VgEx 4	EX 5	ExMt 6	NM 7	NmMt 8	MT 9
Bill Barnes	4	5	5	5	8	12	40	
Don Bosseler	4	5	5	5	8	12	20	60
Sam Huff	4	5	5	8	12	18	30	
Sonny Jurgensen	4	5	5	8	12	20	50	150
Bob Khayat	4	5	5	5	8	12	20	80
Riley Mattson	4	5	5	5	8	12	20	
Bobby Mitchell	4	5	5	8	12	18	30	150
John Nisby	4	5	5	5	8	12	20	80
Vince Promuto	4	5	5	5	8	12	20	80
Joe Rutgens	4	5	5	5	8	12	20	50
Lonnie Sanders	4	5	5	5	8	12	20	
Jim Steffen	4	5	5	5	8	12	20	
Washington Redskins Team	4	5	5	5	8	15	150	
Washington Redskins Play	4	5	5	5	8	12	20	80
Checklist 1	4	5	5	8	15	40	200	
Checklist 2	4	5	6	10	20	60	120	

Bobby Mitchell #189 PSA 10 (Gem Mt) sold for $750 (eBay; 12/14)
Mike Ditka #17 PSA 10 (Gem Mt) sold for $3,353 (eBay; 5/11)
Mike Ditka #17 PSA 10 (Gem Mt) sold for $3,080 (Mile High; 1/07)
Paul Hornung #74 PSA 10 (Gem Mt) sold for $2832.2 (Goodwin; 3/12)
Tommy McDonald #50 PSA 10 (Gem Mt) sold for $970 (eBay; 1/06)
Merlin Olson #91 PSA 10 (Gem Mt) sold for $1,625 (eBay; 01/13)

964 Topps

	GD 2	VG 3	VgEx 4	EX 5	ExMt 6	NM 7	NmMt 8	MT 9
Tommy Addison SP	5	6	8	12	18	35	200	
Houston Antwine RC	4	5	5	5	8	12	80	
Nick Buoniconti	4	5	6	10	15	25	50	
Ron Burton SP	4	5	5	6	10	20	60	120
Gino Cappelletti	4	5	5	5	8	12	40	
Jim Colclough SP	4	5	6	10	15	40	100	
Bob Dee SP	4	5	5	6	10	15	100	
Larry Eisenhauer	4	5	5	5	8	12	30	80
Dick Felt SP	4	5	5	6	10	15	60	
Larry Garron	4	5	5	5	8	12	40	120
Art Graham	4	5	5	5	8	12	40	
Ron Hall DB	4	5	5	5	8	12	30	80
Charles Long	4	5	5	5	8	12	30	
Don McKinnon	4	5	5	5	8	12	30	175
Don Oakes SP	4	5	5	6	10	15	80	
Ross O'Hanley SP	4	5	5	6	10	15	60	225
Babe Parilli SP	4	5	5	6	10	15	40	225
Jesse Richardson SP	4	5	5	6	10	15	100	
Jack Rudolph SP	4	5	5	6	10	15	80	
Don Webb RC	4	5	5	5	8	12	40	250
Boston Patriots Team	4	5	5	6	10	15	40	
Ray Abruzzese	4	5	5	5	8	12	30	80
Stew Barber RC	4	5	5	5	8	12	30	200
Dave Behrman	4	5	5	5	8	12	40	
Al Bemiller	4	5	5	5	8	12	40	150
Elbert Dubenion SP	4	5	5	6	10	15	100	
Jim Dunaway SP RC	4	5	5	6	12	30	225	
Booker Edgerson SP	4	5	5	6	10	15	40	
Cookie Gilchrist SP	4	5	6	10	15	40	250	
Jack Kemp SP	12	15	18	30	40	60	150	400
Daryle Lamonica RC	10	12	15	25	40	60	125	350
Bill Miller	4	5	5	5	8	12	40	80
Herb Paterra RC	4	5	5	5	8	12	40	100
Ken Rice SP	4	5	5	6	10	15	60	120
Ed Rutkowski	4	5	5	5	8	12	40	120
George Saimes RC	4	5	5	5	8	12	30	150
Tom Sestak	4	5	5	5	8	12	30	80
Billy Shaw SP	4	5	5	8	12	20	100	
Mike Stratton	4	5	5	5	8	12	40	
Gene Sykes	4	5	5	5	8	12	30	100
John Tracey SP	4	5	5	6	10	15	120	
Sid Youngelman SP	4	5	5	6	10	15	60	120
Buffalo Bills Team	4	5	5	6	10	15	50	
Eldon Danenhauer SP	4	5	5	6	10	15	40	120
Jim Fraser SP	4	5	5	6	10	15	40	150
Chuck Gavin SP	4	5	5	6	10	15	60	
Goose Gonsoulin SP	4	5	5	6	10	15	60	
Ernie Barnes RC	4	5	5	5	8	12	30	80
Tom Janik	4	5	5	5	8	12	25	80
Billy Joe RC	4	5	5	5	8	12	40	100
Ike Lassiter RC	4	5	5	5	8	12	30	80
John McCormick QB SP	4	5	5	6	10	15	40	100
Bud McFadin SP	4	5	5	6	10	15	120	

		GD 2	VG 3	VgEx 4	EX 5	ExMt 6	NM 7	NmMt 8	MT 9
54	Gene Mingo SP	4	5	5	6	10	15	60	
55	Charlie Mitchell	4	5	5	5	8	12	30	80
56	John Nocera SP	4	5	5	6	10	15	40	▲150
57	Tom Nomina	4	5	5	5	8	12	40	80
58	Harold Olson SP	4	5	6	10	15	40	200	
59	Bob Scarpitto	4	5	5	5	8	12	40	
60	John Sklopan	4	5	5	5	8	12	30	80
61	Mickey Slaughter	4	5	5	5	8	12	60	
62	Don Stone	4	5	5	5	8	12	40	100
63	Jerry Sturm	4	5	5	5	8	12	40	100
64	Lionel Taylor SP	4	5	5	8	12	20	50	
65	Denver Broncos Team SP	4	5	5	8	12	20	175	
66	Scott Appleton RC	4	5	5	5	8	12	40	250
67	Tony Banfield SP	4	5	5	6	10	15	60	
68	George Blanda SP	12	15	18	30	50	80	135	
69	Billy Cannon	4	5	5	6	10	15	60	
70	Doug Cline SP	4	5	5	6	10	15	60	
71	Gary Cutsinger SP	4	5	5	6	10	15	40	
72	Willard Dewveall SP	4	5	5	6	10	15	30	
73	Don Floyd SP	4	5	5	6	10	15	60	
74	Freddy Glick SP	4	5	5	6	10	15	40	100
75	Charlie Hennigan SP	4	5	5	6	10	15	40	
76	Ed Husmann SP	4	5	5	6	10	15	60	
77	Bobby Jancik SP	4	5	5	6	10	15	30	175
78	Jacky Lee SP	4	5	5	6	10	15	80	175
79	Bob McLeod SP	4	5	5	6	10	15	50	
80	Rich Michael SP	4	5	5	6	10	15	60	
81	Larry Onesti RC	4	5	5	8	12	40	200	
82	Checklist Card 1	5	6	8	15	25	50	80	350
83	Bob Schmidt SP	4	5	5	6	10	15	80	
84	Walt Suggs SP	4	5	5	6	10	15	40	
85	Bob Talamini SP	4	5	5	5	8	12	30	150
86	Charley Tolar SP	4	5	5	6	10	15	100	
87	Don Trull RC	4	5	5	5	8	12	30	120
88	Houston Oilers Team	4	5	5	6	10	15	40	100
89	Fred Arbanas	4	5	5	5	8	12	60	
90	Bobby Bell RC	6	8	10	15	25	50	120	1,300
91	Mel Branch SP	4	5	5	6	10	15	60	
92	Buck Buchanan RC	6	8	10	15	25	50	150	800
93	Ed Budde RC	4	5	5	5	8	12	40	
94	Chris Burford SP	4	5	5	6	10	15	60	
95	Walt Corey RC	4	5	5	5	8	12	40	135
96	Len Dawson SP	12	15	18	30	50	75	250	1,200
97	Dave Grayson RC	4	5	5	5	8	12	50	100
98	Abner Haynes	4	5	5	6	10	15	150	
99	Sherrill Headrick SP	4	5	5	6	10	15	120	
100	E.J. Holub	4	5	5	5	8	15	200	
101	Bobby Hunt RC	4	5	5	5	8	12	40	200
102	Frank Jackson SP	4	5	5	6	10	15	40	100
103	Curtis McClinton	4	5	5	5	8	12	30	100
104	Jerry Mays SP	4	5	5	6	10	15	60	
105	Johnny Robinson SP	4	5	5	8	12	20	150	
106	Jack Spikes SP	4	5	5	6	10	25	120	
107	Smokey Stover SP	4	5	5	6	10	20		
108	Jim Tyrer RC	4	5	5	6	10	30	200	
109	Duane Wood SP	4	5	5	8	12	80	250	
110	Kansas City Chiefs Team	4	5	5	6	10	15	40	
111	Dick Christy SP	4	5	5	6	10	20	80	
112	Dan Ficca SP	4	5	5	6	10	15	60	200
113	Larry Grantham	4	5	5	5	8	12	40	
114	Curley Johnson SP	4	5	5	6	10	15	60	
115	Gene Heeter	4	5	5	5	8	12	30	100
116	Jack Klotz	4	5	5	5	8	12	30	120
117	Pete Liske RC	4	5	5	5	8	12	30	80
118	Bob McAdam	4	5	5	5	8	12	30	80
119	Dee Mackey SP	4	5	5	6	10	15	▼80	125
120	Bill Mathis SP	4	5	5	6	10	15	100	
121	Don Maynard	5	6	8	12	20	35	80	300
122	Dainard Paulson SP	4	5	5	6	10	15	60	
123	Gerry Philbin RC	4	5	5	5	8	12	40	120
124	Mark Smolinski SP	4	5	5	6	10	15	40	
125	Matt Snell RC	4	5	5	5	8	12	20	80
126	Mike Taliaferro	4	5	5	5	8	12	40	175
127	Bake Turner SP RC	4	5	5	6	10	15	60	
128	Jeff Ware	4	5	5	5	8	12	40	
129	Clyde Washington	4	5	5	5	8	12	60	
130	Dick Wood RC	4	5	5	5	8	12	30	100
131	New York Jets Team	4	5	5	6	10	15	40	150
132	Dalva Allen SP	4	5	5	6	10	15	100	

		GD 2	VG 3	VgEx 4	EX 5	ExMt 6	NM 7	NmMt 8	MT 9
133	Dan Birdwell	4	5	5	5	8	12	30	80
134	Dave Costa RC	4	5	5	5	8	12	30	80
135	Dobie Craig	4	5	5	5	8	12	40	
136	Clem Daniels	4	5	5	5	8	12	40	150
137	Cotton Davidson SP	4	5	5	6	10	15	100	
138	Claude Gibson	4	5	5	5	8	12	40	
139	Tom Flores SP	4	5	6	10	15	40	200	
140	Wayne Hawkins SP	4	5	5	6	10	15	60	
141	Ken Herock	4	5	5	5	8	12	40	
142	Jon Jelacic SP	4	5	5	6	10	15	175	
143	Joe Krakoski	4	5	5	5	8	12	30	80
144	Archie Matsos SP	4	5	5	6	10	15	60	120
145	Mike Mercer	4	5	5	5	8	12	40	
146	Alan Miller SP	4	5	5	6	10	15	60	
147	Bob Mischak SP	4	5	5	6	10	15	60	175
148	Jim Otto SP	5	6	8	12	20	30	125	
149	Clancy Osborne SP	4	5	5	6	10	15	60	
150	Art Powell SP	4	5	5	8	12	25		
151	Bo Roberson	4	5	5	5	8	12	40	
152	Fred Williamson SP	6	8	10	15	25	40	250	
153	Oakland Raiders Team	4	5	5	6	10	15	60	
154	Chuck Allen SP RC	4	5	5	5	8	12	40	150
155	Lance Alworth	8	10	12	18	35	60	100	400
156	George Blair	4	5	5	5	8	12	40	200
157	Earl Faison	4	5	5	5	8	12	30	150
158	Sam Gruneisen	4	5	5	5	8	12	40	
159	John Hadl RC	6	8	10	15	30	50	▼80	400
160	Dick Harris SP	4	5	5	6	10	15	40	225
161	Emil Karas SP	4	5	5	6	10	20	75	150
162	Dave Kocourek SP	4	5	5	6	10	20	100	
163	Ernie Ladd	4	5	5	6	10	15	40	
164	Keith Lincoln	4	5	5	5	8	12	50	120
165	Paul Lowe SP	4	5	5	8	12	20	60	
166	Charley McNeil	4	5	5	5	8	12	40	
167	Jacque MacKinnon SP RC	4	5	5	6	10	15	60	
168	Ron Mix SP	4	5	5	8	12	25	175	
169	Don Norton SP	4	5	5	6	10	15	80	
170	Don Rogers SP	4	5	5	6	10	15	150	
171	Tobin Rote SP	4	5	5	6	15	20	60	
172	Henry Schmidt SP RC	4	5	5	6	10	15	120	
173	Bud Whitehead	4	5	5	5	8	12	40	
174	Ernie Wright SP	4	5	5	8	12	40	250	
175	San Diego Chargers Team	4	5	5	8	15	30	100	200
176	Checklist Card 2 SP	12	15	20	35	60	150	300	

—Buck Buchanan #92 PSA 10 (Gem) sold for $7,503 (eBay; 1/15)
—Houston Antwine #2 PSA 9 (MT) sold for $515 (eBay; 10/07)
—Ed Budde #93 PSA 9 (MT) sold for $893 (eBay; 5/09)
—Jim Dunaway #27 PSA 8 (NmMt) sold for $1,029 (eBay; 2/10)
—Goose Gonsoulin SP #47 PSA 9 (MT) sold for $1,028.50 (eBay; 10/13)
—E.J. Holub #100 PSA 9 (MT) sold for $559 (eBay; 9/07)
—Frank Jackson #102 PSA 10 (Gem) sold for $1,477 (Mastro; 2/07)
—Daryle Lamonica RC #31 PSA 10 (Gem Mint) sold for $799.95 (eBay; 6/12)
—Don Norton SP #169 PSA 10 (Gem Mint) sold for $1099 (eBay; 11/14)
—Art Powell SP #150 PSA 8 (NM/MT) sold for $598.88 (eBay; 5/12)
—Jack Rudolph SP #19 PSA 9 (Mint) sold for $524.50 (eBay; 2/14)
—Mickey Slaughter #61 PSA 10 (Gem) sold for $1,365 (eBay; 1/07)
—Jim Tyrer RC #108 PSA 9 (Mint) sold for $1,283 (eBay; 11/13)

1965 Philadelphia

		GD 2	VG 3	VgEx 4	EX 5	ExMt 6	NM 7	NmMt 8	MT 9
1	Baltimore Colts Team	4	4	5	8	12	60	135	
2	Raymond Berry	4	4	5	6	10	15	100	
3	Bob Boyd DB	4	4	5	5	8	12	35	120
4	Wendell Harris	4	4	5	5	8	12	20	80
5	Jerry Logan	4	4	5	5	8	12	20	50
6	Tony Lorick	4	4	5	5	8	12	20	60
7	Lou Michaels	4	4	5	5	8	12	20	80
8	Lenny Moore	4	4	5	6	10	15	30	
9	Jimmy Orr	4	4	5	5	8	12	20	80
10	Jim Parker	4	4	5	6	10	15	30	
11	Dick Szymanski	4	4	5	5	8	12	20	80
12	Johnny Unitas	8	10	12	20	30	50	150	400
13	Bob Vogel RC	4	4	5	5	8	12	25	
14	Colts Play/Don Shula	4	4	5	8	12	20	40	
15	Chicago Bears Team	4	4	5	5	8	12	40	
16	Jon Arnett	4	4	5	5	8	12	20	50
17	Doug Atkins	4	4	5	6	10	15	30	80
18	Rudy Bukich RC	4	4	5	5	8	12	20	80

		GD 2	VG 3	VgEx 4	EX 5	ExMt 6	NM 7	NmMt 8	MT 9
19	Mike Ditka	5	6	8	12	20	40	100	
20	Dick Evey	4	4	5	5	8	12	20	80
21	Joe Fortunato	4	4	5	5	8	12	20	
22	Bobby Joe Green RC	4	4	5	5	8	12	20	80
23	Johnny Morris	4	4	5	5	8	12	50	80
24	Mike Pyle	4	4	5	5	8	12	20	
25	Roosevelt Taylor	4	4	5	5	8	12	20	
26	Bill Wade	4	4	5	5	8	12	20	80
27	Bob Wetoska	4	4	5	5	8	12	20	80
28	Bears Play/George Halas	4	4	5	6	10	15	30	100
29	Cleveland Browns Team	4	4	5	5	8	12	20	
30	Walter Beach	4	4	5	5	8	12	20	100
31	Jim Brown	20	25	30	40	80	150	▲350	1,200
32	Gary Collins	4	4	5	5	8	12	20	80
33	Bill Glass	4	4	5	5	8	12	20	80
34	Ernie Green	4	4	5	5	8	12	20	80
35	Jim Houston RC	4	4	6	12	40	60	200	
36	Dick Modzelewski	4	4	5	5	8	12	25	
37	Bernie Parrish	4	4	5	5	8	12	15	80
38	Walter Roberts	4	4	5	5	8	12	20	80
39	Frank Ryan	4	4	5	5	8	12	20	
40	Dick Schafrath	4	4	5	5	8	12	30	
41	Paul Warfield RC	12	20	30	50	100	125	300	1,500
42	Cleveland Browns Play	4	4	5	5	8	12	20	80
43	Dallas Cowboys Team	4	4	5	5	8	20	50	
44	Frank Clarke	4	4	5	5	8	12	20	80
45	Mike Connelly	4	4	5	5	8	12	20	
46	Buddy Dial	4	4	5	5	8	12	20	80
47	Bob Lilly	5	6	8	12	20	35	60	450
48	Tony Liscio RC	4	4	5	5	8	12	20	80
49	Tommy McDonald	4	4	5	6	10	15	30	100
50	Don Meredith	4	5	10	15	20	35	60	200
51	Pettis Norman	4	4	5	5	8	12	20	60
52	Don Perkins	4	4	5	6	10	15	25	80
53	Mel Renfro RC	8	10	15	40	50	80	300	1,200
54	Jim Ridlon	4	4	5	5	8	12	20	80
55	Jerry Tubbs	4	4	5	5	8	12	20	80
56	Cowboys Play/T.Landry	4	4	5	6	10	15	40	150
57	Detroit Lions Team	4	4	5	5	8	12	20	
58	Terry Barr	4	4	5	5	8	12	20	
59	Roger Brown	4	4	5	5	8	12	20	80
60	Gail Cogdill	4	4	5	5	8	12	20	80
61	Jim Gibbons	4	4	5	5	8	12	20	80
62	John Gordy	4	4	5	5	8	12	20	80
63	Yale Lary	4	4	5	6	10	15	30	100
64	Dick LeBeau RC	6	8	12	20	60	80	150	400
65	Earl Morrall	4	4	5	5	8	12	20	60
66	Nick Pietrosante	4	4	5	5	8	12	20	80
67	Pat Studstill	4	4	5	5	8	12	20	80
68	Wayne Walker	4	4	5	5	8	12	20	80
69	Tom Watkins	4	4	5	5	8	12	20	
70	Detroit Lions Play	4	4	5	5	8	12	20	
71	Green Bay Packers Team	4	4	5	6	10	15	50	200
72	Herb Adderley	4	4	5	6	10	15	40	
73	Willie Davis DE	4	4	5	6	10	20	40	
74	Boyd Dowler	4	4	5	6	10	15	25	80
75	Forrest Gregg	4	4	5	6	10	15	60	
76	Paul Hornung	5	6	8	12	20	40	80	200
77	Hank Jordan	4	4	5	6	10	15	50	
78	Tom Moore	4	4	5	5	8	12	40	80
79	Ray Nitschke	4	5	6	10	20	30	100	
80	Elijah Pitts RC	4	4	5	6	10	15	30	100
81	Bart Starr	8	10	15	25	35	80	200	600
82	Jim Taylor	4	5	6	10	15	25	60	300
83	Willie Wood	4	4	5	6	10	15	30	150
84	Packers Play/Lombardi	4	5	6	10	15	25	50	150
85	Los Angeles Rams Team	4	4	5	5	8	12	20	80
86	Dick Bass	4	4	5	5	8	12	20	80
87	Roman Gabriel	4	4	5	6	10	15	30	150
88	Roosevelt Grier	4	4	5	6	10	15	30	80
89	Deacon Jones	4	4	5	6	10	15	40	
90	Lamar Lundy RC	4	4	5	6	10	15	30	80
91	Marlin McKeever	4	4	5	5	8	12	20	50
92	Ed Meador	4	4	5	5	8	12	20	50
93	Bill Munson RC	4	4	5	6	10	15	20	80
94	Merlin Olsen	4	4	5	6	10	15	40	120
95	Bobby Smith	4	4	5	5	8	12	20	50
96	Frank Varrichione	4	4	5	5	8	12	20	50
97	Ben Wilson	4	4	5	5	8	12	20	80

	GD 2	VG 3	VgEx 4	EX 5	ExMt 6	NM 7	NmMt 8	MT 9
Los Angeles Rams Play	4	4	5	5	8	12	20	
Minnesota Vikings Team	4	4	5	5	8	12	20	
Grady Alderman	4	4	5	5	8	12	20	60
Hal Bedsole RC	4	4	5	5	8	12	20	50
Bill Brown	4	4	5	5	8	12	20	80
Bill Butler	4	4	5	5	8	12	20	80
Fred Cox RC	4	4	5	5	8	12	20	100
Carl Eller RC	6	8	10	20	25	50	100	400
Paul Flatley	4	4	5	5	8	12	20	50
Jim Marshall	4	4	5	6	10	15	30	
Tommy Mason	4	4	5	5	8	12	20	125
George Rose	4	4	5	5	8	12	20	80
Fran Tarkenton	4	5	6	10	15	30	80	
Mick Tingelhoff	4	4	5	5	8	12	20	
Vikings Play/Van Brock.	4	4	5	6	10	15	60	
New York Giants Team	4	4	5	5	8	12	20	
Erich Barnes	4	4	5	5	8	15	150	
Roosevelt Brown	4	4	5	6	10	15	40	
Clarence Childs	4	4	5	5	8	12	20	50
Jerry Hillebrand	4	4	5	5	8	12	20	
Greg Larson RC	4	4	5	5	8	12	20	60
Dick Lynch	4	4	5	5	8	12	20	80
Joe Morrison RC	4	4	5	6	10	15	25	60
Lou Slaby	4	4	5	5	8	12	20	80
Aaron Thomas RC	4	4	5	5	8	12	20	
Steve Thurlow	4	4	5	5	8	12	20	
Ernie Wheelwright RC	4	4	5	5	8	12	20	80
Gary Wood RC	4	4	5	5	8	12	20	80
New York Giants Play	4	4	5	5	8	12	20	
Philadelphia Eagles Team	4	4	5	5	8	15	40	
Sam Baker	4	4	5	5	8	15	120	
Maxie Baughan	4	4	5	5	8	12	20	80
Timmy Brown	4	4	5	5	8	12	20	80
Jack Concannon RC	4	4	5	5	8	12	20	50
Irv Cross	4	4	5	5	8	12	20	
Earl Gros	4	4	5	5	8	12	20	50
Dave Lloyd	4	4	5	5	8	12	20	
Floyd Peters RC	4	4	5	5	8	12	20	80
Nate Ramsey	4	4	5	5	8	12	20	80
Pete Retzlaff	4	4	5	5	8	12	20	
Jim Ringo	4	4	5	6	10	15	40	
Norm Snead	4	4	5	6	10	15	40	60
Philadelphia Eagles Play	4	4	5	5	8	12	20	80
Pittsburgh Steelers Team	4	4	5	5	8	12	40	80
John Baker	4	4	5	5	8	12	20	
Gary Ballman	4	4	5	5	8	12	20	80
Charley Bradshaw	4	4	5	5	8	12	20	80
Ed Brown	4	4	5	5	8	12	20	
Dick Haley	4	4	5	5	8	15	80	120
John Henry Johnson	4	4	5	6	10	15	40	
Brady Keys	4	4	5	5	8	12	20	50
Ray Lemek	4	4	5	5	8	12	20	80
Ben McGee	4	4	5	5	8	12	20	50
Clarence Peaks UER	4	4	5	5	8	12	20	50
Myron Pottios	4	4	5	5	8	12	20	80
Clendon Thomas	4	4	5	5	8	12	20	50
Pittsburgh Steelers Play	4	4	5	5	8	12	20	
St. Louis Cardinals Team	4	4	5	5	8	12	20	
Jim Bakken RC	4	4	5	5	8	15	50	100
Joe Childress	4	4	5	5	8	12	20	
Bobby Joe Conrad	4	4	5	5	8	12	20	80
Bob DeMarco	4	4	5	5	8	12	20	80
Pat Fischer RC	4	4	5	6	10	15	50	
Irv Goode	4	4	5	5	8	12	15	60
Ken Gray	4	4	5	5	8	12	20	80
Charlie Johnson.	4	4	5	5	8	12	20	60
Bill Koman	4	4	5	5	8	12	20	
Dale Meinert	4	4	5	5	8	12	20	60
Jerry Stovall RC	4	4	5	5	8	12	20	80
Abe Woodson	4	4	5	5	8	12	20	60
St. Louis Cardinals Play	4	4	5	5	8	12	20	80
San Francisco 49ers Team	4	4	5	5	8	12	30	80
Kermit Alexander	4	4	5	5	8	12	20	80
John Brodie	4	4	5	6	10	15	30	150
Bernie Casey	4	4	5	5	8	12	20	
John David Crow	4	4	5	5	8	12	20	60
Tommy Davis	4	4	5	5	8	12	20	80
Matt Hazeltine	4	4	5	5	8	12	20	80
Jim Johnson	4	4	5	6	10	15	30	100

	GD 2	VG 3	VgEx 4	EX 5	ExMt 6	NM 7	NmMt 8	MT 9
177 Charlie Krueger RC	4	4	5	5	8	12	20	80
178 Roland Lakes	4	4	5	5	8	12	20	60
179 George Mira RC	4	4	5	5	8	12	20	80
180 Dave Parks RC	4	4	5	5	8	12	20	80
181 John Thomas RC	4	4	5	5	8	12	20	
182 49ers Play/Christiansen	4	4	5	5	8	12	20	80
183 Washington Redskins Team	4	4	5	5	8	12	20	80
184 Pervis Atkins	4	4	5	5	8	12	20	
185 Preston Carpenter	4	4	5	5	8	12	20	80
186 Angelo Coia	4	4	5	5	8	12	20	
187 Sam Huff	4	4	5	5	8	10	15	60	125
188 Sonny Jurgensen	4	4	5	6	10	15	60	
189 Paul Krause RC	6	6	10	15	30	60	150	800
190 Jim Martin	4	4	5	5	8	12	20	
191 Bobby Mitchell	4	4	5	6	10	15	30	80
192 John Nisby	4	4	5	5	8	12	20	
193 John Paluck	4	4	5	5	8	12	20	80
194 Vince Promuto	4	4	5	5	8	12	20	80
195 Charley Taylor RC	6	8	10	25	40	100	200	800
196 Washington Redskins Play	4	4	5	5	8	15	40	
197 Checklist 1	4	5	6	10	15	30	60	150
198 Checklist 2	6	8	10	15	25	60	120	

—Raymond Berry #2 PSA 9 (MT) sold for $488 (eBay; 1/08)
—Carl Eller #105 PSA 10 (Gem Mt) sold for $8,284 (Mile High; 6/10)
—Deacon Jones #89 PSA 9 (MT) sold for $465 (eBay; 6/06)
—Tommy Mason #108 PSA 10 (Gem) sold for $795 (eBay; 2/07)
—Ray Nitschke #79 PSA 9 (MT) sold for $525 (eBay; 1/08)
—Fran Tarkenton #110 PSA 9 (MT) sold for $1,228 (eBay; 9/09)
—Fran Tarkenton #110 PSA 9 (Mint) sold for $420 (Bussineau; 4/12)
—Charley Taylor #195 PSA 10 (Gem Mt) sold for $8,284 (Mile High; 10/09)
—Paul Warfield #41 PSA 10 (Gem Mt) sold for $11,027 (Mile High; 6/10)

1965 Topps

		GD 2	VG 3	VgEx 4	EX 5	ExMt 6	NM 7	NmMt 8	MT 9
1	Tommy Addison SP	6	8	10	15	25	40	▲400	
2	Houston Antwine SP	5	6	8	12	20	50	175	
3	Nick Buoniconti SP	6	8	10	15	30	80	500	
4	Ron Burton SP	6	8	10	15	25	80	250	
5	Gino Cappelletti SP	6	8	10	15	▲40	▲50	200	
6	Jim Colclough	5	5	6	8	▲50	▲100		
7	Bob Dee SP	5	5	6	8	12	20	30	60
8	Larry Eisenhauer	5	5	6	8	15	▲30	60	
9	J.D. Garrett	5	5	6	8	15	25	60	
10	Larry Garron	5	5	6	8	15	25	60	
11	Art Graham SP	5	6	8	12	20	30	▲80	
12	Ron Hall DB	5	5	6	8	15	25	125	250
13	Charles Long	5	5	6	8	15	25	50	
14	Jon Morris RC	5	5	6	8	15	25	50	
15	Billy Neighbors SP	5	6	8	12	20	30	60	
16	Ross O'Hanley	5	5	6	8	15	25	100	
17	Babe Parilli SP	6	8	10	15	25	35	150	
18	Tony Romeo SP	5	6	8	12	20	30	60	
19	Jack Rudolph SP	5	6	8	12	20	30	60	
20	Bob Schmidt	5	5	6	8	15	25	60	
21	Don Webb SP	5	6	8	12	20	30	60	
22	Jim Whalen SP	5	6	8	12	20	30	80	
23	Stew Barber	5	5	6	8	15	60	400	
24	Glenn Bass SP	5	6	8	12	20	30	60	
25	Al Bemiller SP	5	6	8	12	20	30	60	
26	Wray Carlton SP	5	6	8	12	▲30	▲40	▲100	
27	Tom Day	5	5	6	8	15	▲30	60	
28	Elbert Dubenion SP	5	6	8	12	20	30	80	
29	Jim Dunaway	5	5	6	8	15	25	60	
30	Pete Gogolak SP RC	6	8	10	15	30	40	150	
31	Dick Hudson SP	5	6	8	12	20	30	60	
32	Harry Jacobs SP	5	6	8	12	20	30	60	
33	Billy Joe SP	5	6	8	12	20	30	100	
34	Tom Keating RC SP	5	6	8	12	20	40	250	
35	Jack Kemp SP	20	25	40	50	80	125	250	
36	Daryle Lamonica SP	8	10	12	20	30	80	150	
37	Paul Maguire SP	6	8	10	15	25	35	▲150	
38	Ron McDole SP RC	5	6	8	12	20	30	100	
39	George Saimes SP	5	6	8	12	20	30	100	
40	Tom Sestak SP	5	6	8	12	20	30	60	
41	Billy Shaw SP	6	8	10	15	25	100	200	
42	Mike Stratton SP	5	6	8	12	20	30	80	300
43	John Tracey SP	5	6	8	12	20	30	60	
44	Ernie Warlick	5	5	6	8	15	25	50	300

FOOTBALL

		GD 2	VG 3	VgEx 4	EX 5	ExMt 6	NM 7	NmMt 8	MT 9
45	Odell Barry	5	5	6	8	15	80		
46	Willie Brown SP RC	20	25	30	50	150	300	500	
47	Gerry Bussell SP	5	6	8	12	20	30	60	
48	Eldon Danenhauer SP	5	6	8	12	20	30	60	
49	Al Denson SP	5	6	8	12	20	30	150	
50	Hewritt Dixon SP RC	5	6	8	12	20	30	200	
51	Cookie Gilchrist SP	6	8	10	15	25	▲50	120	
52	Goose Gonsoulin SP	5	6	8	12	20	30	▼100	
53	Abner Haynes SP	6	8	10	15	25	35	100	
54	Jerry Hopkins	5	5	6	8	15	60	200	
55	Ray Jacobs SP	5	6	8	12	20	30	60	
56	Jacky Lee SP	5	6	8	12	20	40	200	
57	John McCormick QB	5	5	6	8	15	25	50	
58	Bob McCullough SP	5	6	8	12	20	30	120	
59	John McGeever	5	5	6	8	15	25	50	
60	Charlie Mitchell SP	5	6	8	12	20	30	50	
61	Jim Perkins SP	5	6	8	12	20	30	100	
62	Bob Scarpitto SP	5	6	8	12	20	30	100	
63	Mickey Slaughter SP	5	6	8	12	20	30	100	
64	Jerry Sturm SP	5	6	8	12	20	30	200	
65	Lionel Taylor SP	6	8	10	15	25	40	100	300
66	Scott Appleton SP	5	6	8	12	20	30	60	300
67	Johnny Baker SP	5	6	8	12	20	30	60	
68	Sonny Bishop SP	5	6	8	12	20	30	60	
69	George Blanda SP	15	20	25	40	100	125	250	
70	Sid Blanks SP	5	6	8	12	15	30	60	
71	Ode Burrell SP	5	6	8	12	20	30	80	
72	Doug Cline SP	5	6	8	12	20	25	40	250
73	Willard Dewveall	5	5	6	8	15	25	80	300
74	Larry Elkins RC	5	5	6	8	15	25	50	
75	Don Floyd SP	5	6	8	12	20	30	60	
76	Freddy Glick	5	5	6	8	15	25	50	
77	Tom Goode SP	5	6	8	12	20	30	60	
78	Charlie Hennigan SP	6	8	10	15	25	35	100	
79	Ed Husmann	5	5	6	8	15	25	50	
80	Bobby Jancik SP	5	6	8	12	20	30	60	
81	Bud McFadin SP	5	6	8	12	20	30	100	
82	Bob McLeod SP	5	6	8	12	20	30	▲80	300
83	Jim Norton SP	5	6	8	12	20	30	400	
84	Walt Suggs	5	5	6	8	15	25	▲60	
85	Bob Talamini	5	5	6	8	15	25	50	
86	Charley Tolar SP	5	6	8	12	20	30	60	250
87	Checklist SP	20	25	35	60	150	200	▼250	
88	Don Trull SP	5	6	8	12	20	30	▲80	
89	Fred Arbanas SP	5	6	8	12	20	50	120	
90	Pete Beathard SP RC	5	6	8	12	20	80	▲200	
91	Bobby Bell SP	6	8	10	15	25	50	120	
92	Mel Branch SP	5	6	8	12	15	30	▲80	
93	Tommy Brooker SP	5	6	8	12	20	30	60	
94	Buck Buchanan SP	6	8	10	15	25	120		
95	Ed Budde SP	5	6	8	12	20	30	60	
96	Chris Burford SP	5	6	8	12	20	50	120	
97	Walt Corey	5	5	6	8	15	25	50	
98	Jerry Cornelison	5	5	6	8	15	25	50	200
99	Len Dawson SP	15	20	25	40	80	100	250	
100	Jon Gilliam SP	5	6	8	12	20	30	60	
101	Sherrill Headrick SP	5	6	8	12	20	30	150	
102	Dave Hill SP	5	6	8	12	20	30	60	
103	E.J. Holub SP	5	6	8	12	20	30	60	
104	Bobby Hunt SP	5	6	8	12	15	▲40	▲80	
105	Frank Jackson SP	5	6	8	12	20	30	300	
106	Jerry Mays	5	5	6	8	15	25	50	
107	Curtis McClinton SP	5	6	8	12	20	30	60	
108	Bobby Ply SP	5	6	8	12	15	30	60	
109	Johnny Robinson SP	5	6	8	12	20	30	100	
110	Jim Tyrer SP	5	6	8	12	20	30	80	300
111	Bill Baird SP	5	6	8	12	20	30	60	
112	Ralph Baker SP RC	5	6	8	12	20	30	100	400
113	Sam DeLuca SP	5	6	8	12	20	30	50	
114	Larry Grantham SP	5	6	8	12	20	30	80	
115	Gene Heeter SP	5	6	8	12	20	30	60	
116	Winston Hill SP RC	6	8	10	15	25	40	125	
117	John Huarte SP RC	6	8	10	15	25	50	120	
118	Cosmo Iacavazzi SP	5	6	8	12	20	30	60	
119	Curley Johnson SP	5	6	8	12	20	30	60	
120	Dee Mackey	5	5	6	8	15	25	50	300
121	Don Maynard	8	10	12	40	▲80	▲100	250	
122	Joe Namath SP RC	1,000	1,200	1,600	3,000	5,000	10,000	30,000	
123	Dainard Paulson	5	5	6	8	15	25	50	

		GD 2	VG 3	VgEx 4	EX 5	ExMt 6	NM 7	NmMt 8	MT 9
124	Gerry Philbin SP	5	6	8	12	20	30	▲80	
125	Sherman Plunkett SP RC	5	6	8	12	20	30	80	
126	Mark Smolinski	5	5	6	8	15	25	50	300
127	Matt Snell SP	6	8	10	15	25	40	100	▲500
128	Mike Taliaferro SP	5	6	8	12	20	▲40	60	350
129	Bake Turner SP	5	6	8	12	20	30	150	
130	Clyde Washington SP	5	6	8	12	20	30	60	
131	Verlon Biggs SP RC	5	6	8	12	20	40	100	
132	Dalva Allen	5	5	6	8	15	35	200	
133	Fred Biletnikoff SP RC	40	80	80	300	400	600	1,200	10,000
134	Billy Cannon SP	6	8	10	15	25	50	150	
135	Dave Costa SP	5	6	8	12	20	100	300	
136	Clem Daniels SP	5	6	8	12	30	100	300	
137	Ben Davidson SP RC	10	12	20	30	50	100	300	
138	Cotton Davidson SP	5	6	8	12	20	40	60	
139	Tom Flores SP	6	8	10	15	25	40	100	
140	Claude Gibson	5	5	6	8	15	25	50	
141	Wayne Hawkins	5	5	6	8	15	35	50	300
142	Archie Matsos SP	5	6	8	12	20	30	60	
143	Mike Mercer SP	5	6	8	12	20	30	▲80	
144	Bob Mischak SP	5	6	8	12	20	30	80	
145	Jim Otto	6	8	10	15	30	40	150	
146	Art Powell	5	5	6	8	15	50	120	
147	Warren Powers DB SP	5	6	8	12	20	40	▲100	
148	Ken Rice SP	5	6	8	12	20	60	175	
149	Bo Roberson SP	5	6	8	12	20	30	120	
150	Harry Schuh RC	5	5	6	8	15	25	50	
151	Larry Todd SP	5	6	8	12	20	35	▲80	350
152	Fred Williamson SP	6	8	10	15	25	40	120	
153	J.R. Williamson	5	5	6	8	15	25	50	
154	Chuck Allen	5	5	6	8	15	▲40	60	
155	Lance Alworth	12	15	20	30	50	80	300	
156	Frank Buncom	5	5	6	8	15	25	50	
157	Steve DeLong SP RC	5	6	8	12	20	30	60	
158	Earl Faison SP	5	6	8	12	20	40	80	
159	Kenny Graham SP	5	6	8	12	20	30	60	
160	George Gross SP	5	6	8	12	20	30	60	
161	John Hadl SP	6	8	12	20	35	60	135	
162	Emil Karas SP	5	6	8	12	20	30	60	
163	Dave Kocourek SP	5	6	8	12	20	30	150	
164	Ernie Ladd SP	6	8	10	15	25	50	120	
165	Keith Lincoln SP	6	8	10	15	25	40	100	
166	Paul Lowe SP	6	8	10	15	25	35	100	
167	Jacque MacKinnon	5	5	6	8	15	25	50	
168	Ron Mix	6	8	10	15	25	40	100	
169	Don Norton SP	5	6	8	12	20	▲40	60	
170	Bob Petrich	5	5	6	8	15	25	50	
171	Rick Redman SP	5	6	8	12	20	30	60	250
172	Pat Shea	5	5	6	8	15	30	60	
173	Walt Sweeney SP RC	5	6	8	12	20	50	150	
174	Dick Westmoreland RC	5	5	6	10	30	80	150	
175	Ernie Wright SP	6	8	10	15	25	60	150	
176	Checklist SP	30	40	60	100	175	300	600	

—Tommy Addison #1 PSA 9 (MT) sold for $1,735 (Memory Lane; 4/07)
—Willie Brown #46 PSA 9 (MT) sold for $3215 (eBay; 11/14)
—Checklist #87 PSA 9 (MT) sold for $1,485 (Mile High; 3/09)
—Clem Daniels #136 PSA 9 (MT) sold for $2,555 (eBay; 11/08)
—Sam DeLuca SP #113 PSA 9 (Mint) sold for $500.89 (eBay; 8/12)
—Tom Keating SP RC #34 PSA 9 (Mint) sold for $1042 (eBay; 8/12)
—Joe Namath #122 PSA 8.5 (NmMT+) sold for $15,000 (eBay; 1/14)
—Billy Shaw #41 PSA 9 (MT) sold for $1,004 (eBay; 10/08)
—Jim Whalen SP #22 PSA 9 (Mint) sold for $414.89 (eBay; 8/12)

1966 Philadelphia

		GD 2	VG 3	VgEx 4	EX 5	ExMt 6	NM 7	NmMt 8	MT 9
1	Atlanta Falcons Logo	4	6	5	8	12	20	50	
2	Larry Benz	4	5	5	5	12	30		
3	Dennis Claridge	4	5	5	5	8	15	50	
4	Perry Lee Dunn	4	5	5	5	8	15	50	
5	Dan Grimm	4	5	5	5	8	15	50	
6	Alex Hawkins	4	5	5	5	8	15	40	
7	Ralph Heck	4	5	5	5	8	15	50	
8	Frank Lasky	4	5	5	5	8	15	50	
9	Guy Reese	4	5	5	5	8	15	50	
10	Bob Richards	4	5	5	5	8	15	50	
11	Ron Smith RC	4	5	5	5	8	15	50	
12	Ernie Wheelwright	4	5	5	5	8	15	30	
13	Atlanta Falcons Roster	4	5	5	5	8	15	50	

	GD 2	VG 3	VgEx 4	EX 5	ExMt 6	NM 7	NmMt 8	MT 9
Baltimore Colts Team	4	5	5	5	8	15	50	
Raymond Berry	4	5	5	6	10	15	50	150
Bob Boyd DB	4	5	5	5	8	12	50	60
Jerry Logan	4	5	5	5	8	12	50	80
John Mackey	4	5	5	6	10	15	50	
Tom Matte	4	5	5	5	8	15	60	
Lou Michaels	4	5	5	5	8	15	50	
Lenny Moore	4	5	5	6	12	20	50	
Jimmy Orr	4	5	5	5	8	15	50	
Jim Parker	4	5	5	5	8	15	50	
Johnny Unitas	12	15	20	25	50	125	250	
Bob Vogel	4	5	5	5	8	15	50	
Colts Play/Moore/Parker	4	5	5	5	8	15	50	
Chicago Bears Team	4	5	5	5	8	12	25	80
Doug Atkins	4	5	5	5	8	15	50	
Rudy Bukich	4	5	5	5	8	15	50	
Ronnie Bull	4	5	5	5	8	15	50	
Dick Butkus RC	100	125	▲200	250	400	600	2,000	
Mike Ditka	8	12	12	15	25	40	100	400
Joe Fortunato	4	5	5	5	8	15	50	
Bobby Joe Green	4	5	5	5	8	15	50	
Roger LeClerc	4	5	5	5	10	25	100	
Johnny Morris	4	5	5	5	8	15	50	
Mike Pyle	4	5	5	5	8	15	50	
Gale Sayers RC	60	100	125	250	250	500	1,000	3,000
Bears Play/G.Sayers	8	10	12	15	25	40	100	300
Cleveland Browns Team	4	5	5	5	8	15	80	
Jim Brown	20	25	30	50	60	120	600	800
Gary Collins	4	5	5	5	8	15	50	
Ross Fichtner	4	5	5	5	8	15	60	
Ernie Green	4	5	5	5	8	15	50	80
Gene Hickerson RC	8	10	12	15	25	40	120	
Jim Houston	4	5	5	5	8	15	50	
John Morrow	4	5	5	5	8	15	50	100
Walter Roberts	4	5	5	5	8	15	50	
Frank Ryan	4	5	5	5	8	15	50	
Dick Schafrath	4	5	5	5	8	15	50	
Paul Wiggin RC	4	5	5	5	8	12	25	100
Cleveland Browns Play	4	5	5	5	8	15	50	
Dallas Cowboys Team	4	5	5	5	8	15	100	
George Andrie RC	4	5	5	6	10	20	120	
Frank Clarke	4	5	5	5	8	15	50	
Mike Connelly	4	5	5	5	8	15	50	
Cornell Green	4	5	5	5	15	40		
Bob Hayes RC	20	25	30	50	75	200	250	
Chuck Howley RC	6	8	10	20	30	100	250	
Bob Lilly	5	6	6	8	12	20	50	
Don Meredith	6	8	8	10	15	35	60	
Don Perkins	4	5	5	5	15	50		
Mel Renfro	5	6	6	8	12	20	40	
Danny Villanueva	4	5	5	5	8	15	50	
Dallas Cowboys Play	4	5	5	5	8	12	25	80
Detroit Lions Team	4	5	5	5	8	15	50	
Roger Brown	4	5	5	5	8	15	50	
John Gordy	4	5	5	5	15	40		
Alex Karras	5	6	6	8	12	30	50	200
Dick LeBeau	4	5	5	5	8	15	50	
Amos Marsh	4	5	5	5	8	15	50	
Milt Plum	4	5	5	5	8	12	25	80
Bobby Smith	4	5	5	5	8	15	50	
Wayne Rasmussen	4	5	5	5	8	15	50	
Pat Studstill	4	5	5	5	8	15	50	
Wayne Walker	4	5	5	5	8	15	30	
Tom Watkins	4	5	5	5	8	15	30	
Detroit Lions Play	4	5	5	5	8	15	30	
Green Bay Packers Team	4	5	5	6	10	20	50	
Herb Adderley	4	5	5	6	10	15	30	300
Lee Roy Caffey RC	4	5	5	5	8	15	60	
Don Chandler	4	5	5	5	8	15	80	
Willie Davis DE	4	5	5	6	10	25	60	
Boyd Dowler	4	5	5	5	8	20	50	
Forrest Gregg	4	5	5	5	8	15	50	
Tom Moore	4	5	5	5	8	15	50	
Ray Nitschke	5	6	6	8	12	40	150	
Bart Starr	10	12	15	30	40	80	150	600
Jim Taylor	5	6	6	8	12	20	60	
Willie Wood	4	5	5	6	10	15	50	
Green Bay Packers Play	4	5	5	5	8	20	50	
Los Angeles Rams Team	4	5	5	5	8	15	50	

		GD 2	VG 3	VgEx 4	EX 5	ExMt 6	NM 7	NmMt 8	MT 9
93	Willie Brown WR	4	5	5	5	8	15	50	
94	R.Gabriel/D.Bass	4	5	5	5	8	15	50	
95	Bruce Gossett RC	4	5	5	5	8	15	50	
96	Deacon Jones	4	5	5	6	10	15	30	100
97	Tommy McDonald	4	5	5	5	8	12	30	80
98	Marlin McKeever	4	5	5	5	8	15	50	
99	Aaron Martin	4	5	5	5	8	15	50	
100	Ed Meador	4	5	5	5	8	15	50	
101	Bill Munson	4	5	5	5	8	12	25	80
102	Merlin Olsen	4	5	5	6	10	15	40	150
103	Jim Stiger	4	5	5	5	8	12	25	80
104	Rams Play/W.Brown	4	5	5	5	8	15	30	
105	Minnesota Vikings Team	4	5	5	5	8	15	50	
106	Grady Alderman	4	5	5	5	8	15	50	
107	Bill Brown	4	5	5	5	8	12	25	100
108	Fred Cox	4	5	5	5	8	15	60	
109	Paul Flatley	4	5	5	5	8	15	50	
110	Rip Hawkins	4	5	5	5	8	15	30	
111	Tommy Mason	4	5	5	5	15	40		
112	Ed Sharockman	4	5	5	5	8	15	50	
113	Gordon Smith	4	5	5	5	8	15	50	
114	Fran Tarkenton	6	8	10	12	18	60	100	
115	Mick Tingelhoff	4	5	5	5	8	15	120	
116	Bobby Walden RC	4	5	5	5	8	15	40	
117	Minnesota Vikings Play	4	5	5	5	8	15	50	
118	New York Giants Team	4	5	5	5	8	12	25	60
119	Roosevelt Brown	4	5	5	5	8	12	25	80
120	Henry Carr RC	4	5	5	6	12	30	80	
121	Clarence Childs	4	5	5	5	8	15	30	
122	Tucker Frederickson RC	4	5	5	5	8	15	50	
123	Jerry Hillebrand	4	5	5	5	8	15	50	
124	Greg Larson	4	5	5	5	8	15	50	
125	Spider Lockhart RC	4	5	5	5	8	15	60	
126	Dick Lynch	4	5	5	5	8	15	50	
127	E.Morrall/B.Scholtz	4	5	5	5	8	15	50	
128	Joe Morrison	4	5	5	5	8	15	50	
129	Steve Thurlow	4	5	5	5	8	15	60	
130	New York Giants Play	4	5	5	5	8	12	25	50
131	Philadelphia Eagles Team	4	5	5	5	8	12	25	80
132	Sam Baker	4	5	5	5	8	15	50	
133	Maxie Baughan	4	5	5	5	8	15	50	
134	Bob Brown OT RC	5	6	6	8	12	30	250	
135	Timmy Brown	4	5	5	5	8	15	50	
136	Irv Cross	4	5	5	5	15	60		
137	Earl Gros	4	5	5	5	8	15	50	
138	Ray Poage	4	5	5	5	8	15	50	
139	Nate Ramsey	4	5	5	5	8	15	50	
140	Pete Retzlaff	4	5	5	5	8	15	50	
141	Jim Ringo	4	5	5	5	8	15	50	
142	Norm Snead	4	5	5	5	8	15	50	
143	Philadelphia Eagles Play	4	5	5	5	8	15	60	
144	Pittsburgh Steelers Team	4	5	5	5	8	15	50	
145	Gary Ballman	4	5	5	5	8	15	50	
146	Jim Bradshaw	4	5	5	5	15	40		
147	Jim Butler	4	5	5	5	8	15	50	
148	Mike Clark	4	5	5	5	8	15	50	
149	Dick Hoak RC	4	5	5	5	8	15	50	
150	Roy Jefferson RC	4	5	5	5	8	15	50	
151	Frank Lambert	4	5	5	5	8	15	30	
152	Mike Lind	4	5	5	5	8	15	50	
153	Bill Nelsen RC	4	5	5	5	8	15	50	
154	Clarence Peaks	4	5	5	5	8	15	50	
155	Clendon Thomas	4	5	5	5	8	15	50	
156	Pittsburgh Steelers Play	4	5	5	5	8	15	50	
157	St. Louis Cardinals Team	4	5	5	5	8	15	50	
158	Jim Bakken	4	5	5	5	8	15	40	
159	Bobby Joe Conrad	4	5	5	5	8	15	40	80
160	Willis Crenshaw RC	4	5	5	5	8	15	50	
161	Bob DeMarco	4	5	5	5	8	15	50	
162	Pat Fischer	4	5	5	5	8	15	50	
163	Charlie Johnson	4	5	5	5	8	12	25	120
164	Dale Meinert	4	5	5	5	8	15	30	
165	Sonny Randle	4	5	5	5	8	15	50	
166	Sam Silas RC	4	5	5	5	8	15	30	
167	Bill Triplett	4	5	5	5	8	15	50	
168	Larry Wilson	4	5	5	5	8	15	50	
169	St. Louis Cardinals Play	4	5	5	5	8	15	50	
170	San Francisco 49ers Team	4	5	5	5	8	15	50	
171	Kermit Alexander	4	5	5	5	8	15	50	

#	Player	GD 2	VG 3	VgEx 4	EX 5	ExMt 6	NM 7	NmMt 8	MT 9
172	Bruce Bosley	4	5	5	5	8	15	50	
173	John Brodie	4	5	5	6	10	15	50	
174	Bernie Casey	4	5	5	5	8	15	50	
175	John David Crow	4	5	5	5	8	12	25	
176	Tommy Davis	4	5	5	5	8	15	50	
177	Jim Johnson	4	5	5	5	8	15	40	
178	Gary Lewis RC	4	5	5	5	8	15	50	
179	Dave Parks	4	5	5	5	8	15	50	
180	Walter Rock RC	4	5	5	5	8	15	50	
181	Ken Willard RC	4	5	5	5	8	15	50	
182	San Francisco 49ers Play	4	5	5	5	8	12	20	40
183	Washington Redskins Team	4	5	5	5	8	15	50	
184	Rickie Harris	4	5	5	5	8	40		
185	Sonny Jurgensen	4	5	5	6	10	20	50	
186	Paul Krause	4	5	5	6	10	15	50	
187	Bobby Mitchell	4	5	5	6	10	15	60	
188	Vince Promuto	4	5	5	5	8	15	80	
189	Pat Richter RC	4	5	5	5	8	15	50	
190	Joe Rutgens	4	5	5	5	8	15	50	
191	Johnny Sample	4	5	5	5	8	15	50	
192	Lonnie Sanders	4	5	5	5	8	15	50	
193	Jim Steffen	4	5	5	5	8	12	25	100
194	Charley Taylor	5	6	8	12	20	40		
195	Washington Redskins Play	4	5	5	5	8	15	50	
196	Referee Signals	4	5	5	5	8	15	50	
197	Checklist 1	6	8	8	10	15	25	60	175
198	Checklist 2 UER	6	8	10	12	25	80	250	

—George Andrie #54 PSA 9 (MT) sold for $925 (eBay; 8/06)
—Sam Baker #132 PSA 9 (MT) sold for $1,003 (eBay; 1/10)
—Baltimore Colts #14 PSA 10 (Gem Mt) sold for $1,195 (Mile High; 3/09)
—Bob Brown #134 PSA 9 (MT) sold for $1,619 (eBay; 6/13)
—Bob Hayes RC #58 PSA 9 (MT) sold for $4,003 (eBay; 12/14)
—Dick Butkus #31 PSA 9 (MT) sold for $11,166 (Goodwin; 5/08)
—Dick Butkus RC #31 SGC 9 (Mint) sold for $4716 (Memory Lane; 8/12)
—Dick Butkus #31 PSA 8.5 (NmMt+) sold for $1,655 (Mile High; 5/11)
—Dick Butkus #31 SGC 9 (Mint) sold for $4,075 (eBay; 11/13)
—Checklist 2 #198 PSA 9 (MT) sold for $3,058 (eBay; 8/13)
—Irv Cross #136 PSA 8 (NmMt) sold for $715 (eBay; 1/10)
—Dallas Cowboys #53 PSA 9 (MT) sold for $1,060 (eBay; 1/10)
—Bob Hayes #58 PSA 9 (MT) sold for $1,500 (eBay; 9/12)
—Gene Hickerson #45 PSA 9 (MT) sold for $1,580 (eBay; 3/07)
—Chuck Howley #59 PSA 9 (MT) sold for $1,855 (eBay; 8/06)
—Philadelphia Eagles Play #143 PSA 9 (Mint) sold for $801 (eBay; 7/12)
—Gale Sayers #38 GAI 8.5 (NmMt+) sold for $800 (eBay; 1/07)
—Norm Snead #142 PSA 10 (Gem Mt) sold for $1,063 (Andy Madec; 12/08)
—Fran Tarkenton #114 PSA 9 (MT) sold for $1,740 (Memory Lane; 4/07)
—Fran Tarkenton #114 PSA 9 (Mint) sold for $690 (Bussineau; 4/12)
—Johnny Unitas #24 PSA 9 (MT) sold for $1,030 (eBay; 9/06)

1966 Topps

#	Player	GD 2	VG 3	VgEx 4	EX 5	ExMt 6	NM 7	NmMt 8	MT 9
1	Tommy Addison	4	5	8	12	18	25	60	
2	Houston Antwine	4	5	5	8	12	18	60	
3	Nick Buoniconti	4	5	6	10	15	20	40	
4	Gino Cappelletti	4	5	5	8	12	18	35	150
5	Bob Dee	4	5	5	8	12	18	60	
6	Larry Garron	4	5	5	8	12	18	35	150
7	Art Graham	4	5	5	8	12	18	35	150
8	Ron Hall DB	4	5	5	8	12	18	35	
9	Charles Long	4	5	5	8	12	18	35	120
10	Jon Morris	4	5	5	8	12	18	35	
11	Don Oakes	4	5	5	8	12	18	35	
12	Babe Parilli	4	5	5	8	12	18	35	150
13	Don Webb	4	5	5	8	12	18	35	
14	Jim Whalen	4	5	5	8	12	18	35	
15	Funny Ring Checklist	50	60	80	100	175	300	800	
16	Stew Barber	4	5	5	8	12	18	35	120
17	Glenn Bass	4	5	5	8	12	18	35	120
18	Dave Behrman	4	5	5	8	12	18	35	120
19	Al Bemiller	4	5	5	8	12	18	35	120
20	Butch Byrd RC	4	5	5	8	12	18	40	200
21	Wray Carlton	4	5	5	8	12	18	80	
22	Tom Day	4	5	5	8	12	15	35	150
23	Elbert Dubenion	4	5	5	8	12	18	40	
24	Jim Dunaway	4	5	5	8	12	18	25	150
25	Dick Hudson	4	5	5	8	12	18	35	150
26	Jack Kemp	15	20	25	35	▼50	▼60	200	
27	Daryle Lamonica	5	6	8	12	18	25	50	
28	Tom Sestak	4	5	5	8	12	18	35	150
29	Billy Shaw	4	5	6	10	15	20	35	120
30	Mike Stratton	4	5	5	8	12	18	35	150
31	Eldon Danenhauer	4	5	5	8	12	18	35	150
32	Cookie Gilchrist	4	5	6	10	15	20	40	
33	Goose Gonsoulin	4	5	5	8	12	18	35	
34	Wendell Hayes RC	4	5	6	10	15	20	40	200
35	Abner Haynes	4	5	6	10	15	20	40	150
36	Jerry Hopkins	4	5	5	8	12	18	35	
37	Ray Jacobs	4	5	5	8	12	18	30	
38	Charlie Janerette	4	5	5	8	12	18	35	150
39	Ray Kubala	4	5	5	8	12	18	35	200
40	John McCormick QB	4	5	5	8	12	18	80	
41	Leroy Moore	4	5	5	8	12	18	35	120
42	Bob Scarpitto	4	5	5	8	12	15	35	150
43	Mickey Slaughter	4	5	5	8	12	18	35	150
44	Jerry Sturm	4	5	5	8	12	18	35	
45	Lionel Taylor	4	5	5	10	15	20	35	
46	Scott Appleton	4	5	5	8	12	18	35	
47	Johnny Baker	4	5	5	8	12	18	35	
48	George Blanda	8	10	12	18	25	40	80	300
49	Sid Blanks	4	5	5	8	12	18	35	
50	Danny Brabham	4	5	5	8	12	18	35	
51	Ode Burrell	4	5	5	8	12	15	30	120
52	Gary Cutsinger	4	5	5	8	12	18	35	120
53	Larry Elkins	4	5	5	8	12	18	35	
54	Don Floyd	4	5	5	8	12	18	35	
55	Willie Frazier RC	4	5	5	8	12	18	35	
56	Freddy Glick	4	5	5	8	12	18	25	150
57	Charlie Hennigan	4	5	5	8	12	18	25	150
58	Bobby Jancik	4	5	5	8	10	12	25	
59	Rich Michael	4	5	5	8	12	18	35	
60	Don Trull	4	5	5	8	12	18	35	
61	Checklist 1	10	12	15	25	40	80	300	
62	Fred Arbanas	4	5	5	8	12	18	20	200
63	Pete Beathard	4	5	5	8	12	20	35	
64	Bobby Bell	4	5	6	10	15	20	35	150
65	Ed Budde	4	5	5	8	12	18	35	
66	Chris Burford	4	5	5	8	12	18	35	150
67	Len Dawson	10	12	15	20	30	50	120	
68	Jon Gilliam	4	5	5	8	12	18	30	150
69	Sherrill Headrick	4	5	5	8	12	18	30	150
70	E.J. Holub	4	5	5	8	12	18	35	150
71	Bobby Hunt	4	5	5	8	12	15	20	120
72	Curtis McClinton	4	5	5	8	12	18	25	250
73	Jerry Mays	4	5	5	8	12	18	35	150
74	Johnny Robinson	4	5	5	8	12	18	60	
75	Otis Taylor RC	5	6	8	12	18	35	100	350
76	Tom Erlandson	4	5	5	8	12	18	35	
77	Norm Evans RC	4	5	6	10	15	20	50	
78	Tom Goode	4	5	5	8	12	18	35	
79	Mike Hudock	4	5	5	8	12	18	30	200
80	Frank Jackson	4	5	5	8	12	18	60	
81	Billy Joe	4	5	5	8	12	18	35	
82	Dave Kocourek	4	5	5	8	12	18	35	
83	Bo Roberson	4	5	5	8	12	18	35	150
84	Jack Spikes	4	5	5	8	12	18	35	
85	Jim Warren RC	4	5	5	8	12	18	35	200
86	Willie West RC	4	5	5	8	12	18	35	
87	Dick Westmoreland	4	5	5	8	12	18	35	150
88	Eddie Wilson	4	5	5	8	12	18	35	
89	Dick Wood	4	5	5	8	12	18	60	
90	Verlon Biggs	4	5	5	8	12	18	35	120
91	Sam DeLuca	4	5	5	8	12	18	35	
92	Winston Hill	4	5	5	8	12	18	35	
93	Dee Mackey	4	5	5	8	12	18	50	
94	Bill Mathis	4	5	5	8	12	18	35	
95	Don Maynard	6	8	10	15	20	30	60	225
96	Joe Namath	50	60	▲100	125	200	300	600	2,200
97	Dainard Paulson	4	5	5	8	12	18	35	
98	Gerry Philbin	4	5	5	8	12	18	35	
99	Sherman Plunkett	4	5	5	8	12	18	35	80
100	Paul Rochester	4	5	5	8	12	18	50	200
101	George Sauer Jr. RC	4	5	6	10	15	20	35	
102	Matt Snell	4	5	6	10	15	20	35	
103	Jim Turner RC	4	5	5	8	12	18	35	150
104	Fred Biletnikoff	10	12	15	20	▲40	60	175	300
105	Bill Budness	4	5	5	8	12	18	35	60
106	Billy Cannon	4	5	6	10	15	20	35	

	GD 2	VG 3	VgEx 4	EX 5	ExMt 6	NM 7	NmMt 8	MT 9
Clem Daniels	4	5	5	8	12	18	35	
Ben Davidson	4	5	6	10	15	20	50	
Cotton Davidson	4	5	5	8	12	18	35	100
Claude Gibson	4	5	5	8	12	18	35	
Wayne Hawkins	4	5	5	8	12	18	35	100
Ken Herock	4	5	5	8	12	18	50	
Bob Mischak	4	5	5	8	12	18	60	
Gus Otto	4	5	5	8	12	20	50	150
Jim Otto	5	6	8	12	18	25	50	350
Art Powell	4	5	6	10	15	20	35	120
Harry Schuh	4	5	5	8	12	18	35	
Chuck Allen	4	5	5	8	12	18	50	
Lance Alworth	10	12	15	20	30	60	150	
Frank Buncom	4	5	5	8	12	18	100	
Steve DeLong	4	5	5	8	12	18	35	
John Farris	4	5	5	8	12	18	40	
Kenny Graham	4	5	5	8	12	18	30	
Sam Gruneisen	4	5	5	8	12	18	35	
John Hadl	4	5	5	10	15	20	35	
Walt Sweeney	4	5	5	8	15	30	80	
Keith Lincoln	4	5	6	10	15	20	40	200
Ron Mix	4	5	6	10	15	20	40	
Don Norton	4	5	5	8	12	18	40	200
Pat Shea	4	5	5	8	12	18	40	
Ernie Wright	4	5	6	10	15	20	100	
Checklist 2	25	30	40	75	150	300		

Tommy Addison #1 PSA 9 (MT) sold for $756 (Mile High; 11/10)
Bobby Bell #64 PSA 10 (Gem Mt) sold for $1,242 (Mile High; 5/11)
Fred Biletnikoff #104 PSA 9 (MT) sold for $2,545 (Memory Lane; 4/07)
Ed Budde #65 PSA 9 (MT) sold for $700 (eBay; 6/11)
Nick Buoniconti #3 PSA 9 (MT) sold for $425 (eBay; 1/06)
Len Dawson #67 PSA 9 (MT) sold for $925 (eBay; 9/05)
Kenny Graham #123 PSA 10 (Gem Mt) sold for $628 (Mile High; 5/11)
Bobby Hunt #71 PSA 10 (Gem Mt) sold for $1,477 (Mastro; 2/07)
Bobby Hunt #71 PSA 10 (Gem Mt) sold for $1,214 (eBay; 1/10)
Don Maynard #95 PSA 10 (Gem Mt) sold for $1,640 (Mastro; 4/07)
Don Maynard #95 PSA 9 (MT) sold for $795 (eBay; 3/05)
Joe Namath #96 PSA 10 (Gem Mt) sold for $14,771 (Mile High; 11/10)
Jim Otto #115 PSA 9 (MT) sold for $790 (eBay; 4/07)
Willie West RC #86 PSA 10 (Gem Mint) sold for $570 (Bussineau; 7/12)

1967 Philadelphia

	GD 2	VG 3	VgEx 4	EX 5	ExMt 6	NM 7	NmMt 8	MT 9
Atlanta Falcons Team	4	5	5	6	10	20	125	
Junior Coffey RC	4	5	5	5	8	15	30	
Alex Hawkins	4	5	5	5	8	12	35	
Randy Johnson RC	4	5	5	5	8	12	35	80
Lou Kirouac	4	5	5	5	8	12	25	80
Billy Martin RC	4	5	5	5	8	12	35	80
Tommy Nobis RC	5	6	8	10	18	35	80	
Jerry Richardson RC	4	5	5	6	10	15	30	
Marion Rushing	4	5	5	5	8	12	25	80
Ron Smith	4	5	5	5	10	20		
Ernie Wheelwright	4	5	5	5	10	20		
Atlanta Falcons Logo	4	5	5	5	10	20		
Baltimore Colts Team	4	5	5	8	12	25	80	
Raymond Berry	4	5	5	8	12	20	60	
Bob Boyd DB	4	5	5	5	8	12	35	80
Ordell Braase RC	4	5	5	5	8	12	35	80
Alvin Haymond RC	4	5	5	5	8	12	35	250
Tony Lorick	4	5	5	5	8	12	35	
Lenny Lyles	4	5	5	5	8	15	50	
John Mackey	4	5	5	6	10	15	40	120
Tom Matte	4	5	5	5	10	25		
Lou Michaels	4	5	5	5	8	15	30	
Johnny Unitas	15	18	20	25	40	80	300	
Baltimore Colts Logo	4	5	5	5	10	20		
Chicago Bears Team	4	5	5	8	12	25	35	
Rudy Bukich	4	5	5	8	12	25	50	
Ronnie Bull	4	5	5	5	8	12	35	
Dick Butkus	15	18	20	25	50	100	400	
Mike Ditka	8	10	12	15	25	40	100	
Dick Gordon RC	4	5	5	5	8	12	35	80
Roger LeClerc	4	5	5	5	8	15	100	
Bennie McRae	4	5	5	5	8	12	25	
Richie Petitbon	4	5	5	5	8	12	30	80
Mike Pyle	4	5	5	5	8	12	35	80
Gale Sayers	15	20	25	40	50	100	▲300	1,200

		GD 2	VG 3	VgEx 4	EX 5	ExMt 6	NM 7	NmMt 8	MT 9
36	Chicago Bears Logo	4	5	5	5	8	12	35	
37	Cleveland Browns Team	4	5	5	5	8	12	35	100
38	Johnny Brewer	4	5	5	5	8	12	35	80
39	Gary Collins	4	5	5	5	8	12	30	
40	Ross Fichtner	4	5	5	5	8	15	25	
41	Ernie Green	4	5	5	5	8	12	40	
42	Gene Hickerson	4	5	5	5	8	15	100	
43	Leroy Kelly RC	15	18	20	25	35	150	800	
44	Frank Ryan	4	5	5	5	10	20		
45	Dick Schafrath	4	5	5	5	8	12	35	
46	Paul Warfield	4	5	6	8	12	20	50	300
47	John Wooten	4	5	5	6	10	50		
48	Cleveland Browns Logo	4	5	5	5	8	12	35	100
49	Dallas Cowboys Team	4	5	5	5	8	12	35	80
50	George Andrie	4	5	5	5	8	20	80	
51	Cornell Green	4	5	5	5	8	12	35	80
52	Bob Hayes	5	6	8	10	15	25	50	250
53	Chuck Howley	4	5	5	6	10	25	35	
54	Lee Roy Jordan RC	4	5	6	8	12	30	80	300
55	Bob Lilly	4	5	6	8	12	20	50	350
56	Dave Manders RC	4	5	5	5	8	15	200	
57	Don Meredith	6	8	10	12	20	40	175	
58	Dan Reeves RC	10	12	15	20	30	50	300	
59	Mel Renfro	4	5	6	10	30	40		
60	Dallas Cowboys Logo	4	5	5	5	8	12	35	100
61	Detroit Lions Team	4	5	5	5	8	15	30	
62	Roger Brown	4	5	5	5	8	12	35	
63	Gail Cogdill	4	5	5	5	8	12	35	250
64	John Gordy	4	5	5	5	8	12	35	
65	Ron Kramer	4	5	5	5	8	12	25	50
66	Dick LeBeau	4	5	5	5	8	12	35	80
67	Mike Lucci RC	4	5	6	10	15	35	125	
68	Amos Marsh	4	5	5	5	8	12	30	80
69	Tom Nowatzke	4	5	5	5	8	12	30	
70	Pat Studstill	4	5	5	5	8	12	30	
71	Karl Sweetan	4	5	5	5	8	12	30	
72	Detroit Lions Logo	4	5	5	5	8	12	30	80
73	Green Bay Packers Team	4	5	5	6	12	20	500	
74	Herb Adderley	4	5	5	6	10	15	30	100
75	Lee Roy Caffey	4	5	5	5	8	12	80	
76	Willie Davis DE	4	5	5	6	10	15	35	200
77	Forrest Gregg	4	5	5	6	10	15	60	
78	Hank Jordan	4	5	5	6	10	15	35	350
79	Ray Nitschke	4	5	6	8	12	30	60	
80	Dave Robinson RC	12	15	20	30	40	60	175	500
81	Bob Skoronski	4	5	5	5	8	20	100	
82	Bart Starr	15	18	20	25	30	80	300	
83	Willie Wood	4	5	5	6	10	20	100	
84	Green Bay Packers Logo	4	5	5	5	8	12	30	
85	Los Angeles Rams Team	4	5	5	5	8	15	50	
86	Dick Bass	4	5	5	5	8	12	30	40
87	Maxie Baughan	4	5	5	5	8	15	30	
88	Roman Gabriel	4	5	5	6	10	15	25	100
89	Bruce Gossett	4	5	5	5	8	12	30	60
90	Deacon Jones	4	5	5	6	10	15	35	100
91	Tommy McDonald	4	5	5	6	10	15	35	100
92	Marlin McKeever	4	5	5	5	8	15	30	
93	Tom Moore	4	5	5	5	8	15	30	60
94	Merlin Olsen	4	5	5	6	10	15	35	
95	Clancy Williams	4	5	5	5	8	12	30	60
96	Los Angeles Rams Logo	4	5	5	5	8	12	30	80
97	Minnesota Vikings Team	4	5	5	5	8	12	30	80
98	Grady Alderman	4	5	5	5	8	15	30	
99	Bill Brown	4	5	5	5	8	15	30	
100	Fred Cox	4	5	5	5	8	15	30	
101	Paul Flatley	4	5	5	5	8	12	30	80
102	Dale Hackbart RC	4	5	5	5	8	12	30	80
103	Jim Marshall	4	5	5	6	10	15	25	100
104	Tommy Mason	4	5	5	5	8	15	30	
105	Milt Sunde RC	4	5	5	5	8	25		
106	Fran Tarkenton	5	6	8	10	18	30	50	350
107	Mick Tingelhoff	4	5	5	5	8	12	30	
108	Minnesota Vikings Logo	4	5	5	5	8	25		
109	New York Giants Team	4	5	5	5	8	12	30	80
110	Henry Carr	4	5	5	5	10	20		
111	Clarence Childs	4	5	5	5	8	12	30	
112	Allen Jacobs	4	5	5	5	8	15	50	
113	Homer Jones RC	4	5	5	5	8	12	30	80
114	Tom Kennedy	4	5	5	5	8	15	80	

		GD 2	VG 3	VgEx 4	EX 5	ExMt 6	NM 7	NmMt 8	MT 9
115	Spider Lockhart	4	5	5	5	8	15	30	
116	Joe Morrison	4	5	5	5	8	12	25	80
117	Francis Peay	4	5	5	5	8	12	30	80
118	Jeff Smith LB	4	5	5	5	8	12	30	80
119	Aaron Thomas	4	5	5	5	8	12	25	80
120	New York Giants Logo	4	5	5	5	8	12	40	
121	New Orleans Saints Logo	4	5	5	5	8	12	35	80
122	Charley Bradshaw	4	5	5	5	8	12	20	80
123	Paul Hornung	6	8	▲15	▲15	▲30	▲40	200	
124	Elbert Kimbrough	4	5	5	5	8	15	80	
125	Earl Leggett RC	4	5	5	5	8	15	30	
126	Obert Logan	4	5	5	5	8	15	30	
127	Riley Mattson	4	5	5	5	8	15	80	
128	John Morrow	4	5	5	5	8	12	30	
129	Bob Scholtz	4	5	5	5	8	12	40	80
130	Dave Whitsell RC	4	5	5	5	8	12	30	80
131	Gary Wood	4	5	5	5	8	12	20	80
132	NO Saints Roster ERR 121	4	5	5	5	8	12	30	
133	Philadelphia Eagles Team	4	5	5	5	8	12	30	80
134	Sam Baker	4	5	5	5	8	12	20	80
135	Bob Brown OT	4	5	5	6	10	20	60	
136	Timmy Brown	4	5	5	5	8	15	50	
137	Earl Gros	4	5	5	5	8	12	30	
138	Dave Lloyd	4	5	5	5	8	12	30	
139	Floyd Peters	4	5	5	5	8	12	30	
140	Pete Retzlaff	4	5	5	5	8	12	30	80
141	Joe Scarpati	4	5	5	5	8	12	30	
142	Norm Snead	4	5	5	5	8	12	35	120
143	Jim Skaggs	4	5	5	5	8	12	30	
144	Philadelphia Eagles Logo	4	5	5	5	8	15	200	
145	Pittsburgh Steelers Team	4	5	5	5	8	15	40	
146	Bill Asbury	4	5	5	5	8	15	30	
147	John Baker	4	5	5	5	8	15	30	
148	Gary Ballman	4	5	5	5	8	12	30	
149	Mike Clark	4	5	5	5	8	12	30	50
150	Riley Gunnels	4	5	5	5	8	15	50	
151	John Hilton	4	5	5	5	8	12	25	60
152	Roy Jefferson	4	5	5	5	8	15	30	
153	Brady Keys	4	5	5	5	8	15	30	
154	Ben McGee	4	5	5	5	8	12	30	
155	Bill Nelsen	4	5	5	5	8	12	30	
156	Pittsburgh Steelers Logo	4	5	5	5	8	15	30	
157	St. Louis Cardinals Team	4	5	5	5	8	12	30	
158	Jim Bakken	4	5	5	5	8	12	30	
159	Bobby Joe Conrad	4	5	5	5	8	15	30	
160	Ken Gray	4	5	5	5	8	15	30	
161	Charlie Johnson	4	5	5	5	8	15	30	
162	Joe Robb	4	5	5	5	8	15	30	
163	Johnny Roland RC	4	5	5	5	8	12	30	80
164	Roy Shivers	4	5	5	5	8	15	25	
165	Jackie Smith RC	6	8	10	12	20	50	100	
166	Jerry Stovall	4	5	5	5	8	12	30	
167	Larry Wilson	4	5	5	6	10	15	25	
168	St. Louis Cardinals Logo	4	5	5	5	8	12	30	80
169	San Francisco 49ers Team	4	5	5	5	8	15	30	
170	Kermit Alexander	4	5	5	5	8	12	30	
171	Bruce Bosley	4	5	5	5	8	12	30	
172	John Brodie	4	5	5	6	10	▲20	35	
173	Bernie Casey	4	5	5	5	8	15	30	
174	Tommy Davis	4	5	5	5	8	15	30	
175	Howard Mudd	4	5	5	6	10	20	100	
176	Dave Parks	4	5	5	5	8	15	30	
177	John Thomas	4	5	5	5	8	15	30	
178	Dave Wilcox RC	5	6	8	10	20	50	▼100	350
179	Ken Willard	4	5	5	5	8	15	30	
180	San Francisco 49ers Logo	4	5	5	5	8	12	30	
181	Washington Redskins Team	4	5	5	5	8	15	40	
182	Charlie Gogolak RC	4	5	5	5	8	12	25	
183	Chris Hanburger RC	5	6	8	10	20	▲100	200	
184	Len Hauss RC	4	5	5	5	8	15	50	
185	Sonny Jurgensen	4	5	5	6	10	15	35	175
186	Bobby Mitchell	4	5	5	6	10	15	25	80
187	Brig Owens	4	5	5	5	8	12	30	
188	Jim Shorter	4	5	5	5	8	15	35	
189	Jerry Smith RC	4	5	5	5	8	15	80	
190	Charley Taylor	4	5	6	8	12	20	60	
191	A.D. Whitfield	4	5	5	5	8	12	25	50
192	Washington Redskins Logo	4	5	5	5	8	15	50	
193	Browns Play/Leroy Kelly	4	5	5	6	10	15	30	

		GD 2	VG 3	VgEx 4	EX 5	ExMt 6	NM 7	NmMt 8	MT 9
194	Giants Play/Joe Morrison	4	5	5	5	8	12	30	
195	Falcons Play/Wheelwright	4	5	5	5	8	12	25	
196	Referee Signals	4	5	5	5	6	10	35	
197	Checklist 1	4	5	6	8	12	20	35	80
198	Checklist 2	8	10	12	15	40	50	80	300

—Bob Lilly #55 PSA 10 (Gem) sold for $1,232 (eBay; 2/14)
—Raymond Berry #14 PSA 10 (Gem) sold for $1,140 (eBay; 2/07)
—Charley Bradshaw #122 PSA 10 (Gem) sold for $892 (Memory Lane; 5/08)
—Junior Coffey #2 PSA 10 (Gem) sold for $795 (eBay; 5/05)
—Willie Davis #76 PSA 10 (Gem) sold for $803 (eBay; 9/13)
—Chris Hanburger #183 PSA 9 (MT) sold for $4497 (eBay; 11/14)
—Hank Jordan #78 PSA 10 (Gem) sold for $818 (eBay; 8/13)
—Tommy Nobis #7 PSA 9 (MT) sold for $435 (eBay; 9/05)
—Merlin Olsen #94 PSA 9 (MT) sold for $365 (eBay; 1/06)
—Dan Reeves #58 PSA 9 (MT) sold for $1,465 (eBay; 2/07)
—Johnny Unitas #23 PSA 9 (Mint) sold for $2909.55 (Memory Lane; 5/12)
—Ken Willard #179 PSA 10 (Gem) sold for $2,544 (Memory Lane; 5/08)

1967 Topps

		GD 2	VG 3	VgEx 4	EX 5	ExMt 6	NM 7	NmMt 8	MT 9
1	John Huarte	4	5	5	5	10	20	80	200
2	Babe Parilli	4	5	5	5	8	15	100	
3	Gino Cappelletti	4	5	5	5	8	12	25	100
4	Larry Garron	4	5	5	5	8	12	25	80
5	Tommy Addison	4	5	5	5	8	12	25	80
6	Jon Morris	4	5	5	5	8	12	25	80
7	Houston Antwine	4	5	5	5	8	12	35	
8	Don Oakes	4	5	5	5	8	12	35	
9	Larry Eisenhauer	4	5	5	5	8	12	25	
10	Jim Hunt	4	5	5	5	8	12	35	
11	Jim Whalen	4	5	5	5	8	12	25	80
12	Art Graham	4	5	5	5	8	12	25	80
13	Nick Buoniconti	4	5	5	5	8	10	15	40
14	Bob Dee	4	5	5	5	8	12	25	80
15	Keith Lincoln	4	5	5	5	8	15	30	100
16	Tom Flores	4	5	5	5	8	15	30	100
17	Art Powell	4	5	5	5	8	12	25	80
18	Stew Barber	4	5	5	5	8	12	25	80
19	Wray Carlton	4	5	5	5	8	12	25	
20	Elbert Dubenion	4	5	5	5	8	12	25	80
21	Jim Dunaway	4	5	5	5	8	12	25	80
22	Dick Hudson	4	5	5	5	8	12	25	80
23	Harry Jacobs	4	5	5	5	8	12	35	
24	Jack Kemp	12	15	20	25	40	50	60	200
25	Ron McDole	4	5	5	5	8	12	25	50
26	George Saimes	4	5	5	5	8	12	25	100
27	Tom Sestak	4	5	5	5	8	12	25	
28	Billy Shaw	4	5	5	5	8	15	30	100
29	Mike Stratton	4	5	5	5	8	12	25	80
30	Nemiah Wilson RC	4	5	5	5	8	12	25	80
31	John McCormick QB	4	5	5	5	8	12	25	80
32	Rex Mirich	4	5	5	5	8	12	50	150
33	Dave Costa	4	5	5	5	8	12	25	80
34	Goose Gonsoulin	4	5	5	5	8	12	25	80
35	Abner Haynes	4	5	5	5	8	12	25	80
36	Wendell Hayes	4	5	5	5	8	12	25	60
37	Archie Matsos	4	5	5	5	8	12	25	80
38	John Bramlett	4	5	5	5	8	12	25	80
39	Jerry Sturm	4	5	5	5	8	12	30	40
40	Max Leetzow	4	5	5	5	8	12	25	80
41	Bob Scarpitto	4	5	5	5	8	12	25	
42	Lionel Taylor	4	5	5	5	8	15	30	100
43	Al Denson	4	5	5	5	8	12	25	80
44	Miller Farr RC	4	5	5	5	8	12	25	60
45	Don Trull	4	5	5	5	8	12	20	
46	Jacky Lee	4	5	5	5	8	12	20	80
47	Bobby Jancik	4	5	5	5	8	12	25	80
48	Ode Burrell	4	5	5	5	8	12	30	
49	Larry Elkins	4	5	5	5	8	10	30	60
50	W.K. Hicks	4	5	5	5	8	12	25	80
51	Sid Blanks	4	5	5	5	8	12	25	80
52	Jim Norton	4	5	5	5	8	12	25	80
53	Bobby Maples RC	4	5	5	5	8	12	35	100
54	Bob Talamini	4	5	5	5	8	12	35	
55	Walt Suggs	4	5	5	5	8	12	25	80
56	Gary Cutsinger	4	5	5	5	8	12	25	80
57	Danny Brabham	4	5	5	5	8	12	35	80
58	Ernie Ladd	4	5	5	5	8	15	30	100

	GD 2	VG 3	VgEx 4	EX 5	ExMt 6	NM 7	NmMt 8	MT 9
Checklist 1	6	8	10	12	25	50	100	
Pete Beathard	4	5	5	5	8	12	25	80
Len Dawson	6	8	10	12	18	30	80	300
Bobby Hunt	4	5	5	5	8	12	25	80
Bert Coan	4	5	5	5	8	12	25	80
Curtis McClinton	4	5	5	5	8	12	25	80
Johnny Robinson	4	5	5	5	8	12	25	80
E.J. Holub	4	5	5	5	8	12	25	80
Jerry Mays	4	5	5	5	8	12	25	80
Jim Tyrer	4	5	5	5	8	12	35	
Bobby Bell	4	5	5	5	8	15	40	100
Fred Arbanas	4	5	5	5	8	12	35	
Buck Buchanan	4	5	5	5	8	15	30	100
Chris Burford	4	5	5	5	8	12	50	
Otis Taylor	4	5	5	5	8	15	30	100
Cookie Gilchrist	4	5	5	6	10	15	30	100
Earl Faison	4	5	5	5	8	12	50	80
George Wilson Jr.	4	5	5	5	8	12	30	150
Rick Norton	4	5	5	5	8	12	25	120
Frank Jackson	4	5	5	5	8	12	25	80
Joe Auer	4	5	5	5	8	12	40	
Willie West	4	5	5	5	8	12	25	80
Jim Warren	4	5	5	5	8	12	35	
Wahoo McDaniel RC	10	12	15	▲25	▲50	▲60	100	250
Ernie Park	4	5	5	5	8	12	25	80
Billy Neighbors	4	5	5	5	8	12	25	150
Norm Evans	4	5	5	5	8	12	40	120
Tom Nomina	4	5	5	5	8	12	30	100
Rich Zecher	4	5	5	5	8	12	30	100
Dave Kocourek	4	5	5	5	8	12	25	80
Bill Baird	4	5	5	5	8	12	25	80
Ralph Baker	4	5	5	5	8	12	25	80
Verlon Biggs	4	5	5	5	8	12	25	80
Sam DeLuca	4	5	5	5	8	12	25	80
Larry Grantham	4	5	5	5	8	12	25	100
Jim Harris	4	5	5	5	8	12	25	80
Winston Hill	4	5	5	5	8	12	25	
Bill Mathis	4	5	5	5	8	12	25	80
Don Maynard	4	5	6	8	12	20	50	
Joe Namath	20	30	50	60	125	200	350	800
Gerry Philbin	4	5	5	5	8	12	25	50
Paul Rochester	4	5	5	5	8	12	30	
George Sauer Jr.	4	5	5	5	8	12	30	120
Matt Snell	4	5	5	5	8	15	35	
Daryle Lamonica	4	5	5	6	10	30	40	150
Glenn Bass	4	5	5	5	8	12	25	80
Jim Otto	4	5	5	5	8	15	30	120
Fred Biletnikoff	6	8	10	12	18	30	80	300
Cotton Davidson	4	5	5	5	8	12	30	
Larry Todd	4	5	5	5	8	12	30	
Billy Cannon	4	5	5	5	8	15	30	
Clem Daniels	4	5	5	5	8	12	30	
Dave Grayson	4	5	5	5	8	12	25	80
Kent McCloughan RC	4	5	5	5	8	12	25	80
Bob Svihus	4	5	5	5	8	12	25	80
Ike Lassiter	4	5	5	5	8	12	25	80
Harry Schuh	4	5	5	5	8	12	25	80
Ben Davidson	4	5	5	6	10	15	30	200
Tom Day	4	5	5	5	8	12	30	
Scott Appleton	4	5	5	5	8	12	25	80
Steve Tensi RC	4	5	5	5	8	12	30	
John Hadl	4	5	5	5	8	15	30	▼100
Paul Lowe	4	5	5	5	8	12	25	125
Jim Allison	4	5	5	5	8	12	25	80
Lance Alworth	8	10	12	15	20	35	80	400
Jacque MacKinnon	4	5	5	5	8	12	25	80
Ron Mix	4	5	5	5	8	15	30	
Bob Petrich	4	5	5	5	8	12	25	80
Howard Kindig	4	5	5	5	8	12	25	100
Steve DeLong	4	5	5	5	8	12	25	80
Chuck Allen	4	5	5	5	8	12	35	
Frank Buncom	4	5	5	5	8	12	25	80
Speedy Duncan RC	4	5	6	8	12	20	80	350
Checklist 2	12	15	20	25	40	75	150	

–Don Maynard #97 PSA 10 (Gem Mt) sold for $1,206 (Mile High; 10/09)
–Wahoo McDaniel #82 PSA 9 (Mint) sold for $1,205 (eBay; 3/07)
–Wahoo McDaniel #82 PSA 10 (Gem) sold for $768 (Lelands; 6/13)
–Billy Neighbors #84 PSA 10 (Gem Mint) sold for $515.64 (eBay; 9/12)
–Larry Todd #108 PSA 10 (Gem Mint) sold for $912.5 (eBay; 5/12)

1968 Topps

		GD 2	VG 3	VgEx 4	EX 5	ExMt 6	NM 7	NmMt 8	MT 9
1	Bart Starr	8	10	12	20	35	50	300	1,200
2	Dick Bass	4	5	5	5	6	10	20	80
3	Grady Alderman	4	5	5	5	6	10	40	
4	Obert Logan	4	5	5	5	6	10	20	80
5	Ernie Koy RC	4	5	5	5	6	10	40	100
6	Don Hultz	4	5	5	5	6	15	30	150
7	Earl Gros	4	5	5	5	6	10	20	50
8	Jim Bakken	4	5	5	5	6	10	20	80
9	George Mira	4	5	5	5	6	10	30	100
10	Carl Kammerer	4	5	5	5	6	10	20	60
11	Willie Frazier	4	5	5	5	6	10	20	60
12	Kent McCloughan	4	5	5	5	6	10	60	
13	George Sauer Jr.	4	5	5	5	6	10	20	80
14	Jack Clancy	4	5	5	5	6	10	30	
15	Jim Tyrer	4	5	5	5	6	10	30	150
16	Bobby Maples	4	5	5	5	6	10	20	80
17	Bo Hickey	4	5	5	5	6	10	20	80
18	Frank Buncom	4	5	5	5	6	10	30	
19	Keith Lincoln	4	5	5	5	6	10	20	100
20	Jim Whalen	4	5	5	5	6	10	30	
21	Junior Coffey	4	5	5	5	6	10	30	
22	Billy Ray Smith	4	5	5	5	6	10	25	
23	Johnny Morris	4	5	5	5	6	10	20	50
24	Ernie Green	4	5	5	5	6	10	25	60
25	Don Meredith	5	6	8	10	20	25	50	200
26	Wayne Walker	4	5	5	5	6	10	20	50
27	Carroll Dale	4	5	5	5	6	40	250	
28	Bernie Casey	4	5	5	5	6	10	30	
29	Dave Osborn RC	4	5	5	5	6	10	20	80
30	Ray Poage	4	5	5	5	6	10	20	80
31	Homer Jones	4	5	5	5	6	10	20	80
32	Sam Baker	4	5	5	5	6	10	30	
33	Bill Saul	4	5	5	5	6	10	30	100
34	Ken Willard	4	5	5	5	6	10	30	100
35	Bobby Mitchell	4	5	5	5	6	10	30	100
36	Gary Garrison RC	4	5	5	5	6	10	20	125
37	Billy Cannon	4	5	5	5	6	10	30	100
38	Ralph Baker	4	5	5	5	6	10	20	80
39	Howard Twilley RC	4	5	5	5	6	10	30	120
40	Wendell Hayes	4	5	5	5	6	10	20	80
41	Jim Norton	4	5	5	5	6	10	30	100
42	Tom Beer	4	5	5	5	6	10	30	
43	Chris Burford	4	5	5	5	6	10	40	
44	Stew Barber	4	5	5	5	6	10	40	
45	Leroy Mitchell	4	5	5	5	6	10	60	
46	Dan Grimm	4	5	5	5	6	10	30	
47	Jerry Logan	4	5	5	5	6	10	20	80
48	Andy Livingston	4	5	5	5	6	10	30	100
49	Paul Warfield	4	5	5	6	8	12	20	150
50	Don Perkins	4	5	5	5	6	10	30	80
51	Ron Kramer	4	5	5	5	6	10	20	50
52	Bob Jeter RC	4	5	5	5	6	10	30	
53	Les Josephson RC	4	5	5	5	6	10	20	60
54	Bobby Walden	4	5	5	5	6	10	20	80
55	Checklist 1	4	5	5	6	10	20	30	150
56	Walter Roberts	4	5	5	5	6	10	20	80
57	Henry Carr	4	5	5	5	6	10	30	
58	Gary Ballman	4	5	5	5	6	10	30	
59	J.R. Wilburn	4	5	5	5	6	10	20	80
60	Jim Hart RC	4	5	5	5	8	12	30	100
61	Jim Johnson	4	5	5	5	6	10	20	80
62	Chris Hanburger	4	5	5	5	6	10	25	125
63	John Hadl	4	5	5	5	6	10	25	125
64	Hewritt Dixon	4	5	5	5	6	10	30	
65	Joe Namath	20	25	30	50	80	125	250	800
66	Jim Warren	4	5	5	5	6	10	30	100
67	Curtis McClinton	4	5	5	5	6	10	20	80
68	Bob Talamini	4	5	5	5	6	10	30	
69	Steve Tensi	4	5	5	5	6	10	20	80
70	Dick Van Raaphorst	4	5	5	5	6	10	30	
71	Art Powell	4	5	5	5	6	10	25	80
72	Jim Nance RC	4	5	5	5	6	10	30	200
73	Bob Riggle	4	5	5	5	6	10	20	80
74	John Mackey	4	5	5	5	5	10	25	60
75	Gale Sayers	10	12	15	20	40	60	150	600

FOOTBALL

#	Player	GD 2	VG 3	VgEx 4	EX 5	ExMt 6	NM 7	NmMt 8	MT 9
76	Gene Hickerson	4	5	5	5	6	10	30	
77	Dan Reeves	4	5	5	5	8	12	100	
78	Tom Nowatzke	4	5	5	5	6	10	20	80
79	Elijah Pitts	4	5	5	5	6	12	80	
80	Lamar Lundy	4	5	5	5	6	10	30	100
81	Paul Flatley	4	5	5	5	6	10	20	60
82	Dave Whitsell	4	5	5	5	6	10	40	
83	Spider Lockhart	4	5	5	5	6	10	20	80
84	Dave Lloyd	4	5	5	5	6	10	20	80
85	Roy Jefferson	4	5	5	5	6	10	20	80
86	Jackie Smith	4	5	5	5	8	12	40	150
87	John David Crow	4	5	5	5	6	10	30	
88	Sonny Jurgensen	4	5	5	5	8	12	40	
89	Ron Mix	4	5	5	5	6	10	30	
90	Clem Daniels	4	5	5	5	6	10	30	
91	Cornell Gordon	4	5	5	5	6	10	20	60
92	Tom Goode	4	5	5	5	6	10	30	100
93	Bobby Bell	4	5	5	5	6	10	30	150
94	Walt Suggs	4	5	5	5	6	10	40	
95	Eric Crabtree	4	5	5	5	6	10	30	
96	Sherrill Headrick	4	5	5	5	6	10	20	50
97	Wray Carlton	4	5	5	5	6	10	20	80
98	Gino Cappelletti	4	5	5	5	6	10	20	60
99	Tommy McDonald	4	5	5	5	6	10	20	80
100	Johnny Unitas	10	12	15	20	30	50	150	600
101	Richie Petitbon	4	5	5	5	6	10	30	
102	Erich Barnes	4	5	5	5	6	10	30	
103	Bob Hayes	4	5	5	5	8	12	50	
104	Milt Plum	4	5	5	5	6	10	30	80
105	Boyd Dowler	4	5	5	5	6	10	40	
106	Ed Meador	4	5	5	5	6	10	25	100
107	Fred Cox	4	5	5	5	6	10	25	100
108	Steve Stonebreaker RC	4	5	5	5	6	10	20	60
109	Aaron Thomas	4	5	5	5	6	10	20	80
110	Norm Snead	4	5	5	5	6	10	20	60
111	Paul Martha RC	4	5	5	5	10	25	100	
112	Jerry Stovall	4	5	5	5	6	10	20	60
113	Kay McFarland	4	5	5	5	6	10	25	
114	Pat Richter	4	5	5	5	6	10	20	80
115	Rick Redman	4	5	5	5	6	10	30	
116	Tom Keating	4	5	5	5	6	10	20	100
117	Matt Snell	4	5	5	5	6	10	25	100
118	Dick Westmoreland	4	5	5	5	6	10	30	
119	Jerry Mays	4	5	5	5	6	10	30	
120	Sid Blanks	4	5	5	5	6	10	20	80
121	Al Denson	4	5	5	5	6	10	30	
122	Bobby Hunt	4	5	5	5	6	10	30	
123	Mike Mercer	4	5	5	5	6	10	60	
124	Nick Buoniconti	4	5	5	5	6	10	40	
125	Ron Vanderkelen RC	4	5	5	5	6	10	30	
126	Ordell Braase	4	5	5	5	6	10	150	
127	Dick Butkus	10	12	15	20	30	50	100	600
128	Gary Collins	4	5	5	5	6	10	20	80
129	Mel Renfro	4	5	5	5	6	15	40	150
130	Alex Karras	4	5	5	5	6	10	30	▼150
131	Herb Adderley	4	5	5	5	6	15	80	
132	Roman Gabriel	4	5	5	5	6	10	25	80
133	Bill Brown	4	5	5	5	6	10	30	
134	Kent Kramer	4	5	5	5	6	10	30	
135	Tucker Frederickson	4	5	5	5	6	10	40	
136	Nate Ramsey	4	5	5	5	6	10	20	80
137	Marv Woodson	4	5	5	5	6	10	20	50
138	Ken Gray	4	5	5	5	6	10	20	80
139	John Brodie	4	5	5	5	6	10	20	100
140	Jerry Smith	4	5	5	5	6	10	150	
141	Brad Hubbert	4	5	5	5	6	10	20	50
142	George Blanda	4	5	6	8	12	25	40	150
143	Pete Lammons RC	4	5	5	5	6	10	40	120
144	Doug Moreau	4	5	5	5	6	10	20	80
145	E.J. Holub	4	5	5	5	6	10	20	80
146	Ode Burrell	4	5	5	5	6	10	20	80
147	Bob Scarpitto	4	5	5	5	6	10	20	80
148	Andre White	4	5	5	5	6	10	40	
149	Jack Kemp	8	10	12	15	25	40	50	
150	Art Graham	4	5	5	5	6	10	20	50
151	Tommy Nobis	4	5	5	5	8	12	25	100
152	Willie Richardson RC	4	5	5	5	6	10	30	
153	Jack Concannon	4	5	5	5	6	10	50	
154	Bill Glass	4	5	5	5	6	10	20	60

#	Player	GD 2	VG 3	VgEx 4	EX 5	ExMt 6	NM 7	NmMt 8	MT 9
155	Craig Morton RC	4	5	5	5	8	15	80	▲200
156	Pat Studstill	4	5	5	5	6	10	20	80
157	Ray Nitschke	4	5	8	15	30	50	150	400
158	Roger Brown	4	5	5	5	6	10	30	
159	Joe Kapp RC	4	5	5	5	6	10	▲25	125
160	Jim Taylor	5	5	6	8	12	20	40	135
161	Fran Tarkenton	5	6	8	10	15	25	50	200
162	Mike Ditka	6	8	10	12	20	35	60	250
163	Andy Russell RC	4	5	5	5	6	10	30	100
164	Larry Wilson	4	5	5	5	6	10	20	80
165	Tommy Davis	4	5	5	5	6	10	20	100
166	Paul Krause	4	5	5	5	6	10	20	100
167	Speedy Duncan	4	5	5	5	6	10	25	200
168	Fred Biletnikoff	5	6	8	10	15	20	50	200
169	Don Maynard	4	5	5	6	10	15	30	120
170	Frank Emanuel	4	5	5	5	6	10	20	150
171	Len Dawson	5	5	6	8	12	20	40	350
172	Miller Farr	4	5	5	5	6	10	20	80
173	Floyd Little RC	8	10	12	15	30	▼80	150	
174	Lonnie Wright	4	5	5	5	6	10	30	
175	Paul Costa	4	5	5	5	6	10	20	80
176	Don Trull	4	5	5	5	6	10	40	
177	Jerry Simmons	4	5	5	5	6	10	40	
178	Tom Matte	4	5	5	5	6	10	20	50
179	Bennie McRae	4	5	5	5	6	10	30	120
180	Jim Kanicki	4	5	5	5	6	10	20	100
181	Bob Lilly	5	5	6	8	12	20	40	150
182	Tom Watkins	4	5	5	5	6	10	30	100
183	Jim Grabowski RC	4	5	5	5	8	15	▼50	
184	Jack Snow RC	4	5	5	5	6	10	30	150
185	Gary Cuozzo RC	4	5	5	5	6	10	20	50
186	Billy Kilmer	4	5	5	5	6	10	20	
187	Jim Katcavage	4	5	5	5	6	10	20	80
188	Floyd Peters	4	5	5	5	6	10	30	50
189	Bill Nelsen	4	5	5	5	6	10	20	50
190	Bobby Joe Conrad	4	5	5	5	6	10	20	80
191	Kermit Alexander	4	5	5	5	6	10	30	100
192	Charley Taylor	4	5	5	5	8	12	25	100
193	Lance Alworth	5	6	8	10	15	25	50	250
194	Daryle Lamonica	4	5	5	5	6	10	50	
195	Al Atkinson	4	5	5	5	6	10	20	80
196	Bob Griese RC	25	30	35	50	80	100	300	▲1,400
197	Buck Buchanan	4	5	5	5	6	10	20	80
198	Pete Beathard	4	5	5	5	6	10	20	80
199	Nemiah Wilson	4	5	5	5	6	10	20	80
200	Ernie Wright	4	5	5	5	6	10	30	
201	George Saimes	4	5	5	5	6	10	20	50
202	John Charles	4	5	5	5	6	10	20	50
203	Randy Johnson	4	5	5	5	6	10	20	60
204	Tony Lorick	4	5	5	5	6	10	20	60
205	Dick Evey	4	5	5	5	6	10	20	60
206	Leroy Kelly	4	5	5	5	8	15	40	
207	Lee Roy Jordan	4	5	5	5	8	12	40	▼80
208	Jim Gibbons	4	5	5	5	6	10	20	50
209	Donny Anderson RC	4	5	5	5	6	12	60	175
210	Maxie Baughan	4	5	5	8	20	40	250	
211	Joe Morrison	4	5	5	5	6	10	20	120
212	Jim Snowden	4	5	5	5	6	10	30	
213	Lenny Lyles	4	5	5	5	6	10	20	80
214	Bobby Joe Green	4	5	5	5	6	10	25	100
215	Frank Ryan	4	5	5	5	6	10	40	120
216	Cornell Green	4	5	5	5	6	10	25	120
217	Karl Sweetan	4	5	5	5	6	10	30	
218	Dave Williams	4	5	5	5	6	10	20	60
219A	Checklist Green	5	5	6	8	12	25	100	
219B	Checklist Blue	5	5	6	8	12	25	80	

—Donny Anderson RC #209 PSA 10 (Gem Mint) sold for $451.5 (eBay: 5/12)
—George Blanda #142 PSA 10 (Gem Mint) sold for $758.5 (eBay: 8/12)
—Tommy Davis #165 PSA 10 (Gem) sold for $416 (Mile High: 10/09)
—Carroll Dale #27 PSA 9 (Mt) sold for $1028 (eBay: 11/14)
—Mike Ditka #162 PSA 10 (Gem) sold for $8,246 (eBay: 10/07)
—Roy Jefferson #85 PSA 10 (Gem Mint) sold for $616 (eBay: 4/12)
—Floyd Little #173 PSA 9 (Mt) sold for $2407 (eBay: 11/14)
—Floyd Little #173 PSA 9 (Mt) sold for $1007 (eBay: 11/14)
—Bobby Maples #16 PSA 10 (Gem) sold for $765 (eBay: 12/06)
—George Mira #9 PSA 10 (Gem Mint) sold for $284 (eBay: 4/12)
—Carig Morton #155 PSA 10 (Gem) sold for $680 (eBay: 11/06)
—Dan Reeves #77 PSA 10 (Gem) sold for $715 (eBay: 2/07)
—Frank Ryan #215 PSA 10 (Gem) sold for $740 (Mile High: 10/09)

FOOTBALL

orm Snead #110 PSA 10 (Gem) sold for $465 (eBay; 6/06)

nie Wright #200 PSA 10 (Gem) sold for $474 (Mile High; 10/09)

rry Wilson #164 PSA 10 (Gem) sold for $685 (eBay; 1/07)

68 Topps Stand-Ups Inserts

	GD 2	VG 3	VgEx 4	EX 5	ExMt 6	NM 7	NmMt 8	MT 9
COMMON CARD (1-22)	4	5	5	8	12	20	80	
John Brodie	5	6	8	10	15	30	80	
Jack Concannon	5	5	6	8	12	20	100	
Roman Gabriel	5	6	8	10	15	30	80	
Jim Grabowski	5	5	6	8	12	40	80	
John Hadl	5	5	6	8	12	30	60	
Sonny Jurgensen	5	6	8	10	15	40	120	
Alex Karras	5	6	8	10	15	30	60	
Billy Kilmer	5	6	8	10	15	30	120	
Daryle Lamonica	5	6	8	10	15	30	80	
Curtis McClinton	5	5	6	8	12	30	60	
Don Meredith	8	10	12	15	25	50	150	
Joe Namath	15	20	25	35	60	80	250	
Willie Richardson	5	5	6	8	12	30	100	

oman Gabriel #4 PSA 9 (MT) sold for $425 (eBay; 4/07)

omer Jones #9 PSA 10 (Gem Mint) sold for $750 (Bussineau; 7/12)

lex Karras #11 PSA 9 (Mint) sold for $420 (Bussineau; 7/12)

969 Topps

	GD 2	VG 3	VgEx 4	EX 5	ExMt 6	NM 7	NmMt 8	MT 9
Leroy Kelly	4	5	6	8	12	20	80	400
Paul Flatley	4	4	5	6	8	10	20	125
Jim Cadile	4	4	5	6	8	12	60	
Erich Barnes	4	4	5	6	8	10	20	80
Willie Richardson	4	4	5	6	8	10	30	150
Bob Hayes	4	5	6	8	10	12	50	125
Bob Jeter	4	4	5	6	8	10	50	175
Jim Colclough	4	4	5	6	8	10	20	60
Sherrill Headrick	4	4	5	6	8	10	25	
Jim Dunaway	4	4	5	6	8	10	20	
Bill Munson	4	4	5	6	8	10	20	80
Jack Pardee	4	4	5	6	8	10	20	60
Jim Lindsey	4	4	5	6	8	10	25	
Dave Whitsell	4	4	5	6	8	10	20	50
Tucker Frederickson	4	4	5	6	8	10	25	60
Alvin Haymond	4	4	5	6	8	10	25	
Andy Russell	4	4	5	6	8	10	20	80
Tom Beer	4	4	5	6	8	10	20	50
Bobby Maples	4	4	5	6	8	10	20	60
Len Dawson	4	5	6	8	12	15	40	200
Willis Crenshaw	4	4	5	6	8	10	15	60
Tommy Davis	4	4	5	6	8	10	20	60
Rickie Harris	4	4	5	6	8	10	20	60
Jerry Simmons	4	4	5	6	8	10	20	
Johnny Unitas	10	12	15	40	50	60	120	800
Brian Piccolo RC	20	25	30	▲50	60	100	▲300	▲1,400
Bob Matheson	4	4	5	6	8	10	20	60
Howard Twilley	4	4	5	6	8	10	20	80
Jim Turner	4	4	5	6	8	10	20	80
Pete Banaszak RC	4	4	5	6	8	10	20	80
Lance Rentzel RC	4	4	5	6	8	10	20	80
Bill Triplett	4	4	5	6	8	10	20	80
Boyd Dowler	4	4	5	6	8	10	20	80
Merlin Olsen	4	4	5	6	8	10	15	25	100
Joe Kapp	4	4	5	6	8	10	20	80
Dan Abramowicz RC	4	4	5	6	8	10	20	80
Spider Lockhart	4	4	5	6	8	10	20	60
Tom Day	4	4	5	6	8	10	20	60
Art Graham	4	4	5	6	8	10	20	60
Bob Cappadona	4	4	5	6	8	10	20	50
Gary Ballman	4	4	5	6	8	10	20	60
Clendon Thomas	4	4	5	6	8	10	20	100
Jackie Smith	4	5	6	8	10	12	25	100
Dave Wilcox	4	4	5	6	8	10	20	60
Jerry Smith	4	4	5	6	8	10	20	80
Dan Grimm	4	4	5	6	8	10	20	60
Tom Matte	4	4	5	6	8	10	20	80
John Stofa	4	4	5	6	8	10	20	50
Rex Mirich	4	4	5	6	8	10	20	60
Miller Farr	4	4	5	6	8	10	20	60
Gale Sayers	10	12	15	20	▲50	80	200	1,500

	GD 2	VG 3	VgEx 4	EX 5	ExMt 6	NM 7	NmMt 8	MT 9
52	Bill Nelsen	4	4	5	6	8	10	20	80
53	Bob Lilly	4	5	6	8	10	12	40	200
54	Wayne Walker	4	4	5	6	8	10	25	
55	Ray Nitschke	4	5	6	8	12	30	120	
56	Ed Meador	4	4	5	6	8	10	20	60
57	Lonnie Warwick	4	4	5	6	8	10	20	80
58	Wendell Hayes	4	4	5	6	8	10	20	60
59	Dick Anderson RC	4	5	6	8	10	12	40	100
60	Don Maynard	4	5	6	8	10	12	30	100
61	Tony Lorick	4	4	5	6	8	10	25	100
62	Pete Gogolak	4	4	5	6	8	10	20	80
63	Nate Ramsey	4	4	5	6	8	10	20	80
64	Dick Shiner	4	4	5	6	8	10	20	100
65	Larry Wilson	4	4	5	6	8	10	20	60
66	Ken Willard	4	4	5	6	8	10	20	60
67	Charley Taylor	4	5	6	8	10	12	25	100
68	Billy Cannon	4	4	5	6	8	10	25	
69	Lance Alworth	4	5	6	8	12	20	30	200
70	Jim Nance	4	4	5	6	8	10	20	60
71	Nick Rassas	4	4	5	6	8	10	25	
72	Lenny Lyles	4	4	5	6	8	10	20	60
73	Bennie McRae	4	4	5	6	8	10	20	80
74	Bill Glass	4	4	5	6	8	10	25	
75	Don Meredith	5	6	8	10	15	25	60	200
76	Dick LeBeau	4	4	5	6	8	10	20	60
77	Carroll Dale	4	4	5	6	8	10	20	100
78	Ron McDole	4	4	5	6	8	10	20	50
79	Charley King	4	4	5	6	8	10	20	60
80	Checklist 1	4	4	5	6	10	20	60	125
81	Dick Bass	4	4	5	6	8	10	20	60
82	Roy Winston	4	4	5	6	8	10	20	60
83	Don McCall	4	4	5	6	8	10	20	60
84	Jim Katcavage	4	4	5	6	8	10	20	60
85	Norm Snead	4	4	5	6	8	10	20	60
86	Earl Gros	4	4	5	6	8	10	20	60
87	Don Brumm	4	4	5	6	8	10	20	60
88	Sonny Bishop	4	4	5	6	8	10	20	100
89	Fred Arbanas	4	4	5	6	8	10	20	50
90	Karl Noonan	4	4	5	6	8	10	20	80
91	Dick Witcher	4	4	5	6	8	10	20	60
92	Vince Promuto	4	4	5	6	8	10	20	60
93	Tommy Nobis	4	4	5	6	8	10	20	100
94	Jerry Hill	4	4	5	6	8	10	20	150
95	Ed O'Bradovich RC	4	4	5	6	8	12	30	
96	Ernie Kellerman	4	4	5	6	8	10	20	40
97	Chuck Howley	4	4	5	6	8	10	30	100
98	Hewritt Dixon	4	4	5	6	8	10	20	50
99	Ron Mix	4	4	5	6	8	10	25	100
100	Joe Namath	15	20	25	30	80	100	200	1,000
101	Billy Gambrell	4	4	5	6	8	10	25	50
102	Elijah Pitts	4	4	5	6	8	10	30	150
103	Billy Truax RC	4	4	5	6	8	10	20	60
104	Ed Sharockman	4	4	5	6	8	10	25	50
105	Doug Atkins	4	4	5	6	8	10	25	80
106	Greg Larson	4	4	5	6	8	12	30	
107	Israel Lang	4	4	5	6	8	10	20	60
108	Houston Antwine	4	4	5	6	8	10	20	60
109	Paul Guidry	4	4	5	6	8	10	20	60
110	Al Denson	4	4	5	6	8	10	20	80
111	Roy Jefferson	4	4	5	6	8	10	20	80
112	Chuck Latourette	4	4	5	6	8	10	20	60
113	Jim Johnson	4	4	5	6	8	10	20	40
114	Bobby Mitchell	4	5	6	8	10	12	25	80
115	Randy Johnson	4	4	5	6	8	10	20	60
116	Lou Michaels	4	4	5	6	8	10	20	80
117	Rudy Kuechenberg	4	4	5	6	8	10	20	50
118	Walt Suggs	4	4	5	6	8	10	40	
119	Goldie Sellers	4	4	5	6	8	10	20	60
120	Larry Csonka RC	15	20	25	35	60	120	300	2,500
121	Jim Houston	4	4	5	6	8	10	20	80
122	Craig Baynham	4	4	5	6	8	10	20	80
123	Alex Karras	4	5	6	8	10	12	40	125
124	Jim Grabowski	4	4	5	6	8	10	30	
125	Roman Gabriel	4	5	6	8	10	12	60	
126	Larry Bowie	4	4	5	6	8	10	20	60
127	Dave Parks	4	4	5	6	8	10	20	80
128	Ben Davidson	4	4	5	6	8	10	20	80
129	Steve DeLong	4	4	5	6	8	12	30	
130	Fred Hill	4	4	5	6	8	12	40	80

		GD 2	VG 3	VgEx 4	EX 5	ExMt 6	NM 7	NmMt 8	MT 9
131	Ernie Koy	4	4	5	6	8	12	30	
132A	Checklist 2 no border	4	4	5	6	12	25	60	150
132B	Checklist 2 bordered	4	4	5	6	12	25	60	
133	Dick Hoak	4	4	5	6	10	15	80	
134	Larry Stallings RC	4	4	5	6	8	12	80	100
135	Clifton McNeil RC	4	4	5	6	8	12	80	100
136	Walter Rock	4	4	5	6	8		30	80
137	Billy Lothridge	4	4	5	6	8	10	30	50
138	Bob Vogel	4	4	5	6	8	10	25	80
139	Dick Butkus	8	10	12	15	25	40	120	800
140	Frank Ryan	4	4	5	6	8	10	35	150
141	Larry Garron	4	4	5	6	8	10	30	80
142	George Saimes	4	4	5	6	8	10	30	80
143	Frank Buncom	4	4	5	6	8	10	25	80
144	Don Perkins	4	5	6	8	10	12	40	150
145	Johnnie Robinson	4	4	5	6	8	10	30	60
146	Lee Roy Caffey	4	4	5	6	8	10	30	100
147	Bernie Casey	4	4	5	6	8	10	30	60
148	Billy Martin E	4	4	5	6	8	12	40	100
149	Gene Howard	4	4	5	6	8	10	30	100
150	Fran Tarkenton	5	6	8	10	15	30	▲80	300
151	Eric Crabtree	4	4	5	6	8	10	20	100
152	W.K. Hicks	4	4	5	6	8	10	40	80
153	Bobby Bell	4	5	6	8	10	12	30	125
154	Sam Baker	4	4	5	6	8	12	50	100
155	Marv Woodson	4	4	5	6	8	10	30	80
156	Dave Williams	4	4	5	6	8	10	30	80
157	Bruce Bosley	4	4	5	6	8	10	30	100
158	Carl Kammerer	4	4	5	6	8	10	30	100
159	Jim Burson	4	4	5	6	8	10	25	80
160	Roy Hilton	4	4	5	6	8	12	40	150
161	Bob Griese	5	6	8	10	15	30	60	▼500
162	Bob Talamini	4	4	5	6	8	10	30	80
163	Jim Otto	4	4	5	6	8	20	80	175
164	Ronnie Bull	4	4	5	6	8	10	30	100
165	Walter Johnson RC	4	4	5	6	8	12	50	125
166	Lee Roy Jordan	4	4	5	6	10	12	40	200
167	Mike Lucci	4	4	5	6	8	12	40	
168	Willie Wood	4	5	6	8	10	12	40	150
169	Maxie Baughan	4	4	5	6	8	10	25	
170	Bill Brown	4	4	5	6	8	10	25	80
171	John Hadl	4	4	5	6	8	15	80	175
172	Gino Cappelletti	4	4	5	6	8	10	20	80
173	George Butch Byrd	4	4	5	6	8	10	30	80
174	Steve Stonebreaker	4	4	5	6	8	10	30	60
175	Joe Morrison	4	4	5	6	8	10	30	80
176	Joe Scarpati	4	4	5	6	8	12	40	100
177	Bobby Walden	4	4	5	6	8	10	30	80
178	Roy Shivers	4	4	5	6	8	12	25	80
179	Kermit Alexander	4	4	5	6	8	10	30	80
180	Pat Richter	4	4	5	6	8	10	30	80
181	Pete Perreault	4	4	5	6	8	10	30	80
182	Pete Duranko	4	4	5	6	8	10	30	80
183	Leroy Mitchell	4	4	5	6	8	10	20	80
184	Jim Simon	4	4	5	6	8	10	30	80
185	Billy Ray Smith	4	4	5	6	8	10	30	80
186	Jack Concannon	4	4	5	6	8	12	40	80
187	Ben Davis	4	4	5	6	8	10	25	80
188	Mike Clark	4	4	5	6	8	10	40	120
189	Jim Gibbons	4	4	5	6	8	10	25	80
190	Dave Robinson	4	4	5	8	10	20	60	175
191	Otis Taylor	4	4	5	6	8	10	30	60
192	Nick Buoniconti	4	4	5	6	8	10	35	135
193	Matt Snell	4	4	5	6	8	10	30	80
194	Bruce Gossett	4	4	5	6	8	10	30	80
195	Mick Tingelhoff	4	4	5	6	8	10	30	100
196	Earl Leggett	4	4	5	6	8	10	25	50
197	Pete Case	4	4	5	6	8	10	30	80
198	Tom Woodeshick RC	4	4	5	6	8	10	30	80
199	Ken Kortas	4	4	5	6	8	10	30	80
200	Jim Hart	4	4	5	6	8	10	30	80
201	Fred Biletnikoff	4	5	6	8	12	20	50	250
202	Jacque MacKinnon	4	4	5	6	8	10	40	80
203	Jim Whalen	4	4	5	6	8	10	40	
204	Matt Hazeltine	4	4	5	6	8	10	30	80
205	Charlie Gogolak	4	4	5	6	8	10	25	60
206	Ray Ogden	4	4	5	6	8	10	25	50
207	John Mackey	4	5	6	8	10	12	30	60
208	Roosevelt Taylor	4	4	5	6	8	12	40	125
209	Gene Hickerson	4	4	5	6	8	10	25	100
210	Dave Edwards RC	4	4	5	6	8	10	40	80
211	Tom Sestak	4	4	5	6	8	10	30	80
212	Ernie Wright	4	4	5	6	8	10	25	100
213	Dave Costa	4	4	5	6	8	10	30	50
214	Tom Vaughn	4	4	5	6	8	10	30	80
215	Bart Starr	6	8	10	12	20	60	150	▲800
216	Les Josephson	4	4	5	6	8	10	30	80
217	Fred Cox	4	4	5	6	8	10	30	80
218	Mike Tilleman	4	4	5	6	8	10	30	80
219	Darrell Dess	4	4	5	6	8	10	30	80
220	Dave Lloyd	4	4	5	6	8	10	30	80
221	Pete Beathard	4	4	5	6	8	10	20	80
222	Buck Buchanan	4	5	6	8	10	12	35	100
223	Frank Emanuel	4	4	5	6	8	10	30	80
224	Paul Martha	4	4	5	6	8	10	30	80
225	Johnny Roland	4	4	5	6	8	10	30	80
226	Gary Lewis	4	4	5	6	8	10	20	80
227	Sonny Jurgensen	4	5	6	8	10	12	30	▲200
228	Jim Butler	4	4	5	6	8	10	20	60
229	Mike Curtis RC	4	5	6	8	10	12	50	200
230	Richie Petitbon	4	4	5	6	8	10	30	80
231	George Sauer Jr.	4	4	5	6	8	10	30	80
232	George Blanda	4	5	6	8	12	20	50	175
233	Gary Garrison	4	4	5	6	8	10	25	80
234	Gary Collins	4	4	5	6	8	10	30	100
235	Craig Morton	4	4	5	6	8	10	30	175
236	Tom Nowatzke	4	4	5	6	8	10	30	80
237	Donny Anderson	4	4	5	6	8	12	100	200
238	Deacon Jones	4	5	6	8	10	12	50	125
239	Grady Alderman	4	4	5	6	8	10	30	80
240	Billy Kilmer	4	4	5	6	8	10	20	100
241	Mike Taliaferro	4	4	5	6	8	10	30	100
242	Stew Barber	4	4	5	6	8	10	30	80
243	Bobby Hunt	4	4	5	6	8	10	30	60
244	Homer Jones	4	4	5	6	8	10	30	80
245	Bob Brown OT	4	4	5	6	8	15	60	120
246	Bill Asbury	4	4	5	6	8	10	30	100
247	Charlie Johnson	4	4	5	6	8	10	50	80
248	Chris Hanburger	4	4	5	6	8	10	20	80
249	John Brodie	4	5	6	8	10	12	60	80
250	Earl Morrall	4	4	5	6	8	10	40	120
251	Floyd Little	4	5	6	8	10	15	40	120
252	Jerrel Wilson RC	4	4	5	6	8	10	30	100
253	Jim Keyes	4	4	5	6	8	10	30	100
254	Mel Renfro	4	5	6	8	10	12	35	125
255	Herb Adderley	4	5	6	8	10	15	40	150
256	Jack Snow	4	4	5	6	8	10	30	100
257	Charlie Durkee	4	4	5	6	8	10	30	100
258	Charlie Harper	4	4	5	6	8	10	25	80
259	J.R. Wilburn	4	4	5	6	8	10	30	150
260	Charlie Krueger	4	4	5	6	8	10	40	80
261	Pete Jacques	4	4	5	6	8	10	30	80
262	Gerry Philbin	4	4	5	6	10	12	40	100
263	Daryle Lamonica	4	5	6	8	12	20	80	

—John Brodie #249 PSA 10 (Gem Mt) sold for $1,033 (eBay; 2/09)
—Dick Butkus #139 PSA 9 (Mint) sold for $2,007 (eBay; 1/09)
—Dick Butkus #139 PSA 9 (Mint) sold for $1,125 (eBay; 2/10)
—Dick Butkus #139 PSA 9 (Mint) sold for $656 (eBay; 8/12)
—Checklist bordered #132B PSA 9 (Mint) sold for $765 (eBay; 3/08)
—Jim Dunaway #10 PSA 9 (Mint) sold for $1,103 (Mile High; 3/09)
—Wendell Hayes #10 PSA 10 (Gem) sold for $854 (eBay; 11/14)
—Randy Johnson #115 PSA 10 (Gem Mt) sold for $672 (Mile High; 10/09)
—Lou Michaels #116 PSA 10 (Gem Mt) sold for $611 (Mile High; 10/09)
—Leory Mitchell #183 PSA 9 (Mint) sold for $977 (eBay; 10/12)
—Ron Mix #99 PSA 10 (Gem Mt) sold for $1,317 (eBay; 2/13)
—Gayle Sayers #51 PSA 9 (Mint) sold for $1683 (eBay; 8/13)

1969 Topps Four-in-One Inserts

		GD 2	VG 3	VgEx 4	EX 5	ExMt 6	NM 7	NmMt 8	MT 9
	COMMON CARD (1-66)	4	4	4	5	6	10	20	
1	Aldmn/Je.Smith/Sayrs/LeBeau	4	4	5	6	10	15	50	
3	Alwrth/Mynrd/McDle/Cannon	4	4	4	5	8	12	25	60
4	Andrsn/Talifrro/Biltnikff/O/Tylr	4	4	4	5	8	12	25	
6	Bllmn/J.Hill/R.Jeffrsn/Dowler	4	4	4	5	8	10	20	60
8	Bishop/Bnaszk/Guidry/Day	4	4	4	5	6	10	20	60
11	Bnicnti/Saimes/McKinn/Drnko	4	4	4	5	8	10	20	60
13	Carln/Grron/Hicks/Jacques	4	4	4	5	6	10	20	60

	GD 2	VG 3	VgEx 4	EX 5	ExMt 6	NM 7	NmMt 8	MT 9
Dixon/Sell/Namath/Twilley	5	6	8	10	15	25	50	
Durk/McNeil/Bghn/Tarken	4	4	5	6	10	15	30	80
Griese/LeMne/Grysn/Swney	4	4	5	6	10	15	30	100
Hickrsn/D.Andrsn/Butks/Luc	4	4	5	6	10	15	30	
Howrd/Morrisn/B.Mrtin/B.Dvis	4	4	4	5	6	10	20	60
Hwly/Picclo/Hnbrgr/Barnes	5	6	8	10	15	25	50	100
W.John/Frdricksn/Lloyd/Wldn	4	4	4	5	6	10	20	60
Jurgensen/Bass/Martha/Parks	4	4	4	5	8	12	25	
Kelly/Meador/Starr/Ogden	4	4	5	6	10	15	35	120
Lamon/Cnninghm/Hunt/Brbr	4	4	4	5	6	10	20	60
Lang/Lilly/Butler/Brodie	4	4	4	5	8	12	25	
Mrdith/G.Cllins/H.Jnes/Wdsn	4	4	5	6	10	15	30	80
Nance/Dunaway/Csonka/Mix	4	4	5	6	10	15	30	100
Nlsn/Munson/Ramsey/Curtis	4	4	4	5	6	10	20	60
Pard/Snead/Baynham/Jeter	4	4	4	5	6	10	20	60
Rass/Mtte/Rntzl/B.Mitchell	4	4	4	5	6	10	20	60
Rolnd/Mortn/Bi.Brown/Baker	4	4	4	5	6	10	20	60
Rssll/R.Jhnsn/Mthsn/Karras	4	4	4	5	8	12	25	
Sestak/Wright/Moreau/Snell	4	4	4	5	6	10	20	60
Simmns/B.Hyes/Atkns/Lckhrt	4	4	4	5	6	10	20	60
Ja.Smth/Grbw/Ji.Jhnsn/C.Tylr	4	4	4	5	8	12	25	60
Strttn/Rshing/Brnnan/Keyes	4	4	4	5	6	10	20	60
Suggs/Dwsn/Hedrck/Denson	4	4	4	5	8	12	25	80
Talam/Blanda/Whalen/Kemp	4	5	6	8	12	20	40	
Trull/Philbin/Garrison/Buchan	4	4	4	5	6	10	20	60
Unitas/Josephson/Cox/Renfro	4	4	5	6	10	20	40	100
West/Herock/Byrd/Cappell	4	4	4	5	6	10	20	60

Dixon/Sellers/Namath/Twilley #15 PSA 9 (MT) sold for $400 (eBay; 11/06)
Dixon/Sell/Namath/Twilley #15 PSA 10 (Gem Mint) sold for $575.96 (Memory Lane; 5/12)

1970 Kellogg's

	VG 3	VgEx 4	EX 5	ExMt 6	NM 7	NmMt 8	MT 9	Gem 9.5/10
COMMON CARD (1-60)	4	4	5	6	10	12	15	60
Carl Eller	4	5	5	5	6	12	30	80
Len Dawson	4	5	5	5	6	12	20	60
Dick Butkus	4	5	5	6	8	15	30	350
George Sauer Jr.	4	5	5	5	6	10	20	50
Alex Karras	4	5	5	5	6	12	18	50
Bob Griese	4	5	5	5	6	12	25	100
Paul Warfield	4	5	5	5	6	12	20	60
Mike Garrett	4	5	5	5	6	10	25	400
Carl Garrett	4	5	5	5	6	10	20	175
Merlin Olsen	4	5	5	5	6	12	18	60
Lance Alworth	4	5	5	5	6	12	30	300
Larry Csonka	4	5	5	5	6	12	30	300
Bobby Bell	4	5	5	5	6	10	25	
George Webster	4	5	5	5	6	10	20	120
Bubba Smith	4	5	5	5	6	10	20	60
O.J. Simpson	4	5	6	8	12	25	50	200
Fred Biletnikoff	4	5	5	5	6	12	18	60
Gale Sayers	4	5	5	6	8	15	30	100
Sonny Jurgensen	4	5	5	5	6	12	20	80
Bob Lilly	4	5	5	5	6	12	18	80
Johnny Unitas	4	5	6	8	10	20	50	250
Don Maynard	4	5	5	5	6	10	20	60

1970 Topps

	VG 3	VgEx 4	EX 5	ExMt 6	NM 7	NmMt 8	MT 9	Gem 9.5/10
Len Dawson	4	5	6	10	18	40	175	
Doug Hart	4	5	5	5	8	12	60	
Verlon Biggs	4	5	5	5	8	12	40	120
Ralph Neely RC	4	5	5	5	8	20	300	
Harmon Wages	4	5	5	5	8	12	40	
Dan Conners	4	5	5	5	8	12	40	
Gino Cappelletti	4	5	5	5	8	12	150	
Erich Barnes	4	5	5	5	8	12	150	
Checklist 1	4	5	5	6	10	30		
Bob Griese	5	6	8	12	20	40	175	
Ed Flanagan	4	5	5	5	8	12	40	
George Seals	4	5	5	5	8	12	50	
Harry Jacobs	4	5	5	5	8	12	40	
Mike Haffner	4	5	5	5	8	12	50	
Bob Vogel	4	5	5	5	8	12	40	
Bill Peterson	4	5	5	5	8	12	50	
Spider Lockhart	4	5	5	5	8	12	50	
Billy Truax	4	5	5	5	8	12	50	
Jim Beirne	4	5	5	5	8	12	50	

		VG 3	VgEx 4	EX 5	ExMt 6	NM 7	NmMt 8	MT 9	Gem 9.5/10
20	Leroy Kelly	4	5	5	6	10	20	80	
21	Dave Lloyd	4	5	5	5	8	12	40	
22	Mike Tilleman	4	5	5	5	8	12	40	
23	Gary Garrison	4	5	5	5	8	12	50	
24	Larry Brown RC	4	5	5	8	12	30	▼100	
25	Jan Stenerud RC	4	5	6	10	15	40	150	
26	Rolf Krueger	4	5	5	5	8	12	50	
27	Roland Lakes	4	5	5	5	8	12	50	
28	Dick Hoak	4	5	5	5	8	12	50	
29	Gene Washington Vik RC	4	5	5	6	10	15	200	
30	Bart Starr	6	8	10	15	30	80	250	
31	Dave Grayson	4	5	5	5	8	12	50	
32	Jerry Rush	4	5	5	5	8	12	50	
33	Len St. Jean	4	5	5	5	8	20		
34	Randy Edmunds	4	5	5	5	8	12	50	
35	Matt Snell	4	5	5	5	8	12	40	
36	Paul Costa	4	5	5	5	8	12	40	
37	Mike Pyle	4	5	5	5	8	12	50	
38	Roy Hilton	4	5	5	5	8	12	50	
39	Steve Tensi	4	5	5	5	8	12	60	
40	Tommy Nobis	4	5	5	6	10	15	50	
41	Pete Case	4	5	5	5	8	12	40	
42	Andy Rice	4	5	5	5	8	12	50	
43	Elvin Bethea RC	4	5	5	8	15	40	150	600
44	Jack Snow	4	5	5	5	8	12	50	
45	Mel Renfro	4	5	5	6	10	20	60	
46	Andy Livingston	4	5	5	5	8	12	30	120
47	Gary Ballman	4	5	5	5	8	12	40	
48	Bob DeMarco	4	5	5	5	8	12	40	
49	Steve DeLong	4	5	5	5	8	25		
50	Daryle Lamonica	4	5	5	6	10	15	60	300
51	Jim Lynch RC	4	5	5	6	12	25	135	
52	Mel Farr RC	4	5	5	5	8	12	40	
53	Bob Long RC	4	5	5	5	8	12	40	
54	John Elliott	4	5	5	5	8	12	50	
55	Ray Nitschke	4	5	5	6	12	30	100	
56	Jim Shorter	4	5	5	5	8	12	50	
57	Dave Wilcox	4	5	5	6	10	15	60	
58	Eric Crabtree	4	5	5	5	8	12	40	
59	Alan Page RC	6	8	12	20	30	60	200	800
60	Jim Nance	4	5	5	5	8	12	40	
61	Glen Ray Hines	4	5	5	5	8	12	40	120
62	John Mackey	4	5	5	6	10	15	60	
63	Ron McDole	4	5	5	5	8	12	40	
64	Tom Beier	4	5	5	5	8	12	40	120
65	Bill Nelsen	4	5	5	5	8	12	80	
66	Paul Flatley	4	5	5	5	8	12	40	
67	Sam Brunelli	4	5	5	5	8	12	40	
68	Jack Pardee	4	5	5	5	8	12	40	
69	Brig Owens	4	5	5	5	8	12	50	
70	Gale Sayers	6	8	10	15	30	80	400	
71	Lee Roy Jordan	4	5	5	6	10	15	80	
72	Harold Jackson RC	4	5	5	6	10	20	50	
73	John Hadl	4	5	5	6	10	15	100	
74	Dave Parks	4	5	5	5	8	12	40	
75	Lem Barney RC	5	6	8	12	20	40	150	
76	Johnny Roland	4	5	5	5	8	12	40	
77	Ed Budde	4	5	5	5	8	12	50	
78	Ben McGee	4	5	5	5	8	12	40	
79	Ken Bowman	4	5	5	5	8	12	40	
80	Fran Tarkenton	4	5	5	6	10	18	30	100	600
81	G.Washington 49er RC	4	5	5	6	10	20	▲80	
82	Larry Grantham	4	5	5	5	8	12	50	
83	Bill Brown	4	5	5	5	8	12	50	
84	John Charles	4	5	5	5	8	12	40	
85	Fred Biletnikoff	4	5	5	6	10	25	100	
86	Royce Berry	4	5	5	5	8	12	40	
87	Bob Lilly	4	5	5	6	10	20	60	
88	Earl Morrall	4	5	5	5	8	15	50	
89	Jerry LeVias RC	4	5	5	5	8	12	40	
90	O.J. Simpson RC	20	40	60	100	200	500	1,500	
91	Mike Howell	4	5	5	5	8	12	40	
92	Ken Gray	4	5	5	5	8	12	40	100
93	Chris Hanburger	4	5	5	5	8	12	40	
94	Larry Seiple RC	4	5	5	5	8	12	40	250
95	Rich Jackson RC	4	5	5	5	8	12	200	
96	Rockne Freitas	4	5	5	5	8	12	50	
97	Dick Post RC	4	5	5	5	8	12	50	
98	Ben Hawkins RC	4	5	5	5	8	12	40	

#	Player	VG 3	VgEx 4	EX 5	ExMt 6	NM 7	NmMt 8	MT 9	Gem 9.5/10
99	Ken Reaves	4	5	5	5	8	12	50	
100	Roman Gabriel	4	5	5	6	10	15	60	
101	Dave Rowe	4	5	5	5	8	15		
102	Dave Robinson	4	5	5	5	8	12	40	
103	Otis Taylor	4	5	5	5	8	12	60	
104	Jim Turner	4	5	5	5	8	15		
105	Joe Morrison	4	5	5	5	8	12	50	
106	Dick Evey	4	5	5	5	8	12	50	
107	Ray Mansfield	4	5	5	5	8	12	40	
108	Grady Alderman	4	5	5	5	8	12	50	
109	Bruce Gossett	4	5	5	5	8	12	50	
110	Bob Trumpy RC	4	5	5	6	10	20	80	
111	Jim Hunt	4	5	5	5	8	12	40	
112	Larry Stallings	4	5	5	5	8	12	40	
113A	Lance Rentzel Red	4	5	5	5	8	12	40	
113B	Lance Rentzel Black	4	5	5					
114	Bubba Smith RC	5	6	8	12	20	40	150	800
115	Norm Snead	4	5	5	5	8	12	40	
116	Jim Otto	4	5	5	6	10	15	60	
117	Bo Scott RC	4	5	5	5	8	15	60	
118	Rick Redman	4	5	5	5	8	12	40	150
119	George Butch Byrd	4	5	5	5	8	12	40	
120	George Webster RC	4	5	5	5	8	12	40	
121	Chuck Walton RC	4	5	5	5	8	12	40	
122	Dave Costa	4	5	5	5	8	12	40	
123	Al Dodd	4	5	5	5	8	12	40	
124	Len Hauss	4	5	5	5	8	15		
125	Deacon Jones	4	5	5	6	10	20	100	
126	Randy Johnson	4	5	5	5	8	12	40	
127	Ralph Heck	4	5	5	5	8	12	40	
128	Emerson Boozer RC	4	5	5	5	8	12	40	
129	Johnny Robinson	4	5	5	5	8	12	60	
130	John Brodie	4	5	5	6	10	20	90	
131	Gale Gillingham RC	4	5	5	5	8	12	40	
132	Checklist 2 DP	4	5	5	5	8	15	60	
133	Chuck Walker	4	5	5	5	8	12	80	
134	Bennie McRae	4	5	5	5	8	12	50	
135	Paul Warfield	4	5	5	6	10	20	150	
136	Dan Darragh	4	5	5	5	8	12	50	
137	Paul Robinson RC	4	5	5	5	8	12	50	
138	Ed Philpott	4	5	5	5	8	12	40	
139	Craig Morton	4	5	5	5	8	20	100	
140	Tom Dempsey RC	4	5	5	5	8	12	60	
141	Al Nelson	4	5	5	5	8	12	50	
142	Tom Matte	4	5	5	5	8	12	60	
143	Dick Schafrath	4	5	5	5	8	12	50	
144	Willie Brown	4	5	5	5	8	15	100	
145	Charley Taylor	4	5	5	6	10	20	60	
146	John Huard	4	5	5	5	8	12	50	
147	Dave Osborn	4	5	5	5	8	12	50	
148	Gene Mingo	4	5	5	5	8	12	50	
149	Larry Hand	4	5	5	5	8	12	50	
150	Joe Namath	15	20	25	50	100	200	1,300	
151	Tom Mack RC	4	5	5	8	15	60	200	
152	Kenny Graham	4	5	5	5	8	12	50	
153	Don Herrmann	4	5	5	5	8	12	50	
154	Bobby Bell	4	5	5	5	8	20		
155	Hoyle Granger	4	5	5	5	8	12	60	
156	Claude Humphrey RC	4	5	8	12	25	100	250	
157	Clifton McNeil	4	5	5	5	8	12	50	
158	Mick Tingelhoff	4	5	5	5	8	40	200	
159	Don Horn RC	4	5	5	5	8	12	50	
160	Larry Wilson	4	5	5	6	10	30	300	
161	Tom Neville	4	5	5	5	8	12	50	
162	Larry Csonka	5	6	8	12	20	50	300	
163	Doug Buffone RC	4	5	5	5	8	20	80	
164	Cornell Green	4	5	5	5	8	12	50	
165	Haven Moses RC	4	5	5	5	8	12	40	
166	Billy Kilmer	4	5	5	5	8	15	60	
167	Tim Rossovich RC	4	5	5	5	8	12	50	
168	Bill Bergey RC	4	5	5	5	8	15	150	
169	Gary Collins	4	5	5	5	8	12	50	
170	Floyd Little	4	5	5	5	8	15	200	
171	Tom Keating	4	5	5	5	8	20	100	
172	Pat Fischer	4	5	5	5	8	12	50	
173	Walt Sweeney	4	5	5	5	8	20		
174	Greg Larson	4	5	5	5	8	20	80	
175	Carl Eller	4	5	5	6	10	40	300	
176	George Sauer Jr.	4	5	5	5	8	12	50	
177	Jim Hart	4	5	5	5	8	15	60	
178	Bob Brown OT	4	5	5	5	8	15	100	
179	Mike Garrett RC	4	5	5	5	8	25	60	
180	Johnny Unitas	8	10	12	25	40	80	350	
181	Tom Regner	4	5	5	5	8	12	50	
182	Bob Jeter	4	5	5	5	8	12	50	
183	Gail Cogdill	4	5	5	5	8	12	50	
184	Earl Gros	4	5	5	5	8	12	50	
185	Dennis Partee	4	5	5	5	8	12	50	
186	Charlie Krueger	4	5	5	5	8	12	50	
187	Martin Baccaglio	4	5	5	5	8	12	50	
188	Charles Long	4	5	5	5	8	12	50	
189	Bob Hayes	4	5	5	6	12	30		
190	Dick Butkus	8	10	12	20	30	60	250	
191	Al Bemiller	4	5	5	5	8	12	50	
192	Dick Westmoreland	4	5	5	5	8	12	50	
193	Joe Scarpati	4	5	5	5	8	12	50	
194	Ron Snidow	4	5	5	5	8	12	50	
195	Earl McCullouch RC	4	5	5	5	8	12	80	
196	Jake Kupp	4	5	5	5	8	12	50	
197	Bob Lurtsema	4	5	5	5	8	12	50	
198	Mike Current	4	5	5	5	8	12	50	
199	Charlie Smith RB	4	5	5	5	8	12	80	
200	Sonny Jurgensen	4	5	5	6	10	20	100	
201	Mike Curtis	4	5	5	5	8	12	50	
202	Aaron Brown RC	4	5	5	5	8	12	50	
203	Richie Petitbon	4	5	5	5	8	12	50	
204	Walt Suggs	4	5	5	5	8	12	50	
205	Roy Jefferson	4	5	5	5	8	12	100	
206	Russ Washington RC	4	5	5	5	8	12	125	
207	Woody Peoples RC	4	5	5	5	8	12	80	
208	Dave Williams	4	5	5	5	8	12	50	
209	John Zook RC	4	5	5	5	8	12	50	
210	Tom Woodeshick	4	5	5	5	8	12	50	
211	Howard Fest	4	5	5	5	8	12	50	
212	Jack Concannon	4	5	5	5	8	12	50	
213	Jim Marshall	4	5	5	5	8	15	60	
214	Jon Morris	4	5	5	5	8	12	50	
215	Dan Abramowicz	4	5	5	5	8	12	50	
216	Paul Martha	4	5	5	5	8	12	40	
217	Ken Willard	4	5	5	5	8	12	50	
218	Walter Rock	4	5	5	5	8	12	50	
219	Garland Boyette	4	5	5	5	8	12	50	
220	Buck Buchanan	4	5	5	5	8	15	200	
221	Bill Munson	4	5	5	5	10	25	150	
222	David Lee RC	4	5	5	5	8	15		
223	Karl Noonan	4	5	5	5	8	25		
224	Harry Schuh	4	5	5	5	8	12	50	
225	Jackie Smith	4	5	5	5	8	15	60	
226	Gerry Philbin	4	5	5	5	8	12	50	
227	Ernie Koy	4	5	5	5	8	12	50	
228	Chuck Howley	4	5	5	5	8	25	60	
229	Billy Shaw	4	5	5	5	8	15	60	
230	Jerry Hillebrand	4	5	5	5	8	12	50	
231	Bill Thompson RC	4	5	5	5	8	12	50	
232	Carroll Dale	4	5	5	5	8	12	60	
233	Gene Hickerson	4	5	5	5	8	12	50	
234	Jim Butler	4	5	5	5	8	12	50	
235	Greg Cook RC	4	5	5	5	8	12	50	
236	Lee Roy Caffey	4	5	5	5	8	12	50	
237	Merlin Olsen	4	5	5	5	8	25	80	
238	Fred Cox	4	5	5	5	8	12	60	
239	Nate Ramsey	4	5	5	5	8	12	50	
240	Lance Alworth	4	5	5	6	10	25	100	
241	Chuck Hinton	4	5	5	5	8	12	50	
242	Jerry Smith	4	5	5	5	8	12	50	
243	Tony Baker FB	4	5	5	5	8	12	50	
244	Nick Buoniconti	4	5	5	5	8	15	60	
245	Jim Johnson	4	5	5	5	8	15	80	
246	Willie Richardson	4	5	5	5	8	12	100	
247	Fred Dryer RC	4	5	5	8	15	50	200	
248	Bobby Maples	4	5	5	5	8	12	50	
249	Alex Karras	4	5	5	5	8	15	200	
250	Joe Kapp	4	5	5	5	8	12	50	
251	Ben Davidson	4	5	5	5	8	15	60	
252	Mike Stratton	4	5	5	5	8	12	60	
253	Les Josephson	4	5	5	5	8	12	50	
254	Don Maynard	4	5	5	6	10	20	80	
255	Houston Antwine	4	5	5	5	8	25	60	

	VG 3	VgEx 4	EX 5	ExMt 6	NM 7	NmMt 8	MT 9	Gem 9.5/10
Mac Percival RC	4	5	5	5	8	12	80	
George Goeddeke	4	5	5	5	8	12	50	
Homer Jones	4	5	5	5	8	12	50	
Bob Berry	4	5	5	5	8	15		
Calvin Hill Red RC	4	5	6	10	20	40	150	
Calvin Hill RC Black	4	5	10	25	50	100		
Willie Wood	4	5	5	5	8	20	80	
Ed Weisacosky	4	5	5	5	8	25	300	
Jim Tyrer	4	5	5	6	10	30		

m Barney #75 PSA 10 (Gem) sold for $2,011 (eBay; 2/13)
m Barney #75 PSA 10 (Gem) sold for $1440 (eBay; 11/14)
vin Bethea #43 PSA 10 (Gem) sold for $1,280 (eBay; 2/08)
vin Bethea #43 PSA 10 (Gem Mint) sold for $573 (eBay; 6/12)
e Roy Caffey #236 PSA 10 (Gem) sold for $1,252 (Mile High; 10/13)
arry Csonka #162 PSA 10 (Gem) sold for $2,055 (eBay; 3/07)
arry Csonka #162 PSA 10 (Gem Mint) sold for $1517.67 (eBay; 6/12)
arry Csonka #162 PSA 10 (Gem Mint) sold for $2510 (eBay; 6/16)
en Dawson #1 PSA 10 (Gem) sold for $832.69 (eBay; 6/12)
red Dryer RC #247 PSA 10 (Gem Mint) sold for $569.33 (eBay; 6/12)
on Maynard #254 PSA 10 (Gem Mint) sold for $570.03 (eBay; 6/12)
ay Nitschke #55 PSA 10 (Gem) sold for $698 (Andy Madec; 5/07)
erlin Olsen #237 PSA 10 (Gem Mint) sold for $560.43 (eBay; 6/12)
an Page #59 PSA 10 (Gem) sold for $790 (eBay; 4/07)
art Starr #30 PSA 10 (Gem) sold for $720 (eBay; 11/12)
art Starr #30 PSA 10 (Gem) sold for $910 (eBay; 2/07)
art Starr #30 PSA 10 (Gem) sold for $913 (eBay; 4/14)

970 Topps Glossy Inserts

	GD 2	VG 3	VgEx 4	EX 5	ExMt 6	NM 7	NmMt 8	MT 9
COMMON CARD (1-33)	4	4	4	5	6	10	18	80
Tommy Nobis	4	5	5	6	10	15	30	150
Johnny Unitas	6	8	10	12	20	30	50	200
Mac Percival	4	5	5	5	6	10	18	120
Leroy Kelly	4	5	5	5	8	12	20	60
Bob Hayes	4	5	5	5	6	10	18	150
Bart Starr	5	5	6	8	12	20	40	175
Willie Wood	4	5	5	5	8	12	20	80
Dave Osborn	4	5	5	5	6	10	18	120
Fran Tarkenton	4	5	5	5	8	12	40	100
Tom Woodeshick	4	5	5	5	6	10	18	120
Sonny Jurgensen	4	5	5	6	10	15	30	150
Houston Antwine	4	5	5	5	6	10	18	120
O.J. Simpson	4	5	6	8	12	20	40	150
Rich Jackson	4	5	5	5	6	10	18	120
George Webster	4	5	5	5	6	10	18	120
Len Dawson	4	5	5	5	8	12	25	100
Bob Griese	4	5	5	5	8	12	25	100
Joe Namath	8	10	12	15	25	40	60	175
Daryle Lamonica	4	5	5	5	8	12	25	150
Fred Biletnikoff	4	5	5	5	8	12	20	80

971 Kellogg's

	GD 2	VG 3	VgEx 4	EX 5	ExMt 6	NM 7	NmMt 8	MT 9
COMMON CARD (1-60)	4	4	5	5	6	12	25	60
Tom Barrington	4	4	5	5	6	12	50	150
Chris Hanburger	4	4	5	5	6	15	40	80
Fred Dryer	4	4	5	5	6	12	25	60
Larry Brown	4	4	5	5	6	12	25	100
Joe Greene	4	5	6	8	25	30	50	125
Johnny Unitas	8	10	12	15	25	40	125	250
George Blanda	4	5	6	8	12	18	30	100
Dick Butkus	5	6	8	10	15	25	40	200
John Brodie	4	4	5	5	8	15	30	60
Bob Griese	4	5	6	8	12	20	35	100

-Doug Cunningham #58 PSA 10 (Gem) sold for $500 (eBay; 4/07)
-Len Dawson #1 PSA 10 (Gem) sold for $384 (Mile High; 10/09)
-Gary Garrison #110 PSA 10 (Gem) sold for $460 (eBay; 4/07)

1971 Topps

	GD 2	VG 3	VgEx 4	EX 5	ExMt 6	NM 7	NmMt 8	MT 9
Johnny Unitas	5	8	12	▲25	▲40	▲80	200	1,250
Jim Butler	4	4	5	5	6	12	60	
Marty Schottenheimer RC	4	5	6	8	12	20	50	
Joe O'Donnell	4	4	5	5	6	10	20	
Tom Dempsey	4	4	5	5	6	10	20	200
Chuck Allen	4	4	5	5	6	10	20	
Ernie Kellerman	4	4	5	5	6	10	20	100

		GD 2	VG 3	VgEx 4	EX 5	ExMt 6	NM 7	NmMt 8	MT 9
8	Walt Garrison RC	4	4	5	5	6	10	30	150
9	Bill Van Heusen	4	4	5	5	6	10	20	
10	Lance Alworth	4	4	5	5	8	15	25	150
11	Greg Landry RC	4	4	5	5	6	10	20	80
12	Larry Krause	4	4	5	5	6	10	20	80
13	Buck Buchanan	4	4	5	5	6	10	40	
14	Roy Gerela RC	4	4	5	5	6	10	20	80
15	Clifton McNeil	4	4	5	5	6	12	50	
16	Bob Brown OT	4	4	5	5	6	10	20	80
17	Lloyd Mumphord	4	4	5	5	6	10	50	
18	Gary Cuozzo	4	4	5	5	6	12	40	
19	Don Maynard	4	4	5	5	6	12	25	150
20	Larry Wilson	4	4	5	5	6	10	25	
21	Charlie Smith RB	4	4	5	5	6	10	20	80
22	Ken Avery	4	4	5	5	6	10	20	120
23	Billy Walik	4	4	5	5	6	10	20	80
24	Jim Johnson	4	4	5	5	6	10	25	
25	Dick Butkus	5	8	10	12	20	50	125	
26	Charley Taylor	4	4	5	5	6	12	25	100
27	Checklist 1	4	4	5	5	8	30	300	
28	Lionel Aldridge RC	4	4	5	5	6	10	60	150
29	Billy Lothridge	4	4	5	5	6	10	20	80
30	Terry Hanratty RC	4	4	5	5	6	10	20	150
31	Lee Roy Jordan	4	4	5	5	6	10	40	
32	Rick Volk RC	4	4	5	5	6	10	20	
33	Howard Kindig	4	4	5	5	6	10	20	80
34	Carl Garrett RC	4	4	5	5	6	10	20	80
35	Bobby Bell	4	4	5	5	6	20	60	
36	Gene Hickerson	4	4	5	5	6	10	20	100
37	Dave Parks	4	4	5	5	6	10	20	
38	Paul Martha	4	4	5	5	6	10	20	80
39	George Blanda	4	4	5	5	8	15	30	100
40	Tom Woodeshick	4	4	5	5	6	10	20	100
41	Alex Karras	4	4	5	5	6	12	25	100
42	Rick Redman	4	4	5	5	6	10	20	120
43	Zeke Moore	4	4	5	5	6	10	20	
44	Jack Snow	4	4	5	5	6	12	40	120
45	Larry Csonka	4	4	5	6	10	18	40	300
46	Karl Kassulke	4	4	5	5	6	10	20	80
47	Jim Hart	4	4	5	5	6	10	20	80
48	Al Atkinson	4	4	5	5	6	12	100	
49	Horst Muhlmann RC	4	4	5	5	6	10	20	
50	Sonny Jurgensen	4	4	5	5	6	15	30	150
51	Ron Johnson RC	4	4	5	5	6	10	20	
52	Cas Banaszek	4	4	5	5	6	12	60	
53	Bubba Smith	4	4	5	5	6	12	25	150
54	Bobby Douglass RC	4	4	5	5	6	10	20	80
55	Willie Wood	4	4	5	5	6	10	20	
56	Bake Turner	4	4	5	5	6	10	20	
57	Mike Morgan LB	4	4	5	5	6	10	20	
58	George Butch Byrd	4	4	5	5	6	10	40	
59	Don Horn	4	4	5	5	6	12	40	
60	Tommy Nobis	4	4	5	5	6	10	20	135
61	Jan Stenerud	4	4	5	5	6	12	25	100
62	Altie Taylor RC	4	4	5	5	6	10	20	
63	Gary Pettigrew	4	4	5	5	6	10	20	
64	Spike Jones RC	4	4	5	5	6	10	50	
65	Duane Thomas RC	4	4	5	5	6	10	50	
66	Marty Domres RC	4	4	5	5	6	10	20	
67	Dick Anderson	4	4	5	5	6	10	20	150
68	Ken Iman	4	4	5	5	6	10	20	
69	Miller Farr	4	4	5	5	6	12	60	
70	Daryle Lamonica	4	4	5	5	6	12	25	150
71	Alan Page	4	4	5	6	10	18	30	400
72	Pat Matson	4	4	5	5	6	10	20	80
73	Emerson Boozer	4	4	5	5	6	10	20	80
74	Pat Fischer	4	4	5	5	6	12	60	
75	Gary Collins	4	4	5	5	6	10	20	
76	John Fuqua RC	4	4	5	5	8	15	50	
77	Bruce Gossett	4	4	5	5	6	12	50	
78	Ed O'Bradovich	4	4	5	5	6	10	20	80
79	Bob Tucker RC	4	4	5	5	6	12	30	
80	Mike Curtis	4	4	5	5	6	12	50	
81	Rich Jackson	4	4	5	5	6	10	20	100
82	Tom Janik	4	4	5	5	6	10	20	100
83	Gale Gillingham	4	4	5	5	6	10	20	
84	Jim Mitchell TE	4	4	5	5	6	10	20	
85	Charlie Johnson	4	4	5	5	6	10	20	100
86	Edgar Chandler	4	4	5	5	6	10	20	

#	Player	GD 2	VG 3	VgEx 4	EX 5	ExMt 6	NM 7	NmMt 8	MT 9
87	Cyril Pinder	4	4	5	5	6	10	20	
88	Johnny Robinson	4	4	5	5	6	10	20	
89	Ralph Neely	4	4	5	5	6	10	25	
90	Dan Abramowicz	4	4	5	5	6	10	50	
91	Mercury Morris RC	4	4	5	8	12	30	100	
92	Steve DeLong	4	4	5	5	6	10	20	150
93	Larry Stallings	4	4	5	5	6	10	20	
94	Tom Mack	4	4	5	5	6	10	20	
95	Hewritt Dixon	4	4	5	5	6	10	20	120
96	Fred Cox	4	4	5	5	6	12	80	
97	Chris Hanburger	4	4	5	5	6	10	20	
98	Gerry Philbin	4	4	5	5	6	12	30	
99	Ernie Wright	4	4	5	5	6	10	20	
100	John Brodie	4	4	5	5	6	12	40	100
101	Tucker Frederickson	4	4	5	5	6	10	20	
102	Bobby Walden	4	4	5	5	6	10	20	
103	Dick Gordon	4	4	5	5	6	10	25	
104	Walter Johnson	4	4	5	5	6	10	20	
105	Mike Lucci	4	4	5	5	6	10	20	
106	Checklist 2 DP	4	4	5	5	6	10	20	
107	Ron Berger	4	4	5	5	6	10	20	80
108	Dan Sullivan	4	4	5	5	6	10	20	80
109	George Kunz RC	4	4	5	5	6	10	20	80
110	Floyd Little	4	4	5	5	6	12	40	
111	Zeke Bratkowski	4	4	5	5	6	10	40	
112	Haven Moses	4	4	5	5	6	10	20	
113	Ken Houston RC	4	5	6	8	12	20	100	600
114	Willie Lanier RC	4	5	6	8	12	20	80	800
115	Larry Brown	4	4	5	5	6	10	20	120
116	Tim Rossovich	4	4	5	5	6	12	120	
117	Errol Linden	4	4	5	5	6	10	20	
118	Mel Renfro	4	4	5	5	6	10	40	
119	Mike Garrett	4	4	5	5	6	10	40	
120	Fran Tarkenton	4	4	5	6	10	18	50	400
121	Garo Yepremian RC	4	4	5	5	6	10	20	
122	Glen Condren	4	4	5	5	6	10	20	
123	Johnny Roland	4	4	5	5	6	10	30	
124	Dave Herman	4	4	5	5	6	10	20	
125	Merlin Olsen	4	4	5	5	6	12	25	
126	Doug Buffone	4	4	5	5	6	10	30	
127	Earl McCullouch	4	4	5	5	6	10	20	
128	Spider Lockhart	4	4	5	5	6	10	20	100
129	Ken Willard	4	4	5	5	6	10	20	150
130	Gene Washington Vik	4	4	5	5	6	10	20	135
131	Mike Phipps RC	4	4	5	5	6	10	20	150
132	Andy Russell	4	4	5	5	6	12	60	
133	Ray Nitschke	4	4	5	6	8	40	400	
134	Jerry Logan	4	4	5	5	6	12	200	
135	MacArthur Lane RC	4	4	5	5	6	12	80	
136	Jim Turner	4	4	5	5	6	12	175	
137	Kent McCloughan	4	4	5	5	6	12	250	
138	Paul Guidry	4	4	5	5	6	12	150	
139	Otis Taylor	4	4	5	5	6	10	60	
140	Virgil Carter RC	4	4	5	5	6	10	60	
141	Joe Dawkins	4	4	5	5	6	10	25	
142	Steve Preece	4	4	5	5	6	12	30	
143	Mike Bragg RC	4	4	5	5	6	10	50	
144	Bob Lilly	4	4	5	5	6	15	60	
145	Joe Kapp	4	4	5	5	6	10	30	
146	Al Dodd	4	4	5	5	6	12	80	
147	Nick Buoniconti	4	4	5	5	6	10	40	
148	Speedy Duncan	4	4	5	5	6	10	25	
149	Cedrick Hardman RC	4	4	5	5	6	10	150	
150	Gale Sayers	5	8	10	12	20	35	150	800
151	Jim Otto	4	4	5	5	6	10	40	
152	Billy Truax	4	4	5	5	6	10	60	
153	John Elliott	4	4	5	5	6	10	25	
154	Dick LeBeau	4	4	5	5	6	10	60	
155	Bill Bergey	4	4	5	5	6	12	135	
156	Terry Bradshaw RC	35	60	80	125	250	600	▼2,000	10,000
157	Leroy Kelly	4	4	5	5	6	12	30	
158	Paul Krause	4	4	5	5	6	15	50	
159	Ted Vactor	4	4	5	5	6	10	20	80
160	Bob Griese	4	4	5	6	10	18	60	175
161	Ernie McMillan	4	4	5	5	6	10	25	
162	Donny Anderson	4	4	5	5	6	10	30	
163	John Pitts	4	4	5	5	6	12	50	
164	Dave Costa	4	4	5	5	6	10	25	
165	Gene Washington 49er	4	4	5	5	6	10	30	
166	John Zook	4	4	5	5	6	10	25	
167	Pete Gogolak	4	4	5	5	6	10	50	
168	Erich Barnes	4	4	5	5	6	12	80	
169	Alvin Reed	4	4	5	5	6	12	50	
170	Jim Nance	4	4	5	5	6	10	30	80
171	Craig Morton	4	4	5	5	6	10	50	
172	Gary Garrison	4	4	5	5	6	10	30	150
173	Joe Scarpati	4	4	5	5	6	10	25	
174	Adrian Young	4	4	5	5	6	12	120	
175	John Mackey	4	4	5	5	6	15	80	
176	Mac Percival	4	4	5	5	6	12	100	
177	Preston Pearson RC	4	4	5	5	6	12	40	
178	Fred Biletnikoff	4	4	5	5	8	20	80	
179	Mike Battle RC	4	4	5	5	6	10	30	
180	Len Dawson	4	4	5	5	8	15	200	
181	Les Josephson	4	4	5	5	6	10	20	120
182	Royce Berry	4	4	5	5	6	10	60	
183	Herman Weaver	4	4	5	5	6	12	100	
184	Norm Snead	4	4	5	5	6	20	40	
185	Sam Brunelli	4	4	5	5	6	10	25	
186	Jim Kiick RC	4	4	5	5	6	12	80	
187	Austin Denney	4	4	5	5	6	10	20	80
188	Roger Wehrli RC	4	4	5	8	12	25	80	
189	Dave Wilcox	4	4	5	5	6	12	50	
190	Bob Hayes	4	4	5	5	6	10	60	
191	Joe Morrison	4	4	5	5	6	10	50	
192	Manny Sistrunk	4	4	5	5	6	10	100	
193	Don Cockroft RC	4	4	5	5	6	10	25	
194	Lee Bouggess	4	4	5	5	6	12	100	
195	Bob Berry	4	4	5	5	6	10	25	125
196	Ron Sellers	4	4	5	5	6	12	30	
197	George Webster	4	4	5	5	6	12	150	
198	Hoyle Granger	4	4	5	5	6	10	20	150
199	Bob Vogel	4	4	5	5	6	10	40	
200	Bart Starr	4	6	8	15	25	▲80	▲200	800
201	Mike Mercer	4	4	5	5	6	12	30	
202	Dave Smith WR	4	4	5	5	6	12	100	
203	Lee Roy Caffey	4	4	5	5	6	10	25	
204	Mick Tingelhoff	4	4	5	5	6	12	60	
205	Matt Snell	4	4	5	5	6	10	20	125
206	Jim Tyrer	4	4	5	5	6	12	40	
207	Willie Brown	4	4	5	5	6	10	60	
208	Bob Johnson RC	4	4	5	5	6	10	30	
209	Deacon Jones	4	4	5	5	6	12	80	
210	Charlie Sanders RC	4	5	6	10	20	40	250	
211	Jake Scott RC	4	4	6	10	20	25	80	
212	Bob Anderson RC	4	4	5	5	6	10	25	
213	Charlie Krueger	4	4	5	5	6	10	50	
214	Jim Bakken	4	4	5	5	6	15	100	
215	Harold Jackson	4	4	5	5	6	15	100	
216	Bill Brundige	4	4	5	5	6	10	50	300
217	Calvin Hill	4	4	5	5	6	15	60	
218	Claude Humphrey	4	4	5	5	6	12	150	
219	Glen Ray Hines	4	4	5	5	6	12	30	
220	Bill Nelsen	4	4	5	5	6	10	50	80
221	Roy Hilton	4	4	5	5	6	12	150	
222	Don Herrmann	4	4	5	5	6	10	25	
223	John Bramlett	4	4	5	5	6	12	100	
224	Ken Ellis	4	4	5	5	6	30	250	500
225	Dave Osborn	4	4	5	5	6	10	50	
226	Edd Hargett RC	4	4	5	5	6	12	100	
227	Gene Mingo	4	4	5	5	6	12	50	
228	Larry Grantham	4	4	5	5	6	12	100	
229	Dick Post	4	4	5	5	6	25	150	
230	Roman Gabriel	4	4	5	5	6	10	50	300
231	Mike Eischeid	4	4	5	5	6	20	150	
232	Jim Lynch	4	4	5	5	6	10	50	
233	Lemar Parrish RC	4	4	5	5	6	20	135	
234	Cecil Turner	4	4	5	5	6	12	100	
235	Dennis Shaw RC	4	4	5	5	6	10	40	
236	Mel Farr	4	4	5	5	6	12	100	
237	Curt Knight	4	4	5	5	6	10	25	
238	Chuck Howley	4	4	5	5	6	10	50	
239	Bruce Taylor RC	4	4	5	5	6	10	100	
240	Jerry LeVias	4	4	5	5	6	12	100	
241	Bob Lurtsema	4	4	5	5	6	10	25	
242	Earl Morrall	4	4	5	5	6	10	25	
243	Kermit Alexander	4	4	5	5	6	10	25	150
244	Jackie Smith	4	4	5	5	6	10	50	

	GD 2	VG 3	VgEx 4	EX 5	ExMt 6	NM 7	NmMt 8	MT 9
Joe Greene RC	10	15	25	60	100	200	700	
Harmon Wages	4	4	5	5	6	10	50	
Errol Mann	4	4	5	5	6	20	120	
Mike McCoy DT RC	4	4	5	5	6	10	30	
Milt Morin RC	4	4	5	5	6	10	25	
Joe Namath	6	10	12	25	50	125	500	
Jackie Burkett	4	4	5	5	6	10	100	
Steve Chomyszak	4	4	5	5	6	10	35	
Ed Sharockman	4	4	5	5	6	12	200	
Robert Holmes RC	4	4	5	5	6	10	40	100
John Hadl	4	4	5	5	6	10	25	
Cornell Gordon	4	4	5	5	6	12	30	
Mark Moseley RC	4	4	5	5	6	12	30	
Gus Otto	4	4	5	5	6	20	300	
Mike Taliaferro	4	4	5	5	6	12	30	
O.J.Simpson	4	6	8	20	40	▲80	400	
Paul Warfield	4	4	5	5	8	20	250	
Jack Concannon	4	4	5	5	10	20	100	
Tom Matte	4	4	5	5	8	50	150	

Lance Alworth #10 PSA 9 (MT) sold for $760 (eBay; 1/07)
Willie Brown #207 PSA 9 (MT) sold for $710 (eBay; 1/08)
Dick Butkus #25 PSA 9 (MT) sold for $770 (eBay; 7/05)
Dick Butkus #25 PSA 9 (MT) sold for $1,228 (eBay; 9/13)
Joe Greene #245 PSA 10 (Gem) sold for $5115 (eBay; 11/14)
Joe Greene #245 PSA 9 (MT) sold for $2,497 (Mile High; 10/09)
Joe Greene #245 PSA 9 (MT) sold for $2,613 (eBay; 11/13)
John Hadl #255 PSA 9 (MT) sold for $565 (eBay; 1/08)
Ken Houston #113 PSA 10 (Gem Mint) sold for $5,510 (eBay; 2/13)
Les Josephson #181 PSA 9 (MT) sold for $1,335 (eBay; 6/09)
Mike Lucci #105 PSA 10 (Gem Mint) sold for $607 (Memory Lane; 8/12)
John Mackey #175 PSA 9 (MT) sold for $520 (eBay; 10/06)
Mercury Morris #91 PSA 10 (Gem MT) sold for $2,555 (eBay; 12/11)
Craig Morton #171 PSA 10 (Gem MT) sold for $1,228.50 (eBay; 2/14)
Joe Namath #250 PSA 8.5 (NmMT+) sold for $974 (eBay; 12/12)
Ed O'Bradovich #78 PSA 10 (Gem Mint) sold for $552 (Memory Lane; 8/12)
Charlie Sanders #210 PSA 9 (MT) sold for $453 (eBay; 12/12)
Marty Schottenheimer #3 PSA 9 (MT) sold for $550 (eBay; 6/06)
Altie Taylor RC #62 PSA 10 (Gem Mint) sold for $668 (Memory Lane; 8/12)
Duane Thomas #65 PSA 9 (MT) sold for $337 (eBay; 2/13)
Billy Truax #152 PSA 10 (Gem Mint) sold for $889 (Memory Lane; 8/12)
Johnny Unitas #1 PSA 9 (MT) sold for $1,285 (eBay; 3/07)
Roger Wehrli #188 PSA 9 (MT) sold for $1,335 (eBay; 6/09)
Dave Wilcox #189 PSA 10 (Gem Mint) sold for $1,032 (eBay; 7/13)

1971 Topps Game Inserts

	GD 2	VG 3	VgEx 4	EX 5	ExMt 6	NM 7	NmMt 8	MT 9
COMMON CARD (1-53)	4	4	4	5	5	8	15	
Dick Butkus DP	4	4	4	5	6	10	25	
Joe Namath DP	4	4	5	6	8	12	25	100
Mike Curtis	4	4	4	5	5	8	15	80
Jim Nance	4	4	4	5	5	8	12	
O.J. Simpson	4	4	5	6	8	12	30	120
Tommy Nobis	4	4	4	5	5	8	10	80
Gale Sayers	4	4	4	5	6	10	30	60
Floyd Little	4	4	4	5	5	10	25	
Sam Brunelli	4	4	4	5	6	12		
Gene Washington 49er	4	4	4	5	5	8	15	80
Willie Wood	4	4	4	5	5	8	15	80
Charley Johnson	4	4	4	5	5	10	25	
Len Dawson	4	4	4	5	6	10	20	
Merlin Olsen	4	4	4	5	5	8	20	
Roman Gabriel	4	4	4	5	5	10	25	
Bob Griese	4	4	4	5	6	10	30	
Larry Csonka	4	4	4	5	5	15	20	100
Dan Abramowicz	4	4	4	5	5	10	25	
Tom Dempsey	4	4	4	5	5	12		
Fran Tarkenton	4	4	4	5	6	10	20	
Johnny Unitas	4	4	5	6	10	15	40	150
Daryle Lamonica	4	4	4	5	5	8	15	80
Terry Bradshaw	4	4	5	8	12	30	40	200
MacArthur Lane	4	4	4	5	5	8	20	100
Lance Alworth	4	4	4	5	6	10	20	80
John Brodie	4	4	4	5	6	10	30	
Bart Starr DP	4	4	4	5	6	10	30	120
Sonny Jurgensen	4	4	4	5	6	10	15	
Larry Brown	4	4	4	5	6	12		

1972 Topps

	VG 3	VgEx 4	EX 5	ExMt 6	NM 7	NmMt 8	MT 9	Gem 9.5/10
1 Csonka/Little/Hubbard LL	4	5	5	8	15	10	500	
2 Brockington/Owens/Ellison LL	4	5	5	5	8	25	60	
3 Griese/Dawson/Carter LL	4	5	5	5	8	20	120	
4 Staubach/Landry/Kilmer LL	4	5	5	6	10	25	120	
5 Biletnikoff/O.Taylor/Vataha LL	4	5	5	5	8	20	80	
6 Tucker/Kwalick/H.Jack./Jeffer.LL	4	5	5	5	8	15	60	
7 Yepremian/Stenerud/O'Brien LL	4	5	5	5	8	15	50	
8 Knight/Mann/Gossett LL	4	5	5	5	8	12	40	
9 Jim Kiick	4	5	5	5	8	15	50	
10 Otis Taylor	4	5	5	5	8	12	40	
11 Bobby Joe Green	4	5	5	5	8	12	40	
12 Ken Ellis	4	5	5	5	8	12	40	
13 John Riggins RC	8	10	12	15	▲30	▲60	300	
14 Dave Parks	4	5	5	5	8	12	40	
15 John Hadl	4	5	5	5	8	15	40	
16 Ron Hornsby	4	5	5	5	8	15		
17 Chip Myers RC	4	5	5	5	8	12	40	
18 Billy Kilmer	4	5	5	5	8	12	40	
19 Fred Hoaglin	4	5	5	5	8	12	40	
20 Carl Eller	4	5	5	5	8	12	40	
21 Steve Zabel	4	5	5	5	8	12	40	
22 Vic Washington RC	4	5	5	5	8	12	40	
23 Len St. Jean	4	5	5	5	8	12	40	
24 Bill Thompson	4	5	5	5	8	12	40	
25 Steve Owens RC	4	5	5	5	10	25	80	
26 Ken Burrough RC	4	5	5	5	8	12	50	
27 Mike Clark	4	5	5	5	8	12	60	
28 Willie Brown	4	5	5	5	8	12	40	
29 Checklist 1	4	5	5	6	10	20	80	
30 Marlin Briscoe RC	4	5	5	5	8	12	40	
31 Jerry Logan	4	5	5	5	8	12	40	
32 Donny Anderson	4	5	5	5	8	12	40	
33 Rich McGeorge	4	5	5	5	8	12	40	
34 Charlie Durkee	4	5	5	5	8	12	40	
35 Willie Lanier	4	5	5	5	8	12	40	
36 Chris Farasopoulos	4	5	5	5	8	12	40	
37 Ron Shanklin RC	4	5	5	5	8	15		
38 Forrest Blue RC	4	5	5	5	8	12	40	
39 Ken Reaves	4	5	5	5	8	12	40	
40 Roman Gabriel	4	5	5	5	8	12	40	
41 Mac Percival	4	5	5	5	8	12	40	
42 Lem Barney	4	5	5	5	8	12	40	
43 Nick Buoniconti	4	5	5	5	8	15	40	
44 Charlie Gogolak	4	5	5	5	8	12	40	
45 Bill Bradley RC	4	5	5	5	8	12	40	
46 Joe Jones DE	4	5	5	5	8	12	40	
47 Dave Williams	4	5	5	5	8	12	40	
48 Pete Athas	4	5	5	5	8	12	40	
49 Virgil Carter	4	5	5	5	8	12	40	
50 Floyd Little	4	5	5	5	8	20	40	
51 Curt Knight	4	5	5	5	8	12	40	
52 Bobby Maples	4	5	5	5	8	12	40	
53 Charlie West	4	5	5	5	8	12	50	
54 Marv Hubbard RC	4	5	5	5	8	12	40	
55 Archie Manning RC	5	6	10	15	25	50	200	750
56 Jim O'Brien RC	4	5	5	5	8	12	40	
57 Wayne Patrick	4	5	5	5	8	12	40	
58 Ken Bowman	4	5	5	5	8	15		
59 Roger Wehrli	4	5	5	5	8	12	40	
60 Charlie Sanders	4	5	5	5	8	12	40	
61 Jan Stenerud	4	5	5	5	8	12	40	
62 Willie Ellison	4	5	5	5	8	12	40	
63 Walt Sweeney	4	5	5	5	8	12	40	
64 Ron Smith	4	5	5	5	8	12	40	
65 Jim Plunkett RC	5	6	8	12	20	50	175	
66 Herb Adderley	4	5	5	5	8	12	40	
67 Mike Reid RC	4	5	5	5	8	12	50	
68 Richard Caster RC	4	5	5	5	8	12	40	
69 Dave Wilcox	4	5	5	5	8	12	40	
70 Leroy Kelly	4	5	5	5	8	30	60	
71 Bob Lee RC	4	5	5	5	8	12	50	
72 Verlon Biggs	4	5	5	5	8	12	80	
73 Henry Allison	4	5	5	5	8	12	40	
74 Steve Ramsey	4	5	5	5	8	12	40	
75 Claude Humphrey	4	5	5	5	8	12	40	

#	Player	VG 3	VgEx 4	EX 5	ExMt 6	NM 7	NmMt 8	MT 9	Gem 9.5/10
76	Bob Grim RC	4	5	5	5	8	12	40	
77	John Fuqua	4	5	5	5	8	12	100	
78	Ken Houston	4	5	5	5	8	20	40	
79	Checklist 2 DP	4	5	5	5	8	15	40	
80	Bob Griese	4	5	6	8	15	25	120	
81	Lance Rentzel	4	5	5	5	8	12	40	
82	Ed Podolak RC	4	5	5	5	8	12	40	
83	Ike Hill	4	5	5	5	8	12	40	
84	George Farmer	4	5	5	5	8	12	40	
85	John Brockington RC	4	5	5	5	8	12	40	
86	Jim Otto	4	5	5	5	8	12	40	
87	Richard Neal	4	5	5	5	8	12	40	
88	Jim Hart		5	5	5	8	12	40	
89	Bob Babich	4	5	5	5	8	12	40	
90	Gene Washington 49ers	4	5	5	5	8	12	40	
91	John Zook	4	5	5		8	12	40	
92	Bobby Duhon	4	5	5	5	8	12	40	
93	Ted Hendricks RC	4	5	6	8	20	60	▲600	
94	Rockne Freitas	4	5	5	5	8	12	40	
95	Larry Brown	4	5	5	5	8	12	40	
96	Mike Phipps	4	5	5	5	8	12	40	
97	Julius Adams	4	5	5	5	8	12	40	
98	Dick Anderson	4	5	5	5	8	12	40	
99	Fred Willis	4	5	5	5	8	12	40	
100	Joe Namath	10	12	15	25	40	80	200	1,500
101	L.C.Greenwood RC	4	5	6	10	20	50	135	400
102	Mark Nordquist	4	5	5	5	8	12	40	
103	Robert Holmes	4	5	5	5	8	12	40	
104	Ron Yary RC	4	5	6	8	25	50	200	
105	Bob Hayes	4	5	5	5	8	15	50	
106	Lyle Alzado RC	4	5	6	8	15	35	100	
107	Bob Berry	4	5	5	5	8	12	40	
108	Phil Villapiano RC	4	5	5	5	8	12	60	
109	Dave Elmendorf	4	5	5	5	8	12	40	
110	Gale Sayers	5	6	8	12	25	50	200	
111	Jim Tyrer	4	5	5	5	8	12	40	
112	Mel Gray RC	4	5	5	5	8	12	40	
113	Gerry Philbin	4	5	5	5	8	12	40	
114	Bob James	4	5	5	5	8	12	40	
115	Garo Yepremian	4	5	5	5	8	12	50	
116	Dave Robinson	4	5	5	5	8	12	40	
117	Jeff Queen	4	5	5	5	8	12	40	
118	Norm Snead	4	5	5	5	8	25		
119	Jim Nance IA	4	5	5	5	8	12	40	
120	Terry Bradshaw IA	4	5	6	8	12	25	100	300
121	Jim Kiick IA	4	5	5	5	8	12	40	
122	Roger Staubach IA	5	6	8	12	20	30	150	
123	Bo Scott IA	4	5	5	5	8	12	40	
124	John Brodie IA	4	5	5	5	8	12	40	175
125	Rick Volk IA	4	5	5	5	8	12	40	
126	John Riggins IA	4	5	5	6	10	20	30	250
127	Bubba Smith IA	4	5	5	5	8	12	40	
128	Roman Gabriel IA	4	5	5	5	8	12	40	
129	Calvin Hill IA	4	5	5	5	8	12	40	
130	Bill Nelsen IA	4	5	5	5	8	12	40	
131	Tom Matte IA	4	5	5	5	8	12	40	
132	Bob Griese IA	4	5	5	5	8	20	80	
133	AFC Semi-Final	4	5	5	6	10	30	150	
134	NFC Semi-Final	4	5	5	5	8	12	80	
135	AFC Semi-Final	4	5	5	5	8	12	50	
136	NFC Semi-Final	4	5	5	5	8	12	60	
137	AFC Title Game/Unitas	4	5	5	5	10	20	60	
138	NFC Title Game/Lilly	4	5	5	5	8	25		
139	Super Bowl VI/Staubach	4	5	5	6	10	25	100	
140	Larry Csonka	4	5	5	8	15	50	200	
141	Rick Volk	4	5	5	5	8	12	40	
142	Roy Jefferson	4	5	5	5	8	12	40	
143	Raymond Chester RC	4	5	5	5	8	12	60	
144	Bobby Douglass	4	5	5	5	8	12	40	
145	Bob Lilly	4	5	5	5	8	30	150	
146	Harold Jackson	4	5	5	5	8	12	50	
147	Pete Gogolak	4	5	5	5	8	12	40	
148	Art Malone	4	5	5	5	8	12	40	
149	Ed Flanagan	4	5	5	5	8	12	40	
150	Terry Bradshaw	12	15	20	30	40	150	750	
151	MacArthur Lane	4	5	5	5	8	12	40	
152	Jack Snow	4	5	5	5	8	10	40	
153	Al Beauchamp	4	5	5	5	8	12	40	
154	Bob Anderson	4	5	5	5	8	12	40	

#	Player	VG 3	VgEx 4	EX 5	ExMt 6	NM 7	NmMt 8	MT 9	Gem 9.5/1●
155	Ted Kwalick RC	4	5	5	5	8	12	40	
156	Dan Pastorini RC	4	5	5	5	10	20	60	
157	Emmitt Thomas RC	5	6	8	12	20	50	300	
158	Randy Vataha RC	4	5	5	5	8	12	40	
159	Al Atkinson	4	5	5	5	8	12	40	
160	O.J.Simpson	4	5	6	8	15	30	100	
161	Jackie Smith	4	5	5	5	8	12	40	
162	Ernie Kellerman	4	5	5	5	8	15		
163	Dennis Partee	4	5	5	5	8	12	40	
164	Jake Kupp	4	5	5	5	8	12	150	
165	Johnny Unitas	8	10	12	15	25	50	200	
166	Clint Jones RC	4	5	5	5	8	12	40	
167	Paul Warfield	4	5	5	6	10	20	▼80	
168	Roland McDole	4	5	5	5	8	20	60	
169	Daryle Lamonica	4	5	5	5	8	15	125	
170	Dick Butkus	4	5	6	8	20	30	150	
171	Jim Butler	4	5	5	5	8	12	40	
172	Mike McCoy DT	4	5	5	5	8	12	40	
173	Dave Smith WR	4	5	5	5	8	12	40	
174	Greg Landry	4	5	5	5	8	12	40	
175	Tom Dempsey	4	5	5	5	8	15	50	
176	John Charles	4	5	5	5	8	12	150	
177	Bobby Bell	4	5	5	5	8	12	60	
178	Don Horn	4	5	5	5	8	10	40	
179	Bob Trumpy	4	5	5	5	8	15		
180	Duane Thomas	4	5	5	5	8	12	40	
181	Merlin Olsen	4	5	5	5	8	15	60	
182	Dave Herman	4	5	5	5	8	12	40	
183	Jim Nance	4	5	5	5	8	12	40	
184	Pete Beathard	4	5	5	5	8	12	40	
185	Bob Tucker	4	5	5	5	8	12	40	
186	Gene Upshaw RC	4	5	6	10	20	50	400	
187	Bo Scott	4	5	5	5	8	12	40	
188	J.D.Hill RC	4	5	5	5	8	12	40	
189	Bruce Gossett	4	5	5	5	8	12	40	
190	Bubba Smith	4	5	5	5	8	15	40	
191	Edd Hargett	4	5	5	5	8	12	40	
192	Gary Garrison	4	5	5	5	8	12	40	
193	Jake Scott	4	5	5	5	8	12	50	
194	Fred Cox	4	5	5	5	8	25		
195	Sonny Jurgensen	4	5	5	5	8	25	80	
196	Greg Brezina RC	4	5	5	5	8	12	50	
197	Ed O'Bradovich	4	5	5	5	8	12	50	
198	John Rowser	4	5	5	5	8	12	50	
199	Altie Taylor	4	5	5	5	8	12	50	
200	Roger Staubach RC	60	80	100	200	500	▼1,500	10,000	
201	Leroy Keyes RC	4	5	5	5	8	12	40	
202	Garland Boyette	4	5	5	5	8	12	40	
203	Tom Beer	4	5	5	5	8	12	40	
204	Buck Buchanan	4	5	5	5	8	12	40	
205	Larry Wilson	4	5	5	5	8	12	40	
206	Scott Hunter RC	4	5	5	5	8	12	40	
207	Ron Johnson	4	5	5	5	8	12	40	
208	Sam Brunelli	4	5	5	5	8	12	40	
209	Deacon Jones	4	5	5	5	8	12	50	
210	Fred Biletnikoff	4	5	5	6	10	20	80	
211	Bill Nelsen	4	5	5	5	8	20	80	
212	George Nock	4	5	5	5	8	12	40	
213	Dan Abramowicz	4	5	5	5	8	12	40	
214	Irv Goode	4	5	5	5	8	12	40	
215	Isiah Robertson RC	4	5	5	5	8	12	40	
216	Tom Matte	4	5	5	5	8	12	50	
217	Pat Fischer	4	5	5	5	8	15		
218	Gene Washington Vik	4	5	5	5	8	12	50	
219	Paul Robinson	4	5	5	5	8	12	40	
220	John Brodie	4	5	5	5	8	15	50	
221	Manny Fernandez RC	4	5	5	5	8	12	40	
222	Errol Mann	4	5	5	5	8	12	40	
223	Dick Gordon	4	5	5	5	8	12	40	
224	Calvin Hill	4	5	5	5	8	12	120	
225	Fran Tarkenton	4	5	6	8	25	50	200	
226	Jim Turner	4	5	5	5	8	12	40	
227	Jim Mitchell TE	4	5	5	5	8	12	40	
228	Pete Liske	4	5	5	5	8	12	40	
229	Carl Garrett	4	5	5	5	8	12	40	
230	Joe Greene	5	6	8	12	20	50	250	
231	Gale Gillingham	4	5	5	5	8	12	40	
232	Norm Bulaich RC	4	5	5	5	8	20	60	
233	Spider Lockhart	4	5	5	5	8	15		

	VG 3	VgEx 4	EX 5	ExMt 6	NM 7	NmMt 8	MT 9	Gem 9.5/10
Ken Willard	4	5	5	5	8	25	80	
George Blanda	4	5	6	8	15	25	100	
Wayne Mulligan	4	5	5	5	8	12	60	
Dave Lewis	4	5	5	5	8	12	60	
Dennis Shaw	4	5	5	5	8	12	40	
Fair Hooker	4	5	5	5	8	12	40	
Larry Little RC	4	5	6	8	15	50	200	
Mike Garrett	4	5	5	5	8	12	50	
Glen Ray Hines	4	5	5	5	8	15		
Myron Pottios	4	5	5	5	8	12	40	
Charlie Joiner RC	8	10	4	12	5	15 6	25	50 8	200
Len Dawson	4	5	5	8	12	25	80	
W.K. Hicks	4	5	5	5	8	12	40	
Les Josephson	4	5	5	5	8	12	40	
Lance Alworth	4	5	5	8	12	25	100	
Frank Nunley	4	5	5	5	8	12	40	
Mel Farr IA	4	5	5	5	8	12	40	
Johnny Unitas IA	4	5	5	8	15	40	125	
George Farmer IA	4	5	5	5	8	12	40	
Duane Thomas IA	4	5	5	5	8	12	40	
John Hadl IA	4	5	5	5	8	12	40	
Vic Washington IA	4	5	5	5	8	12	40	
Don Horn IA	4	5	5	5	8	12	40	
L.C. Greenwood IA	4	5	5	6	10	25	125	
Bob Lee IA	4	5	5	5	8	12	60	
Larry Csonka IA	4	5	5	5	8	15	60	
Mike McCoy IA	4	5	5	5	8	12	40	
Greg Landry IA	4	5	5	5	8	12	50	
Ray May IA	4	5	5	5	8	20	125	
Bobby Douglass IA	4	5	5	5	8	12	60	
Charlie Sanders AP	8	10	12	15	20	30	60	
Ron Yary AP	8	10	12	15	25	35	60	175
Rayfield Wright AP	10	12	15	30	60	80	100	250
Larry Little AP	8	10	12	15	20	40	75	
John Niland AP	6	8	10	15	25	40	75	
Forrest Blue AP	6	8	10	12	15	30	50	
Otis Taylor AP	6	8	10	12	15	30	50	200
Paul Warfield AP	8	10	12	18	30	50	80	▼300
Bob Griese AP	10	12	15	25	40	60	120	▼600
John Brockington AP	6	8	10	12	15	50	60	
Floyd Little AP	6	8	10	12	15	30	50	200
Garo Yepremian AP	6	8	10	12	15	50	60	
Jerrel Wilson AP	6	8	10	12	15	30	50	150
Carl Eller AP	6	8	10	12	15	40	60	
Bubba Smith AP	8	10	12	15	25	40	80	
Alan Page AP	8	10	12	15	25	40	80	
Bob Lilly AP	8	10	12	18	30	50	80	
Ted Hendricks AP	8	10	12	18	30	50	80	
Dave Wilcox AP	6	8	10	12	15	30	50	
Willie Lanier AP	8	10	12	15	20	35	60	250
Jim Johnson AP	6	8	10	12	15	30	50	200
Willie Brown AP	8	10	12	15	20	35	80	
Bill Bradley AP	6	8	10	12	15	30	50	200
Ken Houston AP	8	10	12	15	20	35	50	250
Mel Farr	6	8	10	12	15	30	50	
Kermit Alexander	6	8	10	12	15	30	50	
John Gilliam RC	6	8	10	12	15	50	120	
Steve Spurrier RC	15	20	50	100	125	200	250	
Walter Johnson	6	8	10	12	15	30	60	
Jack Pardee	6	8	10	12	15	30	60	
Checklist 3	8	10	12	25	40	100	200	
Winston Hill	6	8	10	12	15	30	60	
Hugo Hollas	6	8	10	12	15	30	50	
Ray May RC	6	8	10	12	15	30	50	
Jim Bakken	6	8	10	12	15	30	50	
Larry Carwell	6	8	10	12	15	30	50	
Alan Page	8	10	12	18	40	60	120	
Walt Garrison	6	8	10	12	15	150	200	
Mike Lucci	6	8	10	12	15	30	50	
Nemiah Wilson	6	8	10	12	15	50	60	
Carroll Dale	6	8	10	12	15	30	50	
Jim Kanicki	6	8	10	12	15	30	50	
Preston Pearson	8	10	12	15	18	30	80	
Lemar Parrish	6	8	10	12	15	40	60	
Earl Morrall	6	8	10	12	20	40	80	
Tommy Nobis	6	8	10	12	15	30	60	
Rich Jackson	6	8	10	12	15	30	50	
Doug Cunningham	6	8	10	12	15	30	50	
Jim Marsalis	6	8	10	12	15	30	50	

	VG 3	VgEx 4	EX 5	ExMt 6	NM 7	NmMt 8	MT 9	Gem 9.5/10
313 Jim Beirne	6	8	10	12	15	30	50	
314 Tom McNeill	6	8	10	12	15	30	50	
315 Milt Morin	6	8	10	12	15	30	125	
316 Rayfield Wright RC	12	20	25	30	80	300	400	
317 Jerry LeVias	6	8	10	12	15	30	50	
318 Travis Williams RC	6	8	10	12	15	30	50	
319 Edgar Chandler	6	8	10	12	15	30	50	
320 Bob Wallace	6	8	10	12	15	30	100	
321 Delles Howell	6	8	10	12	15	30	50	
322 Emerson Boozer	6	8	10	12	15	30	50	
323 George Atkinson RC	6	8	10	12	15	50	80	
324 Mike Montler	6	8	10	12	15	30	50	
325 Randy Johnson	6	8	10	12	15	30	50	
326 Mike Curtis	6	8	10	12	15	30	50	
327 Miller Farr	6	8	10	12	15	30	50	
328 Horst Muhlmann	6	8	10	12	15	30	50	
329 John Niland RC	8	10	12	15	30	80	175	
330 Andy Russell	8	10	12	15	20	60	100	
331 Mercury Morris	8	10	12	60	80	125	200	
332 Jim Johnson	8	10	12	15	18	▲40	60	
333 Jerrel Wilson	6	8	10	12	15	30	50	
334 Charley Taylor	8	10	12	15	25	40	▲100	
335 Dick LeBeau	6	8	10	12	15	30	60	
336 Jim Marshall	8	10	12	15	25	40	80	
337 Tom Mack	8	10	12	15	20	30	50	
338 Steve Spurrier IA	10	12	15	20	35	60	100	
339 Floyd Little IA	6	8	10	12	15	50	60	
340 Len Dawson IA	8	10	12	15	25	40	80	
341 Dick Butkus IA	12	15	20	40	80	100	120	
342 Larry Brown IA	6	8	10	12	15	40	60	
343 Joe Namath IA	25	50	60	80	100	200	300	
344 Jim Turner IA	6	8	10	12	15	30	50	
345 Doug Cunningham IA	6	8	10	12	15	30	60	
346 Edd Hargett IA	6	8	10	12	15	30	60	
347 Steve Owens IA	6	8	10	25	30	40	80	
348 George Blanda IA	8	10	12	25	40	60	150	
349 Ed Podolak IA	6	8	10	12	15	30	50	
350 Rich Jackson IA	6	8	10	12	15	30	60	
351 Ken Willard IA	6	8	10	25	40	175	800	

—Csonka/Little Hubbard LL #1 PSA 10 (Gem) sold for $2,205 (eBay; 1/07)
—Yepr/Stenerud/O'Brien LL #7 PSA 10 (Gem) sold for $1,345 (eBay; 11/06)
—Lyle Alzado #106 PSA 10 (Gem) sold for $1411 (eBay; 11/14)
—Dick Anderson #98 PSA 10 (Gem) sold for $1,325 (eBay; 12/07)
—George Blanda IA #348 PSA 10 (Gem) sold for $1,080 (eBay; 9/07)
—Forrest Blue #38 PSA 10 (Gem) sold for $835 (eBay; 12/07)
—Terry Bradshaw #150 PSA 10 (Gem) sold for $1,734 (Mile High; 10/09)
—Nick Buoniconti #43 PSA 10 (Gem) sold for $1,130 (eBay; 4/08)
—Chris Farasopoulis #36 PSA 10 (Gem) sold for $905 (eBay; 4/07)
—Bobby Joe Green #11 PSA 10 (Gem Mint) sold for $717 (eBay: 8/12)
—Bob Griese #272 PSA 10 (Gem) sold for $1,055 (Andy Madec; 10/06)
—Charlie Joiner RC #244 PSA 10 (Gem) sold for $4,059 (eBay 09/14)
—Leroy Kelly #70 PSA 10 (Gem) sold for $563 (eBay; 02/13)
—Floyd Little #50 PSA 10 (Gem) sold for $724 (eBay; 11/14)
—Mercury Morris #331 PSA 10 (Gem) sold for $2,130 (eBay; 3/07)
—Mercury Morris #331 PSA 10 (Gem) sold for $1,025 (eBay; 2/14)
—Joe Namath IA #343 PSA 10 (Gem) sold for $1,535 (eBay; 2/07)
—Joe Namath IA #343 PSA 10 (Gem) sold for $569 (Mile High 10/09)
—Merlin Olsen #181 PSA 10 (Gem) sold for $602 (eBay; 7/07)
—Jim Plunkett #65 PSA 10 (Gem) sold for $1,458 (eBay; 1/09)
—Jim Plunkett #65 PSA 10 (Gem) sold for $1,285 (eBay; 12/07)
—John Riggins #13 PSA 10 (Gem) sold for $4,500 (eBay; 2/07)
—John Riggins #13 PSA 10 (Gem) sold for $4,044 (eBay; 11/14)
—John Riggins #13 PSA 10 (Gem) sold for $1,459 (Mile High; 6/10)
—Charlie Sanders #60 PSA 10 (Gem) sold for $795 (eBay; 4/07)
—Gale Sayers #110 PSA 10 (Gem) sold for $560 (Mile High; 10/09)
—Dennis Shaw #238 PSA 10 (Gem) sold for $835 (eBay; 12/07)
—Steve Spurrier #291 PSA 10 (Gem) sold for $509 (Mile High; 6/10)
—Roger Staubach IA #122 PSA 10 (Gem) sold for $1,225 (eBay; 1/08)
—Roger Staubach IA #122 PSA 10 (Gem) sold for $22,161.37 (Mile High; 12/13)
—Johnny Unitas #165 PSA 10 (Gem) sold for $2,670 (Mile High; 11/10)
—Gene Upshaw #186 PSA 10 (Gem) sold for $3558 (eBay; 11/14)
—Vic Washington #22 PSA 10 (Gem) sold for $1,335 (eBay; 4/07)
—Dave Williams #47 PSA 10 (Gem Mint) sold for $717 (eBay: 8/12)
—Ron Yary #104 PSA 10 (Gem) sold for $2,230 (eBay; 4/08)
—Ron Yary #104 PSA 10 (Gem) sold for $1543 (eBay; 11/14)

1973 Topps

#	Player	VgEx 4	EX 5	ExMt 6	NM 7	NmMt 8	NmMt+ 8.5	MT 9	Gem 9.5/10
1	Simpson/L.Brown LL	5	6	8	12	20	30	150	
2	Snea/Morrall LL	5	6	8	10	15	20	30	
3	H.Jackson/Biletnikoff LL	5	6	8	10	15	20	60	
4	Marcol/Howfield LL	5	6	8	10	15	20	30	
5	Bradley/Sensibaugh LL	5	6	8	10	15	25	60	
6	Capple/J.Wilson LL	5	6	8	10	15	20	50	
7	Bob Trumpy	5	6	8	10	15	20	30	
8	Mel Tom	5	6	8	10	15	20	30	
9	Clarence Ellis	5	6	8	10	15	20	30	
10	John Niland	5	6	8	10	15	20	30	
11	Randy Jackson	5	6	8	10	15	20	30	
12	Greg Landry	5	6	8	10	15	20	30	
13	Cid Edwards	5	6	8	10	15	20	30	
14	Phil Olsen	5	6	8	10	15	20	30	
15	Terry Bradshaw	12	15	20	40	60	80	400	
16	Al Cowlings RC	5	6	8	10	20	25		
17	Walker Gillette	5	6	8	10	15	20	30	
18	Bob Atkins	5	6	8	10	15	20	30	
19	Diron Talbert RC	5	6	8	10	15	20	50	
20	Jim Johnson	5	6	8	10	20	25		
21	Howard Twilley	5	6	8	10	15	20	30	
22	Dick Enderle	5	6	8	10	15	20	30	
23	Wayne Colman	5	6	8	10	15	20	30	
24	John Schmitt	5	6	8	10	15	20	30	
25	George Blanda	5	6	8	10	15	20	35	
26	Milt Morin	5	6	8	10	15	20	30	
27	Mike Current	5	6	8	10	15	20	30	
28	Rex Kern RC	5	6	8	10	15	20	25	
29	MacArthur Lane	5	6	8	10	15	20	30	
30	Alan Page	5	6	8	10	15	20	50	
31	Randy Vataha	5	6	8	10	15	20	25	
32	Jim Kearney	5	6	8	10	20	25		
33	Steve Smith T	5	6	8	10	15	20	30	
34	Ken Anderson RC	8	10	12	20	50	60	300	
35	Calvin Hill	5	6	8	10	15	20	30	
36	Andy Maurer	5	6	8	10	15	20	30	
37	Joe Taylor	5	6	8	10	15	20	30	
38	Deacon Jones	5	6	8	10	15	20	30	
39	Mike Weger	5	6	8	10	20	25		
40	Roy Gerela	5	6	8	10	15	20	30	
41	Les Josephson	5	6	8	10	15	20	30	
42	Dave Washington	5	6	8	10	15	20	30	
43	Bill Curry RC	5	6	8	10	15	20	30	
44	Fred Heron	5	6	8	10	15	20	30	
45	John Brodie	5	6	8	10	15	20	35	
46	Roy Winston	5	6	8	10	15	20	30	
47	Mike Bragg	5	6	8	10	15	20	30	
48	Mercury Morris	5	6	8	10	15	30	50	
49	Jim Files	5	6	8	10	15	20	30	
50	Gene Upshaw	5	6	8	10	15	20	40	
51	Hugo Hollas	5	6	8	10	15	20	30	
52	Rod Sherman	5	6	8	10	15	20	30	
53	Ron Snidow	5	6	8	10	15	20	30	
54	Steve Tannen RC	5	6	8	10	15	20	30	
55	Jim Carter RC	5	6	8	10	15	20	30	
56	Lydell Mitchell RC	5	6	8	10	15	20	30	
57	Jack Rudnay RC	5	6	8	10	20	25		
58	Halvor Hagen	5	6	8	10	15	20	30	
59	Tom Dempsey	5	6	8	10	15	20	30	
60	Fran Tarkenton	5	6	8	10	15	20	80	
61	Lance Alworth	5	6	8	10	15	20	50	
62	Vern Holland	5	6	8	10	15	20	30	
63	Steve DeLong	5	6	8	10	15	20	30	
64	Art Malone	5	6	8	10	15	20	30	
65	Isiah Robertson	5	6	8	10	20	25		
66	Jerry Rush	5	6	8	10	15	20	30	
67	Bryant Salter	5	6	8	10	15	20	30	
68	Checklist 1-132	5	6	8	10	15	20	60	
69	J.D. Hill	5	6	8	10	15	20	30	
70	Forrest Blue	5	6	8	10	15	20	30	
71	Myron Pottios	5	6	8	10	15	20	30	
72	Norm Thompson RC	5	6	8	10	15	20	30	
73	Paul Robinson	5	6	8	10	15	20	30	
74	Larry Grantham	5	6	8	10	15	20	30	
75	Manny Fernandez	5	6	8	10	15	20	30	
76	Kent Nix	5	6	8	10	15	20	30	
77	Art Shell RC	8	10	12	20	60	80	400	
78	George Saimes	5	6	8	10	15	20	30	
79	Don Cockroft	5	6	8	10	15	20	30	
80	Bob Tucker	5	6	8	10	15	20	30	
81	Don McCauley RC	5	6	8	10	15	20	30	
82	Bob Brown DT	5	6	8	10	15	20	30	
83	Larry Carwell	5	6	8	10	15	20	30	
84	Mo Moorman	5	6	8	10	15	20	30	
85	John Gilliam	5	6	8	10	15	20	30	
86	Wade Key	5	6	8	10	15	20	30	
87	Ross Brupbacher	5	6	8	10	15	20	30	
88	Dave Lewis	5	6	8	10	15	20	30	
89	Franco Harris RC	20	30	50	▲100	▲200	▲250	1,200	
90	Tom Mack	5	6	8	10	15	20	30	
91	Mike Tilleman	5	6	8	10	15	20	30	
92	Carl Mauck	5	6	8	10	15	20	30	
93	Larry Hand	5	6	8	10	15	20	30	
94	Dave Foley RC	5	6	8	10	15	20	30	
95	Frank Nunley	5	6	8	10	15	20	30	
96	John Charles	5	6	8	10	15	20	30	
97	Jim Bakken	5	6	8	10	15	20	30	
98	Pat Fischer	5	6	8	10	20	25	35	
99	Randy Rasmussen	5	6	8	10	15	20	30	
100	Larry Csonka	5	6	8	10	25	40	175	
101	Mike Siani RC	5	6	8	10	15	20	30	
102	Tom Roussel	5	6	8	10	15	20	30	
103	Clarence Scott RC	5	6	8	10	15	20	30	
104	Charlie Johnson	5	6	8	10	15	20	30	
105	Rick Volk	5	6	8	10	15	20	30	
106	Willie Young	5	6	8	10	15	20	30	
107	Emmitt Thomas	5	6	8	10	15	20	30	
108	Jon Morris	5	6	8	10	15	20	30	
109	Clarence Williams	5	6	8	10	15	20	30	
110	Rayfield Wright	5	6	8	10	15	20	30	
111	Norm Bulaich	5	6	8	10	15	20	30	
112	Mike Eischeid	5	6	8	10	15	20	30	
113	Speedy Thomas	5	6	8	10	20	25		
114	Glen Holloway	5	6	8	10	15	20	30	
115	Jack Ham RC	15	20	25	40	100	120	400	
116	Jim Nettles	5	6	8	10	15	20	30	
117	Errol Mann	5	6	8	10	15	20	30	
118	John Mackey	5	6	8	10	15	20	30	
119	George Kunz	5	6	8	10	20	25		
120	Bob James	5	6	8	10	15	20	30	
121	Garland Boyette	5	6	8	10	15	20	30	
122	Mel Phillips	5	6	8	10	15	20	30	
123	Johnny Roland	5	6	8	10	15	20	30	
124	Doug Swift	5	6	8	10	15	20	30	
125	Archie Manning	5	6	8	10	15	20	80	
126	Dave Herman	5	6	8	10	15	20	30	
127	Carleton Oats	5	6	8	10	15	20	30	
128	Bill Van Heusen	5	6	8	10	15	20	30	
129	Rich Jackson	5	6	8	10	15	20	30	
130	Len Hauss	5	6	8	10	15	20	30	
131	Billy Parks RC	5	6	8	10	15	20	30	
132	Ray May	5	6	8	10	15	20	30	
133	NFC Semi/R.Staubach	5	6	8	12	30	50	150	
134	AFC Semi/Immac.Rec.	5	6	8	10	15	20	80	
135	NFC Semi-Final	5	6	8	10	15	20	50	
136	AFC Semi/L.Csonka	5	6	8	10	15	20	40	
137	NFC Title Game/Kilmer	5	6	8	10	15	20	40	
138	AFC Title Game	5	6	8	10	15	20	60	
139	Super Bowl VII	5	6	8	10	15	20	80	
140	Dwight White RC	5	6	8	10	40	50	200	
141	Jim Marsalis	5	6	8	10	15	20	30	
142	Doug Van Horn	5	6	8	10	20	25		
143	Al Matthews	5	6	8	10	15	20	30	
144	Bob Windsor	5	6	8	10	15	20	30	
145	Dave Hampton RC	5	6	8	10	15	20	30	
146	Horst Muhlmann	5	6	8	10	15	20	30	
147	Wally Hilgenberg RC	5	6	8	10	15	20	30	
148	Ron Smith	5	6	8	10	15	20	30	
149	Coy Bacon RC	5	6	8	10	15	20	60	
150	Winston Hill	5	6	8	10	15	20	30	
151	Ron Jessie RC	5	6	8	10	15	20	30	
152	Ken Iman	5	6	8	10	15	20	30	
153	Ron Saul	5	6	8	10	15	20	30	
154	Jim Braxton RC	5	6	8	10	15	20	30	

FOOTBALL

	VgEx 4	EX 5	ExMt 6	NM 7	NmMt 8	NmMt+ 8.5	MT 9	Gem 9.5/10
Bubba Smith	5	6	8	10	15	20	35	80
Gary Cuozzo	5	6	8	10	15	20	30	
Charlie Krueger	5	6	8	10	15	20	30	
Tim Foley RC	5	6	8	10	15	20	30	
Lee Roy Jordan	5	6	8	10	15	20	30	
Bob Brown OT	5	6	8	10	15	20	30	
Margene Adkins	5	6	8	10	15	20	30	
Ron Widby	5	6	8	10	15	20	30	
Jim Houston	5	6	8	10	15	20	30	
Joe Dawkins	5	6	8	10	15	20	30	
L.C.Greenwood	5	6	8	10	15	20	35	150
Richmond Flowers RC	5	6	8	10	15	20	30	
Curley Culp RC	8	12	20	30	80	70	150	
Len St. Jean	5	6	8	10	20	25		
Walter Rock	5	6	8	10	15	20	30	
Bill Bradley	5	6	8	10	15	20	30	
Ken Riley RC	5	6	8	10	15	20	50	
Rich Coady	5	6	8	10	15	20	30	
Don Hansen	5	6	8	10	15	20	30	
Lionel Aldridge	5	6	8	10	15	20	30	
Don Maynard	5	6	8	10	15	20	35	
Dave Osborn	5	6	8	10	15	20	30	
Jim Bailey	5	6	8	10	15	20	30	
John Pitts	5	6	8	10	15	20	30	
Dave Parks	5	6	8	10	15	20	30	
Chester Marcol RC	5	6	8	10	15	20	30	
Len Rohde	5	6	8	10	15	20	30	
Jeff Staggs	5	6	8	10	15	20	30	80
Gene Hickerson	5	6	8	10	15	20	30	
Charlie Evans	5	6	8	10	15	20	30	
Mel Renfro	5	6	8	10	15	20	30	
Marvin Upshaw	5	6	8	10	15	20	30	
George Atkinson	5	6	8	10	15	20	50	
Norm Evans	5	6	8	10	15	20	30	
Steve Ramsey	5	6	8	10	15	20	30	80
Dave Chapple	5	6	8	10	15	20	30	
Gerry Mullins	5	6	8	10	15	20	50	
John Didion	5	6	8	10	15	20	30	
Bob Gladieux	5	6	8	10	15	20	30	
Don Hultz	5	6	8	10	15	20	30	
Mike Lucci	5	6	8	10	15	20	30	
John Wilbur	5	6	8	10	15	20	30	
George Farmer	5	6	8	10	15	20	30	
Tommy Casanova RC	5	6	8	10	15	20	40	
Russ Washington	5	6	8	10	15	20	40	
Claude Humphrey	5	6	8	10	15	20	30	
Pat Hughes	5	6	8	10	15	20	30	80
Zeke Moore	5	6	8	10	15	20	30	
Chip Glass	5	6	8	10	15	20	30	
Glenn Ressler	5	6	8	10	15	20	30	
Willie Ellison	5	6	8	10	15	20	30	
John Leypoldt	5	6	8	10	15	20	30	
Johnny Fuller	5	6	8	10	15	20	30	
Bill Hayhoe	5	6	8	10	15	20	30	
Ed Bell	5	6	8	10	15	20	30	
Willie Brown	5	6	8	10	15	20	50	
Carl Eller	5	6	8	10	15	20	30	80
Mark Nordquist	5	6	8	10	15	20	30	
Larry Willingham	5	6	8	10	15	20	30	
Nick Buoniconti	5	6	8	10	15	20	30	
John Hadl	5	6	8	10	15	20	30	80
Jethro Pugh RC	5	6	8	10	20	25	50	
Leroy Mitchell	5	6	8	10	15	20	30	
Billy Newsome	5	6	8	10	15	20	30	
John McMakin	5	6	8	10	15	20	30	
Larry Brown	5	6	8	10	15	20	30	80
Clarence Scott RC	5	6	8	10	15	20	30	
Paul Naumoff	5	6	8	10	15	20	30	
Ted Fritsch Jr.	5	6	8	10	15	20	30	
Checklist 133-264	5	6	8	10	15	20	50	
Dan Pastorini	5	6	8	10	15	20	30	80
Joe Beauchamp	5	6	8	10	15	20	30	
Pat Matson	5	6	8	10	15	20	30	
Tony McGee DT	5	6	8	10	15	20	30	80
Mike Phipps	5	6	8	10	15	20	30	80
Harold Jackson	5	6	8	10	15	20	30	
Willie Williams	5	6	8	10	15	20	30	100
Spike Jones	5	6	8	10	15	20	30	
Jim Tyrer	5	6	8	10	15	20	30	

	VgEx 4	EX 5	ExMt 6	NM 7	NmMt 8	NmMt+ 8.5	MT 9	Gem 9.5/10
234 Roy Hilton	5	6	8	10	15	20	30	
235 Phil Villapiano	5	6	8	10	15	20	30	
236 Charley Taylor	5	6	8	10	15	20	35	
237 Malcolm Snider	5	6	8	10	15	20	30	80
238 Vic Washington	5	6	8	10	15	20	30	80
239 Grady Alderman	5	6	8	10	15	20	30	
240 Dick Anderson	5	6	8	10	15	20	30	
241 Ron Yankowski	5	6	8	10	15	20	30	
242 Billy Masters	5	6	8	10	15	20	30	
243 Herb Adderley	5	6	8	10	15	20	30	
244 David Ray	5	6	8	10	15	20	40	
245 John Riggins	5	6	8	10	15	20	80	
246 Mike Wagner RC	5	6	8	10	35	30	100	
247 Don Morrison	5	6	8	10	15	20	30	
248 Earl McCullouch	5	6	8	10	20	25	50	
249 Dennis Wirgowski	5	6	8	10	15	20	30	
250 Chris Hanburger	5	6	8	10	12	20	30	
251 Pat Sullivan RC	5	6	8	10	15	20	30	
252 Walt Sweeney	5	6	8	10	15	20	30	
253 Willie Alexander	5	6	8	10	15	20	30	
254 Doug Dressler	5	6	8	10	20	25		
255 Walter Johnson	5	6	8	10	15	20	30	
256 Ron Hornsby	5	6	8	10	15	20	25	
257 Ben Hawkins	5	6	8	10	15	20	30	80
258 Donnie Green RC	5	6	8	10	15	20	30	100
259 Fred Hoaglin	5	6	8	10	15	20	30	
260 Jerrel Wilson	5	6	8	10	15	20	30	
261 Horace Jones	5	6	8	10	15	20	30	
262 Woody Peoples	5	6	8	10	15	20	30	
263 Jim Hill RC	5	6	8	10	15	20	30	
264 John Fuqua	5	6	8	10	15	20	30	
265 Donny Anderson KP	5	6	8	10	15	20	30	
266 Roman Gabriel KP	5	6	8	10	15	20	30	
267 Mike Garrett KP	5	6	8	10	15	20	30	
268 Rufus Mayes RC	5	6	8	10	15	20	60	
269 Chip Myrtle	5	6	8	10	15	20	30	
270 Bill Stanfill RC	5	6	8	10	15	20	30	
271 Clint Jones	5	6	8	10	15	20	30	
272 Miller Farr	5	6	8	10	15	20	30	
273 Harry Schuh	5	6	8	10	15	20	30	80
274 Bob Hayes	5	6	8	10	15	20	30	80
275 Bobby Douglass	5	6	8	10	15	20	30	
276 Gus Hollomon	5	6	8	10	15	20	30	
277 Del Williams	5	6	8	10	15	20	30	
278 Julius Adams	5	6	8	10	12	15	20	80
279 Herman Weaver	5	6	8	10	15	20	30	
280 Joe Greene	5	6	8	10	15	20	100	
281 Wes Chesson	5	6	8	10	15	20	30	
282 Charlie Harraway	5	6	8	10	15	20	30	
283 Paul Guidry	5	6	8	10	15	20	30	80
284 Terry Owens RC	5	6	8	10	15	20	30	
285 Jan Stenerud	5	6	8	10	15	20	30	
286 Pete Athas	5	6	8	10	15	20	30	80
287 Dale Lindsey	5	6	8	10	15	20	30	
288 Jack Tatum RC	6	8	10	20	30	40	120	
289 Floyd Little	5	6	8	10	15	20	30	80
290 Bob Johnson	5	6	8	10	15	20	30	
291 Tommy Hart RC	5	6	8	10	15	20	30	
292 Tom Mitchell	5	6	8	10	15	20	30	
293 Walt Patulski RC	5	6	8	10	15	20		
294 Jim Skaggs	5	6	8	10	15	20	30	
295 Bob Griese	5	6	8	10	15	20	50	300
296 Mike McCoy DT	5	6	8	10	15	20	30	
297 Mel Gray	5	6	8	10	15	20	30	80
298 Bobby Bryant	5	6	8	10	15	20	30	
299 Blaine Nye RC	5	6	8	10	15	20	30	
300 Dick Butkus	5	8	10	15	25	30	60	225
301 Charlie Cowan RC	5	6	8	10	15	20	30	
302 Mark Lomas	5	6	8	10	15	20	30	
303 Josh Ashton	5	6	8	10	15	20	30	
304 Happy Feller	5	6	8	10	15	20	30	
305 Ron Shanklin	5	6	8	10	15	20	30	
306 Wayne Rasmussen	5	6	8	10	15	20	30	
307 Jerry Smith	5	6	8	10	15	20	30	80
308 Ken Reaves	5	6	8	10	15	20	30	
309 Ron East	5	6	8	10	15	20	30	
310 Otis Taylor	5	6	8	10	15	20	30	
311 John Garlington	5	6	8	10	15	20	30	
312 Lyle Alzado	5	6	8	10	15	20	40	

FOOTBALL

#	Player	VgEx 4	EX 5	ExMt 6	NM 7	NmMt 8	NmMt+ 8.5	MT 9	Gem 9.5/10
313	Remi Prudhomme	5	6	8	10	15	20	30	
314	Cornelius Johnson	5	6	8	10	15	20	30	
315	Lemar Parrish	5	6	8	10	20	25		
316	Jim Kiick	5	6	8	10	15	20	25	
317	Steve Zabel	5	6	8	10	15	20	30	
318	Alden Roche	5	6	8	10	15	20	30	
319	Tom Blanchard	5	6	8	10	15	20	30	
320	Fred Biletnikoff	5	6	8	10	15	20	40	
321	Ralph Neely	5	6	8	10	15	20	30	80
322	Dan Dierdorf RC	8	10	12	20	40	50	175	
323	Richard Caster	5	6	8	10	15	20	30	
324	Gene Howard	5	6	8	10	15	20	30	
325	Elvin Bethea	5	6	8	10	15	20	30	
326	Carl Garrett	5	6	8	10	15	20	30	
327	Ron Billingsley	5	6	8	10	15	20	30	
328	Charlie West	5	6	8	10	15	20	30	
329	Tom Neville	5	6	8	10	15	20	30	
330	Ted Kwalick	5	6	8	10	15	20	30	
331	Rudy Redmond	5	6	8	10	15	20	30	
332	Henry Davis	5	6	8	10	15	20	30	
333	John Zook	5	6	8	10	15	20	30	
334	Jim Turner	5	6	8	10	15	20	30	60
335	Len Dawson	5	6	8	10	15	20	60	
336	Bob Chandler RC	5	6	8	10	15	20	30	
337	Al Beauchamp	5	6	8	10	15	20	30	80
338	Tom Matte	5	6	8	10	15	20	30	80
339	Paul Laaveg	5	6	8	10	15	20	30	
340	Ken Ellis	5	6	8	10	15	20	30	80
341	Jim Langer RC	5	6	8	12	25	30	80	▲500
342	Ron Porter	5	6	8	10	15	20	30	
343	Jack Youngblood RC	6	8	12	20	50	60	▲200	
344	Cornell Green	5	6	8	10	15	20	30	80
345	Marv Hubbard	5	6	8	10	15	20	30	80
346	Bruce Taylor	5	6	8	10	15	20	30	
347	Sam Havrilak	5	6	8	10	15	20	30	80
348	Walt Sumner	5	6	8	10	15	20	30	
349	Steve O'Neal	5	6	8	10	15	20	30	80
350	Ron Johnson	5	6	8	10	15	20	30	60
351	Rockne Freitas	5	6	8	10	15	20	30	60
352	Larry Stallings	5	6	8	10	15	20	30	
353	Jim Cadile	5	6	8	10	15	20	30	
354	Ken Burrough	5	6	8	10	15	20	30	60
355	Jim Plunkett	5	6	8	10	15	20	100	
356	Dave Long	5	6	8	10	15	20	30	
357	Ralph Anderson	5	6	8	10	15	20	40	
358	Checklist 265-396	5	6	8	10	15	20	40	
359	Gene Washington Vik	5	6	8	10	15	20	30	
360	Dave Wilcox	5	6	8	10	15	20	30	80
361	Paul Smith	5	6	8	10	15	20	30	
362	Alvin Wyatt	5	6	8	10	15	20	30	
363	Charlie Smith RB	5	6	8	10	15	20	30	
364	Royce Berry	5	6	8	10	15	20	30	80
365	Dave Elmendorf	5	6	8	10	15	20	30	
366	Scott Hunter	5	6	8	10	15	20	30	
367	Bob Kuechenberg RC	5	6	8	10	30	30	50	500
368	Pete Gogolak	5	6	8	10	15	20	30	
369	Dave Edwards	5	6	8	10	15	20	30	
370	Lem Barney	5	6	8	10	15	20	30	
371	Verlon Biggs	5	6	8	10	15	20	30	60
372	John Reaves RC	5	6	8	10	15	20	30	80
373	Ed Podolak	5	6	8	10	15	20	30	
374	Chris Farasopoulos	5	6	8	10	15	20	30	60
375	Gary Garrison	5	6	8	10	15	20	30	
376	Tom Funchess	5	6	8	10	15	20	30	80
377	Bobby Joe Green	5	6	8	10	15	20	30	
378	Don Brumm	5	6	8	10	15	20	30	
379	Jim O'Brien	5	6	8	10	15	20	30	
380	Paul Krause	5	6	8	10	15	20	30	
381	Leroy Kelly	5	6	8	10	15	20	30	
382	Ray Mansfield	5	6	8	10	15	20	30	
383	Dan Abramowicz	5	6	8	10	15	20	30	
384	John Outlaw RC	5	6	8	10	15	20	30	
385	Tommy Nobis	5	6	8	10	15	20	30	
386	Tom Domres	5	6	8	10	15	20	30	
387	Ken Willard	5	6	8	10	15	20	30	
388	Mike Stratton	5	6	8	10	15	20	30	80
389	Fred Dryer	5	6	8	10	15	20	30	
390	Jake Scott	5	6	8	10	15	20	30	
391	Rich Houston	5	6	8	10	15	20	30	
392	Virgil Carter	5	6	8	10	15	20	30	
393	Tody Smith	5	6	8	10	15	20	30	
394	Ernie Calloway	5	6	8	10	15	20	30	60
395	Charlie Sanders	5	6	8	10	15	20	30	
396	Fred Willis	5	6	8	10	15	20	30	80
397	Curt Knight	5	6	8	10	15	20	30	
398	Nemiah Wilson	5	6	8	10	15	20	30	
399	Carroll Dale	5	6	8	10	15	20	30	
400	Joe Namath	12	15	25	40	60	80	150	500
401	Wayne Mulligan	5	6	8	10	15	20	30	
402	Jim Harrison	5	6	8	10	15	20	30	
403	Tim Rossovich	5	6	8	10	15	20	30	
404	David Lee	5	6	8	10	15	20	30	
405	Frank Pitts	5	6	8	10	15	20	30	
406	Jim Marshall	5	6	8	10	15	20	30	
407	Bob Brown TE	5	6	8	10	15	20	30	
408	John Rowser	5	6	8	10	15	20	30	
409	Mike Montler	5	6	8	10	20	25		
410	Willie Lanier	5	6	8	10	15	20	30	
411	Bill Bell K	5	6	8	10	15	20	30	
412	Cedrick Hardman	5	6	8	10	15	20	30	80
413	Bob Anderson	5	6	8	10	15	20	30	100
414	Earl Morrall	5	6	8	10	15	20	30	
415	Ken Houston	5	6	8	10	15	20	30	
416	Jack Snow	5	6	8	10	15	20	30	
417	Dick Cunningham	5	6	8	10	15	20	30	
418	Greg Larson	5	6	8	10	15	20	30	
419	Mike Bass	5	6	8	10	15	20	30	80
420	Mike Reid	5	6	8	10	15	20	30	
421	Walt Garrison	5	6	8	10	15	20	30	80
422	Pete Liske	5	6	8	10	15	20	30	
423	Jim Yarbrough	5	6	8	10	15	20	30	
424	Rich McGeorge	5	6	8	10	20	25		
425	Bobby Howfield	5	6	8	10	15	20	30	
426	Pete Banaszak	5	6	8	10	15	20	30	
427	Willie Holman	5	6	8	10	15	20	30	
428	Dale Hackbart	5	6	8	10	15	20	30	
429	Fair Hooker	5	6	8	10	15	20	30	
430	Ted Hendricks	5	6	8	10	15	20	40	
431	Mike Garrett	5	6	8	10	15	20	30	
432	Glen Ray Hines	5	6	8	10	20	25	100	
433	Fred Cox	5	6	8	10	15	20	50	
434	Bobby Walden	5	6	8	10	15	20	30	
435	Bobby Bell	5	6	8	10	15	20	30	
436	Dave Rowe	5	6	8	10	15	20	30	
437	Bob Berry	5	6	8	10	15	20	30	
438	Bill Thompson	5	6	8	10	20	25	100	
439	Jim Beirne	5	6	8	10	15	20	30	
440	Larry Little	5	6	8	10	20	25	80	
441	Rocky Thompson	5	6	8	10	15	20	30	
442	Brig Owens	5	6	8	10	20	25		
443	Richard Neal	5	6	8	10	20	25		
444	Al Nelson	5	6	8	10	15	20	30	
445	Chip Myers	5	6	8	10	15	20	30	
446	Ken Bowman	5	6	8	10	15	20	30	
447	Jim Purnell	5	6	8	10	15	20	30	
448	Altie Taylor	5	6	8	10	15	20	30	
449	Linzy Cole	5	6	8	10	15	20	25	
450	Bob Lilly	5	6	8	10	15	20	40	200
451	Charlie Ford	5	6	8	10	15	20	30	
452	Milt Sunde	5	6	8	10	15	20	30	
453	Doug Wyatt	5	6	8	10	15	20	30	
454	Don Nottingham RC	5	6	8	10	15	20	30	
455	Johnny Unitas	6	8	10	15	35	40	135	
456	Frank Lewis RC	5	6	8	10	15	20	40	
457	Roger Wehrli	5	6	8	10	15	20	30	
458	Jim Cheyunski	5	6	8	10	15	20	30	
459	Jerry Sherk RC	5	6	8	10	15	20	30	
460	Gene Washington 49er	5	6	8	10	15	20	30	
461	Jim Otto	5	6	8	10	15	20	30	
462	Ed Budde	5	6	8	10	15	20	30	
463	Jim Mitchell TE	5	6	8	10	15	20	30	
464	Emerson Boozer	5	6	8	10	15	20	30	
465	Garo Yepremian	5	6	8	10	15	20	40	
466	Pete Duranko	5	6	8	10	15	20	30	
467	Charlie Joiner	5	6	8	10	15	20	60	
468	Spider Lockhart	5	6	8	10	15	20	30	
469	Marty Domres	5	6	8	10	15	20	30	
470	John Brockington	5	6	8	10	15	20	30	

	VgEx 4	EX 5	ExMt 6	NM 7	NmMt 8	NmMt+ 8.5	MT 9	Gem 9.5/10
Ed Flanagan	5	6	8	10	15	20	30	
Roy Jefferson	5	6	8	10	15	20	30	
Julian Fagan	5	6	8	10	15	20	30	
Bill Brown	5	6	8	10	15	20	30	80
Roger Staubach	12	15	25	40	80	100	350	
Jan White RC	5	6	8	10	15	20	40	
Pat Holmes	5	6	8	10	15	20	30	
Bob DeMarco	5	6	8	10	15	20	30	
Merlin Olsen	5	6	8	10	15	20	35	100
Andy Russell	5	6	8	10	15	20	80	
Steve Spurrier	5	6	8	12	20	30	60	
Nate Ramsey	5	6	8	10	20	25		
Dennis Partee	5	6	8	10	20	25	30	
Jerry Simmons	5	6	8	10	15	20	30	
Donny Anderson	5	6	8	10	15	20	30	
Ralph Baker	5	6	8	10	15	20	30	
Ken Stabler RC	20	25	40	80	▼300	400	1,500	
Ernie McMillan	5	6	8	10	15	20	30	
Ken Burrow	5	6	8	10	15	20	30	
Jack Gregory RC	5	6	8	10	15	20	30	
Larry Seiple	5	6	8	10	15	20	30	
Mick Tingelhoff	5	6	8	10	15	20	50	
Craig Morton	5	6	8	10	12	15	20	
Cecil Turner	5	6	8	10	15	20	30	
Steve Owens	5	6	8	10	15	20	30	
Rickie Harris	5	6	8	10	15	20	30	
Buck Buchanan	5	6	8	10	15	20	30	
Checklist 397-528	5	6	8	10	15	20	50	
Billy Kilmer	5	6	8	10	15	20	30	
O.J.Simpson	6	8	10	15	40	50	80	
Bruce Gossett	5	6	8	10	15	20	30	
Art Thoms RC	5	6	8	10	20	25	80	
Larry Kaminski	5	6	8	10	15	20	30	
Larry Smith RB	5	6	8	10	15	20	30	
Bruce Van Dyke	5	6	8	10	15	20	30	
Alvin Reed	5	6	8	10	15	20	30	
Delles Howell	5	6	8	10	15	20	30	
Leroy Keyes	5	6	8	10	15	20	30	
Bo Scott	5	6	8	10	15	20	30	
Ron Yary	5	6	8	10	15	20	60	
Paul Warfield	5	6	8	10	15	20	▼60	
Mac Percival	5	6	8	10	15	20	30	80
Essex Johnson	5	6	8	10	15	25	50	
Jackie Smith	5	6	8	10	15	20	30	
Norm Snead	5	6	8	10	15	20	30	
Charlie Stukes	5	6	8	10	15	20	30	100
Reggie Rucker RC	5	6	8	10	15	20	30	100
Bill Sandeman	5	6	8	10	15	20	30	
Mel Farr	5	6	8	10	15	20	30	
Raymond Chester	5	6	8	10	15	20	30	
Fred Carr RC	5	6	8	10	15	20	30	
Jerry LeVias	5	6	8	10	15	20	30	
Jim Strong	5	6	8	10	15	20	30	
Roland McDole	5	6	8	10	15	20	30	
Dennis Shaw	5	6	8	10	15	20	30	
Dave Manders	5	6	8	10	15	20	40	
Skip Vanderbundt	5	6	8	10	15	20	30	
Mike Sensibaugh RC	5	6	8	10	40	50	250	

Terry Bradshaw #15 BGS 9.5 (Gem) sold for $505 (eBay; 10/07)
Terry Bradshaw #15 PSA 10 (Gem Mint) sold for $2548.98 (Memory Lane; 5/12)
Jack Ham #115 PSA 10 (Gem) sold for $2,185 (Mastro; 12/06)
Jack Ham #115 PSA 10 (Gem) sold for $1,679 (Memory Lane; 5/08)
Jack Ham RC #115 PSA 10 (Gem Mint) sold for $2057.51 (Memory Lane; 5/12)
Larry Little #440 PSA 9 (MT) sold for $480 (eBay; 10/07)
Art Shell RC #77 PSA 10 (Gem Mint) sold for $3158.02 (eBay; 8/12)
O.J. Simpson #500 PSA 10 (Gem Mint) sold for $1657 (eBay; 10/14)

1974 Topps

	VgEx 4	EX 5	ExMt 6	NM 7	NmMt 8	NmMt+ 8.5	MT 9	Gem 9.5/10
O.J.Simpson RB	5	8	12	25	50	60	125	
Blaine Nye	4	5	6	8	10	12	25	
Don Hansen	4	5	6	8	10	12	25	
Ken Bowman	4	5	6	8	10	12	25	
Carl Eller	4	5	6	8	20			
Jerry Smith	4	5	6	8	20			
Ed Podolak	4	5	6	8	10	12	25	
Mel Gray	4	5	6	8	10	12	25	100
Pat Matson	4	5	6	8	20			

		VgEx 4	EX 5	ExMt 6	NM 7	NmMt 8	NmMt+ 8.5	MT 9	Gem 9.5/10
10	Floyd Little	4	5	6	8	10	12	50	
11	Frank Pitts	4	5	6	8	20			
12	Vern Den Herder RC	4	5	6	8	30	40	100	
13	John Fuqua	4	5	6	8	10	12	60	
14	Jack Tatum	4	5	6	8	10	12	30	
15	Winston Hill	4	5	6	8	20			
16	John Beasley	4	5	6	8	10	12	25	
17	David Lee	4	5	6	8	10	12	25	
18	Rich Coady	4	5	6	8	10	12	25	
19	Ken Willard	4	5	6	8	10	12	25	
20	Coy Bacon	4	5	6	8	10	12	25	
21	Ben Hawkins	4	5	6	8	10	12	25	
22	Paul Guidry	4	5	6	8	10	12	25	
23	Norm Snead HOR	4	5	6	8	10	12	25	
24	Jim Yarbrough	4	5	6	8	10	12	25	
25	Jack Reynolds RC	4	5	6	8	25			
26	Josh Ashton	4	5	6	8	10	12	20	
27	Donnie Green	4	5	6	8	10	12	20	
28	Bob Hayes	4	5	6	8	12	12	40	
29	John Zook	4	5	6	8	10	12	15	
30	Bobby Bryant	4	5	6	8	10	12	25	
31	Scott Hunter	4	5	6	8	10	12	25	
32	Dan Dierdorf	4	5	6	10	15	20	50	
33	Curt Knight	4	5	6	8	20			
34	Elmo Wright RC	4	5	6	8	10	12	25	
35	Essex Johnson	4	5	6	8	10	12	25	
36	Walt Sumner	4	5	6	8	10	12	25	80
37	Marv Montgomery	4	5	6	8	10	12	25	
38	Tim Foley	4	5	6	8	10	12	15	
39	Mike Siani	4	5	6	8	10	12	25	
40	Joe Greene	4	5	6	10	30	40	200	
41	Bobby Howfield	4	5	6	8	10	12	25	
42	Del Williams	4	5	6	8	10	12	25	100
43	Don McCauley	4	5	6	8	10	12	25	
44	Randy Jackson	4	5	6	8	10	12	25	100
45	Ron Smith	4	5	6	8	10	12	25	
46	Gene Washington 49er	4	5	6	8	10	12	25	
47	Po James	4	5	6	8	10	12	25	
48	Solomon Freelon	4	5	6	8	10	12	25	
49	Bob Windsor HOR	4	5	6	8	10	12	25	
50	John Hadl	4	5	6	8	10	12	25	
51	Greg Larson	4	5	6	8	10	12	15	
52	Steve Owens	4	5	6	8	20			
53	Jim Cheyunski	4	5	6	8	10	12	20	
54	Rayfield Wright	4	5	6	8	10	12	25	
55	Dave Hampton	4	5	6	8	10	12	25	
56	Ron Widby	4	5	6	8	20			
57	Milt Sunde	4	5	6	8	10		25	
58	Billy Kilmer	4	5	6	8	10	12	25	
59	Bobby Bell	4	5	6	8	10	12	25	
60	Jim Bakken	4	5	6	8	10	12	25	
61	Rufus Mayes	4	5	6	8	20			
62	Vic Washington	4	5	6	8	20			
63	Gene Washington Vik	4	5	6	8	10	12	25	100
64	Clarence Scott	4	5	6	8	20			
65	Gene Upshaw	4	5	6	8	10	20	80	
66	Larry Seiple	4	5	6	8	10	12	25	
67	John McMakin	4	5	6	8	10	12	25	
68	Ralph Baker	4	5	6	8	10	12	25	
69	Lydell Mitchell	4	5	6	8	10	12	20	
70	Archie Manning	4	5	6	8	10		40	
71	George Farmer	4	5	6	8	10	12	25	100
72	Ron East	4	5	6	8	10	12	25	
73	Al Nelson	4	5	6	8	10	12	25	
74	Pat Hughes	4	5	6	8	10	12	25	
75	Fred Willis	4	5	6	8	10	12	25	
76	Larry Walton	4	5	6	8	10	12	25	
77	Tom Neville	4	5	6	8	10	12	25	
78	Ted Kwalick	4	5	6	8	10	12	25	
79	Walt Patulski	4	5	6	8	10	12	20	
80	John Niland	4	5	6	8	10	12	25	
81	Ted Fritsch Jr.	4	5	6	8	10	12	25	
82	Paul Krause	4	5	6	8	10	12	25	
83	Jack Snow	4	5	6	8	15			
84	Mike Bass	4	5	6	8	10	12	25	
85	Jim Tyrer	4	5	6	8	30	50		
86	Ron Yankowski	4	5	6	8	10	12	25	
87	Mike Phipps	4	5	6	8	10	12	25	
88	Al Beauchamp	4	5	6	8	10	12	25	

#	Player	VgEx 4	EX 5	ExMt 6	NM 7	NmMt 8	NmMt+ 8.5	MT 9	Gem 9.5/10
89	Riley Odoms RC	4	5	6	8	15	20	80	
90	MacArthur Lane	4	5	6	8	10	12	25	
91	Art Thoms	4	5	6	8	20			
92	Marlin Briscoe	4	5	6	8	10	12	25	60
93	Bruce Van Dyke	4	5	6	8	10	12	25	
94	Tom Myers RC	4	5	6	8	10	12	25	
95	Calvin Hill	4	5	6	8	10	12	25	
96	Bruce Laird	4	5	6	8	10	12	20	60
97	Tony McGee DT	4	5	6	8	10	12	25	
98	Len Rohde	4	5	6	8	10	12	25	100
99	Tom McNeill	4	5	6	8	10	12	25	
100	Delles Howell	4	5	6	8	10	12	25	
101	Gary Garrison	4	5	6	8	10	12	25	
102	Dan Goich	4	5	6	8	10	12	25	
103	Len St. Jean	4	5	6	8	10	12	25	
104	Zeke Moore	4	5	6	8	10	12	25	
105	Ahmad Rashad RC	6	8	12	20	35	50	80	
106	Mel Renfro	4	5	6	8	10	12	25	
107	Jim Mitchell TE	4	5	6	8	10	12	25	100
108	Ed Budde	4	5	6	8	20		50	
109	Harry Schuh	4	5	6	8	10	12	25	
110	Greg Pruitt RC	4	5	6	8	10	15	135	
111	Ed Flanagan	4	5	6	8	10	12	25	
112	Larry Stallings	4	5	6	8	10	12	25	
113	Chuck Foreman RC	4	6	8	15	25	30	80	
114	Royce Berry	4	5	6	8	10	12	25	
115	Gale Gillingham	4	5	6	8	10	12	25	
116	Charlie Johnson HOR	4	5	6	8	20			
117	Checklist 1-132	4	5	6	8	10	12	25	
118	Bill Butler	4	5	6	8	10	12	25	
119	Roy Jefferson	4	5	6	8	20			
120	Bobby Douglass	4	5	6	8	10	12	25	
121	Harold Carmichael RC	4	6	10	12	25	30	60	
122	George Kunz AP	4	5	6	8	10	15	25	
123	Larry Little	4	5	6	8	10	12	25	
124	Forrest Blue AP	4	5	6	8	20			
125	Ron Yary	4	5	6	8	10	12	25	
126	Tom Mack AP	4	5	6	8	10	12	25	
127	Bob Tucker AP	4	5	6	8	10	12	25	
128	Paul Warfield	4	5	6	8	10	15	60	
129	Fran Tarkenton	4	5	6	10	40	50	200	
130	O.J.Simpson	4	6	8	15	40	50	250	
131	Larry Csonka	4	5	6	10	15	30	120	
132	Bruce Gossett AP	4	5	6	8	10	12	25	
133	Bill Stanfill AP	4	5	6	8	10	12	25	
134	Alan Page	4	5	6	8	10	12	30	
135	Paul Smith AP	4	5	6	8	10	12	25	
136	Claude Humphrey AP	4	5	6	8	10	12	25	
137	Jack Ham	4	6	8	12	30	25	▼60	
138	Lee Roy Jordan	4	5	6	8	10	12	40	
139	Phil Villapiano AP	4	5	6	8	10	12	25	
140	Ken Ellis AP	4	5	6	8	10	12	25	80
141	Willie Brown	4	5	6	8	10	12	40	100
142	Dick Anderson AP	4	5	6	8	10	12	25	
143	Bill Bradley AP	4	5	6	8	10	12	25	
144	Jerrel Wilson AP	4	5	6	8	10	12	25	
145	Reggie Rucker	4	5	6	8	20			
146	Marty Domres	4	5	6	8	10	12	25	80
147	Bob Kowalkowski	4	5	6	8	10	12	25	100
148	John Matuszak RC	4	5	6	10	15	20	50	
149	Mike Adamle RC	4	5	6	8	10	12	25	
150	Johnny Unitas	6	8	12	20	35	50	100	
151	Charlie Ford	4	5	6	8	10	12	20	
152	Bob Klein RC	4	5	6	8	10	12	25	
153	Jim Merlo	4	5	6	8	10	12	25	
154	Willie Young	4	5	6	8	10	12	25	60
155	Donny Anderson	4	5	6	8	10	12	25	60
156	Brig Owens	4	5	6	8	10	12	25	
157	Bruce Jarvis	4	5	6	8	10	12	25	
158	Ron Carpenter RC	4	5	6	8	10	12	25	60
159	Don Cockroft	4	5	6	8	10	12	25	
160	Tommy Nobis	4	5	6	8	10	12	25	80
161	Craig Morton	4	5	6	8	10	12	25	80
162	Jon Staggers	4	5	6	8	20			
163	Mike Eischeid	4	5	6	8	10	12	25	
164	Jerry Sisemore RC	4	5	6	8	10	12	25	
165	Cedrick Hardman	4	5	6	8	20			
166	Bill Thompson	4	5	6	8	20			
167	Jim Lynch	4	5	6	8	10	12	20	

#	Player	VgEx 4	EX 5	ExMt 6	NM 7	NmMt 8	NmMt+ 8.5	MT 9	Gem 9.5/10
168	Bob Moore	4	5	6	8	10	12	25	
169	Glen Edwards	4	5	6	8	10	12	25	100
170	Mercury Morris	4	5	6	8	10	12	25	
171	Julius Adams	4	5	6	8	10	12	20	100
172	Cotton Speyrer	4	5	6	8	10	12	25	100
173	Bill Munson	4	5	6	8	10	12	25	
174	Benny Johnson	4	5	6	8	10	12	25	150
175	Burgess Owens RC	4	5	6	8	10	12	25	80
176	Cid Edwards	4	5	6	8	10	12	25	
177	Doug Buffone	4	5	6	8	10	12	20	100
178	Charlie Cowan	4	5	6	8	10	12	25	60
179	Bob Newland	4	5	6	8	10	12	25	
180	Ron Johnson	4	5	6	8	10	12	25	100
181	Bob Rowe	4	5	6	8	10	12	25	
182	Len Hauss	4	5	6	8	10	12	25	80
183	Joe DeLamielleure RC	6	8	12	15	30	80	60	▲400
184	Sherman White RC	4	5	6	8	10	12	25	
185	Fair Hooker	4	5	6	8	10	12	20	80
186	Nick Mike-Mayer	4	5	6	8	15			
187	Ralph Neely	4	5	6	8	10	12	20	80
188	Rich McGeorge	4	5	6	8	10	12	25	80
189	Ed Marinaro RC	4	5	6	8	10	12	25	100
190	Dave Wilcox	4	5	6	8	10	12	25	80
191	Joe Owens RC	4	5	6	8	10	12	25	80
192	Bill Van Heusen	4	5	6	8	10	12	25	100
193	Jim Kearney	4	5	6	8	20			
194	Otis Sistrunk RC	4	5	6	8	30	50		
195	Ron Shanklin	4	5	6	8	10	12	25	50
196	Bill Lenkaitis	4	5	6	8	10	12	25	
197	Tom Drougas	4	5	6	8	10	12	15	80
198	Larry Hand	4	5	6	8	10	12	25	80
199	Mack Alston	4	5	6	8	10	12	25	80
200	Bob Griese	4	5	6	10	15	20	▲80	
201	Earlie Thomas	4	5	6	8	10	12	25	
202	Carl Gersbach	4	5	6	8	10	12	25	80
203	Jim Harrison	4	5	6	8	10	12	25	80
204	Jake Kupp	4	5	6	8	10	12	20	
205	Merlin Olsen	4	5	6	8	10	12	25	
206	Spider Lockhart	4	5	6	8	10	12	25	
207	Walker Gillette	4	5	6	8	10	12	15	100
208	Verlon Biggs	4	5	6	8	10	12	25	100
209	Bob James	4	5	6	8	10	12	25	100
210	Bob Trumpy	4	5	6	8	20			
211	Jerry Sherk	4	5	6	8	10	12	25	80
212	Andy Maurer	4	5	6	8	10	12	25	80
213	Fred Carr	4	5	6	8	10	12	25	100
214	Mick Tingelhoff	4	5	6	8	10	12	25	100
215	Steve Spurrier	4	5	6	10	15	20	40	
216	Richard Harris	4	5	6	8	10	12	25	100
217	Charlie Greer	4	5	6	8	10	12	15	100
218	Buck Buchanan	4	5	6	8	20			
219	Ray Guy RC	8	10	15	▲50	80	▲150	500	
220	Franco Harris	5	6	8	12	30	40	100	
221	Darryl Stingley RC	4	5	6	8	10	12	25	
222	Rex Kern	4	5	6	8	10	12	25	80
223	Toni Fritsch	4	5	6	8	10	12	25	80
224	Levi Johnson	4	5	6	8	10	12	25	50
225	Bob Kuechenberg	4	5	6	8	10	12	25	
226	Elvin Bethea	4	5	6	8	10	12	25	100
227	Al Woodall RC	4	5	6	8	10	12	25	
228	Terry Owens	4	5	6	8	10	12	25	80
229	Bivian Lee	4	5	6	8	10	12	25	
230	Dick Butkus	5	6	10	15	▲40	▲50	100	
231	Jim Bertelsen RC	4	5	6	8	10	12	25	80
232	John Mendenhall RC	4	5	6	8	15			
233	Conrad Dobler RC	4	5	6	8	10	12	20	100
234	J.D. Hill	4	5	6	8	10	12	25	60
235	Ken Houston	4	5	6	8	10	12	25	
236	Dave Lewis	4	5	6	8	10	12	25	80
237	John Garlington	4	5	6	8	10	12	25	100
238	Bill Sandeman	4	5	6	8	10	12	25	100
239	Alden Roche	4	5	6	8	10	12	25	100
240	John Gilliam	4	5	6	8	10	12	25	80
241	Bruce Taylor	4	5	6	8	10	12	25	
242	Vern Winfield	4	5	6	8	10	12	25	80
243	Bobby Maples	4	5	6	8	10	12	25	100
244	Wendell Hayes	4	5	6	8	10	12	25	
245	George Blanda	4	5	6	10	15	20	50	
246	Dwight White	4	5	6	8	10	12	25	100

Name	VgEx 4	EX 5	ExMt 6	NM 7	NmMt 8	NmMt+ 8.5	MT 9	Gem 9.5/10
Sandy Durko	4	5	6	8	10	12	25	50
Tom Mitchell	4	5	6	8	10	12	25	60
Chuck Walton	4	5	6	8	10	12	25	
Bob Lilly	4	5	6	8	10	15	50	
Doug Swift	4	5	6	8	10	12	25	60
Lynn Dickey RC	4	5	6	8	15	20	25	
Jerome Barkum RC	4	5	6	8	20			100
Clint Jones	4	5	6	8	20			
Billy Newsome	4	5	6	8	10	12	25	100
Bob Asher	4	5	6	8	10	12	25	
Joe Scibelli	4	5	6	8	20		80	
Tom Blanchard	4	5	6	8	10	12	25	80
Norm Thompson	4	5	6	8	10	12	15	60
Larry Brown	4	5	6	8	10	12	25	
Paul Seymour	4	5	6	8	10	12	25	80
Checklist 133-264	4	5	6	8	10	12	25	80
Doug Dieken RC	4	5	6	8	10	12	25	100
Lemar Parrish	4	5	6	8	20		50	
Bob Lee	4	5	6	8	10	12	25	100
Bob Brown DT	4	5	6	8	10	12	25	
Roy Winston	4	5	6	8	10	12	25	
Randy Beisler	4	5	6	8	10	12	25	100
Joe Dawkins	4	5	6	8	10	12	25	
Tom Dempsey	4	5	6	8	10	12	25	
Jack Rudnay	4	5	6	8	10	12	25	
Art Shell	4	5	6	8	12	20	40	
Mike Wagner	4	5	6	8	10	12	25	
Rick Cash	4	5	6	8	10	12	20	
Greg Landry	4	5	6	8	10	12	25	
Glenn Ressler	4	5	6	8	10	12	25	100
Billy Joe DuPree RC	4	5	6	8	10	12	25	
Norm Evans	4	5	6	8	10	12	25	100
Billy Parks	4	5	6	8	10	12	25	
John Riggins	4	5	6	10	15	20	70	
Lionel Aldridge	4	5	6	8	10	12	25	
Steve O'Neal	4	5	6	8	10	12	25	
Craig Clemons	4	5	6	8	10	12	25	100
Willie Williams	4	5	6	8	10	12	25	80
Isiah Robertson	4	5	6	8	10	12	25	
Dennis Shaw	4	5	6	8	10	12	25	
Bill Brundige	4	5	6	8	10	12	25	
John Leypoldt	4	5	6	8	10	12	20	
John DeMarie	4	5	6	8	10	12	25	
Mike Reid	4	5	6	8	10	12	25	
Greg Brezina	4	5	6	8	10	12	25	
Willie Buchanon RC	4	5	6	8	10	12	25	
Dave Osborn	4	5	6	8	10	12	25	
Mel Phillips	4	5	6	8	10	12	25	
Haven Moses	4	5	6	8	10	12	25	
Wade Key	4	5	6	8	10	12	25	50
Marvin Upshaw	4	5	6	8	10	12	25	
Ray Mansfield	4	5	6	8	10	12	25	
Edgar Chandler	4	5	6	8	10	12	25	
Marv Hubbard	4	5	6	8	10	12	25	
Herman Weaver	4	5	6	8	10	12	25	
Jim Bailey	4	5	6	8	10	12	15	80
D.D.Lewis RC	4	5	6	8	10	12	25	100
Ken Burrough	4	5	6	8	10	12	25	
Jake Scott	4	5	6	8	10	12	25	
Randy Rasmussen	4	5	6	8	10	12	25	
Pettis Norman	4	5	6	8	10	12	15	80
Carl Johnson	4	5	6	8	10	12	25	
Joe Taylor	4	5	6	8	10	12	15	
Pete Gogolak	4	5	6	8	10	12	25	100
Tony Baker FB	4	5	6	8	10	12	25	
John Richardson	4	5	6	8	10	12	25	
Dave Robinson	4	5	6	8	10	12	25	100
Reggie McKenzie RC	4	5	6	8	10	12	25	
Isaac Curtis RC	4	5	6	8	10	12	25	100
Thom Darden	4	5	6	8	10	12	25	
Ken Reaves	4	5	6	8	10	12	25	
Malcolm Snider	4	5	6	8	10	12	25	
Jeff Siemon RC	4	5	6	8	10	12	25	100
Dan Abramowicz	4	5	6	8	20			
Lyle Alzado	4	5	6	8	10	12	25	
John Reaves	4	5	6	8	10	12	25	100
Morris Stroud	4	5	6	8	10	12	25	
Bobby Walden	4	5	6	8	10	12	25	60
Randy Vataha	4	5	6	8	10	12	25	

#	Name	VgEx 4	EX 5	ExMt 6	NM 7	NmMt 8	NmMt+ 8.5	MT 9	Gem 9.5/10
326	Nemiah Wilson	4	5	6	8	20			
327	Paul Naumoff	4	5	6	8	10	12	25	80
328	Simpson/Brockington LL	4	5	6	8	10	12	30	
329	Staubach/Stabler LL	4	5	6	8	20	25	40	
330	Carmichael/Willis LL	4	5	6	8	10	12	25	
331	Gerela/Ray LL	4	5	6	8	10	12	25	
332	Interception Leaders	4	5	6	8	10	12	25	
333	J.Wilson/Wittum LL	4	5	6	8	10	12	25	100
334	Dennis Nelson	4	5	6	8	10	12	25	
335	Walt Garrison	4	5	6	8	10	12	25	100
336	Tody Smith	4	5	6	8	10	12	25	80
337	Ed Bell	4	5	6	8	10	12	25	
338	Bryant Salter	4	5	6	8	10	12	25	
339	Wayne Colman	4	5	6	8	10	12	15	80
340	Garo Yepremian	4	5	6	8	10	12	25	
341	Bob Newton	4	5	6	8	10	12	25	
342	Vince Clements RC	4	5	6	8	10	12	25	
343	Ken Iman	4	5	6	8	10	12	20	
344	Jim Tolbert	4	5	6	8	10	12	25	100
345	Chris Hanburger	4	5	6	8	10	12	25	
346	Dave Foley	4	5	6	8	10	12	20	80
347	Tommy Casanova	4	5	6	8	20			
348	John James	4	5	6	8	10	12	25	100
349	Clarence Williams	4	5	6	8	10	12	25	60
350	Leroy Kelly	4	5	6	8	10	12	25	
351	Stu Voigt RC	4	5	6	8	10	12	25	
352	Skip Vanderbundt	4	5	6	8	10	12	25	
353	Pete Duranko	4	5	6	8	20			
354	John Outlaw	4	5	6	8	10	12	25	100
355	Jan Stenerud	4	5	6	8	10	12	25	
356	Barry Pearson	4	5	6	8	10	12	25	100
357	Brian Dowling RC	4	5	6	8	10	12	25	
358	Dan Conners	4	5	6	8	10	12	25	
359	Bob Bell	4	5	6	8	10	12	25	
360	Rick Volk	4	5	6	8	10	12	25	100
361	Pat Toomay	4	5	6	8	10	12	25	
362	Bob Gresham	4	5	6	8	20			
363	John Schmitt	4	5	6	8	10	12	25	
364	Mel Rogers	4	5	6	8	10	12	25	100
365	Manny Fernandez	4	5	6	8	10	12	25	60
366	Ernie Jackson	4	5	6	8	10	12	25	50
367	Gary Huff RC	4	5	6	8	10	12	25	
368	Bob Grim	4	5	6	8	20			
369	Ernie McMillan	4	5	6	8	10	12	25	60
370	Dave Elmendorf	4	5	6	8	10	12	25	
371	Mike Bragg	4	5	6	8	10	12	25	100
372	John Skorupan	4	5	6	8	10	12	25	
373	Howard Fest	4	5	6	8	10	12	25	
374	Jerry Tagge RC	4	5	6	8	10	12	25	
375	Art Malone	4	5	6	8	10	12	25	80
376	Bob Babich	4	5	6	8	20			
377	Jim Marshall	4	5	6	8	10	12	25	
378	Bob Hoskins	4	5	6	8	10	12	25	100
379	Don Zimmerman	4	5	6	8	10	12	25	
380	Ray May	4	5	6	8	10	12	20	
381	Emmitt Thomas	4	5	6	8	10	12	25	100
382	Terry Hanratty	4	5	6	8	10	12	25	
383	John Hannah RC	6	8	12	▲40	▲100	▲125	800	
384	George Atkinson	4	5	6	8	10	12	25	
385	Ted Hendricks	4	5	6	8	10	12	25	
386	Jim O'Brien	4	5	6	8	20			
387	Jethro Pugh	4	5	6	8	10	12	30	
388	Elbert Drungo	4	5	6	8	10	12	15	100
389	Richard Caster	4	5	6	8	10	12	25	
390	Deacon Jones	4	5	6	8	10	12	25	
391	Checklist 265-396	4	5	6	8	10	12	25	
392	Jess Phillips	4	5	6	8	10	12	25	
393	Garry Lyle	4	5	6	8	10	12	25	
394	Jim Files	4	5	6	8	10	12	25	100
395	Jim Hart	4	5	6	8	10	12	25	
396	Dave Chapple	4	5	6	8	20			
397	Jim Langer	4	5	6	8	15	20	25	
398	John Wilbur	4	5	6	8	20			
399	Dwight Harrison	4	5	6	8	10	12	25	
400	John Brockington	4	5	6	8	10	12	25	
401	Ken Anderson	4	5	6	8	10	15	20	50
402	Mike Tilleman	4	5	6	8	10	12	25	
403	Charlie Hall	4	5	6	8	10	12	25	
404	Tommy Hart	4	5	6	8	10	12	25	100

#	Player	VgEx 4	EX 5	ExMt 6	NM 7	NmMt 8	NmMt+ 8.5	MT 9	Gem 9.5/10
405	Norm Bulaich	4	5	6	8	10	12	25	
406	Jim Turner	4	5	6	8	10	12	25	
407	Mo Moorman	4	5	6	8	10	12	25	
408	Ralph Anderson	4	5	6	8	10	12	25	
409	Jim Otto	4	5	6	8	10	12	25	
410	Andy Russell	4	5	6	8	10	12	25	
411	Glenn Doughty	4	5	6	8	10	12	15	50
412	Altie Taylor	4	5	6	8	10	12	25	
413	Marv Bateman	4	5	6	8	10	12	25	
414	Willie Alexander	4	5	6	8	25			
415	Bill Zapalac RC	4	5	6	8	10	12	25	
416	Russ Washington	4	5	6	8	10	12	25	
417	Joe Federspiel	4	5	6	8	10	12	20	
418	Craig Cotton	4	5	6	8	10	12	25	
419	Randy Johnson	4	5	6	8	10	12	25	
420	Harold Jackson	4	5	6	8	10	12	25	80
421	Roger Wehrli	4	5	6	8	10	12	15	100
422	Charlie Harraway	4	5	6	8	20			
423	Spike Jones	4	5	6	8	10	12	15	
424	Bob Johnson	4	5	6	8	20			
425	Mike McCoy DT	4	5	6	8	10	12	15	
426	Dennis Havig	4	5	6	8	10	12	25	
427	Bob McKay RC	4	5	6	8	10	12	25	
428	Steve Zabel	4	5	6	8	10	12	25	
429	Horace Jones	4	5	6	8	10	12	25	
430	Jim Johnson	4	5	6	8	10	12	30	
431	Roy Gerela	4	5	6	8	10	12	25	
432	Tom Graham RC	4	5	6	8	10	12	20	
433	Curley Culp	4	5	6	10	15	20	40	125
434	Ken Mendenhall	4	5	6	8	10	12	20	
435	Jim Plunkett	4	5	6	8	12	15	30	
436	Julian Fagan	4	5	6	8	10	12	25	
437	Mike Garrett	4	5	6	8	10	12	25	
438	Bobby Joe Green	4	5	6	8	10	12	25	
439	Jack Gregory	4	5	6	8	10	12	25	
440	Charlie Sanders	4	5	6	8	10	12	25	100
441	Bill Curry	4	5	6	8	10	12	25	
442	Bob Pollard	4	5	6	8	20			
443	David Ray	4	5	6	8	10	12	25	
444	Terry Metcalf RC	4	5	6	8	20			
445	Pat Fischer	4	5	6	8	10	12	25	100
446	Bob Chandler	4	5	6	8	10	12	25	
447	Bill Bergey	4	5	6	8	10	12	25	100
448	Walter Johnson	4	5	6	8	10	12	25	
449	Charle Young RC	4	5	6	8	20			
450	Chester Marcol	4	5	6	8	10	12	30	
451	Ken Stabler	6	8	12	20	40	50	200	
452	Preston Pearson	4	5	6	8	10	12	25	
453	Mike Current	4	5	6	8	10	12	25	
454	Ron Bolton	4	5	6	8	20			
455	Mark Lomas	4	5	6	8	10	12	25	
456	Raymond Chester	4	5	6	8	10	12	25	
457	Jerry LeVias	4	5	6	8	10	12	25	
458	Skip Butler	4	5	6	8	10	12	25	80
459	Mike Livingston RC	4	5	6	8	15			
460	AFC Semi-Final	4	5	6	8	20	25	125	
461	NFC Semi-Finals/R.Staubach	4	5	6	8	20	30	150	
462	Playoff Champships/Stabler	4	5	6	8	10	12	15	50
463	SB VIII/L.Csonka	4	5	6	8	10	12	120	
464	Wayne Mulligan	4	5	6	8	10	12	25	60
465	Horst Muhlmann	4	5	6	8	10	12	25	
466	Milt Morin	4	5	6	8	10	12	20	
467	Don Parish	4	5	6	8	10	12	25	
468	Richard Neal	4	5	6	8	10	12	25	
469	Ron Jessie	4	5	6	8	10	12	25	
470	Terry Bradshaw	8	10	15	25	50	80	400	
471	Fred Dryer	4	5	6	8	10	12	25	
472	Jim Carter	4	5	6	8	10	12	25	100
473	Ken Burrow	4	5	6	8	10	12	15	60
474	Wally Chambers RC	4	5	6	8	10	12	25	
475	Dan Pastorini	4	5	6	8	20			
476	Don Morrison	4	5	6	8	10	12	25	
477	Carl Mauck	4	5	6	8	10	12	25	100
478	Larry Cole RC	4	5	6	8	10	12	25	
479	Jim Kiick	4	5	6	8	20		120	
480	Willie Lanier	4	5	6	8	10	12	25	100
481	Don Herrmann	4	5	6	8	10	12	25	
482	George Hunt	4	5	6	8	10	12	25	
483	Bob Howard RC	4	5	6	8	10	12	25	

#	Player	VgEx 4	EX 5	ExMt 6	NM 7	NmMt 8	NmMt+ 8.5	MT 9	Gem 9.5,
484	Myron Pottios	4	5	6	8	10	12	25	
485	Jackie Smith	4	5	6	8	10	12	25	100
486	Vern Holland	4	5	6	8	10	12	25	
487	Jim Braxton	4	5	6	8	10	12	20	100
488	Joe Reed	4	5	6	8	20			
489	Wally Hilgenberg	4	5	6	8	10	12	30	
490	Fred Biletnikoff	4	5	6	8	12	15	50	
491	Bob DeMarco	4	5	6	8	20			
492	Mark Nordquist	4	5	6	8	10	12	25	
493	Larry Brooks	4	5	6	8	20			
494	Pete Athas	4	5	6	8	10	12	25	
495	Emerson Boozer	4	5	6	8	10	12	25	
496	L.C.Greenwood	4	5	6	8	10	12	80	
497	Rockne Freitas	4	5	6	8	10	12	25	
498	Checklist 397-528	4	5	6	8	10	12	25	
499	Joe Schmiesing	4	5	6	8	10	12	25	
500	Roger Staubach	8	10	15	▲25	30	40	▲400	
501	Al Cowlings	4	5	6	8	10	12	25	100
502	Sam Cunningham RC	4	5	6	8	10	12	25	
503	Dennis Partee	4	5	6	8	10	12	25	
504	John Didion	4	5	6	8	10	12	25	
505	Nick Buoniconti	4	5	6	8	10	12	25	
506	Carl Garrett	4	5	6	8	10	12	25	
507	Doug Van Horn	4	5	6	8	10	12	25	
508	Jamie Rivers	4	5	6	8	10	12	30	
509	Jack Youngblood	4	5	6	8	10	15	40	
510	Charley Taylor	4	5	6	8	20			
511	Ken Riley	4	5	6	8	10	12	25	
512	Joe Ferguson RC	4	5	6	8	10	20	40	
513	Bill Lueck	4	5	6	8	10	12	25	
514	Ray Brown DB RC	4	5	6	8	10	12	25	
515	Fred Cox	4	5	6	8	20			
516	Joe Jones DE	4	5	6	8	10	12	25	
517	Larry Schreiber	4	5	6	8	10	12	25	
518	Dennis Wirgowski	4	5	6	8	10	12	25	
519	Leroy Mitchell	4	5	6	8	10	12	25	
520	Otis Taylor	4	5	6	8	10	12	25	80
521	Henry Davis	4	5	6	8	20			
522	Bruce Barnes	4	5	6	8	20	20		
523	Charlie Smith RB	4	5	6	8	10	12	25	
524	Bert Jones RC	4	5	6	10	▲40	▲50	125	
525	Lem Barney	4	5	6	8	10	12	25	
526	John Fitzgerald RC	4	5	6	8	10	12	40	
527	Tom Funchess	4	5	6	8	10	12	25	
528	Steve Tannen	4	5	6	8	10	12	20	

—Dick Butkus #230 PSA 10 (Gem) sold for $1,403.65 (eBay; 12/13)
—Billy Joe Dupree #277 PSA 10 (Gem) sold for $1,237 (Andy Madec; 5/07)
—Chuck Foreman RC #113 PSA 10 (Gem Mint) sold for $300 (Bussineau; 4/12)
—Ray Guy #219 PSA 10 (Gem) sold for $3,755 (eBay; 9/13)
—Franco Harris #220 PSA 10 (Gem) sold for $886 (eBay; 12/07)
—Roger Staubach #500 PSA 10 (Gem) sold for $825 (Goodwin; 2/11)
—Roger Staubach #500 PSA 10 (Gem) sold for $1,220.94 (Mile High; 12/13)

1975 Topps

#	Player	VgEx 4	EX 5	ExMt 6	NM 7	NmMt 8	NmMt+ 8.5	MT 9	Gem 9.5,
1	McCutcheon/Armstrong LL	4	4	5	6	10	15		
2	Jurgensen/K.Anderson LL	4	4	5	5	10	15	60	
3	C.Young/L.Mitchell LL	4	4	5	5	10	12	25	
4	Marcol/Gerela LL	4	4	5	5	10	12	30	
5	R.Brown/E.Thomas LL	4	4	5	5	10	12	25	
6	Blanchard/Guy LL	4	4	5	5	10	12	25	
7	George Blanda HL	4	4	5	6	10	12	25	
8	George Blanda HL	4	4	5	6	10	12	25	80
9	Ralph Baker	4	4	5	5	10	12	25	
10	Don Woods	4	4	5	5	10	12	25	
11	Bob Asher	4	4	5	5	10	12	25	60
12	Mel Blount RC	6	8	10	20	50	80	200	1,500
13	Sam Cunningham	4	4	5	5	10	12	25	
14	Jackie Smith	4	4	5	5	10	12	25	80
15	Greg Landry	4	4	5	5	15	20	150	
16	Buck Buchanan	4	4	5	5	10	12	25	60
17	Haven Moses	4	4	5	5	10	12	25	50
18	Clarence Ellis	4	4	5	5	10	12	25	50
19	Jim Carter	4	4	5	5	10	12	25	
20	Charley Taylor	4	4	5	5	10	12	25	50
21	Jess Phillips	4	4	5	5	10	12	25	
22	Larry Seiple	4	4	5	5	10	12	25	
23	Doug Dieken	4	4	5	5	10	12	20	60

	VgEx 4	EX 5	ExMt 6	NM 7	NmMt 8	NmMt+ 8.5	MT 9	Gem 9.5/10
Ron Saul	4	4	5	5	10	12	15	50
Isaac Curtis	4	4	5	5	10	12	25	60
Gary Larsen RC	4	4	5	5	10	12	25	100
Bruce Jarvis	4	4	5	5	10	12	25	60
Steve Zabel	4	4	5	5	10	12	20	50
John Mendenhall	4	4	5	5	10	12	25	60
Rick Volk	4	4	5	5	10	12	25	60
Checklist 1-132	4	4	5	5	10	12	25	
Dan Abramowicz	4	4	5	5	10	12	20	80
Bubba Smith	4	4	5	5	10	12	25	100
David Ray	4	4	5	5	10	12	25	60
Dan Dierdorf	4	4	5	6	10	12	25	
Randy Rasmussen	4	4	5	5	10	12	25	
Bob Howard	4	4	5	5	10	12	20	80
Gary Huff	4	4	5	5	10	12	20	
Rocky Bleier RC	10	12	15	25	40	50	80	
Mel Gray	4	4	5	5	10	12	25	60
Tony McGee DT	4	4	5	5	10	12	25	
Larry Hand	4	4	5	5	10	12	25	60
Wendell Hayes	4	4	5	5	10	12	25	60
Doug Wilkerson RC	4	4	5	5	10	12	25	60
Paul Smith	4	4	5	5	10	12	25	
Dave Robinson	4	4	5	5	10	12	25	80
Bivian Lee	4	4	5	5	10	12	25	80
Jim Mandich RC	4	4	5	5	10	12	80	
Greg Pruitt	4	4	5	5	10	12	25	135
Dan Pastorini	4	4	5	5	10	12	25	60
Ron Pritchard	4	4	5	5	10	12	25	60
Dan Conners	4	4	5	5	10	12	25	
Fred Cox	4	4	5	5	10	12	25	50
Tony Greene	4	4	5	5	10	12	25	
Craig Morton	4	4	5	5	10	12	25	200
Jerry Sisemore	4	4	5	5	10	12	25	60
Glenn Doughty	4	4	5	5	10	12	25	
Larry Schreiber	4	4	5	5	10	12	20	60
Charlie Waters RC	4	4	5	6	15	20	50	
Jack Youngblood	4	4	5	5	10	12	25	80
Bill Lenkaitis	4	4	5	5	10	12	25	
Greg Brezina	4	4	5	5	10	12	25	
Bob Pollard	4	4	5	5	10	12	25	80
Mack Alston	4	4	5	5	10	12	25	
Drew Pearson RC	6	8	10	15	▲40	▲50	100	
Charlie Stukes	4	4	5	5	10	12	25	60
Emerson Boozer	4	4	5	5	10	12	25	
Dennis Partee	4	4	5	5	10	12	20	120
Bob Newton	4	4	5	5	10	12	25	80
Jack Tatum	4	4	5	5	10	12	25	
Frank Lewis	4	4	5	5	10	12	25	
Bob Young	4	4	5	5	10	12	25	60
Julius Adams	4	4	5	5	40	60	150	
Paul Naumoff	4	4	5	5	10	12	25	
Otis Taylor	4	4	5	5	10	12	25	
Dave Hampton	4	4	5	5	10	12	25	60
Mike Current	4	4	5	5	10	12	25	60
Brig Owens	4	4	5	5	10	12	25	80
Bobby Scott	4	4	5	5	10	12	25	
Harold Carmichael	4	4	5	5	10	12	25	
Bill Stanfill	4	4	5	5	10	12	25	80
Bob Babich	4	4	5	5	10	12	25	
Vic Washington	4	4	5	5	10	12	25	
Mick Tingelhoff	4	4	5	5	10	12	25	60
Bob Trumpy	4	4	5	5	10	12	25	60
Earl Edwards	4	4	5	5	10	12	20	60
Ron Hornsby	4	4	5	5	10	12	25	
Don McCauley	4	4	5	5	10	12	20	80
Jim Johnson	4	4	5	5	10	12	25	
Andy Russell	4	4	5	5	10	12	25	80
Cornell Green	4	4	5	5	10	12	25	
Charlie Cowan	4	4	5	5	10	12	15	60
Jon Staggers	4	4	5	5	10	12	25	60
Billy Newsome	4	4	5	5	10	12	20	
Willie Brown	4	4	5	5	10	12	25	60
Carl Mauck	4	4	5	5	10	12	20	60
Doug Buffone	4	4	5	5	10	12	20	60
Preston Pearson	4	4	5	5	15	20	60	
Jim Bakken	4	4	5	5	10	12	25	60
Bob Griese	4	4	5	6	10	12	25	
Bob Windsor	4	4	5	5	10	12	25	
Rockne Freitas	4	4	5	5	10	12	25	

		VgEx 4	EX 5	ExMt 6	NM 7	NmMt 8	NmMt+ 8.5	MT 9	Gem 9.5/10
103	Jim Marsalis	4	4	5	5	10	12	25	
104	Bill Thompson	4	4	5	5	10	12	25	
105	Ken Burrow	4	4	5	5	10	12	20	60
106	Diron Talbert	4	4	5	5	10	12	20	60
107	Joe Federspiel	4	4	5	5	10	12	25	
108	Norm Bulaich	4	4	5	5	10	12	25	50
109	Bob DeMarco	4	4	5	5	10	12	25	50
110	Tom Wittum	4	4	5	5	10	12	25	
111	Larry Hefner	4	4	5	5	10	12	25	80
112	Tody Smith	4	4	5	5	10	12	20	
113	Stu Voigt	4	4	5	5	10	12	25	60
114	Horst Muhlmann	4	4	5	5	10	12	25	60
115	Ahmad Rashad	4	4	5	8	12	15	25	
116	Joe Dawkins	4	4	5	5	10	12	20	
117	George Kunz	4	4	5	5	10	12	25	60
118	D.D.Lewis	4	4	5	5	10	12	25	60
119	Levi Johnson	4	4	5	5	10	12	30	
120	Len Dawson	4	4	5	6	10	15	50	
121	Jim Bertelsen	4	4	5	5	10	12	25	60
122	Ed Bell	4	4	5	5	10	12	25	
123	Art Thoms	4	4	5	5	10	12	25	60
124	Joe Beauchamp	4	4	5	5	10	12	15	60
125	Jack Ham	4	4	5	8	20	30	80	
126	Carl Garrett	4	4	5	5	10	12	25	
127	Roger Finnie	4	4	5	5	10	12	25	
128	Howard Twilley	4	4	5	5	10	12	25	
129	Bruce Barnes	4	4	5	5	10	12	25	
130	Nate Wright	4	4	5	5	10	12	25	
131	Jerry Tagge	4	4	5	5	10	12	25	
132	Floyd Little	4	4	5	5	10	12	25	80
133	John Zook	4	4	5	5	10	12	20	
134	Len Hauss	4	4	5	5	10	12	25	
135	Archie Manning	4	4	5	8	12	15	25	
136	Po James	4	4	5	5	10	12	20	60
137	Walt Sumner	4	4	5	5	10	12	25	
138	Randy Beisler	4	4	5	5	10	12	25	60
139	Willie Alexander	4	4	5	5	10	12	25	
140	Garo Yepremian	4	4	5	5	10	12	20	
141	Chip Myers	4	4	5	5	10	12	25	80
142	Jim Braxton	4	4	5	5	10	12	50	
143	Doug Van Horn	4	4	5	5	10	12	25	
144	Stan White	4	4	5	5	10	12	25	80
145	Roger Staubach	6	8	10	25	▲40	▲50	80	800
146	Herman Weaver	4	4	5	5	10	12	25	60
147	Marvin Upshaw	4	4	5	5	10	12	25	
148	Bob Klein	4	4	5	5	10	12	25	
149	Earlie Thomas	4	4	5	5	10	12	25	60
150	John Brockington	4	4	5	5	10	12	25	80
151	Mike Siani	4	4	5	5	10	12	25	
152	Sam Davis RC	4	4	5	5	10	12	25	
153	Mike Wagner	4	4	5	5	10	12	25	
154	Larry Stallings	4	4	5	5	10	12	25	60
155	Wally Chambers	4	4	5	5	10	12	25	60
156	Randy Vataha	4	4	5	5	10	12	25	
157	Jim Marshall	4	4	5	5	10	12	25	
158	Jim Turner	4	4	5	5	10	12	25	60
159	Walt Sweeney	4	4	5	5	10	12	25	
160	Ken Anderson	4	4	5	6	10	12	35	
161	Ray Brown DB	4	4	5	5	10	12	25	60
162	John Didion	4	4	5	5	10	12	25	
163	Tom Dempsey	4	4	5	5	10	12	15	
164	Clarence Scott	4	4	5	5	10	12	25	60
165	Gene Washington 49er	4	4	5	5	10	12	25	60
166	Willie Rodgers RC	4	4	5	5	10	12	25	80
167	Doug Swift	4	4	5	5	10	12	25	
168	Rufus Mayes	4	4	5	5	10	12	25	80
169	Marv Bateman	4	4	5	5	10	12	25	100
170	Lydell Mitchell	4	4	5	5	10	12	25	60
171	Ron Smith	4	4	5	5	10	12	25	
172	Bill Munson	4	4	5	5	10	12	25	
173	Bob Grim	4	4	5	5	10	12	25	60
174	Ed Budde	4	4	5	5	10	12	15	60
175	Bob Lilly	4	4	5	6	10	12	35	120
176	Jim Youngblood RC	4	4	5	5	10	12	25	60
177	Steve Tannen	4	4	5	5	10	12	25	60
178	Rich McGeorge	4	4	5	5	10	12	20	60
179	Jim Tyrer	4	4	5	5	10	12	25	
180	Forrest Blue	4	4	5	5	10	12	25	
181	Jerry LeVias	4	4	5	5	10	12	15	60

#	Player	VgEx 4	EX 5	ExMt 6	NM 7	NmMt 8	NmMt+ 8.5	MT 9	Gem 9.5/10
182	Joe Gilliam RC	4	4	5	5	10	12	25	60
183	Jim Otis RC	4	4	5	5	10	12	25	
184	Mel Tom	4	4	5	5	10	12	25	60
185	Paul Seymour	4	4	5	5	10	12	20	
186	George Webster	4	4	5	5	10	12	25	50
187	Pete Duranko	4	4	5	5	10	12	20	60
188	Essex Johnson	4	4	5	5	10	12	25	
189	Bob Lee	4	4	5	5	10	12	25	60
190	Gene Upshaw	4	4	5	5	10	12	25	80
191	Tom Myers	4	4	5	5	10	12	25	60
192	Don Zimmerman	4	4	5	5	10	12	25	60
193	John Garlington	4	4	5	5	10	12	25	
194	Skip Butler	4	4	5	5	10	12	25	60
195	Tom Mitchell	4	4	5	5	10	12	25	60
196	Jim Langer	4	4	5	5	10	12	25	
197	Ron Carpenter	4	4	5	5	10	12	25	60
198	Dave Foley	4	4	5	5	10	12	25	
199	Bert Jones	4	4	5	5	10	12	25	80
200	Larry Brown	4	4	5	5	10	12	25	80
201	F.Biletnikoff/C.Taylor AP	4	4	5	5	10	12	25	80
202	R.Wright/R.Washington AP	4	4	5	5	10	12	25	80
203	L.Little/T.Mack AP	4	4	5	5	10	12	25	
204	J.Van Note/J.Rudnay AP	4	4	5	5	10	12	25	60
205	J.Hannah/G.Gillingham AP	4	4	5	5	10	12	25	80
206	D.Dierdorf/W.Hill AP	4	4	5	5	10	12	25	50
207	C.Young/R.Odoms AP	4	4	5	5	10	12	25	
208	F.Tarkenton/K.Stabler AP	4	4	5	6	10	12	35	100
209	O.Simpson/L.McCutchen AP	4	4	5	5	10	12	40	
210	T.Metcalf/O.Armstrong AP	4	4	5	5	10	12	25	
211	M.Gray/I.Curtis AP	4	4	5	5	10	12	25	
212	C.Marcol/R.Gerela AP	4	4	5	5	10	12	25	
213	J.Youngblood/E.Bethea AP	4	4	5	5	10	12	25	
214	A.Page/O.Sistrunk AP	4	4	5	5	10	12	25	
215	M.Olsen/M.Reid AP	4	4	5	5	10	12	25	
216	C.Eller/L.Alzado AP	4	4	5	5	10	12	25	
217	T.Hendricks/P.Villapiano AP	4	4	5	5	10	12	25	
218	W.Lanier/L.Jordan AP	4	4	5	5	10	12	25	60
219	i.Robertson/A.Russell AP	4	4	5	5	10	12	25	
220	N.Wright/E.Thomas AP	4	4	5	5	10	12	25	
221	W.Buchanon/L.Parrish AP	4	4	5	5	10	12	15	80
222	K.Houston/D.Anderson AP	4	4	5	5	10	12	25	80
223	C.Harris/J.Tatum AP	4	4	5	5	10	12	25	80
224	T.Wittum/R.Guy AP	4	4	5	5	10	12	25	
225	T.Metcalf/G.Pruitt AP	4	4	5	5	10	12	20	60
226	Ted Kwalick	4	4	5	5	10	12	20	
227	Spider Lockhart	4	4	5	5	10	12	25	
228	Mike Livingston	4	4	5	5	10	12	25	
229	Larry Cole	4	4	5	5	10	12	25	80
230	Gary Garrison	4	4	5	5	10	12	25	60
231	Larry Brooks	4	4	5	5	10	12	20	60
232	Bobby Howfield	4	4	5	5	10	12	15	60
233	Fred Carr	4	4	5	5	10	12	25	60
234	Norm Evans	4	4	5	5	10	12	20	60
235	Dwight White	4	4	5	5	10	12	40	125
236	Conrad Dobler	4	4	5	5	10	12	25	60
237	Garry Lyle	4	4	5	5	10	12	15	60
238	Darryl Stingley	4	4	5	5	10	12	25	60
239	Tom Graham	4	4	5	5	10	12	25	60
240	Chuck Foreman	4	4	5	5	10	12	50	
241	Ken Riley	4	4	5	5	10	12	30	
242	Don Morrison	4	4	5	5	10	12	25	
243	Lynn Dickey	4	4	5	5	10	12	20	80
244	Don Cockroft	4	4	5	5	10	12	20	
245	Claude Humphrey	4	4	5	5	10	12	50	
246	John Skorupan	4	4	5	5	10	12	25	60
247	Raymond Chester	4	4	5	5	10	12	25	60
248	Cas Banaszek	4	4	5	5	10	12	20	50
249	Art Malone	4	4	5	5	10	12	25	
250	Ed Flanagan	4	4	5	5	10	12	25	60
251	Checklist 133-264	4	4	5	5	10	20	100	
252	Nemiah Wilson	4	4	5	5	10	12	25	60
253	Ron Jessie	4	4	5	5	10	12	25	60
254	Jim Lynch	4	4	5	5	10	12	25	
255	Bob Tucker	4	4	5	5	10	12	25	
256	Terry Owens	4	4	5	5	10	12	25	
257	John Fitzgerald	4	4	5	5	10	12	25	
258	Jack Snow	4	4	5	5	10	12	25	
259	Garry Puetz	4	4	5	5	10	12	25	60
260	Mike Phipps	4	4	5	5	10	12	25	
261	Al Matthews	4	4	5	5	10	12	25	
262	Bob Kuechenberg	4	4	5	5	10	12	20	80
263	Ron Yankowski	4	4	5	5	10	12	25	
264	Ron Shanklin	4	4	5	5	10	12	30	
265	Bobby Douglass	4	4	5	5	10	12	25	
266	Josh Ashton	4	4	5	5	10	12	25	
267	Bill Van Heusen	4	4	5	5	10	12	25	
268	Jeff Siemon	4	4	5	5	10	12	25	60
269	Bob Newland	4	4	5	5	10	12	20	60
270	Gale Gillingham	4	4	5	5	10	12	25	
271	Zeke Moore	4	4	5	5	10	12	25	
272	Mike Tilleman	4	4	5	5	10	12	25	
273	John Leypoldt	4	4	5	5	10	12	15	60
274	Ken Mendenhall	4	4	5	5	10	12	15	60
275	Norm Snead	4	4	5	5	10	12	25	80
276	Bill Bradley	4	4	5	5	10	12	25	60
277	Jerry Smith	4	4	5	5	10	12	20	60
278	Clarence Davis	4	4	5	5	10	12	25	
279	Jim Yarbrough	4	4	5	5	10	12	15	
280	Lemar Parrish	4	4	5	5	10	12	15	60
281	Bobby Bell	4	4	5	5	10	12	25	80
282	Lynn Swann RC	15	30	40	60	125	250	500	2,000
283	John Hicks	4	4	5	5	10	12	25	60
284	Coy Bacon	4	4	5	5	10	12	40	
285	Lee Roy Jordan	4	4	5	5	10	12	25	80
286	Willie Buchanon	4	4	5	5	10	12	25	
287	Al Woodall	4	4	5	5	10	12	25	
288	Reggie Rucker	4	4	5	5	10	12	25	
289	John Schmitt	4	4	5	5	10	12	25	
290	Carl Eller	4	4	5	5	10	12	25	
291	Jake Scott	4	4	5	5	10	12	25	
292	Donny Anderson	4	4	5	5	10	12	20	
293	Charley Wade	4	4	5	5	10	12	20	60
294	John Tanner	4	4	5	5	10	12	20	60
295	Charlie Johnson	4	4	5	5	10	12	25	
296	Tom Blanchard	4	4	5	5	10	12	15	60
297	Curley Culp	4	4	5	5	10	15	40	60
298	Jeff Van Note RC	4	4	5	5	10	12	25	
299	Bob James	4	4	5	5	10	12	25	60
300	Franco Harris	4	5	6	10	15	20	60	200
301	Tim Berra	4	4	5	5	10	12	20	
302	Bruce Gossett	4	4	5	5	10	12	25	
303	Verlon Biggs	4	4	5	5	10	12	20	
304	Bob Kowalkowski	4	4	5	5	10	12	25	
305	Marv Hubbard	4	4	5	5	10	12	25	
306	Ken Avery	4	4	5	5	10	12	25	60
307	Mike Adamle	4	4	5	5	10	12	25	60
308	Don Herrmann	4	4	5	5	10	12	25	60
309	Chris Fletcher	4	4	5	5	10	12	25	60
310	Roman Gabriel	4	4	5	5	10	12	25	60
311	Billy Joe DuPree	4	4	5	5	10	12	20	80
312	Fred Dryer	4	4	5	5	10	12	20	
313	John Riggins	4	4	5	6	10	12	35	
314	Bob McKay	4	4	5	5	10	12	25	60
315	Ted Hendricks	4	4	5	5	10	12	35	80
316	Bobby Bryant	4	4	5	5	10	12	25	100
317	Don Nottingham	4	4	5	5	10	12	20	80
318	John Hannah	4	4	5	6	10	12	25	120
319	Rich Coady	4	4	5	5	10	12	30	60
320	Phil Villapiano	4	4	5	5	10	12	25	
321	Jim Plunkett	4	4	5	5	10	12	25	
322	Lyle Alzado	4	4	5	5	10	12	25	
323	Ernie Jackson	4	4	5	5	10	12	25	
324	Billy Parks	4	4	5	5	10	12	25	
325	Willie Lanier	4	4	5	5	10	12	25	
326	John James	4	4	5	5	10	12	25	60
327	Joe Ferguson	4	4	5	5	10	12	25	60
328	Ernie Holmes RC	4	5	6	12	30	40	80	
329	Bruce Laird	4	4	5	5	10	12	80	
330	Chester Marcol	4	4	5	5	10	12	25	80
331	Dave Wilcox	4	4	5	5	10	12	25	80
332	Pat Fischer	4	4	5	5	10	12	20	
333	Steve Owens	4	4	5	5	10	12	25	
334	Royce Berry	4	4	5	5	10	12	30	
335	Russ Washington	4	4	5	5	10	12	40	
336	Walker Gillette	4	4	5	5	10	12	25	80
337	Mark Nordquist	4	4	5	5	10	12	25	60
338	James Harris RC	4	4	5	6	10	12	50	60
339	Warren Koegel	4	4	5	5	10	12	25	60

Name	VgEx 4	EX 5	ExMt 6	NM 7	NmMt 8	NmMt+ 8.5	MT 9	Gem 9.5/10
Emmitt Thomas	4	4	5	5	10	12	25	
Walt Garrison	4	4	5	5	10	12	25	
Thom Darden	4	4	5	5	10	12	25	100
Mike Eischeid	4	4	5	5	10	12	25	80
Ernie McMillan	4	4	5	5	10	12	20	60
Nick Buoniconti	4	4	5	5	10	12	20	
George Farmer	4	4	5	5	10	12	25	60
Sam Adams OL	4	4	5	5	10	12	25	
Larry Cipa	4	4	5	5	10	12	25	80
Bob Moore	4	4	5	5	10	12	25	
Otis Armstrong RC	4	4	5	5	10	12	25	80
George Blanda RB	4	4	5	5	10	12	40	
Fred Cox RB	4	4	5	5	10	12	25	60
Tom Dempsey RB	4	4	5	5	10	12	25	
Ken Houston RB	4	4	5	5	10	12	25	80
O.J.Simpson RB	4	4	5	6	15	20	50	
Ron Smith RB	4	4	5	5	10	12	25	60
Bob Atkins	4	4	5	5	10	12	40	
Pat Sullivan	4	4	5	5	10	12	25	80
Joe DeLamielleure	4	4	5	5	10	12	25	
Lawrence McCutcheon RC	4	4	5	5	10	12	25	100
David Lee	4	4	5	5	10	12	50	
Mike McCoy DT	4	4	5	5	10	12	20	60
Skip Vanderbundt	4	4	5	5	10	12	25	
Mark Moseley	4	4	5	5	10	12	25	
Lem Barney	4	4	5	5	10	12	25	120
Doug Dressler	4	4	5	5	10	12	25	
Dan Fouts RC	15	20	25	50	80	100	300	1,500
Bob Hyland	4	4	5	5	10	12	25	
John Outlaw	4	4	5	5	10	12	25	60
Roy Gerela	4	4	5	5	10	12	25	
Isiah Robertson	4	4	5	5	10	12	25	60
Jerome Barkum	4	4	5	5	10	12	25	
Ed Podolak	4	4	5	5	10	12	25	60
Milt Morin	4	4	5	5	10	12	25	60
John Niland	4	4	5	5	20	40	60	
Checklist 265-396	4	4	5	5	10	12	30	
Ken Iman	4	4	5	5	10	12	25	80
Manny Fernandez	4	4	5	5	10	12	25	
Dave Gallagher	4	4	5	5	10	12	25	60
Ken Stabler	5	6	8	15	25	30	50	300
Mack Herron	4	4	5	5	10	12	25	
Bill McClard	4	4	5	5	10	12	25	60
Ray May	4	4	5	5	10	12	25	
Don Hansen	4	4	5	5	10	12	25	
Elvin Bethea	4	4	5	5	10	12	25	80
Joe Scibelli	4	4	5	5	10	12	25	60
Neal Craig	4	4	5	5	10	12	25	60
Marty Domres	4	4	5	5	10	12	25	60
Ken Ellis	4	4	5	5	10	12	25	
Charle Young	4	4	5	5	10	12	25	
Tommy Hart	4	4	5	5	10	12	25	
Moses Denson	4	4	5	5	10	12	25	60
Larry Walton	4	4	5	5	10	12	25	60
Dave Green	4	4	5	5	10	12	50	
Ron Johnson	4	4	5	5	10	12	25	80
Ed Bradley RC	4	4	5	5	10	12	25	60
J.T. Thomas	4	4	5	5	10	12	30	175
Jim Bailey	4	4	5	5	10	12	25	60
Barry Pearson	4	4	5	5	10	12	25	
Fran Tarkenton	4	5	6	10	15	20	▲50	400
Jack Rudnay	4	4	5	5	10	12	25	60
Rayfield Wright	4	4	5	5	10	12	30	
Roger Wehrli	4	4	5	5	10	12	40	200
Vern Den Herder	4	4	5	5	10	12	25	60
Fred Biletnikoff	4	4	5	5	10	12	25	
Ken Grandberry	4	4	5	5	10	12	25	
Bob Adams	4	4	5	5	10	12	25	60
Jim Merlo	4	4	5	5	10	12	25	
John Pitts	4	4	5	5	10	12	25	60
Dave Osborn	4	4	5	5	10	12	25	60
Dennis Havig	4	4	5	5	10	12	25	80
Bob Johnson	4	4	5	5	10	12	25	60
Ken Burrough	4	4	5	5	10	12	25	80
Jim Cheyunski	4	4	5	5	10	12	25	60
MacArthur Lane	4	4	5	5	10	12	25	
Joe Theismann RC	8	10	12	20	40	50	150	
Mike Boryla RC	4	4	5	5	10	12	25	60
Bruce Taylor	4	4	5	5	10	12	25	60

#	Name	VgEx 4	EX 5	ExMt 6	NM 7	NmMt 8	NmMt+ 8.5	MT 9	Gem 9.5/10
419	Chris Hanburger	4	4	5	5	10	12	30	
420	Tom Mack	4	4	5	5	10	12	25	
421	Errol Mann	4	4	5	5	10	12	25	
422	Jack Gregory	4	4	5	5	10	12	25	60
423	Harrison Davis	4	4	5	5	10	12	25	
424	Burgess Owens	4	4	5	5	10	12	25	60
425	Joe Greene	4	4	8	15	30	50	125	
426	Morris Stroud	4	4	5	5	10	12	25	60
427	John DeMarie	4	4	5	5	10	12	25	60
428	Mel Renfro	4	4	5	5	10	12	50	
429	Cid Edwards	4	4	5	5	10	12	25	80
430	Mike Reid	4	4	5	5	10	12	25	60
431	Jack Mildren RC	4	4	5	5	10	12	25	80
432	Jerry Simmons	4	4	5	5	10	12	25	
433	Ron Yary	4	4	5	5	10	12	60	
434	Howard Stevens	4	4	5	5	10	12	25	
435	Ray Guy	4	4	5	5	10	12	60	
436	Tommy Nobis	4	4	5	5	10	12	25	100
437	Solomon Freelon	4	4	5	5	10	12	25	
438	J.D. Hill	4	4	5	5	10	12	25	60
439	Toni Linhart	4	4	5	5	10	12	50	
440	Dick Anderson	4	4	5	5	10	12	25	
441	Guy Morriss	4	4	5	5	10	12	25	60
442	Bob Hoskins	4	4	5	5	10	12	25	60
443	John Hadl	4	4	5	5	10	12	50	80
444	Roy Jefferson	4	4	5	5	10	12	25	
445	Charlie Sanders	4	4	5	5	10	12	25	80
446	Pat Curran	4	4	5	5	10	12	25	60
447	David Knight	4	4	5	5	10	12	25	60
448	Bob Brown DT	4	4	5	5	10	12	25	
449	Pete Gogolak	4	4	5	5	10	12	25	
450	Terry Metcalf	4	4	5	5	10	12	25	
451	Bill Bergey	4	4	5	5	10	12	25	60
452	Dan Abramowicz HL	4	4	5	5	10	12	25	60
453	Otis Armstrong HL	4	4	5	5	10	12	25	60
454	Cliff Branch HL	4	4	5	5	10	12	25	60
455	John James HL	4	4	5	5	10	12	25	
456	Lydell Mitchell HL	4	4	5	5	10	12	25	60
457	Lemar Parrish HL	4	4	5	5	10	12	25	
458	Ken Stabler HL	4	4	5	5	10	12	25	
459	Lynn Swann HL	4	5	6	10	15	20	40	200
460	Emmitt Thomas HL	4	4	5	5	10	12	25	
461	Terry Bradshaw	8	10	15	20	30	50	80	1,000
462	Jerrel Wilson	4	4	5	5	10	12	25	
463	Walter Johnson	4	4	5	5	10	12	25	
464	Golden Richards	4	4	5	5	10	12	25	
465	Tommy Casanova	4	4	5	5	10	12	25	
466	Randy Jackson	4	4	5	5	10	12	25	
467	Ron Bolton	4	4	5	5	10	12	25	60
468	Joe Owens	4	4	5	5	10	12	25	
469	Wally Hilgenberg	4	4	5	5	10	12	30	
470	Riley Odoms	4	4	5	5	10	12	25	80
471	Otis Sistrunk	4	4	5	5	10	12	25	
472	Eddie Ray	4	4	5	5	10	12	25	60
473	Reggie McKenzie	4	4	5	5	10	12	25	60
474	Elbert Drungo	4	4	5	5	10	12	35	100
475	Mercury Morris	4	4	5	5	10	12	35	
476	Dan Dickel	4	4	5	5	10	12	25	60
477	Merritt Kersey	4	4	5	5	10	12	25	
478	Mike Holmes	4	4	5	5	10	12	25	
479	Clarence Williams	4	4	5	5	10	12	25	60
480	Billy Kilmer	4	4	5	5	10	12	25	
481	Altie Taylor	4	4	5	5	10	12	25	60
482	Dave Elmendorf	4	4	5	5	10	12	25	60
483	Bob Rowe	4	4	5	5	10	12	30	
484	Pete Athas	4	4	5	5	10	12	25	
485	Winston Hill	4	4	5	5	10	12	25	60
486	Bo Matthews	4	4	5	5	10	12	100	
487	Earl Thomas	4	4	5	5	10	12	25	
488	Jan Stenerud	4	4	5	5	10	12	25	
489	Steve Holden	4	4	5	5	10	12	25	
490	Cliff Harris RC	4	5	6	8	20	40	100	
491	Boobie Clark RC	4	4	5	5	10	12	80	
492	Joe Taylor	4	4	5	5	10	12	40	
493	Tom Neville	4	4	5	5	10	12	25	60
494	Wayne Colman	4	4	5	5	10	12	25	
495	Jim Mitchell TE	4	4	5	5	10	12	25	60
496	Paul Krause	4	4	5	5	10	12	25	80
497	Jim Otto	4	4	5	5	10	12	50	

#	Player	VgEx 4	EX 5	ExMt 6	NM 7	NmMt 8	NmMt+ 8.5	MT 9	Gem 9.5/10
498	John Rowser	4	4	5	5	10	12	25	60
499	Larry Little	4	4	5	5	10	12	100	
500	O.J.Simpson	5	6	8	12	25	30	80	
501	John Dutton RC	4	4	5	5	10	12	25	
502	Pat Hughes	4	4	5	5	10	12	25	80
503	Malcolm Snider	4	4	5	5	10	12	25	60
504	Fred Willis	4	4	5	5	10	12	25	
505	Harold Jackson	4	4	5	5	10	12	25	
506	Mike Bragg	4	4	5	5	10	12	25	
507	Jerry Sherk	4	4	5	5	10	12	25	
508	Mirro Roder	4	4	5	5	10	12	25	
509	Tom Sullivan	4	4	5	5	10	12	25	60
510	Jim Hart	4	4	5	5	10	12	25	
511	Cedrick Hardman	4	4	5	5	10	12	25	
512	Blaine Nye	4	4	5	5	10	12	30	
513	Elmo Wright	4	4	5	5	10	12	25	60
514	Herb Orvis	4	4	5	5	10	12	60	
515	Richard Caster	4	4	5	5	10	12	25	
516	Doug Kotar RC	4	4	5	5	10	12	30	
517	Checklist 397-528	4	4	5	5	10	12	25	
518	Jesse Freitas	4	4	5	5	10	12	25	
519	Ken Houston	4	4	5	5	10	12	25	
520	Alan Page	4	4	5	5	10	12	40	
521	Tim Foley	4	4	5	5	10	12	25	
522	Bill Olds	4	4	5	5	10	12	25	60
523	Bobby Maples	4	4	5	5	10	12	25	
524	Cliff Branch RC	5	6	8	12	25	40	100	
525	Merlin Olsen	4	4	5	5	10	12	50	
526	AFC Champs/Bradshaw/Harris	4	4	5	6	10	12	80	
527	NFC Champs/Foreman	4	4	5	5	10	15	40	
528	Super Bowl IX/Bradshaw	4	5	6	10	25	40	120	

—AFC Champs/Brad/Harris #526 PSA 10 (Gem) sold for $672 (Mile High; 6/10)
—Rocky Bleier RC #39 PSA 10 (Gem Mint) sold for $590.77 (eBay: 6/12)
—Rocky Bleier RC #39 PSA 10 (Gem Mint) sold for $570 (eBay: 6/12)
—Bob Brown DT #448 PSA 10 (Gem Mint) sold for $505 (eBay: 6/12)
—Dan Fouts #367 PSA 10 (Gem) sold for $3,055 (eBay; 4/07)
—Joe Greene #425 PSA 10 (Gem Mint) sold for $839.02 (eBay: 6/12)
—Drew Pearson #65 PSA 10 (Gem) sold for $1,000 (eBay; 11/07)
—O.J.Simpson #500 PSA 10 (Gem Mint) sold for $543 (eBay: 6/12)
—Super Bowl IX/Bradshaw #528 PSA 10 (Gem Mint) sold for $791 (eBay: 6/12)
—Lynn Swann #282 PSA 10 (Gem) sold for $2,809.99 (eBay; 3/14)
—Lynn Swann #282 PSA 10 (Gem) sold for $2,805 (eBay; 4/07)
—Lynn Swann #282 PSA 10 (Gem) sold for $1,767 (Mile High; 10/09)
—Joe Theismann RC #416 PSA 10 (Gem Mint) sold for $2958 (eBay: 8/12)
—Joe Theismann RC #416 PSA 10 (Gem Mint) sold for $3553 (eBay: 10/14)
—Joe Theismann RC #416 PSA 10 (Gem Mint) sold for $3008 (eBay: 10/14)

1976 Topps

#	Player	VgEx 4	EX 5	ExMt 6	NM 7	NmMt 8	NmMt+ 8.5	MT 9	Gem 9.5/10
1	George Blanda RB	4	4	5	8	10	12	60	175
2	Neal Colzie RB	4	4	5	8	20	25	60	
3	Chuck Foreman RB	4	4	5	8	10	12	30	
4	Jim Marshall RB	4	4	5	8	12	15	40	
5	Terry Metcalf RB	4	4	5	8	10	12	30	
6	O.J.Simpson RB	4	4	5	8	12	15	60	
7	Fran Tarkenton RB	4	4	5	8	10	12	25	
8	Charley Taylor RB	4	4	5	8	10	12	30	100
9	Ernie Holmes	4	4	5	8	10	12	30	
10	Ken Anderson	4	4	5	8	15	20	120	
11	Bobby Bryant	4	4	5	8	10	12	25	60
12	Jerry Smith	4	4	5	8	10	12	30	
13	David Lee	4	4	5	8	10	12	25	
14	Robert Newhouse RC	4	4	5	8	20	25	80	
15	Vern Den Herder	4	4	5	8	10	12	25	60
16	John Hannah	4	4	5	8	10	12	30	
17	J.D. Hill	4	4	5	8	10	12	30	
18	James Harris	4	4	5	8	10	12	30	
19	Willie Buchanon	4	4	5	8	10	12	25	60
20	Charle Young	4	4	5	8	10	12	30	
21	Jim Yarbrough	4	4	5	8	10	12	25	
22	Ronnie Coleman	4	4	5	8	10	12	25	
23	Don Cockroft	4	4	5	8	10	12	25	
24	Willie Lanier	4	4	5	8	10	12	30	
25	Fred Biletnikoff	4	4	5	8	10	12	30	
26	Ron Yankowski	4	4	5	8	10	12	25	80
27	Spider Lockhart	4	4	5	8	10	12	25	
28	Bob Johnson	4	4	5	8	10	12	25	
29	J.T. Thomas	4	4	5	8	10	12	25	60
30	Ron Yary	4	4	5	8	10	12	30	
31	Brad Dusek RC	4	4	5	8	10	12	25	
32	Raymond Chester	4	4	5	8	10	12	25	
33	Larry Little	4	4	5	8	10	12	30	
34	Pat Leahy RC	4	4	5	8	10	12	30	
35	Steve Bartkowski RC	4	4	5	8	10	12	40	
36	Tom Myers	4	4	5	8	10	12	25	
37	Bill Van Heusen	4	4	5	8	10	12	25	60
38	Russ Washington	4	4	5	8	10	12	25	
39	Tom Sullivan	4	4	5	8	10	12	25	
40	Curley Culp	4	4	5	8	30	40	100	
41	Johnnie Gray	4	4	5	8	10	12	25	60
42	Bob Klein	4	4	5	8	10	12	25	60
43	Lem Barney	4	4	5	8	10	12	30	
44	Harvey Martin RC	4	4	5	12	20	25	80	
45	Reggie Rucker	4	4	5	8	10	12	30	
46	Neil Clabo	4	4	5	8	10	12	25	
47	Ray Hamilton	4	4	5	8	10	12	25	
48	Joe Ferguson	4	4	5	8	10	12	30	60
49	Ed Podolak	4	4	5	8	10	12	25	
50	Ray Guy	4	4	5	8	10	12	30	
51	Glen Edwards	4	4	5	8	10	12	25	
52	Jim LeClair	4	4	5	8	10	12	25	80
53	Mike Barnes	4	4	5	8	10	12	25	
54	Nat Moore RC	4	4	5	8	10	12	30	
55	Billy Kilmer	4	4	5	8	10	12	30	
56	Larry Stallings	4	4	5	8	10	12	25	60
57	Jack Gregory	4	4	5	8	10	12	25	
58	Steve Mike-Mayer	4	4	5	8	10	12	25	
59	Virgil Livers	4	4	5	8	10	12	25	
60	Jerry Sherk	4	4	5	8	10	12	30	
61	Guy Morriss	4	4	5	8	10	12	25	
62	Barty Smith	4	4	5	8	10	12	25	
63	Jerome Barkum	4	4	5	8	10	12	25	
64	Ira Gordon	4	4	5	8	10	12	25	
65	Paul Krause	4	4	5	8	10	12	30	80
66	John McMakin	4	4	5	8	10	12	25	
67	Checklist 1-132	4	4	5	8	10	12	30	
68	Charlie Johnson	4	4	5	8	10	12	30	60
69	Tommy Nobis	4	4	5	8	10	12	30	80
70	Lydell Mitchell	4	4	5	8	10	12	30	
71	Vern Holland	4	4	5	8	10	12	25	
72	Tim Foley	4	4	5	8	10	12	30	
73	Golden Richards	4	4	5	8	10	12	25	
74	Bryant Salter	4	4	5	5	10	12	25	
75	Terry Bradshaw	6	8	12	20	35	40	150	
76	Ted Hendricks	4	4	5	8	10	12	30	80
77	Rich Saul RC	4	4	5	8	10	12	25	
78	John Smith RC	4	4	5	8	10	12	25	
79	Altie Taylor	4	4	5	8	10	12	25	80
80	Cedrick Hardman	4	4	5	8	10	12	100	
81	Ken Payne	4	4	5	8	10	12	25	
82	Zeke Moore	4	4	5	8	10	12	25	
83	Alvin Maxson	4	4	5	8	10	12	25	
84	Wally Hilgenberg	4	4	5	8	10	12	25	
85	John Niland	4	4	5	8	10	12	25	
86	Mike Sensibaugh	4	4	5	8	10	12	25	
87	Ron Johnson	4	4	5	8	10	12	30	
88	Winston Hill	4	4	5	8	10	12	25	
89	Charlie Joiner	4	4	5	8	10	12	25	100
90	Roger Wehrli	4	4	5	8	10	12	30	
91	Mike Bragg	4	4	5	8	10	12	25	
92	Dan Dickel	4	4	5	8	10	12	25	
93	Earl Morrall	4	4	5	8	10	12	30	
94	Pat Toomay	4	4	5	8	10	12	25	
95	Gary Garrison	4	4	5	8	10	12	25	80
96	Ken Geddes	4	4	5	8	10	12	25	60
97	Mike Current	4	4	5	8	10	12	25	
98	Bob Avellini RC	4	4	5	8	10	12	50	
99	Dave Pureifory	4	4	5	8	10	12	25	
100	Franco Harris	4	4	5	8	15	20	60	
101	Randy Logan	4	4	5	8	10	12	25	
102	John Fitzgerald	4	4	5	8	10	12	25	60
103	Gregg Bingham RC	4	4	5	8	10	12	100	
104	Jim Plunkett	4	4	5	8	10	12	25	
105	Carl Eller	4	4	5	8	10	12	30	
106	Larry Walton	4	4	5	8	10	12	25	
107	Clarence Scott	4	4	5	8	10	12	25	
108	Skip Vanderbundt	4	4	5	8	10	12	25	

	VgEx 4	EX 5	ExMt 6	NM 7	NmMt 8	NmMt+ 8.5	MT 9	Gem 9.5/10
Boobie Clark	4	4	5	8	10	12	30	
Tom Mack	4	4	5	8	10	12	30	60
Bruce Laird	4	4	5	8	10	12	25	
Dave Dalby RC	4	4	5	8	10	12	30	
John Leypoldt	4	4	5	8	10	12	25	
Barry Pearson	4	4	5	8	10	12	25	
Larry Brown	4	4	5	8	10	12	30	
Jackie Smith	4	4	5	8	10	12	30	80
Pat Hughes	4	4	5	8	10	12	25	
Al Woodall	4	4	5	8	10	12	25	80
John Zook	4	4	5	8	15	20	25	
Jake Scott	4	4	5	8	10	12	30	
Rich Glover	4	4	5	8	10	12	25	
Ernie Jackson	4	4	5	8	10	12	25	
Otis Armstrong	4	4	5	8	10	12	30	
Bob Grim	4	4	5	8	10	12	25	60
Jeff Siemon	4	4	5	8	10	12	25	
Harold Hart	4	4	5	8	10	12	25	
John DeMarie	4	4	5	8	10	12	25	
Dan Fouts	4	5	6	10	15	20	40	
Jim Kearney	4	4	5	8	10	12	25	
John Dutton	4	4	5	8	10	12	100	
Calvin Hill	4	4	5	8	10	12	30	80
Toni Fritsch	4	4	5	8	10	12	25	
Ron Jessie	4	4	5	8	10	12	25	60
Don Nottingham	4	4	5	8	10	12	25	
Lemar Parrish	4	4	5	8	10	12	25	60
Russ Francis RC	4	4	5	8	10	12	30	
Joe Reed	4	4	5	8	10	12	25	60
C.L. Whittington	4	4	5	8	10	12	25	50
Otis Sistrunk	4	4	5	8	10	12	30	
Lynn Swann	4	6	10	15	30	30	135	
Jim Carter	4	4	5	8	10	12	25	
Mike Montler	4	4	5	8	10	12	25	100
Walter Johnson	4	4	5	8	10	12	25	
Doug Kotar	4	4	5	8	10	12	25	
Roman Gabriel	4	4	5	8	10	12	30	
Billy Newsome	4	4	5	8	10	12	25	80
Ed Bradley	4	4	5	8	10	12	25	50
Walter Payton RC	125	▲200	▲250	▲400	800	1,000	2,500	15,000
Johnny Fuller	4	4	5	8	10	12	25	
Alan Page	4	4	5	8	10	12	30	
Frank Grant	4	4	5	8	10	12	25	50
Dave Green	4	4	5	8	10	12	25	
Nelson Munsey	4	4	5	8	10	12	25	
Jim Mandich	4	4	5	8	10	12	25	
Lawrence McCutcheon	4	4	5	8	10	12	30	
Steve Ramsey	4	4	5	8	10	12	25	
Ed Flanagan	4	4	5	8	10	12	25	
Randy White RC	5	6	12	25	40	60	250	
Gerry Mullins	4	4	5	8	10	12	25	
Jan Stenerud	4	4	5	8	10	12	30	
Steve Odom	4	4	5	8	10	12	25	60
Roger Finnie	4	4	5	8	10	12	25	
Norm Snead	4	4	5	8	10	12	30	
Jeff Van Note	4	4	5	8	10	12	30	
Bill Bergey	4	4	5	8	10	12	30	
Allen Carter	4	4	5	8	10	12	25	
Steve Holden	4	4	5	8	10	12	25	
Sherman White	4	4	5	8	10	12	25	
Bob Berry	4	4	5	8	10	12	25	80
Ken Houston	4	4	5	8	10	12	25	
Bill Olds	4	4	5	8	10	12	25	
Larry Seiple	4	4	5	8	10	12	25	
Cliff Branch	4	4	5	8	10	12	30	
Reggie McKenzie	4	4	5	8	10	12	25	
Dan Pastorini	4	4	5	8	10	12	30	
Paul Naumoff	4	4	5	8	10	12	25	
Checklist 133-264	4	4	5	8	10	12	30	
Durwood Keeton	4	4	5	8	10	12	25	
Earl Thomas	4	4	5	8	10	12	25	
L.C. Greenwood	4	4	5	10	15	20	50	
John Outlaw	4	4	5	8	10	12	25	
Frank Nunley	4	4	5	8	10	12	25	
Dave Jennings RC	4	4	5	8	10	12	30	
MacArthur Lane	4	4	5	8	10	12	25	
Chester Marcol	4	4	5	8	10	12	25	
J.J. Jones	4	4	5	8	10	12	25	
Tom DeLeone	4	4	5	8	10	12	25	100

	VgEx 4	EX 5	ExMt 6	NM 7	NmMt 8	NmMt+ 8.5	MT 9	Gem 9.5/10
188 Steve Zabel	4	4	5	8	10	12	25	
189 Ken Johnson DT	4	4	5	8	10	12	25	
190 Rayfield Wright	4	4	5	8	10	12	40	
191 Brent McClanahan	4	4	5	8	10	12	25	60
192 Pat Fischer	4	4	5	8	10	12	30	
193 Roger Carr RC	4	4	5	8	10	12	30	
194 Manny Fernandez	4	4	5	8	10	12	30	
195 Roy Gerela	4	4	5	8	10	12	25	
196 Dave Elmendorf	4	4	5	8	10	12	25	
197 Bob Kowalkowski	4	4	5	8	10	12	25	
198 Phil Villapiano	4	4	5	8	10	12	30	
199 Will Wynn	4	4	5	8	10	12	25	60
200 Terry Metcalf	4	4	5	8	10	12	30	
201 F.Tarkenton/K.Anderson LL	4	4	5	8	10	12	30	
202 Rucker/Mitchell/Foreman LL	4	4	5	8	10	12	30	80
203 O.Simpson/J.Otis LL	4	4	5	8	10	12	30	
204 O.Simpson/C.Foreman LL	4	4	5	8	10	12	30	
205 M.Blount/P.Krause LL	4	4	5	8	10	12	30	
206 R.Guy/H.Weaver LL	4	4	5	8	10	12	30	
207 Ken Ellis	4	4	5	8	10	12	25	60
208 Ron Saul	4	4	5	8	10	12	25	80
209 Toni Linhart	4	4	5	8	10	12	25	80
210 Jim Langer	4	4	5	8	10	12	30	
211 Jeff Wright S	4	4	5	8	10	12	25	
212 Moses Denson	4	4	5	8	10	12	25	
213 Earl Edwards	4	4	5	8	10	12	25	
214 Walker Gillette	4	4	5	8	10	12	25	60
215 Bob Trumpy	4	4	5	8	10	12	30	
216 Emmitt Thomas	4	4	5	8	10	12	30	
217 Lyle Alzado	4	4	5	8	10	12	30	
218 Carl Garrett	4	4	5	8	10	12	30	
219 Van Green	4	4	5	8	10	12	25	
220 Jack Lambert RC	12	15	25	50	100	200	▼500	4,000
221 Spike Jones	4	4	5	8	10	12	25	
222 John Hadl	4	4	5	8	10	12	30	
223 Billy Johnson RC	4	4	5	8	12	15	40	
224 Tony McGee DT	4	4	5	8	10	12	25	
225 Preston Pearson	4	4	5	8	10	12	40	
226 Isiah Robertson	4	4	5	8	10	12	30	80
227 Errol Mann	4	4	5	8	10	12	25	
228 Paul Seal	4	4	5	8	10	12	25	60
229 Roland Harper RC	4	4	5	8	10	12	25	
230 Ed White RC	4	4	5	8	10	12	25	
231 Joe Theismann	4	4	5	8	10	12	40	
232 Jim Cheyunski	4	4	5	8	10	12	25	
233 Bill Stanfill	4	4	5	8	10	12	30	
234 Marv Hubbard	4	4	5	8	10	12	25	
235 Tommy Casanova	4	4	5	8	10	12	30	
236 Bob Hyland	4	4	5	8	10	12	25	60
237 Jesse Freitas	4	4	5	8	10	12	25	
238 Norm Thompson	4	4	5	8	10	12	25	
239 Charlie Smith WR	4	4	5	8	10	12	25	
240 John James	4	4	5	8	10	12	25	
241 Alden Roche	4	4	5	8	10	12	25	
242 Gordon Jolley	4	4	5	8	10	12	25	
243 Larry Ely	4	4	5	8	10	12	25	
244 Richard Caster	4	4	5	8	10	12	25	80
245 Joe Greene	4	4	5	8	10	12	50	200
246 Larry Schreiber	4	4	5	8	10	12	25	
247 Terry Schmidt	4	4	5	8	10	12	25	
248 Jerrel Wilson	4	4	5	8	10	12	25	
249 Marty Domres	4	4	5	8	10	12	25	
250 Isaac Curtis	4	4	5	8	10	12	35	
251 Harold McLinton	4	4	5	8	10	12	25	
252 Fred Dryer	4	4	5	8	10	12	30	80
253 Bill Lenkaitis	4	4	5	8	10	12	25	80
254 Don Hardeman	4	4	5	8	10	12	25	
255 Bob Griese	4	4	5	8	10	12	30	
256 Oscar Roan RC	4	4	5	8	10	12	25	
257 Randy Gradishar RC	4	4	5	8	25	30	60	
258 Bob Thomas RC	4	4	5	8	10	12	25	
259 Joe Owens	4	4	5	8	10	12	25	
260 Cliff Harris	4	4	5	8	10	12	30	
261 Frank Lewis	4	4	5	8	10	12	25	
262 Mike McCoy DT	4	4	5	8	10	12	25	60
263 Rickey Young RC	4	4	5	8	10	12	25	60
264 Brian Kelley RC	4	4	5	8	10	12	25	60
265 Charlie Sanders	4	4	5	8	10	12	30	
266 Jim Hart	4	4	5	8	10	12	25	

#	Player	VgEx 4	EX 5	ExMt 6	NM 7	NmMt 8	NmMt+ 8.5	MT 9	Gem 9.5/10
267	Greg Gantt	4	4	5	8	10	12	25	
268	John Ward	4	4	5	8	10	12	25	
269	Al Beauchamp	4	4	5	8	10	12	25	
270	Jack Tatum	4	4	5	8	10	12	30	
271	Jim Lash	4	4	5	8	10	12	25	80
272	Diron Talbert	4	4	5	8	10	12	25	
273	Checklist 265-396	4	4	5	8	10	12	30	
274	Steve Spurrier	4	4	5	8	10	12	30	120
275	Greg Pruitt	4	4	5	8	10	12	30	
276	Jim Mitchell TE	4	4	5	8	10	12	25	
277	Jack Rudnay	4	4	5	8	10	12	25	
278	Freddie Solomon RC	4	4	5	8	10	12	30	
279	Frank LeMaster	4	4	5	8	10	12	25	
280	Wally Chambers	4	4	5	8	10	12	25	
281	Mike Collier	4	4	5	8	10	12	25	
282	Clarence Williams	4	4	5	8	10	12	25	
283	Mitch Hoopes	4	4	5	8	10	12	25	
284	Ron Bolton	4	4	5	8	10	12	25	
285	Harold Jackson	4	4	5	8	10	12	30	
286	Greg Landry	4	4	5	8	10	12	30	
287	Tony Greene	4	4	5	8	10	12	25	
288	Howard Stevens	4	4	5	8	10	12	25	
289	Roy Jefferson	4	4	5	8	10	12	25	
290	Jim Bakken	4	4	5	8	10	12	25	
291	Doug Sutherland	4	4	5	8	10	12	25	
292	Marvin Cobb RC	4	4	5	8	10	12	25	
293	Mack Alston	4	4	5	8	10	12	25	60
294	Rod McNeill	4	4	5	8	10	12	25	80
295	Gene Upshaw	4	4	5	8	10	12	30	
296	Dave Gallagher	4	4	5	8	10	12	25	
297	Larry Ball	4	4	5	8	10	12	25	60
298	Ron Howard	4	4	5	8	10	12	25	
299	Don Strock RC	4	4	5	8	10	12	30	
300	O.J.Simpson	4	4	5	8	20	25	60	
301	Ray Mansfield	4	4	5	8	10	12	25	
302	Larry Marshall	4	4	5	8	10	12	25	
303	Dick Himes	4	4	5	8	10	12	25	
304	Ray Wersching RC	4	4	5	8	10	12	25	
305	John Riggins	4	4	5	8	10	12	30	
306	Bob Parsons	4	4	5	8	10	12	25	
307	Ray Brown DB	4	4	5	8	10	12	25	
308	Len Dawson	4	4	5	8	10	12	30	
309	Andy Maurer	4	4	5	8	10	12	25	60
310	Jack Youngblood	4	4	5	8	10	12	30	80
311	Essex Johnson	4	4	5	8	10	12	25	
312	Stan White	4	4	5	8	10	12	25	
313	Drew Pearson	4	4	5	8	15	20	40	
314	Rockne Freitas	4	4	5	8	10	12	25	60
315	Mercury Morris	4	4	5	8	10	12	30	100
316	Willie Alexander	4	4	5	8	10	12	25	
317	Paul Warfield	4	4	5	8	10	12	30	
318	Bob Chandler	4	4	5	8	10	12	30	
319	Bobby Walden	4	4	5	8	10	12	25	60
320	Riley Odoms	4	4	5	8	10	12	30	
321	Mike Boryla	4	4	5	8	10	12	25	
322	Bruce Van Dyke	4	4	5	8	10	12	25	
323	Pete Banaszak	4	4	5	8	10	12	25	
324	Darryl Stingley	4	4	5	8	10	12	30	60
325	John Mendenhall	4	4	5	8	10	12	40	
326	Dan Dierdorf	4	4	5	8	10	12	30	
327	Bruce Taylor	4	4	5	8	10	12	25	
328	Don McCauley	4	4	5	8	10	12	25	
329	John Reaves	4	4	5	8	10	12	25	100
330	Chris Hanburger	4	4	5	8	10	12	30	
331	NFC Champs/Staubach	4	4	5	8	12	25		
332	AFC Champs/F.Harris	4	4	5	8	10	18	60	
333	Super Bowl X/Bradshaw	4	5	6	12	50	80		
334	Godwin Turk	4	4	5	8	10	12	25	60
335	Dick Anderson	4	4	5	8	10	12	30	
336	Woody Green	4	4	5	8	10	12	25	
337	Pat Curran	4	4	5	8	10	12	25	
338	Council Rudolph	4	4	5	8	10	12	25	60
339	Joe Lavender	4	4	5	8	10	12	25	60
340	John Gilliam	4	4	5	8	10	12	30	80
341	Steve Furness RC	4	4	5	8	10	12	30	
342	D.D. Lewis	4	4	5	8	10	15	60	
343	Duane Carrell	4	4	5	8	10	12	25	
344	Jon Morris	4	4	5	8	10	12	25	
345	John Brockington	4	4	5	8	10	12	30	100

#	Player	VgEx 4	EX 5	ExMt 6	NM 7	NmMt 8	NmMt+ 8.5	MT 9	Gem 9.5/10
346	Mike Phipps	4	4	5	8	10	12	30	
347	Lyle Blackwood RC	4	4	5	8	10	12	25	
348	Julius Adams	4	4	5	8	10	12	25	
349	Terry Hermeling	4	4	5	8	10	12	25	80
350	Rolland Lawrence RC	4	4	5	8	10	12	25	
351	Glenn Doughty	4	4	5	8	10	12	25	
352	Doug Swift	4	4	5	8	10	12	25	
353	Mike Strachan	4	4	5	8	10	12	25	
354	Craig Morton	4	4	5	8	10	12	30	
355	George Blanda	4	4	5	8	10	12	25	150
356	Garry Puetz	4	4	5	8	10	12	25	
357	Carl Mauck	4	4	5	8	10	12	25	
358	Walt Patulski	4	4	5	8	10	12	25	60
359	Stu Voigt	4	4	5	8	10	12	25	60
360	Fred Carr	4	4	5	8	10	12	25	
361	Po James	4	4	5	8	10	12	25	60
362	Otis Taylor	4	4	5	8	10	12	30	
363	Jeff West	4	4	5	8	10	12	25	
364	Gary Huff	4	4	5	8	10	12	30	
365	Dwight White	4	4	5	8	10	12	25	
366	Dan Ryczek	4	4	5	8	10	12	25	
367	Jon Keyworth RC	4	4	5	8	10	12	25	
368	Mel Renfro	4	4	5	8	10	12	30	100
369	Bruce Coslet RC	4	4	5	8	10	12	30	
370	Len Hauss	4	4	5	8	10	12	25	
371	Rick Volk	4	4	5	8	10	12	25	
372	Howard Twilley	4	4	5	8	10	12	25	
373	Cullen Bryant RC	4	4	5	8	10	12	30	
374	Bob Babich	4	4	5	8	10	12	25	
375	Herman Weaver	4	4	5	8	10	12	25	
376	Steve Grogan RC	4	4	5	8	10	15	30	
377	Bubba Smith	4	4	5	8	10	12	30	
378	Burgess Owens	4	4	5	8	10	12	25	
379	Al Matthews	4	4	5	8	10	12	25	80
380	Art Shell	4	4	5	8	10	12	30	
381	Larry Brown	4	4	5	8	10	12	25	
382	Horst Muhlmann	4	4	5	8	10	12	25	
383	Ahmad Rashad	4	4	5	8	10	12	35	
384	Bobby Maples	4	4	5	8	10	12	25	
385	Jim Marshall	4	4	5	8	10	12	30	
386	Joe Dawkins	4	4	5	8	10	12	25	
387	Dennis Partee	4	4	5	8	10	12	25	80
388	Eddie McMillan RC	4	4	5	8	10	12	25	
389	Randy Johnson	4	4	5	8	10	12	25	
390	Bob Kuechenberg	4	4	5	8	10	12	25	
391	Rufus Mayes	4	4	5	8	10	12	25	
392	Lloyd Mumphord	4	4	5	8	10	12	25	60
393	Ike Harris	4	4	5	8	10	12	25	
394	Dave Hampton	4	4	5	8	10	12	25	60
395	Roger Staubach	5	8	12	20	30	35	125	800
396	Doug Buffone	4	4	5	8	10	12	25	
397	Howard Fest	4	4	5	8	10	12	25	
398	Wayne Mulligan	4	4	5	8	10	12	25	
399	Bill Bradley	4	4	5	8	10	12	30	
400	Chuck Foreman	4	4	5	8	10	12	30	
401	Jack Snow	4	4	5	8	10	12	30	
402	Bob Howard	4	4	5	8	10	12	25	60
403	John Matuszak	4	4	5	8	10	12	30	
404	Bill Munson	4	4	5	8	10	12	30	
405	Andy Russell	4	4	5	8	10	12	30	80
406	Skip Butler	4	4	5	8	10	12	25	
407	Hugh McKinnis	4	4	5	8	10	12	25	
408	Bob Penchion	4	4	5	8	10	12	25	
409	Mike Bass	4	4	5	8	10	12	25	60
410	George Kunz	4	4	5	8	10	12	25	
411	Ron Pritchard	4	4	5	8	10	12	25	60
412	Barry Smith	4	4	5	8	10	12	25	
413	Norm Bulaich	4	4	5	8	10	12	25	
414	Marv Bateman	4	4	5	8	10	12	25	
415	Ken Stabler	4	5	6	10	15	20	50	
416	Conrad Dobler	4	4	5	8	10	12	30	
417	Bob Tucker	4	4	5	8	10	12	30	
418	Gene Washington 49er	4	4	5	8	10	12	30	
419	Ed Marinaro	4	4	5	8	10	12	30	60
420	Jack Ham	4	4	5	8	10	12	100	
421	Jim Turner	4	4	5	8	10	12	25	80
422	Chris Fletcher	4	4	5	8	10	12	25	60
423	Carl Barzilauskas	4	4	5	8	10	12	25	
424	Robert Brazile RC	4	4	6	10	15	20	60	

	VgEx 4	EX 5	ExMt 6	NM 7	NmMt 8	NmMt+ 8.5	MT 9	Gem 9.5/10
Harold Carmichael	4	4	5	8	10	12	35	
Ron Jaworski RC	4	4	5	10	25	30	80	
Ed Too Tall Jones RC	5	6	10	20	30	35	100	1,000
Larry McCarren	4	4	5	8	10	12	30	
Mike Thomas RC	4	4	5	8	10	12	25	
Joe DeLamielleure	4	4	5	8	10	12	30	80
Tom Blanchard	4	4	5	8	10	12	25	
Ron Carpenter	4	4	5	8	10	12	25	
Levi Johnson	4	4	5	8	10	12	25	60
Sam Cunningham	4	4	5	8	10	12	30	
Garo Yepremian	4	4	5	8	10	12	25	
Mike Livingston	4	4	5	8	10	12	25	
Larry Csonka	4	4	5	8	10	12	40	
Doug Dieken	4	4	5	8	10	12	30	
Bill Lueck	4	4	5	8	10	12	25	80
Tom MacLeod	4	4	5	8	10	12	25	
Mick Tingelhoff	4	4	5	8	10	12	30	
Terry Hanratty	4	4	5	8	10	12	30	
Mike Siani	4	4	5	8	10	12	25	
Dwight Harrison	4	4	5	8	10	12	25	
Jim Otis	4	4	5	8	10	12	30	
Jack Reynolds	4	4	5	8	10	12	30	
Jean Fugett RC	4	4	5	8	10	12	30	
Dave Beverly	4	4	5	8	10	12	25	
Bernard Jackson RC	4	4	5	8	10	12	30	
Charley Taylor	4	4	5	8	10	12	35	
Atlanta Falcons CL	4	4	5	8	10	12	30	
Baltimore Colts CL	4	4	5	8	10	12		
Buffalo Bills CL	4	4	5	8	12	15	25	
Chicago Bears CL	4	4	5	8	10	12	50	
Cincinnati Bengals CL	4	4	5	8	10	12		
Cleveland Browns CL	4	4	5	8	10	12	30	
Dallas Cowboys CL	4	4	5	8	10	12	40	
Denver Broncos CL	4	4	5	8	10	12		
Detroit Lions CL	4	4	5	8	10	12	25	60
Green Bay Packers CL	4	4	5	8	10	12		
Houston Oilers CL	4	4	5	8	10	12	25	
Kansas City Chiefs CL	4	4	5	8	10	12	30	80
Los Angeles Rams CL	4	4	5	8	10	12		
Miami Dolphins CL	4	4	5	8	10	12	30	
Minnesota Vikings CL	4	4	5	8	10	12		
New England Patriots CL	4	4	5	8	10	12		
New Orleans Saints CL	4	4	5	8	10	12		
New York Giants CL	4	4	5	8	10	12		
New York Jets CL	4	4	5	8	10	12	25	
Oakland Raiders CL	4	4	5	8	10	12	50	
Philadelphia Eagles CL	4	4	5	8	10	12	25	
Pittsburgh Steelers CL	4	4	5	8	10	12	40	
St. Louis Cardinals CL	4	4	5	8	10	12		
San Diego Chargers CL	4	4	5	8	10	12	30	
San Francisco 49ers CL	4	4	5	8	10	12	100	
Seattle Seahawks CL	4	4	5	8	10	12		
Tampa Bay Buccaneers CL	4	4	5	8	10	12	40	
Washington Redskins CL	4	4	5	8	10	12	30	
Fred Cox	4	4	5	8	10	12	25	60
Mel Blount	4	4	5	8	10	12	80	
John Bunting RC	4	4	5	8	10	12	25	60
Ken Mendenhall	4	4	5	8	10	12	25	
Will Harrell	4	4	5	8	10	12	25	
Marlin Briscoe	4	4	5	8	10	12	25	
Archie Manning	4	4	5	8	10	12	25	
Tody Smith	4	4	5	8	10	12	25	
George Hunt	4	4	5	8	10	12	25	80
Roscoe Word	4	4	5	8	10	12	25	
Paul Seymour	4	4	5	8	10	12	25	60
Lee Roy Jordan	4	4	5	8	15	20	35	
Chip Myers	4	4	5	8	10	12	25	
Norm Evans	4	4	5	8	10	12	25	
Jim Bertelsen	4	4	5	8	10	12	25	
Mark Moseley	4	4	5	8	10	12	25	
George Buehler	4	4	5	8	10	12	25	
Charlie Hall	4	4	5	8	10	12	25	
Marvin Upshaw	4	4	5	8	10	12	25	60
Tom Banks RC	4	4	5	8	10	12	80	
Randy Vataha	4	4	5	8	10	12	25	
Fran Tarkenton	4	4	5	8	15	20	100	
Mike Wagner	4	4	5	8	10	12	25	60
Art Malone	4	4	5	8	10	12	25	
Fred Cook	4	4	5	8	10	12	25	

		VgEx 4	EX 5	ExMt 6	NM 7	NmMt 8	NmMt+ 8.5	MT 9	Gem 9.5/10
504	Rich McGeorge	4	4	5	8	10	12	25	
505	Ken Burrough	4	4	5	8	10	12	25	
506	Nick Mike-Mayer	4	4	5	8	10	12	25	
507	Checklist 397-528	4	4	5	8	10	12	30	
508	Steve Owens	4	4	5	8	10	12	25	
509	Brad Van Pelt RC	4	4	5	8	10	12	25	
510	Ken Riley	4	4	5	8	10	12	25	
511	Art Thoms	4	4	5	8	10	12	25	
512	Ed Bell	4	4	5	8	10	12	25	
513	Tom Wittum	4	4	5	8	10	12	25	60
514	Jim Braxton	4	4	5	8	10	12	25	80
515	Nick Buoniconti	4	4	5	10	10	12	30	
516	Brian Sipe RC	4	4	5	8	35	50	100	
517	Jim Lynch	4	4	5	8	10	12	25	
518	Prentice McCray	4	4	5	8	10	12	25	
519	Tom Dempsey	4	4	5	8	10	12	25	
520	Mel Gray	4	4	5	8	10	12	20	
521	Nate Wright	4	4	5	8	10	12	25	
522	Rocky Bleier	4	4	5	8	10	12	40	
523	Dennis Johnson RC	4	4	5	8	10	12	25	
524	Jerry Sisemore	4	4	5	8	10	12	25	
525	Bert Jones	4	4	5	8	10	12	40	
526	Perry Smith	4	4	5	8	10	12	40	
527	Blaine Nye	4	4	5	8	10	12	25	
528	Bob Moore	4	4	5	5	10	12	25	

—Terry Bradshaw #75 BGS 9.5 (Gem Mint) sold for $435.01 (eBay: 5/12)
—L.C.Greenwood #180 PSA 10 (Gem Mint) sold for $532 (eBay: 8/12)
—Jack Lambert #220 PSA 10 (Gem) sold for $1,179 (eBay: 2/10)
—Jack Lambert #220 PSA 10 (Gem) sold for $1,538.65 (eBay: 11/13)
—Jack Lambert #220 BGS 10 (Gem) sold for $6573 (eBay: 09/14)
—Jack Lambert #220 BGS 9.5 (Gem Mint) sold for $840.01 (eBay: 5/12)
—Walter Payton #148 BVG 10 (Pristine) sold for $11,050 (eBay: 11/07)
—Walter Payton #148 PSA 10 (Gem) sold for $10,230 (eBay: 10/14)
—O.J. Simpson #6 PSA 10 (Gem) sold for $695 (eBay: 10/14)
—Fran Tarkenton #500 PSA 10 (Gem Mint) sold for $540 (Bussineau; 4/12)
—Randy White #158 PSA 10 (Gem) sold for $1,476 (eBay; 9/07)
—Super Bowl X/Bradshaw #333 PSA 10 (Gem) sold for $1,037 (eBay; 7/13)

1977 Topps

		VgEx 4	EX 5	ExMt 6	NM 7	NmMt 8	NmMt+ 8.5	MT 9	Gem 9.5/10
1	K.Stabler/J.Harris LL	4	4	5	5	10	15	40	
2	D.Pearson/M.Lane LL	4	4	5	5	10	12	30	
3	W.Payton/O.Simpson LL	4	4	6	10	20	30	120	
4	M.Moseley/T.Linhart LL	4	4	5	5	10	12	25	60
5	M.Jackson/K.Riley LL	4	4	5	5	10	12	25	
6	J.James/M.Bateman LL	4	4	5	5	10	12	25	
7	Mike Phipps	4	4	5	5	10	12	25	
8	Rick Volk	4	4	5	5	10	12	25	
9	Steve Furness	4	4	5	5	10	12	25	
10	Isaac Curtis	4	4	5	5	10	12	25	
11	Nate Wright	4	4	5	5	10	12	25	
12	Jean Fugett	4	4	5	5	10	12	25	80
13	Ken Mendenhall	4	4	5	5	10	12	25	
14	Sam Adams OL	4	4	5	5	10	12	25	
15	Charlie Waters	4	4	5	5	10	12	25	80
16	Bill Stanfill	4	4	5	5	10	12	25	
17	John Holland	4	4	5	5	10	12	25	
18	Pat Haden RC	4	4	5	5	10	12	25	60
19	Bob Young	4	4	5	5	10	12	25	
20	Wally Chambers	4	4	5	5	10	12	25	
21	Lawrence Gaines	4	4	5	5	10	12	25	
22	Larry McCarren	4	4	5	5	10	12	25	
23	Horst Muhlmann	4	4	5	5	10	12	25	60
24	Phil Villapiano	4	4	5	5	10	12	25	60
25	Greg Pruitt	4	4	5	5	10	12	40	
26	Ron Howard	4	4	5	5	10	12	25	
27	Craig Morton	4	4	5	5	10	12	25	
28	Rufus Mayes	4	4	5	5	10	12	50	
29	Lee Roy Selmon RC	4	5	8	15	25	30	▼125	
30	Ed White	4	4	5	5	10	12	25	
31	Harold McLinton	4	4	5	5	10	12	25	50
32	Glenn Doughty	4	4	5	5	10	12	25	60
33	Bob Kuechenberg	4	4	5	5	10	12	25	
34	Duane Carrell	4	4	5	5	10	12	25	
35	Riley Odoms	4	4	5	5	10	12	25	
36	Bobby Scott	4	4	5	5	10	12	25	
37	Nick Mike-Mayer	4	4	5	5	10	12	25	
38	Bill Lenkaitis	4	4	5	5	10	12	25	

#	Player	VgEx 4	EX 5	ExMt 6	NM 7	NmMt 8	NmMt+ 8.5	MT 9	Gem 9.5/10
39	Roland Harper	4	4	5	5	10	12	25	
40	Tommy Hart	4	4	5	5	10	12	25	
41	Mike Sensibaugh	4	4	5	5	10	12	25	
42	Rusty Jackson	4	4	5	5	10	12	25	
43	Levi Johnson	4	4	5	5	10	12	25	
44	Mike McCoy DT	4	4	5	5	10	12	25	60
45	Roger Staubach	5	8	12	25	40	50	200	
46	Fred Cox	4	4	5	5	10	12	25	
47	Bob Babich	4	4	5	5	10	12	25	
48	Reggie McKenzie	4	4	5	5	10	12	25	
49	Dave Jennings	4	4	5	5	10	12	25	
50	Mike Haynes RC	4	5	8	15	30	40	200	
51	Larry Brown	4	4	5	5	10	12	25	
52	Marvin Cobb	4	4	5	5	10	12	25	
53	Fred Cook	4	4	5	5	10	12	25	
54	Freddie Solomon	4	4	5	5	10	12	25	
55	John Riggins	4	4	5	5	12	15	30	
56	John Bunting	4	4	5	5	10	12	25	
57	Ray Wersching	4	4	5	5	10	12	25	
58	Mike Livingston	4	4	5	5	10	12	25	60
59	Billy Johnson	4	4	5	5	10	12	25	
60	Mike Wagner	4	4	5	5	10	12	25	
61	Waymond Bryant	4	4	5	5	10	12	25	
62	Jim Otis	4	4	5	5	10	12	25	60
63	Ed Galigher	4	4	5	5	10	12	25	60
64	Randy Vataha	4	4	5	5	10	12	25	
65	Jim Zorn RC	4	4	5	8	15	20	40	
66	Jon Keyworth	4	4	5	5	10	12	25	
67	Checklist 1-132	4	4	5	5	10	12	25	
68	Henry Childs	4	4	5	5	10	12	25	60
69	Thom Darden	4	4	5	5	10	12	25	
70	George Kunz	4	4	5	5	10	12	25	
71	Lenvil Elliott	4	4	5	5	10	12	25	
72	Curtis Johnson	4	4	5	5	10	12	25	
73	Doug Van Horn	4	4	5	5	10	12	20	80
74	Joe Theismann	4	4	5	8	15	20	40	125
75	Dwight White	4	4	5	5	10	12	30	100
76	Scott Laidlaw	4	4	5	5	10	12	25	
77	Monte Johnson	4	4	5	5	10	12	25	
78	Dave Beverly	4	4	5	5	10	12	25	
79	Jim Mitchell TE	4	4	5	5	10	12	25	60
80	Jack Youngblood	4	4	5	5	10	12	25	60
81	Mel Gray	4	4	5	5	10	12	25	
82	Dwight Harrison	4	4	5	5	10	12	25	60
83	John Hadl	4	4	5	5	10	12	25	
84	Matt Blair RC	4	4	5	5	10	12	100	
85	Charlie Sanders	4	4	5	5	10	12	25	
86	Noah Jackson	4	4	5	5	10	12	25	
87	Ed Marinaro	4	4	5	5	10	12	25	80
88	Bob Howard	4	4	5	5	10	12	25	
89	John McDaniel	4	4	5	5	10	12	25	
90	Dan Dierdorf	4	4	5	5	10	12	40	60
91	Mark Moseley	4	4	5	5	10	12	25	
92	Cleo Miller	4	4	5	5	10	12	25	
93	Andre Tillman	4	4	5	5	10	12	25	60
94	Bruce Taylor	4	4	5	5	10	12	25	60
95	Bert Jones	4	4	5	5	10	12	25	
96	Anthony Davis RC	4	4	5	5	10	12	25	
97	Don Goode	4	4	5	5	10	12	25	
98	Ray Rhodes RC	4	4	5	8	15	20	50	
99	Mike Webster RC	4	5	8	12	30	40	▼60	700
100	O.J.Simpson	4	4	5	8	15	20	80	300
101	Doug Plank RC	4	4	5	5	10	12	25	
102	Efren Herrera	4	4	5	5	10	12	50	
103	Charlie Smith WR	4	4	5	5	10	12	25	60
104	Carlos Brown RC	4	4	5	5	10	12	25	
105	Jim Marshall	4	4	5	5	10	12	25	80
106	Paul Naumoff	4	4	5	5	10	12	25	60
107	Walter White	4	4	5	5	10	12	25	60
108	John Cappelletti RC	4	4	5	5	10	15	40	
109	Chip Myers	4	4	5	5	10	12	25	60
110	Ken Stabler	4	4	6	10	25	30	60	200
111	Joe Ehrmann	4	4	5	5	10	12	25	
112	Rick Engles	4	4	5	5	10	12	25	
113	Jack Dolbin RC	4	4	5	5	10	12	25	60
114	Ron Bolton	4	4	5	5	10	12	25	60
115	Mike Thomas	4	4	5	5	10	12	25	
116	Mike Fuller	4	4	5	5	10	12	25	
117	John Hill	4	4	5	5	10	12	20	
118	Richard Todd RC	4	4	5	5	10	12	30	
119	Duriel Harris RC	4	4	5	5	10	12	30	
120	John James	4	4	5	5	10	12	25	
121	Lionel Antoine	4	4	5	5	10	12	25	
122	John Skorupan	4	4	5	5	10	12	25	
123	Skip Butler	4	4	5	5	10	12	25	
124	Bob Tucker	4	4	5	5	10	12	25	
125	Paul Krause	4	4	5	5	10	12	25	
126	Dave Hampton	4	4	5	5	10	12	25	
127	Tom Wittum	4	4	5	5	10	12	25	60
128	Gary Huff	4	4	5	5	10	12	25	60
129	Emmitt Thomas	4	4	5	5	10	12	25	
130	Drew Pearson	4	4	5	5	10	12	30	
131	Ron Saul	4	4	5	5	10	12	25	
132	Steve Niehaus	4	4	5	5	10	12	25	
133	Fred Carr	4	4	5	5	10	12	25	60
134	Norm Bulaich	4	4	5	5	10	12	25	
135	Bob Trumpy	4	4	5	5	10	12	25	
136	Greg Landry	4	4	5	5	10	12	25	
137	George Buehler	4	4	5	5	10	12	25	
138	Reggie Rucker	4	4	5	5	10	12	25	
139	Julius Adams	4	4	5	5	10	12	25	
140	Jack Ham	4	4	5	5	10	12	80	
141	Wayne Morris RC	4	4	5	5	10	12	25	
142	Marv Bateman	4	4	5	5	10	12	25	
143	Bobby Maples	4	4	5	5	10	12	25	
144	Harold Carmichael	4	4	5	5	10	12	25	
145	Bob Avellini	4	4	5	5	10	12	25	
146	Harry Carson RC	5	8	12	20	50	80	▼250	
147	Lawrence Pillers	4	4	5	5	10	12	25	60
148	Ed Williams RC	4	4	5	5	10	12	25	
149	Dan Pastorini	4	4	5	5	10	12	25	60
150	Ron Yary	4	4	5	5	10	12	25	
151	Joe Lavender	4	4	5	5	10	12	25	60
152	Pat McInally RC	4	4	5	5	10	12	100	
153	Lloyd Mumphord	4	4	5	5	10	12	25	
154	Cullen Bryant	4	4	5	5	10	12	25	
155	Willie Lanier	4	4	5	5	10	12	25	60
156	Gene Washington 49er	4	4	5	5	10	12	25	
157	Scott Hunter	4	4	5	5	10	12	25	60
158	Jim Merlo	4	4	5	5	10	12	25	
159	Randy Grossman	4	4	5	5	10	12	30	
160	Blaine Nye	4	4	5	5	10	12	25	
161	Ike Harris	4	4	5	5	10	12	25	
162	Doug Dieken	4	4	5	5	10	12	25	
163	Guy Morriss	4	4	5	5	10	12	25	60
164	Bob Parsons	4	4	5	5	10	12	25	80
165	Steve Grogan	4	4	5	5	10	12	25	
166	John Brockington	4	4	5	5	10	12	25	
167	Charlie Joiner	4	4	5	5	10	12	30	
168	Ron Carpenter	4	4	5	5	10	12	25	
169	Jeff Wright S	4	4	5	5	10	12	25	
170	Chris Hanburger	4	4	5	5	10	12	25	
171	Roosevelt Leaks RC	4	4	5	5	10	12	25	80
172	Larry Little	4	4	5	5	10	12	25	
173	John Matuszak	4	4	5	5	10	12	25	80
174	Joe Ferguson	4	4	5	5	10	12	25	
175	Brad Van Pelt	4	4	5	5	10	12	25	
176	Dexter Bussey RC	4	4	5	5	10	12	25	60
177	Steve Largent RC	8	15	▲25	▲40	60	100	225	2,500
178	Dewey Selmon	4	4	5	5	10	12	25	80
179	Randy Gradishar	4	4	5	5	10	12	25	80
180	Mel Blount	4	4	5	5	10	12	30	
181	Dan Neal	4	4	5	5	10	12	25	50
182	Rich Szaro	4	4	5	5	10	12	25	
183	Mike Boryla	4	4	5	5	10	12	25	60
184	Steve Jones	4	4	5	5	10	12	25	60
185	Paul Warfield	4	4	5	5	10	12	30	
186	Greg Buttle RC	4	4	5	5	10	12	25	
187	Rich McGeorge	4	4	5	5	10	12	25	
188	Leon Gray RC	4	4	5	5	10	12	25	
189	John Shinners	4	4	5	5	10	12	25	60
190	Toni Linhart	4	4	5	5	10	12	25	60
191	Robert Miller	4	4	5	5	10	12	25	
192	Jake Scott	4	4	5	5	10	12	25	
193	Jon Morris	4	4	5	5	10	12	25	
194	Randy Crowder	4	4	5	5	10	12	25	
195	Lynn Swann	4	5	8	12	20	25	60	
196	Marsh White	4	4	5	5	10	12	25	

#	Player	VgEx 4	EX 5	ExMt 6	NM 7	NmMt 8	NmMt+ 8.5	MT 9	Gem 9.5/10
	Rod Perry RC	4	4	5	5	10	12	25	
	Willie Hall	4	4	5	5	10	12	25	60
	Mike Hartenstine	4	4	5	5	10	12	25	60
	Jim Bakken	4	4	5	5	10	12	25	
	Atlanta Falcons CL	4	4	5	5	10	12	25	
	Baltimore Colts CL	4	4	5	5	10	12	25	
	Buffalo Bills CL	4	4	5	5	10	12	25	
	Chicago Bears CL	4	4	5	5	10	12	25	
	Cincinnati Bengals CL	4	4	5	5	10	12	25	60
	Cleveland Browns CL	4	4	5	5	10	12	25	80
	Dallas Cowboys CL	4	4	5	5	10	12	25	
	Denver Broncos CL	4	4	5	5	10	12	25	
	Detroit Lions CL	4	4	5	5	10	12	25	
	Green Bay Packers CL	4	4	5	5	10	12	25	
	Houston Oilers CL	4	4	5	5	10	12	25	
	Kansas City Chiefs CL	4	4	5	5	10	12	60	
	Los Angeles Rams CL	4	4	5	5	10	12	25	
	Miami Dolphins CL	4	4	5	5	10	12	25	
	Minnesota Vikings CL	4	4	5	5	10	12	25	
	New England Patriots CL	4	4	5	5	10	12	25	
	New Orleans Saints CL	4	4	5	5	10	12	25	
	New York Giants CL	4	4	5	5	10	12	25	50
	New York Jets CL	4	4	5	5	10	12	25	50
	Oakland Raiders CL	4	4	5	5	10	12	25	80
	Philadelphia Eagles CL	4	4	5	5	10	12	25	
	Pittsburgh Steelers CL	4	4	5	5	10	12	25	80
	St. Louis Cardinals CL	4	4	5	5	10	12	25	
	San Diego Chargers CL	4	4	5	5	10	12	25	80
	San Francisco 49ers CL	4	4	5	5	10	12	25	
	Seattle Seahawks CL	4	4	5	5	10	12	40	
	Tampa Bay Buccaneers CL	4	4	5	5	10	12	25	
	Washington Redskins CL	4	4	5	5	10	12	25	
	Sam Cunningham	4	4	5	5	10	12	25	
	Alan Page	4	4	5	5	10	12	40	
	Eddie Brown S	4	4	5	5	10	12	25	
	Stan White	4	4	5	5	10	12	25	60
	Vern Den Herder	4	4	5	5	10	12	25	
	Clarence Davis	4	4	5	5	10	12	25	
	Ken Anderson	4	4	5	5	8	12	25	60
	Karl Chandler	4	4	5	5	10	12	25	
	Will Harrell	4	4	5	5	10	12	25	
	Clarence Scott	4	4	5	5	10	12	25	
	Bo Rather	4	4	5	5	10	12	25	50
	Robert Brazile	4	4	5	5	10	12	25	
	Bob Bell	4	4	5	5	10	12	25	
	Rolland Lawrence	4	4	5	5	10	12	25	
	Tom Sullivan	4	4	5	5	10	12	25	60
	Larry Brunson	4	4	5	5	10	12	25	60
	Terry Bradshaw	4	5	8	20	30	40	100	
	Rich Saul	4	4	5	5	10	12	25	60
	Cleveland Elam	4	4	5	5	10	12	25	
	Don Woods	4	4	5	5	10	12	25	
	Bruce Laird	4	4	5	5	10	12	25	
	Coy Bacon	4	4	5	5	10	12	25	80
	Russ Francis	4	4	5	5	10	12	25	
	Jim Braxton	4	4	5	5	10	12	25	
	Perry Smith	4	4	5	5	10	12	25	
	Jerome Barkum	4	4	5	5	10	12	25	50
	Garo Yepremian	4	4	5	5	10	12	25	
	Checklist 133-264	4	4	5	5	10	12	25	
	Tony Galbreath RC	4	4	5	5	10	12	25	
	Troy Archer	4	4	5	5	10	12	25	
	Brian Sipe	4	4	5	5	10	12	25	
	Billy Joe DuPree	4	4	5	5	10	12	25	60
	Bobby Walden	4	4	5	5	10	12	25	
	Larry Marshall	4	4	5	5	10	12	25	
	Ted Fritsch Jr.	4	4	5	5	10	12	25	
	Larry Hand	4	4	5	5	10	12	25	
	Tom Mack	4	4	5	5	10	12	25	60
	Ed Bradley	4	4	5	5	10	12	25	60
	Pat Leahy	4	4	5	5	10	12	25	
	Louis Carter	4	4	5	5	8	12	25	
	Archie Griffin RC	4	4	5	10	20	25	60	
	Art Shell	4	4	5	5	10	12	25	
	Stu Voigt	4	4	5	5	10	12	25	
	Prentice McCray	4	4	5	5	10	12	25	
	MacArthur Lane	4	4	5	5	10	12	25	
	Dan Fouts	4	4	5	8	12	20	40	
	Charle Young	4	4	5	5	10	12	25	50
276	Wilbur Jackson RC	4	4	5	5	10	12	25	
277	John Hicks	4	4	5	5	10	12	25	
278	Nat Moore	4	4	5	5	10	12	25	60
279	Virgil Livers	4	4	5	5	10	12	25	
280	Curley Culp	4	4	5	5	10	12	25	
281	Rocky Bleier	4	4	5	5	10	12	30	
282	John Zook	4	4	5	5	10	12	25	60
283	Tom DeLeone	4	4	5	5	10	12	25	
284	Danny White RC	4	4	6	12	25	30	60	▲400
285	Otis Armstrong	4	4	5	5	10	12	25	
286	Larry Walton	4	4	5	5	10	12	25	60
287	Jim Carter	4	4	5	5	10	12	25	
288	Don McCauley	4	4	5	5	10	12	25	
289	Frank Grant	4	4	5	5	10	12	25	50
290	Roger Wehrli	4	4	5	5	10	12	25	80
291	Mick Tingelhoff	4	4	5	5	10	12	25	60
292	Bernard Jackson	4	4	5	5	10	12	25	
293	Tom Owen RC	4	4	5	5	10	12	25	
294	Mike Esposito	4	4	5	5	10	12	25	60
295	Fred Biletnikoff	4	4	5	5	10	12	30	
296	Revie Sorey RC	4	4	5	5	10	12	25	
297	John McMakin	4	4	5	5	10	12	25	
298	Dan Ryczek	4	4	5	5	10	12	25	
299	Wayne Moore	4	4	5	5	8	12	25	80
300	Franco Harris	4	4	5	8	25	35	175	
301	Rick Upchurch RC	4	4	5	5	10	12	25	80
302	Jim Stienke	4	4	5	5	10	12	25	
303	Charlie Davis	4	4	5	5	10	12	25	
304	Don Cockroft	4	4	5	5	10	12	25	60
305	Ken Burrough	4	4	5	5	10	12	25	
306	Clark Gaines	4	4	5	5	10	12	25	
307	Bobby Douglass	4	4	5	5	10	12	50	
308	Ralph Perretta	4	4	5	5	10	12	25	
309	Wally Hilgenberg	4	4	5	5	10	12	25	
310	Monte Jackson RC	4	4	5	5	10	12	25	60
311	Chris Bahr RC	4	4	5	5	10	12	25	
312	Jim Cheyunski	4	4	5	5	10	12	25	60
313	Mike Patrick	4	4	5	5	8	12	25	
314	Ed Too Tall Jones	4	4	5	8	20	25	50	
315	Bill Bradley	4	4	5	5	10	12	25	
316	Benny Malone	4	4	5	5	10	12	25	
317	Paul Seymour	4	4	5	5	10	12	25	60
318	Jim Laslavic	4	4	5	5	10	12	25	
319	Frank Lewis	4	4	5	5	10	12	25	60
320	Ray Guy	4	4	5	5	10	12	30	
321	Allan Ellis	4	4	5	5	10	12	25	
322	Conrad Dobler	4	4	5	5	10	12	25	
323	Chester Marcol	4	4	5	5	10	12	25	
324	Doug Kotar	4	4	5	5	10	12	25	
325	Lemar Parrish	4	4	5	5	10	12	25	
326	Steve Holden	4	4	5	5	10	12	25	
327	Jeff Van Note	4	4	5	5	10	12	25	
328	Howard Stevens	4	4	5	5	10	12	25	
329	Brad Dusek	4	4	5	5	10	12	25	
330	Joe DeLamielleure	4	4	5	5	10	12	20	
331	Jim Plunkett	4	4	5	5	10	12	30	
332	Checklist 265-396	4	4	5	5	10	12	25	
333	Lou Piccone	4	4	5	5	10	12	25	60
334	Ray Hamilton	4	4	5	5	10	12	25	
335	Jan Stenerud	4	4	5	5	10	12	25	
336	Jeris White	4	4	5	5	10	12	25	
337	Sherman Smith RC	4	4	5	5	10	12	25	
338	Dave Green	4	4	5	5	10	12	25	
339	Terry Schmidt	4	4	5	5	10	12	25	
340	Sammie White RC	4	4	5	5	10	12	50	
341	Jon Kolb RC	4	4	5	5	8	12	25	
342	Randy White	4	4	5	10	20	25	60	175
343	Bob Klein	4	4	5	5	10	12	40	
344	Bob Kowalkowski	4	4	5	5	10	12	25	60
345	Terry Metcalf	4	4	5	5	10	12	25	
346	Joe Danelo	4	4	5	5	10	12	25	60
347	Ken Payne	4	4	5	5	10	12	25	
348	Neal Craig	4	4	5	5	10	12	25	
349	Dennis Johnson	4	4	5	5	10	12	25	
350	Bill Bergey	4	4	5	5	10	12	25	
351	Raymond Chester	4	4	5	5	10	12	25	
352	Bob Matheson	4	4	5	5	10	12	25	60
353	Mike Kadish	4	4	5	5	10	12	25	60
354	Mark Van Eeghen RC	4	4	5	5	10	12	40	

#	Player	VgEx 4	EX 5	ExMt 6	NM 7	NmMt 8	NmMt+ 8.5	MT 9	Gem 9.5/10
355	L.C.Greenwood	4	4	5	5	10	12	25	
356	Sam Hunt	4	4	5	5	10	12	25	
357	Darrell Austin	4	4	5	5	10	12	25	
358	Jim Turner	4	4	5	5	10	12	25	
359	Ahmad Rashad	4	4	5	5	8	12	25	
360	Walter Payton	8	12	25	35	100	125	600	
361	Mark Arneson	4	4	5	5	10	12	25	
362	Jerrel Wilson	4	4	5	5	10	12	25	
363	Steve Bartkowski	4	4	5	5	10	12	25	
364	John Watson	4	4	5	5	10	12	25	
365	Ken Riley	4	4	5	5	10	12	25	
366	Gregg Bingham	4	4	5	5	10	12	25	60
367	Golden Richards	4	4	5	5	10	12	25	
368	Clyde Powers	4	4	5	5	10	12	25	
369	Diron Talbert	4	4	5	5	10	12	25	
370	Lydell Mitchell	4	4	5	5	10	12	25	
371	Bob Jackson	4	4	5	5	10	12	25	
372	Jim Mandich	4	4	5	5	10	12	25	
373	Frank LeMaster	4	4	5	5	10	12	25	
374	Benny Ricardo	4	4	5	5	10	12	25	
375	Lawrence McCutcheon	4	4	5	5	10	12	25	
376	Lynn Dickey	4	4	5	5	10	12	25	
377	Phil Wise	4	4	5	5	10	12	25	
378	Tony McGee DT	4	4	5	5	10	12	25	
379	Norm Thompson	4	4	5	5	8	12	25	
380	Dave Casper RC	4	5	8	15	50	60	300	
381	Glen Edwards	4	4	5	5	10	12	25	
382	Bob Thomas	4	4	5	5	10	12	25	
383	Bob Chandler	4	4	5	5	10	12	25	
384	Rickey Young	4	4	5	5	10	12	25	
385	Carl Eller	4	4	5	5	10	12	25	
386	Lyle Alzado	4	4	5	5	10	12	25	
387	John Leypoldt	4	4	5	5	10	12	25	
388	Gordon Bell	4	4	5	5	10	12	25	60
389	Mike Bragg	4	4	5	5	10	12	25	
390	Jim Langer	4	4	5	5	10	12	25	
391	Vern Holland	4	4	5	5	10	12	25	
392	Nelson Munsey	4	4	5	5	10	12	25	
393	Mack Mitchell	4	4	5	5	10	12	25	
394	Tony Adams RC	4	4	5	5	10	12	25	
395	Preston Pearson	4	4	5	5	10	12	25	
396	Emanuel Zanders	4	4	5	5	8	12	25	
397	Vince Papale RC	5	8	12	15	25	35	60	
398	Joe Fields RC	4	4	5	5	10	12	25	
399	Craig Clemons	4	4	5	5	10	12	25	80
400	Fran Tarkenton	4	4	5	8	15	20	50	
401	Andy Johnson	4	4	5	5	10	12	25	60
402	Willie Buchanon	4	4	5	5	10	12	25	60
403	Pat Curran	4	4	5	5	10	12	25	
404	Ray Jarvis	4	4	5	5	10	12	25	
405	Joe Greene	4	4	5	5	10	12	40	
406	Bill Simpson	4	4	5	5	10	12	25	
407	Ronnie Coleman	4	4	5	5	10	12	25	
408	J.K. McKay RC	4	4	5	5	10	12	25	60
409	Pat Fischer	4	4	5	5	10	12	25	
410	John Dutton	4	4	5	5	10	12	25	
411	Boobie Clark	4	4	5	5	10	12	25	
412	Pat Tilley RC	4	4	5	5	10	12	25	80
413	Don Strock	4	4	5	5	10	12	25	
414	Brian Kelley	4	4	5	5	10	12	25	
415	Gene Upshaw	4	4	5	5	10	12	25	
416	Mike Montler	4	4	5	5	10	12	25	
417	Checklist 397-528	4	4	5	5	10	12	25	
418	John Gilliam	4	4	5	5	10	12	25	60
419	Brent McClanahan	4	4	5	5	10	12	30	
420	Jerry Sherk	4	4	5	5	10	12	30	
421	Roy Gerela	4	4	5	5	10	12	25	60
422	Tim Fox	4	4	5	5	10	12	25	60
423	John Ebersole	4	4	5	5	10	12	25	
424	James Scott RC	4	4	5	5	10	12	25	60
425	Delvin Williams RC	4	4	5	5	10	12	25	
426	Spike Jones	4	4	5	5	10	12	25	
427	Harvey Martin	4	4	5	5	10	12	25	120
428	Don Herrmann	4	4	5	5	10	12	25	60
429	Calvin Hill	4	4	5	5	10	12	25	
430	Isiah Robertson	4	4	5	5	10	12	25	60
431	Tony Greene	4	4	5	5	10	12	25	
432	Bob Johnson	4	4	5	5	10	12	25	
433	Lem Barney	4	4	5	5	10	12	25	80

#	Player	VgEx 4	EX 5	ExMt 6	NM 7	NmMt 8	NmMt+ 8.5	MT 9	Gem 9.5/
434	Eric Torkelson	4	4	5	5	10	12	25	
435	John Mendenhall	4	4	5	5	10	12	25	
436	Larry Seiple	4	4	5	5	10	12	25	
437	Art Kuehn	4	4	5	5	10	12	60	
438	John Vella	4	4	5	5	10	12	25	
439	Greg Latta	4	4	5	5	10	12	25	100
440	Roger Carr	4	4	5	5	10	12	25	
441	Doug Sutherland	4	4	5	5	10	12	25	80
442	Mike Kruczek RC	4	4	5	5	10	12	25	60
443	Steve Zabel	4	4	5	5	10	12	25	
444	Mike Pruitt RC	4	4	5	5	10	12	25	
445	Harold Jackson	4	4	5	5	10	12	25	
446	George Jakowenko	4	4	5	5	10	12	25	
447	John Fitzgerald	4	4	5	5	10	12	60	
448	Carey Joyce	4	4	5	5	10	12	25	
449	Jim LeClair	4	4	5	5	10	12	25	
450	Ken Houston	4	4	5	5	10	12	50	
451	Steve Grogan RB	4	4	5	5	10	12	25	50
452	Jim Marshall RB	4	4	5	5	10	12	25	
453	O.J.Simpson RB	4	4	5	5	10	12	30	100
454	Fran Tarkenton RB	4	4	5	5	10	12	30	
455	Jim Zorn RB	4	4	5	5	10	12	25	50
456	Robert Pratt	4	4	5	5	10	12	25	50
457	Walker Gillette	4	4	5	5	10	12	25	60
458	Charlie Hall	4	4	5	5	10	12	25	
459	Robert Newhouse	4	4	5	5	10	12	25	
460	John Hannah	4	4	5	5	10	12	25	
461	Ken Reaves	4	4	5	5	10	12	25	
462	Herman Weaver	4	4	5	5	10	12	25	50
463	James Harris	4	4	5	5	10	12	25	80
464	Howard Twilley	4	4	5	5	10	12	30	
465	Jeff Siemon	4	4	5	5	10	12	25	80
466	John Outlaw	4	4	5	5	10	12	25	
467	Chuck Muncie RC	4	4	5	5	12	15	40	
468	Bob Moore	4	4	5	5	10	12	25	80
469	Robert Woods	4	4	5	5	10	12	25	
470	Cliff Branch	4	4	5	5	10	12	25	100
471	Johnnie Gray	4	4	5	5	10	12	25	50
472	Don Hardeman	4	4	5	5	10	12	25	50
473	Steve Ramsey	4	4	5	5	10	12	25	50
474	Steve Mike-Mayer	4	4	5	5	10	12	25	
475	Gary Garrison	4	4	5	5	10	12	25	
476	Walter Johnson	4	4	5	5	10	12	25	50
477	Neil Clabo	4	4	5	5	8	12	25	
478	Len Hauss	4	4	5	5	10	12	25	
479	Darryl Stingley	4	4	5	5	10	12	30	
480	Jack Lambert	4	4	5	10	20	25	▼150	
481	Mike Adamle	4	4	5	5	10	12	25	50
482	David Lee	4	4	5	5	10	12	25	
483	Tom Mullen	4	4	5	5	10	12	25	60
484	Claude Humphrey	4	4	5	5	10	12	25	
485	Jim Hart	4	4	5	5	10	12	25	
486	Bobby Thompson RB	4	4	5	5	10	12	25	
487	Jack Rudnay	4	4	5	5	10	12	25	
488	Rich Sowells	4	4	5	5	10	12	25	
489	Reuben Gant	4	4	5	5	10	12	25	
490	Cliff Harris	4	4	5	5	10	12	25	
491	Bob Brown DT	4	4	5	5	10	12	25	
492	Don Nottingham	4	4	5	5	10	12	25	
493	Ron Jessie	4	4	5	5	10	12	25	
494	Otis Sistrunk	4	4	5	5	10	12	25	60
495	Billy Kilmer	4	4	5	5	10	12	25	
496	Oscar Roan	4	4	5	5	10	12	25	
497	Bill Van Heusen	4	4	5	5	10	12	25	
498	Randy Logan	4	4	5	5	10	12	25	
499	John Smith	4	4	5	5	10	12	25	
500	Chuck Foreman	4	4	5	5	10	12	50	
501	J.T. Thomas	4	4	5	5	10	12	25	
502	Steve Schubert	4	4	5	5	10	12	25	
503	Mike Barnes	4	4	5	5	10	12	25	
504	J.V. Cain	4	4	5	5	10	12	25	
505	Larry Csonka	4	4	5	5	10	12	30	135
506	Elvin Bethea	4	4	5	5	10	12	25	
507	Ray Easterling	4	4	5	5	10	12	25	
508	Joe Reed	4	4	5	5	10	12	25	
509	Steve Odom	4	4	5	5	10	12	25	
510	Tommy Casanova	4	4	5	5	10	12	25	
511	Dave Dalby	4	4	5	5	10	12	25	
512	Richard Caster	4	4	5	5	10	12	25	

	VgEx 4	EX 5	ExMt 6	NM 7	NmMt 8	NmMt+ 8.5	MT 9	Gem 9.5/10
Fred Dryer	4	4	5	5	10	12	40	
Jeff Kinney	4	4	5	5	10	12	25	
Bob Griese	4	4	5	5	10	12	40	
Butch Johnson RC	4	4	5	5	10	12	40	
Gerald Irons	4	4	5	5	10	12	25	
Don Calhoun	4	4	5	5	10	12	25	
Jack Gregory	4	4	5	5	10	12	25	
Tom Banks	4	4	5	5	10	12	25	
Bobby Bryant	4	4	5	5	10	12	25	
Reggie Harrison	4	4	5	5	10	12	25	
Terry Hermeling	4	4	5	5	10	12	25	
David Taylor	4	4	5	5	10	12	25	60
Brian Baschnagel RC	4	4	5	5	10	12	25	
AFC Champ/Stabler	4	4	5	5	10	12	25	120
NFC Championship	4	4	5	5	10	12	35	80
Super Bowl XI	4	4	5	5	12	20	50	

Dave Casper #380 PSA 10 (Gem) sold for $4,275 (eBay; 10/07)
Joe Greene #405 PSA 10 (Gem) sold for $300 (eBay; 1/08)
John Hannah #460 PSA 10 (Gem Mint) sold for $421.26 (Goodwin; 3/12)
Walter Payton #360 PSA 10 (Gem) sold for $4,600 (eBay; 8/08)
Walter Payton #360 PSA 10 (Gem) sold for $5,661 (eBay; 12/13)
Walter Payton #360 PSA 10 (Gem Mint) sold for $4110 (Bussineau; 6/12)
Lee Roy Selmon #29 PSA 10 (Gem) sold for $1,186 (eBay; 2/13)
Lee Roy Selmon #29 PSA 10 (Gem Mint) sold for $4,059 (eBay; 09/14)
Mike Webster #99 PSA 10 (Gem) sold for $504 (eBay; 6/08)

1978 Topps

	VgEx 4	EX 5	ExMt 6	NM 7	NmMt 8	NmMt+ 8.5	MT 9	Gem 9.5/10
Gary Huff HL	4	4	5	5	8	10	25	50
Craig Morton HL	4	4	5	5	8	10	15	50
Walter Payton HL	4	4	5	8	15	20	40	200
O.J.Simpson HL	4	4	5	5	8	10	20	60
Fran Tarkenton HL	4	4	5	5	8	10	20	80
Bob Thomas HL	4	4	5	5	8	10	20	
Joe Pisarcik	4	4	5	5	8	10	20	
Skip Thomas	4	4	5	5	8	10	25	
Roosevelt Leaks	4	4	5	5	8	10	20	
Ken Houston	4	4	5	5	8	10	20	
Tom Blanchard	4	4	5	5	8	10	20	
Jim Turner	4	4	5	5	8	10	20	40
Tom DeLeone	4	4	5	5	8	10	20	
Jim LeClair	4	4	5	5	8	10	20	40
Bob Avellini	4	4	5	5	8	10	20	
Tony McGee DT	4	4	5	5	8	10	20	50
James Harris	4	4	5	5	8	10	20	
Terry Nelson	4	4	5	5	8	10	20	
Rocky Bleier	4	4	5	5	8	10	20	
Joe DeLamielleure	4	4	5	5	8	10	20	
Richard Caster	4	4	5	5	8	10	20	
A.J.Duhe RC	4	4	5	5	8	10	20	
John Outlaw	4	4	5	5	8	10	20	50
Danny White	4	4	5	5	8	10	20	80
Larry Csonka	4	4	5	6	10	12	25	
David Hill RC	4	4	5	5	8	10	20	
Mark Arneson	4	4	5	5	8	10	20	50
Jack Tatum	4	4	5	5	8	10	20	
Norm Thompson	4	4	5	5	8	10	20	50
Sammie White	4	4	5	5	8	10	20	50
Dennis Johnson	4	4	5	5	8	10	20	
Robin Earl	4	4	5	5	8	10	20	40
Don Cockroft	4	4	5	5	8	10	20	50
Bob Johnson	4	4	5	5	8	10	20	50
John Hannah	4	4	5	5	8	10	20	
Scott Hunter	4	5	6	15	30	40	50	
Ken Burrough	4	4	5	5	8	10	20	
Wilbur Jackson	4	4	5	5	8	10	20	50
Rich McGeorge	4	4	5	5	8	10	20	60
Lyle Alzado	4	4	5	5	8	10	15	60
John Ebersole	4	4	5	5	8	10	20	50
Gary Green RC	4	4	5	5	8	10	20	
Art Kuehn	4	4	5	5	8	10	20	40
Glen Edwards	4	4	5	5	8	10	20	40
Lawrence McCutcheon	4	4	5	5	8	10	20	50
Duriel Harris	4	4	5	5	8	10	20	
Rich Szaro	4	4	5	5	8	10	20	50
Mike Washington	4	4	5	5	8	10	20	
Stan White	4	4	5	5	8	10	20	50
Dave Casper	4	4	5	5	8	10	20	

		VgEx 4	EX 5	ExMt 6	NM 7	NmMt 8	NmMt+ 8.5	MT 9	Gem 9.5/10
51	Len Hauss	4	4	5	5	8	10	20	
52	James Scott	4	4	5	5	8	10	20	50
53	Brian Sipe	4	4	5	5	8	10	20	50
54	Gary Shirk	4	4	5	5	8	10	20	50
55	Archie Griffin	4	4	5	5	8	10	15	60
56	Mike Patrick	4	4	5	5	8	10	20	50
57	Mario Clark	4	4	5	5	8	10	20	50
58	Jeff Siemon	4	4	5	5	8	10	20	50
59	Steve Mike-Mayer	4	4	5	5	8	10	20	50
60	Randy White	4	4	5	8	12	15	25	175
61	Darrell Austin	4	4	5	5	8	10	20	50
62	Tom Sullivan	4	4	5	5	8	10	20	40
63	Johnny Rodgers RC	4	4	5	5	15	20	30	
64	Ken Reaves	4	4	5	5	8	10	20	
65	Terry Bradshaw	4	5	6	10	15	20	60	
66	Fred Steinfort	4	4	5	5	8	10	20	50
67	Curley Culp	4	4	5	5	8	10	20	50
68	Ted Hendricks	4	4	5	5	8	10	25	
69	Raymond Chester	4	4	5	5	8	10	20	50
70	Jim Langer	4	4	5	5	8	10	20	50
71	Calvin Hill	4	4	5	5	8	10	20	
72	Mike Hartenstine	4	4	5	5	8	10	20	40
73	Gerald Irons	4	4	5	5	8	10	50	
74	Billy Brooks	4	4	5	5	8	10	20	
75	John Mendenhall	4	4	5	5	8	10	20	50
76	Andy Johnson	4	4	5	5	8	10	20	50
77	Tom Wittum	4	4	5	5	8	10	20	
78	Lynn Dickey	4	4	5	5	8	10	20	60
79	Carl Eller	4	4	5	5	8	10	20	
80	Tom Mack	4	4	5	5	8	10	20	50
81	Clark Gaines	4	4	5	5	8	10	20	50
82	Lem Barney	4	4	5	5	8	10	20	50
83	Mike Montler	4	4	5	5	8	10	20	
84	Jon Kolb	4	4	5	5	8	10	30	
85	Bob Chandler	4	4	5	5	8	10	20	
86	Robert Newhouse	4	4	5	5	8	10	25	
87	Frank LeMaster	4	4	5	5	8	10	25	50
88	Jeff West	4	4	5	5	8	10	20	50
89	Lyle Blackwood	4	4	5	5	8	10	20	
90	Gene Upshaw	4	4	5	5	8	10	40	
91	Frank Grant	4	4	5	5	8	10	20	50
92	Tom Hicks	4	4	5	5	8	10	20	50
93	Mike Pruitt	4	4	5	5	8	10	20	80
94	Chris Bahr	4	4	5	5	8	10	20	50
95	Russ Francis	4	4	5	5	8	10	20	
96	Norris Thomas	4	4	5	5	8	10	20	50
97	Gary Barbaro RC	4	4	5	5	8	10	20	
98	Jim Merlo	4	4	5	5	8	10	20	50
99	Karl Chandler	4	4	5	5	8	10	20	
100	Fran Tarkenton	4	4	5	8	12	15	30	
101	Abdul Salaam	4	4	5	5	8	10	20	50
102	Marv Kellum	4	4	5	5	8	10	20	50
103	Herman Weaver	4	4	5	5	8	10	20	
104	Roy Gerela	4	4	5	5	8	10	20	40
105	Harold Jackson	4	4	5	5	8	10	20	40
106	Dewey Selmon	4	4	5	5	8	10	20	40
107	Checklist 1-132	4	4	5	5	8	10	20	
108	Clarence Davis	4	4	5	5	8	10	20	
109	Robert Pratt	4	4	5	5	8	10	20	50
110	Harvey Martin	4	4	5	5	8	10	20	50
111	Brad Dusek	4	4	5	5	8	10	20	50
112	Greg Latta	4	4	5	5	8	10	20	50
113	Tony Peters	4	4	5	5	8	10	20	50
114	Jim Braxton	4	4	5	5	8	10	20	50
115	Ken Riley	4	4	5	5	8	10	20	
116	Steve Nelson	4	4	5	5	8	10	25	50
117	Rick Upchurch	4	4	5	5	8	10	20	60
118	Spike Jones	4	4	5	5	8	10	20	50
119	Doug Kotar	4	4	5	5	8	10	20	60
120	Bob Griese	4	4	5	6	10	12	20	150
121	Burgess Owens	4	4	5	5	8	10	20	
122	Rolf Benirschke RC	4	4	5	5	8	10	20	
123	Haskel Stanback RC	4	4	5	5	8	10	20	
124	J.T. Thomas	4	4	5	5	8	10	20	60
125	Ahmad Rashad	4	4	5	5	8	10	20	50
126	Rick Kane	4	4	5	5	8	10	20	
127	Elvin Bethea	4	4	5	5	8	10	20	
128	Dave Dalby	4	4	5	5	8	10	20	
129	Mike Barnes	4	4	5	5	8	10	20	

#	Player	VgEx 4	EX 5	ExMt 6	NM 7	NmMt 8	NmMt+ 8.5	MT 9	Gem 9.5/10
130	Isiah Robertson	4	4	5	5	8	10	20	50
131	Jim Plunkett	4	4	5	5	8	10	20	
132	Allan Ellis	4	4	5	5	8	10	20	40
133	Mike Bragg	4	4	5	5	8	10	20	
134	Bob Jackson	4	4	5	5	8	10	20	50
135	Coy Bacon	4	4	5	5	8	10	20	50
136	John Smith	4	4	5	5	8	10	20	50
137	Chuck Muncie	4	4	5	5	8	10	20	
138	Johnnie Gray	4	4	5	5	8	10	20	50
139	Jimmy Robinson	4	4	5	5	8	10	20	50
140	Tom Banks	4	4	5	5	8	10	20	
141	Marvin Powell RC	4	4	5	5	8	10	20	40
142	Jerrel Wilson	4	4	5	5	8	10	20	
143	Ron Howard	4	4	5	5	8	10	20	
144	Rob Lytle RC	4	4	5	5	8	10	20	50
145	L.C.Greenwood	4	4	5	5	10	12	25	50
146	Morris Owens	4	4	5	5	8	10	20	50
147	Joe Reed	4	4	5	5	8	10	20	
148	Mike Kadish	4	4	5	5	8	10	20	50
149	Phil Villapiano	4	4	5	5	8	10	20	100
150	Lydell Mitchell	4	4	5	5	8	10	20	50
151	Randy Logan	4	4	5	5	8	10	20	60
152	Mike Williams RC	4	4	5	5	8	10	20	
153	Jeff Van Note	4	4	5	5	8	10	20	50
154	Steve Schubert	4	4	5	5	8	10	20	50
155	Billy Kilmer	4	4	5	5	8	10	20	60
156	Boobie Clark	4	4	5	5	8	10	20	
157	Charlie Hall	4	4	5	5	8	10	20	
158	Raymond Clayborn RC	4	4	5	5	8	10	20	
159	Jack Gregory	4	4	5	5	8	10	20	50
160	Cliff Harris	4	4	5	5	8	10	20	50
161	Joe Fields	4	4	5	5	8	10	20	50
162	Don Nottingham	4	4	5	5	8	10	20	
163	Ed White	4	4	5	5	8	10	20	50
164	Toni Fritsch	4	4	5	5	8	10	20	50
165	Jack Lambert	4	4	5	10	12	15	25	150
166	NFC Champs/Staubach	4	4	5	5	8	10	25	
167	AFC Champs/Lytle	4	4	5	5	8	10	50	
168	Super Bowl XII/Dorsett	4	4	5	8	10	12	30	
169	Neal Colzie RC	4	4	5	5	8	10	20	
170	Cleveland Elam	4	4	5	5	8	10	20	
171	David Lee	4	4	5	5	8	10	20	50
172	Jim Otis	4	4	5	5	8	10	20	
173	Archie Manning	4	4	5	5	8	10	20	60
174	Jim Carter	4	4	5	5	8	10	20	50
175	Jean Fugett	4	4	5	5	8	10	20	
176	Willie Parker C	4	4	5	5	8	10	20	50
177	Haven Moses	4	4	5	5	8	10	20	50
178	Horace King RC	4	4	5	5	8	10	20	50
179	Bob Thomas	4	4	5	5	8	10	20	
180	Monte Jackson	4	4	5	5	8	10	20	50
181	Steve Zabel	4	4	5	5	8	10	20	
182	John Fitzgerald	4	4	5	5	8	10	20	
183	Mike Livingston	4	4	5	5	8	10	20	50
184	Larry Poole	4	4	5	5	8	10	20	50
185	Isaac Curtis	4	4	5	5	8	10	20	
186	Chuck Ramsey	4	4	5	5	8	10	20	50
187	Bob Klein	4	4	5	5	8	10	20	50
188	Ray Rhodes	4	4	5	5	8	10	20	
189	Otis Sistrunk	4	4	5	5	8	10	20	
190	Bill Bergey	4	4	5	5	8	10	20	
191	Sherman Smith	4	4	5	5	8	10	20	
192	Dave Green	4	4	5	5	8	10	20	
193	Carl Mauck	4	4	5	5	8	10	20	50
194	Reggie Harrison	4	4	5	5	8	10	20	
195	Roger Carr	4	4	5	5	8	10	20	50
196	Steve Bartkowski	4	4	5	5	8	10	20	
197	Ray Wersching	4	4	5	5	8	10	20	60
198	Willie Buchanon	4	4	5	5	8	10	20	
199	Neil Clabo	4	4	5	5	8	10	20	
200	Walter Payton	5	6	12	20	40	50	150	800
201	Sam Adams OL	4	4	5	5	8	10	20	50
202	Larry Gordon	4	4	5	5	8	10	20	50
203	Pat Tilley	4	4	5	5	8	10	20	50
204	Mack Mitchell	4	4	5	5	8	10	20	
205	Ken Anderson	4	4	5	5	8	10	30	
206	Scott Dierking	4	4	5	5	8	10	20	50
207	Jack Rudnay	4	4	5	5	8	10	20	
208	Jim Stienke	4	4	5	5	8	10	20	

#	Player	VgEx 4	EX 5	ExMt 6	NM 7	NmMt 8	NmMt+ 8.5	MT 9	Gem 9.5
209	Bill Simpson	4	4	5	5	8	10	20	50
210	Errol Mann	4	4	5	5	8	10	20	80
211	Bucky Dilts	4	4	5	5	8	10	20	50
212	Reuben Gant	4	4	5	5	8	10	20	50
213	Thomas Henderson RC	4	4	5	5	8	10	20	
214	Steve Furness	4	4	5	5	8	10	100	
215	John Riggins	4	4	5	5	8	10	20	
216	Keith Krepfle RC	4	4	5	5	8	10	20	60
217	Fred Dean RC	4	5	6	10	25	40	100	1,500
218	Emanuel Zanders	4	4	5	5	8	10	20	50
219	Don Testerman	4	4	5	5	8	10	20	60
220	George Kunz	4	4	5	5	8	10	20	
221	Darryl Stingley	4	4	5	5	8	10	20	
222	Ken Sanders	4	4	5	5	8	10	20	50
223	Gary Huff	4	4	5	5	8	10	20	40
224	Gregg Bingham	4	4	5	5	8	10	20	
225	Jerry Sherk	4	4	5	5	8	10	20	50
226	Doug Plank	4	4	5	5	8	10	20	40
227	Ed Taylor	4	4	5	5	8	10	20	
228	Emery Moorehead	4	4	5	5	8	10	20	
229	Reggie Williams RC	4	4	5	5	8	10	20	60
230	Claude Humphrey	4	4	5	5	8	10	20	
231	Randy Cross RC	4	4	5	5	10	12	25	
232	Jim Hart	4	4	5	5	8	10	20	50
233	Bobby Bryant	4	4	5	5	8	10	20	
234	Larry Brown	4	4	5	5	8	10	20	40
235	Mark Van Eeghen	4	4	5	5	8	10	20	
236	Terry Hermeling	4	4	5	5	8	10	20	
237	Steve Odom	4	4	5	5	8	10	20	
238	Jan Stenerud	4	4	5	5	8	10	20	
239	Andre Tillman	4	4	5	5	8	10	20	50
240	Tom Jackson RC	4	4	5	8	12	15	30	150
241	Ken Mendenhall	4	4	5	5	8	10	20	
242	Tim Fox	4	4	5	5	8	10	20	60
243	Don Herrmann	4	4	5	5	8	10	20	
244	Eddie McMillan	4	4	5	5	8	10	20	50
245	Greg Pruitt	4	4	5	5	8	10	20	50
246	J.K. McKay	4	4	5	5	8	10	20	40
247	Larry Keller	4	4	5	5	8	10	20	
248	Dave Jennings	4	4	5	5	8	10	20	40
249	Bo Harris	4	4	5	5	8	10	20	40
250	Revie Sorey	4	4	5	5	8	10	20	50
251	Tony Greene	4	4	5	5	8	10	20	50
252	Butch Johnson	4	4	5	5	8	10	20	
253	Paul Naumoff	4	4	5	5	8	10	20	50
254	Rickey Young	4	4	5	5	8	10	20	50
255	Dwight White	4	4	5	5	8	10	20	
256	Joe Lavender	4	4	5	5	8	10	20	
257	Checklist 133-264	4	4	5	5	8	10	20	
258	Ronnie Coleman	4	4	5	5	8	10	20	50
259	Charlie Smith WR	4	4	5	5	8	10	20	40
260	Ray Guy	4	4	5	5	8	10	20	
261	David Taylor	4	4	5	5	8	10	20	50
262	Bill Lenkaitis	4	4	5	5	8	10	20	50
263	Jim Mitchell TE	4	4	5	5	8	10	20	50
264	Delvin Williams	4	4	5	5	8	10	20	40
265	Jack Youngblood	4	4	5	5	8	10	20	
266	Chuck Crist	4	4	5	5	8	10	20	
267	Richard Todd	4	4	5	5	8	10	20	
268	Dave Logan RC	4	4	5	5	8	10	20	50
269	Rufus Mayes	4	4	5	5	8	10	20	
270	Brad Van Pelt	4	4	5	5	8	10	20	40
271	Chester Marcol	4	4	5	5	8	10	20	40
272	J.V. Cain	4	4	5	5	8	10	20	40
273	Larry Seiple	4	4	5	5	8	10	20	
274	Brent McClanahan	4	4	5	5	8	10	20	
275	Mike Wagner	4	4	5	5	8	10	30	80
276	Diron Talbert	4	4	5	5	8	10	20	
277	Brian Baschnagel	4	4	5	5	8	10	20	40
278	Ed Podolak	4	4	5	5	8	10	20	50
279	Don Goode	4	4	5	5	8	10	20	40
280	John Dutton	4	4	5	5	8	10	20	40
281	Don Calhoun	4	4	5	5	8	10	20	
282	Monte Johnson	4	4	5	5	8	10	20	
283	Ron Jessie	4	4	5	5	8	10	20	
284	Jon Morris	4	4	5	5	8	10	20	50
285	Riley Odoms	4	4	5	5	8	10	20	50
286	Marv Bateman	4	4	5	5	8	10	20	50
287	Joe Klecko RC	4	4	5	5	8	10	25	

Name	VgEx 4	EX 5	ExMt 6	NM 7	NmMt 8	NmMt+ 8.5	MT 9	Gem 9.5/10
Oliver Davis	4	4	5	5	8	10	20	
John McDaniel	4	4	5	5	8	10	20	
Roger Staubach	4	5	6	20	25	30	60	
Brian Kelley	4	4	5	5	8	10	20	
Mike Hogan	4	4	5	5	8	10	20	
John Leypoldt	4	4	5	5	8	10	20	
Jack Novak	4	4	5	5	8	10	20	
Joe Greene	4	4	5	5	10	12	30	
John Hill	4	4	5	5	8	10	20	50
Danny Buggs	4	4	5	5	8	10	20	50
Ted Albrecht	4	4	5	5	8	10	20	40
Nelson Munsey	4	4	5	5	8	10	20	
Chuck Foreman	4	4	5	5	8	10	20	60
Dan Pastorini	4	4	5	5	8	10	20	50
Tommy Hart	4	4	5	5	8	10	20	40
Dave Beverly	4	4	5	5	8	10	20	60
Tony Reed RC	4	4	5	5	8	10	20	
Cliff Branch	4	4	5	5	8	10	20	
Clarence Duren	4	4	5	5	8	10	20	40
Randy Rasmussen	4	4	5	5	8	10	20	
Oscar Roan	4	4	5	5	8	10	20	60
Lenvil Elliott	4	4	5	5	8	10	20	50
Dan Dierdorf	4	4	5	5	8	10	20	
Johnny Perkins	4	4	5	5	8	10	20	
Rafael Septien RC	4	4	5	5	8	10	20	50
Terry Beeson	4	4	5	5	8	10	20	50
Lee Roy Selmon	4	4	5	5	8	10	20	
Tony Dorsett RC	10	12	25	35	80	100	500	
Greg Landry	4	4	5	5	8	10	20	50
Jake Scott	4	4	5	5	8	10	20	40
Dan Peiffer	4	4	5	5	8	10	20	
John Bunting	4	4	5	5	8	10	20	
John Stallworth RC	5	6	8	12	30	40	80	1,000
Bob Howard	4	4	5	5	8	10	20	40
Larry Little	4	4	5	5	8	10	20	50
Reggie McKenzie	4	4	5	5	8	10	20	
Duane Carrell	4	4	5	5	8	10	20	
Ed Simonini	4	4	5	5	8	10	20	
John Vella	4	4	5	5	8	10	20	
Wesley Walker RC	4	4	5	6	10	12	25	200
Jon Keyworth	4	4	5	5	8	10	20	40
Ron Bolton	4	4	5	5	8	10	20	40
Tommy Casanova	4	4	5	5	8	10	20	
R.Staubach/B.Griese LL	4	4	5	8	12	15	30	
A.Rashad/Mitchell LL	4	4	5	5	8	10	30	
W.Payton/VanEeghenLL	4	4	5	6	10	12	50	
W.Payton/E.Mann LL	4	4	5	6	10	12	40	
Interception Leaders	4	4	5	5	8	10	20	
Punting Leaders	4	4	5	5	8	10	30	
Robert Brazile	4	4	5	5	8	10	20	50
Charlie Joiner	4	4	5	5	8	10	20	
Joe Ferguson	4	4	5	5	8	10	20	40
Bill Thompson	4	4	5	5	8	10	20	40
Sam Cunningham	4	4	5	5	8	10	20	50
Curtis Johnson	4	4	5	5	8	10	20	
Jim Marshall	4	4	5	5	8	10	20	100
Charlie Sanders	4	4	5	5	8	10	20	40
Willie Hall	4	4	5	5	8	10	20	
Pat Haden	4	4	5	5	8	10	20	100
Jim Bakken	4	4	5	5	8	10	20	40
Bruce Taylor	4	4	5	5	8	10	20	
Barty Smith	4	4	5	5	8	10	20	50
Drew Pearson	4	4	5	5	8	10	20	
Mike Webster	4	4	5	6	10	12	25	
Bobby Hammond	4	4	5	5	8	10	20	100
Dave Mays	4	4	5	5	8	10	20	40
Pat McInally	4	4	5	5	8	10	20	
Toni Linhart	4	4	5	5	8	10	20	
Larry Hand	4	4	5	5	8	10	20	50
Ted Fritsch Jr.	4	4	5	5	8	10	20	
Larry Marshall	4	4	5	5	8	10	20	50
Waymond Bryant	4	4	5	5	8	10	20	50
Louie Kelcher RC	4	4	5	5	8	10	20	
Stanley Morgan RC	4	4	5	5	8	12	30	200
Bruce Harper RC	4	4	5	5	8	10	20	50
Bernard Jackson	4	4	5	5	8	10	20	40
Walter White	4	4	5	5	8	10	20	50
Ken Stabler	4	4	5	5	8	12	15	25	150
Fred Dryer	4	4	5	5	8	10	20	50
367 Ike Harris	4	4	5	5	8	10	20	40
368 Norm Bulaich	4	4	5	5	8	10	20	
369 Merv Krakau	4	4	5	5	8	10	20	
370 John James	4	4	5	5	8	10	20	
371 Bennie Cunningham RC	4	4	5	5	8	10	20	
372 Doug Van Horn	4	4	5	5	8	10	20	40
373 Thom Darden	4	4	5	5	8	10	20	40
374 Eddie Edwards RC	4	4	5	5	8	10	20	
375 Mike Thomas	4	4	5	5	8	10	20	
376 Fred Cook	4	4	5	5	8	10	20	50
377 Mike Phipps	4	4	5	5	8	10	20	
378 Paul Krause	4	4	5	5	8	10	20	60
379 Harold Carmichael	4	4	5	5	8	10	20	60
380 Mike Haynes	4	4	5	5	8	10	20	
381 Wayne Morris	4	4	5	5	8	10	20	
382 Greg Buttle	4	4	5	5	8	10	20	50
383 Jim Zorn	4	4	5	5	8	10	20	50
384 Jack Dolbin	4	4	5	5	8	10	20	40
385 Charlie Waters	4	4	5	5	8	10	20	50
386 Dan Ryczek	4	4	5	5	8	10	20	40
387 Joe Washington RC	4	4	5	5	8	10	20	50
388 Checklist 265-396	4	4	5	5	8	10	25	40
389 James Hunter	4	4	5	5	8	10	20	40
390 Billy Johnson	4	4	5	5	8	10	20	40
391 Jim Allen RC	4	4	5	5	8	10	20	
392 George Buehler	4	4	5	5	8	10	20	
393 Harry Carson	4	4	5	5	8	10	20	60
394 Cleo Miller	4	4	5	5	8	10	20	40
395 Gary Burley	4	4	5	5	8	10	20	
396 Mark Moseley	4	4	5	5	8	10	20	
397 Virgil Livers	4	4	5	5	8	10	20	40
398 Joe Ehrmann	4	4	5	5	8	10	20	40
399 Freddie Solomon	4	4	5	5	8	10	20	
400 O.J.Simpson	4	4	5	8	12	15	25	
401 Julius Adams	4	4	5	5	8	10	20	40
402 Artimus Parker	4	4	5	5	8	10	20	40
403 Gene Washington 49er	4	4	5	5	8	10	20	
404 Herman Edwards	4	4	5	5	8	10	20	80
405 Craig Morton	4	4	5	5	8	10	20	60
406 Alan Page	4	4	5	5	8	10	20	50
407 Larry McCarren	4	4	5	5	8	10	20	
408 Tony Galbreath	4	4	5	5	8	10	20	40
409 Roman Gabriel	4	4	5	5	8	10	20	60
410 Efren Herrera	4	4	5	5	8	10	30	60
411 Jim Smith RC	4	4	5	5	8	10	20	50
412 Bill Bryant	4	4	5	5	8	10	20	
413 Doug Dieken	4	4	5	5	8	10	20	50
414 Marvin Cobb	4	4	5	5	8	10	20	40
415 Fred Biletnikoff	4	4	5	5	8	10	20	
416 Joe Theismann	4	4	5	6	10	12	20	80
417 Roland Harper	4	4	5	5	8	10	20	50
418 Derrel Luce	4	4	5	5	8	10	20	50
419 Ralph Perretta	4	4	5	5	8	10	20	40
420 Louis Wright RC	4	4	5	5	8	10	20	
421 Prentice McCray	4	4	5	5	8	10	20	40
422 Garry Puetz	4	4	5	5	8	10	20	40
423 Alfred Jenkins RC	4	4	5	5	8	10	20	
424 Paul Seymour	4	4	5	5	8	10	20	50
425 Garo Yepremian	4	4	5	5	8	10	20	50
426 Emmitt Thomas	4	4	5	5	8	10	15	50
427 Dexter Bussey	4	4	5	5	8	10	20	40
428 John Sanders	4	4	5	5	8	10	20	40
429 Ed Too Tall Jones	4	4	5	5	8	10	40	
430 Ron Yary	4	4	5	5	8	10	20	60
431 Frank Lewis	4	4	5	5	8	10	20	
432 Jerry Golsteyn	4	4	5	5	8	10	20	
433 Clarence Scott	4	4	5	5	8	10	20	60
434 Pete Johnson RC	4	4	5	5	8	10	20	80
435 Charle Young	4	4	5	5	8	10	20	40
436 Harold McLinton	4	4	5	5	8	10	20	
437 Noah Jackson	4	4	5	5	8	10	20	40
438 Bruce Laird	4	4	5	5	8	10	20	40
439 John Matuszak	4	4	5	5	8	10	20	50
440 Nat Moore	4	4	5	5	8	10	20	125
441 Leon Gray	4	4	5	5	8	10	20	100
442 Jerome Barkum	4	4	5	5	8	10	20	
443 Steve Largent	4	5	6	10	15	20	40	300
444 John Zook	4	4	5	5	8	10	20	60
445 Preston Pearson	4	4	5	5	8	10	20	50

#	Player	VgEx 4	EX 5	ExMt 6	NM 7	NmMt 8	NmMt+ 8.5	MT 9	Gem 9.5/10
446	Conrad Dobler	4	4	5	5	8	10	20	40
447	Wilbur Summers	4	4	5	5	8	10	20	40
448	Lou Piccone	4	4	5	5	8	10	20	50
449	Ron Jaworski	4	4	5	5	8	10	20	60
450	Jack Ham	4	4	5	5	8	10	25	80
451	Mick Tingelhoff	4	4	5	5	8	10	20	
452	Clyde Powers	4	4	5	5	8	10	20	
453	John Cappelletti	4	4	5	5	8	10	20	40
454	Dick Ambrose	4	4	5	5	8	10	20	
455	Lemar Parrish	4	4	5	5	8	10	20	50
456	Ron Saul	4	4	5	5	8	10	20	
457	Bob Parsons	4	4	5	5	8	10	20	50
458	Glenn Doughty	4	4	5	5	8	10	20	
459	Don Woods	4	4	5	5	8	10	20	50
460	Art Shell	4	4	5	5	8	10	25	
461	Sam Hunt	4	4	5	5	8	10	20	
462	Lawrence Pillers	4	4	5	5	8	10	20	
463	Henry Childs	4	4	5	5	8	10	20	40
464	Roger Wehrli	4	4	5	5	8	10	30	
465	Otis Armstrong	4	4	5	5	8	10	20	80
466	Bob Baumhower RC	4	4	5	5	12	15	25	
467	Ray Jarvis	4	4	5	5	8	10	20	40
468	Guy Morriss	4	4	5	5	8	10	20	40
469	Matt Blair	4	4	5	5	8	10	20	50
470	Billy Joe DuPree	4	4	5	5	8	10	20	
471	Roland Hooks	4	4	5	5	8	10	20	40
472	Joe Danelo	4	4	5	5	8	10	20	
473	Reggie Rucker	4	4	5	5	8	10	20	
474	Vern Holland	4	4	5	5	8	10	20	50
475	Mel Blount	4	4	5	5	8	10	25	
476	Eddie Brown S	4	4	5	5	8	10	20	
477	Bo Rather	4	4	5	5	8	10	20	
478	Don McCauley	4	4	5	5	8	10	20	40
479	Glen Walker	4	4	5	5	8	10	20	40
480	Randy Gradishar	4	4	5	5	8	10	20	50
481	Dave Rowe	4	4	5	5	8	10	20	
482	Pat Leahy	4	4	5	5	8	10	20	50
483	Mike Fuller	4	4	5	5	8	10	20	40
484	David Lewis RC	4	4	5	5	8	10	20	
485	Steve Grogan	4	4	5	5	8	10	20	50
486	Mel Gray	4	4	5	5	8	10	20	
487	Eddie Payton RC	4	4	5	5	8	10	20	
488	Checklist 397-528	4	4	5	5	8	10	20	60
489	Stu Voigt	4	4	5	5	8	10	20	50
490	Rolland Lawrence	4	4	5	5	8	10	20	100
491	Nick Mike-Mayer	4	4	5	5	8	10	20	
492	Troy Archer	4	4	5	5	8	10	20	50
493	Benny Malone	4	4	5	5	8	10	20	40
494	Golden Richards	4	4	5	5	8	12	80	
495	Chris Hanburger	4	4	5	5	8	10	20	80
496	Dwight Harrison	4	4	5	5	8	10	20	
497	Gary Fencik RC	4	4	5	5	8	10	20	80
498	Rich Saul	4	4	5	5	8	10	20	50
499	Dan Fouts	4	4	5	8	12	15	25	
500	Franco Harris	4	4	5	8	12	15	25	150
501	Atlanta Falcons TL	4	4	5	5	8	10	20	40
502	Baltimore Colts TL	4	4	5	5	8	10	20	
503	Bills TL/O.J.Simpson	4	4	5	5	8	10	25	
504	Bears TL/W.Payton	4	4	5	5	8	10	40	
505	Bengals TL/Reg.Williams	4	4	5	5	8	10	25	
506	Cleveland Browns TL	4	4	5	5	8	10	25	
507	Cowboys TL/T.Dorsett	4	4	5	6	10	12	25	
508	Denver Broncos TL	4	4	5	5	8	10	20	
509	Detroit Lions TL	4	4	5	5	8	10	20	
510	Green Bay Packers TL	4	4	5	5	8	10	20	50
511	Houston Oilers TL	4	4	5	5	8	10	20	50
512	Kansas City Chiefs TL	4	4	5	5	8	10	20	60
513	Los Angeles Rams TL	4	4	5	5	8	10	20	50
514	Miami Dolphins TL	4	4	5	5	8	10	20	50
515	Minnesota Vikings TL	4	4	5	5	8	10	20	60
516	New England Patriots TL	4	4	5	5	8	10	20	50
517	New Orleans Saints TL	4	4	5	5	8	10	20	
518	New York Giants TL	4	4	5	5	8	10	20	60
519	Jets TL/Wesley Walker	4	4	5	5	8	10	20	
520	Oakland Raiders TL	4	4	5	5	8	10	20	60
521	Philadelphia Eagles TL	4	4	5	5	8	10	20	
522	Steelers TL/Harris/Blount	4	4	5	5	8	10	50	
523	St.Louis Cardinals TL	4	4	5	5	8	10	20	40
524	San Diego Chargers TL	4	4	5	5	8	10	20	50
525	San Francisco 49ers TL	4	4	5	5	8	10	20	
526	Seahawks TL/S.Largent	4	4	5	5	8	10	25	
527	Tampa Bay Bucs TL	4	4	5	5	8	10	20	50
528	Redskins TL/Ken Houston	4	4	5		12	15	35	60

—Terry Bradshaw #65 PSA 10 (Gem) sold for $577 (Andy Madec; 5/07)
—Terry Bradshaw #65 PSA 10 (Gem) sold for $1,331 (Goodwin; 11/12)
—Fred Dean RC #217 PSA 10 (Gem) sold for $2910 (eBay; 09/14)
—Tony Dorsett #315 PSA 10 (Gem) sold for $4500 (eBay; 1/08)
—Tony Dorsett #315 PSA 10 (Gem) sold for $3825.01 (eBay; 5/12)
—Tony Dorsett #315 PSA 10 (Gem) sold for $6520 (eBay; 09/14)
—Tony Dorsett #315 PSA 10 (Gem) sold for $16,661 (eBay; 07/16)
—Joe Greene #295 PSA 10 (Gem) sold for $575 (eBay; 10/14)
—Roger Staubach #290 PSA 10 (Gem) sold for $812.31 (eBay; 3/14)
—Roger Staubach #290 PSA 10 (Gem) sold for $908 (Mile High; 4/14)

1979 Topps

#	Player	VgEx 4	EX 5	ExMt 6	NM 7	NmMt 8	NmMt+ 8.5	MT 9	Gem 9.5/10
1	Staubach/Bradshaw LL	4	4	5	8	12	15	50	400
2	S.Largent/R.Young LL	4	4	5	5	8	10	20	50
3	E.Campbell/W.Payton LL	4	4	5	6	10	12	30	175
4	F.Corral/P.Leahy LL	4	4	5	5	8	10	20	
5	Buchanon/Stone/Darden LL	4	4	5	5	8	10	20	40
6	T.Skladany/P.McInally LL	4	4	5	5	8	10	20	40
7	Johnny Perkins	4	4	5	5	8	10	20	
8	Charles Phillips	4	4	5	5	8	10	20	
9	Derrel Luce	4	4	5	5	8	10	20	50
10	John Riggins	4	4	5	5	8	10	20	
11	Chester Marcol	4	4	5	5	8	10	20	40
12	Bernard Jackson	4	4	5	5	8	10	20	
13	Dave Logan	4	4	5	5	8	10	20	50
14	Bo Harris	4	4	5	5	8	10	20	
15	Alan Page	4	4	5	5	8	10	20	50
16	John Smith	4	4	5	5	8	10	20	
17	Dwight McDonald	4	4	5	5	8	10	20	40
18	John Cappelletti	4	4	5	5	8	10	20	
19	Steelers TL/Harris/Dungy	4	4	5	8	12	15	25	
20A	Bill Bergey	4	4	5	5	8	10	20	80
21	Jerome Barkum	4	4	5	5	8	10	20	60
22	Larry Csonka	4	4	5	5	8	10	25	80
23	Joe Ferguson	4	4	5	5	8	10	30	50
24	Ed Too Tall Jones	4	4	5	5	8	10	40	
25	Dave Jennings	4	4	5	5	8	10	20	
26	Horace King	4	4	5	5	8	10	20	40
27	Steve Little	4	4	5	5	8	10	20	50
28	Morris Bradshaw	4	4	5	5	8	10	20	
29	Joe Ehrmann	4	4	5	5	8	10	20	60
30	Ahmad Rashad	4	4	5	5	8	10	20	
31	Joe Lavender	4	4	5	5	8	10	20	50
32	Dan Neal	4	4	5	5	8	10	20	
33	Johnny Evans	4	4	5	5	8	10	20	40
34	Pete Johnson	4	4	5	5	8	10	20	
35	Mike Haynes	4	4	5	5	8	10	20	50
36	Tim Mazzetti	4	4	5	5	8	10	20	40
37	Mike Barber RC	4	4	5	5	8	10	20	
38	49ers TL/O.J.Simpson	4	4	5	5	8	10	20	
39	Bill Gregory	4	4	5	5	8	10	20	50
40	Randy Gradishar	4	4	5	5	8	10	20	80
41	Richard Todd	4	4	5	5	8	10	20	60
42	Henry Marshall	4	4	5	5	8	10	20	
43	John Hill	4	4	5	5	8	10	20	
44	Sidney Thornton	4	4	5	5	8	10	20	
45	Ron Jessie	4	4	5	5	8	10	20	40
46	Bob Baumhower	4	4	5	5	8	10	30	
47	Johnnie Gray	4	4	5	5	8	10	20	40
48	Doug Williams RC	4	4	5	6	10	12	30	400
49	Don McCauley	4	4	5	5	8	10	20	
50	Ray Guy	4	4	5	5	8	10	20	
51	Bob Klein	4	4	5	5	8	10	20	
52	Golden Richards	4	4	5	5	8	10	20	
53	Mark Miller QB	4	4	5	5	8	10	20	
54	John Sanders	4	4	5	5	8	10	20	
55	Gary Burley	4	4	5	5	8	10	20	
56	Steve Nelson	4	4	5	5	8	10	20	
57	Buffalo Bills TL	4	4	5	5	8	10	20	40
58	Bobby Bryant	4	4	5	5	8	10	20	
59	Rick Kane	4	4	5	5	8	10	20	
60	Larry Little	4	4	5	5	8	10	20	
61	Ted Fritsch Jr.	4	4	5	5	8	10	20	

	VgEx 4	EX 5	ExMt 6	NM 7	NmMt 8	NmMt+ 8.5	MT 9	Gem 9.5/10
Larry Mallory	4	4	5	5	8	10	20	
Marvin Powell	4	4	5	5	8	10	20	
Jim Hart	4	4	5	5	8	10	20	40
Joe Greene	4	4	5	5	8	10	30	150
Walter White	4	4	5	5	8	10	20	40
Gregg Bingham	4	4	5	5	8	10	20	40
Errol Mann	4	4	5	5	8	10	20	
Bruce Laird	4	4	5	5	8	10	20	
Drew Pearson	4	4	5	5	8	10	20	60
Steve Bartkowski	4	4	5	5	8	10	20	40
Ted Albrecht	4	4	5	5	8	10	20	40
Charlie Hall	4	4	5	5	8	10	20	40
Pat McInally	4	4	5	5	8	10	20	
Bubba Baker RC	4	4	5	5	8	10	20	
New England Pats TL	4	4	5	5	8	10	20	40
Steve DeBerg RC	4	4	5	5	8	10	25	60
John Yarno	4	4	5	5	8	10	20	
Stu Voigt	4	4	5	5	8	10	20	
Frank Corral AP	4	4	5	5	8	10	20	50
Troy Archer	4	4	5	5	8	10	20	
Bruce Harper	4	4	5	5	8	10	20	
Tom Jackson	4	4	5	5	8	10	20	50
Larry Brown	4	4	5	5	8	10	20	
Wilbert Montgomery RC	4	4	5	5	8	10	25	
Butch Johnson	4	4	5	5	8	10	20	
Mike Kadish	4	4	5	5	8	10	20	40
Ralph Perretta	4	4	5	5	8	10	20	40
David Lee	4	4	5	5	8	10	20	40
Mark Van Eeghen	4	4	5	5	8	10	20	
John McDaniel	4	4	5	5	8	10	20	
Gary Fencik	4	4	5	5	8	10	20	40
Mack Mitchell	4	4	5	5	8	10	20	
Cincinnati Bengals TL	4	4	5	5	8	10	20	60
Steve Grogan	4	4	5	5	8	10	20	
Garo Yepremian	4	4	5	5	8	10	20	40
Barty Smith	4	4	5	5	8	10	20	40
Frank Reed	4	4	5	5	8	10	20	40
Jim Clack	4	4	5	5	8	10	20	
Chuck Foreman	4	4	5	5	8	10	20	
Joe Klecko	4	4	5	5	8	10	20	
Pat Tilley	4	4	5	5	8	10	20	80
Conrad Dobler	4	4	5	5	8	10	20	
Craig Colquitt	4	4	5	5	8	10	20	
Dan Pastorini	4	4	5	5	8	10	20	40
Rod Perry AP	4	4	5	5	8	10	20	40
Nick Mike-Mayer	4	4	5	5	8	10	20	
John Matuszak	4	4	5	5	8	10	20	
David Taylor	4	4	5	5	8	10	20	40
Billy Joe DuPree	4	4	5	5	8	10	20	80
Harold McLinton	4	4	5	5	8	10	20	
Virgil Livers	4	4	5	5	8	10	20	
Cleveland Browns TL	4	4	5	5	8	10	20	
Checklist 1-132	4	4	5	5	8	10	20	
Ken Anderson	4	4	5	5	8	10	20	60
Bill Lenkaitis	4	4	5	5	8	10	20	40
Bucky Dilts	4	4	5	5	8	10	20	40
Tony Greene	4	4	5	5	8	10	20	
Bobby Hammond	4	4	5	5	8	10	20	
Nat Moore	4	4	5	5	8	10	20	40
Pat Leahy	4	4	5	5	8	10	20	40
James Harris	4	4	5	5	8	10	20	
Lee Roy Selmon	4	4	5	5	8	10	20	
Bennie Cunningham	4	4	5	5	8	10	20	40
Matt Blair AP	4	4	5	5	8	10	20	
Jim Allen	4	4	5	5	8	10	20	40
Alfred Jenkins	4	4	5	5	8	10	20	
Arthur Whittington	4	4	5	5	8	10	20	40
Norm Thompson	4	4	5	5	8	10	20	
Pat Haden	4	4	5	5	8	10	20	40
Freddie Solomon	4	4	5	5	8	10	20	40
Bears TL/W.Payton	4	4	5	5	8	10	30	
Mark Moseley	4	4	5	5	8	10	20	
Cleo Miller	4	4	5	5	8	10	20	
Ross Browner RC	4	4	5	5	8	10	20	50
Don Calhoun	4	4	5	5	8	10	20	40
David Whitehurst	4	4	5	5	8	10	20	200
Terry Beeson	4	4	5	5	8	10	20	40
Ken Stone	4	4	5	5	8	10	20	
Brad Van Pelt AP	4	4	5	5	8	10	20	

		VgEx 4	EX 5	ExMt 6	NM 7	NmMt 8	NmMt+ 8.5	MT 9	Gem 9.5/10
141	Wesley Walker	4	4	5	5	8	10	20	50
142	Jan Stenerud	4	4	5	5	8	10	20	
143	Henry Childs	4	4	5	5	8	10	20	
144	Otis Armstrong	4	4	5	5	8	10	20	
145	Dwight White	4	4	5	5	8	10	25	
146	Steve Wilson	4	4	5	5	8	10	20	
147	Tom Skladany RC	4	4	5	5	8	10	20	40
148	Lou Piccone	4	4	5	5	8	10	20	40
149	Monte Johnson	4	4	5	5	8	10	30	
150	Joe Washington	4	4	5	5	8	10	20	
151	Eagles TL/W.Montgomery	4	4	5	5	8	10	20	40
152	Fred Dean	4	4	5	5	8		20	50
153	Rolland Lawrence	4	4	5	5	8	10	20	
154	Brian Baschnagel	4	4	5	5	8	10	20	
155	Joe Theismann	4	4	5	5	8	10	25	80
156	Marvin Cobb	4	4	5	5	8	10	20	
157	Dick Ambrose	4	4	5	5	8	10	20	
158	Mike Patrick	4	4	5	5	8	10	20	
159	Gary Shirk	4	4	5	5	8	10	20	
160	Tony Dorsett	4	5	6	10	15	20	40	250
161	Greg Buttle	4	4	5	5	8	10	20	
162	A.J. Duhe	4	4	5	5	8	10	20	50
163	Mick Tingelhoff	4	4	5	5	8	10	20	
164	Ken Burrough	4	4	5	5	8	10	20	40
165	Mike Wagner	4	4	5	5	8	10	30	
166	AFC Champs/F.Harris	4	4	5	5	8	10	20	60
167	NFC Championship	4	4	5	5	8	10	20	50
168	Super Bowl XIII/Harris	4	4	5	5	8	10	20	100
169	Raiders TL/T.Hendricks	4	4	5	5	8	10	20	40
170	O.J. Simpson	4	4	5	5	8	10	40	120
171	Doug Nettles	4	4	5	5	8	10	20	40
172	Dan Dierdorf	4	4	5	5	8	10	20	
173	Dave Beverly	4	4	5	5	8	10	20	
174	Jim Zorn	4	4	5	5	8	10	20	40
175	Mike Thomas	4	4	5	5	8	10	20	40
176	John Outlaw	4	4	5	5	8	10	20	
177	Jim Turner	4	4	5	5	8	10	20	
178	Freddie Scott	4	4	5	5	8	10	20	50
179	Mike Phipps	4	4	5	5	8	10	20	
180	Jack Youngblood	4	4	5	5	8	10	20	
181	Sam Hunt	4	4	5	5	8	10	20	
182	Tony Hill RC	4	4	5	5	8	12	60	250
183	Gary Barbaro	4	4	5	5	8	10	20	
184	Archie Griffin	4	4	5	5	8	10	20	40
185	Jerry Sherk	4	4	5	5	8	10	20	40
186	Bobby Jackson	4	4	5	5	8	10	20	40
187	Don Woods	4	4	5	5	8	10	20	60
188	New York Giants TL	4	4	5	5	8	10	20	
189	Raymond Chester	4	4	5	5	8	10	20	50
190	Joe DeLamielleure AP	4	4	5	5	8	10	20	50
191	Tony Galbreath	4	4	5	5	8	10	20	
192	Robert Brazile AP	4	4	5	5	8	10	20	
193	Neil O'Donoghue	4	4	5	5	8	10	20	
194	Mike Webster	4	4	5	5	8	10	40	150
195	Ed Simonini	4	4	5	5	8	10	20	40
196	Benny Malone	4	4	5	5	8	10	20	
197	Tom Wittum	4	4	5	5	8	10	20	
198	Steve Largent	4	4	5	6	10	12	25	125
199	Tommy Hart	4	4	5	5	8	10	20	50
200	Fran Tarkenton	4	4	5	5	8	10	25	
201	Leon Gray AP	4	4	5	5	8	10	20	40
202	Leroy Harris	4	4	5	5	8	10	20	40
203	Eric Williams LB	4	4	5	5	8	10	20	
204	Thom Darden AP	4	4	5	5	8	10	20	40
205	Ken Riley	4	4	5	5	8	10	20	
206	Clark Gaines	4	4	5	5	8	10	20	40
207	Kansas City Chiefs TL	4	4	5	5	8	10	20	
208	Joe Danelo	4	4	5	5	8	10	20	
209	Glen Walker	4	4	5	5	8	10	20	
210	Art Shell	4	4	5	5	8	10	40	
211	Jon Keyworth	4	4	5	5	8	10	20	40
212	Herman Edwards	4	4	5	5	8	10	20	40
213	John Fitzgerald	4	4	5	5	8	10	20	
214	Jim Smith	4	4	5	5	8	10	20	60
215	Coy Bacon	4	4	5	5	8	10	20	40
216	Dennis Johnson RC	4	4	5	5	8	10	20	
217	John Jefferson RC	4	4	5	5	8	10	30	
218	Gary Weaver	4	4	5	5	8	10	20	
219	Tom Blanchard	4	4	5	5	8	10	20	

FOOTBALL

#	Player	VgEx 4	EX 5	ExMt 6	NM 7	NmMt 8	NmMt+ 8.5	MT 9	Gem 9.5/10
220	Bert Jones	4	4	5	5	8	10	20	
221	Stanley Morgan	4	4	5	5	8	10	20	50
222	James Hunter	4	4	5	5	8	10	20	40
223	Jim O'Bradovich	4	4	5	5	8	10	20	40
224	Carl Mauck	4	4	5	5	8	10	20	40
225	Chris Bahr	4	4	5	5	8	10	20	
226	Jets TL/W.Walker	4	4	5	5	8	10	20	60
227	Roland Harper	4	4	5	5	8	10	20	50
228	Randy Dean	4	4	5	5	8	10	20	40
229	Bob Jackson	4	4	5	5	8	10	20	40
230	Sammie White	4	4	5	5	8	10	20	
231	Mike Dawson	4	4	5	5	8	10	20	
232	Checklist 133-264	4	4	5	5	8	10	20	40
233	Ken MacAfee RC	4	4	5	5	8	10	20	
234	Jon Kolb AP	4	4	5	5	8	10	30	80
235	Willie Hall	4	4	5	5	8	10	20	
236	Ron Saul AP	4	4	5	5	8	10	20	
237	Haskel Stanback	4	4	5	5	8	10	20	
238	Zenon Andrusyshyn	4	4	5	5	8	10	20	
239	Norris Thomas	4	4	5	5	8	10	20	
240	Rick Upchurch	4	4	5	5	8	10	20	
241	Robert Pratt	4	4	5	5	8	10	20	40
242	Julius Adams	4	4	5	5	8	10	20	
243	Rich McGeorge	4	4	5	5	8	10	20	40
244	Seahawks TL/S.Largent	4	4	5	5	8	10	20	100
245	Blair Bush RC	4	4	5	5	8	10	20	
246	Billy Johnson	4	4	5	5	8	10	20	40
247	Randy Rasmussen	4	4	5	5	8	10	20	40
248	Brian Kelley	4	4	5	5	8	10	20	40
249	Mike Pruitt	4	4	5	5	8	10	20	100
250	Harold Carmichael	4	4	5	5	8	10	25	50
251	Mike Hartenstine	4	4	5	5	8	10	20	
252	Robert Newhouse	4	4	5	5	8	10	20	
253	Gary Danielson RC	4	4	5	5	8	10	20	50
254	Mike Fuller	4	4	5	5	8	10	20	
255	L.C.Greenwood	4	4	5	5	8	10	20	
256	Lemar Parrish	4	4	5	5	8	10	20	
257	Ike Harris	4	4	5	5	8	10	20	
258	Ricky Bell RC	4	4	5	5	8	10	20	
259	Willie Parker C	4	4	5	5	8	10	20	
260	Gene Upshaw	4	4	5	5	8	10	30	60
261	Glenn Doughty	4	4	5	5	8	10	20	
262	Steve Zabel	4	4	5	5	8	10	30	
263	Atlanta Falcons TL	4	4	5	5	8	10	20	
264	Ray Wersching	4	4	5	5	8	10	20	40
265	Lawrence McCutcheon	4	4	5	5	8	10	20	
266	Willie Buchanon AP	4	4	5	5	8	10	20	40
267	Matt Robinson	4	4	5	5	8	10	20	40
268	Reggie Rucker	4	4	5	5	8	10	20	40
269	Doug Van Horn	4	4	5	5	8	10	20	
270	Lydell Mitchell	4	4	5	5	8	10	20	
271	Vern Holland	4	4	5	5	8	10	20	40
272	Eason Ramson	4	4	5	5	8	10	20	40
273	Steve Towle	4	4	5	5	8	10	20	
274	Jim Marshall	4	4	5	5	8	10	20	40
275	Mel Blount	4	4	5	5	8	10	20	80
276	Bob Kuziel	4	4	5	5	8	10	20	
277	James Scott	4	4	5	5	8	10	20	40
278	Tony Reed	4	4	5	5	8	10	20	40
279	Dave Green	4	4	5	5	8	10	20	40
280	Toni Linhart	4	4	5	5	8	10	20	40
281	Andy Johnson	4	4	5	5	8	10	20	
282	Los Angeles Rams TL	4	4	5	5	8	10	20	40
283	Phil Villapiano	4	4	5	5	8	10	20	
284	Dexter Bussey	4	4	5	5	8	10	20	
285	Craig Morton	4	4	5	5	8	10	20	
286	Guy Morriss	4	4	5	5	8	10	20	40
287	Lawrence Pillers	4	4	5	5	8	10	20	
288	Gerald Irons	4	4	5	5	8	10	20	40
289	Scott Perry	4	4	5	5	8	10	20	40
290	Randy White	4	4	5	5	8	10	50	
291	Jack Gregory	4	4	5	5	8	10	20	
292	Bob Chandler	4	4	5	5	8	10	20	50
293	Rich Szaro	4	4	5	5	8	10	20	40
294	Sherman Smith	4	4	5	5	8	10	20	40
295	Tom Banks AP	4	4	5	5	8	10	20	40
296	Revie Sorey AP	4	4	5	5	8	10	30	
297	Ricky Thompson	4	4	5	5	8	10	20	
298	Ron Yary	4	4	5	5	8	10	20	40
299	Lyle Blackwood	4	4	5	5	8	10	20	

#	Player	VgEx 4	EX 5	ExMt 6	NM 7	NmMt 8	NmMt+ 8.5	MT 9	Gem 9.5/10
300	Franco Harris	4	4	5	5	8	10	30	200
301	Oilers TL/E.Campbell	4	4	5	5	8	10	25	
302	Scott Bull	4	4	5	5	8	10	40	
303	Dewey Selmon	4	4	5	5	8	10	20	40
304	Jack Rudnay	4	4	5	5	8	10	20	40
305	Fred Biletnikoff	4	4	5	5	8	10	25	
306	Jeff West	4	4	5	5	8	10	20	
307	Shafer Suggs	4	4	5	5	8	10	20	
308	Ozzie Newsome RC	5	6	8	15	30	50	150	400
309	Boobie Clark	4	4	5	5	8	10	20	50
310	James Lofton RC	5	6	8	15	30	40	150	
311	Joe Pisarcik	4	4	5	5	8	10	20	
312	Bill Simpson AP	4	4	5	5	8	10	20	40
313	Haven Moses	4	4	5	5	8	10	20	40
314	Jim Merlo	4	4	5	5	8	10	20	40
315	Preston Pearson	4	4	5	5	8	10	20	
316	Larry Tearry	4	4	5	5	8	10	20	40
317	Tom Dempsey	4	4	5	5	8	10	20	
318	Greg Latta	4	4	5	5	8	10	20	
319	Redskins TL/J.Riggins	4	4	5	5	8	10	20	
320	Jack Ham	4	4	5	5	8	10	20	100
321	Harold Jackson	4	4	5	5	8	10	20	
322	George Roberts	4	4	5	5	8	10	20	
323	Ron Jaworski	4	4	5	5	8	10	20	150
324	Jim Otis	4	4	5	5	8	10	20	
325	Roger Carr	4	4	5	5	8	10	20	40
326	Jack Tatum	4	4	5	5	8	10	20	
327	Derrick Gaffney	4	4	5	5	8	10	20	
328	Reggie Williams	4	4	5	5	8	10	20	
329	Doug Dieken	4	4	5	5	8	10	20	
330	Efren Herrera	4	4	5	5	8	10	20	
331	Earl Campbell RB	4	4	5	6	10	12	30	150
332	Tony Galbreath RB	4	4	5	5	8	10	20	40
333	Bruce Harper RB	4	4	5	5	8	10	20	40
334	John James RB	4	4	5	5	8	10	15	40
335	Walter Payton RB	4	4	5	5	8	10	25	
336	Rickey Young RB	4	4	5	5	8	10	20	
337	Jeff Van Note	4	4	5	5	8	10	20	40
338	Chargers TL/J.Jefferson	4	4	5	5	8	10	20	
339	Stan Walters RC	4	4	5	5	8	10	20	
340	Louis Wright	4	4	5	5	8	10	20	50
341	Horace Ivory	4	4	5	5	8	10	20	50
342	Andre Tillman	4	4	5	5	8	10	20	40
343	Greg Coleman RC	4	4	5	5	8	10	20	40
344	Doug English RC	4	4	5	5	8	10	20	
345	Ted Hendricks	4	4	5	5	8	10	20	
346	Rich Saul	4	4	5	5	8	10	20	40
347	Mel Gray	4	4	5	5	8	10	20	60
348	Toni Fritsch	4	4	5	5	8	10	20	40
349	Cornell Webster	4	4	5	5	8	10	20	
350	Ken Houston	4	4	5	5	8	10	20	
351	Ron Johnson DB RC	4	4	5	5	8	10	20	40
352	Doug Kotar	4	4	5	5	8	10	20	50
353	Brian Sipe	4	4	5	5	8	10	20	50
354	Billy Brooks	4	4	5	5	8	10	20	
355	John Dutton	4	4	5	5	8	10	20	
356	Don Goode	4	4	5	5	8	10	20	
357	Detroit Lions TL	4	4	5	5	8	10	20	
358	Reuben Gant	4	4	5	5	8	10	20	40
359	Bob Parsons	4	4	5	5	8	10	20	40
360	Cliff Harris	4	4	5	5	8	10	40	
361	Raymond Clayborn	4	4	5	5	8	10	20	40
362	Scott Dierking	4	4	5	5	8	10	20	40
363	Bill Bryan	4	4	5	5	8	10	20	
364	Mike Livingston	4	4	5	5	8	10	20	40
365	Otis Sistrunk	4	4	5	5	8	10	20	
366	Charle Young	4	4	5	5	8	10	20	
367	Keith Wortman	4	4	5	5	8	10	20	40
368	Checklist 265-396	4	4	5	5	8	10	20	
369	Mike Michel	4	4	5	5	8	10	20	
370	Delvin Williams AP	4	4	5	5	8	10	20	40
371	Steve Furness	4	4	5	5	8	10	20	
372	Emery Moorehead	4	4	5	5	8	10	20	
373	Clarence Scott	4	4	5	5	8	10	20	40
374	Rufus Mayes	4	4	5	5	8	10	20	
375	Chris Hanburger	4	4	5	5	8	10	20	
376	Baltimore Colts TL	VgEx 4	EX 5	ExMt 6	NM 7	NmMt 8	NmMt+ 8.5	MT 9	
377	Bob Avellini	4	4	5	5	8	10	20	
378	Jeff Siemon	4	4	5	5	8	10	20	50
379	Roland Hooks	4	4	5	5	8	10	20	

	VgEx 4	EX 5	ExMt 6	NM 7	NmMt 8	NmMt+ 8.5	MT 9	Gem 9.5/10
Russ Francis	4	4	5	5	8	10	20	60
Roger Wehrli	4	4	5	5	8	10	20	40
Joe Fields	4	4	5	5	8	10	20	
Archie Manning	4	4	5	5	8	10	20	
Rob Lytle	4	4	5	5	8	10	20	40
Thomas Henderson	4	4	5	5	8	10	80	
Morris Owens	4	4	5	5	8	10	20	
Dan Fouts	4	4	5	5	8	10	25	80
Chuck Crist	4	4	5	5	8	10	20	
Ed O'Neil	4	4	5	5	8	10	20	
Earl Campbell RC	10	12	20	30	60	80	350	2,000
Randy Grossman	4	4	5	5	8	10	20	
Monte Jackson	4	4	5	5	8	10	20	
John Mendenhall	4	4	5	5	8	10	20	
Miami Dolphins TL	4	4	5	5	8	10	20	
Isaac Curtis	4	4	5	5	8	10	20	40
Mike Bragg	4	4	5	5	8	10	20	
Doug Plank	4	4	5	5	8	10	20	
Mike Barnes	4	4	5	5	8	10	20	
Calvin Hill	4	4	5	5	8	10	20	40
Roger Staubach	4	5	6	10	20	30	50	
Doug Beaudoin	4	4	5	5	8	10	20	
Chuck Ramsey	4	4	5	5	8	10	20	40
Mike Hogan	4	4	5	5	8	10	20	
Mario Clark	4	4	5	5	8	10	20	40
Riley Odoms	4	4	5	5	8	10	20	40
Carl Eller	4	4	5	5	8	10	20	50
Packers TL/J.Lofton	4	4	5	5	8	10	20	
Mark Arneson	4	4	5	5	8	10	20	
Vince Ferragamo RC	4	4	5	5	8	10	20	
Cleveland Elam	4	4	5	5	8	10		
Donnie Shell RC	4	4	5	8	15	20	120	
Ray Rhodes	4	4	5	5	8	10	20	40
Don Cockroft	4	4	5	5	8	10	20	40
Don Bass	4	4	5	5	8	10	20	
Cliff Branch	4	4	5	5	8	10	20	
Diron Talbert	4	4	5	5	8	10	20	60
Tom Hicks	4	4	5	5	8	10	20	40
Roosevelt Leaks	4	4	5	5	8	10	20	
Charlie Joiner	4	4	5	5	8	10	20	80
Lyle Alzado	4	4	5	5	8	10	20	60
Sam Cunningham	4	4	5	5	8	10	20	
Larry Keller	4	4	5	5	8	10	20	50
Jim Mitchell TE	4	4	5	5	8	10	20	
Randy Logan	4	4	5	5	8	10	20	40
Jim Langer	4	4	5	5	8	10	20	
Gary Green	4	4	5	5	8	10	20	
Luther Blue	4	4	5	5	8	10	20	
Dennis Johnson	4	4	5	5	8	10	20	
Danny White	4	4	5	5	8	10	20	
Roy Gerela	4	4	5	5	8	10	20	
Jimmy Robinson	4	4	5	5	8	10	20	
Minnesota Vikings TL	4	4	5	5	8	10	60	
Oliver Davis	4	4	5	5	8	10	20	40
Lenvil Elliott	4	4	5	5	8	10	20	
Willie Miller RC	4	4	5	5	8	10	20	40
Brad Dusek	4	4	5	5	8	10	20	
Bob Thomas	4	4	5	5	8	10	20	
Ken Mendenhall	4	4	5	5	8	10	20	
Clarence Davis	4	4	5	5	8	10	20	40
Bob Griese	4	4	5	5	8	10	25	50
Tony McGee DT	4	4	5	5	8	10	20	40
Ed Taylor	4	4	5	5	8	10	20	40
Ron Howard	4	4	5	5	8	10	20	
Wayne Morris	4	4	5	5	8	10	20	
Charlie Waters	4	4	5	5	8	10	20	
Rick Danmeier	4	4	5	5	8	10	20	
Paul Naumoff	4	4	5	5	8	10	20	40
Keith Krepfle	4	4	5	5	8	10	20	
Rusty Jackson	4	4	5	5	8	10	20	40
John Stallworth	4	4	5	5	8	10	25	
New Orleans Saints TL	4	4	5	5	8	10	20	
Ron Mikolajczyk	4	4	5	5	8	10	20	40
Fred Dryer	4	4	5	5	8	10	20	40
Jim LeClair	4	4	5	5	8	10	20	
Greg Pruitt	4	4	5	5	8	10	20	40
Jake Scott	4	4	5	5	8	10	20	
Steve Schubert	4	4	5	5	8	10	20	
George Kunz	4	4	5	5	8	10	20	
Mike Williams	4	4	5	5	8	10	20	40

		VgEx 4	EX 5	ExMt 6	NM 7	NmMt 8	NmMt+ 8.5	MT 9	Gem 9.5/10
460	Dave Casper AP	4	4	5	5	8	10	40	
461	Sam Adams OL	4	4	5	5	8	10	20	40
462	Abdul Salaam	4	4	5	5	8	10	20	40
463	Terdell Middleton	4	4	5	5	8	10	20	40
464	Mike Wood	4	4	5	5	8	10	20	40
465	Bill Thompson AP	4	4	5	5	8	10	20	40
466	Larry Gordon	4	4	5	5	8	10	20	
467	Benny Ricardo	4	4	5	5	8	10	20	40
468	Reggie McKenzie	4	4	5	5	8	10	20	
469	Cowboys TL/T.Dorsett	4	4	5	5	8	10	25	
470	Rickey Young	4	4	5	5	8	10	20	
471	Charlie Smith WR	4	4	5	5	8	10	20	
472	Al Dixon	4	4	5	5	8	10	20	
473	Tom DeLeone	4	4	5	5	8	10	20	
474	Louis Breeden	4	4	5	5	8	10	20	
475	Jack Lambert	4	4	5	5	8	10	30	175
476	Terry Hermeling	4	4	5	5	8	10	20	
477	J.K. McKay	4	4	5	5	8	10	20	
478	Stan White	4	4	5	5	8	10	20	40
479	Terry Nelson	4	4	5	5	8	10	20	40
480	Walter Payton	5	6	12	20	35	40	125	
481	Dave Dalby	4	4	5	5	8	10	20	50
482	Burgess Owens	4	4	5	5	8	10	20	
483	Rolf Benirschke	4	4	5	5	8	10	20	40
484	Jack Dolbin	4	4	5	5	8	10	20	
485	John Hannah	4	4	5	5	8	10	20	
486	Checklist 397-528	4	4	5	5	8	10	50	
487	Greg Landry	4	4	5	5	8	10	20	50
488	St. Louis Cardinals TL	4	4	5	5	8	10	20	
489	Paul Krause	4	4	5	5	8	10	20	50
490	John James	4	4	5	5	8	10	20	40
491	Merv Krakau	4	4	5	5	8	10	20	
492	Dan Doornink	4	4	5	5	8	10	20	
493	Curtis Johnson	4	4	5	5	8	10	20	
494	Rafael Septien	4	4	5	5	8	10	40	
495	Jean Fugett	4	4	5	5	8	10	20	40
496	Frank LeMaster	4	4	5	5	8	10	20	
497	Allan Ellis	4	4	5	5	.8	10	20	40
498	Billy Waddy RC	4	4	5	5	8	10	20	
499	Hank Bauer	4	4	5	5	8	10	20	
500	Terry Bradshaw	4	5	6	10	15	20	40	400
501	Larry McCarren	4	4	5	5	8	10	20	40
502	Fred Cook	4	4	5	5	8	10	20	
503	Chuck Muncie	4	4	5	5	8	10	20	80
504	Herman Weaver	4	4	5	5	8	10	20	40
505	Eddie Edwards	4	4	5	5	8	10	20	40
506	Tony Peters	4	4	5	5	8	10	20	40
507	Denver Broncos TL	4	4	5	5	8	10	20	
508	Jimbo Elrod	4	4	5	5	8	10	20	
509	David Hill	4	4	5	5	8	10	20	
510	Harvey Martin	4	4	5	5	8	10	20	
511	Terry Miller	4	4	5	5	8	10	20	40
512	June Jones RC	4	4	5	5	8	10	20	50
513	Randy Cross	4	4	5	5	8	10	20	40
514	Duriel Harris	4	4	5	5	8	10	20	40
515	Harry Carson	4	4	5	5	8	10	20	
516	Tim Fox	4	4	5	5	8	10	20	
517	John Zook	4	4	5	5	8	10	20	
518	Bob Tucker	4	4	5	5	8	10	20	40
519	Kevin Long RC	4	4	5	5	8	10	20	
520	Ken Stabler	4	4	5	6	10	12	50	
521	John Bunting	4	4	5	5	8	10	20	
522	Rocky Bleier	4	4	5	5	8	10	20	
523	Noah Jackson	4	4	5	5	8	10	20	100
524	Cliff Parsley	4	4	5	5	8	10	20	
525	Louie Kelcher AP	4	4	5	5	8	10	20	50
526	Bucs TL/R.Bell	4	4	5	5	8	10	20	
527	Bob Brudzinski RC	4	4	5	5	8	10	20	
528	Danny Buggs	4	4	5	5	8	10	15	

—James Lofton #310 PSA 10 (Gem Mt) sold for $1,660 (eBay; 10/11)
—James Lofton #310 PSA 10 (Gem Mt) sold for $2,338 (eBay; 1/13)
—Wilbert Montgomery RC #85 PSA 10 (Gem Mint) sold for $519 (eBay; 6/12)
—Walter Payton #480 PSA 10 (Gem Mt) sold for $1,022 (eBay; 4/08)
—Walter Payton #480 PSA 10 (Gem Mt) sold for $905 (eBay; 7/09)
—Walter Payton #480 PSA 10 (Gem Mint) sold for $1869 (eBay; 6/12)
—Walter Payton #480 PSA 10 (Gem Mint) sold for $1350 (Bussineau; 6/12)
—Walter Payton RB #335 PSA 10 (Gem Mint) sold for $769 (eBay; 6/12)
—Roger Staubach #400 PSA 10 (Gem Mint) sold for $530 (eBay; 6/12)
—Roger Staubach #400 PSA 10 (Gem Mint) sold for $497.32 (eBay; 3/14)

FOOTBALL

1980 - Present

1980 Topps

		NmMt 8	NmMt+ 8.5	MT 9	Gem 9.5/10
160	Walter Payton	▲35	▲40	▲100	500
170	Ottis Anderson RC	10	12	20	250
195	Lester Hayes RC	25	30	80	350
200	Terry Bradshaw	15	20	30	400
225	Phil Simms RC	25	40	100	400
330	Tony Dorsett	10	12	30	150
418	Clay Matthews RC	15	20	30	100

—Terry Bradshaw #200 PSA 10 (Gem) sold for $1,003 (eBay; 4/08)

1981 Topps

		NmMt 8	NmMt+ 8.5	MT 9	Gem 9.5/10
100	Billy Sims RC	10	12	30	150
150	Kellen Winslow RC	12	15	40	200
194	Art Monk RC	20	25	50	400
202	Walter Payton SA	10	12	25	
216	Joe Montana RC	250	300	1,000	14,000
316	Dan Hampton RC	15	20	80	225
375	Terry Bradshaw	12	15	25	120
400	Walter Payton	▲25	▲30	▲80	400
422	Dwight Clark RC	▲25	▲30	▲40	
500	Tony Dorsett	10	12	20	60

—Joe Montana #216 BGS 9.5 (GemMt) typically sells for $2,500-$3,500

1982 Topps

		NmMt 8	NmMt+ 8.5	MT 9	Gem 9.5/10
44	Cris Collinsworth RC	10	12	25	60
51	Anthony Munoz RC	15	20	40	200
196	Matt Millen RC	6	8	12	25
204	Terry Bradshaw	10	12	25	80
257	J.Montana/Anderson LL	10	12	20	50
302	Walter Payton	20	25	50	200
303	Walter Payton IA	10	12	20	80
434	Lawrence Taylor RC	60	80	150	1,200
435	Lawrence Taylor IA	10	12	25	125
486	Ronnie Lott RC	25	50	100	400
487	Ronnie Lott IA	10	12	20	80
488	Joe Montana	20	35	50	200
489	Joe Montana IA	10	12	20	100

1983 Topps

		NmMt 8	NmMt+ 8.5	MT 9	Gem 9.5/10
4	Joe Montana RB	8	10	20	80
33	Jim McMahon RC	12	15	30	100
36	Walter Payton	10	12	30	150
38	Mike Singletary RC	▲25	▲30	▲50	350
133	Lawrence Taylor	8	10	15	40
169	Joe Montana DP	12	15	35	200
190	Joe Jacoby RC	12	15	40	200
294	Marcus Allen RC DP	20	25	50	400
356	Gary Anderson K RC DP	6	8	15	60
358	Terry Bradshaw DP	10	12	20	60

1984 Topps

		NmMt 8	NmMt+ 8.5	MT 9	Gem 9.5/10
63	John Elway RC	60	80	300	▼800
98	Marcus Allen	8	10	15	60
111	Howie Long RC	20	25	40	350
120	Mark Duper PB RC	8	10	15	60
123	Dan Marino RC	60	80	200	1,200
124	Dan Marino IR	12	15	30	100
129	Dwight Stephenson RC	8	12	30	120
143	Andre Tippett RC	8	12	25	

(1984 Topps continued)

		NmMt 8	NmMt+ 8.5	MT 9	Gem 9.5/10
162	Terry Bradshaw	8	10	20	60
202	D.Marino/Bartkow. LL	8	10	15	80
228	Walter Payton	25	35	▼150	
280	Eric Dickerson RC	15	25	60	400
286	Jackie Slater RC	8	10	20	150
300	Morten Andersen RC	8	10	20	150
353	Roger Craig RC	10	12	25	200
358	Joe Montana	15	20	35	250
359	Joe Montana IR	8	10	20	120
380	Darrell Green RC	15	20	40	250
381	Russ Grimm PB RC	8	10	25	80

—John Elway #63 BGS 10 (Pristine) sold for $3,615 (eBay; 3/08)
—John Elway #63 BGS 10 (Pristine) sold for $2,924 (eBay; 4/08)
—John Elway #63 in BGS 9.5 (Gem) typically sells for $250-$500
—Dan Marino #123 BGS 10 (Pristine) sold for $2,555 (eBay; 4/08)
—Dan Marino #123 BGS 10 (Pristine) sold for $1,637 (eBay; 8/08)
—Dan Marino #123 BGS 10 (Pristine) sold for $1,040 (eBay; 11/08)
—Dan Marino #123 in BGS 9.5 (Gem) typically sells for $250-$500
—Walter Payton #228 PSA 10 (Gem) sold for $1398 (eBay; 08/14)
—Walter Payton #228 PSA 10 (Gem) sold for $570 (eBay; 11/06)
—Dwight Stephenson #129 PSA 10 (Gem) sold for $2,610 (eBay; 4/07)

1984 Topps USFL

		NmMt 8	NmMt+ 8.5	MT 9	Gem 9.5/10
36	Jim Kelly XRC	100	125	200	1,200
52	Steve Young XRC	150	200	500	3,000
58	Reggie White XRC	80	100	250	
59	Anthony Carter XRC	12	15	25	200
74	Herschel Walker XRC	50	60	80	
76	Marcus Dupree XRC	25	30		

—Herschel Walker #74 PSA 10 (Gem Mt) sold for $565 (eBay; 1/08)

1985 Topps

		NmMt 8	NmMt+ 8.5	MT 9	Gem 9.5/10
4	Dan Marino RB	10	12	25	200
24	Richard Dent RC	12	20	125	
33	Walter Payton	15	20	200	
80	Henry Ellard RC	8	10	20	150
157	Joe Montana	15	20	50	350
192	D.Marino/Montana LL	15	20	30	300
238	John Elway	15	25	80	
251	Warren Moon RC	20	25	▲80	500
253	Mike Munchak RC	15	20	50	
308	Mark Clayton AP RC	8	10	30	
314	Dan Marino	15	20	40	500
325	Irving Fryar RC	10	12	40	150
328	Craig James RC	8	10	30	

—Walter Payton #33 PSA 10 (Gem) sold for $2420 (eBay; 07/14)

1985 Topps USFL

		NmMt 8	NmMt+ 8.5	MT 9	Gem 9.5/10
45	Jim Kelly	20	25	50	150
49	Gary Clark XRC	10	12	25	80
65	Steve Young	30	35	60	300
75	Reggie White	20	25	40	150
80	Doug Flutie XRC	30	40	60	200
86	Herschel Walker	10	12	25	80
105	Marcus Dupree	12	15		

1986 Topps

		NmMt 8	NmMt+ 8.5	MT 9	Gem 9.5/10
11	Walter Payton	10	12	40	300
45	Dan Marino	10	12	30	400
112	John Elway	10	12	30	500
156	Joe Montana	15	20	50	1,000

(1986 Topps continued)

		NmMt 8	NmMt+ 8.5	MT 9	Gem 9.5/10
161	Jerry Rice RC	80	200	700	5,000
187	Bernie Kosar RC	10	12	40	200
255	Boomer Esiason RC	10	12	50	300
275	Reggie White RC	▲25	30	80	400
374	Steve Young RC	▲50	60	500	
388	Andre Reed RC	10	20	40	300
389	Bruce Smith RC	15	20	▲60	600

—Jerry Rice #161 BGS 9.5 (Gem Mt) typically sell for $1,800-$3,000
—Steve Young #374 BGS 9.5 (Gem Mt) sold for $1,350 (Mile High; 3/09)

1987 Topps

		NmMt 8	NmMt+ 8.5	MT 9	Gem 9.5/10
31	John Elway	8	10	15	60
45	Doug Flutie RC	10	12	25	80
46	Walter Payton	10	12	30	100
112	Joe Montana	10	12	25	60
115	Jerry Rice	8	10	15	60
125	Charles Haley RC	8	10	20	120
207	Gary Zimmerman RC	10	12	25	100
233	Dan Marino	8	10	15	60
264	Herschel Walker RC	8	10	15	40
296	Randall Cunningham RC	10	12	25	200
301	Reggie White	8	10	20	50
362	Jim Kelly RC	25	30	40	150
384	Steve Young	8	10	20	60

1988 Topps

		NmMt 8	NmMt+ 8.5	MT 9	Gem 9.5/10
23	John Elway	8	10	15	50
38	Joe Montana	8	10	15	50
43	Jerry Rice	6	8	12	50
144	Brian Bosworth RC	8	10	20	50
157	Chris Doleman RC	10	12	20	50
190	Dan Marino	8	10	15	30
327	Bo Jackson RC	▲25	▲30	▲40	▲300
352	Vinny Testaverde RC	8	10	20	50

1989 Pro Set

		NmMt 8	NmMt+ 8.5	MT 9	Gem 9.5/10
32	Thurman Thomas RC	8	10	12	30
89	Michael Irvin RC	8	10	12	35
183	Tim Brown RC	8	10	12	30
314	Cris Carter RC	8	10	12	30
486	Deion Sanders RC	8	10	12	30
490	Troy Aikman RC	10	12	15	40
494	Barry Sanders RC	10	12	▲20	▲50
498	Derrick Thomas RC	8	10	12	40

1989 Score Supplemental

		NmMt 8	NmMt+ 8.5	MT 9	Gem 9.5/10
333S	Sterling Sharpe RC	8	10	20	40
384S	Bo Jackson FB/BB	8	10	20	50
408S	Dermontti Dawson RC	8	10	15	50

1989 Topps

		NmMt 8	NmMt+ 8.5	MT 9	Gem 9.5/10
45	Thurman Thomas RC	8	10	12	30
121	Cris Carter RC	8	10	12	40
265	Tim Brown RC	8	10	12	40
383	Michael Irvin RC	8	10	12	40

1989 Topps Traded

		NmMt 8	NmMt+ 8.5	MT 9	Gem 9.5/10
30T	Deion Sanders RC	6	8	12	25
54T	Randall McDaniel RC	6	8	10	20

	NmMt 8	NmMt+ 8.5	MT 9	Gem 9.5/10
Troy Aikman RC	8	10	15	▲40
Barry Sanders RC	8	10	15	▲80
Derrick Thomas RC	6	8	10	20

990 Action Packed Rookie Update

	NmMt 8	NmMt+ 8.5	MT 9	Gem 9.5/10
Emmitt Smith RC UER	12	15	30	150
Junior Seau RC	8	10	15	50

990 Fleer Update

	NmMt 8	NmMt+ 8.5	MT 9	Gem 9.5/10
Emmitt Smith RC	15	20	25	50
2 Junior Seau RC	8	10	12	30

990 Pro Set

	NmMt 8	NmMt+ 8.5	MT 9	Gem 9.5/10
Junior Seau RC	6	8	12	40
Emmitt Smith RC	12	15	20	▲60
0 Emmitt Smith/(Offensive ROY) 5		6	10	30

990 Score Supplemental

	NmMt 8	NmMt+ 8.5	MT 9	Gem 9.5/10
Junior Seau	10	12	15	30
T Emmitt Smith RC	40	50	75	400

990 Topps

	NmMt 8	NmMt+ 8.5	MT 9	Gem 9.5/10
Junior Seau RC	6	8	15	40

990 Topps Traded

	NmMt 8	NmMt+ 8.5	MT 9	Gem 9.5/10
Emmitt Smith RC	8	10	20	50
Junior Seau	5	6	8	25

991 Action Packed Rookie Update

	NmMt 8	NmMt+ 8.5	MT 9	Gem 9.5/10
Brett Favre RC	8	10	20	40

991 Pacific

	NmMt 8	NmMt+ 8.5	MT 9	Gem 9.5/10
1 Brett Favre RC	8	10	20	30

991 Pro Set

	NmMt 8	NmMt+ 8.5	MT 9	Gem 9.5/10
62 Brett Favre RC	12	15	25	50
35 John Randle RC	10	12	20	30

991 Pro Set Platinum

	NmMt 8	NmMt+ 8.5	MT 9	Gem 9.5/10
90 Brett Favre RC	10	12	20	40

991 Stadium Club

	NmMt 8	NmMt+ 8.5	MT 9	Gem 9.5/10
4 Brett Favre RC UER	30	35	60	200

—Brett Favre #94 BGS 10 (Pristine) sold for $1,030 (eBay; 8/08)
—Brett Favre #94 BGS 10 (Pristine) sold for $1,000 (eBay; 2/09)

991 Star Pics

	NmMt 8	NmMt+ 8.5	MT 9	Gem 9.5/10
5 Brett Favre	6	8	15	25

1991 Star Pics Autographs

	NmMt 8	NmMt+ 8.5	MT 9	Gem 9.5/10
5 Brett Favre	175	200	250	400

1991 Ultra

	NmMt 8	NmMt+ 8.5	MT 9	Gem 9.5/10
283 Brett Favre RC	10	12	15	30

1991 Ultra Update

	NmMt 8	NmMt+ 8.5	MT 9	Gem 9.5/10
J1 Brett Favre	12	15	25	40

1991 Upper Deck

	NmMt 8	NmMt+ 8.5	MT 9	Gem 9.5/10
13 Brett Favre RC	10	12	20	40
647 Brett Favre	8	10	15	30

1991 Wild Card Draft

	NmMt 8	NmMt+ 8.5	MT 9	Gem 9.5/10
119 Brett Favre	8	10	20	50

1992 Stadium Club

	NmMt 8	NmMt+ 8.5	MT 9	Gem 9.5/10
683 Brett Favre	60	80	120	250

—Brett Favre #683 BGS 10 (Pristine) sold for $1,946 (eBay; 8/08)

1992 Topps

	NmMt 8	NmMt+ 8.5	MT 9	Gem 9.5/10
696 Brett Favre	8	10	20	40

1992 Topps Gold

	NmMt 8	NmMt+ 8.5	MT 9	Gem 9.5/10
696 Brett Favre	25	30	50	120

1993 Action Packed

	NmMt 8	NmMt+ 8.5	MT 9	Gem 9.5/10
163 Drew Bledsoe RC	10	12	25	50
172 Jerome Bettis RC	10	12	25	50

1993 Bowman

	NmMt 8	NmMt+ 8.5	MT 9	Gem 9.5/10
264 Jerome Bettis RC	12	15	25	▼40
280 Drew Bledsoe RC FOIL	12	15	25	60

1993 Playoff

	NmMt 8	NmMt+ 8.5	MT 9	Gem 9.5/10
294 Jerome Bettis RC	10	12	20	30

1993 Playoff Contenders

	NmMt 8	NmMt+ 8.5	MT 9	Gem 9.5/10
124 Jerome Bettis RC	10	12	20	30

1993 Power Update Prospects

	NmMt 8	NmMt+ 8.5	MT 9	Gem 9.5/10
3 Trent Green RC	8	10	12	40
9 Jerome Bettis RC	8	10	12	40

1993 Select

	NmMt 8	NmMt+ 8.5	MT 9	Gem 9.5/10
166 Drew Bledsoe RC	6	8	10	20
172 Jerome Bettis RC	10	12	20	40

1993 SkyBox Premium

	NmMt 8	NmMt+ 8.5	MT 9	Gem 9.5/10
62 Jerome Bettis RC	10	12	20	35

1993 SP

	NmMt 8	NmMt+ 8.5	MT 9	Gem 9.5/10
6 Jerome Bettis RC	40	50	150	▲1,000
9 Drew Bledsoe RC	15	20	40	200
91 Mark Brunell RC	10	12	20	40
259 John Lynch RC	10	12	20	40

1993 Stadium Club

	NmMt 8	NmMt+ 8.5	MT 9	Gem 9.5/10
108 Jerome Bettis RC	10	12	20	40
280A Drew Bledsoe RC ERR	8	10	15	30
280B Drew Bledsoe RC COR	8	10	15	30

1993 Topps

	NmMt 8	NmMt+ 8.5	MT 9	Gem 9.5/10
130 Drew Bledsoe RC	8	10	15	30
166 Jerome Bettis RC	10	12	20	40

1993 Upper Deck

	NmMt 8	NmMt+ 8.5	MT 9	Gem 9.5/10
20 Jerome Bettis RC	10	12	15	25

1993 Upper Deck Rookie Exchange

	NmMt 8	NmMt+ 8.5	MT 9	Gem 9.5/10
RE2 Drew Bledsoe UER	8	10	15	25
RE7 Jerome Bettis	10	12	20	30

1994 Bowman

	NmMt 8	NmMt+ 8.5	MT 9	Gem 9.5/10
2 Marshall Faulk RC	15	20	40	120
68 Isaac Bruce RC	12	15	25	40

1994 Collector's Choice

	NmMt 8	NmMt+ 8.5	MT 9	Gem 9.5/10
14 Marshall Faulk RC	6	8	12	30

1994 Fleer Rookie Exchange

	NmMt 8	NmMt+ 8.5	MT 9	Gem 9.5/10
3 Marshall Faulk	15	20	30	40

1994 Pinnacle

	NmMt 8	NmMt+ 8.5	MT 9	Gem 9.5/10
198 Marshall Faulk RC	8	10	15	40

1994 Playoff

	NmMt 8	NmMt+ 8.5	MT 9	Gem 9.5/10
300 Larry Allen RC	8	40	100	400

1994 Playoff Contenders

	NmMt 8	NmMt+ 8.5	MT 9	Gem 9.5/10
104 Marshall Faulk RC	8	10	15	40

1994 Select

	NmMt 8	NmMt+ 8.5	MT 9	Gem 9.5/10
200 Marshall Faulk RC	8	10	20	40
SR1 Marshall Faulk SR	35	40	50	80

1994 SkyBox Impact

	NmMt 8	NmMt+ 8.5	MT 9	Gem 9.5/10
274 Marshall Faulk RC	8	10	15	25

1994 SkyBox Premium

	NmMt 8	NmMt+ 8.5	MT 9	Gem 9.5/10
158 Marshall Faulk RC	10	12	20	40

1994 SP

	NmMt 8	NmMt+ 8.5	MT 9	Gem 9.5/10
3 Marshall Faulk RC	20	30	▼40	100
5 Trent Dilfer RC	10	12	15	40

1994 SP Die Cuts

	NmMt 8	NmMt+ 8.5	MT 9	Gem 9.5/10
3 Marshall Faulk	20	25	40	400

1994 Stadium Club

	NmMt 8	NmMt+ 8.5	MT 9	Gem 9.5/10
288 Larry Allen RC	8	10	15	30
327 Marshall Faulk RC	8	10	12	40

1994 Topps

	NmMt 8	NmMt+ 8.5	MT 9	Gem 9.5/10
445 Marshall Faulk RC	6	8	12	40

1994 Ultra

	NmMt 8	NmMt+ 8.5	MT 9	Gem 9.5/10
133 Marshall Faulk RC	8	10	15	40

1994 Upper Deck

	NmMt 8	NmMt+ 8.5	MT 9	Gem 9.5/10
7 Marshall Faulk RC	8	10	15	60

1995 Absolute

	NmMt 8	NmMt+ 8.5	MT 9	Gem 9.5/10
182 Steve McNair RC	6	8	12	30

1995 Action Packed

	NmMt 8	NmMt+ 8.5	MT 9	Gem 9.5/10
36 Steve McNair RC	6	8	12	30

1995 Action Packed Rookies/Stars

	NmMt 8	NmMt+ 8.5	MT 9	Gem 9.5/10
90 Curtis Martin RC	6	8	12	30

		NmMt 8	NmMt+ 8.5	MT 9	Gem 9.5/10
92	Terrell Davis RC	6	8	12	30
101	Steve McNair RC	6	8	12	30

1995 Bowman

		NmMt 8	NmMt+ 8.5	MT 9	Gem 9.5/10
3	Steve McNair RC	10	12	20	60
301	Curtis Martin RC	8	10	20	40

1995 Bowman's Best

		NmMt 8	NmMt+ 8.5	MT 9	Gem 9.5/10
R3	Steve McNair RC	10	12	20	40
R5	Kerry Collins RC	8	10	12	30
R8	Joey Galloway RC	8	10	12	30
R74	Curtis Martin RC	12	15	30	80
R90	Antonio Freeman RC	8	10	12	25

1995 Bowman's Best Refractors

		NmMt 8	NmMt+ 8.5	MT 9	Gem 9.5/10
R3	Steve McNair	30	40	60	80
R74	Curtis Martin	40	50	80	100

1995 Crown Royale

		NmMt 8	NmMt+ 8.5	MT 9	Gem 9.5/10
78	Curtis Martin RC	8	10	15	60
126	Steve McNair RC	8	10	15	60
136	Terrell Davis RC	8	10	15	60

1995 Finest

		NmMt 8	NmMt+ 8.5	MT 9	Gem 9.5/10
264	Curtis Martin RC	10	12	20	40

1995 Flair

		NmMt 8	NmMt+ 8.5	MT 9	Gem 9.5/10
83	Steve McNair RC	6	8	12	60
124	Curtis Martin RC	6	8	12	60

1995 Playoff Contenders

		NmMt 8	NmMt+ 8.5	MT 9	Gem 9.5/10
126	Terrell Davis RC	6	8	10	40

1995 Select Certified

		NmMt 8	NmMt+ 8.5	MT 9	Gem 9.5/10
117	Curtis Martin RC	12	15	25	50
126	Terrell Davis RC	10	12	20	50

1995 Select Certified Mirror Gold

		NmMt 8	NmMt+ 8.5	MT 9	Gem 9.5/10
117	Curtis Martin	40	50	80	300
126	Terrell Davis	30	▲40	80	▲200

1995 SP

		NmMt 8	NmMt+ 8.5	MT 9	Gem 9.5/10
3	Steve McNair RC	12	15	30	60
5	Kerry Collins RC	10	12	25	50
6	Joey Galloway RC	10	12	25	50
18	Curtis Martin RC	12	15	40	150
99	Warren Sapp RC	10	12	25	60
103	Derrick Brooks RC	10	12	25	50
130	Terrell Davis RC	10	12	30	80
174	Ty Law RC	8	10	15	25

1995 SP Championship

		NmMt 8	NmMt+ 8.5	MT 9	Gem 9.5/10
14	Terrell Davis RC	10	12	20	80
19	Steve McNair RC	10	12	25	100
29	Curtis Martin RC	10	12	25	100

1996 Bowman's Best

		NmMt 8	NmMt+ 8.5	MT 9	Gem 9.5/10
147	Terrell Owens RC	12	15	25	40
148	Jonathan Ogden RC	12	15	25	40
162	Tedy Bruschi RC	15	20	30	60
164	Ray Lewis RC	40	50	80	150
165	Marvin Harrison RC	8	10	15	30
170	Eddie George RC	10	12	20	40
175	Zach Thomas RC	8	10	12	25
180	Keyshawn Johnson RC	8	10	15	40

1996 Bowman's Best Atomic Refractors

		NmMt 8	NmMt+ 8.5	MT 9	Gem 9.5/10
147	Terrell Owens	50	60	120	300
165	Marvin Harrison	50	60	120	
180	Keyshawn Johnson	25	30	60	150

1996 Bowman's Best Refractors

		NmMt 8	NmMt+ 8.5	MT 9	Gem 9.5/10
147	Terrell Owens	30	40	60	100
162	Tedy Bruschi	60	80	100	250
164	Ray Lewis	175	200	300	500
165	Marvin Harrison	30	40	80	
170	Eddie George	15	20	40	80
180	Keyshawn Johnson	12	15	30	60

1996 Collector's Choice

		NmMt 8	NmMt+ 8.5	MT 9	Gem 9.5/10
20	Ray Lewis RC	12	15	25	40

1996 Collector's Choice Update

		NmMt 8	NmMt+ 8.5	MT 9	Gem 9.5/10
U32	Ray Lewis	10	12	20	40

1996 Crown Royale

		NmMt 8	NmMt+ 8.5	MT 9	Gem 9.5/10
27	Marvin Harrison RC	10	12	20	50
39	Terrell Owens RC	10	12	20	50

1996 Finest

		NmMt 8	NmMt+ 8.5	MT 9	Gem 9.5/10
225	Keyshawn Johnson B RC	6	8	12	25
243	Marvin Harrison B RC	10	12	25	50
338	Terrell Owens B RC	10	12	25	50
344	Brian Dawkins B RC	10	12	80	200

1996 Finest Refractors

		NmMt 8	NmMt+ 8.5	MT 9	Gem 9.5/10
225	Keyshawn Johnson B	20	25	40	150
243	Marvin Harrison B	40	50	80	
338	Terrell Owens B	40	50	60	300

1996 Fleer

		NmMt 8	NmMt+ 8.5	MT 9	Gem 9.5/10
165	Ray Lewis RC	12	15	30	50

1996 Score Board Lasers

		NmMt 8	NmMt+ 8.5	MT 9	Gem 9.5/10
99	Ray Lewis RC	10	12	25	50

1996 Select Certified

		NmMt 8	NmMt+ 8.5	MT 9	Gem 9.5/10
91	Marvin Harrison RC	12	15	25	50
105	Keyshawn Johnson RC	8	10	15	30

1996 SP

		NmMt 8	NmMt+ 8.5	MT 9	Gem 9.5/10
1	Keyshawn Johnson RC	8	10	15	40
4	Jonathan Ogden RC	20	25	60	350
5	Eddie George RC	8	10	20	100
7	Terrell Owens RC	20	25	60	400
18	Marvin Harrison RC	15	20	35	100
126	Mike Alstott RC	8	10	20	40

1996 Stadium Club

		NmMt 8	NmMt+ 8.5	MT 9	Gem 9.5/10
351	Ray Lewis SP RC	20	25	60	100

1996 Topps Chrome

		NmMt 8	NmMt+ 8.5	MT 9	Gem 9.5/10
156	Marvin Harrison RC	15	20	25	60
159	Keyshawn Johnson RC	8	10	20	30
162	Eddie George RC	10	12	20	50
163	Jonathan Ogden RC	10	12	25	80

1996 Topps Chrome Refractors

		NmMt 8	NmMt+ 8.5	MT 9	Gem 9.5/10
156	Marvin Harrison	50	60	80	150
162	Eddie George	40	50	80	

1997 Bowman's Best

		NmMt 8	NmMt+ 8.5	MT 9	Gem 9.5/10
96	Jake Plummer RC	5	6	8	15
101	Tony Gonzalez RC	8	10	15	30
125	Warrick Dunn RC	5	6	8	15

1997 Pacific Philadelphia

		NmMt 8	NmMt+ 8.5	MT 9	Gem 9.5/10
199	Adam Vinatieri RC	80	100	125	▼300

1997 Pinnacle Certified

		NmMt 8	NmMt+ 8.5	MT 9	Gem 9.5/10
129	Tiki Barber RC	10	12	20	25
149	Tony Gonzalez RC	8	10	20	30

1997 Pinnacle Totally Certified Platinum Red

		NmMt 8	NmMt+ 8.5	MT 9	Gem 9.5/10
129	Tiki Barber RC	15	20	25	50
149	Tony Gonzalez RC	12	15	25	60

1997 SP Authentic

		NmMt 8	NmMt+ 8.5	MT 9	Gem 9.5/10
1	Orlando Pace RC	15	20	60	
10	Warrick Dunn RC	12	15	25	80
11	Tony Gonzalez RC	30	40	50	▲250
23	Jake Plummer RC	12	15	25	80
25	Corey Dillon RC	12	15	25	80
116	Jason Taylor RC	20	30	80	400
137	Tiki Barber RC	15	20	25	40
186	Ronde Barber RC	25	30	50	

1997 Topps Chrome

		NmMt 8	NmMt+ 8.5	MT 9	Gem 9.5/10
24	Tony Gonzalez RC	15	20	40	125

1998 Absolute Hobby

		NmMt 8	NmMt+ 8.5	MT 9	Gem 9.5/10
40	Randy Moss RC	15	20	30	120
165	Peyton Manning RC	25	30	50	250

1998 Absolute Retail

		NmMt 8	NmMt+ 8.5	MT 9	Gem 9.5/10
40	Randy Moss RC	8	10	15	40
165	Peyton Manning RC	15	20	25	80

1998 Aurora

		NmMt 8	NmMt+ 8.5	MT 9	Gem 9.5/10
71	Peyton Manning RC	20	25	50	150

1998 Black Diamond Rookies

		NmMt 8	NmMt+ 8.5	MT 9	Gem 9.5/10
91	Peyton Manning RC	25	30	50	100
97	Randy Moss RC	15	20	30	60

1998 Black Diamond Rookies Double

		NmMt 8	NmMt+ 8.5	MT 9	Gem 9.5/10
91	Peyton Manning	20	25	60	120

1998 Black Diamond Rookies Triple

		NmMt 8	NmMt+ 8.5	MT 9	Gem 9.5/10
91	Peyton Manning	60	80	120	250

1998 Bowman

		NmMt 8	NmMt+ 8.5	MT 9	Gem 9.5/10
1	Peyton Manning RC	20	25	30	▲80
27	Hines Ward RC	8	10	20	40
29	Ahman Green RC	8	10	15	25
181	Charles Woodson RC	8	10	15	25
182	Randy Moss RC	10	12	20	40

8 Bowman Interstate

	NmMt 8	NmMt+ 8.5	MT 9	Gem 9.5/10
Peyton Manning	30	40	60	120
Randy Moss	20	25	40	100

8 Bowman Rookie Autographs

	NmMt 8	NmMt+ 8.5	MT 9	Gem 9.5/10
Peyton Manning	450	500	550	1,000

8 Bowman Chrome Preview

	NmMt 8	NmMt+ 8.5	MT 9	Gem 9.5/10
Peyton Manning	25	30	50	100

8 Bowman Chrome Preview Refractors

	NmMt 8	NmMt+ 8.5	MT 9	Gem 9.5/10
Peyton Manning	50	60	100	200

8 Bowman Chrome

	NmMt 8	NmMt+ 8.5	MT 9	Gem 9.5/10
Peyton Manning RC	30	40	60	120
Hines Ward RC	12	15	25	50
Charles Woodson RC	10	12	20	40
Randy Moss RC	12	15	25	50

8 Bowman Chrome Interstate

	NmMt 8	NmMt+ 8.5	MT 9	Gem 9.5/10
Peyton Manning	40	50	60	150
Hines Ward	15	20	30	60
Randy Moss	15	20	30	60

8 Bowman Chrome Interstate Refractors

	NmMt 8	NmMt+ 8.5	MT 9	Gem 9.5/10
Peyton Manning	175	200	350	600
Hines Ward	60	80	100	200
Randy Moss	60	80	120	300

8 Bowman Chrome Refractors

	NmMt 8	NmMt+ 8.5	MT 9	Gem 9.5/10
Peyton Manning	100	125	225	▲800
Hines Ward	40	50	80	125
Randy Moss	35	40	100	200

8 Bowman's Best

	NmMt 8	NmMt+ 8.5	MT 9	Gem 9.5/10
Charles Woodson RC	8	10	15	30
Randy Moss RC	10	12	20	35
Peyton Manning RC	20	25	30	▲60
Hines Ward RC	10	12	20	35

8 Bowman's Best Atomic Refractors

	NmMt 8	NmMt+ 8.5	MT 9	Gem 9.5/10
Randy Moss	100	120	150	300
Peyton Manning	250	300	400	600

8 Bowman's Best Refractors

	NmMt 8	NmMt+ 8.5	MT 9	Gem 9.5/10
Randy Moss	40	50	60	120
Peyton Manning	60	80	100	200

998 Bowman's Best Autographs

	NmMt 8	NmMt+ 8.5	MT 9	Gem 9.5/10
Peyton Manning	350	400	500	650
Peyton Manning	350	400	500	650

998 Bowman's Best Performers

	NmMt 8	NmMt+ 8.5	MT 9	Gem 9.5/10
Peyton Manning	25	30	40	80

998 Collector's Edge First Place

	NmMt 8	NmMt+ 8.5	MT 9	Gem 9.5/10
Matt Hasselbeck RC	20	25	40	60
Peyton Manning RC	12	15	25	50

998 Collector's Edge First Place Rookie Ink

	NmMt 8	NmMt+ 8.5	MT 9	Gem 9.5/10
Peyton Manning Blue	135	150	175	
Peyton Manning Black	135	150	175	

1998 Collector's Edge Masters

		NmMt 8	NmMt+ 8.5	MT 9	Gem 9.5/10
73	Peyton Manning RC	20	25	30	50

1998 Crown Royale

		NmMt 8	NmMt+ 8.5	MT 9	Gem 9.5/10
54	Peyton Manning RC	25	30	50	150
75	Randy Moss RC	12	15	25	80

1998 E-X2001

		NmMt 8	NmMt+ 8.5	MT 9	Gem 9.5/10
54	Peyton Manning RC	20	25	40	80
55	Randy Moss RC	12	15	25	50

1998 E-X2001 Star Date 2001

		NmMt 8	NmMt+ 8.5	MT 9	Gem 9.5/10
15	Peyton Manning	15	20	30	60

1998 Finest

		NmMt 8	NmMt+ 8.5	MT 9	Gem 9.5/10
121	Peyton Manning RC	30	35	50	100
135	Randy Moss RC	12	15	25	50
148	Hines Ward RC	12	15	25	40

1998 Finest No-Protectors

		NmMt 8	NmMt+ 8.5	MT 9	Gem 9.5/10
121	Peyton Manning	35	40	60	120
135	Randy Moss	12	15	25	60

1998 Finest No-Protectors Refractors

		NmMt 8	NmMt+ 8.5	MT 9	Gem 9.5/10
121	Peyton Manning	100	120	175	400
135	Randy Moss	40	50	80	150

1998 Finest Refractors

		NmMt 8	NmMt+ 8.5	MT 9	Gem 9.5/10
121	Peyton Manning	60	80	120	200
135	Randy Moss	25	30	50	100

1998 Finest Undergrads

		NmMt 8	NmMt+ 8.5	MT 9	Gem 9.5/10
U20	Peyton Manning	25	30	35	▲80

1998 Flair Showcase Row 3

		NmMt 8	NmMt+ 8.5	MT 9	Gem 9.5/10
3	Peyton Manning RC	15	20	30	80
5	Randy Moss RC	10	12	20	50

1998 Flair Showcase Row 2

		NmMt 8	NmMt+ 8.5	MT 9	Gem 9.5/10
3	Peyton Manning	15	20	40	80
5	Randy Moss	10	12	25	50

1998 Flair Showcase Row 1

		NmMt 8	NmMt+ 8.5	MT 9	Gem 9.5/10
3	Peyton Manning	60	80	100	175
5	Randy Moss	25	30	40	80

1998 Flair Showcase Row 0

		NmMt 8	NmMt+ 8.5	MT 9	Gem 9.5/10
3	Peyton Manning	100	120	▲300	1,000
5	Randy Moss	50	60	80	200

1998 Fleer Brilliants

		NmMt 8	NmMt+ 8.5	MT 9	Gem 9.5/10
120	Peyton Manning RC	30	40	50	150
140	Randy Moss RC	15	20	30	100

1998 Fleer Brilliants Blue

		NmMt 8	NmMt+ 8.5	MT 9	Gem 9.5/10
120	Peyton Manning	40	50	80	150

1998 Leaf Rookies and Stars

		NmMt 8	NmMt+ 8.5	MT 9	Gem 9.5/10
199	Randy Moss RC	20	25	50	80
202	Hines Ward RC	20	25	40	80
233	Peyton Manning RC	40	50	60	120
270	Peyton Manning PT	25	30	40	80

1998 Leaf Rookies and Stars True Blue

		NmMt 8	NmMt+ 8.5	MT 9	Gem 9.5/10
233	Peyton Manning	40	50	80	200

1998 Metal Universe

		NmMt 8	NmMt+ 8.5	MT 9	Gem 9.5/10
189	Peyton Manning RC	15	20	30	60
190	Randy Moss RC	8	10	15	40

1998 Pacific

		NmMt 8	NmMt+ 8.5	MT 9	Gem 9.5/10
181	Peyton Manning RC	12	15	30	150

1998 Playoff Contenders Leather

		NmMt 8	NmMt+ 8.5	MT 9	Gem 9.5/10
37	Peyton Manning	20	25	40	80
52	Randy Moss	12	15	25	50

1998 Playoff Contenders Ticket

		NmMt 8	NmMt+ 8.5	MT 9	Gem 9.5/10
5	Priest Holmes RC	25	30	60	
87	Peyton Manning AU/200*	4,000	6,000	7,000	8,000
89	Fred Taylor AU/500*	60	80	120	300
92	Randy Moss AU/300*	1,200	1,400	2,000	2,500
94	Hines Ward AU/500*	250	300	500	1,500
97	Ahman Green AU/500*	40	50	100	

1998 Playoff Contenders Ticket Red

		NmMt 8	NmMt+ 8.5	MT 9	Gem 9.5/10
87	Peyton Manning	200	225	350	

1998 Playoff Momentum Hobby

		NmMt 8	NmMt+ 8.5	MT 9	Gem 9.5/10
98	Peyton Manning RC	▼25	▼30	▼40	▼80
131	Randy Moss RC	20	25	40	▼50

1998 Playoff Momentum Retail

		NmMt 8	NmMt+ 8.5	MT 9	Gem 9.5/10
146	Peyton Manning RC	15	20	30	60

1998 Playoff Prestige Hobby

		NmMt 8	NmMt+ 8.5	MT 9	Gem 9.5/10
165	Peyton Manning RC	20	25	40	60
173	Randy Moss RC	12	15	20	

1998 Playoff Prestige Retail

		NmMt 8	NmMt+ 8.5	MT 9	Gem 9.5/10
165	Peyton Manning RC	10	12	20	50
173	Randy Moss RC	6	8	10	30

1998 Revolution

		NmMt 8	NmMt+ 8.5	MT 9	Gem 9.5/10
58	Peyton Manning RC	20	25	40	80

1998 Score

		NmMt 8	NmMt+ 8.5	MT 9	Gem 9.5/10
233	Peyton Manning RC	12	15	30	60
235	Randy Moss RC	8	10	15	30
252	Hines Ward RC	8	10	12	25

1998 Score Showcase Artist's Proofs

		NmMt 8	NmMt+ 8.5	MT 9	Gem 9.5/10
PP123 150	Peyton Manning	60	80	80	

1998 SkyBox Premium

		NmMt 8	NmMt+ 8.5	MT 9	Gem 9.5/10
231	Peyton Manning RC	35	40	50	150
240	Randy Moss RC	12	15	25	60

1998 SkyBox Thunder

		NmMt 8	NmMt+ 8.5	MT 9	Gem 9.5/10
239	Peyton Manning RC	15	20	30	80
242	Randy Moss RC	10	12	20	50

1998 SP Authentic

		NmMt 8	NmMt+ 8.5	MT 9	Gem 9.5/10
14	Peyton Manning RC	600	700	1,200	▼3,000
16	Fred Taylor RC	25	30	40	150
18	Randy Moss RC	300	400	600	2,000
23	Charles Woodson RC	50	60	▲250	600
27	Ahman Green RC	30	40	50	100

—Peyton Manning #14 BGS 10 (PRISTINE) sold for $2460 (eBay; 6/07)

1998 SP Authentic Die Cuts

		NmMt 8	NmMt+ 8.5	MT 9	Gem 9.5/10
11	Brian Griese	30	40	60	100
14	Peyton Manning	700	800	1,000	3,000
16	Fred Taylor	40	50	80	120
18	Randy Moss	250	300	500	800
23	Charles Woodson	50	60	100	250
27	Ahman Green	30	40	60	100

1998 SP Authentic Maximum Impact

		NmMt 8	NmMt+ 8.5	MT 9	Gem 9.5/10
SE11	Peyton Manning	12	15	25	80

1998 SPx Finite

		NmMt 8	NmMt+ 8.5	MT 9	Gem 9.5/10
181	Peyton Manning/1998 RC	200	400	500	1,500
239	Randy Moss/1998 RC	50	60	100	
287	Peyton Manning ET	30	40	60	150

1998 Stadium Club

		NmMt 8	NmMt+ 8.5	MT 9	Gem 9.5/10
182	Hines Ward RC	8	10	20	30
189	Randy Moss RC	10	12	25	40
195	Peyton Manning RC	20	25	40	60

1998 Stadium Club First Day

		NmMt 8	NmMt+ 8.5	MT 9	Gem 9.5/10
195	Peyton Manning	80	100	150	300

1998 Stadium Club Prime Rookies

		NmMt 8	NmMt+ 8.5	MT 9	Gem 9.5/10
PR10	Peyton Manning	12	15	25	50

1998 Topps

		NmMt 8	NmMt+ 8.5	MT 9	Gem 9.5/10
341	Hines Ward RC	10	12	20	40
352	Randy Moss RC	10	12	20	40
360	Peyton Manning RC	15	20	35	200

1998 Topps Autographs

		NmMt 8	NmMt+ 8.5	MT 9	Gem 9.5/10
A1	Randy Moss	80	125	300	400
A10B	Peyton Manning Bronze	450	500	600	900
A10G	Peyton Manning Gold	450	500	600	900

1998 Topps Chrome

		NmMt 8	NmMt+ 8.5	MT 9	Gem 9.5/10
35	Randy Moss RC	12	15	30	80
44	Charles Woodson RC	8	10	15	60
165	Peyton Manning RC	50	60	80	300

1998 Topps Chrome Refractors

		NmMt 8	NmMt+ 8.5	MT 9	Gem 9.5/10
35	Randy Moss	100	125	200	400
44	Charles Woodson	20	25	80	▲300
133	Brian Griese	12	15	30	60
152	Fred Taylor	12	15	30	60
165	Peyton Manning	200	350	500	▲1,600

1998 Topps Gold Label Class 1

		NmMt 8	NmMt+ 8.5	MT 9	Gem 9.5/10
20	Peyton Manning RC	20	25	40	80

1998 Topps Gold Label Class 1 Black

		NmMt 8	NmMt+ 8.5	MT 9	Gem 9.5/10
20	Peyton Manning	50	60	80	120

1998 Topps Gold Label Class 2

		NmMt 8	NmMt+ 8.5	MT 9	Gem 9.5/10
20	Peyton Manning	25	30	50	120

1998 Topps Gold Label Class 2 Black

		NmMt 8	NmMt+ 8.5	MT 9	Gem 9.5/10
20	Peyton Manning	80	100	125	150

1998 Topps Gold Label Class 3

		NmMt 8	NmMt+ 8.5	MT 9	Gem 9.5/10
20	Peyton Manning	30	40	60	120

1998 Topps Season Opener

		NmMt 8	NmMt+ 8.5	MT 9	Gem 9.5/10
1	Peyton Manning RC	15	20	35	80
11	Hines Ward RC	8	10	15	30
22	Randy Moss RC	12	15	25	50

1998 Topps Stars

		NmMt 8	NmMt+ 8.5	MT 9	Gem 9.5/10
67	Peyton Manning RC	15	20	30	100

1998 Topps Stars Bronze

		NmMt 8	NmMt+ 8.5	MT 9	Gem 9.5/10
67	Peyton Manning	15	20	30	150

1998 UD3

		NmMt 8	NmMt+ 8.5	MT 9	Gem 9.5/10
1	Peyton Manning FE	30	35	50	200
91	Peyton Manning FF	40	50	80	200
181	Peyton Manning FR RC	15	20	30	100
197	Randy Moss FR RC	10	12	20	60

1998 UD Choice

		NmMt 8	NmMt+ 8.5	MT 9	Gem 9.5/10
193	Peyton Manning RC	12	15	25	50
200	Randy Moss RC	6	8	12	25
256	Peyton Manning DN	15	20	30	60

1998 Ultra

		NmMt 8	NmMt+ 8.5	MT 9	Gem 9.5/10
201	Peyton Manning RC	30	40	50	120
207	Randy Moss RC	12	15	30	60
416	Peyton Manning	25	30	40	100

1998 Ultra Gold Medallion

		NmMt 8	NmMt+ 8.5	MT 9	Gem 9.5/10
201G	Peyton Manning	40	50	80	300
207G	Randy Moss	25	30	50	125

1998 Upper Deck

		NmMt 8	NmMt+ 8.5	MT 9	Gem 9.5/10
1	Peyton Manning RC	40	50	80	125
17	Randy Moss RC	15	20	25	80

1998 Upper Deck Game Jerseys

		NmMt 8	NmMt+ 8.5	MT 9	Gem 9.5/10
GJ16	Peyton Manning	150	200	300	500

1998 Upper Deck Encore

		NmMt 8	NmMt+ 8.5	MT 9	Gem 9.5/10
1	Peyton Manning RC	30	35	50	125
12	Randy Moss RC	15	20	30	60

1999 Black Diamond

		NmMt 8	NmMt+ 8.5	MT 9	Gem 9.5/10
114	Donovan McNabb RC	15	20	30	100
126	Torry Holt RC	10	12	15	60

1999 Bowman

		NmMt 8	NmMt+ 8.5	MT 9	Gem 9.5/10
168	Donovan McNabb RC	12	15	20	60

1999 Bowman Chrome

		NmMt 8	NmMt+ 8.5	MT 9	Gem 9.5/10
168	Donovan McNabb RC	10	12	25	50
174	Torry Holt RC	10	12	20	40

1999 Bowman Chrome Interstate

		NmMt 8	NmMt+ 8.5	MT 9	Gem 9.5/10
161	Edgerrin James	10	12	20	60
166	Daunte Culpepper	10	12	20	60
168	Donovan McNabb	12	15	30	100
174	Torry Holt	10	12	20	60

1999 Bowman Chrome Refractors

		NmMt 8	NmMt+ 8.5	MT 9	Gem 9.5/10
161	Edgerrin James	12	15	25	125
166	Daunte Culpepper	12	15	25	125
168	Donovan McNabb	25	30	60	300
174	Torry Holt	12	15	25	125

1999 Bowman's Best

		NmMt 8	NmMt+ 8.5	MT 9	Gem 9.5/10
110	Kurt Warner RC	10	12	25	60
118	Donovan McNabb RC	10	12	20	40
120	Torry Holt RC	8	10	15	30

1999 Bowman's Best Atomic Refractors

		NmMt 8	NmMt+ 8.5	MT 9	Gem 9.5/10
118	Donovan McNabb	60	80	120	400

1999 Bowman's Best Refractors

		NmMt 8	NmMt+ 8.5	MT 9	Gem 9.5/10
107	Daunte Culpepper	15	20	30	80
115	Edgerrin James	15	20	30	80
118	Donovan McNabb	40	50	60	150
120	Torry Holt	15	20	30	80

1999 Collector's Edge First Place

		NmMt 8	NmMt+ 8.5	MT 9	Gem 9.5/10
201PG	Kurt Warner Promo Gold	10	12	20	35
201PS	Kurt Warner Promo Silver	10	12	25	40

1999 Donruss

		NmMt 8	NmMt+ 8.5	MT 9	Gem 9.5/10
188	Kurt Warner RC	8	10	20	40

1999 Donruss Elite

		NmMt 8	NmMt+ 8.5	MT 9	Gem 9.5/10
178	Torry Holt RC	10	12	25	80
190	Donovan McNabb RC	15	20	40	120

1999 E-X Century

		NmMt 8	NmMt+ 8.5	MT 9	Gem 9.5/10
64	Donovan McNabb RC	12	15	25	80

1999 Finest

		NmMt 8	NmMt+ 8.5	MT 9	Gem 9.5/10
166	Donovan McNabb RC	10	12	15	40
175	Torry Holt RC	6	8	12	30

1999 Finest Refractors

		NmMt 8	NmMt+ 8.5	MT 9	Gem 9.5/10
151	Daunte Culpepper	8	10	20	40
152	Edgerrin James	10	12	25	▼40
166	Donovan McNabb	15	20	35	60

1999 Flair Showcase

		NmMt 8	NmMt+ 8.5	MT 9	Gem 9.5/10
182	Donovan McNabb RC	50	60	100	

1999 Fleer Focus

		NmMt 8	NmMt+ 8.5	MT 9	Gem 9.5/10
40	Kurt Warner RC	10	12	20	40
118	Donald Driver RC	35	40	80	150
172	Donovan McNabb RC	15	20	40	80

1999 Fleer Mystique

		NmMt 8	NmMt+ 8.5	MT 9	Gem 9.5/10
102	Donovan McNabb RC	▼15	▼20	▼25	▼30
105	Daunte Culpepper RC	10	12	25	80
109	Torry Holt RC	10	12	25	80

99 Fleer Tradition

	NmMt 8	NmMt+ 8.5	MT 9	Gem 9.5/10
Donovan McNabb RC	10	12	20	60

99 Leaf Certified

	NmMt 8	NmMt+ 8.5	MT 9	Gem 9.5/10
Daunte Culpepper RC	10	12	25	50
Donovan McNabb RC	15	20	40	100
Torry Holt RC	10	12	25	50

99 Leaf Rookies and Stars

	NmMt 8	NmMt+ 8.5	MT 9	Gem 9.5/10
Daunte Culpepper RC	10	12	25	50
Donovan McNabb RC	15	20	40	100
Kurt Warner RC	15	20	50	
Torry Holt RC	10	12	25	50

99 Metal Universe

	NmMt 8	NmMt+ 8.5	MT 9	Gem 9.5/10
Donovan McNabb RC	8	10	15	50

99 Pacific

	NmMt 8	NmMt+ 8.5	MT 9	Gem 9.5/10
Kurt Warner RC/Tony Horne	12	15	35	120
Torry Holt RC	6	8	12	40
Donovan McNabb RC	8	10	15	60

99 Paramount

	NmMt 8	NmMt+ 8.5	MT 9	Gem 9.5/10
Edgerrin James RC	6	8	12	30
Donovan McNabb RC	8	10	15	50

99 Playoff Contenders SSD

	NmMt 8	NmMt+ 8.5	MT 9	Gem 9.5/10
Jeff Garcia AU/325* RC	60	80	125	200
Kurt Warner AU/1825* RC	150	175	250	600
R.Williams AU/725* RC	35	40	60	120
D.McNabb AU/525* RC	35	40	50	120
E.James AU/525* RC	30	35	60	200
Torry Holt AU/1025* RC	30	35	60	200
D.Culpepper AU/1025* RC	30	35	50	100
Champ Bailey AU/1725* RC	35	40	60	400

99 Playoff Momentum SSD

	NmMt 8	NmMt+ 8.5	MT 9	Gem 9.5/10
Kurt Warner RC	20	25	40	80
Donovan McNabb RC	20	25	40	80

99 SkyBox Molten Metal

	NmMt 8	NmMt+ 8.5	MT 9	Gem 9.5/10
Kurt Warner RC	10	12	15	30
Donovan McNabb RC	8	10	15	30
Donald Driver RC	25	30	50	100

99 SP Authentic

	NmMt 8	NmMt+ 8.5	MT 9	Gem 9.5/10
Ricky Williams RC	20	25	40	80
Donovan McNabb RC	40	50	100	250
Torry Holt RC	15	20	▲100	▲125
Champ Bailey RC	25	80	100	400

99 SP Authentic Excitement

	NmMt 8	NmMt+ 8.5	MT 9	Gem 9.5/10
Ricky Williams	25	30	60	100
Edgerrin James	20	25	50	100
Donovan McNabb	100	120	200	400
Torry Holt	25	30	60	125

99 SP Signature

	NmMt 8	NmMt+ 8.5	MT 9	Gem 9.5/10
Donovan McNabb RC	20	25	40	80
Torry Holt RC	15	20	30	60

99 SPx

	NmMt 8	NmMt+ 8.5	MT 9	Gem 9.5/10
Champ Bailey AU RC	30	40	60	

		NmMt 8	NmMt+ 8.5	MT 9	Gem 9.5/10
129	Torry Holt AU RC	35	40	50	200
132	Donovan McNabb AU RC	35	40	50	100
134	D.Culpepper AU/500 RC	30	40	50	100
135	Ricky Williams AU/500 RC	50	60	80	120

1999 Stadium Club

		NmMt 8	NmMt+ 8.5	MT 9	Gem 9.5/10
165	Donovan McNabb RC	10	12	25	50
166	Torry Holt RC	8	10	20	40

1999 Stadium Club Chrome

		NmMt 8	NmMt+ 8.5	MT 9	Gem 9.5/10
133	Donovan McNabb RC	12	15	30	60
134	Torry Holt RC	10	12	25	50

1999 Topps

		NmMt 8	NmMt+ 8.5	MT 9	Gem 9.5/10
341	Donovan McNabb RC	12	15	30	60
343	Torry Holt RC	10	12	25	50

1999 Topps Collection

		NmMt 8	NmMt+ 8.5	MT 9	Gem 9.5/10
330	Daunte Culpepper	8	10	20	60
339	Edgerrin James	8	10	20	60
341	Donovan McNabb	10	12	25	80
343	Torry Holt	8	10	20	60

1999 Topps Chrome

		NmMt 8	NmMt+ 8.5	MT 9	Gem 9.5/10
147	Donovan McNabb RC	20	25	40	80
149	Torry Holt RC	12	15	25	40

1999 Topps Chrome Refractors

		NmMt 8	NmMt+ 8.5	MT 9	Gem 9.5/10
135	Ricky Williams	12	15	25	40
147	Donovan McNabb	30	35	50	80

1999 Topps Gold Label Class 1

		NmMt 8	NmMt+ 8.5	MT 9	Gem 9.5/10
71	Torry Holt RC	8	10	15	40
75	Donovan McNabb RC	10	12	20	50

1999 UD Ionix

		NmMt 8	NmMt+ 8.5	MT 9	Gem 9.5/10
65	Donovan McNabb RC	12	15	30	80

1999 Ultra

		NmMt 8	NmMt+ 8.5	MT 9	Gem 9.5/10
265	Torry Holt RC	12	15	30	
266	Donovan McNabb RC	15	20	40	

1999 Upper Deck

		NmMt 8	NmMt+ 8.5	MT 9	Gem 9.5/10
235	Donovan McNabb RC	15	20	40	100
248	Torry Holt RC	12	15	30	60

1999 Upper Deck Encore

		NmMt 8	NmMt+ 8.5	MT 9	Gem 9.5/10
139	Kurt Warner RC	10	12	20	60
190	Donovan McNabb RC	15	20	30	150

1999 Upper Deck MVP

		NmMt 8	NmMt+ 8.5	MT 9	Gem 9.5/10
220	Donovan McNabb RC	8	10	15	50

1999 Upper Deck Retro

		NmMt 8	NmMt+ 8.5	MT 9	Gem 9.5/10
117	Donovan McNabb RC	8	10	15	30

2000 Absolute Coaches Honors

		NmMt 8	NmMt+ 8.5	MT 9	Gem 9.5/10
195	Tom Brady	175	600	700	

2000 Aurora

		NmMt 8	NmMt+ 8.5	MT 9	Gem 9.5/10
84	Tom Brady RC	50	60	100	200

2000 Black Diamond

		NmMt 8	NmMt+ 8.5	MT 9	Gem 9.5/10
126	Tom Brady RC	▲250	▲300	500	▲1,200
166	Brian Urlacher JSY RC	30	40	60	120

2000 Bowman

		NmMt 8	NmMt+ 8.5	MT 9	Gem 9.5/10
177	Shaun Alexander RC	6	8	10	15
178	Brian Urlacher RC	8	10	15	50
236	Tom Brady RC	▲400	▲500	▲600	1,200

2000 Bowman Chrome

		NmMt 8	NmMt+ 8.5	MT 9	Gem 9.5/10
178	Brian Urlacher RC	15	20	50	80
236	Tom Brady RC	600	1,000	1,200	▲3,000

2000 Bowman Chrome Refractors

		NmMt 8	NmMt+ 8.5	MT 9	Gem 9.5/10
236	Tom Brady	6,000	8,000	10,000	20,000

2000 Collector's Edge Supreme

		NmMt 8	NmMt+ 8.5	MT 9	Gem 9.5/10
176	Tom Brady RC	▲400	▲500	600	800
190	Brian Urlacher RC	20	25	30	60

2000 Crown Royale

		NmMt 8	NmMt+ 8.5	MT 9	Gem 9.5/10
110	Tom Brady RC	▲150	▲250	300	800

2000 Crown Royale Retail

		NmMt 8	NmMt+ 8.5	MT 9	Gem 9.5/10
110	Tom Brady RC	40	50	300	500

2000 Crown Royale Rookie Autographs

		NmMt 8	NmMt+ 8.5	MT 9	Gem 9.5/10
110	Tom Brady	550	1,500	1,800	2,500

2000 Crown Royale Rookie Royalty

		NmMt 8	NmMt+ 8.5	MT 9	Gem 9.5/10
2	Tom Brady	▲100	▲125	▲200	500

2000 Donruss

		NmMt 8	NmMt+ 8.5	MT 9	Gem 9.5/10
230	Tom Brady RC	500	600	1,000	2,000

2000 Donruss Elite

		NmMt 8	NmMt+ 8.5	MT 9	Gem 9.5/10
183	Tom Brady RC	400	500	800	2,000

2000 Donruss Elite Rookie Die Cuts

		NmMt 8	NmMt+ 8.5	MT 9	Gem 9.5/10
183	Tom Brady	225	250	400	500

2000 E-X

		NmMt 8	NmMt+ 8.5	MT 9	Gem 9.5/10
122	Tom Brady RC	600	800	1,200	▲4,000
140	Brian Urlacher RC	25	30	60	120

2000 Finest

		NmMt 8	NmMt+ 8.5	MT 9	Gem 9.5/10
151	Brian Urlacher RC	25	30	40	80

2000 Fleer Mystique

		NmMt 8	NmMt+ 8.5	MT 9	Gem 9.5/10
103	Tom Brady RC	400	500	600	2,000

2000 Fleer Tradition

		NmMt 8	NmMt+ 8.5	MT 9	Gem 9.5/10
309	Brian Urlacher RC	8	10	20	
352	T.Brady RC/Stachelski RC	▲60	▲80	100	300

2000 Fleer Tradition Glossy

		NmMt 8	NmMt+ 8.5	MT 9	Gem 9.5/10
352	Tom Brady/Stachelski	40	60	80	500

2000 Impact

		NmMt 8	NmMt+ 8.5	MT 9	Gem 9.5/10
27	Tom Brady RC	80	100	150	300

2000 Leaf Certified

		NmMt 8	NmMt+ 8.5	MT 9	Gem 9.5/10
157	Brian Urlacher RC	15	20	30	50
207	Tom Brady RC	500	800	1,000	2,000

2000 Leaf Certified Mirror Red

		NmMt 8	NmMt+ 8.5	MT 9	Gem 9.5/10
207	Tom Brady	600	800	1,500	3,000

2000 Leaf Certified Rookie Die Cuts

		NmMt 8	NmMt+ 8.5	MT 9	Gem 9.5/10
207	Tom Brady	250	300	1,000	

2000 Leaf Limited

		NmMt 8	NmMt+ 8.5	MT 9	Gem 9.5/10
378	Tom Brady RC	2,000	2,500	3,500	4,000

2000 Leaf Rookies and Stars

		NmMt 8	NmMt+ 8.5	MT 9	Gem 9.5/10
134	Tom Brady RC	1,000	1,000	1,200	
301	Michael Vick XRC	20	25	30	40
302	Drew Brees XRC	60	80	100	250
306	LaDainian Tomlinson XRC	15	20	50	

2000 Metal

		NmMt 8	NmMt+ 8.5	MT 9	Gem 9.5/10
267	Tom Brady RC	200	250	300	700

2000 Metal Emerald

		NmMt 8	NmMt+ 8.5	MT 9	Gem 9.5/10
267	Tom Brady	250	400	500	

2000 Pacific

		NmMt 8	NmMt+ 8.5	MT 9	Gem 9.5/10
403	Tom Brady RC	▲100	▲125	150	400

2000 Pacific Autographs

		NmMt 8	NmMt+ 8.5	MT 9	Gem 9.5/10
403	Tom Brady/200*	450	500	▲1,000	▲3,200

2000 Pacific Omega

		NmMt 8	NmMt+ 8.5	MT 9	Gem 9.5/10
191	Tom Brady RC	200	225	800	▲2,000

2000 Pacific Prism Prospects

		NmMt 8	NmMt+ 8.5	MT 9	Gem 9.5/10
156	Tom Brady RC	400	800	1,000	

2000 Paramount

		NmMt 8	NmMt+ 8.5	MT 9	Gem 9.5/10
138	Tom Brady RC	80	100	125	350

2000 Paramount Draft Picks 325

		NmMt 8	NmMt+ 8.5	MT 9	Gem 9.5/10
138	Tom Brady	300	400	500	1,000

2000 Playoff Contenders

		NmMt 8	NmMt+ 8.5	MT 9	Gem 9.5/10
103	Brian Urlacher AU RC	100	125	250	
113	Shaun Alexander AU RC	20	25	40	
144	Tom Brady AU RC	8,000	10,000	16,000	18,000

2000 Playoff Contenders Round Numbers Autographs

		NmMt 8	NmMt+ 8.5	MT 9	Gem 9.5/10
11	M.Bulger/T.Brady	350	2,000	2,200	

2000 Playoff Momentum

		NmMt 8	NmMt+ 8.5	MT 9	Gem 9.5/10
180	Tom Brady RC	1,200	1,600	2,000	5,000

2000 Playoff Prestige

		NmMt 8	NmMt+ 8.5	MT 9	Gem 9.5/10
286	Tom Brady RC	200	250	400	800

2000 Press Pass Gold Zone

		NmMt 8	NmMt+ 8.5	MT 9	Gem 9.5/10
37	Tom Brady	60	80	125	300

2000 Press Pass Autographs

		NmMt 8	NmMt+ 8.5	MT 9	Gem 9.5/10
3	Tom Brady	800	1,000	1,500	3,000

2000 Private Stock

		NmMt 8	NmMt+ 8.5	MT 9	Gem 9.5/10
128	Tom Brady RC	400	600	800	1,500

2000 Private Stock Retail

		NmMt 8	NmMt+ 8.5	MT 9	Gem 9.5/10
128	Tom Brady RC	▲300	▲400	▲500	▲1,000

2000 Private Stock Premiere Date

		NmMt 8	NmMt+ 8.5	MT 9	Gem 9.5/10
128	Tom Brady	350	400	500	800

2000 Quantum Leaf

		NmMt 8	NmMt+ 8.5	MT 9	Gem 9.5/10
343	Tom Brady RC	125	150	400	2,000

2000 Revolution

		NmMt 8	NmMt+ 8.5	MT 9	Gem 9.5/10
128	Tom Brady RC	1,200	1,800	3,000	4,000

2000 Revolution First Look

		NmMt 8	NmMt+ 8.5	MT 9	Gem 9.5/10
22	Tom Brady	40	50	100	

2000 Score

		NmMt 8	NmMt+ 8.5	MT 9	Gem 9.5/10
288	Brian Urlacher RC	8	10	15	25
316	Tom Brady RC	150	200	300	1,000

2000 Score Scorecard

		NmMt 8	NmMt+ 8.5	MT 9	Gem 9.5/10
316	Tom Brady	300	400	500	

2000 SkyBox Dominion

		NmMt 8	NmMt+ 8.5	MT 9	Gem 9.5/10
234	T.Brady RC/Carmazzi RC	40	50	80	125

2000 SkyBox Dominion Extra

		NmMt 8	NmMt+ 8.5	MT 9	Gem 9.5/10
234	G.Carmazzi/T.Brady			100	350

2000 SP Authentic

		NmMt 8	NmMt+ 8.5	MT 9	Gem 9.5/10
118	Tom Brady RC	5,000	6,000	8,000	20,000
122	Brian Urlacher RC	50	60	100	300
140	Shaun Alexander RC	12	15	25	80

2000 SPx

		NmMt 8	NmMt+ 8.5	MT 9	Gem 9.5/10
130	Tom Brady RC	1,000	2,000	3,000	4,000
134	Brian Urlacher JSY AU RC	125	150	225	

2000 Stadium Club

		NmMt 8	NmMt+ 8.5	MT 9	Gem 9.5/10
170	Shaun Alexander RC	10	12	20	40

2000 Topps

		NmMt 8	NmMt+ 8.5	MT 9	Gem 9.5/10
383	Brian Urlacher RC	10	12	20	40

2000 Topps Chrome

		NmMt 8	NmMt+ 8.5	MT 9	Gem 9.5/10
241	Shaun Alexander RC	12	15	25	40
253	Brian Urlacher RC	40	50	80	125

2000 UD Graded

		NmMt 8	NmMt+ 8.5	MT 9	Gem 9.5/10
104	Tom Brady RC	800	1,000	1,200	1,500
111	Brian Urlacher RC	25	30	40	50
157	Shaun Alexander AU RC	35	40	60	100

2000 UD Ionix

		NmMt 8	NmMt+ 8.5	MT 9	Gem 9.5/10
77	Tom Brady RC	500	600	800	1,300

2000 Ultimate Victory

		NmMt 8	NmMt+ 8.5	MT 9	Gem 9.5/10
146	Tom Brady RC	250	300	400	1,000

2000 Ultimate Victory Parallel

		NmMt 8	NmMt+ 8.5	MT 9	Gem 9.5/10
146	Tom Brady	▲400	▲500	600	

2000 Ultra

		NmMt 8	NmMt+ 8.5	MT 9	Gem 9.5/10
234	Tom Brady RC	100	125	400	500
240	LaVar Arrington RC SP	50	60	100	175

2000 Ultra Gold Medallion

		NmMt 8	NmMt+ 8.5	MT 9	Gem 9.5/10
234	Tom Brady	200	300	500	▲1,000

2000 Upper Deck

		NmMt 8	NmMt+ 8.5	MT 9	Gem 9.5/10
254	Tom Brady RC	200	250	300	600

2000 Upper Deck Exclusives Gold

		NmMt 8	NmMt+ 8.5	MT 9	Gem 9.5/10

2000 Upper Deck Encore

		NmMt 8	NmMt+ 8.5	MT 9	Gem 9.5/10
254	Tom Brady RC	200	250	400	1,000

2000 Upper Deck Gold Reserve

		NmMt 8	NmMt+ 8.5	MT 9	Gem 9.5/10
215	Tom Brady RC	400	500	800	2,000

2000 Upper Deck MVP

		NmMt 8	NmMt+ 8.5	MT 9	Gem 9.5/10
192	Brian Urlacher RC	10	12	20	30

2000 Upper Deck Pros and Prospects

		NmMt 8	NmMt+ 8.5	MT 9	Gem 9.5/10
93	Brian Urlacher RC	30	40	60	100
124	Tom Brady RC	225	400	800	2,000

2000 Upper Deck Victory

		NmMt 8	NmMt+ 8.5	MT 9	Gem 9.5/10
326	Tom Brady RC	125	150	200	300

2000 Upper Deck Vintage Previews

		NmMt 8	NmMt+ 8.5	MT 9	Gem 9.5/10
14	T.Brady/J.R.Redmond	50	250	300	

2000 Vanguard

		NmMt 8	NmMt+ 8.5	MT 9	Gem 9.5/10
139	Tom Brady RC	▲500	▲600	▲800	▲1,800

2001 Bowman

		NmMt 8	NmMt+ 8.5	MT 9	Gem 9.5/10
164	Drew Brees RC	▲50	▲60	▲250	
200	Michael Vick RC	15	20	40	
210	LaDainian Tomlinson RC	15	20	35	

2001 Bowman Chrome

		NmMt 8	NmMt+ 8.5	MT 9	Gem 9.5/10
144	Drew Brees RC	▲600	▲800	▲1,000	▲1,200
180	Michael Vick RC	25	30	40	125
190	LaDainian Tomlinson RC	40	50	100	150

01 Bowman Chrome Gold Refractors

	NmMt 8	NmMt+ 8.5	MT 9	Gem 9.5/10
Drew Brees	▲2,500	▲2,800	▲5,000	▲6,000
Michael Vick	200	225	300	500
LaDainian Tomlinson	200	225	300	500

01 Bowman Chrome Xfractors

	NmMt 8	NmMt+ 8.5	MT 9	Gem 9.5/10
Drew Brees	▲1,200	▲1,500	▲2,000	▲2,200
Michael Vick	125	150	200	300
LaDainian Tomlinson	125	150	200	300

01 Bowman's Best

	NmMt 8	NmMt+ 8.5	MT 9	Gem 9.5/10
Drew Brees RC	100	200	300	800
LaDainian Tomlinson RC	25	30	50	100
Michael Vick RC	25	30	50	100

01 Crown Royale

	NmMt 8	NmMt+ 8.5	MT 9	Gem 9.5/10
Michael Vick AU/250 RC	80	120	100	
Drew Brees AU/250 RC	150	175	300	350

01 Crown Royale Crown Rookies

	NmMt 8	NmMt+ 8.5	MT 9	Gem 9.5/10
Drew Brees	10	12	25	40

01 Donruss Elite

	NmMt 8	NmMt+ 8.5	MT 9	Gem 9.5/10
Michael Vick RC	15	25	50	
Drew Brees RC	125	200	400	500
LaDainian Tomlinson RC	25	30	100	

01 eTopps

	NmMt 8	NmMt+ 8.5	MT 9	Gem 9.5/10
Drew Brees/1290	25	30	80	150
Michael Vick/5721	25	30	40	50
LaDainian Tomlinson/1536	20	25	30	40

01 E-X

	NmMt 8	NmMt+ 8.5	MT 9	Gem 9.5/10
L.Tomlinson/1000 RC	30	40	60	100
Michael Vick/1000 RC	20	25	50	80

01 Finest

	NmMt 8	NmMt+ 8.5	MT 9	Gem 9.5/10
Drew Brees RC	100	200	300	600
LaDainian Tomlinson RC	25	30	40	100
Michael Vick RC	20	25	30	40
Reggie Wayne RC	15	20	40	50

01 Fleer Authority

	NmMt 8	NmMt+ 8.5	MT 9	Gem 9.5/10
Michael Vick RC	12	15	25	40
Drew Brees RC	▲30	▲50	▲80	200
LaDainian Tomlinson RC	12	15	25	40

01 Fleer Legacy Rookie Postmarks Autographs

	NmMt 8	NmMt+ 8.5	MT 9	Gem 9.5/10
Michael Vick	200	250	300	450

01 Leaf Rookies and Stars Rookie Autographs

	NmMt 8	NmMt+ 8.5	MT 9	Gem 9.5/10
Drew Brees	175	200	350	

2001 Pacific

	NmMt 8	NmMt+ 8.5	MT 9	Gem 9.5/10
Drew Brees AU/1000 RC	350	500	600	1,500
L.Tomlinson AU/1500 RC	50	60	100	200

2001 Pacific Dynagon

	NmMt 8	NmMt+ 8.5	MT 9	Gem 9.5/10
Drew Brees AU RC	400	500	1,000	
LaDainian Tomlinson AU RC	80	100	150	

2001 Pacific Dynagon Retail

		NmMt 8	NmMt+ 8.5	MT 9	Gem 9.5/10
102	Drew Brees RC	10	12	20	30
108	LaDainian Tomlinson RC	10	12	20	30

2001 Playoff Contenders

		NmMt 8	NmMt+ 8.5	MT 9	Gem 9.5/10
124	Drew Brees AU/500* RC	4,000	6,000	10,000	15,000
150	L.Tomlinson AU/600* RC	200	250	450	800
157	Michael Vick AU/327* RC	175	200	400	700
166	Reggie Wayne AU/400* RC	125	150	200	400
190	Steve Smith AU/300* RC	120	150	300	450

2001 Quantum Leaf

		NmMt 8	NmMt+ 8.5	MT 9	Gem 9.5/10
201	Michael Vick RC	10	12	20	30
202	Drew Brees RC	30	40	80	200
210	LaDainian Tomlinson RC	8	10	15	25

2001 SAGE HIT

		NmMt 8	NmMt+ 8.5	MT 9	Gem 9.5/10
5	LaDainian Tomlinson	6	8	12	20
7	Michael Vick	6	8	12	20
15	Drew Brees	8	10	15	25

2001 SP Authentic

		NmMt 8	NmMt+ 8.5	MT 9	Gem 9.5/10
91	Michael Vick JSY AU RC	400	500	600	1,200
101	Drew Brees JSY RC	150	200	1,000	2,500
120	L.Tomlinson JSY/500 RC	200	250	400	700
146	Steve Smith AU RC	60	100	150	200

2001 SP Authentic Sign of the Times

		NmMt 8	NmMt+ 8.5	MT 9	Gem 9.5/10
DBR	Drew Brees	500	800	1,200	1,600

2001 SP Game Used Edition

		NmMt 8	NmMt+ 8.5	MT 9	Gem 9.5/10
91	Michael Vick JSY RC	50	60	120	200
93	Drew Brees JSY RC	50	80	125	200
96	LaDainian Tomlinson JSY RC	50	60	120	200

2001 SPx

		NmMt 8	NmMt+ 8.5	MT 9	Gem 9.5/10
95B	M.Vick JSY AU/250 RC	80	100	175	300
95G	M.Vick JSY AU/250 RC	80	100	175	300
101B	D.Brees JSY AU/250 RC	275	300	400	600
101G	D.Brees JSY AU/250 RC	275	300	400	600
122B	L.Tomlinson JSY/250 RC	50	60	100	
122G	L.Tomlinson JSY/250 RC	50	60	100	

2001 Topps

		NmMt 8	NmMt+ 8.5	MT 9	Gem 9.5/10
311	Michael Vick RC	12	15	25	50
328	Drew Brees RC	60	80	100	300
350	LaDainian Tomlinson RC	12	15	25	60

2001 Topps Rookie Premier Autographs

		NmMt 8	NmMt+ 8.5	MT 9	Gem 9.5/10
RPDB	Drew Brees	350	400	500	
RPMV	Michael Vick	350	400	600	

2001 Topps Chrome

		NmMt 8	NmMt+ 8.5	MT 9	Gem 9.5/10
221	LaDainian Tomlinson RC	250	300	500	600
229	Drew Brees RC	1,500	2,000	3,000	4,000
250	Reggie Wayne RC	100	120	300	
262	Michael Vick RC	100	120	150	

2001 Topps Chrome Refractors

		NmMt 8	NmMt+ 8.5	MT 9	Gem 9.5/10
221	LaDainian Tomlinson	125	300	500	1,200
229	Drew Brees	2,000	2,500	4,000	
262	Michael Vick	60	80	200	

2001 Topps Debut

		NmMt 8	NmMt+ 8.5	MT 9	Gem 9.5/10
101	Drew Brees AU RC	200	300	500	1,200
103	LaDainian Tomlinson AU RC	80	100	200	300
108	Michael Vick AU RC	40	80	150	200

2001 Topps Gallery

		NmMt 8	NmMt+ 8.5	MT 9	Gem 9.5/10
101	Michael Vick RC	10	12	15	30
103	LaDainian Tomlinson RC	10	12	15	30
115	Drew Brees RC	25	30	40	▲125

2001 Topps Heritage

		NmMt 8	NmMt+ 8.5	MT 9	Gem 9.5/10
116	Drew Brees RC	▲80	▲100	▲125	600
133	Michael Vick RC	25	30	40	60
136	LaDainian Tomlinson RC	25	30	40	80

2001 UD Game Gear

		NmMt 8	NmMt+ 8.5	MT 9	Gem 9.5/10
107	Drew Brees RC	20	25	50	80
108	LaDainian Tomlinson RC	25	30	50	100

2001 UD Graded

		NmMt 8	NmMt+ 8.5	MT 9	Gem 9.5/10
47	Drew Brees Action RC	35	40	100	300
47P	Drew Brees Portrait RC	35	40	100	300
53	L.Tomlinson Action RC	20	25	50	80
53P	L.Tomlinson Portrait RC	20	25	50	80
54	Michael Vick Action RC	15	20	40	80
54P	Michael Vick Portrait RC	15	20	40	80
56	Reggie Wayne Action RC	12	15	25	50
56P	Reggie Wayne Portrait RC	12	15	25	50

2001 Upper Deck

		NmMt 8	NmMt+ 8.5	MT 9	Gem 9.5/10
206	Drew Brees RC	25	30	80	150
230	LaDainian Tomlinson RC	20	25	40	60
239	Michael Vick RC	20	25	40	60

2001 UD Graded Rookie Autographs

		NmMt 8	NmMt+ 8.5	MT 9	Gem 9.5/10
47	Drew Brees	300	500	800	1,500
53	LaDainian Tomlinson	60	80	100	250
54	Michael Vick	▼40	▼50	▼60	▼80

2001 Upper Deck MVP

		NmMt 8	NmMt+ 8.5	MT 9	Gem 9.5/10
283	Michael Vick RC	10	12	20	30
287	Drew Brees RC	30	40	50	100
294	LaDainian Tomlinson RC	8	10	12	25

2001 Upper Deck Pros and Prospects

		NmMt 8	NmMt+ 8.5	MT 9	Gem 9.5/10
95	Drew Brees RC	40	80	100	250
104	LaDainian Tomlinson RC	40	50	60	80
135	Michael Vick JSY RC	40	50	60	120

2001 Upper Deck Top Tier

		NmMt 8	NmMt+ 8.5	MT 9	Gem 9.5/10
184	Michael Vick/1500 RC	20	25	40	60
227	L.Tomlinson/1500 RC	20	25	40	60

2001 Upper Deck Victory

		NmMt 8	NmMt+ 8.5	MT 9	Gem 9.5/10
374	Michael Vick RC	10	12	15	25
415	Drew Brees RC	25	30	50	100
416	LaDainian Tomlinson RC	10	12	15	25

2001 Upper Deck Vintage

		NmMt 8	NmMt+ 8.5	MT 9	Gem 9.5/10
204	Michael Vick RC	8	10	20	35
251	Drew Brees RC	▲40	▲50	▲60	▲100
252	LaDainian Tomlinson RC	10	12	20	40

2002 Bowman Chrome

		NmMt 8	NmMt+ 8.5	MT 9	Gem 9.5/10
223	Brian Westbrook AU C RC	15	25	40	60
227	Dwight Freeney AU D RC	35	40	50	80
230	Ed Reed AU A RC	50	60	80	

2002 Finest

		NmMt 8	NmMt+ 8.5	MT 9	Gem 9.5/10
77	Julius Peppers RC	8	10	15	25
92	Dwight Freeney RC	8	10	12	20
102	Brian Westbrook RC	10	12	20	40
109	Ed Reed RC	12	15	40	50

2002 Finest Refractors

		NmMt 8	NmMt+ 8.5	MT 9	Gem 9.5/10
87	Jeremy Shockey	12	15	25	50
122	Clinton Portis AU	40	50	100	200

2002 Playoff Contenders

		NmMt 8	NmMt+ 8.5	MT 9	Gem 9.5/10
128	Dwight Freeney AU/410 RC	50	60	80	
129	Ed Reed AU/550 RC	80	100	150	

2002 SP Authentic

		NmMt 8	NmMt+ 8.5	MT 9	Gem 9.5/10
157	Brian Westbrook RC	25	30	40	60
195	Ed Reed AU RC	50	60	80	150

2002 SPx

		NmMt 8	NmMt+ 8.5	MT 9	Gem 9.5/10
99	Ed Reed RC	15	20	30	50

2002 Topps Chrome

		NmMt 8	NmMt+ 8.5	MT 9	Gem 9.5/10
208	Ed Reed RC	25	30	100	250
214	Julius Peppers RC	15	20	60	400

2002 Upper Deck

		NmMt 8	NmMt+ 8.5	MT 9	Gem 9.5/10
245	Clinton Portis RC	15	20	25	50

2003 Bowman

		NmMt 8	NmMt+ 8.5	MT 9	Gem 9.5/10
111	Carson Palmer RC	8	10	20	
171	Tony Romo RC	20	25	50	80
257	Troy Polamalu RC	15	20	35	60

2003 Bowman Chrome

		NmMt 8	NmMt+ 8.5	MT 9	Gem 9.5/10
144	Tony Romo RC	25	30	50	▲100
180	Rex Grossman RC	8	10	15	30
195	Andre Johnson RC	10	12	20	▲50
206	Willis McGahee RC	8	10	15	30
230	Jason Witten AU D RC	60	80	200	400
235	Larry Johnson AU B RC	35	40	80	
237	Carson Palmer AU A RC	▼40	▼50	▼60	

2003 Bowman Chrome Refractors

		NmMt 8	NmMt+ 8.5	MT 9	Gem 9.5/10
144	Tony Romo	50	60	120	200
195	Andre Johnson	20	25	40	80

2003 Finest

		NmMt 8	NmMt+ 8.5	MT 9	Gem 9.5/10
61	Troy Polamalu RC	▲30	▲40	▲50	▲100
119	Carson Palmer AU/399 RC	60	80	150	
127	Willis McGahee AU/399 RC	40	50	80	
139	Jason Witten AU RC	40	50	80	

2003 Fleer Tradition

		NmMt 8	NmMt+ 8.5	MT 9	Gem 9.5/10
299	Kings RC/Romo RC/St.P RC	12	15	20	30

2003 Leaf Limited

		NmMt 8	NmMt+ 8.5	MT 9	Gem 9.5/10
123	Tony Romo RC	40	50	60	100
145	Andre Johnson AU RC	60	80	120	

2003 Leaf Rookies and Stars

		NmMt 8	NmMt+ 8.5	MT 9	Gem 9.5/10
205	Tony Romo RC	40	50	80	125

2003 Playoff Contenders

		NmMt 8	NmMt+ 8.5	MT 9	Gem 9.5/10
117	Jason Witten AU/599 RC	175	250	400	800
126B	C.Palmer Blue AU/158 RC	200	250	400	600
127	Byron Leftwich AU/169 RC	50	60	100	175
134	Larry Johnson AU/344 RC	25	30	40	60
135	Will McGahee AU/369 RC	40	50	80	175
146	Anquan Boldin AU/524 RC	35	40	80	120
150	Dallas Clark AU/539 RC	35	40	50	60
156	Tony Romo AU/999 RC	250	300	350	600
190	Troy Polamalu AU/989 RC	300	350	500	

2003 Score

		NmMt 8	NmMt+ 8.5	MT 9	Gem 9.5/10
276	Carson Palmer RC	10	12	20	40

2003 SP Authentic

		NmMt 8	NmMt+ 8.5	MT 9	Gem 9.5/10
120	Troy Polamalu RC	40	50	80	200
199	Jason Witten RC	35	40	100	250
217	Tony Romo AU RC	225	250	300	▼400
244	Willis McGahee JSY RC	15	20	35	60
270	Carson Palmer JSY AU RC	125	150	400	

2003 SP Game Used Edition

		NmMt 8	NmMt+ 8.5	MT 9	Gem 9.5/10
91	Carson Palmer RC	20	25	40	60
111	Willis McGahee RC	12	15	25	40

2003 SP Signature

		NmMt 8	NmMt+ 8.5	MT 9	Gem 9.5/10
106	Tony Romo RC	30	40	50	60

2003 SPx

		NmMt 8	NmMt+ 8.5	MT 9	Gem 9.5/10
114	Tony Romo RC	35	40	60	120
184	Troy Polamalu RC	40	50	80	▼100
202	A.Johnson JSY AU/250 RC	150	175	250	350
207	B.Leftwich JSY AU/250 RC	25	30	50	60
208	McGahee JSY AU/450 RC	35	40	60	120
210	C.Palmer JSY AU/250 RC	40	50	80	120

2003 Topps

		NmMt 8	NmMt+ 8.5	MT 9	Gem 9.5/10
311	Carson Palmer RC	8	10	20	35

2003 Topps Chrome

		NmMt 8	NmMt+ 8.5	MT 9	Gem 9.5/10
166	Carson Palmer RC	12	15	25	50
215	Willis McGahee RC	8	10	20	30
227	Jason Witten RC	12	30	60	150
235	Andre Johnson RC	12	15	20	40
274	Troy Polamalu RC	50	60	80	100

2003 Topps Pristine

		NmMt 8	NmMt+ 8.5	MT 9	Gem 9.5/10
75	Carson Palmer C RC	10	12	20	35
76	Carson Palmer U	12	15	25	40
77	Carson Palmer R	15	20	30	50

2003 Topps Pristine Refractors

		NmMt 8	NmMt+ 8.5	MT 9	Gem 9.5/10
75	Carson Palmer C	12	15	25	40
76	Carson Palmer U	15	20	30	50
77	Carson Palmer R	35	40	60	100

		NmMt 8	NmMt+ 8.5	MT 9	Gem 9.5/10
111	Larry Johnson C	20	25	40	60
112	Larry Johnson U	25	30	50	80
113	Larry Johnson R	12	15	25	40

2003 Ultimate Collection

		NmMt 8	NmMt+ 8.5	MT 9	Gem 9.5/1
58	Tony Romo/750 RC	35	40	60	100
85	Carson Palmer AU/250 RC	100	120	150	250
95	Willis McGahee AU/250 RC	35	40	60	100
105	Andre Johnson/750 RC	15	20	30	60

2003 Ultra

		NmMt 8	NmMt+ 8.5	MT 9	Gem 9.5/10
161	Carson Palmer RC	8	10	20	30
164	Andre Johnson RC	10	12	15	25
182	Tony Romo RC	25	30	40	50

2003 Upper Deck

		NmMt 8	NmMt+ 8.5	MT 9	Gem 9.5/10
241	Carson Palmer RC	15	20	30	50
251	Willis McGahee RC	10	12	20	30
253	Andre Johnson RC	15	20	30	50
256	Tony Romo RC	25	30	50	80

2004 Absolute Memorabilia

		NmMt 8	NmMt+ 8.5	MT 9	Gem 9.5/10
225	Eli Manning RPM RC	40	50	80	120
227	Ben Roethlisberger RPM RC	50	60	100	150

2004 Bazooka

		NmMt 8	NmMt+ 8.5	MT 9	Gem 9.5/10
200	Eli Manning RC	10	12	15	30
210	Ben Roethlisberger RC	15	15	20	40

2004 Bowman

		NmMt 8	NmMt+ 8.5	MT 9	Gem 9.5/10
111	Eli Manning RC	12	15	25	40
114	Ben Roethlisberger RC	15	20	25	50

2004 Bowman Chrome

		NmMt 8	NmMt+ 8.5	MT 9	Gem 9.5/10
111	Roethlisberger AU/199 RC	250	300	350	600
114	Matt Schaub RC	8	10	20	35
118	Larry Fitzgerald RC	10	12	20	40
179	Wes Welker RC	15	20	30	40
223	Philip Rivers AU/199 RC	100	125	150	200
225	Eli Manning AU/199 RC	200	225	300	500
238	Michael Turner AU D RC	20	25	40	60

2004 Bowman Chrome Refractors

		NmMt 8	NmMt+ 8.5	MT 9	Gem 9.5/10
118	Larry Fitzgerald	20	25	80	100
179	Wes Welker	35	40	50	60

2004 Bowman Chrome Super Bowl XXXIX Unsigned Draft Picks

		NmMt 8	NmMt+ 8.5	MT 9	Gem 9.5/10
111	Ben Roethlisberger	60	80	100	150
225	Eli Manning	40	50	60	100

2004 Bowman's Best

		NmMt 8	NmMt+ 8.5	MT 9	Gem 9.5/10
126	Eli Manning AU/199 RC	125	150	200	
130	Roethlisberger AU/199 RC	175	200	350	500

2004 eTopps

		NmMt 8	NmMt+ 8.5	MT 9	Gem 9.5/10
35	Ben Roethlisberger/2500	15	20	50	80
44	Eli Manning/3750	20	25	30	50

2004 E-X Rookie Die Cuts

		NmMt 8	NmMt+ 8.5	MT 9	Gem 9.5/10
41	Eli Manning No Ser.#	25	30	40	50
46	Ben Roethlisberger No Ser.#	35	40	50	60

04 Finest

	NmMt 8	NmMt+ 8.5	MT 9	Gem 9.5/10
Larry Fitzgerald RC	10	12	20	40
Roethlisberger AU/399 RC	200	225	250	350
Philip Rivers AU/399 RC	60	80	200	300
Eli Manning AU/399 RC	125	150	200	250

04 Finest Refractors

	NmMt 8	NmMt+ 8.5	MT 9	Gem 9.5/10
Ben Roethlisberger AU	250	300	400	500
Philip Rivers AU	80	100	200	400
Eli Manning AU	150	200	250	450

04 Finest Gold Refractors

	NmMt 8	NmMt+ 8.5	MT 9	Gem 9.5/10
Ben Roethlisberger AU	350	400	600	1,500
Eli Manning AU	350	400	500	800

04 Fleer Showcase

	NmMt 8	NmMt+ 8.5	MT 9	Gem 9.5/10
Eli Manning RC	25	30	40	60
Ben Roethlisberger RC	30	40	50	80

04 Fleer Tradition

	NmMt 8	NmMt+ 8.5	MT 9	Gem 9.5/10
Eli Manning RC	10	12	20	35
Larry Fitzgerald RC	8	10	12	25
Ben Roethlisberger RC	10	12	20	40
Philip Rivers RC	8	10	12	25
Eli/Rivers/Roethlisberger	20	20	25	80
Fitz/Will/Ro.Will.WR	8	10	15	30

04 Leaf Rookies and Stars

	NmMt 8	NmMt+ 8.5	MT 9	Gem 9.5/10
Willie Parker RC	6	8	12	20

04 Playoff Contenders

	NmMt 8	NmMt+ 8.5	MT 9	Gem 9.5/10
Roethlisberger AU/541* RC	300	600	1,200	2,000
Eli Manning AU/372* RC	400	450	600	1,000
Philip Rivers AU/556* RC	500	600	800	1,000
Roy Williams AU/564* RC	25	30	60	
Steven Jackson AU/333* RC	50	60	100	150
Willie Parker Blk AU RC	20	25	50	
Wes Welker AU RC	125	135	175	

04 Playoff Prestige

	NmMt 8	NmMt+ 8.5	MT 9	Gem 9.5/10
Eli Manning RC	12	15	20	40
Ben Roethlisberger RC	15	20	30	60
Mike Williams SP RC	15	20	50	100

04 SAGE

	NmMt 8	NmMt+ 8.5	MT 9	Gem 9.5/10
Ben Roethlisberger	10	12	15	25

04 Score

	NmMt 8	NmMt+ 8.5	MT 9	Gem 9.5/10
Eli Manning RC	10	12	15	25
Philip Rivers RC	6	8	12	20
Ben Roethlisberger RC	10	12	20	30

04 Score Glossy

	NmMt 8	NmMt+ 8.5	MT 9	Gem 9.5/10
Eli Manning	12	15	20	30
Ben Roethlisberger	20	20	25	40

04 SP Authentic

	NmMt 8	NmMt+ 8.5	MT 9	Gem 9.5/10
Wes Welker RC	25	30	60	120
Michael Turner AU RC	50	60	80	120
Matt Schaub JSY AU RC	175	200	250	350
Ben Roethlisberger JSY AU RC	▲1,000	▲1,200	1,500	
Philip Rivers JSY AU RC	150	400	500	
Larry Fitzgerald JSY AU RC	250	300	400	
Eli Manning JSY AU RC	600	1,000		

2004 SP Game Used Edition

	NmMt 8	NmMt+ 8.5	MT 9	Gem 9.5/10
171 Ben Roethlisberger RC	50	60	80	120
184 Eli Manning RC	50	60	80	150

2004 SPx

	NmMt 8	NmMt+ 8.5	MT 9	Gem 9.5/10
220 Roethlisberger JSY AU/375 RC	175	200	300	500
221 Eli Manning JSY AU/375 RC	150	175	250	500

2004 Topps

	NmMt 8	NmMt+ 8.5	MT 9	Gem 9.5/10
311 Ben Roethlisberger RC	12	20	40	100
350 Eli Manning RC	10	12	20	35
356 Matt Schaub RC	8	10	15	25
360 Larry Fitzgerald RC	8	10	15	25
375 Philip Rivers RC	8	10	15	25

2004 Topps Rookie Premiere Autographs

	NmMt 8	NmMt+ 8.5	MT 9	Gem 9.5/10
RPBR Ben Roethlisberger	250	300	500	

2004 Topps Chrome

	NmMt 8	NmMt+ 8.5	MT 9	Gem 9.5/10
166 Ben Roethlisberger RC	50	80	100	300
205 Eli Manning RC	25	30	50	250
211 Matt Schaub RC	10	12	20	35
215 Larry Fitzgerald RC	20	30	50	200
230 Philip Rivers RC	20	25	100	200

2004 Topps Chrome Gold Xfractors

	NmMt 8	NmMt+ 8.5	MT 9	Gem 9.5/10
166 Ben Roethlisberger	100	200	250	400
205 Eli Manning	100	120	150	300
230 Philip Rivers	50	125	300	400

2004 Topps Chrome Refractors

	NmMt 8	NmMt+ 8.5	MT 9	Gem 9.5/10
166 Ben Roethlisberger	80	200	250	400
180 Steven Jackson	15	20	35	60
205 Eli Manning	60	80	100	
230 Philip Rivers	60	80	300	350

2004 Topps Draft Picks and Prospects

	NmMt 8	NmMt+ 8.5	MT 9	Gem 9.5/10
150 Eli Manning RC	12	15	20	30
165 Ben Roethlisberger RC	15	20	25	30

2004 Topps Draft Picks and Prospects Chrome

	NmMt 8	NmMt+ 8.5	MT 9	Gem 9.5/10
150 Eli Manning	20	25	30	50
165 Ben Roethlisberger	25	30	40	75

2004 Topps Draft Picks and Prospects Gold Chrome

	NmMt 8	NmMt+ 8.5	MT 9	Gem 9.5/10
150 Eli Manning	60	60	80	120
165 Ben Roethlisberger	80	80	100	150

2004 Topps Pristine

	NmMt 8	NmMt+ 8.5	MT 9	Gem 9.5/10
51 Ben Roethlisberger C RC	20	25	35	60
52 Ben Roethlisberger U	25	30	50	80
53 Ben Roethlisberger R	30	35	50	80
87 Eli Manning C RC	15	20	25	40
88 Eli Manning U	20	25	35	60
89 Eli Manning R	25	30	40	60
108 Larry Fitzgerald C RC	10	12	15	30
109 Larry Fitzgerald U	12	15	20	40
110 Larry Fitzgerald R	15	20	25	50
129 Philip Rivers C RC	10	12	15	30
130 Philip Rivers U	12	15	20	40
131 Philip Rivers R	15	20	25	50

2004 Topps Pristine Refractors

	NmMt 8	NmMt+ 8.5	MT 9	Gem 9.5/10
51 Ben Roethlisberger C	35	40	50	60
52 Ben Roethlisberger U	40	50	80	125
53 Ben Roethlisberger R	100	120	150	250
87 Eli Manning C	35	40	50	80
88 Eli Manning U	40	50	60	100
89 Eli Manning R	80	100	125	175

2004 Topps Signature

	NmMt 8	NmMt+ 8.5	MT 9	Gem 9.5/10
80 Philip Rivers AU/299 RC	80	150	200	500
90 Eli Manning AU/299 RC	150	175	250	450
93 Roethlisberger AU/299 RC	200	250	300	500

2004 Topps Total

	NmMt 8	NmMt+ 8.5	MT 9	Gem 9.5/10
331 Philip Rivers RC	8	10	15	30
350 Eli Manning RC	10	12	20	40
375 Ben Roethlisberger RC	12	15	25	50

2004 Ultimate Collection

	NmMt 8	NmMt+ 8.5	MT 9	Gem 9.5/10
124 Steven Jackson AU RC	80	100	120	200
127 Ben Roethlisberger AU RC	300	350	450	800
128 Philip Rivers AU RC	80	100	125	500
129 Larry Fitzgerald AU RC	125	150	200	250
130 Eli Manning AU RC	150	200	400	500

2004 Ultimate Collection Ultimate Signatures

	NmMt 8	NmMt+ 8.5	MT 9	Gem 9.5/10
USBR Roethlisberger/100	225	250	300	800
USEM E.Manning/100	175	200	250	350
USPR Philip Rivers/275	60	80	250	300

2004 Ultra Gold Medallion

	NmMt 8	NmMt+ 8.5	MT 9	Gem 9.5/10
201 Eli Manning L13	35	40	50	80
213 Ben Roethlisberger L13	25	30	40	60

2004 Upper Deck

	NmMt 8	NmMt+ 8.5	MT 9	Gem 9.5/10
201 Eli Manning RC	20	25	30	40
202 Larry Fitzgerald RC	12	15	25	40
204 Ben Roethlisberger RC	25	30	40	80
205 Philip Rivers RC	15	20	30	50

2004 Upper Deck Rookie Premiere

	NmMt 8	NmMt+ 8.5	MT 9	Gem 9.5/10
1 Eli Manning	8	10	15	30
2 Ben Roethlisberger	10	12	20	40
25 Matt Schaub	6	8	10	20

2005 Absolute Memorabilia

	NmMt 8	NmMt+ 8.5	MT 9	Gem 9.5/10
180 Aaron Rodgers RC	▲60	▲80	▲100	▲150

2005 Bazooka

	NmMt 8	NmMt+ 8.5	MT 9	Gem 9.5/10
190 Aaron Rodgers RC	10	12	20	30

2005 Bowman

	NmMt 8	NmMt+ 8.5	MT 9	Gem 9.5/10
112 Aaron Rodgers RC	15	30	80	250
114 Alex Smith QB RC	8	10	15	25

2005 Bowman Chrome

	NmMt 8	NmMt+ 8.5	MT 9	Gem 9.5/10
221 Aaron Rodgers AU/199 RC	700	750	1,000	1,800
259 Frank Gore AU B RC	40	50	80	120

2005 Donruss Classics

	NmMt 8	NmMt+ 8.5	MT 9	Gem 9.5/10
210 Aaron Rodgers RC	40	50	80	250

FOOTBALL

2005 Donruss Elite

		NmMt 8	NmMt+ 8.5	MT 9	Gem 9.5/10
101	Aaron Rodgers RC	100	120	150	

2005 Exquisite Collection

		NmMt 8	NmMt+ 8.5	MT 9	Gem 9.5/10
93	Frank Gore JSY AU RC	175	200	300	600
106	A.Rodgers JSY AU RC	2,000	2,200	2,800	5,000
114	R.Brown JSY AU/99 RC	250	300	500	800
117	C.Williams JSY AU/99 RC	100	125	200	300
118	A.Smith QB JSY AU/99 RC	300	350	450	

2005 Finest

		NmMt 8	NmMt+ 8.5	MT 9	Gem 9.5/10
121	Frank Gore RC	6	8	12	20
150	Marion Barber RC	10	12	15	25
151	Aaron Rodgers AU/299	450	500	800	1,500
152	Alex Smith QB AU/299 RC	80	100	125	175
163	Brandon Jacobs AU RC	20	25	40	60

2005 Leaf Certified Materials

		NmMt 8	NmMt+ 8.5	MT 9	Gem 9.5/10
162	Aaron Rodgers RC	35	40	60	125

2005 Playoff Contenders

		NmMt 8	NmMt+ 8.5	MT 9	Gem 9.5/10
101	A.Rodgers AU/530* RC	1,300	1,500	3,200	6,000
106	Alex Smith AU/401* RC	80	100	125	250
110	Brandon Jacobs AU RC	25	30	50	80
129	Darren Sproles AU/454* RC	25	30	50	100
133	DeMarcus Ware AU RC	35	40	60	200
139	Frank Gore AU RC	▲125	▲150	▲200	▲250
164	R.Brown AU/550* RC	20	25	35	60

2005 SAGE

		NmMt 8	NmMt+ 8.5	MT 9	Gem 9.5/10
37	Aaron Rodgers	6	8	10	15
50	Cadillac Williams	6	8	12	18

2005 SAGE HIT

		NmMt 8	NmMt+ 8.5	MT 9	Gem 9.5/10
8	Aaron Rodgers	6	8	12	20
24	Cadillac Williams	6	8	10	15

2005 Score

		NmMt 8	NmMt+ 8.5	MT 9	Gem 9.5/10
335	Cadillac Williams RC	6	8	12	20
352	Aaron Rodgers RC	12	15	30	60

2005 Score Glossy

		NmMt 8	NmMt+ 8.5	MT 9	Gem 9.5/10
352	Aaron Rodgers	20	25	40	60

2005 SP Authentic

		NmMt 8	NmMt+ 8.5	MT 9	Gem 9.5/10
188	Marion Barber AU RC	12	15	25	50
190	Derek Anderson AU RC	12	15	25	40
217	Matt Cassel AU RC	20	25	40	80
219	DeMarcus Ware AU RC	40	50	80	150
224	Frank Gore JSY/899 AU RC	60	80	120	200
243	Ro.Brown JSY/299 AU RC	25	30	50	80
248	A.Smith QB JSY/299 AU RC	225	250	350	500
249	C.Williams JSY/299 AU RC	25	30	50	80
252	A.Rodgers JSY/99/AU RC	2,250	2,500	3,000	

2005 SPx

		NmMt 8	NmMt+ 8.5	MT 9	Gem 9.5/10
198B	Kyle Orton JSY AU RC	25	30	50	
200B	Frank Gore JSY AU RC	35	40	60	125
222	A.Smith QB JSY AU/250 RC	100	120	150	200
223	A.Rodgers JSY AU/250 RC	600	1,000	1,600	2,600

2005 Topps

		NmMt 8	NmMt+ 8.5	MT 9	Gem 9.5/10
431	Aaron Rodgers RC	30	40	60	150
438	Cadillac Williams RC	8	10	12	20

2005 Topps Rookie Premiere Autographs

		NmMt 8	NmMt+ 8.5	MT 9	Gem 9.5/10
RPAS	Alex Smith QB	80	100	125	175

2005 Topps Chrome

		NmMt 8	NmMt+ 8.5	MT 9	Gem 9.5/10
171	Jason Campbell RC	8	10	15	25
177	Frank Gore RC				
183	Heath Miller RC	10	12	20	35
190	Aaron Rodgers RC	200	250	400	1,000
194	Alex Smith QB RC	12	20	60	80
197	Cadillac Williams RC	8	10	15	25
223	Marion Barber RC	8	10	15	25

2005 Topps Chrome Black Refractors

		NmMt 8	NmMt+ 8.5	MT 9	Gem 9.5/10
194	Alex Smith QB	60	80	100	150
197	Cadillac Williams	30	40	60	100

2005 Topps Chrome Gold Xfractors

		NmMt 8	NmMt+ 8.5	MT 9	Gem 9.5/10
170	Ronnie Brown	15	20	30	50
190	Aaron Rodgers AU	1,000	2,000	2,200	5,000
194	Alex Smith QB	40	50	60	100
197	Cadillac Williams	12	15	20	30

2005 Topps Chrome Refractors

		NmMt 8	NmMt+ 8.5	MT 9	Gem 9.5/10
170	Ronnie Brown	10	12	20	30
190	Aaron Rodgers	250	400	1,200	1,500
194	Alex Smith QB	25	30	40	50
197	Cadillac Williams	8	10	20	30

2005 Topps Draft Picks and Prospects

		NmMt 8	NmMt+ 8.5	MT 9	Gem 9.5/10
150	Cadillac Williams RC	8	10	12	20
152	Aaron Rodgers RC	12	15	20	40

2005 Topps Draft Picks and Prospects Chrome

		NmMt 8	NmMt+ 8.5	MT 9	Gem 9.5/10
152	Aaron Rodgers	25	30	50	80

2005 Topps Heritage

		NmMt 8	NmMt+ 8.5	MT 9	Gem 9.5/10
344A	Aaron Rodgers SP RC	25	30	50	80

2005 Topps Turkey Red

		NmMt 8	NmMt+ 8.5	MT 9	Gem 9.5/10
221	Aaron Rodgers RC	25	30	50	100

2005 Ultimate Collection

		NmMt 8	NmMt+ 8.5	MT 9	Gem 9.5/10
216	Frank Gore AU RC	30	40	50	100
232	Jason Campbell AU/150 RC	50	60	100	150
241	Alex Smith QB AU/99 RC	125	135	150	250
242	Aaron Rodgers AU/99 RC	800	900	1,500	3,500

2005 Ultra

		NmMt 8	NmMt+ 8.5	MT 9	Gem 9.5/10
201	Alex Smith QB L13 RC	25	30	40	60
202	Aaron Rodgers L13 RC	100	120	175	250
248	Frank Gore RC	8	10	15	25

2005 Upper Deck

		NmMt 8	NmMt+ 8.5	MT 9	Gem 9.5/10
202	Aaron Rodgers RC	35	40	60	125

2005 Upper Deck Kickoff

		NmMt 8	NmMt+ 8.5	MT 9	Gem 9.5/10
91	Aaron Rodgers RC	12	15	25	60

2005 Upper Deck Legends

		NmMt 8	NmMt+ 8.5	MT 9	Gem 9.5/10
101	Aaron Rodgers RC	40	50	100	300

2005 Upper Deck Rookie Debut

		NmMt 8	NmMt+ 8.5	MT 9	Gem 9.5/10
110	Cadillac Williams RC	10	12	15	30
126	Aaron Rodgers RC	15	20	30	100

2005 Upper Deck Rookie Materials

		NmMt 8	NmMt+ 8.5	MT 9	Gem 9.5/10
91	Aaron Rodgers RC		30	40	50

2005 Upper Deck Rookie Premiere

		NmMt 8	NmMt+ 8.5	MT 9	Gem 9.5/10
4	Cadillac Williams	8	6	15	15
16	Aaron Rodgers	12	15	30	80

2005 Upper Deck Rookie Premiere Gold

		NmMt 8	NmMt+ 8.5	MT 9	Gem 9.5/10
16	Aaron Rodgers	25	30	40	100

2006 Bowman

		NmMt 8	NmMt+ 8.5	MT 9	Gem 9.5/10
112	Matt Leinart RC	8	8	12	25
114	Jay Cutler RC	8	10	15	30

2006 Bowman Chrome

		NmMt 8	NmMt+ 8.5	MT 9	Gem 9.5/10
222	Jay Cutler RC	10	12	25	40
224	Matt Leinart RC	8	10	20	30
253	Brandon Marshall RC	8	10	25	40

2006 Bowman Chrome Blue Refractors

		NmMt 8	NmMt+ 8.5	MT 9	Gem 9.5/10
222	Jay Cutler	25	30	40	80
223	Reggie Bush	25	30	40	60

2006 Bowman Chrome Refractors

		NmMt 8	NmMt+ 8.5	MT 9	Gem 9.5/10
222	Jay Cutler	15	20	30	50
223	Reggie Bush	15	20	30	50

2006 Bowman Chrome Rookie Autographs

		NmMt 8	NmMt+ 8.5	MT 9	Gem 9.5/10
224	Matt Leinart/199	20	25	40	80
227	Santonio Holmes/199	20	25	40	
253	Brandon Marshall D	20	25	35	50

2006 Bowman Sterling

		NmMt 8	NmMt+ 8.5	MT 9	Gem 9.5/10
DHE	Devin Hester AU RC	40	50	60	80
ML	Matt Leinart JSY RC	20	25	40	50

2006 Finest

		NmMt 8	NmMt+ 8.5	MT 9	Gem 9.5/10
152	Matt Leinart AU/199 RC	25	30	50	80
153	Vince Young AU/199 RC	25	30	50	80
154	Jay Cutler AU/199 RC	40	60	100	125

2006 Fleer

		NmMt 8	NmMt+ 8.5	MT 9	Gem 9.5/10
146	Jay Cutler RC	6	8	12	20
173	Matt Leinart RC	6	8	12	20
197	Vince Young RC	6	10	12	20

2006 Playoff Contenders

		NmMt 8	NmMt+ 8.5	MT 9	Gem 9.5/10
115	Santonio Holmes AU RC	20	25	35	60
165	Devin Hester AU RC	30	40	50	60

2006 Playoff Prestige

		NmMt 8	NmMt+ 8.5	MT 9	Gem 9.5/10
198	Jay Cutler RC	8	10	15	
223	Matt Leinart RC	8	10	12	25
246	Vince Young RC	10	12	15	30

2006 SAGE

		NmMt 8	NmMt+ 8.5	MT 9	Gem 9.5/10
59	Vince Young	8	10	15	25

06 SAGE HIT

	NmMt 8	NmMt+ 8.5	MT 9	Gem 9.5/10
Vince Young	8	10	15	25
Matt Leinart	8	10	12	20

06 Score

	NmMt 8	NmMt+ 8.5	MT 9	Gem 9.5/10
Matt Leinart RC	6	8	10	15
Vince Young RC	8	10	12	20
Jay Cutler RC	6	8	10	15
Jay Cutler fact set	6	8	10	15

06 SP Authentic

	NmMt 8	NmMt+ 8.5	MT 9	Gem 9.5/10
Jay Cutler AU/99 RC	800	1,000	1,500	
M.Drew JSY/999 AU RC	50	60	120	
R.Bush JSY/299 AU RC	100	120	200	

06 SPx

	NmMt 8	NmMt+ 8.5	MT 9	Gem 9.5/10
Vince Young JSY AU RC	25	30	40	60
S.Holmes JSY AU RC	25	30	50	80
Matt Leinart JSY AU RC	25	30	50	80
Maurice Drew JSY AU RC	25	30	40	50
Brandon Marshall JSY AU RC	20	25	40	60

06 SPx Rookie Autographs Gold

	NmMt 8	NmMt+ 8.5	MT 9	Gem 9.5/10
Jay Cutler	80	100	125	200

06 Topps

	NmMt 8	NmMt+ 8.5	MT 9	Gem 9.5/10
Vince Young RC	8	10	15	25
Matt Leinart RC	8	10	15	25
Jay Cutler RC	10	12	20	35

06 Topps Chrome

	NmMt 8	NmMt+ 8.5	MT 9	Gem 9.5/10
Vince Young RC	8	10	20	30
Matt Leinart RC	8	10	20	30
Jay Cutler RC	10	12	25	40
Santonio Holmes RC	8	10	20	30
Maurice Drew RC	10	12	20	30
Devin Hester RC	10	12	25	35

06 Topps Chrome Black Refractors

	NmMt 8	NmMt+ 8.5	MT 9	Gem 9.5/10
Reggie Bush	25	30	40	60
Jay Cutler	25	30	40	60

06 Topps Chrome Refractors

	NmMt 8	NmMt+ 8.5	MT 9	Gem 9.5/10
Reggie Bush	15	20	30	50
Matt Leinart	10	12	20	35
Jay Cutler	20	25	40	50
Vernon Davis	12	15	25	40
Santonio Holmes	10	12	20	35
Maurice Drew	15	20	30	40
Brandon Marshall	12	15	25	40
Joseph Addai	12	15	25	40

06 Topps Chrome Special Edition Rookies

	NmMt 8	NmMt+ 8.5	MT 9	Gem 9.5/10
Reggie Bush	10	12	20	35
Vince Young	8	10	20	30
Matt Leinart	8	10	20	30
Laurence Maroney	15	20	30	50
DeAngelo Williams	8	10	20	30
Jay Cutler	12	15	25	40
Maurice Drew	10	12	20	35
Joseph Addai	15	20	30	50

06 Topps Chrome Rookie Autographs

	NmMt 8	NmMt+ 8.5	MT 9	Gem 9.5/10
Reggie Bush A	40	50	60	80
Brandon Marshall D	▼15	▼20	▼25	▼40

2006 Topps Heritage

	NmMt 8	NmMt+ 8.5	MT 9	Gem 9.5/10
320 Vince Young SP RC	10	12	20	30

2006 Topps Turkey Red

	NmMt 8	NmMt+ 8.5	MT 9	Gem 9.5/10
183A Vince Young PS RC	8	10	18	30
229A Matt Leinart TIB RC	8	10	15	25

2006 Ultra

	NmMt 8	NmMt+ 8.5	MT 9	Gem 9.5/10
201 Matt Leinart L13 RC	25	30	50	100
202 Vince Young L13 RC	25	30	50	100
206 Jay Cutler L13 RC	50	60	100	175

2006 Ultra Target Exclusive Rookies

	NmMt 8	NmMt+ 8.5	MT 9	Gem 9.5/10
201 Matt Leinart L13	25	30	40	50
202 Vince Young L13	25	30	40	50
203 Reggie Bush L13	30	40	50	60
206 Jay Cutler L13	30	40	50	60

2006 Upper Deck

	NmMt 8	NmMt+ 8.5	MT 9	Gem 9.5/10
210 Jay Cutler RC	15	20	30	50
216 Matt Leinart RC	10	12	20	35
225 Vince Young RC	10	12	20	35

2006 Upper Deck Exclusive Edition Rookies

	NmMt 8	NmMt+ 8.5	MT 9	Gem 9.5/10
210 Jay Cutler	8	10	12	20
216 Matt Leinart	6	8	12	20
219 Reggie Bush	8	10	15	25
225 Vince Young	8	10	15	25

2006 Upper Deck Rookie Premiere

	NmMt 8	NmMt+ 8.5	MT 9	Gem 9.5/10
2 Reggie Bush	8	10	15	25
15 Matt Leinart	8	10	12	20
26 DeAngelo Williams	6	8	10	15
30 Vince Young	8	10	15	25

2007 Artifacts

	NmMt 8	NmMt+ 8.5	MT 9	Gem 9.5/10
152 Adrian Peterson RC	20	25	40	60

2007 Bowman

	NmMt 8	NmMt+ 8.5	MT 9	Gem 9.5/10
126 Adrian Peterson RC	15	20	25	30

2007 Bowman Chrome

	NmMt 8	NmMt+ 8.5	MT 9	Gem 9.5/10
BC65 Adrian Peterson RC	20	25	30	40
BC66 Marshawn Lynch RC		8	12	20
BC75 Calvin Johnson RC	12	15	25	▼40

2007 Bowman Chrome Refractors

	NmMt 8	NmMt+ 8.5	MT 9	Gem 9.5/10
BC65 Adrian Peterson	▼25	▼30	▼40	▼80
BC66 Marshawn Lynch	10	12	15	25
BC75 Calvin Johnson	20	25	40	60

2007 Bowman Chrome Uncirculated Rookies

	NmMt 8	NmMt+ 8.5	MT 9	Gem 9.5/10
BC65 Adrian Peterson	25	30	60	100
BC75 Calvin Johnson	20	25	30	40

2007 Bowman Sterling

	NmMt 8	NmMt+ 8.5	MT 9	Gem 9.5/10
APE1 Adrian Peterson JSY RC	40	50	60	100
CJ01 Calvin Johnson JSY RC	20	25	35	60

2007 Donruss Elite

	NmMt 8	NmMt+ 8.5	MT 9	Gem 9.5/10
105 Adrian Peterson RC	40	50	80	
118 Calvin Johnson RC	25	30	50	

2007 Finest

	NmMt 8	NmMt+ 8.5	MT 9	Gem 9.5/10
112 Adrian Peterson RC	15	20	30	40
135 Calvin Johnson RC	10	12	20	40

2007 Finest Blue Refractors

	NmMt 8	NmMt+ 8.5	MT 9	Gem 9.5/10
102 Brady Quinn	12	15	25	40
112 Adrian Peterson	30	35	50	80

2007 Finest Refractors

	NmMt 8	NmMt+ 8.5	MT 9	Gem 9.5/10
112 Adrian Peterson	40	50	60	80
135 Calvin Johnson	15	20	35	60

2007 Finest Rookie Autographs

	NmMt 8	NmMt+ 8.5	MT 9	Gem 9.5/10
112 Adrian Peterson A	250	300	500	

2007 Playoff Contenders

	NmMt 8	NmMt+ 8.5	MT 9	Gem 9.5/10
104 A.Peterson AU/355* RC	300	350	400	700
123 C.Johnson AU/525* RC	▼150	▼200	▼250	500

2007 Playoff Prestige

	NmMt 8	NmMt+ 8.5	MT 9	Gem 9.5/10
155 Adrian Peterson RC	20	25	30	50

2007 SAGE HIT

	NmMt 8	NmMt+ 8.5	MT 9	Gem 9.5/10
28 Adrian Peterson	8	10	15	25

2007 Score

	NmMt 8	NmMt+ 8.5	MT 9	Gem 9.5/10
341 Adrian Peterson RC	8	10	15	25
351 Calvin Johnson RC	8	10	12	30

2007 SP Authentic

	NmMt 8	NmMt+ 8.5	MT 9	Gem 9.5/10
289 Adrian Peterson JSY AU RC	500	600		

2007 SP Chirography

	NmMt 8	NmMt+ 8.5	MT 9	Gem 9.5/10
101 Adrian Peterson AU/199 RC	125	150	200	300

2007 SPx

	NmMt 8	NmMt+ 8.5	MT 9	Gem 9.5/10
218 A.Peterson JSY AU/299 RC	250	300	400	
220 Ca.Johnson JSY AU/299 RC	100	120	200	

2007 Topps

	NmMt 8	NmMt+ 8.5	MT 9	Gem 9.5/10
301 Adrian Peterson RC	10	12	20	60
320 Calvin Johnson RC	8	10	15	25

2007 Topps Rookie Premiere Autographs

	NmMt 8	NmMt+ 8.5	MT 9	Gem 9.5/10
AP Adrian Peterson	175	200	350	500

2007 Topps Chrome

	NmMt 8	NmMt+ 8.5	MT 9	Gem 9.5/10
TC181 Adrian Peterson RC	25	30	40	100
TC200 Calvin Johnson RC	15	20	30	60

2007 Topps Chrome Blue Refractors

	NmMt 8	NmMt+ 8.5	MT 9	Gem 9.5/10
TC181 Adrian Peterson	50	60	100	150

2007 Topps Chrome Red Refractors Uncirculated

	NmMt 8	NmMt+ 8.5	MT 9	Gem 9.5/10
TC181 Adrian Peterson	125	150	175	250

2007 Topps Chrome Refractors

	NmMt 8	NmMt+ 8.5	MT 9	Gem 9.5/10
TC181 Adrian Peterson	50	60	80	100
TC200 Calvin Johnson	30	40	50	80

2007 Topps Chrome White Refractors

	NmMt 8	NmMt+ 8.5	MT 9	Gem 9.5/10
TC181 Adrian Peterson	60	80	100	150
TC200 Calvin Johnson	40	50	60	100

2007 Topps Chrome Xfractors

	NmMt 8	NmMt+ 8.5	MT 9	Gem 9.5/10
TC181 Adrian Peterson	50	60	80	135
TC200 Calvin Johnson	50	60	80	100

2007 Topps Draft Picks and Prospects

	NmMt 8	NmMt+ 8.5	MT 9	Gem 9.5/10
135 Adrian Peterson RC	10	12	15	25

2007 Topps Draft Picks and Prospects Chrome Black

	NmMt 8	NmMt+ 8.5	MT 9	Gem 9.5/10
132 Calvin Johnson	8	10	15	25
135 Adrian Peterson	12	15	20	30

2007 Topps Draft Picks and Prospects Chrome Bronze

	NmMt 8	NmMt+ 8.5	MT 9	Gem 9.5/10
135 Adrian Peterson	15	20	25	40

2007 Ultimate Collection

	NmMt 8	NmMt+ 8.5	MT 9	Gem 9.5/10
101 Adrian Peterson AU/99 RC	250	300	400	500
103 Calvin Johnson AU/99 RC	150	175	200	250

2007 Ultra

	NmMt 8	NmMt+ 8.5	MT 9	Gem 9.5/10
205 Adrian Peterson L13 RC	25	30	40	60

2007 Ultra Retail

	NmMt 8	NmMt+ 8.5	MT 9	Gem 9.5/10
205 Adrian Peterson L13 RC	25	30	40	50

2007 Upper Deck

	NmMt 8	NmMt+ 8.5	MT 9	Gem 9.5/10
277 Calvin Johnson RC	12	15	25	40
279 Adrian Peterson RC	15	20	30	50

2007 Upper Deck Exclusive Edition Rookies

	NmMt 8	NmMt+ 8.5	MT 9	Gem 9.5/10
279 Adrian Peterson	8	10	15	25

2007 Upper Deck First Edition

	NmMt 8	NmMt+ 8.5	MT 9	Gem 9.5/10
104 Adrian Peterson RC	10	12	20	30

2007 Upper Deck Rookie Premiere

	NmMt 8	NmMt+ 8.5	MT 9	Gem 9.5/10
15 Calvin Johnson	8	10	12	25
21 Adrian Peterson	10	12	15	30

2008 Bowman Chrome

	NmMt 8	NmMt+ 8.5	MT 9	Gem 9.5/10
BC59 Matt Ryan RC	12	15	30	▲50
BC61 Joe Flacco RC	▼8	▼10	▼15	▼20

2008 Bowman Chrome Refractors

	NmMt 8	NmMt+ 8.5	MT 9	Gem 9.5/10
BC59 Matt Ryan	15	20	50	100
BC61 Joe Flacco	15	20	35	50
BC76 Chris Johnson	12	15	25	40

2008 Bowman Sterling Blue Refractor Rookie Autographs

	NmMt 8	NmMt+ 8.5	MT 9	Gem 9.5/10
BA1 Matt Ryan	80	100	125	150

2008 Bowman Sterling Gold Rookie Autographs

	NmMt 8	NmMt+ 8.5	MT 9	Gem 9.5/10
156 Chris Johnson/400	12	15	25	50

2008 Bowman Sterling Rookie Blue Refractors

	NmMt 8	NmMt+ 8.5	MT 9	Gem 9.5/10
BS1 Matt Ryan	12	15	25	50
BS2 Joe Flacco	12	15	25	▼40
BS7 Chris Johnson	8	10	15	30

2008 Donruss Classics

	NmMt 8	NmMt+ 8.5	MT 9	Gem 9.5/10
219 Joe Flacco AU/399 RC	30	40	50	60

2008 Donruss Elite

	NmMt 8	NmMt+ 8.5	MT 9	Gem 9.5/10
101 Matt Ryan AU/199 RC	80	100	125	175
105 Joe Flacco AU/299 RC	80	100	125	150

2008 Exquisite Collection

	NmMt 8	NmMt+ 8.5	MT 9	Gem 9.5/10
148 Jamaal Charles JSY AU RC	60	80	·200	
168 Matt Ryan JSY AU RC	750	800	1,200	
170 Joe Flacco JSY AU RC	▼300	▼400	▼500	

2008 Finest

	NmMt 8	NmMt+ 8.5	MT 9	Gem 9.5/10
109 Matt Ryan RC	15	20	30	50
116 Chris Johnson RC	10	12	20	30

2008 Playoff Contenders

	NmMt 8	NmMt+ 8.5	MT 9	Gem 9.5/10
112 Chad Henne AU RC	20	25	40	60
115 Chris Johnson AU RC	25	30	60	120
123 Darren McFadden AU RC	30	35	60	100
151 Joe Flacco AU/220* RC	80	100	250	400
178 Matt Forte AU RC	35	40	50	80
179 Matt Ryan AU/246* RC	400	500	600	1,000

2008 Playoff National Treasures

	NmMt 8	NmMt+ 8.5	MT 9	Gem 9.5/10
111 Matt Ryan JSY AU RC	300	350	400	500

2008 Playoff Prestige

	NmMt 8	NmMt+ 8.5	MT 9	Gem 9.5/10
151 Joe Flacco RC	8	10	15	25
179 Matt Ryan RC	8	10	15	25

2008 Score

	NmMt 8	NmMt+ 8.5	MT 9	Gem 9.5/10
333 Matt Ryan RC	10	12	15	25
344 Joe Flacco RC	8	10	12	20
348 Chris Johnson RC	8	10	12	20

2008 SP Authentic

	NmMt 8	NmMt+ 8.5	MT 9	Gem 9.5/10
129 Danny Amendola RC	35	40	60	
228 Matt Flynn AU RC	35	40	60	80
279 Jordy Nelson JSY AU RC	40	50	60	
290 DeSean Jackson JSY AU RC	40	50	80	
293 Jamaal Charles JSY AU RC	30	40	60	100
295 Joe Flacco JSY AU RC	60	80	100	200
300 Matt Ryan JSY AU/499 RC	▼125	▼150	▼200	
302 Chad Henne JSY AU/499 RC	40	50	80	
304 Mendenhall JSY AU/499 RC	35	40	80	

2008 SP Rookie Edition

	NmMt 8	NmMt+ 8.5	MT 9	Gem 9.5/10
127 Joe Flacco RC	8	10	15	25
143 Matt Ryan RC	10	12	20	30
196 Matt Ryan 93	10	12	20	30

2008 SPx

	NmMt 8	NmMt+ 8.5	MT 9	Gem 9.5/10
153 Chris Johnson JSY AU RC	20	25	50	
162 Joe Flacco JSY AU RC	50	60	100	150

2008 Topps Rookie Premiere Autographs

	NmMt 8	NmMt+ 8.5	MT 9	Gem 9.5/10
RPADM Darren McFadden	80	100	125	200

	NmMt 8	NmMt+ 8.5	MT 9	Gem 9.5/1
RPAJF Joe Flacco	80	100	125	200
RPAJS Jonathan Stewart	40	50	60	80
RPAMF Matt Forte	40	50	60	80
RPAMR Matt Ryan	80	100	120	150

2008 Topps Chrome

	NmMt 8	NmMt+ 8.5	MT 9	Gem 9.5/*
TC166 Matt Ryan RC	12	15	▼50	▼80
TC170 Joe Flacco RC	10	12	20	30

2008 Topps Chrome Copper Refractors

	NmMt 8	NmMt+ 8.5	MT 9	Gem 9.5/*
TC166 Matt Ryan	20	25	40	100

2008 Topps Chrome Refractors

	NmMt 8	NmMt+ 8.5	MT 9	Gem 9.5/*
TC166 Matt Ryan	15	20	30	60
TC170 Joe Flacco	12	15	25	50
TC186 Chris Johnson	8	10	20	40

2008 Topps Chrome Rookie Autographs

	NmMt 8	NmMt+ 8.5	MT 9	Gem 9.5/*
TC186 Chris Johnson E	20	25	40	50
TC187 Ray Rice B	25	30	40	50
TC191 Matt Forte E	25	30	40	50

2008 Upper Deck

	NmMt 8	NmMt+ 8.5	MT 9	Gem 9.5/10
219 Chris Johnson RC	8	10	15	20
251 Joe Flacco RC	10	12	15	25
305 Matt Ryan SP RC	20	25	35	50

2008 Upper Deck Draft Edition

	NmMt 8	NmMt+ 8.5	MT 9	Gem 9.5/1
50 Joe Flacco RC	10	12	15	25
74 Matt Ryan RC	10	12	15	25

2008 Upper Deck Rookie Premiere

	NmMt 8	NmMt+ 8.5	MT 9	Gem 9.5/1
4 Matt Ryan	8	10	15	25

2009 Bowman Chrome

	NmMt 8	NmMt+ 8.5	MT 9	Gem 9.5/1
111 Matthew Stafford RC	12	15	20	40
112 Josh Freeman RC	8	10	12	20
138 Percy Harvin RC	8	10	12	20

2009 Bowman Chrome Rookie Autographs

	NmMt 8	NmMt+ 8.5	MT 9	Gem 9.5/1
111 Matthew Stafford A	125	150	200	250

2009 Bowman Draft

	NmMt 8	NmMt+ 8.5	MT 9	Gem 9.5/10
111 Matthew Stafford RC	10	12	20	30
183 Arian Foster RC	10	12	15	25

2009 Bowman Sterling

	NmMt 8	NmMt+ 8.5	MT 9	Gem 9.5/10
115 Arian Foster AU/599 RC	125	150	175	250

2009 Finest

	NmMt 8	NmMt+ 8.5	MT 9	Gem 9.5/10
61 Josh Freeman RC	8	10	12	20
73 Percy Harvin RC	8	10	12	20
80 Mark Sanchez RC	10	12	15	25
100 Matthew Stafford RC	12	15	20	▼40

2009 Playoff Contenders

	NmMt 8	NmMt+ 8.5	MT 9	Gem 9.5/10
101 M.Stafford AU/540* RC	100	125	150	300
124 Mike Wallace AU RC	25	30	40	50
156 Clay Matthews AU RC	80	100	125	150
176 Julian Edelman AU RC	80	100	120	200

2009 Playoff National Treasures

	NmMt 8	NmMt+ 8.5	MT 9	Gem 9.5/10
119 LeSean McCoy JSY AU RC	60	125	150	200

	NmMt 8	NmMt+ 8.5	MT 9	Gem 9.5/10
Matthew Stafford JSY AU RC	▼250	▼300	▼400	600
Clay Matthews AU RC	80	100	125	▼150

009 Playoff Prestige

	NmMt 8	NmMt+ 8.5	MT 9	Gem 9.5/10
Matthew Stafford RC	12	15	25	40

009 Score

	NmMt 8	NmMt+ 8.5	MT 9	Gem 9.5/10
Chris Wells RC	10	12	15	25
Matthew Stafford RC	12	15	20	30

009 SP Authentic

	NmMt 8	NmMt+ 8.5	MT 9	Gem 9.5/10
Julian Edelman AU RC	100	125	200	400
Clay Matthews AU/299 RC	60	80	100	150
M.Stafford JSY AU/499 RC	▼150	▼200	▼250	

009 Topps

	NmMt 8	NmMt+ 8.5	MT 9	Gem 9.5/10
A Matthew Stafford RC	12	15	20	35

009 Topps Chrome

	NmMt 8	NmMt+ 8.5	MT 9	Gem 9.5/10
55 Percy Harvin RC	8	10	15	25
10 Matthew Stafford RC	15	20	30	50

009 Topps Chrome Blue Refractors

	NmMt 8	NmMt+ 8.5	MT 9	Gem 9.5/10
10 Matthew Stafford	30	40	50	60
20 Mark Sanchez	15	20	30	40

009 Topps Chrome Refractors

	NmMt 8	NmMt+ 8.5	MT 9	Gem 9.5/10
*10 Matthew Stafford	20	25	40	80
*20 Mark Sanchez	12	15	30	60

009 Topps Chrome Xfractors

	NmMt 8	NmMt+ 8.5	MT 9	Gem 9.5/10
10 Matthew Stafford	25	30	50	80
20 Mark Sanchez	15	20	30	50

009 Topps Chrome Rookie Autographs

	NmMt 8	NmMt+ 8.5	MT 9	Gem 9.5/10
210 Matthew Stafford B	100	125	150	250
220 Mark Sanchez B	60	80	80	120

009 Topps Platinum

	NmMt 8	NmMt+ 8.5	MT 9	Gem 9.5/10
Matthew Stafford RC	10	12	20	30

009 Upper Deck

	NmMt 8	NmMt+ 8.5	MT 9	Gem 9.5/10
Matthew Stafford RC	12	15	20	30

010 Bowman Chrome Rookie Preview Inserts

	NmMt 8	NmMt+ 8.5	MT 9	Gem 9.5/10
R1 Tim Tebow	8	10	15	25
R3 Dez Bryant	8	10	15	25

010 Donruss Rated Rookies

	NmMt 8	NmMt+ 8.5	MT 9	Gem 9.5/10
Tim Tebow	8	10	15	25
Victor Cruz	8	10	12	20

010 Exquisite Collection Draft Picks

	NmMt 8	NmMt+ 8.5	MT 9	Gem 9.5/10
AD Andy Dalton	50	60	80	100
CN Cam Newton	125	150	200	300

010 Finest

	NmMt 8	NmMt+ 8.5	MT 9	Gem 9.5/10
Tim Tebow RC	10	12	20	30
Dez Bryant RC	8	10	15	25

010 Finest Atomic Refractor Rookies

	NmMt 8	NmMt+ 8.5	MT 9	Gem 9.5/10
325 Tim Tebow	15	20	30	50

2010 Playoff Contenders

		NmMt 8	NmMt+ 8.5	MT 9	Gem 9.5/10
56	Danny Woodhead RC	8	10	15	30
105	Antonio Brown AU RC	250	300	500	▼800
142	James Starks AU RC	12	15	25	40
151	Jimmy Graham AU/358* RC	60	80	100	125
186	Sean Lee AU RC	25	30	40	60
199	Victor Cruz AU RC	40	50	60	80
204A	Ben Tate Cut AU RC	15	20	30	50
204B	Ben Tate Stnd AU RC	15	20	30	50
206A	C.J. Spiller BJ AU/372* RC	50	60	80	100
206B	C.J. Spiller WJ AU/372* RC	60	80	100	100
207A	Colt McCoy BJ AU/394* RC	25	30	50	80
207B	Colt McCoy WJ AU/394* RC	25	30	50	80
209A	D.Thomas Cut AU RC	40	50	80	120
209B	D.Thomas Fwd AU RC	40	50	80	120
211A	Dez Bryant BJ AU/360* RC	80	100	125	200
211B	Dez Bryant WJ AU/360* RC	80	100	125	200
214A	Eric Decker BJ AU/492* RC	30	40	50	60
214B	Eric Decker OJ AU/492* RC	30	40	50	60
228A	N.Suh BJ AU/326* RC	40	50	60	80
228B	N.Suh WJ AU/326* RC	40	50	60	80
229A	Gronkowski BJ AU/499* RC	60	80	100	300
229B	Gronkowski WJ AU/499* RC	60	80	100	300
232A	Bradford Fwd AU/377* RC	60	80	100	125
232B	Bradford Lft AU/377* RC	60	80	100	125
234A	Tim Tebow BJ AU/400* RC	60	80	150	250
234B	T.Tebow WJ AU/400* RC	60	80	150	250

2010 Playoff National Treasures

		NmMt 8	NmMt+ 8.5	MT 9	Gem 9.5/10
311	Dez Bryant JSY AU RC	250	300	400	
329	Rob Gronkowski JSY AU RC	225	250	500	
332	Sam Bradford JSY AU RC	500	600	700	
334	Tim Tebow JSY AU RC	250	300	400	

2010 Score

		NmMt 8	NmMt+ 8.5	MT 9	Gem 9.5/10
323	Colt McCoy RC	8	10	12	20
334	Dez Bryant RC	8	10	15	25
377	Ndamukong Suh RC	6	8	10	20
387	Sam Bradford RC	10	12	20	30
396	Tim Tebow RC	10	12	20	35

2010 SP Authentic

		NmMt 8	NmMt+ 8.5	MT 9	Gem 9.5/10
102	Colt McCoy JSY AU/299 RC	25	30	35	
103	Dez Bryant JSY AU/299 RC	▼60	▼80	▼100	150
107	Bradford JSY AU/299 RC	40	50	60	80
108	Tim Tebow JSY AU/299 RC	100	125	150	200
128	Gronkowski JSY AU/499 RC	60	100	▼125	200

2010 SPx

		NmMt 8	NmMt+ 8.5	MT 9	Gem 9.5/10
101	Sam Bradford JSY AU RC	350	400	500	600
102	Tim Tebow JSY AU RC	175	200	250	400
121	Rob Gronkowski JSY AU RC	50	60	80	100

2010 Topps

		NmMt 8	NmMt+ 8.5	MT 9	Gem 9.5/10
148A	Rob Gronkowski RC				
	Cutting to his right	8	10	12	20
194A	Colt McCoy RC helmet	8	10	15	25
300A	Sam Bradford RC passing	10	12	20	30
300B	Sam Bradford SP snap	60	80	100	125
425A	Dez Bryant RC leaping	8	10	15	25
440A	Tim Tebow RC leaping	10	12	20	40

2010 Topps Chrome

		NmMt 8	NmMt+ 8.5	MT 9	Gem 9.5/10
C60A	Dez Bryant RC	10	12	15	25
C67	Jimmy Graham RC	8	10	15	25
C70A	Colt McCoy helm RC	10	12	15	25
C100A	Tim Tebow leap RC	8	10	15	25
C150A	Sam Bradford run RC	12	15	20	30
C150B	Sam Bradford snap SP	60	80	100	150
C160A	Ndamukong Suh RC	8	10	15	25

2010 Topps Chrome Purple Refractors

		NmMt 8	NmMt+ 8.5	MT 9	Gem 9.5/10
C150	Sam Bradford	25	30	40	50

2010 Topps Chrome Refractors

		NmMt 8	NmMt+ 8.5	MT 9	Gem 9.5/10
C3	Jahvid Best	12	15	20	30
C60	Dez Bryant	10	12	25	40
C70	Colt McCoy	10	12	20	30
C100	Tim Tebow	15	20	30	50
C150	Sam Bradford	15	20	30	40
C160	Ndamukong Suh	10	12	20	30

2010 Topps Chrome Rookie Autographs

		NmMt 8	NmMt+ 8.5	MT 9	Gem 9.5/10
C60	Dez Bryant A	80	100	125	200
C70	Colt McCoy A	15	20	25	30
C100	Tim Tebow A	60	80	100	125
C110	Demaryius Thomas A	40	50	60	100
C112	Rob Gronkowski B	80	100	150	300
C150	Sam Bradford A	25	30	40	50
C160	Ndamukong Suh A	35	40	50	100

2010 Topps Platinum Rookie Autographs

		NmMt 8	NmMt+ 8.5	MT 9	Gem 9.5/10
103	Jimmy Graham/999	25	30	40	60

2011 Bowman Chrome Rookie Preview Inserts

		NmMt 8	NmMt+ 8.5	MT 9	Gem 9.5/10
BCR3	Cam Newton	10	12	20	40
BCR18	Cam Newton	10	12	20	40

2011 Donruss Elite

		NmMt 8	NmMt+ 8.5	MT 9	Gem 9.5/10
115	Cam Newton RC	20	25	30	50

2011 Exquisite Collection

		NmMt 8	NmMt+ 8.5	MT 9	Gem 9.5/10
152	Cam Newton JSY AU	500	600	800	1,000
154	Julio Jones JSY AU		250	400	600

2011 Exquisite Collection Draft Picks Bronze

		NmMt 8	NmMt+ 8.5	MT 9	Gem 9.5/10
ERRW	Russell Wilson	100	125	150	175

2011 Finest

		NmMt 8	NmMt+ 8.5	MT 9	Gem 9.5/10
125	Cam Newton RC	10	12	15	40

2011 Finest Refractors

		NmMt 8	NmMt+ 8.5	MT 9	Gem 9.5/10
52	Colin Kaepernick	25	30	50	80
125	Cam Newton	20	25	40	60

2011 Finest Xfractors

		NmMt 8	NmMt+ 8.5	MT 9	Gem 9.5/10
52	Colin Kaepernick	30	40	50	80
125	Cam Newton	25	30	50	80

2011 Finest Atomic Refractor Rookies

		NmMt 8	NmMt+ 8.5	MT 9	Gem 9.5/10
FARAG	A.J. Green	8	10	12	20
FARCN	Cam Newton	15	20	25	50
FARDM	DeMarco Murray	8	10	12	20

2011 Finest Rookie Patch Autographs

		NmMt 8	NmMt+ 8.5	MT 9	Gem 9.5/10
RAPCN	Cam Newton/100	125	150	175	250

2011 Finest Rookie Patch Autographs Refractors

		NmMt 8	NmMt+ 8.5	MT 9	Gem 9.5/10
RAPAD	Andy Dalton	80	100	125	150
RAPCN	Cam Newton	125	150	175	300

2011 Leaf Metal Draft

	NmMt 8	NmMt+ 8.5	MT 9	Gem 9.5/10
RCCN1 Cam Newton	60	80	100	150

2011 Panini Plates and Patches

	NmMt 8	NmMt+ 8.5	MT 9	Gem 9.5/10
201 C.Newton JSY AU/299 RC	80	100	125	150
222 D.Murray JSY AU/499 RC	30	40	60	80

2011 Panini Threads

	NmMt 8	NmMt+ 8.5	MT 9	Gem 9.5/10
255 Cam Newton AU/300 RC	100	120	150	200

2011 Playoff Contenders

	NmMt 8	NmMt+ 8.5	MT 9	Gem 9.5/10
137 J.J. Watt AU RC	150	200	225	400
203A Ryan Mallett AU RC				
205A Christian Ponder AU RC				
220A Von Miller AU RC	40	50	60	80
221A Julio Jones AU RC	100	125	150	300
222A A.J. Green AU RC	50	60	80	100
225A Andy Dalton AU RC	35	40	60	80
228A Cam Newton AU RC	▼125	▼200	▼250	400
231A DeMarco Murray AU RC	▼20	▼25	▼30	▼40

2011 Playoff National Treasures

	NmMt 8	NmMt+ 8.5	MT 9	Gem 9.5/10
243 J.J. Watt AU RC	300	400	500	600
307 Von Miller JSY AU RC	60	80	100	400
323 Julio Jones JSY AU RC	250	300	400	600
326 Andy Dalton JSY AU RC	60	80	100	250
327 Kaepernick JSY AU RC	▼125	▼150	▼200	▼250
328 Cam Newton JSY AU RC	600	700	800	1,200
329 A.J. Green JSY AU RC	150	200	250	300

2011 Rookies and Stars

	NmMt 8	NmMt+ 8.5	MT 9	Gem 9.5/10
251 Cam Newton AU RC	60	80	100	125

2011 Score

	NmMt 8	NmMt+ 8.5	MT 9	Gem 9.5/10
315A Cam Newton RC	8	10	15	25
320A Colin Kaepernick RC	10	12	20	30

2011 SP Authentic

	NmMt 8	NmMt+ 8.5	MT 9	Gem 9.5/10
89 A.J. Green	8	10	15	25
94 Cam Newton	10	12	20	30
100 Julio Jones	8	10	15	25
151 Cam Newton FW	8	10	15	25
203 A.J. Green JSY AU/299	60	80	100	
204 Cam Newton JSY AU/299	125	150	200	250
207 Julio Jones JSY AU/299	80	100	125	200
216 D.Murray JSY AU/699	20	30	40	50

2011 SPx

	NmMt 8	NmMt+ 8.5	MT 9	Gem 9.5/10
48 D.Murray JSY AU/225	20	25	30	50
64 Julio Jones JSY AU/150	60	80	100	120
67 A.J. Green JSY AU/150	▼50	▼60	▼80	▼100
68 Cam Newton JSY AU/150	▼80	▼100	▼125	200

2011 Topps

	NmMt 8	NmMt+ 8.5	MT 9	Gem 9.5/10
200A Cam Newton RC	10	12	20	30

2011 Topps Rookie Refractors

	NmMt 8	NmMt+ 8.5	MT 9	Gem 9.5/10
TMB1 Cam Newton	10	12	20	30

2011 Topps Chrome

	NmMt 8	NmMt+ 8.5	MT 9	Gem 9.5/10
1A Cam Newton RC	10	12	20	40
104 J.J. Watt RC	10	12	20	40
131A Julio Jones RC	8	10	12	25
150A A.J. Green RC	8	10	12	25
173A DeMarco Murray RC	8	10	12	25

2011 Topps Chrome Blue Refractors

	NmMt 8	NmMt+ 8.5	MT 9	Gem 9.5/10
1 Cam Newton	60	80	100	150

2011 Topps Chrome Orange Refractors

	NmMt 8	NmMt+ 8.5	MT 9	Gem 9.5/10
1 Cam Newton	25	30	50	80
25 Colin Kaepernick	20	25	40	80
51 Andy Dalton	12	15	25	40
150 A.J. Green	10	12	20	25
173 DeMarco Murray	10	12	20	40

2011 Topps Chrome Refractors

	NmMt 8	NmMt+ 8.5	MT 9	Gem 9.5/10
1 Cam Newton	15	20	30	60
25 Colin Kaepernick	15	20	30	40
51 Andy Dalton	12	15	25	40
131 Julio Jones	10	12	20	30
150 A.J. Green	10	12	20	30
173 DeMarco Murray	10	12	20	30

2011 Topps Chrome Sepia Refractors

	NmMt 8	NmMt+ 8.5	MT 9	Gem 9.5/10
1 Cam Newton	100	125	150	250

2011 Topps Chrome Xfractors

	NmMt 8	NmMt+ 8.5	MT 9	Gem 9.5/10
1 Cam Newton	25	30	50	80
25 Colin Kaepernick	30	40	50	60
51 Andy Dalton	15	20	25	30
104 J.J. Watt	20	30	40	50

2011 Topps Chrome Finest Freshman

	NmMt 8	NmMt+ 8.5	MT 9	Gem 9.5/10
FFCM Cam Newton	10	12	15	30

2011 Topps Chrome Rookie Autographs

	NmMt 8	NmMt+ 8.5	MT 9	Gem 9.5/10
1 Cam Newton A	125	150	200	250

2011 Topps Chrome Rookie Autographs Refractors

	NmMt 8	NmMt+ 8.5	MT 9	Gem 9.5/10
1 Cam Newton	▼200	▼250	▼300	▼400

2011 Topps Legends

	NmMt 8	NmMt+ 8.5	MT 9	Gem 9.5/10
75 Cam Newton RC	10	12	20	30

2011 Topps Platinum

	NmMt 8	NmMt+ 8.5	MT 9	Gem 9.5/10
1 Cam Newton RC	10	12	25	40
86 J.J. Watt RC	6	10	20	40

2011 Topps Platinum Xfractors

	NmMt 8	NmMt+ 8.5	MT 9	Gem 9.5/10
1 Cam Newton	15	20	25	30
59 Colin Kaepernick	25	30	40	60
132 Andy Dalton	10	12	20	30

2011 Upper Deck

	NmMt 8	NmMt+ 8.5	MT 9	Gem 9.5/10
198 Cam Newton	10	12	20	35

2012 Bowman

	NmMt 8	NmMt+ 8.5	MT 9	Gem 9.5/10
150A Andrew Luck RC	10	12	20	35

2012 Bowman Gold

	NmMt 8	NmMt+ 8.5	MT 9	Gem 9.5/10
150 Andrew Luck	15	20	30	60

2012 Bowman Sterling

	NmMt 8	NmMt+ 8.5	MT 9	Gem 9.5/10
5 Russell Wilson RC	10	12	20	30
100 Andrew Luck RC	15	20	30	50

2012 Certified

	NmMt 8	NmMt+ 8.5	MT 9	Gem 9.5/10
316 Andrew Luck JSY AU/299 RC	100	125	150	200
346 Russell Wilson JSY AU/499 RC	50	60	80	100

2012 Elite

	NmMt 8	NmMt+ 8.5	MT 9	Gem 9.5/10
101 Andrew Luck/699 RC	35	40	50	80

2012 Elite Turn of the Century Autographs

	NmMt 8	NmMt+ 8.5	MT 9	Gem 9.5/10
101 Andrew Luck/99	80	125	200	300

2012 Finest

	NmMt 8	NmMt+ 8.5	MT 9	Gem 9.5/10
110 Andrew Luck RC	12	15	25	50
140 Russell Wilson RC	8	10	15	30

2012 Finest Blue Refractors

	NmMt 8	NmMt+ 8.5	MT 9	Gem 9.5/10
110 Andrew Luck	60	80	100	150

2012 Finest Prism Refractors

	NmMt 8	NmMt+ 8.5	MT 9	Gem 9.5/10
110 Andrew Luck	35	40	80	100
140 Russell Wilson	30	35	40	60

2012 Finest Refractors

	NmMt 8	NmMt+ 8.5	MT 9	Gem 9.5/10
110 Andrew Luck	20	25	30	40
140 Russell Wilson	20	25	35	50

2012 Finest Atomic Refractor Rookies

	NmMt 8	NmMt+ 8.5	MT 9	Gem 9.5/10
FARAL Andrew Luck	20	25	30	50

2012 Leaf Draft Army All-American Bowl

	NmMt 8	NmMt+ 8.5	MT 9	Gem 9.5/10
AABAL1 Andrew Luck	10	12	15	25

2012 Leaf Metal Draft

	NmMt 8	NmMt+ 8.5	MT 9	Gem 9.5/10
TR1 Trent Richardson	15	20	25	40

2012 Leaf Metal Draft Prismatic Silver

	NmMt 8	NmMt+ 8.5	MT 9	Gem 9.5/10
TR1 Trent Richardson	20	25	30	50

2012 Leaf Ultimate Draft

	NmMt 8	NmMt+ 8.5	MT 9	Gem 9.5/10

2012 Leaf Valiant Draft

	NmMt 8	NmMt+ 8.5	MT 9	Gem 9.5/10
RW1 Russell Wilson	40	50	80	150

2012 Leaf Valiant Draft Blue

	NmMt 8	NmMt+ 8.5	MT 9	Gem 9.5/10
RW1 Russell Wilson	40	50	80	120

2012 Leaf Valiant Draft Army All-American Bowl Green

	NmMt 8	NmMt+ 8.5	MT 9	Gem 9.5/10
AL1 Andrew Luck	20	25	30	40

2012 Leaf Valiant Draft Army All-American Bowl Purple

	NmMt 8	NmMt+ 8.5	MT 9	Gem 9.5/10
AL1 Andrew Luck/125		40	60	80

2012 Leaf Young Stars Draft Autographs

	NmMt 8	NmMt+ 8.5	MT 9	Gem 9.5/10
RW1 Russell Wilson SP	40	50	80	120

2012 Momentum

	NmMt 8	NmMt+ 8.5	MT 9	Gem 9.5/10
101 A.Luck JSY AU/399 RC	▼100	▼125	▼150	300

012 Panini Contenders

	NmMt 8	NmMt+ 8.5	MT 9	Gem 9.5/10
Richard Sherman RC	10	12	15	30
Kirk Cousins AU RC	80	100	200	▼300
Andrew Luck AU/550* RC	500	600	750	1,000
Andrew Luck AU SP/75*	850	1,000	1,200	2,000
R.Tannehill AU/550* RC	80	100	125	175
R.Tannehill AU SP/200*	80	100	125	200
Doug Martin AU/550* RC	20	25	35	60
Nick Foles AU/550* RC	80	100	125	150
R.Wilson AU/550* RC	200	250	350	500
Andrew Luck AU/550* RC				

all in right hand only) #201A BGS 10 (Pristine) sold for $3,110 (eBay; 3/15)

012 Panini Contenders Playoff Ticket

	NmMt 8	NmMt+ 8.5	MT 9	Gem 9.5/10
Andrew Luck AU	1,000	1,200	1,500	2,500
Nick Foles AU	150	200	250	▼300
Russell Wilson AU	600	650	700	1,000

012 Panini Contenders Rookie Stallions

	NmMt 8	NmMt+ 8.5	MT 9	Gem 9.5/10
Andrew Luck	10	12	20	35

012 Panini National Treasures

	NmMt 8	NmMt+ 8.5	MT 9	Gem 9.5/10
Kirk Cousins AU RC	125	150	200	400
Russell Wilson JSY AU RC	1,000	1,200	1,600	2,000

012 Panini Prizm

	NmMt 8	NmMt+ 8.5	MT 9	Gem 9.5/10
A Andrew Luck RC	12	15	25	40
A Russell Wilson RC	8	12	15	30

012 Panini Prizm Autographs

Andrew Luck/250
Kirk Cousins/499

012 Panini Prizm Autographs Prizms

	NmMt 8	NmMt+ 8.5	MT 9	Gem 9.5/10	Pristine
Russell Wilson/99	200	250	300	350	400

012 Prestige

	NmMt 8	NmMt+ 8.5	MT 9	Gem 9.5/10
A Andrew Luck RC	12	15	25	50

012 Rookies and Stars

	NmMt 8	NmMt+ 8.5	MT 9	Gem 9.5/10
Andrew Luck JSY AU RC	▼50	▼60	▼80	▼100

012 Score

	NmMt 8	NmMt+ 8.5	MT 9	Gem 9.5/10
A Andrew Luck RC	8	10	15	25

012 SP Authentic

	NmMt 8	NmMt+ 8.5	MT 9	Gem 9.5/10
Russell Wilson	10	12	20	30
Nick Foles JSY AU/885	40	50	60	100
Kirk Cousins JSY AU/885	100	125	150	250
Russell Wilson JSY AU/885	60	80	100	200

012 Topps

	NmMt 8	NmMt+ 8.5	MT 9	Gem 9.5/10
A Andrew Luck RC	10	12	20	40
B A.Luck SP rabbit foot	200	225	300	400
D A.Luck FS twst pass	10	12	20	40
A Russell Wilson RC	10	12	15	30

012 Topps Rookie Refractors

	NmMt 8	NmMt+ 8.5	MT 9	Gem 9.5/10
HMAL Andrew Luck	12	15	20	30

012 Topps Chrome

	NmMt 8	NmMt+ 8.5	MT 9	Gem 9.5/10
A.Luck RC passing	25	30	40	100
Andrew Luck SP drop	80	100	135	250

	NmMt 8	NmMt+ 8.5	MT 9	Gem 9.5/10
23A T.Rchardson RC cut	8	10	15	30
40A R.Wilson RC stands	15	20	30	50

2012 Topps Chrome Black Refractors

	NmMt 8	NmMt+ 8.5	MT 9	Gem 9.5/10
1 Andrew Luck	▼40	▼50	▼60	▼80
40 Russell Wilson	60	80	100	150

2012 Topps Chrome Blue Refractors

	NmMt 8	NmMt+ 8.5	MT 9	Gem 9.5/10
1 Andrew Luck	▼50	▼60	▼80	▼100
40 Russell Wilson	60	80	100	150

2012 Topps Chrome Camo Refractors

	NmMt 8	NmMt+ 8.5	MT 9	Gem 9.5/10
1 Andrew Luck	▼12	▼15	▼25	▼30
40 Russell Wilson	40	50	60	▲125

2012 Topps Chrome Orange Refractors

	NmMt 8	NmMt+ 8.5	MT 9	Gem 9.5/10
1 Andrew Luck	▼12	▼15	▼20	▼25
40 Russell Wilson	15	20	30	▲80

2012 Topps Chrome Pink Refractors

	NmMt 8	NmMt+ 8.5	MT 9	Gem 9.5/10
1 Andrew Luck	▼25	▼30	▼40	▼50
40 Russell Wilson	40	50	60	100

2012 Topps Chrome Prism Refractors

	NmMt 8	NmMt+ 8.5	MT 9	Gem 9.5/10
1 Andrew Luck	▼20	▼30	▼40	▼60
40 Russell Wilson	40	50	60	150

2012 Topps Chrome Purple Refractors

	NmMt 8	NmMt+ 8.5	MT 9	Gem 9.5/10
1 Andrew Luck	▼12	▼15	▼20	▼25
40 Russell Wilson	40	50	60	80

2012 Topps Chrome Refractors

	NmMt 8	NmMt+ 8.5	MT 9	Gem 9.5/10
1A Andrew Luck/passing pose	▼12	▼20	▼25	▼30
40 Russell Wilson	▲30	▲40	▲50	100
147 Doug Martin	8	10	15	25

2012 Topps Chrome Sepia Refractors

	NmMt 8	NmMt+ 8.5	MT 9	Gem 9.5/10
1 Andrew Luck	▼30	▼40	▼50	▼60
40 Russell Wilson	▲125	▲150	▲200	▲250

2012 Topps Chrome Xfractors

	NmMt 8	NmMt+ 8.5	MT 9	Gem 9.5/10
1 Andrew Luck	▼12	▼15	▼20	▼25
40 Russell Wilson	20	25	35	50

2012 Topps Chrome 1957

	NmMt 8	NmMt+ 8.5	MT 9	Gem 9.5/10
1 Andrew Luck	12	15	25	50
2 Andrew Luck	12	15	25	50

2012 Topps Chrome 1965

	NmMt 8	NmMt+ 8.5	MT 9	Gem 9.5/10
1 Andrew Luck	12	15	25	50
12 Russell Wilson	8	10	15	30

2012 Topps Chrome 1984

	NmMt 8	NmMt+ 8.5	MT 9	Gem 9.5/10
1 Andrew Luck	12	15	25	50
14 Russell Wilson	8	10	15	30

2012 Topps Chrome Red Zone Rookies Refractors

	NmMt 8	NmMt+ 8.5	MT 9	Gem 9.5/10
RZDC1 Andrew Luck	15	20	25	50
RZDC14 Russell Wilson	12	15	20	30

2012 Topps Chrome Rookie Autographs

	NmMt 8	NmMt+ 8.5	MT 9	Gem 9.5/10
40 Russell Wilson	175	200	250	300

	NmMt 8	NmMt+ 8.5	MT 9	Gem 9.5/10
147 Doug Martin	20	25	40	60
153 Nick Foles	40	50	60	80

2012 Topps Chrome Rookie Autographs Pink Refractors

	NmMt 8	NmMt+ 8.5	MT 9	Gem 9.5/10
1 Andrew Luck		600	800	1,200

2012 Topps Chrome Rookie Autographs Prism Refractors

	NmMt 8	NmMt+ 8.5	MT 9	Gem 9.5/10
1 Andrew Luck		▼150	▼200	▼300

2012 Topps Chrome Rookie Autographs Refractors

	NmMt 8	NmMt+ 8.5	MT 9	Gem 9.5/10
40 Russell Wilson	175	200	250	400
153 Nick Foles	60	80	100	150

2012 Topps Chrome Rookie Autographs Refractors Variations

	NmMt 8	NmMt+ 8.5	MT 9	Gem 9.5/10
1 Andrew Luck	400	450	1,200	1,500
40 Russell Wilson	225	250	300	500

2012 Topps Magic

	NmMt 8	NmMt+ 8.5	MT 9	Gem 9.5/10
1 Andrew Luck RC	10	12	20	40
181 Russell Wilson RC	8	10	15	30

2012 Topps Platinum

	NmMt 8	NmMt+ 8.5	MT 9	Gem 9.5/10
138 Russell Wilson RC	15	20	25	40
150 Andrew Luck RC	12	15	25	40

2012 Topps Platinum Orange Refractors

	NmMt 8	NmMt+ 8.5	MT 9	Gem 9.5/10
120 Robert Griffin III	15	20	25	35
150 Andrew Luck	15	20	50	35

2012 Topps Platinum Xfractors

	NmMt 8	NmMt+ 8.5	MT 9	Gem 9.5/10
120 Robert Griffin III	20	25	30	50
138 Russell Wilson	15	20	25	40
150 Andrew Luck	▼8	▼10	▼12	▼15

2012 Topps Platinum Rookie Die Cut

	NmMt 8	NmMt+ 8.5	MT 9	Gem 9.5/10
PDCAL Andrew Luck	25	30	40	60

2013 Topps Chrome Rookie Autographs

	NmMt 8	NmMt+ 8.5	MT 9	Gem 9.5/10
198 Le'Veon Bell/600	50	60	100	125

2014 Bowman

R8 Odell Beckham Jr. RC

2014 Bowman Chrome Rookie Autographs College Refractors

	NmMt 8	NmMt+ 8.5	MT 9	Gem 9.5/10
79 Odell Beckham Jr.	100	125	150	200

2014 Bowman Chrome Rookie Autographs College Blue Refractors

	NmMt 8	NmMt+ 8.5	MT 9	Gem 9.5/10
12 Johnny Manziel	80	100	125	150
14 Teddy Bridgewater	80	100	125	150
79 Odell Beckham Jr.	125	150	200	400

2014 Bowman Chrome

	NmMt 8	NmMt+ 8.5	MT 9	Gem 9.5/10
190A Odell Beckham Jr. RC	8	10	12	20

2014 Bowman Chrome Rookie Autographs Refractors

	NmMt 8	NmMt+ 8.5	MT 9	Gem 9.5/10
RCRAAD Aaron Donald	40	50	80	100
RCRADC Derek Carr	50	60	80	200
RCRAJG Jimmy Garoppolo	100	125	150	200
RCRAJM Johnny Manziel	60	80	100	125
RCRAOB Odell Beckham Jr.	60	80	100	150

2014 Bowman Chrome Rookie Autographs Blue Refractors

	NmMt 8	NmMt+ 8.5	MT 9	Gem 9.5/10
RCRAOB Odell Beckham Jr.	80	100	125	150

2014 Finest

	NmMt 8	NmMt+ 8.5	MT 9	Gem 9.5/10
116 Jimmy Garoppolo RC	8	12	25	40

2014 Panini Contenders

	NmMt 8	NmMt+ 8.5	MT 9	Gem 9.5/10
208A Carlos Hyde AU RC (ball in right arm)		50	60	80
214A Derek Carr AU RC (ball at right shoulder)		125	400	500
221A Jimmy Garoppolo AU RC (looking left)		500	600	▼1,000
227A Odell Beckham Jr. AU RC (ball in left arm)	125	150	200	250
227B Odell Beckham Jr. AU 206*/looking straight)	125	150	200	250
235A Kelvin Benjamin AU RC (ball in left arm)	40	50	60	125
236A Mike Evans AU RC (looking right)	40	50	60	100
237A Sammy Watkins AU RC (ball in left arm)	▼30	▼40	▼50	▼60

2014 Panini National Treasures

	NmMt 8	NmMt+ 8.5	MT 9	Gem 9.5/10
221 Martavis Bryant AU RC	40	50	60	80
274 Jimmy Garoppolo JSY AU RC	2,000	2,500	▼2,800	▼3,000
296 Derek Carr JSY AU RC	500	600	700	800

2014 SP Authentic

	NmMt 8	NmMt+ 8.5	MT 9	Gem 9.5/10
231 Jimmy Garoppolo JSY AU/350	150	200	300	600

2014 Topps

	NmMt 8	NmMt+ 8.5	MT 9	Gem 9.5/10
355A Odell Beckham Jr. RC	3	4	5	10

2014 Topps Chrome

	NmMt 8	NmMt+ 8.5	MT 9	Gem 9.5/10
117A Odell Beckham Jr. RC	12	15	20	30

2014 Topps Chrome Refractors

	NmMt 8	NmMt+ 8.5	MT 9	Gem 9.5/10
115 Derek Carr	10	12	20	50
117 Odell Beckham Jr.	25	30	40	50
150 Jimmy Garoppolo	25	30	40	100
173 Teddy Bridgewater	8	10	15	25

2014 Topps Chrome Rookie Autographs

	NmMt 8	NmMt+ 8.5	MT 9	Gem 9.5/10
115 Derek Carr SP	200	250	300	500
117 Odell Beckham Jr.	▼60	▼80	▼100	▼150
150 Jimmy Garoppolo	▲150	▲200	▲250	▼400
169 Johnny Manziel SP	50	60	80	100
175 Aaron Donald	20	25	50	100

2014 Topps Chrome Rookie Autographs Refractors

	NmMt 8	NmMt+ 8.5	MT 9	Gem 9.5/10
115 Derek Carr	100	120	300	400
117 Odell Beckham Jr.	150	200	250	400
150 Jimmy Garoppolo	150	200	250	500
173 Teddy Bridgewater	60	80	100	125

2015 Bowman

	NmMt 8	NmMt+ 8.5	MT 9	Gem 9.5/10
R22 Marcus Mariota RC	6	10	15	30
R23 Jameis Winston RC	5	8	12	25

2015 Bowman Chrome Rookie Autographs Refractors

	NmMt 8	NmMt+ 8.5	MT 9	Gem 9.5/10
RCRAAC Amari Cooper	60	80	100	150
RCRAJW Jameis Winston	50	60	80	100
RCRAMM Marcus Mariota	60	80	100	150
RCRATG Todd Gurley	60	80	100	150

2015 Panini Contenders

	NmMt 8	NmMt+ 8.5	MT 9	Gem 9.5/10
228A Amari Cooper AU RC	60	80	100	125
238A Todd Gurley AU RC	80	100	125	150

2015 Panini Contenders Draft Picks

	NmMt 8	NmMt+ 8.5	MT 9	Gem 9.5/10
122A Jameis Winston AU RC SP1 (red jsy)			120	200
131A Marcus Mariota AU RC SP1 (white jsy)	150	200	300	400

2015 Panini National Treasures

	NmMt 8	NmMt+ 8.5	MT 9	Gem 9.5/10
107 Jameis Winston JSY AU RC	400	500	600	800
128 Todd Gurley JSY AU RC	400	500	600	800
140 Marcus Mariota JSY AU RC	400	500	600	800

2015 Topps Chrome Rookie Autographs

	NmMt 8	NmMt+ 8.5	MT 9	Gem 9.5/10
177 David Johnson	25	30	40	50

2015 Topps Chrome Rookie Autographs Camo Refractors

	NmMt 8	NmMt+ 8.5	MT 9	Gem 9.5/10
110 Todd Gurley	100	125	150	200

2015 Topps Chrome Rookie Autographs Pink Refractors

	NmMt 8	NmMt+ 8.5	MT 9	Gem 9.5/10
110 Todd Gurley	100	125	150	200

2015 Topps Chrome Rookie Autographs Refractors

	NmMt 8	NmMt+ 8.5	MT 9	Gem 9.5/10
110 Todd Gurley	60	80	100	125
150 Marcus Mariota	100	125	150	200

2016 Donruss Optic

	NmMt 8	NmMt+ 8.5	MT 9	Gem 9.5/10
156 Carson Wentz RR RC	15	20	25	40
162 Dak Prescott RR RC	12	15	20	25
168 Ezekiel Elliott RR RC	▼8	10	12	▲30

2016 Donruss Optic Holo

	NM 7	NmMt+ 8.5	MT 9	Gem 9.5/10
156 Carson Wentz RR		25	30	▲60
168 Ezekiel Elliott RR		40	50	60

2016 Donruss Optic Rated Rookies Autographs

	NmMt 8	NmMt+ 8.5	MT 9	Gem 9.5/10
156 Carson Wentz	150	200	250	400
162 Dak Prescott			150	▼250
168 Ezekiel Elliott			150	▼250

2016 Elite Pen Pals

	NM 7	NmMt+ 8.5	MT 9	Gem 9.5/10
PPCW Carson Wentz			150	300
PPDP Dak Prescott			150	300
PPEE Ezekiel Elliott			150	300

2016 Panini Contenders Draft Picks

	NmMt 8	NmMt+ 8.5	MT 9	Gem 9.5/10
105A Ezekiel Elliott AU RC (white jsy)			150	400
125A Dak Prescott AU RC (throwing)			150	300
127A Carson Wentz AU RC (white jsy)			150	400

2016 Panini National Treasures

	NmMt 8	NmMt+ 8.5	MT 9	Gem 9.5/10
102 Carson Wentz JSY AU RC			3,000	5,000

2016 Panini Prizm

	NmMt 8	NmMt+ 8.5	MT 9	Gem 9.5/10
218 Carson Wentz RC	10	15	▲40	▲125

	NmMt 8	NmMt+ 8.5	MT 9	Gem 9.5/10
231 Dak Prescott RC	5	10	12	▲60
238 Ezekiel Elliott RC	5	10	20	▲60

2017 Classics

	NmMt 8	NmMt+ 8.5	MT 9	Gem 9.5/1
274 Patrick Mahomes II RC	12	15	30	▲60

2017 Classics Glossy

	NmMt 8	NmMt+ 8.5	MT 9	Gem 9.5/1
274 Patrick Mahomes II	20	25	50	▲100

2017 Crown Royale

	NmMt 8	NmMt+ 8.5	MT 9	Gem 9.5/1
84 Patrick Mahomes II RC	30	50	100	150

2017 Donruss

	NmMt 8	NmMt+ 8.5	MT 9	Gem 9.5/1
327 Patrick Mahomes II RR RC	25	50	80	100

2017 Donruss The Elite Series Rookies

	NmMt 8	NmMt+ 8.5	MT 9	Gem 9.5/1
7 Patrick Mahomes II	30	40	50	200

2017 Donruss The Rookies

	NmMt 8	NmMt+ 8.5	MT 9	Gem 9.5/1
7 Patrick Mahomes II	30	40	100	150

2017 Donruss Optic

	NmMt 8	NmMt+ 8.5	MT 9	Gem 9.5/1
177 Patrick Mahomes II RR RC	40	50	60	200

2017 Donruss Optic Holo

	NmMt 8	NmMt+ 8.5	MT 9	Gem 9.5/1
177 Patrick Mahomes II RR	80	100	125	200

2017 Donruss Optic Pink

	NmMt 8	NmMt+ 8.5	MT 9	Gem 9.5/1
195 Deshaun Watson RR	10	12	30	50

2017 Panini Contenders Optic

	NmMt 8	NmMt+ 8.5	MT 9	Gem 9.5/10
102 Deshaun Watson AU RC			▲400	▲600
103 Patrick Mahomes II AU RC	▲1,000	▲1,200	▲3,000	▲6,000
127 JuJu Smith-Schuster AU RC	60	80	100	125

2017 Panini Prizm

	NmMt 8	NmMt+ 8.5	MT 9	Gem 9.5/10
269 Patrick Mahomes II RC	▲80	▲100	▲150	▲400
279 Deshaun Watson RC	60	80	▲100	▲200

2017 Panini Prizm Rookie Autographs Prizm

	NmMt 8	NmMt+ 8.5	MT 9	Gem 9.5/10
RAPM Patrick Mahomes II	▲300	▲400	▲500	▲1,200

2018 Donruss

	NmMt 8	NmMt+ 8.5	MT 9	Gem 9.5/10
301 Sam Darnold RR RC	6	10	15	20
303 Baker Mayfield RR RC	▲15	▲20	▲30	50
306 Saquon Barkley RR RC	8	12	25	40
317 Lamar Jackson RR RC	12	20	50	80

2018 Donruss Optic

	NmMt 8	NmMt+ 8.5	MT 9	Gem 9.5/10
151 Sam Darnold RR RC	6	15	25	50
153 Baker Mayfield RR RC	25	40	▼50	100
156 Saquon Barkley RR RC	12	15	25	50
167 Lamar Jackson RR RC	8	15	25	50

2018 Panini Contenders Optic

	NmMt 8	NmMt+ 8.5	MT 9	Gem 9.5/10
101 Baker Mayfield AU RC		600	800	1,000

2018 Panini Prizm

	NmMt 8	NmMt+ 8.5	MT 9	Gem 9.5/10
201 Baker Mayfield RC	15	25	60	▲150
202 Saquon Barkley RC	10	15	▲40	▲50
203 Sam Darnold RC	10	15	▲40	▲50

GOLF
1927 - Present

1927 Churchman's Famous Golfers Large

		VgEx 4	EX 5	ExMt 6	NM 7
	Walter Hagen	100	200	350	500
	Bobby Jones	200	350	700	1,200

1927 Churchman's Famous Golfers Small

		EX 5	ExMt 6	NM 7	NmMt 8
3	Walter Hagen 13	50	100	250	750
4	Walter Hagen 14	50	100	250	750
7	Bobby Jones 27	125	250	600	1,000
3	Bobby Jones 28	125	250	600	1,000
3	Tom Morris	75	125	300	600
4	Edward Ray 34	15	25	50	150
5	Edward Ray 35	15	25	50	150
0	Freddie Tait	15	25	50	150
1	John Henry Taylor 41	20	30	60	150
2	John Henry Taylor 42	20	30	60	150
3	Cyril Tolley	15	25	50	150
4	Harry Vardon 44	30	50	150	300
5	Harry Vardon 45	30	50	150	300
6	Harry Vardon 46	30	50	150	300
7	Harry Vardon 47	30	50	150	300

1928 J.Millhoff and Co. Famous Golfers

		EX 5	ExMt 6	NM 7	NmMt 8
	Walter Hagen	60	100	175	400
	Harry Vardon	30	50	100	300
0	Bobby Jones	175	275	500	900

1930 Wills Cigarettes Famous Golfers

		EX 5	ExMt 6	NM 7	NmMt 8
	Walter Hagen	75	125	150	300

1931 Churchman's Prominent Golfers Large

		EX 5	ExMt 6	NM 7	NmMt 8
3	Henry Cotton	25	60	100	
4	Walter Hagen	100	175	250	
5	Bobby Jones	150	250	500	800
6	Abe Mitchell	25	60	100	
3	Cyril Tolley	20	40	80	
11	Roger Wethered	25	60	100	

—Walter Hagen #4 PSA 8.5 (NmMt+) sold for $1,540 (eBay; 2/10)
—Walter Hagen #4 PSA 8 (NmMt) sold for $461 (eBay; 10/08)
—Harry Vardon #9 PSA 9 (MT) sold for $1,490 (eBay; 11/11)
—Harry Vardon #9 PSA 8 (NmMt) sold for $300 (eBay; 05/09)

1931 Churchman's Prominent Golfers Small

		VgEx 4	EX 5	ExMt 6	NM 7
16	Walter Hagen	25	40	75	200
25	Bobby Jones	60	100	175	325
35	Gene Sarazen	40	60	75	125

1981 Donruss

		NM 7	NmMt 8	MT 9	Gem 9.5/10
	COMMONS & MINOR STARS	5	10	15	60
1	Tom Watson RC	10	15	25	250
2	Lee Trevino RC	8	12	20	125
3	Curtis Strange RC	5	10	15	75
5	Ben Crenshaw RC	5	12	20	125
10	Raymond Floyd RC	5	10	15	200
13	Jack Nicklaus RC	15	40	40	225
20	Tom Kite RC	5	10	15	75
21	Jim Colbert RC	5	10	20	200
27	David Graham RC	5	10	30	175
29	Lon Hinkle RC	5	10	15	150
30	Johnny Miller RC	5	10	15	100
31	Dave Eichelberger RC	5	10	15	125
32	Wayne Levi SP RC	5	10	15	200
35	Jay Haas RC	5	10	15	150
36	Dan Halldorson SP RC	5	10	20	200
39	Mark Lye RC	5	10	20	125
47	Tom Weiskopf RC	5	10	15	150
48	Jim Simons RC	5	10	30	200
NNO	Jack Nicklaus SL	8	15	30	150
NNO	Tom Watson SL	5	10	40	250

1982 Donruss

		NM 7	NmMt 8	MT 9	Gem 9.5/10
	COMMONS & MINOR STARS	5	10	25	
1	Tom Kite	10	15	30	
3	Tom Watson	10	15	40	
16	Jack Nicklaus	15	30	50	
23	Lee Trevino	8	15	40	
53	Fred Couples RC	10	20	100	
55	Mark O'Meara RC	8	20	60	

—Jack Nicklaus #16 BGS 9.5 (Gem) sold for $145 (Mastro; 02/08)

1990 Pro Set

		NmMt 8	NmMt+ 8.5	MT 9	Gem 9.5/10
20	Payne Stewart RC	4	6	10	20
80	Arnold Palmer RC	4	6	10	
93	Jack Nicklaus	3	5	8	15

1992 Pro Set

		NmMt 8	NmMt+ 8.5	MT 9	Gem 9.5/10
E6	Vijay Singh RC	10	15	30	

1996 Niketown Promo

		NmMt 8	NmMt+ 8.5	MT 9	Gem 9.5/10
NNO	Tiger Woods	70	125	200	350

—Tiger Woods BGS 9.5 (Gem) sold for $4,155 (eBay; 5/09)

1996 Sports Illustrated for Kids II

		NmMt 8	NmMt+ 8.5	MT 9	Gem 9.5/10
536	Tiger Woods/Golf	400	500	750	2,500

1997-98 Grand Slam Ventures Masters Collection

		NmMt 8	NmMt+ 8.5	MT 9	Gem 9.5/10
1997	Tiger Woods XRC	60	75	350	500

1997-98 Grand Slam Ventures Masters Collection Gold Foil

		NmMt 8	NmMt+ 8.5	MT 9	Gem 9.5/10
1997	Tiger Woods	150	250	750	

—Tiger Woods #1997 BGS 9.5 (Gem) sold for $2,560 (eBay; 07/07)
—Tiger Woods #1997 BGS 9.5 (Gem) sold for $3,000 (eBay; 11/07)

2001 SP Authentic Preview

		NmMt 8	NmMt+ 8.5	MT 9	Gem 9.5/10
21	Tiger Woods STAR	15	20	25	50

2001 SP Authentic Preview Red

—Tiger Woods STAR #21 BGS 9 (Mint) sold for $1,505 (eBay; 06/08)

2001 SP Authentic

		NmMt 8	NmMt+ 8.5	MT 9	Gem 9.5/10
45	Tiger Woods AS AU/900 RC	2,000	5,000	6,000	10,000
46	D.Duval AS AU/900 RC	25	40	60	100
47	J.Parnevik AS AU/900 RC	15	30	40	75
62	S.Garcia AS AU/900 RC	20	40	60	100
78	R.Goosen AS AU/900 RC	20	40	60	100
136	David Toms AS AU/900	15	30	50	100

—#45 Tiger Woods BGS 10 (Pristine) sold for $16,610 (eBay; 3/08)
—#45 Tiger Woods BGS 10 (Pristine) sold for $10,417 (eBay; 5/09)

2001 SP Authentic Gold

—Tiger Woods #45 BGS 10 (Pristine) sold for $5,890 (eBay; 1/10)
—Tiger Woods #45 PSA 10 (Gem) sold for $4,540 (eBay; 11/07)
—Tiger Woods #45 PSA 10 (Gem) sold for $15,000 (eBay; 05/08)
—Tiger Woods #45 PSA 10 (Gem) sold for $10,000 (eBay; 10/09)
—Tiger Woods #45 PSA 10 (Gem) sold for $12,000 (eBay; 07/12)
—Tiger Woods #45 BGS 9.5 (Gem) sold for $10,000 (eBay; 02/08)
—Tiger Woods #45 BGS 9.5 (Gem) sold for $8,500 (eBay; 02/08)
—Tiger Woods #45 BGS 9.5 (Gem) sold for $4,533 (eBay; 10/09)
—Tiger Woods #45 BGS 9.5 (Gem) sold for $3,892 (eBay; 10/11)
—Tiger Woods #45 BGS 9.5 (Gem) sold for $4,999 (eBay; 4/13)
—Tiger Woods #45 BGS 9.5 (Gem) sold for $4,161 (eBay; 9/13)
—Tiger Woods #45 BGS 9.5 (Gem) sold for $3,870 (eBay; 9/13)
—Tiger Woods #45 BGS 9 (MT) sold for $8,900 (eBay; 02/08)
—Tiger Woods #45 BGS 9 (MT) sold for $8,500 (eBay; 06/08)
—Tiger Woods #45 BGS 9 (MT) sold for $6,000 (eBay; 08/08)
—Tiger Woods #45 BGS 9 (MT) sold for $4,500 (eBay; 04/08)
—Retief Goosen #78 BGS 9.5 (Gem) sold for $130 (eBay; 02/08)
—Retief Goosen #78 BGS 9.5 (Gem) sold for $125 (eBay; 03/08)
—Retief Goosen #78 BGS 9.5 (Gem) sold for $120 (eBay; 04/08)

2001 SP Authentic Sign of the Times

—Tiger Woods #TW BGS 9.5 (Gem) sold for $2,930 (eBay; 04/08)
—Tiger Woods #TW BGS 9.5 (Gem) sold for $750 (eBay; 05/11)
—Tiger Woods #TW PSA 10 (Gem) sold for $1,850 (eBay; 10/11)
—Tiger Woods #TW BGS 9 (Mint) sold for $1,900 (eBay; 06/08)
—Tiger Woods #TW BGS 9 (Mint) sold for $1,400 (eBay; 05/08)
—Tiger Woods #TW BGS 9 (Mint) sold for $999 (eBay; 5/09)
—Tiger Woods #TW BGS 9 (Mint) sold for $795 (eBay; 3/13)

2001 SP Authentic Sign of the Times Red

		NM 7	NmMt 8	NmMt+ 8.5	MT 9
TW1	T.Woods Bay Hill/273	250	400	600	800
TW2	T.Woods Player's/274	250	400	600	800

—Tiger Woods #TW1 PSA 10 (Gem) sold for $2,515 (eBay; 06/08)
—Tiger Woods #TW1 BGS 9.5 (Gem) sold for $2,025 (eBay; 06/08)
—Tiger Woods #TW1 SGC 10 (Gem) sold for $1,627 (eBay; 12/08)
—Tiger Woods #TW1 BGS 9.5 (Gem) sold for $1,230 (eBay; 11/08)
—Tiger Woods #TW1 BGS 9.5 (Gem) sold for $1,188 (eBay; 10/09)
—Tiger Woods #TW1 BGS 9 (Mint) sold for $1,190 (eBay; 06/08)
—Tiger Woods #TW1 BGS 9 (Mint) sold for $1,032 (eBay; 01/09)
—Tiger Woods #TW1 BGS 9 (Mint) sold for $807 (eBay; 5/09)
—Tiger Woods #TW2 BGS 10 (Pristine) sold for $3,300 (eBay; 12/08)
—Tiger Woods #TW2 BGS 10 (Pristine) sold for $3,030 (eBay; 2/10)
—Tiger Woods #TW2 BGS 9.5 (Gem) sold for $1,125 (eBay; 10/08)
—Tiger Woods #TW2 BGS 9.5 (Gem) sold for $762 (eBay; 09/26)
—Tiger Woods #TW2 BGS 9 (Mint) sold for $1,000 (eBay; 05/08)
—Tiger Woods #TW4 BGS 9.5 (Gem) sold for $2,220 (eBay; 08/12)
—Tiger Woods #TW5 BGS 9.5 (Gem) sold for $12,200 (eBay; 09/09)
—Tiger Woods #TW5 BGS 9.5 (Gem) sold for $9,560 (eBay; 05/08)
—Tiger Woods #TW7 BGS 9 (Mint) sold for $1,800 (eBay; 9/09)

2001 Upper Deck Promos

		NmMt 8	NmMt+ 8.5	MT 9	Gem 9.5/10
NNO	Tiger Woods	25	50	100	200

2001 Upper Deck

		NmMt 8	NmMt+ 8.5	MT 9	Gem 9.5/10
1	Tiger Woods RC	8	12	20	35

—Tiger Woods #1 BGS 10 (Pristine) sold for $1,010 (eBay; 04/08)
—Tiger Woods #1 BGS 10 (Pristine) sold for $550 (eBay; 02/09)
—Tiger Woods #1 BGS 10 (Pristine) sold for $500 (eBay; 03/08)
—Tiger Woods #1 BGS 10 (Pristine) sold for $500 (eBay; 05/09)
—Tiger Woods #1 BGS 10 (Pristine) sold for $493 (eBay; 03/09)
—Tiger Woods #1 BGS 10 (Pristine) sold for $485 (eBay; 03/08)
—Tiger Woods #1 BGS 10 (Pristine) sold for $430 (eBay; 06/08)
—Tiger Woods #1 BGS 10 (Pristine) sold for $415 (eBay; 06/08)
—Tiger Woods #1 BGS 10 (Pristine) sold for $409 (eBay; 04/09)
—Tiger Woods #1 BGS 10 (Pristine) sold for $375 (eBay; 06/08)
—Tiger Woods #1 BGS 10 (Pristine) sold for $305 (eBay; 05/08)
—Tiger Woods #1 BGS 10 (Pristine) sold for $235 (eBay; 11/07)
—Tiger Woods #1 BGS 10 (Pristine) sold for $230 (eBay; 06/08)
—Tiger Woods #1 BGS 10 (Pristine) sold for $215 (eBay; 11/07)
—Tiger Woods #1 BGS 10 (Pristine) sold for $215 (eBay; 11/07)
—Tiger Woods #1 BGS 10 (Pristine) sold for $215 (eBay; 01/08)
—Tiger Woods #1 BGS 10 (Pristine) sold for $205 (eBay; 01/08)
—Tiger Woods #1 BGS 10 (Pristine) sold for $155 (eBay; 01/08)
—Tiger Woods VM #151 BGS 10 (Pristine) sold for $181 (eBay; 02/09)
—Tiger Woods VM #151 BGS 10 (Pristine) sold for $124 (eBay; 03/09)

2001 Upper Deck Gallery

		NmMt 8	NmMt+ 8.5	MT 9	Gem 9.5/10
GG4	Tiger Woods	5	8	10	20

—Tiger Woods #GG4 BGS 10 (Pristine) sold for $105 (eBay; 06/08)
—Tiger Woods #GG4 BGS 10 (Pristine) sold for $32 (eBay; 5/11)

2001 Upper Deck Player's Ink

		NmMt 8	NmMt+ 8.5	MT 9	Gem 9.5/10
TW	Tiger Woods	600	800	1,000	1,200

—Tiger Woods #TW BGS 10 (Pristine) sold for $5,500 (eBay; 10/09)
—Tiger Woods #TW BGS 10 (Pristine) sold for $3,303 (eBay; 10/09)
—Tiger Woods #TW BGS 10 (Pristine) sold for $3,187 (eBay; 9/09)

2001 Upper Deck Stat Leaders

		NmMt 8	NmMt+ 8.5	MT 9	Gem 9.5/10
SL2	Tiger Woods	5	8	10	40
SL7	Tiger Woods	5	8	10	40
SL11	Tiger Woods	5	8	10	40
SL17	Tiger Woods	5	8	10	40

2001 Upper Deck Tiger's Tales

	NmMt 8	NmMt+ 8.5	MT 9	Gem 9.5/10
COMMON CARD (TT1-TT30)	5	5	5	15

2001 Upper Deck Heroes of Golf National Convention Promos

		NmMt 8	NmMt+ 8.5	MT 9	Gem 9.5/10
1TW	Tiger Woods	8	12	20	50

2001 Upper Deck Tiger Jam IV

		NmMt 8	NmMt+ 8.5	MT 9	Gem 9.5/10
TJ1	Tiger Woods	20	30	50	75
TJ2	Tiger Woods Silver	30	50	75	150

2002 SP Authentic

		NmMt 8	NmMt+ 8.5	MT 9	Gem 9.5/10
110	Phil Mickelson AU RC	100	125	175	300

2002 SP Authentic Limited

—Phil Mickelson #110 BGS 9 (MT) sold for $330 (eBay; 03/08)

2002 SP Game Used

		NmMt 8	NmMt+ 8.5	MT 9	Gem 9.5/10
80	Phil Mickelson AU Jsy T3 RC	150	200	250	400

2002 SP Game Used 01 Buybacks

—Tiger Woods #1 UD/18 PSA 9 (Mint) sold for $11,005 (eBay; 03/08)

2002 Upper Deck

		NmMt 8	NmMt+ 8.5	MT 9	Gem 9.5/10
41	Phil Mickelson RC	5	6	8	30

2003 SP Authentic

		NmMt 8	NmMt+ 8.5	MT 9	Gem 9.5/10
110	Annika Sorenstam AU/799 RC	40	50	75	125
125	Natalie Gulbis AU/1999 RC	15	20	25	40
127	Lorena Ochoa AU/1999 RC	15	20	25	50

2003 Upper Deck

		NmMt 8	NmMt+ 8.5	MT 9	Gem 9.5/10
48	Annika Sorenstam FL RC	6	8	10	25
57	Lorena Ochoa FL RC	6	8	10	25

—Tiger Woods #1 BGS 10 (Pristine) sold for $132 (eBay; 05/09)

2005 SP Authentic

		NmMt 8	NmMt+ 8.5	MT 9	Gem 9.5/10
104	Paula Creamer AU L1 RC	60	80	100	150

2005 SP Authentic Sign of the Times Single

		NmMt 8	NmMt+ 8.5	MT 9	Gem 9.5/10
TW	Tiger Woods	200	250	300	500

2015 Sports Illustrated for Kids

		NmMt 8	NmMt+ 8.5	MT 9	Gem 9.5/10
430	Jordan Spieth Golf	40	50	60	

HOCKEY

1910 - 1980

1910-11 C56

		PrFr 1	GD 2	VG 3	VgEx 4	EX 5	ExMt 6	NM 7	NmMt 8
1	Frank Patrick RP	250	400	500	1,000	2,000			
2	Percy Lesueur RC	▲300	▲400	500	800	3,000			
3	Gordon Roberts RC	100	150	250	400	600			
4	Barney Holden RC	80	120	200	300	500			
5	Frank(Pud) Glass RC	80	▲200	▲250	300	500			
6	Edgar Dey RC	80	120	200	300	500			
7	Marty Walsh RC	100	150	250	300	600	800		
8	Art Ross RC	500	800	1,000	1,500	5,000			
9	Angus Campbell RC	80	120	200	300	600			
10	Harry Hyland RC	125	175	300	400	800			
11	Herb Clark RC	60	150	200	300				
12	Art Ross RC	500	800	1,000	1,500	2,500	5,000		
13	Ed Decary RC	▲80	▲150	▲200	▲300	▲500	▲800		
14	Tom Dunderdale RC	150	200	300	500	800			
15	Fred Taylor RC	550	800	1,200	2,000	3,000	5,000		
16	Jos. Cattarinich RC	80	120	200	400	600			
17	Bruce Stuart RC	125	175	300	400	600	1,000		
18	Nick Bawlf RC	60	100	150	250	400	800		
19	Jim Jones RC	80	120	200	300	500	1,000		
20	Ernest Russell RC	125	175	300	400	800	1,500		
21	Jack Laviolette RC	80	120	200	300	600			
22	Riley Hern RC	100	150	250	400	600			
23	Didier(Pit) Pitre RC	125	200	250	400	600			
24	Skinner Poulin RC	60	100	▲200	▲300	400	800		
25	Art Bernier RC	60	▲150	▲250	▲300	500			
26	Lester Patrick RC	200	350	500	800	2,000			
27	Fred Lake RC	60	100	150	200	400			
28	Paddy Moran RC	200	400	500	700	1,250			
29	C.Toms RC	60	120	150	250	400			
30	Ernest(Moose) Johnson RC	150	250	400	600	800			
31	Horace Gaul RC	60	100	150	250	400			
32	Harold McNamara RC	100	150	200	300	500			
33	Jack Marshall RC	100	150	200	600	1,000			
34	Bruce Ridpath RC	60	150	200	250	500	1,000		
35	Jack Marshall RC	100	175	300	400	600			
36	Newsy Lalonde RC	500	600	1,000	2,500	3,000			

—Nick Bawlf #18 PSA 7 (NM) sold for $1,792.77 (eBay; 3/16)
—Art Bernier #25 PSA 6 (ExMt) sold for $1,366 (eBay; 3/16)
—Joesph Cattarinich #16 PSA 6 (ExMt) sold for $1,144 (eBay; 3/16)
—Frank Glass #5 PSA 6 (ExMt) sold foe $896 (eBay; 3/16)
—Harry Hyland RC #10 PSA 6 (ExMt) sold for $1,910 (eBay; 1/14)
—Skinner Poulin #24 PSA 7 (NrMt) sold for $2,911 (Mastro; 4/07)

1911-12 C55

		PrFr 1	GD 2	VG 3	VgEx 4	EX 5	ExMt 6	NM 7	NmMt 8
1	Paddy Moran	100	200	250	400	800			
2	Joe Hall RC	60	100	200	300	500			
3	Barney Holden	40	80	125	200	300	650		
4	Joe Malone RC	200	300	400	▲700	1,500	2,250		
5	Ed Oatman RC	60	100	125	200	300	800		
6	Tom Dunderdale	50	80	125	250	400	600		
7	Ken Mallen RC	50	80	125	200	300	500		
8	Jack MacDonald RC	100	120	150	200	300	800		
9	Fred Lake	60	80	125	200	300	600		
10	Albert Kerr RC	50	80	125	200	300	500		
11	Marty Walsh	50	80	125	250	400	800		
12	Hamby Shore RC	60	80	125	200	300	600		
13	Alex Currie RC	60	100	125	200	300	600		
14	Bruce Ridpath	50	80	125	200	300	400		
15	Bruce Stuart	50	80	125	250	400	600		
16	Percy Lesueur	80	150	200	300	400	600		
17	Jack Darragh RC	60	100	150	300	400	800		
18	Steve Vair RC	50	80	100	150	200	400		
19	Don Smith RC	50	80	125	150	300	600		
20	Fred Taylor	300	400	500	800	1,500	2,400		
21	Bert Lindsay RC	40	100	▲150	▲250	350	600		
22	H.L.(Larry) Gilmour RC	50	80	125	250	400	600		
23	Bobby Rowe RC	40	60	100	150	250	600		
24	Sprague Cleghorn RC	75	150	300	400	800	1,200		
25	Odie Cleghorn RC	50	80	125	250	300	600		

		PrFr 1	GD 2	VG 3	VgEx 4	EX 5	ExMt 6	NM 7	NmMt
26	Skene Ronan RC	50	▲100	▲150	200	300	800		
27A	W.Smail RC Hand on stk	120	200	300	600	1,200			
27B	W.Smail RC Hand on hip	150	300	800	1,200				
28	Ernest(Moose) Johnson	60	100	125	200	400	800		
29	Jack Marshall	50	80	150	200	400	800		
30	Harry Hyland	50	80	125	250	350	600		
31	Art Ross	300	500	700	1,000	1,500	2,000		
32	Riley Hern	60	100	▲150	▲250	▲350			
33	Gordon Roberts	60	100	150	200	400	800		
34	Frank Glass	50	80	125	200	300	500		
35	Ernest Russell	60	100	150	250	300	600		
36	James Gardner UER RC	50	80	125	250	400			
37	Art Bernier	40	60	100	150	250	500		
38	Georges Vezina RC	1,200	2,000	3,500	5,000	8,000	10,000		
39	G.(Henri) Dallaire RC	60	100	150	250	400	600		
40	R.(Rocket) Power RC	50	80	125	200	300	600		
41	Didier(Pit) Pitre	80	120	250	300	500			
42	Newsy Lalonde	250	400	500	800	1,000	2,000		
43	Eugene Payan RC	50	80	125	250	300	500		
44	George Poulin RC	50	80	125	200	300	600		
45	Jack Laviolette	80	120	150	300	500	2,200		

—Jack Darragh RC #17 PSA 7 (NM MT) sold for $1,085 (eBay, 1/14)
—Bert Lindsay #21 PSA 8 (NM MT) sold for $4,176 (eBay, 8/13)
—Ed Oatman RC #5 PSA 8 (NM MT) sold for $2,010 (eBay, 8/13)
—Walter Smaill #27A PSA 8 (NM MT) sold for $7,620 (eBay, 8/13)
—Fred Taylor #20 SCG 8 (NM MT) sold for $3,438 (Mile High; 1/16)
—Fred Taylor #20 PSA 6 (NM) sold for $1,812.50 (eBay, 2/14)
—George Vezina #38 SGC 6 (ExMt) sold for $1,910 (eBay, 07/09)
—George Vezina #38 SGC 96 (MT) sold for $100,000 (BMW, private sale)
—George Vezina #38 PSA 7 (NM) sold for $11,000 (Mastro, 12/08)
—George Vezina #38 SGC 20 (Fair) sold for $1,535 (eBay, 05/08)
—George Vezina #38 PSA 7 (NM) sold for $20,698.50 (eBay, 03/14)

1933-34 O-Pee-Chee V304A

		PrFr 1	GD 2	VG 3	VgEx 4	EX 5	ExMt 6	NM 7	NmM
1	Danny Cox RC	35	60	100	150	250			
2	Joe Lamb RC	30	40	80	100	200			
3	Eddie Shore RC	200	350	450	1,000	1,800	3,000		
4	Ken Doraty RC	30	40	60	100	200			
5	Fred Hitchman RC	30	40	60	125	200	600		
6	Nels Stewart RC	120	200	300	500	800			
7	Walter Galbraith RC	▲50	▲80	▲100	▲150	▲200	400		
8	Dit Clapper RC	100	150	250	500	800			
9	Harry Oliver RC	60	100	150	250	400	600		
10	Red Horner RC	50	80	120	200	300			
11	Alex Levinsky RC	30	40	60	100	200	400		
12	Joe Primeau RC	100	150	200	300	600	1,000		
13	Ace Bailey RC	▲150	▲200	▲300	▲400	▲500	600		
14	George Patterson RC	30	40	60	100	150			
15	George Hainsworth RC	60	100	150	300	500			
16	Ott Heller RC	30	40	60	100	150			
17	Art Somers RC	30	40	60	100	150			
18	Lorne Chabot RC	60	100	125	250	400			
19	Johnny Gagnon RC	30	40	60	100	200	400		
20	Pit Lepine RC	30	40	60	100	150			
21	Wildor Larochelle RC	30	40	60	120	150	400		
22	Georges Mantha RC	30	40	60	120	175			
23	Howie Morenz	250	400	1,000	1,500	2,500			
24	Syd Howe RC	50	150	200	250	300	500		
25	Frank Finnigan RC	30	40	60	100	150			
26	Bill Touhey RC	30	40	60	100	150			
27	Cooney Weiland RC	▲80	▲100	▲150	▲250	▲350	500		
28	Leo Bourgeault RC	35	50	80	125	250			
29	Normie Himes RC	35	50	75	135	200	400		
30	Johnny Sheppard RC	30	40	60	100	150			
31	King Clancy RC	100	150	250	400	600	1,000		
32	Hap Day RC	▲50	▲80	▲150	▲200	▲300			
33	Busher Jackson RC	100	150	250	300	500	1,000		
34	Charlie Conacher RC	100	150	250	350	800			
35	Harold Cotton RC	50	60	100	150	200	350		
36	Butch Keeling RC	30	40	60	100	150			
37	Murray Murdoch RC	35	40	60	100	200			
38	Bill Cook	35	50	100	150	350	500		

	PrFr 1	GD 2	VG 3	VgEx 4	EX 5	ExMt 6	NM 7	NmMt 8
Ching Johnson RC	60	100	150	250	500	900		
Hap Emms RC	30	40	60	100	150			
Bert McInenly RC	30	40	60	100	150			
John Sorrell RC	50	100	150	200	250			
Bill Phillips RC	30	40	60	100	150	300		
Charley McVeigh RC	30	40	60	100	150			
Roy Worters RC	60	100	150	250	400			
Albert Leduc RC	35	60	80	120	200			
Nick Wasnie RC	30	40	60	100	150	500		
Armand Mondou RC	▲50	▲80	▲100	▲150	200			

Bailey #13 PSA 7 (NM) sold for $1,154 (eBay; 6/13)
Clapper #8 PSA 8 (NmMt) sold for $5,008 (eBay; 5/12)
Clapper #8 PSA 7.5 (NmMt) sold for $854 (eBay; 9/14)
tch Keeling #36 PSA 7 (NM) sold for $1,475 (eBay; 2/13)
ooney Weiland #27 PSA 7 (NM) sold for $1,283 (eBay; 2/16)

933-34 O-Pee-Chee V304B

	PrFr 1	GD 2	VG 3	VgEx 4	EX 5	ExMt 6	NM 7	NmMt 8
Babe Siebert RC	50	80	120	200	300			
Aurel Joliat	125	200	300	400	600			
Larry Aurie RC	▲50	▲80	100	150	250	400		
Ebbie Goodfellow RC	35	60	100	150	250			
John Roach	30	50	80	125	200			
Bill Beveridge RC	30	50	80	125	200			
Earl Robinson RC	25	▲50	▲100	▲150	▲200	500		
Jimmy Ward RC	▲30	▲50	▲80	100	150			
Archie Wilcox RC	25	40	60	100	150	350		
Lorne Duguid RC	25	40	60	100	150	350		
Dave Kerr RC	▲30	▲80	▲100	▲150	200			
Baldy Northcott RC	30	50	80	125	200	400		
Marvin Wentworth RC	30	50	80	125	200	400		
Dave Trottier RC	30	50	80	125	150	250		
Wally Kilrea RC	25	40	60	100	150	350		
Glen Brydson RC	30	50	80	125	200			
Vernon Ayres RC	25	40	60	100	150			
Bob Gracie RC	25	40	60	100	150	400		
Vic Ripley RC	30	50	80	125	250			
Tiny Thompson RC	60	100	150	250	800			
Alex Smith RC	25	40	60	100	150			
Andy Blair RC	25	40	60	100	150			
Cecil Dillon RC	25	40	60	125	200	600		
Bun Cook RC	50	80	120	200	800			

ny Thompson #68 PSA 7 (NM) sold for $1,865 (eBay; 4/16)

933-34 V357 Ice Kings

	PrFr 1	GD 2	VG 3	VgEx 4	EX 5	ExMt 6	NM 7	NmMt 8
Dit Clapper RC	40	75	125	250	400	1,500		
Bill Brydge RC	25	30	50	80	150			
Aurel Joliat UER	50	100	200	300	400	700		
Andy Blair	25	30	50	80	100	150		
Earl Robinson RC	25	30	50	80	100	150		
Paul Haynes RC	25	30	50	80	100	150		
Ronnie Martin RC	25	30	50	80	100	150		
Babe Siebert RC	25	50	100	150	200	500		
Archie Wilcox RC	25	30	50	80	100	150		
Hap Day	35	50	80	125	250			
Roy Worters RC	50	80	150	200	350			
Nels Stewart RC	40	60	100	200	300	500		
King Clancy	40	80	120	200	300	600		
Marty Burke RC	30	40	60	100	200			
Cecil Dillon RC	25	30	50	80	100			
Red Horner RC	50	60	100	150	300			
Armand Mondou RC	25	30	50	80	100	150		
Paul Raymond RC	25	30	50	80	100			
Dave Kerr RC	25	30	50	80	100	150	250	
Butch Keeling RC	25	30	50	80	100	150	300	
Johnny Gagnon RC	25	30	50	80	100	150	250	
Ace Bailey RC	40	80	120	200	300			
Harry Oliver RC	30	40	60	100	150	250	400	
Gerald Carson RC	25	30	50	80	100	150	200	
Red Dutton RC	25	35	50	80	125	200		
Georges Mantha RC	25	30	50	80	100	200		
Marty Barry RC	40	50	80	125	175	250		
Wildor Larochelle RC	25	30	50	80	100	150		
Red Beattie RC	25	30	50	80	100	150		
Bill Cook	40	50	80	125	175	250		
Hooley Smith	50	60	100	150	200	350		
Art Chapman RC	25	30	50	80	100	150		
Harold Cotton RC	30	50	80	100	150	250		
Lionel Hitchman RC	30	40	60	100	150	250		
George Patterson RC	25	30	50	80	100	150		
Howie Morenz	150	250	400	800				
Jimmy Ward RC	25	30	50	80	100	150		
Charley McVeigh RC	25	35	50	80	125	175		
Glen Brydson RC	25	35	50	80	125	175		
Joe Primeau RC	100	125	200	300	500	800		
Joe Lamb RC	25	40	60	100	150	200	350	
Sylvio Mantha	50	60	100	150	225	350		
Cy Wentworth RC	30	40	60	100	200	400		

	PrFr 1	GD 2	VG 3	VgEx 4	EX 5	ExMt 6	NM 7	NmMt 8
44 Normie Himes RC	25	35	50	80	125	175		
45 Doug Brennan RC	25	30	50	80	100	150		
46 Pit Lepine RC	25	30	50	80	100			
47 Alex Levinsky RC	25	35	50	80	125	175		
48 Baldy Northcott RC	25	35	50	80	125	175		
49 Ken Doraty RC	25	35	50	80	125			
50 Bill Thoms RC	25	35	50	80	125			
51 Vernon Ayres RC	25	35	60	100	150			
52 Lorne Duguid RC	25	35	50	80	125			
53 Wally Kilrea RC	25	35	50	80	125			
54 Vic Ripley RC	25	35	50	80	125			
55 Hap Emms RC	25	35	50	80	125			
56 Duke Dutkowski RC	25	35	50	80	125			
57 Tiny Thompson RC	200	250	300	400	500			
58 Charlie Sands RC	25	35	50	80	125			
59 Larry Aurie RC	25	35	50	80	125			
60 Bill Beveridge RC	25	35	50	80	125			
61 Bill McKenzie RC	25	35	50	80	125			
62 Earl Roche RC	25	35	50	80	125			
63 Bob Gracie RC	25	35	50	80	125			
64 Hec Kilrea RC	25	35	50	80	125			
65 Cooney Weiland RC	125	150	200	250	400			
66 Bun Cook RC	40	60	100	150	300			
67 John Roach	25	35	50	80	125	175		
68 Murray Murdoch RC	25	35	50	80	125			
69 Danny Cox RC	25	35	50	80	125			
70 Desse Roche RC	25	35	50	80	150			
71 Lorne Chabot RC	125	150	200	300	400			
72 Syd Howe RC	40	60	100	150				

Ace Bailey #22 PSA 7 (NrMt) sold for $756 (eBay; 9/12)
Armand Mondou #17 PSA 8 (NmMt) sold for $1,127 (eBay; 9/12)
Aurel Joliat #3 PSA 7 (NrMt) sold for $1,153 (eBay; 9/12)
Bill Brydge #2 PSA 8 (NmMt) sold for $1,143 (eBay; 9/12)
Hap Day #10 PSA 8 (NmMt) sold for $592 (eBay; 9/12)
King Clancy #13 PSA 8 (NmMt) sold for $2,385 (Mile High; 1/12)
Nels Stewart #12 PSA 8 (NmMt) sold for $1,432 (eBay; 9/14)

1935-36 O-Pee-Chee V304C

	PrFr 1	GD 2	VG 3	VgEx 4	EX 5	ExMt 6	NM 7	NmMt 8
73 Wilfred Cude RC	50	80	125	200	600			
74 Jack McGill RC	30	50	100	150				
75 Russ Blinco RC	30	50	80	150				
76 Hooley Smith	50	80	125	200				
77 Herb Cain RC	30	50	80	125	250			
78 Gus Marker RC	30	50	80	200				
79 Lynn Patrick RC	50	80	125	200				
80 Johnny Gottselig	30	50	80	125				
81 Marty Barry	35	60	100	150	300			
82 Sylvio Mantha	50	80	125	250				
83 Flash Hollett RC	30	50	80	200	500			
84 Nick Metz RC	30	50	80	125				
85 Bill Thoms	30	50	80	125				
86 Hec Kilrea	30	50	80	125				
87 Pep Kelly RC	30	50	80	125				
88 Art Jackson RC	30	50	80	125				
89 Allan Shields RC	30	50	80	125				
90 Buzz Boll	30	50	80	125				
91 Jean Pusie RC	30	50	80	125				
92 Roger Jenkins RC	30	50	80	125	400			
93 Arthur Coulter RC	30	50	125	200	400			
94 Art Chapman	30	50	80	125				
95 Paul Haynes	35	60	100	150				
96 Leroy Goldsworthy RC	50	80	125	200	250	300		

1936-37 O-Pee-Chee V304D

	PrFr 1	GD 2	VG 3	VgEx 4	EX 5	ExMt 6	NM 7	NmMt 8
97 Turk Broda RC	150	300	600	1,000	2,500			
98 Sweeney Schriner RC	40	100	150	200	300	500		
99 Jack Shill RC	25	40	60	100	150	200		
100 Bob Davidson RC	35	60	80	100	250	400		
101 Syl Apps RC	80	200	300	500	600	2,500		
102 Lionel Conacher	60	150	250	400	500			
103 Jimmy Fowler RC	35	60	100	150	250	400		
104 Al Murray RC	25	40	60	100	150			
105 Neil Colville RC	35	100	150	250	300	450		
106 Paul Runge RC	25	40	60	100	150	200		
107 Mike Karakas RC	30	50	80	125	175	250		
108 John Gallagher RC	25	40	60	100	150	250		
109 Alex Shibicky RC	35	60	100	150	200	300		
110 Herb Cain	35	60	100	150	200	300		
111 Bill McKenzie	25	40	60	100	150	200		
112 Harold Jackson RC	40	60	80	125	200	300		
113 Art Wiebe RC	25	40	60	100	150			
114 Joffre Desilets RC	25	40	60	100	150			
115 Earl Robinson	25	40	60	100	200	300		
116 Cy Wentworth	35	60	80	125	200	250		
117 Ebbie Goodfellow	25	40	60	100	175	300		
118 Eddie Shore	200	400	600	800	1,500			
119 Buzz Boll	25	40	60	100	150			

#	Player	PrFr 1	GD 2	VG 3	VgEx 4	EX 5	ExMt 6	NM 7	NmMt 8
120	Wilfred Cude	30	50	80	120	200			
121	Howie Morenz	250	400	600	800	1,500	2,000		
122	Red Horner	40	100	150	250	300	500		
123	Charlie Conacher	100	250	350	500	600			
124	Busher Jackson	50	120	200	250	300	400		
125	King Clancy	100	250	400	500	750	1,000		
126	Dave Trottier	30	50	80	125	200	300		
127	Russ Blinco	25	40	60	100	150			
128	Lynn Patrick	50	120	200	300	400			
129	Aurel Joliat	80	200	300	500	600	800		
130	Baldy Northcott	25	50	100	150	200	250		
131	Larry Aurie	25	40	100	150	225	300		
132	Hooley Smith	40	80	120	200	300	400		

—Turk Broda #97 PSA 8 (NmMt) sold for $3,6192.00 (eBay; 11/11)
—Charlie Conacher #123 SGC 9 (Mint) sold for $4,633.86.00 (Goodwin; 7/12)
—Aurel Joliat #129 SGC 8 (NRMint) sold for $1,036 (eBay; 3/14)
—Aurel Joliat #129 SGC 7 (NRMint) sold for $837 (eBay; 9/14)

1937-38 O-Pee-Chee V304E

#	Player	PrFr 1	GD 2	VG 3	VgEx 4	EX 5	ExMt 6	NM 7	NmMt 8
133	Turk Broda	100	150	250	400				
134	Red Horner	30	50	80	120				
135	Jimmy Fowler	25	35	50	60				
136	Bob Davidson	25	35	50	60				
137	Reg. Hamilton RC	25	35	50	60	200			
138	Charlie Conacher	80	120	200	300				
139	Busher Jackson	60	100	150	250				
140	Buzz Boll	25	35	50	60	200			
141	Syl Apps	60	100	150	250				
142	Gordie Drillon RC	60	100	200	300	400			
143	Bill Thoms	25	35	50	60				
144	Nick Metz	25	35	50	60				
145	Pep Kelly	25	35	50	60				
146	Murray Armstrong RC	25	35	50	60				
147	Murph Chamberlain RC	25	35	50	60				
148	Des Smith RC	25	35	50	60	200			
149	Wilfred Cude	30	50	80	100				
150	Babe Siebert	30	50	80	120				
151	Bill MacKenzie	25	40	60	80				
152	Aurel Joliat	80	120	200	300				
153	Georges Mantha	25	35	50	60				
154	Johnny Gagnon	25	35	50	60	200			
155	Paul Haynes	25	35	50	60				
156	Joffre Desilets	25	35	50	60				
157	George Allen Brown RC	25	35	50	60				
158	Paul Drouin RC	25	35	50	60				
159	Pit Lepine	25	50	60	80				
160	Toe Blake RC	150	250	300	500				
161	Bill Beveridge	30	50	80	100				
162	Allan Shields	25	35	50	60				
163	Cy Wentworth	30	50	80	120				
164	Stew Evans RC	25	35	50	60				
165	Earl Robinson	25	35	50	60				
166	Baldy Northcott	30	50	80	100				
167	Paul Runge	25	35	50	60				
168	Dave Trottier	25	35	50	60				
169	Russ Blinco	25	35	50	60	200			
170	Jimmy Ward	25	35	50	60				
171	Bob Gracie	25	35	50	60				
172	Herb Cain	30	50	80	120	250			
173	Gus Marker	25	35	50	60				
174	Walter Buswell RC	25	35	50	60				
175	Carl Voss	30	50	80	120				
176	Rod Lorraine RC	25	35	50	60				
177	Armand Mondou	25	35	50	60				
178	Cliff(Red) Goupille RC	25	35	50	60	200			
179	Jerry Shannon RC	25	35	50	60				
180	Tom Cook RC	30	50	80	120				

—Carl Voss #175 PSA 7 (NM) sold for $902 (eBay; 3/16)

1939-40 O-Pee-Chee V301-1

#	Player	PrFr 1	GD 2	VG 3	VgEx 4	EX 5	ExMt 6	NM 7	NmMt 8
1	Reg Hamilton	15	25	35	60				
2	Turk Broda	▲100	▲150	▲200	▲250	300			
3	Bingo Kampman RC	15	25	35	50				
4	Gordie Drillon	20	25	40	80				
5	Bob Davidson	15	25	35	50				
6	Syl Apps	30	50	80	120				
7	Pete Langelle RC	15	▲30	▲50	▲100				
8	Don Metz RC	15	25	35	50				
9	Pep Kelly	15	25	35	50				
10	Red Horner	20	30	50	80				
11	Wally Stanowsky RC	15	25	35	50				
12	Murph Chamberlain	15	25	35	50				
13	Bucko MacDonald	15	25	35	50				
14	Sweeney Schriner	20	30	50	80				
15	Billy Taylor RC	15	25	35	50				
16	Gus Marker	15	25	35	50				
17	Hooley Smith	20	30	50	80				

#	Player	PrFr 1	GD 2	VG 3	VgEx 4	EX 5	ExMt 6	NM 7	NmM
18	Art Chapman	15	25	35	50				
19	Murray Armstrong	15	25	35	50				
20	Busher Jackson	20	30	50	80	150			
21	Buzz Boll	15	25	35	50				
22	Cliff(Red) Goupille	15	25	35	50				
23	Rod Lorraine	15	25	35	50				
24	Paul Drouin	15	25	35	50				
25	Johnny Gagnon	15	25	35	50				
26	Georges Mantha	15	25	40	60				
27	Armand Mondou	15	25	40	60				
28	Claude Bourque RC	15	25	40	60				
29	Ray Getliffe RC	15	25	40	60				
30	Cy Wentworth	15	25	40	60				
31	Paul Haynes	15	25	35	50				
32	Walter Buswell	15	25	35	50				
33	Ott Heller	15	25	35	50				
34	Arthur Coulter	15	25	35	60				
35	Clint Smith RC	20	30	50	80				
36	Lynn Patrick	20	30	50	80				
37	Dave Kerr	15	25	40	60				
38	Murray Patrick RC	15	25	35	50				
39	Neil Colville	20	30	50	80				
40	Jack Portland RC	15	25	35	50				
41	Flash Hollett	15	25	35	50				
42	Herb Cain	20	30	50	80				
43	Mud Bruneteau	15	25	35	50				
44	Joffre DeSilets	15	25	35	50				
45	Mush March	15	25	35	50				
46	Cully Dahlstrom RC	15	25	35	50				
47	Mike Karakas	15	25	35	60				
48	Bill Thoms	15	25	35	50				
49	Art Wiebe	15	25	35	50				
50	Johnny Gottselig	15	25	35	50				
51	Nick Metz	15	25	35	50				
52	Jack Church RC	15	25	35	50				
53	Bob Heron RC	15	25	35	50				
54	Hank Goldup RC	15	25	35	50	80			
55	Jimmy Fowler	15	25	35	50				
56	Charlie Sands	15	25	35	50				
57	Marty Barry	15	25	35	60				
58	Doug Young	15	25	35	50				
59	Charlie Conacher	30	60	100	150	250			
60	John Sorrell	15	25	35	50				
61	Tommy Anderson RC	15	25	35	50	135			
62	Lorne Carr	15	25	35	50				
63	Earl Robertson RC	15	25	60	80				
64	Wilfy Field RC	15	25	35	50				
65	Jimmy Orlando RC	15	25	35	50				
66	Ebbie Goodfellow	15	▲30	▲50	▲80	100			
67	Jack Keating RC	15	25	35	50	80			
68	Sid Abel RC	60	100	120	200	300			
69	Gus Giesebrecht RC	15	25	35	50				
70	Don Deacon RC	15	25	35	50	80			
71	Hec Kilrea	15	25	35	50				
72	Syd Howe	20	30	50	80				
73	Eddie Wares RC	15	25	35	50	80			
74	Carl Liscombe RC	15	25	35	50				
75	Tiny Thompson	20	30	50	80	150			
76	Earl Seibert RC	15	25	35	50				
77	Des Smith RC	15	25	35	50	80			
78	Les Cunningham RC	15	25	35	50				
79	George Allen RC	15	25	35	50				
80	Bill Carse RC	15	25	35	50				
81	Bill McKenzie	15	25	35	50				
82	Ab DeMarco RC	15	▲30	▲50	▲80	150			
83	Phil Watson	15	25	35	50				
84	Alf Pike RC	15	25	35	50				
85	Babe Pratt RC	15	25	40	60				
86	Bryan Hextall Sr. RC	15	25	40	60				
87	Kilby MacDonald RC	15	25	35	50				
88	Alex Shibicky	15	25	35	50	100			
89	Dutch Hiller RC	15	25	35	50				
90	Mac Colville	15	25	35	50				
91	Roy Conacher RC	20	30	50	80	125			
92	Cooney Weiland	20	30	50	80	125			
93	Art Jackson	15	25	35	50				
94	Woody Dumart RC	20	30	50	80	250			
95	Dit Clapper	30	50	80	120	200			
96	Mel Hill RC	15	25	35	50				
97	Frank Brimsek RC	50	80	120	200	300			
98	Bill Cowley RC	▲50	▲80	▲100	▲200	250			
99	Bobby Bauer RC	40	60	100	200				
100	Eddie Shore	100	150	250	400				

—Bryan Hextall #86 SGC 9 (Mint) sold for $1,705 (Mile High; 10/12)
—Bryan Hextall #86 PSA 8 (NM Mt) sold for $837 (eBay; 2/16)
—Rod Lorraine #23 SGC 9 (Mint) sold for $1,025 (Mile High; 5/12)
—Wally Stanowsky #11 SGC 8.5 (NmMt+) sold for $567 (Mile High; 5/12)

1951-52 Parkhurst

	GD 2	VG 3	VgEx 4	EX 5	ExMt 6	NM 7	NmMt 8	NmMt+ 8.5
Elmer Lach	80	150	▲300	▲400	650	▲1,250	4,000	
Paul Meger RC	25	60	100	200	250	400	3,500	
Butch Bouchard RC	▲80	▲150	▲200	▲250	▲500	650	1,500	
Maurice Richard RC	1,000	1,250	1,750	2,000	2,500	3,500	7,000	7,500
Bert Olmstead RC	40	▲100	150	200	300	600	1,250	
Bud MacPherson RC	15	25	40	80	125	250	700	
Tom Johnson RC	▲30	▲50	▲80	▲100	▲200	350	600	
Paul Masnick RC	15	25	40	80	100	200	300	
Calum Mackay RC	25	40	80	100	150	200	500	
Doug Harvey RC	200	250	300	400	500	800	2,000	2,500
Ken Mosdell RC	15	25	40	80	125	200	800	
Floyd Curry RC	12	20	30	60	100	150	400	
Billy Reay RC	15	25	40	60	100	150	500	
Bernie Geoffrion RC	▲250	▲300	▲400	▲500	▲750	1,000	1,500	
Gerry McNeil RC	30	60	100	200	300	600	2,000	
Dick Gamble RC	15	30	50	80	120	200	350	
Gerry Couture RC	15	30	40	60	100	200	600	
Ross Robert Lowe RC	20	25	40	60	100	200	500	1,000
Jim Henry RC	20	30	50	60	100	175	400	
Victor Ivan Lynn RC	15	25	40	60	100	150	300	
Walter(Gus) Kyle RC	12	20	30	50	80	120	250	
Ed Sandford RC	12	20	30	50	100	150	250	
John Henderson RC	12	20	30	50	80	120	250	
Dunc Fisher RC	15	25	40	60	80	120	400	
Hal Laycoe RC	15	25	40	50	80	120	250	
Bill Quackenbush RC	20	30	50	80	120	200	400	
George Sullivan RC	12	20	30	50	80	120	250	
Woody Dumart RC	20	30	50	60	100	150	250	
Milt Schmidt	25	40	100	200	300	400	500	
Adam Brown RC	12	20	50	80	100	150	250	500
Pentti Lund RC	15	25	40	60	100	150	400	850
Ray Barry RC	12	20	30	50	80	100	250	
Ed Kryznowski UER RC	12	20	30	50	80	100	300	
Johnny Peirson RC	12	20	30	50	80	120	250	
Lorne Ferguson RC	12	20	30	50	80	120	250	
Clare(Rags) Raglan	12	20	30	50	80	120	350	
Bill Gadsby RC	50	80	150	200	250	350	600	
Al Dewsbury RC	12	20	40	50	80	120	400	
George Clare Martin RC	12	20	40	50	80	120	250	
Gus Bodnar RC	20	30	40	80	150	200	300	
Jim Peters RC	12	20	30	50	80	125	250	
Bep Guidolin RC	12	20	30	50	80	150	350	
George Gee RC	12	20	30	50	80	120	250	
Jim McFadden RC	▲15	▲30	▲50	▲80	▲150	▲200	300	
Fred Hucul RC	12	20	30	50	80	120	200	
Lee Fogolin	12	20	30	50	80	100	250	
Harry Lumley RC	50	60	100	150	250	300	600	900
Doug Bentley RC	25	50	80	100	200	400	800	
Bill Mosienko RC	30	60	80	100	150	250	500	
Roy Conacher	20	40	60	80	120	200	300	
Pete Babando RC	15	25	40	80	100	200	500	
B.Barilko/G.McNeil IA	80	150	250	300	400	500	1,400	
Jack Stewart	25	30	60	80	150	200	400	
Marty Pavelich RC	12	20	30	50	80	150	800	
Red Kelly RC	100	250	300	400	500	800	1,500	2,000
Ted Lindsay RC	▲100	▲200	▲300	400	500	600	1,000	
Glen Skov RC	12	20	30	50	80	250	1,200	
Benny Woit RC	12	20	30	50	80	175	400	
Tony Leswick RC	15	25	40	80	120	200	400	
Fred Glover RC	15	25	40	60	120	200	400	
Terry Sawchuk RC	▲400	▲600	▲700	▲900	▲1,250	1,500	3,500	
Vic Stasiuk RC	12	20	30	60	100	150	300	
Alex Delvecchio RC	80	150	250	300	500	800	1,500	2,000
Sid Abel	25	40	60	100	200	400	600	
Metro Prystai RC	12	20	30	50	80	150	400	
Gordie Howe RC	▲3,000	▲4,500	▲5,500	▲6,500	▲7,500	12,000	40,000	
Bob Goldham RC	15	25	40	60	125	200	500	
Marcel Pronovost RC	25	40	60	100	150	250	500	
Leo Reise	12	20	30	50	80	100	200	
Harry Watson RC	60	80	100	150	200	450	1,400	
Danny Lewicki RC	12	20	30	50	80	150	400	
Howie Meeker RC	50	100	150	250	300	350	800	
Gus Mortson RC	12	25	40	60	100	200	300	
Joe Klukay RC	15	30	50	80	120	250	1,000	
Turk Broda	60	100	200	250	400	1,000	3,000	
Al Rollins RC	25	40	60	80	100	350	1,500	
Bill Juzda RC	12	20	30	50	80	150	350	
Ray Timgren RC	12	20	30	50	80	150	300	
Hugh Bolton RC	12	20	60	80	120	150	600	
Fern Flaman RC	25	50	80	100	200	300	550	
Max Bentley	20	30	50	80	120	200	800	
Jim Thomson	12	20	30	50	80	150	300	
Fleming Mackell RC	▲15	▲30	▲50	▲80	▲100	▲200	400	
Sid Smith RC	20	30	50	80	125	250	400	
Cal Gardner RC	15	30	50	80	125	200	400	
Teeder Kennedy RC	40	60	100	150	250	400	750	2,400

		GD 2	VG 3	VgEx 4	EX 5	ExMt 6	NM 7	NmMt 8	NmMt+ 8.5
87	Tod Sloan RC	15	25	40	80	125	200	300	
88	Bob Solinger	▲15	▲30	▲50	▲80	▲100	▲200	300	
89	Frank Eddolls RC	12	20	30	50	80	150	300	
90	Jack Evans RC	12	20	30	60	80	120	250	
91	Hy Buller RC	12	20	30	80	80	150	700	
92	Steve Kraftcheck	12	20	30	50	80	100	300	
93	Don Raleigh	12	25	50	80	100	150	300	
94	Allan Stanley RC	40	60	80	100	150	200	500	
95	Paul Ronty RC	15	25	40	60	80	120	300	
96	Edgar Laprade RC	20	40	60	100	150	250	500	
97	Nick Mickoski RC	12	20	30	50	80	120	300	
98	Jack McLeod RC	12	20	30	50	80	150	300	
99	Gaye Stewart	12	20	30	50	80	150	300	
100	Wally Hergesheimer RC	▲15	▲30	▲50	▲80	▲100	150	300	
101	Ed Kullman RC	25	40	60	80	100	150	400	
102	Ed Slowinski RC	25	40	60	80	100	200	1,000	
103	Reg Sinclair RC	15	25	40	100	150	300	550	
104	Chuck Rayner RC	25	50	100	150	200	300	600	
105	Jim Conacher RC	25	40	60	100	200	300	800	

—Pete Babando #51 PSA 7.5 (NrMt) sold for $2,030 (eBay; 7/08)
—Bill Barilko/Gerry McNeil #53 PSA 9 (MT) sold for $5,612 (Memory Lane; 4/12)
—Bill Barilko/Gerry McNeil #53 PSA 8.5 (NmMt+) sold for $2,427 (Mile High; 5/12)
—Ray Barry #32 PSA 9 (MT) sold for $3,312 (Memory Lane; 7/12)
—Ray Barry #32 PSA 9 (MT) sold for $1,721 (eBay; 3/16)
{ %%Doug Bentley #48 PSA 8.5 (NmMt+) sold for $1,332 (Mile High; 5/12)
—Doug Bentley #48 PSA 8.5 (NmMt+) sold for $7,200 (eBay; 8/08)
—Butch Bouchard #3 PSA 8.5 (NmMt+) sold for $7,200 (Mastro; 8/08)
—Turk Broda #75 PSA 8 (NmMt) sold for $3,065 (eBay; 3/14)
—Adam Brown #30 PSA 10 (Gem) sold for $6,000 (Mastro; 8/08)
—Adam Brown #30 PSA 9 (MT) sold for $1,256.50 (eBay; 5/16)
—Hy Buller #91 PSA 9 (MT) sold for $2,608.50 (eBay; 5/16)
—Roy Conacher #50 PSA 9 (MT) sold for $4,524 (eBay; 7/15)
—Gerry Couture RC #17 PSA 9 (Mt) sold for $2,216 (Memory Lane; 12/13)
—Alex Delvecchio #63 PSA 8 (NmMt) sold for $4,859 (eBay; 8/12)
—Alex Delvecchio #63 PSA 9 (MT) sold for $3,708 (eBay; 3/13)
—Jack Evans #90 PSA 9 (NmMt) sold for $2,379 (eBay; 6/12)
—Bill Gadsby #37 PSA 9 (MT) sold for $2,549 (Memory Lane; 5/13)
—George Gee #43 PSA 9 (MT) sold for $2,489 (Memory Lane; 7/12)
—Bob Goldman #67 PSA 10 (GEM) sold for $6,000 (Mastro; 8/08)
—Bep Guidolin #42 PSA 8.5 (NmMt+) sold for $6,000 (Mastro; 8/08)
—Doug Harvey #10 PSA 9 (MT) sold for $5,620 (eBay; 3/13)
—Doug Harvey #10 PSA 9 (MT) sold for $3,000 (eBay; 9/08)
—Jim Henry #19 PSA 9 (MT) sold for $2,005 (Mile High; 5/12)
—Jim Henry #19 PSA 9 (MT) sold for $3,204 (eBay; 10/08)
—Gordie Howe #66 SGC 9 (MT) sold for $29,372 (Goodwin; 9/15)
—Gordie Howe #66 SGC 8.5 (NmMt+) sold for $21,493 (Mile High; 7/15)
—Gordie Howe #66 PSA 8.5 (NmMt+) sold for $26,300 (eBay; 3/13)
—Fred Hucul #45 PSA 9 (MT) sold for $1,307 (eBay; 1/07)
—Fred Hucul #45 PSA 9 (MT) sold for $1,840 (eBay; 3/16)
—Tom Johnson #7 PSA 9 (MT) sold for $4,191 (eBay; 10/15)
—Ed Kryznowski #33 PSA 9 (Mint) sold for $1,034 (Memory Lane; 7/12)
—Hal Laycoe #25 PSA 9 (MT) sold for $1,367 (Mile High; 5/12)
—Hal Laycoe #25 PSA 9 (MT) sold for $2,480 (Mile High; 1/07)
—Danny Lewicki #71 PSA 9 (MT) sold for $2,263 (Memory Lane; 4/12)
—Ted Lindsay #56 PSA 9 (MT) sold for $7,714 (Memory Lane; 12/06)
—Ted Lindsay #56 SGC 9 (MT) sold for $2,323 (Goodwin; 3/13)
—Robert Lowe #18 PSA 9 (MT) sold for $2,738 (Mile High; 5/12)
—Harry Lumley #47 PSA 9 (MT) sold for $1,923 (eBay; 3/13)
—Jim McFadden #44 PSA 9 (MT) sold for $1,830 (eBay; 7/08)
—George Martin #39 PSA 9 (MT) sold for $1,627 (Memory Lane; 7/12)
—George Martin #39 PSA 9 (MT) sold for $2,534 (Memory Lane; 4/07)
—George Martin #39 PSA 9 (MT) sold for $1,704 (eBay; 10/08)
—Paul Meger #2 PSA 8 (NmMt) sold for $3,844 (Goodwin; 9/11)
—Ken Mosdell #11 PSA 9 (MT) sold for $3,300 (eBay; 9/08)
—Bill Mosienko #49 PSA 9 (MT) sold for $2,670 (Mile High; 5/12)
—Marcel Pronovost #68 PSA 8.5 (NmMt+) sold for $2,167 (Mile High; 5/12)
—Bill Quackenbush #26 PSA 9 (MT) sold for $3,600 (eBay; 9/08)
—Don Raleigh #93 PSA 9 (MT) sold for $1,700 (Memory Lane; 4/12)
—Maurice Richard #4 PSA 9 (MT) sold for $30,100 (eBay; 3/13)
—Maurice Richard #4 PSA 9 (MT) sold for $9,008 (eBay; 11/14)
—Maurice Richard #4 PSA 9 (MT) sold for $8,295 (Robert Edward; Fall 2013)
—Maurice Richard #4 PSA 5 (Ex) sold for $1,369 (eBay; 1/14)
—Maurice Richard #4 PSA 9 (MT) sold for $30,100 (eBay; 3/13)
—Maurice Richard #4 PSA 9 (MT) sold for $9,008 (eBay; 11/14)
—Maurice Richard #4 PSA 9 (MT) sold for $8,295 (Robert Edward; Fall 2013)
—Maurice Richard #4 PSA 5 (Ex) sold for $1,369 (eBay; 1/14)
—Paul Ronty #95 PSA 9 (MT) sold for $2,489 (Memory Lane; 4/12)
—Paul Ronty #95 PSA 9 (MT) sold for $1,262 (eBay; 3/20)
—Terry Sawchuk #61 PSA 9 (MT) sold for $6,600 (Mastro; 8/08)
—Terry Sawchuk #61 PSA 8.5 (NmMt+) sold for $4,041 (eBay; 11/15)
—Milt Schmidt #29 PSA 9 (MT) sold for $1,902 (Memory Lane; 7/12)
—Milt Schmidt #29 SGC 9 (MT) sold for $2,750 (eBay; 1/16)
—Allen Stanley #94 PSA 9 (MT) sold for $3,232 (Mile High; 5/12)
—Jack Stewart #53 PSA 9 (MT) sold for $2,520 (Mastro; 8/08)
—Jack Stewart #53 PSA 8.5 (NrMt) sold for $772 (eBay; 2/14)

1952-53 Parkhurst

#	Name	PrFr 1	GD 2	VG 3	VgEx 4	EX 5	ExMt 6	NM 7	NmMt 8
1	Maurice Richard	150	250	300	500	800	1,000	1,500	
2	Billy Reay	5	10	15	25	40	80	150	
3	Bernie Geoffrion UER	30	60	100	120	150	200	300	
4	Paul Meger	5	8	12	15	20	30	80	300
5	Dick Gamble	5	10	15	20	25	40	120	
6	Elmer Lach	8	15	25	30	40	60	120	300
7	Floyd(Busher) Curry	5	10	15	20	25	40	120	300
8	Ken Mosdell	5	10	15	20	25	40	80	200
9	Tom Johnson	5	10	15	20	25	40	80	300
10	Dickie Moore RC	30	60	100	150	150	225	300	1,200
11	Bud MacPherson	5	8	12	15	20	30	80	200
12	Gerry McNeil	12	25	40	50	60	80	175	
13	Butch Bouchard	5	10	20	30	40	50	200	300
14	Doug Harvey	25	40	50	80	100	200	300	600
15	John McCormack	5	8	12	15	20	30	80	
16	Pete Babando	5	8	12	15	20	30	100	300
17	Al Dewsbury	5	8	12	15	20	30	80	
18	Ed Kullman	5	8	12	15	20	25	80	200
19	Ed Slowinski	5	8	12	15	20	25	80	250
20	Wally Hergesheimer	5	10	15	20	25	40	80	250
21	Allan Stanley	10	20	30	40	50	60	120	250
22	Chuck Rayner	8	15	25	30	40	80	120	200
23	Steve Kraftcheck	5	8	12	15	25	40	80	200
24	Paul Ronty	5	8	12	15	20	30	80	175
25	Gaye Stewart	5	8	12	15	20	30	80	250
26	Fred Hucul	5	8	12	15	20	40	80	
27	Bill Mosienko	6	12	20	30	50	60	120	300
28	Jim Morrison RC	5	8	12	15	20	30	80	
29	Ed Kryznowski	5	8	12	15	20	30	80	300
30	Cal Gardner	5	10	15	20	25	40	60	200
31	Al Rollins	8	15	25	30	40	60	100	200
32	Enio Sclisizzi RC	5	8	12	15	20	30	100	
33	Pete Conacher RC	5	10	15	20	40	50	100	250
34	Leo Boivin RC	8	15	25	30	60	100	200	850
35	Jim Peters	5	8	12	15	20	30	80	200
36	George Gee	5	8	12	20	40	60	100	200
37	Gus Bodnar	5	10	15	20	25	40	60	150
38	Jim McFadden	5	8	12	15	20	25	80	200
39	Gus Mortson	5	10	15	20	25	40	80	200
40	Fred Glover	5	8	12	15	20	25	60	225
41	Gerry Couture	5	8	12	25	50	80	150	250
42	Howie Meeker	12	20	30	40	60	80	120	500
43	Jim Thomson	5	8	12	15	20	30	80	250
44	Teeder Kennedy	12	25	40	50	60	100	200	
45	Sid Smith	5	10	15	20	25	40	80	400
46	Harry Watson	6	12	20	25	30	50	100	400
47	Fern Flaman	5	10	15	20	25	40	150	250
48	Tod Sloan	5	10	15	20	25	40	60	250
49	Leo Reise	5	8	12	15	25	40	80	200
50	Bob Solinger	5	8	12	15	25	50	150	250
51	George Armstrong RC	30	60	100	150	200	250	500	1,500
52	Dollard St.Laurent RC	5	10	15	20	25	50	100	300
53	Alex Delvecchio	20	25	40	80	100	150	250	
54	Gord Hannigan RC	5	8	12	15	20	30	80	250
55	Lee Fogolin	5	8	12	15	20	30	80	250
56	Bill Gadsby	6	12	20	25	30	50	100	225
57	Herb Dickenson RC	5	8	12	15	25	40	100	
58	Tim Horton RC	150	250	350	500	650	1,250	3,000	3,500
59	Harry Lumley	12	25	40	50	60	100	150	350
60	Metro Prystai	12	10	20	25	50	80	100	200
61	Marcel Pronovost	5	10	15	20	25	50	120	
62	Benny Woit	5	8	12	15	20	40	100	250
63	Glen Skov	5	8	12	20	40	50	100	300
64	Bob Goldham	5	8	12	15	20	25	60	
65	Tony Leswick	5	8	12	15	20	40	80	250
66	Marty Pavelich	5	8	12	15	25	40	80	200
67	Red Kelly	20	30	40	60	100	120	175	300
68	Bill Quackenbush	6	12	20	25	30	50	80	
69	Ed Sandford	5	8	12	15	20	30	80	250
70	Milt Schmidt	8	15	25	30	40	60	150	
71	Hal Laycoe	5	10	15	20	25	40	80	175
72	Woody Dumart	5	10	15	20	25	40	80	225
73	Zellio Toppazzini	5	10	15	20	25	30	80	175
74	Jim Henry	5	10	15	20	25	50	80	200
75	Joe Klukay	5	8	12	15	20	30	80	200
76	Dave Creighton RC	5	10	15	20	25	40	80	200
77	Jack McIntyre	5	8	12	15	25	50	80	125
78	Johnny Peirson	5	8	12	15	20	40	100	
79	George Sullivan	5	10	15	20	25	40	80	200
80	Real Chevrefils RC	5	10	15	20	25	40	80	225
81	Leo Labine RC	6	12	20	25	30	50	80	400
82	Fleming Mackell	5	10	15	20	25	40	80	250
83	Pentti Lund	5	8	12	15	20	25	125	300
84	Bob Armstrong RC	5	8	12	15	20	25	60	
85	Warren Godfrey RC	5	8	12	15	20	25	60	
86	Terry Sawchuk	50	80	150	200	300	400	500	2,000
87	Ted Lindsay	20	40	60	80	100	120	200	
88	Gordie Howe	200	300	350	400	500	800	1,500	3,0
89	Johnny Wilson RC	5	10	15	20	25	40	100	
90	Vic Stasiuk	5	10	15	20	25	40	80	
91	Larry Zeidel	5	8	12	15	20	30	80	
92	Larry Wilson RC	5	8	12	15	20	50	100	
93	Bert Olmstead	5	10	15	25	40	40	80	
94	Ron Stewart RC	5	10	15	25	40	60	120	
95	Max Bentley	6	12	20	25	30	50	150	
96	Rudy Migay RC	5	8	12	15	20	30	60	
97	Jack Stoddard	5	8	12	15	20	25	80	
98	Hy Buller	5	8	12	15	20	50	100	
99	Don Raleigh UER	5	8	12	15	20	30	80	
100	Edgar Laprade	5	10	15	20	25	50	80	
101	Nick Mickoski	5	8	12	15	20	30	80	
102	Jack McLeod UER	5	8	12	15	20	25	80	
103	Jim Conacher	6	10	15	20	25	50	100	
104	Reg Sinclair	5	8	12	15	20	35	100	
105	Bob Hassard RC	15	30	40	60	80	100	350	

—Bob Armstrong #84 PSA 8 (NmMt) sold for $430.05 (Mile High; 11/11)
—George Armstrong #51 PSA 8 (NmMt) sold for $1,932.38 (eBay; 5/12)
—George Armstrong #51 PSA 8 (NmMt) sold for $1,221 (Mile High; 10/12)
—Dick Gamble #5 PSA 8 (NmMt) sold for $667 (eBay; 7/11)
—Bernie Geoffrion #5 PSA 8.5 (NmMt+) sold for $1,152 (eBay; 2/13)
—Tim Horton #58 PSA 8.5 (NmMt+) sold for $3,406.33 (eBay; 9/12)
—Tim Horton #58 PSA 8 (NmMt) sold for $3,270 (eBay; 2/14)
—Gordie Howe #88 SGC 9 (MT) sold for $3,828 (eBay; 7/12)
—Howie Meeker #42 PSA 9 (MT) sold for $1,096 (eBay; 3/16)
—Dickie Moore #10 PSA 8 (NmMt) sold for $1,377 (eBay; 7/11)

1953-54 Parkhurst

#	Name	PrFr 1	GD 2	VG 3	VgEx 4	EX 5	ExMt 6	NM 7	NmM
1	Harry Lumley	35	50	100	150	250	400	500	
2	Sid Smith	5	6	12	20	25	50	150	
3	Gord Hannigan	5	6	12	20	25	40	60	
4	Bob Hassard	5	6	12	20	25	40	60	
5	Tod Sloan	5	6	12	20	25	40	60	
6	Leo Boivin	5	6	12	20	25	40	100	1
7	Teeder Kennedy	10	15	25	40	60	100	150	25
8	Jim Thomson	5	6	12	20	25	40	60	22
9	Ron Stewart	5	6	12	20	25	40	60	2
10	Eric Nesterenko RC	6	10	20	30	40	60	▲150	40
11	George Armstrong	10	15	30	50	60	100	150	3
12	Harry Watson	6	10	20	30	40	60	80	30
13	Tim Horton	30	50	100	150	200	300	400	7
14	Fern Flaman	5	8	15	25	30	50	80	5
15	Jim Morrison	5	6	12	20	25	40	80	1
16	Bob Solinger	5	6	12	20	25	40	60	15
17	Rudy Migay	5	6	12	20	25	40	60	15
18	Dick Gamble	5	6	12	20	25	40	75	2
19	Bert Olmstead	5	8	15	25	30	50	80	30
20	Eddie Mazur RC	5	6	12	20	25	40	60	20
21	Paul Meger	5	6	12	20	25	40	60	15
22	Bud MacPherson	5	6	12	20	25	40	60	20
23	Dollard St.Laurent	5	6	12	20	25	40	60	30
24	Maurice Richard	60	100	150	300	500	650	800	3,50
25	Gerry McNeil	8	12	25	40	60	100	150	25
26	Doug Harvey	20	30	60	100	120	150	250	4
27	Jean Beliveau RC	▲350	▲450	▲650	▲750	▲900	▲2,500	3,000	6,50
28	Dickie Moore UER	12	20	40	60	80	125	200	4
29	Bernie Geoffrion	20	30	60	80	120	200	250	50
30	E.Lach/M.Richard	20	30	60	80	100	200	300	50
31	Elmer Lach	6	10	20	30	40	80	100	25
32	Butch Bouchard	5	8	15	25	30	50	80	30
33	Ken Mosdell	5	6	12	20	25	40	80	15
34	John McCormack	5	6	12	20	25	40	80	15
35	Floyd (Busher) Curry	5	6	12	20	25	40	60	15
36	Earl Reibel RC	5	6	12	20	25	40	80	20
37	Bill Dineen UER RC	8	12	25	40	50	80	120	40
38	Al Arbour UER RC	10	15	30	50	60	100	150	30
39	Vic Stasiuk	5	6	12	20	25	40	60	15
40	Red Kelly	10	15	30	50	60	100	150	25
41	Marcel Pronovost	5	8	15	25	30	50	80	30
42	Metro Prystai	5	6	12	20	25	40	60	15
43	Tony Leswick	5	6	12	20	25	40	60	▲20
44	Marty Pavelich	5	6	12	20	25	40	60	15
45	Benny Woit	5	6	12	20	25	40	60	15
46	Terry Sawchuk	50	60	80	150	200	350	500	85
47	Alex Delvecchio	10	25	30	50	60	100	175	30
48	Glen Skov	5	6	12	20	25	40	60	15
49	Bob Goldham	5	6	12	20	25	40	60	20
50	Gordie Howe	100	120	250	350	550	600	1,500	5,00
51	Johnny Wilson	5	6	12	20	25	40	60	15
52	Ted Lindsay	10	15	30	50	60	100	150	30
53	Gump Worsley RC	60	100	150	200	250	350	500	1,20
54	Jack Evans	5	6	12	20	25	40	60	20
55	Max Bentley	6	10	20	30	40	60	100	30
56	Andy Bathgate RC	15	25	40	60	100	200	300	55
57	Harry Howell RC	15	25	50	80	100	120	200	40

	PrFr 1	GD 2	VG 3	VgEx 4	EX 5	ExMt 6	NM 7	NmMt 8
Hy Buller	5	6	12	20	25	40	60	150
Chuck Rayner	5	8	15	40	45	50	80	200
Jack Stoddard	5	6	12	20	▲30	▲50	▲100	200
Ed Kullman	5	6	12	20	25	50	120	300
Nick Mickoski	5	6	12	20	25	40	60	150
Paul Ronty	5	6	12	20	25	40	60	200
Allan Stanley	6	10	20	30	40	60	100	250
Leo Reise	5	6	12	20	25	40	60	150
Aldo Guidolin RC	5	6	12	20	25	40	60	200
Wally Hergesheimer	5	6	12	20	25	40	60	200
Don Raleigh	5	6	12	20	25	40	60	250
Jim Peters	5	6	12	20	25	40	60	300
Pete Conacher	5	6	12	20	25	40	60	200
Fred Hucul	5	6	12	20	25	40	60	250
Lee Fogolin	5	6	12	20	25	40	60	200
Larry Zeidel	5	6	12	20	25	40	50	200
Larry Wilson	5	6	12	20	25	50	100	150
Gus Bodnar	5	6	12	20	25	40	80	200
Bill Gadsby	6	10	20	30	40	60	100	250
Jim McFadden	5	6	12	20	25	40	60	200
Al Dewsbury	5	6	12	20	25	40	50	200
Clare Raglan	5	6	12	20	25	40	60	200
Bill Mosienko	6	10	20	30	40	60	80	200
Gus Mortson	5	6	12	20	25	40	60	200
Al Rollins	5	20	40	30	50	100	200	350
George Gee	5	6	12	20	25	40	60	200
Gerry Couture	5	6	12	20	25	40	60	150
Dave Creighton	5	6	12	20	25	40	60	175
Jim Henry	5	8	15	25	30	50	80	200
Hal Laycoe	5	6	12	20	25	40	60	200
Johnny Peirson UER	5	8	15	25	30	50	80	200
Real Chevrefils	5	6	12	20	25	40	60	150
Ed Sandford	5	6	12	20	25	40	60	150
Fleming Mackell NoBio	5	8	15	25	30	50	80	150
Fleming Mackell COR	200	250	350	450	600			
Milt Schmidt	6	10	20	30	40	100	150	300
Leo Labine	5	6	12	20	25	40	60	200
Joe Klukay	5	6	12	20	25	40	60	150
Warren Godfrey	5	6	12	20	25	50	100	200
Woody Dumart	5	8	15	25	30	50	80	350
Frank Martin RC	5	6	12	20	25	40	60	250
Jerry Toppazzini RC	5	6	12	20	25	50	150	300
Cal Gardner	5	6	12	20	25	40	60	500
Bill Quackenbush	15	25	50	80	100	150	300	900

Andy Bathgate #56 PSA 8 (Mint) sold for $2,709 (Mile High; 1/12)
Jean Beliveau RC #27 PSA 5.5 (Ex+) sold for $910 (eBay; 4/14)
Alex Delvecchio #47 PSA 9 (MT) sold for $1,033 (eBay; 12/15)
Al Dewsbury #78 PSA 10 (Gem) sold for $3,732 (Memory Lane; 4/12)
Fern Flaman #14 PSA 9 (Mint) sold for $1,515 (Mile High; 1/12)
Aldo Guidolin RC #66 PSA 9 (Mint) sold for $962 (eBay; 2/14)
Red Kelly #40 PSA 9 (Mint) sold for $1,790 (Mile High; 1/12)
Leo Labine #93 PSA 9 (Mint) sold for $562 (eBay; 1/12)
Hal Laycoe #87 PSA 10 (Gem Mt) sold for $3,023 (Mile High; 5/12)
Harry Lumley #1 PSA 8 (NmMt) sold for $4,3034 (Mile High; 1/12)
Harry Lumley #1 PSA 8 (NmMt) sold for $2,390 (eBay; 3/14)
Bill Mosienko #1 PSA 9 (Mint) sold for $1,516 (eBay; 2/15)
Eric Nesterenko #10 PSA 9 (Mint) sold for $825 (Mile High; 1/12)
Bert Olmsted #19 PSA 9 (Mint) sold for $619 (Mile High; 1/12)
Marty Pavelich #44 PSA 9 (Mint) sold for $494 (eBay; 1/08)
Marcel Pronovost #41 PSA 9 (MT) sold for $896.99 (eBay; 3/16)
Al Rollins #82 PSA 9 (Mint) sold for $619 (Mile High; 1/12)
Sid Smith #2 PSA 8 (NmMt) sold for $704 (Mile High; 1/12)
Vic Stassiuk #39 PSA 9 (MT) sold for $626.79 (eBay; 4/16)
Johnny Wilson #51 PSA 9 (Mint) sold for $1,099 (Mile High; 1/12)
Gump Worsley #82 PSA 8.5 (NmMt+) sold for $2,015 (eBay; 11/14)

1954-55 Parkhurst

	PrFr 1	GD 2	VG 3	VgEx 4	EX 5	ExMt 6	NM 7	NmMt 8
Gerry McNeil	40	50	60	100	150	300	800	3,500
Dickie Moore	10	15	25	40	50	100	150	350
Jean Beliveau	40	60	100	150	200	300	600	1,600
Eddie Mazur	5	8	12	20	25	40	80	
Bert Olmstead	5	8	12	20	25	40	150	
Butch Bouchard	8	12	20	25	40	60	120	
Maurice Richard	50	75	120	200	250	300	400	1,200
Bernie Geoffrion	15	25	40	60	80	100	200	
John McCormack	5	8	12	20	25	40	80	
Tom Johnson	5	8	12	20	25	40	80	
Calum Mackay	8	10	15	25	40	80	150	
Ken Mosdell	5	8	12	20	25	40	100	
Paul Masnick	8	10	15	25	40	60	100	400
Doug Harvey	15	25	40	60	80	100	150	
Floyd(Busher) Curry	5	8	12	20	25	40	80	
Harry Lumley	8	12	15	25	35	60	80	
Harry Watson	10	15	20	25	40	50	80	
Jim Morrison	5	8	12	15	20	40	100	
Eric Nesterenko	5	8	12	15	20	40	80	
Fern Flaman	5	8	12	20	25	40	80	
Rudy Migay	5	8	12	20	25	30	60	
Sid Smith	5	8	12	20	25	30	60	

		PrFr 1	GD 2	VG 3	VgEx 4	EX 5	ExMt 6	NM 7	NmMt 8
23	Ron Stewart	5	8	12	20	25	40	80	150
24	George Armstrong	10	15	25	40	50	60	80	200
25	Earl Balfour RC	5	8	12	20	25	40	80	200
26	Leo Boivin	5	8	12	20	25	40	80	
27	Gord Hannigan	5	8	12	20	25	40	100	300
28	Bob Bailey RC	5	8	12	20	25	40	100	200
29	Teeder Kennedy	8	12	15	20	30	50	80	
30	Tod Sloan	5	8	12	20	25	40	80	250
31	Tim Horton	35	50	60	80	125	150	300	800
32	Jim Thomson	5	8	12	20	25	40	100	
33	Terry Sawchuk	40	60	80	100	150	250	350	800
34	Marcel Pronovost	5	8	12	20	25	40	80	
35	Metro Prystai	5	8	12	20	25	30	60	
36	Alex Delvecchio	10	15	25	40	50	60	100	300
37	Earl Reibel	5	8	12	20	25	40	80	
38	Benny Woit	5	8	12	20	25	40	80	
39	Bob Goldham	5	8	12	20	25	40	80	
40	Glen Skov	5	8	12	20	25	60	80	300
41	Gordie Howe	60	100	150	200	300	400	600	1,200
42	Red Kelly	10	15	25	40	50	60	80	250
43	Marty Pavelich	5	8	12	20	25	40	80	250
44	Johnny Wilson	5	8	12	20	25	40	80	250
45	Tony Leswick	5	8	12	20	25	30	60	150
46	Ted Lindsay	10	15	25	40	50	60	150	300
47	Keith Allen RC	5	8	12	20	25	40	60	
48	Bill Dineen	5	8	12	20	25	40	60	
49	Jim Henry	8	12	15	25	30	40	60	
50	Fleming Mackell	5	8	12	20	25	40	60	250
51	Bill Quackenbush	8	12	15	25	30	40	80	
52	Hal Laycoe	5	8	12	20	25	40	80	250
53	Cal Gardner	5	8	12	20	25	40	80	250
54	Joe Klukay	5	8	12	20	25	40	100	
55	Bob Armstrong	5	8	12	20	25	40	80	
56	Warren Godfrey	8	10	15	25	40	60	100	
57	Doug Mohns RC	8	12	15	25	30	40	80	
58	Dave Creighton	15	25	40	60	80	100	200	
59	Milt Schmidt	8	12	15	25	35	50	100	
60	Johnny Peirson	5	8	12	20	25	30	60	
61	Leo Labine	8	10	15	25	40	60	120	
62	Gus Bodnar	5	8	12	20	25	40	80	
63	Real Chevrefils	5	8	12	20	25	40	80	
64	Ed Sandford	8	10	15	25	40	50	80	120
65	Johnny Bower UER RC	40	120	150	250	300	400	600	2,000
66	Paul Ronty	5	8	12	20	25	30	60	
67	Leo Reise	5	8	12	20	25	30	50	150
68	Don Raleigh	5	8	12	20	25	40	120	
69	Bob Chrystal	5	8	12	20	25	40	80	
70	Harry Howell	8	12	20	30	40	50	125	
71	Wally Hergesheimer	5	8	12	20	25	30	60	
72	Jack Evans	5	8	12	20	25	30	60	200
73	Camille Henry RC	5	8	12	20	25	40	80	
74	Dean Prentice RC	8	12	15	25	30	40	80	
75	Nick Mickoski	5	8	12	15	20	30	60	120
76	Ron Murphy RC	5	8	12	15	20	30	60	120
77	Al Rollins	8	12	15	25	30	50	100	
78	Al Dewsbury	5	8	12	20	25	40	60	
79	Lou Jankowski	5	8	12	20	25	30	60	200
80	George Gee	5	8	12	15	20	30	40	
81	Gus Mortson	5	8	12	15	20	30	60	200
82	Fred Saskamoose UER RC	15	25	40	60	80	125	200	400
83	Ike Hildebrand RC	5	8	12	20	25	40	60	
84	Lee Fogolin	5	8	12	20	25	40	60	150
85	Larry Wilson	5	8	12	20	25	40	80	
86	Pete Conacher	5	8	12	20	25	40	80	
87	Bill Gadsby	5	8	12	25	25	40	80	150
88	Jack McIntyre	5	8	12	20	25	40	80	
89	Busher Curry goes/up and over	5	8	12	20	25	40	60	
90	Delvecchio/Defense	8	12	15	25	35	50	120	
91	R.Kelly/H.Lumley	8	12	15	25	25	40	100	200
92	Lumley/Howe/Stewart	12	20	30	50	60	80	150	400
93	H.Lumley/R.Murphy	5	8	12	15	20	30	60	200
94	P.Meger/J.Morrison	5	8	12	15	20	30	60	250
95	D.Harvey/E.Nesterenko	8	12	15	25	35	50	80	200
96	T.Sawchuk/T.Kennedy	12	20	30	50	60	80	125	400
97	Plante/B.Bouchard/Reibel	12	20	30	50	60	80	100	400
98	J.Plante/Harvey/Sloan	12	20	30	50	60	80	100	400
99	J.Plante/T.Kennedy	12	20	30	50	60	80	125	400
100	T.Sawchuk/B.Geoffrion	25	40	60	80	120	150	400	1,000

—Alex Delvecchio #90 PSA 8 (NM) sold for $365 (eBay; 4/16)
—Camille Henry #73 PSA 9 (Mint) sold for $393 (eBay; 8/12)
—Ted Lindsay #46 PSA 9 (Mint) sold for $1,303 (eBay; 4/12)
—Gerry McNeil #1 PSA 8 (NrMt) sold for $3,633 (eBay; 8/12)

1954-55 Topps

		PrFr 1	GD 2	VG 3	VgEx 4	EX 5	ExMt 6	NM 7	NmMt 8
1	Dick Gamble	20	30	50	100	150	225	1,000	4,000
2	Bob Chrystal	6	10	15	25	40	100	600	2,000
3	Harry Howell	12	20	30	40	60	80	150	600
4	Johnny Wilson	6	10	15	20	30	▲80	100	400
5	Red Kelly	20	30	60	100	150	200	300	550
6	Real Chevrefils	6	10	15	20	30	50	150	450

#	Player	PrFr 1	GD 2	VG 3	VgEx 4	EX 5	ExMt 6	NM 7	NmMt 8
7	Bob Armstrong	6	10	15	20	30	40	100	250
8	Gordie Howe	200	300	500	800	1,000	2,000	▲3,000	4,000
9	Benny Woit	6	10	15	20	30	40	150	250
10	Gump Worsley	25	40	80	100	150	200	350	500
11	Andy Bathgate	12	20	30	80	100	150	200	400
12	Bucky Hollingworth RC	6	10	15	20	30	40	120	400
13	Ray Timgren	6	10	15	20	30	80	150	250
14	Jack Evans	6	10	15	20	30	40	100	300
15	Paul Ronty	6	15	20	30	40	60	125	200
16	Glen Skov	6	10	15	20	40	80	100	250
17	Gus Mortson	6	10	15	20	30	40	100	250
18	Doug Mohns RC	15	25	40	50	80	150	200	350
19	Leo Labine	10	12	20	30	40	80	200	600
20	Bill Gadsby	10	12	25	50	80	100	200	650
21	Jerry Toppazzini	8	12	20	30	60	80	100	350
22	Wally Hergesheimer	6	10	15	20	30	40	100	300
23	Danny Lewicki	6	10	15	20	30	60	150	300
24	Metro Prystai	6	10	15	20	30	▲50	▲150	200
25	Fern Flaman	8	12	20	40	50	100	150	350
26	Al Rollins	10	15	25	50	80	150	250	500
27	Marcel Pronovost	10	15	25	50	80	▲150	200	350
28	Lou Jankowski	6	10	15	20	30	60	150	300
29	Nick Mickoski	6	10	15	20	30	40	150	300
30	Frank Martin	6	15	30	40	50	100	200	300
31	Lorne Ferguson	6	10	15	20	30	40	100	300
32	Camille Henry RC	10	15	25	40	60	80	200	500
33	Pete Conacher	8	12	20	30	50	50	100	250
34	Marty Pavelich	6	10	15	20	40	▲100	▲150	300
35	Don McKenney RC	10	15	25	40	50	80	120	400
36	Fleming Mackell	8	12	20	30	40	50	100	300
37	Jim Henry	10	15	25	40	60	80	▲150	300
38	Hal Laycoe	6	10	15	20	50	100	200	300
39	Alex Delvecchio	20	30	40	60	80	100	200	550
40	Larry Wilson	6	10	15	20	30	40	100	250
41	Allan Stanley	12	20	30	50	80	100	175	650
42	George Sullivan	6	10	15	20	30	60	150	350
43	Jack McIntyre	6	10	15	20	30	40	100	300
44	Ivan Irwin RC	6	10	15	20	30	50	120	300
45	Tony Leswick	8	10	25	40	60	100	300	600
46	Bob Goldham	6	10	15	20	50	80	150	350
47	Cal Gardner	8	12	20	30	50	50	150	300
48	Ed Sandford	6	10	15	20	30	40	100	300
49	Bill Quackenbush	10	15	25	40	60	100	175	400
50	Warren Godfrey	6	10	15	25	50	80	150	300
51	Ted Lindsay	20	25	40	60	100	150	300	500
52	Earl Reibel	5	10	15	25	30	60	100	300
53	Don Raleigh	6	10	15	25	40	60	150	800
54	Bill Mosienko	10	15	25	40	60	100	200	500
55	Larry Popein	8	12	▲25	▲50	▲80	▲150	375	
56	Edgar Laprade	8	12	20	30	40	60	150	800
57	Bill Dineen	8	12	20	30	▲50	▲100	▲150	800
58	Terry Sawchuk	75	80	100	150	300	▲500	▲1,250	▲2,500
59	Marcel Bonin RC	10	15	25	50	150	250	600	2,000
60	Milt Schmidt	30	50	80	150	250	350	1,200	3,000

—Marcel Bonin #59 PSA 8 (NmMt) sold for $4,800 (Memory Lane; 5/08)
—Dick Gamble #1 PSA 8 (NmMt) sold for $5,141 (Goodwin & Co.; 12/08)
—Wally Hergesheimer #22 PSA 9 (MT) sold for $4,195 (Memory Lane; 9/07)
—Gordie Howe #8 SGC 96 (MT) sold for $13,200 (Mastro; 8/08)
—Gordie Howe #8 SGC 8.5 (NrMt+) sold for $2,398 (eBay; 4/14)
—Gordie Howe #8 SGC 7.5 (ExMt+) sold for $1,750 (eBay; 4/14)
—Red Kelly #5 SGC 96 (MT) sold for $6,955 (Memory Lane; 5/08)
—Edgar Laprade #56 PSA 8 (NmMt) sold for $4,365 (Memory Lane; 12/06)
—Edgar Laprade #56 PSA8 (NmMt) sold for $1,530 (Memory Lane; 9/07)
—Edgar Laprade #56 PSA 8 (NmMt) sold for $865 (Memory Lane; 5/08)
—Tony Leswick #42 PSA 8 (NmMt) sold for $2,035 (Memory Lane; 9/07)
—Ted Lindsay #51 PSA 9 (MT) sold for $2,726 (eBay; 6/12)
—Frank Martin #30 SGC 9 (MT) sold for $670 (eBay; 8/12)
—Nick Mickoski #29 PSA 9 (MT) sold for $810 (eBay; 7/08)
—Gus Mortson #17 PSA 9 (MT) sold for $3,466 (Memory Lane; 9/07)
—Gus Mortson #17 SGC 9 (MT) sold for $346.02 (eBay; 2/16)
—Larry Popein #55 PSA 7 (NM) sold for $560 (eBay; 11/07)
—Don Raleigh #53 PSA 9 (MT) sold for $9,650 (Mile High; 1/07)
—Don Raleigh #53 PSA 9 (MT) sold for $2,980 (Memory Lane; 5/07)
—Milt Schmidt #60 PSA 8 (NmMt) sold for $5,447 (Mile High; 1/07)
—Milt Schmidt #60 PSA 7.5 (NrMt+) sold for $1,752 (Goodwin & Co.; 12/08)
—Allan Stanley #41 SGC 96 (MT) sold for $3,600 (Memory Lane; 7/08)
—Jerry Toppazzini #21 PSA 9 (MT) sold for $2,252 (eBay; 3/13)

1955-56 Parkhurst

#	Player	PrFr 1	GD 2	VG 3	VgEx 4	EX 5	ExMt 6	NM 7	NmMt 8
1	Harry Lumley	40	60	100	200	400	900	3,000	
2	Sid Smith	6	8	10	15	30	100	300	
3A	Tim Horton	30	50	80	100	200	200	350	
4	George Armstrong	10	15	25	40	60	120	300	
5	Ron Stewart	6	8	10	15	30	100	300	
6	Joe Klukay	5	8	12	15	25	60	100	200
7	Marc Reaume	5	5	8	12	25	100	200	
8	Jim Morrison	5	6	8	12	25	60	▲1,000	300
9	Parker MacDonald RC	5	6	8	12	20	50	100	

#	Player	PrFr 1	GD 2	VG 3	VgEx 4	EX 5	ExMt 6	NM 7	NmMt 8
10	Tod Sloan	6	8	10	12	30	80	150	
11	Jim Thomson	5	6	8	12	20	50	100	
12	Rudy Migay	5	6	8	12	20	50	100	300
13	Brian Cullen RC	6	8	10	15	25	50	120	
14	Hugh Bolton	5	6	8	12	20	50	100	
15	Eric Nesterenko	6	8	10	20	40	150	400	
16	Larry Cahan RC	5	6	8	12	20	50	100	400
17	Willie Marshall	5	6	8	12	20	50	200	
18	Dick Duff RC	12	20	30	50	80	175	800	
19	Jack Caffery RC	5	6	8	12	20	50	100	
20	Billy Harris RC	6	8	10	15	25	50	150	
21	Lorne Chabot OTG	8	8	10	15	25	50	100	
22	Harvey Jackson OTG	6	10	15	25	40	80	150	
23	Turk Broda OTG	12	20	30	40	60	100	250	
24	Joe Primeau OTG	6	8	12	20	30	60	150	300
25	Gordie Drillon OTG	6	8	10	15	25	50	150	500
26	Chuck Conacher OTG	6	8	12	20	30	100	150	300
27	Sweeney Schriner OTG	6	8	10	15	30	80	200	
28	Syl Apps OTG	6	8	12	20	30	80	150	
29	Teeder Kennedy OTG	8	12	20	30	40	80	150	
30	Ace Bailey OTG	8	12	20	30	50	80	175	350
31	Babe Pratt OTG	6	8	10	15	30	100	200	
32	Harold Cotton OTG	6	8	10	15	30	80	150	
33	King Clancy CO	12	20	30	50	80	150	250	
34	Hap Day	6	10	15	25	40	100	175	
35	Don Marshall RC	6	8	10	15	25	40	80	150
36	Jackie LeClair RC	6	8	10	15	30	100	200	
37	Maurice Richard	60	80	120	200	300	400	600	1,000
38	Dickie Moore	10	15	25	40	60	100	200	
39	Ken Mosdell	6	8	10	15	30	100	200	
40	Floyd(Busher) Curry	5	6	8	12	20	50	150	
41	Calum Mackay	5	6	8	12	20	50	100	400
42	Bert Olmstead	6	8	10	15	25	50	100	150
43	Bernie Geoffrion	15	25	50	100	150	200	300	600
44	Jean Beliveau	50	80	120	200	250	300	500	1,000
45	Doug Harvey	15	25	40	60	100	125	200	600
46	Butch Bouchard	6	8	10	15	25	50	120	200
47	Bud MacPherson	6	8	10	15	20	50	100	200
48	Dollard St.Laurent	5	6	8	12	20	50	100	300
49	Tom Johnson	6	8	10	15	25	50	100	200
50	Jacques Plante RC	200	300	400	600	750	1,500	3,500	5,000
51	Paul Meger	5	6	8	12	20	50	100	400
52	Gerry McNeil	6	8	12	20	30	60	100	200
53	Jean-Guy Talbot RC	6	8	10	15	30	100	250	
54	Bob Turner	5	6	8	12	25	80	150	400
55	Newsy Lalonde OTG	8	12	20	30	50	120	250	500
56	Georges Vezina OTG	15	25	40	60	100	125	250	
57	Howie Morenz OTG	12	20	30	50	80	150	250	600
58	Aurel Joliat OTG	8	12	20	30	40	80	200	
59	George Hainsworth OTG	12	20	30	50	80	100	200	
60	Sylvio Mantha OTG	6	8	10	15	30	100	250	
61	Battleship Leduc OTG	6	8	10	15	30	100	200	
62	Babe Siebert OTG UER	6	8	12	20	30	50	100	200
63	Bill Durnan OTG RC	8	12	20	30	50	150	300	600
64	Ken Reardon OTG RC	8	12	20	30	50	50	150	300
65	Johnny Gagnon OTG	6	8	10	15	25	60	150	500
66	Billy Reay OTG	6	8	10	15	30	50	100	400
67	Toe Blake CO	6	10	15	25	40	150	250	
68	Frank Selke MG	6	8	12	20	30	80	200	
69	H.Bolton/C.Hodge	6	8	10	15	25	50	150	
70	H.Lumley/B.Geoffrion	8	12	20	30	50	150	300	
71	B.Bouchard/T.Johnson	10	15	25	40	60	100	250	
72	Rocket (Richard) Roars	10	15	30	50	80	200	500	
73	M.Richard/H.Lumley	12	20	30	40	60	150	300	
74	J.Beliveau/H.Lumley	8	12	20	30	50	80	200	500
75	Nesterenko/Smith/Plante	10	15	25	40	60	100	250	
76	Curry/Lumley/Morrison	6	8	10	15	30	100	300	500
77	Sloan/MacD/Harvey/Beliv	10	15	25	40	60	150	400	
78	Montreal Forum	40	60	100	120	200	450	1,200	
79	Maple Leaf Gardens	40	60	100	150	250	600	1,000	

—Tim Horton #3 SGC 9 (MT) sold for $12,103 (eBay; 4/11)
—Dick Duff #18 PSA 8 (NmMt) sold for $1,633 (eBay; 5/12)
—Harold Cotton OTG #32 PSA 9 (MT) sold for $4,118 (eBay; 8/12)
—Newsy Lalonde OTG #55 PSA 9 (MT) sold for $4,874 (Mile High; 10/12)
—Sloan/Macdonald/Harvey/Beliviau #77 PSA 8 (NmMt) sold for $2,782 (eBay; 8/12)

1957-58 Parkhurst

#	Player	PrFr 1	GD 2	VG 3	VgEx 4	EX 5	ExMt 6	NM 7	NmMt 8
M1	Doug Harvey	30	50	80	120	200	250	600	200
M2	Bernie Geoffrion	12	25	40	60	100	200	700	2,000
M3	Jean Beliveau	30	50	80	120	200	250	400	1,500
M4	Henri Richard RC	200	250	300	400	600	800	1,200	3,750
M5	Maurice Richard	40	60	100	150	250	400	550	1,250
M6	Tom Johnson	5	5	6	10	15	25	80	150
M7	Andre Pronovost RC	5	6	10	15	25	40	80	250
M8	Don Marshall	5	5	8	8	12	20	50	100
M9	Jean-Guy Talbot	5	5	5	8	12	20	50	100
M10	Dollard St.Laurent	5	5	5	8	12	20	50	100
M11	Phil Goyette RC	5	6	10	15	25	40	100	350

	PrFr 1	GD 2	VG 3	VgEx 4	EX 5	ExMt 6	NM 7	NmMt 8
Claude Provost RC	5	6	10	15	25	50	150	250
Bob Turner	5	5	5	8	12	20	50	120
Dickie Moore	6	10	15	25	40	60	100	250
Jacques Plante	40	60	100	150	200	300	500	1,250
Toe Blake CO	5	6	10	15	25	40	100	200
Charlie Hodge RC	8	12	20	30	50	80	150	300
Marcel Bonin	5	6	8	10	15	25	60	120
Bert Olmstead	5	5	6	10	15	25	80	120
Floyd (Busher) Curry	5	5	5	8	12	20	50	100
Len Broderick IA RC	5	6	10	15	25	40	80	200
Brian Cullen scores	5	5	5	8	12	20	50	200
Broderick/Harvey IA	5	6	10	15	25	40	60	150
Geoffrion/Chadwick IA	5	8	12	20	30	50	100	200
Olmstead/Chadwick IA	5	6	10	15	25	40	60	200
George Armstrong	10	15	25	50	100	200	500	
Ed Chadwick RC	30	40	60	100	135	225	600	
Dick Duff	5	10	15	25	50	120	700	1,800
Bob Pulford RC	30	40	60	125	200	250	750	1,000
Tod Sloan	5	8	15	25	60	80	175	800
Rudy Migay	5	5	6	10	15	25	60	175
Ron Stewart	5	5	6	8	12	25	60	100
Gerry James RC	5	5	6	10	15	25	80	120
Brian Cullen	5	5	5	8	12	20	50	120
Sid Smith	5	5	6	8	15	20	60	150
Jim Morrison	5	5	5	8	12	20	50	100
Marc Reaume	5	5	5	8	12	20	50	120
Hugh Bolton	5	5	6	8	12	20	60	100
Pete Conacher	5	5	5	8	12	20	50	100
Billy Harris	5	5	5	8	12	20	50	150
Mike Nykoluk RC	5	5	5	8	12	20	50	100
Frank Mahovlich RC	▲150	▲200	▲300	▲400	▲500	▲800	▲1,000	▲1,750
Ken Girard RC	5	5	5	8	12	20	50	100
Al MacNeil RC	5	5	5	8	12	20	60	150
Bob Baun RC	10	15	25	40	60	100	300	500
Barry Cullen RC	5	5	8	12	20	40	80	150
Tim Horton	25	30	50	80	120	200	350	500
Gary Collins RC	5	5	5	8	12	20	50	100
Gary Aldcorn RC	5	5	5	8	12	20	50	150
Billy Reay CO	5	6	10	15	25	40	80	250

—George Armstrong #T1 PSA 8 (NmMt) sold for $3,570 (eBay; 9/15)
—Pete Conacher #T14 PSA 9 (MT) sold for $410 (eBay; 8/12)
—Tom Johnson #M6 PSA 9 (MT) sold for $799 (eBay; 1/08)
—Don Marshall #M8 PSA 9 (MT) sold for $799 (eBay; 1/08)
—Rudy Migay #T6 PSA 10 (Gem MT) sold for $1,500 (eBay; 3/13)
—Bert Olmstead #M19 PSA 10 (Gem MT) sold for $1,317 (eBay; 4/15)
—Claude Provost #M12 PSA 10 (Gem MT) sold for $1,331 (eBay; 4/15)
—Billy Reay CO #T25 PSA 8.5 (NMMT+) sold for $356 (eBay; 7/12)

1957-58 Topps

	PrFr 1	GD 2	VG 3	VgEx 4	EX 5	ExMt 6	NM 7	NmMt 8
Real Chevrefils	6	8	12	20	25	60	400	1,000
Jack Bionda RC	5	6	8	12	20	30	60	500
Bob Armstrong	5	5	6	10	12	20	50	200
Fern Flaman	6	8	20	25	30	40	80	300
Jerry Toppazzini	6	8	10	40	50	60	80	250
Larry Regan RC	6	8	10	20	25	30	60	150
Bronco Horvath RC	6	8	10	15	25	40	100	450
Jack Caffery	5	5	6	12	15	20	80	150
Leo Labine	5	6	8	12	15	25	30	100
Johnny Bucyk RC	25	40	60	100	150	400	500	2,000
Vic Stasiuk	5	6	8	12	20	25	50	100
Doug Mohns	6	8	12	20	30	40	60	500
Don McKenney	5	6	8	12	20	30	50	250
Don Simmons RC	6	8	10	15	25	40	120	600
Allan Stanley	5	6	8	12	20	30	50	250
Fleming Mackell	5	6	8	12	15	25	30	200
Larry Hillman RC	5	6	8	12	15	50	100	200
Leo Boivin	5	6	8	12	15	25	30	100
Bob Bailey	5	5	6	10	12	20	40	100
Glenn Hall RC	100	125	200	250	300	450	550	1,200
Ted Lindsay	8	12	20	30	40	60	80	200
Pierre Pilote RC	10	15	25	50	80	150	250	550
Jim Thomson	5	6	8	12	20	25	60	200
Eric Nesterenko	5	6	8	12	20	25	60	200
Gus Mortson	5	6	8	12	20	30	80	400
Ed Litzenberger RC	5	6	8	12	20	30	60	200
Elmer Vasko RC	5	6	8	12	20	30	40	100
Jack McIntyre	5	6	8	10	12	20	30	100
Ron Murphy	5	6	8	12	15	25	40	300
Glen Skov	5	5	6	10	12	20	50	135
Hec Lalande RC	5	5	6	10	12	20	40	175
Nick Mickoski	5	6	8	10	12	20	60	150
Wally Hergesheimer	5	6	8	12	15	25	50	120
Alex Delvecchio	6	8	12	20	25	50	120	300
Terry Sawchuk UER	25	40	60	80	100	200	250	1,000
Guyle Fielder RC	5	6	8	12	15	25	30	150
Tom McCarthy	5	5	6	10	12	20	30	100
Al Arbour	6	8	10	15	25	35	50	120
Billy Dea	5	5	6	10	12	25	60	150

	PrFr 1	GD 2	VG 3	VgEx 4	EX 5	ExMt 6	NM 7	NmMt 8
40 Lorne Ferguson	5	5	6	10	12	25	50	200
41 Warren Godfrey	5	6	8	12	15	25	40	120
42 Gordie Howe	80	100	135	175	250	350	550	2,250
43 Marcel Pronovost	6	8	15	20	25	30	40	120
44 Bill McNeil RC	5	6	8	12	20	25	40	120
45 Earl Reibel	5	6	8	12	20	25	40	150
46 Norm Ullman RC	40	60	80	120	150	200	250	800
47 Johnny Wilson	5	5	6	10	12	30	50	120
48 Red Kelly	6	8	12	20	25	50	80	300
49 Bill Dineen	6	8	12	20	25	50	80	120
50 Forbes Kennedy RC	6	8	12	20	25	30	50	175
51 Harry Howell	8	12	20	25	30	40	60	200
52 Jean-Guy Gendron RC	5	6	8	12	15	25	40	100
53 Gump Worsley	10	15	25	40	50	80	100	250
54 Larry Popein	5	6	8	12	20	25	40	120
55 Jack Evans	5	5	6	10	12	20	30	120
56 George Sullivan	5	6	8	12	15	25	60	250
57 Gerry Foley RC	5	6	8	12	15	25	60	250
58 Andy Hebenton RC	5	6	8	12	15	25	50	120
59 Larry Cahan	5	6	8	10	12	20	40	150
60 Andy Bathgate	6	8	12	20	30	50	100	400
61 Danny Lewicki	5	6	8	12	25	30	50	150
62 Dean Prentice	6	8	10	15	25	30	60	250
63 Camille Henry	6	8	10	15	25	30	60	250
64 Lou Fontinato RC	6	8	12	20	25	40	60	250
65 Bill Gadsby	6	8	10	15	20	30	60	200
66 Dave Creighton	6	8	12	20	35	60	250	600

—Glenn Hall #20 SGC 9 (MT) sold for $1,860 (Greg Bussineau; Fall 2014)
—Ted Lindsay #21 PSA 9 (MT) sold for $1,346 (eBay; 3/13)
—Pierre Pilote #22 SGC 9 (MT) sold for $4,613 (Goodwin; 7/12)
—Pierre Pilote #22 PSA 8.5 (NmMt+) sold for $2,208 (eBay; 3/13)
—Terry Sawchuk UER #35 PSA 9 (MT) sold for $1,380 (Greg Bussineau; Fall 2013)
—Allan Stanley #15 PSA 9 (MT) sold for $1,803 (eBay; 3/14)
—Elmer Vasko #27 PSA 9 (MT) sold for $802 (eBay; 8/12)
—Elmer Vasko #27 PSA 9 (MT) sold for $672.78 (eBay; 2/14)

1958-59 Parkhurst

	PrFr 1	GD 2	VG 3	VgEx 4	EX 5	ExMt 6	NM 7	NmMt 8
1 Bob Pulford IA	5	8	12	20	30	50	150	600
2 Henri Richard	20	30	50	80	120	200	250	1,000
3 Andre Pronovost	5	5	6	10	15	20	80	120
4 Billy Harris	5	5	6	10	15	25	60	175
5 Albert Langlois RC	5	5	6	10	15	20	60	120
6 Noel Price RC	5	5	6	10	15	20	60	100
7 G.Armstrong/Johnson IA	5	6	8	12	20	30	50	120
8 Dickie Moore	5	6	10	15	25	40	60	175
9 Toe Blake CO	5	6	8	12	20	30	60	175
10 Tom Johnson	5	5	6	10	15	25	60	120
11 J.Plante/G.Armstrong	10	12	15	20	30	50	80	150
12 Ed Chadwick	5	6	10	15	25	40	60	150
13 Bob Nevin RC	5	6	8	12	20	30	60	175
14 Ron Stewart	5	5	6	10	15	25	50	120
15 Bob Baun	5	6	10	15	25	40	60	120
16 Ralph Backstrom RC	5	8	12	20	30	50	80	250
17 Charlie Hodge	5	6	8	12	25	40	60	120
18 Gary Aldcorn	5	5	6	10	15	20	50	120
19 Willie Marshall	5	5	6	10	15	20	50	120
20 Marc Reaume	5	5	6	10	15	20	50	100
21 Jacques Plante IA	10	15	20	25	40	60	80	200
22 Jacques Plante	40	50	80	120	150	250	300	600
23 Allan Stanley UER	5	6	8	12	20	30	50	120
24 Ian Cushenan RC	5	5	6	10	15	25	50	120
25 Billy Reay CO	5	5	6	10	15	20	50	120
26 Jacques Plante IA	10	15	20	30	40	60	80	200
27 Bert Olmstead	5	5	6	10	15	25	50	120
28 Bernie Geoffrion	8	12	20	35	50	80	120	250
29 Dick Duff	5	5	6	10	15	25	50	100
30 Ab McDonald RC	5	5	6	10	15	20	60	100
31 Barry Cullen	5	5	6	10	15	20	50	100
32 Marcel Bonin	5	5	6	10	15	20	50	120
33 Frank Mahovlich	20	30	50	60	100	150	200	350
34 Jean Beliveau	20	30	50	80	100	▲150	▲250	▲500
35 J.Plante/Canadiens IA	6	10	15	25	40	60	80	150
36 Brian Cullen Shoots	5	5	6	10	15	20	50	150
37 Steve Kraftcheck	5	5	6	10	15	20	50	150
38 Maurice Richard	40	50	▲100	▲150	▲250	▲300	▲500	▲650
39 Jacques Plante IA	6	10	15	25	40	60	80	200
40 Bob Turner	5	5	6	10	15	20	50	100
41 Jean-Guy Talbot	5	5	6	10	15	25	50	100
42 Tim Horton	12	20	30	50	80	100	200	350
43 Claude Provost	5	5	6	10	15	25	50	120
44 Don Marshall	5	5	6	10	15	25	50	200
45 Bob Pulford	5	6	8	12	20	30	50	120
46 Johnny Bower UER	15	25	40	60	100	120	150	350
47 Phil Goyette	5	5	6	10	15	25	50	120
48 George Armstrong	5	6	10	15	25	40	60	150
49 Doug Harvey	8	12	20	30	50	80	100	250
50 Brian Cullen	5	6	10	15	25	40	100	200

1958-59 Topps

		PrFr 1	GD 2	VG 3	VgEx 4	EX 5	ExMt 6	NM 7	NmMt 8
1	Bob Armstrong	5	6	10	15	25	100	300	
2	Terry Sawchuk	25	30	50	80	120	175	300	500
3	Glen Skov	5	5	5	8	12	20	80	300
4	Leo Labine	5	5	6	10	15	25	60	150
5	Dollard St.Laurent	5	5	5	8	12	20	100	250
6	Danny Lewicki	5	5	5	8	12	20	25	150
7	John Hanna RC	5	5	5	8	12	20	100	400
8	Gordie Howe UER	60	80	120	150	250	300	600	1,200
9	Vic Stasiuk	5	5	5	8	12	20	40	400
10	Larry Regan	5	5	5	8	12	20	30	100
11	Forbes Kennedy	5	5	5	8	12	20	60	200
12	Elmer Vasko	5	5	6	10	15	25	100	400
13	Glenn Hall	15	25	40	60	80	100	200	500
14	Ken Wharram RC	5	5	6	10	15	25	100	300
15	Len Lunde RC	5	5	5	8	12	20	60	200
16	Ed Litzenberger	5	5	6	10	15	25	40	100
17	Norm Johnson RC	5	5	5	8	12	20	50	120
18	Earl Ingarfield RC	5	5	5	8	12	20	60	300
19	Les Colwill RC	5	5	5	8	12	20	60	120
20	Leo Boivin	5	5	6	10	15	25	40	150
21	Andy Bathgate	6	10	15	25	40	60	250	
22	Johnny Wilson	5	5	5	8	12	20	60	250
23	Larry Cahan	5	5	5	8	12	20	30	100
24	Marcel Pronovost	5	5	6	10	15	25	40	120
25	Larry Hillman	5	5	6	10	15	25	60	150
26	Jim Bartlett RC	5	5	5	8	12	20	30	120
27	Nick Mickoski	5	5	5	8	12	20	80	650
28	Larry Popein	5	5	5	8	12	20	100	1,000
29	Fleming Mackell	5	5	6	10	15	25	50	150
30	Eddie Shack RC	25	40	80	100	200	250	300	400
31	Jack Evans	5	5	5	8	12	20	50	120
32	Dean Prentice	5	5	6	10	15	25	60	500
33	Claude Laforge RC	5	5	5	8	12	20	60	300
34	Bill Gadsby	5	5	8	12	20	50	80	150
35	Bronco Horvath	5	5	6	10	15	25	50	120
36	Pierre Pilote	5	8	15	40	60	80	100	200
37	Earl Balfour	5	5	5	8	12	20	60	350
38	Gus Mortson	5	5	8	12	20	30	60	200
39	Gump Worsley	8	12	20	30	40	60	100	250
40	Johnny Bucyk	12	20	25	40	60	80	150	300
41	Lou Fontinato	5	5	6	10	15	25	80	200
42	Tod Sloan	5	5	5	8	12	20	60	300
43	Charlie Burns RC	5	5	5	8	12	20	100	400
44	Don Simmons	5	5	6	10	15	25	80	250
45	Jerry Toppazzini	5	5	5	8	12	20	60	150
46	Andy Hebenton	5	5	5	8	12	25	60	
47	Pete Goegan UER	5	5	5	8	12	25	100	
48	George Sullivan	5	5	5	8	12	20	60	200
49	Hank Ciesla RC	5	5	5	8	12	20	100	1,000
50	Doug Mohns	5	5	5	8	12	20	40	100
51	Jean-Guy Gendron	5	5	5	8	12	20	40	100
52	Alex Delvecchio	5	6	10	15	25	40	80	200
53	Eric Nesterenko	5	5	6	10	15	40	100	900
54	Camille Henry	5	5	6	10	15	25	60	400
55	Lorne Ferguson	5	5	5	8	12	20	60	150
56	Fern Flaman	5	5	6	10	15	25	60	150
57	Earl Reibel	5	5	5	8	15	40	100	
58	Warren Godfrey	5	5	5	8	12	20	60	300
59	Ron Murphy	5	5	5	8	12	30	80	300
60	Harry Howell	5	5	8	12	20	30	100	250
61	Red Kelly	5	6	10	15	25	40	80	250
62	Don McKenney	5	5	5	8	12	20	50	200
63	Ted Lindsay	5	6	10	15	25	40	100	550
64	Al Arbour	5	5	6	10	15	25	50	150
65	Norm Ullman	10	15	25	40	50	80	120	400
66	Bobby Hull RC	500	1,000	1,500	2,500	3,500	4,000	6,000	

1959-60 Parkhurst

		VG 3	VgEx 4	EX 5	ExMt 6	NM 7	NmMt 8	NmMt+ 8.5	MT
1	Canadiens On Guard	40	60	70	80	200	350	450	8
2	Maurice Richard	100	120	150	▲250	▲400	▲800	▲1,000	▲2,0
3	Carl Brewer RC	20	30	40	60	80	150		
4	Phil Goyette	8	12	15	25	30	80	150	3
5	Ed Chadwick	10	15	20	30	40	100		
6	Jean Beliveau	50	80	100	150	200	350	450	1,5
7	George Armstrong	10	15	20	30	40	100	125	25
8	Doug Harvey	25	50	60	80	100	200	250	40
9	Billy Harris	8	15	25	40	50	100	150	25
10	Tom Johnson	8	12	15	25	40	100		
11	Marc Reaume	8	12	15	25	30	100	150	2
12	Marcel Bonin	8	12	15	25	30	80		
13	Johnny Wilson	8	12	15	25	30	120	150	20
14	Dickie Moore	12	20	30	50	80	150	250	4
15	Punch Imlach CO RC	12	20	25	40	50	120		
16	Charlie Hodge	10	15	25	50	80	150	200	30
17	Larry Regan	8	12	20	30	50	120	150	25
18	Claude Provost	8	12	15	25	30	120	150	25
19	Gerry Ehman RC	8	12	15	25	30	100	150	30
20	Ab McDonald	8	12	15	25	40	100	125	25
21	Bob Baun	8	12	15	25	30	100	125	30
22	Ken Reardon VP	8	12	15	25	30	100		
23	Tim Horton	30	50	60	80	100	250	350	60
24	Frank Mahovlich	40	60	80	100	150	250	300	50
25	Johnny Bower IA	12	20	25	40	50	150		
26	Ron Stewart	8	12	15	25	30	250		
27	Toe Blake CO	8	12	15	25	30	100		
28	Bob Pulford	8	12	15	25	30	100		
29	Ralph Backstrom	8	12	15	25	30	150		
30	Action Around the Net	10	15	20	30	40	150		
31	Bill Hicke RC	10	15	20	25	30	80		
32	Johnny Bower	30	50	60	80	120	250		
33	Bernie Geoffrion	20	30	40	60	80	200		
34	Ted Hampson RC	8	12	15	25	30	120		
35	Andre Pronovost	8	12	15	25	40	200		
36	Stafford Smythe CHC	8	12	15	25	▲50	▲150	▲200	25
37	Don Marshall	8	12	15	25	30	100		
38	Dick Duff	8	12	15	25	30	150		
39	Henri Richard	40	60	80	120	150	250	300	50
40	Bert Olmstead	8	12	15	25	30	100		
41	Jacques Plante	60	100	120	200	250	400	600	1,500
42	Noel Price	8	12	15	25	30	80		
43	Bob Turner	8	12	15	25	30	120		
44	Allan Stanley	12	20	25	40	50	100	125	300
45	Albert Langlois	8	12	15	25	▲50	▲150		
46	Officials Intervene	8	12	15	25	30	80		
47	Frank Selke MD	8	12	15	25	30	120		
48	Gary Edmundson RC	8	12	15	25	30	100	125	350
49	Jean-Guy Talbot	8	12	15	25	30	150		
50	King Clancy AGM	25	40	50	60	120	300		

1959-60 Topps

		PrFr 1	GD 2	VG 3	VgEx 4	EX 5	ExMt 6	NM 7	NmMt 8
1	Eric Nesterenko	5	8	12	20	30	50	150	850
2	Pierre Pilote	5	6	10	15	25	40	60	150
3	Elmer Vasko	5	5	6	10	15	25	50	300
4	Peter Goegan	5	5	5	8	12	20	50	250
5	Lou Fontinato	5	5	6	10	15	25	50	150
6	Ted Lindsay	5	6	10	15	25	40	60	200
7	Leo Labine	5	5	6	10	15	25	80	300
8	Alex Delvecchio	5	6	10	15	25	40	60	175
9	Don McKenney UER	5	5	5	8	12	20	50	120
10	Earl Ingarfield	5	5	5	8	12	20	50	120
11	Don Simmons	5	5	6	10	15	25	60	100
12	Glen Skov	5	5	5	8	12	20	50	120
13	Tod Sloan	5	5	5	8	12	25	80	350
14	Vic Stasiuk	5	5	5	8	12	20	50	120
15	Gump Worsley	6	10	15	25	40	60	80	200
16	Andy Hebenton	5	5	6	10	15	25	50	120
17	Dean Prentice	5	5	5	8	12	20	50	120
18	Action/Pronovost/Bartlett	5	5	5	8	12	20	60	200
19	Fleming Mackell	5	5	6	10	15	25	50	100
20	Harry Howell	5	5	6	10	15	25	60	120
21	Larry Popein	5	5	5	8	12	20	50	100

	PrFr 1	GD 2	VG 3	VgEx 4	EX 5	ExMt 6	NM 7	NmMt 8
Len Lunde	5	5	5	8	12	20	50	150
Johnny Bucyk	6	10	15	25	40	60	80	250
Jean-Guy Gendron	5	5	5	8	12	20	50	150
Barry Cullen	5	5	5	8	12	20	50	100
Leo Boivin	5	5	6	10	15	25	50	100
Warren Godfrey	5	5	5	8	12	20	50	100
G.Hall/C.Henry IA	5	6	10	15	25	40	50	200
Fern Flaman	5	5	6	10	15	25	50	120
Jack Evans	5	5	5	8	12	20	50	100
John Hanna	5	5	5	8	12	20	50	120
Glenn Hall	10	15	25	30	40	60	100	200
Murray Balfour RC	5	5	6	10	15	25	50	120
Andy Bathgate	5	6	10	15	25	40	60	250
Al Arbour	5	5	6	10	15	25	50	150
Jim Morrison	5	5	5	8	12	20	50	100
Nick Mickoski	5	5	5	8	12	20	40	150
Jerry Toppazzini	5	5	5	8	12	20	50	120
Bob Armstrong	5	5	5	8	12	20	50	100
Charlie Burns UER	5	5	5	8	20	50	80	150
Bill McNeil	5	5	5	8	12	20	50	200
Terry Sawchuk	20	25	40	60	80	10	150	600
Dollard St.Laurent	5	5	5	8	12	20	60	150
Marcel Pronovost	5	5	6	10	15	25	50	300
Norm Ullman	6	10	15	25	40	60	60	200
Camille Henry	5	5	6	10	15	30	100	300
Bobby Hull	50	80	100	150	250	350	550	850
G.Howe/Jack Evans IA	8	12	20	30	50	80	120	400
Lou Marcon RC	5	5	5	8	12	20	50	100
Earl Balfour	5	5	5	8	12	20	50	250
Jim Bartlett	5	5	5	8	12	20	50	200
Forbes Kennedy	5	5	5	8	12	20	50	200
Action Picture	5	5	5	8	12	20	50	120
G.Worsley/H.Howell IA	5	6	10	15	25	40	50	120
Brian Cullen	5	5	5	8	12	20	50	200
Bronco Horvath	5	5	6	10	15	25	50	150
Eddie Shack	10	15	25	40	50	60	100	200
Doug Mohns	5	5	6	10	15	25	80	350
George Sullivan	5	5	5	8	12	20	50	150
Pierre Pilote/Flem Mackell IA	5	5	5	8	12	20	50	120
Ed Litzenberger	5	5	5	8	12	20	▲80	150
Bill Gadsby	5	5	8	12	20	30	50	120
Gordie Howe	40	80	100	100	150	250	350	600
Claude Laforge	5	5	5	8	12	20	50	150
Red Kelly	5	6	10	15	25	40	100	250
Ron Murphy	5	8	12	20	35	50	150	

John Bucyk #23 SGC 9 (MT) sold for $467 (Goodwin; 1/12)
Bill Gadsby #62 PSA 9 (Mint) sold for $249.50 (eBay; 4/16)
Glenn Hall #32 SGC 9 (MT) sold for $467 (Goodwin; 1/12)
Ed Litzenberger #61 PSA 9 (MT) sold for $732 (eBay; 5/12)
Terry Sawchuk #42 PSA 9 (MT) sold for $1,365 (eBay; 2/14)
Eddie Shack #57 PSA 9 (MT) sold for $897 (eBay; 6/12)
Tod Sloan #13 PSA 9 (MT) sold for $797.50 (eBay; 2/14)
Norm Ullman #45 PSA 9 (MT) sold for $1,221 (eBay; 2/13)
Norm Ullman #45 SGC 9 (MT) sold for $464 (Goodwin; 1/12)

1960-61 Parkhurst

	VG 3	VgEx 4	EX 5	ExMt 6	NM 7	NmMt 8	NmMt+ 8.5	MT 9
Tim Horton	30	50	80	100	250	500		
Frank Mahovlich	25	30	50	80	125	350	400	800
Johnny Bower	15	20	30	50	100	200	600	
Bert Olmstead	8	10	12	20	30	100	125	200
Gary Edmundson	8	10	12	20	30	60	80	175
Ron Stewart	8	10	12	20	30	80	100	175
Gerry James	8	10	12	20	30	80	100	175
Gerry Ehman	8	10	12	20	30	60	80	175
Red Kelly	12	15	20	30	50	80	125	225
Dave Creighton	8	10	12	20	30	80	100	150
Bob Baun	8	10	12	20	30	80	100	175
Dick Duff	8	10	12	20	30	80	100	175
Larry Regan	8	10	12	20	25	60	80	175
Johnny Wilson	8	10	12	20	30	80	100	150
Billy Harris	8	10	12	20	30	80	100	150
Allan Stanley	8	10	12	20	30	60	80	120
George Armstrong	8	10	12	20	30	80	100	150
Carl Brewer	8	10	12	20	40	80	100	200
Bob Pulford	8	10	12	20	50	100	120	175
Gordie Howe	60	100	150	250	300	500	800	1,500
Val Fonteyne	8	10	12	20	25	60	80	175
Murray Oliver RC	8	10	12	20	30	80	100	150
Sid Abel CO	8	10	12	20	30	60	80	200
Jack McIntyre	8	10	12	20	25	60	80	175
Marc Reaume	8	10	12	20	30	80	100	175
Norm Ullman	15	20	30	50	80	150	200	150
Brian Smith	8	10	12	20	30	80	100	150
Gerry Melnyk UER RC	8	10	12	20	30	60	80	175
Marcel Pronovost	8	10	12	20	30	80	120	250
Warren Godfrey	8	10	12	20	30	80	125	200
Terry Sawchuk	30	40	60	80	150	200	250	400
Barry Cullen	8	10	12	20	30	60	80	150

	VG 3	VgEx 4	EX 5	ExMt 6	NM 7	NmMt 8	NmMt+ 8.5	MT 9
33	Gary Aldcorn	8	10	12	20	30	60	80	200
34	Pete Goegan	8	10	12	20	30	80	100	225
35	Len Lunde	8	10	12	20	30	80	100	175
36	Alex Delvecchio	12	15	20	30	60	100	150	300
37	John McKenzie RC	10	12	15	25	40	80	100	250
38	Dickie Moore	10	12	15	25	40	80	100	350
39	Albert Langlois	8	10	12	20	30	80	100	175
40	Bill Hicke	8	10	12	20	30	80	100	175
41	Ralph Backstrom	8	10	12	20	30	80	100	300
42	Don Marshall	8	10	12	20	30	80	100	200
43	Bob Turner	8	10	12	25	50	100	200	300
44	Tom Johnson	8	10	12	20	30	80	100	300
45	Maurice Richard	60	80	100	150	250	400	600	2,000
46	Bernie Geoffrion	15	20	30	50	80	120	150	400
47	Henri Richard	25	30	50	80	100	250	300	500
48	Doug Harvey	20	25	40	60	100	150	200	550
49	Jean Beliveau	25	40	50	80	125	250	300	600
50	Phil Goyette	8	10	12	20	30	80	125	250
51	Marcel Bonin	8	10	12	20	30	60	80	150
52	Jean-Guy Talbot	8	10	12	20	30	80	100	175
53	Jacques Plante	30	50	60	100	200	350	400	600
54	Claude Provost	8	10	12	20	30	80	100	250
55	Andre Pronovost	8	10	12	20	40	100		
56	Hicke/McDonald/Backstrom	8	10	12	20	30	80	125	200
57	Marsh/H.Richard/Moore	15	20	30	40	60	100	150	400
58	Provost/Pronovost/Goyette	8	10	12	20	30	80	100	300
59	Boom/Marshall/Beliveau	15	20	30	50	100	150	200	500
60	Ab McDonald	8	10	12	20	40	100	125	300
61	Jim Morrison	25	35	60	100	150	500		

Gary Aldcorn #33 PSA 9 (MT) sold for $350 (eBay; 1/08)
Johnny Bower #3 PSA 10 (GemMt) sold for $875 (eBay; 2/16)
Phil Goyette #50 PSA 9 (MT) sold for $350 (eBay; 1/08)
Bill Hicke #40 PSA 9 (MT) sold for $205 (eBay; 1/08)
Albert Langlois #39 PSA 10 (GemMt) sold for $1005.00 (eBay; 8/12)
John McKenzie #37 PSA 9 (MT) sold for $290 (eBay; 8/12)
Allan Stanley #16 PSA 10 (GemMt) sold for $308.50 (eBay; 1/16)
Norm Ullman #26 PSA 9 (MT) sold for $262 (eBay; 1/08)

1960-61 Topps

		VG 3	VgEx 4	EX 5	ExMt 6	NM 7	NmMt 8	NmMt+ 8.5	MT 9
1	Lester Patrick ATG	20	25	50	80	200	800		
2	Paddy Moran ATG	8	10	15	20	30	80		
3	Joe Malone ATG	10	12	20	30	40	80		
4	Ernest (Moose) Johnson ATG	6	8	12	20	30	80		
5	Nels Stewart ATG	10	12	20	30	50			
6	Bill Hay RC	6	8	12	20	40	150		
7	Eddie Shack	20	25	30	50	100	300		
8	Cy Denneny ATG	6	8	12	20	30	80	125	300
9	Jim Morrison	5	6	10	15	30	80		
10	Bill Cook ATG	6	8	12	25	50	100	150	225
11	Johnny Bucyk	15	20	25	40	80	250		
12	Murray Balfour	5	6	8	10	15	30	120	
13	Leo Labine	5	6	10	15	30	80		
14	Stan Mikita RC	150	250	350	550	600	1,800		
15	George Hay ATG	6	8	12	20	30	80		
16	Mervyn(Red) Dutton ATG	6	8	12	20	30	80		
17	Dickie Boon ATG UER	5	6	10	15	30	80		
18	George Sullivan	5	6	10	15	30	80		
19	Georges Vezina ATG	15	20	25	35	60	100	125	225
20	Eddie Shore ATG	15	20	25	30	50	100		
21	Ed Litzenberger	5	6	10	15	30	80		
22	Bill Gadsby	8	10	15	20	30	80		
23	Elmer Vasko	5	6	15	30	225			
24	Charlie Burns	5	6	10	30	60	250		
25	Glenn Hall	20	25	30	50	80	300		
26	Dit Clapper ATG	10	12	20	30	40	80	100	300
27	Art Ross ATG	15	20	25	40	60	100		
28	Jerry Toppazzini	5	6	10	15	30	80		
29	Frank Boucher ATG	6	8	12	20	30	80	100	225
30	Jack Evans	5	6	10	15	30	80		
31	Jean-Guy Gendron	5	6	10	15	40	120		
32	Chuck Gardiner ATG	8	10	15	25	40	80	100	250
33	Ab McDonald	5	6	12	20	30	80		
34	Frank Frederickson ATG	6	8	12	25	50	100	150	300
35	Frank Nighbor ATG	8	10	15	25	40	100		
36	Gump Worsley	20	25	40	50	80	250		
37	Dean Prentice	6	8	12	20	30	80		
38	Hugh Lehman ATG	6	8	12	20	30	80		
39	Jack McCartan RC	10	12	20	30	100	300		
40	Don McKenney UER	5	6	10	15	30	80		
41	Ron Murphy	5	6	10	15	30	80		
42	Andy Hebenton	8	10	15	20	40	120		
43	Don Simmons	8	12	20	30	100			
44	Herb Gardiner ATG	6	8	12	20	30	80		
45	Andy Bathgate	8	10	15	25	40	150		
46	Cyclone Taylor ATG	10	12	30	40	60	150		
47	King Clancy ATG	15	20	25	40	80	200		
48	Newsy Lalonde ATG	10	12	20	30	100	125		250
49	Harry Howell	6	8	15	25	60	150		

		VG 3	VgEx 4	EX 5	ExMt 6	NM 7	NmMt 8	NmMt+ 8.5	MT 9
50	Ken Schinkel RC	5	6	10	15	50	200		
51	Tod Sloan	5	8	12	20	40	100		
52	Doug Mohns	8	10	15	25	60			
53	Camille Henry	6	8	12	20	30	125		
54	Bronco Horvath	5	6	10	15	30	150		
55	Tiny Thompson ATG	12	15	25	30	50	80		
56	Bob Armstrong	5	6	10	15	30	80		
57	Fern Flaman	6	8	12	20	50	150		
58	Bobby Hull	100	120	250	300	400	800	1,200	
59	Howie Morenz ATG	20	25	30	40	60	150		
60	Dick Irvin ATG	10	12	20	30	40	80		
61	Lou Fontinato	5	6	10	15	60			
62	Leo Boivin	6	8	12	20	40	100		
63	Moose Goheen ATG	6	8	12	20	30	80		
64	Al Arbour	6	8	12	20	50	120		
65	Pierre Pilote	10	12	20	40	50	120		
66	Vic Stasiuk	12	15	20	30	80	150		

—Johnny Bucyk #11 PSA 9 (MT) sold for $989 (eBay; 2/07)
—George Sullivan #18 PSA 9 (MT) sold for $502 (eBay; 4/12)
—Glenn Hall #25 PSA 9 (MT) sold for $636 (Goodwin; 2/07)
—Hugh Lehman #38 PSA 9 (MT) sold for $882 (eBay; 4/09)
—Lou Fontinato #61 PSA 8 (NMMT) sold for $908 (eBay; 8/12)
—Pierre Pilote #65 PSA 9 (MT) sold for $1,968.00 (Memory Lane; 6/12)

1961-62 Parkhurst

		VG 3	VgEx 4	EX 5	ExMt 6	NM 7	NmMt 8	NmMt+ 8.5	MT 9
1	Tim Horton	30	50	120	150	250	800		
2	Frank Mahovlich	25	30	40	80	100	300		
3	Johnny Bower	20	25	35	60	100	200		
4	Bert Olmstead	8	10	12	20	30	60		
5	Dave Keon RC	125	200	300	400	500	800	1,000	1,600
6	Ron Stewart	8	10	12	20	30	80	120	300
7	Eddie Shack	20	25	40	60	80	150	200	350
8	Bob Pulford	8	10	12	25	40	80		
9	Red Kelly	10	12	15	25	40	80		
10	Bob Nevin	8	10	12	20	25	60	100	175
11	Bob Baun	8	10	12	20	30	80	125	200
12	Dick Duff	8	10	12	25	40	80	100	175
13	Larry Keenan	8	10	12	20	30	80	125	200
14	Larry Hillman	8	10	12	20	25	60	100	200
15	Billy Harris	8	10	12	20	25	60	100	200
16	Allan Stanley	8	10	12	20	25	60	100	175
17	George Armstrong	8	10	12	20	30	80	125	175
18	Carl Brewer	8	10	12	20	25	60	100	200
19	Howie Glover	8	10	12	20	25	60	100	175
20	Gordie Howe	60	80	100	150	▲300	▲450	600	▲1,500
21	Val Fonteyne	8	10	12	20	30	80		
22	Al Johnson	8	10	12	20	30	80		
23	Pete Goegan	8	10	12	20	30	60	100	600
24	Len Lunde	8	10	12	20	30	80		
25	Alex Delvecchio	10	12	15	25	40	100	125	200
26	Norm Ullman	15	20	25	40	60	100	125	200
27	Bill Gadsby	8	10	12	20	30	80		175
28	Ed Litzenberger	8	10	12	20	30	80	100	200
29	Marcel Pronovost	8	10	12	20	30	80		
30	Warren Godfrey	8	10	12	20	25	60	100	175
31	Terry Sawchuk	25	30	▲50	▲80	▲150	▲250	▲300	400
32	Vic Stasiuk	8	10	12	20	30	80	100	175
33	Leo Labine	8	10	12	20	30	80	100	175
34	John McKenzie	8	10	12	20	30	80	100	175
35	Bernie Geoffrion	20	25	30	40	60	120	150	250
36	Dickie Moore	8	10	12	20	30	80	100	175
37	Albert Langlois	8	10	12	20	25	80	100	175
38	Bill Hicke	8	10	12	20	25	60	100	200
39	Ralph Backstrom	8	10	12	20	25	60	100	200
40	Don Marshall	8	10	12	20	30	80	100	175
41	Bob Turner	8	10	12	20	30	80	100	200
42	Tom Johnson	8	10	12	20	30	80	100	200
43	Henri Richard	20	25	35	60	80	150	200	350
44	Wayne Connelly UER RC	8	10	12	20	30	80	100	175
45	Jean Beliveau	25	30	50	100	150	200	250	400
46	Phil Goyette	8	10	12	20	30	80	100	175
47	Marcel Bonin	8	10	12	20	30	80	100	175
48	Jean-Guy Talbot	8	10	12	20	30	80	120	250
49	Jacques Plante	30	50	80	150	200	300	400	650
50	Claude Provost	8	10	12	20	30	80	125	250
51	Andre Pronovost UER	15	20	25	40	60	150		

—Bill Gadsby #27 PSA 9 (GmMt) sold for $1,025 (eBay; 8/12)
—Dave Keon #5 PSA 9 (Mint) sold for $1,365 (eBay; 2/13)
—Bert Olmstead #4 PSA 9 (Mint) sold for $186.50 (eBay; 3/16)
—Andre Pronovost #61 PSA 10 (GmMt) sold for $3,643.78 (Memory Lane; 4/12)

1961-62 Topps

		VG 3	VgEx 4	EX 5	ExMt 6	NM 7	NmMt 8	NmMt+ 8.5	MT 9
1	Phil Watson CO	20	25	40	60	100	550		
2	Ted Green RC	15	20	30	40	80	200		
3	Earl Balfour	6	8	10	12	30	80		
4	Dallas Smith RC	12	15	20	25	40	100		
5	Andre Pronovost UER	12	15	20	25	30	80		

		VG 3	VgEx 4	EX 5	ExMt 6	NM 7	NmMt 8	NmMt+ 8.5	MT
6	Dick Meissner	6	8	10	12	30	80		
7	Leo Boivin	8	10	12	15	30	60		
8	Johnny Bucyk	15	20	30	40	50	150		
9	Jerry Toppazzini	6	8	10	12	25	60	80	1
10	Doug Mohns	8	10	12	15	30	80		
11	Charlie Burns	6	8	10	12	25	60		
12	Don McKenney	6	8	10	20	100	250		
13	Bob Armstrong	6	8	10	15	40	150		
14	Murray Oliver	6	8	10	12	25	60		
15	Orland Kurtenbach RC	10	12	15	20	30	80	100	30
16	Terry Gray	6	8	10	12	25	60	80	1
17	Don Head	8	10	12	15	30	80		
18	Pat Stapleton RC	12	15	25	50	100	200	300	4
19	Cliff Pennington	6	8	10	12	25	60	125	30
20	Bruins Team Picture	15	20	30	40	50	100	135	40
21	E.Balfour/F.Flaman IA	8	12	20	25	50	120		
22	A.Bathgate/G.Hall IA	12	15	20	25	60	175		
23	Rudy Pilous CO RC	8	12	20	25	50	200		
24	Pierre Pilote	12	15	20	25	40	80	125	40
25	Elmer Vasko	6	8	10	12	25	60	125	35
26	Reg Fleming RC	8	10	12	15	30	80		
27	Ab McDonald	6	8	10	12	25	60	100	17
28	Eric Nesterenko	8	10	12	15	30	80	100	20
29	Bobby Hull	75	100	150	200	300	500	600	1,00
30	Ken Wharram	8	10	12	30	80	100		17
31	Dollard St.Laurent	6	8	10	12	25	60	100	25
32	Glenn Hall	20	25	40	60	100	200	300	40
33	Murray Balfour	6	8	10	12	25	60	80	17
34	Ron Murphy	6	8	10	12	25	60		
35	Bill(Red) Hay	6	8	10	12	25	60		
36	Stan Mikita	30	40	60	100	150	300	400	75
37	Denis DeJordy RC	15	20	30	40	60	120		
38	Wayne Hillman	8	10	12	15	30	120		
39	Rino Robazzo	6	8	10	12	25	60		
40	Bronco Horvath	6	8	10	12	25	60		
41	Bob Turner	6	8	10	12	25	60		
42	Blackhawks Team Picture	15	20	30	40	60	120		
43	Ken Wharram IA	10	15	20	25	40	150		
44	St.Laurent/G.Hall IA	12	15	20	25	60	200	250	400
45	Doug Harvey CO	15	20	30	40	60	100	150	300
46	Junior Langlois	6	8	10	12	25	60	100	175
47	Irv Spencer	6	8	10	12	25	60	100	200
48	George Sullivan	6	8	10	12	25	60		
49	Earl Ingarfield	6	8	10	12	25	60	100	175
50	Gump Worsley	15	20	30	40	60	100	150	250
51	Harry Howell	8	10	12	15	30	80	100	175
52	Larry Cahan	6	8	10	12	25	60	100	175
53	Andy Bathgate	10	12	15	20	30	80	125	400
54	Dean Prentice	8	10	12	15	30	80	100	175
55	Andy Hebenton	6	8	10	12	25	60	100	175
56	Camille Henry	8	10	12	15	30	60	100	200
57	Jean-Guy Gendron	6	8	10	12	25	60		
58	Pat Hannigan	6	8	10	12	30	80	100	200
59	Ted Hampson	6	8	10	12	25	60		
60	Jean Ratelle RC	40	60	80	135	200	600	750	1,600
61	Al Lebrun	6	8	10	15	25	60	125	350
62	Rod Gilbert RC	40	50	100	125	200	400	600	2,000
63	Rangers Team Picture	15	20	30	40	80	800		
64	Meissner/Worsley IA	10	12	20	40	200			
65	Gump Worsley IA	15	20	30	80	150			
66	Checklist Card	50	60	80	120	200	600		

—Bob Armstrong #13 PSA 8.5 (NM MT+) sold for $173.99 (eBay; 3/16)
—Earl Balfour #3 PSA 9 (MT) sold for $305 (eBay; 8/08)
—Bruins Team Picture #20 PSA 9 (MT) sold for $648 (eBay; 3/07)
—Charlie Burns #11 PSA 9 (MT) sold for $279 (eBay; 2/16)
—Camile Henry #56 PSA 9 (MT) sold for $305 (eBay; 8/08)
—Camile Henry #56 PSA 10 (GemMT) sold for $639 (eBay; 3/17)
—Don McKenney #12 PSA 9 (MT) sold for $929 (eBay; 2/16)
—Stan Mikita #36 PSA 9 (MT) sold for $685 (ebay; 3/14)
—Stan Mikita #36 PSA 9 (MT) sold for $662 (ebay; 2/14)
—Stan Mikita #36 SGC 9 (MT) sold for $467.67 (Goodwin; 3/12)
—Dallas Smith #4 PSA 9 (MT) sold for $269.10 (eBay; 3/16)
—Jean Ratelle #60 SGC 10 (Gem) sold for $2,427 (Goodwin; 3/12)
—D.St.Laurent/G.Hall #44 PSA 9 (MT) sold for $940 (eBay; 8/09)
—Pat Stapleton #18 PSA 9 (MT) sold for $435 (eBay; 8/12)
—Bob Turner #41 PSA 9 (MT) sold for $299 (eBay; 2/16)
—Phil Watson #1 PSA 9 (MT) sold for $1,030 (eBay; 8/12)

1962-63 Parkhurst

		VG 3	VgEx 4	EX 5	ExMt 6	NM 7	NmMt 8	NmMt+ 8.5	MT 9
1	Billy Harris	10	12	20	30	50	120	150	350
2	Dick Duff	6	10	12	20	30	60	80	120
3	Bob Baun	6	10	12	20	30	60	80	120
4	Frank Mahovlich	12	15	30	50	80	125	200	300
5	Red Kelly	8	10	15	25	40	100	120	150
6	Ron Stewart	6	8	10	15	25	50	80	120
7	Tim Horton	12	15	25	40	75	150	225	350
8	Carl Brewer	6	8	10	15	25	50	80	120
9	Allan Stanley	6	8	10	20	30	60	80	120

364 www.beckett.com/price-guide

	VG 3	VgEx 4	EX 5	ExMt 6	NM 7	NmMt 8	NmMt+ 8.5	MT 9
Bob Nevin	6	8	10	15	25	60	80	120
Bob Pulford	6	8	10	15	25	50	80	120
Ed Litzenberger	6	8	10	15	25	50	100	
George Armstrong	6	8	10	15	25	50	80	120
Eddie Shack	10	12	20	30	50	100	150	225
Dave Keon	12	15	25	40	75	125	150	250
Johnny Bower	10	12	20	30	50	100	150	200
Larry Hillman	6	8	10	15	25	50	60	100
Frank Mahovlich	12	15	25	40	60	100	125	250
Hank Bassen	6	8	10	15	25	50	80	120
Gerry Odrowski	6	8	10	15	25	50	60	100
Norm Ullman	6	8	10	20	30	60	100	150
Vic Stasiuk	6	8	10	15	25	50	80	120
Bruce MacGregor	6	8	10	15	25	50	80	120
Claude Laforge	6	8	10	15	25	50	80	120
Bill Gadsby	6	8	10	15	25	50	80	120
Leo Labine	6	8	10	15	25	50	80	120
Val Fonteyne	6	8	10	15	25	50	80	120
Howie Glover	6	8	10	15	25	50	80	120
Marc Boileau	6	8	10	15	25	50	80	120
Gordie Howe	60	80	100	150	300	400	500	900
Gordie Howe	60	80	100	150	200	300	400	800
Alex Delvecchio	8	10	15	25	40	80	100	150
Marcel Pronovost	6	8	10	15	25	50	80	120
Sid Abel CO	6	8	10	15	25	50	80	120
Len Lunde	6	8	10	15	25	50	80	100
Warren Godfrey	6	8	10	15	25	50	80	100
Phil Goyette	6	8	10	15	25	50	80	120
Henri Richard	12	15	25	40	100	175	200	250
Jean Beliveau	12	15	25	40	75	150	250	300
Bill Hicke	6	8	10	15	25	50	80	120
Claude Provost	6	8	10	15	25	100	120	150
Dickie Moore	6	8	10	15	25	50	80	120
Don Marshall	6	8	10	15	25	50	80	120
Ralph Backstrom	6	8	10	20	25	50	80	120
Marcel Bonin	6	8	10	15	25	50	80	120
Gilles Tremblay RC	10	12	20	30	50	80	125	175
Bobby Rousseau RC	8	10	15	25	40	100	150	200
Bernie Geoffrion	10	12	20	30	50	100	150	200
Jacques Plante	25	30	50	75	125	200	300	350
Tom Johnson	6	8	10	15	25	50	80	120
Jean-Guy Talbot	6	8	10	15	25	50	80	120
Lou Fontinato	6	8	10	15	25	100	120	150
Bernie Geoffrion	10	12	20	30	50	80	125	175
J.C.Tremblay RC	12	15	25	35	60	150	200	500
Zip Entry Game Card	60	80	100	150	250	400	500	600
Checklist Card	50	75	125	250	400	500		

—Sid Able #34 PSA 10 (Gem) sold for $192.50 (eBay; 12/15)
—Bob Baun #3 PSA 10 (Gem) sold for $219.50 (eBay; 12/15)
—Warren Godfrey #36 PSA 10 (Gem) sold for $1,031 (eBay; 9/12)
—Frank Mahovlich #4 PSA 10 (Gem) sold for $1,100 (eBay; 9/12)
—Frank Mahovlich #4 PSA 10 (Gem) sold for $637 (eBay; 3/14)
—Don Marshall #43 PSA 10 (Gem) sold for $797 (eBay; 8/07)
—Bob Nevin #10 PSA 10 (Gem) sold for $585 (eBay; 2/13)
—Jaques Plante #10 PSA 10 (Gem) sold for $1,099 (eBay; 3/13)
—Bobby Rousseau #47 PSA 9 (MT) sold for $515 (eBay; 12/06)
—Ron Stewart #6 PSA 10 (Gem) sold for $376 (eBay; 2/16)

1962-63 Topps

	VG 3	VgEx 4	EX 5	ExMt 6	NM 7	NmMt 8	NmMt+ 8.5	MT 9
Phil Watson CO	10	15	25	35	80	200		
Bob Perreault	10	15	25	35	60	200		
Bruce Gamble RC	10	15	25	35	60	300		
Warren Godfrey	6	8	10	15	30	80	100	150
Leo Boivin	8	10	12	15	30	80		
Doug Mohns	8	10	12	15	30	80	100	150
Ted Green	8	10	12	15	30	80		
Pat Stapleton	8	10	12	15	30	80		
Dallas Smith	8	10	12	15	30	60		
Don McKenney	6	8	10	15	30	80		
Johnny Bucyk	15	20	25	30	50	100	125	400
Murray Oliver	6	8	10	15	30	60		
Jerry Toppazzini	6	8	10	15	30	80		
Cliff Pennington	6	8	10	15	30	80		
Charlie Burns	6	8	10	15	30	100		
Jean-Guy Gendron	6	8	10	15	30	100		
Irv Spencer	6	8	10	15	30	60	100	300
Wayne Connelly	6	8	10	15	30	60	80	150
Andre Pronovost	6	8	10	15	30	80		
Terry Gray	6	8	10	15	30	80		
Tom Williams RC	8	10	12	15	30	80	100	150
Bruins Team	20	25	30	40	50	80		
Rudy Pilous CO	6	8	10	15	30	80		
Glenn Hall	25	30	35	50	100	150	200	400
Denis DeJordy	8	10	12	15	30	80	100	200
Jack Evans	6	8	10	15	30	80		
Elmer Vasko	6	8	10	15	30	60		
Pierre Pilote	10	12	15	20	30	80	100	200
Bob Turner	6	8	10	15	30	60	80	150

	VG 3	VgEx 4	EX 5	ExMt 6	NM 7	NmMt 8	NmMt+ 8.5	MT 9
30	Dollard St.Laurent	6	8	10	15	30	80		
31	Wayne Hillman	8	10	12	20	30	60		
32	Al McNeil	6	8	10	15	30	80		
33	Bobby Hull	50	60	80	150	300	350	450	1,000
34	Stan Mikita	30	40	50	80	150	200	250	400
35	Bill(Red) Hay	6	8	10	15	30	80		
36	Murray Balfour	6	8	10	15	30	80		
37	Chico Maki RC	10	12	15	20	40	80		
38	Ab McDonald	6	8	10	15	30	80		
39	Ken Wharram	8	10	12	15	30	80		
40	Ron Murphy	6	8	10	15	30	250		
41	Eric Nesterenko	6	8	10	15	30	80		
42	Reg Fleming	6	8	10	12	15	30	80	
43	Murray Hall	6	8	10	15	30	80	100	250
44	Blackhawks Team	20	25	30	40	50	100		
45	Gump Worsley	20	25	30	40	60	120		
46	Harry Howell	6	8	10	15	30	80	100	200
47	Albert Langlois	6	8	10	15	30	60	100	250
48	Larry Cahan	6	8	10	15	30	80		
49	Jim Neilson UER RC	10	12	15	20	30	80		
50	Al Lebrun	6	8	10	15	30	80		
51	Earl Ingarfield	6	8	10	15	30	60		
52	Andy Bathgate	10	12	15	20	30	80	100	200
53	Dean Prentice	8	10	12	15	30	80	100	175
54	Andy Hebenton	6	8	10	15	30	60		
55	Ted Hampson	6	8	10	15	30	60		
56	Dave Balon	6	8	10	15	30	60		400
57	Bert Olmstead	8	10	12	15	30	60	80	150
58	Jean Ratelle	25	30	35	50	60	120		
59	Rod Gilbert	25	30	35	50	▲80	▲150		
60	Vic Hadfield RC	25	30	35	50	80	150	200	300
61	Frank Paice RC TR	6	8	10	15	30	80		
62	Camille Henry	8	10	12	15	30	80		
63	Bronco Horvath	6	8	10	15	30	60		
64	Pat Hannigan	6	8	10	▲25	▲50	80		
65	Rangers Team	15	20	25	30	40	60	100	
66	Checklist Card	60	80	100	150	225	500		

—Denis DeJordy #25 PSA 10 (Gem) sold for $2,064.65 (Goodwin; 3/12)
—Vic Hadfield #60 PSA 10 (Gem) sold for $840 (ebay; 2/14)
—Bobby Hull #33 PSA 10 (Gem) sold for $5,118 (Mastro; 2/07)

1963-64 Parkhurst

		VG 3	VgEx 4	EX 5	ExMt 6	NM 7	NmMt 8	NmMt+ 8.5	MT 9
1	Allan Stanley	12	15	30	40	60	80	135	450
2	Don Simmons	6	8	10	20	30	60	80	150
3	Red Kelly	10	12	20	25	40	80	100	200
4	Dick Duff	6	8	10	20	30	50	80	120
5	Johnny Bower	15	20	25	50	80	100	150	250
6	Ed Litzenberger	6	8	10	20	30	60	80	120
7	Kent Douglas	6	8	10	▲30	▲50	▲80	▲100	200
8	Carl Brewer	6	8	10	20	30	60	80	120
9	Eddie Shack	15	20	25	40	80	120	150	250
10	Bob Nevin	6	8	10	20	30	60	80	120
11	Billy Harris	6	8	15	20	30	60	80	120
12	Bob Pulford	6	8	10	20	30	60	80	120
13	George Armstrong	6	8	10	20	40	60	100	300
14	Ron Stewart	6	8	10	20	30	60	80	250
15	John McMillan	6	8	10	20	30	50	60	120
16	Tim Horton	20	40	50	60	80	150	200	350
17	Frank Mahovlich	20	25	30	50	80	150	200	350
18	Bob Baun	6	8	10	20	30	60	80	120
19	Punch Imlach ACO/GM	10	12	15	25	40	80	100	250
20	King Clancy ACO	10	12	15	25	50	100		
21	Gilles Tremblay	6	8	10	20	30	60	80	135
22	Jean-Guy Talbot	6	8	10	20	30	60	80	120
23	Henri Richard	20	25	30	50	100	150	175	300
24	Ralph Backstrom	6	8	10	20	30	60	80	250
25	Bill Hicke	6	8	10	20	30	50	80	200
26	Red Berenson RC	12	15	20	30	50	80	100	200
27	Jacques Laperriere RC	15	20	25	50	100	200	250	600
28	Jean Gauthier	6	8	10	20	30	60	80	120
29	Bernie Geoffrion	12	15	20	30	50	80	125	200
30	Jean Beliveau	20	25	30	60	100	200	300	350
31	J.C.Tremblay	6	8	10	20	30	60	80	120
32	Terry Harper RC	10	12	15	25	40	100	120	200
33	John Ferguson RC	20	25	30	60	100	175	225	400
34	Toe Blake CO	10	12	15	25	40	80	100	175
35	Bobby Rousseau	6	8	10	20	30	60	80	120
36	Claude Provost	6	8	10	20	30	60	80	120
37	Marc Reaume	6	8	10	20	30	60	100	150
38	Dave Balon	6	8	10	20	30	60		
39	Gump Worsley	12	15	20	30	50	100	175	300
40	Cesare Maniago RC	15	20	25	50	60	100	150	250
41	Bruce MacGregor	6	8	10	20	30	60	80	150
42	Alex Faulkner RC	50	60	100	150	200	400	500	900
43	Pete Goegan	6	8	10	20	30	60	80	120
44	Parker MacDonald	6	8	10	20	30	60	80	120
45	Andre Pronovost	6	8	10	20	30	60	80	120
46	Marcel Pronovost	6	8	10	20	30	60	80	120

#	Player	VG 3	VgEx 4	EX 5	ExMt 6	NM 7	NmMt 8	NmMt+ 8.5	MT 9
47	Bob Dillabough	6	8	10	20	30	80		
48	Larry Jeffrey	6	8	10	20	30	60		
49	Ian Cushenan	6	8	10	20	30	60	80	120
50	Alex Delvecchio	10	12	15	25	40	100	125	250
51	Hank Ciesla	6	8	10	20	30	60	80	120
52	Norm Ullman	10	12	15	25	40	80	100	150
53	Terry Sawchuk	25	30	40	75	125	250		
54	Ron Ingram	6	8	10	20	30	60	80	150
55	Gordie Howe	80	100	150	250	400	600	800	1,800
56	Billy McNeil	6	8	10	20	30	60	80	150
57	Floyd Smith	6	8	10	20	30	60	80	120
58	Vic Stasiuk	6	8	10	20	30	60	80	120
59	Bill Gadsby	6	8	10	20	30	60	80	150
60	Doug Barkley	6	8	10	20	30	45	60	120
61	Allan Stanley	6	8	10	20	30	60	80	120
62	Don Simmons	6	8	10	20	30	50	60	100
63	Red Kelly	10	12	15	25	40	80	100	200
64	Dick Duff	6	8	10	20	30	80	100	350
65	Johnny Bower	15	20	25	50	80	100	200	400
66	Ed Litzenberger	6	8	10	20	30	50	60	100
67	Kent Douglas	6	8	10	20	30	60	80	120
68	Carl Brewer	6	8	10	20	30	50	60	100
69	Eddie Shack	15	20	25	40	80	100	150	200
70	Bob Nevin	6	8	10	20	30	60	80	120
71	Billy Harris	6	8	10	20	30	50	60	100
72	Bob Pulford	6	8	10	20	30	60	80	120
73	George Armstrong	6	8	10	20	30	60	80	120
74	Ron Stewart	6	8	10	20	30	50	60	100
75	Dave Keon	15	25	40	60	80	120	200	250
76	Tim Horton	15	20	25	40	80	120	200	400
77	Frank Mahovlich	15	20	25	40	60	100	120	300
78	Bob Baun	6	8	10	20	30	60	80	120
79	Punch Imlach ACO/GM	10	12	15	25	40	60	100	225
80	Gilles Tremblay	6	8	10	20	30	60	80	200
81	Jean-Guy Talbot	6	8	10	20	30	60	80	150
82	Henri Richard	20	25	30	60	80	100	150	300
83	Ralph Backstrom	6	8	10	20	30	50	80	100
84	Bill Hicke	6	8	10	20	30	50	60	120
85	Red Berenson RC	12	15	20	30	50	100	150	200
86	Jacques Laperriere RC	12	20	30	50	80	200		
87	Jean Gauthier	6	8	10	20	30	80	100	400
88	Bernie Geoffrion	12	15	20	30	50	125	150	200
89	Jean Beliveau	20	25	30	50	80	150	200	300
90	J.C.Tremblay	6	8	10	20	30	45	60	100
91	Terry Harper RC	10	12	15	25	40	60	80	150
92	John Ferguson RC	15	20	25	50	80	150		
93	Toe Blake CO	10	12	15	25	40	80	125	400
94	Bobby Rousseau	6	8	10	20	30	60	80	120
95	Claude Provost	6	8	10	20	30	50		100
96	Marc Reaume	6	8	10	20	30	60	80	100
97	Dave Balon	6	8	10	20	30	80	100	150
98	Gump Worsley	12	15	20	30	50	100	150	200
99	Cesare Maniago RC	30	40	60	100	175	300		800

—George Armstrong #73 PSA 10 (Gem) sold for $428.79 (eBay; 2/16)
—Ralph Backstrom #83 PSA 10 (Gem) sold for $560 (eBay; 7/08)
—Bob Baun #18 PSA 10 (Gem) sold for $852 (eBay; 9/12)
—Jean Beliveau #89 PSA 10 (Gem) sold for $2,260 (eBay; 7/08)
—Red Berenson #85 PSA 10 (Gem) sold for $1,683.33 (eBay; 9/12)
—Johnny Bower #5 PSA 10 (Gem) sold for $1,533.60 (eBay; 5/12)
—Johnny Bower #5 PSA 10 (Gem) sold for $673 (eBay; 3/14)
—Johnny Bower #65 PSA 10 (Gem) sold for $1,930.33 (eBay; 6/12)
—Bob Dillabough #47 PSA 9 (MT) sold for $803 (eBay; 3/14)
—Kent Douglas #7 PSA 10 (Gem) sold for $1,197 (eBay; 6/12)
—Alex Faulkner #42 PSA 10 (Gem) sold for $2,409 (eBay; 2/13)
—Alex Faulkner #42 PSA 10 (Gem) sold for $1,533 (eBay; 3/13)
—Alex Faulkner #42 PSA 10 (Gem) sold for $1,319 (eBay; 3/14)
—John Ferguson #33 PSA 10 (Gem) sold for $1,609.44 (eBay; 9/12)
—Glenn Hall #23 PSA 10 (Gem) sold for $3159 (eBay 4/27)
—Billy Harris #71 PSA 10 (Gem) sold for $259.90 (eBay; 2/16)
—Tim Horton #76 PSA 9 (MT) sold for $466.78 (eBay; 9/12)
—Gordie Howe #55 SGC 8.5 (NmMt) sold for $372 (eBay; 3/14)
—Gordie Howe #55 PSA 9 (MT) sold for $1,856 (eBay; 2/16)
—Ed Litzenberger #6 PSA 10 (Gem) sold for $873 (eBay; 2/14)
—Frank Mahovlich #77 PSA 10 (Gem) sold for $2,180 (Memory Lane; 4/12)
—Cesare Maniago #40 PSA 10 (Gem) sold for $1,533.33 (eBay; 9/12)
—Cesare Maniago #99 PSA 9 (MT) sold for $668 (eBay; 3/14)
—Marcel Pronovost #46 PSA 10 (Gem) sold for $259 (eBay; 2/16)
—Henri Richard #82 PSA 10 (Gem) sold for $1,109 (eBay; 4/12)
—Henri Richard #82 PSA 10 (Gem) sold for $973 (eBay; 12/12)
—Henri Richard #82 PSA 10 (Gem) sold for $508 (eBay; 2/16)
—Terry Sawchuk #53 PSA 9 (MT) sold for $436 (eBay; 2/16)
—Don Simmons #62 PSA 10 (Gem) sold for $1,297 (eBay; 6/12)
—Jean-Guy Talbot #81 PSA 9 (MT) sold for $514 (eBay; 12/06)
—Norm Ullman #52 PSA 10 (Gem) sold for $1,395 (eBay; 6/12)
—Norm Ullman #52 PSA 10 (Gem) sold for $342.76 (eBay; 2/16)
—Gump Worsley #98 PSA 10 (Gem) sold for $2,032 (eBay; 9/12)

1963-64 Topps

#	Player	VG 3	VgEx 4	EX 5	ExMt 6	NM 7	NmMt 8	NmMt+ 8.5	MT
1	Milt Schmidt CO	12	15	20	30	40	200		
2	Ed Johnston RC	15	20	25	35	50	80	100	30
3	Doug Mohns	8	10	12	15	30	80		
4	Tom Johnson	8	10	12	15	30	100		
5	Leo Boivin	8	10	12	15	30	80		
6	Bob McCord	6	8	10	12	25	60		
7	Ted Green	8	10	12	15	40	80		
8	Ed Westfall RC	15	20	25	30	40	80		
9	Charlie Burns	6	8	10	15	40	80		
10	Murray Oliver	8	10	12	15	30	60		
11	Johnny Bucyk	12	15	20	25	40	200		
12	Tom Williams	8	10	12	15	30	80		
13	Dean Prentice	8	10	12	15	30	80		
14	Bob Leiter	6	8	10	12	25	50	80	15
15	Andy Hebenton	6	8	10	12	25	50		
16	Jean-Guy Gendron	6	8	10	12	25	50		
17	Wayne Rivers	6	8	10	12	25	50		
18	Jerry Toppazzini	6	8	10	12	25	50		
19	Forbes Kennedy	6	8	10	12	25	50		
20	Orland Kurtenbach	8	10	12	15	30	80		
21	Bruins Team	20	25	30	40	60	200		
22	Billy Reay CO	8	10	12	15	30	80		
23	Glenn Hall	20	25	30	40	50	150	200	35
24	Denis DeJordy	8	10	12	15	30	80		
25	Pierre Pilote	8	10	12	15	30	80	120	30
26	Elmer Vasko	6	8	10	12	30	80		
27	Wayne Hillman	8	10	12	15	30	60	80	17
28	Al McNeil	6	8	10	12	25	50		
29	Howie Young	6	8	10	12	25	50		
30	Ed Van Impe RC	8	10	12	20	30	175		
31	Reg Fleming	8	10	12	15	30	80		
32	Bob Turner	6	8	10	12	25	50	60	200
33	Bobby Hull	50	60	▲100	▲150	▲250	350	▲450	50
34	Bill(Red) Hay	6	8	10	12	25	50		
35	Murray Balfour	6	8	10	12	25	50		
36	Stan Mikita	25	30	35	50	80	150	300	50
37	Ab McDonald	6	8	10	12	25	50	100	25
38	Ken Wharram	8	10	12	15	30	80		
39	Eric Nesterenko	8	10	12	15	30	80	100	35
40	Ron Murphy	6	8	10	12	25	50		
41	Chico Maki	6	8	10	12	25	50	60	200
42	John McKenzie	8	10	12	15	30	80		
43	Blackhawks Team	15	20	25	30	40	120		
44	George Sullivan	10	12	15	20	50	300		
45	Jacques Plante	25	30	40	60	100	200		
46	Gilles Villemure RC	15	20	25	30	40	100		
47	Doug Harvey	15	20	25	30	40	100		350
48	Harry Howell	8	10	12	15	30	80		
49	Albert Langlois	6	8	10	12	25	50	60	150
50	Jim Neilson	8	10	12	15	30	80		
51	Larry Cahan	6	8	10	12	25	50	60	150
52	Andy Bathgate	8	10	12	15	30	80	100	225
53	Don McKenney	8	10	12	15	25	50		
54	Vic Hadfield	8	10	12	15	30	80	100	175
55	Earl Ingarfield	6	8	10	12	25	50		
56	Camille Henry	6	8	10	12	25	50		
57	Rod Gilbert	15	20	25	30	40	100		
58	Phil Goyette	8	10	12	15	30	80	100	250
59	Don Marshall	8	10	12	15	30	60	80	150
60	Dick Meissner	6	8	10	12	25	50		
61	Val Fonteyne	6	8	10	12	25	50		
62	Ken Schinkel	8	10	12	15	25	50		
63	Jean Ratelle	15	20	25	30	40	80	100	300
64	Don Johns	6	8	10	12	25	50		
65	Rangers Team	20	25	30	40	50	125		
66	Checklist Card	40	50	80	100	200	400		

—Ab McDonald #37 PSA 9 (Mt) sold for $255 (eBay; 05/08)
—Glenn Hall #23 PSA 10 (GEM) sold for $3,195 (eBay; 4/16)
—Chico Maki #41 PSA 9 (Mt) sold for $365.28 (eBay; 5/12)
—Billy Reay #22 PSA 10 (GEM) sold for $1092 (eBay; 2/14)

1964-65 Topps

#	Player	VG 3	VgEx 4	EX 5	ExMt 6	NM 7	NmMt 8	NmMt+ 8.5	MT 9
1	Pit Martin RC	50	60	100	125	250	600	800	
2	Gilles Tremblay	12	15	20	25	50	225		
3	Terry Harper	12	15	20	30	80	150		
4	John Ferguson	20	25	30	40	60	120	250	
5	Elmer Vasko	10	12	15	20	60	150		
6	Terry Sawchuk UER	30	40	60	80	150	300		
7	Bill(Red) Hay	10	12	15	25	60	200		
8	Gary Bergman RC	15	25	40	70	100	300		
9	Doug Barkley	10	12	15	20	50	120	175	400
10	Bob McCord	10	12	15	20	50	100	150	400
11	Parker MacDonald	10	12	15	25	50	120		
12	Glenn Hall	25	30	50	100	200	350		
13	Albert Langlois	10	12	15	20	50	150		

	VG 3	VgEx 4	EX 5	ExMt 6	NM 7	NmMt 8	NmMt+ 8.5	MT 9
Camille Henry	20	30	50	80	150	350		
Norm Ullman	15	20	25	40	60	150		
Ab McDonald	10	15	25	40	60	120		
Charlie Hodge	10	12	15	20	60	175		
Orland Kurtenbach	10	12	15	25	60	150		
Dean Prentice	10	12	15	20	50	100		
Bobby Hull	100	150	200	350	500	800		
Ed Johnston	12	15	20	25	50	150		
Denis DeJordy	10	12	15	25	50	175		
Claude Provost	10	12	15	20	60	120		
Rod Gilbert	20	25	30	50	80	200		
Doug Mohns	10	12	25	40	60	100	150	300
Al McNeil	10	12	20	▲30	▲80	▲150		
Billy Harris	12	15	30	60	175	400		
Ken Wharram	12	15	25	50	120	400		
George Sullivan	10	12	15	20	50	80		
John McKenzie	10	12	15	40	50	100	150	450
Stan Mikita	40	50	60	100	150	300		
Ted Green	12	15	25	80	150	450		
Jean Beliveau	50	60	100	200	300	1,000		
Arnie Brown	10	12	15	20	50	100	150	400
Reg Fleming	10	12	15	20	40	120	175	400
Jim Mikol	10	12	15	20	50	80	125	400
Dave Balon	10	12	15	20	50	100		
Billy Reay CO	10	12	15	20	50	100	150	400
Marcel Pronovost	20	30	40	60	150	800		
Johnny Bower	25	30	40	50	80	175		
Wayne Hillman	10	12	15	20	50	80	125	700
Floyd Smith	10	12	15	25	50	80		
Toe Blake CO	15	20	25	▲50	▲100	▲200		
Red Kelly	15	20	25	30	50	120	175	400
Punch Imlach CO	15	20	25	30	50	120		
Dick Duff	15	20	25	30	50	120	150	250
Roger Crozier RC	25	30	40	60	100	225		
Henri Richard	40	60	100	150	250	1,200		
Larry Jeffrey	10	12	15	20	50	100		
Leo Boivin	10	12	15	20	50	100		
Ed Westfall	12	20	40	80	175	400		
Jean-Guy Talbot	10	12	15	20	40	135	175	400
Jacques Laperriere	12	15	20	25	50	135	175	500
1st Checklist	100	120	150	225	300	1,000		
2nd Checklist	120	200	350	600	1,200	1,500		
Ron Murphy	25	30	40	80	175	300		
Bob Baun	25	30	40	50	100	250		
Tom Williams SP	60	80	100	200	750	1,000		
Pierre Pilote SP	100	120	150	250	400	800		
Bob Pulford	25	30	35	50	100	250		
Red Berenson	25	30	35	50	100	200		
Vic Hadfield	25	30	35	50	100	300		
Bob Leiter	25	30	40	50	80	225		
Jim Pappin RC	25	30	40	60	150	250		
Earl Ingarfield	25	30	40	60	120	600		
Lou Angotti RC	25	30	40	60	175	600		
Rod Seiling RC	25	30	35	50	120	400		
Jacques Plante	60	80	100	175	250	500		
George Armstrong UER	40	50	60	80	120	250		
Milt Schmidt CO	25	30	35	50	100	250		
Eddie Shack	40	50	60	100	250	500		
Gary Dornhoefer SP RC	80	100	150	250	500	800		
Chico Maki SP	80	125	150	250	325	700		
Gilles Villemure SP	80	100	125	200	400	600		
Carl Brewer	25	30	35	50	100	300		
Bruce MacGregor	25	30	40	60	120	400		
Bob Nevin	25	30	40	60	120	300		
Ralph Backstrom	30	35	50	80	150	300		
Murray Oliver	25	30	40	60	100	250		
Bobby Rousseau SP	60	80	125	200	400			
Don McKenney	25	30	40	60	125	400		
Ted Lindsay	30	40	50	80	150	400		
Harry Howell	25	30	40	60	120	500		
Doug Robinson	25	30	40	60	120	300		
Frank Mahovlich	40	50	60	120	200	400		
Andy Bathgate	25	30	50	80	150	300		
Phil Goyette	25	30	40	60	100	250		
J.C. Tremblay	25	30	40	60	100	300		
Gordie Howe	200	250	300	400	600	1,750		
Murray Balfour	25	30	40	60	120	300		
Eric Nesterenko SP	60	100	120	175	400	1,000		
Marcel Paille SP RC	100	150	225	300	600	1,200		
Sid Abel CO	25	30	50	80	120	300		
Dave Keon	40	50	60	100	200	400		
Alex Delvecchio	30	40	50	80	150	400		
Bill Gadsby	25	30	40	60	175	350		
Don Marshall	25	30	35	50	100	500		
Bill Hicke SP	100	120	150	175	400	600		
Ron Stewart	25	30	40	60	120	300		
Johnny Bucyk	30	40	50	80	200	450		
Tom Johnson	25	30	35	50	100	250		
Tim Horton	70	80	100	150	350	700		

		VG 3	VgEx 4	EX 5	ExMt 6	NM 7	NmMt 8	NmMt+ 8.5	MT 9
103	Jim Neilson	25	30	35	50	100	250		
104	Allan Stanley	25	30	35	60	135	400		
105	Tim Horton AS SP	120	150	225	350	600	1,200		
106	Stan Mikita AS SP	100	120	150	250	400	750		
107	Bobby Hull AS	60	80	125	200	300	650		
108	Ken Wharram AS	25	30	40	60	150	500		
109	Pierre Pilote AS	25	30	40	80	120	250		
110	Glenn Hall AS	50	60	75	150	300	1,000		

—George Armstrong UER #69 PSA 9 sold for $698 (eBay; 12/15)
—Ralph Backstrom #78 PSA 9 sold for $483 (eBay; 2/07)
—Bob Baun #57 PSA 10 (Gem) sold for $4,207 (Memory Lane; 9/07)
—Toe Blake CO #43 PSA 9 (MT) sold for $359.10 (eBay; 3/16)
—Leo Boivin #50 PSA 9 sold for $491 (eBay; 12/15)
—Johnny Bucyk #100 PSA 9 (MT) sold for $1,617 (Memory Lane; 4/07)
—Checklist Card #54 PSA 9 (MT) sold for $3,271 (Memory Lane; 12/06)
—2nd Checklist Card #55 PSA 8.5 (NmMt+) sold for $2,032 (eBay; 9/12)
—John Ferguson #4 PSA 9 (MT) sold for $1,042 (eBay; 3/07)
—Ted Green #32 PSA 8 (NmMt) sold for $890 (eBay; 2/07)
—Terry Harper #3 PSA 10 (Gem) sold for $1,789 (Memory Lane; 12/13)
—Terry Harper #3 PSA 9 (MT) sold for $519 (eBay; 12/06)
—Camille Henry #14 PSA 9 sold for $1,949 (eBay; 11/15)
—Wayne Hillman #41 PSA 9 sold for $545 (eBay; 12/06)
—Charlie Hodge #17 PSA 9 sold for $498 (eBay; 3/07)
—Harry Howell #83 PSA 9 sold for $1,013 (Goodwin; 2/07)
—Punch Imlach CO #45 PSA 9 (MT) sold for $607 (eBay; 12/06)
—Tom Johnson #101 PSA 9 sold for $1,241 (eBay; 9/12)
—Ed Johnston #21 PSA 9 (MT) sold for $775 (eBay; 6/12)
—Ed Johnston #21 PSA 9 (MT) sold for $675 (eBay; 3/16)
—Dave Keon #94 PSA 9 (MT) sold for $678.88 (eBay; 2/16)
—Bob Leiter #63 PSA 9 (MT) sold for $1,184 (Memory Lane; 6/12)
—Parker MacDonald #11 PSA 9 (MT) sold for $1,187 (Memory Lane; 4/07)
—Frank Mahovlich #85 PSA 9 (MT) sold for $2,563 (eBay; 9/12)
—Pit Martin #1 SGC 9 (MT) sold for $1,549 (Goodwin; 3/12)
—Jim Pappin #64 PSA 9 (MT) sold for $1,305 (Memory Lane; 4/07)
—Claude Provost #23 PSA 9 (MT) sold for $593 (eBay; 2/16)
—Bob Pulford #60 PSA 9 (MT) sold for $470 (eBay; 12/15)
—Terry Sawchuk #6 PSA 9 (MT) sold for $1,504 (eBay; 6/12)
—Milt Schmidt CO #70 PSA 9 (MT) sold for $888 (eBay; 2/16)
—Gilles Tremblay #2 PSA 9 (MT) sold for $1,435 (Memory Lane; 4/07)
—Norm Ullman #15 PSA 9 (MT) sold for $1,609 (eBay; 12/15)
—Ken Wharram AS #108 PSA 8.5 (NM MT+) sold for $569.99 (eBay; 12/15)
—Ken Wharram #28 PSA 9 (MT) sold for $1,024 (eBay; 3/16)

1965-66 Topps

		VG 3	VgEx 4	EX 5	ExMt 6	NM 7	NmMt 8	NmMt+ 8.5	MT 9
1	Toe Blake CO	25	35	40	60	150	700		
2	Gump Worsley	15	20	25	40	125	400		
3	Jacques Laperriere	6	8	10	12	25	60	80	135
4	Jean-Guy Talbot	6	8	10	20	50	200		
5	Ted Harris	6	8	20	50	80	200		
6	Jean Beliveau	25	30	35	50	80	150	200	400
7	Dick Duff	6	8	10	15	30	100		
8	Claude Provost DP	6	8	10	12	25	60		
9	Red Berenson	6	8	10	12	25	80		
10	John Ferguson	6	8	10	12	30	60		
11	Punch Imlach CO	6	8	10	12	40	120		
12	Terry Sawchuk	25	30	35	50	80	150	225	350
13	Bob Baun	6	8	10	12	25	50	80	150
14	Kent Douglas	6	8	10	12	25	60	80	150
15	Red Kelly	10	12	15	20	30	80	100	175
16	Jim Pappin	6	8	10	12	25	60	80	120
17	Dave Keon	15	20	25	30	60	100		
18	Bob Pulford	6	8	10	12	25	100		
19	George Armstrong	8	10	12	15	30	80	100	175
20	Orland Kurtenbach	6	8	10	12	25	60	80	150
21	Ed Giacomin RC	40	50	80	120	200	500		1,200
22	Harry Howell	6	8	10	12	25	60		500
23	Rod Seiling	6	8	10	12	25	80		
24	Mike McMahon	6	8	10	12	25	60		
25	Jean Ratelle	12	15	20	25	40	100		200
26	Doug Robinson	6	8	10	12	30	80		
27	Vic Hadfield	6	8	10	12	25	60	80	120
28	Garry Peters UER RC	6	8	10	12	25	60	80	120
29	Don Marshall	6	8	10	12	25	60	80	120
30	Bill Hicke	6	8	10	12	25	60	80	120
31	Gerry Cheevers RC	80	100	125	200	300	500		
32	Leo Boivin	6	8	10	12	25	60		
33	Albert Langlois	6	8	10	12	25	60		
34	Murray Oliver DP	6	8	10	12	25	60	80	150
35	Tom Williams	6	8	10	12	25	60	80	120
36	Ron Schock	6	8	10	12	25	100		
37	Ed Westfall	6	8	10	12	25	60		
38	Gary Dornhoefer	6	8	10	12	25	60		
39	Bob Dillabough	6	8	10	12	25	80		
40	Paul Popiel	6	8	10	12	25	60	80	150
41	Sid Abel CO	6	8	10	12	25	60		
42	Roger Crozier	6	8	10	15	30	100		
43	Doug Barkley	6	8	10	12	25	125		
44	Bill Gadsby	6	8	10	12	25	60	100	175

#	Player	VG 3	VgEx 4	EX 5	ExMt 6	NM 7	NmMt 8	NmMt+ 8.5	MT 9
45	Bryan Watson RC	8	10	12	15	30	80	100	200
46	Bob McCord	6	8	10	12	25	60		
47	Alex Delvecchio	8	10	12	15	30	80		
48	Andy Bathgate	8	10	12	15	30	80	100	300
49	Norm Ullman	8	10	12	15	30	100		
50	Ab McDonald	6	8	10	12	25	60		200
51	Paul Henderson RC	20	25	40	60	350	600		1,200
52	Pit Martin	6	8	10	12	25	60		
53	Billy Harris DP	6	8	10	12	25	80		
54	Billy Reay CO	6	8	15	20	25	60	100	200
55	Glenn Hall	15	20	30	50	120	400		
56	Pierre Pilote	8	10	12	15	30	100	120	200
57	Al McNeil	6	8	10	12	25	80		
58	Camille Henry	6	8	10	12	25	60	80	120
59	Bobby Hull	60	80	100	125	150	300	400	500
60	Stan Mikita	25	30	35	50	60	120	150	250
61	Ken Wharram	6	8	10	25	50	120		
62	Bill(Red) Hay	6	8	10	12	25	60		
63	Fred Stanfield RC	6	8	10	12	25	60	80	120
64	Dennis Hull RC DP	15	20	25	40	80	120	175	300
65	Ken Hodge RC	25	30	35	50	200	500		
66	Checklist Card	40	80	120	175	250	450		
67	Charlie Hodge	6	8	10	15	30	100		
68	Terry Harper	6	8	10	12	25	60		
69	J.C. Tremblay	6	8	10	12	25	100		
70	Bobby Rousseau DP	6	8	10	12	25	60		
71	Henri Richard	25	30	35	50	80	150	175	300
72	Dave Balon	6	8	10	12	25	60		
73	Ralph Backstrom	6	8	10	12	25	60	100	175
74	Jim Roberts RC	6	8	10	12	25	60		200
75	Claude Larose	6	8	10	12	25	60	80	150
76	Y.Cournoyer UER RC DP	▲50	▲80	▲100	▲200	▲350	500		
77	Johnny Bower DP	12	15	20	25	40	100	150	350
78	Carl Brewer	6	8	10	12	25	80	120	225
79	Tim Horton	25	30	35	50	100	250		
80	Marcel Pronovost	6	8	10	12	25	60		
81	Frank Mahovlich	25	30	35	50	80	120	175	300
82	Ron Ellis RC	15	20	25	40	60	150		
83	Larry Jeffrey	6	8	10	12	25	60	80	120
84	Peter Stemkowski RC	6	8	10	12	25	60	100	400
85	Eddie Joyal	6	8	10	12	25	60		120
86	Mike Walton RC	6	8	10	12	25	60	80	150
87	George Sullivan	6	8	10	12	25	60		
88	Don Simmons	6	8	10	12	25	60	100	175
89	Jim Neilson	6	8	10	12	25	60		
90	Arnie Brown	6	8	10	12	25	60		
91	Rod Gilbert	12	15	20	25	40	100	150	300
92	Phil Goyette	6	8	10	12	25	100		
93	Bob Nevin	6	8	10	12	25	60	100	175
94	John McKenzie	6	8	10	12	25	60	80	150
95	Ted Taylor RC	6	8	10	12	25	60		
96	Milt Schmidt CO DP	6	8	10	▲25	▲50	▲100	▲200	400
97	Ed Johnston	6	8	10	15	40	120		
98	Ted Green	6	8	10	15	40	120		
99	Don Awrey RC	6	8	10	20	50	200		
100	Bob Woytowich DP	6	8	10	12	25	60	100	250
101	Johnny Bucyk	10	12	15	20	50	100		
102	Dean Prentice	6	8	10	12	25	60		
103	Ron Stewart	6	8	10	12	25	60		
104	Reg Fleming	6	8	10	15	50	200		
105	Parker MacDonald	6	8	10	15	40	120		
106	Hank Bassen	6	8	10	12	25	60	80	150
107	Gary Bergman	6	8	10	12	25	60	80	250
108	Gordie Howe DP	40	50	60	100	175	600		
109	Floyd Smith	6	8	10	12	25	60		
110	Bruce MacGregor	6	8	10	12	25	60	80	150
111	Ron Murphy	6	8	10	12	25	80		
112	Don McKenney	6	8	10	12	25	60		
113	Denis DeJordy DP	6	8	10	12	25	60	100	250
114	Elmer Vasko	6	8	10	12	50	120		
115	Matt Ravlich	6	8	10	12	25	60	100	200
116	Phil Esposito RC	150	200	300	400	700	1,000	1,800	4,500
117	Chico Maki	6	8	10	12	25	60		
118	Doug Mohns	6	8	10	12	25	80		
119	Eric Nesterenko	6	8	10	12	25	60	100	250
120	Pat Stapleton	6	8	10	12	25	75	100	250
121	Checklist Card	50	75	125	200	250	400		
122	Gordie Howe 600 SP	125	200	225	250	400	800		
123	Toronto Maple Leafs SP	20	25	30	60	100	175		
124	Chicago Blackhawks SP	20	25	30	60	80	150		
125	Detroit Red Wings SP	30	40	50	80	150	350		
126	Montreal Canadiens SP	30	40	50	80	100	150	250	750
127	New York Rangers SP	30	40	50	80	200			
128	Boston Bruins SP	60	▲100	▲150	▲250	▲300	▲450		

—Toe Blake CO #1 PSA 9 (Mint) sold for $390 (eBay; 1/16)
—Gerry Cheevers #31 SGC 9 (Mint) sold for $3,149 (Goodwin; 3/12)
—Gerry Cheevers #31 PSA 9 (Mint) sold for $3,715 (eBay; 2/16)
—Yvan Cournoyer #76 PSA 10 (Gem) sold for $3,269 (eBay; 12/11)
—Yvan Cournoyer #76 PSA 9 (Mint) sold for $2,756 (eBay; 3/14)
—Yvan Cournoyer #76 PSA 9 (Mint) sold for $2,632.89 (eBay; 4/16)
—Kent Douglas #14 PSA 10 (Gem) sold for $426.99 (eBay; 3/16)
—Ron Ellis #82 PSA 10 (Gem) sold for $818 (eBay; 3/13)
—Ed Giacomin #21 SGC 8.5 (NrMt+) sold for $1,627 (Goodwin; 3/12)
—Phil Doyette #92 PSA 9 (Mint) sold for $415 (eBay; 3/16)

—Paul Henderson #51 PSA 9 (MT) sold for $1,419 (eBay; 10/15)
—Punch Imlach CO #11 PSA 8.5 (NrMt+) sold for $293.98 (eBay; 12/15)
—Pit Martin #53 PSA 10 (Gem) sold for $556.99 (eBay; 3/16)
—Mike McMahon #24 PSA 10 (Gem) sold for $528 (eBay; 2/07)
—Terry Sawchuk #12 SGC 9 (Mint) sold for $382 (Goodwin; 3/12)
—Pat Stapleton #120 PSA 9 (Mint) sold for $323 (eBay; 3/08)
—Peter Stemkowski #84 PSA 10 (Gem) sold for $719 (eBay; 3/16)
—George Sullivan #87 PSA 9 (Mint) sold for $388 (eBay; 3/08)
—Ted Taylor #95 PSA 9 (MT) sold for $278 (eBay; 12/06)

1966-67 Topps

#	Player	VG 3	VgEx 4	EX 5	ExMt 6	NM 7	NmMt 8	NmMt+ 8.5	MT
1	Toe Blake CO	25	30	40	80	500	1,250		
2	Gump Worsley	12	20	30	40	135	750		
3	Jean-Guy Talbot	6	8	10	40	150	▲800		
4	Gilles Tremblay	6	8	10	15	40	120		
5	J.C. Tremblay	8	10	12	20	50	200		
6	Jim Roberts	8	10	15	30	80			
7	Bobby Rousseau	6	8	10	15	100	250		
8	Henri Richard	20	25	30	50	80	350		
9	Claude Provost	6	8	10	12	40	200		
10	Claude Larose	8	10	12	15	60	300		
11	Punch Imlach CO	8	10	12	15	40	300		
12	Johnny Bower	15	20	25	30	80	400		
13	Terry Sawchuk	30	40	50	60	80	250		
14	Mike Walton	8	10	12	15	40	120		
15	Pete Stemkowski	6	8	10	15	30	120		
16	Allan Stanley	8	10	12	15	40	120		
17	Eddie Shack	20	25	30	40	60	150		
18	Brit Selby RC	8	10	12	15	40	100		
19	Bob Pulford	8	10	12	15	40	100		
20	Marcel Pronovost	8	10	12	15	40	250		
21	Emile Francis RC CO	12	15	20	25	60	350		
22	Rod Seiling	6	8	10	15	30	100		
23	Ed Giacomin	30	40	50	60	100	250		
24	Don Marshall	8	10	12	15	40	100		
25	Orland Kurtenbach	6	8	10	15	100	600		
26	Rod Gilbert	12	15	20	25	60	200		
27	Bob Nevin	6	8	10	15	30	100		
28	Phil Goyette	6	8	10	15	30	100		
29	Jean Ratelle	12	15	20	25	60	135		
30	Earl Ingarfield	6	8	10	15	30	300		
31	Harry Sinden RC CO	25	30	40	50	150	400		
32	Ed Westfall	8	10	12	15	40	150		
33	Joe Watson RC	8	10	12	15	40	150		
34	Bob Woytowich	6	8	10	15	30	100		
35	Bobby Orr RC	2,000	▲2,750	▲3,250	▲4,250	6,500	22,000		
36	Gilles Marotte RC	8	10	12	20	60	175		
37	Ted Green	8	10	12	15	40	200		
38	Tom Williams	6	8	10	15	30	200		
39	Johnny Bucyk	15	20	25	40	60	150		
40	Wayne Connelly	6	8	10	15	60	400		
41	Pit Martin	8	10	12	15	40	100		
42	Sid Abel CO	6	8	10	30	50	120		
43	Roger Crozier	8	10	12	15	40	200		
44	Andy Bathgate	8	10	12	15	40	120		
45	Dean Prentice	6	8	10	15	30	175		
46	Paul Henderson	10	12	15	20	80	150		
47	Gary Bergman	6	8	10	15	30	100		
48	Bryan Watson	8	10	12	15	40	120		
49	Bob Wall	6	8	10	15	30	150		
50	Leo Boivin	8	10	12	15	40	120		
51	Bert Marshall	6	10	15	25	150	350		
52	Norm Ullman	10	12	15	20	50	100		
53	Billy Reay CO	8	10	12	15	40	120		
54	Glenn Hall	15	20	25	30	60	300		
55	Wally Boyer	6	8	10	15	30	200		
56	Fred Stanfield	6	8	10	15	40	150		
57	Pat Stapleton	8	10	12	15	40	150		
58	Matt Ravlich	6	8	10	15	30	100		
59	Pierre Pilote	8	10	12	15	40	120		
60	Eric Nesterenko	8	10	12	15	40	200		
61	Doug Mohns	8	10	12	15	40	100		
62	Stan Mikita	25	30	40	50	100	400		
63	Phil Esposito	40	50	60	100	150	300		
64	Bobby Hull LL	40	50	60	100	200	450		
65	C.Hodge/Worsley	15	20	25	30	80	300		
66	Checklist Card	100	125	200	400	500	2,000		
67	Jacques Laperriere	8	10	12	15	100	400		
68	Terry Harper	6	8	10	15	30	135		
69	Ted Harris	6	8	10	15	30	120		
70	John Ferguson	8	10	12	25	80	300		
71	Dick Duff	8	10	12	20	60	120		
72	Yvan Cournoyer	25	30	40	50	100	200		
73	Jean Beliveau	30	40	50	60	150	300		
74	Dave Balon	6	8	10	15	30	100		
75	Ralph Backstrom	8	10	12	15	40	120		
76	Jim Pappin	6	8	10	15	40	100		
77	Frank Mahovlich	20	25	30	40	80	600		

HOCKEY

	VG 3	VgEx 4	EX 5	ExMt 6	NM 7	NmMt 8	NmMt+ 8.5	MT 9
Dave Keon	20	25	30	40	80	200		
Red Kelly	12	15	20	25	50	100		
Tim Horton	25	30	40	50	80	200		
Ron Ellis	8	10	12	15	50	100		
Kent Douglas	6	8	10	15	40	150		
Bob Baun	8	10	15	15	50	100		
George Armstrong	10	12	15	20	50	120		
Bernie Geoffrion	15	20	25	30	50	250		
Vic Hadfield	8	10	12	15	40	200		
Wayne Hillman	6	8	10	15	30	120		
Jim Neilson	6	8	10	15	30	120		
Al McNeil	6	8	10	15	30	120		
Arnie Brown	6	8	10	15	30	200		
Harry Howell	8	10	12	15	40	120		
Red Berenson	8	10	12	15	40	100		
Reg Fleming	6	8	10	15	30	100		
Ron Stewart	6	8	10	15	30	120		
Murray Oliver	6	8	10	15	30	200		
Ron Murphy	6	8	10	15	30	100		
John McKenzie	8	10	12	15	50	200		
Bob Dillabough	6	8	10	15	30	100		
Ed Johnston	8	10	12	15	40	100		
Ron Schock	6	8	10	15	40	450		
Dallas Smith	6	8	10	15	30	100		
Alex Delvecchio	15	20	30	40	60	200		
Peter Mahovlich RC	20	25	30	40	80	200		
Bruce MacGregor	6	8	10	15	30	300		
Murray Hall	6	8	10	15	30	100		
Floyd Smith	6	8	10	15	30	120		
Hank Bassen	8	10	12	15	40	175		
Val Fonteyne	6	8	10	15	30	100		
Gordie Howe	80	100	150	250	350	1,500		
Chico Maki	6	8	10	15	30	175		
Doug Jarrett	6	8	12	20	60	150		
Bobby Hull	50	60	80	125	200	400		
Dennis Hull	8	10	12	15	60	200		
Ken Hodge	10	12	15	20	50	200		
Denis DeJordy	8	10	12	15	40	100		
Lou Angotti	6	8	10	15	30	150		
Ken Wharram	6	8	10	15	30	150		
Montreal Canadiens/Team Card	15	20	25	40	100	250		
Detroit Red Wings/Team Card	15	20	25	30	80	400		
Checklist Card	100	125	200	300	500			
Gordie Howe AS	40	50	60	80	225	700		
Jacques Laperriere AS	8	10	12	30	80	300		
Pierre Pilote AS	8	10	12	15	40	500		
Stan Mikita AS	15	20	▲50	▲100	▲250	▲350		
Bobby Hull AS	40	50	60	80	100	250		
Glenn Hall AS	20	25	30	40	80	250		
Jean Beliveau AS	20	25	40	80	150	500		
Allan Stanley AS	8	10	15	25	80	500		
Pat Stapleton AS	8	10	12	20	175	400		
Gump Worsley AS	20	25	30	60	150	350		
Frank Mahovlich AS	25	30	50	100	400			
Bobby Rousseau AS	25	30	40	120	400	2,500		

Andy Bathgate #44 PSA 9 (MT) sold for $891 (ebay; 3/14)
-Jean Beliveau #73 PSA 8.5 (NmMt+) sold for $1,500 (ebay; 3/14)
-Jean Beliveau AS #127 PSA 8 (NmMT) sold for $1,149 (Memory Lane; 9/07)
-Wally Boyer #55 PSA 9 (Mint) sold for $829 (eBay; 3/16)
-Gerry Cheevers #31 PSA 10 (Gem) sold for $3,558 (eBay; 5/09)
-Wayne Connelly #40 PSA 8 (NmMt) sold for $774 (eBay; 5/12)
-Denis DeJordy #115 PSA 9 (MT) sold for $1,812 (Mile High; 10/15)
-Bernie Geoffrion #85 PSA 9 (MT) sold for $3,630 (Mile High; 10/15)
-Bobby Hull AS #125 PSA 9 (MT) sold for $1,834 (eBay; 10/15)
-Doug Jarrett #111 PSA 9 (MT) sold for $1,994 (Mile High; 10/15)
-Frank Mahovlich AS #131 PSA 8 (NmMt) sold for $1,278 (eBay; 4/12)
-Al McNeil #89 PSA 9 (Mint) sold for $844.95 (eBay; 3/16)
-Stan Mikita AS #124 PSA 9 (MT) sold for $2,948 (Mile High; 10/15)
-Bobby Orr #35 PSA 9 (MT) sold for $47,923 (Mastro; 4/07)
-Bobby Orr #35 BGS 9.5 (GEM) sold for $5,789.44 (eBay; 5/12)
-Pierre Pilote AS #123 PSA 9 (Mt) sold for $3,537 (Mile High; 10/15)
-Pierre Pilote AS #123 PSA 9 (Mt) sold for $1,118.88 (eBay; 1/16)
--Jim Roberts #6 PSA 9 (MT) sold for $2,228 (Mile High; 10/15)
-Bobby Rousseau #132 PSA 8 (NmMt) sold for $2,720 (eBay; 1/13)
- Terry Sawchuk #13 PSA 9 (MT) sold for $1,312 (ebay; 1/14)
- Terry Sawchuk #13 PSA 9 (MT) sold for $1,187 (Memory Lane; 9/07)
-Eddie Shack #17 PSA 9 (MT) sold for $490 (eBay; 7/08)

1967-68 Topps

		VG 3	VgEx 4	EX 5	ExMt 6	NM 7	NmMt 8	NmMt+ 8.5	MT 9
1	Gump Worsley	20	25	35	60	100	300	500	
2	Dick Duff	6	8	10	30	150	500		
3	Jacques Lemaire RC	25	30	60	100	200	350		
4	Claude Larose	8	10	12	15	40	80		
5	Gilles Tremblay	6	8	10	12	25	40	50	120
6	Terry Harper	6	8	10	12	25	40	50	120
7	Jacques Laperriere	6	8	10	12	25	50	60	200
8	Garry Monahan	6	8	10	12	25	40	50	100
9	Carol Vadnais RC	6	8	10	12	25	40	50	100

		VG 3	VgEx 4	EX 5	ExMt 6	NM 7	NmMt 8	NmMt+ 8.5	MT 9
10	Ted Harris	6	8	10	12	25	40	50	100
11	Dave Keon	10	12	15	20	30	60	80	150
12	Pete Stemkowski	6	8	10	12	25	40	50	150
13	Allan Stanley	6	8	10	12	25	40	50	120
14	Ron Ellis	6	8	10	12	25	50	60	150
15	Mike Walton	6	8	10	12	25	40	50	100
16	Tim Horton	15	20	25	30	50	100		
17	Brian Conacher	6	8	10	12	25	40	50	100
18	Bruce Gamble	6	8	10	12	25	40	50	100
19	Bob Pulford	6	8	10	12	25	50		
20	Duane Rupp	6	8	10	12	25	40		
21	Larry Jeffrey	6	8	10	12	25	40		
22	Wayne Hillman	6	8	10	12	25	40		
23	Don Marshall	6	8	10	12	25	50		
24	Red Berenson	6	8	10	12	25	40	50	120
25	Phil Goyette	6	8	10	12	25	40	50	100
26	Camille Henry	6	8	10	12	25	40	50	80
27	Rod Seiling	6	8	10	12	25	40		
28	Bob Nevin	6	8	10	12	25	40	50	120
29	Bernie Geoffrion	15	20	25	30	40	50	60	120
30	Reg Fleming	6	8	10	12	25	40	60	120
31	Jean Ratelle	8	10	12	15	30	50	60	120
32	Phil Esposito	25	30	40	60	80	150	175	300
33	Derek Sanderson RC	30	40	50	80	125	300		
34	Eddie Shack	12	15	20	25	40	60	80	120
35	Ross Lonsberry RC	6	8	10	12	25	50	60	150
36	Fred Stanfield	6	8	10	12	25	40	50	100
37	Don Awrey UER	6	8	10	12	25	40	50	80
38	Glen Sather RC	15	20	25	30	50	100	125	250
39	John McKenzie	6	8	10	12	25	40	50	100
40	Tom Williams	6	8	10	12	25	40	50	100
41	Dallas Smith	6	8	10	12	25	40	60	120
42	Johnny Bucyk	10	12	15	20	30	60	100	175
43	Gordie Howe	30	40	50	80	125	350	450	800
44	Gary Jarrett	6	8	10	12	25	40		
45	Dean Prentice	6	8	10	12	25	40		
46	Bert Marshall	6	8	10	12	25	40		
47	Gary Bergman	6	8	10	12	25	40	60	120
48	Roger Crozier	6	8	10	12	25	50		
49	Howie Young	6	8	10	12	25	40	50	100
50	Doug Roberts	6	8	10	12	25	40	60	120
51	Alex Delvecchio	10	12	15	20	30	60		
52	Floyd Smith	6	8	10	12	25	40	60	120
53	Doug Shelton	6	8	10	12	25	40		
54	Gerry Goyer	6	8	10	12	25	40	50	150
55	Wayne Maki	6	8	10	12	25	40	60	120
56	Dennis Hull	6	8	10	12	25	50		
57	Dave Dryden RC	8	10	12	15	30	60	80	200
58	Paul Terbenche	6	8	10	12	25	40	50	200
59	Gilles Marotte	6	8	10	12	25	40	60	120
60	Eric Nesterenko	6	8	10	12	25	50	60	120
61	Pat Stapleton	6	8	10	12	30	60	80	120
62	Pierre Pilote	6	8	10	12	25	40		
63	Doug Mohns	6	8	10	12	25	40		
64	Stan Mikita Triple	15	20	25	30	50	100		
65	G.Hall/D.DeJordy	10	12	15	20	30	60		
66	Checklist Card	50	60	100	150	250	450		
67	Ralph Backstrom	6	8	10	12	25	50		
68	Bobby Rousseau	6	8	10	12	25	40	60	120
69	John Ferguson	6	8	10	15	30	80	100	200
70	Yvan Cournoyer	15	20	25	30	50	80	100	200
71	Claude Provost	6	8	10	12	25	40	60	120
72	Henri Richard	12	15	20	25	40	80	100	200
73	J.C. Tremblay	6	8	10	12	25	50	60	150
74	Jean Beliveau	20	25	30	40	60	135	150	350
75	Rogatien Vachon RC	25	30	40	60	125	300	300	800
76	Johnny Bower	10	12	15	20	30	80	100	200
77	Wayne Carleton	6	8	10	12	25	40	60	120
78	Jim Pappin	6	8	10	12	25	40	50	100
79	Frank Mahovlich	12	15	20	25	40	100	120	200
80	Larry Hillman	6	8	10	12	25	40	50	100
81	Marcel Pronovost	6	8	10	12	25	60	80	120
82	Murray Oliver	6	8	10	12	25	40	60	120
83	George Armstrong	8	10	12	15	30	50	60	100
84	Harry Howell	6	8	10	12	25	40	60	100
85	Ed Giacomin	15	20	25	30	40	80	100	175
86	Gilles Villemure	6	8	10	12	40	80	100	150
87	Orland Kurtenbach	6	8	10	12	25	40	50	80
88	Vic Hadfield	6	8	10	12	25	40	50	100
89	Arnie Brown	6	8	10	12	25	40	60	120
90	Rod Gilbert	8	10	12	15	30	80	100	175
91	Jim Neilson	6	8	10	12	25	40	50	100
92	Bobby Orr	250	400	500	600	800	▲2,250	▲3,000	5,500
93	Skip Krake UER RC	6	8	10	12	25	40	50	100
94	Ted Green	6	8	10	12	25	40	50	100
95	Ed Westfall	6	8	10	12	25	40	50	100
96	Ed Johnston	6	8	10	12	25	40	50	100
97	Gary Doak RC	6	8	10	12	25	40	50	100
98	Ken Hodge	6	8	10	12	25	50		

#	Player	VG 3	VgEx 4	EX 5	ExMt 6	NM 7	NmMt 8	NmMt+ 8.5	MT 9
99	Gerry Cheevers	20	25	30	40	60	100	120	250
100	Ron Murphy	6	8	10	12	25	40	50	100
101	Norm Ullman	8	10	12	15	30	50	60	100
102	Bruce MacGregor	6	8	10	12	25	40	50	100
103	Paul Henderson	6	8	10	12	25	50		
104	Jean-Guy Talbot	6	8	10	12	25	40	60	120
105	Bart Crashley	6	8	10	12	25	40	50	100
106	Roy Edwards	6	8	10	12	25	50	60	135
107	Jim Watson	6	8	10	12	25	40	50	100
108	Ted Hampson	6	8	10	12	30	100		
109	Bill Orban	6	8	10	12	25	40	50	100
110	Geoffrey Powis	6	8	10	12	25	40	50	150
111	Chico Maki	6	8	10	12	25	40	50	100
112	Doug Jarrett	6	8	10	12	25	40	50	135
113	Bobby Hull	30	40	50	80	▲150	200	250	800
114	Stan Mikita	20	25	30	40	60	120	150	300
115	Denis DeJordy	6	8	10	12	25	40	50	100
116	Pit Martin	6	8	10	12	25	50		
117	Ken Wharram	6	8	10	12	25	40	50	100
118	Bobby Orr Calder	80	100	125	200	300	500	600	800
119	Harry Howell Norris	6	8	10	12	25	40	60	135
120	Checklist Card	60	80	100	150	250	400	500	800
121	Harry Howell AS	6	8	10	12	25	40	50	175
122	Pierre Pilote AS	6	8	10	12	30	60	75	120
123	Ed Giacomin AS	8	10	12	15	30	50	60	120
124	Bobby Hull AS	30	40	50	60	100	150	175	300
125	Ken Wharram AS	6	8	10	12	25	40	60	120
126	Stan Mikita AS	12	15	20	25	40	80	120	250
127	Tim Horton AS	10	12	15	20	30	80	100	150
128	Bobby Orr AS	125	150	200	250	▲350	▲500	▲800	▲1,500
129	Glenn Hall AS	10	12	15	20	30	50	60	120
130	Don Marshall AS	6	8	10	12	25	40	50	200
131	Gordie Howe AS	30	40	50	80	125	200	250	400
132	Norm Ullman AS	10	12	15	20	40	175		

—Checklist Card #66 PSA 9 (Mint) sold for $1,013 (eBay; 3/16)
—Ron Ellis #14 PSA 9 (Mint) sold for $365 (eBay; 3/08)
—Reg Flemming #30 PSA 10 (Gem) sold for $434 (eBay; 2/14)
—Harry Howell #84 PSA 10 (Gem) sold for $505 (eBay; 10/08)
—Harry Howell Norris #119 PSA 10 (Gem) sold for $640 (eBay; 8/12)
—Bruce MacGregor ##102 PSA 10 (Gem) sold for $364.44 (eBay; 2/16)
—Stan Mikita AS #126 PSA 10 (Gem) sold for $571.20 (Mile High 5/12)
—Bobby Orr AS #128 PSA 10 (Gem) sold for $6,655 (eBay; 2/12)
—Pierre Pilote AS #122 PSA 10 (Gem) sold for $711 (eBay; 8/07)
—Jean Ratelle #31 PSA 10 (Gem) sold for $298.98 (eBay; 8/12)
—Fred Stanfield #36 PSA 9 (Mint) sold for $359 (eBay; 3/08)
—J.C. Tremblay #73 PSA 10 (Gem) sold for $1,034 (eBay; 3/16)

1968-69 O-Pee-Chee

#	Player	VG 3	VgEx 4	EX 5	ExMt 6	NM 7	NmMt 8	NmMt+ 8.5	MT 9
1	Doug Harvey	25	30	40	80	350	400		
2	Bobby Orr	150	200	300	450	1,600			
3	Don Awrey UER	6	8	10	15	30	60		
4	Ted Green	6	8	10	15	30	60		
5	Johnny Bucyk	10	15	50	80	150			
6	Derek Sanderson	20	25	30	40	60	120		
7	Phil Esposito	20	25	30	40	60	120		
8	Ken Hodge	6	8	10	15	40	175		
9	John McKenzie	6	8	10	15	30	60	80	150
10	Fred Stanfield	6	8	10	20	30	80		
11	Tom Williams	6	8	10	15	30	50	60	175
12	Denis DeJordy	6	8	10	15	60	200		
13	Doug Jarrett	6	8	10	15	30	60		
14	Gilles Marotte	6	8	10	15	30	60		
15	Pat Stapleton	6	8	10	15	40	125		
16	Bobby Hull	30	40	50	60	150	250		
17	Chico Maki	6	8	10	15	100	175		
18	Pit Martin	6	8	10	15	30	135		
19	Doug Mohns	6	8	10	15	40	150		
20	John Ferguson	6	8	12	30	80	600		
21	Jim Pappin	6	8	10	15	80	100		
22	Ken Wharram	6	8	10	15	30	60		
23	Roger Crozier	6	8	10	25	100			
24	Bob Baun	6	8	10	20	50	120		
25	Gary Bergman	6	8	12	30	80			
26	Kent Douglas	6	8	12	30	150	250		
27	Ron Harris	6	8	10	15	30	60		
28	Alex Delvecchio	8	10	12	20	60	200		
29	Gordie Howe	50	60	80	100	150	600	800	1,600
30	Bruce MacGregor	6	8	10	15	30	50	80	150
31	Frank Mahovlich	10	12	15	20	80	200		
32	Dean Prentice	6	8	10	15	30	60		
33	Pete Stemkowski	6	8	10	15	30	60		
34	Terry Sawchuk	20	25	30	50	100	200		
35	Larry Cahan	6	8	10	15	30	60		
36	Real Lemieux	6	8	10	15	30	60		
37	Bill White RC	6	8	10	15	30	60		
38	Gord Labossiere RC	6	8	10	15	30	60		
39	Ted Irvine RC	6	8	10	15	30	60		
40	Eddie Joyal	6	8	10	15	30	50	60	100

#	Player	VG 3	VgEx 4	EX 5	ExMt 6	NM 7	NmMt 8	NmMt+ 8.5	M
41	Dale Rolfe	6	8	10	15	30	60		
42	Lowell MacDonald RC	6	8	10	15	30	60		
43	Skip Krake UER	6	8	10	15	30	60		
44	Terry Gray	6	8	10	25	60	200		
45	Cesare Maniago	6	8	10	15	40	80	100	1
46	Mike McMahon	6	8	10	15	30	60		
47	Wayne Hillman	6	8	10	15	25	60		
48	Larry Hillman	6	8	10	15	30	60		
49	Bob Woytowich	6	8	15	30	125	250		
50	Wayne Connelly	6	8	10	15	30	60		
51	Claude Larose	6	8	10	15	30	175		
52	Danny Grant RC	10	12	15	25	80	175		
53	Andre Boudrias	6	8	10	15	30	60		
54	Ray Cullen RC	6	8	10	15	30	60	80	1
55	Parker MacDonald	6	8	10	15	30	300		
56	Gump Worsley	8	10	15	40	200	400		
57	Terry Harper	6	8	10	15	30	60		
58	Jacques Laperriere	6	8	10	15	30	60		
59	J.C. Tremblay	6	8	10	15	30	80		
60	Ralph Backstrom	6	8	10	20	60	120		
61	Checklist 2	60	80	150	250	350	600		
62	Yvan Cournoyer	10	12	15	20	50	175		
63	Jacques Lemaire	12	15	20	25	60	200		
64	Mickey Redmond RC	30	40	50	80	150	350		
65	Bobby Rousseau	6	8	10	15	30	60		
66	Gilles Tremblay	6	8	10	15	30	60		
67	Ed Giacomin	10	12	15	20	40	80		
68	Arnie Brown	6	8	10	15	30	60		
69	Harry Howell	6	8	12	25	60	200		
70	Al Hamilton	6	8	10	15	30	60		
71	Rod Seiling	6	8	12	25	100	300		
72	Rod Gilbert	6	8	10	15	40	80		
73	Phil Goyette	6	8	10	15	30	100		
74	Larry Jeffrey	6	8	10	15	30	80		
75	Don Marshall	6	8	10	15	30	60		
76	Bob Nevin	6	8	10	15	30	60		
77	Jean Ratelle	6	8	10	15	30	60		
78	Charlie Hodge	6	8	10	15	30	150		
79	Bert Marshall	6	8	10	15	30	100		
80	Billy Harris	6	8	10	15	30	100		
81	Carol Vadnais	6	8	10	15	30	60		
82	Howie Young	6	8	10	15	30	60		
83	John Brenneman	6	8	10	15	30	80		
84	Gerry Ehman	6	8	10	15	30			
85	Ted Hampson	6	8	10	15	30	60		
86	Bill Hicke	6	8	10	15	30	80		
87	Gary Jarrett	6	8	10	15	30	60		
88	Doug Roberts	6	8	10	15	30	50		
89	Bernie Parent RC	125	200	250	350	1,300	2,000		
90	Joe Watson	6	8	10	15	30	60		
91	Ed Van Impe	6	8	10	15	30	80		
92	Larry Zeidel	6	8	10	15	30	120		
93	John Miszuk	6	8	10	15	30	50		
94	Gary Dornhoefer	6	8	10	15	30	60		
95	Leon Rochefort	6	8	10	15	30	60		
96	Brit Selby	6	8	10	15	30	60		
97	Forbes Kennedy	6	8	10	15	30	60		
98	Ed Hoekstra RC	6	8	10	15	60	150		
99	Garry Peters	6	8	10	20	30	60		
100	Les Binkley RC	10	12	15	25	100	120		
101	Leo Boivin	6	8	10	15	30	80		
102	Earl Ingarfield	6	8	10	15	30	60		
103	Lou Angotti	6	8	10	15	30	80		
104	Andy Bathgate	6	8	10	15	40	100		
105	Wally Boyer	6	8	10	15	30	80		
106	Ken Schinkel	6	8	10	15	30	60		
107	Ab McDonald	6	8	10	15	30	150		
108	Charlie Burns	6	8	10	15	40	80		
109	Val Fonteyne	6	8	10	15	30	60	80	200
110	Noel Price	6	8	10	15	30	50	60	200
111	Glenn Hall	10	12	15	20	40	100		
112	Bob Plager RC	12	15	20	25	50	100		
113	Jim Roberts	6	8	10	15	30	60		
114	Red Berenson	6	8	10	15	30	60		
115	Larry Keenan	6	8	10	15	30	60		
116	Camille Henry	6	8	10	15	30	150		
117	Gary Sabourin	6	8	10	15	40	60		
118	Ron Schock	6	8	15	50	150	300		
119	Gary Veneruzzo	6	8	10	15	30	60		
120	Gerry Melnyk	6	8	10	15	30	100		
121	Checklist 2	80	125	250	400	550			
122	Johnny Bower	8	15	15	20	80	300		
123	Tim Horton	12	15	20	25	50	100		
124	Pierre Pilote	6	8	10	15	40	200		
125	Marcel Pronovost	6	8	10	15	30	60		
126	Ron Ellis	6	8	10	15	30	80		
127	Paul Henderson	6	8	10	15	30	80		
128	Al Arbour	8	10	15	30	60	150		
129	Bob Pulford	6	8	10	15	30	80		

	VG 3	VgEx 4	EX 5	ExMt 6	NM 7	NmMt 8	NmMt+ 8.5	MT 9
Floyd Smith	6	8	10	15	30	80		
Norm Ullman	6	8	20	25	80			
Mike Walton	6	8	12	25	80			
Ed Johnston	6	8	12	25	150			
Glen Sather	8	10	12	20	60	120		
Ed Westfall	6	8	10	15	30	80		
Dallas Smith	6	8	10	15	30	60		
Eddie Shack	6	8	10	15	30	60		
Gary Doak	6	8	10	15	25	60	80	100
Ron Murphy	6	8	10	15	80	200		
Gerry Cheevers	10	12	15	20	50	100		
Bob Falkenberg	6	8	10	15	30	60		
Garry Unger DP RC	15	20	25	30	80	150		
Peter Mahovlich	6	8	10	15	30	60		
Roy Edwards	6	8	10	15	30	80		
Gary Bauman	6	8	10	15	100	200		
Bob McCord	6	8	10	15	30	60		
Elmer Vasko	6	8	10	15	30	60		
Bill Goldsworthy RC	6	8	10	15	30	100		
Jean-Paul Parise RC	6	8	10	15	40	120		
Dave Dryden	6	8	10	15	30	100		
Howie Young	6	8	10	15	25	50		
Matt Ravlich	6	8	10	15	30	120		
Dennis Hull	6	8	10	15	50	100		
Eric Nesterenko	6	8	10	15	30	60		125
Stan Mikita	15	20	25	30	50	100		
Bob Wall	6	8	10	15	30	80		
Dave Amadio	6	8	10	15	30	60		
Howie Hughes	6	8	10	15	60	120		
Bill Flett RC	6	8	10	15	30	80		
Doug Robinson	6	8	10	15	30	60		125
Dick Duff	6	8	10	15	25	40		
Ted Harris	6	8	10	15	30	60		
Claude Provost	6	8	10	15	25	50		
Rogatien Vachon	20	25	30	40	100	200		
Henri Richard	10	12	15	20	80	150		
Jean Beliveau	20	25	30	40	60	200		
Reg Fleming	6	8	10	15	30	80		
Ron Stewart	6	8	10	15	30	80		
Dave Balon	6	8	10	15	30	80		
Orland Kurtenbach	6	8	10	15	30	80		
Vic Hadfield	6	8	10	15	30	60		
Jim Neilson	6	8	10	15	25	40	50	120
Bryan Watson	6	8	10	15	30	60		
George Swarbrick	6	8	10	15	30	80		
Joe Szura	6	8	10	15	30	80		
Gary Smith RC	12	15	20	25	60	200		
Barclay Plager UER RC	8	10	12	15	40	80		
Tim Ecclestone	6	8	10	12	30	60		
Jean-Guy Talbot	6	8	10	15	25	50		
Ab McDonald	6	8	10	15	30	80		
Jacques Plante	20	25	30	40	50	120		
Bill McCreary	6	8	10	15	30	150		
Allan Stanley	6	8	10	15	25	50		
Andre Lacroix RC	6	8	10	15	60	175		
Jean-Guy Gendron	6	8	10	15	25	40	60	100
Jim Johnson RC	6	8	10	15	30	60		
Simon Nolet RC	6	8	10	15	60	80		
Joe Daley RC	6	8	12	20	80	150		
John Arbour	6	8	10	15	50	100		
Billy Dea	6	8	10	15	30	80		
Bob Dillabough	6	8	10	15	30	60		
Bob Woytowich	6	8	10	15	30	50	60	100
Keith McCreary RC	6	8	10	15	30	60		
Murray Oliver	6	8	10	15	30	60		
Larry Mickey	6	8	10	15	40	80		
Bill Sutherland	6	8	10	15	50	100		
Bruce Gamble	6	8	10	25	50	100		
Dave Keon	8	10	12	25	50	150		
Gump Worsley AS1	6	8	12	25	80			
Bobby Orr AS1	60	80	100	150	250	400	500	800
Tim Horton AS1	8	10	15	30	80	175		
Stan Mikita AS1	8	10	12	30	60	400		
Gordie Howe AS1	30	40	50	60	100	175	200	450
Bobby Hull AS1	25	30	40	50	80	175		
Ed Giacomin AS2	8	10	12	20	80	350		
J.C. Tremblay AS2	6	8	12	25	250	400		
Jim Neilson AS2	6	8	10	15	30	135		
Phil Esposito AS2	12	15	20	40	120	300		
Rod Gilbert AS2	6	8	12	30	100	500		
Johnny Bucyk AS2	6	8	10	15	80	250		
Stan Mikita Triple	8	10	12	30	60	200		
Worsley/Vachon Vezina	20	25	30	60	120	200		
Derek Sanderson Calder	25	30	40	50	100	250		
Bobby Orr Norris	60	80	100	150	250	800		
Glenn Hall Smythe	6	8	10	15	100	200		
Claude Provost Mast	8	10	12	15	80	200		

- Ralph Backstrom #5 PSA 9 (MT) sold for $1,132 (eBay; 8/15)
- Johnny Bucyk #5 PSA 9 (MT) sold for $626 (eBay; 8/12)
- Checklist #61 PSA 9 (MT) sold for $833 (eBay; 10/12)
- Roger Crozier #23 PSA 9 (MT) sold for $694 (eBay; 8/12)
- Alex Delvecchio #28 PSA 10 (Gem) sold for $1,490 (eBay; 4/15)
- Dave Dryden #150 PSA 9 (MT) sold for $1,040 (eBay; 2/13)
- Doug Harvey #1 PSA 8 (NmMt) sold for $1,649 (eBay; 2/13)
- Gordie Howe #29 PSA 9 (MT) sold for $1,584 (eBay; 3/15)
- Larry Hillman #48 PSA 9 (MT) sold for $611 (eBay; 3/14)
- Gordie Howe AS1#203 PSA 9 (MT) sold for $460 (eBay; 8/12)
- Gordie Howe #29 PSA 9 (MT) sold for $1,130 (eBay; 8/12)
- John McKenzie #9 PSA 10 (Gem) sold for $453 (eBay; 2/07)
- Bobby Orr #2 PSA 9 (Mt) sold for $13,547 (Mile High; 12/13)
- Bobby Orr Norris #214 PSA 9 (Mt) sold for $1,775 (Mile High; 12/13)
- Bobby Orr Norris #214 PSA 9 (Mt) sold for $1,258 (eBay;2/16)
- Jim Pappin #21 PSA 9 (Mt) sold for $1040 (eBay; 2/13)
- Mickey Redmond RC #64 PSA 8 (NmMt) sold for $703.44 (eBay; 8/12)
- Mike Walton #132 PSA 9 (MT) sold for $465 (eBay; 8/12)

1968-69 Topps

		VG 3	VgEx 4	EX 5	ExMt 6	NM 7	NmMt 8	NmMt+ 8.5	MT 9
1	Gerry Cheevers	10	12	15	20	30	125		
2	Bobby Orr	80	100	▲200	▲300	400	1,200		
3	Don Awrey UER	6	8	10	12	15	30		
4	Ted Green	6	8	10	12	15	30		
5	Johnny Bucyk	6	8	10	15	30	100		
6	Derek Sanderson	12	15	20	25	30	80	100	175
7	Phil Esposito	15	20	25	30	40	80	120	300
8	Ken Hodge	6	8	10	12	15	150		
9	John McKenzie	6	8	10	12	15	30		
10	Fred Stanfield	6	8	10	12	15	30		
11	Tom Williams	6	8	10	12	15	30	40	100
12	Denis DeJordy	6	8	10	12	15	30	40	80
13	Doug Jarrett	6	8	10	12	15	30	40	80
14	Gilles Marotte	6	8	10	12	15	30		
15	Pat Stapleton	6	8	10	12	15	30		
16	Bobby Hull	25	25	▲50	▲80	150	200	300	
17	Chico Maki	6	8	10	15	30	60		
18	Pit Martin	6	8	10	12	15	30	40	175
19	Doug Mohns	6	8	10	12	15	30	40	175
20	Stan Mikita	10	12	15	20	30	150		
21	Jim Pappin	6	8	10	12	15	30		
22	Ken Wharram	6	8	10	12	15	30		
23	Roger Crozier	6	8	10	12	25	40		
24	Bob Baun	6	8	10	12	15	30		
25	Gary Bergman	6	8	10	12	25	50		
26	Kent Douglas	6	8	10	5	25	60		
27	Ron Harris	6	8	10	12	15	30	40	80
28	Alex Delvecchio	6	8	10	12	15	40		
29	Gordie Howe	30	40	▲60	▲80	▲100	200		
30	Bruce MacGregor	6	8	10	12	15	30	40	80
31	Frank Mahovlich	8	10	12	15	20	50	75	135
32	Dean Prentice	6	8	10	12	15	30		
33	Pete Stemkowski	6	8	10	12	15	30	35	60
34	Terry Sawchuk	20	25	30	40	50	▲100	▲150	300
35	Larry Cahan	6	8	10	12	15	30	40	80
36	Real Lemieux	6	8	10	12	15	30		
37	Bill White RC	6	8	10	12	15	30		
38	Gord Labossiere	6	8	10	12	15	30	40	80
39	Ted Irvine	6	8	10	12	15	30	35	60
40	Eddie Joyal	6	8	10	12	15	30	35	60
41	Dale Rolfe	6	8	10	12	15	30	35	80
42	Lowell MacDonald RC	6	8	10	12	15	30	35	60
43	Skip Krake UER	6	8	10	12	15	30	40	80
44	Terry Gray	6	8	10	12	20	60		
45	Cesare Maniago	6	8	10	12	15	30	40	80
46	Mike McMahon	6	8	10	12	15	30		
47	Wayne Hillman	6	8	10	12	15	30		
48	Larry Hillman	6	8	10	12	15	30		
49	Bob Woytowich	6	8	10	12	15	30	40	80
50	Wayne Connelly	6	8	10	12	15	30		
51	Claude Larose	6	8	10	12	15	30		
52	Danny Grant RC	6	8	10	12	15	80	120	150
53	Andre Boudrias	6	8	10	12	15	30	50	125
54	Ray Cullen RC	6	8	10	12	15	30	40	100
55	Parker MacDonald	6	8	10	12	15	30		
56	Gump Worsley	8	10	12	15	30	50		
57	Terry Harper	6	8	10	12	15	30	40	80
58	Jacques Laperriere	6	8	10	12	15	▲50	▲80	▲100
59	J.C. Tremblay	6	8	10	12	15	30	40	80
60	Ralph Backstrom	6	8	10	12	15	30		
61	Jean Beliveau	10	12	15	20	30	80	100	250
62	Yvan Cournoyer	8	10	12	15	20	50		
63	Jacques Lemaire	10	12	15	20	25	60		
64	Henri Richard	8	10	12	15	20	50		
65	Bobby Rousseau	6	8	10	12	15	30	40	80
66	Gilles Tremblay	6	8	10	12	15	30		
67	Ed Giacomin	8	10	12	15	30	50	60	120
68	Arnie Brown	6	8	10	12	15	30		

#	Player	VG 3	VgEx 4	EX 5	ExMt 6	NM 7	NmMt 8	NmMt+ 8.5	MT 9
69	Harry Howell	6	8	10	12	20	50		
70	Jim Neilson	6	8	10	12	20	50		
71	Rod Seiling	6	8	10	12	20	50		
72	Rod Gilbert	6	8	10	12	15	▲60	▲80	100
73	Phil Goyette	6	8	10	12	15	30	40	80
74	Vic Hadfield	6	8	10	12	15	35	50	100
75	Don Marshall	6	8	10	12	15	40		
76	Bob Nevin	6	8	10	12	15	40	50	80
77	Jean Ratelle	6	8	10	12	15	40	50	80
78	Charlie Hodge	6	8	10	12	15	30		
79	Bert Marshall	6	8	10	12	15	30	40	80
80	Billy Harris	6	8	10	12	15	30		
81	Carol Vadnais	6	8	10	12	15	30		
82	Howie Young	6	8	10	12	15	30		
83	John Brenneman	6	8	10	12	15	30	40	80
84	Gerry Ehman	6	8	10	12	15	30		
85	Ted Hampson	6	8	10	12	15	40		
86	Bill Hicke	6	8	10	12	15	40	50	80
87	Gary Jarrett	6	8	10	12	15	30		
88	Doug Roberts	6	8	10	12	15	40		
89	Bernie Parent RC	30	40	50	60	100	175	225	500
90	Joe Watson	6	8	10	12	15	30		
91	Ed Van Impe	6	8	10	12	15	40		
92	Larry Zeidel	6	8	10	12	15	30		
93	John Miszuk	6	8	10	12	15	30		
94	Gary Dornhoefer	6	8	10	12	15	30	50	150
95	Leon Rochefort	6	8	10	12	15	40	50	80
96	Brit Selby	6	8	10	12	15	40		
97	Forbes Kennedy	6	8	10	12	15	30	40	150
98	Ed Hoekstra	6	8	10	12	15	30		
99	Garry Peters	6	8	10	12	15	30	40	120
100	Les Binkley RC	8	10	12	15	20	50		
101	Leo Boivin	6	8	10	12	15	30		
102	Earl Ingarfield	6	8	10	12	15	30	40	135
103	Lou Angotti	6	8	10	12	15	30		
104	Andy Bathgate	6	8	10	12	15	30	40	80
105	Wally Boyer	6	8	10	12	15	40	50	100
106	Ken Schinkel	6	8	10	12	15	30	50	100
107	Ab McDonald	6	8	10	12	15	30		
108	Charlie Burns	6	8	10	12	15	30	50	100
109	Val Fonteyne	6	8	10	12	15	30	40	80
110	Noel Price	6	8	10	12	15	30	40	80
111	Glenn Hall	8	10	12	15	20	40	50	100
112	Bob Plager RC	8	10	12	15	▲30	▲60	▲80	100
113	Jim Roberts	6	8	10	12	15	30		
114	Red Berenson	6	8	10	12	15	30	40	80
115	Larry Keenan	6	8	10	12	15	30	40	80
116	Camille Henry	6	8	10	15	30	50		
117	Gary Sabourin	6	8	10	12	15	30		
118	Ron Schock	6	8	10	12	15	40		
119	Gary Veneruzzo	6	8	10	12	15	30	40	80
120	Gerry Melnyk	6	8	10	12	15	30	35	60
121	Checklist Card	40	50	60	80	150	200	250	350
122	Johnny Bower	8	10	12	15	20	80	60	150
123	Tim Horton	10	12	15	20	25	40	60	200
124	Pierre Pilote	6	8	10	12	15	30		
125	Marcel Pronovost	6	8	10	12	15	30	40	80
126	Ron Ellis	6	8	10	12	15	30		
127	Paul Henderson	6	8	10	12	30	40		
128	Dave Keon	6	8	10	12	15	40	50	100
129	Bob Pulford	6	8	10	12	20	50		
130	Floyd Smith	6	8	10	12	15	30	40	80
131	Norm Ullman	6	8	10	12	15	40		
132	Mike Walton	6	8	10	12	15	30		

—Bobby Hull #16 PSA 9 (MT) sold for $430 (eBay; 8/09)

1969-70 O-Pee-Chee

#	Player	VG 3	VgEx 4	EX 5	ExMt 6	NM 7	NmMt 8	NmMt+ 8.5	MT 9
1	Gump Worsley	20	25	40	50	150	400	500	800
2	Ted Harris	5	6	10	15	60	200		
3	Jacques Laperriere	5	6	10	15	50	200	250	350
4	Serge Savard RC	30	50	120	200	325	1,000		
5	J.C. Tremblay	5	6	8	10	25	100		
6	Yvan Cournoyer	5	6	8	10	25	50		
7	John Ferguson	5	6	8	10	30	120	135	250
8	Jacques Lemaire	5	6	8	15	50	200		
9	Bobby Rousseau	5	6	8	15	40	150		
10	Jean Beliveau	10	12	15	25	40	100	250	
11	Dick Duff	5	6	8	15	50	350		
12	Glenn Hall	6	8	10	12	25	60	80	120
13	Bob Plager	5	6	8	10	25	50	60	120
14	Ron Anderson	5	6	8	10	25	50	60	120
15	Jean-Guy Talbot	5	6	8	10	25	50		
16	Andre Boudrias	5	6	8	10	25	50	60	120
17	Camille Henry	5	6	8	10	25	50		
18	Ab McDonald	5	6	8	10	25	50	60	120
19	Gary Sabourin	5	6	8	10	25	50		
20	Red Berenson	5	6	8	15	50	120		
21	Phil Goyette	5	6	8	10	25	50	60	120

#	Player	VG 3	VgEx 4	EX 5	ExMt 6	NM 7	NmMt 8	NmMt+ 8.5	MT 9
22	Gerry Cheevers	8	10	12	15	30	80		
23	Ted Green	5	6	8	10	25	50		
24	Bobby Orr	80	100	▲150	▲250	▲400	▲800		
25	Dallas Smith	5	6	8	10	25	50	60	1
26	Johnny Bucyk	6	8	10	12	25	50	80	
27	Ken Hodge	5	6	8	10	25	50		
28	John McKenzie	5	6	8	10	25	50	60	
29	Ed Westfall	5	6	8	10	▲40	▲80		
30	Phil Esposito	15	20	25	30	50	80	100	
31	Checklist 2	50	60	100	150	275	400	450	7
32	Fred Stanfield	5	6	8	10	25	50		
33	Ed Giacomin	8	10	12	15	▲60	▲100		
34	Arnie Brown	5	6	8	10	25	50		
35	Jim Neilson	5	6	8	10	25	50	60	1
36	Rod Seiling	5	6	8	10	25	50		
37	Rod Gilbert	5	6	8	12	40	150		
38	Vic Hadfield	5	6	8	10	30	80		
39	Don Marshall	5	6	8	10	25	50		
40	Bob Nevin	5	6	8	10	25	50		
41	Ron Stewart	5	6	8	10	25	50	60	1
42	Jean Ratelle	5	6	8	10	25	▲80		
43	Walt Tkaczuk RC	5	6	8	10	25	50		
44	Bruce Gamble	5	6	8	10	25	50	60	12
45	Jim Dorey	5	6	8	10	25	50		
46	Ron Ellis	5	6	8	10	▲40	▲60		
47	Paul Henderson	5	6	8	10	25	150		
48	Brit Selby	5	6	8	10	25	50		13
49	Floyd Smith	5	6	8	10	25	50		
50	Mike Walton	5	6	8	10	25	50		
51	Dave Keon	5	6	8	15	50	120		
52	Murray Oliver	5	6	8	10	25	50		
53	Bob Pulford	5	6	8	10	25	50		
54	Norm Ullman	5	6	8	10	25	50	60	12
55	Roger Crozier	5	6	8	10	25	50		
56	Roy Edwards	5	6	8	10	25	50	60	12
57	Bob Baun	5	6	8	10	25	50		
58	Gary Bergman	5	6	8	10	25	▲60	▲80	▲15
59	Carl Brewer	5	6	8	10	25	50	60	12
60	Wayne Connelly	5	6	8	10	25	50	60	12
61	Gordie Howe	30	50	80	100	300	500	600	800
62	Frank Mahovlich	6	8	10	12	▲80	▲100	▲150	▲20
63	Bruce MacGregor	5	6	8	15	40	150		
64	Ron Harris	5	6	8	10	25	50	60	120
65	Pete Stemkowski	5	6	8	10	25	50		
66	Denis DeJordy	5	6	8	10	25	50	60	120
67	Doug Jarrett	5	6	8	10	25	50		
68	Gilles Marotte	5	6	8	10	25	50	60	120
69	Pat Stapleton	5	6	8	10	25	50	60	135
70	Bobby Hull	30	40	50	80	150	200	250	350
71	Dennis Hull	5	6	8	10	25	50		
72	Doug Mohns	5	6	8	15	50	200		
73	Howie Menard	5	6	8	10	25	50	60	120
74	Ken Wharram	5	6	8	10	25	50	60	120
75	Pit Martin	5	6	8	10	25	50		
76	Stan Mikita	10	12	15	25	60	250		
77	Charlie Hodge	5	6	8	10	25	50	60	120
78	Gary Smith	5	6	8	10	25	50		
79	Harry Howell	5	6	8	10	25	50	60	135
80	Bert Marshall	5	6	8	10	25	50	60	120
81	Doug Roberts	5	6	8	10	25	50		
82	Carol Vadnais	5	6	8	10	30	80		
83	Gerry Ehman	5	6	8	10	25	50		
84	Brian Perry	5	6	8	10	25	50	60	120
85	Gary Jarrett	5	6	8	10	25	50	60	120
86	Ted Hampson	5	6	8	10	25	50	60	120
87	Earl Ingarfield	5	6	8	10	25	50		
88	Doug Favell RC	8	10	12	15	50	175		
89	Bernie Parent	20	25	30	40	50	100	100	300
90	Larry Hillman	5	6	8	10	25	50		
91	Wayne Hillman	5	6	8	10	25	50		
92	Ed Van Impe	5	6	8	10	25	50	60	135
93	Joe Watson	5	6	8	10	25	50	60	120
94	Gary Dornhoefer	5	6	8	10	30	80		
95	Reg Fleming	5	6	8	10	25	50	60	120
96	Ralph McSweyn	5	6	8	10	25	50		
97	Jim Johnson	5	6	8	10	25	50		
98	Andre Lacroix	5	6	8	10	25	50		
99	Gerry Desjardins RC	6	8	10	12	25	50		
100	Dale Rolfe	5	6	8	10	25	50		
101	Bill White	5	6	8	10	25	50	60	150
102	Bill Flett	5	6	8	10	25	50		
103	Ted Irvine	5	6	8	10	25	▲80		
104	Ross Lonsberry	5	6	8	10	25	50		
105	Leon Rochefort	5	6	8	10	25	50		
106	Bryan Campbell	5	6	8	12	30	60		
107	Dennis Hextall RC	5	6	8	10	25	50		
108	Eddie Joyal	5	6	8	10	25	50		
109	Gord Labossiere	5	6	8	10	25	50		
110	Les Binkley	5	6	8	10	30	150	175	250

	VG 3	VgEx 4	EX 5	ExMt 6	NM 7	NmMt 8	NmMt+ 8.5	MT 9
Tracy Pratt	5	6	8	10	25	60	80	150
Bryan Watson	5	6	8	10	25	50		
Bob Blackburn	5	6	8	10	25	50		
Keith McCreary	5	6	8	10	25	50		
Dean Prentice	5	6	8	10	25	50		
Glen Sather	5	6	8	10	25	50		
Ken Schinkel	5	6	8	10	25	50	60	135
Wally Boyer	5	6	8	10	25	50		
Val Fonteyne	5	6	8	10	25	50		
Ron Schock	5	6	8	10	25	50	60	120
Cesare Maniago	5	6	8	10	25	50	60	120
Leo Boivin	5	6	8	10	25	50		
Bob McCord	5	6	8	10	30	100		
John Miszuk	5	6	8	10	25	50		
Danny Grant	5	6	8	10	25	60		
Bill Collins	5	6	8	10	25	50		
Jean-Paul Parise	5	6	8	10	25	50	60	135
Tom Williams	5	6	8	10	25	50		
Charlie Burns	5	6	8	10	25	50	75	175
Ray Cullen	5	6	8	10	25	50		
Danny O'Shea	5	6	8	10	50	135		
Checklist 1	125	175	250	400	500			
Jim Pappin	5	6	8	10	12	25	30	50
Lou Angotti	5	6	8	10	12	15	20	30
Terry Caffery RC	5	6	8	10	12	15	20	30
Eric Nesterenko	5	6	8	10	12	30	40	80
Chico Maki	5	6	8	10	12	15	20	30
Tony Esposito RC	40	80	100	150	250	350	400	600
Eddie Shack	5	6	8	10	12	15	20	30
Bob Wall	5	6	8	10	12	30	40	60
Skip Krake RC	5	6	8	10	12	15	20	30
Howie Hughes	5	6	8	10	12	15	20	30
Jimmy Peters RC	5	6	8	10	12	20	30	50
Brent Hughes RC	5	6	8	10	12	25	30	50
Bill Hicke	5	6	8	10	12	15	20	30
Norm Ferguson RC	5	6	8	10	12	15	20	40
Dick Mattiussi RC	5	6	8	10	12	25	30	60
Mike Laughton RC	5	6	8	10	12	25	30	50
Gene Ubriaco RC	5	6	8	10	12	15	20	30
Bob Dillabough	5	6	8	10	12	20	30	50
Bob Woytowich	5	6	8	10	12	25	30	60
Joe Daley	5	6	8	10	12	25	30	60
Duane Rupp	5	6	8	10	12	30	30	60
Bryan Hextall RC	5	6	8	10	12	15	20	30
Jean Pronovost RC	5	6	8	10	12	20	25	40
Jim Morrison	5	6	8	10	12	20	25	40
Alex Delvecchio	6	8	10	12	12	25	30	50
Paul Popiel	5	6	8	10	12	20	25	40
Garry Unger	5	6	8	10	12	15	20	30
Garry Monahan	5	6	8	10	12	15	20	30
Matt Ravlich	5	6	8	10	12	20	25	40
Nick Libett RC	5	6	8	10	12	20	25	40
Henri Richard	6	8	10	12	12	30	40	175
Terry Harper	5	6	8	10	12	30	40	120
Rogatien Vachon	8	10	12	15	20	30	40	100
Ralph Backstrom	5	6	8	10	12	15	20	40
Claude Provost	5	6	8	10	12	15	20	30
Gilles Tremblay	5	6	8	10	12	15	40	50
Jean-Guy Gendron	5	6	8	10	12	20	25	40
Earl Heiskala RC	5	6	8	10	15	40		
Garry Peters	5	6	8	10	15	40		
Bill Sutherland	5	6	8	10	12	15	20	30
Dick Cherry RC	5	6	8	10	12	15	20	30
Jim Roberts	5	6	8	10	12	20	25	40
Noel Picard RC	5	6	8	10	15	40		
Barclay Plager RC	5	6	8	10	12	15	20	30
Frank St. Marseille RC	5	6	8	10	12	15	20	30
Al Arbour	5	6	8	10	12	15	20	30
Tim Ecclestone	5	6	8	10	12	20	25	40
Jacques Plante	15	20	25	35	50	60	80	120
Bill McCreary	5	6	8	10	12	15	20	30
Tim Horton	8	10	12	15	20	30	40	60
Rick Ley RC	5	6	8	10	12	15	20	50
Wayne Carleton	5	6	8	10	12	15	20	30
Marv Edwards RC	5	6	8	10	12	20	25	40
Pat Quinn RC	8	10	12	15	20	60	80	135
Johnny Bower	6	8	10	12	15	50	80	100
Orland Kurtenbach	5	6	8	10	12	20	25	40
Terry Sawchuk UER	10	12	15	20	30	80	100	150
Real Lemieux	5	6	8	10	12	15	20	30
Dave Balon	5	6	8	10	12	15	20	30
Al Hamilton	5	6	8	10	12	30	40	80
3A G.Howe Mr. HK ERR	30	40	50	60	80	100	150	250
3B G.Howe Mr. HK COR	50	60	80	100	150	200		
Claude Larose	5	6	8	10	12	20	25	40
Bill Goldsworthy	5	6	8	10	12	30	40	80
Bob Barlow	5	6	8	10	12	30	40	80
Ken Broderick RC	5	6	8	10	12	30	40	60
Lou Nanne RC	5	6	8	10	12	20	25	40
Tom Polonic RC	5	6	8	10	12	15	20	30
Ed Johnston	5	6	8	10	12	15	20	30
Derek Sanderson	10	12	15	20	25	40	50	80

		VG 3	VgEx 4	EX 5	ExMt 6	NM 7	NmMt 8	NmMt+ 8.5	MT 9
202	Gary Doak	5	6	8	10	12	15	20	50
203	Don Awrey	5	6	8	10	12	20	20	30
204	Ron Murphy	5	6	8	10	12	25	30	60
205A	P.Esposito Double ERR	12	15	20	25	60			
205B	P.Esposito Double COR	12	15	20	50				
206	Alex Delvecchio Byng	5	6	8	10	12	25	30	50
207	J.Plante/G.Hall Vezina	15	20	25	30	40	50		
208	Danny Grant Calder	5	6	8	10	12	20	25	40
209	Bobby Orr Norris	30	40	50	▲80	▲150	▲200	▲250	▲350
210	Serge Savard Smythe	5	6	8	10	12	20	25	40
211	Glenn Hall AS	8	10	12	15	30	150		
212	Bobby Orr AS	30	40	50	60	80	120	150	250
213	Tim Horton AS	10	12	15	20	25	40	50	120
214	Phil Esposito AS	10	12	15	20	40	80		
215	Gordie Howe AS	25	30	40	50	80	120		
216	Bobby Hull AS	15	20	25	30	50	80		
217	Ed Giacomin AS	6	8	10	12	20	40		
218	Ted Green AS	5	6	8	10	12	20	25	40
219	Ted Harris AS	5	6	8	10	12	20	25	50
220	Jean Beliveau AS	10	12	15	30	80	400		
221	Yvan Cournoyer AS	5	6	8	12	25	50		
222	Frank Mahovlich AS	5	6	8	15	40	135		
223	Art Ross Trophy	5	6	12	20	60	250		
224	Hart Trophy	5	6	8	10	12	20	30	60
225	Lady Byng Trophy	5	6	8	12	25	100		
226	Vezina Trophy	5	6	8	10	12	30	35	40
227	Calder Trophy	5	6	8	12	30	200		
228	James Norris Trophy	5	6	8	12	25	80		
229	Conn Smythe Trophy	5	6	8	12	25	50		
230	Prince of Wales Trophy	5	6	8	10	12	20	25	50
231	The Stanley Cup	15	20	25	40	60	75	140	175

—Jean Beliveau #10 PSA 9 (MT) sold for $410 (eBay; 4/07)
—Checklist #31 PSA 10 (Gem) sold for $2,375 (Memory Lane; 4/07)
—Checklist #132 PSA 8 (Gem) sold for $1,454 (eBay; 11/14)
—Gordie Howe #193A PSA 10 (Gem) sold for $3,216 (Memory Lane; 12/13)
—Bobby Hull #70 PSA 10 (Gem) sold for $2,092 (Memory Lane; 12/13)
—Eddie Joyal #108 PSA 10 (Gem) sold for $446 (eBay; 4/07)
—Cesare Maniago PSA 10 (Gem) sold for $265 (eBay; 05/08)
—Pit Martin #75 PSA 9 (MT) sold for $321 (3/08)
—Keith Mcreary #114 PSA 10 (Gem) sold for $446 (eBay; 4/07)
—Bobby Orr #24 PSA 9 (MT) sold for $2,624 (Mile High; 12/13)
—Serge Savard RC #4 PSA 8 (NmMt) sold for $1,044 (eBay; 5/12)
—Gump Worsley #1 PSA 9 (MT) sold for $919 (eBay; 3/07)

1969-70 Topps

		VG 3	VgEx 4	EX 5	ExMt 6	NM 7	NmMt 8	NmMt+ 8.5	MT 9
1	Gump Worsley	8	10	12	15	25			
2	Ted Harris	5	6	8	10	15	30		
3	Jacques Laperriere	5	6	8	10	15	25	30	80
4	Serge Savard RC	10	12	15	20	40	120		
5	J.C. Tremblay	5	6	8	10	15	25	30	80
6	Yvan Cournoyer	5	6	8	10	15	40		
7	John Ferguson	5	6	8	10	15	25	30	80
8	Jacques Lemaire	5	6	8	10	15	40	50	100
9	Bobby Rousseau	5	6	8	10	15	80		
10	Jean Beliveau	8	10	12	15	60	100	135	300
11	Henri Richard	5	6	8	10	30	50	60	135
12	Glenn Hall	5	6	8	10	20	60		
13	Bob Plager	5	6	8	10	15	30		
14	Jim Roberts	5	6	8	10	15	30		
15	Jean-Guy Talbot	5	6	8	10	15	25	30	80
16	Andre Boudrias	5	6	8	10	15	25	30	80
17	Camille Henry	5	6	8	10	15	30		
18	Ab McDonald	5	6	8	10	15	30		
19	Gary Sabourin	5	6	8	10	15	50		
20	Red Berenson	5	6	8	10	15	30		
21	Phil Goyette	5	6	8	10	15	30		
22	Gerry Cheevers	6	8	10	12	20	50		
23	Ted Green	5	6	8	10	15	50		
24	Bobby Orr	50	60	▲100	▲150	▲200	▲300	▲350	1,400
25	Dallas Smith	5	6	8	10	15	25	30	80
26	Johnny Bucyk	5	6	8	10	15	35	50	125
27	Ken Hodge	5	6	8	10	15	50		
28	John McKenzie	5	6	8	10	15	50		
29	Ed Westfall	5	6	8	10	15	50		
30	Phil Esposito	10	12	15	20	35	60	80	200
31	Derek Sanderson	8	10	12	15	25	50		
32	Fred Stanfield	5	6	8	10	15	30		
33	Ed Giacomin	6	8	10	12	20	40	50	135
34	Arnie Brown	5	6	8	10	15	30		
35	Jim Neilson	5	6	8	10	15	25	30	60
36	Rod Seiling	5	6	8	10	15	25	30	60
37	Rod Gilbert	5	6	8	10	15	25	30	60
38	Vic Hadfield	5	6	8	10	15	40		
39	Don Marshall	5	6	8	10	15	60		
40	Bob Nevin	5	6	8	10	15	50		
41	Ron Stewart	5	6	8	10	15	30		
42	Jean Ratelle	5	6	8	10	15	30	35	80
43	Walt Tkaczuk RC	5	6	8	10	15	30		
44	Bruce Gamble	5	6	8	10	15	30		

(1969-70 O-Pee-Chee continued)

#	Player	VG 3	VgEx 4	EX 5	ExMt 6	NM 7	NmMt 8	NmMt+ 8.5	MT 9
45	Tim Horton	8	10	12	15	25	60	80	175
46	Ron Ellis	5	6	8	10	15	30		
47	Paul Henderson	5	6	8	10	15	30	35	80
48	Brit Selby	5	6	8	10	15	30		
49	Floyd Smith	5	6	8	10	15	25	30	60
50	Mike Walton	5	6	8	10	15	30		
51	Dave Keon	5	6	8	10	15	40		
52	Murray Oliver	5	6	8	10	15	40		
53	Bob Pulford	5	6	8	10	15	25	30	60
54	Norm Ullman	5	6	8	10	15	30	40	80
55	Roger Crozier	5	6	8	10	15	50		
56	Roy Edwards	5	6	8	10	15	30		
57	Bob Baun	5	6	8	10	15	30	35	80
58	Gary Bergman	5	6	8	10	15	25	30	60
59	Carl Brewer	5	6	8	10	15	30	35	80
60	Wayne Connelly	5	6	8	10	15	30		
61	Gordie Howe	12	15	25	35	50	80	125	500
62	Frank Mahovlich	5	6	8	10	20	50	60	100
63	Bruce MacGregor	5	6	8	10	15	25	30	60
64	Alex Delvecchio	5	6	8	10	20	40	40	80
65	Pete Sternkowski	5	6	8	10	15	25	30	60
66	Denis DeJordy	5	6	8	10	15	30	35	80
67	Doug Jarrett	5	6	8	10	15	30	35	80
68	Gilles Marotte	5	6	8	10	15	30	35	80
69	Pat Stapleton	5	6	8	10	15	25	30	60
70	Bobby Hull	12	15	20	40	50	80	120	300
71	Dennis Hull	5	6	8	10	15	30	35	80
72	Doug Mohns	5	6	8	10	15	30		
73	Jim Pappin	5	6	8	10	15	40		
74	Ken Wharram	5	6	8	10	15	30	35	80
75	Pit Martin	5	6	8	10	15	30		
76	Stan Mikita	8	10	12	15	25	80	100	175
77	Charlie Hodge	5	6	8	10	15	30	35	80
78	Gary Smith	5	6	8	10	15	25	30	60
79	Harry Howell	5	6	8	10	15	30	35	80
80	Bert Marshall	5	6	8	10	15	30	35	80
81	Doug Roberts	5	6	8	10	15	25	30	60
82	Carol Vadnais	5	6	8	10	15	30		
83	Gerry Ehman	5	6	8	10	15	30		
84	Bill Hicke	5	6	8	10	15	25	30	60
85	Gary Jarrett	5	6	8	10	15	25	30	60
86	Ted Hampson	5	6	8	10	15	25	30	60
87	Earl Ingarfield	5	6	8	10	15	25	30	60
88	Doug Favell RC	6	8	10	12	25	60		
89	Bernie Parent	10	12	15	18	25	40	50	80
90	Larry Hillman	5	6	8	10	20	80		
91	Wayne Hillman	5	6	8	10	15	60		
92	Ed Van Impe	5	6	8	10	15	25	30	60
93	Joe Watson	5	6	8	10	15	30		
94	Gary Dornhoefer	5	6	8	10	15	30		
95	Reg Fleming	5	6	8	10	15	25	30	60
96	Jean-Guy Gendron	5	6	8	10	15	25	30	60
97	Jim Johnson	5	6	8	10	15	25	30	60
98	Andre Lacroix	5	6	8	10	15	30	35	80
99	Gerry Desjardins RC	5	6	8	10	15	30	35	80
100	Dale Rolfe	5	6	8	10	15	25	30	60
101	Bill White	5	6	8	10	15	25	30	60
102	Bill Flett	5	6	8	10	15	30		
103	Ted Irvine	5	6	8	10	15	25	30	60
104	Ross Lonsberry	5	6	8	10	15	40		
105	Leon Rochefort	5	6	8	10	15	25	30	60
106	Eddie Shack	5	6	8	10	15	40		
107	Dennis Hextall RC	5	6	8	10	15	30	35	60
108	Eddie Joyal	5	6	8	10	15	25	30	60
109	Gord Labossiere	5	6	8	10	15	25	30	60
110	Les Binkley	5	6	8	10	15	30	35	80
111	Tracy Pratt	5	6	8	10	15	30		
112	Bryan Watson	5	6	8	10	15	40		
113	Bob Woytowich	5	6	8	10	15	25	30	60
114	Keith McCreary	5	6	8	10	15	60		
115	Dean Prentice	5	6	8	10	15	30		
116	Glen Sather	5	6	8	10	15	30		
117	Ken Schinkel	5	6	8	10	15	50		
118	Wally Boyer	5	6	8	10	15	30	35	80
119	Val Fonteyne	5	6	8	10	15	30		
120	Ron Schock	5	6	8	10	15	25	30	60
121	Cesare Maniago	5	6	8	10	15	50		
122	Leo Boivin	5	6	8	10	15	30		
123	Bob McCord	5	6	8	10	15	50		
124	John Miszuk	5	6	8	10	15	30		
125	Danny Grant	5	6	8	10	15	30		
126	Claude Larose	5	6	8	10	15	50		
127	Jean-Paul Parise	5	6	8	10	15	30		
128	Tom Williams	5	6	8	10	15	25	30	60
129	Charlie Burns	5	6	8	10	15	80		
130	Ray Cullen	5	6	8	10	20	100		
131	Danny O'Shea	5	6	8	10	20	100		
132	Checklist Card	15	25	40	50	80	250		

—Bobby Hull #70 PSA 10 (GEM) sold for $780 (Mastro; 8/08)
—Bobby Orr #24 PSA 9 (MT) sold for $1,211780 (Mile High; 12/13)

1970-71 O-Pee-Chee

#	Player	VG 3	VgEx 4	EX 5	ExMt 6	NM 7	NmMt 8	NmMt+ 8.5	MT
1	Gerry Cheevers	20	25	35	50	80	300	350	8
2	Johnny Bucyk	4	5	6	10	30	80		
3	Bobby Orr	60	80	125	200	400	800	1,600	2,2
4	Don Awrey	4	4	8	20	40	100		
5	Fred Stanfield	4	5	6	12	30	250		
6	John McKenzie	4	5	6	10	30	80		
7	Wayne Cashman RC	12	15	20	30	40	150	175	25
8	Ken Hodge	4	5	6	10	30	80		
9	Wayne Carleton	4	4	5	10	20	80		
10	Garnet Bailey RC	4	5	6	12	30	400		
11	Phil Esposito	20	25	30	40	50	100		
12	Lou Angotti	4	4	5	10	20	60	80	15
13	Jim Pappin	4	4	5	10	25	100		
14	Dennis Hull	4	5	8	15	25	100		
15	Bobby Hull	40	45	50	60	100	200	250	35
16	Doug Mohns	4	4	5	8	15	30	50	12
17	Pat Stapleton	4	5	6	10	30	300		
18	Pit Martin	4	4	5	10	20	50	80	13
19	Eric Nesterenko	4	5	6	10	20	40	50	20
20	Stan Mikita	15	20	20	30	40	80	125	22
21	Roy Edwards	4	5	6	10	20	40	50	8
22	Frank Mahovlich	10	12	15	25	50	250		
23	Ron Harris	4	4	5	8	15	30		
24	Checklist 1	150	200	250	300	400	600	800	1,00
25	Pete Sternkowski	4	4	5	8	15	25	40	12
26	Garry Unger	4	4	5	8	15	80		
27	Bruce MacGregor	4	4	5	8	15	50		
28	Larry Jeffrey	4	4	5	8	15	30		
29	Gordie Howe	30	40	60	80	100	200	300	60
30	Billy Dea	4	4	5	8	15	30	40	10
31	Denis DeJordy	4	5	6	10	20	50		
32	Matt Ravlich	4	5	8	12	40	135		
33	Dave Amadio	4	4	5	8	15	30	40	8
34	Gilles Marotte	4	4	5	10	30	60		
35	Eddie Shack	10	12	15	25	40	60	80	200
36	Bob Pulford	4	5	6	10	20	30		
37	Ross Lonsberry	4	5	6	10	20	40	50	120
38	Gord Labossiere	4	4	5	8	15	30	40	120
39	Eddie Joyal	4	4	5	8	15	30	40	100
40	Gump Worsley	10	12	15	25	40	80	125	250
41	Bob McCord	4	4	5	8	15	30		
42	Leo Boivin	4	5	6	10	20	30	40	80
43	Tom Reid RC	4	4	5	8	15	30	40	80
44	Charlie Burns	4	4	5	8	15	50		
45	Bob Barlow	4	4	5	8	15	30	40	80
46	Bill Goldsworthy	4	4	5	6	10	20	40	80
47	Danny Grant	4	5	6	10	20	30	40	100
48	Norm Beaudin RC	4	4	5	8	20	40	50	120
49	Rogatien Vachon	10	12	15	25	35	50	60	200
50	Yvan Cournoyer	10	12	15	25	35	60	80	135
51	Serge Savard	10	12	15	25	40	150		
52	Jacques Laperriere	4	8	10	15	30	100	125	175
53	Terry Harper	4	4	5	8	15	30	40	120
54	Ralph Backstrom	4	5	6	10	20	60		
55	Jean Beliveau	10	12	15	25	40	100		
56	Claude Larose	4	4	5	8	80	300		
57	Jacques Lemaire	10	12	15	25	40	80		
58	Peter Mahovlich	4	5	6	10	20		40	120
59	Tim Horton	12	15	20	30	40	80	100	200
60	Bob Nevin	4	4	5	8	15	30		
61	Dave Balon	4	4	5	8	15	60		
62	Vic Hadfield	4	5	6	10	20	30		
63	Rod Gilbert	10	12	15	25	40	80		
64	Ron Stewart	4	4	5	8	15	25		
65	Ted Irvine	4	4	5	8	15	40		
66	Arnie Brown	4	4	5	8	15	120		
67	Brad Park RC	20	25	30	60	75	250	300	1,400
68	Ed Giacomin	10	12	15	20	30	80		
69	Gary Smith	4	5	6	10	20	30		
70	Carol Vadnais	4	5	6	10	20		40	120
71	Doug Roberts	4	4	5	8	15	30		
72	Harry Howell	4	5	6	10	20	30		
73	Joe Szura	4	4	5	8	15	30	40	100
74	Mike Laughton	4	4	5	8	15	150		
75	Gary Jarrett	4	4	5	8	15	30	40	100
76	Bill Hicke	4	4	5	8	15	50		
77	Paul Andrea RC	4	4	5	8	20	80		
78	Bernie Parent	20	25	30	40	60	200		
79	Joe Watson	4	4	5	8	15	30	40	100
80	Ed Van Impe	4	4	5	8	15	60		
81	Larry Hillman	4	4	5	8	15	60		
82	George Swarbrick	4	4	5	8	15	60		
83	Bill Sutherland	4	4	5	8	15	40		
84	Andre Lacroix	4	4	5	10	20	80		
85	Gary Dornhoefer	4	5	6	10	20	30	50	100
86	Jean-Guy Gendron	4	4	5	8	15	30		

Left table:

	VG 3	VgEx 4	EX 5	ExMt 6	NM 7	NmMt 8	NmMt+ 8.5	MT 9
Al Smith RC	4	5	6	10	25	50		
Bob Woytowich	4	4	5	8	15	30		
Duane Rupp	4	4	5	8	15	30		
Jim Morrison	4	4	5	8	15	50		
Ron Schock	4	4	5	8	15	60		
Ken Schinkel	4	4	5	8	15	30	40	120
Keith McCreary	4	4	5	8	15	40		
Bryan Hextall	4	5	6	10	25	60		
Wayne Hicks RC	4	4	5	8	15	40		
Gary Sabourin	4	4	5	8	15	30		
Ernie Wakely RC	4	5	6	10	20	80		
Bob Wall	4	4	5	8	15	40	50	100
Barclay Plager	4	5	6	10	20	40	50	100
Jean-Guy Talbot	4	4	5	8	15	30		
Gary Veneruzzo	4	4	5	8	15	30		
Tim Ecclestone	4	4	5	8	15	30	40	100
Red Berenson	4	5	6	10	20	60		
Larry Keenan	4	4	5	8	15	30	40	100
Bruce Gamble	4	5	6	10	20	100		
Jim Dorey	4	4	5	8	15	30		
Mike Pelyk RC	4	4	5	8	30	150		
Rick Ley	4	4	5	10	20	60		
Mike Walton	4	4	5	8	15	30		
Norm Ullman	10	12	15	25	40	100	125	175
Brit Selby no trade	4	4	5	8	15	30	40	80
Brit Selby trade	15	20	20	30	40	100		
Garry Monahan	4	4	5	8	15	100		
George Armstrong	10	12	15	25	40	125	150	300
Gary Doak	4	5	10	15	30	150		
Darryl Sly RC	4	4	5	8	15	30		
Wayne Maki	4	4	5	8	15	125		
Orland Kurtenbach	4	4	5	8	20	60		
Murray Hall	4	4	5	8	15	30		
Marc Reaume	4	4	5	8	15	30	40	350
Pat Quinn	10	12	15	25	40	60	80	200
Andre Boudrias	4	4	5	15	60	100		
Paul Popiel	4	4	5	8	15	150		
Paul Terbenche	4	4	5	8	15	40	50	80
Howie Menard	4	4	5	8	15	30		
Gerry Meehan RC	4	5	6	10	20	60		
Skip Krake	4	4	5	8	15	30		
Phil Goyette	4	4	5	8	15	50	60	150
Reg Fleming	4	4	5	8	15	30	40	100
Don Marshall	4	5	6	10	20	40		
Bill Inglis RC	4	4	5	8	15	40	50	100
Gilbert Perreault RC	50	80	125	250	400	1,750		
Checklist 2	50	100	150	300	350	1,200	1,350	1,500
Ed Johnston	4	5	6	10	40	50		
Ted Green	4	5	6	10	20	40		
Rick Smith RC	4	4	5	8	15	40		
Derek Sanderson	15	20	20	30	40	100	150	
Dallas Smith	4	5	8	20	30	100		
Don Marcotte RC	4	5	6	10	20	40	50	150
Ed Westfall	4	5	6	10	20	60		
Floyd Smith	4	4	5	8	15	30	35	60
Randy Wyrozub RC	4	4	5	8	15	30		
Cliff Schmautz RC	4	4	5	8	15	30		
Mike McMahon	4	4	5	8	15	30	40	150
Jim Watson	4	4	5	8	15	30		
Roger Crozier	4	5	6	10	20	40		
Tracy Pratt	4	4	5	8	15	30		
Cliff Koroll RC	4	5	6	10	20	30		
Gerry Pinder RC	4	5	6	10	20	30	40	60
Chico Maki	4	4	5	8	15	30	40	135
Doug Jarrett	4	4	5	8	15	30		
Keith Magnuson RC	10	12	15	20	30	50	60	150
Gerry Desjardins	4	5	6	10	20	30		
Tony Esposito	20	25	30	40	60	150	200	300
Gary Bergman	4	4	5	8	15	30	40	80
Tom Webster RC	4	5	6	10	20	30	40	60
Dale Rolfe	4	4	5	8	15	30		
Alex Delvecchio	10	12	15	20	25	40	50	100
Nick Libett	4	4	5	8	15	30		
Wayne Connelly	4	4	5	8	15	30	40	60
Mike Byers RC	4	4	5	8	15	30		
Bill Flett	4	4	5	8	15	30	40	60
Larry Mickey	4	4	5	8	15	30	40	80
Noel Price	4	4	5	8	15	30		
Larry Cahan	4	4	5	8	15	50		
Jack Norris RC	4	5	6	10	20	30	40	80
Ted Harris	4	4	5	8	15	30	40	60
Murray Oliver	4	4	5	8	15	30	40	80
Jean-Paul Parise	4	5	6	10	20	40	50	80
Tom Williams	4	4	5	8	15	30		
Bobby Rousseau	4	4	5	8	15	30		
Jude Drouin RC	4	5	6	10	20	30		
Walt McKechnie RC	4	5	6	10	20	30		
Cesare Maniago	4	5	6	10	20	100		
Rejean Houle RC	10	12	15	20	25	40	50	100

Right table:

		VG 3	VgEx 4	EX 5	ExMt 6	NM 7	NmMt 8	NmMt+ 8.5	MT 9
175A	M.Redmond trade	4	5	6	10	25	40	50	80
175B	M.Redmond no trade	12	15	20	30	40	150		
176	Henri Richard	10	12	15	20	30	60	80	200
177	Guy Lapointe RC	15	20	30	40	50	125	150	250
178	J.C. Tremblay	4	5	6	10	20	30	40	60
179	Marc Tardif RC	10	12	15	20	50	60	80	100
180	Walt Tkaczuk	4	5	6	10	20	30	40	50
181	Jean Ratelle	6	8	12	15	25	60	80	100
182	Pete Stemkowski	4	4	5	8	15	30		
183	Gilles Villemure	4	5	6	10	20	30	35	60
184	Rod Seiling	4	4	5	8	15	30	35	60
185	Jim Neilson	4	4	5	8	15	30	35	60
186	Dennis Hextall	4	5	6	10	20	30	35	60
187	Gerry Ehman	4	4	5	8	15	30		
188	Bert Marshall	4	4	5	8	15	50		
189	Gary Croteau RC	4	4	5	8	15	30		
190	Ted Hampson	4	4	5	8	15	30		
191	Earl Ingarfield	4	4	5	8	15	30	40	60
192	Dick Mattiussi	4	4	5	8	15	30		
193	Earl Heiskala	4	4	5	8	15	30	40	80
194	Simon Nolet	4	4	5	8	15	30	40	60
195	Bobby Clarke RC	▲50	▲80	▲100	▲150	200	400	500	1,000
196	Garry Peters	4	4	5	8	15	30		
197	Lew Morrison RC	4	4	5	8	15	30	40	80
198	Wayne Hillman	4	4	5	8	15	40		
199	Doug Favell	10	12	15	25	40	150		
200	Les Binkley	4	5	6	10	20	40	50	150
201	Dean Prentice	4	4	5	8	15	30		
202	Jean Pronovost	4	5	6	10	25	80		
203	Wally Boyer	4	4	5	8	15	30		
204	Bryan Watson	4	4	5	8	15	30		
205	Glen Sather	4	5	6	10	25	40	50	80
206	Lowell MacDonald	4	4	5	8	15	30	40	80
207	Andy Bathgate	4	5	6	10	20	40	40	80
208	Val Fonteyne	4	4	5	8	15	30		
209	Jim Lorentz RC	4	4	5	8	15	30		
210	Glenn Hall	10	12	20	30	50	60	100	
211	Bob Plager	4	5	6	10	20	40	50	60
212	Noel Picard	4	4	5	8	15	30	40	80
213	Jim Roberts	4	5	6	10	25	40		
214	Frank St.Marseille	4	4	5	8	15	30	40	60
215	Ab McDonald	4	4	5	8	15	30		
216	Brian Glennie RC	4	4	5	8	15	30	40	80
217	Paul Henderson	4	5	6	10	20	30	50	80
218	Darryl Sittler RC	60	80	100	▲150	▲300	▲550	600	1,600
219	Dave Keon	8	10	12	20	35	50	60	125
220	Jim Harrison RC	4	4	5	8	15	30	40	125
221	Ron Ellis	4	5	6	10	20	30		
222	Jacques Plante	20	25	30	40	60	150		
223	Bob Baun	4	5	10	20	30	120		
224	George Gardner RC	4	4	5	8	15	30	40	60
225	Dale Tallon RC	4	5	6	10	20	40	50	80
226	Rosaire Paiement RC	4	4	5	8	15	30		
227	Mike Corrigan RC	4	4	5	8	15	30	40	80
228	Ray Cullen	4	4	5	8	15	30		
229	Charlie Hodge	4	5	6	10	20	40		
230	Len Lunde	4	4	5	8	15	30	40	80
231	Terry Sawchuk Mem	30	40	50	60	80	100	125	200
232	Bruins Team Champs	10	12	15	25	40	80	100	150
233	Espo/Cashmn/Hodge	15	20	20	25	35	60	80	150
234	Tony Esposito AS1	20	25	30	40	60	120		
235	Bobby Hull AS1	20	25	30	40	50	80		
236	Bobby Orr AS1	40	50	60	80	120	300	400	750
237	Phil Esposito AS1	12	15	20	30	40	80	100	200
238	Gordie Howe AS1	20	30	40	50	80	100		
239	Brad Park AS1	12	15	20	30	40	80		
240	Stan Mikita AS2	10	12	15	25	40	100		
241	John McKenzie AS2	4	5	8	10	25	125	150	200
242	Frank Mahovlich AS2	4	4	5	8	15	30	50	150
243	Carl Brewer AS2	4	4	5	8	15	30		
244	Ed Giacomin AS2	4	5	6	20	40	200		
245	J.Laperriere AS2	4	4	6	10	20	80		
246	Bobby Orr Hart	40	50	60	80	150	250	300	700
247	Tony Esposito Calder	20	25	30	40	60	100		
248A	B.Orr Norris Howe	50	60	80	120	200	350	500	
248B	B.Orr Norris no Howe	50	60	80	120	200	350	500	
249	Bobby Orr Ross	35	50	60	80	100	350	500	
250	Tony Esposito Vezina	20	25	30	40	60	120		
251	Phil Goyette Byng Trophy	4	4	5	8	15	30		
252	Bobby Orr Smythe	50	60	80	120	150	225	350	600
253	P.Martin Mastrtn Trophy	4	5	6	8	15	30		
254	Stanley Cup	12	15	20	30	40	50	60	100
255	Prince of Wales Trophy	4	5	6	10	20	30		
256	Conn Smythe Trophy	4	5	6	10	20	40	60	80
257	James Norris Trophy	4	5	6	10	20	30	40	80
258	Calder Trophy	4	5	6	10	20	30	40	80
259	Vezina Trophy	4	5	6	10	20	40		
260	Lady Byng Trophy	4	5	6	10	20	30	40	80
261	Hart Trophy	4	5	6	10	20	30	35	60

#		VG 3	VgEx 4	EX 5	ExMt 6	NM 7	NmMt 8	NmMt+ 8.5	MT 9
262	Art Ross Trophy	4	5	6	10	20	40		
263	Clarence Campbell Bowl	4	5	6	10	25	40		
264	John Ferguson	10	12	15	25	50	250		

—Art Ross Trophy #262 PSA 9 (MT) sold for $408 (eBay; 4/07)
—Bobby Orr Hart #246 PSA 9 (MT) sold for $681 (Mile High; 12/13)
—Bruins Team Champs #232 PSA 10 (Gem) sold for $929 (eBay; 1/14)
—Checklist 2 #132 PSA 10 (Gem) sold for $2,385 (Mile High; 12/13)
—Guy LaPointe #177 PSA 10 (Gem) sold for $1,209 (eBay; 9/15)
—Peter Mahovlich #58 PSA 10 (Gem) sold for $204 (eBay; 2/07)
—Bobby Orr #3 PSA 10 (Gem) sold for $7,036 (eBay; 5/12)
—Bobby Orr Norris #214 PSA 9 (MT) sold for $1,775 (Mile High; 12/13)
—Bobby Orr Norris no Howe #248B PSA 10 (Gem) sold for $1,710 (eBay; 2/13)
—Bobby Orr Smythe #252 PSA 10 (Gem) sold for $1,955 (Memory Lane; 5/08)
—Jacques Plante #222 PSA 9 (MT) sold for $460 (eBay; 2/14)
—Terry Sawchuk Mem #231 PSA 10 (gem) sold for $1,135 (eBay; 2/16)
—Brad Park RC #67 PSA 9 (MT) sold for $1,730 (eBay; 4/09)

1970-71 Topps

#		VG 3	VgEx 4	EX 5	ExMt 6	NM 7	NmMt 8	NmMt+ 8.5	MT 9
1	Gerry Cheevers	10	12	15	20	25	50		
2	Johnny Bucyk	5	6	8	10	12	30		
3	Bobby Orr	25	40	60	80	150	300	400	1,400
4	Don Awrey	5	6	8	10	12	15	25	40
5	Fred Stanfield	5	6	8	10	12	15	25	40
6	John McKenzie	5	6	8	10	12	15	25	40
7	Wayne Cashman RC	6	8	10	12	15	25	40	60
8	Ken Hodge	5	6	8	10	12	15	25	40
9	Wayne Carleton	5	6	8	10	12	15	25	40
10	Garnet Bailey RC	5	6	8	10	12	15	25	40
11	Phil Esposito	10	12	15	20	25	60	80	100
12	Lou Angotti	5	6	8	10	12	15	25	40
13	Jim Pappin	5	6	8	10	12	15	25	40
14	Dennis Hull	5	6	8	10	12	15	25	40
15	Bobby Hull	12	15	20	25	30	60	80	175
16	Doug Mohns	5	6	8	10	12	15	25	40
17	Pat Stapleton	5	6	8	10	12	15	20	30
18	Pit Martin	5	6	8	10	12	15	25	40
19	Eric Nesterenko	5	6	8	10	12	15	25	40
20	Stan Mikita	8	10	12	15	20	30	50	200
21	Roy Edwards	5	6	8	10	12	15	25	40
22	Frank Mahovlich	5	6	8	10	15	30	40	150
23	Ron Harris	5	6	8	10	12	15	25	40
24	Bob Baun	5	6	8	10	12	15	25	40
25	Pete Stemkowski	5	6	8	10	12	15	25	40
26	Garry Unger	5	6	8	10	12	15	25	40
27	Bruce MacGregor	5	6	8	10	12	15	25	40
28	Larry Jeffrey	5	6	8	10	12	15	25	40
29	Gordie Howe	20	25	40	50	60	80	100	150
30	Billy Dea	5	6	8	10	12	15	25	40
31	Denis DeJordy	5	6	8	10	12	15	25	40
32	Matt Ravlich	5	6	8	10	12	20	30	50
33	Dave Amadio	5	6	8	10	12	15	25	40
34	Gilles Marotte	5	6	8	10	12	15	20	30
35	Eddie Shack	5	6	8	10	12	15	25	50
36	Bob Pulford	5	6	8	10	12	15	25	40
37	Ross Lonsberry	5	6	8	10	12	15	20	30
38	Gord Labossiere	5	6	8	10	12	15	25	40
39	Eddie Joyal	5	6	8	10	12	15	25	40
40	Gump Worsley	5	6	8	10	12	20		
41	Bob McCord	5	6	8	10	12	15	20	30
42	Leo Boivin	5	6	8	10	12	15	25	40
43	Tom Reid	5	6	8	10	12	15	25	40
44	Charlie Burns	5	6	8	10	12	15	25	40
45	Bob Barlow	5	6	8	10	12	15	20	30
46	Bill Goldsworthy	5	6	8	10	12	15	20	30
47	Danny Grant	5	6	8	10	12	15	25	40
48	Norm Beaudin	5	6	8	10	12	15	20	30
49	Rogatien Vachon	6	8	10	12	12	20	25	50
50	Yvan Cournoyer	5	6	8	10	12	15	25	50
51	Serge Savard	5	6	8	10	12	15	30	50
52	Jacques Laperriere	5	6	8	10	12	15	20	30
53	Terry Harper	5	6	8	10	12	15	20	30
54	Ralph Backstrom	5	6	8	10	12	15	25	40
55	Jean Beliveau	8	10	12	15	20	50	60	80
56	Claude Larose UER	5	6	8	10	12	15	25	40
57	Jacques Lemaire	5	6	8	10	12	20	25	50
58	Peter Mahovlich	5	6	8	10	12	15	25	40
59	Tim Horton	8	10	12	15	▲25	▲40	▲50	▲80
60	Bob Nevin	5	6	8	10	12	15	25	40
61	Dave Balon	5	6	8	10	12	15	25	40
62	Vic Hadfield	5	6	8	10	12	15	25	40
63	Rod Gilbert	5	6	8	10	12	20	25	50
64	Ron Stewart	5	6	8	10	12	15	25	40
65	Ted Irvine	5	6	8	10	12	15	25	40
66	Arnie Brown	5	6	8	10	12	15	20	30
67	Brad Park RC	12	15	20	25	25	40	50	200
68	Ed Giacomin	5	6	8	10	12	20	25	50
69	Gary Smith	5	6	8	10	12	15	20	30
70	Carol Vadnais	5	6	8	10	12	15	20	30

#		VG 3	VgEx 4	EX 5	ExMt 6	NM 7	NmMt 8	NmMt+ 8.5	
71	Doug Roberts	5	6	8	10	12	15	25	
72	Harry Howell	5	6	8	10	12	15	25	
73	Joe Szura	5	6	8	10	12	15	20	
74	Mike Laughton	5	6	8	10	12	15	20	
75	Gary Jarrett	5	6	8	10	12	15	25	
76	Bill Hicke	5	6	8	10	12	20		
77	Paul Andrea	5	6	8	10	12	15	25	
78	Bernie Parent	8	10	12	15	20	40	50	
79	Joe Watson	5	6	8	10	12	15	25	
80	Ed Van Impe	5	6	8	10	12	15	25	
81	Larry Hillman	5	6	8	10	12	15	25	
82	George Swarbrick	5	6	8	10	12	15	25	
83	Bill Sutherland	5	6	8	10	12	15	25	
84	Andre Lacroix	5	6	8	10	12	15	25	
85	Gary Dornhoefer	5	6	8	10	12	15	25	
86	Jean-Guy Gendron	5	6	8	10	12	15	25	
87	Al Smith	5	6	8	10	12	15	25	
88	Bob Woytowich	5	6	8	10	12	15	25	
89	Duane Rupp	5	6	8	10	12	15	25	
90	Jim Morrison	5	6	8	10	12	15	25	
91	Ron Schock	5	6	8	10	12	15	25	
92	Ken Schinkel	5	6	8	10	12	15	25	
93	Keith McCreary	5	6	8	10	12	15	25	
94	Bryan Hextall	5	6	8	10	12	15	25	
95	Wayne Hicks	5	6	8	10	12	15	25	
96	Gary Sabourin	5	6	8	10	12	15	25	
97	Ernie Wakely	5	6	8	10	12	15	25	
98	Bob Wall	5	6	8	10	12	15	25	
99	Barclay Plager	5	6	8	10	12	15	25	
100	Jean-Guy Talbot	5	6	8	10	12	20		
101	Gary Veneruzzo	5	6	8	10	12	20		
102	Tim Ecclestone	5	6	8	10	12	15	25	
103	Red Berenson	5	6	8	10	12	15	25	
104	Larry Keenan	5	6	8	10	12	15	20	
105	Bruce Gamble	5	6	8	10	12	20		
106	Jim Dorey	5	6	8	10	12	15	25	
107	Mike Pelyk	5	6	8	10	12	15	25	
108	Rick Ley	5	6	8	10	12	15	25	
109	Mike Walton	5	6	8	10	12	15	25	
110	Norm Ullman	5	6	8	10	12	20	25	
111	Brit Selby	5	6	8	10	12	15	25	
112	Garry Monahan	5	6	8	10	12	15	20	
113	George Armstrong	5	6	8	10	12	20	25	
114	Gary Doak	5	6	8	10	12	15	25	
115	Darryl Sly	5	6	8	10	12	15	20	
116	Wayne Maki	5	6	8	10	12	20		
117	Orland Kurtenbach	5	6	8	10	12	15	25	
118	Murray Hall	5	6	8	10	12	15	20	
119	Marc Reaume	5	6	8	10	12	15	25	
120	Pat Quinn	5	6	8	10	12	30	40	
121	Andre Boudrias	5	6	8	10	12	15	25	
122	Paul Popiel	5	6	8	10	12	15	25	
123	Paul Terbenche	5	6	8	10	12	15	25	
124	Howie Menard	5	6	8	10	12	15	25	
125	Gerry Meehan RC	5	6	8	10	12	25	30	
126	Skip Krake	5	6	8	10	12	15	25	
127	Phil Goyette	5	6	8	10	12	15	25	
128	Reg Fleming	5	6	8	10	12	20		
129	Don Marshall	5	6	8	10	12	15	25	
130	Bill Inglis	5	6	8	10	12	15	25	
131	Gilbert Perreault RC	20	25	30	▲50	▲100	150	250	40
132	Checklist Card	25	25	30	40	80	150		

—Jean Beliveau #55 PSA 10 (GmMT) sold for $665 (eBay; 1/07)
—Gary Doak #114 PSA 10 (GmMT) sold for $535 (Memory Lane; 5/08)
—Gordie Howe #29 PSA 10 (GmMT) sold for $1,630 (eBay; 1/07)
—Orland Kurtenbach #117 PSA 10 (GmMT) sold for $535 (Memory Lane; 5/08)
—Gilbert Perreault RC #131 PSA 8 (NrMt) sold for $3,442.99 (eBay; 2/14)
—Doug Mohns #16 PSA 9 (MT) sold for $258 (eBay; 7/12)
—Brad Park #67 PSA 10 (GmMT) sold for $921.50 (eBay; 8/12)

1971-72 O-Pee-Chee

#		VG 3	VgEx 4	EX 5	ExMt 6	NM 7	NmMt 8	NmMt+ 8.5	MT
1	Paul Popiel	6	8	10	15	30	200		
2	Pierre Bouchard RC	5	8	15	40	100	250		
3	Don Awrey	4	4	5	8	15	40	60	150
4	Paul Curtis RC	4	4	5	8	15	80		
5	Guy Trottier RC	4	4	5	10	20	50	60	135
6	Paul Shmyr RC	4	4	5	10	20	50	60	135
7	Fred Stanfield	4	4	5	10	20	50	60	120
8	Mike Robitaille RC	4	4	5	8	15	50	60	100
9	Vic Hadfield	4	5	6	10	20	30	60	100
10	Jim Harrison	4	4	5	8	15	40	60	100
11	Bill White	4	4	5	8	15	40	50	80
12	Andre Boudrias	4	4	5	8	25	60		
13	Gary Sabourin	4	4	5	8	15	60	80	150
14	Arnie Brown	5	6	10	15	30	80		
15	Yvan Cournoyer	6	8	10	15	30	60	80	175
16	Bryan Hextall	4	5	6	10	20	40	50	80
17	Gary Croteau	4	4	5	8	15	80		

	VG 3	VgEx 4	EX 5	ExMt 6	NM 7	NmMt 8	NmMt+ 8.5	MT 9
Gilles Villemure	4	5	6	10	20	60		
Serge Bernier RC	4	5	6	10	20	50		
Phil Esposito	15	20	25	40	80	100	125	200
Tom Reid	4	4	5	8	15	40	60	120
Doug Barrie RC	4	4	5	8	15	50	60	80
Eddie Joyal	4	4	5	8	15	50		
Dunc Wilson RC	6	8	10	15	30	100	125	250
Pat Stapleton	4	5	6	10	20	60		
Garry Unger	4	5	10	20	50	300		
Al Smith	4	5	6	10	20	40	50	80
Bob Woytowich	4	5	6	8	40	80		
Marc Tardif	4	5	6	10	20	60	80	150
Norm Ullman	6	8	10	15	30	80		
Tom Williams	4	4	5	8	40	250		
Ted Harris	4	4	5	8	15	40	50	80
Andre Lacroix	4	5	6	10	20	50		
Mike Byers	4	4	5	8	15	40	50	100
Johnny Bucyk	6	8	10	15	30	150	200	400
Roger Crozier	4	5	6	10	20	50	60	120
Alex Delvecchio	8	10	12	20	30	80		
Frank St.Marseille	4	4	5	8	15	50	60	100
Pit Martin	4	5	6	10	20	40	50	80
Brad Park	12	15	15	25	35	50	60	120
Greg Polis RC	4	4	5	8	15	50		
Orland Kurtenbach	4	4	5	8	15	50	60	100
Jim McKenny RC	4	4	5	8	15	50	60	100
Bob Nevin	4	4	5	8	15	60	80	135
Ken Dryden RC	100	120	250	400	500	1,000	1,500	3,500
Carol Vadnais	4	5	6	10	20	50	60	100
Bill Flett	4	4	5	8	15	40	50	80
Jim Johnson	4	4	5	8	15	50	60	100
Al Hamilton	4	4	5	8	15	50		
Bobby Hull	30	40	50	60	80	100	125	300
Chris Bordeleau RC	4	4	5	8	15	60	80	175
Tim Ecclestone	4	4	5	8	15	40	50	80
Rod Seiling	4	4	5	8	15	40		
Gerry Cheevers	8	10	12	20	40	80		
Bill Goldsworthy	4	5	6	10	20	50	60	100
Ron Schock	4	4	5	8	15	50	60	100
Jim Dorey	4	4	5	8	15	40	50	80
Wayne Maki	4	4	5	8	15	40		
Terry Harper	4	4	5	8	15	50		
Gilbert Perreault	20	25	30	50	80	100	125	225
Ernie Hicke RC	4	4	5	8	15	40	50	80
Wayne Hillman	4	4	5	8	20	80	100	175
Denis DeJordy	4	5	6	10	20	80		
Ken Schinkel	4	4	5	8	15	50	60	100
Derek Sanderson	10	12	15	25	40	80	125	225
Barclay Plager	4	5	6	10	20	50	60	100
Paul Henderson	4	5	6	10	20	60	80	200
Jude Drouin	4	4	5	8	15	80	100	175
Keith Magnuson	4	5	6	10	20	40	50	80
Ron Harris	4	4	5	8	15	40	50	80
Jacques Lemaire	6	8	10	15	30	60	80	150
Doug Favell	4	5	6	10	20	60	80	150
Bert Marshall	4	4	5	8	15	30	40	80
Ted Irvine	4	4	5	8	15	30	40	80
Walt Tkaczuk	4	5	6	10	25	40	50	100
Bob Berry RC	6	8	10	15	30	60		
Syl Apps RC	6	8	10	15	30	60	80	150
Tom Webster	4	5	6	10	20	40	50	100
Danny Grant	4	5	6	10	20	60	80	150
Dave Keon	6	8	10	15	30			350
Ernie Wakely	4	5	6	10	20			150
John McKenzie	4	5	6	10	20	50	60	100
Ron Stackhouse RC	4	4	5	8	15			100
Peter Mahovlich	4	5	6	10	20			300
Dennis Hull	4	5	6	10	20	50	80	175
Juha Widing RC	4	4	5	8	15	50	60	100
Gary Doak	4	4	5	8	15	50	60	100
Phil Goyette	4	4	5	8	15	40	50	80
Lew Morrison	4	4	5	8	15	40	50	80
Ab DeMarco RC	4	4	5	8	15	40	50	80
Red Berenson	4	5	6	10	20	40	50	80
Mike Pelyk	4	4	5	8	15	50		
Gary Jarrett	4	4	5	8	15	30	40	60
Bob Pulford	4	5	6	10	20	40	50	100
Dan Johnson RC	4	4	5	8	15	30	40	60
Eddie Shack	6	8	10	15	30	50	60	120
Jean Ratelle	6	8	10	15	30	60	80	150
Jim Pappin	4	4	5	8	15	50	60	100
Roy Edwards	4	5	6	10	25	40	50	80
Bobby Orr	40	50	60	100	200	800		
Ted Hampson	4	5	6	8	15	40	50	80
Mickey Redmond	6	8	10	15	30	80		
Bob Plager	6	8	10	15	30	50	60	100
Barry Ashbee RC	4	5	6	10	20	50	60	150
Frank Mahovlich	8	10	12	20	40	100		
Dick Redmond RC	4	4	5	8	15	30	40	80
Tracy Pratt	4	4	5	8	15	30	40	80

	VG 3	VgEx 4	EX 5	ExMt 6	NM 7	NmMt 8	NmMt+ 8.5	MT 9
108 Ralph Backstrom	4	5	6	10	15	30	40	80
109 Murray Hall	4	4	5	8	15	30	40	80
110 Tony Esposito	25	30	40	50	60	100	125	250
111 Checklist Card	250	300	400	700	900	2,000		
112 Jim Neilson	4	4	5	8	15	50	60	100
113 Ron Ellis	4	5	6	10	20	80		
114 Bobby Clarke	30	35	40	50	80	100	125	300
115 Ken Hodge	4	5	6	10	30	60		
116 Jim Roberts	4	5	6	10	30	80	100	175
117 Cesare Maniago	4	5	6	10	20	50	60	100
118 Jean Pronovost	4	5	6	10	20	50		
119 Gary Bergman	4	4	5	8	15	40	50	80
120 Henri Richard	8	10	12	20	30	80	100	175
121 Ross Lonsberry	4	4	5	8	15	50	60	100
122 Pat Quinn	4	5	6	10	20	60	80	150
123 Rod Gilbert	6	8	10	15	30	50	60	100
124 Walt McKechnie	4	5	6	10	20	50		
125 Stan Mikita	12	15	15	25	40	60	80	250
126 Ed Van Impe	4	4	5	8	15	30	40	60
127 Terry Crisp RC	8	10	12	20	30	40	50	80
128 Fred Barrett RC	4	4	5	8	15	40	50	80
129 Wayne Cashman	6	8	10	15	30	80		
130 J.C. Tremblay	4	5	6	10	40	80		
131 Bernie Parent	15	20	25	40	80	120	135	250
132 Bryan Watson	4	5	6	10	20	60		
133 Marcel Dionne RC	50	▲80	▲100	▲150	▲250	350	450	1,250
134 Ab McDonald	4	5	6	10	20	60	80	150
135 Leon Rochefort	4	5	6	10	20	30	40	60
136 Serge Lajeunesse RC	4	5	6	10	20	30	40	60
137 Joe Daley	5	6	8	12	25	40	50	80
138 Brian Conacher	4	5	6	10	20	60		
139 Bill Collins	4	5	6	10	20	60		
140 Nick Libett	4	5	6	10	20	60	80	150
141 Bill Sutherland	4	5	6	10	20	30	40	60
142 Bill Hicke	4	5	6	10	20	50	60	100
143 Serge Savard	8	10	12	20	40	80	80	150
144 Jacques Laperriere	5	6	8	12	40	100	120	175
145 Guy Lapointe	5	6	8	12	25	60		
146 Claude Larose UER	4	5	6	10	20	60		
147 Rejean Houle	5	6	8	12	25	60	80	120
148 Guy Lafleur UER RC	60	100	▲150	▲250	▲350	▲650	▲800	▲1,250
149 Dale Hoganson RC	4	5	6	10	20	30	40	80
150 Al McDonough RC	4	5	6	10	20	30	40	100
151 Gilles Marotte	4	5	6	10	20	30	40	100
152 Butch Goring RC	8	10	12	20	50	120		
153 Harry Howell	5	6	8	12	25	60	80	150
154 Real Lemieux	4	5	6	10	20	30	35	60
155 Gary Edwards RC	5	6	8	12	25	40	50	100
156 Rogatien Vachon	8	10	12	20	30	40	60	120
157 Mike Corrigan	4	5	6	10	20	60	80	150
158 Floyd Smith	4	5	6	10	20	40	50	100
159 Dave Dryden	5	6	8	12	25	60	80	150
160 Gerry Meehan	5	6	8	12	25	50		
161 Richard Martin RC	15	20	25	30	50	60	80	175
162 Steve Atkinson RC	4	5	6	10	20	60		
163 Ron Anderson	4	5	6	10	20	30	35	60
164 Dick Duff	5	6	8	12	25	50	60	100
165 Jim Watson	4	5	6	10	20	30	35	60
166 Don Luce RC	4	5	6	10	20	60		
167 Larry Mickey	4	5	6	10	20	60		
168 Larry Hillman	4	5	6	10	20	30	35	60
169 Ed Westfall	5	6	8	12	25	30	40	100
170 Dallas Smith	4	5	6	10	20	40	50	100
171 Mike Walton	4	5	6	10	20	40	50	100
172 Ed Johnston	5	6	8	12	25	40	50	80
173 Ted Green	5	6	8	12	25	50	60	100
174 Rick Smith	4	5	6	10	20	40	50	80
175 Reggie Leach RC	15	20	25	40	80	120		
176 Don Marcotte	4	5	6	10	20	50		
177 Bobby Sheehan RC	4	5	6	10	20	60		
178 Wayne Carleton	4	5	6	10	20	40	50	120
179 Norm Ferguson	4	5	6	10	20	30	35	60
180 Don O'Donoghue RC	4	5	6	10	20	30	40	80
181 Gary Kurt RC	5	6	8	12	25	40	50	120
182 Joey Johnston RC	4	5	6	10	20	60		
183 Stan Gilbertson RC	4	5	6	10	20	60	80	150
184 Craig Patrick RC	8	10	12	20	40	50	60	120
185 Gerry Pinder	4	5	6	10	20	30	35	60
186 Tim Horton	10	12	15	25	35	50	60	100
187 Darryl Edestrand RC	4	5	6	10	20	60		
188 Keith McCreary	4	5	6	10	20	50	60	100
189 Val Fonteyne	4	5	6	10	20	50	60	100
190 S.Kannegiesser RC	4	5	6	10	20	30	35	60
191 Nick Harbaruk RC	4	5	6	10	20	60		
192 Les Binkley	5	6	8	10	20	30	35	60
193 Darryl Sittler	18	20	25	30	50	100	120	200
194 Rick Ley	4	5	6	10	20	60	80	150
195 Jacques Plante	25	30	35	40	50	100	120	200
196 Bob Baun	5	6	10	15	50	250		
197 Brian Glennie	4	5	6	10	20	40	50	80
198 Brian Spencer RC	8	10	12	20	35	50	60	175
199 Don Marshall	5	6	8	12	25	40	50	100
200 Denis Dupere RC	5	6	8	12	25	30	35	60
201 Bruce Gamble	5	6	8	12	25	30	35	60

#	Player	VG 3	VgEx 4	EX 5	ExMt 6	NM 7	NmMt 8	NmMt+ 8.5	MT 9
202	Gary Dornhoefer	4	5	6	10	20	30	40	80
203	Bob Kelly RC	5	6	8	12	25	60		
204	Jean-Guy Gendron	4	5	6	10	20	30	35	60
205	Brent Hughes	4	5	6	10	20	35	40	100
206	Simon Nolet	4	5	6	10	20	40	50	80
207	Rick MacLeish RC	15	20	25	30	40	60	80	150
208	Doug Jarrett	4	5	6	10	20	30	35	60
209	Cliff Koroll	4	5	6	10	20	40	50	80
210	Chico Maki	4	5	6	10	20	30	35	60
211	Danny O'Shea	4	5	6	10	20	30	40	80
212	Lou Angotti	4	5	6	10	20	30	40	880
213	Eric Nesterenko	5	6	8	12	25	30	35	60
214	Bryan Campbell	4	5	6	10	20	30	40	80
215	Bill Fairbairn RC	4	5	6	10	20	40	50	80
216	Bruce MacGregor	4	5	6	10	20	30	35	60
217	Pete Stemkowski	4	5	6	10	20	30	40	80
218	Bobby Rousseau	4	5	6	10	20	30	40	80
219	Dale Rolfe	4	5	6	10	20	30	35	60
220	Ed Giacomin	8	10	12	20	40	40	50	120
221	Glen Sather	5	6	8	12	25	30	50	80
222	Carl Brewer	5	6	8	12	25	30	40	80
223	George Morrison RC	4	5	8	15	50	200		
224	Noel Picard	4	5	6	10	20	30	35	60
225	Peter McDuffe RC	5	6	8	12	30	80		
226	Brit Selby	4	5	6	10	20	40	50	80
227	Jim Lorentz	4	5	6	10	20	30	40	80
228	Phil Roberto RC	4	5	6	10	20	40	50	80
229	Dave Balon	4	5	6	10	20	30	40	100
230	Barry Wilkins RC	4	5	6	10	20	35	40	80
231	Dennis Kearns RC	4	5	6	10	20	30	40	80
232	Jocelyn Guevremont RC	5	6	8	12	25	30	40	80
233	Rosaire Paiement	4	5	6	10	20	80	100	175
234	Dale Tallon	4	5	6	10	20	80		
235	George Gardner	4	5	6	10	20	50	60	100
236	Ron Stewart	4	5	6	10	20	30	35	60
237	Wayne Connelly	4	5	6	10	20	40	50	80
238	Charlie Burns	4	5	6	10	30	200		
239	Murray Oliver	4	5	6	10	20	30	40	80
240	Lou Nanne	5	6	8	12	25	30	40	100
241	Gump Worsley	8	10	12	20	35	50	60	100
242	Doug Mohns	4	5	6	10	20	50	60	100
243	Jean-Paul Parise	4	5	6	10	20	35	40	80
244	Dennis Hextall	5	6	8	15	60	250		
245	Bobby Orr Double	25	30	40	50	80	150	175	350
246	Gilbert Perreault Calder	12	15	15	25	40	80		
247	Phil Esposito Ross	8	10	12	20	30	60		
248	Giacmn/Ville Vezina	5	8	15	30	150	500		
249	Johnny Bucyk Byng	5	6	8	12	25	40	50	100
250	Ed Giacomin AS1	5	6	8	12	25	50	60	100
251	Bobby Orr AS1	25	30	35	40	80	150	250	500
252	J.C. Tremblay AS1	5	8	15	30	125	200		
253	Phil Esposito AS1 UER	10	12	15	25	40	60	80	200
254	Ken Hodge AS1	5	6	8	12	25	60		
255	Johnny Bucyk AS1	5	6	8	15	30	80		
256	Jacques Plante AS2 UER	12	15	15	30	50	80	100	200
257	Brad Park AS2	5	6	8	12	25	40	60	100
258	Pat Stapleton AS2	5	6	8	12	25	35		
259	Dave Keon AS2	5	6	8	15	30	200		
260	Yvan Cournoyer AS2	5	6	8	12	25	50	60	100
261	Bobby Hull AS2	15	20	25	30	40	80	100	200
262	Gordie Howe Retires	25	30	40	60	80	100	175	300
263	Jean Beliveau Retires	25	30	40	60	80	120	150	300
264	Checklist Card	60	80	120	150	200	300	400	1,000

—Jean Beliveau Retires #263 PSA 10 (Gem) sold for $1,499 (eBay; 2/14)
—Checklist Card #111 PSA 9 (MT) sold for $2,800 (eBay; 2/07)
—Checklist Card #264 PSA 9 (Mt) sold for $1,034 (eBay; 2/14)
—Marcel Dionne RC #133 BGS 9.5 (GemMT) sold for $1,629.30 (eBay; 12/15)
—Ted Hampson #101 PSA 10 (Gem) sold for $311 (eBay; 8/12)
—Bobby Hull #50 PSA 10 (Gem) sold for $1,063 (eBay; 11/15)
—Ed Johnston #172 PSA 10 (Gem) sold for $425 (eBay; 4/07)
—Andre Lacroix #33 PSA 10 (Gem) sold for $425 (eBay; 8/12)
—Peter Mahovlich #84 PSA 10 (Gem) sold for $684 (eBay; 8/12)
—Chico Maki #210 PSA 10 (Gem) sold for $375 (eBay; 8/07)
—Murray Oliver #239 PSA 10 (Gem) sold for $505 (eBay; 4/07)
—Bobby Orr #100 PSA 9 (MT) sold for $3.354 (eBay; 12/12)
—Bobby Orr #100 PSA 9 (MT) sold for $2,887 (Mile High; 12/13)
—Mike Pelyk #92 PSA 10 (Gem) sold for $526 (eBay; 8/12)
—Frank St.Marseille #38 PSA 10 (Gem) sold for $266 (eBay; 8/12)
—Gary Sabourin #13 PSA 10 (Gem) sold for $444 (eBay; 8/12)
—Serge Savard #143 PSA 10 (Gem) sold for $570 (eBay; 7/12)
—Ken Schinkel #64 PSA 10 (Gem) sold for $540 (eBay; 8/12)
—Jim Watson #165 PSA 10 (Gem) sold for $408 (eBay; 4/07)

1971-72 Topps

#	Player	VG 3	VgEx 4	EX 5	ExMt 6	NM 7	NmMt 8	NmMt+ 8.5	MT 9
1	Espo/Bucyk/B.Hull LL	12	15	30	50	60	80		
2	Orr/Espo/Bucyk LL	15	20	25	30	40	60	80	200
3	Espo/Orr/Bucyk LL	8	10	12	15	20	30	40	60
4	Espo/EJ/Cheev/Giaco LL	5	6	8	10	12	20	25	60
5	Giaco/Espo/Maniago LL	4	5	6	8	12	20	25	100
6	Plante/Giaco/T.Espo LL	6	8	10	12	15	25	30	80
7	Fred Stanfield	4	5	6	8	12	15	20	40
8	Mike Robitaille RC	4	5	6	8	10	12	15	30

#	Player	VG 3	VgEx 4	EX 5	ExMt 6	NM 7	NmMt 8	NmMt+ 8.5	M
9	Vic Hadfield	4	5	6	8	12	15	20	
10	Jacques Plante	8	10	12	15	20	25	30	
11	Bill White	4	5	6	8	12	15	30	
12	Andre Boudrias	4	5	6	8	10	12	15	
13	Jim Lorentz	4	5	6	8	10	12	15	
14	Arnie Brown	4	5	6	8	12	15	20	
15	Yvan Cournoyer	4	5	6	8	12	15	20	
16	Bryan Hextall	4	5	6	8	12	15	20	
17	Gary Croteau	4	5	6	8	10	12	15	
18	Gilles Villemure	4	5	6	8	12	15	20	
19	Serge Bernier RC	4	5	6	8	12	15	20	
20	Phil Esposito	6	8	10	12	15	25	30	
21	Charlie Burns	4	5	6	8	12	15	20	
22	Doug Barrie RC	4	5	6	8	12	15	20	
23	Eddie Joyal	4	5	6	8	12	15	20	
24	Rosaire Paiement	4	5	6	8	12	15	20	
25	Pat Stapleton	4	5	6	8	12	15	20	
26	Garry Unger	4	5	6	8	12	15	20	
27	Al Smith	4	5	6	8	12	15	20	
28	Bob Woytowich	4	5	6	8	12	15	20	
29	Marc Tardif	4	5	6	8	12	15	20	
30	Norm Ullman	4	5	6	8	12	15	20	
31	Tom Williams	4	5	6	8	12	15	20	
32	Ted Harris	4	5	6	8	12	15	20	
33	Andre Lacroix	4	5	6	8	10	12	15	
34	Mike Byers	4	5	6	8	12	15	20	
35	Johnny Bucyk	4	5	6	8	12	15	30	1
36	Roger Crozier	4	5	6	8	12	15	20	
37	Alex Delvecchio	4	5	6	8	12	15	20	
38	Frank St.Marseille	4	5	6	8	12	15	20	
39	Pit Martin	4	5	6	8	12	15	20	
40	Brad Park	5	6	8	10	12	15	25	
41	Greg Polis RC	4	5	6	8	12	15	20	
42	Orland Kurtenbach	4	5	6	8	10	12	15	
43	Jim McKenny RC	4	5	6	8	10	12	15	
44	Bob Nevin	4	5	6	8	12	15	20	
45	Ken Dryden RC	40	▲80	▲100	▲150	▲200	▲300	▲350	▲5
46	Carol Vadnais	4	5	6	8	12	15	20	
47	Bill Flett	4	5	6	8	12	15	20	
48	Jim Johnson	4	5	6	8	12	15	20	
49	Al Hamilton	4	5	6	8	12	15	30	
50	Bobby Hull	12	15	20	30	▲50	▲80	▲100	▲15
51	Chris Bordeleau RC	4	5	6	8	12	15	20	
52	Tim Ecclestone	4	5	6	8	10	12	15	3
53	Rod Seiling	4	5	6	8	12	15	20	
54	Gerry Cheevers	4	5	6	8	12	15	30	20
55	Bill Goldsworthy	4	5	6	8	12	15	20	
56	Ron Schock	4	5	6	8	10	12	15	3
57	Jim Dorey	4	5	6	8	10	12	15	3
58	Wayne Maki	4	5	6	8	12	15	20	4
59	Terry Harper	4	5	6	8	12	15	20	4
60	Gilbert Perreault	8	10	12	15	20	25	30	8
61	Ernie Hicke RC	4	5	6	8	10	12	15	3
62	Wayne Hillman	4	5	6	8	10	12	15	3
63	Denis DeJordy	4	5	6	8	12	15	20	4
64	Ken Schinkel	4	5	6	8	12	15	25	6
65	Derek Sanderson	4	5	6	8	12	15	25	6
66	Barclay Plager	4	5	6	8	12	15	20	3
67	Paul Henderson	4	5	6	8	12	15	20	4
68	Jude Drouin	4	5	6	8	10	12	15	3
69	Keith Magnuson	4	5	6	8	10	12	15	3
70	Gordie Howe	12	15	20	50	80	100	150	20
71	Jacques Lemaire	4	5	6	8	12	15	30	6
72	Doug Favell	4	5	6	8	12	15	30	8
73	Bert Marshall	4	5	6	8	12	15	20	4
74	Gerry Meehan	4	5	6	8	12	15	20	4
75	Walt Tkaczuk	4	5	6	8	12	15	20	4
76	Bob Berry RC	4	5	6	8	12	15	20	4
77	Syl Apps Jr. RC	4	5	6	8	12	15	20	4
78	Tom Webster	4	5	6	8	10	12	15	30
79	Danny Grant	4	5	6	8	12	15	20	3
80	Dave Keon	4	5	6	8	10	12	15	30
81	Ernie Wakely	4	5	6	8	12	15	20	4
82	John McKenzie	4	5	6	8	12	15	25	80
83	Doug Roberts	4	5	6	8	10	12	15	30
84	Peter Mahovlich	4	5	6	8	10	12	15	30
85	Dennis Hull	4	5	6	8	12	15	30	60
86	Juha Widing RC	4	5	6	8	10	12	15	30
87	Gary Doak	4	5	6	8	12	15	20	4
88	Phil Goyette	4	5	6	8	12	15	20	4
89	Gary Dornhoefer	4	5	6	8	12	15	20	4
90	Ed Giacomin	4	5	6	8	12	15	30	4
91	Red Berenson	4	5	6	8	10	12	15	3
92	Mike Pelyk	4	5	6	8	10	12	15	3
93	Gary Jarrett	4	5	6	8	12	15	20	4
94	Bob Pulford	4	5	6	8	12	15	25	6
95	Dale Tallon	4	5	6	8	12	15	20	4
96	Eddie Shack	4	5	6	8	12	15	20	4
97	Jean Ratelle	4	5	6	8	12	15	30	4

	VG 3	VgEx 4	EX 5	ExMt 6	NM 7	NmMt 8	NmMt+ 8.5	MT 9
Jim Pappin	4	5	6	8	12	15	20	40
Roy Edwards	4	5	6	8	12	15	20	40
Bobby Orr	15	20	▲30	▲50	▲100	▲150	▲200	350
Ted Hampson	4	5	6	8	12	15	20	40
Mickey Redmond	4	5	6	8	12	15	20	40
Bob Plager	4	5	6	8	12	15	40	60
Bruce Gamble	4	5	6	8	12	15	20	40
Frank Mahovlich	4	5	6	8	12	15	20	40
Tony Featherstone RC	4	5	6	8	12	15	20	40
Tracy Pratt	4	5	6	8	12	15	20	40
Ralph Backstrom	4	5	6	8	12	15	20	40
Murray Hall	4	5	6	8	12	15	20	40
Tony Esposito	12	15	20	25	30	40	50	100
Checklist Card	12	15	20	30	50	100	150	250
Jim Neilson	4	5	6	8	12	15	20	40
Ron Ellis	4	5	6	8	12	15	20	40
Bobby Clarke	12	15	20	25	▲50	▲80	▲100	▲150
Ken Hodge	4	5	6	8	12	15	30	100
Jim Roberts	4	5	6	8	12	15	20	40
Cesare Maniago	4	5	6	8	12	15	20	40
Jean Pronovost	4	5	6	8	10	12	15	30
Gary Bergman	4	5	6	8	10	12	15	30
Henri Richard	4	5	6	8	12	15	20	40
Ross Lonsberry	4	5	6	8	12	15	20	40
Pat Quinn	4	5	6	8	12	15	25	60
Rod Gilbert	4	5	6	8	12	15	20	40
Gary Smith	4	5	6	8	10	12	15	30
Stan Mikita	5	6	8	10	12	20	25	80
Ed Van Impe	4	5	6	8	12	15	30	60
Wayne Connelly	4	5	6	8	12	15	20	60
Dennis Hextall	4	5	6	8	12	15	20	40
Wayne Cashman	4	5	6	8	12	20	30	60
J.C. Tremblay	4	5	6	8	12	15	20	40
Bernie Parent	4	5	6	8	12	40	50	100
Dunc McCallum RC	5	6	8	10	20	40	50	150

spo/Bucyk/B. Hull LL #1 PSA 10 (Gem) sold for $2,000 (eBay; 7/08)
spo/Bucyk/B. Hull LL #1 PSA 9 (MT) sold for $367 (eBay; 3/08)
en Dryden #45 PSA 10 (MT) sold for $2,375 (eBay; 9/12)

972-73 0-Pee-Chee

	VG 3	VgEx 4	EX 5	ExMt 6	NM 7	NmMt 8	NmMt+ 8.5	MT 9
Johnny Bucyk DP	6	8	12	20	25	100	120	250
Rene Robert RC	4	5	10	12	20	50		
Gary Croteau	4	5	6	10	15	30		
Pat Stapleton	4	5	6	10	15	25	30	60
Ron Harris	4	5	6	10	15	25	30	60
Checklist 1	30	40	50	60	80	100		
Playoff Game 1	4	5	10	15	30	150		
Marcel Dionne	12	15	20	25	35	50	60	200
Bob Berry	4	5	6	10	15	30		
Lou Nanne	4	5	6	10	15	30		
Marc Tardif	4	5	6	10	15	30		
Jean Ratelle	4	5	6	10	15	30		
Craig Cameron RC	4	5	6	10	15	30		
Bobby Clarke	25	30	40	40	50	60	80	150
Jim Rutherford RC	8	10	20	25	30			
Andre Dupont RC	4	5	6	10	15	30	40	60
Mike Pelyk	4	5	6	10	15	25	30	60
Dunc Wilson	4	5	6	10	15	30		
Checklist 2	30	40	50	60	80	100		
Playoff Game 2	4	5	6	10	15	30		
Dallas Smith	4	5	6	10	15	30		
Gerry Meehan	4	5	6	10	15	30		
Rick Smith UER	4	5	6	10	15	25	30	60
Pit Martin	4	5	6	10	15	30		
Keith McCreary	4	5	6	10	15	30		
Alex Delvecchio	4	5	6	10	15	30		
Gilles Marotte	4	5	6	10	15	30	30	60
Gump Worsley	4	5	6	10	15	40		
Yvan Cournoyer	4	5	6	10	15	40		
Playoff Game 3	4	5	6	10	15	30		
Vic Hadfield	4	5	6	10	15	25	30	60
Tom Miller RC	4	5	6	10	15	25	30	60
Ed Van Impe	4	5	6	10	15	30		
Greg Polis	4	5	6	10	15	30		
Barclay Plager	4	5	6	10	15	25	30	60
Ron Ellis	4	5	6	10	15	30		
Jocelyn Guevremont	4	5	6	10	15	30		
Playoff Game 4	4	5	6	10	15	25	30	80
Carol Vadnais	4	5	6	10	15	30		
Steve Atkinson	4	5	6	10	15	30		
Ivan Boldirev RC	4	5	6	10	15	30		
Jim Pappin	4	5	6	10	15	25	30	60
Phil Myre RC	6	8	12	20	25	40	50	80
Yvan Cournoyer IA	4	5	6	10	15	30	40	60
Nick Libett	4	5	6	10	15	30		
Juha Widing	4	5	6	10	15	30		
Jude Drouin	4	5	6	10	15	25	30	60
Jean Ratelle IA Defense	4	5	6	10	15	30	40	60

		VG 3	VgEx 4	EX 5	ExMt 6	NM 7	NmMt 8	NmMt+ 8.5	MT 9
48B	Jean Ratelle IA Centre	4	5	6	10	15	30	40	60
49	Ken Hodge	4	5	6	10	15	40		
50	Roger Crozier	4	5	6	10	25	30		
51	Reggie Leach	4	5	6	10	15	30	40	60
52	Dennis Hull	4	5	6	10	15	30		
53	Larry Hale RC	4	5	6	10	15	30		
54	Playoff Game 5	4	5	6	10	15	30		
55	Tim Ecclestone	4	5	6	10	15	25	30	60
56	Butch Goring	4	5	6	10	15	30	40	60
57	Danny Grant	4	5	6	10	15	30		
58	Bobby Orr IA	25	30	40	50	50	80	100	300
59	Guy Lafleur	30	40	50	60	80	120	200	400
60	Jim Neilson	4	5	6	10	15	30		
61	Brian Spencer	4	5	6	10	15	25	30	60
62	Joe Watson	4	5	6	10	15	25	30	60
63	Playoff Game 6	4	5	6	10	15	25	30	80
64	Jean Pronovost	4	5	6	10	15	30		
65	Frank St.Marseille	4	5	6	10	15	30		
66	Bob Baun	4	5	6	10	15	30		
67	Paul Popiel	4	5	6	10	15	25	30	60
68	Wayne Cashman	4	5	6	10	15	30		
69	Tracy Pratt	4	5	6	10	15	30		
70	Stan Gilbertson	4	5	6	10	15	20	25	50
71	Keith Magnuson	4	5	6	10	15	30		
72	Ernie Hicke	4	5	6	10	15	30		
73	Gary Doak	4	5	6	10	15	30		
74	Mike Corrigan	4	5	6	10	15	30		
75	Doug Mohns	4	5	6	10	15	25	30	60
76	Phil Esposito IA	6	8	12	20	25	40	50	100
77	Jacques Lemaire	4	5	6	10	15	30	40	80
78	Pete Stemkowski	4	5	6	10	15	30		
79	Bill Mikkelson RC	4	5	6	10	15	25	30	60
80	Rick Foley RC	4	5	6	10	15	25	30	60
81	Ron Schock	4	5	6	10	15	25	30	60
82	Phil Roberto	4	5	6	10	15	25	30	60
83	Jim McKenny	4	5	6	10	15	30		
84	Wayne Maki	4	5	6	10	15	25	30	60
85A	Brad Park IA Centre	6	8	12	20	25	40		
85B	Brad Park IA Defense	4	5	8	12	20	40		
86	Guy Lapointe	4	5	6	10	15	30	40	60
87	Bill Fairbairn	4	5	6	10	15	25	30	60
88	Terry Crisp	4	5	6	10	15	25	30	60
89	Doug Favell	4	5	6	10	15	25	30	60
90	Bryan Watson	4	5	6	10	15	20	25	50
91	Gary Sabourin	4	5	6	10	15	25	30	60
92	Jacques Plante	10	12	15	20	25	40	50	100
93	Andre Boudrias	4	5	6	10	15	20	25	50
94	Mike Walton	4	5	6	10	15	20	25	50
95	Don Luce	4	5	6	10	15	30		
96	Joey Johnston	4	5	6	10	15	20	25	50
97	Doug Jarrett	4	5	6	10	15	25	30	60
98	Bill MacMillan RC	4	5	6	10	15	30		
99	Mickey Redmond	4	5	6	10	15	30		
100	Rogatien Vachon UER	4	5	6	10	15	30	40	60
101	Barry Gibbs RC	4	5	6	10	15	30		
102	Frank Mahovlich DP	4	5	6	10	15	30	40	60
103	Bruce MacGregor	4	5	6	10	15	25	30	60
104	Ed Westfall	4	5	6	10	15	25	30	60
105	Rick MacLeish	4	5	8	12	20	35	40	80
106	Nick Harbaruk	4	5	6	10	15	25	30	60
107	Jack Egers RC	4	5	6	10	15	20	25	50
108	Dave Keon	4	5	6	10	15	30	40	80
109	Barry Wilkins	4	5	6	10	20	50		
110	Walt Tkaczuk	4	5	6	10	15	25	30	60
111	Phil Esposito	8	10	12	15	25	50	60	100
112	Gilles Meloche RC	6	8	12	20	25	40		
113	Gary Edwards	4	5	6	10	15	30	40	
114	Brad Park	8	10	20	25	30	40	50	80
115	Syl Apps DP	4	5	6	10	15	30		
116	Jim Lorentz	4	5	6	10	15	20	25	50
117	Gary Smith	4	5	6	10	15	20	25	50
118	Ted Harris	4	5	6	10	15	30		
119	Gerry Desjardins DP	4	5	6	10	15	25	30	60
120	Garry Unger	4	5	6	10	15	20	25	50
121	Dale Tallon	4	5	6	10	15	30		
122	Bill Plager RC	4	5	6	10	15	20	25	50
123	Red Berenson DP	4	5	6	10	15	20	25	50
124	Peter Mahovlich DP	4	5	6	10	15	20	25	50
125	Simon Nolet	4	5	6	10	15	30	35	60
126	Paul Henderson	4	5	6	10	15	30		
127	Hart Trophy Winners	4	5	6	10	15	20	25	50
128	Frank Mahovlich IA	4	5	6	10	15	30	35	60
129	Bobby Orr	35	40	50	▲80	▲100	▲250	▲350	800
130	Bert Marshall	4	5	6	10	15	30		
131	Ralph Backstrom	4	5	6	10	15	20	25	50
132	Gilles Villemure	4	5	6	10	15	20	25	50
133	Dave Burrows RC	4	5	6	10	15	20	25	50
134	Calder Trophy Winners	4	5	6	10	15	30	35	60
135	Dallas Smith IA	4	5	6	10	15	20	25	50

#	Player	VG 3	VgEx 4	EX 5	ExMt 6	NM 7	NmMt 8	NmMt+ 8.5	MT 9
136	Gilbert Perreault DP	8	10	12	15	20	30	35	60
137	Tony Esposito DP	8	10	12	15	25	40	50	100
138	Cesare Maniago DP	4	5	6	10	15	30		
139	Gerry Hart RC	4	5	6	10	15	20	25	50
140	Jacques Caron RC	4	5	6	10	15	30	40	60
141	Orland Kurtenbach	4	5	6	10	15	30		
142	Norris Trophy Winners	4	5	6	10	15	80		
143	Lew Morrison	4	5	6	10	15	30		
144	Arnie Brown	4	5	6	10	15	20	25	50
145	Ken Dryden DP	12	15	20	25	35	50	60	120
146	Gary Dornhoefer	4	5	6	10	15	20	25	50
147	Norm Ullman	4	5	8	12	20	30	35	80
148	Art Ross Trophy/Winners	4	5	6	10	15	20	25	50
149	Orland Kurtenbach IA	4	5	6	10	15	30	35	60
150	Fred Stanfield	4	5	6	10	15	30		
151	Dick Redmond DP	4	5	6	10	15	20	25	50
152	Serge Bernier	4	5	6	10	15	20	25	50
153	Rod Gilbert	4	5	8	12	20	30	35	60
154	Duane Rupp	4	5	6	10	15	20	25	50
155	Vezina Trophy Winners	4	5	6	10	15	30		
156	Stan Mikita IA	4	5	8	12	20	40	50	80
157	Richard Martin DP	4	5	8	12	20	30	40	80
158	Bill White DP	4	5	6	10	15	20	25	50
159	Bill Goldsworthy DP	4	5	6	10	15	25	30	60
160	Jack Lynch RC	4	5	6	10	15	30		
161	Bob Plager DP	4	5	6	10	15	25	30	60
162	Dave Balon UER	4	5	6	10	15	30		
163	Noel Price	4	5	6	10	15	30		
164	Gary Bergman DP	4	5	6	10	15	20	25	50
165	Pierre Bouchard	4	5	6	10	15	30		
166	Ross Lonsberry	4	5	6	10	15	20	25	50
167	Denis Dupere	4	5	6	10	15	30		
168	Byng Trophy Winners DP	4	5	6	10	15	20	25	50
169	Ken Hodge	4	5	6	10	15	30		
170	Don Awrey DP	4	5	6	10	15	25		
171	Marshall Johnston DP RC	4	5	6	10	15	40		
172	Terry Harper	4	5	6	10	15	30		
173	Ed Giacomin	4	5	8	10	15	25	35	60
174	Bryan Hextall DP	4	5	6	10	15	20	25	50
175	Conn Smythe/Trophy Winners	4	5	6	10	20	30	35	60
176	Larry Hillman	4	5	6	10	15	30		
177	Stan Mikita DP	6	8	12	20	25	40	50	80
178	Charlie Burns	4	5	6	10	15	30		
179	Brian Marchinko	4	5	6	10	15	30		
180	Noel Picard DP	4	5	6	10	15	20	25	50
181	Bobby Schmautz RC	4	5	6	10	15	30		
182	Richard Martin IA UER	4	5	6	10	15	30	40	80
183	Pat Quinn	4	5	6	10	15	30		
184	Denis DeJordy UER	4	5	6	10	15	20	25	50
185	Serge Savard	4	5	8	12	20	40		
186	Eddie Shack IA	4	5	6	10	15	30		
187	Bill Flett	4	5	6	10	15	30		
188	Darryl Sittler	15	20	25	30	40			
189	Gump Worsley IA	4	5	6	10	15	30	40	60
190	Checklist	25	30	40	50	60	80	100	200
191	Garnet Bailey DP	4	5	6	10	15	20	25	50
192	Walt McKechnie	4	5	6	10	15	20	25	50
193	Harry Howell	4	5	6	10	15	30		
194	Rod Seiling	4	5	6	10	15	30	35	60
195	Darryl Edestrand	4	5	6	10	15	30		
196	Tony Esposito IA	6	8	12	20	25	40		
197	Tim Horton	6	8	12	20	25	40		
198	Chico Maki DP	4	5	6	10	15	20	25	50
199	Jean-Paul Parise	4	5	6	10	15	30		
200	Germaine Gagnon UER RC	4	5	6	10	15	30		
201	Danny O'Shea	4	5	6	10	15	20	25	50
202	Richard Lemieux RC	4	5	6	10	15	30		
203	Dan Bouchard RC	8	10	20	25	30	40	50	100
204	Leon Rochefort	4	5	6	10	15	30		
205	Jacques Laperriere	4	5	6	10	15	25	30	60
206	Barry Ashbee	4	5	6	10	15	30		
207	Garry Monahan	4	5	6	10	15	30		
209	Dave Keon IA	4	5	8	12	20	40	50	80
210	Rejean Houle	4	5	6	10	15	30		
211	Dave Hudson RC	4	5	6	10	20	60		
212	Ted Irvine	4	5	6	10	15	25	30	60
213	Don Saleski RC	4	5	8	12	20	50		
214	Lowell MacDonald	4	5	6	10	15	20	25	50
215	Mike Murphy RC	4	5	6	10	15	30		
216	Brian Glennie	4	5	6	10	15	30		
217	Bobby Lalonde RC	4	5	6	10	15	30		
218	Bob Leiter	4	5	6	10	15	30		
219	Don Marcotte	4	5	6	10	25	60		
220	Jim Schoenfeld RC	10	12	20	25	30	60	80	125
221	Craig Patrick	4	5	6	10	15	30		
222	Cliff Koroll	4	5	6	10	15	30		
223	Guy Charron RC	4	5	6	10	15	20	25	50
224	Jim Peters	4	5	6	10	15	40		
225	Dennis Hextall	4	5	6	10	15	30		

#	Player	VG 3	VgEx 4	EX 5	ExMt 6	NM 7	NmMt 8	NmMt+ 8.5	MT 9
226	Tony Esposito AS1	12	15	20	25	30			
227	Orr/Park AS1	25	30	40	60	80	150	250	5
228	Bobby Hull AS1	25	30	40	50	80	100	200	2
229	Rod Gilbert AS1	4	5	6	10	20	50		
230	Phil Esposito AS1	8	10	20	25	30	100		
231	Claude Larose UER	4	5	6	10	15	20	25	
232	Jim Mair RC	4	5	6	10	15	20	25	
233	Bobby Rousseau	4	5	6	10	15	20	25	
234	Brent Hughes	4	5	6	10	15	30		
235	Al McDonough	4	5	6	10	15	20	25	
236	Chris Evans RC	4	5	6	10	15	30		
237	Pierre Jarry RC	4	5	6	10	15	30		
238	Don Tannahill RC	4	5	6	10	15	60		
239	Rey Comeau RC	4	5	6	10	15	30		
240	Gregg Sheppard UER RC	4	5	6	10	15	30		
241	Dave Dryden	4	5	6	10	15	40	50	1
242	Ted McAneeley RC	4	5	6	10	15	30	40	1
243	Lou Angotti	4	5	6	10	15	30		
244	Len Fontaine RC	4	5	6	10	15	30		
245	Bill Lesuk RC	4	5	6	10	15	30		
246	Fred Harvey	4	5	6	10	15	30	35	
247	Ken Dryden AS2	15	20	25	30	60	125		
248	Bill White AS2	4	5	6	10	15	30		
249	Pat Stapleton AS2	4	5	6	10	15	20	25	
250	Ratelle/Cour/Hadfld LL	5	6	10	12	20	80		
251	Henri Richard	4	5	6	10	25	80		
252	Bryan Lefley RC	4	5	6	10	15	30	40	
253	Stanley Cup Trophy	12	15	20	25	40	150		
254	Steve Vickers RC	6	8	12	20	25	40		
255	Wayne Hillman	4	5	6	10	15	30		
256	Ken Schinkel UER	4	5	6	10	15	30		
257	Kevin O'Shea RC	4	5	6	10	15	30		
258	Ron Low RC	12	15	20	25	40	60	80	1
259	Don Lever RC	8	12	20	25	80	150		
260	Randy Manery RC	4	5	6	10	15	30		
261	Ed Johnston	4	5	6	10	20	40		
262	Craig Ramsay RC	5	6	10	12	25	80		
263	Pete Laframboise RC	4	5	6	10	15	25	30	
264	Dan Maloney RC	4	5	8	12	20	40		
265	Bill Collins	4	5	6	10	15	30		
266	Paul Curtis	4	5	6	10	15	30		
267	Bob Nevin	4	5	6	10	15	60		
268	Watson/Magnuson LL	4	5	6	10	20	50		
269	Jim Roberts	4	5	6	10	15	30		
270	Brian Lavender RC	4	5	6	10	20	30	50	
271	Dale Rolfe	4	5	6	10	15	30		
272	Espo/Hadf/B.Hull LL	15	20	25	30	40			
273	Michel Belhumeur RC	6	8	12	20	25	40		
274	Eddie Shack	4	5	6	10	15	30		
275	W.Stephenson UER RC	8	10	20	25	30	50	60	1
276	Bruins Team	6	8	12	20	25	60		
277	Rick Kehoe RC	6	8	12	20	25	60		
278	Gerry O'Flaherty RC	4	5	6	10	15	40		
279	Jacques Richard RC	4	5	6	10	15	30		
280	Espo/Orr/Ratelle LL	20	25	30	40	60			
281	Nick Beverley RC	5	6	10	12	20	40	50	10
282	Larry Carriere RC	4	5	6	10	15	30		
283	Orr/Espo/Ratelle LL	20	25	30	40	60	250		
284	Rick Smith IA	4	5	6	10	15	30		
285	Jerry Korab RC	4	5	8	12	25	80		
286	Espo/Villem/Worsley LL	10	12	20	25	30			
287	Ron Stackhouse	4	5	6	10	15	30		
288	Barry Long RC	4	5	6	10	15	30		
289	Dean Prentice	4	4	6	10	15	100		
290	Norm Beaudin	6	8	12	20	25	40		
291	Mike Amodeo RC	6	8	12	20	25	40		
292	Jim Harrison	6	8	12	20	25	40	50	10
293	J.C. Tremblay	6	8	12	20	25	50	80	
294	Murray Hall	6	8	12	20	25	40		
295	Bart Crashley	6	8	12	20	25	40		
296	Wayne Connelly	6	8	12	20	25	40		
297	Bobby Sheehan	6	8	12	20	25	40		
298	Ron Anderson	6	8	12	20	25	40		
299	Chris Bordeleau	6	8	12	20	25	40		
300	Les Binkley	6	8	15	20	25	40	50	10
301	Ron Walters	6	8	15	20	25	40		
302	Jean-Guy Gendron	6	8	15	20	25	40		
303	Gord Labossiere	6	8	15	20	25	30	40	6
304	Gerry Odrowski	6	8	15	20	25	40	50	8
305	Mike McMahon	6	8	15	20	25	40		
306	Gary Kurt	6	8	15	20	25	40		
307	Larry Cahan	6	8	15	20	25	40	50	8
308	Wally Boyer	6	8	15	20	25	80		
309	Bob Charlebois RC	6	8	15	20	25	40		
310	Bob Falkenberg	6	8	15	20	25	40		
311	Jean Payette RC	6	8	15	20	25	40		
312	Ted Taylor	6	8	15	20	25	40		
313	Joe Szura	6	8	15	20	25	40		
314	George Morrison	6	8	15	20	25	40		

	VG 3	VgEx 4	EX 5	ExMt 6	NM 7	NmMt 8	NmMt+ 8.5	MT 9
Wayne Rivers	6	8	15	20	25	50		
Reg Fleming	6	8	15	20	25	60		
Larry Hornung RC	6	8	15	20	25	40		
Ron Climie RC	6	8	15	20	25	30	40	80
Val Fonteyne	6	8	15	20	25	40		
Michel Archambault RC	6	8	15	20	25	40	50	100
Ab McDonald	6	8	15	20	25	40		
Bob Leduc RC	6	8	15	20	25	40		
Bob Wall	6	8	15	20	25	40	50	80
Alain Caron RC	6	8	15	20	25	40		
Bob Woytowich	6	8	15	20	25	40	50	100
Guy Trottier	6	8	15	20	25	40		
Bill Hicke	6	8	15	20	25	40	50	100
Guy Dufour RC	6	8	15	20	25	30	40	60
Wayne Rutledge RC	6	8	15	20	25	40	50	80
Gary Veneruzzo	6	8	15	20	25	40	50	100
Fred Speck RC	6	8	15	20	25	40	50	100
Ron Ward RC	6	8	15	20	25	40		
Rosaire Paiement	6	8	15	20	25	40	50	100
Checklist 3 ERR	60	80	100	120	150			
Checklist 3 COR	50	60	80	100	125			
Michel Parizeau RC	6	8	15	20	25	40		
Bobby Hull	40	50	60	80	100	150	350	
Wayne Carleton	6	8	15	20	25	40		
John McKenzie	6	8	15	20	25	40		
Jim Dorey	6	8	15	20	25	50		
Gerry Cheevers	20	25	30	40	50	60	80	150
Gerry Pinder	15	20	25	30	50	120	150	150

Guy Lafleur #59 PSA 10 (Gem) sold for $408 (eBay; 12/06)
Brad Park #114 PSA 10 (Gem) sold for $127.50 (eBay; 8/12)
Bobby Orr #129 PSA 10 (Gem) sold for $3,327.24 (Mile High; 12/13)
Craig Ramsay #262 PSA 9 (MT) sold for $237.50 (eBay; 8/12)
Rick Kehoe #277 PSA 10 (Gem) sold for $203.48 (eBay; 7/11)

1972-73 Topps

	VgEx 4	EX 5	ExMt 6	NM 7	NmMt 8	NmMt+ 8.5	MT 9	Gem 9.5/10
Bruins Team DP	5	6	8	12	20	25	30	250
Playoff Game 1	5	6	8	10	12	15	30	
Playoff Game 2	5	6	8	10	12	20	50	
Playoff Game 3	5	6	8	10	12	20	60	
Playoff Game 4 DP	5	6	8	10	12	15	20	60
Playoff Game 5 DP	5	6	8	10	12	15	20	60
Playoff Game 6 DP	5	6	8	10	12	15	20	60
Stanley Cup Trophy	5	6	8	10	12	15	30	150
Ed Van Impe DP	5	6	8	10	10	12	15	50
Yvan Cournoyer DP	5	6	8	10	12	15	20	120
Syl Apps DP	5	6	8	10	10	12	15	50
Bill Plager RC	5	6	8	10	10	12	15	50
Ed Johnston DP	5	6	8	10	12	15	40	
Walt Tkaczuk	5	6	8	10	12	15	50	
Dale Tallon DP	5	6	8	10	10	12	15	50
Gerry Meehan	5	6	8	10	12	15	20	60
Reggie Leach	5	6	8	10	10	12	15	50
Marcel Dionne DP	6	8	10	12	15	20	50	100
Andre Dupont RC	5	6	8	10	12	15	20	
Tony Esposito	6	8	10	15	25	30	40	100
Bob Berry DP	5	6	8	10	10	12	15	50
Craig Cameron	5	6	8	10	10	12	15	40
Ted Harris	5	6	8	10	12	15	20	
Jacques Plante	6	8	10	15	20	25	40	120
Jacques Lemaire DP	5	6	8	10	10	12	15	50
Simon Nolet DP	5	6	8	10	10	12	15	50
Keith McCreary DP	5	6	8	10	10	12	15	40
Duane Rupp	5	6	8	10	10	12	15	50
Wayne Cashman	5	6	8	10	12	15	20	
Brad Park	5	6	8	10	12	15	20	
Roger Crozier	5	6	8	10	10	12	15	50
Wayne Maki	5	6	8	10	10	12	15	50
Tim Ecclestone	5	6	8	10	12	15	20	
Rick Smith	5	6	8	10	10	12	15	50
Garry Unger DP	5	6	8	10	10	12	15	50
Serge Bernier DP	5	6	8	10	10	12	15	50
Brian Glennie	5	6	8	10	12	15	20	
Gerry Desjardins DP	5	6	8	10	10	12	15	50
Danny Grant	5	6	8	10	10	12	15	50
Bill White DP	5	6	8	10	10	12	15	50
Gary Dornhoefer DP	5	6	8	10	12	15	20	
Peter Mahovlich	5	6	8	10	12	15	20	60
Greg Polis DP	5	6	8	10	10	12	15	50
Larry Hale DP RC	5	6	8	10	10	12	15	50
Dallas Smith	5	6	8	10	10	12	15	50
Orland Kurtenbach DP	5	6	8	10	10	12	15	50
Steve Atkinson	5	6	8	10	12	15	20	
Joey Johnston DP	5	6	8	10	10	12	15	50
Gary Bergman	5	6	8	10	12	15	20	
Jean Ratelle	5	6	8	10	12	15	20	
Rogatien Vachon DP	5	6	8	10	10	12	15	50
Phil Roberto DP	5	6	8	10	12	15	20	
Brian Spencer DP	5	6	8	10	10	12	15	50

	VgEx 4	EX 5	ExMt 6	NM 7	NmMt 8	NmMt+ 8.5	MT 9	Gem 9.5/10
54	Jim McKenny DP	5	6	8	10	10	12	15	50
55	Gump Worsley	5	6	8	10	12	15	30	80
56	Stan Mikita DP	5	6	8	10	12	15	50	100
57	Guy Lapointe	5	6	8	10	12	15	20	
58	Lew Morrison DP	5	6	8	10	10	12	15	50
59	Ron Schock DP	5	6	8	10	10	12	15	50
60	Johnny Bucyk	5	6	8	10	12	15	25	60
61	Espo/Hadf/B.Hull LL	6	8	10	15	20	25	40	
62	Orr/Espo/Ratelle LL DP	6	8	10	15	20	25	40	
63	Espo/Orr/Ratelle LL DP	6	8	10	15	20	25	40	
64	Espo/Villem/Worsley LL	5	6	8	10	12	15	20	
65	Wtsn/Magn/Dorn LL	5	6	8	10	12	15	20	
66	Jim Neilson	5	6	8	10	12	15	20	
67	Nick Libett DP	5	6	8	10	10	12	15	50
68	Jim Lorentz	5	6	8	10	10	12	15	50
69	Gilles Meloche RC	5	6	8	10	12	15	25	60
70	Pat Stapleton	5	6	8	10	10	12	15	50
71	Frank St.Marseille DP	5	6	8	10	10	12	15	50
72	Butch Goring FTC	5	6	8	10	10	12	15	50
73	Paul Henderson DP	5	6	8	10	10	12	15	50
74	Doug Favell	5	6	8	10	10	12	15	50
75	Jocelyn Guevremont DP	5	6	8	10	10	12	15	50
76	Tom Miller RC	5	6	8	10	10	12	15	50
77	Bill MacMillan	5	6	8	10	12	15	20	
78	Doug Mohns	5	6	8	10	12	15	20	50
79	Guy Lafleur DP	6	10	12	15	20	25	80	150
80	Rod Gilbert DP	5	6	8	10	10	12	15	50
81	Gary Doak	5	6	8	10	10	12	15	50
82	Dave Burrows DP RC	5	6	8	10	10	12	15	50
83	Gary Croteau	5	6	8	10	12	15	20	
84	Tracy Pratt DP	5	6	8	10	12	15	20	
85	Carol Vadnais DP	5	6	8	10	10	12	15	50
86	Jacques Caron DP RC	5	6	8	10	10	12	15	50
87	Keith Magnuson	5	6	8	10	12	25	40	100
88	Dave Keon	5	6	8	10	12	15	30	80
89	Mike Corrigan	5	6	8	10	10	12	15	40
90	Bobby Clarke	10	12	15	20	25	30	60	
91	Dunc Wilson DP	5	6	8	10	10	12	15	50
92	Gerry Hart RC	5	6	8	10	10	12	15	50
93	Lou Nanne	5	6	8	10	12	15	20	
94	Checklist 1-176 DP	8	10	12	15	20	25	40	175
95	Red Berenson DP	5	6	8	10	10	12	15	
96	Bob Plager	5	6	8	10	10	12	15	50
97	Jim Rutherford RC	5	6	8	10	12	15	20	
98	Rick Foley DP RC	5	6	8	10	10	12	15	50
99	Pit Martin DP	5	6	8	10	10	12	15	50
100	Bobby Orr DP	15	▲25	▲40	▲80	▲100	▲150	▲200	450
101	Stan Gilbertson	5	6	8	10	10	12	15	50
102	Barry Wilkins	5	6	8	10	10	12	15	50
103	Terry Crisp DP	5	6	8	10	10	12	15	50
104	Cesare Maniago DP	5	6	8	10	10	12	15	50
105	Marc Tardif	5	6	8	10	10	12	15	50
106	Don Luce DP	5	6	8	10	10	12	15	50
107	Mike Pelyk	5	6	8	10	12	15	20	
108	Juha Widing DP	5	6	8	10	12	15	20	
109	Phil Myre DP RC	5	6	8	10	10	12	15	50
110	Vic Hadfield	5	6	8	10	10	12	15	50
111	Arnie Brown DP	5	6	8	10	10	12	15	50
112	Ross Lonsberry DP	5	6	8	10	10	12	15	50
113	Dick Redmond	5	6	8	10	10	12	15	50
114	Gary Smith	5	6	8	10	12	15	20	
115	Bill Goldsworthy	5	6	8	10	12	15	20	
116	Bryan Watson	5	6	8	10	12	15	20	
117	Dave Balon DP	5	6	8	10	10	12	15	50
118	Bill Mikkelson DP RC	5	6	8	10	10	12	15	50
119	Terry Harper DP	5	6	8	10	10	12	15	50
120	Gilbert Perreault DP	5	6	8	10	12	20	40	80
121	Tony Esposito AS1	5	6	8	10	12	20	30	60
122	Bobby Orr AS1	12	15	20	30	50	60	100	80
123	Brad Park AS1	5	6	8	10	10	12	15	50
124	Phil Esposito AS1	5	6	8	10	12	15	30	60
125	Rod Gilbert AS1	5	6	8	10	12	15	20	
126	Bobby Hull AS1	10	12	15	25	40	50	50	
127	Ken Dryden AS2 DP	8	10	12	15	20	25	40	100
128	Bill White AS2 DP	5	6	8	10	10	12	15	50
129	Pat Stapleton AS2 DP	5	6	8	10	12	15	20	
130	Jean Ratelle AS2 DP	5	6	8	10	10	12	15	50
131	Yvan Cournoyer AS2 DP	5	6	8	10	10	12	15	50
132	Vic Hadfield AS2 DP	5	6	8	10	12	15	20	
133	Ralph Backstrom DP	5	6	8	10	10	12	15	
134	Bob Baun DP	5	6	8	10	10	12	15	50
135	Fred Stanfield DP	5	6	8	10	10	12	15	50
136	Barclay Plager DP	5	6	8	10	10	12	15	50
137	Gilles Villemure	5	6	8	10	10	12	15	50
138	Ron Harris DP	5	6	8	10	10	12	15	50
139	Bill Flett DP	5	6	8	10	10	12	15	50
140	Frank Mahovlich	5	6	8	10	12	15	20	50
141	Alex Delvecchio DP	5	6	8	10	12	15	20	50
142	Paul Popiel	5	6	8	10	12	15	20	50

HOCKEY

#	Player	VgEx 4	EX 5	ExMt 6	NM 7	NmMt 8	NmMt+ 8.5	MT 9	Gem 9.5/10
143	Jean Pronovost DP	5	6	8	10	10	12	15	50
144	Denis DeJordy DP	5	6	8	10	10	12	15	50
145	Richard Martin DP	5	6	8	10	10	12	15	40
146	Ivan Boldirev RC	5	6	8	10	12	15	20	
147	Jack Egers RC	5	6	8	10	10	12	15	50
148	Jim Pappin	5	6	8	10	10	12	15	50
149	Rod Seiling	5	6	8	10	10	12	15	50
150	Phil Esposito	6	8	10	15	25	30	50	150
151	Gary Edwards	5	6	8	10	10	12	15	50
152	Ron Ellis DP	5	6	8	10	10	12	15	50
153	Jude Drouin	5	6	8	10	10	12	15	40
154	Ernie Hicke DP	5	6	8	10	10	12	15	40
155	Mickey Redmond	5	6	8	10	10	12	15	50
156	Joe Watson DP	5	6	8	10	10	12	15	50
157	Bryan Hextall	5	6	8	10	10	12	15	50
158	Andre Boudrias	5	6	8	10	10	12	15	50
159	Ed Westfall	5	6	8	10	10	12	15	50
160	Ken Dryden	12	15	20	30	30	40	50	80
161	Rene Robert DP RC	5	6	8	10	10	12	15	50
162	Bert Marshall DP	5	6	8	10	10	12	15	50
163	Gary Sabourin	5	6	8	10	10	12	15	50
164	Dennis Hull	5	6	8	10	12	15	20	100
165	Ed Giacomin DP	5	6	8	10	12	15	20	60
166	Ken Hodge	5	6	8	10	10	12	15	50
167	Gilles Marotte DP	5	6	8	10	10	12	15	50
168	Norm Ullman DP	5	6	8	10	10	12	15	40
169	Barry Gibbs RC	5	6	8	10	10	12	15	50
170	Art Ross Trophy	5	6	8	10	12	15	20	
171	Hart Memorial Trophy	5	6	8	10	10	12	15	50
172	James Norris Trophy	5	6	8	12	12	15	30	
173	Vezina Trophy DP	5	6	8	12	15	20	25	60
174	Calder Trophy DP	5	6	8	12	15	20	25	
175	Lady Byng Trophy DP	5	6	8	12	20	25	30	
176	Conn Smythe Trophy DP	5	6	8	12	20	25	40	

—Bruins Team #1 PSA 10 (Gem) sold for $901 (eBay; 7/07)
—Bruins Team #1 PSA 10 (Gem) sold for $704 (eBay; 10/14)
—Espo/Orr/Ratelle LL #62 PSA 10 (Gem) sold for $323 (eBay; 9/12)
—Espo/Orr/Ratelle LL #63 PSA 10 (Gem) sold for $2,040 (eBay; 4/12)
—Playoff Game 3 PSA 10 (Gem) sold for $704 (Mile High; 10/12)

1973-74 O-Pee-Chee

#	Player	VG 3	VgEx 4	EX 5	ExMt 6	NM 7	NmMt 8	NmMt+ 8.5	MT 9
1	Alex Delvecchio	5	6	8	12	15	20	25	40
2	Gilles Meloche	4	5	6	10	15	60		
3	Phil Roberto	4	5	6	10	15	20		
4	Orland Kurtenbach	4	5	6	10	15	20		
5	Gilles Marotte	4	5	6	10	15	20		
6	Stan Mikita	5	6	8	12	15	30		
7	Paul Henderson	4	5	6	10	15	20	30	50
8	Gregg Sheppard	4	5	6	10	12	15	20	35
9	Rod Seiling	4	5	6	10	15	20		
10	Red Berenson	4	5	6	10	15	20		
11	Jean Pronovost	4	5	6	10	12	15	20	35
12	Dick Redmond	4	5	6	10	15	20	25	40
13	Keith McCreary	4	5	6	10	15	20		
14	Bryan Watson	4	5	6	10	15	20		
15	Garry Unger	4	5	6	10	15	20		
16	Neil Komadoski RC	4	5	6	10	15	20	25	40
17	Marcel Dionne	6	8	10	15	20	30	35	60
18	Ernie Hicke	4	5	6	10	12	15	20	30
19	Andre Boudrias	4	5	6	10	15	20	25	40
20	Bill Flett	4	5	6	10	15	20		
21	Marshall Johnston	4	5	6	10	12	15	20	30
22	Gerry Meehan	4	5	6	10	15	20		
23	Ed Johnston	4	5	6	10	15	20	30	40
24	Serge Savard	5	6	8	12	15	30	35	60
25	Walt Tkaczuk	4	5	6	10	12	15	20	35
26	Ken Hodge	4	5	6	10	15	20	25	40
27	Norm Ullman	5	6	8	12	15	30		
28	Cliff Koroll	4	5	6	10	15	20		
29	Rey Comeau	4	5	6	10	15	20	30	50
30	Bobby Orr	15	20	30	40	60	100	150	
31	Wayne Stephenson	4	5	6	10	15	20		
32	Dan Maloney	4	5	6	10	15	20		
33	Henry Boucha RC	4	5	6	10	15	20	25	40
34	Gerry Hart	4	5	6	10	12	15	20	35
35	Bobby Schmautz	4	5	6	10	15	20	25	40
36	Ross Lonsberry	4	5	6	10	15	20		
37	Ted McAneeley	4	5	6	10	15	20	25	40
38	Don Luce	4	5	6	10	12	15	20	35
39	Jim McKenny	4	5	6	10	15	20	25	40
40	Jacques Laperriere	4	5	6	10	12	15	20	30
41	Bill Fairbairn	4	5	6	10	15	20		
42	Craig Cameron	4	5	6	10	12	15	20	35
43	Bryan Hextall	4	5	6	10	12	15	20	35
44	Chuck Lefley RC	4	5	6	10	15	20		
45	Dan Bouchard	4	5	6	10	15	20		
46	Jean-Paul Parise	4	5	6	10	12	15	20	35
47	Barclay Plager	4	5	6	10	12	15	20	35

#	Player	VG 3	VgEx 4	EX 5	ExMt 6	NM 7	NmMt 8	NmMt+ 8.5	
48	Mike Corrigan	4	5	6	10	12	15	20	
49	Nick Libett	4	5	6	10	15	20		
50	Bobby Clarke	6	8	10	15	25	35	40	
51	Bert Marshall	4	5	6	10	15	20		
52	Craig Patrick	4	5	6	10	12	15	20	
53	Richard Lemieux	4	5	6	10	15	20		
54	Tracy Pratt	4	5	6	10	12	15	20	
55	Ron Ellis	4	5	6	10	15	20		
56	Jacques Lemaire	5	6	8	12	15	30	35	
57	Steve Vickers	4	5	6	10	12	15	20	
58	Carol Vadnais	4	5	6	10	15	20	25	
59	Jim Rutherford	4	5	6	10	15	20		
60	Rick Kehoe	4	5	6	10	15	20	25	
61	Pat Quinn	4	5	6	10	15	20		
62	Bill Goldsworthy	4	5	6	10	15	20	25	
63	Dave Dryden	4	5	6	10	15	20	30	
64	Rogatien Vachon	5	6	8	12	15	30	35	
65	Gary Bergman	4	5	6	10	15	20		
66	Bernie Parent	6	8	10	15	20	30	40	
67	Ed Westfall	4	5	6	10	15	20		
68	Ivan Boldirev	4	5	6	10	12	15	20	
69	Don Tannahill	4	5	6	10	15	20	25	
70	Gilbert Perreault	6	8	10	15	20	40	50	
71	Mike Pelyk	4	5	6	10	15	20	25	
72	Guy Lafleur	8	10	12	20	30	40	60	
73	Pit Martin	4	5	6	10	15	20		
74	Gilles Gilbert RC	5	6	8	12	15	30	40	
75	Jim Lorentz	4	5	6	10	12	15	20	
76	Syl Apps	4	5	6	10	12	15	20	
77	Phil Myre	4	5	6	10	15	20		
78	Bill White	4	5	6	10	12	15	20	
79	Jack Egers	4	5	6	10	12	15	20	
80	Terry Harper	4	5	6	10	15	20		
81	Bill Barber RC	6	8	10	15	25	40	50	
82	Roy Edwards	4	5	6	10	15	20	25	
83	Brian Spencer	4	5	6	10	12	15	20	
84	Reggie Leach	4	5	6	10	15	20		
85	Wayne Cashman	4	5	6	10	12	15	20	
86	Jim Schoenfeld	5	6	8	12	15	20		
87	Henri Richard	5	6	8	12	15	30		
88	Dennis O'Brien RC	4	5	6	10	12	15	20	
89	Al McDonough	4	5	6	10	12	15	20	
90	Tony Esposito	6	8	10	15	20	30	40	
91	Joe Watson	4	5	6	10	12	15	20	
92	Flames Team	4	5	6	10	12	15	20	
93	Bruins Team	4	5	6	10	15	20		
94	Sabres Team	4	5	6	10	12	15	20	
95	Golden Seals Team	4	5	6	10	12	15	20	
96	Blackhawks Team	4	5	6	10	15	20		
97	Red Wings Team	4	5	6	10	12	15	20	
98	Kings Team	4	5	6	10	15	20		
99	North Stars Team	4	5	6	10	12	15	20	
100	Canadiens Team	4	5	6	10	15	30	35	
101	Islanders Team	4	5	6	10	12	15	20	
102	Rangers Team	4	5	6	10	12	15	20	
103	Flyers Team	4	5	6	10	15	20	25	
104	Penguins Team	4	5	6	10	15	20	25	
105	Blues Team	4	5	6	10	15	20		
106	Maple Leafs Team	4	5	6	10	15	20	30	
107	Canucks Team	4	5	6	10	15	20		
108	Vic Hadfield	4	5	6	10	15	20	25	
109	Tom Reid	4	5	6	10	15	20	25	
110	Hilliard Graves RC	4	5	6	10	15	20		
111	Don Lever	4	5	6	10	15	20		
112	Jim Pappin	4	5	6	10	15	20	25	
113	Andre Dupont	4	5	6	10	15	20		
114	Guy Lapointe	4	5	6	10	15	20		
115	Dennis Hextall	4	5	6	10	15	20	25	
116	Checklist 1	8	12	20	35	40	80		
117	Bob Leiter	4	5	6	10	15	20		
118	Ab DeMarco	4	5	6	10	15	20		
119	Gilles Villemure	4	5	6	10	15	20		
120	Phil Esposito	6	8	10	15	20	30	40	
121	Mike Robitaille	4	5	6	10	15	20		
122	Real Lemieux	4	5	6	10	12	15	20	
123	Jim Neilson	4	5	6	10	15	20		
124	Steve Durbano RC	4	5	6	10	12	15	20	
125	Jude Drouin	4	5	6	10	12	15	20	
126	Gary Smith	4	5	6	10	12	15	20	
127	Cesare Maniago	4	5	6	10	12	15	20	
128	Lowell MacDonald	4	5	6	10	15	20		
129	Checklist 2	8	12	20	25	30	40	50	
130	Billy Harris RC	4	5	6	10	15	20		
131	Randy Manery	4	5	6	10	15	20		
132	Darryl Sittler	6	8	10	15	20	40		
133	P.Espo/MacLeish LL	4	5	6	10	15	20	30	
134	P.Espo/B.Clarke LL	4	5	6	10	15	20	25	
135	P.Espo/B.Clarke LL	4	5	6	10	15	20		
136	K.Dryden/T.Espo LL	6	8	10	12	15	30	30	

	VG 3	VgEx 4	EX 5	ExMt 6	NM 7	NmMt 8	NmMt+ 8.5	MT 9
Schultz/Schnfeld LL	4	5	6	10	15	20		
P.Espo/MacLeish LL	4	5	6	10	15	20	30	60
Rene Robert	4	5	6	10	15	20		
Dave Burrows	4	5	6	10	12	15	20	35
Jean Ratelle	5	6	8	12	15	30		
Billy Smith RC	15	20	25	35	50	125	225	700
Jocelyn Guevremont	4	5	6	10	15	20		
Tim Ecclestone	4	5	6	10	12	15	20	35
Frank Mahovlich	5	6	8	12	15	30	25	40
Rick MacLeish	5	6	8	12	15	20	25	40
Johnny Bucyk	5	6	8	12	15	30		
Bob Plager	4	5	6	10	15	20	25	40
Curt Bennett RC	4	5	6	10	12	15	20	35
Dave Keon	5	6	8	12	15	30		
Keith Magnuson	4	5	6	10	15	20	25	40
Walt McKechnie	4	5	6	10	15	20		
Roger Crozier	4	5	6	10	15	20		
Ted Harris	4	5	6	10	15	20		
Butch Goring	4	5	6	10	15	20	25	40
Rod Gilbert	5	6	8	12	15	40	50	60
Yvan Cournoyer	5	6	8	12	15	30	40	50
Doug Favell	4	5	6	10	15	20		
Juha Widing	4	5	6	10	12	15	20	35
Ed Giacomin	5	6	8	12	15	30		
Germaine Gagnon UER	4	5	6	10	12	15	20	35
Dennis Kearns	4	5	6	10	15	20		
Bill Collins	4	5	6	10	15	20		
Peter Mahovlich	4	5	6	10	15	20	30	60
Brad Park	5	6	8	12	15	30	35	60
Dave Schultz RC	6	8	10	15	20	30	40	60
Dallas Smith	4	5	6	10	15	20		
Gary Sabourin	4	5	6	10	15	20		
Jacques Richard	4	5	6	10	15	20	25	40
Brian Glennie	4	5	6	10	15	20	25	50
Dennis Hull	4	5	6	10	15	20	25	40
Joey Johnston	4	5	6	10	15	20		
Richard Martin	5	6	8	12	15	30		
Barry Gibbs	4	5	6	10	12	15	20	30
Bob Berry	4	5	6	10	15	20		
Greg Polis	4	5	6	10	15	20		
Dale Rolfe	4	5	6	10	15	20		
Gerry Desjardins	4	5	6	10	15	20	25	40
Bobby Lalonde	4	5	6	10	15	20		
Mickey Redmond	4	5	6	10	15	30		
Jim Roberts	4	5	6	10	15	20		
Gary Dornhoefer	4	5	6	10	15	20		
Derek Sanderson	5	6	8	12	15	30	35	60
Brent Hughes	4	5	6	10	12	15	20	30
Larry Romanchych RC	4	5	6	10	15	20		
Pierre Jarry	4	5	6	10	15	20		
Doug Jarrett	4	5	6	10	12	15	20	35
Bob Stewart RC	4	5	6	10	15	20		
Tim Horton	5	6	8	12	15	40	50	60
Fred Harvey	4	5	6	10	15	20		
Series A/Cand/Sabr	4	5	6	10	15	20	25	50
Series B/Flyrs/Stars	4	5	6	10	12	15	20	35
Series C/Hwks/Blues	4	5	6	10	15	20	25	40
Series D/Rngr/Bruins	4	5	6	10	15	40		
Series E/Cndn/Flyr	4	5	6	10	15	20		
Series F/Blckh/Rngr	4	5	6	10	15	20	25	40
Series G/Cndn/Hawk	4	5	6	10	15	25	30	60
Canadiens Champs	5	6	8	12	15	30		
Gary Edwards	4	5	6	10	15	20		
Ron Schock	4	5	6	10	15	20		
Bruce MacGregor	4	5	6	10	12	15	20	35
Bob Nystrom RC	4	5	6	10	15	20	30	50
Jerry Korab	4	5	6	10	12	15	20	30
Thommie Bergman RC	4	5	6	10	12	15	20	30
Bill Lesuk	4	5	6	10	15	20		
Ed Van Impe	4	5	6	10	12	15	20	30
Doug Roberts	4	5	6	10	12	15	20	35
Chris Evans	4	5	6	10	12	15	20	35
Lynn Powis RC	4	5	6	10	12	15	20	35
Denis Dupere	4	5	6	10	15	20	25	40
Dale Tallon	4	5	6	10	15	20		
Stan Gilbertson	4	5	6	10	15	20		
Craig Ramsay	4	5	6	10	15	20	25	40
Danny Grant	4	5	6	10	15	20		
Doug Volmar RC	4	5	6	10	12	15	20	35
Darryl Edestrand	4	5	6	10	15	20		
Pete Stemkowski	4	5	6	10	12	15	20	30
Lorne Henning RC	4	5	6	10	15	20		
Bryan McSheffrey RC	4	5	6	10	12	15	20	30
Guy Charron	4	5	6	10	15	20	25	40
Wayne Thomas RC	5	6	8	12	15	40	50	60
Simon Nolet	4	5	6	10	12	15	20	30
Fred O'Donnell RC	4	5	6	10	15	20	25	40
Lou Angotti	4	5	6	10	15	20		
Arnie Brown	4	5	6	10	15	20		

#		VG 3	VgEx 4	EX 5	ExMt 6	NM 7	NmMt 8	NmMt+ 8.5	MT 9
226	Garry Monahan	4	5	6	10	15	20	25	40
227	Chico Maki	4	5	6	10	12	15	20	35
228	Gary Croteau	4	5	6	10	12	15	20	30
229	Paul Terbenche	4	5	6	10	15	20		
230	Gump Worsley	5	6	8	12	15	20	30	50
231	Jim Peters	4	5	6	10	12	15	20	40
232	Jack Lynch	4	5	6	10	12	15	20	35
233	Bobby Rousseau	4	5	6	10	15	20		
234	Dave Hudson	4	5	6	10	12	15	20	30
235	Gregg Boddy RC	4	5	6	10	15	20	25	40
236	Ron Stackhouse	4	5	6	10	12	15	20	35
237	Larry Robinson RC	20	25	40	60	100	200	225	500
238	Bobby Taylor RC	5	6	8	12	15	30	40	60
239	Nick Beverley	4	5	6	10	15	20		
240	Don Awrey	4	5	6	10	12	15	20	35
241	Doug Mohns	4	5	6	10	15	20	25	40
242	Eddie Shack	5	6	8	12	15	20	25	40
243	Phil Russell RC	4	5	6	10	12	15	25	35
244	Pete Laframboise	4	5	6	10	15	20		
245	Steve Atkinson	4	5	6	10	15	20		
246	Lou Nanne	4	5	6	10	15	20	25	40
247	Yvon Labre RC	4	5	6	10	15	20		
248	Ted Irvine	4	5	6	10	15	20		
249	Tom Miller	4	5	6	10	15	20	25	50
250	Gerry O'Flaherty	4	5	6	10	15	20	25	40
251	Larry Johnston RC	4	5	6	10	15	20		
252	Michel Plasse RC	5	6	8	12	15	30	40	80
253	Bob Kelly	4	5	6	10	12	15	20	30
254	Terry O'Reilly RC	15	20	25	40	80	200		
255	Pierre Plante RC	4	5	6	10	15	20	25	40
256	Noel Price	4	5	6	10	15	20		
257	Dunc Wilson	4	5	6	10	15	20		
258	J.P. Bordeleau RC	4	5	6	10	15	20		
259	Terry Murray RC	4	5	6	10	15	20	30	60
260	Larry Carriere	4	5	6	10	15	20		
261	Pierre Bouchard	4	5	6	10	15	30		
262	Frank St.Marseille	4	5	6	10	15	20		
263	Checklist 3	8	12	20	35	50	120		
264	Fred Barrett	4	5	6	10	15	30	35	60

—Bob Nystrom RC #202 PSA 10 (MT) sold for $1,017 (eBay; 2/14)
—Larry Robinson #237 PSA 10 (MT) sold for $1,387.54 (Mile High; 5/12)
—Terry O'Reilly #254 PSA 9 (MT) sold for $145 (eBay; 2/07)

1973-74 Topps

#		VG 3	VgEx 4	EX 5	ExMt 6	NM 7	NmMt 8	NmMt+ 8.5	MT 9
1	P.Espo/MacLeish LL	4	5	6	8	15	25	35	80
2	P.Espo/B.Clarke LL	4	5	6	8	12	20		60
3	P.Espo/B.Clarke LL	4	5	6	8	12	20	25	40
4	K.Dryden/T.Espo LL	4	5	6	8	12	20	25	40
5	Schultz/Schoenfeld LL	4	5	6	8	12	20	25	35
6	P.Espo/MacLeish LL	4	5	6	8	12	20	25	40
7	Paul Henderson DP	4	5	6	8	12	20	25	60
8	Gregg Sheppard DP UER	4	5	6	8	12	18		
9	Rod Seiling DP	4	5	6	8	12	18	20	30
10	Ken Dryden	10	15	20	25	30	40	60	120
11	Jean Pronovost DP	4	5	6	8	12	18	20	30
12	Dick Redmond	4	5	6	8	12	18		
13	Keith McCreary DP	4	5	6	8	12	18		
14	Ted Harris DP	4	5	6	8	12	18	20	30
15	Garry Unger	4	5	6	8	12	18		
16	Neil Komadoski RC	4	5	6	8	12	18	20	30
17	Marcel Dionne	5	6	8	10	15	25	30	50
18	Ernie Hicke DP	4	5	6	8	12	18	20	30
19	Andre Boudrias	4	5	6	8	12	18	25	50
20	Bill Flett	4	5	6	8	12	18	25	50
21	Marshall Johnston	4	5	6	8	12	18	20	30
22	Gerry Meehan	4	5	6	8	12	18		
23	Ed Johnston DP	4	5	6	8	12	18	20	30
24	Serge Savard	4	5	6	8	12	18	20	30
25	Walt Tkaczuk	4	5	6	8	12	18		
26	Johnny Bucyk	4	5	6	8	12	18		
27	Dave Burrows	4	5	6	8	12	18	20	30
28	Cliff Koroll	4	5	6	8	12	18		
29	Rey Comeau DP	4	5	6	8	12	18		
30	Barry Gibbs	4	5	6	8	12	18		
31	Wayne Stephenson	4	5	6	8	12	18	20	30
32	Dan Maloney DP	4	5	6	8	12	18	20	30
33	Henry Boucha DP	4	5	6	8	12	18	20	30
34	Gerry Hart	4	5	6	8	12	18		
35	Bobby Schmautz	4	5	6	8	12	18	20	30
36	Ross Lonsberry DP	4	5	6	8	12	18		
37	Ted McAneeley	4	5	6	8	12	18		
38	Don Luce DP	4	5	6	8	12	18		
39	Jim McKenny DP	4	5	6	8	12	18		
40	Frank Mahovlich	4	5	6	8	12	20	30	80
41	Bill Fairbairn	4	5	6	8	12	18	20	30
42	Dallas Smith	4	5	6	8	12	18		
43	Bryan Hextall	4	5	6	8	12	18	20	30
44	Keith Magnuson	4	5	6	8	12	18	20	30

#	Player	VG 3	VgEx 4	EX 5	ExMt 6	NM 7	NmMt 8	NmMt+ 8.5	MT 9
45	Dan Bouchard	4	5	6	8	12	18	20	30
46	Jean-Paul Parise DP	4	5	6	8	12	18	20	30
47	Barclay Plager	4	5	6	8	12	18		
48	Mike Corrigan	4	5	6	8	12	18	20	30
49	Nick Libett DP	4	5	6	8	12	18	20	30
50	Bobby Clarke	5	6	8	10	15	25		
51	Bert Marshall DP	4	5	6	8	12	18	20	30
52	Craig Patrick	4	5	6	8	12	18	20	30
53	Richard Lemieux	4	5	6	8	12	18		
54	Tracy Pratt DP	4	5	6	8	12	18		
55	Ron Ellis DP	4	5	6	8	12	18		30
56	Jacques Lemaire	4	5	6	8	12	18		
57	Steve Vickers DP	4	5	6	8	12	18	20	30
58	Carol Vadnais	4	5	6	8	12	18	20	30
59	Jim Rutherford DP	4	5	6	8	12	18	20	30
60	Dennis Hull	4	5	6	8	12	18		
61	Pat Quinn DP	4	5	6	8	12	18		
62	Bill Goldsworthy DP	4	5	6	8	12	18		
63	Fran Huck RC	4	5	6	8	12	18		
64	Rogatien Vachon DP	4	5	6	8	12	18	20	30
65	Gary Bergman DP	4	5	6	8	12	18		
66	Bernie Parent	4	5	6	8	12	20		
67	Ed Westfall	4	5	6	8	12	18		
68	Ivan Boldirev	4	5	6	8	12	18	20	30
69	Don Tannahill DP	4	5	6	8	12	18		
70	Gilbert Perreault	4	5	6	8	12	20	25	60
71	Mike Pelyk DP	4	5	6	8	12	18		
72	Guy Lafleur DP	5	6	8	10	15	30	40	80
73	Jean Ratelle	4	5	6	8	12	18		
74	Gilles Gilbert DP RC	4	5	6	8	12	20	25	50
75	Greg Polis	4	5	6	8	12	18		
76	Doug Jarrett DP	4	5	6	8	12	18		
77	Phil Myre DP	4	5	6	8	12	18	20	30
78	Fred Harvey DP	4	5	6	8	12	18	20	30
79	Jack Egers	4	5	6	8	12	18		
80	Terry Harper	4	5	6	8	12	18		
81	Bill Barber RC	5	6	8	10	15	25	30	50
82	Roy Edwards DP	4	5	6	8	12	18		
83	Brian Spencer	4	5	6	8	12	18	20	30
84	Reggie Leach DP	4	5	6	8	12	18	20	30
85	Dave Keon	4	5	6	8	12	18		
86	Jim Schoenfeld	4	5	6	8	12	18		
87	Henri Richard DP	4	5	6	8	12	18	20	30
88	Rod Gilbert DP	4	5	6	8	12	18	20	30
89	Don Marcotte DP	4	5	6	8	12	18	20	30
90	Tony Esposito	4	5	6	8	12	18		
91	Joe Watson	4	5	6	8	12	18	20	30
92	Flames Team	4	5	6	8	12	20	25	40
93	Bruins Team	4	5	6	8	12	20	25	40
94	Sabres Team DP	4	5	6	8	12	20	25	40
95	Golden Seals Team DP	4	5	6	8	12	18		
96	Blackhawks Team	4	5	6	8	12	20	25	40
97	Red Wings Team DP	4	5	6	8	12	20	30	100
98	Kings Team DP	4	5	6	8	12	18		
99	North Stars Team	4	5	6	8	12	20	25	40
100	Canadiens Team	4	5	6	8	12	20	25	40
101	Islanders Teams	4	5	6	8	12	20	25	40
102	Rangers Team DP	4	5	6	8	12	20	25	40
103	Flyers Team DP	4	5	6	8	12	18		
104	Penguins Team	4	5	6	8	12	20	25	40
105	Blues Team	4	5	6	8	12	18		
106	Maple Leafs Team	4	5	6	8	12	20	25	40
107	Canucks Team	4	5	6	8	12	20	25	40
108	Roger Crozier DP	4	5	6	8	12	18	20	30
109	Tom Reid	4	5	6	8	12	18	20	30
110	Hilliard Graves RC	4	5	6	8	12	18		
111	Don Lever	4	5	6	8	12	18		
112	Jim Pappin	4	5	6	8	12	18	20	30
113	Ron Schock DP	4	5	6	8	12	18	20	30
114	Gerry Desjardins	4	5	6	8	12	18	20	30
115	Yvan Cournoyer DP	4	5	6	8	12	18	20	30
116	Checklist Card	6	8	10	12	20	40		
117	Bob Leiter	4	5	6	8	12	18		
118	Ab DeMarco	4	5	6	8	12	18		
119	Doug Favell	4	5	6	8	12	18	20	30
120	Phil Esposito	4	5	6	8	12	18		
121	Mike Robitaille	4	5	6	8	12	18	20	30
122	Real Lemieux	4	5	6	8	12	18	20	30
123	Jim Neilson	4	5	6	8	12	18	20	30
124	Tim Ecclestone DP	4	5	6	8	12	18	20	30
125	Jude Drouin	4	5	6	8	12	18		
126	Gary Smith DP	4	5	6	8	12	18	20	30
127	Walt McKechnie	4	5	6	8	12	18	20	30
128	Lowell MacDonald	4	5	6	8	12	18		
129	Dale Tallon DP	4	5	6	8	12	18		
130	Billy Harris RC	4	5	6	8	12	18	20	30
131	Randy Manery DP	4	5	6	8	12	18	20	30
132	Darryl Sittler DP	4	5	6	8	12	20	25	40
133	Ken Hodge	4	5	6	8	12	18		

#	Player	VG 3	VgEx 4	EX 5	ExMt 6	NM 7	NmMt 8	NmMt+ 8.5	N
134	Bob Plager	4	5	6	8	12	18	20	
135	Rick MacLeish	4	5	6	8	12	18	20	
136	Dennis Hextall	4	5	6	8	12	18	20	
137	Jacques Laperriere DP	4	5	6	8	12	18	20	
138	Butch Goring	4	5	6	8	12	18	20	
139	Rene Robert	4	5	6	8	12	18		
140	Ed Giacomin	4	5	6	8	12	18	20	
141	Alex Delvecchio DP	4	5	6	8	12	18	20	
142	Jocelyn Guevremont	4	5	6	8	12	18		
143	Joey Johnston	4	5	6	8	12	18	20	
144	Bryan Watson DP	4	5	6	8	12	18	20	
145	Stan Mikita	4	5	6	8	12	20	25	
146	Cesare Maniago	4	5	6	8	12	18		
147	Craig Cameron	4	5	6	8	12	18	20	
148	Norm Ullman DP	4	5	6	8	12	18	20	
149	Dave Schultz RC	5	6	8	10	15	25		
150	Bobby Orr	10	15	20	25	35	50	60	
151	Phil Roberto	4	5	6	8	12	18		
152	Curt Bennett	4	5	6	8	12	18	20	
153	Gilles Villemure DP	4	5	6	8	12	18	20	
154	Chuck Lefley	4	5	6	8	12	18	20	
155	Richard Martin	4	5	6	8	12	18		
156	Juha Widing	4	5	6	8	12	18		
157	Orland Kurtenbach	4	5	6	8	12	18		
158	Bill Collins DP	4	5	6	8	12	18		
159	Bob Stewart	4	5	6	8	12	18	20	
160	Syl Apps	4	5	6	8	12	18		
161	Danny Grant	4	5	6	8	12	18		
162	Billy Smith RC	8	10	12	▲20	▲40	▲80		
163	Brian Glennie	4	5	6	8	12	18		
164	Pit Martin DP	4	5	6	8	12	18		
165	Brad Park	4	5	6	8	12	18		
166	Wayne Cashman DP	4	5	6	8	12	18		
167	Gary Dornhoefer	4	5	6	8	12	18		
168	Steve Durbano RC	4	5	6	8	12	18		
169	Jacques Richard	4	5	6	8	12	18	20	
170	Guy Lapointe	4	5	6	8	12	18		
171	Jim Lorentz	4	5	6	8	12	18		
172	Bob Berry DP	4	5	6	8	12	18	20	
173	Dennis Kearns	4	5	6	8	12	18		
174	Red Berenson	4	5	6	8	12	18		
175	Gilles Meloche DP	4	5	6	8	12	18	20	
176	Al McDonough	4	5	6	8	12	18	20	
177	Dennis O'Brien RC	4	5	6	8	12	18	20	
178	Germaine Gagnon UER DP	4	5	6	8	12	18		
179	Rick Kehoe DP	4	5	6	8	12	18		
180	Bill White	4	5	6	8	12	18		
181	Vic Hadfield DP	4	5	6	8	12	18		
182	Derek Sanderson	4	5	6	8	12	20	25	
183	Andre Dupont DP	4	5	6	8	12	18		
184	Gary Sabourin	4	5	6	8	12	18		
185	Larry Romanchych RC	4	5	6	8	12	18	20	
186	Peter Mahovlich	4	5	6	8	12	18		
187	Dave Dryden	4	5	6	8	12	18	20	
188	Gilles Marotte	4	5	6	8	12	18		
189	Bobby Lalonde	4	5	6	8	12	18	20	
190	Mickey Redmond	4	5	6	8	12	18		
191	Series A/Can 4/Sabres 2	4	5	6	8	12	18		
192	Series B/Flyers 4/Stars 2	4	5	6	8	12	18		
193	Series C/Hawks 4/Blues 1	4	5	6	8	12	18		
194	Series D/Rangrs 4/Bruins	4	5	6	8	12	18	20	
195	Series E/Canad 4/Flyers 1	4	5	6	8	12	18		
196	Series F/Hawks 4/Rangrs 1	4	5	6	8	12	18		
197	Series G/Canad 4/'Hawks 2	4	5	6	8	12	20		
198	Canadiens Champs		5	6	8	15	20		

—Paul Henderson #7 PSA 9 (MT) sold for $110.50 (eBay; 7/12)
—Gary Bergman #65 PSA 9 (MT) sold for $211.75 (eBay; 8/12)
—Bobby Orr #150 PSA 9 (MT) sold for $640.34 (eBay; 2/14)

1974-75 O-Pee-Chee

#	Player	VG 3	VgEx 4	EX 5	ExMt 6	NM 7	NmMt 8	NmMt+ 8.5	MT
1	P.Espo/Gldswrthy LL	5	6	8	12	30	80		
2	B.Orr/D.Hextall LL	6	8	10	15	30	135	150	25
3	P.Espo/B.Clarke LL	5	6	8	12	15	40		
4	Favell/B.Parent LL	4	5	6	10	12	20		
5	Watson/D.Schulz LL	4	5	6	10	12	20		
6	Redmond/MacLsh LL	4	5	6	10	12	20	25	
7	Gary Bromley	4	5	6	10	12			
8	Bill Barber	5	6	8	12	20			
9	Emile Francis CO	4	5	6	10	12	30		
10	Gilles Gilbert	4	5	6	10	12	20		
11	John Davidson RC	6	8	10	15	20	40	50	10
12	Ron Ellis	4	5	6	10	12			
13	Syl Apps	4	5	6	10	12	20		
14	Richard/Lysiak TL	4	5	6	10	12	20	25	
15	Dan Bouchard	4	5	6	10d	12	25		
16	Ivan Boldirev	4	5	6	10	12	20		
17	Gary Coalter RC	4	5	6	10	12	20		
18	Bob Berry	4	5	6	10	12	20		

	VG 3	VgEx 4	EX 5	ExMt 6	NM 7	NmMt 8	NmMt+ 8.5	MT 9
Red Berenson	4	5	6	10	12	20		
Stan Mikita	5	6	8	12	15	40	50	120
Fred Shero CO RC	5	6	10	15	25	80		
Gary Smith	4	5	6	10	12	20		
Bill Mikkelson	4	5	6	10	12	20		
Jacques Lemaire UER	4	5	6	10	12			
Gilbert Perreault	5	6	8	12	15	30	35	60
Cesare Maniago	4	5	6	10	12			
Bobby Schmautz	4	5	6	10	12	20		
Espo/Orr/Bucyk TL	6	8	10	15	20	50	60	150
Steve Vickers	4	5	6	10	12	20		
Lowell MacDonald UER	4	5	6	10	25	80		
Fred Stanfield	4	5	6	10	12	20		
Ed Westfall	4	5	6	10	12			
Curt Bennett	4	5	6	10	12	20		
Bep Guidolin CO	4	5	6	10	12	20		
Cliff Koroll	4	5	6	10	12			
Gary Croteau	4	5	6	10	12	20		
Mike Corrigan	4	5	6	10	12			
Henry Boucha	4	5	6	10	12			
Ron Low	4	5	6	10	12	20		
Darryl Sittler	6	8	10	12	15	30		
Tracy Pratt	4	5	6	10	12	20		
Martin/Robert TL	4	5	6	10	12	20	25	40
Larry Carriere	4	5	6	10	12	20		
Gary Dornhoefer	4	5	6	10	12			
Denis Herron RC	5	6	8	12	15	25	30	60
Doug Favell	4	5	6	10	12	20		
Dave Gardner RC	4	5	6	10	12	20		
Morris Mott RC	4	5	6	10	12	20		
Marc Boileau CO	4	5	6	10	12	20		
Brad Park	5	6	8	12	15	30		
Bob Leiter	4	5	6	10	12	20		
Tom Reid	4	5	6	10	12	20		
Serge Savard	4	5	6	10	15	40		
Checklist 1-132 UER	12	20	25	40	100			
Terry Harper	4	5	6	10	12	20		
Joey Johnston LL	4	5	6	10	12	20	25	40
Guy Charron	4	5	6	10	12	20		
Pit Martin	4	5	6	10	12			
Chris Evans	4	5	6	10	12	20		
Bernie Parent	5	6	8	12	15			
Jim Lorentz	4	5	6	10	12	20		
Dave Kryskow RC	4	5	6	10	12	20		
Lou Angotti CO	4	5	6	10	12	20		
Bill Flett	4	5	6	10	12	20		
Vic Hadfield	4	5	6	10	12	20		
Wayne Merrick RC	4	5	6	10	12			
Andre Dupont	4	5	6	10	12			
Tom Lysiak RC	4	5	6	10	12	20		
Pappin/Mikita/Bord TL	4	5	6	10	12	20		
Guy Lapointe	4	5	6	10	12	20		
Gerry O'Flaherty	4	5	6	10	12	20		
Marcel Dionne	6	8	10	15	30			
Butch Deadmarsh RC	4	5	6	25	60			
Butch Goring	4	5	6	10	12	20		
Keith Magnuson	4	5	6	10	12	20		
Red Kelly CO	4	5	6	10	15	80		
Pete Stemkowski	4	5	6	10	12	20		
Jim Roberts	4	5	6	10	12	20		
Don Luce	4	5	6	10	12	20		
Don Awrey	4	5	6	10	12	20		
Rick Kehoe	4	5	6	10	12	20		
Billy Smith	6	8	10	12	15			
Jean-Paul Parise	4	5	6	10	12	20		
Rdmnd/Dnne/Hoga TL	4	5	6	10	12	20		
Ed Van Impe	4	5	6	10	12	20		
Randy Manery	4	5	6	10	12	20		
Barclay Plager	4	5	6	10	12	20		
Inge Hammarstrom RC	4	5	6	10	12	20		
Ab DeMarco	4	5	6	10	12	25	30	50
Bill White	4	5	6	10	12	20		
Al Arbour CO	4	5	6	10	12	20	30	60
Bob Stewart	4	5	6	10	12	20		
Jack Egers	4	5	6	10	12	20		
Don Lever	4	5	6	10	12	20		
Reggie Leach	4	5	6	10	12	20		
Dennis O'Brien	4	5	6	10	12	20		
Peter Mahovlich	4	5	6	10	12	20		
Grng/St.Mrsle/Kzk TL	4	5	6	10	12	20		
Gerry Meehan	4	5	6	10	12	20		
Bobby Orr	25	30	50	100	125	450	500	800
Jean Potvin RC	4	5	6	10	12	20		
Rod Seiling	4	5	6	10	12	20	25	50
Keith McCreary	4	5	6	10	12	20	25	60
Phil Maloney CO RC	4	5	6	10	12	20		
Denis Dupere	4	5	6	10	12	20		
Steve Durbano	4	5	6	10	12	20		
Bob Plager UER	4	5	6	10	12	20	25	50

		VG 3	VgEx 4	EX 5	ExMt 6	NM 7	NmMt 8	NmMt+ 8.5	MT 9
108	Chris Oddleifson RC	4	5	6	10	12	20	25	60
109	Jim Neilson	4	5	6	10	12	20		
110	Jean Pronovost	4	5	6	10	12	20		
111	Don Kozak RC	4	5	6	10	12	20		
112	Gldswrthy/Hxtall TL	4	5	6	10	12	20	25	50
113	Jim Pappin	4	5	6	10	12	20		
114	Richard Lemieux	4	5	6	10	12	20		
115	Dennis Hextall	4	5	6	10	12			
116	Bill Hogaboam RC	4	5	6	10	12	20		
117	Vrgrt/Schmt/Boud TL	4	5	6	10	12	20	25	50
118	Jimmy Anderson CO	4	5	6	10	12	20		
119	Walt Tkaczuk	4	5	6	10	12	20		
120	Mickey Redmond	4	5	6	10	12			
121	Jim Schoenfeld	4	5	6	10	12	20		
122	Jocelyn Guevremont	4	5	6	10	12	20		
123	Bob Nystrom	4	5	6	10	12	20		
124	Cour/F.Mahov/Lrse TL	4	5	6	10	12	20	25	60
125	Lew Morrison	4	5	6	10	12	20		
126	Terry Murray	4	5	6	10	12	20		
127	Richard Martin AS	4	5	6	10	12	20		
128	Ken Hodge AS	4	5	6	10	12			
129	Phil Esposito AS	4	5	6	10	12	20	30	80
130	Bobby Orr AS	8	10	12	▲40	▲80	200	225	350
131	Brad Park AS	4	5	6	10	12	20		
132	Gilles Gilbert AS	4	5	6	10	12			
133	Lowell MacDonald AS	4	5	6	10	12	20	25	40
134	Bill Goldsworthy AS	4	5	6	10	12	20		
135	Bobby Clarke AS	5	6	8	15	25	100		
136	Bill White AS	4	5	6	10	12			
137	Dave Burrows AS	4	5	6	10	12	20		
138	Bernie Parent AS	4	5	6	10	12	35		
139	Jacques Richard	4	5	6	10	12	20		
140	Yvan Cournoyer	4	5	6	10	12	20		
141	R.Gilbert/B.Park TL	4	5	6	10	12	20		
142	Rene Robert	4	5	6	10	12	20		
143	J. Bob Kelly RC	4	5	6	10	12	25		
144	Ross Lonsberry	4	5	6	10	12	20		
145	Jean Ratelle	4	5	6	10	12	20		
146	Dallas Smith	4	5	6	10	12	20		
147	Bernie Geoffrion CO	4	5	6	10	12	20	25	40
148	Ted McAneeley	4	5	6	10	12	20		
149	Pierre Plante	4	5	6	10	12	20		
150	Dennis Hull	4	5	6	10	12	20		
151	Dave Keon	4	5	6	10	12			
152	Dave Dunn RC	4	5	6	10	12	20		
153	Michel Belhumeur	4	5	6	10	12	20	25	40
154	Clarke/D.Schultz TL	4	5	6	10	12	20		
155	Ken Dryden	10	12	15	25	40	150		
156	John Wright RC	4	5	6	10	12	20		
157	Larry Romanchych	4	5	6	10	12	20		
158	Ralph Stewart RC	4	5	6	10	12	20		
159	Mike Robitaille	4	5	6	10	12	20		
160	Ed Giacomin	4	5	6	10	12	20		
161	Don Cherry CO RC	15	20	30	60	75	125	150	300
162	Checklist 133-264	10	12	20	30	50	100		
163	Rick MacLeish	4	5	6	10	12	20		
164	Greg Polis	4	5	6	10	12	20		
165	Carol Vadnais	4	5	6	10	12	20		
166	Pete Laframboise	4	5	6	10	12	20		
167	Ron Schock	4	5	6	10	12	20		
168	Lanny McDonald RC	10	12	20	40	60	300	500	800
169	Scouts Emblem	4	5	6	10	12	20		
170	Tony Esposito	5	6	8	12	15	40		
171	Pierre Jarry	4	5	6	10	12	20	25	40
172	Dan Maloney	4	5	6	10	12	20		
173	Peter McDuffe	4	5	6	10	12	20		
174	Danny Grant	4	5	6	10	12			
175	John Stewart RC	4	5	6	10	12	20		
176	Floyd Smith CO	4	5	6	10	12	20		
177	Bert Marshall	4	5	6	10	12			
178	Chuck Lefley UER	4	5	6	10	15	60		
179	Gilles Villemure	4	5	6	10	12	20		
180	Borje Salming RC	10	12	25	30	80	200		
181	Doug Mohns	4	5	6	10	12	20		
182	Barry Wilkins	4	5	6	10	12	20		
183	MacDonald/Apps TL	4	5	6	10	12	20	25	40
184	Gregg Sheppard	4	5	6	10	12	20	25	40
185	Joey Johnston	4	5	6	10	12			
186	Dick Redmond	4	5	6	10	12	20		
187	Simon Nolet	4	5	6	10	12	20		
188	Ron Stackhouse	4	5	6	10	12	20		
189	Marshall Johnston	4	5	6	10	12	20		
190	Richard Martin	4	5	6	10	12	20		
191	Andre Boudrias	4	5	6	10	12	20		
192	Steve Atkinson	4	5	6	10	12	20		
193	Nick Libett	4	5	6	10	12	20	25	40
194	Bob Murdoch Kings RC	4	5	6	10	12	20		
195	Denis Potvin RC	15	20	25	50	100	300	400	1,200
196	Dave Schultz	4	5	6	10	12	20		

#	Name	VG 3	VgEx 4	EX 5	ExMt 6	NM 7	NmMt 8	NmMt+ 8.5	MT 9
197	Unger/Plante TL	4	5	6	10	12	20		
198	Jim McKenny	4	5	6	10	12	20		
199	Gerry Hart	4	5	6	10	12			
200	Phil Esposito	5	6	8	12	15	30	40	100
201	Rod Gilbert	4	5	6	10	12	20	25	60
202	Jacques Laperriere	4	5	6	10	12	25		
203	Barry Gibbs	4	5	6	10	12	20	30	100
204	Billy Reay CO	4	5	6	10	12	20		
205	Gilles Meloche	4	5	6	10	12	20		
206	Wayne Cashman	4	5	6	10	12	20		
207	Dennis Ververgaert	4	5	6	10	12	20		
208	Phil Roberto	4	5	6	10	12	20		
209	Quarter Finals	4	5	6	10	12			
210	Quarter Finals	4	5	6	10	12	20		
211	Quarter Finals	4	5	6	10	12	20		
212	Quarter Finals	4	5	6	10	12	20		
213	Semi-Finals	4	5	6	10	12	20		
214	Semi-Finals	4	5	6	10	12	25		
215	Stanley Cup Finals	4	5	6	10	12	20		
216	Flyers Champions	4	5	6	10	12	25		
217	Joe Watson	4	5	6	10	12	20	25	50
218	Wayne Stephenson	4	5	6	10	12	20		
219	Sittl/Ullmn/Hend TL	4	5	6	10	12	20		
220	Bill Goldsworthy	4	5	6	10	12	20		
221	Don Marcotte	4	5	6	10	12	20		
222	Alex Delvecchio CO	4	5	6	10	12			
223	Stan Gilbertson	4	5	6	10	12	20		
224	Mike Murphy	4	5	6	10	12			
225	Jim Rutherford	4	5	6	10	12			
226	Phil Russell	4	5	6	10	12	20		
227	Lynn Powis	4	5	6	10	12	20		
228	Billy Harris	4	5	6	10	12	20	25	50
229	Bob Pulford CO	4	5	6	10	12	25		
230	Ken Hodge	4	5	6	10	12			
231	Bill Fairbairn	4	5	6	10	12	20		
232	Guy Lafleur	6	8	10	15	20	40		
233	Harr/Stw/Ptvn TL UER	4	5	6	10	12	20		
234	Fred Barrett	4	5	6	10	12	20	25	40
235	Rogatien Vachon	4	5	6	10	12	20		
236	Norm Ullman	4	5	6	10	12	20		
237	Garry Unger	4	5	6	10	12	20		
238	Jack Gordon CO RC	4	5	6	10	12	20		
239	Johnny Bucyk	4	5	6	10	12	20	25	50
240	Bob Dailey RC	4	5	6	10	12	20		
241	Dave Burrows	4	5	6	10	12	20		
242	Len Frig RC	4	5	6	10	12	20	25	40
243	Henri Richard Mstrsn	4	5	6	10	25	100		
244	Phil Esposito Hart	4	5	6	10	12	20		
245	Johnny Bucyk Byng	4	5	6	10	12	20		
246	Phil Esposito Ross	4	5	6	12	20			
247	Wales Trophy	4	5	6	10	12	20		
248	Bobby Orr Norris	8	10	12	25	40	80	125	
249	Bernie Parent Vezina	4	5	6	10	15	40		
250	Philadelphia Flyers SC	4	5	6	10	12	20	30	60
251	Bernie Parent Smythe	4	5	6	10	12	40		
252	Denis Potvin Calder	6	8	10	12	15	30		
253	Campbell Trophy	4	5	6	10	12	20		
254	Pierre Bouchard	4	5	6	10	12	20		
255	Jude Drouin	4	5	6	10	12	20		
256	Capitals Emblem	4	5	6	10	12	20		
257	Michel Plasse	4	5	6	10	12	20		
258	Juha Widing	4	5	6	10	12			
259	Bryan Watson	4	5	6	10	12			
260	Bobby Clarke UER	6	8	10	15	20	60	80	150
261	Scotty Bowman CO RC	15	20	30	60	75	150		
262	Craig Patrick	4	5	6	10	12			
263	Craig Cameron	4	5	6	10	12			
264	Ted Irvine	4	5	6	10	12	20		
265	Ed Johnston	4	5	6	10	12	20		
266	Dave Forbes RC	4	5	6	10	12	20		
267	Red Wings Team CL	4	5	6	10	12	20	25	50
268	Rick Dudley RC	4	5	6	10	12	30		
269	Darcy Rota RC	4	5	6	10	12	20	25	50
270	Phil Myre	4	5	6	10	12	20		
271	Larry Brown RC	4	5	6	10	12	20		
272	Bob Neely RC	4	5	6	10	12			
273	Jerry Byers RC	4	5	6	10	12			
274	Penguins Team CL	4	5	6	10	12	20		
275	Glenn Goldup RC	4	5	6	10	12			
276	Ron Harris	4	5	6	10	12	20		
277	Joe Lundrigan RC	4	5	6	10	12	30		
278	Mike Christie RC	4	5	6	10	12	20		
279	Doug Rombough RC	4	5	6	10	12	20		
280	Larry Robinson	8	10	12	15	25	50		
281	Blues Team CL	4	5	6	10	12	20	25	40
282	John Marks RC	4	5	6	10	12	20		
283	Don Saleski	4	5	6	10	12	20	25	40
284	Rick Wilson RC	4	5	6	10	12	20		
285	Andre Savard RC	4	5	6	10	12			

#	Name	VG 3	VgEx 4	EX 5	ExMt 6	NM 7	NmMt 8	NmMt+ 8.5	MT 9
286	Pat Quinn	4	5	6	10	12	20		
287	Kings Team CL	4	5	6	10	12			
288	Norm Gratton	4	5	6	10	12	20		
289	Ian Turnbull RC	4	5	6	10	12	60		
290	Derek Sanderson	4	5	6	10	12	20		
291	Murray Oliver	4	5	6	10	12	20		
292	Wilf Paiement RC	4	5	6	10	12	20		
293	Nelson Debenedet RC	4	5	6	10	12	20		
294	Greg Joly RC	4	5	6	10	12	25	30	
295	Terry O'Reilly	4	5	6	10	12	20		
296	Rey Comeau	4	5	6	10	12	20	25	
297	Michel Larocque RC	5	6	8	12	15	80		
298	Floyd Thomson RC	4	5	6	10	12	20		
299	Jean-Guy Lagace RC	4	5	6	10	12			
300	Flyers Team CL	4	5	6	10	12	30		
301	Al MacAdam RC	4	5	6	10	12	20		
302	George Ferguson RC	4	5	6	10	12	20		
303	Jimmy Watson RC	4	5	6	10	20	50		
304	Rick Middleton RC	8	10	12	25	40	100	120	3
305	Craig Ramsay UER	4	5	6	10	12	20		
306	Hilliard Graves	4	5	6	10	12			
307	Islanders Team CL	4	5	6	10	12	20		
308	Blake Dunlop RC	4	5	6	10	12	20		
309	J.P. Bordeleau	4	5	6	10	12			
310	Brian Glennie	4	5	6	10	12			
311	Checklist 265-396 UER	10	12	20	35	60	120		
312	Doug Roberts	4	5	6	10	12	20		
313	Darryl Edestrand	4	5	6	10	12			
314	Ron Anderson	4	5	6	10	12	20		
315	Blackhawks Team CL	4	5	6	10	12	20		
316	Steve Shutt RC	10	12	15	25	50	300	400	6
317	Doug Horbul RC	4	5	6	10	12	20	25	
318	Billy Lochead RC	4	5	6	10	12	20		
319	Fred Harvey	4	5	6	10	12			
320	Gene Carr RC	4	5	6	10	12			
321	Henri Richard	4	5	6	10	12	50		
322	Canucks Team CL	4	5	6	10	12	20	25	
323	Tim Ecclestone	4	5	6	10	12	20		
324	Dave Lewis RC	4	5	6	10	12	25		
325	Lou Nanne	4	5	6	10	12	20		
326	Bobby Rousseau	4	5	6	10	12	20		
327	Dunc Wilson	4	5	6	10	12	20		
328	Brian Spencer	4	5	6	10	12	20		
329	Rick Hampton RC	4	5	6	10	12	20		
330	Canadiens Team CL UER	4	5	6	10	12	30	35	
331	Jack Lynch	4	5	6	10	12			
332	Garnet Bailey	4	5	6	10	12	20		
333	Al Sims RC	4	5	6	10	12	25		
334	Orest Kindrachuk RC	4	5	6	10	12	40		
335	Dave Hudson	4	5	6	10	12	20		
336	Bob Murray RC	4	5	6	10	12	20		
337	Sabres Team CL	4	5	6	10	12	20		
338	Sheldon Kannegiesser	4	5	6	10	12			
339	Bill MacMillan	4	5	6	10	12			
340	Paulin Bordeleau RC	4	5	6	10	12			
341	Dale Rolfe	4	5	6	10	12	20		
342	Yvon Lambert RC	4	5	6	10	12	50		
343	Bob Paradise RC	4	5	6	10	12	20		
344	Germaine Gagnon UER	4	5	6	10	12			
345	Yvon Labre	4	5	6	10	12	20		
346	Chris Ahrens RC	4	5	6	10	12	20		
347	Doug Grant RC	4	5	6	10	12	20		
348	Blaine Stoughton RC	4	5	6	10	12	20		
349	Gregg Boddy	4	5	6	10	12	25	30	6
350	Bruins Team CL	4	5	6	10	12	20		
351	Doug Jarrett	4	5	6	10	12	20	25	5
352	Terry Crisp	4	5	6	10	12	20	25	5
353	Glenn Resch UER RC	8	10	12	15	25	50	60	10
354	Jerry Korab	4	5	6	10	12	20		
355	Stan Weir RC	4	5	6	10	12	20		
356	Noel Price	4	5	6	10	12	20		
357	Bill Clement RC	6	8	10	20	30	60	80	13
358	Neil Komadoski	4	5	6	10	12			
359	Murray Wilson RC	4	5	6	10	12			
360	Dale Tallon UER	4	5	6	10	12	20		
361	Gary Doak	4	5	6	10	12			
362	Randy Rota RC	4	5	6	10	12	20		
363	North Stars Team CL	4	5	6	10	12	20		
364	Bill Collins	4	5	6	10	12	20		
365	Thommie Bergman UER	4	5	6	10	12	20		
366	Dennis Kearns	4	5	6	10	12	20		
367	Lorne Henning	4	5	6	10	12	20		
368	Gary Sabourin	4	5	6	10	12	20		
369	Mike Bloom RC	4	5	6	10	12	20		
370	Rangers Team CL	4	5	6	10	12	20		
371	Gary Simmons RC	5	6	8	12	15			
372	Dwight Bialowas RC	4	5	6	10	12	20		
373	Gilles Marotte	4	5	6	10	12			
374	Frank St.Marseille	4	5	6	10	12			

	VG 3	VgEx 4	EX 5	ExMt 6	NM 7	NmMt 8	NmMt+ 8.5	MT 9
Garry Howatt RC	4	5	6	10	12	30		
Ross Brooks RC	4	5	6	10	12	20	25	60
Flames Team CL	4	5	6	10	12	20		
Bob Nevin	4	5	6	10	12	20		
Lyle Moffat RC	4	5	6	10	12	20		
Bob Kelly	4	5	6	10	12	20		
John Gould RC	4	5	6	10	12	20		
Dave Fortier RC	4	5	6	10	12	20		
Jean Hamel RC	4	5	6	10	12	20		
Bert Wilson RC	4	5	6	10	12	20		
Chuck Arnason RC	4	5	6	10	12	20		
Bruce Cowick RC	4	5	6	10	12	20		
Ernie Hicke	4	5	6	10	12	20		
Bob Gainey RC	10	12	20	30	60	125	200	550
Vic Venasky RC	4	5	6	10	12	20		
Maple Leafs Team CL	4	5	6	10	12	25	30	60
Eric Vail RC	4	5	6	10	12	20		
Bobby Lalonde	4	5	6	10	12	20		
Jerry Butler RC	4	5	6	10	12	20		
Tom Williams	4	5	6	10	12	20		
Chico Maki	4	5	6	10	12	30		
Tom Bladon RC	4	5	6	12	20	40		

Scotty Bowman CO RC #61 PSA 9 (MT) sold for $351.95 (eBay; 8/12)
Bill Clement RC #357 PSA 9 (MT) sold for $305 (eBay; 8/12)
Espo/Orr/Bucyk TL #28 PSA 10 (Gem) sold for $1,491 (eBay; 3/07)
Espo/Orr/Bucyk TL #28 PSA 10 (Gem) sold for $562 (Mile High; 12/13)
Espo/Orr/Bucyk TL #28 PSA 10 (Gem) sold for $510 (eBay; 12/06)
Bob Gainey RC #388 PSA 10 (Gem) sold for $1,079 (eBay; 9/15)
Rick Middleton RC #304 PSA 10 (Gem) sold for $764 (eBay; 7/12)
Bobby Orr AS #130 PSA 10 (Gem) sold for $2,025 (eBay; 8/12)
Bobby Orr AS #130 PSA 10 (Gem) sold for $1,952 (Mile High; 10/12)
Bobby Orr AS #130 PSA 10 (Gem) sold for $1,626.73 (Mile High; 12/13)
Bobby Orr Norris #248 BVG 10 (Gem) sold for $507.99 (eBay; 2/16)
Denis Potvin RC #195 BVG 9.5 (GemMT) sold for $652.50 (eBay; 4/16)
Steve Schutt RC #316 PSA 9 (MT) sold for $569 (eBay; 7/12)
Billy Smith #82 PSA 10 (Gem) sold for $488 (eBay; 7/15)

1974-75 O-Pee-Chee WHA

	VG 3	VgEx 4	EX 5	ExMt 6	NM 7	NmMt 8	NmMt+ 8.5	MT 9
COMMON CARD (1-66)	5	5	5	8	10	15	20	30
Gord/Mark/Marty Howe	15	20	25	40	60	100	120	200
Bruce MacGregor	5	5	5	8	10	15		
Ulf Nilsson RC	5	6	8	12	15	25	30	50
Rosaire Paiement	5	5	5	8	10	15		
Tom Webster	5	5	5	8	10	15		
Norm Beaudin	5	5	5	8	10	15	25	40
Anders Hedberg RC	5	6	8	12	15	30	40	60
Mike Pelyk	5	5	5	8	10	15	20	40
Danny Lawson RC	5	5	5	8	10	15	20	40
Gene Peacosh RC	5	5	5	8	10	15		
Fran Huck	5	5	5	8	10	15		
Al Hamilton	5	5	5	8	10	15	20	40
Gerry Cheevers	5	8	10	15	20	30	40	60
Pat Stapleton	5	6	8	12	15	25	30	50
Joe Daley	5	5	5	8	10	15	20	40
Frank Mahovlich	5	6	8	12	15	30	40	60
Rejean Houle	5	5	5	8	10	15	20	40
Ron Chipperfield RC	5	5	6	10	12	20		
Don McLeod RC	5	5	5	8	10	15	20	40
Vaclav Nedomansky RC	5	5	6	10	12	20	25	40
Bobby Hull	8	10	15	20	25	40	50	120
Checklist	6	10	15	20	25	40	50	80
Wayne Connelly	5	5	5	8	10	15		
Dennis Sobchuk RC	5	5	5	8	10	15	20	40
Paul Henderson	5	5	5	8	10	15	20	40
Andy Brown RC	5	5	6	10	12	20	25	50
Andre Lacroix	5	5	5	8	10	15	20	40
Gary Jarrett	5	5	5	8	10	15	20	40
Claude St.Sauveur RC	5	5	5	8	10	15		
Real Cloutier RC	5	5	6	10	12	20	25	50
Jacques Plante	8	10	15	20	25	40	50	100
Gilles Gratton RC	5	6	8	12	15	25		
Lars-Erik Sjoberg RC	5	6	8	12	25	40		

Gordie/Mark/Marty Howe #1 PSA 10 (Gem) sold for $1,633 (eBay; 12/15)

1974-75 Topps

	VG 3	VgEx 4	EX 5	ExMt 6	NM 7	NmMt 8	NmMt+ 8.5	MT 9
P.Espo/Goldsworthy LL	4	5	6	8	15	40		
B.Orr/D.Hextall LL	4	5	6	8	20	25	30	50
P.Espo/B.Clarke LL	4	5	6	8	12	20	25	50
D.Favell/B.Parent LL	4	5	6	8	12	20		
B.Watson/D.Schultz LL	4	5	6	8	12	18		
M.Redmond/R.Mac LL	4	5	6	8	10	12	15	30
Gary Bromley RC	4	5	6	8	10	12	15	30
Bill Barber	4	5	6	8	12	20		
Emile Francis CO	4	5	6	8	12	18		
Gilles Gilbert	4	5	6	8	12	20		
John Davidson RC	5	6	8	10	15	25		
Ron Ellis	4	5	6	8	12	18		

	VG 3	VgEx 4	EX 5	ExMt 6	NM 7	NmMt 8	NmMt+ 8.5	MT 9
13	Syl Apps	4	5	6	8	10	12	15	30
14	Richard/Lysiak/McCrry TL	4	5	6	8	12	18		
15	Dan Bouchard	4	5	6	10	15	50		
16	Ivan Boldirev	4	5	6	8	12	18		
17	Gary Coalter RC	4	5	6	8	12	18		
18	Bob Berry	4	5	6	8	12	18		
19	Red Berenson	4	5	6	10	15			
20	Stan Mikita	4	5	6	8	12	20		
21	Fred Shero CO RC	4	5	6	8	12	15	20	35
22	Gary Smith	4	5	6	8	10	12	15	30
23	Bill Mikkelson	4	5	6	8	12	18		
24	Jacques Lemaire UER	4	5	6	8	12	20		
25	Gilbert Perreault	4	5	6	8	12	20	25	50
26	Cesare Maniago	4	5	6	8	10	12	15	30
27	Bobby Schmautz	4	5	6	8	12	18		
28	Espo/Orr/Bucyk TL	5	6	8	10	15	25	30	60
29	Steve Vickers	4	5	6	8	12	18		
30	Lowell MacDonald	4	5	6	8	12	18		
31	Fred Stanfield	4	5	6	8	10	12	15	30
32	Ed Westfall	4	5	6	10	15			
33	Curt Bennett	4	5	6	8	10	12	15	30
34	Bep Guidolin CO	4	5	6	8	12	18		
35	Cliff Koroll	4	5	6	8	10	12	15	30
36	Gary Croteau	4	5	6	8	10	12	15	30
37	Mike Corrigan	4	5	6	8	10	12	15	30
38	Henry Boucha	4	5	6	10	15			
39	Ron Low	4	5	6	8	10	12	15	30
40	Darryl Sittler	4	5	6	8	12	15	20	40
41	Tracy Pratt	4	5	6	8	12	18		
42	R.Martin/R.Robert TL	4	5	6	8	12	18		
43	Larry Carriere	4	5	6	8	10	12	15	30
44	Gary Dornhoefer	4	5	6	8	12	18		
45	Denis Herron RC	4	5	6	8	12	15	20	35
46	Doug Favell	4	5	6	8	10	12	15	30
47	Dave Gardner RC	4	5	6	8	10	12	15	30
48	Morris Mott RC	4	5	6	8	10	12	15	30
49	Marc Boileau CO	4	5	6	8	10	12	15	30
50	Brad Park	4	5	6	8	12	20		
51	Bob Leiter	4	5	6	8	10	12	15	30
52	Tom Reid	4	5	6	8	12	18		
53	Serge Savard	4	5	6	8	12	15	20	35
54	Checklist 1-132	5	6	8	10	15	25		
55	Terry Harper	4	5	6	8	10	12	15	30
56	Johnston/McKechnie TL	4	5	6	8	10	12	15	30
57	Guy Charron	4	5	6	8	10	12	15	30
58	Pit Martin	4	5	6	8	12	18		
59	Chris Evans	4	5	6	8	12	18		
60	Bernie Parent	4	5	6	8	12	20		
61	Jim Lorentz	4	5	6	8	12	18		
62	Dave Kryskow RC	4	5	6	8	12	18		
63	Lou Angotti CO	4	5	6	10	15	30		
64	Bill Flett	4	5	6	8	12	18		
65	Vic Hadfield	4	5	6	10	15	30		
66	Wayne Merrick RC	4	5	6	10	15	35		
67	Andre Dupont	4	5	6	10	15	35		
68	Tom Lysiak RC	4	5	6	8	12	20		
69	Pappin/Mikita/Bord TL	4	5	6	8	12	18		
70	Guy Lapointe	4	5	6	8	10	12	15	30
71	Gerry O'Flaherty	4	5	6	8	12	18		
72	Marcel Dionne	4	5	6	8	12	20		
73	Butch Deadmarsh RC	4	5	6	10	15	35		
74	Butch Goring	4	5	6	8	10	12	15	30
75	Keith Magnuson	4	5	6	8	12	18		
76	Red Kelly CO	4	5	6	8	12	18		
77	Pete Stemkowski	4	5	6	8	12	18		
78	Jim Roberts	4	5	6	8	10	12	15	30
79	Don Luce	4	5	6	8	10	12	15	30
80	Don Awrey	4	5	6	8	12	18		
81	Rick Kehoe	4	5	6	8	10	12	15	30
82	Billy Smith	4	5	6	8	12	15	20	40
83	Jean-Paul Parise	4	5	6	8	12	18		
84	Redmnd/Dionne/Hog TL	4	5	6	8	12	18		
85	Ed Van Impe	4	5	6	8	12	18		
86	Randy Manery	4	5	6	8	12	15	20	30
87	Barclay Plager	4	5	6	10	15	30		
88	Inge Hammarstrom RC	4	5	6	8	12	18		
89	Ab DeMarco	4	5	6	8	12	18		
90	Bill White	4	5	6	8	10	12	15	30
91	Al Arbour CO	4	5	6	8	12	20		
92	Bob Stewart	4	5	6	8	12	18		
93	Jack Egers	4	5	6	8	12	18		
94	Don Lever	4	5	6	8	10	12	15	30
95	Reggie Leach	4	5	6	8	12	18		
96	Dennis O'Brien	4	5	6	8	10	12	15	30
97	Peter Mahovlich	4	5	6	8	12	18		
98	Goring/St.Mars/Kozak TL	4	5	6	8	10	12	15	30
99	Gerry Meehan	4	5	6	8	10	12	15	30
100	Bobby Orr	12	15	20	25	40	60	80	120
101	Jean Potvin RC	4	5	6	8	12	18		

#	Player	VG 3	VgEx 4	EX 5	ExMt 6	NM 7	NmMt 8	NmMt+ 8.5	MT 9
102	Rod Seiling	4	5	6	8	12	18		
103	Keith McCreary	4	5	6	8	10	12	15	30
104	Phil Maloney CO RC	4	5	6	8	10	12	15	30
105	Denis Dupere	4	5	6	8	12	18		
106	Steve Durbano	4	5	6	8	12	18		
107	Bob Plager UER	4	5	6	8	10	12	15	30
108	Chris Oddleifson RC	4	5	6	8	12	18		
109	Jim Neilson	4	5	6	8	12	18		
110	Jean Pronovost	4	5	6	8	10	12	15	30
111	Don Kozak RC	4	5	6	8	10	12	15	30
112	Goldswrthy/Grant/Hex	4	5	6	8	12	18		
113	Jim Pappin	4	5	6	8	12	18		
114	Richard Lemieux	4	5	6	8	10	12	15	30
115	Dennis Hextall	4	5	6	8	12	18		
116	Bill Hogaboam	4	5	6	8	12	18		
117	Canucks Leaders	4	5	6	8	12	18		
118	Jimmy Anderson CO	4	5	6	8	12	18		
119	Walt Tkaczuk	4	5	6	8	12	18		
120	Mickey Redmond	4	5	6	10	15			
121	Jim Schoenfeld	4	5	6	8	12	20		
122	Jocelyn Guevremont	4	5	6	8	10	12	15	30
123	Bob Nystrom	4	5	6	8	12	20		
124	Cour./F.Mahv/Larose TL	4	5	6	8	12	15	20	35
125	Lew Morrison	4	5	6	10	15	25		
126	Terry Murray	4	5	6	8	12	18		
127	Richard Martin	4	5	6	8	12	18		
128	Ken Hodge AS	4	5	6	8	12	18		
129	Phil Esposito AS	4	5	6	8	12	20		
130	Bobby Orr AS	5	6	8	10	15	30	40	100
131	Brad Park AS	4	5	6	10	15			
132	Gilles Gilbert AS	4	5	6	10	15	80		
133	Lowell MacDonald AS	4	5	6	8	10	12	15	30
134	Bill Goldsworthy AS	4	5	6	8	12	18		
135	Bobby Clarke AS	4	5	6	8	12	20		
136	Bill White AS	4	5	6	10	15	25		
137	Dave Burrows AS	4	5	6	8	12	18		
138	Bernie Parent AS	4	5	6	8	12	20		
139	Jacques Richard	4	5	6	8	10	12	15	30
140	Yvan Cournoyer	4	5	6	8	10	12	15	30
141	R.Gilbert/B.Park TL	4	5	6	8	12	15	20	35
142	Rene Robert	4	5	6	8	10	12	15	30
143	J. Bob Kelly RC	4	5	6	10	15	25		
144	Ross Lonsberry	4	5	6	8	12	18		
145	Jean Ratelle	4	5	6	8	12	20		
146	Dallas Smith	4	5	6	8	10	12	15	30
147	Bernie Geoffrion CO	4	5	6	8	12	15	20	35
148	Ted McAneeley	4	5	6	8	10	12	15	30
149	Pierre Plante	4	5	6	8	12	18		
150	Dennis Hull	4	5	6	8	12	18		
151	Dave Keon	4	5	6	8	12	15	20	35
152	Dave Dunn RC	4	5	6	8	10	12	15	30
153	Michel Belhumeur	4	5	6	8	12	18		
154	B.Clarke/D.Schultz TL	4	5	6	8	12	20		
155	Ken Dryden	6	8	10	12	20	30	35	50
156	John Wright RC	4	5	6	8	12	18		
157	Larry Romanchych	4	5	6	8	10	12	15	30
158	Ralph Stewart	4	5	6	10	15			
159	Mike Robitaille	4	5	6	8	10	12	15	30
160	Ed Giacomin	4	5	6	8	12	15	20	35
161	Don Cherry CO RC	8	10	12	15	25	30	35	50
162	Checklist 133-264	5	6	8	10	15	25		
163	Rick MacLeish	4	5	6	8	10	12	15	30
164	Greg Polis	4	5	6	10	15	25		
165	Carol Vadnais	4	5	6	8	12	18		
166	Pete Laframboise	4	5	6	8	10	12	15	30
167	Ron Schock	4	5	6	8	10	12	15	30
168	Lanny McDonald RC	5	6	8	10	15	40	50	80
169	Scouts Emblem	4	5	6	8	12	18		
170	Tony Esposito	4	5	6	8	12	25	30	60
171	Pierre Jarry	4	5	6	8	12	18		
172	Dan Maloney	4	5	6	8	10	12	15	30
173	Peter McDuffe	4	5	6	8	10	12	15	30
174	Danny Grant	4	5	6	8	10	12	15	30
175	John Stewart	4	5	6	8	10	12	15	30
176	Floyd Smith CO	4	5	6	8	10	12	15	30
177	Bert Marshall	4	5	6	8	12	18		
178	Chuck Lefley UER	4	5	6	8	12	18		
179	Gilles Villemure	4	5	6	8	10	12	15	30
180	Borje Salming RC	5	6	8	12	20	25	30	80
181	Doug Mohns	4	5	6	8	12	18		
182	Barry Wilkins	4	5	6	8	10	12	15	30
183	MacDonald/S.Apps TL	4	5	6	8	12	18		
184	Gregg Sheppard	4	5	6	8	10	12	15	30
185	Joey Johnston	4	5	6	8	12	18		
186	Dick Redmond	4	5	6	8	10	12	15	30
187	Simon Nolet	4	5	6	8	10	12	15	30
188	Ron Stackhouse	4	5	6	8	12	18		
189	Marshall Johnston	4	5	6	8	10	12	15	30
190	Richard Martin	4	5	6	8	12	15	20	35
191	Andre Boudrias	4	5	6	8	12	18		
192	Steve Atkinson	4	5	6	10	12	20		
193	Nick Libett	4	5	6	8	12	18		

#	Player	VG 3	VgEx 4	EX 5	ExMt 6	NM 7	NmMt 8	NmMt+ 8.5	M
194	Bob Murdoch RC	4	5	6	8	10	12	15	
195	Denis Potvin RC	10	12	15	20	30	50		
196	Dave Schultz	4	5	6	8	12	20		
197	G.Unger/P.Plante TL	4	5	6	8	12	18		
198	Jim McKenny	4	5	6	8	12	18		
199	Gerry Hart	4	5	6	8	12	18		
200	Phil Esposito	4	5	6	8	12	20	30	
201	Rod Gilbert	4	5	6	8	12	20		
202	Jacques Laperriere	4	5	6	8	10	12	15	
203	Barry Gibbs	4	5	6	8	10	12	15	
204	Billy Reay CO	4	5	6	8	10	12	15	
205	Gilles Meloche	4	5	6	8	12	18		
206	Wayne Cashman	4	5	6	8	10	12	15	
207	Dennis Ververgaert RC	4	5	6	8	12	18		
208	Phil Roberto	4	5	6	8	10	12	15	
209	Quarter Finals	4	5	6	8	12	18		
210	Quarter Finals	4	5	6	8	12	18		
211	Quarter Finals	4	5	6	8	10	12	15	
212	Quarter Finals	4	5	6	8	10	12	15	
213	Stanley Cup Semifinals	4	5	6	8	10	12	15	
214	Stanley Cup Semifinals	4	5	6	8	12	18		
215	Stanley Cup Finals	4	5	6	8	12	18		
216	Flyers Champions	4	5	6	8	12	15	20	
217	Joe Watson	4	5	6	8	12	18		
218	Wayne Stephenson	4	5	6	10	15	25		
219	Sittler/Ullman/Hend TL	4	5	6	8	12	20		
220	Bill Goldsworthy	4	5	6	8	12	18		
221	Don Marcotte	4	5	6	8	12	18		
222	Alex Delvecchio CO	4	5	6	8	12	20		
223	Stan Gilbertson	4	5	6	8	10	12	15	
224	Mike Murphy	4	5	6	8	10	12	15	
225	Jim Rutherford	4	5	6	8	12	18		
226	Phil Russell	4	5	6	8	10	12	15	
227	Lynn Powis	4	5	6	8	10	12	15	
228	Billy Harris	4	5	6	8	10	12	15	
229	Bob Pulford CO	4	5	6	8	10	12	15	
230	Ken Hodge	4	5	6	8	12	18		
231	Bill Fairbairn	4	5	6	8	10	12	15	
232	Guy Lafleur	5	6	8	10	15	30	40	10
233	Harris/Stew/Potvin TL	4	5	6	8	12	20		
234	Fred Barrett	4	5	6	8	10	12	15	
235	Rogatien Vachon	4	5	6	8	12	15	20	3
236	Norm Ullman	4	5	6	8	12	20		
237	Garry Unger	4	5	6	10	15			
238	Jack Gordon CO RC	4	5	6	8	10	12	15	3
239	Johnny Bucyk	4	5	6	8	12	15	20	3
240	Bob Dailey RC	4	5	6	8	10	12	15	3
241	Dave Burrows	4	5	6	8	12	18		
242	Len Frig RC	4	5	6	8	12	12	15	3
243	Henri Richard Mast.	4	5	6	10	15	30		
244	Phil Esposito Hart	4	5	6	8	12	15	20	4
245	Johnny Bucyk Byng	4	5	6	8	12	18		
246	Phil Esposito Ross	4	5	6	8	12	20		
247	Prince of Wales Trophy	4	5	6	8	12	18		
248	Bobby Orr Norris	5	6	8	10	15	25	25	4
249	Bernie Parent Vezina	4	5	6	8	12	15	20	4
250	Flyers Stanley Cup	4	5	6	8	12	15	20	4
251	Bernie Parent Smythe	4	5	6	8	12	15	20	4
252	Denis Potvin Calder	4	5	6	8	12	20		
253	Flyers Campbell Trophy	4	5	6	8	12	18		
254	Pierre Bouchard	4	5	6	8	12	18		
255	Jude Drouin	4	5	6	8	12	18		
256	Capitals Emblem	4	5	6	8	12	20		
257	Michel Plasse	4	5	6	8	12	18		
258	Juha Widing	4	5	6	10	12	20		
259	Bryan Watson	4	5	6	10	12	20		
260	Bobby Clarke	5	6	8	10	15	25		
261	Scotty Bowman CO RC	8	10	12	15	25	30	40	8
262	Craig Patrick	4	5	6	10	15	25		
263	Craig Cameron	4	5	6	10	15			
264	Ted Irvine	4	5	6	12	20			

1975-76 O-Pee-Chee

#	Player	VG 3	VgEx 4	EX 5	ExMt 6	NM 7	NmMt 8	NmMt+ 8.5	MT 9
1	Stanley Cup Finals	4	5	6	12	20	50		
2	Semi-Finals/Phil/Isln	4	5	6	10	12	25		
3	Semi-Finals/Buf/Mont	4	5	6	10	12	25	30	50
4	Quarter Finals/Isln/Pitt	4	5	6	10	12	20		
5	Quarter Finals/Mont/Van	4	5	6	10	12	20		
6	Quarter Finals/Buf/Chi	4	5	6	10	12	20	30	80
7	Quarter Finals/Phil/Tor	4	5	6	10	12	30		
8	Curt Bennett	4	5	6	10	12	20		
9	Johnny Bucyk	4	5	6	10	12	20		
10	Gilbert Perreault	5	6	8	12	15	25		
11	Darryl Edestrand	4	5	6	10	12	20		
12	Ivan Boldirev	4	5	6	10	12	20	25	4
13	Nick Libett	4	5	6	10	12	20	25	4
14	Jim McElmury RC	4	5	6	10	12	20		
15	Frank St.Marseille	4	5	6	10	12	20		
16	Blake Dunlop	4	5	6	10	12	20		
17	Yvon Lambert	4	5	6	10	12	20		

	VG 3	VgEx 4	EX 5	ExMt 6	NM 7	NmMt 8	NmMt+ 8.5	MT 9
Gerry Hart	4	5	6	10	12	20		
Steve Vickers	4	5	6	10	12	20		
Rick MacLeish	4	5	6	10	12	20		
Bob Paradise NoTR	4	5	6	10	12	20	25	40
Bob Paradise TR	4	5	6	10				
Red Berenson	4	5	6	10	12	20		
Lanny McDonald	5	6	8	12	15	25	35	60
Mike Robitaille	4	5	6	10	12	20		
Ron Low	4	5	6	10	12	20	25	40
Bryan Hextall NoTR	4	5	6	10	12	20		
Bryan Hextall TR	4	5	6	10	12			
Carol Vadnais NoTR	4	5	6	10	12	20		
Carol Vadnais TR	4	5	6	10	12	20		
Jim Lorentz	4	5	6	10	12	20	25	40
Gary Simmons	4	5	6	10	12	20		
Stan Mikita	4	5	6	10	12	20		
Bryan Watson	4	5	6	10	12	20		
Guy Charron	4	5	6	10	12	20		
Bob Murdoch	4	5	6	10	12	20		
Norm Gratton	4	5	6	10	12	20		
Ken Dryden	10	12	15	25	35	60	75	135
Jean Potvin	4	5	6	10	12	20	25	40
Rick Middleton	4	5	6	10	12	20		
Ed Van Impe	4	5	6	10	12	20		
Rick Kehoe	4	5	6	10	12	20	25	40
Garry Unger	4	5	6	10	12	20		
Ian Turnbull	4	5	6	10	12	20		
Dennis Ververgaert	4	5	6	10	12	20		
Mike Marson RC	4	5	6	10	12	20	25	50
Randy Manery	4	5	6	10	12	20		
Gilles Gilbert	4	5	6	10	12	20		
Rene Robert	4	5	6	10	12	20	25	40
Bob Stewart	4	5	6	10	12	20		
Pit Martin	4	5	6	10	12	20	25	40
Danny Grant	4	5	6	10	12	20	25	40
Peter Mahovlich	4	5	6	10	12	20		
Dennis Patterson RC	4	5	6	10	12	20	25	40
Mike Murphy	4	5	6	10	12	20	25	40
Dennis O'Brien	4	5	6	10	12	20	25	40
Garry Howatt	4	5	6	10	12	20		
Ed Giacomin	4	5	6	10	12	20		
Andre Dupont	4	5	6	10	12	20		
Chuck Arnason	4	5	6	10	12	20		
Bob Gassoff RC	4	5	6	10	12	20		
Ron Ellis	4	5	6	10	12	20		
Andre Boudrias	4	5	6	10	12	20		
Yvon Labre	4	5	6	10	12	20		
Hilliard Graves	4	5	6	10	12	20	25	40
Wayne Cashman	4	5	6	10	12	20		
Danny Gare RC	4	5	6	10	12	20		
Rick Hampton	4	5	6	10	12	20	25	40
Darcy Rota	4	5	6	10	12	20		
Bill Hogaboam	4	5	6	10	12	20		
Denis Herron	4	5	6	10	12	20		
Sheldon Kannegiesser	4	5	6	10	12	20		
Yvan Cournoyer UER	4	5	6	10	12	20	30	50
Ernie Hicke	4	5	6	10	12	20		
Bert Marshall	4	5	6	10	12	20	25	40
Derek Sanderson NoTR	4	5	6	10	12	20		
Tom Bladon	4	5	6	10	12	20		
Ron Schock	4	5	6	10	12	20		
Larry Sacharuk RC	4	5	6	10	12	20		
George Ferguson	4	5	6	10	12	20		
Ab DeMarco	4	5	6	10	12	20		
Tom Williams	4	5	6	10	12	20	25	40
Phil Roberto	4	5	6	10	12	20		
Bruins Team CL	4	5	6	10	12	20		
Seals Team CL	4	5	6	10	12	20	25	50
Sabres Team CL	4	5	6	10	12	20		
Blackhawks Team CL	4	5	6	10	12	20		
Flames Team CL	4	5	6	10	12	20		
Kings Team CL	4	5	6	10	12	20		
Red Wings Team CL	4	5	6	10	12	20		
Scouts Team CL	4	5	6	10	12	20		
North Stars Team CL	4	5	6	10	12	20		
Canadiens Team CL	4	5	6	10	15	60		
Maple Leafs Team CL	4	5	6	10	12	40		
Islanders Team CL	4	5	6	10	12	20		
Penguins Team CL	4	5	6	10	12	20		
Rangers Team CL	4	5	6	10	12	20		
Flyers Team CL	4	5	6	10	12	20		
Blues Team CL	4	5	6	10	12	20		
Canucks Team CL	4	5	6	10	12	20		
Capitals Team CL	4	5	6	10	12			
Checklist 1-110	6	8	10	15	40	80		
Bobby Orr	15	20	25	30	▲50	▲100	▲150	300
Germain Gagnon UER	4	5	6	10	12	20		
Phil Russell	4	5	6	10	12	20		
Billy Lochead	4	5	6	10	12	20		
Robin Burns RC	4	5	6	10	12	20	25	40
Gary Edwards	4	5	6	10	12	20	25	40
Dwight Bialowas	4	5	6	10	12	20		

		VG 3	VgEx 4	EX 5	ExMt 6	NM 7	NmMt 8	NmMt+ 8.5	MT 9
107	Doug Risebrough UER RC	4	5	6	10	15	35	50	80
108	Dave Lewis	4	5	6	10	12	20		
109	Bill Fairbairn	4	5	6	10	12	20		
110	Ross Lonsberry	4	5	6	10	12	20		
111	Ron Stackhouse	4	5	6	10	12	20		
112	Claude Larose	4	5	6	10	12	20	25	40
113	Don Luce	4	5	6	10	12	20	25	40
114	Errol Thompson RC	4	5	6	10	12	20	25	40
115	Gary Smith	4	5	6	10	12	20		
116	Jack Lynch	4	5	6	10	12			
117	Jacques Richard	4	5	6	10	12	20		
118	Dallas Smith	4	5	6	10	12	20		
119	Dave Gardner	4	5	6	10	12	20		
120	Mickey Redmond	4	5	6	10	12	20		
121	John Marks	4	5	6	10	12	20		
122	Dave Hudson	4	5	6	10	12	20		
123	Bob Nevin	4	5	6	10	12	20		
124	Fred Barrett	4	5	6	10	12	20		
125	Gerry Desjardins	4	5	6	10	12	20		
126	Guy Lafleur UER	6	8	10	15	25	50	60	100
127	Jean-Paul Parise	4	5	6	10	12	20		
128	Walt Tkaczuk	4	5	6	10	12	20		
129	Gary Dornhoefer	4	5	6	10	12	20	25	40
130	Syl Apps	4	5	6	10	12	20		
131	Bob Plager	4	5	6	10	12	20		
132	Stan Weir	4	5	6	10	12	20		
133	Tracy Pratt	4	5	6	10	12	20		
134	Jack Egers	4	5	6	10	12	20	25	40
135	Eric Vail	4	5	6	10	12	20		
136	Al Sims	4	5	6	10	12	20		
137	Larry Patey RC	4	5	6	10	12	20	25	40
138	Jim Schoenfeld	4	5	6	10	12	20		
139	Cliff Koroll	4	5	6	10	12	20	25	40
140	Marcel Dionne	5	6	8	12	15	25		
141	Jean-Guy Lagace	4	5	6	10	12	20		
142	Juha Widing	4	5	6	10	12	20	25	40
143	Lou Nanne	4	5	6	10	12	20		
144	Serge Savard	4	5	6	10	12	20		
145	Glenn Resch	4	5	6	10	12	20		
146	Ron Greschner RC	4	5	6	10	12	20		
147	Dave Schultz	4	5	6	10	12	20		
148	Barry Wilkins	4	5	6	10	12	20		
149	Floyd Thomson	4	5	6	10	12	20		
150	Darryl Sittler	5	6	8	12	15	30	35	60
151	Paulin Bordeleau	4	5	6	10	12	20	25	40
152	Ron Lalonde RC	4	5	6	10	12	20	25	40
153	Larry Romanchych	4	5	6	10	12	20		
154	Larry Carriere	4	5	6	10	12	20	25	40
155	Andre Savard	4	5	6	10	12	20		
156	Dave Hrechkosy RC	4	5	6	10	12	20		
157	Bill White	4	5	6	10	12	20		
158	Dave Kryskow	4	5	6	10	12	20		
159	Denis Dupere	4	5	6	10	12	20		
160	Rogatien Vachon	4	5	6	10	12	20	25	50
161	Doug Rombough	4	5	6	10	12	20		
162	Murray Wilson	4	5	6	10	12	20		
163	Bob Bourne RC	4	5	6	10	12	25	30	50
164	Gilles Marotte	4	5	6	10	12	20		
165	Vic Hadfield	4	5	6	10	12	20	25	50
166	Reggie Leach	4	5	6	10	12	20		
167	Jerry Butler	4	5	6	10	12	20		
168	Inge Hammarstrom	4	5	6	10	12	20		
169	Chris Oddleifson	4	5	6	10	12	20		
170	Greg Joly	4	5	6	10	12	20		
171	Checklist 111-220	6	8	10	12	25	80		
172	Pat Quinn	4	5	6	10	12	20		
173	Dave Forbes	4	5	6	10	12	20	25	40
174	Len Frig	4	5	6	10	12	20		
175	Richard Martin	4	5	6	10	12	20		
176	Keith Magnuson	4	5	6	10	12	20	25	40
177	Dan Maloney	4	5	6	10	12	20		
178	Craig Patrick	4	5	6	10	12	20		
179	Tom Williams	4	5	6	10	12	20		
180	Bill Goldsworthy	4	5	6	10	12	20		
181	Steve Shutt	4	5	6	10	12	20	30	60
182	Ralph Stewart	4	5	6	10	12	20	25	40
183	John Davidson	4	5	6	10	12			
184	Bob Kelly	4	5	6	10	12	20		
185	Ed Johnston	4	5	6	10	12	20		
186	Dave Burrows	4	5	6	10	12	20		
187	Dave Dunn	4	5	6	10	12	20		
188	Dennis Kearns	4	5	6	10	12	20		
189	Bill Clement	4	5	6	10	12	20		
190	Gilles Meloche	4	5	6	10	12	20	25	40
191	Bob Leiter	4	5	6	10	12	20	25	40
192	Jerry Korab	4	5	6	10	12	20		
193	Joey Johnston	4	5	6	10	12	20		
194	Walt McKechnie	4	5	6	10	12	20		
195	Wilf Paiement	4	5	6	10	12	20		
196	Bob Berry	4	5	6	10	12	20	25	40
197	Dean Talafous RC	4	5	6	10	12	20		
198	Guy Lapointe	4	5	6	10	12	20		

HOCKEY

#	Player	VG 3	VgEx 4	EX 5	ExMt 6	NM 7	NmMt 8	NmMt+ 8.5	MT 9
199	Clark Gillies RC	5	6	12	40	60	150	200	300
200A	Phil Esposito NoTR	5	6	8	12	15			
200B	Phil Esposito TR	4	5	6	10	12	30		
201	Greg Polis	4	5	6	10	12	20		
202	Jimmy Watson	4	5	6	10	12	20		
203	Gord McRae RC	4	5	6	10	12	20	25	40
204	Lowell MacDonald	4	5	6	10	12	20		
205	Barclay Plager	4	5	6	10	12	20		
206	Don Lever	4	5	6	10	12	20		
207	Bill Mikkelson	4	5	6	10	12	20		
208	Espo/Lafleur/Martin LL	4	5	6	10	12	20		
209	Clarke/Orr/P.Mahv LL	5	6	8	12	60	150	250	500
210	Orr/Espo/Dionne LL	5	8	12	30	50	350		
211	Schltz/Dupnt/Rssll LL	4	5	6	10	12	25		
212	Espo/Martin/Grant LL	4	5	6	10	12	20		
213	Parnt/Vach/Drydn LL	5	6	8	12	15	30		
214	Barry Gibbs	4	5	6	10	12	20		
215	Ken Hodge	4	5	6	10	12	20		
216	Jocelyn Guevremont	4	5	6	10	12	20		
217	Warren Williams RC	4	5	6	10	12	20		
218	Dick Redmond	4	5	6	10	12	20		
219	Jim Rutherford	4	5	6	10	12	20		
220	Simon Nolet	4	5	6	10	12	20		
221	Butch Goring	4	5	6	10	12	20		
222	Glen Sather	4	5	6	10	12	20		
223	Mario Tremblay UER RC	4	5	6	10	20	60		
224	Jude Drouin	4	5	6	10	12	20		
225	Rod Gilbert	4	5	6	10	12	20		
226	Bill Barber	4	5	6	10	12	20		
227	Gary Inness RC	4	5	6	10	12	20	25	40
228	Wayne Merrick	4	5	6	10	12	20		
229	Rod Seiling	4	5	6	10	12	20		
230	Tom Lysiak	4	5	6	10	12	20		
231	Bob Dailey	4	5	6	10	12	20		
232	Michel Belhumeur	4	5	6	10	12	20		
233	Bill Hajt RC	4	5	6	10	12	20		
234	Jim Pappin	4	5	6	10	12	20		
235	Gregg Sheppard	4	5	6	10	12	20		
236A	Gary Bergman NoTR	4	5	6	10	12			
236B	Gary Bergman TR	4	5	6	10	12			
237	Randy Rota	4	5	6	10	12	20	25	40
238	Neil Komadoski	4	5	6	10	12			
239	Craig Cameron	4	5	6	10	12	20		
240	Tony Esposito	5	6	8	12	15	25	30	60
241	Larry Robinson	5	6	8	12	20	40	50	80
242	Billy Harris	4	5	6	10	12	20		
243A	Jean Ratelle NoTR	4	5	6	10	12			
243B	Jean Ratelle TR	4	5	6	10	12	20		
244	Ted Irvine UER	4	5	6	10	12	20	25	40
245	Bob Neely	4	5	6	10	12	20		
246	Bobby Lalonde	4	5	6	10	12	20	25	40
247	Ron Jones RC	4	5	6	10	12	20		
248	Rey Comeau	4	5	6	10	12	20		
249	Michel Plasse	4	5	6	10	12	20		
250	Bobby Clarke	5	6	8	12	20	40		
251	Bobby Schmautz	4	5	6	10	12	20		
252	Peter McNab RC	4	5	6	10	12	20	25	50
253	Al MacAdam	4	5	6	10	12	20		
254	Dennis Hull	4	5	6	10	12	20		
255	Terry Harper	4	5	6	10	12	20		
256	Peter McDuffe	4	5	6	10	12	20	25	40
257	Jean Hamel	4	5	6	10	12	20		
258	Jacques Lemaire	4	5	6	10	12	20		
259	Bob Nystrom	4	5	6	10	12	20		
260A	Brad Park NoTR	4	5	6	10	12	20		
260B	Brad Park TR	4	5	6	10	12	20		
261	Cesare Maniago	4	5	6	10	12	20	25	40
262	Don Saleski	4	5	6	10	12	20	25	40
263	J. Bob Kelly	4	5	6	10	12	20		
264	Bob Hess RC	4	5	6	10	12	20		
265	Blaine Stoughton	4	5	6	10	12	20	25	40
266	John Gould	4	5	6	10	12	20		
267A	Checklist 221-330	6	8	10	15	30	80		
267B	Checklist 331-396	6	8	10	15	30	80		
268	Dan Bouchard	4	5	6	10	12	20		
269	Don Marcotte	4	5	6	10	12	20		
270	Jim Neilson	4	5	6	10	12	20		
271	Craig Ramsay	4	5	6	10	12	20		
272	Grant Mulvey RC	4	5	6	10	12	30		
273	Larry Giroux RC	4	5	6	10	12	20		
274	Real Lemieux	4	5	6	10	12	20		
275	Denis Potvin	5	6	8	12	20	30	35	50
276	Don Kozak	4	5	6	10	12	20		
277	Tom Reid	4	5	6	10	12	20		
278	Bob Gainey	5	6	8	12	15	25		
279	Nick Beverley	4	5	6	10	12	20		
280	Jean Pronovost	4	5	6	10	12	20		
281	Joe Watson	4	5	6	10	12	20		
282	Chuck Lefley	4	5	6	10	12			
283	Borje Salming	5	6	8	12	15	30	35	60
284	Garnet Bailey	4	5	6	10	12	20	25	40
285	Gregg Boddy	4	5	6	10	12	20		

#	Player	VG 3	VgEx 4	EX 5	ExMt 6	NM 7	NmMt 8	NmMt+ 8.5	MT
286	Bobby Clarke AS1	4	5	6	10	12	25		
287	Denis Potvin AS1	4	5	6	10	12	20		
288	Bobby Orr AS1	10	12	15	25	40	80	100	2
289	Richard Martin AS1	4	5	6	10	12	20	30	5
290	Guy Lafleur AS1	5	6	8	12	15	30		
291	Bernie Parent AS1	4	5	6	10	12	20		
292	Phil Esposito AS2	4	5	6	10	12	20		
293	Guy Lapointe AS2	4	5	6	10	12	20		
294	Borje Salming AS2	4	5	6	10	12	20		
295	Steve Vickers AS2	4	5	6	10	12	20		
296	Rene Robert AS2	4	5	6	10	12	20		
297	Rogatien Vachon AS2	4	5	6	10	12	25		
298	Buster Harvey RC	4	5	6	10	12	20		
299	Gary Sabourin	4	5	6	10	12	20		
300	Bernie Parent	4	5	6	10	12	20		
301	Terry O'Reilly	4	5	6	10	12	20		
302	Ed Westfall	4	5	6	10	12	20		
303	Pete Stemkowski	4	5	6	10	12	20		
304	Pierre Bouchard	4	5	6	10	12	20		
305	Pierre Larouche RC	5	6	8	12	15	30		
306	Lee Fogolin RC	4	5	6	10	12	20	25	4
307	Gerry O'Flaherty	4	5	6	10	12	20		
308	Phil Myre	4	5	6	10	12	20		
309	Pierre Plante	4	5	6	10	12	20		
310	Dennis Hextall	4	5	6	10	12	20		
311	Jim McKenny	4	5	6	10	12	20		
312	Vic Venasky	4	5	6	10	12	20		
313	Vail/Lysiak TL	4	5	6	10	12	20		
314	P.Espo/Orr/Bucyk TL	10	12	15	20	30	50	60	13
315	R.Martin/R.Robert TL	4	5	6	10	12	20		
316	Hrchsy/Ptey/Weir TL	4	5	6	10	12	20		
317	S.Mikita/J.Pappin TL	4	5	6	10	12	20		
318	D.Grant/M.Dionne TL	4	5	6	10	12	20		
319	Nolet/Pmnt/Charn TL	4	5	6	10	12	20		
320	Nevin/Wdng/Brry TL	4	5	6	10	12	20	25	4
321	Gldswrthy/Hextall TL	4	5	6	10	12	20		
322	Lafleur/P.Mahov TL	4	5	6	10	12	20		
323	Nystrom/Potvin/Gill TL	4	5	6	10	12	20		
324	Vick/Gilbert/Ratelle TL	4	5	6	10	12	20		
325	R.Leach/B.Clarke TL	4	5	6	10	12	20	30	5
326	Pronovost/Schock TL	4	5	6	10	12	20		
327	G.Unger/L.Sacharuk TL	4	5	6	10	12	20		
328	Darryl Sittler TL	4	5	6	10	12	25	30	5
329	Lever/Boudrias TL	4	5	6	10	12	20		
330	Williams/Bailey TL	4	5	6	10	12	20		
331	Noel Price	4	5	6	10	12	20		
332	Fred Stanfield	4	5	6	10	12	20		
333	Doug Jarrett	4	5	6	10	12	20	25	4
334	Gary Coalter	4	5	6	10	12	20		
335	Murray Oliver	4	5	6	10	12	20		
336	Dave Fortier	4	5	6	10	12	20		
337	Terry Crisp UER	4	5	6	10	12	20		
338	Bert Wilson	4	5	6	10	12	20	25	40
339	John Grisdale RC	4	5	6	10	12	20	25	4
340	Ken Broderick	4	5	6	10	12	20		
341	Frank Spring RC	4	5	6	10	12	20		
342	Mike Korney RC	4	5	6	10	12	20		
343	Gene Carr	4	5	6	10	12	20		
344	Don Awrey	4	5	6	10	12	20		
345	Pat Hickey	4	5	6	10	12	20		
346	Colin Campbell RC	4	5	6	10	12	20		
347	Wayne Thomas	4	5	6	10	12	20		
348	Bob Gryp RC	4	5	6	10	12	20		
349	Bill Flett	4	5	6	10	12	20		
350	Roger Crozier	4	5	6	10	12	20	25	40
351	Dale Tallon	4	5	6	10	12	20		
352	Larry Johnston	4	5	6	10	12	20		
353	John Flesch RC	4	5	6	10	12	20		
354	Lorne Henning	4	5	6	10	12	20		
355	Wayne Stephenson	4	5	6	10	12	20	25	40
356	Rick Wilson	4	5	6	10	12	20		
357	Garry Monahan	4	5	6	10	12	20		
358	Gary Doak	4	5	6	10	12	20	25	40
359A	Pierre Jarry NoTR	4	5	6	10	12			
359B	Pierre Jarry TR	4	5	6	10	12	20		
360	George Pesut RC	4	5	6	10	12	20		
361	Mike Corrigan	4	5	6	10	12	20		
362	Michel Larocque	4	5	6	10	12	20		
363	Wayne Dillon	4	5	6	10	12	20		
364	Pete Laframboise	4	5	6	10	12	20	25	40
365	Brian Glennie	4	5	6	10	12	20		
366	Mike Christie	4	5	6	10	12	20		
367	Jean Lemieux RC	4	5	6	10	12	20		
368	Gary Bromley	4	5	6	10	12	20	25	50
369	J.P. Bordeleau	4	5	6	10	12	20		
370	Ed Gilbert RC	4	5	6	10	12	20		
371	Chris Ahrens	4	5	6	10	12	20		
372	Billy Smith	5	6	8	12	15	25		
373	Larry Goodenough RC	4	5	6	10	12	20		
374	Leon Rochefort	4	5	6	10	12	20		
375	Doug Gibson RC	4	5	6	10	12	20		
376	Mike Bloom	4	5	6	10	12	20		

	VG 3	VgEx 4	EX 5	ExMt 6	NM 7	NmMt 8	NmMt+ 8.5	MT 9
Larry Brown	4	5	6	10	12	20		
Jim Roberts	4	5	6	10	12	20		
Gilles Villemure	4	5	6	10	12	20	25	40
Dennis Owchar RC	4	5	6	10	12	20		
Doug Favell	4	5	6	10	12	20		
Stan Gilbertson UER	4	5	6	10	12	20		
Ed Kea RC	4	5	6	10	12	20		
Brian Spencer	4	5	6	10	12	20		
Mike Veisor RC	4	5	6	10	12	20		
Bob Murray	4	5	6	10	12	20		
Andre St.Laurent RC	4	5	6	10	12	20	25	40
Rick Chartraw RC	4	5	6	10	12	20		
Orest Kindrachuk	4	5	6	10	12	20	25	40
Dave Hutchinson RC	4	5	6	10	12	20		
Glenn Goldup	4	5	6	10	12	20		
Jerry Holland RC	4	5	6	10	12	20		
Peter Sturgeon RC	4	5	6	10	12	20		
Alain Daigle RC	4	5	6	10	12	20		
Harold Snepsts RC	10	12	15	25	40	80		

Espo/Orr/Bucyk TL #314 PSA 10 (Gem) sold for $1,531 (eBay; 3/07)
Espo/Orr/Bucyk TL #314 PSA 10 (Gem) sold for $510 (eBay; 12/06)
Orr/Espo/Dionne LL #210 PSA 10 (Gem) sold for $618.80 (Mile High; 12/13)

1975-76 O-Pee-Chee WHA

	VG 3	VgEx 4	EX 5	ExMt 6	NM 7	NmMt 8	NmMt+ 8.5	MT 9
COMMON CARD (1-132)	5	5	6	8	10	15		
Bobby Hull	8	12	20	30	40	60		
Dale Hoganson	5	5	6	8	10	20		
Ron Chipperfield	5	5	6	8	10	20		
Paul Shmyr	5	5	6	8	10	15	20	30
Mark Howe RC	20	25	30	40	50	150		
Bryon Baltimore	5	5	6	8	10	15	20	30
Nick Harbaruk	5	5	6	8	10	20		
John Garrett RC	6	8	10	12	15	25	30	60
Lou Nistico	5	5	6	8	10	15	20	30
Veli-Pekka Ketola RC	5	6	8	10	12	20	25	40
Real Cloutier	5	5	6	8	10	15	20	30
Duane Rupp	5	5	6	8	10	15	20	30
Robbie Ftorek RC	6	8	12	15	20	30	35	60
Gerry Cheevers	6	8	12	15	20	30	35	80
Bruce MacGregor	5	5	6	8	10	15	20	30
Gene Peacosh	5	5	6	8	10	15	20	30
C.Abrahamsson RC	5	6	8	10	12	20	25	40
Bryan Campbell	5	5	6	8	10	15	20	30
Al McDonough	5	5	6	8	10	15		30
Jacques Plante	6	10	15	25	40	60		
Ken Baird	5	5	6	8	10	15	20	30
Anders Hedberg	5	5	6	8	10	15	20	40
Rick Smith	5	5	6	8	10	15	20	30
Richard Brodeur RC	6	8	10	12	15	25	30	60
Jim Harrison	5	5	6	8	10	15	20	30
Murray Heatley	5	5	6	8	10	15	20	30
Jim Shaw	5	5	6	8	10	15	20	30
Larry Pleau RC	5	5	6	8	10	15	20	30
Butch Deadmarsh	5	5	6	8	10	15	20	30
J.C. Tremblay AS	5	5	6	8	10	15	20	30
Kevin Morrison AS	5	5	6	8	10	15	20	30
Andre Lacroix AS	5	5	6	8	10	15	20	30
Bobby Hull AS	6	10	15	20	25	40	50	80
Gordie Howe AS	6	10	15	20	25	60		
Gerry Cheevers AS	5	6	8	10	12	20		
Barry Long AS	5	5	6	8	10	15	20	30
Serge Bernier AS	5	5	6	8	10	15	20	30
Kevin Morrison	5	5	6	8	10	15	20	30
Ulf Nilsson	5	5	6	8	10	15	20	40
N.Lapointe RC UER	5	5	6	8	10			
Al McLeod	5	5	6	8	10	15	20	30
Barry Long	5	5	6	8	10	15	20	40
Dave Keon	5	5	6	8	10	15	20	40
Rick Jodzio	5	5	6	8	10	15	20	30
Gordie Howe	12	15	20	30	50	80	100	150
Joe Daley	5	5	6	8	10	15	20	40
Wayne Muloin	5	5	6	8	10	15	20	30
Rosaire Paiement	5	5	6	8	10	15	20	30
John Sheridan RC	5	6	8	10	12	20		
Nick Fotiu RC	6	8	10	12	15	25		
Frank Mahovlich	5	5	6	8	12	25	30	60
Jack Norris	5	5	6	8	10	15	20	40
Cam Newton	5	5	6	8	10	15	20	30
Fran Huck	5	5	6	8	10	15	20	30
Tony Featherstone	5	5	6	8	10	15	20	30
Heikki Riihiranta	5	5	6	8	10	15	20	50
Jacques Locas	5	5	6	8	10	15		
Checklist Card	10	12	20	30	50	80	100	150
Ernie Wakely	5	5	6	8	10	12	20	

Gordie Howe AS #66 PSA 10 (Gem) sold for $668 (eBay; 8/12)
Dave Keon #97 PSA 10 (Gem) sold for $99 (Sirius Sports; 6/12)
Jacques Plante #34 PSA 9 (MT) sold for $110 (Sirius Sports; 6/12)

1975-76 Topps

		VG 3	VgEx 4	EX 5	ExMt 6	NM 7	NmMt 8	NmMt+ 8.5	MT 9
1	Stanley Cup Finals	4	5	6	8	15	25		
2	Semi-Finals	4	5	6	8	12	18		
3	Semi-Finals	4	5	6	8	12	18		
4	Quarter Finals	4	5	6	8	12	15	20	30
5	Quarter Finals	4	5	6	10	15			
6	Quarter Finals	4	5	6	8	12	15	20	30
7	Quarter Finals	4	5	6	8	12	15	20	30
8	Curt Bennett	4	5	6	8	10	12	15	25
9	Johnny Bucyk	4	5	6	8	10	12	15	25
10	Gilbert Perreault	4	5	6	8	12	20		
11	Darryl Edestrand	4	5	6	8	10	12	15	25
12	Ivan Boldirev	4	5	6	8	10	12	15	25
13	Nick Libett	4	5	6	8	10	12	15	25
14	Jim McElmury RC	4	5	6	8	10	12	15	25
15	Frank St.Marseille	4	5	6	8	10	12	15	25
16	Blake Dunlop	4	5	6	10	15			
17	Yvon Lambert	4	5	6	8	10	12	15	25
18	Gerry Hart	4	5	6	8	10	12	15	25
19	Steve Vickers	4	5	6	8	12	18		
20	Rick MacLeish	4	5	6	10	15			
21	Bob Paradise	4	5	6	8	10	12	15	25
22	Red Berenson	4	5	6	8	10	12	15	25
23	Lanny McDonald	4	5	6	8	12	20	30	50
24	Mike Robitaille	4	5	6	8	10	12	15	25
25	Ron Low	4	5	6	8	12	18		
26	Bryan Hextall	4	5	6	8	10	12	15	25
27	Carol Vadnais	4	5	6	8	10	12	15	25
28	Jim Lorentz	4	5	6	8	10	12	15	25
29	Gary Simmons	4	5	6	10	15			
30	Stan Mikita	4	5	6	8	12	20	25	40
31	Bryan Watson	4	5	6	8	10	12	15	25
32	Guy Charron	4	5	6	8	10	12	15	25
33	Bob Murdoch	4	5	6	8	10	12	15	25
34	Norm Gratton	4	5	6	8	10	12	15	25
35	Ken Dryden	6	8	10	12	20	30	40	60
36	Jean Potvin	4	5	6	8	12	18		
37	Rick Middleton	4	5	6	10	15			
38	Ed Van Impe	4	5	6	8	10	12	15	25
39	Rick Kehoe	4	5	6	8	10	12	15	25
40	Garry Unger	4	5	6	8	10	12	15	25
41	Ian Turnbull	4	5	6	8	10	12	15	25
42	Dennis Ververgaert	4	5	6	8	12	18		
43	Mike Marson	4	5	6	8	10	12	15	25
44	Randy Manery	4	5	6	10	15			
45	Gilles Gilbert	4	5	6	8	10	12	15	25
46	Rene Robert	4	5	6	8	10	12	15	25
47	Bob Stewart	4	5	6	8	10	12	15	25
48	Pit Martin	4	5	6	8	12	18		
49	Danny Grant	4	5	6	8	10	12	15	25
50	Peter Mahovlich	4	5	6	10	15			
51	Dennis Patterson RC	4	5	6	8	10	12	15	25
52	Mike Murphy	4	5	6	8	10	12	15	25
53	Dennis O'Brien	4	5	6	8	10	12	15	25
54	Garry Howatt	4	5	6	8	10	12	15	25
55	Ed Giacomin	4	5	6	8	12	20	25	35
56	Andre Dupont	4	5	6	10	15			
57	Chuck Arnason	4	5	6	8	10	12	15	25
58	Bob Gassoff RC	4	5	6	10	15			
59	Ron Ellis	4	5	6	8	10	12	15	25
60	Andre Boudrias	4	5	6	8	10	12	15	25
61	Yvon Labre	4	5	6	8	10	12	15	25
62	Hilliard Graves	4	5	6	8	10	12	15	25
63	Wayne Cashman	4	5	6	8	12	18		
64	Danny Gare RC	4	5	6	8	12	20	25	35
65	Rick Hampton	4	5	6	8	10	12	15	25
66	Darcy Rota	4	5	6	8	10	12	15	25
67	Bill Hogaboam	4	5	6	8	10	12	15	25
68	Denis Herron	4	5	6	8	10	12	15	25
69	Sheldon Kannegiesser	4	5	6	8	10	12	15	25
70	Yvan Cournoyer UER	4	5	6	8	10	12	15	25
71	Ernie Hicke	4	5	6	8	10	15		
72	Bert Marshall	4	5	6	8	10	12	15	25
73	Derek Sanderson	4	5	6	8	12	20	25	35
74	Tom Bladon	4	5	6	8	10	12	15	25
75	Ron Schock	4	5	6	8	10	12	15	25
76	Larry Sacharuk RC	4	5	6	8	10	12	15	25
77	George Ferguson	4	5	6	8	10	12	15	25
78	Ab DeMarco	4	5	6	8	10	12	15	25
79	Tom Williams	4	5	6	8	12	18		
80	Phil Roberto	4	5	6	8	10	15		
81	Bruins Team CL	4	5	6	8	12	20	25	35
82	Seals Team CL	4	5	6	8	12	20	25	35
83	Sabres Team CL UER	4	5	6	8	12	20	25	35
84	Blackhawks CL UER	4	5	6	8	12	20	25	35
85	Flames Team CL	4	5	6	8	12	20	25	35
86	Kings Team CL	4	5	6	8	12	20	25	35

HOCKEY

#	Name	VG 3	VgEx 4	EX 5	ExMt 6	NM 7	NmMt 8	NmMt+ 8.5	MT 9
87	Red Wings Team CL	4	5	6	8	12	20	25	35
88	Scouts Team CL UER	4	5	6	8	12	20	25	35
89	North Stars Team CL	4	5	6	8	12	20	25	35
90	Canadiens Team CL	4	5	6	8	12	20	25	35
91	Maple Leafs Team CL	4	5	6	8	12	20	25	35
92	Islanders Team CL	4	5	6	8	12	20	25	35
93	Penguins Team CL	4	5	6	8	12	20	25	35
94	Rangers Team CL	4	5	6	8	12	20	25	35
95	Flyers Team CL UER	4	5	6	8	12	20	25	35
96	Blues Team CL	4	5	6	8	12	20	25	35
97	Canucks Team CL	4	5	6	8	12	20	25	35
98	Capitals Team CL	4	5	6	8	12	20	25	35
99	Checklist 1-110	5	6	8	10	15	25		
100	Bobby Orr	8	10	12	15	25	40	60	100
101	Germaine Gagnon UER	4	5	6	8	10	12	15	25
102	Phil Russell	4	5	6	8	10	12	15	25
103	Billy Lochead	4	5	6	8	10	12	15	25
104	Robin Burns	4	5	6	10	15			
105	Gary Edwards	4	5	6	8	10	12	15	25
106	Dwight Bialowas	4	5	6	8	10	12	15	25
107	D.Risebrough UER RC	4	5	6	8	12	20	25	35
108	Dave Lewis	4	5	6	10	15			
109	Bill Fairbairn	4	5	6	10	15			
110	Ross Lonsberry	4	5	6	8	10	12	15	25
111	Ron Stackhouse	4	5	6	8	12	18		
112	Claude Larose	4	5	6	8	10	12	15	25
113	Don Luce	4	5	6	8	10	12	15	25
114	Errol Thompson RC	4	5	6	8	10	12	15	25
115	Gary Smith	4	5	6	8	10	12	15	25
116	Jack Lynch	4	5	6	8	10	12	15	25
117	Jacques Richard	4	5	6	10	15			
118	Dallas Smith	4	5	6	10	15			
119	Dave Gardner	4	5	6	8	10	12	15	25
120	Mickey Redmond	4	5	6	8	10	12	15	25
121	John Marks	4	5	6	8	10	12	15	25
122	Dave Hudson	4	5	6	8	10	12	15	25
123	Bob Nevin	4	5	6	8	12	18		
124	Fred Barrett	4	5	6	8	10	12	15	25
125	Gerry Desjardins	4	5	6	10	15			
126	Guy Lafleur UER	5	6	8	10	15	25	30	40
127	Jean-Paul Parise	4	5	6	8	10	12	15	25
128	Walt Tkaczuk	4	5	6	8	10	12	15	25
129	Gary Dornhoefer	4	5	6	8	10	12	15	25
130	Syl Apps	4	5	6	8	10	12	15	25
131	Bob Plager	4	5	6	8	10	12	15	25
132	Stan Weir	4	5	6	8	10	12	15	25
133	Tracy Pratt	4	5	6	8	10	12	15	25
134	Jack Egers	4	5	6	8	10	12	15	25
135	Eric Vail	4	5	6	8	10	12	15	25
136	Al Sims	4	5	6	8	10	12	15	25
137	Larry Patey	4	5	6	8	10	12	15	25
138	Jim Schoenfeld	4	5	6	8	10	12	15	25
139	Cliff Koroll	4	5	6	8	10	12	15	25
140	Marcel Dionne	4	5	6	8	12	20	30	50
141	Jean-Guy Lagace	4	5	6	8	10	12	15	25
142	Juha Widing	4	5	6	8	10	12	15	25
143	Lou Nanne	4	5	6	8	10	12	15	25
144	Serge Savard	4	5	6	8	10	12	15	25
145	Glenn Resch	4	5	6	8	12	20	25	40
146	Ron Greschner RC	4	5	6	8	12	20	25	35
147	Dave Schultz	4	5	6	8	10	12	15	25
148	Barry Wilkins	4	5	6	8	10	12	15	25
149	Floyd Thomson	4	5	6	8	10	12	15	25
150	Darryl Sittler	4	5	6	8	10	12	15	25
151	Paulin Bordeleau	4	5	6	8	10	12	15	25
152	Ron Lalonde RC	4	5	6	8	10	12	15	25
153	Larry Romanchych	4	5	6	8	10	12	15	25
154	Larry Carriere	4	5	6	8	12	18		
155	Andre Savard	4	5	6	8	10	12	15	25
156	Dave Hrechkosy RC	4	5	6	8	12	15		25
157	Bill White	4	5	6	8	10	12	15	25
158	Dave Kryskow	4	5	6	8	10	12	15	25
159	Denis Dupere	4	5	6	8	12	18		
160	Rogatien Vachon	4	5	6	8	12	20	25	35
161	Doug Rombough	4	5	6	8	10	12	15	25
162	Murray Wilson	4	5	6	8	10	12	15	25
163	Bob Bourne RC	4	5	6	8	12	20	25	35
164	Gilles Marotte	4	5	6	10	15			
165	Vic Hadfield	4	5	6	10	15			
166	Reggie Leach	4	5	6	8	10	12	15	25
167	Jerry Butler	4	5	6	10	15			
168	Inge Hammarstrom	4	5	6	8	12	18		
169	Chris Oddleifson	4	5	6	8	12	18		
170	Greg Joly	4	5	6	8	10	12	15	25
171	Checklist 111-220	5	6	10	12	20			
172	Pat Quinn	4	5	6	10	15			
173	Dave Forbes	4	5	6	8	10	12	15	25
174	Len Frig	4	5	6	8	10	12	15	25
175	Richard Martin	4	5	6	8	10	12	15	25

#	Name	VG 3	VgEx 4	EX 5	ExMt 6	NM 7	NmMt 8	NmMt+ 8.5	MT
176	Keith Magnuson	4	5	6	8	10	12	15	
177	Dan Maloney	4	5	6	8	10	12	15	
178	Craig Patrick	4	5	6	8	10	12	15	
179	Tom Williams	4	5	6	10	15			
180	Bill Goldsworthy	4	5	6	8	10	12	15	
181	Steve Shutt	4	5	6	8	10	12	15	
182	Ralph Stewart	4	5	6	8	12	18		
183	John Davidson	4	5	6	8	12	20	25	
184	Bob Kelly	4	5	6	8	10	12	15	
185	Ed Johnston	4	5	6	8	10	12	15	
186	Dave Burrows	4	5	6	8	10	12	15	
187	Dave Dunn	4	5	6	8	10	12	15	
188	Dennis Kearns	4	5	6	8	10	12	15	
189	Bill Clement	4	5	6	8	12	20	25	
190	Gilles Meloche	4	5	6	8	10	12	15	
191	Bob Leiter	4	5	6	8	10	12	15	
192	Jerry Korab	4	5	6	8	10	12	15	
193	Joey Johnston	4	5	6	8	10	12	15	
194	Walt McKechnie	4	5	6	8	10	12	15	
195	Wilf Paiement	4	5	6	8	10	12	15	
196	Bob Berry	4	5	6	8	10	12	15	
197	Dean Talafous RC	4	5	6	8	10	12	15	
198	Guy Lapointe	4	5	6	8	10	12	15	
199	Clark Gillies RC	4	5	6	8	12	20	30	
200	Phil Esposito	4	5	6	8	12	20	25	
201	Greg Polis	4	5	6	8	10	12	15	2
202	Jimmy Watson	4	5	6	10	15			
203	Gord McRae RC	4	5	6	8	12	18		
204	Lowell MacDonald	4	5	6	8	10	12	15	2
205	Barclay Plager	4	5	6	8	10	12	15	2
206	Don Lever	4	5	6	8	12	18		
207	Bill Mikkelson	4	5	6	8	10	12	15	2
208	Espo/Lafleur/Martin LL	4	5	6	8	12	20	25	4
209	Clarke/Orr/P.Mahov LL	4	5	6	8	12	25	30	12
210	Orr/Espo/Dionne LL	4	5	6	8	12	30		
211	Schultz/Dupont/Rusl LL	4	5	6	8	10	12	15	2
212	Espo/Martin/Grant LL	4	5	6	10	15			
213	Parent/Vach/Dryden LL	4	5	6	8	12	25	30	5
214	Barry Gibbs	4	5	6	10	15			
215	Ken Hodge	4	5	6	8	10	12	15	2
216	Jocelyn Guevremont	4	5	6	8	10	12	15	2
217	Warren Williams RC	4	5	6	8	10	12	15	2
218	Dick Redmond	4	5	6	8	10	12	15	2
219	Jim Rutherford	4	5	6	8	10	12	15	2
220	Simon Nolet	4	5	6	8	10	12	15	2
221	Butch Goring	4	5	6	8	10	12	15	2
222	Glen Sather	4	5	6	8	10	12	15	2
223	Mario Tremblay RC	4	5	6	8	12	20		
224	Jude Drouin	4	5	6	10	15			
225	Rod Gilbert	4	5	6	8	10	12	15	2
226	Bill Barber	4	5	6	8	10	12	15	2
227	Gary Inness RC	4	5	6	8	10	12	15	2
228	Wayne Merrick	4	5	6	8	10	12	15	2
229	Rod Seiling	4	5	6	8	10	12	15	2
230	Tom Lysiak	4	5	6	8	10	12	15	2
231	Bob Dailey	4	5	6	8	10	12	15	2
232	Michel Belhumeur	4	5	6	10	15			
233	Bill Hajt RC	4	5	6	8	10	12	15	2
234	Jim Pappin	4	5	6	8	10	12	15	2
235	Gregg Sheppard	4	5	6	8	10	12	15	2
236	Gary Bergman	4	5	6	8	10	12	15	25
237	Randy Rota	4	5	6	8	10	12	15	25
238	Neil Komadoski	4	5	6	10	15			
239	Craig Cameron	4	5	6	8	10	12	15	2
240	Tony Esposito	4	5	6	8	12	20		
241	Larry Robinson	4	5	6	10	15			
242	Billy Harris	4	5	6	8	10	12	15	25
243	Jean Ratelle	4	5	6	8	10	12	15	25
244	Ted Irvine UER	4	5	6	8	10	12	15	25
245	Bob Neely	4	5	6	8	10	12	15	25
246	Bobby Lalonde	4	5	6	8	10	12	15	25
247	Ron Jones RC	4	5	6	8	10	12	15	25
248	Rey Comeau	4	5	6	8	10	12	15	25
249	Michel Plasse	4	5	6	8	10	12	15	25
250	Bobby Clarke	4	5	6	8	12	25	30	50
251	Bobby Schmautz	4	5	6	8	10	12	15	25
252	Peter McNab RC	4	5	6	8	12	20	25	35
253	Al MacAdam	4	5	6	8	10	12	15	25
254	Dennis Hull	4	5	6	8	10	12	15	25
255	Terry Harper	4	5	6	8	10	12	15	25
256	Peter McDuffe	4	5	6	8	10	12	15	25
257	Jean Hamel	4	5	6	10	15			
258	Jacques Lemaire	4	5	6	10	15			
259	Bob Nystrom	4	5	6	8	10	12	15	25
260	Brad Park	4	5	6	8	12	20		
261	Cesare Maniago	4	5	6	8	10	12	15	25
262	Don Saleski	4	5	6	8	10	12	15	25
263	J. Bob Kelly	4	5	6	8	12	18		
264	Bob Hess RC	4	5	6	8	10	12	15	25

	VG 3	VgEx 4	EX 5	ExMt 6	NM 7	NmMt 8	NmMt+ 8.5	MT 9
Blaine Stoughton	4	5	6	8	12	18		
John Gould	4	5	6	8	10	12	15	25
Checklist 221-330	5	6	8	10	15	25	40	60
Dan Bouchard	4	5	6	8	10	12	15	25
Don Marcotte	4	5	6	8	12	18		
Jim Neilson	4	5	6	8	10	12	15	25
Craig Ramsay	4	5	6	8	10	12	15	25
Grant Mulvey RC	4	5	6	8	10	12	15	25
Larry Giroux RC	4	5	6	8	10	12	15	25
Real Lemieux	4	5	6	10	15			
Denis Potvin	4	5	6	8	12	25	30	50
Don Kozak	4	5	6	10	15			
Tom Reid	4	5	6	8	12	18		
Bob Gainey	4	5	6	8	12	20	30	50
Nick Beverley	4	5	6	10	15			
Jean Pronovost	4	5	6	8	10	12	15	25
Joe Watson	4	5	6	10	15			
Chuck Lefley	4	5	6	8	10	12	15	25
Borje Salming	4	5	6	8	12	25	30	50
Garnet Bailey	4	5	6	8	10	12	15	25
Gregg Boddy	4	5	6	8	10	12	15	25
Bobby Clarke AS1	4	5	6	8	12	20		
Denis Potvin AS1	4	5	6	8	12	20	25	40
Bobby Orr AS1	5	6	8	12	20	40	80	300
Richard Martin AS1	4	5	6	8	10	12	15	25
Guy Lafleur AS1	4	5	6	8	12	20	30	50
Bernie Parent AS1	4	5	6	8	10	12	15	25
Phil Esposito AS2	4	5	6	8	12	20	25	35
Guy Lapointe AS2	4	5	6	8	10	12	15	25
Borje Salming AS2	4	5	6	8	12	20	25	35
Steve Vickers AS2	4	5	6	8	10	12	15	25
Rene Robert AS2	4	5	6	8	10	12	15	25
Rogatien Vachon AS2	4	5	6	8	12	20	25	35
Buster Harvey RC	4	5	6	8	10	12	15	25
Gary Sabourin	4	5	6	8	10	12	15	25
Bernie Parent	4	5	6	8	10	12	15	25
Terry O'Reilly	4	5	6	8	10	12	15	25
Ed Westfall	4	5	6	8	10	12	15	25
Pete Stemkowski	4	5	6	10	15			
Pierre Bouchard	4	5	6	8	12	18		
Pierre Larouche RC	4	5	6	8	12	20	30	50
Lee Fogolin RC	4	5	6	8	10	12	15	25
Gerry O'Flaherty	4	5	6	8	10	12	15	25
Phil Myre	4	5	6	8	10	12	15	25
Pierre Plante	4	5	6	8	10	12	15	25
Dennis Hextall	4	5	6	10	15			
Jim McKenny	4	5	6	8	10	12	15	25
Vic Venasky	4	5	6	8	10	12	15	25
Flames Leaders	4	5	6	8	12	15	20	30
Espo/Orr/Bucyk TL	4	5	6	8	12	25	30	50
Sabres Leaders	4	5	6	8	12	15	20	30
Seals Leaders	4	5	6	8	12	15	20	30
S.Mikita/J.Pappin TL	4	5	6	8	12	15	20	30
D.Grant/M.Dionne TL	4	5	6	8	12	15	20	30
Scouts Leaders	4	5	6	8	12	15	20	30
Kings Leaders	4	5	6	8	12	15	20	30
North Stars Leaders	4	5	6	8	12	15	20	30
Lafleur/P.Mahov TL	4	5	6	8	12	20	25	35
Nystrom/Potvin/Gill TL	4	5	6	8	12	20		
Vick/Gilbert/Ratelle TL	4	5	6	10	15			
R.Leach/B.Clarke TL	4	5	6	8	12	15	20	30
Penguins Leaders	4	5	6	10	15			
Blues Leaders	4	5	6	10	15			
Darryl Sittler TL	4	5	6	10	15			
Canucks Leaders	4	5	6	8	12	15	20	30
Capitals Leaders	4	5	6	8	12	18	20	30

-Stan Mikita #30 PSA 10 (Gem) sold for $99.98 (eBay; 4/12)
-Bobby Orr #100 PSA 10 (Gem) sold for $1,047 (eBay; 5/12)
-Bobby Orr #100 PSA 10 (Gem) sold for $564 (eBay; 11/15)
-Bobby Orr AS #288 PSA 10 (Gem) sold for $924.63 (Memory Lane; 4/12)

1976-77 O-Pee-Chee

	VG 3	VgEx 4	EX 5	ExMt 6	NM 7	NmMt 8	NmMt+ 8.5	MT 9
Leach/Lafleur/Larou LL	5	6	8	12	15	60		
Clarke/Lafleur/Perr LL	5	6	8	12	15	25	30	50
Lafleur/Clarke/Perr LL	5	6	8	10	12	25		
Durbno/Watsn/Schltz LL	4	5	6	10	12	20		
Espo/Lafleur/Potvin LL	5	6	8	10	12	30		
Dryden/Resch/Laroc LL	5	6	8	10	12	20	30	60
Gary Doak	4	5	6	10	12	20		
Jacques Richard	4	5	6	10	12	20		
Wayne Dillon	4	5	6	10	12	20	25	50
Bernie Parent	4	5	6	10	12	20		
Ed Westfall	4	5	6	10	12	15	20	30
Dick Redmond	4	5	6	10	12	20		
Bryan Hextall	4	5	6	10	12	20		
Jean Pronovost	4	5	6	10	12	15	20	30
Peter Mahovlich	4	5	6	10	12	20		
Danny Grant	4	5	6	10	12	15	20	30

		VG 3	VgEx 4	EX 5	ExMt 6	NM 7	NmMt 8	NmMt+ 8.5	MT 9
17	Phil Myre	4	5	6	10	12	15	20	30
18	Wayne Merrick	4	5	6	10	12	20		
19	Steve Durbano	4	5	6	10	12	15	20	30
20	Derek Sanderson	4	5	6	10	12	20		
21	Mike Murphy	4	5	6	10	12	15	20	30
22	Borje Salming	5	6	8	10	12	20	30	60
23	Mike Walton	4	5	6	10	12	20		
24	Randy Manery	4	5	6	10	12	15	20	30
25	Ken Hodge	4	5	6	10	12	15	20	30
26	Mel Bridgman RC	4	5	6	10	12	20	25	50
27	Jerry Korab	4	5	6	10	12	20		
28	Gilles Gratton	4	5	6	10	12	20		
29	Andre St.Laurent	4	5	6	10	12	20		
30	Yvan Cournoyer	4	5	6	10	12	20	25	50
31	Phil Russell	4	5	6	10	12	20		
32	Dennis Hextall	4	5	6	10	12	20		
33	Lowell MacDonald	4	5	6	10	12	20		
34	Dennis O'Brien	4	5	6	10	12	20		
35	Gerry Meehan	4	5	6	10	12	15	20	30
36	Gilles Meloche	4	5	6	10	12	15	20	30
37	Wilf Paiement	4	5	6	10	12	15	20	30
38	Bob MacMillan RC	4	5	6	10	12	20		
39	Ian Turnbull	4	5	6	10	12	20		
40	Rogatien Vachon	4	5	6	10	12	20	25	50
41	Nick Beverley	4	5	6	10	12	20		
42	Rene Robert	4	5	6	10	12	15	20	30
43	Andre Savard	4	5	6	10	12	15	20	30
44	Bob Gainey	5	6	8	10	12	20	25	50
45	Joe Watson	4	5	6	10	12	20		
46	Billy Smith	5	6	8	10	12	20	25	40
47	Darcy Rota	4	5	6	10	12	20		
48	Rick Lapointe RC	4	5	6	10	12	15	20	30
49	Pierre Jarry	4	5	6	10	12	20		
50	Syl Apps	4	5	6	10	12	15	20	30
51	Eric Vail	4	5	6	10	12	15	20	30
52	Greg Joly	4	5	6	10	12	15	20	30
53	Don Lever	4	5	6	10	12	20		
54	Bob Murdoch Seals	4	5	6	10	12	20		
55	Denis Herron	4	5	6	10	12	15	20	30
56	Mike Bloom	4	5	6	10	12	15	20	30
57	Bill Fairbairn	4	5	6	10	12	20		
58	Fred Stanfield	4	5	6	10	12	20		
59	Steve Shutt	4	5	6	10	12	20		
60	Brad Park	4	5	6	10	12	20		
61	Gilles Villemure	4	5	6	10	12	20		
62	Bert Marshall	4	5	6	10	12	20		
63	Chuck Lefley	4	5	6	10	12	20		
64	Simon Nolet	4	5	6	10	12	15	20	30
65	Reggie Leach RB	4	5	6	10	12	20		
66	Darryl Sittler RB	4	5	6	10	12	20		
67	Bryan Trottier RB	5	6	8	10	15	30	40	60
68	Garry Unger RB	4	5	6	10	12	15	20	30
69	Ron Low	4	5	6	10	12	20		
70	Bobby Clarke	5	6	8	10	12	25	30	50
71	Michel Bergeron RC	4	5	6	10	12	15	20	30
72	Ron Stackhouse	4	5	6	10	12	15	20	30
73	Bill Hogaboam	4	5	6	10	12	20		
74	Bob Murdoch Kings	4	5	6	10	12	20		
75	Steve Vickers	4	5	6	10	12	20		
76	Pit Martin	4	5	6	10	12	15	20	30
77	Gerry Hart	4	5	6	10	12	15	20	30
78	Craig Ramsay	4	5	6	10	12	20		
79	Michel Larocque	4	5	6	10	12	20		
80	Jean Ratelle	4	5	6	10	12	20		
81	Don Saleski	4	5	6	10	12	15	20	30
82	Bill Clement	4	5	6	10	12	20		
83	Dave Burrows	4	5	6	10	12	15	20	30
84	Wayne Thomas	4	5	6	10	12	15	20	30
85	John Gould	4	5	6	10	12	20		
86	Dennis Maruk RC	5	6	8	10	12	20	25	50
87	Ernie Hicke	4	5	6	10	12	20		
88	Jim Rutherford	4	5	6	10	12	15	20	30
89	Dale Tallon	4	5	6	10	12	20		
90	Rod Gilbert	4	5	6	10	12	20		
91	Marcel Dionne	5	6	8	10	12	25	30	40
92	Chuck Arnason	4	5	6	10	12	15	20	30
93	Jean Potvin	4	5	6	10	12	20		
94	Don Luce	4	5	6	10	12	20		
95	Johnny Bucyk	4	5	6	10	12	20	25	40
96	Larry Goodenough	4	5	6	10	12	20		
97	Mario Tremblay	4	5	6	10	12	20		
98	Nelson Pyatt	4	5	6	10	12	20		
99	Brian Glennie	4	5	6	10	12	20		
100	Tony Esposito	5	6	8	10	12	25	30	50
101	Dan Maloney	4	5	6	10	12	15	20	30
102	Dunc Wilson	4	5	6	10	12	20		
103	Dean Talafous	4	5	6	10	12	20		
104	Ed Staniowski	4	5	6	10	12	15	20	30
105	Dallas Smith	4	5	6	10	12	15	20	30

#	Player	VG 3	VgEx 4	EX 5	ExMt 6	NM 7	NmMt 8	NmMt+ 8.5	MT 9
106	Jude Drouin	4	5	6	10	12	15	20	30
107	Pat Hickey	4	5	6	10	12	20		
108	Jocelyn Guevremont	4	5	6	10	12	15	20	30
109	Doug Risebrough	4	5	6	10	12	20		
110	Reggie Leach	4	5	6	10	12	20		
111	Dan Bouchard	4	5	6	10	12	15	20	30
112	Chris Oddleifson	4	5	6	10	12	20		
113	Rick Hampton	4	5	6	10	12	20		
114	John Marks	4	5	6	10	12	15	20	30
115	Bryan Trottier RC	15	25	40	60	80	150	200	600
116	Checklist 1-132	6	8	10	12	20	35	50	80
117	Greg Polis	4	5	6	10	12	20		
118	Peter McNab	4	5	6	10	12	20	25	40
119	Jim Roberts Mont	4	5	6	10	12	15	20	30
120	Gerry Cheevers	5	6	8	10	12	20	25	40
121	Rick MacLeish	4	5	6	10	12	20		
122	Billy Lochead	4	5	6	10	12	15	20	30
123	Tom Reid	4	5	6	10	12	15	20	30
124	Rick Kehoe	4	5	6	10	12	15	20	30
125	Keith Magnuson	4	5	6	10	12	20		
126	Clark Gillies	4	5	6	10	12	20	25	40
127	Rick Middleton	4	5	6	10	12	20		
128	Bill Hajt	4	5	6	10	12	20		
129	Jacques Lemaire	4	5	6	10	12	20		
130	Terry O'Reilly	4	5	6	10	12	20		
131	Andre Dupont	4	5	6	10	12	20		
132	Flames Team	5	6	8	10	12	20		
133	Bruins Team	5	6	8	10	12	20		
134	Sabres Team	5	6	8	10	12	20		
135	Seals Team	5	6	8	10	12	20		
136	Blackhawks Team	5	6	8	10	12	20	25	40
137	Red Wings Team	5	6	8	10	12	20	25	40
138	Scouts Team	5	6	8	10	12	20		
139	Kings Team	5	6	8	10	12	20		
140	North Stars Team	5	6	8	10	12	20		
141	Canadiens Team	5	6	8	10	12	20	25	40
142	Islanders Team	5	6	8	10	12	20		
143	Rangers Team	5	6	8	10	12	20	25	40
144	Flyers Team	5	6	8	10	12	20	25	40
145	Penguins Team	5	6	8	10	12	20		
146	Blues Team	5	6	8	10	12	20	25	40
147	Maple Leafs Team	5	6	8	10	12	20		
148	Canucks Team	5	6	8	10	12	20		
149	Capitals Team	5	6	8	10	12	20		
150	Dave Schultz	4	5	6	10	12	20	25	50
151	Larry Robinson	5	6	8	10	12	25	30	40
152	Al Smith	4	5	6	10	12	15	20	30
153	Bob Nystrom	4	5	6	10	12	15	20	30
154	Ron Greschner	4	5	6	10	12	20		
155	Gregg Sheppard	4	5	6	10	12	20		
156	Alain Daigle	4	5	6	10	12	15	20	30
157	Ed Van Impe	4	5	6	10	12	20		
158	Tim Young RC	4	5	6	10	12	15	20	30
159	Bryan Lefley	4	5	6	10	12	20		
160	Ed Giacomin	4	5	6	10	12	20	25	50
161	Yvon Labre	4	5	6	10	12	20		
162	Jim Lorentz	4	5	6	10	12	15	20	30
163	Guy Lafleur	6	8	10	12	20	40	50	80
164	Tom Bladon	4	5	6	10	12	20		
165	Wayne Cashman	4	5	6	10	12	20		
166	Pete Stemkowski	4	5	6	10	12	20		
167	Grant Mulvey	4	5	6	10	12	15	20	30
168	Yves Belanger	4	5	6	10	12	15	20	30
169	Bill Goldsworthy	4	5	6	10	12	15	20	30
170	Denis Potvin	5	6	8	10	12	25	30	40
171	Nick Libett	4	5	6	10	12	15	20	30
172	Michel Plasse	4	5	6	10	12	20		
173	Lou Nanne	4	5	6	10	12	20		
174	Tom Lysiak	4	5	6	10	12	15	20	30
175	Dennis Ververgaert	4	5	6	10	12	15	20	30
176	Gary Simmons	4	5	6	10	12	20		
177	Pierre Bouchard	4	5	6	10	12	15	20	30
178	Bill Barber	4	5	6	10	12	20	25	40
179	Darryl Edestrand	4	5	6	10	12	20		
180	Gilbert Perreault	5	6	8	10	12	20		
181	Dave Maloney RC	4	5	6	10	12	20	25	40
182	Jean-Paul Parise	4	5	6	10	12	20		
183	Jim Harrison	4	5	6	10	12	20		
184	Pete Lopresti	4	5	6	10	12	15	20	30
185	Don Kozak	4	5	6	10	12	15	20	30
186	Guy Charron	4	5	6	10	12	15	20	30
187	Stan Gilbertson	4	5	6	10	12	20		
188	Bill Nyrop	4	5	6	10	12	20		
189	Bobby Schmautz	4	5	6	10	12	15	20	30
190	Wayne Stephenson	4	5	6	10	12	20		
191	Brian Spencer	4	5	6	10	12	15	20	30
192	Gilles Marotte	4	5	6	10	12	15	20	30
193	Lorne Henning	4	5	6	10	12	15	20	30
194	Bob Neely	4	5	6	10	12	15	20	30

#	Player	VG 3	VgEx 4	EX 5	ExMt 6	NM 7	NmMt 8	NmMt+ 8.5	MT 9
195	Dennis Hull	4	5	6	10	12	15	20	3
196	Walt McKechnie	4	5	6	10	12	15	20	30
197	Curt Ridley	4	5	6	10	12	20		
198	Dwight Bialowas	4	5	6	10	12	15	20	30
199	Pierre Larouche	4	5	6	10	12	20		
200	Ken Dryden	6	8	10	15	30	60	80	15
201	Ross Lonsberry	4	5	6	10	12	20		
202	Curt Bennett	4	5	6	10	12	20		
203	Hartland Monahan	4	5	6	10	12	20		
204	John Davidson	5	6	8	10	12	20	25	5
205	Serge Savard	4	5	6	10	12	20		
206	Garry Howatt	4	5	6	10	12	15	20	3
207	Darryl Sittler	5	6	8	10	12	20	25	4
208	J.P. Bordeleau	4	5	6	10	12	15	20	30
209	Henry Boucha	4	5	6	10	12	20		
210	Richard Martin	4	5	6	10	12	20		
211	Vic Venasky	4	5	6	10	12	15	20	3
212	Buster Harvey	4	5	6	10	12	20		
213	Bobby Orr	15	20	25	30	50	120	135	30
214	Martin/Perreault/Robert	5	6	8	10	12	20	25	5
215	Barber/Clarke/Leach	5	6	8	10	12	20	30	
216	Gillies/Trottier/Harris	5	6	8	10	12	20	25	4
217	Gainey/Jarvis/Roberts	4	5	6	10	12	20		
218	Bicentennial Line	4	5	6	10	12	20		
219	Bob Kelly	4	5	6	10	12	20		
220	Walt Tkaczuk	4	5	6	10	12	15	20	3
221	Dave Lewis	4	5	6	10	12	15	20	30
222	Danny Gare	4	5	6	10	12	20		
223	Guy Lapointe	4	5	6	10	12	20		
224	Hank Nowak	4	5	6	10	12	15	20	3
225	Stan Mikita	5	6	8	10	12	20	25	5
226	Vic Hadfield	4	5	6	10	12	20		
227	Bernie Wolfe	4	5	6	10	12	15	20	30
228	Bryan Watson	4	5	6	10	12	15	20	30
229	Ralph Stewart	4	5	6	10	12	20		
230	Gerry Desjardins	4	5	6	10	12	20		
231	John Bednarski	4	5	6	10	12	20		
232	Yvon Lambert	4	5	6	10	12	20		
233	Orest Kindrachuk	4	5	6	10	12	20		
234	Don Marcotte	4	5	6	10	12	15	20	30
235	Bill White	4	5	6	10	12	20		
236	Red Berenson	4	5	6	10	12	20		
237	Al MacAdam	4	5	6	10	12	20		
238	Rick Blight	4	5	6	10	12	15	20	30
239	Butch Goring	4	5	6	10	12	20		
240	Cesare Maniago	4	5	6	10	12	20		
241	Jim Schoenfeld	4	5	6	10	12	20		
242	Cliff Koroll	4	5	6	10	12	20		
243	Scott Garland	4	5	6	10	12	20		
244	Rick Chartraw	4	5	6	10	12	20		
245	Phil Esposito	5	6	8	10	12	20	25	40
246	Dave Forbes	4	5	6	10	12	15	20	30
247	Jimmy Watson	4	5	6	10	12	20		
248	Ron Schock	4	5	6	10	12	20		
249	Fred Barrett	4	5	6	10	12	15	20	3
250	Glenn Resch	5	6	8	10	12	20	25	50
251	Ivan Boldirev	4	5	6	10	12	20		
252	Billy Harris	4	5	6	10	12	15	20	3
253	Lee Fogolin	4	5	6	10	12	15	20	3
254	Murray Wilson	4	5	6	10	12	15	20	30
255	Gilles Gilbert	4	5	6	10	12	20		
256	Gary Dornhoefer	4	5	6	10	12	20		
257	Carol Vadnais	4	5	6	10	12	15	20	30
258	Checklist 133-264	10	15	20	30	40	200		
259	Errol Thompson	4	5	6	10	12	20		
260	Garry Unger	4	5	6	10	12	20		
261	J. Bob Kelly	4	5	6	10	12	20		
262	Terry Harper	4	5	6	10	12	15	20	30
263	Blake Dunlop	4	5	6	10	12	20		
264	Canadiens Champs	4	5	6	10	12	20		
265	Richard Mulhern	4	5	6	10	12	15	20	30
266	Gary Sabourin	4	5	6	10	12	20		
267	Bill McKenzie UER RC	4	5	6	10	12	20		
268	Mike Corrigan	4	5	6	10	12	15	20	30
269	Rick Smith	4	5	6	10	12	20		
270	Stan Weir	4	5	6	10	12	15	20	30
271	Ron Sedlbauer	4	5	6	10	12	15	20	30
272	Jean Lemieux	4	5	6	10	12	20		
273	Hilliard Graves	4	5	6	10	12	20		
274	Dave Gardner	4	5	6	10	12	20		
275	Tracy Pratt	4	5	6	10	12	15	20	30
276	Frank St.Marseille	4	5	6	10	12	15	20	30
277	Bob Hess	4	5	6	10	12	15	20	30
278	Bobby Lalonde	4	5	6	10	12	15	20	30
279	Tony White	4	5	6	10	12	20		
280	Rod Seiling	4	5	6	10	12	20		
281	Larry Romanchych	4	5	6	10	12	20		
282	Ralph Klassen	4	5	6	10	12	15	20	30
283	Gary Croteau	4	5	6	10	12	15	20	30

Player	VG 3	VgEx 4	EX 5	ExMt 6	NM 7	NmMt 8	NmMt+ 8.5	MT 9
Neil Komadoski	4	5	6	10	12	15	20	30
Ed Johnston	4	5	6	10	12	20		
George Ferguson	4	5	6	10	12	20		
Gerry O'Flaherty	4	5	6	10	12	20		
Jack Lynch	4	5	6	10	12	15	20	30
Pat Quinn	4	5	6	10	12	15	20	30
Gene Carr	4	5	6	10	12	15	20	30
Bob Stewart	4	5	6	10	12	15	20	30
Doug Favell	4	5	6	10	12	15	20	30
Rick Wilson	4	5	6	10	12	20		
Jack Valiquette	4	5	6	10	12	15	20	30
Garry Monahan	4	5	6	10	12	20		
Michel Belhumeur	4	5	6	10	12	20		
Larry Carriere	4	5	6	10	12	15	20	30
Fred Ahern	4	5	6	10	12	20		
Dave Hudson	4	5	6	10	12	20		
Bob Berry	4	5	6	10	12	15	20	30
Bob Gassoff	4	5	6	10	12	15	20	30
Jim McKenny	4	5	6	10	12	20		
Gord Smith	4	5	6	10	12	15	20	30
Garnet Bailey	4	5	6	10	12	15	20	30
Bruce Affleck	4	5	6	10	12	20		
Doug Halward	4	5	6	10	12	20		
Lew Morrison	4	5	6	10	12	20		
Bob Sauve RC	5	6	8	10	12	20	25	50
Bob Murray RC	4	5	6	10	12	20		
Claude Larose	4	5	6	10	12	15	20	30
Don Awrey	4	5	6	10	12	15	20	30
Bill MacMillan	4	5	6	10	12	20		
Doug Jarvis RC	4	5	6	10	12	30	35	80
Dennis Owchar	4	5	6	10	12	15	20	30
Jerry Holland	4	5	6	10	12	15	20	30
Guy Chouinard RC	4	5	6	10	12	20	25	40
Gary Smith	4	5	6	10	12	20		
Pat Price	4	5	6	10	12	15	20	30
Tom Williams	4	5	6	10	12	15	20	30
Larry Patey	4	5	6	10	12	15	20	30
Claire Alexander	4	5	6	10	12	15	20	30
Larry Bolonchuk	4	5	6	10	12	15	20	
Bob Sirois	4	5	6	10	12	20		
Joe Zanussi	4	5	6	10	12	20		
Joey Johnston	4	5	6	10	12	15	20	30
J.P. LeBlanc	4	5	6	10	12	15	20	30
Craig Cameron	4	5	6	10	12	15	20	30
Dave Fortier	4	5	6	10	12	15	20	30
Ed Gilbert	4	5	6	10	12	15	20	30
John Van Boxmeer	4	5	6	10	12	15	20	30
Gary Inness	4	5	6	10	12	20		
Bill Flett	4	5	6	10	12	15	20	30
Mike Christie	4	5	6	10	12	20		
Denis Dupere	4	5	6	10	12	20		
Sheldon Kannegiesser	4	5	6	10	12	15	20	30
Jerry Butler	4	5	6	10	12	15	20	30
Gord McRae	4	5	6	10	12	15	20	30
Dennis Kearns	4	5	6	10	12	15	20	30
Ron Lalonde	4	5	6	10	12	20		
Jean Hamel	4	5	6	10	12	15	20	30
Barry Gibbs	4	5	6	10	12	20		
Mike Pelyk	4	5	6	10	12	20		
Rey Comeau	4	5	6	10	12	15	20	30
Jim Neilson	4	5	6	10	12	20		
Phil Roberto	4	5	6	10	12	20		
Dave Hutchinson	4	5	6	10	12	20		
Ted Irvine	4	5	6	10	12	15	20	30
Lanny McDonald UER	5	6	8	10	12	20	30	60
Jim Moxey	4	5	6	10	12	15	20	30
Bob Dailey	4	5	6	10	12	15	20	30
Tim Ecclestone	4	5	6	10	12	20		
Len Frig	4	5	6	10	12	20		
Randy Rota	4	5	6	10	12	20		
Juha Widing	4	5	6	10	12	15	20	30
Larry Brown	4	5	6	10	12	20		
Floyd Thomson	4	5	6	10	12	20		
Richard Nantais	4	5	6	10	12	20		
Inge Hammarstrom	4	5	6	10	12	15	20	30
Mike Robitaille	4	5	6	10	12	20		
Rejean Houle	4	5	6	10	12	15	20	30
Ed Kea	4	5	6	10	12	15	20	30
Bob Girard	4	5	6	10	12	15	20	30
Bob Murray Vancv	4	5	6	10	12	15	20	30
Dave Hrechkosy	4	5	6	10	12	15	20	30
Gary Edwards	4	5	6	10	12	15	20	30
Harold Snepsts	5	6	8	10	12	20	25	40
Pat Boutette RC	4	5	6	10	12	20	25	40
Bob Paradise	4	5	6	10	12	15	20	30
Bob Plager	4	5	6	10	12	15	20	30
Tim Jacobs	4	5	6	10	12	15	20	30
Pierre Plante	4	5	6	10	12	15	20	30
Colin Campbell	4	5	6	10	12	15	20	30

#	Player	VG 3	VgEx 4	EX 5	ExMt 6	NM 7	NmMt 8	NmMt+ 8.5	MT 9
373	Dave Williams RC	8	10	15	20	30	60	100	200
374	Ab DeMarco	4	5	6	10	12	20		
375	Mike Lampman	4	5	6	10	12	15	20	30
376	Mark Heaslip	4	5	6	10	12	15	20	30
377	Checklist Card	6	8	10	12	20	50	60	100
378	Bert Wilson	4	5	6	10	12	20		
379	Bntt/Lysk/Qnn/St.S TL	4	5	6	10	12	20		
380	Gre/Perrlt/Mrtin TL	4	5	6	10	12	15	20	30
381	Bucyk/Ratle/O'Rei TL	4	5	6	10	12	20		
382	Mrtn/Tln/Rsll/Kroll TL	4	5	6	10	12	20		
383	Seals/McAd/Mrdch TL	4	5	6	10	12	20		
384	Charron/Durbano TL	4	5	6	10	12	20		
385	Brgrn/McKch/Wtsn TL	4	5	6	10	12	20		
386	Dione/Htch/Corrig TL	4	5	6	10	12	15	20	30
387	Hoga/Yng/O'Brien TL	4	5	6	10	12	15	20	30
388	Laflr/P.Mahv/Rise TL	5	6	8	10	12	20	25	50
389	Gillies/Potvin/How TL	4	5	6	10	12	20		50
390	Gilbert/Vick/Espo TL	4	5	6	10	12	20		
391	Leach/Clarke/Barber TL	4	5	6	10	12	20		
392	Lrch/Apps/Schck TL	4	5	6	10	12	20		
393	Lefly/Ungr/Gssf TL	4	5	6	10	12	20		
394	Thmpsn/Sittlr/Will TL	4	5	6	10	12	20		
395	Vgrt/Odl/Krns/Snpst TL	4	5	6	10	12	20		
396	Pyatt/Mhn/Lbr/Whte TL	4	5	6	10	12	20		

—Guy Lafleur #163 PSA 10 (Gem) sold for $262 (Memory Lane; 4/12)
—Bobby Orr #213 PSA 10 (Gem) sold for $949 (Memory Lane; 4/07)
—Bobby Orr #213 PSA 10 (Gem) sold for $756.84 (Mile High; 12/13)
—Brian Trottier RC #155 PSA 10 (Gem) sold for $2,033 (eBay; 3/13)

1976-77 O-Pee-Chee WHA

#	Player	GD 2	VG 3	VgEx 4	EX 5	ExMt 6	NM 7	NmMt 8	MT 9
	COMMON CARD (1-132)	4	4	5	6	8	10	12	
2	Tardit/Trembl/Nils LL	4	4	5	6	10	12		
3	Tardit/B.Hull/Nils LL	4	5	6	8	12	15	20	40
9	Ulf Nilsson	4			6	10	12	15	
14	Tom Webster	4	4	5	6	8	10	12	25
15	Marty Howe	4	4	5	6	8	12	15	30
20	Joe Daley	4	4	5	6	8	12	15	
21	Gary Veneruzzo	4	4	5	6	8	10	12	25
23	Mike Antonovich	4	4	5	6	8	10	12	30
27	Poul Popiel	4	4	5	6	8	10	12	25
28	Renald Leclerc	4	4	5	6	8	10	12	25
30	Lars-Erik Sjoberg	4	4	5	6	8	10	12	25
33	Tim Sheehy	4	4	5	6	8	10	12	25
34	Brent Hughes	4	4	5	6	8	10	12	25
37	Rosaire Paiement	4	4	5	6	8	10	12	25
39	Hugh Harris	4	4	5	6	8	10	12	25
41	Rich Leduc	4	4	5	6	8	10	12	25
46	Joe Noris RC	4	4	5	6	8	10	12	25
50	Gordie Howe	8	10	15	20	25	30	40	80
52	Dave Keon	4			6	10	12	15	
54	Bryan Maxwell	4	4	5	6	8	10	12	
60	Gene Peacosh	4	4	5	6	8	10	12	25
62	J.C. Tremblay AS	4	4	5	6	8	10	12	25
63	Lars-Erik Sjoberg AS	4	4	5	6	8	10	12	25
65	Bobby Hull AS	6	8	10	12	20	25	35	80
67	Chris Abrahamsson AS	4	4	5	6	8	10	12	25
72	Gordie Howe AS	6	8	10	12	20	25	40	150
73	Bob Nevin	4	4	5	6	8	10	12	25
81	Frank Hughes	4	4	5	6	8	10	12	25
82	Reg Thomas	4	4	5	6	8	10	12	25
84	Paul Henderson	4			6	10	12	15	
91	Garry Swain	4	4	5	6	8	10	12	25
95	Mark Howe	5	6	8	10	12	15	20	40
96	Peter Marrin RC	4	4	5	6	10	12	15	
98	Paulin Bordeleau	4	4	5	6	8	10	12	25
100	Bobby Hull	6	8	10	12	20	25	40	80
101	Rick Ley	4	4	5	6	8	10	12	25
105	John French	4	4	5	6	8	10	12	25
106	John Hughes	4	4	5	6	8	10		
111	Frank Mahovlich	5	6	8	10	15	20	30	60
115	Rich Preston	4	4	5	6	8	10	12	25
117	Checklist Card	4	5	6	8	12	20	40	100
125	Anders Hedberg	4	4	5	6	8	10	12	15
126	Norm Ullman	4	4	5	6	8	10	15	35
127	Steve Sutherland	4	4	5	6	8	10	12	25
128	John Schella	4	4	5	6	8	10	12	25
129	Don McLeod	4	4	5	6	8	10	12	25
130	Canadian Finals	4	5	6	8	12	15	20	40
132	World Trophy Final	5	6	8	10	12	15	20	40

1976-77 Topps

#	Player	VG 3	VgEx 4	EX 5	ExMt 6	NM 7	NmMt 8	NmMt+ 8.5	MT 9
1	Leach/Lafleur/Larou LL	4	5	6	8	10	20	25	
2	Clarke/Lafleur/Perr/ LL	4	5	6	8	10	20	25	
3	Lafleur/Clarke/Perr LL	4	5	6	8	10	15	20	
4	Durbno/Watsn/Schultz LL	4	5	6	8	10	15	20	
5	Espo/Lafleur/Potvin LL	4	5	6	8	10	12	15	
6	Dryden/Resch/Laroc LL	4	5	6	8	10	12	15	

#	Player	VG 3	VgEx 4	EX 5	ExMt 6	NM 7	NmMt 8	NmMt+ 8.5	MT 9
7	Gary Doak	4	5	6	8	10	12	15	
8	Jacques Richard	4	5	6	8	10	12	15	
9	Wayne Dillon	4	5	6	8	10	12	15	20
10	Bernie Parent	4	5	6	8	10	12	15	25
11	Ed Westfall	4	5	6	8	10	12	15	20
12	Dick Redmond	4	5	6	8	10	12	15	
13	Bryan Hextall	4	5	6	8	10	12	15	20
14	Jean Pronovost	4	5	6	8	10	12	15	20
15	Peter Mahovlich	4	5	6	8	10	12	15	20
16	Danny Grant	4	5	6	8	10	12	15	
17	Phil Myre	4	5	6	8	10	12	15	20
18	Wayne Merrick	4	5	6	8	10	12	15	
19	Steve Durbano	4	5	6	8	10	12	15	
20	Derek Sanderson	4	5	6	8	10	12	15	
21	Mike Murphy	4	5	6	8	10	12	15	
22	Borje Salming	4	5	6	8	10	12	15	25
23	Mike Walton	4	5	6	8	10	12	15	20
24	Randy Manery	4	5	6	8	10	12	15	20
25	Ken Hodge	4	5	6	8	10	12	15	
26	Mel Bridgman RC	4	5	6	8	10	12	15	20
27	Jerry Korab	4	5	6	8	10	12	15	20
28	Gilles Gratton	4	5	6	8	10	12	15	20
29	Andre St.Laurent	4	5	6	8	10	12	15	
30	Yvan Cournoyer	4	5	6	8	10	12	15	
31	Phil Russell	4	5	6	8	10	12	15	20
32	Dennis Hextall	4	5	6	8	10	12	15	
33	Lowell MacDonald	4	5	6	8	10	12	15	20
34	Dennis O'Brien	4	5	6	8	10	12	15	
35	Gerry Meehan	4	5	6	8	10	12	15	
36	Gilles Meloche	4	5	6	8	10	12	15	
37	Wilf Paiement	4	5	6	8	10	12	15	
38	Bob MacMillan RC	4	5	6	8	10	12	15	
39	Ian Turnbull	4	5	6	8	10	12	15	
40	Rogatien Vachon	4	5	6	8	10	12	15	
41	Nick Beverley	4	5	6	8	10	12	15	
42	Rene Robert	4	5	6	8	10	12	15	20
43	Andre Savard	4	5	6	8	10	12	15	20
44	Bob Gainey	4	5	6	8	10	12	15	
45	Joe Watson	4	5	6	8	10	12	15	20
46	Billy Smith	4	5	6	8	10	12	15	25
47	Darcy Rota	4	5	6	8	10	12	15	
48	Rick Lapointe RC	4	5	6	8	10	12	15	20
49	Pierre Jarry	4	5	6	8	10	12	15	
50	Syl Apps	4	5	6	8	10	12	15	20
51	Eric Vail	4	5	6	8	10	12	15	20
52	Greg Joly	4	5	6	8	10	12	15	
53	Don Lever	4	5	6	8	10	12	15	
54	Bob Murdoch Seals	4	5	6	8	10	12	15	
55	Denis Herron	4	5	6	8	10	12	15	
56	Mike Bloom	4	5	6	8	10	12	15	20
57	Bill Fairbairn	4	5	6	8	10	12	15	
58	Fred Stanfield	4	5	6	8	10	12	15	
59	Steve Shutt	4	5	6	8	10	12	15	25
60	Brad Park	4	5	6	8	10	12	15	25
61	Gilles Villemure	4	5	6	8	10	12	15	
62	Bert Marshall	4	5	6	8	10	12	15	20
63	Chuck Lefley	4	5	6	8	10	12	15	
64	Simon Nolet	4	5	6	8	10	12	15	
65	Reggie Leach RB	4	5	6	8	10	12	15	
66	Darryl Sittler RB	4	5	6	8	10	12	15	
67	Bryan Trottier RB	5	6	8	10	12	15	20	30
68	Garry Unger RB	4	5	6	8	10	12	15	20
69	Ron Low	4	5	6	8	10	12	15	
70	Bobby Clarke	5	6	8	10	12	15	20	25
71	Michel Bergeron RC	4	5	6	8	10	12	15	
72	Ron Stackhouse	4	5	6	8	10	12	15	20
73	Bill Hogaboam	4	5	6	8	10	12	15	20
74	Bob Murdoch Kings	4	5	6	8	10	12	15	
75	Steve Vickers	4	5	6	8	10	12	15	
76	Pit Martin	4	5	6	8	10	12	15	20
77	Gerry Hart	4	5	6	8	10	12	15	
78	Craig Ramsay	4	5	6	8	10	12	15	20
79	Michel Larocque	4	5	6	8	10	12	15	20
80	Jean Ratelle	4	5	6	8	10	12	15	20
81	Don Saleski	4	5	6	8	10	12	15	20
82	Bill Clement	4	5	6	8	10	12	15	20
83	Dave Burrows	4	5	6	8	10	12	15	
84	Wayne Thomas	4	5	6	8	10	12	15	20
85	John Gould	4	5	6	8	10	12	15	20
86	Dennis Maruk RC	4	5	6	8	10	12	15	25
87	Ernie Hicke	4	5	6	8	10	12	15	20
88	Jim Rutherford	4	5	6	8	10	12	15	
89	Dale Tallon	4	5	6	8	10	12	15	
90	Rod Gilbert	4	5	6	8	10	12	15	
91	Marcel Dionne	4	5	6	8	10	15	20	25
92	Chuck Arnason	4	5	6	8	10	12	15	
93	Jean Potvin	4	5	6	8	10	12	15	20
94	Don Luce	4	5	6	8	10	12	15	20
95	Johnny Bucyk	4	5	6	8	10	12	15	20
96	Larry Goodenough	4	5	6	8	10	12	15	20
97	Mario Tremblay	4	5	6	8	10	12	15	
98	Nelson Pyatt RC	4	5	6	8	10	12	15	

#	Player	VG 3	VgEx 4	EX 5	ExMt 6	NM 7	NmMt 8	NmMt+ 8.5	MT
99	Brian Glennie	4	5	6	8	10	12	15	
100	Tony Esposito	4	5	6	8	10	12	15	30
101	Dan Maloney	4	5	6	8	10	12	15	20
102	Barry Wilkins	4	5	6	8	10	12	15	
103	Dean Talafous	4	5	6	8	10	12	15	20
104	Ed Staniowski RC	4	5	6	8	10	12	15	20
105	Dallas Smith	4	5	6	8	10	12	15	
106	Jude Drouin	4	5	6	8	10	12	15	
107	Pat Hickey	4	5	6	8	10	12	15	
108	Jocelyn Guevremont	4	5	6	8	10	12	15	20
109	Doug Risebrough	4	5	6	8	10	12	15	20
110	Reggie Leach	4	5	6	8	10	12	15	
111	Dan Bouchard	4	5	6	8	10	12	15	20
112	Chris Oddleifson	4	5	6	8	10	12	15	
113	Rick Hampton	4	5	6	8	10	12	15	
114	John Marks	4	5	6	8	10	12	15	
115	Bryan Trottier RC	10	12	15	25	30	▲80	▲100	▲150
116	Checklist 1-132	5	6	8	10	15	20	30	
117	Greg Polis	4	5	6	8	10	12	15	
118	Peter McNab	4	5	6	8	10	12	15	20
119	Jim Roberts	4	5	6	8	10	12	15	
120	Gerry Cheevers	4	5	6	8	10	12	15	
121	Rick MacLeish	4	5	6	8	10	12	15	20
122	Billy Lochead	4	5	6	8	10	12	15	
123	Tom Reid	4	5	6	8	10	12	15	20
124	Rick Kehoe	4	5	6	8	10	12	15	20
125	Keith Magnuson	4	5	6	8	10	12	15	20
126	Clark Gillies	4	5	6	8	10	12	15	20
127	Rick Middleton	4	5	6	8	10	12	15	20
128	Bill Hajt	4	5	6	8	10	12	15	
129	Jacques Lemaire	4	5	6	8	10	12	15	
130	Terry O'Reilly	4	5	6	8	10	12	15	20
131	Andre Dupont	4	5	6	8	10	12	15	
132	Flames Team CL	4	5	6	8	10	12	15	
133	Bruins Team CL	4	5	6	8	10	12	15	
134	Sabres Team CL	4	5	6	8	10	12	15	
135	Seals Team CL	4	5	6	8	10	12	15	40
136	Blackhawks Team CL	4	5	6	8	10	12	15	
137	Red Wings Team CL	4	5	6	8	10	12	15	40
138	Scouts Team CL	4	5	6	8	10	12	15	
139	Kings Team CL	4	5	6	8	10	12	15	
140	North Stars Team CL	4	5	6	8	10	12	15	
141	Canadiens Team CL	4	5	6	8	10	12	15	
142	Islanders Team CL	4	5	6	8	10	12	15	
143	Rangers Team CL	4	5	6	8	10	12	15	
144	Flyers Team CL	4	5	6	8	10	12	15	
145	Penguins Team CL	4	5	6	8	10	12	15	
146	Blues Team CL	4	5	6	8	10	12	15	
147	Maple Leafs Team CL	4	5	6	8	10	12	15	
148	Canucks Team CL	4	5	6	8	10	12	15	
149	Capitals Team CL	4	5	6	8	10	12	15	
150	Dave Schultz	4	5	6	8	10	12	15	20
151	Larry Robinson	5	6	8	10	12	15	20	25
152	Al Smith	4	5	6	8	10	12	15	
153	Bob Nystrom	4	5	6	8	10	12	15	20
154	Ron Greschner UER	4	5	6	8	10	12	15	
155	Gregg Sheppard	4	5	6	8	10	12	15	
156	Alain Daigle	4	5	6	8	10	12	15	20
157	Ed Van Impe	4	5	6	8	10	12	15	20
158	Tim Young RC	4	5	6	8	10	12	15	20
159	Gary Bergman	4	5	6	8	10	12	15	
160	Ed Giacomin	4	5	6	8	10	12	15	20
161	Yvon Labre	4	5	6	8	10	12	15	20
162	Jim Lorentz	4	5	6	8	10	12	15	20
163	Guy Lafleur	5	6	8	10	12	15	20	50
164	Tom Bladon	4	5	6	8	10	12	15	
165	Wayne Cashman	4	5	6	8	10	12	15	
166	Pete Stemkowski	4	5	6	8	10	12	15	
167	Grant Mulvey	4	5	6	8	10	12	15	
168	Yves Belanger RC	4	5	6	8	10	12	15	
169	Bill Goldsworthy	4	5	6	8	10	12	15	
170	Denis Potvin	5	6	8	10	15	20	25	40
171	Nick Libett	4	5	6	8	10	12	15	
172	Michel Plasse	4	5	6	8	10	12	15	
173	Lou Nanne	4	5	6	8	10	12	15	20
174	Tom Lysiak	4	5	6	8	10	12	15	20
175	Dennis Ververgaert	4	5	6	8	10	12	15	
176	Gary Simmons	4	5	6	8	10	12	15	20
177	Pierre Bouchard	4	5	6	8	10	12	15	
178	Bill Barber	4	5	6	8	10	12	15	25
179	Darryl Edestrand	4	5	6	8	10	12	15	
180	Gilbert Perreault	4	5	6	8	10	12	15	30
181	Dave Maloney RC	4	5	6	8	10	12	15	
182	Jean-Paul Parise	4	5	6	8	10	12	15	20
183	Bobby Sheehan	4	5	6	8	10	12	15	20
184	Pete Lopresti RC	4	5	6	8	10	12	15	20
185	Don Kozak	4	5	6	8	10	12	15	
186	Guy Charron	4	5	6	8	10	12	15	
187	Stan Gilbertson	4	5	6	8	10	12	15	
188	Bill Nyrop RC	4	5	6	8	10	12	15	
189	Bobby Schmautz	4	5	6	8	10	12	15	20
190	Wayne Stephenson	4	5	6	8	10	12	15	

	VG 3	VgEx 4	EX 5	ExMt 6	NM 7	NmMt 8	NmMt+ 8.5	MT 9
Brian Spencer	4	5	6	8	10	12	15	
Gilles Marotte	4	5	6	8	10	12	15	
Lorne Henning	4	5	6	8	10	12	15	20
Bob Neely	4	5	6	8	10	12	15	
Dennis Hull	4	5	6	8	10	12	15	
Walt McKechnie	4	5	6	8	10	12	15	20
Curt Ridley RC	4	5	6	8	10	12	15	
Dwight Bialowas	4	5	6	8	10	12	15	20
Pierre Larouche	4	5	6	8	10	12	15	
Ken Dryden	6	8	10	12	15	▲30	▲40	▲80
Ross Lonsberry	4	5	6	8	10	12	15	
Curt Bennett	4	5	6	8	10	12	15	
Hartland Monahan RC	4	5	6	8	10	12	15	20
John Davidson	4	5	6	8	10	12	15	
Serge Savard	4	5	6	8	10	12	15	
Garry Howatt	4	5	6	8	10	12	15	20
Darryl Sittler	4	5	6	8	10	15	20	25
J.P. Bordeleau	4	5	6	8	10	12	15	20
Henry Boucha	4	5	6	8	10	12	15	
Richard Martin	4	5	6	8	10	12	15	20
Vic Venasky	4	5	6	8	10	12	15	20
Buster Harvey	4	5	6	8	10	12	15	
Bobby Orr	8	10	12	15	20	30	40	80
Martin/Perrit/Robert	4	5	6	8	10	12	15	30
Barber/Clarke/Leach	4	5	6	8	10	12	15	
Gillies/Trottier/Harris	4	5	6	8	10	15	20	
Gainey/Jarvis/Roberts	4	5	6	8	10	12	15	
MacDon/Apps/Pronvst	4	5	6	8	10	12	15	
Bob Kelly	4	5	6	8	10	12	15	20
Walt Tkaczuk	4	5	6	8	10	12	15	20
Dave Lewis	4	5	6	8	10	12	15	
Danny Gare	4	5	6	8	10	12	15	
Guy Lapointe	4	5	6	8	10	12	15	
Hank Nowak RC	4	5	6	8	10	12	15	
Stan Mikita	4	5	6	8	10	15	20	30
Vic Hadfield	4	5	6	8	10	12	15	
Bernie Wolfe RC	4	5	6	8	10	12	15	
Bryan Watson	4	5	6	8	10	12	15	
Ralph Stewart	4	5	6	8	10	12	15	
Gerry Desjardins	4	5	6	8	10	12	15	20
John Bednarski RC	4	5	6	8	10	12	15	
Yvon Lambert	4	5	6	8	10	12	15	
Orest Kindrachuk	4	5	6	8	10	12	15	
Don Marcotte	4	5	6	8	10	12	15	
Bill White	4	5	6	8	10	12	15	
Red Berenson	4	5	6	8	10	12	15	20
Al MacAdam	4	5	6	8	10	12	15	
Rick Blight RC	4	5	6	8	10	12	15	20
Butch Goring	4	5	6	8	10	12	15	
Cesare Maniago	4	5	6	8	10	12	15	
Jim Schoenfeld	4	5	6	8	10	12	15	20
Cliff Koroll	4	5	6	8	10	12	15	
Mickey Redmond	4	5	6	8	10	12	15	
Rick Chartraw	4	5	6	8	10	12	15	
Phil Esposito	4	5	6	8	10	15	20	30
Dave Forbes	4	5	6	8	10	12	15	20
Jimmy Watson	4	5	6	8	10	12	15	
Ron Schock	4	5	6	8	10	12	15	20
Fred Barrett	4	5	6	8	10	12	15	
Glenn Resch	4	5	6	8	10	12	15	
Ivan Boldirev	4	5	6	8	10	12	15	20
Billy Harris	4	5	6	8	10	12	15	
Lee Fogolin	4	5	6	8	10	12	15	
Murray Wilson	4	5	6	8	10	12	15	
Gilles Gilbert	4	5	6	8	10	12	15	
Gary Dornhoefer	4	5	6	8	10	12	15	
Carol Vadnais	4	5	6	8	10	12	15	
Checklist 133-264	5	6	8	10	15	20	30	
Errol Thompson	4	5	6	8	10	12	15	
Garry Unger	4	5	6	8	10	12	15	
J. Bob Kelly	4	5	6	8	10	12	15	
Terry Harper	4	5	6	8	10	12	15	
Blake Dunlop	4	5	6	8	10	12	15	
Canadiens Champs	4	5	6	8	12	15	20	

1977-78 O-Pee-Chee

	VG 3	VgEx 4	EX 5	ExMt 6	NM 7	NmMt 8	NmMt+ 8.5	MT 9
COMMON CARD (1-396)	4	5	6	8	10	15		
Shutt/Lafleur/Dionne LL	4	5	6	8	10	15	20	40
Lafleur/Dionne/Sal/ LL	4	5	6	8	10	15	20	35
Lafleur/Dionne/Shutt LL	4	5	6	8	10	15	20	35
Williams/Polonich/Gassoff LL	4	5	6	8	10	12	15	25
McDonald/Espo/Will LL	4	5	6	8	10	12	15	25
Laroc/Dryden/Resch LL	4	5	6	8	10	15	20	40
Perr/Shutt/Lafleur/ LL	4	5	6	8	10	15	20	35
Dryden/Vach/Parent/ LL	4	5	6	8	10	15	20	40
Brian Spencer	4	5	6	8	10	12	15	
Denis Potvin	4	5	6	8	10	15	20	40
Nick Fotiu	4	5	6	8	10	12	15	25
Bob Murray	4	5	6	8	10	12	15	25
Pete Lopresti	4	5	6	8	10	15	20	

		VG 3	VgEx 4	EX 5	ExMt 6	NM 7	NmMt 8	NmMt+ 8.5	MT 9
14	J. Bob Kelly	4	5	6	8	10	12	15	25
15	Rick MacLeish	4	5	6	8	10	12	15	25
16	Terry Harper	4	5	6	8	10	15	20	
17	Willi Plett RC	4	5	6	8	10	12	15	40
18	Peter McNab	4	5	6	8	10	12	15	25
19	Wayne Thomas	4	5	6	8	10	12	15	25
20	Pierre Bouchard	4	5	6	8	10	12	15	
21	Dennis Maruk	4	5	6	8	10	15	20	
22	Mike Murphy	4	5	6	8	10	15	20	
23	Cesare Maniago	4	5	6	8	10	12	15	25
24	Paul Gardner RC	4	5	6	8	10	12	15	25
25	Rod Gilbert	4	5	6	8	10	12	15	25
26	Orest Kindrachuk	4	5	6	8	10	12	15	25
27	Bill Hajt	4	5	6	8	10	12	15	25
28	John Davidson	4	5	6	8	10	15	20	35
29	Jean-Paul Parise	4	5	6	8	10	15	20	40
30	Larry Robinson	4	5	6	8	10	12	15	25
31	Yvon Labre	4	5	6	8	10	12	15	25
32	Walt McKechnie	4	5	6	8	10	12	15	25
33	Rick Kehoe	4	5	6	8	10	12	15	25
34	Randy Holt	4	5	6	8	10	12	15	25
35	Garry Unger	4	5	6	8	10	15	20	
36	Lou Nanne	4	5	6	8	10	12	15	25
37	Dan Bouchard	4	5	6	8	10	12	15	25
38	Darryl Sittler	4	5	6	8	10	15	20	40
39	Bob Murdoch	4	5	6	8	10	12	15	25
40	Jean Ratelle	4	5	6	8	10	12	15	25
41	Dave Maloney	4	5	6	8	10	12	15	25
42	Danny Gare	4	5	6	8	10	15	20	
43	Jimmy Watson	4	5	6	8	10	12	15	25
44	Tom Williams	4	5	6	8	10	15	20	
45	Serge Savard	4	5	6	8	10	12	15	25
46	Derek Sanderson	4	5	6	8	10	15	20	
47	John Marks	4	5	6	8	10	15	20	
48	Al Cameron	4	5	6	8	10	12	15	25
49	Dean Talafous	4	5	6	8	10	15	20	35
50	Glenn Resch	4	5	6	8	10	12	15	25
51	Ron Schock	4	5	6	8	10	12	15	25
52	Gary Croteau	4	5	6	8	10	12	15	25
53	Gerry Meehan	4	5	6	8	10	12	15	25
54	Ed Staniowski	4	5	6	8	10	12	15	25
55	Phil Esposito UER	4	5	6	8	10	15	20	40
56	Dennis Ververgaert	4	5	6	8	10	12	15	25
57	Rick Wilson	4	5	6	8	10	12	15	25
58	Jim Lorentz	4	5	6	8	10	12	15	25
59	Bobby Schmautz	4	5	6	8	10	12	15	25
60	Guy Lapointe AS2	4	5	6	8	10	12	15	25
61	Ivan Boldirev	4	5	6	8	10	12	15	25
62	Bob Nystrom	4	5	6	8	10	15	20	
63	Rick Hampton	4	5	6	8	10	12	15	25
64	Jack Valiquette	4	5	6	8	10	12	15	25
65	Bernie Parent	4	5	6	8	10	15	20	
66	Dave Burrows	4	5	6	8	10	15	20	
67	Butch Goring	4	5	6	8	10	12	15	25
68A	Checklist 1-132 ERR	4	5	6	8	10	20	30	
68B	Checklist 1-132 COR								
69	Murray Wilson	4	5	6	8	10	12	15	25
70	Ed Giacomin	4	5	6	8	10	15	20	35
71	Flames Team/(checklist back)	4	5	6	8	10	15	20	35
72	Bruins Team/(checklist back)	4	5	6	8	10	15	20	
73	Sabres Team/(checklist back)	4	5	6	8	10	15	20	
74	Blackhawks Team/(checklist back)	4	5	6	8	10	15	20	
75	Barons Team/(checklist back)	4	5	6	8	10	15	20	
76	Rockies Team/(checklist back)	4	5	6	8	10	15	20	35
77	Red Wings Team/(checklist back)	4	5	6	8	10	15	20	35
78	Kings Team/(checklist back)	4	5	6	8	10	15	20	
79	North Stars Team/(checklist back)	4	5	6	8	10	15	20	35
80	Canadiens Team/(checklist back)	4	5	6	8	10	15	20	35
81	Islanders Team/(checklist back)	4	5	6	8	10	15	20	35
82	Rangers Team/(checklist back)	4	5	6	8	10	15	20	35
83	Flyers Team/(checklist back)	4	5	6	8	10	15	20	35
84	Penguins Team/(checklist back)	4	5	6	8	10	15	20	
85	Blues Team/(checklist back)	4	5	6	8	10	15	20	
86	Maple Leafs Team/(checklist back)	4	5	6	8	10	15	20	35
87	Canucks Team/(checklist back)	4	5	6	8	10	15	20	35
88	Capitals Team/(checklist back)	4	5	6	8	10	15	20	35
89	Keith Magnuson	4	5	6	8	10	12	15	25
90	Walt Tkaczuk	4	5	6	8	10	12	15	25
91	Bill Nyrop	4	5	6	8	10	12	15	25
92	Michel Plasse	4	5	6	8	10	12	15	25
93	Bob Bourne	4	5	6	8	10	12	15	25
94	Lee Fogolin	4	5	6	8	10	15	20	
95	Gregg Sheppard	4	5	6	8	10	15	20	
96	Hartland Monahan	4	5	6	8	10	12	15	25
97	Curt Bennett	4	5	6	8	10	15	20	
98	Bob Dailey	4	5	6	8	10	12	15	25
99	Bill Goldsworthy	4	5	6	8	10	12	15	25
100	Ken Dryden	4	5	6	8	10	40	50	150
101	Grant Mulvey	4	5	6	8	10	12	15	25

#	Player	VG 3	VgEx 4	EX 5	ExMt 6	NM 7	NmMt 8	NmMt+ 8.5	MT 9
102	Pierre Larouche	4	5	6	8	10	12	15	25
103	Nick Libett	4	5	6	8	10	15	20	
104	Rick Smith	4	5	6	8	10	12	15	25
105	Bryan Trottier	5	6	8	10	15	20	25	50
106	Pierre Jarry	4	5	6	8	10	12	15	25
107	Red Berenson	4	5	6	8	10	12	15	25
108	Jim Schoenfeld	4	5	6	8	10	12	15	25
109	Gilles Meloche	4	5	6	8	10	12	15	25
110	Lanny McDonald	4	5	6	8	10	15	20	35
111	Don Lever	4	5	6	8	10	12	15	25
112	Greg Polis	4	5	6	8	10	12	15	25
113	Gary Sargent RC	4	5	6	8	10	15	20	
114	Earl Anderson	4	5	6	8	10	12	15	25
115	Bobby Clarke	4	5	6	8	10	15	25	40
116	Dave Lewis	4	5	6	8	10	12	15	25
117	Darcy Rota	4	5	6	8	10	12	15	25
118	Andre Savard	4	5	6	8	10	12	15	25
119	Denis Herron	4	5	6	8	10	15	20	
120	Steve Shutt	4	5	6	8	10	15	20	35
121	Mel Bridgman	4	5	6	8	10	15	20	
122	Buster Harvey	4	5	6	8	10	15	20	
123	Roland Eriksson	4	5	6	8	10	12	15	25
124	Dale Tallon	4	5	6	8	10	12	15	25
125	Gilles Gilbert	4	5	6	8	10	12	15	25
126	Billy Harris	4	5	6	8	10	12	15	25
127	Tom Lysiak	4	5	6	8	10	12	15	25
128	Jerry Korab	4	5	6	8	10	12	15	25
129	Bob Gainey	4	5	6	8	10	15	20	35
130	Wilf Paiement	4	5	6	8	10	15	20	
131	Tom Bladon	4	5	6	8	10	15	20	25
132	Ernie Hicke	4	5	6	8	10	15	20	
133	J.P. LeBlanc	4	5	6	8	10	15	20	
134	Mike Milbury RC	4	5	8	10	15	25	30	80
135	Pit Martin	4	5	6	8	10	12	15	25
136	Steve Vickers	4	5	6	8	10	15	20	
137	Don Awrey	4	5	6	8	10	12	15	25
138	Bernie Wolfe	4	5	6	8	10	12	15	25
139	Doug Jarvis	4	5	6	8	10	12	15	25
140	Borje Salming	4	5	6	8	10	15	20	
141	Bob MacMillan	4	5	6	8	10	12	15	25
142	Wayne Stephenson	4	5	6	8	10	15	20	
143	Dave Forbes	4	5	6	8	10	12	15	25
144	Jean Potvin	4	5	6	8	10	12	15	25
145	Guy Charron	4	5	6	8	10	12	15	25
146	Cliff Koroll	4	5	6	8	10	12	15	25
147	Danny Grant	4	5	6	8	10	12	15	25
148	Bill Hogaboam	4	5	6	8	10	12	15	25
149	Al MacAdam	4	5	6	8	10	12	15	25
150	Gerry Desjardins	4	5	6	8	10	12	15	25
151	Yvon Lambert	4	5	6	8	10	12	15	25
152	Rick Lapointe	4	5	6	8	10	15	20	
153	Ed Westfall	4	5	6	8	10	15	20	
154	Carol Vadnais	4	5	6	8	10	15	20	
155	Johnny Bucyk	4	5	6	8	10	15	20	
156	J.P. Bordeleau	4	5	6	8	10	12	15	25
157	Ron Stackhouse	4	5	6	8	10	15	20	
158	Glen Sharpley	4	5	6	8	10	15	20	
159	Michel Bergeron	4	5	6	8	10	15	20	
160	Rogatien Vachon	4	5	6	8	10	15	20	35
161	Fred Stanfield	4	5	6	8	10	12	15	25
162	Gerry Hart	4	5	6	8	10	15	20	
163	Mario Tremblay	4	5	6	8	10	12	15	25
164	Andre Dupont	4	5	6	8	10	12	15	25
165	Don Marcotte	4	5	6	8	10	12	15	25
166	Wayne Dillon	4	5	6	8	10	12	15	25
167	Claude Larose	4	5	6	8	10	15	20	
168	Eric Vail	4	5	6	8	15	25	30	
169	Tom Edur	4	5	6	8	10	12	15	25
170	Tony Esposito	4	5	6	8	10	15	20	40
171	Andre St.Laurent	4	5	6	8	10	15	20	
172	Dan Maloney	4	5	6	8	10	12	15	25
173	Dennis O'Brien	4	5	6	8	10	12	15	25
174	Blair Chapman	4	5	6	8	10	12	15	25
175	Dennis Kearns	4	5	6	8	10	12	15	25
176	Wayne Merrick	4	5	6	8	10	15	20	
177	Michel Larocque	4	5	6	8	10	12	15	25
178	Bob Kelly	4	5	6	8	10	12	15	25
179	Dave Farrish	4	5	6	8	10	15	20	
180	Richard Martin AS2	4	5	6	8	10	12	15	25
181	Gary Doak	4	5	6	8	10	15	20	
182	Jude Drouin	4	5	6	8	10	12	15	25
183	Barry Dean	4	5	6	8	10	12	15	25
184	Gary Smith	4	5	6	8	10	15	20	
185	Reggie Leach	4	5	6	8	10	12	15	25
186	Ian Turnbull	4	5	6	8	10	12	15	25
187	Vic Venasky	4	5	6	8	10	15	20	
188	Wayne Bianchin	4	5	6	8	10	12	15	25
189	Doug Risebrough	4	5	6	8	10	15	20	
190	Brad Park	4	5	6	8	10	15	20	35

#	Player	VG 3	VgEx 4	EX 5	ExMt 6	NM 7	NmMt 8	NmMt+ 8.5	MT
191	Craig Ramsay	4	5	6	8	10	12	15	2
192	Ken Hodge	4	5	6	8	10	12	15	2
193	Phil Myre	4	5	6	8	10	15	20	
194	Garry Howatt	4	5	6	8	10	12	15	2
195	Stan Mikita	4	5	6	8	10	15	20	4
196	Garnet Bailey	4	5	6	8	10	12	15	2
197	Dennis Hextall	4	5	6	8	10	15	20	
198	Nick Beverley	4	5	6	8	10	15	20	
199	Larry Patey	4	5	6	8	10	15	20	
200	Guy Lafleur	4	5	6	10	15	25	30	100
201	Don Edwards RC	4	5	6	8	10	15	20	8
202	Gary Dornhoefer	4	5	6	8	10	12	15	25
203	Bob Paradise	4	5	6	8	10	12	15	25
204	Alex Pirus	4	5	6	8	10	12	15	25
205	Peter Mahovlich	4	5	6	8	10	12	15	25
206	Bert Marshall	4	5	6	8	10	12	15	25
207	Gilles Gratton	4	5	6	8	10	12	15	25
208	Alain Daigle	4	5	6	8	10	15	20	
209	Chris Oddleifson	4	5	6	8	10	12	15	25
210	Gilbert Perreault	4	5	6	8	10	15	20	60
211	Mike Palmateer RC	4	5	6	10	15	30	40	80
212	Billy Lochead	4	5	6	8	10	12	15	25
213	Dick Redmond	4	5	6	8	10	15	20	
214	Guy Lafleur RB	4	5	6	8	10	15	20	35
215	Ian Turnbull RB	4	5	6	8	10	12	15	25
216	Guy Lafleur RB	4	5	6	8	10	15	20	35
217	Steve Shutt RB	4	5	6	8	10	12	15	25
218	Guy Lafleur RB	4	5	6	8	10	15	20	35
219	Lorne Henning	4	5	6	8	10	12	15	25
220	Terry O'Reilly	4	5	6	8	10	12	15	25
221	Pat Hickey	4	5	6	8	10	12	15	25
222	Rene Robert	4	5	6	8	10	12	15	25
223	Tim Young	4	5	6	8	10	12	15	25
224	Dunc Wilson	4	5	6	8	10	15	20	
225	Dennis Hull	4	5	6	8	10	12	15	25
226	Rod Seiling	4	5	6	8	10	15	20	
227	Bill Barber	4	5	6	8	10	12	15	25
228	Dennis Polonich	4	5	6	8	10	12	15	25
229	Billy Smith	4	5	6	8	10	15	20	35
230	Yvan Cournoyer	4	5	6	8	10	15	20	
231	Don Luce	4	5	6	8	10	12	15	25
232	Mike McEwen RC	4	5	6	8	10	15	20	
233	Don Saleski	4	5	6	8	10	12	15	25
234	Wayne Cashman	4	5	6	8	10	12	15	25
235	Phil Russell	4	5	6	8	10	12	15	25
236	Mike Corrigan	4	5	6	8	10	12	15	25
237	Guy Chouinard	4	5	6	8	10	12	15	25
238	Steve Jensen	4	5	6	8	10	12	15	25
239	Jim Rutherford	4	5	6	8	10	12	15	25
240	Marcel Dionne	4	5	6	8	10	15	20	40
241	Rejean Houle	4	5	6	8	10	12	15	25
242	Jocelyn Guevremont	4	5	6	8	10	12	15	25
243	Jim Harrison	4	5	6	8	10	12	15	25
244	Don Murdoch	4	5	6	8	10	15	20	
245	Rick Green RC	4	5	6	8	10	12	15	25
246	Rick Middleton	4	5	6	8	10	15	20	
247	Joe Watson	4	5	6	8	10	12	15	25
248	Syl Apps	4	5	6	8	10	15	20	
249	Checklist 133-264	4	5	6	10	20	40		
250	Clark Gillies	4	5	6	8	10	15	20	
251	Bobby Orr	6	10	12	15	25	60	80	150
252	Nelson Pyatt	4	5	6	8	10	12	15	25
253	Gary McAdam	4	5	6	8	10	12	15	25
254	Jacques Lemaire	4	5	6	8	10	12	15	25
255	Bob Girard	4	5	6	8	10	12	15	25
256	Ron Greschner	4	5	6	8	10	12	15	25
257	Ross Lonsberry	4	5	6	8	10	12	15	25
258	Dave Gardner	4	5	6	8	10	12	15	25
259	Rick Blight	4	5	6	8	10	12	15	25
260	Gerry Cheevers	4	5	6	8	10	15	20	35
261	Jean Pronovost	4	5	6	8	10	15	20	
262	Cup Semi-Finals	4	5	6	8	10	12	15	25
263	Cup Semi-Finals	4	5	6	8	10	12	15	25
264	Canadiens Champs	4	5	6	8	10	12	15	25
265	Rick Bowness RC	4	5	6	8	12	20	25	40
266	George Ferguson	4	5	6	8	10	12	15	25
267	Mike Kitchen RC	4	5	6	8	10	12	15	25
268	Bob Berry	4	5	6	8	10	12	15	25
269	Greg Smith RC	4	5	6	8	10	12	15	25
270	Stan Jonathan RC	4	5	6	8	10	15	20	40
271	Dwight Bialowas	4	5	6	8	10	12	15	25
272	Pete Stemkowski	4	5	6	8	10	12	15	25
273	Greg Joly	4	5	6	8	10	12	15	25
274	Ken Houston RC	4	5	6	8	10	12	15	25
275	Brian Glennie	4	5	6	8	10	12	15	25
276	Ed Johnston	4	5	6	8	10	12	15	25
277	John Grisdale	4	5	6	8	10	12	15	25
278	Craig Patrick	4	5	6	8	10	12	15	25
279	Ken Breitenbach RC	4	5	6	8	10	12	15	25
280	Fred Ahern	4	5	6	8	10	12	15	25
281	Jim Roberts	4	5	6	8	10	12	15	25
282	Harvey Bennett RC	4	5	6	8	10	15	20	25
283	Ab DeMarco	4	5	6	8	10	12	15	25

#	Player	VG 3	VgEx 4	EX 5	ExMt 6	NM 7	NmMt 8	NmMt+ 8.5	MT 9
	Pat Boutette	4	5	6	8	10	12	15	25
	Bob Plager	4	5	6	8	10	12	15	25
	Hilliard Graves	4	5	6	8	10	12	15	25
	Gordie Lane RC	4	5	6	8	10	12	15	25
	Ron Andruff	4	5	6	8	10	12	15	25
	Larry Brown	4	5	6	8	10	12	15	25
	Mike Fidler	4	5	6	8	10	12	15	25
	Fred Barrett	4	5	6	8	10	12	15	25
	Bill Clement	4	5	6	8	10	12	15	25
	Errol Thompson	4	5	6	8	10	12	15	25
	Doug Grant	4	5	6	8	10	15	20	35
	Harold Snepsts	4	5	6	8	10	15	20	35
	Rick Bragnalo	4	5	6	8	10	15	20	
	Bryan Lefley	4	5	6	8	10	12	15	25
	Gene Carr	4	5	6	8	10	12	15	25
	Bob Stewart	4	5	6	8	10	15	20	
	Lew Morrison	4	5	6	8	10	12	15	25
	Ed Kea	4	5	6	8	10	12	15	25
	Scott Garland	4	5	6	8	10	15	20	
	Bill Fairbairn	4	5	6	8	10	12	15	25
	Larry Carriere	4	5	6	8	10	12	15	25
	Ron Low	4	5	6	8	10	12	15	25
	Tom Reid	4	5	6	8	10	12	15	25
	Paul Holmgren RC	4	5	6	8	10	15	20	40
	Pat Price	4	5	6	8	10	12	15	25
	Kirk Bowman	4	5	6	8	10	15	20	
	Bobby Simpson	4	5	6	8	10	12	15	25
	Ron Ellis	4	5	6	8	10	12	15	25
	R.Bourbonnais (Federko)	4	5	6	8	10	15	20	35
	Bobby Lalonde	4	5	6	8	10	12	15	25
	Tony White	4	5	6	8	10	12	15	25
	John Van Boxmeer	4	5	6	8	10	12	15	25
	Don Kozak	4	5	6	8	10	12	15	25
	Jim Neilson	4	5	6	8	10	12	15	25
	Terry Martin	4	5	6	8	10	15	20	
	Barry Gibbs	4	5	6	8	10	12	15	25
	Inge Hammarstrom	4	5	6	8	10	12	15	25
	Darryl Edestrand	4	5	6	8	10	15	20	35
	Flames Logo	4	5	6	8	10	15	20	35
	Bruins Logo	4	5	6	8	10	15	20	35
	Sabres Logo	4	5	6	8	10	15	20	35
	Blackhawks Logo	4	5	6	8	10	15	20	35
	Barons Logo	4	5	6	8	10	15	20	35
	Rockies Logo	4	5	6	8	10	15	20	35
	Red Wings Logo	4	5	6	8	10	15	20	35
	Kings Logo	4	5	6	8	10	15	20	35
	North Stars Logo	4	5	6	8	10	15	20	35
	Canadiens Logo	4	5	6	8	10	15	20	35
	Islanders Logo	4	5	6	8	10	15	20	35
	Rangers Logo	4	5	6	8	10	15	20	35
	Flyers Logo	4	5	6	8	10	15	20	35
	Penguins Logo	4	5	6	8	10	15	20	35
	Blues Logo	4	5	6	8	10	15	20	35
	Maple Leafs Logo	4	5	6	8	10	15	20	35
	Canucks Logo	4	5	6	8	10	15	20	35
	Capitals Logo	4	5	6	8	10	15	20	35
340	Chuck Lefley	4	5	6	8	10	12	15	25
341	Garry Monahan	4	5	6	8	10	12	15	25
342	Bryan Watson	4	5	6	8	10	12	15	25
343	Dave Hudson	4	5	6	8	10	12	15	25
344	Neil Komadoski	4	5	6	8	10	12	15	25
345	Gary Edwards	4	5	6	8	10	12	15	25
346	Rey Comeau	4	5	6	8	10	15	20	
347	Bob Neely	4	5	6	8	10	12	15	25
348	Jean Hamel	4	5	6	8	10	12	15	25
349	Jerry Butler	4	5	6	8	10	15	20	
350	Mike Walton	4	5	6	8	10	12	15	25
351	Bob Sirois	4	5	6	8	10	12	15	25
352	Jim McElmury	4	5	6	8	10	12	15	25
353	Dave Schultz	4	5	6	8	10	12	15	25
354	Doug Palazzari	4	5	6	8	10	12	15	25
355	David Shand	4	5	6	8	10	12	15	25
356	Stan Weir	4	5	6	8	10	12	15	25
357	Mike Christie	4	5	6	8	10	12	15	25
358	Floyd Thomson	4	5	6	8	10	15	20	
359	Larry Goodenough	4	5	6	8	10	12	15	25
360	Bill Riley	4	5	6	8	10	15	20	
361	Doug Hicks	4	5	6	8	10	15	20	
362	Dan Newman	4	5	6	8	10	15	20	
363	Rick Chartraw	4	5	6	8	10	15	20	
364	Tim Ecclestone	4	5	6	8	10	12	15	25
365	Don Ashby	4	5	6	8	10	12	15	25
366	Jacques Richard	4	5	6	8	10	12	15	25
367	Yves Belanger	4	5	6	8	10	12	15	25
368	Ron Sedlbauer	4	5	6	8	10	12	15	25
369	Jack Lynch UER (Collins)	4	5	6	8	10	15	20	
370	Doug Favell	4	5	6	8	10	12	15	25
371	Bob Murdoch	4	5	6	8	10	12	15	25
372	Ralph Klassen	4	5	6	8	10	15	20	
373	Richard Mulhern	4	5	6	8	10	12	15	25
374	Jim McKenny	4	5	6	8	10	15	20	
375	Mike Bloom	4	5	6	8	10	12	15	25
376	Bruce Affleck	4	5	6	8	10	15	20	
377	Gerry O'Flaherty	4	5	6	8	10	12	15	25

#	Player	VG 3	VgEx 4	EX 5	ExMt 6	NM 7	NmMt 8	NmMt+ 8.5	MT 9
378	Ron Lalonde	4	5	6	8	10	12	15	25
379	Chuck Arnason	4	5	6	8	10	12	15	25
380	Dave Hutchinson	4	5	6	8	10	12	15	25
381A	Checklist ERR Topps	4	5	6	10	20	35	40	
381B	Checklist COR No Topps	4	5	6	10	20	25	30	60
382	John Gould	4	5	6	8	10	15	20	40
383	Dave Williams	4	5	6	8	10	12	15	25
384	Len Frig	4	5	6	8	10	12	15	25
385	Pierre Plante	4	5	6	8	10	12	15	25
386	Ralph Stewart	4	5	6	8	10	12	15	25
387	Gord Smith	4	5	6	8	10	12	15	25
388	Denis Dupere	4	5	6	8	10	12	15	25
389	Randy Manery	4	5	6	8	10	12	15	25
390	Lowell MacDonald	4	5	6	8	10	12	15	25
391	Dennis Owchar	4	5	6	8	10	12	15	25
392	Jim Roberts RC	4	5	6	8	10	12	15	25
393	Mike Veisor	4	5	6	8	10	15	20	
394	Bob Hess	4	5	6	8	10	12	15	25
395	Curt Ridley	4	5	6	8	10	12	15	25
396	Mike Lampman	4	5	6	8	10	15	20	

Mike Milbury RC #134 PSA 10 (Gem) sold for $169.66 (eBay; 4/12)

1977-78 O-Pee-Chee WHA

#	Player	VG 3	VgEx 4	EX 5	ExMt 6	NM 7	NmMt 8	NmMt+ 8.5	MT 9
	COMMON CARD (1-66)	4	5	6	8	10		15	25
1	Gordie Howe	15	20	25	30	40	100		
2	Jean Bernier RC	5	6	8	10	12	20		
3	Anders Hedberg	5	8	10	12	15	50		
4	Ken Broderick	4	5	6		10	12		
5	Joe Noris	5	6	8	10	12	20		
6	Blaine Stoughton	5	6	8	10	12	20		
7	Claude St.Sauveur	5	6	8	10	12	20		
8	Real Cloutier	4	5	6	8	10	15	20	30
9	Joe Daley	4	5	6	8	10	15	20	30
11	Wayne Rutledge	4	5	6	8	10	15	20	30
12	Mark Napier	4	5	6	8	10	15	20	30
14	Don McLeod	4	5	6	8	10	15		
15	Ulf Nilsson	4	5	6	8	10	12		
16	Blair MacDonald	4	5	6	8	10	12		
17	Mike Rogers	4	5	6	8	10	12	15	30
18	Gary Inness	4	5	6	8	10	12		
19	Larry Lund	4	5	6	8	10	12		
20	Marc Tardif	4	5	6	8	10	12	15	30
21	Lars-Erik Sjoberg	4	5	6	8	10	12		
22	Bryan Campbell	4	5	6	8	10	12		
23	John Garrett	4	5	6	8	10	12	15	30
27	Mark Howe	5	6	8	10	12	20	25	40
28	Dave Dryden	4	5	6	8	10	12		
29	Reg Thomas	4	5	6	8	10	12		
30	Andre Lacroix	4	5	6	8	10	12	15	30
32	Paul Henderson	4	5	6	8	10	12		
33	Juha Widing	4	5	6	8	10	12	15	30
35	Robbie Ftorek	4	5	6		10	12		
37	Terry Ruskowski	4	5	6	8	10	12		
38	Richard Brodeur	4	5	6	8	10	15	20	40
39	Willy Lindstrom RC	4	5	6	8	10	15	20	50
40	Al Hamilton	4	5	6		10	12		
41	John McKenzie	4	5	6	8	10	12	15	30
42	Wayne Wood	4	5	6	8	10	12		
44	J.C. Tremblay	4	5	6	8	10	12		
45	Gary Bromley	4	5	6		10	12		
47	Bobby Sheehan	4	5	6	8	10	12		
48	Ron Larway RC	4	5	6	8	10	12		
49	Al Smith	4	5	6	8	10	12	15	30
50	Bobby Hull	6	8	10	12	20	40		
56	Jim Park RC	4	5	6	8	10	12	15	30
57	Dan Labraaten RC	4	5	6	8	10	12		
58	Checklist Card	5	6	8	10	12	25		
59	Paul Shmyr	4	5	6	8	10	12		
60	Serge Bernier	4	5	6	8	10	12	15	30
61	Frank Mahovlich	5	6	8	10	12	20	25	80
62	Michel Dion	4	5	6	8	10	12		
63	Poul Popiel	4	5	6		10	12		
64	Lyle Moffat	4	5	6		10	12		
65	Marty Howe	5	6	8	10	12	20		
66	Don Burgess	5	8	10	12	15	40		

1977-78 Topps

#	Player	VG 3	VgEx 4	EX 5	ExMt 6	NM 7	NmMt 8	NmMt+ 8.5	MT 9
1	Shutt/Lafleur/Dionne LL	4	5	6	8	10	15	20	40
2	Lafleur/Dionne/Sal LL	4	5	6	8	10	12	15	25
3	Lafleur/Dionne/Shutt LL	4	5	6	8	10	12	15	20
4	Williams/Polnch/Gasfl LL	4	5	6	8	10	12	15	20
5	McDonald/Espo/Will LL	4	5	6	8	10	12	15	20
6	Laroc/Dryden/Resch LL	4	5	6	8	10	12	15	20
7	Perr/Shutt/Lafleur LL	4	5	6	8	10	12	15	20
8	Dryden/Vach/Parent LL	4	5	6	8	10	12	15	20
9	Brian Spencer	4	5	6	8	10	12	15	20
10	Denis Potvin AS2	4	5	6	8	10	12	15	20
11	Nick Fotiu	4	5	6	8	10	12	15	20

HOCKEY

#	Player	VG 3 / 4	VgEx 4 / 5	EX 5 / 6	ExMt 6 / 8	NM 7 / 10	NmMt 8 / 12	NmMt+ 8.5 / 15	MT 9 / 20
12	Bob Murray	4	5	6	8	10	12	15	20
13	Pete Lopresti	4	5	6	8	10	12	15	20
14	J. Bob Kelly	4	5	6	8	10	12	15	20
15	Rick MacLeish	4	5	6	8	10	12		
16	Terry Harper	4	5	6	8	10	12	15	20
17	Willi Plett RC	4	5	6	8	10	12	15	20
18	Peter McNab	4	5	6	8	10	12	15	20
19	Wayne Thomas	4	5	6	8	10	12	15	20
20	Pierre Bouchard	4	5	6	8	10	12	15	20
21	Dennis Maruk	4	5	6	8	10	12	15	20
22	Mike Murphy	4	5	6	8	10	12	15	20
23	Cesare Maniago	4	5	6	8	10	12	15	20
24	Paul Gardner RC	4	5	6	8	10	12	15	20
25	Rod Gilbert	4	5	6	8	10	12	15	20
26	Orest Kindrachuk	4	5	6	8	10	12	15	20
27	Bill Hajt	4	5	6	8	10	12	15	20
28	John Davidson	4	5	6	8	10	12	15	20
29	Jean-Paul Parise	4	5	6	8	10	12	15	20
30	Larry Robinson AS1	4	5	6	8	10	12	15	20
31	Yvon Labre	4	5	6	8	10	12	15	20
32	Walt McKechnie	4	5	6	8	10	12	15	20
33	Rick Kehoe	4	5	6	8	10	12	15	20
34	Randy Holt RC	4	5	6	8	10	12	15	20
35	Garry Unger	4	5	6	8	10	12	15	20
36	Lou Nanne	4	5	6	8	10	12		
37	Dan Bouchard	4	5	6	8	10	12	15	20
38	Darryl Sittler	4	5	6	8	10	12	15	25
39	Bob Murdoch	4	5	6	8	10	12	15	20
40	Jean Ratelle	4	5	6	8	10	12	15	20
41	Dave Maloney	4	5	6	8	10	12	15	20
42	Danny Gare	4	5	6	8	10	12		
43	Jimmy Watson	4	5	6	8	10	12	15	20
44	Tom Williams	4	5	6	8	10	12	15	20
45	Serge Savard	4	5	6	8	10	12	15	20
46	Derek Sanderson	4	5	6	8	10	12		
47	John Marks	4	5	6	8	10	12		
48	Al Cameron RC	4	5	6	8	10	12	15	20
49	Dean Talafous	4	5	6	8	10	12	15	20
50	Glenn Resch	4	5	6	8	10	12	15	20
51	Ron Schock	4	5	6	8	10	12	15	20
52	Gary Croteau	4	5	6	8	10	12		
53	Gerry Meehan	4	5	6	8	10	12	15	20
54	Ed Staniowski	4	5	6	8	10	12	15	20
55	Phil Esposito	4	5	6	8	10	12	15	25
56	Dennis Ververgaert	4	5	6	8	10	12	15	20
57	Rick Wilson	4	5	6	8	10	12	15	20
58	Jim Lorentz	4	5	6	8	10	12	15	20
59	Bobby Schmautz	4	5	6	8	10	12		
60	Guy Lapointe AS2	4	5	6	8	10	12	15	20
61	Ivan Boldirev	4	5	6	8	10	12	15	20
62	Bob Nystrom	4	5	6	8	10	12	15	20
63	Rick Hampton	4	5	6	8	10	12	15	20
64	Jack Valiquette	4	5	6	8	10	12	15	20
65	Bernie Parent	4	5	6	8	10	12		
66	Dave Burrows	4	5	6	8	10	12		
67	Butch Goring	4	5	6	8	10	12	15	20
68	Checklist 1-132	4	5	6	10	12	15		
69	Murray Wilson	4	5	6	8	10	12	15	20
70	Ed Giacomin	4	5	6	8	10	12	15	20
71	Flames Team CL	4	5	6	8	10	12	15	20
72	Bruins Team CL	4	5	6	8	10	12	15	20
73	Sabres Team CL	4	5	6	8	10	12	15	20
74	Blackhawks Team CL	4	5	6	8	10	12	15	20
75	Barons Team CL	4	5	6	8	10	12	15	20
76	Rockies Team CL	4	5	6	8	10	12	15	20
77	Red Wings Team CL	4	5	6	8	10	12	15	20
78	Kings Team CL	4	5	6	8	10	12		
79	North Stars Team CL	4	5	6	8	10	12	15	20
80	Canadiens Team CL	4	5	6	8	10	12	15	20
81	Islanders Team CL	4	5	6	8	10	12	15	20
82	Rangers Team CL	4	5	6	8	10	12	15	20
83	Flyers Team CL	4	5	6	8	10	12	15	20
84	Penguins Team CL	4	5	6	8	10	12	15	20
85	Blues Team CL	4	5	6	8	10	12	15	20
86	Maple Leafs Team CL	4	5	6	8	10	12	15	20
87	Canucks Team CL	4	5	6	8	10	12	15	20
88	Capitals Team CL	4	5	6	8	10	12	15	20
89	Keith Magnuson	4	5	6	8	10	12	15	20
90	Walt Tkaczuk	4	5	6	8	10	12	15	20
91	Bill Nyrop	4	5	6	8	10	12	15	20
92	Michel Plasse	4	5	6	8	10	12	15	20
93	Bob Bourne	4	5	6	8	10	12		
94	Lee Fogolin	4	5	6	8	10	12	15	20
95	Gregg Sheppard	4	5	6	8	10	12	15	20
96	Hartland Monahan	4	5	6	8	10	12	15	20
97	Curt Bennett	4	5	6	8	10	12	15	20
98	Bob Dailey	4	5	6	8	10	12	15	20
99	Bill Goldsworthy	4	5	6	8	10	12	15	20
100	Ken Dryden AS1	4	5	6	8	10	12	15	25

#	Player	VG 3 / 4	VgEx 4 / 5	EX 5 / 6	ExMt 6 / 8	NM 7 / 10	NmMt 8 / 12	NmMt+ 8.5 / 15	MT 9 / 20
101	Grant Mulvey	4	5	6	8	10	12	15	2
102	Pierre Larouche	4	5	6	8	10	12	15	2
103	Nick Libett	4	5	6	8	10	12		
104	Rick Smith	4	5	6	8	10	12	15	2
105	Bryan Trottier	5	6	8	10	12	15	20	2
106	Pierre Jarry	4	5	6	8	10	12	15	2
107	Red Berenson	4	5	6	8	10	12	15	2
108	Jim Schoenfeld	4	5	6	8	10	12	15	2
109	Gilles Meloche	4	5	6	8	10	12	15	2
110	Lanny McDonald AS2	4	5	6	8	10	12	15	20
111	Don Lever	4	5	6	8	10	12		
112	Greg Polis	4	5	6	8	10	12	15	2
113	Gary Sargent RC	4	5	6	8	10	12	15	2
114	Earl Anderson RC	4	5	6	8	10	12	15	2
115	Bobby Clarke	4	5	6	8	10	12		
116	Dave Lewis	4	5	6	8	10	12	15	20
117	Darcy Rota	4	5	6	8	10	12		
118	Andre Savard	4	5	6	8	10	12	15	20
119	Denis Herron	4	5	6	8	10	12		
120	Steve Shutt AS1	4	5	6	8	10	12	15	20
121	Mel Bridgman	4	5	6	8	10	12		
122	Buster Harvey	4	5	6	8	10	12	15	20
123	Roland Eriksson RC	4	5	6	8	10	12	15	20
124	Dale Tallon	4	5	6	8	10	12		
125	Gilles Gilbert	4	5	6	8	10	12	15	20
126	Billy Harris	4	5	6	8	10	12	15	20
127	Tom Lysiak	4	5	6	8	10	12	15	20
128	Jerry Korab	4	5	6	8	10	12	15	20
129	Bob Gainey	4	5	6	8	10	12	15	20
130	Wilf Paiement	4	5	6	8	10	12	15	20
131A	Tom Bladon Standing	4	5	6	8	10	12	15	25
131B	Tom Bladon Skating	4	5	6	8	10	12	15	20
132	Ernie Hicke	4	5	6	8	10	12	15	20
133	J.P. LeBlanc	4	5	6	8	10	12	15	20
134	Mike Milbury RC	4	5	6	8	10	12	15	25
135	Pit Martin	4	5	6	8	10	12		
136	Steve Vickers	4	5	6	8	10	12	15	20
137	Don Awrey	4	5	6	8	10	12	15	20
138A	Bernie Wolfe MacAdam	4	5	6	8	10	12		
138B	Bernie Wolfe COR	4	5	6	8	10	12	15	20
139	Doug Jarvis	4	5	6	8	10	12	15	20
140	Borje Salming AS1	4	5	6	8	10	12		
141	Bob MacMillan	4	5	6	8	10	12	15	20
142	Wayne Stephenson	4	5	6	8	10	12	15	20
143	Dave Forbes	4	5	6	8	10	12	15	20
144	Jean Potvin	4	5	6	8	10	12	15	20
145	Guy Charron	4	5	6	8	10	12	15	20
146	Cliff Koroll	4	5	6	8	10	12	15	20
147	Danny Grant	4	5	6	8	10	12	15	20
148	Bill Hogaboam UER	4	5	6	8	10	12	15	20
149A	Al MacAdam ERR Wolfe	4	5	6	8	10	12		
149B	Al MacAdam COR	4	5	6	8	10	12	15	20
150	Gerry Desjardins	4	5	6	8	10	12	15	20
151	Yvon Lambert	4	5	6	8	10	12	15	20
152A	Rick Lapointe ERR	4	5	6	8	10	12		
152B	Rick Lapointe COR	4	5	6	8	10	12	15	20
153	Ed Westfall	4	5	6	8	10	12	15	20
154	Carol Vadnais	4	5	6	8	10	12	15	20
155	Johnny Bucyk	4	5	6	8	10	12		
156	J.P. Bordeleau	4	5	6	8	10	12	15	20
157	Ron Stackhouse	4	5	6	8	10	12	15	20
158	Glen Sharpley RC	4	5	6	8	10	12		
159	Michel Bergeron	4	5	6	8	10	12	15	20
160	Rogatien Vachon AS2	4	5	6	8	10	12	15	20
161	Fred Stanfield	4	5	6	8	10	12	15	20
162	Gerry Hart	4	5	6	8	10	12	15	20
163	Mario Tremblay	4	5	6	8	10	12	15	20
164	Andre Dupont	4	5	6	8	10	12	15	20
165	Don Marcotte	4	5	6	8	10	12	15	20
166	Wayne Dillon	4	5	6	8	10	12	15	20
167	Claude Larose	4	5	6	8	10	12	15	20
168	Eric Vail	4	5	6	8	10	12		
169	Tom Edur	4	5	6	8	10	12	15	20
170	Tony Esposito	4	5	6	8	10	12	15	20
171	Andre St.Laurent	4	5	6	8	10	12	15	20
172	Dan Maloney	4	5	6	8	10	12	15	20
173	Dennis O'Brien	4	5	6	8	10	12	15	20
174	Blair Chapman RC	4	5	6	8	10	12	15	20
175	Dennis Kearns	4	5	6	8	10	12	15	20
176	Wayne Merrick	4	5	6	8	10	12	15	20
177	Michel Larocque	4	5	6	8	10	12	15	20
178	Bob Kelly	4	5	6	8	10	12	15	20
179	Dave Farrish RC	4	5	6	8	10	12		
180	Richard Martin AS2	4	5	6	8	10	12	15	20
181	Gary Doak	4	5	6	8	10	12	15	20
182	Jude Drouin	4	5	6	8	10	12	15	20
183	Barry Dean RC	4	5	6	8	10	12	15	20
184	Gary Smith	4	5	6	8	10	12		
185	Reggie Leach	4	5	6	8	10	12	15	20

#	Player	VG 3	VgEx 4	EX 5	ExMt 6	NM 7	NmMt 8	NmMt+ 8.5	MT 9
186	Ian Turnbull	4	5	6	8	10	12		
187	Vic Venasky	4	5	6	8	10	12	15	20
188	Wayne Bianchin RC	4	5	6	8	10	12	15	20
189	Doug Risebrough	4	5	6	8	10	12	15	20
190	Brad Park	4	5	6	8	10	12	15	20
191	Craig Ramsay	4	5	6	8	10	12	15	20
192	Ken Hodge	4	5	6	8	10	12	15	20
193	Phil Myre	4	5	6	8	10	12		
194	Garry Howatt	4	5	6	8	10	12	15	20
195	Stan Mikita	4	5	6	8	10	12	15	30
196	Garnet Bailey	4	5	6	8	10	12		
197	Dennis Hextall	4	5	6	8	10	12	15	20
198	Nick Beverley	4	5	6	8	10	12	15	20
199	Larry Patey	4	5	6	8	10	12	15	20
200	Guy Lafleur AS1	4	5	6	8	10	12	15	25
201	Don Edwards RC	4	5	6	8	10	12	15	30
202	Gary Dornhoefer	4	5	6	8	10	12		
203	Stan Gilbertson	4	5	6	8	10	12	15	20
204	Alex Pirus RC	4	5	6	8	10	12	15	20
205	Peter Mahovlich	4	5	6	8	10	12	15	20
206	Bert Marshall	4	5	6	8	10	12	15	20
207	Gilles Gratton	4	5	6	8	10	12	15	20
208	Alain Daigle	4	5	6	8	10	12	15	20
209	Chris Oddleifson	4	5	6	8	10	12	15	20
210	Gilbert Perreault AS2	4	5	6	8	10	12	15	40
211	Mike Palmateer RC	4	5	6	8	12	20		
212	Billy Lochead	4	5	6	8	10	12	15	20
213	Dick Redmond	4	5	6	8	10	12	15	25
214	Guy Lafleur RB	4	5	6	8	10	12	15	20
215	Ian Turnbull RB	4	5	6	8	10	12	15	20
216	Guy Lafleur RB	4	5	6	8	10	12	15	25
217	Steve Shutt RB	4	5	6	8	10	12	15	20
218	Guy Lafleur RB	4	5	6	8	10	12	15	25
219	Lorne Henning	4	5	6	8	10	12	15	20
220	Terry O'Reilly	4	5	6	8	10	12	15	20
221	Pat Hickey	4	5	6	8	10	12	15	20
222	Rene Robert	4	5	6	8	10	12		
223	Tim Young	4	5	6	8	10	12	15	20
224	Dunc Wilson	4	5	6	8	10	12		
225	Dennis Hull	4	5	6	8	10	12		
226	Rod Seiling	4	5	6	8	10	12		
227	Bill Barber	4	5	6	8	10	12	15	20
228	Dennis Polonich RC	4	5	6	8	10	12	15	20
229	Billy Smith	4	5	6	8	10	12	15	25
230	Yvan Cournoyer	4	5	6	8	10	12	15	20
231	Don Luce	4	5	6	8	10	12	15	20
232	Mike McEwen RC	4	5	6	8	10	12	15	20
233	Don Saleski	4	5	6	8	10	12	15	20
234	Wayne Cashman	4	5	6	8	10	12	15	20
235	Phil Russell	4	5	6	8	10	12		
236	Mike Corrigan	4	5	6	8	10	12	15	20
237	Guy Chouinard	4	5	6	8	10	12	15	20
238	Steve Jensen RC	4	5	6	8	10	12		
239	Jim Rutherford	4	5	6	8	10	12	15	20
240	Marcel Dionne AS1	4	5	6	8	10	12	15	25
241	Rejean Houle	4	5	6	8	10	12		
242	Jocelyn Guevremont	4	5	6	8	10	12		
243	Jim Harrison	4	5	6	8	10	12		
244	Don Murdoch RC	4	5	6	8	10	12		
245	Rick Green RC	4	5	6	8	10	12	15	20
246	Rick Middleton	4	5	6	8	10	12	15	20
247	Joe Watson	4	5	6	8	10	12	15	20
248	Syl Apps	4	5	6	8	10	12		
249	Checklist 133-264	4	5	6	10	12	15	20	25
250	Clark Gillies	4	5	6	8	10	12		
251	Bobby Orr	6	8	10	12	15	25	30	50
252	Nelson Pyatt	4	5	6	8	10	12	15	20
253	Gary McAdam RC	4	5	6	8	10	12	15	20
254	Jacques Lemaire	4	5	6	8	10	12	15	20
255	Bill Fairbairn	4	5	6	8	10	12	15	20
256	Ron Greschner	4	5	6	8	10	12	15	20
257	Ross Lonsberry	4	5	6	8	10	12	15	20
258	Dave Gardner	4	5	6	8	10	12	15	20
259	Rick Blight	4	5	6	8	10	12	15	20
260	Gerry Cheevers	4	5	6	8	10	12	15	20
261	Jean Pronovost	4	5	6	8	10	12	15	20
262	Mon/NYI Semi-Finals	4	5	6	8	10	12	15	20
263	Bruins Semi-Finals	4	5	6	8	10	12	15	20
264	Canadiens Champs	4	5	6	8	10	12	15	20

1978-79 O-Pee-Chee

#	Card	VG 3	VgEx 4	EX 5	ExMt 6	NM 7	NmMt 8	NmMt+ 8.5	MT 9
	COMMON CARD (1-396)	4	4	5	8	10	15	20	
1	Mike Bossy HL	6	8	12	15	40	120	135	200
2	Phil Esposito HL	4	5	6	8	10	15	20	
3	Guy Lafleur HL	4	5	6	8	10	15	20	
4	Darryl Sittler HL	4	5	6	8	10	15	20	
5	Garry Unger HL	4	5	6	8	10	15	20	
6	Gary Edwards	4	5	6	8	10	15	20	

#	Player	VG 3	VgEx 4	EX 5	ExMt 6	NM 7	NmMt 8	NmMt+ 8.5	MT 9
7	Rick Blight	4	5	6	8	10	15	20	
8	Larry Patey	4	5	6	8	10	15	20	
9	Craig Ramsay	4	5	6	8	10	15	20	30
10	Bryan Trottier	5	6	8	10	12	15	20	40
11	Don Murdoch	4	5	6	8	10	15	20	
12	Phil Russell	4	5	6	8	10	15	20	
13	Doug Jarvis	4	5	6	8	10	15	20	
14	Gene Carr	4	5	6	8	10	15	20	
15	Bernie Parent	4	5	6	8	10	15	20	35
16	Perry Miller	4	5	6	8	10	15	20	
17	Kent-Erik Andersson RC	4	5	6	8	10	15	20	
18	Gregg Sheppard	4	5	6	8	10	15	20	
19	Dennis Owchar	4	5	6	8	10	15	20	
20	Rogatien Vachon	4	5	6	8	10	15	20	
21	Dan Maloney	4	5	6	8	10	15	20	
22	Guy Charron	4	5	6	8	10	15	20	
23	Dick Redmond	4	5	6	8	10	15	20	
24	Checklist 1-132	5	6	8	10	12	20	30	60
25	Anders Hedberg	4	5	6	8	10	15	20	
26	Mel Bridgman	4	5	6	8	10	15	20	
27	Lee Fogolin	4	5	6	8	10	15	20	
28	Gilles Meloche	4	5	6	8	10	15	20	
29	Garry Howatt	4	5	6	8	10	15	20	
30	Darryl Sittler	4	5	6	8	10	15	20	
31	Curt Bennett	4	5	6	8	10	15	20	
32	Andre St.Laurent	4	5	6	8	10	15	20	
33	Blair Chapman	4	5	6	8	10	15	20	
34	Keith Magnuson	4	5	6	8	10	15	20	35
35	Pierre Larouche	4	5	6	8	10	15	20	
36	Michel Plasse	4	5	6	8	10	15	20	
37	Gary Sargent	4	5	6	8	10	15	20	
38	Mike Walton	4	5	6	8	10	15	20	
39	Robert Picard RC	4	5	6	8	10	15	20	
40	Terry O'Reilly	4	5	6	8	10	15	20	
41	Dave Farrish	4	5	6	8	10	15	20	
42	Gary McAdam	4	5	6	8	10	15	20	
43	Joe Watson	4	5	6	8	10	15	20	
44	Yves Belanger	4	5	6	8	10	15	20	35
45	Steve Jensen	4	5	6	8	10	15	20	
46	Bob Stewart	4	5	6	8	10	15	20	
47	Darcy Rota	4	5	6	8	10	15	20	
48	Dennis Hextall	4	5	6	8	10	15	20	
49	Bert Marshall	4	5	6	8	10	15	20	
50	Ken Dryden	5	6	10	12	20	50	60	80
51	Peter Mahovlich	4	5	6	8	10	15	20	
52	Dennis Ververgaert	4	5	6	8	10	15	20	30
53	Inge Hammarstrom	4	5	6	8	10	15	20	30
54	Doug Favell	4	5	6	8	10	15	20	30
55	Steve Vickers	4	5	6	8	10	15	20	
56	Syl Apps	4	5	6	8	10	15	20	
57	Errol Thompson	4	5	6	8	10	15	20	
58	Don Luce	4	5	6	8	10	15	20	30
59	Mike Milbury	4	5	6	8	10	15	20	
60	Yvan Cournoyer	4	5	6	8	10	15	20	35
61	Kirk Bowman	4	5	6	8	10	15	20	
62	Billy Smith	4	5	6	8	10	15	20	
63	Lafleur/Bossy/Shutt LL	5	6	8	10	12	20	30	
64	Trott/Lafleur/Sitt LL	4	5	6	8	10	15	20	
65	Lafleur/Trott/Sitt LL	4	5	6	8	10	15	20	40
66	Schitz/Will/Polnich LL	4	5	6	8	10	15	20	35
67	Bossy/Espo/Shutt LL	5	6	8	10	12	20	25	40
68	Dryden/Parent/Gilb LL	5	6	8	10	12	20	25	40
69	Lafleur/Barber/Sitt LL	4	5	6	8	10	15	20	40
70	Parent/Dryden/Espo LL	5	6	8	10	12	20	25	40
71	Bob Kelly	4	5	6	8	10	15	20	
72	Ron Stackhouse	4	5	6	8	10	15	20	
73	Wayne Dillon	4	5	6	8	10	15	20	
74	Jim Rutherford	4	5	6	8	10	15	20	
75	Stan Mikita	4	5	6	8	10	15	20	35
76	Bob Gainey	4	5	6	8	10	15	20	35
77	Gerry Hart	4	5	6	8	10	15	20	
78	Lanny McDonald	4	5	6	8	10	15	20	
79	Brad Park	4	5	6	8	10	15	20	
80	Richard Martin	4	5	6	8	10	15	20	30
81	Bernie Wolfe	4	5	6	8	10	15	20	
82	Bob MacMillan	4	5	6	8	10	15	20	
83	Brad Maxwell RC	4	5	6	8	10	15	20	
84	Mike Fidler	4	5	6	8	10	15	20	
85	Carol Vadnais	4	5	6	8	10	15	20	
86	Don Lever	4	5	6	8	10	15	20	
87	Phil Myre	4	5	6	8	10	15	20	
88	Paul Gardner	4	5	6	8	10	15	20	30
89	Bob Murray	4	5	6	8	10	15	20	30
90	Guy Lafleur	5	6	8	10	12	20	25	50
91	Bob Murdoch	4	5	6	8	10	15	20	30
92	Ron Ellis	4	5	6	8	10	15	20	
93	Jude Drouin	4	5	6	8	10	15	20	
94	Jocelyn Guevremont	4	5	6	8	10	15	20	
95	Gilles Gilbert	4	5	6	8	10	15	20	30

#	Player	VG 3	VgEx 4	EX 5	ExMt 6	NM 7	NmMt 8	NmMt+ 8.5	MT 9
96	Bob Sirois	4	5	6	8	10	15	20	30
97	Tom Lysiak	4	5	6	8	10	15	20	
98	Andre Dupont	4	5	6	8	10	15	20	
99	Per-Olov Brasar RC	4	5	6	8	10	15	20	30
100	Phil Esposito	4	5	6	8	10	15	20	
101	J.P. Bordeleau	4	5	6	8	10	15	20	
102	Pierre Mondou RC	4	5	6	8	10	15	20	
103	Wayne Bianchin	4	5	6	8	10	15	20	
104	Dennis O'Brien	4	5	6	8	10	15	20	30
105	Glenn Resch	4	5	6	8	10	15	20	35
106	Dennis Polonich	4	5	6	8	10	15	20	
107	Kris Manery RC	4	5	6	8	10	15	20	
108	Bill Hajt	4	5	6	8	10	15	20	
109	Jere Gillis RC	4	5	6	8	10	15	20	30
110	Garry Unger	4	5	6	8	10	15	20	
111	Nick Beverley	4	5	6	8	10	15	20	
112	Pat Hickey	4	5	6	8	10	15	20	
113	Rick Middleton	4	5	6	8	10	15	20	
114	Orest Kindrachuk	4	5	6	8	10	15	20	
115	Mike Bossy RC	12	20	25	40	80	200	250	650
116	Pierre Bouchard	4	5	6	8	10	15	20	30
117	Alain Daigle	4	5	6	8	10	15	20	
118	Terry Martin	4	5	6	8	10	15	20	30
119	Tom Edur	4	5	6	8	10	15	20	
120	Marcel Dionne	4	5	6	8	10	20	25	40
121	Barry Beck RC	4	5	6	8	10	15	20	
122	Billy Lochead	4	5	6	8	10	15	20	
123	Paul Harrison RC	4	5	6	8	10	15	20	30
124	Wayne Cashman	4	5	6	8	10	15	20	
125	Rick MacLeish	4	5	6	8	10	15	20	
126	Bob Bourne	4	5	6	8	10	15	20	30
127	Ian Turnbull	4	5	6	8	10	15	20	
128	Gerry Meehan	4	5	6	8	10	15	20	
129	Eric Vail	4	5	6	8	10	15	20	30
130	Gilbert Perreault	4	5	6	8	10	15	20	30
131	Bob Dailey	4	5	6	8	10	15	20	
132	Dale McCourt RC	4	5	6	8	10	15	20	
133	John Wensink RC	4	5	6	8	10	15	20	
134	Bill Nyrop	4	5	6	8	10	15	20	
135	Ivan Boldirev	4	5	6	8	10	15	20	30
136	Lucien DeBlois RC	4	5	6	8	10	15	20	
137	Brian Spencer	4	5	6	8	10	15	20	
138	Tim Young	4	5	6	8	10	15	20	
139	Ron Sedlbauer	4	5	6	8	10	15	20	30
140	Gerry Cheevers	4	5	6	8	10	15	20	
141	Dennis Maruk	4	5	6	8	10	15	20	
142	Barry Dean	4	5	6	8	10	15	20	
143	Bernie Federko RC	5	6	10	15	30	60	100	300
144	Stefan Persson RC	4	5	6	8	10	15	20	30
145	Wilf Paiement	4	5	6	8	10	15	20	
146	Dale Tallon	4	5	6	8	10	15	20	30
147	Yvon Lambert	4	5	6	8	10	15	20	
148	Greg Joly	4	5	6	8	10	15	20	
149	Dean Talafous	4	5	6	8	10	15	20	
150	Don Edwards	4	5	6	8	10	15	20	
151	Butch Goring	4	5	6	8	10	15	20	
152	Tom Bladon	4	5	6	8	10	15	20	
153	Bob Nystrom	4	5	6	8	10	15	20	
154	Ron Greschner	4	5	6	8	10	15	20	
155	Jean Ratelle	4	5	6	8	10	15	20	
156	Russ Anderson RC	4	5	6	8	10	15	20	
157	John Marks	4	5	6	8	10	15	20	
158	Michel Larocque	4	5	6	8	10	15	20	
159	Paul Woods RC	4	5	6	8	10	15	20	
160	Mike Palmateer	4	5	6	8	10	15	20	30
161	Jim Lorentz	4	5	6	8	10	15	20	
162	Dave Lewis	4	5	6	8	10	15	20	
163	Harvey Bennett	4	5	6	8	10	15	20	
164	Rick Smith	4	5	6	8	10	15	20	
165	Reggie Leach	4	5	6	8	10	15	20	
166	Wayne Thomas	4	5	6	8	10	15	20	30
167	Dave Forbes	4	5	6	8	10	15	20	
168	Doug Wilson RC	5	6	8	10	12	30	40	100
169	Dan Bouchard	4	5	6	8	10	15	20	
170	Steve Shutt	4	5	6	8	10	15	20	
171	Mike Kaszycki RC	4	5	6	8	10	15	20	
172	Denis Herron	4	5	6	8	10	15	20	
173	Rick Bowness	4	5	6	8	10	15	20	
174	Rick Hampton	4	5	6	8	10	15	20	
175	Glen Sharpley	4	5	6	8	10	15	20	
176	Bill Barber	4	5	6	8	10	15	20	
177	Ron Duguay RC	5	6	8	10	12	25	30	80
178	Jim Schoenfeld	4	5	6	8	10	15	20	
179	Pierre Plante	4	5	6	8	10	15	20	
180	Jacques Lemaire	4	5	6	8	10	15	20	
181	Stan Jonathan	4	5	6	8	10	15	20	
182	Billy Harris	4	5	6	8	10	15	20	
183	Chris Oddleifson	4	5	6	8	10	15	20	
184	Jean Pronovost	4	5	6	8	10	15	20	

#	Player	VG 3	VgEx 4	EX 5	ExMt 6	NM 7	NmMt 8	NmMt+ 8.5	MT 9
185	Fred Barrett	4	5	6	8	10	15	20	
186	Ross Lonsberry	4	5	6	8	10	15	20	3
187	Mike McEwen	4	5	6	8	10	15	20	
188	Rene Robert	4	5	6	8	10	15	20	
189	J. Bob Kelly	4	5	6	8	10	15	20	
190	Serge Savard	4	5	6	8	10	15	20	
191	Dennis Kearns	4	5	6	8	10	15	20	
192	Flames Team	4	5	6	8	10	15	20	3
193	Bruins Team	4	5	6	8	10	15	20	
194	Sabres Team	4	5	6	8	10	15	20	
195	Blackhawks Team	4	5	6	8	10	15	20	30
196	Rockies Team	4	5	6	8	10	15	20	30
197	Red Wings Team	4	5	6	8	10	15	20	
198	Kings Team	4	5	6	8	10	15	20	30
199	North Stars Team	4	5	6	8	10	15	20	
200	Canadiens Team	4	5	6	8	10	15	20	30
201	Islanders Team	4	5	6	8	10	15	20	
202	Rangers Team	4	5	6	8	10	15	20	
203	Flyers Team	4	5	6	8	10	15	20	
204	Penguins Team	4	5	6	8	10	15	20	30
205	Blues Team	4	5	6	8	10	15	20	30
206	Maple Leafs Team	4	5	6	8	10	15	20	30
207	Canucks Team	4	5	6	8	10	15	20	
208	Capitals Team	4	5	6	8	10	15	20	30
209	Danny Gare	4	5	6	8	10	15	20	
210	Larry Robinson	4	5	6	8	10	15	20	
211	John Davidson	4	5	6	8	10	15	20	
212	Peter McNab	4	5	6	8	10	15	20	
213	Rick Kehoe	4	5	6	8	10	15	20	30
214	Terry Harper	4	5	6	8	10	15	20	
215	Bobby Clarke	4	5	6	8	10	15	20	30
216	Bryan Maxwell UER	4	5	6	8	10	15	20	
217	Ted Bulley RC	4	5	6	8	10	15	20	
218	Red Berenson	4	5	6	8	10	15	20	
219	Ron Grahame	4	5	6	8	10	15	20	30
220	Clark Gillies	4	5	6	8	10	15	20	
221	Dave Maloney	4	5	6	8	10	15	20	
222	Derek Smith RC	4	5	6	8	10	15	20	30
223	Wayne Stephenson	4	5	6	8	10	15	20	
224	John Van Boxmeer	4	5	6	8	10	15	20	
225	Dave Schultz	4	5	6	8	10	15	20	
226	Reed Larson RC	4	5	6	8	10	15	20	
227	Rejean Houle	4	5	6	8	10	15	20	
228	Doug Hicks	4	5	6	8	10	15	20	30
229	Mike Murphy	4	5	6	8	10	15	20	
230	Pete Lopresti	4	5	6	8	10	15	20	
231	Jerry Korab	4	5	6	8	10	15	20	
232	Ed Westfall	4	5	6	8	10	15	20	30
233	Greg Malone RC	4	5	6	8	10	15	20	
234	Paul Holmgren	4	5	6	8	10	15	20	
235	Walt Tkaczuk	4	5	6	8	10	15	20	30
236	Don Marcotte	4	5	6	8	10	15	20	
237	Ron Low	4	5	6	8	10	15	20	30
238	Rick Chartraw	4	5	6	8	10	15	20	30
239	Cliff Koroll	4	5	6	8	10	15	20	
240	Borje Salming	4	5	6	8	10	15	20	
241	Roland Eriksson	4	5	6	8	10	15	20	
242	Ric Seiling RC	4	5	6	8	10	15	20	
243	Jim Bedard RC	4	5	6	8	10	15	20	
244	Peter Lee RC	4	5	6	8	10	15	20	
245	Denis Potvin	4	5	6	8	10	15	20	30
246	Greg Polis	4	5	6	8	10	15	20	
247	Jimmy Watson	4	5	6	8	10	15	20	
248	Bobby Schmautz	4	5	6	8	10	15	20	
249	Doug Risebrough	4	5	6	8	10	15	20	
250	Tony Esposito	4	5	6	8	10	15	20	40
251	Nick Libett	4	5	6	8	10	15	20	
252	Ron Zanussi RC	4	5	6	8	10	15	20	
253	Andre Savard	4	5	6	8	10	15	20	
254	Dave Burrows	4	5	6	8	10	15	20	
255	Ulf Nilsson	4	5	6	8	10	15	20	
256	Richard Mulhern	4	5	6	8	10	15	20	
257	Don Saleski	4	5	6	8	10	15	20	
258	Wayne Merrick	4	5	6	8	10	15	20	30
259	Checklist 133-264	5	6	8	10	12	20	30	
260	Guy Lapointe	4	5	6	8	10	15	20	
261	Grant Mulvey	4	5	6	8	10	15	20	
262	Stanley Cup Semifinals	4	5	6	8	10	15	20	40
263	Stanley Cup Semifinals	4	5	6	8	10	15	20	
264	Stanley Cup Finals	4	5	6	8	10	15	20	30
265	Bob Sauve	4	5	6	8	10	15	20	
266	Randy Manery	4	5	6	8	10	15	20	
267	Bill Fairbairn	4	5	6	8	10	15	20	
268	Garry Monahan	4	5	6	8	10	15	20	
269	Colin Campbell	4	5	6	8	10	15	20	
270	Dan Newman	4	5	6	8	10	15	20	30
271	Dwight Foster RC	4	5	6	8	10	15	20	30
272	Larry Carriere	4	5	6	8	10	15	20	
273	Michel Bergeron	4	5	6	8	10	15	20	30

	VG 3	VgEx 4	EX 5	ExMt 6	NM 7	NmMt 8	NmMt+ 8.5	MT 9
Scott Garland	4	5	6	8	10	15	20	
Bill McKenzie	4	5	6	8	10	15	20	
Garnet Bailey	4	5	6	8	10	15	20	
Ed Kea	4	5	6	8	10	15	20	
Dave Gardner	4	5	6	8	10	15	20	
Bruce Affleck	4	5	6	8	10	15	20	
Bruce Boudreau RC	4	5	6	8	10	15	20	
Jean Hamel	4	5	6	8	10	15	20	
Kurt Walker RC	4	5	6	8	10	15	20	
Denis Dupere	4	5	6	8	10	15	20	
Gordie Lane	4	5	6	8	10	15	20	
Bobby Lalonde	4	5	6	8	10	15	20	
Pit Martin	4	5	6	8	10	15	20	
Jean Potvin	4	5	6	8	10	15	20	
Jimmy Jones RC	4	5	6	8	10	15	20	
Dave Hutchinson	4	5	6	8	10	15	20	
Pete Stemkowski	4	5	6	8	10	15	20	
Mike Christie	4	5	6	8	10	15	20	30
Bill Riley	4	5	6	8	10	15	20	
Rey Comeau	4	5	6	8	10	15	20	
Jack McIlhargey RC	4	5	6	8	10	15	20	
Tom Younghans RC	4	5	6	8	10	15	20	
Mario Faubert RC	4	5	6	8	10	15	20	
Checklist Card	5	6	8	10	12	20	30	
Rob Palmer RC	4	5	6	8	10	15	20	
Dave Hudson	4	5	6	8	10	15	20	
Bobby Orr	6	8	12	20	35	80	100	175
Lorne Stamler RC	4	5	6	8	10	15	20	
Curt Ridley	4	5	6	8	10	15	20	
Greg Smith	4	5	6	8	10	15	20	
Jerry Butler	4	5	6	8	10	15	20	
Gary Doak	4	5	6	8	10	15	20	30
Danny Grant	4	5	6	8	10	15	20	30
Mark Suzor RC	4	5	6	8	10	15	20	
Rick Bragnalo	4	5	6	8	10	15	20	
John Gould	4	5	6	8	10	15	20	
Sheldon Kannegiesser	4	5	6	8	10	15	20	
Bobby Sheehan	4	5	6	8	10	15	20	
Randy Carlyle RC	5	6	8	10	15	40		
Lorne Henning	4	5	6	8	10	15	20	
Tom Williams	4	5	6	8	10	15	20	30
Ron Andruff	4	5	6	8	10	15	20	
Bryan Watson	4	5	6	8	10	15	20	
Willi Plett	4	5	6	8	10	15	20	
John Grisdale	4	5	6	8	10	15	20	
Brian Sutter RC	5	6	10	12	25	30	60	
Trevor Johansen RC	4	5	6	8	10	15	20	30
Vic Venasky	4	5	6	8	10	15	20	
Rick Lapointe	4	5	6	8	10	15	20	
Ron Delorme RC	4	5	6	8	10	15	20	
Yvon Labre	4	5	6	8	10	15	20	
Bryan Trottier AS UER	5	6	8	10	12	20	25	40
Guy Lafleur AS	4	5	6	8	10	15	20	35
Clark Gillies AS	4	5	6	8	10	15	20	30
Borje Salming AS	4	5	6	8	10	15	20	30
Larry Robinson AS	4	5	6	8	10	15	20	30
Ken Dryden AS	5	6	8	10	12	25	30	40
Darryl Sittler AS	4	5	6	8	10	15	20	53
Terry O'Reilly AS	4	5	6	8	10	15	20	30
Steve Shutt AS	4	5	6	8	10	15	20	30
Denis Potvin AS	4	5	6	8	10	15	20	30
Serge Savard AS	4	5	6	8	10	15	20	30
Don Edwards AS	4	5	6	8	10	15	20	30
Glenn Goldup	4	5	6	8	10	15	20	
Mike Kitchen	4	5	6	8	10	15	20	
Bob Girard	4	5	6	8	10	15	20	
Guy Chouinard	4	5	6	8	10	15	20	
Randy Holt	4	5	6	8	10	15	20	
Jim Roberts	4	5	6	8	10	15	20	
Dave Logan RC	4	5	6	8	10	15	20	
Walt McKechnie	4	5	6	8	10	15	20	
Brian Glennie	4	5	6	8	10	15	20	
Ralph Klassen	4	5	6	8	10	15	20	
Gord Smith	4	5	6	8	10	15	20	
Ken Houston	4	5	6	8	10	15	20	
Bob Manno RC	4	5	6	8	10	15	20	
Jean-Paul Parise	4	5	6	8	10	15	20	
Don Ashby	4	5	6	8	10	15	20	
Fred Stanfield	4	5	6	8	10	15	20	
Dave Taylor RC	6	10	15	20	25	50	60	100
Nelson Pyatt	4	5	6	8	10	15	20	
Blair Stewart RC	4	5	6	8	10	15	20	
David Shand	4	5	6	8	10	15	20	
Hilliard Graves	4	5	6	8	10	15	20	
Bob Hess	4	5	6	8	10	15	20	
Dave Williams	4	5	6	8	10	15	20	
Larry Wright RC	4	5	6	8	10	15	20	
Larry Brown	4	5	6	8	10	15	20	
Gary Croteau	4	5	6	8	10	15	20	

		VG 3	VgEx 4	EX 5	ExMt 6	NM 7	NmMt 8	NmMt+ 8.5	MT 9
363	Rick Green	4	5	6	8	10	15	20	
364	Bill Clement	4	5	6	8	10	15	20	
365	Gerry O'Flaherty	4	5	6	8	10	15	20	
366	John Baby RC	4	5	6	8	10	15	20	
367	Nick Fotiu	4	5	6	8	10	15	20	
368	Pat Price	4	5	6	8	10	15	20	
369	Bert Wilson	4	5	6	8	10	15	20	
370	Bryan Lefley	4	5	6	8	10	15	20	
371	Ron Lalonde	4	5	6	8	10	15	20	
372	Bobby Simpson	4	5	6	8	10	15	20	
373	Doug Grant	4	5	6	8	10	15	20	
374	Pat Boutette	4	5	6	8	10	15	20	
375	Bob Paradise	4	5	6	8	10	15	20	
376	Mario Tremblay	4	5	6	8	10	15	20	
377	Darryl Edestrand	4	5	6	8	10	15	20	
378	Andy Spruce RC	4	5	6	8	10	15	20	
379	Jack Brownschidle RC	4	5	6	8	10	15	20	
380	Harold Snepsts	4	5	6	8	10	15	20	30
381	Al MacAdam	4	5	6	8	10	15	20	
382	Neil Komadoski	4	5	6	8	10	15	20	
383	Don Awrey	4	5	6	8	10	15	20	
384	Ron Schock	4	5	6	8	10	15	20	
385	Gary Simmons	4	5	6	8	10	15	20	30
386	Fred Ahern	4	5	6	8	10	15	20	
387	Larry Bolonchuk	4	5	6	8	10	15	20	
388	Brad Gassoff RC	4	5	6	8	10	15	20	
389	Chuck Arnason	4	5	6	8	10	15	20	
390	Barry Gibbs	4	5	6	8	10	15	20	
391	Jack Valiquette	4	5	6	8	10	15	20	
392	Doug Halward	4	5	6	8	10	15	20	
393	Hartland Monahan	4	5	6	8	10	15	20	
394	Rod Seiling	4	5	6	8	10	15	20	
395	George Ferguson	4	5	6	8	10	15	20	
396	Al Cameron	4	5	6	8	10	15	20	

—Randy Carlye RC #312 PSA 9 (Mt) sold for $643.99 (eBay; 2/14)
—Randy Carlye RC #312 PSA 10 (Gem) sold for $512 (eBay; 4/12)
—Bernie Federko RC #143 PSA 10 (Gem) sold for $1,830 (eBay; 3/12)
—Doug Wilson RC #168 PSA 10 (Gem) sold for $714 (eBay; 9/15)

1978-79 Topps

		VG 3	VgEx 4	EX 5	ExMt 6	NM 7	NmMt 8	NmMt+ 8.5	MT 9
1	Mike Bossy HL	6	8	10	12	15	30		
2	Phil Esposito HL	4	5	6	8	10	12	15	20
3	Guy Lafleur HL	4	5	6	8	10	12	15	20
4	Darryl Sittler HL	4	5	6	8	10	12	15	20
5	Garry Unger HL	4	5	6	8	10	12	15	20
6	Gary Edwards	4	5	6	8	10	12	15	20
7	Rick Blight	4	5	6	8	10	12	15	20
8	Larry Patey	4	5	6	8	10	12	15	20
9	Craig Ramsay	4	5	6	8	10	12		
10	Bryan Trottier	5	6	8	10	12	15	20	25
11	Don Murdoch	4	5	6	8	10	12	15	20
12	Phil Russell	4	5	6	8	10	12	15	20
13	Doug Jarvis	4	5	6	8	10	12	15	20
14	Gene Carr	4	5	6	8	10	12	15	20
15	Bernie Parent	4	5	6	8	10	12	15	20
16	Perry Miller	4	5	6	8	10	12	15	20
17	Kent-Erik Andersson RC	4	5	6	8	10	12	15	20
18	Gregg Sheppard	4	5	6	8	10	12	15	20
19	Dennis Owchar	4	5	6	8	10	12	15	
20	Rogatien Vachon	4	5	6	8	10	12	15	
21	Dan Maloney	4	5	6	8	10	12	15	
22	Guy Charron	4	5	6	8	10	12	15	20
23	Dick Redmond	4	5	6	8	10	12	15	20
24	Checklist 1-132	4	5	6	8	10	12	15	25
25	Anders Hedberg	4	5	6	8	10	12	15	20
26	Mel Bridgman	4	5	6	8	10	12	15	20
27	Lee Fogolin	4	5	6	8	10	12	15	
28	Gilles Meloche	4	5	6	8	10	12	15	20
29	Garry Howatt	4	5	6	8	10	12	15	20
30	Darryl Sittler	4	5	6	8	10	12	15	20
31	Curt Bennett	4	5	6	8	10	12	15	20
32	Andre St.Laurent	4	5	6	8	10	12	15	
33	Blair Chapman	4	5	6	8	10	12	15	20
34	Keith Magnuson	4	5	6	8	10	12	15	20
35	Pierre Larouche	4	5	6	8	10	12	15	20
36	Michel Plasse	4	5	6	8	10	12	15	
37	Gary Sargent	4	5	6	8	10	12	15	20
38	Mike Walton	4	5	6	8	10	12	15	20
39	Robert Picard RC	4	5	6	8	10	12	15	20
40	Terry O'Reilly	4	5	6	8	10	12	15	20
41	Dave Farrish	4	5	6	8	10	12	15	20
42	Gary McAdam	4	5	6	8	10	12	15	
43	Joe Watson	4	5	6	8	10	12	15	
44	Yves Belanger	4	5	6	8	10	12	15	20
45	Steve Jensen	4	5	6	8	10	12	15	20
46	Bob Stewart	4	5	6	8	10	12	15	20
47	Darcy Rota	4	5	6	8	10	12	15	
48	Dennis Hextall	4	5	6	8	10	12	15	20

#	Player	VG 3	VgEx 4	EX 5	ExMt 6	NM 7	NmMt 8	NmMt+ 8.5	MT 9
49	Bert Marshall	4	5	6	8	10	12	15	20
50	Ken Dryden	5	6	8	10	12	15	20	25
51	Peter Mahovlich	4	5	6	8	10	12	15	20
52	Dennis Ververgaert	4	5	6	8	10	12	15	20
53	Inge Hammarstrom	4	5	6	8	10	12	15	
54	Doug Favell	4	5	6	8	10	12	15	20
55	Steve Vickers	4	5	6	8	10	12	15	
56	Syl Apps	4	5	6	8	10	12	15	20
57	Errol Thompson	4	5	6	8	10	12	15	20
58	Don Luce	4	5	6	8	10	12	15	20
59	Mike Milbury	4	5	6	8	10	12	15	20
60	Yvan Cournoyer	4	5	6	8	10	12	15	20
61	Kirk Bowman	4	5	6	8	10	12	15	20
62	Billy Smith	4	5	6	8	10	12	15	20
63	Lafleur/Bossy/Shutt LL	4	5	6	8	10	12	20	25
64	Trott/Lafleur/Sitt LL	4	5	6	8	10	12	15	
65	Lafleur/Trott/Sitt LL	4	5	6	8	10	12	15	20
66	Schltz/Wil/Polnich LL	4	5	6	8	10	12	15	20
67	Bossy/Espo/Shutt LL	4	5	6	8	10	12	15	20
68	Dryden/Parent/Gilb LL	4	5	6	8	10	12	15	20
69	Lafleur/Barber/Sitt LL	4	5	6	8	10	12	15	20
70	Parent/Dryden/Espo LL	4	5	6	8	10	12	15	20
71	Bob Kelly	4	5	6	8	10	12	15	20
72	Ron Stackhouse	4	5	6	8	10	12	15	20
73	Wayne Dillon	4	5	6	8	10	12	15	20
74	Jim Rutherford	4	5	6	8	10	12	15	20
75	Stan Mikita	4	5	6	8	10	12	15	25
76	Bob Gainey	4	5	6	8	10	12	15	20
77	Gerry Hart	4	5	6	8	10	12	15	20
78	Lanny McDonald	4	5	6	8	10	12	15	20
79	Brad Park	4	5	6	8	10	12	15	20
80	Richard Martin	4	5	6	8	10	12	15	
81	Bernie Wolfe	4	5	6	8	10	12	15	20
82	Bob MacMillan	4	5	6	8	10	12	15	20
83	Brad Maxwell RC	4	5	6	8	10	12	15	20
84	Mike Fidler	4	5	6	8	10	12	15	20
85	Carol Vadnais	4	5	6	8	10	12	15	
86	Don Lever	4	5	6	8	10	12	15	20
87	Phil Myre	4	5	6	8	10	12	15	20
88	Paul Gardner	4	5	6	8	10	12	15	20
89	Bob Murray	4	5	6	8	10	12	15	20
90	Guy Lafleur	4	5	6	8	10	12	20	25
91	Bob Murdoch	4	5	6	8	10	12	15	20
92	Ron Ellis	4	5	6	8	10	12	15	
93	Jude Drouin	4	5	6	8	10	12	15	20
94	Jocelyn Guevremont	4	5	6	8	10	12	15	20
95	Gilles Gilbert	4	5	6	8	10	12	15	20
96	Bob Sirois	4	5	6	8	10	12	15	20
97	Tom Lysiak	4	5	6	8	10	12	15	20
98	Andre Dupont	4	5	6	8	10	12	15	20
99	Per-Olov Brasar RC	4	5	6	8	10	12	15	20
100	Phil Esposito	4	5	6	8	10	12	15	25
101	J.P. Bordeleau	4	5	6	8	10	12	15	20
102	Pierre Mondou RC	4	5	6	8	10	12	15	20
103	Wayne Bianchin	4	5	6	8	10	12	15	20
104	Dennis O'Brien	4	5	6	8	10	12	15	20
105	Glenn Resch	4	5	6	8	10	12	15	20
106	Dennis Polonich	4	5	6	8	10	12	15	20
107	Kris Manery RC	4	5	6	8	10	12	15	
108	Bill Hajt	4	5	6	8	10	12	15	20
109	Jere Gillis RC	4	5	6	8	10	12	15	20
110	Garry Unger	4	5	6	8	10	12	15	20
111	Nick Beverley	4	5	6	8	10	12	15	20
112	Pat Hickey	4	5	6	8	10	12	15	20
113	Rick Middleton	4	5	6	8	10	12	15	20
114	Orest Kindrachuk	4	5	6	8	10	12	15	20
115	Mike Bossy RC	10	12	15	30	50	60	80	120
116	Pierre Bouchard	4	5	6	8	10	12	15	20
117	Alain Daigle	4	5	6	8	10	12	15	20
118	Terry Martin	4	5	6	8	10	12	15	20
119	Tom Edur	4	5	6	8	10	12	15	20
120	Marcel Dionne	4	5	6	8	10	12	15	25
121	Barry Beck RC	4	5	6	8	10	12	15	20
122	Billy Lochead	4	5	6	8	10	12	15	20
123	Paul Harrison	4	5	6	8	10	12	15	20
124	Wayne Cashman	4	5	6	8	10	12	15	
125	Rick MacLeish	4	5	6	8	10	12	15	20
126	Bob Bourne	4	5	6	8	10	12	15	20
127	Ian Turnbull	4	5	6	8	10	12	15	20
128	Gerry Meehan	4	5	6	8	10	12	15	20
129	Eric Vail	4	5	6	8	10	12	15	20
130	Gilbert Perreault	4	5	6	8	10	12	15	20
131	Bob Dailey	4	5	6	8	10	12	15	20
132	Dale McCourt RC	4	5	6	8	10	12	15	20
133	John Wensink RC	4	5	6	8	10	12	15	20
134	Bill Nyrop	4	5	6	8	10	12	15	
135	Ivan Boldirev	4	5	6	8	10	12	15	20
136	Lucien DeBlois RC	4	5	6	8	10	12	15	20
137	Brian Spencer	4	5	6	8	10	12	15	20

#	Player	VG 3	VgEx 4	EX 5	ExMt 6	NM 7	NmMt 8	NmMt+ 8.5	MT 9
138	Tim Young	4	5	6	8	10	12	15	20
139	Ron Sedlbauer	4	5	6	8	10	12	15	20
140	Gerry Cheevers	4	5	6	8	10	12	15	20
141	Dennis Maruk	4	5	6	8	10	12	15	20
142	Barry Dean	4	5	6	8	10	12	15	
143	Bernie Federko RC	5	6	8	10	12	15	20	30
144	Stefan Persson RC	4	5	6	8	10	12	15	20
145	Wilf Paiement	4	5	6	8	10	12	15	20
146	Dale Tallon	4	5	6	8	10	12	15	20
147	Yvon Lambert	4	5	6	8	10	12	15	20
148	Greg Joly	4	5	6	8	10	12	15	20
149	Dean Talafous	4	5	6	8	10	12	15	
150	Don Edwards AS2	4	5	6	8	10	12	15	20
151	Butch Goring	4	5	6	8	10	12	15	20
152	Tom Bladon	4	5	6	8	10	12	15	20
153	Bob Nystrom	4	5	6	8	10	12	15	20
154	Ron Greschner	4	5	6	8	10	12	15	20
155	Jean Ratelle	4	5	6	8	10	12	15	20
156	Russ Anderson RC	4	5	6	8	10	12	15	20
157	John Marks	4	5	6	8	10	12	15	20
158	Michel Larocque	4	5	6	8	10	12	15	20
159	Paul Woods RC	4	5	6	8	10	12	15	20
160	Mike Palmateer	4	5	6	8	10	12	15	20
161	Jim Lorentz	4	5	6	8	10	12	15	20
162	Dave Lewis	4	5	6	8	10	12	15	
163	Harvey Bennett	4	5	6	8	10	12	15	20
164	Rick Smith	4	5	6	8	10	12	15	20
165	Reggie Leach	4	5	6	8	10	12	15	20
166	Wayne Thomas	4	5	6	8	10	12	15	20
167	Dave Forbes	4	5	6	8	10	12	15	20
168	Doug Wilson RC	5	6	8	10	12	15	20	25
169	Dan Bouchard	4	5	6	8	10	12	15	20
170	Steve Shutt	4	5	6	8	10	12	15	20
171	Mike Kaszycki RC	4	5	6	8	10	12	15	20
172	Denis Herron	4	5	6	8	10	12	15	20
173	Rick Bowness	4	5	6	8	10	12	15	
174	Rick Hampton	4	5	6	8	10	12	15	20
175	Glen Sharpley	4	5	6	8	10	12	15	20
176	Bill Barber	4	5	6	8	10	12	15	20
177	Ron Duguay RC	4	5	6	8	10	12	15	25
178	Jim Schoenfeld	4	5	6	8	10	12	15	20
179	Pierre Plante	4	5	6	8	10	12	15	20
180	Jacques Lemaire	4	5	6	8	10	12	15	20
181	Stan Jonathan	4	5	6	8	10	12	15	20
182	Billy Harris	4	5	6	8	10	12	15	20
183	Chris Oddleifson	4	5	6	8	10	12	15	20
184	Jean Pronovost	4	5	6	8	10	12	15	20
185	Fred Barrett	4	5	6	8	10	12	15	20
186	Ross Lonsberry	4	5	6	8	10	12	15	20
187	Mike McEwen	4	5	6	8	10	12	15	20
188	Rene Robert	4	5	6	8	10	12	15	20
189	J. Bob Kelly	4	5	6	8	10	12	15	20
190	Serge Savard AS2	4	5	6	8	10	12	15	20
191	Dennis Kearns	4	5	6	8	10	12	15	20
192	Flames Team CL	4	5	6	8	10	12	15	20
193	Bruins Team CL	4	5	6	8	10	12	15	20
194	Sabres Team CL	4	5	6	8	10	12	15	20
195	Blackhawks Team CL	4	5	6	8	10	12	15	20
196	Rockies Team CL	4	5	6	8	10	12	15	20
197	Red Wings Team CL	4	5	6	8	10	12	15	20
198	Kings Team CL	4	5	6	8	10	12	15	20
199	North Stars Team CL	4	5	6	8	10	12	15	20
200	Canadiens Team CL	4	5	6	8	10	12	15	20
201	Islanders Team CL	4	5	6	8	10	12	15	20
202	Rangers Team CL	4	5	6	8	10	12	15	20
203	Flyers Team CL	4	5	6	8	10	12	15	20
204	Penguins Team CL	4	5	6	8	10	12	15	20
205	Blues Team CL	4	5	6	8	10	12	15	20
206	Maple Leafs Team CL	4	5	6	8	10	12	15	20
207	Canucks Team CL	4	5	6	8	10	12	15	20
208	Capitals Team CL	4	5	6	8	10	12	15	20
209	Danny Gare	4	5	6	8	10	12	15	20
210	Larry Robinson	4	5	6	8	10	12	15	25
211	John Davidson	4	5	6	8	10	12	15	20
212	Peter McNab	4	5	6	8	10	12	15	20
213	Rick Kehoe	4	5	6	8	10	12	15	20
214	Terry Harper	4	5	6	8	10	12	15	20
215	Bobby Clarke	4	5	6	8	10	12	15	25
216	Bryan Maxwell UER	4	5	6	8	10	12	15	20
217	Ted Bulley	4	5	6	8	10	12	15	20
218	Red Berenson	4	5	6	8	10	12	15	
219	Ron Grahame	4	5	6	8	10	12	15	20
220	Clark Gillies AS1	4	5	6	8	10	12	15	20
221	Dave Maloney	4	5	6	8	10	12	15	20
222	Derek Smith RC	4	5	6	8	10	12	15	20
223	Wayne Stephenson	4	5	6	8	10	12	15	20
224	John Van Boxmeer	4	5	6	8	10	12	15	
225	Dave Schultz	4	5	6	8	10	12	15	20
226	Reed Larson RC	4	5	6	8	10	12	15	20

	VG 3	VgEx 4	EX 5	ExMt 6	NM 7	NmMt 8	NmMt+ 8.5	MT 9
Rejean Houle	4	5	6	8	10	12	15	20
Doug Hicks	4	5	6	8	10	12	15	20
Mike Murphy	4	5	6	8	10	12	15	20
Pete Lopresti	4	5	6	8	10	12	15	20
Jerry Korab	4	5	6	8	10	12	15	
Ed Westfall	4	5	6	8	10	12	15	20
Greg Malone RC	4	5	6	8	10	12	15	20
Paul Holmgren	4	5	6	8	10	12	15	20
Walt Tkaczuk	4	5	6	8	10	12	15	20
Don Marcotte	4	5	6	8	10	12	15	20
Ron Low	4	5	6	8	10	12	15	20
Rick Chartraw	4	5	6	8	10	12	15	20
Cliff Koroll	4	5	6	8	10	12	15	20
Borje Salming	4	5	6	8	10	12	15	20
Roland Eriksson	4	5	6	8	10	12	15	20
Ric Seiling RC	4	5	6	8	10	12	15	20
Jim Bedard RC	4	5	6	8	10	12	15	20
Peter Lee RC	4	5	6	8	10	12	15	20
Denis Potvin	4	5	6	8	10	12	15	25
Greg Polis	4	5	6	8	10	12	15	
Jimmy Watson	4	5	6	8	10	12	15	20
Bobby Schmautz	4	5	6	8	10	12	15	
Doug Risebrough	4	5	6	8	10	12	15	20
Tony Esposito	4	5	6	8	10	12	15	20
Nick Libett	4	5	6	8	10	12	15	
Ron Zanussi RC	4	5	6	8	10	12	15	20
Andre Savard	4	5	6	8	10	12	15	20
Dave Burrows	4	5	6	8	10	12	15	20
Ulf Nilsson	4	5	6	8	10	12	15	20
Richard Mulhern	4	5	6	8	10	12	15	20
Don Saleski	4	5	6	8	10	12	15	20
Wayne Merrick	4	5	6	8	10	12	15	20
Checklist 133-264	4	5	6	8	10	12	15	25
Guy Lapointe	4	5	6	8	10	12	15	20
Grant Mulvey	4	5	6	8	10	12	15	20
Stanley Cup: Semis	4	5	6	8	10	12	15	20
Stanley Cup: Semis	4	5	6	8	10	12	15	20
Stanley Cup Finals	4	5	6	8	10	12	15	20

Mike Bossy RC #115 BGS 9.5 (Gem) sold for $302 (eBay; 6/12)
Mike Bossy RC #115 PSA 10 (Gem) sold for $1,302 (Memory Lane; 6/12)

1979-80 O-Pee-Chee

	VG 3	VgEx 4	EX 5	ExMt 6	NM 7	NmMt 8	NmMt+ 8.5	MT 9
Bossy/Dionne/Lafleur LL	6	10	12	15	40	135		
Trott/Lafleur/Dionne LL	4	5	6	8	15	25	30	
Trott/Dionne/Lafleur LL	4	6	8	10	15	60	80	
Williams/Holt/Schultz LL	4	4	5	6	10	25		
Bossy/Dionne/Gardner LL	4	6	8	12	20	30	50	150
Dryden/Resch/Parent LL	4	5	6	8	15	25	30	100
Lafleur/Bossy/Trott/ LL	4	5	6	8	15	25	30	
Dryden/Espo/Parent LL	4	5	6	8	15	60	80	120
Greg Malone	4	4	5	6	10	15	20	
Rick Middleton	4	4	5	6	10	15	20	50
Greg Smith	4	4	5	6	10	15	20	35
Rene Robert	4	4	5	6	10	15	20	
Doug Risebrough	4	4	5	6	10	15	20	
Bob Kelly	4	4	5	6	10	15	20	
Walt Tkaczuk	4	4	5	6	10	15	20	35
John Marks	4	4	5	6	10	15	20	
Willie Huber RC	4	4	5	6	10	15	20	35
Wayne Gretzky UER RC#{80 GP not 60	▲800	1,000	1,500	▲2,000	2,500	▲6,500	▲12,000	▲40,000
Ron Sedlbauer	4	4	5	6	10	15	20	35
Glenn Resch AS2	4	4	5	6	10	15	20	35
Blair Chapman	4	4	5	6	10	15	20	
Ron Zanussi	4	4	5	6	10	15	20	
Brad Park	4	5	6	8	12	30		
Yvon Lambert	4	4	5	6	10	15	20	35
Andre Savard	4	4	5	6	10	15	20	
Jimmy Watson	4	4	5	6	10	15	20	
Hal Philipoff RC	4	4	5	6	10	15	20	
Dan Bouchard	4	4	5	6	10	15	20	
Bob Sirois	4	4	5	6	10	15	20	35
Ulf Nilsson	4	4	5	6	10	15	20	
Mike Murphy	4	4	5	6	10	15	20	
Stefan Persson	4	4	5	6	10	15	20	
Garry Unger	4	4	5	6	10	15	20	35
Rejean Houle	4	4	5	6	10	15	20	35
Barry Beck	4	4	5	6	10	15	20	
Tim Young	4	4	5	6	10	15	20	
Rick Dudley	4	4	5	6	10	15	20	35
Wayne Stephenson	4	4	5	6	10	15	20	
Peter McNab	4	4	5	6	10	15	20	35
Borje Salming AS2	4	4	5	6	10	15	20	
Tom Lysiak	4	4	5	6	10	15	20	
Don Maloney RC	4	4	5	6	10	15	20	40
Mike Rogers	4	4	5	6	10	15	20	
Dave Lewis	4	4	5	6	10	15	20	
Peter Lee	4	4	5	6	10	15	20	35
Marty Howe	4	4	5	6	10	15	20	40

		VG 3	VgEx 4	EX 5	ExMt 6	NM 7	NmMt 8	NmMt+ 8.5	MT 9
47	Serge Bernier	4	4	5	6	10	15	20	
48	Paul Woods	4	4	5	6	10	15	20	
49	Bob Sauve	4	4	5	6	10	15	20	
50	Larry Robinson AS1	4	5	6	8	12	40		
51	Tom Gorence RC	4	4	5	6	10	15	20	35
52	Gary Sargent	4	4	5	6	10	15	20	
53	Thomas Gradin RC	4	4	5	6	10	15	20	
54	Dean Talafous	4	4	5	6	10	15	20	
55	Bob Murray	4	4	5	6	10	15	20	35
56	Bob Bourne	4	4	5	6	10	15	20	
57	Larry Patey	4	4	5	6	10	15	20	
58	Ross Lonsberry	4	4	5	6	10	15	20	35
59	Rick Smith UER	4	4	5	6	10	15	20	35
60	Guy Chouinard	4	4	5	6	10	15	20	35
61	Danny Gare	4	4	5	6	10	15	20	
62	Jim Bedard	4	4	5	6	10	15	20	
63	Dale McCourt UER	4	4	5	6	10	15	20	
64	Steve Payne RC	4	4	5	6	10	30		
65	Pat Hughes RC	4	4	5	6	10	15	20	35
66	Mike McEwen	4	4	5	6	10	15	20	35
67	Reg Kerr RC	4	4	5	6	10	15	20	35
68	Walt McKechnie	4	4	5	6	10	15	20	
69	Michel Plasse	4	4	5	6	10	15	20	
70	Denis Potvin AS1	4	4	5	6	10	15	20	
71	Dave Dryden	4	4	5	6	10	15	20	40
72	Gary McAdam	4	4	5	6	10	15	20	35
73	Andre St.Laurent	4	4	5	6	10	15	20	
74	Jerry Korab	4	4	5	6	10	15	20	
75	Rick MacLeish	4	4	5	6	10	15	20	40
76	Dennis Kearns	4	4	5	6	10	15	20	
77	Jean Pronovost	4	4	5	6	10	15	20	35
78	Ron Greschner	4	4	5	6	10	15	20	
79	Wayne Cashman	4	4	5	6	10	15	20	35
80	Tony Esposito	4	5	6	8	12	15	20	35
81	Jets Logo CL	5	8	10	12	20	30	40	80
82	Oilers Logo CL	6	10	12	20	25	40	50	150
83	Stanley Cup Finals	4	5	6	30	40	50		
84	Brian Sutter	4	4	5	6	10	15	20	40
85	Gerry Cheevers	4	4	5	6	10	15	20	
86	Pat Hickey	4	4	5	6	10	15	20	
87	Mike Kaszycki	4	4	5	6	10	15	20	35
88	Grant Mulvey	4	4	5	6	10	15	20	
89	Derek Smith	4	4	5	6	10	15	20	35
90	Steve Shutt	4	4	5	6	10	15	20	
91	Robert Picard	4	4	5	6	10	15	20	
92	Dan Labraaten	4	4	5	6	10	15	20	
93	Glen Sharpley	4	4	5	6	10	15	20	
94	Denis Herron	4	4	5	6	10	15	20	
95	Reggie Leach	4	4	5	6	10	15	20	
96	John Van Boxmeer	4	4	5	6	10	15	20	
97	Tiger Williams	4	4	5	6	10	20	25	50
98	Butch Goring	4	4	5	6	10	15	20	35
99	Don Marcotte	4	4	5	6	10	15	20	
100	Bryan Trottier AS1	4	5	6	8	12	30	40	
101	Serge Savard AS2	4	4	5	6	10	15	20	
102	Cliff Koroll	4	4	5	6	10	15	20	
103	Gary Smith	4	4	5	6	10	15	20	
104	Al MacAdam	4	4	5	6	10	15	20	35
105	Don Edwards	4	4	5	6	10	15	20	
106	Errol Thompson	4	4	5	6	10	15	20	
107	Andre Lacroix	4	4	5	6	10	15	20	35
108	Marc Tardif	4	4	5	6	10	15	20	35
109	Rick Kehoe	4	4	5	6	10	15	20	
110	John Davidson	4	4	5	6	10	15	20	
111	Behn Wilson RC	4	4	5	6	10	15	20	35
112	Doug Jarvis	4	4	5	6	10	15	20	35
113	Tom Rowe RC	4	4	5	6	10	15	20	35
114	Mike Milbury	4	4	5	6	10	15	20	
115	Billy Harris	4	4	5	6	10	15	20	
116	Greg Fox RC	4	4	5	6	10	15	20	
117	Curt Fraser RC	4	4	5	6	10	15	20	35
118	Jean-Paul Parise	4	4	5	6	10	15	20	
119	Ric Seiling	4	4	5	6	10	15	20	35
120	Darryl Sittler	4	4	5	6	10	15	20	
121	Rick Lapointe	4	4	5	6	10	15	20	
122	Jim Rutherford	4	4	5	6	15	30	20	
123	Mario Tremblay	4	4	5	6	10	15	20	40
124	Randy Carlyle	4	4	5	6	10	15	20	40
125	Bobby Clarke	4	5	6	8	12	20	25	
126	Wayne Thomas	4	4	5	6	10	20	20	
127	Ivan Boldirev	4	4	5	6	10	15	20	35
128	Ted Bulley	4	4	5	6	10	15	20	
129	Dick Redmond	4	4	5	6	10	15	20	35
130	Clark Gillies AS1	4	4	5	6	10	30		
131	Checklist 1-132	6	10	15	25	40	60		
132	Vaclav Nedomansky	4	4	5	6	10	15	20	
133	Richard Mulhern	4	4	5	6	10	15	20	
134	Dave Schultz	4	4	5	6	10	15	20	
135	Guy Lapointe	4	4	5	6	10	15	20	

#	Player	VG 3	VgEx 4	EX 5	ExMt 6	NM 7	NmMt 8	NmMt+ 8.5	MT 9
136	Gilles Meloche	4	4	5	6	10	15	20	
137	Randy Pierce RC	4	4	5	6	10	15	20	35
138	Cam Connor	4	4	5	6	10	15	20	
139	George Ferguson	4	4	5	6	10	15	20	35
140	Bill Barber	4	4	5	6	10	15	20	
141	Terry Ruskowski UER	4	4	5	6	10	15	20	
142	Wayne Babych RC	4	4	5	6	10	15	20	35
143	Phil Russell	4	4	5	6	10	15	20	
144	Bobby Schmautz	4	4	5	6	10	15		80
145	Carol Vadnais	4	4	5	6	10	30		
146	John Tonelli RC	4	6	8	10	15	40	50	80
147	Peter Marsh RC	4	4	5	6	10	15	20	35
148	Thommie Bergman	4	4	5	6	10	15	20	35
149	Richard Martin	4	4	5	6	10	15	20	
150	Ken Dryden AS1	5	8	10	12	15	50	60	200
151	Kris Manery	4	4	5	6	10	15	20	35
152	Guy Charron	4	4	5	6	10	15	20	
153	Lanny McDonald	4	4	5	6	10	15	20	40
154	Ron Stackhouse	4	4	5	6	10	15	20	
155	Stan Mikita	4	5	6	8	12	20	25	40
156	Paul Holmgren	4	4	5	6	10	15	20	35
157	Perry Miller	4	4	5	6	10	15	20	
158	Gary Croteau	4	4	5	6	10	15	20	
159	Dave Maloney	4	4	5	6	10	15	20	
160	Marcel Dionne AS2	4	5	6	8	12	20	25	
161	Mike Bossy RB	4	5	6	8	20	25		
162	Don Maloney RB	4	4	5	6	10	15	20	
163	Whalers Logo CL	5	8	10	12	15	25	40	80
164	Brad Park RB	4	4	5	6	10	15	20	
165	Bryan Trottier RB	4	4	5	6	10	15	20	
166	Al Hill RC	4	4	5	6	10	15	20	35
167	Gary Bromley UER	4	4	5	6	10	15	20	35
168	Don Murdoch	4	4	5	6	10	15	20	35
169	Wayne Merrick	4	4	5	6	10	15	20	
170	Bob Gainey	4	4	5	6	10	20	25	40
171	Jim Schoenfeld	4	4	5	6	10	15	20	
172	Gregg Sheppard	4	4	5	6	10	15	20	35
173	Dan Bolduc RC	4	4	5	6	10	15	20	
174	Blake Dunlop	4	4	5	6	10	25		
175	Gordie Howe	6	10	12	20	25	50	75	350
176	Richard Brodeur	4	4	5	6	10	15	20	40
177	Tom Younghans	4	4	5	6	10	15	20	35
178	Andre Dupont	4	4	5	6	10	15	20	35
179	Ed Johnstone RC	4	4	5	6	10	15	20	
180	Gilbert Perreault	4	4	5	6	10	20		
181	Bob Lorimer RC	4	4	5	6	10	15	20	
182	John Wensink	4	4	5	6	10	15	20	
183	Lee Fogolin	4	4	5	6	10	15	20	
184	Greg Carroll RC	4	4	5	6	10	15	20	
185	Bobby Hull	6	10	12	15	20	60		
186	Harold Snepsts	4	4	5	6	10	15	20	
187	Peter Mahovlich	4	4	5	6	10	15	20	
188	Eric Vail	4	4	5	6	10	15	20	35
189	Phil Myre	4	4	5	6	10	15	20	
190	Wilf Paiement	4	4	5	6	10	15	20	
191	Charlie Simmer RC	5	8	10	12	20	30	40	60
192	Per-Olov Brasar	4	4	5	6	10	15	20	35
193	Lorne Henning	4	4	5	6	10	15	20	
194	Don Luce	4	4	5	6	10	15	20	
195	Steve Vickers	4	4	5	6	10	15	20	35
196	Bob Miller RC	4	4	5	6	10	15	20	
197	Mike Palmateer	4	4	5	6	10	15	20	
198	Nick Libett	4	4	5	6	10	15	20	
199	Pat Ribble RC	4	4	5	6	10	15	20	
200	Guy Lafleur AS1	5	8	10	12	20	60	80	
201	Mel Bridgman	4	4	5	6	10	30		
202	Morris Lukowich RC	4	4	5	6	10	15	20	35
203	Don Lever	4	4	5	6	10	15	20	
204	Tom Bladon	4	4	5	6	10	15	20	35
205	Garry Howatt	4	4	5	6	10	15	20	
206	Bobby Smith RC	5	8	10	12	20	40	50	150
207	Craig Ramsay	4	4	5	6	10	15	20	
208	Ron Duguay	4	4	5	6	10	15	20	35
209	Gilles Gilbert	4	4	5	6	10	15	20	
210	Bob MacMillan	4	4	5	6	10	15	20	
211	Pierre Mondou	4	4	5	6	10	15	20	
212	J.P. Bordeleau	4	4	5	6	10	15	20	35
213	Reed Larson	4	4	5	6	10	15	20	35
214	Dennis Ververgaert	4	4	5	6	10	15	20	
215	Bernie Federko	4	5	6	8	15	25	30	
216	Mark Howe	4	6	8	10	15	25		
217	Bob Nystrom	4	4	5	6	10	15	20	
218	Orest Kindrachuk	4	4	5	6	10	15	20	
219	Mike Fidler	4	4	5	6	10	15	20	35
220	Phil Esposito	4	4	5	6	10	15	20	
221	Bill Hajt	4	4	5	6	10	15	20	35
222	Mark Napier	4	4	5	6	10	30		
223	Dennis Maruk	4	4	5	6	10	15	20	
224	Dennis Polonich	4	4	5	6	10	15	20	35

#	Player	VG 3	VgEx 4	EX 5	ExMt 6	NM 7	NmMt 8	NmMt+ 8.5	MT 9
225	Jean Ratelle	4	4	5	6	10	15	20	
226	Bob Dailey	4	4	5	6	10	15	20	
227	Alain Daigle	4	4	5	6	10	15	20	
228	Ian Turnbull	4	4	5	6	10	15	20	
229	Jack Valiquette	4	4	5	6	10	15	20	
230	Mike Bossy AS2	5	8	10	12	20	40	60	
231	Brad Maxwell	4	4	5	6	10	15	20	
232	Dave Taylor	4	5	6	8	15	25	30	
233	Pierre Larouche	4	4	5	6	10	15	20	4
234	Rod Schutt RC	4	4	5	6	10	15	20	
235	Rogatien Vachon	4	4	5	6	10	15	20	
236	Ryan Walter RC	4	4	5	6	10	15	20	6
237	Checklist 133-264 UER	8	12	25	50	80	250		
238	Terry O'Reilly	4	4	5	6	10	15	20	
239	Real Cloutier	4	4	5	6	10	15	20	
240	Anders Hedberg	4	4	5	6	10	15	20	
241	Ken Linseman RC	4	5	6	8	15	25	30	
242	Billy Smith	4	4	5	6	10	15	20	
243	Rick Chartraw	4	4	5	6	10	15	20	
244	Flames Team	4	5	6	8	12	20	25	
245	Bruins Team	4	5	6	8	12	20	25	
246	Sabres Team	4	5	6	8	12	20	25	
247	Blackhawks Team	4	5	6	8	12	20	25	
248	Rockies Team	4	5	6	8	12	20	25	
249	Red Wings Team	4	5	6	8	12	20	25	5
250	Kings Team	4	5	6	8	12	20	25	
251	North Stars Team	4	5	6	8	12	20	25	5
252	Canadiens Team	5	8	10	12	20	40		
253	Islanders Team	4	5	6	8	15	100		
254	Rangers Team	4	5	6	8	12	20	25	
255	Flyers Team	4	5	6	8	12	20	25	5
256	Penguins Team	4	5	6	8	12	20	25	
257	Blues Team	4	5	6	8	12	20	25	
258	Maple Leafs Team	4	5	6	8	15	25	30	
259	Canucks Team	4	5	6	8	15	25	30	
260	Capitals Team	4	5	6	8	12	30	40	
261	Nordiques Team	5	8	10	12	30	40	50	8
262	Jean Hamel	4	4	5	6	10	15	20	
263	Stan Jonathan	4	4	5	6	10	15	20	
264	Russ Anderson	4	4	5	6	10	15	20	35
265	Gordie Roberts RC	4	4	5	6	10	15	20	35
266	Bill Flett	4	4	5	6	10	15	20	35
267	Robbie Ftorek	4	4	5	6	10	15	20	
268	Mike Amodeo	4	4	5	6	10	15	20	35
269	Vic Venasky	4	4	5	6	10	15	20	
270	Bob Manno	4	4	5	6	10	15	20	
271	Dan Maloney	4	4	5	6	10	15	20	
272	Al Sims	4	4	5	6	10	15	20	
273	Greg Polis	4	4	5	6	10	15	20	
274	Doug Favell	4	4	5	6	15	20	25	
275	Pierre Plante	4	4	5	6	10	15	20	
276	Bob Murdoch	4	4	5	6	10	15	20	35
277	Lyle Moffat	4	4	5	6	10	30		
278	Jack Brownschidle	4	4	5	6	10	15	20	
279	Dave Keon	4	4	5	6	15	20	25	35
280	Darryl Edestrand	4	4	5	6	10	15	20	35
281	Greg Millen RC	4	6	8	10	20	30		
282	John Gould	4	4	5	6	10	15	20	
283	Rich Leduc	4	4	5	6	10	15	20	
284	Ron Delorme	4	4	5	6	10	15	20	40
285	Gord Smith	4	4	5	6	10	15	20	
286	Nick Fotiu	4	4	5	6	10	15	20	
287	Kevin McCarthy RC	4	4	5	6	10	15	20	90
288	Jimmy Jones	4	4	5	6	10	15	20	
289	Pierre Bouchard	4	4	5	6	10	15	20	
290	Wayne Bianchin	4	4	5	6	10	15	20	50
291	Garry Lariviere	4	4	5	6	10	15	20	
292	Steve Jensen	4	4	5	6	10	15	20	
293	John Garrett	4	4	5	6	10	15	20	
294	Hilliard Graves	4	4	5	6	10	15	20	35
295	Bill Clement	4	4	5	6	10	15	20	
296	Michel Larocque	4	4	5	6	10	30		40
297	Bob Stewart	4	4	5	6	10	15	20	
298	Doug Patey RC	4	4	5	6	10	15	20	35
299	Dave Farrish	4	4	5	6	10	15	20	
300	Al Smith	4	4	5	6	10	15	20	
301	Billy Lochead	4	4	5	6	15	20	25	
302	Dave Hutchison	4	4	5	6	10	15	20	
303	Bill Riley	4	4	5	6	10	15	20	
304	Barry Gibbs	4	4	5	6	10	15	20	
305	Chris Oddleifson	4	4	5	6	10	15	20	
306	J. Bob Kelly UER	4	4	5	6	10	30		
307	Al Hangsleben RC	4	4	5	6	10	15	20	40
308	Curt Brackenbury RC	4	4	5	6	10	15	20	35
309	Rick Green	4	4	5	6	10	15	20	
310	Ken Houston	4	4	5	6	10	15	20	
311	Greg Joly	4	4	5	6	10	15	20	35
312	Bill Lesuk	4	4	5	6	10	15	20	
313	Bill Stewart RC	4	4	5	6	10	15	20	40

	VG 3	VgEx 4	EX 5	ExMt 6	NM 7	NmMt 8	NmMt+ 8.5	MT 9
Rick Ley	4	4	5	6	10	15	20	
Brett Callighen RC	4	4	5	6	10	15	20	35
Michel Dion	4	4	5	6	10	15	20	
Randy Manery	4	4	5	6	10	15	20	35
Barry Dean	4	4	5	6	10	20	25	
Pat Boutette	4	4	5	6	10	15	20	
Mark Heaslip	4	4	5	6	10	15	20	
Dave Inkpen	4	4	5	6	10	15	20	
Jere Gillis	4	4	5	6	10	15	20	
Larry Brown	4	4	5	6	10	15	20	
Alain Cote RC	4	4	5	6	10	15	20	35
Gordie Lane	4	4	5	6	10	15	20	
Bobby Lalonde	4	4	5	6	10	15	20	
Ed Staniowski	4	4	5	6	10	20	25	
Ron Plumb	4	4	5	6	10	15	20	
Jude Drouin	4	4	5	6	10	15	20	
Rick Hampton	4	4	5	6	10	15	20	35
Stan Weir	4	4	5	6	10	15	20	
Blair Stewart	4	4	5	6	10	15	20	
Mike Polich RC	4	4	5	6	10	15	20	35
Jean Potvin	4	4	5	6	10	15	20	35
Jordy Douglas RC	4	4	5	6	10	15	20	35
Joel Quenneville RC	4	4	5	6	10	15	20	
Glen Hanlon RC	4	5	6	8	10	20	25	
Dave Hoyda RC	4	4	5	6	10	15	20	
Colin Campbell	4	4	5	6	10	15	20	
John Smrke	4	4	5	6	10	15	20	
Brian Glennie	4	4	5	6	10	15	20	
Don Kozak	4	4	5	6	10	15	20	
Yvon Labre	4	4	5	6	10	15	20	
Curt Bennett	4	4	5	6	10	15	20	
Mike Christie	4	4	5	6	10	20	25	
Checklist 265-396	5	8	12	40	60			
Pat Price	4	4	5	6	10	15	20	35
Ron Low	4	4	5	6	10	15	20	
Mike Antonovich	4	4	5	6	10	15	20	35
Roland Eriksson	4	4	5	6	10	15	20	
Bob Murdoch	4	4	5	6	10	15	20	
Rob Palmer	4	4	5	6	10	15	20	
Brad Gassoff	4	4	5	6	10	15	20	35
Bruce Boudreau	4	4	5	6	10	15	20	35
Al Hamilton	4	4	5	6	10	15	20	
Blaine Stoughton	4	4	5	6	10	15	20	35
John Baby	4	4	5	6	10	15	20	
Gary Inness	4	4	5	6	10	30		35
Wayne Dillon	4	4	5	6	10	15	20	
Darcy Rota	4	4	5	6	10	15	20	
Brian Engblom RC	4	4	5	6	10	30		
Bill Hogaboam	4	4	5	6	10	15	20	
Dave Debol RC	4	4	5	6	10	15	20	
Pete Lopresti	4	4	5	6	10	15	20	
Gerry Hart	4	4	5	6	10	15	20	
Syl Apps	4	4	5	6	10	15	20	
Jack McIlhargey	4	4	5	6	10	15	20	
Willy Lindstrom	4	4	5	6	10	15	20	35
Don Laurence RC	4	4	5	6	10	15	20	35
Chuck Luksa RC	4	4	5	6	10	15	20	
Dave Semenko RC	5	8	10	12	15	40	60	100
Paul Baxter RC	4	4	5	6	10	15	20	
Ron Ellis	4	4	5	6	10	15	20	
Leif Svensson RC	4	4	5	6	10	15	20	60
Dennis O'Brien	4	4	5	6	10	15	20	
Glenn Goldup	4	4	5	6	10	15	20	
Terry Richardson	4	4	5	6	10	15	20	
Peter Sullivan	4	4	5	6	10	15	20	35
Doug Hicks	4	4	5	6	10	15	20	
Jamie Hislop RC	4	4	5	6	10	15	20	30
Jocelyn Guevremont	4	4	5	6	10	15	20	
Willi Plett	4	4	5	6	10	15	20	
Larry Goodenough	4	4	5	6	10	15	20	35
Jim Warner RC	4	4	5	6	10	15	20	40
Rey Comeau	4	4	5	6	10	15	20	
Barry Melrose RC	4	6	8	10	12	30	40	100
Dave Hunter RC	4	4	5	6	10	15	20	40
Wally Weir RC	4	4	5	6	10	15	20	35
Mario Lessard RC	4	4	5	6	10	15	20	40
Ed Kea	4	4	5	6	10	15	20	35
Bob Stephenson RC	4	4	5	6	10	15	20	30
Dennis Hextall	4	4	5	6	10	15	20	35
Jerry Butler	4	4	5	6	10	15	20	
David Shand	4	4	5	6	10	15	20	
Rick Blight	4	4	5	6	10	15	20	
Lars-Erik Sjoberg	4	4	5	6	8	12	25	30

Wayne Gretzky RC #18 BGS 9.5 (Gem) sold for $50,000 (eBay; 7/08)
Wayne Gretzky RC #18 BGS 9.5 (Gem) sold for $11,789 (Memory Lane; 6/12)
Billy Harris #115 PSA 10 (Gem Mt) sold for $11,789 (Memory Lane; 6/12)
Billy Harris #115 PSA 10 (Gem Mt) sold for $3,174 (eBay; 1/13)

1979-80 Topps

		VG 3	VgEx 4	EX 5	ExMt 6	NM 7	NmMt 8	NmMt+ 8.5	MT 9
1	Bossy/Dionne/Lafleur LL	4	4	5	6	8	25		
2	Trott/Lafleur/Dionne LL	4	4	5	6	8	12	15	
3	Trott/Dionne/Lafleur LL	4	4	5	6	10	15	25	
4	Williams/Holt/Schultz LL	4	4	5	6	8	12	15	
5	Bossy/Dionne/Gardner LL	4	4	5	6	8	12	15	
6	Dryden/Resch/Parent LL	4	4	5	6	8	12	15	
7	Lafleur/Bossy/Trott/ LL	4	4	5	6	8	12	15	
8A	Dryden/Espo/Par LL ERR	4	4	5	8	15	40		
8B	Dryden/Espo/Par LL COR	4	4	5	6	10	25	35	
9	Greg Malone	4	4	5	6	10	15	20	
10	Rick Middleton	4	4	5	6	8	12	15	
11	Greg Smith	4	4	5	6	8	12	15	30
12	Rene Robert	4	4	5	6	8	12	15	
13	Doug Risebrough	4	4	5	6	8	12	15	30
14	Bob Kelly	4	4	5	6	8	12	15	
15	Walt Tkaczuk	4	4	5	6	8	12	15	30
16	John Marks	4	4	5	6	8	12	15	
17	Willie Huber RC	4	4	5	6	8	12	15	30
18	Wayne Gretzky RC	▲400	▲500	▲600	▲800	▲1,000	▲2,000	2,500	7,000
19	Ron Sedlbauer	4	4	5	6	8	12	15	30
20	Glenn Resch AS2	4	4	5	6	8	12	15	
21	Blair Chapman	4	4	5	6	8	12	15	
22	Ron Zanussi	4	4	5	6	8	12	15	30
23	Brad Park	4	4	5	6	10	15	20	
24	Yvon Lambert	4	4	5	6	8	12	15	
25	Andre Savard	4	4	5	6	8	12	15	
26	Jimmy Watson	4	4	5	6	10	15	20	
27	Hal Philipoff RC	4	4	5	6	8	12	15	
28	Dan Bouchard	4	4	5	6	8	12	15	
29	Bob Sirois	4	4	5	6	8	12	15	30
30	Ulf Nilsson	4	4	5	6	10	15	20	
31	Mike Murphy	4	4	5	6	10	15	20	
32	Stefan Persson	4	4	5	6	8	12	15	
33	Garry Unger	4	4	5	6	8	12	15	30
34	Rejean Houle	4	4	5	6	8	12	15	30
35	Barry Beck	4	4	5	6	8	12	15	
36	Tim Young	4	4	5	6	8	12	15	30
37	Rick Dudley	4	4	5	6	8	12	15	
38	Wayne Stephenson	4	4	5	6	8	12	15	30
39	Peter McNab	4	4	5	6	10	15	20	
40	Borje Salming AS2	4	4	5	6	8	12	15	
41	Tom Lysiak	4	4	5	6	8	12	15	30
42	Don Maloney RC	4	4	5	6	8	12	15	30
43	Mike Rogers	4	4	5	6	10	15	20	
44	Dave Lewis	4	4	5	6	8	12	15	
45	Peter Lee	4	4	5	6	8	12	15	30
46	Marty Howe	4	4	5	6	8	12	15	30
47	Serge Bernier	4	4	5	6	8	12	15	30
48	Paul Woods	4	4	5	6	10	15	20	
49	Bob Sauve	4	4	5	6	8	12	15	30
50	Larry Robinson AS1	4	4	5	6	8	12	15	
51	Tom Gorence RC	4	4	5	6	8	12	15	30
52	Gary Sargent	4	4	5	6	8	12	15	30
53	Thomas Gradin RC	4	4	5	6	10	15	20	
54	Dean Talafous	4	4	5	6	8	12	15	
55	Bob Murray	4	4	5	6	8	12	15	30
56	Bob Bourne	4	4	5	6	8	12	15	
57	Larry Patey	4	4	5	6	8	12	15	30
58	Ross Lonsberry	4	4	5	6	10	15	20	
59	Rick Smith	4	4	5	6	8	12	15	30
60	Guy Chouinard	4	4	5	6	8	12	15	30
61	Danny Gare	4	4	5	6	8	12	15	
62	Jim Bedard	4	4	5	6	8	12	15	
63	Dale McCourt	4	4	5	6	10	15	20	
64	Steve Payne RC	4	4	5	6	8	12	15	
65	Pat Hughes RC	4	4	5	6	10	15	20	
66	Mike McEwen	4	4	5	6	8	12	15	30
67	Reg Kerr RC	4	4	5	6	8	12	15	
68	Walt McKechnie	4	4	5	6	8	12	15	30
69	Michel Plasse	4	4	5	6	8	12	15	
70	Denis Potvin AS1	4	4	5	6	8	12	15	
71	Dave Dryden	4	4	5	6	8	12	15	
72	Gary McAdam	4	4	5	6	8	12	15	30
73	Andre St.Laurent	4	4	5	6	8	12	15	
74	Jerry Korab	4	4	5	6	10	15	20	
75	Rick MacLeish	4	4	5	6	8	12	15	30
76	Dennis Kearns	4	4	5	6	8	12	15	
77	Jean Pronovost	4	4	5	6	8	12	15	30
78	Ron Greschner	4	4	5	6	10	15	20	
79	Wayne Cashman	4	4	5	6	8	12	15	30
80	Tony Esposito	4	4	5	6	8	15	25	30
81	Cup Semi-Finals	4	4	5	6	8	40		
82	Cup Semi-Finals	4	4	5	6	8	12	15	
83	Stanley Cup Finals	4	4	5	6	10	15	20	
84	Brian Sutter	4	4	5	6	8	12	15	
85	Gerry Cheevers	4	4	5	6	8	12	15	30
86	Pat Hickey	4	4	5	6	10	15	20	
87	Mike Kaszycki	4	4	5	6	8	12	15	

HOCKEY

#	Name	VG 3	VgEx 4	EX 5	ExMt 6	NM 7	NmMt 8	NmMt+ 8.5	MT 9
88	Grant Mulvey	4	4	5	6	8	12	15	30
89	Derek Smith	4	4	5	6	8	12	15	
90	Steve Shutt	4	4	5	6	8	12	15	
91	Robert Picard	4	4	5	6	10	15	20	
92	Dan Labraaten	4	4	5	6	8	12	15	
93	Glen Sharpley	4	4	5	6	8	12	15	30
94	Denis Herron	4	4	5	6	8	12	15	
95	Reggie Leach	4	4	5	6	8	12	15	
96	John Van Boxmeer	4	4	5	6	8	12	15	
97	Tiger Williams	4	4	5	6	8	12	15	
98	Butch Goring	4	4	5	6	8	12	15	30
99	Don Marcotte	4	4	5	6	8	12	15	30
100	Bryan Trottier AS1	4	4	5	6	8	12	15	
101	Serge Savard AS2	4	4	5	6	10	15	20	
102	Cliff Koroll	4	4	5	6	8	12	15	30
103	Gary Smith	4	4	5	6	8	12	15	30
104	Al MacAdam	4	4	5	6	10	15	20	
105	Don Edwards	4	4	5	6	8	12	15	30
106	Errol Thompson	4	4	5	6	8	12	15	
107	Andre Lacroix	4	4	5	6	8	12	15	
108	Marc Tardif	4	4	5	6	8	12	15	30
109	Rick Kehoe	4	4	5	6	8	12	15	30
110	John Davidson	4	4	5	6	8	12	15	
111	Behn Wilson RC	4	4	5	6	8	12	15	30
112	Doug Jarvis	4	4	5	6	8	12	15	30
113	Tom Rowe RC	4	4	5	6	10	15	20	
114	Mike Milbury	4	4	5	6	8	12	15	
115	Billy Harris	4	4	5	6	8	12	15	30
116	Greg Fox RC	4	4	5	6	8	12	15	30
117	Curt Fraser RC	4	4	5	6	8	12	15	
118	Jean-Paul Parise	4	4	5	6	8	12	15	
119	Ric Seiling	4	4	5	6	8	12	15	30
120	Darryl Sittler	4	4	5	6	8	12	15	
121	Rick Lapointe	4	4	5	6	8	12	15	
122	Jim Rutherford	4	4	5	6	8	12	15	
123	Mario Tremblay	4	4	5	6	8	12	15	30
124	Randy Carlyle	4	4	5	6	8	12	15	
125	Bobby Clarke	4	4	5	6	10	15	20	
126	Wayne Thomas	4	4	5	6	8	12	15	30
127	Ivan Boldirev	4	4	5	6	8	12	15	
128	Ted Bulley	4	4	5	6	8	12	15	
129	Dick Redmond	4	4	5	6	8	12	15	30
130	Clark Gillies AS1	4	4	5	6	8	12	15	
131	Checklist 1-132	4	4	5	8	10	30		
132	Vaclav Nedomansky	4	4	5	6	8	12	15	30
133	Richard Mulhern	4	4	5	6	10	15	20	
134	Dave Schultz	4	4	5	6	10	15	20	
135	Guy Lapointe	4	4	5	6	8	12	15	
136	Gilles Meloche	4	4	5	6	8	12	15	
137	Randy Pierce RC	4	4	5	6	8	12	15	30
138	Cam Connor	4	4	5	6	8	12	15	30
139	George Ferguson	4	4	5	6	10	15	20	30
140	Bill Barber	4	4	5	6	8	12	15	
141	Mike Walton	4	4	5	6	8	12	15	
142	Wayne Babych RC	4	4	5	6	8	12	15	30
143	Phil Russell	4	4	5	6	8	12	15	
144	Bobby Schmautz	4	4	5	6	10	15	20	
145	Carol Vadnais	4	4	5	6	10	15	20	
146	John Tonelli RC	4	4	5	8	10	15	25	60
147	Peter Marsh RC	4	4	5	6	8	12	15	
148	Thommie Bergman	4	4	5	6	8	12	15	
149	Richard Martin	4	4	5	6	8	12	15	30
150	Ken Dryden AS1	4	4	5	8	10	15	30	100
151	Kris Manery	4	4	5	6	8	12	15	30
152	Guy Charron	4	4	5	6	10	15	20	
153	Lanny McDonald	4	4	5	6	8	12	15	30
154	Ron Stackhouse	4	4	5	6	8	12	15	
155	Stan Mikita	4	4	5	6	8	12	15	
156	Paul Holmgren	4	4	5	6	10	15	20	
157	Perry Miller	4	4	5	6	8	12	15	30
158	Gary Croteau	4	4	5	6	8	12	15	30
159	Dave Maloney	4	4	5	6	8	12	15	30
160	Marcel Dionne AS2	4	4	5	6	8	12	15	80
161	Mike Bossy RB	4	4	5	6	8	12	15	
162	Don Maloney RB	4	4	5	6	10	15	20	
163	Ulf Nilsson RB	4	4	5	6	8	12	15	
164	Brad Park RB	4	4	5	6	8	12	15	
165	Bryan Trottier RB	4	4	5	6	10	15	20	
166	Al Hill RC	4	4	5	6	8	12	15	30
167	Gary Bromley	4	4	5	6	8	12	15	30
168	Don Murdoch	4	4	5	6	10	15	20	
169	Wayne Merrick	4	4	5	6	10	15	20	
170	Bob Gainey	4	4	5	6	8	12	15	
171	Jim Schoenfeld	4	4	5	6	8	12	15	30
172	Gregg Sheppard	4	4	5	6	8	12	15	
173	Dan Bolduc RC	4	4	5	6	8	12	15	
174	Blake Dunlop	4	4	5	6	8	12	15	30
175	Gordie Howe	5	6	8	▲15	▲25	▲50	▲60	80
176	Richard Brodeur	4	4	5	6	8	12	15	30
177	Tom Younghans	4	4	5	6	8	12	15	
178	Andre Dupont	4	4	5	6	10	15	20	
179	Ed Johnstone RC	4	4	5	6	8	12	15	30

#	Name	VG 3	VgEx 4	EX 5	ExMt 6	NM 7	NmMt 8	NmMt+ 8.5	MT
180	Gilbert Perreault	4	4	5	6	8	12	15	
181	Bob Lorimer RC	4	4	5	6	10	15	20	
182	John Wensink	4	4	5	6	8	12	15	
183	Lee Fogolin	4	4	5	6	10	15	20	
184	Greg Carroll RC	4	4	5	6	8	12	15	3
185	Bobby Hull	4	5	6	10	15	25	30	5
186	Harold Snepsts	4	4	5	6	8	12	15	3
187	Peter Mahovlich	4	4	5	6	8	12	15	
188	Eric Vail	4	4	5	6	8	12	15	3
189	Phil Myre	4	4	5	6	10	15	20	
190	Wilf Paiement	4	4	5	6	10	15	20	
191	Charlie Simmer RC	4	4	5	8	10	15	25	
192	Per-Olov Brasar	4	4	5	6	10	15	20	3
193	Lorne Henning	4	4	5	6	8	12	15	
194	Don Luce	4	4	5	6	8	12	15	
195	Steve Vickers	4	4	5	6	8	12	15	3
196	Bob Miller RC	4	4	5	6	8	12	15	
197	Mike Palmateer	4	4	5	6	8	12	15	
198	Nick Libett	4	4	5	6	10	15	20	
199	Pat Ribble RC	4	4	5	6	8	12	15	
200	Guy Lafleur AS1	4	4	5	6	8	30	40	
201	Mel Bridgman	4	4	5	6	10	15	20	
202	Morris Lukowich RC	4	4	5	6	8	12	15	
203	Don Lever	4	4	5	6	10	15	20	
204	Tom Bladon	4	4	5	6	8	12	15	3
205	Garry Howatt	4	4	5	6	8	12	15	3
206	Bobby Smith RC	4	4	5	6	10	15	20	
207	Craig Ramsay	4	4	5	6	8	12	15	3
208	Ron Duguay	4	4	5	6	8	12	15	3
209	Gilles Gilbert	4	4	5	6	10	15	20	3
210	Bob MacMillan	4	4	5	6	8	12	15	
211	Pierre Mondou	4	4	5	6	8	12	15	
212	J.P. Bordeleau	4	4	5	6	10	15	20	3
213	Reed Larson	4	4	5	6	10	15	20	3
214	Dennis Ververgaert	4	4	5	6	8	12	15	
215	Bernie Federko	4	4	5	6	8	12	15	
216	Mark Howe	4	4	5	6	8	12	15	
217	Bob Nystrom	4	4	5	6	8	12	15	3
218	Orest Kindrachuk	4	4	5	6	10	15	20	
219	Mike Fidler	4	4	5	6	8	12	15	3
220	Phil Esposito	4	4	5	6	8	12	15	
221	Bill Hajt	4	4	5	6	8	12	15	3
222	Mark Napier	4	4	5	6	8	12	15	3
223	Dennis Maruk	4	4	5	6	10	15	20	
224	Dennis Polonich	4	4	5	6	8	12	15	
225	Jean Ratelle	4	4	5	6	8	12	15	30
226	Bob Dailey	4	4	5	6	8	12	15	
227	Alain Daigle	4	4	5	6	8	12	15	
228	Ian Turnbull	4	4	5	6	8	12	15	
229	Jack Valiquette	4	4	5	6	10	15	20	
230	Mike Bossy AS2	4	4	5	10	12	20	30	80
231	Brad Maxwell	4	4	5	6	8	12	15	30
232	Dave Taylor	4	4	5	8	10	15	20	
233	Pierre Larouche	4	4	5	6	10	15	20	30
234	Rod Schutt RC	4	4	5	6	10	15	20	
235	Rogatien Vachon	4	4	5	6	10	15	20	
236	Ryan Walter RC	4	4	5	6	8	12	15	
237	Checklist 133-264	4	4	5	8	10	60		
238	Terry O'Reilly	4	4	5	6	8	12	15	30
239	Real Cloutier	4	4	5	6	8	12	15	30
240	Anders Hedberg	4	4	5	6	10	15	20	
241	Ken Linseman RC	4	4	5	6	8	12	15	
242	Billy Smith	4	4	5	6	10	15		
243	Rick Chartraw	4	4	5	6	8	12	15	
244	Flames Team	4	4	5	6	8	12	15	
245	Bruins Team	4	4	5	6	8	12	15	35
246	Sabres Team	4	4	5	6	8	12	15	
247	Blackhawks Team	4	4	5	6	8	12	15	
248	Rockies Team	4	4	5	6	8	12	15	
249	Red Wings Team	4	4	5	6	8	12	15	35
250	Kings Team	4	4	5	6	8	12	15	
251	North Stars Team	4	4	5	6	8	12	15	
252	Canadiens Team	4	4	5	6	8	20	25	
253	Islanders Team	4	4	5	6	8	12	15	
254	Rangers Team	4	4	5	6	8	12	15	
255	Flyers Team	4	4	5	6	8	12	15	
256	Penguins Team	4	4	5	6	8	12	15	35
257	Blues Team	4	4	5	6	10	15		
258	Maple Leafs Team	4	4	5	6	8	12	15	
259	Canucks Team	4	4	5	6	8	12	15	
260	Capitals Team	4	4	5	6	8	12	15	35
261	New NHL Entries CL	4	5	6	10	20	40	50	
262	Jean Hamel	4	4	5	6	8	12	15	
263	Stan Jonathan	4	4	5	6	8	12	15	30
264	Russ Anderson	4	4	5	6	8	12	15	35

—Wayne Gretzky #18 PSA 10 (Gem) sold for $30,209 (Mastro; 4/07)
—Wayne Gretzky #18 BGS 9.5 (Gem) sold for $22,000 (eBay; 1/14)

HOCKEY

1980 - Present

1980-81 O-Pee-Chee

	NmMt 8	NmMt+ 8.5	MT 9	Gem 9.5/10
Ray Bourque RB	20	25	60	120
Wayne Gretzky RB	50	60	150	250
Ken Morrow OLY RC	12	15	25	60
Mike Liut RC	30	40	80	100
Brian Propp RC	20	30	100	
Michel Goulet RC	50	80	150	700
Wayne Gretzky AS2	40	50	100	300
Ray Bourque RC	200	250	600	800
Gretzky/Dionne/Lafleur LL	20	25	60	125
Dionne/Gretzky/Lafleur LL	20	25	80	125
Wayne Gretzky TL	20	25	60	250
Mike Foligno RC	20	30	50	
Mike Gartner RC	50	100	150	300
Rick Vaive RC	30	40	80	
Wayne Gretzky	250	350	600	750
Pete Peeters RC	20	30	60	
Mark Messier UER RC	300	350	650	850
Rod Langway RC	30	40	125	
Richard Sevigny RC	20	30	60	

1980-81 Topps

	NmMt 8	NmMt+ 8.5	MT 9	Gem 9.5/10
Ray Bourque RB#(65 Points.;	12	25	40	
Record for#(Rookie Defenseman				
Wayne Gretzky	30	50	80	
RB#(Youngest 50-goal Scorer				
Michel Goulet RC	10	15	30	
Wayne Gretzky AS2	30	50	80	
Ray Bourque RC	40	60	250	
Gretz/Dion/Lafl LL	10	15	30	
Gretz/Dion/Lafl LL	15	30	50	
Wayne Gretzky TL	15	25	50	
Oilers Scoring Leaders#((checklist back)				
Mike Gartner RC	20	30	40	
Wayne Gretzky UER	s80	s100	s150	
(1978-79 GP should#(be 80 not 60)				

1981-82 O-Pee-Chee

	NmMt 8	NmMt+ 8.5	MT 9	Gem 9.5/10
Ray Bourque	30	40	175	300
Denis Savard RC	40	60	120	300
Wayne Gretzky	60	80	200	400

	NmMt 8	NmMt+ 8.5	MT 9	Gem 9.5/10
107	Jari Kurri RC	80	100	250	350
108	Glenn Anderson RC	20	30	120	250
111	Paul Coffey RC	200	250	350	550
117	Kevin Lowe RC	25	30	100	
118	Mark Messier	25	30	80	135
120	Andy Moog RC	s60	s80	s100	250
125	Wayne Gretzky SA	50	80	100	300
126	Wayne Gretzky TL	15	20	40	80
148	Larry Murphy RC	25	30	150	
161	Dino Ciccarelli RC	50	80	100	s300
269	Peter Stastny RC	40	60	120	200
277	Dale Hunter RC	25	30	50	80
383	Wayne Gretzky LL	15	25	100	
384	Wayne Gretzky LL	15	25	100	
392	Wayne Gretzky RB	20	30	60	

1981-82 Topps

	NmMt 8	NmMt+ 8.5	MT 9	Gem 9.5/10
5	Ray Bourque	6	12	25	40
16	Wayne Gretzky	25	50	80	100
18	Jari Kurri RC	6	15	40	60
W75	Denis Savard RC	10	15	20	40
W100	Larry Murphy RC	6	10	20	30
W105	Dino Ciccarelli RC	10	15	25	

1982-83 O-Pee-Chee

	NmMt 8	NmMt+ 8.5	MT 9	Gem 9.5/10
1	Wayne Gretzky HL	10	12	25	60
99	Wayne Gretzky TL	8	10	20	50
105	Grant Fuhr RC	60	80	150	300
106	Wayne Gretzky	50	80	150	
107	Wayne Gretzky IA	25	50	80	
111	Jari Kurri	8	10	20	40
117	Mark Messier	10	12	20	40
123	Ron Francis RC	50	60	120	300
164	Neal Broten RC	10	15	25	100
235	Wayne Gretzky LL	8	10	20	60
237	W.Gretzky/M.Goulet LL	8	10	20	50
240	Wayne Gretzky LL	8	10	20	50
242	Wayne Gretzky LL	8	10	20	60
243	Wayne Gretzky LL	8	10	20	60
307	Joe Mullen RC	10	15	40	150
380	Dale Hawerchuk RC	20	25	30	150

1983-84 O-Pee-Chee

	NmMt 8	NmMt+ 8.5	MT 9	Gem 9.5/10
22	Wayne Gretzky TL			15	40
23	M.Messier/W.Gretzky HL	40	50	80	150
29	Wayne Gretzky	s50	s80	s150	200
65	Phil Housley RC	8	12	30	100
160	Bernie Nicholls RC	8	10	s50	s80
185	Guy Carbonneau RC	12	15	s60	s100
203	Wayne Gretzky Hart	8	10	15	40
204	Wayne Gretzky Ross	8	10	15	40
212	Wayne Gretzky RB	8	10	15	40
215	Wayne Gretzky LL	8	10	20	80
216	Wayne Gretzky LL	8	10	20	100
217	Wayne Gretzky LL	8	10	20	60
268	Pelle Lindbergh RC	50	60	80	300
376	Scott Stevens RC	15	25	60	150

1984-85 O-Pee-Chee

	NmMt 8	NmMt+ 8.5	MT 9	Gem 9.5/10
17	Dave Andreychuk RC	10	15	40	200
18	Tom Barrasso RC	10	15	40	150
67	Steve Yzerman RC	150	200	300	1,250
121	Pat Verbeek RC	12	15	30	60
129	Pat LaFontaine RC	15	20	40	150
185	Doug Gilmour RC	50	80	150	400
208	Wayne Gretzky AS	12	15	25	150
243	Wayne Gretzky	20	30	60	150
259	Chris Chelios RC	50	80	100	250
327	Cam Neely RC	80	100	150	250
357	Wayne Gretzky TL	8	12	20	50
373	Wayne Gretzky Ross	6	12	20	50
374	Wayne Gretzky Hart	6	12	20	50
380	Wayne Gretzky TL	10	12	20	50
381	Wayne Gretzky LL	10	12	20	40
382	Wayne Gretzky LL	10	12	20	40
383	Wayne Gretzky LL	10	12	20	40
385	Steve Yzerman LL	20	25	60	150
388	Wayne Gretzky RB	8	15	25	60

—Steve Yzerman #67 BGS 10 (Pristine) sold for $2,465 (eBay; 7/08)

—Steve Yzerman #67 BGS 10 (Pristine) sold for $2,300 (eBay; 7/07)

—Chris Chelios #259 BGS 10 (Pristine) sold for $410 (eBay, 05/08)

1984-85 Topps

		NmMt 8	NmMt+ 8.5	MT 9	Gem 9.5/10
13	Dave Andreychuk SP RC	8	10	15	40
14	Tom Barrasso RC	8	10	15	40
49	Steve Yzerman RC	80	100	150	300
51	Wayne Gretzky	8	12	25	

1985-86 O-Pee-Chee

		NmMt 8	NmMt+ 8.5	MT 9	Gem 9.5/10
9	Mario Lemieux RC	400	500	700	8,000
29	Steve Yzerman	25	40	60	120
110	Pelle Lindbergh Mem.	20	25	40	80
120	Wayne Gretzky	40	60	80	225
122	Kelly Hrudey RC	12	15	25	50
210	Al Iafrate RC	15	20	30	60
237	Al MacInnis RC	30	40	80	
257	Wayne Gretzky LL	15	25	50	100
258	Wayne Gretzky LL	15	25	50	100
259	Wayne Gretzky LL	15	25	50	100
262	Mario Lemieux LL	40	60	80	500

1985-86 Topps

		NmMt 8	NmMt+ 8.5	MT 9	Gem 9.5/10
9	Mario Lemieux RC	200	250	350	800
29	Steve Yzerman	15	20	30	
110	Pelle Lindbergh SP	12	15	30	
120	Wayne Gretzky	20	30	50	

1986-87 O-Pee-Chee

		NmMt 8	NmMt+ 8.5	MT 9	Gem 9.5/10
3	Wayne Gretzky	30	40	100	200
9	John Vanbiesbrouck RC	20	30	50	120
11	Steve Yzerman	25	30	60	150
53	Patrick Roy RC	300	350	500	1,750
122	Mario Lemieux	40	50	100	200
149	Wendel Clark RC	50	80	150	200
259	Wayne Gretzky LL	10	15	25	50
260	Wayne Gretzky LL	10	15	25	50

1986-87 Topps

		NmMt 8	NmMt+ 8.5	MT 9	Gem 9.5/10
3	Wayne Gretzky	20	30	50	
9	John Vanbiesbrouck DP RC	12	20	40	
53	Patrick Roy RC	150	200	300	2,500
122	Mario Lemieux	25	40	75	
149	Wendel Clark DP RC	12	20	40	

1987-88 O-Pee-Chee

		NmMt 8	NmMt+ 8.5	MT 9	Gem 9.5/10
15	Mario Lemieux	25	30	50	100
42	Luc Robitaille RC	30	40	60	200
53	Wayne Gretzky	25	50	100	250
56	Steve Yzerman	12	15	25	60

		NmMt 8	NmMt+ 8.5	MT 9	Gem 9.5/10
123	Adam Oates RC	15	20	40	100
163	Patrick Roy	20	25	40	100
169	Ron Hextall RC	15	20	30	120
215	Mike Vernon RC	15	20	35	80
227	Claude Lemieux RC	12	20	30	80
243	Vincent Damphousse RC	12	20	30	80

1987-88 Topps

		NmMt 8	NmMt+ 8.5	MT 9	Gem 9.5/10
15	Mario Lemieux	15	25	30	50
42	Luc Robitaille RC	15	20	25	40
53	Wayne Gretzky	10	20	30	
123	Adam Oates RC	10	15	25	
163	Patrick Roy	20	25	30	60
169	Ron Hextall RC	10	15	40	

1988-89 O-Pee-Chee

		NmMt 8	NmMt+ 8.5	MT 9	Gem 9.5/10
1	Mario Lemieux	10	12	25	100
16	Joe Nieuwendyk RC	10	15	40	100
66	Brett Hull RC	30	40	80	300
116	Patrick Roy	12	15	25	35
120	Wayne Gretzky UER	15	20	30	200
122	Brendan Shanahan RC	50	80	100	250
181	Bob Probert RC	12	20	30	100
194	Pierre Turgeon RC	10	12	25	120
196	Steve Yzerman	8	12	25	50

1988-89 Topps

		NmMt 8	NmMt+ 8.5	MT 9	Gem 9.5/10
1	Mario Lemieux DP	6	10	20	
16	Joe Nieuwendyk RC	10	15	30	
66	Brett Hull DP RC	30	50	80	
116	Patrick Roy DP	8	12	25	
120	Wayne Gretzky Sweater	15	25	40	250
122	Brendan Shanahan RC	15	20	50	
181	Bob Probert DP RC	10	15	30	
194	Pierre Turgeon RC	10	12	25	

1989-90 O-Pee-Chee

		NmMt 8	NmMt+ 8.5	MT 9	Gem 9.5/10
89	Trevor Linden RC	10	12	20	40
113	Joe Sakic RC	15	20	50	100
136	Brian Leetch RC	10	12	20	75
156	Wayne Gretzky	8	10	20	
232	Theo Fleury RC	10	12	30	50

1989-90 Topps

		NmMt 8	NmMt+ 8.5	MT 9	Gem 9.5/10
113	Joe Sakic RC	15	20	50	
136	Brian Leetch RC	8	12	20	60

1990-91 O-Pee-Chee

		NmMt 8	NmMt+ 8.5	MT 9	Gem 9.5/
7	Jeremy Roenick RC	5	5	12	25
120	Wayne Gretzky	2	4	6	15
348	Mike Modano RC				

1990-91 OPC Premier

		NmMt 8	NmMt+ 8.5	MT 9	Gem 9.5/1
30	Sergei Fedorov RC	8	10	15	80
38	Wayne Gretzky	5	6	12	40
50	Jaromir Jagr RC	15	30	80	200
51	Curtis Joseph RC	5	8	15	30
74	Mike Modano RC	5	8	25	50
100	Jeremy Roenick RC	6	8	20	40
114	Mats Sundin RC	6	8	12	30

1990-91 Score Rookie Traded

		NmMt 8	NmMt+ 8.5	MT 9	Gem 9.5/1
20T	Sergei Fedorov RC	5	6	8	15
70T	Jaromir Jagr	6	8	10	20
88T	Eric Lindros	8	10	12	25

1990-91 Topps

		NmMt 8	NmMt+ 8.5	MT 9	Gem 9.5/1
171	Curtis Joseph RC	8	10	15	25
348	Mike Modano RC	8	10	15	25

1990-91 Upper Deck

		NmMt 8	NmMt+ 8.5	MT 9	Gem 9.5/1
24	Alexander Mogilny RC	5	6	10	15
46	Mike Modano RC	6	8	12	20
55	Ed Belfour RC	6	8	12	20
63	Jeremy Roenick RC	5	6	10	15
178	Mark Recchi RC	5	6	10	15
356	Jaromir Jagr RC	8	10	15	60
365	Mats Sundin RC	5	6	10	20
458	Felix Potvin RC	6	8	12	25
525	Sergei Fedorov YG RC UER	6	8	12	20
526	Pavel Bure YG RC	8	10	30	60

1990-91 Upper Deck French

		NmMt 8	NmMt+ 8.5	MT 9	Gem 9.5/1
356	Jaromir Jagr RC	10	12	20	40
525	Sergei Fedorov YG RC UER	8	10	15	40
526	Pavel Bure YG RC	12	15	25	50

1991-92 OPC Premier

		NmMt 8	NmMt+ 8.5	MT 9	Gem 9.5/1
117	Nicklas Lidstrom RC	5	10	15	40
118A	V.Konstantinov ERR RC	10	15	25	40

1991-92 Upper Deck

		NmMt 8	NmMt+ 8.5	MT 9	Gem 9.5/1
21	Teemu Selanne CC RC	8	10	15	30
26	Nicklas Lidstrom CC RC	8	10	15	30

	NmMt 8	NmMt+ 8.5	MT 9	Gem 9.5/10
Peter Forsberg RC	8	10	15	30
Dominik Hasek RC	8	10	15	30
John LeClair RC	6	8	12	20
Nikolai Khabibulin RC	6	8	12	20
Alexei Kovalev RC	6	8	12	20
Keith Tkachuk RC	6	8	12	20

991-92 Upper Deck French

	NmMt 8	NmMt+ 8.5	MT 9	Gem 9.5/10
Teemu Selanne RC CC	8	10	15	30
Nicklas Lidstrom RC CC	8	10	15	30
Peter Forsberg RC	8	10	15	30
Dominik Hasek RC	8	10	15	30

992-93 Upper Deck

	NmMt 8	NmMt+ 8.5	MT 9	Gem 9.5/10
Markus Naslund RC	6	8	10	15
Paul Kariya RC	8	10	12	40
Chris Pronger RC	6	8	15	30
Saku Koivu RC	6	8	12	20

994-95 Finest

	NmMt 8	NmMt+ 8.5	MT 9	Gem 9.5/10
Wayne Gretzky	10	12	20	30
Miikka Kiprusoff RC	20	20	25	50

994-95 SP

	NmMt 8	NmMt+ 8.5	MT 9	Gem 9.5/10
Jarome Iginla RC	12	15	50	175
Wayne Gretzky 2500	10	15	25	50

996-97 Black Diamond

	NmMt 8	NmMt+ 8.5	MT 9	Gem 9.5/10
Joe Thornton RC	250	300	400	

997-98 Black Diamond

	NmMt 8	NmMt+ 8.5	MT 9	Gem 9.5/10
Daniel Sedin RC	12	20	30	60
Roberto Luongo RC	12	15	25	50
Henrik Sedin RC	12	20	30	60
Vincent Lecavalier RC	12	15	25	40

1997-98 SP Authentic

	NmMt 8	NmMt+ 8.5	MT 9	Gem 9.5/10
Zdeno Chara RC	35	40	60	250

1997-98 Zenith

	NmMt 8	NmMt+ 8.5	MT 9	Gem 9.5/10
Patrik Elias RC	5	5	20	
Vincent Lecavalier RC	25	50	100	175
Roberto Luongo RC	25	40	80	150
Alex Tanguay RC	6	12	25	40

1998-99 SP Authentic

	NmMt 8	NmMt+ 8.5	MT 9	Gem 9.5/10
95 Milan Hejduk RC	20	25	30	60

1998-99 Upper Deck

	NmMt 8	NmMt+ 8.5	MT 9	Gem 9.5/10
234 Martin St. Louis RC	10	12	20	30

2000-01 SP Game Used

	NmMt 8	NmMt+ 8.5	MT 9	Gem 9.5/10
70 Marian Gaborik RC	35	40	50	80

2000-01 Upper Deck

	NmMt 8	NmMt+ 8.5	MT 9	Gem 9.5/10
198 Dany Heatley YG RC	15	20	30	50
229 Marian Gaborik YG RC	25	30	50	150

2001-02 SP Authentic

	NmMt 8	NmMt+ 8.5	MT 9	Gem 9.5/10
145 Pavel Datsyuk RC	60	80	100	200
175 Ilya Kovalchuk AU RC	135	150	175	300

2001-02 Upper Deck

	NmMt 8	NmMt+ 8.5	MT 9	Gem 9.5/10
211 Ilya Kovalchuk YG RC	50	60	80	200
422A Pavel Datsyuk YG RC	60	80	200	300
422B Pavel Datsyuk YG RC	60	80	100	200

2002-03 Pacific Exclusive

	NmMt 8	NmMt+ 8.5	MT 9	Gem 9.5/10
196 Rick Nash AU RC	30	40	50	80
197 Henrik Zetterberg AU RC	30	40	50	100

2002-03 SP Authentic

	NmMt 8	NmMt+ 8.5	MT 9	Gem 9.5/10
184 Rick Nash AU RC	30	50	80	
186 Henrik Zetterberg AU RC	40	60	100	
191 Jason Spezza AU RC	40	60	80	140

2002-03 SP Game Used

	NmMt 8	NmMt+ 8.5	MT 9	Gem 9.5/10
73 Rick Nash RC	10	20	25	40
75 Henrik Zetterberg RC	8	15	25	35
82 Jason Spezza RC	10	20	25	40
97 Ryan Miller RC	10	20	25	40

2002-03 Upper Deck

	NmMt 8	NmMt+ 8.5	MT 9	Gem 9.5/10
232 Rick Nash YG RC	175	200	250	400
234 Henrik Zetterberg YG RC	150	175	200	300

—Henrik Zetterberg #234 BGS 10 (Pristine) sold for $675 (eBay; 4/15)

—Rick Nash #232 BGS 10 (Pristine) sold for $456.44 (eBay; 4/12)

2003-04 Black Diamond

	NmMt 8	NmMt+ 8.5	MT 9	Gem 9.5/10
198 Marc-Andre Fleury RC	35	40	50	80

2003-04 SP Authentic

	NmMt 8	NmMt+ 8.5	MT 9	Gem 9.5/10
137 Eric Staal AU RC	40	50	100	150
146 Patrice Bergeron AU RC	40	50	80	120
153 Marc-Andre Fleury AU RC	60	80	125	200
158 Alexander Semin AU RC	20	25	30	50

2003-04 Upper Deck

	NmMt 8	NmMt+ 8.5	MT 9	Gem 9.5/10
204 Patrice Bergeron YG RC	40	80	100	300
206 Eric Staal YG RC	40	50	60	100
221 Brent Burns YG RC	30	40	50	100
234 Marc-Andre Fleury YG RC	60	80	100	175
454 Ryan Kesler YG RC	25	30	40	60

2003-04 Upper Deck Trilogy

	NmMt 8	NmMt+ 8.5	MT 9	Gem 9.5/10
143 Patrice Bergeron RC	15	20	25	40
180 Marc-Andre Fleury RC	25	30	35	50

2004-05 SP Authentic Rookie Redemptions

	NmMt 8	NmMt+ 8.5	MT 9	Gem 9.5/10
RR5 Dion Phaneuf	20	30	60	100
RR24 Sidney Crosby	150	200	250	400
RR30 Alexander Ovechkin	100	125	150	200
RR40 Mike Richards	15	20	25	40
RR45 Ryan Getzlaf	20	25	30	50

2005-06 Artifacts

	NmMt 8	NmMt+ 8.5	MT 9	Gem 9.5/10
224 Sidney Crosby RC	135	150	200	300
230 Alexander Ovechkin RC	60	80	100	150

2005-06 Beehive

	NmMt 8	NmMt+ 8.5	MT 9	Gem 9.5/10
101 Sidney Crosby RC UER	40	50	80	150
Typo 'talent it tow'				
102 Alexander Ovechkin RC	20	25	40	60

2005-06 Black Diamond

	NmMt 8	NmMt+ 8.5	MT 9	Gem 9.5/10
155 Duncan Keith RC	15	20	30	60
156 Henrik Lundqvist RC	20	25	30	50
191 Alexander Ovechkin RC	50	60	80	120
192 Zach Parise RC	20	25	35	50
193 Sidney Crosby RC	150	200	250	600
194 Dion Phaneuf RC	15	20	30	50
195 Jeff Carter RC	15	20	25	50
196 Corey Perry RC	25	30	35	50
199 Mike Richards RC	20	25	30	50

2005-06 Parkhurst

		NmMt 8	NmMt+ 8.5	MT 9	Gem 9.5/10
657	Sidney Crosby RC	35	40	50	120
669	Alexander Ovechkin RC	20	25	30	40

2005-06 SP Authentic

		NmMt 8	NmMt+ 8.5	MT 9	Gem 9.5/10
131	Ryan Getzlaf AU RC	35	40	60	100
132	Corey Perry AU RC	35	40	50	80
139	Thomas Vanek AU RC	30	35	40	60
140	Dion Phaneuf AU RC	30	35	40	80
142	Cam Ward AU RC	15	20	25	40
145	Brent Seabrook AU RC	25	30	40	80
147	Duncan Keith AU RC	60	80	100	175
155	Jim Howard AU RC	30	35	40	60
167	Zach Parise AU RC	35	40	50	100
171	Henrik Lundqvist AU RC	60	80	100	200
177	Jeff Carter AU RC	30	35	40	80
178	Mike Richards AU RC	20	25	30	50
181	Sidney Crosby AU RC	600	700	1,000	2,250
188	Alexander Steen AU RC	25	30	35	60
190	Alex Ovechkin AU RC	300	350	400	600

—Sidney Crosby #190 BGS 10 (Pristine) sold for $2,010 (eBay, 06/13)
—Alexander Ovechkin #190 BGS 10 (Pristine) sold for $1,280 (eBay, 05/08)

2005-06 SP Game Used

		NmMt 8	NmMt+ 8.5	MT 9	Gem 9.5/10
101	Sidney Crosby RC	125	150	200	300
111	Alexander Ovechkin RC	60	80	100	200

2005-06 SPx

		NmMt 8	NmMt+ 8.5	MT 9	Gem 9.5/10
164	Dion Phaneuf JSY AU RC	35	40	60	
173	Henrik Lundqvist JSY AU RC	50	60	80	125
190	Alex Ovechkin JSY AU/499 RC	300	350	500	750
191	Sidney Crosby JSY AU/499 RC	400	500	600	1,250

2005-06 UD Rookie Class

		NmMt 8	NmMt+ 8.5	MT 9	Gem 9.5/10
1	Sidney Crosby	10	12	20	50
2	Alexander Ovechkin	6	8	12	20

2005-06 Ultimate Collection

		NmMt 8	NmMt+ 8.5	MT 9	Gem 9.5/10
91	Sidney Crosby AU RC	650	700	800	1,200
92	Alexander Ovechkin AU RC	350	400	600	800
97	Henrik Lundqvist AU RC	60	80	125	250
101	Ryan Getzlaf AU RC	35	40	50	100
105	Dion Phaneuf AU RC	30	40	50	100

2005-06 Ultra

		NmMt 8	NmMt+ 8.5	MT 9	Gem 9.5/10
251	Sidney Crosby RC	50	60	100	200
252	Alexander Ovechkin RC	30	40	50	100
269	Henrik Lundqvist RC	12	15	20	40

2005-06 Upper Deck

		NmMt 8	NmMt+ 8.5	MT 9	Gem 9.5/10
201	Sidney Crosby YG RC	250	300	1,500	2,000
216	Henrik Lundqvist YG RC	25	30	50	120
443	Alexander Ovechkin YG RC	100	150	250	450
452	Ryan Getzlaf YG RC	12	15	20	60

2005-06 Upper Deck Ice

		NmMt 8	NmMt+ 8.5	MT 9	Gem 9.5/10
103	Alexander Ovechkin RC	800	900	1,000	
105	Corey Perry RC	250	300	400	
106	Sidney Crosby RC	3,000	3,200	3,500	
107	Ryan Getzlaf RC	25	30	40	80
109	Dion Phaneuf RC	15	20	30	50
110	Cam Ward RC	12	15	25	40
115	Zach Parise RC	25	30	40	60
117	Mike Richards RC	20	25	30	50
123	Brent Seabrook RC	10	12	25	50
137	Henrik Lundqvist RC	25	30	40	60
148	Duncan Keith RC	12	15	20	30
251	Pekka Rinne RC	12	15	30	50
260	Corey Crawford RC	12	15	30	30

2005-06 Upper Deck MVP

		NmMt 8	NmMt+ 8.5	MT 9	Gem 9.5/10
393	Sidney Crosby RC	35	40	50	80
394	Alexander Ovechkin RC	20	25	30	50

2005-06 Upper Deck Trilogy

		NmMt 8	NmMt+ 8.5	MT 9	Gem 9.5/10
211	Sidney Crosby RC	100	125	150	250
220	Alexander Ovechkin RC	40	60	80	125

2005-06 Upper Deck Victory

		NmMt 8	NmMt+ 8.5	MT 9	Gem 9.5/10
264	Alexander Ovechkin RC	12	15	20	35
285	Sidney Crosby RC	15	20	30	50

2006-07 Black Diamond

		NmMt 8	NmMt+ 8.5	MT 9	Gem 9.5/10
200	Anze Kopitar RC	20	25	30	50
202	Phil Kessel RC	20	25	30	50
205	Jordan Staal RC	20	25	30	50
206	Paul Stastny RC	25	30	40	50
210	Evgeni Malkin RC	50	60	80	150

2006-07 Flair Showcase

		NmMt 8	NmMt+ 8.5	MT 9	Gem 9.5/10
322	Evgeni Malkin RC	25	30	40	60

2006-07 SP Authentic

		NmMt 8	NmMt+ 8.5	MT 9	Gem 9.5/10
163	Phil Kessel AU RC	40	50	60	100
184	Anze Kopitar AU RC	50	60	80	125
196	Evgeni Malkin AU RC	150	175	200	300

		NmMt 8	NmMt+ 8.5	MT 9	Gem 9.5/10
198	Jordan Staal AU RC	30	35	50	100
200	Kristopher Letang AU RC	35	40	50	80

2006-07 The Cup

		NmMt 8	NmMt+ 8.5	MT 9	Gem 9.5/
169	Jordan Staal JSY AU/99 RC	250	400	600	750
170	Phil Kessel JSY AU/99 RC	250	350	500	700
171	Evgeni Malkin JSY AU/99 RC	1,400	1,800	2,400	3,200
172	Paul Stastny JSY AU/99 RC	300	500	700	900
173	Anze Kopitar JSY AU/99 RC	400	600	750	1,000

2006-07 Ultra

		NmMt 8	NmMt+ 8.5	MT 9	Gem 9.5/
251	Evgeni Malkin RC	8	10	15	50

2006-07 Upper Deck

		NmMt 8	NmMt+ 8.5	MT 9	Gem 9.5/1
204	Phil Kessel YG RC	25	30	40	80
216	Anze Kopitar YG RC	25	30	40	80
222	Shea Weber YG RC	15	20	25	40
239	Jordan Staal YG RC	15	20	25	40
240	Kristopher Letang YG RC	20	25	30	80
486	Evgeni Malkin YG RC	80	100	120	300
487	Joe Pavelski YG RC	12	15	25	40
495	Evgeni Malkin YG CL	15	20	25	50

2006-07 Upper Deck Trilogy

		NmMt 8	NmMt+ 8.5	MT 9	Gem 9.5/1
149	Evgeni Malkin RC	50	60	80	120

2007-08 Black Diamond

		NmMt 8	NmMt+ 8.5	MT 9	Gem 9.5/1
191	Jonathan Toews RC	40	50	80	100
194	Carey Price RC	40	50	60	100
200	Patrick Kane RC	30	40	50	80

2007-08 O-Pee-Chee

		NmMt 8	NmMt+ 8.5	MT 9	Gem 9.5/1
517	Jonathan Toews RC	12	20	40	60
518	Patrick Kane RC	10	15	25	40

2007-08 SP Authentic

		NmMt 8	NmMt+ 8.5	MT 9	Gem 9.5/10
177	Jonathan Quick RC	125	150	175	250
203	Jonathan Toews AU RC	175	200	250	400
204	Patrick Kane AU RC	135	150	175	250
225	Carey Price AU RC	100	125	150	500

2007-08 SP Authentic Sign of the Times

		NmMt 8	NmMt+ 8.5	MT 9	Gem 9.5/10
STGP	Carey Price	40	50	75	125
STJT	Jonathan Toews	80	100	125	175

HOCKEY

007-08 Ultra

	NmMt 8	NmMt+ 8.5	MT 9	Gem 9.5/10
Carey Price RC	30	35	50	80
Jonathan Toews RC	35	40	50	100
Patrick Kane RC	30	35	50	80

007-08 Upper Deck

	NmMt 8	NmMt+ 8.5	MT 9	Gem 9.5/10
Bobby Ryan YG RC	12	15	20	40
Milan Lucic YG RC	10	12	15	40
David Krejci YG RC	12	15	20	50
Patrick Kane YG RC	60	80	150	300
Jonathan Bernier YG RC	15	20	25	50
Carey Price YG RC	100	125	200	300
Jaroslav Halak YG RC	8	10	12	40
Nicklas Backstrom YG RC	8	10	12	40
Ondrej Pavelec YG RC	12	15	20	30
Tuukka Rask YG RC	20	25	35	60
Jonathan Toews YG RC	100	150	200	300

007-08 Upper Deck Ice

	NmMt 8	NmMt+ 8.5	MT 9	Gem 9.5/10
Jonathan Toews/99 RC	500	600	700	1,250
Carey Price/99 RC	700	800	900	1,250
Nicklas Backstrom/99 RC	100	125	150	250
Patrick Kane/99 RC	300	350	400	600

008-09 Black Diamond

	NmMt 8	NmMt+ 8.5	MT 9	Gem 9.5/10
Claude Giroux RC	12	15	20	40
Steven Stamkos RC	40	50	80	150

008-09 SP Authentic

	NmMt 8	NmMt+ 8.5	MT 9	Gem 9.5/10
Max Pacioretty RC	50	60	80	150
Claude Giroux AU RC	50	60	80	125
T.J. Oshie AU RC	20	25	30	80
Drew Doughty AU RC	50	60	80	150
Steven Stamkos AU RC	175	200	250	350

008-09 Ultra

	NmMt 8	NmMt+ 8.5	MT 9	Gem 9.5/10
Steven Stamkos RC	20	25	35	50

008-09 Upper Deck

	NmMt 8	NmMt+ 8.5	MT 9	Gem 9.5/10
Blake Wheeler YG RC	6	8	12	40
Jakub Voracek YG RC	12	20	25	40
T.J. Oshie YG RC	12	15	20	30
Drew Doughty YG RC	20	25	30	80
Claude Giroux YG RC	25	30	50	80
Steven Stamkos YG RC	60	80	120	200

2008-09 Upper Deck Ice

	NmMt 8	NmMt+ 8.5	MT 9	Gem 9.5/10
161 Claude Giroux RC	40	50	60	100

2008-09 Upper Deck Trilogy

	NmMt 8	NmMt+ 8.5	MT 9	Gem 9.5/10
163 Steven Stamkos RC	40	50	60	100

2009-10 Black Diamond

	NmMt 8	NmMt+ 8.5	MT 9	Gem 9.5/10
222 John Tavares RC	30	40	50	100

2009-10 SP Authentic

	NmMt 8	NmMt+ 8.5	MT 9	Gem 9.5/10
201 John Tavares AU RC	125	150	200	300
203 Matt Duchene AU RC	40	50	60	100
209 Erik Karlsson AU RC	60	80	100	150
223 Jamie Benn AU RC	40	50	60	100
259 Logan Couture AU RC	35	40	50	100

2009-10 The Cup

	NmMt 8	NmMt+ 8.5	MT 9	Gem 9.5/10
178 Matt Duchene JSY AU RC/99	650	700	800	1,200
180 John Tavares JSY AU RC/99	1,800	2,000	2,500	4,000

2009-10 Upper Deck

	NmMt 8	NmMt+ 8.5	MT 9	Gem 9.5/10
201 John Tavares YG RC	60	100	150	350
202 Victor Hedman YG RC	12	15	20	60
203 Matt Duchene YG RC	20	25	30	60
210 Erik Karlsson YG RC	25	30	40	200
212 Jamie Benn YG RC	30	40	50	120
214 Tyler Myers YG RC	8	10	20	40
452 Brad Marchand YG RC	20	25	30	60
487 Logan Couture YG RC	10	12	20	40
493 James Reimer YG RC	15	20	30	50
494 Michael Grabner YG RC	10	12	20	40
499 Braden Holtby YG RC	12	15	25	40

2009-10 Upper Deck Ice

	NmMt 8	NmMt+ 8.5	MT 9	Gem 9.5/10
170 Jamie Benn RC	175	200	250	400
183 Matt Duchene RC	175	200	250	350
184 John Tavares RC	500	600	700	800

2009-10 Upper Deck MVP

	NmMt 8	NmMt+ 8.5	MT 9	Gem 9.5/10
377 John Tavares RC	30	35	40	60

2009-10 Upper Deck Victory

	NmMt 8	NmMt+ 8.5	MT 9	Gem 9.5/10
318 John Tavares RC	10	12	15	25

2010-11 Black Diamond

	NmMt 8	NmMt+ 8.5	MT 9	Gem 9.5/10
218 P.K. Subban RC	25	30	40	60
220 Jordan Eberle RC	30	35	50	80
221 Tyler Seguin RC	25	30	40	60
222 Taylor Hall RC	20	25	50	100

2010-11 SP Authentic

	NmMt 8	NmMt+ 8.5	MT 9	Gem 9.5/10
271 P.K. Subban AU RC	50	80	100	150
277 Brayden Schenn AU RC	20	25	30	60
280 Taylor Hall AU RC	80	100	120	200
281 Jordan Eberle AU RC	60	80	100	200
301 Tyler Seguin AU RC	80	100	125	225

2010-11 The Cup

	NmMt 8	NmMt+ 8.5	MT 9	Gem 9.5/10
176 P.K. Subban JSY AU RC	700	800	1,000	
178 Jordan Eberle JSY AU RC	1,000	1,200	1,500	
179 Tyler Seguin JSY AU RC	1,600	1,800	2,000	
180 Taylor Hall JSY AU RC	1,000	1,200	1,600	

2010-11 Upper Deck

	NmMt 8	NmMt+ 8.5	MT 9	Gem 9.5/10
211 Jeff Skinner YG RC	20	25	30	60
219 Taylor Hall YG RC	40	50	60	150
220 Jordan Eberle YG RC	30	40	50	100
231 P.K. Subban YG RC	25	40	60	100
240 Sergei Bobrovsky YG RC	8	12	15	60
247 Nazem Kadri YG RC	20	25	30	80
456 Tyler Seguin YG RC	60	80	100	150
466 Magnus Paajarvi YG RC	12	15	20	30
486 Robin Lehner YG RC	10	12	15	30

—Taylor Hall #219 BGS 10 (Pristine) sold for $269 (eBay; 9/12)

—Jordan Eberle #220 BGS 10 (Pristine) sold for $217 (eBay; 10/12)

—Tyler Seguin #456 BGS 10 (Pristine) sold for $239 (eBay; 7/12)

2010-11 Upper Deck 20th Anniversary Parallel

	NmMt 8	NmMt+ 8.5	MT 9	Gem 9.5/10
219 Taylor Hall YG	60	80	100	150
456 Tyler Seguin YG	60	80	100	150
549 Jordan Eberle CWJ	60	80	100	150

2010-11 Upper Deck Exclusives

	NmMt 8	NmMt+ 8.5	MT 9	Gem 9.5/10
219 Taylor Hall YG	175	200	250	
456 Tyler Seguin YG	275	300	325	450

2010-11 Upper Deck Ice

	NmMt 8	NmMt+ 8.5	MT 9	Gem 9.5/10
102 Derek Stepan/99 B RC	80	100	125	200
103 P.K. Subban/99 B RC	300	350	400	500
104A Tyler Seguin/99 B RC	350	400	450	600
105 Taylor Hall/99 B RC	600	650	700	900
110 Jordan Eberle/99 S RC	350	400	450	550

2011-12 Black Diamond

		NmMt 8	NmMt+ 8.5	MT 9	Gem 9.5/10
250	Ryan Nugent-Hopkins RC	25	30	40	80

2011-12 Panini Contenders

		NmMt 8	NmMt+ 8.5	MT 9	Gem 9.5/10
218	Ryan Nugent-Hopkins AU RC	40	50	80	100

2011-12 SP Authentic

		NmMt 8	NmMt+ 8.5	MT 9	Gem 9.5/10
221	Gustav Nyquist AU RC	30	40	50	80
228	Mark Scheifele AU RC	20	25	30	40
238	Brandon Saad AU RC	25	30	35	50
245	Ryan Johansen AU RC	25	30	40	60
247	Gabriel Landeskog AU RC	50	60	80	120
248	Nugent-Hopkins AU RC	80	100	150	200

2011-12 The Cup

		NmMt 8	NmMt+ 8.5	MT 9	Gem 9.5/10
180	Nugent-Hopkins JSY AU/99 RC	1,000	1,300	2,000	2,500

2011-12 Ultimate Collection

		NmMt 8	NmMt+ 8.5	MT 9	Gem 9.5/10
121	Ryan Nugent-Hopkins AU/99 RC	150	200	250	300

2011-12 Upper Deck

		NmMt 8	NmMt+ 8.5	MT 9	Gem 9.5/10
207	Brandon Saad YG RC	12	15	20	60
208	Gabriel Landeskog YG RC	20	25	30	60
214	Ryan Nugent-Hopkins YG RC	35	40	50	120
226	Adam Henrique YG RC	15	20	25	40
234	Sean Couturier YG RC	15	20	25	40
245	Cody Hodgson YG RC	15	20	25	30
248	Mark Scheifele YG RC	12	15	25	80
465	Ryan Johansen YG RC	15	20	25	35
468	Gustav Nyquist YG RC	15	25	30	40
476	Louis Leblanc YG RC	12	15	25	35

—Ryan Nugent-Hopkins #214 BGS 10 (Pristine) sold for $385 (eBay; 9/12)

—Ryan Nugent-Hopkins #214 BGS 10 (Pristine) sold for $412 (eBay; 2/12)

2011-12 Upper Deck Canvas

		NmMt 8	NmMt+ 8.5	MT 9	Gem 9.5/10
C98	Ryan Nugent-Hopkins YG	50	60	80	120

2011-12 Upper Deck Ice

		NmMt 8	NmMt+ 8.5	MT 9	Gem 9.5/10
98	Gabriel Landeskog RC	200	225	250	350
100	Ryan Nugent-Hopkins RC	500	550	600	800

2012-13 Upper Deck Ice

		NmMt 8	NmMt+ 8.5	MT 9	Gem 9.5/10
46	Chris Kreider/99 RC	80	100	125	150

2013-14 Black Diamond

		NmMt 8	NmMt+ 8.5	MT 9	Gem 9.5/10
229	Nathan MacKinnon RC	25	30	50	100

2013-14 SP Authentic

		NmMt 8	NmMt+ 8.5	MT 9	Gem 9.5/10
249	Tyler Johnson RC	15	20	25	50
265	Nail Yakupov AU RC	30	40	50	80
268	Morgan Rielly AU RC	20	25	30	60
269	Filip Forsberg AU RC	50	60	80	100
274	Tyler Toffoli AU RC	20	25	30	50
276	Vladimir Tarasenko AU RC	50	80	150	300
312	Nathan MacKinnon AU RC	125	150	200	250
313	Jacob Trouba AU RC	20	25	30	50
319	Mikael Granlund AU RC	20	25	30	60

2013-14 Upper Deck

		NmMt 8	NmMt+ 8.5	MT 9	Gem 9.5/10
230	Vladimir Tarasenko YG RC	35	40	50	150
238	Nathan MacKinnon YG RC	30	40	80	150
242	Sean Monahan YG RC	15	20	25	40
246	Tyler Toffoli YG RC	12	15	25	35
451	Filip Forsberg YG RC	25	30	35	50
466	Petr Mrazek YG RC	12	15	20	30
470	Aleksander Barkov YG RC	12	15	20	30
477	Brendan Gallagher YG RC	15	20	25	40
483	Nikita Kucherov YG RC	30	40	60	150
485	Martin Jones YG RC	12	15	20	30
486	John Gibson YG RC	15	20	30	60
492	Tyler Johnson YG RC	15	20	25	40

2013-14 Upper Deck Canvas

		NmMt 8	NmMt+ 8.5	MT 9	Gem 9.5/10
C114	Nathan MacKinnon YG	60	80	100	150
C119	Tomas Hertl YG	20	25	30	50
C257	Nathan MacKinnon POE	100	125	150	200

2013-14 Upper Deck Ice

		NmMt 8	NmMt+ 8.5	MT 9	Gem 9.5/10
119	Filip Forsberg/99 RC	150	200	250	300
123	Nathan MacKinnon/99 RC	600	700	800	1,000
124	Vladimir Tarasenko/99 RC	300	350	400	500
128	Nail Yakupov/99 RC	200	250	300	350
129	Alex Galchenyuk/99 RC	400	450	500	600
130	Aleksander Barkov/99 RC	150	175	200	300
131	Tomas Hertl/99 RC	150	175	200	300
133	Seth Jones/99 RC	100	125	150	200

2014-15 Black Diamond

		NmMt 8	NmMt+ 8.5	MT 9	Gem 9.5/10
231	Johnny Gaudreau RC	25	30	50	100

2014-15 SP Authentic

		NmMt 8	NmMt+ 8.5	MT 9	Gem 9.5/10
294	Kevin Hayes AU RC	25	30	50	100
309	Aaron Ekblad AU RC	40	50	60	100
313	Jonathan Drouin AU RC	50	60	100	150

2014-15 Upper Deck

		NmMt 8	NmMt+ 8.5	MT 9	Gem 9.5/10
211	Johnny Gaudreau YG RC	35	40	80	120
214	Teuvo Teravainen YG RC	15	20	25	40
223	Leon Draisaitl YG RC	50	60	80	200
225	Aaron Ekblad YG RC	25	30	40	80
236	Anthony Duclair YG RC	10	12	20	40
248	Evgeny Kuznetsov YG RC	12	15	30	60
457	Darnell Nurse YG RC	10	12	20	40
477	Jonathan Drouin YG RC	40	50	60	150
478	Andrei Vasilevskiy YG RC	10	12	20	40
494	Bo Horvat YG RC	20	30	40	60
495	David Pastrnak YG RC	30	40	60	120

2014-15 Upper Deck Canvas

		NmMt 8	NmMt+ 8.5	MT 9	Gem 9.5/10
C94	Sam Reinhart YG	20	25	30	50
C96	Johnny Gaudreau YG	40	50	60	100
C98	Teuvo Teravainen YG	35	40	50	80
C104	Leon Draisaitl YG	25	30	35	60
C105	Aaron Ekblad YG	35	40	50	80
C110	Anthony Duclair YG	15	20	25	40
C117	Evgeny Kuznetsov YG	25	30	35	60
C214	Jonathan Drouin YG	35	40	50	80
C225	David Pastrnak YG	35	40	50	80

2014-15 Upper Deck Ice

		NmMt 8	NmMt+ 8.5	MT 9	Gem 9.5/10
157	Anthony Duclair/249 RC	20	25	40	80
158	Evgeny Kuznetsov/249 RC	35	40	60	125
159	David Pastrnak/99 RC	200	250	300	400
160	Sam Reinhart/99 RC	200	250	300	350
161	Leon Draisaitl/99 RC	125	150	175	200
162	Aaron Ekblad/99 RC	200	250	300	400
163	Curtis Lazar/99 RC	125	150	175	200
164	Bo Horvat/99 RC	150	200	225	250
165	Teuvo Teravainen/99 RC	150	200	225	250
166	Jonathan Drouin/99 RC	200	250	300	400
167	Johnny Gaudreau/99 RC	400	450	500	600
168	Andre Burakovsky/99 RC	125	150	175	200

2015-16 Upper Deck

		NmMt 8	NmMt+ 8.5	MT 9	Gem 9.5/10
201	Connor McDavid YG RC	200	300	400	600
206	Mikko Rantanen YG RC	25	50	80	100
451	Jack Eichel YG RC	50	80	150	250

2016-17 Upper Deck

		NmMt 8	NmMt+ 8.5	MT 9	Gem 9.5/10
201	Auston Matthews YG RC	100	150	250	400
205	Brayden Point YG RC	20	25	50	80
451	Patrik Laine YG RC	20	30	100	250
458	Mathew Barzal YG RC	25	50	80	150
468	Mitch Marner YG RC	25	50	100	150

HOCKEY

GAMING

1993 Magic The Gathering Alpha

		NmMt 8	NmMt+ 8.5	MT 9	Gem 9.5/10
1	Air Elemental U :B:	40	▲120	▲175	600
2	Ancestral Recall R :B:	3,500	4,500	▲9,000	▲12,000
3	Animate Artifact U :B:	▲60	▲75	▲100	250
4	Animate Dead U :K:	200	▲350	▲400	▲600
5	Animate Wall R :W:	150	▲300	▲350	500
6	Ankh of Mishra R :A:	300	▲400	▲950	▲2,400
7	Armageddon R :W:	▲800	▲950	▲1,700	
8	Aspect of Wolf R :G:	150	200	▲500	1,800
9	Bad Moon R :K:	200	300	▲1,000	1,300
10	Badlands R :L:	1,500	▲3,800	▲4,000	▲5,300
11	Balance R :W:	800	900	▲2,300	10,000
12	Basalt Monolith U :A:	150	▲300	▲450	▲900
13	Bayou R :L:	▲2,000	▲3,000	▲4,000	▲7,000
15	Berserk U :G:	t200	▲450	▲700	▲900
16	Birds of Paradise R :G:	1,500	1,800		30,000
17	Black Knight U :K:	200	▲300	▲500	1,200
18	Black Lotus R :A:	18,000	▲45,000	▲80,000	▲120,000
19	Black Vise U :A:	200	500	800	1,000
20	Black Ward U :W:	40	60	▲250	400
21	Blaze of Glory R :W:	300	▲400	▲600	▲2,300
22	Blessing R :W:	200	▲300	▲500	▲1,400
24	Blue Ward U :W:	30	▲60	▲100	▲300
25	Bog Wraith U :K:	▲75	▲100	200	1,500
26	Braingeyser R :B:	▲900	▲1,000	▲2,600	4,300
27	Burrowing U :R:	▲50	▲75	150	300
28	Camouflage U :G:	60	100	▲250	300
29	Castle U :W:	30	50	▲125	▲250
30	Celestial Prism U :A:	30	▲60	▲120	200
31	Channel U :G:	▲120	150	▲400	
32	Chaos Orb R :A:	4,000	4,500	5,000	
33	Chaoslace R :R:	▲200	▲250	500	▲1,000
38	Clockwork Beast R :A:	150	175	▲800	
39	Clone U :B:	100	150	250	400
40	Cockatrice R :G:	150	200	350	
41	Consecrate Land U :W:	30	40	60	
42	Conservator U :A:	40	60	80	300
43	Contract from Below R :K:	250	300	500	
44	Control Magic U :B:	200	250		
45	Conversion U :W:	40	50	75	175
46	Copper Tablet U :A:	100	150	200	250
47	Copy Artifact R :B:	400	500	600	
48	Counterspell U :B:	400	600	900	
51	Crusade R :W:	400	500	600	
52	Crystal Rod U :A:	50	75	100	
53	Cursed Land U :K:	35	50	150	
54	Cyclopean Tomb R :A:	300	400	600	
56	Darkpact R :K:	200	300	400	
58	Deathgrip U :K:	50	80	150	200
59	Deathlace R :K:	150	200	300	900
60	Demonic Attorney R :K:	200	300	500	
61	Demonic Hordes R :K:	150	200	300	650
62	Demonic Tutor U :K:	500	700	900	
63	Dingus Egg R :A:	80	120	250	
66	Disrupting Scepter R :A:	400	600	700	800
67	Dragon Whelp U :R:	80	150	250	
69	Drain Power R :B:	200	300	400	
71	Dwarven Demolition Team U :R:	50	100	200	750
73	Earth Elemental U :R:	40	60	100	200
75	Earthquake R :R:	250	300	400	500
76	Elvish Archers R :G:	200	250	350	
77	Evil Presence U :K:	30	50	85	
79	Farmstead R :W:	300	350	400	450
80	Fastbond R :G:	400	500	700	
82	Feedback U :B:	30	50	200	350
83	Fire Elemental U :R:	30	50	80	
86	Flashfires U :R:	70	125		
89	Force of Nature R :G:	500	700	1,000	
90	Forcefield R :A:	600	800	1,200	▲10,000
93	Fork R :R:	550	700	900	1,000
95	Fungusaur R :G:	200	250		
96	Gaea's Liege R :G:	200	250		
97	Gauntlet of Might R :A:	1,000	1,200		
100	Glasses of Urza U :A:	40	50		
101	Gloom U :K:	60	100	125	
102	Goblin Balloon Brigade U :R:	40	60	80	200
103	Goblin King R :R:	350	500	650	
104	Granite Gargoyle R :R:	250	300	450	600
106	Green Ward U :W:	30	40	60	
110	Helm of Chatzuk R :A:	100	150	400	
112	Hive, The R :A:	300	400	500	
116	Howling Mine R :A:	400	500	700	900
118	Hurricane U :G:	80	100		
119	Hypnotic Specter U :K:	400	500	600	
120	Ice Storm U :G:	100	140	150	300
121	Icy Manipulator U :A:	300	400	500	800
122	Illusionary Mask R :A:	350	400	750	
123	Instill Energy U :G:	150	200	250	
125	Iron Star U :A:	40	60	80	100
128	Island Sanctuary R :W:	200	250	300	1,000
131	Ivory Cup U :A:	20	30	40	200
132	Jade Monolith R :A:	100	150	325	
133	Jade Statue U :A:	100	130		
134	Jayemdae Tome R :A:	500	700	1,100	
135	Juggernaut U :A:	150	200	300	
137	Karma U :W:	50	80	100	200
138	Keldon Warlord U :R:	150	200	300	
139	Kormus Bell R :A:	200	300	500	1,000
140	Kudzu R :G:	150	200		
141	Lance U :W:	60	100	150	
142	Ley Druid U :G:	30	50	100	180
143	Library of Leng U :A:	60	80	100	
144	Lich R :K:	400	500	600	
145	Lifeforce U :G:	30	50	100	175
146	Lifelace R :G:	100	200	300	
147	Lifetap U :B:	40	80	100	125
149	Living Artifact R :G:	100	150	300	800
150	Living Lands R :G:	100	150	200	
151	Living Wall U :A:	30	50	150	450
153	Lord of Atlantis R :B:	300	500	600	
154	Lord of the Pit R :K:	300	500	700	3,000
155	Lure U :G:	60	80	100	
156	Magical Hack R :B:	150	200	500	
157	Mahamoti Djinn R :B:	275	325	500	
158	Mana Flare R :R:	125	180	400	600
159	Mana Short R :B:	300	400	800	
160	Mana Vault R :A:	▲1,400	▲1,500	2,000	▲3,700
161	Manabarbs R :R:	100	150	300	1,300
162	Meekstone R :A:	200	250	400	600
165	Mind Twist R :K:	400	450	750	
169	Mox Emerald R :A:	2,000	▲5,000	▲9,000	▲16,000
170	Mox Jet R :A:	▲2,500	▲6,000	▲9,000	▲40,000
171	Mox Pearl R :A:	▲5,800	▲8,000	▲12,000	▲15,000
172	Mox Ruby R :A:	2,000	3,000	▲10,000	▲20,000
173	Mox Sapphire R :A:	▲3,200	▲7,000	▲13,000	
174	Natural Selection R :G:	150	200	300	
175	Nether Shadow R :K:	150	200	300	500
176	Nettling Imp U :K:	20	30	75	
177	Nevinyrral's Disk R :A:	400	▲1,000	▲1,700	4,000
178	Nightmare R :K:	400	500	600	
179	Northern Paladin R :W:	145	200	500	
180	Obsianus Golem U :A:	15	25	50	
181	Orcish Artillery U :R:	25	30	70	
182	Orcish Oriflamme U :R:	20	35	50	
185	Personal Incarnation R :W:	200	300	500	
187	Phantasmal Forces U :B:	30	50	100	
189	Phantom Monster U :B:	20	30	60	100
190	Pirate Ship R :B:	150	200	500	
194	Plateau R :L:	1,000	▲2,000	▲2,500	▲3,100
197	Power Surge R :R:	100	125	170	
199	Psionic Blast U :B:	80	100	200	
201	Purelace R :W:	75	125	200	500
202	Raging River R :R:	200	250	500	1,000
205	Red Ward U :W:	20	30	60	
207	Regrowth U :G:	50	70	160	
208	Resurrection U :W:	30	45	100	250
209	Reverse Damage R :W:	100	150	500	
210	Righteousness R :W:	150	200	300	400
211	Roc of Kher Ridges R :R:	300	400	500	
212	Rock Hydra R :R:	150	200	250	
213	Rod of Ruin U :A:	20	30	80	
214	Royal Assassin R :K:	300	400	1,100	1,800
215	Sacrifice U :K:	20	30	80	
217	Savannah Lions R :W:	450	600	800	1,000
218	Savannah R :L:	800	1,100	▲2,000	▲5,000
220	Scavenging Ghoul U :K:	20	30	60	
221	Scrubland R :L:	1,000	▲2,500	▲2,700	▲6,300
224	Sedge Troll R :R:	400	500	800	
225	Sengir Vampire U :K:	75	90	200	
226	Serra Angel U :W:	400	600	800	
229	Shivan Dragon R :R:	1,000	1,500	3,000	9,000
230	Simulacrum U :K:	20	35	80	
232	Siren's Call U :B:	20	40	80	180
233	Sleight of Mind R :B:	100	150	300	600
234	Smoke R :R:	100	150	200	
235	Sol Ring U :A:	150	400	1,000	2,000
236	Soul Net U :A:	40	80	200	
238	Stasis R :B:	200	300	400	
239	Steal Artifact U :B:	20	35	50	
240	Stone Giant U :R:	20	35	50	
243	Sunglasses of Urza R :A:	100	150	170	
246	Swords to Plowshares U :W:	200	250	500	
247	Taiga R :L:	1,500	▲2,500	4,000	8,000
249	Thicket Basilisk U :G:	20	30	50	
250	Thoughtlace R :B:	150	180	300	
251	Throne of Bone U :A:	20	30	50	
252	Timber Wolves R :G:	150	200	400	600
253	Time Vault R :A:	900	▲2,000	▲3,000	▲4,000
254	Time Walk R :B:	▲3,000	▲6,200	▲6,000	▲14,000
255	Timetwister R :B:	2,000	▲5,900	▲11,000	▲25,000
257	Tropical Island R :L:	▲3,000	▲3,500	▲4,000	▲6,000
258	Tsunami U :G:	20	35	50	
259	Tundra R :L:	▲2,300	▲2,500	3,000	5,000
260	Tunnel U :R:	20	40	60	
262	Two-Headed Giant of Foriys R :R:	125	180	300	
263	Underground Sea R :L:	▲5,000	▲6,300	▲8,400	▲21,000
266	Uthden Troll U :R:	30	60	100	250
267	Verduran Enchantress R :G:	150	200	500	1,000
268	Vesuvan Doppelganger R :B:	800	1,000	2,000	3,500
269	Veteran Bodyguard R :W:	150	200	250	
270	Volcanic Eruption R :B:	100	150	300	
271	Wall of Air U :B:	20	30	40	120
272	Wall of Bone U :K:	20	30	40	
273	Wall of Brambles U :G:	20	30	40	
274	Wall of Fire U :R:	20	30	40	
275	Wall of Ice U :G:	20	30	40	
276	Wall of Stone U :R:	20	30	40	
277	Wall of Swords U :W:	20	30	40	
278	Wall of Water U :B:	20	30	40	
280	Wanderlust U :G:	20	30	50	
282	Warp Artifact R :K:	100	120	150	
283	Water Elemental U :B:	30	40	60	
285	Web R :G:	100	150	200	
286	Wheel of Fortune R :R:	800	1,000	▲3,500	
287	White Knight U :W:	50	100	150	250
288	White Ward U :W:	20	30	40	180
290	Will-O'-The-Wisp R :K:	150	200	500	700
291	Winter Orb R :A:	300	400	500	
292	Wooden Sphere U :A:	30	40	80	
293	Word of Command R :K:	200	250	400	
294	Wrath of God R :W:	400	600	800	1,200
295	Zombie Master R :K:	250	300	400	500

1993 Magic The Gathering Beta

		NmMt 8	NmMt+ 8.5	MT 9	Gem 9.5/10
1	Air Elemental U :B:	8	10	15	20
2	Ancestral Recall R :B:	2,000	2,500	3,000	5,000
3	Animate Artifact U :B:	8	15	20	
4	Animate Dead U :K:	20	40	70	90
5	Animate Wall R :W:	15	25	30	75
6	Ankh of Mishra R :A:	50	120	150	350
7	Armageddon R :W:	150	225	300	500
8	Aspect of Wolf R :G:	20	30	40	100
9	Bad Moon R :K:	100	150	200	400
10	Badlands R :L:	800	1,000	1,200	1,500
11	Balance R :W:	150	180	200	500
12	Basalt Monolith U :A:	10	20	30	60
13	Bayou R :L:	1,000	1,300	1,500	2,000
14	Benalish Hero C :W:	5	10	15	25
15	Berserk U :G:	130	150	180	250
16	Birds of Paradise R :G:	400	500	600	800
17	Black Knight U :K:	20	30	50	
18	Black Lotus R :A:	7,500	8,000	12,000	15,000
19	Black Vise U :A:	20	35	50	
20	Black Ward U :W:	8	15	20	
21	Blaze of Glory R :W:	40	100	125	350
22	Blessing R :W:	20	40	60	125
23	Blue Elemental Blast C :B:	8	15	20	30
24	Blue Ward U :W:	8	15	20	30
25	Bog Wraith U :K:	8	15	20	
26	Braingeyser R :B:	130	150	200	350
27	Burrowing U :R:	8	15	20	
28	Camouflage U :G:	12	20	25	
29	Castle U :W:	12	20	25	50
30	Celestial Prism U :A:	8	15	20	
31	Channel U :G:	15	25	30	
32	Chaos Orb R :A:	400	450	500	700
33	Chaoslace R :R:	15	25	30	60
34	Circle of Protection Black C :W:	8	15	20	30
35	Circle of Protection Blue C :W:	8	15	20	40
36	Circle of Protection Green C :W:	8	15	20	30
37	Circle of Protection Red C :W:	8	15	20	30
38	Circle of Protection White C :W:	8	15	20	30
39	Clockwork Beast R :A:	20	30	40	100
40	Clone U :B:	20	40	50	
41	Cockatrice R :G:	25	40	50	
42	Consecrate Land U :W:	15	25	30	75
43	Conservator U :A:	8	15	20	
44	Contract from Below R :K:	40	80	100	250
45	Control Magic U :B:	15	25	30	
46	Conversion U :W:	8	15	20	
47	Copper Tablet U :A:	10	20	30	60
48	Copy Artifact R :B:	50	120	150	400
49	Counterspell U :B:	40	80	100	
50	Craw Wurm C :G:	8	15	20	40
51	Creature Bond C :B:	8	15	20	30
52	Crusade R :W:	50	100	125	500
53	Crystal Rod U :A:	8	15	20	
54	Cursed Land U :K:	8	15	20	30
55	Cyclopean Tomb R :A:	75	125	150	400
56	Dark Ritual C :K:	20	50	60	150
57	Darkpact R :K:	20	40	50	
58	Death Ward C :W:	8	15	20	30
59	Deathgrip U :K:	8	15	20	
60	Deathlace R :K:	20	30	40	100
61	Demonic Attorney R :K:	20	30	40	100
62	Demonic Hordes R :K:	50	100	125	400
63	Demonic Tutor U :K:	100	125	200	300
64	Dingus Egg R :A:	20	40	50	
65	Disenchant C :W:	15	20	25	40
66	Disintegrate C :R:	8	15	20	30
67	Disrupting Scepter R :A:	40	80	100	250
68	Dragon Whelp U :R:	20	40	60	125
69	Drain Life C :K:	8	15	20	30
70	Drain Power R :B:	20	50	60	150
71	Drudge Skeletons C :K:	8	15	20	30
72	Dwarven Demolition Team U :R:	10	20	30	
73	Dwarven Warriors C :R:	8	15	20	30
74	Earth Elemental U :R:	8	15	20	
75	Earthbind C :R:	8	15	20	30
76	Earthquake R :R:	40	80	100	250
77	Elvish Archers R :G:	40	100	125	350
78	Evil Presence U :K:	8	15	20	30
79	False Orders C :R:	8	15	20	30
80	Farmstead R :W:	20	40	50	125
81	Fastbond R :G:	80	150	175	450
82	Fear C :K:	8	15	20	30
83	Feedback U :B:	8	15	20	30
84	Fire Elemental U :R:	8	15	20	30
85	Fireball C :R:	10	20	25	40

#	Card	NmMt 8	NmMt+ 8.5	MT 9	Gem 9.5/10
86	Firebreathing C :R:	8	15	20	30
87	Flashfires U :R:	10	20	30	60
88	Flight C :B:	8	15	20	30
89	Fog C :G:	8	15	20	
90	Force of Nature R :G:	80	150	175	400
91	Forcefield R :A:	350	400	500	
92	Forest (blue) C :L:	8	15	20	30
93	Forest (black) C :L:	8	15	20	30
94	Forest (with trail) v3 C :L:	8	15	20	30
95	Fork R :R:	80	150	200	350
96	Frozen Shade C :K:	8	15	20	30
97	Fungusaur R :G:	20	30	40	
98	Gaea's Liege R :G:	20	40	50	125
99	Gauntlet of Might R :A:	100	175	225	650
100	Giant Growth C :G:	8	15	20	30
101	Giant Spider C :G:	8	15	20	30
102	Glasses of Urza U :A:	8	15	20	30
103	Gloom U :K:	8	15	20	30
104	Goblin Balloon Brigade U :R:	8	15	20	40
105	Goblin King R :R:	50	100	125	350
106	Granite Gargoyle R :R:	30	50	60	175
107	Gray Ogre C :R:	8	15	20	30
108	Green Ward U :W:	8	15	20	
109	Grizzly Bears C :G:	10	15	25	50
110	Guardian Angel C :W:	8	15	20	30
111	Healing Salve C :W:	8	15	20	30
112	Helm of Chatzuk R :A:	15	25	30	60
113	Hill Giant C :R:	8	15	20	30
114	Hive, The R :A:	20	30	40	100
115	Holy Armor C :W:	8	15	20	30
116	Holy Strength C :W:	8	15	20	30
117	Howl from Beyond C :K:	8	15	20	30
118	Howling Mine R :A:	100	175	200	500
119	Hurloon Minotaur C :R:	8	15	20	30
120	Hurricane U :G:	10	20	25	
121	Hypnotic Specter U :K:	50	80	100	225
122	Ice Storm U :G:	30	60	80	150
123	Icy Manipulator U :A:	50	80	100	350
124	Illusionary Mask R :A:	150	300	400	850
125	Instill Energy U :G:	8	15	20	40
126	Invisibility C :B:	8	15	20	30
127	Iron Star U :A:	8	15	20	30
128	Ironclaw Orcs C :R:	8	15	20	30
129	Ironroot Treefolk C :G:	8	15	20	30
130	Island Sanctuary R :W:	20	50	60	150
131	Island v1 C :L:	8	15	20	30
132	Island v2 C :L:	8	15	20	30
133	Island v3 C :L:	8	15	20	30
134	Ivory Cup U :A:	8	15	20	30
135	Jade Monolith R :A:	20	30	40	100
136	Jade Statue U :A:	15	25	30	75
137	Jayemdae Tome R :A:	25	40	50	125
138	Juggernaut U :A:	25	40	50	125
139	Jump C :B:	8	15	20	30
140	Karma U :W:	8	15	20	
141	Keldon Warlord U :R:	8	15	20	
142	Kormus Bell R :A:	20	30	40	100
143	Kudzu R :G:	20	30	40	100
144	Lance U :W:	8	15	20	
145	Ley Druid U :G:	8	15	20	30
146	Library of Leng U :A:	8	15	20	30
147	Lich R :K:	75	125	150	400
148	Lifeforce U :G:	8	15	20	30
149	Lifelace R :G:	15	25	30	
150	Lifetap U :B:	8	15	20	30
151	Lightning Bolt C :R:	20	50	120	150
152	Living Artifact R :G:	20	30	40	100
153	Living Lands R :G:	20	30	40	100
154	Living Wall U :A:	8	15	20	
155	Llanowar Elves C :G:	20	50	60	150
156	Lord of Atlantis R :B:	50	120	150	350
157	Lord of the Pit R :K:	75	125	150	400
158	Lure U :G:	8	15	20	30
159	Magical Hack R :B:	20	40	50	
160	Mahamoti Djinn R :B:	50	100	125	400
161	Mana Flare R :R:	75	125	150	400
162	Mana Short R :B:	50	100	125	350
163	Mana Vault R :A:	100	200	250	600
164	Manabarbs R :R:	20	30	40	
165	Meekstone R :A:	30	50	60	175
166	Merfolk of the Pearl Trident C :B:	8	15	20	
167	Mesa Pegasus C :W:	8	15	20	30
168	Mind Twist R :K:	125	225	300	750
169	Mons's Goblin Raiders C :R:	8	15	20	30
170	Mountain v1 C :L:	8	15	20	30
171	Mountain v2 C :L:	8	15	20	30
172	Mountain v3 C :L:	8	15	20	30
173	Mox Emerald R :A:	1,500	2,500	4,000	5,000
174	Mox Jet R :A:	1,500	2,500	4,000	10,000
175	Mox Pearl R :A:	1,500	1,800	2,000	4,500
176	Mox Ruby R :A:	1,500	2,000	2,500	4,500
177	Mox Sapphire R :A:	2,000	2,500	3,000	5,000
178	Natural Selection R :G:	50	100	125	350
179	Nether Shadow R :K:	40	80	100	250
180	Nettling Imp U :K:	8	15	20	30
181	Nevinyrral's Disk R :A:	150	275	350	750
182	Nightmare R :K:	50	100	150	400
183	Northern Paladin R :W:	40	80	100	250
184	Obsianus Golem U :A:	8	15	20	
185	Orcish Artillery U :R:	10	20	25	40
186	Orcish Oriflamme U :R:	10	20	25	40
187	Paralyze C :K:	8	15	20	
188	Pearled Unicorn C :W:	8	15	20	30
189	Personal Incarnation R :W:	20	30	40	
190	Pestilence C :K:	8	15	20	30
191	Phantasmal Forces U :B:	8	15	20	
192	Phantasmal Terrain C :L:	8	15	20	30
193	Phantom Monster U :B:	8	15	20	30
194	Pirate Ship R :B:	20	40	50	125
195	Plague Rats C :K:	8	15	20	30

#	Card	NmMt 8	NmMt+ 8.5	MT 9	Gem 9.5/10
196	Plains v1 C :L:	8	15	20	30
197	Plains v2 C :L:	8	15	20	30
198	Plains v3 C :L:	8	15	20	30
199	Plateau R :L:	650	800	1,000	2,000
200	Power Leak C :B:	8	15	20	30
201	Power Sink C :B:	8	15	20	30
202	Power Surge R :R:	20	40	60	150
203	Prodigal Sorcerer C :B:	8	15	20	30
204	Psionic Blast U :B:	40	80	100	250
205	Psychic Venom C :B:	8	15	20	
206	Purelace R :W:	12	20	25	50
207	Raging River R :R:	40	80	100	250
208	Raise Dead C :K:	8	15	20	30
209	Red Elemental Blast C :R:	10	20	25	40
210	Red Ward U :W:	8	15	20	30
211	Regeneration C :G:	8	15	20	30
212	Regrowth U :G:	40	80	100	250
213	Resurrection U :W:	8	15	20	30
214	Reverse Damage R :W:	20	40	50	125
215	Righteousness R :W:	20	40	50	125
216	Roc of Kher Ridges R :R:	20	40	50	125
217	Rock Hydra R :R:	30	50	60	175
218	Rod of Ruin U :A:	8	15	20	
219	Royal Assassin R :K:	100	200	250	650
220	Sacrifice U :K:	8	15	20	
221	Samite Healer C :W:	8	15	20	30
222	Savannah Lions R :W:	80	100	150	500
223	Savannah R :L:	800	850	950	1,100
224	Scathe Zombies C :K:	8	15	20	30
225	Scavenging Ghoul U :K:	8	15	20	
226	Scrubland R :L:	800	1,000	1,200	1,500
227	Scryb Sprites C :G:	8	15	20	30
228	Sea Serpent C :B:	8	15	20	30
229	Sedge Troll R :R:	40	80	100	
230	Sengir Vampire U :K:	30	60	70	150
231	Serra Angel U :W:	80	150	175	400
232	Shanodin Dryads C :G:	8	15	20	30
233	Shatter C :R:	8	15	20	30
234	Shivan Dragon R :R:	175	250	300	750
235	Simulacrum U :K:	8	15	20	
236	Sinkhole C :K:	40	100	125	300
237	Siren's Call U :B:	8	15	20	30
238	Sleight of Mind R :B:	20	30	40	100
239	Smoke R :R:	20	40	50	125
240	Sol Ring U :A:	90	150	200	500
241	Soul Net U :A:	8	15	20	30
242	Spell Blast C :B:	8	15	20	30
243	Stasis R :B:	50	100	125	350
244	Steal Artifact U :B:	8	15	20	
245	Stone Giant U :R:	8	15	20	
246	Stone Rain C :R:	8	15	20	30
247	Stream of Life C :G:	8	15	20	30
248	Sunglasses of Urza R :A:	20	30	40	100
249	Swamp v1 C :L:	8	15	20	30
250	Swamp v2 C :L:	8	15	20	30
251	Swamp v3 C :L:	8	15	20	30
252	Swords to Plowshares U :W:	30	75	100	300
253	Taiga R :L:	600	750	900	1,100
254	Terror C :K:	8	15	20	30
255	Thicket Basilisk U :G:	8	15	20	30
256	Thoughtlace R :B:	20	30	40	100
257	Throne of Bone U :A:	8	15	20	30
258	Timber Wolves R :G:	15	25	30	75
259	Time Vault R :A:	600	800	1,000	1,250
260	Time Walk R :A:	1,500	2,000	2,500	3,000
261	Timetwister R :B:	1,000	1,750	2,500	3,000
262	Tranquility C :G:	8	15	20	30
263	Tropical Island R :L:	1,000	1,500	2,000	3,000
264	Tsunami U :G:	8	15	20	30
265	Tundra R :L:	1,800	2,000	2,500	3,500
266	Tunnel U :R:	8	15	20	30
267	Twiddle C :B:	8	15	20	30
268	Two-Headed Giant of Foriys R :R:	50	100	125	350
269	Underground Sea R :L:	3,000	4,000	4,500	5,000
270	Unholy Strength C :K:	8	15	20	30
271	Uncommon C :B:	8	15	20	30
272	Uthden Troll U :R:	8	15	20	
273	Verduran Enchantress R :G:	40	80	100	250
274	Vesuvan Doppelganger R :B:	100	200	250	
275	Veteran Bodyguard R :W:	20	30	40	
276	Volcanic Eruption R :B:	15	25	30	75
277	Volcanic Island R :L:	3,000	4,000	5,000	10,000
278	Wall of Air U :B:	8	15	20	
279	Wall of Bone U :K:	8	15	20	30
280	Wall of Brambles U :G:	8	15	20	
281	Wall of Fire U :R:	8	15	20	
282	Wall of Ice U :G:	8	15	20	30
283	Wall of Stone U :R:	8	15	20	
284	Wall of Swords U :W:	8	15	20	30
285	Wall of Water U :B:	8	15	20	
286	Wall of Wood C :G:	8	15	20	30
287	Wanderlust U :G:	8	15	20	
288	War Mammoth C :G:	8	15	20	
289	Warp Artifact R :K:	15	25	30	60
290	Water Elemental U :B:	8	15	20	
291	Weakness C :K:	8	15	20	
292	Web R :G:	15	25	30	60
293	Wheel of Fortune R :R:	150	300	400	800
294	White Knight U :W:	20	30	40	
295	White Ward U :W:	8	15	20	30
296	Wild Growth C :G:	8	15	20	30
297	Will-O'-The-Wisp R :K:	50	100	125	350
298	Winter Orb R :A:	75	125	175	500
299	Wooden Sphere U :A:	8	15	20	30
300	Word of Command R :K:	75	125	150	400
301	Wrath of God R :W:	300	400	500	600
302	Zombie Master R :K:	50	80	100	250

1999 Pokemon Base 1st Edition Thick Stamp

#	Card	NmMt 8	NmMt+ 8.5	MT 9	Gem 9.5/1
1	Alakazam HOLO R	300	400	500	2,000
2	Blastoise HOLO R	600	800	1,500	7,000
3	Chansey HOLO R	200	250	500	5,000
4	Charizard HOLO R	3,500	4,000	5,500	18,000
5	Clefairy HOLO R	200	300	400	2,000
6	Gyarados HOLO R	250	350	500	2,000
7	Hitmonchan HOLO R	250	350	450	1,800
8	Machamp HOLO R	200	300	400	1,000
9	Magneton HOLO R	200	300	400	1,800
10	Mewtwo HOLO R	200	300	700	6,000
11	Nidoking HOLO R	200	300	400	2,000
12	Ninetales HOLO R	200	300	500	3,000
13	Poliwrath HOLO R	200	300	500	5,000
14	Raichu HOLO R	200	300	500	5,000
15	Venusaur HOLO R	400	500	700	4,500
16	Zapdos HOLO R	200	300	500	2,500
17	Beedrill R	80	100	150	800
18	Dragonair R	40	60	80	800
19	Dugtrio R	30	40	50	450
20	Electabuzz R	30	40	50	400
21	Electrode R	30	40	75	600
22	Pidgeotto R	20	30	40	350
23	Arcanine U	20	30	40	100
24	Charmeleon U	25	40	60	450
25	Dewgong U	15	20	30	65
26	Dratini U	15	20	25	450
27	Farfetch'd U	15	20	30	75
28	Growlithe U	20	30	35	300
29	Haunter U	20	25	30	250
30	Ivysaur U	20	30	40	150
31	Jynx U	15	20	25	300
32	Kadabra U	20	30	40	200
33	Kakuna (UER) U	10	15	20	50
34	Machoke U	15	20	30	70
35	Magikarp U	15	20	30	70
36	Magmar U	15	20	25	70
37	Nidorino U	10	15	20	70
38	Poliwhirl U	15	20	30	75
39	Porygon U	20	25	30	70
40	Raticate U	20	30	40	70
41	Seel U	15	20	25	40
42	Wartortle U	30	40	75	800
43	Abra C	5	10	15	45
44	Bulbasaur (UER) C	30	45	55	200
45	Caterpie (UER) C	10	15	20	80
46	Charmander C	20	25	35	100
47	Diglett C	10	15	20	30
48	Doduo C	10	15	20	40
49	Drowzee C	10	15	20	45
50	Gastly C	10	15	20	45
51	Koffing C	10	15	20	40
52	Machop C	10	15	20	45
53	Magnemite C	10	15	20	40
54	Metapod (UER) C	10	15	20	45
55	Nidoran-M C	10	15	20	40
56	Onix C	10	15	20	40
57	Pidgey C	10	15	20	40
58	Pikachu (Red cheeks Error) C	50	60	75	350
59	Pikachu (Yellow cheeks Corr.) C	20	30	50	150
60	Poliwag C	10	15	20	40
61	Ponyta C	10	15	20	40
62	Rattata C	10	15	20	40
63	Sandshrew C	15	20	30	80
64	Squirtle C	15	20	30	80
65	Starmie C	10	15	20	40
66	Staryu C	10	15	20	40
67	Tangela C	10	15	20	45
68	Voltorb (UER) C	10	15	20	45
69	Vulpix (UER) C	15	20	25	45
70	Weedle C	10	15	20	45
71	Clefairy Doll R	20	30	45	500
72	Computer Search R	60	80	100	450
73	Devolution Spray R	20	30	40	750
74	Impostor Professor Oak R	30	40	60	350
75	Item Finder R	15	20	25	500
76	Lass R	60	80	100	1,000
77	Pokemon Breeder R	20	25	35	300
78	Pokemon Trader R	20	30	40	350
79	Scoop Up R	20	25	35	200
80	Super Energy Removal R	20	30	40	300
81	Defender U	5	10	15	20
82	Energy Retrieval U	10	15	20	200
83	Full Heal U	10	15	20	80
84	Maintenance U	10	15	20	70
85	Plus Power U	10	15	20	120
86	Pokemon Center U	10	15	20	300
87	Pokemon Flute U	10	15	20	300
88	Pokédex U	10	15	20	120
89	Professor Oak U	15	20	30	450
90	Revive U	10	15	20	80
91	Super Potion U	10	15	25	80
92	Bill C	10	15	20	45
93	Energy Removal C	10	15	20	45
94	Gust of Wind C	10	15	20	80
95	Potion C	10	15	20	30
96	Switch C	10	15	25	60
97	Double Colorless Energy U	10	15	20	100
98	Fighting Energy	5	10	15	45
99	Fire Energy	5	10	15	45
100	Grass Energy	5	10	15	45
101	Lightning Energy	5	10	15	20
102	Psychic Energy	5	10	15	20
103	Water Energy	5	10	15	20